W9-BVN-745

With this new 1985 edition of The Answer Book—

- students do better classwork (and *faster* homework)
- parents can answer the 1,001 questions that children ask
- executives can find basic business data quickly
- Crossword fans can solve more difficult puzzles
- *anyone* can answer the little questions of daily living (postage, taxes, metrics, distances, sports, celebrity birthdates)—and the larger questions, too (history, science, statistics, world affairs).

If you need to know, turn to

INFORMATION PLEASE!

READER SURVEY

Could we have some information, please?

We want **Information Please** to be as useful as possible to you. The more we know about our readers and their requirements, the better we, in "The Answer Book," can supply the answers you need.

Would you, therefore, take a moment to give *us* some answers, about yourself and the way you use this Almanac? We'll read your replies carefully, and use them to create an even more helpful book for you in future years.

Please check the sections you find most useful:

_____ Special articles
_____ Election of 1984
_____ Current Events
_____ Headline History
_____ Business and the Economy
_____ Energy
_____ Environment
_____ World Statistics
_____ U.S. Statistics
_____ Countries of the World
_____ Canada
_____ Calendar and Holidays
_____ Weights and Measures
_____ Weather and Climate
_____ Science
_____ Astronomy
_____ Space
_____ Religion
_____ Travel
_____ Structures
_____ United Nations
_____ Aviation
_____ Military
_____ Disasters
_____ First Aid
_____ Nutrition and Health
_____ Where to Find Out More
_____ Toll-Free Numbers
_____ Writer's Guide
_____ Crossword Puzzle Guide
_____ Geography and Maps
_____ U.S. History & Government
_____ Postage
_____ U.S. Societies
_____ Awards
_____ People
_____ Guide to Growing Older
_____ Taxes
_____ Media
_____ Education
_____ Sports
_____ Entertainment and Culture

Where do you use **Information Please** the most?

_____At home _____At work _____In school _____In college

Your age?

_____under 18 _____18–25 _____26–45 _____46–60 _____over 60

Your education?

_____now in school _____high school graduate _____some college
_____college graduate

Your occupation? _______________

Have you bought Information Please before? _______________

How often do you buy an almanac? (every year, every 2 years, etc.)? _______________

We would be very pleased to have you make any other comments you think would be helpful.

Please return this information to the Editor, Information Please Almanac, Houghton Mifflin Company, 149 Madison Avenue, New York, N.Y., 10016.

INFORMATION PLEASE ALMANAC

ATLAS & YEARBOOK

1985

38TH EDITION

HOUGHTON MIFFLIN COMPANY BOSTON

1985

Executive Editor
Otto T. Johnson
Associate Editor
Vera Dailey
Contributing Editors
Arthur Reed, Jr. (Current Events)
Stan Carter (Countries of the World)
Dennis M. Lyons (Sports)
Staff
Editorial Assistants:
Roy Murphy, III, and
Rhona Peyser
Maps
Maps copyright © Hammond Incorporated.
Requests for maps should be sent to Hammond Incorporated, Maplewood, New Jersey 07040.

The Information Please Almanac invites comments and suggestions from readers. Because of the many letters received, however, it is not possible to respond personally to every correspondent. Nevertheless, all suggestions are most welcome, and the editors will consider them carefully. (Information Please Almanac does not rule on bets or wagers.)

ISBN (Hardcover): 0-395-36698-4
ISBN (Paperback): 0-395-36699-2
ISSN: 0073-7860

Previous editions of INFORMATION PLEASE were published in 1982 by A&W Publishing Company, and in 1981, 1980, and 1979 by Simon & Schuster, in 1978 and 1977 by Information Please Publishing, Inc., and from 1947–1976 by Dan Golenpaul Associates.

INFORMATION PLEASE ALMANAC®
Editorial Office
Houghton Mifflin Company
149 Madison Avenue
New York, N.Y. 10016

Printed in the United States of America

WP 10 9 8 7 6 5 4 3 2 1

CONTENTS

A Consumer's Guide to VCR's

Source: "Video—Your New Window on the World" published by the Electronic Industries Association/Consumer Electronics Group.

The Video Cassette Recorder (VCR)

It happens to all of us. There's a program on television that we want to see, but we can't watch it. We're not home, or it's aired too late, or maybe we're even watching another program at the time. Until the advent of the VCR we were out of luck. But the VCR gives us the ability to "timeshift," to record a program at one time and play it back at another. Almost all video cassette recorders have the necessary tuner/timer either built-in or available as an accessory.

Another advantage of the VCR is the large selection of prerecorded tapes that is available to the consumer. They include everything from tennis and golf lessons to speed reading and cooking courses. There are thousands of older films available and an increasing number of new films are being offered for sale to the VCR user.

Formats

There are several different formats of video cassette recorders available, each with its own combination of features and benefits. The different VCR formats use different tape cartridges, or cassettes.

Most home VCR buyers will make their choice between the two major half-inch (named for the width of the tape) formats—BETA and VHS.[1] Tapes used on the BETA system cannot be run on the VHS system and vice versa. Here is a brief rundown of some of the key features available in both systems:

Multiple speeds. Most decks can be set to run at two or three different speeds. At slower speeds, recording time is extended—up to three or six hours with standard videocassette tape, five to eight hours with thinner tape. Why include faster speeds then? Picture and sound quality can be somewhat superior at the faster speeds. Even at the slowest speeds, however, picture quality has been judged as more than acceptable.

Picture search-and-scan. On a tape that lasts as long as five or eight hours, it can be tough to find the part you're looking for. That's why search-and-scan features are so desirable. They let you whiz through the tape at high speed, while the picture remains visible. You'll see some interference lines on the screen during the high-speed search (which can work in both forward and reverse directions) but the lines don't get in the way of this feature's function—to make it possible for you to find quickly the section of the tape you're looking for.

[1]The JVC-developed VHS format is currently outselling the Sony-developed Beta format by about three to one. Sony was the first manufacturer to introduce video home recorders to the public in the late 1970s.—Ed.

Tuners/Timers. All home VCR's except portables have tuner/timers built-in. They let you set the machine to record any available station at the time you select, operating much as the clock in a clock radio. To save weight and reduce their size, portable, battery-operated VCR's usually don't have built-in tuner/timers. For these units, a separate tuner/timer is usually available, and most often packaged in one carton as a complete system. The tuner/timer has a power supply to recharge the portable's battery and to run the deck on regular AC wall-outlet power when it's used indoors at home.

Programmable Tuner/Timers. More sophisticated than standard units, these let you preset your machine to record several different programs at different times, on different channels. You can set the machine from one day to two weeks or more in advance, and then take off on vacation, knowing that all your choices, up to the capacity of the tape and speed you've selected, will be recorded while you're gone.

Freeze-Frame Stills. This feature allows you to freeze the on-screen picture for closer study.

Slow Motion. Anyone who watches TV sports knows what a slow motion replay looks like. With this feature, VCR's give you the ability to see any scene in slow motion. Some units with this feature let you vary the speed of the slow motion, from slow to very slow, to freeze-frame stills.

Fast Motion. With this feature the picture runs at two or three times normal speed. It can be used for humorous, "Keystone Kops" effects and, more seriously, when someone wants to "get the message" in one half to one third the time (especially good for sports events). This should not be confused with picture search-and-scan features that are much faster, speeding the picture at speeds which can be ten or twenty times normal.

Remote Control. Most VHS and BETA VCR's come with a remote pause control, to momentarily stop the machine during record or playback, from a distance. But many models have remotes that do much more. Some of these let you control most or all of the special effects listed above from your easy chair.

Choosing Between BETA and VHS

Because both are excellent designs, it's hard to go wrong with either. Both systems offer a similar roster of attractive features and excellent performance. However, there are differences between the two formats, just as there are differences between units of the same format, depending upon the manufacturer. Check with your dealer to determine the best combination of features for your needs. And actually try operating different models to see which is most comfortable for you.

Incidentally, people often wonder why tapes from VHS and BETA formats are not interchangeable, since both formats use one-half inch tape. The answer is that the cassettes have different physical dimensions, and the electronic recording and playback characteristics of the two formats differ as well.

Keep in mind, though, that if you have two machines available, you can copy or dub a tape made on one format to the other. For example, your VHS machine can be hooked up to a friend's BETA deck so that a VHS tape played on your machine can be transferred to a BETA tape inserted into your friend's deck. Of course, the reverse is also true.

Other VCR Formats

Besides BETA and VHS, there are several other formats available for home video. While these are not compatible with the more widely used one-half-inch formats, and playing time is usually shorter, these formats do offer unique advantages of their own. Quarter-inch tape systems, for example, are available in portable systems that are smaller and lighter than one-half-inch units.[2]

Buying Tapes

It's important to avoid off-brand and no-name tapes. Inside your machine, the tape heads rotate against the tape at hundreds of revolutions per minute. Any imperfections on the tape can clog these fast-moving heads. Tape oxides, if not properly bonded to the backing, can flake off and clog moving parts. The extra slow speeds and special effects on the new VCR's put greater demand on the tape. Reputable tape manufacturers take extra care to insure that their product is reliable and dependable, and won't harm the VCR. Fly-by-night, off-brand manufacturers don't take this care. Most tape purchasers know this and look for well-known brand names. Because of this, some unscrupulous tape makers have actually produced counterfeit tapes—bearing well-known brand names, but of markedly inferior quality. How to protect yourself? Look at the packages closely. The counterfeit tape usually looks imperfect, with sloppy printing and flimsy packaging.

[2]In March 1983, electronic and tape manufacturers agreed on a quarter-inch tape format as the common standard for the industry. These tapes can be played for 60 or 90 minutes. In the near future, the half-inch format will continue to coexist with the quarter-inch tapes. It is expected that the quarter-inch format will be used mainly for movie making.—Ed.

Portable Video

Just think, you can make hours of "video movies" for the cost of a single video cassette—under twenty dollars. Old fashioned home movies, including film and developing, can cost up to fifty times as much for the same running time—up to a thousand dollars! And cost isn't the only benefit to video movies. Unlike film, you see the results right away, no waiting days for the film to be developed. In fact, you can check the results right in the field; many TV cameras let you play back the picture you've recorded through their mini-TV set viewfinders.

Another advantage of video over film is convenience. There's no fumbling with projectors and screens, and no darkened rooms are needed. Just pop the video cassette into the deck and watch your home video movies right on the TV.

Tips For Getting the Most From Your VCR

1. If you're using your VCR with cable TV, be sure to let your dealer know. You may need a special but simple hookup to retain the ability to tape one channel while watching another.

2. One VCR can easily serve two TV sets in different rooms, with little, if any, picture degradation. Ask your dealer for a two-set coupler or A/B switch and cable.

3. When setting your VCR's timer be sure to note whether you're setting AM or PM. On programmable timers, double check which day (and, on some models, which week) you've selected. Simple advice, but worth heeding. Timer setting errors are the leading cause of failure to tape the show you want.

4. Unless you're running short of time on a tape, it's a good idea to set the timer to record for a few minutes longer than the show you want to tape. That way, if a news bulletin or technical malfunction causes a show to run long, you won't miss the ending.

5. Similarly, TV station schedules tend to be less accurate during the late-night time periods. If you're recording a late movie by using the timer, it's a good idea to set it to start recording a few minutes early and continue recording five minutes after the show is supposed to end.

6. Do you have a video game hooked up to your TV? Well, you can record your highest scoring games if you wish.

Playing the software—Using the Hardware

7. Don't leave tapes in the stillframe mode longer than necessary. The rotating tape heads go over and over the same track on the tape in this mode. Clogged heads and damaged video tape can result from overlong use of stillframe (Most machines automatically take the machine out of stillframe/pause after a few minutes for this reason.)

8. The counter on your deck reads in arbitrary digits rather than minutes. But you can make a chart that will convert the number into minutes. Just set the counter to zero, start a tape, and note the counter reading every five minutes. If you do this at the slowest speed, you can multiply the time reading to make the chart accurate at faster speeds too.

9. Portable VCR batteries last between one and two hours on each charge. It's a good idea to get

an extra battery pack to extend the recording time. You can charge one battery while using the other.

10. In a portable VCR and camera combination, the camera takes the most power, especially if it has an electronic viewfinder. To extend battery life on each charge, turn the camera off between scenes. Some cameras have a standby switch for this purpose.

11. When dubbing a video tape (or disc) to another tape machine, the best results will be obtained by going from the direct video and audio outputs (found on most machines) to the direct inputs on the second machine. Results will be superior to an R.F. output to tuner input hookup. Your dealer has the inexpensive direct hookup cables you'll need.

12. TV cameras are rugged devices but don't point them directly at a bright source of light. If you do, you may "burn" the pickup tube, causing a dark spot or streak to appear in the picture where the point of light shone. In many cases, where the light source was not too strong, and exposure brief, the burn will disappear in a few seconds or minutes. In serious cases, for example pointing the camera at the sun, the damage will be permanent.

Caring For Your VCR and Camera

13. VCR's can't function properly with too much moisture in the air. Most have a DEW light to signal excessive moisture. The machines won't play when the DEW light is on.

14. Don't leave a portable VCR or camera in a car trunk. Summertime temperatures in a trunk can reach 130° F, which can damage equipment and tapes.

15. Tape used over and over again can, as it wears, shed some of the oxide coating and gum up the head assembly. When reusing tapes for timeshift recording and viewing, discard them after about 200 recording/playback cycles to avoid possibly clogging or damaging the video head assembly.

16. Just as phonograph cartridges may wear out and require replacement at intervals, depending on usage, so the VCR head mechanisms may require cleaning or replacement from time to time. Unlike the phono cartridges, however, the VCR head assembly is not designed for user maintenance or replacement. This should be done only by a manufacturer's or distributor's authorized service facility.

Using and Caring For Tapes

17. Keep video cassettes, both blank and prerecorded, in their jackets and stored upright. Dust and dirt are a video cassette's Number 1 enemy.

18. When not in use, keep one of the blank video cassettes with your machine so you are always ready to record. That way, if you're called away from the TV while watching a program, the VCR can be turned on immediately so you don't have to miss the rest of the show.

19. How do you edit material from a tape after it's been recorded? Speed search features let you skip through unwanted portions of a tape in a hurry. But to permanently eliminate material, use two decks (your home unit and portable, for example, or your deck and a friend's). Copy the tape from one deck to another, pausing the second deck while the unwanted material goes by. That's the way to edit video tape. Don't even think about cutting the tape.

20. You can transfer your old home movies to video tape with a telecine adapter that fits between your film projector and video camera. Or, for an even easier transfer, there are commercial services that do the job for you. The service is available for 35-mm slides too. Costs are very reasonable for these services.

Some Top Career Opportunities for 1985

The following employment information was taken from *The Guidance Information System™*, a product of TSC· Division, Houghton Mifflin Company, the U.S. Bureau of Labor, and *Information Please Almanac* Questionnaires to trade associations.

Keep in mind that no one can predict future employment with perfect accuracy. This listing is only a selection of careers with good employment potential and is not intended to be complete.

Because salaries not only vary widely from small businesses to large organizations, but also in different geographic locations of the United States, they are to be taken as a comparative guide.

Accountants and Auditors

Accountants and auditors prepare, analyze, and verify financial information and reports. This includes auditing contracts, orders, and vouchers, and preparing balance sheets to reflect a company's assets, liabilities, and capital.

Estimated employment: Over 800,000. About 40% are women. More than 200,000 are certified public accountants.

Average starting salary in private industry with an accounting degree: $15,000 to 19,000. Beginning auditors average $18,700 a year.

Qualifications: Most employers consider a bachelor's degree in accounting or a related field as the minimum entry level requirement. Obtaining a CPA certificate is useful. A master's degree may be preferred. Familiarity with computers and their applications in accounting and internal auditing is desireable.

For Additional Information: American Institute of Certified Public Accountants, 1211 Avenue of the Americas, New York, N.Y. 10036.

Institute of Internal Auditors, Inc., International Headquarters, 249 Maitland Ave., Altamonte Springs, Fla. 32701.

Bank Officers and Managers

Bank officers and managers supervise and oversee operation of bank services and departments. They direct the bank within the policy structure set by the board of directors and existing laws and regulations.

Estimated employment: Over 400,000. Almost 50% of these positions are held by women. Average starting salary: $21,000 to 28,000. Master degree holders generally higher.

Qualifications: Bank officer and management positions are filled by management trainees, and by promotion from within the company from outstanding bank clerks and tellers who demonstrate the potential. College graduation is usually required for management trainees. A business administration major in finance or a liberal arts curriculum, including accounting, economics, commercial law, political science, and statistics serves as excellent preparation for trainee positions. Knowledge of computers and their applications is also important to managerial skills.

For Additional Information: American Bankers Association, 1120 Connecticut Ave., N.W., Washington, D.C., 20036.

Computer Operating Personnel

All computer systems require specialized workers to enter data and instructions, operate the computer, and retrieve the results. **Computer operators** monitor and control the computer to process business, scientific, engineering, or other data according to operating instructions. **Computer-peripheral-equipment operators** use peripheral machines to transfer data from one form to another, print output, and read data into and out of a distant computer. Also watch the machine operation for malfunctions. **Data entry operators** or **typists** operate a special-purpose electric typewriter to convert alphabetic, numeric, and symbolic data into coded form on punch cards or tapes. Proofread and correct typed copy.

Estimated employment: Over 500,000. About one out of seven data typists works part-time. Average starting salary: Computer operators, at least $14,781; peripheral equipment operators, at least $14,800; and data entry typists, at least $10,893.

Qualifications: Most employers recruit workers who already have some of the necessary skills to operate the equipment, especially in data processing. A high school education is required. Specialized training in private vocational and business schools and in junior colleges may be preferred for computer operators and some peripheral-equipment operators.

For Additional Information: American Federation of Information Processing Societies, Inc., 1899 Preston White Drive, Reston, Va. 22091.

Computer Programmers

Because computers are machines that cannot think for themselves, computer programmers must write detailed instructions called programs that list in a logical order the steps the machine must follow to organize data, solve a problem, or do some other task.

Estimated employment: Over 250,000. About one third of programmers are women. Average starting salary: $19,000 to 23,000 per year.

Qualifications: There are no universal training requirements because employer's needs vary. Job prospects are best for college graduates with a bachelor's degree who have computer-related courses. A graduate degree is required for some advance positions. Graduates of two-year colleges, or less than a two-year degree, are expected to have more difficulty in finding employment than in the past.

For Additional Information: American Federation of Information Processing Societies, Inc., 1899 Preston White Drive, Reston, Va. 22091.

Computer Service Technicians

Computer service technicians keep computer systems operating efficiently. They perform necessary maintenance. They repair computer equipment when it breaks down. Technicians often help install new computer equipment.

Estimated employment: About 55,000. Estimated median earnings: Over $22,000 a year.

Qualifications: Most employers require applicants to have one to two years post-high school training in basic electronics or electrical engineering at vocational schools, colleges, or junior colleges. Newly hired technicians usually have to complete six months to two years on-the-job training.

For Additional Information: Contact your state department of education and personnel departments of computer manufacturers and maintenance firms in your area.

Computer Systems Analysts

Systems analysts plan and develop methods for computerizing business and scientific tasks, or improve computer systems already in use.

Estimated employment: Over 200,000. About 25% are women. Average starting salary: $28,000 to 35,000 a year.

Qualifications: There is no universally accepted way of preparing for this career because employer's preferences depend on the work being done. College graduates are generally sought and, for some of the more complex jobs, persons with graduate degrees are preferred. Familiarity with computer languages and prior work experience is important.

Seven out of ten persons entering into this field transfer from other occupations such as engineer, manager, and computer programmer.

For Additional Information: American Federation of Information Processing Societies, Inc., 1899 Preston White Drive, Reston, Va. 22091.

Dental Hygienists

Dental hygienists, working under the direction of a dentist, provide direct patient care such as cleaning teeth, exposing and developing dental X-ray films, and other preventive and therapeutic services.

Estimated employment: 69,000, of which 98% are women. Average earnings: $15,000 to 20,000.

Qualifications: A license is necessary. Minimum educational requirement is two academic years of college in an accredited dental hygiene program. A bachelor's degree is required to do research, teach, and work in a public school or health program. A master's degree is necessary to work as a teacher or administrator in dental hygiene and dental assisting training programs, public health agencies, and in associated research.

Because multiple job holding is common to this field, the number of positions exceeds the number of individuals at work. Because dentists frequently hire hygienists to work only two or three days a week, hygienists who want full-time employment may have to hold more than one job.

For Additional Information: American Dental Hygienists Association, 444 North Michigan Ave.-3400, Chicago, Ill. 60611.

Dietitians

Dietitians provide nutritional counseling to individuals and groups, set up and supervise food service systems for institutions such as hospitals and schools, and promote sound eating habits through education and research.

Chief dietitians direct food service and nutritional care activities in hospitals, universities, and other institutions; **research dietitions** conduct nutritional research in one or more areas of dietetics; and **consultant dietitians** advise and assist institutions such as hospital, child-care centers, and schools in providing quality food service and nutritional care for clients.

Estimated employment: 44,000, of which about 98% are women. Average starting salary: At least $14,500 for chief dietitians, $17,064 for research dietitians, and $17,064 for consultant dietitians. Some experienced dietitians earn over $40,000 a year.

Qualifications: A bachelor's degree, with a major in foods and nutrition or institutional management, is the basic requirement. Experienced dietitians may advance to assistant or associate director of a dietetic department. Advancement to a higher level position in teaching and research requires graduate education.

For Additional Information: American Dietetic Association, 430 North Michigan Ave., Chicago, Ill. 60611.

Legal Secretaries

A legal secretary has the skills and knowledge required of a secretary in any office. In addition to these duties, a legal secretary prepares papers and correspondence of a legal nature such as summonses, complaints, motions, and subpoenas.

There is a vast difference between the duties of a legal secretary in a one-lawyer office and the duties in a large firm employing perhaps a hundred attorneys. In some firms, the duties of a legal secretary overlap with those of a legal assistant (paralegal). In a general way, the duties of a legal secretary tend to be of a more supportive nature to the employer, whereas the duties of a legal assistant tend to be more in the area of research.

Average national starting salary: At least $14,820.

Qualifications: A high school diploma is required. A beginner who has completed a legal secretarial course at a business school or two-year college can usually expect a higher initial salary than one who enters the field without specialized training. Among the usual skills required are the ability to take dictation at 100 words per minute and to type accurately at 60 words per minute.

For Additional Information: National Association of Legal Secretaries, 3005 East Skelly Drive, Suite 120, Tulsa, Okla. 74105.

Licensed Practical Nurses (LPN/VN's)

Licensed practical nurses help care for the physically or mentally ill and infirm. Under the direction of physicians and registered nurses, they provide nursing care that requires technical knowledge but not the professional education and training of a registered nurse. In California and Texas, the title "licensed vocational nurse" (LVN) is the equivalent of "licensed practical nurse" used in all other states.

Estimated employment: 600,000. Average full-time earnings at least $13,160 a year. About 10% earn over $18,000 a year. Over half of the salaried jobs are in hospitals. About 10% of LPN/VN's are self-employed. About three in ten work part-time.

Qualifications: All states and the District of Columbia require a license. Applicants must complete a state-approved program in practical nursing offered by hospitals, vocational schools, and two-year colleges. A high school diploma is preferred but not always required. **NOTE:** A person cannot become a licensed practical/vocational nurse by taking correspondence courses.

For Additional Information: National League for

Nursing, 10 Columbus Circle, New York, N.Y. 10010.

Occupational Therapists

Occupational therapists plan, organize, and conduct occupational therapy programs in hospitals, institutions, or community settings to help rehabilitate the mentally, physically, or emotionally handicapped. They usually work as a member of a medical team which may include a physician, clinical psychologist, social worker, and others.

The largest number of jobs is in hospitals; a growing number of therapists are engaged in private practice. Many work part-time.

Estimated employment: 25,000, of which 23,000 are women. Average starting salary: At least $15,000 a year. Some administrators earn at least $34,000 a year.

Qualifications: A bachelor's degree in occupational therapy is required. Entry to educational programs is highly competitive and applicants are screened carefully. In addition, twenty-one states require a license. A master's degree is often necessary for teaching, research, or administrative work.

For Additional Information: American Occupational Therapy Association, 1383 Piccard Drive, Rockville, Md. 20850.

Radiologic (X-Ray) Technologists

Most technologists operate equipment that is used for diagnostic imaging: X-ray machines, fluoroscopes, and ultrasonic scanners, for example. They assist in treating diseased areas with specified concentrations of X-rays, under a physician's supervision.

Radiologic technologists take X-ray films of the human body for use in diagnosing medical problems. **Nuclear medical technologists** participate in or direct various activities involving radiopharmaceuticals in medical diagnosis and treatment. **Radiation therapy technologists** treat cancer patients. **Ultrasound technologists** use special equipment to transmit sound waves into a patient's body to obtain information and images for diagnosis by physicians.

About seven out of ten jobs are in hospitals. Many technologists work part-time.

Estimated employment: over 110,000. National average starting salary: at least $16,900 per year.

Qualifications: Post-high completion of a formal education program in radiography is required for entry in this field. A bachelor's or master's degree is helpful for specialized positions and advancement.

For Additional Information: National Health Council, Inc., Health Careers Program, 70 West 40th St., New York, N.Y. 10018.

Registered Nurses (RN's)

Registered nurses perform a wide variety of health care functions. The work setting usually determines the scope of the RN's responsibilities. In general, they observe, assess, and record symptoms, reactions, and progress of patients, and administer medication.

Nurse practitioners provide general medical care and treatment to patients in clinics, health centers, or public health agencies. Their duties include performing physical examinations, and recommending drugs and other forms of treatment.

General duty nurses provide general nursing care to patients in a hospital, infirmary, sanitarium, or similar institution.

Community health nurses instruct individuals and families in health education and disease prevention in community health agencies. Duties include visiting homes and teaching home nursing and child care.

Occupational health nurses provide nursing service to employees or persons who become ill or have accidents at department stores, factories, or other establishments.

Estimated employment: 1,400,000, of which 97% are women. Average earnings: $19,600. The top 10% of nurses earned over $27,000 a year. Between one fourth and one third of all nursing jobs are part-time.

Qualifications: A license is required by all states and the District of Columbia. Applicants must be graduates of a state-approved school of nursing, and pass the state board examination. Nurses' training varies in length from two to five years, depending on the nature of the program—associate degree, diploma, or bachelor's degree. A bachelor's degree in nursing is required for top jobs and advancement.

For Additional Information: National League for Nursing, 10 Columbus Circle, New York, N.Y. 10019.

Secretaries

Secretaries perform a variety of administrative and clerical duties so that their employers can work on other matters. This includes scheduling appointments, taking dictation, typing letters, and filing correspondence and other records.

Estimated employment: 3,891,000, of which 99% are women. The national average starting salary is at least $13,468. Some secretaries in advanced positions earn over $30,000 a year.

Qualifications: High school graduates with basic office skills qualify for many positions. Typing proficiency and good spelling, punctuation, grammar, and oral communication skills are needed. Shorthand is necessary for some positions. Applicants who have had secretarial training in a two- and four-year college, or business school, are preferred by employers. Those with word processing experience are usually paid higher.

Highly qualified secretaries are in great demand. Opportunities are also excellent for part-time work in the secretarial field. Office automation is not expected to have an adverse effect upon the employment of secretaries.

For Additional Information: Professional Secretaries International, Crown Center, Suite G-10, 2440 Pershing Road, Kansas City, Mo. 64108.

Walter Frederick Mondale

Democratic Presidential Candidate

Walter Frederick Mondale, known as a cautious and wary politician, exercised daring, blunt, and aggressive tactics in winning the Democratic Party's mantle as its 28th Presidential candidate. In the protracted and bitter primary campaign, he regained the lead dramatically after unexpected early defeats by Senator Gary Hart of Colorado. Then, at the party's convention in July, he electrified the delegates and nationwide TV viewers by his historic and decisive choice of Representative Geraldine A. Ferraro of Queens, N.Y., as the first woman to be named Vice-Presidential candidate on a major party ticket.

Mondale was born in the village of Ceylon in southern Minnesota, Jan. 5, 1928, one of seven children of Theodore Sigvaard Mondale, a Methodist minister, who steeped his children in the "social gospel." The son became an all-round athlete in the high school at Elmore. In 1948 he enrolled at the small liberal arts college of Macalester in St. Paul and later studied at the University of Minnesota.

After two years as an Army corporal, Mondale entered the University's law school under the G.I. bill and practiced law for four years. Gov. Orville L. Freeman appointed him State Attorney General in 1960, and in the same year he was elected in his own right and later re-elected. In 1964 he was appointed to the Senate seat held by his mentor and ideal, Hubert H. Humphrey, when Humphrey became Vice President.

As a Senator, Mondale fought for civil rights and liberal legislation, including open housing, child nutrition, Indian education, and improved migrant worker conditions, proving himself a liberal in the Democratic tradition. In his convention acceptance speech, the nominee branded Reagan policies a threat to the nation's long-term economic security and the physical survival of its families.

As Vice President, Mondale was an influential adviser to President Carter. He helped shape the Chrysler Corporation bailout and was the first to urge a boycott of the Moscow Olympic Games. Mondale headed the joint-agency panel that shaped the President's $2-billion youth employment program in 1980. Friction with Senator Edward M. Kennedy developed over budgetary and foreign policy, and Mondale's critics dubbed him the Administration's "hatchet man."

After the Democratic defeat in 1980, Mondale joined the law firm of Winston & Strawm in Washington and lectured at three Minnesota universities. On Feb. 21, 1983, in St. Paul he announced his candidacy for the Presidency.

Mondale married Joan Adams, daughter of a Presbyterian minister, in St. Paul in 1955. Their three children are: Ted, 26, a Mondale campaign worker; Eleanor, 24, a Hollywood actress; and William, 22, a sophomore at Brown University.

Geraldine A. Ferraro

Democratic Vice-Presidential Candidate

Geraldine A. Ferraro entered the history books in July 1984 when a cheering Democratic convention accepted her by acclamation as the first woman candidate for Vice President on a major party ticket. She was also unusual in being a Roman Catholic of Italian ancestry and working-class background.

In her years in Congress and as assistant district attorney in her home borough of Queens, N.Y., she won a high place in Democratic councils as a tough politician.

Geraldine Anne Ferraro was born in Newburgh, N.Y., Aug. 26, 1935, the only daughter of Dominick Ferraro, a native of Italy, and Antonetta, born in New York. Her parents operated a small restaurant and a business.

After her father's death at 44, the mother and Geraldine, then 8, moved to the Bronx, where the child attended parochial school. In 1952 she graduated from Marymount school in Tarrytown and won a B.A. degree in 1956 from Marymount Manhattan College. After working as a legal secretary, she attended Fordham Law School while teaching at a Queens elementary school by day.

Upon graduation in 1960, she was married to John A. Zaccaro, head of a prominent real estate concern. She practiced law in her husband's business, at the same time caring for their three children at home.

Through her cousin, Nicholas Ferraro, Queens District Attorney, she became an assistant district attorney in 1974, and saw the seamy side of life as head of a bureau handling child abuse, sex crimes, and crimes against the elderly.

She won the Democratic primary for a House of Representatives seat in 1978 and defeated Alfred A. Dellabovi, Republican and Conservative, in the election. Ferraro kept the seat in the elections of 1980 and 1982.

One of her major roles in Congress has been as a member of the House Budget Committee, where she sponsored a bipartisan Economic Equity Act and authored sections reforming private pensions for women and allowing homemakers to deposit as much as their husbands in individual retirement accounts. In 1984 Ferraro voted for the Black Caucus's budget calling for large cuts in defense spending and increases in domestic outlays. To improve her knowledge of foreign affairs, she traveled to the Middle East, Central America, Taiwan, and Japan. While she is a Catholic, she supports government financing of abortions for poor women and does not favor outlawing abortion.

The Zaccaros have three children: Laura, 18, a graduate of The Spence School in Manhattan; John, Jr., 20, a student at Middlebury College; and Donna, 22, a financial analyst.

—A.P.R., Jr.

(NOTE: The biographies of Ronald Reagan and George Bush appear on pp. 635 to 636.)

ELECTIONS

The Ninety-Ninth Congress

The Senate

Unofficial results as of 2:57 P.M., Nov. 7, 1984. Source: News Election Service, New York, N.Y.

Senior Senator is listed first. The dates in the first column indicate period of service. The date given in parentheses after the Senator's name is year of birth. All terms are for six years and expire in January. Mailing address of Senators: The Senate, Washington, D.C. 20510.

ALABAMA
1979-91 Howell T. Heflin (D) (1921)
1981-87 Jeremiah A. Denton, Jr. (R) (1924)
ALASKA
1968-91 Ted Stevens (R) (1923)
1981-87 Frank H. Murkowski (R) (1933)
ARIZONA
1969-87 Barry Goldwater (R) (1909)
1977-89 Dennis DeConcini (D) (1937)
ARKANSAS
1975-87 Dale Bumpers (D) (1925)
1979-91 David H. Pryor (D) (1934)
CALIFORNIA
1969-87 Alan Cranston (D) (1914)
1983-89 Pete Wilson (R) (1933)
COLORADO
1975-87 Gary Hart (D) (1937)
1979-91 William L. Armstrong (R) (1937)
CONNECTICUT
1971-89 Lowell P. Weicker, Jr. (R) (1931)
1981-87 Christopher Dodd (D) (1944)
DELAWARE
1971-89 William V. Roth (R) (1921)
1973-91 Joseph R. Biden, Jr. (D) (1942)
FLORIDA
1971-89 Lawton Chiles (D) (1930)
1981-87 Paula Hawkins (R) (1927)
GEORGIA
1973-91 Sam Nunn (D) (1938)
1981-87 Mack Mattingly (R) (1931)
HAWAII
1963-87 Daniel K. Inouye (D) (1924)
1977-89 Spark M. Matsunaga (D) (1916)
IDAHO
1973-91 James A. McClure (R) (1924)
1981-87 Steven D. Symms (R) (1938)
ILLINOIS
1981-87 Alan J. Dixon (D) (1927)
1985-91 Paul Simon (D) (1929)
INDIANA
1977-89 Richard G. Lugar (R) (1932)
1981-87 Dan Quayle (R) (1947)
IOWA
1981-87 Charles E. Grassley (R) (1933)
1985-91 Tom Harkin (D) (1939)
KANSAS
1969-87 Robert J. Dole (R) (1923)
1979-91 Nancy Landon Kassebaum (R) (1932)
KENTUCKY
1975-87 Wendell H. Ford (D) (1924)
1985-91 Mitch McConnell (R) (1942)
LOUISIANA
1948-87 Russell B. Long (D) (1918)
1973-91 J. Bennett Johnston (D) (1932)
MAINE
1979-91 William S. Cohen (R) (1940)
1980-89 George J. Mitchell (D) (1933)
MARYLAND
1969-87 Charles McC. Mathias, Jr. (R) (1922)
1977-89 Paul S. Sarbanes (D) (1933)
MASSACHUSETTS
1962-89 Edward M. Kennedy (D) (1932)
1985-91 John F. Kerry (D) (1944)
MICHIGAN
1977-89 Donald W. Riegle, Jr. (D) (1938
1979-91 Carl Levin (D) (1934)
MINNESOTA
1978-89 David F. Durenberger (R) (1943)
1979-91 Rudy Boschwitz (R) (1930)
MISSISSIPPI
1947-87 John C. Stennis (D) (1901)
1978-91 Thad Cochran (R) (1937)
MISSOURI
1968-87 Thomas F. Eagleton (D) (1929)
1977-89 John C. Danforth (R) (1936)
MONTANA
1977-89 John Melcher (D) (1924)
1979-91 Max Baucus (D) (1941)
NEBRASKA
1977-89 Edward Zorinsky (D) (1928)
1979-91 J. James Exon (D) (1921)
NEVADA
1975-87 Paul Laxalt (R) (1922)
1983-89 Chic Hecht (R) (1928)
NEW HAMPSHIRE
1979-91 Gordon J. Humphrey (R) (1940)
1981-87 Warren Rudman (R) (1930)
NEW JERSEY
1979-91 Bill Bradley (D) (1943)
1983-89 Frank R. Lautenberg (D) (1924)
NEW MEXICO
1973-91 Pete V. Domenici (R) (1932)
1983-89 Jeff Bingaman (D) (1943)
NEW YORK
1977-89 Daniel P. Monynihan (D) (1927)
1981-87 Alfonse M. D'Amato (R) (1937)
NORTH CAROLINA
1973-91 Jesse Helms (R) (1921)
1981-87 John P. East (R) (1931)
NORTH DAKOTA
1960-89 Quentin N. Burdick (D) (1908)
1981-87 Mark Andrews (R) (1926)
OHIO
1975-87 John H. Glenn, Jr. (D) (1921)
1977-89 Howard M. Metzenbaum (D) (1917)
OKLAHOMA
1979-91 David L. Boren (D) (1941)
1981-87 Don Nickles (R) (1948)
OREGON
1967-91 Mark O. Hatfield (R) (1922)
1969-87 Bob Packwood (R) (1932)
PENNSYLVANIA
1977-89 John Heina (R) (1938)
1981-87 Arlen Specter (R) (1930)
RHODE ISLAND
1961-91 Claiborne Pell (D) (1918)
1977-89 John H. Chafee (R) (1922)
SOUTH CAROLINA
1956-91 Strom Thurmond (R) (1902)
1966-87 Ernest F. Hollings (D) (1922)
SOUTH DAKOTA
1979-91 Larry Pressler (R) (1942)
1981-87 James Abdnor (R) (1923)
TENNESSEE
1977-89 James R. Sasser (D) (1936)
1985-91 Albert Gore, Jr. (D) (1948)
TEXAS
1971-89 Lloyd M. Bentsen (D) (1921)
1985-91 Phil Gramm (R) (1942)
UTAH
1975-87 E. J. (Jake) Garn (R) (1932)
1977-89 Orrin G. Hatch (R) (1934)

VERMONT
1971-89 Robert T. Stafford (R) (1913)
1975-87 Patrick J. Leahy (D) (1940)
VIRGINIA
1979-91 John W. Warner (R) (1927)
1983-89 Paul S. Trible, Jr. (D) (1946)
WASHINGTON
1953-89 Henry M. Jackson (D) (1912)
1981-87 Slade Gorton (R) (1928)

WEST VIRGINIA
1959-89 Robert C. Byrd (D) (1918)
1985-91 John D. (Jay) Rockefeller IV (D) (1937)
WISCONSIN
1957-89 William Proxmire (D) (1915)
1981-87 Robert W. Kasten, Jr. (R) (1942)
WYOMING
1977-89 Malcolm Wallop (R) (1933)
1979-91 Alan K. Simpson (R) (1931)

The House of Representatives

Unofficial results as of 2:57 P.M., Nov. 7, 1984. Source: News Election Service, New York, N.Y.

The numerals indicate the Congressional Districts of the states; the designation AL means At-Large. All terms end January 1987. Mailing address of Representatives: House of Representatives, Washington, D.C. 20515

ALABAMA
(7 Representatives)
1. H.L. (Sonny) Callahan (R)
2. William L. Dickinson (R)
3. William Nichols (D)
4. Thomas Bevill (D)
5. Ronald G. Flippo (D)
6. Ben Erdreich (D)
7. Richard C. Shelby (D)

ALASKA
(1 Representative)
AL Don Young (R)

ARIZONA
(5 Representatives)
1. John McCain (R)
2. Morris K. Udall (D)
3. Bob Stump (R)
4. Eldon Rudd (R)
5. Jim Kolbe (R)

ARKANSAS
(4 Representatives)
1. Bill Alexander (D)
2. Tommy Robinson (D)
3. John Paul Hammerschmidt (R)
4. Beryl Anthony, Jr. (D)

CALIFORNIA
(45 Representatives)
1. Douglas H. Bosco (D)
2. Gene Chappie (R)
3. Robert T. Matsui (D)
4. Vic Fazio (D)
5. Sala Burton (D)
6. Barbara Boxer (D)
7. George Miller (D)
8. Ronald V. Dellums (D)
9. Fortney H. (Pete) Stark (D)
10. Don Edwards (D)
11. Tom Lantos (D)
12. Ed Zschau (R)
13. Norman Y. Mineta (D)
14. Norman D. Shumway (R)
15. Tony Coelho (D)
16. Leon E. Panetta (D)
17. Charles Pashayan (R)
18. Richard H. Lehman (D)
19. Robert J. Lagomarsino (R)
20. William M. Thomas (R)
21. Bobbi Fiedler (R)
22. Carlos J. Moorhead (R)
23. Anthony C. Beilenson (D)
24. Henry A. Waxman (D)
25. Edward R. Roybal (D)
26. Howard L. Berman (D)
27. Mel Levine (D)
28. Julian C. Dixon (D)
29. Augustus F. Hawkins (D)
30. Matthew G. Martinez (D)
31. Mervyn M. Dymally (D)
32. Glenn M. Anderson (D)
33. David Dreier (R)
34. Esteban Edward Torres (D)
35. Jerry Lewis (R)
36. George E. Brown, Jr. (D)
37. Al McCandless (R)
38. Robert K. Dornan (R)
39. William E. Dannemeyer (R)
40. Robert E. Badham (R)
41. William Lowery (R)
42. Dan E. Lungren (R)
43. Ron Packard (R)
44. James Bates (D)
45. Duncan L. Hunter (R)

COLORADO
(6 Representatives)
1. Patricia Schroeder (D)
2. Timothy E. Wirth (D)
3. Michael L. Strang (R)
4. Hank Brown (R)
5. Kenneth B. Kramer (R)
6. Daniel L. Schaefer (R)

CONNECTICUT
(6 Representatives)
1. Barbara B. Kennelly (D)
2. Sam Gejdenson (D)
3. Bruce A. Morrison (D)
4. Steward B. McKinney (R)
5. John G. Rowland (R)
6. Nancy L. Johnson (R)

DELAWARE
(1 Representative)
AL Thomas R. Carper (D)

FLORIDA
(19 Representatives)
1. Earl D. Hutto (D)
2. Don Fuqua (D)
3. Charles E. Bennett (D)
4. William V. Chappell, Jr. (D)
5. Bill McCollum (R)
6. Kenneth H. MacKay (D)
7. Sam M. Gibbons (D)
8. C.W. Bill Young (R)
9. Michael Bilirakis (R)
10. Andy Ireland (R)
11. Bill Nelson (D)
12. Tom Lewis (R)
13. Connie Mack (R)
14. Daniel A. Mica (D)
15. E. Clay Shaw, Jr. (R)
16. Larry Smith (D)
17. William Lehman (D)
18. Claude D. Pepper (D)
19. Dante B. Fascell (D)

GEORGIA
(10 Representatives)
1. Lindsay Thomas (D)
2. Charles F. Hatcher (D)
3. Richard Ray (D)
4. Patrick Lynn Swindall (R)
5. Wyche Fowler, Jr. (D)
6. Newt Gingrich (R)
7. George (Buddy) Darden (D)
8. J. Roy Rowland (D)
9. Edgar L. Jenkins (D)
10. Doug Barnard, Jr. (D)

HAWAII
(2 Representatives)
1. Cecil Heftel (D)
2. Daniel K. Akaka (D)

IDAHO
(2 Representatives)
1. Larry E. Craig (R)
2. Richard Stallings (D)

ILLINOIS
(22 Representatives)
1. Charles A. Hayes (D)
2. Gus Savage (D)
3. Marty Russo (D)
4. George M. O'Brien (R)
5. William O. Lipinski (D)
6. Henry J. Hyde (R)
7. Cardiss Collins (D)
8. Dan Rostenkowski (D)
9. Sidney R. Yates (D)
10. John Edward Porter (R)
11. Frank Annunzio (D)
12. Philip M. Crane (R)
13. Harris W. Fawell (R)
14. John E. Grotberg (R)
15. Edward R. Madigan (R)
16. Lynn Martin (R)
17. Lane Evans (D)
18. Robert H. Michel (R)
19. Terry L. Bruce (D)
20. Richard Durbin (D)
21. Melvin Price (D)
22. Kenneth J. Gray (D)

INDIANA
(10 Representatives)
1. Peter Visclosky (D)
2. Philip R. Sharp (D)
3. John Hiler (R)
4. Daniel Coats (R)
5. Elwood Hillis (R)
6. Daniel L. Burton (R)
7. John T. Meyers (R)
8. Richard D. McIntyre (R)
9. Lee H. Hamilton (D)
10. Andrew Jacobs, Jr. (D)

IOWA
(6 Representatives)
1. Jim Leach (R)
2. Thomas J. Tauke (R)
3. Cooper Evans (R)
4. Neal Smith (D)
5. Jim Ross Lightfoot (R)
6. Berkley Bedell (D)

KANSAS
(5 Representatives)
1. Pat Roberts (R)

2. James Slattery (D)
3. Jan Meyers (R)
4. Dan Glickman (D)
5. Bob Whittaker (R)

KENTUCKY
(7 Representatives)
1. Carroll Hubbard, Jr. (D)
2. William H. Natcher (D)
3. Romano L. Mazzoli (D)
4. Gene Snyder (R)
5. Harold Rogers (R)
6. Larry J. Hopkins (R)
7. Carl C. (Chris) Perkins (D)

LOUISANA
(8 Representatives)
1. Robert L. Livingston, Jr. (R)
2. Corrine C. (Lindy) Boggs (D)
3. W.J. (Billy) Tauzin (D)
4. Buddy Roemer (D)
5. Thomas J. Huckaby (D)
6. W. Henson Moore (R)
7. John B. Breaux (D)
8. Gillis W. Long (D)

MAINE
(2 Representatives)
1. John R. McKernan, Jr. (R)
2. Olympia J. Snowe (R)

MARYLAND
(8 Representatives)
1. Roy Dyson (D)
2. Helen Delich Bentley (R)
3. Barbara A. Mikulski (D)
4. Marjorie S. Holt (R)
5. Steny H. Hoyer (D)
6. Beverly B. Byron (D)
7. Parren J. Mitchell (D)
8. Michael D. Barnes (D)

MASSACHUSETTS
(11 Representatives)
1. Silvio O. Conte (R)
2. Edward P. Boland (D)
3. Joseph D. Early (D)
4. Barney Frank (D)
5. Chester G. Atkins (D)
6. Nicholas Mavroules (D)
7. Edward J. Markey (D)
8. Thomas P. O'Neill, Jr. (D)
9. John J. Moakley (D)
10. Gerry E. Studds (D)
11. Brian J. Donnelly (D)

MICHIGAN
(18 Representatives)
1. John Conyers, Jr. (D)
2. Carl D. Pursell (R)
3. Howard Wolpe (D)
4. Mark D. Siljander (R)
5. Paul B. Henry (R)
6. Bob Carr (D)
7. Dale E. Kildee (D)
8. Bob Traxler (D)
9. Guy Vander Jagt (R)
10. Bill Schuette (R)
11. Robert W. Davis (R)
12. David E. Bonior (D)
13. George W. Crockett, Jr. (D)
14. Dennis M. Hertel (D)
15. William D. Ford (D)
16. John D. Dingell (D)
17. Sander M. Levin (D)
18. William S. Broomfield (R)

MINNESOTA
(8 Representatives)
1. Timothy J. Penny (D)
2. Vin Weber (R)
3. Bill Frenzel (R)
4. Bruce F. Vento (D)
5. Martin Olav Sabo (D)
6. Gerry Sikorski (D)
7. Arlan Strangeland (R)
8. James L. Oberstar (D)

MISSISSIPPI
(5 Representatives)
1. Jamie L. Whitten (D)
2. Webb Franklin (R)
3. G.V. (Sonny) Montgomery (D)
4. Wayne Dowdy (D)
5. Trent Lott (R)

MISSOURI
(9 Representatives)
1. William L. Clay (D)
2. Robert A. Young (D)
3. Richard A. Gephardt (D)
4. Ike Skelton (D)
5. Alan Wheat (D)
6. E. Thomas Coleman (R)
7. Gene Taylor (R)
8. William Emerson (R)
9. Harold L. Volkmer (D)

MONTANA
(2 Representatives)
1. Pat Williams (D)
2. Ron Marlenee (R)

NEBRASKA
(3 Representatives)
1. Douglas K. Bereuter (R)
2. Hal Daub (R)
3. Tom Vickers (D)

NEVADA
(2 Representatives)
1. Harry Reid (D)
2. Barbara F. Vucanovich (R)

NEW HAMPSHIRE
(2 Representatives)
1. Robert C. Smith (R)
2. Judd Gregg (R)

NEW JERSEY
(14 Representatives)
1. James J. Florio (D)
2. William J. Hughes (D)
3. James J. Howard (D)
4. Christopher H. Smith (R)
5. Marge Roukema (R)
6. Bernard J. Dwyer (D)
7. Matthew J. Rinaldo (R)
8. Robert A. Roe (D)
9. Robert G. Torricelli (D)
10. Peter W. Rodino, Jr. (D)
11. Dean A. Gallo (R)
12. Jim Courter (R)
13. H. James Saxton (R)
14. Frank J. Guarini (D)

NEW MEXICO
(3 Representatives)
1. Manuel Lujan, Jr. (R)
2. Joseph R. Skeen (R)
3. William Richardson (D)

NEW YORK
(34 Representatives)
1. William Carney (R)
2. Thomas J. Downey (D)
3. Robert J. Mrazek (D)
4. Norman F. Lent (R)
5. Raymond J. McGrath (R)
6. Joseph P. Addabbo (D)
7. Gary L. Ackerman (D)
8. James H. Scheuer (D)
9. Thomas J. Manton (D)
10. Charles E. Schumer (D)
11. Edolphus Towns (D)
12. Major R. Owens (D)
13. Stephen J. Solarz (D)
14. Guy V. Molinari (R)
15. Bill Green (R)
16. Charles B. Rangel (D)
17. Ted Weiss (D)
18. Robert Garcia (D)
19. Mario Biaggi (D)
20. Joseph D. DioGuardi (R)
21. Hamilton Fish, Jr. (R)
22. Benjamin A. Gilman (R)
23. Samuel S. Stratton (D)
24. Gerald B.H. Solomon (R)
25. Sherwood Boehlert (R)
26. David O'B. Martin (R)
27. George C. Wortley (R)
28. Matthew F. McHugh (D)
29. Frank Horton (R)
30. Fred J. Eckert (R)
31. Jack F. Kemp (R)
32. John J. LaFalce (D)
33. Henry J. Nowak (D)
34. Stan Lundine (D)

NORTH CAROLINA
(11 Representatives)
1. Walter B. Jones (D)
2. Tim Valentine (D)
3. Charles Whitley (D)
4. William Cobey, Jr. (R)
5. Stephen L. Neal (D)
6. Howard Coble (R)
7. Charlie Rose (D)
8. W.G. (Bill) Hefner (D)
9. J. Alex McMillan (R)
10. James T. Broyhill (R)
11. Bill Hendon (R)

NORTH DAKOTA
(1 Representative)
AL Byron L. Dorgan (D)

OHIO
(21 Representatives)
1. Thomas A. Luken (D)
2. Willis D. Gradison, Jr. (R)
3. Tony P. Hall (D)
4. Michael G. Oxley (R)
5. Delbert L. Latta (R)
6. Bob McEwen (R)
7. Michael DeWine (R)
8. Thomas N. Kindness (R)
9. Marcy Kaptur (D)
10. Clarence E. Miller (R)
11. Dennis E. Eckart (D)
12. John R. Kasich (R)
13. Don J. Pease (D)
14. John F. Seiberling (D)
15. Chalmers P. Wylie (R)
16. Ralph Regula (R)
17. James A. Traficant, Jr. (D)
18. Douglas Applegate (D)
19. Edward F. Feighan (D)
20. Mary Rose Oakar (D)
21. Louis Stokes (D)

OKLAHOMA
(6 Representatives)
1. James R. Jones (D)
2. Mike Synar (D)
3. Wesley W. Watkins (D)
4. Dave McCurdy (D)
5. Mickey Edwards (R)
6. Glenn English (D)

OREGON
(5 Representatives)
1. Les AuCoin (D)
2. Robert F. Smith (R)
3. Ronald L. Wyden (D)
4. James Weaver (D)
5. Denny Smith (R)

PENNSYLVANIA
(23 Representatives)
1. Thomas M. Foglietta (D)
2. William H. Gray III (D)
3. Robert A. Borski (D)
4. Joseph P. Kolter (D)
5. Richard T. Schulze (R)

6. Gus Yatron (D)
7. Bob Edgar (D)
8. Peter H. Kostmayer (D)
9. Bud Shuster (R)
10. Joseph M. McDade (R)
11. Paul E. Kanjorski (D)
12. John P. Murtha (D)
13. Lawrence Coughlin (R)
14. William J. Coyne (D)
15. Don Ritter (R)
16. Robert S. Walker (R)
17. George W. Gekas (R)
18. Doug Walgren (D)
19. William F. Goodling (R)
20. Joseph M. Gaydos (D)
21. Tom Ridge (R)
22. Austin J. Murphy (D)
23. Bill Clinger (R)

RHODE ISLAND
(2 Representatives)
1. Fernand J. St. Germain (D)
2. Claudine Schneider (R)

SOUTH CAROLINA
(6 Representatives)
1. Thomas F. Hartnett (R)
2. Floyd Spence (R)
3. Butler Derrick (D)
4. Carroll A. Campbell, Jr. (R)
5. John M. Spratt, Jr. (D)
6. Robin Tallon (D)

SOUTH DAKOTA
(1 Representative)
AL Thomas A. Daschle (D)

TENNESSEE
(9 Representatives)
1. James H. Quillen (R)
2. John J. Duncan (R)
3. Marilyn Lloyd (D)
4. James Cooper (D)
5. William H. Boner (D)
6. Bart Gordon (D)
7. Don Sundquist (R)
8. Ed Jones (D)
9. Harold E. Ford (D)

TEXAS
(27 Representatives)
1. Sam B. Hall (D)
2. Charles Wilson (D)
3. Steven Bartlett (R)
4. Ralph M. Hall (D)
5. John Bryant (D)
6. Joe Barton (R)
7. Bill Archer (R)
8. Jack Fields (R)
9. Jack Brooks (D)
10. J.J. Pickle (D)
11. Marvin Leath (D)
12. Jim Wright (D)
13. Beau Boulter (R)
14. Mac Sweeney (R)
15. E. (Kika) de la Garza (D)
16. Ronald Coleman (D)
17. Charles W. Stenholm (D)
18. George T. (Mickey) Leland (D)
19. Larry Combest (R)
20. Henry B. Gonzalez (D)
21. Tom Loeffler (R)
22. Tom DeLay (R)
23. Albert G. Bustamante (D)
24. Martin Frost (D)
25. Michael A. Andrews (D)
26. Richard Armey (R)
27. Solomon P. Ortiz (D)

UTAH
(3 Representatives)
1. James V. Hansen (R)
2. David S. Monson (R)
3. Howard C. Nielson (R)

VERMONT
(1 Representative)
AL James M. Jeffords (R)

VIRGINIA
(10 Representatives)
1. Herbert H. Bateman (R)
2. G. Williams Whitehurst (R)
3. Thomas J. Bliley, Jr. (R)
4. Norman Sisisky (D)
5. Dan Daniel (D)
6. James R. Olin (D)
7. French Slaughter (R)
8. Stan Parris (R)
9. Frederick C. Boucher (D)
10. Frank R. Wolf (R)

WASHINGTON
(8 Representatives)
1. John Miller (R)
2. Al Swift (D)
3. Don L. Bonker (D)
4. Sid W. Morrison (R)
5. Thomas S. Foley (D)
6. Norman D. Dicks (D)
7. Mike Lowry (D)
8. Rodney Chandler (R)

WEST VIRGINIA
(4 Representatives)
1. Alan B. Mollohan (D)
2. Hartley O. Staggers, Jr. (D)
3. Robert Wise (D)
4. Nick J. Rahall II (D)

WISCONSIN
(9 Representatives)
1. Les Aspin (D)
2. Robert W. Kastenmeier (D)
3. Steve Gunderson (R)
4. Gerald D. Kleczka (D)
5. James Moody (D)
6. Thomas E. Petri (R)
7. David P. Obey (D)
8. Toby Roth (R)
9. F. James Sensenbrenner, Jr. (R)

WYOMING
(1 Representative)
AL Dick Cheney (R)

The Governors of the Fifty States

State	Governor	Year of birth	Current term[1]	State	Governor	Year of birth	Current term[1]
Ala.	George C. Wallace, D	1919	1983-87	Mont.	Ted Schwinden, D	1925	1985-89
Alaska	William Sheffield, D	1928	1982-86[2]	Neb.	Robert Kerrey, D	1943	1983-87
Ariz.	Bruce E. Babbitt, D	1938	1983-87	Nev.	Richard H. Byran, D	1937	1983-87
Ark.	Bill Clinton, D	1946	1985-87	N.H.	John H. Sununu, R	1939	1985-89
Calif.	George Deukmejian, R	1928	1983-87	N.J.	Thomas H. Kean, R	1935	1982-86
Colo.	Richard D. Lamm, D	1935	1983-87	N.M.	Toney Anaya, D	1941	1983-87
Conn.	William A. O'Neill, D	1930	1983-87	N.Y.	Mario M. Cuomo, D	1932	1983-87
Del.	Michael N. Castle, R	1940	1985-89	N.C.	James G. Martin, R	1936	1985-89
Fla.	Robert Graham, D	1936	1983-87	N.D.	George Sinner, D	1928	1985-89
Ga.	Joe Frank Harris, D	1936	1983-87	Ohio	Richard F. Celeste, D	1937	1985-87
Hawaii	George R. Ariyoshi, D	1926	1982-86[2]	Okla.	George P. Nigh, D	1927	1983-87
Idaho	John V. Evans, D	1925	1983-87	Ore.	Victor G. Atiyeh, R	1923	1983-87
Ill.	James R. Thompson, R	1936	1983-87	Pa.	Richard L. Thornburg, R	1932	1983-87
Ind.	Robert D. Orr, R	1917	1985-89	R.I.	Edward D. DiPrete, R	1935	1985-87
Iowa	Terry E. Branstad, R	1946	1983-87	S.C.	Richard W. Riley, D	1933	1983-87
Kan.	John W. Carlin, D	1940	1983-87	S.D.	William J. Janklow, R	1939	1983-87
Ky.	Martha Layne Collins, D	1936	1983-87[2]	Tenn.	Lamar Alexander, R	1940	1983-87
La.	Edwin W. Edwards, D	1927	1984-86[3]	Tex.	Mark W. White, Jr., D	1940	1983-87
Me.	Joseph E. Brennen, D	1934	1983-87	Utah	Norman H. Bangerter, R	1933	1985-89
Md.	Harry R. Hughes, D	1926	1983-87	Vt.	Madeline M. Kunin, D	1933	1985-89
Mass.	Michael S. Dukakis, D	1934	1983-87	Va.	Charles S. Robb, D	1939	1982-86
Mich.	James J. Blanchard, D	1942	1983-87	Wash.	Booth Gardner, D	1939	1985-89
Minn.	Rudy Pepich, D	1929	1983-87	W.Va.	Arch A. Moore, Jr., R	1923	1985-89
Miss.	Bill Allain, D		1984-88	Wis.	Anthony S. Earl, D	1936	1983-87
Mo.	John Ashcroft, R	1942	1985-89	Wyo.	Ed. C. Herschler, D	1918	1983-87

1. Except where indicated, all terms begin in January. 2. December. 3. March.

Presidential Election of 1984

Principal Candidates for President and Vice President
Republican: Ronald W. Reagan; George Bush
Democratic: Walter F. Mondale; Geraldine A. Ferraro

	Ronald W. Reagan			Walter F. Mondale		
State	**Popular Vote**	**%**	**Electoral Vote**	**Popular Vote**	**%**	**Electoral Vote**
Alabama	851,609	60	9	545,925	39	–
Alaska	115,390	67	3	51,169	30	–
Arizona	676,524	66	7	330,771	33	–
Arkansas	529,756	61	6	336,406	39	–
California	5,305,434	58	47	3,815,992	42	–
Colorado	768,711	63	8	434,560	36	–
Connecticut	883,461	61	8	561,387	39	–
Delaware	151,494	60	3	100,632	40	–
D.C.	26,803	13	–	172,459	87	3
Florida	2,582,980	65	21	1,397,097	35	–
Georgia	1,060,680	60	12	701,605	40	–
Hawaii	185,050	55	4	146,654	44	–
Idaho	296,687	73	4	108,447	26	–
Illinois	2,687,112	57	24	2,066,580	43	–
Indiana	1,332,681	61	12	814,659	38	–
Iowa	700,779	54	8	603,810	46	–
Kansas	675,366	67	7	332,476	33	–
Kentucky	816,580	60	9	535,559	40	–
Louisiana	1,030,091	61	10	648,040	39	–
Maine	336,113	61	4	212,190	39	–
Maryland	836,395	52	10	759,205	48	–
Massachusetts	1,297,737	51	13	1,226,490	49	–
Michigan	2,247,058	59	20	1,528,558	41	–
Minnesota	1,024,631	50	–	1,039,904	50	10
Mississippi	585,052	62	7	351,677	38	–
Missouri	1,268,408	60	11	838,599	40	–
Montana	214,269	61	4	135,071	38	–
Nebraska	447,810	71	5	184,058	29	–
Nevada	188,794	67	4	91,654	32	–
New Hampshire	255,140	69	4	116,284	31	–
New Jersey	1,914,942	60	16	1,255,115	40	–
New Mexico	304,323	60	5	200,703	39	–
New York	3,553,762	54	36	3,021,719	46	–
North Carolina	1,340,274	62	13	821,364	38	–
North Dakota	199,352	66	3	103,957	34	–
Ohio	2,655,395	59	23	1,805,845	41	–
Oklahoma	861,757	68	8	384,918	31	–
Oregon	639,755	56	7	508,516	44	–
Pennsylvania	2,572,472	54	25	2,213,429	46	–
Rhode Island	204,450	52	4	191,914	48	–
South Carolina	561,963	64	8	316,746	36	–
South Dakota	198,119	63	3	114,967	37	–
Tennessee	1,002,722	59	11	705,820	41	–
Texas	3,351,589	64	29	1,897,190	36	–
Utah	467,214	75	5	155,098	25	–
Vermont	134,252	58	3	94,518	41	–
Virginia	1,338,378	63	12	798,553	37	–
Washington	945,052	56	10	736,260	44	–
West Virginia	400,261	55	6	324,073	45	–
Wisconsin	1,198,379	55	11	992,807	45	–
Wyoming	132,073	71	3	53,272	28	–
Total	**53,355,081**	**59**	**525**	**36,884,702**	**41**	**13**

Note: Unofficial results as of 2:57 p.m., Nov. 7, 1984. Source: News Election Service, New York, N.Y.

Senate and House Standing Committees, 98th Congress

Committees of the Senate

Agriculture, Nutrition, and Forestry (18 members)
Chairman: Jesse Helms (N.C.)
Ranking Dem.: Walter D. Huddleston (Ky.)
Appropriations (29 members)
Chairman: Mark O. Hatfield (Ore.)
Ranking Dem.: William Proxmire (Wis.)
Armed Services (18 members)
Chairman: John Tower (Tex.)
Ranking Dem.: Henry M. Jackson (Miss.)
Banking, Housing, and Urban Affairs (18 members)
Chairman: E.J. (Jake) Garn (Utah)
Ranking Dem.: William Proxmire (Wis.)
Budget (22 members)
Chairman: Pete V. Domenici (N.M.)
Ranking Dem.: Lawton Chiles (Fla.)
Commerce, Science, and Transportation (17 members)
Chairman: Bob Packwood (Ore.)
Ranking Dem.: Ernest F. Hollings (S.C.)
Energy and Natural Resources (20 members)
Chairman: James A. McClure (Idaho)
Ranking Dem.: J. Bennett Johnston (La.)
Environment and Public Works (16 members)
Chairman: Robert T. Stafford (Vt.)
Ranking Dem.: Jennings Randolph (W.Va.)
Finance (20 members)
Chairman: Robert J. Dole (Kan.)
Ranking Dem.: Russell B. Long (La.)
Foreign Relations (17 members)
Chairman: Charles H. Percy (Ill.)
Ranking Dem.: Claiborne Pell (R.I.)
Governmental Affairs (18 members)
Chairman: William V. Roth, Jr. (Del.)
Ranking Dem.: Thomas F. Eagleton (Mo.)
Judiciary (18 members)
Chairman: Strom Thurmond (S.C.)
Ranking Dem.: Joseph R. Biden, Jr. (Del.)
Labor and Human Resources (18 members)
Chairman: Orrin G. Hatch (Utah)
Ranking Dem.: Edward M. Kennedy (Mass.)
Rules and Administration (12 members)
Chairman: Charles McC. Mathias, Jr. (Md.)
Ranking Dem.: Wendell H. Ford (Ky.)
Small Business (19 members)
Chairman: Lowell P. Weicker, Jr. (Conn.)
Ranking Dem.: Sam Nunn (Ga.)
Veterans' Affairs (12 members)
Chairman: Alan K. Simpson (Wyo.)
Ranking Dem.: Alan Cranston (Calif.)

Select and Special Committees

Aging (15 members)
Chairman: John Heinz (Pa.)
Ranking Dem.: Lawton Chiles (Fla.)
Ethics (6 members)
Chairman: Ted Stevens (Alas.)
Vice Chairman: Howell T. Heflin (Ala.)
Indian Affairs (7 members)
Chairman: Mark Andrews (N.D.)
Ranking Dem.: John Melcher (Mont.)
Intelligence (15 members)
Chairman: Barry Goldwater (Ariz.)
Vice Chairman: Daniel Patrick Moynihan (N.Y.)

Committees of the House

Agriculture (41 members)
Chairman: E. (Kika) de la Garza (Tex.)
Ranking Repub.: Edward R. Madigan (Ill.)
Appropriations (57 members)
Chairman: Jamie L. Whitten (Miss.)
Ranking Repub.: Silvio O. Conte (Mass.)
Armed Services (45 members)
Chairman: Melvin Price (Ill.)
Ranking Repub.: William L. Dickinson (Ala.)
Banking, Finance, and Urban Affairs (47 members)
Chairman: Fernand J. St. Germain (R.I.)
Ranking Repub.: Chalmers P. Wylie (Ohio)
Budget (31 members)
Chairman: James R. Jones (Okla.)
Ranking Repub.: Delbert L. Latta (Ohio)
District of Columbia (12 members)
Chairman: Ronald V. Dellums (Calif.)
Ranking Repub.: Stewart B. McKinney (Conn.)
Education and Labor (30 members)
Chairman: Carl D. Perkins (Ky.)
Ranking Repub.: John N. Erienborn (Ill)
Energy and Commerce (42 members)
Chairman: John D. Dingell (Mich.)
Ranking Repub.: James T. Broyhill (N.C.)
Foreign Affairs (37 members)
Chairman: Clement J. Zablocki (Wis.)
Ranking Repub.: William S. Broomfield (Mich.)
Government Operations (38 members)
Chairman: Jack Brooks (Tex.)
Ranking Repub.: Frank Horton (N.Y.)
House Administration (19 members)
Chairman: Augustus F. Hawkins (Calif.)
Ranking Repub.: Bill Frenzel (Minn.)
Interior and Insular Affairs (42 members)
Chairman: Morris K. Udall (Ariz.)
Ranking Repub.: Manuel Lujan, Jr. (N.M.)
Judiciary (31 members)
Chairman: Peter W. Rodino, Jr. (N.J.)
Ranking Repub.: Hamilton Fish, Jr. (N.Y.)
Merchant Marine and Fisheries (40 members)
Chairman: Walter B. Jones (N.C.)
Ranking Repub.: Edwin B. Forsythe (N.J.)
Post Office and Civil Service (24 members)
Chairman: William D. Ford (Mich.)
Ranking Repub.: Gene Taylor (Miss.)
Public Works and Transportation (50 members)
Chairman: James J. Howard (N.J.)
Ranking Repub.: Gene Snyder (Ky.)
Rules (13 members)
Chairman: Claude Pepper (Fla.)
Ranking Repub.: James H. Quillen (Tenn.)
Science and Technology (41 members)
Chairman: Don Fuqua (Fla.)
Ranking Repub.: Larry Winn, Jr. (Kan.)
Small Business (40 members)
Chairman: Parren J. Mitchell (Md.)
Ranking Repub.: Joseph M. McDade (Pa.)
Standards of Official Conduct (12 members)
Chairman: Louis Stokes (Ohio)
Ranking Repub.: Floyd D. Spence (S.C.)
Veterans' Affairs (33 members)
Chairman: G.V. (Sonny) Montgomery (Miss.)
Ranking Repub.: John P. Hammerschmidt (Ark.)
Ways and Means (35 members)
Chairman: Dan Rostenkowski (Ill.)
Ranking Repub.: Barber B. Conable, Jr. (N.Y.)

Select Committees

Aging (60 members)
Chairman: Edward Roybal (Calif.)
Ranking Repub.: Matthew J. Renaldo (N.J.)

Intelligence (16 members)
Chairman: Edward P. Boland (Mass.)
Ranking Repub.: J. Kenneth Robinson (Va.)

Narcotics Abuse and Control (25 members)
Chairman: Charles B. Rangel (N.Y.)
Ranking Repub.: Benjamin A. Gilman (N.Y.)

Speakers of the House of Representatives

Dates served	Congress	Name and state
1789–1791	1	Frederick A. C. Muhlenberg (Pa.)
1791–1793	2	Jonathan Trumbull (Conn.)
1793–1795	3	Frederick A. C. Muhlenberg (Pa.)
1795–1799	4–5	Jonathan Dayton (N.J.)[1]
1799–1801	6	Theodore Sedgwick (Mass.)
1801–1807	7–9	Nathaniel Macon (N.C.)
1807–1811	10–11	Joseph B. Varnum (Mass.)
1811–1814	12–13	Henry Clay (Ky.)[2]
1814–1815	13	Langdon Cheves (S.C.)
1815–1820	14–16	Henry Clay (Ky.)[3]
1820–1821	16	John W. Taylor (N.Y.)
1821–1823	17	Philip P. Barbour (Va.)
1823–1825	18	Henry Clay (Ky.)
1825–1827	19	John W. Taylor (N.Y.)
1827–1834	20–23	Andrew Stevenson (Va.)[4]
1834–1835	23	John Bell (Tenn.)
1835–1839	24–25	James K. Polk (Tenn.)
1839–1841	26	Robert M. T. Hunter (Va.)
1841–1843	27	John White (Ky.)
1843–1845	28	John W. Jones (Va.)
1845–1847	29	John W. Davis (Ind.)
1847–1849	30	Robert C. Winthrop (Mass.)
1849–1851	31	Howell Cobb (Ga.)
1851–1855	32–33	Linn Boyd (Ky.)
1855–1857	34	Nathaniel P. Banks (Mass.)
1857–1859	35	James L. Orr (S.C.)
1859–1861	36	Wm. Pennington (N.J.)
1861–1863	37	Galusha A. Grow (Pa.)
1863–1869	38–40	Schuyler Colfax (Ind.)
1869–1869	40	Theodore M. Pomeroy (N.Y.)[5]
1869–1875	41–43	James G. Blaine (Me.)
1875–1876	44	Michael C. Kerr (Ind.)[6]
1876–1881	44–46	Samuel J. Randall (Pa.)
1881–1883	47	J. Warren Keifer (Ohio)
1883–1889	48–50	John G. Carlisle (Ky.)
1889–1891	51	Thomas B. Reed (Me.)
1891–1895	52–53	Charles F. Crisp (Ga.)
1895–1899	54–55	Thomas B. Reed (Me.)
1899–1903	56–57	David B. Henderson (Iowa)
1903–1911	58–61	Joseph G. Cannon (Ill.)
1911–1919	62–65	Champ Clark (Mo.)
1919–1925	66–68	Frederick H. Gillett (Mass.)
1925–1931	69–71	Nicholas Longworth (Ohio)
1931–1933	72	John N. Garner (Tex.)
1933–1934	73	Henry T. Rainey (Ill.)[7]
1935–1936	74	Joseph W. Byrns (Tenn.)[8]
1936–1940	74–76	William B. Bankhead (Ala.)[9]
1940–1947	76–79	Sam Rayburn (Tex.)
1947–1949	80	Joseph W. Martin, Jr. (Mass.)
1949–1953	81–82	Sam Rayburn (Tex.)
1953–1955	83	Joseph W. Martin, Jr. (Mass.)
1955–1961	84–87	Sam Rayburn (Tex.)[10]
1962–1971	87–91	John W. McCormack (Mass.)[11]
1971–1977	92–94	Carl Albert (Okla.)[12]
1977–	95–	Thomas P. O'Neill, Jr. (Mass.)

1. George Dent (Md.) was elected Speaker pro tempore for April 20 and May 28, 1798. 2. Resigned during second session of 13th Congress. 3. Resigned between first and second sessions of 16th Congress. 4. Resigned during first session of 23rd Congress. 5. Elected Speaker and served the day of adjournment. 6. Died between first and second sessions of 44th Congress. During first session, there were two Speakers pro tempore: Samuel S. Cox (N.Y.), appointed for Feb. 17, May 12, and June 19, 1876, and Milton Sayler (Ohio), appointed for June 4, 1876. 7. Died in 1934 after adjournment of second session of 73rd Congress. 8. Died during second session of 74th Congress. 9. Died during third session of 76th Congress. 10. Died between first and second sessions of 87th Congress. 11. Not a candidate in 1970 election. 12. Not a candidate in 1976 election. *Source: Congressional Directory.*

Floor Leaders of the Senate

Democratic

Gilbert M. Hitchcock, Neb. (Min. 1919–20)
Oscar W. Underwood, Ala. (Min. 1920–23)
Joseph T. Robinson, Ark. (Min. 1923–33, Maj. 1933–37)
Alben W. Barkley, Ky. (Maj. 1937–46, Min. 1947–48)
Scott W. Lucas, Ill. (Maj. 1949–50)
Ernest W. McFarland, Ariz. (Maj. 1951–52)
Lyndon B. Johnson, Tex. (Min. 1953–54, Maj. 1955–60)
Mike Mansfield, Mont. (Maj. 1961–77)
Robert C. Byrd, W. Va. (Maj. 1977–81, Min. 1981–)

Republican

Charles Curtis, Kan. (Maj. 1925–29)
James E. Watson, Ind. (Maj. 1929–33)
Charles L. McNary, Ore. (Min. 1933–44)
Wallace H. White, Jr., Me. (Min. 1944–47, Maj. 1947–48)
Kenneth S. Wherry, Neb. (Min. 1949–51)
Styles Bridges, N. H. (Min. 1951–52)
Robert A. Taft, Ohio (Maj. 1953)
William F. Knowland, Calif. (Maj. 1953–54, Min. 1955–58)
Everett M. Dirksen, Ill. (Min. 1959–69)
Hugh Scott, Pa. (Min. 1969–1977)
Howard H. Baker, Jr., Tenn. (Min. 1977–81, Maj. 1981–)

NOTE: Min. = Minority Leader; Maj. = Majority Leader. *Source:* United States Senate, Secretary for the Majority.

Plurality and Majority

In order to win a plurality, a candidate must receive a greater number of votes than anyone running against him. If he receives 50 votes, for example, and two other candidates receive 49 and 2, he will have a plurality of one vote over his closest opponent.

However, a candidate does not have a majority unless he receives more than 50% of the total votes cast. In the example above, the candidate does not have a majority, because his 50 votes are less than 50% of the 101 votes cast.

CURRENT EVENTS

What Happened in 1983–84

The important events of the year from September 1983 to August 1984, organized month by month, in three categories for easy reference. The Countries of the World section (starting on page 140) covers specific international events, country by country.

1983–84

SEPTEMBER 1983

International

Reagan Authorizes Aggressive Self-Defense Tactics in Lebanon (Sept. 12): The President authorizes the use of naval planes and guns if necessary to protect U.S. marines under fire at the Beirut International Airport.

2,000 More Marines Arrive in Lebanon (Sept. 12): An additional force of 2,000 Marines arrives off Lebanon to bolster the Marine's 1,400-man peacekeeping contingent in Beirut.

Soviet Union Cancels Gromyko's U.N. Trip (Sept. 17): The Soviet Government cancels plans for Foreign Minister Andrei A. Gromyko to attend 38th session of the United Nations General Assembly, claiming that the U.S. cannot guarantee his safety or properly service his special plane. It will be the first time that Gromyko will miss the meeting since he became Foreign Minister in 1957. Moscow accuses the U.S. of violating generally recognized international norms.

Syria Warns U.S. of Open Conflict in Beirut (Sept. 17): Syria warns the United States that if any shells from U.S. forces on land, sea, or in the air hit areas occupied by Syrian troops, Syria will retaliate by shelling their source.

Iraqi Leader Seeks Peace With Iran (Sept. 17): President Saddam Hussein of Iraq tells the Islamic Conference Organization's Peace Committee that Iraq wants peace and good relations with Iran. Hussein says that he would welcome any new effort by the group to end the war.

Mrs. Gandhi Says India Does Not Have Atomic Bomb (Sept. 18): Prime Minister Indira Gandhi tells attendees at the opening of the World Energy Conference in New Delhi, that India does not possess an atomic bomb and is opposed to nuclear weapons. She says that India is pursuing nuclear development for peaceful purposes.

New President of U.N. General Assembly Elected (Sept. 20): Jorge E. Illueca, the Vice President of Panama, is elected President of the U.N. General Assembly.

Andropov Appeals to Bonn to Reject U.S. Missiles (Sept. 20): Yuri V. Andropov asks West German legislators to resist the deployment of the 572 U.S. missiles scheduled to be placed in West Germany in December 1983. The Atlantic Alliance decided to deploy them in 1979 to counter Soviet SS-20 missiles aimed at Western Europe.

Seven Die in Anti-Marcos Riot in Manila (Sept. 21): About 500,000 anti-government demonstrators clash with security forces in Manila at the end of a long rally marking the 11th anniversary of martial law, and the death of Benigno S. Aquino. At least seven people are killed and more than 150 wounded. The violence is said to be the worst since Pres. Marcos took office 18 years ago.

Cease-Fire Announced in Lebanon (Sept. 25): The Syrian and Lebanese governments announce their agreement of a Saudi-Arabian-sponsored cease-fire accord. The U.S. says that it regards the agreement as a first step to bringing about a strong central government in Lebanon and the withdrawal of all Syrian, Israeli, and Palestinian forces from that country. An important point of the accord is that the cease-fire is to be supervised by neutral observers.

38 Irish Terrorists Escape Belfast Prison (Sept. 25): Thirty-eight Irish nationalists break out of Maze prison in Belfast after a gun battle and hand-to-hand combat with the guards. One guard is stabbed and five wounded. At least ten prisoners captured. The maximum security prison is supposed to be escape proof.

Pres. Reagan Addresses the U.N. on Arms Control (Sept. 26): Speaking in the opening debate of the 38th U.N. General Assembly, Pres. Reagan calls on the Soviets to reduce tensions it "heaped on the world," and offers to make concessions to achieve a nuclear weapons accord. He says that "the door to an agreement is open. It is time for the Soviet Union to walk through it." **(Sept. 28):** Yuri V. Andropov says that Pres. Reagan's new nuclear disarmament proposals are unacceptable.

Brazil to Get $11 Billion From IMF (Sept. 26): The International Monetary Fund announces that an accord was reached to provide Brazil with $11 billion in credits until the end of 1984 to help the nation close the gap in meeting its international payments.

Mitterand Rejects Soviet Arms Demand (Sept. 28): In an address to the U.N. General Assembly, Pres. François Mitterand rejects the Soviet Union's long-standing demand that French nuclear missiles be counted as part of NATO's nuclear weapons. Mitterand says that France has only 98 nuclear warheads for its national defense as compared to the 8,000 to 9,000 each possessed by the U.S. and the Soviet Union.

National

Former Governor to Fill Senator Jackson's Seat (Sept. 9): Republican Gov. John Spellman of Washington, appoints former governor Daniel J. Evans, 57, also a Republican, to temporarily fill the vacant seat of the late Senator Jackson. Mr. Evans is president of Evergreen State College in Olympia.

Chrysler Buys Back Stock Rights (Sept. 12): The Treasury

Department announces that Chrysler agreed to pay $311.1 million to the government to buy back the rights to purchase 14.4 million shares of the corporation's stock.

Congress and President Compromise on War Powers Resolution (Sept. 20): Leaders of both houses of Congress and Pres. Reagan agree on a compromise resolution that would authorize keeping the U.S. Marine peacekeeping force in Lebanon for another 18 months under the War Powers Resolution. **(Sept. 28):** The House of Representatives votes 270 to 161 to approve legislation to invoke the War Powers Act in Lebanon according to the compromise resolution. **(Sept. 29):** The Senate passes bill 54 to 46.

Watt Apologizes for Remarks About Coal Panel (Sept. 21): Interior Secretary James G. Watt apologizes for saying that he had a mixed advisory panel comprising "a black, a woman, two Jews, and a cripple," while speaking to trade association members at the U.S. Chamber of Commerce. He states that his choice of words was unfortunate. **(Oct. 9):** Watt resigns after much congressional and public reaction to his unguarded remarks.

Continental Air Lines Files for Bankruptcy (Sept. 24): Continental Air Lines files for reorganization under chapter 11 of the Federal Bankruptcy Act, suspends all domestic flights, and lays off 12,000 employees. The carrier lost $84 million in 1983, and $471.9 million since January 1979. **(Sept. 26):** Continental resumes operation to 25 U.S. cities and rehires about 4,200 of its former workers who have to take sharp cuts in salaries and benefits.

Almost 600 Banks in Trouble Over Bad Loans (Sept. 28): Federal bank regulators report that the number of banks in deep trouble because of bad loans made during the 1981–82 recession had risen to 597, the highest level ever recorded by the Federal Deposit Insurance Corporation.

Teachers Association Backs Mondale (Sept. 30): The board of directors of the National Educational Association votes 9 to 1 to support Walter Mondale in state primaries and caucuses. The NEA has a membership of 1.7 million.

General

Union Approves Chrysler Workers Pay Hike (Sept. 6): The United Automobile Workers reach a tentative contract with Chrysler Corporation giving the autoworkers a $2.42 an hour wage increase over the next two years. The agreement also restores the 3% annual wage increase and cost of living adjustments that the workers gave up as part of the terms for the federal loan guarantees to save Chrysler from bankruptcy.

Czech Family Flees to Austria in Balloon (Sept. 8): A former member of the Czechoslovakian national cycling team and his wife and two children escape at night to Drasenhofen, Austria, in a makeshift balloon sewn out of raincoats. They ask for political asylum.

South African Coal Mine Blast Kills 64 (Sept. 12): A methane gas explosion at the Hlobane coal mine in Natal Province kills 64 miners and injures four others.

First Black Woman Wins Miss America Contest (Sept. 17): Miss New York, Vanessa Williams, 20, of Millwood, N.Y., becomes the first black woman to hold the title of Miss America. A musical theater major at Syracuse University, Miss Williams wins a $25,000 scholarship and the chance to earn over $100,000 during her reign. Black leaders throughout the country praise her selection.

Japanese Car Rated Most Fuel Efficient by EPA (Sept. 17): The 1984 Honda Civic coupe is rated by the Environmental Protection Agency as the top fuel-efficient car sold domestically with an average of 51 miles per gallon of gasoline.

August Weather Broke Nation's Heat Records (Sept. 20): The National Climate Analysis Center says that August 1983 was the hottest month on record for the United States and was also one of the driest. The agency says that the heat and drought killed at least 220 people and ruined $10 billion in crops.

Dying Girl Gets Medical Treatment Over Parent's Religious Objections (Sept. 21): A state appeals court in Knoxville, Tenn., rules that Pamela Hamilton, 12, who is suffering from bone cancer, must undergo treatment to save her life despite her family's objections on religious grounds. The girl and her parents are members of the Church of God of the Union Assembly which does not believe in using medicine to heal.

NASA Selects Two Women Physicians for Space Shuttle Missions (Sept. 21): Dr. Rhea Seddon, 35, and Dr. Anna A. Fisher, 33, astronauts, are selected by NASA as the third and fourth women to fly on the space shuttle. Dr. Seddon is assigned to the June 1984 mission and Dr. Fisher to the August 1984 flight.

King Leopold of the Belgians Dies (Sept. 25): King Leopold III of the Belgians, 81, dies after an emergency heart operation at a Brussels University Hospital following a heart attack.

Australia II Wins the America Cup (Sept. 26): Australia II becomes the first challenger in 132 years to win the America's Cup by defeating Liberty by 41 seconds in the seventh and final race in Rhode Island Sound.

New Grimm Fairy Tale to be Published (Sept. 27): A story written by Wihelm Grimm for a little girl in 1816 and never published before will be published by Farrar, Straus & Giroux and illustrated by Maurice Sendak.

"A Chorus Line" sets a Theater Milestone (Sept. 29): "A Chorus Line" becomes Broadway's longest-running show with its 3,389th performance, surpassing "Grease", which had 3,388 performances.

OCTOBER 1983

International

British Labor Party Elects Youngest Leader (Oct. 2): Neil Kinnock, 41, is chosen to succeed Michael Foot as leader at the party's annual conference. Mr. Kinnock wins more than two thirds of the votes cast and would become Prime Minister in the event of a Labor victory. He is the youngest leader in the Labor party's history.

Argentine Labor Strike Disrupts Nation (Oct. 4): A 24-hour strike called by the Peronist-dominated labor federations over low wages and high inflation paralyzes the nation's businesses, industry, and public transportation. The inflation rate in Argentina was 571% in August 1983.

Lebanon Agrees to Nonaligned Countries as Truce Observers (Oct. 5): President Amin Gemayel agrees to accept observers from neutral countries to oversee the Lebanese cease-fire that began on September 25th.

British Labor Party Seeks to Give Up All Nuclear Arms (Oct. 5): The Labor Party adopts a resolution at its annual conference that states that the next Labor government will unconditionally scrap all nuclear weapon systems, including cruise, Trident, and

Polaris missiles, and remove all American nuclear bases from Britain.

Indian Government Takes Control of Punjab (Oct. 6): The Indian government imposes the President's rule on the Punjab state government and takes direct control of the state in an effort to check political and religious violence by Sikh separatists who seek greater autonomy for their homeland. The action is taken after militants killed six Hindu passengers on a bus and two officials on a train. More than 175 people have died in Punjab as a result of religious strife.

China and Soviet Union Hold Arms Talks (Oct. 6): Soviet and Chinese delegations meet in Peking for talks aimed at normalizing relations between the two countries and to discuss the reduction of Soviet troops and SS-20 nuclear missiles deployed against China along the Chinese-Soviet border.

Banks Agree to Lend Brazil an Additional $12 Billion (Oct. 6): Sixty major U.S. and European banks agree to give Brazil a five-year grace period to repay its $90 billion foreign debt. Under the agreement, Brazil will get a new $12 billion loan to be repaid over four years beginning in 1988.

Reagan Asserts Soviets Are Arming Syria With SS-21's (Oct. 8): President Reagan says the Soviet Union is preparing to supply Syria with the 75-mile range SS-21's which have been deployed only by Warsaw Pact forces in Europe.

Burma Bomb Explosion Kills Korean Ministers (Oct. 9): A terrorist bomb explodes at a wreath-laying ceremony at the Martyrs Mausoleum in Rangoon, Burma, killing at least 21 people including two advisors to the president of South Korea and four of his cabinet ministers. South Korean President Chun Doo Hwan escapes from harm because he is five minutes late in arriving at the ceremony. President Chun cuts short his trip to six Asian and Pacific countries and returns home. He blames North Korean agents for the killing. No terrorist group claims responsibility for the bombing.

Israel Devaluates Currency (Oct. 11): Prime Minister Yitzhak Shamir's new government devaluates the Shekel by 23% as one of several emergency measures to stop panicky selling of Israeli currency.

Ex-Premier of Japan Found Guilty of Bribery (Oct. 12): Former Prime Minister Kakuei Tanaka is found guilty of having accepted $2.1 million in bribes to arrange the purchase of Lockheed Aircraft for Japan's airline. He is sentenced to four years in jail and ordered to pay a fine equal to the amount of the bribes. Tanaka plans to appeal the conviction.

Moscow Plans to Counter U.S. Missiles in Europe (Oct. 13): Marshal Viktor G. Kulikov, commander-in-chief of the Warsaw Pact forces, and also a Soviet First Deputy Defense Minister, says that if American medium-range missiles are placed in Western Europe in December 1983, the Soviet Union will deploy additional nuclear weapons to counter them.

Grenada's Prime Minister Killed in Coup (Oct. 19): Maurice Bishop, 39, Prime Minister of Grenada is killed by rebel soldiers after a military coup. **(Oct. 20):** A 16-member military council is installed as the new government.

Terrorist Explosion Kills 237 Marines in Beirut (Oct. 23): A truck laden with explosives crashes into a four-story U.S. Marine headquarters at the Beirut airport in a predawn attack, killing at least 237 sleeping Marines and Navy personnel and wounding many others. At almost the same time, another truck packed with explosives crashes into an eight-story French military post three miles away, killing 31 French paratroopers and wounding at least 12 others. An unknown group calling itself the Free Islamic Revolutionary Movement claims responsibility for the suicide attacks. The two men who drove the explosive trucks are killed in the blasts.

Soviets Prepare to Deploy New Missiles in Eastern Europe (Oct. 24): The official Soviet news agency, Tass, reports that the Soviet Union is beginning preparatory work to install Soviet missiles in East Germany and Czechoslovakia to counter the missiles NATO plans to deploy in Western Europe in December 1983.

U.S. and Caribbean Allies Invade Grenada (Oct. 25): President Reagan orders a predawn invasion of Grenada, site of the Oct. 19 coup, by U.S. marine and airborne troops to protect some 1,000 American citizens on the island, and to help restore democratic institutions in that country. He launches the attack after receiving an urgent request from five members of the Organization of Eastern Caribbean States (O.E.C.S.). Over 1,900 U.S. troops form the major forces of the joint-action that includes soldiers from Barbados, Dominica, Jamaica, St. Lucia, and St. Vincent. The island's two airfields are seized. The invading troops meet strong resistance from about 800 Cuban personnel on the island. **(Oct. 27):** Twenty-four Cubans are reported killed and 59 wounded. **(Oct. 30):** The American death toll is placed at 18 dead and 116 wounded. Although sniper action continues, the capital, St. George's, returns to an almost normal life. **(Nov. 3):** House Speaker, Thomas O'Neill, Jr., says he is convinced that the invasion was justified to rescue endangered American citizens, after hearing the report of a 14-member House fact-finding mission. **(Nov. 9):** Governor General Paul Scoon names Alister McIntyre, a U.N. official, to head a nine-member provisional government until elections can be held. **(Dec. 15):** The last of the American combat forces fly home. A detachment of about 300 American noncombat soldiers remains to give support to the Caribbean peacekeeping force there.

Soviets Urge Press Curbs at UNESCO Conference (Oct. 25): The Soviet Union calls for international curbs on freedom of the press at a UNESCO conference in Paris as part of a "new world information and communication order." The Soviets ask members to "ban the mass media for building up world tension and disseminating tendentious and slanderous messages that sow the seeds of alienation and enmity."

Peronist Party Defeated in Argentina (Oct. 31): Raúl Alfonsín, 56, leader of the middle-class Radical Civic Union, is the surprise winner in the nation's presidential elections, handing the Peronists their first defeat since the party was founded in 1945.

Lebanese Peace Conference Opens in Geneva (Oct. 31): At the opening session of the National Reconciliation Conference in Geneva, Pres. Amin Gemayel of Lebanon appeals to all of his country's warring leaders to set aside differences because the "country is dying."

National

AFL–CIO Backs Mondale in Unprecedented Move (Oct. 1): The AFL–CIO leadership votes overwhelmingly to endorse Walter Mondale as the 1984 Democratic presidential candidate. **(Oct. 5):** AFL–CIO delegates endorse Mondale at their convention in

Hollywood, Fla.

Supreme Court Upholds Local Anti-Gun Law (Oct. 3): The Court lets stand a local ordinance adopted in 1981 by the village of Morton Grove, Ill., that bans the possession of privately owned handguns. The Court rules that the ban does not violate the Constitution's Second Amendment, which guarantees the right of the people to keep and bear arms.

New U.S. Treasurer Takes Oath of Office (Oct. 3): Katherine Davalos Ortega, a Mexican-American and former bank president, is sworn-in as Treasurer of the United States.

Reagan Announces New Compromise Arms Proposals (Oct. 4): President Reagan formally announces a new proposal in which more nuclear warheads would be linked to the destruction of old ones. In addition, there would be fewer nuclear warheads on U.S. bombers and cruise missiles if the Soviet Union were willing to destroy some of their powerful land-based missiles. Under the plan, more old warheads would be destroyed if fixed land-base missile were deployed than if sea-based or mobile missiles were deployed.

William P. Clark Chosen to Succeed James Watt (Oct. 13): President Reagan names his national security advisor, William P. Clark, 51, to replace James Watt as Secretary of the Interior.

Reagan Legally Becomes a Candidate for 1984 (Oct. 17): The President signs two letters authorizing his candidacy. One of them authorizes Sen. Paul Laxalt, Republican of Nevada, to establish a campaign committee, and the other informs the Federal Election Committee that this will be his principal campaign committee.

Reagan Names McFarlane as National Security Adviser (Oct. 17): President Reagan appoints Robert C. McFarlane, 46, as his national security adviser, replacing William P. Clark. Mr. McFarlane recently had served as the President's special Middle East envoy.

General

Floods Sweep Arizona (Oct. 2): At least seven storm-related deaths are caused by flooding resulting from desert rainstorms in southeastern Arizona. The governor had declared a statewide emergency earlier in the week.

Volcano Devastates Japanese Island (Oct. 3): Mount Oyama, situated on the Japanese island of Miyakejima in the Pacific, 100 miles south of Tokyo, erupts and destroys one village with lava and another by fire. The population of about 4,500 people are evacuated. The eruption is accompanied by an earthquake measuring 6.1 on the Richter scale.

Chicago Teachers Go On Strike (Oct. 3): The Chicago Teachers Union along with 18 other unions strikes in a dispute over pay. Chicago is the nation's third largest school system. **(Oct. 23):** The Chicago Teachers Union and the Board of Education reach a settlement to end the strike.

Price of Gold Drops Below $400 (Oct. 3): For the first time in 1983, the price of gold bullion in New York closes at $390.90, touching off widespread selling.

Quake Shakes Northeastern U.S. and Canada (Oct. 8): An earthquake measuring 5.2 on the Richter Scale originates in northern New York's Adirondack Mountains, sending tremors throughout the northeastern U.S. and Quebec and Ontario, Canada. No deaths, injuries, or major damage are reported. The earthquake is the largest in New York State since Sept. 4, 1944.

New Bible Text Eliminates Male God Terminology (Oct. 14): A new Bible translation is released by the National Council of Churches that eliminates references to God as a male only. The new readings were prepared for voluntary, experimental use in services by Protestant churches. The translations are called "The Inclusive Language Lectionary," and were prepared by a committee of 11 biblical scholars from various religious denominations including the Roman Catholic Church.

First Image of Sun's Rings Photographed (Oct. 14): Japanese astronomers take a picture of two rings of dust around the Sun during the eclipse of the Sun in Indonesia, June 1983, with a special video camera suspended from a balloon. The dust rings are 900,000 to 1,500,000 miles above the Sun's surface.

Pope Proclaims Croatian Priest as New Saint (Oct. 16): Pope John Paul proclaims Leopold Mandic, a Croatian Capuchin Monk, as a new saint of the Catholic Church. Mandic is credited with performing many miracles since his death in 1942.

American Charged With Selling Missile Secrets to Poland (Oct. 17): James Durward Harper, Jr., 49, a power supply engineer at Selectron Corp., San Francisco, is arrested on charges that he sold sensitive ballistic missile research data to a Polish spy for $250,000. The government says that the source of the documents was his late wife, Ruby, who worked at Systems Control, Inc., Palo Alto, Calif.

E.P.A. Warns Earth Will Heat Up by 1990s (Oct. 17): A report released by the Environmental Protection Agency warns that a warming of the Earth by a buildup of carbon dioxide in the atmosphere known as the "greenhouse effect," will occur by the 1990s, and will cause major changes in the world's climate. It is predicted that the changes will disrupt food production and raise the coastal waters significantly. The report states that the warming trend is imminent and inevitable. Not even a total ban on the use of fossil fuels can prevent it. **(Oct. 20):** A National Academy of Sciences report on the "greenhouse effect" agrees that the earth is warming up, but says that there is sufficient time to prepare for its impact. President Reagan's science advisor, George A. Keyworth, 3rd praises the Academy's report and calls the E.P.A. report "unwarranted" and "alarmist."

G.M. Makes Record Job Bias Settlement (Oct. 18): The General Motors Corp. agrees to pay $42 million to settle out of court a 10-year complaint charging job discrimination by the company against blacks, women, and hispanic people. It is the largest out-of-court settlement in a job discrimination case. The accord sets numerical goals for the hiring, training, and promotion of women and minorities. Under a provision of the agreement, G.M. will give $15 million in endowments and scholarships to colleges and schools to help G.M. employees and family members.

Senate Designates Martin Luther King's Birthday a National Holiday (Oct. 19): The Senate voted 78 to 22 to honor Dr. Martin Luther King, Jr., by making his birthday a new national holiday. This makes Dr. King the only other American besides George Washington whose birthday is celebrated as a national holiday. Dr. King was born on Jan. 15th, but the first King holiday will be celebrated on Jan. 20, 1986. The new legislation designates the third Monday in January as the legal public date to commemorate Dr. King's birthday.

New Zealander Wins New York City Marathon (Oct. 23): Rod Dixon, 33, wins the 14th annual New York City

Marathon with a time of two hours, eight minutes, and 59 seconds. More than 17,000 runners competed in the 26.2-mile race.

Arrest 1,100 Antinuclear Demonstrators (Oct. 24): At least 1,100 anti-nuclear protesters at military installations in New York, Minnesota, South Carolina, New Mexico, California, and at the Pentagon are arrested while protesting against the planned deployment of new missiles in Western Europe.

Huge Quake Strikes Western States (Oct. 28): An earthquake measuring 7.2 on the Richter scale rocks eight western states, killing two children in Challis, Idaho. The earthquake is felt in Idaho, Washington, Montana, Oregon, Nevada, Wyoming, North Dakota, Utah, and the Canadian provinces of British Columbia and Alberta.

Eastern Turkey Hit by Earthquake (Oct. 30): A major earthquake measuring 7.1 on the Richter scale shakes eastern Turkey, destroying 44 villages and killing 1,233 people, and injuring 534 others.

NOVEMBER 1983

International

Military-Backed Party Loses Turkish Elections (Nov. 6): The independent conservative Motherland Party, led by 56-year old economist Turgut Ozal, wins a majority 212 of the 400 seats in Parliament in the general election held Nov. 6th. The Populist Party wins 117 seats, and the Nationalist Democracy Party finishes last with 71 seats.

President Reagan Visits Japan (Nov. 10): President Reagan meets with Japanese Prime Minister Yasuhiro Nakasone in Tokyo to resolve trade differences. In a speech, Reagan warns Japanese leaders that rising protectionism is threatening U.S. and Japanese relations. **(Nov. 11)**: Reagan becomes the first American president to address the Japanese Parliament. He calls on Japan to join the U.S. in a "powerful partnership for good."

Reagan Addresses South Korean National Assembly (Nov. 13): President Reagan tells assembly that the U.S. will back South Korea in its stand against the aggression of Communist North Korea. **(Nov. 14)**: Reagan concludes visit to Seoul and says that he would strengthen U.S. forces in that country.

First U.S. Missiles Arrive in England (Nov. 14): The first American cruise missiles are delivered to the Greenham Common air base, England, as part of NATO's new medium-range missiles to be deployed in Western Europe.

Turkish Cypriots Declare Independent Nation (Nov. 15): Turkish Cypriot leader Rauf Raif Denktash, 59, declares their part of Cyprus an independent republic. The Turkish government gives the first formal recognition to the new state. The action is condemned by Greek Cypriot President Spyros Kyprianov and other world leaders.

U.S. Navy Officer Assassinated in Greece (Nov. 15): Two gunmen kill Capt. George Tsantes, 53, head of the naval section of the Joint U.S. Military Assistance Group, Greece, and his Greek chauffeur in Athens, as Tsantes is being driven to work. The left-wing terrorist group "November 17" claims responsibility for the killing.

Israel Bombs Suspected Terrorist Base in Lebanon (Nov. 16): Four Israeli fighters bomb a pro-Iranian Shiite training base reportedly belonging to the group that attacked U.S. marine, French, and Italian barracks in Beirut.

French Jets Raid Lebanese Shiite Bases (Nov. 17): French warplanes attack pro-Iranian Shiite militia installations in central Lebanon in order to prevent new terrorist attacks against French forces there. Fifty-nine French paratroopers were killed in the Oct. 23, 1983, terrorist attack.

Argentina Announces Nuclear Capacity (Nov. 18): Rear Adm. Carlos Madero, president of the Argentina National Atomic Energy Council, announces that his country has developed the technology to make enriched uranium and can make fuel for atomic weapons. He says that Argentina would only use its nuclear capability for peaceful ends. Madero also says that Argentina will not allow inspections called for in international treaties against the spread of nuclear weapons. Argentina has not signed these agreements. Argentina is now the eighth nation to produce enriched uranium, joining the United States, the Soviet Union, France, Britain, West Germany, The Netherlands, and China.

Moscow Offers to Reduce its Missiles in Half (Nov. 18): The Soviet chief arms negotiator in Geneva, Yuli A. Kvitsinsky, makes an informal offer to the U.S. negotiator, Paul H. Nitze, to reduce the number of Soviet SS-20 missiles in Europe if NATO agrees to stop its plans to deploy 572 new U.S. missiles in Europe. The proposal is turned down as unacceptable by the Reagan administration because the Russians would still have about 360 warheads on 120 SS-20 aimed at Western Europe and the same number of SS-20's aimed at Asia. The proposal would not permit the U.S. to have a similar missile capability.

West German Party Opposes New American Missiles (Nov. 19): The West German Social Democratic Party ignores an appeal by former Chancellor Helmut Schmidt, and says that it cannot accept the deployment of new U.S. medium-range missiles in West Germany. The Party demands that the United States and the Soviet Union continue their nuclear arms talks in Geneva.

Gunmen Kill Three in Ulster Church (Nov. 20): Two gunmen, using automatic weapons, attack worshipers in a Protestant church in Darkley, Northern Ireland, killing three and wounding seven others. A group calling itself the Catholic Reaction Force claims responsibility for the murders.

Bonn Approves U.S. Missile Deployment (Nov. 22): The West German Parliament votes 286 to 226 in favor of deploying U.S. Pershing 2 and cruise missiles in West Germany starting November 23, 1983. Chancellor Helmut Kohl's coalition of Christian Democrats and Free Democrats endorses the decision to deploy the missiles because of the stalemate at the arms talks in Geneva.

Joint U.S.-Israeli Military Cooperation Announced (Nov. 29): After meeting in Washington, D.C. for two days of talks, Pres. Reagan and Israeli Prime Minister Yitzhak Shamir announce a plan to create a joint committee to coordinate American and Israeli military planning, maneuvers, and the stockpiling of U.S. arms in Israel. The joint panel is being planned to deal with the increased Soviet involvement with Syria and the rest of the Middle East.

National

The Chicago Sun-Times Purchased by Murdock (Nov. 1): Rupert Murdock, the Australian publisher of seven U.S. newspapers, buys the Chicago *Sun-Times*, the nation's ninth largest newspaper, for $90 million.

House Rejects Fund Cutting for MX and B1 Bomber (Nov. 1): The House of Representatives votes 217 to 208 against deleting funds for the MX missile. It also votes 247 to 175 to finance the B1 bomber for more than a year.

Jackson Announces His Presidential Candidacy (Nov. 3): The Rev. Jesse Jackson, 42, civil rights leader, formally declares his candidacy for the Democratic presidential nomination in a 45-minute speech at the Washington Convention Center. He says, "I seek the Presidency to serve the nation at a level where I can help restore a moral tone, a redemptive spirit, and a sensitivity to the poor and the dispossessed of this nation."

Bomb Explodes in Capitol (Nov. 7): A small bomb explodes about 30 feet from the Senate chamber inside the Capitol. No one is injured. A group calling itself the Armed Resistance Unit claims responsibility for the explosion, which is in reaction to the invasion of Grenada and the U.S. presence in Lebanon and South America.

Senate Approves Nerve Gas Funds (Nov. 8): The Senate votes 47 to 46, with Vice President George Bush breaking the tie, to approve $252 billion for nerve gas production. **(Nov. 15):** House of Representatives votes 258 to 165 to oppose the Senate's measure.

Philadelphia Elects First Black Mayor (Nov. 8): W. Wilson Goode, 44, a Democrat, is elected the first black Mayor of Philadelphia, the fourth largest city in the nation.

Kentucky Elects First Woman Governor (Nov. 8): Martha Layne Collins, 46, a Democrat, becomes the first woman to be elected Governor of Kentucky.

Revived Equal Rights Amendment Defeated in House (Nov. 15): The House of Representatives defeats a plan to revive the proposed Equal Rights Amendment by only six votes short of the two-thirds majority needed.

Senate Defeats Reagan's Tuition Tax Aid Bill (Nov. 16): The Senate votes 59 to 38 against a bill that would give tax credits to the parents of children who attend private schools.

Millions Watch T.V. Nuclear War (Nov. 20): An estimated 100 million viewers, half of them adults, watched the controversial ABC-TV drama "The Day After," which depicts the nuclear destruction of Kansas City and its aftermath in Lawrence, Kan. Viewers are left with mixed emotions concerning the use of nuclear weapons and the government's policy of securing arms reductions. In over 1,000 calls received by the network, 662 persons supported the film and 392 opposed its showing.

Reagan Signs Non-Milk Production Farm Bill (Nov. 29): President Reagan signs a bill that will pay farmers not to produce milk. He had opposed the measure as too costly, but yielded to pressure from his political allies in Congress.

General

Earthquake in China Kills 30 (Nov. 7): An earthquake measuring 5.9 on the Richter scale strikes an agricultural area of eastern China, killing at least 30 people and damaging thousands of houses and buildings.

Belgium Earthquake Kills Two (Nov. 8): An earthquake measuring 5 on the Richter scale strikes Liege, Belgium, killing at least two people, injuring at least ten, and causing much damage in that city. The last severe earthquake in Belgium was in 1938.

Angolan Plane Crash Kills 150 (Nov. 8): A 737 Angolan national jetliner carrying about 150 passengers and crew members crashes after takeoff in Lubango, Angola, killing all aboard.

East Germany Celebrates Luther's 500th Birthday (Nov. 10): Protestant clergymen from 37 countries, along with Roman Catholics, Jews, and East German officials, gathers in Eisleben, East Germany, to honor Martin Luther on the 500th anniversary of his birth there.

Pope Urges Scientists to End War Research (Nov. 12): Pope John Paul II speaking at a special audience of the Pontifical Academy of Sciences asks scientists to abandon their "laboratories and factories of death" and to insure that "the discoveries of science are not placed at the service of war, tyranny, and terror."

Hawaiian Earthquake Injures Four (Nov. 15): An earthquake measuring 6.7 on the Richter scale jolts Hilo, Hawaii, damaging houses and disrupting power, telephone, and gas service. At least four persons suffer minor injuries.

Smoking-Related Heart Disease Kills 170,000 (Nov. 17): A government report by the Surgeon General said that 170,000 Americans will die of heart disease caused by cigarette smoking. According to the study, cigarette smoking is responsible for up to 30% of all heart disease in the United States. The report also says that cigar and pipe smokers do not appear to have substantially greater risks of heart disease than nonsmokers.

Breakup of Black Families Hurts Economic Gains (Nov. 19): In the past 18 years, fatherless black families with children have increased from 25% to 50%, headed by women, and 55% of black babies are born to unmarried mothers. Politicians and scholars agree that this development has reached proportions that can undo the economic gains that black Americans have made over the last three decades and that the problem must be resolved. It is believed to be an important cause of poverty because no man is providing for the family and that women on an average earn less than men.

Colombian Jetliner Crashes Near Madrid (Nov. 26): A Colombian Avianca Boeing 747 airliner with 194 people aboard crashes near Mejorada del Campó, Spain, as it is preparing to land in Madrid, killing 183 persons. Eleven people survive the accident.

Largest Theft of Gold Bullion in Britain (Nov. 26): Six masked gunmen steal about $400 million in gold bullion bars from a security warehouse of Brinks-Mat Ltd. near Heathrow Airport near London. It is the largest theft in British history.

Record Blizzard Hits Seven Mid-Western States (Nov. 28): Severe snowstorms in Colorado, Iowa, Kansas, Nebraska, Minnesota, South Dakota, and Wyoming strand thousands of travelers and bring many mid-Western cities to a standstill. At least 61 deaths are attributed to the winter storms.

Columbia Carries Spacelab Into Orbit (Nov. 28): The space shuttle *Columbia* is launched from Cape Canaveral, Fla., at 11 A.M. E.S.T. into a scheduled nine-day orbit. It carries the European-built research laboratory in the cargo bay, and a crew of six men, including the first non-astronauts, Dr. Byron K. Lichtenberg, 35, of M.I.T., and Dr. Ulf Merbold, 42, of Max Planck Institute, Stuttgart, West Germany. The mission pilots are John W. Young, 53, and Air Force Major, Brewster H. Shaw, Jr., 38. Other payload specialists are Dr. Owen K. Garriott, 53, and Dr. Robert A.R. Parker, 47. The 17-ton, 23-foot-long *Spacelab* was built in West Germany for the European Space Agency at a cost of $1 billion. The experiments in the *Spacelab* were scheduled to be performed around the clock by the four scientists. **(Dec.**

8): After a 10-day record flight, the *Columbia* lands safely at Edwards Air Force Base, Calif., at 6:47 P.M. E.S.T., eight hours late after a series of computer malfunctions struck the navigation systems.

DECEMBER 1983

International

Venezuelan Presidential Election Won by Former President (Dec. 4): Jaime Lusinchi, 53, the opposition candidate from the Democratic Action Party, easily defeats his leading opponent, Rafael Caldera of the Social Christian Party. Lusinchi is the first candidate to win re-election after the legally mandated 10-year waiting period.

Lech Walesa's Wife Accepts His Nobel Prize (Dec. 10): Mrs. Danuta Walesa, 35, wife of Poland's outlawed Solidarity union's founder, accepts the 1983 Nobel Peace Prize awarded him on his behalf in ceremonies at Oslo, Norway.

Terrorist Bombings in Kuwait Blast Six Sites (Dec. 12): Two terrorists riding in a truck laden with explosives crash into the U.S. Embassy compound and blow it up, injuring 37 people. Terrorists also explode remote-control car bombs at the French Embassy and four other sites. At least seven persons are killed in the attacks.

U.S. Renews Azores Air Base Agreement (Dec. 13): The U.S. and Portugal sign agreements giving the U.S. rights to use the Lajes Air Base on Teceira Island. In return, the U.S. pledges to increase military and economic assistance to Portugal.

U.S. Battleship *New Jersey* Shells Syrian Missile Sites (Dec. 14): The *New Jersey* fires its 16-inch guns at Syrian anti-aircraft missile targets in Lebanon after two U.S. Navy reconnaissance planes are fired upon from the Syrian positions. The U.S. orders the tour of duty for the battleship to be extended until spring 1984.

New U.S. Arms Policy for Israel, Egypt (Dec. 15): The U.S. government grants Israel $1.4 billion in military aid during fiscal 1984 and gives Egypt $1.1 billion in military grants. Under the Reagan Administration's new policy, none of the military assistance has to be repaid.

Trudeau Discusses East-West Peace Initiative With Reagan (Dec. 15): Prime Minister Pierre Elliott Trudeau of Canada meets with Pres. Reagan at the White House and receives encouragement from Reagan on his plan to travel to Moscow and seek renewed arms control talks.

Argentina to Investigate Civil Rights Abuses (Dec. 16): Argentina's new president, Raúl Alfonsín, sets up a panel to investigate the disappearances of over 6,000 Argentines during the past military government's rule. He has pledged to punish civil rights abuses and has ordered a court-martial of nine former junta members.

Arafat's P.L.O. Evacuates Tripoli (Dec. 20): Yasir Arafat, P.L.O. leader, and about 4,000 of his loyalist forces are evacuated from Tripoli aboard five Greek ships, ending a six-week siege against his supporters by a Syrian-backed P.L.O. rebellion. **(Dec. 22):** Arafat arrives in Cairo for talks and a reconciliation with Egyptian President Hosni Mubarak. **(Dec. 26):** Yasir Arafat arrives in Yemen with 1,000 of his guerrillas.

Nakasone Re-Elected as Japan's Prime Minister (Dec. 26): Yasuhiro Nakasone is formally re-elected to a second term as Prime Minister of Japan after he is able to form a coalition government. His victory comes a week after his Liberal Democratic Party suffered one of its worst election defeats.

Andropov Unable to Attend Communist Party Meeting (Dec. 26): Soviet leader Yuri V. Andropov fails to attend a regular meeting of the Communist Party's Central Committee in Moscow. He is believed to be seriously ill and has not been seen in public for over four months.

Pope Meets His Attacker in Prison (Dec. 27): Pope John Paul II meets his assailant, Mehmet Ali Agca, 25, for 20 minutes in Rebibbia Prison, Rome, where they have a private talk "as brothers." The meeting is a highlight of the Pope's visit to the jail as part of his Christmas season celebration.

National

EPA's Lavelle Found Guilty of Perjury (Dec. 1): Rita Lavelle, former head of the Superfund Toxic Waste Program, is convicted of perjury and of obstructing an investigation into her management of the Environmental Protection Agency's $1.6-billion toxic waste cleanup program by a U.S. District Court jury in Washington, D.C.

Northeast Governors Ask for Uniform Drinking Age (Dec. 5): The governors of New York, New Jersey, Massachusetts, New Hampshire, Rhode Island, Connecticut, and Pennsylvania unanimously adopt a resolution at a meeting of the Northeast Governor's Conference calling for a uniform legal drinking age for the seven-state region.

Greyhound Strikers Approve Contract (Dec. 19): Greyhound employees approve a new three-year contract, ending a seven-week strike that was marked with violence.

Record Sub-Zero Weather Grips U.S. Cities (Dec. 24): Record low temperatures are reported in 21 states and 60 U.S. cities. According to the National Weather Service, it was the coldest December in 50 years.

Reagan Accepts Blame for Marine Security Failure (Dec. 27): President Reagan says that he accepts the responsibility for the lack of proper security measures in the terrorist truck bombing of the Marine compound in Beirut, which killed 241 American servicemen on Oct. 23, 1983.

U.S. Steel Announces Closing of Three Plants (Dec. 27): U.S. Steel Corp., the nation's largest steel producer announces that it will close plants in Chicago, Cleveland, Trenton, and sections of other plants in April 1984, thereby eliminating 15,430 jobs.

Special Commission Blames Commanders and Policy in Marine Deaths (Dec. 28): A special five-man Defense Department commission concludes a seven-week investigation of the terrorist bombing of the Marine headquarters in Beirut, and reports that major failures of command, inadequate intelligence, and policy contributed to vulnerability of the Marine defenses there.

General

Vatican Issues New Guidelines on Sex Education (Dec. 1): A new 36-page booklet entitled "Educational Guidance in Human Love," published after several years of study initiated by Pope John Paul II, condemns sexual relations by the unmarried, masturbation, and homosexuality, and urges the courts to protect the young from pornography. Virginity is also praised as rendering "the heart more free to love God."

German Pay $11.7 Million for Rare Medieval Book (Dec. 6): A West German consortium purchases a rare Medieval masterpiece created about 1174, entitled the "Gospels of Henry the Lion," for more than

$11.7 million at a London auction.

90 Killed in Madrid Jetliner Collision (Dec. 7): An Iberia Airlines Boeing 727 bound for Rome with 93 people aboard collides in a heavy fog on a takeoff runway with an Aviaco DC-9 bound for Santander, Spain, with 42 people aboard. All persons on the Aviaco plane are killed and 48 passengers on the Iberia Airliner die in the crash. Both planes had permission from the control tower to move at the time, but apparently the Aviaco pilot did not follow the proper departure route.

Court Denies Paralyzed Woman's Request to Starve Self (Dec. 16): A California Superior Court judge ruled that Elizabeth Bouvia, 26, paralyzed from birth by cerebral palsy, had a fundamental right to terminate her life, but not with the aid of society. She has requested the right to starve to death in a hospital where she is a patient.

Hundreds Die in Guinea Earthquake (Dec. 21): An earthquake strikes Guinea, West Africa, killing at least 300 people and destroying at least 16 villages.

Propane Blast Kills Six in Buffalo (Dec. 27): A sixteen-block area in Buffalo, N.Y., is devastated when a tank containing propane illegally stored in a warehouse explodes, killing six and injuring over 70 others.

JANUARY 1984

International

Rebels Blow Up Major El Salvador Bridge (Jan. 1): Leftist guerrillas destroy Cuscatlan Bridge spanning Lempa River. It was the last suspension bridge for carrying traffic between East and West.

Soviet Gas Arrives in France (Jan. 1): Nation gets first deliveries under 25-year contract with Soviet Union. Officials doubt that the gas flows through new pipelines from Siberia to Western Europe.

Cruise Missiles Operational in Britain (Jan. 1): Defense Minister announces first 16, based at Greenham Common Air Base, are in operating condition.

Brunei Gains Independence (Jan. 1): Sultanate becomes independent of Britain, with name of Brunei Darussalam, "Brunei, Abode of Peace."

Syria Frees Captured Navy Pilot (Jan. 3): Releases Navy Lieut. Robert O. Goodman, Jr., after dramatic personal appeal by Rev. Jesse Jackson to Syrian President Hafez al-Assad. Reagan praises Democratic Presidential aspirant for his success.

France Cuts Lebanon Force (Jan. 3): Announces it will remove 482 troops from multinational peacekeeping contingent in Beirut by end of January.

Nigeria Names Ruling Military Council (Jan. 3): Major Gen. Mohammed Buhari, new military leader, announces formation of Supreme Military Council to succeed government of former President Shehu Shagari, ousted in military coup Dec. 31, 1983.

Price Increase Canceled in Tunisia (Jan. 6): President Habib Bourguiba, in nationally televised address, announces he is reversing dramatic increase in price of bread and other grain products that had triggered week of rioting throughout country.

Brunei Joins Association (Jan. 7): Newly independent sultanate is first new member of Association of Southeast Asian Nations since group was formed in 1967 by Indonesia, Malaysia, Singapore, the Philippines, and Thailand.

Argentina's 1983 Inflation Sets Record (Jan. 7): National Statistics Institute of nation reports rate reached a record high of 433.7%.

South Africa Withdraws Angola Troops (Jan. 8): Begins action after month-long offensive. Withdrawal follows South African offer to sanction negotiations between South African administrator of Namibia (South-West Africa) and guerrillas of South-West Africa People's Organization (SWAPO).

U.S. and Vatican Establish Diplomatic Ties (Jan. 10): Establish full relations after hiatus of 116 years. Congress had repealed prohibition against use of federal funds for a Vatican Embassy.

Ex-President Arrested in Argentina (Jan. 10): Reynaldo Bignone charged with complicity in disappearances and presumed murders of two Communists. Separately, 482 unidentified bodies are discovered, those of people who had disappeared during military campaign against leftists.

Soviet Calls for Ban on Chemical Arms (Jan. 10): Urges negotiations between Warsaw Pact and North Atlantic Treaty Organization to outlaw such weapons in Europe.

U.S. Panel Cites Threat to Central America (Jan. 11): National Bipartisan Commission appointed by President recommends $8-billion economic aid program and substantial increase in military aid for El Salvador. Commission endorses most major elements of the Administration's regional policy.

Nicaragua Downs U.S. Helicopter in Honduras (Jan. 11): Gunfire kills pilot, Chief Warrant Officer Jeffrey C. Schwab, first U.S. soldier to be killed by hostile fire in Honduras since joint maneuvers began in 1983.

China and U.S. Sign Agreements (Jan. 12): Reach new accord on industrial cooperation and renew pact on science and technology. News is highlight of visit to Washington by Chinese Premier Zhao Ziyang, first by a Chinese premier and first by a top Chinese official since then Vice Premier Deng Xiaoping visited U.S. in 1979.

Nicaragua Schedules Election (Jan. 14): Government announces balloting for president, vice president, and 90-member legislative assembly, which will take place early in 1985.

U.S. Report on El Salvador (Jan. 16): State Department tells Congress human rights are still a major problem despite recent improvements. It is first Administration report since President Reagan vetoed legislation in November 1983 tying U.S. aid to improvements by El Salvadoran regime.

Islamic Group Readmits Egypt (Jan. 19): Organization of the Islamic Conference, at summit meeting in Casablanca, votes move to end isolation of Egypt, suspended in 1979 after peace treaty with Israel.

Soviet President Eases Criticism of U.S. (Jan. 24): Yuri V. Andropov, in interview with *Pravda*, moderates attack by Foreign Minister Andrei Gromyko. Andropov is critical of Reagan's call for improved relations and urges U.S. to take concrete steps.

Vatican Aid to Nazis Charged (Jan. 26): Report in 1947 by State Department asserted that in the years after World War II, Vatican had been "the largest single organization involved in the illegal movement of emigrants," including Nazis. A historian of Holocaust, Charles R. Allen, obtained copy of report. It charges Vatican used influence to apply pressure on some nations for entry of Nazis, former Fascists, or members of other anti-Communist groups. Vatican doubts official sanction was given for what aid may have occurred.

Newfoundland Bans Offshore Drilling (Jan. 26): Charges Canadian Government had not provided adequate search-and-rescue facilities in response to hazardous winter conditions. Ottawa warns oil companies of loss of federal incentive payments if they comply with ban on offshore exploration.

Brazil Financial Package Set (Jan. 27): Nation and foreign creditor banks sign four-part financial arrangement that includes $6.5 billion in new loans.

China Halts "Spiritual Pollution" Drive (Jan. 28): Ends campaign against Western ideas and trends viewed as threatening to Chinese socialism.

Soviet Charges Arms Treaty Violations (Jan. 29): Protests alleged conduct in diplomatic note following release to Congress of classified Administration report on alleged Soviet arms violations.

National

Walter Mondale Kicks Off Campaign (Jan. 3): Former Vice President begins five-day trip through South with address in Washington. He criticizes Reagan's foreign policy and urges a more competitive economy.

Defense Aide Resigns in Stock Inquiry (Jan. 4): Paul Thayer quits as deputy secretary amid allegations that he had illegally supplied associates with confidential stock trading information. Thayer, 64, calls charges "without merit." One inquiry was begun by Securities and Exchange Commission, the other by Justice Department.

"Test Tube" Babies Born (Jan. 6): Woman in Australia, 31, is mother of first quadruplets to be conceived in a laboratory and planted in her womb.

Rita Lavelle Gets Six-Month Term (Jan. 9): Former official of Environmental Protection Agency also fined $10,000 for conviction of lying to Congressional committee investigating agency's program for cleaning up sites for disposal of hazardous wastes.

U.S.I.A. Chief Apologizes for Taping (Jan. 9): Director Charles Z. Wick says he's sorry for secretly taping telephone conversations while in office. Concedes he gave misinformation about taping when story broke.

New Rules for "Baby Doe" Cases (Jan. 9): Reagan Administration permits voluntary infant care committees of medical professionals, lawyers, clergy, and community members to decide on withholding treatment from seriously handicapped babies. New rules ease provisions that had drawn severe criticism.

Federal Panel Doubts Widespread Hunger (Jan. 10): Advisory commission recommends steps for alleviating hunger that does exist in nation. Forty-two national and antipoverty organizations condemn panel's program.

Supreme Court Backs Damages in Nuclear Case (Jan. 11): Justices, 5-4, rule courts can impose punitive damages on nuclear power industry for safety violations. Ruling a victory for states and partly one for family of Karen Silkwood, killed in car crash, who had been contaminated by plutonium at Kerr-McGee plant in Oklahoma.

High Court Curbs States on Offshore Oil Leasing (Jan. 11): Rules, 5-4, that states cannot block attempts by federal government to sell offshore oil and natural gas leases. Suit was brought by California.

Study Links Cholesterol and Heart Disease (Jan. 12): National Heart, Lung, and Blood Institute reports study of 3,806 men with high cholesterol levels showed that lowering cholesterol in blood stream reduced possibility of heart ailments in middle-aged men.

Reagan Calls for Arms Talk Resumption (Jan. 16): In major foreign policy speech, President urges return to parallel sets of nuclear-weapon negotiations in Geneva and talks in Vienna on reducing conventional forces in Europe. Speech modifies tone of President's previous statements on Soviet Union.

U.S. Panel Renounces Racial Quotas (Jan. 17): New Commission on Civil Rights, 6-2, calls such preferences "another form of unjust discrimination . . . and [they] offend constitutional principle of equal protection." Panel disappointed with Supreme Court decision not to review Detroit Police Department plan for affirmative action to equalize promotion of blacks and whites.

Justices Approve Video Recorders in Homes (Jan. 17): Supreme Court rules, 5-4, that noncommercial use of video cassette recorders does not violate Federal Copyright Act of 1976. Ruling a victory for Sony Corp. and defeat for film studios, which argued that home taping of copyrighted films and television productions violated property rights and deprived them of revenue.

Orwell's "1984" Popular in 1984 (Jan. 18): 1948 book by Eric Blair, whose pen name was George Orwell, becomes fastest selling book in U.S. *New York Times* reports three soft-cover editions and one hard-cover edition have been selling 50,000 copies for several weeks.

Telephone Access Fees Delayed (Jan. 19): Federal Communications Commission holds up until mid-1985 imposition of long-distance access fee on residential and small-business customers starting at $2 a month per user.

Attorney General Resigns (Jan. 22): William French Smith, 66, a longtime friend and adviser of President Reagan, expresses desire to return to private practice of law. White House chooses, Edwin Meese, 3rd, its counselor, to replace him.

Thousands Join Rally Against Abortion (Jan. 23): Demonstration in Washington draws 30,000 to 50,000 for "March for Life" marking 11th anniversary of Supreme Court decision legalizing abortion. Members of National Organization for Women picket Republican Party offices in Washington to protest Reagan's stand against abortion.

Ruling on Death Penalty Reviews (Jan. 23): Supreme Court, 7-2, decides a state does not have to review a death sentence to determine if it was comparable to punishments meted out in similar cases in that state. Ruling directly affects Robert Alton Harris, convicted murderer, who had challenged California for allegedly violating constitutional ban on cruel and unusual punishment by failing to conduct review.

Inflation Rate Lowest Since 1972 (Jan. 24): Labor Department reports Consumer Price Index rose only 3.8% during 1983, smallest gain since 3.4% in 1972. Decrease in price of energy helped hold down costs.

Reagan's State of the Union Address (Jan. 25): President reports nation "much improved" in message to Congress and nationwide television and radio audience. He appeals for bipartisan approach to reduction of huge federal deficits. Asks negotiations toward that end and a goal of $100-billion reduction over three years. Plans study to simplify tax code. Democrats challenge Administration policies as cutting Medicare and welfare while ordering huge increases in defense budget and retreating on civil rights.

Nation's Trade Deficit Sets Record (Jan. 27): Gap on merchandise trade overseas set by Commerce Dept. at $69.4 billion for 1983. Previous record gap was $42.7 billion in 1982.

Arab Support for Jackson Group Revealed (Jan. 29): Arab League reported to have contributed $100,000 to PUSH Foundation, an affiliate of Operation PUSH, civil rights organization led by Rev. Jesse Jackson before his campaign for Democratic Presidential nomination.

President Reagan Announces Re-Election Bid (Jan. 29): Supports Vice President George Bush as running mate. Reagan cites Administration accomplishments in economy and defense and says nation is "back and standing tall."

General

Bell System Divestiture Takes Place (Jan. 1): Twenty-two local telephone companies of American Telegraph & Telephone organized into several regional holding companies. AT&T divided into AT&T Communications and AT&T Technologies, Inc.

Miami No. 1 in Football (Jan. 3): University chosen national champion of college football in separate polls conducted by Associated Press and United Press International.

Auto Sales in U.S. Up 15.1% in Year (Jan. 5): Total of 9,155,-741 imported and domestic cars sold during year, up from 7,955,970 in 1982.

Texaco, Inc. Buys Getty Oil Corp. (Jan. 8): Agrees on purchase price of $9.98 billion. Texaco is the nation's third-largest oil company.

Carnegie Grants Aimed at Nuclear Risks (Jan. 4): Carnegie Corporation of New York awards more than $1.4 million to Stanford University and Harvard's John F. Kennedy School of Government to help develop strategies for reducing risk of nuclear war.

Christine Craft Awarded $325,000 (Jan. 13): Federal jury in Joplin, Mo., grants fraud damages in retrial of case against station KMBC-TV, Kansas City. Ms. Craft had contended that station had purported to hire her as news anchor based on skills but demoted her because of dissatisfaction with appearance.

Unions Lose Continental Court Fight (Jan. 17): Federal bankruptcy judge in Houston rules Continental Air Lines did not act in bad faith when it filed for bankruptcy for protection from creditors. Unions contended management had conspired to throw company into bankruptcy to break union contracts covering 4,000 employees.

New Apple Personal Computer Introduced (Jan. 24): Apple Computer, Inc. formally presents the Macintosh, latest challenge to International Business Machines' growing control over market for personal computers.

FEBRUARY 1984

International

Australia Gets Medicare Plan (Feb. 1): Health insurance program in effect despite rift between Labor Government and Medical Association. Plan would cover 85% of medical fees and provide free hospital treatment.

Reagan Proposes Central American Aid (Feb. 3): Calls for five-year, $8-billion package and supplementary aid for current fiscal year. Warns that "if we don't help now we'll surely pay dearly in the future." Plan follows recommendations of National Bipartison Commission on Central America.

Reagan Orders Marines Out of Beirut (Feb. 7): Decides on withdrawal of U.S. units of international peacekeeping force because of rapidly worsening conditions. Decision follows resignation of President Amin Gemayel's Lebanese Cabinet and military collapse, leaving Moslem militiamen in control of western and southern Beirut. Permits naval and air attacks on anti-government forces. Congressional relief at order is evident, but criticism widens on U.S. role in support of Gemayel.

Three Soviet Astronauts Launched (Feb. 8): Along with the five *Challenger* astronauts, a record is set for number of persons in space at one time. **(Feb. 9):** Soviet *Soyuz-10* spaceship docks with *Salyut-7* orbiting space station.

Soviet Union Gets New Leader (Feb. 9): Yuri V. Andropov, 69, general secretary of Communist Party Central Committee, dead of complications from chronic kidney ailment. **(Feb. 13):** Konstantin U. Chernenko, 72, member of ruling Politburo and a Central Committee secretary, elected to succeed Andropov. Chernenko pledges to continue program of economic and political reforms. He is the oldest man to be party leader and is described as intellectually limited and without foreign or domestic experience.

Survey Finds Improvement in Human Rights (Feb. 10): State Dept. report to Congress says violations continued through 1983 but finds improvement in more than two dozen Latin-American countries, Argentina foremost. Report is critical of Soviet Union, Afghanistan, Cambodia, Cuba, and Nicaragua.

China-Soviet Trade Treaty Signed (Feb. 10): Two nations approve $1.2-billion trade agreement providing for 50% trade increase in 1984.

U.S. Seizes Eight in China Smuggling Plot (Feb. 12): Customs Service reveals arrest on charges of conspiring to smuggle classified high-technology to China.

Argentina Revises Code of Military Justice (Feb. 14): President Raúl Alfonsín decrees civilian review of military court sentences. Under decree, findings by military courts on human rights violations in 1970s will be open to civilian review.

Italy and Vatican Sign New Accord (Feb. 18): Roman Catholicism ceases to be state religion. Teaching of Catholicism now optional in schools. Church annulments made subject to state's approval. Parliament must ratify accord.

Nicaragua Advances Election Date (Feb. 21): Announces ballot will be held in November instead of in 1985.

Former Grenada Leaders Accused (Feb. 22): Interim government charges 18 former military and political leaders in connection with killing in October 1983 of Prime Minister Maurice Bishop.

National

Reagan's New Budget (Feb. 1): President hands Congress $925.5-billion budget for fiscal 1985 with $180.4-billion deficit. Proposals continue Reagan-era military buildup. Pentagon outlays would increase $33 billion, a 14.5% rise. Nondefense spending would fall about $5 billion with increases in some areas, such as space program and environmental protection. Tax revenue expected to increase $8 billion.

Administration's Economic Report (Feb. 2): Seven-page section signed by President, stressing Administration's accomplishments. Rest, by Council of Economic Advisers under Chairman Martin Feldstein, reiterates concern over huge deficits and repeats Reagan's call for $100-billion down payment on deficit.

High Court Rules on Labor Agreements (Feb. 22): Justices decide, 5-4, that failing company can unilaterally cancel labor contracts. Case involves New Jersey building supply company and Teamsters Union.

Supreme Court Upholds Reagan Rights Stand (Feb. 28): Justices, 6-3, rule Title IX of Education Amendments of 1972 is enforceable only upon programs that specifically receive federal funds. Under previous broad interpretations, college or university risked cutoff of funds for entire institution if any program was in violation. Case involved Grove City (Pa.) College, which did not receive aid but where a few students had loans or grants.

General

Tenth Mission for Space Shuttle Program (Feb. 3): *Challenger* begins fourth flight carrying crew of five astronauts: Vance Brand, mission commander; Navy Comdr. Robert Gibson, pilot; and mission specialists Ronald McNair, Navy Capt. Bruce McCandless, and Army Lieut. Col. Robert Stewart. McNair, a physicist, is second American black in space. **(Feb. 7):** McCandless and Stewart leave shuttle and float in space without lifelines attached to spaceship and driven by jet propulsion backpacks designed by McCandless. Mission experiences three major failures of projects. **(Feb. 11):** *Challenger* lands at Cape Canaveral, Fla., after eight-day mission. It is first landing by a space shuttle at base from which it was launched. Brake damage in landing is revealed later. NASA plans to redesign braking system.

Baby Born From Donated Embryo (Feb. 3): Doctors in Long Beach, Calif., report first birth from infertile woman with transplanted embryo. Baby boy reported healthy. Embryo transferred from woman in whom it had been conceived by artificial insemination.

Four Sentenced in Brink's Case (Feb. 18): Federal judge in Manhattan metes out maximum sentences in robbery of Brink's armored car in Rockland County, N.Y., in which guard and two policemen were killed. Sekou Odinga and Silvia Baraldini each get 40 years in prison and are fined $50,000. Cecil Ferguson and Edward L. Joseph get 12 1/2-year sentences as accessories.

MARCH 1984

International

Two Leaders End Talks on Middle East Peace (March 1): King Hussein of Jordan and Yasir Arafat, chairman of Palestine Liberation Organization, report after five-day conference that they agreed to continue discussion "on joint stand based on an organized, firmly established and balanced basis, which will allow them to move together with support of the Arab nation."

Chernenko Critical of U.S. (March 2): In first major policy address since taking office, General Secretary of Soviet Communist Party calls for U.S. to take concrete actions that could bring "real drastic change" in relations. U.S. welcomes apparent softening of Soviet attitude.

D'Aubuisson Linked to Death Squads (March 3): Former Salvadoran military official quoted as saying Roberto D'Aubuisson, presidential candidate in El Salvador, had organized and directed right-wing death squads. D'Aubuisson and other officials deny the charges.

West German Chancellor Visits U.S. (March 3–7): Helmut Kohl meets Reagan and press in diplomatic visit. He urges that U.S.-Soviet arms talks be resumed and informs Reagan of European concerns about U.S. deficit and high interest rates.

Hundreds Perish in Nigerian Rioting (March 4): One-thousand reported dead in week of fighting between members of outlawed Moslem sect and police, soldiers, and civilian vigilantes in northern area.

U.S. Charges Chemical Warfare by Iraq (March 5): Backs Iranian charges that Iraqis were using chemical gas against Iranian forces in 42-month Persian Gulf War. U.S. cites "available evidence" gathered by International Red Cross.

G.M.-South Korea Agreement (March 6): General Motors confirms "memorandum of understanding" with Daewoo Corp. of South Korea to jointly produce small cars in Korea. Under the $500 million agreement, G.M. would begin importing 60,000 subcompacts during the 1987 model year.

Women's Rights Bill Voted in Australia (March 7): Parliament acts to eliminate discrimination on basis of sex, marital status, or pregnancy. Proposal had bipartisan support.

Newfoundland Loses Offshore Claim (March 8): Supreme Court of Canada rules unanimously that the federal government owns the oil-rich Hibernian area, 190 miles east of Newfoundland, ending a long dispute between Ottawa Government and the province.

Irish Prime Minister Visits U.S. (March 9 et seq.): Garret FitzGerald, on week-long visit, addresses joint session of Congress. He calls on U.S. to cut off all aid to Irish guerrillas, saying America seems to be prime outside source of arms and funds for terrorists.

Lebanese Factions Meet in Switzerland (March 12): New round of talks aimed at reconciliation is under way after government cancels the accord reached with Israel in 1983 for withdrawal of troops. **(March 20):** Lebanese national reconciliation talks in Lausanne, under Syrian sponsorship, end without accord after nine days.

Jordan Holds First Election Since 1967 (March 12): Nationwide balloting fills eight vacant seats in 60-member Council of Delegates, lower house of Parliament. Women are allowed to vote for first time.

Hussein Scores U.S. Mideast Policy (March 14): In interview with The New York Times, Jordan's king rejects peace talks with Israel in statement viewed as serious blow to Reagan policy in Middle East. Hussein charges one-sided support of Israel has impugned U.S. credibility as a mediator in disputes in the region.

Argentine President Suffers Major Defeat (March 15): Senate rejects Raul Alfonsin's labor reform bill in his first setback since taking office in December 1983. Bill had called for government-supervised union elections, proportional representation and government supervision of union assets.

U.S. Photographer Killed in El Salvador (March 16): John Hoagland caught in crossfire between leftists and government troops northeast of San Salvador.

U.S. Diplomat Kidnapped in Beirut (March 16): William F. Buckley, first secretary of embassy's political section, abducted upon setting out for work. He is third American to have disappeared within three weeks. Earlier victims were Frank Regier, professor at American University, and Jeremy Levin, bureau chief of Cable News Network.

South Africa and Mozambique Sign Pact (March 16): Nonaggression treaty is designed to end long-standing hostilities. "Accord of Nkomati" is first such agreement between a black southern African nation and white South Africa.

E.C. Summit Fails to Settle Disputes (March 20): Two-day meeting at Brussels of leaders of European Community nations ends without settling issue of

Britain's contribution to budget. In another obstacle to progress, Prime Minister Garret FitzGerald of Ireland walks out to protest refusal to exempt Ireland from milk production cuts.

Mine Damages Soviet Ship Off Nicaragua (March 20): Five crewmen injured off Puerto Sandino. Nicaraguan rebel Democratic Revolutionary Alliance had said it had mined ports. (**March 21**): Soviet note to U.S. charges U.S. complicity in latest incident. Washington rejects charge.

Mitterand Confers in U.S. (March 21 et seq.): French President arrives in Washington for eight-day visit and is received warmly by President Reagan, who praises Mitterand's "courage and decisiveness" in handling international challenges. Visitor addresses joint session of Congress. Talks with leaders emphasize areas of agreement and mutual respect.

Sale of Missiles to Jordan Canceled (March 21): Reagan calls off transfer of 1,600 Stinger missiles to Jordan and sale of another 1,200 shoulder-fired weapons to Saudi Arabia. Missile deal had been opposed by Israel and in United States Congress.

Soviet Sub Collides With U.S. Carrier (March 21): Nuclear-powered Soviet vessel strikes glancing blow at *Kitty Hawk*. No injuries or serious damage reported. Carrier had been trailed by sub in routine surveillance.

French Troops Leave Lebanon (March 24): France announces it is withdrawing remaining 1,250 soldiers. France is last member of multi-national peacekeeping force to evacuate forces.

$21.8 Million Robbery in Rome (March 24): Four armed men loot Brink's security vault in what police call biggest single theft in Italy's history. Red Brigades guerrillas reported to have taken responsibility, but police suspect common criminals.

Coal Strike Shuts 80% of British Mines (March 25): Walkout, begun March 12 in nation's 172 pits, protests announced layoffs and closings of mines.

$500 Million Package for Argentina (March 30): U.S., banks, and Latin nations join in move to rescue nation's tottering economy. (**March 31**): U.S. announces participation with $300 million loan to help President Raul Alfonsin over "crisis of government." Argentina can now make interest payments due since January on foreign debts.

Queen Elizabeth Visits Jordan (March 30): British monarch ends five-day visit, held under tight security. She expressed sympathy with the Palestinians and disapproval of Israeli occupation of West Bank. (**April 2**): President Chaim Herzog of Israel, after six-day visit to Britain, invites Queen to visit Israel.

Reagan Ends U.S. Role in Beirut (March 30): Releases Sixth Fleet from multi-nation peacekeeping force for duty elsewhere in Mediterranean. Number of warships off Lebanon had already been reduced. (**March 31**): Last French forces ferried from Beirut, in final action of 19-month multi-national force.

India Gives Sikhs Concession (March 31): Announces Government will amend constitution to recognize Sikhism as a separate religion. Sikhs in northern state of Punjab had waged campaign of violence in support of their separatist cause.

Honduran Commander Forced Out (March 31): Gen. Gustavo Alvarez Martinez, supporter of U.S. military presence, resigns and is flown out of country. President Roberto Suazo Cordova takes charge of armed forces.

National

Senate Votes Export Act Revision (March 1): Approves measure revising Export Administration Act of 1979. Law outlines executive branch trade powers in relation to foreign policy and national security considerations.

Supreme Court Backs Nativity Scene (March 5): Rules, 5-4, that a city can constitutionally use public funds for Christmas crèche. Reverses Court of Appeals in upholding display in Pawtucket, R.I., as not violating separation of church and state. Chief Justice Warren E. Burger, for majority, stresses "legitimate secular" purpose of Christmas displays as reminder of "significant historical religious event."

Compromise on Deficit Reduction (March 15): Reagan and Republican Congressional leaders agree on revised budget plan to cut deficit by $150 billion by fiscal 1987. President agrees to $57 billion slash in defense spending.

Record Deficit in Balance of Payments (March 19): Commerce Dept. reports gap of $40.78 billion for 1983, more than double previous shortfall of $15.5 billion recorded for 1978.

Senate Blocks School Prayer Amendment (March 20): Vote is 56–44, 11 short of two-thirds required for passage. Amendment would have permitted organized spoken prayer in public schools.

Justices Back Judgment Against Monsanto (March 20): Supreme Court, 8–0, upholds $10.5 million award to Spray-Rite Service Corp., which had charged "vertical price-fixing" conspiracy. Court rejects Administration plea to overturn 73-year-old antitrust "per se" rule that price agreements between producers and distributors are a violation.

Supreme Court Widens Libel Suit Rights (March 20): Rules unanimously in two cases that plaintiffs can sue publication or its employees in any state in which publication circulates, giving them latitude to seek favorable jurisdiction for suits. Cases involved Hustler magazine and two employees of National Enquirer.

Congress Votes Bankruptcy Reform (March 21): House, following Senate, acts ten days before expiration of temporary authority under which Federal Bankruptcy Court was operating. Measure would make it difficult for companies in reorganization to escape obligations of labor union contracts.

General

Braniff Resumes Service to 20 Cities (March 1): Restructured airline is much smaller than when it filed for bankruptcy protection in 1982. Hyatt Corp. now owns 80% of Braniff.

$13.5 Billion Merger Offer (March 5): Standard Oil Co. of California and Gulf Corp. negotiate for Standard to purchase Gulf for $80 a share. If approved by Federal antitrust regulators, it would be biggest merger in U.S. history.

Major Drug Seizure in Colombia (March 10): Police seize cocaine valued at $1.2 billion on street in raid on a cocaine-processing center. Lewis Tambs, U.S. Ambassador, calls it "largest drug raid in the world." Embassy says plant was protected by Colombian Revolutionary Armed Forces, the military wing of the Colombia Communist Party.

Miami Policeman Acquitted in Death (March 15): All-white jury clears Hispanic officer, Luis Alvarez, of manslaughter charge in 1982 shooting death of black messenger. Rioting in black Miami neighborhoods rages 24 hours without injuries or deaths.

Four Men Sentenced in Barroom Rape (March 17 and 26): Get prison terms after separate trials found them guilty of joining in 1983 attack on woman in a Bedford, Mass., tavern. Sentences handed down in Falls River, Mass., Superior Court. Two others acquitted. Case drew national attention and stirred protests among women's groups and Portuguese-American community.

Black Engineer Cleared in Robbery (March 26): Lenell Geter acquitted in second trial in Texas after sentence to life in first trial drew national attention. He had charged that arrest was result of racism and poor police work.

Canadian Wins Steelworkers Election (March 30): Lynn Williams, 59, secretary of United Steelworkers, wins over treasurer, Frank McKee, 63, in union balloting.

APRIL 1984

International

3 Arabs Wound 48 in Jerusalem (April 2): With guns and grenades, they attack crowds of shoppers in heart of city. One person injured critically. One of attackers fatally wounded, two others caught.

First Indian Astronaut in Space (April 3): Rakesh Sharma, 35, Air Force pilot, joins Soviet astronauts for eight-day visit to *Salyut 7* space station, where three other Soviet astronauts have lived since Feb. 8.

Armed Forces Seize Power in Guinea (April 3): Military seal off West African nation a week after death of President Ahmed Sékou Touré ends what they call a "bloody and ruthless dictatorship."

New Army Chief in Honduras (April 4): Congress elects Gen. Walter López Reyes, 43, a friend of U.S. to replace ousted Gen. Gustav Alvarez Martinez.

U.S. and Japan Agree on Trade Quotas (April 7): Reach new export accord to allow American farmers to sell significantly more beef and citrus products to Japan.

Anti-Soviet Olympic Bias Charged (April 9): Soviet Olympic Committee says anti-Soviet campaign is taking shape for summer games in Los Angeles. Calls for emergency session of International Olympic Committee to examine security and demand U.S. adherence to Olympic charter.

Nicaragua Goes to World Court (April 9): Asks International Court of Justice to declare illegal support by U.S. for guerrilla raids on its territory and what it called U.S. role in mining of harbors.

Pope Receives U.S. Envoy (April 9): John Paul II accepts credentials of William A. Wilson, first American ambassador to Vatican in more than 100 years.

Chernenko Becomes Soviet President (April 11): Party leader Konstantin U. Chernenko, 72, completes consolidation of top offices in only two months. Action taken on opening day of session of Supreme Soviet, the nation's nominal legislature.

Arabs Hijack Bus in Israel (April 12): Terrorists force vehicle to occupied Gaza Strip. **(April 13):** Israeli troops storm bus and kill all four terrorists. A woman dies and seven passengers are injured. Army demolishes four houses of families of Palestinian terrorists.

Beirut Militia Free U.S. Professor (April 15): Shiite Moslems storm West Beirut house to release American kidnapped more than two months previously, Prof. Frank Regier of American University. They also free a Frenchman, Christian Joubert.

Briton Guilty of Spying Attempt (April 16): Michael Bettaney, 34, officer of MI5, Britain's domestic intelligence service, sentenced to 23 years in prison for attempted espionage for Soviet Union. Supersensitive material is found in home.

Embassy Employee Slain in El Salvador (April 16): Five armed men shoot Joaquim Alfredo Zapata Romero, 59, senior security Salvadoran officer of U.S. Embassy in San Salvador.

Two Americans Killed in South-West Africa (April 16): Bomb fatal to members of U.S. mission monitoring peace efforts in neighboring Angola. South Africa charges guerrillas carried out bombing.

Libyan Embassy Gunman Fires Into London Crowd (April 17): Machine-gun fire rakes Libyans protesting government of Muammar el-Qaddafi and kills policewoman. **(April 22):** Britain breaks diplomatic relations with Libya and orders embassy staff to leave. **(April 27):** After 11-day siege of embassy by British police, 30 diplomats and other occupants leave and fly home.

Two Senators Downed on Honduras Flight (April 18): Aboard unarmed Army helicopter attacked with another on flight near El Salvador border. They were Lawton Chiles of Florida and J. Bennett Johnston of Louisiana, both Democrats.

U.S. Bars Nicaraguan as Envoy (April 19): White House rejects Nora Astorga, Deputy Foreign Minister, at insistence of Central Intelligence Agency. She had major role in 1978 slaying of officer in Nicaraguan National Guard, Gen. Reynaldo Peréz Vega, a key C.I.A. operative.

29 Dead in Dominican Price Rioting (April 24): Mobs battle police in four cities after violence breaks out during 24-hour strike by businesses to protest government-ordered price increases on imports and on many foodstuffs.

U.S. Fines Swedish Exporter $3 Million (April 27): Federal judge in Washington finds "treacherous conduct" by electronics company in illegally shipping strategic American material to the Soviet Union. Company, Datasaab Contracting A.B., bought radar parts in U.S. and forwarded them to Soviet Union in violation of license.

China Signs Coal Accord (April 29): Agrees with Occidental Petroleum Corp. to begin developing what could be world's largest open-pit coal mine.

National

Justices Uphold Warrantless Test (April 2): Supreme Court, 7–2, rules police do not need search warrant to conduct chemical test on suspected narcotic discovered and exposed by a private party.

Supreme Court to Decide on Silent Prayer (April 2): Justices agree to rule on constitutionality of "moment of silence" laws for public schools. They reaffirm ruling that organized prayer violates Constitution.

Counsel Named for Meese Inquiry (April 2): Three-judge panel appoints Jacob A. Stein, 59, prominent Washington lawyer, to investigate charges against Edwin Meese 3rd, counselor to President Reagan and appointee for Attorney General.

Georgia Honors Dr. Martin Luther King, Jr. (April 3): Governor of home state signs bill creating holiday a day before 16th anniversary of assassination of civil rights leader.

Reagan for World Ban on Chemical Arms (April 4): President says rise in such weapons has "serious implications for our own security." U.S. will submit proposed treaty in Geneva to ban production, possession, and use of weapons.

Former U.S. Agent Held in Spy Case (April 4): Richard Craig Smith, 40, formerly of Army counterintelligence, charged with selling to Soviets information about American double agent operation.

Congress Rebukes Reagan on Harbor Mining (April 10): Senate, 84–12, adopts nonbinding resolution opposing use of federal funds to mine Nicaraguan waters. (April 12): House approves resolution, 281–111.

Space Shuttle Ends Seven-Day Mission (April 13): *Challenger* astronauts land at Edwards Air Force Base, Calif., because of bad weather at Cape Canaveral, Fla. After a first failure, crew rendezvoused with and captured *Solar Max* satellite, repaired and returned it to orbit for telescopic observations in space. It was first time disabled satellite had been visited and repaired in orbit.

Supreme Court Backs Searches for Aliens (April 17): Rules, 7-2, that immigration officials may conduct unannounced raids on factories and businesses to look for illegal aliens. Overturns lower court ruling.

Indiana Standard Liable in Oil Spill (April 19): Federal judge in Chicago rules company and two subsidiaries liable for damages in 1978 spill from tanker *Amoco Cadiz*, biggest such accident in tanker transportation history. Tanker ran aground on rocks off French coast.

Jesse Jackson Bars Convention Walkout (April 23): Reaches accord with Democratic leaders in exchange for promise by national chairman, Charles T. Manatt, to consider demands for changes in party rules that he says reduce his number of delegates and result in discrimination against minority candidates.

General Killed in Nevada Crash (April 27): Lieut. Gen. Robert M. Bond, vice commander of Air Force Systems Command, was reported flying Soviet MIG-23 jet that has been used in tests against American planes equipped with radar-evading technology.

Supreme Court Resolves Libel Issue (April 30): Rules, 6-3, that First Amendment guarantee of freedom of press requires appellate courts to conduct especially careful reviews of judgments. Finds inadequate evidence to justify finding against Consumers Union for inaccurate review of stereo speaker.

General

Idaho Congressman Convicted (April 2): Republican Rep. George Hansen, 53, a conservative, found guilty by Federal Court jury of filing false financial disclosure by omitting $87,000 silver deal and loans involving Texas billionaire Nelson Bunker Hunt.

Two Suspended Players Reinstated (April 3): Richard Bloch, baseball's impartial arbiter, orders Jerry Martin of Mets and Willie Wilson of Kansas City Royals reinstated by May 15. They had been suspended by Commissioner Bowie Kuhn for cocaine-related convictions.

Two Convicted Killers Executed in South (April 4): Inmates in Florida and Louisiana electrocuted as 17th and 18th to be executed since Supreme Court lifted ban on capital punishment in 1976.

RCA Cancels Videodisk Player (April 4): Losses ascribed to competition from video cassette recorder, which unlike the Videodisk player, can both record and play material.

Federal Reserve Raises Interest Rate (April 6): Board increases charge on loans to banks by half point to 9% in move to tighten credit during economic recovery.

First Baby From Frozen Embryo (April 10): Zoe, 5 1/2 pounds, world's first infant produced from embryo frozen two months, scientists announce in Melbourne, Australia. Healthy baby was delivered by Caesarean section.

Shearson American Express Acquiring Lehman Brothers Kuhn Loeb Inc. (April 10): Shearson to pay $360 million for one of Wall Street's oldest and most powerful investment banking concerns.

New Football Players' Union (April 12): Players of United States Football League vote decisively to form U.S.F.L. Players Association, part of Federation of Professional Athletes.

Canadian Heads Steelworkers' Union (April 12): Lynn R. Williams, 59, defeats Frank McKee to become first Canadian president of million-member United Steelworkers of America.

Texas Repeals Curb on Science Textbooks (April 14): Board of Education drops rule requiring texts in state's public schools to describe evolution as only one explanation of origin of humans and as theory, not established fact.

Nine Cleared in Anti-Klan Rally Deaths (April 15): All-white jury in Winston-Salem, N.C., acquits six Ku Klux Klansmen and three American Nazi Party members in federal trial on charges of civil rights violations in deaths of five Communists and wounding of seven others in 1979.

First Lexicon of Earliest Writing (April 17): Scholars at University of Pennsylvania announce plans to issue first volume of world's first dictionary of cuneiform, or wedge-shaped, Sumerian writing of ancient Mesopotamia.

Two Baseball Players Reinstated (April 17): Commissioner Bowie Kuhn rules Pascual Pérez of Atlanta Braves and Willie Aikens of Toronto Blue Jays, both convicted of drug charges, would be allowed to play May 16.

Chrysler's Earnings Set Record (April 18): Auto maker reports net for first quarter of $705.8 million, higher than any quarter or full year in its 60 years. Gain follows five years of restructuring, in which bankruptcy threatened.

G.N.P. Up 8.3% in First Quarter (April 19): Annual rate of economic growth well above 5% of last 1983 quarter.

Virus Believed Cause of AIDS (April 21): Virus discovered in France is called LAV, for lymphadenopathy-associated virus. Dr. James O. Mason, head of Federal Centers for Disease Control in Atlanta, terms it cause of acquired immune deficiency syndrome. Additional finds made at Atlanta centers and National Institutes of Health in Bethesda, Md.

Earthquake Shakes San Francisco Region (April 24): Damage greatest at center, 12 miles southeast of San Jose, measured 6.0 to 6.2 on Richter scale. Twelve persons injured and many shops are closed.

Robert Kennedy's Son David Found Dead (April 25): David Anthony Kennedy, 28, found in room at Palm Beach hotel in Florida. His life had been troubled by heroin and alcohol addiction after assassination of father in 1968, which son viewed on television.

Substance Vital to Blood Clotting Is Created (April 25): Genentech Inc. of South San Francisco announces production of factor VIII, largest and most complex protein ever created artificially in laboratory through cloning and transplanting of genes.

Kathy Boudin Switches Plea to Guilty (April 26): Prisoner, 40, pleads to murder and robbery charges in 1981 Brink's holdup in Rockland County, N.Y., in which guard and two policemen were slain. She expresses remorse for her part. Judge decides on sentence of 20 years to life in prison in agreement with state's prosecutors.

Claus Von Bülow's Conviction Voided (April 27): Rhode Island Supreme Court overrules jury verdict, in long and dramatic trial, that he twice tried to murder his wealthy wife. Judge finds some evidence tainted and orders a new trial.

MAY 1984

International

Justice Minister Slain in Colombia (May 1): President Belisario Betancur Cuartas declares state of siege after assassination April 30 of Rodrigo Lara Bonilla by one of two men on a motorcycle as he was being driven in Bogota. Minister had campaigned against drug traffickers and had received death threats.

Solidarity Disrupts May Day Parade (May 1): Lech Walesa and thousands of supporters shout slogans as they slip into official march in Gdansk and pass official reviewing stand. Communist officials appear stunned. Demonstrations develop into street clashes in Warsaw and other major cities.

Pope Visits Far East (May 2): President Reagan joins 5,000 Alaskans in welcoming John Paul II and hearing his plea for "openness of heart." The two confer at start of Pontiff's visit to South Korea, Papua New Guinea, the Solomon Islands, and Thailand. **(May 6):** At Seoul, Pope canonizes 93 Koreans and 10 French missionaries who died for faith between 1839 and 1867. It is first such canonization outside Rome since Middle Ages. Pope calm despite breach of security when young man brandished a cap gun near him. **(May 11):** John Paul visits Indochinese refugee camp in Thailand and tells thousands they are "free people who have rightful place in world." Flies home to Rome from Bangkok.

Warsaw Signs Economic Pact With Soviet (May 4): Fifteen-year agreement appears to offer renewed Russian assistance to Poland's failing economy in return for tighter linking of Poland to Soviet economic orbit.

Soviet Union Quits Olympic Games; Others Follow (May 7): Soviet National Olympic Committee calls participation of its athletes in 1984 games in Los Angeles "impossible" in light of "cavalier attitude of U.S. authorities" and charges no intention to "insure security of all sportsmen." Bulgaria and East Germany soon announce withdrawals. **(May 11–17):** Poland, Vietnam, Mongolia, Czechoslovakia, Laos, Afghanistan, and Hungary quit Olympic games.

Gunman Kills Three in Quebec Legislature (May 8): Canadian soldier fires volleys with submachine gun into Quebec National Assembly. Thirteen wounded.

World Court Rules Against U.S. (May 10): International Court of Justice rules unanimously that nation should immediately halt any attempts to blockade or mine Nicaraguan waters. Grants Nicaragua's request for preliminary restraining order to protect sovereign rights.

Denmark Stops Payments for Missile Deployment (May 10): Action by Parliament leads to withdrawal of first NATO country from program to deploy 572 missiles in West Germany, Britain, Italy, The Netherlands, and Belgium.

José Napoleón Duarte Declared El Salvador Winner (May 11): Central Elections Council finds moderate candidate winner of presidential election with almost 54% of vote. Washington reports CIA had provided $2.1 million in effort to prevent election of Roberto d'Aubuisson of opposition party.

Attacks Grow on Oil Shipping in Persian Gulf (May 14–16): U.S. officials report that for first time there is evidence that Iranian planes were striking at foreign-owned shipping in apparent fulfillment of threat to retaliate against Iraqi attacks on Iranian oil exports. Air attacks have set ablaze oil tankers in northern Persian Gulf in series of attacks in late April and early May.

Panama President Elected (May 16): Election tribunal names Nicolas Ardito winner of election May 6.

Arab League Condemns Iran (May 20): Majority resolution accuses nation of aggression in Persian Gulf and denounces Iranian attacks on Arab shipping. Resolution voted by foreign ministers at emergency meeting in Tunis.

Salvador Calls on U.S. for More Aid (May 21): President-elect José Napoleón Duarte appeals to U.S. Congress for more military assistance. He pledges his government to follow principles of Universal Declaration of Human Rights and vows he will never ask U.S. to send troops to fight in El Salvador. Following conference with Reagan, joint communiqué emphasizes that free elections provide "only access to power."

Philippine Opposition Makes Strong Showing (May 23): Tally of vote for National Assembly May 14 shows government of President Ferdinand E. Marcos and New Society Movement the victor, but with opponents much stronger than expected. Voting reported to have been orderly, but by May 16 at least 91 had been killed in clashes between Communist guerrillas and government forces.

Iran Resumes Attacks on Ships (May 24): After five-day lull, announces air hits on two large naval targets in vicinity of Kharg Island, Iranian oil-loading port.

National

Seven Agent Orange Makers Settle Lawsuit (May 7): Agree to create $180-million fund for thousand of Vietnam veterans and their families who said the herbicide had harmed them. Accord in Brooklyn Federal District Court follows more than five years' litigation. Award called largest ever won by class of claimants who sued for wrongful injury.

Ban on Yarmulkes in Military Upheld (May 8): U.S. Court of Appeals in Washington reverses, 3–0, lower court ruling that military could not prevent Jews from wearing prayer skullcaps without violating their religious freedom.

U.S. Supports Chicago Bank (May 17): Banking regulators pledge full support for Continental Illinois Corp., huge holding company. Package aimed to stop run on deposits at ailing institution. Company to seek merger to restore confidence in deposits.

General

1,000 Works Given 19 Art Museums (May 3): Mark Rothko Foundation announces donation of most of collection of works by Rothko, a leading artist of twentieth century. National Gallery in Washington gets core of collection.

Baseball Agreement on Drug Problem (May 3): Player-owner drug committee reaches accord for handling cases involving problem. Program provides discipline in some instances, with loss of some pay for players undergoing treatment.

Esmark Inc. Accepts Takeover Offer (May 4): Big Chicago conglomerate agrees to $2.4-billion deal with Kohlberg, Kravis, Roberts & Co., a leading New York investment house.

Four Connecticut Students Expelled in Cocaine Inquiry (May 4): Penalized by Choate Rosemary Hall School after one is arrested on charges of trying to smuggle $300,000 worth of the drug into country.

Unknown Donizetti Opera Unearthed (May 5): Three-act work, "Elisabeth," found as result of discoveries in London and Paris. Composed to French words sometime between 1840 and 1844.

1984 Olympic Pageantry Begins (May 8): Runners at United Nations in New York start Olympic torch on 9,000-mile cross-country relay to Los Angeles. Olympic officials, heroes of past games, and mayors of New York and Los Angeles join in ceremonies.

Fire Kills Eight at Amusement Park (May 11): Teen-agers perish when flames destroy Haunted Castle at Six Flags Great Adventure at Jackson Township, N.J.

Lorin Maazel Takes Pittsburgh Post (May 13): Named music consultant of Symphony Orchestra after resigning as director of Vienna State Opera in controversy with management and reported unwarranted criticism.

Martin Feldstein Quits Reagan Administration (May 9): Chairman of President's Council of Economic Advisers returning to Harvard University. He had frequently differed with White House over budget deficits and Federal Reserve policies.

Reagan Wins Test on Salvadoran Arms Aid (May 10): House of Representatives, 212–208, approves request for military aid that would give President discretion in spending money. Vote follows Reagan's TV address that some believed influenced votes.

U.S. Ruled Negligent in Atomic Tests (May 10): Federal judge in Salt Lake City finds radioactive fallout from above-ground testing in 1950s caused nine persons to die of cancer as result of way government conducted tests. Verdict is first time that explosions at Nevada Test Site from 1951 to 1962 had been legally found responsible for causing cancer.

Louisiana World Exposition Opens (May 12): Fair begins six-month run in New Orleans. Fair cost $350 million and was 10 years in preparation.

Sun Myung Moon's Appeal Blocked (May 14): Supreme Court refuses to review conviction for income tax evasion. Founder of Unification Church faces having to serve 18-month prison sentence.

Justices Define "Ineffective Counsel" (May 14): Supreme Court, 8–1, for first time sets standard in criminal appeals, ruling in Florida case.

Senate Votes Reagan Deficit-Reduction Plan (May 17): Party-line tally, 65–32. Senate version calls for cuts of about $142 billion through 1987.

JUNE 1984

International

Reagan Visits Ireland and England (June 4): President tells Irish Parliament in Dublin he would be willing to discuss with Soviet Union renunciation of force if Moscow would agree to arms limitations in Europe. Culminating his three-day visit, 5,000 demonstrators march through central Dublin to protest Reagan's visit and his foreign policies, particularly in Central America. Four-day visit to Ireland included stop at ancestral home of Ballyporeen. His speeches focused on nuclear arms talks and ending sectarian strife in Ulster. In London, President confers with Prime Minister Margaret Thatcher with emphasis on measures to counter terrorism, in preparation for conference of Western leaders. Reagans are luncheon guests of Queen Elizabeth at Buckingham Palace and have dinner with Mrs. Thatcher.

Saudis Down Two Iranian Fighters (June 5): Two pilots shoot down American-built F-4's. Saudi Arabians fly American-built F-15's with help from U.S. aerial tanker planes and surveillance craft. Iran reports 600 killed in Iraqi air raid on town of Baneh.

Soviet Scholar Returns From U.S. (June 6): Sergei M. Kozlov, mathematician, allowed to leave after indecision about leaving America produced a freeze in Soviet-United States scholarly exchanges.

300 Slain in Attack on Sikh Temple (June 6): Perish as Indian Army occupies Golden Temple, holiest shrine of Sikh religion, in northern city of Amritsar, in attempt to end terrorist campaign that has ravaged Punjab state for nearly two years. Fresh eruptions of violence have thwarted attempts at agreements between the Sikh party, Akali Dal, and government of Prime Minister Mrs. Indira Gandhi. **(June 7):** Twenty-seven die as Sikh protests against army's attack on temple erupt in sev eral Indian cities. **(June 10):** Some 500–600 Sikh troops desert in northeastern India, apparently angered by Army's raid on Golden Temple. A top Indian Army commander is slain. **(June 11):** Most of deserters arrested. More defections reported. **(June 13):** Prime Minister Gandhi declares rebellion is under control.

40th Anniversary of D-Day Observed (June 6): Veterans of Britain, U.S., Canada, and other nations return to beaches of Normandy to commemorate one of history's great invasions. Facing graves of those who died, President Reagan calls for rededication to unity of democracies and "a firm resolve to keep the peace." At Caen, Queen Elizabeth welcomes President François Mitterand of France. Eight heads of state honor dead at Utah Beach.

Summit Pledges Aid to Debtor Nations (June 7): Tenth conference of seven leaders of most powerful industrial democracies opens in London. President Reagan meets individually with leaders, who represent U.S., Britain, France, West Germany, Canada, Japan, and Italy. **(June 8):** Leaders disagree over new appeal to Soviet Union to resume nuclear arms talks, and on impact of U.S. deficit. **(June 9):** Conference pledges to make it easier for third-world countries to repay debts, promises continued fight on inflation and supports "precise commitments" to nonuse of force by both East and West.

Bulgaria Linked to Attack on Pope (June 9): Italian prosecutor reports to court that Bulgarian secret services recruited Mehmet Ali Agca, Turk convicted of shooting John Paul II in 1981, in plot to weaken Solidarity movement in Poland. Secret report asks trial of three Bulgarians and six Turks.

Pope on Six-Day Visit to Switzerland (June 12 et seq.): John Paul II's trip is 22nd abroad since becoming Pontiff. He addresses Roman Catholic, Protestant, and Orthodox groups. He renews pledge to seek Christian unity in talk at Geneva Headquarters of Protestant World Council of Churches.

Chernenko Rejects Nuclear Arms Talks (June 13): Soviet leader answers call by leaders of industrial democracies for renewed discussions. Says proposal is "not backed up by anything tangible."

Dutch Approve Delay on Missiles (June 14): Parliament approves government plan to delay stationing of U.S. cruise missiles on Dutch soil for two years after deadline scheduled for 1986.

Reagan Offers to Meet Russians (June 14): Tells televised news conference he is willing to "meet and talk any time" with Konstantin U. Chernenko, Soviet leader, to discuss broad range of issues for improved mutual understanding. In Moscow, spokesman says Russians favor idea of summit conference, but timing depends on preparations of issues to be discussed.

New Canadian Liberal Party Leader (June 16): John Napier Turner, 55, succeeds Pierre Elliott Trudeau as head of ruling party. Trudeau headed party for 16 years and was Prime Minister for all but nine months.

Polish Voting Is Quiet (June 17): Balloting for local councils is first election since martial law was imposed in December 1981. Appeals for boycott by Solidarity underground have some effect, but demonstrations are few and perfunctory.

Europe Votes Rebuff Governments (June 18): Parties of left and right defeated in balloting for European Parliament in ten member countries of Common Market. French Communists make worst showing. British Conservatives and West German Christian Democrats lose ground.

Mrs. Thatcher Condemns Strikers (June 19): British Prime Minister denounces "scenes of mob rule" in 100-day-old coal mine tie-up. Speaks in Commons day after worst outbreak of nation's industrial violence.

French and Soviet Leaders Clash (June 21): François Mitterand, French President, argues over human rights with Konstantin U. Chernenko. At Kremlin dinner, French President defies convention to raise case of Andrei D. Sakharov, physicist and rights activist.

Plot on U.S. Ambassador Exposed (June 22): Officials in Washington and El Salvador report plan by right-wing Salvadoran extremists to kill Thomas R. Pickering.

Bonn Mission in East Berlin Cut Off (June 25): West Germans close diplomatic post to East Germans seeking refuge and emigration to the West.

Congress Bars Aid to Nicaragua Rebels (June 25): Senate, 88–1, ends deadlock with House over move to delete funds from bill which also provided $100 million for summer youth jobs. Administration accepts action.

Common Market Dispute Settled (June 26): Five-year old budget disagreement ends in move to clear way for greater European political and economic unity. Leaders of ten nations, meeting in France, agree to compromise on size of Britain's contribution.

Jackson Wins Release of Cuban Prisoners (June 27): President Fidel Castro agrees to plea and frees 26 political prisoners and 22 U.S. citizens, most of them held in Cuban jails on drug-trafficking charges.

Russians Propose Space Weapons Talks (June 29): Suggests conference in September at Vienna and offers reciprocal moratorium on testing of weapons for use in outer space, effective with the opening of the sessions. Soviet statement urges a comprehensive ban on pace weapons "of any kind." In Washington, Soviet Ambassador is told U.S. is willing to discuss ban but in the context of restrictions on all missile systems.

Argentina Reaches Accord in Debt Crisis (June 29): Agrees with international banks on $350 million payment of overdue interest on $45 billion debt, third largest in the developing world. Government has adopted austerity measures to ease crisis.

Bolivian President Kidnapped in Abortive Coup (June 30): Group of army and police officers abduct Hernán Siles Zuazo, release him hours later. Civilian coalition cabinet controls nation. **(July 2):** Two former cabinet ministers and 100 right-wing military officers arrested in coup attempt. Leader, still in hiding, identified as Col. Rolando Saravia. **(July 10):** In embarrassment for U.S., kidnappers prove to be leaders of new narcotics police unit financed and equipped by U.S.

17th Canadian Prime Minister Sworn in (June 30): Sixteen-year era dominated by Pierre Elliott Trudeau ends with induction of John N. Turner, 55, until recently a corporate lawyer, who had pledged a more businesslike government.

National

High Court Backs Youth Detention (June 4): Ruling, 6–3, reinstates New York law, similar to those in 50 states, under which juveniles charged with delinquency may be held before trial to prevent them from committing additional crimes. Justices reverse two lower Federal courts.

Severe Drought Plagues Wide Southwest Area (June 5): For second year, crops are ruined and ranchers are forced to sell breeding stock.

High Court Allows Illegal Evidence (June 11): Justices, 7–2, rule that illegally obtained evidence may be admitted at trial if prosecution can prove it would "inevitably" have been discovered by lawful means.

Justices Restrict Rights of Suspects (June 12): Supreme Court rules, 5–4, that in cases of "overriding consideration of public safety," police may question a suspect without the "Miranda warning" of his right not to incriminate himself.

Supreme Court Upholds Seniority in Layoffs (June 12): Decision, 6–3, holds a court may not order employer to protect jobs of recently hired black employees at expense of whites with greater seniority. Court overturns lower courts' orders protecting black officers of Memphis Fire Department from layoffs.

Congress Votes Immigration Bill (June 20): House, 216–211, passes comprehensive measure to stem flow of illegal immigrants. Senate has voted similar bill by 4–1 margin. Landmark House bill would prohibit employment of illegal aliens and offer legal status to others who can prove they have been living in U.S. since January 1982.

Congress Votes $50 Billion Tax Increases (June 23): House and Senate conferees approve four-year package, including $11 billion in benefit cuts, in step toward program to reduce deficit. Many rules changed. Major part of spending cuts is nearly $8 billion saved in Medicare, including premium increase and 15-month freeze in physicians' fees.

"Bubble" Policy for Clear Air Reinstated (June 25): Supreme Court, 6–0, overrules lower court and decides Clean Air Act permits extension of policy allowing companies to increase pollutants in one area if they are offset by decreases elsewhere.

Appeals Court Rejects Special Counsel Move (June 25): Eight judges in Washington rule no court has power to appoint independent counsel over objection of Attorney General. Reverse lower court order that Attorney General William French Smith have such counsel investigate how 1980 Reagan campaign got documents from Carter White House and campaign.

Supreme Court Halts N.C.A.A. TV Control (June 27): Justices, 7–2, rules 33-year power by National Collegiate Athletic Association to regulate number of appearances by a football team is "unreasonable restraint of trade," violating Sherman Antitrust Act.

Overhaul of Bankruptcy System Approved (June 28): House-Senate conferees agree to major overhaul. In victory for labor, conferees limit employers' freedom to escape union contracts by declaring bankruptcy. Changes also affect lenders and consumers, farmers, and small businesses.

Jesse Jackson Rejects Black Muslim's Views (June 28): Democratic Presidential candidate brands "reprehensible" words of Louis Farrakhan, who had called creation of Israel an "outlaw act" and referred to Judaism as a "gutter religion."

General

One Dead, 18 Missing as Sailing Ship Capsizes (June 2): Nine survivors say rogue wind from "out of nowhere" sunk *Marques* north of Bermuda. The 117-foot British square-rigged bark had been racing with 41 other sailing vessels from Bermuda to Halifax, Nova Scotia.

Genes From Extinct Animal Reproduced (June 4): Scientists report cloning in laboratory of University of California at Berkeley. Say genetic material DNA was extracted from dried muscle tissue of animal called quagga, relative of zebra and horse. Skin had been preserved for 140 years in West Germany.

Tornadoes Kill at Least 16 in Wisconsin (June 8): Forty-nine tornadoes sweep Plains and upper Middle West. One town flattened and damage is heavy.

Wall Street Journal Settles Libel Suit (June 8): Dow Jones & Company to pay $800,000 in $5 million action brought by two former Federal prosecutors who said they were defamed by articles in 1979. Payment is largest reported settlement in libel suit that did not go to trial.

Treatment for Herpes Attacks Reported (June 13): Daily oral doses of drug acyclovir said to suppress or prevent recurring attacks of genital herpes in people infected with fast-spreading, sexually transmitted disease. Scientist at medical virology section of National Institute of Allergy and Infectious Diseases says treatment is not a cure but a major accomplishment over past therapies.

Kentucky Derby Winner Drops Dead (June 17): Swale, three-year-old who won Derby in May and Belmont Stakes nine days previously, collapses suddenly outside stable at Belmont Park. **(June 20):** Veterinarians announce after preliminary laboratory reports that Swale did not suffer heart failure and that cause of death remains a mystery. **(July 10):** Area of fibrosis on heart which can cause fatal arrhythmia, reported after tests at University of Pennsylvania's School of Veterinary Science.

Radio Talk-Show Host Shot Dead (June 18): Alan Berg, 50, controversial radio host known for irritating listeners, killed outside his Denver home.

Hollywood Negotiates a New Rating (June 19): Motion picture industry develops new rating of PG-13, to put some movies off limits for children under 13 unless accompanied by parent or guardian. It is first major change in code in 16 years of system.

Suspect Held in Murder of Ten (June 20): Christopher Thomas, 34, charged with killings in Brooklyn, called New York City's largest mass murder.

Businessman Sentenced in Slaying of Two (June 21): Irwin M. Margolies, 49, gets 50 years to life in prison for murders of two women in bungled plot. Three CBS technicians were also slain in New York. The former owner of Manhattan diamond company charged with hiring a gunman to kill two employees he feared had alerted U.S. agencies to a fraud scheme.

Baseball Owners Approve Drug Program (June 21): Major league managements ratify management-union program to deal with drug abuse among players. Players had already accepted the control proposals.

Space Shuttle Flight Aborted (June 25): Computer malfunction forces delay of launching at Cape Canaveral, Fla. **(June 26):** Engines of *Discovery* begin firing and then cut off, forcing long postponement of mission. Computers detected apparent valve failure. Six-member crew unharmed. No previous shuttle had failed. It was second such aborted flight for an American-manned spacecraft.

New Test for Liver Cancer (June 26): Scientists at Massachusetts General Hospital report rapid, highly sensitive screening method. Can detect cancers arising in liver cells after long infection with hepatitis B virus.

JULY 1984

International

Iraquis Report Sinking Five Ships (July 1): Says Air Force also shot down an Iranian F-14 jet in northern Persian Gulf. Renewal of ground fighting with Iran also reported east of southern port of Basra.

Head of Argentine Army Ousted (July 5): President Raúl Alfonsín dismisses Chief of Staff, Gen. Jorge H. Arguindegui and three other generals in reported move to quell dissent inside army over prosecution of military men for abuses of human rights.

Nigerian Exile Kidnapped in London (July 6): Umaro Dikko, former government official called Nigeria's "most wanted man," seized at gunpoint, drugged, and sealed in crate ready to be loaded on plane and addressed to official in Lagos. British antiterrorist police free him. **(July 7):** Authorities in Britain and Nigeria agree to allow each other's aircraft to return home, ending diplomatic standoff. **(July 10):** British charge Nigerian and three Israelis with kidnapping. Nigerian government has repeatedly denied involvement in it.

Lebanese Army Takes Over Beirut (July 6): Completes transfer of capital from militia forces. Security plan aimed at unifying city under control of Prime Minister Rashid Karami.

Fire Damages York Minister Cathedral (July 9): Lightning believed cause of blaze at York, England. Damage to ancient structure estimated at $1.3 million. Cathedral's windows contain half of all medieval stained glass found in Britain.

General Strike Paralyzes Beirut (July 9): Protesters demand action to free kidnapped relatives. They shut down roads and crossing points between Moslem and Christian sections. Force closing of Beirut International Airport only hours after it had been reopened for first time in five months.

Crippling Soviet Naval Blast Reported July (10): Authoritative British publication says explosion May 13 in ammunition depot at Severomorsk, northeast of Murmansk, impaired fighting capacity of Northern Fleet, strongest of Soviet Navy's four high-sea fleets. Nearly 300 persons reported killed. Carelessness blamed as cause of explosion.

World Population of 10 Billion Seen (July 10): World Bank projects doubling by year 2050. Most of increase expected to come from poorer countries.

Roosevelt-Churchill Friction Reported (July 11): Complete correspondence between wartime leaders reveals serious strains after military alliance was forged. Princeton University Press will publish the correspondence.

Pope Rebukes Nicaragua Government (July 11): Pope John Paul II denounces expulsion of 10 missionaries and calls on Sandinista regime to reverse decision.

New Church Council Official (July 12): Rev. Emilio Castro of Uruguay elected general secretary of World Council of Churches. He left Roman Catholic Church to join small Evangelical Methodist Church.

Train Crash Kills 36 in Yugoslavia (July 14): Freight train crashes into holiday express with 1,500 passengers, mostly youngsters at siding at Divaca.

21 Salvador Police Killed (July 14): Treasury officers die as leftist guerrillas attack cargo train 25 miles north of capital. Three civilians wounded.

Conservatives Ousted in New Zealand (July 14): Labor Party defeats National Party in general election. Labor, led by David Lange, has 17-seat margin over Sir Robert Muldoon's party. Labor wants to bar U.S. nuclear-armed and -powered naval vessels. **(July 16):** To avoid Pacific crisis, U.S. Navy plans not to send Navy ships to New Zealand until mid-1985.

Danube Power Project Protested (July 15): Thousands of Hungarians petition against plan to dam or divert 138-mile stretch for hydroelectric power. It is reported to be biggest environmental protest in Soviet bloc.

U.S. and Soviet Agree on New Hot Line (July 17): Officials in Washington initial diplomatic note upgrading 21-year-old hot-line link between Washington and Moscow for communication in times of crisis.

Cabinet Shaken Up in France (July 17): Prime Minister Pierre Mauroy and Cabinet resign. President François Mitterand appoints Industry Minister, Laurent Fabius, to form new government. At 37 he is youngest Prime Minister in modern French history. **(July 19):** Communists quit Government, charging Socialist policies would eliminate jobs and crush industry.

Earthquake Shakes Areas in Britain (July 19): Most powerful one ever recorded there rocks buildings in western areas and along east coast of Ireland. Last major quake reported in 1884.

Reagan Reports Laos Agreement (July 20): President says it will let U.S. officials excavate a site to seek remains of 13 American servicemen whose plane crashed there nearly 13 years previously.

Dockworkers End British Tie-Up (July 21): Union leaders approve agreement with port employers ending 10-day strike that had paralyzed most of Britain's trade. Strike grew out of 18-week-old miners' strike and protested use of nonunion labor to load iron ore.

Warsaw Grants Political Amnesty (July 21): Parliament votes bill to release 652 within 30 days, marking 40th anniversary of Communist rule in Poland. Measure also extends amnesty to 35,000 common criminals.

Israeli Election Indecisive (July 24): Parties negotiate for coalition partners after Labor alignment wins 44 or 45 seats in Parliament and ruling right-wing Likud bloc 40 or 41.

President Lifts Ban on Soviet Fishing (July 25): Action taken under policy of improving relations with Soviet Union. President Carter had imposed embargo in 1980 in response to Soviet invasion of Afghanistan.

Woburn Abbey Booty Discovered (July 28): Workmen stumble on $6.6-million worth of silver and heirlooms stolen from Duke of Bedford's stately home, 20 miles from London. Thieves evaded security system March 14.

Train Crash in Scotland Kills 14 (July 30): Forty injured as crowded commuter express hits cow and derails between Edinburgh and Glasgow.

Leftist Guerrillas Kill 58 in Salvador (July 31): Slay 39 civil defense troops and 19 civilians in attack on two farming cooperatives and village.

79 Rescued from Hijacked Plane (July 31): Commandos storm hijacked Venezuelan DC-9 jetliner at Wilemstad, Curaçao, and kill both hijackers.

JULY 1984

National

Mrs. Burford Named to Environment Panel (July 2): President chooses Anne M. Burford to head National Advisory Committee on Oceans and Atmosphere. She had been forced to resign in 1983 as head of Environmental Protection Agency. **(July 3):** Environmental leaders express outrage at appointment. **(Aug. 1):** At Mrs. Burford's request, White House withdraws appointment. She cites "furor" over it.

High Court Lifts Broadcast Editorial Ban (July 2): Justices, 5–4, uphold District bench in ruling unconstitutional a federal law forbidding the broadcasting of editorials by hundreds of public radio and television stations that get funds from Corporation for Public Broadcasting. Court also rules that anyone in police custody, even for minor crime, must be formally advised of right against self-incrimination.

Supreme Court Rules Against Jaycees (July 3): Justices, 7–0, decide state laws can force all-male organization to accept women as members, overruling lower court.

Link of Scholarship Aid to Draft Upheld (July 5): Supreme Court, 6–2, overturns lower court ruling against federal law making college men who fail to register ineligible for federal educational assistance.

Curb on Evidence Relaxed (July 5): Supreme Court, 6–3, rules some evidence gathered with defective search warrants could be used in criminal prosecutions. It is a victory for Reagan Administration in controversy.

U.S. Life Expectancy at Record High (July 8): Government statistics show age-adjusted death rate at a low. Life expectancy reported at 74.2 years for 1981.

Deadline for Car Air Bags Is Set (July 11): U.S. Government says bags or automatic seat belts must be provided on all new passenger cars unless two-thirds of states require seat belt use before April 1, 1989.

The 39th Democratic National Convention (July 16–19): Meeting in San Francisco, 3,944 delegates nominated former Vice President Walter F. Mondale of Minnesota as candidate for President on the first ballot, then chose Rep. Geraldine A. Ferraro of Queens, N.Y., by acclamation for Vice President, the first woman to be named for the office on a major party ticket. An exuberant convention ended with a display of unity and a determination to defeat President Reagan for re-election. The party platform moved away from some Democratic traditions of liberalism, favoring less expensive social policies and stressing centrist and "family" values. Specific points included: reduction of "intolerable deficits"; tax reform; equal rights for women; a reversal of "automatic militarization" of foreign policy, and pursuit of peace in the Middle East. Major speakers included New York Gov. Mario Cuomo, the Rev. Jesse H. Jackson, and Gary Hart, unsuccessful contenders for the nomination, and Senator Edward M. Kennedy, who pledged support for the ticket. Mondale, accepting the nomination, branded Reagan policies a threat to the nation's economic security and the physical survival of its families. Mrs. Ferraro called her nomination a triumph for the feminist movement and those with immigrant backgrounds. Mondale encountered party opposition to his abortive attempt to remove Charles T. Manatt as chairman of the Democratic National Committee and his appointment of Bert Lance as general chairman of his campaign. (Lance later withdrew from the post.)

Reagan Signs Bill for Higher Drinking Age (July 17): Approves legislation to deny some Federal highway funds to states that keep their drinking age under 21. President appeals for cooperation in ending "crazy quilt" of different laws in the states.

Congress Votes School Prayer Meetings (July 25): House, 337–77, approves bill passed by Senate allowing students to hold religious meetings in public high schools outside regular school hours. President Reagan enthusiastically supports bill. It would also affirm students' rights to political and philosophical meetings.

Senate Strengthens Waste Disposal Law (July 25): Votes, 93–0, to reauthorize statute regulating handling, transportation, and disposal of toxic wastes. House has approved similar measure.

U.S. Rescues Bank from Insolvency (July 26): Three agencies agree on $4.5 billion to save Continental Illinois National Trust and Bank Company of Chicago, largest package of federal support for any private enterprise. Bank, with billions in bad loans, threatened with outflow of deposits. Move also taken to avoid possibility of major international financial crisis.

JULY 1984

General

Journalist Jailed for Concealing Source (July 3): Richard Hargraves, 34, gets indefinite contempt sentence in Belleville, Ill., court for refusing to reveal source for an editorial that led to a libel suit. **(July 5):** Writer freed after official reveals he was source.

Air Florida Files in Bankruptcy (July 3): Carrier, once successful under airline deregulation, fails as result of fare wars and competition.

Woman Reports 10th Set of Twins (July 4): Maria Gonçalves Moreira of Rio de Janeiro leaves hospital with identical twin boys, 4 pounds 8 ounces and 4 pounds 4 ounces. Miss Moreira says double births run in family and expects to have more.

Gene Fragment Called Widespread (July 5): Researchers in U.S. and Switzerland find substance that appears to be common to human beings, flies, earthworms, chickens, and frogs. Dr. Gary Struhl of Harvard University thinks discovery may be "major breakthrough in understanding vertebrate development."

World's Second Embryo Birth (July 6): Birth of 8-pound, 14-ounce boy developed from frozen embryo is announced by physician in Holland. Baby in good condition.

11 Killed on Tennessee River (July 7): Perish as triple-deck riverboat capsizes in 70-mile-an-hour wind. Seven reported rescued on excursion trip.

Five Killed in Vermont Train Crash (July 8): Amtrak passenger train with 275 aboard derails while crossing washed-out culvert at Wiliston, Vt., injuring 153. "Extraordinary" local disaster plan praised by federal officials for saving many lives.

A.T.&T. Freezes Management Pay (July 10): Will keep present levels through 1985 for 114,000 management-level salaries in move expected to save $184 million in coming year.

New York Gets First Seat-Belt Law (July 11): Gov. Mario Cuomo signs legislation requiring automobile drivers and front seat passengers to wear belts, and passengers under 10 to wear belts or sit in special seats. Saving of life predicted. Measure first of kind in country.

Train-Truck Crash Kills Two (July 11): Five others injured when Amtrak passenger train crashes into gasoline carrier at crossing near McBee, S.C. It is third fatal Amtrak crash within a week.

$80,000 Ring Found on Jetliner (July 11): Two cleaning women recover engagement ring lost by Elize Botha, wife of Prime Minister P.W. Botha of South Africa, on plane that flew couple to Britain.

$7.5 Million Auto Accident Verdict (July 12): Jury in Los Angeles awards compensatory damages to New York teacher who lost use of arms and legs in van accident on family vacation in New Mexico in 1978. She had charged defective design on a wheel in suit against Rockwell International Corp. and its Western Wheel Division.

Three Hippopotamuses Die in Zoo Mishap (July 15): Neighboring elephant blamed for opening valve and allowing 140-degree water to flow into their pool at Karlsruhe, West Germany.

"Quiet Man" Kills 21 in McDonald's (July 19): James Oliver Huberty, 41, wounds 19 in San Ysidro restaurant gunfire before police sharpshooter kills him. Huberty revealed as unemotional neighbor who had accumulated arsenal of weapons and sometimes turned violent, beating his daughter.

Abducted Mexican Woman Freed (July 20): Edith Rosenkranz, wife of one of wealthiest Mexicans, kidnapped at gunpoint from Washington hotel during national bridge championships. **(July 22):** Three suspects arrested after she is freed unharmed after 46 hours in captivity. Money called motive.

Photos Cost Miss America Her Title (July 20): Officials of Miss America Pageant vote to ask reigning queen, Vanessa Williams, 21, to resign because she had posed before her selection for sexually explicit pictures published in *Penthouse* magazine. **(July 23):** Miss Williams agrees to yield crown. Suzette Charles, Miss New Jersey, runner-up, succeeds to title.

Amtrak Trains Collide Head-on in New York (July 23): One killed and 125 injured on viaduct 80 feet above Queens street. Train service snarled. **(July 26):** Amtrak president says error by signal operator is likeliest cause of crash.

Rev. Sun Myung Moon Enters Prison (July 21): Leader of Unification Church, 64, starts serving 18-month sentence for income-tax evasion. Korean evangelist reported adjusting well in Danbury, Conn., federal prison.

F.C.C. Raises Limit on TV Station Ownership (July 26): Repealing 31-year-old rule, it decides individual or company may own 12 instead of 7. Will remove all restrictions on ownership in 1990.

Cheating at Bridge Tournament Alleged (July 30): Five young players from Boston area suspected of using illegal signals. Suspended by American Contract Bridge League after withdrawing from national tournament in Washington, where video tapes were taken.

AUGUST 1984

International

Britain-China Accord on Hong Kong (Aug. 1): Nations settle on draft agreement outlining terms under which colony will be turned over to China in 1997. For 50 years, accord will "provide for preservation of all rights and freedoms" of Hong Kong people.

Former Argentinian President Jailed (Aug. 2): Jorge Rafael Videla indicted by military's top court on charges related to thousands of deaths and disappearances under his rule.

Congress Boosts Aid to El Salvador (Aug. 10): Approves compromise to give extra $70 million in military assistance in current fiscal year.

U.S. Copters Seek Mines in Middle East (Aug. 13): Three minesweeping craft sent to Saudi Arabia to widen search for source of explosions in Gulf of Suez and Red Sea. U.S. move to clear channels made at request from Saudi government.

Russians Test Cruise Missiles (Aug. 25): Soviet Defense Ministry says it has conducted successful tests of long-range, ground-launched weapons in response to what it called widespread deployment of such missiles by U.S.

National

Bert Lance Quits as Mondale Chairman (Aug. 2): Resigns Presidential campaign post less than three weeks after appointment. Mondale had asked Lance to join campaign to underscore political interest in South.

Reagan Signs Child Support Bill (Aug. 16): Approves measure to enforce payment of obligations, denouncing "devil-may-care" attitude of some parents. Law, passed unanimously by both houses of Congress, requires some withholding of child support payments when a parent falls one month behind.

Ferraro Defends Her Finances (Aug. 20): Democratic Vice-Presidential nominee releases mass of records intended to quiet controversy. They answer some questions, but raise others as to whether she had met ethics requirements of House of Representatives. **(Aug. 21):** In two-hour news conference she vigorously defends propriety of affairs, admitting some sloppy recordkeeping and technical mistakes by others.

The 33rd Republican National Convention (Aug. 20–23): Delegates at Dallas, Texas, renominate Ronald Reagan and George Bush by acclamation in riotous "coronation" ceremony at otherwise lackluster conclave, with conservatives in control. Convention opens with party leaders attacking Mondale ticket as having "nothing to offer." Week's speakers include: Senator Howard H. Baker of Tennessee; Jeane J. Kirkpatrick, chief U.S. delegate to United Nations; Margaret M. Heckler, Secretary of Health and Human Services; Katherine Davalos Ortega, treasurer of U.S. and first woman to keynote a G.O.P. convention, and Senator Barry Goldwater of Arizona, "Mr. Conservative." In his acceptance speech President Reagan appeals for party's help in finishing "unfinished agenda" of a conservative reformation of Government. Party platform, adopted without debate, is most conservative in decades. It pledges even lower and more simplified tax rates, increased tax shelters to protect incomes, and reduction of federal deficit through expanding a strong economic recovery credited to Administration's policies. It also opposes abortion, promotes school prayer, and denounces pornography.

B-1 Prototype Crashes in Test Flight (Aug. 29): One crewman killed, two others injured as bomber bursts into flames in Mojave Desert. **(Aug. 30):** Air Force says craft was on mission to test slow flight control. **(Aug. 31):** Officials say bomber stalled when pilot banked sharply to avoid observation plane.

Former Reagan Aide Indicted (Aug. 30): U.S. charges Thomas C. Reed, former national security official, with using inside information to reap $431,000 profit in stock market. He faces five years in prison on each charge of fraud, perjury, and obstruction of justice.

General

Games of XXIII Olympiad Held (July 29): Competition in Summer Games begins in Los Angeles with U.S. winning four gold medals in swimming and one in cycling. **(Aug. 12):** As Games end, U.S. has won 83 gold medals and Romania is second with 20. U.S. has won total of 174 medals; West Germany is second with 59. Speculation arises as to possible results if 14 Soviet bloc nations had competed instead of boycotting games.

Widow Wins Right to Husband's Sperm (Aug. 1): Paris court rules for Corinne Parpalaix, ruling that widow has right to use sperm deposited by her husband, who later died, in effort to have his child. Sperm bank had objected to her claim in case that had aroused international interest in new legal issue.

New York State Curbs Acid Rain (Aug. 14): Governor Cuomo signs nation's first law to curb the pollution. It requires reductions in emission of sulfur dioxide, one of prime contributors to acid rain.

Skin Patches Save Burn Victims (Aug. 15): Medical team in Boston takes tiny sections of skin from bodies of two young brothers, growing the patches into sheets and grafting them back over the burns. New technique called major advance in therapy.

Jaycees Admit Women Members (Aug. 16): All-male civic organization bows to Supreme Court decision.

Youngest Heart Transplant Patient Dies (Aug. 17): Hollie Roffey, 28 days old, develops respiratory problems in London hospital. Child born with left side of heart missing. She was given heart of three-day-old Dutch infant dead of brain damage.

Reporters Backed at Combat Scenes (Aug. 23): Defense Department panel recommends access to military operations for news organizations. Secretary Caspar W. Weinberger orders it put into effect. Military security to remain major consideration in guidelines.

Space Shuttle Fired After Three Delays (Aug. 30): *Discovery* rockets into orbit at Cape Canaveral, Fla., and deploys first of three communications satellites. Intruding private plane delays launching. Two other satellites to be deployed. Crew to test extendable solar-power panel and drug-processing unit. Commander of *Discovery* is Henry W. Hartsfield, Jr. Other crew members are: Comdr. Michael L. Coats of Navy; Lieut. Col. Richard M. Mullane of Air Force; and Dr. Steven A. Hawley, Dr. Judith A. Resnik, and Charles D. Walker. **(Aug. 31):** Crew reports $1.2-billion spaceship performing well, launches another communications satellite, and begins drug test. **(Sept. 5):** *Discovery* returns to a safe landing at Edwards Air Force Base, Calif., after completing its successful six-day maiden flight.

Late Events

Three Russians Equal Space Longevity Record (Sept. 5): Astronauts in orbit since Feb. 8, 1984, demonstrate Soviet commitment to long-term space flight by endurance record of 211 days in space.

Suicide Driver Blasts U.S. Lebanon Embassy (Sept. 20): Bomber devastates building at Aukar, with at least 23 reported dead and scores injured. Two Americans among dead and Ambassador is slightly injured. **(Sept. 22):** Administration officials acknowledge that security of structure near East Beirut was inadequate.

Inquiry Clears Edwin Meese 3rd (Sept. 20): Jacob A. Stein, court-appointed investigator, finds "no basis" for prosecuting President Reagan's counselor, the President's nominee for Attorney General. Stein reports mandate did not permit him to evaluate "propriety" or "ethics" of Meese's financial dealings.

Gromyko and Reagan Confer Three Hours (Sept. 28): President and Soviet Foreign Minister hold "forceful and direct" discussion of differences. Administration officials call meeting successful, with results uncertain.

Raiders Seize Mafia Figures in Italy (Sept. 30): Police round up organized crime figures in one of nation's most-sweeping anti-Mafia operations. Raids follow Mafia leader's informing on more than 100 crimes.

Labor Secretary Donovan Indicted (Oct. 1): Bronx grand jury names him, his former company, and seven company executives on charges of scheme to defraud New York City Transit Authority. **(Oct. 2):** Donovan pleads not guilty to 137-count indictment.

Space Shuttle Has Successful Voyage (Oct. 5-13): Challenger lands safely at Cape Canaveral, Fla., after trip marked by technical breakdowns and shrewd problem solving. Carries largest crew in history of space flight, five men and two women.

I.R.A. Bomb Blasts Mrs. Thatcher's Hotel (Oct. 12): Two are killed and 34 wounded in explosion in seafront building at Brighton, England, scene of Conservative Party conference. Irish Republican Army claims responsibility. Senior Cabinet member narrowly escapes.

Baboon's Heart Transplanted in Infant (Oct. 26): A surgical team headed by Dr. Leonard L. Bailey at Loma Linda University Medical Center near Riverside, Calif., transplanted a baboon's heart into a dying two-week old girl known as "Baby Fae." Baby Fae suffered from a severe birth defect known as hypoplastic heart syndrome.

Indira Gandi Assassinated (Oct. 30): Indian Prime Minister, Indira Gandi, 66, shot outside her home in New Delhi by two or three of her own security guards. She dies about two hours after the attack. Her son, Rajiv chosen to succeed her as Prime Minister.

1984 Nobel Prize Winners

Peace: Bishop Desmond Tutu (South African), general secretary of the South African Council of Churches, because the means by which the campaign to end apartheid "is conducted is of vital importance for the whole of the continent of Africa and in the cause of peace in the world."

Medicine: Dr. Cesar Milstein (dual British/Argentine) of the British Medical Research Council's Cambridge laboratory; Dr. Georges J. F. Kohler (West German) of the Basel Institute of Immunology in Switzerland; and Dr. Niels K. Jerne (dual British/Danish), professor emeritus of the Basel Institute, all for their work in immunology.

Physics: Dr. Carlo Rubbia (Italian), on the faculty of Harvard University and the staff of CERN, and Dr. Simon van der Meer (Dutch) senior engineer at CERN, outside Geneva, for their role in discovering three subatomic particles, a step toward developing a single theory to account for all natural forces.

Chemistry: Dr. R. Bruce Merrifield (American), professor at Rockefeller University, New York City, for research that revolutionized the study of proteins and has practical importance in the development of new drugs.

Economics: Sir Richard Stone (British), retired Cambridge University professor, for his work to develop the systems widely used to measure the performance of national economics.

Literature: Jaroslav Seifert, a Czechoslovak poet, for work which, "endowed with freshness, sensuality and rich inventiveness, provides a liberating image of the indomitable spirit and versatility of man."

Major Emmy Awards for TV, 1984

Drama series: *Hill Street Blues (NBC)*
- **Actress:** Tyne Daly, *Cagney & Lacey* (CBS)
- **Actor:** Tom Selleck, *Magnum, P.I.* (CBS)
- **Supporting actress:** Alfre Woodard, *Hill Street Blues* (NBC)
- **Supporting actor:** Bruce Weitz, *Hill Street Blues* (NBC)

Comedy series: *Cheers* (NBC)
- **Actress:** Jane Curtin, *Kate & Allie* (CBS)
- **Actor:** John Ritter, *Three's Company* (ABC)
- **Supporting actress:** Rhea Perlman, *Cheers* (NBC)
- **Supporting actor:** Pat Harrington, *One Day at a Time* (CBS)

Comedy, variety, or music program: *The Sixth Annual Kennedy Center Honors: A Celebration of the Performing Arts* (CBS)

Limited series or special: *Concealed Enemies,* American Playhouse (PBS)
- **Actress:** Jane Fonda, *The Dollmaker* (ABC)
- **Actor:** Sir Laurence Olivier, *Laurence Olivier's King Lear* (Syn.)
- **Supporting actress:** Roxana Zal, *Something About Amelia* (ABC)
- **Supporting actor:** Art Carney, *Terrible Joe Moran* (CBS)

Drama special: *Something About Amelia* (ABC)

Individual performance in a variety or music program: Cloris Leachman, *Screen Actors Guild 50th Anniversary Celebration* (CBS)

Children's program: *He Makes Me Feel Like Dancin'* (NBC)

Animated program: *Garfield on the Town* (CBS)

Information special: *America Remembers John F. Kennedy (Syn.)*

Information series: *A Walk Through the 20th Century with Bill Moyers* (PBS)

Classical program in the performing arts: *Placido Domingo Celebrates Seville,* Great Performances (PBS)

Governors Award: Bob Hope

Network totals: NBC, 20, CBS, 18, ABC, 16, PBS, 10

Deaths in 1983–1984

Adams, Ansel, 82: photographer known for clarity and precision of black-and-white landscapes of American West. April 22, 1984.

Atkinson, Brooks, 89: former *New York Times* drama critic and Pulitzer Prize-winning foreign correspondent. Jan. 13, 1984.

Basie, Count (William), 79: jazz pianist with distinctive style and leader of one of most influential groups in Big Band era. April 26, 1984.

Bellonte, Maurice, 87: French flier was navigator and radio operator on first nonstop transatlantic airplane flight from Paris to New York in 1930. Jan. 14, 1984.

Berlinguer, Enrico, 62: Italian Communist leader who started movement for greater independence from Moscow by Western European Communists. June 11, 1984.

Bright, Johnny, 53: college football star at Drake University in the 1950s, of a heart attack. Dec. 15, 1983.

Burton, Richard, 58: British actor famed for Shakespearean roles and performances in other plays and more than 40 movies. Aug. 5, 1984.

Capote, Truman, 59: author, best known for his novels "Breakfast at Tiffany's" and "In Cold Blood." Aug. 25, 1984.

Church, Frank, 59: Idaho Senator for 24 years and for a time chairman of Foreign Relations Committee. Led movement against war in Vietnam. April 7, 1984.

Clark, Gen. Mark W., 87: key Army commander in World War II and Korean War. Prominent in planning and execution of North African campaign. Capture of Rome highlighted sometimes controversial career. April 17, 1984.

Cole, Kenneth, 83: winner of National Medal of Science and pioneer in study of electrical properties of nerves and other living cells. April 18, 1984.

Coogan, Jackie, 69: In 1919 became first major child star in American cinema history as foundling in "The Kid," with Charlie Chaplin. In later years known as Uncle Fester on television series "The Addams Family." March 1, 1984.

Cooke, Terrence, 62: Cardinal and spiritual head of the New York Archdiocese and Military Vicar of the United States, of leukemia. Oct. 6, 1983.

Conrad, Michael, 58: film and TV actor who won two Emmy Awards for his portrayal of Sgt. Phillip Esterhaus in the TV drama "Hill Street Blues," of cancer. Nov. 22, 1983.

Corridan, Rev. John M., 73: Jesuit known as "the Waterfront Priest" for crusade against crime on New York docks. July 1, 1984.

Coveleski, Stan, 94: won at least 20 games in 5 of his 14 seasons as American League pitcher and was later elected to Baseball Hall of Fame. March 20, 1984.

Demarest, William, 91: well-known TV and film actor, best known for his roles in comedies. Dec. 28, 1983.

Demaret, Jimmy, 73: first golfer to win the Masters Tournament three times, and host of golf TV series during the 1960s. Dec. 28, 1983.

Dolin, Sir Anton, 79: internationally famous British ballet star and founder of major ballet companies in Britain and the U.S. Nov. 26, 1983.

Donohue, Jack, 75: director and dancer whose work ranged from MGM musicals with Shirley Temple to pioneering efforts in live television. March 27, 1984.

Dunham, Dr. Theodore, Jr., 86: Astronomer who was co-discoverer of fact that atmosphere of Venus contains a large amount of carbon dioxide. April 2, 1984.

Egan, William A., 69: Alaska's first elected governor after leading drive for statehood. May 6, 1984.

Engel, Samuel G., 79: three-time president of Screen Producers Guild, who started televising of Academy Awards ceremonies. April 7, 1984.

Farrar, Margaret, 87: pioneering crossword-puzzle editor for *New York Times* from 1942 to 1969, and editor of crossword-puzzle books. June 11, 1984.

Fisher, Sir John, 91: organized the evacuation of Allied troops from Dunkirk in 1940, in a suicide pact with his wife, **Maria,** 78. Both died. Nov. 8, 1983.

Fixx, James F., 52: encouraged jogging with best-selling books about health benefits of running. July 20, 1984.

Flowers, Walter, 51: conservative Democrat, Alabama Representative in Congress from 1968 to 1976. Member of House Judiciary Committee during Watergate hearings. April 12, 1984.

Foreman, Carl, 69: screen writer, author of "High Noon," "The Guns of Navarone," and "The Bridge on the River Kwai." Blacklisted in 1951 after refusing to testify before House Un-American Activities Committee. June 26, 1984.

Friendly, Alfred, 71: former managing editor of the *Washington Post* who won a Pulitzer Prize in 1968. Nov. 7, 1983.

Gallup, Dr. George H., 82: pioneer in public opinion polling, making techniques key tool of politics, government, business, and scholarship. July 26, 1984.

Gobbi, Tito, 68: Italian operatic baritone known especially for character portrayals. March 5, 1984.

Grimm, Charlie, 85: former major league first baseman and manager, of cancer. Nov. 15, 1983.

Guillen, Jorge, 91: one of Spain's best-known lyric poets and outspoken critic of Generalissimo Francisco Franco. Feb. 6, 1984.

Halas, George, 88: one of the founders and organizers of professional football in 1920, and coach and owner of the Chicago Bears. Oct. 31, 1983.

Hamey, Roy H., 81: former general manager of the Yankees, and other major league clubs, of a heart attack. Dec. 16, 1983.

Hathaway, Dr. Starke R., 80: co-developer of Minnesota Multiphasic Personality Inventory Test, world's most widely used psychological test. July 4, 1984.

Hellman, Lillian, 77: author and playwright who wrote "The Children's Hour," "The Little Foxes," and "Watch on the Rhine." Was successful film scenarist and wrote three books of memoirs. Defied House Un-American Activities Committee in 1952. June 30, 1984.

Huu, Tran Van, 87: Prime Minister of Vietnam from 1950 to 1952, sponsor of self-rule movement. Jan. 17, 1984.

Jacoby, Oswald, 81: champion bridge player, key member of Four Aces in 1930s, which won string of national titles. Wrote books and a syndicated column. June 27, 1984.

Kapitsa, Pyotr L., 89: Nobel Prize-winning Soviet physicist and outspoken advocate of free scientific thought. April 8, 1984.

Kastler, Dr. Alfred, 81: won Nobel Prize in 1966 for research leading to invention of the laser. Jan. 7, 1984.

Klein, Brig. Gen. Julius, 82: former publicist, journalist, and politician. Helped arrange negotiations on treaty settling war claims against West Germany by Holocaust victims. April 6, 1984.

Knopf, Alfred A., 91: outstanding American publisher whose authors included more Nobel laureates in literature than any other American publisher. Aug. 11, 1984.

Kotar, Doug, 32: former New York Giants star running back, of a brain tumor. Dec. 16, 1983.

Low, George M., 58: president of Rensselaer Polytechnic Institute and a leader in the *Apollo* moon-landing project and other space activities. July 17, 1984.

Martin, Freddy, 76: tenor saxophonist and popular Big Band leader for over 50 years. Sept. 30, 1983.

Mason, James, 75: British-born film actor known for portrayals of suave aristocrats and scoundrels. July 27, 1984.

McBride, Lloyd, 67: president of the United Steelworkers of America. Nov. 6, 1983.

Medeiros, Humberto Sousa, 67: Cardinal of Boston. Sept. 17, 1983.

Mehegan, John F., 67: jazz pianist, teacher, and author of widely used four-volume work "Jazz Improvisation." April 3, 1984.

Mercer, Mabel, 84: singer of popular music who influenced Frank Sinatra and other prominent figures. April 20, 1984.

Merrill, Dr. John Putnam, 67: leader of team that performed world's first successful kidney transplant. Was flight surgeon for B-29 that dropped first atomic bomb over Hiroshima. April 4, 1984.

Messmer, Otto, 91: film-animator who created Felix the Cat in 1919. The character starred in over 300 films and in a TV cartoon series. Oct. 28, 1983.

Middleton, Ray, 77: baritone, leading man of Broadway musical theater for three decades who also appeared in more than 20 Hollywood films. April 10, 1984.

Miró, Joan, 90: world famous Spanish Surrealist artist. Dec. 25, 1983.

Mitchell, Clarence, 73: former chief Washington lobbyist for National Association for Advancement of Colored People. Prominent in passage of landmark civil rights legislation. March 18, 1984.

Niemoller, Rev. Martin, 92: German pacifist and theologian who spent eight years in Nazi concentration camps for leading Protestant opposition to Hitler. President of World Council of Churches from 1961 to 1968. March 6, 1984.

O'Brien, Pat (Joseph), 83: famous actor whose films included "Angels With Dirty Faces," and "Fighting 69th," of a heart attack. Oct. 15, 1983.

Partch, Virgil, 67: cartoonist whose work appeared in *New Yorker* and other magazines, creator of comic strip "Big George." Aug. 10, 1984.

Peers, Lieut. Gen. William R., 69: headed inquiry into Army's handling of 1968 My Lai massacre in Vietnam. April 6, 1984.

Perkins, Carl Dewey, 71: Kentucky Democratic liberal Representative in Congress, sponsored key social legislation, including federal aid to schools and child nutrition. Aug. 3, 1984.

Phouma, Prince Souvanna, 84: former prime minister of Laos. For 20 years, he kept on neutral course between right and left. Jan. 9, 1984.

Pollock, Lee Krasner, 75: a leading Abstract Expressionist painter, wife and artistic partner of Jackson Pollock. June 19, 1984.

Powell, William, 91: actor who played suave and sophisticated roles in films of 1930s and 1940s. "Thin Man" series one of best-known films. March 5, 1984.

Price, T. Rowe, 83: money-market expert who popularized the "growth stock" investment concept. Sept. 20, 1983.

Priestley, J.B., 89: British novelist and playwright wrote character portraits with sharp and humorous political overtones. Aug. 14, 1984.

Renault, Mary, 78: best-selling historical novelist whose works on the history and legends of ancient Greece included "The King Must Die" and "The Bull From the Sea." Dec. 13, 1983.

Richardson, Sir Ralph, 80: renowned English actor-knight whose career spanned more than 60 years. Oct. 10, 1983.

Robson, Dame Flora, 82: a leading British actress, popular in U.S. Made Dame Commander of Order of British Empire in 1960. July 7, 1984.

Savitch, Jessica, 35: NBC News anchorwoman, drowned as a result of a car accident. Oct. 24, 1983.

Schacht, Alexander (Al), 91: major league player who became known as Clown Prince of Baseball. July 14, 1984.

Schneider, Alan, 66: innovative American theatrical director of plays by Beckett, Albee, Pinter, Brecht, and others. Fatally injured in traffic accident. May 3, 1984.

Sholokhov, Mikhail, 78: Russian author of "And Quiet Flows the Don" and other works that won Nobel Prize for Literature in 1965. Feb. 21, 1984.

Stapleton, Ruth Carter, 54: the younger sister of Pres. Jimmy Carter, and Baptist evangelist and spiritual healer, of cancer. Sept. 26, 1983.

Stewart, Reginald, 84: Scottish-born conductor and pianist, conductor of Baltimore Symphony and director of Peabody Conservatory. July 8, 1984.

Touré, Ahmed Sékou, 62: president of Guinea and black Africa's longest-ruling head of state. March 27, 1984.

Ulam, Stanislaw M., 75: played key role in developing hydrogen bomb and known as one of greatest contemporary mathematicians. May 13, 1984.

Vorster, John B., 67: South African Prime Minister from 1966–1978 who was a symbol of apartheid. Sept. 10, 1983.

Wadsworth, James J., 78: former head of U.S. delegation to United Nations. Represented U.S. at nuclear-test ban talks with Soviet Union in Geneva from 1958 to 1960. March 13, 1984.

Wallace, Lila Acheson, 94: co-founder and longtime chairman of *Reader's Digest* whose philantropic donations totaled scores of millions of dollars. May 8, 1984.

Waring, Fred, 84: conductor of choral and orchestral groups as one of last great conductors of Big Band era. Inventor of Waring Blendor. July 29, 1984.

Weissmuller, Johnny, 79: Olympic swimming champion who won fame as Tarzan of the Jungle in a series of movies. Jan. 20, 1984.

West, Jessamyn, 81: author of popular short stories and novels about Quakers set in her native Indiana. Feb. 23, 1984.

Willson, Meredith, 82: composer, author of Broadway hit "The Music Man." June 15, 1984.

Winwood, Estelle, 101: actress for nearly a century with hundreds of appearances on stage, screen, and television. June 20, 1984.

Yadin, Yigael, 67: hero of Israel's war of independence in 1948, Deputy Prime Minister in 1977–81, and an archeologist devoted to discovering roots of Jewish history. June 28, 1984.

BUSINESS & THE ECONOMY

Consumer Price Indexes

(1967 = 100)

Year	Commodities	Services	Housing	All items	Percent change[1]	Year	Commodities	Services	Housing	All items	Percent change[1]
1940	40.6	43.6	52.4	42.0	1.0	1975	158.4	166.6	166.8	161.2	8.9
1945	56.3	48.2	59.1	53.9	2.3	1977	174.7	194.3	186.5	181.5	6.5
1950	78.8	58.7	72.8	72.1	1.0	1979	208.4	234.2	227.6	217.4	11.3
1955	85.1	70.9	82.3	80.2	−0.4	1980	233.9	270.3	263.3	246.8	13.6
1960	91.5	83.5	90.2	88.7	1.6	1981	253.6	305.7	293.5	272.4	10.4
1965	95.7	92.2	94.9	94.5	1.7	1982	263.8	333.3	314.7	289.1	6.1
1970	113.5	121.6	118.9	116.3	5.9	1983	270.9	342.6	322.0	297.1	3.5

1. Over previous year. *Source:* Department of Labor, Bureau of Labor Statistics.

Consumer Price Index for All Urban Consumers

(1967 = 100)

Group	Feb. 1984	% increase Oct.–Feb.	Group	Feb. 1984	% increase Oct.–Feb.
All items	306.6	1.4	Fuel oil, coal, bottled gas	688.6	9.3
Food	302.1	3.1	House operation[1]	240.4	0.5
Alcoholic beverages	219.9	0.5	House furnishings	197.6	−0.2
Apparel and upkeep	196.2	−2.3	Transportation	305.8	0.0
Men's and boys' apparel	187.9	−2.2	Medical care	373.2	2.8
Women's and girls' apparel	159.0	−6.0	Personal care	267.9	1.8
Footwear	206.4	−1.1	Tobacco products	305.4	2.1
Housing, total	331.0	1.3	Entertainment	251.5	0.1
Rent	243.6	1.4	Personal and educational expenses	354.4	0.1
Gas and electricity	429.0	−1.5			

1. Combines house furnishings and operation. *Source:* Department of Labor, Bureau of Labor Statistics.

Consumer Price Index for Urban Wage Earners and Clerical Workers

(1967 = 100)

Effective January 1978, the Consumer Price Index was revised, with two indexes now being produced: A new index for All Urban Consumers covers 80% of the non-institutional population; the other index, the Consumer Price Index for Urban Wage Earners and Clerical Workers, covers about half of those included in the new index and is a major revision of the one that had been published for many years.

	1984[1]	1983	1980	1975	1970	1965	1960	1955	1950
All items	303.3	301.5	247.0	161.2	116.3	94.5	88.7	80.2	72.1
Food total	302.1	292.6	255.3	175.4	114.9	94.4	88.0	81.6	—
Apparel and upkeep	195.4	198.1	177.4	142.3	116.1	93.7	89.6	84.1	79.0
Housing total	324.2	324.2	263.2	166.8	118.9	94.9	90.2	82.3	72.8
Rent	242.9	241.3	191.3	137.3	110.1	96.9	91.7	84.3	70.4
Gas and electricity	427.9	426.7	301.2	169.6	107.3	99.4	98.6	87.5	81.2
Fuel oil, coal, bottled gas	691.4	626.4	557.2	253.3	110.1	94.6	89.2	82.3	72.7
House operation[2]	237.4	237.3	202.9	158.1	113.4	95.3	93.8	89.9	—
House furnishings	196.0	196.9	172.6	144.4	111.4	97.1	99.3	99.2	95.5
Transportation	307.7	308.2	250.5	150.6	112.7	95.9	89.6	77.4	68.2
Medical care	371.3	364.3	267.2	168.6	120.6	89.5	79.1	64.8	53.7
Personal care	266.1	264.4	212.7	150.7	113.2	95.2	90.1	77.9	68.3
Entertainment	247.7	245.8	203.7	144.4	113.4	95.9	87.3	76.7	74.4

1. May 1984. 2. Combines house furnishings and operation. *Source:* Department of Labor, Bureau of Labor Statistics.

Per Capita Personal Income

Year	Amount	Year	Amount	Year	Amount	Year	Amount	Year	Amount
1929	$705	1960	$2,219	1966	$2,987	1972	$4,493	1978	$7,729
1935	474	1961	2,269	1967	3,167	1973	4,980	1979	8,638
1940	593	1962	2,373	1968	3,433	1974	5,428	1980	9,511
1945	1,223	1963	2,460	1969	3,667	1975	5,851	1981	10,517
1950	1,501	1964	2,592	1970	3,893	1976	6,402	1982	11,100
1955	1,881	1965	2,773	1971	4,132	1977	7,043	1983	11,675

Source: Department of Commerce, Bureau of Economic Analysis.

Median Earnings of Full-Time Women Workers

(persons 15 years and over)

Major occupation group	1982 earnings	As percent of men's earnings
Professional and technical workers	$18,423	65.9
Nonfarm managers and administrators	17,326	60.1
Clerical workers	12,693	61.9
Sales workers	11,002	50.2
Operatives (including transport)	11,369	79.6
Service workers (except private household)	8,565	59.2
All occupations	13,014	61.7

Source: U.S. Department of Commerce, Bureau of the Census.

Median Family Income

(in current dollars)

Year	Income	Percent change	Year	Income	Percent change
1960	$ 5,620	—	1978	$17,640	10.2
1970	9,867	—	1979	19,661	11.5
1972	11,116	—	1980	21,023	6.9
1973	12,051	8.4	1981	22,388	6.5
1974	12,902	7.1	1982	23,433	4.7
1975	13,719	6.3	1983	24,580	4.9

Source: Department of Commerce, Bureau of the Census. NOTE: Figures are latest available.

Median Weekly Earnings of Full-Time Workers by Occupation and Sex

(For third-quarter of 1983)

	MEN		WOMEN		TOTAL	
Occupation	Number of workers (in thousands)	Median weekly earnings	Number of workers (in thousands)	Median weekly earnings	Number of workers (in thousands)	Median weekly earnings
Managerial and professional specialty	10,204	$550	7,094	$363	17,298	$445
Executive, administrative, and managerial	5,407	568	2,746	347	8,153	476
Professional specialty	4,797	533	4,348	371	9,145	431
Technical, sales, and administrative support	8,372	402	14,014	247	22,386	287
Technicians and related support	1,472	444	1,228	304	2,700	367
Sales occupations	3,969	407	2,517	208	6,486	316
Administrative support, including clerical	2,931	370	10,269	248	13,200	266
Service occupations	3,945	258	3,849	176	7,793	208
Private household	13	(1)	288	112	302	113
Protective service	1,400	356	155	241	1,555	345
Service, except private household and protective	2,532	223	3,405	179	5,937	194
Precision production, craft, and repair	9,718	404	782	243	10,500	392
Mechanics and repairers	3,544	396	110	365	3,654	394
Construction trades	3,265	396	50	(1)	3,315	392
Other precision production, craft, and repair	2,909	417	622	237	3,531	390
Operators, fabricators, and laborers	10,349	316	3,523	207	13,873	279
Machine operators, assemblers, and inspectors	4,350	327	2,830	205	7,180	266
Transportation and material moving occupations	3,267	345	157	239	3,424	341
Handlers, equipment cleaners, helpers, and laborers	2,733	243	536	211	3,269	239
Farming, forestry, and fishing	1,324	198	215	175	1,539	194

1. Data not shown where base is less than 100,000. *Source:* U.S. Department of Labor, Bureau of Labor Statistics, "Employment and Earnings," January 1984.

Brief Explanation of the Consumer Price Index

The Consumer Price Index (CPI) is a measure of the average change in prices over time in a fixed market basket of goods and services. Effective with the January 1978 index, the Bureau of Labor Statistics began publishing CPI's for two population groups: (1) a new CPI for All Urban Consumers (CPI-U) which covers approximately 80% of the total noninstitutional civilian population; and (2) a revised CPI for Urban Wage Earners and Clerical Workers (CPI-W) which represents about half the population covered by the CPI-U. The CPI-U includes, in addition to wage earners and clerical workers, groups that historically have been excluded from CPI coverage, such as professional, managerial, and technical workers, the self-employed, short-term workers, the unemployed, and retirees and others not in the labor force.

The CPI is based on prices of food, clothing, shelter, and fuels, transportation fares, charges for doctors' and dentists' services, drugs, and the other goods and services that people buy for day-to-day living. Prices are collected in 85 urban areas across the country from about 18,000 tenants, 18,000 housing units for property taxes, and about 24,000 establishments—grocery and department stores, hospitals, filling stations, and other types of stores and service establishments. All taxes directly associated with the purchase and the use of items are included in the index. Prices of food, fuels, and a few other items are obtained every month in all 85 locations. Prices of most other commodities and services are collected every month in the five largest geographic areas and every other month in other areas. Prices of most goods and services are obtained by personal visits of the Bureau's trained representatives. Mail questionnaires are used to obtain public utility rates, some fuel prices, and certain other items.

In calculating the index, price changes for the various items in each location are averaged together with weights that represent their importance in the spending of the appropriate population group. Local data are then combined to obtain a U.S. city average. Separate indexes are also published by size of city, by region of the country, for cross-classification of regions and population-size classes, and for 28 local areas. Area indexes do not measure differences in the level of prices among cities; they measure only the average change in prices for each area since the base period.

The index measures price changes from a designated reference date—1967—which equals 100.0. An increase of 122%, for example, is shown as 222.0. This change can also be expressed in dollars as follows: The price of a base period "market basket" of goods and services in the CPI has risen from $10 in 1967 to $22.20.

Gross National Product or Expenditure

(in billions)

Item	1983	1982	1981	1980	1979	1978	1975	1970	1965	1960	1955	1950	1946	1938	1933	1929
Gross national product	$3,311	$3,073	$2,926	$2,626	$2,414	$2,128	$1,529	$982	$688	$506	$399	$286	$210	$85	$56	$103
GNP in constant (1972) dollars	1,538	1,485	1,510	1,481	1,483	1,399	1,202	1,075	926	737	655	534	477	312	222	315
Personal consumption expenditures	2,157	1,992	1,858	1,673	1,511	1,351	980	619	430	325	254	192	144	64	46	77
Durable goods	279	245	232	212	212	200	133	85	63	43	39	31	16	6	3	9
Nondurable goods	804	761	743	676	602	531	409	265	189	151	123	98	83	34	22	38
Services	1,074	986	883	785	696	620	438	269	179	131	92	63	45	24	20	30
Gross private domestic investment	471	414	451	395	416	352	189	141	112	76	68	54	31	6	1	16
Residential structures	131	91	106	105	119	108	52	36	31	24	24	20	7	2	1	4
Nonresidential structures	349	348	126	109	96	77	53	38	26	18	14	9	7	2	1	5
Producers' durable equipment	3.6	3.2	206	190	186	145	96	64	46	30	24	18	10	3	1	6
Change in business inventories	−8.7	−24.5	16	−6	18	22	−11	4	10	4	6	7	6	−1	−2	2
Net export of goods and services	−7.1	17.4	26	23	13	−10	20	4	8	4	2	2	8	1	(1)	1
Government purchases	690	649	591	535	474	436	339	219	138	100	75	38	28	13	8	8
Federal	690	649	230	199	168	153	123	96	67	54	44	19	18	5	2	1
National defense	275	259	154	132	111	99	84	74	49	44	38	14	15	n.a.	n.a.	n.a.
Other	200	179	76	67	57	54	39	22	18	9	6	5	3	n.a.	n.a.	n.a.
State and local	75	79	361	336	306	283	216	123	71	47	31	20	10	8	6	7
Implicit price deflator	391	415	194	177	163	150	127	91	74	69	61	54	44	27	25	33

1. Less than $500 million. NOTE: n.a. = not available. *Source:* Department of Commerce, Bureau of Economic Analysis.

Total Family Income
(figures in percent)

Income range	White 1982	1980	1970	1960	Black and other races 1982	1980	1970	1960
Families (thousands)[1]	53,407	52,710	46,535	41,123	7,987	7,599	5,413	4,333
Under $2,500	1.9	1.6	5.6	15.1	4.9	5.0	15.6	39.8
$2,500 to $7,499	7.1	8.6	25.8	52.9	21.0	22.5	41.4	48.9
$7,500 to $12,400	11.1	13.1	33.4	24.6	17.5	18.5	25.6	9.9
$12,500 to $14,999	5.9	6.8	11.5	3.3	6.2	7.4	6.5	0.9
$15,000 to $19,999	12.3	14.1	13.8	2.2	11.1	12.8	7.4	0.3
$20,000 to $24,999	12.6	14.2	4.9	0.9	10.7	10.6	2.1	0.3
$25,000 to $34,999	20.3	20.8	3.2	—	14.5	12.9	1.1	—
$35,000 to $49,999	16.9	13.6	1.2	1.1	9.6	7.6	0.3	—
$50,000 and over	11.9	7.2	0.6	—	4.6	2.8	0.1	—
Median income	$24,603	$21,904	$10,236	$5,835	$15,211	$13,843	$6,516	$3,230

1. As of March 1984. *Source:* Department of Commerce, Bureau of the Census.

Producer Price Indexes by Major Commodity Groups
(1967 - 100)

Commodity	1983	1980	1975	1970	1965	1960	1955
All commodities	303.1	268.8	174.9	110.4	96.6	94.9	87.8
Farm products	248.2	249.4	186.7	111.0	98.7	97.2	98.2
Processed foods	256.0	241.2	182.6	112.1	95.5	89.5	85.0
Textile products and apparel	204.9	183.5	137.9	107.1	99.8	99.5	98.7
Hides, skins, and leather products	271.4	248.9	148.5	110.3	94.3	90.8	77.3
Fuels and related products and power	665.9	574.0	245.1	106.2	95.5	96.1	91.2
Chemicals and allied products	292.9	260.3	181.3	102.2	99.0	101.8	98.5
Rubber and plastic products	243.4	217.4	150.2	108.3	95.9	103.1	102.4
Lumber and wood products	307.3	288.9	176.9	113.6	95.9	95.3	97.1
Pulp, paper, and allied products	297.7	249.2	170.4	108.2	96.2	98.1	87.8
Metals and metal products	307.1	286.4	185.6	116.6	96.4	92.4	82.1
Machinery and equipment	286.4	239.8	161.4	111.4	93.9	92.0	75.7
Furniture and household durables	213.9	187.7	139.7	107.5	96.9	99.0	93.3
Nonmetallic mineral products	325.3	283.0	174.0	112.9	97.5	97.2	87.5
Transportation equipment (Dec. 1968 - 100)	256.7	207.0	141.5	104.6	98.5	98.8	—
Miscellaneous products	289.5	258.8	147.7	109.9	95.9	93.0	86.5

Source: Department of Labor, Bureau of Labor Statistics.

Life Insurance in Force
(in millions of dollars)

As of Dec. 31	Ordinary	Group	Industrial	Credit	Total
1915	$16,650	$100	$4,279	—	$21,029
1930	78,756	9,801	17,693	73	106,413
1945	101,550	22,172	27,675	365	151,762
1950	149,071	47,793	33,415	3,844	234,168
1955	216,812	101,345	39,682	14,493	373,332
1960	341,881	175,903	39,563	29,101	586,448
1965	499,638	308,078	39,818	53,020	900,554
1970	734,730	551,357	38,644	77,392	1,402,123
1980	1,760,474	1,579,355	35,994	165,215	3,541,038
1981	1,978,080	1,888,612	34,547	162,356	4,063,595
1982	2,216,388	2,066,361	32,766	161,144	4,476,659
1983	2,544,275	2,219,573	31,354	170,659	4,965,861

Source: American Council of Life Insurance.

Farm Indexes
(1977 - 100)

Year	Prices paid by farmers[1]	Prices rec'd by farmers[2]	Ratio
1950	37	56	151
1955	40	51	128
1960	44	52	118
1965	47	54	115
1970	55	60	109
1975	89	101	113
1980	138	134	97
1981	150	139	93
1982	156	133	85

1. Commodities, interest, and taxes, and wage rates. 2. All crops and livestock. *Source:* Department of Agriculture, Statistical Reporting Service.

Terms on Conventional First Mortgages: All Major Types of Lenders

Type of homes and year	Contract rate (percent)	Fees and charges (percent)	Effective rate (percent)	Maturity (years)	Loan amount	Purchase price	Loan-to-price ratio (percent)
New homes: 1983	12.11	2.39	12.57	26.7	70.6	93.9	77.3
1982	14.49	2.96	15.14	27.5	69.5	94.1	76.6
1981	14.13	2.66	14.70	27.7	65.2	90.3	74.8
1980	12.25	2.09	12.65	28.2	59,200	83,400	73.2
1979	10.48	1.66	10.77	28.5	53,300	74,400	73.9
1975	8.75	1.54	—	26.8	33,300	44,600	76.1
1970	8.27	1.03	—	25.1	25,200	35,500	71.7
Existing homes: 1983	12.29	2.40	12.75	25.9	56.8	79.3	74.3
1982	14.78	2.55	15.33	24.9	48.7	70.7	71.9
1981	14.51	2.27	15.00	25.9	47.7	68.5	72.9
1980	12.58	1.90	12.95	26.8	48,000	68,000	73.3
1979	10.66	1.45	10.92	27.1	46,300	64,600	74.0
1975	9.01	1.19	—	24.0	27,400	38,200	73.4
1970	8.20	0.92	—	22.8	21,000	30,000	71.1

Source: Federal Home Loan Bank Board.

Consumer Credit

(non-installment credit; in millions of dollars)

End of year	Service credit	Charge accounts	Single-payment loans	Total credit outstanding
1950	$ 1,638	$ 4,858	$ 3,642	$ 10,138
1955	2,316	6,761	6,002	15,079
1960[1]	3,734	7,235	9,084	20,053
1965	5,545	8,319	15,462	29,326
1970	9,106	9,156	19,323	37,585
1975	12,027	11,739	27,378	51,144
1980	19,280	13,135	42,352	74,767
1981	22,270	14,403	43,496	80,663
1982	24,346	14,381	47,144	85,871
1983	28,635	15,790	52,485	96,910

1. Beginning with 1960, data include Alaska and Hawaii. *Source:* Federal Reserve Board.

Estimated Annual Retail and Wholesale Sales by Kind of Business

(in millions of dollars)

Kind of business	1983	1980
Retail trade, total	$1,173,966	$951,902
Building materials, hardware, garden supply, and mobile home dealers	59,873	49,616
Automotive dealers	221,687	162,309
Furniture, home furnishings, and equipment stores	51,774	43,416
General merchandise group stores	142,997	117,227
Food stores	259,441	217,047
Gasoline service stations	103,121	93,624
Apparel and accessory stores	54,005	44,426
Eating and drinking places	115,710	85,842
Drug stores and proprietary stores	38,766	30,504
Liquor stores	19,690	17,083
Merchant wholesale trade, total	1,183,790	1,055,168
Total, (excluding farm-product raw materials)	(S)	932,941
Durable goods, total	504,810	448,040
Motor vehicles and automotive parts and supplies	98,814	84,227
Furniture and home furnishings	18,572	15,321
Lumber and other construction materials	(S)	34,514
Electrical goods	66,143	47,542
Hardware, plumbing, heating and supplies	31,187	27,136
Machinery, equipment, supplies	138,952	130,282
Scrap and waste materials	(S)	17,220
Nondurable goods, total	678,980	607,128
Total (excluding farm-product raw materials)	(S)	484,901
Paper and paper products	26,532	21,296
Drugs, drug proprietaries, and druggists' sundries	(S)	13,626
Apparel, piece goods, and notions	(S)	25,121
Groceries and related products	199,836	152,551
Beer, wine, distilled alcoholic beverages	36,945	32,554
Miscellaneous nondurable goods	84,744	68,382
Tobacco and tobacco products	(S)	11,366

NOTE: (S) = does not meet publication standards. *Source:* Department of Commerce, Bureau of the Census.

Expenditures for New Plant and Equipment[1]

(in millions of dollars)

Year	Manufacturing and mining	Transportation	All other[2]	Total
1950	$8,570	$2,380	$14,370	$25,320
1955	13,810	2,600	20,170	36,580
1960	17,650	3,190	27,800	48,630
1965	26,770	5,460	38,200	70,430
1970	39,010	6,950	59,650	105,610
1975	61,020	8,680	88,010	157,710
1978	89,930	10,680	130,630	231,240
1979	110,060	12,350	148,050	270,460
1980	129,320	12,090	154,220	295,630
1981	143,650	12,050	165,790	321,490
1982	135,130	11,950	169,360	316,430
1983	123,180	11,250	168,750	303,200
1984[3]	139,460	10,960	182,900	333,320

1. Data exclude agriculture. 2. Includes electric and gas utilities, trade, service, communications, construction, and finance. 3. Planned capital expenditures. NOTE: This series was revised in January 1984. *Source:* Department of Commerce, Bureau of Economic Analysis.

New Housing Starts[1] and Mobile Homes Shipped

(in thousands)

Year	No. of units started	Year	No. of units started	Year	Mobile homes shipped
1900	189	1965	1,510	1965	217
1910	387	1970	1,469	1970	401
1920	247	1975	1,171	1975	213
1925	937	1976	1,548	1976	246
1930	330	1977	2,002	1977	277
1935	221	1978	2,036	1978	275
1940	603	1979	1,760	1979	277
1945	326	1980	1,313	1980	222
1950	1,952	1981	1,100	1981	241
1955	1,646	1982	1,072	1982	240
1960[1]	1,296	1983	1,712	1983	296

1. Prior to 1960, starts limited to nonfarm housing; from 1960 on, figures include farm housing. *Sources:* Department of Commerce, Housing Construction Statistics, 1900–1965, and Construction Reports, Housing Starts, 1970–83, Manufactured Housing Institute, 1965–76; National Conference of States on Building Codes and Standards.

Shareholders in Public Corporations

Characteristic	1983	1980	1975	1970	1965	1959	1952
Individual shareholders (thousands)	42,360	30,200	25,270	30,850	20,120	12,490	6,490
Owners of shares listed on New York Stock Exchange (thousands)	26,029	23,804	17,950	18,290	12,430	8,510	n.a.
Adult shareowner incidence in population	1 in 4	1 in 5	1 in 6	1 in 4	1 in 6	1 in 8	1 in 16
Median household income	$33,200	$27,750	$19,000	$13,500	$9,500	$7,000	$7,100
Adult shareowners with household income: under $10,000 (thousands)	1,460	1,742	3,420	8,170	10,080	9,340	n.a.
$10,000 and over (thousands)	36,261	25,715	19,970	20,130	8,410	2,740	n.a.
Adult female shareowners (thousands)	20,385	13,696	11,750	14,290	9,430	6,350	3,140
Adult male shareowners (thousands)	19,226	14,196	11,630	14,340	9,060	5,740	3,210
Median age	45	46	53	48	49	49	51

NOTE: n.a. = not available. *Source:* New York Stock Exchange.

50 Most Active Stocks in 1983

Stock	Share volume	Stock	Share volume	Stock	Share volume
American Tel. & Tel.	420,502,900	Atlantic Richfield	97,006,700	Standard Oil (Indiana)	75,719,300
Int'l Business Machines	186,294,000	Sony Corp.	96,055,800	Morris (Philip)	75,504,200
Exxon Corp.	166,494,600	Diamond Shamrock	94,775,500	Pepsi Co, Inc.	73,962,900
Chrysler Corporation	158,081,300	Ford Motor	94,170,100	Halliburton Co.	73,520,700
Merrill Lynch	127,643,200	General Electric	93,151,700	Int'l Tel. & Tel.	70,926,300
General Motors	126,271,600	AMR Corp.	92,136,600	National Semiconductor	70,264,200
American Express	112,792,580	RCA Corp.	92,057,600	Boeing Co.	70,234,900
Pan American World Airways	112,434,100	Johnson & Johnson	88,146,900	Prime Computer	69,947,900
Schlumberger, N.V.	112,353,700	K mart Corp.	88,068,800	Phillips Petroleum	69,067,500
Citicorp	111,945,900	Dow Chemical	81,958,300	Unocal Corp.	68,431,800
Eastman Kodak	111,325,100	Phibro-Salomon	81,885,200	GTE Corp.	67,491,300
Tandy Corp.	109,085,600	Hewlett-Packard	79,972,200	Archer-Daniels-Midland	67,332,800
Sears, Roebuck	103,730,400	Federal Nat'l Mortgage	79,688,645	Amerada Hess	66,828,100
Mobil Corp.	102,291,000	Warner Communications	79,051,700	BankAmerica	64,709,700
Digital Equipment	101,313,900	Goodyear Tire	79,040,500	Xerox Corp.	64,368,400
Gulf Oil	98,481,300	Coleco Industries	76,203,600	American Motors	64,334,100
Superior Oil	97,404,800	Standard Oil Co. of Cal.	75,841,100		

Source: New York Stock Exchange.

50 Companies With Largest Number of Stockholders

Company	Stockholders	Company	Stockholders
American Tel. & Tel.	2,960,000	Middle South Utilities	218,000
General Motors	998,000	United States Steel	216,000
Exxon Corporation	890,000	Dominion Resources	213,000
International Business Machines	770,000	Niagara Mohawk Power	209,000
General Electric	501,000	Consolidated Edison	207,000
GTE Corporation	476,000	Ohio Edison	204,000
Imperial Chemical	366,000	Northeast Utilities	201,000
Texaco Inc.	354,000	Eastman Kodak	200,000
Sears, Roebuck	340,000	RCA Corporation	200,000
Southern Company	340,000	Atlantic Richfield	198,000
American Electric Power	338,000	Union Electric	193,000
Bell Canada Enterprises	304,000	Standard Oil (Indiana)	190,000
Commonwealth Edison	301,000	Consumers Power	189,000
Ford Motor	291,000	Occidental Petroleum	185,000
Philadelphia Electric	276,000	International Tel. & Tel.	181,000
Mobil Corp.	272,000	Long Island Lighting	180,000
Pacific Gas & Electric	268,000	Pennsylvania Power & Light	169,000
Detroit Edison	254,000	Chrysler Corporation	169,000
Gulf Oil	253,000	BankAmerica	161,000
British Petroleum	251,000	Southern California Edison	158,000
duPont de Nemours	246,000	Duquesne Light	144,000
Hitachi, Ltd.	240,000	Westinghouse Electric	144,000
Standard Oil of California	236,000	Dow Chemical	136,000
Public Service Electric & Gas	232,000	Cleveland Electric	132,000
Tenneco Inc.	224,000	Matsushita Electric	129,000

Note: As of early 1984. *Source:* New York Stock Exchange.

50 Leading Stocks in Market Value

Stock	Market value (millions)	Listed shares (millions)	Stock	Market value (millions)	Listed shares (millions)
International Business Machines	$74,013	604.8	Merck & Co.	6,861	75.9
American Telephone & Telegraph	57,371	936.7	Dow Chemical	6,819	205.9
Exxon Corp.	33,877	906.4	American Express	6,746	207.6
General Electric	27,139	462.9	Reynolds (R.J.) Inds.	6,359	104.7
General Motors	23,375	314.3	International Telephone & Telegraph	6,140	137.2
Standard Oil (Indiana)	15,407	304.3	Union Pacific	5,813	114.5
Schlumberger, N.V.	15,218	302.8	Bristol-Myers	5,761	135.9
Sears, Roebuck	13,367	361.3	Tenneco Inc.	5,716	139.4
Eastman Kodak	12,658	165.7	Sun Co.	5,698	130.2
duPont de Nemours	12,392	238.3	Pfizer Inc.	5,696	159.3
Shell Oil	12,370	309.3	Abbott Laboratories	5,615	124.1
Mobil Corp.	12,282	427.2	Unocal Corp.	5,493	173.7
Standard Oil of California	11,888	342.1	Standard Oil (Ohio)	5,443	121.6
Atlantic Richfield	10,719	247.8	Teledyne, Inc.	5,385	32.3
Hewlett-Packard	10,681	252.1	Phillips Petroleum	5,329	154.4
Texaco Inc.	9,875	274.3	Bell Canada Enterprises	5,295	196.1
Minnesota Mining & Manufacturing	9,735	118.0	Wal-Mart Stores	5,271	135.1
Procter & Gamble	9,545	167.8	Motorola, Inc.	5,215	38.3
Gulf Oil	9,139	211.9	Rockwell International	5,098	154.5
Morris (Philip)	9,048	126.1	Citicorp	5,081	136.9
Getty Oil	8,687	88.5	Texas Oil & Gas	5,010	104.9
American Home Products	8,373	168.7	Westinghouse Electric	4,932	90.1
GTE Corp.	8,131	185.9	Superior Oil	4,880	132.8
Johnson & Johnson	7,800	190.8	Halliburton Co.	4,785	118.5
Coca-Cola Co.	7,300	136.4	**Total**	**$571,897**	**11,134.6**
Ford Motor	7,066	166.3			

NOTE: As of Dec. 31, 1983. Of the 1,518 common stocks listed on the New York Stock Exchange at the end of 1983, the 50 issues with the largest market value totaled $572 billion, or 37% of the total value of common stocks listed. The five largest common issues were valued at $216 billion, or 16% of the total. *Source:* New York Stock Exchange.

Largest Businesses, 1983

(in thousands of dollars)

Source: Fortune magazine.

50 LARGEST INDUSTRIAL CORPORATIONS

	Sales	Assets
Exxon	$88,561,134	$62,962,990
General Motors	74,581,600	45,694,500
Mobil	54,607,000	35,072,000
Ford Motor	44,454,600	23,868,900
International Business Machines	40,180,000	37,243,000
Texaco	40,068,000	27,199,000
E.I. du Pont de Nemours	35,378,000	24,432,000
Standard Oil (Indiana)	27,635,000	25,805,000
Standard Oil of California	27,342,000	24,010,000
General Electric	26,797,000	23,288,000
Gulf Oil	26,581,000	20,964,000
Atlantic Richfield	25,147,036	23,282,307
Shell Oil	19,678,000	22,169,000
Occidental Petroleum	19,115,700	11,775,400
U.S. Steel	16,869,000	19,314,000
Phillips Petroleum	15,249,000	13,094,000
Sun	14,730,000	12,466,000
United Technologies	14,669,265	8,720,059
Tenneco	14,353,000	17,994,000
ITT	14,155,408	13,966,744
Chrysler	13,240,399	6,772,300
Proctor & Gamble	12,452,000	8,135,000
R.J. Reynolds Industries	11,957,000	9,874,000
Getty Oil	11,600,024	10,385,050
Standard Oil (Ohio)	11,599,000	16,362,000
AT&T Technologies	11,154,700	9,087,500
Boeing	11,129,000	7,471,000
Dow Chemical	10,951,000	11,981,000
Allied	10,351,000	7,647,000
Eastman Kodak	10,170,000	10,928,000
Unocal	10,065,600	9,228,000
Goodyear Tire & Rubber	9,735,800	5,985,500
Dart & Kraft	9,714,000	5,418,100
Westinghouse Electric	9,532,600	8,569,000
Philip Morris	9,465,600	9,667,000
Beatrice Foods	9,188,200	4,731,700
Union Carbide	9,001,100	10,295,300
Xerox	8,463,500	9,296,900
Amerada Hess	8,368,946	6,217,098
Union Pacific	8,352,585	10,218,416
General Foods	8,256,433	4,309,598
McDonnell Douglas	8,111,000	4,791,800
Rockwell International	8,097,900	5,231,100
PepsiCo	7,895,936	4,638,340
Ashland Oil	7,852,299	4,107,839
General Dynamics	7,146,300	2,836,200
Minnesota Mining & Manufacturing	7,039,000	5,760,000
Coca-Cola	6,990,992	5,227,822
Consolidated Foods	6,572,298	2,616,340
Lockheed	6,490,300	2,829,600

50 LARGEST RETAILING COMPANIES

	Sales	Assets
Sears Roebuck	$35,882,900	$46,176,100
K mart	18,597,900	8,183,100
Safeway Stores	18,585,217	4,174,363
Kroger	15,236,013	3,502,278
J.C. Penney	12,078,000	7,438,000
Southland	8,772,067	3,309,455
Frederated Department Stores	8,689,579	4,901,346
Lucky Stores	8,388,155	1,713,206
American Stores	7,983,677	1,626,695
Household International	7,911,900	8,446,000
Winn-Dixie Stores	7,018,605	1,158,666
Dayton Hudson	6,963,255	3,586,411
Montgomery Ward	6,003,000	4,149,000
Jewel Companies	5,723,522	1,562,195
BATUS	5,523,191	3,903,125
F. W. Woolworth	5,456,000	2,364,000
Wal-Mart Stores	4,743,744	1,652,254
Great Atlantic & Pacific Tea	4,607,817	1,087,395
Albertson's	4,279,331	935,660
May Department Stores	4,229,400	2,844,900
Melville	3,923,220	1,492,553
Associated Dry Goods	3,717,827	2,003,876
Allied Stores	3,675,873	2,530,375
Carter Hawley Hale Stores	3,632,662	2,028,818
Grand Union	3,519,341	764,539
Supermarkets General	3,517,548	750,900
R.H. Macy	3,468,144	1,893,443
ARA Services	3,056,593	1,336,171
Marriott	3,036,703	2,501,428
McDonald's	3,001,146	3,727,307
Wickes Companies	2,875,085	1,638,945
Publix Super Markets	2,835,440	540,555
Stop & Shop Companies	2,790,799	801,558
Zayre	2,613,667	908,005
Tandy	2,475,188	1,581,908
Walgreen	2,360,614	718,022
Rapid-American	2,340,000	1,553,000
Jack Eckerd	2,325,044	864,885
Best Products	2,081,328	1,213,412
Trans World	1,889,233	1,473,048
Giant Food	1,852,134	451,170
Revco D.S.	1,792,756	597,862
Mercantile Stores	1,625,958	928,426
Waldbaum	1,586,895	314,214
U.S. Shoe	1,507,773	670,263
Brown Group	1,500,504	645,415
Service Merchandise	1,458,098	756,069
Lowe's Companies	1,430,576	520,910
Evans Products	1,352,114	871,674
Toys "R" Us	1,319,642	820,228

10 LARGEST COMMERCIAL BANKS

	Assets	Deposits
Citicorp	$134,655,000	$79,794,000
BankAmerica Corp.	121,175,689	95,750,672
Chase Manhattan Corp.	81,921,449	56,299,557
Manufacturers Hanover Corp.	64,332,306	42,284,115
J.P. Morgan & Co.	58,023,000	38,070,000
Chemical New York Corp.	51,164,860	32,452,401
First Interstate Bancorp.	44,422,997	32,030,652
Continental Illinois Corp.	42,097,371	29,431,468
Security Pacific Corp.	40,382,185	27,842,915
Bankers Trust New York Corp.	40,003,359	22,829,079

10 LARGEST LIFE INSURANCE COMPANIES

	Assets	Premium and annuity income
Prudential	$72,248,810	$9,514,847
Metropolitan	60,598,562	5,947,671
Equitable Life Assurance	43,305,559	1,102,684
Aetna Life	31,414,088	3,693,699
New York Life	24,228,095	3,554,362
John Hancock Mutual	23,458,537	2,397,284
Travelers	20,741,507	3,976,185
Connecticut General Life	17,425,833	3,036,377
Teachers Insurance & Annuity	16,143,856	1,641,832
Northwestern Mutual	14,480,689	2,012,505

10 LARGEST TRANSPORTATION COMPANIES

	Operating revenues	Assets
Santa Fe Southern Pacific	$6,273,400	$11,387,800
UAL	6,021,849	5,133,643
United Parcel Service	6,015,210	2,575,793
CSX	5,786,700	10,834,600
AMR	4,763,307	4,728,165
Burlington Northern	4,508,217	10,901,059
Eastern Air Lines	3,942,134	3,757,708
Pan American World Airways	3,789,381	2,910,526
Delta Air Lines	3,616,413	3,246,960
Trans World Airlines	3,354,305	2,738,523

10 LARGEST UTILITIES

	Assets	Operating revenues
American Telephone & Telegraph	$149,529,800	$69,403,200
GTE	24,222,856	13,086,559
Pacific Gas & Electric	14,721,533	6,646,699
Commonwealth Edison	13,591,137	4,634,021
Southern Company	13,475,388	5,418,043
American Electric Power	12,831,843	4,368,430
Middle South Utilities	11,100,667	2,909,657
Southern California Edison	11,035,060	4,464,256
Texas Utilities	8,780,954	3,487,916
Public Service Electric & Gas	8,565,433	3,962,932

10 LARGEST DIVERSIFIED FINANCIAL COMPANIES

	Assets	Revenues
Federal National Mortgage Assoc.	$78,917,537	$8,381,589
Aetna Life & Casualty	47,626,200	14,410,600
American Express	43,981,000	9,770,000
CIGNA	35,116,800	12,563,800
Travelers Corp.	32,875,800	12,002,100
Merrill Lynch & Co.	26,139,084	5,686,906
Financial Corp. of America	22,700,448	1,827,100
First Boston	22,003,316	515,434
H.F. Ahmanson	20,226,213	2,213,357
Great Western Financial	18,639,336	1,991,023

20 Largest Black-Owned Businesses

Company	1983 Sales
Johnson Publishing Company, Inc.	$118,000,000
Motown Industries	108,200,000
H.J. Russell Construction, Inc.	95,600,000
Thacker Construction Company	86,200,000
Fedco Foods Corporation	85,000,000
Wardoco, Inc.	78,247,000
Vanguard Oil & Service Company, Inc.	65,000,000
Soft Sheen Products, Inc.	64,667,000
The Jackson Oil Company	61,750,000
Dick Griffey Productions	50,300,000
M&M Products Company, Inc.	47,300,000
Johnson Products Company, Inc.	45,775,000
Porterfield Wilson Pontiac–GMC Truck, Inc.	40,000,000
Systems and Applied Sciences Corporation	37,000,000
Porterfield Wilson Mazda, Inc.	33,000,000
G&M Oil Company, Inc.	31,200,000
Systems Management American Corporation	31,000,000
American Development Corporation	28,000,000
Teleport Oil Company	27,700,000
Bob Ross Buick, Inc.	26,619,000

Source: *Black Enterprise* magazine.

Effective Wage Adjustments in Collective Bargaining Units Covering 1,000 Workers or More

Measure	1984[1]	1983	1982	1981	1980	1979
Average percent adjustments						
All industries	0.9	4.0	6.8	9.5	9.9	9.1
Manufacturing	1.2	2.7	5.2	9.4	10.2	9.6
Nonmanufacturing	0.7	4.8	7.9	9.5	9.7	8.8
For settlements reached in period	0.1	0.8	1.7	2.5	3.6	3.0
Deferred from settlements reached in earlier periods	0.4	2.5	3.6	3.8	3.5	3.0
From cost-of-living clauses	0.4	0.6	1.4	3.2	2.8	3.1
Total number of workers receiving wage change (in thousands)[2]	2,926	6,530	7,852	8,648	—	—
From settlements reached in period	272	2,327	1,907	2,270	—	—
Deferred from settlements reached in earlier periods	1,049	3,260	4,846	6,267	—	—
From cost-of-living clauses	1,640	2,327	3,830	4,593	—	—
Number of workers receiving no adjustments (in thousands)	4,791	1,187	483	145	—	—

1. Preliminary. 2. The total number of workers who received adjustments does not equal the sum of workers that received each type of adjustment, because some workers received more than one type of adjustment during the period. *Source:* U.S. Department of Labor, *Monthly Labor Review*, June, 1984.

National Labor Organizations With Membership Over 100,000

Members[1]	Union
96,000	Automobile, Aerospace and Agricultural Implement Workers of America, International Union, United
129,000	Bakery, Confectionary, and Tobacco Workers International Union
131,000	Boilermakers, Iron Ship Builders, Blacksmiths, Forgers and Helpers, International Brotherhood of
105,000	Bricklayers and Allied Craftsmen, International Union of
105,000	California State Employees' Association (Ind.)
609,000	Carpenters and Joiners of America, United Brotherhood of
n.a.	Classified School Employees, American Association of (Ind.)
233,000	Clothing and Textile Workers Union, Amalgamated
526,000	Communications Workers of America
1,684,000	Education Association, National (Ind.)
223,000	Electrical, Radio and Machine Workers, International Union of
162,000	Electrical, Radio and Machine Workers of America, United (Ind.)
834,000	Electrical Workers, International Brotherhood of
144,000	Fire Fighters, International Association of
1,034,000	Food and Commercial Workers International Union, United
223,000	Government Employees, American Federation of
200,000	Government Employees, National Association of (Ind.)
362,000	Hotel and Restaurant Employees and Bartenders, International Union
473,000	Laborers' International Union of North America
296,000	Ladies' Garment Workers' Union, International
151,000	Letter Carriers, National Association of
680,000	Machinists and Aerospace Workers, International Association of
78,000	Maintenance of Way Employes, Brotherhood of
245,000	Mine Workers of America, United (Ind.)
206,000	Musicians, American Federation of
180,000	Nurses' Association; American (Ind.)
84,000	Office and Professional Employees International Union
141,000	Oil, Chemical and Atomic Workers International Union
423,000	Operating Engineers, International Union of
160,000	Painters and Allied Trades of the United States and Canada, International Brotherhood of
257,000	Paper Workers International Union, United
228,000	Plumbing and Pipe Fitting Industry of the United States and Canada, United Association of Journeymen and Apprentices of the
150,000	Police, Fraternal Order of (Ind.)
125,000	Postal and Federal Employees, National Alliance of (Ind.)
249,000	Postal Workers Union, American
93,000	Printing and Graphic Communications Union, International
127,000	Railway, Airline and Steamship Clerks, Freight Handlers, Express and Station Employees, Brotherhood of
118,000	Retail, Wholesale and Department Store Union
131,000	Rubber, Cork, Linoleum and Plastic Workers of America, United
579,000	Service Employees International Union
120,000	Sheet Metal Workers' International Association
957,000	State, County and Municipal Employees of America, American Federation of
913,000	Steelworkers of America, United
461,000	Teachers, American Federation of
1,891,000	Teamsters, Chauffeurs, Warehousemen and Helpers of America, International Brotherhood of (Ind.)
95,000	Transit Union, Amalgamated
85,000	Transport Workers Union of America
117,000	Transportation Union, United
45,000	Woodworkers of America, International

1. Data for independent (Ind.) unions are for 1980. Data for AFL-CIO affiliated unions are based on a 2-year period ending August 1981. NOTE: n.a. = not available. *Source:* Directory of U.S. Labor Organizations, 1982–83 edition, Bureau of National Affairs.

New Business Concerns and Business Failures

Formations and Failures	1983	1982	1981	1980	1979	1978	1975	1970
Business formations								
Index, net formations (1967 = 100)	n.a.	113.0	118.6	122.4	128.3	128.2	107.0	106.4
New Incorporations (1,000)	600	567	581	534	525	478	326	264
Failures, number (1,000)	31.3	25.3	16.8	11.7	7.7	6.6	11.4	10.7
Rate per 10,000 concerns	n.a.	n.a.	61	42	28	24	43	44

NOTE: n.a. = not available. *Sources:* U.S. Bureau of Economic Analysis and Dun & Bradstreet Corporation.

Corporate Profits
(in billions of dollars)

Item	1984[1]	1983	1982	1981	1980	1975	1970
Domestic industries	209.7	176.9	144.1	179.7	161.9	107.6	62.4
Financial	31.1	31.5	20.9	20.3	26.9	11.8	12.1
Nonfinancial	178.6	145.5	123.2	159.4	134.9	95.8	50.2
Manufacturing	92.3	72.0	59.0	86.7	72.9	52.6	26.6
Wholesale and retail trade	41.2	34.7	27.6	32.8	23.6	21.3	9.5
Other	20.4	18.0	36.6	39.8	38.4	21.9	14.1
Rest of world	22.1	21.4	21.8	23.7	29.9	13.0	6.5
Total	**231.8**	**198.3**	**165.9**	**203.3**	**191.7**	**120.6**	**68.9**

1. Preliminary. *Source:* U.S. Bureau of Economic Analysis, *Survey of Current Business,* June 1984.

National Income by Type
(in billions of dollars)

Type of share	1983	1983 % of total	1980	1979	1975	1970	1965	1960	1950
National income	$2,646.9	100.0	$2,121.4	$1,963.3	$1,215.0	$800.5	$564.3	$414.5	$241.1
Compensation of employees	1,990.1	75.2	1,596.5	1,460.9	931.1	603.9	393.8	294.2	154.6
Wages and salaries	1,664.0	62.9	1,343.6	1,235.9	805.9	542.0	358.9	270.8	146.8
Supplements to wages and salaries	326.1	12.3	252.9	225.0	125.2	61.9	35.0	23.4	7.8
Proprietors' income	128.6	4.9	130.6	131.6	87.0	66.9	57.3	46.2	37.5
Business and professional	107.6	4.1	107.2	100.7	63.5	50.0	42.4	34.2	24.0
Farm	21.0	0.8	23.4	30.8	23.5	16.9	14.8	12.0	13.5
Rental income of persons	54.8	2.1	31.8	30.5	22.4	23.9	19.0	15.8	9.4
Corporate profits[1]	226.3	8.5	182.7	196.8	95.9	69.4	76.1	49.9	37.7
Net interest	247.2	9.3	179.8	143.4	78.6	36.4	18.2	8.4	2.0

1. Includes inventory valuation adjustment. *Source:* Department of Commerce, Bureau of Economic Analysis.

The Federal Budget—Receipts and Outlays
(in billions of dollars)

Description	1982	1983 (Estimated)	1984 (Estimated)
RECEIPTS BY SOURCE			
Individual income taxes	$297.7	$285.2	$295.6
Corporation income taxes	49.2	35.3	51.8
Social insurance taxes and contributions:	201.5	210.3	242.9
Employment taxes and contributions	180.7	186.4	213.3
Unemployment insurance	16.6	19.5	24.1
Other retirement contributions	4.2	4.4	5.5
Excise taxes	36.3	37.3	40.4
Estate and gift taxes	8.0	6.1	5.9
Customs duties	8.9	8.8	9.1
Miscellaneous receipts	16.2	14.5	14.0
Total receipts	**617.8**	**597.5**	**659.7**
OUTLAYS BY FUNCTION			
National defense	187.4	214.8	245.3
International affairs	10.0	11.9	13.2
General science, space, and technology	7.1	7.8	8.2
Energy	4.7	4.5	3.3

Description	1982	1983 (Estimate)	1984 (Estimate)
Natural resources and environment	12.9	12.1	9.8
Agriculture	14.9	21.1	12.1
Commerce and housing credit	3.9	1.9	0.4
Transportation	20.6	21.9	25.1
Community and regional development	7.2	7.4	7.0
Education, training, employment, and social services	26.3	26.7	25.3
Health	74.0	82.4	90.6
Income security	248.3	282.5	282.4
Veterans benefits and services	24.0	24.4	25.7
Administration of justice	4.7	5.3	5.5
General government	4.7	5.8	6.0
General purpose fiscal assistance	6.4	6.4	7.0
Net interest	84.7	88.9	103.2
Allowances	—	—	0.9
Undistributed offsetting receipts	−13.3	−20.4	−22.8
Total outlays	**728.4**	**805.2**	**848.5**
Total deficit	**110.6**	**207.7**	**188.8**

NOTE: The fiscal year is from Oct. 1 to Sept. 30. *Source:* Executive Office of the President, Office of Management and Budget.

Work Stoppages Involving 1,000 Workers or More[1]

Year	Work stop-pages	Workers involved (thousands)	Man-days idle (thousands)	Year	Work stop-pages	Workers involved (thousands)	Man-days idle (thousands)
1950	424	1,698	30,390	1974	424	1,796	31,809
1955	363	2,055	21,180	1975	235	965	17,563
1960	222	896	13,260	1976	231	1,519	23,962
1965	268	999	15,140	1977	298	1,212	21,258
1968	392	1,855	35,567	1978	219	1,006	23,774
1969	412	1,576	29,397	1979	235	1,021	20,409
1970	381	2,468	52,761	1980	187	795	20,844
1971	298	2,516	35,538	1981	145	729	16,908
1972	250	975	16,764	1982	96	656	9,061
1973	317	1,400	16,260	1983	81	909	17,461

1. The number of stoppages and workers relate to stoppages that began in the year. Days of idleness include all stoppages in effect. Workers are counted more than once if they were involved in more than one stoppage during the year. *Source:* U.S. Department of Labor, Bureau of Labor Statistics, *Handbook of Labor Statistics, December 1984.*

Persons in the Labor Force

Year	Labor force[1] Number (thousands)	Labor force[1] % working-age population	Percent of labor force in Farm occupation	Percent of labor force in Nonfarm occupation	Year	Labor force[1] Number (thousands)	Labor force[1] % working-age population	Percent of labor force in Farm occupation	Percent of labor force in Nonfarm occupation
1830	3,932	45.5	70.5	29.5	1910	37,371	52.2	31.0	69.0
1840	5,420	46.6	68.6	31.4	1920	42,434	51.3	27.0	73.0
1850	7,697	46.8	63.7	36.3	1930	48,830	49.5	21.4	78.6
1860	10,533	47.0	58.9	41.1	1940	52,966	52.4	17.0	83.0
1870	12,925	44.4	53.0	47.0	1950	59,671	53.4	11.5	88.5
1880	17,392	47.3	49.4	50.6	1960	69,877	55.3	5.9	94.1
1890	23,318	49.2	42.6	57.4	1970	82,049	58.2	3.1	96.9
1900	29,073	50.2	37.5	62.5	1980	106,085	68.2	2.2	97.8

1. For 1830 to 1930, the data relate to the population and gainful workers at ages 10 and over. For 1940 to 1960, the data relate to the population and labor force at ages 14 and over; for 1970 and 1980, the data relate to the population and labor force at age 16 and over. The farm and nonfarm percentages relate only to the experienced civilian labor force. *Source:* Department of Commerce, Bureau of the Census.

Women in the Labor Force

(16 years of age and over; in thousands)

Labor force status	1983	1982	1981	1980	1979	1978
In the labor force:	48,503	47,755	46,696	45,487	44,235	42,631
16 to 19 years of age	3,868	4,056	4,211	4,381	4,527	4,503
20 years and over	44,635	43,699	42,485	41,106	39,708	38,128
Employed	44,047	43,256	43,000	42,117	41,217	39,569
16 to 19 years of age	3,043	3,170	3,410	3,625	3,783	3,733
20 years and over	41,004	40,086	39,590	38,492	37,434	35,836
Unemployed	4,457	4,499	3,696	3,370	3,018	3,061
16 to 19 years of age	825	886	801	755	742	769
20 years and over	3,632	3,613	2,895	2,615	2,276	2,292
Not in the labor force:	43,181	42,993	42,922	42,861	42,608	42,703
Women as percent of labor force	43.5	43.3	43.0	42.5	42.1	41.7
Total civilian noninstitutional population	91,684	90,748	89,618	88,348	86,843	85,334

Source: Department of Labor, Bureau of Labor Statistics, 1984.

Single Bliss is a Viable Alternative to Marriage

According to a study conducted by University of Michigan researchers, most American young people no longer consider it better to be married than single. Only 25% of the young people questioned reported that it would bother them a great deal if they didn't marry and another 25% said it wouldn't bother them at all. Moreover, 40% of the mothers queried indicated that it wouldn't bother them at all if their son or daughter didn't marry and only 10% said it would trouble them a great deal.

Employed Persons 16 Years and Over, by Race and Occupational Groups

Race and occupational group	1983 Number	1983 Percent distribution	1980 Number	1980 Percent distribution
WHITE				
White-collar workers	49,767,000	56.0	47,267,000	53.9
Professional and technical workers	14,281,000	16.0	14,444,000	16.5
Managers and administrators, except farm	10,016,000	11.3	10,512,000	12.0
Sales workers	10,999,000	12.4	5,963,000	6.8
Clerical workers	14,471,000	16.3	16,350,000	18.6
Blue-collar workers	24,663,000	27.7	27,327,000	31.2
Craft and kindred workers	11,219,000	12.6	11,683,000	13.3
Operatives, except transport	6,414,000	7.2	8,884,000	10.1
Transport equipment operatives	3,592,000	4.0	2,984,000	3.4
Nonfarm laborers	3,438,000	3.9	3,776,000	4.3
Private household workers	2,105,000	2.4	706,000	.8
Service workers, except private household	9,019,000	10.1	9,887,000	11.3
Farm workers	3,339,000	3.8	2,527,000	2.9
Total	**88,893,000**	**100.0**	**87,715,000**	**100.0**
BLACK AND OTHER				
White-collar workers	3,704,000	39.6	41,614,000	39.8
Professional and technical workers	1,071,000	11.4	1,524,000	13.2
Managers and administrators, except farm	504,000	5.4	627,000	5.4
Sales workers	558,000	6.0	340,000	2.9
Clerical workers	1,571,000	16.8	2,124,000	18.3
Blue-collar workers	3,097,000	33.0	4,124,000	35.6
Craft and kindred workers	841,000	9.0	1,105,000	9.5
Operatives, except transport	1,081,000	11.5	1,680,000	14.5
Transport equipment operatives	547,000	5.8	548,000	4.7
Nonfarm laborers	628,000	6.7	791,000	6.8
Private household workers	500,000	5.3	358,000	3.1
Service workers, except private household	1,795,000	19.1	2,277,000	19.6
Farm workers	279,000	3.0	214,000	1.8
Total	**9,375,000**	**100.0**	**11,588,000**	**100.0**

Source: Department of Labor, Bureau of Labor Statistics.

Mothers Participating in Labor Force

(figures in percentage)

Year	Mothers with children: Under 18 years	6 to 17 years	Under 6 years[1]
1950	21.6	32.8	13.6
1955	27.0	38.4	18.2
1965	35.0	45.7	25.3
1975	47.4	54.8	38.9
1977	50.7	58.3	40.9
1979	54.5	61.6	45.4
1980	56.6	64.4	46.6
1981	58.1	65.5	48.9
1982	58.5	65.8	49.9
1983	58.9	66.3	50.5

1. May also have older children. NOTE: For 1950 and 1955 data are for April; for 1965 and 1975–83, data are for March. *Source:* Department of Labor, Bureau of Labor Statistics.

Women in the Working Population

Year[1]	Number (thousands)	Percent of female population aged 10 and over[1]	Percent of total working population aged 10 and over[1]
1900	5,319	18.8	18.3
1910	7,445	21.5	19.9
1920	8,637	21.4	20.4
1930	10,752	22.0	22.0
1940	12,845	25.4	24.3
1950	18,408	33.9	29.0
1960[2]	23,268	37.8	32.5
1970	31,580	43.4	37.2
1980	45,611	51.6	42.0
1981	46,829	52.2	42.5
1982	47,894	52.7	42.8
1983	48,646	53.0	43.0

1. For 1900–1930, data relate to population and gainful workers at ages 10 and over; for 1940, to ages 14 and over; for 1950–78, to population at ages 16 and over. 2. Beginning in 1960, figures include Alaska and Hawaii. *Sources:* Department of Commerce, Bureau of the Census, and Department of Labor, Bureau of Labor Statistics.

Employed Persons by Major Occupations, 1983

(in thousands)

Occupations	Total employed	Percent distribution: Female	Percent distribution: Black and other
White-collar workers	**75,679**	**50.8**	**11.3**
Professional and technical	12,820	48.1	8.9
Accountants	1,105	38.7	8.8
Architects	103	12.7	3.1
Computer programmers	443	32.5	6.5
Computer systems analysts	276	27.8	8.9
Engineers	1,572	5.8	4.9
Aeronautical and astronautical engineers	80	6.9	3.6
Civil engineers	211	4.0	5.1
Electrical and electronic engineers	450	6.1	6.5
Industrial engineers	210	11.0	5.7
Mechanical engineers	259	2.8	4.3
Lawyers and judges	651	15.8	3.7
Librarians, archivists, and curators	213	84.4	9.4
Life and physical scientists	55	40.8	4.2
Operators and systems researchers and analysts	142	31.3	7.1
Personnel and labor relations workers	106	43.9	7.5
Dentists	126	6.7	3.4
Pharmacists	158	26.7	6.4
Physicians, medical and osteopathic	519	15.8	7.7
Registered nurses	1,372	95.8	8.5
Therapists	247	76.3	10.3
Health technologists and technicians	1,111	84.3	15.8
Clergy	293	5.6	6.3
Economists	98	37.9	9.0
Psychologists	135	57.1	9.7
Social workers	407	64.3	24.5
Recreation workers	65	71.9	17.7
Teachers, college and university	606	36.3	6.2
Teachers, except college and university	3,365	70.9	11.8
Adult education teachers	425	64.5	7.7
Elementary school teachers	1,350	83.3	14.2
Prekindergarten and kindergarten teachers	299	98.2	15.2
Secondary school teachers	1,209	51.8	9.5
Engineering and science technicians	822	18.4	9.6
Airplane pilots	69	2.1	1.6
Vocational and educational counselors	184	53.1	17.1
Writers, artists, and entertainers	1,544	42.7	7.7
Athletes and kindred workers	58	17.6	11.1
Designers	393	52.7	5.8
Editors and reporters	204	48.4	5.0
Musicians and composers	155	28.0	12.3
Painters and sculptors	186	47.4	4.4
Photographers	113	20.7	7.4
Public relations specialists and publicity writers	157	50.1	8.1
Managers and administrators, except farm	2,966	40.3	9.3
Bank officials and financial managers	357	38.6	6.6
Buyers and purchasing agents	82	23.6	6.5
Buyers, wholesale and retail trade	191	47.2	8.3
Health administration	91	57.0	7.0
Office managers, n.e.c.	646	80.6	17.9
Officials and administrators, public administration, n.e.c.	417	38.5	12.1
Restaurant, cafeterias, and bar managers	239	63.5	15.6
Sales managers and department heads, retail trade	5,511	69.7	11.5
Sales managers, except retail trade	1,442	15.1	13.7
School administration, elementary and secondary	415	41.4	13.7

Occupations	Total employed	Percent distribution: Female	Percent distribution: Black and other
Sales workers, except clerks, retail trade	11,818	47.5	8.4
Clerical workers	2,397	85.2	18.4
Bank tellers	480	91.0	11.8
Billing clerks	146	88.4	10.1
Bookkeepers	1,970	91.0	7.6
Cashiers	2,009	84.4	15.5
Counter clerks, except food	648	80.6	17.9
File clerks	287	83.5	22.5
Insurance adjusters, examiners, and investigators	199	65.0	14.8
Library attendants and assistants	147	81.9	17.9
Mail carriers, post office	259	17.1	15.2
Computer and peripheral equipment operators	605	63.9	18.5
Key punch operators	311	93.6	24.2
Payroll and timekeeping clerks	192	82.2	10.9
Postal clerks	248	36.7	31.4
Receptionists	602	96.8	14.1
Secretaries	3,891	99.0	9.8
Shipping and receiving clerks	421	22.6	20.2
Statistical clerks	96	75.7	10.9
Stock clerks and storekeepers	532	38.7	18.8
Teachers aides, except school monitors	348	93.7	30.4
Telephone operators	244	90.4	21.3
Typists	906	95.6	20.2
Blue-collar workers	**123,759**	**30.9**	**18.1**
Craft and kindred workers	3,784	1.0	13.2
Carpenters	1,160	1.4	10.0
Brickmasons and stonemasons	156	0.3	21.4
Electricians	602	1.5	9.5
Excavating, grading, and machinery operations	196	2.3	9.3
Painters, construction, and maintenance	473	4.9	17.5
Plumbers and pipefitters	443	1.1	12.6
Structural metal craft workers	63	1.2	7.1
Roofers and slaters	133	0.1	15.2
Blue-collar workers, supervisors, n.e.c.	504	1.3	7.8
Metal craft workers, except mechanics, machinists, and job setters	3,685	21.5	14.7
Job setters and machinists	5,235	43.1	24.8
Sheetmetal workers and tinsmiths	127	4.5	9.7
Tool and die makers	148	1.2	5.0
Automobile body repairers	199	0.7	13.1
Automobile mechanics	800	0.5	13.8
Mechanics, except automobiles	12,328	8.1	13.0
Heavy equipment mechanics, including diesel	162	0.7	10.3
Household appliance and accessory installers and mechanics	200	0.5	11.3
Compositors and typesetters	76	64.1	4.0
Printing press operators	459	25.6	11.7
Bakers	105	44.4	16.6
Crane, derrick, and hoist operators	93	1.3	18.2
Stationary engineers	119	2.1	11.9
Telephone installers and repairers	247	9.9	11.5
Operatives, excluding transport	16,091	26.6	22.3
Assemblers	953	46.4	22.4
Checkers, examiners and inspectors, manufacturing	794	53.8	20.7
Garage workers and gas station attendants	293	4.6	16.1
Packers and wrappers, except meat and produce	396	63.1	32.3

Precision machine operatives	7,714	42.1	23.4
Sewers and stitchers	806	94.0	30.0
Textile operatives	1,414	82.1	31.2
Welders and flame cutters	543	5.0	16.9
Transport equipment operators	4,201	7.8	18.9
Bus drivers	365	45.5	29.2
Taxicab drivers and chauffeurs	148	10.4	28.2
Truck drivers	2,195	9.7	36.6
Nonfarm laborers	4,147	16.8	23.7
Service workers	**13,857**	**60.1**	**23.4**
Private households	980	96.1	36.3
Service workers, except private	11,205	64.0	22.9
Households	646	54.0	26.7
Cleaning workers	2,736	38.8	33.6
Food service workers	4,860	63.3	17.3
Bartenders	338	48.4	7.1
Cooks	1,359	50.8	22.8
Waiters	1,357	87.8	7.7
Health service workers	1,739	89.2	28.3
Dental assistants	154	98.1	11.8
Health aides, excluding nursing	316	86.8	21.3
Nursing aides, orderlies, and attendants	1,269	88.7	32.0
Personal service workers	1,870	79.2	17.1
Protective service workers	1,672	12.8	18.2
Fire fighters	189	1.0	10.8
Guards	711	20.6	22.6
Police and detectives	645	9.4	17.1
Farm workers	**3,700**	**16.0**	**15.7**
Farmers and farm managers	1,450	12.1	2.0
Farm laborers, wage workers	1,149	24.8	27.5
Total employed	**199,438**	**42.1**	**14.3**

NOTE: n.e.c. = "not elsewhere classified" and designates broad categories of occupations that cannot be more specifically identified. *Source:* Department of Labor, Bureau of Labor Statistics.

Manufacturing Industries—Gross Average Weekly Earnings and Hours Worked

	1984		1983		1980		1975		1970		1958	
Industry	**Earnings**	**Hours worked**	**Earnings**	**Hours worked**	**Earnings**	**Hours worked**	**Earnings**	**Hours worked**	**Earnings**	**Hours worked**	**Earnings**	**Hours worked**
All manufacturing[2]	$370.78	40.7	$346.10	39.6	$288.62	39.7	$189.51	39.4	$133.73	39.8	$82.71	39.2
Durable goods	400.75	41.4	372.53	40.1	310.78	40.1	205.09	39.9	143.07	40.3	89.27	39.5
Primary metal industries	480.06	42.0	446.23	39.7	391.78	40.1	246.80	40.0	159.17	40.5	101.11	38.3
Iron and steel foundries	423.26	41.7	381.42	39.0	328.00	40.0	220.99	40.4	151.03	40.6	86.86	37.6
Nonferrous foundries	381.43	42.1	358.57	40.7	291.27	39.9	190.03	39.1	138.16	39.7	90.85	39.5
Fabricated metal products	385.74	41.3	361.10	39.9	300.98	40.4	201.60	40.0	143.67	40.7	89.78	39.9
Hardware, cutlery, hand tools	371.69	40.8	346.66	39.8	275.89	39.3	187.07	39.3	132.33	40.1	82.92	39.3
Other hardware	385.40	41.3	363.41	38.1	286.21	39.1	195.42	39.4	133.46	40.2	84.32	39.4
Structural metal products	354.16	40.2	344.08	39.1	291.85	40.2	202.61	40.2	142.61	40.4	92.63	40.1
Electric and electronic equipment	364.90	41.0	344.00	40.0	276.21	39.8	180.91	39.5	130.54	39.8	83.95	39.6
Machinery, except electrical	416.91	41.9	378.40	40.0	328.00	41.0	219.22	40.9	154.95	41.1	94.33	39.8
Transportation equipment	522.02	43.0	480.28	41.8	379.61	40.6	242.61	40.3	163.22	40.3	100.40	40.0
Motor vehicles and equipment	562.93	44.5	505.33	42.5	394.00	40.0	262.68	40.6	170.07	40.3	101.24	39.7
Lumber and wood products	312.83	39.8	302.59	39.4	252.18	38.5	167.35	39.1	117.51	39.7	69.09	38.6
Furniture and fixtures	266.34	39.4	251.29	38.6	209.17	38.1	142.13	37.9	108.58	39.2	69.95	39.3
Nondurable goods	327.10	39.6	311.20	38.9	255.45	39.0	168.78	38.8	120.43	39.1	74.11	38.8
Textile mill products	261.06	40.6	242.57	39.7	203.31	40.1	133.28	39.2	97.76	39.9	57.51	38.6
Apparel and other textile products	200.75	36.7	190.28	35.7	161.42	35.4	111.97	35.1	84.37	35.3	54.05	35.1
Leather and leather products	205.25	36.2	197.06	35.7	169.09	36.7	120.80	37.4	92.63	37.2	57.25	36.7
Food and kindred products	328.94	39.3	316.61	38.8	271.95	39.7	184.17	40.3	127.98	40.5	79.15	40.8
Tobacco manufactures	414.77	37.0	378.61	36.3	294.89	38.1	171.38	38.0	110.00	37.8	62.17	39.1
Paper and allied products	437.68	42.7	406.14	42.0	330.85	42.2	207.58	41.6	144.14	41.9	87.99	41.9
Printing and publishing	353.78	38.0	338.63	37.5	279.36	37.1	198.32	37.0	147.78	37.7	94.62	38.0
Chemicals and allied products	456.46	41.8	428.07	41.2	344.45	41.5	219.63	40.9	153.50	41.6	93.20	40.7
Petroleum and allied products	584.64	44.0	584.32	43.5	422.18	41.8	267.07	41.6	182.76	42.7	111.66	40.9

1. March preliminary. *Source:* Department of Labor, Bureau of Labor Statistics.

Nonmanufacturing Industries—Gross Average Weekly Earnings and Hours Worked

Industry	1984 Earnings	1984 Hours worked	1983 Earnings	1983 Hours worked	1975 Earnings	1975 Hours worked	1970 Earnings	1970 Hours worked	1958 Earnings	1958 Hours worked
Bituminous coal and lignite mining	$606.92	41.4	$523.48	39.3	$284.53	39.2[2]	$186.41	40.8	$97.57	33.3
Metal mining	522.12	40.6	490.46	39.3	250.72	42.3	165.68	42.7	94.96	38.6
Nonmetallic minerals	413.95	43.3	378.06	42.1	213.09	43.4	155.11	44.7	88.33	43.3
Telephone communications	464.11	39.6	442.46	39.4	221.18	38.4	131.60	39.4	78.72	38.4
Radio and TV broadcasting	342.62	37.0	320.02	36.7	214.50	39.0	147.45	38.2	100.70	38.0
Electric, gas, and sanitary services	493.99	41.2	463.30	41.0	246.79	41.2	172.64	41.5	98.57	40.9
Local and suburban transportation	315.63	37.8	317.20	39.7	196.89	40.1	142.30	42.1	87.29	43.0
Wholesale trade	333.80	38.5	316.74	38.3	188.75	38.6	137.60	40.0	84.02	40.2
Retail trade	173.76	29.5	166.42	29.3	108.22	32.4	82.47	33.8	54.10	38.1
Hotels, tourist courts, motels	163.86	30.4	156.22	30.1	89.64	31.9	68.16	34.6	40.89	39.7
Laundries and dry cleaning plants	186.48	33.6	179.90	33.5	106.05	35.0	77.47	35.7	45.28	38.7
General building contracting	384.08	36.2	388.77	36.3	254.88	36.0	184.40	36.3	96.92	35.5

1. March preliminary. 2. 11-month average. *Source:* Department of Labor, Bureau of Labor Statistics.

Median Income Comparisons of Year-Round Workers by Educational Attainment 1983

(persons 25 years and over)

Years of school completed	Median income: Women	Median income: Men	Income gap in dollars	Women's income as a percent of men's	Percent men's income exceeded women's
Elementary school:					
Less than 8 years	$9,385	$14,093	$4,708	66.6	50.2
8 years	10,337	16,438	6,101	62.9	59.0
High School:					
1 to 3 years	11,131	17,685	6,554	62.9	58.9
4 years	13,787	21,823	8,036	63.2	58.3
College:					
1 to 3 years	16,536	24,613	8,077	67.2	48.8
4 years or more	20,251	31,800	11,549	63.7	57.0

Source: Department of Commerce, Bureau of the Census.

Characteristics of Households With Female Householder, 1982

Characteristics	Number of households	Income bracket	number of households
All female householders	24,557,000	3 persons	3,365,000
MARITAL STATUS		4 persons or more	3,366,000
Married, husband present	2,103,000	**RELATED CHILDREN UNDER 18**	
Married, husband absent	2,625,000	No related children	17,105,000
Widowed	9,169,000	1 or more related children	7,452,000
Divorced	5,655,000	**TOTAL HOUSEHOLD INCOME**	
Single (never married)	5,005,000	Under $2,500	1,379,000
RACE AND SPANISH ORIGIN		$2,500 to $4,999	4,433,000
OF HOUSEHOLDER		$5,000 to $7,499	3,616,000
White	19,808,000	$7,500 to $9,999	2,639,000
Black	4,349,000	$10,000 to $14,999	4,289,000
Spanish origin[1]	1,174,000	$15,000 to $24,999	4,777,000
SIZE OF HOUSEHOLD		$25,000 to $49,000	2,960,000
1 person	11,872,000	$50,000 and over	464,000
2 persons	5,954,000	Median income	$10,220
		Mean income	$13,797

1. Persons of Spanish origin may be of any race. *Source:* Department of Commerce, Bureau of the Census.

Occupations of Employed Women

(16 years of age and over)

Occupations	1983[1] (percent)	1982[1] (percent)	1981[1] (percent)	1980[1] (percent)	1979[1] (percent)	1978[1] (percent)
Professional and technical workers	17.3	17.1	17.0	16.8	16.1	15.6
Managers and administrators (except farm)	7.9	7.8	7.4	6.9	6.4	6.1
Sales workers	12.8	11.9	6.8	6.8	6.9	6.9
Clerical workers	29.7	30.7	34.7	35.1	35.0	34.6
Craft and kindred workers	2.3	1.9	1.9	1.8	1.8	1.8
Operatives, except transport	9.4	10.3	9.7	10.0	10.8	11.1
Transport equipment operatives	.7	.7	.7	.7	.7	.7
Nonfarm laborers	.5	.4	1.2	1.2	1.3	1.3
Private household workers	2.1	2.3	2.3	2.5	2.6	2.9
Service workers	16.3	16.3	17.1	17.0	17.2	17.7
Farmers and farm managers	1.3	1.4	.4	.4	.3	.3
Farm laborers and supervisors	1.6	2.0	.7	.8	.9	1.0

1. Annual averages. NOTE: Details may not add up to totals because of rounding. *Source:* Department of Labor, Bureau of Labor Statistics.

Employment by Marital Status and Sex, March 1983

(in thousands)

Marital status and sex (persons 16 years and over)	Population	Civilian labor force: Number	Labor force participation rate	Employed	Unemployed: Number	Unemployed: Percent of labor force
Men	83,142	62,035	75.4	54,638	7,397	11.9
Never married	23,672	16,468	69.9	13,203	3,265	19.8
Married, wife present	50,665	39,589	79.2	36,371	3,218	8.1
Other ever married	8,804	5,978	68.6	5,064	914	15.3
Married, wife absent	2,243	1,718	78.6	1,405	314	18.3
Widowed	1,938	514	26.6	467	47	9.2
Divorced	4,624	3,745	81.5	3,192	553	14.8
Women	91,395	47,779	52.3	43,165	4,614	9.7
Never married	19,617	12,282	62.6	10,620	1,661	13.5
Married, husband present	50,659	26,227	51.8	24,335	1,893	7.2
Other ever married	21,119	9,270	43.9	8,210	1,060	11.4
Married, husband absent	3,258	1,913	58.7	1,549	365	19.1
Widowed	10,895	2,161	19.8	1,995	166	7.7
Divorced	6,966	5,196	74.6	4,667	529	10.2
Total: Both sexes	**174,537**	**109,814**	**63.2**	**97,804**	**12,011**	**10.9**

1. Male members of the Armed Forces living off-post or with their families on post are included in the population figures. NOTE: Due to rounding sums may not equal totals. *Source:* U.S. Department of Labor, Bureau of Labor Statistics.

Earnings Distribution of Year-Round, Full-Time Workers, by Sex, 1982

(persons 15 years old and over as of March 1983)

Earnings group	Number: Women	Number: Men	Distribution (percent): Women	Distribution (percent): Men	Likelihood of a woman in each earnings group (percent)[1]
Less than $3,000	549,000	963,000	2.3	2.4	1.0
$3,000 to $4,999	489,000	452,000	2.1	1.1	1.9
$5,000 to $6,999	1,379,000	917,000	5.8	2.3	2.5
$7,000 to $9,999	4,030,000	2,404,000	17.0	6.0	2.8
$10,000 to $14,999	7,800,000	6,527,000	32.9	16.3	2.0
$15,000 to $19,999	4,936,000	7,006,000	20.8	17.5	1.2
$20,000 to $24,999	2,615,000	6,643,000	11.0	16.6	0.7
$25,000 to $49,9999	1,763,000	12,751,000	7.4	31.8	0.2
$50,000 and over	142,000	2,444,000	0.6	6.1	0.1
Total with earnings	**23,703,000**	**40,107,000**	**100.0**	**100.0**	**1.0**

1. Figures obtained by dividing percentages for women by percentages for men. *Source:* Department of Commerce, Bureau of the Census.

Comparison of Median Earnings of Year-Round, Full-Time Workers; 15 Years and Over, by Sex, 1960 to 1982

Year	Median earnings: Women	Median earnings: Men	Earnings gap in current dollars	Women's earnings as a percent of men's	Percent men's earnings exceeded women's	Earnings gap in constant 1982 dollars
1960	$3,257	$5,368	$2,111	60.7	64.8	$6,880
1965	3,828	6,388	2,560	60.0	66.9	7,832
1970	5,323	8,966	3,643	59.4	68.4	9,056
1974	6,970	11,889	4,919	58.6	70.6	9,628
1975	7,504	12,758	5,254	58.8	70.0	9,423
1976	8,099	13,455	5,356	60.2	66.1	9,082
1977	8,618	14,626	6,008	58.9	69.7	9,570
1978	9,350	15,730	6,380	59.4	68.2	9,439
1979	10,169	17,045	6,876	59.7	67.6	9,144
1980	11,197	18,612	7,415	60.2	66.2	8,686
1981	12,001	20,260	8,259	59.2	68.8	8,765
1982	13,014	21,077	8,063	61.7	62.0	8,063

Source: Department of Commerce, Bureau of the Census.

Composition of the Civilian Labor Force and Unemployment

Race, sex, and age	July 1983 Civilian labor force: Number (thousands)	Percent distribution	July 1983 Unemployed: Number (thousands)	Percent distribution	Rate	July 1982 Civilian labor force: Number (thousands)	Percent distribution	July 1982 Unemployed: Number (thousands)	Percent distribution	Rate
White	97,255	64.4	7,995	59.1	8.2	96,493	87.3	8,356	77.4	8.7
Men, 20 years and older	51,901	34.4	4,010	29.6	7.7	51,292	46.4	4,037	37.4	7.9
Women, 20 years and older	38,161	25.3	2,587	19.1	6.8	37,845	34.2	2,777	25.7	7.3
Teenagers, 16 to 19 years	7,193	4.8	1,398	10.3	19.4	7,356	6.7	1,542	14.3	21.0
Black and other	11,741	35.6	2,298	40.9	19.6	14,027	12.7	2,433	22.6	17.3
Men, 20 years and older	5,599	17.0	1,040	18.5	18.6	6,784	6.1	1,063	10.0	15.7
Women, 20 years and older	5,317	16.1	859	15.3	16.2	6,247	5.7	897	8.3	14.4
Teenagers, 16 to 19 years	825	2.5	399	7.1	48.4	997	0.9	473	4.4	47.4
All races										
Men, 20 years and older	57,500	51.4	5,050	48.2	8.8	58,076	52.5	5,100	47.3	8.8
Women, 20 years and older	43,478	41.4	3,446	34.4	7.9	44,092	40.0	3,674	34.1	8.3
Teenagers, 16 to 19 years	8,018	7.3	1,797	17.4	22.4	8,353	7.6	2,015	18.7	24.1
Total	**108,996**	**100.0**	**10,293**	**100.0**	**9.4**	**110,520**	**100.0**	**10,789**	**100.0**	**9.8**

NOTE: Totals may not add due to rounding. *Source:* Department of Labor, Bureau of Labor Statistics.

Advertising Expenditures by Medium

(in Millions)

Medium	1982 Amt.	1982 % of total	1981 Amt.	1981 % of total	1980 Amt.	1980 % of total	1975 Amt.	1975 % of total	1970 Amt.	1970 % of total	1960 Amt.	1960 % of total
Newspapers	$17.7	26.6	$16.5	27.3	$14.8	27.7	$8.2	29.5	$5.7	29.2	$3.7	31.0
Magazines	3.7	5.6	3.5	5.8	3.1	5.9	1.5	5.2	1.3	6.6	0.9	7.9
Business Papers	1.9	2.8	1.8	3.0	1.7	3.1	0.9	3.3	0.7	3.8	0.6	5.1
Radio	4.7	7.0	4.2	7.0	3.7	6.9	2.0	7.1	1.3	6.7	0.7	5.8
Television	14.3	21.5	12.7	21.0	11.4	21.2	5.3	18.9	3.6	18.4	1.6	13.3
Direct mail	10.3	15.5	8.9	14.7	7.6	14.2	4.1	14.8	2.8	14.1	1.8	15.3
Outdoor	0.7	1.1	0.7	1.2	0.6	1.1	0.3	1.2	0.2	1.2	0.2	1.7
Miscellaneous[2]	13.3	19.9	12.1	20.0	10.7	19.9	5.6	20.0	3.9	20.0	2.4	19.8
Total	**66.6**	**100.0**	**60.4**	**100.0**	**53.6**	**100.0**	**27.9**	**100.0**	**19.5**	**100.0**	**11.9**	**100.0**

1. Preliminary. 2. Includes regional farm papers. *Sources:* McCann-Erickson, Inc., and *Advertising Age*.

Leading Advertising Agencies in World Billings

(in millions of dollars)

Agency	1983	1982
Young & Rubicam	$2,761.4	$2,511.7
Ted Bates Worldwide	2,586.1	2,374.0
J. Walter Thompson Co.	2,524.1	2,315.2
Ogilvy & Mather	2,360.4	2,151.0
McCann-Erickson	1,993.1	1,841.4
BBDO International	1,949.0	1,605.5
Saatchi & Saatchi Compton	1,710.6	1,302.6
Leo Burnett Co.	1,485.3	1,487.4
Foote Cone & Belding	1,405.6	1,211.4
SSC&B: Lintas Worldwide	1,321.5	1,305.5

Source: Reprinted with permission from the March 28, 1984, issue of *Advertising Age.* Copyright © 1984 by Crain Communications, Inc.

Unemployment Rate, 1983

Race and age	Women[1]	Men[1]
All races:	9.2	9.9
16 to 19 years	21.3	23.3
20 years and over	8.1	8.9
White	7.9	8.8
16 to 19 years	18.3	20.2
20 years and over	6.9	7.9
Minority races:	17.0	18.5
16 to 19 years	44.6	44.9
20 years and over	15.2	16.5

1. Annual averages. *Source:* Department of Labor, Bureau of Labor Statistics.

Percent Unemployed in the Civilian Labor Force

Year	Percent Unemployed	Year	Percent Unemployed
1920	5.2	1972	5.6
1922	6.7	1974	5.6
1924	5.0	1976	7.7
1926	1.8	1978	6.0
1928	4.2	1979	5.8
1930	8.7	1980	7.1
1932	23.6	1981	7.6
1934	21.7	1982	9.7
1936	16.9	1983	9.6
1938	19.0	Jan.	10.4
1940	14.6	Feb.	10.4
1942	4.7	March	10.3
1944	1.2	April	10.2
1946	3.9	May	10.1
1948	3.8	June	10.0
1950	5.3	July	9.5
1952	3.0	Aug.	9.5
1954	5.5	Sept.	9.2
1956	4.1	Oct.	8.8
1958	6.8	Nov.	8.4
1960	5.5	Dec.	8.2
1962	5.5	1984	
1964	5.2	Jan.	8.0
1966	3.8	Feb.	7.8
1968	3.6	March	7.8
1970	4.9	April	7.8

NOTE: Estimates prior to 1940 are based on sources other than direct enumeration. *Source:* Department of Labor, Bureau of Labor Statistics.

Employment and Unemployment

(in millions of persons)

Category	1983	1980	1979	1975	1970	1959	1950	1945	1941	1932	1929
EMPLOYMENT STATUS[1]											
Total noninstitutional population	174.2	169.8	167.0	155.3	140.3	117.9	106.6	105.5	101.5	—	—
Total labor force	—	109.0	107.0	96.0	86.0	70.9	63.9	65.3	57.5	51.3	49.4
Percent of population	64.0	64.2	64.1	61.8	61.3	60.2	59.9	61.9	56.7	—	—
Civilian labor force	111.6	106.9	105.0	93.8	82.8	68.4	62.2	53.9	55.9	51.0	49.2
Employed	100.8	99.3	98.8	85.8	78.7	64.6	58.9	52.8	50.4	38.9	47.6
Agriculture	3.4	3.4	3.3	3.4	3.5	5.6	7.2	8.6	9.1	10.2	10.5
Nonagricultural industries	97.5	95.9	95.5	82.4	75.2	59.1	51.8	44.2	41.3	28.8	37.2
Unemployed	10.7	7.6	6.1	7.9	4.1	3.7	3.3	1.0	5.6	12.1	1.6
Percent of labor force	9.6	7.1	5.8	8.5	4.9	5.5	5.3	1.9	9.9	23.6	3.2
Not in labor force	62.7	60.8	59.9	59.4	54.3	47.0	42.8	40.2	44.0	—	—
INDUSTRY											
Total nonagricultural employment	90.1	90.4	89.8	76.9	70.9	53.3	45.2	40.4	36.5	23.6	31.3
Goods-producing industries	23.4	25.7	26.5	22.6	23.6	20.4	18.5	17.5	16.0	8.6	13.3
Mining	1.0	1.0	1.0	0.8	0.6	0.7	0.9	0.8	1.0	0.7	1.1
Construction	3.9	4.3	4.5	3.5	3.6	3.0	2.4	1.1	1.8	1.0	1.5
Manufacturing: Durable goods	10.8	12.2	12.8	10.7	11.2	9.4	8.1	9.1	7.0	—	—
Nondurable goods	7.7	8.1	8.3	7.6	8.2	7.3	7.1	6.5	6.2	—	—
Services-producing industries	66.7	64.7	63.4	54.3	47.3	32.9	26.7	22.9	20.6	15.0	18.0
Transportation and public utilities	5.0	5.1	5.1	4.5	4.5	4.0	4.0	3.9	3.3	2.8	3.9
Trade: Wholesale	5.3	5.3	5.1	4.4	4.0	3.1	2.6	1.9	2.0	—	—
Retail	15.5	15.0	15.0	12.6	11.0	8.0	6.8	5.4	5.3	—	—
Finance, insurance, and real estate	5.5	5.2	5.0	4.2	3.6	2.5	1.9	1.5	1.5	1.3	1.5
Services	19.7	17.9	17.9	13.9	11.5	7.1	5.4	4.2	3.9	2.9	3.4
Federal government	2.8	2.9	2.8	2.7	2.7	2.2	1.9	2.8	1.3	0.6	0.5
State and local government	13.1	13.4	13.2	11.9	9.8	5.9	4.1	3.1	3.3	2.7	2.5

1. For 1929–45, figures on employment status relate to persons 14 years and over; beginning in 1950, 16 years and over. NOTE: Figures may not add to totals because of rounding. *Source:* Department of Labor, Bureau of Labor Statistics.

Livestock on Farms

(in thousands)

Type	1984	1983	1980	1975	1970	1965	1960	1950	1945
Cattle[1]	114,040	115,199	111,192	132,028	112,369	109,000	96,236	77,963	85,573
Dairy cows[1]	11,140	11,076	10,779	11,220	13,303	16,981	19,527	23,853	27,770
Sheep[1]	9,703	10,385	11,065	14,515	20,423	25,127	33,170	29,826	39,609
Swine[2]	55,819	53,935	67,353	54,693	57,046	56,106	59,026	58,937	59,373
Chickens[2]	364,584	378,609	400,585	384,101	422,000	401,000	369,000	457,000	516,000
Turkeys[3]	3,155	3,429	3,705	3,014	6,715	6,100	5,633	5,124	7,082

1. As of Jan. 1. 2. As of Jan. 1 the previous year for 1945–60 and Dec. 1 for 1965–81. 3. Turkey breeder hens for 1975–81 as of Dec. 1. *Source:* Department of Agriculture, Statistical Reporting Service.

Agricultural Output by States, 1982 Crops

State	Corn (1,000 bu)	Wheat (1,000 bu)	Cotton (1,000 ba[1])	Potatoes (1,000 cwt)	Tobacco (1,000 lb)	Cattle[2] (1,000 head)	Swine[3] (1,000 head)
Alabama	29,700	26,400	460.0	2,004	—	1,910	480
Alaska	—	—	—	—	—	9.0	3.5
Arizona	3,430	12,407	1,160.9	1,434	—	1,000	170
Arkansas	2,460	72,200	534.0	—	—	1,900	490
California	43,900	81,625	3,073.0	21,145	—	4,900	160
Colorado	110,390	87,504	—	14,489	—	3,040	290
Connecticut	—	—	—	423	4,244	106	8.0
Delaware	18,564	2,058	—	1,566	—	36	33
Florida	15,190	—	19.6	6,744	20,972	2,425	290
Georgia	69,275	48,840	235.0	—	105,500	1,875	1,400
Hawaii	—	—	—	—	—	230	49
Idaho	7,800	94,200	—	91,710	—	1,950	105
Illinois	1,513,540	67,500	—	583	—	2,800	5,600
Indiana	815,280	46,440	—	1,342	20,210	1,700	4,400
Iowa	1,578,000	3,000	—	308	—	6,450	14,400
Kansas	140,220	462,000	0.1	—	—	5,750	1,670
Kentucky	157,940	26,325	—	—	589,350	2,700	960
Louisiana	3,120	19,000	870.0	88	—	1,350	135
Maine	—	—	—	27,030	—	144	9.4
Maryland	70,620	6,120	—	328	37,530	375	200
Massachusetts	—	—	—	735	887	96	46
Michigan	307,380	24,600	—	9,645	—	1,500	800
Minnesota	734,500	126,809	—	13,401	—	3,610	3,900
Mississippi	5,580	39,900	1,760.0	—	—	1,800	300
Missouri	204,880	75,820	204.0	—	5,945	5,500	3,500
Montana	1,400	183,560	—	1,924	—	2,990	154
Nebraska	770,340	101,500	—	2,307	—	7,200	3,600
Nevada	—	—	0.9	4,095	—	650	14
New Hampshire	—	—	—	—	—	71	8.4
New Jersey	11,424	1,968	—	2,054	—	100	50
New Mexico	7,475	13,250	88.0	1,274	—	1,450	38
New York	67,160	5,438	—	12,015	—	2,025	100
North Carolina	158,570	21,600	102.0	2,657	700,689	1,100	2,150
North Dakota	35,360	330,785	—	17,250	—	2,100	210
Ohio	475,020	55,000	—	2,628	31,860	1,900	1,830
Oklahoma	6,000	227,700	238.0	—	—	5,350	200
Oregon	5,100	64,500	—	21,105	—	1,650	90
Pennsylvania	126,100	8,208	—	5,758	25,885	2,000	870
Rhode Island	—	—	—	720	—	8.0	4.3
South Carolina	30,600	19,800	155.0	—	124,195	660	440
South Dakota	192,720	99,630	—	1,550	—	4,060	1,580
Tennessee	61,100	33,660	339.0	257	178,117	2,675	750
Texas	119,700	144,000	2,722.8	3,228	—	15,000	575
Utah	2,006	9,572	—	1,305	—	950	32
Vermont	—	—	—	129	—	379	7.9
Virginia	62,475	14,060	0.4	2,228	125,384	1,700	500
Washington	23,200	138,880	—	52,800	—	1,570	51
West Virginia	6,900	324	—	—	3,591	580	42
Wisconsin	361,800	5,596	—	22,575	20,136	4,400	1,220
Wyoming	5,145	8,628	—	988	—	1,475	29
U.S. Total	**8,362,364**	**2,810,407**	**11,962.7**	**351,822**	**1,994,495**	**115,199**	**53,944.5**

1. 480-lb net-weight bales. 2. Number on farms as of Jan. 1, 1983. 3. Number on farms as of Dec. 1, 1982. *Source:* Department of Agriculture, Statistical Reporting Service.

Farm Income

(in millions of dollars)

Year	Cash receipts from marketings: Crops	Livestock, livestock products	Government payments	Total cash income
1920	$6,644	$5,956	—	$12,600
1925	5,545	5,476	—	11,021
1930	3,868	5,187	—	9,055
1935	2,977	4,143	$573	7,693
1940	3,469	4,913	723	9,105
1945	9,655	12,008	742	22,405
1950	12,356	16,105	283	28,744
1955	13,523	15,967	229	29,719
1960	15,259	18,989	702	34,950
1965	17,479	21,886	2,463	41,828
1970	20,977	29,532	3,717	54,226
1975	45,813	43,089	807	89,709
1977	48,600	47,635	1,819	98,054
1978	53,708	59,162	3,030	115,900
1979	63,174	68,594	1,375	133,143
1980	72,707	67,800	1,286	141,793
1981	73,342	69,215	1,932	144,489
1982	74,623	70,139	3,492	148,254
1983	69,516	69,203	9,294[1]	148,013

1. Includes value of PIK commodities. *Source:* Department of Agriculture, Economic Research Service. NOTE: Figures are latest available.

Consumption of Principal Foods[1]

(in pounds per capita)

Foods	1983[1]	1982	1981
Red meats	144.2	139.4	145.1
Poultry	63.8	64.1	62.4
Eggs	33.1	33.4	33.6
Fluid milk and cream[2]	240.0	242.2	245.7
Cheese	22.4	20.1	19.9
Butter	5.1	4.5	4.3
Margarine	10.3	11.1	11.2
Fats and oils	62.7	56.3	60.6
Fresh fruits	91.8	81.2	84.0
Processed fruits	48.6	50.4	55.0
Fresh vegetables	102.1	150.9	96.2
Processed vegetables	56.4	56.3	59.2
Potatoes, sweet potatoes[3]	n.a.	119.3	114.8
Sugar	71.0	75.2	79.4
Corn products[4]	130.2	125.6	119.9
Wheat flour	116.0	114.0	115.9
Coffee	7.6	7.5	7.7
Cocoa products	3.3	3.0	2.9

1. As of August 1984. Except where noted, consumption is from commercial sources and is in terms of retail weight. 2. Includes milk and cream produced and consumed on farms. 3. Farm-weight equivalent of fresh and processed use. 4. Farm-weight equivalent of corn for all food use except fresh. NOTE: n.a. = not available. *Source:* Department of Agriculture, Economic Research Service.

Government Employment and Payrolls

Year and function	Employees (in thousands): Total	Federal[1]	State	Local	October payrolls (in millions): Total	Federal[1]	State	Local
1940	4,474	1,128	3,346		566	$177	$389	
1945	6,556	3,375	3,181		1,110	642	468	
1950	6,402	2,117	1,057	3,228	1,528	613	218	96
1955	7,432	2,378	1,199	1,436	2,265	846	326	1,093
1960	8,808	2,421	1,527	4,860	3,333	1,118	524	1,691
1965	10,589	2,588	2,028	5,973	4,884	1,484	849	2,551
1970	13,028	2,881	2,755	7,392	8,334	2,428	1,612	4,294
1972	13,759	2,795	2,957	8,007	9,950	2,710	1,937	5,303
1973	14,139	2,786	3,013	8,339	11,027	3,102	2,158	5,857
1975	14,973	2,890	3,271	8,813	13,224	3,584	2,653	6,987
1976	15,012	2,843	3,343	8,826	13,924	3,565	2,894	7,465
1977	15,614	2,848	3,491	9,274	15,338	3,918	3,195	8,225
1978	15,628	2,885	3,539	9,204	16,483	4,344	3,483	8,656
1979	15,971	2,869	3,699	9,403	18,077	4,728	3,869	9,480
1980	16,213	2,898	3,753	9,562	19,935	5,205	4,285	10,445
1981	15,976	2,865	3,726	9,385	21,199	5,245	4,667	11,287
1982	15,918	2,848	3,747	9,324	23,124	5,959	5,028	12,137
1983, total	16,034	2,875	3,816	9,344	$24,525	6,301	5,346	12,878
National defense and international relations	1,042	1,042	(2)	(2)	2,155	2,155	(2)	(2)
Postal service	669	669	(2)	(2)	1,512	1,512	(2)	(2)
Education	6,807	16	1,666	5,125	9,045	37	1,989	7,018
Instructional employees	n.a.	n.a.	n.a.	n.a.	n.a.	n.a.	n.a.	n.a.
Highways	532	5	243	284	789	11	393	384
Health and hospitals	1,668	269	670	730	2,415	533	953	929
Police protection	735	64	76	595	1,306	161	145	1,000
Local fire protection	n.a.	n.a.	n.a.	n.a.	n.a.	n.a.	n.a.	n.a.
Sewerage and sanitation	n.a.	n.a.	n.a.	n.a.	n.a.	n.a.	n.a.	n.a.
Local parks and recreation	n.a.	n.a.	n.a.	n.a.	n.a.	n.a.	n.a.	n.a.
Natural resources	440	244	159	37	836	560	232	44
Financial administration	414	108	119	187	633	216	184	233
All other	3,096	376	756	1,965	4,890	894	1,206	2,790

1. Civilians only. 2. Not applicable. NOTE: n.a. = not available. *Source:* Department of Commerce, Bureau of the Census.

Receipts and Outlays of the Federal Government

(in millions of dollars)

From 1789 to 1842, the federal fiscal year ended Dec. 31; from 1844 to 1976, on June 30; and beginning 1977, on Sept. 30.

	Receipts						Outlays					
		Internal revenue										
Year	Customs (including tonnage tax)[1]	Income and profits tax	Other	Miscel-laneous taxes and receipts	Total receipts	Net receipts[2]	Department of Defense (Army, 1789–1950)	Department of the Navy	Interest on public debt	All other	Net outlays[3]	Surplus (+) or deficit (–)
1789–1791	$ 4	—	—	—	$ 4	$ 4	$ 1	—	$ 2	$ 1	$ 4	—
1800	9	—	$ –1	$ 1	11	11	3	$ 3	3	1	11	—
1810	9	—	—	1	9	9	2	2	3	1	8	$ +1
1820	15	—	—	3	18	18	3	4	5	6	18	—
1830	22	—	—	3	25	25	5	3	2	5	15	+10
1840	14	—	—	6	20	20	7	6	—	11	24	–4
1850	40	—	—	4	44	44	9	8	4	18	40	+4
1860	53	—	—	3	56	56	16	12	3	32	63	–7
1865	85	—	209	39	334	334	1,031	123	77	66	1,298	–964
1870	195	—	185	32	411	411	58	22	129	101	310	+101
1880	187	—	124	23	334	334	38	14	96	120	268	+66
1890	230	—	143	31	403	403	45	22	36	215	318	+85
1900	233	—	295	39	567	567	135	56	40	290	521	+46
1910	334	—	290	52	675	675	190	123	21	359	694	–19
1915	210	$ 80	335	72	698	683	202	142	23	379	746	–63
1918	180	2,314	872	299	3,665	3,645	4,870	1,279	190	6,339	12,677	–9,032
1929	602	2,331	607	493	4,033	3,862	426	365	678	1,658	3,127	+734
1933	251	746	858	225	2,080	1,997	435	349	689	3,125	4,598	–2,602
1939	319	2,189	2,972	188	5,668	4,979	695	673	941	6,533	8,841	–3,862
1943	324	16,094	6,050	934	23,402	21,947	42,526	20,888	1,808	14,146	79,368	–57,420
1944	431	34,655	7,030	3,325	45,441	43,563	49,438	26,538	2,609	16,401	94,986	–51,423
1945	355	35,173	8,729	3,494	47,750	44,362	50,490	30,047	3,617	14,149	98,303	–53,941
1950	423	28,263	11,186	1,439	41,311	36,422	5,789	4,130	5,750	23,875	39,544	–3,122
1956[4]	705	56,639	20,564	389	78,297	74,547	35,693	—	6,787	27,981	70,460	+4,087
1960	1,123	67,151	28,266	1,190	97,730	92,492	43,969	—	9,180	39,075	92,223	+269
1965	1,478	79,792	39,996	1,598	122,863	116,833	47,179	—	11,346	59,904	118,430	–1,596
1970	2,494	138,689	65,276	3,424	209,883	193,743	78,360	—	19,304	98,924	196,588	–2,845
1975	3,782	202,146	108,371	6,711	321,010	280,997	87,471	—	32,665	205,969	326,105	–45,108
1980	7,482	359,927	192,436	12,797	572,641	520,050	136,138	—	74,860	368,013	579,011	–58,961
1981	8,523	406,583	235,088	13,796	663,991	602,612	159,183	—	95,589	405,772	660,544	–57,932
1982	9,278	418,600	246,355	16,188	690,421	617,766	185,821	—	117,404	425,199	728,424	–110,658
1983	9,060	411,410	251,491	15,620	687,581	600,563	207,939	—	128,813	459,165	795,917	–195,354

1. Beginning 1933, tonnage tax is included in "Other receipts." 2. Net receipts equal total receipts less (a) appropriations to federal old-age and survivors' insurance trust fund beginning fiscal year 1939 and (b) refunds of receipts beginning fiscal year 1933. 3. Includes Air Force 1950–65 (in millions): 1950—$3,521; 1956—$16,750; 1960—$19,065; 1965—$18,471. 4. Beginning 1956, computed on unified budget concepts; not strictly comparable with preceding figures. *Source:* Department of the Treasury, Bureau of Government Financial Operations.

Social Welfare Expenditures Under Public Programs

(in millions of dollars)

Year and source of funds	Social insurance	Public aid	Health and medical programs	Veterans' programs	Education	Housing	Other social welfare	All health and medical care[1]	Total social welfare	Total social welfare as: Percent of gross national product	Percent of total gov't outlays
FEDERAL											
1950	$2,103	$1,103	$604	$6,386	$157	$15	$174	$1,362	$10,541	4.0	26.2
1955	6,385	1,504	1,150	4,772	485	75	252	1,948	14,623	3.9	22.3
1960	14,307	2,117	1,737	5,367	868	144	417	2,918	24,957	5.0	28.1
1965	21,807	3,594	2,781	6,011	2,470	238	812	4,625	37,712	5.7	32.6
1970	45,246	9,649	4,775	8,952	5,876	582	2,259	16,600	77,337	8.1	40.1
1975	99,715	27,205	8,513	16,570	8,629	2,541	4,264	34,645	167,436	11.5	53.8
1978	147,252	40,013	11,566	19,570	10,884	4,887	5,949	53,851	240,121	11.8	55.3
1979	163,879	43,384	11,707	20,412	12,108	5,069	6,649	59,009	263,634	10.9	54.1
1980	191,162	48,666	12,886	21,254	13,452	6,608	8,786	68,989	303,276	11.5	53.2
1981[2]	224,541	55,946	14,309	23,229	13,372	6,045	7,304	80,990	344,747	11.7	52.9
1982[2]	249,304	52,402	15,073	24,463	11,917	7,176	6,247	91,008	366,582	11.9	51.0
STATE AND LOCAL											
1950	2,844	1,393	1,460	480	6,518	(3)	274	1,704	12,967	4.9	59.2
1955	3,450	1,499	1,953	62	10,672	15	367	2,473	18,017	4.7	55.3
1960	4,999	1,984	2,727	112	16,758	33	723	3,478	27,337	5.5	60.1
1965	6,316	2,690	3,466	20	25,638	80	1,254	4,911	39,464	6.0	60.4
1970	9,446	6,839	5,132	127	44,970	120	1,886	8,791	68,519	7.1	64.0
1975	23,298	14,122	9,195	449	72,234	631	2,683	17,847	122,612	8.4	63.7
1978	27,683	19,381	11,364	174	90,708	337	4,614	24,441	154,261	7.6	62.7
1979	30,408	20,940	13,256	190	97,154	424	4,192	27,814	166,563	6.9	65.6
1980	38,592	23,133	14,771	212	107,597	601	4,813	31,309	189,720	7.2	66.5
1981[2]	42,822	26,477	15,813	212	114,773	688	4,914	34,955	205,729	7.0	65.3
1982[2]	51,437	28,384	17,819	245	121,957	778	5,349	39,338	225,969	7.4	64.6
TOTAL											
1950	4,947	2,496	2,064	6,866	6,674	15	448	3,065	23,508	8.9	37.4
1955	9,835	3,003	3,103	4,834	11,157	89	619	4,421	32,640	8.6	32.7
1960	19,307	4,101	4,464	5,479	17,626	177	1,139	6,395	52,293	10.5	38.4
1965	28,123	6,283	6,246	6,031	28,108	318	2,066	9,535	77,175	11.7	42.2
1970	54,691	16,488	9,907	9,078	50,846	701	4,145	25,391	145,856	15.2	48.2
1975	123,013	41,326	17,708	17,019	80,863	3,172	6,947	52,492	290,047	20.0	57.4
1978	174,935	59,394	22,930	19,744	101,592	6,133	10,563	78,292	394,383	19.3	57.8
1979	194,288	64,324	24,963	20,602	109,262	5,493	10,841	86,823	429,710	17.8	57.8
1980	229,754	71,799	27,657	21,466	121,050	7,210	13,599	100,298	492,534	18.7	57.4
1981[2]	267,363	82,424	30,122	23,441	128,146	6,734	12,248	115,914	550,476	18.6	56.8
1982[2]	300,741	80,786	32,892	32,892	133,874	7,952	11,596	130,346	592,551	19.3	55.3
PERCENT OF TOTAL, BY TYPE											
1950	21.0	10.6	8.8	29.2	28.4	0.1	1.9	13.0	100.0	(3)	(3)
1955	30.1	9.2	9.5	14.8	34.2	0.3	1.9	13.5	100.0	(3)	(3)
1960	36.9	7.8	8.5	10.5	33.7	0.3	2.2	12.2	100.0	(3)	(3)
1965	36.4	8.1	8.1	7.8	36.4	0.4	2.7	12.4	100.0	(3)	(3)
1970	37.5	11.3	6.7	6.2	34.9	0.5	3.0	17.2	100.0	(3)	(3)
1975	42.4	14.2	6.1	5.9	27.9	1.1	2.4	18.1	100.0	(3)	(3)
1978	44.4	15.1	5.8	5.0	25.8	1.3	2.7	19.8	100.0	(3)	(3)
1979	45.2	15.0	5.8	4.8	25.4	1.3	2.5	20.2	100.0	(3)	(3)
1980	46.6	14.6	5.6	4.4	24.6	1.5	2.8	20.4	100.0	(3)	(3)
1981[2]	48.6	15.0	5.5	4.3	23.3	1.2	2.2	21.1	100.0	(3)	(3)
1982[2]	50.8	13.6	5.6	4.2	22.6	1.3	2.0	22.0	100.0	(3)	(3)
FEDERAL PERCENT OF TOTAL											
1950	42.5	44.2	29.2	93.0	2.3	100.0	38.9	44.4	44.8	(3)	(3)
1955	64.9	50.1	37.1	98.7	4.3	83.7	40.7	44.1	44.8	(3)	(3)
1960	74.1	51.6	38.9	98.0	4.9	81.2	36.6	45.6	47.7	(3)	(3)
1965	77.5	57.2	44.5	99.7	8.8	74.9	39.3	48.5	48.9	(3)	(3)
1970	82.7	58.5	48.2	98.6	11.6	82.9	54.5	65.4	53.0	(3)	(3)
1975	81.1	65.8	48.1	97.4	10.7	80.1	61.4	66.0	57.7	(3)	(3)
1978	84.2	67.4	50.4	99.2	10.7	93.5	56.3	68.8	60.9	(3)	(3)
1979	84.3	67.4	46.9	99.1	11.1	92.3	61.3	68.0	61.4	(3)	(3)
1980	83.2	67.8	46.6	99.0	11.1	91.7	64.6	68.8	61.6	(3)	(3)
1981[2]	84.0	67.9	47.5	99.1	10.4	89.8	59.6	69.9	62.6	(3)	(3)
1982[2]	82.9	64.9	45.8	99.0	8.9	90.2	53.9	69.8	61.9	(3)	(3)

1. Combines health and medical programs with medical services provided in connection with social insurance, public aid, veterans, and other social welfare programs. 2. Preliminary. 3. Not applicable. NOTE: Figures are latest available. *Source:* Department of Health and Human Services. *Social Security Bulletin,* July 10, 1984.

Contributions to International Organizations

(for fiscal year 1983 in millions of dollars)

Organization	Amount[1]
United Nations and Specialized Agencies	$319.78
United Nations	151.90
Food and Agricultural Organization	35.07
International Atomic Energy Agency	8.48
International Civil Aviation Organization	3.14
International Labor Union	30.23
International Telecommunications Union	2.54
UNESCO	39.10
World Health Organization	45.08
World Meteorological Organization	2.82
Others	1.42
United Nations Peacekeeping Forces	96.40
United Nations Force in Cyprus	9.00
United Nations Disengagement Observer Force	65.30
Multinational Forces and Observers	22.10
Inter-American Organizations	88.71
Organization of American States	46.45
Pan American Health Organization	28.57
Inter-American Institute for Cooperation on Agriculture	11.32
Inter-American Tropical Tuna Commission	1.85
Others	.52
Regional Organizations	21.36
NATO Civilian Headquarters	11.87
Organization for Economic Cooperation and Development	7.72
Others	1.77
Other International Organizations	10.48
Customs Cooperation Council	1.29
General Agreement on Tariffs and Trade	1.36
International Institute for Cotton	2.73
Others	5.10
Special Voluntary Programs	578.32
Consultative Group on International Agricultural Research	43.75
Intergovernmental Committee for Migration—Special Voluntary	6.17
International Atomic Energy Agency—Technical Assistance Fund	14.44[2]
Organization of American States—Special Development Assistance Fund	6.00
Organization of American States—Special Multilateral Fund (education and science)	6.50
United Nations Children's Fund	42.48
United Nations Development Program	139.33
United Nations Environmental Program	7.83
UN/FAO World Food Program	33.90[3]
United Nations Fund for Drug Abuse Control	2.00
United Nations Fund for Population Activities	33.76
United Nations High Commissioner for Refugees (5 programs)	98.37
8 Special programs	9.22
United Nations Relief and Works Agency	67.00
World Health Organization—Special Programs	3.25
Others	64.32
Total	**1,115.05**

1. Estimated. 2. Includes cash, commodities and services and $5.1 million for Safeguard Program. 3. Includes cash, commodities, and services. *Source:* Department of State.

Per Capita Personal Income by States

State	1983	1982	1981	1980
Alabama	$ 9,242	$ 8,684	$ 8,235	$ 7,465
Alaska	17,194	16,854	14,979	13,007
Arizona	10,656	10,053	9,820	8,854
Arkansas	8,967	8,444	8,018	7,113
California	13,257	12,617	12,105	11,021
Colorado	12,770	12,239	11,444	10,143
Connecticut	14,895	13,939	12,895	11,532
Delaware	12,665	11,912	11,070	10,059
D.C.	15,744	14,743	13,659	12,251
Florida	11,593	10,929	10,387	9,246
Georgia	10,379	9,637	8,946	8,021
Hawaii	12,114	11,590	11,090	10,129
Idaho	9,555	9,012	8,947	8,105
Illinois	12,405	12,027	11,598	10,454
Indiana	10,476	10,019	9,810	8,914
Iowa	10,705	10,635	10,523	9,226
Kansas	12,247	11,850	11,158	9,880
Kentucky	9,397	9,122	8,602	7,679
Louisiana	10,270	10,065	9,565	8,412
Maine	9,847	9,264	8,625	7,760
Maryland	12,994	12,280	11,546	10,394
Massachusetts	13,264	12,287	11,287	10,103
Michigan	11,466	10,751	10,456	9,801
Minnesota	11,913	11,290	10,725	9,673
Mississippi	8,098	7,733	7,261	6,573
Missouri	10,969	10,403	9,819	8,812
Montana	9,949	9,617	9,254	8,342
Nebraska	11,212	10,886	10,453	8,895
Nevada	12,451	11,919	11,771	10,848
New Hampshire	12,021	11,131	10,219	9,150
New Jersey	14,122	13,164	12,203	10,966
New Mexico	9,640	9,285	8,774	7,940
New York	12,990	12,204	11,346	10,179
North Carolina	9,787	9,147	8,659	7,780
North Dakota	11,666	10,866	10,766	8,642
Ohio	11,216	10,659	10,221	9,399
Oklahoma	10,963	11,071	10,331	9,018
Oregon	10,740	10,148	9,938	9,309
Pennsylvania	11,448	10,928	10,323	9,353
Rhode Island	11,670	10,930	10,244	9,227
South Carolina	9,187	8,613	8,169	7,392
South Dakota	9,847	9,332	9,019	7,800
Tennessee	9,549	9,029	8,554	7,711
Texas	11,685	11,380	10,807	9,439
Utah	8,993	8,693	8,325	7,671
Vermont	9,979	9,518	9,030	7,957
Virginia	12,116	11,353	10,553	9,413
Washington	12,177	11,694	11,254	10,256
West Virginia	9,159	8,966	8,395	7,764
Wisconsin	11,352	10,774	10,262	9,364
Wyoming	11,911	12,222	12,111	11,018
United States	**11,685**	**11,113**	**10,544**	**9,494**

Source: U.S. Department of Commerce, Bureau of Economic Analysis.

Foreign Assistance

(in millions of dollars)

Calendar years	Economic Assistance (net)				Military grants (net)	Net assistance[1]
	Net new grants	Net new credits	Net other assistance	Total		
July 1945–50[2]	$18,413	$ 8,086	—	$ 26,498	$ 1,981	$ 28,479
1951–55	10,459	556	$ 541	11,556	14,464	26,020
1956–60	8,291	1,503	2,226	12,021	11,327	23,348
1961–65	9,384	5,522	576	15,482	7,831	23,313
1966–70	8,803	9,430	−564	17,674	12,028	29,702
1971–75	12,939	7,524	−725	19,737	16,693	36,430
1976–80	14,266	17,748	−286	31,729	5,645	37,374
1981	4,134	4,136	−15	8,256	1,150	9,407
1982	4,668	4,787	1	9,456	1,491	10,947
1983	5,126	3,570	−3	8,693	1,295	9,988
Total postwar period	**96,488**	**62,863**	**1,752**	**161,104**	**73,905**	**235,009**

1. Excludes investment in international nonmonetary financial institutions of $11,713 million. 2. Includes transactions after V-J Day (Sept. 2, 1945). NOTE: Detail may not add to total due to rounding. *Source:* Department of Commerce, Bureau of Economic Analysis.

The Public Debt

Year	Gross debt		Year	Gross debt	
	Amount (in millions)	Per capita		Amount (in millions)	Per capita
1800 (Jan. 1)	$ 83	$ 15.87	1950	$256,087[2]	$1,688.30
1860 (June 30)	65	2.06	1955	272,807[2]	1,650.63
1865	2,678	75.01	1960	284,093[2]	1,572.31
1900	1,263	16.60	1965	313,819[2]	1,612.70
1920	24,299	228.23	1970	370,094[2]	1,807.09
1925	20,516	177.12	1975	533,189	2,496.90
1930	16,185	131.51	1980	907,701	3,969.55
1935	28,701	225.55	1981	997,855	4,329.48
1940	42,968	325.23	1982	1,142,034	4,907.71
1945	258,682	1,848.60	1983[1]	1,377,210	5,863.59

1. Preliminary, Sept. 30, 1983. 2. Adjusted to exclude issues to the international Monetary Fund and other international lending institutions to conform to the budget presentation. *Source:* Department of the Treasury, Bureau of Government Financial Operations.

Domestic Freight Traffic by Major Carriers

(in millions of ton-miles)[1]

Year	Railroads		Inland waterways[2]		Motor trucks		Oil pipelines		Air carriers	
	Ton-miles	% of total	Ton-miles	% of total	Ton-miles	% of total	Ton-miles	% of total	Ton-miles	% of total
1940	379,201	61.3	118,057	19.1	62,043	10.0	59,277	9.6	14	—
1945	690,809	67.3	142,737	13.9	66,948	6.5	126,530	12.3	91	—
1950	596,940	56.2	163,344	15.4	172,860	16.3	129,175	12.1	318	—
1955	631,385	49.5	216,508	17.0	223,254	17.5	203,244	16.0	481	—
1960	579,130	44.1	220,253	16.8	285,483	21.7	228,626	17.4	778	—
1965	708,700	43.3	262,421	16.0	359,218	21.9	306,393	18.7	1,910	0.1
1970	771,168	39.8	318,560	16.4	412,000	21.3	431,000	22.3	3,274	0.2
1975	759,000	36.7	342,210	16.5	454,000	22.0	507,300	24.6	3,732	0.2
1976	799,876	36.3	372,865	16.9	510,000	23.2	515,100	23.4	3,900	0.2
1977	833,994	36.1	368,275	15.9	555,000	24.1	546,000	23.7	4,181	0.2
1978	867,982	35.1	409,316	16.6	602,000	24.4	585,800	23.7	4,630	0.2
1979	927,000	35.7	431,000	16.6	628,000	24.2	605,000	23.3	4,439	0.2
1980	932,000	37.2	420,000	16.9	567,000	22.6	588,000	23.1	4,528	0.2
1981	926,000	37.5	423,000	17.1	565,000	22.9	553,000	22.4	4,657	0.2
1982[3]	812,000	36.3	—	—	—	—	—	—	—	—

1. Mail and express included, except railroads for 1970. 2. Rivers, canals, and domestic traffic on Great Lakes. 3. Preliminary. *Sources:* Interstate Commerce Commission; Civil Aernautics Board; Association of American Railroads, and Transportation Association of America.

Intercity Passenger Traffic
(in millions of passenger miles)

Year	Railroads Miles	Buses Miles	Air carriers Miles	Inland waterways[1] Miles	Total commercial	Private airplanes
1945	93,535	27,027	3,362	2,056	125,980	—
1950	32,481	26,436	10,072	1,190	70,179	—
1955	28,695	25,519	22,741	1,738	78,693	—
1960	21,574	19,327	31,730	2,688	75,319	2,228
1965	17,557	23,775	53,719	3,101	98,152	4,364
1970	10,903	25,300	109,499	4,000	149,702	9,101
1975	10,075	25,000	136,432	4,000	175,507	11,500
1976	11,000	25,000	150,000	4,000	190,000	13,000
1977	10,400	25,900	164,200	4,000	204,500	12,100
1978	10,500	25,400	189,100	4,000	229,000	12,700
1979	11,600	26,600	210,300	4,000	252,500	15,500
1980	11,500	27,700	204,368	4,000	243,600	15,600
1981	11,800	26,900	201,400	4,000	244,100	14,600
1982[2]	10,900	28,000	213,000	n.a.	251,900	14,500

1. Rivers, canals, and Great Lakes. 2. Preliminary. NOTE: Beginning in 1970, data include Alaska and Hawaii. n.a. = not available. *Sources:* Interstate Commerce Commission; Civil Aeronautics Board; Association of American Railroads, and Transportation Association of America.

Tonnage Handled by Principal U.S. Ports
(Over 10 million tons annually; in thousands of tons)

Port	1982	1981	Port	1982	1981
New Orleans	177,302	188,850	St. Louis (Metropolitan)	22,398	22,666
New York	149,255	156,551	Paulsboro, N.J.	18,756	20,581
Houston	94,649	100,966	Toledo Harbor, Ohio	16,394	22,962
Valdez Harbor, Alaska	90,138	84,842	Boston	17,593	20,306
Baton Rouge, La.	68,556	72,044	Seattle	17,805	20,514
Norfolk Harbor, Va.	55,294	52,897	Newport News, Va.	20,911	18,249
Beaumont, Tex.	33,286	40,358	Freeport, Tex.	14,989	23,357
Baltimore Harbor	40,830	49,804	Detroit	13,176	17,839
Tampa Harbor, Fla.	38,079	44,978	Huntington, W. Va.	13,748	18,561
Philadelphia	31,936	41,583	Conneault Harbor, Ohio	10,968	16,150
Corpus Christi Ship Chnl, Tex.	37,974	41,980	Richmond, Calif.	15,394	18,019
Duluth-Superior, Minn.	27,436	39,425	Tacoma Harbor, Wash.	13,246	15,170
Corpus Christi, Tex.	36,186	39,148	Indiana, Ind.	12,303	18,374
Long Beach, Calif.	42,010	43,537	Jacksonville, Fla.	12,707	15,843
Mobile, Ala.	32,320	37,611	Cleveland	8,941	13,903
Pittsburgh	28,251	32,294	Everglades, Fla.	11,487	12,031
Lake Charles, La.	18,876	20,705	Portland, Me.	10,455	14,752
Chicago	26,819	31,599	Savannah, Ga.	10,975	12,707
Los Angeles	33,099	31,526	New Castle, Del.	9,819	11,732
Port Arthur, Tex.	19,945	26,037	Memphis, Tenn.	11,686	11,403
Portland, Ore.	25,129	27,624	Escanaba, Mich.	6,507	10,061
Texas City, Tex.	33,370	27,852	Cincinnati	18,120	15,084
Marcus Hook, Pa.	23,880	24,550	St. Paul	8,998	10,315
Pascagoula, Miss.	19,157	26,632	Astabula, Ohio	6,832	9,947

Source: Department of the Army, Corps of Engineers.

Annual Railroad Carloadings

Year	Total	Year	Total	Year	Total	Year	Total
1920	33,754,000	1945	41,918,000	1970	27,160,000	1978	23,373,000
1925	34,783,000	1950	38,903,000	1974	26,184,000	1979	23,876,000
1930	30,173,000	1955	37,636,000	1975	23,217,000	1980	22,598,000
1935	22,015,000	1960	30,441,000	1976	23,457,000	1981	21,612,000
1940	36,358,000	1965	29,248,000	1977	23,173,000	1982	18,550,199

Source: Association of American Railroads.

Estimated Motor Vehicle Registration, 1983

(in thousands; including publicly owned vehicles)

State	Autos[1]	Trucks and buses	Motor-cycles	Total
Alabama	2,197	881	69	3,147
Alaska	214	126	11	351
Arizona	1,648	660	106	2,414
Arkansas	955	511	24	1,490
California	14,016	3,782	714	18,512
Colorado	1,847	669	118	2,634
Connecticut	2,119	161	77	2,357
Delaware	339	84	12	435
D.C.	211	18	6	235
Florida	7,299	1,655	233	9,187
Georgia	3,031	941	117	4,089
Hawaii	532	61	7	600
Idaho	530	360	52	942
Illinois	5,840	1,416	293	7,549
Indiana	2,873	1,009	157	4,039
Iowa	1,664	692	239	2,595
Kansas	1,398	699	130	2,227
Kentucky	1,817	816	64	2,697
Louisiana	2,036	782	69	2,887
Maine	568	202	48	818
Maryland	2,453	480	75	3,008
Massachusetts	3,298	451	99	3,848
Michigan	5,007	1,331	223	6,561
Minnesota	2,347	980	173	3,500
Mississippi	1,230	380	29	1,639
Missouri	2,565	874	98	3,537
Montana	477	306	47	830
Nebraska	814	415	45	1,274
Nevada	519	200	24	743
New Hampshire	666	115	59	840
New Jersey	4,402	538	104	5,044
New Mexico	806	428	63	1,297
New York	7,180	1,097	192	8,469
North Carolina	3,468	1,120	117	4,705
North Dakota	386	279	32	697
Ohio	6,305	1,291	282	7,878
Oklahoma	1,811	1,029	134	2,974
Oregon	1,463	622	89	2,174
Pennsylvania	5,613	1,123	233	6,969
Rhode Island	505	80	29	614
South Carolina	1,594	451	35	2,080
South Dakota	384	243	39	666
Tennessee	2,746	607	83	3,436
Texas	8,110	3,517	338	11,965
Utah	723	325	66	1,114
Vermont	271	82	22	375
Virginia	3,144	545	79	3,768
Washington	2,286	931	136	3,353
West Virginia	802	340	56	1,198
Wisconsin	2,570	633	210	3,413
Wyoming	303	219	22	544
Total	**125,382**	**36,557**	**5,779**	**167,718**

1. Includes taxicabs. NOTE: Figures are latest available. *Source:* Department of Transportation, Federal Highway Administration.

Passenger Car Production by Makes

Companies and models	1983	1982	1980	1975	1970	1965
American Motors Corporation	200,385	109,549	164,765	323,704	276,127	346,367
Chrysler Corporation						
Plymouth	310,824	241,225	293,100	443,550	699,031	679,539
Dodge	358,813	244,833	326,506	354,482	405,699	547,531
Chrysler	234,649	114,444	82,440	102,940	158,614	224,061
Imperial	—	—	—	1,930	10,111	16,422
Total	**904,286**	**600,502**	**638,535**	**902,902**	**1,273,455**	**1,467,553**
Ford Motor Company						
Ford	1,008,799	690,645	929,627	1,301,414	1,647,918	2,164,902
Mercury	432,353	315,789	324,528	405,104	310,463	355,404
Lincoln	106,528	97,620	52,793	101,520	58,771	45,470
Total	**1,547,680**	**1,104,054**	**1,306,948**	**1,808,038**	**2,017,152**	**2,565,776**
General Motors Corporation						
Chevrolet	1,279,106	994,251	1,760,030	1,687,091	1,504,614	2,587,509
Pontiac	429,920	421,317	575,365	523,469	422,212	860,652
Oldsmobile	1,050,846	759,637	783,230	654,342	439,632	650,801
Buick	905,608	751,338	783,575	535,820	459,931	653,838
Cadillac	309,811	246,602	203,991	278,404	152,859	196,595
Total	**3,975,291**	**3,173,145**	**4,106,191**	**3,679,126**	**2,979,248**	**4,949,395**
Checker Motors Corporation	55,335	2,000	3,340	3,181	4,146	6,136
Volkswagen of America	98,207	84,246	197,106	—	—	—
Industry total	**6,781,184**	**5,073,496**	**6,416,885**	**6,716,951**	**6,550,128**	**9,335,227**

Source: Automotive News, Feb. 17, 1983, and Motor Vehicle Manufacturers Association of the United States.

Passenger Car Data

	1982	1980	1970	1960	1950
U.S. passenger cars and taxis registered (thousands)	123,697,863	121,724	89,280	61,671	40,339
Total mileage of U.S. passenger cars (millions)	1,133,883	1,111,950	901,000	588,083	363,613
Total fuel consumption of U.S. passenger cars (millions of gallons)	69,430	73,375	65,784	41,169	24,305
World registration of cars, trucks, and buses (thousands)	436,532	411,113	248,900	126,908	70,424
U.S. registration of cars, trucks, and buses (thousands)	159,510	155,890	108,407	73,858	49,162
U.S. share of world registration of cars, trucks, and buses	36.5%	37.9%	44.0%	58.2%	69.8%

Source: Motor Vehicle Manufacturers Association of the U.S.

Domestic Passenger Car Sales

Company and model	1983	1982	1981
American Motors	193,351	112,433	136,682
Total Renault	146,190	30,178	—
Alliance	126,008	30,173	—
Encore	20,182	—	—
Total AMC	47,161	82,260	136,682
Spirit	4,441	16,182	33,504
Concord	11,513	30,872	59,846
Pacer	—	—	111
Eagle	31,207	35,206	43,221
Chrysler Corp.	841,622	691,703	729,873
Total Plymouth	265,608	251,628	325,598
Horizon	56,763	46,907	75,377
Turismo/TC3	36,497	39,704	51,815 [1]
Reliant/Volare	157,247 [2]	146,762	196,997
Plymouth	15,101	18,255	1,409
Total Chrysler	260,884	176,369	93,869
Laser	11,097	—	—
LeBaron	—	—	36,311
LeBaron K	80,309	88,575	10,680
Cordoba	10,375	15,828	23,904
New Yorker 5th Ave.	73,729	62,725	5,894 [3]
E-Class	35,283	9,122	—
New Yorker E	50,091	119	—
Total Imperial	1,153	2,601	4,649
Total Dodge	313,977	261,105	305,757
Omni	50,451	40,002	56,038
Charger/024	45,975	41,275	51,743 [4]
Daytona	8,761	—	—
Aries	119,400	113,076	149,653
600 Coupe/400	28,488	28,946 [5]	3,150 [5]
Diplomat	22,603	24,866	25,598
Mirada/Magnum	4,417 [6]	7,316	13,947
Dodge 600	33,882	5,624	5,628
Ford Motor	1,571,321	1,345,698	1,380,600
Ford Division	1,060,315	925,490	977,220
EXP	19,574	39,021	54,502
Escort	326,333	337,667	284,907
Mustang	116,976	119,526	154,985
Tempo	136,148	—	—
Fairmont	37,521	139,056	182,909
Granada	3,751	94,750	106,996
Thunderbird	134,710	42,585	69,775
LTD '83	165,396	26,820	—
Ford Crown Victoria	119,905	126,065	113,109 [7]
L-M Division	511,007	420,208	403,380
Total Mercury	409,433	327,142	339,550
Bobcat	—	—	2,169
LN7	4,694	13,107	18,217
Lynx	78,876	95,959	92,809
Topaz	41,796	—	—
Zephyr	11,583	42,363	50,603
Cougar/Monarch	906	40,829	46,750 [8]
XR7	87,027	15,609	28,706
Capri	22,708	31,280	47,151
Marquis '83	65,184	10,645	—
Mercury Grand Marquis	96,659	77,348	53,145 [9]
Total Lincoln	101,574	93,068	68,830
Continental/Versailles	13,691 [10]	22,611	4,919
Lincoln	59,626	42,537	29,178
Mark VII	28,257	27,920 [11]	29,733 [11]
General Motors	4,053,561	3,515,660	3,796,696
Buick Division	845,083	723,011	722,617
Skyhawk	72,998	46,942	—
Skylark	102,763	141,766	200,460
Century FD	150,280	99,873	2,691
Regal Sedan/Coupe	234,035	222,169	332,005
LaSabre	151,555	108,989	82,263
Electra	80,106	59,599	57,234
Riviera	53,346	43,673	47,964
Cadillac Division	300,337	249,295	230,665
Cimarron	19,188	13,774	14,604
Seville	33,522	24,029	22,724
Cadillac	176,003	154,229	138,948
Eldorado	71,624	57,263	54,389
Chevrolet Division	1,347,447	1,260,620	1,442,281
Chevette	178,759	231,927	346,307
Cavalier/Monza	259,397 [12]	121,392	88,072
Citation	92,379	186,782 [13]	300,184
Camaro	178,266	182,848	94,606
Celebrity	180,354	101,311	1,361
Malibu	85,421	110,736	211,130
Monte Carlo	105,797	98,954	161,158
Chevrolet	238,930	204,193	210,424
Corvette	28,144	22,477	29,039
Oldsmobile Division	1,007,559	799,585	848,739
Firenza	44,753	28,282	—
Omega	49,818	72,392	109,981
Cutlass Ciera	191,720	113,921	2,882
Cutlass/Supreme	331,179	280,566 [14]	454,022
Olds 88	228,770	180,840	158,662
Olds 98	119,526	89,222	84,583
Toronado	41,791	34,362	38,609
Pontiac Division	553,135	483,149	552,394
Fiero	22,591	—	—
1000	34,173	51,257	55,868
2000/Sunbird	88,313	57,048	75,884
Phoenix	24,362	49,527	82,825
Firebird	90,777	105,686	52,188
6000	92,513	55,794	1,325
Bonneville/LeMans	84,122	76,063	73,988
Grand Prix	89,355	83,598	128,236
Parisienne	26,929	—	—
Pontiac	—	4,176	82,620
Volkswagen	85,045	91,166	162,445
Honda	50,402	—	—
Industry total	**9,177,777**	**7,978,058**	**6,206,296**

1. TC3. 2. Reliant only. 3. New Yorker. 4. 024. 5. 400. 6. Mirada only. 7. Ford. 8. Cougar only. 9. Mercury. 10. Continental only. 11. Mark VI. 12. Cavalier only. 13. Citation/Nova. 14. Supreme only. 15. Bonneville only. *Source: Automotive News,* Jan. 9, 1984.

Domestic and Export Factory Sales of Motor Vehicles

(in thousands)

	From plants in United States								
	Passenger cars			Motor trucks and buses			Total motor vehicles		
Year	Total	Domestic	Exports	Total	Domestic	Exports	Total	Domestic	Exports
1965	9,306	9,101	205	1,752	1,616	136	11,058	10,717	341
1970	6,547	6,187	360	1,692	1,566	126	8,239	7,753	486
1975	6,713	6,073	640	2,272	2,003	269	8,985	8,076	909
1979	8,419	7,678	741	3,037	2,741	296	11,456	10,419	1,037
1980	6,400	5,840	560	1,667	1,464	203	8,067	7,304	763
1981	6,255	5,749	506	1,701	1,513	188	7,956	7,262	694
1982	5,049	4,696	353	1,906	1,779	127	6,955	6,475	480
1983	6,739	6,201	538	2,414	2,260	154	9,153	8,461	692

Source: Motor Vehicle Manufacturers Association of the U.S.

Balance of International Payments

(in billions of dollars)

Item	1983	1980	1979	1975	1970	1965	1960	1955	1949
Exports of goods and services (excluding transfers under military grants)	$334.2	$344.7	$228.9	$155.7	$65.7	$41.1	$28.9	$19.9	$15.8
Merchandise, adjusted, excluding military	200.2	224.0	184.5	107.1	42.5	26.5	19.7	14.4	12.2
Transfers under U.S. military agency sales contracts	12.7	8.2	6.6	3.9	1.5	0.8	0.3	0.2	n.s.s.
Receipts of income on U.S. investments abroad	22.2	75.9	66.7	25.4	11.8	7.4	4.6	2.6	1.5
Other services	55.9	36.5	31.1	19.3	9.9	6.4	4.3	2.7	2.1
Imports of goods and services	−366.4	−333.9	−281.9	−132.6	−60.0	−32.8	−23.7	−17.8	−9.6
Merchandise, adjusted, excluding military	−260.7	−249.3	−211.8	−98.0	−39.9	−21.5	−14.8	−11.5	−6.9
Direct defense expenditures	−12.2	−10.7	−8.6	−4.8	4.9	−3.0	−3.1	−2.9	−0.6
Payments of income on foreign assets in U.S.	−7.2	−43.2	−33.2	−12.6	−5.5	−2.1	−1.2	−0.5	−0.3
Other services	−47.3	−30.7	−28.3	−17.2	−9.8	−6.2	−4.6	−2.8	−1.8
Unilateral transfers, excluding military grants, net	−8.6	−7.0	−5.6	−4.6	−3.3	−2.9	−2.3	−2.5	−5.6
U.S. Government assets abroad, net	−49.3	−84.8	−62.6	−3.5	−1.6	−1.6	−1.1	−0.3	−0.7
U.S. private assets abroad, net	−43.2	−71.5	−57.7	−35.4	−10.2	−5.3	−5.1	−1.3	−0.6
U.S. assets abroad, official reserve, net	−1.2	−8.2	−1.1	−0.6	2.5	1.2	2.1	0.2	−0.3
Foreign assets in U.S., net	83.0	50.3	38.9	15.6	6.4	0.7	2.3	−1.4	0.2
Statistical discrepancy	7.0	29.6	21.1	5.5	−0.2	−0.5	−1.0	0.4	0.7
Balance on goods and services	−32.2	10.8	7.1	23.1	5.7	8.3	5.1	2.2	6.2
Balance on goods, services, and remittances	−34.8	8.4	5.0	21.3	4.1	7.2	4.5	1.6	5.6
Balance on current account	−40.8	3.7	1.4	18.4	2.4	5.4	2.8	−0.3	0.6

NOTE: n.s.s. = not shown separately. – denotes debits. *Source:* Department of Commerce, Bureau of Economic Analysis.

Foreign Investors in U.S. Business Enterprises

	Number				Investment outlays (millions of dollars)			
	1983[1]	1982	1981	1980	1983[1]	1982	1981	1980
Investments, total	629	1,108	1,332	1,659	$6,962	$10,817	$23,219	$12,172
Acquisitions	242	395	462	721	4,473	6,563	18,151	8.974
Establishments	387	713	870	938	2,489,	4,254	5,067	3,198
Investors, total	632	1,218	1,521	1,833	6,962	10,817	23,219	12,172
Foreign direct investors	365	720	979	1,188	2,113	3,954	6,158	4,129
U.S. affilates	317	498	542	645	4,849	6,863	17,060	8,043

1. Figures are preliminary. *Source:* U.S. Department of Commerce, *Survey of Current Business*, May 1984.

Imports of Leading Commodities

(value in millions of dollars)

Commodity	1983	1982
Food and live animals	$15,412	$14,453
Cattle, except for breeding	301	289
Meat and preparations	2,034	2,075
Dairy products and eggs	403	371
Fish	3,594	3,143
Grains and feed for animals	483	437
Vegetables and fruit	2,920	2,816
Sugar, cane or beet	1,047	863
Coffee, green	2,590	2,730
Cocoa beans	349	323
Tea	132	129
Beverages and tobacco	3,408	3,364
Alcoholic beverages	2,626	2,513
Tobacco, unmanufactured	464	445
Crude materials, inedible, except fuels	9,590	8,589
Hides and skins, except fur skins	64	71
Fur skins, undressed	126	127
Crude rubber	655	535
Wood—simply worked	2,719	1,737
Wood pulp	1,470	1,485
Textile fibers and wastes	312	264
Industrial diamonds	96	90
Ores and metal scrap	2,500	2,684
Iron ore and concentrates	452	497
Nonferrous metal ores and concentrates	1,306	1,552
Precious metal ores and concentrates, except gold	418	356
Mineral fuels and related materials	57,952	65,409
Petroleum products	52,325	59,396
Natural gas	5,530	5,934
Animal and vegetable oils and fats	495	406
Chemicals	10,779	9,494
Organic chemicals	3,477	2,960
Inorganic chemicals	2,568	2,645
Medicinal and pharmaceutical products	703	563
Fertilizers, manufactured	997	963
Machinery and transport equipment	86,131	73,320
Machinery	46,075	39,457
Transport equipment	39,156	33,863
Automobiles, buses, trucks	28,736	24,989
Motor vehicle parts	6,299	4,372
Aircraft and parts	2,051	2,481
Other manufactured goods	31,706	33,148
Paper and manufactures	4,215	3,848
Glass, glassware, and pottery	1,602	1,351
Gem diamonds	2,275	1,917
Metals and manufactures	16,396	15,806
Iron and steel-mill products	6,338	9,184
Nonferrous metals	7,422	5,321
Precious metals, except gold	2,636	1,301
Other metal manufactures	4,504	4,294
Textile yarn and fabrics	3,225	2,808
Clothing	9,583	8,165
Footwear	4,010	3,438
Scientific and controlling instruments	1,911	1,692
Clocks and watches	1,058	991
Baby carriages, toys, games, and sporting goods	2,506	2,786
Artworks and antiques	2,017	1,100
Other transactions	7,742	7,708
Total	**$292,396**	**$243,952**

Exports of Leading Commodities

(value in millions of dollars)

Commodity	1983	1982
Food and live animals	$24,166	$23,950
Meat and preparations	1,191	1,285
Dairy products and eggs	373	409
Grains and preparations	15,152	14,747
Wheat, including wheat flour	6,509	6,869
Rice	926	997
Vegetables and fruit	2,444	2,716
Feed for animals	2,802	2,473
Beverages and tobacco	2,813	3,026
Cigarettes	1,126	1,235
Beverages	351	245
Crude materials, inedible, except fuels	18,596	19,248
Hides and skins, except fur skins	807	778
Soybeans, other oilseeds, peanuts	5,925	6,240
Synthetic rubber	543	553
Logs and lumber	2,104	2,095
Pulpwood and wood pulp	1,916	1,964
Raw cotton, excluding wastes	1,817	1,955
Ores and metal scrap	2,276	2,174
Mineral fuels and related materials	9,500	12,729
Coal	4,115	6,072
Petroleum and products	4,557	5,947
Animal and vegetable oils and fats	1,459	1,541
Soybean oil	429	497
Chemicals	19,751	18,891
Chemical elements and compounds	8,378	8,541
Medicines and pharmaceuticals	2,494	2,275
Fertilizers	1,267	1,386
Plastic materials and resins	3,732	3,650
Machinery and transport equipment	82,578	87,148
Machinery	54,309	59,324
Power generating machinery	8,718	9,461
Aircraft engines, parts	1,638	910
Automotive engines, parts	1,042	942
Agricultural machinery, including tractors, and parts	1,589	2,389
Office machines, computers	11,669	10,206
Metalworking machinery	1,121	1,611
Textile and leather machinery	453	554
Transport equipment	28,269	27,824
Motor vehicles and parts	14,463	13,907
Aircraft, spacecraft, accessories	12,189	11,775
Other manufactured goods	15,246	16,739
Tires and tubes	304	372
Paper and manufactures	2,553	2,653
Nonmetallic mineral manufactures	1,770	1,805
Metals and manufactures	1,478	7,850
Iron and steel-mill products	1,415	2,101
Nonferrous base metals	2,302	1,768
Other manufactures of metals	2,086	3,981
Textile yarns and fabrics	2,368	2,784
Clothing	818	952
Scientific instruments	5,856	6,003
Photographic supplies	1,366	1,396
Printed matter	1,324	1,341
Other transactions	7,009	6,924
Total	**$266,983**	**$212,275**

Source: Department of Commerce, Bureau of the Census, Foreign Trade Division.

The following material was submitted to and reviewed by the American Red Cross, the American Heart Association, and Edumed, Inc.

First aid is the rendering of prompt and knowledgeable treatment to a person who has been injured or suddenly taken ill and for whom no immediate medical attention is available. Depending on circumstances, effective first aid can mean the difference between life and death or between temporary and permanent disability. Artificial respiration and treatment for shock that sets in after a serious accident are also important factors in the success of first aid. The best course of action to follow after taking emergency measures is to summon assistance from the local police or fire department or from the nearest available hospital.

Burns

Burns are classified according to first degree (reddened skin), second degree (blisters develop), and third degree (deep tissue damage). Face, feet, groin, and hands are critical areas. For first-degree and small second-degree burns, if the skin is intact, submerge affected area in cold water until pain subsides. Apply protective bandage. *Do not break blisters.* For third-degree burns, apply thick, sterile dressing, elevate the extremities, and obtain medical help immediately.

Eye Burns: For burns of the eye, wash thoroughly with water for five minutes—hold the eyelid open and pour the water from the inside corner out. Put a clean pad over both closed eyelids (not only injured eye), bandage, and get medical help.

Poisoning

Speed and a clear head are vital in first aid for poison intake. If the victim loses consciousness, call for an emergency squad and give artificial respiration or cardiopulmonary resuscitation (CPR) if needed. If the victim is conscious and not in convulsions, dilute the swallowed poison with a glass of water or milk, but stop at signs of nausea.

Next, call your physician or local poison-control center or hospital emergency department. Be ready to supply information on what poison, and how much of it, was taken and the weight and age of the victim, and to take down instructions for treatment and antidotes. (Antidotes suggested on a poison-container label should not be given without approval by your physician or poison-control center.)

If vomiting occurs, save a vomit specimen along with the container label for the attending physician.

Shock

Shock is caused by many types of severe injuries and severe illnesses—poisoning, damage to the respiratory system, and loss of body fluids resulting from vomiting, dysentery, or burns. It is prudent to give shock care to seriously injured individuals.

The symptoms of shock are: pale or bluish skin that is cool to the touch (in the case of dark-skinned persons, examine the color of the mucous membranes inside the mouth or under the eyelids, or of the nail beds); moist or clammy skin; weakness of the injured person; rapid pulse; increased rate of breathing, which may be shallow, possibly deep, and irregular; severe thirst; vomiting or retching from nausea.

With possible neck or back injury, a victim should not be moved. Otherwise, a person in shock should be kept lying down and covered only enough to keep him from losing body heat. (*Do not* add extra heat, because raising the body's surface temperature is harmful.)

A patient with severe injuries of the lower face and jaw or who is unconscious should be placed on the side, with care taken to prevent suffocation from vomit and blood. When in doubt about the proper position, keep the person lying flat. Fluids may be given by mouth if the victim has no head or abdominal injury, if the victim would probably not need surgery and if medical help will not be available for an hour or more. But fluids *should not* be given to persons who are unconscious, are vomiting, or are having convulsions.

Severe Bleeding

Shock and loss of consciousness may occur from the rapid loss of as little as a quart of blood. A preferred technique is to direct pressure by hand over a dressing since it prevents loss of blood from the body without interference with normal blood circulation. In an emergency, in the absence of compresses, the bare hand or fingers may be used, but only until a compress can be applied.

Apply direct pressure by placing the palm of the hand on a dressing directly over the entire area of an open wound on any surface part of the body. In most instances this technique will stop the bleeding.

A thick pad of cloth held between the hand and the wound helps to control the bleeding by absorbing the blood and allowing it to clot.

Do not disturb blood clots after they have formed within the cloth. If blood soaks through the entire pad without clotting, do not remove the pad, but add additional thick layers of cloth and continue to direct pressure even more firmly.

Tourniquet Warning. The use of a tourniquet is dangerous, and the tourniquet should be used only for a severe life-threatening hemorrhage that cannot be controlled by other means. Once a tourniquet is applied, care by a physician is imperative.

Cardiac Pulmonary Resuscitation (CPR) for Cardiac Arrest[1]

The most common signal of a heart attack is uncomfortable pressure, squeezing, fullness, or pain in the center of the chest behind the breastbone; others may be sweating, nausea, shortness of breath or a feeling of weakness. These signals may subside and return. If these signals persist, activate the emergency medical services system or take the victim to the nearest hospital with 24-hour emergency cardiac care.

Airway: Determine if the collapsed person is conscious by shaking his shoulder and shouting

"Are you all right?" If there is no response, you must open his airway. Be sure he is lying flat on his back. If you have to roll him over, move his entire body as a total unit.

To open the airway, lift up his chin (or neck) gently with one hand while pushing down on the forehead with the other to tilt the head back. Place your ear close to the victim's mouth. Look at his chest and stomach for movement. Listen for sounds of breathing. Feel for breath on your cheek.

If none of these signs is present, the victim is not breathing.

Breathing: Use the mouth-to-mouth technique. Turn the hand on the victim's forehead and pinch his nose shut while maintaining the head tilt with the heel of the hand. The other hand should remain under the victim's chin (or neck) lifting up.

Immediately give four quick, full breaths in rapid succession.

Check Pulse: After giving four quick breaths, locate the victim's carotid pulse to see if his heart is beating. Take the hand that is lifting the victim's chin or neck and locate the voice box. Slide the tips of your index and middle fingers into the groove beside the voice box. Feel for the pulse.

If you cannot find the pulse, you must provide artificial circulation in addition to rescue breathing. Activate the emergency medical services system.

Chest Compression: To perform external chest compression, kneel at the victim's side near his chest. Locate the notch at the lowest portion of the sternum (breastbone). Place the heel of one hand about 1 to 1 1/2 inches from that tip and the other on top of the first. Be sure to keep the fingers off the chest wall. You may find it easier to do by interlocking the fingers.

Bring your shoulders directly over the victim's sternum as you compress downward, keeping your arms straight. Depress the sternum about 1 1/2 to 2 inches for an adult victim. Relaxation must follow compression immediately and be of equal time. Do *not* remove your hands from the sternum.

If you are the only rescuer, you must provide both rescue breathing and chest compression at the ratio of 15 chest compressions to 2 quick breaths. You must compress at the rate of 80 times per minute, since you will lose compressions when you take time to interpose these breaths.

If there is another rescuer, position yourselves on opposite sides of the victim. One should interpose a breath after every fifth compression; the other should compress the chest at a rate of 60 compressions per minute.

For Infants and Small Children: Do not exaggerate the backward position of the head tilt because it might block breathing passages.

Do not try to pinch off the nose. Cover both the mouth and nose if the victim is not breathing. Use small breaths with less volume to inflate the lungs. Give one breath every 3 seconds.

Only one hand is used for compression. The other can be slipped under the child to provide a firm support for his back.

For infants, use only the *tips* of the index and middle fingers to compress the chest at midsternum, depressing between 1/2 to 1 inch at a rate of 100 times per minute.

For small children, use only the *heel* of one hand to compress the chest at midsternum, depressing between 1 inch and 1 1/2 inches, depending on the size of the child. The rate should be 80 times per minute.

For both infants and small children, breaths should be interposed after every fifth chest compression.

Neck Fracture: If the victim is injured in a diving or automobile accident, the possibility of a neck fracture should be considered. The airway should be opened by using a modified jaw thrust, keeping the victim's head in a fixed, neutral position.

The Heimlich Maneuver[2]

Food-Choking

Food-choking is caused by a piece of food lodging in the throat creating a blockage of the airway, making it impossible for the victim to breathe or speak. The victim will die of strangulation in four minutes if you do not act to save him.

Using the Heimlich Maneuver, you exert pressure that forces the diaphragm upward, compresses the air in the lungs, and expels the object blocking the breathing passage.

The victim should see a physician immediately after the rescue. Performing the maneuver could result in injury to the victim. However, he will survive only if his airway is quickly cleared.

If no help is at hand, victims should attempt to perform the Heimlich Maneuver on themselves by pressing their own fists upward into the abdomen as described.

What to Look for: The victim of food-choking: (1) Cannot speak or breathe, (2) turns blue, (3) collapses.

Performing the Heimlich Maneuver with the rescuer standing and the victim standing or sitting: Stand behind the victim and wrap your arms around his waist.

Place your fist thumb side against the victim's abdomen, slightly above the navel and below the rib cage.

Grasp your fist with your other hand and press into the victim's abdomen with a **quick upward thrust**.

(When the victim is sitting, the rescuer stands behind the victim's chair and performs the Maneuver in the same manner.)

With the rescuer kneeling and the victim lying face up: Facing the victim, kneel astride his hips.

With one of your hands on top of the other, place the heel of your bottom hand on the abdomen slightly above the navel and below the rib cage.

Press into the victim's abdomen with a **quick upward thrust**.

Repeat several times if necessary.

Drowning

The Heimlich Maneuver is the first step used to treat drowning in order to get water out of the victim's lungs.

With the rescuer kneeling and the victim lying face up: Facing the victim, kneel astride his or her

(Continued on page 82)

 HEIMLICH MANEUVER is a registered service mark of EDUMED, INC. which reserves all rights to its use. Teaching slides, posters, wallet cards, and other instructional materials on the Heimlich Maneuver are now available. To obtain these send a self-addressed, stamped envelope to: Edumed, Inc., Box 52, Cincinnati, Ohio 45201. Heimlich Maneuver instruction for the treatment of choking and drowning can be found in the book, "Dr. Heimlich's Home Guide to Emergency Medical Situations" by Henry J. Heimlich, M.D. and Lawrence Galton (Simon and Schuster).

Sources of Sodium in the Diet

Source: "Technical Paper of Sources of Sodium in the Diet," Water Quality Association

Introduction

Sodium is essential in human nutrition. It plays a vital role in growth, development, and in the maintenance of many bodily functions. Further, though our total sodium intake is usually far larger than the body requires, a person in normal health readily excretes the excess.

In certain physiological conditions, however, normal control functions fail, or are unable to deal with otherwise ordinary amounts of sodium. In such cases, certain drugs may be useful. In addition, the physician may also restrict the amount of sodium ingested.

A typical normal adult takes in 3000 to 6000 milligrams of sodium a day, which is approximately 1/10 to 1/5 ounce. Most of it comes from common salt (sodium chloride). But even unsalted foods, and some everyday medicinals, may contain substantial amounts.

Sodium in Natural Water Supplies

Every natural water supply contains sodium, with the concentration depending upon the exposure of the water to soluble sodium compounds present in the earth or in the atmosphere. Rainwater may contain only a few milligrams per liter (mg/1) of sodium, while water from brackish or saline wells may contain several thousand mg/1. A liter is the equivalent of 1.0567 quarts or just over four 8-ounce glassfuls.

The sodium content of a natural water supply can be determined only by an actual analysis of that supply, but the sodium added by ion exchange water softening can be calculated from the hardness in the supply.

Water Softening and Sodium

It is well known that in ion exchange water softening the chief components of water hardness (calcium and magnesium ions) are removed along with other heavy metal cations and are exchanged for sodium.

Sodium is exchanged not only in household ion exchange softening, but significantly, in ion exchange softening conducted **on a community or municipal basis**. In municipal softening, each milligram of hardness as $CaCO_3$ is replaced by 0.46 milligrams of sodium as Na.

Compared to the sodium added by softening the "average" water **cow's milk** (517 mg/1) and **skim milk** (541 mg/1) contain over ten times this much sodium; **low fat milk**, with 2% dry milk solids added (636 mg/1), contains over 12 times this much sodium, and **human milk** (170 mg/1) contains over three times this much sodium.

Sodium in Common Foods and Beverages

The data in the following table demonstrate the usual range of sodium in common foods. Despite the care with which the table was prepared, it cannot be totally accurate. Variations in sodium content may be even greater than indicated. However, the table does show an important principle: The amount of sodium almost invariably increases with the degree of preparation.

Typical Sodium Contents of Some Common Foods

Food	*Degree of prep.	mg. Sodium per serving	Serving or measure	Weight basis
Apples	R	0.5–3.5	1 medium	3 per lb
Apricots, fresh	R	0.9	2 medium	10 per lb
Asparagus, spears	R	3.5	1/2 cup	2 cups cooked per lb
Asparagus, spears, canned	O	560	1/2 cup	1 1/2 cup/14.5 oz
Asparagus, frozen	O	1.3–12	1/2 cup	2 cups/10 oz
Bacon, raw	O	103	1 slice	30 slices per lb
Baking Powder, Phosphate	O	243	1 teaspoon	1 teasp./2.7 g
Bananas	R	0.6–6	1 medium	3 per lb
Beans, baked Navy and Pork	O	950	3/4 cup	1 1/2 cup/14 oz
Beans, canned, baked	O	1130	3/4 cup	2 cups/18 oz
Beans, w/tomato sauce	O	796	3/4 cup	1 1/2 cup/14 oz
Beans, green	R	0.1–2.3	1/2 cup	3 cups cooked per lb
Beans, green, canned	O	465	1/2 cup	2 cups/lb
Beans, green, frozen	O	1.0–1.5	1/2 cup	3 cups/lb
Beans, lima	R	0.2	1/2 cup	3 cups/lb

Food	*Degree of prep.	mg. Sodium per serving	Serving or measure	Weight basis
Beans, lima, canned	O	235	1/2 cup	3 cups/lb
Beans, lima, frozen	O	114–235	1/2 cup	3 cups/lb
Beef, corned	O	1850	5 oz.	—
Beef, hash, corned, canned	O	610	1/2 cup	2 cups/lb
Beef, dried	O	1220	1 oz	—
Beef, lean	R	72–92	5 oz	—
Beef, lean, Koshered	R	2270	5 oz	—
Beef, steak	R	98	5 oz	—
Beef, stew, canned	D	22	1 cup	2 cups/lb
Beets	R	32–124	1/2 cup	2 cups/lb
Beets, canned	O	41	1/2 cup	2 cups/lb
Beverages, alcoholic				
Beer	O	28	12 fl oz	—
Beer, dark	O	15	12 fl oz	—
Beer, light	O	56	12 fl oz	—
Beer & ale, various	O	3.1–80	12 fl oz	—
Brandy	O	0.9	1 fl oz	—
Gin	O	.24	1 fl oz	—
Rum	O	0.6	1 fl oz	—
Whiskey, blended	O	.09	1 fl oz	—
Whiskey, bonded	O	.03	1 fl oz	—
Wine (average)	O	2.1	1 fl oz	—
Wine Port	O	1.2	1 fl oz	—
Wine, Sauterne	O	3.0	1 fl oz	—
Beverages, carbonated*				
Coca-Cola		3.5–7.0	12 fl oz	—
Creme Soda		3.5	12 fl oz	—
Dr. Pepper		10.5	12 fl oz	—
Ginger Ale		7–28	12 fl oz	—
Canada Dry		63	12 fl oz	—
Grape Soda		42	12 fl oz	—
Lemon-Lime Soda		24.5	12 fl oz	—
Orange Crush		7	12 fl oz	—
Orange Soda		81	12 fl oz	—
Pepsi-Cola		35–49	12 fl oz	—
Root Beer		3.5–28	12 fl oz	—
Royal Crown Cola		17.5	12 fl oz	—
Seven-Up		3.5	12 fl oz	—
Strawberry Soda		17.5	12 fl oz	—
White Rock		3.5	12 fl oz	—
Blueberries	R	1	1 cup	1 cup/5 oz
Bouillon cube, beef	O	908	1 cube	15 cubes/2 oz
Bread, Rye & Wheat	O	112	1 slice	24 slices/lb
Bread, White	O	112	1 thin slice	21 slices/lb
Bread, White	O	129	1 reg. slice	18 slices/lb
Bread, White enriched	O	161	1 reg. slice	18 slices/lb
Bread, Whole Wheat	O	152–211	1 slice	20 slices/lb
Broccoli	R	11–18	3/4 cup	8 stalks/lb
Broccoli, frozen	O	15	3/4 cup	2 cups/10 oz
Brussels Sprouts	R	6.4–8.5	1/2 cup	2 cups/10 oz
Brussels Sprouts, frozen	O	6.4–23	1/2 cup	2 cups/10 oz
Butter, salted	O	42	1 pat	96 pats or teasp./lb
Butter, sweet	O	1	1 pat	96 pats or teasp./lb
Cabbage	R	3.2–14	1/2 cup shredded R	3 1/2 cups shredded/lb
Cabbage		4.5–19	1/2 cup cooked	2 1/2 cups cooked/lb
Candy				
Caramel, soft	D	16	1 pc.	50 pcs./14 oz
Milk Chocolate	O	18	1 bar-3/4 oz	
Gum Drops	O	36	1/2 cup	2 1/2 cups/lb
Bar, Baby Ruth	O	60	1 bar-1 1/4 oz	—
Bar, Milky Way	O	78	1 bar-1 1/4 oz	—
Carrots	R	68	1/2 cup	2 1/4 cups diced or shredded/lb
Carrots		75	1/2 cup cooked	2 cups cooked/lb
Carrots, canned	O	318	1/2 cup	2 cups/lb
Cashew nuts, roasted in oil, salted	O	226	4 oz	—
Catsup, tomato	O	204	1 tablespoon	—
Celery	R	172–259	1 cup raw diced	2 1/2 cups/lb
Celery flakes, dehyd.	O	34.5	1 tablespoon	—

Food	*Degree of prep.	mg. Sodium per serving	Serving or measure	Weight basis
Celery Salt	O	672	1 teaspoon	—
Celery Seed	O	3	1 teaspoon	—
Cereals				
Bran, all-bran	O	340–395	1 oz	1 pkg./1 oz
Cornflakes	O	186	1 cup-1 oz	1 cup/oz
Oats, Oatmeal	R	0.2	1/4 cup uncooked	5 1/2 cups/lb
Rice, Puffed	O	.13	1/2 oz.-1 cup	2 cups/oz
Wheat Flakes	O	367	1 cup-1 oz	1 cup/oz
Grape Nuts	O	186	1/4 cup-1 oz	1/4 cup/oz
Muffets	O	1.5	2 biscuits	24 biscuits/lb
Puffed Wheat	O	.56	1/2 oz.-1 cup	2 cups/oz
Shredded Wheat	O	0.5	2 biscuits	19 biscuits/lb
Cheese, Am. Swiss	O	201	1 slice	16 slices/lb
Cheese, Cheddar	O	173–198	1 slice	16 slices/lb
Cheese, Cottage	O	330	1/2 cup	16 fl. oz./lb
Cheese, Cream, Phila.	O	212	3 oz pkg.	—
Cheese, Parmesan powd.	O	14.3	1 teaspoon	—
Cheese, Velveeta Cheese	O	910	1″×1 1/4″×2″	—
Cherries	R	4.5	1 cup	3 cups/lb
Cherries, sweet, dark canned	D	1.2	1/2 cup	16 fl oz/1 lb 1 oz
Chicken	R	106	5 oz	—
Chicken, light meat	R	77	5 oz	—
Chicken, light meat breast	R	111	5 oz	—
Chicken, dark meat	R	114	5 oz	—
Chicken, leg meat	R	156	5 oz	—
Chocolate syrup, Hershey	O	10.6	1 tablespoon	13 fl oz/lb
Cloves, whole	O	1.4	10 whole	—
Coffee, instant, Nescafe, dry	O	.84	1 teaspoon	—
Coffee, reg. roasted dry	O	0.2	2 tablespoons	—
Corn, sweet	R	.15–.7	1/2 cup	—
Corn, sweet, frozen	R	65–80	1/2 cup	3 cups/lb
Corn, sweet yellow, canned	O	252	1/2 cup	2 cups/lb
Crackers, Graham	O	100	1 dbl. cracker	32 dbl. crackers/lb
Crackers, Rye, Ry-Krisp	O	95	1 triple cracker	36 triple crackers/8 oz
Crackers, Soda	O	138	1–4 pc. cracker	36×4 crackers/lb
Cucumber, pickle, dill	O	318	1 pickle 1/2″ diam. × 2 1/2″	—
Duck, breast	R	97	5 oz	—
Duck, leg	R	136	5 oz	—
Eggs, whole	R	36–62	1 med.	10 avg. eggs w/out shell/lb
Frankfurters	O	610	1 med.	8/lb
Fruit cocktail, canned in syrup	O	10	1/2 cup	2 cups/lb
Goose, breast	R	108	5 oz	—
Goose, leg	R	136	5 oz	—
Ham, cured	O	1560	5 oz	—
Ice Cream	O	43–68	1/4 pt	1 pt/9.5 oz
Lamb (Lean)	R	128	5 oz	—
Lamb chop	R	129–139	5 oz	—
Lamb leg	R	111	5 oz	—
Liver, beef	R	75–492	5 oz	—
Liver, calf	R	156	5 oz	—
Liver, chicken	R	119	5 oz	—
Margarine	O	52	1 pat	96 pats or teasp./lb
Mayonnaise	O	560	1/2 cup	2 1/2 cups/lb
Milk, Cows				
Milk, Condensed, sweeted	O	444	1 cup	—
Milk, Evaporated	O	246	1 cup	—
Milk, Whole	R	122–127	1 cup	—
Mushrooms, sliced	R	3–7	1/4 cup	1 1/4 cup/lb
Mushrooms, canned	O	283	1/4 cup	1 1/4 cup/lb
Mustard, Prep paste	O	57	1 teaspoon	—
Olives, ripe, pickled	O	33	1 medium	8/oz
Olives, stuffed, pickled	O	70	1 medium	11/oz
Onion, cooked	O	8–11	1/2 cup	2 cups/lb
Onion Soup, cream of, canned	D	72	1 cup	—
Parsley flakes	O	4.4	1 tablespoon	—
Parsnips	R	9–11	1/2 cup	2 cups/lb
Peanut butter	O	16	1 tablespoon	—

Food	*Degree of prep.	mg. Sodium per serving	Serving or measure	Weight basis
Peanuts, roasted in oil and salted	O	520	1/4 lb	—
Peas	R	1.1–9.1	1/4 cup	1 cup/lb
Peas, frozen	O	27–295	1/2 cup	1 cup/lb
Peas, canned, less liquor	O	306	1/2 cup	2 cups/lb
Pea, Soup, canned	D	28–69	1 cup	—
Pork, lean	R	82	5 oz	—
Pork, med. lean	R	97	5 oz	—
Pork, 10% protein	R	60	5 oz	—
Potatoes	R	7.5–9.8	1 medium	3/lb
Potato chips	O	384	1/4 lb	—
Pretzels	O	1925	1/4 lb	—
Raisins, seedless	O	30	1 cup	3 1/4 cups/lb
Salmon, canned	O	1190	1–7 3/4 oz can	—
Sardines, canned, various	O	424–806	1–3 3/4 oz can	—
Sauerkraut, canned	O	690	1/2 cup	2 cups/lb
Sausage-breakfast	O	1000	1/4 lb	—
Sausage-bolona		370	1 slice	16 slices/lb
Sausage-pork		840–870	1/4 lb or 4 links	—
Shrimp	R	159	1/4 lb	—
Spinach	R	24–165	1/2 cup	1 1/2 to 2 cups/lb
Spinach, frozen	O	30–43	1/2 cup	3 cups/lb
Sweet Potatoes	R	13.4	1/2 cup	2 1/2 cups/lb
Sweet Potatoes, canned	O	66	1/2 cup	—
Tomato juice	O	250	1/2 cup	—
Tomato Soup, canned diluted as served	O	900	1 cup	—
Tuna, canned	O	1580	7 oz can	—
Turkey, breast	R	57	5 oz	—
Turkey, leg meat	R	131	5 oz	—
Veal, fillet	R	152	5 oz	—
Veal, lean	R	68	5 oz	—
Veal, muscle	R	163–278	5 oz	—
Worcestershire Sauce	O	84	1 teaspoon	—

NOTE: 1 level teaspoon of table salt weighs approximately 7,000 milligrams. This amount of salt would contain approx. 2800 mg. of sodium. R = Raw or fresh foods, O = Ordinary commercial production processes, D = Dietetic foods. Also note that in beverages, considerable variation may be found between bottling plants, depending on the sodium content of the local water. *Source:* "Technical Paper of Sources of Sodium in the Diet," Water Quality Association.

Physicians, Dentists, and Nurses

(numbers in thousands)

Profession	1981	1980	1979	1978	1975	1970	1965	1960
Physicians, number	505	487	473	454	409	348	305	275
Rate per 100,000 resident population[1]	217	211	210	204	188	166	153	148
Active (exc. physicians in Federal serv.)	425	418	399	381	338	282	255	n.a.
Rate per 100,000 resident population[1]	184	182	177	172	155	135	129	n.a.
Doctors of medicine[2]	485	468	455	437	394	334	292	260
Doctors of osteopathy	20	19[3]	18	17	15[3]	14	13	14
Physicians admitted to U.S. as immigrants[4]	n.a.	n.a.	3.0	4.4	7.1	3.2	2.0	1.6
Dentists, number[5]	144	141	124	121	n.a.	116	109	103
Active (excl. dentists in Federal service)	124[3]	121	118	115	108	96	86	85
Rate per 100,000 resident population[1]	54	54	54	53	50	47	45	47
Nurses, number (active registered)	n.a.	1,273	1,075	1,059	906	700	613	504
Rate per 100,000 resident population[1]	n.a.	506	490	487	427	345	319	282

1. Based on Bureau of the Census population estimates. 2. Excludes non-Federal physicians with temporary foreign addresses. 3. Estimated. 4. Immigration and Naturalization Service figures. 5. Beginning 1960, excludes graduates of year stated. Beginning in 1976, excludes inactive dentists. NOTE: n.a. = not available. *Source: Statistical Abstract of the United States, 1983–84.*

DROWNING

(Continued from page 78)

hips. Turn the victim's head to the side. This allows water to drain out of the victim's mouth when you perform the Heimlich Maneuver.

With one of your hands on top of the other, place the heel of your bottom hand on the abdomen slightly above the navel and below the rib cage.

Press into the victim's abdomen with a **quick upward thrust**.

Repeat until water no longer flows out. If the victim has not started breathing, proceed with mouth to mouth resuscitation.

Estimated Safe and Adequate Daily Dietary Intakes of Additional Selected Vitamins and Minerals[1]

		Vitamins			Trace Elements[2]					Electrolytes		
	Age (years)	Vitamin K (μg)	Biotin (μg)	Pantothenic Acid (mg)	Copper (mg)	Manganese (mg)	Fluoride (mg)	Chromium (mg)	Selenium (mg)	Molybdenum (mg)	Sodium (mg)	Potassium (mg)	Chloride (mg)
Infants	0–0.5	12	35	2	0.5–0.7	0.5–0.7	0.1–0.5	0.01–0.04	0.01–0.04	0.03–0.06	115–350	350–925	275–700
	0.5–1	10–20	50	3	0.7–1.0	0.7–1.0	0.2–1.0	0.02–0.06	0.02–0.06	0.04–0.08	250–750	425–1275	400–1200
Children	1–3	15–30	65	3	1.0–1.5	1.0–1.5	0.5–1.5	0.02–0.08	0.02–0.08	0.05–0.1	325–975	550–1650	500–1500
and	4–6	20–40	85	3–4	1.5–2.0	1.5–2.0	1.0–2.5	0.03–0.12	0.03–0.12	0.06–0.15	450–1350	775–2325	700–2100
Adolescents	7–10	30–60	120	4–5	2.0–2.5	2.0–3.0	1.5–2.5	0.05–0.2	0.05–0.2	0.1–0.3	600–1800	1000–3000	925–2775
	11+	50–100	100–200	4–7	2.0–3.0	2.5–5.0	1.5–2.5	0.05–0.2	0.05–0.2	0.15–0.5	900–2700	1525–4575	1400–4200
Adults		70–140	100–200	4–7	2.0–3.0	2.5–5.0	1.5–4.0	0.05–0.2	0.05–0.2	0.15–0.5	1100–3300	1875–5625	1700–1500

1. Because there is less information on which to base allowances, these figures are not given in the main table of the RDA and are provided in the form of ranges of recommended intakes.
2. Since the toxic levels for many trace elements may be only several times usual intakes, the upper levels for the trace elements given in this table should not be habitually exceeded. NOTE: μg—microgram; mg—milligram. *Source: Recommended Dietary Allowances,* Ninth Edition (1980), with the permission of the National Academy of Sciences, Washington, D.C.

Recommended Dietary Allowances

The Recommended Dietary Allowances (RDA) given in the tables are the latest established by the National Academy of Sciences Committee on Dietary Allowances as recommendations for the average daily amounts of nutrients for healthy population groups. They should not be confused with requirements for a specific individual.

Differences in the nutrient requirements of individuals are ordinarily unknown. Therefore, RDA (except for energy) are estimated to exceed the requirements of most individuals. Intake below the recommended allowance for a nutrient is not necessarily inadequate, but the risk of its being inadequate is increased if intake falls below the level recommended as safe.

Special needs for nutrients arising from such problems as premature birth, inherited metabolic disorders, infections, chronic diseases, and the use of medications are not covered by the RDA.

These dietary allowances form the basis for the RDA set by the Food and Drug Administration and are found on food labels as "U.S.R.D.A." The nutritional label lists the percentage of the RDA for protein and any of 17 vitamins and minerals found in the product. This does not represent all the required nutrients.

Because individual foods are not nutritionally complete, RDA should be met by eating a wide variety of selected foods in your diet.

Allowance for Energy

The recommended allowances for energy are estimates of the average needs of population groups, not recommended intakes for individuals. These needs vary from person to person and are not easily predictable without detailed information about physical characteristics and activity of the individual. Hence, the average energy needs for each age and sex are provided only as guidelines and are not repeated in the general table of recommended allowances.

Adjustments in RDA

The RDA does not take into account special needs that may require special attention. Some of these considerations are:

Physical Activity. This increases energy expenditure. Here, the increased need for a nutrient that may be related to carbohydrate utilization is generally met by consuming a larger amount of food. Attention must be given to salt and water losses due to sweating, which if prolonged, may lead to a loss of other nutrients.

Climate. There is little evidence that nutrient requirements, other than those for energy, are altered when individuals are exposed to heat or cold. Therefore, adjustments in dietary allowances to compensate for temperature changes are not considered necessary. However, exposures to temperatures that increase sweating will also increase the need for water and salt.

Aging. It is evident from studies of adult populations that body composition changes throughout life, with fat increasing and metabolically active tissues being slowly reduced. This reduction accounts for the fall in basal energy metabolism, often with an even greater reduction in physical activity.

As a result, less food is needed to meet energy requirements, and, unless food choices are made with great care, the amounts of essential nutrients may fall below desirable levels. It is important for older people to make sure that the smaller quantities of food that they eat are selected to provide the needed amounts of essential nutrients.

It is also important that physical activity be continued in adult life and into old age.

Mean Heights and Weights and Recommended Energy Intake

Category	Age (years)	Weight (lb)	Weight (kg)	Height (in.)	Height (cm)	Energy needs (with range) (kcal)	Energy needs (MJ)
Infants	0.0–0.5	13	6	24	60	kg × 115 (95–145)	kg × .48
	0.5–1.0	20	9	28	71	kg × 105 (80–135)	kg × .44
Children	1-3	29	13	35	90	1300 (900–1800)	5.5
	4-6	44	20	44	112	1700 (1300–2300)	7.1
	7-10	62	28	52	132	2400 (1650–3300)	10.1
Males	11-14	99	45	62	157	2700 (2000–3700)	11.3
	15-18	145	66	69	176	2800 (2100–3900)	11.8
	19-22	154	70	70	177	2900 (2500–3300)	12.2
	23-50	154	70	70	178	2700 (2300–3100)	11.3
	51-75	154	70	70	178	2400 (2000–2800)	10.1
	76 +	154	70	70	178	2050 (1650–2450)	8.6
Females	11-14	101	46	62	157	2200 (1500–3000)	9.2
	15-18	120	55	64	163	2100 (1200–3000)	8.8
	19-22	120	55	64	163	2100 (1700–2500)	8.8
	23-50	120	55	64	163	2000 (1600–2400)	8.4
	51-75	120	55	64	163	1800 (1400–2200)	7.6
	76 +	120	55	64	163	1600 (1200–2000)	6.7
Pregnancy						+ 300	
Lactation						+ 500	

The energy allowances for the young adults are for men and women doing light work. The allowances for the two older age groups represent mean energy needs over these age spans, allowing for a 2% decrease in basal (resting) metabolic rate per decade and a reduction in activity of 200 kcal/day for men and women between 51 and 75 years, 500 kcal for men over 75 years, and 400 kcal for women over 75. The customary range of daily energy output is shown for adults in parentheses, and is based on a variation in energy needs of ± 400 kcal at any one age, emphasizing the wide range of energy intakes appropriate for any group of people. Energy allowances for children through age 18 are based on median energy intakes of children these ages followed in longitudinal growth studies. The values in parentheses are 10th and 90th percentile of energy intake, to indicate the range of energy consumption among children of these ages. NOTE: kg—kilogram; cm—centimeter; kcal—kilocalorie; MJ—megajoule. 1 kcal is equivalent to 4.18 kilojoules. 1 megajoule is equal to 1000 kilojoules. *Source: Recommended Dietary Allowances,* Ninth Edition (1980), with the permission of the National Academy of Sciences, Washington, D.C.

Desirable Weights[1]

Height[2]		Weight[3]			
		Men		Women	
in.	cm	lb	kg	lb	kg
58	147	— —	— —	102 (92–119)	46 (42–54)
60	152	— —	— —	107 (96–125)	49 (44–57)
62	158	123 (112–141)	56 (51–64)	113 (102–131)	51 (46–59)
64	163	130 (118–148)	59 (54–67)	120 (108–138)	55 (49–63)
66	168	136 (124–156)	62 (56–71)	128 (114–146)	58 (52–66)
68	173	145 (132–166)	66 (60–75)	136 (122–154)	62 (55–70)
70	178	154 (140–174)	70 (64–79)	144 (130–163)	65 (59–74)
72	183	162 (148–184)	74 (67–84)	152 (138–173)	69 (63–79)
74	188	171 (156–194)	78 (71–88)	— —	— —
76	193	181 (164–204)	82 (74–93)	— —	— —

1. Desirable weights for men and women of different heights, based on evidence from insurance statistics of weight in relation to longevity. According to the National Center for Health Statistics, the average American male adult is 70 in. tall (178 cm) and the average female is 64 in. tall (163 cm). Accordingly, the average desirable weights are 154 lb (70 kg) and 120 lb (55 kg) throughout adult life. 2. Without shoes. 3. Without clothes. Average weight ranges in parentheses. *Source: Recommended Dietary Allowances,* 9th Edition (1980), with permission of the National Academy of Sciences, Washington, D.C.

Sunbathing and Skin Cancer

Scientists agree that ultraviolet radiation from the sun is the leading cause of skin cancer, which is responsible for an estimated 6,500 to 7,500 deaths in the United States every year.

People can reduce the potential hazard from the sun by not exposing themselves to it unnecessarily for extended periods between 10 a.m. and 2 p.m. when most ultraviolet radiation is strongest.

New Height and Weight Tables for Longevity

According to the Metropolitan Life Insurance Company's new height and weight tables, today's adults can weigh more than their 1959 counterparts and still expect favorable longevity.

These tables, which indicate the weights associated with lowest mortality, generally show higher weights than Metropolitan's previous tables, published in 1959.

Please note that the tables are not used for underwriting and do not necessarily indicate the weights that reduce the likelihood of illness. Nor are the weights those that optimize job performance or at which a person looks the best. It also does not mean that people have a license to gain. It simply indicates that many people may have fewer pounds to lose.

According to Metropolitan Life, for the greatest longevity people should aim for the weights shown on the new tables. The company no longer labels these weights "ideal" or "desirable" because these adjectives mean different things to different people.

How to Determine Your Body Frame by Elbow Breadth

In order to use these tables, you need to know your body frame. Here's how to make a simple approximation of your frame size:

Extend your arm and bend the forearm upward at a 90-degree angle. Keep the fingers straight and turn the inside of your wrist away from the body. Place the thumb and index finger of your other hand on the two prominent bones on *either side* of your elbow. Measure the space between your fingers against a ruler or a tape measure.* Compare the measurements on the following tables.

These tables list the elbow measurements for medium-framed men and women of various heights. Measurements lower than those listed indicate you have a small frame and higher measurements indicate a large frame.

*For the most accurate measurement, have your physician measure your elbow breadth with a caliper.

Men

Height in 1-in. heels	Elbow breadth
5 ft 2 in.—5 ft 3 in.	2 1/2 in.—2 7/8 in.
5 ft 4 in.—5 ft 7 in.	2 5/8 in.—2 7/8 in.
5 ft 8 in.—5 ft 11 in.	2 3/4 in.—3 in.
6 ft 0 in.—6 ft 3 in.	2 3/4 in.—3 1/8 in.
6 ft 4 in.	2 7/8 in.—3 1/4 in.

Women

Height in 1-in. heels	Elbow breadth
4 ft 10 in.—4 ft. 11 in.	2 1/4 in.—2 1/2 in.
5 ft 0 in.—5 ft 3 in.	2 1/4 in.—2 1/2 in.
5 ft 4 in.—5 ft 7 in.	2 3/8 in.—2 5/8 in.
5 ft 8 in.—5 ft 11 in.	2 3/8 in.—2 5/8 in.
6 ft 0 in.	2 1/2 in.—2 3/4 in.

Metropolitan's Height and Weight Tables for Longevity

MEN[1]

Height Feet	Height Inches	Small frame	Medium frame	Large frame
5	2	128–134	131–141	138–150
5	3	130–136	133–143	140–153
5	4	132–138	135–145	142–156
5	5	134–140	137–148	144–160
5	6	136–142	139–151	146–164
5	7	138–145	142–154	149–168
5	8	140–148	145–157	152–172
5	9	142–151	148–160	155–176
5	10	144–154	151–163	158–180
5	11	146–157	154–166	161–184
6	0	149–160	157–170	164–188
6	1	152–164	160–174	168–192
6	2	155–168	164–178	172–197
6	3	158–172	167–182	176–202
6	4	162–176	171–187	181–207

WOMEN[2]

Height Feet	Height Inches	Small frame	Medium frame	Large frame
4	10	102–111	109–121	118–131
4	11	103–113	111–123	120–134
5	0	104–115	113–126	122–137
5	1	106–118	115–129	125–140
5	2	108–121	118–132	128–143
5	3	111–124	121–135	131–147
5	4	114–127	124–138	134–151
5	5	117–130	127–141	137–155
5	6	120–133	130–144	140–159
5	7	123–136	133–147	143–163
5	8	126–139	136–150	146–167
5	9	129–142	139–153	149–170
5	10	132–145	142–156	152–173
5	11	135–148	145–159	155–176
6	0	138–151	148–162	158–179

1. Weights at ages 25–59 based on lowest mortality. Weight in pounds according to frame (in indoor clothing weighing 5 lb., shoes with 1 in. heels). 2. Weights at ages 25–59 based on lowest mortality. Weight in pounds according to frame (in indoor clothing weighing 3 lb., shoes with 1-in. heels). *Source of basic data: 1979 Build Study*, Society of Actuaries and Association of Life Insurance Medical Directors of America, 1980.

Recommended Daily Dietary Allowances[1]

Designed for the maintenance of good nutrition of practically all healthy persons in the U.S. (revised 1980)

						Fat-Soluble Vitamins			Water-Soluble Vitamins							Minerals					
Persons	Age (years)	Wgt. (lbs)	Wgt. (kg)	Hgt. (in.)	Hgt. (cm)	Vitamin A μg R.E.[2]	Vitamin D (μg)[3]	Vitamin E (mgα T.E.)[4]	Ascorbic Acid (mg)	Folacin (μg)	Niacin[5] (mg)	Riboflavin (mg)	Thiamin (mg)	Vitamin B_1 (mg)	Vitamin B_{12} (μg)	Calcium (mg)	Phosphorus (mg)	Iodine (μg)	Iron (mg)	Magnesium (mg)	Zinc (mg)
Infants	0.0–0.5	13	6	24	60	420	10	3	35	30	6	0.4	0.3	0.3	0.5[6]	360	240	40	10	50	3
	0.5–1.0	20	9	28	71	400	10	4	35	45	8	0.6	0.5	0.6	1.5	540	360	50	15	70	5
Children	1–3	29	13	35	90	400	10	5	45	100	9	0.8	0.7	0.9	2.0	800	800	70	15	150	10
	4–6	44	20	44	112	500	10	6	45	200	11	1.0	0.9	1.3	2.5	800	800	90	10	200	10
	7–10	62	28	52	132	700	10	7	45	300	16	1.4	1.2	1.6	3.0	800	800	120	10	250	10
Males	11–14	99	45	62	157	1,000	10	8	50	400	18	1.6	1.4	1.8	3.0	1,200	1,200	150	18	350	15
	15–18	145	66	69	176	1,000	10	10	60	400	18	1.7	1.4	2.0	3.0	1,200	1,200	150	18	400	15
	19–22	154	70	70	177	1,000	7.5	10	60	400	19	1.7		2.2	3.0	800	800	150	10	350	15
	23–50	154	70	70	178	1,000	5	10	60	400	18	1.6	1.4	2.2	3.0	800	800	150	10	350	15
	51+	154	70	70	178	1,000	5	10	60	400	16	1.4	1.2	2.2	3.0	800	800	150	10	350	15
Females	11–14	101	46	62	157	800	10	8	50	400	15	1.3	1.1	1.8	3.0	1,200	1,200	150	18	300	15
	15–18	120	55	64	163	800	10	8	60	400	14	1.3	1.1	2.0	3.0	1,200	1,200	150	18	300	15
	19–22	120	55	64	163	800	7.5	8	60	400	14	1.3	1.1	2.0	3.0	800	800	150	18	300	15
	23–50	120	55	64	163	800	5	8	60	400	13	1.2	1.0	3.0	800	800	150	150	18	300	15
	51+	120	55	64	163	800	5	8	60	400	13	1.2	1.0	2.0	3.0	800	800	150	10	300	15
Pregnant	—	—	—	—	—	+200	+5	+2	+20	+400	+2	+0.3	+0.4	+0.6	+1.0	+400	+400	+25	[7]	+150	+5
Lactating	—	—	—	—	—	+400	+5	+3	+40	+100	+5	+0.5	+0.5	+0.5	+1.0	+400	+400	+50	[7]	+150	+10

1. Allowances provide for individual variances among most normal persons living in the United States under usual environmental stresses. 2. Retinol equivalents. 1. Retinol equivalent = 1 μg retinol. 3. As cholecalciferol. 10 μg cholecalciferol = 400 I.U. vitamin D. 4. αtocopherol equivalents. 1 mg d-α-tocopherol = 1 α T.E. 5. 1 NE (niacin equivalent) is equal to 1 mg of niacin or 60 mg of dietary tryptophan. 6. The RDA for vitamin B12 in infants is based on average concentration of the vitamin in human milk. 7. Cannot be met by ordinary diets: use of supplemental iron is recommended. NOTE: mg—milligram; μg—microgram; IU—International Units; lbs—pounds; Wgt.—Weight; Hgt.—Height. *Source: Recommended Dietary Allowances,* Ninth Edition (1980), with the permission of the National Academy of Sciences, Washington, D.C.

Calories, Minerals, and Vitamins of Selected Foods

Food and amount	Energy (calories)	Nutrients		Minerals		Vitamins				
		Protein (gm)	Fat (gm)	Calcium (mg)	Iron (mg)	Vitamin A (IU)	Vitamin B_1 (thiamin) (mg)	Vitamin B_2 (riboflavin) (mg)	Niacin (mg)	Vitamin C (ascorbic acid) (mg)
Apple, 1 medium, raw	80	—	1	10	.4	120	.04	.03	.1	6
Applesauce, 1 cup, canned, unsweetened	100	—	—	10	1.2	100	.05	.02	.1	2
Bacon, 2 slices, crisp	85	4	8	2	.5	—	.08	.05	.8	—
Banana, 1 medium	100	1	—	10	.8	230	.06	.07	.8	12
Beans, snap green, 1 cup cooked	30	2	—	63	.8	680	.09	.11	.6	15
Beans, red kidney, 1 cup canned	230	15	1	74	4.6	10	.13	.10	1.5	—
Beans, baked, pork and molasses, 1 cup	385	16	12	161	5.9	—	.15	.10	1.3	—
Beef cuts, cooked: Chuck, boned, 3 ounces	245	23	16	10	2.9	30	.04	.18	3.6	—
Hamburger, 3 ounces	235	20	17	9	2.6	30	.07	.17	4.4	—
Rib roast, 3 ounces boned	375	17	33	8	2.2	70	.05	.13	3.1	—
Round, 3 ounces boned	220	24	13	10	3.0	20	.07	.19	4.8	—
Sirloin, 3 ounces boned	330	20	27	9	2.5	50	.05	.15	4.0	—
Beef stew with vegetables, 1 cup	220	16	11	29	2.9	2,400	.15	.17	4.7	17
Beets, 1 cup cooked	55	2	—	24	.9	30	.05	.07	.5	10
Breads: Cracked wheat, average slice	65	2	1	22	.5	—	.08	.06	.8	—
Italian, average slice, enriched	85	3	—	.5	.7	—	.12	.07	1.0	—
Raisin, average slice enriched	65	2	1	18	.6	—	.09	.06	.6	—
Rye (American), average slice	60	2	—	19	.5	—	.07	.05	.7	—
White, average slice enriched	70	2	1	21	.6	—	.10	.06	.8	—
Whole wheat, average slice	65	3	1	24	.8	—	.09	.03	.8	—
Butter, 1 tbsp	100	—	12	3	—	430	—	—	—	—
Cabbage, 1 cup, raw, coarsely shredded	15	1	—	34	.3	90	.04	.04	.2	33
Cake: Sponge, average slice	195	5	4	20	1.1	300	.09	.14	.6	—
Pound, average slice	160	2	10	6	.5	80	.05	.06	.4	—
Candies: Caramels, 1 ounce	115	1	3	42	.4	—	.01	.05	.1	—
Chocolate, milk, 1 ounce	145	2	9	65	.3	80	.02	.10	.1	—
Cantaloupe, 1/2 melon	80	2	—	38	1.1	9,240	.11	.08	1.6	90
Carrot, raw, 1 average size	30	1	—	27	.5	7,930	.04	.04	.4	6
Catsup, 1 tbsp	15	—	—	3	.1	210	.01	.01	.2	2
Cheese: Cheddar, 1 ounce	115	7	9	204	.2	300	.01	.11	—	—
Cottage, creamed, 1 cup	235	28	10	135	.3	370	.05	.37	.3	—
Cottage, uncreamed, 1 cup	125	25	1	46	.3	40	.04	.21	.2	—
Cream cheese, 1 ounce	100	2	10	23	.3	400	—	.06	—	—
Swiss, natural, 1 ounce	105	8	8	272	—	240	.01	.10	—	—
Swiss, process, 1 ounce	95	7	7	219	.2	230	—	.08	—	—
Chicken, broiled, 3 ounces	115	20	3	8	1.4	80	.05	.16	7.4	—

Food and amount	Energy (calories)	Nutrients: Protein (gm)	Nutrients: Fat (gm)	Minerals: Calcium (mg)	Minerals: Iron (mg)	Vitamins: Vitamin A (IU)	Vitamins: Vitamin B₁ (thiamin) (mg)	Vitamins: Vitamin B₂ (riboflavin) (mg)	Vitamins: Niacin (mg)	Vitamins: Vitamin C (ascorbic acid) (mg)
Chicken, fried, 1/2 breast, 3.3 ounces	160	26	5	9	1.3	70	.04	.17	11.6	—
Chicken, canned, boned, 3 ounces	170	18	10	18	1.3	200	.03	.11	3.7	3
Clams, raw, 3 ounces	65	11	1	59	5.2	90	.08	.15	1.1	8
Cocoa, 1 cup, homemade	220	9	9	298	.8	320	.10	.44	.4	2
Coffee; black, 1 cup	—	—	—	—	—	—	—	—	—	—
Cola, carbonated, 12 ounces	145	—	—	—	—	—	—	—	—	—
Corn, average ear	70	2	1	2	.5	310	.09	.08	1.1	7
Corn flakes, 1 cup	95	2	—	3	.6	1,180	.29	.35	2.9	9
Crabmeat, canned, 3 ounces	85	15	2	38	.7	—	.07	.07	1.6	—
Crackers, Graham, 4	110	2	3	11	1.0	—	.04	.16	1.0	—
Saltines, 4	50	1	1	2	.5	—	.05	.05	.4	—
Cream: Light, table, 1 cup	470	6	46	231	.1	1,730	.08	.36	.1	2
Heavy, whipping, 1 cup	820	5	88	154	.1	3,500	.05	.26	.1	1
Sour, 1 cup	495	7	48	268	.1	1,820	.08	.34	.2	2
Whipped topping (pressurized), 1 cup	155	2	13	61	—	550	.02	.04	—	—
Doughnut, 1 plain	100	1	5	10	.4	20	.05	.05	.4	—
Egg: Raw or cooked in shell, 1	80	6	6	28	1.0	260	.04	.14	—	—
Omelet, scrambled, 1	95	6	7	47	.9	310	.04	.16	—	—
Frankfurter, 1	170	7	15	3	.8	—	.08	.11	1.4	—
Fruit cocktail, 1 cup canned	195	1	—	23	1.0	360	.05	.03	1.0	5
Grapefruit: Raw, 1/2	45	1	—	19	.5	10	.05	.02	.2	44
Canned, syrup, 1 cup	180	2	—	33	.8	30	.08	.05	.5	76
Juice, fresh, 1 cup	95	1	—	22	.5	20	.10	.05	.5	93
Haddock, breaded, fried, 3 ounces	140	17	5	34	1.0	—	.03	.06	2.7	2
Honey, strained, 1 tbsp.	65	—	—	1	.1	—	—	.01	.1	—
Ice cream, 1 cup	270	5	14	176	.1	540	.05	.33	.1	1
Jellies, 1 tbsp	50	—	—	4	.3	—	—	.01	—	1
Lamb: Rib chop, boned, 4 ounces	400	25	33	10	1.5	—	.14	.25	5.6	—
Leg roast, 3 ounces, boned	235	22	16	9	1.4	—	.13	.23	4.7	—
Lemon, 1 medium	20	1	—	19	.4	10	.03	.01	.1	39
Liver: Beef, fried, 2 ounces	130	15	6	6	5.0	30,280	.15	2.37	9.4	15
Luncheon meat: Boiled ham, 2 ounces	135	11	10	6	1.6	—	.25	.09	1.5	—
Canned, spiced or unspiced, 2 ounces	165	8	14	5	1.2	—	.18	.12	1.6	—
Macaroni, enriched, 1 cup	155	5	1	11	1.3	—	.20	.11	1.5	—
Macaroni and cheese, 1 cup	430	17	22	362	1.8	860	.20	.40	1.8	—
Margarine, 1 tbsp	100	—	12	3	—	470	—	—	—	—
Mayonnaise, 1 tbsp	100	—	11	3	.1	40	—	.01	—	—
Milk: Whole, 1 cup	150	8	8	291	.1	310	.09	.40	.2	2
Skim (non-fat), 1 cup	85	8	—	302	.1	500	.09	.34	.2	2

Buttermilk, 1 cup	100	8	2	285	.1	80	.08	.38	.1	2
Mushrooms, canned, 1 cup	40	5	—	15	1.2	—	.04	.60	4.8	4
Nuts: Almonds, 1 cup shelled	850	26	77	332	6.7	—	.34	1.31	5.0	—
Peanuts, roasted, 1 cup	840	37	72	107	3.0	—	.46	.19	24.8	—
Oatmeal, 1 cup cooked	130	5	2	22	1.4	—	.19	.05	.2	—
Oils, salad, cooking, 1 tbsp	120	—	14	—	—	—	—	—	—	—
Orange, 1 medium	65	1	—	54	.5	260	.13	.05	.5	66
Orange juice, fresh, 1 cup	110	2	—	27	.5	500	.22	.07	1.0	124
Frozen, diluted with 3 parts water, 1 cup	120	2	—	25	.2	540	.23	.03	.9	120
Oysters, raw, 1 cup	160	20	4	226	13.2	740	.34	.43	6.0	—
Pancake, wheat, 1 average	60	2	2	27	.4	30	.06	.07	.5	—
Peach, raw, 1 medium	40	1	—	9	.5	1,330	.02	.05	1.0	7
Peanut butter, 1 tbsp	95	4	8	9	.3	—	.02	.02	2.4	—
Peas, green, 1 cup	110	8	—	30	3.0	960	.43	.14	2.7	21
Pie: Apple, 4-inch wedge	345	3	15	11	.9	40	.15	.11	1.3	2
Cherry, 4-inch wedge	350	4	15	19	.9	590	.16	.12	1.4	—
Lemon meringue, 4-inch wedge	305	4	12	17	1.0	200	.09	.12	.7	4
Pineapple, raw, 1 cup diced	80	1	—	26	.8	110	.14	.05	.3	26
Pineapple juice, canned, 1 cup	140	1	—	38	.8	130	.13	.05	.5	23
Pizza (cheese), 4 3/4-inch wedge	145	6	4	86	1.1	230	.16	.18	1.6	4
Pork: Roast, 3 ounces	310	21	24	9	2.7	—	.78	.22	4.8	—
Chop, with bone, 2.7 ounces	305	19	25	9	2.7	—	.75	.22	4.5	—
Potatoes: Baked, 1 medium	145	4	—	14	1.1	—	.15	.07	2.7	31
French fried, deep fat, 10 pieces	135	2	7	8	.7	—	.07	.04	1.6	11
Mashed with milk, 1 cup	135	4	2	50	.8	40	.17	.11	2.1	21
Potato chips, 10	115	1	8	8	.4	—	.04	.01	1.0	3
Prune juice, 1 cup canned	195	1	—	36	1.8	—	.03	.03	1.0	5
Rice: White, enriched, 1 cup cooked	225	4	—	21	1.8	—	.23	.02	2.1	—
Puffed, 1 cup	60	1	—	3	.3	—	.07	.01	.7	—
Salad dressings: Mayonnaise type, 1 tbsp	65	—	6	2	—	30	—	—	—	—
French, 1 tbsp	65	—	6	2	.1	—	—	—	—	—
French, low calorie, 1 tbsp	15	—	1	2	.1	—	—	—	—	—
Salmon: Canned, 3 ounces	120	17	5	167	.7	60	.03	.16	6.8	—
Sardines, canned, 3 ounces	175	20	9	372	2.5	190	.02	.17	4.6	—
Spaghetti, 1 cup cooked	155	5	1	11	1.3	—	.20	.11	1.5	—
Spinach, 1 cup cooked	40	5	1	167	4.0	14,580	.13	.25	.9	50
Sugar, 1 teaspoon	15	—	—	—	—	—	—	—	—	—
Tomato juice, canned, 1 cup	45	2	—	17	2.2	1,940	.12	.07	1.9	39
Tuna fish, 3 ounces	170	24	7	7	1.6	70	.04	.10	10.1	—
Veal, 3-ounce cutlet	185	23	9	9	2.7	—	.06	.21	4.6	—
Yogurt, from lowfat milk, 8-oz. container, plain	145	12	4	415	.2	150	.10	.49	.3	2

NOTE: GM—gram; MG—milligram; IU—International Unit. A dash in a column indicates little or no basis for assigning value. *Source:* Department of Agriculture, Science and Education Administration.

Communicable Diseases

Disease	Incubation period[1]	Period of communicability
Chickenpox (varicella)	2 to 3 weeks	From 5 days before appearance of vesicles to 6 days after
Common Cold	12 to 72 hours; usually 24 hrs	From 1 day before onset to 5 days after
Conjunctivitis	1 to 3 days	During course of active infection
Diphtheria	2 to 5 days	Usually 2 weeks or less; seldom more than 4 weeks
Dysentery, amebic	2 to 4 weeks (varies widely)	During intestinal infection; possibly for years if untreated
Enterobiasis (pinworm)	3 to 6 weeks	Not directly transmitted
Food poisoning: Botulism	12 to 36 hours	Not applicable
Salmonella infection	6 to 72 hours; usually 36	3 days to 3 weeks (extremely variable)
Staphylococcus intoxication	2 to 4 hours	Not applicable
German measles (rubella)	8 to 10 days; usually 14	1 week before and at least 4 days after onset of rash
Gonorrhea	2 to 5 days; sometimes longer	Indefinite unless treated
Hepatitis (serum)	45 to 160 days; usually 80 to 100	Many weeks before onset of symptoms
Herpes Simplex	Up to 2 weeks	As long as 7 weeks after recovery
Impetigo contagiosa	4 to 10 days; sometimes longer	Until lesions are healed
Infectious mononucleosis	Varies 2 to 6 weeks	Unknown
Influenza	Usually 1 to 3 days	Probably limited to 3 days from clinical onset
Measles (rubeola)	10 days (to onset): 14 days (to rash)	From beginning of prodromal period to 4 days after onset of rash
Meningitis, meningococcal	2 to 10 days	Usually 1 day after appropriate medication
Mumps	12 to 26 days; commonly 18	From 6 days before distinctive symptoms up to 9 days after
Pediculosis	Apprx. 2 weeks	While lice remain alive
Pneumonia: Bacterial	Usually 1 to 3 days	Unknown
Viral	Believed to be 1 to 3 days	Unknown
Poliomyelitis	3 to 21 days; commonly 7 to 12	7 to 10 days before and after onset of symptoms
Rabies	2 to 8 weeks or longer	From animals, 3 to 5 days before onset and during course of the disease
Respiratory (acute viral)	Few days to 1 week or more	Duration of active disease
Ringworm (of body)	4 to 10 days	As long as lesions are present
(Athlete's foot)	Unknown	As long as lesions are present
Scarlet fever and streptococcal sore throat	1 to 3 days	Uncomplicated cases apprx. 10 to 21 days; in untreated cases, weeks or months
Smallpox	7 to 17 days; commonly 10 to 12	During first week
Syphilis	10 days to 10 weeks; usually 3 weeks	Variable and indefinite
Tetanus	4 days to 3 weeks	Not applicable
Trichinosis	2 to 28 days after ingestion of infected meat; usually 9 days	Not directly transmitted
Tuberculosis	4 to 12 weeks (to primary phase)	As long as tubercle bacilli are discharged by patient
Typhoid fever	1 to 3 weeks, average 2 weeks	As long as typhoid bacilli appear in excreta; 2 to 5% of patients become permanent carriers
Whooping cough (pertussis)	Commonly 7 days, almost uniformly within 10 days, and not exceeding 21 days	From 7 days after exposure to 3 weeks after onset of typical paroxysms

1. Usual limits. NOTE: This list is incomplete, but includes those diseases that are most common and widespread.

Scientists Seek Alternate Foods in Case of Emergencies

The food and nutrition scientists of the U.S. Dept. of Agriculture's Agricultural Research Service aren't predicting a nutritional doomsday because they expect food supplies to sustain most of America's eating habits for decades to come. However, they consider it prudent to be ready for any disaster that might cripple the food chain in the future. In case that happens, the scientists are looking for new uses of existing plants as well as little-known crops that could help fill food bins.

For example, researchers have learned that beef tallow, cottonseed, animal hides, clover, and blades of grass can be added to the human diet in new nutritional forms you may not recognize.

Amaranth, a staple of Mayan and Aztec Indians in the distant past may make a comeback as a hot weather vegetable and as a grain crop.

From leaf tobacco, a food that resembles soybean, curd can be made. Protein extracted from leaf tobacco has a nutritional value comparable to milk and is easy to store. About 40 pounds per acre could be obtained as a byproduct of tobacco production at current yield levels.

History of the Income Tax in the United States

Source: Touche Ross & Co.

The nation had few taxes in its early history. From 1791 to 1802, the United States Government was supported by internal taxes on distilled spirits, carriages, refined sugar, tobacco and snuff, property sold at auction, corporate bonds, and slaves. The high cost of the War of 1812 brought about the nation's first sales taxes on gold, silverware, jewelry, and watches. In 1817, however, Congress did away with all internal taxes, relying on tariffs on imported goods to provide sufficient funds for running the Government.

In 1862, in order to support the Civil War effort, Congress enacted the nation's first income tax law. It was a forerunner of our modern income tax in that it was based on the principles of graduated, or progressive, taxation and of withholding income at the source. During the Civil War, a person earning from $600 to $10,000 per year paid tax at the rate of 3%. Those with incomes of more than $10,000 paid taxes at a higher rate. Additional sales and excise taxes were added, and an "inheritance" tax also made its debut. In 1866, internal revenue collections reached their highest point in the nation's 90-year history—more than $310 million, an amount not reached again until 1911.

The Act of 1862 established the office of Commissioner of Internal Revenue. The Commissioner was given the power to assess, levy, and collect taxes, and the right to enforce the tax laws through seizure of property and income and through prosecution. His powers and authority remain very much the same today.

In 1868, Congress again focused its taxation efforts on tobacco and distilled spirits and eliminated the income tax in 1872. It had a short-lived revival in 1894 and 1895. In the latter year, the U.S. Supreme Court decided that the income tax was unconstitutional because it was not apportioned among the states in conformity with the Constitution.

By 1913, with the 16th Amendment to the Constitution, the income tax had become a permanent fixture of the U.S. tax system. The amendment gave Congress legal authority to tax income and resulted in a revenue law that taxed incomes of both individuals and corporations. In fiscal year 1918, annual internal revenue collections for the first time passed the billion-dollar mark, rising to $5.4 billion by 1920. With the advent of World War II, employment increased, as did tax collections—to $7.3 billion. The withholding tax on wages was introduced in 1943 and was instrumental in increasing the number of taxpayers to 60 million and tax collections to $43 billion by 1945.

In 1981, Congress enacted the largest tax cut in U.S. history, including a 25% reduction in individual tax rates over a three-year period. The Economic Recovery Tax Act of 1981 has resulted in numerous changes in the tax law, including the reduction of total taxes for individuals and businesses by approximately $750 billion over a six-year period.

Internal Revenue Service

The Internal Revenue Service (IRS), a bureau of the U.S. Treasury Department, is the federal agency charged with the administration of the tax laws passed by Congress. The IRS functions through a national office in Washington, 7 regional offices, 63 district offices, and 10 service centers.

Operations involving most taxpayers are carried out in the district offices and service centers. District offices are organized into Resources Management, Examination, Collection, Taxpayer Service, Employee Plans and Exempt Organizations, and Criminal Investigation. All tax returns are filed with the service centers, where the IRS computer operations are located.

Auditing Tax Returns

Most taxpayers' contacts with IRS arise through the auditing of their tax returns. The Service has been empowered by Congress to inquire about all persons who may be liable for any tax and to obtain for review the books and/or records pertinent to those taxpayers' returns. A wide-ranging audit operation is carried out in the 63 district offices by some 13,500 field agents and 4,000 office auditors.

Selecting Returns for Audit

The primary method used by the IRS in selecting returns for audits is a computer program that measures the probability of tax error in each return. The data base (established by an in-depth audit of randomly selected returns in various income categories) consists of approximately 200–250 individual items of information taken from each return. These 200–250 variables individually or in combination are weighted as relative indicators of potential tax change. Returns are then scored according to the weights given the combinations of variables as they appear on each return. The higher the score, the greater the tax change potential. Other returns are selected for examination on the basis of claims for refund, multi-year audits, related

Internal Revenue Service

	1983	1982	1981	1970	1960	1950
U.S. population (in thousands)	234,875	232,634	225,865	204,878	180,671	152,271
Number of IRS employees	85,379	82,857	86,156	68,098	50,199	55,551
Cost to govt. of collecting $100 in taxes	$0.47	$0.42	$0.41	$0.45	$0.40	$0.59
Tax per capita	$2,670.56	$2,717.75	$2,686.55	$955.31	$507.96	$255.84
Collections by principal sources (in thousands of dollars)						
Total IRS collections	$627,246,793	$632,240,506	$606,799,120	$195,722,096	$91,744,803	$38,957,132
Income and profits taxes						
Individual	349,627,967	352,608,936	332,850,146	103,651,585	44,945,711	17,153,308
Corporation	61,779,556	65,990,832	73,733,156	35,036,983	22,179,414	10,854,351
Employment taxes	173,847,854	168,717,936	152,885,816	37,449,188	11,158,589	2,644,575
Estate and gift taxes	6,225,877	8,143,373	6,910,386	3,680,076	1,626,348	706,227
Alcohol taxes	5,634,853	5,459,810	5,688,413	4,746,382	3,193,714	2,219,202
Tobacco taxes	4,139,810	2,539,495	2,583,857	2,094,212	1,931,504	1,328,464
Manufacturers' excise taxes	6,776,023	6,382,900	6,089,000	6,683,061	4,735,129	1,836,053
All other taxes	19,214,853	22,397,223	26,058,329	2,380,609	2,004,394	2,214,951

NOTE: For fiscal year ending September 30th.

return audits, and other audits initiated by the IRS as a result of informants' information, special compliance programs, and the information document matching program.

During 1980, the IRS initiated a new method to group individual returns for examination selection purposes. Total positive income, the sum of all positive income amounts appearing on a return, with losses treated as zero is the newly utilized factor. This new method replaces the adjusted gross income method of classifying returns. In a similar manner, total gross receipts is used for business returns.

The Appeals Process

The IRS attempts to resolve tax disputes through an administrative appeals system. Taxpayers who, after audit of their tax returns, disagree with a proposed change in their tax liabilities are entitled to an independent review of their cases. Taxpayers are able to seek an immediate, informal appeal with the Appeals Office. If, however, the dispute arises from a field audit and the amount in question exceeds $2,500, a taxpayer must submit a written protest. Alternatively, the taxpayer can wait for the examiner's report and then request consideration by the Appeals Office and file a protest if necessary. Taxpayers may represent themselves or be represented by an attorney, accountant, or any other advisor authorized to practice before the IRS. Taxpayers can forego their right to the above process and await receipt of a deficiency notice. At this juncture, taxpayers can either (1) not pay the deficiency and petition the Tax Court by a required deadline or (2) pay the deficiency and file a claim for refund with the District Director's office. If the claim is denied, a suit for refund may be brought either in the District Court or the Court of Claims within a specified period. A third option is to let the IRS assess the tax and then submit a compromise offer on Form 656. In 1983, over 76,400 taxpayers requested appeals to resolve disputed tax cases administratively. The Tax Court tried 2,125 cases, and the U.S. District Courts and the Court of Claims tried 242 cases.

Federal Individual Income Tax

The Federal individual income tax is levied on the world-wide income of U.S. citizens and resident aliens and on certain types of U.S. source income of non-residents. A new term, "tax table income," was introduced by the Tax Reduction and Simplification Act of 1977. For a non-itemizer, "tax table income" is adjusted gross income *(see below)* less $1,000 for each personal exemptions and 25% of the first $300 of charitable contributions (a maximum of $75). If a taxpayer itemizes, tax table income is adjusted gross income minus excess itemized deductions and personal exemptions. Excess itemized deductions are the excess of a taxpayer's itemized deductions on Schedule A, Form 1040, over the zero bracket amount. The zero bracket amount is $2,300 for unmarried individuals and heads of household; $3,400 for married individuals filing jointly and for surviving spouses; $1,700 for married individuals filing separately. The tax tables apply to individuals with taxable income of less than $50,000. Taxpayers with taxable income of $50,000 or more must use Tax Rate Schedule X, Y, or Z to compute their tax. For this purpose tax rates are graduated, for joint returns, from a minimum of 11% on the first $2,100 of taxable income above $3,400 to a maximum of 50% of taxable income above $162,400 (1984 rates).

Who Must File a Return[1]

You must file a return if you are:	and your gross income is at least:
Single (legally separated, divorced, or married living apart from spouse with dependent child) and are under 65	$3,300
Single (legally separated, divorced, or married living apart from spouse with dependent child) and are 65 or older	$4,300
A person who can be claimed as a dependent on your parent's return, and who has taxable dividends, interest, or other unearned income	$1,000
A qualifying widow(er) with a dependent child and under 65	$4,400
A qualifying widow(er) with a dependent child and are 65 or older	$5,400
Married, filing jointly, living together at end of year (or at date of death of spouse), and both are under 65	$5,400
Married, filing jointly, living together at end of year (or at date of death of spouse), and one is 65 or older	$6,400
Married, filing jointly, living together at end of year (or at date of death of spouse), and both are 65 or older	$7,400
Married, filing separate return, or married but not living together at end of year	$1,000
A person with income from sources within U.S. possessions	$1,000
Self-employed and your net earnings from self-employment were at least $400	
A person who received any advance earned income credit payments from their employer during 1983	
A person who owes minimum tax, individual retirement arrangement tax, investment credit recapture tax or social security tax on unreported tips	

1. In 1984.

Adjusted Gross Income

Gross income consists of wages and salaries, tips and gratuities, interest, dividends, annuities, rents and royalties, up to 1/2 of Social Security Benefits if the recipient's income exceeds a base amount, and certain other types of income. Among the items excluded from gross income, and thus not subject to tax, are federal and state unemployment compensation (phased out above a base amount), public assistance benefits, interest on exempt securities (mostly state and local bonds), and 60 percent of net capital gains. Net capital gain is the excess of net long-term capital gain over the net short-term capital loss for the year. In addition, the first $100 (up to $200 on a joint return) of eligible dividends received is excluded from gross income. *Adjusted gross income* is determined by subtracting from gross income certain business-type expenses considered necessary in earning income, job-related moving expenses, alimony, payments to an I.R.A. or Keogh, disability income, penalties on early withdrawal of savings, and the deduction for a married couple when both work.

Deductions

Taxpayers may itemize deductions or, as previously discussed, take the benefit of the zero bracket amount incorporated in the tax tables and tax rate schedules. In itemizing deductions, the following are the major items that may be deducted (with limits, in some instances): interest payments; state and local general sales, income, and property taxes; medical expenses; charitable contributions; and casualty losses.

Personal Exemptions

Personal exemptions are available to the taxpayer, his spouse, and his dependents. The amount is $1,000 for each individual. Additional exemptions of $1,000 each are granted for persons 65 and over and for the blind.

Credits

The Revenue Act of 1978 grants a credit (a reduction of tax owed) for certain lower-income households with dependent children, with a maximum credit of $500 ($550 after 1984) on $5,000 of earned income. This maximum credit will be reduced if earned income or adjusted gross income exceeds $6,000 ($6,500 after 1984), and the credit will be zero for families with incomes over $10,000 ($11,000 after 1984).

The Tax Reform Act of 1976 provided for the credit for Child and Dependent Care Expense. The credit is between 20% and 30% (depending on adjusted gross income) of up to $2,400 of employment-related expenses for one qualifying child or dependent and up to $4,800 of expenses for two or more qualifying individuals.

The Revenue Act of 1978 extended the child care credit to include payments to grandparents for care of their grandchildren, provided that the parents are not also entitled to a dependency deduction for the grandparents.

The Tax Reform Act of 1976 also provided for a new expanded and simplified credit for the elderly. A credit of as much as $375 (if single) or $562.50 (if married and filing jointly) could be claimed by persons 65 or older who have retirement income. This credit, however, phases out for married couples with adjusted gross income over $10,000 and single persons with adjusted gross income over $7,500. In 1984, the maximum base amount eligible for the credit is doubled and the credit is extended to include taxpayers under 65 who retired under total disability.

Expenditures for insulation, other energy-conserving components, and for renewable energy source equipment are eligible for residential energy credits. The residential insulation and energy conservation credit is 15% of the first $2,000 of qualifying expenditures, with a maximum $300 credit. The residential renewable energy source equipment credit is 40% of the first $10,000 of expenditures, with a maximum credit of $4,000.

Other tax credits available to taxpayers include the targeted jobs credit, contributions to candidates for public office credit, the investment tax credit, and the foreign tax credit.

Recent Legislation

Economic Recovery Tax Act of 1981. The Economic Recovery Tax Act of 1981, enacted on August 13, 1981, had as its chief objective the stimulation of economic growth through the reduction of individual income taxes. The Act sought to encourage savings and provide investment incentives to both individuals and businesses.

In addition to reducing both the minimum and

Federal Individual Income Tax Rates Effective January 1, 1984

MARRIED INDIVIDUALS FILING JOINT RETURNS AND SURVIVING SPOUSES:

If taxable income is:	*The tax is:*
Not over $3,400	No tax.
Over $3,400 but not over $5,500	11% of the excess over $3,400
Over $5,500 but not over $7,600	$231, plus 12% of the excess over $5,500
Over $7,600 but not over $11,900	$483, plus 14% of the excess over $7,600
Over $11,900 but not over $16,000	$1,085, plus 16% of the excess over $11,900
Over $16,000 but not over $20,200	$1,741, plus 18% of the excess over $16,000
Over $20,200 but not over $24,600	$2,497, plus 22% of the excess over $20,200
Over $24,600 but not over $29,900	$3,465, plus 25% of the excess over $24,600
Over $29,900 but not over $35,200	$4,790, plus 28% of the excess over $29,900
Over $35,200 but not over $45,800	$6,274, plus 33% of the excess over $35,200
Over $45,800 but not over $60,000	$9,772, plus 38% of the excess over $45,800
Over $60,000 but not over $85,600	$15,168, plus 42% of the excess over $60,000
Over $85,600 but not over $109,400	$25,920, plus 45% of the excess over $85,600
Over $109,400 but not over $162,400	$36,630, plus 49% of the excess over $109,400
Over $162,400	$62,600, plus 50% of the excess over $162,400

HEADS OF HOUSEHOLDS:

If taxable income is:	*The tax is:*
Not over $2,300	No tax.
Over $2,300 but not over $4,400	11% of the excess over $2,300
Over $4,400 but not over $6,500	$231, plus 12% of the excess over $4,400
Over $6,500 but not over $8,700	$483, plus 14% of the excess over $6,500
Over $8,700 but not over $11,800	$791, plus 17% of the excess over $8,700
Over $11,800 but not over $15,000	$1,318, plus 18% of the excess over $11,800
Over $15,000 but not over $18,200	$1,894, plus 20% of the excess over $15,000
Over $18,200 but not over $23,500	$2,534, plus 24% of the excess over $18,200
Over $23,500 but not over $28,800	$3,806, plus 28% of the excess over $23,500
Over $28,800 but not over $34,100	$5,290, plus 32% of the excess over $28,800
Over $34,100 but not over $44,700	$6,986, plus 35% of the excess over $34,100
Over $44,700 but not over $60,600	$10,696, plus 42% of the excess over $44,700
Over $60,600 but not over $81,800	$17,374, plus 45% of the excess over $60,600
Over $81,800 but not over $108,300	$26,914, plus 48% of the excess over $81,800
Over $108,300	$39,634, plus 50% of the excess over $108,300

maximum marginal rates of tax for individuals, the Act reduced the maximum tax on capital gains from 28% to 20% for sales or exchanges as of June 10, 1981. Starting in 1983, the Act provides for a marriage tax offset deduction of 5% (10% after 1982) of the lower-paid spouse's salary up to $1,500 ($3,000 after 1982) and permits an adjustment to gross income for contributions to Individual Retirement Accounts of up to $2,000 per working spouse regardless of pension coverage by an employer. The Act revived the stock option as a compensation technique by providing that qualified incentive stock options exercised after 1980 will not be taxed, to the employee until sold. Individuals who earn income abroad are allowed an exclusion from gross income ($80,000 in 1984). In addition, reasonable housing expenses in excess of a base amount can be excluded from gross income.

The Act also increased the amount of depreciation deduction for real property acquired after 1980 by allowing an accelerated 15-year recovery period. The Accelerated Cost Recovery System section of the Act provides for a faster writeoff of capital expenditures for property acquired or placed in service retroactive to January 1, 1981. For tangible personal property, assets are grouped into four classes with recovery periods of 3, 5, 10, and 15 years. As an incentive for research and experimentation, the Act provides for a 25% tax credit for such expenditures made after June 30, 1981.

Tax Equity and Fiscal Responsibility Act of 1982. Congress enacted the Tax Equity and Fiscal Responsibility Act of 1982 (TEFRA) in an attempt to raise additional revenue and improve compliance with the tax laws. Most of TEFRA's provisions became effective in 1983.

To improve compliance, TEFRA requires more information reporting, imposes new penalties, and essentially requires the registration of most bonds, including tax-exempt municipal bonds. Brokers are required to report customer transactions, state governments must report refunds paid to taxpayers, and most restaurants must report additional information relating to the tip income of their waiters. TEFRA also expands the reporting requirements relating to payments of interest and payments for goods and services. In addition, taxpayers who substantially understate the tax liability on their returns and those who aid taxpayers in substantially understating tax liability face new penalties.

Federal Individual Income Tax Rates Effective January 1, 1984

UNMARRIED INDIVIDUALS:

If taxable income is:	*The tax is:*
Not over $2,300	No tax
Over $2,300 but not over $3,400	11% of the excess over $2,300
Over $3,400 but not over $4,400	$121, plus 12% of the excess over $3,400
Over $4,400 but not over $6,500	$241, plus 14% of the excess over $4,400
Over $6,500 but not over $8,500	$535, plus 15% of the excess over $6,500
Over $8,500 but not over $10,800	$835, plus 16% of the excess over $8,500
Over $10,800 but not over $12,900	$1,203, plus 18% of the excess over $10,800
Over $12,900 but not over $15,000	$1,581, plus 20% of the excess over $12,900
Over $15,000 but not over $18,200	$2,001, plus 23% of the excess over $15,000
Over $18,200 but not over $23,500	$2,737, plus 26% of the excess over $18,200
Over $23,500 but not over $28,800	$4,115, plus 30% of the excess over $23,500
Over $28,800 but not over $34,100	$5,705, plus 34% of the excess over $28,800
Over $34,100 but not over $41,500	$7,507, plus 38% of the excess over $34,100
Over $41,500 but not over $55,300	$10,319, plus 42% of the excess over $41,500
Over $55,300 but not over $81,800	$16,115, plus 48% of the excess over $55,300
Over $81,800	$28,835, plus 50% of the excess over $81,800

MARRIED INDIVIDUALS FILING SEPARATE RETURNS:

If taxable income is:	*The tax is:*
Not over $1,700	No tax
Over $1,700 but not over $2,750	11% of the excess over $1,700
Over $2,750 but not over $3,800	$115.50, plus 12% of the excess over $2,750
Over $3,800 but not over $5,950	$241.50, plus 14% of the excess over $3,800
Over $5,950 but not over $8,000	$542.50, plus 16% of the excess over $5,950
Over $8,000 but not over $10,100	$870.50, plus 18% of the excess over $8,000
Over $10,100 but not over $12,300	$1,248.50, plus 22% of the excess over $10,100
Over $12,300 but not over $14,950	$1,732.50, plus 25% of the excess over $12,300
Over $14,950 but not over $17,600	$2,395, plus 28% of the excess over $14,950
Over $17,600 but not over $22,900	$3,137, plus 33% of the excess over $17,600
Over $22,900 but not over $30,000	$4,886, plus 38% of the excess over $22,900
Over $30,000 but not over $42,800	$7,584, plus 42% of the excess over $30,000
Over $42,800 but not over $54,700	$12,960, plus 45% of the excess over $42,800
Over $54,700 but not over $81,200	$18,315, plus 49% of the excess over $54,700
Over $81,200	$31,300, plus 50% of the excess over $81,200

As originally enacted, TEFRA required income tax withholding on interest and dividends. The Internal Revenue Service had estimated that approximately 11% of interest income and 15% of dividend income was going unreported by taxpayers each year. This measure, however, was repealed on August 5, 1983. In its place, "Backup Withholding" provisions were enacted requiring all payors of interest subject to information reporting to withold 20% of interest payments to a payee if the payee fails to furnish a tax identification number to the payor.

TEFRA reduces various deductions and tax benefits for both individuals and businesses. Individuals may now deduct casualty losses only to the extent that the loss, after a $100 minimum, exceeds 10 percent of the taxpayers' adjusted gross income. Also, medical expenses are now deductible only to the extent they exceed 5% of adjusted gross income. (Formerly the limitation was 3%). The separate $150 deduction for health insurance premiums has been eliminated.

For businesses, TEFRA reduces the ceiling on the amount of investment tax credit that may be used, accelerates the payment of income taxes, and places new restrictions on the tax rules governing corporate mergers and liquidations.

Finally, TEFRA makes significant changes in the pension and benefit rules. Special restrictions are imposed on plans that mainly benefit key employees. Also, the limitations on the contributions to and benefits from corporate pension plans are greatly reduced. The limitations on non-corporate plans, however, are increased to the new levels governing corporate plans.

Tax Reform Act of 1984. The Deficit Reduction Act, enacted July 18, 1984, was the fifth major amendment to the Internal Revenue Code in the past nine years. It attempts to raise over $50 billion of revenue by altering hundreds of provisions including those affecting compliance, tax accounting, depreciation, individual taxation, and the taxation of investments.

The Act imposes additional record-keeping requirements on taxpayers by requiring that they keep contemporaneous diaries to substantiate their business use of automobiles and other business property. Taxpayers claiming charitable donations of property of more than $5,000 must attach independent appraisals to their returns. Tax shelter promoters must register certain shelters with the IRS prior to offering them to investors.

The Act introduces new tax accounting rules by recharacterizing interest-free and below market loans to attribute the interest income to the lender and a gift, dividend, or compensation, depending on the parties involved, to the recipient. The recipient will also receive a potentially deductible expense equal in amount to the income attributable to him. Additional requirements are placed on accrual basis taxpayers which prevent them from prematurely deducting expenses.

The Act extends the ACRS life for depreciating most real property from 15 to 18 years. The depreciable life of automobiles costing more than

Federal Income Tax Comparisons

Taxes at Selected Rate Brackets After Standard Deductions/Zero Bracket Amounts[2]

Adjusted gross income	Single return listing no dependents				Joint return listing two dependents			
	1984	1980	1972[1]	1967	1984	1980	1972[1]	1967
$ 5,000	$ 193	$ 250	$ 495	$ 667	$ –500[3]	$–500[3]	$ 102	$ 286
10,000	915	1,177	1,545	1,742	291	374	901	1,114
15,000	1,801	2,345	2,703	3,334	959	1,242	1,820	2,172
20,000	2,945	3,837	4,255	5,350	1,741	2,265	3,010	3,428
25,000	4,265	5,562	6,090	7,730	2,673	3,497	4,380	4,892
30,000	5,773	7,522	8,152	10,938	3,815	4,953	6,020	6,596

1. A 2.5% surcharge was in effect. 2. For comparison purposes, tax rate schedules were used. 3. Refund based on Earned Income credit for families with dependent children.

Returns Filed and Examined

Internal Revenue Service

Category	Returns filed for calendar year 1982	Returns examined 1983	Percent coverage
Individual, total	95,419,000	1,427,690	1.50
1040A, TPI[1] under $10,000	25,168,000	81,636	.32
Non 1040A, TPI under $10,000	7,862,000	61,042	.78
TPI $10,000 under $25,000, simple	21,412,000	136,817	.64
TPI $10,000 under $25,000, complex	10,663,000	228,936	2.15
TPI $25,000 under $50,000	20,332,000	530,920	2.61
TPI $50,000 and over	4,425,000	218,338	4.93
Schedule C-TGR[2] under $25,000	1,756,000	28,563	1.63
Schedule C-TGR $25,000 under $100,000	1,797,000	58,893	3.28
Schedule C-TGR $100,000 and over	945,000	57,849	6.12
Schedule F-TGR[3] under $25,000	328,000	4,963	1.52
Schedule F-TGR $25,000 under $100,000	501,000	10,137	2.02
Schedule F-TGR $100,000 and over	231,000	9,564	4.14
Fiduciary	1,962,000	8,303	.42
Partnerships	1,499,000	36,115	2.41
Corporation, total[3]	2,364,000	85,980	3.64
Assets not reported	140,000	3,893	2.77
Under $100,000[4]	1,092,000	21,418	1.96
$100,000 under $1 million	887,000	30,617	3.45
$1 mil under $10 mil	193,000	19,139	9.90
$10 mil under $100 mil	32,000	7,098	22.47
$100 mil and over	6,600	3,815	57.83
Small business corporations	567,000	7,428	1.31
Form 1120 DISC	13,000	1,416	10.61
Estate, total	127,000	21,517	16.94
Gross estate under $1 mil	119,000	15,873	13.36
Gross estate $1 mil under $5 mil	8,000	5,120	66.87
Gross estate $5 mil and over	1,000	524	90.81
Gift	84,000	3,028	3.59
Income, estate and gift, total	102,037,000	1,591,447	1.56
Excise	798,000	51,935	6.51
Employment	25,736,000	25,902	.10
Windfall profit	13,000	6,611	50.85
Miscellaneous	—	127	—
Service center corrections	—	930,215	—

NOTE: Totals may not add due to rounding. 1. Total positive income. 2. Total gross receipts. 3. Includes 13,000 Forms 1120F not allocated to corporation classes. 4. Balance sheet assets.

$16,000 is also extended and the investment tax credit is limited to a maximum of $1,000 per vehicle.

The Act drastically overhauls the area of domestic relations by simplifying the taxation of property settlements, alimony, and child support. Individuals are further affected by the Act's restricting the benefits of an income tax saving technique known as income averaging.

Finally, the taxation of investments is affected by the Act's extension of the original issue discount rules to more obligations including leases with deferred rents and certain obligations issued by individuals and the reduction in the holding period for long-term capital gain or loss treatment to six months for assets acquired after June 22, 1984.

Returns Received

In 1983, the IRS Service Centers processed 171.2 million federal tax returns; 56% (95.3 million) of these returns were filed by individual taxpayers. Nearly 15 million taxpayers filed Form 1040EZ, 21.1 million taxpayers filed Form 1040A, and 59.2 million taxpayers filed Form 1040.

Federal Corporation Taxes

Corporations are taxed under a graduated tax rate structure as shown in the chart below. For taxable years beginning after 1983, the benefits of the lower rates are phased out for corporations with taxable income between $1,000,000 and $1,405,000 and totally eliminated for corporations with incomes equal to or in excess of $1,405,000.

If the corporation qualifies, it may elect to be an S corporation. If it makes this election, the corporation will not (with certain exceptions) pay corporate tax on its income. Its income is instead passed through and taxed to its shareholders. There are several requirements a corporation must meet to qualify as an S corporation including having 35 or fewer shareholders, and having only one class of stock.

1984

Taxable income	Tax	Percent over excess
$0 to $25,000	$ 0	15% over $0
$25,000 to $50,000	$ 3,750	18% over $25,000
$50,000 to $75,000	$ 8,250	30% over $50,000
$75,000 to $100,000	$ 15,750	40% over $75,000
$100,000 and over	$ 25,750	46% over $100,000

State Corporation Income and Franchise Taxes

All states but Nevada, South Dakota, Texas, Washington, and Wyoming impose a tax on corporation net income. The majority of states impose the tax at flat rates ranging from 2.35% to 11.5%. Several states have adopted a graduated basis of rates for corporations.

Nearly all states follow the federal law in defining net income. However, many states provide for varying exclusions and adjustments.

A state is empowered to tax all of the net income of its domestic corporations. With regard to nonresident corporations, however, it may only tax the net income on business carried on within its boundaries. Corporations are, therefore, required to apportion their incomes among the states where they do business and pay a tax to each of these states. Nearly all states provide an apportionment to their domestic corporations, too, in order that they not be unduly burdened.

Several states tax unincorporated businesses separately.

Federal Estate and Gift Taxes

A Federal Estate Tax Return must be filed for the estate of every U.S. citizen or resident whose gross estate, if the decedent died in 1984, exceeds $325,000. The gross estate filing requirement is increased and phased in from 1984 to 1987 from the present $325,000 to $600,000. An estate tax return must also be filed for the estate of a non-resident, if the value of his gross estate in the U.S. is more than $60,000 at the date of death. The estate tax return is due nine months after the date of death of the decedent, but a reasonable extension of time to file may be obtained for good reason. Tax due is to be paid when the return is filed. The executor of an estate with an interest in closely held business that comprises at least 35% of the adjusted gross estate may pay estate tax attributable to the business in from two to ten equal annual installments. In such a case, a 5-year extension for the payment of estate taxes may be exercised for that portion of the tax attributable to a closely held business.

Under the unified federal estate and gift tax structure, individuals who made taxable gifts during the calendar year are required to file a gift tax return by April 15 of the following year.

The Tax Reform Act of 1976 replaced the old $30,000 gift tax exemption and $60,000 estate tax exemption with a unified credit. This credit is used for both estate and gift taxes. Any part of the credit used to offset gift taxes is not available to offset estate taxes. As a result, although they are still taxable as gifts, lifetime transfers no longer cushion the impact of progressive estate tax rates. Lifetime transfers and transfers made at death are cumulated for estate tax rate purposes. Gift taxes are computed by applying the uniform rate schedule to lifetime taxable transfers (after deducting the unified credit) and subtracting the taxes payable for prior taxable periods. In general, estate taxes are computed by applying the uniform rate schedule to cumulated transfers and subtracting the gift taxes paid. An appropriate adjustment is made for taxes on lifetime transfers—such as certain gifts within three years of death—in a decedent's estate.

Unified Credit—Estate & Gift Taxes

Year	Credit
1981	$47,000
1982	62,800
1983	79,300
1984	96,300
1985	121,800
1986	155,800
1987 and after	192,800

Among the deductions allowed in computing the amount of the estate subject to tax are funeral expenditures, administrative costs, claims and bequests to religious, charitable, and fraternal organizations or government welfare agencies, and state inheritance taxes. For transfers made after 1981 during life or death, there is an unlimited marital deduction. An annual gift tax exclusion is provided that permits tax-free gifts to each donee of $10,000 for each year. A husband and wife who agree to treat gifts to third persons as joint gifts can exclude up to $20,000 a year to each donee. An unlimited exclusion for medical expenses and school tuition paid for the benefit of any donee is also available.

Federal Estate and Gift Taxes

Unified Rate Schedule, 1984[1]

If the net amount is:		Tentative tax is:		
From	To	Tax +	%	On excess over
$ 0	$ 10,000	$ 0	18	$ 0
10,000	20,000	1,800	20	10,000
20,000	40,000	3,800	22	20,000
40,000	60,000	8,200	24	40,000
60,000	80,000	13,000	26	60,000
80,000	100,000	18,200	28	80,000
100,000	150,000	23,800	30	100,000
150,000	250,000	38,800	32	150,000
250,000	500,000	70,800	34	250,000
500,000	750,000	155,800	37	500,000
750,000	1,000,000	248,300	39	750,000
1,000,000	1,250,000	345,800	41	1,000,000
1,250,000	1,500,000	448,300	43	1,250,000
1,500,000	2,000,000	555,800	45	1,500,000
2,000,000	2,500,000	780,800	49	2,000,000
2,500,000	3,000,000	1,025,800	53	2,500,000
3,000,000 and up	—	1,290,800	55	3,000,000

1. The estate and gift tax rates are combined in the single rate schedule effective for the estates of decedents dying, and for gifts made, after Dec. 31, 1976.

Family Size Determines Per Child Cost

According to a recent study by Thomas J. Espenshade, a population economist for the Urban Institute, a middle-income family spends about 54% more on an only child than a similar family with three children spends per child. In a "typical" two-child, middle-income family, it would cost $149,000 to raise the first child from birth until graduation from a four-year public college.

Dual Income Families Growing

The number of two-income households in the United States has increased significantly since 1960. More than three fifths of all married couples (62%) had two incomes in 1981, the latest year for which statistics are available. This was up from 50.1% in 1970 and 40% in 1960, according to a Census Bureau report.

The Year of the Octogenarian

Nearly a quarter of the elderly will be 85 years old or older by 2050—24% of them—according to Census Bureau projections. At present only 9.2% of the elderly are 85 or older.

Sales Tax Rates in Selected Cities[1]

City	Percent rate	City	Percent rate	City	Percent rate
Amarillo, Tex.	1	Ithaca, N.Y.[2]	3	Richmond, Va.	1
Anaheim, Calif.[2]	1.25	Jefferson City, Mo.	1	Roanoke, Va.	1
Austin, Tex.	1	Lincoln, Neb.	1	Sacramento, Calif.[2]	1.25
Baton Rouge, La.[3]	3	Los Angeles[2]	1.25	St. Louis	1
Berkeley, Calif.[2,4]	1.75	Lynchburg, Va.	1	San Antonio, Tex.	1
Birmingham, Ala.	1	Mobile, Ala.	2	San Diego, Calif.[2]	1.25
Boulder, Colo.	2.15	Montgomery, Ala.	2	San Francisco[2 4]	1.75
Chicago[2]	3	New Orleans[3]	3.5	Seattle[2]	0.925
Dallas	1	New York	4.25	Shreveport, La.[3]	3
Denver	3	Nome, Alaska	3	Spokane, Wash.[2]	0.925
Duluth, Minn.	1	Norfolk, Va.	1	Springfield, Ill.[2]	2
El Paso	1	Oakland, Calif.[2,4]	1.75	Topeka, Kan.	0.1
Fort Worth	1	Oklahoma City	2	Troy, N.Y.[2]	3
Fresno, Calif.[2]	1.25	Omaha, Neb.	1.5	Tucson, Ariz.	2
Glendale, Calif.[2]	1.75	Pasadena, Calif.[2]	1.25	Tulsa, Okla.	3
Houston	1	Phoenix, Ariz.	1	Washington, D.C.	6
Huntsville, Ala.	2	Rapid City, S.D.	2	Yonkers, N.Y.[2]	4

1. Excludes state and county sales taxes unless otherwise indicated. 2. Combined city and county rate. 3. Includes Parish School Board tax. 4. Includes 0.5% imposed for public transit. *Source:* Tax Foundation, Inc.

State General Sales and Use Taxes[1]

(as of May 1, 1984)

State	Percent rate	State	Percent rate	State	Percent rate
Alabama	4	Kentucky	5	Ohio	5
Arizona	5	Louisiana	4	Oklahoma	3
Arkansas	4	Maine	5	Pennsylvania	6
California	4.75	Maryland	5	Rhode Island	6
Colorado	3	Massachusetts	5	South Carolina	5
Connecticut	7.5	Michigan	4	South Dakota	4
D.C.	6	Minnesota	6	Tennessee	5.5
Florida	5	Mississippi	6	Texas	4
Georgia	3	Missouri	4.125	Utah	4.625
Hawaii	4	Nebraska	3.5	Vermont	4
Idaho	4	Nevada	5.75	Virginia	3
Illinois	5	New Jersey	6	Washington	6.5
Indiana	5	New Mexico	3.75	West Virginia	5
Iowa	4	New York	4	Wisconsin	5
Kansas	3	North Carolina	3	Wyoming	3
		North Dakota	4		

1. Local and county taxes, if any, are additional. NOTE: Alaska, Delaware, Montana, New Hampshire and Oregon have no statewide sales and use taxes. *Source: Information Please Almanac* questionnaires to the states, and Tax Foundation, Inc.

Old Magic and New Science

Over 1,000 years ago, certain "magic" stones protected people against many illnesses including arsenic poisoning—or so Persian pharmacists believed. These "bezoar" stones (*bezoar* meant "to protect against poison") were used by royalty, always afraid of poisoned wine. It is said that Queen Elizabeth I set these stones in her rings; other monarchs wore them on necklaces.

Bezoar stones are really bits of non-digestible hair and other substances, in the stomachs of cud-chewing animals, around which a mineral (sodium hydrogen phosphate) collects. The curative properties of these stones were considered yet another ancient myth—but recent research concerned with arsenic metabolism in the ocean at the Scripps Institution of Oceanography discovered that the partly digested animal hair really *did* absorb arsenite, one form of th epoison, like a "chemical sponge." Earlier research at Scripps had discovered that the mineral accumulated in these stones switched phosphate for arsenate, another form of the poison, by means of ion exchange.

Income Tax Rates in Selected Cities

(Population exceeding 50,000)

City	Percent rate	Year begun	City	Percent rate	Year begun
Akron, Ohio	2	1962	Lakewood, Ohio	1.5	1968
Allentown, Pa.	1	1958	Lancaster, Pa.	0.5	1959
Altoona, Pa.	1	1948	Lansing, Mich.	1	1968
Baltimore	(1)	1966	Lexington, Ky.	2	1952
Bethlehem, Pa.	1	1957	Lima, Ohio	1.5	1959
Birmingham, Ala.	1	1970	Lorain, Ohio	1	1967
Canton, Ohio	2	1954	Louisville, Ky.	2.2	1948
Cincinnati	2	1954	Mansfield, Ohio	1	1966
Cleveland	2	1967	New York	0.9–4.3	1966
Cleveland Heights, Ohio	2	1968	Owensboro, Ky.	1	1960
Columbus, Ohio	2	1947	Parma, Ohio	2	1967
Covington, Ky.	2.5	1956	Philadelphia	4.96	1939
Dayton, Ohio	2.25	1949	Pontiac, Mich.	1	1968
Detroit	2	1965	Reading, Pa.	1	1969
District of Columbia	2–11	1947	Saginaw, Mich.	1	1965
Elyria, Ohio	1	1969	St. Louis	1	1948
Erie, Pa.	1	1948	Scranton, Pa.	2.5	1948
Euclid, Ohio	2	1967	Springfield, Ohio	2	1948
Flint, Mich.	1	1965	Toledo, Ohio	2.25	1946
Gadsden, Ala.	2	1956	Warren, Ohio	1.5	1952
Grand Rapids, Mich.	1	1967	Wilkes-Barre, Pa.	3	1966
Hamilton, Ohio	1.5	1960	Wilmington, Del.	1.25	1970
Harrisburg, Pa.	1	1966	York, Pa.	1	1965
Kansas City, Mo.	1	1964	Youngstown, Ohio	2	1948
Kettering, Ohio	1.75	1968			

1. Tax is 50% of state income tax. NOTE: Rates are for residents only, except in Kentucky, Ohio, and Pennsylvania cities, where non-resident rate is the same. *Source:* Tax Foundation, Inc.

Higher Literacy—Lower Birth Rates

As female illiteracy goes down, so does the birth rate. Studies by the World Fertility Survey show that throughout the developing world, women with secondary schooling tend to have two or three fewer children than the uneducated. The influence of literacy on the success of a country's birth control program is greater than the country's gnp. Where the use of contraception appears higher than income levels seem to predict—as in Indonesia and Thailand—relatively high literacy is the reason.

National Clearinghouse for Health Information

The Department of Health and Human Services has opened a National Health Information Clearinghouse to help consumers locate specific information about health. The project has a number of referral specialists to work with questions, get in touch with resource organizations, and refer those sources to the caller or writer. The center will not give medical advice or provide referrals to individual physicians.

For information, write: National Health Information Clearinghouse, P.O. Box 1133, Washington, D.C. 20013, or call 800-336-4797 (in Virginia, 703-522-2590).

U.S. Crime Down

According to the Justice Department, the number of households falling victim to crime dropped 29% in 1982 to 27% in 1983—the largest decline in nine years. Fewer households were affected by almost every type of crime. Those experiencing robbery dropped by 19%, burglary by 11%, and aggravated assault by 9%.

Although the number of households has increased by 18% since 1975, the number that were burglarized in 1983 were 7% fewer than in 1975.

The Stages of Invention

Alexander von Humbolt (1769–1859), the German naturalist, said that an invention goes through three stages: doubt of its existence, denial of its importance, and, finally, credit for its discovery going to someone else.

One example of the truth in this perception is the invention of the "Pullman," the railroad sleeping car. The first sleeper was built by Richard Imlay of Philadelphia. It ran between Chambersburg and Harrisburg, Pa., in 1838. At least eight railroads advertised some kind of sleeping car before 1850. Pullman's first car was not built until 1859. George M. Pullman and his friend Ben Field patented the folding upper berth in 1864. Pullman seems to have been a better businessman and a better promoter.

HEADLINE HISTORY

In any broad overview of history, arbitrary compartmentalization of facts is self-defeating (and makes locating interrelated people, places, and things that much harder). Therefore, Headline History is designed as a "timeline"—a chronology that highlights both the march of time and interesting, sometimes surprising, juxtapositions.

Also see related sections of *Information Please,* particularly the Statistical History of the United States, Inventions and Discoveries, Countries of the World, etc.

B.C.

Before Christ or Before Common Era (B.C.E.)

4500–3000 B.C. Sumerians in the Tigris and Euphrates valleys develop a city-state civilization; first phonetic writing (**c.3500 B.C.**). Egyptian agriculture develops. Western Europe is neolithic, without metals or written records. Earliest recorded date in Egyptian calendar (**4241 B.C.**). First year of Jewish calendar (**3760 B.C.**). Copper used by Egyptians and Sumerians.

3000–2000 B.C. Pharaonic rule begins in Egypt. Cheops, 4th dynasty (**2700–2675 B.C.**). The Great Sphinx of Giza. Earliest Egyptian mummies. Papyrus. Phoenician settlements on coast of what is now Syria and Lebanon. Semitic tribes settle in Assyria. Sargon, first Akkadian king, builds Mesopotamian empire. The Gilgamesh epic (**c.3000 B.C.**). Abraham leaves Ur (**c.2000 B.C.**). Systematic astronomy in Egypt, Babylon, India, China.

2000–1500 B.C. Hyksos invaders drive Egyptians from Lower Egypt (**17th century B.C.**). Amosis I frees Egypt from Hyksos (**c.1600 B.C.**). Assyrians rise to power—cities of Ashur and Nineveh. Twenty-four-character alphabet in Egypt. Israelites enslaved in Egypt. Cuneiform inscriptions used by Hittites. Peak of Minoan culture on Isle of Crete—earliest form of written Greek. Hammurabi, king of Babylon, develops oldest existing code of laws (**18th century B.C.**). In Britain, Stonehenge erected on some unknown astronomical rationale.

1500–1000 B.C. Ikhnaton develops monotheistic religion in Egypt (**c.1375 B.C.**). His successor, Tutankhamen, returns to earlier gods. Moses leads Israelites out of Egypt into Canaan—Ten Commandments. Greeks destroy Troy (**c.1193 B.C.**). End of Greek civilization in Mycenae with invasion of Dorians. Chinese civilization develops under Shang dynasty. Olmec civilization in Mexico—stone monuments; picture writing.

1000–900 B.C. Solomon succeeds King David, builds Jerusalem temple. After Solomon's death, kingdom divided into Israel and Judah. Hebrew elders begin to write Old Testament books of Bible. Phoenicians colonize Spain with settlement at Cadiz.

900–800 B.C. Phoenicians establish Carthage (**c.810 B.C.**). The *Iliad* and the *Odyssey,* perhaps composed by Greek poet Homer.

800–700 B.C. Prophets Amos, Hosea, Isaiah. First recorded Olympic games (**776 B.C.**). Legendary founding of Rome by Romulus (**753 B.C.**). Assyrian king Sargon II conquers Hittites, Chaldeans, Samaria (end of Kingdom of Israel). Earliest written music. Chariots introduced into Italy by Etruscans.

700–600 B.C. End of Assyrian Empire (**616 B.C.**)—Nineveh destroyed by Chaldeans (Neo-Babylonians) and Medes (**612 B.C.**). Founding of Byzantium by Greeks (**c.660 B.C.**). Building of the Acropolis in Athens. Solon, Greek lawgiver (**640–560 B.C.**). Sappho of Lesbos, Greek poetess, Lao-Tse, Chinese philosopher and founder of Taoism (born **c.604 B.C.**).

600–500 B.C. Babylonian king Nebuchadnezzar builds empire, destroys Jerusalem (**586 B.C.**). Babylonian Captivity of the Jews (starting **587 B.C.**). Hanging Gardens of Babylon. Cyrus the Great of Persia creates great empire, conquers Babylon (**539 B.C.**), frees the Jews. Athenian democracy develops. Aeschylus, Greek dramatist (**525–465 B.C.**). Confucius (**551–479 B.C.**) develops philosophy-religion in China. Buddha (**563–483 B.C.**) founds Buddhism in India.

500–400 B.C. Greeks defeat Persians: battles of Marathon (**490 B.C.**), Thermop-

Some Ancient Civilizations

Name	Approximate dates	Location	Major cities
Akkadian	2350–2230 B.C.	Mesopotamia, parts of Syria, Asia Minor, Iran	Akkad, Ur, Erich
Assyrian	1800–889 B.C.	Mesopotamia, Syria	Assur, Nineveh, Calah
Babylonian	1728–1686 B.C. (old) 625–539 B.C. (new)	Mesopotamia, Syria, Palestine	Babylon
Cimmerian	750–500 B.C.	Caucasus, northern Asia Minor	—
Egyptian	2850–715 B.C.	Nile valley	Thebes, Memphis, Tanis
Etruscan	900–396 B.C.	Northern Italy	—
Greek	900–200 B.C.	Greece	Athens, Sparta, Thebes, Mycenae, Corinth
Hittite	1640–1200 B.C.	Asia Minor, Syria	Hattusas, Nesa
Lydian	700–547 B.C.	Western Asia Minor	Sardis, Miletus
Mede	835–550 B.C.	Iran	Media
Minoan	3000–1100 B.C.	Crete	Knossos
Persian	559-330 B.C.	Iran, Asia Minor, Syria	Persepolis, Pasargadae
Phoenician	1100–332 B.C.	Palestine (colonies: Gibralter, Carthage Sardinia)	Tyre, Sidon, Byblos
Phrygian	1000–547 B.C.	Central Asia Minor	Gordion
Roman	500 B.C.–A.D. 300	Italy, Mediterranean region, Asia Minor, western Europe	Rome, Byzantium
Scythian	800–300 B.C.	Caucasus	—
Sumerian	3200–2360 B.C.	Mesopotamia	Ur, Nippur

ylae (**480** B.C.), Salamis (**480** B.C.). Peloponnesian Wars between Athens and Sparta (**431–404** B.C.)—Sparta victorious. Pericles comes to power in Athens (**462** B.C.). Flowering of Greek culture during the Age of Pericles (**450–400** B.C.). Sophocles, Greek dramatist (**496–c.406** B.C.). Hippocrates, Greek "Father of Medicine" (born **460** B.C.). Xerxes I, king of Persia (rules **485–465** B.C.).

400–300 B.C. Pentateuch—first five books of the Old Testament evolve in final form. Philip of Macedon assassinated (**336** B.C.) after conquering Greece; succeeded by son, Alexander the Great (**356–323** B.C.), who destroys Thebes (**335** B.C.), conquers Tyre and Jerusalem (**332** B.C.), occupies Babylon (**330** B.C.), invades India, and dies in Babylon. His empire is divided among his generals; one of them, Seleucis I, establishes Middle East empire with capitals at Antioch (Syria) and Seleucia (in Iraq). Trial and execution of Greek philosopher Socrates (**399** B.C.). Dialogues recorded by his student, Plato. Euclid's work on geometry (**323** B.C.). Aristotle, Greek philosopher (**354–322** B.C.). Demosthenes, Greek orator (**384–322** B.C.). Praxiteles, Greek sculptor (**400–330** B.C.).

300–251 B.C. First Punic War (**264–241** B.C.): Rome defeats the Carthaginians and begins its domination of the Mediterranean. Temple of the Sun at Teotihuacan, Mexico (**c.300** B.C.). Invention of Mayan calendar in Yucatán—more exact than older calendars. First Roman gladiatorial games (**264** B.C.). Archimedes, Greek mathematician (**287–212** B.C.).

250–201 B.C. Second Punic War (**219–201** B.C.): Hannibal, Carthaginian general (**246–142** B.C.), crosses the Alps (**218** B.C.), reaches gates of Rome (**211** B.C.), retreats, and is defeated by Scipio Africanus at Zama (**202** B.C.). Great Wall of China built (**c.215** B.C.).

200–151 B.C. Romans defeat Seleucid King Antiochus III at Thermopylae (**191** B.C.)—beginning of Roman world domination. Maccabean revolt against Seleucids (**167** B.C.).

150–101 B.C. Third Punic War (**149–146** B.C.): Rome destroys Carthage, killing 450,000 and enslaving the remaining 50,000 inhabitants. Roman armies conquer Macedonia, Greece, Anatolia, Balearic Islands, and southern France. Venus de Milo (**c.140** B.C.). Cicero, Roman orator (**106–43** B.C.).

100–51 B.C. Julius Caesar (**100–44** B.C.) invades Britain (**55** B.C.) and conquers Gaul (France) (**c.50** B.C.). Spartacus leads slave revolt against Rome (**71** B.C.). Romans conquer Seleucid empire. Roman general Pompey conquers Jerusalem (**63 B.C.**). Cleopatra on Egyptian throne (**51–31 B.C.**). Chinese develop use of paper (**c.100 B.C.**). Virgil, Roman poet (**70–19 B.C.**). Horace, Roman poet (**65–8 B.C.**).

50–1 B.C. Caesar crosses Rubicon to fight Pompey (**50 B.C.**). Herod made Roman governor of Judea (**47 B.C.**). Caesar murdered (**44 B.C.**). Caesar's nephew, Octavian, defeats Mark Antony and Cleopatra at Battle of Actium (**31 B.C.**), and establishes Roman empire as Emperor Augustus—rules **27 B.C.—A.D.** 14. Birth of Jesus Christ (variously given from **4 B.C. to A.D.** 7). Ovid, Roman poet (**43 B.C.—A.D. 18**).

A.D.

The Christian or Common Era (C.E.)

1–49 After Augustus, Tiberius becomes emperor (dies, **37**), succeeded by Caligula (assassinated, **41**), who is followed by Claudius. Crucifixion of Jesus (probably **30**). Han dynasty in China founded by Emperor Kuang Wu Ti. Buddhism introduced to China.

50–99 Claudius poisoned (**54**), succeeded by Nero (commits suicide, **68**). Missionary journeys of Paul the Apostle (**34–60**). Jews revolt against Rome; Jerusalem destroyed (**70**). Roman persecutions of Christians begin (**64**). Colosseum built in Rome (**71–80**). Trajan (rules **98–116**); Roman empire extends to Mesopotamia, Arabia, Balkans. First Gospels of St. Mark, St. John, St. Matthew.

100–149 Hadrian rules Rome (**117–138**); codifies Roman law, establishes postal system, builds wall between England and Scotland. Jews revolt under Bar Kokhba (**122–135**); final *Diaspora* (dispersion) of Jews begins.

150–199 Marcus Aurelius (rules Rome **161–180**). Oldest Mayan temples in Central America (**c.200**)., Mayan civilization develops writing, astronomy, mathematics.

200–249 Goths invade Asia Minor (**c.220**). Roman persecutions of Christians increase. Persian (Sassanid) empire re-established. End of Chinese Han dynasty.

250–299 Increasing invasions of the Roman empire by Franks and Goths. Buddhism spreads in China.

300–349 Constantine the Great (rules **312–337**) reunites eastern and western Roman empires, with new capital (Constantinople) on site of Byzantium (**330**); issues Edict of Milan legalizing Christianity (**313**); becomes a Christian on his deathbed (**337**). Council of Nicaea (**325**) defines orthodox Christian doctrine. First Gupta dynasty in India (**c.320**).

350–399 Huns (Mongols) invade Europe (**c.360**). Theodosius the Great (rules **392–395**)—last emperor of a united Roman empire. Roman empire permanently divided in **395**: western empire ruled from Rome; eastern empire ruled from Constantinople.

400–449 Western Roman empire disintegrates under weak emperors. Alaric, king of the Visigoths, sacks Rome (**410**). Attila, Hun chieftain, attacks Roman provinces (**433**). St. Patrick returns to Ireland (**432**). St. Augustine's *City of God* (**411**).

450–499 Vandals destroy Rome (**455**). Western Roman empire ends as Odoacer, German chieftain, overthrows last Roman emperor, Romulus Augustulus, and becomes king of Italy (**476**). Ostrogothic kingdom of Italy established by Theodoric the Great (**493**). Clovis, ruler of the Franks, is converted to Christianity (**496**). First schism between western and eastern churches (**484**). Peak of Mayan culture in Mexico (**c.460**).

500–549 Eastern and western churches reconciled (**519**). Justinian I, the Great (**483–565**), becomes Byzantine emperor (**527**), issues his first code of civil laws (**529**), conquers North Africa, Italy, and part of Spain. Plague spreads through Europe (from **542**). Arthur, semi-legendary king of the Britons (killed, **c.537**). Boëthius, Roman scholar (executed, **524**).

550–599 Beginnings of European silk industry after Justinian's missionaries smuggle silkworms out of China (**553**). Mohammed, founder of Islam (**570–632**). Buddhism in Japan (**c.560**). St. Augustine of Canterbury brings Christianity to Britain (**597**). After killing about half the population, plague in Europe subsides (**594**).

600–649 Mohammed flees from Mecca to Medina (the *Hegira*); first year of the Muslim calendar (**622**). Muslim empire grows (**634**). Arabs conquer Jerusalem (**637**), destroy Alexandrian library (**641**), conquer Persians (**641**). Fatima, Mohammed's daughter (**606–632**).

650–699 Arabs attack North Africa (**670**), destroy Carthage (**697**). Venerable Bede, English monk (**672–735**).

700–749 Arab empire extends from Lisbon to China (by **716**). Charles Martel,

Frankish leader, defeats Arabs at Tours/Poitiers, halting Arab advance in Europe (732). Charlemagne (742–814).

750–799 Caliph Harun al-Rashid rules Arab empire (786–809): the "golden age" of Arab culture. Vikings begin attacks on Britain (790), land in Ireland (795). Charlemagne becomes king of the Franks (771). City of Machu Picchu flourishes in Peru.

800–849 Charlemagne (Charles the Great) crowned first Holy Roman Emperor in Rome (800). Arabs conquer Crete, Sicily, and Sardinia (826–827). Charlemagne dies (814), succeeded by his son, Louis the Pious, who divides France among his sons (817).

850–899 Norsemen attack as far south as the Mediterranean but are repulsed (859), discover Iceland (861). Alfred the Great becomes king of Britain (871), defeats Danish invaders (878). Russian nation founded by Vikings under Prince Rurik, establishing capital at Novgorod (855–879).

900–949 Vikings discover Greenland (c.900). Arab Spain under Abd ar-Rahman III becomes center of learning (912–961).

950–999 Eric the Red establishes first Viking colony in Greenland (982). Mieczyslaw I becomes first ruler of Poland (960). Hugh Capet elected King of France in 987; Capetian dynasty to rule until 1328. Musical notation systematized (c.990). Vikings and Danes attack Britain (988–999). Holy Roman Empire founded by Otto I, King of Germany since 936, crowned by Pope John XII in 962.

---

c.1000 Hungary and Scandinavia converted to Christianity. Viking raider Leif Ericson discovers North America, calls it *Vinland*. Chinese invent gunpowder. *Beowulf*, Old English epic.

1009 Moslems destroy Holy Sepulchre in Jerusalem.

1013 Danes control England. Canute takes throne (1016), conquers Norway (1028), dies (1035); kingdom divided among his sons: Harold Harefoot (England), Sweyn (Norway), Hardecanute (Denmark).

1040 Macbeth murders Duncan, king of Scotland.

1053 Robert Guiscard, Norman invader, establishes kingdom in Italy, conquers Sicily (1072).

1054 Final separation between Eastern (Orthodox) and Western (Roman) churches.

1055 Seljuk Turks, Asian nomads, move west, capture Baghdad, Armenia (1064), Syria, and Palestine (1075).

1066 William of Normandy invades England, defeats last Saxon king, Harold II, at Battle of Hastings, crowned William I of England ("the Conqueror").

1073 Emergence of strong papacy when Gregory VII is elected. Conflict with English and French kings and German emperors will continue throughout medieval period.

1095 (*See* special material on "The Crusades.")

1150–67 Universities of Paris and Oxford founded in France and England.

1162 Thomas à Becket named Archbishop of Canterbury, murdered by Henry II's men (1170). Troubadours (wandering minstrels) glorify romantic concepts of feudalism.

1189 Richard I ("the Lionhearted") succeeds Henry II in England, killed in France (1199), succeeded by King John.

1211 Genghis Khan invades China, captures Peking (1214), conquers Persia (1218), invades Russia (1223), dies (1227).

1215 King John forced by barons to sign Magna Carta at Runneymede, limiting royal power.

1233 The Inquisition begins as Pope Gregory IX assigns Dominicans responsibility for combatting heresy. Torture used (1252). Ferdinand and Isabella establish Spanish Inquisition (1478). Tourquemada, Grand Inquisitor, forces conversion or expulsion of Spanish Jews (1492). Forced

Omar Khayyám, *Persian poet* (1027?–1123)
El Cid, *Spanish national hero* (1040–1099)
Peter Abelard, *French theologian* (1079–1142)
Judah Halevi, *Jewish poet* (1085–1140)

Thomas á Becket, *English prelate and martyr* (1118–1170)
Moses Maimonides, *Jewish philosopher* (1135–1204)
Genghis Khan, *Mongol emperor* (1162–1227)
St. Francis of Assisi, *founder of Franciscans* (1182–1226)
Roger Bacon, *English scientist* (1214–1294)
Kublai Khan, *Mongol ruler* (1216–1294)
St. Thomas Aquinas, *Catholic theologian* (1225–1274)
Marco Polo, *Venetian explorer* (1254–1323)
Dante Alighieri, *Italian poet* (1265–1321)

THE CRUSADES (1096–1291)

In 1095 Pope Urban II calls for war to rescue Holy Land from Moslem infidels at Council of Clermont. *First Crusade* (1096)—about 500,000 peasants led by Peter the Hermit prove so troublesome that Byzantine Emperor Alexius ships them to Asia Minor; only 25,000 survive return after massacre by Seljuk Turks. Followed by organized army, led by nobility, which reaches Constantinople (1097), conquers Jerusalem (1099), Acre (1104), establishes Latin Kingdom protected by Knights of St. John the Hospitaller (1100), and Knights Templar (1123). Seljuk Turks start series of counterattacks (1144). *Second Crusade* (1146) led by King Louis VIII of France and Emperor Conrad III. Crusaders perish in Asia Minor (1147).

Saladin controls Egypt (1171), unites Islam in Holy War (*Jihad*) against Christians, recaptures Jerusalem (1187). *Third Crusade* (1189) under kings of France, England, and Germany fails to reduce Saladin's power. *Fourth Crusade* (1200–1204)—French knights sack Greek Christian Constantinople, establish Latin empire in Byzantium. Greeks reestablish Orthodox faith (1262).

Children's Crusade (1212)—Only 1 of 30,000 French children and about 200 of 20,000 German children survive to return home. Other Crusades—against Egypt (1217), *Sixth* (1228), *Seventh* (1248), *Eighth* (1270). Mamelukes conquer Acre; end of the Crusades (1291).

conversion of Moors (**1499**). Inquisition in Portugal (**1531**). First Protestants burned at the stake in Spain (**1543**). Spanish Inquisition abolished (**1834**).

1241 Mongols defeat Germans in Silesia, invade Poland and Hungary, withdraw from Europe after Ughetai, Mongol leader, dies.

1251 Kublai Khan governs China, becomes ruler of Mongols (1259), establishes Yuan dynasty in China (1280), invades Burma (1287), dies (1294).

1271 Marco Polo of Venice travels to China, in court of Kublai Khan (1275–1292), returns to Genoa (1295) and writes *Travels.*

1295 English King Edward I summons the Model Parliament.

1312-37 Mali Empire reaches its height in Africa under King Mansa Musa.

1337-1453 Hundred Years' War—English and French kings fight for control of France.

c.1325 The beginning of the Renaissance in Italy: writers Dante, Petrarch, Boccaccio; painter Giotto. Development of *No* drama in Japan. Aztecs establish capital on site of modern Mexico City. Peak of Moslem culture in Spain. Small cannon in use.

1347-1351 At least 25 million people die in Europe's "Black Death" (bubonic plague).

1368 Ming dynasty begins in China.

1376-82 John Wycliffe, pre-Reformation religious reformer and followers translate Latin Bible into English.

1378 The Great Schism (to 1417)—rival popes in Rome and Avignon, France, fight for control of Roman Catholic Church.

c.1387 Chaucer's *Canterbury Tales.*

1415 Henry V defeats French at Agincourt. Jan Hus, Bohemian preacher and follower of Wycliffe, burned at stake in Constance as heretic.

1418-60 Portugal's Prince Henry the Navigator sponsors exploration of Africa's coast.

1428 Joan of Arc leads French against English, captured by Burgundians (1430) and turned over to the English, burned at the stake as a witch after ecclesiastical trial (1431).

1438 Inca rule in Peru.

1450 Florence becomes center of Renaissance arts and learning under the Medicis.

1453 Turks conquer Constantinople, end of the Byzantine empire. Hundred Years' War between France and England ends.

1455 The Wars of the Roses, civil wars between rival noble factions, begin in England (to 1485). Having invented printing with movable type at Mainz, Germany, Johann Gutenberg completes first Bible.

1462 Ivan the Great rules Russia until 1505 as first czar; ends payment of tribute to Mongols.

1492 Moors conquered in Spain by troops of Ferdinand and Isabella. Columbus discovers Caribbean islands, returns to Spain (1493). Second voyage to Dominica, Jamaica, Puerto Rico (1493–1496). Third voyage to Orinoco (1498). Fourth voyage to Honduras and Panama (1502–1504).

Duns Scotus, *Scottish theologian* (1265–1308)
Giotto, *Italian painter* (1276–1337)
Guillaume de Machaut, *French composer* (1300–1377)
Petrarch (Francesco Petrarca), *Italian poet* (1304–1374)
Giovanni Boccaccio, *Florentine novelist* (1313–1375)
John Wycliffe, *English church reformer* (1320–1384)
Geoffrey Chaucer, *English writer* (c.1340–1400)
Jan Hus, *Bohemian religious reformer* (c.1369–1415)
Thomas á Kempis, *German mystic* (1380–1471)
Donatello, *Italian sculptor* (1386–1466)
Fra Angelico, *Italian painter* (1387–1455)
Johann Gutenberg, *inventor of movable type* (1398–1468)
Luca della Robbia, *Italian sculptor* (1400–1482)
Guillaume Dufay, *French composer* (c.1400–1474)
Fra Filippo Lippi, *Italian painter* (1406–1469)
Joan of Arc, *French saint and national heroine* (1412–1431)
Tomas de Torquemada, *Spanish Inquisitor* (1420–1498)
Giovanni Bellini, *Italian painter* (1430–1516)
François Villon, *French poet* (1431–1465?)
Sandro Botticelli, *Italian painter* (1444–1510)
Lorenzo de'Medici, *Renaissance ruler* (1449–1492)
Hieronymus Bosch, *Dutch painter* (1450–1516)
Josquin des Prés, *Dutch composer* (1450–1521)
Isabella I, *Queen of Spain* (1451–1504)
Christopher Columbus, *Italian explorer* (1451–1506)
Amerigo Vespucci, *Italian navigator* (1451–1512)
Savonarola, *Italian churchman* (1452–1498)

Leonardo da Vinci, *Renaissance artistic and scientific genius* (1452–1519)
Vasco da Gama, *Portuguese explorer* (1460–1524)
Juan Ponce de León, *Spanish explorer* (1460–1521)
Hans Holbein (the Elder), *German painter* (1465?–1524)
Niccolo Machiavelli, *Italian author* (1468–1527)
Albrecht Dürer, *German painter* (1471–1528)
Nicolaus Copernicus, *Polish scientist* (1473–1543)
Michelangelo Buonarroti, *Italian painter, sculptor, architect* (1475–1564)

Cesare Borgia, *Renaissance prince* (1476–1507)
Titian, *Italian painter* (1477–1576)
Sir Thomas More, *English statesman* (1478–1535)
Lucrezia Borgia, *Italian patron of the arts* (1480–1519)
Ferdinand Magellan, *Portuguese explorer* (1480–1521)
Martin Luther, *German Reformation leader* (1483–1546)
Raphael, *Italian painter* (1483–1520)

Ulrich Zwingli, *Swiss humanist* (1484–1531)
Hernando Cortes, *Spanish Conquistador* (1485–1547)
Andrea del Sarto, *Florentine painter* (1486–1531)
Thomas Cranmer, *English churchman* (1489–1556)
François Rabelais, *French writer* (1490–1553)
Jacques Cartier, *French explorer* (1491–1557)
St. Ignatius de Loyola, *founder of Jesuits* (1491–1556)
Paracelsus, *Swiss physician* (1493–1541)
Correggio, *Italian painter* (1494–1534)
Hans Holbein (the Younger) *German painter* (1497–1543)
Hernando De Soto, *Spanish explorer* (1499–1542)

1497 Vasco da Gama sails around Africa and discovers sea route to India (1498). Establishes Portuguese colony in India (1502). John Cabot, employed by England, reaches and explores Canadian coast. Michelangelo's *Bacchus* sculpture.

1501 First black slaves in America brought to Spanish colony of Santo Domingo.
c.1503 Leonardo da Vinci paints the *Mona Lisa.*
1506 St. Peter's Church started in Rome; designed and decorated by such artists and architects as Bramante, Michelangelo, da Vinci, Raphael, and Bernini before its completion in **1626.**
1509 Henry VIII ascends English throne. Michelangelo paints the ceiling of the Sistine Chapel.
1517 Turks conquer Egypt, control Arabia. Martin Luther posts his 95 theses denouncing church abuses on church door in Wittenberg—start of the Reformation in Germany.
1519 Ulrich Zwingli begins Reformation in Switzerland. Hernando Cortes conquers Mexico for Spain. Charles I of Spain is chosen Holy Roman Emperor Charles V. Portuguese explorer Fernando Magellan sets out to circumnavigate the globe.
1520 Luther excommunicated by Pope Leo X. Suleiman I ("the Magnificent") becomes Sultan of Turkey, invades Hungary (**1521**), Rhodes (**1522**), attacks Austria (**1529**), annexes Hungary (**1541**), Tripoli (**1551**), makes peace with Persia (**1553**), destroys Spanish fleet (**1560**), dies (**1566**). Magellan reaches the Pacific, is killed by Philippine natives (**1521**). One of his ships under Juan Sebastián del Cano continues around the world, reaches Spain (**1522**).
1524 Verrazano, sailing under the French flag, explores the New England coast and New York Bay.
1527 Troops of the Holy Roman Empire attack Rome, imprison Pope Clement VII—the end of the Italian Renaissance. Castiglione writes *The Courtier.* The Medici expelled from Florence.
1532 Pizarro marches from Panama to Peru, kills the Inca chieftain, Atahualpa, of Peru (**1533**). Machiavelli's *Prince* published posthumously.
1535 Reformation begins as Henry VIII makes himself head of English Church after being excommunicated by Pope. Sir Thomas More executed as traitor for refusal to acknowledge king's religious authority. Jacques Cartier sails up the St. Lawrence River, basis of French claims to Canada.
1536 Henry VIII executes second wife, Anne Boleyn. John Calvin establishes Presbyterian form of Protestantism in Switzerland, writes *Institutes of the Christian Religion.* Danish and Norwegian Reformations. Michelangelo's *Last Judgment.*
1541 John Knox leads Reformation in Scotland, establishes Presbyterian church (**1560**).
1543 Publication of *On the Revolution of Heavenly Bodies* by Polish scholar Nicolaus Copernicus—giving his theory that the earth revolves around the sun.
1545 Council of Trent to meet intermittently until **1563** to define Catholic dogma and doctrine, reiterate papal authority.
1547 Ivan IV ("the Terrible") crowned as Czar of Russia, begins conquest of Astrakhan and Kazan (**1552**), battles nobles (boyars) for power (**1564**), kills his son (**1580**), dies, and is succeeded by a son who gives power to Boris Godunov (**1584**).
1553 Roman Catholicism restored in England by Queen Mary I, who rules until **1558.** Religious radical Michael Servetus burned as heretic in Geneva by order of John Calvin.
1554 Benvenuto Cellini completes the bronze *Perseus.*
1556 Akbar the Great becomes Mogul emperor of India, conquers Afghanistan (**1581**), continues wars of conquest (until **1605**).
1558 Queen Elizabeth I ascends the throne (rules to **1603**). Restores Protestantism, establishes state Church of England (Anglicanism). Renaissance will reach height in England—Shakespeare, Marlowe, Spenser.
1561 Persecution of Huguenots in France stopped by Edict of Orleans. French religious wars begin again with massacre of Huguenots at Vassy. St. Bartholomew's Day Massacre—thousands of Huguenots murdered (**1572**). Amnesty granted (**1573**). Persecution continues periodically until Edict of Nantes (**1598**) gives Huguenots religious freedom (until **1685**).
1568 Protestant Netherlands revolts against Catholic Spain; independence will be acknowledged by Spain in **1648.** High point of Dutch Renaissance—painters Rubens, Van Dyck, Hals, and Rembrandt.

Benvenuto Cellini, *Florentine sculptor* (1500–1571)
Nostradamus, *French astrologer* (1503–1566)
John Knox, *Scottish church reformer* (1505–1572)
St. Francis Xavier, *Jesuit missionary* (1506–1552)
John Calvin, *Swiss theologian* (1509–1564)
Giorgio Vasari, *Italian art historian* (1511–1574)
Andreas Vesalius, *Dutch anatomist* (1515–1564)
Andrea Palladio, *Italian architect* (1518–1580)
Tintoretto (Jacopo Robusti), *Italian painter* (1518–1594)
Pieter Brueghel (the Elder), *Dutch painter* (1520–1569)
Pierre de Ronsard, *French poet* (1524–1585)
Giovanni Palestrina, *Italian composer* (1526–1594)
Paolo Veronese, *Italian painter* (1528–1588)
Queen Elizabeth, *English ruler* (1533?–1603)
Michel de Montaigne, *French author* (1533–1592)
El Greco, *Spanish-Greek painter* (1542–1614)
Tycho Brahe, *Danish astronomer* (1546–1601)
Miguel de Cervantes, *Spanish writer* (1547–1616)
Giordano Bruno, *Italian philosopher* (1548–1600)
Sir Walter Raleigh, *English courtier* (1552–1618)
Edmund Spenser, *English poet* (1552–1599)
Giovanni Gabrieli, *Italian composer* (c.1557–1612)
Francis Bacon, *English philosopher* (1561–1626)
Christopher Marlowe, *English dramatist* (1564–1593)
Galileo Galilei, *Italian scientist* (1564–1642)
William Shakespeare, *English dramatist and poet* (1564–1616)
Michelangelo da Caravaggio, *Italian painter* (c.1565–1609)
Claudio Monteverdi, *Italian composer* (1567–1643)
Johannes Kepler, *German astronomer* (1571–1630)
John Donne, *English poet* (1573–1631)
Inigo Jones, *English architect* (1573–1652)
Ben Jonson, *English dramatist* (1573–1637)
Peter Paul Rubens, *Flemish painter* (1577–1652)
William Harvey, *English physician and anatomist* (1578–1657)

1570 Japan permits visits of foreign ships. Queen Elizabeth I excommunicated by Pope. Turks attack Cyprus and war on Venice. Turkish fleet defeated at Battle of Lepanto by Spanish and Italian fleets (**1571**). Peace of Constantinople (**1572**) ends Turkish attacks on Europe.

1580 Francis Drake returns to England after circumnavigating the globe. Knighted by Queen Elizabeth I (**1581**). Montaigne's *Essays* published.

1583 William of Orange rules The Netherlands; assassinated on orders of Philip II of Spain (**1584**).

1587 Mary, Queen of Scots, executed for treason by order of Queen Elizabeth I. Monteverdi's *First Book of Madrigals.*

1588 Defeat of the Spanish Armada by English. Henry, King of Navarre and Protestant leader, recognized as Henry IV, first Bourbon king of France. Converts to Roman Catholicism in **1593** in attempt to end religious wars.

1590 Henry IV enters Paris, wars on Spain (**1595**), marries Marie de Medici (**1600**), assassinated (**1610**). Spenser's *The Faerie Queen,* El Greco's *St. Jerome.* Galileo's experiments with falling objects.

1598 Boris Godunov becomes Russian Czar. Tycho Brahe describes his astronomical experiments.

1600 Giordano Bruno burned as a heretic. Ieyasu rules Japan, moves capital to Edo (Tokyo). Shakespeare's *Hamlet* begins his most productive decade. English East India Company established to develop overseas trade.

1607 Jamestown, Virginia, established—first permanent English colony on American mainland.

1609 Samuel de Champlain establishes French colony of Quebec.

1611 Gustavus Adolphus elected King of Sweden. King James Version of the Bible published in England. Rubens paints his *Descent from the Cross.*

1614 John Napier discovers logarithms.

1618 Start of the Thirty Years' War (to **1648**)—Protestant revolt against Catholic oppression; Denmark, Sweden, and France will invade Germany in later phases of war. Kepler proposes his Third Law of planetary motion.

1620 Pilgrims, after three-month voyage in *Mayflower,* land at Plymouth Rock. Francis Bacon's *Novum Organum.*

1633 Inquisition forces Galileo to recant his belief in Copernican theory.

1642 English Civil War. Cavaliers, supporters of Charles I, against Roundheads, parliamentary forces. Oliver Cromwell defeats Royalists (**1646**). Parliament demands reforms. Charles I offers concessions, brought to trial (**1648**), beheaded (**1649**). Cromwell becomes Lord Protector (**1653**). Rembrandt paints his *Night Watch.*

1644 End of Ming Dynasty in China—Manchus come to power. Descartes' *Principles of Philosophy.* John Milton's *Areopagitica* on the freedom of the press.

1648 End of the Thirty Years' War. German population about half of what it was in **1618** because of war and pestilence.

1658 Cromwell dies; his son, Richard, resigns and Puritan government collapses.

1660 English Parliament calls for the restoration of the monarchy; invites Charles II to return from France.

1661 Charles II is crowned King of England. Louis XIV begins personal rule

Frans Hals, *Dutch painter* (1581–1666)
Phineas Fletcher, *English dramatist* (1582–1650)
Francis Beaumont, *English dramatist* (1584–1616)
Cardinal Richelieu, *French prelate* (1585–1642)
Thomas Hobbes, *English philosopher* (1588–1679)
John Winthrop, *first governor of Massachusetts* (1588–1649)
Robert Herrick, *English poet* (1591–1674)
Johann Amos Comenius, *Moravian educational reformer* (1592–1670)
Peter Stuyvesant, *Dutch administrator in America* (1592–1672)
George Herbert, *English poet* (1593–1633)
Izaak Walton, *English biographer* (1593–1683)
Nicola Amati, *Italian violin maker* (1594–1684)
Nicolas Poussin, *French painter* (1594–1665)
Pocahontas, *Indian princess* (1595–1617)
René Descartes, *French philosopher* (1596–1650)
Oliver Cromwell, *English general and statesman* (1599–1658)
Anthony Van Dyck, *Flemish painter* (1599–1641)
Diego Velázquez, *Spanish painter* (1599–1660)
Pedro Calderón de la Barca, *Spanish dramatist* (1600–1681)
Roger Williams, *American religious leader* (1604–1683)
Pierre Corneille, *French dramatist* (1606–1684)
Rembrandt van Rijn, *Dutch painter* (1606–1669)

THE FOUNDING OF THE AMERICAN NATION

Colonization of America begins: Jamestown, Va. **(1607)**; Pilgrims in Plymouth **(1620)**; Massachusetts Bay Colony **(1630)** New Netherland founded by Dutch West India Company **(1623)**, captured by English **(1664)**. Delaware established by Swedish trading company **(1638)**, absorbed later by Penn family. Proprietorships by royal grants to Lord Baltimore (Maryland, **1632**); Captain John Mason (New Hampshire, **1635**); Sir William Berkeley and Sir George Carteret (New Jersey, **1663**); friends of Charles II (the Carolinas, **1663**); William Penn (Pennsylvania, **1682**); James Oglethorpe and others (Georgia, **1732**).

Increasing conflict between colonists and Britain on western frontier because of royal edict limiting western expansion **(1763)**, and regulation of colonial trade and increased taxation of colonies (Writs of Assistance allow search for illegal shipments, **1761**; Sugar Act, **1764**; Currency Act, **1764**; Stamp Act, **1765**; Quartering Act, **1765**; Duty Act, **1767**.) Boston Massacre **(1770)**. Lord North attempts conciliation **(1770)**. Boston Tea Party **(1773)**, followed by punitive measures passed by Parliament—the "Intolerable Acts."

First Continental Congress **(1774)** sends "Declaration of Rights and Grievances" to king, urges colonies to form Continental Association. Paul Revere's Ride and Lexington and Concord battle between Massachusetts minutemen and British **(1775)**.

Second Continental Congress **(1775)**, while sending "olive branch" to the king, begins to raise army, appoints Washington commander-in-chief, and seeks alliance with France. Some colonial legislatures urge their delegates to vote for independence. Declaration of Independence **(July 4, 1776)**.

Major Battles of the Revolutionary War: *Long Island:* Howe defeats Putnam's division of Washington's Army in Brooklyn Heights, but Americans escape across East River **(1776)**. *Trenton and Princeton:* Washington defeats Hessians at Trenton. British at Princeton, winters at Morristown **(1776–77)**. Howe winters in Philadelphia; Washington at Valley Forge **(1777–78)**. Burgoyne surrenders British army to General Gates at *Saratoga* **(1777)**.

France recognizes American independence **(1778)**. The War moves south: Savannah captured by British **(1778)**; Charleston occupied **(1780)**; Americans fight successful guerrilla actions under Marion, Pickens, and Sumter. In the West, George Rogers Clark attacks Forts Kaskaskia and Vincennes **(1778–1779)**, defeating British in the region. Cornwallis surrenders at *Yorktown,* Virginia **(Oct. 19, 1781)**. By **1782**, Britain is eager for peace because of conflicts with European nations. *Peace of Paris* **(1783)**: Britain recognizes American independence.

as absolute monarch; starts to build Versailles.

1664 British take New Amsterdam from the Dutch. English limit "Nonconformity" with re-established Anglican Church. Isaac Newton's experiments with gravity.

1665 Great Plague in London kills 75,000.

1666 Great Fire of London. Molière's *Misanthrope.*

1683 War of European powers against the Turks (to **1699**). Vienna withstands three-month Turkish siege; high point of Turkish advance in Europe.

1685 James II succeeds Charles II in England, calls for freedom of conscience (**1687**). Protestants fear restoration of Catholicism and demand "Glorious Revolution." William of Orange invited to England and James II escapes to France (**1688**). William III and his wife, Mary, crowned. In France, Edict of Nantes of **1598,** granting freedom of worship to Huguenots (French Protestants), is revoked by Louis XIV; thousands of Protestants flee.

John Milton, *English poet* (1608–1674)
François de La Rouchefoucauld, *French author* (1613–1680)
Henry More, *English philosopher* (1614–1687)
Cyrano de Bergerac, *French poet* (1619–1655)
Andrew Marvell, *English poet* (1621–1678)
Molière (Jean-Baptiste Poquelin), *French dramatist* (1622–1673)
Blaise Pascal, *French philosopher* (1623–1662)
Robert Boyle, *English scientist* (1627–1691)
John Bunyan, *English author* (1628–1688)
John Dryden, *English dramatist* (1631–1700)
John Locke, *English philosopher* (1631–1704)
Luca Giordano, *Italian painter* (1632–1705)
Anton van Leeuwenhoek, *Dutch zoologist* (1632–1723)

Jan Vermeer, *Dutch painter* (1632–1675)
Baruch Spinoza, *Dutch philosopher* (1632–1677)
Christopher Wren, *English architect* (1632–1723)
Samuel Pepys, *English diarist* (1633–1703)
Jean Baptiste Lully, *French composer* (1639–1687)
Jean Racine, *French dramatist* (1639–1699)
Sir Isaac Newton, *English philosopher and mathematician* (1642–1727)
William Penn, *founder of Pennsylvania* (1644–1718)
Antonio Stradivari, *Italian violin maker* (1644–1737)
Gottfried W. von Leibniz, *German scientist* (1646–1716)
Arcangelo Corelli, *Italian composer* (1653–1713)
Jacques Bernoulli, *Swiss scientist* (1654–1705)

Edmund Halley, *English astronomer* (1656–1742)
Henry Purcell, *English composer* (1658–1695)
Daniel Defoe, *English author* (1659–1731)
Alessandro Scarlatti, *Italian composer* (1659–1725)
Cotton Mather, *Massachusetts churchman* (1663–1728)
François Couperin, *French composer* (1668–1733)
Giovanni Battista Vico, *Italian philosopher* (1668–1744)
William Congreve, *English dramatist* (1670–1730)
Peter the Great, *Russian czar* (1672–1725)
Antonio Vivaldi, *Italian composer* (1678–1741)

George Phillip Telemann, *German composer* (1681–1767)
Jean Philippe Rameau, *French composer* (1683–1764)
Jean Antoine Watteau, *French painter* (1684–1721)
J.S. Bach, *German composer* (1685–1750)
George Frederick Handel, *German-English composer* (1685–1759)
Domenico Scarlatti, *Italian composer* (1685–1757)
Gabriel Fahrenheit, *German physicist* (1686–1736)
Alexander Pope, *English poet* (1688–1744)
Emanuel Swedenborg, *Swedish mystic* (1688–1772)
Baron de Montesquieu, *French philosopher* (1689–1755)
François de Voltaire, *French philosopher* (1694–1778)
Canaletto (Antonio Canale), *Italian painter* (1697–1768)
William Hogarth, *English painter* (1697–1764)

1689 Peter the Great becomes Czar of Russia—attempts to westernize nation and build Russia as a military power. Defeats Charles XII of Sweden at Poltava (**1709**). Beginning of the French and Indian Wars (to **1763**), campaigns in America linked to a series of wars between France and England for domination of Europe.

1690 William III of England defeats former King James II and Irish rebels at Battle of the Boyne in Ireland. John Locke's *Human Understanding.*

1701 War of the Spanish Succession begins—the last of Louis XIV's wars for domination of the continent. The Peace of Utrecht (**1714**) will end the conflict and mark the rise of the British Empire. Called Queen Anne's War in America, it ends with the British taking New Foundland, Acadia, and Hudson's Bay Territory from France, and Gibraltar and Minorca from Spain.

1704 Deerfield (Conn.) Massacre of English colonists by French and Indians. Bach's first cantata. Jonathan Swift's *Tale of a Tub. Boston News Letter*—first newspaper in America.

1707 United Kingdom of Great Britain formed—England, Wales, and Scotland joined by parliamentary Act of Union.

1729 J. S. Bach's *St. Matthew Passion.* Isaac Newton's *Principia* translated from Latin into English.

1735 John Peter Zenger, New York editor, acquitted of libel in New York, establishing press freedom.

1740 Capt. Vitus Bering, Dane employed by Russia, discovers Alaska.

François Boucher, *French painter* (1703–1770)
Jonathan Edwards, *American theologian* (1703–1758)
John Wesley, *founder of Methodism* (1703–1791)
Benjamin Franklin, *American statesman* (1706–1790)
Henry Fielding, *English novelist* (1707–1754)
Leonhard Euler, *Swiss mathematician* (1707–1783)
Linnaeus (Carl von Linné), *Swedish botanist* (1707–1778)
Samuel Johnson, *English author* (1709–1784)
William Boyce, *English composer* (1710–1779)
Giovanni Pergolesi, *Italian composer* (1710–1736)
David Hume, *Scottish philosopher* (1711–1776)

1746 British defeat Scots under Stuart Pretender Prince Charles at Culloden Moor. Last battle fought on British soil.
1751 Publication of the *Encyclopédie* begins in France, the "bible" of the Enlightenment.
1755 Samuel Johnson's *Dictionary* first published. Great earthquake in Lisbon, Portugal—over 60,000 die.
1756 Seven Years' War (French and Indian War in America) (to **1763**), in which Britain and Prussia defeat France, Spain, Austria, and Russia. France loses North American colonies; Spain cedes Florida to Britain in exchange for Cuba. In India, over 100 British prisoners die in "Black Hole of Calcutta."
1757 Beginning of British Empire in India as Robert Clive, British commander, defeats Nawab of Bengal at Plassey.
1759 British capture Quebec from French. Voltaire's *Candide.* Haydn's *Symphony No. 1.*
1762 Catherine II ("the Great") becomes Czarina of Russia. J. J. Rousseau's *Social Contract.* Mozart tours Europe as six-year-old prodigy.
1765 James Watt invents the steam engine.
1769 Sir William Arkwright patents a spinning machine—an early step in the Industrial Revolution.
1772 Joseph Priestley and Daniel Rutherford independently discover nitrogen. Partition of Poland—in **1772, 1793,** and **1795,** Austria, Prussia, and Russia divide land and people of Poland, end its independence.
1775 The American Revolution (*see* "The Founding of the American Nation"). Priestley discovers hydrochloric and sulfuric acids.
1776 Adam Smith's *Wealth of Nations.* Edward Gibbon's *Decline and Fall of the Roman Empire.* Thomas Paine's *Common Sense.* Fragonard's *Washerwoman.* Mozart's *Haffner Serenade.*
1778 Capt. James Cook discovers Hawaii. Franz Mesmer uses hypnotism.
1781 Immanuel Kant's *Critique of Pure Reason.* Herschel discovers Uranus.
1783 End of Revolutionary War (*see* special material on "The Founding of the American Nation"). William Blake's poems. Beethoven's first printed works.
1784 Crimea annexed by Russia. John Wesley's *Deed of Declaration,* the basic work of Methodism.
1785 Russians settle Aleutian Islands.
1787 The Constitution of the United States signed. Lavoisier's work on chemical nomenclature. Mozart's *Don Giovanni.*

Jean-Jacques Rousseau, *French philosopher* (1712–1778)
Denis Diderot, *French encyclopedist* (1713–1784)
Laurance Sterne, *English novelist* (1713–1768)
K.P.E. Bach, *German composer* (1714–1788)
David Garrick, *English actor* (1717–1779)
Horace Walpole, *English statesman and novelist* (1717–1797)
Thomas Chippendale, *English artisan* (1718?–1779)
Bernardo Canaletto, *Italian painter* (1720–1780)
Giambattista Piranesi, *Italian artist* (1720–1778)
Baron von Münchhausen, *German anecdotist* (1720–1797)
Mme. de Pompadour, *French courtesan* (1721–1764)
Tobias Smollet, *English novelist* (1721–1771)
Samuel Adams, *American patriot* (1722–1803)
Joshua Reynolds, *English painter* (1723–1792)
Adam Smith, *English economist* (1723–1790)
Immanuel Kant, *German philosopher* (1724–1804)
Giovanni Casanova, *Italian adventurer* (1725–1798)
Thomas Gainsborough, *English painter* (1727–1788)
Oliver Goldsmith, *English writer* (1728–1774)
Catherine II (Catherine the Great), *Russian empress* (1729–1796)
Edmund Burke, *English statesman* (1729–1797)
William Cowper, *English poet* (1731–1800)

George Washington, *first American President* (1732–1799)
J.H. Fragonard, *French painter* (1732–1800)
Josef Haydn, *Austrian composer* (1732–1809)
Franz Anton Mesmer, *Austrian hypnotist* (1733–1815)
Joseph Priestley, *English scientist* (1733–1804)
John Adams, *American President* (1735–1826)
Daniel Boone, *American frontiersman* (1735–1820)
Patrick Henry, *American patriot* (1736–1799)
James Watt, *Scottish inventor* (1736–1819)
John S. Copley, *American painter* (1737–1815)
Edward Gibbon, *English historian* (1737–1794)

Thomas Paine, *American author and patriot* (1737–1809)
William Herschel, *English astronomer* (1738–1822)
Prince Potemkin, *Russian statesman* (1739–1791)
James Boswell, *Scottish writer* (1740–1795)
Marquis de Sade, *French libertine and writer* (1741–1814)
Benedict Arnold, *American general and traitor* (1741–1801)
Luigi Boccherini, *Italian composer* (1743–1805)
Antoine Lavoisier, *French chemist* (1743–1794)

Jean-Paul Marat, *French revolutionist* (1743–1793)
Thomas Jefferson, *American President* (1743–1826)
Jean-Baptiste de Lamark, *French scientist* (1744–1829)
Alessandro Volta, *Italian scientist* (1745–1827)
Francisco de Goya, *Spanish painter* (1746–1828)
Johann Pestalozzi, *Swiss educator* (1746–1827)
John Paul Jones, *American naval officer* (1747–1792)
Jeremy Bentham *English economist* (1748–1832)
Jacques David, *French painter* (1748–1825)
Count Casimir Pulaski, *Polish-American patriot* (1748–1779)
Johann Wolfgang von Goethe, *German writer* (1749–1832)

FRENCH REVOLUTION (1789–1799)

Revolution begins when Third Estate (Commons) delegates swear not to disband until France has a constitution. Paris mob storms Bastille, symbol of royal power **(July 14, 1789).** National Assembly votes for Constitution, Declaration of the Rights of Man, a limited monarchy, and other reforms **(1789–90).** Legislative Assembly elected, Revolutionary Commune formed, and French Republic proclaimed **(1792).** War of the First Coalition—Austria, Prussia, Britain, Netherlands, and Spain fight to restore French nobility **(1792–97).** Start of series of wars between France and European powers that will last, almost without interruption, for 23 years. Louis XVI and Marie Antoinette executed. Committee of Public Safety begins Reign of Terror as political control measure. Interfactional rivalry leads to mass killings. Danton and Robespierre executed. Third French Constitution sets up Directory government **(1795).**

1788 French *Parlement* presents grievances to Louis XVI who agrees to convening of Estates-General in **1789**—not called since **1613.** Goethe's *Egmont.* Laplace's *Laws of the Planetary System.*

1789 French Revolution (*see* special material on the "French Revolution"). In U.S., George Washington elected President with all 69 votes of the Electoral College, takes oath of office in New York City. Vice President: John Adams. Secretary of State: Thomas Jefferson. Secretary of Treasury: Alexander Hamilton.

1790 H.M.S. *Bounty* mutineers settle on Pitcairn Island. Aloisio Galvani experiments on electrical stimulation of the muscles. Philadelphia temporary capital of U.S. as Congress votes to establish new capital on Potomac. U.S. population about 3,929,000, including 698,000 slaves. Lavoisier formulates *Table of 31 chemical elements.*

1791 U.S. Bill of Rights ratified. Boswell's *Life of Johnson.*

1794 Kosciusko's uprising in Poland quelled by the Russians. In U.S., Whiskey Rebellion in Pennsylvania as farmers object to liquor taxes. U.S. Navy and Post Office Department established.

James Madison, *American President* (1751–1836)
Richard Brinsley Sheridan, *Irish dramatist* (1751–1816)
Fanny Burney, *English writer* (1752–1840)
Betsy Ross, *American flagmaker* (1752–1836)
C. de Talleyrand-Périgord, *French statesman* (1754–1838)
Marie Antoinette, *French queen* (1755–1793)
Alexander Hamilton, *American statesman* (1755–1804)
Gilbert Stuart, *American painter* (1755–1828)
Aaron Burr, *American statesman* (1756–1836)
Wolfgang Amadeus Mozart, *Austrian composer* (1756–1791)
William Blake, *English poet* (1757–1827)
Marquis de Lafayette, *French general in America* (1757–1834)

James Monroe, *American President* (1758–1831)
Horatio Nelson, *English admiral* (1758–1805)
Maximilien de Robespierre, *French revolutionist* (1758–1794)
Noah Webster, *American lexicographer* (1758–1843)
Robert Burns, *Scottish poet* (1759–1796)
Katsuhika Hokusai, *Japanese artist* (1760–1849)
Luigi Cherubini, *Italian composer* (1760–1842)
Robert Fulton, *American inventor* (1765–1815)
Eli Whitney, *American inventor* (1765–1825)
John Dalton, *English chemist* (1766–1844)
T. R. Malthus, *English economist* (1766–1834)
John Quincy Adams, *American President* (1767–1848)
Andrew Jackson, *American President* (1767–1845)

Jacques Lafitte, *French pirate* (1767–1844)
Tecumseh, *American Indian chief* (1768?–1813)
Napoleon Bonaparte, *French emperor* (1769–1821)
Duke of Wellington, *English general* (1769–1852)
Ludwig van Beethoven, *German composer* (1770–1827)
G. W. F. Hegel, *German philosopher* (1770–1831)
William Wordsworth, *English writer* (1770–1850)
Robert Owen, *English social reformer* (1771–1858)
Walter Scott, *Scottish novelist* (1771–1832)
Friedrich von Schlegel, *German philosopher* (1772–1829)

Prince K. von Metternich, *Austrian statesman* (1773–1859)
Jane Austen, *English novelist* (1775–1817)
J. W. Turner, *English painter* (1775–1851)
John Constable, *English painter* (1776–1837)
Henry Clay, *American statesman* (1777–1852)
Heinrich von Kleist, *German poet* (1777–1811)
Karl von Clausewitz, *German military strategist* (1780–1831)
J.A. Ingres, *French painter* (1780–1867)
Nicolo Paganini, *Italian composer* (1782–1840)
Daniel Webster, *American statesman* (1782–1852)
Simón Bolívar, *Latin American patriot* (1783–1830)
Washington Irving, *American writer* (1783–1859)
Stendhal (Marie Henri Beyle), *French novelist* (1783–1842)
J. J. Audubon, *American naturalist* (1785–1851)

1796 Napoleon Bonaparte, French general, defeats Austrians. In the U.S., Washington's Farewell Address (**Sept. 17**); John Adams elected President; Thomas Jefferson, Vice President. Edward Jenner introduces smallpox vaccination.

1798 Napoleon extends French conquests to Rome and Egypt.

1799 Napoleon leads coup that overthrows Directory, becomes First Consul—one of three who rule France.

1800 Napoleon conquers Italy, firmly establishes himself as First Consul in France. In the U.S., Federal Government moves to Washington. Robert Owen's social reforms in England. William Herschel discovers infrared rays. Alessandro Volta produces electricity.

1801 Austria makes temporary peace with France. United Kingdom of Great Britain and Ireland established with one monarch and one parliament; Catholics excluded from voting.

1803 U.S. negotiates Louisiana Purchase from France: For $15 million, U.S. doubles its domain, increasing its territory by 827,000 sq. mi. (2,144,500 sq km), from Mississippi River to Rockies and from Gulf of Mexico to British North America.

1804 Haiti declares independence from France; first black nation to gain freedom from European colonial rule. Napoleon proclaims himself emperor of France, systematizes French law under *Code Napoleon.* In the U.S.,

Davy Crockett, *American frontiersman* (1786–1836)
Carl Maria von Weber, *German composer* (1786–1826)
Louis Daguerre, *French photographic pioneer* (1787–1851)
Lord Byron, *English poet* (1788–1824)
Arthur Schopenhauer, *German philosopher* (1788–1860)
James Fenimore Cooper, *American writer* (1789–1851)
Michael Faraday, *English physicist* (1791–1867)
Samuel F. B. Morse, *American inventor* (1791–1872)

Alexander Hamilton is mortally wounded in duel with Aaron Burr. Lewis and Clark expedition begins exploration of what is now northwestern U.S.

1805 Lord Nelson defeats the French-Spanish fleets in the Battle of Trafalgar. Napoleon victorious over Austrian and Russian forces at the Battle of Austerlitz.

1807 Robert Fulton makes first successful steamboat trip on *Clermont* between New York City and Albany.

1808 French armies occupy Rome and Spain, extending Napoleon's empire. Britain begins aiding Spanish guerrillas against Napoleon in Peninsular War. In the U.S., Congress bars importation of slaves. Beethoven's *Fifth* and *Sixth Symphonies* performed.

1812 Napoleon's Grand Army invades Russia in June. Forced to retreat in winter, most of Napoleon's 600,000 men are lost. In the U.S., war with Britain declared over freedom of the seas for U.S. vessels. U.S.S. *Constitution* sinks British frigate. (*See* special material on the "War of 1812.")

1814 French defeated by allies (Britain, Austria, Russia, Prussia, Sweden, and Portugal) in War of Liberation. Napoleon exiled to Elba, off Italian coast. Bourbon King Louis XVIII takes French throne. George Stephenson builds first practical steam locomotive.

1815 Napoleon returns: "Hundred Days" begin. Napoleon defeated by Wellington at Waterloo, banished again to St. Helena in South Atlantic. Congress of Vienna: victorious allies change the map of Europe.

1817 Simón Bolívar establishes independent Venezuela, as Spain loses hold on South American countries. Bolívar named President of Colombia (**1819**). Peru, Guatemala, Panama, and Santo Domingo proclaim independence from Spain (**1821**).

1820 Missouri Compromise—Missouri admitted as slave state but slavery barred in rest of Louisiana Purchase north of 36°30′ N.

1822 Greeks proclaim a republic and independence from Turkey. Turks invade Greece. Russia declares war on Turkey (**1828**). Greece also aided by France and Britain. War ends and Turks recognize Greek independence (**1829**). Brazil becomes independent of Portugal. Schubert's *Eighth Symphony* ("The Unfinished").

1823 U.S. Monroe Doctrine warns European nations not to interfere in Western Hemisphere.

1824 Mexico becomes a republic, three years after declaring independence from Spain. Beethoven's *Ninth Symphony.*

1825 First passenger-carrying railroad in England.

1830 French invade Algeria. Louis Philippe becomes "Citizen King" as revolution forces Charles X to abdicate. Mormon church formed in U.S. by Joseph Smith.

1831 Polish revolt against Russia fails. Belgium separates from the Netherlands. In U.S., Nat Turner leads unsuccessful slave rebellion.

1833 Slavery abolished in British Empire.

1834 Charles Babbage invents "analytical engine," precursor of computer. McCormick patents reaper.

1836 Boer farmers start "Great Trek"—Natal, Transvaal, and Orange Free State founded in South Africa. Mexican army besieges Texans in Alamo. Entire garrison, including Davy Crockett and Jim Bowie, wiped out. Texans gain independence from Mexico after winning Battle of San Jacinto. Dicken's *Pickwick Papers.*

1837 Victoria becomes Queen of Great Britain. Mob kills Elijah P. Lovejoy, Illinois abolitionist publisher.

1839 First Opium War (to **1842**) between Britain and China, over importation of drug into China.

1840 Lower and Upper Canada united.

1841 U.S. President Harrison dies (**April 4**) one month after inauguration; John Tyler becomes first Vice President to succeed to Presidency.

1844 Democratic convention calls for annexation of Texas and acquisition of Oregon ("Fifty-four-forty-or-fight"). Five Chinese ports opened to U.S. ships. Samuel F. B. Morse patents telegraph.

1845 Congress adopts joint resolution for annexation of Texas.

1846 Failure of potato crop causes famine in Ireland. U.S. declares war on Mexico. California and New Mexico annexed by U.S. Brigham Young leads Mormons to Great Salt Lake. W.T. Morton uses ether as anesthetic. Sewing machine patented by Elias Howe.

Percy Bysshe Shelley, *English poet* (1792–1822)
Gioacchino Rossini, *Italian composer* (1792–1868)
Sam Houston, *Texas political leader* (1793–1863)
John Keats, *English poet* (1795–1821)
Thomas Carlyle, *British historian* (1795–1881)
Heinrich Heine, *German poet* (1797–1856)
Ando Hiroshige, *Japanese painter* (1797–1858)
Franz Schubert, *Austrian composer* (1797–1828)
Adam Mickiewicz, *Polish poet* (1798–1855)
Auguste Comte, *French philosopher* (1798–1857)
Ferdinand Delacroix, *French painter* (1798–1863)
Honoré de Balzac, *French novelist* (1799–1850)
Aleksander Pushkin, *Russian poet* (1799–1837)
John Henry Newman, *English prelate* (1801–1890)
Brigham Young, *Mormon leader* (1801–1877)
Lajos Kossuth, *Hungarian patriot* (1802–1894)
Alexander Dumas, père, *French novelist* (1802–1870)
Victor Hugo, *French novelist* (1802–1885)
Ralph Waldo Emerson, *American philosopher* (1803–1882)
Hector Berlioz, *French composer* (1803–1869)
Benjamin Disraeli, *British statesman* (1804–1881)
Nathaniel Hawthorne, *American novelist* (1804–1864)
George Sand, *French writer* (1804–1876)
Giuseppe Mazzini, *Italian patriot* (1805–1872)
Hans Christian Andersen, *Danish writer* (1805–1875)
Alexis de Tocqueville, *French writer* (1805–1859)
Elizabeth Barrett Browning, *English poet* (1806–1861)
John Stuart Mill, *English philosopher* (1806–1873)
Giuseppe Garibaldi, *Italian patriot* (1807–1882)
Henry Wadsworth Longfellow, *American poet* (1807–1882)
Honoré Daumier, *French artist* (1808–1879)

WAR OF 1812

British interference with American trade, impressment of American seamen, and "War Hawks" drive for western expansion lead to war. American attacks on Canada foiled; U.S. Commodore Perry wins battle of Lake Erie (**1813**). British capture and burn Washington (**1814**) but fail to take Fort McHenry at Baltimore. Andrew Jackson repulses assault on New Orleans after treaty of Ghent ends war (**1815**). War settles little but strengthens U.S. as independent nation.

1848 Revolt in Paris: Louis Philippe abdicates; Louis Napoleon elected President of French Republic. Revolutions in Vienna, Venice, Berlin, Milan, Rome, and Warsaw. Put down by royal troops in **1848–49.** U.S.-Mexico War ends; Mexico cedes claims to Texas, California, Arizona, New Mexico, Utah, Nevada. U.S. treaty with Britain sets Oregon Territory boundary at 49th parallel. Karl Marx and Friedrich Engels' *Communist Manifesto.*
1849 California gold rush begins.
1850 Henry Clay opens great debate on slavery, warns South against secession.
1851 Herman Melville's *Moby Dick.* Harriet Beecher Stowe's *Uncle Tom's Cabin.*
1852 South African Republic established. Louis Napoleon proclaims himself Napoleon III ("Second Empire").
1853 Crimean War begins as Turkey declares war on Russia. Commodore Perry reaches Tokyo.
1854 Britain and France join Turkey in war on Russia. In U.S., Kansas-Nebraska Act permits local option on slavery; rioting and bloodshed. Japanese allow American trade. Antislavery men in Michigan form Republican Party. Tennyson's *Charge of the Light Brigade.* Thoreau's *Walden.*
1855 Armed clashes in Kansas between pro- and anti-slavery forces. Florence Nightingale nurses wounded in Crimea. Walt Whitman's *Leaves of Grass.*
1856 Flaubert's *Madame Bovary.*
1857 Supreme Court, in Dred Scott decision, rules that a slave is not a citizen. Financial crisis in Europe and U.S. Great Mutiny (Sepoy Rebellion) begins in India. India placed under crown rule as a result.
1858 Pro-slavery constitution rejected in Kansas. Abraham Lincoln makes strong antislavery speech in Springfield, Ill.: ". . . this Government cannot endure permanently half slave and half free." Lincoln-Douglas debates. First trans-Atlantic telegraph cable completed by Cyrus W. Field.
1859 John Brown raids Harpers Ferry; is captured and hanged. Work begins on Suez Canal. Unification of Italy starts under leadership of Count Cavour, Sardinian premier. Joined by France in war against Austria. Edward Fitzgerald's *Rubaiyat of Omar Khayyam.* Charles Darwin's *Origin of Species.* J. S. Mill's *On Liberty*
1861 U.S. Civil War begins as attempts at compromise fail (*see* special material on "The Civil War"). Congress creates Colorado, Dakota, and Nevada territories; adopts income tax; Lincoln inaugurated. Serfs emancipated in Russia. Pasteur's theory of germs. Independent Kingdom of Italy proclaimed under Sardinian King Victor Emmanuel II.
1863 French capture Mexico City; proclaim Archduke Maximilian of Austria emperor.
1865 Lincoln fatally shot at Ford's Theater by John Wilkes Booth. Vice President Johnson sworn as successor. Booth caught and dies of gunshot wounds; four conspirators are hanged. Joseph Lister begins antiseptic surgery. Gregor Mendel's Law of Heredity. Lewis Carroll's *Alice's Adventures in Wonderland.*
1866 Alfred Nobel invents dynamite. Seven Weeks' War: Austria defeated by

Abraham Lincoln, *American president* (1809–1865)
Nicolai Gogol, *Russian writer* (1809–1852)
Edgar Allan Poe, *American writer* (1809–1849)
Alfred, Lord Tennyson, *English poet* (1809–1892)
William Ewart Gladstone, *British statesman* (1809–1898)
Charles Darwin, *English scientist* (1809–1882)
Felix Mendelssohn, *German composer* (1809–1847)
Louis Braille, *French inventor of touch alphabet for blind* (1809–1852)
Frédéric Chopin, *Polish composer* (1810–1849)
Robert Schumann, *German composer* (1810–1856)
Phineas T. Barnum, *American showman* (1810–1891)
Harriet Beecher Stowe, *American writer* (1811–1896)
William M. Thackeray, *English novelist* (1811–1863)
Franz Liszt, *Hungarian composer* (1811–1896)
Robert Browning, *English poet* (1812–1889)
Charles Dickens, *English novelist* (1812–1870)
Alfred Krupp, *German munitions magnate* (1812–1887)
Sören Kierkegaard, *Danish philosopher* (1813–1855)
Giuseppe Verdi, *Italian composer* (1813–1901)
Richard Wagner, *German composer* (1813–1883)
Otto von Bismarck, *Prussian statesman* (1815–1898)
Charlotte Brontë, *English writer* (1816–1855)

THE CIVIL WAR
(The War Between the States or the War of the Rebellion)

Apart from the matter of slavery, the Civil War arose out of both the economic and political rivalry between an agrarian South and an industrial North and the issue of the right of states to secede from the Union.

1861 After South Carolina secedes **(Dec. 20, 1860),** Mississippi, Florida, Alabama, Georgia, Louisiana, and Texas follow, forming the Confederate States of America, with Jefferson Davis as president **(Jan.-March).** War begins as Confederates fire on Fort Sumter **(April 12).** Lincoln calls for 75,000 volunteers. Southern ports blockaded by superior Union naval forces. Virginia, Arkansas, Tennessee, and North Carolina secede to complete 11-state Confederacy. Union army advancing on Richmond repulsed at first Battle of Bull Run **(July).**

1862 Edwin M. Stanton named Secretary of War **(Jan.).** Grant wins first important Union victory in West, at Fort Donelson; Nashville falls **(Feb.).** Ironclads, Union's *Monitor* and Confederate's *Virginia (Merrimac)* duel at Hampton Roads **(March).** New Orleans falls to Union fleet under Farragut; city occupied **(April).** Grant's army escapes defeat at Shiloh. Memphis falls as Union gunboats control upper Mississippi **(June).** Confederate general Robert E. Lee victorious at second Battle of Bull Run **(Aug.).** Union army under McClellan halts Lee's attack on Washington in the Battle Antietam **(Sept.).** Lincoln removes McClellan for lack of aggressiveness. Burnside's drive on Richmond fails at Fredericksburg **(Dec.).** Union forces under Rosecrans chase Bragg through Tennessee; battle of Murfreesboro **(Oct.-Jan. 1863).**

1863 Lee defeats Hooker at Chancellorsville; "Stonewall" Jackson, Confederate general, dies **(May).** Confederate invasion of Pennsylvania stopped at Gettysburg by George Meade—Lee loses 20,000 men—the greatest battle of the War **(July).** It and the Union victory at Vicksburg mark the war's turning point. Union general George H. Thomas, the "Rock of Chickamauga," holds Bragg's forces on Georgia-Tennessee border **(Sept.).** Sherman, Hooker, and Thomas drive Bragg back to Georgia. Tennessee restored to the Union **(Nov.).**

1864 Ulysses S. Grant named commander-in-chief of Union forces **(March).** In the Wilderness campaign, Grant forces Lee's Army of Northern Virginia back toward Richmond **(May-June).** Sherman's Atlanta campaign and "march to the sea" **(May-Sept.).** Farragut's victory at Mobile Bay **(Aug.).** Hood's Confederate army defeated at Nashville. Sherman takes Savannah **(Dec.).**

1865 Sheridan defeats Confederates at Five Forks; Confederates evacuate Richmond **(April).** On **April 9,** Lee surrenders to Grant at Appomattox.

Prussia and Italy.

1867 Austria-Hungary Dual Monarchy established. French leave Mexico; Maximilian executed. Dominion of Canada established. U.S. buys Alaska from Russia for $7,200,000. South African diamond field discovered. Volume I of Marx's *Das Kapital.* Strauss's *Blue Danube.*

1868 Revolution in Spain; Queen Isabella deposed, flees to France. In U.S., Fourteenth Amendment giving civil rights to blacks is ratified. Georgia under military government after legislature expels blacks.

1869 First U.S. transcontinental rail route completed. James Fisk and Jay Gould attempt to control gold market causes Black Friday panic. Suez Canal opened. Mendeleev's periodic table of elements.

1870 Franco-Prussian War (to **1871**): Napoleon III capitulates at Sedan. Revolt in Paris; Third Republic proclaimed.

1871 France surrenders Alsace-Lorraine to Germany; war ends. German Empire proclaimed with Prussian King as Kaiser Wilhelm I. Fighting with Apaches begins in American West. Boss Tweed corruption exposed in New York. The Chicago Fire, with 250 deaths and $196-million damage. Stanley meets Livingston in Africa.

1872 Congress gives amnesty to most Confederates. Jules Verne's *Around the World in 80 Days.*

1873 Economic crisis in Europe. U.S. establishes gold standard.

1875 First Kentucky Derby.

1876 Sioux kill Gen. George A. Custer and 264 troopers at Little Big Horn River. Alexander Graham Bell patents the telephone.

1877 After Presidential election of **1876**, Electoral Commission gives disputed Electoral College votes to Rutherford B. Hayes despite Tilden's popular majority. Russo-Turkish war (ends in **1878** with power of Turkey in Europe broken). Reconstruction ends in the American South. Thomas Edison patents phonograph.

1878 Congress of Berlin revises Treaty of San Stefano ending Russo-Turkish War; makes extensive redivision of southeastern Europe. First commercial telephone exchange opened in New Haven, Conn.

1880 U.S.-China treaty allows U.S. to restrict immigration of Chinese labor.

1881 President Garfield fatally shot by assassin; Vice President Arthur succeeds him. Charles J. Guiteau convicted and executed (in **1882**).

1882 Terrorism in Ireland after land evictions. Britain invades and conquers Egypt. Germany, Austria, and Italy form Triple Alliance. In U.S., Congress adopts Chinese Exclusion Act. Rockefeller's Standard Oil Trust is first industrial monopoly. In Berlin, Robert Koch announces discovery of tuberculosis germ.

1883 Congress creates Civil Service Commission. Brooklyn Bridge and Metropolitan Opera House completed.

1885 British Gen. Charles G. "Chinese" Gordon killed at Khartoum in Egyptian Sudan.

1886 Bombing at Haymarket Square, Chicago, kills seven policemen and injures many others. Eight alleged anarchists accused—three imprisoned, one commits suicide, four hanged. (In **1893**, Illinois Governor Altgeld, critical of trial, pardons three survivors.) Statue of Liberty dedicated. Geronimo, Apache Indian chief, surrenders.

1887 Queen Victoria's Golden Jubilee. Sir Arthur Conan Doyle's first Sherlock Holmes story, "A Study in Scarlet."

1888 Historic March blizzard in Northeast U.S.—many perish, property damage exceeds $25 million. George Eastman's box camera (the Kodak). J.B. Dunlop invents pneumatic tire. Jack the Ripper murders in London.

1889 Second (Socialist) International founded in Paris. Indian Territory in Oklahoma opened to settlement. Thousands die in Johnstown, Pa., flood. Mark Twain's *A Connecticut Yankee in King Arthur's Court.*

1890 Congress votes Sherman Antitrust Act. Sitting Bull killed in Sioux uprising.

1892 Battle between steel strikers and Pinkerton guards at Homestead, Pa.; union defeated after militia intervenes. Silver mine strikers in Idaho fight non-union workers; U.S. troops dispatched. Diesel engine patented.

1894 Sino-Japanese War begins (ends in **1895** with China's defeat). In France,

Henry David Thoreau, *American writer* (1817–1862)
Ivan Turgenev, *Russian writer* (1818–1883)
Karl Marx, *German political philosopher* (1818–1883)
Queen Victoria, *British monarch* (1819–1901)
George Eliot, *English novelist* (1819–1880)
Walt Whitman, *American poet* (1819–1892)
Friedrich Engels, *German political philosopher* (1820–1895)
Florence Nightingale, *English nurse* (1820–1910)
Charles Baudelaire, *French poet* (1821–1867)
Feodor Dostoevsky, *Russian writer* (1821–1881)
Gustave Flaubert, *French novelist* (1821–1880)
Mary Baker Eddy, *founder of Christian Science* (1821–1910)
Ulysses S. Grant, *American President* (1822–1885)
Gregor Mendel, *Austrian scientist* (1822–1884)
Louis Pasteur, *French scientist* (1822–1895)
Alexandre Dumas, fils, *French writer* (1824–1895)
Johann Strauss, *Austrian "waltz king"* (1825–1899)
Stephen Foster, *American composer* (1826–1864)
Joseph Lister, *English surgeon* (1827–1912)
Henrik Ibsen, *Norwegian dramatist* (1828–1906)
Leo Tolstoi, *Russian novelist* (1828–1910)
Jules Verne, *French author* (1828–1905)
William Booth, *Salvation Army founder* (1829–1912)
Emily Dickinson, *American poet* (1830–1886)
James Clerk Maxwell, *Scottish astronomer and physicist* (1831–1879)
Louisa May Alcott, *American author* (1832–1888)
Horatio Alger, *American author* (1834–1899)
Lewis Carroll (Charles Lutwidge Dodgson), *English author* (1832–1898)

SPANISH-AMERICAN WAR (1898–1899)

War fires stoked by "jingo journalism" as American people support Cuban rebels against Spain. American business sees economic gain in Cuban trade and resources and American power zones in Latin America. Outstanding events: Submarine mine explodes U.S. battleship *Maine* in Havana Harbor **(Feb. 15)**; 260 killed; responsibility never fixed. Congress declares independence of Cuba **(April 19)**. Spain declares war on U.S. **(Apr. 24)**; Congress **(Apr. 25)** formally declares nation has been at war with Spain since Apr. 21. Commodore George Dewey wins seven-hour battle of Manila Bay **(May 1)**. Spanish fleet destroyed off Santiago, Cuba **(July 3)**; city surrenders **(July 17)**. Treaty of Paris (ratified by Senate **1899**) ends war. U.S. given Guam and Puerto Rico and agrees to pay Spain $20 million for Philippines. Cuba independent of Spain; under U.S. military control for three years until **May 20, 1902**. Yellow fever is eradicated and political reforms achieved.

Capt. Alfred Dreyfus convicted on false treason charge (pardoned in **1906**). In U.S., Jacob S. Coxey of Ohio leads "Coxey's Army" of unemployed on Washington. Eugene V. Debs calls general strike of rail workers to support Pullman Company strikers; strike broken, Debs jailed for six months. Thomas A. Edison's kinetoscope given first public showing in New York City.

1895 X-rays discovered by German physicist, Wilhelm Roentgen.

1896 Supreme Court's *Plessy v. Ferguson* decision—"separate but equal" doctrine. Alfred Nobel's will establishes prizes for peace, science, and literature. Marconi receives first wireless patent in Britain. William Jennings Bryan delivers "Cross of Gold" speech at Democratic Convention in Chicago. First modern Olympic games held in Athens, Greece.

1898 Chinese "Boxers," anti-foreign organization, established. They stage uprisings against Europeans in **1900;** U.S. and other Western troops relieve Peking legations. Spanish-American War (*see* special material on the "Spanish-American War"). Pierre and Marie Curie discover radium and polonium.

1899 Boer War (or South African War). Conflict between British and Boers (descendants of Dutch settlers of South Africa). Causes rooted in long-standing territorial disputes and in friction over political rights for English and other "uitlanders" following 1886 discovery of vast gold deposits in Transvaal. (British victorious as war ends in **1902.**) Casualties: 5,774 British dead, about 4,000 Boers. Union of South Africa established in **1908** as confederation of colonies; becomes British dominion in **1910.**

1900 Hurricane ravages Galveston, Tex.; 6,000 drown. Sigmund Freud's *The Interpretation of Dreams.*

1901 Queen Victoria dies; succeeded by son, Edward VII. As President McKinley begins second term, he is shot fatally by anarchist Leon Czolgosz. Theodore Roosevelt sworn in as successor.

1902 Enrico Caruso's first gramophone recording.

1903 Wright brothers, Orville and Wilbur, fly first powered, controlled, heavier-than-air plane at Kitty Hawk, N.C. Henry Ford organizes Ford Motor Company.

1904 Russo-Japanese War—competition for Korea and Manchuria: In **1905,** Port Arthur surrenders to Japanese and Russia suffers other defeats; President Roosevelt mediates Treaty of Portsmouth, N.H., ending war with concessions for Japan. *Entente Cordiale:* Britain and France settle their international differences. General theory of radioactivity by Rutherford and Soddy. New York City subway opened.

1905 General strike in Russia; first workers' soviet set up in St. Petersburg. Sailors on battleship *Potemkin* mutiny; reforms including first Duma (parliament) established by Czar's "October Manifesto." Albert Einstein's special theory of relativity and other key theories in physics. Franz Lehar's *Merry Widow.*

1906 San Francisco earthquake and three-day fire; 500 dead. Roald Amundsen, Norwegian explorer, fixes magnetic North Pole.

1907 Second Hague Peace Conference, of 46 nations, adopts 10 conventions on rules of war. Financial panic of **1907** in U.S.

1908 Earthquake kills 150,000 in southern Italy and Sicily. U.S. Supreme Court, in Danbury Hatters' case, outlaws secondary union boycotts.

1909 North Pole reached by American explorers Robert E. Peary and Matthew Henson.

1910 Boy Scouts of America incorporated.

1911 First use of aircraft as offensive weapon in Turkish-Italian War. Italy defeats Turks and annexes Tripoli and Libya. Chinese Republic proclaimed after revolution overthrows Manchu dynasty. Sun Yat-sen named president. Mexican Revolution: Porfirio Diaz, president since 1877, replaced by Francisco Madero. Triangle Shirtwaist Company fire in New York; 145 killed. Richard Strauss's *Der Rosenkavalier.* Irving Berlin's *Alexander's Ragtime Band.* Amundsen reaches South Pole.

1912 Balkan Wars (**1912–13**) resulting from territorial disputes: Turkey defeated by alliance of Bulgaria, Serbia, Greece, and Montenegro; London peace treaty (**1913**) partitions most of European Turkey among the victors. In second war (**1913**), Bulgaria attacks Serbia and Greece and is defeated after Romania intervenes and Turks recapture Adrianople. *Titanic* sinks on maiden voyage; over 1,500 drown.

1913 Suffragettes demonstrate in London. Garment workers strike in New York and Boston; win pay raise and shorter hours. Sixteenth Amendment (income tax) and 17th (popular election of U.S. senators) adopted. Bill creating U.S. Federal Reserve System becomes law. Stravinsky's *The Rite of Spring.*

Edouard Manet, *French painter* (1832-1883)
Johannes Brahms, *German composer* (1833-1897)
Alfred Nobel, *Swedish industrialist* (1833-1896)
Edgar Dégas, *French painter* (1834-1917)
James McNeill Whistler, *American painter* (1834-1903)
Dmitri Mendeleev, *Russian chemist* (1834-1907)
Mark Twain (Samuel L. Clemens), *American author* (1835-1910)
Camille Saint-Saëns, *French composer* (1835-1910)
Andrew Carnegie, *American industrialist* (1835-1919)
W. S. Gilbert, *English librettist* (1836-1911)
Bret Harte, *American novelist* (1836-1902)
Winslow Homer, *American painter* (1836-1910)
Sitting Bull, *American Indian chief* (1837-1890)
J. P. Morgan, *American financier* (1837-1913)
Georges Bizet, *French composer* (1838-1875)
Paul Cézanne, *French painter* (1839-1906)
John D. Rockefeller, *American industrialist* (1839-1937)
Thomas Hardy, *English novelist* (1840-1928)
Emile Zola, *French novelist* (1840-1902)
Claude Monet, *French painter* (1840-1926)
Pierre Renoir, *French painter* (1840-1919)
Auguste Rodin, *French sculptor* (1840-1917)
Peter Ilich Tchaikovsky, *Russian composer* (1840-1893)
Ambrose Bierce, *American author* (1842-1914)
William James, *American philosopher* (1842-1910)
Arthur Sullivan, *English composer* (1842-1900)
Henry James, *American novelist* (1843-1916)
Edvard Grieg, *Norwegian composer* (1843-1907)
Sarah Bernhardt, *French actress* (1844-1923)
Anatole France (Jacques Anatole Thibault), *French author* (1844-1924)
Gerard Manley Hopkins, *English poet* (1844-1899)
Friedrich Nietzsche, *German philosopher* (1844-1900)
Nikolai Rimski-Korsakov, *Russian composer* (1844-1908)

1914 World War I begins (*see* special material on "World War I"). Panama Canal officially opened. Congress sets up Federal Trade Commission, passes Clayton Antitrust Act. U.S. Marines occupy Veracruz, Mexico, intervening in civil war to protect American interests.

1915 U.S. protests German submarine actions and British blockade of Germany. U.S. banks lend $500 million to France and Britain. D. W. Griffith's film *Birth of a Nation*. Albert Einstein's *General Theory of Relativity*.

1916 Congress expands armed forces. Tom Mooney arrested for San Francisco bombing (pardoned in **1939**). Pershing fails in raid into Mexico in quest of rebel Pancho Villa. U.S. buys Virgin Islands from Denmark for $25 million. President Wilson re-elected with "he kept us out of war" slogan. "Black Tom" explosion at munitions dock in Jersey City, N.Y., $40,000,000 damages; traced to German saboteurs. Margaret Sanger opens first birth control clinic. Easter Rebellion in Ireland put down by British troops.

1917 First U.S. combat troops in France as U.S. declares war (**April 6**). Russian Revolution—climax of long unrest under czars. February Revolution—Czar forced to abdicate, liberal government created. Kerensky becomes prime minister and forms provisional government (**July**). In October Revolution, Bolsheviks seize power in armed coup d'état led by Lenin and Trotsky. Kerensky flees. Revolutionaries execute the czar and his family (**1918**). Reds set up Third International in Moscow (**1919**). Balfour Declaration promises Jewish homeland in Palestine. Sigmund Freud's *Introduction to Psychoanalysis*.

1918 Russian Civil War between Reds (Bolsheviks) and Whites (anti-Bolsheviks); Reds win in **1920**. Allied troops (U.S., British, French) intervene (**March**); leave in **1919**. Japanese hold Vladivostok until **1922**. World-wide influenza epidemic strikes; by **1920**, nearly 20 million are dead. In U.S. alone, 500,000 perish.

1919 Third International (Comintern) establishes Soviet control over international Communist movements. Paris peace conference. Versailles Treaty, incorporating Wilson's draft Covenant of League of Nations, signed by Allies and Germany; rejected by U.S. Senate. Congress formally ends war in **1921**. Eighteenth (Prohibition) Amendment adopted. Alcock and Brown make first trans-Atlantic non-stop flight.

1920 League of Nations holds first meeting at Geneva, Switzerland. U.S. Dept. of Justice "red hunt" nets thousands of radicals; aliens deported. Women's suffrage (19th) amendment ratified. First Agatha Christie mystery. Sinclair Lewis's *Main Street*.

1921 Reparations Commission fixes German liability at 132 billion gold marks. German inflation begins. Major treaties signed at Washington Disarmament Conference limit naval tonnage and pledge to respect territorial integrity of China. Irish Free State formed in southern Ireland as self-governing dominion of British Empire. In U.S., Nicola Sacco and Bartolomeo Vanzetti, Italian-born anarchists, convicted of armed robbery murder; case stirs world-wide protests; they are executed in **1927**.

1922 Mussolini marches on Rome; forms Fascist government. Irish Free State officially proclaimed.

Wilhelm Conrad Roentgen, *German discoverer of X-rays* (1845–1923)
Gabriel Fauré, *French composer* (1845–1924)
Thomas Alva Edison, *American inventor* (1847–1931)
Alexander Graham Bell, *American inventor* (1847–1922)
Paul Gauguin, *French painter* (1848–1903)
August Strindberg, *Swedish dramatist* (1849–1912)
Luther Burbank, *American horticulturist* (1849–1926)
Guy de Maupassant, *French author* (1850–1893)
Robert Louis Stevenson, *English author* (1850–1894)
Vincent van Gogh, *Dutch painter* (1853–1890)
George Eastman, *American photographic pioneer* (1854–1932)
George Bernard Shaw, *Irish dramatist* (1856–1950)
Oscar Wilde, *Anglo-Irish author* (1856–1900)
Sigmund Freud, *Austrian founder of psychoanalysis* (1856–1939)
Robert E. Peary, *American explorer* (1856–1920)
Booker T. Washington, *American educator* (1856–1915)
Joseph Conrad, *Anglo-Polish novelist* (1857–1924)
Giacomo Puccini, *Italian composer* (1858–1924)
Theodore Roosevelt, *American President* (1858–1919)
Max Planck, *German physicist* (1858–1947)

WORLD WAR I (1914–1918)

Imperial, territorial, and economic rivalries lead to the "Great War" between the Central Powers (Austria-Hungary, Germany, Bulgaria, and Turkey) and the Allies (U.S., Britain, France, Russia, Belgium, Serbia, Greece, Romania, Montenegro, Portugal, Italy, Japan). About 10 million combatants killed, 20 million wounded.

1914 Austrian Archduke Francis Ferdinand and wife assassinated in Sarajevo by Serbian nationalist, Gavrilo Princip **(June 28)**. Austria declares war on Serbia **(July 28)**. Germany declares war on Russia **(Aug. 1)**, on France **(Aug. 3)**, invades Belgium **(Aug. 4)**. Britain declares war on Germany **(Aug. 4)**. Germans defeat Russians in Battle of Tannenberg on Eastern Front **(Aug.)**. First Battle of the Marne **(Sept.)**. German drive stopped 25 miles from Paris. By end of year, war on the Western Front is "positional" in the trenches.

1915 German submarine blockade of Great Britain begins **(Feb.)**. Dardanelles Campaign—British land in Turkey **(April)**, withdraw from Gallipoli **(Dec. to Jan. 1916)**. Germans use gas at second Battle of Ypres **(April–May)**. *Lusitania* sunk by German submarine—1,198 lost, including 128 Americans **(May 7)**. On Eastern Front, German and Austrian "great offensive" conquers all of Poland and Lithuania; Russians lose 1 million men (by **Sept. 6**). "Great Fall Offensive" by Allies results in little change from 1914 **(Sept.–Oct.)**. Britain and France declare war on Bulgaria **(Oct. 14)**.

1916 Battle of Verdun—Germans and French each lose about 350,000 men **(Feb.)**. Extended submarine warfare begins **(March)**. British-German sea battle of Jutland **(May)**; British lose more ships, but German fleet never ventures forth again. On Eastern front, the Brusilov offensive demoralizes Russians, costs them 1 million men **(June–Sept.)**. Battle of the Somme—British lose over 400,000; French, 200,000; Germans, about 450,000; all with no strategic results **(July–Nov.)**. Romania declares war on Austria-Hungary **(Aug. 27)**. Bucharest captured **(Dec.)**.

1917 U.S. declares war on Germany **(April 6)**. Submarine warfare at peak **(April)**. On Italian Front, Battle of Caporetto—Italians retreat, losing 600,000 prisoners and deserters **(Oct.–Dec.)**. On Western Front, Battles of Arras, Champagne, Ypres (third battle), etc. First large British tank attack **(Nov.)**. U.S. declares war on Austria-Hungary **(Dec. 7)**. Armistice between new Russian Bolshevik government and Germans **(Dec. 15)**.

1918 Great offensive by Germans **(March–June)**. Americans' first important battle role at Château-Thierry—as they and French stop German advance **(June)**. Second Battle of the Marne **(July–Aug.)**—start of Allied offensive at Amiens, St. Mihiel, etc. Battles of the Argonne and Ypres panic German leadership **(Sept.–Oct.)**. British offensive in Palestine **(Sept.)**. Germans ask for armistice **(Oct. 4)**. British armistice with Turkey **(Oct.)**. German Kaiser abdicates **(Nov.)**. Hostilities cease on Western Front **(Nov. 11)**.

1923 Adolf Hitler's "Beer Hall Putsch" in Munich fails; in **1924** he is sentenced to five years in prison where he writes *Mein Kampf;* released after eight months. Occupation of Ruhr by French and Belgian troops to enforce reparations payments. Widespread Ku Klux Klan violence in U.S. George Gershwin's *Rhapsody in Blue.*

1924 Death of Lenin; Stalin wins power struggle, rules as Soviet dictator until death in **1953.** Italian Fascists murder Socialist leader Giacomo Matteotti. Interior Secretary Albert B. Fall and oilmen Harry Sinclair and Edward L. Doheny are charged with conspiracy and bribery in the Teapot Dome scandal, involving fraudulent leases of naval oil reserves. In **1931,** Fall is sentenced to year in prison; Doheny and Sinclair acquitted of bribery. Nathan Leopold and Richard Loeb convicted in "thrill killing" of Bobby Franks in Chicago; defended by Clarence Darrow; sentenced to life imprisonment. (Loeb killed by fellow convict in **1936;** Leopold paroled in **1958,** dies in **1971.**)

1925 Nellie Tayloe Ross elected governor of Wyoming; first woman governor elected in U.S. Locarno conferences seek to secure European peace by mutual guarantees. John T. Scopes convicted and fined for teaching evolution in a public school in Tennessee "Monkey Trial"; sentence set aside. John Logie Baird, Scottish inventor, transmits human features by television. Adolf Hitler publishes Volume I of *Mein Kampf.*

1926 General strike in Britain brings nation's activities to standstill. U.S. marines dispatched to Nicaragua during revolt; they remain until **1933.** Gertrude Ederle of U.S. is first woman to swim English Channel.

1927 German economy collapses. Socialists riot in Vienna; general strike follows acquittal of Nazis for political murder. Trotsky expelled from Russian Communist Party. Charles A. Lindbergh flies first successful solo non-stop flight from New York to Paris. Ruth Snyder and Judd Gray convicted of murder of Albert Snyder; they are executed at Sing Sing prison in **1928.** *The Jazz Singer,* with Al Jolson, first part-talking motion picture.

1928 Kellogg-Briand Pact, outlawing war, signed in Paris by 65 nations. Alexander Fleming discovers penicillin. Richard E. Byrd starts expedition to Antarctic; returns in **1930.**

1929 Trotsky expelled from U.S.S.R. Lateran Treaty establishes independent Vatican City. In U.S., stock market prices collapse, with U.S. securities losing $26 billion—first phase of Depression and world economic crisis. St. Valentine's Day gangland massacre in Chicago.

1930 Britain, U.S., Japan, France, and Italy sign naval disarmament treaty. Nazis gain in German elections. Cyclotron developed by Ernest O. Lawrence, U.S. physicist.

1931 Spain becomes a republic with overthrow of King Alfonso XIII. German industrialists finance 800,000-strong Nazi party. British parliament enacts statute of Westminster, legalizing dominion equality with Britain. Mukden Incident begins Japanese occupation of Manchuria. In U.S., Hoover proposes one-year moratorium of war debts. Harold C. Urey discovers heavy hydrogen. Gangster Al Capone sentenced to 11 years in prison for tax evasion (freed in **1939;** dies in **1947**).

1932 Nazis lead in German elections with 230 Reichstag seats. Famine in U.S.S.R. In U.S., Congress sets up Reconstruction Finance Corporation to stimulate economy. Veterans march on Washington—most leave after Senate rejects payment of cash bonuses; others removed by troops under Douglas MacArthur. U.S. protests Japanese aggression in Manchuria. Amelia Earhart is first woman to fly Atlantic solo. Charles A.

Arthur Conan Doyle, *English writer* (1859–1930)
Knut Hamsun, *Norwegian novelist* (1859–1952)
Henri Bergson, *French philosopher* (1859–1941)
John Dewey, *American philosopher* (1859–1952)
Georges Seurat, *French painter* (1859–1891)
Pierre Curie, *French physicist* (1859–1906)
Anton Chekhov, *Russian dramatist* (1860–1904)
Gustav Mahler, *German composer* (1860–1911)
Rabindranath Tagore, *Indian poet* (1861–1941)
Alfred North Whitehead, *British philosopher-mathematician* (1861–1947)
Edith Wharton, *American author* (1862–1937)
Claude Debussy, *French composer* (1862–1918)
David Lloyd George, *British statesman* (1863–1945)
Henry Ford, *American automobile pioneer* (1863–1947)
William Randolph Hearst, *American newspaper magnate* (1863–1951)
Henri Toulouse-Lautrec, *French painter* (1864–1901)
George Washington Carver, *American botanist* (1864–1943)
Richard Strauss, *German composer* (1864–1949)
Rudyard Kipling, *English writer* (1865–1936)
William Butler Yeats, *Irish poet* (1865–1939)
Jean Sibelius, *Finnish composer* (1865–1957)
Sun Yat-sen, *Chinese statesman* (1866–1927)
Benedetto Croce, *Italian philosopher* (1866–1952)

THE HOLOCAUST (1933–1945)

"Holocaust" is the term describing the Nazi annihilation of about 6 million Jews (two thirds of the pre-World War II European Jewish population), including 4,500,000 from Russia, Poland, and the Baltic; 750,000 from Hungary and Romania; 290,000 from Germany and Austria; 105,000 from The Netherlands; 90,000 from France; 54,000 from Greece, etc.

The Holocaust was unique in its being *genocide*—the systematic destruction of a people solely because of religion, race, ethnicity, or nationality—on an unmatched scale. Along with the Jews, another 9 to 10 million people—Gypsies, Slavs (Poles, Ukrainians, and Belorussians)—were exterminated.

The only comparable act of genocide in modern times was launched in April 1915, when an estimated 600,000 Armenians were massacred by the Turks.

1933 Hitler named German Chancellor **(Jan.).** Dachau, first concentration camp, established **(March).** Boycotts against Jews begin **(April).**

1935 Anti-Semitic Nuremberg Laws passed by Reichstag **(Sept.).**

1937 Buchenwald concentration camp opens **(July).**

1938 Extenstion of anti-Semitic laws to Austria after annexation **(March).** *Kristallnacht* (Night of Broken Glass)—anti-Semitic riots in Germany and Austria **(Nov. 9).** 26,000 Jews sent to concentration camps; Jewish children expelled from schools **(Nov.).** Expropriation of Jewish property and businesses **(Dec.).**

1940 As war continues, Nazi acts against Jews extended to German-conquered areas.

1941 Deportation of German Jews begins; massacres of Jews in Odessa and Kiev—68,000 killed **(Nov.);** in Riga and Vilna—almost 60,000 killed **(Dec.).**

1942 Unified Jewish resistance in ghettos begins **(Jan.).** 300,000 Jews from Warsaw Ghetto deported to Treblinka death camp **(July).**

1943 Warsaw Ghetto uprisings **(Jan.** and **April);** Ghetto exterminated **(May).**

1944 476,000 Hungarian Jews sent to Auschwitz **(May–June).** D-day **(June 6).** Soviet Army liberates Maidanek death camp **(July).** Nazis try to hide evidence of death camps **(Nov.).**

1945 Americans liberate Buchenwald, Bergen-Belsen camps **(April).** Nuremberg War Crimes Trial **(Nov. 1945** to **Oct. 1946).**

Lindbergh's baby son kidnapped, killed. (Bruno Richard Hauptmann arrested in **1934**, convicted in **1935**, executed in **1936**.)

1933 Hitler appointed German chancellor, gets dictatorial powers. Reichstag fire in Berlin; Nazi terror begins. (*See* special material on "The Holocaust.") Germany and Japan withdraw from League of Nations. Giuseppe Zangara executed for attempted assassination of President-elect Roosevelt in which Chicago Mayor Cermak is fatally shot. Roosevelt inaugurated ("the only thing we have to fear is fear itself"); launches New Deal. Prohibition repealed. U.S.S.R. recognized by U.S.

1934 Chancellor Dollfuss of Austria assassinated by Nazis. Hitler becomes Führer. U.S.S.R. admitted to League of Nations. Dionne sisters, first quintuplets to survive beyond infancy, born in Canada.

1935 Saar incorporated into Germany after plebiscite. Nazis repudiate Versailles Treaty, introduce compulsory military service. Mussolini invades Ethiopia; League of Nations invokes sanctions. Roosevelt opens second phase of New Deal in U.S., calling for social security, better housing, equitable taxation, and farm assistance. Huey Long assassinated in Louisiana.

1936 Germans occupy Rhineland. Italy annexes Ethiopia. Rome-Berlin Axis proclaimed (Japan to join in **1940**). Trotsky exiled to Mexico. King George V dies; succeeded by son, Edward VIII, who soon abdicated to marry American-born divorcée, and is succeeded by brother, George VI. Spanish civil war begins. (Franco's fascist forces defeat Loyalist forces by **1939**, when Madrid falls.) War between China and Japan begins, to continue through World War II. Japan and Germany sign anti-Commintern pact; joined by Italy in **1937**.

1937 Hitler repudiates war guilt clause of Versailles Treaty; continues to build German power. Italy withdraws from League of Nations. U.S. gunboat *Panay* sunk by Japanese in Yangtze River. Japan invades China, conquers most of coastal area. Amelia Earhart lost somewhere in Pacific on round-the-world flight.

1938 Hitler marches into Austria; political and geographical union of Germany and Austria proclaimed. Munich Pact—Britain, France, and Italy agree to let Germany partition Czechoslovakia. Douglas "Wrong-Way" Corrigan flies from New York to Dublin.

1939 Germany occupies Bohemia and Moravia; renounces pacts with Poland and England and concludes 10-year non-aggression pact with U.S.S.R. Russo-Finnish War begins; Finns to lose one tenth of territory in **1940** peace treaty. World War II begins (*see* special material on "World War II"). In U.S., Roosevelt submits $1,319-million defense budget, proclaims U.S. neutrality, and declares limited emergency. Einstein writes

Wilbur Wright, *American aviation pioneer* (1867–1912)
Arturo Toscanini, *Italian conductor* (1867–1957)
Marie (Sklodowska) Curie, *Polish-French scientist* (1867–1937)
Maxim Gorki, *Russian writer* (1868–1936)
Robert A. Millikan, *American physicist* (1869–1953)
Mohandas Gandhi, *Indian leader* (1869–1948)
André Gide, *French author* (1869–1951)
Henri Matisse, *French painter* (1869–1954)
Frank Lloyd Wright, *American architect* (1869–1959)
Nikolai Lenin, *Russian revolutionist* (1870–1924)
Orville Wright, *American aviation pioneer* (1871–1948)
Rasputin, *Russian monk* (1871–1916)
Stephen Crane, *American author* (1871–1900)
Theodore Dreiser, *American novelist* (1871–1945)
Marcel Proust, *French author* (1871–1922)
Bertrand Russell, *English philosopher* (1872–1970)
Enrico Caruso, *Italian tenor* (1873–1921)
Chaim Weizmann, *first president of Israel* (1874–1952)

WORLD WAR II (1939–1945)

Axis powers (Germany, Italy, Japan, Hungary, Romania, Bulgaria) *vs.* Allies (U.S., Britain, France, U.S.S.R., Australia, Belgium, Brazil, Canada, China, Denmark, Greece, Netherlands, New Zealand, Norway, Poland, South Africa, Yugoslavia).

1939 Germany invades Poland and annexes Danzig; Britain and France give Hitler ultimatum **(Sept. 1)**, declare war **(Sept. 3)**. Disabled German pocket battleship *Admiral Graf Spee* blown up off Montevideo, Uruguay, on Hitler's orders **(Dec. 17)**. Limited activity ("Sitzkrieg") on Western Front.

1940 Nazis invade Netherlands, Belgium, and Luxembourg **(May 10)**. Chamberlain resigns as Prime Minister; Churchill takes over **(May 10)**. Germans cross French frontier **(May 12)** using air/tank/infantry "Blitzkrieg" tactics. Dunkerque evacuation—about 335,000 out of 400,000 Allied soldiers rescued from Belgium by British civilian and naval craft **(May 26–June 3)**. Italy declares war on France and Britain; invades France **(June 10)**. Germans enter Paris; city undefended **(June 14)**. France and Germany sign armistice at Compiègne **(June 22)**. Nazis bomb Coventry, England **(Nov. 14)**.

1941 Germans launch attacks in Balkans. Yugoslavia surrenders—General Mihajlovic continues guerrilla warfare; Tito leads left-wing guerrillas **(April 17)**. Nazi tanks enter Athens; remnants of British Army quit Greece **(April 27)**. Hitler attacks Russia **(June 22)**. Atlantic Charter—FDR and Churchill agree on war aims **(Aug. 14)**. Japanese attacks on Pearl Harbor, Philippines, Guam force U.S. into war; U.S. Pacific fleet crippled **(Dec. 7)**. U.S. and Britain declare war on Japan. Germany and Italy declare war on U.S.; Congress declares war on those countries **(Dec. 11)**.

1942 British surrender Singapore to Japanese **(Feb. 15)**. U.S. forces on Bataan peninsula in Philippines surrender **(April 9)**. U.S. and Filipino troops on Corregidor island in Manila Bay surrender to Japanese **(May 6)**. Village of Lidice in Czechoslovakia razed by Nazis **(June 10)**. U.S. and Britain land in French North Africa **(Nov. 8)**.

1943 Casablanca Conference—Churchill and FDR agree on unconditional surrender goal **(Jan. 14–24)**. German 6th Army surrenders at Stalingrad—turning point of war in Russia **(Feb. 1–2)**. Remnants of Nazis trapped on Cape Bon, ending war in Africa **(May 12)**. Mussolini deposed; Badoglio named premier **(July 25)**. Allied troops land on Italian mainland after conquest of Sicily **(Sept. 3)**. Italy surrenders **(Sept. 8)**. Nazis seize Rome **(Sept. 10)**. Cairo Conference: FDR, Churchill, Chiang Kai-shek pledge defeat of Japan, free Korea **(Nov. 22–26)**. Teheran Conference: FDR, Churchill, Stalin agree on invasion plans **(Nov. 28–Dec. 1)**.

1944 U.S. and British troops land at Anzio on west Italian coast and hold beachhead **(Jan. 22)**. U.S. and British troops enter Rome **(June 4)**. D-Day—Allies launch Normandy invasion **(June 6)**. Hitler wounded in bomb plot **(July 20)**. Paris liberated **(Aug. 25)**. Athens freed by Allies **(Oct. 13)**. Americans invade Philippines **(Oct. 20)**. Germans launch counter-offensive in Belgium—Battle of Bulge **(Dec. 16)**.

1945 Yalta Agreement signed by FDR, Churchill, Stalin—establishes basis for occupation of Germany, returns to Soviet Union lands taken by Germany and Japan; U.S.S.R. agrees to friendship pact with China **(Feb. 11)**. Mussolini killed at Lake Como **(April 28)**. Admiral Doenitz takes command in Germany; suicide of Hitler announced **(May 1)**. Berlin falls **(May 2)**. V-E Day—Germany signs unconditional surrender terms at Rheims **(May 7)**. Potsdam Conference—Truman, Churchill, Atlee (after **July 28**), Stalin establish council of foreign ministers to prepare peace treaties; plan German postwar government and reparations **(July 17–Aug. 2)**. A-bomb blasts Hiroshima **(Aug. 6)**. U.S.S.R. declares war on Japan **(Aug. 8)**. Nagasaki hit by A-bomb **(Aug. 9)**. Japan surrenders **(Aug. 14)**. V-J Day—Japanese sign surrender terms aboard battleship *Missouri* **(Sept. 2)**.

FDR about feasibility of atomic bomb. New York World's Fair opens.

1940 Trotsky assassinated in Mexico. Estonia, Latvia, and Lithuania annexed by U.S.S.R. U.S. trades 50 destroyers for leases on British bases in Western Hemisphere. Selective Service Act signed.

1941 Japanese surprise attack on U.S. fleet at Pearl Harbor brings U.S. into World War II. Manhattan Project (atomic bomb research) begins. Roosevelt enunciates "four freedoms," signs lend-lease act, declares national emergency, promises aid to U.S.S.R.

1942 Declaration of United Nations signed in Washington. Women's military services established. Enrico Fermi achieves nuclear chain reaction. Japanese and persons of Japanese ancestry moved inland from Pacific Coast. Coconut Grove nightclub fire in Boston kills 491.

1943 President freezes prices, salaries, and wages to prevent inflation. Income tax withholding introduced.

1944 G.I. Bill of Rights enacted. Bretton Woods Conference creates International Monetary Fund and World Bank. Dumbarton Oaks Conference—U.S., British Commonwealth, and U.S.S.R. propose establishment of United Nations.

1945 Yalta Conference (Roosevelt, Churchill, Stalin) plans final defeat of Germany (**Feb.**). Germany surrenders (**May 7**). San Francisco Conference establishes U.N. (**April–June**). FDR dies (April 12). Potsdam Conference (Truman, Churchill, Stalin) establishes basis of German reconstruction (**July–Aug**). Japan surrenders (**Sept. 2**).

1946 First meeting of U.N. General Assembly opens in London (**Jan. 10**). League of Nations dissolved (**April**). Italy abolishes monarchy (**June**). Verdict in Nuremberg war trial: 12 Nazi leaders (including 1 tried in absentia) sentenced to hang; 7 imprisoned; 3 acquitted (**Oct. 1**). Goering commits suicide a few hours before 10 other Nazis are executed (**Oct. 15**). Winston Churchill's "Iron Curtain" speech warns of Soviet expansion.

1947 Britain nationalizes coal mines (**Jan. 1**). Peace treaties for Italy, Romania, Bulgaria, Hungary, Finland signed in Paris (**Feb. 10**). Soviet Union rejects U.S. plan for U.N. atomic-energy control (**March 4**). Truman Doctrine proposed—the first significant U.S. attempt to "contain" communist expansion (**March 12**). Marshall Plan for European recovery proposed—a coordinated program to help European nations recover from ravages of war (**June**). (By **1951**, this "European Recovery Program" had cost $11 billion.) India and Pakistan gain independence from Britain (**Aug. 15**). Cominform (Communist Information Bureau) founded under Soviet auspices to rebuild contacts among European Communist parties, missing since dissolution of Comintern in **1943** (**Sept.**). (Yugoslav party expelled in **1948** and Cominform disbanded in **1956**.)

1948 Gandhi assassinated in New Delhi by Hindu fanatic (**Jan. 30**). Communists seize power in Czechoslovakia (**Feb. 23–25**). Burma and Ceylon granted independence by Britain. Organization of American States (OAS) Charter signed at Bogotá, Colombia (**April 30**). Nation of Israel proclaimed; British end Mandate at midnight; Arab armies attack (**May 14**). Berlin airlift begins (**June 21**); ends **May 12, 1949.** Stalin and Tito break (**June 28**). Independent Republic of Korea is proclaimed, following election supervised by U.N. (**Aug. 15**). Verdict in Japanese war trial: Tojo and six others sentenced to hang (hanged Dec. 23); 18 imprisoned (**Nov. 12**). United States of Indonesia established as Dutch and Indonesians settled conflict (**Dec. 27**). Alger Hiss, former U.S. State Department official, indicted on perjury charges after denying passing secret documents to communist spy ring. Convicted in second trial (**1950**) and sentenced to five-year prison term.

1949 Cease-fire in Palestine (**Jan. 7**). Truman proposes Point Four Program to help world's backward areas (**Jan. 20**). Israel signs armistice with Egypt (**Feb. 24**). Start of North Atlantic Treaty Organization (NATO)—treaty signed by 12 nations (**April 4**). German Federal Republic (West Germany) established (**Sept. 21**). Truman discloses Soviet Union has set off atomic explosion (**Sept. 23**). Communist People's Republic of China formally proclaimed (**Oct. 1**).

Winston Churchill, *British statesman* (1874–1965)
Gertrude Stein, *American writer* (1874–1946)
Arnold Schönberg, *Austrian composer* (1874–1951)
Guglielmo Marconi, *Italian physicist* (1874–1935)
Thomas Mann, *German novelist* (1875–1955)
Carl G. Jung, *Swiss psychiatrist* (1875–1961)
Carl Sandburg, *American poet* (1878–1967)
Martin Buber, *Jewish philosopher* (1878–1965)
Joseph Stalin, *Russian dictator* (1879–1953)
Leon Trotsky, *Russian revolutionist* (1879–1940)
Paul Klee, *Swiss painter* (1879–1940)
Albert Einstein, *German-American physicist* (1879–1955)
Douglas MacArthur, *American general* (1880–1964)
Pablo Picasso, *Spanish-born French painter* (1881–1973)
Béla Bartók, *Hungarian composer* (1881–1945)
Alexander Fleming, *English scientist* (1881–1955)
Franklin D. Roosevelt, *American President* (1882–1945)
Eamon de Valera, *Irish statesman* (1882–1975)
James Joyce, *Irish author* (1882–1941)
Georges Braque, *French painter* (1882–1963)
Igor Stravinsky, *Russian composer* (1882–1971)
Benito Mussolini, *Italian dictator* (1883–1945)
Franz Kafka, *Czechoslovakian-born Austrian author* (1883–1924)
John Maynard Keynes, *English economist* (1883–1946)
Walter Gropius, *German architect* (1883–1969)
Harry S. Truman, *American President* (1884–1972)
Eduard Benes, *Czechoslovakian statesman* (1884–1948)
D. H. Lawrence, *English writer* (1885–1930)

KOREAN WAR (1950–1953)

1950 North Korean Communist forces invade South Korea (June 25). U.N. calls for cease-fire and asks U.N. members to assist South Korea (June 27). Truman orders U.S. forces into Korea (June 27). North Koreans capture Seoul (June 28). Gen. Douglas MacArthur designated commander of unified U.N. forces (July 8). Pusan Beachhead—U.N. forces counterattack and capture Seoul (Aug.–Sept.), capture Pyongyang, North Korean capital (**Oct.**). Chinese Communists enter war (**Oct. 26**), force U.N. retreat toward 39th parallel (**Dec.**).

1951 Gen. Matthew B. Ridgeway replaces MacArthur after he threatens Chinese with massive retaliation (**April 11**). Armistice negotiations (**July**) continue with interruptions until **June 1953.**

1953 Armistice signed (**June 26**). Chinese troops withdraw from North Korea (**Oct. 26, 1958**), but over 200 violations of armistice noted to **1959.**

1950 Truman orders development of hydrogen bomb (**Jan. 31**). Korean War (*see* special material on the "Korean War"). Assassination attempt on President Truman by Puerto Rican nationalists (**Nov. 1**). Brink's robbery in Boston; almost $3 million stolen (**Jan. 17**).

1951 Six nations agree to Schuman Plan to pool European coal and steel (**March 19**)—in effect **Feb. 10, 1953**. Julius and Ethel Rosenberg sentenced to death for passing atomic secrets to Russians (**March**). Japanese peace treaty signed in San Francisco by 49 nations (**Sept. 8**). Color television introduced in U.S.

1952 George VI dies; his daughter becomes Elizabeth II (**Feb. 6**). NATO conference approves European army (**Feb.**). AEC announces "satisfactory" experiments in hydrogen-weapons research; eyewitnesses tell of blasts near Enewetak (**Nov.**).

1953 Gen. Dwight D. Eisenhower inaugurated President of United States (**Jan. 20**). Stalin dies (**March 5**). Malenkov becomes Soviet Premier; Beria, Minister of Interior; Molotov, Foreign Minister (**March 6**). Dag Hammarskjold begins term as U.N. Secretary-General (**April 10**). Edmund Hillary, of New Zealand, and Tenzing Norkay, of Nepal, reach top of Mt. Everest (**May 29**). East Berliners rise against Communist rule; quelled by tanks (**June 17**). Egypt becomes republic ruled by military junta (**June 18**). Julius and Ethel Rosenberg executed in Sing Sing prison (**June 19**). Korean armistice signed (**July 27**). Moscow announces explosion of hydrogen bomb (**Aug. 20**).

1954 First atomic submarine *Nautilus,* launched (**Jan. 21**). Five U.S. Congressmen shot on floor of House as Puerto Rican nationalists fire from spectators' gallery; all five recover (**March 1**). Army *vs.* McCarthy inquiry—Senate subcommittee report blames both sides (**Apr. 22–June 17**). Dien Bien Phu, French military outpost in Vietnam, falls to Vietminh army (**May 7**). (*see* special material on the "Vietnam War.") U.S. Supreme Court (in *Brown* v. *Board of Education of Topeka*) unanimously bans racial segregation in public schools (**May 17**). Eisenhower launches world atomic pool without Soviet Union (**Sept. 6**). Eight-nation Southeast Asia defense treaty (SEATO) signed at Manila (**Sept. 8**). West Germany is granted sovereignty, admitted to NATO and Western European Union (**Oct. 23**). Dr. Jonas Salk starts innoculating children against polio. Algerian War of Independence against France begins (**Nov.**); France struggles to maintain colonial rule until 1962 when it agrees to Algeria's independence.

1955 Nikolai A. Bulganin becomes Soviet Premier, replacing Malenkov (**Feb. 8**). Churchill resigns; Anthony Eden succeeds him (**April 6**). Federal Republic of West Germany becomes a sovereign state (**May 5**). Warsaw

Ezra Pound, *American poet* (1885–1972)
Sinclair Lewis, *American novelist* (1885–1951)
Alban Berg, *Austrian composer* (1885–1935)
Niels Bohr, *Danish physicist* (1885–1962)
David Ben-Gurion, *Israeli statesman* (1886–1973)
Chiang Kai-shek, *Chinese statesman* (1887–1975)
Le Corbusier (C.E. Jeanneret), *Swiss-born French architect* (1887–1965)
T. S. Eliot, *Anglo-American poet* (1888–1965)
Eugene O'Neill, *American dramatist* (1888–1953)
Ludwig Wittgenstein, *Austrian philosopher* (1889–1951)
Adolf Hitler, *German dictator* (1889–1945)
Charles Chaplin, *English screen actor-director* (1889–1977)
Dwight D. Eisenhower, *American President* (1890–1969)
Charles de Gaulle, *French soldier and statesman* (1890–1970)
Sergei Prokofiev, *Russian composer* (1891–1953)
Frederick Banting, *Canadian discoverer of insulin* (1891–1941)

VIETNAM WAR (1950–1975)

U.S., South Vietnam, and Allies versus North Vietnam and National Liberation Front (Viet Cong). Outstanding events:

1950 President Truman sends 35-man military advisory group to aid French fighting to maintain colonial power in Vietnam.

1954 After defeat of French at Dienbienphu, Geneva Agreements (**July**) provide for withdrawal of French and Vietminh to either side of demarcation zone (DMZ) pending reunification elections, which are never held. Presidents Eisenhower and Kennedy (from **1954** onward) send civilian advisors and, later, military personnel to train South Vietnamese.

1960 Communists from National Liberation Front in South.

1963 Ngo Dinh Diem, South Vietnam's premier, slain in coup (**Nov. 1**).

1961–1963 U.S. military advisors rise from 2,000 to 15,000.

1964 North Vietnamese torpedo boats reportedly attack U.S. destroyers in Gulf of Tonkin (**Aug. 2**). President Johnson orders retaliatory air strikes. Congress approves Gulf of Tonkin resolution (**Aug. 7**) authorizing President to take necessary steps to "maintain peace."

1965 U.S. planes begin combat missions over South Vietnam. In **June,** 23,000 American advisors committed to combat. By end of year over 184,000 U.S. troops in area.

1966 B-52s bomb DMZ, reportedly used by North Vietnam for entry into South (**July 31**).

1967 South Vietnam National Assembly approves election of Nguyen Van Thieu as President (**Oct. 21**).

1968 U.S. has almost 525,000 men in Vietnam. In Tet offensive (**Jan.–Feb.**), Viet Cong guerrillas attack Saigon, Hue, and some provincial capitals. President Johnson orders halt to U.S. bombardment of North Vietnam (**Oct. 31**). Saigon and N.L.F. join U.S. and North Vietnam in Paris peace talks.

1969 President Nixon announces Vietnam peace offer (**May 14**)—begins troop withdrawals (**June**). Viet Cong forms Provisional Revolutionary Government. U.S. Senate calls for curb on commitments (**June 25**). Ho Chi Minh, 79, North Vietnam president, dies (**Sept. 3**); collective leadership chosen. Some 6,000 U.S. troops pulled back from Thailand and 1,000 marines from Vietnam (announced **Sept. 30**). Massive demonstrations in U.S. protest or support war policies (**Oct. 15**).

1970 Nixon announces sending of troops to Cambodia (**April 30**). Last U.S. troops removed from Cambodia (**June 29**).

1971 Congress bars use of combat troops, but not air power, in Laos and Cambodia (**Jan. 1**). South Vietnamese troops, with U.S. air cover, fail in Laos thrust. Many American ground forces withdrawn from Vietnam combat. *New York Times* publishes Pentagon papers, classified material on expansion of war (**June**).

1972 Nixon responds to North Vietnamese drive across DMZ by ordering mining of North Vietnam ports and heavy bombing of Hanoi-Haiphong area (**April 1**). Nixon orders "Christmas bombing" of north to get North Vietnamese back to conference table (**Dec.**).

1973 President orders halt to offensive operations in North Vietnam (**Jan. 15**). Representatives of North and South Vietnam, U.S., and N.L.F. sign peace pacts in Paris, ending longest war in U.S. history (**Jan. 27**).

1974 Both sides accuse each other of frequent violations of cease-fire agreement.

1975 Full-scale warfare resumes. Communists victorious (**April 30**). South Vietnam Premier Nguyen Van Thieu resigns (**April 21**). American troops evacuated (**April 30**). More than 140,000 Vietnamese refugees leave by air and sea, many to settle in U.S. Provisional Revolutionary Government takes control (**June 6**).

1976 Election of National Assembly paves way for reunification of North and South.

Pact, east European mutual defense agreement, signed (**May 14**). Argentina ousts Perón (**Sept. 19**). President Eisenhower suffers coronary thrombosis in Denver (**Sept. 24**). Martin Luther King, Jr., leads black boycott of Montgomery, Ala., bus system (**Dec. 1**); desegregated service begun (**Dec. 21**). AFL and CIO become one organization—AFL-CIO (**Dec. 5**).

1956 Nikita Khrushchev, First Secretary of U.S.S.R. Communist Party, denounces Stalin's excesses (**Feb. 24**). First aerial H-bomb tested over Namu islet, Bikini Atoll—10 million tons TNT equivalent (**May 21**). Worker's uprising against Communist rule in Poznan, Poland, is crushed (**June 28–30**). Egypt takes control of Suez Canal (**July 26**). Israel launches attack on Egypt's Sinai peninsula and drives toward Suez Canal (**Oct. 29**). British and French invade Egypt at Port Said (**Nov. 5**). Cease-fire forced by U.S. pressure stops British, French, and Israeli advance (**Nov. 6**). Revolt starts in Hungary—Soviet troops and tanks crush anti-Communist rebellion (**Nov.**).

1957 Eisenhower Doctrine calls for aid to Mideast countries which resist armed aggression from Communist-controlled nations (**Jan. 5**). Eisenhower sends troops to Little Rock, Ark., to quell mob and protect school integration (**Sept. 24**). Russians launch *Sputnik I*, first earth-orbiting satellite—the Space Age begins (**Oct. 4**).

1958 Army's Jupiter-C rocket fires first U.S. earth satellite, *Explorer I*, into orbit (**Jan. 31**). Egypt and Syria merge into United Arab Republic (**Feb. 1**). European Economic Community (Common Market) established by Rome Treaty becomes effective **Jan. 1, 1958.** Khrushchev becomes Premier of Soviet Union as Bulganin resigns (**Mar. 27**). Gen. Charles de Gaulle becomes French premier (**June 1**), remaining in power until **1969.** New French constitution adopted (**Sept. 28**), de Gaulle elected president of 5th Republic (**Dec. 21**). Eisenhower orders U.S. Marines into Lebanon at request of President Chamoun, who fears overthrow (**July 15**).

1959 Cuban President Batista resigns and flees—Castro takes over (**Jan. 1**). Tibet's Dalai Lama escapes to India (**Mar. 31**). St. Lawrence Seaway opens, allowing ocean ships to reach Midwest (**April 25**).

1960 American U-2 spy plane, piloted by Francis Gary Powers, shot down over Russia (**May 1**). Khrushchev kills Paris summit conference because of U-2 (**May 16**). Powers sentenced to prison for 10 years (**Aug. 19**)—freed in **February 1962** in exchange for Soviet spy. Top Nazi murderer of Jews, Adolf Eichmann, captured by Israelis in Argentina (**May 23**)—executed in Israel in **1962.** Communist China and Soviet Union split in conflict over Communist ideology. Belgium starts to break up its African colonial empire, gives independence to Belgian Congo (Zaire) on **June 30.** Cuba begins confiscation of $770 million of U.S. property (**Aug. 7**).

1961 U.S. breaks diplomatic relations with Cuba (**Jan. 3**). John F. Kennedy inaugurated President of U.S. (**Jan. 20**). Kennedy proposes Alliance for Progress—10-year plan to raise Latin American living standards (**Mar. 13**). Moscow announces putting first man in orbit around earth, Maj. Yuri A. Gagarin (**April 12**). Cuba invaded at Bay of Pigs by an estimated 1,200 anti-Castro exiles aided by U.S.; invasion crushed (**April 17**). First U.S. spaceman, Navy Cmdr. Alan B. Shepard, Jr., rockets 116.5 miles up in 302-mile trip (**May 5**). Virgil Grissom becomes second American astronaut, making 118-mile-high, 303-mile-long rocket flight over Atlantic (**July 21**). Gherman Stepanovich Titov is launched in Soviet spaceship *Vostok II:* makes 17 1/2 orbits in 25 hours, covering 434,960 miles before landing safely (**Aug. 6**). East Germans erect Berlin Wall between East and West Berlin to halt flood of refugees (**Aug. 13**). U.S.S.R. fires 50-megaton hydrogen bomb, biggest explosion in history (**Oct. 29**).

1962 Lt. Col. John H. Glenn, Jr., is first American to orbit earth—three times in 4 hr 55 min (**Feb. 20**). Adolf Eichmann hanged in Israel for his part in Nazi extermination of six million Jews (**May 31**). France transfers sovereignty to new republic of Algeria (**July 3**). Cuban missile crisis—U.S.S.R. to build missile bases in Cuba; Kennedy orders Cuban blockade, lifts blockade after Russians back down (**Aug.–Nov.**). James H. Meredith, escorted by Federal marshals, registers in University of Mississippi (**Oct. 1**). Pope John XXIII opens Second Vatican Council (Oct. 11)—Council holds four sessions, finally closing Dec. 8, 1965. Cuba releases 1,113 prisoners of 1961 invasion attempt (**Dec. 24**).

1963 France and West Germany sign treaty of cooperation ending four centuries of conflict (**Jan. 22**). Pope John XXIII dies (**June 3**)—succeeded June 21 by Cardinal Montini, who becomes Paul VI. U.S. Supreme Court rules no locality may require recitation of Lord's Prayer or Bible verses in public schools (**June 17**). Civil rights rally held by 200,000 blacks and whites in Washington, D.C. (**Aug. 28**). Washington-to-Moscow "hot line"

Tito (Josip Broz), *Yugoslavian President* (1892–1980)
Haile Selassie, *Ethiopian emperor* (1892–1975)
Hermann Goering, *Nazi leader* (1893–1946)
Mao Zedong, *Chinese Communist leader* (1893–1976)
Nikita Khrushchev, *Russian leader* (1894–1971)
Martha Graham, *American dancer* (1894–)
Paul Hindemith, *German-American composer* (1895–1963)
Bertolt Brecht, *German dramatist* (1898–1956)
Ernest Hemingway, *American author* (1898–1961)
Federico García Lorca, *Spanish author* (1899–1936)
Francis Poulenc, *French composer* (1899–1963)
Kurt Weill, *German-American composer* (1900–1950)
Aaron Copland, *American composer* (1900–)
Werner Heisenberg, *German physicist* (1901–)
Walt Disney, *American cartoonist* (1901–1966)
Enrico Fermi, *Italian-American physicist* (1901–1954)
John Steinbeck, *American novelist* (1902–1968)
Dmitri Shostakovich, *Russian composer* (1906–1975)
W. H. Auden, *English poet* (1907–1973)
Albert Camus, *French author* (1913–1960)
John F. Kennedy, *American President* (1917–1963)

communications link opens, designed to reduce risk of accidental war (**Aug. 30**). President Kennedy shot and killed by sniper in Dallas, Tex. Lyndon B. Johnson becomes President same day (**Nov. 22**). Lee Harvey Oswald, accused assassin of President Kennedy, is shot and killed by Jack Ruby, Dallas nightclub owner (**Nov. 24**).

1964 U.S. Supreme Court rules that Congressional districts should be roughly equal in population (**Feb. 17**). Jack Ruby convicted of murder in slaying of Lee Harvey Oswald; sentenced to death by Dallas jury (**March 14**)—conviction reversed **Oct. 5, 1966;** Ruby dies **Jan. 3, 1967,** before second trial can be held. Three civil rights workers—Schwerner, Goodman, and Cheney—murdered in Mississippi (**June**). Twenty-one arrests result in trial and conviction of seven by Federal jury. President's Commission on the Assassination of President Kennedy issues Warren Report concluding that Lee Harvey Oswald acted alone.

1965 Rev. Dr. Martin Luther King, Jr., and more than 2,600 other blacks arrested in Selma, Ala., during three-day demonstrations against voter-registration rules (**Feb. 1**). Malcolm X, black-nationalist leader, shot to death at Harlem rally in New York City (**Feb. 21**). U.S. Marines land in Dominican Republic as fighting persists between rebels and Dominican army (**April 28**). Medicare, senior citizens' government medical assistance program, begins (**July 1**). Blacks riot for six days in Watts section of Los Angeles: 34 dead, over 1,000 injured, nearly 4,000 arrested, fire damage put at $175 million (**Aug. 11–16**). Power failure in Ontario plant blacks out parts of eight northeastern states of U.S. and two provinces of southeastern Canada (**Nov. 9**).

1966 Black teen-agers riot in Watts, Los Angeles; two men killed and at least 25 injured (**March 15**). Michael E. De Bakey implants artificial heart in human for first time at Houston hospital; plastic device functions and patient lives (**April 21**).

1967 Three Apollo astronauts—Col. Virgil I. Grissom, Col. Edward White II, and Lt. Cmdr. Roger B. Chaffee—killed in spacecraft fire during simulated launch (**Jan. 27**). Israeli and Arab forces battle; six-day war ends with Israel occupying Sinai Peninsula, Golan Heights, Gaza Strip, and east bank of Suez Canal (**June 5**). Red China announces explosion of its first hydrogen bomb (**June 17**). Racial violence in Detroit; 7,000 National Guardsmen aid police after night of rioting. Similar outbreaks occur in New York City's Spanish Harlem, Rochester, N.Y., Birmingham, Ala., and New Britain, Conn. (**July 23**). Thurgood Marshall sworn in as first black U.S. Supreme Court justice (**Oct. 2**). Dr. Christian N. Barnard and team of South African surgeons perform world's first successful human heart transplant (**Dec. 3**)—patient dies 18 days later.

1968 North Korea seizes U.S. Navy ship *Pueblo;* holds 83 on board as spies (**Jan. 23**). President Johnson announces he will not seek or accept presidential renomination (**March 31**). Martin Luther King, Jr., civil rights leader, is slain in Memphis (**April 4**)—James Earl Ray, indicted in murder, captured in London on **June 8.** In **1969** Ray pleads guilty and is sentenced to 99 years. Sen. Robert F. Kennedy is shot and critically wounded in Los Angeles hotel after winning California primary (**June 5**)—dies **June 6.** Sirhan B. Sirhan convicted **1969.** Czechoslovakia is invaded by Russians and Warsaw Pact forces to crush liberal regime (**Aug. 20**).

1969 Richard M. Nixon is inaugurated 37th President of the U.S. (**Jan. 20**). Apollo 11 astronauts—Neil A. Armstrong, Edwin E. Aldrin, Jr., and Michael Collins—take man's first walk on moon (**July 20**). Sen. Edward M. Kennedy pleads guilty to leaving scene of fatal accident at Chappaquiddick, Mass. (**July 18**) in which Mary Jo Kopechne was drowned—gets two-month suspended sentence (**July 25**).

1970 Biafra surrenders after 32-month fight for independence from Nigeria (**Jan. 12**). Rhodesia severs last tie with British Crown and declares itself a racially segregated republic (**March 1**). Four students at Kent State University in Ohio slain by National Guardsmen at demonstration protesting April 30 incursion into Cambodia (**May 4**). Senate repeals Gulf of Tonkin resolution (**June 24**).

1971 Supreme Court rules unanimously that busing of students may be ordered to achieve racial desegregation (**April 20**). Anti-war militants attempt to disrupt government business in Washington (**May 3**)—police and military units arrest as many as 12,000; most are later released. Twenty-sixth Amendment to U.S. Constitution lowers voting age to 18. U.N. seats Communist China and expels Nationalist China (**Oct. 25**).

1972 President Nixon makes unprecedented eight-day visit to Communist China (**Feb.**). Britain takes over direct rule of Northern Ireland in bid for peace (**March 24**). Gov. George C. Wallace of Alabama is shot by Arthur H. Bremer at Laurel, Md., political rally (**May 15**). Five men are apprehended by police in attempt to bug Democratic National Committee headquarters in Washington D.C.'s Watergate complex—start of the Watergate scandal (**June 17**). Supreme Court rules that death penalty is unconstitutional (**June 29**). Eleven Israeli athletes at Olympic Games in Munich are killed after eight members of an Arab terrorist group invade Olympic Village; five guerrillas and one policeman are also killed (**Sept. 5**).

1973 Great Britain, Ireland, and Denmark enter European Common Market (**Jan. 1**). Nixon, on national TV, accepts responsibility, but not blame, for Watergate; accepts resignations of advisers H. R. Haldeman and John D. Ehrlichman, fires John W. Dean III as counsel. (**April 30**). Greek military junta abolishes monarchy and proclaims republic (**June 1**). U.S. bombing of Cambodia ends, marking official halt to 12 years of combat activity in Southeast Asia (**Aug. 15**). Fourth and biggest Arab-Israeli War begins as Egyptian and Syrian forces attack Israel as Jews mark Yom Kippur, holiest day in their calendar. (**Oct. 6**). Spiro T. Agnew resigns as Vice President and then, in Federal Court in Baltimore, pleads no contest to charges of evasion of income taxes on $29,500 he received in 1967, while Governor of Maryland. He is fined $10,000 and put on three years' probation (**Oct. 10**). In the "Saturday Night Massacre," Nixon fires special Watergate prosecutor Archibald Cox and Deputy Attorney General William D. Ruckelshaus; Attorney General Elliot L. Richardson resigns (**Oct. 20**). Egypt and Israel sign U.S.-sponsored cease-fire accord (**Nov. 11**).

1974 Patricia Hearst, 19-year-old daughter of publisher Randolph Hearst, kidnapped by Symbionese Liberation Army. (**Feb. 5**). House Judiciary Committee adopts three articles of impeachment charging President Nixon with obstruction of justice, failure to uphold laws, and refusal to produce material subpoenaed by the committee (**July 30**). Richard M. Nixon announces he will resign the next day, the first President to do so (**Aug. 8**). Vice President Gerald R. Ford of Michigan is sworn in as 38th President of the U.S. (**Aug. 9**). Ford grants "full, free, and absolute pardon" to ex-President Nixon (**Sept. 8**).

1975 John N. Mitchell, H. R. Haldeman, John D. Ehrlichman, and Robert C. Mardian found guilty of Watergate cover-up. Mitchell, Haldeman, and Ehrlichman are sentenced on Feb. 21 to 30 months-8 years in jail and Mardian to 10 months-3 years (**Jan. 1**). American merchant ship *Mayaguez,* seized by Cambodian forces, is rescued in operation by U.S. Navy and Marines, 38 of whom are killed (**May 15**). *Apollo* and *Soyuz* spacecraft take off for U.S.-Soviet link-up in space (**July 15**). President Ford escapes assassination attempt in Sacramento, Calif., (**Sept. 5**). President Ford escapes second assassination attempt in 17 days. (**Sept. 22**).

1976 Supreme Court rules that blacks and other minorities are entitled to retroactive job seniority (**March 24**). Ford signs Federal Election Campaign Act (**May 11**). Supreme Court rules that death penalty is not inherently cruel or unusual and is a constitutionally acceptable form of punishment (**July 3**). Nation celebrates Bicentennial (**July 4**). Israeli airborne commandos attack Uganda's Entebbe Airport and free 103 hostages held by pro-Palestinian hijackers of Air France plane; one Israeli and several Ugandan soldiers killed in raid (**July 4**). Mysterious disease that eventually claims 29 lives strikes American Legion convention in Philadelphia (**Aug. 4**). Jimmy Carter elected U.S. President (**Nov. 2**).

1977 First woman Episcopal priest ordained (**Jan. 1**). Scientists identify previously unknown bacterium as cause of mysterious "legionnaire's disease" (**Jan. 18**). Astronomers discover water outside of Earth's galaxy, indicating possibility of life in outer space (**Jan. 19**). New Chinese Government allows films, plays, and artists previously banned by Cultural Revolution (**Jan. 21**). Carter pardons Vietnam draft evaders (**Jan. 21**). Spain legalizes Communist Party after 38-year ban (**April 9**). Scientists report using bacteria in lab to make insulin (**May 23**). Soviets charge Anatoly Shcharansky, Jewish human-rights activist, with treason (**June 4**). Laetrile found useless as cancer cure (**June 15**). Supreme Court rules that states are not required to spend Medicaid funds on elective abortions (**June 20**). Deng Xiaoping, purged Chinese leader, restored to power as "Gang of Four" is expelled from Communist Party (**July 22**). Nuclear-proliferation pact, curbing spread of nuclear weapons, signed by 15 countries, including U.S. and U.S.S.R. (**Sept. 21**). Inquiry into prison death of Steven Biko, black leader, absolves South African security police; U.S. State Department expresses shock. (**Dec. 2**).

1978 President chooses Federal Appeals Court Judge William H. Webster as FBI director (**Jan. 19**). Soviet spy satellite with atomic reactor breaks up over northwest Canada (**Jan. 24**); Rhodesia's Prime Minister Ian D. Smith and three black leaders agree on transfer to black majority rule (**Feb. 15**). Former Italian Premier Aldo Moro kidnapped by left-wing terrorists, who kill five bodyguards (**March 16**); he is found slain (**May**

9). U.S. Senate approves Panama Canal neutrality treaty (**March 16**); votes treaty to turn canal over to Panama by year 2000 (**April 18**). Supreme Court upholds corporate spending in elections under constitutional right of free speech (**April 26**). All 51 construction workers killed in collapse of power plant cooling tower under construction at St. Mary's, W. Va. (**April 27**). David Berkowitz pleads guilty and gets 25 years to life in each of New York's six "Son of Sam" killings (**May 8**). Californians in referendum approve Proposition 13 for nearly 60% slash in property tax revenues (**June 6**). Supreme Court, in Bakke case, bars quota system in college admissions, but affirms constitutionality of programs giving advantage to minorities (**June 28**). Baby girl born in England from egg fertilized outside womb in what is believed world's first such case (**July 26**). Pope Paul VI, dead at 80, mourned (**Aug. 6**); new Pope, John Paul I, 65, dies unexpectedly after 34 days in office (**Sept. 28**); succeeded by Karol Cardinal Wojtyla of Poland as John Paul II (**Oct. 16**). "Framework for Peace" in Middle East signed by Egypt's President Anwar el-Sadat and Israeli Premier Menachem Begin after 13-day conference at Camp David led by President Carter (**Sept. 17**). 911 in cult die in mass murder-suicide in Guyanan jungle after California Congressman and four others perish in ambush (**Nov. 20**). U.S. and China agree to begin diplomatic relations; Carter reassures Taiwan (**Dec. 15**).

1979 Oil spills pollute ocean waters in Atlantic and Gulf of Mexico (**Jan. 1, June 8, July 21**). Ohio agrees to pay $675,000 to families of dead and injured in Kent State University shootings (**Jan. 4**). Vietnam and Cambodian insurgents it backs announce fall of Phnom Penh, Cambodian capital, and collapse of Pol Pot regime (**Jan. 7**). Shah leaves Iran after year of turmoil (**Jan. 16**); revolutionary forces under Moslem leader Ayatollah Ruhollah Khomeini, take over (**Feb. 1**, et seq.). Chinese invade Vietnam (**Feb. 18**); withdraw troops (**March 5**); report 20,000 casualties, with probably 5,000 deaths (**May 2**). Conservatives win British election; Margaret Thatcher new Prime Minister (**March 28**). Nuclear power plant accident at Three Mile Island, Pa., releases radioactivity (**March 28**). Bishop Abel T. Muzorewa wins interracial Rhodesia election (**April 24**). Carter and Brezhnev sign SALT II agreement (**June 14**). Supreme Court upholds Federal ban on controversial cancer drug laetrile (**June 18**). China signs three-year trade treaty with U.S. (**July 7**). Nicaraguan President Gen. Anastasio Somoza Debayle resigns and flees to Miami (**July 17**); Sandinists form government (**July 19**). Andrew Young resigns as U.N. delegate from U.S. after reprimand for unauthorized talks with P.L.O. (**Aug 15**). Earl Mountbatten of Burma, 79, British World War II hero, and three others killed by blast on fishing boat off Irish coast (**Aug. 27**); two I.R.A. members accused (**Aug. 30**). Spacecraft *Pioneer II* gets first close photos of Saturn (**Sept. 1**). Carter approves controversial Tellico hydroelectric dam on Little Tennessee River (Sept. 25). Vietnamese start offensive against Pol Pot regime in Cambodia (**Sept. 25**). Thousands cheer Pope on visit to Ireland and U.S. (**Sept. 29–Oct. 7**). Park Chung Hee, 62, South Korean President for 18 years, assassinated by intelligence chief (**Oct. 26**). Iranian militants seize U.S. embassy in Teheran and hold hostages (**Nov. 4**). Lane Kirkland succeeds George Meany as AFL-CIO president (**Nov. 19**). Soviet invasion of Afghanistan stirs world protests. (**Dec. 27**).

1980 Six U.S. Embassy aides escape from Iran with Canadian help (**Jan. 29**). FBI's two-year undercover operation "Abscam" (for Arab scam) implicates public officials (**Feb. 2**). U.S. breaks diplomatic ties with Iran (**April 7**). Eight U.S. servicemen are killed and five are injured as helicopter and cargo plane collide in abortive desert raid to rescue American hostages in Teheran (**April 25**). Cyrus R. Vance resigns as Secretary of State (**April 28**). Senator Edmund S. Muskie of Maine succeeds him (**April 29**). Georgia Federal court jury acquits Bert Lance, former U.S. Budget Director, on nine bank fraud charges (**April 30**). First women graduate from service academies (**May 21, 28**). Congress votes $20-billion synthetic fuels program (**June 26**). Supreme Court upholds limits on Federal aid for abortions (**June 30**). Justices approve affirmative action for minority contractors in Federal works program (**July 2**). Olympic games open in Moscow, boycotted by U.S. and other nations (**July 19**). Shah of Iran dies at 60 (**July 27**). Anastasio Somoza Debayle, ousted Nicaragua ruler, and two aides assassinated in Asunción, Paraguay capital (**Sept. 17**). Iraq troops hold 90 square miles of Iran after invasion (**Sept. 19**). New law gives Gandhi Government in India power to imprison without trial (**Sept. 23**). Aleksei N. Kosygin, 76, ailing Soviet Prime Minister, resigns (**Oct. 23**). Ronald Reagan elected President in Republican sweep (**Nov. 4**). *Voyager I* discovers 15th Saturn moon (**Nov. 8**). 300,000 greet Pope on visit to West Germany (**Nov. 15**). Three U.S. nuns and lay workers found slain in El Salvador (**Dec. 4**). John Lennon of Beatles shot dead in New York City (**Dec. 8**). Justice Department drops case against L. Patrick Gray, 3rd, former FBI head accused of authorizing illegal break-ins (**Dec. 11**).

1981 U.S.-Iran agreement frees 52 hostages held in Tehran since Nov. 4, 1979 (**Jan. 18**); hostages welcomed back in U.S. (**Jan. 25**). Ronald Reagan takes oath as 40th President (**Jan. 20**). President Reagan wounded by gunman, with press secretary, and two law-enforcement officers (**March 30**). Space shuttle *Columbia* succeeds in test flight (**April 12**). Supreme Court widens restrictions on search of homes (**April 21**). Senator Harrison A. Williams of New Jersey convicted in Abscam case (**May, 1**). Hunger strikers die in Belfast prison protest (**May 5–July 13**). Congress approves $695.5-billion Reagan budget (**May 14**) Pope John Paul II wounded by gunman (**May 14**). Supreme Court expands protection for criminal defendants against self-incrimination (**May 18**). Israeli planes destroy Iraqi atomic reactor (**June 8**). Iran's President Abolhassan Bani-Sadr removed from office (**June 22**); he flees to France and is granted asylum (**July 29**). Supreme Court rules, 4–4, that former President Nixon and three top aides may be required to pay monetary damages for unconstitutional wiretap of home telephone of former national security aide (**June 22**). Court, 6–3, decides that registration for draft can exclude women (**June 23**). Congress supports Reagan's $35.5-billion budget cuts designed to reverse government's expansion (**June 26–July 31**). United Auto Workers Union rejoins A.F.L.-C.I.O. 13 years after split (**July 1**). Reagan nominates Judge Sandra Day O'Connor, 51, of Arizona as first woman on Supreme Court (**July 7**). More than 110 die in collapse of aerial walkways in lobby of Hyatt Regency Hotel in Kansas City; 188 injured (**July 18**). *Washington Star* ends publication (**July 23**). Millions around world view wedding of Prince Charles of Britain, 32, and Lady Diana Spencer, 20 (**July 29**). Congress backs Reagan on tax reductions (**July 29–Aug. 4**). Major league baseball strike ends after seven weeks (**July 31**). Air controllers strike, disrupting flights (**Aug. 3**). Government dismisses strikers (**Aug. 11**). President orders production of neutron weapons (**Aug. 6**). Three former Congressmen are first defendants sentenced in Federal Abscam investigation into political corruption (**Aug. 13**). President Anwar el-Sadat of Egypt assassinated (**Oct. 6**). First test-tube baby born in U.S. hospital (**Dec. 28**).

1982 *Philadelphia Bulletin* ceases publication (**Jan. 29**). British overcome Argentina in Falklands war (**April 2–June 15**). British Queen gives Canada its Constitution (**April 17**). Israel completes withdrawal from Sinai (**April 25**). Israel invades Lebanon in attack on P.L.O. (**June 4**). John W. Hinckley, Jr., found not guilty because of insanity in shooting of President Reagan (**June 21**). Princess of Wales gives birth to a boy (**June 21**). Alexander M. Haig, Jr., resigns as Secretary of State (**June 25**). Equal rights amendment fails ratification (**June 30**). Mexico nationalizes private banking institutions (**Sept. 1**). Bomb blast kills Lebanon President-elect, Bashir Gemayel (**Sept. 14**). His brother, Amin Gemayel, is elected to succeed him (**Sept. 21**). Lebanese Christian Phalangists kill hundreds of people in two Palestinian refugee camps in West Beirut (**Sept. 15**). Reagan orders return of U.S. troops to join French and Italian peacekeeping force (**Sept. 22**). Princess Grace, 52, dies of injuries when car plunges off mountain road. Daughter Stephanie, 17, suffers serious injuries (**Sept. 14**). Polish Parliament outlaws Solidarity and all existing labor unions (**Oct. 8**). Cyanide-laced Tylenol, placed by a madman in store shelves, kills seven in Chicago (**Oct. 6**). Leonid I. Brezhnev, Soviet leader, dies at 75 (**Nov. 10**). Yuri V. Andropov, 68, chosen as his successor (**Nov. 15**). Thousands of Vietnam War veterans march proudly past White House toward Vietnam War Memorial (**Nov. 13**). Space shuttle *Columbia* lands at Edwards Air Force Base, Calif., after successful five-day inaugural trip (**Nov. 16**). Football strike ends after 57 days (**Nov. 21**). Artificial heart implanted for first time in Dr. Barney B. Clark, 61, at University of Utah Medical Center in Salt Lake City (**Dec. 2**). Barney Clark dies (**March 23, 1983**). House votes to kill MX missile (**Dec. 7**). 117 nations sign sea law treaty; U.S. and Britain refuse to approve it (**Dec. 10**).

1983 George C. Wallace becomes the first man to be inaugurated for fourth term as Governor of Alabama (**Jan. 19**). Jim Thorpe's Olympic gold medals won in 1912 are posthumously returned to him at Los Angeles (**Jan. 18**). Pope John Paul II signs new Roman Catholic code incorporating changes brought about by Second Vatican Council (**Jan. 25**). Key subatomic "W" particle discovered after 40-year search by scientific team at CERN research center near Geneva (**Jan. 26**). Snowstorm paralyzes Northeast, fourteen deaths reported (**Feb. 12**). Congressional commission charges internment of 120,000 Japanese citizens and resident aliens in World War II was a grave injustice (**Feb. 24**). Queen Elizabeth and Prince Philip arrive at San Diego, Calif., on first stop of North American tour (**Feb. 26**). Supreme Court votes 5–4 to uphold age bias law (**March 2**). Final episode of CBS-TV series, M*A*S*H*, draws an estimated 125 million viewers (**March 2**). EPA head, Anne McGill Burford, resigns in dispute over investigation of environmental agency (**March 9**). Pope John Paul II completes visit to seven Central American countries (**March 10**). Employees agree to buy National Steel's Weirton Steel Works for $66 million (**March 13**). OPEC members agree to cut oil prices for first time (**March 14**). Congress votes $4.6 billion for emergency jobs bill (**March 21**). More than 200 people are killed in Popauan, Columbia, earthquake (**March 31**). Thousands of demonstrators in Europe protest nuclear weapons on European soil (**April 1**). U.S. grants asylum to Chinese tennis star, Hu Na, 19, who defected during tournament in California, July 1982 (**April 4**). Second space shuttle *Challenger* makes successful maiden voyage which included the first U.S. space walk in nine years (**April 4**). More than 27,000 people are displaced and at least 10 killed after 20 inches of rain fall in Gulf Coast states (**April 8**). Harold Washington, 60, becomes the first black mayor elected in Chicago (**April 12**). Severe earthquake shakes Coalinga, Calif., injuring 47, and causing an estimated $31 million in property damage (**May 2**). U.S. bishops denounce the testing, manufacture, and deployment of nuclear weapons (**May 3**). West German Interior Ministry declares Hitler diaries published in *Stern* magazine a hoax (**May 6**). New York celebrates 100th anniversary of the Brooklyn Bridge (**May 24**). Lt. Cmdr. Albert Schaufelberger, 3rd, American military advisor in San Salvador, killed by four assassins (**May 25**). Death toll over 200 after a Nile steamer burns and sinks (**May 25**). Earthquake strikes Northern Japan, killing almost 100 people (**May 26**). *Pioneer 10* spacecraft launched March 3, 1972, crosses the orbit of Neptune and departs the planetary system (**June 13**). U.S. Supreme Court declares many local legislative abortion restrictions unconstitutional (**June 15**). Pope John Paul II makes eight-day trip to Poland (**June 16–23**). Sally K. Ride, 32, becomes the first U.S. woman astronaut in space as a crew member aboard the space shuttle *Challenger* (**June 18**). Supreme Court votes, 7–2, to restrict rights of Congress to overrule actions by the Executive Branch (**June 23**). Yasir Arafat, P.L.O. leader, is expelled from Syria by Syrian army head (**June 24**). Proposed anti-abortion constitutional amendment rejected by Senate in 50–40 vote (**June 28**). Supreme Court declares life prison sentence without possibility of parole for minor crime is unconstitutional (**June 28**). Ecuadorean jetliner crashes in mountain near Cuenca, killing 119 (**July 11**). Armenian terrorists explode bomb at Orly Airport, Paris, killing six, and injuring 56 others (**July 15**). Polish Government lifts martial law (**July 22**). $2.25-billion default made by Washington Public Power System is largest in history of municipal bond market (**July 25**). New long-term U.S.-Soviet grain purchase accord reached (**July 28**). Bettino Craxi, 49, is sworn in as Italy's first Socialist Prime Minister (**Aug. 4**). Nationwide strike by almost 675,000 telephone workers against American Telephone and Telegraph System after contract negotiations fail. (**Aug. 7**). Tentative contract agreement with unions reached (**Aug. 27**). Nation's poverty rate in 1982 reported to be 15% (**Aug. 8**). Space Telescope finds evidence that there might be another solar system (**Aug. 9**). El Salvador and Guatemala agree on closer military cooperation (**Aug. 14**). U.S. admits shielding former Nazi Gestapo Chief, Klaus Barbie, 69, the "Butcher of Lyons," wanted by the French Government for war crimes (**Aug. 15**). Benigo S. Aquino, Jr., 50, political rival of Philippine President Marcos, slain in Manila (**Aug. 21**). Iran makes $419.5-million payment to Export-Import Bank in settlement of claims arising as a result of seizure of American hostages in 1979 (**Aug. 23**). Drug scandal among athletes rocks Pan American Games in Caracas (**Aug. 23**). Almost 250,000 civil rights demonstrators gather in Washington, D.C. to celebrate 20th anniversary of Dr. Martin Luther King, Jr.'s historic march on Washington (**Aug. 27**). Two marines killed by mortor fire are first combat fatalities in the American peacekeeping force in Lebanon (**Aug. 29**). Air Force Col. Guion S. Bluford, Jr., 40, becomes the first black astronaut in space as a crew member of the space shuttle *Challenger* (**Aug. 30**). A South Korean Boeing 747 jetliner bound for Seoul, apparently strays off course into Soviet air space and is shot down by a Soviet SU-15 fighter after it had tracked the airliner for two hours. All 269 people aboard are killed, including 61 Americans, among them Rep. Larry McDonald of Georgia (**Aug. 30**).

(For later events, *See* Current Events, 1983–84, in Table of Contents.)

Some Labor Market Contrasts: U.S. and Europe

Source: U.S. Department of Labor, Bureau of Labor Statistics.

Fewer Women Work in Europe

More than half of all American women of working age are now in the labor force. In Europe, only Scandinavian women exceed this level. Economic activity by women in the rest of Europe is rising but, in general, remains well below the U.S. level. A transformation of major proportions in the role of women in working life has been occurring here and is beginning to accelerate in most of Europe.

Only one of five American married women with children under the age of six was in the labor force in 1960; now about half are. In Sweden, the proportion is even higher.

Youth Unemployment High

Youth unemployment rates are at very high levels in both Europe and in the United States. More than one of five teenagers in the U.S. labor force is unemployed, as is one of seven young adults. Italian and Dutch youth now meet or surpass these high U.S. levels, while West Germany manages to maintain much lower rates, especially for teenagers.

Since the late 1970s, the traditional gap between the U.S. and European youth unemployment rates has narrowed or disappeared. During the early to mid-1960s, when the U.S. birth rate began to fall, European birth rates began to rise. These young Europeans started to enter the labor market in the latter half of the 1970s. After many years of decline, youth participation rates in Europe also began to stabilize or even increase. Further, more European youth were beginning to adopt the American pattern of seeking work while in school, and increasing educational enrollments in post-compulsory schooling brought a rising tide of youth into the school vacation job market. The labor markets in Europe have not been able to absorb the greater supply of student jobseekers or the greater supply of new college graduates.

In the United States, the teenage population began to decline in 1978, as the baby-boom generation moved into older age groups. This development is expected to exert downward pressure on the unemployment rate throughout the present decade and into the 1990s. In Europe, the teenage population has only recently begun to decline; the 20- to 24-year-old age group, however, continues to increase. Youth are expected to exert upward pressure on European unemployment rates for several years to come.

The Role of Older Workers

During the last two decades, the U.S. and European population over the age of 65 has grown by one half. Compounding the normal increase in "dependency" that would accompany an aging population has been the decline in labor market activity of older workers.

In Europe, the changes in older worker labor market status preceded ours in timing and have been more serious. Not only has the older population of Europe been consistently a higher proportion of the total population, but their labor force participation rates have been substantially lower, and currently are less than half those in the U.S.

In the face of high unemployment rates, a new emphasis in many European countries has been placed on encouraging persons to retire early or to work part time while receiving a pension. The rationale is to create more opportunities for younger workers.

Minorities

Many of the European countries have experienced an inflow of foreign "guestworkers" who came to meet the labor shortages of the 1960s. Originally, the European guestworker flows were cyclical; foreign nationals flowed into the Northern European countries when demand was high and left when it was low, with little effect on the unemployment rate in the host country. As work contracts were renewed, however, many guestworkers began to put down roots in the host countries, marrying locally or bringing their wives and children from home. When the recession struck in 1974, increased job competition caused bans to be placed on new immigration by the host countries. While some guestworkers returned home, most stayed, and many entered the unemployment rolls. The children and wives of the guestworkers also entered the labor market, more than offsetting the numbers who had returned to their homelands. Further, there was a growing influx of illegal migrants.

These new problems that Europe has had to confront sound familiar to us. They include language as well as social and cultural differences. Foreigners tend to live in the large urban areas. The foreign youth of working age constitute a substantial and growing part of the youth unemployment problem in Europe.

Unemployment Duration

In the United States, even during the recent period of recession, the mean duration of unemployment is only about four months; in Europe, the average ranges from seven to ten months for most countries. On average, in 1982, one of three of the British and French unemployed were out of work for one year or longer. In contrast, fewer than one of ten of the American unemployed had been jobless that long. American workers tend to move into and out of employment and unemployment, whereas European joblessness tends to reflect a much larger group of long-term unemployed.

Job Security

In Europe, employers often cut working hours during periods of reduced orders; the lost hours are reimbursed by government-subsidized benefits. When the 1974–75 recession came, these short-time work mechanisms saved thousands of European workers from becoming unemployed.

Most of the European-style job security and job continuity practices are absent or are much weaker in the United States. American employers are quicker to respond to labor market conditions by hiring or dismissing workers. In general, American workers must be fully unemployed to collect unemployment benefits.

WORLD STATISTICS

Area and Population by Country

Mid-1983 Estimates

Country	Area[1]	Population
Afghanistan	251,000	17,220,000
Albania	11,100	2,840,000
Algeria	919,595	20,000,000
Andorra	175	35,000
Angola	481,350	7,450,000
Antigua and Barbuda	171	80,000
Argentina	1,072,067	29,630,000
Australia	2,966,150	15,370,000
Austria	32,375	7,550,000
Bahamas	5,382	220,000
Bahrain	254	375,000
Bangladesh	55,598	94,650,000
Barbados	166	250,000
Belgium	11,781	9,860,000
Belize	8,867	160,000
Benin	43,483	3,725,000
Bhutan	18,000	1,350,000
Bolivia	424,162	6,080,000
Botswana	222,000	900,000
Brazil	3,286,470	129,660,000
Bulgaria	42,823	8,940,000
Burma	261,789	37,500,000
Burundi	10,747	4,420,000
Cambodia	69,884	7,000,000
Cameroon	183,569	9,160,000
Canada	3,851,809	24,910,000
Cape Verde	1,557	340,000
Central African Republic	241,313	2,500,000
Chad	495,752	4,650,000
Chile	292,132	11,680,000
China, People's Republic of[2]	3,691,521	1,020,000,000
China, Republic of[3]	13,895	18,350,000
Colombia	455,355	28,575,000
Comoros	719	420,000
Congo	132,046	1,625,000
Costa Rica	19,652	2,440,000
Cuba	44,218	9,890,000
Cyprus	3,572	650,000
Czechoslovakia	49,374	15,420,000
Denmark[4]	16,631	5,110,000
Djibouti	8,996	330,000
Dominica	290	85,000
Dominican Republic	18,704	5,960,000
Ecuador	109,484	9,250,000
Egypt	385,227	44,750,000
El Salvador	8,260	5,150,000
Equatorial Guinea	10,830	380,000
Ethiopia	472,432	33,680,000
Fiji	7,078	670,000
Finland	130,119	4,860,000
France	211,208	54,650,000
Gabon	103,346	560,000
Gambia	4,093	640,000
Germany, East[5]	41,767	16,700,000
Germany, West[6]	96,010	61,420,000
Ghana	92,100	12,700,000
Greece	50,961	9,800,000
Grenada	133	110,000
Guatemala	42,042	7,700,000
Guinea	94,925	5,300,000
Guinea-Bissau	13,948	590,000
Guyana	83,000	925,000
Haiti	10,714	5,200,000
Honduras	43,277	4,090,000
Hungary	35,919	10,690,000
Iceland	39,709	235,000
India[7]	1,229,737	700,000,000
Indonesia[8]	735,268	153,000,000
Iran	636,293	41,640,000
Iraq	169,284	14,000,000
Ireland	26,600	3,510,000
Israel	7,992[9]	4,100,000
Italy	116,311	56,500,000
Ivory Coast	124,502	8,500,000
Jamaica	4,411	2,250,000
Japan	143,574	119,260,000
Jordan	37,297	3,475,000
Kenya	224,960	18,780,000
Kiribati	264	60,000
Korea, North	46,768	18,750,000
Korea, South	38,031	39,950,000
Kuwait	7,780	1,670,000
Laos	91,429	3,900,000
Lebanon	4,015	2,700,000
Lesotho	11,720	1,400,000
Liberia	43,000	2,150,000
Libya	679,536	3,250,000
Liechtenstein	61	30,000
Luxembourg	999	370,000
Madagascar	230,035	9,400,000
Malawi	45,747	6,430,000
Malaysia	128,328	14,750,000
Maldives	115	160,000
Mall	478,819	7,530,000
Malta	122	375,000
Mauritania	397,573	1,725,000
Mauritius	787	960,000
Mexico	761,600	72,900,000
Monaco	([10])	30,000
Mongolia	604,250	1,725,000
Morocco	177,116	21,275,000
Mozambique	303,073	11,100,000
Nauru	8.2	8,000
Nepal	54,463	15,325,000
Netherlands	13,104	14,360,000
New Zealand[11]	103,884	3,200,000
Nicaragua	57,143	3,060,000
Niger	489,206	5,650,000
Nigeria	356,700	82,250,000
Norway	125,056	4,130,000
Oman[12]	105,000	950,000
Pakistan[13]	310,400	89,730,000
Panama	29,761	2,090,000
Papua New Guinea	178,704	3,190,000
Paraguay	157,047	3,470,000
Peru	496,222	18,710,000
Philippines	115,830	51,960,000
Poland	120,727	36,570,000
Portugal	34,340	10,100,000
Qatar	4,000	260,000
Romania	91,700	22,550,000
Rwanda	10,169	5,200,000
St. Lucia	238	125,000
St. Vincent and the Grenadines	250	150,000
San Marino	23.6	20,500
São Tomé and Príncipe	372	90,000

Country	Area[1]	Population
Saudi Arabia	873,000	9,700,000
Senegal	75,954	6,320,000
Seychelles	171	60,000
Sierra Leone	27,925	3,675,000
Singapore	238	2,500,000
Solomon Islands	11,500	250,000
Somalia	246,199	5,150,000
South Africa[14]	440,355	23,500,000
Spain[15]	194,885	38,230,000
Sri Lanka	25,332	15,420,000
Sudan	967,491	19,150,000
Suriname	63,251	410,000
Swaziland	6,704	610,000
Sweden	173,229	8,330,000
Switzerland	15,941	6,510,000
Syria	71,498	9,610,000
Tanzania[16]	364,900	20,380,000
Thailand	198,455	49,460,000
Togo	21,925	2,800,000
Tonga	290	100,000
Trinidad and Tobago	1,980	1,150,000
Tunisia	63,379	6,890,000
Turkey	300,947	47,280,000
Tuvalu	10	7,000
Uganda	91,343	14,000,000
U.S.S.R.	8,649,489	269,850,000
United Arab Emirates	32,000	1,210,000
United Kingdom	94,249	55,850,000
United States	3,540,939	233,700,000
Upper Volta	105,870	7,170,000
Uruguay	68,548	2,970,000
Vanuatu	5,700	120,000
Vatican City State	([17])	1,000
Venezuela	352,143	16,390,000
Vietnam	127,246	56,250,000
Western Samoa	1,093	160,000
Yemen, People's Democratic Republic of[18]	111,000	2,160,000
Yemen Arab Republic	75,290	8,575,000
Yugoslavia	98,766	22,860,000
Zaire	905,365	28,150,000
Zambia	290,586	6,240,000
Zimbabwe	150,699	7,740,000

1. Square miles. 2. Including Manchuria and Tibet. 3. Excluding Quemoy and Matsu. 4. Excluding Faeroe Islands and Greenland. 5. Including East Berlin. 6. Excluding West Berlin. 7. Including Jammu and Kashmir and Sikkim. 8. Including Portuguese East Timor, annexed in 1976, and Irian Jaya (former Netherlands New Guinea and later West Irian). 9. Excluding territory occupied in 1967 war. 10. 0.65 square mile. 11. Excluding dependencies. 12. Excluding Kuria Muria Islands. 13. Excluding Jammu and Kashmir. 14. Excluding South-West Africa (Namibia), Bophuthatswana, Transkei, Venda, and Ciskei. 15. Including Balearic and Canary Islands. 16. Including Zanzibar. 17. 0.17 square mile. 18. Excluding Perim and Kamaran Islands.

Largest Cities of the World

Census figures and population estimates in the following table are based on data reflecting different years. Some cities include metropolitan areas or contiguous suburbs, while others report only those residing within precise geographical or physical boundaries. Therefore, the ratings in this listing must be considered approximate.

City	Population	Year
Shanghai	10,820,000	1970E
Mexico City	9,191,295	1979E
Calcutta	9,165,650	1981C
Seoul, South Korea	8,364,379	1980C
Tokyo	8,334,860	1981E
Moscow	8,302,000	1982E
Bombay	8,227,332	1981C
Peking	7,570,000	1970E
New York	7,071,639	1980C
São Paulo	7,033,529	1980C
London	6,696,008	1981C
Jakarta, Indonesia	6,503,449	1980C
Rio de Janeiro	5,093,232	1980C
Cairo	5,074,016	1976C
Leningrad	4,722,000	1982E
Teheran	4,530,233	1976C
Santiago	4,039,287	1982E
Lima	3,968,972	1981C
Karachi, Pakistan	3,498,634	1972C
Sydney	3,280,900	1981E

Source: United Nations *Demographic Yearbook, 1982* and official estimates. NOTE: E = estimate: C = census.

Some Other Large Foreign Cities

City	Population	Year[1]
Addis Ababa, Ethiopia	1,408,068	1982E
Ahmedabad, India	2,515,195[1]	1981C
Alexandria, Egypt	2,317,705	1976C
Algiers	2,500,000	1982E
Amman, Jordon	650,000	1981E
Amsterdam	715,000	1982E
Ankara, Turkey	2,561,765	1980C
Antwerp, Belgium	190,000	1982E
Athens	855,136	1981C
Auckland, New Zealand	825,000	1982E
Baghdad, Iraq	3,300,000	1982E
Baku, U.S.S.R.	1,650,000	1982E
Badung, Indonesia	1,462,637	1980C
Bangalore, India	2,913,537	1981C
Barcelona	1,750,000	1983E
Barranquilla, Colombia	865,000	1982E
Beirut, Lebanon	750,000	1981E
Belfast, Northern Ireland	345,800	1980E
Belgrade, Yugoslavia	1,000,000	1982E
Belo Horizonte, Brazil	1,442,483	1980C
Berlin[3]	3,046,000	1980E
Bern, Switzerland	147,300	1981E
Birmingham, England	1,006,000	1981E
Bogotá, Colombia	4,250,000	1982E
Bonn, West Germany	290,000	1982E
Brasilia, Brazil	411,305	1980C
Brisbane, Australia	1,086,500	1981C
Brussels	1,000,000	1982E
Bucharest	1,929,360	1981E
Budapest	2,100,000	1982E

City	Population	Year[1]
Buenos Aires	3,000,000	1983E
Calgary, Canada	592,743[2]	1981C
Cali, Colombia	1,300,000	1982E
Canton, China	3,250,000	1983E
Cape Town, South Africa	220,000	1982E
Caracas, Venezuela	3,000,000[2]	1981E
Casablanca, Morocco	2,350,000	1979E
Chongqing (Chungking), China	3,225,000	1983E
Cologne, West Germany	971,403	1981E
Copenhagen	650,000	1982E
Córdoba, Argentina	1,000,000	1983E
Dacca, Bangladesh	2,500,000	1982E
Damascus, Syria	1,251,028	1981C
Delhi, India	5,713,581[2]	1981C
Dnepropetrovsk, U.S.S.R.	1,110,000	1982E
Donetsk, U.S.S.R.	1,045,000	1982E
Dresden, East Germany	516,604	1981E
Dublin	525,360	1981C
Düsseldorf, West Germany	590,000	1982E
Edinburgh, Scotland	446,361	1981E
Edmonton, Canada	657,057[2]	1981C
Florence, Italy	453,293	1981C
Frankfurt, West Germany	630,000	1982E
Fukuoka, Japan	1,104,483[2]	1981E
Geneva	153,000	1982E
Genoa, Italy	760,300	1981C
Glasgow, Scotland	767,456	1981E
Gorki, U.S.S.R.	1,375,000	1982E
Guadalajara, Mexico	1,906,145	1979E
Guatemala City	1,250,000	1980E
Guayaquil, Ecuador	1,278,908	1982E
The Hague	460,000	1982E
Haifa, Israel	250,000	1981E
Hamburg, West Germany	1,650,000	1982E
Harbin, China	2,750,000	1983E
Havana	2,000,000	1982E
Helsinki, Finland	484,000	1981E
Ho Chi Minh City (Saigon), Vietnam	3,450,000	1979E
Hyderabad, India	1,607,396	1971C
Hyderabad, Pakistan	795,000	1981C
Ibadan, Nigeria	847,000	1975E
Istanbul	2,909,455[2]	1980C
Jerusalem	412,000	1981E
Johannesburg, South Africa	1,550,000	1982E
Kanpur, India	1,688,242[2]	1981C
Kharkov, U.S.S.R.	1,490,000	1982E
Kiev, U.S.S.R.	2,450,000	1982E
Kinshasa, Zaire	2,500,000	1979E
Kobe, Japan	1,375,000	1981E
Kuala Lumpur, Malaysia	1,000,000	1980E
Kuibyshev, U.S.S.R.	1,240,000	1982E
Kunming, China	1,750,000	1983E
Lagos, Nigeria	4,000,000[2]	1980E
Lahore, Pakistan	2,900,000	1981C
La Paz, Bolivia	800,000	1983E
Lausanne, Switzerland	130,000	1982E
Leipzig, East Germany	561,867	1981E
Liège, Belgium	218,000	1982E
Lisbon	812,400	1981C
Liverpool, England	510,300	1981C
Lódz, Poland	850,800	1982E
Lyons, France	456,716	1975C
Madras, India	4,276,635[2]	1981C
Madrid	3,188,297	1981C
Manchester, England	449,200	1981C
Marseilles, France	908,600	1975C
Mecca, Saudi Arabia	500,000	1980E
Medellin, Colombia	1,500,000	1982E
Melbourne	2,775,000[2]	1982E
Milan, Italy	1,634,638	1981C
Minsk, U.S.S.R.	1,335,000	1982E
Monterrey, Mexico	1,100,000	1982E
Montevideo, Uruguay	1,325,000	1982E
Montreal	2,828,349[2]	1981C
Munich, West Germany	1,291,828	1981E
Nagoya, Japan	2,089,103	1981E
Nanjing (Nanking), China	2,250,000	1983E
Nantes, France	255,093	1975C
Naples, Italy	1,210,503	1981C
Nice, France	344,481	1975C
Novosibirsk, U.S.S.R.	1,350,000	1982E
Odessa, U.S.S.R.	1,075,000	1982E
Osaka, Japan	2,635,211	1981E
Oslo	455,000	1983E
Ottawa	717,978[2]	1981C
Paris	2,150,000	1983E
Port-au-Prince, Haiti	790,000	1980E
Porto Alegre, Brazil	1,108,883	1980C
Prague	1,195,000	1982E
Pusan, South Korea	3,159,766	1980C
Pyongyang, North Korea	1,550,000	1982E
Quebec	576,075[2]	1981C
Quezon City, Philippines	1,175,000	1981E
Quito, Ecuador	800,000	1983E
Rangoon, Burma	2,250,000	1983E
Recife, Brazil	1,184,215	1980C
Riyadh, Saudi Arabia	1,250,000	1980E
Rome	2,830,569	1981C
Rosario, Argentina	950,000	1983E
Rotterdam	580,000	1982E
Salvador, Brazil	1,496,276	1980C
San José, Costa Rica	850,000	1982E
Santiago, Chile	4,039,287	1982E
Santo Domingo, Dominican Republic	1,250,000	1982E
Sapporo, Japan	1,433,355	1981E
Seville, Spain	650,000	1983E
Sheffield, England	477,142	1981C
Shenyang, China	3,500,000	1983E
Singapore, Singapore	2,471,800	1982E
Sofia, Bulgaria	1,052,433	1980E
Stockholm	650,000	1982E
Stuttgart, West Germany	583,001	1981E
Surabaja, Indonesia	2,100,000	1982E
Sverdlovsk, U.S.S.R.	1,245,000	1982E
Sydney, Australia	3,280,900	1981E
Taipei, Taiwan	2,300,000	1982E
Tashkent, U.S.S.R.	1,865,000	1982E
Tbilisi, U.S.S.R.	1,100,000	1982E
Tel Aviv-Jaffa, Israel	350,000	1981E
Tianjin (Tientsin), China	5,000,000	1983E
Toronto	2,998,947[2]	1981C
Tunis, Tunisia	1,000,000	1981E
Turin, Italy	1,103,520	1981C
Valparaiso, Chile	266,577	1982E
Valencia, Spain	751,734	1981C
Vancouver, Canada	1,268,183[2]	1981C
Venice	117,149	1980E
Vienna	1,550,600	1983E
Volgograd, U.S.S.R.	929,000	1979C
Warsaw	1,625,000	1982E
Wellington, New Zealand	345,000	1982E
Winnipeg, Canada	584,842[2]	1981C
Yokohama, Japan	2,806,523	1981E
Zurich	371,600	1981E

1. E = estimated; C = census. 2. Figure is for metropolitan area and may include suburbs or some rural population. 3. West Berlin, 1,900,000; East Berlin, 1,046,000. NOTE: The population of many other cities will be found throughout the World History section under individual countries. *See* Table of Contents.

Expectation of Life by Age and Sex for Selected Countries

		Average future lifetime in years at stated age											
		Males						Females					
Country	Period	0	1	10	20	40	60	0	1	10	20	40	60
NORTH AMERICA													
United States	1979	70.0	70.1	61.4	51.9	33.7	17.5	77.8	77.7	69.0	59.2	40.0	22.6
Canada	1975–77	70.2	70.2	61.6	52.1	33.6	17.2	77.5	77.4	68.7	58.9	39.7	22.0
Mexico	1979	62.1	—	—	—	—	—	66.0	—	—	—	—	—
Trinidad and Tobago	1970	64.1	65.6	57.3	47.8	29.5	13.6	68.1	69.3	60.9	51.3	32.7	16.3
CENTRAL AND SOUTH AMERICA													
Brazil	1960–70	57.6	—	56.2	47.0	30.0	15.0	61.1	—	58.9	49.7	32.5	16.6
Chile	1975–80	61.3	65.2	57.7	48.3	30.9	15.9	67.6	70.6	62.8	53.2	35.2	18.9
Costa Rica	1972–74	66.3	69.1	61.3	51.8	33.8	17.4	70.5	72.7	64.9	55.2	36.5	19.2
Ecuador[1]	1974–79	59.5	63.3	57.4	48.6	32.1	16.5	61.8	65.4	59.2	50.3	33.5	17.4
Guatemala	1972–73	53.7	—	55.3	46.5	30.5	16.2	55.5	—	56.6	47.8	31.6	16.6
Panama[2]	1970	64.3	66.4	59.9	50.8	33.4	17.0	67.5	69.4	62.7	53.6	36.1	19.9
Peru	1975–80	55.1	—	—	—	—	—	58.0	—	—	—	—	—
Uruguay	1975–80	66.3	—	—	—	—	—	72.8	—	—	—	—	—
Venezuela	1975	65.0	67.3	59.6	50.2	32.6	17.1	69.7	71.5	63.8	54.2	35.6	18.9
EUROPE													
Austria	1980	69.0	69.1	60.4	51.0	32.5	16.4	76.1	76.1	67.3	57.7	38.3	20.4
Belgium	1972–76	68.6	68.9	60.3	50.7	32.0	15.5	75.1	75.2	66.5	56.7	37.5	19.7
Cyprus	1979–81	72.3	—	63.8	54.0	34.6	17.3	76.0	—	67.2	57.3	37.7	19.5
Czechoslovakia	1981	67.0	67.3	58.8	49.1	30.5	14.9	74.3	74.4	65.9	56.0	36.7	19.0
Denmark[3]	1980–81	71.1	70.8	62.1	52.4	33.7	17.0	77.2	76.8	68.0	58.2	38.9	21.5
Finland	1981	69.5	69.0	60.3	50.6	32.0	16.0	77.8	77.2	68.4	58.5	39.0	20.7
France	1978–80	70.1	69.9	61.2	51.6	33.1	17.1	78.2	77.9	69.1	59.4	40.1	22.2
Germany, East[4]	1981	69.0	68.9	60.3	50.7	32.1	15.6	74.8	74.6	65.9	56.1	36.7	19.0
Germany, West[4]	1979–81	69.9	69.9	61.2	51.6	33.0	16.4	76.6	76.5	67.8	58.0	38.7	20.7
Greece	1970	70.1	72.2	63.8	54.1	35.1	17.5	73.6	75.3	66.9	57.1	37.8	19.3
Hungary	1981	66.0	66.5	57.8	48.2	30.0	15.2	73.4	73.7	64.9	55.1	36.1	19.0
Ireland	1970–72	68.8	69.2	60.6	51.0	32.1	15.6	73.5	73.8	65.1	55.3	36.0	18.7
Italy	1974–77	69.7	70.3	61.6	52.0	33.0	16.5	75.9	76.3	67.6	57.7	38.3	20.3
Netherlands	1980	72.4	72.2	63.4	53.7	34.6	17.4	79.2	78.8	70.0	60.2	40.7	22.5
Norway	1980–81	72.5	72.1	63.4	53.7	34.8	17.8	79.2	78.8	69.9	60.1	40.6	22.3
Poland	1981	67.1	67.7	59.0	49.5	31.2	15.8	75.2	75.6	66.8	57.0	37.7	20.1
Portugal	1975	65.1	67.0	58.8	49.4	31.4	15.6	72.9	74.5	66.2	56.5	37.3	19.6
Spain	1975	70.4	70.9	62.3	52.6	33.8	17.1	76.2	76.5	67.8	58.0	38.6	20.6
Sweden	1981	73.0	72.6	63.8	54.0	35.1	17.9	79.1	78.6	69.7	59.9	40.4	22.1
Switzerland	1977–78	72.0	71.7	63.1	53.5	34.8	17.8	78.7	78.3	69.5	59.7	40.3	22.1
U.S.S.R.	1971–72	64.0	—	—	—	—	—	74.0	—	—	—	—	—
United Kingdom													
England and Wales	1978–80	70.4	70.4	61.7	52.0	32.9	17.1	76.6	76.4	67.6	57.8	38.4	20.7
Northern Ireland	1976–78	67.8	68.0	59.4	49.8	31.2	15.0	74.1	74.3	65.7	55.8	36.5	19.1
Scotland	1979–81	68.6	68.5	59.8	50.2	31.2	15.1	74.9	74.7	65.9	56.1	36.7	19.5
Yugoslavia	1970–72	65.4	68.0	59.7	50.1	31.8	15.7	70.2	72.8	64.6	54.9	35.8	18.2
ASIA													
Bangladesh	1974	45.8	53.5	50.5	42.5	28.1	14.4	46.6	53.5	50.3	42.2	27.7	14.1
India	1961–70	46.4	52.3	48.8	41.1	25.9	13.6	44.7	50.2	47.7	39.9	25.4	13.8
Iran	1973–76	57.6	63.5	59.1	49.7	31.4	16.1	57.4	64.0	60.9	51.6	33.7	17.9
Israel[5]	1981	72.7	72.9	64.2	54.5	35.4	18.3	75.9	76.0	67.3	57.4	38.0	19.9
Japan[6]	1981	73.8	73.4	64.7	54.9	35.9	18.5	79.1	78.6	69.9	60.0	40.5	22.2
Korea, South	1978–79	62.7	63.7	55.6	46.2	28.1	12.7	69.1	71.0	63.5	53.9	35.0	17.9
Pakistan	1975–80	51.9	—	—	—	—	—	51.7	—	—	—	—	—
Sri Lanka	1975–80	62.0	—	—	—	—	—	65.0	—	—	—	—	—
Syria	1981	63.8	66.9	59.9	50.7	32.7	16.2	64.7	67.0	60.1	50.9	32.8	16.2
AFRICA													
Egypt	1975–81	53.6	—	—	—	—	—	56.1	—	—	—	—	—
Kenya	1975–80	53.9	—	—	—	—	—	57.5	—	—	—	—	—
South Africa	1975–80	58.9	—	—	—	—	—	61.7	—	—	—	—	—
OCEANIA													
Australia[7]	1981	71.4	71.2	62.5	52.9	34.1	17.3	78.4	78.1	69.3	59.5	40.1	22.1
New Zealand	1975–77	69.0	69.2	60.6	51.2	32.6	16.1	75.4	75.4	66.7	57.0	37.8	20.4

1. Excluding nomadic Indian tribes. 2. Excluding data for the former Canal Zone. Excluding tribal Indian population. 3. Excluding data for Faeroe Islands and Greenland. 4. Including relevant data relating to Berlin. No separate data have been supplied. 5. Including data for East Jerusalem and Israeli residents in certain other territories under occupation by Israeli military forces since June 1967. 6. Japanese nationals in Japan only. 7. Excluding full-blooded aborigines. NOTE: Figures are latest available. *Source:* United Nations *Demographic Yearbook, 1982.*

Estimates of World Population by Regions

Year	North America[1]	Latin America[2]	Europe[3]	U.S.S.R.	Asia[4]	Africa	Oceania	World total
	Estimated population in millions							
1650	1	7	103	([5])	257	100	2	470
1750	1	10	144	([5])	437	100	2	694
1850	26	33	274	([5])	656	100	2	1,091
1900	81	63	423	([5])	857	141	6	1,571
1930	134	108	355[6]	179	1,120[7]	164	10	2,070
1950	166	164	392[6]	180	1,380[7]	219	13	2,513
1960	199	215	425[6]	214	1,683[7]	275	16	3,027
1970	226	283	460[6]	244	2,091[7]	354	19	3,678
1975	236	323	474[6]	254	2,319[7]	406	21	4,033
1980	252	365	484	266	2,618	472	23	4,478
1981	254	370	487[6]	268	2,691[7]	484	23	4,577
1982	257	381	487	270	2,720	501	23	4,640
1983	259	390	489	272	2,771	516	24	4,722

1. U.S. (including Alaska and Hawaii), Bermuda, Canada, Greenland, and St. Pierre and Miquelon. 2. Mexico, Central and South America, and Caribbean Islands. 3. Includes Russia 1650–1900. 4. Excludes Russia (U.S.S.R.). 5. Included in Europe. 6. Excludes European Turkey, which is included in Asia. 7. Includes both Asian and European Turkey. NOTE: Figures are latest available. *Sources:* W.F. Willcox, 1650–1900; United Nations, 1930–79. United States Department of Commerce, Bureau of the Census, 1981, 1982, and 1983.

Crude Birth and Death Rates for Selected Countries

(per 1,000 population)

Country	Birth rates					Death rates				
	1982	1980	1975	1970	1965	1982	1980	1975	1970	1965
Australia	15.8	15.3	16.9	20.6	19.6	7.6	7.4	7.9	9.0	8.8
Austria	12.5	12.0	12.5	15.2	17.9	12.0	12.2	12.8	13.4	13.0
Belgium	12.2	12.7	12.2	14.7	16.4	11.4	11.6	12.2	12.3	12.5
Canada	15.1	15.4	15.8	17.4	21.4	7.1	7.2	7.4	7.3	7.5
Czechoslovakia	15.2	16.4	19.6	15.9	16.4	11.7	12.1	11.5	11.6	10.0
Denmark	10.3	11.2	14.2	14.4	18.2	10.8	10.9	10.1	9.8	10.1
El Salvador	31.4	34.7	38.9	40.0	46.5	6.7	7.9	7.9	9.9	10.6
Finland	13.7	13.1	13.9	14.0	17.0	9.0	9.3	9.3	9.6	7.9
France	14.7	14.8	14.1	16.8	17.7	10.1	10.2	10.6	10.7	11.1
Germany, East	14.4	14.6	10.8	13.9	16.5	13.7	14.2	14.3	14.1	13.3
Germany, West	10.1	10.0	9.7	11.4	17.9	11.6	11.6	12.1	12.1	11.2
Greece	14.3	15.4	15.7	16.5	17.7	8.7	9.1	8.9	8.4	7.9
Hungary	12.5	13.9	18.4	14.7	13.1	13.5	13.6	12.4	11.6	10.7
Ireland	20.3	21.9	21.5	21.8	22.2	9.4	9.7	10.6	11.4	11.5
Israel	n.a.	24.1	28.2	26.9	25.4	n.a.	6.7	7.1	7.1	6.2
Italy	10.9	11.2	14.8	16.8	19.2	9.4	9.7	9.9	9.7	10.0
Japan	12.9	13.7	17.2	18.9	18.6	6.1	6.2	6.4	6.9	7.1
Luxembourg	12.0	11.5	11.2	13.2	15.6	11.6	11.5	12.2	12.3	11.8
Malta	16.0	16.0	18.3	16.3	17.6	9.5	8.8	8.8	9.4	9.4
Mauritius	22.4	27.0	25.1	26.0	35.4	6.7	7.2	8.1	7.8	8.6
Mexico	n.a.	n.a.	37.5	42.1	45.3	n.a.	n.a.	7.2	9.6	9.5
Netherlands	12.0	12.8	13.0	18.3	19.9	8.2	8.1	8.3	8.4	8.0
New Zealand	15.8	n.a.	18.4	22.1	22.8	8.1	n.a.	8.1	8.8	8.7
Norway	12.4	12.5	14.1	16.6	17.5	10.0	10.1	9.9	10.0	9.1
Panama	25.5	26.8	32.3	37.2	39.1	n.a.	n.a.	n.a.	8.8[1]	7.3
Poland	19.4	19.5	18.9	16.8	17.3	9.2	9.8	8.7	8.2	7.4
Portugal	n.a.	16.4	19.1	20.0	22.9	n.a.	9.9	10.4	10.8	10.1
Singapore	17.3	17.3	17.8	23.0	31.1	5.2	5.2	5.1	5.2	5.6
Spain	13.4	16.1	19.1	19.5	21.3	7.4	7.7	8.2	8.3	8.7
Sweden	11.1	11.7	12.6	13.7	15.9	10.9	11.0	10.8	9.9	10.1
Switzerland	n.a.	11.3	12.3	15.8	18.7	n.a.	9.2	8.7	9.1	9.3
Tunisia	n.a.	n.a.	36.6	36.4	44.3	n.a.	n.a.	n.a.	17.6[1]	11.8
United Kingdom	12.8	13.5	12.5	16.3	18.4	11.8	11.8	11.9	11.8	11.5
United States	16.0	16.2	14.8	18.3	19.4	8.6	8.9	8.9	9.4	9.4
Yugoslavia	14.9	17.0	18.2	17.8	20.9	8.9	9.0	8.7	8.9	8.7

1. 1969–70 figure. NOTE: n.a. = not available. *Source:* United Nations, *Monthly Bulletin of Statistics,* May 1984.

Suicide Rates for Selected Countries by Sex and Age Group, 1981

(Rate per 100,000 population)

	Male					Female				
Country	15–24 years	25–44 years	45–64 years	65 and over	Total[1]	15–24 years	24–44 years	45–64 years	65 and over	Total[1]
Australia[2]	17.6	23.1	23.1	25.3	16.4	4.5	8.1	8.6	7.9	5.6
Austria	30.1	43.2	61.9	85.7	40.4	10.5	14.0	19.9	29.3	15.1
Canada[2]	27.8	30.3	30.2	28.6	22.3	5.7	10.1	12.8	8.7	7.3
Denmark[2]	17.3	45.4	63.7	74.5	38.8	5.1	21.6	40.5	36.1	21.3
France[2]	14.0	25.5	38.2	62.3	24.7	5.2	9.1	14.9	21.8	10.0
West Germany	21.2	33.1	40.5	59.0	29.6	6.4	12.5	21.3	27.3	14.4
Ireland[2]	6.2	11.1	12.1	4.3	6.4	2.5	4.8	8.4	3.6	3.5
Israel[2,3]	10.8	9.4	12.9	23.4	8.1	1.2	4.3	6.6	15.9	3.8
Japan[2]	16.6	26.8	32.9	51.3	22.2	8.2	11.9	16.3	44.4	13.1
Netherlands	5.3	14.5	20.7	28.2	12.2	3.8	8.7	12.9	15.9	7.9
Norway	20.2	22.5	32.0	22.3	19.1	3.3	8.0	13.4	6.5	6.5
Poland[2]	19.5	31.8	34.9	24.7	21.8	4.3	4.6	6.3	5.8	4.0
Sweden[2]	16.9	35.3	39.4	42.7	27.6	5.8	13.6	19.6	13.2	11.3
Switzerland[2]	34.8	39.1	53.1	66.1	36.6	12.5	16.0	21.1	25.2	15.2
United Kingdom[4]	7.0	14.8	17.6	18.3	11.4	2.1	5.8	11.1	12.5	6.5
United States[2]	20.2	24.0	23.7	35.0	18.6	4.3	7.7	8.9	6.1	5.5

1. Includes other age groups not shown separately. 2. 1981 data not available. 1980 data shown for U.S., Australia, Denmark, Israel, Japan, Sweden, and Switzerland; 1979 data shown for Poland; 1978 data shown for Canada, France, and Ireland. 3. Jewish population. 4. England and Wales only. *Source: Statistical Abstract of the United States, 1984.*

Cost of Living of United Nations Personnel in Selected Cities as Reflected by Index of Retail Prices, 1983

(New York City, December 1983 = 100)

City	Index	City	Index	City	Index
Addis Ababa, Ethiopia	93	Dar es Salaam, Tanzania	105	New Dehli, India	81
Algiers, Algeria	119	Geneva	111	Nicosia, Cyprus	64
Amman, Jordan	98	Guatemala City, Guatemala	83	Paris	90
Ankara, Turkey	63	The Hague, the Netherlands	92	Port-au-Prince, Hati	95
Athens	90	Havana	67	Quito, Ecuador	59
Baghdad, Iraq	104	Islamabad, Pakistan	72	Rabat, Morocco	76
Bangkok, Thailand	84	Jakarta, Indonesia	97	Rangoon, Burma	72
Beirut, Lebanon	106	Kabul, Afghanistan	70	Rio de Janeiro	62
Belgrade, Yugoslavia	68	Katmandu, Nepal	81	Rome	78
Bogotá, Colombia	90	Kingston, Jamaica	73	San José, Costa Rica	67
Bonn, West Germany	92	Kinshasa, Zaire	83	San Salvador, El Salvador	69
Brazzaville, Congo	82	La Paz, Bolivia	83	Santiago, Chile	85
Brussels, Belgium	85	Lagos, Nigeria	102	Seoul, South Korea	91
Budapest	51	Lima, Peru	91	Sofia, Bulgaria	92
Buenos Aires	80	London	95	Sydney, Australia	88
Cairo	107	Madrid	75	Tokyo	137
Caracas, Venezuela	59	Manila	74	Tripoli, Libya	114
Colombo, Sri Lanka	70	Mexico City	61	Tunis, Tunisia	100
Copenhagen	96	Montevideo, Uruguay	70	Vienna	95
Dacca, Bangladesh	71	Montreal	81	Vientiane, Laos	94
Dakar, Senegal	80	Nairobi, Kenya	78	Warsaw	65
Damascus, Syria	141	Nassau, Bahamas	107	Washington, D.C.	94

Source: United Nations, *Monthly Bulletin of Statistics, March 1984.*

World Bank Loans Reach Record High

The World Bank reported that it extended $15.5 billion in loans and credits to developing countries for fiscal 1984—$1.1 billion more than in fiscal 1983. South Asian countries received the largest share—24 percent.

The poorest countries in sub-Saharan Africa received about 34% of the total financing approved by the International Development Association (IDA), the Bank's concessionary lending affiliate. Its activities accounted for $3.6 billion of the $15.5 billion total. About 92 percent of IDA credits went to countries with individual incomes of less than $410.

Value of Exports and Imports

(in millions of U.S. dollars)

Country	Exports[1]	Imports[1]
Afghanistan	708	695
Algeria	14,143[2]	11,031[2]
Argentina	7,798	5,337
Australia	22,002	24,187
Austria	15,685	19,557
Bahamas	6,546[3]	7,014[3]
Bahrain	3,789	3,730
Bangladesh	769	2,300
Barbados	257	551
Belgium-Luxenbourg	52,381	58,037
Benin	27[4]	312[4]
Bolivia	832	496
Brazil	18,627	19,936
Bulgaria	11,428	11,527
Burma	380	408
Burundi	88	214
Cameroon	998	1,205
Canada	68,499	55,091
Cape Verde	4[3]	68[3]
Central African Republic	117[2]	148[2]
Chile	3,822	3,529
Colombia	3,095	5,478
Congo	814[2]	442[2]
Costa Rica	872	887
Cuba	5,536[3]	6,293[3]
Cyprus	555	1,215
Czechoslovakia	15,637	15,403
Denmark	15,527	17,162
Dominican Republic	768	1,256
Ecuador	2,341	2,189
Egypt	3,120	9,078
El Salvador	704	883
Ethiopia	404	787
Fiji	286	515
Finland	13,132	13,387
France	92,629	115,645
Gabon	2,161	724
Gambia	44	97
Germany, East	21,743	20,196
Germany, West	176,428	155,856
Ghana	873	705
Greece	4,297	10,023
Guatemala	1,120	1,362
Guinea-Bissau	12	50
Guyana	256	283
Haiti	154[2]	461[2]
Honduras	654	712
Hungary	8,767	8,814
Iceland	685	942
India	8,446	14,088
Indonesia	22,294	16,859
Iran	12,505[2]	12,156[2]
Iraq	11,061[4]	4,213[4]
Ireland	7,982	9,618
Israel	5,017	7,960
Italy	73,490	86,213
Ivory Coast	2,235	2,090
Jamaica	726	1,372
Japan	138,911	131,932
Jordan	753	3,241
Kenya	979	1,683
Korea, South	21,853	24,251
Kuwait	16,298[2]	6,969[2]
Liberia	531[2]	477[2]
Libya	15,576[2]	8,382[2]
Madagascar	402[3]	600[3]
Malawi	262	314
Malaysia	12,884[2]	13,132[2]
Mali	146	332
Malta	411	789
Mauritania	232	273
Mauritius	362	463
Mexico	21,006	15,042
Morocco	2,059	4,315
Netherlands	66,322	62,583
New Zealand	5,539	5,825
Nicaragua	406	776
Nigeria	19,484[2]	20,821[2]
Norway	17,595	15,479
Oman	4,421	2,682
Pakistan	2,403	5,396
Panama	309	1,569
Papua-New Guinea	799	1,029
Paraguay	330	581
Peru	3,230	3,787
Philippines	5,722[2]	7,946[2]
Poland	11,208	10,248
Portugal	4,111	9,313
Qatar	4,252	1,949
Romania	11,714	9,836
Rwanda	90	286
Saudi Arabia	79,123	40,654
Senegal	477	974
Sierra Leone	111	298
Singapore	20,788	28,167
Solomon Islands	66[2]	76[2]
Somalia	317	378
Spain	20,522	31,535
Sri Lanka	1,015	1,771
Sudan	499	1,285
Suriname	474[2]	568[2]
Sweden	26,817	27,591
Switzerland	26,024	28,670
Syria	2,026	4,015
Tanzania	566[2]	1,152[2]
Thailand	6,945	8,548
Togo	208[2]	435[2]
Tonga	5	47
Trinidad and Tobago	3,072	3,697
Tunisia	1,960	3,294
Turkey	5,685	8,812
Uganda	345[3]	293[3]
U.S.S.R.	86,912	77,752
United Arab Emirates	16,883	9,419
United Kingdom	97,026	99,723
United States	212,275	254,884
Upper Volta	56	346
Uruguay	1,023	1,042
Vanuatu	23	59
Venezuela	16,443	11,670
Western Samoa	13	50
Yemen, People's Democratic Republic of	779[3]	1,527[3]
Yemen Arab Republic	47[2]	1,609[2]
Yugoslavia	10,265	13,346
Zaire	569	480
Zambia	1,059	831
Zimbabwe	1,273	1,430

1. 1982 unless otherwise indicated. 2. 1981. 3. 1980. 4. 1978. *Source:* United Nations, *Monthly Bulletin of Statistics,* March 1984.

Consumer Price Indexes for Selected Countries

(1967=100)

Country	Total Indexes 1982	1981	1980	1975	Average annual percent change 1975–1982	Indexes for Selected Items, 1982: Food[1]	Clothing	Housing[2]	Transportation
Australia	360.3	328.9	295.5	178.7	10.2	343.1	345.8	396.5	n.a.
Austria	229.0	217.1	203.3	175.2	5.4	206.3	188.2	271.4	247.2
Canada	303.4	273.9	243.5	160.1	9.4	346.4	221.0	307.2	314.9
France	373.1	333.6	294.2	178.9	11.3	378.6	319.4	402.3	431.7
Germany, West	196.1	186.1	175.8	144.1	4.5	177.1	196.2	217.4	206.1
Italy	553.2	481.8	403.2	186.9	17.2	517.7	594.3	539.1	660.8
Japan	303.8	295.7	281.8	204.5	5.5	309.0	310.6	242.8	274.6
Netherlands	268.7	253.8	237.4	175.3	6.1	220.4	277.9	289.6	253.9
Sweden	329.3	303.3	270.6	164.3	10.3	364.5	219.6	398.1	n.a.
United Kingdom	514.7	473.9	423.6	216.5	11.9	547.3	314.0	538.5	535.8
United States	289.1	272.4	246.8	161.2	7.8	285.7	191.8	314.7	291.5

1. Restaurant meals, alcohol, and tobacco are included for some countries, excluded for others. 2. Includes shelter, utilities, and household furnishings and operations. However, actual coverage and measurements vary significantly from country to country. NOTE: n.a. = not available. *Source:* United States Department of Labor, Bureau of Labor Statistics.

Energy, Petroleum, and Coal, by Country

Country	Energy consumed[1] (coal equiv.): Total (mil. metric tons) 1981	Total 1970	Per capita (kilograms) 1981	Per capita 1970	Electric energy production[2] (bil. kwh) 1980	1970	Crude petroleum production[3] (mil. metric tons) 1980	1970	Coal production[4] (mil. metric tons) 1980	1970
Algeria	28.0	4.6	1,429	316	6.2	2.0	54.9	49.0	z	z
Argentina	48.3	37.9	1,718	1,595	40.6	21.7	25.3	20.0	.4	.6
Australia	89.4	60.6	5,987	4,843	95.9	53.9[6]	18.9	8.5[7]	75.6	45.2
Austria	30.2	24.4	4,020	3,283	42.0	30.0	1.5	2.8	—	—
Bahrain	5.3	.6	16,543	2,698	1.3	.2[8]	2.4	3.8	n.a.	n.a.
Bangladesh	4.2	n.a.	46	n.a.	2.6	n.a.	z[9]	n.a.	—	—
Belgium	52.5	54.1	5,329	5,603	53.6	30.5	—	—	6.3	11.4
Brazil	92.0	41.7	757	450	137.4[5]	45.5[5]	8.8	8.0	5.2	2.4
Bulgaria	47.7	32.1	5,261	3,775	34.8	19.5	.3[9]	.3	.3	.4
Burma	2.3	1.6	63	59	1.4	.6	1.7[9]	.8	z	z
Canada	243.8	188.8	10,070	8,852	366.7[5]	204.7[5]	70.4	60.4	20.2	11.6
Chile	10.4	10.8	925	1,152	11.5	7.6	1.5	1.5	1.0	1.4
China, People's Republic of	571.8	297.8	578	367	300.6[8]	107.0[8]	106.0	23.9	594.0	360.0[10,11]
China, Republic of[12]	36.1[13]	37.9[13]	1,992[13]	2,127[13]	42.0	14.0	n.a.	n.a.	2.6	4.5
Colombia	20.9	12.0	752	586	20.6	8.8	6.5[9]	11.3	5.0	2.3
Cuba	13.5	8.5	1,382	997	9.8	4.9	.3[9]	.2	—	—
Czechoslovakia	98.1	77.4	6,403	5,403	74.1	45.2	.1	.2	28.2[14]	28.2[14]
Denmark	29.0	26.8	5,653	5,442	25.4	20.0	.3	—	—	—
Ecuador	5.4	1.7	630	282	3.2	.9	10.4	.2	n.a.	n.a.
Egypt	22.4	8.7	516	260	18.5	7.6	29.4	16.4	—	—
Ethiopia	.8	.7	26	27	.7	.5[15]	—	—	n.a.	n.a.
Finland	22.9	18.7	4,761	4,068	38.6[5]	21.2[5]	—	—	—	—
France[16]	220.3	193.3	4,081	3,806	257.8	147.0	1.4	2.3	19.1[14]	37.8[14]
Germany, East	124.0	104.5	7,409	6,128	98.8	67.7	.1[9]	.1	—	1.0
Germany, West	346.2	313.9	5,614	5,170	368.8	242.6	4.6	7.5	94.5	116.3[17]
Greece	19.5	9.7	2,013	1,108	22.4	9.8	n.a.	n.a.	—	—
Hong Kong	7.7	3.8	1,487	952	12.6[8]	5.1[8]	n.a.	n.a.	—	—
Hungary	40.8	29.1	3,809	2,815	23.9	14.5	2.0	1.9	3.1[14]	4.2[14]
India	136.2	76.4	199	142	116.3	61.2[18]	9.4	6.8	109.1	73.7
Indonesia	36.4	13.8	242	116	7.1	2.3	77.6	42.6	.3	.2
Iran	34.4	27.2	874	947	17.2	7.0	77.9	191.3	.9	.5[10,19]
Iraq	5.7	8.0	595	603	8.0	2.8	133.0	76.5[20]	.3	n.a.
Ireland	11.0	7.6	3,206	2,588	10.9	6.1[18]	—	—	.1	.2
Israel	8.9	6.4	2,255	2,139	12.5	6.9	z	5.0[21]	—	—
Italy	187.3[22]	142.0[22]	3,273[22]	2,646[22]	186.3[22]	117.4[22]	1.8	1.4	—	.3
Japan	420.6	317.4	3,575	3,098	612.0	359.5[18]	.4	.8	18.0	39.7[23]
Korea, North	48.8	28.5	2,666	2,050	35.0[8]	16.5[8]	—	—	36.0	21.8[10]

Country	Energy consumed[1] (coal equiv.) Total (mil. metric tons) 1981	1970	Per capita (kilograms) 1981	1970	Electric energy production[2] (bil. kwh) 1980	1970	Crude petroleum production[3] (mil. metric tons) 1980	1970	Coal production[4] (mil. metric tons) 1980	1970
Korea, South	54.8	20.9	1,416	648	40.0	9.6	—	—	18.6	12.4
Kuwait	6.7[24]	3.6[20]	4,548[24]	4,847[24]	9.3[24]	2.7[24]	80.5[24]	150.6[24]	n.a.	n.a.
Libya	6.6	1.3	2,134	672	3.1[8]	.4[8]	88.5	159.8	n.a.	n.a.
Malaysia	14.2	6.0	987	574	9.0	3.5	13.2	.9	—	—
Mexico	125.7	53.1	1,687	1,048	64.2[5]	28.7[5]	99.9	21.5	7.4	3.0
Morocco	7.0	2.9	339	187	4.8	1.9	z[9]	z	.7	.4
Netherlands	80.5	59.8	5,652	4,589	64.8	40.9	1.3	1.9	—	4.3
Nigeria	17.5	2.7	220	49	5.0	1.6	104.2	54.2	.2	.1
Norway	24.4	17.6	5,950	4,546	84.0	57.6	24.4	—	.3	.5
Pakistan	18.7	10.6[25]	221	82[25]	16.1	8.7[6 25]	.5	.5	1.8	1.3[6 11]
Peru	10.9	8.0	595	596	9.8	5.5	9.6	3.6	z	.2
Philippines	17.5	10.0	353	272	18.0	8.7	.5	—	.3	z
Poland	161.8	116.3	4,507	3,574	121.9	64.5	.3	.4	193.1	140.1
Portugal	12.4	6.4	1,250	706	15.0	7.5	—	—	.2	.3
Romania	99.3	61.0	4,420	3,013	67.5	35.1	11.5	13.4	8.1	6.4
Saudi Arabia	15.7[24]	2.7[24]	1,680[24]	432[24]	9.0[24]	1.1[24]	488.7[24]	188.4[24]	n.a.	n.a.
South Africa[26]	91.7	56.9	2,694	2,250	95.8	50.8	—	—	115.0	54.6
Soviet Union	1,535.9	998.7	5,738	4,114	1,295.0	740.9	603.0	353.0[7]	493.0	432.7
Spain	90.3	49.6	2,397	1,467	110.2	56.5	1.6	.2	13.1[14]	10.8[14]
Sudan	1.7	2.1	89	148	1.0	.4	—	—	n.a.	n.a.
Sweden	42.9	46.4	5,156	5,769	96.3	60.6	z	n.a.	z	z
Switzerland	22.7[27]	20.2[27]	3,488[27]	3,211[27]	48.2[5 27]	33.2[5 27]	—	—	—	—
Syria	7.8	2.4	836	386	3.4	.9	8.6[9]	4.2	n.a.	n.a.
Tanzania	.9	.8	48	57	.7	.5	—	—	z	z
Thailand	16.0	6.7	333	183	15.0	4.5	z[9]	z[10]	—	—
Trinidad and Tabago	6.6	4.5	5,601	4,398	1.8	1.2	11.0	7.2	n.a.	n.a.
Tunisia	4.3	1.5	662	288	2.8	.8	5.6	4.2	—	—
Turkey	32.5	16.8	702	476	23.3	8.6	2.3	3.5	3.6	4.6
United Arab Emirates	5.8	.6	7,558	2,476	4.5[8]	.1[8 28]	83.6	37.7	n.a.	n.a.
United Kingdom	259.1	271.3	4,641	4,895	285.1	249.0	78.8	.1	130.0[14]	147.1[14]
United States	2,344.8	2,216.9	10,204	10,811	2,356.0[5]	1,640.0[5]	424.0	475.3	714.5	550.4
Venezuela	45.1	24.6	3,153	2,392	31.0	12.7	114.4	194.3	z	z
Vietnam	8.1	12.6	148	300	3.9	2.1	n.a.	n.a.	6.3	3.0
Yugoslavia	51.6	28.7	2,290	1,408	58.9	26.0	4.2	2.9	.4	.6
Zaire	2.0	1.5	74	68	4.4	3.2	1.0	—	.1	.1
Zambia	2.2	1.6	373	380	8.9[5]	.9[5]	—	—	.6	.6
World total	**8,493.4**	**6,446.3**	**1,893**	**1,762**	**8,239**	**4,923**	**2,986**	**2,277**	**2,733**	**2,143**

1. Based on apparent consumption of coal, lignite, petroleum products, natural gas, and hydro and nuclear electricity. 2. Comprises production by utilities generating primarily for public use, and production by industrial establishments generating primarily for own use. Relates to production at generating centers, including station use and transmission losses. 3. Includes shale oil, but excludes natural gasoline. 4. Excludes lignite and brown coal, except as noted. 5. Net production, i.e. excluding station use. 6. Year ending June 30. 7. Includes gas condensates. 8. Excludes production by industrial establishments for own use. 9. United Nations Statistical Office estimate. 10. Data from U.S. Bureau of Mines. 11. Includes lignite and brown coal. 12. *Source:* U.S. Bureau of the Census. Data from Republic of China publications. 13. Estimated on the basis of the conversion coefficients in the U.N. *Statistical Yearbook.* 14. Includes slurries. 15. Year ending Sept. 10. 16. Includes Monaco. 17. Includes low-grade coal at its hard-coal equivalent. 18. Year beginning April. 19. Year beginning March 21. 20. Data from Organization of Petroleum Exporting Countries (OPEC). 21. Includes estimated production in the occupied Sinai Peninsula (1970, 4.9 million metric tons). 22. Includes San Marino. 23. Includes brown coal. 24. Includes share of production in the Neutral Zone. 25. Includes Bangladesh. 26. Includes Botswana, Lesotho, Namibia, and Swaziland. 27. Includes Liechtenstein. 28. Abu Dhabi only. NOTES: metric ton = 1.1023 short tons. n.a. = not available. z = less than 50,000 metric tons. A dash equals zero or not applicable. *Sources:* Except as noted, Statistical Office of the United Nations, New York, N.Y., *Statistical Yearbook* (copyright); and *1980 Yearbook of World Energy Statistics* (copyright).

Wheat and Rice—Production by Country

(in thousands of metric tons)[1]

Country	Wheat 1981	1980	1979	1978	1977	Rice[1] 1981	1980	1979	1978	1977
Afghanistan	3,000	2,700	2,663	2,813	2,652	475	461	439	428	400
Argentina	8,100	7,780	8,100	8,100	5,390	286	266	312	310	320
Australia	16,400	10,870	16,188	18,086	9,370	761	613	692	490	530
Austria	1,025	1,201	850	1,195	1,072	n.a.	n.a.	n.a.	n.a.	([1])

Country	Wheat					Rice[1]				
	1981	**1980**	**1979**	**1978**	**1977**	**1981**	**1980**	**1979**	**1978**	**1977**
Bangladesh	1,093	823	494	348	259	20,000	20,822	19,599	19,582	19,441
Belgium	943[2]	906[2]	1,015[2]	1,022[2]	795[2]	n.a.	n.a.	n.a.	n.a.	(1)
Brazil	2,207	2,708	2,927	2,691	2,066	8,261	9,748	7,595	7,296	8,994
Bulgaria	4,429	3,847	3,355	3,466	3,028	71	67	73	61	68
Burma	80[3]	74	41	92	75	14,636	13,107	10,448	10,500	9,462
Cambodia	n.a.	n.a.	n.a.	n.a.	(1)	1,160	1,000[3]	850	1,500[3]	1,800[3]
Canada	24,519	19,157	17,185	21,146	19,862	n.a.	n.a.	n.a.	n.a.	(1)
Chile	686	966	995	893	1,219	100	95	181	105	120
China, People's Republic of[3]	57,003	54,158	62,733	52,002	45,001	146,087	142,338	146,959	138,202	129,470
Colombia	62	46	42	38	29	1,799	1,798	1,932	1,715	1,307
Cuba	n.a.	n.a.	n.a.	n.a.	(1)	518[3]	478	425	458	459
Czechoslovakia	4,400[3]	5,386	3,736	5,601	5,214	n.a.	n.a.	n.a.	n.a.	(1)
Denmark	792	652	590	642	606	n.a.	n.a.	n.a.	n.a.	(1)
Ecuador	41	31	31	29	40	402	381	318	233	328
Egypt	1,850	1,796	1,856	1,943	1,699	2,500	2,350	2,517	2,358	2,275
Ethiopia	491	469	449	429	605	n.a.	n.a.	n.a.	n.a.	(1)
Finland	235	357	208	241	295	n.a.	n.a.	n.a.	n.a.	(1)
France	22,782	23,683	19,522	20,970	17,350	21	24	24	35	23
Germany, East	3,000[3]	3,098	3,116	3,147	2,914	n.a.	n.a.	n.a.	n.a.	(1)
Germany, West	8,314	8,156	8,061	8,118	7,235	n.a.	n.a.	n.a.	n.a.	(1)
Greece	2,750	2,951	2,407	2,660	1,766	74	80	87	93	94
Hungary	4,800[3]	6,077	3,709	5,677	5,319	85[3]	24	41	23	35
India	36,460	31,830	35,508	31,749	29,010	82,000[3]	79,930	63,476	80,660	79,006
Indonesia	n.a.	n.a.	n.a.	n.a.	(1)	33,000	29,774	26,283	25,781	23,356
Iran	5,800	5,700	5,500	5,700	5,517	1,400	1,212	1,420	1,280	1,400
Iraq	1,100	1,300	1,492	910	696	250[3]	250[3]	284	172	199
Ireland	240	235	245	247	250	n.a.	n.a.	n.a.	n.a.	(1)
Israel	215	253	133	169	220	n.a.	n.a.	n.a.	n.a.	(1)
Italy	8,921	9,150	8,980	9,332	6,347	931	950	1,107	979	693
Japan	612	583	541	367	236	12,824	12,189	14,948	16,349	17,000
Korea, North[3]	400	380	370	350	310	4,900	4,800	4,800	4,500	4,610
Korea, South	57	92	42	36	45	7,032	5,311	7,881	8,352	8,291
Laos	n.a.	n.a.	n.a.	n.a.	(1)	1,155[3]	1,053	867	796	847
Madagascar	(1)	(1)	(1)	(1)	(1)	1,999	2,109	2,045	1,914	2,154
Malaysia	n.a.	n.a.	n.a.	n.a.	(1)	2,147	2,171	2,095	1,498	1,922
Mexico	3,189	2,785	2,339	2,785	2,456	644	456	500	402	567
Nepal	477	440	415	411	362	2,407	2,464	2,060	2,339	2,282
Netherlands	882	882	836	792	661	n.a.	n.a.	n.a.	n.a.	(1)
New Zealand	373	306	295	329	354	n.a.	n.a.	n.a.	n.a.	(1)
Pakistan	11,340	10,805	9,950	8,367	9,144	5,093	4,679	4,824	4,908	4,424
Panama	n.a.	n.a.	n.a.	n.a.	(1)	192	156	170	162	186
Peru	117	77	102	113	120	684	420	560	468	587
Philippines	n.a.	n.a.	n.a.	n.a.	(1)	7,720	7,840	7,504	7,198	6,895
Poland	4,229	4,175	4,187	6,029	5,308	n.a.	n.a.	n.a.	n.a.	(1)
Portugal	310	430	252	255	229	112	155	145	135	112
Romania	5,800[3]	6,427	4,676	6,243	6,463	65	39	60	58	47
South Africa	2,090	1,470	2,086	1,690	1,860	3[3]	3[3]	3[3]	3[3]	3[3]
Soviet Union	88,000[3]	98,185	90,207	120,824	92,165	2,400[3]	2,791	2,394	2,096	2,217
Spain	3,356	5,849	4,101	4,806	4,064	441	433	421	401	379
Sri Lanka	n.a.	n.a.	n.a.	n.a.	(1)	2,020	2,133	1,917	1,890	1,677
Sweden	1,034	1,193	1,030	1,290	1,522	n.a.	n.a.	n.a.	n.a.	(1)
Switzerland	391	394	423	408	323	n.a.	n.a.	n.a.	n.a.	(1)
Syria	2,086	2,226	1,319	1,651	1,217	n.a.	n.a.	n.a.	n.a.	(1)
Thailand	n.a.	n.a.	n.a.	n.a.	(1)	19,000	17,366	15,758	17,530	13,921
Turkey	17,040	16,554	17,569	16,764	16,720	290	234	363	305	270
United Kingdom	8,465	8,470	7,168	6,613	5,274	n.a.	n.a.	n.a.	n.a.	(1)
United States	76,026	64,619	58,081	48,322	55,420	8,408	6,629	5,985	6,040	4,501
Uruguay	400	307	430	174	173	326	290	248	226	228
Venezuela	1	1	1	1	1	708	712	653	502	496
Vietnam	n.a.	n.a.	n.a.	n.a.	(1)	12,570	11,679	10,758	10,040	10,885
Yugoslavia	4,270	5,091	4,512	5,355	5,595	40[3]	42	34	34	36
World total	**458,195**	**444,603**	**428,777**	**449,372**	**390,697**	**413,785**	**397,597**	**377,394**	**385,885**	**369,729**

1. Rice data cover rough and paddy, except as noted. Data for each country pertain to the calendar year in which all or most of the crop was harvested. 2. Includes Luxembourg. 3. FAO estimate. NOTES: metric ton = 1.1023 short tons, n.a. = not available. *Source:* Food and Agriculture Organization of the United Nations, Rome, *1981 FAO Production Yearbook,* vol. 35 (copyright).

Corn, Meat, and Sugar—Production by Country

(in thousands of metric tons)

Country	Corn			Meat[1]			Sugar[3]		
	1981	1980	1979	1980[2]	1979	1978	1981	1980	1979
Argentina	13,500	6,400	8,700	3,286	3,486	3,544	1,624	1,716	1,411
Australia	118	151	169	2,313[4]	2,708[4]	2,897[4]	3,450	3,329	2,963
Austria	1,374	1,293	1,347	529	535	504	490	456	408
Belgium[5]	25	39	37	994	951	912	1,100	870	993
Brazil	21,098	20,374	16,306	3,302	3,058	3,218	8,500	8,547	7,027
Bulgaria	2,477	2,256	3,223	450	487	455	150[6]	180[6]	240
Canada	6,214	5,434	4,983	1,845	1,700	1,684	125	89	106
Chile	518	405	489	256	236	224	250	63	104
China, People's Republic of	61,601[6]	61,105	60,149	19,563	18,604	17,518	4,031[6]	3,615	3,587
Colombia	880	813	870	744	731	695	1,185	1,247	1,105
Cuba	95[6]	95[6]	95[6]	210	207	206	7,359	6,787	8,048
Czechoslovakia	800	745	949	1,201	1,183	1,174	870	830	910
Denmark	n.a.	n.a.	n.a.	1,199	1,153	1,050	522	470	486
Dominican Republic	50	49	38	55	62	61	1,032	1,039	1,200
Egypt	2,700	3,231	2,938	291	284	282	679	662	668
El Salvador	487	527	523	44	46	47	174	179	277
Ethiopia	1,100[6]	1,144	1,067	346	344	343	165	167	171
France	9,100	9,358	10,413	3,856	3,840	3,584	5,600	4,253	4,332
Germany, East	2[6]	4	6	1,552	1,549	1,523	740	600	679
Germany, West	832	672	741	4,274	4,194	4,040	3,600	2,994	3,088
Ghana	420	300	380	33	32	31	6	8	6
Greece	1,250	1,158	711	359	353	369	340	198	311
Guatemala	1,052	1,041	941	99	96	85	448	385	377
Hungary	6,500	6,673	7,396	1,042	1,029	998	587	480	510
India	7,000[6]	6,804	5,603	669	658	653	5,587	4,191	6,367
Indonesia	3,991	4,012	3,606	314	306	304	1,449[6]	1,403	1,307
Iran	50[6]	60[6]	57	450	445	437	400	380	600
Ireland	n.a.	n.a.	n.a.	596	579	567	196	161	192
Italy	7,250	6,403	6,197	2,268	2,207	2,051	2,170	1,932	1,707
Japan	3	4	5	1,894	1,832	1,688	770	822	762
Kenya	2,250	1,768	1,800	234	232	230	440	438	322
Malaysia	8	8	8	89[1]	88[7]	85[7]	64	40	75
Mexico	14,766	12,383	8,124	1,120	1,058	1,100	2,518	2,765	3,078
Morocco	90	333	312	136	133	135	352	359	372
Netherlands	2[6]	2	2	1,549	1,528	1,440	1,139	951	915
Nigeria	1,580[6]	1,550[6]	1,500[6]	456	446	414	60	46	41
Pakistan	1,004	947	875	657	628	601	928	624	663
Peru	628	443	621	183	191	191	493	552	716
Philippines	3,176	3,117	3,167	541	507	499	2,394	2,343	2,342
Poland	79	58	181	2,421	2,549	2,505	1,872	1,186	1,782
Portugal	417	534	506	290	278	278	7	10	12
Romania	11,200[6]	11,153	12,425	1,330	1,346	1,223	640	553	571
South Africa	14,650	10,790	8,240	832	884	829	2,050	1,606	2,079
Soviet Union	8,000[6]	9,454	8,373	12,553	13,218	13,309	6,100	7,150	4,700
Spain	2,151	2,208	2,205	1,523	1,465	1,336	1,054	1,010	750
Sweden	n.a.	n.a.	n.a.	475	470	459	374	327	350
Switzerland	117	91	134	466	428	411	136	105	118
Thailand	3,700	3,150	3,300	454	447	429	1,641	1,098	1,862
Turkey	1,100	1,240	1,350	692	655	577	1,300	930	1,052
Uganda	342	286	453	116	114	114	5	5	4
United Kingdom	1[6]	1	1	2,247	2,218	2,133	1,200	1,202	1,255
United States	208,314	168,787	201,655	17,683	17,065	17,498	5,771	5,331	5,061
Uruguay	196	119	71	378	318	377	79	102	73
Venezuela	486	662	848	438	410	400	291	374	351
Vietnam	540[6]	418	475	508	533	505	120[6]	130[6]	102
Yugoslavia	9,800	9,317	10,084	1,119	1,145	1,185	850	709	814
Zaire	520[6]	516	509	60	58	57	50	48	55
Zimbabwe	2,880	1,539	1,200	140	153	164	390	358	300
World total	**451,704**	**394,056**	**418,357**	**109,483**	**108,024**	**106,092**	**92,046**	**84,212**	**88,984**

1. Beef and veal (incl. buffalo meat), pork (incl. bacon and ham), and mutton and lamb (incl. goat meat). Refers to meat from animals slaughtered within the national boundaries irrespective of origin of animals, and relates to commercial and farm slaughter. In terms of carcass weight. Excludes lard, tallow, and edible offals, except as noted. 2. Estimated. 3. Beef and cane. Data generally in terms of raw sugar. 4. Year ending June 30. 5. Includes Luxembourg. 6. FAO estimate. 7. West Malaysia only. NOTES: Data for each country pertain to the calendar year in which all or most of the crop was harvested. Metric ton = 1.1023 short tons. n.a. = not available. *Sources:* Statistical Office of the United Nations, New York, *Statistical Yearbook* (copyright), and Food and Agriculture Organization of the United Nations, Rome, *1981 FAO Production Yearbook*, vol. 35 (copyright).

Communications

(telephones, mail, newspapers, radio, and television)

Country	Telephones, in use[1] 1980 (1,000)	Telephones per 100 population, 1980	Daily newspapers,[2] 1979: Number	Daily newspapers,[2] 1979: Circulation: Total (1,000)	Daily newspapers,[2] 1979: Circulation: Copies per 1,000 population	Receiving sets, 1980: Number (1000)	Receiving sets, 1980: TV sets per 1,000 population	Receiving sets, 1980: Number (1,000)	Receiving sets, 1980: Radios per 1,000 population
Algeria	485	2.5	4	425	22	975	52	3,230	174
Argentina	2,588	9.3	133	2,556[5]	n.a.	5,140	190	9,000[6]	379[6]
Australia	7,153	48.9	63	4,851	336	5,525	378	15,000	1,026
Austria	3,010	40.1	31	2,634	351	2,225	296	3,322[7]	443[7]
Bangladesh	104[8]	1[8]	30	404	5	80	1	710	8
Belgium	3,636	36.9	26	2,242	228	3,500[7]	395[7]	4,500[7]	457[7]
Bolivia	49[9]	9[9]	14	214	39	300	54	500	89
Brazil	7,496	6.3	828[5]	5,094[5]	44[5]	15,000	122	35,000	284
Bulgaria	1,255	14.1	12	2,093	234	1,652[7]	186[7]	2,149[7,10]	242[7,10]
Burma	37[8]	.1[6]	7	329	10	n.a.	22[11]	700	20
Cambodia	n.a.	n.a.	17[12]	n.a.	n.a.	30[18]	4[18]	110[18]	14[18]
Canada	16,531	68.6	126	5,700	241	11,280	471	26,551	1,109
Chile	551	5.0	37	945	87	1,225	110	3,250	293
China, People's Republic of	4,355	.4	n.a.	n.a.	n.a.	4,000	4	55,000	57
China, Republic of	3,166	17.9	31	n.a.	n.a.	n.a.	90[12]	n.a.	226
Colombia	1,718	6.4	38	1,273[13]	48[13]	2,250	83	3,010	111
Costa Rica	236	10.7	4	155	70	162	72	180	80
Cuba	362[8]	3.7[8]	9	891	91	1,273	129	2,914	295
Cyprus	113	17.9	12	67[14]	n.a.	150[7]	238[7]	313	498
Czechoslovakia	3,150	20.6	30	4,641	304	4,292[7]	280[7]	4,432[7]	289[7]
Denmark	3,283	64.1	49	1,876	367	1,886[7]	368[7]	1,950[7]	381[7]
Dominican Republic	165	2.9	7	220	42	385	71	220	41
Ecuador	272	3.3	38	400	49	500	60	2,650	317
Egypt	534	1.2	9	2,475[15]	n.a.	1,400	33	6,000	143
El Salvador	86	1.9	12	334[14]	n.a.	300	62	1,550	322
Ethiopia	86	.3	5	52	2	30	1	250	8
Finland	2,374	49.6	62	2,289	480	1,780[8]	374[8]	4,000	837
France	24,686	45.9	96[11]	10,863[11]	205[11]	19,000	354	48,050	895
Germany, East	3,156	18.9	39	8,658	517	5,731[7]	342[7]	6,409[7]	383[7]
Germany, West	28,554	46.4	412[11]	25,968[11]	423[11]	20,762[7]	337[7]	22,750[7]	370[7]
Ghana	67[8]	.7[8]	5	345[5,16]	31[5,16]	57	5	1,870	163
Greece	2,796	28.9	116	n.a.	n.a.	1,500[7]	156[7]	3,310	345
Guatemala	71[11]	1.2[11]	9	91[17]	n.a.	175	24	289	40
Honduras	27[8]	.8[8]	7	223	63	49	13	176	48
Hong Kong	1,676	32.6	41	n.a.	n.a.	1,114	220	2,550	503
Hungary	1,261	11.8	27	2,585	242	2,766[7]	258[7]	2,700	252
Iceland	109	47.7	6	127	557	63[7]	275[7]	140[7]	614[7]
India	2,424[8]	.4[8]	1,087	13,033	20	1,150[7]	2[7]	30,000[7]	45[7]
Indonesia	487	.3	178[12]	2,358[12]	n.a.	1,405	9	6,200	41
Iran	1,227	3.2	23[12]	473[12]	n.a.	2,085	56	2,050[18]	62[18]
Iraq	320[11]	2.6[11]	5	325[16]	n.a.	650	50	2,000	153
Ireland	650	18.7	7	770	229	757[8]	225[8]	1,250[8]	371[8]
Israel	1,130	29.3	24[12]	801[12]	231[12]	581[7]	150[7]	802	207
Italy	19,277	33.7	75	5,308	93	22,000	386	13,781[7]	242[7]
Jamaica	119	6.0	3	128	59	167	76	719	328
Japan	53,634	46.0	178	65,880	569	62,976	539	79,200	678
Kenya	192	2.1	3	156	10	65	4	540	33
Korea, South	2,898[8]	7.7[8]	29	6,496[11,19]	197[11,19]	6,280[7]	164[7]	15,000	393
Kuwait	215	15.9	7	180[11]	159[11]	542	400	525	387
Lebanon	192[6]	6.8[6]	251	n.a.	n.a.	750	237	2,000	633
Luxembourg	199[8]	54.7[8]	51	1,301	358	89[8]	245[8]	186[8]	512[8]
Madagascar	37[8]	.4[8]	12[5]	n.a.	n.a.	45	5	1,700	194
Malaysia	598	4.5	44	1,796[20]	n.a.	850[8]	64[8]	2,000	149
Mexico	4,992	7.2	352[11]	3,994[11]	n.a.	7,500	104	20,500	285
Morocco	231	1.2	9	230[15]	n.a.	749[7]	37[7]	3,000	148
Netherlands	7,230	50.9	80	4,553	325	4,181[7]	296[7]	4,376[7]	309[7]
New Zealand	1,730	55.0	37	1,067	345	862	278	2,755	889
Nigeria	128[11]	.2[11]	15	527[11]	n.a.	450	6	5,600	73
Norway	1,852	45.2	83	1,859	456	1,195[7]	292[7]	1,335	327
Pakistan	367	.4	119	1,094	14	800	10	5,500	67
Panama	173	9.5	6	148	79	220	120	285	155

Country	Telephones, in use[1] 1980 (1,000)	Telephones per 100 population, 1980	Daily newspapers,[2] 1979: Number	Circulation: Total (1,000)	Circulation: Copies per 1,000 population	Receiving sets, 1980: TV sets Number (1000)	TV sets per 1,000 population	Radios Number (1,000)	Radios per 1,000 population
Paraguay	59	1.8	5	88[14]	n.a.	60	20	190	62
Peru	475	2.7	59	828[11]	51[11]	850	48	2,750	155
Philippines	702	1.5	19	972[21]	n.a.	1,000	21	2,100	43
Poland	3,387	9.5	44	8,433	237	7,953[7]	224[7]	10,500[8]	295[8]
Portugal	1,372	13.8	22	492	50	1,400	141	1,576	159
Puerto Rico	631	20.3	4	475	139	800	233	2,000	582
Romania	1,196[8]	5.6[8]	35	3,998	181	3,714[7]	167[7]	3,205[7]	144[7]
Saudi Arabia	443	5.3	12	143[11]	n.a.	2,100	251	2,500	299
Singapore	702	29.1	11	587	249	397[7]	166[7]	459[7]	192[7]
South Africa	2,662	11.2	24[11]	1,728[11]	66[11]	2,000	68	8,000	273
Soviet Union	23,707[22]	8.9[22]	686[11]	102,462[11]	396[11]	80,000[8]	303[8]	130,000	490
Spain	11,945	31.5	105	4,710[11]	128[11]	9,424	252	9,600	256
Sri Lanka	84	.6	22	n.a.	n.a.	35	2	1,454	99
Sudan	65	.3	3	18	1	105	6	1,330	71
Sweden	6,621	79.6	112	4,359	526	3,165[7]	381[7]	3,140[7,18]	383[7,18]
Switzerland	4,632	72.7	88	2,501	395	2,000[7]	314[7]	2,300[7]	361[7]
Syria	287	3.2	6	104	12	385	43	1,367[6]	218[6]
Thailand	497	1.1	18	1,943[23]	n.a.	810	17	5,910	125
Trinidad and Tobago	77[5]	6.8[5]	4	193	171	210	184	300	263
Tunisia	189	3.0	5	271	44	300	47	1,000	157
Turkey	1,902	4.2	1,115[24]	3,880[24]	n.a.	3,348[7]	75[7]	4,284[7]	95[7]
United Kingdom	26,651	47.7	120	25,221[24]	n.a.	22,600	404	53,000	947
United States	180,424	78.8	1,787	62,223	282	142,000	624	477,800	2,099
Uruguay	287	9.9	28	n.a.	n.a.	363	125	1,630	582
Venezuela	789[8]	5.8[8]	69	2,383	176	1,710	123	5,350	385
Vietnam	47[9,26]	.3[9,26]	3	500[27]	n.a.	n.a.	n.a.	n.a.	n.a.
Yugoslavia	2,139	9.5	27	2,282	103	4,300[7]	192[7]	4,635[7]	207[7]
Zimbabwe	214[8]	2.8[8]	2	111	16	76	10	315	43
World total	**508,286**	**11.5**	n.a.	n.a.	n.a.	n.a.	n.a.	n.a.	n.a.

1. Comprises public and private telephones installed which can be connected to a central exchange. 2. Publications containing general news and appearing at least 4 times a week; may range in size from a single sheet to 50 or more pages. Circulation data refer to average circulation per issue or number of printed copies per issue and include copies sold outside the country. 3. Estimated number of sets in use, except as noted. 4. Data cover estimated number of receivers in use, except as noted, and apply to all types of receivers for radio broadcasts to the public, including receivers connected to a radio "redistribution system" but excluding television sets. 5. For 1978. 6. For 1970. 7. Number of licenses issued. 8. For 1979. 9. For 1973. 10. Excludes licenses for receivers connected by wire to a redistribution system. 11. For 1977. 12. For 1976. 13. 33 dailies. 14. 9 dailies. 15. 8 dailies. 16. 4 dailies. 17. 3 dailies. 18. For 1975. 19. 26 dailies. 20. 32 dailies. 21. 18 dailies. 22. Excludes telephone systems of the military forces. 23. 17 dailies. 24. Data include non-daily newspapers. 25. 117 dailies. 26. Date are for former Rep. of South Vietnam. 27. 2 dailies. NOTE: n.a. = not available. *Sources:* Except Taiwan, Statistical Office of the United Nations, New York, N.Y., *Statistical Yearbook* (copyright) and United Nations Educational, Scientific, and Cultural Organization, Paris, *Statistical Yearbook* (copyright); Taiwan, United States Bureau of the Census. Data from Republic of China publications.

World Population Growth Is Slowing

For the first time in history the global birth rate is declining. National family planning programs are credited with aiding in the slowdown which began in 1965. By 1975 two thirds of the world's governments had taken action to limit births. Cuba and China have experienced the most dramatic declines. The birth rate in Cuba fell 47% from 1965 to 1980 and in China it fell 67% from 1971 to 1979. Only in Africa has the birth rate failed to fall.

The Role of Third World Women

Although women in the Third World perform more than half of all agricultural labor, the image of the male farmer persists. In rural areas, where the men have migrated in large numbers to seek work, women manage the farm and continue performing their household-maintance tasks.

In transportation, due to high transportation costs and few tertiary roads and paths, it is the women who play an important role in the marketing of produce. They carry the foods on their heads.

In areas where there is no piped water supply, it is up to the women to fetch water, assisted by their children. The quantity of water available for the use of the family is determined by the distance, time, and capacity of women to carry it. They also must carry water for needs other than the use of their family. It is needed for agriculture, food processing at the household level, and for watering livestock.

COUNTRIES OF THE WORLD

International Treaties, Agreements, and Organizations

Association of Southeast Asian Nations

A non-military alliance of Thailand, Malaysia, Singapore, Indonesia, and the Philippines, formed in Bangkok in 1967. Its goal of regional economic integration along the lines of the European Economic Community has not been achieved. However, cooperation on international, political, and economic issues has been evolving. ASEAN took its first major political stand in January 1979 when it condemned Vietnam's invasion of Cambodia.

Papua New Guinea now has observer status in the ASEAN.

Alliance for Progress Agreement

Embodied in the Declaration of Punta del Este, adopted Aug. 17, 1961, by the U.S. and 19 other American republics, Cuba abstaining. The U.S. agreed to provide most of $20 billion needed over the next 10 years for Latin-American economic development. The other nations pledged themselves to increase their own contributions to economic and social development and to make the reforms necessary for all to share fully in the benefits gained under the Alliance for Progress.

Central Treaty Organization (CENTO)

Created in 1955 to provide a defense shield on the northern tier of the Middle East against Soviet penetration. Its original members were Turkey, Iran, U.K., Pakistan, and Iraq (which withdrew in 1959). In 1958, the U.S. signed a declaration of collective security to cooperate with the member states. CENTO was known as the Baghdad Pact until 1958, when its headquarters were moved to Ankara, Turkey. Iran and Pakistan withdrew in 1979.

Commonwealth of Nations

An association of equal and independent nations and subordinate areas formerly part of the old British Empire and united by their symbolic allegiance to the Crown. Member nations gained equal status with the U.K. under the Statute of Westminster of 1931, which formally initiated the Commonwealth. Its members consult and cooperate and share trade and other economic benefits. For a list of members, *see* Countries of the World by Groupings.

Arab League

Formed at Cairo on March 22, 1945, as a loose confederation of Arab states seeking Arab unity. Founding members were Egypt, Iraq, Jordan, Lebanon, Saudi Arabia, Syria, and the Yemen Arab Republic, joined later by Algeria, Bahrain, Djibouti, Kuwait, Libya, Mauritania, Morocco, Oman, Qatar, Somalia, the Sudan, Tunisia, the United Arab Emirates, the Yemen People's Democratic Republic, and the Palestine Liberation Organization. Military cooperation has been hampered by differences among the members, except in the Suez Canal crisis of 1956. The league has proved more effective in economic and cultural affairs. A permanent secretariat was set up at Cairo.

The European Community

In 1950, the then French Foreign Minister, Robert Schumann, proposed a "Community" of the French and German coal and steel industries, with membership open to other European countries. The *European Coal and Steel Community (ECSC)* was established in 1952; it eliminated customs duties and reduced currency and trade restrictions on coal, iron ore, and scrap. Original members were France, Germany, Italy, Belgium, the Netherlands, and Luxembourg.

By 1955, discussions began on other ways of increasing European economic integration. The *European Economic Community* (the *Common Market* or *EEC*) was established by a treaty, signed in Rome in 1957, by the original members of the ECSC. In 1970, the U.K., Ireland, Denmark, and Norway were invited to join. All except Norway did so in 1972; the enlarged "Community of the Nine" formally came into existence on January 1, 1973. Greece became the tenth EEC member in 1979 and joined formally Jan. 1, 1981.

The purposes of the EEC include the removal of trade barriers, coordination of economic policies, and increased mobility of labor and capital among its members—much of which had been achieved by 1978. Its aim is eventual economic union of the member nations and ultimate political confederation.

A second treaty was signed in Rome in 1957 establishing the *European Atomic Energy Community (Euratom)* to integrate activities of member nations concerned with nuclear power and technology.

The three Communities (ECSC, EEC, and Euratom) make up the *European Community*, with a Council of Ministers and a European Parliament. A European Court of Justice and the European Investment Bank also function within the European Community. (*See* R.C. Mowat, *Creating the European Community*, 1973.)

European Free Trade Association (EFTA)

Formed in 1959 (formally begun 1960) to promote economic growth and fair competition, equalize the supply of raw materials among the member states, and to expand world trade. Members now include Austria, Iceland, Norway, Portugal, Sweden, Switzerland, and Finland (associate). Denmark and the U.K., originally members, withdrew before becoming members of the EEC in 1973: at that time a new trade agreement was made between the EFTA and the Common Market. By 1966, custom duties between members had virtually been eliminated. The EFTA is based in Geneva.

Marshall Plan (European Recovery Program)

Proposed in June 1947 by Gen. George C. Marshall, U.S. Secretary of State, to meet the need for integrated recovery efforts against "hunger, poverty, desperation, and chaos" in Europe. A July conference of 16 nations (the U.S.S.R. and its satellites refusing to participate) estimated four-year-aid requirements at $22.4 billion. In April 1948, Congress appropriated $5.4 billion. The U.S. established the Economic Cooperation Administration; European nations set up the Organization for European Economic Cooperation (OEEC). Each participating country set aside, in its own currency, sums matching the aid it received. The ERP ended in December 1951, a year ahead of schedule, with a total cost of $11 billion. Emphasis by then had been shifted to rearmament. (*See* S.E. Harris, ed., *Foreign Economic Policy for the U.S.*, 1948, 1968.)

The Helsinki Agreement

Popular name for declaration adopted Aug. 1, 1975, by 35 nations—including the United States and the Soviet Union—participating in the Conference on Security and Cooperation in Europe held at Helsinki, Finland. The declaration particularly stressed "fundamental rights, economic and social progress and well-being for all peoples," as well as the need for joint action to promote world peace and security. The participating states reaffirmed their full support for the United Nations and pledged to respect each other's "sovereign equality and individuality. . . ." They pledged to broaden and deepen détente, and renounced the "threat or use of force" and subversion in settling international disputes.

Outstanding in the declaration was the section on cooperation in humanitarian and cultural fields. The signers pledged themselves to respect "fundamental freedoms, including the freedom of thought, conscience, religion or belief."

Among the stated objectives were: Freer movement among persons, institutions, and organizations; wider exchange of information; increased cultural exchanges and broader dissemination of books, films, other media, and artistic works. The agreement was reviewed in an eight-month conference at Belgrade, Yugoslavia, ending in March 1978, which was attended by representatives of the U.S. and Canada, 32 European countries, and the Vatican. After bitter debate, the conference adopted a summary document that did not mention human rights or other issues dividing East and West.

Another review conference began in Madrid in the autumn of 1980 and adjourned the following July 24 until Oct. 27 without reaching agreement on the major issues of human rights or military security. The protracted negotiations ranged from terrorism to measures to ease emigration, and a proposal to hold a later conference on military security in Europe. The Madrid conference resumed as scheduled but adjourned March 12, 1982, with East and West at loggerheads over the issue of martial law in Poland. The parting exchange of charges reflected widely varying interpretations of the 1975 Helsinki accords that were under review.

Nonaligned Movement

The Nonaligned Movement is a formal association of Third World states designed to promote the political and economic interests of developing and dependent nations. It supports efforts to remove colonial rule and stands behind the U.N. General Assembly's 1974 Declaration on the New International Economic Order, calling for transfer of economic resources to the Third World. The term "nonaligned" originally referred to the position of neutrality between East and West adoptd by many new and developing countries in the 1950s. The present organization dates from the 1961 Belgrade conference sponsored by Yugoslavia, Egypt, and India.

The movement's membership is not open to all developing countries. Although North Korea was granted membership in 1975, South Korea and the Philippines were rejected on the grounds of their close alignment with the United States.

North Atlantic Treaty Organization (NATO)

Set up April 4, 1949, under a regional defense treaty for the North Atlantic area stating that "an armed attack against one . . . shall be considered an attack against . . . all" and that participating nations will take necessary joint counteraction under the United Nations Charter, including the use of armed force. The founding members were the U.S., Canada, Iceland, Norway, Great Britain, the Netherlands, Denmark, Belgium, Luxembourg, Portugal, France, and Italy. Greece, Turkey, and West Germany were added later. Spain formally became the 16th member on May 30, 1982. NATO marked the first time that the United States pledged to go to war to support allies before the outbreak of hostilities. The member nations are represented on the governing NATO Council. Its organization comprises their top foreign, economic, defense, and financial ministers. Its major military commands are SACEUR for Europe and SACLANT for the Atlantic Ocean area. (*See* James Huntley, *The NATO Story*, 1969.)

Organization of American States (OAS)

Created in April 1948 as a regional agency working with the UN to promote peace, justice, hemispheric solidarity, and economic development; and to defend the sovereignty of member nations. Original members were Argentina, Bolivia, Brazil, Chile, Colombia, Costa Rica, Cuba, Dominica, the

Dominican Republic, Ecuador, El Salvador, Guatemala, Haiti, Honduras, Mexico, Nicaragua, Panama, Paraguay, Peru, the U.S., Uruguay, and Venezuela. Barbados, Grenada, Jamaica, Santa Lucia, Surinam, and Trinidad and Tobago were admitted later. In 1962 Cuba was suspended. The permanent body of the OAS is the General Secretariat, formerly the Pan-American Union Headquarters, Washington, D.C.

Organization of African Unity (OAU)

Founded in May 1963 by 32 African countries, the OAU has grown to include most independent African countries; South Africa is specifically excluded; as was Rhodesia; Zimbabwe, formerly Rhodesia, was admitted as 50th member upon gaining independence in 1980. On Feb. 22, 1982, the Polisario Front (guerrillas fighting Morocco) was admitted as the 51st member. Its charter reflects historical Pan-African concern for the political sovereignty, economic advancement, and cultural cooperation of all African peoples. The charter affirms allegiance to United Nations principles; its key section emphasizes the eradication of colonialism and promotion of international cooperation. The OAU has assisted in the relaxation or settlement of border disputes and helped resolve internal crises. In economic cooperation, it has stressed transportation and telecommunications. It maintains a close relationship with the U.N. OAU headquarters are at Addis Ababa, Ethiopia.

Organization for Economic Cooperation and Development (OECD)

Founded in 1961 to encourage world trade and economic progress and aid underdeveloped nations. The OECD superseded the Organization for European Economic Cooperation, which had been established under the Marshall Plan in 1948. Members are Australia, Austria, Belgium, Canada, Denmark, Finland, France, West Germany, Greece, Iceland, Ireland, Italy, Japan, Luxembourg, the Netherlands, New Zealand, Norway, Portugal, Spain, Sweden, Switzerland, Turkey, the U.K. and the U.S. (Yugoslavia has a special association). Its structure is consultative; its decisions, not binding.

Organization of Petroleum Exporting Countries (OPEC)

Founded in 1960 at Baghdad, Iraq, to advance its members' interests in trade and development and in relations with other oil-producing nations. Venezuela took the initiative; other founders were Iran, Iraq, Kuwait, and Saudi Arabia. They were joined by Algeria, Ecuador, Gabon, Indonesia, Libya, Nigeria, Qatar, and the United Arab Emirates. Through such practices as the 1973–74 embargo, OPEC has maintained high oil prices and has generally fixed the price of oil in international trade.

Panama Canal Treaties

Approved by the U.S. Senate in March and April of 1978. The basic treaty provides for turning the canal over to Panama by the year 2000. Until noon Dec. 31, 1999, the canal will be operated by a new U.S. agency, the Panama Canal Commission, with five Americans and four Panamanians on the board. Until 2000 the U.S. will have primary responsibility for defending the canal; Panama will assume jurisdiction over the 533-square-mile Canal Zone.

The Neutrality Treaty, also effective Dec. 31, 1999, provides that the U.S. and Panama will each have the right to defend the canal against threats to its neutrality or the peaceful passage of ships. A Senate reservation gave the U.S. the unilateral right to use force if necessary to reopen the canal or restore its operations. The Senate specified that any intervention would be only to keep the canal open, not to interfere in Panama's internal affairs. (See *Panama.*)

The Potsdam Declaration

Issued at Potsdam, Germany, July 26, 1945, after a conference of President Truman, Prime Minister Churchill (later, Clement Attlee), and Prime Minister Stalin. Pending entry of the U.S.S.R. into the war against Japan, it was issued in the names of Truman, Churchill, and Chiang Kai-shek (reached by radio). The declaration, designed to clarify and implement the Yalta Agreement, demanded unconditional surrender of Japan and outlined surrender terms. It called for elimination of "irresponsible militarism" and for Allied occupation until Japan's war-making power was destroyed. Other major points included "stern justice" for war criminals, democratic reforms, and respect for fundamental human rights. Successful U.S. testing of the atom bomb was revealed to Stalin at Potsdam.

The Rio Treaty

Signed at Rio de Janeiro on September 2, 1947, by 19 American states. Formally the Inter-American Treaty of Mutual Assistance, it provides for peaceful settlement of disputes in the Western Hemisphere and common action against aggressors, whether American or an outside nation, within a defense zone encircling North and South America and including Greenland and Antarctica. Canada, Ecuador, and Nicaragua did not sign, but Ecuador, Nicaragua, and Trinidad-Tobago joined later. In 1964 the members suspended Cuba. Countries in alliance now total 21.

Strategic Arms Limitation Talks (SALT I)

Two agreements limiting American and Soviet nuclear weapons were signed in Moscow in 1972 after three years of negotiations. One was a five-year interim pact limiting some offensive strategic weapons and the number of launchers for intercontinental ballistic missiles carrying nuclear warheads. The other, a treaty of indefinite duration, restricted antiballistic or defensive missiles to 200 on each side. (That number was reduced to 100 in a 1974 amendment.) The agreements were signed by President Richard M. Nixon and Leonid I. Brezhnev, the Soviet Communist Party leader. The talks originated with discussions at Glassboro, N.J., in 1967 between President Lyndon B. Johnson and the Soviet Prime Minister, Aleksei N. Kosygin. On Nov. 24, 1974, President Gerald R. Ford reached agreement in principle with Mr. Brezhnev at Vladivostok on limiting the numbers of all offensive strategic weapons and delivery systems until Dec. 31, 1985.

(SALT II)

A treaty resulting from the second round of strategic arms limitation talks was signed in Vienna on June 18, 1979, by President Carter and Soviet leader Brezhnev and went to the U.S. Senate for ratification. The treaty runs to 1985 and limits each side to 2,400 intercontinental ballistic missile launchers and long-range bombers within six months. The U.S. is already under this ceiling, but the Russians will have to destroy 100 of their launchers or bombers. By the end of 1981, a new ceiling of 2,250 is to come into effect. The treaty allows each country to develop one new missile and to modernize its existing weapons within certain restrictions. Each side would verify the other's compliance by its own technical means. The agreement ran into sharp opposition in the Senate. A substantial increase in spending on armaments appeared to be the price many senators would set for their affirmative votes. President Carter delayed ratification efforts indefinitely following the Soviet invasion of Afghanistan in December 1979. Controversy over the treaty continued well into the Reagan Administration and it remained unratified.

Treaty for a Partial Nuclear Test Ban

Agreement, effective Oct. 10, 1963, signed in Moscow Aug. 8, 1963, by the U.S., U.K., and the U.S.S.R. Although over 100 nations have since signed, France and China have not. The treaty banned nuclear testing in the atmosphere, in outer space, or under water. The signatories can withdraw under certain conditions.

Warsaw Pact

Signed May 14, 1955, by Albania, Bulgaria, Czechoslovakia, East Germany, Hungary, Poland, Romania, and the U.S.S.R. Albania, barred from meetings in 1962, withdrew in 1968 after ideological differences. The pact is the Communist equivalent of NATO, providing that an attack on one shall be regarded as an attack on all.

The Yalta Agreement

Signed Feb. 11, 1945, at conference of President Roosevelt and Prime Ministers Churchill and Stalin. The U.S., U.K., and the U.S.S.R. agreed to require Germany's unconditional surrender and on dividing Germany into separate zones for occupation, with France invited to join as the fourth occupying power. The agreement pledged disarmament of Germany, breakup of the arms industry, punishment of war criminals, reparations for destruction by the Germans, and the wiping out of nazism and militarism. The conference also agreed on terms for Russia to enter the war against Japan. (See R.F. Fenno, ed., *The Yalta Conference,* 2nd ed., 1972.)

START

Strategic Arms Reduction Talks between representatives of the United States and the Soviet Union began in Geneva on June 29, 1982. The meeting was the first on strategic weapons between the two powers in more than three years. Washington had wanted to delay negotiations until it could build up a wide range of weapons. Rising antinuclear sentiment in the United States and Europe, however, prompted it to enter the talks earlier. The START discussions deal basically with intercontinental ballistic missiles and long-range bombers, and are a complement to Soviet-American talks on European-based intermediate-range missiles, which began in Geneva in November, 1981. In opening the talks, the U.S. delegation presented a letter from President Reagan appealing for a reversal of the trend toward increasingly unstable strategic relations, blaming a Soviet buildup for the instability but terming the talks an opportunity "to reverse this process and to reduce substantially both the numbers and destructive potential of nuclear forces." The President said the discussions "must immediately focus on the most destabilizing elements of the strategic balance," which the United States has defined as land-based missiles.

America has proposed that each side reduce its missile warheads to no more than 5,000, roughly a one-third reduction. The Soviet Union would have to make greater cuts in its intercontinental ballistic missile force than would the United States. But the Americans say they would have to cut back on sea-launched missiles to a similar degree.

In response to the American proposals, the Soviet offered to make substantial cuts in long-range missile and bomber forces. But in return Moscow demanded that the United States agree to forgo the deployment of new medium-range missiles in Europe and to accept stringent restrictions on all future cruise missile deployment. Administration officials branded the Soviet proposals unacceptable, but neither side formally rejected the other's proposals.

As the negotiations went on toward autumn, it became evident to Administration officials that the principal Soviet goal in the Geneva talks was to limit American cruise missiles while preparing to deploy large numbers of its own. The cruise missile is of critical importance because of its versatility and relative safety to its operators. Basically, it is an uncrewed aircraft with more features of an aircraft than of a missile, having wings and a turbine engine. It has a range of from 200 miles to over 1,200. The cruise can be launched from ships, submarines, ground stations and crewed aircraft.

A Moscow spokesman said no arms control agreement could be of "any value" if the United States began a new race in cruise missiles while seeking to reduce the heavy land-based missiles in which the Soviet Union has an advantage. United States programs called for the deployment of 8,000 land-, sea- and air-based cruise missiles, beginning in December, 1982. Several Washington officials said the U.S.S.R. was still several years from being able to deploy this weapon. Thus, the Soviet is trying to curtail American cruise missiles while stepping up their own program, which has closed the gap with the United States from ten years to five.

In the Moscow START proposals, all 3,800 prospective U.S. air-launched cruise missiles and some sea-launched ones are counted within an unspecified limit on nuclear warheads and bombs. The American proposals for a limit of 5,000 nuclear warheads includes only missile warheads, and not bombs or cruise missiles.

The START talks were suspended in Geneva on Dec. 8, 1983, with the Soviet negotiators declining to set a date for their resumption. The Russians cited the deployment of U.S. intermediate-range missiles as a "change in the over-all strategic situation" calling for a "re-examination" of issues. The U.S. delegate did not agree with this assessment.

—A.P.R.

Countries of the World by Groupings

KEY

1—Member of the Organization of American States (OAS)
2—Member of the Organization of African Unity (OAU)
3—Member of the Organization of Petroleum Exporting Countries (OPEC)
4—Member of the North Atlantic Treaty Organization (NATO)
5—Member of the Association of Southeast Asian Nations (ASEAN)
6—Member of the Central Treaty Organization (CENTO)
7—Member of the Arab League
8—Member of the Warsaw Pact
9—Member of the European Economic Community (EEC)
10—Member of the European Free Trade Association (EFTA)
11—Member of British Commonwealth of Nations
12—Member of the Economic Community of West African States (ECOWAS)
13—Member of the Organization for Economic Cooperation and Development (OECD)
14—Member of Inter-American Treaty of Reciprocal Assistance (Rio Pact)
15—Member of the Nonaligned Movement

NORTH AMERICA

Canada: 4, 11, 13
Mexico: 1, 14
United States: 1, 4, 13, 14

SOUTH AMERICA

Argentina: 1, 14, 15
Bolivia: 1, 14, 15
Brazil: 1, 14
Chile: 1, 14
Colombia: 1, 14
Ecuador: 1, 3, 14, 15
Guyana: 11, 15
Paraguay: 1, 14
Peru: 1, 14, 15
Suriname: 1, 15
Uruguay: 1, 14
Venezuela: 1, 3, 14

CENTRAL AMERICA

Belize: 11, 15
Costa Rica: 1, 14
El Salvador: 1, 14
Guatemala: 1, 14
Honduras: 1, 14
Nicaragua: 1, 14, 15
Panama: 1, 14, 15

CARIBBEAN REGION

Antigua and Barbuda: 11
Bahamas: 11
Barbados: 1, 11, 15
Cuba: 15
Dominica: 1, 11
Dominican Republic: 1, 14
Grenada: 1, 11, 15
Haiti: 1, 14
Jamaica: 1, 11, 15
St. Lucia: 1, 11, 15
St. Vincent and the Grenadines: 11
Trinidad and Tobago: 1, 11, 14, 15

EUROPE

Albania
Andorra
Austria: 10, 13
Belgium: 4, 9, 13
Bulgaria: 8
Cyprus: 11
Czechoslovakia: 8
Denmark: 4, 9, 13
Finland: 10 (assoc. mem.), 13
France: 4, 9, 13
Germany, East: 8
Germany, West: 4, 9, 13
Greece: 4, 9, 13
Hungary: 8
Iceland: 4, 10, 13
Ireland: 9, 13
Italy: 4, 9, 13
Liechtenstein
Luxembourg: 4, 9, 13
Malta: 11, 15
Monaco
Netherlands: 4, 9, 13
Norway: 4, 10, 13
Poland: 8
Portugal: 4, 10, 13
Romania: 8
San Marino
Spain: 4, 13
Sweden: 10, 13
Switzerland, 10, 13
U.S.S.R.: 8
United Kingdom: 4, 6, 9, 11, 13
Vatican City State
Yugoslavia: 15

MIDDLE EAST

Bahrain: 7, 15
Iran: 3, 15
Iraq: 3, 7, 15
Israel: 15
Jordan: 7, 15
Kuwait: 3, 7, 15
Lebanon: 7, 15
Oman: 7, 15
Qatar: 3, 7, 15
Saudi Arabia: 3, 7, 15
Syria: 7, 15
Turkey: 4, 6, 13
United Arab Emirates: 3, 7, 15
Yemen, People's Democratic Republic of: 7, 15
Yemen Arab Republic: 7, 15

FAR EAST

China, People's Republic of
China, Republic of
Japan: 13
Korea, North: 15
Korea, South
Mongolia
Philippines: 5

SOUTHEAST ASIA

Cambodia
Indonesia: 3, 5, 15
Laos: 15
Malaysia: 5, 11, 15
Singapore: 5, 11, 15
Thailand: 5
Vietnam: 15

SOUTH ASIA

Afghanistan: 15
Bangladesh: 11, 15
Bhutan: 15
Burma
India: 11, 15
Maldives: 15
Nepal: 15
Pakistan: 15
Sri Lanka: 11, 15

OCEANIA

Australia: 11
Fiji: 11
Kiribati: 11
Nauru: 11
New Zealand: 11, 13
Papua New Guinea: 11
Solomon Islands: 11
Tonga: 11
Tuvalu: 11
Vanuatu (New Hebrides)
Western Samoa: 11

AFRICA

Algeria: 2, 3, 7, 15
Angola: 2, 15
Benin: 2, 12, 15
Bophuthatswana
Botswana: 2, 11, 15
Burundi: 2, 15
Cameroon: 2, 12, 15
Cape Verde: 2, 15
Central African Republic: 2, 15
Chad: 2, 12, 15
Comoro Islands: 2, 15
Congo: 2, 15
Djibouti: 7, 15
Egypt: 2, 7, 15
Equatorial Guinea: 2, 15
Ethiopia: 2, 15
Gabon: 2, 3, 15
Gambia: 2, 11, 12, 15
Ghana: 2, 11, 12, 15
Guinea: 12, 15
Guinea-Bissau: 2, 12, 15
Ivory Coast: 2, 12, 15
Kenya: 2, 11, 15
Lesotho: 2, 11, 15
Liberia: 2, 12, 15
Libya: 2, 3, 7, 15
Madagascar: 2, 15
Malawi: 2, 11, 15
Mali: 2, 12, 15
Mauritania: 2, 7, 12, 15
Mauritius: 2, 11, 15
Morocco: 2, 7, 15
Mozambique: 2, 15
Niger: 2, 12, 15
Nigeria: 2, 3, 11, 12, 15
Rwanda: 2, 15
São Tomé and Príncipe: 2, 15
Senegal: 2, 12, 15
Seychelles: 11, 15
Sierra Leone: 2, 11, 12, 15
Somalia: 2, 7, 15
South Africa, Rep. of: 15
Sudan: 2, 7, 15
Swaziland: 2, 11, 15
Tanzania: 2, 11, 15
Togo: 2, 12, 15
Transkei
Tunisia: 2, 7, 15
Uganda: 2, 11, 15
Upper Volta: 2, 12, 15
Venda
Zaire: 2, 15
Zambia: 2, 11, 15
Zimbabwe: 2, 11, 15

Countries, Territories, and Dependencies

For later developments, *see* Current Events

Economic data for each country have been drawn from reports of the United States State Department, the World Bank, the National Foreign Assessment Center, and other sources. Unless noted otherwise.

AFGHANISTAN

Democratic Republic of Afghanistan
President: Babrak Karmal (1979)
Premier: Sultan Ali Kishtmand (1981)
Area: 251,000 sq mi. (650,090 sq km)
Population (est. 1983): 14,177,000 (average annual growth rate: −0.2)
Density per square mile: 68.5
Capital: Kabul
Largest cities (est. 1983): Kabul, 750,000; Kandahar, 225,000; Herat, 150,000
Monetary unit: Afghani
Languages: Pushtu and Dari Persian (both official)
Religion: Islam (Sunni, 80%; Shiite, 20%)
National name: Jamhouri Democratike Afghanistan
Literacy rate (1981): 10%
Economic summary: Gross national product (1979): $2.8 billion. Average annual growth rate (1976–79): 2.5%. Per capita income (1979): $225. Land used for agriculture: 12%; labor force: 68%; principal products: wheat, grains, cotton, fruits, nuts. Labor force in industry: 10%; major products: carpets and textiles. Natural resources: natural gas, oil, coal, copper, sulfur, lead, zinc, iron, salt, precious and semi-precious stones. Exports: fresh and dried fruits, natural gas, carpets. Imports: petroleum products and food supplies. Major trading partners: U.S.S.R., and Soviet bloc countries.

Geography. Afghanistan, approximately the size of Texas, lies wedged between the U.S.S.R., China, Pakistan, and Iran. The country is split east to west by the Hindu Kush mountain range, rising in the east to heights of 24,000 feet (7,315 m). With the exception of the southwest, most of the country is covered by high snow-capped mountains and is traversed by deep valleys.

Government. A Marxist "people's republic" was created by the coup of April 27, 1978. Pending adoption of a new Constitution, a 35-member Revolutionary Council is headed by Babrak Karmal, general secretary of the Central Committee of the People's Democratic Party of Afghanistan, the only authorized political party.

History. Darius I and Alexander the Great were the first conquerors to use Afghanistan as the gateway to India. Islamic conquerors arrived in the 7th century and Genghis Khan and Tamerlane followed in the 13th and 14th centuries. Tamerlane's descendant, Baber, used Kabul as the base for the campaign that created the Mogul empire in India. Afghanistan was torn by tribal warfare until Ahmed Shah of Persia established an emirate in 1747 that unified the country.

In the 19th century, Afghanistan became a battleground in the rivalry of imperial Britain and Czarist Russia for the control of Central Asia. The Afghan Wars (1838–42 and 1878–81) fought against the British by Dost Mohammed and his son and grandson ended in victory for the invaders despite the 1840 massacre of the British at Kabul and later fierce battles in the Khyber Pass.

Afghanistan regained autonomy by the Anglo-Russian agreement of 1907 and full independence by the Treaty of Rawalpindi in 1919. Emir Amanullah founded the kingdom in 1926.

The 1973 coup that ousted King Mohammed Zahir Shah also cut off a 10-year experiment in democracy when Mohammed Daud seized all powers. A coup on April 27, 1978, brought Noor Mohammed Taraki to power and resulted in Daud's death.

Taraki's attempts to create a Marxist state with Soviet aid brought armed resistance from conservative Muslim opposition. Rebels kidnapped U.S. Ambassador Adolph Dubs in an attempt to ransom comrades held by the Taraki government. Dubs was killed on Feb. 14, 1979, when Afghan police attacked his captors.

Taraki resigned on Sept. 16, 1979, reportedly because of poor health, and was succeeded by Prime Minister Hafizullah Amin. As disorder spread, it was announced on Dec. 28 that Amin had been killed and replaced by Babrak Karmal, who had called for Soviet troops under a mutual defense treaty. Pakistan and other Moslem nations called for a U.N. Security Council session and charged that Amin had been executed on Dec. 27 by Soviet troops already present in Kabul. The Council's call for immediate withdrawal of an estimated 40,000 Soviet troops was vetoed by the U.S.S.R. on Jan. 8, 1980.

With 85,000 reported in the invasion force by June, the U.S.S.R. and government forces were still unable to quell the rebels. Despite cuts in U.S. exports of high-technology goods and restrictions on food exports, together with a boycott of the Moscow Olympics by Western and Moslem nations, the Soviet Union refused to withdraw its troops.

The United States charged the Soviet Union with the use of chemical weapons in Afghanistan. Deputy Secretary of State Walter J. Stoessel testified in 1982 that at least 3,000 Afghans had been killed by chemical weapons.

Despite the Soviets' helicopter gunships, heavy artillery and mechanized infantry, the Afghan guerrillas continued to resist, some armed only with 19th-century flintlock rifles. With the fighting in its fifth year, Soviet forces in mid-1984 were estimated at 105,000, and the total number of Soviet casualties was estimated in the tens of thousands. Three million Afghan refugees had fled to Pakistan, another half million to Iran, and at least another half million Afghans had been killed, wounded, or driven from their homes, according to foreign intelligence estimates.

ALBANIA

People's Socialist Republic of Albania
President of Presidium: Ramiz Alia (1982)
Premier: Adil Carcani (1982)
Area: 11,100 sq mi. (28,748 sq km)
Population (est. 1982): 2,875,000 (average annual growth rate: 2.1%)

Density per square mile: 259.0
Capital and largest city (est. 1983): Tirana, 200,000
Monetary unit: Lek
Language: Albanian
Religions: Historically Islam 70%; Greek Orthodox, 20%; Roman Catholic, 10%
National name: Republika Popullore Socialiste e Shqipërisë
Literacy rate (1981): 70%
Economic summary: Gross national product (1979): $2.15 billion. Average annual growth rate (1970–78): 4.2%. Per capita income (1979): $830. Land used for agriculture: 43%; labor force: 61%; principal products: wheat, corn, potatoes, sugar beets, cotton, tobacco. Labor force in industry: 18%; major products: textiles, timber, construction materials, fuels, semi-processed minerals. Exports: minerals, metals, fuels, foodstuffs, agricultural materials. Imports: machinery, equipment, and spare parts, minerals, metals, fuels, construction materials, foodstuffs. Major trading partners: East European countries.

Geography. Albania is situated on the eastern shore of the Adriatic Sea, with Yugoslavia to the north and east and Greece to the south. Slightly larger than Maryland, it is a mountainous country, mostly over 3,000 feet (914 m) above sea level, with a narrow, marshy coastal plain crossed by several rivers. The centers of population are contained in the interior mountain plateaus and basins.

Government. Under the Constitution that Albania adopted in 1946, supreme power is vested in the popularly elected National Assembly, to which the Cabinet, headed by the Premier, is responsible. The 240 members of the National Assembly all belong to the Labor Party and Democratic Front. The only political party is Labor (Communist), led by First Secretary Enver Hoxha.

History. Albania proclaimed its independence on Nov. 28, 1912, after a history of Roman, Byzantine, and Turkish domination.

A battlefield in World War I, Albania reasserted its independence in 1920. A chief, Ahmet Zogu, proclaimed himself president in 1925 and monarch (King Zog) in 1928. Italy, under Benito Mussolini, drove him into exile in 1939 and annexed the country. The Communists under Enver Hoxha established a government in 1944, issuing a Constitution in 1946 (amended in 1950) declaring the country a people's republic. Close relations with the U.S.S.R. ended in 1961 with the Soviet-Chinese rupture. Thereafter, Albania functioned as a Peking satellite, receiving massive Chinese aid to offset the Soviet boycott.

In 1967, the regime closed all of the nation's 2,169 churches and mosques in a move to make the country "the first atheist state in the world."

Albania's long alliance with China ended with the announcement in 1978, that China was cutting off all aid to its one-time partner. Albanian criticism of Peking following the death of Mao Zedong was cited as the reason, but Tirana called the action "arbitrary." There was no indication from Tirana that Albania was ready to return to the Soviet sphere.

ALGERIA

Democratic and Popular Republic of Algeria
President: Chadli Bendjedid (1979)
Prime Minister: Mohammed Benahmed Abdelghani (1979)
Area: 919,595 sq mi. (2,381,751 sq km)
Population (est. 1982): 20,000,000 (average annual growth rate: 3.1%)
Density per square mile: 21.7
Capital: Algiers
Largest cities (est. 1982): Algiers, 2,500,000; Oran, 600,000; Constantine, 500,000; Annaba, 300,000
Monetary unit: Dinar
Languages: Arabic (official), French
Religion: Islam
National name: République Algérienne Democratique et Populaire—El Djemhouria El Djazaïria Demokratia Echaabia
Literacy rate (1981): 25%
Economic summary: Gross national product (1982): $42.9 billion. Average annual growth rate (1970–79): 2.8%. Per capita income (1982): $2,142. Land used for agriculture: 3%; labor force: 19%; principal products: wheat, barley, oats, wine, fruits, olives, vegetables, livestock. Labor force in industry: 20%; major products: petroleum, gas, petrochemicals, fertilizers, iron and steel, textiles, transport equipment. Natural resources: petroleum, natural gas, iron ore, phosphates, lead, zinc, mercury. Exports: petroleum and gas. Imports: food, capital and consumer goods. Major trading partners: U.S., West Germany, France, Italy.

Geography. Nearly four times the size of Texas, Algeria is bordered on the west by Morocco and on the east by Tunisia and Libya. To the south are Mauritania, Mali, and Niger. Low plains cover small areas near the Mediterranean coast, with 68% of the country a plateau between 2,625 and 5,250 feet (800 and 1,600 m) above sea level. The highest point is Mount Tahat in the Sahara, which rises 9,850 feet (3,000 m).

Government. Algeria is governed by the President, whose term runs for 5 years. A new Constitution was approved on Nov. 19, 1976.

A National Popular Assembly of 281 members exercises legislative power, serving for a five-year term. The National Liberation Front, which led the struggle for independence from France, is the only legal party.

History. As ancient Numidia, Algeria became a Roman colony at the close of the Punic Wars (145 B.C.). Conquered by the Vandals about A.D. 440, it fell from a high state of civilization to virtual barbarism, from which it partly recovered after invasion by the Moslems about 650.

In 1492 the Moors and Jews, who had been expelled from Spain, settled in Algeria. Falling under Turkish control in 1518, Algiers served for three centuries as the headquarters of the Barbary pirates. The French took Algeria in 1830 and made it a part of France in 1848.

The fight by Algerian nationalists for independence had widespread political, diplomatic, military, and financial repercussions in France. Politically, it brought Gen. Charles de Gaulle to power when the army and extremist French colonist virtually seceded, set up a "Committee of Public Safety," and demanded that de Gaulle be given power. Ironically, it was de Gaulle who resolved to end the fighting by granting Algeria self-determination and independence, while his former army and French colonial supporters in Algeria joined to create the Secret Army Organization (OAS), a terrorist group that tried to block independence. But metropolitan France, weary of continued warfare, voted by some 15 million to 5 million in January

1961 to approve de Gaulle's proposals.

On July 5, 1962, Algeria was proclaimed independent. In October 1963, Ahmed Ben Bella was elected President. He began to nationalize foreign holdings and aroused opposition. He was overthrown in a military coup on June 19, 1965, by Col. Houari Boumediène, who suspended the Constitution and sought to restore financial stability. While retaining close economic and financial relations with France and the U.S., Algeria entered the Arab bloc and joined the war against Israel in 1967. Thereafter, the U.S.S.R. stepped up development aid.

Friction with Morocco intensified in 1976 as Algeria opposed the annexation of the Spanish Sahara by Morocco and Mauritania following a mass invasion of the former Spanish colony by Moroccan civilians. Algeria formally recognized a Saharan Arab Democratic Republic—composed of Polisario front leaders who fought unsuccessfully for an independent Sahara—on Feb. 27, 1976. The move was accompanied by a break in diplomatic relations with Morocco.

From an agricultural economy closely linked to France even after independence, Algeria became an exporter of energy in the form of petroleum products and then liquefied natural gas. The U.S. replaced France as Algeria's chief trading partner in 1976, buying 40% of Algerian crude oil production. In common with other oil-exporting countries in 1977 and 1978, however, Algeria slowed its general industrial expansion and shifted investment toward increasing oil and gas output and strengthening agriculture. Non-energy industry had proved too costly in relation to income produced and agricultural imports had become a drain on a weakened economy.

Boumediène died in December 1978 after a long illness. Chadli Bendjedid, Secretary-General of the National Liberation Front, took the presidency in a smooth transition of power. On July 4, 1979, he released from house arrest former President Ahmed Ben Bella, who had been confined for 14 years since his overthrow.

Algeria, chosen by Iran to represent it in negotiations in November 1980 with the United States, was able to secure the eventual release of 52 Americans who had been held hostage in the U.S. Embassy in Teheran. The hostages were flown to Algiers on Jan. 20, 1981, and turned over to U.S. custody, ending 444 days in captivity.

ANDORRA

Principality of Andorra
Episcopal Co-Prince: Msgr. Joan Martí y Alanis, Bishop of Seo de Urgel, Spain
French Co-Prince: François Mitterrand, President of France (1981)
First Syndic: Oscar Ribas Reig (1982)
Area: 175 sq mi. (453 sq km)
Population (est. 1982): 35,000 (average annual growth rate: 4.1%)
Density per square mile: 200.0
Capital (est. 1983): Andorra la Vella, 15,000
Monetary units: French franc and Spanish peseta
Languages: Catalán (official); French, Spanish
Religion: Roman Catholic
National names: Les Vallées d'Andorre-Valls d'Andorra
Literacy rate (1981): 10–15%
Economic summary: Land used for agriculture: 4%; labor force: 20%; principal products: oats, barley, cattle, sheep. Labor force in industry: 80%; major products: tobacco products and electric power; tourism. Natural resources: water power, mineral water. Major trading partners: Spain and France.

Geography. Andorra lies high in the Pyrenees Mountains on the French-Spanish border. The country is drained by the Valira River.

Government. A General Council of 28 members, elected for four years, chooses the First Syndic and Second Syndic. In 1976 the Andorran Democratic Party, the principality's first political party, was formed.

History. An autonomous and semi-independent coprincipality, Andorra has been under the joint suzerainty of the French state and the Spanish bishops of Urgel since 1278.

ANGOLA

People's Republic of Angola
President: José Eduardo dos Santos (1979)
Area: 481,350 sq mi. (1,246,700 sq km)
Population (est. 1982): 7,450,000 (average annual growth rate: 2.5%)
Density per square mile: 15.5
Capital and largest city (est. 1983): Luanda, 525,000
Monetary unit: Kwanza
Languages: Bantu, Portuguese (official)
Religions: Roman Catholic, 69%; Protestant, 20%; Animist, 10%
Literacy rate (1981): 15%
Economic summary: Gross national product (1980): $3.3 billion. Average annual growth rate (1970–79): –9.6%. Per capita income (1980): $470. Principal agricultural products: coffee, sisal, corn, cotton, sugar, tobacco, bananas. Major industrial products: oil, diamonds, processed fish, tobacco, textiles, cement, processed food and sugar. Natural resources: diamonds, gold, iron, oil. Exports: oil, coffee, diamonds, fish and fish products, iron ore, timber, corn. Imports: machinery and electrical equipment, bulk iron, steel and metals, textiles, clothing. Major trading partners: Cuba, U.S.S.R., Portugal, U.S.

Geography. Angola, more than three times the size of California, extends for more than 1,000 miles (1,609 km) along the South Atlantic in southwestern Africa. Zaire is to the north and east; Zambia to the east, and South-West Africa (Namibia) to the south. A plateau averaging 6,000 feet (1,829 m) above sea level rises abruptly from the coastal lowlands. Nearly all the land is desert or savanna, with hardwood forests in the northeast.

Government. A Marxist "people's republic" is the recognized government, but large areas in the east and south are held by the Union for the Total Independence of Angola (Unita), led by Jonas Savimbi. President José Eduardo dos Santos heads the only official party, the Popular Movement for the Liberation of Angola-Workers Party. The Popular Movement won out over Savimbi's group and a third element in an internal struggle after Portugal granted its former colony independence on Nov. 11, 1975. Elections promised at the time of independence have never taken place, and the government relies heavily on Soviet support and Cuban troops, while Savimbi receives aid from South Africa.

History. Discovered by the Portuguese navigator Diego Cao in 1482, Angola became a link in trade with India and the Far East. Later it was a major source of slaves for Portugual's New World colony of Brazil. Development of the interior began after the Treaty of Berlin in 1885 fixed the colony's borders, and British and Portuguese investment pushed mining, railways, and agriculture.

Following World War II, independence movements began but were sternly suppressed by military force. The April revolution of 1974 brought about a reversal of Portugal's policy, and the next year President Francisco da Costa Gomes signed an agreement to grant independence to Angola. The plan called for election of a constituent assembly and a settlement of differences by the MPLA and the National Front for the Liberation of Angola (FNLA) and the National Union for the Total Independence of Angola (UNITA).

Despite covert aid to FNLA by the U.S. and open support by neighboring Zaire for the Front's leader, Holden Roberto, the MPLA had the initial advantage of strength in the capital region. Cuban troops were introduced in October and soon routed the poorly trained and equipped FNLA and UNITA forces.

The Organization of African Unity, split over the issue earlier, recognized the MPLA government led by Agostinho Neto on Feb. 11, 1976, and the People's Republic of Angola became the 47th member of the organization.

The new government nationalized 19 major industries on May 19, mostly Portuguese-owned. This, together with Lisbon's objection to the refueling of Cuban troop transports in the Azores, led to a break between the former mother country and Angola.

Although militarily victorious, Neto's regime had yet to consolidate its power in opposition strongholds in the east and south. Less militantly Marxist than their colleagues in the former East African colony of Mozambique, the new leaders sought help from both the Western and Eastern worlds.

In March 1977, Zairean refugees in Angola invaded Zaire's Shaba Province, bringing charges by Zairean President Mobutu Sese Seko that the unsuccessful invasion was Soviet-backed with the collaboration of Angola. The Neto regime, the U.S.S.R., and Cuba all denied complicity. In May 1978, another invasion took place, and this time the U.S. and France joined Mobutu in accusing Angola, the U.S.S.R., and Cuba, all of which again denied guilt.

Neto died in Moscow of cancer on Sept. 10, 1979. The Planning Minister, José Eduardo dos Santos, was named President.

In March 1981, President Reagan asked Congress to repeal a 1976 ban on military aid to UNITA rebels led by Joseph Savimbi but strong opposition caused the administration to abandon its efforts. U.S. firms doing business with Angola, led by Gulf Oil, which has exploited the Cabinda oil field since its discovery, have supported the central government and urged establishment of diplomatic relations between Washington and Luanda.

Portugal's estrangement ended in April 1982 with the visit of Portuguese President Antonio Ramalho Eanes, the first Western head of state to visit Luanda since independence, who denounced South Africa's "undeclared war" against Angola. Chester A. Crocker, U.S. Assistant Secretary of State, came to Luanda in January to discuss Namibian independence with Angolan officials but Washington made it clear that diplomatic recognition must await withdrawal of Cuban troops.

ANTIGUA AND BARBUDA

Sovereign: Queen Elizabeth II
Governor-General: Sir Wilfred E. Jacobs (1981)
Prime Minister: Vere Bird (1981)
Area: 171 sq mi. (442 sq km)
Population (est. 1982): 80,000 (average annual growth rate: 1.3%)
Density per square mile: 467.8
Capital and largest city (est. 1983): St. John's, 25,000
Monetary unit: East Caribbean dollar
Language: English
Religions: Anglican and Roman Catholic
Literacy rate: 88%
Member of Commonwealth of Nations
Economic summary: Gross national product (1980): $100 million. Average annual growth rate (1970–79): –2.6%. Per capita income (1980): $1,270. Land used for agriculture: 54%; principal product: cotton. Major industry: tourism. Exports: clothing, rum, lobsters. Imports: fuel, food, machinery. Major trading partners: U.K., U.S.

Geography. Antigua, the larger of the two main islands, is low-lying except for a range of hills in the south that rise to their highest point at Boggy Peak (1,319 ft; 402 m). Deforested and without major streams, the island is subject to droughts despite a mean annual rainfall of 44 inches. Barbuda is a coral island, well wooded.

Government. Executive power is held by the Governor-General acting for the sovereign, but actual power is held by the Prime Minister. A 17-member Parliament is elected by universal suffrage. The Antigua Labor Party, led by Prime Minister Bird, holds 14 seats and the remainder are held by the opposition Progressive Labor Movement.

History. Antigua was discovered by Christopher Columbus in 1493 and named for the Church of Santa Maria la Antigua in Seville. Colonized by Britain in 1632, it joined the West Indies Federation in 1958. With the breakup of the Federation, it became one of the West Indies Associated States in 1967, self-governing in internal affairs. Full independence was granted Nov. 1, 1981.

ARGENTINA

Argentine Republic
President: Rául Alfonsín (1983)
Area: 1,072,067 sq mi. (2,776,654 sq km)
Population (est. 1983): 28,750,000 (average annual growth rate: 1.6%)
Density per square mile: 26.8
Capital: Buenos Aires
Largest cities (est. 1983): Buenos Aires, 3,000,000; Córdoba, 1,000,000; Rosario, 950,000; La Plafa, 450,-000; San Miguel de Tucumán, 400,000
Monetary unit: Peso
Language: Spanish
Religion: Predominantly Roman Catholic
National name: República Argentina
Literacy rate (1981): 85%
Economic summary: Gross national product (1980): $66.4 billion. Average annual growth rate (1970–79): 1.0%. Per capita income (1980): $2,390. Land used for agriculture: 57%; labor force: 19%; principal products:

grains, oilseeds, livestock products. Labor force in industry: 25%; major products: processed foods, motor vehicles, consumer durables, textiles, chemicals. Natural resources: minerals, lead, zinc, tin, copper, iron, manganese, oil, uranium. Exports: meats, corn, wheat, wool, hides. Imports: machinery, fuel and lubricating oils, iron and steel. Major trading partners: U.S., Brazil, Italy, West Germany, Japan, Soviet Union.

Geography. With an area slightly less than one third of the United States and second in South America only to its eastern neighbor, Brazil, in size and population, Argentina is a plain, rising from the Atlantic to the Chilean border and the towering Andes peaks. Aconcagua (23,034 ft.; 7,021 m) is the highest peak in the world outside Asia. It is bordered also by Bolivia and Paraguay on the north, and by Uruguay on the east.

The northern area is the swampy and partly wooded Gran Chaco, bordering on Bolivia and Paraguay. South of that are the rolling, fertile pampas, rich for agriculture and grazing and supporting most of the population. Next southward is Patagonia, a region of cool, arid steppes with some wooded and fertile sections.

Government. Argentina is a federal union of 22 provinces, one national territory, and the Federal District. Under the Constitution of 1853 (restored by a Constituent National Convention in 1957 and amended in 1972), the President and Vice President are elected every six years by direct vote. The President appointed his Cabinet. The Vice President presides over the Senate but has no other powers. The Congress consists of two houses: a 69-member Senate and a 243-member Chamber of Deputies.

After almost eight years of military government, Argentina returned to elections and democracy with the inauguration of President Raúl Alfonsín's civilian government in December 1983.

History. Discovered in 1516 by Juan Díaz de Solis, Argentina developed slowly under Spanish colonial rule. Buenos Aires was settled in 1580; the cattle industry was thriving as early as 1600.

Invading British forces were expelled in 1806–07, and when Napoleon conquered Spain, the Argentinians set up their own government in the name of the Spanish King in 1810. On July 9, 1816, independence was formally declared.

As in World War I, Argentina proclaimed neutrality at the outbreak of World War II, but in the closing phase declared war on the Axis on March 27, 1945, and became a founding member of the United Nations. Juan D. Perón, an army colonel, emerged as the strongman of the postwar era, winning the Presidential elections of 1946 and 1951.

Opposition to Perón's increasing authoritarianism, led to a coup by the armed forces that sent Perón into exile in 1955. The Peronist Party and Congress dissolved, and Argentina entered a long period of military dictatorships with brief intervals of constitutional government.

In the first free election since 1951, a Perón-endorsed candidate, Hector Campora, won the Presidency in 1973. He resigned July 13, seven weeks after his inauguration, in an effort to hand power back to Perón. The former dictator returned from exile and, with his third wife, Maria Estela (Isabel) Martinez de Perón, as Vice-Presidential candidate, swept the election on Sept. 23, 1973.

Perón died of a heart attack at the age of 78 on July 1, 1974. His widow became the hemisphere's first woman chief of state and was re-elected head of the Peronist movement Aug. 24, 1975. In mid-September she announced she would take a month-long leave of absence to recover from nervous strain and turned the presidential duties over to Italo A. Luder, president of the Senate.

Returning on October 16, Mrs. Perón was greeted with demands for her resignation as both the economic recession and terrorism increased.

The long-anticipated military revolt came March 24, 1976, with a junta taking power. Mrs. Perón and her closest advisers were arrested. Army Lt. Gen. Jorge Rafael Videla took office as president and suspended all political parties, decreed new security laws and censorship.

Political murders and terrorism under the Videla regime mounted, together with allegations of police torture. The economy deteriorated and inflation soared.

Gen. Roberto Eduardo Viola, former Army Chief of Staff, was sworn in as President on March 29, 1981. On July 6, Viola released Mrs. Perón from house arrest and she left for Spain.

The deteriorating economy was believed to have led the junta to depose Viola in December 1981. Lt. Gen. Leopoldo Galtieri, commander of the army, was named president with economic reform as his first priority. However, Galtieri's austerity program brought protestors into the streets, denouncing military government.

Hostile crowds changed to cheering mobs, however, after Galtieri landed thousands of troops on the Falkland Islands on April 2, 1982, and reclaimed the Malvinas, their Spanish name, as national territory. The cheering died when Britain reacted with unexpected force, shooting down Argentine planes and torpedoing the ancient *General Belgrano,* flagship of the fleet. By May 21, when 5,000 British marines and paratroops landed from the British armada, the superior power of an industrialized European nation had made the outcome clear to even the most patriotic Argentines.

Galtieri resigned three days after the surrender of the island garrison on June 14. Maj. Gen. Reynaldo Bignone, took office as President on July 1. Civilian rule was promised by early 1984 and on July 16 Bignone lifted the six-year ban on political parties.

In the presidential election of October 1983, Raúl Alfonsín, leader of the middle-class Radical Civic Union was the surprise winner, handing the Peronist Party its first defeat since its founding.

One of Alfonsín's first acts after his inauguration in December was to order trials of former President Viola and eight other former junta members on charges related to the deaths, disappearances and tortures of thousands of people while the military was in power. Former President Bignone, also was indicted—and held briefly under barracks arrest—on charges brought by the families of two missing servicemen even though he was not on the list of those charged by the government.

Among the enormous problems facing Alfonsín after eight years of mismanagement under military rule was a $45-billion foreign debt, the developing world's third largest. In some circles, fears were voiced that the new civilian government might repudiate the debt, triggering a wholesale repudiation by debtor countries that could bring on a worldwide financial collapse. But after cliff-hanging negotiations with American, European, and Japanese banks representing the country's private creditors, the Alfonsín government agreed on June 29, 1984, to pay $350 million in overdue interest and was moving toward austerity measures.

AUSTRALIA

Commonwealth of Australia
Sovereign: Queen Elizabeth II
Governor-General: Sir Ninian Stephen (1982)
Prime Minister: Robert J. L. Hawke (1983)
Area: 2,966,150 sq mi. (7,682,329 sq km)
Population (est. 1983): 15,410,000 (average annual growth rate: 1.3%)
Density per square mile: 5.1
Capital (est. 1983): Canberra, 251,000
Largest cities (est. 1983 for metropolitan area): Sydney, 3,310,500; Melbourne, 2,836,800; Brisbane, 1,124,200; Adelaide, 960,000; Perth, 948,000
Monetary unit: Australian dollar
Language: English
Religions: Roman Catholic, 30%; Anglican, 28%; Uniting Church (combined Methodist-Presbyterian), 14%
Literacy rate (1981): 99%
Member of Commonwealth of Nations
Economic summary: Gross national product (1980): $142.2 billion. Average annual growth rate (1970–79): 1.4%. Per capita income (1980): $9,820. Land used for agriculture: 64%; labor force: 6.4%; principal products: wool, meat, cereals, sugar, wine grapes, sheep, cattle, dairy products. Labor force in industry: 32%; major products: machinery, motor vehicles, iron and steel, textiles, chemicals. Natural resources: gold, iron ore, bauxite, zinc, lead, tin, coal, oil, gas, copper, nickel, diamonds, uranium, timber. Exports: agricultural products, metal ores, wool, coal. Imports: manufactured raw materials, capital equipment, consumer goods. Major trading partners: Japan, U.S., U.K., New Zealand, EEC, ASEAN, China.

Geography. The continent of Australia, with the island state of Tasmania, is approximately equal in area to the United States (excluding Alaska and Hawaii), and is nearly 50% larger than Europe (excluding the U.S.S.R.).

Mountain ranges run from north to south along the east coast, reaching their highest point in Mount Kosciusko (7,308 ft; 2,228 m). The western half of the continent is occupied by a desert plateau that rises into barren, rolling hills near the west coast. It includes the Great Victoria Desert to the south and the Great Sandy Desert to the north. The Great Barrier Reef, extending about 1,245 miles (2,000 km), lies along the northeast coast.

The island of Tasmania (26,178 sq mi.; 67,800 sq km) is off the southeastern coast.

Government. The Federal Parliament consists of a bicameral legislature. The House of Representatives has 125 members elected for three years by popular vote. The Senate has 64 members elected by popular vote for six years. One half of the Senate is elected every three years. Voting is compulsory at 18. Supreme federal judicial power is vested in the High Court of Australia in the Federal Courts, and in the State Courts invested by Parliament with Federal jurisdiction. The High Court consists of seven justices, appointed by the Governor-General in Council. Each of the states has its own judicial system.

The major political parties are the Australian Labor Party (75 seats in the House of Representatives), led by Prime Minister R.J.L. (Bob) Hawke; Liberal Party (33 seats) led by Andrew S. Peacock; National Country Party (17 seats), led by Ian M. Sinclair.

History. Dutch, Portuguese, and Spanish ships sighted Australia in the 17th century; the Dutch landed at the Gulf of Carpentaria in 1606. In 1642, Abel Tasman (for whom Tasmania was named) proved that Australia was not part of the Antarctic Continent. Australia was called New Holland, Botany Bay, and New South Wales until about 1820.

Captain James Cook, in 1770, claimed possession for Great Britain. A British penal colony was set up at what is now Sydney, then Port Jackson, in 1788, and about 161,000 transported English convicts were settled there until the system was suspended in 1839.

Free settlers established six colonies: New South Wales (1786), Tasmania (then Van Diemen's Land) (1825), Western Australia (1829), South Australia (1834), Victoria (1851), and Queensland (1859).

Sheep raising and wheat growing built the economy, and the white population, which had dwindled to 34,000 in 1820, grew to 400,000 by 1850. Discovery of gold in Victoria in 1851 led immigrants to pour in. The six colonies became states and in 1901 federated into the Commonwealth of Australia with a Constitution that incorporated British parliamentary tradition and U.S. federal experience. Australia became known for liberal legislation: free compulsory education, protected trade unionism with industrial conciliation and arbitration, the "Australian" ballot facilitating selection, the secret ballot, women's suffrage, maternity allowances, and sickness and old age pensions.

The Labor Government of Prime Minister Gough Whitlam, elected in 1972, was itself a victim of the twin economic troubles that hit Australia along with most of the rest of the world—inflation and recession. Opposition parties blocked passage of government budget requests to force Whitlam to resign and, in what was called an unconstitutional action, Governor-General Sir John Kerr dissolved both houses of Parliament in November, 1975. Kerr asked Malcolm Fraser, the Liberal Party chief, to form a caretaker government until a new general election in December. Kerr resigned in 1977.

Following a narrow re-election victory in October 1980, Fraser embarked on a program of spending cuts and incentive to private industry. R.J.L. Hawke succeeded Fraser as Liberal Party leader and Prime Minister in March 1983.

By mid-1982, however, world recession was slowing the resources boom and for the first time in years Australia reported a drop in employment and a record $3.4-billion trade deficit for the year ending June 30.

Australian External Territories

Norfolk Island (13 sq mi.; 36.3 sq km) was placed under Australian administration in 1914. Population in 1982 was 1,800.

The Ashmore and Cartier Islands (.8 sq mi.), situated in the Indian Ocean off the northwest coast of Australia, came under Australian administration in 1934. In 1938 the islands were annexed to the Northern Territory. On the attainment of self-government by the Northern Territory in 1978, the islands which are uninhabited were retained as Commonwealth Territory.

The Australian Antarctic Territory (2,360,000 sq mi.; 6,112,400 sq km), comprises all the islands and territories, other than Adélie Land, situated south of lat. 60° S and lying between long. 160° to 45° E. It came under Australian administration in 1936.

Heard Island and the McDonald Islands (158 sq mi.; 409.2 sq km), lying in the sub-Antarctic, were placed under Australian administration in 1947. The islands are uninhabited.

The Cocos (Keeling) Islands (5.5 sq mi.; 14.2 sq. km) consist of 27 small coral islands lying in the Indian Ocean. Administered by Australia since 1955, the 546 islanders voted in a U.N.-observed Act of Self-Determination, in April 1984, for integration with Australia.

Christmas Island (52 sq mi.; 134.7 sq km) is situated in the Indian Ocean. It came under Australian administration in 1958. Population in 1982 was 3,018.

Coral Sea Islands (400,000 sq mi.; 1,036,000 sq km, but only a few sq mi. of land) became a territory of Australia in 1969. There is no permanent population on the islands.

AUSTRIA

Republic of Austria
President: Rudolf Kirchschläger (1974)
Chancellor: Fred Sinowatz (1983)
Area: 32,375 sq mi. (83,851 sq km)
Population (est. 1983): 7,574,000 (average annual growth rate: 0.0%)
Density per square mile: 232.1
Capital: Vienna
Largest cities (est. 1983): Vienna, 1,550,000; Graz, 240,000; Linz, 200,000; Salzburg, 135,000; Innsbruck, 115,000; Klagenfurt, 85,000
Monetary unit: Schilling
Language: German
Religion: Roman Catholic, 89%
Literacy rate (1981): 98%
National name: Republik Österreich
Economic summary: Gross national product (1981): $66.6 billion. Average annual growth rate (1980): 0.5%. Per capita income (1981): $10,995. Land used for agriculture: 20%; labor force: 18%; principal products: livestock, forest products, grains, sugar beets, potatoes. Labor force in industry: 49%; principal products: iron and steel, chemicals, machinery, paper and pulp. Natural resources: iron ore, petroleum, timber, magnesite, aluminum, coal, lignite, cement, copper. Exports: iron and steel products, timber, paper, textiles, electrotechnical machines, chemical products. Imports: machinery, chemicals, iron and steel, textiles and clothing, petroleum. Major trading partners: West Germany, Italy, Switzerland, U.K., U.S.

Geography. Slightly smaller than Maine, Austria includes much of the mountainous territory of the eastern Alps (about 75% of the area). The country contains many snowfields, glaciers, and snow-capped peaks, the highest being the Grossglockner (12,530 ft; 3,819 m). The Danube is the principal river. Forests and woodlands cover about 40% of the land area.

Almost at the heart of Europe, Austria has as its neighbors Italy, Switzerland, West Germany, Czechoslovakia, Hungary, Yugoslavia, and Liechtenstein.

Government. Austria is a federal republic composed of nine provinces (Bundesländer), including Vienna. The President is elected by the people for a term of six years. The bicameral legislature consists of the Bundesrat, with 58 members chosen by the provincial assemblies, and the Nationalrat, with 183 members popularly elected for four years. Presidency of the Bundesrat revolves every six months, going to the provinces in alphabetical order.

The major political parties are the Social Democratic Party (90 of 183 seats in Nationalrat), led by Chancellor Fred Sinowatz; People's Party (81 seats); Freiheitliche Partei (12 seats).

History. Settled in prehistoric times, the Central European land that is now Austria was overrun in pre-Roman times by various tribes, including the Celts. Charlemagne conquered the area in 788 and encouraged colonization and Christianity. In 1252, Ottokar, King of Bohemia, gained possession, only to lose the territories to Rudolf of Hapsburg in 1278. Thereafter, until World War I, Austria's history was largely that of its ruling house, the Hapsburgs.

Austria emerged from the Congress of Vienna in 1815 as the Continent's dominant power. The *Ausgleich* of 1867 provided for a dual sovereignty, the empire of Austria and the kingdom of Hungary, under Francis Joseph I, who ruled until his death on Nov. 21, 1916. He was succeeded by his grandnephew, Charles I.

During World War I, Austria-Hungary was one of the Central Powers with Germany, Bulgaria, and Turkey, and the conflict left the country in political chaos and economic ruin. Austria, shorn of Hungary, was proclaimed a republic in 1918, and the monarchy was dissolved in 1919.

A parliamentary democracy was set up by the Constitution of Nov. 10, 1920. To check the power of Nazis advocating union with Germany, Chancellor Engelbert Dollfuss in 1933 established a dictatorship, but was assassinated by the Nazis on July 25, 1934. Kurt von Schuschnigg, his successor, struggled to keep Austria independent, but on March 12, 1938, German troops occupied the country, and Hitler proclaimed its *Anschluss* (union) with Germany, annexing it to the Third Reich.

After World War II, the U.S. and Britain declared the Austrians a "liberated" people. But the Russians prolonged the occupation. Finally Austria concluded a state treaty with the U.S.S.R. and the other occupying powers and regained its independence on May 15, 1955. The second Austrian republic, established Dec. 19, 1945, on the basis of the 1920 Constitution (amended in 1929), was declared by the federal parliament to be permanently neutral. Austria became a member of the Council of Europe in 1956.

Vienna has become a headquarters for international organizations, such as the International Atomic Energy Agency and the Organization of Petroleum Exporting Countries (OPEC). In June 1979, Presidents Jimmy Carter and Leonid Brezhnev met in Vienna to sign the second U.S.-Soviet Strategic Arms Limitation Treaty—SALT II.

BAHAMAS

Commonwealth of the Bahamas
Sovereign: Queen Elizabeth II
Governor-General: Sir Gerald Cash (1979)
Prime Minister: Lynden O. Pindling (1967)
Area: 5,380 sq mi. (13,939 sq km)
Population (est. 1984): 235,000 (average annual growth rate: 2.8%)
Density per square mile: 56.8
Capital and largest city (est. 1984 for metropolitan area): Nassau, 139,000
Monetary unit: Bahamian dollar
Language: English
Religions: Baptist, 29%; Anglican, 23%; Roman Catholic, 23%; Methodist, 7%
Literacy rate: Not known
Member of Commonwealth of Nations
Economic summary: Gross national product (1983): $900 million. Average annual growth rate (1970–82): 4.1%. Per capita income (1980): $3,300. Principal agricultural products: fruits, vegetables. Major industrial products: fish, petroleum, pharmaceutical products; tourism. Natural resources: salt, aragonite. Exports: lobster, fish, petroleum products, pharmaceuticals, cement, rum. Imports: foodstuffs, manufactured goods. Major trading partners: U.S., U.K., Canada.

Geography. The Bahamas are an archipelago of about 700 islands and 2,400 uninhabited islets and cays lying 50 miles off the east coast of Florida. They extend from northwest to southeast for about 760 miles (1,223 km). Only 22 of the islands are inhabited; the most important is New Providence (80 sq mi.; 207 sq km), on which Nassau is situated. Other islands include Grand Bahama, Abaco, Eleuthera, Andros, Cat Island, San Salvador (or Watling's Island), Exuma, Long Island, Crooked Island, Acklins Island, Mayaguana, and Inagua.

The islands are mainly flat, few rising above 200 feet (61 m). There are no fresh water streams. There are several large brackish lakes on several islands including Inagua and New Providence.

Government. The Bahamas moved toward greater autonomy in 1968 after the overwhelming victory in general elections of the Progressive Liberal Party, led by Prime Minister Lynden O. Pindling. The black leader's party won 29 seats in the House of Assembly to only 7 for the predominantly white United Bahamians, who had controlled the islands for decades before Pindling became Premier in 1967.

With its new mandate from the 85%-black population, Pindling's government negotiated a new Constitution with Britain under which the colony became the Commonwealth of the Bahama Islands in 1969. On July 10, 1973, The Bahamas became an independent nation as the Commonwealth of the Bahamas.

In the 1982 election, Pindling's Progressive Liberal Party won 32 of 43 seats in Parliament; the Free National Movement, 11.

History. The islands were reached by Columbus in October 1492, and were a favorite pirate area in the early 18th century. The Bahamas were a crown colony from 1717 until they were granted internal self-government in 1964.

BAHRAIN

State of Bahrain
Amir: Sheik Isa bin-Sulman al-Khalifa (1961)
Prime Minister: Khalifa bin Sulman al-Khalifa (1970)
Area: 254 sq mi. (659 sq km)
Population (est. 1982): 375,000 (average annual growth rate: 4.7%)
Density per square mile: 1,562.5
Capital (est. 1982): Manama, 150,000
Monetary unit: Bahrain dinar
Languages: Arabic (official), English, French
Religion: Islam
Literacy rate (1981): 40%
Economic summary: Gross national product (1980): $2.4 billion. Average annual growth rate (1970–79): 0.7%. Per capita income (1980): $5,560. Land used for agriculture: 5%; labor force: 5%; principal products: eggs, vegetables, fruits. Labor force in industry: 90%; major products: oil, aluminum, fish. Natural resources: oil, fish. Exports: oil, aluminum, fish. Imports: machinery, oil-industry equipment, motor vehicles, foodstuffs. Major trading partners: Saudi Arabia, U.S., U.K., Japan.

Geography. Bahrain is an archipelago in the Persian Gulf off the coast of Saudi Arabia. The islands for the most part are level expanses of sand and rock.

Government. A new Constitution was approved in 1973. It created the first elected parliament in the country's history. Called the National Council, it consisted of 30 members elected by male citizens for four-year terms, plus up to 16 Cabinet ministers as ex-officio members. In August 1975, the Amir dissolved the National Council.

History. A sheikdom that passed from the Persians to the al-Khalifa family from Arabia in 1782, Bahrain became, by treaty, a British protectorate in 1820. It has become a major Middle Eastern oil center and, through use of oil revenues, is one of the most developed of the Persian Gulf sheikdoms. The Amir, Sheik Isa bin-Sulman al-Khalifa, who succeeded to the post in 1961, is a member of the original ruling family. Bahrain announced its independence on Aug. 14, 1971.

BANGLADESH

People's Republic of Bangladesh
President: Lieut. Gen. H. M. Ershad (1983)
Area: 55,598 sq mi. (143,998 sq km)
Population (est. 1983): 94,600,000 (average annual growth rate: 2.6%)
Density per square mile: 1,710.5
Capital and largest city (est 1982): Dacca, 3,500,000
Monetary unit: Taka
Principal languages: Bengali (official), English
Religions: Islam, 87%; Hindu, 11%
Literacy rate (1980): 23%
Member of Commonwealth of Nations
Economic summary: Gross national product (1980): $11.2 billion. Average annual growth rate (1970–79): 0.8%. Per capita income (1980): $120. Land used for agriculture: 66%; labor force, 75%; principal products: rice, jute, tea, sugar, wheat. Labor force in industry, 11%;

major products: jute goods, textiles, leather, sugar, fertilizer, paper, pharmaceuticals. Natural resources: natural gas. Exports: jute goods, jute, tea, leather, seafood. Imports: food grains, fuels, raw cotton, yarn, manufactured goods. Major trading partners: U.S., U.S.S.R., Japan.

Geography. Bangladesh, on the northern coast of the Bay of Bengal, is surrounded by India, with a small common border with Burma in the southeast. It is approximately the size of Wisconsin. The country is low-lying riverine land traversed by the many branches and tributaries of the Ganges and Brahmaputra rivers. Elevation averages less than 600 feet (183 m) above sea level. Tropical monsoons and frequent floods and cyclones inflict heavy damage in the delta region.

Government. On March 24, 1982, Gen. Hossain Mohammed Ershad ousted President Abdus Sattar, ending three years of civilian rule. He suspended the Constitution and declared himself Martial Law Administrator, appointing former Chief Justice A. F. N. Ahsanuddin Chowdhury as ceremonial President. Gen. Ershad later announced that military rule would continue for at least two years.

History. Like West Pakistan and India, the former East Pakistan was part of imperial British India until Britain withdrew in 1947. The two Pakistans were united by religion (Islam), but their peoples were separated by culture, physical features, and 1,000 miles of Indian territory. Bangladesh consists primarily of East Bengal (West Bengal is part of India and its people are primarily Hindu) plus the Sylhet district of the Indian state of Assam. For almost 25 years after independence from Britain, its history was as part of Pakistan (*see* Pakistan).

The East Pakistanis unsuccessfully sought greater autonomy from West Pakistan. The first general elections in Pakistani history, in December 1970, saw virtually all 171 seats of the region (out of 300 for both East and West Pakistan) go to Sheik Mujibur Rahman's Awami League, with the rest to other similarly independence-minded minor parties.

Attempts to write an all-Pakistan Constitution to replace the military regime of Gen. Yahya Khan failed. General strikes in East Pakistan followed at Mujibur's direction; he also told his followers to stop paying taxes. Yahya bloodily put down his revolt in March 1971. An estimated one million Bengalis were killed in the fighting or later slaughtered. Ten million more took refuge in India.

In December 1971, India invaded East Pakistan, routed the West Pakistani occupation forces, and created Bangladesh. The U.S. opposed its violent creation, but recognized Bangladesh in April 1972 and provided several hundred million dollars in relief aid. In February 1974, Pakistan agreed to recognize the independence of Bangladesh.

The charismatic Mujibur had a following of millions and near-dictatorial powers, but he failed to cope with poverty, starvation, sporadic political violence, and widespread government corruption.

Before dawn on Aug. 15, 1975, Mujibur, his wife, and several relatives were assassinated in a coup led by young Army officers. As president, they installed Khondakar Mushtaque Ahmed, a founder of the Awami League who was then Minister of Foreign Trade and Commerce.

A military coup forced Ahmed from power Nov. 6, 1975, and installed former Supreme Court Chief Justice Abu Sadat Mohammed Sayem as president and "chief martial law administrator." On Nov. 30, 1976, Gen Ziaur Rahman, Army Chief of Staff, took over Sayem's powers and blocked the national elections scheduled for early 1977. On April 21, 1977, Ziaur became president following Sayem's resignation. Two years later, Ziaur ended the martial law originally imposed in 1975 and in 1979 permitted parliamentary elections, in which his Bangladesh Nationalist Party won an absolute majority.

On May 30, 1981, Ziaur was killed by a group of army officers in an attempted coup. Vice President Abdus Sattar assumed power and was elected President Nov. 15. On March 24, 1982, Gen. Hossain Mohammad Ershad, army chief of staff, took control in a bloodless coup. Ershad assumed the office of President in 1983.

BARBADOS

Sovereign: Queen Elizabeth II
Governor-General: Sir Deighton L. Ward (1976)
Prime Minister: J. M. G. Adams (1976)
Area: 166 sq. mi. (431 sq km)
Population (est. 1982): 275,000 (average annual growth rate: 0.5%)
Density per square mile: 1,656.6
Capital and largest city (est. 1982): Bridgetown, 8,000
Monetary unit: Barbados dollar
Language: English
Religions: Anglican, 53%; Methodist, 9%; Roman Catholic, 4%
Literacy rate (1981): 90%
Member of Commonwealth of Nations
Economic summary: Gross national product (1980): $760 million. Average annual growth rate (1970–79): 2.1%. Per capita income (1980): $3,040. Land used for agriculture: 60%; principal products: sugar cane, subsistence foods. Major industrial products: light manufactures, sugar milling, tourism. Exports: sugar and sugar cane byproducts, clothing. Imports: foodstuffs, machinery, manufactured goods. Major trading partners: U.S., Caribbean nations, U.K., Canada.

Geography. An island in the Atlantic about 300 miles (483 km) north of Venezuela, Barbados is only 21 miles long (34 km) and 14 miles across (23 km) at its widest point. It is circled by fine beaches and narrow coastal plains. The highest point is Mount Hillaby (1,105 ft; 337 m) in the north central area.

Government. The Barbados legislature dates from 1627. It is bicameral, with a Senate of 21 appointed members and an Assembly of 27 elected members.

The major political parties are the Barbados Labor Party (17 seats in Assembly), led by Prime Minister J. M. G. Adams; Democratic Labor Party (10 seats), led by Errol Barrow.

History. Barbados, with a population 90% black, was settled by the British in 1627. It became a crown colony in 1885. It was a member of the Federation of the West Indies from 1958 to 1962. Britain granted the colony independence on Nov. 30, 1966, and it became a parliamentary democracy.

While retaining membership in the Commonwealth of Nations and economic ties with Britain, Barbados seeks broader economic and political relations with Western Hemisphere countries. Diplomatic ties with Cuba were established in 1972.

BELGIUM

Kingdom of Belgium
Sovereign: King Baudouin I (1951)
Premier: Wilfried Martens (1981)
Area: 11,781 sq mi. (30,513 sq km)
Population (est. 1982): 9,870,000 (average annual growth rate: 0.1%)
Density per square mile: 837.8
Capital: Brussels
Largest cities (est. 1982): Brussels, 1,000,000; Ghent, 240,000; Charleroi, 220,000; Liège, 218,000; Antwerp, 190,000; Bruges, 120,000
Monetary unit: Belgian franc
Languages: Dutch, 56%; French, 32%; bilingual (Brussels), 11% Germany, 1%.
Religion: Roman Catholic, 97%
National name: Royaume de Belgique—Koninkrijk van België
Literacy rate (1981): 97%
Economic summary: Gross national product (1982): $83.0 billion. Average annual growth rate (1970–79): 2.9%. Per capita income (1980): $12,180. Land used for agriculture: 28%; labor force: 2.8%; principal products: livestock, poultry, grain, sugar beets, flax, tobacco, potatoes, vegetables, fruits. Labor force in industry: 35%; major products: fabricated metal, iron and steel, coal, textiles, chemicals. Exports: iron and steel products, precious stones, textile products. Imports: nonelectrical machinery, motor vehicles, textiles, chemicals, fuels. Major trading partners: West Germany, France, Netherlands, U.K., U.S., Italy.

Geography. A neighbor of France, West Germany, the Netherlands, and Luxembourg, Belgium has about 40 miles of seacoast on the North Sea at the Strait of Dover. In area, it is approximately the size of Maryland. The northern third of the country is a plain extending eastward from the seacoast. North of the Sambre and Meuse Rivers is a low plateau; to the south lies the heavily wooded Ardennes plateau, attaining an elevation of about 2,300 feet (700 m).

The Schelde River, which rises in France and flows through Belgium, emptying into the Schelde estuaries, enables Antwerp to be an ocean port.

Government. Belgium, a parliamentary democracy under a constitutional monarch, consists of nine provinces. Its bicameral legislature has a Senate, with its 181 members elected for four years—106 by general election, 50 by provincial councillors and 25 by the Senate itself. The 212-member Chamber of Representatives is directly elected for four years by proportional representation. There is universal suffrage, and those who do not vote are fined.

Belgium joined the North Atlantic Alliance in 1949 and is a member of the European Community. NATO and the European Community have their headquarters in Brussels.

The sovereign, Baudouin I, was born Sept. 7, 1930, the son of King Leopold III and Queen Astrid. He became King on July 17, 1951, after the abdication of his father. He married Doña Fabiola de Mora y Aragón on Dec. 15, 1960. Since he has no children, his brother, Prince Albert, is heir to the throne.

The major political parties are the Flemish-Speaking Social Christian Party (40 Senators, 43 Representatives); French-Speaking Social Christian Party (16 Senators, 18 Representatives); Flemish-Speaking Socialist Party (21 Senators, 26 Representatives); French-Speaking Socialist Party (31 Senators, 35 Representatives); Flemish-Speaking Liberal Party (23 Senators, 28 Representatives); Flemish People's Party (17 Senators, 20 Representatives); French-Speaking Liberal Party (20 Senators, 24 Representatives).

History. Belgium occupies part of the Roman province of Belgica, named after the Belgae, a people of ancient Gaul. The area was conquered by Julius Caesar in 57–50 B.C., then was overrun by the Franks in the 5th century. It was part of Charlemagne's empire in the 8th century, then in the next century was absorbed into Lotharingia and later into the Duchy of Lower Lorraine. In the 12th century it was partitioned into the Duchies of Brabant and Luxembourg, the Bishopric of Liège, and the domain of the Count of Hainaut, which included Flanders.

The rise of the wool industry brought prosperity and power to the country, particularly to the semi-independent cities—Ghent, Bruges, and Ypres. In the 16th century, Belgium, with most of the area of the Low Countries, passed to the Duchy of Burgundy and was the marriage portion of Archduke Maximilian of Hapsburg and the inheritance of his grandson, Charles V, who incorporated it into his empire. Then, in 1555, they were united with Spain.

By the treaty of Utrecht in 1713, the country's sovereignty passed to Austria. During the wars that followed the French Revolution, Belgium was occupied and later annexed to France. But with the downfall of Napoleon, the Congress of Vienna in 1815 gave the country to the Netherlands. The Belgians revolted in 1830 and declared their independence.

Germany's invasion of Belgium in 1914 set off World War I. The Treaty of Versailles (1919) gave the areas of Eupen, Malmédy, and Moresnet to Belgium. Leopold III succeeded Albert, King during World War I, in 1934. In World War II, Belgium was overwhelmed by Nazi Germany, and Leopold III was made prisoner. When he attempted to return in 1950, Socialists and Liberals revolted. He abdicated July 16, 1951, and his son, Baudouin, became King the next day.

The country has long been torn by language disputes between the Dutch-speaking Flemish people and the French-speaking Walloons. In 1972, a major clash occurred over transferring six small hamlets from Flemish to Walloon administrative jurisdiction. When a balancing change was not implemented, the government fell. A new one under Edmond Leburton was formed; this, in turn, was replaced in 1974 by one under Léo Tindemans of the Flemish Social Christian party.

A financial crisis, building for more than a year, brought down the government on March 31, 1981, when Socialists in the majority coalition opposed the suspension of the automatic linkage of wage increases to rising prices. Premier Wilfried Martens proposed that after the suspension, wage increases should be given in fixed amounts, eliminating the indexing system which Belgium pioneered. Mark Eyskens, taking office on April 6, retained Socialist support by instituting a temporary price freeze, thus blocking wage hikes without dismantling the wage-price linkage.

Eyskens' government fell on Sept. 21 in a dispute over the management of the state-controlled Cockerill-Sambre steel company, with French-speaking Socialists in his coalition insisting on maintenance of employment, despite heavy losses. Liberal gains and Socialist losses in the ensuing elections brought a new Christian Democratic-Liberal coalition headed by former Premier Wilfried Martens to office on Dec. 17. Faced with unemployment above 10%, Martens won Parliamentary approval of special powers permitting him to deal with the economic crisis with tax cuts and other special measures.

BELIZE

Sovereign: Queen Elizabeth II
Governor-General: Minita Gordon (1981)
Prime Minister: George C. Price (1981)
Area: 8,867 sq mi. (22,965 sq km)
Population (est. 1982): 175,000 (average annual growth rate: 1.8%)
Density per sq mi.: 19.7
Capital (est. 1982): Belmopan, 4,500
Largest city (est. 1982): Belize City, 43,000
Monetary unit: Belize dollar
Languages: English (official) and Spanish
Religions: Roman Catholic, 67%; Anglican, 14%; Methodist, 13%
Literacy rate (1981): 80%
Member of Commonwealth of Nations
Economic summary: Gross national product (1981): $176 million. Average annual growth rate (1981): 1.3%. Per capita income (1981 est. $1,000). Land used for agriculture: 35%; labor force: 39%; principal products: sugar cane, citrus fruits, corn, molasses, rice, bananas, livestock. Labor force in industry: 20%; major products: timber, processed foods, furniture, rum, soap. Natural resource: timber. Exports: sugar, molasses, clothing, lumber, citrus fruits, fish. Imports: fuels, transportation equipment, foodstuffs, textiles, machinery. Major trading partners: U.S. U.K. Trinidad and Tobago.

Geography. Belize (formerly British Honduras) is situated on the Caribbean Sea south of Mexico and east and north of Guatemala. In area, it is about the size of New Hampshire. Most of the country is heavily forested with mahogany, cedar, and logwood. Mangrove swamps and cays along the coast give way to hills and mountains in the interior. The highest point is Victoria Peak, 3,681 feet (11,220 m).

Government. Formerly the colony of British Honduras, Belize became a fully independent commonwealth on Sept. 21, 1981, after having been self-governing since 1964. Executive power is nominally wielded by Queen Elizabeth II through an appointed Governor-General but effective power is held by the Prime Minister, who is responsible to an 18-member parliament elected by universal suffrage. The major parties are the People's United Party (13 of 18 seats), led by Prime Minister George Price, and the United Democratic Party (5 seats), led by Dean Russell Lindo.

History. Once a part of the Mayan empire, the area was deserted until British timber cutters began exploiting valuable hardwoods in the 17th century. Efforts by Spain to dislodge British settlers, including a major naval attack in 1798, were defeated. The territory was formally named a British colony in 1862 but administered by the Governor of Jamaica until 1884.

Guatemala has long made claims to the territory and refused to recognize Britain's efforts to grant independence to Belize. Fear of Guatemala caused many inhabitants to oppose independence until a tentative agreement was reached between Britain, Belize, and Guatemala in March 1981 that would offer access to the Caribbean through Belizean territory for Guatemala. The agreement broke down, however, and 1,600 British troops remained to protect the new state after the flag-raising ceremony on Sept. 21, 1981.

BENIN

People's Republic of Benin
President: Col. Mathieu Kerekou (1972)
Area: 43,483 sq mi. (112,622 sq km)
Population (est. 1983): 3,725,000 (average annual growth rate: 2.6%)
Density per square mile: 85.7
Capital (est. 1980): Porto-Novo, 125,000
Largest city (est. 1982): Cotonou, 225,000
Monetary unit: Franc CFA
Ethnic groups: Fons and Adjas, Baribas, Yorubas, Mahis
Languages: French, African languages
Religions: Animist, Christian, Islam
National name: Republique Populaire du Benin
Literacy rate (1981): 20%
Economic summary: Gross national product (1980): $1.1 billion. Average annual growth rate (1970–79): 0.6%. Per capita income (1980): $300. Labor force in agriculture: 70%; principal products: oil palms, peanuts, cotton, coffee, tobacco, corn, rice, livestock, fish. Major industrial products: processed palm oil, palm kernel oil. Natural resources: low-grade iron ore, limestone, some offshore oil. Exports: palm and agricultural products. Imports: clothing, consumer goods, lumber, fuels, foodstuffs, machinery, transportation equipment. Major trading partners: France and other Western European countries.

Geography. This West African nation on the Gulf of Guinea, between Togo on the west and Nigeria on the east, is about the size of Tennessee. It is bounded also by Upper Volta and Niger on the north. The land consists of a narrow coastal strip that rises to a swampy, forested plateau and then to highlands in the north. A hot and humid climate blankets the entire country.

Government. The change in name from Dahomey to Benin was announced by President Mathieu Kerekou in November 1975. Benin commemorates an African kingdom that flourished in the 17th century. At the same time, Kerekou announced the formation of a political organization, the Party of the People's Revolution of Benin, to mark the first anniversary of his declaration of a "new society" guided by Marxist-Leninist principles.

History. One of the smallest and most densely populated states in Africa, Benin was annexed by the French in 1893. The area was incorporated into French West Africa in 1904. It became an autonomous republic within the French Community in 1958, and on Aug. 1, 1960, was granted its independence within the Community.

Gen. Christophe Soglo deposed the first president, Hubert Maga, in an army coup in 1963. He dismissed the civilian government in 1965, proclaiming himself chief of state. A group of young army officers seized power in December 1967, deposing Soglo. They promulgated a new Constitution in 1968.

In December 1969, Benin had its fifth coup of the decade, with the army again taking power. In May 1970, a three-man presidential commission was created to take over the government. The commission had a six-year term; each member serves as president for two years. Maga turned over power as scheduled to Justin Ahomadegbe in May 1972, but six months later yet another army coup ousted the triumvirate and installed Lt. Col. Mathieu Kerekou as President.

BHUTAN

Kingdom of Bhutan
Ruler: King Jigme Singye Wangchuk (1972)
Area: 18,000 sq mi. (46,620 sq km)
Population (est. 1982): 1,200,000 (average annual growth rate: 2%)
Density per square mile: 66.7
Capital (est. 1982): Thimphu, 12,000
Monetary unit: Ngultrum
Language: Dzongkha
Religions: Buddhist, 69%; Hindu, 25%; Islam, 5%
National name: Druk-yul
Literacy rate: 10%
Economic summary: Gross national product (1981): $129 million. Average annual growth rate (1970–79): –0.1%. Per capita income (1981): $116 Labor force in agriculture: 95%; principal products: rice, barley, wheat, potatoes, fruit. Major industrial product: handicrafts. Natural resources: timber, hydroelectric power. Exports: fruits and vegetables, timber, coal, cement. Imports: textiles, cereals, vehicles. Major trading partner: India.

Geography. Mountainous Bhutan, half the size of Indiana, is situated on the southeast slope of the Himalayas, bordered on the north and east by Tibet and on the south and west by India. The landscape consists of a succession of lofty and rugged mountains running generally from north to south and separated by deep valleys. In the north, towering peaks reach a height of 24,000 feet (7,315 m).

Government. Bhutan is a constitutional monarchy. The King rules with a Council of Ministers and a nine-member Advisory Council, of whom five are elected by the people; two represent the monastic order and two are named by the King. There is a National Assembly (Parliament), which meets semiannually, but no political parties.

History. After almost a century of conflict, British troops invaded the country in 1865 and negotiated an agreement under which Britain undertook to pay an annual allowance to Bhutan on condition of good behavior. A treaty with India in 1949 increased this subsidy and placed Bhutan's foreign affairs under Indian control.

In the 1960s, Bhutan undertook modernization, abolishing slavery and the caste system, emancipating women, breaking up estates, and limiting farms to 30 acres.

BOLIVIA

Republic of Bolivia
President: Hernán Siles Zuazo (1982)
Area: 424,162 sq mi. (1,098,581 sq km)
Population (est. 1982): 5,900,000 (average annual growth rate, 2.6%) (Indian, 53%; mestizo, 32%; white, 15%)
Density per square mile: 13.9
Judicial capital (est. 1973): Sucre, 90,000
Administrative capital (est. 1983): La Paz, 800,000
Largest cities (est. 1982): Santa Cruz, 335,000; Cochabamba, 245,000; Oruro, 145,000
Monetary unit: Peso boliviano
Languages: Spanish, Quechua, Aymara
Religion: Roman Catholic, 94%
National name: República de Bolivia
Literacy rate (1981): 40%
Economic summary: Gross national product (1981): $7 billion. Average annual growth rate (1980): 1%. Per capita income (1981): $1,217. Labor force in agriculture: 70%; principal products: potatoes, corn, rice, sugar cane, bananas. Labor force in industry: 10%; major products: refined petroleum, processed foods, tin, textiles, clothing. Natural resources: petroleum, natural gas, tin, lead, zinc, copper, tungsten, bismuth, antimony, gold, sulfur, silver, iron ore. Exports: tin, petroleum, lead, zinc, silver, antimony, gold, coffee, sugar, cotton, natural gas. Imports: foodstuffs, chemicals, capital goods, pharmaceuticals, transport equipment. Major trading partners: Western European and Latin American countries, U.S., Japan.

Geography. Landlocked Bolivia, equal in size to California and Texas combined, lies to the west of Brazil. Its other neighbors are Peru and Chile on the west and Argentina and Paraguay on the south.

The country is a low alluvial plain throughout 60% of its area toward the east, drained by the Amazon and Plata river systems. The western part, enclosed by two chains of the Andes, is a great plateau—the Altiplano, with an average altitude of 12,000 feet (3,658 m). More than 80% of the population lives on the plateau, which also contains La Paz. At an altitude of 11,910 feet (3,630 m), it is the highest capital city in the world.

Lake Titicaca, half the size of Lake Ontario, is one of the highest large lakes in the world, at an altitude of 12,507 feet (3,812 m). Islands in the lake hold ruins of the ancient Incas.

Government. President Hernán Siles Zuazo, who took office in 1982 after a series of military regimes, heads the first freely elected government in 19 years. There is a bicameral National Congress. The two traditional political parties, the Nationalist Revolutionary Movement and the Bolivian Socialist Falange, are both seriously factionalized.

History. Famous since Spanish colonial days for its mineral wealth, modern Bolivia was once a part of the ancient Incan Empire. After the Spaniards defeated the Incas in the 16th century, Bolivia's predominantly Indian population was reduced to slavery. The country won its independence in 1825 and was named after Simón Bolívar, the famed liberator.

Since 1825 Bolivia has had more than 60 revolutions, 70 Presidents, and 11 Constitutions.

Harassed by internal strife, Bolivia lost great slices of territory to three neighbor nations. Several thousand square miles and its outlet to the Pacific were taken by Chile after the War of the Pacific (1879–84). In 1903 a piece of Bolivia's Acre province, rich in rubber, was ceded to Brazil. And in 1938, after a war with Paraguay, Bolivia gave up claim to nearly 100,000 square miles of the Gran Chaco.

Great prosperity came with World War II and its demand for two important Bolivian products, tin and wolframite. But rising prices provoked strikes that were ruthlessly broken and promoted growth of the leftist National Revolutionary Movement. The movement seized power in 1943 but was ousted by a moderate government in 1947.

In 1965 a guerrilla movement mounted from Cuba and headed by Maj. Ernesto (Ché) Guevara began a revolutionary war. With the aid of U.S. military advisers, the Bolivian army, helped by the peasants, smashed the guerrilla movement, wounding and capturing Guevara on Oct. 8, 1967, and shooting him to death the next day.

Faltering steps toward restoration of civilian government were halted abruptly on July 17, 1980, when Gen. Luis Garcia Meza Tejada seized power. The coup was the 189th in Bolivia's 155 years of independence and took place after a national election on June 29 chose Hernán Siles Zuazo as President of a civilian government but before the planned August inauguration. A series of military leaders followed before the military moved, in 1982, to return the government to civilian rule. The Congress, which had been elected in 1980, then selected Siles to head the new government and he was inaugurated President on Oct. 10, 1982.

The near collapse of the economy and several coup plots weakened the civilian government. On June 30, 1984, a group of armed men abducted the 72-year-old President from his bed before dawn and held him for 10 hours, with his arms and legs tied, in a warehouse in the center of the capital. To the embarrassment of the United States, the kidnappers turned out to be the leaders of a new narcotics police unit, financed and trained by the U.S. Drug Enforcement Administration. The President was rescued and the coup attempt failed.

The incident, however, drew attention to the failure thus far of a $5-million anti-drug trafficking program agreed upon by the U.S. and Bolivia's civilian government. Bolivia is the world's largest producer of coca leaf, the basic ingredient of cocaine. A year after the U.S.-Bolivian program began, no major traffickers had been arrested and U.S. officials said there had been a significant increase in the flow of cocaine paste to processing laboratories in Colombia, Peru, and Brazil.

BOPHUTHATSWANA

See South Africa

BOTSWANA

Republic of Botswana

President: Quett Masire (1980)
Area: 222,000 sq mi. (576,000 sq km)
Population (est. 1983): 1,000,000 (average annual growth rate: 3.6%)
Density per square mile: 4.5
Capital and largest city (est. 1982): Gaborone, 60,000
Monetary unit: Pula
Languages: English, Setswana
Religions: Christian, 60%; Animist
Member of Commonwealth of Nations
Literacy rate (1981): 54%
Economic summary: Gross national product (1980): $730 million. Average annual growth rate (1970–79): 12.0%. Per capita income (1980): $910. Land used for agriculture: 1%; principal products: livestock, sorghum, corn, millet, cowpeas, beans. Major industrial products: diamonds, copper, nickel, salt, soda ash, potash, coal, frozen beef; tourism. Natural resources: diamonds, copper, nickel, salt, soda ash, potash, coal. Exports: diamonds, cattle, animal products, copper, nickel. Imports: foodstuffs, vehicles, textiles, petroleum products. Major trading partners: South Africa, U.K.

Geography. Twice the size of Arizona, Botswana is in south central Africa, bounded by South-West Africa, Zambia, Zimbabwe, and South Africa. Most of the country is near-desert, with the Kalahari occupying the western part of the country. The eastern part is hilly, with salt lakes in the north.

Government. The Botswana Constitution provides, in addition to the unicameral National Assembly, for a House of Chiefs, which has a voice on bills affecting tribal affairs. There is universal suffrage.

The major political parties are the Democratic Party (29 of 32 elective seats in 36-man Legislative Assembly), led by President Quett Masire; National Front (2 seats), led by Kenneth Koma; People's Party (1 seat), led by Kenneth Nkhwa.

History. Botswana is the land of the Batawana tribes, which, when threatened by the Boers in Transvaal, asked Britain in 1885 to establish a protectorate over the country, then known as Bechuanaland. In 1961, Britain granted a Constitution to the country. Self-government began in 1965, and on Sept. 30, 1966, the country became independent. Since 1975, it has been an associate member of the European Common Market.

BOURKINA FASSO

See Upper Volta

BRAZIL

Federative Republic of Brazil

President: Gen. João Baptista de Oliveira Figueiredo (1979)
Area: 3,286,470 sq mi. (8,511,957 sq km)
Population (est. 1983): 131,305,000 (average annual growth rate, 2.3%) (approx.: white, 60%; mestizo, 26%; black, 11%)
Density per square mile: 37.9
Capital (1980 census): Brasilia, 411,305
Largest cities (1980 census): São Paulo, 7,033,529; Rio de Janeiro, 5,093,529; Salvador, 1,496,276; Belo Horizonte, 1,442,483; Recife, 1,184,215; Porto Alegre, 1,108,883
Monetary unit: Cruzeiro
Language: Portuguese
Religion: Roman Catholic, 90%
National name: Brasil
Literacy rate (1981): 45%
Economic summary: Gross national product (1981): $250 billion. Average annual growth rate (est. 1981): 1%. Per capita income (1980): $2,050. Land used for agriculture; 4%; labor force: 36%; principal products: coffee, rice, beef, corn, milk, sugar cane, soybeans, cocoa. Labor force in industry: 23%; major products: steel, chemicals, petrochemicals, machinery, motor vehicles, cement, lumber. Natural resources: iron ore, manganese, bauxite, nickel, other industrial metals. Exports: coffee, iron ore, soybeans, sugar, wood, beef, cocoa beans, footwear. Imports: wheat, copper, aluminum, petroleum, machinery, chemicals, pharmaceuticals. Major trading partners: U.S. West Germany, Argentina, Japan.

Geography. Brazil covers nearly half of South America, extends 2,965 miles (4,772 km) north-south, 2,691 miles (4,331 km), east-west, and borders every nation on the continent except Chile and Ecuador. It is the fifth largest country in the world, ranking after the U.S.S.R., Canada, China, and the U.S.

More than a third of Brazil is drained by the Amazon and its more than 200 tributaries. The Amazon is navigable for ocean steamers to Iquitos, Peru, 2,300 miles (3,700 km) upstream. Southern Brazil is drained by the Plata system—the Paraguay, Uruguay, and Paraná Rivers. The most important stream entirely within Brazil is the Sao Francisco, navigable for 1,000 miles (1,903 km), but broken near its mouth by the 275-foot (84 m) Paulo Afonso Falls.

Government. Under the Constitution, Brazil is a union of 22 states, 4 territories, and 1 federal district. The President is elected for a six-year term by an electoral college made up of members of the National Congress. The National Congress is composed of two houses—the Senate, whose members serve eight-year terms, and the Chamber of Deputies, elected for four-year terms. Members of Congress are elected by equal, direct, compulsory, and secret suffrage under proportional representation.

The military took control in 1964, ousting the last elected civilian President and installing a series of military men (with the Congress ratifying the junta's choice). Election of a civilian President by the 686-member electoral college is scheduled in January 1985.

The major political parties are the Partido Democrático Social, led by Senator José Sarney (the progovernment party formerly called ARENA, for Aliança Renovadora Nacional); Partido do Movimento Democrático Brasileiro, led by Representative Ulysses Guimarães; Partido Popular, led by Senator Tancredo Neves; Partido Trabalhista Brasileiro, led by Yvette Vargas; Partido Democrático Trabalhista, led by Leonel Brizolla; and Partido dos Trabalhadores, led by Luiz Inacio Silva.

History. Brazil is the only Latin American nation deriving its language and culture from Portugal. Adm. Pedro Alvares Cabral claimed the territory for the Portuguese in 1500. He brought to Portugal a cargo of wood, pau-brasil, from which the land received its name. Portugal began colonization in 1532 and made the area a royal colony in 1549.

During the Napoleonic wars, King João VI, then Prince Regent, fled the country in 1807 in advance of the French armies and in 1808 set up his court in Rio de Janeiro. João was drawn home in 1820 by a revolution, leaving his son as Regent. When Portugal sought to reduce Brazil again to colonial status, the prince declared Brazil's independence on Sept. 7, 1822, and became Pedro I, Emperor of Brazil.

Harassed by his parliament, Pedro I abdicated in 1831 in favor of his five-year-old son, who became Emperor in 1840 as Pedro II. The son was a popular monarch, but discontent built up and, in 1889, following a military revolt, he had to abdicate. Although a republic was proclaimed, Brazil was under two military dictatorships during the next four years. A revolt permitted a gradual return to stability under civilian Presidents.

The President during World War I, Wenceslau Braz, cooperated with the Allies and declared war on Germany. The President from 1926 to 1930, Washington Luiz Pereira da Souza, was overthrown by a revolutionary group under Getulio Vargas, who took over as provisional President.

Vargas' 1934 Constitution curtailed states' rights and established a nationalistic policy. In 1937, Vargas seized absolute power and adopted another Constitution, extending his term indefinitely. In World War II, Brazil cooperated with the Western Allies, welcoming Allied air bases, patrolling the South Atlantic, and joining the invasion of Italy after declaring war on the Axis.

Vargas was overthrown on Oct. 29, 1945. Succeeding presidents were Gen. Eurico Gaspar Dutra (1945–50); Getulio Vargas (1950–54); João Cafe Filho (1954–55); Juscelino Kubitschek de Oliveira (1955–60); Janio Quadros (1960); João Goulart (1960–63); Gen. Humberto de Alencar Castelo Branco (1963–66); Gen. Arthur Costa e Silva (1966–69); Gen. Emilio Garrastazu Médici (1970–74).

In 1974, Gen. Ernesto Geisel was elected President and relations with the U.S. remained cool.

National elections on Nov. 15, 1978, saw the ruling ARENA party lose its majority by a slight margin in popular voting but it retained control of both houses of Congress by a narrow edge. In the 1979 presidential election, Geisel's hand-picked candidate, Gen. João Baptista de Oliveira Figueiredo, was elected.

Figueiredo pledged a return to democracy by 1985, and granted amnesty to 5,000 political exiles, but he aroused international protest when his government sentenced Luiz da Silva, leader of a strike that shut down automobile production in 1980, to a three-and-a-half-year term in 1981. Da Silva was freed in March 1982.

Economically, Brazil's $93-billion foreign debt was the Third World's largest, and inflation reached a staggering 229% annual rate in 1984, almost double the 115% rate in 1983. But tough austerity measures imposed by the International Monetary Fund appeared to be taking hold and, by mid-1984, Brazilian economists said the country's recession had ended and Brazil was on the road to recovery.

BRUNEI

State of Brunei
Sultan: Hassanal Bolkiah
Area: 2,226 sq mi. (5,765 sq km)
Population (est. 1983): 209,000 (average annual growth rate: 4.0%)
Density per square mile: 93.9
Capital and largest city (est. 1978): Bandar Seri Begawan, 70,000
Monetary unit: Brunei dollar
Ethnic groups: Malay, 65%; Chinese, 24%; other, 11%
Languages: Malay and English official; Chinese
Religions: Islam, 60%; Christian, 8%; other (Buddhist and animist), 32%
Literacy rate (1983): 45%
Member of Commonwealth of Nations
Economic summary: Gross national product (1980): $2.6 billion. Average annual growth rate (1970–79): 4.6%. Per capita income (1980): $11,890. Land used for agriculture: 3%; labor force: 31%; principle agricultural

products: rubber, rice, pepper. Labor force in industry: 33%; major industrial products: crude petroleum, liquified natural gas. Natural resources: petroleum, natural gas. Exports: crude petroleum, liquified natural gas. Imports: machinery, transport equipment, manufactured goods, foodstuffs. Major trading partners: Japan, U.S., U.K., Singapore.

Geography. About the size of Delaware, Brunei is an independent sultanate on the northwest coast of the island of Borneo in the South China Sea, wedged between the Malaysian states of Sabah and Sarawak. Three quarters of the thinly populated country is covered with tropical rain forest; there are rich oil and gas deposits.

Government. Sultan Hassanal Bolkiah is ruler of the state, a former British protectorate which became fully sovereign and independent on New Year's Day, 1984. presiding over a Privy Council and Council of Ministers appointed by himself. Brunei remains a member of the Commonwealth, of which Queen Elizabeth II is the nominal head, but the British monarch has no political role. The Constitution provides for a three-tiered system of indirect elections, but the last elections were held in 1965. The only known opposition leader is in exile.

History. Brunei (pronounced broon-eye) was a powerful state from the 16th to the 19th century, ruling over the northern part of Borneo and adjacent island chains. But it fell into decay and lost Sarawak in 1841, becoming a British protectorate in 1888 and a British dependency in 1905.

The Sultan regained control over internal affairs in 1959, but Britain retained responsibility for the state's defense and foreign affairs until the end of 1983, when the sultanate became fully independent.

Sultain Bolkiah was crowned in 1968 at the age of 22, succeeding his father, Sir Omar Ali Saifuddin, who had abdicated. During his reign, exploitation of the rich Seria oilfield has made the sultanate wealthy. The majority of the population lives in and around the capital, situated on the Brunei River nine miles from its mouth.

BULGARIA

People's Republic of Bulgaria
Chairman of the State Council: Todor Zhivkov (1971)
Prime Minister (Chairman of Council of Ministers): Grisha Filipov (1981)
Area: 42,823 sq mi. (110,912 sq km)
Population (est. 1983): 8,944,000 (average annual growth rate: 0.3%)
Density per square mile: 208.4
Capital: Sofia
Largest cities (est. 1982): Sofia, 1,000,000; Plovdiv, 335,000; Varna, 285,000; Ruse, 175,000; Burgas, 175,000; Stara Zagora, 165,000
Monetary unit: Lev
Language: Bulgarian
Religions: Reliable figures not available
National name: Narodna Republika Bulgariya
Literacy rate (1981): 95%
Economic summary: Gross national product (1980): $34 billion. Average annual growth rate (1970–1980): 3.0%. Per capita income (1980): $3,820. Labor force in agriculture: 23%; principal products: grains, tobacco, fruits, vegetables. Labor force in industry: 35%; major products: processed agricultural products, machinery, textiles, clothing. Natural resources: metals, minerals, lumber. Exports: machinery and transport equipment, fuels, minerals, raw materials, agricultural products. Imports: machinery and transportation equipment, fuels, raw materials, metals, agricultural raw materials. Major trading partners: U.S.S.R., Soviet bloc countries.

Geography. Two mountain ranges and two great valleys mark the topography of Bulgaria, a country the size of Tennessee. Situated on the Black Sea in the eastern part of the Balkan peninsula, it shares borders with Yugoslavia, Romania, Greece, and Turkey. The Balkan belt crosses the center of the country, almost due east-west, rising to a height of 7,800 feet (2,377 m). The Rhodope range breaks off from the Balkans in the west, curves, and then straightens out to run nearly parallel along the southern border. Between the two ranges, is the valley of the Maritsa, Bulgaria's principal river. Between the Balkan range and the Danube, which forms most of the northern boundary with Romania, is the Danubian tableland.

Southern Dobruja, a fertile region of 2,900 square miles (7,511 sq km), below the Danube delta, is an area of low hills, fens, and sandy steppes.

Government. The present Constitution has been in effect since May 18, 1971. The National Assembly, consisting of 400 members elected for five-year terms, is the governing body. It elects the State Council and the Council of Ministers.

The Communist Party is led by the chairman of the State Council, Todor Zhivkov.

History. The first Bulgarians, a tribe of wild horsemen akin to the Huns, crossed the Danube from the north in A.D. 679 and subjugated the Slavic population of Moesia. They adopted a Slav dialect and Slavic customs and twice conquered most of the Balkan peninsula between 893 and 1280. After the Serbs subjected their kingdom in 1330, the Bulgars gradually fell prey to the Turks, and from 1396 to 1878 Bulgaria was a Turkish province. In 1878, Russia forced Turkey to give the country its independence; but the European powers, fearing that Bulgaria might become a Russian dependency, intervened. By the Treaty of Berlin in 1878, Bulgaria became autonomous under Turkish sovereignty.

In 1887, Prince Ferdinand of Saxe-Coburg-Gotha was elected ruler of Bulgaria; on Oct. 5, 1908, he declared the country independent and took the title of Tsar.

Bulgaria joined Germany in World War I and lost. On Oct. 3, 1918, Tsar Ferdinand abdicated in favor of his son, Tsar Boris III. Boris assumed dictatorial powers in 1934–35. When Hitler awarded Bulgaria southern Dobruja, taken from Romania in 1940, Boris joined the Nazis in war the next year and occupied parts of Yugoslavia and Greece. Later the Germans tried to force Boris to send his troops against the Russians. Boris resisted and died under mysterious circumstances on Aug. 28, 1943.

Simeon II, infant son of Boris, became nominal ruler under a regency. Russia declared war on Bulgaria on Sept. 5, 1944. An armistice was agreed to three days later, after Bulgaria had declared war on Germany. Russian troops streamed in the next day.

A Soviet-stype people's republic was established in 1947. Since then, Bulgaria acquired the reputation of being the most slavishly loyal to Moscow of all the East European Communist countries. An Italian prosecutor's report in 1984 charged that Bulgaria, possibly with Soviet support, masterminded the 1981 attempt by Turkish gunman Mehmet Ali Agca to assassinate Pope John Paul II.

BURMA

Socialist Republic of the Union of Burma
President: San Yu (1981)
Prime Minister: U Maung Maung Kha (1977)
Area: 261,789 sq mi. (678,036 sq km)
Population (est. 1982): 37,500,000 (average annual growth rate: 2.5%)
Density per square mile: 143.2
Capital: Rangoon
Largest cities (est. 1983): Rangoon, 2,250,000 **(est. 1977 for metropolitan area by U.N.):** Mandalay, 458, 000; Moulmein, 188,000; Bassein, 138,000; Pegu, 135, 000
Monetary unit: Kyat
Language: Burmese
Religions: Buddhist, 87%; Christian, Islam, Hindu
National name: Pyidaungsu Socialist Thammada Myanma Naingngandau
Literacy rate (1981): 70%
Economic summary: Gross national product (1980): $5.9 billion. Average annual growth rate (1970–79): 2.0%. Per capita income (1980): $180. Labor force in agriculture: 67%; principal products: sugar cane, corn, rice, peanuts. Labor force in industry: 9%; major products: textiles, footwear, processed agricultural products, wood and wood products, refined petroleum. Natural resources: timber, nickel, cobalt, copper, gold, rubies, sapphires, jade. Exports: rice, teak. Imports: machinery and transportation equipment, textiles, manufactured goods. Major trading partners: Singapore, Western European countries, China, U.K., Japan.

Geography. Burma occupies the northwest portion of the Indochinese peninsula. India lies to the northwest and China to the northeast. Bangladesh, Laos, and Thailand are also neighbors. The Bay of Bengal touches the southwestern coast.

Slightly smaller than Texas, the country is divided into three natural regions: the Arakan Yoma, a long, narrow mountain range forming the barrier between Burma and India; the Shan Plateau in the east, extending southward into Tenasserim; and the Central Basin, running down to the flat fertile delta of the Irrawaddy in the south. This delta contains a network of intercommunicating canals and nine principal river mouths.

Government. On March 2, 1962, the government of U Nu was overthrown and replaced by a Revolutionary Council, which assumed all power in the state. Gen. U Ne Win, as chairman of the Revolutionary Council, became the chief executive.

A new Constitution was approved in 1973 and took effect Jan. 4, 1974. Under it, Burma is a Socialist Democratic Republic with a 475-seat unicameral legislature called the People's Congress. In 1972, Ne Win and his colleagues resigned their military titles and thereafter ruled as "civilians." In 1974, Ne Win dissolved the Revolutionary Council and became President under the new Constitution. He voluntarily relinquished the presidency on Nov. 9, 1981, but retained leadership of the Burmese Socialist Program Party, the only legal party. San Yu was elected President by the People's Congress.

History. In 1612, the British East India Company sent agents to Burma, but the Burmese long resisted efforts of British traders, and Dutch and Portuguese as well, to establish posts on the Bay of Bengal. By the Anglo-Burmese War in 1824–26 and two following wars, the British East India Company expanded to the whole of Burma by 1886. Burma was annexed to India. It became a separate colony in 1937.

During World War II, Burma was a key battleground; the 800-mile Burma Road was the Allies' vital supply line to China. The Japanese invaded the country in December 1941, and by May 1942 had occupied most of it, cutting the Burma Road. After one of the most difficult campaigns of the war, Allied forces liberated most of Burma prior to the Japanese surrender in August 1945.

Burma became independent on Jan. 4, 1948. The new government was soon faced by armed uprisings of Communists and of Karen tribesmen. In 1949 the Karen rebels won a large degree of autonomy. In 1951 and 1952 the Socialists achieved power, and Burma became the first Asian country to introduce social legislation.

In 1968, after the government had made headway against the Communist rebels, the military regime adopted a policy of strict nonalignment and followed "the Burmese Way" to socialism. But the insurgents, reportedly numbering several thousand and armed by China, continued active.

BURUNDI

Republic of Burundi
Head of Government: Col. Jean-Baptiste Bagaza (1978)
Area: 10,747 sq mi. (27,834 sq km)
Population (est. 1983): 4,561,000 (average annual growth rate: 2.7%)
Density per square mile: 414.1
Capital and largest city (1982): Bujumbura, 175,000
Monetary unit: Burundi franc
Languages: Kirundi (official), French
Religions: Roman Catholic, 78%; Protestant, 5%
National name: Republika Y'Uburundi
Literacy rate (1981): 20% (est.)
Economic summary: Gross national product (1980): $830 million. Average annual growth rate (1970–79): 1.5%. Per capita income (1980): $200. Principal agricultural products: coffee, tea, cotton, food crops. Major industrial products: light consumer goods. Natural resources: nickel, uranium, cobalt, unexploited copper and platinum deposits. Exports: coffee, tea, hides. Imports: textiles, food, transport equipment, petroleum products. Major trading partners: U.S., Belgium, West Germany, France.

Geography. Wedged among Tanzania, Zaire, and Rwanda in east central Africa, Burundi occupies a high plateau divided by several deep valleys. It is equal in size to Maryland.

Government. Legislative and executive power is vested in the president.

Burundi's first Constitution, approved July 11, 1974, placed UPRONA (Unity and National Progress), the only political party, in control of national policy and automatically made Lt. Gen. Michel Micombero president.

History. Burundi was once part of German East Africa. An integrated society developed among the Watusi, a tall, warlike people and nomad cattle raisers, and the Bahutu, a Bantu people, who were subject farmers. Belgium won a League of Nations mandate in 1923, and subsequently Burundi, with Rwanda, was transferred to the status of a United Nations trust territory.

In 1962, Burundi gained independence and became a kingdom under Mwami Mwambutsa IV, with his son, Louis Rwangasore, as premier. Shortly after, the son was assassinated. The second man to succeed him, Pierre Ngendandumwe, who took office in 1963, was assassinated in 1965 when an unsuccessful coup against the Watusi led to the massacre of many Bahutus.

Crown Prince Charles, returning from Europe, rallied Watusi extremists, ousted the premier, suspended the Constitution, and renewed relations with Communist China. He deposed his father in 1966, reigned as Ntare V, with Micombero as premier. Three months later, Micombero, in a military coup, overthrew the Mwami and established a republic, installing himself as president.

One of Africa's worst tribal wars, which became genocide, occurred in Burundi in April 1972, following the return of Ntare. He was given a safe-conduct promise in writing by Micombero but was "judged and immediately executed" by the Burundi leader. His return was apparently attended by an invasion of exiles of Burundi's Hutu tribe. Although Hutus make up 85% of the population, they have been dominated for centuries by the minority Tutsi tribe of Micombero. Whether Hutus living in Burundi joined the invasion is unclear, but after it failed, the victorious Tutsis proceeded to massacre some 100,000 persons in six weeks, with possibly 100,000 more slain by summer.

On Nov. 1, 1976, a military coup led by Lt. Col. Jean-Baptiste Bagaza ousted Micombero, who was serving his second term. Bagaza assumed the presidency Nov. 3, suspended the Constitution, and announced that a 30-member Supreme Revolutionary Council would be the governing body.

Bagaza was elected head of the only legal political party in 1979 and re-elected to a second five-year term as party chieftain in 1984.

CAMBODIA

People's Republic of Kampuchea
President: Heng Samrin (1979)
Prime Minister: Chan Sy (1982)
Area: 69,884 sq mi. (181,000 sq km)
Population (est. 1983): 5,996,000 (average annual growth rate: 1.9%)
Density per square mile: 100.0
Capital and largest city (est. 1980 for metropolitan area): Phnom Penh, 500,000
Monetary unit: Riel
Ethnic groups: Khmer, 93%; Vietnamese, 4%; Chinese, 3%
Languages: Khmer (official), French, Vietnamese, Chinese
Religion: Theravada Buddhist
Literacy rate: Not known
Economic summary: Gross national product (1971): $500 million. Principal agricultural products: rice, rubber, corn. Major industrial products: fish, wood and wood products, milled rice. Natural resources: timber, gemstones, iron ore, manganese, phosphate. Exports: natural rubber, rice, pepper, wood. Imports: foodstuffs, fuel, machinery. Major trading partners: China, North Korea, Vietnam, U.S.S.R.

Geography. Situated on the Indochinese peninsula, Cambodia is bordered by Thailand and Laos on the north and Vietnam on the east and south. The Gulf of Siam is off the western coast. The country, the size of Missouri, consists chiefly of a large alluvial plain ringed in by mountains and on the east by the Mekong River. The plain is centered on Lake Tonle Sap, which is a natural storage basin of the Mekong.

Government. A bloodless coup toppled Prince Sihanouk in 1970. It was led by Lon Nol and Prince Sisowath Sirik Matak, Sihanouk's cousin. Sihanouk moved to Peking to head a government-in-exile. On Oct. 9, 1970, Lon Nol proclaimed himself President.

The Lon Nol regime was overthrown in April 1975 by Pol Pot, a leader of the Communist Khmer Rouge forces, who instituted a xenophobic reign of terror. Pol Pot was in turn ousted on Jan. 8, 1979, by Heng Samrin, a dissident backed by strong Vietnamese forces.

History. Cambodia came under Khmer rule about A.D. 600. Under the Khmers, magnificent temples were built at Angkor. The Khmer kingdom once ruled over most of Southeast Asia, but attacks by the Thai and the Vietnamese almost annihilated the empire until the French joined Cambodia, Laos, and Vietnam into French Indochina.

Under Norodom Sihanouk, enthroned in 1941, and particularly under Japanese occupation during World War II, nationalism revived. After the ouster of the Japanese, the Cambodians sought independence, but the French returned in 1946, granting the country a Constitution in 1947 and independence within the French Union in 1949. Sihanouk won full military control during the French-Indochinese War in 1953. He abdicated in 1955 in favor of his parents, remaining head of the government, and when his father died in 1960, became chief of state without returning to the throne. In 1963, he sought a guarantee of Cambodia's neutrality from all parties to the Vietnam War.

Sihanouk first favored the Communist-backed Vietcong in Vietnam, but in 1967 he accused the Communists of planning a revolt and veered away from them.

On March 18, 1970, while Sihanouk was abroad trying to get North Vietnamese and the Vietcong out of border sanctuaries near Vietnam, anti-Vietnamese riots occurred, and Sihanouk was overthrown, a move legalized by the legislature. The historically anti-Vietnamese Cambodians largely stayed with the government.

North Vietnamese and Vietcong units in border sanctuaries began moving deeper into Cambodia, threatening rapid overthrow of Lon Nol. President Nixon sent South Vietnamese and U.S. troops across the border on April 30. U.S. ground forces, limited to 30-kilometer penetration, withdrew by June 30.

The Vietnam peace agreement of 1973 stipulated withdrawal of foreign forces from Cambodia, but fighting continued between Hanoi-backed insurgents and U.S.-supplied government troops. U.S. air support for the government forces was ended by Congress on Aug. 15, 1973.

Fighting continued through 1974, then reached a quick climax early in 1975. In January, the rebels cut off the Mekong River as a supply route to Phnom Penh and fought their way to the outskirts of the capital and began shelling it. In February, the U.S. Congress ignored a request from President Ford for $222 million to supplement Phnom Penh's dwindling arms stores, but a U.S. food airlift to the besieged capital went forward.

As government troops fell back in bitter fighting, Lon Nol fled by air April 1, leaving the government under the interim control of Premier Long Boret. On April 16, the government's capitulation ended the five-year war, but not the travails of war-ravaged Cambodia.

Khieu Samphan, an early Khmer Rouge leader, appeared to be the strong man of the new regime. Sihanouk, the nominal chief of state, returned from exile in Peking in 1975 for the first time since the 1970 coup. A new Constitution was proclaimed in December 1975, establishing a 250-member People's Assembly, a State Presidium headed by Pol Pot, and a Supreme Judicial Tribunal. Samphan replaced Sihanouk as head of state in April 1976, and the former monarch became a virtual prisoner.

In the next two years, from 2 million to 4 million Cambodians are estimated to have died under the brutality of the regime. Border clashes with Vietnam developed into a Vietnamese invasion and by the end of 1978 the Pol Pot government appeared to be collapsing.

Sihanouk, held under house arrest since 1976, was freed by Pol Pot early in 1979 and sent as a spokesman for the regime to protest the Vietnamese invasion before the U.N. Security Council. Sihanouk eloquently attacked Vietnam while conceding that the Pol Pot regime was inhumane. His call for Vietnam's withdrawal was barred only by a Soviet veto.

Despite the capture of Phnom Penh on Jan. 8 by Heng Samrin, a dissident Khmer Rouge backed by Vietnamese troops, fighting continued in isolated areas. Retreating Pol Pot forces and refugees totaling 40,000 were driven into Thailand by May.

Due largely to the support of China and the Association of Southeast Asian Nations, the defeated regime retained the Cambodian seat at the United Nations. A conference on Cambodia met at the United Nations, July 13–17, 1981, and approved unanimously a resolution calling for Vietnamese withdrawal.

Vietnam and the Soviet Union, together with all Soviet bloc supporters, boycotted the conference.

On June 22, 1982, meeting in Kuala Lumpur, Malaysia, Sihanouk signed an agreement with San Son, his former prime minister, and Khieu Samphan to form a government of national unity. Sihanouk was to be head of state of Democratic Kampuchea, the rebel regime that still holds Cambodia's United Nations seat; Khieu was to be vice president, and Son prime minister. Sihanouk said of his partnership with his old foes, the Khmer Rouge, "We have to choose between letting the Vietnamese colonize Cambodia or working with the Khmer Rouge."

Two years later, in mid-1984, a mixed force of about 50,000 Pol Pot and other insurgents of the Sihanouk coalition was reported still holding out in isolated jungle camps and causing "military problems" for the estimated 160,000 Vietnamese troops still in Cambodia.

CAMEROON

Republic of Cameroon
President: Paul Biya (1982)
Prime Minister: Bello Bouba Maigari (1982)
Area: 183,569 sq mi. (475,442 sq km)
Population (est. 1982): 8,800,000 (average annual growth rate: 2.9%)
Density per square mile: 47.9
Capital: Yaoundé
Largest cities (est. 1982): Douala, 500,000; Yaoundé, 450,000
Monetary unit: Franc CFA
Languages: French and English (both official); Foulbé, Bamiléke, Ewondo, Donala, Mungaka, Bassa
Religions: Roman Catholic, 35%; Animist, 25%; Islam, 22%; Protestant, 18%
National name: République Unie du Cameroun
Literacy rate (1981): 50%
Economic summary: Gross national product (1980): $5.7 billion. Average annual growth rate (1970–79): 3.1%. Per capita income (1980): $675. Land used for agriculture: 35%; labor force: 80%; principal products: coffee, cocoa, tropical agricultural products. Labor force in industry: 10–15%. Major products: small manufacturing, consumer goods, aluminum. Natural resources: timber, some oil, bauxite. Exports: cocoa, coffee, timber, aluminum, cotton. Imports: consumer goods, machinery, food, beverages, tobacco, fuel. Major trading partners: France, U.S., Western European nations.

Geography. Cameroon is a West African nation on the Gulf of Guinea, bordered by Nigeria, Chad, the Central African Republic, the Congo, Equatorial Guinea, and Gabon. It is nearly twice the size of Oregon.

The interior consists of a high plateau, rising to 4,500 feet (1,372 m), with the land descending to a lower, densely wooded plateau and then to swamps and plains along the coast. Mount Cameroon (13,350 ft.; 4,069 m), near the coast, is the highest elevation in the country. The main rivers are the Benue, Nyong, and Sanaga.

Government. After a 1972 plebiscite, a unitary nation was formed out of East and West Cameroon to replace the former Federal Republic. A Constitution was adopted, providing for election of a president every five years and of a 150-seat National Assembly, whose nominal five-year term can be extended or shortened by the president. The Cameroon National Union is the only political party.

History. The Republic of Cameroon is inhabited by Hamitic and Semitic peoples in the north, where Islam is the principal religion, and by Bantu peoples in the central and southern regions, where native animism prevails. The tribes were conquered by many invaders.

The land escaped colonial rule until 1884, when treaties with tribal chiefs brought the area under German domination. After World War I, the League of Nations gave the French a mandate over 80% of the area, and the British 20% adjacent to Nigeria. After World War II, when the country came under a U.N. trusteeship in 1946, self-government was granted, and the Cameroun People's Union emerged as the dominant party by campaigning for reunification of French and British Cameroon and for independence. Accused of being under Communist control, it waged a campaign of revolutionary terror from 1955 to 1958, when it was crushed. In British Cameroon, unification was pressed also by the leading party, the Kamerun National Democratic Party, led by John Foncha.

France set up Cameroun as an autonomous state in 1957, and the next year its legislative assembly voted for independence by 1960. In 1959 a fully autonomous government of Cameroun was formed under Ahmadou Ahidjo. Cameroun became an independent republic on Jan. 1, 1960, adopted a Constitution in a referendum in February, and chose a National Assembly in April. The Assembly elected Ahidjo president. A federal Constitution was approved in 1961, and the Federal Republic of Cameroon came into being in October, headed by Ahidjo and Foncha.

CANADA

See separate Canada section

CAPE VERDE

Republic of Cape Verde
President: Aristides Pereira (1975)
Premier: Maj. Pedro Pires (1975)
Area: 1,557 sq mi. (4,033 sq km)
Population: (est. 1982): 340,000 (average annual growth rate: 2.6%)
Density per square mile: 218.4
Capital (est. 1982): Praia, 35,000
Largest city (est. 1982): Mindelo, 50,000
Monetary unit: Cape Verde escudo
Language: Portuguese
Religion: Roman Catholic, 96%
National name: República de Cabo Verde
Literacy rate (1981): 20% (est.)
Economic summary: Gross national product (1980): $100 million. Average annual growth rate (1970–79): 4.8%. Per capita income (1980): $300. Principal agricultural products: bananas, corn, sugar cane, sweet potatoes. Major industry: fishing, salt mining. Natural resources: salt, siliceous rock, minerals. Exports: fish and shellfish, bananas, salt. Imports: machinery, textiles, petroleum products. Major trading partners: Portugal, U.K., Japan, neighboring African states.

Geography: Cape Verde, only slightly larger than Rhode Island, is an archipelago in the Atlantic 385 miles (620 km) west of Dakar, Senegal.

The islands are divided into two groups: Barlavento in the north, comprising Santo Antão (291 sq mi.; 754 sq km), Boa Vista (240 sq mi.; 622 sq km), São Nicolau (132 sq mi.; 342 sq km), São Vicente (88 sq mi.; 246 sq km), Sal (83 sq mi.; 298 sq km), and Santa Luzia (13 sq mi.; 34 sq km); and Sotavento in the south, consisting of São Tiago (383 sq mi.; 992 sq km), Fogo (184 sq mi.; 477 sq km), Maio (103 sq mi.; 267 sq km), and Brava (25 sq mi.; 65 sq km). The islands are mostly mountainous, with the land deeply scarred by erosion. There is an active volcano on Fogo.

Government. The islands became independent on July 5, 1975, under an agreement negotiated with Portugal in 1974. The 56-member National Assembly chose Aristides Pereira as President and Maj. Pedro Pires as Premier. All members of the Assembly belong to the African Party for the Independence of Portuguese Guinea and Cape Verde, then the only party that entered candidates in the election. It is committed to union with Guinea-Bissau, another former Portuguese colony.

History. Uninhabited upon their discovery in 1456, the Cape Verde islands became part of the Portuguese empire in 1495. A majority of their modern inhabitants are of mixed Portuguese and African ancestry. A coaling station developed during the 19th century on the island of São Vicente has grown in recent years to an oil and gasoline storage depot for ships and aircraft.

CENTRAL AFRICAN REPUBLIC

Head of Government: Gen. André Kolingba (1981)
Area: 241,313 sq mi. (625,000 sq km)
Population (est. 1982): 2,500,000 (average annual growth rate, 2.6%)
Density per square mile: 10.4
Capital and largest city (est. 1981): Bangui, 375,000
Monetary unit: Franc CFA
Ethnic groups: Mandja-Baya, Banda, Mbaka, Azande, Yakoma
Languages: French (official) and Sango
Religions: Protestant, 50%; Roman Catholic, 33%; Animist, 12%, Islam, 3%
National name: République Centrafricaine
Member of French Community
Literacy rate (1981): 20% (est.)
Economic summary: Gross national product (1980): $680 million. Average annual growth rate (1970–79): 0.9%. Per capita income (1980): $300. Land used for agriculture: 15%; labor force: 80%; principal products: cotton, coffee, peanuts, food crops, livestock. Major industrial products: timber, textiles, soap, cigarettes, processed food. Natural resources: diamonds, uranium, timber. Exports: diamonds, cotton, timber, coffee. Imports: machinery and electrical equipment, petroleum products, textiles. Major trading partners: France, Yugoslavia, Japan, U.S.

Geography. Situated about 500 miles north (805 km) of the equator, the Central African Republic is a landlocked nation bordered by Cameroon, Chad, the Sudan, Zaire, and the Congo. Twice the size of New Mexico, it is covered by tropical forests in the south and semidesert land in the east. The Ubangi and Shari are the largest of many rivers.

Government. On Dec. 4, 1976, the Central African Republic became the Central African Empire. Marshal Jean-Bédel Bokassa, who had ruled the republic since he took power in a military coup Dec. 31, 1965, was declared Emperor Bokassa I. He was overthrown in a coup on Sept. 20, 1979. Former President David Dacko, returned to power and changed the country's name back to the Central African Republic. An army coup on Sept. 1, 1981, deposed Dacko and suspended the Constitution and all political parties. A Military Committee of National Redress was set up to run the country.

History. As the colony of Ubangi-Shari, what is now the Central African Republic was united with Chad in 1905 and joined with Gabon and the Middle Congo in French Equatorial Africa in 1910. After World War II a rebellion in 1946 forced the French to grant self-government. In 1958 the territory voted to become an autonomous republic within the French Community, but on Aug. 13, 1960, President David Dacko proclaimed the republic's independence from France.

Dacko undertook to move the country into Peking's orbit, but was overthrown in a coup on Dec. 31, 1965, by the then Col. Jean-Bédel Bokassa, Army Chief of Staff. In August 1977, the U.S. State Department protested the Emperor's jailing of American and British newsmen.

Bokassa staged an elaborate coronation ceremony on the first anniversary of the Empire, inviting 3,500 guests to see him place a diamond-studded crown on his head and sit on a 2.5-ton gilded bronze throne in the shape of an eagle. The cost of the ceremony was one fourth of the annual foreign-exchange earnings of the country, one of the 25 poorest in the world.

CHAD

Republic of Chad
President: Hissen Habré (1982)
Area: 495,752 sq mi. (1,284,000 sq km)
Population (est. 1982): 4,650,000 (average annual growth rate, 2.3%)
Density per square mile: 9.4
Capital and largest city (est. 1982): N'djamena, 325,000
Monetary unit: Franc CFA
Ethnic groups: Baguirmiens, Kanembous, Saras, Massas, Arabs, Toubous, Goranes
Languages: French and Arabic (official), Sara, Kanembou, Ouddai, Massa, Gorane
Religions: Islam, 44%; Christian, 33%; Animist, 23%
National name: République de Tchad
Literacy rate (1981): 10%
Economic summary: Gross national product (1980): $530 million. Average annual growth rate (1970–79): –2.4%. Per capita income (1980): $120. Land used for agriculture: 17%; labor force: 90%; principal products: cotton, cattle, fish, sugar, subsistence crops. Labor force in industry: 4%; major products: livestock and livestock products, beer, bicycle and radio assembly, textiles, cigarettes. Natural resources: petroleum, unexploited uranium, kaolin. Exports: cotton, livestock and animal products. Imports: food, motor vehicles and parts, petroleum products, machinery, cement, textiles. Major trading partners: France and central African countries.

Geography. A landlocked country in north central Africa, Chad is about 85% the size of Alaska. Its neighbors are Niger, Libya, the Sudan, the Central African Empire, Cameroon, and Nigeria.

Lake Chad, from which the country gets its name, lies on the western border with Niger and Nigeria. In the north is a desert that runs into the Sahara.

Government. Hissen Habré became president of Chad on June 7, 1982, by overthrowing Goukouni Oueddi.

History. Chad was absorbed into the colony of French Equatorial Africa, as part of Ubangi-Shari, in 1910. France began the country's development after 1920, when it became a separate colony. In 1946, French Equatorial Africa was admitted to the French Union. By referendum in 1958 the Chad territory became an autonomous republic within the French Union.

An independence movement led by the first Premier and President, François (later Ngarta) Tombalbaye, achieved complete independence on Aug. 11, 1960.

A six-year sub-Sahara drought caused mass migrations, thousands of deaths, and famine conditions for some 2 million Chadians in 1974. International relief efforts were disrupted October 25, when President Tombalbaye ordered rejection of U.S. grain shipments.

Tombalbaye was killed in the 1975 coup and was succeeded by Gen. Félix Malloum, who faced a Libyan-financed rebel movement, the Chadian National Liberation Front (Frolinat), throughout his tenure in office. A ceasefire backed by Libya, Niger, and the Sudan early in 1978 failed to end the fighting, and French military aid, both troops and supplies, was increased.

Nine rival groups meeting in Lagos, Nigeria, in March 1979 agreed to form a provisional government headed by Goukouni Oueddi, a former Frolinat leader. Fighting broke out again in Chad in March 1980, when Defense Minister Hissen Habré challenged Goukouni and seized the capital. By the year's end, Libyan troops supporting Goukouni recaptured N'djamena, and Libyan President Muammar el-Qaddafi, in January 1981, proposed a merger of Chad with Libya.

The Libyan merger proposal was rejected and Libyan troops withdrew from Chad under pressure from other African countries, but in 1983 poured back into the barren northern part of the country in support of Goukouni. France, in turn, sent troops to the southern part of Chad in support of Habré, resulting in defacto division of the country. Intermittent fighting continued through 1984.

CHILE

Republic of Chile
President: Gen. Augusto Pinochet Ugarte (1973)
Area: 292,132 sq mi. (756,622 sq km)
Population (est. 1983): 11,700,000 (average annual growth rate: 1.3%)
Density per square mile: 40.1
Capital: Santiago
Largest cities (est. 1982): Santiago, 4,000,000; Viña del Mar, 290,000; Valparaiso, 275,000; Talcahuano, 210, 000; Concepción, 210,000; Antofagasta, 175,000
Monetary unit: Peso
Language: Spanish
Religion: Roman Catholic
National name: República de Chile
Literacy rate (1977): 90%
Economic summary: Gross national product (1980): $24.0 billion. Average annual growth rate (1970–79): 0.8%. Per capita income (1980): $2,160. Land used for agriculture: 21%; labor force 20%; principal products: grains, fruits, potatoes, vegetables, wine, livestock. Labor force in industry: 22%; major products: processed fish, transportation equipment, iron and steel, pulp, paper. Natural resources: copper, timber, iron ore, nitrates. Exports: copper, iron ore, paper and wood products, fruits. Imports: sugar, wheat, vehicles, petroleum, capital goods. Major trading partners: U.S., Japan, West Germany and Brazil.

Geography. Situated south of Peru and west of Bolivia and Argentina, Chile fills a narrow 1,800-

mile (2,897 km) strip between the Andes and the Pacific. Its area is nearly twice that of Montana.

One third of Chile is covered by the towering ranges of the Andes. In the north is the mineral-rich Atacama Desert, between the coastal mountains and the Andes. In the center is a 700-mile-long (1,127 km) valley, thickly populated, between the Andes and the coastal plateau. In the south, the Andes border on the ocean.

At the southern tip of Chile's mainland is Punta Arenas, the southernmost city in the world, and beyond that lies the Strait of Magellan and Tierra del Fuego, an island divided between Chile and Argentina. The southernmost point of South America is Cape Horn, a 1,390-foot (424-m) rock on Horn Island in the Wollaston group, which belongs to Chile.

The Juan Fernández Islands, in the South Pacific about 400 miles (644 km) west of the mainland, and Easter Island, about 2,000 miles (3,219 km) west, are Chilean possessions.

Government. Under the pre-coup Constitution, the nation elected a President every six years, a Senate of 50 members every eight years (one-half renewable every four years), and a Chamber of Deputies of 150 members every four years.

Leftist parties were abolished immediately after the 1973 military coup that ousted President Salvador Allende Gossens. Other parties were placed "in recess," and on March 12, 1977, the government officially dissolved them.

History. Chile was originally under the control of the Incas in the north and the fierce Araucanian people in the south. In 1541, a Spaniard, Pedro de Valdivia, founded Santiago. Chile won its independence from Spain in 1818 under Bernardo O'Higgins and an Argentinian, José de San Martin. O'Higgins, dictator until 1823, laid the foundations of the modern state with a two-party system and a centralized government.

The dictator from 1830 to 1837, Diego Portales, fought a war with Peru in 1836–39 that expanded Chilean territory. The Conservatives were in power from 1831 to 1861. Then the Liberals, winning a share of power for the next 30 years, disestablished the church and limited presidential power. Chile fought the War of the Pacific with Peru and Bolivia from 1879 to 1883, winning Antofagasta, Bolivia's only outlet to the sea, and extensive areas from Peru. A revolt in 1890 led by Jorge Montt overthrew, in 1891, José Balmaceda and established a parliamentary dictatorship that existed until a new Constitution was adopted in 1925. Industrialization began before World War I and led to the formation of Marxist groups.

Juan Antonio Ríos, President during World War II, was originally pro-Nazi but in 1944 led his country into the war on the side of the U.S. After the war, Gabriel González Videla, elected by a coalition including the Communists, turned on them. The Communist Party was outlawed until 1958.

A small abortive army uprising in 1969 raised fear of military intervention to prevent a Marxist, Salvador Allende Gossens, from taking office after his election to the presidency on Sept. 4, 1970, with 36.3% of the vote in a three-way battle. Dr. Allende was the first President in a non-Communist country freely elected on a Marxist-Leninist program.

Allende quickly established relations with Cuba and the People's Republic of China and nationalized several American companies. He promised compensation but imposed retroactive taxes to cancel out most claims, leading to cool but proper relations with the U.S. By 1972, inflation was running over 100% annually.

A middle-class general strike led to a military coup Sept. 11, 1973, then to Allende's overthrow and mysterious death in an army assault on the presidential palace. More than 2,700 deaths were reported in the coup, and many thousands were arrested. The coup ended a 46-year era of constitutional government in Chile, which had boasted the longest such record in Latin America.

The takeover was led by a four-man junta headed by Army Chief of Staff Augusto Pinochet Ugarte, who assumed the office of President and governed under a state of siege that was kept in force by extensions every six months. In March 1978, Pinochet lifted the state of siege because of "support for government" by the public, reported by a Gallup poll to be 75%.

Committed to "exterminate Marxism," the junta embarked on a right-wing dictatorship. It suspended parliament, banned political activity, and broke relations with Cuba.

The Human Rights Commission of the Organization of American States charged the junta with "most grave violations" of basic liberties, but the O.A.S. voted in May 1975 not to hear the report until further evidence was supplied. In July, Chile denied entry to a U.N. investigatory panel. On June 9, 1978, the government reversed that policy to permit the U.N. Human Rights Commission to send an investigative mission to Cuba.

In 1974, it was disclosed that the U.S. Central Intelligence Agency had secretely aided Allende's opponents before his election and had later worked covertly to "destabilize" his government.

In 1977, Pinochet, in a speech marking his fourth year in power, promised elections by 1985 if conditions warranted. Earlier, he had abolished DINA, the secret police, and decreed an amnesty for political prisoners, an action Amnesty International said might affect only 200–400 of some 1,500 political prisoners. In 1978, Pinochet permitted the deportation of Michael V. Townley to the U.S., where he and three Cuban exiles were charged with the murder of Orlando Letellier, a former Chilean foreign minister who had taken refuge in Washington.

Townley, given a reduced sentence in May 1979 because he gave evidence to convict the Cubans, testified that all four had been ordered to act by the secret police. A Chilean court refused to extradite three Chilean officers the U.S. accused of complicity in the assassination.

Pinochet was inaugurated on March 11, 1981, for an eight-year term as President, at the end of which, according to the Constitution adopted six months earlier, the junta would nominate a civilian as successor.

CHINA

People's Republic of China
President: Li Xiannian (1983)
Premier: Zhao Ziyang (1980)
Area: 3,691,521 sq mi. (9,561,000 sq km)[1]
Population (est. 1982): 1,060,000,000 (average annual growth rate, 1.4%)
Density per square mile: 276.3

Capital: Peking
Largest cities (est. 1983): Shanghai, 12,500,000; Peking, 9,500,000; Tianjin (Tientsin) 5,000,000; Shenyang (Mukden), 3,500,000; Canton 3,250,000, Wuhan, 3,000,000; Chongqing (Chungking), 3,225,000; Harbin; 2,750,000; Nanjing (Nanking), 2,250,000
Monetary unit: Yuan
Languages: Chinese, (Mandarin, Cantonese, and local dialects)
Religions: Principally Confucianist, Buddhist, and Taoist
National name: Zhonghua Renmin Gongheguo
Literacy rate (1981): 25%
Economic summary: Gross national product (1982); $350 billion. Average annual growth rate (1970–79): 2.8%. Per capita income (1982): $347. Land used for agriculture: 11%; labor force: 75%; principal products: rice, wheat, grains, cotton. Major industrial products: iron and steel, textiles, armaments, petroleum. Natural resources: coal, natural gas, limestone, marble. Exports: agricultural products, oil, minerals, metals, manufactured goods. Imports: grains, chemical fertilizer, steel, industrial raw materials, machinery and equipment. Major trading partners: Japan, Hong Kong, U.S., West Germany, Australia, Romania, Canada, U.S.S.R., U.K., France.

1. Including Manchuria and Tibet.

Geography. China, which occupies the eastern part of Asia, is slightly larger in area than the U.S. Its coastline is roughly a semicircle, about 2,150 miles (3,460 km) long. The greater part of the country is mountainous, and only in the lower reaches of the Yellow and Yangtze Rivers are there extensive low plains.

The principal mountain ranges are the Tien Shan, to the northwest; the Kunlun chain, running south of the Taklimakan and Gobi Deserts; and the Trans-Himalaya, connecting the Kunlun with the borders of China and Tibet. Manchuria is largely an undulating plain connected with the north China plain by a narrow lowland corridor. Inner Mongolia contains the relatively fertile southern and eastern portions of the Gobi. The large island of Hainan (13,500 sq mi.; 34,965 sq km) lies off the southern coast.

Hydrographically, China proper consists of three great river systems. The northern part of the country is drained by the Yellow River (Huang Ho), 2,900 miles long (4,667 km) and mostly unnavigable. The central part is drained by the Chang Jiang (Yangtze Kiang), the fourth longest river in the world 3,602 miles (5,797 km). The Xi Jiang (Si Kiang) in the south is 1,236 miles long (1,989 km) and navigable for a considerable distance. In addition, the Amur (2,704 sq mi.; 4,352 km) forms part of the northeastern boundary.

Government. With 3,040 deputies, elected for four-year terms by universal suffrage, the National People's Congress is the chief legislative organ. A State Council has the executive authority. The Congress elects the Premier and Deputy Premiers. All ministries are under the Stae Council, headed by the Premier.

The Communist Party controls the government.

History. By 2000 B.C.; the Chinese were living in the Hwang Ho basin, and they had achieved an advanced stage of civilization by 1200 B.C. The great philosophers Lao-tse, Confucius Mo Ti, and Mencius lived during the Chou dynasty (1122–249 B.C.). The warring feudal states were first united under Emperor Ch'in Shih Huang Ti, during whose reign (246–210 B.C.) work was begun on the Great Wall. Under the Han dynasty (206 B.C.–A.D. 220), China prospered and traded with the West.

In the T'ang dynasty (618–907), often called the golden age of Chinese history, painting, sculpture, and poetry flourished, and printing made its earliest known appearance.

The Mings, last of the native rulers (1368–1644), overthrew the Mongol, or Yuan, dynasty (1280–1368) established by Kublai Khan. The Mings in turn were overthrown in 1644 by invaders from the north, the Manchus.

China closely restricted foreign activities, and by the end of the 18th century only Canton and the Portuguese port of Macao were open to European merchants. Following the Anglo-Chinese War of 1839–42, however, several treaty ports were opened, and Hong Kong was ceded to Britain. Treaties signed after further hostilities (1856–60) weakened Chinese sovereignty and removed foreigners from Chinese jurisdiction. The disastrous Chinese-Japanese War of 1894–95 was followed by a scramble for Chinese concessions by European powers, leading to the Boxer Rebellion (1900), suppressed by an international force.

The death of the Empress Dowager Tzu Hsi in 1908 and the accession of the infant Emperor Hsüan T'ung (Pu-Yi) were followed by a nationwide rebellion led by Dr. Sun Yat-sen, who became first President of the Provisional Chinese Republic in 1911. The Manchus abdicated on Feb. 12, 1912. Dr. Sun resigned in favor of Yuan Shih-k'ai, who suppressed the republicans but was forced by a serious rising in 1915–16 to abandon his intention of declaring himself Emperor. Yuan's death in June 1916 was followed by years of civil war between rival militarists and Dr. Sun's republicans.

Nationalist forces, led by Gen. Chiang Kai-shek and with the advice of Communist experts, soon occupied most of China, setting up a Kuomintang regime in 1928. Internal strife continued, however, and Chiang broke with the Communists.

An alleged explosion on the South Manchurian Railway on Sept. 18, 1931, brought invasion of Manchuria by Japanese forces, who installed the last Manchu Emperor, Henry Pu-Yi, as nominal ruler of the puppet state of "Manchukuo." Japanese efforts to take China's northern provinces in July 1937 were resisted by Chiang, who meanwhile had succeeded in uniting most of China behind him. Within two years, however, Japan seized most of the ports and railways. The Kuomintang government retreated first to Hankow and then to Chungking, while the Japanese set up a puppet government at Nanking headed by Wang Jingwei.

Japan's surrender in 1945 touched off civil war between Nationalist forces under Chiang and Communist forces led by Mao Zedong, the party chairman. Despite U. S. aid, the Chiang forces were overcome by the Maoists, backed by the Soviet bloc, and were expelled from the mainland. The Mao regime, established in Peking as the new capital, proclaimed the People's Republic of China on Oct. 1, 1949, with Zhou Enlai as Premier.

The soviet-type government, after prolonged negotiations, signed a 30-year treaty of friendship and mutual aid with the U.S.S.R. on Feb. 14, 1950. Its published terms provided for return of the Changchun railroad to China and the eventual return of Port Arthur and Dairen, occupied by Soviet troops. Later in the year, Chinese troops invaded Tibet and began its subjugation, a campaign that brought China into conflict with India. After the

Provinces and Regions of China

Name	Area (sq mi.)	Area (sq km)	Capital
Provinces			
Anhui (Anhwei)	54,015	139,900	Hefei (Hofei)
Fujian (Fukien)	47,529	123,100	Fuzhou (Fukien)
Gansu (Kansu)	137,104	355,100	Lanzhou (Lanchow)
Guangdong (Kwangtung)	89,344	231,400	Canton
Guizhou (Kweichow)	67,181	174,000	Guiyang (Kweiyang)
Hebei (Hopei)	81,479	211,030	Shijiazhuang (Shitikiachwang)
Heilongjiang (Heilungkiang)[1]	178,996	463,600	Harbin
Henan (Honan)	64,479	167,000	Zhengzhou (Chengchow)
Hubei (Hupeh)	72,394	187,500	Wuhan
Hunan	81,274	210,500	Changsha
Jiangsu (Kiangsu)	40,927	106,000	Nanjing (Nanking)
Jiangxi (Kiangsi)	63,629	164,800	Nanchang
Jilin (Kirin)[1]	72,201	187,000	Changchun
Liaoning[1]	53,301	138,050	Shenyang
Quinghai (Chinghai)	278,378	721,000	Xining (Sining)
Shaanxi (Shensi)	75,598	195,800	Xian (Sian)
Shandong (Shantung)	59,189	153,300	Jinan (Tsinan)
Shanxi (Shansi)	60,656	157,100	Taiyuan
Sichuan (Szechwan)	219,691	569,000	Chengdu (Chengtu)
Yunnan	168,417	436,200	Kunming
Zhejiang (Chekiang)	39,305	101,800	Hangzhou (Hangchow)
Autonomous Region			
Guangxi Zhuang (Kwangsi Chuang)	85,096	220,400	Nanning
Nei Monggol (Inner Mongolia)[1]	454,633	1,177,500	Hohhot (Huhehot)
Ningxia Hui	30,039	77,800	Yinchuan (Yinchwan)
Xinjiang Uygur (Sinkiang Uighur)[1]	635,829	1,646,800	Urumqi (Urumchi)
Xizang (Tibet)	471,660	1,221,600	Lhasa

1. Together constitute (with Taiwan) what has been traditionally known as Outer China, the remaining territory forming the historical China Proper. NOTE: Names are in Pinyin, with conventional spelling in parentheses.

Korean War began in June 1950, China led the Communist block in supporting North Korea, and on Nov. 26, 1950, the Mao regime intervened openly.

A deterioration of relations between Peking and Moscow was indicated in 1958 when Peking emerged as an independent center of Communist power, challenging the leadership role of the U.S.S.R. in the Soviet bloc.

In 1958, Mao undertook the "Great Leap Forward" campaign, which combined the establishment of rural communes with a crash program of village industrialization. These efforts also failed, causing Mao to lose influence to Liu Shaoqi, who became President in 1959, to Premier Zhou, and to Party Secretary Deng Xiaoping. Meanwhile China's backing of subversive movements in Asia soured relations with India and Burma, although it very nearly achieved the conquest of Indonesia, and culminated in war on the borders of India late in 1962. By the next year, the break with the U.S.S.R. was complete.

Zhou proposed the movement that became known as the Cultural Revolution at the party congress in 1964, the same year China exploded its first atomic (fission) bomb (it produced a fusion bomb in 1967).

Mao moved to Shanghai, and from that base he and his supporters waged their own Cultural Revolution. President Liu and the party secretary, Deng, took over, and their followers denounced hundreds of party and government officials at rallies and in wall posters. Then, in 1966, Chen became director of the Cultural Revolution; the Army Chief of Staff, Lo Ruiqing, was purged; and Lin replaced Liu as second in the hierarchy. In the spring of 1966 the Mao group formed Red Guard units dominated by youths and students, closing the schools to free the students for agitation.

The Red Guards campaigned against "old ideas, old culture, old habits, and old customs." Often they were no more than uncontrolled mobs, and brutality was frequent. Early in 1967 efforts were made to restore control. The Red Guards were urged to return home. Schools started opening. But the height of violence was only reached in September 1967 when in Canton the opposing factions used tanks and artillery against each other.

Persistent overtures by the Nixon Administration (relaxed trade and travel restrictions) abruptly climaxed in an invitation to a U.S. table tennis team to visit Peking in April 1971. This was followed by the dramatic announcement in July that Henry Kissinger, President Richard M. Nixon's national security adviser, had secretly visited Peking and reached agreement on a visit by the President to China.

The movement toward reconciliation, which signaled the end of the U.S. containment policy toward China, provided irresistible momentum for Chinese admission to the U.N. Despite U.S. opposition to expelling Taiwan (Nationalist China), the world body overwhelmingly ousted Chiang in seating Peking.

President Nixon went to Peking for a week early in 1972, meeting Mao as well as Zhou. The summit ended with a historic communiqué on February 28, in which both nations promised to work toward improved relations. They differed over Vietnam as well as Taiwan, although the U.S. noted it was withdrawing from Vietnam and said its ultimate goal was withdrawal from Taiwan as well, with interim reductions of those forces as tension in the area diminished.

In 1973, the U.S. and China agreed to set up "liaison offices" in each other's capitals, which constituted de facto diplomatic relations. Full diplomatic relations were barred by China as long as the U.S. continued to recognize Nationalist China.

The National People's Congress held its first meeting in a decade in Peking, Jan. 13–17, 1975. With Mao absent, it re-elected Zhou as Premier. It approved a government realignment that placed Marshal Ye Jianying in the post of Defense Minister, vacant since Lin's death. It revised the 1954 Constitution to reassert the primacy of the Communist Party and to specify limited rights of citizens to strike and demonstrate, to hold private farm plots, and to work for themselves.

Zhou predicted in a keynote address that "fierce contention" between the U.S. and the U.S.S.R. "is bound to lead to world war some day." He said there is "no détente, let alone lasting peace in the world today."

The same warnings against détente were made during President Ford's visit to China, Dec. 8–12, 1975, by Vice Premier Deng Xiaoping. Deng served as chief host because Zhou was now seriously ill with cancer and Mao, visibly failing, saw the visitor only briefly.

On Jan. 8, 1976, amid a national outpouring of grief, Zhou died. Demonstrations in the capital turned into near riots when mourners suspected the government of trying to suppress the display of emotion. Deng, who had been rehabilitated by Zhou and designated as his successor, was supplanted within a month by Hua Guofeng, former Minister of Public Security. Hua, believed to be a compromise between radicals and the moderates represented by the ousted Deng, became permanent Premier in April. In October he was named successor to Mao as Chairman of the Communist Party.

Mao died September 10, apparently of Parkinson's disease, and China for the second time in a year went into a period of national mourning. Almost immediately afterward, a campaign against his widow, Jiang Qing, and three of her "radical" colleagues began. The "Gang of Four" was denounced for having undermined the party, the government, and the economy.

Jiang was brought to trial in 1980 and sentenced on Jan. 25, 1981, to die within two years unless she showed repentance, in which case she would be imprisoned for life. She showed no remorse at the trial, shouting defiance as she was taken away.

While the despised four were reviled throughout China, there was evidence by late 1976 that Deng was to be rehabilitated. At the Central Committee meeting of 1977, Deng was reinstated as Deputy Premier, Chief of Staff of the Army, and member of the Central Committee of the Politburo. He was ranked behind Ye Jianying, the Defense Minister, in the third-ranking place in the government.

At the same time, Jiang Qing, Wang Hongwen, Zhang Chunqiao, and Yao Wenyuan—the notorious "Gang of Four"—were removed from all official posts and banished from the party. The final resolution of the committee meeting declared national unity restored and "a new leap forward taking shape in the national economy."

In August 1977, the 11th national Communist Party Congress and the election of a new Politburo took place as U.S. Secretary of State Cyrus Vance visited China to call for efforts by both China and the U.S. to normalize relations.

The Fifth National People's Congress adopted a new Constitution on March 5, 1978, strengthening civil rights such as free speech and the right to file complaints against the government. The Congress also approved a 10-year plan to increase farm production and add 120 industrial complexes to the nation's industrial base. Hua Guofeng was affirmed as Premier despite rumors that Deputy Premier Deng might take the post.

In May 1978, expulsion of ethnic Chinese by Vietnam produced an open rupture. China withdrew aid technicians and announced a complete cutoff, disclosing for the first time that it had given $10 billion to Vietnam in the past 20 years. Peking sided with Cambodia in the border fighting that flared between Vietnam and Cambodia, charging Hanoi with aggression.

On Aug. 12, 1978, China and Japan signed a treaty of peace and friendship, a treaty attacked by Moscow as hostile to the Soviet Union. Peking and Washington then announced that they would open full diplomatic relations on Jan. 1, 1979. Over Congressional objections, the Carter Administration abrogated the Taiwan defense treaty, the last obstacle to full relations. Deputy Premier Deng sealed the agreement with a visit to the United States that coincided with the opening of embassies in both capitals on March 1.

Peking protested Congressional guarantees of Taiwan's defense that were inserted in legislation governing future U.S. relations with the island. The Chinese nevertheless went ahead with the drafting of a trade pact that gave them most-favored-nation status. China agreed to pay $80 million compensation for American property seized after the 1949 Communist take-over of the mainland.

A near proxy war with the Soviet Union erupted on Deng's return from the U.S. as 200,000 to 300,000 Chinese troops invaded Vietnam to avenge alleged violations of Chinese territory. The action was seen as more a reaction to Vietnam's invasion of Cambodia, where China had been the dominant outside influence since 1975. While the Soviet Union stepped up supply airlifts, the Chinese inflicted damage on the northern border, then withdrew.

At home, a political trend that had seen a "freedom wall" in Peking where individuals could publish their opinions without censorship was dampened. But if individual expression was curbed, the leadership encouraged a radical shift from traditional Marxism toward private enterprise in every phase of the national economy.

The first People's Congress in five years marked the culmination of Deng's post-Mao modernization efforts. On Sept. 10, the Congress confirmed Zhao Ziyang, an economic planner, as Premier replacing Hua Guofeng, who had held the post since 1976. Hua retained his chairmanship of the Communist Party.

At the Central Committee meeting of June 27–29, 1981, another Deng protégé, Hu Yaobang, was elevated to the party chairmanship and Hua retired. The 66-year-old Hu had served as party Secretary-General, a post he retained. Deng became chairman of the military commission of the central committee, giving him control over the army. The committee's 215 members concluded the session with a statement holding Mao Zedong responsible for the "grave blunder" of the Cultural Revolution.

Deng's triumph was somewhat dulled by the recognition that his modernization program had outpaced Chinese resources. The 1981 budget had to be reduced by $9.8 billion to $64.6 billion, cutting capital spending for oil and coal production and even for defense. Inflation was blamed for casualties such as the Baoshan steel plant in Shanghai, which was to have been a showpiece of industrial modernization.

Despite economic problems, foreign investment gained during 1981 and, on Dec. 16 of that year Japan signed a $1.4-billion aid agreement providing funds to complete the first phase of the Baoshan plant, a refinery at Daqing and four other projects.

In April 1982, a new draft constitution proposed the re-establishment of the office of president, last held by Liu, and the return of the military to parliamentary rather than party control. It also proposed the removal of political power of the communes, leaving them as economic units, with political functions restored to elected town officials.

A clash with the United States over the continuation of U.S. arms to Taiwan required a peacemaking visit by Vice President George Bush to Peking, but despite Chinese protests, incoming Secretary of State George Schultz affirmed in July that U.S. F-5E fighter planes would continue to be made in Taiwan under license. On Aug. 17, however, the United States signed a joint communiqué with China pledging that arms sales to Taiwan would not be increased and would instead be gradually decreased pending a "final resolution" of the Taiwan problem.

On June 18, 1983, the Chinese Parliament elected Li Xiannian, an economics and financial specialist, as the first national president since 1969. Previously an outspoken critic of the United States, he was the official host when President Ronald Reagan visited China in April 1984.

CHINA (TAIWAN)

Republic of China
President: Chiang Ching-kuo (1978)
Premier: Sun Yun-hsuan (1978)
Area: 13,895 sq mi. (35,988 sq km)[1]
Population (est. 1982): 18,350,000 (average annual growth rate: 1.8%)
Density per square mile: 1,350.1
Capital: Taipei
Largest cities (est. 1982): Taipei, 2,300,000; Kaohsiung, 1,250,000; Taichung, 595,000; Tainan, 585,000; Chilung (Keelung), 350,000
Monetary unit: New Taiwan dollar
Languages: Chinese (Mandarin) and various dialects
Religions: Confucianist, Buddhist, Christian, Taoist
Literacy rate (1981): 90%
Economic summary: Gross national product (1982): $46 billion. Average annual growth rate (1970–77): 5.5%. Per capital income (1982): $2,143. Land used for agriculture: 24%; labor force: 22%; principal products: rice, sweet potatoes, sugar cane, bananas, pineapples, citrus fruits. Labor force in industry: 42%; major products: textiles, clothing, chemicals, processed foods, electronic equipment, cement, ships, plywood. Natural resources: timber, camphor. Exports: textiles, electrical machinery, plywood. Imports: machinery, basic metals, crude oil, chemicals. Major trading partners: U.S., Japan.

1. Excluding Quemoy and Matsu.

Geography. The Republic of China today consists of the island of Taiwan, an island 100 miles (161 km) off the Asian mainland in the Pacific; two offshore islands, Quemoy and Matsu; and the nearby islets of the Pescadores chain. It is slightly larger than the combined areas of Massachusetts and Connecticut.

Taiwan is divided by a central mountain range that runs from north to south, rising sharply on the east coast and descending gradually to a broad western plain, where cultivation is concentrated.

Government. The President and the Vice President are elected by the National Assembly for a term of six years. There are five major governing bodies called Yuans: Executive, Legislative, Judicial, Control, and Examination. Taiwan's internal affairs are administered by the Taiwan Provincial Government under the supervision of the Provincial Assembly, which is popularly elected.

The majority and ruling party is the Kuomintang (Nationalist Party) led by President Chiang Ching-kuo. There are also two minority parties: the China Democratic Socialist Party and the Young China Party.

History. Taiwan was inhabited by aborigines of Malayan descent when Chinese from the areas now designated as Fukien and Kwangtung began settling it beginning in the 7th century, becoming the majority.

The Portuguese explored the area in 1590, naming it The Beautiful (Formosa). In 1624 the Dutch set up forts in the south, the Spanish in the North. The Dutch threw out the Spanish in 1641 and controlled the island until 1661, when the Chinese General Koxinga took it over, established an independent kingdom, and expelled the Dutch. The Manchus seized the island in 1683 and held it until 1895, when it passed to Japan after the first Sino-Japanese War. Japan developed and exploited it, and it was heavily bombed by American planes during World War II, after which it was restored to China.

After the defeat of its armies on the mainland, the Nationalist Government of Generalissimo Chiang Kai-shek retreated to Taiwan in December 1949. With only 15% of the population consisting of the 1949 immigrants, Chiang dominated the island, maintaining a 600,000-man army in the hope of eventually recovering the mainland. Japan renounced its claim to the island by the San Francisco Peace Treaty of 1951.

By stationing a fleet in the Strait of Formosa the U.S. prevented a mainland invasion in 1953.

The "China seat" in the U.N., which the Nationalists held with U.S. help for over two decades was lost in October 1971, when the People's Republic of China was admitted and Taiwan ousted by the world body.

President Nixon's summit meeting with Chinese leaders and the 1972 Sino-American communiqué further eroded Taiwan's position. In it, the U.S. said its eventual goal was complete withdrawal of its forces from Taiwan and progressive cutbacks as tensions in the area eased. With the end of U.S. participation in the war in Vietnam, withdrawal of U.S. air-support forces on the island began in 1973.

Chiang died at 87 of a heart attack on April 5, 1975. His son, Chiang Ching-kuo, continued as Premier and dominant power in the Taipei regime. He assumed the presidency in 1978, and Sun Yunhsuan became Premier.

President Carter's announcement that the U.S. would recognize only the People's Republic of China after Jan. 1, 1979, and that the U.S. defense treaty with the Nationalists would end aroused protests in Taiwan and in the U.S. Congress. Against Carter's wishes, Congress, in a bill governing future relations with Taiwan, guaranteed U.S. action in the event of an attack on the island. The legislation also provided for the continuation of trade and other relations through an American Institute in Taipei, housed in the former American Embassy.

Although the U.S. had assured Taiwan of continuing arms aid, a communiqué on Aug. 17, 1982, signed by Washington and Peking and promising a gradual reduction of such aid, cast a shadow over Taiwan. The Nationalist government protested that the communiqué contradicted the "letter and the spirit" of the Taiwan Relations Act by which the U.S. Congress sought to assure Taiwan's defense.

COLOMBIA

Republic of Colombia
President: Belisario Betancur Cuartas (1982)
Area: 455,355 sq mi. (1,179,369 sq km)
Population (est. 1982): 28,575,000 (average annual growth rate, 1.6%) (mestizo, 68%; white, 20%; Indian, 7%; black, 5%)
Density per square mile: 62.8
Capital: Bogotá
Largest cities (est. 1982): Bogotá, 4,250,000; Medellín, 1,500,000; Cali, 1,300,000; Baranquilla, 865,000; Cartagena, 450,000; Bucaramanga, 400,000
Monetary unit: Peso
Language: Spanish
Religion: Roman Catholic
National name: República de Colombia
Literacy rate (1981): 75%
Economic summary: Gross national product (est. 1981): \$39.8. billion. Average annual growth rate (1970–79): 3.7%. Per capita income (est. 1981): \$1,370. Land used for agriculture: 30%; labor force: 30%; principal products: coffee, bananas, rice, corn, sugar cane, cotton, tobacco, flowers. Labor force in industry: 15%; major products: textiles, processed food, clothing and footwear, beverages, chemicals, metal products, cement. Natural resources: petroleum, natural gas, coal, iron ore, nickel, gold, copper, emeralds. Exports: coffee, fuel oil, cotton, tobacco, sugar, textiles. Imports: machinery, electrical equipment, chemical products, metals and metal products, transportation equipment. Major trading partners: U.S., West Germany, Japan, Venezuela, Netherlands.

Geography. Colombia, in the northwestern part of South America, is the only country on that continent that borders on both the Atlantic and Pacific Oceans. It is nearly equal to the combined areas of California and Texas.

Through the western half of the country, three Andean ranges run north and south, merging into one at the Ecuadorean border. The eastern half is a low, jungle-covered plain, drained by spurs of the Amazon and Orinoco, inhabited mostly by isolated, tropical-forest Indian tribes. The fertile plateau and valley of the eastern range are the most densely populated parts of the country.

Government. Colombia's President, who appoints his own Cabinet, serves for a four-year term. The Senate, the upper house of Congress, has 114 members elected for four years by direct vote. The House of Representatives of 199 members is directly elected for four years.

The major political parties are the Liberal Party (60 of 114 seats in Senate, 114 of 199 seats in House), Conservative Party (51 seats in Senate, 84 seats in House), and a leftist coalition (1 seat in Senate, 1 seat in House).

History. Spaniards in 1510 founded Darien, the first permanent European settlement on the American mainland. In 1538 the Spaniards established the colony of New Granada, the area's name until 1861. After a 14-year struggle, in which Simón Bolívar's Venezuelan troops won the battle of Boyacá in Colombia on Aug. 7, 1819, independence was attained in 1824. Bolívar united Colombia, Venezuela, Panama, and Ecuador in the Republic of Greater Colombia (1819–30), but lost Venezuela and Ecuador to separatists. Bolívar's Vice President, Francisco de Paula Santander, founded the Liberal Party as the Federalists while Bolívar established the Conservatives as the Centralists.

Santander's presidency (1832–36) re-established order, but later periods of Liberal dominance (1849–57 and 1861–80), when the Liberals sought to disestablish the Roman Catholic Church, were marked by insurrection and even civil war. Rafael Nuñez, in a 15-year-presidency, restored the power of the central government and the church, which led in 1899 to a bloody civil war and the loss in 1903 of Panama over ratification of a lease to the U.S. of the Canal Zone. For 21 years, until 1930, the Conservatives held power as revolutionary pressures built up.

The Liberal administrations of Enrique Olaya Herrera and Alfonso López (1930–38) were marked by social reforms that failed to solve the country's problems, and in 1946, insurrection and banditry broke out, claiming hundreds of thousands of lives by 1958. Laureano Gómez (1950–53); the Army Chief of Staff, Gen. Gustavo Rojas Pinilla (1953–56), and a military junta (1956–57) sought to curb disorder by repression.

Subsequent Presidents were Alberto Lleras Camargo (1957–62); Guillermo León Valencia (1962–66); Carlos Lleras Restrepo (1966–70); Misael Pastrana Borrero (1970–74); and Alfonso López Michelson (1974–78).

Julio César Turbay Ayala, Liberal Party candidate in 1978, won a narrow victory—approximately 140,000 of a total of nearly 2.5 million votes—over the Conservative Party candidate. The Liberals also retained control of both the Senate and House.

Government efforts to stamp out the Movement of April 19 (M-19), an urban guerrilla organization, intensified in 1981 with the capture of some of the leaders. A general amnesty failed to bring an end to the movement, but its efforts to impede the 1982 national elections on March 14 had little effect as the voting was called the most peaceful in years. Although the Liberals won a solid majority, a party split enabled Belisario Betancur Cuartas, the Conservative candidate, to win the presidency on May 31. After his inauguration, he ended the state of siege that had existed almost continuously for 34 years and renewed Turbay's amnesty offer.

COMOROS

Federal and Islamic Republic of the Comoros
President: Ahmed Abdallah (1978)
Premier: Ali Mroudjae (1982)
Area: 719 sq mi. (1,862 sq km)
Population (est. 1983): 442,000 (average annual growth rate: 2.8%)
Density per square mile: 541.9
Capital and largest city (est. 1980): Moroni (on Grande Comoro), 20,000
Monetary unit: Franc CFA
Language: French
Religions: Islam and Christian
National name: État Comorien
Literacy rate (1981): 20%
Economic summary: Gross national product (1980): $100 million. Average annual growth rate (1970–79): –4.3%. Per capita income (1980): $300. Principal agricultural products: perfume essences, copra, coconuts, cloves, vanilla, cinnamon, yams; major industrial products: perfume distillations. Exports: perfume essences, vanilla, copra, cloves. Imports: foodstuffs, fuels, chemicals, cotton textiles, cement. Major trading partners: France, Madagascar, West Germany, Kenya, Italy.

Geography. The Comoros Islands—Grande Comoro, Anjouan, Mohéli, and Mayotte (which retains ties to France)—are an archipelago of volcanic origin in the Indian Ocean between Mozambique and Madagascar.

Government. A coup by foreign mercenaries on May 13, 1978, deposed President Ali Soilih, who had held power since 1975. A "political and military directorate" headed by Ahmed Abdallah and Mohammed Ahmed governed until the adoption of a constitution on Oct. 1 ushered in a republic. With the resignation of Ahmed two days later, Abdallah became president.

History. Under French rule since 1886, the Comoros declared themselves independent July 6, 1975. However, Mayotte, with a Christian majority, voted against joining the other, mainly Islamic, islands, in the move to independence and remains French.

A month after independence, Justice Minister Ali Soilih staged a coup with the help of mercenaries, overthrowing the new nation's first president, Ahmed Abdallah. Soilih lowered the voting age to 14, destroyed all records and killed many Comorans. He was overthrown on May 13, 1978, when a small boatload of French mercenaries, some of whom had aided him three years earlier, seized government headquarters.

CONGO

People's Republic of the Congo
President: Col. Denis Sassou-Nguessou (1979)
Prime Minister: Ange Edouard Poungui (1984)
Area: 132,046 sq mi. (342,000 sq km)
Population (est. 1982): 1,625,000 (average annual growth rate, 2.8%)
Density per sq mile: 12.3
Capital and largest city (est. 1982): Brazzaville, 450,000
Monetary unit: Franc CFA
Ethnic groups: Vilis, Bakongo, Batekes, Mbochis
Languages: French, Lingala, Kokongo
Religions: Animist, 47%; Roman Catholic, 41%; Protestant, 10%
National name: République Populaire du Congo
Literacy rate (1981): 10% (est.)
Economic summary: Gross national product (1980): $1.1 billion. Average annual growth rate (1970–79): –0.2%. Per capita income (1980): $730. Principal agricultural products: sugar cane, wood, coffee, cocoa, peanuts, tobacco. Labor force in industry: 20%; major products: crude oil, cigarettes, soap, beverages, milled sugar. Natural resources: wood, potash, petroleum, natural gas. Exports: oil, lumber, tobacco, veneer and plywood. Imports: machinery, transportation equipment, manufactured consumer goods, iron and steel, foodstuffs. Major trading partners: France and other Western European countries.

Geography. The Congo is situated in west Central Africa astride the Equator. It borders on Gabon, Cameroon, the Central African Republic, Zaire, and the Angola exclave of Cabinda, with a short stretch of coast on the South Atlantic. Its area is nearly three times that of Pennsylvania.

Most of the inland is tropical rain forest, drained by tributaries of the Zaire (Congo) River, which flows south along the eastern border with Zaire to Stanley Pool. The narrow coastal plain rises to highlands separated from the inland plateaus by the 200-mile-wide Niari River Valley, which gives passage to the coast.

Government. Since the coup of September 1968 the country has been governed by a military regime. The Congolese Labor Party is the only party.

History. The inhabitants of the former French Congo, mainly Bantu peoples with Pygmies in the north, were subjects of several kingdoms in earlier times.

The Frenchman Pierre Savorgnan de Brazza signed a treaty with Makoko, ruler of the Bateke people, in 1880, which established French control. The area, with Gabon and Ubangi-Shari, was constituted the colony of French Equatorial Africa in 1910. It joined Chad in supporting the Free French cause in World War II. The Congo proclaimed its independence without leaving the French Community in 1960.

Maj. Marien Ngouabi, head of the National Council of the Revolution, took power as president on Jan. 1, 1969. He was sworn in for a second five-year term in 1975. A visit to Moscow by Ngouabi in March ended with the signing of a Soviet-Congolese economic and technical aid pact.

A four-man commando squad assassinated Ngouabi in Brazzaville on March 18, 1977. Five days later the assassination of Émile Cardinal Biayenda, Archbishop of Brazzaville, was announced. Former President Alphonse Massamba-Débat, accused of plotting both deaths, was executed.

Col. Joachim Yhombi-Opango, Army Chief of Staff, assumed the presidency on April 4. In June, the new government agreed to resume diplomatic relations with the U.S., ending a 12-year rift. Yombhi-Opango resigned on Feb. 4, 1979, and was replaced by Col. Denis Sassou-Neguessou.

COSTA RICA

Republic of Costa Rica
President: Luis Alberto Monge Alvarez (1982)
Area: 19,652 sq mi. (50,898 sq km)
Population (est. 1983): 2,375,000 (average annual growth rate, 2.9%)
Density per square mile: 120.9
Capital and largest city (est. 1982): San José, 265,000
Monetary unit: Colón
Language: Spanish
Religion: Roman Catholic
National name: República de Costa Rica
Literacy rate (1981): 90%
Economic summary: Gross national product (1980): $3.8 billion. Average annual growth rate (1970–79): 3.2%. Per capita income (1980): $1,730. Land used for agriculture: 8%; labor force: 33%; principal products: bananas, coffee, sugar cane, rice, corn, cocoa, livestock. Labor force in industry: 20%; major products: processed foods, textiles and clothing, construction materials, fertilizer. Natural resource: timber. Exports: coffee, bananas, beef, sugar, cacao. Imports: manufactured products, machinery, transportation equipment, chemicals, foodstuffs, fuels, fertilizer. Major trading partners: U.S., Central American countries, West Germany, Japan.

Geography. This Central American country lies between Nicaragua to the north and Panama to the south. Its area slightly exceeds that of Vermont and New Hampshire combined.

Most of Costa Rica is tableland, from 3,000 to 6,000 feet (914 to 1,829 m) above sea level. Cocos Island (10 sq mi.; 26 sq km), about 300 miles (483 km) off the Pacific Coast, is under Costa Rican sovereignty; it is of potential strategic importance in defense of the Panama Canal.

Government. Under the 1949 Constitution, the president and the one-house Legislative Assembly of 57 members are elected for terms of four years.

The army was abolished in 1949. There is a civil guard of 3,000 and a rural guard of 2,500.

The major political parties are the National Liberation Party (33 of 57 seats in the Legislative Assembly), led by Armando Arauz; Unity Party (18 seats), led by Rafael A. Grillo; Communist Party (4 seats); Pueblo Unido Party (1 seat); Movimiento Nacional Party (1 seat).

History. Costa Rica was inhabited by 25,000 Indians when Columbus discovered it and probably named it in 1502. Few of the Indians survived the Spanish conquest, which began in 1563. The region was administered as a Spanish province. Costa Rica achieved independence in 1821 but was absorbed for two years by Agustín de Iturbide in his Mexican Empire. It was established as a republic in 1848.

Except for the military dictatorship of Tomás Guardia from 1870 to 1882, Costa Rica has enjoyed one of the most democratic governments in Latin America.

Rodrigo Carazo Odio, leader of a four-party coalition called the Unity Party, won the presidency in February 1978, campaigning on the government's having allowed Robert L. Vesco, a fugitive U.S. financier, to find asylum in Costa Rica. His tenure was marked by a disastrous decline in the economy, which forced postponement of foreign debt payments at the end of 1981. Luis Alberto Monge Alvarez, a former union organizer and cofounder of the National Liberation Party, swept to victory in the Feb. 7, 1982, national elections.

CUBA

Republic of Cuba
President (1976) and head of government (1959): Fidel Castro
Area: 44,218 sq mi. (114,524 sq km)
Population (est. 1982): 9,850,000 (average annual growth rate, 0.8%)
Density per square mile: 222.8
Capital: Havana
Largest cities (est. 1982): Havana, 2,000,000; Santiago de Cuba, 565,000; Santa Clara, 525,000; Camagüey, 480,000; Holguin, 460,000; Matanzas, 425,000
Monetary unit: Peso
Language: Spanish
Religion: Roman Catholic
National name: República de Cuba
Literacy rate (1981): 96%
Economic summary: Gross national product (1979): $13.9 billion. Average annual growth rate (1970–78): 4.7%. Land used for agriculture: 35%; labor force: 33%; principal products: sugar, tobacco, coffee, rice, meat, vegetables, fruits. Labor force in industry: 17%; major products: refined oil products, textiles, chemicals, processed food, metals, light consumer products. Natural resources: metals, primarily nickel. Exports: sugar, nickel, shellfish, tobacco. Imports: capital goods, industrial raw materials, petroleum, foodstuffs. Major trading partners: U.S.S.R., other Communist bloc countries, Mexico, Argentina, Canada.

Geography. The largest island of the West Indies group (equal in area to Pennsylvania), Cuba is also the westernmost—just west of Hispaniola (Haiti and the Dominican Republic), and 90 miles (145 km) south of Key West, Fla., at the entrance to the Gulf of Mexico.

The island is mountainous in the southeast and south central area (Sierra Maestra). Elsewhere it is flat or rolling.

Government. Since 1976, elections have been held every five years to elect the National Assembly, which in turn elects the 31-member Council of States, its President, First Vice-President, five Vice-Presidents, and Secretary. Fidel Castro is President of the Council of State and of the government.

The only political party is the Communist Party of Cuba.

History. Arawak Indians inhabiting Cuba when Columbus discovered the island in 1492 died off from diseases brought by sailors and settlers. By 1511, Spaniards under Diego Velásquez were founding settlements that served as bases for Spanish exploration. Cuba soon after served as an assembly point for treasure looted by the conquistadores, attracting French and English pirates.

Black slaves and free laborers were imported to work sugar and tobacco plantations, and waves of chiefly Spanish immigrants maintained a European character in the island's culture. Early slave rebellions and conflicts between colonials and Spanish rulers laid the foundation for an independence movement that turned into open warfare from 1867 to 1878. The poet, José Marti, in 1895 led the struggle that finally ended Spanish rule, thanks largely to U.S. intervention in 1898 after the sinking of the battleship *Maine* in Havana harbor.

A treaty in 1899 made Cuba an independent republic under U.S. protection. The U.S. occupation, which ended in 1902, suppressed yellow fever and brought large American investment. From 1906 to 1909, Washington invoked the Platt Amendment to the treaty, which gave it the right to intervene in order to suppress any revolt. U.S. troops came back in 1912 and again in 1917 to restore order. The Platt Amendment was abrogated in 1934.

Gerardo Machado, President during the Depression, planned vast social reforms but abandoned them. Fulgencio Batista, an army sergeant, led a revolt in 1934 that overthrew the Machado regime and developed into a Batista dictatorship. A succession of constitutionally elected Presidents—Ramón Grau San Martín, Carlos Mendieta, Miguel Mariano Gómez, Carlos Prío Sacarrás—pushed through social reforms, hampered by overwhelming corruption manipulated by Batista, who seized power in 1952.

Fidel Castro staged a hopeless revolt in 1953. Captured and paroled, he went to Oriente Province and, aided by an Argentinian adventurer, Ernesto (Ché) Guevara, rebuilt his forces and waged a guerrilla war. The U.S. withdrew support from Batista in 1958. With funds from Soviet sources, Castro bought off the leaders of Batista's army. This and popular support from the intellectual and laboring classes demoralized the army, and Castro's forces grew as he marched on Havana. Batista fled to the Dominican Republic on Jan. 1, 1959.

Executions and torture by the new Castro regime caused a world outcry. Castro antagonized the U.S. in 1959 by confiscating U.S. investments in banks and industries and by seizing large U.S. landholdings, turning them at first into collective farms, then into Soviet-type state farms.

The U.S. broke off relations on Jan. 3, 1961, and Castro disclosed his alliance with the U.S.S.R. and the Soviet bloc. Thousands of Cubans fled to the U.S. From their ranks an invasion force was recruited by an all-party coalition financed and guided by the U.S. Central Intelligence Agency and trained in Florida and Guatemala. A landing in the Bay of Pigs, Cuba, on April 17, 1961, failed when President Kennedy refused it air support under Soviet and Latin American pressure.

In 1962 the U.S.S.R. built missile sites in Cuba and provided Castro's army with troops, planes, and submarines. Alarmed, Kennedy on Oct. 22, 1962, served notice that the U.S. was willing to risk war to enforce a demand that the Soviet Union remove weapons and troops threatening U.S. security. The U.S. confronted Soviet vessels with U.S. warships. Soviet Premier Nikita Khrushchev agreed to remove the missiles, and the blockade was lifted on November 20. Shortly before Christmas, Castro released 1,113 Bay of Pigs prisoners.

U.S.-Cuban relations began to thaw with negotiation of a 1973 agreement to end air hijacking. Except for political refugees, criminal hijackers will be extradited to their home country or tried for the crime where they land; also, both nations pledged to forbid attacks on the other to be mounted from their territory.

U.S. curbs on travel by Cuba's United Nations delegation were eased in 1975 and the U.S. joined 15 Latin American republics in voting to scrap economic and diplomatic sanctions the O.A.S. had imposed against Cuba in 1964.

Despite Cuba's intervention in Africa, the Carter administration signed fishing agreements with Havana in 1977, removed restrictions on travel to the island, and eased the 1960 embargo to permit Cuba to buy essential goods.

In September 1977, Cuban diplomats opened an interests section in the old Cuban embassy in Washington and 10 Americans—later 20—opened a similar office in the former U.S. embassy in Havana. Hopes that full diplomatic relations would be restored were shattered early in 1978 when Washington charged that 10,000 to 11,000 Cubans were fighting for the Marxist government of Ethiopia.

Emigration increased dramatically after April 1, 1980, when Castro, irritated at the granting of asylum to would-be refugees by the Peruvian embassy, removed the guards and allowed 10,000 Cubans to swarm into the embassy grounds. As an airlift began taking them to Costa Rica for distribution to other countries, Castro insisted that they must go directly to their final destination. He ordered the port of Mariel opened and a "freedom flotilla" of small boats from the U.S. arrived to find that the government had consigned criminals, homosexuals, and others considered undesirable to be taken along with relatives of Cuban-Americans. Departures soared past 125,000 despite efforts by the Carter Administration to halt the traffic and they stopped only when Castro, embarrassed by the reported application of 1 million Cubans to join the exodus, closed the port Sept. 26.

At the second Party Congress in December, Castro voiced willingness to improve relations with the new Reagan Administration, but was rebuffed by Secretary of State Alexander M. Haig, Jr., who denounced Cuba in January 1981 as a proxy for Soviet subversion in the Caribbean. Haig later named Cuba as the source of arms and training for leftist guerrillas in El Salvador and threatened to "go to the source," a threat that Castro used as justification for mustering a new territorial force of 500,000 as a supplement to regular forces.

Despite a report by the U.S. Congress' Joint Economic Committee in April 1982 that the 20-year embargo against Cuba had served only to drive the island into greater dependence on Moscow, the Reagan Administration banned tourist travel to Cuba and tightened the embargo. Secret contacts—a meeting between Haig and Cuban Vice President Carlos Rafael Rodriguez and another between Castro and U.S. Ambassador at Large Vernon Walters—brought no improvement in relations.

In a dramatic exercise in personal diplomacy, the Rev. Jesse Jackson, a candidate for the Democratic Presidential nomination, flew to Cuba in June 1984, met with Castro, and obtained his agreement to free 22 American citizens held in Cuban jails and 26 Cuban political prisoners, and flew home with them. Most of the Americans had been imprisoned on drug-related charges. In a speech on July 26, Castro said he sincerely wanted better relations with the United States but recited a litany of complaints against the U.S.

CYPRUS

Republic of Cyprus
President: Spyros Kyprianou (1977)
Area: 3,572 sq mi (9,251 sq km)
Population (est. 1983): 660,000 (average annual growth rate: 1.0%) (Greek, 81%; Turkish, 19%)
Density per square mile: 184.8
Capital and largest city (est. 1980): Nicosia, 160,000
Monetary unit: Cyprus pound
Languages: Greek, Turkish, English
Religions: Greek Orthodox, 76%; Islam, 19%

National name: Kypriaki Dimokratia—Kibris Cumhuriyeti
Member of Commonwealth of Nations
Literacy rate (1981): 89%
Economic summary: Gross national product (1980): $2.2 billion. Average annual growth rate (1970–78): 1.4%. Per capita income (1980): $3,560. Land used for agriculture: 47%; labor force: 36%; principal products: vine products, citrus, potatoes, other vegetables. Labor force in industry: 47%; major products: beverages, footwear, clothing, cement, asbestos mining. Natural resources: copper, asbestos, gypsum, building stone, marble, clay, salt. Exports: asbestos, copper, pyrites, citrus, raisins. Imports: manufactured goods, machinery and transportation equipment, petroleum products, foodstuffs. Major trading partners: U.K., Lebanon, Libya.

Geography. The third largest island in the Mediterranean (one and one half times the size of Delaware), Cyprus lies off the southern coast of Turkey and the western shore of Syria. Most of the country consists of a wide plain lying between two mountain ranges that cross the island. The highest peak is Mount Olympus at 6,406 feet (1,953 m).

Government. Under the republic's Constitution, for the protection of the Turkish minority the vice president as well as three of the 10 Cabinet ministers must be from the Turkish community, while the House of Representatives is elected by each community separately, 70% Greek Cypriote and 30% Turkish Cypriote representatives.

The Greek and Turkish communities are self-governing in questions of religion, education, and culture. Other governmental matters are under the jurisdiction of the central government. Each community is entitled to a Communal Chamber.

The Greek Communal Chamber, which had 23 members, was abolished in 1965 and its function was absorbed by the Ministry of Education. The Turkish Communal Chamber, however, has continued to function.

The following is a breakdown of the 35 seats held by Greeks: Democratic Front of Spyros Kyprianou (8); AKEL Progressive Party of the Working People (12); Democratic Rally (12); Socialist Party of Dr. Vassos Lyssarides (3). The 15 Turkish members have not attended sessions of the House since 1964.

History. Cyprus was the site of early Phoenician and Greek colonies. For centuries its rule passed through many hands. It fell to the Turks in 1571, and a large Turkish colony settled on the island.

In World War I, on the outbreak of hostilities with Turkey, Britain annexed the island. It was declared a crown colony in 1925.

For centuries the Greek population, regarding Greece as its mother country, has sought self-determination and reunion with it *(enosis).* The resulting quarrel with Turkey threatened NATO. Cyprus became an independent nation on Aug. 16, 1960, with Britain, Greece, and Turkey as guarantor powers.

After troubled years, a crisis was averted in 1968 when an American mediator, Cyrus R. Vance, induced Turkey, Greece, and Cyprus to accept a solution proposed by U.N. Secretary General U Thant for withdrawal of the Greek troops and the dismantling of Turkish invasion forces. The ethnic blocs began long direct negotiations for a new Constitution.

Archbishop Makarios, president since 1959, was overthrown July 15, 1974, by a military coup led by the Cypriot National Guard. The new regime named Nikos Giorgiades Sampson as president and Bishop Gennadios as head of the Cypriot Church to replace Makarios. The rebels were led by rightist Greek officers who supported *enosis.*

Diplomacy failed to resolve the crisis. Turkey invaded Cyprus by sea and air July 20, 1974, asserting its right to protect the Turkish Cypriote minority. Greece rejected a Turkish demand for withdrawal of the 650 Greek officers who had engineered the coup. The crisis forced resignation of the military junta that had ruled Greece for seven years.

Geneva talks involving Greece, Turkey, Britain, and the two Cypriote factions failed in mid-August, and the Turks subsequently gained control of 40% of the island. Greece made no armed response to the superior Turkish force, but bitterly suspended military participation in the NATO alliance.

On Cyprus, U.S. Ambassador Rodger P. Davies was shot to death in August during Greek Cypriote riots. The tension continued after Makarios returned to become President on Dec. 7, 1974. He offered self-government to the Turkish minority, but rejected any solution "involving transfer of populations and amounting to partition of Cyprus."

Turkish Cypriots proclaimed a separate state in the northern part of the island and proposed a "biregional federation." Some 200,000 Greek Cypriots demanded return to their homes in the Turkish zone and an estimated three fourths of the 45,000 ethnic Turks in the Greek zone crossed into the Turkish area.

Makarios died on Aug. 3, 1977, and Spyros Kiprianou was elected to serve the remaining five months of his term. Kiprianou, running unopposed, won a full five-year term in 1978. In February 1983, President Kiprianou was re-elected for another five-year term, polling 57% of the vote.

CZECHOSLOVAKIA

Czechoslovak Socialist Republic
President: Gustav Husak (1975)
Premier: Lubomir Strougal (1970)
Area: 49,374 sq mi. (127,896 sq km)
Population (est. 1982): 15,400,000 (average annual growth rate: 0.4%) (Czech, 64%; Slovak, 30%)
Density per square mile: 311.9
Capital: Prague
Largest cities (est. 1982): Prague, 1,185,000; Bratislava, 395,000; Brno, 375,000; Ostrova, 325,000; Kosice, 210,000; Plzěn, 173,000
Monetary unit: Koruna
Languages: Czech, Slovak, Hungarian
Religions: Roman Catholic, 70%; Czechoslovak Church, 8%; Protestant, 7%; Greek Orthodox, 5%
National name: Ceskoslovenská Socialistická Republika
Literacy rate (1981): 100%
Economic summary: Gross national product (1981); 90.9 billion. Average annual growth rate (1980–81); 3.9%. Per capita income (1980): $5,820. Labor force in agriculture: 14%; principal products: wheat, rye, oats, corn, barley, potatoes, sugar beets, hogs, cattle, horses. Labor force in industry: 39%; major products: iron and steel, machinery and equipment, cement, textiles, motor vehicles, armaments, chemicals, ceramics. Natural resources: coal/coke, timber, lignite, uranium, magnesite. Exports: machinery, fuels and raw materials, consumer goods. Imports: machinery, equipment, fuels, raw materials, food, consumer goods. Major trading partners: U.S.S.R. and Soviet bloc, West Germany, Austria, U.K.

Geography. Czechoslovakia lies in central Europe, a neighbor of East and West Germany, Poland, the U.S.S.R., Hungary, and Austria. It is equal in size to New York State. The principal rivers—the Elbe, Danube, Oder, and Moldau—are vital commercially to this landlocked country, for both waterborne commerce and agriculture, which flourishes in fertile valleys irrigated by these rivers and their tributaries.

Government. Since 1969 the supreme organ of the state has been the Federal Assembly, which has two equal chambers: the Chamber of People, with 200 deputies, and the Chamber of Nations, with 150 deputies (75 from the Czech Socialist Republic and 75 from the Slovak Socialist Republic). The chief executive is the President, who is elected by the Federal Assembly for a five-year term. The Premier and his Cabinet are appointed by the President but are responsible to the Federal Assembly.

The major political parties are the Communist Party, led by First Secretary Gustav Husak in both republics; Socialist Party; People's Party in the Czech Socialist Republic; Slovak Freedom Party and Slovak Reconstruction Party in the Slovak Socialist Republic. Together with trade unions, youth organizations, and other organizations, they form the National Front.

History. Probably about the 5th century A.D., Slavic tribes from the Vistula basin settled in the region of modern Czechoslovakia. Slovakia came under Magyar domination. The Czechs founded the kingdom of Bohemia, the Premyslide dynasty, which ruled Bohemia and Moravia from the 10th to the 16th century. One of the Bohemian kings, Charles IV, Holy Roman Emperor, made Prague an imperial capital and a center of Latin scholarship. The Hussite movement founded by Jan Hus (1369?–1415) linked the Slavs to the Reformation and revived Czech nationalism, previously under German domination. A Hapsburg, Ferdinand I, ascended the throne in 1526. The Czechs rebelled in 1618. Defeated in 1620, they were ruled for the next 300 years as part of the Austrian Empire.

In World War I, Czech and Slovak patriots, notably Thomas G. Masaryk and Milan Stefanik, promoted Czech-Slovak independence from abroad while their followers fought against the Central Powers. On Oct. 28, 1918, Czechoslovakia proclaimed itself a republic. Shortly thereafter Masaryk was unanimously elected first President.

Hitler provoked the country's German minority in the Sudetenland, led by Konrad Henlein, to agitate for autonomy. At the Munich Conference on Sept. 30, 1938, France and the U.K., seeking to avoid World War II, agreed that the Nazis could take the Sudetenland. Dr. Eduard Beneš, who had succeeded Masaryk, resigned on Oct. 5, 1938, and fled to London. Czechoslovakia became a state within the German orbit and was known as Czecho-Slovakia. In March 1939, the Nazis occupied the country. Beneš organized a government-in-exile in London in 1940.

Soon after Czechoslovakia was liberated in World War II and the government returned in April 1945, it was obliged to cede Ruthenia to the U.S.S.R. In 1946, a Communist, Klement Gottwald, formed a six-party coalition Cabinet. Pressure from Moscow increased until Feb. 23–25, 1948, when the Communists seized complete control in a coup. Following constituent assembly elections in which the Communists and their allies were unopposed, a new Constitution was adopted.

Beneš refused to sign it and resigned; he died mysteriously on Sept. 3, 1948. The Constitution was promulgated June 9. Thereafter, agriculture was collectivized, industry almost completely socialized, and foreign trade conducted chiefly with the Soviet bloc. Industrialization was intensified and concentrated upon heavy industry. The "people's democracy" was converted into a "socialist" state by a new Constitution adopted June 11, 1960.

After the death of Stalin and the relaxing of Soviet controls, Czechoslovakia witnessed a nationalist awakening. In 1968 conservative Stalinists were driven from power and replaced by more liberal, reform-minded Communists.

In more orthodox circles of the U.S.S.R. and its European satellites, fears arose that the trend was undermining Communist rule. Soviet military maneuvers on Czechoslovak soil in May 1968 were followed in July by a meeting of the U.S.S.R. with Poland, Bulgaria, East Germany, and Hungary in Warsaw that demanded an accounting, which Prague refused. Czechoslovak-Soviet talks on Czechoslovak territory, at Cierna, in late July led to an accord. But the Russians charged that the Czechoslovaks had reneged on pledges to modify their policies, and on Aug. 20–21, troops of the five powers, estimated at 600,000, executed a lightning invasion and occupation.

Soviet secret police seized the top Czechoslovak leadership and detained it for several days in Moscow. But Soviet efforts to establish a puppet regime failed. President Ludvik Svoboda negotiated an accord providing for a gradual troop withdrawal in return for "normalization" of political policy.

The purge of liberals was virtually completed in 1970. Only Svoboda remained from 1968. Husak, who became Secretary General of the Communist Party in 1969, promised no show trials, but most liberals were punished. Czechoslovakia signed a new friendship treaty with the U.S.S.R. that codified the "Brezhnev doctrine," under which Russia can invade any Eastern European socialist nation that threatens to leave the satellite camp.

Continuing ferment surfaced early in 1975 with publication in the West of a long letter of protest against repression written by Alexander Dubcek, First Secretary of the Czechoslovak Communist Party during the 1968 "Prague Spring." The letter, addressed to the Presidium of Czechoslovakia's Federal Assembly, charged that the regime had purged thousands of creative workers. Dubcek was later reported transferred to a menial forester's job.

One of the most vigorous of the Eastern European groups formed to support human rights in the wake of the 1975 Helsinki Conference on Security and Cooperation in Europe was the Czech "Charter 77," an association of 240 intellectuals who signed a New Year manifesto protesting the suppression of freedom. Detentions of the signers began immediately, and a second manifesto appeared on January 8 with 300 signatures condemning the official reaction to the first. On Jan. 28, the government offered to let five of the dissidents leave the country, but they refused.

Charter 77 adherents marked their first anniversary with a manifesto Jan. 1, 1978, calling for open debate on the observance of human rights in Czechoslovakia. Enough of the group remained in May 1981 for the government to jail 36 persons in the biggest roundup of dissidents since 1971, as part of the precautions against any show of sympathy for Polish workers. The Czech Communist Party was among the most severe of the Eastern European states in condemning what Husak called an attempted "counterrevolutionary coup" in Poland.

DENMARK

Kingdom of Denmark
Sovereign: Queen Margrethe II (1972)
Premier: Poul Schlüter (1982)
Area: 16,631 sq mi. (43,075 sq km)[1]
Population (est. 1982): 5,130,000[1] (average annual growth rate: 0.1%)
Density per square mile: 308.8
Capital: Copenhagen
Largest cities (est. 1982): Copenhagen, 650,000; Aarhus, 250,000; Odense, 170,000; Alborn, 155,000
Monetary unit: Krone
Language: Danish
Religion: Lutheran (established)
National name: Kongeriget Danmark
Literacy rate (1981): 99%
Economic summary: Gross national product (1980): $66.4 billion. Average annual growth rate (1970–79): 2.1%. Per capita income (1980): $12,950. Labor force in agriculture: 9%; principal products: meat, dairy products, fish, fur. Labor force in industry: 33%; major products; industrial and construction equipment, electronics, furniture, textiles. Natural resources: oil and gas, zinc, lead, iron ore, coal, molybdenum, cryolite, uranium. Exports: meat and dairy products, industrial machinery, textiles and clothing, chemical products, transportation equipment. Imports: industrial raw materials, fuel, machinery and equipment, transport equipment, petroleum, chemicals, textile fibers. Major trading partners: West Germany, Sweden, U.K., U.S.

1. Excluding Faeroe Islands and Greenland.

Geography. Smallest of the Scandinavian countries (half the size of Maine), Denmark occupies the Jutland peninsula, which extends north from Germany between the tips of Norway and Sweden. To the west is the North Sea and to the east the Baltic.

The country also consists of several Baltic islands; the two largest are Sjaelland, the site of Copenhagen, and Fyn. The narrow waters off the north coast are called the Skagerrak and those off the east, the Kattegat.

Government. Denmark has been a constitutional monarchy since 1849. Legislative power is held jointly by the Sovereign and parliament. The Constitution of 1953 provides for a unicameral parliament called the Folketing, consisting of 179 popularly elected members who serve for four years. The Cabinet is presided over by the Sovereign, who appoints the Prime Minister.

The Sovereign, Queen Margrethe II, was born April 16, 1940, and became Queen—the first in Denmark's history—Jan. 15, 1972, the day after her father, King Frederik IX, died at 72 in the 25th year of his reign. Margrethe was the eldest of his three daughters (by Princess Ingrid of Sweden). The nation's Constitution was amended in 1953 to permit her to succeed her father in the absence of a male heir to the throne. (Denmark was ruled six centuries ago by Margrethe I, but she was never crowned Queen since there was no female right of succession.) Margrethe's sisters are Benedikte (born 1944) and Anne Marie (born 1946), now the former Queen of Greece.

The major political parties are the Social Democratic Party (56 seats in the Folketing), led by former Premier Anker Jørgensen; Conservative People's Party (42 seats), led by Premier Poul Schlüter; Socialist People's Party (21 seats), led by Gert Petersen; Liberal Party (22 seats), led by Henning Christophersen; Radical Liberal Party (10 seats); Center Democrats (8 seats); Progress Party (6 seats), Christian People's Party (5 seats); Leftwing Socialists (5 seats).

History. Denmark emerged with establishment of the Norwegian dynasty of the Ynglinger in Jutland at the end of the 8th century. Danish mariners played a major role in the raids of the Vikings, or Norsemen, on Western Europe and particularly England. The country was Christianized by St. Ansgar and Harald Blaatand (Bluetooth)—the first Christian king—in the 10th century. Harald's son, Sweyn, conquered England in 1013. His son, Canute the Great, who reigned from 1014 to 1035, united Denmark, England, and Norway under his rule; the southern part of Sweden was part of Denmark until the 17th century. On Canute's death, civil war tore the country until Waldemar I (1157–82) re-established Danish hegemony over the north.

In 1282, the nobles won the Great Charter, and Eric V was forced to share power with parliament and a Council of Nobles. Waldemar IV (1340–75) restored Danish power, checked only by the Hanseatic League of north German cities allied with ports from Holland to Poland. His daughter, Margrethe, in 1397 united under her rule Denmark, Norway, and Sweden. But Sweden later achieved autonomy and in 1523, under Gustavus I, independence.

Denmark supported Napoleon, for which it was punished at the Congress of Vienna in 1815 by the loss of Norway to Sweden. In 1864, Bismarck, together with the Austrians, made war on the little country as an initial step in the unification of Germany. Denmark was neutral in World War I.

In 1939, Denmark signed a 10-year pact with Hitler, but less than a year later it was invaded by the Nazis. King Christian X reluctantly cautioned his countrymen to accept the occupation, but there was widespread resistance against the Nazis. In 1944, Iceland declared its independence from Denmark, ending a union that had existed since 1380.

Liberated by British troops in May 1945, the country staged a fast recovery in both agriculture and manufacturing and was a leader in liberalizing trade. It joined the United Nations in 1945 and NATO in 1949.

The Social Democrats largely ran Denmark after the war but were ousted in 1973 when, in an election dominated by protests against high taxes, all established parties lost heavily. The big winner was the new Progress Party. A minority government was formed by the Liberal Democrats, with their leader, Poul Hartling, as Premier. After losing a vote of confidence in January 1975, Hartling resigned and was succeeded by Anker Jørgensen, a Social Democrat who was Premier in 1972–73.

Outlying Territories of Denmark

FAEROE ISLANDS

Status: Autonomous part of Denmark
Commissioner: L. Groth (1972)

Area: 540 sq mi. (1,399 sq km)
Population (est. 1982): 43,000 (average annual growth rate: 1.8%)
Density per square mile: 79.9
Capital (est. 1982): Thorshavn, 12,750
Monetary unit: Faeroese krone
Literacy rate (1981): 80%
Economic summary: Gross national product (1980): $440 million. Average annual growth rate (1970–79): 5.6 %. Per capita income (1980): $10,620. Principal agricultural products: sheep and cattle. Major industrial product: fish. Exports: fish and fish products. Imports: machinery and transport equipment, foodstuffs, petroleum and petroleum products. Major trading partners: Denmark, U.S., Norway, U.K.

This group of 21 islands, lying in the North Atlantic about 200 miles (322 km) northwest of the Shetland Islands, joined Denmark in 1386 and has since been part of the Danish kingdom. The islands were occupied by British troops during World War II, after the German occupation of Denmark.

The Faeroes have home rule under a bill enacted in 1948; they also have two representatives in the Danish Folketing.

GREENLAND

Status: Autonomous part of Denmark
Premier: Jonathan Motzfeldt
Area: 840,000 sq mi. (incl. 708,069 sq mi. covered by icecap) (2,175,600 sq km)
Population (est. 1982): 50,000 (average annual growth rate: 0.6%)
Capital (est. 1982): Godthaab, 10,000
Monetary unit: Krone
Literacy rate (1981): 99%
Economic summary: Gross national product (1980): $430 million. Average annual growth rate (1970–79): 4.4%. Per capita income (1980): $8,290. Principal agricultural products: hay, sheep, garden produce. Major industries: mining, slaughtering, fishing, sealing. Natural resource: cryolite. Exports: fish and fish products, metalic ores and concentrates. Imports: petroleum and petroleum products, machinery and transport equipment, foodstuffs. Major trading partners: Denmark, U.S., Finland, West Germany, U.K.

Greenland, the world's largest island, was colonized in 985–86 by Eric the Red. Danish sovereignty, which covered only the west coast, was extended over the whole island in 1917. In 1941 the U.S. signed an agreement with the Danish minister in Washington, placing it under U.S. protection during World War II but maintaining Danish sovereignty. A definitive agreement for the joint defense of Greenland within the framework of NATO was signed in 1951. A large U.S. air base at Thule in the far north was completed in 1953.

Under 1953 amendments to the Danish Constitution, Greenland became part of Denmark, with two representatives in the Danish Folketing. On May 1, 1979, Greenland gained home rule, with its own local parliament (Landsting), replacing the Greenland Provincial Council.

In February 1982, Greenlanders voted to withdraw from the European Community, which they had joined as part of Denmark in 1973. Danish Premier Anker Jørgensen said he would support the request, but with reluctance.

Greenland is the world's only source of natural cryolite, important in making aluminum.

DJIBOUTI

Republic of Djibouti
President: Gouled Aptidon Hassan (1977)
Prime Minister: Gourad Hamadou Barkat (1978)
Area: 8,996 sq mi. (23,300 sq km)
Population (est. 1982): 335,000 (average annual growth rate: 4.1%)
Density per sq mile: 37.2
Capital (est. 1980): Djibouti, 150,000
Monetary unit: Djibouti franc
Languages: Arabic, French, Afar, Somali
Religions: Islam. 91%; Christian, 9%
National name: Jumhouriyya Djibouti
Literacy rate (1981): 15%
Economic summary: Gross national product (1980): $170 million. Average annual growth rate (1970–79): –4.9%. Per capita income (1980): $480. Principal agricultural products: goats, sheep, camels. Industries: port and maritime support, construction. Exports: hides, cattle, coffee (in transit from Ethiopia). Imports: machinery, transport equipment, foodstuffs. Major trading partners: France, Ethiopia, Japan, Belgium, U.K.

Geography. Djibouti lies in northeastern Africa on the Gulf of Aden at the southern entrance to the Red Sea. It borders on Ethiopia and Somalia. The country, the size of Massachusetts, is mainly a stony desert, with scattered plateaus and highlands.

Government. On May 8, 1977, the population of the French Territory of the Afars and Issas voted by more than 98% for independence. Voters also approved a 65-member interim Constituent Assembly. France transferred sovereignty to the new nation of Djibouti on June 27. Later in the year it became a member of the Organization of African Unity and the Arab League. The People's Progress Assembly is the only legal political party.

History. The territory that is now Djibouti was acquired by France between 1843 and 1886 by treaties with the Somali sultans. Small, arid, and sparsely populated, Djibouti is important chiefly because of the capital city's port, the terminal of the Djibouti-Addis Ababa railway that carries 60% of Ethiopia's foreign trade.

Originally known as French Somaliland, the colony voted in 1958 and 1967 to remain under French rule. It was renamed the Territory of the Afars and Issas in 1967 and took the name of its capital city on attaining independence.

Somali rebels in Ethiopia's Ogaden Province cut the railway to Djibouti in June 1977 and there was fear that the new nation might be absorbed by Somalia. In July 1980, Djibouti granted base rights to United States ships and planes in exchange for undisclosed amounts of aid.

DOMINICA

Commonwealth of Dominica
President: Aurelius Marie (1980)
Prime Minister: Mary Eugenia Charles (1980)
Area: 290 sq mi. (751 sq km)
Population: (est. 1983): 74,000 (average annual growth rate: –0.2%)
Density per square mile: 283.3
Capital and largest city (est. 1981): Roseau, 20,000
Monetary unit: East Caribbean dollar
Languages: English and French patois
Religions: Roman Catholic, Anglican, Methodist

National name: Republica Dominicana
Member of Commonwealth of Nations
Literacy rate (1981): 80%
Economic summary: Gross national product (1981): $65 million. Average annual growth rate (1981): 9.5%. Per capita income (1981): $883. Labor force in agriculture: 50%; principal products: bananas, citrus fruits, coconuts, cocoa. Major industries: agricultural processing; tourism. Exports: bananas, lime juice, oil, cocoa. Imports: machinery and equipment, foodstuffs, manufactured goods, cement. Major trading partners: U.K. and Caribbean countries.

Geography. Dominica is an island of the Lesser Antilles in the Caribbean south of Guadeloupe and north of Martinique.

Government. Dominica is a republic, with a president elected by the House of Assembly as head of state and a prime minister appointed by the president on the advice of the Assembly. The Freedom Party (17 of 21 seats in the Assembly) is led by Prime Minister Mary Eugenia Charles. The Opposition Democratic Labor Party holds two seats and independents the remaining two.

History. Discovered by Columbus in 1493, Dominica was claimed by Britain and France until 1815, when Britain asserted sovereignty. Dominica, along with other Windward Isles, became a self-governing member of the West Indies Associated States in free association with Britain in 1967.

Full independence was granted on Nov. 3, 1978, in ceremonies at which the first Prime Minister, Patrick R. John, declared a socialist course for the new republic. John aroused strong opposition when he proposed laws curbing the right to strike and freedom of the press. During a demonstration in Roseau in May 1979, police fired at the crowd, killing three. After a general strike, John dissolved the Assembly and set new elections for Dec. 1, but continued disorder forced his resignation and replacement by Oliver Seraphin.

Dissatisfaction over the slow pace of reconstruction after Hurricane David struck the island in September 1979 brought a landslide victory for the opposition Freedom Party in July 1980. The vote gave the prime ministership to Mary Eugenia Charles, a strong advocate of free enterprise.

DOMINICAN REPUBLIC

President: Salvador Jorge Blanco (1982)
Area: 18,704 sq mi. (48,442 sq km)
Population (1982): 5,647,977 (average annual growth rate: 2.7%) (approx.): mestizo, 75%; white, 15%; Negro, 10%
Density per square mile: 298.1
Capital: Santo Domingo
Largest cities (est. 1982): Santo Domingo, 1,250,000; Santiago de los Caballeros, 300,000
Monetary unit: Peso
Language: Spanish
Religion: Roman Catholic
National name: República Dominicana
Literacy rate (1981): 68%
Economic summary: Gross national product (1980): $6.6 billion. Average annual growth rate (1970–79): 3.7%. Per capital income (1980): $1,224. Land used for agriculture: 14%; labor force: 79%; principal products: sugar cane, coffee, cocoa, tobacco, rice, corn. Labor force in industry: 19%; major products: processed sugar, textiles, cement, nickel, bauxite, and gold mining. Natural resources: nickel, bauxite, gold, silver. Exports: sugar, nickel, coffee, tobacco, cocoa, bauxite. Imports: foodstuffs, petroleum, industrial raw materials, capital equipment. Major trading partner: U.S.

Geography. The Dominican Republic in the West Indies, occupies the eastern two thirds of the island of Hispaniola, which it shares with Haiti. Its area equals that of Vermont and New Hampshire combined.

Crossed from northwest to southeast by a mountain range with elevations exceeding 10,000 feet (3,048 m), the country has fertile, well-watered land in the north and east, where nearly two thirds of the population lives. The southwest part is arid and has poor soil, except around Santo Domingo.

Government. The president is elected by direct vote every four years. Legislative powers rest with a Senate and a Chamber of Deputies, both elected by direct vote, also for four years. All citizens must vote when they reach 18 years of age, or even earlier if they are married.

The major political parties are the Dominican Revolutionary Party, the party of the Administration, led by Dr. José Francisco Peña Gomez; the Reformist Party, led by former President Joaquín Balaguer; Dominican Liberation Party, led by Juan Bosch; Partido Quisquellano Demócrata, led by Elías Wessin y Wessin; Movimiento de Integración Democrática Anti-Releccionista, led by Augusto Lora.

History. The Dominican Republic was discovered by Columbus in 1492. He named it La Española, and his son, Diego, was its first viceroy. The capital, Santo Domingo, founded in 1496, is the oldest European settlement in the Western Hemisphere. Spain ceded the colony to France in 1795, and Haitian blacks under Toussaint L'Ouverture conquered it in 1801.

In 1808 the people revolted and the next year captured Santo Domingo, setting up the first republic. Spain regained title to the colony in 1814. In 1821 the people overthrew Spanish rule, but in 1822 they were reconquered by the Haitians. They revolted again in 1844, threw out the Haitians, and established the Dominican Republic, headed by Pedro Santana. Uprisings and Haitian attacks led Santana to make the country a province of Spain from 1861 to 1865. The U.S. Senate refused to ratify a treaty of annexation. Disorder continued until the dictatorship of Ulíses Heureaux; in 1916, when disorder broke out again, the U.S. sent in a contingent of marines, who remained until 1934.

A sergeant in the Dominican army trained by the marines, Rafaél Leonides Trujillo Molina, overthrew Horacio Vásquez in 1930 and established a dictatorship that lasted until his assassination 31 years later.

After Trujillo's assassination on May 30, 1961, disorders forced out the President, Joaquín Balaguer, but a governing council, in spite of an abortive military coup, steered the country to a return to constitutional government.

A new Constitution was adopted in 1962, and the first free elections since 1924 put Juan Bosch, a leftist leader, in office. A planned program of reforms with U.S. support was cut off by a right-wing military coup that replaced Bosch with a civilian triumvirate.

Leftists rebelled April 24, 1965, and President Lyndon Johnson sent in 400 marines to help evacuate U.S. citizens. After an OAS ceasefire request May 6, a compromise installed Hector Garcia-Godoy as provisional president. Balaguer won in free elections in 1966 against Bosch, and an OAS force of 9,000 U.S. troops and 2,000 from other countries withdrew. Balaguer restored political and economic stability program.

Balaguer's longtime support for free elections faltered in May 1978, when the army suspended the counting of ballots as he trailed in a fourth-term bid. After a warning from President Jimmy Carter, however, Balaguer accepted the victory of Antonio Guzmán of the opposition Dominican Revolutionary Party.

Guzman began a rural development and land reform program. In June 1981, Guzmán announced that he would not seek re-election at the end of his term in August 1982.

Salvador Jorge Blanco of the Dominican Revolutionary Party was elected President on May 16, 1982, defeating Balaguer and Bosch. Austerity measures imposed by the International Monetary Fund, including sharply higher prices for food and gasoline, provoked rioting in the spring of 1984 that left dozens dead.

ECUADOR

Republic of Ecuador
President: León Febres Condero (1984)
Area: 109,484 sq mi. (283,561 sq km)
Population (est. 1982): 8,950,000 (average annual growth rate: 3.1%)
Density per square mile: 81.6
Capital: Quito
Largest cities (est. 1983): Guayaquil, 1,250,000; Quito, 800,000; Cuenca, 135,000
Monetary unit: Sucre
Languages: Spanish, Quéchua, Jibaro
Religion: Roman Catholic
National name: República del Ecuador
Literacy rate (1981): 57%
Economic summary: Gross national product (1981). $13.0 billion. Average annual growth rate (1975–81): 6.3%. Per capita income (1981): $1,504. Land used for agriculture: 15%; labor force: 56%; principal products: bananas, coffee, cocoa, sugar cane, fruits, corn, potatoes, rice. Labor force in industry: 18%; major products: processed foods, textiles, chemicals, fish, petroleum. Natural resources: petroleum, fish, timber, minerals. Exports: petroleum, bananas, coffee, cocoa, fish products. Imports: agricultural and industrial machinery, industrial raw materials, building supplies, chemical products, transportation and communication equipment. Major trading partners: U.S., Latin American and Western European countries, Japan.

Geography. Ecuador, equal in area to Nevada, is in the northwest part of South America fronting on the Pacific. To the north is Colombia and to the east and south is Peru. Two high and parallel ranges of the Andes, traversing the country from north to south, are topped by tall volcanic peaks. The highest is Chimborazo at 20,577 feet (6,272 m).

The Galápagos Islands (or Colón Archipelago) (3,029 sq mi.; 7,845 sq km) in the Pacific Ocean about 600 miles (966 km) west of the South American mainland, became part of Ecuador in 1832.

Government. A 1978 Constitution returned Ecuador to civilian government after eight years of military rule. Under its terms, the President is elected by universal suffrage to a term of five years and a House of Representatives of 69 members popularly elected for the same period.

History. The tribes in the northern highlands of Ecuador formed the Kingdom of Quito around A.D. 1000 It was absorbed, by conquest and marriage, into the Inca Empire. Pizarro conquered the land in 1532, and through the 17th century a thriving colony was built by exploitation of the Indians. The first revolt against Spain occurred in 1809. Ecuador then joined Venezuela, Colombia, and Panama in a confederacy founded by Simón Bolívar and known as Greater Colombia.

On the collapse of this union in 1830, Ecuador became independent. Subsequent history was one of revolts and dictatorships; it had 48 presidents during the first 131 years of the republic. Conservatives ruled until the Revolution of 1895 ushered in nearly a half century of Radical Liberal rule, during which the church was disestablished and freedom of worship, speech, and press was introduced.

In 1970, following six months of strife between university students and police, President José María Velasco Ibarra, who was elected in 1968 for the fifth time, took supreme powers to "avoid social and economic chaos." He closed universities, jailed some professors and businessmen, and demanded "reform" of the Supreme Court. Opposition political leaders were arrested and a military shake-up ensued.

Velasco was ousted nine months later by a junta, which sharply increased fees charged to foreign oil companies.

A three-man military junta headed by Vice Adm. Alfredo Poveda, which had taken power in a 1976 coup, agreed to a free presidential election on July 16, 1978. Jaime Roldós Aguilera won the runoff on April 29, 1979, backed by a "center leftist" coalition, the Concentration of Popular Forces.

The 40-year-old President, his wife and Ecuador's minister of defense died in the crash of a small plane May 24, 1981. Vice President Osvaldo Hurtado Larrea became President. León Febres Cordero, leader of the National Reconstruction Front, narrowly won two rounds of voting in 1984 elections and was installed President in August. Combined opposition parties won a majority in the 71-member Congress large enough to block significant action.

EGYPT

Arab Republic of Egypt
President: Hosni Mubarak (1981)
Premier: Kamal Hassan Ali (1984)
Area: 385,227 sq mi. (997,739 sq km)
Population (est. 1983): 45,851,000 (average annual growth rate: 2.8%)
Density per square mile: 115.7
Capital: Cairo
Largest cities (est. 1979): Cairo, 5,423,000; **(1976 census):** Alexandria, 2,317,705; Giza, 1,246,713; Shubra el Khema, 393,700; El Mahalla el Kubra, 292,853; Tanta, 284,636; Port Said, 262,620; Mansura, 257,866
Monetary unit: Egyptian pound
Language: Arabic
Religions: Islam, 82%, Christian (mostly Copt), 18%
Literacy rate (1981): 44%
Economic summary: Gross national product (1981): $30.8 billion. Average annual growth rate (1982): 6%. Per capita income (1982): $690. Land used for agriculture: 3%; labor force: 50%; principal products: cotton, wheat,

rice, corn. Labor force in industry: 13%; major products: textiles, processed foods, tobacco manufactures, chemicals, fertilizer, petroleum and petroleum products. Natural resources: manganese ore, phosphates, petroleum, gold, nickel, tungsten. Exports: cotton, rice, petroleum, cement, potatoes. Imports: foodstuffs, machinery, fertilizers, woods. Major trading partners: West Germany, Italy, France, U.K., U.S.

Geography. Egypt, at the northeast corner of Africa on the Mediterranean Sea, is bordered on the west by Libya, on the south by the Sudan, and on the east by the Red Sea and Israel. It is nearly one and one half times the size of Texas.

The historic Nile flows through the eastern third of the country. On either side of the Nile valley are desert plateaus, spotted with oases. In the north, toward the Mediterranean, plateaus are low, while south of Cairo they rise to a maximum of 1,015 feet (309 m) above sea level. At the head of the Red Sea is the Sinai Peninsula, between the Suez Canal and Israel.

Navigable throughout its course in Egypt, the Nile is used largely as a means of cheap transport for heavy goods. The principal port is Alexandria.

The Nile delta starts 100 miles (161 km) south of the Mediterranean and fans out to a sea front of 155 miles between the cities of Alexandria and Port Said. From Cairo north, the Nile branches into many streams, the principal ones being the Damietta and the Rosetta.

Except for a narrow belt along the Mediterranean, Egypt lies in an almost rainless area, in which high daytime temperatures fall quickly at night.

Government. Executive power is held by the President, who can appoint one or more Vice Presidents.

The National Democratic Party, led by President Hosni Mubarak, is the dominant political party. As expected, it won a huge majority (391 of the 448 contested seats) in the new Parliament chosen May 27, 1984, in Egypt's first free, multiparty election since 1952. The New Wafd, a rebirth of Egypt's oldest and most respected political party, ran second (57 seats).

History. Egyptian history dates back to about 4000 B.C., when the kingdoms of upper and lower Egypt, already highly civilized, were united. Egypt's "Golden Age" coincided with the 18th and 19th dynasties (16th to 13th centuries B.C.), during which the empire was established. Persia conquered Egypt in 525 B.C.; Alexander the Great subdued it in 332 B.C.; and then the dynasty of the Ptolemies ruled the land until 30 B.C., when Cleopatra, last of the line, committed suicide and Egypt became a Roman province. From 641 to 1517 the Arab caliphs ruled Egypt, and then the Turks took it for their Ottoman Empire.

Napoleon's armies occupied the country from 1798 to 1801. In 1805, Mohammed Ali, leader of a band of Albanian soldiers, became Pasha of Egypt. After completion of the Suez Canal in 1869, the French and British took increasing interest in Egypt.

British troops occupied Egypt in 1882, and British resident agents became its actual administrators, though it remained under nominal Turkish sovereignty. In 1914, this fiction was ended, and Egypt became a protectorate of Britain.

Egyptian nationalism forced Britain to declare Egypt an independent, sovereign state on Feb. 28, 1922, although the British reserved rights for the protection of the Suez Canal and the defense of Egypt. In 1936, by an Anglo-Egyptian treaty of alliance, all British troops and officials were to be withdrawn, except from the Suez Canal Zone. When World War II started, Egypt remained neutral. British imperial troops finally ended the Nazi threat to Suez in 1942 in the battle of El Alamein, west of Alexandria.

In 1951, Egypt abrogated the 1936 treaty and the 1899 Anglo-Egyptian condominium of the Sudan (*See* Sudan). Rioting and attacks on British troops in the Suez Canal Zone followed, reaching a climax in January 1952. The army, led by Gen. Mohammed Naguib, seized power on July 23, 1952. Three days later, King Farouk abdicated in favor of his infant son. The monarchy was abolished and a republic proclaimed on June 18, 1953, with Naguib holding the posts of Provisional President and Premier. He relinquished the latter in 1954 to Gamal Abdel Nasser, leader of the ruling military junta. Naguib was deposed seven months later and Nasser confirmed as President in a referendum on June 23, 1956.

Nasser's policies embroiled his country in continual conflict. In 1956, the U.S. and Britain withdrew their pledges of financial aid for the building of the Aswan High Dam. In reply, Nasser nationalized the Suez Canal and expelled British oil and embassy officials. Israel, barred from the Canal and exasperated by terrorist raids, invaded the Gaza Strip and the Sinai Peninsula. Britain and France, after demanding Egyptian evacuation of the Canal Zone, attacked Egypt on Oct. 31, 1956. Worldwide pressure forced Britain, France, and Israel to halt the hostilities. A U.N. emergency force occupied the Canal Zone, and all troops were evacuated in the spring of 1957.

On Feb. 1, 1958, Egypt and Syria formed the United Arab Republic, which was joined by Yemen in an association known as the United Arab States. However, Syria withdrew from the United Arab Republic in 1961 and Egypt dissolved its ties with Yemen in the United Arab States. On Sept. 2, 1971, Egypt finally shed the name United Arab Republic.

On June 5, 1967, Israel invaded the Sinai Peninsula, the East Bank of the Jordan River, and the zone around the Gulf of Aqaba. Only a U.N. cease-fire on June 10 saved the Arabs from complete rout.

Nasser declared the 1967 cease-fire void along the Canal in April 1969 and began a war of attrition. Egyptian artillery fire across the canal sparked Israeli "deep penetration" raids that attempted to topple Nasser. He went to Moscow in January 1970, and by March, Russians were flying planes with Egyptian markings to defend the Nile delta and were manning some antiaircraft missiles. An estimated 10,000 to 12,000 Russians were in Egypt in 1970. Missiles were moved into the Canal Zone, challenging Israeli air superiority. The U.S. peace plan of June 19, 1970, resulted in Egypt's agreement to reinstate the cease-fire for at least three months, (from August) and to accept Israel's existence within "recognized and secure" frontiers that might emerge from U.N.-mediated talks. In return, Israel accepted the principle of withdrawing from occupied territories.

Then, on Sept. 28, 1970, Nasser died, at 52, of a heart attack. The new President was Anwar el-Sadat, an associate of Nasser and a former newspaper editor.

The Aswan High Dam, whose financing by the U.S.S.R. was its first step into Egypt, was completed and dedicated in January 1971.

In July 1972, Sadat ordered the expulsion of Soviet "advisors and experts" from Egypt because the Russians had not provided the sophisticated weapons he felt were needed to retake territory lost to Israel in 1967. Moscow pulled out virtually all of its 18,000 men.

The fourth Arab-Israeli war broke out Oct. 6, 1973, while Israelis were commemorating Yom Kippur, the Jewish high holy day. Egypt swept deep into the Sinai, while Syria strove to throw Israel off the Golan Heights. Arab oil-producing countries cut off shipments to the U.S. and other Western nations, precipitating a worldwide energy crisis.

A U.N.-sponsored truce was accepted on October 22 after an Israeli thrust across the Suez into Egypt itself cut off Egyptian forces in the Sinai. In January 1974, both sides agreed to a settlement negotiated by U.S. Secretary of State Henry A. Kissinger that gave Egypt a narrow strip along the entire Sinai bank of the Suez Canal. In June, President Nixon made the first visit by a U.S. President to Egypt and full diplomatic relations were established. The Suez Canal was cleared and reopened on June 5, 1975.

Kissinger pursued "shuttle diplomacy" between Cairo and Jerusalem to extend areas of agreement. Israel yielded on three points—the possession of the Mitla and Giddi passes in the Sinai and the Abu Rudeis oil field in the peninsula—and both sides committed themselves to annual renewal of the U.N. peacekeeping force in the Sinai.

In the most audacious act of his career, Sadat flew to Jerusalem at the invitation of Prime Minister Menachem Begin and pleaded before Israel's Knesset on Nov. 20, 1977, for a permanent peace settlement. The Arab world reacted with fury—only Morocco, Tunisia, Sudan, and Oman approved—and Egyptian Foreign Minister Ismail Fahmy resigned. Hope for progress cooled when political talks in Jerusalem snagged, and Sadat ordered his negotiators home Jan. 17, 1978. The Egyptian was angered by Begin's defense of new settlements on the West Bank and his refusal to discuss the ultimate status of the West Bank and Gaza Strip, which Sadat proposed be placed under Jordanian and Egyptian administration, respectively.

Egypt and Israel signed a formal peace treaty on March 26, 1979. The pact ended 30 years of war and established diplomatic and commercial relations.

Egyptian and Israeli officials met in the Sinai desert on April 26, 1979, to implement the peace treaty calling for the phased withdrawal of occupation forces from the peninsula. On May 27, ahead of schedule, Israel turned over the gateway town of El Arish to Egyptian administration. By mid-1980, two thirds of the Sinai was transferred, but progress here was not matched in the other area covered by the treaty—the negotiation of Arab autonomy in the Gaza Strip and the West Bank.

Sadat halted further autonomy talks in August 1980 because of continued Israeli settlement of the West Bank. A year later he went to Washington to urge President Reagan to recognize the Palestine Liberation Organization as a means of resuming the talks. There were indications that the Reagan Administration might yield, but the process was arrested on Oct. 6, 1981, with the assassination of Sadat by extremist Muslim soldiers at a parade in Cairo. Vice President Hosni Mubarak, a former Air Force chief of staff, was confirmed by the parliament as president the next day.

Although feared unrest in Egypt did not occur in the wake of the assassination, and Israel completed the return of the Sinai to Egyptian control on April 25, 1982, Mubarak was unable to revive the autonomy talks. Israel's invasion of Lebanon in June imposed a new strain on him, and brought a marked cooling in Egyptian-Israeli relations, but not a disavowal of the peace treaty.

During 1983 and 1984, President Mubarak tried to cement relations with his Arab neighbors, most of whom had severed relations with Egypt when it signed the 1979 peace treaty with Israel. In April 1983, Egypt and Jordan resumed trade relations.

Suez Canal. The Suez Canal, in Egyptian territory between the Arabian Desert and the Sinai Peninsula, is an artificial waterway about 100 miles (161 km) long between Port Said on the Mediterranean and Suez on the Red Sea. Construction work, directed by the French engineer Ferdinand de Lesseps, was begun April 25, 1859, and the Canal was opened Nov. 17, 1869. The cost was 432,807,882 francs. The concession was held by an Egyptian joint stock company, *Compagnie Universelle du Canal Maritime de Suez*, in which the British government held 353,504 out of a total of 800,000 shares. The concession was to expire Nov. 17, 1968, but the company was nationalized July 26, 1956, by unilateral action of the Egyptian government.

The Canal was closed in June 1967 after the Arab-Israeli conflict. With the help of the U.S. Navy, work was begun on clearing the Canal in 1974, after the cease-fire ending the Arab-Israeli war. It was reopened to traffic June 5, 1975.

EL SALVADOR

Republic of El Salvador
President: José Napoleón Duarte (1984)
Area: 8,260 sq mi. (21,393 sq km)
Population (est. 1982): 5,150,000 (average annual growth rate: −2.4%)
Density per square mile: 623.5
Capital: San Salvador
Largest cities (est. 1982): San Salvador, 430,000; Santa Ana, 175,000
Monetary unit: Colón
Language: Spanish
Religion: Roman Catholic
National name: República de El Salvador
Literacy rate (1981): 40%
Economic summary: Gross national product (1980): $2.7 billion. Average annual growth rate (1970–79): 1.4%. Per capita income (1980): $590. Land used for agriculture: 32%; labor force: 50%; principal products: coffee, cotton, corn, sugar, rice, beans. Labor force in industry: 14%; major products: processed foods, clothing and textiles, petroleum products. Natural resources: timber, balsam, gold, silver, coal, copper, iron, zinc, mercury, sulfur. Exports: coffee, cotton, sugar. Imports: machinery, automotive vehicles, petroleum, foodstuffs, fertilizer. Major trading partners: U.S., Caribbean countries, Japan.

Geography. Situated on the Pacific coast of Central America, El Salvador has Guatemala to the west and Honduras to the north and east. It is the smallest of the Central American countries, its area equal to that of Massachusetts, and the only one without an Atlantic coastline.

Most of the country is a fertile volcanic plateau about 2,000 feet (607 m) high. There are some active volcanoes and many scenic crater lakes.

Government. The Constitution provides for a President, popularly elected for five years and ineligible to succeed himself, and a unicameral legislature, the National Assembly, consisting of 52 members elected by popular suffrage for two years.

A 60-member Constituent Assembly was elected on March 28, 1982, charged with the drafting of a new Constitution. A coalition of rightist parties won 36 seats and the opposition Christian Democrats won 24. José Napoleón Duarte, a Christian Democrat regarded as a moderate, was elected President in 1984.

History. Pedro de Alvarado, a lieutenant of Cortés, conquered El Salvador in 1525. El Salvador, with the other countries of Central America, declared its independence from Spain on Sept. 15, 1821, and was part of a federation of Central American states until that union was dissolved in 1838. Its independent career for several decades thereafter was marked by numerous revolutions and wars against other Central American republics.

In 1931, the first free election in 20 years was held, but Gen. Maximiliano Hernández Martínez took power in December of that year and maintained a dictatorship until he was ousted in 1944. For nearly two decades, politics remained turbulent and unstable, until the 1962 elections.

The new President, Julio Adalberto Rivera, restored free elections. In 1968, a drop in exports of coffee and cotton produced a slump. Widespread unemployment in El Salvador and land hunger in Honduras resulted in a conflict between the two nations in 1969. Deportation from Honduras of several thousand Salvadorans led to an invasion by El Salvador. Under threats of economic sanctions and military intervention, El Salvador withdrew its troops.

Presidential elections in 1972 gave none of four candidates a clear majority; therefore, the National Assembly, in which the National Conciliation Party had an overwhelming majority, proclaimed its candidate, Col. Arturo Armando Molina, as President.

The 1977 presidential elections were marked by at least eight deaths and massive protest demonstrations by the National Opposition Union, which charged extensive voter fraud. Gen. Carlos Humberto Romero, candidate of the governing National Conciliation Party, claimed victory over Lt. Col. Ernesto Claramount, the National Opposition Union candidate, who chose exile rather than prison after the election.

On Oct. 15, 1979, a junta composed of two army officers and three civilians deposed the President, Gen. Carlos Humberto Romero, seeking to halt increasingly violent clashes between leftist and rightist forces. The junta strove to halt civil strife but found itself attacked from the left as too conservative and from the right as too liberal, with bloody conflicts continuing.

On Dec. 4, 1980, three American nuns and an American lay worker were killed in an ambush near San Salvador, causing the Carter Administration to suspend all aid pending an investigation. The naming of José Napoleón Duarte, a moderate civilian, as head of the governing junta brought a resumption of U.S. aid.

Leftist guerrillas announced a "final offensive" aimed at victory before the Reagan Administration took office Jan. 20, but Salvadoran forces beat down rebel attacks. The new U.S. administration sent 56 military advisers and increased military and economic aid to the beleaguered government and launched a campaign to dissuade other countries from supporting the rebels, asserting that the guerrillas were receiving Soviet arms via Cuba and Nicaragua. Violence from both the right and left continued, with the death toll averaging 1,000 a month.

Defying guerrilla threats, voters on March 28, 1982, elected a rightist majority to a constituent assembly that dismissed Duarte and replaced him with a centrist physician, Dr. Alvaro Alfredo Magaña. The rightist majority repealed the laws permitting expropriation of land, and critics charged that the land-reform program begun under Duarte was dead. Even though fighting continued, with reports of government violations of human rights, the Reagan Administration asked certification of El Salvador's eligibility for resumed foreign aid, and this was approved by Congress.

In an election closely monitored by American and other foreign observers, Duarte was elected President in May 1984, and took office in June, succeeding Magaña. Visiting Washington in late July, Duarte appealed to President Reagan and Congressional leaders for increased U.S. economic and security assistance.

EQUATORIAL GUINEA

Republic of Equatorial Guinea
Head of junta: Lieut. Col. Teodoro Obiang Nguema Mbasogo (1979)
Area: 10,830 sq mi. (28,051 sq km)
Population (est. 1982): 380,000 (average annual growth rate: 2.1%)
Density per square mile: 35.1
Capital and largest city (est. 1980): Malabo, 35,000
Monetary unit: Ekuele
Languages: Spanish, Fang, Bubi
Religions: Roman Catholic, Protestant, Animist
National name: Républica de Guinea Ecuatorial
Literacy rate (1981): 38%
Economic summary: Gross national product (1980): $100 million. Per capita income (1980): $417. Land used for agriculture: 85–90%; labor force: 95%; principal products: cocoa, wood, coffee. Natural resource: wood. Exports: cocoa, wood, coffee. Imports: foodstuffs, chemicals, textiles, machinery. Major trading partner: Spain.

Geography. Equatorial Guinea, formerly Spanish Guinea, consists of Rio Muni (10,045 sq mi.; 26,117 sq km), on the western coast of Africa, and several islands in the Gulf of Guinea, the largest of which is Bioko (formerly Fernando Po) (785 sq mi.; 2,033 sq km). The other islands are Pagalu (formerly Annobón), Corisco, Elobey Grande, and Elobey Chico. The total area is twice that of Connecticut.

Government. The Constitution of 1973 was suspended after a coup on Aug. 3, 1979. A Supreme Military Council, headed by the president, exercises all power. Political parties are banned.

History. Fernando Po and Annobón came under Spanish control in 1778. From 1827 to 1844, with Spanish consent, Britain administered Fernando Po, but in the latter year Spain reclaimed the island. Río Muni was given to Spain in 1885 by the Treaty of Berlin.

Negotiations with Spain led to independence on Oct. 12, 1968.

In 1969, anti-Spanish incidents in Río Muni, including the tearing down of a Spanish flag by national troops, caused 5,000 Spanish residents to flee for their safety, and diplomatic relations between the two nations became strained. A month later, President Masie Nguema Biyogo Negue Ndong charged that a coup had been attempted against him. He seized dictatorial powers and arrested 80 opposition politicians and even several of his Cabinet ministers and the secretary of the National Assembly.

A coup on Aug. 3, 1979, deposed Masie, and a junta led by Lieut. Col. Teodoro Obiang Nguema Mbasogo took over the government. Obiang expelled Soviet technicians and reinstated cooperation with Spain.

ETHIOPIA

Head of State: Col. Mengistu Haile Mariam (1977)
Area: 472,432 sq mi. (1,223,600 sq km)
Population (est. 1983): 33,450,000 (average annual growth rate: 1.9%)
Density per square mile: 70.8
Capital: Addis Ababa
Largest cities (est. 1980): Addis Ababa, 1,275,000; Asmara, 425,000
Monetary unit: Birr
Languages: Amharic (official), Galligna, Tigrigna
Religions: Ethiopian Orthodox, 57%; Islam, 31%; Animist, 11%
Literacy rate (1981): 15%
Economic summary: Gross national product (1980): $4.3 billion. Average annual growth rate (1970–79): 0.3%. Per capita income (1980): $140. Land used for agriculture: 65%; labor force: 90%; principal products: coffee, barley, wheat, corn, sugar cane, cotton, oilseeds, livestock. Labor force in industry: 10%; Major industrial products: cement, cotton textiles, refined sugar, processed foods, refined oil. Natural resources: potash, salt, gold, copper, platinum. Exports: coffee, hides and skins, oilseeds. Imports: petroleum. Major trading partners: Saudi Arabia, Japan, Italy, West Germany, Iran, U.K., France, U.S.

Geography. Ethiopia is in east central Africa, bordered on the west by the Sudan, the east by Somalia and Djibouti, the south by Kenya, and the north by the Red Sea. It is nearly three times the size of California.

Over its main plateau land, Ethiopia has several high mountains, the highest of which is Ras Dashan at 15,158 feet (4,620 m). The Blue Nile, or Abbai, rises in the northwest and flows in a great semicircle east, south, and northwest before entering the Sudan. Its chief reservoir, Lake Tana, lies in the northwestern part of the plateau.

Government. A provisional military government headed by a 120-member officers' committee (the Dirgue) deposed Ethiopia's traditional monarchy in 1974, suspended parliament, and ruled by decree. It proclaimed Ethiopia a socialist state.

History. Black Africa's oldest state, Ethiopia can trace 2,000 years of recorded history. Its nowdeposed royal line claimed descent from King Menelik I, traditionally believed to have been the son of the Queen of Sheba and King Solomon. The present nation is a consolidation of smaller kingdoms that owed feudal allegiance to the Ethiopian Emperor.

Hamitic peoples migrated to Ethiopia from Asia Minor in prehistoric times. Semitic traders from Arabia penetrated the region in the 7th century B.C. Its Red Sea ports were important to the Roman and Byzantine Empires. Coptic Christianity came to the country in A.D. 341, and a variant of that communion became Ethiopia's state religion.

Ancient Ethiopia reached its peak in the 5th century, then was isolated by the rise of Islam and weakened by feudal wars. Modern Ethiopia emerged under Emperor Menelik II, who established its independence by routing an Italian invasion in 1896. He expanded Ethiopia by conquest.

Disorders that followed Menelik's death brought his daughter to the throne in 1917, with his cousin, Tafari Makonnen, as Regent, heir presumptive, and strongman. When the Empress died in 1930, Tafari was crowned Emperor Haile Selassie I.

As Regent, Haile Selassie outlawed slavery. As Emperor, he worked for centralization of his diffuse realm, in which 70 languages are spoken, and for moderate reform. In 1931, he granted a Constitution, revised in 1955, that created a parliament with an appointed Senate and an elected Chamber of Deputies, and a system of courts. But basic power remained with the Emperor.

Bent on colonial empire, fascist Italy invaded Ethiopia on Oct. 3, 1935, forcing Haile Selassie into exile in May 1936. Ethiopia was annexed to Eritrea, then an Italian colony, and Italian Somaliland to form Italian East Africa, losing its independence for the first time in recorded history. In 1941, British troops routed the Italians, and Haile Selassie returned to Addis Ababa.

The Emperor's gradual reforms failed to make headway against key problems. Although 85% of Ethiopians were subsistence farmers, feudal laws vested ownership of 55% of its land in the crown, the church, and the nobility; there was strong pressure for land reform. There was also mounting insurgency in Eritrea, a culturally distinct province where Christians and Moslems have long vied for control, which the United Nations placed under Ethiopian rule in 1952. Violent agitation for Eritrean independence was begun in 1969 by the Moslem-led Eritrean Liberation Front, which used Arab-supplied arms to field a 4,000-man guerrilla force.

Deep discontent erupted in the fall of 1973. A long drought had caused famine that killed 100,000 peasants and drove thousands of others to cities, where food was scarce and inflation was rampant. Charges of mismanagement of drought relief sparked riots in Addis Ababa in 1974, and unpaid troops in Asmara, capital of Eritrea, mutinied to protest conditions.

The Emperor named Endalkachew Makonnen, a moderate, as Prime Minister and agreed to call a constitutional convention. But there was a general strike, students rioted, and mutiny spread to the air force.

Endalkachew was ousted on July 24, arrested and later executed. Under his successor, Michael Imru, a draft Constitution proposing a constitutional monarchy was put forward, but power shifted relentlessly to a new Armed Forces Committee.

In August, the Armed Forces Committee nationalized Haile Selassie's palace and estates and directed him not to leave Addis Ababa. On Sept. 12, 1974, He was peacefully deposed after nearly 58 years as Regent and Emperor. The 82-year-old "Lion of Judah" was placed under guard. Parliament was dissolved and the Constitution suspended.

On Aug. 27, 1975, Haile Selassie died in a small apartment in his former Addis Ababa palace where he had been treated as a state prisoner. He was 83.

After the coup, revolt in Eritrea escalated from guerrilla conflict to open war. The Eritrean Liberation Front, armed by Libya and other Arab states, demanded full independence. The regime tried and failed to negotiate with the Front and then began vigorous military action. Some 22,000 government troops were in combat in Eritrea by February 1975, and 6,000 deaths, mostly of civilians, were said to have resulted in March.

U.S. military aid, which had been going to Ethiopia since World War II, was suspended after the 1974 coup and only briefly resumed in 1976 as the military government turned increasingly toward the U.S.S.R.

Lt. Col. Mengistu Haile Mariam was named head of state Feb. 2, 1977, to replace Brig. Gen. Teferi Benti, who was killed in a factional fight of the Dirgue after having ruled since 1974. The government was losing its fight to hold Eritrea and in the southeastern region of Ogaden, Somali guerrillas backed by Somali regular forces threatened the ancient city of Harar. In October, the U.S.S.R. announced it would end military aid to Somalia and henceforth back its new ally, Ethiopia. This, together with the intervention of Cuban troops in Ogaden, turned the tide for Mengistu. By March 1978, the badly beaten Somalis had retreated to their homeland. This brought an end to large-scale fighting with Somalia, but border skirmishing continued intermittently through 1984.

The Marxist government still had not quelled the Eritrean secessionists in the north by 1984. In addition, a secessionist struggle was going on in Tigre, the province adjoining Eritrea.

A Communist regime was formally proclaimed on Sept. 10, 1984, with Mengistu as party leader. After enduring years of drought, the country was in the throes of the worst famine in more than a decade, with tens of thousands of Ethiopians reported dying of starvation and related diseases and 6 million in dire need of food.

FIJI

Sovereign: Queen Elizabeth II
Governor General: Sir George Cakobau (1973)
Prime Minister: Sir Kamisese Mara (1970)
Area: 7,078 sq mi. (18,333 sq km)
Population (est. 1983): 676,000 (average annual growth rate: 2.1%)
Density per square mile: 92.1
Capital (1981): Suva (on Viti Levu), 65,000
Monetary unit: Fijian dollar
Languages: Fijian, Hindustani, English
Religions: Christian, 50%; Hindu, 41%; Islam, 8%
Member of Commonwealth of Nations
Literacy rate (1981): 80%
Economic summary: Gross national product (1980): $1.2 billion. Average annual growth rate (1970–79): 3.0%. Per capita income (1980): $1,850. Average rate of inflation (1975–77): 9.3%. Labor force in agriculture: 44%; principal products: sugar, copra, bananas, ginger. Labor force in industry: 16%; major industrial products: refined sugar, gold, lumber. Natural resources: timber, fish, gold, copper. Exports: sugar, copra. Imports: foodstuffs, machinery, manufactured goods, fuels, chemicals. Major trading partners: U.K., New Zealand, U.S.

Geography. Fiji consists of more than 500 islands in the southwestern Pacific Ocean about 1,960 miles (3,152 km) from Sydney, Australia. The two largest islands are Viti Levu (4,109 sq mi.; 10,642 sq km) and Vanua Levu (2,242 sq mi.; 5,807 sq km). The island of Rotuma (18 sq mi.; 47 sq km), about 400 miles (644 km) to the north, is a dependency of Fiji. Overall, Fiji is nearly as large as New Jersey.

The largest islands in the group are mountainous and volcanic, with the tallest peak being Mount Victoria (4,341 ft; 1,323 m) on Viti Levu. The islands in the south have dense forests on the windward side and grasslands on the leeward.

Government. Executive authority is vested in the Cabinet and legislative authority in a bicameral 74-member Parliament. The major political parties are the Alliance Party, led by Prime Minister Sir Kamisese Mara; National Federation Party, led by Jai Ram Reddy, and Fijian Nationalist Party, led by Sakeasi Butadroka.

History. In 1874, an offer of cession by the Fijian chiefs was accepted, and Fiji was proclaimed a possession and dependency of the British Crown.

During World War II, the archipelago was an important air and naval station on the route from the U.S. and Hawaii to Australia and New Zealand.

Fiji became independent on Oct. 10, 1970. The next year it joined the five-island South Pacific Forum, which intends to become a permanent regional group to promote collective diplomacy of the newly independent members. The Forum also includes Western Samoa, Tonga, Nauru, and the self-governing segments of the Cook Islands.

FINLAND

Republic of Finland
President: Mauno H. Koivisto (1982)
Premier: Kalevi Sorsa (1982)
Area: 130,119 sq mi. (337,009 sq km)
Population (est. 1982): 4,825,000 (average annual growth rate: 0.4%) (Finnish, 93%; Swedish, 6%)
Density per square mile: 37.0
Capital: Helsinki
Largest cities (est. 1981): Helsinki, 484,000; Tampere, 167,300; Turku, 163,500
Monetary unit: Markka
Languages: Finnish, Swedish
Religions: Lutheran, 97%; Orthodox, 1%
National name: Suomen Tasavalta—Republiken Finland
Literacy rate (1981): 99%
Economic summary: Gross national product (1983): $47.4 billion. Average annual growth rate (1970–79): 2.2%. Per capita income (1980): $9,720. Land used for agriculture: 8%; labor force: 12%; principal products:

dairy products, cereals, sugar beets, potatoes. Labor force in industry: 33%; major products: metal manufactures, forestry and wood products, refined copper, ships. Natural resource: timber. Exports: timber, paper and pulp, ships, machinery, iron and steel, clothing, footwear. Imports: foodstuffs, petroleum and petroleum products, chemicals, transportation equipment, iron and steel, machinery, textile yarns. Major trading partners: Western European countries, U.S.S.R., Sweden.

Geography. Finland stretches 700 miles (1,127 km) from the Gulf of Finland on the south to Soviet Petsamo, north of the Arctic Circle. The U.S.S.R. extends along the entire eastern frontier. In area, Finland is three times the size of Ohio.

Off the southwest coast are the Aland Islands, controlling the entrance to the Gulf of Bothnia. Finland has more than 60,000 lakes. Of the few rivers, only the Oulu (Ulea) is navigable to any important extent.

The Swedish-populated Aland Islands (581 sq mi.; 1,505 sq km) have an autonomous status under a law passed in 1951.

Government. The president, chosen for six years by the popularly elected Electoral College of 300 members, appoints the Cabinet. The one-chamber Diet, the Eduskunta, consists of 200 members elected for four-year terms by proportional representation.

The major political parties are the Social Democratic Party (57 seats in the Eduskanta), led by Premier Kalevi Sorsa; Conservative Party (44 seats); Center Party (38 seats); People's Democratic League (Communist) (27 seats); Finnish Rural Party (17 seats); Swedish People's Party (11 seats); Christian League (3 seats). Premier Sorsa leads a coalition of Social Democratic, Center, Swedish People's Party, and Finnish Rural Party members totaling 106 seats.

History. At the end of the 7th century, the Finns came to Finland from their Volga settlements, taking the country from the Lapps, who retreated northward. The Finns' repeated raids on the Scandinavian coast impelled Eric IX, the Swedish King, to conquer the country in 1157 and bring it into contact with Western Christendom. By 1809 the whole of Finland was conquered by Alexander I of Russia, who set up Finland as a Grand Duchy.

The first period of Russification (1809–1905) resulted in a lessening of the powers of the Finnish Diet. The Russian language was made official, and the Finnish military system was superseded by the Russian. The pace of Russification was intensified from 1908 to 1914. When Russian control was weakened as a consequence of the March Revolution of 1917, the Diet on July 20, 1917, proclaimed Finland's independence, which became complete on Dec. 6, 1917.

Finland rejected Soviet territorial demands, and the U.S.S.R. attacked on Nov. 30, 1939. The Finns made an amazing stand of three months and finally capitulated, ceding 16,000 square miles (41,440 sq km) to the U.S.S.R. Under German pressure, the Finns joined the Nazis against Russia in 1941, but were defeated again and ceded the Petsamo area to the U.S.S.R. In 1948, a 20-year treaty of friendship and mutual assistance was signed by the two nations and renewed for another 20 years in 1970.

In 1970 Finland entered into a trade agreement with the enlarged European Economic Community (Common Market) and also with Comecom, the Communist East European Economic Group.

Helsinki was the site in 1975 of a summit conference of 35 heads of government convened for the signing of a European security agreement.

After 25 years in office, President Urho K. Kekkonen resigned in October 1981 because of ill health. Premier Mauno Koivisto, leader of the Social Democratic Party, was elected President on Jan. 26, 1982, and was sworn in the next day. Radio Moscow hailed Koivisto's victory as a "clear shift to the left" because he won decisively over a conservative rival with support from Finnish Communists. On Feb. 17, Kalevi Sorsa, a Social Democrat, took office as Premier, heading the same center-left coalition Koivisto had led.

FRANCE

French Republic
President: François Mitterrand (1981)
Premier: Laurent Fabius (1984)
Area: 211,208 sq mi. (547,026 sq km)
Population (est. 1983): 54,604,000 (average annual growth rate: 0.5%)
Density per square mile: 254.7
Capital: Paris
Largest cities (est. 1983): Paris, 2,150,000; **(1975 census):** Marseilles, 908,600; Lyons, 456,716; Toulouse, 373,796; Nice, 344,481; Nantes, 255,093; Strasbourg, 253,384; Bordeaux, 223,131
Monetary unit: Franc
Religion (est.): Roman Catholic, 90%; Protestant, Jewish, Islam, and others, 10%
National name: République Française
Literacy rate (1981): 97%
Economic summary: Gross national product (1981): $569 billion. Average annual growth rate (1972–81): 3.1%. Per capita income (1981): $10,552. Land used for agriculture, 35%; labor force: 9%; principal products: cereals, feed grains, livestock and dairy products, wine, fruits, vegetables. Labor force in industry: 35%; major products: chemicals, automobiles, processed foods, iron and steel, aircraft, textiles, clothing. Natural resources: coal, iron ore, bauxite, fish, forests. Exports: textiles and clothing, iron and steel products, machinery and transport equipment, agricultural products. Imports: machinery, crude petroleum, iron and steel products, chemicals, foodstuffs, agricultural products. Major trading partners: West Germany, Italy, U.S., Belgium-Luxembourg, U.K., Netherlands.

Geography. France (80% the size of Texas) is second in size to the U.S.S.R. among Europe's nations. In the Alps near the Italian and Swiss borders is Europe's highest point—Mont Blanc (15,781 ft; 4,810 m). The forest-covered Vosges Mountains are in the northeast, and the Pyrenees are along the Spanish border.

Except for extreme northern France, which is part of the Flanders plain, the country may be described as four river basins and a plateau. Three of the streams flow west—the Seine into the English Channel, the Loire into the Atlantic, and the Garonne into the Bay of Biscay. The Rhône flows south into the Mediterranean. For about 100 miles (161 km), the Rhine is France's eastern border.

West of the Rhône and northeast of the Garonne

Rulers of France

Name	Born	Ruled[1]
CAROLINGIAN DYNASTY		
Pepin the Short	c. 714	751–768
Charlemagne[2]	742	768–814
Louis I the Debonair[3]	778	814–840
Charles I the Bald[4]	823	840–877
Louis II the Stammerer	846	877–879
Louis III[5]	c. 863	879–882
Carloman[5]	?	879–884
Charles II the Fat[6]	839	884–887
Eudes (Odo), Count of Paris	?	888–898
Charles III the Simple[8]	879	893–923[9]
Robert I[10]	c. 865	922–923
Rudolf (Raoul), Duke of Burgundy	?	923–936
Louis IV d'Outremer	c. 921	936–954
Lothair	941	954–986
Louis V the Sluggard	c. 967	986–987
CAPETIAN DYNASTY		
Hugh Capet	c. 940	987–996
Robert II the Pious[11]	c. 970	996–1031
Henry I	1008	1031–1060
Philip I	1052	1060–1108
Louis VI the Fat	1081	1108–1137
Louis VII the Young	c.1121	1137–1180
Philip II (Philip Augustus)	1165	1180–1223
Louis VIII the Lion	1187	1223–1226
Louis IX (St. Louis)	1214	1226–1270
Philip III the Bold	1245	1270–1285
Philip IV the Fair	1268	1285–1314
Louis X the Quarreler	1289	1314–1316
John I[12]	1316	1316
Philip V the Tall	1294	1316–1322
Charles IV the Fair	1294	1322–1328
HOUSE OF VALOIS		
Philip VI	1293	1328–1350
John II the Good	1319	1350–1364
Charles V the Wise	1337	1364–1380
Charles VI the Well-Beloved	1368	1380–1422
Charles VII	1403	1422–1461
Louis XI	1423	1461–1483
Charles VIII	1470	1483–1498
Louis XII the Father of the People	1462	1498–1515
Francis I	1494	1515–1547
Henry II	1519	1547–1559
Francis II	1544	1559–1560
Charles IX	1550	1560–1574
Henry III	1551	1574–1589
HOUSE OF BOURBON		
Henry IV of Navarre	1553	1589–1610
Louis XIII	1601	1610–1643
Louis XIV the Great	1638	1643–1715
Louis XV the Well-Beloved	1710	1715–1774
Louis XVI	1754	1774–1792[13]
Louis XVII (Louis Charles de France)[14]	1785	1793–1795
FIRST REPUBLIC		
National Convention	—	1792–1795
Directory (Directoire)	—	1795–1799
CONSULATE		
Napoleon Bonaparte[15]	1769	1799–1804
FIRST EMPIRE		
Napoleon I	1769	1804–1815[16]
RESTORATION OF HOUSE OF BOURBON		
Louis XVIII le Désiré	1755	1814–1824
Charles X	1757	1824–1830[17]
BOURBON-ORLEANS LINE		
Louis Philippe ("Citizen King")	1773	1830–1848[18]
SECOND REPUBLIC		
Louis Napoleon[19]	1808	1848–1852
SECOND EMPIRE		
Napoleon III (Louis Napoleon)	1808	1852–1870[20]
THIRD REPUBLIC (PRESIDENTS)		
Louis Adolphe Thiers	1797	1871–1873
Marie E. P. M. de MacMahon	1808	1873–1879
François P. J. Grévy	1807	1879–1887
Sadi Carnot	1837	1887–1894
Jean Casimir-Périer	1847	1894–1895
François Félix Faure	1841	1895–1899
Émile Loubet	1838	1899–1906
Clement Armand Fallières	1841	1906–1913
Raymond Poincaré	1860	1913–1920
Paul E. L. Deschanel	1856	1920–1920
Alexandre Millerand	1859	1920–1924
Gaston Doumergue	1863	1924–1931
Paul Doumer	1857	1931–1932
Albert Lebrun	1871	1932–1940
VICHY GOVERNMENT (CHIEF OF STATE)		
Henri Philippe Pétain	1856	1940–1944
PROVISIONAL GOVERNMENT (PRESIDENTS)		
Charles de Gaulle	1890	1944–1946
Félix Gouin	1884	1946–1946
Georges Bidault	1899	1946–1947
FOURTH REPUBLIC (PRESIDENTS)		
Vincent Auriol	1884	1947–1954
René Coty	1882	1954–1959
FIFTH REPUBLIC (PRESIDENTS)		
Charles de Gaulle	1890	1959–1969
Georges Pompidou	1911	1969–1974
Valéry Giscard d'Estaing	1926	1974–1981
François Mitterrand	1916	1981–

1. For Kings and Emperors through the Second Empire, year of end of rule is also that of death, unless otherwise indicated. 2. Crowned Emperor of the West in 800. His brother, Carloman, ruled as King of the Eastern Franks from 768 until his death in 771. 3. Holy Roman Emperor 814–840. 4. Holy Roman Emperor 875–877 as Charles II. 5. Ruled jointly 879–882. 6. Holy Roman Emperor 881–887 as Charles III. 7. Died 888. 8. King 893–898 in opposition to Eudes. 9. Died 929. 10. Not counted in regular line of Kings of France by some authorities. Elected by nobles but killed in Battle of Soissons. 11. Sometimes called Robert I. 12. Posthumous son of Louis X; lived for only five days. 13. Executed 1793. 14. Titular King only. He died in prison according to official reports, but many pretenders appeared during the Bourbon restoration. 15. As First Consul, Napoleon held the power of government. In 1804, he became Emperor. 16. Abdicated first time June 1814. Re-entered Paris March 1815, after escape from Elba; Louis XVIII fled to Ghent. Abdicated second time June 1815. He named as his successor his son, Napoleon II, who was not acceptable to the Allies. He died 1821. 17. Died 1836. 18. Died 1850. 19. President; became Emperor in 1852. 20. Died 1873.

lies the central plateau, covering about 15% of France's area and rising to a maximum elevation of 6,188 feet (1,886 m). In the Mediterranean, about 115 miles (185 km) east-southeast of Nice, is Corsica (3,367 sq mi.; 8,721 sq km).

Government. The president is elected for seven years by universal suffrage. He appoints the premier, and the Cabinet is responsible to Parliament. The president has the right to dissolve the National Assembly or to ask Parliament for reconsideration of a law. The Parliament consists of two houses: the National Assembly and the Senate.

The major political parties are the Socialists (267 of 491 seats in the National Assembly), led by Pierre Joxe; Rally for the Republic (79 seats), led by Claude Labbe; Union for French Democracy (52 seats), led by Jean-Claude Gaudin, and Communists (43 seats), led by André Lajoinie. Forty-two other members are affiliated with the various parties, while the remainder do not belong to any group.

History. The history of France, as distinct from ancient Gaul, begins with the Treaty of Verdun (843), dividing the territories corresponding roughly to France, Germany, and Italy among the three grandsons of Charlemagne. Julius Caesar had conquered part of Gaul in 57–52 B.C., and it remained Roman until Franks invaded it in the 5th century.

Charles the Bald, inheritor of *Francia Occidentalis,* founded the Carolingian dynasty, which ruled over a kingdom increasingly feudalized. By 987, the crown passed to Hugh Capet, a princeling who controlled only the Ile-de-France, the region surrounding Paris. For 350 years, an unbroken Capetian line added to its domain and consolidated royal authority until the accession in 1328 of Philip VI, first of the Valois line. France was then the most powerful nation in Europe, with a population of 15 million.

The missing pieces in Philip's domain were the French provinces still held by the Plantagenet kings of England, who also claimed the French crown. Beginning in 1338, the Hundred Years' War eventually settled the contest. English longbows defeated French armored knights at Crécy (1346) and the English also won the second landmark battle at Agincourt (1415), but the final victory went to the French peasant girl, Joan of Arc, at Orléans (1429).

Absolute monarchy reached its apogee in the reign of Louis XIV (1643–1715), the Sun King, whose brilliant court was the center of the Western world. Neither Louis XV, nor his grandson, Louis XVI, could sustain the role, however, and the Ancien Régime tottered under the weight of an outmoded society, crushing taxes, and the infiltration of egalitarian philosophy. The monarchy lost French Canada in the Battle of Quebec Sept. 13, 1759, and in its last gasp under Louis XVI aided the American British colonists to gain their freedom.

Revolution plunged France into a blood bath beginning in 1789 and ending with a new authoritarianism under Napoleon Bonaparte, who had successfully defended the infant republic from foreign attack and then made himself First Consul in 1799 and Emperor in 1804. Napoleon set patterns in government, education, and law visible today, and his conquests spread them throughout Europe.

The Congress of Vienna (1815) sought to restore the pre-Napoleonic order in the person of Louis XVIII, but industrialization and the middle class, both fostered under Napoleon, built pressure for change, and a revolution in 1848 drove Louis Philipe, last of the Bourbons, into exile.

A second republic elected as its president Prince Louis Napoleon, a nephew of Napoleon I, who declared the Second Empire in 1852 and took the throne as Napoleon III. His opposition to the rising power of Prussia ignited the Franco-Prussian War (1870–71), ending in his defeat and abdication.

A new France emerged from World War I as the continent's dominant power. But four years of hostile occupation had reduced northeast France to ruins. The postwar Third Republic was plagued by political instability and economic chaos.

From 1919, French foreign policy aimed at keeping Germany weak through a system of alliances, but it failed to halt the rise of Adolf Hitler and the Nazi war machine. On May 10, 1940, mechanized Nazi troops attacked, and, as they approached Paris, Italy joined with Germany. The Germans marched into an undefended Paris and Marshal Henri Philippe Pétain signed an armistice June 22. France was split into an occupied north and an unoccupied south, the latter becoming a totalitarian state with Pétain as its chief.

Allied armies liberated France in August 1944. The French Committee of National Liberation, formed in Algiers in 1943, established a provisional government in Paris headed by Gen. Charles de Gaulle. The Fourth Republic was born Dec. 24, 1946.

The Empire became the French Union; the National Assembly was strengthened and the presidency weakened; and France joined the North Atlantic Treaty Organization. A war against communist insurgents in Indochina was abandoned after the defeat at Dien Bien Phu. A new rebellion in Algeria (*see* Algeria) threatened a military coup, and on June 1, 1958, the Assembly invited de Gaulle to return as premier with extraordinary powers. He drafted a new Constitution for a Fifth Republic, adopted Sept. 28, which strengthened the presidency and reduced legislative power. He was elected president Dec. 21.

The new president negotiated the independence of Algeria on July 5, 1962. De Gaulle cultivated the former colonies along with other new nations of what he called the Third World—nations aligned with neither the West nor the Soviet bloc—as a base for French leadership. In 1960, de Gaulle exploded an atomic bomb; in 1963 he negotiated a Franco-German friendship treaty; and the following year he recognized Peking, at the same time improving relations with the U.S.S.R.

De Gaulle took France out of the NATO military command in 1967 and expelled all foreign-controlled troops from the country. He later went on to attempt to achieve a long-cherished plan of regional reform. This, however, aroused wide opposition. He decided to stake his fate on a referendum. At the voting in April 1969, the electorate defeated the plan. His successor, Georges Pompidou continued the de Gaulle policies of seeking to expand France's influence in the Mideast and Africa, selling arms to South Africa (despite the U.N. embargo), to Libya, and to Greece, and in 1971 he endorsed British entry into the Common Market.

Pompidou died of cancer in April 1974 and the special election to choose a successor was won by Valéry Giscard d'Estaing, who had served as de Gaulle's Finance Minister but was not a Gaullist party member.

A surprise victory in parliamentary elections in 1978, resulting from a split between Socialists and Communists, gave Giscard a solid majority, but the following year a cut in subsidies to industry generated a wave of strikes and the worst rioting in Paris since the student rebellion of 1968. Giscard concentrated on foreign policy, attacking the U.S. at the Tokyo economic summit of 1979 for failing to conserve oil and continuing his criticism at the Venice summit the following year. To the further annoyance of the Carter Administration, he met with Soviet President Leonid I. Brezhnev in Warsaw earlier without prior consultation with Washington.

Giscard's African strongman image began to fade with the collapse of his one-time protégé, Jean-Bedel Bokassa, whose Central African Empire dissolved in a cloud of scandal in 1979. The defeat of President Goukouni Oueddi of Chad by Libyan-aided dissidents in January 1981, despite the presence of French troops, added no luster to Giscard's African record.

Socialist François Mitterand's stunning victory in the May 10, 1981, Presidential election over the Gaullist alliance that had held power since 1958 was attributed to the challenger's skill in maintaining the Communists' support while holding them at arm's length and Giscard's failure to hold Gaullist support.

Mitterrand's ultimate triumph came in the final round of parliamentary voting when his Socialist Party, which in 1971 had polled only 5% of the votes in a similar election, swept to absolute power in the Assembly with 285 of the 491 seats. The Gaullist Rassemblement pour la République (Rally for the Republic) was cut in half, together with its allied Union pour la Democratie Française (Union for French Democracy), and the Communists fell to their lowest strength since World War II.

Although Communist support was not needed, Mitterrand named four Communist ministers to his 44-member Cabinet, the first since the postwar period and the cause for some alarm among NATO allies. Mitterrand reassured Vice President George Bush in June, pointing to the statement signed by the Communist Party as the price of joining the government, endorsing Western European defense against the Soviet Union and calling for Soviet withdrawal from Afghanistan. Mitterrand also met with German Chancellor Helmut Schmidt to support the stationing of U.S. nuclear weapons in Western Europe.

The victors immediately moved to carry out campaign pledges to nationalize major industries, halt nuclear testing, suspend nuclear power plant construction, and impose new taxes on the rich. Premier Pierre Mauroy called for the nationalization of military production of the Dassault-Breguet aircraft corporation, the Sacinor and Usinor steel companies, some remaining privately owned commercial banks, and the major manufacturing companies in generators, chemicals, glass appliances, and nonferrous metals.

On Feb. 11, 1982, the nationalization bills became law. Acquisition of the five major industries targeted by the law was estimated to cost $7 billion and the government announced an immediate program to spend $1.6 billion to aid the weakest of the five—the steel, electronics, and textile-chemical conglomerates. A reaction to the Socialist innovations brought opposition victories in four parliamentary by-elections in January and an opposition sweep in local elections in March, when the Socialist-Communist-alliance won majorities in only 37 of France's 95 departments.

At the Versailles summit of the industrialized nations in June, overshadowed by war in the Falkland Islands and Lebanon, Mitterrand sought U.S. agreement to the extension of French credit and technology for the construction of a Soviet gas pipeline to supply Western Europe. Despite U.S. disapproval, Mitterrand ordered French manufacturers to supply even U.S.-licensed technology to the project.

The Socialists' policies during Mitterand's first two years left a trail of economic disaster—a 12% inflation rate, a huge trade deficit, and three successive devaluations of the franc. In early 1983, Mitterand shifted course, embarking on an unpopular austerity program to control inflation and reduce the trade deficit. He increased taxes and slashed government spending. A halt in economic growth, declining purchasing power for the average Frenchman, and an increase in unemployment to 10% of the work force followed. Mitterand sank lower and lower in the opinion polls.

In mid-1984, Mitterand shifted course again—this time toward the political center. He accepted Mauroy's resignation and replaced him with Laurent Fabius, at 37 the youngest French Premier in a century. Fabius, a pragmatic moderate who had been Industry Minister, appointed a new Cabinet of all Socialists, ending the Socialist-Communist coalition. He proposed cuts that would reduce the average French worker's income and social security taxes by 5 to 8%. Mitterand promised that further tax cuts would be "the rule for the rest of my seven-year term of office."

Overseas Departments and Territories of France

FRENCH GUIANA (including ININI)

Status: Overseas Department
Prefect: Maxime Gonzalvo (1981)
Area: 35,135 sq mi. (91,000 sq km)
Population (est. 1983): 70,000 (average annual growth rate: 2.5%)
Capital (est. 1982): Cayenne, 40,000
Monetary unit: Franc
Language: Creole
Religion: Roman Catholic
Literacy rate (1981): 73%
Economic summary: Gross national product (1980): $180 million. Average annual growth rate (1970–79): 0.4%. Per capita income (1980): $2,880. Labor force in agriculture: 21%; principal agricultural products: rice, corn, manioc, cocoa, bananas, sugar cane. Labor force in industry: 8%; major industrial products: timber, rum, rosewood essence, gold mining. Natural resources: bauxite, timber, cinnabar, low-grade iron ore. Exports: shrimp, timber, rum, rosewood essence. Imports: food, consumer and producer goods, petroleum. Major trading partners: U.S., France, Martinique.

French Guiana, lying north of Brazil and east of Suriname on the northeast coast of South America, was first settled in 1604. Penal settlements, embracing the area around the mouth of the Maroni River and the Iles du Salut (including Devil's Island), were founded in 1852; they have since been abolished.

During World War II, French Guiana at first adhered to the Vichy government, but the Free French took over in 1943. French Guiana accepted in 1958 the new Constitution of the French Fifth Republic and remained an Overseas Department of the French Republic.

FRENCH POLYNESIA

Status: Overseas Territory
High Commissioner: Paul Noirot-Cosson
Area: 1,544 sq mi. (4,000 sq km)
Population (est. 1983): 160,000 (average annual growth rate: 2.2%)
Monetary unit: Pacific financial community franc
Language: French
Religions: Protestant, 55%; Roman Catholic, 32%
Capital (est. 1980): Papeete (on Tahiti), 25,000
Economic summary: Gross national product (1980): $1.0 billion. Average annual growth rate (1970–78): 2.8%. Per capita income (1980): $6,780. Principal agricultural product: coconuts. Major industries: tourism, maintenance of French nuclear test base. Exports: coconut products, mother of pearl, vanilla. Imports: fuels, foodstuffs, equipment. Major trading partners: France, U.S.

The term French Polynesia is applied to the scattered French possessions in the South Pacific—Mangareva (Gambier), Makatea, the Marquesas Islands, Rapa, Rurutu, Rimatara, the Society Islands, the Tuamotu Archipelago, Tubuai, Raivavae, and the island of Clipperton—which were organized into a single colony in 1903. There are 120 islands, of which 25 are uninhabited.

The High Commissioner is assisted by a Council of Government and a popularly elected Territorial Assembly. The principal and most populous island—Tahiti, in the Society group—was claimed as French in 1768. In 1958, French Polynesia voted in favor of the new Constitution of the French Fifth Republic and remained an Overseas Territory of the French Republic. The natives are mostly Maoris.

The Pacific Nuclear Test Center on the atoll of Mururoa, 744 miles (1,200 km) from Tahiti, was completed in 1966.

GUADELOUPE

Status: Overseas Department
Prefect: Robert Miguet (1982)
Area: 687 sq mi. (1,779 sq km)
Population (est. 1982): 330,000 (average annual growth rate: −0.7%)
Capital (est. 1982): Basse-Terre, 20,000
Largest city (est. 1982): Pointe-à-Pitre, 50,000
Monetary unit: Franc
Language: French, Creole patois
Religions: Roman Catholic
Literacy rate (1981): 70%
Economic summary: Gross national product (1980): $1.3 billion. Average annual growth rate (1970–79): 5.1%. Per capita income (1980): $3,870. Land used for agriculture: 24%; labor force: 25%; principal agricultural products: sugar cane, bananas, rum, pineapples. Major industries: construction, public works. Exports: sugar, fruits and vegetables, bananas. Imports: foodstuffs, clothing, consumer goods, petroleum. Major trading partner: France.

Guadeloupe, in the West Indies about 300 miles (483 km) southeast of Puerto Rico, was discovered by Columbus in 1493. It consists of the twin islands of Basse-Terre and Grande-Terre and five dependencies—Marie-Galante, Les Saintes, La Désirade, St. Barthélemy, and the northern half of St. Martin. The volcano Soufrière (4,813 ft; 1,467 m), also called La Grande Soufrière, is the highest point on Guadeloupe. Violent activity in 1976 and 1977 caused thousands to flee their homes.

French colonization began in 1635. In 1958, Guadeloupe voted in favor of the new Constitution of the French Fifth Republic and remained an Overseas Department of the French Republic.

MAHORÉ

Status: Territorial collectivity
Prefect: Christian Pellerin (1983)
Area: 146 sq mi. (378 sq km)
Population (est. 1980): 48,600
Capital: Dzaoudzi (about 4,100)
Principal products: vanilla, essential oils, copra

The most populous of the Comoro Islands in the Indian Ocean, with a Christian majority, Mahoré (formerly Mayotte) voted in 1974 and 1976 against joining the other, predominantly Moslem islands, in declaring themselves independent. It continues to retain its ties to France.

MARTINIQUE

Status: Overseas Department
Prefect: Jean Chevance (1981)
Area: 431 sq mi. (1,116 sq km)
Population (est. 1982): 326,536 (average annual growth rate: −0.8%)
Capital (est. 1982): Fort-de-France, 100,000
Monetary unit: Franc
Languages: French, Creole patois
Religion: Roman Catholic
Literacy rate (1981): 70%
Economic summary: Gross national product (1980): $1.5 billion. Average annual growth rate (1970–79): 4.3%. Per capita income (1980): $4,640. Land used for agriculture: 31%; labor force: 23%; principal agricultural products: sugar cane, bananas, rum, pineapples. Labor force in industry: 9%; major industries: sugar, rum, oil, cement, tourism. Natural resource: fish. Exports: bananas, refined petroleum products, rum, sugar, pineapples. Imports: foodstuffs, clothing and other consumer goods, petroleum products. Major trading partners: France, U.S.

Martinique, lying in the Lesser Antilles about 300 miles (483 km) northeast of Venezuela, was probably discovered by Columbus in 1502 and was taken for France in 1635. Following the Franco-German armistice of 1940, it had a semiautonomous status until 1943, when authority was relinquished to the Free French. The area, administered by a Prefect assisted by an elected council, is represented in the French Parliament. In 1958, Martinique voted in favor of the new Constitution of the French Fifth Republic and remained an Overseas Department of the French Republic.

NEW CALEDONIA AND DEPENDENCIES

Status: Overseas Territory
High Commissioner: Jacques Roynette (1982)
Area: 7,374 sq mi. (19,103 sq km)[1]

Population (est. 1982): 150,000 (average annual growth rate: 0.5%)
Capital (est. 1982): Nouméa, 50,000
Monetary unit: Pacific financial community franc
Languages: Melanesian and Polynesian dialects
Religion: Christian
Literacy rate: Not known
Economic summary: Gross national product (1980): $1.1 billion. Average annual growth rate (1970–78): –4.9%. Per capita income (1980): $7,830. Principal agricultural products: coffee, vegetables, beef. Major industrial product: nickel. Natural resources: nickel, chromite, iron ore. Exports: nickel, coffee. Imports: mineral fuels, machinery, transport equipment, foodstuffs. Major trading partners: France, Japan, U.S., Australia.

1. Including dependencies.

New Caledonia (6,466 sq mi.; 16,747 sq km), about 1,070 miles (1,722 km) northeast of Sydney, Australia, was discovered by Capt. James Cook in 1774 and annexed by France in 1853. The government also administers the Isle of Pines, the Loyalty Islands (Uvéa, Lifu, and Maré), the Belep Islands, the Huon Island group, and the Chesterfield Islands.

The natives are Melanesians; about one third of the population is white and one fifth Indochinese and Javanese. The French National Assembly on July 31, 1984, voted a bill into law that granted internal autonomy to New Caledonia and opened the way to possible independence.

RÉUNION

Status: Overseas Department
Prefect: Michel Levallois (1981)
Area: 970 sq mi. (2,510 sq km)
Population (est. 1982): 500,000 (average annual growth rate, 1975–79: 0.7%)
Capital (est. 1981): Saint-Denis, 105,000
Monetary unit: Franc
Languages: French, Creole
Religion: Roman Catholic
Economic summary: Gross national product (1980): $2.0 billion. Average annual growth rate (1970–79): –0.9%. Principal agriculatural products: sugar cane, vanilla, bananas, perfume plants. Major industrial products: rum, cigarettes, processed sugar. Exports: sugar, perfume essences, rum, molasses. Imports: manufactured goods, foodstuffs, beverages, machinery and transportation equipment, petroleum products. Major trading partners: France, Mauritius.

Discovered by Portuguese navigators in the 16th century, the island of Réunion, then uninhabited, was taken as a French possession in 1642. It is located about 450 miles (724 km) east of Madagascar, in the Indian Ocean. In 1958, Réunion approved the Constitution of the Fifth French Republic and remained an Overseas Department of the French Republic.

ST. PIERRE AND MIQUELON

Status: Overseas Department
Prefect: Philippe Parant (1982)
Area: 93 sq mi. (242 sq km)
Population (est. 1982): 6,000
Capital (est. 1981): Saint Pierre, 5,800
Economic summary: Major industries: fishing, canneries. Exports: petroleum products, cattle, fish. Major trading partners: Canada, France, U.S.

The sole remnant of the French colonial empire in North America, these islands were first occupied by the French in 1604. Their only importance arises from proximity to the Grand Banks, located 10 miles south of Newfoundland, making them the center of the French Atlantic cod fisheries. On July 19, 1976, the islands became an Overseas Department of the French Republic.

SOUTHERN AND ANTARCTIC LANDS

Status: Overseas Territory
Administrator: Claude Pieri
Area: 169,614 sq mi. (439,300 sq km)
Capital: Port-au-Français

This territory is uninhabited except for the personnel of scientific bases. It consists of Adélie Land (166,752 sq mi.; 431,888 sq km) on the Antarctic mainland and the following islands in the southern Indian Ocean: the Kerguelen and Crozet archipelagos and the islands of Saint-Paul and New Amsterdam.

WALLIS AND FUTUNA ISLANDS

Status: Overseas Territory
Administrator Superior: Robert Thill (1982)
Area: 77 sq mi. (200 sq km)
Population (est. 1982): 9,200
Capital (1980): Wallis (on Uvea), 600

The two islands groups in the South Pacific between Fiji and Samoa were settled by French missionaries at the beginning of the 19th century. A protectorate was established in the 1880s. Following a referendum by the Polynesian inhabitants, the status was changed to that of an Overseas Territory in 1961.

GABON

Gabonese Republic
President: Omar Bongo (1967)
Premier: Léon Mébiame (1975)
Area: 103,346 sq mi. (267,667 sq km)
Population (est. 1983): 921,000 (average annual growth rate: 4.6%)
Density per square mile: 5.5
Capital and largest city (est. 1980): Libreville, 250,000
Monetary unit: Franc CFA
Ethnic groups: Bateke, Obamba, Bakota, Shake, Pongwés, Adumas, Chiras, Punu, and Lumbu
Languages: French (official) and Bantu dialects
Religions: Animist, Christian, Islam
National name: République Gabonaise
Member of French Community
Literacy rate (1981): 20%
Economic summary: Gross national product (1981): $3.3 billion. Average annual growth rate (1970–79): 5.2%. Per capita income (1980): $5,500. Labor force in agriculture: 70%; principal products: cocoa, coffee, wood, palm, rice, bananas, peanuts. Labor force in industry: 30%; major products: petroleum, natural gas, processed wood, manganese, uranium. Natural resources: wood, petroleum, iron ore, manganese, uranium. Exports: crude petroleum, wood and wood products, minerals, coffee.

Imports: mining and road-building machinery, electrical equipment, foodstuffs, textiles, transport vehicles. Major trading partners: France, U.S., West Germany.

Geography. This West African land with the Atlantic as its western border is also bounded by Equatorial Guinea, Cameroon, and the Congo. Its area is slightly less than Kentucky's.

From mangrove swamps on the coast, the land becomes divided plateaus in the north and east and mountains in the north. Most of the country is covered by a dense tropical forest.

Government. The president is elected for a seven-year term. Legislative powers are exercised by a National Assembly, which is elected for a seven-year term. After his conversion to Islam in 1973, President Bongo changed his given name, Albert Bernard, to Omar. The Parti Démocratique Gabonais (all National Assembly seats) is led by President Bongo. He was re-elected without opposition in 1973 and in 1980.

History. Little is known of Gabon's history, even in oral tradition, but Pygmies are believed to be the original inhabitants. Now there are many tribal groups in the country, the largest being the Fang people who constitute a third of the population.

Gabon was first visited by the Portuguese navigator Diego Cam in the 15th century. In 1839, the French founded their first settlement on the left bank of the Gabon Estuary and gradually occupied the hinterland during the second half of the 19th century. It was organized as a French territory in 1888 and became an autonomous republic within the French Union after World War II and an independent republic on Aug. 17, 1960.

Immense resources in oil, uranium, manganese, and iron help give Gabon's inhabitants a per capita annual income of $5,500, the highest in black Africa. To speed exploitation of a billion-ton iron ore reserve in the Belinga-Mekambo region, the government began work in 1969 on a 350-mile railroad leading from the coast into the area. The project was initiated by President León Mba, who died in 1967, and has been continued by his hand-picked successor, Omar Bongo.

In 1974, Bongo negotiated 60% control of an iron-ore venture half-owned by the Bethlehem Steel Corp. In October of that year, he visited Peking and concluded an economic and technical agreement with China.

GAMBIA

Republic of the Gambia
President: Sir Dawda K. Jawara (1970)
Area: 4,093 sq mi. (10,600 sq km)
Population (est. 1982): 640,000 (average annual growth rate: 2.8%)
Density per square mile: 159.4
Capital and largest city (est. 1980): Banjul, 48,000
Monetary unit: Dalasi
Languages: Native tongues, English (official)
Religions: Islam, Christian, Animist
Member of Commonwealth of Nations
Literacy rate (1981): 10%
Economic summary: Gross national product (1980): $150 million. Average annual growth rate (1970–79): 0.4%. Per capita income (1980): $250. Land used for agriculture: 55%; labor force: 85%; principal products: peanuts, rice, palm kernels. Major industrial products: processed peanuts. Natural resources: fish. Exports: peanuts and peanut products, fish. Imports: textiles, foodstuffs, tobacco, machinery, petroleum products. Major trading partners: Western European countries.

Geography. Situated on the Atlantic coast in westernmost Africa and surrounded on three sides by Senegal, Gambia is twice the size of Delaware. The Gambia River flows for 200 miles (322 km) through Gambia on its way to the Atlantic. The country, the smallest on the continent, averages only 20 miles (32 km) in width.

Government. The president's five-year term is linked to the 35-member unicameral House of Representatives, from which he appoints his Cabinet members and the vice president.

The major political party is the People's Progressive Party (29 seats in House of Representatives), led by President Jawara.

History. During the 17th century, Gambia was settled by various companies of English merchants. Slavery was the chief source of revenue until it was abolished in 1807. Gambia became a crown colony in 1843 and an independent nation within the Commonwealth of Nations on Feb. 18, 1965.

Full independence was approved in a 1970 referendum, and on April 24 of that year Gambia proclaimed itself a republic.

President Dawda K. Jawara won overwhelming re-election to his fifth term on May 5, 1982, in a vote that was also seen as an endorsement of his proposal for a confederation with Senegal.

GERMANY, EAST

German Democratic Republic
Chairman of Council of State: Erich Honecker (1976)
Chairman of Council of Ministers: Willi Stoph (1976)
Area: 41,767 sq mi. (108,177 sq km)[1]
Population (est. 1982): 16,750,000 (average annual growth rate: 0.0%)
Density per square mile: 41.2
Capital: Berlin (eastern sector)
Largest cities (est. 1980): East Berlin, 1,146,000; Leipzig, 563,000; Dresden, 516,000; Karl-Marx Stadt, 317,000; Magdeburg, 289,000; Halle, 232,000; Rostock, 230,000; Erfurt, 230,000
Monetary unit: Mark of the Deutsche Demokratische Republik
Language: German
Religions: Protestant, 53%; Roman Catholic, 8%
National name: Deutsche Demokratische Republik
Literacy rate (1981): 99%
Economic summary: Gross national product (1980): $120.9 billion. Average annual growth rate (1970–79): 4.7%. Per capita income (1980): $7,180. Land used for agriculture: 43%; labor force: 9%; principal products: grains, potatoes, sugar beets, meat and dairy products. Labor force in industry: 39%; major products: steel, chemicals, machinery, electrical and precision engineer-

ing products, fishing vessels. Natural resources: brown coal, potash, uranium. Exports: machinery and equipment, chemical products, textiles, clothing. Imports: raw materials, fuels, agricultural products, machinery and equipment. Major trading partners: U.S.S.R., Soviet bloc, West Germany.

1. Including East Berlin (156 square miles), which has been incorporated into the German Democratic Republic.

Geography. East Germany lies on the Baltic Sea with Poland to the east and Czechoslovakia to the south. The border with West Germany is roughly a line running south from Lübeck for about 250 miles. The main river is the Elbe, which flows from Dresden in the southeast to the North Sea in the northwest. The Oder and Neisse Rivers form the border with Poland. Most of the country, which is the size of Tennessee, is situated in the north German plain.

Government. The People's Chamber, composed of 500 deputies elected for five-year terms, chooses the chairman and Council of State and the chairman and Council of Ministers, which carries on executive functions.

The major political party is the Socialist Unity (Communist) Party, led by Secretary General Erich Honecker. Others are Christian Democratic Union, Liberal Democratic Party, Democratic Farmers' Party, National Democratic Party.

History. (For history before 1945, *see* Germany, West.) The area now occupied by East Germany, as well as adjacent areas in Eastern Europe, consists of Mecklenburg, Brandenburg, Lusatia, Saxony, and Thuringia. Soviet armies conquered the five territories by 1945. In the division of 1945 they were allotted to the U.S.S.R. Soviet forces created a State controlled by the secret police with a single party, the Socialist Unity (Communist) Party. The Russians appropriated East German plants to restore their war-ravaged industry.

When the Federal Republic of Germany was established in West Germany, the East German states adopted a more centralized constitution for the Democratic Republic of Germany, and it was put into effect on Oct. 7, 1949. The U.S.S.R. thereupon dissolved its occupation zone, but Soviet troops remained. The Western Allies declared that the East German Republic was a Soviet creation undertaken without self-determination and refused to recognize it. It was recognized only within the Soviet bloc.

In 1953, the U.S.S.R. transferred control of East Germany from the military commander to a civilian commissioner and announced a more liberal policy. Continued austerity and political repression led to workers' riots in East Berlin and other cities, allegedly instigated by the Soviet secret police as part of a power struggle within the Kremlin. Soviet troops ruthlessly reestablished order.

In 1955, Walter Ulbricht, hard-line dictator, won Soviet recognition of the East German republic and joined the Warsaw Treaty Organization, organizing troops under the guise of police forces. In the middle and late 1960s, East Germany also came to enjoy economic prosperity.

East German troops took part in the Soviet-bloc occupation of Czechoslovakia in August 1968, but reportedly were withdrawn after the U.S.S.R. questioned whether the 1945 Potsdam agreements permitted German troops on foreign soil.

A constitution adopted in April 1968 reaffirmed one-party rule and narrowed civil rights. Ulbricht continued pressure on West Berlin, opposed liberalization in Czechoslovakia and other parts of the Soviet bloc, impeded Bonn's establishment of ties with East Europe, and pressured Bonn to acknowledge the existence of the two German states.

Talks between the two German states on normalization began in 1970, with the East seeking recognition of its existence and the West wanting easing of pressure on Berlin. West Germany's nonaggression treaty with the U.S.S.R. was cooly received by Ulbricht. In 1971 he resigned and rapprochement between the two Germanys accelerated with agreement on a variety of issues (for details, *see* Germany, West). By 1973, normal relations were established, and the two states entered the United Nations.

A new Constitution unanimously approved by the East German parliament on Sept. 27, 1974, pointedly deleted any reference to eventual reunification of the two Germanys, a principle maintained in the West German constitution.

The 25-year diplomatic hiatus between East Germany and the U.S. ended Sept. 4, 1974, with the establishment of formal relations.

The East German government has repeatedly challenged the Western powers' right of access to Berlin, most recently at the time of President Carter's July 15, 1978, visit to West Berlin. Autobahn traffic between the city and West Germany was deliberately slowed and, as in a similar 1977 case, the U.S., U.K., and France protested to the U.S.S.R. and the East Germans that such action was illegal under the 1971 Four Power Agreement.

Increased Soviet action in Africa in 1978 revealed that East Germany as well as Cuba was actively engaged as a Soviet agent. Defense Minister Heinz Hoffmann visited Angola just before the invasion of Zaire's Shaba Province was launched in May. In Angola, 1,000 East German troops were reported serving with the army, and a small number of pilots were flying combat strikes.

Chairman of the Council of State Erich Honecker gave strong backing to the Soviet Union's stern policy toward Poland as the workers' demand for democratic rights advanced in 1980 and 1981. On Oct. 28, 1980, he closed the border, which had been open between the two states for 10 years, permitting only certified relatives or invited friends to visit. Five million Poles had visited East Germany in the previous year, largely to find cheaper and more abundant consumer goods.

In February 1981, Honecker, in a surprise gesture, declared at his party's 16th Congress that German reunification might eventually be possible, something the Communist regime had ruled out 10 years earlier. He also eased border restrictions on exchanges with West Germany imposed a few months before.

GERMANY, WEST

Federal Republic of Germany
President: Richard von Weizsäcker (1984)
Chancellor: Helmut Kohl (1982)
Area: 96,010 sq mi. (248,667 sq km)[1]
Population (est. 1983): 61,600,000 (average annual growth rate: 0.0%)
Density per square mile: 641.6
Capital (est. 1982): Bonn, 292,000

Largest cities (est. 1982): Hamburg, 1,630,400; Munich, 1,288,000; Cologne, 967,700; Essen, 642,000; Frankfurt, 623,000; Dordmund, 603,000; Düsseldorf, 586,000; Stuttgart, 575,000; Bremen, 551,000; Hannover, 528,000
Monetary unit: Deutsche Mark
Language: German
Religions: Protestant, 49%; Roman Catholic, 45%
National name: Bundesrepublik Deutschland
Literacy rate (1980): 99%
Economic summary: Gross national product (1982): $657.9 billion. Average annual growth rate (1980–82) 0.2%. Per capita income (1981): $11,130. Land used for agriculture: 33%; labor force: 5%; principal products: grains, potatoes, sugar beets. Labor force in industry: 43%; major products: iron, steel, coal, cement, chemicals, machinery, ships, vehicles. Natural resources: timber, coal, potash. Exports: machines and machine tools, chemicals, motor vehicles, iron and steel products. Imports: manufactured and agricultural products, raw materials, fuels. Major trading partners: France, Netherlands, Belgium-Luxembourg, Italy, U.S., U.K.

1. Excluding West Berlin (184 square miles with 1981 population of 1,890,300).

Geography. The Federal Republic of Germany occupies the western half of the central European area historically regarded as German. This was the part of Germany occupied by the United States, Britain, and France after World War II, when the eastern half of prewar Germany was split roughly between a Soviet-occupied zone, which became the present German Democratic Republic, and an area annexed by Poland.

West Germany's neighbors are France, Belgium, Luxembourg, and the Netherlands on the west, Switzerland and Austria on the south, Czechoslovakia and East Germany on the east, and Denmark on the north.

The northern plain, the central hill country, and the southern mountain district constitute the main physical divisions of West Germany, which is slightly smaller than Oregon. The Bavarian plateau in the southwest averages 1,600 feet (488 m) above sea level, but it reaches 9,721 feet (2,963 m) in the Zugspitze Mountains, the highest point in the country.

Important navigable rivers are the Danube, rising in the Black Forest and flowing east across Bavaria into Austria, and the Rhine, which rises in Switzerland and flows across the Netherlands in two channels to the North Sea and is navigable by smaller vessels as far as Cologne. The Rhine and the Elbe, which also empties into the North Sea, are navigable within Germany for ships of 400 tons. The Weser, flowing into the North Sea, and the Main and Mosel (Moselle), both tributaries of the Rhine, are also important.

Government. Under the Constitution of May 23, 1949, the Federal Republic was established as a parliamentary democracy. The Parliament consists of the Bundesrat, an upper chamber representing and appointed by the 10 Länder, or states (plus West Berlin), and the Bundestag, a lower house elected for four years by universal suffrage. Each house has non-voting representatives from West Berlin. The entire legislature elects the President of the Republic for a five-year term; the Bundestag alone chooses the Chancellor, or Prime Minister. Each of the Länder and West Berlin have a legislature popularly elected for a four-year or five-year term.

The major political parties are the Christian Democratic Union-Christian Social Union (244 of 498 seats in the Bundestag), led by Chancellor Helmut Kohl; Social Democratic Party (193 seats) led by former Chancellor Willy Brandt; and the Free Democratic Party (34 seats), led by Foreign Minister Hans-Dietrich Genscher; the Greens (27 seats). Kohl's government is a coalition with the Free Democrats.

History. Immediately before the Christian era, when the Roman Empire had pushed its frontier to the Rhine, what is now Germany was inhabited by several tribes believed to have migrated from Central Asia between the 6th and 4th centuries B.C. One of these tribes, the Franks, attained supremacy in western Europe under Charlemagne, who was crowned Holy Roman Emperor A.D. 800. By the Treaty of Verdun (843), Charlemagne's lands east of the Rhine were ceded to the German Prince Louis. Additional territory acquired by the Treaty of Mersen (870) gave Germany approximately the area it maintained throughout the Middle Ages. For several centuries after Otto the Great was crowned King in 936, the German rulers were also usually heads of the Holy Roman Empire.

Relations between state and church were changed by the Reformation, which began with Martin Luther's 95 theses, and came to a head in 1547, when Charles V scattered the forces of the Protestant League at Mühlberg. Freedom of worship was guaranteed by the Peace of Augsburg (1555), but a Counter Reformation took place later, and a dispute over the succession to the Bohemian throne brought on the Thirty Years' War (1618–48), which devastated Germany and left the empire divided into hundreds of small principalities virtually independent of the Emperor.

Meanwhile, Prussia was developing into a state of considerable strength. Frederick the Great (1740–86) reorganized the Prussian army and defeated Maria Theresa of Austria in a struggle over Silesia. After the defeat of Napoleon at Waterloo (1815), the struggle between Austria and Prussia for supremacy in Germany continued, reaching its climax in the defeat of Austria in the Seven Weeks' War (1866) and the formation of the Prussian-dominated North German Confederation (1867).

The architect of German unity was Otto von Bismarck, a conservative, monarchist, and militaristic Prussian Junker who had no use for "empty phrase-making and constitutions." From 1862 until his retirement in 1890 he dominated not only the German but also the entire European scene. He unified all Germany in a series of three wars against Denmark (1864), Austria (1866), and France (1870–71), which many historians believe were instigated and promoted by Bismarck in his zeal to build a nation through "blood and iron."

On Jan. 18, 1871, King Wilhelm I of Prussia was proclaimed German Emperor in the Hall of Mirrors at Versailles. The North German Confederation, created in 1867, was abolished, and the Second German Reich, consisting of the North and South German states, was born. With a powerful army, an efficient bureaucracy, and a loyal bourgeoisie, Chancellor Bismarck consolidated a powerful centralized state.

Wilhelm II dismissed Bismarck in 1890 and embarked upon a "New Course," stressing an intensified colonialism and a powerful navy. His chaotic foreign policy culminated in the diplomatic isolation of Germany and the disastrous defeat in World War I (1914–18).

The Second German Empire collapsed following the defeat of the German armies in 1918, the naval mutiny at Kiel, and the flight of the Kaiser to the Netherlands on November 10. The Social Democrats, led by Friedrich Ebert and Philipp Scheidemann, crushed the Communists and established a moderate republic with Ebert as President.

The Weimar Constitution of 1919 provided for a President to be elected for seven years by universal suffrage and a bicameral legislature, consisting of the Reichsrat, representing the states, and the Reichstag, representing the people. It contained a model Bill of Rights. It was weakened, however, by a provision that enabled the President to rule by decree.

President Ebert died Feb. 28, 1925, and on April 26, Field Marshal Paul von Hindenburg was elected president.

The mass of Germans regarded the Weimar Republic as a child of defeat, imposed upon a Germany whose legitimate aspirations to world leadership had been thwarted by a world conspiracy. Added to this were a crippling currency debacle, a tremendous burden of reparations, and acute economic distress.

Adolf Hitler, an Austrian war veteran and a fanatical nationalist, fanned discontent by promising a Greater Germany, abrogation of the Treaty of Versailles, restoration of Germany's lost colonies, and destruction of the Jews. When the Social Democrats and the Communists refused to combine against the Nazi threat, President Hindenburg made Hitler chancellor on Jan. 30, 1933.

With the death of Hindenburg on Aug. 2, 1934, Hitler repudiated the Treaty of Versailles and began full-scale rearmament. In 1935 he withdrew Germany from the League of Nations, and the next year he reoccupied the Rhineland and signed the anti-Comintern pact with Japan, at the same time strengthening relations with Italy. Austria was annexed in March 1938. By the Munich agreement in September 1938 he gained the Czech Sudetenland, and in violation of this agreement he completed the dismemberment of Czechoslovakia in March 1939. But his invasion of Poland on Sept. 1, 1939, precipitated World War II.

On May 8, 1945, Germany surrendered unconditionally to Allied and Soviet military commanders, and on June 5 the four-nation Allied Control Council became the *de facto* government of Germany.

(For details of World War II, *see* Headline History.)

At the Berlin (or Potsdam) Conference (July 17–Aug. 2, 1945) President Truman, Premier Stalin, and Prime Minister Clement Attlee of Britain set forth the guiding principles of the Allied Control Council. They were Germany's complete disarmament and demilitarization, destruction of its war potential, rigid control of industry, and decentralization of the political and economic structure. Pending final determination of territorial questions at a peace conference, the three victors agreed in principle to the ultimate transfer of the city of Königsberg (now Kaliningrad) and its adjacent area to the U.S.S.R. and to the administration by Poland of former German territories lying generally east of the Oder-Neisse Line.

For purposes of control Germany was divided in 1945 into four national occupation zones, each headed by a Military Governor.

The Western powers were unable to agree with the U.S.S.R. on any fundamental issue. Work of the Allied Control Council was hamstrung by repeated Soviet vetoes; and finally, on March 20, 1948, Russia walked out of the Council. Meanwhile, the U.S. and Britain had taken steps to merge their zones economically (Bizone); and on May 31, 1948, the U.S., Britain, France, and the Benelux countries agreed to set up a German state comprising the three Western Zones.

The U.S.S.R. reacted by clamping a blockade on all ground communications between the Western Zones and Berlin, an enclave in the Soviet Zone. The Western Allies countered by organizing a gigantic airlift to fly supplies into the beleaguered city, assigning 60,000 men to it. The U.S.S.R. was finally forced to lift the blockade on May 12, 1949.

The Federal Republic of Germany was proclaimed on May 23, 1949, with its capital at Bonn. In free elections, West German voters gave a majority in the Constituent Assembly to the Christian Democrats, with the Social Democrats largely making up the opposition. Konrad Adenauer became chancellor, and Theodor Heuss of the Free Democrats was elected first president.

With admission into the European Coal and Steel Community and later into the Common Market, West Germany prospered. In 1950 a West Berlin Constitution provided for autonomous municipal government and representation in the Bundestag.

Agreements in Paris in 1954 giving the Federal Republic full independence and complete sovereignty came into force on May 5, 1955. Under it, West Germany and Italy became members of the Brussels treaty organization created in 1948 and renamed the Western European Union. West Germany also became a member of NATO. In 1955 the U.S.S.R. recognized the Federal Republic. The Saar territory, under an agreement between France and West Germany, held a plebiscite and despite economic links to France voted to rejoin West Germany. It became a state of West Germany on Jan. 1, 1957.

In 1963, Chancellor Adenauer concluded a treaty of mutual cooperation and friendship with France and then retired. He was succeeded by his chief inner-party critic, Ludwig Erhard, who was followed in 1966 by Kurt Georg Kiesinger. He, in turn, was succeeded in 1969 by Willy Brandt, former mayor of West Berlin.

The division between West Germany and East Germany was intensified when the Communists erected the Berlin Wall in 1961. In 1968, the East German Communist leader, Walter Ulbricht, imposed restrictions on West German movements into West Berlin. The Soviet-bloc invasion of Czechoslovakia in August 1968 added to the tension.

A treaty with the U.S.S.R. was signed in Moscow in August 1970 in which force was renounced and respect for the "territorial integrity" of present European states declared.

Three months later, West Germany signed a similar treaty with Poland, renouncing force and setting Poland's western border as the Oder-Neisse Line. It subsequently resumed formal relations with Czechoslovakia in a pact that "voided" the Munich treaty that gave Nazi Germany the Sudetenland.

Both German states were admitted to the United Nations in 1973.

Brandt, winner of a Nobel Peace Prize for his foreign policies, was forced to resign in 1974 when an East German spy was discovered to be one of his top staff members. Succeeding him was a moderate Social Democrat, Helmut Schmidt.

Rulers of Germany and Prussia

Name	Born	Ruled[1]
KINGS OF PRUSSIA		
Frederick I[2]	1657	1701–1713
Frederick William I	1688	1713–1740
Frederick II the Great	1712	1740–1786
Frederick William II	1744	1786–1797
Frederick William III	1770	1797–1840
Frederick William IV	1795	1840–1861
William I	1797	1861–1871[3]
EMPERORS OF GERMANY		
William I	1797	1871–1888
Frederick III	1831	1888–1888
William II	1859	1888–1918[4]
HEADS OF THE REICH		
Friedrich Ebert[5]	1871	1919–1925
Paul von Hindenburg[5]	1847	1925–1934
Adolf Hitler[6] [7]	1889	1934–1945
Karl Doenitz[6]	1891	1945–1945
GERMAN FEDERAL REPUBLIC (WEST) (PRESIDENTS)		
Theodor Heuss	1884	1949–1959[9]
Heinrich Luebke	1895	1959–1969[8]
Gustav Heinemann[10]	1899	1969–1974
Walter Scheel	1919	1974–1979
Karl Carstens	1914	1979–1984
Richard von Weizsäcker	1920	1984–
GERMAN DEMOCRATIC REPUBLIC (EAST)		
Wilhelm Pieck[5]	1876	1949–1960
Walter Ulbricht[11]	1893	1960–1973
Willi Stoph[12]	1914	1973–1976
Erich Honecker[12]	1912	1976–

1. Year of end of rule is also that of death, unless otherwise indicated. 2. Was Elector of Brandenburg (1688–1701) as Frederick III. 3. Became Emperor of Germany in 1871. 4. Died 1941. 5. President. 6. Führer. 7. Named Chancellor by President Hindenburg in 1933. 8. Died 1972. 9. Died 1963. 10. Died 1976. 11. Chairman of Council of State. Died 1973. 12. Chairman of Council of State.

In 1980, Chancellor Schmidt, campaigning on a tough policy of stationing U.S. nuclear weapons in West Germany despite Soviet threats, won the Oct. 5 contest easily with a new coalition majority of 271.

Schmidt had made an unsuccessful trip to Moscow four months before the vote to urge President Leonid I. Brezhnev to withdraw from Afghanistan. He canceled a scheduled visit to East Germany in August because of the Soviet and East bloc pressure on the Polish labor movement.

At the "big seven" economic summit in Ottawa in July 1981 Schmidt forcefully presented European demands for lower U.S. interest rates, without success. A year later when the eighth economic summit convened at Versailles, he was no more successful despite the serious decline in the German economy. Schmidt staunchly backed U.S. military strategy in Europe nevertheless, staking his political fate on the strategy of placing U.S. nuclear missiles in Germany unless the Soviet Union reduced its arsenal of intermediate missiles.

The chancellor also strongly opposed nuclear freeze proposals and won 2-1 support for his stand at the convention of Social Democrats in April. But the nuclear issue, as well as economic problems, contributed to a Social Democratic defeat in Schmidt's hometown bastion, Hamburg, in which state elections in June put the opposition Christian Democrats in first place. The anti-nuclear "Greens" ran third and the Free Democrats, partners in Schmidt's federal coalition, lost many of their seats. The Free Democrats then deserted the Socialists and joined with the Christian Democrats to unseat Schmidt and install Helmut Kohl as chancellor in 1982.

BERLIN

Status: West Berlin: State of West Germany; East Berlin: capital of East Germany
Governing Mayor, West Berlin: Eberhard Diepgen (1984)
Mayor, East Berlin: Erhard Krack
Area: 340 square miles (West Berlin, 184; East Berlin, 156
Population (est. 1981) 3,036,300 (West Berlin, 1,890, 300; East Berlin, 1,146,000)

Berlin, the capital of prewar Germany, lies entirely within the borders of East Germany. After the war, the city was occupied by the forces of the U.S., Britain, France, and the U.S.S.R. The three western sectors, now known as West Berlin, contain 55% of the area and two thirds of the population.

West Berlin is a state of the Federal Republic of Germany, but supreme authority remains in the hands of the three Western powers in accordance with postwar agreements. The government is composed of the governing mayor, the 11-member Senate (his Cabinet), and the House of Representatives, a popularly elected legislative body that elects the governing mayor and the Senate.

East Berlin is governed by a City Assembly elected by Communist Party members, and a Magistrate (City Council) chosen by the Assembly and headed by the mayor. In violation of the Four Power Agreements, the Soviet Sector has been incorporated into the German Democratic Republic and is now the capital of that country.

Major anti-Communist riots broke out in East Berlin in June 1953 and, since Aug. 13, 1961, the Soviet Sector has been virtually sealed off by a Communist-built wall, 26 1/2 miles (43 km) long, running through the city. It was built to stem the flood of refugees seeking freedom in the West, 200, 000 having fled in 1961 before the wall was erected.

GHANA

Republic of Ghana
Chairman of Provisional National Defense Council: Flight Lt. Jerry Rawlings (1981)
Area: 92,100 sq mi. (238,537 sq km)
Population (est. 1983): 13,367,000 (average annual growth rate: 2.6%)

Density per square mile: 134.6
Capital: Accra
Largest cities (est. 1983): Accra, 1,500,000
Monetary unit: Cedi
Languages: Native tongues (Twi, Fanti, Ga, Ewe, Dagbani); English
Religions: Christian and Islam
Literacy rate (1981): 40% (in English)
Member of Commonwealth of Nations
Economic summary: Gross national product (1981): $9.4 billion. Average annual growth rate (1970–79): –3.0%. Per capita income (1981): $752. Land used for agriculture: 19%; labor force: 60%; principal products: cocoa, timber, coconuts, coffee, subsistence crops, rubber. Labor force in industry: 17%; major products: mining products, lumber, light manufactured goods, fish, aluminum. Natural resources: gold, diamonds, bauxite, manganese, fish. Exports: cocoa beans and products, gold, timber, manganese ore. Imports: textiles and manufactured goods, food, fuels, transport equipment. Major trading partners: U.K., Western European countries, U.S.

Geography. A West African country bordering on the Gulf of Guinea, Ghana has the Ivory Coast to the west, Upper Volta to the north, and Togo to the east. It compares in size to Oregon.

The coastal belt, extending about 270 miles (435 km), is sandy, marshy, and generally exposed. Behind it is a gradually widening grass strip. The forested plateau region to the north is broken by ridges and hills. The largest river is the Volta.

Government. Ghana returned to military rule after two years of constitutional government when Flight Lt. Jerry Rawlings, who led a coup in 1979 and stepped down voluntarily, seized power on Dec. 31, 1981. Rawlings heads a Provisional National Defense Council, which exercises all power.

History. Created an independent country on March 6, 1957, Ghana is the former British colony of the Gold Coast. The area was first seen by Portuguese traders in 1470. They were followed by the English (1553), the Dutch (1595), and the Swedes (1640). British rule over the Gold Coast began in 1820, but it was not until after quelling the severe resistance of the Ashanti in 1901 that it was firmly established. British Togoland, formerly a colony of Germany, was incorporated into Ghana by referendum in 1956. As the result of a plebiscite, Ghana became a republic on July 1, 1960.

Premier Kwame Nkrumah attempted to take leadership of the Pan-African Movement, holding the All-African People's Congress in his capital, Accra, in 1958 and organizing the Union of African States with Guinea and Mali in 1961. But he oriented his country toward the Soviet Union and China and built an autocratic rule over all aspects of Ghanaian life.

In February 1966, while Nkrumah was visiting Peking and Hanoi, he was deposed by a military coup led by Gen. Emmanuel K. Kotoka. The U.S. recognized the new regime and gave it financial aid. In April 1967, a military junta was crushed, but Kotoka was killed. The military leaders took steps to restore civilian rule and a new Constitution was approved in May 1969.

Another military group took over in January 1972. Its leader, Col. Ignatius Acheampong, proclaimed himself Head of State and chairman of the National Redemption Council, which replaced Parliament. The new regime proposed a union government of military, police, and civilian elements in a referendum approved by the voters in March 1978. Before the plan could be implemented, however, Lt. Gen. Frederick W. K. Akuffo of the military governing council ousted Acheampong on July 5. The shift was apparently related to food shortages and Ghana's raging inflation, running at an annual rate of more than 100%.

A military coup led by Flight Lieutenant Jerry Rawlings, imprisoned after an earlier attempt, overthrew Akuffo on June 4, 1979. Rawlings promised that the election of a civilian president would go ahead as scheduled, and Hilla Limann, candidate of the People's National Party, became President-elect in July.

Rawlings, who had been retired from the Air Force by Limann, staged a coup on Dec. 31, 1981, charging the civilian government with corruption and repression. As chairman of the Provisional National Defense Council, Rawlings instituted an austerity program aimed at "total economic independence" by reducing budget deficits and slowing the 116% inflation rate recorded in 1981.

GREECE

Hellenic Republic
President: Constantine Karamanlis (1980)
Premier: Andreas Papandreou (1981)
Area: 50,961 sq mi. (131,990 sq km)
Population (est. 1982): 9,800,000 (average annual growth rate: 0.7%)
Density per square mile: 193.9
Capital: Athens
Largest cities (1981 census): Athens, 855,136; Salonika, 402,443; Patras, 140,878; Larissa, 103,263; Heraklion, 101,668
Monetary unit: Drachma
Language: Greek
Religion: Greek Orthodox
National name: Elliniki Dimokratia
Literacy rate (1981): 90%
Economic summary: Gross national product (1980): $42.2 billion. Average annual growth rate (1970–79): 4.1%. Per capita income (1980): $4,520. Land used for agriculture: 29%; labor force: 31%; principal products: grains, fruits, vegetables, olives, olive oil, tobacco, cotton, livestock, dairy products. Labor force in industry: 30%; major products: textiles, metals, chemicals, electrical equipment, cement, glass. Natural resources: bauxite, lignite, forests. Exports: fruits, minerals, textiles, tobacco. Imports: machinery and automotive equipment, petroleum, consumer goods, chemicals, meat, live animals. Major trading partners: West Germany, Italy, France, Saudi Arabia, U.S.A.

Geography. Greece, on the Mediterranean Sea, is the southernmost country on the Balkan Peninsula in Eastern Europe. It is bordered on the north by Albania, Yugoslavia, and Bulgaria; on the west by the Ionian Sea; and on the east by the Aegean Sea and Turkey. It is slightly smaller than Alabama.

North central Greece, Epirus, and western Macedonia all are mountainous. The main chain of the Pindus Mountains rises to 9,000 feet (2,743 m) in places, separating Epirus from the plains of Thessaly. Mt. Olympus, rising to 9,570 feet (2,909

m) in the north near the Aegean Sea, is the highest point in the country. Greek Thrace is mostly a lowland region separated from European Turkey by the lower Evros River.

Among the many islands are the Ionian group off the west coast; the Cyclades group to the southeast; other islands in the eastern Aegean, including the Dodecanese Islands, Euboea, Lesbos, Samos, and Chios; and Crete, the fourth largest Mediterranean island.

Government. A referendum in December 1974, five months after the collapse of a military dictatorship, ended the Greek monarchy and established a republic. Ceremonial executive power is held by the president; the Premier heads the government and is responsible to a 300-member unicameral Parliament.

The major political parties are the Panhellenic Socialist Movement (172 of 300 seats in Parliment), led by Premier Andreas Papandreou; New Democracy Party (115 seats), led by Evangelos Averoff-Tossiza; and Communist Party (13 seats), led by Harilaos Florakis.

History. Greece, with a recorded history going back to 766 B.C., reached the peak of its glory in the 5th century B.C., and by the middle of the 2nd century B.C., it had declined to the status of a Roman province. It remained within the Eastern Roman Empire until Constantinople fell to the Crusaders in 1204.

In 1453, the Turks took Constantinople, and by 1460 Greece was a Turkish province. The insurrection made famous by the poet Lord Byron broke out in 1821, and in 1827 Greece won independence with sovereignty guaranteed by Britain, France, and Russia.

The protecting powers chose Prince Otto of Bavaria as the first king of modern Greece in 1832 to reign over an area only slightly larger than the Peloponnese Peninsula. Chiefly under the next king, George I, chosen by the protecting powers in 1863, Greece acquired much of its present territory. During his 57-year reign, a period in which he encouraged parliamentary democracy, Thessaly, Epirus, Macedonia, Crete, and most of the Aegean islands were added from the disintegrating Turkish empire. An unsuccessful war against Turkey after World War I brought down the monarchy, to be replaced by a republic in 1923.

Two military dictatorships and a financial crisis brought George II back from exile, but only until 1941, when Italian and German invaders defeated tough Greek resistance. After British and Greek troops liberated the country in October 1944, Communist guerrillas staged a long campaign in which the government received U.S. aid under the Truman Doctrine, the predecessor of the Marshall Plan.

A military junta seized power in April 1967, sending young King Constantine II into exile December 14. Col. George Papadopoulos, as premier, converted the government to republican form in 1973 and as President ended martial law. He was moving to restore democracy when he was ousted in November of that year by his military colleagues. The regime of the "colonels," which had tortured its opponents and scoffed at human rights, resigned July 23, 1974, after having bungled an attempt to seize Cyprus.

Former Premier Karamanlis returned from exile to become premier of Greece's first civilian government since 1967. The election in November gave him 54% backing, and a new republican Constitution was adopted June 7, 1975.

Greece cut its military ties with the North Atlantic Treaty Organization in 1974 because of U.S. failure to restrain Turkey from invading Cyprus. It was not until Oct. 20, 1980, that Greece returned as a military partner in NATO, even then with some public protest. A lengthy dispute with Turkey over air and sea rights in the Aegean advanced toward settlement with the return to the alliance.

On Jan. 1, 1981, Greece became the 10th member of the European Community. On Oct. 18, the first Socialist government in Greek history won power, and the new Premier, Andreas Papandreou, immediately called for the removal of U.S. bases and threatened to end Greek military participation in NATO because of the alliance's alleged failure to guarantee Greek borders adjoining Turkey. By May 1982, however, Papandreou had retreated from his stand. In July 1983, an agreement was reached with the Greek government to allow the U.S. bases to remain for another five years.

GRENADA

State of Grenada
Sovereign: Queen Elizabeth II
Governor General: Paul Scoon (1978)
Prime Minister: to be elected
Area: 133 sq mi. (344 sq km)
Population (est. 1982): 110,000 (black, 84%; mixed, 11%) (average annual growth rate, 1.0%)
Density per square mile: 827.1
Capital and largest city (est. 1980): St. George's, 32,000
Monetary unit: East Caribbean dollar
Ethnic groups: Caribs and Indians
Language: English
Religions: Roman Catholic, 64%; Anglican, 22%
Member of Commonwealth of Nations
Literacy rate: Not known
Economic summary: Gross national product (1980): $80 million. Average annual growth rate (1970–79): –1.3%. Per capita income (1980): $690. Land used for agriculture: 44%; labor force: 40%; principal products: spices, cocoa, bananas. Exports: nutmeg, cocoa beans, bananas, mace. Imports: foodstuffs, machinery, building materials. Major trading partners: U.K., West Indies countries, West Germany, Netherlands, U.S.

Geography. Grenada (the first "a" is pronounced as in "gray") is the most southerly of the Windward Islands, about 100 miles (161 km) from the South American coast. It is a volcanic island traversed by a mountain range, the highest peak of which is Mount St. Catherine (2,756 ft.; 840 m).

History. Grenada was discovered by Columbus in 1498. After more than 200 years of British rule, most recently as part of the West Indies Associated States, it became independent Feb. 7, 1974, with Eric M. Gairy as Prime Minister.

The government of Prime Minister Gairy was ousted March 13, 1979, by the New Jewel Movement of Maurice Bishop. Bishop, a protégé of Cuban President Fidel Castro, invited Cuban military advisers to Grenada and on June 20, 1980, called on Grenadians to join a "people's militia" to fight a "people's war" against imperialism.

Bishop was killed in a military coup on Oct. 19, 1983. At the request five members of the Organization of Eastern Caribbean States, President Reagan ordered an invasion of Grenada on Oct. 25 involving over 1,900 U.S. troops and a small military force from Barbados, Dominica, Jamaica, St. Lucia, and St. Vincent. The troops met strong resistance from Cuban military personnel on the island. Reagan said he ordered the invasion to protect some 1,000 American citizens on the island, and to help restore democratic institutions in that country. New elections were promised before the end of 1984.

GUATEMALA

Republic of Guatemala
President: Gen. Oscar Mejía Victores (1983)
Area: 42,042 sq mi. (108,889 sq km)
Population (est. 1982): 7,700,000 (average annual growth rate: 3.1%)
Density per square mile: 183.2
Capital and largest city (est. 1982): Guatemala City, 1, 250,000
Monetary unit: Quetzal
Languages: Spanish, Indian dialects
Religion: Roman Catholic
National name: República de Guatemala
Literacy rate (1981): 30%
Economic summary: Gross national product (1981): $8.8 billion. Average annual growth rate (1975–80) 5.7%. Per capita income (1981) $1,114. Land used for agriculture: 14%; labor force. 53%; principal products: corn, beans, coffee, cotton, cattle, sugar, bananas, essential oils, timber. Labor force in industry: 12%; principal products: prepared foods, textiles, construction materials, tires, pharmaceuticals. Natural resources: nickel, timber, shrimp. Exports: coffee, cotton, sugar, meat,.bananas. Imports: manufactured products, machinery, transportation equipment, chemicals, fuels. Major trading partners: U.S., Central American nations, West Germany, Japan, Venezuela.

Geography. The northernmost of the Central American nations, Guatemala is the size of Tennessee. Its neighbors are Mexico on the north, west, and east and Belize, Honduras, and El Salvador on the east. The country consists of two main regions—the cool highlands with the heaviest population and the tropical area along the Pacific and Caribbean coasts. The principal mountain range rises to the highest elevation in Central America and contains many volcanic peaks. Volcanic eruptions are frequent.

The Petén region in the north contains important resources and archaeological sites of the Mayan civilization.

Government. The Constitution was suspended and political parties banned by a military junta that seized power on March 23, 1982. Gen. Oscar Majía Victores seized power in a palace coup in August 1983.

History. Once the site of the ancient Mayan civilization, Guatemala, conquered by Spain in 1524, set itself up as a republic in 1839. From 1898 to 1920, the dictator Manuel Estrada Cabrera ran the country, and from 1931 to 1944, Gen. Jorge Ubico Castaneda was the strongman. In 1944 the National Assembly elected Gen. Federico Ponce president, but he was overthrown in October. In December, Dr. Juan José Arévalo was elected as the head of a leftist regime that continued to press its reform program. Jacobo Arbenz Guzmán, administration candidate with pro-Communist leanings, won the 1950 elections.

Arbenz expropriated the large estates, including plantations of the United Fruit Company, and exterminated his political enemies. With covert U.S. backing, a revolt was led by Col. Carlos Castillo Armas, and Arbenz took refuge in Havana. Castillo Armas became president but was assassinated in 1957. Constitutional government was restored in 1958, and Gen. Miguel Ydigoras Fuentes was elected president. He was host to the Cuban force that trained for the disastrous landing at the Bay of Pigs in April 1961.

In 1963 the Ydigoras government was overthrown by Enrique Peralta Azurdia, who ruled until 1966, when elections, under a new Constitution, led to Congress's choice of Dr. Julio César Méndez Montenegro.

A wave of terrorism, by left and right, began in 1967, and in August 1968 U.S. Ambassador John Gordon Mein was killed when he resisted kidnappers. Fear of anarchy led to the election in 1970 of Army Chief of Staff Carlos Araña Osorio, who had put down a rural guerrilla movement at the cost of nearly 3,000 lives. Araña, surprisingly, pledged social reforms when he took office. Another military candidate, Gen. Kjell Laugerud, won the presidency in 1974 amid renewed political violence.

A devastating earthquake on Feb. 4, 1976, killed 22,000 and injured 74,000, doing little damage to the country's growing industrial base, however.

The administration of Gen. Romeo Lucas Garcia, elected president in 1978, ended in a coup by a three-man military junta on March 23, 1982. Lucas Garcia was charged by Amnesty International with responsibility for at least 5,000 political murders in a reign of brutality and corruption that brought a cutoff of U.S. military aid in 1978. Hopes for improvement under the junta faded when Gen. José Efraín Ríos Montt took sole power in June and declared a state of siege on July 1 to pursue a war of extermination against the newly unified leftist guerrillas. Amid reports of massacres, thousands of Guatemalans sought refuge in Mexico.

President Oscar Mejía Victores, another general, seized power from Rios Montt in an August 1983 coup and pledged to turn over power to an elected civilian President in 1985. A constituent assembly was elected on July 1, 1984, to write a new Constitution.

GUINEA

Revolutionary People's Republic of Guinea
President: Ahmed Sékou Touré (1958)
Premier: Louis Lansana Béavogui (1972)
Area: 94,925 sq mi. (245,857 sq km)
Population (est. 1982): 5,300,000 (average annual growth rate: 1.9%)
Density per square mile: 55.8
Capital and largest city (est. 1980): Conakry, 765,000
Monetary unit: Syli
Languages: French (official), native tongues (Malinké, Susu, Fulani)
Religions: Islam, 69%; Animist, 30%
National name: République Populaire Revolutionnaire de Guinée
Literacy rate (1981): 20%
Economic summary: Gross national product (1980): $1.6 billion. Average annual growth rate (1970–79): 0.6%.

Per capita income (1980): $290. Principal agricultural products: rice, cassava, millet, corn, coffee, bananas, palm products, pineapples. Major industrial products: bauxite, alumina, light manufactured and processed goods. Natural resources: bauxite, iron ore, diamonds, gold, water power. Exports: bauxite, alumina, pineapples, bananas, coffee. Imports: petroleum, machinery, transport equipment, foodstuffs, textiles. Major trading partners: Communist bloc, Western Europe, U.S.

Geography. Guinea, in West Africa on the Atlantic, is also bordered by Guinea-Bissau, Senegal, Mali, the Ivory Coast, Liberia, and Sierra Leone. Slightly smaller than Oregon, the country consists of a coastal plain, a mountainous region, a savanna interior, and a forest area in the Guinea Highlands. The highest peak is Mount Nimba at about 6,000 feet (1,829 m).

Government. The National Assembly has 150 members elected by universal suffrage from a list prepared and presented by the Parti Démocratique de Guinée, the only political party, led by President Ahmed Sékou Touré, Secretary General of the party.

History. Previously part of French West Africa, Guinea achieved independence by rejecting the new French Constitution, and on Oct. 2, 1958, became an independent state with Sékou Touré as president. Touré led the country into being the first avowedly Marxist state in Africa. Diplomatic relations with France were suspended in 1965, with the Soviet Union replacing France as the country's chief source of economic and technical assistance.

In 1966, when a Ghanaian military coup deposed Kwame Nkrumah as President, Touré welcomed him to Guinea and declared him joint president and party leader. The titles proved to be only honorary. Touré accused Ghana of being an American imperialist puppet, and the U.S. Embassy in his capital, Conakry, was sacked. In retaliation the United States ended financial aid. An exchange of letters between the Guinean and U.S. presidents restored relations.

Prosperity came in 1969 after the start of exploitation of bauxite deposits. Touré was re-elected to a seven-year term in 1974 and again in 1981.

GUINEA-BISSAU

Republic of Guinea-Bissau
President of Revolutionary Council: Joao Bernardo Vieira (1980)
Area: 13,948 sq mi. (36,125 sq km)
Population (est. 1982): 768,000 (average annual growth rate: 2.2%)
Density per square mile: 42.3
Capital and largest city (est. 1980): Bissau, 110,000
Monetary unit: Guinea-Bissau peso
Language: Portugese
Religions: Animist, 52%; Islam, 38%; Christian, 10%
National name: Guiné Bissau
Literacy rate (1981): 5%
Economic summary: Gross national product (1980): $130 million. Average annual growth rate (1970–78): 2.9%. Per capita income (1980): $160. Labor force in agriculture: 90%; principal products: palm oil, root crops, rice, coconuts, peanuts. Natural resources: potential bauxite deposits. Exports: peanuts, coconuts, shrimp. fish, wood. Imports: foodstuffs, manufactured goods, fuels, transportation equipment. Major trading partner: Portugal.

Geography. A neighbor of Senegal and Guinea in West Africa, on the Atlantic coast, Guinea-Bissau is about half the size of South Carolina.

The country is a low-lying coastal region of swamps, rain forests, and mangrove-covered wetlands, with about 25 islands off the coast. The Bijagos archipelago extends 30 miles (48 km) out to sea. Internal communications depend mainly on deep estuaries and meandering rivers, since there are no railroads. Bissau, the capital, is the main port.

Government. After the overthrow of Louis Cabral in November 1980, the nine-member Council of the Revolution formed an interm government. In 1982, they formed a new government consisting of the President, the Prime Minister, 13 ministers, 2 vice-ministers, and 5 state secretaries.

History. Guinea-Bissau was discovered in 1446 by the Portuguese Nuno Tristao, and colonists in the Cape Verde Islands obtained trading rights in the territory. In 1879 the connection with the Cape Verde Islands was broken. Early in the 1900s the Portuguese managed to pacify some tribesmen, although resistance to colonial rule remained.

The African Party for the Independence of Guinea-Bissau and Cape Verde was founded in 1956 and several years later began guerrilla warfare that grew increasingly effective. By 1974 the rebels controlled most of the countryside, where they formed a government that was soon recognized by scores of countries. The military coup in Portugal in April 1974 brightened the prospects for freedom, and in August the Lisbon government signed an agreement granting independence to the province as of Sept. 10. The new republic took the name Guinea-Bissau. Its government was immediately recognized by the United States.

In November 1980, Prémier Joao Bernardo Vieira headed a coup that deposed Luis Cabral, President since 1974. A Revolutionary Council assumed the powers of government, with Vieira as its head.

GUYANA

Cooperative Republic of Guyana
President: Forbes Burnham (1980)
Prime Minister: Ptolemy A. Reid (1980)
Area: 83,000 sq mi. (214,969 sq km)
Population (est. 1982): 925,000 (average annual growth rate: 1.5%) (East Indian, 50%; African, 31%; mixed 10%; Amerindian, 5%)
Density per square mile: 11.1
Capital and largest city (est. 1981): Georgetown, 200,000
Monetary unit: Guyana dollar
Languages: English (official), Hindi, Urdu
Religions: Hindu, 34%; Protestant, 34%; Islam, 9%; Roman Catholic, 8%
Member of Commonwealth of Nations
Literacy rate (1981): 86%
Economic summary: Gross national product (1980): $550 million. Average annual growth rate (1970–79): 0.0%. Per capita income (1980): $690. Labor force in agriculture: 29%; principal products: sugar, rice. Labor force in industry: 31%; major products: bauxite, alumina. Natural resources: bauxite, gold, diamonds, hardwood timber, shrimp. Exports: sugar, bauxite, alumina, rice,

shrimp. Imports: consumer and manufactured goods. Major trading partners: U.K., U.S., Caribbean nations.

Geography. Guyana is situated on the northern coast of South America east of Venezuela, west of Suriname, and north of Brazil. The country consists of a low coastal area and the Guiana Highlands in the south. There is an extensive north-south network of rivers. Guyana is the size of Idaho.

Government. Guyana, formerly British Guiana, proclaimed itself a republic on Feb. 23, 1970, ending its tie with Britain while remaining in the Commonwealth.

Guyana has a unicameral legislature, the National Assembly, with 53 members directly elected for five-year terms and 12 elected by local councils. A 24-member Cabinet is headed by the President.

The major political parties are the People's National Congress (41 of 53 seats in National Assembly), led by President Forbes Burnham; People's Progressive Party (10 seats), led by Dr. Cheddi B. Jagan.

History. British Guiana won internal self-government in 1952. The next year the People's Progressive Party, headed by Cheddi B. Jagan, an East Indian dentist, won the elections and Jagan became Prime Minister. British authorities deposed him for alleged Communist connections. A coalition ousted Jagan in 1964, installing a moderate Socialist, Forbes Burnham, a black, as Prime Minister. On May 26, 1966, the country became an independent member of the Commonwealth and resumed its traditional name, Guyana.

The government nationalized mining operations of the U.S.-owned Reynolds Metals Co. in 1975.

In 1978, the International Monetary Fund approved an $18.7-million loan for Guyana, which is trying to overcome a $60-million deficit in balance of payments.

One of the most bizarre incidents in modern history occurred when 911 persons died in a mass murder-suicide on Nov. 19, 1978, at a remote settlement in Guyana founded by a U.S. sect known as the People's Temple. The victims were either shot or forced to drink poisoned Kool-Aid by the Rev. Jim Jones, for whom the site, Jonestown, was named.

Jones ordered his followers to die after his aides had killed U.S. Representative Leo J. Ryan of California and three newsmen who accompanied Ryan on an investigative trip to the colony.

HAITI

Republic of Haiti
Life President: Jean-Claude Duvalier (1971)
Area: 10,714 sq mi. (27,750 sq km)
Population (est. 1983): 5,666,000 (average annual growth rate: 2.0%)
Density per square mile: 485.3
Capital and largest city (est. 1980): Port-au-Prince, 790,000
Monetary unit: Gourde
Languages: French, Creole
Religion: Roman Catholic
National name: République d'Haïti
Literacy rate (1981): 12%
Economic summary: Gross national product (1982): $1.6 billion. Average annual growth rate (1970–79): 1.8%. Per capita income (1980): $270. Land used for agriculture: 31%; labor force: 79%; principal products: coffee, sugar cane, rice, corn, sorghum. Labor force in industry: 7%; major products: refined sugar, textiles, flour, cement, bauxite, light assembly products. Natural resource: bauxite. Exports: coffee, light industrial products, bauxite, sugar, essential oils, sisal. Imports: consumer goods, foodstuffs, industrial equipment, petroleum products, construction materials. Major trading partner: U.S.

Geography. Haiti, in the West Indies, occupies the western third of the island of Hispaniola, which it shares with the Dominican Republic. About the size of Maryland, Haiti is two thirds mountainous, with the rest of the country marked by great valleys, extensive plateaus, and small plains. The most densely populated region is the Cul-de-Sac plain near Port-au-Prince.

Government. In 1964, the late President, François Duvalier, known as "Papa Doc," made himself president for life. His son, Jean-Claude, then 19, known as "Baby Doc," inherited the title on his father's death on April 21, 1971. Under a Constitution revised in 1964, the president in periods of crisis may dismiss the National Assembly and Cabinet and govern by decree. The Parti d'Unité Nationale (57 of the 58 seats in the National Assembly), led by President Duvalier, is the only legal party in the country.

History. Discovered by Columbus, who landed at Môle Saint Nicolas on Dec. 6, 1492, Haiti in 1697 became a French possession known as Saint Domingue. An insurrection among a slave population of 500,000 in 1791 ended with a declaration of independence by Pierre-Dominique Toussaint l'Ouverture in 1801. Napoleon Bonaparte suppressed the independence movement, but it eventually triumphed in 1804 under Jean-Jacques Dessalines, who gave the new nation the aboriginal name Haiti.

Its prosperity dissipated in internal strife as well as disputes with neighboring Santo Domingo during a succession of 19th-century dictatorships, a bankrupt Haiti accepted a U.S. customs receivership from 1905 to 1941. Direct U.S. rule from 1915 to 1930 brought a measure of stability and a population growth that made Haiti the most densely populated nation in the hemisphere.

In 1949, after four years of democratic rule by President Dumarsais Estimé, dictatorship returned under Gen. Paul Magloire, who was succeeded by François Duvalier in 1957.

Duvalier established a dictatorship based on secret police, known as the "Ton-ton Macoutes," who gunned down opponents of the regime. Duvalier's son, Jean-Claude, or "Baby Doc," succeeded his father in 1971 as ruler of the poorest nation in the Western Hemisphere.

Limited economic improvement followed an increase in foreign investment under the new regime as 150 foreign companies established Haitian branches to take advantage of low wages. A steady exodus of refugees continued toward the United States, reaching a high of 15,000 in 1980. Previously denied refugee status, Haitian "boat people" were accorded the same temporary entrance rights as Cubans who arrived by boat.

On May 27, 1980, Duvalier married Michelle Bennett in a wedding attended by 5,000 guests and estimated to cost from $3 million to $5 million.

HONDURAS

Republic of Honduras
President: Dr. Roberto Suazo Córdova (1982)
Area: 43,277 sq mi. (112,088 sq km)
Population (est. 1982): 4,129,000 (average annual growth rate: 3.9%) (60% mestizo)
Density per square mile: 91.3
Capital and largest city (est. 1982): Tegucigalpa, 533,600
Monetary unit: Lempira
Languages: Spanish, some Indian dialects, English in Bay Islands Department
Religion: Roman Catholic
National name: República de Honduras
Literacy rate (1970): 59%
Economic summary: Gross national product (1982): $2.6 billion. Average annual growth rate (1981–82): 4.7%. Per capita income (1982): $744. Labor force in agriculture: 59%; principal products: bananas, coffee, corn, beans, cotton, sugar cane, tobacco. Labor force in industry: 14%; major products: processed agricultural products, textiles and clothing, wood products. Natural resources: timber, gold, silver, lead, zinc, antimony. Exports: bananas, coffee, lumber, meat, petroleum products. Imports: manufactured goods, machinery, transportation equipment, chemicals, petroleum. Major trading partners: U.S., Caribbean countries, West Germany, Venezuela, Japan, Spain, Netherlands.

Geography. Honduras, in the north central part of Central America, has a 400-mile (644-km) Caribbean coastline and a 40-mile (64-km) Pacific frontage. Its neighbors are Guatemala to the west, El Salvador to the south, and Nicaragua to the east. Honduras is slightly larger than Tennessee.

Generally mountainous, the country is marked by fertile plateaus, river valleys, and narrow coastal plains.

Government. The elected President, Roberto Suazo Córdova, ended a decade of military rule when he took office on Jan. 29, 1982.

History. Columbus discovered Honduras on his last voyage in 1502. Honduras, with four other countries of Central America, declared its independence from Spain in 1821 and was part of a federation of Central American states until 1838. In that year it seceded from the federation and became a completely independent country.

U.S. Marines intervened in 1903 and 1923. In 1931, 1932, and 1937, major revolutions were crushed by force.

In July 1969, El Salvador invaded Honduras after Honduran landowners had deported several thousand Salvadorans. The fighting left 1,000 dead and tens of thousands homeless. By threatening economic sanctions and military intervention, the OAS induced El Salvador to withdraw.

Although parliamentary democracy returned with the election of Roberto Suazo Córdova as President in 1982 after a decade of military rule, Honduras faced severe economic problems and tensions along its border with Nicaragua. An estimated 12,000 "contra" rebels, waging a guerrilla war against the Sandinista regime in Nicaragua, used Honduras as a training and staging area. At the same time, the United States used Honduras as a site for military exercises and built bases to train both Honduran and Salvadoran troops. Honduras received $125 million in U.S. economic and military aid in 1984.

HUNGARY

Hungarian People's Republic
President: Pál Losonczi (1967)
Premier: Gyorgy Lazar (1975)
Area: 35,919 sq mi. (93,030 sq km)
Population (est. 1982): 10,725,000 (average annual growth rate: 0.0%)
Density per square mile: 298.6
Capital: Budapest
Largest cities (est. 1982): Budapest, 2,100,000; Miskolc, 225,000; Debrecen, 215,000; Szeged, 200,000; Pécs, 195,000; Györ, 150,000
Monetary unit: Forint
Language: Magyar
Religions: Roman Catholic, 54%; Protestant, 22%; atheist, 7%
National name: Magyar Népköztársaság
Literacy rate (1981): 97%
Economic summary: Gross national product (1981): $22.5 billion. Average annual growth rate (1975–80): 4%. Per capita income (1980): $4,180. Land used for agriculture: 75%; labor force: 20%; principal products: corn, wheat, potatoes, sugar beets, vegetables, wine grapes, fruits. Labor force in industry: 33%; major products: precision and measuring equipment, pharmaceuticals, textiles, transport equipment. Natural resources: some bauxite and brown coal. Exports: machinery and tools, industrial and consumer goods, raw materials. Imports: machinery, raw materials. Major trading partners: U.S.S.R., Warsaw Pact countries, West Germany, Yugoslavia, Austria, and Italy.

Geography. This central European country the size of Indiana is bordered by Austria to the west, Czechoslovakia to the north, the U.S.S.R. and Romania to the east, and Yugoslavia to the south.

Most of Hungary is a fertile, rolling plain lying east of the Danube River and drained by the Danube and Tisza rivers. In the extreme northwest is the Little Hungarian Plain. South of that area is Lake Balaton (250 sq mi.; 648 sq km).

Government. Hungary is a People's Republic with legislative power vested in the unicameral National Assembly, whose 352 members are elected directly for four-year terms. The supreme body of state power is the 21-member Presidential Council elected by the National Assembly. The supreme administrative body is the Council of Ministers, headed by the Premier.

The Hungarian Socialist Workers (Communist) Party, led by János Kádár, is the only political party.

History. About 2,000 years ago, Hungary was part of the Roman provinces of Pannonia and Dacia. In A.D. 896 it was invaded by the Magyars, who founded a kingdom. Christianity was accepted during the reign of Stephen I (St. Stephen) (997–1038).

The peak of Hungary's great period of medieval power came during the reign of Louis I the Great (1342–82), whose dominions touched the Baltic, Black, and Mediterranean seas.

War with the Turks broke out in 1389, and for more than 100 years the Turks advanced through the Balkans. When the Turks smashed a Hungarian army in 1526, western and northern Hungary accepted Hapsburg rule to escape Turkish occupation. Transylvania became independent under Hungarian princes. Intermittent war with the Turks was waged until a peace treaty was signed in 1699.

After the suppression of the 1848 revolt against Hapsburg rule, led by Louis Kossuth, the dual monarchy of Austria-Hungary was set up in 1867.

The dual monarchy was defeated with the other Central Powers in World War I. After a short-lived republic in 1918, the chaotic Communist rule of 1919 under Béla Kun ended with the Romanians occupying Budapest on Aug. 4, 1919. When the Romanians left, Adm. Nicholas Horthy entered the capital with a national army. The Treaty of Trianon of June 4, 1920, cost Hungary 68% of its land and 58% of its population. Meanwhile, the National Assembly had restored the legal continuity of the old monarchy; and, on March 1, 1920, Horthy was elected Regent.

Following the German invasion of Russia on June 22, 1941, Hungary joined the attack against the Soviet Union, but the war was not popular and Hungarian troops were almost entirely withdrawn from the eastern front by May 1943. German occupation troops set up a puppet government after Horthy's appeal for an armistice with advancing Soviet troops on Oct. 15, 1944, had resulted in his overthrow. The German regime soon fled the capital, however, and on December 23 a provisional government was formed in Soviet-occupied eastern Hungary. On Jan. 20, 1945, it signed an armistice in Moscow. Early the next year, the National Assembly approved a constitutional law abolishing the thousand-year-old monarchy and establishing a republic.

By the Treaty of Paris (1947), Hungary had to give up all territory it had acquired since 1937 and to pay $300 million reparations to the U.S.S.R., Czechoslovakia, and Yugoslavia. In 1948 the Communist Party, with the support of Soviet troops seized control. Hungary was proclaimed a People's Republic and one-party state in 1949. Industry was nationalized, the land collectivized into state farms, and the opposition terrorized by the secret police.

The terror, modeled after that of the U.S.S.R., reached its height with the trial of Jozsef Cardinal Mindszenty, Roman Catholic primate. He confessed to fantastic charges under duress of drugs or brainwashing and was sentenced to life imprisonment in 1949. Protests were voiced in all parts of the world.

On Oct. 23, 1956, anti-Communist revolution broke out in Budapest. To cope with it, the Communists set up a coalition government and called former Premier Imre Nagy back to head it. But he and most of his ministers were swept by the logic of events into the anti-Communist opposition, and he declared Hungary a neutral power, withdrawing from the Warsaw Treaty and appealing to the United Nations for help.

One of his ministers, János Kádár, established a counter-regime and asked the U.S.S.R. to send in military power. Soviet troops and tanks suppressed the revolution in bloody fighting after 190,000 people had fled the country and Mindszenty, freed from jail, had taken refuge in the U.S. Embassy. By treachery, Nagy and some of his ministers were abducted by the Soviet occupation troops and executed.

Kádár was succeeded as Premier, but not party secretary, by Gyula Kallai in 1965. Continuing his program of national reconciliation, Kádár emptied prisons, reformed the secret police, and eased travel restrictions.

Hungary developed the reputation of being the freest East European state, with Kádár's new motto—"If you're not against us, you're with us"—replacing previous police state suspicions. Significant Western capitalist investment was welcomed and some capitalistic methods embraced.

After 15 years' asylum in the U.S. Embassy, Mindszenty, under an agreement between the Vatican and the Hungarian regime, was allowed to travel into exile to Rome in 1971. In a move applauded by Kádár, Pope Paul VI removed Mindszenty from his honorary post as Primate of Hungary in 1974. The Cardinal died in Vienna in 1975.

Relations with the U.S. improved in 1972 when World War II debt claims between the two nations were settled. On Jan. 6, 1978, the U.S. returned to Hungary, over anti-Communist protests, the 977-year-old crown of St. Stephen, held at Fort Knox since World War II.

ICELAND

Republic of Iceland
President: Vigdis Finnbogadottir (1980)
Prime Minister: Steingrimur Hermannsson (1983)
Area: 39,709 sq mi. (102,846 sq km)
Population (est. 1982): 235,000 (average annual growth rate: 1.0%)
Density per square mile: 5.9[1]
Capital and largest city (est. 1982): Reykjavik, 85,700
Monetary unit: New króna
Language: Icelandic
Religion: Evangelical Lutheran
National name: Lydveldid Island
Literacy rate (1981): 99%
Economic summary: Gross national product (1980): $2.6 billion. Average annual growth rate (1977–81): 3.9%. Per capita income (1980): $11,330. Labor force in agriculture: 7.9%; fishing and fish processing: 14.6%; principal agricultural products: livestock, hay, fodder, cheese. Labor force in industry: 29%; major products: processed aluminum, fish. Natural resources: fish, diatomite, hydroelectric and geothermal power. Exports: fish, animal products, aluminum. Imports: petroleum products, machinery and transportation equipment, petroleum, food, textiles. Major trading partners: U.S., U.S.S.R., Western European countries.

1. Including some offshore islands.

Geography. Iceland, a bleak island about the size of Kentucky, lies in the north Atlantic Ocean east of Greenland and just touches the Arctic Circle. It is one of the most volcanic regions in the world.

Small fresh-water lakes are to be found throughout the island, and there are many natural phenomena, including hot springs, geysers, sulfur beds, canyons, waterfalls, and swift rivers. More than 13% of the area is covered by snowfields and glaciers, and most of the people live in the 7% of the island comprising fertile coastlands.

Government. The president is elected for four years by popular vote. Executive power resides in the prime minister and his Cabinet. The Althing (Parliament) is composed of 60 members in two houses. They elect 20 of themselves to constitute the Upper House, the remaining 40 representing the Lower House.

The major political parties are the Independence Party (23 of 60 seats in the Althing), led by Thorsteinn Pálsson; Progressive Party (14 seats), led by Steingrimur Hermannsson; People's Alliance (10 seats), led by Svavar Gestsson; Social

Democratic Party (6 seats), led by Kjartan Jóhannsson; Social Democratic Alliance (4 seats), and the Women's League (3 seats). Prime Minister Steingrimur Hermannsson of the Progressives leads a coalition of his party and the Independence Party.

History. Iceland was first settled shortly before 900, mainly by Norse. A Constitution drawn up about 930 created a form of democracy and provided for an Althing, or General Assembly.

In 1262–64, Iceland came under Norwegian rule and passed to ultimate Danish control through the formation of the Union of Kalmar in 1483. In 1874, Icelanders obtained their own Constitution. In 1918, Denmark recognized Iceland as a separate state with unlimited sovereignty but still nominally under the Danish king.

On June 17, 1944, after a popular referendum, the Althing proclaimed Iceland an independent republic.

The British occupied Iceland in 1940, immediately after the German invasion of Denmark. In 1942, the U.S. took over the burden of protection. Iceland refused to abandon its neutrality in World War II and thus forfeited charter membership in the United Nations, but it cooperated with the Allies throughout the conflict. Iceland joined the North Atlantic Treaty Organization in 1949.

Iceland unilaterally extended its territorial waters from 12 to 50 nautical miles in 1972, precipitating a running dispute with Britain known as the "cod war." Icelandic warships harassed British trawlers, which then received aid from British gunboats; some trawlers were shelled, and Icelandic and British warships collided in 1973. The World Court ruled in 1974 and that the 50-mile limit could not be applied unilaterally, but Iceland rejected the ruling.

An agreement calling for registration of all British trawlers fishing within 200 miles of Iceland and a 24-hour time limit on incursions was finally reached in 1976.

INDIA

Republic of India
President: Giani Zail Singh (1982)
Prime Minister: Indira Gandhi (1980)
Area: 1,229,737 sq mi. (3,185,019 sq km)
Population (1983): 740,000,000 (average annual growth rate: 2.2%)
Density per square mile: 569.2
Capital (1980 census): New Delhi, 619,417
Largest cities (1980 census): Calcutta, 9,165,650; Greater Bombay, 8,202,759; Delhi, 6,196,414; Madras, 4,276,635; Bangalore, 2,913,537; Ahmedabad, 2,515,195; Kanpur, 1,685,308
Monetary unit: Rupee
Principal languages; Hindi (official), Bengali, Sindhi, Gujarati, Kannarese, Kashmiri, Malayalam, Marathi, Oriya, Punjabi, Tamil, Telugu, Urdu, Kannada, Assamese (all recognized by the Constitution)
Religions: Hindu, 83%; Islam, 11%; Christian, 3%; Sikh, 2%
National name: Bharat
Literacy rate (1981): 36%
Member of Commonwealth of Nations
Economic summary: Gross national product (1980): $159.4 billion. Average annual growth rate (1970–80): 4.2%. Per capita income (1981): $260. Land used for agriculture: 50%; labor force: 70%; principal products: rice, wheat, oilseeds, cotton, tea. Major industrial products: jute, processed food, steel, machinery, transport machinery, cement. Natural resources: Iron ore, coal, manganese, mica, bauxite, limestone. Exports: engineering goods, textiles and clothing, tea. Imports: machinery and transport equipment, petroleum, edible oils, fertilizers. Major trading partners: U.S., U.K., U.S.S.R., Japan.

Geography. One third the area of the United States, the Republic of India occupies most of the subcontinent of India in south Asia. It borders on China in the northeast. Other neighbors are Pakistan on the west. Nepal and Bhutan on the north, and Burma and Bangladesh on the east.

The country contains a large part of the great Indo-Gangetic plain, which extends from the Bay of Bengal on the east to the Afghan frontier on the Arabian Sea on the west. This plain is the richest and most densely settled part of the subcontinent. Another distinct natural region is the Deccan, a plateau of 2,000 to 3,000 feet (610 to 914 m) in elevation, occupying the southern portion of the subcontinent.

Forming a part of the republic are several groups of islands—the Laccadives (14 islands) in the Arabian Sea and the Andamans (204 islands) and the Nicobars (19 islands) in the Bay of Bengal.

India's three great river systems, all rising in the Himalayas, have extensive deltas. The Ganges flows south and then east for 1,540 miles (2,478 km) across the northern plain to the Bay of Bengal; part of its delta, which begins 220 miles (354 km) from the sea, is within the republic. The Indus, starting in Tibet, flows northwest for several hundred miles in the Kashmir before turning southwest toward the Arabian Sea; it is important for irrigation in Pakistan. The Brahmaputra, also rising in Tibet, flows eastward, first through India and then south into Bangladesh and the Bay of Bengal.

Government. India is a federal republic. It is also a member of the Commonwealth of Nations, a status defined at the 1949 London Conference of Prime Ministers, by which India recognizes the Queen as head of the Commonwealth. Under the Constitution effective Jan. 26, 1950, India has a parliamentary type of government.

The constitutional head of the state is the President, who is elected every five years. He is advised by the Prime Minister and a Cabinet based on a majority of the bicameral Parliament, which consists of a Council of States (Rajya Sabha), representing the constituent units of the republic and a House of the People (Lok Sabha), elected every five years by universal suffrage.

The major political parties are Congress Party I (351 of 542 seats in the Lok Sabha), led by Prime Minister Indira Gandhi; Lok Dal (secular Janata) Party (41 seats), led by former Prime Minister Charan Singh; Congress II (anti-Gandhi) Party (13 seats); Communist (Marxist independent) Party (35 seats); Communist (pro-Soviet) Party of India (10 seats).

History. The Aryans, or Hindus, who invaded India between 2400 and 1500 B.C. from the northwest found a land already well civilized. Buddhism was founded in the 6th century B.C. and spread through northern India. The earliest exact date in Indian history is 327 B.C., when Alexander the Great invaded India.

In 1526, Moslem invaders founded the great Mogul empire, centered on Delhi, which lasted, at

Political Subdivisions of Republic of India

Subdivisions	Area sq mi.	Population 1981 census
STATES		
Andhra Pradesh	106,052	53,403,619
Assam	30,400	19,902,826
Bihar	67,198	69,823,154
Gujarat	72,154	33,960,905
Haryana	16,670	12,850,902
Himachal Pradesh	10,880	4,237,569
Jammu and Kashmir[1]	85,861	5,981,600
Karnataka	74,122	37,043,451
Kerala	15,003	25,403,217
Madhya Pradesh	171,210	52,131,117
Maharashtra	118,530	62,693,898
Manipur	8,628	1,433,691
Meghalaya	8,700	1,327,874
Nagaland	6,236	773,287
Orissa	60,182	26,272,054
Punjab	21,630	16,609,755
Rajasthan	132,151	34,102,912
Sikkim	2,744	315,682
Tamil Nadu	50,132	48,297,456
Tripura	4,022	2,060,189
Uttar Pradesh	113,452	110,858,019
West Bengal	33,928	54,485,560
UNION TERRITORIES		
Andaman and Nicobar Islands	3,215	188,254
Arunachal Pradesh	31,400	628,050
Chandigath	44	450,061
Dadra and Nagar-Haveli	189	103,677
Delhi	573	6,196,414
Goa, Daman, and Diu	1,619	1,082,117
Lakshadweep	11	40,237
Mizoram	8,100	487,774
Pondicherry	196	604,136

1. Status in dispute with Pakistan.

least in name, until 1857. Akbar the Great (1542–1605) strengthened this empire and became the ruler of a greater portion of India than had ever before acknowledged the suzerainty of one man. The long reign of his great-grandson, Aurangzeb (1658–1707), represents both the culmination of Mogul power and the beginning of its decay.

Vasco da Gama, the Portuguese explorer, visited India first in 1498, and for the next 100 years the Portuguese had a virtual monopoly on trade with the subcontinent. Meanwhile, the English founded the East India Company, which set up its first factory at Surat in 1612 and began expanding its influence, fighting the Indian rulers and the French, Dutch, and Portuguese traders simultaneously.

Bombay, taken from the Portuguese, became the seat of English rule in 1687. The defeat of French and Islamic armies by Lord Clive in the decade ending in 1760 laid the foundation of the British Empire in India. From then until 1858, when the administration of India was formally transferred to the British Crown following the Sepoy Mutiny of native troops in 1857, the East India Company suppressed native uprisings and extended British rule.

After World War I, in which the Indian states sent more than 6 million troops to fight beside the Allies, Indian nationalist unrest rose to new heights under the leadership of a little Hindu lawyer, Mohandas K. Gandhi, called Mahatma Gandhi. His tactics called for nonviolent revolts against British authority. He soon became the leading spirit of the All-India Congress Party, which was the spearhead of revolt. In 1919 the British gave added responsibility to Indian officials, and in 1935 India was given a federal form of government and a measure of self-rule.

In 1942, with the Japanese pressing hard on the eastern borders of India, the British War Cabinet tried and failed to reach a political settlement with nationalist leaders. The Congress Party took the position that the British must quit India. In 1942, fearing mass civil disobedience, the government of India carried out widespread arrests of Congress leaders, including Gandhi.

Gandhi was released in 1944 and negotiations for a settlement were resumed. Finally, in February 1947, the Labor government announced its determination to transfer power to "responsible Indian hands" by June 1948 even if a Constitution had not been worked out.

Lord Mountbatten as Viceroy, by June 1947, achieved agreement on the partitioning of India along religious lines (a plan previously opposed by the predominant Hindus and by Britain) and on the splitting of the provinces of Bengal and the Punjab, which the Moslems had claimed.

The Indian Independence Act, passed quickly by the British Parliament, received royal assent on July 18, 1947, and on August 15 the Indian Empire passed into history.

Jawaharlal Nehru, leader of the Congress Party, was made Prime Minister. Before an exchange of populations could be arranged, bloody riots occurred among the communal groups, and armed conflict broke out over rival claims to the princely state of Jammu and Kashmir. Peace was restored only with the greatest difficulty. In 1949 a Constitution, along the lines of the U.S. Constitution, was approved making India a sovereign republic. Under a federal structure the states were organized on linguistic lines.

The dominance of the Congress Party contributed to stability. In 1956 the republic absorbed the former French settlements. Five years later, it forcibly annexed the Portuguese enclaves of Goa, Damao, and Diu.

Communist China provoked a border dispute in 1957 that proceeded by local skirmishes until Oct. 20, 1962, when the Chinese mounted a massive offensive against Ladakh in the Kashmir and against the North East Frontier Agency. After gaining much territory claimed by India, the

Chinese announced a cease-fire on Nov. 20, 1962.

Nehru died in 1964. His successor, Lal Bahadur Shastri, died on Jan. 10, 1966, a few hours after having concluded talks with President Ayub Khan of Pakistan. Nehru's daughter, Indira Gandhi, became Prime Minister, and she continued his policy of nonalignment.

In 1971 the Pakistani Army moved in to quash the independence movement in East Pakistan that was supported by clandestine aid from India, and some 10 million Bengali refugees poured across the border into India, creating social, economic, and health problems. In August, India signed a friendship treaty with the U.S.S.R. and quantities of Soviet arms began to enter India. After numerous border incidents, India invaded East Pakistan and in two weeks forced the surrender of the Pakistani army and took 93,000 prisoners. East Pakistan was established as an independent state and renamed Bangladesh.

India startled the world in 1974 by exploding an atomic device made of plutonium it had surreptitiously removed from a peaceful reactor given by Canada.

In the summer of 1975, the world's largest democracy veered suddenly toward authoritarianism when a judge in Allahabad, Mrs. Gandhi's home constituency, found her landslide victory in the 1971 elections invalid because civil servants had illegally aided her campaign. Amid demands for her resignation, Mrs. Gandhi decreed a state of emergency on June 26 and ordered mass arrests of her critics, including all opposition party leaders except the Communists.

Legislation extending the emergency indefinitely passed Parliament July 23. Opposition members walked out after the vote. Unhampered Congress Party majorities successively enacted: a bill forbidding courts to invalidate the government's emergency decrees; a constitutional amendment retroactively barring lawsuits challenging the elections of high government officers, including the Prime Minister, and a bill retroactively wiping out Mrs. Gandhi's conviction in the 1971 election case.

In 1976, India and Pakistan formally renewed diplomatic relations.

Despite strong opposition to her repressive measures and particularly the resentment against compulsory birth control programs, Mrs. Gandhi in 1977 announced parliamentary elections for March. At the same time, she freed most political prisoners, including her former Deputy Prime Minister, Morarji R. Desai, and L. K. Advani, a rightwing Hindu nationalist.

The landslide victory of Desai and his allies unseated Mrs. Gandhi and also defeated a bid for office by her son, Sanjay, himself a focus of much criticism as the recipient of official favors. Taking office, the 81-year-old Desai promised to "drive fear from the society" and restore morality to government.

Desai moved away from Mrs. Gandhi's pro-Soviet policy, receiving a visit from President Carter Jan. 1–3, 1978, and himself visiting Carter in June.

Mrs. Gandhi staged a spectacular comeback in elections in January 1980. Returned to power, Mrs. Gandhi showed a less hostile attitude toward the United States, condemning the Soviet invasion of Afghanistan and obtaining from the Carter administration approval for continued uranium shipments for India's nuclear program. She suffered a personal blow in the death of her son, Sanjay, a close personal aide, in a plane crash on June 23.

The visit of Soviet President Leonid I. Brezhnev to India in December 1980 altered Mrs. Gandhi's stand on Afghanistan to an acceptance of the Soviet assertion that its troops were there only because of U.S. and Chinese "interference" in that country. A joint statement called for dismantling all foreign bases in the Indian Ocean but named only one, the U.S. naval base on Diego Garcia Island.

A dispute with Washington over nuclear fuel supplies for a U.S. reactor at Tarapur was resolved in July 1982 when Mrs. Gandhi visited President Reagan. The U.S. Senate had previously barred aid to India and Pakistan if they exploded a nuclear device, and India had balked at inspection of Tarapur. To circumvent the problem, Reagan approved the sale of fuel by France, which would insure international inspection of the reactor, but not of a reprocessing plant, which would have been covered if the fuel were supplied by the United States.

In 1984, Mrs. Gandhi ordered the Indian Army to root out a band of Sikh holy men and gunmen who were using the holiest shrine of the Sikh religion, the Golden Temple in Amritsar, as a base for terrorist raids in a violent campaign for greater political autonomy in the strategic Punjab border state. As many as 1,000 people were reported killed in the June 5–6 battle, including Jarnall Singh Bhindranwale, the Khomeini-like militant leader, and 93 soldiers. The perceived sacrilege to the Golden Temple kindled outrage among many of India's 14 million Sikhs and brought a spasm of mutinies and desertions by Sikh officers and soldiers in the army. Mrs. Gandhi said mistakes had been made in the government crackdown on Sikh violence but there had been no choice but to take action against terrorism, which had been blamed for 400 deaths in Punjab.

Native States. Most of the 560-odd native states and subdivisions of pre-1947 India acceded to the new nation, and the central government pursued a vigorous policy of integration. This took three forms: merger into adjacent provinces, conversion into centrally administered areas, and grouping into unions of states. Finally, under a controversial reorganization plan effective Nov. 1, 1956, the unions of states were abolished and merged into adjacent states, and India became a union of 15 states and 8 centrally administered areas. A 16th state was added in 1962, and in 1966, the Punjab was partitioned into two states.

The status of the large princely state of Jammu and Kashmir on the northwest frontier is in dispute with Pakistan. It is 85% Islamic, but its Hindu ruling prince acceded to India, which took over administration following invasion by Moslem troops in late 1947. The part occupied by India was incorporated into India in 1957.

The controversy over Jammu and Kashmir was waged in the halls of the U.N. until 1965, when India announced that its civil servants would assume administration of the state. Pakistan sent guerrillas into the territory, and India, in response, invaded in August 1965. In September the U.N. sponsored a cease-fire and stationed observers to make sure it was honored, but there were violations.

The U.S.S.R. intervened and arranged a meeting in Tashkent between Prime Minister Shastri of India and President Ayub Khan of Pakistan. With the U.S.S.R. as mediator, they reached an interim settlement, the Declaration of Tashkent, in January 1966. It provided for the withdrawal of troops, observance of the U.N. cease-fire, and continued attempts to resolve their disputes by diplomatic means.

Resolution of the territorial dispute over Kashmir grew out of peace negotiations following the two-week India-Pakistan war of 1971. After sporadic skirmishing, an accord reached July 3, 1972, committed both powers to withdraw troops from a temporary cease-fire line after the border was fixed. Agreement on the border was reached Dec. 7, 1972.

In April 1975, the Indian Parliament voted to make the 300-year-old kingdom of Sikkim a full-fledged Indian state, and the annexation took effect May 16.

Situated in the Himalayas, Sikkim was a virtual dependency of Tibet until the early 19th century. Under an 1890 treaty between China and Great Britain, it became a British protectorate, and was made an Indian protectorate after Britain quit the subcontinent.

INDONESIA

Republic of Indonesia
President and Prime Minister: General Suharto (1969)[1]
Area: 735,268 sq mi. (1,904,344 sq km)[2]
Population (est. 1983): 160,000,000 (average annual growth rate: 2.1%)
Density per square mile: 208.1
Capital: Jakarta
Largest cities (est. 1982): Jakarta, 6,500,000; Surabaja, 2,100,000; Bandung, 1,500,000; Medan, 1,400,000; Semarang, 1,100,000; Palembang, 800,000
Monetary unit: Rupiah
Languages: Bahasa Indonesia (official), Dutch, and more than 60 regional languages
Religions: Islam, 89%; Christian, 7%; Hindu, Buddhist
National name: Republik Indonesia
Literacy rate (1981): 60% (est.)
Economic summary: Gross national product (1980): $61.8 billion. Average annual growth rate (1970–79): 4.6%. Per capita income (1980): $420. Land used for agriculture: 11%; labor force: 64%; principal products: rice, cassava, soybeans, copra, rubber, coffee, palm oil, tea. Labor force in industry: 7%; major products: textiles, food and beverages, light manufactures, cement, fertilizer. Natural resources: oil, timber, nickel, natural gas, tin, bauxite, copper. Exports: petroleum and liquid natural gas, timber, rubber, coffee, tin. Imports: rice, wheat, textiles, chemicals, iron and steel. Major trading partners: Japan, U.S., Saudi Arabia, West Germany.

1. General Suharto served as Acting President of Indonesia from 1967 to 1969. 2. Includes West Iran (former Netherlands New Guinea), renamed Iran Jaya in March 1973 (159,355 sq mi.; 412,731 sq km), and former Portuguese Timor (5,763 sq mi.; 14,925 sq km), annexed in 1976.

Geography. Indonesia is part of the Malay archipelago in Southeast Asia with an area nearly three times that of Texas. It consists of the islands of Sumatra, Java, Madura, Borneo (except Sarawak in the north), the Celebes, the Moluccas, and about 30 smaller archipelagos, totaling 13,677 islands, of which about 6,000 are inhabited. Its neighbor to the north is Malaysia and to the east Papua New Guinea.

A backbone of mountain ranges extends throughout the main islands of the archipelago. Earthquakes are frequent, and there are many active volcanoes.

Government. The President is elected by the People's Consultative Assembly, whose 920 members include the functioning legislative arm, the 464-member House of Representatives. Meeting at least once every five years, the Assembly has broad policy functions. The House, 100 of whose members are appointed by the President, meets at least once annually. General Suharto was elected unopposed to a fourth five-year term in 1983.

The major political parties are Sekber Golkar, 246 of 464 contested seats in the House; Islamic United Development Party, 94 seats; Democratic Party, 24 seats.

History. Indonesia is inhabited by Malayan and Papuan peoples ranging from the more advanced Javanese and Balinese to the more primitive Dyaks of Borneo. Invasions from China and India contributed Chinese and Indian admixtures.

During the first few centuries of the Christian era, most of the islands came under the influence of Hindu priests and traders, who spread their culture and religion. Moslem invasions began in the 13th century, and most of the area was Moslem by the 15th. Portuguese traders arrived early in the 16th century but were ousted by the Dutch about 1595. After Napoleon subjugated the Netherlands homeland in 1811, the British seized the islands but returned them to the Dutch in 1816. In 1922 the islands were made an integral part of the Netherlands kingdom.

In World War II, the Japanese military occupation with nominal native self-government continued until August 1945. About the time of the Japanese surrender, a self-styled Indonesian Republic headed by Achmed Sukarno took over effective control of parts of Sumatra and Java. Allied forces, mostly British Indian troops, moved in, and fought the nationalists until November 1946, when Dutch-Indonesian parleys resulted in a draft agreement that contemplated the formation by Jan. 1, 1949, of a Netherlands-Indonesian Union. This would consist on the one hand of the Netherlands, the Netherlands Antilles, and Surinam and on the other of the United States of Indonesia, which was to be a sovereign nation composed of three equal states—the Republic of Indonesia, East Indonesia, and Borneo. Differences of interpretation ensued, and the Dutch resorted to force in July 1947. Both sides issued cease-fire orders the next month in response to a call from the U.N. Security Council.

On Nov. 2, 1949, Dutch and Indonesian leaders agreed upon the terms of union. Sukarno was elected president of the federation and the first all-Indonesian Cabinet was formed with Mohammed Hatta as premier. The transfer of sovereignty took place at Amsterdam on December 27, 1949.

In 1963, Netherlands New Guinea was transferred to Indonesia, and renamed West Irian. In 1973 it became Irian Jaya.

Sukarno, who had himself declared "President for Life," launched a series of guerrilla raids in 1963 to scuttle formation of the new Federation of Malaysia. A treaty between Indonesia and Malaysia in 1966 ended the open conflict.

Early in 1966, Moslem students led an anti-Communist campaign that is believed to have assassinated more than 300,000 Indonesians suspected of Communist ties. Sukarno was forced in

March 1966 to yield power to General Suharto, army Chief of Staff. The Communist Party was outlawed and Sukarno was forced to give up all power. Suharto became acting President in March 1967.

He ended hostilities with Malaysia and established close ties with the West. Suharto introduced a "New Order" emphasizing austerity and fiscal responsibility and with Western aid of $200 million—one third provided by the U.S.—began rebuilding the country. In 1968, the Consultative Assembly elected Suharto president for a five-year term.

Suharto also permitted national elections, which moved the nation back toward representative government. The Consultative Assembly elected him unanimously for a second five-year term in 1973.

In 1975, tightening of world money markets put serious pressures on ambitious industrial development plans underwritten by Pertamina, the state-owned oil company. Communist triumphs in Vietnam and Cambodia encouraged Jakarta toward a policy of non-alignment with any great power and toward closer relationships with other members of the Association of Southeast Asian Nations.

Indonesia invaded the former Portuguese half of the island of Timor in 1975, and annexed the territory in 1976. On a visit to Jakarta in July 1984, Secretary of State George P. Shultz expressed concern about reports of human rights abuses being carried out by Indonesian forces in East Timor. More than 100,000 Timorese, a sixth of the mostly Catholic population, was reported to have died from famine, disease, and fighting since the annexation.

IRAN

Islamic Republic of Iran
President: Hojatolislam Mohammed Ali Khamenei (1981)
Prime Minister: Mir Hussein Moussavi Khamenei (1981)
Area: 636,293 sq mi. (1,648,000 sq km)
Population (est. 1983): 41,450,000 (average annual growth rate: 3.1%) (Iranian, Kurdish, Azerbaijani)
Density per square mile: 65.1
Capital: Teheran
Largest cities (est. 1982): Teheran, 6,000,000; Isfahan, 725,000; Mashed, 725,000; Tabriz, 650,000
Monetary unit: Rial
Languages: Farsi (Persian), Kurdish, Azerbaijani
Religions: Shi'ite Moslem, 93%; Sunni Moslem, 5%
Literacy rate (1976): 37% (est.)
Economic summary: Gross national product (1982): $66.5 billion. Per capita income (1982): $1,621. Land used for agriculture: 14%; Labor force: 33%; principal products: wheat, barley, rice, sugar beets, cotton, dates, raisins, sheep, goats. Labor force in industry: 21%; major products: crude and refined oil, textiles, cement, processed foods, steel and copper fabrication. Natural resources: oil, gas, iron, copper. Exports: petroleum, carpets, fruits and nuts. Imports: machinery, military supplies, foodstuffs, pharmaceuticals. Major trading partners: Japan, West Germany, U.K., Italy, Netherlands, Spain.

Geography. Iran, a Middle Eastern country south of the Caspian Sea and north of the Persian Gulf, is three times the size of Arizona. It shares borders with Iraq, Turkey, the U.S.S.R., Afghanistan, and Pakistan.

In general, the country is a plateau averaging 4,000 feet (1,219 m) in elevation. There are also maritime lowlands along the Persian Gulf and the Caspian Sea. The Elburz Mountains in the north rise to 18,603 feet (5,670 m) at Mt. Damavend. From northwest to southeast, the country is crossed by a desert 800 miles (1,287 km) long.

Government. The Pahlavi dynasty was overthrown on Feb. 11, 1979, by followers of the Ayatollah Ruhollah Khomeini. After a referendum endorsed the establishment of a republic, Khomeini drafted a Constitution calling for a President to be popularly elected every four years, an appointed Prime Minister, and a unicameral National Consultative Assembly, popularly elected every four years.

Khomeini also instituted a Revolutionary Council to insure the adherence to Islamic principles in all phases of Iranian life. The Council formally handed over its powers to the Assembly after the organization of the legislature in July 1980, but continued to exercise power as a sort of shadow government.

History. Oil-rich Iran was called Persia before 1935. Its key location blocks the lower land gate to Asia and also stands in the way of traditional Russian ambitions for access to the Indian Ocean. After periods of Assyrian, Median, and Achaemenidian rule, Persia became a powerful empire under Cyrus the Great, reaching from the Indus to the Nile at its zenith in 525 B.C. It fell to Alexander in 331–30 B.C. and to the Seleucids in 312–02 B.C., and a native Persian regime arose about 130 B.C. Another Persian regime arose about A.D. 224, but it fell to the Arabs in 637. In the 12th century, the Mongols took their turn ruling Persia, and in the early part of the 18th century, the Turks occupied the country.

An Anglo-Russian convention of 1907 divided Persia into two spheres of influence. British attempts to impose a protectorate over the entire country were defeated in 1919. Two years later, Gen. Reza Pahlavi seized the government and was elected hereditary Shah in 1925. Subsequently he did much to modernize the country and abolished all foreign extraterritorial rights.

Increased pro-Axis activity led to Anglo-Russian occupation of Iran in 1941 and deposition of the Shah in favor of his son, Mohammed Reza Pahlavi.

Ali Razmara became premier in 1950 and pledged to restore efficient and honest government, but he was assassinated after less than nine months in office and Mohammed Mossadegh took over. Mossadegh was ousted in August 1953, by Fazollah Zahedi, whom the Shah had named premier.

Iran established closer relations with the U.S. and the West, and the U.S. began a vast program of economic and military aid. In 1955 the country joined the Central Treaty Organization. The government undertook a broad program of reform, especially agrarian land reform, distributing crown lands and estates to the landless peasants.

Iran's oil profits financed an extraordinary modernization program of education, industrialization, and construction.

Opposition to the Shah spread, despite the imposition of martial law in September 1978, and massive demonstrations demanded the return of the exiled Ayatollah Ruhollah Khomeini. Riots and strikes continued despite the appointment of an opposition leader, Shahpur Bakhtiar, as premier on Dec. 29. The Shah and his family left Iran on Jan. 16, 1979, for a "vacation," leaving power in the hands of a regency council.

Khomeini returned on Feb. 1 to a nation in turmoil as military units loyal to the Shah continued to support Bakhtiar and clashed with revolutionaries. Khomeini appointed Mehdi Bazargan as premier of the provisional government and in two days of fighting, revolutionaries forced the military to capitulate on Feb. 11.

The new government began a program of nationalization of insurance companies, banks, and industries both locally and foreign-owned. Oil production fell amid the political confusion.

Khomeini, ignoring opposition, proceeded with his plans for revitalizing Islamic traditions. He urged women to return to the veil, or chador; banned alcohol and mixed bathing, and prohibited music from radio and television broadcasting, declaring it to be "no different from opium."

Revolutionary militants invaded the U.S. Embassy in Teheran on Nov. 4, 1979, seized staff members as hostages, and precipitated an international crisis.

Khomeini refused all appeals, even a unanimous vote by the U.N. Security Council demanding immediate release of the hostages. On a New Year's trip to Teheran, U.N. Secretary-General Kurt Waldheim never saw Khomeini, and a subsequent U.N. commission of inquiry met a similar rebuff.

Election of Abolhassan Bani-Sadr as President on Jan. 25, 1980, raised hopes that his moderate stance might bring a change.

Iranian hostility toward Washington was reinforced by the Carter administration's ineffective economic boycott and deportation order against Iranian students in the U.S., the break in diplomatic relations and ultimately an aborted U.S. raid in April aimed at rescuing the hostages.

Even the death of the deposed Shah Mohammed Reza Pahlavi on July 17 had no effect. As the first anniversary of the embassy seizure neared, Khomeini and his followers insisted on their original conditions: guarantee by the U.S. not to interfere in Iran's affairs, cancellation of U.S. damage claims against Iran, release of $8 billion in frozen Iranian assets, an apology, and the return of the assets held by the former imperial family.

These conditions were largely met in an agreement signed by Deputy Secretary of State Warren Christopher on Jan. 19 and the 52 American hostages were released the following day, ending 444 days in captivity. The $8 billion was subject to claims of U.S. creditors, however, and the delivery of the late Shah's assets under U.S. control was made subject to court decisions.

From the release of the hostages onward, Bani-Sadr and the conservative clerics of the dominant Islamic Republican Party clashed with growing frequency. He was stripped of his command of the armed forces by Khomeini on June 6 and ousted as President on June 22. Bani-Sadr went into hiding and emerged in Paris, vowing to fight Khomeini. On June 28, four Cabinet members and 68 other prominent Khomeini backers were killed by a bomb planted in the Islamic Republican Party headquarters. On July 24, Prime Minister Mohammed Ali Rajai was elected overwhelmingly to the Presidency.

Rajai and Prime Minister Mohammed Javad Bahonar were killed on Aug. 30 by a bomb in Bahonar's office.

Hojatolislam Mohammed Ali Khamenei, a clergyman, leader of the Islamic Republican Party and spokesman for Khomeini, was elected President on Oct. 2, 1981. The insurgent Mujahedeen-i-Khalq, accused by the government of killing 300 officials in pre-election violence, announced a government in exile, headquartered in Paris with Bani-Sadr as provisional president.

The sporadic war with Iraq regained momentum in 1982, as Iran launched an offensive in March and regained much of the border area occupied by Iraq in late 1980. On May 24, Iran claimed the recapture of Khurramshahr, the last sizable Iranian town in Iraqi hands, and in July Iranian troops were moving into Iraqi territory. Khomeini rejected Iraqi bids for a truce, insisting that Iraq's President Saddam Hussein must leave office first.

Iran continued to be at war with Iraq well into 1984 without either side achieving any great military success. Although Iraq has expressed its willingness to cease fighting, Iran has stated that it will not stop the war until Iraq agrees to withdraw its troops to the prewar border, make payment for war damages to Iran, and punish the Iraqi government leaders involved in the conflict. The fighting, previously mostly on the ground, spread into the Persian Gulf in 1984, with Iraq using French-made Exocet air-to-surface missiles to attack tankers loading at Iran's Kargh Island, and Iran striking back at tankers calling at Saudi Arabia and the smaller, oil-rich Arab Gulf states.

IRAQ

Republic of Iraq
President: Saddam Hussein (1979)
Area: 169,284 sq mi. (438,446 sq km)
Population (est. 1982): 14,000,000 (average annual growth rate: 3.3%) (Arab, 77%; Kurds, 19%)
Density per square mile: 81.4
Capital: Baghdad
Largest cities (est. 1982): Baghdad, 3,300,000; Basra, 375,000; Mosul, 350,000; Kirkuk, 250,000; An Najaf, 225,000
Monetary unit: Iraqi dinar
Languages: Arabic and Kurdish
Religions: Islam, 96%; Christian, 3%
National name: Al Jumhouriya Al Iraqia
Literacy rate (1981): 30%
Economic summary: Gross national product (1981): $31.3 billion. Average annual growth rate (1970–79): 9.3%. Per capita income (1981): $2,300. Average rate of inflation (1976–78): 10%. Land used for agriculture, 18%; labor force, 30%; principal products: livestock, wheat, barley, cotton, fruits, vegetables. Labor force in industry: 27%; major products: petroleum, cement, textiles. Natural resources: oil, natural gas, phosphates, sulfur. Exports: petroleum, dates. Imports: manufactured goods, food grains, machinery, construction materials, livestock. Major trading partners: France, Italy, U.S.S.R., Japan, West Germany, Turkey, Brazil, U.K.

Geography. Iraq, a triangle of mountains, desert, and fertile river valley, is bounded on the east by Iran, on the north by Turkey, the west by Syria and Jordan, and the south by Saudi Arabia and Kuwait. It is twice the size of Idaho.

The country has arid desertland west of the Euphrates, a broad central valley between the Euphrates and Tigris, and mountains in the northeast. The fertile lower valley is formed by the delta of the two rivers, which join about 120 miles (193 km) from the head of the Persian Gulf. The gulf coastline is 26 miles (42 km) long. The only port for seagoing vessels is Basra, which is on the Shatt-al-Arab River near the head of the Persian Gulf.

Government. Since the coup d'etat of July 1968, Iraq has been governed by the Arab Ba'ath Socialist Party through a Council of Command of the Revolution headed by the President. There is also a Council of Ministers headed by the President.

History. From earliest times Iraq was known as Mesopotamia—the land between the rivers—for it embraces a large part of the alluvial plains of the Tigris and Euphrates.

An advanced civilization existed by 4000 B.C. Sometime after 2000 B.C. the land became the center of the ancient Babylonian and Assyrian empires. It was conquered by Cyrus the Great of Persia in 538 B.C., and by Alexander in 331 B.C. After an Arab conquest in A.D. 637–40, Baghdad became capital of the ruling caliphate. The country was cruelly pillaged by the Mongols in 1258, and during the 16th, 17th, and 18th centuries was the object of repeated Turkish-Persian competition.

Nominal Turkish suzerainty imposed in 1638 was replaced by direct Turkish rule in 1831. In World War I, an Anglo-Indian force occupied most of the country, and Britain was given a mandate over the area in 1920. The British recognized Iraq as a kingdom in 1922 and terminated the mandate in 1932 when Iraq was admitted to the League of Nations. In World War II, Iraq generally adhered to its 1930 treaty of alliance with Britain, but in 1941, British troops were compelled to put down a pro-Axis revolt led by Premier Rashid Ali.

Iraq became a charter member of the Arab League in 1945, and Iraqi troops took part in the Arab invasion of Palestine in 1948.

Faisal II, born on May 2, 1935, succeeded his father, Ghazi I, who was killed in an automobile accident on April 4, 1939. Faisal and his uncle, Crown Prince Abdul-Ilah, were assassinated in August 1958 in a swift revolutionary coup that brought to power a military junta headed by Abdul Karem Kassim. Kassim, in turn, was overthrown and killed in a coup staged March 8, 1963, by the Ba'ath Socialist Party.

President Abdel Salam Arif, a leader in the March coup, staged another coup in November, driving the Ba'ath members of the revolutionary council from power. He adopted a new constitution in 1964. In 1966, he, two Cabinet members, and other supporters died in a helicopter crash. His brother, Gen. Abdel Rahman Arif, assumed the presidency, crushed the opposition, and won an indefinite extension of his term in 1967. His regime was ousted in July 1968 by a junta led by Maj. Gen. Ahmed Hassan al-Bakr.

In 1970, the Baghdad government announced a settlement of the 8 1/2-year sporadic war with the Kurds of northeastern Iraq (who spread over the border into Turkey and Iran). The Kurdish rebellion flared anew in 1974, following collapse of an Iraqi plan for Kurdish self-rule. The rebels, armed and reinforced from Iran, withstood Soviet-supplied Iraqi forces for 11 months until Iran ended its aid under an agreement with Iraq and 200,000 Kurds fled to Iran.

A long-standing dispute over control of the Shatt al-Arab waterway between Iraq and Iran broke into full-scale war on Sept. 20, 1980. Iraqi planes attacked Iranian airfields and the Abadan refinery, and Iraqi ground forces moved into Iranian territory.

Despite the smaller size of its armed forces, Iraq took and held the initiative by seizing Abadan and Khurramshahr together with substantial Iranian territory by December and beating back Iranian counterattacks in January. Peace efforts by the Islamic nations, the nonaligned, and the United Nations failed as 1981 wore on and the war stagnated.

Despite strong Arab support in the war against Iran—financial contributions from Saudi Arabia and other oil producers were estimated in 1982 to have reached $22 billion—the balance of the war appeared to be tipping against the smaller Iraqi army in midyear. Syria, which had openly sided with Iran in the war, closed its border in April and shut down the pipeline carrying Iraqi oil to the Mediterranean.

The Iraqis fell back to their own country and dug themselves in behind sandbagged defensive fortifications. With massive firepower, they turned back wave after wave of attacking Iranian troops and revolutionary guards, many of them in their teens. From the beginning of the war in September 1980 to September 1984, foreign military analysts estimated that more than 100,000 Iranians and perhaps 50,000 Iraqis had been killed.

The Iraqis, trying to cut off the flow of Iranian oil as Syria had cut their oil off from foreign markets, acquired sophisticated Exocet missiles from France and used them to attack foreign tankers loading at Iran's Kharg Island terminal, but failed to halt Iranian exports.

The Iraqis clearly wanted to end the war, but the Iranians refused.

IRELAND

President: Patrick J. Hiliery (1976)
Taoiseach (Prime Minister): Garret FitzGerald (1982)
Area: 26,600 sq mi. (68,394 sq km)
Population (est. 1982): 3,480,000 (average annual growth rate, 1.5%)
Density per square mile: 130.8
Capital: Dublin
Largest cities (est. 1982): Dublin, 550,000; Cork, 140,000; Limerick, 60,000
Monetary unit: Irish pound (punt)
Languages: Irish, English
Religions: Roman Catholic, 94%; Protestant, 5%
National name: Eire
Literacy rate (1981): 99%
Economic summary: Gross national product (1980): $17.8 billion. Average annual growth rate (1975–80): 3.9%; Per Capita Income (1980): $5,190. Land used for agriculture, 67%; labor force in agriculture and fishing: 19.1%; principal products: cattle and dairy products, potatoes, barley, sugar beets, hay, silage, wheat. Labor force in industry: 32.4%; major products: processed foods, beverages, textiles, chemicals and pharmaceuticals, machinery and construction equipment. Natural resources: zinc, lead, natural gas, barite, copper, gypsum, limestone, dolomite, peat, silver. Exports: livestock, meat, dairy products, machinery, chemicals, textiles, and clothing. Imports: grains, petroleum products, machinery, chemicals, textile yarn, cereals. Major trading partners: U.K., Western European countries, U.S., Canada.

Geography. Ireland is situated in the Atlantic

Ocean and separated from Britain by the Irish Sea. Half the size of Arkansas, it occupies the entire island except for the six northern counties of Ulster.

Ireland resembles a basin—a central plain rimmed with mountains, except in the Dublin region. The mountains are low, with the highest peak, Carrantuohill in County Kerry, rising to 3,415 feet (1,041 m).

The principal river is the Shannon, which begins in the north central area, flows south and southwest for about 240 miles (386 km), and empties into the Atlantic.

Government. Ireland is a parliamentary democracy. The National Parliament (Oireachtas) consists of the president and two Houses, the House of Representatives (Dáil Éireann) and the Senate (Seanad Éireann), whose members serve for a maximum term of five years. The House of Representatives has 166 members elected by proportional representation; the Senate has 60 members of whom 11 are nominated by the prime minister, 6 by the universities and the remaining 43 from five vocational panels. The prime minister (Taoiseach), who is the head of government, is appointed by the president on the nomination of the House of Representatives, to which he is responsible.

The major political parties are Fianna Fáil (75 of 166 seats in the Dáil), led by former Prime Minister Charles J. Haughey; Fine Gael (70 seats), led by Prime Minister Garret FitzGerald; Labor Party (16 seats), led by Dick Spring; Workers Party (2 seats) led by Thomas MacGiolla; Independents (3 seats). The government is a coalition of the Fine Gael and Labor Parties.

History. In the Stone and Bronze Ages, Ireland was inhabited by Picts in the north and a people called the Erainn in the south, the same stock, apparently, as in all the isles before the Anglo-Saxon invasion of Britain. About the fourth century B.C., tall, red-haired Celts arrived from Gaul or Galicia. They subdued and assimilated the inhabitants and established a Gaelic civilization.

By the beginning of the Christian Era, Ireland was divided into five kingdoms—Ulster, Connacht, Leinster, Meath, and Munster. St. Patrick introduced Christianity in 432 and the country developed into a center of Gaelic and Latin learning. Irish monasteries, the equivalent of universities, attracted intellectuals as well as the pious and sent out missionaries to many parts of Europe and, some believe, to North America.

Norse depredations along the coasts, starting in 795, ended in 1014 with Norse defeat at the Battle of Clontarf by forces under Brian Borv. In the the 12th century, the Pope gave all Ireland to the English Crown as a papal fief. In 1171, Henry II of England was acknowledged "Lord of Ireland," but local sectional rule continued for centuries, and English control over the whole island was not reasonably absolute until the 17th century. By the Act of Union (1800), England and Ireland became the "United Kingdom of Great Britain and Ireland."

A steady decline in the Irish economy followed in the next decades. The population had reached 8.25 million when the great potato famine of 1846–48 took many lives and drove millions to emigrate to America. By 1921 it was down to 4.3 million.

In the meantime, anti-British agitation continued along with demands for Irish home rule. The advent of World War I delayed the institution of home rule and resulted in the Easter Rebellion in Dublin (April 24–29, 1916), in which Irish nationalists unsuccessfully attempted to throw off British rule. Guerrilla warfare against British forces followed proclamation of a republic by the rebels in 1919.

The Irish Free State was established as a dominion on Dec. 6, 1921, with the six northern counties as part of the United Kingdom. Ireland was neutral in World War II.

In 1948, Éamon de Valera, American-born leader of the Sinn Fein, who had won establishment of the Free State in 1921 in negotiations with Britain's David Lloyd George, was defeated by John A. Costello, who demanded final independence from Britain. The Republic of Ireland was proclaimed on April 18, 1949. It withdrew from the Commonwealth but in 1955 entered the United Nations. Since 1949 the prime concern of successive governments has been economic development.

De Valera, who retired in 1973 after two terms in the largely ceremonial presidency, died Aug. 29, 1975, at the age of 92.

Through the 1960s, two antagonistic currents dominated Irish politics. One sought to bind the wounds of the rebellion and civil war. The other was the effort of the outlawed extremist Irish Republican Army to bring Northern Ireland into the republic. Despite public sympathy for unification of Ireland, the Dublin government dealt rigorously with IRA guerrillas caught inside the republic's borders.

The 1973 election brought to power Liam Cosgrave, at the head of a coalition of the Fine Gael and the Labor Party, unseating the Fianna Fáil, which had governed for 35 of 41 years of the republic. Cosgrave cooperated with the British government in attempts to control IRA terrorism and, after the assassination of the British Ambassador to Ireland in 1976, pushed through an Emergency Powers Act to strengthen police and court powers in combating terrorists.

The 1977 election gave the Fianna Fáil a record 84 seats in the Dáil and put John Lynch into the prime minister's post.

Although Lynch drew protests from Britain and Ulster for publicly advocating unification in 1978, he resigned on Dec. 5, 1979, amid intra-party complaints that he was too conciliatory on the issue.

Elections on June 11, 1981, failed to provide Charles J. Haughey, the party's choice to succeed Lynch, with a majority and Garret M. D. FitzGerald, leader of the Fine Gael, was elected Prime Minister by 81 to 78 with the support of 15 Labor Party members and one independent Socialist added to his own party's 65 members. Other independents abstained, among them Kieran Doherty, a prisoner in Northern Ireland's Maze Prison, who with another prisoner had won election to the Southern Parliament (the Republic's Constitution extends citizenship to anyone born in Northern Ireland). Doherty died after a hunger strike on Aug. 3, one of nine Maze prisoners to do so.

FitzGerald resigned Jan. 27, 1982, after his presentation of an austerity budget aroused the opposition of independents who had backed him previously. His party lost two seats in the subsequent election and the opposition Fianna Fail won eight but still required support of a splinter party and independents to achieve a majority. Former Prime Minister Haughey was sworn in on March 9 and presented a budget with nearly a $1 billion deficit, with additional public spending aimed at stimulating the lagging economy. FitzGerald was re-elected Prime Minister on Dec. 14, 1982. He called for "strenous efforts and great sacrifices" to be made by the country in order to mitigate the problems of unemployment and its effects on the nation.

ISRAEL

State of Israel
President: Chaim Herzog (1983)
Prime Minister: Shimon Peres (1984)
Area: 7,992 sq mi. (20,699 sq km)
Population (est. 1983): 4,100,000 (average annual growth rate: 1.9%)
Density per square mile: 513.0
Capital: Jerusalem
Largest cities (est. 1981): Jerusalem, 412,000[1], Tel Aviv, 350,000; Haifa, 235,000; Holon, 130,000; Ramat Gan, 125,000
Monetary unit: Shekel
Languages: Hebrew, Arabic, English
Religions: Jewish, 83%, Islam 13.1%, Christian 2.3%, Druze and others, 1.6%
National name: Medinat Israel
Literacy rate (1981): Jews 94%, non-Jews 83.2%
Economic summary: Gross national product (1983): $24.3 Average annual growth rate (1972–82): 2.88%. Per capita income (1982): $4,470. Land used for agriculture: 20%; labor force: 6%; principal products: citrus and other fruits, vegetables, beef, dairy and poultry products. Labor force in industry: 25%; major products: processed foods, cut diamonds, clothing and textiles, chemicals, metal products, transport and electrical equipment, plastics. Natural resources: sulfur, limestone, rock salt, phosphates, potash, bromine. Exports: polished diamonds, citrus and other fruits, clothing and textiles, processed foods, high technology products, computerized medical equipment, military hardware, fertilizer and chemical products. Imports: military equipment, rough diamonds, chemicals, oil, machinery, iron and steel, cereals, textiles, vehicles, ships, aircraft. Major trading partners: U.S., West Germany, U.K., Switzerland, France, Italy.

1. Includes East Jerusalem.

Geography. Israel, slightly smaller than Massachusetts, lies at the eastern end of the Mediterranean Sea. It is bordered by Egypt on the west, Syria and Jordan on the east, and Lebanon on the north.

Northern Israel is largely a plateau traversed from north to south by mountains and broken by great depressions, also running from north to south.

The maritime plain of Israel is remarkably fertile. The southern Negev region, which comprises almost half the total area, is largely a wide desert steppe area. The National Water Project irrigation scheme is now transforming it into fertile land. The Jordan, the only important river, flows from the north through Lake Hule (Waters of Merom) and Lake Kinneret (Sea of Galilee or Sea of Tiberias), finally entering the Dead Sea, 1,290 feet (393 m) below sea level. This "sea," which is actually a salt lake (394 sq mi.; 1,020 sq km), has no outlet, its water balance being maintained by evaporation.

Government. Israel, which does not have a written constitution, has a republican form of government headed by a president elected for a five-year term by the Knesset. He may serve no more than two terms. The Knesset has 120 members elected by universal suffrage under proportional representation for four years. The government is administered by the Cabinet, which is headed by the prime minister.

The Knesset decided in June 1950 that Israel would acquire a constitution gradually through the years by the enactment of fundamental laws. Israel grants automatic citizenship to every Jew who desires to settle within its borders, subject to control of the Knesset.

The major political parties are Labor Alignment (44 of 120 seats in the Knesset), led by Prime Minister Shimon Peres; Likud (41 seats), led by Deputy Prime Minister Yitzhak Shamir; Tehiya-Tzomet (5 seats); National Religious Party (4 seats); Democratic Movement for Peace and Equality (Communist) (4 seats); Sephardi Torah Guardians (4 seats); Shinui (3 seats); Movement for Citizens Rights and Peace (3 seats); Yahad (3 seats); other parties (9 seats).

History. Palestine, cradle of two great religions and homeland of the modern state of Israel, was known to the ancient Hebrews as the "Land of Canaan." Palestine's name derives from the Philistines, a people who occupied the southern coastal part of the country in the 12th century B.C.

A Hebrew kingdom established in 1000 B.C. was later split into the kingdoms of Judah and Israel; they were subsequently invaded by Assyrians, Babylonians, Egyptians, Persians, Macedonians, Romans, and Byzantines. The Arabs took Palestine from the Byzantine Empire A.D. 634–40. With the exception of a Frankish Crusader kingdom from 1099 to 1187, Palestine remained under Moslem rule until the 20th century (Turkish rule from 1516), when British forces under Gen. Sir Edmund Allenby defeated the Turks and captured Jerusalem Dec. 9, 1917. The League of Nations granted Britain a mandate to govern Palestine, effective in 1923.

Jewish colonies—Jews from Russia established one as early as 1882—multiplied after Theodor Herzl's 1897 call for a Jewish state. The Zionist movement received official approval with the publication of a letter Nov. 2, 1917, from Arthur Balfour, British Foreign Secretary, to Lord Rothschild, a British Jewish leader. Balfour promised support for the establishment of a Jewish homeland in Palestine on the understanding that the civil and religious rights of non-Jewish Palestinians would be safeguarded.

A 1937 British proposal called for an Arab and a Jewish state separated by a mandated area incorporating Jerusalem and Nazareth. Arabs opposed this, demanding a single state with minority rights for Jews, and a 1939 British White Paper retreated, offering instead a single state with further Jewish immigration to be limited to 75,000. Although the White Paper satisfied neither side, further discussion ended on the outbreak of World War II, when the Jewish population stood at nearly 500,000, or 30% of the total. Illegal and legal immigration during the war brought the Jewish population to 678, 000 in 1946, compared with 1,269,000 Arabs. Unable to reach a compromise, Britain turned the problem over to the United Nations in 1947, which on November 29 voted for partition—despite strong Arab opposition.

Britain did not help implement the U.N. decision and withdrew on expiration of its mandate May 14, 1948. Zionists had already seized control of areas designated as Jewish, and, on the day of British departure, the Jewish National Council proclaimed the State of Israel.

U.S. recognition came within hours. The next day, Jordanian and Egyptian forces invaded the new nation. At the cease-fire Jan. 7, 1949, Israel increased its original territory by 50%, taking western Galilee, a broad corridor through central Palestine to Jerusalem, and part of modern Jerusalem. (In April 1950, Jordan annexed areas of eastern and central Palestine that had been designated for an Arab state, together with the old city of Jerusalem.)

Chaim Weizmann and David Ben-Gurion, became Israel's first president and prime minister. The new government was admitted to the U.N. May 11, 1949.

The next clash with Arab neighbors came when Egypt nationalized the Suez Canal in 1956 and barred Israeli shipping. Coordinating with an Anglo-French force, Israeli troops seized the Gaza Strip and drove through the Sinai to the east bank of the Suez Canal, but withdrew under U.S. and U.N. pressure. In 1967, Israel threatened retaliation against Syrian border raids, and Syria asked Egyptian aid. Egypt demanded the removal of U.N. peace-keeping forces from Suez, staged a national mobilization, closed the Gulf of Aqaba, and moved troops into the Sinai. On June 5, with a simultaneous air attack against Syrian, Jordanian, and Egyptian bases and in a six-day war totally defeated its Arab enemies. Expanding its territory by 200%, Israel at the cease-fire held the Golan Heights, the West Bank of the Jordan River, the Old City, and all of the Sinai and the east bank of the Suez Canal.

Israel insisted that Jerusalem remain a unified city and that peace negotiations be conducted directly, something the Arab states had refused to do because it would constitute a recognition of their Jewish neighbor.

Egypt's President Gamal Abdel Nasser renounced the 1967 cease-fire in 1969 and began a "war of attrition" against Israel, firing Soviet artillery at Israeli forces on the east bank of the canal. Nasser died of a heart attack on Sept. 28, 1970, and was succeeded by Anwar el-Sadat.

In the face of Israeli reluctance even to discuss the return of occupied territories, the fourth Mideast war erupted Oct. 6, 1973, with a surprise Egyptian and Syrian assault on the Jewish high holy day of Yom Kippur. Initial Arab gains were reversed when a cease-fire took effect two weeks later, but Israel suffered heavy losses in manpower.

U.S. Secretary of State Henry A. Kissinger arranged a disengagement of forces on both the Egyptian and Syrian fronts. Geneva talks, aimed at a lasting peace, foundered, however, when Israel balked at inclusion of the Palestine Liberation Organization, a guerrilla front increasingly active in terrorism directed against Israel.

At home, criticism of the ruling Labor Party's lack of preparedness cost it five seats in 1973 election, and Prime Minister Golda Meir was forced to head a minority government until her retirement on April 10, 1974. Yitzhak Rabin, a former general formed a successor government, which won narrow approval in the Knesset and, in October assembled a majority coalition.

In the same month, the PLO won recognition as the "representative of the Palestine people" in a resolution passed by the U.N. General Assembly and at an Arab summit meeting in Rabat, Morocco.

A second-stage Sinai withdrawal signed by Israel and Egypt in September 1975 required Israel to give up the strategic Mitla and Gidi passes and to return the captured Abu Rudeis oil fields. Egypt guaranteed passage of Israeli cargoes through the reopened Suez Canal, and both sides renounced force in the settlement of disputes. Two hundred U.S. civilian technicians were stationed in a widened U.N. buffer zone to monitor and warn either side of truce violations.

A U.S. commitment to give Israel $400 million in economic aid and $1 billion in weapons was then disclosed, along with the assurance of a coordinated U.S.-Israeli position in any renewed Geneva negotiations.

With no progress toward permanent peace and rampant inflation causing severe economic strain, the malaise in the Labor Party deepened in early 1977 when Rabin confessed to maintaining an illegal bank account in the United States. He resigned April 8 and Defense Minister Shimon Peres was named the party's leader for general elections May 17, in which the Labor Party was defeated for the first time since Israel's founding.

Menachem Begin, 63, took office June 21 as the leader of the Likud, a coalition of conservative parties. Begin founded the Irgun Zvai Leumi (National Military Organization) to fight British rule during the Palestine Mandate.

A dramatic breakthrough in the tortuous history of Mideast peace efforts occurred Nov. 9, 1977, when Egypt's President Sadat declared his willingness to go anywhere to talk peace. Begin on Nov. 15 extended an invitation to the Egyptian leader to address the Knesset. Sadat's arrival in Israel four days later raised worldwide hopes. But optimism ebbed even before Begin was invited to Ismailia by Sadat, December 25–26.

An Israeli peace plan unveiled by Begin on his return, and approved by the Knesset, offered to end military administration in the West Bank and the Gaza Strip, with a degree of Arab self-rule but no relinquishment of sovereignty by Israel. Sadat severed talks on Jan. 18 and, despite U.S. condemnation, Begin approved new West Bank settlements by Israelis. Dissidents within the cabinet, notably Defense Minister Ezer Weizman, kept the door open for negotiations, however, and a foreign ministerial meeting of the two antagonists with U.S. Secretary of State Cyrus Vance took place in England on July 18.

A PLO raid on Israel's coast on March 11, 1978, killed 30 civilians and provoked a full-scale invasion of southern Lebanon by Israel three days later to attack PLO bases. Israel withdrew three months later, turning over strongpoints to Lebanese Christian militia wherever possible rather than to a U.N. peacekeeping force installed in the area.

Peace talks resumed their painful progress in October as Israeli Foreign Minister Moshe Dayan and Egyptian Defense Minister Kamel Hassan Ali, with the participation of President Carter, agreed on a U.S. draft treaty.

On March 14, 1979, after a visit by Carter, the Knesset approved a final treaty, and 12 days later Begin and Sadat signed the document, together with Carter, in a White House ceremony. Israel began its withdrawal from the Sinai on May 25 by handing over the coastal town of El Arish and the two countries opened their border on May 29.

On Palestinian autonomy, there was little progress. On Feb. 10, 1980, Israel inflamed Arab opinion with the Cabinet's approval of Jewish settlements in Hebron, until then an exclusively Arab West Bank city. A right-wing Israeli terrorist campaign that maimed three Arab West Bank mayors and finally, the Knesset's passage of a law annexing East Jerusalem further antagonized the Arabs and stalled the autonomy talks.

One of the most difficult periods in Israel's history began with a confrontation with Syria over the placing by Syria of Soviet surface-to-air missiles in the Bekaa Valley of Lebanon in April 1981. President Reagan dispatched Philip C. Habib to prevent a clash. While Habib was seeking a settlement, Begin ordered a bombing raid against an Iraqi nuclear reactor on June 7, invoking the theory of preemptive self-defense because he said Iraq was planning to make nuclear weapons to attack Israel.

Begin's belligerency was credited with his narrow victory over Shimon Peres' Labor Party on June 30. He followed it with a bombing raid against PLO headquarters in Beirut on July 17 that killed 300 persons and injured 700.

Although Israel withdrew its last settlers from the Sinai in April 1982 and agreed to a Sinai "peace patrol" composed of troops from four West European nations, the fragile peace engineered by Habib in Lebanon was shattered on June 9 by a massive Israeli assault on southern Lebanon. The attack was in retaliation for what Israel charged was a PLO attack that critically wounded the Israeli ambassador to London six days earlier.

Israeli armor swept through UNIFIL lines in southern Lebanon, destroyed PLO strongholds in Tyre and Sidon, and reached the suburbs of Beirut on June 10. Air strikes destroyed Syrian missile sites in the Bekaa Valley and resulted in Israeli claims of downing 25 Soviet-made Syrian jets. As Israeli troops ringed Moslem East Beirut, where 5,000 PLO guerrillas were believed trapped, Habib sought to negotiate a safe exit for them. The Arab world loudly protested the entire action, estimated by Lebanon to have cost the lives of 10,000 civilians by mid-July, but no Arab nation would accept the Palestinian militants Israel insisted must leave Lebanon.

Begin's belligerence for the first time brought large antiwar demonstrations in Israel and a hostile reception by the U.S. Congress when he visited President Reagan in mid-June.

A U.S.-mediated accord between Lebanon and Israel, signed on May 17, 1983, provided for Israeli withdrawal from Lebanon, Israeli participation in security patrols in southern Lebanon under Lebanese officers, and gradual normalization of relations between the two countries based on "sovereignty, political independence and territorial integrity." Israeli withdrawal was conditioned on withdrawal of Syrian troops from the Bekaa Valley, however, and the Syrians refused to leave. Israel eventually withdrew its troops from the Beirut area, but kept them in southern Lebanon. Lebanon, under pressure from Syria, canceled the accord in March 1984.

Prime Minister Begin resigned on Sept. 15, 1983. On Oct. 10, Likud Party stalwart Yitzhak Shamir was elected Prime Minister. In parliamentary elections on July 23, 1984, the opposition Labor Alignment, under Shimon Peres, emerged with the largest vote of any single party and 44 seats in the Knesset, to Likud's 41. Since both major parties were far short of the 61-seat majority needed to govern, they began negotiating with other parties to try to form a governing coalition.

After seven weeks of wrangling, the two major parties worked out a carefully balanced power-sharing agreement and the Knesset, on Sept. 14, approved a national unity government including both the Labor Alignment and the Likud bloc. Under the terms, Labor leader Peres was to serve as Prime Minister for the first half of a 50-month term and Shamir, the Likud leader, was to be Deputy Prime Minister and Foreign Minister. For the second half of the term, the two men were to reverse roles. The 25-member Cabinet, largest in Israeli history, included 12 Likud ministers, 12 Labor ministers, and a minister from the National Religious Party.

Within days, the unity government took steps to deal with Israel's severe economic problems, announcing a 9% devaluation of the shekel and plans for stiff budget cuts. Peres also said the government was committed to withdrawing Israeli troops from Lebanon "in a matter of several months."

On a visit to Washington in October, Peres made a detailed plea for billions of dollars in additional American aid over several years. President Reagan promised that the United States would "cooperate the best way we can" to help resolve Israel's economic problems.

ITALY

Italian Republic

President: Sandro Pertini (1978)
Premier: Bettino Craxi (1983)
Area: 116,500 sq mi. (301,278 sq km)
Population (est. 1982): 56,500,000 (average annual growth rate: 0.3%)
Density per square mile: 485.8
Capital: Rome
Largest cities (1982): Rome, 2,834,094; Milan, 1,580,810; Naples, 1,209,086; Turin, 1,093,384; Genoa, 754,432; Palermo, 707,721; Bologna, 454,703; Florence, 444,294; Catania, 382,784; Bari, 370,308
Monetary unit: Lira
Language: Italian
Religion: Roman Catholic
National name: Repubblica Italiana
Literacy rate: Not known
Economic summary: Gross national product (1980): \$369.0 billion. Average annual growth rate (1970–79): 2.2%. Per capita income (1980): \$6,480. Land used for agriculture: 50%; labor force: 14%; principal products: wheat, rice, grapes, olives, citrus fruits. Labor force in industry: 38%; major products: automobiles, machinery, chemicals, textiles, shoes. Natural resources: fish, dwindling natural gas reserves. Exports: machinery and transport equipment, textiles, foodstuffs, chemicals, footwear. Imports: machinery and transport equipment, foodstuffs, ferrous and nonferrous metals, wool, cotton, petroleum. Major trading partners: West Germany, France, Netherlands, U.K.

Geography. Italy is a long peninsula shaped like a boot bounded on the west by the Tyrrhenian Sea and on the east by the Adriatic. Slightly larger than Arizona, it has for neighbors France, Switzerland, Austria, and Yugoslavia.

Approximately 600 of Italy's 708 miles (1,139 km) of length are in the long peninsula that projects into the Mediterranean from the fertile basin of the Po River. The Apennine Mountains, branching off from the Alps between Nice and Genoa, form the peninsula's backbone, and rise to a maximum height of 9,560 feet (2,912 m) at the Gran Sasso d'Italia (Corno). The Alps form Italy's northern boundary.

Several islands form part of Italy. Sicily (9,926 sq mi.; 25,708 sq km) lies off the toe of the boot, across the Strait of Messina, with a steep and rockbound northern coast and gentler slopes to the sea in the west and south. Mount Etna, an active volcano, rises to 10,741 feet (3,274 m), and most of Sicily is more than 500 feet (3,274 m) in elevation. Sixty-two miles (100 km) southwest of Sicily lies Pantelleria (45 sq mi.; 117 sq km), and south of that are Lampedusa and Linosa. Sardinia (9,301 sq mi.; 24,090 sq km), which is just south of Corsica and about 125 miles (200 km) west of the mainland, is mountainous, stony, and unproductive.

Italy has many northern lakes, lying below the snow-covered peaks of the Alps. The largest are Garda (143 sq mi.; 370 sq km), Maggiore (83 sq mi.; 215 sq km), and Como (55 sq mi.; 142 sq km).

The Po, the principal river, flows from the Alps on Italy's western border and crosses the Lombard plain to the Adriatic.

Government. The president is elected for a term of seven years by Parliament in joint session with regional representatives. The president nominates the premier and, upon the premier's recommendations, the members of the Cabinet. Parliament is composed of two houses: a Senate with 315 elective members and a Chamber of Deputies of 630 members elected by the people for a five-year term.

The major political parties are: Christian Democratic Party (225 seats of 630 in Chamber of Deputies), led by Ciriaco De Mita; Communist Party (198 seats), led by Alessandro Natta; Socialist Party (73 seats), led by Premier Bettino Craxi; Italian Social Movement (42 seats), led by Giorgio Almirante; Republican Party (29 seats), led by Giovanni Spadolini; Social Democratic Party (23 seats), led by Pietro Longo; Liberal Party (16 seats), led by Valerio Zanone; Radical Party (11 seats), led by Roberto Cicciomessere; Proletarian Democracy (7 seats), led by Lucio Magri; South Tyrol Popular Party (3 seats), led by Silvius Magnago; and other groups (3 seats).

History. Until A.D. 476, when the German Odoacer became head of the Roman Empire in the west, the history of Italy was largely the history of Rome. From A.D. 800 on, the Holy Roman Emperors, Popes, Normans, and Saracens all vied for control over various segments of the Italian peninsula. Numerous city states, such as Venice and Genoa, and many small principalities flourished in the late Middle Ages.

In 1713, after the War of the Spanish Succession, Milan, Naples, and Sardinia were handed over to Austria, which lost some of its Italian territories in 1735. After 1800, Italy was unified by Napoleon, who crowned himself King of Italy in 1805; but with the Congress of Vienna in 1815, Austria once again became the dominant power in Italy.

Austrian armies crushed Italian uprisings in 1820, 1821, and 1831. In the 1830s Giuseppe Mazzini, brilliant liberal nationalist, organized the Risorgimento (Resurrection), which laid the foundation for Italian unity.

Disappointed Italian patriots looked to the House of Savoy for leadership. Count Camille di Cavour (1810–61), Premier of Sardinia in 1852 and the architect of a united Italy, joined England and France in the Crimean War (1853–56), and in 1859, helped France in a war against Austria, thereby obtaining Lombardy. By plebiscite in 1860, Modena, Parma, Tuscany, and the Romagna voted to join Sardinia. In 1860, Giuseppe Garibaldi conquered Sicily and Naples and turned them over to Sardinia. Victor Emmanuel II, King of Sardinia, was proclaimed King of Italy in 1861.

Allied with Germany and Austria-Hungary in the Triple Alliance of 1882, Italy declared its neutrality upon the outbreak of World War I on the ground that Germany had embarked upon an offensive war. In 1915, Italy entered the war on the side of the Allies.

Benito (Il Duce) Mussolini, a former Socialist, organized discontented Italians in 1919 into the Fascist Party to "rescue Italy from Bolshevism." He led his Black Shirts in a march on Rome and, on Oct. 28, 1922, became premier. He transformed Italy into a dictatorship, embarking on an expansionist foreign policy with the invasion and annexation of Ethiopia in 1935 and allying himself with Adolf Hitler in the Rome-Berlin Axis in 1936. He was executed by Partisans on April 28, 1945 at Dongo on Lake Como.

Following the overthrow of Mussolini's dictatorship and the armistice with the Allies (Sept. 3, 1943), Italy joined the war against Germany as a co-belligerent. King Victor Emmanuel III abdicated May 9, 1946, and left the country after having installed his son as King Humbert II. A plebiscite rejected monarchy, however, and on June 13, King Humbert followed his father into exile.

The peace treaty of Sept. 15, 1947, required Italian renunciation of all claims in Ethiopia and Greece and the cession of the Dodecanese to Greece and of five small Alpine areas to France. Much of the Istrian Peninsula, including Fiume and Pola, went to Yugoslavia.

The Trieste area west of the new Yugoslav territory was made a free territory (until 1954, when the city and a 90-square-mile zone were transferred to Italy and the rest to Yugoslavia).

The government of Mario Rumor fell in 1974. After a 51-day crisis, a government was formed under Aldo Moro, a left-centrist Christian Democrat who had been Premier three times before.

Withdrawal of the Socialists from Moro's coalition—the 32nd government since World War II—brought his resignation Jan. 7, 1976. In the June elections, the Communists gained but the Christian Democrats still led and, warned by the U.S. and West Germany against a Communist coalition, they chose to govern as a minority under Giulio Andreotti. Petro Ingrao, a Communist, became President of the Chamber of Deputies, however, and Communists won 7 of 26 parliamentary chairmanships.

Andreotti had Communist cooperation in imposing wage limits and taxes to meet International Monetary Fund conditions for a $530-million loan. He also got Communist backing to combat a wave of kidnappings and political terrorism that culminated in the seizure of former Premier Moro in Rome on March 16, 1978, by the ultra-left Red Brigades. The discovery on May 9 of Moro's bullet-ridden body near the site of his kidnapping caused worldwide shock.

A second political shock was the resignation of President Giovanni Leone on June 15, six months before the end of his term, because of his involvement in Lockheed bribery scandals. Eighty-one-year-old Sandro Pertini became Italy's first Socialist president.

Tacit Communist support that had enabled Andreotti to govern ended on March 31, 1979, as the Communists insisted on seats in Andreotti's fifth cabinet and joined with the Socialists to defeat the government.

Disaster and scandal brought the long reign of the Christian Democrats to an end when Italy's 40th premier since World War II, Arnaldo Forlani, was forced to resign in the wake of disclosure that many high-ranking Christian Democrats and civil servants belonged to a secret Masonic lodge known as "P-2." The scandal followed the disastrous earthquake that struck southern Italy on Nov. 23, 1980, killing 3,105, injuring 7,671, and leaving 1,575 missing and presumed dead. Delay in providing relief for survivors, amid reports of theft of supplies, cast a pall over the nation.

When the Socialists deserted the coalition, Forlani was forced to resign on May 26, 1981, leaving to Giovanni Spadolini of the small Republican Party the task of forming a new government. He was succeeded by Amintore Fanfani, a Christian Democrat, the following year. Bettino Craxi, a Socialist, became Premier in 1983.

A resurgence of terrorism occurred with the kidnapping of Brig. Gen. James L. Dozier, U.S. commander of the NATO land forces headquarters in Verona. He was freed by Italian commandos on Jan. 28, 1982, after 42 days of captivity in a Red Brigade hideout. A total of 385 terrorists were arrested in a nationwide crackdown.

Religion. Although Italy is predominantly Roman Catholic, religious freedom is permitted. Catholic religious teaching is given in all elementary and intermediate schools. Relations with the Church were regulated until 1977, by the treaty with the Holy See of Feb. 11, 1929, which established the temporal power of the Pope over Vatican City. In November 1977, a new accord replaced the 1929 Corcordat; Catholicism is no longer to be considered as the state religion and Vatican influence on education and marriage has been reduced.

IVORY COAST

Republic of Ivory Coast
President: Félix Houphouët-Boigny (1960)
Area: 124,502 sq mi. (322,462 sq km)
Population (est. 1982): 8,500,000 (average annual growth rate: 3.3%)
Density per square mile: 68.3
Capital and largest city (est. 1981): Abidjan, 1,500,000
Monetary unit: Franc CFA
Ethnic groups: Agnis, Baoulés, Senoufos, Kroumen, Mandes, Dan-Gouros, Akié
Languages: French and African languages
Religions: Animist, 44%; Christian, 32%; Islam, 24%
National name: République de la Côte d'Ivoire
Literacy rate: 65%
Economic summary: Gross national product (1980): $9.9 billion. Average annual growth rate (1970–79): 1.3%. Per capita income (1980): $1,150. Labor force in agriculture: 85%; principal products: coffee, cocoa, timber, palm oil, sugar, bananas. Major industrial products: food, textiles, shoes, metals. Natural resources: petroleum, iron ore. Exports: coffee, cocoa, tropical woods. Imports: raw materials, consumer goods, fuels. Major trading partners: France, U.S., Western European countries.

Geography. The Ivory Coast, in western Africa on the Gulf of Guinea, is a little larger than New Mexico. Its neighbors are Liberia, Guinea, Mali, Upper Volta, and Ghana.

The country consists of a coastal strip in the south, dense forests in the interior, and savannas in the north. Rainfall is heavy, especially along the coast.

Government. The government is headed by a President who is elected every five years by popular vote, together with a National Assembly of 147 members.

The Parti Démocratique de la Côte d'Ivoire, a member of the Rassemblement Démocratique Africain, is the only political party.

History. The Ivory Coast attracted both French and Portuguese merchants in the 15th century. French traders set up establishments early in the 19th century, and in 1842, the French obtained territorial concessions from local tribes, gradually extending their influence along the coast and inland. The area was organized as a territory in 1893, became an autonomous republic in the French Union after World War II, and achieved independence on Aug. 7, 1960.

The Ivory Coast formed a customs union in 1959 with Dahomey (Benin), Niger, and Upper Volta. The country is one of the most prosperous and stable in West Africa.

JAMAICA

Sovereign: Queen Elizabeth II
Governor-General: Sir Florizel Glasspole (1973)
Prime Minister: Edward P. G. Seaga (1980)
Area: 4,411 sq mi. (11,424 sq km)
Population (est. 1982): 2,250,000 (average annual growth rate: 1.2%)
Density per square mile: 510.1
Capital and largest city (est. 1981): Kingston, 200,000
Monetary unit: Jamaican dollar
Language: English
Religions: Anglican, Baptist, Roman Catholic
Member of Commonwealth of Nations
Literacy rate (1981): 40%
Economic summary: Gross national product (1980): $2.3 billion. Average annual growth rate (1970–79): –3.7%. Per capita income (1980): $1,030. Land used for agriculture: 21%; labor force: 30% (includes fishing and mining); principal products: sugar cane, citrus fruits, bananas, pimentos, coconuts, coffee, cocoa. Labor force in industry: 12%; major products: bauxite, textiles, processed foods, light manufactures. Natural resources: bauxite, gypsum, limestone. Exports: alumina, bauxite, sugar, bananas, citrus fruits, rum, cocoa. Imports: fuels, machinery, transport and electrical equipment, food, fertilizer. Major trading partners: U.S., U.K., Canada.

Geography. Jamaica is an island in the West Indies, 90 miles (145 km) south of Cuba and 100 miles (161 km) west of Haiti. It is a little smaller than Connecticut.

The island is made up of a plateau and the Blue Mountains, a group of volcanic hills, in the east. Blue Mountain (7,402 ft.; 2,256 m) is the tallest peak.

Government. The legislature is a 60-member House of Representatives elected by universal suffrage and an appointed Senate of 21 members. The Prime Minister is appointed by the Governor-General and must, in the Governor-General's opinion, be the person best able to command the confidence of a majority of the members of the House of Representatives.

The major political parties are the Jamaica Labor Party (all 60 seats in the House of Representatives), led by Prime Minister Edward P. G. Seaga; and the People's National Party (no seats), led by former Prime Minister Michael Manley.

History. Jamaica was inhabited by Arawak Indians when Columbus discovered it in 1494 and named it St. Iago. It remained under Spanish rule until 1655, then became a British possession. The island prospered from wealth brought by buccaneers to their base, Port Royal, the capital, until the city disappeared in the sea in 1692 after an earthquake. The Arawaks died off from disease and exploitation, and slaves, mostly black, were imported to work sugar plantations. Abolition of the slave trade (1807), emancipation of the slaves (1833), and a gradual drop in sugar prices led to depressed economic conditions that resulted in an uprising in 1865.

The following year Jamaica's status was changed to that of a colony, and conditions improved considerably. Introduction of banana cultivation made the island less dependent on the sugar crop for its well-being. Overpopulation and problems inherited from the colonial era, such as illiteracy, produced chronic substantial unemployment, leading to much emigration to the Caribbean countries and to the U.S.

On May 5, 1953, Jamaica attained internal autonomy, and in 1958 it led in organizing the West Indies Federation. This effort at Caribbean unification failed. A nationalist labor leader, Sir Alexander Bustamente, led a campaign for withdrawal from the Federation. As the result of a popular referendum in 1961, Jamaica became independent on Aug. 6, 1962.

Michael Manley became Prime Minister in 1972 and initiated a socialist program and in 1977, the government bought 51% of the Kaiser and Reynolds bauxite operations.

Elections on Oct. 30, 1980, offered a sharp contrast between Manley's socialism trending toward the Cuban model of his friend, Fidel Castro, and the aggressive capitalism of Labor Party leader Edward P. G. Seaga. A campaign marked by violence ended with 57% of the popular vote and 51 of 60 House seats for Seaga, who immediately banished the Cuban ambassador. Seaga was the first foreign head of government to visit the newly installed President Reagan, on Jan. 28, 1981, to appeal for aid. The International Monetary Fund granted a loan of $650 million in April and a group of industrialized nations, together with the Interamerican Development Bank, offered credits of $350,000.

Manley's People's National Party boycotted an election in 1983, leading to a sweep by Seaga's Labor Party of all 60 seats in the House of Representatives.

JAPAN

Emperor: Hirohito (1926)
Prime Minister: Yasuhiro Nakasone (1982)
Area: 143,574 sq mi. (371,367 sq km)
Population (est. 1982): 118,693,000 (average annual growth rate: 0.7%)
Density per square mile: 825.4
Capital: Tokyo
Largest cities (est. 1981)[1] Tokyo, 8,335,000; Yokohama, 2,807,000; Osaka, 2,635,000; Nagoya, 2,089,000; Kyoto, 1,477,000; Sapporo, 1,433,000; Fukuoka, 1,104,000
Monetary unit: Yen
Language: Japanese
Religions: Shintoist, Buddhist, Christian
National name: Nippon
Literacy rate (1981): 99%
Economic summary: Gross national product (1981): $1,060.0 billion. Average annual growth rate (1972–81): 4.85%. Per capita income (1981): $9,864. Land used for agriculture, 16%; labor force, including fishing, 11%; principal products: rice, vegetables, fruits, meat, natural silk. Labor force in industry: 34%; major products: machinery and equipment, metals and metal products, textiles, autos, chemicals, electrical and electronic equipment. Natural resource: fish. Exports: machinery and equipment, automobiles, metals and metal products, textiles. Imports: fossil fuels, metal ore, raw materials, foodstuffs, machinery and equipment. Major trading partners: U.S., Southeast Asian, Middle Eastern, and Western European countries.

1. Except for Tokyo, figures refer to *shi*, a minor division that may include some scattered or rural population as well as an urban center.

Geography. An archipelago extending more than 1,744 miles (2,790 km) from northeast to southwest in the Pacific, Japan is separated from the east coast of Asia by the Sea of Japan. It is approximately the size of Montana.

Japan's four main islands are Honshu, Hokkaido, Kyushu, and Shikoku. The Ryukyu chain to the southwest was U.S.-occupied and the Kuriles to the northeast are Russian-occupied. The surface of the main islands consists largely of mountains separated by narrow valleys. There are about 60 more or less active volcanoes, of which the best-known is Mount Aso. Mount Fuji, seen on postcards, is not active.

Government. Japan's Constitution, promulgated on Nov. 3, 1946, replaced the Meiji Constitution of 1889. The 1946 Constitution, sponsored by the U.S. during its occupation of Japan, brought fundamental changes to the Japanese political system, including the abandonment of the Emperor's divine rights. The Diet (Parliament) consists of a House of Representatives of 511 members, elected for four years, and a House of Councilors of 252 members, half of whom are elected every three years for six-year terms. Executive power is vested in the Cabinet, which is headed by a Prime Minister, nominated by the Diet from its members.

Emperor Hirohito, who was born April 29, 1901, succeeded his father, Yoshihito, on Dec. 25, 1926. He was married on Jan. 26, 1924, to Princess Nagako, born in 1903. They have two sons—Crown Prince Akihito (born Dec. 23, 1933) and Prince Hitachi (born Nov. 28, 1935)—and four daughters. Succession to the Japanese throne is in the male line only.

The major political parties are the Liberal Democratic Party (284 of 511 seats in the House of Representatives), led by Prime Minister Yasuhiro Nakasme; Socialist Party (102 seats), led by Masatsugu Ishibashi; Clean Government (Komeito) Party (34 seats), led by Yoshikatsu Takeiri; Communist Party (29 seats), led by Kenji Miyamoto; Democratic Socialist Party (31 seats), led by Riyosaku Sasaki; New Liberal Club (13 seats).

History. A series of legends attributes creation of Japan to the sun goddess, from whom the later emperors were allegedly descended. The first of them was Jimmu Tenno, supposed to have ascended the throne in 660 B.C.

Recorded Japanese history begins with the first contact with China in the 5th century A.D. Japan was then divided into strong feudal states, all nominally under the Emperor, but with real power often held by a court minister or clan. In 1185, Yoritomo, chief of the Minamoto clan, was designated Shogun (Generalissimo) with the administration of the islands under his control. A dual government system—Shogun and Emperor—continued until 1867.

First contact with the West came about 1542, when a Portuguese ship off course arrived in Japanese waters. Portuguese, traders, Jesuit missionaries, and Spanish, Dutch, and English traders followed. Suspicious of Christianity and of Portuguese support of a local Japanese revolt, the shoguns prohibited all trade with foreign countries; only a Dutch trading post at Nagasaki was permitted. Western attempts to renew trading relations failed until 1853, when Commodore Matthew Perry sailed an American fleet into Tokyo Bay.

Japan now quickly made the transition from a medieval to a modern power. Feudalism was abolished and industrialization was speeded. An imperial army was established with conscription. The shogun system was abolished in 1868 by Emperor Meiji, and parliamentary government was established in 1889. After a brief war with China in 1894–95, Japan acquired Formosa (Taiwan), the Pescadores Islands, and part of southern Manchuria. China also recognized the independence of Korea (Chosen), which Japan later annexed (1910).

In 1904–05, Japan defeated Russia in the Russo-Japanese War, gaining the territory of southern Sakhalin (Karafuto) and Russia's port and rail rights in Manchuria. In World War I, Japan, which took a negligible part in military operations, seized Germany's Pacific islands and leased areas in China. The Treaty of Versailles then awarded it a mandate over the islands.

At the Washington Conference of 1921–22, Japan agreed to respect Chinese national integrity. The series of Japanese aggressions that was to lead to the nation's downfall began in 1931 with the invasion of Manchuria. The following year, Japan set up this area as a puppet state, "Manchukuo," under Emperor Henry Pu-Yi, last of China's Manchu dynasty. On Nov. 25, 1936, Japan joined the Axis by signing the anti-Comintern pact. The invasion of China came the next year and the Pearl Harbor attack on the U.S. on Dec. 7, 1941.

(For details of World War II (1939–45), *see* Headline History.)

Japan surrendered formally on Sept. 2, 1945, aboard the battleship *Missouri* in Tokyo Bay after atomic bombs had hit Hiroshima and Nagasaki. Southern Sakhalin and the Kurile Islands reverted to the U.S.S.R., and Formosa (Taiwan) and Manchuria to China. The Pacific islands remained under U.S. occupation. General of the Army Douglas MacArthur was appointed Supreme Commander for the Allied Powers on Aug. 14, 1945.

A new Japanese Constitution went into effect in 1947. In 1949, many of the responsibilities of government were returned to the Japanese. Full sovereignty was granted to Japan by the Japanese Peace Treaty in 1951.

The treaty took effect on April 28, 1952, when Japan returned to full status as a nation. It was admitted into the United Nations in 1958.

Following the visit of Prime Minister Eisaku Sato to Washington in 1969, the U.S. agreed to return Okinawa and other Ryukyu Islands to Japan in 1972, and both nations renewed the security treaty in 1970.

When President Nixon opened a dialogue with Peking in 1972, Prime Minister Kakuei Tanaka, who succeeded Sato in 1972, quickly established diplomatic relations with the mainland Chinese and severed ties with Formosa.

President Ford visited Japan Nov. 18–24, 1974, the first U.S. President to do so. Substantive results were minimized by Tanaka's domestic political troubles. Tanaka resigned two days after Ford's departure, and was succeeded by Takeo Miki, a compromise choice from the progressive wing of the Liberal Democrats.

While economic recovery continued in 1976, the Lockheed scandal pursued the ruling Liberal Democrats. With the disclosure by the U.S. Senate that $6.3 million in "promotion" money had been paid by the aircraft company to Yoshio Kodama, a rightwing political "fixer," Miki was placed under strong pressure to investigate the ultimate recipients. The scandal cost the party its control of the House of Representatives in the December election, but nine independents affiliated with the Liberal Democrats to provide a narrow majority. Miki resigned, turning over leadership to Takeo Fukuda.

Fukuda, concentrating on economic recovery, achieved a record year in 1977, with exports exceeding imports by $9 billion, nearly twice the previous record of $5.1 billion in 1972.

Visiting Washington in May 1978, Fukuda promised "massive efforts" to reduce Japan's surplus, by cutting automobile, color television, and steel exports and by buying U.S. aircraft. In return, like other U.S. trade partners, he urged Washington to curb inflation at home and support the dollar in foreign markets.

On Aug. 12, 1978, Japan and China signed a treaty of peace and friendship. This pact followed an 8-year, $20-billion economic pact in which Japanese business leaders agreed to provide China with modern technology in return for Chinese natural resources.

Despite pledges to its economic partners at the Bonn summit of industrial powers in July 1978 that it would reduce its trade surplus, Japan reported an all-time high figure of $18.3 billion for the year.

But, Japan's oil bill of $39.5 billion for the year ended March 31, 1980, produced a record trade deficit of $14.4 billion in contrast to a $13.4 billion surplus the previous year.

A $6-billion favorable balance in trade with the U.S. brought strong pressure from the U.S. auto industry and unions for a reduction in exports of Japanese cars although an earlier voluntary restraint on television exports was dropped.

Masayoshi Ohira, Prime Minister since November 1978, died on June 12, 1980, and in national elections held June 22, the ruling Liberal Democrats reversed an eight-year decline in public support, winning a firm parliamentary majority. The party chose Zenko Suzuki, a little-known 66-year-old follower of Ohira, as the new Prime Minister.

Suzuki's first contact with the Reagan Administration, in May 1981, went badly as reports of a U.S.-Japan "alliance" and weapons build-up emerged from the White House, causing the resignation of Masayoshi Ito as Foreign Minister for "misinterpreting" events. The sinking of a Japanese freighter by a U.S. nuclear submarine in the China Sea on April 9 and the statement by Former U.S. Ambassador Edwin O. Reischauer that U.S. ships carrying nuclear weapons regularly entered Japanese ports in the 1960s despite the Constitutional ban so aroused public opinion that Secretary of State Alexander M. Haig, Jr., canceled plans to visit Tokyo on his Far East tour in June.

Announcement on June 19 that Japan's gross national product grew at a rate of nearly 5% for the fiscal year ending March 31 brought new demands for increased imports of manufactured goods by Japan, which international trade experts charged was still creating barriers against trade despite repeated promises by Tokyo to relax such restrictions. To placate the ailing U.S. automobile industry, Japan announced that it would limit exports of cars to the United States to 1,680,000 units for the year ending March 31, 1982.

The same figure was agreed to by Japan for the following year, and for the first time, Japanese automobile exports declined for the 12-month period ending March 31, 1982. In an effort to remove non-tariff trade barriers, which U.S. businessmen held responsible for their inability to increase sales in Japan, the Suzuki government appointed a special ombudsman with authority to cut red tape. Despite this, Japan registered an average monthly trade surplus with the U.S. of $1.77 billion for the first half of 1982.

Under continued U.S. prodding, Tokyo announced a $707-million increase in defense spending for fiscal 1982 and $745 million for fiscal 1983, still below the target figure of 1% of the gross national product, which Suzuki pledged would be reached by 1985.

Suzuki was defeated in 1982 by Yasuhiro Nakasone who is considered pro-Western and better relations with the United States have ensued.

JORDAN

The Hashemite Kingdom of Jordan
Ruler: King Hussein I (1952)
Prime Minister: Ahmad Obeidat (1984)
Area: 37,297 sq mi. (96,599 sq km)[1]
Population (est. 1982): 3,475,000 (average annual growth rate: 3.2%)
Density per square mile: 93.2
Capital: Amman
Largest cities (est. 1981): Amman, 650,000; Zarka, 215,000; Irbid, 115,000
Monetary unit: Jordanian dinar
Language: Arabic
Religions: Islam, 93%; Christian, 5%
National name: Al Mamlaka al Urduniya al Hashemiyah
Literacy rate (1981): 55%
Economic summary: Gross national product (1980): $3.3 billion (East Bank only). Average annual growth rate (1970–79): 6.0%. Per capita income (1980): $1,420. Land used for agriculture: 11%; labor force: 23%; principal products: wheat, fruits, vegetables, olive oil. Labor force in industry: 67%; major products: phosphate, refined petroleum products, cement. Natural resources: phosphate, potash. Exports: fruits, vegetables, phosphate. Imports: petroleum products, textiles, capital goods, motor vehicles, foodstuffs. Major trading partners: U.S., U.K., West Germany, Japan, Lebanon, Saudi Arabia.

1. Includes territory occupied by Israel in 1967 war.

Geography. The Middle East kingdom of Jordan is bordered on the west by Israel and the Dead Sea, on the north by Syria, on the east by Iraq, and on the south Saudi Arabia. It is comparable in size to Indiana.

Arid hills and mountains make up most of the country. The southern section of the Jordan River flows through the country.

Government. Jordan is a constitutional monarchy with a bicameral parliament. Its Chamber of Deputies of 60 members is elected for four years by the people, and the 30 members of the Senate are appointed by the King.

All political parties were banned in 1957.

History. In biblical times, the country that is now Jordan contained the lands of Edom, Moab, Ammon, and Bashan. In A.D. 106 it became part of the Roman province of Arabia and in 633–36 was conquered by the Arabs.

Taken from the Turks by the British in World War I, Jordan (formerly known as Transjordan) was separated from the Palestine mandate in 1920, and in 1921, placed under the rule of Abdullah ibn Hussein.

In 1923, Britain recognized Jordan's independence, subject to the mandate. In 1946, grateful for Jordan's loyalty in World War II, Britain abolished the mandate. That part of Palestine occupied by Jordanian troops was formally incorporated by action of the Jordanian Parliament in 1950.

King Abdullah was assassinated in 1951. His son Talal was deposed as mentally ill the next year. Talal's son Hussein, born Nov. 14, 1935, succeeded him.

From the beginning of his reign, Hussein had to steer a careful course between his powerful neighbor to the west, Israel, and rising Arab nationalism, frequently a direct threat to this throne. Riots erupted when he joined the Central Treaty Organization (the Baghdad Pact) in 1955, and he incurred further unpopularity when Britain, France, and Israel attacked the Suez Canal in 1956, forcing him to place his army under nominal command of the United Arab Republic of Egypt and Syria.

The 1961 breakup of the UAR eased Arab national pressure on Hussein, who was the first to recognize Syria after it reclaimed its independence. Jordan was swept into the 1967 Arab-Israeli war, however, and lost the old city of Jerusalem and all of its territory west of the Jordan river, the West Bank. Embittered Palestinian guerrilla forces virtually took over sections of Jordan in the aftermath of defeat, and open warfare broke out between the Palestinians and government forces in 1970.

Despite intervention of Syrian tanks, Hussein's Bedouin army defeated the Palestinians, suffering heavy casualties. A U.S. military alert and Israeli armor massed on the Golan Heights contributed psychological weight, but the Jordanians alone drove out the Syrians and invited the departure of 12,000 Iraqui troops who had been in the country since the 1967 war. Ignoring protests from other Arab states, Hussein by mid-1971 crushed Palestinian strength in Jordan and shifted the problem to Lebanon, where many of the guerrillas had fled.

In October 1974, Hussein concurred in an Arab summit resolution calling for an independent Palestinian state and endorsing the Palestine Liberation Organization as the "sole legitimate representative of the Palestinian people." This apparent reversal of policy changed with the growing disillusion of Arab states with the P.L.O., however, and by 1977 Hussein referred again to the unity of people on both banks of the Jordan.

As Egypt and Israel neared final agreement on a peace treaty early in 1979, Hussein met with Yassir Arafat, the PLO leader, on March 17 and issued a joint statement of opposition. Although the U.S. pressed Jordan to break Arab ranks on the issue, Hussein elected to side with the great majority, cutting ties with Cairo and joining the boycott against Egypt.

On June 15, 1978, Hussein, who had celebrated his 25th anniversary on the throne, married Elizabeth Halaby, 26, daughter of Najeeb Halaby, former president of Pan American World Airways. In an unexpected gesture, the monarch's fourth wife—his previous wife was killed and the first two divorced—was proclaimed Queen and given the name Noor al-Hussein.

In September 1980, Jordan declared itself with Iraq in its conflict with Iran and, despite threats from Syria, opened ports to war shipments for Iraq unable to go directly to Baghdad because of the blocking of the Shatt al-Arab waterway.

In April 1983, Jordan rejected the American-sponsored Palestine peace plan proposed by President Reagan.

KAMPUCHEA

See Cambodia

KENYA

Republic of Kenya
President: Daniel Arap Moi (1978)
Area: 224,960 sq mi. (582,646 sq km)
Population (est. 1982): 17,600,000 (average annual growth rate: 4.1%)
Density per square mile: 78.2
Capital: Nairobi
Largest cities (est. 1980): Nairobi, 835,000; Mombasa, 400,000
Monetary unit: Kenyan shilling
Languages: Swahili (official), Bantu, Kikuyu, English
Religions: Protestant, 27%; Roman Catholic, 26%; Animist, 19%; Islam, 6%
Literacy rate (1981): 27%
Member of Commonwealth of Nations
Economic summary: Gross national product (1980): $6.6 billion. Average annual growth rate (1970–79): 2.6%. Per capita income (1980): $420. Land used for agriculture: 10–15%; labor force in agriculture: 23%; principal products: coffee, sisal, tea, pyrethrum, cotton, livestock. Labor force in industry: 14%; major products: plastic goods, furniture, batteries, textiles, soap, cigarettes, refined oil. Natural resources: wildlife. Exports: coffee, tea, livestock products, pyrethrum, tanning extract. Imports: machinery, transport equipment, crude oil, paper and paper products, iron and steel products, textiles. Major trading partners: Western European countries, Japan, Iran, U.S., Zambia, Uganda.

Geography. Kenya lies on the equator in east central Africa on the coast of the Indian Ocean. It is twice the size of Nevada. Kenya's neighbors are Tanzania, Uganda, the Sudan, Ethiopia, and Somalia.

In the north, the land is arid; the southwestern corner is in the fertile Lake Victoria Basin; and a length of the eastern depression of Great Rift Valley separates western highlands from those that rise from the lowland coastal strip. Large game reserves have been developed.

Government. Under its Constitution of 1963, amended in 1964, Kenya has a one-house National Assembly of 171 members, elected for five years by universal suffrage. Since 1969, the president has been chosen by a general election.

The Kenya African National Union, led by the president, is the only political party.

President Jomo Kenyatta died in his sleep on Aug. 22, 1978. Vice President Daniel Arap Moi was elected to succeed him on Oct. 10.

History. Kenya, formerly a British colony and protectorate, was made a crown colony in 1920. The whites' domination of the rich plateau area, the White Highlands, long regarded by the Kikiyu people as their territory, was a factor leading to native terrorism, called the Mau Mau movement, in 1952. In 1954 the British began preparing the territory for African rule and independence. In 1961 Jomo Kenyatta was freed from banishment to become leader of the Kenya African National Union.

Internal self-government was granted in 1963; Kenya became independent on Dec. 12, 1963, with Kenyatta the first president. Kenya obtained economic and technical assistance from Communist China beginning in 1964 and later a World Bank loan.

KIRIBATI

Republic of Kiribati
Sovereign: Queen Elizabeth II
Governor General: Reginald J. Wallace (1980)
President: Ieremia Tabai (1979)
Area: 264 sq mi. (683 sq km)
Population (est. 1982): 60,000 (average annual growth rate: 1.1%)
Density per square mile: 227.3
Capital (est. 1974): Bairiki (on Tarawa Atoll), 17,100
Monetary unit: Australian dollar
Language: English
Religions: Roman Catholic, 48%; Protestant, 45%
Member of Commonwealth of Nations
Literacy rate: Not known
Economic summary: Gross national product (1980): $50 million. Per capita income (1980): $770. Principal agricultural products: copra, vegetables. Exports: phosphates, copra. Imports: foodstuffs, fuel, transportation equipment. Major trading partners: New Zealand, Australia.

Geography. Kiribati, formerly the Gilbert Islands, consists of three widely separated main groups of Southwest Pacific islands, the Gilberts on the equator, the Phoenix Islands to the east, and the Line Islands further east. Ocean Island, producer of phosphates, which constitute 99% of the new nation's annual income of $18 million, is also included in the two million square miles of ocean, which will give Kiribati an important fishery resource.

Government. The president holds executive power. The legislature consists of a House Assembly with 37 members.

History. A British protectorate since 1892, the Gilbert and Ellice Islands became a colony in 1915–

16. The two island groups were separated in 1975 and given internal self-government.

Tarawa and others of the Gilbert group were occupied by Japan during World War II. Tarawa was the site of one of the bloodiest battles in U.S. Marine Corps history when Marines landed in November 1943 to dislodge the Japanese defenders.

Princess Anne, representing Queen Elizabeth II, presented the independence documents to the new government on July 12, 1979.

KOREA, NORTH

Democratic People's Republic of Korea
President: Marshal Kim Il Sung (1972)
Premier: Yi Chong Ok (1977)
Area: 46,768 sq mi. (121,129 sq km)
Population (est. 1982): 18,802,000 (average annual growth rate: 1.7%)
Density per square mile: 400.9
Capital and largest city (est. 1982): Pyongyang, 1,500,000
Monetary unit: Won
Language: Korean
Religions: None
National name: Democratic People's Republic of Korea
Literacy rate (1981): 90% (est.)
Economic summary: Gross national product (1982): $16.2 billion. Average annual growth rate (1970–79): 3.8%. Per capita income (1982): $786. Land used for agriculture: 17%; labor force, 48%; principal products: corn, rice, vegetables. Major industrial products: machines, electric power, chemicals, textiles, processed foods, metallurgical products. Natural resources: coal, iron ore. Exports: minerals, chemical and metallurgical products. Imports: machinery and equipment, petroleum, foodstuffs, coking coal. Major trading partners: U.S.S.R., China, Japan.

Geography. Korea is a 600-mile (966 km) peninsula jutting from Manchuria and China (and a small portion of the U.S.S.R.) into the Sea of Japan and the Yellow Sea off eastern Asia. North Korea occupies an area slightly smaller than Pennsylvania north of the 38th parallel.

The country is almost completely covered by a series of north-south mountain ranges separated by narrow valleys. The Yalu River forms part of the northern border with Manchuria.

Government. The elected Supreme People's Assembly, as the chief organ of government, chooses a Presidium and a Cabinet. The Cabinet, which exercises executive authority, is subject to approval by the Assembly and the Presidium.

The Korean Workers (Communist) Party, led by President Kim Il Sung, is the only political party.

History. According to myth, Korea was founded in 2333 B.C. by Tangun. In the 17th century, it became a vassal of China and was isolated from all but Chinese influence and contact until 1876, when Japan forced Korea to negotiate a commercial treaty, opening the land to the U. S. and Europe. Japan achieved control as the result of its war with China (1894–95) and with Russia (1904–05) and annexed Korea in 1910. Japan developed the country but never won over the Korean nationalists.

After the Japanese surrender in 1945, the country was divided into two occupation zones, the U.S.S.R. north of and the U.S. south of the 38th parallel. When the cold war developed between the U.S. and U.S.S.R., trade between the zones was cut off. In 1948, the division between the zones was made permanent with the establishment of separate regimes in the north and south. By mid-1949, the U.S. and U.S.S.R. withdrew all troops. The Democratic People's Republic of Korea (North Korea) was established on May 1, 1948. The Communist Party, headed by Kim Il Sung, was established in power.

On June 25, 1950, the North Korean army launched a surprise attack on South Korea. On June 26, the U.N. Security Council condemned the invasion as aggression and ordered withdrawal of the invading forces. On June 27, President Harry S. Truman ordered air and naval units into action to enforce the U.N. order. The British government did the same, and soon a multinational U.N. command was set up to aid the South Koreans. The North Korean invaders took Seoul and pushed the South Koreans into the southeast corner of their country.

Gen. Douglas MacArthur, U.N. commander, made an amphibious landing at Inchon on September 15 behind the North Korean lines, which resulted in the complete rout of the North Korean army. The U.N. forces drove north across the 38th parallel, approaching the Yalu River. Then Communist China entered the war, forcing the U.N. forces into headlong retreat. Seoul was lost again, then regained; ultimately the war stabilized near the 38th parallel but dragged on for two years while the belligerents negotiated. An armistice was agreed to on July 27, 1953.

North Korea became embroiled with the U.S. again on Jan. 23, 1968, when it seized the American intelligence ship *Pueblo* and its crew of 83. After more than a year, the crew was released.

When a U.S. helicopter strayed across the 38th parallel July 13, 1977, and was shot down by North Koreans, with the loss of three crewmen, the reaction was much more restrained. President Carter acknowledged U.S. error and, after seven hours of talks at Panmunjom, the North Koreans sent back the three bodies and the lone survivor.

Although Kim appears to be revered, economic troubles have beset his rigidly collectivist country. World bankers say a record of unpaid accounts due the U.S.S.R., as well as non-Communist states, has demolished North Korea's international credit standing. Its armed forces, numbering 467,000, are about three fourths of the South's military establishment, but the North's 600-plane air force holds a 3-to-1 edge over its potential foe, who has relied on U.S. air support in the event of war.

President Carter, visiting Seoul from June 29 to July 1, 1979, proposed that the U.S., North Korea, and South Korea meet "to promote dialogue and reduce tensions in the area," possibly leading to reunification of the two Koreas. Pyongyang's official party newspaper rejected the proposal, saying the North favors reunification talks but without the "alien interference" of the U.S.

Kim again rejected as a "foolish burlesque" an invitation on Jan. 12, 1981, by South Korea's military chief, Chun Doo Hwan, to hold reunification talks in Seoul. Kim refused again when Chun repeated the invitation on March 3 during his inauguration as President of the Southern republic.

KOREA, SOUTH

Republic of Korea
President: Chun Doo Hwan (1980)
Premier: Chin lee Chong (1984)
Area: 38,031 sq mi. (98,500 sq km)
Population (est. 1983): 40,000,000 (average annual growth rate: 1.6%)
Density per square mile: 1,046
Capital: Seoul
Largest cities (est. 1983): Seoul, 9,000,000; Pusan, 3,400,000; Taegu, 2,000,000; Inchon, 1,200,000
Monetary unit: Won
Language: Korean
Religions: Buddhist, 19%; Protestant, 13.4%; Roman Catholic, 4%; Confucian, 1.9%
National name: Dae Han Min Kook
Literary rate (1981): 90%
Economic summary: Gross national product (1983): $75.1 billion. Average annual growth rate (1974–83): 7.35%. Per capita income (1983): $1,880. Land used for agriculture: 23%; labor force, including fishing, 21.8%; principal products: rice, barley. Labor force in industry: 24%; major products: clothing and textiles, processed foods, chemical fertilizers, chemicals, plywood, steel, electronics equipment. Natural resources: iron and copper ore, tungsten, graphite, limestone, coal, gold, silver. Exports: clothing and textiles, electric machinery, footwear, steel. Imports: oil, steel, grains, textiles, organic chemicals, machinery. Major trading partners: U.S., Japan.

Geography. Slightly larger than Indiana, South Korea lies below the 38th parallel on the Korean peninsula. It is mountainous in the east; in the west and south are many harbors on the mainland and offshore islands.

Government. A national referendum in October 1980 approved a new Constitution that provides for election of the President by an electoral college chosen by popular vote. The term of office is for seven years, limited to one term. A unicameral National Assembly has 276 members, 184 elected directly by popular vote, the remainder appointed in proportion to party strength in the selection.

Major parties are the Democratic Justice Party (152 of 276 National Assembly seats), led by President Chun Doo Hwan; the opposition Democratic Korea Party (81 seats), led by Yoo Chi Song, and the Korea National Party (25 seats), led by Kim Chong Chull; Independents hold 11 seats and the remaining seven are held by splinter parties.

History. South Korea came into being in the aftermath of World War II as the result of a 1945 agreement making the 38th parallel the boundary between a northern zone occupied by the U.S.S.R. and a southern zone occupied by U.S. forces. (For details, *see* North Korea.)

Elections were held in the U.S. zone in 1948 for a national assembly, which adopted a republican Constitution and elected Syngman Rhee president. The new republic was proclaimed on August 15 and was recognized as the legal government of Korea by the U.N. on Dec. 12, 1948.

On June 25, 1950, South Korea was attacked by North Korean Communist forces. U.S. armed intervention was ordered on June 27 by President Harry S. Truman, and on the same day the U.N. invoked military sanctions against North Korea. Gen. Douglas MacArthur was named commander of the U.N. forces. U.S. and South Korean troops fought a heroic holding action but, by the first week of August, they had been forced back to a 4,000-square-mile beachhead in southeast Korea.

There they stood off superior North Korean forces until September 15, when a major U.N. amphibious attack was launched far behind the Communist lines at Inchon, port of Seoul. By September 30, U.N. forces were in complete control of South Korea. They then invaded North Korea and were nearing the Manchurian and Siberian borders when several hundred thousand Chinese Communist troops entered the conflict in late October. U.N. forces were then forced to retreat below the 38th parallel.

On May 24, 1951, U.N. forces recrossed the parallel and had made important new inroads into North Korea when truce negotiations began on July 10. An armistice was finally signed at Panmunjom on July 27, 1953, leaving a devastated Korea in need of large-scale rehabilitation.

The U.S. and South Korea signed a mutual-defense treaty on Oct. 1, 1953.

Rhee, president since 1948, resigned in 1960 in the face of rising disorders. PoSun Yun was elected to succeed him, but political instability continued. In 1961, Gen. Park Chung Hee took power and subsequently built up the country. The U.S. stepped up military aid, building up South Korea's armed forces to 600,000 men. The South Koreans sent 50,000 troops to Vietnam, at U.S. expense.

In mid-1972, following President Nixon's summit meetings in Moscow and Peking, the two Kôreas issued a mutual declaration setting a goal of peaceful reunification. (For details, *see* Korea, North).

In 1977, tension between Seoul and Washington also arose over human rights as South Korean dissidents appealed for U.S. support in their demands that Park rescind both the 1972 Constitution and his 1975 emergency powers. Park responded to pressure by releasing 14 political detainees.

A growing scandal over Korean bribery of U.S. Congressmen accelerated in 1977 with testimony by a defecting ex-Director of the KCIA who named a Washington influence man, Tongsun Park, as a KCIA agent. Two former Democratic Representatives, Richard T. Hanna of California and Otto E. Passman of Louisiana, were indicted in 1978 for accepting bribes, with Hanna sentenced to six months in prison.

A Congressional investigation in 1978 charged four Democratic Representatives, Charles H. Wilson, Edward R. Roybal, and John J. McFall of California, and Edward J. Patten of New Jersey, with having accepted money improperly from Park.

Park's assassination on Oct. 26, 1979, by Kim Jae Kyu, head of the Korean Central Intelligence Agency, brought a liberalizing trend as Choi Kyu Hah, the new President, freed imprisoned dissidents. The release of opposition leader Kim Dae Jung in February 1980 generated anti-government demonstrations that turned into riots by May. Choi resigned on Aug. 16. Chun Doo Wha, head of a military Special Committee for National Security Measures, was the sole candidate as the electoral college confirmed him as President on Aug. 27. On Sept. 17, Kim Dae Jung was sentenced to death by a military court on charges of high treason. Chun commuted the sentence on Jan. 23, 1981, and lifted martial law the next day.

Elected to a full seven-year term on Feb. 11, Chun had visited Washington on Feb. 2 to receive President Reagan's assurance that U.S. troops would remain in South Korea and that the sale of U.S. F-16 jet aircraft would be authorized to modernize the Republic's air force. General elections on March 25 gave the ruling Democratic Justice Party a solid majority of the National Assembly.

Chun marked his first anniversary in March 1982 by freeing 2,863 political prisoners, but renewed political unrest in Pusan two weeks later brought a government crackdown. For the first time since the Korean War, curfew was lifted in Seoul in preparation for the nation's role as host of the 1988 Summer Olympic Games, as a major refurbishing of the capital began.

KUWAIT

State of Kuwait
Emir: Sheik Jaber al-Ahmad al-Sabah (1977)
Prime Minister: Sheik Sa'ad Abdullah al-Sabah (1978)
Area: 7,780 sq mi. (20,150 sq km)
Population (est. 1983): 1,650,000 (average annual growth rate: 6.2%)
Density per square mile: 212.1
Capital (est. 1982): Kuwait, 182,000
Largest city (est. 1980): Hawalli, 752,000
Monetary unit: Kuwaiti dinar
Languages: Arabic and English
Religions: Islam, 92%; Christian 6%
National name: Dowlat al Kuwait
Literacy rate (1981): 60%
Economic summary: Gross national product (1980): $30.9 billion. Average annual growth rate (1970–79): 1.4%. Per capita income (1980): $22,840. Land used for agriculture: 1%. Labor force in industry: 22%; major products: crude and refined oil, fertilizer, chemicals, building materials, shrimp. Natural resources: petroleum, fish, shrimp. Exports: crude and refined petroleum, shrimp. Imports: foodstuffs, automobiles, building materials, machinery, textiles. Major trading partners: U.S., Japan, U.K., West Germany.

Geography. Kuwait is situated northeast of Saudi Arabia at the northern end of the Persian Gulf, south of Iraq. It is slightly larger than Hawaii. The low-lying land is mainly sandy and barren.

Government. Sheik Jaber al-Ahmad al-Sabah rules as Emir of Kuwait and appoints the Prime Minister, who appoints his Cabinet (Council of Ministers). The National Assembly, consists of 50 members elected by adult males. There are no political parties in Kuwait.

History. Kuwait obtained British protection in 1897 when the Sheik feared that the Turks would take over the area. In 1961, Britain ended the protectorate, giving Kuwait independence, but agreed to give military aid on request. Iraq immediately threatened to occupy the area and Sheik Sabah al-Salem al-Sabah called in British troops in 1961. Soon afterward the Arab League sent in troops, replacing the British. The prize was oil.

Oil was discovered in the 1930s. Kuwait proved to have 20% of the world's known oil resources. It has been a major producer since 1946, the world's second largest oil exporter, with the main concession held by a British-American concern. The Sheik, who gets half the profits, devotes most of them to the education, welfare, and modernization of his kingdom. In 1966, Sheik Sabah designated a relative, Jaber al-Ahmad al-Sabah, as his successor.

By 1968, the sheikdom had established a model welfare state, and it sought to establish dominance among the sheikdoms and emirates of the Persian Gulf.

In 1975, the government nationalized Kuwaiti operations of Gulf Oil and British Petroleum. The acquisition, which cost about $180 million, gave Kuwait full control of an estimated 60 billion barrels of petroleum reserves.

In 1981, the World Bank classed Kuwait as the world's richest country, with a per capita gross national product of $15,970.

The Kuwaitis became greatly alarmed in mid-1984 by the possibility they might become embroiled in the nearby fighting between Iran and Iraq. After the United States refused to sell them antiaircraft missiles, they initialed a $327-million deal to buy missiles, tanks and other military equipment from the Soviet Union.

LAOS

Lao People's Democratic Republic
President: Souphanouvong (1975)
Premier: Kaysone Phomvihane (1975)
Area: 91,429 sq mi. (236,800 sq km)
Population (est. 1982): 3,900,000 (average annual growth rate: 1.7%)
Density per square mile: 42.7
Capital and largest city (est. 1980): Vientiane, 250,000
Monetary unit: Kip
Languages: Lao (official), French, English
Religions: Buddhist, 58%; tribal, 34%
Literacy rate (1981): 15%
Economic summary: Gross national product: (1980): $300 million. Per capita income (1977): $70. Land used for agriculture, 8%; labor force, 85%; principal products: rice, corn, vegetables. Major industrial products: tin, timber, tobacco, textiles, electric power. Natural resources: tin, timber, hydroelectric power. Exports: electric power, forest products, tin concentrates, coffee. Imports: rice, foodstuffs, petroleum products, machinery, transport equipment. Major trading partners: Thailand, U.S.S.R., Malaysia, France, Vietnam.

Geography. A landlocked nation in Southeast Asia occupying the northwestern portion of the Indochinese peninsula, Laos is surrounded by China, Vietnam, Cambodia, Thailand, and Burma. It is twice the size of Pennsylvania.

Laos is a mountainous country, especially in the north, where peaks rise above 8,000 feet (2,438 m). Dense forests cover the northern and eastern areas. The Mekong River, which forms the boundary with Burma and Thailand, flows entirely through the country for 300 miles (483 km) of its course.

Government. Laos is a people's democratic republic with executive power in the hands of the premier. The monarchy was abolished Dec. 2, 1975, when the Pathet Lao ousted a coalition government and King Sisavang Vatthana abdicated. The King was appointed "Supreme Adviser" to the President, the former Prince Souphanouvong. Former Prince Souvanna Phouma, Premier since 1962, was made an "adviser" to the government. The Lao People's Revolutionary Party (Pathet Lao), led by Premier Kaysone Phomvihane, is the only political party.

History. Laos became a French protectorate in 1893, and the territory was incorporated into the union of Indochina. A strong nationalist movement developed during World War II, but France reestablished control in 1946 and made the King of Luang Prabang constitutional monarch of all Laos. France granted semiautonomy in 1949 and then, spurred by the Viet Minh rebellion in Vietnam, full independence within the French Union in 1950. In 1951, Prince Souphanouvong organized the Pathet Lao, a Communist independence movement, in North Vietnam. The Viet Minh in 1953 established the Pathet Lao in power at Samneua. Viet Minh and Pathet Lao forces invaded central Laos, and civil war resulted.

By the Geneva agreements of 1954 and an armistice of 1955, two northern provinces were given the Pathet Lao, the royal regime the rest. Full sovereignty was given the kingdom by the Paris agreements of Dec. 29, 1954. In 1957, Prince Souvanna Phouma, the royal Premier, and the Pathet Lao leader, Prince Souphanouvong, the Premier's half-brother, agreed to reestablishment of a unified government, with Pathet Lao participation and integration of Pathet Lao forces into the royal army. The agreement broke down in 1959, and armed conflict broke out again.

In 1960, the struggle became three-way as Gen. Phoumi Nosavan, controlling the bulk of the royal army, set up in the south a pro-Western revolutionary government headed by Prince Boun Gum. General Phoumi took Vientiane in December, driving Souvanna Phouma into exile in Cambodia. The Soviet bloc supported Souvanna Phouma. In 1961, a cease-fire was arranged and the three princes agreed to a coalition government headed by Souvanna Phouma.

But North Vietnam, the U.S. (in the form of Central Intelligence Agency personnel), and China remained active in Laos after the settlement. North Vietnam used a supply line (Ho Chi Minh trail) running down the mountain valleys of eastern Laos into Cambodia and South Vietnam, particularly after the U.S.-South Vietnamese incursion into Cambodia in 1970 stopped supplies via Cambodian seaports.

An agreement, reached in 1973 revived coalition government. The Communist Pathet Lao seized complete power in 1975, installing Souphanouvong as president and Kaysone Phomvihane as premier. Since then other parties and political groups have been moribund and most of their leaders have fled the country.

Laotian officials confirmed in March 1979 the presence of 30,000 Vietnamese troops in Laos and their use of the country as a staging area for the Vietnamese invasion of Cambodia. They also confirmed that 1,000 Laotian troops were in Cambodia in support of the Heng Samrin regime, which overthrew the Pol Pot government in January.

LEBANON

Republic of Lebanon
President: Amin Gemayel (1982)
Premier: Rashid Karami (1984)
Area: 4,015 sq mi. (10,400 sq km)
Population (est. 1983): 1,598,000 (average annual growth rate: −0.5%)
Density per square mile: 672.5
Capital: Beirut
Largest cities (est. 1981): Beirut, 750,000; Tripoli, 200,-000
Monetary unit: Lebanese pound
Languages: Arabic (official), French, English
Religions: Christian and Islam
National name: Al-Joumhouriya al-Lubnaniya
Literacy rate (1981): 86%
Economic summary: Gross national product (1980 est.): $4.1 billion. Per capita income: n.a. Land used for agriculture: 27%; labor force: 49%; principal products: fruits, wheat, corn, barley, potatoes, tobacco, olives, onions. Labor force in industry: 11%; major products: processed foods, textiles, cement, chemicals, refined oil; tourism. Exports: fruits, vegetables, textiles. Imports: metals, machinery, foodstuffs. Major trading partners: U.S., Western European and Arab countries.

Geography. Lebanon lies at the eastern end of the Mediterranean Sea north of Israel and west of Syria. It is four fifths the size of Connecticut.

The Lebanon Mountains, which parallel the coast on the west, cover most of the country, while on the eastern border is the Anti-Lebanon range. Between the two lies the El Bika Valley, the principal agricultural area.

Government. Lebanon is governed by a President, elected by Parliament for a six-year term, and a Cabinet of Ministers appointed by the President but responsible to Parliament.

Parliament has 99 members elected for a four-year term by universal suffrage and chosen by proportional division of religious groups.

Party breakdown of the Chamber of Deputies is difficult because of the religious groupings required by law and because many deputies join in major parliamentary blocs.

History. In ancient times Lebanon was the mountainous hinterland of the Phoenician coast towns. From the 7th to the 11th century there infiltrated into southern Lebanon the heretics of Islam, who finally coalesced into the Druse community.

In the 19th century the Turkish Sultanate encouraged the Druses to wage civil war against the Christian Maronites. After a massacre of 2,500 Christians in 1860, Lebanon was occupied by the French for a year. From 1864 to 1914, a Christian military government ruled the area under nominal Turkish sovereignty. After World War I, France received a League of Nations mandate over Syria and Lebanon. The French drew a Lebanese border in 1920 to offset predominantly Moslem Syria and proclaimed the area a republic under French control on May 23, 1926. Complete independence came on Nov. 26, 1941. Lebanon joined the Arab League and took part in the invasion of Palestine on May 15, 1948.

In 1958, a civil war broke out, with the Moslems Kamal Jumblatt and Saeb Salam leading the opposition to the Maronite Christian government. Threatened with defeat, President Camille Chamoun obtained the intervention of U.S. military forces. In September, a Maronite Christian military man, Gen. Fouad Chehab, took over the presidency. After a U.N. resolution demanded it, the U.S. forces withdrew.

Palestinian guerrillas using Lebanese territory drew Lebanon into conflict with Israel. Terrorist assaults on Israel's northern settlements drew punitive raids against guerrillas in Lebanon by Israeli.

Intensifying civil war through 1976 led to the ousting of President Suleiman Franjieh by Parliament in May. Franjieh refused to step down until the end of his six-year term in October when his successor, Elias Sarkis, took office.

At the time of Sarkis' inauguration, Lebanon was divided into a northern sector, controlled by Syrian troops who had entered the country to restore order, and a coastal region under Christian control, with enclaves where leftist Moslems and the Palestine Liberation Organization dominated.

A new crisis began for Lebanon on March 14, 1978, with the invasion of Israeli forces across the entire 60-mile northern border. The invasion was in retaliation for a PLO terrorist raid on Israel and the chief targets were PLO bases in southern Lebanon. On March 19, the U.N. Security Council called for immediate withdrawal and authorized a 4,000-man peacekeeping force to occupy the area, a force later enlarged to 6,000.

Israeli troops withdrew by June but turned over more strongpoints to Lebanese Christian militia than to UNIFIL, the U.N. force.

Tension escalated in April 1981 when Israeli jets intervened for the first time in fighting between Syrian troops and Christian militia east of Beirut. While a special U.S. Mideast peace envoy, Philip C. Habib, sought to mediate, Israel on July 17 bombed a densely populated section of Beirut, claiming that it was done in retaliation for PLO rockets and artillery fired from Lebanon into northern Israel.

The bombing left 300 dead and 800 wounded and brought an appeal by the Security Council for a cease-fire. Not until July 24 was Habib able to win Begin's consent to a cease-fire, difficult to arrange because the Israeli Prime Minister refused to negotiate with the PLO.

On June 6, 1982, Lebanon suffered a total invasion by Israel, bent on revenge for a PLO attack on the Israeli ambassador to London. Within four days, the invaders had surrounded Beirut after destroying Tyre and Sidon, two coastal strongholds of the Palestinian guerrillas. The Israelis laid siege to Moslem West Beirut, where some 5,000 or 6,000 PLO guerrillas were trapped, and pounded the city with bombs and artillery.

Habib was finally able to negotiate the dispersal of most of the PLO to other Arab nations and Israel pulled back some of its forces. The violence seemed to have come to an end when, on Sept. 14, Bashir Gemayel, the 34-year-old President-elect, was killed when a bomb destroyed his Phalangist Party headquarters, resulting in the death of 26 others.

The day after Gemayel's assassination, Israel troops moved into west Beirut in force. On Sept. 17 it was revealed that hundreds of Palestinians had been massacred in two refugee camps, reportedly by Christian militiamen. Israel denied responsibility for the killings although its troops had been stationed in the area.

On Sept. 20, Amin Gemayel, older brother of Bashir Gemayel, was elected President by the parliament.

The massacre in the refugee camps prompted the return of a multinational peacekeeping force composed of U.S. Marines and British, French, and Italian soldiers. Their mandate was to support the central Lebanese government, but they soon found themselves drawn into the struggle for power between different Lebanese factions. During their stay in Lebanon, 260 U.S. Marines and about 60 French soldiers were killed, most of them in suicide bombings of the Marine and French Army compounds on Oct. 23, 1983. The multinational force left in the spring of 1984.

During 1984, Israeli troops remained in southern Lebanon and Syrian troops remained in the Bekaa Valley. Fighting between Lebanese factions erupted sporadically but the capital, Beirut, began to calm down as a government security plan was gradually put into effect and barricades dividing the city's Moslem and Christian sectors were torn down.

LESOTHO

Kingdom of Lesotho
Sovereign: King Moshoeshoe II (1966)
Prime Minister: Chief Leabua Jonathan (1966)
Area: 11,720 sq mi. (30,355 sq km)
Population (est. 1982): 1,300,000 (average annual growth rate: 2.2%)
Density per square mile: 119.5
Capital and largest city (est. 1981): Maseru, 45,000
Monetary unit: Loti
Languages: English and Sesotho (official)
Religions: Roman Catholic, 44%; Lesotho Evangelical Church, 30%; Anglican, 12%
Member of Commonwealth of Nations
Literacy rate (1981): 40%
Economic summary: Gross national product (1980): $520 million. Average annual growth rate (1970–79): 9.5%. Per capita income (1980): $390. Land used for agriculture: 15%; labor force: 87%; principal products: corn, wheat, sorghum, barley, livestock. Labor force in industry: 2%. Natural resources: diamonds. Exports: wool, mohair, wheat, cattle, diamonds, hides and skins. Imports: corn, building materials, clothing, vehicles, machinery. Major trading partner: South Africa.

Geography. Mountainous Lesotho, the size of Maryland, is surrounded by the Republic of South Africa in the east central part of that country except for short borders on the east and south with two discontinuous units of the Republic of Transkei. The Drakensberg Mountains in the east are Lesotho's principal chain. Elsewhere the region consists of rocky tableland.

Government. There is a 93-member interim National Assembly made up of 60 representatives of various political parties, 22 leading chiefs, and 11 appointees.

The major political parties are the Basotho National Party, led by Prime Minister Leabua Jonathan and the Basutoland Congress Party, led by G. P. Ramoreboli.

History. Lesotho (formerly Basutoland) was constituted a native state under British protection by a treaty signed with the native chief Moshesh in 1843. It was annexed to Cape Colony in 1871, but in 1884 it was restored to direct control by the Crown.

The colony of Basutoland became the independent nation of Lesotho on Oct. 4, 1966.

In the 1970 elections, Ntsu Mokhehle, head of the Basutoland Congress Party, claimed a victory, but Jonathan declared a state of emergency, suspended the Constitution, and arrested Mokhehle. The major issue in the election was relations with South Africa, with Jonathan for close ties to the surrounding white nation, while Mokhehle was for a more independent policy. Jonathan jailed 45 opposition politicians, declared the King had "technically abdicated" by siding with the opposition party, exiled him to the Netherlands, and named his Queen and her seven-year-old son as Regent.

The King returned after a compromise with Jonathan in which the new Constitution would name him head of state but forbid his participation in politics.

LIBERIA

Republic of Liberia
President: Gen. Samuel K. Doe (1980)
Area: 43,000 sq mi. (111,370 sq km)
Population (est. 1982): 2,150,000 (average annual growth rate: 3.2%)
Density per square mile: 50.0
Capital and largest city (est. 1981): Monrovia, 245,000
Monetary unit: Liberian dollar
Languages: English (official) and tribal dialects
Religions: Animist, 44%; Christian, 35%; Islam, 21%
Literacy rate (1981): 24%
Economic summary: Gross national product (1980): $980 million. Average annual growth rate (1970–79): 0.5%. Per capita income (1980): $520. Land used for agriculture: 20%; labor force: 75%; principal products: rubber, rice, palm oil, cassava, coffee, cocoa. Labor force in industry: 25%; major products: iron ore, diamonds, processed rubber, processed food, construction materials. Natural resources: iron ore, rubber, timber, diamonds. Exports: iron ore, rubber, timber, diamonds. Imports: machinery, petroleum products, transport equipment, foodstuffs. Major trading partners: U.S., West Germany, Netherlands, Italy, Belgium.

Geography. Lying on the Atlantic in the southern part of West Africa, Liberia is bordered by Sierra Leone, Guinea, and the Ivory Coast. It is comparable in size to Tennessee.

Most of the country is a plateau covered by dense tropical forests, which thrive under an annual rainfall of about 160 inches a year.

Government. Since April 25, 1980, Liberia had been under military rule by the 17-member People's Redemptive Council, which suspended the Constitution after overthrowing the civilian government. On July 22, 1984, the Council was replaced with an interim, appointed National Assembly in a step toward return of civilian rule.

History. Liberia was founded in 1822 as a result of the efforts of the American Colonization Society to settle freed American slaves in West Africa. In 1847, it became the Free and Independent Republic of Liberia.

The government of Africa's first republic was modeled after that of the United States, and Joseph J. Roberts of Virginia was elected the first president. He laid the foundations of a modern state and initiated efforts, never too successful but pursued for more than a century, to bring the aboriginal inhabitants of the territory to the level of the emigrants. The English-speaking descendants of U.S. blacks, known as Americo-Liberians, were the intellectual and ruling class. The indigenous inhabitants, divided, constitute 99% of the population.

The country's only big enterprises are the million-acre concession granted in 1925 to the Firestone Plantations Co. for rubber cultivation, and a large iron ore concession developed by the Republic Steel Corp., beginning in 1951. After 1920, considerable progress was made toward opening up the interior, a process that was spurred in 1951 by the establishment of a 43-mile (69-km) railroad to the Bomi Hills from Monrovia.

In July 1971, while serving his sixth term as president, William V. S. Tubman died following surgery and was succeeded by his long-time associate, Vice President William R. Tolbert, Jr.

Tolbert was ousted in a military coup carried out April 12, 1980, by army enlisted men led by Master Sgt. Samuel K. Doe. Tolbert and 27 other high officials were executed. Doe and his colleagues based their action on the grievances of "native" Liberians against corruption and misrule by the Americo-Liberians who had ruled the country since its founding.

LIBYA

Socialist People's Libyan Arab Jamahiriya
Head of State: Col. Muammar el-Qaddafi (1969)
Secretary-General of the General People's Congress: Muhammad al-Zarruq Rajah (1981)
Premier: Jadallah Azzuz et Talhi (1979)
Area: 679,536 sq mi. (1,759,998 sq km)
Population (est. 1983): 3,498,000 (average annual growth rate: 5.0%)
Density per square mile: 4.8
Capital: Tripoli
Largest cities (est. 1980): Tripoli, 1,000,000; Benghazi, 400,000
Monetary unit: Libyan dinar
Language: Arabic
Religion: Islam
National name: Al-Jumhuria al-Arabia al-Libya
Literacy rate (1981): 35%
Economic summary: Gross national product (1982): $25.3 billion. Average annual growth rate (1970–79): –1.6%. Per capita income (1982): $7,918. Land used for agriculture: 7%; labor force: 20%; principal products: wheat, barley, olives, dates, citrus fruits, peanuts. Labor force in industry: 10%; major products: petroleum, processed foods, textiles, handicrafts. Natural resources: petroleum, natural gas. Export: petroleum. Imports: machinery, foodstuffs, manufactured goods. Major trading partners: Italy, West Germany, U.S., U.K., France.

Geography. Libya stretches along the northeastern coast of Africa between Tunisia and Algeria on the west and Egypt on the east; to the south are the Sudan, Chad, and Niger. It is one sixth larger than Alaska.

A greater part of the country lies within the Sahara. Along the Mediterranean coast and farther inland is arable plateau land.

Government. In a bloodless coup d'etat on Sept. 1, 1969, the military seized power in Libya. King Idris I, who had ruled since 1951, was deposed and the Libyan Arab Republic proclaimed. The official name was changed in 1977 to the Socialist People's Libyan Arab Jamahiriya. The Revolutionary Council that had governed since the coup was renamed the General Secretariat of the General People's Congress. The Arab Socialist Union Organization is the only political party.

History. Libya was a part of the Turkish dominions from the 16th century until 1911. Following the outbreak of hostilities between Italy and Turkey in that year, Italian troops occupied Tripoli; Italian sovereignty was recognized in 1912.

Libya was the scene of much desert fighting during World War II. After the fall of Tripoli on Jan. 23, 1943, it came under Allied administration. In 1949, the U.N. voted that Libya should become independent by 1952.

Discovery of oil in the Libyan Desert promised financial stability and funds for economic development.

On July 21, 1977, a four-day war broke out between Libya and Egypt, with Egypt charging that Libyans had attacked a frontier post. Superior Egyptian air power and armor inflicted losses on their opponents and the clash ended after Algerian President Houari Boumediène intervened as peacemaker.

Another military adventure by President Muammar el-Qaddafi ended ignominiously in April 1979 with the defeat of a Libyan force of 2,000 sent to the aid of Uganda's President Idi Amin against Ugandan rebels and Tanzanian forces. Qaddafi offered asylum to the ousted Amin and his family.

The United States closed its embassy in Tripoli on Feb. 7 amid growing U.S.-Libyan tension. Four members of the Libyan embassy in Washington were expelled on May 11 for threatening Libyan students in the United States.

The Reagan Administration, accusing Libya of supporting international terrorism, closed the Libyan embassy in Washington on May 6, 1981. After talks with Libyan officials in July, the U.S. concluded that no improvement in relations was possible, although U.S. oil companies remained active in Libya and 2,000 U.S. citizens continued to work there.

On Aug. 19, 1981, two U.S. Navy F-14's shot down two Soviet-made SU-22's of the Libyan air force that had attacked them in air space above the Gulf of Sidra, claimed by Libya but held to be international by the U.S. In December, Washington asserted that Libyan "hit squads" had been dispatched to the U.S. and security was drastically tightened around President Reagan and other officials. Reagan requested remaining American citizens to leave Libya and nearly all did by Dec. 15. When the Mobil Oil Company abandoned its operations in April 1962, only four U.S. firms were still in Libya, using Libyan or third-country personnel.

Qaddafi's troops also supported rebels in Chad.

In a bizarre incident in the spring of 1984, Libyan exiles demonstrating against Qaddafi outside the Libyan embassy in London were sprayed with machinegun fire from a window of the embassy. A British policewoman was killed and about 15 anti-Qaddafi Libyans wounded. After a standoff of nearly a week, the Libyan embassy in London and the British embassy in Tripoli were closed and diplomatic relations suspended. Along with the other Libyans in the London embassy, the unidentified gunman returned to Tripoli unpunished.

LIECHTENSTEIN

Principality of Liechtenstein
Ruler: Prince Franz Josef II (1938)
Prime Minister: Hans Brunhart (1978)
Area: 61 sq mi. (157 sq km)
Population (est. 1982): 30,000 (average annual growth rate: 1.7%)
Density per square mile: 491.8
Capital and largest city (est. 1980): Vaduz, 4,600
Monetary unit: Swiss franc
Language: German (Alemannish dialect)
Religions: Roman Catholic, 88%; Protestant, 11%
Literacy rate (1981): 100%
Economic summary: Per capita income (1978): $14,000. Labor force in agriculture: 4%; principal products: livestock, vegetables, corn, wheat, potatoes, grapes. Labor force in industry: 55%; major products: high-technology products, building equipment, food products, machinery, industrial goods. Natural resources: timber, hydroelectric power, salt. Exports: manufactured metal products, machines and instruments, textiles, chemical products. Imports: raw materials, machinery, processed foods and goods. Major trading partners: Finland, Switzerland and other Western European countries.

Geography. Tiny Liechtenstein, not quite as large as Washington, D.C., lies on the east bank of the Rhine River south of Lake Constance between Austria and Switzerland. It consists of low valley land and Alpine peaks. Falknis (8,401 ft; 2,561 m) and Naatkopf (8,432 ft; 2,570 m) are the tallest.

Government. The Constitution of 1921, amended in 1972, provides for a legislature, the Landtag, of 15 members elected by direct male suffrage.

Prince Hans Adam has been defacto ruler since 1984, when his father, Prince Franz Josef II, relinquished his responsibilities but not his title to the throne.

The major political parties are the Homeland Union (8 of 15 seats in the Landtag) and the Progressive Citizens Party (7 seats).

History. Founded in 1719, Liechtenstein was a member of the German Confederation from 1815 to 1866, when it became an independent principality. It abolished its army in 1868 and has managed to stay neutral and undamaged in all European wars since then. In a referendum on July 1, 1984, male voters granted women the right to vote, a victory for Prince Hans Adam.

LUXEMBOURG

Grand Duchy of Luxembourg
Ruler: Grand Duke Jean (1964)
Premier: Jacques Santer (1984)
Area: 999 sq mi. (2,586 sq km)
Population (est. 1983): 366,000 (Luxembourgian, French, German) (average annual growth rate: 0.1%)
Density per square mile: 365.4
Capital and largest city (est. 1982): Luxembourg, 80,000
Monetary unit: Luxembourg franc
Languages: Letzeburgesch, French, German
Religion: Mainly Roman Catholic
National name: Grand-Duché de Luxembourg
Literacy rate (1981): 98%
Economic summary: Gross national product (1981): $3.9 billion. Average annual growth rate (1981): –2.0%. Per capita income (1981): $10,785. Land used for agriculture: 25%; labor force: 6%; principal products: livestock, dairy products, wine. Labor force in industry: 46%; major products: steel, rubber, synthetic fibers. Natural resource: Iron ore. Export: steel. Imports: machinery, textiles, transport equipment, plastics. Major trading partners: European Common Market countries.

Geography. Luxembourg is a neighbor of Belgium on the west, West Germany on the east, and France on the south. The Ardennes Mountains extend from Belgium into the northern section of Luxembourg.

Government. Luxembourg's unicameral legislature, the Chamber of Deputies, consists of 59 members elected for five years.

The major political parties are the Christian Social Party (25 of 59 seats in Chamber of Deputies), led by Prime Minister Jacques Santer; Socialist-Labor (21 seats), led by Robert Krieps; Democratic Party (14 seats), led by Colette Flesch; Communist Party (2 seats); Green Party (2 seats).

History. Sigefroi, Count of Ardennes, an offspring of Charlemagne, was Luxembourg's first sovereign ruler. In 1060, the country came under the rule of the House of Luxembourg. From the 15th to the 18th century, Spain, France, and Austria held it in turn. The Congress of Vienna in 1815 made it a Grand Duchy and gave it to William I, King of the Netherlands. In 1839 the Treaty of London ceded the western part of Luxembourg to Belgium.

The eastern part, continuing in personal union with the Netherlands and a member of the German Confederation, became autonomous in 1848 and a neutral territory by decision of the London Conference of 1867, governed by its Grand Duke. Germany occupied the duchy in World Wars I and II. Allied troops liberated the enclave in 1944.

In 1961, Prince Jean, son and heir of Grand Duchess Charlotte, was made head of state, acting for his mother. She abdicated in 1964, and Prince Jean became Grand Duke.

By a customs union between Belgium and Luxembourg, which came into force on May 1, 1922, to last for 50 years, customs frontiers between the two countries were abolished. On Jan. 1, 1948, a customs union with Belgium and the Netherlands (Benelux) came into existence. On Feb. 3, 1958, it became an economic union.

MADAGASCAR

Democratic Republic of Madagascar

President and Head of State: Comdr. Didier Ratsiraka (1975)
Prime Minister: Lt. Col. Desiré Rakotoarijaona (1977)
Area: 230,035 sq mi. (595,791 sq km)
Population (est. 1982): 9,190,000 (average annual growth rate: 2.8%)
Density per square mile: 40.1
Capital and largest city (est. 1983): Antananarivo, 700,000
Monetary unit: Malagasy franc
Languages: Malagasy, French
Ethnic groups: Merina (or Hova), Betsimisaraka, Betsileo, Tsimihety, Antaisaka, Sakalava, Antandroy
Religions: Animist, 45%; Roman Catholic, 25%; Protestant, 25%; Islam, 5%
National name: Repoblika Demokratika Malagasy
Literacy rate (1981): 45%
Economic summary: Gross national product (1983): $3 billion. Average annual growth rate (1970–79): 3.0%. Per capita income (1980): $350. Land used for agriculture: 63%; labor force: 26%; principal products: rice, livestock, coffee, vanilla, sugar, cloves, cotton, sisal, peanuts, tobacco. Labor force in industry: 15%; major products: processed food, textiles, refined petroleum products, assembled automobiles, soap, mining products. Natural resources: graphite, chromium, coal, bauxite, ilmenite, tar sands, semiprecious stones. Exports: coffee, cloves, vanilla, chromium, graphite, shellfish, cotton products. Imports: consumer goods, foodstuffs, crude petroleum, rice. Major trading partners: France, U.S.

Geography. Madagascar lies in the Indian Ocean off the southeast coast of Africa opposite Mozambique. The world's fourth-largest island, it is twice the size of Arizona. The country's low-lying coastal area gives way to a central plateau. The once densely wooded interior has largely been cut down.

Government. The Constitution of Dec. 30, 1975, approved by referendum following a military coup, provides for direct election by universal suffrage of a president for a seven-year term, a Supreme Council of the Revolution as a policy-making body, a unicameral People's National Assembly of 137 members (elected for five-year terms), and a military Committee for Development. The new constitution followed a period of martial rule that began with the suspension of the republic's original bicameral legislature in 1972.

History. The present population is of black and Malay stock, with perhaps some Polynesian, called Malagasy. The French took over a protectorate in 1885, and then in 1894–95 ended the monarchy, exiling Queen Rànavàlona III to Algiers. A colonial administration was set up, to which the Comoro Islands were attached in 1908, and other territories later. In World War II, the British occupied Madagascar, which retained ties to Vichy France.

An autonomous republic within the French Community since 1958, Madagascar became an independent member of the Community in 1960. In May 1973, an army coup led by Maj. Gen. Gabriel Ramanantsoa ousted Philibert Tsiranana, president since 1959.

With unemployment and inflation both high, Ramanantsoa resigned Feb. 5, 1975. His leftist-leaning successor, Interior Minister Richard Ratsimandrava, an Army lieutenant colonel, was killed six days later by a machine-gun ambush in Antananarivo, the capital.

On June 15, 1975, Comdr. Didier Ratsiraka was named President. He announced that he would follow a socialist course and, after nationalizing banks and insurance companies, declared all mineral resources nationalized.

MALAWI

Republic of Malawi

Life President: Hastings Kamuzu Banda (1966)
Area: 45,747 sq mi. (118,484 sq km)
Population (est. 1982): 6,275,000 (average annual growth rate: 2.6%)
Density per square mile: 137.2
Capital (est. 1982): Lilongwe, 125,000
Largest city (est. 1982): Blantyre, 250,000
Monetary unit: Kwacha
Languages: English (official) and Chichewa (National)
Religions: Christian, 65%; Animist, 19%; Islam, 16%
Member of Commonwealth of Nations
Literacy rate (1981): 15%
Economic summary: Gross national product (1980): $1.4 billion. Average annual growth rate (1979–82): 2.5%. Per capita income (1982): $222,000. Average rate of

inflation (1974–78): 10%. Land used for agriculture: 30%; labor force: 48%; principal products: tobacco, tea, sugar, corn, peanuts. Labor force in industry: 21%; major products: food, beverages, tobacco, textiles, footwear, cement. Natural resource: limestone. Exports: tobacco, sugar, peanuts. Imports: machinery, transport equipment, building and construction materials, fuel. Major trading partners: U.K., U.S., Zimbabwe, Netherlands, Japan, West Germany.

Geography. Malawi is a landlocked country the size of Pennsylvania in southeastern Africa, surrounded by Mozambique, Zambia, and Tanzania. Lake Malawi, formerly Lake Nyasa, occupies most of the country's eastern border. The north-south Rift Valley is flanked by mountain ranges and high plateau areas.

Government. Under a Constitution that came into effect on July 6, 1966, the president is the sole head of state; there is neither a prime minister nor a vice president. The National Assembly has 107 members.

There is only one national party—the Malawi Congress Party led by President Hastings K. Banda.

History. The first European to make extensive explorations in the area was David Livingstone in the 1850s and 1860s. In 1884, Cecil Rhodes's British South African Company received a charter to develop the country. The company came into conflict with the Arab slavers in 1887–89. After Britain annexed the Nyasaland territory in 1891, making it a protectorate in 1892, Sir Harry Johnstone, the first high commissioner, using Royal Navy gunboats, wiped out the slavers.

Nyasaland became the independent nation of Malawi on July 6, 1964. Two years later, it became a republic within the Commonwealth of Nations.

Dr. Hastings K. Banda, Malawi's first Prime Minister, became its first President. He pledged to follow a policy of "discretionary nonalignment." Banda alienated much of Black Africa by maintaining good relations with such white-ruled nations as South Africa and Rhodesia. He argued that his landlocked country had to rely on white-ruled countries for access to the sea and trade.

MALAYSIA

Paramount Ruler: Almutawakkil Alallah Sultan Iskandar Alhaj D.K., Sultan of Johore (1984)
Prime Minister: Mahathir Bin Mohamed (1981)
Area: 128,328 sq mi. (332,370 sq km)
Population (est. 1982): 14,750,000 (average annual growth rate: 2.3%)
Density per square mile: 114.9
Capital: Kuala Lumpur
Largest cities (est. 1980 by U.N.): Kuala Lumpur, 1,000,000; George Town (Pinang), 300,000; Ipoh, 275,000
Monetary unit: Ringgit
Languages: Malay (official), Chinese, Tamil, English
Religions: Islam, (official), Buddhist, Hindu, Christian, Confucian, Taoist
Member of Commonwealth of Nations
Literacy rate (1981): 72%
Economic summary: Gross national product (1981): $12.3 billion. Average annual growth rate (1970–79): 5.4%. Per capita income (1981): $1,796. Labor force: 12%; principal products: natural rubber, palm oil, tin, petroleum, rice, timber. Major industrial products: processed rubber, timber, and palm oil, tin, petroleum, light manufactures, electronics equipment. Natural resources: tin, oil, copper, timber. Exports: natural rubber, palm oil, tin, timber, petroleum. Imports: machinery, transport equipment, chemicals. Major trading partners: Japan, Singapore, U.S., Western European countries.

Geography. Malaysia is at the southern end of the Malay Peninsula in southeast Asia. The nation also includes Sabah and Sarawak on the island of Borneo to the southeast. Its area slightly exceeds that of New Mexico.

Most of Malaysia is covered by dense jungle and swamps, with a mountain range running the length of the peninsula. Extensive forests provide ebony, sandalwood, teak, and other woods.

Government. Malaysia is a sovereign constitutional monarchy within the Commonwealth of Nations. The Paramount Ruler is elected for a five-year term by the hereditary rulers of the states from among themselves. He is advised by the prime minister and his cabinet. There is a bicameral legislature. The Senate, whose role is comparable more to that of the British House of Lords than to the U.S. Senate, has 68 members, partly appointed by the Paramount Ruler to represent minority and special interests, and partly elected by the legislative assemblies of the various states.

The House of Representatives, or lower house, is made up of 154 members, who are elected for five-year terms.

The major political parties are the National Front, a coalition of 10 parties (132 of 154 seats in the House of Representatives); Democratic Action Party (9 seats); Islamic Party (5 seats); Independents (8 seats).

History. Malaysia came into existence on Sept. 16, 1963, as a federation of Malaya, Singapore, Sabah (North Borneo), and Sarawak. In 1965, Singapore withdrew from the federation. Since 1966, the 11 states of former Malaya have been known as West Malaysia, and Sabah and Sarawak have been known as East Malaysia.

The Union of Malaya was established April 1, 1946, being formed from the Federated Malay States of Negri Sembilan, Pahang, Perak, and Selangor; the Unfederated Malay States of Johore, Kedah, Kelantan, Perlis, and Trengganu; and two of the Straits Settlements—Malacca and Penang. The Malay states had been brought under British administration during the late 19th and early 20th centuries.

It became the Federation of Malaya on Feb. 1, 1948, and the Federation attained full independence within the Commonwealth of Nations in 1957.

Sabah, constituting the extreme northern portion of the island of Borneo, was a British protectorate administered under charter by the British North Borneo Company from 1881 to 1946, when it assumed the status of a colony. It was occupied by Japanese troops from 1942 to 1945.

Sarawak extends along the northwestern coast of Borneo for about 500 miles (805 km). In 1841, part of the present territory was granted by the Sultan of Brunei to Sir James Brooke. Sarawak continued to be ruled by members of the Brooke family until the Japanese occupation.

From 1963, when Malaysia became independent, it was the target of guerrilla infiltration from

Indonesia, but beat off invasion attempts. In 1966, when Sukarno fell and the Communist Party was liquidated in Indonesia, hostilities ended.

In the late 1960s, the country was torn by communal rioting directed against Chinese and Indians, who controlled a disproportionate share of the country's wealth. Beginning in 1968, the government moved to achieve greater economic balance through a rural development program.

Malaysia felt the impact of the "boat people" fleeing Vietnam early in 1978. Because the refugees were mostly ethnic Chinese, the government was apprehensive about any increase of a minority that previously had been the source of internal conflict in the country. In November, authorities banned landings and reversed the order only after several hundred refugees drowned when their fragile boats were towed offshore by Malaysian police. By August 1980, the number of refugees was reported down to 20,000 from a high of 76,500 in July 1979.

MALDIVES

Republic of Maldives
President: Maumoon Abdul Gayoom (1978)
Area: 115 sq mi. (298 sq km)
Population (est. 1982): 168,000 (average annual growth rate: 3.0%)
Density per square mile: 1,391.3
Capital and largest city (est. 1980): Malé, 30,000
Monetary unit: Maldivian rupee
Language: Divehi
Religion: Islam
Literacy rate: Largely illiterate
Economic summary: Gross national product (1981 est.): $51.2 million. Average annual growth rate (1970–79): −0.7%. Per capita income (est. 1981): $352. Principal agricultural products: coconuts, millet. Labor force in industry: 42%, major products: fish, processed coconuts. Natural resource: fish, coconuts. Export: fish, sharkfins Imports: rice, sugar. Major trading partners: Japan, Sri Lanka, Singapore.

Geography. The Republic of Maldives is a group of atolls in the Indian Ocean about 417 miles (671 km) southwest of Sri Lanka. Its 1,300 coral islets stretch over an area of 35,200 square miles (90,000 sq km).

Government. The 9-member Cabinet is headed by the president. The Majlis (Parliament) is a unicameral legislature consisting of 48 members. Eight of these are appointed by the president. The others are elected for five-year terms, 2 from the capital island of Malé and 2 from each of the 19 administrative atolls.

There are no political parties in the Maldives.

History. The Maldives (formerly called the Maldive Islands) are inhabited by an Islamic seafaring people. Originally the islands were under the suzerainty of Ceylon. They came under British protection in 1887 and were a dependency of the then colony of Ceylon until 1948. The independence agreement with Britain was signed July 26, 1965.

For centuries a sultanate, the islands adopted a republican form of government in 1952, but the sultanate was restored in 1954. In 1968, however, as the result of a referendum, a republic was again established in the islands.

Ibrahim Nasir, president since 1968, was removed from office by the Majlis in November 1978 and replaced by Maumoon Abdul Cayoom. A national referendum confirmed the new leader.

MALI

Republic of Mali
Chief of State (1968) and Head of Government (1969): Gen. Moussa Traoré
Area: 478,819 sq mi. (1,240,142 sq km)
Population (est. 1982): 7,350,000 (average annual growth rate, 2.7%)
Density per square mile: 15.8
Capital and largest city (est. 1981): Bamako, 450,000
Monetary unit: Franc CFA
Ethnic groups: Bambara, Peul, Soninke, Malinke, Songhai, Dogon, Senoufo, Minianka, Berbers, and Moors
Languages: French (official), African languages
Religions: Islam, 65%; Animist, 30%; Christian, 5%
National name: République de Mali
Literacy rate (1981): 5%
Economic summary: Gross national product (1980): $1.3 billion. Average annual growth rate (1970–79): 2.5%. Per capita income (1980): $190. Principal agricultural products: millet, sorghum, corn, rice, sugar, cotton, peanuts, livestock. Major industrial products: processed foods, textiles, cigarettes, fish. Natural resources: bauxite, iron ore, maganese, lithium, phosphate, kaolin, salt, limestone, gold. Exports: livestock, peanuts, dried fish, cotton, skins. Imports: textiles, vehicles, petroleum products, machinery, sugar. Major trading partners: Western European countries, U.S.S.R., China.

Geography. Most of Mali, in West Africa, lies in the Sahara. A landlocked country four fifths the size of Alaska, it is bordered by Guinea, Senegal, Mauritania, Algeria, Niger, Upper Volta, and the Ivory Coast.

The only fertile area is in the south, where the Niger and Senegal Rivers provide irrigation.

Government. The army overthrew the government on Nov. 19, 1968, and formed a provisional government. The Military Committee of National Liberation consists of 14 members and forms the decision-making body.

In late 1969 an attempted coup was foiled, and Lt. Moussa Traoré, president of the Military Committee took over as chief of state and later as head of government, ousting Capt. Yoro Diakité as Premier.

The Malian People's Democratic Union, established in 1976, is the only political party.

History. Subjugated by France by the end of the 19th century, this area became a colony in 1904 (named French Sudan in 1920) and in 1946 became part of the French Union. On June 20, 1960, it became independent and, under the name of Sudanese Republic, was federated with the Republic of Senegal in the Mali Federation. However, Senegal seceded from the Federation on Aug. 20, 1960, and the Sudanese Republic then changed its name to the Republic of Mali on September 22.

In the 1960s, Mali concentrated on economic development, continuing to accept aid from both Soviet bloc and Western nations, as well as international agencies. In the late 1960s, it began retreating from close ties with China. But a purge of conservative opponents brought greater power to President Modibo Keita, and in 1968 the influence of the Chinese and their Malian sympathizers increased. By a treaty signed in Peking in 1968, China agreed to help build a railroad from Mali to Guinea, providing Mali with vital access to the sea.

Mali, with Mauritania, the Ivory Coast, Senegal, Dahomey (Benin), Niger, and Upper Volta signed a treaty establishing the Economic Community for West Africa to promote economic development among the seven nations. It came into force on Jan. 1, 1973.

A six-year sub-Sahara drought devastated Mali before disastrously heavy rains began in 1974. Emergency shipments from a dozen nations and international organizations helped alleviate a famine that affected 1.8 million Malians and killed thousands.

MALTA

Republic of Malta
President: Agatha Barbara (1982)
Prime Minister: Dom Mintoff (1971)
Area: 122 sq mi. (316 sq km)
Population (est. 1982): 315,000 (average annual growth rate: 1.6%)
Density per square mile: 3,073.8
Capital (est. 1982): Valetta, 15,000
Largest city (est. 1982): Sliema, 20,500
Monetary unit: Maltese pound
Languages: Maltese and English
Religion: Roman Catholic
National name: Repubblika Ta Malta
Member of Commonwealth of Nations
Literacy rate (1981): 83%
Economic summary: Gross national product (1980): $1.2 billion. Average annual growth rate (1970–79): 11.0%. Per capita income (1980): $3,470. Land used for agriculture, 45%; labor force: 6%; principal products: fodder crops, potatoes, onions, fruits and vegetables. Labor force in industry: 27%; major products: textiles, yarn, knitted goods, processed foods, plastics, electronic equipment. Natural resources: limestone, salt. Exports: textiles, yarns, manufactured goods, ships. Imports: manufactured goods, machinery, transport equipment. Major trading partners: West Germany, U.K., Italy.

Geography. The five Maltese islands—with a combined land area smaller than Philadelphia—are in the Mediterranean about 60 miles (97 km) south of the southeastern tip of Sicily.

Government. The government is headed by a Prime Minister, responsible to a 65-member House of Representatives elected by universal suffrage.

The major political parties are Malta Labor Party (34 of 65 seats in House of Representatives), led by Prime Minister Dom Mintoff; Nationalist Party (31 seats), led by Edward Fenech Adami.

History. The strategic importance of Malta was recognized by the Phoenicians, who occupied it, as did in their turn the Greeks, Carthaginians, and Romans. The apostle Paul was shipwrecked there in A.D. 58.

The Knights of St. John (Malta), who obtained the three habitable Maltese islands of Malta, Gozo, and Comino from Charles V in 1530, reached their highest fame when they withstood an attack by superior Turkish forces in 1565.

Napoleon seized Malta in 1798, but the French forces were ousted by British troops the next year, and British rule was confirmed by the Treaty of Paris in 1814.

Malta was heavily attacked by German and Italian aircraft during World War II, but was never invaded by the Axis.

Malta became an independent nation on Sept. 21, 1964, and a republic Dec. 13, 1974, but remained in the British Commonwealth. The Governor-General, Sir Anthony Mamo, was sworn in as first president and Dom Mintoff remained prime minister.

The new government proposed a seven-year plan to end economic dependence on foreign military bases by 1980. It called for a $568-million investment program to create 20,000 new jobs. Britain withdrew its last troops from Malta in 1979, thus ending its annual subsidy of $33 million for use of the island's port facilities.

For a time, Libya appeared to be substituting for Britain as a source of outside income, as President Muammar el-Qaddafi extended generous credits and concessionary prices for oil on condition that Malta's Labor government keep the North Atlantic Treaty Organization from using the island's port facilities. But a conflict over oil rights, in which Libyan ships threatened a Maltese-licensed drilling rig in the waters between Malta and Libya in August 1980 forced Mintoff to break with Qaddafi, expel most of the Libyan military advisers, and negotiate a treaty of friendship and aid with Italy.

MAURITANIA

Islamic Republic of Mauritania
Chief of State and Head of Government: Lt. Col. Mohamed Khouna Ould Haydalla (1980)
Premier: Lieut. Col. Maaouya Ould Sidi Ahmed Taya (1981)
Area: 397,953 sq mi. (1,030,700 sq km)
Population (est. 1982): 1,725,000 (average annual growth rate: 1.9%)
Density per square mile: 4.1
Capital and largest city (est. 1981): Nouakchott, 175,000
Monetary unit: Ouguyia
Ethnic groups: Moors; a black minority (Poulars, Soninkes, and Wolofs)
Languages: Arabic and French
Religion: Islam
National name: République Islamique de Mauritanie
Literacy rate (1981): 17%
Economic summary: Gross national product (1981): $800 million. Average annual growth rate (1970–79):—0.7%. Per capita income (1982): $536. Principal agricultural products: livestock, millet, maize, wheat, dates, rice. Major industrial products: iron ore, processed fish. Natural resources: copper, iron ore, gypsum, fish. Exports: iron ore, fish, copper. Imports: foodstuffs, petroleum, capital goods. Major trading partners: France, Spain, U.S., U.K., Italy.

Geography. Mauritania, three times the size of Arizona, is situated in northwest Africa with about 350 miles (592 km) of coastline on the Atlantic Ocean. It is bordered by Morocco on the north, Algeria and Mali on the east, and Senegal on the south.

The country is mostly desert, with the exception of the fertile Senegal River valley in the south and grazing land in the north.

Government. An Army coup on July 10, 1978, deposed Moktar Ould Daddah, who had been President since Mauritania's independence in 1960. Since then, a 13-man Committee for National Recovery has exercised executive and legislative power, having replaced the National Assembly and the single political party that existed before the coup.

History. Mauritania was first explored by the Portuguese. The French organized the area as a territory in 1904.

Mauritania became an independent nation on Nov. 28, 1960, and was admitted to the United Nations in 1961 over the strenuous opposition of Morocco, which claimed the territory. With Moors, Arabs, Berbers, and blacks frequently in conflict, the government in the late 1960s sought to make Arab culture dominant to unify the land.

Mauritania acquired administrative control of the former Spanish Sahara when the colonial administration withdrew in 1975, under an agreement with Morocco and Spain. Mauritanian troops moved into the territory but encountered resistance from the Polisario Front, a Saharan independence movement backed by Algeria. The task of trying to pacify the area proved a heavy burden. Mauritania signed a peace agreement with the Polisario insurgents in August 1979, withdrew from the territory and renounced territorial claims.

Increased military spending and rising casulaties in Western Sahara contributed to the discontent that brought down the civilian government of Ould Daddah in 1978. His military replacement, Lt. Col. Moustapha Saleck, was forced to resign after Premier Ahmed Bouceif and other military leaders were killed in a plane crash on May 27, 1979. Lt. Col. Mohamed Mahmoud Ould Louly held power for only six months and was removed by the junta on Jan. 4, 1980, for unsatisfactory performance. Lt. Col. Mohamed Khouna Ould Haydalla was named new chief of state and government.

MAURITIUS

Sovereign: Queen Elizabeth II
Governor-General: Sir Dayendranath Burrenchobay (1978)
Prime Minister: Sir Seewoosagur Ramgoolam (1983)
Area: 787 sq mi. (2,040 sq km)
Population (est. 1984): 1,000,000 (average annual growth rate: 1.7%) (Indian, 51%; Creole, 33%)
Density per square mile: 1,207.1
Capital and largest city (est. 1980): Port Louis, 155,000
Monetary unit: Mauritian rupee
Languages: English (official), French, Creole, Hindi, Urdu, Chinese
Religions: Hindu, 46%, Christian (mainly Roman Catholic), 35%; Islam, 16%; Buddhist, 3%
Member of Commonwealth of Nations
Literacy rate (1981): 70%
Economic summary: Gross national product (1980): $1.0 billion. Average annual growth rate (1970–79): 6.4%. Per capita income (1980): $1,060. Land used for agriculture: 50%; labor force: 50%; principal products: sugar cane, rice. Labor force in industry: 6%; major products: processed sugar and tea, tobacco, cut diamonds, textiles, electronic equipment. Natural resources: iron ore, gypsum, fish. Exports: sugar, tea, molasses. Imports: foodstuffs, manufactured goods. Major trading partners: Western European countries, U.S., U.K.

Geography. Mauritius is a mountainous island in the Indian Ocean east of Madagascar.

Government. Mauritius is a member of the British Commonwealth, with Queen Elizabeth II as head of state. She is represented by a governor-general, who chooses the prime minister from the unicameral Legislative Assembly. The Legislative Assembly has 70 members, 62 of whom are elected by direct suffrage. The remaining 8 are chosen from among the unsuccessful candidates.

The major parties are the governing Alliance Party coalition, composed of the Mouvement Socialiste Mauricien, the Parti Mauricien Social Democrate, the Labor Party, and the Organisation du Peuple Rodriguais (48 of 70 seats in the Legislative Assembly, led by Prime Minister Sir Seewoosagur Ramgoolam, and the opposition Mouvement Militant Mauricien, led by former Prime Minister Aneerood Jugnauth).

History. Mauritius was seized from France by British troops in 1810 and ceded to Britain by the Treaty of Paris in 1814. Until 1903, Mauritius and the Seychelles were administered as a single colony. The colony of Mauritius became an independent nation on March 12, 1968.

The nation has an Indian majority, descendants of laborers imported from India to work the sugar plantations after the abolition of slavery in 1834. The native blacks speak French and are Roman Catholics.

The Labor Party government of Sir Seewoosagur Ramgoolam, who had ruled Mauritius since independence, was toppled in a 1982 election by the Movement Militant Mauricien, which had campaigned for recovery of Diego Garcia island, separated from Mauritius during the colonial period and leased by Britain to the United States for a naval base. But an Alliance Party coalition, including the Labor Party, regained power at the end of 1983 and brought back Ramgoolam as Prime Minister.

MEXICO

United Mexican States
President: Miguel de la Madrid Hurtado (1982)
Area: 761,600 sq mi. (1,972,547 sq km)
Population (est. 1983): 75,702,000 (average annual growth rate: 2.6%) (55% mestizo; 29% Indian)
Density per square mile: 95.7
Capital: Mexico City
Largest cities (1980 census): Mexico City, 12,900,000; Guadalajara, 3,000,000; Monterrey, 2,700,000; Ciudad Juarez, 1,120,000; Puebla de Zaragoza, 1,100,000; Leon, 1,000,000
Monetary unit: Peso
Languages: Spanish, Indian languages
Religion: Mainly Roman Catholic
National name: Estados Unidos Mexicanos
Literacy rate (1983): 74%
Economic summary: Gross national product (1980): $144.0 billion. Average annual growth rate (1970–79): 1.9%. Per capita income (1980): $2,130. Land used for agriculture, 12%; labor force: 33%; principal products: corn, cotton, coffee, sugar cane, vegetables. Labor force in industry: 33%; major products: processed foods, chemicals, basic metals and metal products, petroleum. Natural resources: petroleum, silver, copper, gold, lead, zinc, natural gas, timber. Exports: coffee, cotton, sugar, shrimp, cattle and meat, petroleum, sulfur. Imports: machinery, equipment, industrial vehicles, intermediate goods. Major trading partners: U.S., Japan, Western European countries.

Geography. The United States' neighbor to the south, Mexico is about one fifth its size. Baja California in the west, an 800-mile (1,287-km) peninsula, forms the Gulf of California. In the east are the Gulf of Mexico and the Bay of Campeche, which is formed by Mexico's other peninsula, the Yucatán.

Mexico is a great, high plateau, open to the north, with mountain chains on east and west and with ocean-front lowlands lying outside of them.

Government. The President, who is popularly elected for six years and is ineligible to succeed himself, governs with a Cabinet of ministers. Congress has two houses—a 400-member Chamber of Deputies, elected for three years, and a 64-member Senate, elected for six years.

Each of the 31 states has considerable autonomy, with a popularly elected governor, a legislature, and a local judiciary. The President of Mexico appoints the governor of the Federal District.

The major parties are the Partido Revolucionario Institucional (all 64 seats in the Senate and 299 of 400 seats in the Chamber of Deputies); Partido Acción Nacional (56 of 400 seats in Chamber); Partido Socialista Unificado de Mexico (16 seats); Partido Popular Socialista (10 seats); Partido Socialista de los Trabajadores (Socialist Workers Party) (10 seats); and Partido Democrata Mexicano (9 seats). The formerly separate Communist Party merged in 1981 with others to form the Partido Socialista Unificado de Mexico.

History. At least two civilized races—the Mayas and later the Toltecs—preceded the wealthy Aztec empire, conquered in 1519–21 by the Spanish under Hernando Cortés. Spain ruled for the next 300 years until 1810 (the date was Sept. 16 and is now celebrated as Independence Day), when the Mexicans first revolted. They continued the struggle and finally won independence in 1821.

From 1821 to 1877, there were two emperors, several dictators, and enough presidents and provisional executives to make a new government on the average of every nine months. Mexico lost Texas (1836), and after defeat in the war with the U.S. (1846–48) it lost the area comprising the present states of California, Nevada, and Utah, most of Arizona and New Mexico, and parts of Wyoming and Colorado.

In 1855, the Indian patriot Benito Juárez began a series of liberal reforms, including the disestablishment of the Catholic Church, which had acquired vast property. A subsequent civil war was interrupted by the French invasion of Mexico (1861), the crowning of Maximilian of Austria as Emperor (1864), and then his overthrow and execution by forces under Juárez, who again became President in 1867.

The years after the fall of the dictator Porfirio Diaz (1877–80 and 1884–1911) were marked by bloody political-military strife and trouble with the U.S., culminating in the punitive expedition into northern Mexico (1916–17) in unsuccessful pursuit of the revolutionary Pancho Villa. Since a brief period of civil war in 1920, Mexico has enjoyed a period of gradual agricultural, political, and social reforms. Relations with the U.S. were again disturbed in 1938 when all foreign oil wells were expropriated. Agreement on compensation was finally reached in 1941.

Lázaro Cardenas (1934–40), president during the oil seizures, also began a program of distributing land to the peasants and of broad labor reforms. Manuel Avila Camacho, president during World War II, followed Cardenas' policy at home but cooperated closely with the United Nations, and established cordial relations with the U.S. His policy was followed by his immediate successors, Miguel Alemán, Adolfo Ruíz Cortines, and Adolfo López Mateos. López Mateos redefined Mexican foreign policy as "independent" rather than neutral or partial, a course followed by Gustavo Díaz Ordaz, who became president in 1964.

Luis Echeverría Alvarez, who was elected president in 1970, worked vigorously in Latin America and elsewhere in the underdeveloped world to promote more benefits for developing nations from the raw materials they export.

Mexico and Venezuela proposed formation of a Latin American economic system (SELA) to promote regional economic development, and the first meeting in Caracas was held in 1976.

The country's oil reserves were estimated to be the world's fifth largest in 1981, following the discovery of a huge offshore field in the Gulf of Mexico. It was here that the world's biggest oil spill was capped in March 1980 after 3.1 million barrels were lost. The disaster caused a dispute with the United States when Mexico refused to pay the cost of cleaning up Texas beaches.

With the election of Ronald Reagan as U.S. President, a new era of "personal relationship" was proclaimed by him and López Portillo at a border meeting on Jan. 5, 1981. López Portillo came to Washington in June, and after a long meeting with Reagan at Camp David, a new U.S. immigration policy designed to ease Mexican concerns was disclosed.

López Portillo also pressed for economic, rather than military, aid to combat Communist penetration of the Caribbean area. With Venezuela, he led the way in pledging oil to help poor nations in the region. He urged Reagan to follow his policy and invited him to a 22-nation conference on aid for developing nations sponsored by Mexico at Cancun in October 1981. Reagan accepted after assurances that Cuba, with which López Portillo maintained friendly relations, would not be invited.

The last year of López Portillo's presidency was shadowed by economic problems caused by falling oil prices. Instead of an expected $20 billion in oil export earnings for 1981, the actual figure was only $12 billion. In February 1982, a 41% devaluation of the peso pushed the inflation rate to 75% the following month. Cuts of $5.7 billion in the 1982 budget of $72 billion and the suspension of a $30-billion nuclear energy program were projected to reduce the economic growth rate to zero through mid-1983, in contrast to recent annual growth rates of 8%.

Miguel de la Madrid Hurtado, candidate of the ruling Partido Revolucionario Institucional, won the July 4 election for the presidential term beginning Dec. 1. De la Madrid, 47, was formerly Secretary of Planning and Budget and Deputy Director General of Pemex.

During 1983 and 1984, Mexico suffered its worst financial crisis in 50 years, leading to critically high unemployment and widespread dissatisfaction with the Institutional Revolutionary Party. Its inability to make payments on its $89.8-billion foreign debt as they came due triggered a worldwide debt crisis. Although the country remained calm politically, it was uncertain in mid-1984 how long President de la Madrid could maintain belt-tightening measures.

MONACO

Principality of Monaco
Ruler: Prince Rainier III (1949)
Minister of State: Jean Herly (1981)
Area: 0.73 sq mi. (465 acres)
Population (est. 1982): 30,000, of whom 5,500 are Monégasque citizens (average annual growth rate: 0.8%)
Density per square mile: 41,095.9
Capital: Monaco-Ville
Monetary unit: French franc
Languages: French and Monégasque
Religion: Roman Catholic
National name: Principauté de Monaco
Literacy rate (1981): 99%

Geography. Monaco is a tiny, hilly wedge driven into the French Mediterranean coast nine miles east of Nice.

Government. Prince Albert of Monaco gave the principality a Constitution in 1911, creating a National Council of 18 members popularly elected for five years. The head of government is the Minister of State.

Prince Rainier III, born May 31, 1923, succeeded his grandfather, Louis II, on the latter's death, May 9, 1949. Rainier was married April 18, 1956, to Grace Kelly, U.S. actress. A daughter, Princess Caroline Louise Marguerite, was born on Jan. 23, 1957 (married to Philippe Junot June 28, 1978 and divorced in 1980; married to Stefano Casiraghi Dec. 29, 1983, and gave birth to a son, Andrea Albert, June 9, 1984); a son, Prince Albert Louis Pierre, on March 14, 1958; and Princess Stéphanie Marie Elisabeth, on Feb. 1, 1965. Princess Grace died Sept. 14, 1982, of injuries received the day before when the car she was driving went off the road near Monte Carlo. She was 52. Her daughter Stéphanie suffered neck injuries.

The special significance attached to the birth of descendants to Prince Rainier stems from a clause in the Treaty of July 17, 1919, between France and Monaco stipulating that in the event of vacancy of the Crown, the Monégasque territory would become an autonomous state under a French protectorate.

The National and Democratic Union (all 18 seats in National Council), led by Auguste Medecin, is the only political party.

History. The Phoenicians, and after them the Greeks, had a temple on the Monacan headland honoring Hercules. From *Monoikos,* the Greek surname for this mythological strong man, the principality took its name. After being independent for 800 years, Monaco was annexed to France in 1793 and was placed under Sardinia's protection in 1815. In 1861, it went under French guardianship but continued to be independent.

By a treaty in 1918, France stipulated that the French government be given a veto over the succession to the throne.

Monaco is a little land of pleasure with a tourist business that runs as high as 1.5 million visitors a year. It had popular gaming tables as early as 1856. Five years later, a 50-year concession to operate the games was granted to François Blanc, of Bad Homburg. This concession passed into the hand of a private company in 1898.

Monaco's practice of providing a tax shelter for French businessmen resulted in a dispute between the countries. When Rainier refused to end the practice, France retaliated with a customs tax. In 1967, Rainier took control of the Société des Bains de Mer, operator of the famous Monte Carlo gambling casino, in a program to increase hotel and convention space. He paid $8 million to Greek shipping magnate Aristotle Onassis for his shares.

MONGOLIA

Mongolian People's Republic
Chairman of Presidium of the Great People's Khural (President): Yumjaagiin Tsedenbal (1974)
Chairman of Council of Ministers (Premier): Jambyn Batmunkh (1974)
Area: 604,250 sq mi. (1,565,000 sq km)
Population (est. 1982): 1,820,000 (average annual growth rate: 2.9%)
Density per square mile: 2.9
Capital and largest city (est. 1981): Ulan Bator, 440,000
Monetary unit: Tugrik
Language: Mongolian
Religion: Lamaistic Buddhism
National name: Bugd Nairamdakh Mongol Ard Uls
Literacy rate (1981): 80%
Economic summary: Gross national product (1981): $1.5 billion. Average annual growth rate (1970–81): 3.1%. Per capita income: n.a. Principal agricultural products: livestock, wheat, oats, barley. Major industrial products: animal products, building materials, minerals. Natural resources: coal, copper, molybdenum. Exports: livestock, animal products, nonferrous metals. Imports: machinery and equipment, clothing, petroleum, sugar, tea. Major trading partners: U.S.S.R. and Soviet bloc countries.

Geography. Mongolia lies in eastern Asia between Soviet Siberia on the north and China on the south. It is slightly larger than Alaska.

The productive regions of Mongolia—a tableland ranging from 3,000 to 5,000 feet (914 to 1,524 m) in elevation—are in the north, which is well drained by numerous rivers, including the Hovd, Onon, Selenga, and Tula.

Much of the Gobi Desert falls within Mongolia.

Government. The Mongolian People's Republic is a socialist state. The highest organ of state power is the Great People's Khural (Parliament), which is elected for a term of four years and is convened once a year. The Great People's Khural elects the Presidium, which consists of a chairman, two vice chairmen, a secretary, and six members. The Council of Ministers is set up by the Great People's Khural and consists of a chairman, vice chairmen, and ministers.

The Mongolian People's Revolutionary Party, led by President Yumjaagiin Tsedenbal, is the only political party.

History. The Mongolian People's Republic, formerly known as Outer Mongolia, is a Soviet satellite. It contains the original homeland of the historic Mongols, whose power reached its zenith during the 13th century under Kublai Khan. The area accepted Manchu rule in 1689, but after the Chinese Revolution of 1911 and the fall of the Manchus in 1912, the northern Mongol princes expelled the Chinese officials and declared independence under the Khutukhtu, or "Living Buddha."

In 1921, Soviet troops entered the country and

facilitated the establishment of a republic by Mongolian revolutionaries in 1924 after the death of the last Living Buddha. China, meanwhile, continued to claim Outer Mongolia but was unable to back the claim with any strength. Under the 1945 Chinese-Russian Treaty, China agreed to give up Outer Mongolia, which, after a plebiscite, became a nominally independent country.

Allied with the U.S.S.R. in its dispute with China, Mongolia has mobilized troops along its borders since 1968 when the two powers became involved in border clashes on the Kazakh-Sinkiang frontier to the west and on the Amur and Ussuri Rivers. A 20-year treaty of friendship and cooperation, signed in 1966, entitled Mongolia to call upon the U.S.S.R. for military aid in the event of invasion.

MOROCCO

Kingdom of Morocco
Ruler: King Hassan II (1961)
Premier: Maati Bouabid (1981)
Area: 177,116 sq mi. (458,730 sq km)
Population (1982): 20,419,555 (average annual growth rate: 2.9%)
Density per square mile: 123.7
Capital: Rabat
Largest cities (1982): Casablanca, 2,139,204; Rabat, 518,616; Fez, 448,823; Marrakech, 439,728; Meknes, 319,783
Monetary unit: Dirham
Languages: Arabic, French, Spanish
Religions: Chiefly Islam
National name: al-Mamlaka al-Maghrebia
Literacy rate (1981): 38%
Economic summary: Gross national product (1980): $17.4 billion. Average annual growth rate (1970–79): 3.5%. Per capita income (1980): $860. Land used for agriculture; 32%; labor force: 50%; products: barley, wheat, citrus fruits, vegetables, sugar beets, wool. Labor force in industry, 15%; major products: textiles, fish, chemicals. Natural resources: phosphates, iron, manganese, lead, fisheries. Exports: phosphates, citrus fruits, vegetables, canned fruits and vegetables, canned fish, carpets. Imports: capital goods, fuels, food stuffs, petroleum products. Major trading partners: France, West Germany, Italy.

Geography. Morocco, about one tenth larger than California, is just south of Spain across the Strait of Gibraltar and looks out on the Atlantic from the northwest shoulder of Africa. Algeria is to the east and Mauritania to the south.

On the Atlantic coast there is a fertile plain. The Mediterranean coast is mountainous. The Atlas Mountains, running northeastward from the south to the Algerian frontier, average 11,000 feet (3,353 m) in elevation.

Government. The King, after suspending the 1962 Constitution and dissolving Parliament in 1965, promulgated a new Constitution in 1972. He continued to rule by decree until June 3, 1977, when the first free elections since 1962 took place. The 264-member Chamber of Deputies has 176 elected seats, with the balance chosen by local councils and groups.

A coalition of independents loyal to the King and small right-wing parties has 114 of the 176 elected seats in the Chamber of Deputies; Istiqlal, which participates in the government, 45 seats; Socialist Union of Popular Forces, 16 seats; and the Communist Party of Progress and Socialism, one seat.

History. Morocco was once the home of the Berbers, who helped the Arabs invade Spain in A.D. 711 and then revolted against them and gradually won control of large areas of Spain for a time after 739.

The country was ruled successively by various native dynasties and maintained regular commercial relations with Europe, even during the 17th and 18th centuries when it was the headquarters of the famous Salé pirates. In the 19th century, there were frequent clashes with the French and Spanish. Finally, in 1904, France and Spain divided Morocco into zones of French and Spanish influence, and these were established as protectorates in 1912.

Meanwhile, Morocco had become the object of big-power rivalry, which almost led to a European war in 1905 when Germany attempted to gain a foothold in the rich mineral country. By terms of the Algeciras Conference (1906), Morocco was internationalized economically, and France's privileges were limited.

The Tangier Statute, concluded by Britain, France, and Spain in 1923, created an international zone at the port of Tangier, permanently neutralized and demilitarized. In World War II, Spain occupied the zone, ostensibly to ensure order, but was forced to withdraw in 1945.

Sultan Mohammed V was deposed by the French in 1953 and replaced by his uncle, but nationalist agitation forced his return in 1955. On his death on Feb. 26, 1961, his son, Hassan, became King.

France and Spain recognized the independence and sovereignty of Morocco in 1956. Later the same year, the Tangier international zone was abolished.

In 1975, tens of thousands of Moroccans crossed the border into Spanish Sahara to back their government's contention that the northern part of the territory was historically part of Morocco. At the same time, Mauritania occupied the southern half of the territory in defiance of Spanish threats to resist such a takeover. Abandoning its commitment to self-determination for the territory, Spain withdrew, and only Algeria protested. Algerian recognition of a Saharan republic in 1976 led to a break in relations among the three North African states, and Algerian-backed Polisario Front guerrillas continued to fight Moroccan and Mauritanian forces, preventing exploitation of the region's rich phosphate deposits.

When Mauritania signed a peace treaty with the Polisario Front in August 1979, Morocco occupied and assumed administrative control of the southern part of the Western Sahara, in addition to the northern part it already occupied. Under pressure from other African leaders, Hassan agreed in mid-1981 to a cease-fire with a referendum under international supervision to decide the fate of the Sahara territory, but the referendum was never carried out. Moroccan troups still occupied the territory in 1984, fending off occasional raids by Polisario guerrillas based in Algeria.

King Hassan, startled the Reagan Administration in mid-August 1984 by signing a treaty of union with Col. Muammar el-Qaddafi, the Libyan leader.

The Moroccans described the treaty as the culmination of a process in which Libya had withdrawn its support for the Polisario in the Western Sahara, and Morocco had agreed to refrain from sending troops to help the French in Chad. Shortly after the treaty signing, the Polisario guerillas were reported on the verge of being quelled. Libya and France later signed an agreement to withdraw their forces that had been supporting opposite sides in the Chad civil war.

MOZAMBIQUE

People's Republic of Mozambique
President: Samora Moises Machel (1975)
Area: 303,073 sq mi. (784,959 sq km)
Population (est. 1982): 11,100,000 (average annual growth rate: 2.7%)
Density per square mile: 36.6
Capital and largest city (est. 1980): Maputo, 750,000
Monetary unit: Metical
Languages: Portuguese (official), Bantu languages
Religions: Animist, 66%; Christian, 22%; Islam, 11%
National name: República Popular de Moçambique
Literacy rate (1974): 15% (est.)
Economic summary: Gross national product (1980): $2.8 billion. Average annual growth rate (1970–79): −5.3%. Per capita income (1980): $270. Principal agricultural products: cotton, cashew nuts, sugar, tea, copra, wheat, peanuts. Labor force in industry: 5%; major products: processed foods, petroleum products, beverages, textiles, tobacco. Natural resources: coal, iron ore, fluorite, tantalite, timber. Exports: cashew nuts, cotton, sugar, mineral and timber products, tea, copra. Imports: machinery and electrical equipment, cotton textiles, vehicles, petroleum products, iron and steel. Major trading partners: Portugal, South Africa, U.S., U.K., West Germany.

Geography. Mozambique stretches for 1,535 miles (2,470 km) along Africa's southeast coast. It is nearly twice the size of California. Tanzania is to the north; Malawi, Zambia, and Zimbabwe to the west; and South Africa and Swaziland to the south.

The country is generally a low-lying plateau broken up by 25 sizable rivers that flow into the Indian Ocean. The largest is the Zambezi; which provides access to central Africa. The principal ports are Maputo and Beira, which is the port for Zimbabwe.

Government. After having been under Portuguese colonial rule for 470 years, Mozambique became independent on June 25, 1975. It is a Marxist state. The first President, Samora Moises Machel, is a former nurse who headed the National Front for the Liberation of Mozambique (FRELIMO) in its 10-year guerrilla war for independence.

History. Mozambique was discovered by Vasco da Gama in 1498, although the Arabs had penetrated into the area as early as the 10th century. It was first colonized in 1505, and by 1510, the Portuguese had control of all the former Arab sultanates on the east African coast.

FRELIMO was organized in 1963. Guerrilla activity had become so extensive by 1973 that Portugal was forced to dispatch 40,000 troops to fight the rebels. A cease-fire was signed in September 1974, when Portugal agreed to grant Mozambique independence.

After a brief period of cooperation with neighboring white-ruled Rhodesia, Mozambique closed its border in 1976, cutting off Rhodesia's most direct link to the sea. A series of border clashes between Rhodesian forces and guerrillas based in Mozambique continued until Zimbabwe achieved independence in April 1980, when rail and highway communications between the two countries were reopened.

NAMIBIA

See South Africa

NAURU

Republic of Nauru
President and Head Chief: Hammer DeRoburt (1968)
Area: 8.2 sq mi. (21 sq km)
Population (est. 1982): 8,000 (average annual growth rate: 1.7%)
Density per square mile: 1,000.0
Capital: Yaren
Monetary unit: Australian dollar
Languages: Nauruan and English
Religions: Protestant, 58%; Roman Catholic, 24%; Confucian and Taoist, 8%
Special relationship within the Commonwealth of Nations
Literacy rate (1981): 99%
Economic summary: Gross national product (1977): $155 million. Per capita income (1977): $21,400. Major industrial products: phosphates. Natural resources: phosphates. Exports: phosphates. Imports: foodstuffs, fuel. Major trading partners: Australia, New Zealand, U.K., Japan.

Geography. Nauru (pronounced NAH oo roo) is an island in the Pacific just south of the equator, about 2,500 miles (4,023 km) southwest of Honolulu.

Government. Legislative power is invested in a popularly elected 18-member Parliament, which elects the President from among its members. Executive power rests with the President, who is assisted by a five-member Cabinet.

History. Nauru was annexed by Germany in 1888. It was placed under joint Australian, New Zealand, and British mandate after World War I, and in 1947 it became a U.N. trusteeship administered by the same three powers. On Jan. 31, 1968, Nauru became an independent republic.

NEPAL

Kingdom of Nepal
Ruler: King Birendra Bir Bikram Shah Dev. (1972)
Prime Minister: Lokendra Bahadur Chand (1983)
Area: 54,463 sq mi. (141,059 sq km)
Population (est. 1982): 15,325,000 (average annual growth rate: 2.4%)
Density per square mile: 281.9
Capital and largest city (est. 1980): Katmandu, 300,000
Monetary unit: Nepalese rupee
Languages: Nepali (official), Newari, Bhutia
Religions: Hindu, 90%; Buddhist, 6%; Islam, 3%
Literacy rate (1981): 12%
Economic summary: Gross national product (1980): $2.0 billion. Average annual growth rate (1970–79): 0.3%. Per capita income (1980): $140. Labor force in agriculture: 95%; principal products: rice, maize, wheat, millet, jute, sugar cane, oilseed, potatoes. Labor force in industry: 5%; major products: cigarettes, bricks, sugar, lumber, jute, hydroelectric power, cement. Natural resources: water, timber, hydroelectric potential. Exports:

rice and food products, and timber. Imports: textiles, manufactured goods, construction materials, fuel. Major trading partner: India.

Geography. A landlocked country the size of Arkansas, lying between India and the Tibetan Autonomous Region of China, Nepal contains Mount Everest (29,028 ft.; 8,848 m), the tallest mountain in the world. Along its southern border, Nepal has a strip of level land that is partly forested, partly cultivated. North of that is the slope of the main section of the Himalayan range, including Everest and many other peaks higher than 20,000 feet (6,096 m).

Government. A new Constitution promulgated by King Mahendra in 1962 provided for a unicameral legislature called the National Panchayat. All political parties were banned in 1960.

History. The Kingdom of Nepal was unified in 1768 by King Prithwi Narayan Shah. A commercial treaty was signed with Britain in 1792, and in 1816, after more than a year's hostilities, the Nepalese agreed to allow British residents to live in Katmandu, the capital. In 1923, Britain recognized the absolute independence of Nepal. Between 1846 and 1951, the country was ruled by the Rana family, which always held the office of prime minister. In 1951, however, the King took over all power and proclaimed a constitutional monarchy.

Mahendra Bir Bikram Shah became King in 1955. Nepal and China settled their differences in 1956, and thereafter Nepal accepted economic aid from the Chinese. The U.S. and the U.S.S.R. also provide aid.

After Mahendra, who had ruled since 1955, died of a heart attack in 1972, Prince Birendra, at 26, succeeded to the throne.

In the first election in 22 years, on May 2, 1980, voters approved the continued autocratic rule by the King with the advice of a partyless Parliament. The King promised, however, that he would eventually permit the election of a new legislature to which the Prime Minister and Cabinet would be responsible.

THE NETHERLANDS

Kingdom of the Netherlands
Sovereign: Queen Beatrix (1980)
Premier: Ruud Lubbers (1982)
Area: 13,104 sq mi. (33,940 sq km)
Population (est. 1982): 14,350,000 (average annual growth rate: 0.4%)
Density per square mile: 1,027.4
Capital: Amsterdam; seat of government: The Hague
Largest cities (est. 1983): Rotterdam, 1,024,700; Amsterdam, 936,400; The Hague, 674,500; Utrecht, 498,800.
Monetary unit: Guilder
Language: Dutch
Religions: Roman Catholic, 38%; Dutch Reformed, 31%; unaffiliated, 27%; Islam, 2%
National name: Koninkrijk der Nederlanden
Literacy rate (1981): 98%
Economic summary: Gross national product (1980): $161.4 billion. Average annual growth rate (1970–79): 2.2%. Per capita income (1980): $11,470. Land used for agriculture: 70%; labor force, 10%; principal products: wheat, barley, sugar beets, potatoes, flax, bulbs, meat and dairy products. Labor force in industry: 30%; major products: metal fabrication, textiles, chemicals, electronic equipment. Exports: foodstuffs, machinery, natural gas, chemicals, petroleum products, textiles. Imports: machinery, crude petroleum, chemicals, textiles, mineral ores. Major trading partners: West Germany, Belgium, France, U.K.

Geography. The Netherlands, on the coast of the North Sea, has West Germany to the east and Belgium to the south. It is twice the size of New Jersey.

Part of the great plain of north and west Europe, the Netherlands has maximum dimensions of 190 by 160 miles (360 by 257 km) and is low and flat except in Limburg in the southeast, where some hills rise to 300 feet (92 m). About half the country's area is below sea level, making the famous Dutch dikes a requisite to the use of much land. Reclamation of land from the sea through dikes has continued through recent times.

All drainage reaches the North Sea, and the principal rivers—Rhine, Maas (Meuse), and Schelde—have their sources outside the country. The Rhine is the most heavily used waterway in Europe.

Government. The Netherlands and its former colony of the Netherlands Antilles form the Kingdom of the Netherlands.

The Netherlands is a constitutional monarchy with a bicameral Parliament. The Upper Chamber has 75 members elected for six years by representative bodies of the provinces, half of the members retiring every three years. The Lower Chamber has 150 members elected by universal suffrage for four years. The two Chambers have the right of investigation and interpellation; the Lower Chamber can initiate legislation and amend bills.

The Sovereign, Queen Beatrix Wilhelmina Armgard, born Jan. 31, 1938, was married on March 11, 1966, to Claus von Amsberg, a former West German diplomat. The marriage drew public criticism because of the bridegroom's service in the German army during World War II. In 1967, Beatrix gave birth to a son, Wilhem-Alexander Claus George Ferdinand, the first male heir to the throne since 1884. She also has two other sons, Johan Friso Bernhard Christian David, born in 1968, and Constantijn Christof Frederik Aschwin, born the next year.

Premier Ruud Lubber heads a coalition of Christian Democrats (43 of 150 seats in the Lower Chamber), and Liberals (36 seats). Other major parties are the opposition Labor Party (47 seats), and Democrats '66 (6 seats).

History. Julius Caesar found the low-lying Netherlands inhabited by Germanic tribes—the Nervii, Frisii, and Batavi. The Batavi on the Roman frontier did not submit to Rome's rule until 13 B.C., and then only as allies.

A part of Charlemagne's empire in the 8th and 9th centuries A.D., the area later passed into the hands of Burgundy and the Austrian Hapsburgs, and finally in the 16th century came under Spanish rule.

When Philip II of Spain suppressed political liberties and the growing Protestant movement in the Netherlands, a revolt led by William of Orange broke out in 1568. Under the Union of Utrecht (1579), the seven northern provinces became the

Republic of the United Netherlands.

The Dutch East India Company was established in 1602, and by the end of the 17th century Holland was one of the great sea and colonial powers of Europe.

The nation's independence was not completely established until after the Thirty Years' War (1618–48), after which the country's rise as a commercial and maritime power began. In 1814, all the provinces of Holland and Belgium were merged into one kingdom, but in 1830 the southern provinces broke away to form the Kingdom of Belgium. A liberal Constitution was adopted by the Netherlands in 1848.

In spite of its neutrality in World War II, the Netherlands was invaded by the Nazis in May 1940, and the East Indies were later taken by the Japanese. The nation was liberated in May 1945. In 1948, after a reign of 50 years, Queen Wilhelmina resigned and was succeeded by her daughter Juliana.

In 1949, after a four-year war, the Netherlands granted independence to the East Indies, which became the Republic of Indonesia. In 1963, it turned over the western half of New Guinea to the new nation, ending 300 years of Dutch presence in Asia. Attainment of independence by Suriname on Nov. 25, 1975, left the Dutch Antilles as the Netherlands' only overseas territory.

Prime Minister Andries van Agt ended a seven-month constitutional crisis in December 1977 when he was able to form a center-right majority coalition. Early in 1980, Queen Juliana announced her intention to abdicate on her 71st birthday, April 30, in favor of the 42-year-old Crown Princess Beatrix: Beatrix was invested as Queen on April 30 in a ceremony marred by protests of Amsterdam squatters against eviction.

Van Agt lost his narrow majority in elections on May 26, 1981, in which the major issue was the deployment of U.S. cruise missiles on Dutch soil. Public opposition to the missiles forced the Netherlands, along with Belgium, to reverse its position in 1982 despite the Prime Minister's personal support for the NATO decision to deploy the new weapons in Western Europe. Van Agt lost his centrist coalition in May 1982 in a dispute over economic policy, and was succeeded by Ruud Lubber as Premier. Lubber put off any decision on missile deployment until 1985.

Netherlands Autonomous Country

NETHERLANDS ANTILLES

Status: Part of the Kingdom of the Netherlands
Governor: Bernardito M. Leito (1970)
Premier: Domenico F. Martina
Area: 383 sq mi. (993 sq km)
Population (est. 1982): 260,000 (average annual growth rate: 1.0%)
Capital (est. 1978): Willemstad, 152,000
Literacy rate (1981): 95%
Economic summary: Gross national product (1980): $1.1 billion. Average annual growth rate (1970–79): 0.9%. Per capita income: $4,290. Principal agricultural products: pigs, goats. Major industries: oil refining, tourism. Natural resource: phosphate. Export: petroleum. Import: petroleum. Major trading partners: U.S., Venezuela.

Geography. The Netherlands Antilles comprise two groups of Caribbean islands 500 miles (805 km) apart: one, about 40 miles (64 km) off the Venezuelan coast, consists of Curaçao (173 sq mi.; 448 sq km), Bonaire (95 sq mi.; 246 sq km), and Aruba (69 sq mi.; 179 sq km); the other, lying to the northeast, consists of three small islands with a total area of 34 square miles (88 sq km). The Dutch acquired Curaçao from Spain in 1643.

Government. There is a constitutional government formed by the Governor and Cabinet and an elected Legislative Council. The area has complete autonomy in domestic affairs.

NEW ZEALAND

Dominion of New Zealand
Sovereign: Queen Elizabeth II
Governor-General: David R. Lange (1984)
Prime Minister: Robert D. Muldoon (1975)
Area: 103,884 sq mi. (269,062 sq km) (excluding dependencies)
Population (est. 1982): 3,175,000 (average annual growth rate: 0.1%) (European, 90%; Maori and other Polynesian, 10%)
Density per square mile: 30.6
Capital: Wellington
Largest cities (est. 1982): Aukland, 825,000; Wellington, 345,000; Christchurch, 325,000; Hamilton, 160,000; Dunedin, 115,000
Monetary unit: New Zealand dollar
Languages: English, Maori
Religions: Church of England, 35%; Presbyterian, 22%; Roman Catholic, 16%
Member of Commonwealth of Nations
Literacy rate (1981): 98%
Economic summary: Gross national product (1980): $23.2 billion. Average annual growth rate (1970–79): 0.5%. Per capita income (1980): $7,090. Labor force in agriculture: 13%; principal products: wool, meat, dairy products, livestock. Labor force in industry: 33%; major products: processed foods, textiles, machinery, transport equipment, wood and paper products. Natural resources: forests, coal, gold, tungsten, iron ore, asbestos. Exports: meat, dairy products, wool. Imports: machinery, minerals, chemicals, consumer goods. Major trading partners: Australia, U.K., Japan, U.S.

Geography. New Zealand, about 1,250 miles (2,012 km) east of Australia, consists of two main islands and a number of smaller, outlying islands so scattered that they range from the tropical to the antarctic. The country is the size of Colorado.

New Zealand's two main components are North Island and South Island, separated by Cook Strait, which varies from 16 to 190 miles (26 to 396 km) in width. North Island (44,281 sq mi.; 114,688 sq km) is 515 miles (829 km) long and volcanic in its south-central part. It contains many hot springs and beautiful geysers. South Island (58,093 sq mi.; 150,461 sq km) has the Southern Alps along its west coast, with Mount Cook (12,349 ft; 3,764 m) the highest point.

The largest of the outlying islands are the Auckland Islands (234 sq mi.; 606 sq km), Campbell Island (44 sq mi.; 114 sq km), the Antipodes Islands (24 sq mi.; 62 sq km), and the Kermadec Islands (13 sq mi.; 34 sq km).

Government. New Zealand was granted self-government in 1852, a full parliamentary system and ministries in 1856, and dominion status in 1907. The Queen is represented by a Governor-General, and the Cabinet is responsible to a unicameral Parliament of 92 members, who are elected by popular vote for three years.

The major political parties are the Labor Party (56 of 95 seats in the House of Representatives), led by Prime Minister David R. Lange; the National Party (37 seats), led by former Prime Minister Sir Robert D. Muldoon; and the Social Credit Party (2 seats).

History. New Zealand was discovered and named in 1642 by Abel Tasman, a Dutch navigator. Captain James Cook explored the islands in 1769. In 1840, Britain formally annexed them.

From the first, the country has been in the forefront in instituting social welfare legislation. It adopted old age pensions (1898); a national child welfare program (1907); social security for the aged, widows, and orphans, along with family benefit payments; minimum wages; a 40-hour week and unemployment and health insurance (1938); and socialized medicine (1941).

The New Zealand Labor Party, headed by David Lange, swept Sir Robert Muldoon's conservative National Party from power in Parliamentary elections on July 14, 1984, that could cause major problems for the U.S. military commitments in the region. One of the Labor campaign promises was to ban American nuclear-powered and nuclear-armed naval vessels from New Zealand waters. At a meeting with visiting U.S. Secretary of State George Shultz after the election, both stressed their desire to avoid any crisis in the 33-year-old Anzus alliance of the United States, New Zealand and Australia.

Cook Islands and Overseas Territories

The Cook Islands (93 sq mi.; 241 sq km) were placed under New Zealand administration in 1901. They achieved self-governing status in association with New Zealand in 1965. Population in 1978 was about 19,600. The seat of government is on Rarotonga Island.

The island's chief exports are citrus juice, clothing, canned fruit, and pineapple juice. Nearly all of the trade is with New Zealand.

Niue (100 sq mi.; 259 sq km) was formerly administered as part of the Cook Islands. It was placed under separate New Zealand administration in 1901 and achieved self-governing status in association with New Zealand in 1974. The capital is Alofi. Population in 1980 was about 3,300.

Niue export passion fruit, copra, plaited ware, honey, and limes. Its principal trading partner is New Zealand.

The Ross Dependency (160,000 sq mi.; 414,400 sq km), an Antarctic region, was placed under New Zealand administration in 1923.

Tokelau (4 sq mi.; 10 sq km) was formerly administered as part of the Gilbert and Ellice Islands colony. It was placed under New Zealand administration in 1925. Its population is about 1,600.

NICARAGUA

Republic of Nicaragua

Executive power is held by the nine-member Directorate of the Sandinista Front (1979)

Area: 57,143 sq mi. (148,000 sq km)

Population (est. 1982): 2,900,000 (average annual growth rate: 3.2%) (mestizo, 70%; white, 17%; black, 9%; Indian, 4%)

Density per square mile: 50.7

Capital and largest city (est. 1981): Managua, 550,000

Monetary unit: Cordoba

Language: Spanish

Religion: Roman Catholic

National name: República de Nicaragua

Literacy rate (1981): 87%

Economic summary: Gross national product (1980): $1.9 billion. Average annual growth rate (1970–79): −1.6%. Per capita income (1980): $720. Land used for agriculture: 7%; labor force: 43%; principal products: cotton, coffee, sugar cane, rice, corn, beans, cattle. Labor force in industry: 13%; major products: processed foods, chemicals, metal products, clothing and textiles. Natural resources: timber, fisheries. Exports: cotton, coffee, chemical products, meat, sugar. Imports: food and non-food agricultural products, chemicals and pharmaceuticals, transport equipment, clothing, petroleum. Major trading partners: U.S., Caribbean and Western European countries.

Geography. Largest but most sparsely populated of the Central American nations, Nicaragua borders on Honduras to the north and Costa Rica to the south. It is slightly larger than New York State.

Nicaragua is mountainous in the west, with fertile valleys. A plateau slopes eastward toward the Caribbean.

Two big lakes—Nicaragua, about 100 miles long (161 km), and Managua, about 38 miles long (61 km)—are connected by the Tipitapa River. The Pacific coast is bald and rocky. The Caribbean coast, swampy and indented, is aptly called the "Mosquito Coast."

Government. A nine-member Directorate for the Sandinista National Liberation Front has replaced the five-member junta that took power July 19, 1979, with the overthrow of President Anastasio Somoza Debayle. Although members of the Directorate share authority in principle, Daniel Ortega Saavedra, a member of the original junta, dominates the Directorate as its "coordinator."

History. Nicaragua, which established independence in 1838, was first visited by the Spaniards in 1522. The chief of the country's leading Indian tribe at that time was called Nicaragua, from whom the nation derived its name. A U.S. naval force intervened in 1909 after two American citizens had been executed, and a few U.S. Marines were kept in the country from 1912 to 1925. The Bryan-Chamorro Treaty of 1916 (terminated in 1970) gave the U.S. an option on a canal route through Nicaragua, and naval bases. Disorder after the 1924 elections brought in the marines again.

A guerrilla leader, Gen. César Augusto Sandino, began fighting the occupation force in 1927. He fought the U.S. troops until their withdrawal in 1933. They trained Gen. Anastasio (Tacho) Somoza García to head a National Guard. In 1934, Somoza assassinated Sandino and overthrew the Liberal President Juan Batista Sacassa, establishing a military dictatorship with himself as president. He spurred the economic development of the country, meanwhile enriching his family through estates in the countryside and investments in air and shipping lines. On his assassination in 1956, he was succeeded by his son Luis, who alternated with trusted family friends in the presidency until his death in 1967. Another son, Maj. Gen. Anastasio Somoza Debayle, became President in 1967.

One of the worst earthquakes in Nicaragua's history struck Managua on Dec. 23, 1972, destroying an estimated 90% of its commercial establishments and 70% of its housing. Over 6,000 were killed, 20,000 injured, and 300,000 made homeless, and 60,000 were jobless as a result. Rebuilding costs were put at $772 million. Somoza obtained loans from the U.S. and international banks totaling $127 million for the reconstruction of Managua. Shortly afterward, he declared martial law after leftist guerrillas had kidnapped 14 prominent officials.

Sandinista guerrillas, leftists who took their name from Gen. Sandino, launched a civil war in May 1979, occupying parts of Managua and holding several provincial towns. Somoza ordered bombings to drive the rebels out, an action that embittered Nicaraguans of all classes. He defied appeals by the U.S. and the Organization of American States to step down and permit a peaceful transition to an all-party government.

After seven weeks of fighting, Somoza fled the country on July 17, 1979. The Sandinistas assumed power on July 19, promising to maintain a mixed economy, a non-aligned foreign policy, and a pluralist political system. However, the prominence of Cuban President Fidel Castro at the celebration of the first anniversary of the revolution and a delay of more than five years in holding elections strengthened debate over the true political color of the Sandinistas.

On Jan. 23, 1981, the Reagan Administration suspended U.S. aid, charging that Nicaragua, with the aid of Cuba and the Soviet Union, was supplying arms to rebels in El Salvador. The Sandinistas denied the charges. Later that year, Nicaraguan guerrillas known as "contras," or counterrevolutionaries, began a war to overthrow the Sandinistas. The guerrilla groups included both former members of Somoza's National Guard and disillusioned former Sandinistas. They received millions of dollars in covert assistance from the U.S. Central Intelligence Agency before Congress ordered a cutoff of the clandestine aid, following disclosure in early 1984 that contras had mined Nicaraguan harbors, using speedboats dispatched from a CIA mother ship. Several foreign ships, including a Soviet freighter, were damaged.

The long-promised Nicaraguan elections were scheduled for Nov. 4, 1984, with Daniel Ortega Saavedra, the junta coordinator, running as the Sandinista candidate for President and the heavy favorite to win. President Reagan dismissed the voting in advance as "a Soviet-style sham election."

NIGER

Republic of Niger
Chief of State: Gen. Seyni Kountché (1974)
Area: 489,206 sq mi. (1,267,044 sq km)
Population (est. 1982): 5,650,000 (average annual growth rate: 2.9%)
Density per square mile: 11.5
Capital and largest city (est. 1982): Niamey, 363,000
Monetary unit: Franc CFA
Ethnic groups: Hausa, 54%; Djerma and Songhai, 24%; Peul, 11%
Languages: French (official); Hausa, Songhai; Arabic
Religions: Islam, 85%; Animist, 15%, Christian
National name: République du Niger
Literacy rate (1981): 6%
Economic summary: Gross national product (1980): $1.8 billion. Average annual growth rate (1970–79): –1.2%. Per capita income (1980): $330. Land used for agriculture: 3%; labor force: 90%; principal products: peanuts, cotton, livestock, millet, sorghum, vegetables. Major industrial products: uranium, cement, bricks, light industrial products. Natural resources: uranium, coal, iron. Exports: uranium, peanuts, livestock, hides, skins. Imports: fuels, machinery, transport equipment, foodstuffs, consumer goods. Major trading partners: France, other Western European countries, Nigeria.

Geography. Niger, in West Africa's Sahara region, is four fifths the size of Alaska. It is surrounded by Mali, Algeria, Libya, Chad, Nigeria, Benin, and Upper Volta.

The Niger River in the southwest flows through the country's only fertile area. Elsewhere the land is semiarid.

Government. After a military coup on April 15, 1974, Col. Seyni Kountché suspended the Constitution and instituted rule by decree. Previously, the President was elected by direct universal suffrage for a five-year term and a National House of Assembly of 50 members was elected for the same term.

The Parti Progressiste Nigérien-Rassemblement Démocratique Africain, the only political party, was dissolved in 1974.

History. Niger was incorporated into French West Africa in 1896. There were frequent rebellions, but when order was restored in 1922, the French made the area a colony. In 1958, the voters approved the French Constitution and voted to make the territory an autonomous republic within the French Community. The republic adopted a Constitution in 1959 and the next year withdrew from the Community, proclaiming its independence.

The 1974 army coup ousted President Hamani Diori, who had held office since 1960. He was charged with having mishandled relief for the terrible drought that had devastated Niger and five neighboring sub-Saharan nations for several years. An estimated 2 million people were starving in Niger, but 200,000 tons of imported food, half U.S.-supplied, substantially ended famine conditions by the year's end. The new President, Lt. Col. Seyni Kountché, Chief of Staff of the army, installed a 12-man military government. A predominantly civilian government was formed by Kountché in 1976.

NIGERIA

Federal Republic of Nigeria
President: Maj. Gen. Muhammad Buhari (1983)
Area: 356,700 sq mi. (923,853 sq km)
Population (est. 1983): 91,117,500 (average annual growth rate: 3.3%)

Density per square mile: 230.6
Capital: Lagos
Largest cities (est. 1980): Lagos (metropolitan area): 4,000,000; **(est. 1975 by U.N.):** Ibadan, 847,000; Ogbomosho, 432,000; Kano, 399,000
Monetary unit: Naira
Languages: English (official) and native tongues
Religions: Islam, 47%; Christian, 34%; Animist
Member of Commonwealth of Nations
Literacy rate (1981): 25% (est.)
Economic summary: Gross national product (1980): $85.5 billion. Average annual growth rate (1970–79): 5.3%. Per capita income (1980): $1,010. Land used for agriculture: 13%; labor force: 70%; principal products: peanuts, cotton, cocoa, rubber, yams, cassava, livestock. Labor force in industry: 10%; major products: crude oil, natural gas, coal, tin, processed rubber, cotton, petroleum, wood, hides, textiles, cement, footwear, chemicals. Natural resources: petroleum, tin, columbite, iron ore, coal, limestone, lead, zinc, timber. Exports: oil, cocoa, palm products, rubber, timber, tin. Imports: machinery and transport equipment, manufactured goods, chemicals. Major trading partners: U.K., Western European countries, U.S.

Geography. Nigeria, one third larger than Texas and black Africa's most populous nation, is situated on the Gulf of Guinea in West Africa. Its neighbors are Benin, Niger, Cameroon, and Chad.

The lower course of the Niger River flows south through the western part of the country into the Gulf of Guinea. Swamps and mangrove forests border the southern coast; inland are hardwood forests.

Government. After 12 years of military rule, a new Constitution re-established democratic government in 1979, but it lasted less than four years. The military again took over from the democratically elected civilian government on Dec. 31, 1983. The arms of the military government include a Supreme Military Council and a National Council of State. The various ministers make up the Federal Executive Council. There are state military governors.

History. Between 1879 and 1914, private colonial developments by the British, with reorganizations of the Crown's interest in the region, resulted in the formation of Nigeria as it exists today. During World War I, native troops of the West African frontier force joined with French forces to defeat the German garrison in the Cameroons.

Nigeria became independent on Oct. 1, 1960.

Organized as a loose federation of self-governing states, the independent nation faced an overwhelming task of unifying a country with 250 ethnic and linguistic groups.

Rioting broke out again in 1966, the military commander was seized, and Col. Yakubu Gowon took power. Also in that year, the Moslem Hausas in the north massacred the predominantly Christian Ibos in the east, many of whom had been driven from the north. Thousands of Ibos took refuge in the Eastern Region. The military government there asked Ibos to return to the region and, in May 1967, the assembly voted to secede from the federation and set up the Republic of Biafra. Civil war broke out.

In January 1970, after 31 months of civil war, Biafra surrendered to the federal government.

Gowon's nine-year rule was ended in 1975 by a bloodless coup that made Army Brigadier Muritala Rufai Mohammed the new chief of state. Mohammed was assassinated the next year 1976 by a group of seven young officers, who failed to seize control of the government.

The return of civilian leadership was established with the election of Alhaji Shehu Shagari, as president in 1979.

A coup on December 31, 1983, restored military rule. In a bizarre incident on July 5, 1984, British customs officials broke into two crates aboard a Nigerian cargo plane at Stansted Airport, 30 miles north of London. The crates were labeled diplomatic baggage and addressed to the Nigerian Foreign Ministry in Lagos.

A Nigerian exile, Umaru Dikko, who had been transport minister in Shagari's government and was wanted by the military regime on charges of amassing great wealth through theft and corruption, was found in a drugged stupor in one of the crates. Crated with him was a man equipped with drugs and a syringe, who was identified as an Israeli. Two other men, who may have helped kidnap Dikko from his luxurious London home, were in the other crate. Maj. Gen. Mohammed Buhari's military government denied any involvement and hinted that Dikko may have faked his own abduction as a publicity stunt.

NORWAY

Kingdom of Norway
Sovereign: King Olav V (1957)
Prime Minister: Kåre Willoch (1981)
Area: 125,056 sq mi. (323,895 sq km)
Population (est. 1982): 4,125,000 (average annual growth rate: 0.3%)
Density per square mile: 33.0
Capital: Oslo
Largest cities (est. 1983): Oslo, 455,000; Bergen, 210,000; Trondheim, 135,000; Stavanger, 90,000
Monetary unit: Krone
Language: Norwegian
Religion: Evangelical Lutheran (state), 98%
National name: Kongeriket Norge
Literacy rate (1981): 100%
Economic summary: Gross national product (1981): $46.2 billion. Average annual growth rate (1970–79): 3.7%. Per capita income (1981): $11,255. Land used for agriculture: 3%; labor force, including fishing: 7%; principal products: dairy products, livestock, grain, vegetables, fruits, furs, wool. Labor force in industry: 29%; major products: oil and gas, fish, pulp and paper, ships, aluminum, iron, steel, nickel, fertilizers, transportation equipment, hydroelectric power, petrochemicals, electronic equipment. Natural resources: fish, timber, hydroelectric power, ores, oil, gas. Exports: oil, natural gas, ships, fish products, chemicals, pulp and paper. Imports: machinery, motor vehicles, foodstuffs, iron and steel, textiles and clothing. Major trading partners: U.K., Sweden, West Germany, U.S., Denmark.

Geography. Norway is situated in the western part of the Scandinavian peninsula. It extends about 1,100 miles (1,770 km) from the North Sea along the Norwegian Sea to more than 300 miles (483 km) above the Arctic Circle, the farthest north of any European country. It is slightly larger than New Mexico. Sweden borders on most of the eastern frontier, with Finland and the U.S.S.R. in the northeast.

Nearly 70% of Norway is uninhabitable and covered by mountains, glaciers, moors, and rivers. The hundreds of deep fiords that cut into the coastline give Norway an overall oceanfront of more than 12,000 miles (19,312 km). Nearly 150,000 islands off the coast form a breakwater and make a safe coastal shipping channel.

Government. Norway is a constitutional hereditary monarchy. Executive power is vested in the King together with a Cabinet, or Council of State, consisting of a Prime Minister and at least seven other members. The Storting, or Parliament, is composed of 156 members elected by the people under proportional representation. The Storting discusses and votes on political and financial questions, but divides itself into two sections (Lagting and Odelsting) to discuss and pass on legislative matters. The King cannot dissolve the Storting before the expiration of its term.

The sovereign is Olav V, born July 2, 1903, only son of Haakon VII and Princess Maud (1869–1938), third daughter of Edward VII of England. He succeeded to the throne on the death of his father Sept. 20, 1957. He married Princess Märtha of Sweden (1901–1954) on March 21, 1929. Their children are Princess Ragnhild Alexandra (born 1930), Princess Astrid (born 1932), and Crown Prince Harald (born 1937). In 1968, the Crown Prince married Sonja Haraldsen, a commoner.

The major political parties are the Labor Party (66 of 156 seats in the Storting), led by former Prime Minister Gro Harlem Brundtland; Conservative Party (53 seats), led by Prime Minister Kåre Willoch; Christian Democratic Party (16 seats), led by Kjell Magne Bondevik; Center Party (11 seats), led by Johan J. Jakobsen; Socialist Left Party (4 seats), led by Hanna Kvanmo; Party of Progress (4 seats), led by Carl I. Hagen; and Liberal Party (2 seats), led by Odd-Einar Dorum.

History. Norwegians, like the Danes and Swedes, are of Teutonic origin. The Norsemen, also known as Vikings, ravaged the coasts of northwestern Europe from the 8th to the 11th century.

In 1815, Norway fell under the control of Sweden. The union of Norway, inhabited by fishermen, sailors, merchants, and peasants, and Sweden, an aristocratic country of large estates and tenant farmers, was not a happy one, but it lasted for nearly a century. In 1905, the Norwegian Parliament arranged a peaceful separation and invited a Danish prince to the Norwegian throne—King Haakon VII. A treaty with Sweden provided that all disputes be settled by arbitration and that no fortifications be erected on the common frontier.

When World War I broke out, Norway joined with Sweden and Denmark in a decision to remain neutral and to cooperate in the joint interest of the three countries. In World War II, Norway was invaded by the Germans on April 9, 1940. It resisted for two months before the Nazis took over complete control. King Haakon and his government fled to London, where they established a government-in-exile. Maj. Vidkun Quisling, whose name is now synonymous with traitor or fifth columnist, was the most notorious Norwegian collaborator with the Nazis. He was executed by the Norwegians on Oct. 24, 1945.

Despite severe losses in the war, Norway recovered quickly. The country led the world in social experimentation. A neighbor of the U.S.S.R., Norway sought to retain good relations with the Soviet Union without losing its identity with the West. It entered the North Atlantic Treaty Organization in 1949.

Verification of U.S. and Soviet oil strikes in separated areas of Norway's sector of the North Sea bottom led the Storting in 1975 to impose stiff tax and royalty rates on concession holders. Following discovery of a North Sea field expected to produce 900,000 barrels a day by 1984, Parliament in 1976 approved establishment of a national refining and distributing company to market petroleum products at home and abroad.

Dependencies of Norway

Svalbard (23,957 sq mi.; 62,049 sq km), in the Arctic Ocean about 360 miles north of Norway, consists of the Spitsbergen group and several smaller islands, including Bear Island, Hope Island, King Charles Land, and White Island (or Gillis Land). It came under Norwegian administration in 1925. The population in 1979 was 3,640.

Bouvet Island (23 sq mi.; 60 sq km), in the South Atlantic about 1,600 miles south-southwest of the Cape of Good Hope, came under Norwegian administration in 1928.

Jan Mayen Island (144 sq mi.; 273 sq km), in the Arctic Ocean between Norway and Greenland, came under Norwegian administration in 1929.

Peter I Island (96 sq mi.; 249 sq km), lying off Antarctica in the Bellinghausen Sea, came under Norwegian administration in 1931.

Queen Maud Land, a section of Antarctica, came under Norwegian administration in 1939.

OMAN

Sultanate of Oman
Sultan: Qabus Bin Said (1970)
Area: 105,000 sq mi. (271,950 sq km)[1]
Population (est. 1984): 1,500,000 (average annual growth rate: 3.1%)
Density per square mile: 11.6
Capital and largest city (est. 1981): Muscat, 50,000
Monetary unit: Omani rial
Language: Arabic
Religion: Islam
National name: Sultanate of Oman
Literacy rate (1981): 10%
Economic summary: Gross national product (1980): $3.9 billion. Average annual growth rate (1970–79): 3.8%. Per capita income (1980): $4,380. Principal agricultural products: dates, alfalfa, onions, wheat, tobacco, bananas. Major industries: petroleum drilling, fishing, construction. Natural resources: oil, asbestos, marble, copper, limestone, chromium, manganese, iron. Exports: oil. Imports: machinery and transport equipment, food, mineral fuels, tobacco. Major trading partners: U.K., U.S., India, Australia, China, Japan, West Germany.

1. Excluding the Kuria Muria Islands.

Geography. Oman is a 1,000-mile-long (1,700-km) coastal plain at the southeastern tip of the Arabian peninsula lying on the Arabian Sea and the Gulf of Oman. The interior is a plateau. The country is the size of Kansas.

Government. The Sultan of Oman (formerly called Muscat and Oman), an absolute monarch, is assisted by a council of ministers, six specialized councils, a consultative council and personal advisers.

There are no political parties.

History. Although Oman is an independent state under the rule of the Sultan, it has been under British protection since the early 19th century.

Muscat, the capital of the geographical area known as Oman, was occupied by the Portuguese from 1508 to 1648. Then it fell to Persian princes and later was regained by the Sultan.

The Kuria Muria Islands, formerly part of Aden, were given to Oman by the British in 1967.

In a palace coup on July 23, 1970, the Sultan, Sa'id bin Taimur, who had ruled since 1932, was overthrown by his son, who promised to establish a modern government and use new-found wealth to aid the people of this very isolated state.

PAKISTAN

Islamic Republic of Pakistan
President: Gen. Mohammad Zia ul-Han (1978)
Area: 310,400 sq mi. (803,936 sq km)[1]
Population (est. 1983): 89,850,000[2] (average annual growth rate: 2.9%)
Density per square mile: 289.5
Capital (1981 census): Islamabad, 150,000
Largest cities (1981 census for metropolitan area): Karachi, 5,100,000; Lahore, 2,900,000; Faisalabad, (Lyallpur) 1,920,000; Rawalpindi, 920,000; Hyderabad, 795,000
Monetary unit: Pakistan rupee
Principal languages: Urdu (national), English (official), Punjabi, Sindhi, Pashtu, and Baluchi
Religions: Islam, 97%; Hindu, Christian
Literacy rate (1980): 28%
Economic summary: Gross national product (1980): $24.9 billion. Average annual growth rate (1970–79): 1.5%. Per capita income (1980): $300. Land used for agriculture: 24%; labor force: 52%; principal products: wheat, rice, cotton. Labor force in industry: 21%; major products: cotton textiles, processed foods, tobacco, chemicals, natural gas. Natural resources: natural gas, limited petroleum, iron ore. Exports: raw and manufactured cotton, rice, carpets, leather, petroleum products. Imports: food grains, edible oil, crude oil, machinery, chemicals, transport equipment. Major trading partners: U.S., U.K., West Germany, Saudi Arabia, Japan, China.

1. Excluding Kashmir and Jammu. 2. Does not include about 3 million refugees from Afghanistan.

Geography. Pakistan is situated in the western part of the Indian subcontinent, with Afghanistan and Iran on the west, India on the east, and the Arabian Sea on the south.

Nearly twice the size of California, Pakistan consists of towering mountains, including the Hindu Kush in the west, a desert area in the east, the Punjab plains in the north, and an expanse of alluvial plains. The 1,000-mile-long (1,609 km) Indus River flows through the country from the Kashmir to the Arabian Sea.

Government. On July 5, 1977, Gen. Mohammad Zia ul-Haq, Army Chief of Staff, ousted the civilian government of Prime Minister Zulfikar Ali Bhutto. Zia declared himself Chief Administrator of Martial Law as head of a four-man council. The national and state assemblies were dissolved and all political parties banned, while the Chief Justices of the four states replaced the governors.

History. Pakistan was one of the two original successor states to British India. For almost 25 years following independence in 1947, it consisted of two separate regions East and West Pakistan, but now comprises only the western sector. It consists of Sind, Baluchistan, the former North-West Frontier Province, western Punjab, the princely state of Bahawalpur, and several other smaller native states.

The British became the dominant power in the region in 1797 following Lord Clive's military victory, but rebellious tribes kept the northwest in turmoil. In the northeast, the formation of the Moslem League in 1906 estranged the Moslems from the Hindus. In 1930, the league, led by Mohammed Ali Jinnah, demanded creation of a Moslem state wherever Moslems were in the majority. He supported Britain during the war. Afterward, the league received almost a unanimous Moslem vote in 1946 and Britain agreed to the formation of Pakistan as a separate dominion.

Pakistan was proclaimed a republic March 23, 1956. Iskander Mirza, then Governor General, was elected Provisional President and H. S. Suhrawardy became the first non-Moslem League Prime Minister.

In 1958, Mirza surrendered his power to Gen. Ayub Khan, who purged corrupt and inefficient officeholders, broke up the feudal land system, eliminated much of the black market, tax evasion, and hoarding, and revolutionized education. In 1969, Gen. Yahya Khan ousted Ayub and took over as President.

The election of 1970 set the stage for civil war when Sheik Muuibur called general strikes, which turned bloody, and told East Pakistanis to stop paying taxes to the central government. West Pakistan troops moved in and fighting began. The independent state of Bangladesh, or Bengali nation, was proclaimed March 26, 1971.

The intervention of Indian troops protected the new state and brought Yahya down. Bhutto took over and accepted Bangladesh as an independent entity.

Diplomatically, 1976 saw the resumption of formal relations between India and Pakistan. At the same time, civilian air traffic between the two nations was restored after an 11-year interruption.

Pakistan's first elections under civilian rule took place in March 1977 and provoked bitter opposition protest when Bhutto's party was declared to have won 155 of the 200 elected seats in the 216-member National Assembly. A rising tide of violent protest and political deadlock led to a military takeover on July 5. Gen. Mohammed Zia ul-Haq became Chief Martial Law Administrator.

Bhutto was tried and convicted for the 1974 murder of a political opponent, and despite worldwide protests was executed on April 4, 1979, touching off riots by his supporters. Zia declared himself President on Sept. 16, 1978, a month after Fazel Elahi Chaudhry left office upon the completion of his 5-year term.

In April 1981, a five-year U.S. military and economic aid program, with $500 million to be delivered in the first year, was accepted by Pakistan, which had rejected a two-year, $400-million package offered by the Carter administration as inadequate to meet the Soviet threat. While Zia continued to repress political opposition at home, he became increasingly active in world affairs. Pakistan took the leadership in Islamic efforts to settle the war between Iran and Iraq and in opposing the Soviet presence in Afghanistan and the Soviet-backed Vietnamese invasion of Cambodia.

In January 1982, Saudi Arabia was reported to have pledged $500 million to Pakistan to help pay for the first six of a total of 40 U.S. F-16 jet fighters. In February, Zia extended the 28-month ban on all political activity and the next month announced that general elections—once expected to take place before the end of 1982—would be indefinitely postponed.

PANAMA

Republic of Panama
President: Nicolás Ardito Barletta (1984)
Area: 29,761 sq mi. (77,082 sq km)
Population (est. 1982): 2,000,000 (average annual growth rate: 2.3%) (mestizo, 65%; black, 13%; white, 11%; Indian, 10%)
Density per square mile: 68.2
Capital and largest city (est. 1980): Panama City, 400,-000
Monetary unit: Balboa
Language: Spanish (official)
Religions: Roman Catholic, 92%; Islam, 5%
National name: República de Panamá
Literacy rate (1981): 82%
Economic summary: Gross national product (1980): $3.2 billion. Average annual growth rate (1970–79): 1.3%. Per capita income (1980): $1,730. Land used for agriculture: 24%; labor force: 29%; principal products: bananas, corn, sugar, rice, cattle. Labor force in industry: 18%; major industrial products: refined petroleum, sugar. Natural resources: copper (unexploited). Exports: bananas, refined petroleum, sugar, shrimp. Imports: crude oil, crude petroleum, chemicals, food. Major trading partners: U.S., West Germany, Ecuador.

Geography. The southernmost of the Central American nations, Panama is south of Costa Rica and north of Colombia. The Panama Canal bisects the isthmus at its narrowest and lowest point, allowing passage from the Caribbean Sea to the Pacific Ocean.

Panama is slightly smaller than South Carolina. It is marked by a chain of volcanic mountains in the west, moderate hills in the interior, and a low range on the east coast. There are extensive forests in the fertile Caribbean area.

Government. In 1972, a new Constitution was approved by a new 505-seat National Assembly of Community Representatives (corregidores), which was created in the first election in five years. The Charter provides for indirect election of the President by the Assembly for a six-year term.

History. Visited by Columbus in 1502 on his fourth voyage and explored by Balboa in 1513, Panama was the principal transshipment point for Spanish treasure and supplies to and from South and Central America in colonial days. In 1821, when Central America revolted against Spain, Panama joined Colombia, which already had declared its independence. For the next 82 years, Panama attempted unsuccessfully to break away from Colombia. After U. S. proposals for canal rights over the narrow isthmus had been rejected by Colombia, Panama proclaimed its independence with U.S. backing in 1903.

For canal rights in perpetuity, the U.S. paid Panama $10 million and agreed to pay $250,000 each year, increased to $430,000 after devaluation of the U.S. dollar in 1933 and was further increased under a revised treaty signed in 1955. In exchange, the U.S. got the Canal Zone—a 10-mile-wide strip across the isthmus—and a considerable degree of influence in Panama's affairs.

In 1968, Dr. Arnulfo Arias was elected President for the third time in three decades. And for the third time, he was thrown out of office by the military. A two-man junta, Col. José M. Pinilla and Col. Bolivar Urrutia, took control. They were ousted by Gen. Omar Torrijos Herrera, who named a new junta, with Demetrio Lakas Bahas as President.

Panama and the U.S. agreed in 1974 to negotiate the eventual reversion of the canal to Panama, despite strongly expressed opposition in the U.S. Congress. The texts of two treaties—one governing the transfer of the canal and the other guaranteeing its neutrality after transfer—were negotiated by August 1977 and were signed by Torrijos and President Carter in Washington on September 7. A Panamanian referendum approved the treaties by more than two thirds on October 23, but further changes were insisted upon by the U.S. Senate.

The principal change was a reservation sponsored by Senator Dennis De Concini, an Arizona Democrat, specifying that despite the neutrality treaty's specification that only Panama shall maintain forces in its territory after transfer of the canal Dec. 31, 1999, the U.S. should have the right to use military force to keep the canal operating if it should become obstructed. After lengthy debate, the Senate approved the neutrality treaty on March 16, 1978, by 68–32 and by the same vote approved the basic treaty governing the transfer on April 18. On June 16, Carter and Torrijos exchanged instruments of ratification in Panama City.

The basic treaty provides an increase from the present $2.3 million a year in royalties to $10 million a year during the transition period, with an additional annual payment of $10 million if it can be obtained from tolls. It also requires the use of more Panamanians as canal employees in the interim and pledges the U.S. not to pursue the development of another canal without the agreement of Panama.

The death of Torrijos in a plane crash on July 31, 1981, left a power vacuum. President Aristides Royo, named by Torrijos in 1978 to a six-year term, clashed with the leadership of the National Guard and was unable to harmonize factions within the ruling Democratic Revolutionary Party. On July 30, 1982, Royo resigned in favor of Vice President Ricardo de la Espriella. Nicolas Ardito Barletta, Panama's first directly elected President in 16 years, was inaugurated on Oct. 11, 1984, for a five-year term.

Panama Canal. First conceived by the Spaniards in 1534, when King Charles V of Spain ordered a survey of a waterway across the Isthmus, a construction concession was granted by the Colombian government in 1878 to St. Lucien N. B. Wyse, representing a French company. Two years later, the French Canal Company, inspired by Ferdinand de Lesseps, began construction of what was to have been a sea-level canal. The effort ended in bankruptcy nine years later and the United States ultimately paid the French $40 million for their rights and assets.

The U.S. project, built on territory controlled by the United States, and calling for the creation of an interior lake connected to both oceans by locks, got under way in 1904. Completed in 1914, the Canal is 40.27 miles long and lifts ships 85 feet above sea level through a series of three locks on the Pacific and Atlantic sides. Enlarged in later years, each lock now measures 1,000 feet in length, 110 feet in width, and 40 feet in depth of water.

PAPUA NEW GUINEA

Sovereign: Queen Elizabeth II
Governor General: Sir Kingsford Díbela (1983)
Prime Minister: Michael Somare (1982)
Area: 178,704 sq mi. (462,840 sq km)
Population (est. 1982): 3,250,000 (average annual growth rate: 2.2%)
Density per square mile: 17.7
Capital and largest city (est. 1982): Port Moresby, 150,-000
Monetary unit: Kina
Languages: English, Melanesian pidgin, and 717 distinct native languages
Religions: Protestant, 64%; Roman Catholic, 33%
Member of Commonwealth of Nations
Literacy rate (1982): 15%
Economic summary: Gross national product (1980): $2.4 billion. Average annual growth rate (1970–79): 0.3%. Per capita income (1980): $780. Labor force in agriculture, including fishing: 85%; principal products: sweet potatoes, coffee, copra, palm oil, cocoa, tea, rubber, cattle. Major industrial products: soap, concrete products, clothing, light fabricated metal products, paint, furniture. Natural resources: copper, gold, silver, timber, tuna. Exports: copper, coffee and cocoa beans, copra, timber. Imports: food, machinery, transport equipment, fuels, chemicals. Major trading partners: Australia, U.K., Japan.

Geography. Papua New Guinea occupies the eastern half of the island of New Guinea, just north of Australia, and many outlying islands. The Indonesian province of Irian Jaya is to the west. To the north and east are the islands of Manus, New Britain, New Ireland, and Bougainville, all part of Papua New Guinea.

Papua New Guinea is about one tenth larger than California. Its mountainous interior has only recently been explored. The high-plateau climate is temperate, in contrast to the tropical climate of the coastal plains. Two major rivers, the Sepik and the Fly, are navigable for shallow-draft vessels.

Government. Papua New Guinea attained independence Sept. 16, 1975, ending a United Nations trusteeship under the administration of Australia. Parliamentary democracy was established by a Constitution that invests power in a 109-member national legislature.

The Pangu Party, People's Progress Party, National Party, and United Party are the largest of half a dozen political parties.

History. The eastern half of New Guinea was first visited by Spanish and Portuguese explorers in the 16th century, but a permanent European presence was not established until 1884, when Germany declared a protectorate over the northern coast and Britain took similar action in the south. Both nations formally annexed their protectorates and, in 1901, Britain transferred its rights to a newly independent Australia. Australian troops invaded German New Guinea in World War I and retained control under a League of Nations mandate that eventually became a United Nations trusteeship, incorporating a territorial government in the southern region, known as Papua.

Australia granted limited home rule in 1951 and, in 1964, organized elections for the first House of Assembly. Autonomy in internal affairs came nine years later.

Just before independence, dissidents on the island of Bougainville, whose copper resources provide the chief foreign earnings for the central government, declared their intention to secede. The central government responded by taking direct control in October 1975, amid warnings from Australia that it would oppose secession. Prime Minister Michael Somare met with pro-secessionists early in 1976 and, after conceding extra powers for a restored provincial government, resolved the dispute.

Somare lost a vote of confidence on March 11, 1980, and was succeeded by Sir Julius Chan, head of the People's Progress Party and former Finance Minister. After the elections of June 1982, he was chosen prime minister by the new legislature.

PARAGUAY

Republic of Paraguay
President: Gen. Alfredo Stroessner (1954)
Area: 157,047 sq mi. (406,752 sq km)
Population (est. 1983): 3,475,000 (average annual growth rate: 2.4%) (mestizo, 95%; white, 3%; Indian, 2%)
Density per square mile: 22.1
Capital and largest city (est. 1980): Asunción, 530,000
Monetary unit: Guaraní
Languages: Spanish (official), Guaraní
Religion: Roman Catholic (official)
National name: República del Paraguay
Literacy rate (1981): 40%
Economic summary: Gross national product (1980): $4.1 billion. Average annual growth rate (1970–79): 5.3%. Per capita income (1980): $1,340. Labor force in agriculture: 53%; principal products: oilseeds, cotton, wheat, sweet potatoes, tobacco, corn, rice, sugar cane. Labor force in industry: 19%; major products: packed meats, crushed oilseeds, beverages, textiles, light consumer goods, cement. Natural resource: timber. Exports: cotton, oilseeds, meat products, tobacco, timber, coffee, essential oils. Imports: fuels and lubricants, machinery and motors, motor vehicles, beverages, tobacco, foodstuffs. Major trading partners: Argentina, Brazil, West Germany, U.S., Netherlands.

Geography. California-size Paraguay is surrounded by Brazil, Bolivia, and Argentina in south central

South America. Eastern Paraguay, between the Paraná and Paraguay Rivers, is upland country with the thickest population settled on the grassy slope that inclines toward the Paraguay River. The greater part of the Chaco region to the west is covered with marshes, lagoons, dense forests, and jungles.

Government. The President is elected by popular vote for five years. The legislature is bicameral, consisting of a Senate of 30 members and a Chamber of Representatives of 60 members. There is also a Council of State, whose members are nominated by the government.

The governing Partido Colorado was further strengthened in 1977 when the Partido Liberal Unido, a merger of the Partido Liberal Radical and Partido Liberal, was declared illegal.

History. In 1526 and again in 1529, Sebastian Cabot explored Paraguay when he sailed up the Paraná and Paraguay Rivers. From 1608 until their expulsion from the Spanish dominions in 1767, the Jesuits maintained an extensive establishment in the south and east of Paraguay. In 1811, Paraguay revolted against Spanish rule and became a nominal republic under two Consuls.

Actually, Paraguay was governed by three dictators during the first 60 years of independence. The third, Francisco López, waged war against Brazil and Argentina in 1864–65, a conflict in which the male population was almost wiped out. A new Constitution in 1870, designed to prevent dictatorships and internal strife, failed to do so, and not until 1912 did a period of comparative economic and political stability begin. The dispute between Paraguay and Bolivia over the Chaco region led to war in 1932 and was finally settled by the 1935 Buenos Aires Peace Conference, which gave most of the Chaco to Paraguay.

After World War II, politics became particularly unstable. Juan Natalicio González was elected President in 1948. Successive revolts on Jan. 30 and Feb. 26, 1949, ousted him and his successor. The leader of the second revolt, Felipe Molas López, was elected President in April but gave way to Federico Chaves. Re-elected in 1953, Chaves was ousted by the army, and Gen. Alfredo Stroessner was elected to complete his term.

Stroessner ruled under a state of siege until 1965, when the dictatorship was relaxed and exiles returned. The Constitution was revised in 1967 to permit Stroessner to be re-elected, and press freedom was briefly restored before the regime again moved to repress opposition.

Although oil exploration begun by U.S. companies in the Chaco boreal in 1974 has been fruitless, Paraguay found prosperity in another form of energy when construction started in 1978 on the Itaipu Dam on the Parana River as a joint Paraguayan-Brazilian project. The largest hydroelectric development in the world when completed in 1988, Itaipu will generate 12.6 megawatts of electricity, surpassing the U.S. Grand Coulee Dam. With 40,000 Paraguayans working around the clock building the $12-billion project, unemployment has virtually disappeared.

The Stroessner regime was criticized by the U.S. State Department during the Carter administration as a violator of human rights, but unlike Argentina and Uruguay, Paraguay did not suffer cuts in U.S. military aid. The criticism is credited with having reduced the number of political prisoners to a "few hundred."

PERU

Republic of Peru
President: Fernando Belaúnde Terry (1980)
Premier: Sandro Mariategui (1984)
Area: 496,222 sq mi. (1,285,216 sq km)
Population (1983): 19,300,000 (average annual growth rate: 2.8%) (white and mestizo, 52%; Indian, 46%)
Density per square mile: 38.9
Capital: Lima
Largest cities (est. 1979 for metropolitan area): Lima, 4,900,000; **(est. 1978):** Arequipa, 410,000; Trujillo, 350,000; Chiclayo, 260,000; Piura, 165,000; Cuzco, 150,000
Monetary unit: Sol
Languages: Spanish and Quéchua
Religion: Roman Catholic
National name: República del Perú
Literacy rate (1981): 45%
Economic summary: Gross national product (1980): $16.5 billion. Average annual growth rate (1970–79): 0.2%. Per capita income (1980): $930. Land used for agriculture: 2%; labor force: 42%; principal products: corn, sugar, cotton, coffee, wool. Labor force in industry: 13%; major products: processed minerals, fish meal, refined petroleum, textiles. Natural resources: minerals and metals, fish, petroleum, timber. Exports: copper, fish products, cotton, sugar, coffee, lead, silver, zinc, wool, iron ore. Imports: machinery, foodstuffs, chemicals, pharmaceuticals. Major trading partners: U.S., Japan, Western European, and Latin American countries.

Geography. Peru, in western South America, extends for nearly 1,500 miles (2,414 km) along the Pacific Ocean. Colombia and Ecuador are to the north, Brazil and Bolivia to the east, and Chile to the south.

Five sixths the size of Alaska, Peru is divided by the Andes Mountains into three sharply differentiated zones. To the west is the coastline, much of it arid, extending 50 to 100 miles (80 to 160 km) inland. The mountain area, with peaks over 20,000 feet (6,096 m), lofty plateaus, and deep valleys, lies centrally. Beyond the mountains to the east is the heavily forested slope leading to the Amazonian plains.

Government. The President, elected by universal suffrage for a five-year term, holds executive power. A Senate of 60 members and a Chamber of Deputies of 180 members, both elected for five-year terms, share legislative power.

The major political parties are: Acción Popular (98 of 180 seats in the Chamber and 26 of 60 seats in the Senate), led by President Fernando Belaúnde Terry; Partido Popular Cristiano (10 Chamber seats and 6 Senate seats), led by Luis Bedoya Reyes; and the opposition Partido Aprista Peruano (58 Chamber seats and 18 Senate seats), led by Luis Alberto Sanchez. The Partido Popular Cristiano is allied with Belaúnde.

History. Peru was once part of the great Incan empire and later the major vice-royalty of Spanish South America. It was conquered in 1531–33 by Francisco Pizarro. On July 28, 1821, Peru proclaimed its independence, but the Spanish were not finally defeated until 1824. For a hundred years thereafter, revolutions were frequent, and a new war was fought with Spain in 1864–66.

Peru emerged from 20 years of dictatorship in 1945 with the inauguration of President José Luis Bustamente y Rivero after the first free election in many decades. But he served for only three years and was succeeded in turn by Gen. Manual A. Odria, Manuel Prado y Ugarteche, and Fernando Belaúnde Terry. On Oct. 3, 1968, Belaúnde was overthrown by Gen. Juan Velasco Alvarado.

Velasco nationalized the nation's second biggest bank and turned two large newspapers over to Marxists in 1970, but he also allowed a new agreement with a copper-mining consortium of four American firms.

On May 31, 1970, the country suffered the hemisphere's worst natural disaster, an earthquake which, together with a mud slide it caused, took an estimated 50,000 lives.

The World Bank granted Peru $470 million in credits in 1973, which appeared to end a boycott by international financial institutions in which the U.S. has a strong influence. American copper and fishing firms were seized in 1974, but compensation was paid. Peru also became in 1974 the first nation in the Western Hemisphere to receive Soviet military advisers.

On Aug. 29, 1975, Velasco was replaced in a bloodless coup by his Premier, Gen. Francisco Morales Bermúdez. To meet International Monetary Fund requirements for the extension of credit, Morales decreed a severe economic austerity program in 1977, touching off student and leftist demonstrations. Even stiffer measures, ranging from 50% to 100% increases in the prices of essentials, were ordered in 1978.

Fulfilling a pledge to restore civilian government, Morales scheduled elections for May 18, 1980, in which Belaúnde Terry, the last civilian President, won 43% of the vote in a field of 15 candidates. Allied with the small Partido Popular Cristiano, Belaúnde Terry's Acción Popular party was assured of a parliamentary majority. In one of his first moves, the new President returned to private ownership newspapers that had been seized under the Morales regime.

THE PHILIPPINES

Republic of the Philippines
President: Ferdinand E. Marcos (1965)
Prime Minister: César Virata (1981)
Area: 115,830 sq mi. (300,000 sq km)
Population (est. 1982): 50,500,000 (average annual growth rate: 2.5%)
Density per square mile: 436.4
Capital: Manila
Largest cities (est. 1981): Manila, 1,750,000[1]; Quezon City, 1,175,000; Davao, 625,000; Cebu, 500,000
Monetary unit: Peso
Languages: Pilipino, English, Spanish; dialects: Tagalog, Visayan, Ilocano
Religions: Roman Catholic, 85%; Islam, 4%; Aglipayan (Independent Philippine Christian), 4%; Protestant, 3%
National name: Republika ng Pilipinas
Literacy rate (1981): 83%
Economic summary: Gross national product (1982): $39 billion. Growth rate (1982): 2.6%. Per capita income (1982): $772. Land used for agriculture: 53%; labor force: 47%; principal products: rice, corn, coconuts, sugar cane, bananas, tobacco. Labor force in industry: 12%; major products: processed agricultural products, textiles, chemicals and chemical products. Natural resources: forests, metallic and non-metallic minerals. Exports: coconut products, sugar, logs and lumber, copper concentrates, bananas, garments, nickel. Imports: petroleum, industrial equipment, wheat. Major trading partners: U.S., Japan.

1. Metropolitan area population is 7,500,000.

Geography. The Philippine Islands are an archipelago of over 7,000 islands lying about 500 miles (805 km) off the southeast coast of Asia. The overall land area is comparable to that of Arizona. The northernmost island, Y'Ami, is 65 miles (105 km) from Taiwan, while the southernmost, Saluag, is 40 miles (64 km) east of Borneo.

Only about 7% of the islands are larger than one square mile, and only one third have names. The largest are Luzon in the north (40,420 sq mi.; 104,687 sq km) Mindanao in the south (36,537 sq mi.; 94,631 sq km), Samar (5,124 sq mi.; 13,271 sq km), Negros (4,903 sq mi.; 12,699 sq km), and Palawan (4,550 sq km).

The islands are of volcanic origin, with the larger ones crossed by mountain ranges. The highest peak is Mount Apo (9,690 ft; 2,954 m) on Mindanao.

Government. President Ferdinand E. Marcos proclaimed a new Constitution in 1973, replacing the previous presidential style of government with a parliamentary system. This was changed in 1981 to a semiparliamentary system with a strong president. Marcos ruled by decree from 1972 until 1978 when an interim parliament with limited powers was elected. A regular parliament with greater powers was elected on May 14, 1984, with the ruling New Society Movement winning a clear majority (110 elected seats, plus 17 appointed by Marcos, in the 200-member National Assembly), but opponents scoring substantial gains (71 elected seats). The opposition consists of many small parties united only in their dislike of Marcos.

History. Fernando Magellan, the Portuguese navigator in the service of Spain, discovered the Philippines in 1521. Twenty-one years later, a Spanish exploration party named the group of islands in honor of Prince Philip, later Philip II of Spain. Spain retained possession of the islands for the next 350 years.

The Philippines were ceded to the U.S. in 1899 by the Treaty of Paris after the Spanish-American War. Meanwhile, the Filipinos, led by Emilio Aguinaldo, had declared their independence. They continued guerrilla warfare against U.S. troops until the capture of Aguinaldo in 1901. By 1902, peace was established except among the Moros.

The first U.S. civilian Governor-General was William Howard Taft (1901–04). The Jones Law (1916) provided for the establishment of a Philippine Legislature composed of an elective Senate and House of Representatives. The Tydings-McDuffie Act (1934) provided for a transitional period until 1946, at which time the Philippines would become completely independent.

Under a Constitution approved by the people of the Philippines in 1935, the Commonwealth of the Philippines came into being, with Manuel Quezon y Molina as president.

On Dec. 8, 1941, the Philippines were invaded by Japanese troops. Following the fall of Bataan and Corregidor, Quezon established a government-in-exile, which he headed until his death in 1944. He was succeeded by Vice President Sergio Osmeña.

U.S. forces led by Gen. Douglas MacArthur reinvaded the Philippines in October 1944 and, after the liberation of Manila in February 1945, Osmeña re-established the government.

The Philippines achieved full independence on July 4, 1946. Manual A. Roxas y Acuña was elected first president. Subsequent presidents have been Elpidio Quirino (1948–53), Ramón Magsaysay (1953–57). Carlos P. García (1957–61), Diosdado Macapagal (1961–65), and Ferdinand E. Marcos (since Dec. 30, 1965).

Marcos became the first president in Philippine history to win re-election in 1969, when he overwhelmingly defeated Sergio Osmeña, Jr., with campaign promises to become less dependent on the U.S. and to establish ties with Communist countries. The campaign violence led to 59 deaths.

Political, civil, and religious unrest was responsible for the deaths of almost 500 persons in 1971, and disastrous month-long rains that caused enormous flooding added to the toll in 1972. In September 1972, Marcos declared martial law and arrested hundreds of political opponents; journalists, and leftists.

Nearly 8,000 persons died Aug. 17, 1976, when an earthquake measuring 8 on the Richter scale hit Mindanao and other southern islands. The disaster temporarily quelled a rebellion by the Moslem majority in Mindanao, but fighting resumed.

The Philippines was one of six nations criticized by the U.S. State Department for human-rights violations in a report made public in 1977, although the department recommended continuing aid because of the importance of U.S. bases in the Philippines.

Marcos, who had freed the last of the national leaders still in detention, former Senator Benigno S. Aquino, Jr., in 1980 and permitted him to go to the United States, ended eight years of martial law on January 17, 1981. On April 7, a plebiscite approved changes to the 1973 Constitution establishing a ministerial government and authorizing reelection of the President. On June 16, Marcos won a second six-year term with 86% of the vote as most opposition parties boycotted the election.

Despite having been warned by First Lady Imelda Marcos that he risked being killed if he came back, opposition leader Aquino returned to the Philippines from self-exile on Aug. 21, 1983. He was shot to death as he was being escorted from his plane by military police at Manila International Airport. The government contended the assassin was Rolando Galman, a small-time hoodlum allegedly hired by communists, who was in turn shot dead by Filipino troops, but there was widespread suspicion that the Marcos government was somehow involved in the murder.

The assassination sparked huge anti-government rallies and violent clashes between demonstrators and police, which continued intermittently through most of 1984, and helped the fragmented opposition parties score substantial gains in the May 14, 1984, elections for a National Assembly with greater power than a previous interim parliament.

Social and economic pressures also were building, as was a communist insurgency by armed guerrillas calling themselves the New People's Army. In May, Marcos said the N.P.A. had increased by 25% since 1982, to 6,800 armed insurgents. Western analysts used higher figures.

POLAND

Polish People's Republic

President of the Council of State: Henryk Jablonski (1972)
Premier: Gen. Wojciech Jaruzelski (1981)
Area: 120,727 sq mi. (312,683 sq km)
Population (est. 1982): 36,300,000 (average annual growth rate: 0.9%)
Density per square mile: 301.6
Capital: Warsaw
Largest cities (est. 1982): Warsaw, 1,625,000; Lodz, 850,000; Krakow, 725,000; Wroclaw, 625,000; Poznan, 560,000; Gdansk, 460,000; Szczecin, 390,000
Monetary unit: Zloty
Language: Polish (more than 90%)
Religions: Roman Catholic, Greek Orthodox, Protestant, Jewish
National name: Polska Rzeczpospolita Ludowa
Literacy rate (1981): 98%
Economic summary: Gross national product (1980): $139.8 billion. Average annual growth rate (1970–79): 5.2%. Per capita income (1980): $3,900. Labor force in agriculture: 27%; principal products: grains, sugar beets, potatoes, hogs and other livestock. Labor force in industry: 32%; major products: iron and steel, chemicals, textiles, processed foods, transport equipment. Natural resources: coal, sulfur, copper, natural gas. Exports: fuels, machinery and equipment, agricultural products, light industrial products. Imports: machinery and equipment, fuels, raw materials, agricultural and food products. Major trading partners: Communist bloc countries, U.K., Italy, U.S., West Germany, France.

Geography. Poland, a country the size of New Mexico in north central Europe, borders on East Germany to the west, Czechoslovakia to the south, and the U.S.S.R. to the east. In the north is the Baltic Sea.

Most of the country is a plain with no natural boundaries except the Carpathian Mountains in the south and the Oder and Neisse Rivers in the east. Other major rivers, which are important to commerce, are the Vistula, Warta, and Bug.

Government. The 1952 Constitution describes Poland as a people's republic. The supreme organ of state authority is the Sejm (Parliament), which is composed of 460 members elected for four years.

The major political parties are the Polish United Workers' (Communist) Party (255 of 460 seats in the Sejm), led by First Secretary Wojciech Jaruzelski; United Peasant Party (117 seats), led by Stefan Malinowski; Democratic Party (39 seats), led by Edward Kowalczyk; non-party members and Catholic organizations (49 seats).

History. Little is known about Polish history before the 11th century, when King Boleslaus I (the Brave) ruled over Bohemia, Saxony, and Moravia. Mongol invasions in 1241 and 1259 were repelled. Meanwhile, the Teutonic knights of Prussia conquered part of Poland and barred the latter's access to the Baltic. The knights were defeated by Wladislaus II at Tannenberg in 1410 and became Polish vassals, and Poland regained a Baltic shoreline. Poland reached the peak of power between the 14th and 16th centuries, scoring military successes against the Russians and Turks. In 1683, John III (John Sobieski) turned back the Turkish tide at Vienna.

An elective monarchy failed to produce strong central authority, and Prussia, and Austria were able to carry out a first partition of the country in

1772, a second in 1792, and a third in 1795–96. For more than a century thereafter, there was no Polish state, but the Poles never ceased their efforts to regain their independence.

Poland was formally reconstituted in November 1918, with Marshal Josef Pilsudski as Chief of State. In 1919, Ignace Paderewski, the famous pianist and patriot, became the first premier. In 1926, Pilsudski seized complete power in a coup and ruled dictatorially until his death on May 12, 1935, when he was succeeded by Marshal Edward Smigly-Rydz.

Despite a 10-year nonaggression pact signed in 1934, Hitler attacked Poland on Sept. 1, 1939. Russian troops invaded from the east on September 17, and on September 28 a German-Russian agreement divided Poland between Russia and Germany. Wladyslaw Raczkiewicz formed a government-in-exile in France, which moved to London after France's defeat in 1940.

All of Poland was occupied by Germany after the Nazi attack on the U.S.S.R. in June 1941.

The legal Polish government soon fell out with the Russians, and, in 1944, a Communist-dominated Polish Committee of National Liberation received Soviet recognition. Moving to Lublin after that city's liberation, it proclaimed itself the Provisional Government of Poland. Some former members of the Polish government in London joined with the Lublin government to form the Polish Government of National Unity, which Britain and the U.S. recognized.

On Aug. 2, 1945, in Berlin, President Harry S. Truman, Joseph Stalin and Prime Minister Clement Attlee of Britain established a new *de facto* western frontier for Poland along the Oder and Neisse Rivers. (The border was finally agreed to by West Germany in a nonagression pact signed Dec. 7, 1970.) On Aug. 16, 1945, the U.S.S.R. and Poland signed a treaty delimiting the Soviet-Polish frontier. Under these agreements, Poland was shifted westward. In the east it lost 69,860 square miles (180,934 sq km) with 10,772,000 inhabitants; in the west it gained (subject to final peace-conference approval) 38,986 square miles (100,973 sq km) with a prewar population of 8,621,000.

In 1946, a unicameral Parliament was established by referendum. Then, in 1947, the government bloc won a huge majority in government-controlled elections, opposition was suppressed and the Sovietization of Poland begun, with Soviet Marshal Konstantin Rokossovsky as Defense Minister and army commander.

A New Constitution in 1952 made Poland a "people's democracy" of the Soviet type. In 1955, Poland, which had joined the Council for Economic Mutual Assistance in 1949, became a member of the Warsaw Treaty Organization, and its foreign policy became identical with that of the U.S.S.R. The government undertook persecution of the Roman Catholic Church as a remaining source of opposition and in 1953 arrested the primate, Stefan Cardinal Wyszynski. But in June 1956, worker and student riots in Poznan forced reconsideration of the repression.

Wladyslaw Gomulka was elected leader of the United Workers (Communist) Party in 1956. He denounced the Stalinist terror, ousted many Stalinists, relieved Rokossovsky, freed Wyszynski, and improved relations with the church. Most collective farms were dissolved, and the press became freer.

Much as the Poznan bread riots of 1956 brought Gomulka to power, so pre-Christmas rioting in 1970 in Gdansk and other Baltic coastal towns caused Gomulka to fall and elevated Edward Gierek to the key post of party boss. Cause of the worker riots was steep rises in food prices.

An event of profound importance to Poland's 90% Catholic population was the election in October 1978 of Karol Cardinal Wojtila of Krakow as Pope John Paul II. His visit to his homeland from June 2 to June 11, 1979, was the first papal journey to a Marxist state.

A strike that began in shipyards and spread to other industries in August 1980 produced a stunning victory for workers when the economically hard-pressed government accepted for the first time in a Marxist state the right of workers to organize in independent unions.

The strike also led to major changes in Polish leadership. Edward Babuich, who became Premier early in 1980, was replaced by Jozef Pinkowski, and Edward Gierek, longtime Communist Party head, was ousted in favor of Stanislaw Kania.

Led by Solidarity, a free union founded by Lech Walesa, workers launched a drive for liberty and improved conditions. A national strike for a five-day week in January 1981 led to the dismissal of Premier Pinkowski and the naming of the fourth Premier in less than a year, Gen. Wojciech Jaruzelski. The deteriorating economy required Western creditors in April to defer repayment of $2.6 billion of $27 billion in foreign debt.

The new freedom was short-lived. Pressed by Moscow, the Communist Party's central committee ousted Kania on Oct. 18 and replaced him with Jaruzelski, who now held the posts of first secretary of the party, premier, defense minister, and commander in chief of the armed forces.

Antistrike legislation was approved on Dec. 2 and martial law declared on Dec. 13, when Walesa and other Solidarity leaders were arrested. Ten days later, President Reagan ordered sanctions against the Polish government, stopping food shipments and cutting commercial air traffic. In a New Year message, Pope John Paul II criticized military rule and Polish bishops formally protested the government's action.

Despite demands for declaring Poland in default, Congress in February authorized payment of $3.5 million in interest charges to U.S. banks that had given loans to Poland for food purchases. Poland's economic situation remained desperate and its internal political climate so tense that the government postponed indefinitely a papal visit set for August.

The Pope eventually made the visit, the second to his native Poland of his Pontificate, on June 16–23, 1983. While there, he confered with Premier Jaruzelski, urging him to seek peaceful solutions to the nation's problems and end martial law and met privately with Lech Walesa.

Martial law was formally ended in 1984 but the government retained emergency powers. On July 21, 1984, the Parliament marked the 40th anniversary of Communist rule in Poland by enacting an amnesty bill authorizing the release of 652 political prisoners—virtually all except for those charged with high treason, espionage, and sabotage—and 35,000 common criminals. In Washington, Administration officials indicated President Reagan would soon approve further easing of the economic sanctions against Poland.

PORTUGAL

Portuguese Republic
President: Gen. António Ramalho Eanes (1976)
Premier: Mário Soares (1983)
Area: 34,340 sq mi. (88,941 sq km)
Population (est. 1982): 10,000,000 (average annual growth rate: 0.6%)
Density per square mile: 283.0
Capital: Lisbon
Largest cities (est. 1982): Lisbon, 900,000; Opporto, 400,000
Monetary unit: Escudo
Language: Portuguese
Religion: Roman Catholic
National name: República Portuguesa
Literacy rate (1981): 70%
Economic summary: Gross national product (1980): $23.1 billion. Average annual growth rate (1970–79): 1.1%. Per capita income (1980): $2,350. Land used for agriculture: 48%; labor force: 31%; principal products: grains, potatoes, olives, wine grapes. Labor force in industry: 35%; major products: textiles, footwear, wood pulp, paper, cork, metal products, refined oil, chemicals, canned fish, wine. Natural resources: fish, cork, tungsten ore. Exports: cotton, textiles, cork and cork products, canned fish, wine, timber and timber products, resin. Imports: petroleum, cotton, industrial machinery, iron and steel, chemicals. Major trading partners: Western European countries, U.S.

Geography. Portugal occupies the western part of the Iberian Peninsula, bordering on the Atlantic Ocean to the west and Spain to the north and east. It is slightly smaller than Indiana.

The country is crossed by many small rivers, and also by three large ones that rise in Spain, flow into the Atlantic, and divide the country into three geographic areas. The Minho (Miño in Spain) River, part of the northern boundary, cuts through a mountainous area that extends south to the vicinity of the Douro (Duero) River. South of the Douro, the mountains slope to the plains about the Tagus (Tejo) River. The remaining division is the southern one of Alentejo.

The Azores, stretching over 340 miles (547 km) in the Atlantic, consist of nine islands divided into three groups, with a total area of 902 square miles (2,335 sq km). The nearest continental land is Cape da Roca, Portugal, about 900 miles (1,448 km) to the east. The Azores are an important station on Atlantic air routes, and Britain and the U.S. established air bases there during World War II.

Madeira, consisting of two inhabited islands, Madeira and Porto Santo, and two groups of uninhabited islands, lies in the Atlantic about 535 miles (861 km) southwest of Lisbon. The Madeiras are 307 square miles (796 sq km) in area.

Government. A new Constitution, adopted in April 1976, provides for popular election of a President for a five-year term and for a legislature, the Assembly of the Republic, for four years.

The major political parties are the Socialist Party (99 of 250 seats in the Assembly), led by Mário Soares; the Social Democrat Party (73 seats), led by Euríco de Melo, Carlos Mota Pinta, and Henrique N. Rodrigues; the United People Alliance (44 seats); and the Central Social Democrats (29 seats) led by Francisco Lucas Pires.

History. Portugal was a part of Spain until it won its independence in the middle of the 12th century. King John I (1385–1433) unified his country at the expense of the Castilians and the Moors of Morocco. The expansion of Portugal was brilliantly coordinated by John's son, Prince Henry the Navigator. In 1488, Bartolomew Diaz reached the Cape of Good Hope, proving that the Far East was accessible by sea. In 1498, Vasco da Gama reached the west coast of India. By the middle of the 16th century, the Portuguese Empire included West and East Africa, Brazil, Persia, Indochina, and Malaya.

In 1581, Philip II of Spain invaded Portugal and held it for 60 years, precipitating a catastrophic decline of Portuguese commerce. Courageous and shrewd explorers, the Portuguese proved to be inefficient and corrupt colonizers. By the time the Portuguese dynasty was restored in 1640, Dutch, English, and French competitors began to seize the lion's share of the world's colonies and commerce. Portugal retained Angola and Mozambique in Africa, and Brazil (until 1822).

The corrupt King Carlos, who ascended the throne in 1889, made Joao Franco the Premier with dictatorial power in 1906. In 1908, Carlos and his heir were shot dead on the streets of Lisbon. The new King, Manoel II, was driven from the throne in the Revolution of 1910 and Portugal became a French-style republic.

Traditionally friendly to Britain, Portugal fought in World War I on the Allied side in Africa as well as on the Western Front. Weak postwar governments and a revolution in 1926 brought Antonio Oliveira Salazar to power. He kept Portugal neutral in World War II but gave the Allies naval and air bases after 1943.

Portugal lost the tiny remnants of its Indian empire—Goa, Daman, and Diu—to Indian military occupation in 1961, the year an insurrection broke out in Angola. For the next 13 years, Salazar, who died in 1970, and his successor, Marcello Caetano, fought independence movements amid growing world criticism. Leftists in the armed forces, weary of a losing battle, launched the "Happy Revolution" of April 25, 1974. They installed Gen. António de Spínola as Provisional President with promises of peace in Africa and reforms at home.

Spínola's moderate left Cabinet failed to satisfy the military leadership, who named Col. Vasco dos Santos Gonçalves as Premier on July 14. After Spínola's resignation on Sept. 30, Gen, Francisco da Costa Gomez, Chief of Staff of the armed forces, became President of an increasingly leftist regime.

Anti-Communist violence in rural areas and pressure from non-Communists in the government and military forced Gonçalves out on Aug. 29, 1975, and he was replaced by the more moderate Vice Adm. José Pinheiro. Elections under a new Constitution in 1976 gave Gen. António Ramalho Eanes, Army Chief of Staff, a landslide victory even though he campaigned for a program of economic austerity. With Mário Soares as Premier, tough economic policies slowed inflation but proved unpopular with legislators, who forced Soares out on July 27, 1978.

Pursuit of economic austerity measures brought down Soares' centrist successor, Carlos Alberto Mota Pinto, less than a year later, giving Portugal its first woman Premier, Maria Lurdes Pintassilgo, who acted as caretaker until the victory of Francisco Manoel Lumbrales de Sá Carneiro's Democratic Alliance on Dec. 2, 1979. Sá Carneiro's coalition of his own Social Democratic Party, the

Christian Democrats and the small Popular Monarchist Party won a majority of three seats, the first absolute majority for a governing party since the 1974 revolution.

On Dec. 4, 1980, Sá Carneiro, who had increased his coalition's majority in parliamentary elections in October, died in an air crash while campaigning against the re-election of President Eanes. Three days later, Eanes won a second four-year term with 57% of the popular vote, a victory for the left-leaning general that countered the rightward trend led by Sá Carneiro.

Francisco Pinto Balsemao, the new Premier, continued the drafting of a permanent Constitution. Balsemao was defeated in the elections of April 1983 by Mário Soares, the Socialist party leader.

Portuguese Overseas Territory

After the April 1974 revolution, the military junta moved to grant independence to the territories, beginning with Portuguese Guinea in September 1974, which became the Republic of Guinea-Bissau.

Mozambique and Angola followed, leaving only Portuguese Timor and Macao of the former Empire. Despite Lisbon's objections, Indonesia annexed Timor.

MACAO

Status: Territory
Governor: Adm. Vasco Almeida Costa (1981)
Area: 6 sq mi. (15.5 sq km)
Population (est. 1982): 300,000 (average annual growth rate: 1.7%)
Capital (1970 census): Macao, 241,413
Monetary unit: Patacá
Literacy rate (1981): 99% (excluding Chinese)
Economic summary: Gross national product (1980): $550 million. Annual average growth rate (1970–79): 15%. Land used for agriculture: 10%; labor force: 5%; principal products: rice and vegetables; Labor force in industry: 30%; major products: textiles, fireworks, fish products. Exports: textiles and clothing, manufactured goods, foodstuffs. Imports: consumer goods, foodstuffs. Major trading partners: Hong Kong, China, U.S., West Germany, France.

Macao comprises the peninsula of Macao and the two small islands of Taipa and Colôane on the South China coast, about 35 miles (53 km) from Hong Kong. Established by the Portuguese in 1557, it is the oldest European outpost in the China trade, but Portugal's sovereign rights to the port were not recognized by China until 1887, and its boundaries are still not delimited. The port has been eclipsed in importance by Hong Kong, but it is still a busy distribution center and also has an important fishing industry.

QATAR

State of Qatar
Ruler: Sheik Khalifa bin Hamad al-Thani (1972)
Area: 4,000 sq mi. (11,437 sq km)
Population (est. 1982): 260,000 (average annual growth rate: 4.0%)
Density per square mile: 65.0
Capital (est. 1981): Doha, 190,000
Monetary unit: Qatari riyal
Language: Arabic
Religion: Islam
Literacy rate (1981): 25%
Economic summary: Gross national product (1980): $6.0 billion. Average annual growth rate (1970–79): –1.2%. Per capita income (1980): $26,080. Major industrial product: oil. Natural resource: oil. Export: oil. Major trading partners: U.K., U.S., France, Japan, West Germany.

Geography. Qatar occupies a small peninsula that extends into the Persian Gulf from the east side of the Arabian Peninsula. Saudi Arabia is to the west and the United Arab Emirates to the south. The country is mainly barren.

Government. Qatar, one of the Persian Gulf states, lies between Bahrain and United Arab Emirates. For a long time, it was under Turkish protection, but in 1916, the sultan accepted British protection. After the discovery of oil in the 1940s and its exploitation in the 1950s and 1960s, political unrest spread to the sheikdoms. Qatar declared its independence in 1971. The next year the current Sheik, Khalifa bin Hamad al-Thani, ousted his cousin in a bloodless coup.

ROMANIA

Socialist Republic of Romania
President: Nicolae Ceausescu (1974)
Premier: Constantin Dascalescu (1982)
Area: 91,700 sq mi. (237,500 sq km)
Population (est. 1983): 22,477,707 (Romanian, 87.1%, Hungarian 7.7%, Germans, 1.5%) (average annual growth rate: 0.7%)
Density per square mile: 245.7
Capital: Bucharest
Largest cities (est. 1982): Bucharest, 1,979,076; Brasov, 334,136; Timisoara, 301,612; Constanta, 306,879; Cluj-Napoca, 300,677; Iasi, 294,784; Galati, 278,637
Monetary unit: Leu
Languages: Romanian, Hungarian, Serbian, German, Turkish
Religions: Romanian Orthodox, 70%; Greek Orthodox, 10%
National name: Republica Socialista România
Literacy rate (1981): 99%
Economic summary: Gross national product (1981): $94.7 billion. Average annual growth rate (1981): 1.0%. Per capita income (1981): $4,238. Land used for agriculture: 63%; labor force: 36%; principal products: corn, wheat, oil, seeds, potatoes. Labor force in industry: 26%; major products: power, mining, forestry, metal production and processing, chemicals, food processing, textiles. Natural resources: oil, timber, natural gas, coal. Exports: machinery, minerals and metals, foodstuffs, lumber, fuel, manufactures. Imports: machinery, rolled steel, iron ore, coke and coking coal, minerals. Major trading partners: U.S.S.R., East Germany, West Germany, Iran, Iraq, U.S.A.

Geography. A country in southeastern Europe slightly smaller than Oregon, Romania is bordered on the west by Hungary and Yugoslavia, on the north and east by the U.S.S.R., on the east by the Black Sea, and on the south by Bulgaria.

The Carpathian Mountains divide Romania's upper half from north to south and connect near the center of the country with the Transylvanian Alps, running east and west.

North and west of these ranges lies the Transylvanian plateau, and to the south and east are the plains of Moldavia and Walachia. In its last 190 miles (306 km), the Danube River flows through Romania only. It enters the Black Sea in northern Dobruja, just south of the border with the Soviet Union.

Government. The supreme body of state power and the sole legislative body is the Grand National Assembly, with 465 members elected for five-year terms. It elects a State Council, which provides for the continuity of state power and settles problems between sessions of the Assembly. The supreme executive and administrative body is the Council of Ministers elected by the Assembly.

The Communist Partry, led by Secretary General Nicolae Ceausescu, is the only political party.

History. Most of Romania was the Roman province of Dacia from about A.D. 100 to 275. From the 6th to the 12th century, wave after wave of barbarian conquerors—Vlachs, Bulgars, and others—passed over the area. By the 15th century, the main Romanian principalities of Moldavia and Walachia had become satellites within the Ottoman Empire, although they retained much independence. After the Russo-Turkish War of 1828–29, they became Russian protectorates. In 1848, the Romanians rebelled but were suppressed by the Russians. The nation became a kingdom in 1881 after the Congress of Berlin.

King Ferdinand ascended the throne in 1914. At the start of World War I, Romania proclaimed its neutrality, but later joined the Allied side and in 1916 declared war on the Central Powers. The armistice of Nov. 11, 1918, gave Romania vast territories from Russia and the Austro-Hungarian Empire.

The gains of World War I, making Romania the largest Balkan state, included Bessarabia, Transylvania, and Bukovina. The Banat, a Hungarian area, was divided with Yugoslavia.

In 1925, Crown Prince Carol renounced his rights to the throne, and when King Ferdinand died in 1927, Carol's son, Michael (Mihai) became King under a regency. However, Carol returned from exile in 1930, was crowned King Carol II, and gradually became a powerful political force in the country. In 1938, he abolished the democratic Constitution of 1923.

In 1940, the country was reorganized along Fascist lines, and the Fascist Iron Guard became the nucleus of the new totalitarian party. On June 27, the Soviet Union occupied Bessarabia and northern Bukovina. By the Axis-dictated Vienna Award of 1940, two fifths of Transylvania went to Hungary, after which Carol dissolved Parliament and granted the new premier, Ion Antonescu, full power. He abdicated and again went into exile.

Romania subsequently signed the Axis Pact on Nov. 23, 1940, and the following June joined in Germany's attack on the Soviet Union, reoccupying Bessarabia. Following the invasion of Romania by the Red Army in August 1944, King Michael led a coup that ousted the Antonescu government. An armistice with the Soviet Union was signed in Moscow on Sept. 12, 1944.

A Communist-dominated government bloc won elections in 1946, Michael abdicated on Dec. 30, 1947, and Romania became a "people's republic." In 1955, Romania joined the Warsaw Treaty Organization and the United Nations. A decade later, with the adoption of a new Constitution emphasizing national autonomy, and especially after Nicolae Ceausescu came to power in 1967, Bucharest became an increasingly dissident voice in the Soviet bloc.

Alone of the Warsaw Pact members, Romania maintained ties with China and Albania after the two broke with Moscow. Almost as annoying to the Soviet leadership was Ceausescu's continuing of ties with Israel, a relationship that made possible the secret preparations for the visit to Israel by Egypt's President Anwar el-Sadat in November 1977. Ceausescu also exchanged cultural and scientific accords with Washington in 1974 and visited the United States in 1978. Romania was the only Warsaw Pact country that sent a team to the 1984 Summer Olympic Games in Los Angeles, declining to join the Moscow-led Soviet bloc boycott.

Despite his liberal international record, at home Ceausescu has harshly suppressed dissidents calling for freedom of expression in the wake of the Helsinki agreements.

RWANDA

Republic of Rwanda
President: Maj. Gen. Juvénal Habyarimana (1973)
Area: 10,169 sq mi. (26,338 sq km)
Population (est. 1983): 5,644,000 (average annual growth rate: 3.3%)
Density per square mile: 511.4
Capital and largest city (est. 1981): Kigali, 155,000
Monetary unit: Rwanda franc
Languages: Kinyarwanda and French
Religions: Roman Catholic, 56%; Protestant, 12%; Islam, 9%; Animist
Literacy rate (1981): 25%
Economic summary: Gross national product (1980): $1.0 billion. Average annual growth rate (1970–79): 1.6%. Per capita income (1980): $200. Land used for agriculture: 33%; labor force: 95%; principal products: coffee, tea, pyrethrum, beans, potatoes. Labor force in industry: less than 5%; major products: processed foods, light consumer goods, minerals. Natural resources: cassiterite, wolfram. Exports: coffee, tea, pyrethrum, wolfram. Imports: textiles, foodstuffs, machinery, and equipment. Major trading partners: U.S., Belgium, West Germany, Kenya.

Geography. Rwanda, in east central Africa, is surrounded by Zaire, Uganda, Tanzania, and Burundi. It is slightly smaller than Maryland.

Steep mountains and deep valleys cover most of the country. Lake Kivu in the northwest, at an altitude of 4,829 feet (1,472 m) is the highest lake in Africa. Extending south of it are the Virunga Mountains, which include Volcan Karisimbi (14,187 ft.; 4,324 m), Rwanda's highest point.

Government. Grégoire Kayibanda was President from 1962 until he was overthrown in a bloodless coup on July 5, 1973, by the military led by Gen.

Juvénal Habyarimana.

In a plebiscite in December 1978, Habyarimana was elected to a five-year term as president and a new constitution adopted that provides for an elected Assembly and a single official party, the National Revolutionary Development Movement.

History. Rwanda, which was part of German East Africa, was first visited by European explorers in 1854. During World War I, it was occupied in 1916 by Belgian troops. After the war, it became a Belgian League of Nations mandate, along with Burundi, under the name of Ruanda-Urundi. The mandate was made a U.N. trust territory in 1946. Until the Belgian Congo achieved independence in 1960, Ruanda-Urundi was administered as part of that colony.

Ruanda became the independent nation of Rwanda on July 1, 1962.

ST. CHRISTOPHER-NEVIS

Prime Minister: Kennedy Alphonse Simmonds
Area: St. Christopher (Kitts) 65 sq mi. (169 sq km); Nevis 35 sq mi. (93 sq km)
Population (1980): St. Christopher (Kitts) 35,104; Nevis 9,300; Total 44,404
Capital: Basseterre (on St. Kitts), 14,725
Largest town on Nevis: Charlestown, 1,771
Monetary unit: East Caribbean dollar
Economic summary: St. Christopher-Nevis: Gross domestic product (1977): $32 million. Per capita income: $580. Principal agricultural products: sugar, cotton. Major industries: sugar processing, salt extraction. Exports: sugar, molasses. Imports: foodstuffs, manufactured goods. Major trading partners: U.S., U.K., Japan.

St. Christopher-Nevis was formerly part of the West Indies Associated States which were established in 1967 and consisted of Antigua and St. Kitts-Nevis-Anguilla of the Leeward Islands, and Dominica, Grenada, St. Lucia, and St. Vincent of the Windward Islands. Statehood for St. Vincent was held up until 1969 because of local political uncertainties. (Grenada, became independent in 1974, Dominica in 1978, St. Lucia and St. Vincent in 1979, and Antigua (known as Antigua and Barbuda) in 1981.) Anguilla's association with St. Christopher-Nevis ended in 1980 and it remains a British dependency.

Two members of the Leeward group—the British Virgin Islands and Montserrat—did not become Associated States.

St. Christopher-Nevis became independent on September 19, 1983.

ST. LUCIA

Sovereign: Queen Elizabeth II
Governor-General: Sir Allen Lewis (1982)
Prime Minister: John Compton (1982)
Area: 238 sq mi. (616 sq km)
Population (est. 1982): 125,000 (average annual growth rate: 1.4%)
Density per square mile: 525.2
Capital (est. 1972): Castries, 45,000
Monetary unit: East Caribbean dollar
Languages: English and patois
Religions: Roman Catholic, 91%; Anglican, 3%; Seventh-day Adventist, 2%
Member of Commonwealth of Nations
Literacy rate (1981): 80%
Economic summary: Gross national product (1980): $110 million. Average annual growth rate (1970–79): 2.8%. Per capita income (1980): $850. Labor force in agriculture: 50%; principal products: bananas, coconuts, sugar, cocoa, spices. Major industrial products: processed limes. Exports: bananas, cocoa. Imports: foodstuffs, machinery and equipment, fertilizers, petroleum products. Major trading partners: U.K., U.S., Canada.

Geography. One of the Windward Isles of the Eastern Caribbean, St. Lucia lies just south of Martinique. It is of volcanic origin. A chain of wooded mountains runs from north to south, and from them flow many streams into fertile válleys.

Government. A Governor-General represents the sovereign, Queen Elizabeth II. A Prime Minister is head of government, chosen by a 17-member House of Assembly elected by universal suffrage for a maximum term of five years.

History. Discovered by Spain in 1503 and ruled by Spain and then France, St. Lucia became a British territory in 1803. With other Windward Isles, St. Lucia was granted home rule in 1967 as one of the West Indies Associated States. On Feb. 22, 1979, St. Lucia achieved full independence in ceremonies boycotted by the opposition St. Lucia Labor Party, which had advocated a referendum before cutting ties with Britain.

Unrest and a strike by civil servants forced Prime Minister John Compton to hold elections in July, in which his United Workers Party lost its majority for the first time in 15 years.

A Labor Party government was ousted in turn by Compton and his followers, who won 14 of 17 seats in elections in May 1982. Labor seats fell from 12 to 2, with one seat won by the Progressive Labor Party.

Formerly dependent on a single crop, bananas, St. Lucia has sought to lower its chronic unemployment and payments deficit. The government provided tax incentives to a U.S. corporation, Amerada Hess, to facilitate location of a $150-million oil refinery and transshipment terminal on the island.

ST. VINCENT AND THE GRENADINES

Sovereign: Queen Elizabeth II
Governor-General: Sir Sydney Gunn-Munro (1979)
Prime Minister: James Mitchell (1984)
Area: 150 sq mi. (389 sq km)
Population (est. 1982): 130,000 (average annual growth rate: 2.9%)
Density per square mile: 1,000.0
Capital and largest city (est. 1981): Kingstown, 30,000
Monetary unit: East Caribbean dollar
Language: English
Religions: Anglican, 47%; Methodist, 28%; Roman Catholic, 13%

Member of Commonwealth of Nations
Literacy rate (1981): 85%
Economic summary: Gross national product (1980): $60 million. Average annual growth rate (1970–79): –1.7%. Per capita income (1980): $520. Land used for agriculture: 50%; labor force: 40%; principal products: bananas, arrowroot, coconuts. Major industry: food processing. Exports: bananas, arrowroot, copra. Imports: fertilizers, machinery and equipment, chemicals, fuels, clothing. Major trading partners: U.K., U.S., Canada, Caribbean nations.

Geography. St. Vincent, chief island of the chain, is 18 miles (29 km) long and 11 miles (18 km) wide. One of the Windward Islands in the Lesser Antilles, it is 100 miles (161 km) west of Barbados. The island is mountainous and well forested. The Grenadines, a chain of nearly 600 islets with a total area of only 17 square miles (27 sq km), extend for 60 miles (96 km) from northeast to southwest between St. Vincent and Grenada, southernmost of the Windwards.

St. Vincent is dominated by the volcano La Soufrière, part of a volcanic range running north and south, which rises to 4,048 feet (1,234 m). The volcano erupted over a 10-day period in April 1979, causing the evacuation of the northern two thirds of the island. (There is also a volcano of the same name on Basse-Terre, Guadeloupe, which became violently active in 1976 and 1977.)

Government. A Governor-General represents the sovereign, Queen Elizabeth II. A Prime Minister, elected by a 13-member unicameral legislature, holds executive power. Major political parties are the New Democrats (9 of the 13 seats), led by Prime Minister James Mitchell; and the Labor Party (4 seats), led by former Prime Minister Milton Cato.

History. Discovered by Columbus in 1498, and alternately claimed by Britain and France, St. Vincent became a British colony by the Treaty of Paris in 1783. The islands won home rule in 1969 as part of the West Indies Associated States and achieved full independence Oct. 26, 1979. Prime Minister Milton Cato's government quelled a brief rebellion Dec. 8, 1979 attributed to economic problems following the eruption of La Soufrière in April, 1979. Unlike a 1902 eruption which killed 2,000, there was no loss of life but widespread losses to agriculture.

SAN MARINO

Most Serene Republic of San Marino
Co-Regents: Two selected every six months by Grand and General Council
Area: 23.6 sq mi. (62 sq km)
Population (est. 1983): 22,200 (mostly Italian) (average annual growth rate: 1.6%)
Density per square mile: 868.6
Capital and largest city (est. 1982 for metropolitan area): San Marino, 4,500
Monetary unit: Italian lira
Language: Italian
Religion: Roman Catholic
National name: Repubblica di San Marino
Literacy rate (1983): 98%
Economic summary: Land used for agriculture: 74%; principal products: wheat and other grains, grapes, fruits, vegetables. Major industrial products: textiles, paper, leather, cement and other building materials. Exports: building stone, lime, chestnuts, wheat, hides, baked goods. Imports: manufactured consumer goods. Major trading partner: Italy.

Geography: One tenth the size of New York City, San Marino is surrounded by Italy. It is situated in the Apennines, a little inland from the Adriatic Sea near Rimini.

Government. The country is governed by two co-regents. Executive power is exercised by ten ministers. In 1959, the Grand Council granted women the vote.

The major political parties are the Christian Democratic Party (26 of 60 seats in the Grand and General Council); Communist Party (15 seats); Socialist Party (9 seats); United Socialist Party (8 seats); Democratic Socialist Party (1 seat); and Republican Party (1 seat).

History. According to tradition, San Marino was founded about A.D. 350 and had good luck for centuries in staying out of the many wars and feuds on the Italian peninsula. It is the oldest republic in the world.

A person born in San Marino remains a citizen and can vote no matter where he lives.

SÃO TOMÉ AND PRÍNCIPE

Democratic Republic of São Tomé and Principe
President: Manuel Pinto da Costa (1975)
Area: 372 sq mi. (964 sq km)
Population (est. 1982): 90,000 (average annual growth rate: 1.1%)
Density per square mile: 241.9
Capital and largest city (est. 1981): São Tomé, 30,000
Monetary unit: Dobra
Language: Portuguese
Religions: Roman Catholic, Evangelical Protestant, Seventh-Day Adventist
Literacy rate (1981): 10%
Economic summary: Gross national product (1980): $60 million. Average annual growth rate (1970–79): –0.2%. Per capita income (1980): $490. Principal agricultural products: cocoa, copra, coconuts, palm oil, coffee, bananas. Major industrial products: timber, copra. Exports: cocoa, coffee, copra, palm oil. Imports: foodstuffs, textiles, machinery, electrical equipment, fuels, lubricants. Major trading partners: Netherlands, Portugal, U.S., West Germany.

Geography. The tiny volcanic islands of São Tomé and Príncipe lie in the Gulf of Guinea about 150 miles (241 km) off West Africa. São Tomé (about 330 sq mi.; 855 sq km) is covered by a dense mountainous jungle, out of which have been carved large plantations. Príncipe (about 40 sq. mi.; 104 sq km) consists of jagged mountains. Other islands in the republic are Pedras Tinhosas and Rolas.

Government. The Constitution grants supreme power to a People's Assembly composed of members elected for four years. The Assembly chooses the President of the republic from candidates named by the Movement for the Liberation of São Tomé and Príncipe, the only legal party.

History. São Tomé and Príncipe were discovered, by Portuguese navigators in 1471 and settled by the end of the century. Intensive cultivation by slave labor made the islands a major producer of sugar during the 17th century but output declined until the introduction of coffee and cacao in the 19th century brought new prosperity. The island of São Tomé was the world's largest producer of cacao in 1908 and the crop is still the most important. An exile liberation movement was formed in 1953 after Portuguese landowners quelled labor riots by killing several hundred African workers.

The Portuguese revolution of 1974 brought the end of the overseas empire and the new Lisbon government transferred power to the liberation movement on July 12, 1975. Most of the 4,000 Portuguese inhabitants departed during the transition period.

SAUDI ARABIA

Kingdom of Saudi Arabia

Ruler and Prime Minister: King Fahd bin 'Abd-al-Aziz (1982)
Area: 873,000 sq mi. (2,261,070 sq km)
Population (est. 1983): 10,400,000 (average annual growth rate: 3.4%)
Density per square mile: 11.1
Capital: Riyadh
Largest cities (est. 1980): Riyadh, 1,250,000; Jeddah, 750,000; Mecca, 500,000
Monetary unit: Riyal
Language: Arabic
Religion: Islam
National name: Al-Mamlaka al-'Arabiya as-Sa'udiya
Literacy rate (1981): 20% (est.)
Economic summary: Gross national product (1981): $145 billion. Average annual growth rate (1970–79): 9.6%. Per capita income (1981): $9,500. Labor force in agriculture: 28%; principal products: dates, grains, livestock. Labor force in industry: 39%; major products: petroleum, cement, plastic products, furniture. Natural resource: oil. Exports: petroleum and petroleum products. Imports: manufactured goods, transport equipment, construction materials, processed food. Major trading partners: U.S., Western European countries, Japan, West Germany.

Geography. The Middle East oil-producing country of Saudi Arabia occupies most of the Arabian Peninsula, with the Red Sea and the Gulf of Aqaba on the west and the Persian Gulf on the east. Neighbors are Jordan, Iraq, and Kuwait in the north, and, along the perimeter from southwest to east, the two Yemens, Oman, and the United Arab Emirates. The country is more than three times the size of Texas.

Saudi Arabia's oil region lies along the Persian Gulf. The country is mostly desert. The Asir Mountains inland rise to a height of 9,000 feet (2,743 m).

Government. Saudi Arabia is a monarchy whose legitimacy rests on *Shariah* (the Law of Islam) and custom. A Council of Ministers was formed in 1953. It acts as a Cabinet under the leadership of the King and is composed of 21 ministries.

Royal and ministerial decrees account for most of the promulgated legislation, treaties, and conventions.

There are no political parties in Saudi Arabia.

History. Mohammed united the Arabs in the 7th century, and his followers, led by the caliphs, founded a great empire, with its capital at Medina. Later, the caliphate capital was transferred to Damascus and then Baghdad, but Arabia retained its importance because of the holy cities of Mecca and Medina. In the 16th and 17th centuries, the Turks established at least nominal rule over much of Arabia, and in the middle of the 18th century, it was divided into separate principalities.

The Kingdom of Saudi Arabia is almost entirely the creation of King Ibn Saud (1882–1953). A descendant of earlier Wahabi rulers, he seized Riyadh, the capital of Nejd, in 1901 and set himself up as leader of the Arab nationalist movement. By 1906 he had established Wahabi dominance in Nejd. He conquered Hejaz in 1924–25, consolidating it and Nejd into a dual kingdom in 1926. In 1932, Hejaz and Nejd became a single kingdom, which was officially named Saudi Arabia. A year later the region of Asir was incorporated into the kingdom.

Oil was discovered in 1936, and commercial production began during World War II. Saudi Arabia was neutral until nearly the end of the war, but it was permitted to be a charter member of the United Nations. The country joined the Arab League in 1945 and took part in the 1948–49 war against Israel, but followed a moderate policy afterward.

On Ibn Saud's death in 1953, his eldest son, Saud, began an 11-year reign marked by an increasing hostility toward the radical Arabism of Egypt's Gamal Abdel Nasser. In 1964, the ailing Saud was deposed and replaced by the Premier, Crown Prince Faisal, who gave vocal support but no military help to Egypt in the 1967 Mideast war.

Faisal's assassination by a deranged kinsman in 1975 shook the Middle East, but failed to alter his kingdom's course. His successor was his brother, Prince Khalid. Khalid gave influential support to Egypt during negotiations on Israeli withdrawal from the Sinai desert.

A takeover by an unknown group of the Grand Mosque in Mecca on Nov. 20, 1979, spread fears that the Saudi monarchy might be under internal threat. On Jan. 9, 1980, 63 persons—41 Saudis and the remainder aliens—were beheaded for their participation in the takeover. A tightening of Islamic law and a shakeup in the Army's top command were linked to the incident.

Saudi concern over possible Iranian attack after the outbreak of the war between Iran and Iraq, added to the tension created by the Soviet invasion of Afghanistan, prompted a Saudi request for U.S. arms. Despite Israeli protests, Washington announced on April 21, 1981, that it would sell five Advance Warning and Command Systems (AWAC) planes to the Saudis, together with seven KC-135 tanker planes, which would increase the range of 62 F-15 fighter-interceptors already delivered.

Sheik Ahmed Zaki Yamani, the oil minister, earlier announced that this government would maintain the 10.3-million-barrels-a-day oil production rate it set when the Iran-Iraq war cut the output of those countries. The Saudi action was a key element in the reduction of world oil prices—part of the arms deal—but Congressional approval of the controversial plane sales did not come until Oct. 28. By then, a cut in Saudi production resulted in a total for 1981 of only 9.8 million barrels per day, a decrease from the 9.9 million rate of 1980.

King Khalid died of a heart attack June 13, 1982, and was succeeded by his half-brother, Prince Fahd bin 'Abd-al-Aziz, 60, who had exercised the real power throughout Khalid's reign. King Fahd, a pro-Western modernist, chose his 58-year-old half-brother, Abdullah, as Crown Prince.

Saudi Arabia and the smaller, oil-rich Arab states on the Persian Gulf, fearful that they might become Ayatollah Ruhollah Khomeini's next targets if Iran conquered Iraq, made large financial contributions to the Iraqi war effort. They began being dragged into the conflict themselves in the spring of 1984, when Iraq and Iran extended their ground war to attacks on Gulf shipping. First, Iraq attacked tankers loading at Iran's Kharg Island terminal with air-to-ground missiles, then Iran struck back at tankers calling at Saudi Arabia and other Arab countries.

President Reagan ordered the sale, at the end of May, of 400 Stinger antiaircraft missiles to Saudi Arabia, using his emergency authority without waiting for the normal 30-day waiting period in Congress. Shortly afterward, Saudi fighter planes shot down two Iranian planes as they approached a foreign tanker over the Gulf. The Saudis were directed to the targets by a U.S. Air Force AWAC plane.

SENEGAL

Republic of Senegal
President: Abdou Diouf (1981)
Premier: Moustapha Niasse (1983)
Area: 75,954 sq mi. (196,722 sq km)
Population (est. 1982): 6,335,000 (average annual growth rate: 3.2%)
Density per square mile: 78.2
Capital and largest city (est. 1982): Dakar, 975,000
Monetary unit: Franc CFA
Ethnic groups: Wolofs, Sereres, Peuls, Tukulers, and others
Languages: French (official); Wolof, Serer, other tribal dialects
Religions: Islam, 91%; Christian, 6%
National name: République du Sénegal
Literacy rate (1981): 60%
Economic summary: Gross national product (1980): $2.6 billion. Average annual growth rate (1970–79): 0.1%. Per capita income (1980): $450. Land used for agriculture: 12%; labor force: 80%; principal products: peanuts, millet, cotton, rice, sorghum. Labor force in industry: 8%; major products: peanut oil, fertilizer, cement, processed food and fish, refined petroleum. Natural resources: fish, phosphate. Exports: peanuts, phosphate rock, canned fish. Imports: foodstuffs, consumer goods, machinery, transport equipment. Major trading partners: France, Western European countries, African neighbors.

Geography. The capital of Senegal, Dakar, is the westernmost point in Africa. The country, slighty smaller than South Dakota, surrounds Gambia on three sides and is bordered on the north by Mauritania, on the east by Mali, and on the south by Guinea and Guinea-Bissau.

Senegal is mainly a low-lying country, with a semidesert area in the north and northeast and forests in the southwest. The largest rivers include the Senegal in the north and the Gambia in the central region.

Government. There is a National Assembly of 100 members, elected every five years. There is universal suffrage and a constitutional guarantee of equality before the law.

The major political party is the Socialist Party, led by President Abdou Diouf. Legal opposition was reconstituted in 1974 with formation of the Senegalese Democratic Party, headed by Abdoulaye Wade, which urged reduction in French and Western influences. Other opposition parties include the African Independence Party and the Republican Party.

History. The Portuguese had some stations on the banks of the Senegal River in the 15th century, and the first French settlement was made at Saint-Louis about 1650. The British took parts of Senegal at various times, but the French gained possession in 1840 and organized the Sudan as a territory in 1904. In 1946, together with other parts of French West Africa, Senegal became part of the French Union. On June 20, 1960, it became an independent republic federated with the Sudanese Republic inthe Mali Federation, from which it withdrew two months later.

On Jan. 1, 1973, Senegal joined with six other states to create the West African Economic Community to promote economic development within the region.

SEYCHELLES

Republic of Seychelles
President: Albert René (1977)
Area: 171 sq mi. (443 sq km)
Population (est. 1983): 65,000 (average annual growth rate: 1.1%)
Density per square mile: 380.1
Capital (est. 1981): Victoria, 24,000
Monetary unit: Seychelles rupee
Languages: Creole (official), English, French
Religions: Roman Catholic, 90%; Anglican, 8%
Member of Commonwealth of Nations
Literacy rate (1981): 65%
Economic summary: Gross national product (1980): $120 million. Average annual growth rate (1970–79): 3.8%. Per capita income (1980): $1,770. Land used for agriculture: 54%; labor force: 27%; principal products: vanilla, copra, cinnamon. Labor force in industry: 55%; major products: processed copra and vanilla, coconut oil. Exports: cinnamon, vanilla, copra. Imports: food, tobacco, manufactured goods, machinery, petroleum products, textiles, transport equipment. Major trading partners: U.K., Kenya, India, Singapore.

Geography. Seychelles consists of an archipelago of about 100 islands in the Indian Ocean northeast of Madagascar. The principal islands are Mahé (55 sq mi.; 142 sq km), Praslin (15 sq mi.; 38 sq km), and La Digue (4 sq mi.; 10 sq km). The Aldabra, Farquhar, and Desroches groups are included in the territory of the republic.

Government. Seized from France by Britain in 1810, the Seychelles Islands remained a colony until June 29, 1976. The state is an independent republic within the Commonwealth.

On June 5, 1977, Prime Minister Albert René ousted the islands' first President, James Mancham, suspending the Constitution and the 25-member National Assembly. Mancham, whose "lavish spending" and flamboyance were cited by René in seizing power, charged that Soviet influence was at work. The new president denied this and, while more left than his predecessor, pledged to keep the Seychelles in the Commonwealth.

An unsuccessful attempted coup against René attracted international attention when a group of 50 South African mercenaries posing as rugby players attacked the Victoria airport on Nov. 25, 1981. They caused extensive damage before they hijacked an Air India plane and returned to South Africa, where all but five were freed. Only after widespread African protest did the Pretoria government, which denied any responsibility for the attack, reverse the decision and order all the mercenaries tried as hijackers.

SIERRA LEONE

Republic of Sierra Leone
President: Dr. Siaka P. Stevens (1971)
Area: 27,925 sq mi. (72,326 sq km)
Population (est. 1983): 3,705,000 (average annual growth rate: 2.6%)
Density per square mile: 131.6
Capital and largest city (est. 1980): Freetown, 375,000
Monetary unit: Leone
Languages: English (official), Mende, Temne, Creole
Religions: Animist, 52%; Islam, 40%; Christian, 9%
Member of Commonwealth of Nations
Literacy rate (1981): 10%
Economic summary: Gross national product (1981): $800 million. Average annual growth rate (1970–79): —1.2%. Per capita income (1981): $232. Land used for agriculture: 6%; labor force: 75%; principal products: coffee, cocoa, ginger, rice. Labor force in industry: 15%; major products: diamonds, bauxite, beverages, cigarettes, construction goods. Natural resources: diamonds, bauxite, chromite, iron ore, rutile. Exports: diamonds, iron ore, palm kernels, cocoa, coffee. Imports: food, petroleum products, chemicals, machinery. Major trading partners: U.K., U.S., Western European and Communist countries, Japan.

Geography. Sierra Leone, on the Atlantic Ocean in West Africa, is half the size of Illinois. Guinea, in the north and east, and Liberia, in the south, are its neighbors.

Mangrove swamps lie along the coast, with wooded hills and a plateau in the interior. The eastern region is mountainous.

Government. Sierra Leone became an independent nation on April 27, 1961, and declared itself a republic, with former Prime Minister Siaka P. Stevens as president for a seven-year term, on April 19, 1971.

Sierra Leone became a one party state under the aegis of the All People's Congress Party in April 1978.

History. The coastal area of Sierra Leone was ceded to English settlers in 1788 as a home for blacks discharged from the British armed forces and also for runaway slaves who had found asylum in London. The British protectorate over the hinterland was proclaimed in 1896.

After elections in 1967, the British Governor-General replaced Sir Albert Margai, head of SLPP, which had held power since independence, with Dr. Stevens, head of APC, as prime minister. The Army took over the government; then another coup in April 1968 restored civilian rule and put the military leaders in jail.

A coup attempt early in 1971 by the army commander was apparently foiled by loyal army officers, but the then Prime Minister Stevens called in troops of neighboring Guinea's army, under a 1970 mutual defense pact, to guard his residence. After perfunctorily blaming the U.S. for the coup attempt, Stevens switched Governors-General, changed the Constitution, and ended up with a republic, of which he was first president. He was accused of taking "sweeping dictatorial powers," but was re-elected in 1978.

SINGAPORE

Republic of Singapore
President: C.V. Devan Nair (1981)
Prime Minister: Lee Kuan Yew (1959)
Area: 238 sq mi. (616 sq km)
Population (est. 1982): 2,500,000 (average annual growth rate: 1.2%) (Chinese, 76%; Malay, 15%; Indian, 7%)
Density per square mile: 10,504.2
Capital (est. 1982): Singapore, 2,450,000
Monetary unit: Singapore dollar
Languages: Malay, Chinese (Mandarin), Tamil, English
Religions: Islam, Christian, Buddhist, Hindu, Confucianist, Taoist
Member of Commonwealth of Nations
Literacy rate (1982): 84.8%
Economic summary: Gross national product (1983): $16.4 billion. Average annual growth rate (1969–79): 9.4%. Per capita income (1980): $4,480. Land used for agriculture: 11%; labor force; 1.1%; principal products: poultry, hogs, orchids, vegetables, fruits. Labor force in industry: 29.4%; major industries: petroleum refining, oil exploration, ship repair, rubber processing, electronics and other light industry. Exports: petroleum products, rubber, manufactured goods. Imports: capital equipment, manufactured goods, petroleum. Major trading partners: U.S., Japan, Malaysia, Hong Kong, Indonesia, Saudi Arabia, West Germany.

Geography. The Republic of Singapore consists of the main island of Singapore, off the southern tip of the Malay Peninsula between the South China Sea and the Indian Ocean, and 54 nearby islands.

There are extensive mangrove swamps extending inland from the coast, which is broken by many inlets.

Government. The head of state is the President. There is a Cabinet, headed by the Prime Minister, and a Parliament of 75 members elected by universal suffrage.

The People's Action Party, led by Prime Minister Lee Kuan Yew, is the ruling political party in Parliament, holding all but one seat.

History. Singapore, founded in 1819 by Sir Stamford Raffles, became a separate crown colony of Britain in 1946, when the former colony of the Straits Settlements was dissolved. The other two settlements—Penang and Malacca—were transferred to the Union of Malaya, and the small island of Labuan was transferred to North Borneo. The Cocos (or Keeling) Islands were transferred to Australia in 1955 and Christmas Island in 1958.

Singapore attained full internal self-government in 1959. On Sept. 16, 1963, it joined Malaya, Sabah (North Borneo), and Sarawak in the Federation of Malaysia. It withdrew from the Federation on Aug. 9, 1965, and proclaimed itself a republic the next month.

SOLOMON ISLANDS

Sovereign: Queen Elizabeth II
Governor-General: Baddeley Devesi (1978)
Prime Minister: Solomon Mamaloni (1981)
Area: 11,500 sq mi. (29,785 sq km)
Population (est. 1982): 250,000 (average annual growth rate: 3.4%)
Density per square mile: 21.7
Capital and largest city (est. 1981): Honiara (on Guadalcanal), 20,000
Monetary unit: Solomon Islands dollar
Languages: Pidgin English, English, Melanesian dialects
Religions: Anglican, 34%; Roman Catholic, 19%; South Seas Evangelical, 25%; other Protestant, 15%
Member of British Commonwealth
Literacy rate (1981): 60%
Economic summary: Gross national product (1980): $110 million. Average annual growth rate (1970–79): 2.3%. Per capita income (1980): $460. Principal agricultural products: copra, palm oil, rice, cocoa, cattle, spices. Major industrial products: processed fish, timber, jute, soap, canned meat, handicrafts. Natural resources: fish, timber. Exports: fish, timber, copra, palm oil. Imports: machinery and transport equipment, foodstuffs, fuel, manufactured goods. Major trading partners: Japan, Australia, U.K.

Geography: Lying east of New Guinea, this island nation consists of the southern islands of the Solomon group: Guadalcanal, Malaita, Santa Isabel, San Cristóbal, Choiseul, New Georgia, and numerous smaller islands.

Government. After 85 years of British rule, the Solomons achieved independence July 7, 1978. The Crown is represented by a Governor-General and legislative power is vested in a unicameral legislature of 38 members, led by the Prime Minister.

History. Discovered in 1567 by Alvaro de Mendana, the Solomons were not visited again for about 200 years. In 1886, Great Britain and Germany divided the islands between them. In 1914, Australian forces took over the German islands and the Solomons became an Australian mandate in 1920. In World War II, most of the islands were occupied by the Japanese. American forces landed on Guadalcanal on Aug. 7, 1942. The islands were the scene of several important U.S. naval and military victories. They are still largely undeveloped, with only 60 miles of paved road and fewer than 1,000 motor vehicles.

SOMALIA

Somali Democratic Republic
President: Maj. Gen. Mohamed Siad Barre (1969)
Area: 246,199 sq mi. (637,655 sq km)
Population (est. 1983): 6,248,000 (average annual growth rate: 2.0%)
Density per square mile: 20.9
Capital and largest city (est. 1982): Mogadishu, 500,000
Monetary unit: Somali shilling
Language: Somali
Religion: Islam
National name: Al Jumhouriya As-Somalya Dimocradia
Literacy rate (1981): 10%
Economic summary: Gross national product (1978): $470 million. Average annual growth rate (1970–77): —1.1%. Per capita income (1978): $187. Labor force in agriculture: 30%; principal products: livestock, bananas, sorghum, peanuts, sugar cane, cotton, maize. Labor force in industry: 3%; major products: textiles, meat, fish, canned fruit juices. Natural resources: timber, uranium. Exports: livestock, skins and hides, bananas. Imports: textiles, construction materials and equipment, machinery, manufactured goods, transport equipment. Major trading partners: Arab countries, Italy.

Geography. Somalia, situated in the Horn of Africa, lies along the Gulf of Aden and the Indian Ocean. It is bounded by Djibouti in the northwest, Ethiopia in the east, and Kenya in the southwest. In area it is slightly smaller than Texas.

Generally arid and barren, Somalia has two chief rivers, the Shebeli and the Juba.

Government. Maj. Gen. Mohamed Siad Barre took power on Oct. 21, 1969, in a bloodless coup that established a Supreme Revolutionary Council as the governing body, replacing a parliamentary government. On July 1, 1976, Barre dissolved the Council, naming its members to the Somali Socialist Party, organized that day as the nation's only legal political party. In December 1979, a 171-member People's Assembly was elected under a new Constitution adopted in August. The Assembly confirmed Barre as President for a six-year term.

History. From the 7th to the 10th century, Arab and Persian trading posts were established along the coast of present-day Somalia. Nomadic tribes occupied the interior, occasionally pushing into Ethiopian territory. In the 16th century, Turkish rule extended to the northern coast and the Sultans of Zanzibar gained control in the south.

After British occupation of Aden in 1839, the Somali coast became its source of food. The French established a coaling station in 1862 at the site of Djibouti and the Italians planted a settlement in Eritrea. Egypt, which for a time-claimed Turkish rights in the area, was succeeded by Britain. By 1920, a British protectorate and an Italian protectorate occupied what is now Somalia. The British ruled the entire area after 1941, with Italy returning in 1950 to serve as United Nations trustee for its former territory.

In mid-1960, Britain and Italy granted independence to their respective sectors, enabling the two to join as the Republic of Somalia on July 1. Somalia broke diplomatic relations with Britain in 1963 when the British granted the Somali-populated Northern Frontier District of Kenya to the Republic of Kenya.

On Oct. 15, 1969, President Abdi Rashid Ali

Shermarke was assassinated and the army seized power, dissolving the legislature and arresting all government leaders. Maj. Gen. Mohamed Siad Barre, as President of a renamed Somali Democratic Republic, leaned heavily toward the U.S.S.R.

In 1977, Somalia openly backed rebels in the westernmost area of Ethiopia, the Ogaden desert, which had been seized by Ethiopia at the turn of the century. The action was an embarrassment to the U.S.S.R., which was heavily involved in Ethiopia's new Marxist government after the ouster of Emperor Haile Selassie in 1974.

After denying Barre's pleas for aid, the U.S.S.R. announced in 1977 the cutoff of military aid to Somalia and the providing of "defensive weapons" to Ethiopia. Somalia then expelled an estimated 1,500 Soviet military and civilian aides and broke diplomatic relations with Cuba, which had furnished military advisers to the Ethiopian troops fighting in the Ogaden.

Somalia acknowledged defeat in an eight-month war against the Ethiopians, having lost many of what had become a 32,000-man army and most of its tanks and planes. In March 1978, the U.S. agreed to supply $7 million in food over six months, in addition to $6 million in emergency food relief provided in December. The U.S. refused to consider weapons sales, however, unless Somalia gave up all claims to northern Kenya, the Ogaden, and the Republic of Djibouti, all once claimed as "Greater Somalia." Barre refused to do this.

A U.S. announcement on Jan. 9, 1980, that bases for U.S. ships and planes in the Indian Ocean would be sought in Somalia, Oman, and Kenya, brought a request from Somalia for $1 billion worth of modern arms and an equal amount of economic aid. In August, an agreement was signed giving the U.S. use of military bases in Somalia in return for $25 million in military aid in 1981 and more in subsequent years.

SOUTH AFRICA

Republic of South Africa
President: Pieter W. Botha (1984)
Area: 437,876 sq mi. (1,134,100 sq km)
Population (est. 1982): 23,500,000[1] (average annual growth rate: 2.5%) (black, 67%; white, 19%; colored [mixed], 11%; Asian, 3%)
Density per square mile: 54.3[1]
Administrative capital: Pretoria
Legislative capital: Cape Town
Judicial capital: Bloemfontein
Largest cities (est. 1984): Johannesburg, 1,700,000; Cape Town, 1,000,000; Durban, 1,000,000; Pretoria, 700,000; Port Elizabeth, 600,000; Bloemfontein, 200,000.
Monetary unit: Rand
Languages: English, Afrikaans, 9 Bantu languages
Religions (1984): Dutch Reformed, 40%; Anglican, 11%; Roman Catholic, 8%; other Christian, 25%
National name: Repubilek van Suid-Afrika
Literacy rate (1981): 99% (whites), 50% (Africans)
Economic summary: Gross national product (1983): 69.0 billion. Average annual growth rate (1970–79): 0.6%. Per capita income (1980): $2,290. Labor force in agriculture: 53%; principal products: corn, wool, wheat, sugar cane, tobacco, citrus fruits. Labor force in industry: 15%; major products: assembled automobiles, machinery, textiles, iron and steel, chemicals, fertilizer, fish. Natural resources: gold, diamonds, platinum, uranium, coal, iron ore, asbestos, manganese. Exports: gold, wool, diamonds, corn, uranium, sugar, fruits, hides and skins, asbestos, fish products. Imports: motor vehicles, machinery, metals, petroleum products, chemicals, textiles. Major trading partners: U.S., West Germany, Japan, U.K.

1. Excluding South-West Africa (Namibia), Transkei, Bophuthatswana, Venda, and Ciskei.

Geography. South Africa, on the continent's southern tip, is washed by the Atlantic Ocean on the west and by the Indian Ocean on the south and east. Its neighbors are South-West Africa (Namibia) in the northwest, Zimbabwe and Botswana in the north, and Mozambique and Swaziland in the northeast. Bophuthatswana, Transkei, Ciskei, and Venda are independent states within South Africa, which occupies an area nearly three times that of California.

The country has a high interior plateau, or veld, nearly half of which averages 4,000 feet (1,219 m) in elevation.

There are no important mountain ranges, although the Great Escarpment, separating the veld from the coastal plain, rises to over 11,000 feet (3,350 m) in the Drakensberg Mountains in the east. The principal river is the Orange, rising in Lesotho and flowing westward for 1,300 miles (2,092 km) to the Atlantic.

The southernmost point of Africa is Cape Agulhas, located in Cape Province about 100 miles (161 km) southeast of the Cape of Good Hope.

Government. A new Constitution in 1984 created a new office of Executive State President, with potentially authoritarian powers, in place of the previous parliamentary form of government headed by a Prime Minister. Previously, the Presidency was only ceremonial. Pieter W. Botha, Prime Minister since 1978, was sworn in as President on Sept. 14, 1984.

The new Constitution brought Indian and mixed-race people into a racially divided Parliament made up of three separate chambers for different racial groups. It continued to exclude blacks, who make up 73% of the population. It provides for selection of the President by an Electoral College made up of representatives from the three chambers, with the white chamber controlling the election. It empowers him to veto legislation, declare war, summon Parliament, and dismiss it.

Ten "Bantustans," or black homelands, have unicameral legislatures elected by black voters.

History. The Dutch East India Company landed the first settlers on the Cape of Good Hope in 1652, launching a colony that by the end of the 18th century numbered only about 15,000. Known as Boers or Afrikaners, speaking a Dutch dialect known as Afrikaans, the settlers as early as 1795 tried to establish an independent republic.

After occupying the Cape Colony in that year, Britain took permanent possession in 1814 at the end of the Napoleonic wars, bringing in 5,000 settlers. Anglicization of government and the freeing of slaves in 1833 drove about 12,000 Afrikaners to make the "great trek" north and east into African tribal territory, where they established the republics of the Transvaal and the Orange Free State.

The discovery of diamonds in 1867 and gold nine years later brought an influx of "outlanders" into the republics and spurred Cecil Rhodes to plot annexation. Rhodes's scheme of sparking an "out lander" rebellion to which an armed party under Leander Starr Jameson would ride to the rescue misfired in 1895, forcing Rhodes to resign as prime minister of the Cape colony. What British expansionists called the "inevitable" war with the Boers eventually broke out on Oct. 11, 1899.

The defeat of the Boers in 1902 led in 1910 to the Union of South Africa, composed of four provinces, the two former republics and the old Cape and Natal colonies. Louis Botha, the first Prime Minister and a Boer, allied the dominion with Britain in World War I. The Unionist Party, led by Jan Christiaan Smuts, advocated a pro-British line and a more liberal racial policy in the period between wars, while the Afrikaner Nationalist Party urged withdrawal from the Commonwealth and racial separation.

Smuts brought the nation into World War II on the Allied side against Nationalist opposition, and South Africa became a charter member of the United Nations in 1945, but refused to sign the Universal Declaration of Human Rights. Apartheid—racial separation—dominated domestic politics as the Nationalists gained power and imposed greater restrictions on Bantus, Coloreds, and Asians.

Afrikaner hostility to Britain triumphed in 1961 with the declaration on May 31 of the Republic of South Africa and the severing of ties with the Commonwealth. Nationalist Prime Minister H. F. Verwoerd's government in 1963 asserted the power to restrict freedom of those who opposed rigid racial laws. Three years later, amid increasing racial tension and criticism from the outside world, Verwoerd was assassinated. His Nationalist successor, Balthazar J. Vorster, launched a campaign of conciliation toward conservative black African states, offering development loans and trade concessions.

A critical issue was South-West Africa, where South African rule was challenged by the United Nations when it asserted responsibility for the territory in 1974 under the name Namibia. African demands for immediate freedom for Namibia led to an attempt to expel South Africa from the U.N. in 1974, a move blocked by a U.S., British, and French veto. The General Assembly barred South Africa from its seat anyway, and the seat has remained empty.

Economic restrictions tightened on South Africa following a vote by the Security Council imposing a mandatory embargo on arms in retaliation for South Africa's crackdown on opponents of apartheid. Although the U.S., Britain, and France vetoed mandatory economic sanctions against South Africa, U.S. and European businesses, unions, and church groups acted to cut trade with it.

Scandal rocked the Nationalist government in 1979 with the disclosure of the diversion of secret propaganda funds by former Information Minister Connie Mulder. Mulder's linking of Vorster with the scandal forced Vorster's resignation on June 4, 1979, from the State Presidency to which he had been elected after leaving the prime ministership in September.

The new Prime Minister, Peter W. Botha, moved toward a more liberal racial policy by easing job restrictions on blacks and extending black union rights. He appointed a multiracial advisory council, to assist in a proposed Constitutional revision and to replace the largely ceremonial Senate. The new group, composed of 39 whites, 15 Asians and mixed bloods, but including no blacks, met for the first time on Feb. 3, 1981.

Botha's policy brought right-wing defection from the ruling party in parliamentary elections on April 29, 1981, as the Nationalist popular vote dropped from nearly 65% in 1977 to 55% and the number of seats from 137 to 131. The plan was embodied in a new Constitution that took effect in September 1984. Botha was elected President under the new system and sworn in on Sept. 14. During the two weeks prior to his inauguration, unrest in black townships claimed more than 40 lives in riots over rent increases and educational grievances.

In a split over future parliamentary representation, 18 right-wing Nationalists were expelled by Botha when they opposed sharing power with nonwhites. They formed a new party, the Conservatives. On July 30, Botha presented to the Nationalist party convention in Bloemfontein a plan for separate white, colored, and Asian chambers in order to give 2.5 million South Africans of mixed blood and 800,000 Asians a political voice. There was no provision for national representation of the 21 million black South Africans. The government also proposed that a new president with full executive powers be chosen by the three chambers, with the white chamber controlling the election.

BOPHUTHATSWANA

Republic of Bophuthatswana
President: Chief Lucas Mangope (1977)
Area: 15,573 sq mi. (40,333 sq km)
Population (est. 1982): 1,325,000 (average annual growth rate: 2.4%)
Density per square mile: 80.4
Capital: Mmabatho
Largest city (est. 1981): Ga-Rankuwa, 50,000
Monetary unit: South African rand
Languages: Setswana, English, Afrikaans
Religions: Methodist, Lutheran, Anglican, and Bantu Christian

Geography. Bophuthatswana consists of seven discontinuous areas within the boundaries of South Africa, most of them in the northern sector near Botswana.

Government. The republic has a 103-member Legislative Assembly, three quarters of whom are elected and the others appointed. President Mangope's Democratic Party is the majority party.

History. Bophuthatswana was given independence by South Africa on Dec. 6, 1977, following Transkei as the second "homeland" to be established by Pretoria. The new state and Transkei are recognized only by South Africa and each other.

Mangope, as chief minister in the pre-independence period, sought linkage of the six units into a consolidated area, but was unable to achieve his objective. A second issue, the citizenship of Tswanas in South Africa who wished to remain South African nationals, was settled by enabling them to have citizenship in South African homelands not yet independent.

About two thirds of the population of Bophuthatswana live permanently or as migrants in white areas of South Africa.

Economy. Bophuthatswana is richer than many other South African homelands, as it has more than half of the republic's platinum deposits. All foreign trade is included with South Africa's, and it is economically dependent at present on that country.

CISKEI

Republic of Ciskei
President: Chief Lennox Leslie Wongama Sebe (1981)
Area: 3,282 sq mi. (8,500 sq km)
Population (est. 1982): 675,000
Density per square mile: 21.1
Capital (est. 1980): Zwelitsha, 30,750
Largest city (est. 1981): Mdantsane, 159,000
Monetary unit: South African rand
Languages: Xhosa (official) and English
Religions: Methodist, Lutheran, Anglican, and Bantu Christian

Geography. Ciskei is surrounded by South Africa on three sides, with the Indian Ocean on the south. From a subtropical coastal strip, the land rises through grasslands to the mountainous escarpment that edges the South African interior plateau.

Government. Legislative power is vested in a National Assembly with 22 elected seats. Thirty-three hereditary chiefs complete the membership of the Assembly. The President holds executive power. South Africa's State President retains the power to legislate by proclamation and has veto power over the budget. The Ciskei National Independence Party holds all elective seats in the Assembly.

History. Oral tradition ascribes the origin of the Cape Nguni peoples to the central lakes area of Africa. They arrived in what is now Ciskei in the mid-17th century. White settlers from the Cape Colony first entered the territory a century later, but the Dutch East India Colony sought unsuccessfully to discourage white penetration. Nine wars between whites and the inhabitants, by now known as Xhosas, occurred between 1779 and 1878.

A Ciskeian territorial authority was established in 1961, with 84 chiefs and an executive council exercising limited self-government. In 1972, 20 elected members were added to the legislative assembly and a chief minister and six cabinet members elected by the assembly to function as an executive.

A proposed Constitution was approved by referendum on Oct. 30, 1980, and independence ceremonies held on Dec. 4. No government outside South Africa recognized the new state. A new capital was to be built at Bisho, formerly a settlement called Yellow-wood, and the South African government was expected to cede additional territory that will double Ciskei's area.

Economy. A subsistence agricultural economy has been superseded by commuter and migratory labor, which accounted for 64% of national income in 1977. There is some light industry and a potential for exploitation of limestone and other minerals.

SOUTH-WEST AFRICA (NAMIBIA)

Status: Mandate
Area: 318,261 sq mi. (824,296 sq km)
Population (est. 1982): 1,000,000 (average annual growth rate: 3.0%)
Density per square mile: 3.1
Administrator-General: Dr. Willie van Niekerk (1983)
Capital (est. 1980): Windhoek, 85,000
Summer capital (est. 1980): Swakopmund, 17,500
Monetary unit: South African rand
National name: Suidwes-Afrika/Namibië; South-West Africa/Namibia
Literacy rate: Not known
Economic summary: Gross national product (1980): $1.4 billion. Average annual growth rate (1970–79); 0.3%. Land used for agriculture: 30%; labor force: 68%; principal products: corn, millet, sorghum, livestock. Labor force in industry: 4%; major products: canned meat, dairy products, tanned leather, textiles, clothing. Natural resources: diamonds, copper, lead, zinc, uranium, fish. Exports: diamonds, copper, lead, zinc, beef cattle, karakul pelts. Imports: construction materials, fertilizer, grain, foodstuffs. Major trading partner: South Africa.

Geography. The mandate, bounded on the north by Angola and Zambia and on the east by Botswana and South Africa, was discovered by the Portuguese explorer Diaz in the late 15th century. It is for the most part a portion of the high plateau of southern Africa with a general elevation of from 3,000 to 4,000 feet.

History. The territory became a German colony in 1884 but was taken by South African forces in 1915, becoming a South African mandate by the terms of the Treaty of Versailles.

South Africa's application for incorporation of the territory was rejected by the U.N. General Assembly in 1946 and South Africa was invited to prepare a trusteeship agreement instead. By a law passed in 1949, however, the territory was brought into much closer association with South Africa—including representation in its Parliament.

In 1969, South Africa extended its laws to the mandate over the objection of the U.N., particularly its black African members. When South Africa refused to withdraw them, the Security Council condemned it.

Under a 1974 Security Council resolution, South Africa was required to begin the transfer of power to the Namibians by May 30, 1975, or face U.N. action, but 10 days before the deadline Prime Minister Balthazar J. Vorster rejected U.N. supervision. He said, however, that his government was prepared to negotiate Namibian independence, but not with the South-West African People's Organization, the principal black separatist group. Meanwhile, the all-white legislature of South-West Africa eased several laws on apartheid in public places.

Despite international opposition, the Turnhalle Conference in Windhoek drafted a constitution to organize an interim government based on racial divisions, a proposal overwhelmingly endorsed by white voters in the territory in 1977. At the urging of ambassadors of the five Western members of the Security Council—the U.S., Britain, France, West Germany, and Canada—South Africa on June 11 announced rejection of the Turnhalle constitution and acceptance of the Western proposal to include the South-West Africa People's Organization (SWAPO) in negotiations.

Although negotiations continued between South Africa, the western powers, neighboring black African states, and internal political groups, there was still no agreement on a final independence plan. A new round of talks aimed at resolving the 18-year-old conflict ended in a stalemate on July 25, 1984. Dr. Willie van Niekerk, South Africa's Administrator-General in the territory, met in the remote Cape Verde Islands with leaders of the insurgents, including SWAP leader Sam Nujoma, to "explore the possibilities of bringing about a cessation of violent and armed activities in South-West Africa." South Africa said the insurgents' "inflexible attitude" made it impossible to reach an agreement on a cease-fire.

TRANSKEI

Republic of Transkei
President: Paramount Chief Daliwonga Matanzima (1980)
Prime Minister: Paramount Chief George Matanzima (1979)
Area: 15,831 sq mi. (41,002 sq km)
Population (est. 1982): 2,400,000 (growth rate: 2.2%)
Density per square mile: 157.9
Capital (est. 1980): Umtala, 32,500
Monetary unit: South African rand
Languages: English, Xhosa, Southern Sotho
Religions: Christian, 66%; tribal, 24%
Freedom House classifications: Capitalist pre-industrial, dominant party
Economic summary: Gross domestic product: $150 million. Per capita income: $86. Principal agricultural products: tea, corn, sorghum, dry beans. Major industrial products: timber, textiles. Natural resource: timber. Exports: timber, tea, sacks. Imports: foodstuffs, machines, equipment. Major trading partner: South Africa.

Geography. Transkei occupies three discontinuous enclaves within southeast South Africa that add up to twice the size of Massachusetts. It has a 270-mile (435 km) coastline on the Indian Ocean. A port is being developed at Port St. Johns. The capital, Umtala, is connected by rail to the South African port of East London, 100 miles (161 km) to the southwest.

Government. Transkei was granted independence by South Africa as of Oct. 26, 1976. A constitution called for organization of a parliament composed of 75 representative chiefs and 75 elected members, with a ceremonial president and executive power in the hands of a prime minister.

The Organization of African States and the chairman of the United Nations Special Committee Against Apartheid denounced the new state as a sham and urged governments not to recognize it.

History. British rule was established over the Transkei region between 1866 and 1894, and the Transkeian Territories were formed in 1903. Under the Native Land Act of 1913, the Territories were reserved for black occupation. In 1963, Transkei was given internal self-government and a legislature that elected Paramount Chief Kaiser Matanzima as Chief Minister, a post he retained in elections in 1968 and 1973.

Economy. Some 60% of Transkei is cultivated, producing corn, wheat, beans, and sorghum. Grazing is important. Some light industry has been established.

VENDA

Republic of Venda
President: Chief Patrick R. Mphephu (1979)
Area: 2,510 sq mi. (6,500 sq km)
Population (est. 1982): 400,000 (average annual growth rate: 2.4%)
Density per square mile: 214.5
Capital: Thohoyandou
Largest town (est. 1980): Makearela, 2,500
Monetary unit: South African rand
Languages: Venda, English, Afrikaans
Religions: Christian, tribal
Economic summary: Gross domestic product: $156 million. Per capita income: $312. Principal agricultural products: meat, tea, fruit, sisal, corn. Major industrial products: timber, graphite, magnetite.

Geography. Venda is composed of two noncontiguous territories in northeast South Africa with a total area of about half that of Connecticut. It is mountainous but fertile, well-watered land, with a climate ranging from tropical to subtropical.

Government. The third of South Africa's homelands to be granted independence, Venda became a separate republic on Sept. 13, 1979, unrecognized by any government other than South Africa and its sister homelands, Transkei and Bophuthatswana. The President is popularly elected. An 84-seat legislature is half elected, half appointed.

History. The first European reached Venda in 1816, but the isolation of the area prevented its involvement in the wars of the 19th century between blacks and whites and with other tribes. Venda came under South African administration after the Boer War in 1902. Limited home rule was granted in 1962. Chief Patrick R. Mphephu, leader of one of the 27 tribes that historically made up the Venda nation, became Chief Minister of the interim government in 1973 and President upon independence in 1979.

SOVIET UNION

Union of Soviet Socialist Republics
Chairman of Presidium (President): Konstantin U. Chernenko (1984)
Chairman of Council of Ministers (Premier): Nikolai A. Tikhonov (1980)
Area: 8,649,489 sq mi. (22,402,200 sq km)
Population (est. 1983): 272,308,000 (average annual growth rate: 0.8%) (Russian, 52%; Ukrainian, 17%; Uzbek, 5%; Byelorussian, 4%; Kazak, 3%; Tatar, 2%)
Density per square mile: 31.2
Capital: Moscow
Largest cities (est. 1982): Moscow, 8,225,000; Leningrad, 4,680,000; Kiev, 2,450,000; Tashkent, 1,865,000; Baku, 1,650,000; Kharkov, 1,490,000; Gorki, 1,375,000; Novosibirsk, 1,350,000; Minsk, 1,335,000; Sverdlovsk, 1,245,000; Kuibyshev, 1,240,000; Dnepropetrovsk, 1,110,000; Tbilisi, 1,100,000; Odessa, 1,075,000; Chelyabinsk, 1,060,000; Yerevan, 1,055,000; Omsk, 1,050,000; Donetsk, 1,045,000
Monetary unit: Ruble
Languages: *See* Population, above
Religions: Russian Orthodox (predominant), Islam, Roman Catholic, Jewish, Lutheran
National name: Soyuz Sovyetskikh Sotsialisticheskikh Respublik
Literacy rate (1981): 95%
Economic summary: Gross national product (1980): $1,212.0 billion. Average annual growth rate (1970–79): 4.1%. Per capita income (1980): $4,550. Land used for agriculture: 10%; labor force: 22%; principal products: wheat, rye, corn, oats, potatoes, sugar beets, cotton and flax, cattle, pigs, sheep. Labor force in industry: 78%; major products: ferrous and nonferrous metals, fuels and

power, building materials, chemicals, machinery. Natural resources: fossil fuels, water power, timber, manganese, lead, zinc, nickel, mercury, potash, phosphate. Exports: petroleum and petroleum products, natural gas, machinery and equipment, manufactured goods. Imports: grain, machinery and equipment, foodstuffs, raw materials, consumer manufactures. Major trading partners: Soviet bloc, Western industrialized countries.

Geography. The U.S.S.R. is the largest unbroken political unit in the world unit in the world, occupying more than one seventh of the land surface of the globe. The greater part of its territory is a vast plain stretching from eastern Europe to the Pacific Ocean. This plain, relieved only occasionally by low mountain ranges (notably the Urais), consists of three zones running east and west: the frozen marshy tundra of the Arctic; the more temperate forest belt; and the steppes or prairies to the south, which in sourthern Soviet Asia become sandy deserts.

The topography is more varied in the south, particularly in the Caucasus between the Caspian and Black Seas, and in the Tien-Pamir mountain system bordering Afghanistan, Sinkiang, and Mongolia. Mountains (Stanovoi and Kolyma) and great rivers (Amur, Yenisei, Lena) also break up the sweep of the plain in Siberia.

In the west, the major rivers are the Volga, Dnieper, Don, Kama, and Southern Bug.

Government. Legislative authority is vested in the Supreme Soviet of the U.S.S.R., which consists of two chambers—the Soviet of the Union, with 767 members, and the Soviet of Nationalities, with 750 members. All members of the Supreme Soviet are elected for five years by the people.

A Presidium is elected by the Supreme Soviet to deal with state matters when the latter is not in session. It consists of a chairman, first vice chairman, 15 vice chairmen (one for each union republic), 21 members, and a secretary. The chairman of the Presidium is sometimes referred to as the President.

Executive authority rests with the Council of Ministers. It is appointed by the Supreme Soviet and includes a chairman, a first vice chairman, and various vice chairmen, chairmen of state committees, ministers, etc. The chairman of the Council of Ministers is often referred to as the Premier.

Judicial authority is vested in the Supreme Court of the U.S.S.R. It consists of a chairmen, vice chairman, members, and people's assessors, who are elected by the Supreme Soviet for five years.

Each of the 15 union republics and the 20 autonomous republics has a Supreme Soviet (with a Presidium), a Council of Ministers, and a Supreme Court. Each of the eight autonomous regions has a Soviet of People's Deputies.

The Communist Party of the Soviet Union is the only party. It is the basic power in the country and has a membership of 18,500,000.

The supreme organ of the party is the Party Congress, which meets at least once in five years. It elects a Central Committee, consisting of 320 members and 151 candidate members, to carry on party work between sessions of the Congress.

Within the Central Committee is a Political Bureau (Politburo), which was called the Presidium from 1952 to 1966. It functions between sessions of the Central Committee. Also within the Central Committee is the Secretariat. The present General Secretary of the Central Committee, Konstantin U. Chernenko, has served since Feb. 13, 1984. Named President in April 11, 1984, to succeed Yuri V. Andropov, he is the third man in Soviet history to hold both posts simultaneously.

Republics of the U.S.S.R.

Republic and capital	Area sq mi.	Population est. 1981 (thousands)
Russian S.F.S.R. (Moscow)	6,593,391	139,150
Ukraine (Kiev)	233,089	50,130
Kazakhstan (Alma-Ata)	1,064,092	15,050
Byelorussia (Minsk)	80,154	9,660
Uzbekistan (Tashkent)	158,069	16,160
Georgia (Tbiksi)	26,872	5,070
Azerbaijan (Baku)	33,475	6,205
Lithuania[1] (Vilnius)	25,174	3,445
Moldavia (Kishinev)	13,012	4,000
Latvia[1] (Riga)	24,595	2,540
Kirghizia (Frunze)	76,641	3,655
Tadzhikistan (Duschambe)	55,019	4,010
Armenia (Erevan)	11,506	3,120
Turkmenistan (Ashkhabad)	188,417	2,900
Estonia[1] (Tallin)	17,413	1,485

1. Soviet jurisdiction not recognized by the United States.

History. Tradition says the Viking Rurik came to Russia in A.D. 862 and founded the first Russian dynasty in Novgorod. The various tribes were united by the spread of Christianity in the 10th and 11th centuries; Vladimir "the Saint" was converted in 988. During the 11th century, the grand dukes of Kiev held such centralizing power as existed. In 1240, Kiev was destroyed by the Mongols, and the Russian territory was split into numerous smaller dukedoms, out of which three large centers emerged—Galicia, Moscow, and Novgorod. The early dukes of Moscow extended their dominions through their office of tribute collector for the Mongols.

In the late 15th century, Duke Ivan III acquired Novgorod and Tver and threw off the Mongol yoke. Ivan IV, the Terrible (1533–84), first Muscovite Tsar, is considered to have founded the Russian state. He crushed the power of rival princes and boyars (great landowners), but Russia remained largely medieval until the reign of Peter the Great (1682–1725), grandson of the first Romanov Tsar, Michael (1613–45). Peter made extensive reforms aimed at westernization and, through his defeat of Charles XII of Sweden at the Battle of Poltava in 1709, he extended Russia's boundaries to the west.

Catherine the Great (1762–96) continued Peter's westernization program and also expanded Russian territory, acquiring the Crimea and part of Poland. During the reign of Alexander I (1801–25), Napoleon's attempt to subdue Russia was defeated (1812–13), and new territory was gained, including Finland (1809) and Bessarabia (1812). Alexander originated the Holy Alliance, which for a time crushed Europe's rising liberal movement.

Alexander II (1855–81) pushed Russia's borders to the Pacific and into central Asia. Serfdom was abolished in 1861, but heavy restrictions were imposed on the emancipated class. Revolutionary strikes following Russia's defeat in the war with Japan forced Nicholas II (1894–1917) to grant a representative national body (Duma), elected by narrowly limited suffrage. It met for the first time in 1906, little influencing Nicholas in his reactionary course.

World War I demonstrated tsarist corruption and inefficiency and only patriotism held the poorly equipped army together for a time. Disorders broke out in Petrograd (now Leningrad) in March 1917, and defection of the Petrograd garrison launched the revolution. Nicholas II was forced to abdicate on March 15, 1917, and he and his family were killed by revolutionists on July 16, 1918.

A provisional government under the successive premierships of Prince Lvov and a moderate, Alexander Kerensky, lost ground to the radical, or Bolshevik, wing of the Socialist Democratic Labor Party. On Nov. 7, 1917, the Bolshevik revolution, engineered by N. Lenin[1] and Leon Trotsky, overthrew the Kerensky government and authority was vested in a Council of People's Commissars, with Lenin as Premier.

The humiliating Treaty of Brest-Litovsk (March 3, 1918) concluded the war with Germany, but civil war and foreign intervention delayed Communist control of all Russia until 1920. A brief war with Poland in 1920 resulted in Russian defeat.

The Union of Soviet Socialist Republics was established as a federation on Dec. 30, 1922.

The death of Lenin on Jan. 21, 1924, precipitated an intraparty struggle between Joseph Stalin, General Secretary of the party, and Trotsky, who favored swifter socialization at home and fomentation of revolution abroad. Trotsky was dismissed as Commissar of War in 1925 and banished from the Soviet Union in 1929. He was murdered in Mexico City on Aug. 21, 1940, by a political agent.

Stalin further consolidated his power by a series of purges in the late 1930s, liquidating prominent party leaders and military officers. Stalin assumed the premiership May 6, 1941.

Soviet foreign policy, at first friendly toward Germany and antagonistic toward Britain and France and then, after Hitler's rise to power in 1933, becoming anti-Fascist and pro-League of Nations, took an abrupt turn on Aug. 24, 1939, with the signing of a nonaggression pact with Nazi Germany. The next month, Moscow joined in the German attack on Poland, seizing territory later incorporated into the Ukrainian and Byelorussian S.S.R.'s. The war with Finland, 1939–40, added territory to the Karelian S.S.R. set up March 31, 1940; the annexation of Bessarabia and Bukovina from Romania became part of the new Moldavian S.S.R. on Aug. 2, 1940; and the annexation of the Baltic republics of Estonia, Latvia, and Lithuania in June 1940 (still unrecognized by the U.S.) created the 14th, 15th, and 16th Soviet Republics. (The number of so-called "Union" republics was reduced to 15 in 1956 when the Karelian S.S.R. became one of the 20 Autonomous Soviet Socialist Republics based on ethnic groups.)

The Soviet-German collaboration ended abruptly with a lightning attack by Hitler on June 22, 1941, which seized 500,000 square miles of Russian territory before Soviet defenses, aided by U.S. and British arms, could halt it. The Soviet resurgence at Stalingrad from November 1942 to February 1943 marked the turning point in a long battle, ending in the final offensive of January 1945.

Then, after denouncing a 1941 nonaggression pact with Japan in April 1945, when Allied forces were nearing victory in the Pacific, the Soviet Union declared war on Japan on Aug. 8, 1945, and quickly occupied Manchuria, Karafuto, and the Kurile islands.

Postwar territorial acquisitions include the Carpatho-Ukraine (12,617 sq mi.; 32,678 sq km) ob-

1. N. Lenin was the pseudonym taken by Vladimir Ilich Ulyanov. It is sometimes given as Nikolai Lenin or V.

Rulers of Russia Since 1533

Name	Born	Ruled[1]
Ivan IV the Terrible	1530	1533–1584
Theodore I	1557	1584–1598
Boris Godunov	c.1551	1598–1605
Theodore II	1589	1605–1605
Demetrius I[2]	?	1605–1606
Basil IV Shuiski	?	1606–1610[3]
"Time of Troubles"	—	1610–1613
Michael Romanov	1596	1613–1645
Alexis I	1629	1645–1676
Theodore III	1656	1676–1682
Ivan V[4]	1666	1682–1689[5]
Peter I the Great[4]	1672	1682–1725
Catherine I	c.1684	1725–1727
Peter II	1715	1727–1730
Anna	1693	1730–1740
Ivan VI	1740	1740–1741[5]
Elizabeth	1709	1741–1762
Peter III	1728	1762–1762
Catherine II the Great	1729	1762–1796
Paul I	1754	1796–1801
Alexander I	1777	1801–1825
Nicholas I	1796	1825–1855
Alexander II	1818	1855–1881
Alexander III	1845	1881–1894
Nicholas II	1868	1894–1917[7]
PROVISIONAL GOVERNMENT (PREMIERS)		
Prince Georgi Lvov	1861	1917–1917
Alexander Kerensky	1881	1917–1917
POLITICAL LEADERS		
N. Lenin	1870	1917–1924
Aleksei Rykov	1881	1924–1930
Vyacheslav Molotov	1890	1930–1941
Joseph Stalin[8]	1879	1941–1953
Georgi M. Malenkov	1902	1953–1955
Nikolai A. Bulganin	1895	1955–1958
Nikita S. Khrushchev	1894	1958–1964
Leonid I. Brezhnev	1906	1964–1982
Yuri V. Andropov	1914	1982–1984
Konstantin U. Chernenko	1912	1984–

1. For Tsars through Nicholas II, year of end of rule is also that of death, unless otherwise indicated. 2. Also known as Pseudo-Demetrius. 3. Died 1612. 4. Ruled jointly until 1689, when Ivan was deposed. 5. Died 1696. 6. Died 1764. 7. Killed 1918. 8. General Secretary of Communist Party, 1924–53.

tained from Czechoslovakia June 29, 1945, incorporated into the Ukrainian S.S.R.; the Republic of Tannu Tuva in central Asia (64,000 sq mi.; 165,760 sq km), incorporated early in 1945 into the Russian Soviet Federal Socialist Republic (R.S.F.S.R.); Karafuto or southern Sakhalin (13,935 sq mi.; 36,092 sq km) and the Kurile Islands (3,944 sq mi.; 10,215 sq km), occupied by Soviet troops in August 1945 and incorporated into the R.S.F.S.R.; the northern part of eastern Prussia (about 7,000 sq mi.; 18,130 sq km), placed under *de facto* Soviet administration at the Potsdam Conference and incorporated into the R.S.F.S.R.; the Petsamo district of Finland, obtained *de jure* under the 1947 treaty and incorporated into the R.S.F.S.R.; and Poland east of the Curzon Line (69,860 sq mi.; 180,937 sq km), under terms of the Soviet-Polish treaty of Aug. 16, 1945, incorporated into the Ukrainian and Byelorussian S.S.R.'s.

The U.S.S.R. built a cordon of Communist states running from Poland in the north to Albania and Bulgaria in the south, including East Germany, Czechoslovakia, Hungary, and Romania, composed of the territories Soviet troops occupied at the war's end. With its Eastern front solidified, the Soviet Union launched a political offensive against the non-Communist West, moving first to block the Western access to Berlin. The Western powers countered with an airlift, completed unification of West Germany, and organized the defense of Western Europe in the North Atlantic Treaty Organization.

Stalin died on March 6, 1953, and was succeeded the next day by G. M. Malenkov as Premier. His chief rivals for power—Lavrenti P. Beria (chief of the secret police), Nikolai A. Bulganin, and Lazar M. Kaganovich—were named first deputies. Beria was purged in July and executed on Dec. 23, 1953.

The new power in the Kremlin was Nikita S. Khrushchev, First Secretary of the party. He replaced Malenkov with Bulganin in the premiership and then removed Malenkov, Kaganovich, and Vyacheslav M. Molotov from the Politburo. At the 20th Party Congress in 1956, Khrushchev denounced the "personality cult" of Stalin and in 1958 unseated Bulganin to become head of the government as well as of the party.

Khrushchev formalized the Eastern European system into a Council for Mutual Economic Assistance (Comecon) and a Warsaw Pact Treaty Organization as a counterweight to NATO. Tiny Albania was allowed to break away to join China in contesting Soviet domination of the Communist world, as Yugoslavia had done earlier. However, no mercy was shown to the Hungarians who rebelled in 1956, nor to the Czechs in their political struggle for liberation 12 years later.

In its technological race with the U.S., the Soviet Union exploded a hydrogen bomb in 1953, developed an intercontinental ballistic missile by 1957, sent the first satellite into space (Sputnik I) in 1957, and put Yuri Gagarin in the first orbital flight around the earth in 1961. On July 24, 1975, the 44-hour linkup of a Soviet Soyuz space vehicle (and two crewmen) with a U.S. Apollo spacecraft (and its crew of three) demonstrated—for the first time openly—the level of Soviet space capability.

Khrushchev's downfall stemmed from his decision to place Soviet nuclear missiles in Cuba and then, when challenged by the U.S., backing down and removing the weapons. He was also blamed for the ideological break with China after 1963.

Khrushchev was forced into retirement on Oct. 15, 1964, and was replaced by Leonid I. Brezhnev as First Secretary of the Party and Aleksei N. Kosygin as Premier.

President Nixon visited the U.S.S.R. for summit talks in May 1972, concluding agreements on strategic-arms limitation and a declaration of principles on future U.S.-Soviet relations. The welcome given Nixon at a time when the U.S. was bombing North Vietnam, a Soviet ally, was regarded as proof that 25 years of cold war had ended.

The 1972 Strategic Arms Limitation Treaty (SALT I) set a ceiling of 200 anti-ballistic missiles (ABM's) for each side and the U.S.S.R. was frozen at 1,618 land-based intercontinental missiles (ICBM's), with the U.S. held to 1,054. Submarine-based missiles were restricted by a complicated formula giving the U.S.S.R. a numerical advantage, balanced by permitting the U.S. more warheads for its more reliable and accurate missiles.

Brezhnev visited the U.S. in 1973 to discuss further arms limitations, but a return visit to Moscow by Nixon the following year failed to produce an expected permanent treaty. The two sides agreed to reduce ABM's to 100 each and to restrict underground nuclear testing (air, sea, and space tests were already prohibited), but there was no agreement to stop the proliferation of multi-warhead missiles (MIRV's).

Presidents Gerald R. Ford and Brezhnev met in Vladivostok in November 1974 and reached tentative agreements to be incorporated into a treaty at the Geneva SALT talks in 1975. They proposed a ceiling of 2,400 ICBM's for each side, of which no more than 1,320 could have MIRV's. There was hard bargaining but no decision on verification methods nor on whether the new U.S. subsonic Cruise missile and the Soviet Backfire bomber should be covered.

President Carter, actively pursuing both human rights and disarmament, joined with the Soviet Union in September 1977 to declare that the SALT I accord, which would have expired Oct. 1 without further action, be maintained in effect while the two sides sought a new agreement (SALT II).

Desire for détente appeared to moderate the Kremlin's policies toward the U.S. after the 1972 summit. There was a near-confrontation during the Arab-Israeli war of October 1973, when a Soviet threat to intervene to aid trapped Egyptian forces led Washington to call a world-wide nuclear alert, but the crisis was eased when the United Nations approved a U.S.-U.S.S.R. truce plan. The Kremlin made no overt move to capitalize on the fall of U.S.-backed governments in Indochina in the spring of 1975, but hailed the war's end as an incentive to improvement in relations with the U.S.

Brezhnev's 1977 election to the presidency followed publication of a new Constitution supplanting the one adopted in 1936. It specified the dominance of the Communist Party, previously unstated, and in what was taken to be a weapon against dissidents, declared that "rights and freedoms shall be inseparable from the performance by citizens of their duties." This was thought to restrict dissidents when they cited constitutional guarantees of individual freedom.

Although Brezhnev promised an end to the "illegal repressions" of the Stalin era, the issue of human rights remained a major one in both domestic and foreign policy. Dissidents continued to cite the Helsinki Agreement, and Carter's public support for Anatoly Shcharansky drew the angry charge from Brezhnev that Carter was conducting "ideological warfare" against the U.S.S.R. Amid the verbal fireworks, there was serious concern about the extent to which human rights might become an obstacle to SALT negotiations and to Soviet-U.S. relations in general.

The State Department warned, after Brezhnev had complained of SALT delays, that Soviet military aid to Ethiopia threatened all U.S.-Soviet relations. The Soviet news agency, Tass, said on February 26 that Soviet aid to Ethiopia was to counter Somali aggression and would end with a ceasefire. Similar friction occurred following the invasion of Zaire in May by rebels from Soviet-allied Angola, culminating in a speech by Carter to graduates of the U.S. Naval Academy telling the Russians they must "choose either confrontation or cooperation."

A crisis arose July 10 when, despite warnings from the Carter Administration, the government brought two prominent Jewish dissidents to trial, only two days before the opening of a new round of SALT negotiations in Geneva. Amid worldwide protest, a Moscow judge sentenced Anatoly Scharansky to three years in prison and 10 years in a forced labor camp on charges of treason. Scharansky, a leading spokesman for Jews seeking to emigrate to Israel, was accused of passing classified information to U.S. agents.

Aleksandr Ginzburg, manager of a fund established by exiled writer Aleksandr Solzhenytsin to aid political prisoners, was sentenced to eight years in a labor camp. Ginzburg was found guilty of "anti-Soviet agitation."

Carter condemned the action and temporarily halted the export of high technology goods to the Soviet Union. In April 1979, the issue was partly resolved with the exchange of Ginzburg and four other dissidents for two Soviet spies held by the United States. For 1979, the final count of Soviet Jews allowed to emigrate was 51,320, the highest number since emigration was permitted.

Carter and the ailing Brezhnev signed the SALT II treaty in Vienna on June 18, 1979, setting ceilings on each nation's arsenal of intercontinental ballistic missiles. Doubts about Senate ratification grew, and became a certainty on Dec. 27, when Soviet troops invaded Afghanistan. Despite protests from the Moslem and Western worlds, Moscow insisted that Afghan President Hafizullah Amin had asked for aid in quelling a rebellion.

In the face of evidence that Amin had been liquidated by Soviet advisers before the troops arrived, the Soviet Union vetoed a Security Council resolution on Jan. 7, 1980, that called for a withdrawal. Carter ordered a freeze on grain exports and high-technology equipment and stated that his "opinion of the Russians has changed more drastically in the last week than even in the previous two-and-a-half years."

On Jan. 20, Carter called for a world boycott of the Summer Olympic Games scheduled for Moscow. The boycott, less than complete, nevertheless marred the first Olympics to be held in Moscow as the United States, Canada, Japan, and to a partial extent all the western allies except France and Italy shunned the event.

Through 1981, an estimated 100,000 Soviet troops remained in Afghanistan, with guerrilla resistance continuing, and Moscow's motives still unclear. The invasion was regarded by some U.S. theoreticians as having been prompted by the weak response of the Carter Administration to the seizure of the U.S. Embassy in Teheran. Others suggested that Soviet leaders were only routinely backing a Marxist regime threatened with overthrow. With Iran racked by internal struggles, there was also the opportunity for Soviet military power to intervene from a flanking position, possibly gaining for Moscow both Iranian oil and the access to the Indian Ocean, coveted since tsarist days.

While the Soviet Union maintained a stony defense in the face of criticism from Western Europe and the U.S., and a summit meeting of 37 Islamic nations that unanimously condemned the "imperialist invasion" of Afghanistan, the growing crisis in Poland increasingly drew world attention. The Kremlin adopted an equally unyielding policy, sternly warning Warsaw against concessions to Polish workers and threatening military intervention.

The Reagan Administration took an initial hard line, with Secretary of State Alexander M. Haig, Jr., talking of a total trade embargo in the event of a Soviet military move into Poland. But at the Party's 26th Congress on Feb. 23, 1981, Brezhnev appeared to soften his approach with a call for an East-West summit and new arms-control talks.

Making no direct response, Reagan lifted the Carter-imposed embargo on grain sales to the Soviet Union on April 24.

In reaction to Soviet repression in Poland in December 1981, Reagan ordered economic sanctions aimed at blocking construction of a gas pipeline between the Soviet Union and Western Europe and Japan. Despite the tension between Moscow and Washington, Strategic Arms Reduction Talks (START) began in Geneva between U.S. and Soviet delegations in mid-1982. Negotiations on intermediate missile reduction also continued in Geneva.

On November 10, 1982, Soviet radio and television announced the death of Leonid Brezhnev. Yuri V. Andropov, who formerly headed the K.G.B., was chosen to succeed Brezhnev as General Secretary. By mid-June 1983, Andropov had assumed all of Brezhnev's three titles.

After months of illness, Andropov died in February 1984. Konstantin U. Chernenko, a 72-year-old party stalwart who had been close to Brezhnev, succeeded him as General Secretary and, by mid-April, had also assumed the title of President. In the months following Chernenko's assumption of power, the Kremlin took on a hostile mood toward the West of a kind rarely seen since the height of the cold war 30 years before. Led by Moscow, all the Soviet bloc countries except Romania boycotted the 1984 Summer Olympic Games in Los Angeles—tit-for-tat for the U.S.-led boycott of the 1980 Moscow Games, in the view of most observers.

SPAIN

Spanish State

Ruler: King Juan Carlos I (1975)

Prime Minister: Felipe González Márquez (1982)

Area: 194,885 sq mi. (504,750 km)[1]

Population (est. 1983): 38,000,000 (average annual growth rate: 0.7%) (Spanish, Basque, Catalan, Galician)

Density per square mile: 195.0

Capital: Madrid

Largest cities (est. 1983): Madrid, 3,175,000; Barcelona, 1,750,000; Valencia, 750,000; Seville, 650,000; Zaragoza, 575,000; Vizcaya (Bilbao), 440,000

Monetary unit: Peseta

Languages: Spanish, Basque, Catalan, Galician

Religion: Roman Catholic
National name: Estado Español
Literacy rate (1981): 97%
Economic summary: Gross national product (1980): $199.8 billion. Average annual growth rate (1970–79): 3.0%. Per capita income (1980): $5,350. Land used for agriculture: 41%; labor force: 19%; principal products: cereals, vegetables, citrus fruits, wine, olives and olive oil, livestock. Labor force in industry: 37%; major products: processed foods, textiles, footwear, petro-chemicals, steel, automobiles, ships. Natural resources: coal, lignite, water power, uranium, mercury, pyrites, fluorospar, gypsum, iron ore, zinc, lead, tungsten, copper. Exports: fresh fruits, iron and steel products, textiles, footwear, automobiles, fruits and vegetables. Imports: machinery and transportation equipment, chemicals, fuels, automobiles, iron, steel. Major trading partners: Western European nations, U.S.

1. Including the Balearic and Canary Islands.

Geography. Spain occupies 85% of the Iberian Peninsula in southwestern Europe, which it shares with Portugal; France is to the northeast, separated by the Pyrenees. The Bay of Biscay lies to the north, the Atlantic Ocean to the west, and the Mediterranean Sea to the south and east: Africa is less than 10 miles (16 km) south at the Strait of Gibraltar.

A broad central plateau slopes to the south and east, crossed by a series of mountain ranges and river valleys.

Principal rivers are the Ebro in the northeast, the Tajo in the central region, and the Guadalquivir in the south.

Off Spain's east coast in the Mediterranean are the Balearic Islands (1,936 sq mi.; 5,014 sq km), the largest of which is Majorca. Sixty miles (97 km) west of Africa are the Canary Islands (2,808 sq mi.; 7,273 sq km).

Government. King Juan Carlos I (born Jan. 5, 1938) succeeded Generalissimo Francisco Franco Bahamonde as Chief of State Nov. 22, 1975.

The Cortes, or Parliament, consists of a Chamber of Deputies of 350 members and a Senate of 208, all elected by universal suffrage. The new Cortes, replacing one that was largely appointed or elected by special constituencies, was organized under a constitution adopted by referendum Dec. 6, 1978.

The major political parties are the Spanish Socialist Workers Party (201 of 350 seats in the Chamber of Deputies, 134 of 208 elected Senate seats), led by Prime Minister Felipe González Márquez; Popular Alliance (105 seats in Chamber, 54 in Senate), led by Manuel Fraga Iribarne; Union of the Democratic Center (12 seats in Chamber, 4 in Senate); Communist Party (4 seats in Chamber, none in Senate), led by Gerardo Iglesias; Social and Democratic Center (2 seats in Chamber, none in Senate), led by Adolfo Suárez; Convergencia i Unió (Catalonian Party) (12 seats in Chamber, 8 in Senate); Basque Party (8 seats in Chamber, 7 in Senate).

History. Spain, originally inhabited by Celts, Iberians and Basques, became a part of the Roman Empire in 201 B.C., when it was conquered by Scipio Africanus. In A.D. 412, the barbarian Visigothic leader Ataulf crossed the Pyrenees and ruled Spain, first in the name of the Roman emperor and then independently. In 711, the Moslems under Tariq entered Spain from Africa and within a few years completed the subjugation of the country. In 732, the Franks, led by Charles Martel, defeated the Moslems near Poitiers, thus preventing the further expansion of Islam in southern Europe. Internal dissension of Spanish Islam invited a steady Christian conquest from the north.

Aragon and Castile were the most important Spanish states from the 13th to the 15th century, consolidated by the marriage of Ferdinand II and Isabella I in 1469. The last Moslem stronghold, Granada, was captured in 1492. Roman Catholicism was established as the official state religion and the Jews (1492) and the Moslems (1502) expelled.

In the era of exploration, discovery, and colonization, Spain amassed tremendous wealth and a vast colonial empire through the conquest of Peru by Pizarro (1532–33) and of Mexico by Cortés (1519–21). The Spanish Hapsburg monarchy became for a time the most powerful in the world.

In 1588, Philip II sent his Invincible Armada to invade England, but its destruction cost Spain its supremacy on the seas and paved the way for England's colonization of America. Spain then sank rapidly to the status of a second-rate power and never again played a major role in European politics. Its colonial empire in the Americas and the Philippines vanished in wars and revolutions during the 18th and 19th centuries.

In World War I, Spain maintained a position of neutrality. In 1923, Gen. Miguel Primo de Rivera became dictator. In 1930, King Alfonso XIII revoked the dictatorship, but a strong antimonarchist and republican movement led to his leaving Spain in 1931.[2] The new Constitution declared Spain a workers' republic, broke up the large estates, separated church and state, and secularized the schools. The elections held in 1936 returned a strong Popular Front majority, with Manuel Azaña as President.

On July 18, 1936, a conservative army officer in Morocco, Francisco Franco Bahamonde, led a mutiny against the government. The civil war that followed lasted three years and cost the lives of nearly a million people. Franco was aided by Fascist Italy and Nazi Germany, while Soviet Russia helped the Loyalist side. Several hundred leftist Americans served in the Abraham Lincoln Brigade on the side of the republic. The war ended when Franco took Madrid on March 28, 1939.

Franco became head of the state, national chief of the Falange Party (the governing party), and Premier and Caudillo (leader). In a referendum in 1947, the Spanish people approved a Franco-drafted succession law declaring Spain a monarchy again. Franco, however, continued as Chief of State.

In 1969, Franco and the Cortes designated Prince Juan Carlos Alfonso Victor María de Borbón (who married Princess Sophia of Greece on May 14, 1962) to become King of Spain when the provisional government headed by Franco came to an end. He is the grandson of Alfonso XIII and the son of Don Juan, pretender to the throne.

In 1967 Spain concluded its first economic-social development plan, which had raised levels of living dramatically within a decade and, combined with Spanish migration to higher-wage countries in Western Europe, had virtually eradicated unemployment. A new Constitution, adopted in 1966,

2. However, he did not abdicate. In 1941, shortly before his death, he renounced his claim to the throne in favor of his third son, Don Juan.

allowed for the direct election of one fourth of the Cortes.

Franco died of a heart attack on Nov. 20, 1975, after more than a year of ill health, and Juan Carlos was proclaimed King two days later.

Over strong rightist opposition, the government legalized the Communist Party in advance of the 1977 elections. Premier Adolfo Suaraz Gonzalez's Union of the Democratic Center, a coalition of a dozen centrist and rightist parties, claimed 34.3% of the popular vote in the election.

Under pressure from Catalonian and Basque nationalists, Suárez granted home rule to these regions in 1979, but centrists backed by him did poorly in the 1980 elections for local assemblies in the two areas. Economic problems persisted, along with new incidents of terrorism, and Suárez resigned on Jan. 29, 1981, recommending Leopoldo Calvo Sotelo as his successor.

While the Cortes was debating Calvo's confirmation, 200 right-wing Civil Guardsmen invaded the chamber on Feb. 23 and held the Cabinet and 350 legislators hostage. King Juan Carlos made a televised appeal for support of the government, the attempt failed and the Prime Minister was subsequently confirmed by a vote of 186–158.

Reflecting the end of the economic boom years in which Spain had been catching up with industrialized Europe, unemployment rose from 14% in 1981 to 16% in 1982 to 17% in 1983. The 1983 inflation rate was 15%.

With the overwhelming election of Prime Minister Felipe González Márquez and his Spanish Socialist Workers Party in the Oct. 20, 1982, parliamentary elections, the Franco past was finally buried. The thrust of Gonzalez, a pragmatic moderate, was to modernize rather than radicalize Spain. As promised, the Socialists did not carry out widespread nationalization of private industry, but did seek to nationalize the high-tension power grid.

González continued to press for full Spanish membership in the European Economic Community, while postponing a decision on joining NATO.

SRI LANKA

Democratic Socialist Republic of Sri Lanka
President: J. R. Jayewardene (1978)
Prime Minister: Ranasinghe Premadasa (1978)
Area: 25,332 sq mi. (65,610 sq km)
Population (est. 1982): 15,250,000 (average annual growth rate: 1.8%)
Density per square mile: 602.0
Capital: Sri Jayewardenapura Kotte (Colombo)
Largest cities (est. 1982): Sri Jayewardenapura Kotte, 590,000; Dehiwela, 180,000; Jaffna, 125,000
Monetary unit: Sri Lanka rupee
Languages: Sinhala, Tamil, English
Religions: Buddhist, 69%; Hindu, 16%; Islam, 8%; Christian, 8%
Member of Commonwealth of Nations
Literacy rate (1980): 86.5% (est.)
Economic summary: Gross national product (1980): $4.0 billion. Average annual growth rate (1970–79): 2.5%. Per capita income (1980): $270. Land used for agriculture: 25%; labor force: 53%; principal products: tea, coconuts, rubber, rice, spices. Labor force in industry: 15%; major products: consumer goods, textiles, chemicals, paper and paper products. Natural resources: limestone, graphite, gems. Exports: tea, rubber, petroleum products. Imports: petroleum, machinery, transport equipment, sugar. Major trading partners: Saudi Arabia, Iran, Pakistan.

Geography. An island in the Indian Ocean off the southeast tip of India, Sri Lanka is about half the size of Alabama. Most of the land is flat and rolling; mountains in the south central region rise to over 8,000 feet (2,438 m).

Government. After 24 years as a British dominion, Ceylon became an independent republic and reverted to the traditional name Sri Lanka (resplendent island) on May 22, 1972. A new Constitution was adopted, replacing that of 1948.

The new Constitution set up the National State Assembly, a 168-member unicameral legislature that serves for six years unless dissolved earlier.

The major political parties are the United National Party (141 of 168 seats in the National Assembly), led by President J.R. Jayewardene: Tamil United Liberation Front (17 seats); Sri Lanka Freedom Party (9 seats), led by Anura Bandaranaike. A split in the Freedom Party has resulted in the formation of the Sri Lanka Mahajaua Party (SLMP).

History. Following Portuguese and Dutch rule, Ceylon became an English crown colony in 1798. The British developed coffee, tea, and rubber plantations and granted six Constitutions between 1798 and 1924. The Constitution of 1931 gave a large measure of self-government.

Ceylon became a self-governing dominion of the Commonwealth of Nations in 1948. Rioting by the Tamils seeking a separate state within a federal system occurred in 1958 and 1961, resulting in the outlawing of their party. In 1962, the Prime Minister, Mrs. Sirimavo R.D. Bandaranaike, a radical, nationalized Western oil and other business facilities and became embroiled with the U.S. and Britain over compensation. She was ousted in the 1965 elections by a multiparty coalition.

Following considerable pre-election violence, Mrs. Bandaranaike was returned to power in a landslide victory in 1970, with her three-party leftist coalition capturing over two thirds of parliament. An important factor was the 800,000 youths 18-to-21 years old given the vote for the first time; they proved largely left-leaning.

Worsening economic conditions and charges of corruption combined to produce a crushing defeat for Mrs. Bandaranaike in general elections of 1977. Junius Richard Jayawardene, 73-year-old leader of the small United National Party, became Prime Minister.

Amid opposition criticism, Jayawardene was sworn in as president on Feb. 3, 1978, in a constitutional change to the presidential system of government.

Presidential elections were held in December 1982, and won by J.R. Jayewardene.

Tension between the Tamil minority and the Sinhalese majority continued to build and erupted in bloody violence in 1983 and 1984. There are about 2.6 million Tamils in Sri Lanka, while the Sinhalese make up about three-quarters of the 15-million population. Tamil extremists are fighting for a separate nation. About 400 people, mainly Tamils living in the nothern part of Sri Lanka, were killed in the violence in 1983. Tamil extremists kidnapped and held an American married couple as hostages for a brief period in the spring of 1984, but released them unharmed.

SUDAN

Democratic Republic of the Sudan
President: (1971) Field Marshal Gaafar Mohamed Nimeiri
Area: 967,491 sq mi. (2,505,802 sq km)
Population (est. 1983): 20,585,000 (average annual growth rate: 2.9%)
Density per square mile: 19.8
Capital: Khartoum
Largest cities (est. 1981): Khartoum, 1,250,000; Omdurman, 350,000; Port Sudan, 250,000
Monetary unit: Sudanese pound
Languages: Arabic, English, tribal dialects
Religions: Islam, 73%; Animist, 18%; Christian, 9%
National name: Jamhuryat es-Sudan Al Demogratia
Literacy rate (1981): 20%
Economic summary: Gross national product (1981): $5.0 billion. Average annual growth rate (1970–79): 1.5%. Per capita income (1981): $478. Land used for agriculture: 3%; labor force: 78%; principal products: cotton, peanuts, sesame seeds, gum arabic, sorghum, wheat sugar cane. Labor force in industry: 10%; major products: cement, textiles, pharmaceuticals, shoes, processed foods. Natural resources: some iron ore, copper, chrome, industrial metals. Exports: cotton, peanuts, gum arabic, livestock. Imports: textiles, petroleum products, vehicles, tea, wheat. Major trading partners: U.K., West Germany, Italy, India, China, France, Japan.

Geography. The Sudan, in northeast Africa, is the largest country on the continent, measuring about one fourth the size of the United States. Its neighbors are Chad and the Central African Republic on the west, Egypt and Libya on the north, Ethiopia on the east, and Kenya, Uganda, and Zaire on the south. The Red Sea washes about 500 miles of the eastern coast.

The country extends from north to south about 1,200 miles (1,931 km) and west to east about 1,000 miles (1,609 km). The northern region is a continuation of the Libyan Desert. The southern region is fertile, abundantly watered, and, in places, heavily forested. It is traversed from north to south by the Nile, all of whose great tributaries are partly or entirely within its borders.

Government. Republic under military rule since coup in May 1969.

History. The early history of the Sudan (known as the Anglo-Egyptian Sudan between 1898 and 1955) is linked with that of Nubia, where a powerful local kingdom was formed in Roman times with its capital at Dongola. After conversion to Christianity in the 6th century, it joined with Ethiopia and resisted Mohammedanization until the 14th century. Thereafter the area was broken up into many small states until 1820–22, when it was conquered by Mohammed Ali, Pasha of Egypt. Egyptian forces were evacuated during the Mahdist revolt (1881–98), but the Sudan was reconquered by the Anglo-Egyptian expeditions of 1896–98, and in 1899 became an Anglo-Egyptian condominium, which was reaffirmed by the Anglo-Egyptian treaty of 1936.

Egypt and Britain agreed in 1953 to grant self-government to the Sudan under an appointed Governor-General. An all-Sudanese Parliament was elected in November-December 1953, and an all-Sudanese government was formed. In December 1955, the Parliament declared the independence of the Sudan, which, with the approval of Britain and Egypt, was proclaimed on Jan. 1, 1956.

In October 1969, Maj. Gen. Gaafar Mohamed Nimeiri, the president of the Council for the Revolution, took over as prime minister. He was elected the nation's first president in 1971 by a reported 98.6% of the vote in a national referendum.

On March 2, 1973, eight Palestinian terrorists invaded the Saudi Arabian embassy in Khartoum and killed one Belgian and two American diplomats after their demands for the release of Arab terrorist prisoners in different countries were refused.

The terrorists were convicted of murder June 24, 1974, but Nimeiri freed them the next day and turned them over to the Palestine Liberation Army, which flew them to Cairo. The U.S. withdrew its Ambassador in protest, but he returned in October 1974 after the men were imprisoned in Egypt.

In 1976, a third attempted coup against Nimeiri left 1,000 rebels and loyal troops dead after a fierce battle in Khartoum. Nimeiri accused President Muammar el Qaddafi of Libya of having instigated the attempt and broke relations with Libya. Firing squads executed 81 convicted rebels.

Nimeiri also charged Soviet involvement in the attempt and in 1977 expelled 90 Soviet advisers. He moved closer to Egypt—he was one of the few Arab leaders who supported Sadat's dramatic visit to Israel in November 1977—and the U.S.

In June 1984, Nimeiri said neighboring Ethiopia and Libya and the Soviet Union were waging a "secret war" against Sudan. He accused Ethiopia of helping rebels in the south to sow dissension and unrest. In July Nimeiri announced that Sudanese forces had regained control of the country's southeastern border and driven rebels back into Ethiopia.

SURINAME

Republic of Suriname
President: L. F. Ramdat Misier (1982)
Prime Minister: Wim Udenhout (1984)
Area: 63,251 sq mi. (163,820 sq km)
Population (est. 1983): 360,000 (average annual growth rate: –1.5%) (Hindi, 37%; Creole, 31%; Indonesian, 15%; Bush Negro, 10%)
Density per square mile: 2.2
Capital and largest city (est. 1982): Paramaribo, 100,000
Monetary unit: Suriname guilder
Languages: Dutch, Surinamese (lingua franca)
Religions: Protestant, Roman Catholic, Hindu, Islam
Literacy rate (1981): 80%
Economic summary: Gross national product (1980): $1 billion. Average annual growth rate (1970–79): 6.4%. Per capita income (1980): $2,840. Land used for agriculture: 0.3%; labor force: 29%; principal products: rice, citrus fruits, sugar, coffee. Labor force in industry: 15%; major products: aluminum, alumina, processed foods, lumber, bricks, cigarettes. Natural resources: bauxite, iron ore, timber, fish, shrimp. Exports: bauxite, alumina, aluminum, rice, shrimp, lumber and wood products. Imports: capital equipment, petroleum, iron and steel, cotton, flour, meat, dairy products. Major trading partners: U.S., Western European countries.

Geography. Suriname lies on the northeast coast of South America, with Guyana to the west, French Guiana to the east, and Brazil to the south. It is about one tenth larger than Michigan. The principal rivers are the Corantijn on the Guyana border, the Marowijne in the east, and the Suriname, on which the capital city of Paramaribo is situated. The Tumuc-Humac Mountains are on the border with Brazil.

Government. Suriname, formerly known as Dutch Guiana, became an independent republic on Nov. 25, 1975. The first prime minister, Henck A. E. Arron, was ousted by a 16-man military junta on Feb. 25, 1980, and replaced by Dr. Henk R. Chin A Sen.

Chin A Sen was elevated to the office of President by the junta on Aug. 14, 1980, and the 39-member National Assembly was abolished and replaced by a military cabinet. In 1982, L.F. Ramdat Missier replaced Sen as president.

History. England established the first European settlement on the Suriname River in 1650 but transferred sovereignty to the Dutch in 1667 in the Treaty of Breda, by which the British acquired New York. Colonization was confined to a narrow coastal strip, and until the abolition of slavery in 1863, African slaves furnished the labor for the plantation economy. After 1870, laborers were imported from British India and the Dutch East Indies.

In 1948, the colony was integrated into the Kingdom of the Netherlands and two years later was granted full home rule in other than foreign affairs and defense. After race rioting over unemployment and inflation, the Netherlands offered complete independence in 1973. Henck A. E. Arron, leader of a coalition of Creole (Surinamese of African descent) parties, advocated independence, while Jaggernath Lachmon, leader of the Surinamese of East Indian descent, urged delay.

Arron retained power in the first post-independence elections in 1977 but held only a one-seat margin over Lachmon's group early in 1980. He had promised early elections when Army sergeants and a lieutenant staged a coup on Feb. 25 and installed a civilian, Dr. Henk R. Chin A Sen, as Prime Minister. A subsequent military intervention made Chin A Sen president, abolishing the legislature and instituting a military government.

SWAZILAND

Kingdom of Swaziland
Ruler: Queen Regent Dzeliwe Shongwe (1982)
Prime Minister: Prince Bhekimpi Dlamini (1983)
Area: 6,704 sq mi. (17,363 sq km)
Population (est. 1983): 610,000 (average annual growth rate: 2.8%)
Density per square mile: 91.0
Capital and largest city (est. 1982): Mbabane, 32,000
Monetary unit: Lilangeni
Languages: English and Siswati (official)
Religions: Christian, 77%; Animist, 23%
Member of Commonwealth of Nations
Literacy rate (1981): 25%
Economic summary: Gross national product (1980): $380 million. Average annual growth rate (1970–79): 4.4%. Per capita income (1980): $680. Land used for agriculture: 8%; labor force: 31%; principal products: corn, livestock, sugar cane, citrus fruits, cotton, rice, pineapples. Labor force in industry: 25%; major products: milled sugar, ginned cotton, processed meat and wood, iron ore. Natural resources: iron ore, asbestos, coal. Exports: sugar, wood products, iron ore, asbestos, citrus fruits, meat products, cotton. Imports: motor vehicles, fuels and lubricants, foodstuffs, clothing. Major trading partners: South Africa, U.K., U.S.

Geography. Swaziland, 85% the size of New Jersey, is surrounded by South Africa and Mozambique. The country consists of a high veld in the west and a series of plateaus descending from 6,000 feet (1,829 m) to a low veld of 1,500 feet (457 m).

Government. In 1967, a new Constitution established King Sobhuza II as head of state and provided for an Assembly of 24 members elected by universal suffrage, together with a Senate of 12 members—half appointed by the Assembly and half by the King. In 1973, the King renounced the Constitution, suspended political parties, and took total power for himself. In 1977, he replaced the Parliament with an assembly of tribal leaders. The Parliament reconvened in 1979.

History. Bantu peoples migrated southwest to the area of Mozambique in the 16th century. A number of clans broke away from the main body in the 18th century and settled in Swaziland. In the 19th century they organized as a tribe, partly because they were in constant conflict with the Zulu. Their ruler, Mswazi, applied to the British in the 1840s for help against the Zulu. The British and the Transvaal governments guaranteed the independence of Swaziland in 1881.

South Africa held Swaziland as a protectorate from 1894 to 1899, but after the Boer War, in 1902, Swaziland was transferred to British administration. The Paramount Chief was recognized as the native authority in 1941.

In 1963, the territory was constituted a protectorate, and on Sept. 6, 1968, it became the independent nation of Swaziland.

King Sobhuza died in August 1982, the world's longest-reigning monarch.

SWEDEN

Kingdom of Sweden
Sovereign: King Carl XVI Gustaf (1973)
Prime Minister: Olof Palme (1982)
Area: 173,229 sq mi. (448,661 sq km)
Population (est. 1983): 8,340,000 (average annual growth rate: 0.1%)
Density per square mile: 52
Capital: Stockholm
Largest cities (est. 1982): Stockholm, 650,000; Göteborg, 435,000; Malmö, 235,000; Uppsala, 150,000
Monetary unit: Krona
Language: Swedish
Religion: Swedish Lutheran, 95%
National name: Konungariket Sverige
Literacy rate (1981): 99%
Economic summary: Gross national product (1982): $100

billion. Average annual growth rate (1970–1982): 2.0%. Per capita income (1982): $11,900. Principal agricultural products: dairy products, grains, sugar beets, potatoes, wood. Labor force in industry: 31%; major products: machinery, instruments, metal products, automobiles. Natural resources: forests, iron ore, hydroelectric power, unmined uranium. Exports: machinery, motor vehicles, wood pulp, paper products, iron and steel products. Imports: machinery, petroleum, yarns, foodstuffs, iron and steel, chemicals. Major trading partners: Norway, West Germany, U.K., Denmark, Finland, U.S.

Geography. Sweden occupies the eastern part of the Scandinavian peninsula, with Norway to the west, Finland and the Gulf of Bothnia to the east, and Denmark and the Baltic Sea in the south. It is one tenth larger than California.

The country slopes eastward and southward from the Kjólen Mountains along the Norwegian border, where the peak elevation is Kebnekaise at 6,965 feet (2,123 m) in Lapland. In the north are mountains and many lakes. To the south and east are central lowlands and south of them are fertile areas of forest, valley, and plain.

Along Sweden's rocky coast, chopped up by bays and inlets, are many islands, the largest of which are Gotland and Oland.

Government. Sweden is a constitutional monarchy. Under the 1975 Constitution, the Riksdag is the sole governing body. The prime minister is the political chief executive.

In 1967, agreement was reached on part of a new Constitution after 13 years of work. It provided for a single-house Riksdag of 350 members (later amended to 349 seats) to replace the 104-year old bicameral Riksdag. The members are popularly elected for three years. Ninety-two present members of the Riksdag are women.

The King, Carl XVI Gustaf, was born April 30, 1946, and succeeded to the throne Sept. 19, 1973, on the death at 90 of his grandfather, Gustaf VI Adolf. Carl Gustaf was married on June 19, 1976, to Silvia Sommerlath, a West German commoner. They have three children: Princess Victoria, born July 14, 1977; Prince Carl Philip, born May 13, 1979; and Princess Madeline, born June 10, 1982. Under the new Act of Succession, effective Jan. 1, 1980, the first child of the reigning monarch, regardless of sex, is heir to the throne.

The major political parties are the Social Democratic Party (166 seats in the Riksdag), led by Prime Minister Olof Palme; Conservative Party (86 seats), led by Ulf Adelsohn; Center Party (56 seats), led by former Prime Minister Thorbjörn Fälldin; Liberal Party (21 seats), led by Bengt Westerberg; Communist Party (20 seats), led by Lars Werner.

History. The earliest historical mention of Sweden is found in Tacitus' *Germania,* where reference is made to the powerful king and strong fleet of the Suiones. Toward the end of the 10th century, Olaf Sköttkonung established a Christian stronghold in Sweden. Around 1400, an attempt was made to unite the northern nations into one kingdom, but this led to bitter strife between the Danes and the Swedes.

In 1520, the Danish King, Christian II, conquered Sweden and in the "Stockholm Bloodbath" put leading Swedish personalities to death. Gustavus Vasa (1523–60) broke away from Denmark and fashioned the modern Swedish state.

Sweden played a leading role in the second phase (1630–35) of the Thirty Years' War (1618–48). By the Treaty of Westphalia (1648), Sweden obtained western Pomerania and some neighboring territory on the Baltic. In 1700, a coalition of Russia, Poland, and Denmark united against Sweden and by the Peace of Nystad (1721) forced it to relinquish Livonia, Ingria, Estonia, and parts of Finland.

Sweden emerged from the Napoleonic Wars with the acquisition of Norway from Denmark and with a new royal dynasty stemming from Marshal Jean Bernadotte of France, who became King Charles XIV (1818–44). The artificial union between Sweden and Norway led to an uneasy relationship, and the union was finally dissolved in 1905.

Sweden maintained a position of neutrality in both World Wars.

An elaborate structure of welfare legislation, imitated by many larger nations, began with the establishment of old-age pensions in 1911. Economic prosperity based on its neutralist policy enabled Sweden, together with Norway, to pioneer in public health, housing, and job security programs.

Forty-four years of Socialist government were ended in 1976 with the election of a conservative coalition headed by Thorbjörn Fälldin, a 50-year-old sheep farmer. The surprise conservative victory was credited to public opposition to a nuclear power program backed by the Socialists and to a program that would have given control of all businesses to labor unions within 20 years.

Nuclear-power policy dominated Swedish policy in the ensuing years. Fälldin resigned on Oct. 5, 1978, when his conservative parties partners demanded less restrictions on nuclear power, and his successor, Ola Ullsten, resigned a year later after failing to achieve a consensus on the issue. Returned to office by his coalition partners, Fälldin said he would follow the course directed by a national referendum. On March 23, 1980, voters backed the development of 12 nuclear plants and use of them for at least 25 years to supply 40% of national energy needs while the search for alternative sources continued.

SWITZERLAND

Swiss Confederation
President: Leon Schlumpf (1984)
Vice President: Kurt Furgler (1984)
Area: 15,941 sq mi. (41,288 sq km)
Population (est. 1982): 6,384,000 (average annual growth rate: –0.3%) (Swiss, 85%; Italian, 8%; German, 2%; Spanish, 2%; French, 1%—figures by place of birth)
Density per square mile: 406.2
Capital: Bern
Largest cities (est. 1982): Zurich, 380,000; Basel, 182,000; Geneva, 153,000; Bern, 145,000; Lausanne, 130,000
Monetary unit: Swiss franc
Languages: German, 65%; French, 18%; Italian, 10%; Romansch, 1%
Religions: Roman Catholic, 48%; Protestant, 44%
National name: Schweiz/Suisse/Svizzera
Literacy rate (1981): 98%
Economic summary: Gross national product (1980): $106.3 billion. Average annual growth rate (1970–79): 0.2%. Per capita income (1980): $16,440. Land used for agriculture: 26%; labor force: 7%; principal products:

cheese and other dairy products, livestock, fruits, grains, wine. Labor force in industry: 38%; major products: watches and clocks, precision instruments, machinery, chemicals, pharmaceuticals, textiles, generators, turbines. Natural resources: water power, timber, salt. Exports: electrical machinery, chemicals, precision instruments, textiles, foodstuffs, textile yarns, dyestuffs, chemicals. Imports: transport equipment, metals and metal products, foodstuffs, chemicals, textile yarns. Major trading partners: West Germany, France, U.S., Italy, U.K.

Geography. Switzerland, in central Europe, is the land of the Alps. Its tallest peak is the Dufourspitze at 15,203 feet (4,634 m) on the Swiss side of the Italian border, one of 10 summits of the Monte Rose massif in the Pennine Alps. The tallest peak in all of the Alps, Mont Blanc (15,771 ft; 4,807 m), is actually in France.

Most of Switzerland comprises a mountainous plateau bordered by the great bulk of the Alps on the south and by the Jura Mountains on the northwest. About one fourth of the total area is covered by mountains and glaciers.

The country's largest lakes—Geneva, Constance (Bodensee), and Maggiore—straddle the French, German-Austrian, and Italian borders, respectively.

The Rhine, navigable from Basel to the North Sea, is the principal inland waterway. Other rivers are the Aare and the Rhône.

Switzerland, twice the size of New Jersey, is surrounded by France, West Germany, Austria, Liechtenstein, and Italy.

Government. The Swiss Confederation consists of 23 sovereign cantons, of which three are divided into six half-cantons. Federal authority is vested in a bicameral legislature. The Ständerat, or State Council, consists of 46 members, two from each canton. The lower house, the Nationalrat, or National Council, has 200 deputies, elected for four-year terms.

Executive authority rests with the Bundesrat, or Federal Council, consisting of seven members chosen by parliament. The parliament elects the President, who serves for one year and is succeeded by the Vice President. The federal government regulates foreign policy, railroads, postal service, and the national mint. Each canton reserves for itself important local powers.

A constitutional amendment adopted in 1971 by referendum gave women the vote in federal elections and the right to hold federal office. An equal rights amendment passed in a national referendum June 14, 1981, barring discrimination against women under canton as well as federal law.

The major political parties are the Social Democratic Party (51 of 200 seats in National Council), led by Helmut Hubacher; Radical Democratic Party (51 seats), led by Yann Richter; Christian-Democratic Party (44 seats), led by Hans Wyer; People's Party (23 seats), led by Fritz Hofmann. These four parties constitute the ruling coalition.

History. Called Helvetia in ancient times, Switzerland in the Middle Ages was a league of cantons of the Holy Roman Empire. Fashioned around the nucleus of three German forest districts of Schwyz, Uri, and Unterwalden, the Swiss Confederation slowly added new cantons. In 1648 the Treaty of Westphalia gave Switzerland its independence from the Holy Roman Empire.

French revolutionary troops occupied the country in 1798 and named it the Helvetic Republic, but Napoleon in 1803 restored its federal government. By 1815, the French- and Italian-speaking peoples of Switzerland had been granted political equality.

In 1815, the Congress of Vienna guaranteed the neutrality and recognized the independence of Switzerland. In the revolutionary period of 1847, the Catholic cantons seceded and organized a separate union called the *Sonderbund.* In 1848 the new Swiss Constitution established a union modeled upon that of the U.S. The Federal Constitution of 1874 established a strong central government while maintaining large powers of control in each canton.

National unity and political conservatism grew as the country prospered from its neutrality. Its banking system became the world's leading repository for international accounts. Strict neutrality was its policy in World Wars I and II. Geneva was the seat of the League of Nations (later the European headquarters of the United Nations) and of a number of international organizations.

In 1971, the Swiss Supreme Court ruled that Swiss banks must show U.S. tax officials records of U.S. citizens suspected of tax fraud, thus significantly modifying a 1934 law that had seemed to forbid any bank disclosures.

SYRIA

Syrian Arab Republic
President: Hafez al-Assad (1971)
Premier: Abdel Raouf al-Kasm (1980)
Area: 71,498 sq mi. (185,180 sq km)
Population (est. 1983): 10,000,000 (average annual growth rate: 3.4%)
Density per square mile: 139.9
Capital: Damascus
Largest cities (est. 1981): Damascus, 1,200,000; Aleppo, 895,000; Homs, 315,000; Hama, 190,000; Latakia, 175,000
Monetary unit: Syrian pound
Language: Arabic
Religions: Islam, 85%; Christian, 14%
National name: Al-Jamhouriya al Arabiya As-Souriya
Literacy rate (1981): 40%
Economic summary: Gross national product (1981): $16.2 billion. Average annual growth rate (1970–79): 4.6%. Per capita income (1981): $1,735. Land used for agriculture: 47%; labor force: 32%; principal products: cotton, wheat, sugar beets, sheep, goats. Labor force in industry: 29%; major products: textiles, cement, glass, petroleum, processed food, soap. Natural resources: chrome, manganese, asphalt, iron ore, rock salt, phosphate, oil, natural gas. Exports: petroleum, textiles, tobacco, fruits and vegetables, cotton. Imports: machinery and metal products, textiles, fuels, foodstuffs. Major trading partners: Italy, Romania, West Germany, U.S.S.R., U.S., Iraq.

Geography. Slightly larger than North Dakota, Syria lies at the eastern end of the Mediterranean Sea. It is bordered by Lebanon and Israel on the west, Turkey on the north, Iraq on the east, and Jordan on the south.

Coastal Syria is a narrow plain, in back of which is a range of coastal mountains, and still farther inland a steppe area. In the east is the Syrian

Desert, and in the south is the Jebel Druze Range. The highest point in Syria is Mount Hermon (9,232 ft; 2,814 m) on the Lebanese border.

Government. Syria's first permanent Constitution was approved in 1973, replacing a provisional charter that had been in force for 10 years. It provided for an elected People's Council as the legislature. No national religion is specified, although Islamic law is the basis of the state law.

In the first election in 10 years, in 1973, the Ba'ath Arab Socialist Party of President Hafez al-Assad, running on a unified National Progressive ticket with the Communist and Socialist parties, won 70% of the vote and a commensurate proportion of the seats in the People's Assembly. In 1977 and 1981 elections, the ruling Ba'athists won by similar margins.

History. Ancient Syria was conquered by Egypt about 1500 B.C., and after that by Hebrews, Phoenicians, Assyrians, Chaldeans, Persians, and Greeks. From 64 B.C. until the Arab conquest in A.D. 636, it was part of the Roman Empire except during brief periods. The Arabs made it a trade center for their extensive empire, but it suffered severely from the Mongol invasion in 1260 and fell to the Ottoman Turks in 1516. Syria remained a Turkish province until World War I.

A secret Anglo-French pact of 1916 put Syria in the French zone of influence. The League of Nations gave France a mandate over Syria after World War I, but the French were forced to put down several nationalist uprisings. In 1930, France recognized Syria as an independent republic, but still subject to the mandate. After nationalist demonstrations in 1939, the French High Commissioner suspended the Syrian Constitution. In 1941, British and Free French forces invaded Syria to eliminate Vichy control. During the rest of World War II, Syria was an Allied base.

Again in 1945, nationalist demonstrations broke into actual fighting, and British troops had to restore order. Syrian forces met a series of reverses while participating in the Arab invasion of Palestine in 1948. In 1958, Egypt and Syria formed the United Arab Republic, with Gamal Abdel Nasser of Egypt as President. However, Syria became independent again on Sept. 29, 1961, following a revolution.

In the war of 1967, Israel quickly vanquished the Syrian army. Before acceding to the U.N. ceasefire, the Israeli forces took over control of the fortified Golan Heights commanding the Sea of Galilee.

Syria joined Egypt in attacking Israel in October 1973 in the fourth Arab-Israeli war, but was pushed back from initial successes on the Golan Heights to end up losing more land. However, in the settlement worked out by U.S. Secretary of State Henry A. Kissinger in 1974, the Syrians recovered all the territory lost in 1973 and a token amount of territory, including the deserted town of Quneitra, lost in 1967.

Resumption of relations with the U.S. in 1974 moderated Syria's tone, but not the goals of its policy toward Israel. Syria initiated a resolution declaring the Palestine Liberation Organization to be the sole representative of the Palestinian people, a measure that was adopted by the U.N. General Assembly in October 1974 and became the vehicle for legitimizing the insurgent organization. As Israeli-Egyptian peace negotiations continued, Syria's hostility toward Egypt increased.

Syrian troops, in Lebanon since 1976 as part of an Arab peacekeeping force whose other members subsequently departed, intervened increasingly during 1980 and 1981 on the side of Moslem Lebanese in their clashes with Christian militants supported by Israel. When Israeli jets shot down Syrian helicopters operating in Lebanon in April 1981, Syria moved Soviet-built surface-to-air (SAM 6) missiles into Lebanon's Bekaa Valley. Israel demanded that the missiles be removed because they violated a 1976 understanding between the governments. The demand, backed up by bombing raids, prompted the Reagan Administration to send veteran diplomat Philip C. Habib as a special envoy to avert a new conflict between the nations.

Habib's carefully engineered cease-fire was shattered by a new Israeli invasion in June 1982, when Israeli aircraft bombed Bekaa Valley missile sites, claiming to destroy all of them along with 25 Syrian planes that had sought to defend the sites. On the ground, Syrian army units were driven back by Israeli armor along the Lebanese coast. The Syrians, who were equipped with Soviet weapons, were outfought everywhere by U.S.-equipped Israelis. The Israeli army gained control of all key points in Lebanon.

At the request of the Lebanese Cabinet, a joint U.S.-French-Italian peacekeeping force was established. Syria refused to withdraw its troops from Lebanon. The multi-national peacekeeping force left in early 1984, leaving Israeli forces still occupying Southern Lebanon and Syrian troops still in the Bekaa Valley.

TANZANIA

United Republic of Tanzania
President: Julius K. Nyerere (1964)
Prime Minister: Edward Moringe Sokoine (1983)
Area: 364,900 sq mi. (945,087 sq km)[1]
Population (est. 1983): 20,524,000 (average annual growth rate: 3.2%)
Density per square mile: 52.4
Capital and largest city (est. 1980): Dar es Salaam, 900,-000
Monetary unit: Tanzanian shilling
Languages: Swahili, Bantu, Arabic, English
Religions: Christian, 44%; Islam, 33%; Animist, 23%
Member of Commonwealth of Nations
Literacy rate (1981): 61%
Economic summary: Gross national product (1980): $4.8 billion. Average annual growth rate (1970–79): 0.8%. Per capita income (1980): $260. Land used for agriculture: 60%; labor force: 90%; Principal products: sugar, maize, rice, wheat, cotton, coffee, sisal, cashew nuts, tea, tobacco, pyrethrum, cloves. Major industrial products: textiles, light manufactures, refined oil, processed agricultural products, diamonds, cement, fertilizer. Natural resources: hydroelectric potential, unexploited iron and coal, natural gas. Exports: coffee, cotton, sisal, diamonds, cloves, cashew nuts. Imports: manufactured goods, textiles, machinery and transport equipment, crude oil, foodstuffs. Major trading partners: U.K., China, India, Hong Kong, West Germany, U.S., Japan.

1. Including Zanzibar.

Geography. Tanzania is in East Africa on the Indian Ocean. To the north are Uganda and Kenya; to the west, Burundi, Rwanda, and Zaire; and to the south, Mozambique, Zambia, and Malawi. Its area is three times that of New Mexico.

Tanzania contains three of Africa's best-known lakes—Victoria in the north, Tanganyika in the west, and Nyasa in the south. Mount Kilimanjaro in the north, 19,340 feet (5,895 m), is the highest point on the continent.

Government. Under the republican form of government, Tanzania has a President elected by universal suffrage who appoints the Cabinet ministers. The 218-member National Assembly is composed of 96 elected members from the mainland, 10 members appointed by the President (from both Tanganyika and Zanzibar), 35 national members (elected by the National Assembly after nomination by various national institutions), 32 members of the Zanzibar Revolutionary Council, 20 other Zanzibar members appointed by the President in agreement with the President of Zanzibar, and up to 20 other Zanzibar members appointed by the President in agreement with the first Vice President, who represents Zanzibar.

The Tanganyika African National Union, the only authorized party on the mainland, and the Afro-Shirazi Party, the only party in Zanzibar and Pemba, merged in 1977 as the Revolutionary Party (Chama Cha Mapinduzi) and elected Julius K. Nyerere as its head.

History. Arab traders first began to colonize the area in A.D. 700. Portuguese explorers reached the coastal regions in 1500 and held some control until the 17th century, when the Sultan of Oman took power. With what are now Burundi and Rwanda, Tanganyika became the colony of German East Africa in 1885. After World War I, it was administered by Britain under a League of Nations mandate and later as a U.N. trust territory.

Although not mentioned in old histories until the 12th century, Zanzibar was believed always to have had connections with southern Arabia. The Portuguese made it one of their tributaries in 1503 and later established a trading post, but they were driven out by Arabs from Oman in 1698. Zanzibar was declared independent of Oman in 1861 and, in 1890, it became a British protectorate.

Tanganyika became independent on Dec. 9, 1961; Zanzibar, on Dec. 10, 1963. On April 26, 1964, the two nations merged into the United Republic of Tanganyika and Zanzibar. The name was changed to Tanzania six months later.

In 1975, the 1,163-mile (1,872 km) Tanzam railway linking the Tanzanian port of Dar es Salaam with Zambia was officially opened. Built and financed by China, the railway provided a direct route for Zambian copper exports to the sea, replacing a longer route through white-ruled Rhodesia to Mozambique.

In 1977, Tanzania closed its border with Kenya because of a dispute over the operation of East African Airways, an entity of the East African Community. The breakup of the airline left the East African Posts and Telecommunications Corporation as the only community agency still functioning.

An invasion by Ugandan troops in November 1978 was followed by a counterattack in January 1979, in which 5,000 Tanzanian troops were joined by 3,000 Ugandan exiles opposed to President Idi Amin. Within a month, full-scale war developed and the Tanzania/exile force pushed north and captured Kampala on April 11.

Nyerere kept troops in Uganda in open support of former Ugandan President Milton Obote, despite protests from opposition groups, until the national elections in December 1980. Although Obote asked that the Tanzanians remain after his victory in order to control guerrilla resistance, Nyerere ordered their withdrawal in May 1981, citing the $1-million-a-month drain on his precarious finances.

THAILAND

Kingdom of Thailand
Ruler: King Bhumibol Adulyadej (1946)
Prime Minister: Gen. Prem Tinsulanonda (1980)
Area: 198,455 sq mi. (514,000 sq km)
Population (est. 1983): 49,500,000 (average annual growth rate: 2.1%) (incl. 2.5 million of Chinese descent born in Thailand)
Density per square mile: 249.4
Capital and largest city (est. 1983): Bangkok, 5,018,300
Monetary unit: Baht
Languages: Thai (Siamese), Chinese, English
Religions: Buddhist, 95%; Islam, 4%
National name: Muang Thai
Literacy rate (1981): 82%
Economic summary: Gross national product (1983): $39.2 billion. Average annual growth rate (1979–83): 5.6%. Per capita income (1983): $791. Land used for agriculture: 71%; labor force; 78%; principal products: rice, rubber, corn, tapioca, sugar, pineapples. Labor force in industry: 7%; major products: processed food, textiles, wood, cement, tin, tungsten. Natural resources: fish, natural gas, forests, fluorite, tin, tungsten. Exports: rice, tapioca, sugar, rubber, tin, textiles. Imports: machinery and transport equipment, fertilizer, crude oil, fuels and lubricants, base metals, chemicals. Major trading partners: Japan, U.S., Singapore, West Germany, Netherlands, U.K., Hong Kong.

Geography. Thailand occupies the western half of the Indochinese peninsula and the northern two thirds of the Malay peninsula in southeast Asia. Its neighbors are Burma on the north and west, Laos on the east, and Cambodia and Malaysia on the south. Thailand is about three fourths the size of Texas.

Most of the population is supported in the fertile central alluvial plain, which is drained by the Chao Phnaya River and its tributaries.

Government. King Bhumibol Adulyadej, who was born Dec. 5, 1927, second son of Prince Mahidol of Songkhla, succeeded to the throne on June 9, 1946, when his brother, King Ananda Mahidol, died of a gunshot wound. He was married on April 28, 1950, to Queen Sirikit; their son, Vajiralongkorn, born July 28, 1952, is the Crown Prince.

After three years of civilian government ended with a military coup on Oct. 6, 1976, Thailand reverted to military rule. Political parties, banned after the coup, gained limited freedom in 1980. The same year, the National Assembly elected Gen. Prem Tinsulanonda as prime minister. A general election on April 18, 1983, resulted in a new coalition government being formed, with Prem continuing as prime minister.

History. The Thais first began moving down into their present homeland from the Asiatic continent in the 6th century A.D. and by the end of the 13th century ruled most of the western portion. During the next 400 years, the Thais fought sporadically with the Cambodians and the Burmese. The British obtained recognition of paramount interest in Thailand in 1824, and in 1896 an Anglo-French accord guaranteed the independence of Thailand.

A coup in 1932 changed the absolute monarchy into a representative government with universal suffrage. After five hours of token resistance on Dec. 8, 1941, Thailand yielded to Japanese occupation and became one of the springboards in World War II for the Japanese campaign against Malaya.

After the fall of its pro-Japanese puppet government in July 1944, Thailand pursued a policy of passive resistance against the Japanese, and after the Japanese surrender, Thailand repudiated the declaration of war it had been forced to make against Britain and the U.S. in 1942. By a treaty signed with Britain and India in 1946, Thailand renounced all wartime acquisitions of Malayan territory.

Thailand's major problem in the late 1960s was suppressing guerrilla action by Communist invaders in the north.

Although Thailand had received $2 billion in U.S. economic and military aid since 1950 and had sent troops (paid by the U.S.) to Vietnam while permitting U.S. bomber bases on its territory, the collapse of South Vietnam and Cambodia in the spring of 1975 brought rapid changes in the country's diplomatic posture.

At the Thai government's insistence, the U.S. agreed to withdraw all 23,000 U.S. military personnel remaining in Thailand by March 1976. Diplomatic relations with China were established in 1975. Meanwhile, overtures toward an accommodation with the new regime in South Vietnam were initiated.

Thailand protested vigorously when 1,100 U.S. Marines were airlifted to Thai bases May 14, 1975, for use in the rescue of the crew of the cargo ship Mayaguez after its seizure by a Cambodian gunboat. The marines were withdrawn the next day, and Thailand later accepted a U.S. apology for unauthorized use of its territory.

In 1973, when Field Marshal Thanom Kittikachorn resigned under the pressure of massive student demonstrations, Thailand returned to a civilian government and in 1975 had its first general elections. Premier Seni Pramoj, was ousted in 1976 by Admiral Sa-Ngad Chaloryu and the National Administrative Reform Council after rioting by leftist students. The junta appointed Thanin Kraivichien, a supreme court justice, as premier and appointed a 340-member National Assembly, 110 of them military officers.

As insurgent activity increased and skirmishes along the Cambodian border continued despite Thai efforts to make peace with the Communist regime in Phnom Penh, the military, in 1977, ousted Thanin as "weak," replacing him with Gen. Kriangsak Chamanan. Chamanan resigned in 1980. The National Assembly elected Gen. Prem Tinsulanonda to succeed him.

Refugees from Laos, Cambodia, and Vietnam flooded into Thailand in 1978 and 1979, and despite efforts by the United States and other Western countries to resettle them, a total of 130,000 Laotian and Vietnamese refugees were living in camps along the Cambodian border in mid-1980. A drive by Vietnamese occupation forces on western Cambodian areas loyal to the Pol Pot government, culminating in invasions of Thai territory in late June, drove an estimated 100,000 Cambodians across the line as refugees, adding to the 200,000 of their countrymen already in Thailand. The total of 430,000 were being fed by United Nations and church relief organizations but the Thai government complained of the burden of their presence.

The Vietnamese incursions, notwithstanding Hanoi's claim that the troops were only seeking guerrillas hidden in the refugee camps, prompted a Thai appeal to Washington for military aid. In July, 35 reconditioned tanks and other weapons were flown to Thailand, and the Carter administration pledged its help in the event of a larger attack.

On April 3, 1981, a military coup against the Prem government failed. King Bhumibol Adulyadej took refuge outside Bangkok with Prem and his cabinet and the rebels found neither public nor sufficient military support.

TOGO

Republic of Togo
President: Gen. Gnassingbé Eyadema (1967)
Area: 21,925 sq mi. (56,785 sq km)
Population (est. 1982): 2,800,000 (average annual growth rate: 3.0%)
Density per square mile: 128.1
Capital and largest city (est. 1982): Lomé, 285,000
Monetary unit: Franc CFA
Languages: Ewé, Mina (south), Kabyé, Cotocoli (north), French (official), and many dialects
Religions: Animist, 46%; Christian, 37%; Islam, 17%
National name: République Togolaise
Literacy rate: Not known
Economic summary: Gross national product (1980): $1.0 billion. Average annual growth rate (1970–79): 1.2%. Per capita income (1980): $410. Land used for agriculture: 15%; labor force: 90%; principal products: yams, manioc, millet, sorghum, cocoa, coffee, rice, cotton. Labor force in industry: 22%; major products: phosphate, textiles. Natural resources: marble, iron, manganese, phosphate, limestone. Exports: phosphate, cocoa, coffee. Imports: consumer goods, fuels, machinery, foodstuffs. Major trading partners: France, U.K., West Germany, Netherlands.

Geography. Togo, twice the size of Maryland, is on the south coast of West Africa bordering on Ghana to the west, Upper Volta to the north and Benin to the east.

The Gulf of Guinea coastline, only 32 miles long (51 km), is low and sandy. The only port is at Lomé. The Togo hills traverse the central section.

Government. The government of Nicolas Grunitzky was overthrown in a bloodless coup on Jan. 13, 1967, led by Lt. Col. Etienne Eyadema (now Gen. Gnassingbé Eyadema). A National Reconciliation Committee was set up to rule the country. In April, however, Eyadema dissolved the Committee and took over as President. In December 1979, a 67-member National Assembly was voted in by national referendum. The Assembly of the Togolese People is the only political party.

History. Brazilians were the first traders to settle in Togo. Established as a German colony (Togoland) in 1884, the area was split between the British and the French as League of Nations mandates after World War I and subsequently administered as U. N. trusteeships. The British portion voted for incorporation with Ghana.

Togo became independent on April 27, 1960. Sylvanus Olympio, its first President, was assassinated in 1963 and succeeded by Nicolas Grunitzky.

TONGA

Kingdom of Tonga
Sovereign: King Taufa'ahau Tupou IV (1965)
Prime Minister: Prince Fatafehi Tu'ipelehake (1965)
Area: 290 sq mi. (751 sq km)
Population (est. 1982): 100,000 (average annual growth rate: 2.1%)
Density per square mile: 370.4
Capital (est. 1981): Nuku'alofa, 20,000
Monetary unit: Pa'anga
Languages: Tongan, English
Religions: Free Wesleyan, 47%; Roman Catholic, 16%; Free Church of Tonga, 14%; Mormon, 9%; Church of Tonga, 9%
Member of Commonwealth of Nations
Literacy rate (1981): 95%
Economic summary: Gross national product (1980): $50 million. Average annual growth rate (1970–78): 1.2%. Per Capita Income (1980): $520. Land used for agriculture: 80%; labor force: 75%; principal products: yams, taro, papaya, pineapples, coconuts, tobacco, peanuts, bananas, copra. Major industrial products: copra, desiccated coconut. Natural resources: fish, timber. Exports: copra, coconut products, bananas. Imports: manufactures, foodstuffs, machinery, petroleum. Major trading partners: New Zealand, Australia, Netherlands, Norway.

Geography. Situated east of the Fiji Islands in the South Pacific, Tonga (also called the Friendly Islands) consists of some 150 islands, of which 36 are inhabited.

Most of the islands contain active volcanic craters; others are coral atolls.

Government. Tonga is a constitutional monarchy. Executive authority is vested in the Sovereign, a Privy Council, and a Cabinet headed by the Prime Minister. Legislative authority is vested in the Legislative Assembly.

History. The present dynasty of Tonga was founded in 1831 by Taufa'ahau Tupou, who took the name George I. He consolidated the kingdom by conquest and in 1875 granted a Constitution.

In 1900, his great-grandson, George II, signed a treaty of friendship with Britain, and the country became a British protected state. The treaty was revised in 1959.

Queen Salote Tupou reigned from 1918 to 1964 and was succeeded by her son, who became King Taufa'ahau Tupou IV.

Tonga became independent on June 4, 1970.

TRANSKEI

See South Africa

TRINIDAD AND TOBAGO

Republic of Trinidad and Tobago
President: Ellis Clarke (1976)
Prime Minister: George M. Chambers (1981)
Area: 1,980 sq mi. (5,128 sq km)
Population (est. 1982): 1,200,000 (average annual growth rate: 1.5%) (black, 43%; East Indian, 40%; mixed, 14%)
Density per square mile: 606.1
Capital and largest city (est. 1981): Port-of-Spain, 125,000
Monetary unit: Trinidad and Tobago dollar
Languages: English (official); Hindi, French, Spanish
Religions: Christian, 64%; Hindu, 25%; Islam, 6%
Member of Commonwealth of Nations
Literacy rate (1981): 95%
Economic summary: Gross national product (1981): $6.1 billion. Average annual growth rate (1970–79): 4.5%. Per capita income (1980): $4,370. Land used for agriculture: 26%; labor force: 13%; principal products: sugar cane, cocoa, coffee, rice, bananas. Labor force in industry: 33%; major products: petroleum, processed food, cement; tourism. Natural resources: petroleum. Exports: petroleum, ammonia, fertilizer. Imports: crude oil, foodstuffs, machinery and equipment. Major trading partners: U.S., U.K., Saudi Arabia, Japan.

Geography. Trinidad and Tobago lies in the Caribbean Sea off the northeast coast of Venezuela. The area of the two islands is slightly less than that of Delaware.

Trinidad, the larger, is mainly flat and rolling, with mountains in the north that reach a height of 3,085 feet (940 m) at Mount Aripo. Tobago is heavily forested with hardwood trees.

Government. The legislature consists of a 24-member Senate and a 36-member House of Representatives.

The major political parties are the People's National Movement, led by Prime Minister George M. Chambers (26 seats in the House of Representatives); United Labor Front (8 seats), led by Basdeo Panday; Democratic Action Congress (2 seats).

History. Trinidad was discovered by Columbus in 1498 and remained in Spanish possession, despite raids by other European nations, until it capitulated to the British in 1797 during a war between Britain and Spain.

Trinidad was ceded to Britain in 1802, and in 1899 it was united with Tobago as a colony. From 1958 to 1962, Trinidad and Tobago was a part of the West Indies Federation, and on Aug, 31, 1962, it became independent.

On Aug. 1, 1976, Trinidad and Tobago cut its ties with Britain and became a republic, remaining within the Commonwealth and recognizing Queen Elizabeth II only as head of that organization.

TUNISIA

Republic of Tunisia
President: Habib Bourguiba (1957)
Premier: Mohamed Mzali (1980)
Area: 63,379 sq mi. (164,152 sq km)
Population (est. 1982); 6,650,000 (average annual growth rate: 2.7%)
Density per square mile: 104.9
Capital and largest city (est. 1981): Tunis, 1,000,000

Monetary unit: Tunisian dinar
Languages: Arabic, French
Religions: Predominantly Islam; Roman Catholic, Jewish, Greek Orthodox
National name: Al-Joumhouria Attunsia
Literacy rate (1981): 50%
Economic summary: Gross national product (1980): $8.3 billion. Average annual growth rate (1973–83): 3.7%. Per capital income (1983): $1,320. Land used for agriculture: 28%; labor force: 40%; principal products: wheat, olives, citrus fruits, grapes, dates. Labor force in industry: 21%; major products: crude oil, olive oil, textiles, and leather, chemical fertilizers, petroleum. Natural resources: oil, phosphates, iron ore, lead, zinc. Exports: petroleum, phosphates, textiles. Imports: machinery and equipment, consumer goods, foodstuffs. Major trading partners: France, West Germany, Italy, Greece.

Geography. Tunisia, at the northernmost bulge of Africa, thrusts out toward Sicily to mark the division between the eastern and western Mediterranean Sea. Twice the size of South Carolina, it is bordered on the west by Algeria and by Libya on the south.

Coastal plains on the east rise to a north-south escarpment which slopes gently to the west. Saharan in the south, Tunisia is more mountainous in the north, where the Atlas range continues from Algeria.

Government. Executive power is vested by the Constitution in the president, elected for five years and eligible for re-election to two additional terms. Legislative power is vested in a National Assembly elected by universal suffrage.

In 1975, the National Assembly amended the Constitution to make Habib Bourguiba president for life. At 71, Bourguiba was re-elected to a fourth five-year term when he ran unopposed in 1974. There are four political parties, the Socialist Destourian, led by Bourguiba, the Social Democratic Movement, the Popular Unity Movement and the Communist Party.

History. Tunisia was settled by the Phoenicians and Carthaginians in ancient times. Except for an interval of Vandal conquest in A.D. 439–533, it was part of the Roman Empire until the Arab conquest of 648–69. It was ruled by various Arab and Berber dynasties until the Turks took it in 1570–74. French troops occupied the country in 1881, and the Bey signed a treaty acknowledging a French protectorate.

Nationalist agitation forced France to grant internal autonomy to Tunisia in 1955 and to recognize Tunisian independence and sovereignty in 1956. The Constituent Assembly deposed the Bey on July 25, 1957, declared Tunisia a republic, and elected Habib Bourguiba as president.

Bourguiba maintained a pro-Western foreign policy that earned him enemies. Tunisia refused to break relations with the U.S. during the Israeli-Arab war in June 1967, and it cracked down on anti-U.S. demonstrators.

Tunisia ended its traditionally neutral role in the Arab world when it joined with the majority of Arab League members to condemn Egypt for concluding a peace treaty with Israel. The Tunisian capital was offered as the temporary headquarters of the League, following the expulsion of Egypt. At the League's first sesion in Tunis on June 28, 1979, Tunisian Minister of Information Chedli Klibi was elected Secretary-General to replace Mahmoud Riad of Egypt, who resigned.

TURKEY

Republic of Turkey
President: Gen. Kenan Evren (1982)
Prime Minister: Turgut Özal (1983)
Area: 300,947 sq mi. (incl. 9,121 in Europe) (779,452 sq km)
Population (est. 1983): 47,250,000 (average annual growth rate: 2.2%)
Density per square mile: 157.0
Capital: Ankara
Largest cities (1980 census): Istanbul, 2,990,680; Ankara, 2,561,765; Izmir, 1,049,000; Adana, 834,050; Bursa, 657,500; Gaziantep, 510,650
Monetary unit: Turkish Lira
Language: Turkish
Religion: Islam
National name: Türkiye Cumhuriyeti
Literacy rate (1981): 72%
Economic summary: Gross national product (1980): $66.1 billion. Average annual growth rate (1970–79): 3.5%. Per capita income (1980): $1,460. Land used for agriculture: 35%; labor force: 60%; principal products: cotton, tobacco, cereals, sugar beets, fruits, nuts. Labor force in industry: 16%; major products: textiles, processed foods, steel, petroleum. Natural resources: coal, chromite, copper, boron, oil. Exports: cotton, tobacco, fruits, nuts, livestock products, textiles. Imports: crude oil, machinery, transport equipment, metals, mineral fuels, fertilizer, chemicals, crude oil. Major trading partners: Iran, West Germany, Iraq, France, Italy, U.S.S.R., U.S.

Geography. Turkey is at the northeastern end of the Mediterranean Sea in southeast Europe and southwest Asia. To the north is the Black Sea and to the west the Aegean Sea. Its neighbors are Greece and Bulgaria to the west, the U.S.S.R. to the north, Iran to the east, and Syria and Iraq to the south. Overall, it is more than twice the size of Montana.

The Dardanelles, the Sea of Marmara, and the Bosporus divide the country.

Turkey in Europe comprises an area about equal to the state of Massachusetts. It is hilly country drained by the Maritsa River and its tributaries.

Turkey in Asia, or Anatolia, about the size of Texas, is roughly a rectangle in shape with its short sides on the east and west. Its center is a treeless plateau rimmed by mountains.

Government. The President is elected by the Grand National Assembly for a seven-year term and is not eligible for re-election.

In a military coup on Sept. 11, 1980, led by Gen. Kenan Evren, the Army Chief of Staff, Premier Süleyman Demirel was ousted, the Grand National Assembly dissolved and the Constitution suspended. Demirel, former Premier Bülent Ecevit, and some 100 legislators and political figures were detained. Martial law was declared and all political parties were dissolved.

Following the adoption of a new Constitution in 1982, parliamentary elections were held in 1983. Prime Minister Turgut Özal's Motherland Party came to power with a 211-seat majority in the 400-

seat Grand National Assembly. In local elections in 1984, the Motherland Party also won a majority of municipal posts with about 42% of the total vote.

History. The Ottoman Turks first appeared in the early 13th century in Anatolia, subjugating Turkish and Mongol bands pressing against the eastern borders of Byzantium. They gradually spread through the Near East and Balkans, capturing Constantinople in 1453 and storming the gates of Vienna two centuries later. At its height, the Ottoman Empire stretched from the Persian Gulf to western Algeria.

Defeat of the Turkish navy at Lepanto by the Holy League in 1571 and failure of the siege of Vienna heralded the decline of Turkish power. By the 18th century, Russia was seeking to establish itself as the protector of Christians in Turkey's Balkan territories. Russian ambitions were checked by Britain and France in the Crimean War (1854–56), but the Russo-Turkish War (1877–78) gave Bulgaria virtual independence and Romania and Serbia liberation from their nominal allegiance to the Sultan.

Turkish weakness stimulated a revolt of young liberals known as the Young Turks in 1909. They forced Sultan Abdul Hamid to grant a constitution and install a liberal government. Reforms were no barrier to further defeats, however, in a war with Italy (1911–12) and the Balkan Wars (1912–13). Under the influence of German military advisors, Turkey signed a secret alliance with Germany on Aug. 2, 1914, that led to a declaration of war by the Allied powers and the ultimate humiliation of the occupation of Turkish territory by Greek and other Allied troops.

In 1919, the new Nationalist movement, headed by Mustafa Kemal, was organized to resist the Allied occupation and, in 1920, a National Assembly elected him President of both the Assembly and the government. Under his leadership, the Greeks were driven out of Smyrna, and other Allied forces were withdrawn.

The present Turkish boundaries (with the exception of Alexandretta, ceded to Turkey by France in 1939) were fixed by the Treaty of Lausanne (1923) and later negotiations. The caliphate and sultanate were separated, and the sultanate was abolished in 1922. On Oct. 29, 1923, Turkey formally became a republic, with Mustafa Kemal, who took the name Kemal Atatürk, as its first President. The caliphate was abolished in 1924, and Atatürk proceeded to carry out an extensive program of reform, modernization, and industrialization.

Gen. Ismet Inönü was elected to succeed Atatürk in 1938 and was re-elected in 1939, 1943, and 1946. Defeated in 1950, he was succeeded by Celâl Bayar. In 1939, a mutual assistance pact was concluded with Britain and France. Neutral during most of World War II Turkey, on Feb. 23, 1945, declared war on Germany and Japan, but took no active part in the conflict.

Turkey became a full member of NATO in 1952.

In 1971, the Turkish military demanded the ouster of Süleyman Demirel, Premier since 1965, who was replaced by Nihat Erim. He pushed through a law that forbade growing of opium poppies after 1972.

After Bülent Ecevit, a liberal, became Premier in 1974, the government required bulk-harvesting of all poppies and consignment of dried "poppy hay" to legal refineries abroad, maintaining that the method would prevent farmers from diverting raw opium to illicit channels. The system was continued after Demirel took over the government in 1975.

Turkey invaded Cyprus by sea and air July 20, 1974, following the failure of diplomatic efforts to resolve the crisis caused by the ouster of Archbishop Makarios.

Talks in Geneva involving Greece, Turkey, Britain, and Greek Cypriot and Turkish Cypriot leaders brokers down in mid-August. Turkey unilaterally announced a cease-fire August 16, after having gained control of 40% of the island. Turkish Cypriots established their own state in the north on Feb. 13, 1975.

U.S.-Turkish relations, excellent for a generation, were seriously damaged when Congress voted to end arms sales to Turkey in 1975 because arms the U.S. had supplied for mutual defense had been used in the invasion of Cyprus. Congress maintained the ban despite warnings from President Ford that it would imperil the future of 20 U.S. air and intelligence bases in Turkey and could affect Turkey's role as NATO's anchor in the Eastern Mediterranean.

In July 1975, after a 30-day warning, Turkey took over control of all the installations except the big joint defense base at Incirlik, which it reserved for "NATO tasks alone." Some 7,000 U.S. military men remained on duty under Turkish orders, but relations between Ankara and Washington hit a 30-year low. In August 1978, the Carter administration won a reluctant Congressional reversal of the arms embargo.

Economic problems and civil disturbances plagued the government in 1979, and a $1.45-billion aid package organized by the U.S. and Western European nations—conditioned on economic reforms—was advanced to help Turkey finance imports. Meanwhile, the Soviet Union agreed to build an atomic power plant for Turkey and supply fuel for it, the first such agreement with a NATO member. Moscow also increased its oil shipments to Turkey.

After conservative gains in the elections of Oct. 14, 1979, Ecevit resigned and Demirel returned to power at the head of a minority government. Strikes and terrorism, stimulated by continuing inflation and rising unemployment, brought Turkey to the brink of anarchy in 1980.

The establishment of military government in September 1980 brought greater internal stability and some improvement in the economy. The military regime was criticized, however, for suppression of human rights.

A Constituent Assembly, consisting of the six-member National Security Council and members appointed by them, drafted a new Constitution that was approved by an overwhelming (91.5%) majority of the voters in a Nov. 6, 1982, referendum. Prime Minister Turgut Özal's Motherland Party came to power in parliamentary elections held in late 1983.

TUVALU

Sovereign: Queen Elizabeth II
Governor-General: Sir Fiatau Penitala Teo (1978)
Prime Minister: Tomasi Puapua (1981)
Area: 10 sq mi. (26 sq km)
Population (est. 1982): 7,000 (average annual growth rate: 1.4%)
Density per square mile: 700.0
Capital and largest city (est. 1981): Funafuti, 2,500
Monetary unit: Australian dollar

Languages: Samoan and Gilbertese
Member of the Commonwealth of Nations
Literacy rate (1981): 50%
Economic summary: Gross national product (1980): $4 million. Per Capita Income (1980): $570. Principal agricultural products: copra and coconuts. Export: copra. Imports: food and mineral fuels. Major trading partners: Australia, U.K.

Geography. Formerly the Ellice Islands, Tuvalu consists of nine small islands scattered over 500,000 square miles of the western Pacific, just south of the equator.

Government. Official executive power is vested in a Governor-General, representing the Queen, who is appointed by her on the recommendation of the Tuvalu government. Actual executive power lies with a Prime Minister, who is responsible to a House of Assembly composed of eight elected members.

History. The Ellice Islands became a British protectorate in 1892 and were annexed by Britain in 1915–16 as part of the Gilbert and Ellice Islands Colony. The Ellice Islands were separated in 1975, given home rule, and renamed Tuvalu. Full independence was granted on Sept. 30, 1978.

UGANDA

Republic of Uganda
President: Milton Obote (1980)
Prime Minister: Otema Alimadi (1980)
Area: 91,343 sq mi. (236,880 sq km)
Population (est. 1982): 14,000,000 (average annual growth rate: 3.2%)
Density per square mile: 153.6
Capital and largest city (est. 1980): Kampala, 500,000
Monetary unit: Ugandan shilling
Languages: English (official), Swahili, Luganda, Ateso, Luo
Religions: Christian, 63%; Islam, 6%
Member of Commonwealth of Nations
Literacy rate (1981): 40%
Economic summary: Gross national product (1980): $3.8 billion. Average annual growth rate (1970–79): −3.5%. Per capita income (1980): $280. Land used for agriculture: 21%; labor force: 90%; principal products: coffee, tea, cotton, tobacco, sugar, fish. Labor force in industry: 3%; major products: processed agricultural products, copper, cement, shoes, fertilizer, sheet iron, beverages. Natural resources: copper, sugar, skins and hides. Exports: coffee, cotton, tea. Imports: petroleum products, machinery, transport equipment, metals, food. Major trading partners: U.S., U.K., Kenya.

Geography. Uganda, twice the size of Pennsylvania, is in the east central Africa. It is bordered on the west by Zaire, on the north by the Sudan, on the east by Kenya, and on the south by Tanzania and Rwanda.

The country, which lies across the Equator, is divided into three main areas—swampy lowlands, a fertile plateau with wooded hills, and a desert region. Lake Victoria forms part of the southern border.

Government. Executive power is held by the President, chosen for a five-year term by the party winning a majority in parliamentary elections. Legislative power is held by the National Assembly. Major parties are the Uganda People's Congress, led by Dr. A. M. Obote; the Democratic Party; and the Uganda Patriotic Movement.

History. Uganda was first visited by European explorers as well as Arab traders in 1844. An Anglo-German agreement of 1890 declared it to be in the British sphere of influence in Africa, and the Imperial British East Africa Company was chartered to develop the area. The company did not prosper financially, and in 1894 a British protectorate was proclaimed.

Uganda became independent on Oct. 9, 1962.

As its first president, the country chose Mutesa II, King of the ancient kingdom of Buganda. Dr. Milton Obote had been Prime Minister. In 1965, he suspended the Constitution and assumed the powers of the government, later abolishing the offices of President and Vice President.

Obote in 1970 passed laws declaring that 40,000 British Asians—Asian-born persons, mostly Indian, who lived in Uganda but chose British citizenship in 1962 rather than Ugandan—needed a variety of passes and permits to remain in the country. In 1971, Idi Amin, an unpredictable army sergeant, ousted Obote and made himself President. The next year, he began expelling the Asians. He also expelled Israeli advisors rather than pay Israel's military aid bill and applauded Hitler's treatment of Jews.

With his country's potentially rich agricultural economy in turmoil, partly because of large purchases of weapons for its 20,000-man army, Amin nationalized all land in 1975, without compensation to former owners.

In 1976, Amin had himself proclaimed President for Life by the Defense Council, which replaced the Council of Ministers as Uganda's ruling body.

An Israeli commando raid against Entebbe airport on July 4, 1976, freed 103 hostages in a hijacked French airliner that had been held at the airport for a week by Palestinian guerrillas. Hostages, and the government of Israel, charged that Amin had collaborated with the hijackers.

The world condemned Amin's atrocities—Amnesty International reported in 1977 that 300,000 may have died under his rule, including Cabinet ministers and church leaders. Few African leaders denounced him, however, until President Julius K. Nyerere of Tanzania launched an invasion in November 1978, with the tacit acquiescence of most of Africa. Libya's chief, Muammar el-Qaddafi, came to Amin's defense with troops and arms, but the Libyans only temporarily halted the invaders. Kampala was taken on April 11, 1979, and Amin fled to Libya.

A brief interim government in which Yusufe Lule and Godfrey Binaisa served as President in rapid succession ended when a Military Commission, headed by Paulo Muwanga, took power on May 12, 1980. Elections on Dec. 10–11, the first in 18 years, restored constitutional government.

UNION OF SOVIET SOCIALIST REPUBLICS

See Soviet Union

UNITED ARAB EMIRATES

Head of State: Sheik Zayed Bin Sultan Al-Nahayan (1971)
Prime Minister: Sheik Rashid Bin Said al-Maktoum (1979)
Area: 32,000 sq mi. (82,880 sq km)

Population (est. 1982): 800,000 (Arab, 42%; South Asian, 50%) (average annual growth rate: 11.3%)
Density per square mile: 25.0
Capital and largest city (est. 1981): Abu Dhabi, 225,000
Monetary unit: Dirham
Language: Arabic
Religion: Islam
Literacy rate (1975): 25% (est.)
Economic summary: Gross national product (1980): $26.9 billion. Average annual growth rate (1970–79): 2.4%. Per capita income (1980): $30,070. Land used for agriculture: 8%; labor force: 10%; principal products: vegetables, meats, dates, tobacco, fruit. Labor force in industry: 65%; major products: fish, light manufactures, petroleum, construction materials. Natural resources: oil. Exports: petroleum, pearls, fish. Imports: consumer goods, food. Major trading partners: U.K., Japan, U.S., India.

Geography. The United Arab Emirates, in the eastern part of the Arabian Peninsula, extends along part of the Gulf of Oman and the southern coast of the Persian Gulf. The nation is the size of Maine. Its neighbors are Saudi Arabia in the west and south, Qatar in the north, and Oman in the east. Most of the land is barren and sandy.

Government. The United Arab Emirates was formed in 1971 by seven emirates known as the Trucial States—Abu Dhabi (the largest), Dubai, Sharjah, Ajman, Fujairah, Ras al Khaimah and Umm al-Qaiwain.

The loose federation allows joint policies in foreign relations, defense, and development, with each member state keeping its internal local system of government headed by its own ruler. A 40-member legislature consists of eight seats each for Abu Dhabi and Dubai, six seats each for Ras al Khaimah and Sharjah, and four each for the others. It is a member of the Arab League.

History. Originally the area was inhabited by a seafaring people who were converted to Islam in the seventh century. Later, a dissident sect, the Carmathians, established a powerful sheikdom, and its army conquered Mecca. After the sheikdom disintegrated, its people became pirates.

Threatening the sultanate of Muscat and Oman early in the 19th century, the pirates provoked the intervention of the British, who in 1820 enforced a partial truce and in 1853 a permanent truce. Thus what had been called the Pirate Coast was renamed the Trucial Coast.

UNITED KINGDOM

United Kingdom of Great Britain and Northern Ireland

Sovereign: Queen Elizabeth II (1952)
Prime Minister: Margaret Thatcher (1979)
Area: 94,247 sq mi. (244,100 sq km)
Population (est. mid-1982): 56,340,000 (average annual growth rate: 0.1%) (English, Scottish, Welsh, Northern Irish)
Density per square mile: 598
Capital: London, England
Largest cities (est. mid-1982): Greater London, 6,765,100; Birmingham, 1,017,300; Glasgow, 761,000; Leeds, 716,100; Sheffield, 545,800; Liverpool, 510,700; Bradford 464,700; Manchester, 458,600; Edinburgh, 444,700; Bristol, 399,600
Monetary unit: Pound sterling (£)
Languages: English, Welsh, Gaelic
Religions: Church of England (established church); Church of Wales (disestablished); Church of Scotland (established church—Presbyterian); Church of Ireland (disestablished); Roman Catholic; Methodist; Congregational; Baptist; Jewish
Literacy rate (1983): 99%
Economic summary: Gross national product (1982): $348.8 billion. Average annual growth rate (1980–82): 1%. Per capita income (1982): $6,191. Land used for agriculture: 75%, principal products: cereals, livestock, and livestock products. Major industrial products: steel, heavy engineering and metal manufactures, textiles, motor vehicles and aircraft, electronics, chemicals. Natural resources: coal, oil, gas. Exports: machinery, transport equipment, chemicals, petroleum, foodstuffs. Imports: foodstuffs, petroleum, machinery, chemicals, crude materials. Major trading partners: Western European nations, U.S., West Germany, France.

Geography. The United Kingdom, consisting of England, Wales, Scotland, and Northern Ireland, is twice the size of New York State. England, in the southeast part of the British Isles, is separated from Scotland on the north by the granite Cheviot Hills; from them the Pennine chain of uplands extends south through the center of England, reaching its highest point in the Lake District in the northwest. To the west along the border of Wales—a land of steep hills and valleys—are the Cambrian Mountains, while the Cotswolds, a range of hills in Gloucestershire, extend into the surrounding shires.

The remainder of England is plain land, though not necessarily flat, with the rocky sand-topped moors in the southwest, the rolling downs in the south and southeast, and the reclaimed marshes of the low-lying fens in the east central districts.

Scotland is divided into three physical regions—the Highlands, the Central Lowlands, containing two-thirds of the population, and the Southern Uplands. The western Highland coast is intersected throughout by long, narrow sea-lochs, or fiords. Scotland also includes the Outer and Inner Hebrides and other islands off the west coast and the Orkney and Shetland Islands off the north coast.

Wales is generally hilly; the Snowdon range in the northern part culminates in Mount Snowdon (3,560 ft, 1,085 m), highest in both England and Wales.

Important rivers flowing into the North Sea are the Thames, Humber, Tees, and Tyne. In the west are the Severn and Wye, which empty into the Bristol Channel and are navigable, as are the Mersey and Ribble.

Government. The United Kingdom is a constitutional monarchy, with a Queen and a Parliament that has two houses: the House of Lords with about 830 hereditary peers, 26 spiritual peers, about 270 life peers and peeresses, and 9 law-lords, who are hereditary, or life, peers, and the House of Commons, which since 1974 has had 635 popularly elected members. Supreme legislative power is vested in Parliament, which sits for five years unless sooner dissolved.

The executive power of the Crown is exercised by the Cabinet, headed by the Prime Minister. The latter, normally the head of the party commanding a majority in the House of Commons, is appointed by the Sovereign, with whose consent he or she in turn appoints the rest of the Cabinet. All ministers must be members of one or the other house of Parliament; they are individually and collectively re-

Area and Population of United Kingdom

Subdivision	Area sq mi	Area sq km	Population (est. mid-1982)
England and Wales	58,381	151,207	49,607,000
Scotland	30,414	78,772	5,166,000
Northern Ireland	5,452	14,121	1,567,000
Total	**94,247**	**244,100**	**56,340,000**

sponsible to the Crown and Parliament. The Cabinet proposes bills and arranges the business of Parliament, but it depends entirely on the votes in the House of Commons. The Lords cannot hold up "money" bills, but they can delay other bills for a maximum of one year.

By the Act of Union (1707), the Scottish Parliament was assimilated with that of England, and Scotland is now represented in Commons by 71 members. The Secretary of State for Scotland, a member of the Cabinet, is responsible for the administration of Scottish affairs.

The major political parties are the Conservative Party (397 of the 650 seats in the House of Commons), led by Prime Minister Margaret Thatcher; Labor Party (209 seats), led by Michael Foote; Social Democrats (6 seats), led by Roy Jenkins; Liberal Party (17 seats), led by David Steel; Ulster Unionists and other Northern Irish parties (17 seats); Scottish Nationalist Party (2 seats); Welsh Nationalist Party (2 seats). The Speaker and three deputies do not normally vote.

Ruler: Queen Elizabeth II, born April 21, 1926, elder daughter of King George VI and Queen Elizabeth, succeeded to the throne on the death of her father on Feb. 6, 1952; married Nov. 20, 1947, to Prince Philip, Duke of Edinburgh, born June 10, 1921; their children are Prince Charles[1] (heir presumptive), born Nov. 14, 1948; Princess Anne, born Aug. 15, 1950; Prince Andrew, born Feb. 19, 1960; and Prince Edward, born March 10, 1964. The Queen's sister is Princess Margaret, born Aug. 21, 1930. Prince William Arthur Philip Louis, son of the Prince and Princess of Wales and second in line to the throne, was born June 21, 1982. A second son, Prince Henry Charles Albert David, was born Sept. 15, 1984, and is third in line.

History. Roman invasions of the 1st century B.C. brought Britain into contact with the Continent. When the Roman legions withdrew in the 5th century A.D., Britain fell easy prey to the invading hordes of Angles, Saxons, and Jutes from Scandinavia and the Low Countries. Seven large kingdoms were established, and the original Britons were forced into Wales and Scotland. It was not until the 11th century that the country finally became united under the Danish King Canute. Following the death of Edward the Confessor (1066), a dispute about the succession arose, and William, Duke of Normandy, invaded England, defeating Saxon King, Harold II, at the Battle of Hastings (1066). The Norman conquest introduced Norman law and feudalism.

1. The title Prince of Wales, which is not inherited, was conferred on Prince Charles by his mother on July 26, 1958. The investiture ceremony took place on July 1, 1969. The previous Prince of Wales was Prince Edward Albert, who held the title from 1911 to 1936 before he became Edward VIII.

The reign of Henry II (1154–89), first of the Plantagenets, saw an increasing centralization of royal power at the expense of the nobles, but in 1215 John (1199–1216) was forced to sign the Magna Carta, which awarded the people, especially the nobles, certain basic rights. Edward I (1272–1307) continued the conquest of Ireland, reduced Wales to subjection and made some gains in Scotland. In 1314, however, English forces led by Edward II were ousted from Scotland after the Battle of Bannockburn. The late 13th and early 14th centuries saw the development of a separate House of Commons with tax-raising powers.

Edward III's claim to the throne of France led to the Hundred Years' War (1338–1453) and the loss of almost all the large English territory in France. In England, the great poverty and discontent caused by the war were intensified by the Black Death, a plague that reduced the population by about one third. The Wars of the Roses (1455–85), a struggle for the throne between the House of York and the House of Lancaster, ended in the victory of Henry Tudor (Henry VII) at Bosworth Field (1485).

During the reign of Henry VIII (1509–47), the Church in England asserted its independence from the Roman Catholic Church. Under Edward VI and Mary, the two extremes of religious fanaticism were reached, and it remained for Henry's daughter, Elizabeth I (1558–1603), to set up the Church of England on a moderate basis. In 1588, the Spanish Armada, a fleet sent out by Catholic King Philip II of Spain, was defeated by the English and destroyed during a storm. During Elizabeth's reign, England became a world power.

Elizabeth's heir was a Stuart—James VI of Scotland—who joined the two crowns as James I (1603–25). The Stuart kings incurred large debts and were forced either to depend on Parliament for taxes or to raise money by illegal means. In 1642, war broke out between Charles I and a large segment of the Parliament; Charles was defeated and executed in 1649, and the monarchy was then abolished. After the death in 1658 of Oliver Cromwell, the Lord Protector, the Puritan Commonwealth fell to pieces and Charles II was placed on the throne in 1660. The struggle between the King and Parliament continued, but Charles II knew when to compromise. His brother, James II (1685–88), possessed none of his ability and was ousted by the Revolution of 1688, which confirmed the primacy of Parliament. James's daughter, Mary, and her husband, William of Orange, were now the rulers.

Queen Anne's reign (1702–14) was marked by the Duke of Marlborough's victories over France at Blenheim, Oudenarde, and Malplaquet in the War of the Spanish Succession. England and Scotland meanwhile were joined by the Act of Union (1707). Upon the death of Anne, the distant claims of the elector of Hanover were recognized, and he became King of Great Britain and Ireland as George I.

The unwillingness of the Hanoverian kings to rule resulted in the formation by the royal ministers of a Cabinet, headed by a Prime Minister, which directed all public business. Abroad, the constant wars with France expanded the British Empire all over the globe, particularly in North America and India. This imperial growth was checked by the revolt of the American colonies (1775–81).

Struggles with France broke out again in 1793 and, during the Napoleonic Wars, which ended at

Rulers of England and Great Britain

Name	Born	Ruled[1]
SAXONS[2]		
Egbert[3]	c.775	828–839
Ethelwulf	?	839–858
Ethelbald	?	858–860
Ethelbert	?	860–866
Ethelred I	?	866–871
Alfred the Great	849	871–899
Edward the Elder	c.870	899–924
Athelstan	895	924–939
Edmund I the Deed-doer	921	939–946
Edred	c.925	946–955
Edwy the Fair	c.943	955–959
Edgar the Peaceful	943	959–975
Edward the Martyr	c.962	975–979
Ethelred II the Unready	968	979–1016
Edmund II Ironside	c.993	1016–1016
DANES		
Canute	995	1016–1035
Harold I Harefoot	c.1016	1035–1040
Hardecanute	c.1018	1040–1042
SAXONS		
Edward the Confessor	c.1004	1042–1066
Harold II	c.1020	1066–1066
HOUSE OF NORMANDY		
William I the Conqueror	1027	1066–1087
William II Rufus	c.1056	1087–1100
Henry I Beauclerc	1068	1100–1135
Stephen of Blois	c.1100	1135–1154
HOUSE OF PLANTAGENET		
Henry II	1133	1154–1189
Richard I Coeur de Lion	1157	1189–1199
John Lackland	1167	1199–1216
Henry III	1207	1216–1272
Edward I Longshanks	1239	1272–1307
Edward II	1284	1307–1327
Edward III	1312	1327–1377
Richard II	1367	1377–1399[4]
HOUSE OF LANCASTER		
Henry IV Bolingbroke	1367	1399–1413
Henry V	1387	1413–1422
Henry VI	1421	1422–1461[5]
HOUSE OF YORK		
Edward IV	1442	1461–1483[5]
Edward V	1470	1483–1483
Richard III	1452	1483–1485
HOUSE OF TUDOR		
Henry VII	1457	1485–1509
Henry VIII	1491	1509–1547
Edward VI	1537	1547–1553
Jane (Lady Jane Grey)[6]	1537	1553–1553
Mary I ("Bloody Mary")	1516	1553–1558
Elizabeth I	1533	1558–1603
HOUSE OF STUART		
James I[7]	1566	1603–1625
Charles I	1600	1625–1649
COMMONWEALTH		
Council of State	—	1649–1653
Oliver Cromwell[8]	1599	1653–1658
Richard Cromwell[8]	1626	1658–1659[9]
RESTORATION OF HOUSE OF STUART		
Charles II	1630	1660–1685
James II	1633	1685–1688[10]
William III[11]	1650	1689–1702
Mary II[11]	1662	1689–1694
Anne	1665	1702–1714
HOUSE OF HANOVER		
George I	1660	1714–1727
George II	1683	1727–1760
George III	1738	1760–1820
George IV	1762	1820–1830
William IV	1765	1830–1837
Victoria	1819	1837–1901
HOUSE OF SAXE-COBURG[12]		
Edward VII	1841	1901–1910
HOUSE OF WINDSOR[12]		
George V	1865	1910–1936
Edward VIII	1894	1936–1936[13]
George VI	1895	1936–1952
Elizabeth II	1926	1952–

1. Year of end of rule is also that of death, unless otherwise indicated. 2. Dates for Saxon kings are still subject of controversy. 3. Became King of West Saxons in 802; considered (from 828) first King of all England. 4. Died 1400. 5. Henry VI reigned again briefly 1470–71. 6. Nominal Queen for 9 days; not counted as Queen by some authorities. She was beheaded in 1554. 7. Ruled in Scotland as James VI (1567–1625). 8. Lord Protector. 9. Died 1712. 10. Died 1701. 11. Joint rulers (1689–1694). 12. Name changed from Saxe-Coburg to Windsor in 1917. 13. Was known after his abdication as the Duke of Windsor, died 1972.

Waterloo in (1815).

The Victorian era, named after Queen Victoria (1837–1901), saw the growth of a democratic system of government that had begun with the Reform Bill of 1832. The two important wars in Victoria's reign were the Crimean War against Russia (1853–56) and the Boer War (1899–1902), the latter enormously extending Britain's influence in Africa.

Increasing uneasiness at home and abroad marked the reign of Edward VII (1901–10). Within four years after the accession of George V in 1910, Britain entered World War I when Germany invaded Belgium. The nation was led by coalition Cabinets, headed first by Herbert Asquith and then, starting in 1916, by the Welsh statesman David Lloyd George. Postwar labor unrest culminated in the general strike of 1926.

King Edward VIII succeeded to the throne on Jan. 20, 1936, at his father's death, but abdicated on Dec. 11, 1936 (in order to marry an American divorcee, Wallis Warfield Simpson) in favor of his brother, who became George VI.

The efforts of Prime Minister Neville Chamberlain to stem the rising threat of Nazism in Germany failed with the German invasion of Poland on Sept. 1, 1939, which was followed by Britain's entry into World War II on September 3. Allied reverses in the spring of 1940 led to Chamberlain's resignation and the formation of another coalition war Cabinet by the Conservative leader, Winston Churchill,

British Prime Ministers Since 1770

Name	Term
Lord North (Tory)	1770–1782
Marquis of Rockingham (Whig)	1782–1782
Earl of Shelburne (Whig)	1782–1783
Duke of Portland (Coalition)	1783–1783
William Pitt, the Younger (Tory)	1783–1801
Henry Addington (Tory)	1801–1804
William Pitt, the Younger (Tory)	1804–1806
Baron Grenville (Whig)	1806–1807
Duke of Portland (Tory)	1807–1809
Spencer Perceval (Tory)	1809–1812
Earl of Liverpool (Tory)	1812–1827
George Canning (Tory)	1827–1827
Viscount Goderich (Tory)	1827–1828
Duke of Wellington (Tory)	1828–1830
Earl Grey (Whig)	1830–1834
Viscount Melbourne (Whig)	1834–1834
Sir Robert Peel (Tory)	1834–1835
Viscount Melbourne (Whig)	1835–1841
Sir Robert Peel (Tory)	1841–1846
Earl Russell (Whig)	1846–1852
Earl of Derby (Tory)	1852–1852
Earl of Aberdeen (Coalition)	1852–1855
Viscount Palmerston (Liberal)	1855–1858
Earl of Derby (Conservative)	1858–1859
Viscount Palmerston (Liberal)	1859–1865
Earl Russell (Liberal)	1865–1866
Earl of Derby (Conservative)	1866–1868
Benjamin Disraeli (Conservative)	1868–1868
William E. Gladstone (Liberal)	1868–1874
Benjamin Disraeli (Conservative)	1874–1880
William E. Gladstone (Liberal)	1880–1885
Marquis of Salisbury (Conservative)	1885–1886
William E. Gladstone (Liberal)	1886–1886
Marquis of Salisbury (Conservative)	1886–1892
William E. Gladstone (Liberal)	1892–1894
Earl of Rosebery (Liberal)	1894–1895
Marquis of Salisbury (Conservative)	1895–1902
Earl Balfour (Conservative)	1902–1905
Sir H. Campbell-Bannerman (Liberal)	1905–1908
Herbert H. Asquith (Liberal)	1908–1915
Herbert H. Asquith (Coalition)	1915–1916
David Lloyd George (Coalition)	1916–1922
Andrew Bonar Law (Conservative)	1922–1923
Stanley Baldwin (Conservative)	1923–1924
James Ramsay MacDonald (Labor)	1924–1924
Stanley Baldwin (Conservative)	1924–1929
James Ramsay MacDonald (Labor)	1929–1931
James Ramsay MacDonald (Coalition)	1931–1935
Stanley Baldwin (Coalition)	1935–1937
Neville Chamberlain (Coalition)	1937–1940
Winston Churchill (Coalition)	1940–1945
Clement R. Attlee (Labor)	1945–1951
Sir Winston Churchill (Conservative)	1951–1955
Sir Anthony Eden (Conservative)	1955–1957
Harold Macmillan (Conservative)	1957–1963
Sir Alec Frederick Douglas-Home (Conservative)	1963–1964
Harold Wilson (Labor)	1964–1970
Edward Heath (Conservative)	1970–1974
Harold Wilson (Labor)	1974–1976
James Callaghan (Labor)	1976–1979
Margaret Thatcher (Conservative)	1979–

who led Britain through most of World War II. Churchill resigned shortly after V-E Day, May 7, 1945, but then formed a "caretaker" government that remained in office until after the parliamentary elections in July, which the Labor Party won overwhelmingly. The government formed by Clement R. Attlee began a moderate socialist program.

For details of World War II (1939–45), *see* Headline History.

In 1951, Churchill again became Prime Minister at the head of a Conservative government. George VI died Feb. 6, 1952, and was succeeded by his daughter Elizabeth II.

Churchill stepped down in 1955 in favor of Sir Anthony Eden, who resigned on grounds of ill health in 1957, and was succeeded by Harold Macmillan and Sir Alec Douglas-Home. In 1964, Harold Wilson led the Labor Party to victory.

Wilson, the first Labor Prime Minister in 13 years, was a skilled strategiest from the party's center who instituted no great changes domestically. His ambition for success abroad was thwarted by the French veto of Britain's bid for entry into the European Economic Community and by his own inept handling of the unilateral declaration of independence by Southern Rhodesia, the last sizable British colony.

A lagging economy brought the Conservatives back to power in 1970. Prime Minister Edward Heath won Britain's admission to the European Community, a move affirmed by 67.2% in the nation's first referendum. Heath narrowly lost a February 1974 election overshadowed by a coal strike, returning Wilson to the leadership and the first minority government since 1929.

Party elections after Wilson's announcement of his intention to retire elevated James Callaghan from the Foreign Ministry to the Prime Minister's office in 1976.

Despite economic troubles, unemployment, and continuing conflict in Northern Ireland and Rhodesia, Britons in June 1977 celebrated the Silver Jubilee of Queen Elizabeth II with genuine affection. The Queen's first grandchild, Peter Mark Andrew Phillips, son of Princess Anne, was born November 14. On May 24, 1978, the first divorce in the immediate royal family in more than 150 years took place when Princess Margaret's 18-year marriage to the Earl of Snowdon was legally ended.

Margaret Thatcher became Britain's first woman Prime Minister as the Conservatives won 339 seats for a 43-seat majority in elections on May 3, 1979. The 53-year-old, Oxford-educated daughter of a grocer campaigned for lower taxes, curbs on labor unions, and less government at home coupled with a more decisive foreign policy.

Mrs. Thatcher moved quickly to implement her domestic program but was blocked by African and U.S. resistance from granting early recognition to the Muzorewa government in Zimbabwe (Rhodesia). In September 1979, a bold initiative by her foreign minister, Lord Carrington, brought all parties in the conflict to a conference in London at which she threatened and cajoled the white minority and black factions until all agreed on a new Constitution. The successful conduct of elections in February and the transfer of sovereignty on April 18, 1980, was a political triumph for the Conservatives.

A similar gamble, with Mrs. Thatcher threatening to pull Britain out of the European Economic Community, brought a major reduction in the British contribution to the E.E.C.

Despite rising income from North Sea oil production, the economy sagged in 1980 and continued to slide in 1981 as the government pursued a harsh deflationary policy. With unemployment nearing 2.5 million, rioting broke out in London, Liverpool, Manchester, and other cities. Continuing labor unrest, including strikes by dock and coal workers, and the threat it posed to the national economy helped push the British pound to an all-time low of $1.3040 in July of 1984.

An Argentine invasion of the Falkland Islands on April 2, 1982, involved Britain in a war 8,000 miles from the home islands. Although Argentina had long claimed the Falklands, known as the Malvinas in Spanish, negotiations were in progress until a month before the invasion. The Thatcher government responded to the invasion with a 40-ship task force, which sailed from Portsmouth on April 5. U.S. efforts to settle the dispute failed and United Nations efforts collapsed as the Argentine military government ignored Security Council resolutions calling for a withdrawal of its forces.

The war came only 10 days after the Royal Navy had announced plans to cut its strength by 10,000 men—to 62,000 by 1986—and to rely more on submarines than surface ships.

When more than 11,000 Argentine troops on the Falklands surrendered on June 14, 1982, Mrs. Thatcher declared her intention to garrison the islands indefinitely, together with a naval presence. Although four ships were lost to Argentine air attack during the fighting, they were expected to be replaced.

The military victory bolstered Conservative fortunes at least temporarily, but economic problems continued for the government. Unemployment rose to a record 2.91 million in mid-June and a strike by British Railways workers paralyzed the state-owned system in July.

In the general election of June 9, 1982, Prime Minister Thatcher and her Conservative party won a landslide victory over the Laborites and other opponents. The Tories sized 140-seats in the House of Commons, giving the Labor party its worst defeat since 1922.

NORTHERN IRELAND

Status: Part of United Kingdom
Secretary of State: James Prior (1981)
Area: 5,452 sq mi. (14,121 sq km)
Population (est. mid-1982): 1,567,000
Density per square mile: 279.7
Capital and largest city (est. mid-1982): Belfast, 324,900
Monetary unit: British pound sterling
Languages: English, Gaelic
Religions: Roman Catholic, 35%; Presbyterian, 29%; Church of Ireland, 24%; Methodist, 5%

Geography. Northern Ireland comprises the counties of Antrim, Armagh, Down, Fermanagh, Londonderry, and Tyrone, which make up predominantly Protestant Ulster and form the northern part of the island of Ireland, westernmost of the British Isles. It is slightly larger than Connecticut.

Government. Northern Ireland is an integral part of the United Kingdom (it has 12 representatives in the British House of Commons), but under the terms of the government of Ireland Act in 1920, it had a semiautonomous government. But in 1972, after three years of internal strife which resulted in over 400 dead and thousands injured, Britain suspended the Ulster parliament. The Ulster counties became governed directly from London after an attempt to return certain powers to an elected Assembly in Belfast.

The Northern Ireland Assembly was dissolved in 1975 and a Constitutional Convention was elected to write a Constitution acceptable to Protestants and Catholics. The convention failed to reach agreement and closed down the next year.

The major political parties are the United Ulster Unionist Coalition (Protestant) (46 of 78 delegates to the Constitutional Convention); Social Democratic Labor Party (Catholic) (17 delegates); Alliance Party (8 delegates); New Unionist Party of Northern Ireland (Protestant) (5 delegates).

History. Ulster was part of Catholic Ireland until the reign of Elizabeth I (1558–1603) when, after crushing three Irish rebellions, the crown confiscated lands in Ireland and settled in Ulster the Scot Presbyterians who became rooted there. Another rebellion in 1641–51, crushed as brutally by Oliver Cromwell, resulted in the settlement of Anglican Englishmen in Ulster. Subsequent political policy favoring Protestants and disadvantaging Catholics encouraged further settlement in Northern Ireland.

But the North did not separate from the South until William Gladstone presented in 1886 his proposal for home rule in Ireland as a means of settling the Irish Question. The Protestants in the North, although they had grievances like the Catholics in the South, feared domination by the Catholic majority. Industry, moreover, was concentrated in the north and dependent on the British market.

When World War I began, civil war threatened between the regions. Northern Ireland, however, did not become a political entity until the six counties accepted the Home Rule Bill of 1920. This set up a semiautonomous Parliament in Belfast and a Crown-appointed Governor advised by a Cabinet of the Prime Minister and eight ministers, as well as a 12-member representation in the House of Commons in London.

As the Republic of Ireland gained its sovereignty, relations improved between North and South, although the Irish Republican Army, outlawed in recent years, continued the struggle to end the partition of Ireland. In 1966–69, communal rioting and street fighting between Protestants and Catholics occurred in Londonderry, fomented by extremist nationalist Protestants, who feared the Catholics might attain a local majority, and by Catholics demonstrating for civil rights.

Rioting, terrorism, and sniping killed more than 2,200 people from 1969 through 1984 and the religious communities, Catholic and Protestant, became hostile armed camps. British troops were brought in to separate them but themselves became a target of Catholics.

In 1973, a new British charter created a 78-member Assembly elected by proportional representation that gave more weight to Catholic strength. It created a Province Executive with committee chairmen of the Assembly heading all government departments except law enforcement, which remained under London's control. Assembly elections in 1973 produced a majority for the new Constitution that included Catholic assemblymen.

Ulster's leaders agreed in 1973 to create an 11-member Executive Body with six seats assigned to Unionists (Protestants) and four to members of Catholic parties. Unionist leader Brian Faulkner headed the Executive. Also agreed to was a Council of Ireland, with 14 seats evenly divided between Dublin and Belfast, which could act only by unanimous vote.

Although the Council lacked real authority, its creation sparked a general strike by Protestant extremists in 1974. The two-week strike caused Faulkner's resignation from the Executive and resumption of direct rule from London.

In April 1974, London instituted a new program that responded to some Catholic grievances, but assigned more British troops to cut off movement of arms and munitions to Ulster's violence-racked cities.

Violence continued unabated, with new heights reached early in 1976 when the Brtish government announced the end of special privileges for political prisoners in Northern Ireland. British Prime Minister James Callaghan visited Belfast in July and pledged that Ulster would remain part of the United Kingdom unless a clear majority wished to separate.

In October 1977, the 1976 Nobel Prize for Peace was awarded to Mairead Corrigan and Betty Williams for their campaign for peace in Northern Ireland. Intermittent violence continued, however, and on Aug. 27, 1979, an I.R.A. bomb killed Earl Mountbatten as he was sailing off southern Ireland. The death of the 79-year-old cousin of the Queen, a World War II hero and the last Viceroy of India, shocked the world. Mrs. Thatcher visited Ulster two days later and denounced terrorism. After Mountbatten's state funeral in Westminster Abbey on Sept. 5, Mrs. Thatcher met with Irish Premier John Lynch to discuss security measures against the I.R.A. Lynch urged an attack on the "root cause," the division of Ireland.

New talks aimed at a restoration of home rule in Northern Ireland began and quickly ended in January 1980. In May, Mrs. Thatcher met with the new Prime Minister of the Irish Republic, Charles Haughey, but she insisted that the future of Ulster must be decided only by its people and the British Parliament. Haughey declared that an internal solution "cannot and will not succeed."

Civil disturbances reached new heights in the summer of 1981 as Irish nationalist prisoners went on hunger strikes in Maze Prison to attain their demands for "political" status.

Ten nationalists died before the strike ended in August as families of fasters asked that they be fed. Although the government rejected any compromise, new prison rules promulgated in November permitted all prisoners to wear their own clothing and all but a handful of the I.R.A. convicts ended their five-year "blanket protest" in which they had worn blankets rather than prison-issue clothing.

In April 1982, Northern Ireland Secretary of State James Prior announced plans for reorganizing an elected assembly with proportional representation and a 70% majority in the Assembly to insure adequate representation of the Catholic minority. It was denounced by Protestant political leaders, who insisted on simple majority rule and by the Republic of Ireland, which called it "unworkable."

Dependencies of the United Kingdom

ANGUILLA

Status: Dependency
Commissioner: C.H. Godden
Area: 35 sq mi. (91 sq km)
Population (1980): 6,500
Monetary unit: East Caribbean dollar

Anguilla was originally part of the West Indies Associated States as a component of St. Kitts-Nevis-Anguilla.

In 1967, Anguilla declared its independence from the St. Kitts-Nevis-Anguilla federation. Britain however, did not recognize this action. In February 1969, Anguilla voted to cut all ties with Britain and become an independent republic. In March, Britain landed troops on the island and, on March 30, a truce was signed. In July 1971, Anguilla became a dependency of Britain and two months later Britain ordered the withdrawal of all its troops.

A new Constitution for Anguilla, effective in February 1976, provides for separate administration and a government of elected representatives. The Associated State of St. Kitts-Nevis-Anguilla ended Dec. 19, 1980.

BERMUDA

Status: Self-governing dependency
Governor: Viscount Dunrossil (1983)
Prime Minister: J. David Gibbons (1977)
Area: 20 sq mi. (52 sq km)
Population (est. 1982): 60,000 (average annual growth rate: 2.6%)
Capital (est. 1982): Hamilton, 3,000
Monetary unit: Bermuda dollar
Literacy rate (1981): 98%
Economic summary: Gross national product (1980): $660 million. Average annual growth rate (1970–79): 1.6%. Per capita income (1980): $11,050. Land used for agriculture: 8%; labor force: 1%; principal products: bananas, vegetables, citrus fruits, dairy products. Labor force in industry: 6.2%; major products: structural concrete, paints, perfumes, furniture. Natural resource: limestone. Exports: semi-tropical produce, light manufactures. Imports: foodstuffs, fuel, machinery. Major trading partners: U.S., U.K., Canada.

Bermuda is an archipelago of about 360 small islands, 580 miles (934 km) east of North Carolina. The largest is (Great) Bermuda, or Long Island. Discovered by Juan de Bermúdez, a shipwrecked Spaniard, early in the 16th century, the islands were settled in 1612 by an offshoot of the Virginia Company and became a crown colony in 1684.

In 1940, sites on the islands were leased for 99 years to the U.S. for air and navy bases. Bermuda is also the headquarters of the West Indies and Atlantic squadron of the Royal Navy.

In 1968, Bermuda was granted a new Constitution, its first Prime Minister, and autonomy, except for foreign relations, defense, and internal security.

The predominantly white United Bermuda Party has retained power in three elections against the opposition—the black-led Progressive Laborites—although Bermuda's population is 60% black. Serious rioting occurred in December 1977 after two blacks were hanged for a series of murders, including the 1973 assassination of the Governor, Sir Richard Sharples, and British troops were summoned to restore order.

BRITISH ANTARCTIC TERRITORY

Status: Dependency
High Commissioner: Rex Masterson Hunt (1980)
Area: 500,000 sq mi. (1,395,000 sq km)
Population (1976): 55

The British Antarctic Territory consists of the South Shetland Islands, South Orkney Islands, and Nearby Graham Land on the Antarctic continent, largely uninhabited. They are dependencies of the British crown colony of the Falkland Islands but received a separate administration in 1962, being governed by a British-appointed High Commissioner who is Governor of the Falklands.

BRITISH INDIAN OCEAN TERRITORY

Status: Dependency
Commissioner: W. N. Wenban-Smith
Administrator: D.H. Doble
Administrative headquarters: Victoria, Seychelles
Area: 85 sq mi, (220 sq km)

This dependency, consisting of the Chagos Archipelago and other small island groups, was formed in 1965 by agreement with Mauritius and the Seychelles. There is no permanent civilian population in the territory.

BRITISH VIRGIN ISLANDS

Status: Dependency
Governor: D. R. Barwick
Area: 59 sq mi. (153 sq km)
Population (est. 1982): 11,000
Capital (est. 1975): Road Town (on Tortola): 3,500
Monetary unit: U.S. dollar

Some 36 islands in the Caribbean Sea northeast of Puerto Rico and west of the Leeward Islands, the British Virgin Islands are economically interdependent with the U.S. Virgin Islands to the south. They were formerly part of the administration of the Leeward Islands. They received a separate administration in 1956 as a crown colony. In 1967 a new Constitution was promulgated that provided for a ministerial system of government headed by the Governor. The principal islands are Tortola, Virgin Gorda, Anegada and Jost Van Dyke.

CAYMAN ISLANDS

Status: Dependency
Governor: G. P. Lloyd
Area: 100 sq mi. (259 sq km)
Population (est. 1983): 17,000
Capital (est. 1980): Georgetown (on Grand Cayman), 7,600
Monetary unit: Cayman Islands dollar

This dependency consists of three islands—Grand Cayman (76 sq mi; 197 sq km), Cayman Brac (22 sq mi; 57 sq km), and Little Cayman (20 sq mi; 52 sq km)—situated about 180 miles (290 km) northwest of Jamaica. They were dependencies of Jamaica until 1959, when they became a unit territory within the Federation of the West Indies. In 1962, upon the dissolution of the Federation, the Cayman Islands became a British dependency.

The islands' chief export is turtle products.

CHANNEL ISLANDS

Status: Crown dependencies
Lieutenant Governor of Jersey: Gen. Sir Peter Whiteley (1980)
Lieutenant Governor of Guernsey: Sir Alexander Boswell
Area: 75 sq mi. (194 sq km)
Population (est. 1982): 130,000
Capital of Jersey: St. Helier
Capital of Guernsey: St. Peter Port
Monetary units: Guernsey pound; Jersey pound

This group of islands, lying in the English Channel off the northwest coast of France, is the only portion of the Duchy of Normandy belonging to the English Crown, to which it has been attached since the conquest of 1066. It was the only British possession occupied by Germany during World War II.

For purposes of government, the islands are divided into the Bailiwick of Jersey (45 sq mi.; 117 sq km) and the Bailiwick of Guernsey (30 sq mi.; 78 sq km), including Alderney (3 sq mi.; 7.8 sq km); Sark (2 sq mi.; 5.2 sq km), Herm, Jethou, etc. The islands are administered according to their own laws and customs by local governments. Acts of Parliament in London are not binding on the islands unless they are specifically mentioned. The Queen is represented in each Bailiwick by a Lieutenant Governor.

English is now the language in daily use, although the French patois is still spoken by some people. New legislation is drafted in English, but French has been retained for ceremonial purposes in the legislative bodies.

FALKLAND ISLANDS AND DEPENDENCIES

Status: Dependency
Civil Commissioner: Rex Masterson Hunt (1980)
Area: 4,700 sq mi. (12,173 sq km)
Population est. (1982): 2,000
Capital (est. 1978): Stanley (on East Falkland), 1,100
Monetary unit: Falkland Island pound

This sparsely inhabited dependency consists of a group of islands in the South Atlantic, about 250 miles (402 km) east of the South American mainland. The largest islands are East Falkland and West Falkland. Dependencies are South Georgia Island (1,450 sq mi.; 3,756 sq km), the South Sandwich Islands, and other islets. Three former dependencies—Graham Land, the South Shetland Islands, and the South Orkney Islands—were established as a new British dependency, the British Antarctic Territory, in 1962.

The chief industry is sheep raising and, apart from the production of wool, hides and skins, and tallow, there are no known resources. The whaling industry is carried on from South Georgia Island.

The chief export is wool.

GIBRALTAR

Status: Self-governing dependency
Governor: Admiral Sir David Williams
Chief Minister: Sir Joshua Hassan
Area: 2.25 sq mi. (5.8 sq km)
Population (est. 1982): 30,000 (average annual growth rate: 0.8%)
Monetary unit: Gibraltar pound
Literacy rate: Negligible
Economic summary: Gross national product (1980): $150 million. Average annual growth rate (1970–79): 4.6%. Exports: re-exports of tobacco, petroleum, wine. Imports: manufactured goods, fuels, foodstuffs. Major trading partners: U.K., Morocco, Portugal, Netherlands.

Gibraltar, at the south end of the Iberian Peninsula, is a rocky promonotory commanding the western entrance to the Mediterranean. Aside from its strategic importance, it is also a free port, naval base, and coaling station. It was captured by the Arabs crossing from Africa into Spain in A.D. 711. In the 15th century, it passed to the Moorish ruler of Granada and later became Spanish. It was captured by an Anglo-Dutch force in 1704 during the War of the Spanish Succession and passed to Great Britain by the Treaty of Utrecht in 1713. Most of the inhabitants of Gibraltar are of Spanish, Italian, and Maltese descent.

Spanish efforts to recover Gibraltar culminated in a referendum in 1967 in which the residents voted overwhelmingly to retain their link with Britain. Spain sealed Gibraltar's land border in 1969 and did not open communications until April 1980, after the two governments had agreed to solve their dispute in keeping with a United Nations resolution calling for restoration of the "Rock" to Spain.

HONG KONG

Status: Dependency
Governor: Sir Edward Youde (1982)
Area: 398 sq mi. (1,031 sq km)
Population (est. 1982): 5,250,000 (average annual growth rate: 2.3%)
Density per sq mi.: 13,191.0
Capital (1976 census): Victoria (Hong Kong Island), 501,700
Monetary unit: Hong Kong dollar
Literacy rate (1981): 75%
Economic summary: Gross national product (1980): $21.5 billion. Average annual growth rate (1970–79): 6.5%. Per capita income (1980): $4,210. Land used for agriculture: 14%. labor force, 3%; principal products: vegetables, rice, dairy products. Labor force in industry: 51%; major industrial products: textiles, clothing, toys, transistor radios, watches, electronic components. Exports: clothing, textiles, toys, watches, transistor radios, electronic components. Imports: raw materials, consumer goods, food. Major trading partners: U.S., U.K., Japan, West Germany, China.

The crown colony of Hong Kong comprises the island of Hong Kong (32 sq mi.; 83 sq km), Stonecutters' Island, Kowloon Peninsula, and the New Territories on the adjoining mainland. The island of Hong Kong, located at the mouth of the Pearl River about 90 miles (145 km) southeast of Canton, was ceded to the Britain in 1841.

Stonecutters' Island and Kowloon were annexed in 1860, and the New Territories, which are mainly agricultural lands, were leased from China in 1898 for 99 years. Hong Kong was attacked by Japanese troops Dec. 7, 1941, and surrendered the following Christmas. It remained under Japanese occupation until August 1945.

Possessing an excellent natural harbor, the only safe deep-sea anchorage between Shanghai and Southeast Asia, Hong Kong is the transshipment center for trade throughout southern China and the western Pacific.

The cities of Victoria and Kowloon contain the greater part of the population, which is overwhelmingly Chinese. Besides those Chinese engaged in agriculture or industry, many live in sampans or junks either in Victoria harbor or neighboring bays, supporting themselves by fishing or by performing labor on the wharves.

In 1974, Hong Kong rescinded a policy of accepting illegal immigrants from China that had, since 1968, made the crowded city a sanctuary for thousands of Chinese refugees.

ISLE OF MAN

Status: Dependency
Lieutenant Governor: Rear-Adm. Sir Nigel Cecil (1980)
Area: 227 sq mi. (588 sq km)
Population (est. 1982): 70,000
Capital (est. 1976): Douglas, 20,300
Monetary unit: Isle of Man pound

Situated in the Irish Sea, equidistant from Scotland, Ireland, and England, the Isle of Man is administered according to its own laws by a government composed of the Lieutenant Governor, a Legislative Council, and a House of Keys, one of the most ancient legislative assemblies in the world.

The chief exports are beef and lamb, fish, and livestock.

LEEWARD ISLANDS

See British Virgin Islands; Montserrat

MONTSERRAT

Status: Dependency
Governor: D. K. H. Dale
Area: 40 sq mi. (104 sq km)
Population (est. 1978): 13,500
Capital (est. 1982): Plymouth, 3,500
Monetary unit: East Caribbean dollar

The island of Montserrat is in the Lesser Antilles of the West Indies. Until 1956, it was a division of the Leeward Islands. It did not join the West Indies Associated States established in 1967.

The chief exports are cattle, potatoes, cotton, lint, recapped tires, mangoes, tomatoes.

PITCAIRN ISLAND

Status: Dependency
Governor: R. J. Stratton (1980)

Island Magistrate: Ivan Christian
Area: 1.75 sq mi. (4.5 sq km)
Population (est. 1980): 63
Capital: Adamstown

Pitcairn Island, in the South Pacific about midway between Australia and South America, consists of the island of Pitcairn and the three uninhabited islands of Henderson, Duicie, and Oeno. The island of Pitcairn was settled in 1790 by British mutineers from the ship *Bounty*, commanded by Capt. William Bligh. It was annexed as a British colony in 1838. Overpopulation forced removal of the settlement to Norfolk Island in 1856, but about 40 persons soon returned.

The colony is governed by a 10-member Council presided over by the Island Magistrate, who is elected for a three-year term.

ST. HELENA

Status: Dependency
Governor: J. D. Massingham
Area: 47 sq mi. (122 sq km)
Population (est 1983): 5,250
Capital (est. 1982): Jamestown, 1,500
Monetary unit: Pound sterling

St. Helena is a volcanic island in the South Atlantic about 1,100 miles (1,770 km) from the west coast of Africa. It is famous as the place of exile of Napoleon (1815–21).

It was taken for England in 1659 by the East India Company and was brought under the direct government of the Crown in 1834.

St. Helena has two dependencies: Ascension (34 sq mi.; 88 sq km), an island about 700 miles (1,127 km) northwest of St. Helena; and Tristan da Cunha (40 sq mi.; 104 sq km), a group of six islands about 1,500 miles (2,414 km) south-southwest of St. Helena.

TURKS AND CAICOS ISLANDS

Status: Dependency
Governor: Christopher Turner
Area: 193 sq mi. (500 sq km)
Population (est. 1983): 7,500
Capital (est. 1982): Grand Turk, 3,150
Monetary unit: U.S. dollar

These two groups of islands are situated at the southeast end of the Bahamas. The principal islands in the Turks group are Grand Turk and Salt Cay; the principal ones in the Caicos group are South Caicos, East Caicos, Middle (or Grand) Caicos, North Caicos, Providenciales, and West Caicos.

The Turks and Caicos Islands were dependencies of Jamaica until 1959, when they became a unit territory within the Federation of the West Indies. In 1962, when Jamaica became independent, the Turks and Caicos became a British crown colony. The present Constitution has been in force since 1969.

Chief exports in 1974 were crayfish (73%) and conch (25%).

VIRGIN ISLANDS

See British Virgin Islands

UNITED STATES

The United States of America
President: Ronald Reagan (1981)
Area: 3,540,939 sq mi. (9,171,032 sq km)
Population (est. Jan. 1983): 233,200,000 (average annual growth rate: 1%)
Density per sq mi.: 65.9
Capital (1982 est.): Washington, D.C., 633,425
Largest cities (1982 est.): New York, 7,086,096; Los Angeles, 3,022,247; Chicago, 2,997,155; Houston, 1,-725,617; Philadelphia, 1,665,382; Detroit, 1,138,717
Monetary unit: Dollar
Language: English
Religions: Protestant (73.5 million members); Roman Catholic (51.2 million members); Jewish (5.9 million members)
Literacy rate (1982): 99.5%
Economic summary: Gross national product (1983): $3,-310.5 million; per capita income (1982): $8,980. Labor force in agriculture: 2.7%; principal products: corn, wheat, barley, oats, sugar, potatoes, soybeans, fruits, beef, veal, pork. Labor force in non-agricultural occupations: 97.3%. Major industrial products: petroleum products, fertilizers, cement, pig iron and steel, plastics and resins, newsprint, motor vehicles, machinery, natural gas, electricity. Natural resources: coal, oil, water power, copper, gold, silver, minerals, timber. Exports: machinery, chemicals, aircrafts, military equipment, cereals, motor vehicles, grains. Imports: crude and partly refined petroleum, machinery, automobiles. Major trading partners: Canada, Japan, United Kingdom, West Germany, Mexico, Saudi Arabia, Nigeria.

Government. The president is elected for a four-year term and may be re-elected only once. In 1983, the bicameral Congress consisted of the 100-member Senate (45 Democrats, 55 Republicans) and the 435-member House of Representatives (266 Democrats, 168 Republicans, 1 vacancy) which is elected every two years. The minimum voting age is 18.

UPPER VOLTA

Bourkina Fasso
President of National Council of the Revolution: Capt. Thomas Sankara (1983)
Area: 105,870 sq mi. (274,200 sq km)
Population (est. 1982): 7,170,000 (average annual growth rate, 0.6%)
Density per square mile: 67.7
Capital and largest city (est. 1980): Ouagadougou, 235,-000
Monetary unit: Franc CFA
Ethnic groups: Mossis, Bobos
Languages: French, African languages
Religions: Animist, 50%; Islam, 17%; Roman Catholic, 8%
National name: Bourkina Fasso
Literacy rate (1981): 10%
Economic summary: Gross national product (1980): $1.1 billion. Average annual growth rate (1970–79): —1.2%. Per capita income (1980): $190. Labor force in agriculture: 95%; principal products: millet, sorghum, corn, rice, livestock, peanuts, sugar cane, cotton. Major industrial products: processed agricultural products, light industrial items, brick, brewed products. Natural resources: manganese, limestone, marble, gold, uranium, bauxite, copper. Exports: livestock, peanuts, cotton. Imports: textiles, food and consumer goods, transport equipment, machinery, fuels. Major trading partners: Ivory Coast, France, Ghana, Western European nations.

Togo, and Ghana. The country consists of extensive plains, low hills, high savannas, and a desert area in the north.

Government. Upper Volta has been governed by a series of military leaders since a coup in November 1980 overthrew the last elected president. All political parties were banned and the political process suspended following the coup.

History. Upper Volta consists chiefly of the lands of the Mossi Empire, where France established a protectorate over the Kingdom of Ouagadougou in 1897. Upper Volta became a separate colony in 1919, was partitioned among Niger, the Sudan, and the Ivory Coast in 1933 and was reconstituted in 1947. An autonomous republic within the French Community, it became independent on Aug. 5, 1960.

President Maurice Yameogo was deposed on Jan. 3, 1966, by a military coup led by Col. Sangoulé Lamizana, who dissolved the National Assembly and suspended the Constitution. A new Constitution was adopted later that year and a new Assembly was elected. However, dissension within the Volta Democratic Union, the major party, led to renewed military rule. Constitutional rule returned in 1978 with the election of an Assembly and a presidential vote in June in which Gen. Lamizana won by a narrow margin over three other candidates.

On Nov. 25, 1980, there was a bloodless coup which placed Gen. Lamizana under house arrest. Col. Sayé Zerbo took charge as the President of the Military Committee of Reform for National Progress. Maj. Jean-Baptiste Ouedraogo toppled Zerbo in another coup on Nov. 7, 1982. Captain Thomas Sankara, in turn, deposed Ouedraogo a year later. His government changed the country's name on Aug. 3, 1984, to Bourkina Fasso (the "land of upright men") to sever ties with its colonial past.

URUGUAY

Oriental Republic of Uruguay
President: Gen. Gregorio Alvarez (1981)
Area: 72,172 sq mi. (186,926 sq km)
Population (est. 1982): 2,950,000 (average annual growth rate: 0.6%)
Density per square mile: 43.0
Capital and largest city (est. 1982): Montevideo, 1,325,000
Monetary unit: New peso
Language: Spanish
Religion: Roman Catholic, 60%
National name: Republica Oriental del Uruguay
Literacy rate (1981): 90%
Economic summary: Gross national product (1980): $8.2 billion. Average annual growth rate (1970–79): 2.9%. Per capita income (1980): $2,820. Land used for agriculture: 85%; labor force: 20%; principal products: livestock, grains. Labor force in industry: 29%; major products: processed meats, wool and hides, textiles, shoes, handbags and leather wearing apparel, cement, refined petroleum. Natural resources: hydroelectric power potential. Exports: meat, hides, wool, textiles. Imports: crude petroleum, transportation equipment, chemicals, machinery, metals. Major trading partners: U.S., Brazil, Argentina.

Geography. Uruguay, on the east coast of South America south of Brazil and east of Argentina, is comparable in size to the State of Washington.

The country consists of a low, rolling plain in the south and a low plateau in the north. It has a 120-mile (193 km) Atlantic shore line, a 235-mile (378 km) frontage on the Rio de la Plata, and 270 miles (435 km) on the Uruguay River, its western boundary.

Government. The President serves for a term of five years. He appoints a Council of 11 ministers to assist him. Before it was dissolved, Congress consisted of the Senate and the House of Deputies. Members remained in office for five years.

In June 1973, President Juan María Bordaberry yielded to military pressure and dissolved Congress, thus ending 40 years of constitutional rule. His decree announced creation of a Council of State to perform Congressional functions, oversee presidential activities, and formulate constitutional reforms for a national plebiscite.

There are two major parties: The Blancos and the Colorados, and a small conservative Union Civica. In the November 1982 poll, the Blancos received 60.5% of the vote, the Colorados 39.7%, and the Union Civica only 1.9 percent.

History. Juan Díaz de Solis, a Spaniard, discovered Uruguay in 1516, but the Portuguese were first to settle it when they founded Colonia in 1680. After a long struggle, Spain wrested the country from Portugal in 1778. Uruguay revolted against Spain in 1811, only to be conquered in 1816–20 by the Portuguese from Brazil. Independence was reasserted with Argentine help in 1825, and the republic was set up in 1830.

Independence, however, did not restore order, and a revolt in 1836 touched off nearly 50 years of factional strife, with occasional armed intervention from Argentina and Brazil.

Alberto Heber, who became President in 1966, vigorously championed reform, and a referendum authorized revision of the Constitution to vest executive powers in a President and a Cabinet of Ministers. Oscar Diego Gestido, elected President later that year, devoted much effort to improving the ailing economy. But he died the next year and was succeeded by Jorge Pacheco Areco.

Siege-state regulations were instituted after the Tupámaros first urban guerrilla organization launched a series of spectacular kidnappings, bank and casino robberies (one gold haul netted over $250,000), and arms raids on military arsenals to embarrass what was then the most democratic government in South America. In 1970, the Tupámaros kidnapped a U.S. aid adviser, Dan Mitrione, and killed him when their ransom demands were not met.

The continuing economic, political, and guerrilla problems precipitated impeachment proceedings against Pacheco in 1971. A bitterly fought election followed, with Juan María Bordaberry, Pacheco's hand-picked choice, the winner.

Disputes between the government and the military, coupled with worsening economic problems (the peso was devalued 32 times during Bordaberry's first three years in office), led to a military revolt in February 1973 that ended in an agreement with Bordaberry in which the military promised to maintain the constitutional system but virtually took over control of the government.

Military leaders, citing Bordaberry's opposition

to the return of constitutional government, removed him from office in 1976. The National Council of 25 military officers and 21 civilians designated Aparicio Méndez to take over the Presidency for a five-year term.

Although the government in 1977 reported that sentences for political prisoners would be reduced, Amnesty International estimated that 5,000 such prisoners were being held in Uruguay, more than in any other Latin nation.

In November 1980, voters rejected a draft Constitution that would have given the military permanent power. The Council designated Gen. Gregorio Alvarez, retired commander in chief of the army, as President in September 1981, and shortly afterward a promised discussion of the restoration of a civilian government foundered in a dispute between military leaders and politicians.

The eleven-year prohibition of assembly for political parties was revolved in September 1982. Parliamentary and presidential elections were promised for November 1984, but opposition leaders feared the military would put them off.

VANUATU

Republic of Vanuatu
President: George Sokomanu (1980)
Prime Minister: Rev. Walter Lini (1980)
Area: 5,700 sq mi. (14,763 sq km)
Population (est. 1982): 125,000 (average annual growth rate: 2.7%)
Density per square mile: 21.9
Capital (est. 1982): Vila, 17,500
Monetary unit: Vatu
Religions: Presbyterian, 37%; Roman Catholic, 15%; Anglican, 15%; other Christian, 10%
Literacy rate (1981): 15%
Economic Summary: Gross national product (1980): $60 million. Per Capita Income (1980): $530. Average annual growth rate (1970–78): 1.9%. Principal agricultural products: copra, cocoa, coffee, livestock. Exports: copra, cocoa, coffee, frozen fish. Imports: food. Major trading partners: France, U.S., Japan.

Geography. Formerly known as the New Hebrides, Vanuatu is an archipelago of some 80 islands lying between New Caledonia and Fiji in the South Pacific. Largest of the islands is Espiritu Santo (875 sq mi.; 2,266 sq km); others are Efate, Malekula, Malo, Pentecost, and Tanna. The population is largely Melanesian of mixed blood.

Government. The constitution by which Vanuatu achieved independence on July 30, 1980, vests executive authority in a President, elected by an electoral college for a five-year term. A unicameral legislature of 39 members exercises legislative power. The Vanuaaku party, led by Prime Minister Walter Lini, holds 26 seats.

History. The islands were discovered by Pedro Fernandes de Queiros of Portugal in 1606 and were charted and named by the British navigator James Cook in 1774. Conflicting British and French interests were resolved by a joint naval commission that administered the islands from 1887. A condominium government was established in 1906.

The islands' plantation economy, based on imported Vietnamese labor, was prosperous until the 1920s, when markets for its products declined. The New Hebrides escaped Japanese occupation in World War II and the French population was among the first to support the Gaullist Free French movement.

A brief rebellion by French settlers and plantation workers on Espiritu Santo led by Jimmy Stevens in May 1980 threatened the scheduled independence of the islands. Britain sent a company of Royal Marines and France a contingent of 50 policemen to quell the revolt, which the new government said was financed by the Phoenix Foundation, a right-wing U.S. group. With the British and French forces replaced by soldiers from Papua New Guinea, independence ceremonies took place on July 30. The next month it was reported that Stevens had been arrested and the revolt quelled.

VATICAN CITY STATE

Ruler: Pope John Paul II (1978)
Area: 0.17 sq mi. (0.44 sq km)
Population (est. 1982): 1,000 (Italian, 85%; Swiss and others, 15%)
Density per square mile: 5,882.4
Monetary unit: Lira
Languages: Latin and Italian
Religion: Roman Catholic
National name: Stato della Città del Vaticano

Geography. The Vatican City State is situated on the Vatican hill, on the right bank of the Tiber River, within the commune of Rome.

Government. The Pope has full legal, executive, and judicial powers. Executive power over the area is in the hands of a Commission of Cardinals appointed by the Pope. The College of Cardinals is the Pope's chief advisory body, and upon his death the cardinals elect his successor for life. The cardinals themselves are created for life by the Pope.

In the Vatican the central administration of the Roman Catholic Church throughout the world is carried on by 11 congregations, three tribunals, three main secretariats, and numerous councils, committees, and commissions. In its diplomatic relations, the Holy See is represented by the Papal Secretary of State.

History. The Vatican City State, sovereign and independent, is the survivor of the papal states that in 1859 comprised an area of some 17,000 square miles (44,030 sq km). During the struggle for Italian unification, from 1860 to 1870, most of this area became part of Italy.

By an Italian law of May 13, 1871, the temporal power of the Pope was abrogated, and the territory of the Papacy was confined to the Vatican and Lateran palaces and the villa of Castel Gandolfo. The Popes consistently refused to recognize this arrangement and, by the Lateran Treaty of Feb. 11, 1929, between the Vatican and the Kingdom of Italy, the exclusive dominion and sovereign jurisdiction of the Holy See over the city of the Vatican was again recognized, thus restoring the Pope's temporal authority over the area.

The first session of Ecumenical Council Vatican II was opened by John XXIII on Oct. 11, 1962, to plan and set policies for the modernization of the Roman Catholic Church. Pope Paul VI continued the Council, opening the second session on Sept. 29, 1963.

On Aug. 26, 1978, Cardinal Albino Luciani was chosen by the College of Cardinals to succeed Paul VI, who had died of a heart attack on Aug. 6. The new Pope, who took the name John Paul I, was born on Oct. 17, 1912, at Forno di Canale in Italy.

(For a listing of all the Popes, *see* the Index.)

Only 34 days after his election, John Paul I died of a heart attack, ending the shortest reign in 373 years. On Oct. 16, Cardinal Karol Wojtyla, 58, was chosen Pope and took the name John Paul II. The first Polish Pope was also the first to have been named from a communist nation.

John Paul II visited his homeland in June 1979, exhorting millions to "never lose your spiritual freedom" and telling workers that Christ would not accept that man be considered "merely as a means of production." The trip was a triumph for the warm, outgoing Pontiff despite the Polish government's undisguised efforts to dampen the public impact of his visit.

A visit to the Irish Republic and to the United States in September and October 1979, followed by a 12-nation African tour in May 1980 and a visit in July to Brazil, the most populous Catholic nation, further established John Paul's image as a "people's" Pope. But he also used his travels to preach a more conservative doctrine, cautioning U.S. nuns against seeking priestly functions and sternly opposing abortion and contraception. During his African journey, he reaffirmed long-ignored canon laws against political roles for the clergy. On May 13, 1981, a Turkish terrorist shot the Pope in St. Peter's Square, the first assassination attempt against the Pontiff in modern times. Mehmet Ali Agca was sentenced on July 22 to life imprisonment by an Italian Court.

A controversial trip to Britain, the first by a reigning Pope, was almost canceled in June 1982 because of the war with Argentina over the Falkland Islands. To offset criticism in Catholic Argentina, the Pontiff also made a hastily arranged visit to Buenos Aires.

On June 16–23, the Pontiff made an eight-day visit to his native Poland. While there, he called upon the Polish government to end martial law and to seek peaceful solutions to the nation's problems.

VENEZUELA

Republic of Venezuela
President: Jaime Lusinchi (1984)
Area: 352,143 sq mi. (912,050 sq km)
Population (est. 1982): 14,700,000 (average annual growth rate: 2.8%) (mestizo, 69%; white, 20%; black, 9%; Indian, 2%)
Density per square mile: 41.7
Capital: Caracas
Largest cities (est. 1981 for metropolitan area): Caracas, 3,000,000; Maracaibo, 875,000; Valencia, 475,000; Barquisimento, 465,000
Monetary unit: Bolivar
Language: Spanish
Religion: Roman Catholic
National name: Republica de Venezuela
Literacy rate (1970): 70%
Economic summary: Gross national product (1980): $54.2 billion. Average annual growth rate (1970–79): 2.7%. Per capita income (1980): $3,630. Land used for agriculture, 4%; labor force, 24%; principal products: rice, coffee, corn, sugar, bananas, dairy, meat, and poultry products. Labor force in industry, 23%; principal products: refined petroleum products, iron and steel, paper products, aluminum, textiles, transport equipment. Natural resources: petroleum, natural gas, iron ore, gold, hydroelectric power. Exports: petroleum, iron ore, coffee. Imports: industrial machinery and equipment, manufactures, chemicals, foodstuffs. Major trading partners: U.S., Canada, West Germany, Japan.

Geography. Venezuela, a third larger than Texas, occupies most of the northern coast of South America on the Caribbean Sea. It is bordered by Colombia to the west, Guyana to the east, and Brazil to the south.

Mountain systems break Venezuela into four distinct areas: (1) the Maracaibo lowlands; (2) the mountainous region in the north and northwest; (3) the Orinoco basin, with the llanos (vast grass-covered plains) on its northern border and great forest areas in the south and southeast; (4) the Guiana Highlands, south of the Orinoco, accounting for nearly half the national territory. About 80% of Venezuela is drained by the Orinoco and its tributaries.

Government. Venezuela is a federal republic consisting of 20 states, the Federal District, two territories and 72 islands in the Caribbean. There is a bicameral Congress, the 52 members of the Senate and the 213 members of the Chamber of Deputies being elected by popular vote to five-year terms. The President is also elected for five years. He must be a Venezuelan by birth and over 30 years old. He is not eligible for re-election until 10 years after the end of his term.

The major political parties are the Democratic Action Party, with 23 of 52 Senate seats and 83 of 213 seats in the Chamber of Deputies; Social Christian Party, with 22 Senate seats and 83 Chamber seats, People's Electoral Movement, Democratic Republican Union.

History. Columbus discovered Venezuela on his third voyage in 1498. A subsequent Spanish explorer gave the country its name, meaning "Little Venice." There were no important settlements until Caracas was founded in 1567. Simón Bolívar, who led the liberation of much of the continent from Spain, was born in Caracas in 1783. With Bolívar taking part, Venezuela was one of the first South American colonies to revolt against Spain, in 1810, but it was not until 1821 that independence was won. Federated at first with Colombia and Ecuador, the country set up a republic in 1830 and then sank for many decades into a condition of revolt, dictatorship, and corruption.

From 1908 to 1935, Gen. Juan Vicente Gómez ruled tyrannically, picking satellites to alternate with him in the presidential palace. Thereafter, there was a struggle between democratic forces and those backing a return to strong-man rule. Dr. Rómulo Betancourt and the liberal Acción Democrática Party won a majority of seats in a constituent assembly to draft a new Constitution in 1946. A well-known writer, Rómulo Gallegos, candidate of Betancourt's party, easily won the presidential election of 1947. But, the army ousted Gallegos the next year and instituted a military junta.

The country overthrew the dictatorship in 1958 and thereafter enjoyed democratic government. Rafael Caldera Rodríguez, President from 1969 to 1974, legalized the Communist Party and established diplomatic relations with Moscow.

Venezuela and neighboring Guyana in 1970 called a 12-year moratorium on their border dispute (Venezuela claims 50,000 square miles of Guyana's 83,000).

As a charter member of the Organization of Petroleum Exporting Countries (OPEC), Venezuela shared the benefits of the tripled oil prices engineered by OPEC, but did not join the 1973 Arab oil boycott. President Carlos Andrés Pérez took office in 1974, committed to give all Venezuelans a stake in the oil bonanza that made his country the richest in South America.

In 1976, Venezuela nationalized 21 oil companies, mostly subsidiaries of U.S. firms, offering compensation of $1.28 billion. Oil income in that year was $9.9 billion, and although production decreased 2.2%, revenue remained at the same level in 1977 because of higher prices, largely financing an ambitious social welfare program.

Despite his difficulties at home, Pérez continued to play an active foreign role in extending economic aid to Latin neighbors, in backing the human-rights policy of President Carter, and in supporting Carter's return of the Panama Canal to Panama.

Opposition Christian Democrats capitalized on Pérez's domestic problems to elect Luis Herrera Campíns President in Venezuela's fifth consecutive free election, on Dec. 3, 1978.

Herrera Campins at first supported U.S. policy in Central America, lining up with the majority of Latin nations behind the Christian Democratic government of José Napoleón Duarte in El Salvador, but he later shifted toward a "political solution" that would include the insurgents. In March 1982, he assailed Reagan's policy as "interventionist."

When the Falklands war broke out, Venezuela became one of the most vigorous advocates of the Argentine cause and one of the sharpest critics of the U.S. decision to back Britain.

Jaime Lusinchi of the Democratic Action party won the country's sixth consecutive free election, on Dec. 4, 1983, and was inaugurated President in March 1984.

VIETNAM

Socialist Republic of Vietnam
President: Truong Chinh (1981)
Premier: Pham Van Dong (1976)
Area: 127,246 sq mi. (329,566 sq km)
Population (est. 1982): 56,250,000 (average annual growth rate: 2.5%)
Density per square mile: 444.9
Capital: Hanoi
Largest cities (est. 1979): Ho Chi Minh City (Saigon),[1] 3,450,000; Hanoi, 2,600,000; Haiphong, 1,280,000; (est. 1973); Da Nang, 492,200; Nha Trang, 216,200; Qui Nho'n, 213,750; Hué 209,000
Monetary unit: Dong
Language: Vietnamese
Religions: Buddhist, Roman Catholic, Cao-Dai, Hoa-Hao, Confucian, Animist
National name: Công Hòa Xa Hôi Chú Nghia Viêt Nam
Literacy rate: 78%
Economic summary: Gross national product (1978): $8.9 billion. Per capita income (1980): n.a. Land used for agriculture: 14%; labor force: 70%; principal products: rice, rubber, fruits and vegetables, corn, sugar cane, fish. Labor force in industry, 8%; major products: processed foods, textiles, cement, chemical fertilizers, glass, tires. Natural resources: forests, coal, oil. Exports: agricultural products, coal, mineral ores. Imports: petroleum, steel products, railroad equipment, chemicals, medicines, raw cotton, fertilizer, grain. Major trading partners: U.S.S.R., Soviet bloc nations, Japan.

1. Includes suburb of Cholon.

Geography. Vietnam occupies the eastern and southern part of the Indochinese peninsula in Southeast Asia, with the South China Sea along its entire coast. China is to the north and Laos and Cambodia to the west. Long and narrow on a north-south axis, Vietnam is about twice the size of Arizona.

The Mekong River delta lies in the south and the Red River delta in the north. Heavily forested mountain and plateau regions make up most of the country.

Government. Less than a year after the capitulation of the former Republic of Vietnam (South Vietnam) on April 30, 1975, a joint National Assembly convened with 249 deputies representing the North and 243 representing the South. The Assembly set July 2, 1976, as the official reunification date. Hanoi became the capital, with North Vietnamese President Ton Duc Thang becoming President of the new Socialist Republic of Vietnam and North Vietnamese Premier Pham Van Dong becoming its head of government. By 1981, the National Assembly had increased to 496 members. Truong Chinh succeeded Thang in 1981.

Dang Cong san Vietnam (Communist Party), led by First Secretary Le Duan, is the ruling political party. There are also the Socialist Party and the Democratic Party.

History. The Vietnamese are descendants of Mongoloid nomads from China and migrants from Indonesia. They recognized Chinese suzerainty until the 15th century, an era of nationalistic expansion, when Cambodians were pushed out of the southern area of what is now Vietnam.

A century later, the Portuguese were the first Europeans to enter the area. France established its influence early in the 19th century and within 80 years conquered the three regions into which the country was then divided—Cochin-China in the south, Annam in the center, and Tonkin in the north.

France first unified Vietnam in 1887, when a single governor-generalship was created, followed by the first physical links between north and south—a rail and road system. Even at the beginning of World War II, however, there were internal differences among the three regions.

Japan took over military bases in Vietnam in 1940 and a pro-Vichy French administration remained until 1945. A veteran Communist leader, Ho Chi Minh, organized an independence movement known as the Vietminh to exploit a confused situation. At the end of the war, Ho's followers seized Hanoi and declared a short-lived republic, which ended with the arrival of French forces in 1946.

Paris proposed a unified government within the French Union under the former Annamite emperor, Bao Dai. Cochin-China and Annam accepted the proposal, and Bao Dai was proclaimed emperor of all Vietnam in 1949. Ho and the Vietminh withheld support, and the revolution in China gave them the outside help needed for a war of resistance against French and Vietnamese troops armed largely by the U.S.

A bitter defeat at Dien Bien Phu in northwest Vietnam on May 5, 1954, broke the French military campaign and brought the division of Vietnam at the conference of Geneva that year.

In the new South, Ngo Dinh Diem, Premier under Bao Dai, deposed the monarch in 1955 and established a republic with himself as President. Diem used strong U.S. backing to create an authoritarian regime that suppressed all opposition but could not eradicate the Northern-supplied Communist Viet Cong.

Skirmishing grew into a full-scale war, with escalating U.S. involvement. A military coup, U.S.-inspired in the view of many, ousted Diem Nov. 1, 1963, and a kaleidoscope of military governments followed. The most savage fighting of the war occurred in early 1968, during the Tet holidays.

Although the Viet Cong failed to overthrow the Saigon government, U.S. public reaction to the apparently endless war forced a limitation of U.S. troops to 550,000 and a new emphasis on shifting the burden of further combat to the South Vietnamese. Ho Chi Minh's death on Sept. 3, 1969, brought a quadrumvirate to replace him but no flagging in Northern will to fight.

U.S. bombing and invasion of Cambodia in the summer of 1970—an effort to destroy Viet Cong bases in the neighboring state—marked the end of major U.S. participation in the fighting. Most American ground troops were withdrawn from combat by mid-1971 as heavy bombing of the Ho Chi Minh trail from North Vietnam appeared to cut the supply of men and matériel to the South.

Secret negotiations for peace by Secretary of State Henry A. Kissinger with North Vietnamese officials during 1972 after heavy bombing of Hanoi and Haiphong brought the two sides near agreement in October. When the Northerners demanded the removal of the South's President Nguyen Van Thieu as their price, President Nixon ordered the "Christmas bombing" of the North. The conference resumed and a peace settlement was signed in Paris on Jan. 27, 1973. It called for release of all U.S. prisoners, withdrawal of U.S. forces, limitation of both sides' forces inside South Vietnam, and a commitment to peaceful reunification.

Despite Chinese and Soviet endorsement, the agreement foundered. U.S. bombing of Communist-held areas in Cambodia was halted by Congress in August 1973, and in the following year Communist action in South Vietnam increased.

An armored attack across the 17th parallel in January 1975 panicked the South Vietnamese army and brought the invasion within 40 miles of Saigon by April 9. Thieu resigned on April 21 and fled, to be replaced by Vice President Tran Van Huong, who quit a week later, turning over the office to Gen. Duong Van Minh. "Big Minh" surrendered Saigon on April 30, ending a war that took 1.3 million Vietnamese and 56,000 American lives, at the cost of $141 billion in U.S. aid.

"Re-education" of former South Vietnamese government and army personnel began immediately. By mid-1976, virtually all foreigners were expelled, even those married to Vietnamese.

On May 3, 1977, the U.S. and Vietnam opened negotiations in Paris to normalize relations. One of the first results was the withdrawal of U.S. opposition to Vietnamese membership in the United Nations, formalized in the Security Council on July 20. Two major issues remained to be settled, however: the return of the bodies of some 2,500 U.S. servicemen missing in the war and the claim by Hanoi that former President Nixon had promised reconstruction aid under the 1973 agreement.

Negotiations failed to resolve these issues, and the question of recognition appeared to have been shelved indefinitely when the U.S. expelled the Vietnamese Ambassador to the United Nations, Dinh Ba Thi, early in 1978. This was accused of complicity in an espionage case in which a U.S. citizen and a Vietnamese refugee were later convicted of delivering U.S. intelligence to Hanoi.

The new year also brought an intensification of border clashes between Vietnam and Cambodia and accusations by China that Chinese residents of Vietnam were being subjected to persecution. Peking cut off all aid and withdrew 800 technicians.

By June, 133,000 ethnic Chinese were reported to have fled Vietnam, and a year later as many as 500,000 of the 1.8 million Vietnamese of Chinese ancestry were believed to have escaped. Half of these had gone by land or sea to China. Tens of thousands more had survived boat passage to Thailand, Malaysia, Indonesia, or Hong Kong. U.S. officials said 100,000 may have died. Survivors said they had paid up to $5,000 in bribes to leave Vietnam, and U.S. and British officials charged Hanoi with a deliberate extortion policy.

Hanoi was undoubtedly preoccupied with a continuing war in Cambodia, where 60,000 Vietnamese troops were aiding the Heng Samrin regime in suppressing the last forces of the pro-Chinese Pol Pot regime. In early 1979, Vietnam was conducting a two-front war, defending its northern border against a Chinese invasion and at the same time supporting its army in Cambodia.

Only a Soviet veto prevented Vietnam from being labeled an aggressor by the U.N. Security Council as Prince Shihanouk of Cambodia, released from house arrest by the Pol Pot regime, presented the case against Hanoi after the fall of Phnom Penh. Vietnam's ambassador, backed by the Soviet Union and the Soviet bloc, sought condemnation of Peking's invasion but could find no sympathizers.

Despite Hanoi's claims of total victory, resistance in Cambodia continued through 1984. Vietnam's second conflict, on its border with China, also flared sporadically.

Hanoi permitted four U.S. veterans of the Indochina war to visit Vietnam in December 1981 to discuss the missing U.S. servicemen and the effects of Agent Orange, a defoliant used during the war that veterans have claimed caused permanent damage to their health.

The Hanoi government agreed in July 1984 to resume technical talks with U.S. officials on the possible whereabouts of the 2,490 Americans still listed as missing, most of them believed dead.

Economic troubles continued, with the government seeking to reschedule its $1.4-billion foreign hard-currency debt, owed mainly to Japan and the International Monetary Fund. The exodus of the Vietnamese boat people also continued, despite a growing tendency by passing ships not to help the Vietnamese fleeing their country by boat. In one incident in 1984, 68 refugees died of starvation, thirst, or disease aboard a 39-foot fishing boat that drifted in the South China Sea for 32 days, apparently ignored by at least 40 passing ships. Sixteen survivors eventually were rescued off the Philippines.

(For a Vietnam War chronology, see Headline History.)

WESTERN SAMOA

Independent State of Western Samoa
Head of State: Malietoa Tanumafili II (1962)
Prime Minister: Tofilau Et Alesana (1982)
Area: 1,093 sq mi. (2,831 sq km)
Population (est. 1982): 160,000 (average annual growth rate: 0.7%)
Density per square mile: 141.2
Capital and largest city (1980): Apia, 33,400
Monetary unit: Tala
Languages: Samoan and English
Religions: Congregational, 50%; Roman Catholic, 22%; Methodist, 16%
National name: Samoa i Sisifo
Member of Commonwealth of Nations
Literacy rate (1981): 90%
Economic summary: Gross national product (1978): $70 million. Per capita income (1978): $450. Land used for agriculture: 50%; labor force: 50%; principal products: copra, cocoa, bananas, timber. Labor force in industry: 10%; major products: timber, light industrial products. Natural resource: timber. Exports: copra, cocoa, bananas, timber. Imports: food, manufactured goods, machinery. Major trading partners: West Germany, New Zealand, Australia, Japan.

Geography. Western Samoa, the size of Rhode Island, is in the South Pacific Ocean about 2,200 miles (3,540 km) south of Hawaii midway to Sydney, Australia, and about 800 miles (1,287 km) northeast of Fiji. The larger islands in the Samoan chain are mountainous and of volcanic origin. There is little level land except in the coastal areas, where most cultivation takes place.

Government. Western Samoa has a 47-member Legislature, consisting mainly of the titleholders (chiefs) of family groups, with two members elected by universal suffrage to represent those not belonging to such groups. When the present Head of State dies, successors will be elected by the Legislature.

History. The Samoan islands were discovered in the 18th century and visited by Dutch and French traders. Toward the end of the 19th century, conflicting interests of the U.S., Britain, and Germany resulted in a treaty signed in 1899. It recognized the paramount interests of the U.S. in those islands east of 171° west longitude (American Samoa) and Germany's interests in the other islands (Western Samoa); the British withdrew in return for recognition of their rights in Tonga and the Solomons.

New Zealand occupied Western Samoa in 1914, and was granted a League of Nations mandate. In 1947, the islands became a U.N. trust territory administered by New Zealand.

Western Samoa became independent on Jan. 1, 1962.

YEMEN

People's Democratic Republic of Yemen
President: Ali Nasir Muhammad al-Hasani (1980)
Area: 111,000 sq mi. (287,490 sq km)[1]
Population (est. 1982): 2,100,000 (average annual growth rate: 2.8%)
Density per square mile: 18.9[1]
National capital and largest city (est. 1980): Aden, 343,000
Administrative capital: Madinat ash Sha'b
Monetary unit: Yemen dinar
Language: Arabic
Religion: Islam
National name: Jumhurijah al-Yemen al Dimuqratiyah al Sha'abijah
Literacy rate (1983): 25%
Economic summary: Gross national product (1980): $810 million. Average annual growth rate (1973–78): 12.7%. Per capita income (1980): $420. Land used for agriculture: 0.3%; labor force: 80%; principal products: sorghum, millet, wheat, cotton, coffee. Labor force in industry: 2–3%; major products: refined oil products, salt, fish meal, cloth. Natural resource: fish. Exports: petroleum products, textiles, cotton. Imports: crude oil, foodstuffs, manufactured goods. Major trading partners: U.K., Japan, Yemen Arab Republic.

1. Excluding Perim and Kamaran islands.

Geography. Formerly known as Southern Yemen, the People's Democratic Republic of Yemen extends along the southern part of the Arabian Peninsula on the Gulf of Aden and the Indian Ocean. It is comparable in size to Nevada. The Yemen Arab Republic is to the northwest, Saudi Arabia to the north, and Oman to the east.

A 700-mile (1,130-km) narrow coastal plain gives way to a mountainous region and then a plateau area.

Government. On June 22, 1969, President Qahtan Mohammed al Shaabi resigned and was replaced by a five-man Presidential Council.

A Constitution published in 1970 changed the state's name from Southern Yemen and established a 111-seat legislature, the People's Supreme Council of which al-Hasani is chairman, and thus head of state. The only legal political party is the Yemeni Socialist Party.

History. The People's Republic of Southern Yemen was established Nov. 30, 1967, when Britain granted independence to the Federation of South Arabia. This Federation consisted of the state (once the colony) of Aden and 16 of the 20 states of the Protectorate of South Arabia (once the Aden Protectorate). The four states of the Protectorate that did not join the Federation later became part of Southern Yemen.

Salim Robea Ali, chairman of the Presidential Council since its establishment in 1969, was ousted and executed June 26, 1978, two days after the assassination of President Ahmed Hussein al-Ghashmi of the Yemen Arab Republic. Premier Ali

Nasir Muhammad al-Husani assumed the added duty of Council head.

Abdul Fattah Ismail, Secretary General of the ruling party who was elected President by the Supreme Council on Dec. 27, 1978, reversed Robea's movement toward reconciliation with the Yemen Arab Republic and an accommodation with Saudi Arabia. Despite Fattah Ismail's acquiescence to the continuing build-up of Soviet military strength in the country in conjunction with the Soviet invasion of Afghanistan, he proved to be an embarrassment to Moscow. His sudden resignation on April 21, 1980, was reported to have stemmed from the new Soviet desire to win friends in the Yemen Arab Republic and Saudi Arabia.

YEMEN ARAB REPUBLIC

President: Col. Ali Abdullah Saleh (1978)
Premier: Abdel Karim al-Iriani (1980)
Area: 75,290 sq mi. (195,000 sq km)
Population (est. 1983): 5,744,000 (average annual growth rate: 2.7%)
Density per square mile: 113.9
Capital and largest city (est. 1982): San'a', 275,000
Monetary unit: Rial
Language: Arabic
Religion: Islam
National name: Al Jamhuriya al Arabiya Yamaniya
Literacy rate (1981): 15% (est.)
Economic summary: Gross national product (1980): $2.7 billion. Per capita income (1980): $460. Land used for agriculture: 20%; labor force: 95%; principal products: wheat, sorghum, cattle, sheep, cotton, fruits. Major industrial products: consumer goods, construction materials. Natural resources: traces of copper, sulfur, coal, quartz. Exports: cotton, coffee, hides and skins. Imports: textiles and other manufactured consumer goods, petroleum and petroleum products, sugar, grain, flour. Major trading partners: China, Yemen (Aden), U.S.S.R., Japan, U.K., Australia.

Geography. The Yemen Arab Republic, also known as North Yemen, occupies the southwestern tip of the Arabian Peninsula, with its western coast on the Red Sea opposite Ethiopia. Its neighbors are Saudi Arabia to the north and east and the People's Democratic Republic of Yemen to the south. Its area is slightly less than that of South Dakota.

A north-south coastal plain 20–50 miles wide (32–80 km) lies in the west; eastward, there are the interior highlands, which attain a height of 12,000 feet (3,660 m), and the expanse of the Rub 'al-Khali Desert.

Government. The country's first permanent Constitution was submitted to the National Assembly in 1971. It provided for a 179-member legislature, the Consultative Council, 20 of whose members would be chosen by the President and the rest elected every four years. A five-man executive Presidential Council was to be chosen by the Consultative Council.

In 1974, the army ousted the government in a bloodless coup and suspended the Constitution and its various legislative bodies.

History. The history of Yemen dates back to the Minaean kingdom (1200–650 B.C.). It accepted Islam in A.D. 628, and in the 10th century came under the control of the Rassite dynasty of the Zaidi sect. The Turks occupied the area from 1538 to 1630 and from 1849 to 1918. The sovereign status of Yemen was confirmed by treaties signed with Saudi Arabia and Britain in 1934.

Yemen joined the Arab League in 1945 and established diplomatic relations with the U.S. in 1946.

In 1962, a military revolt of elements favoring President Gamal Abdel Nasser of Egypt broke out. A ruling junta proclaimed a republic, and Yemen became an international battleground, with Egypt and the U.S.S.R. supporting the revolutionaries, and King Saud of Saudi Arabia and King Hussein of Jordan the royalists. The civil war continued until the war between the Arab states and Israel broke out in June 1967. Nasser had to pull out many of his troops and agree to a cease-fire and withdrawal of foreign forces. The war finally ended with the defeat of the royalists in mid-1969.

In 1977, Col. Ibrahim al-Hamidi was assassinated after three years as head of government and was succeeded by Lt. Col. Ahmed Hussein al-Ghashmi as head of the Presidential Council. On June 24, 1978, al-Ghashmi was killed by a bomb as he received the credentials of a new ambassador from the People's Democratic Republic of Yemen. The People's Council elected Col. Ali Abdullah Saleh as President on July 17.

In 1984, the Hunt Oil Co. of Dallas discovered oil in North Yemen, the first time it has been found in the desolate Arab state, one of the world's poorest nations. The company said it was too early to determine the size of the discovery or when production might start. Middle East analysts found news of the oil strike intriguing, partly because North Yemen lies on the Red Sea, far from the war-troubled Persian Gulf and Straits of Hormuz.

YUGOSLAVIA

Socialist Federal Republic of Yugoslavia
President: Veselin Djuronovic (1984)
President of Federal Executive Council (Premier): Milka Planinc (1980)
Area: 98,766 sq mi. (255,804 sq km)
Population (1982 census): 22,412,000 (average annual growth rate: 0.8%) (Serbian, 36%; Croatian, 18%; Moslem, 9%; Slovene, 8%; Albanian, 8%; Macedonian, 6%)
Density per square mile: 226.9
Capital: Belgrade
Largest cities (est. 1982): Belgrade, 1,250,000; Zagreb, 765,000; Skopje, 505,000; Sarajevo, 450,000; Ljubljana, 255,000; Split, 200,000
Monetary unit: Dinar
Languages: Serbo-Croatian, Slovene, Macedonian (all official)
Religions: Greek Orthodox, 41%; Roman Catholic, 32%; Islam, 12%
National name: Socijalisticka Federativna Republika Jugoslavija
Literacy rate (1961): 85%
Economic summary: Gross national product (1980): $58.6 billion. Average annual growth rate (1970–79): 5.4%. Per capita income (1980): $2,620. Land used for agriculture: 33%; labor force: 29%; principal products: corn, wheat, tobacco, sugar beets. Labor force in industry: 52%; major products: wood, processed food, nonferrous metals, machinery, textiles. Natural resources: bauxite,

timber, anitmony, chromium, lead, zinc, asbestos, mercury, cadmium. Exports: raw materials, equipment, consumer goods. Imports: raw materials, equipment, consumer goods. Major trading partners: U.S.S.R., West Germany, Italy, U.S.

Geography. Yugoslavia fronts on the eastern coast of the Adriatic Sea opposite Italy. Its neighbors are Austria, Italy, and Hungary to the north, Romania and Bulgaria to the east, and Greece and Albania to the south. It is slightly larger than Wyoming.

About half of Yugoslavia is mountainous. In the north, the Dinaric Alps rise abruptly from the sea and progress eastward as a barren limestone plateau called the Karst. Montenegro is a jumbled mass of mountains, containing also some grassy slopes and fertile river valleys. Southern Serbia, too, is mountainous. A rich plain in the north and northeast, drained by the Danube, is the most fertile area of the country.

Government. Yugoslavia is a federal republic composed of six socialist republics—Serbia (which includes the provinces of Vojvodina and Kosovo), Croatia, Slovenia, Bosnia-Herzegovina, Macedonia, and Montenegro. Actual administration is carried on by the Federal Executive Council and its secretaries.

The League of Communists and the Socialist Alliance of the Working People are the major political parties.

History. Yugoslavia was formed Dec. 1, 1918, from the patchwork of Balkan states and territories where World War I began with the assassination of Archduke Ferdinand of Austria at Sarajevo on June 28, 1914. The new Kingdom of Serbs, Croats, and Slovenes included the former kingdoms of Serbia and Montenegro; Bosnia-Herzegovina, previously administered jointly by Austria and Hungary; Croatia-Slavonia, a semi-autonomous region of Hungary, and Dalmatia, formerly administered by Austria. King Peter I of Serbia became the first monarch, his son acting as Regent until his accession as Alexander I on Aug. 16, 1921.

Croatian demands for a federal state forced Alexander to assume dictatorial powers in 1929 and to change the country's name to Yugoslavia. Serbian dominance continued despite his efforts, amid the resentment of other regions. A Macedonian associated with Croatian dissidents assassinated Alexander in Marseilles, France, on Oct. 9, 1934, and his cousin, Prince Paul, became Regent for the King's son, Prince Peter.

Paul's pro-Axis policy brought Yugoslavia to sign the Axis Pact on March 25, 1941, and opponents overthrew the government two days later. On April 6 the Nazis occupied the country, and the young King and his government fled. Two guerrilla armies—the Chetniks under Draza Mihajlovic supporting the monarchy and the Partisans under Tito (Josip Broz) leaning toward the U.S.S.R.—fought the Nazis for the duration of the war. In 1943, Tito established an Executive National Committee of Liberation to function as a provisional government.

Tito won the election held in the fall of 1945, as monarchists boycotted the vote. A new Assembly abolished the monarchy and proclaimed the Federal People's Republic of Yugoslavia, with Tito as Prime Minister.

Ruthlessly eliminating opposition, the Tito government executed Mihajlovic in 1946. With Soviet aid, Tito annexed the greater part of Italian Istria under the 1947 peace treaty with Italy but failed in his claim to the key port of Trieste. Zone B of the former free territory of Trieste went to Yugoslavia in 1954.

Tito broke with the Soviet bloc in 1948 and Yugoslavia has since followed a middle road, combining orthodox Communist control of politics and general overall economic policy with a varying degree of freedom in the arts, travel, and individual enterprise. Tito, who became President in 1953 and President for life under a revised Constitution adopted in 1963, has played a major part in the creation of a "non-aligned" group of states, the so-called "third world."

The Marshal supported his one-time Soviet mentors in their quarrel with Communist China, but even though he imprisoned the writer Mihajlo Mihajlov and other dissenters at home, he criticized Soviet repression of Czecholovakia in 1968.

Tito welcomed President Nixon to Yugoslavia in 1970 for the first U.S. Presidential visit, and he went to the U.S. the following year, but the relationship has been touchy.

Tito's death on May 4, 1980, three days before his 88th birthday, removed from the scene the last World War II leader. A rotating presidency designed to avoid internal dissension was put into effect immediately, and the feared clash of Yugoslavia's multiple nationalities and regions appeared to have been averted. A collective presidency, rotated annually among the six republics and two autonomous provinces of the federal republic, continued to govern according to a constitutional change made in 1974.

In March 1981, the Albanian minority, which forms 80 per cent of the population of the autonomous province of Kosovo, backed Albanian students demonstrating against conditions at the university. By April, the demonstrations had swelled to riots in which 11 were killed as 100,000 people demanded the status of a separate republic, which would enable Kosovo to secede from the Yugoslav federation. Unrest continued in 1982, with 1,700 ethnic Albanians arrested by midyear for "anti-Yugoslav activities."

ZAIRE

Republic of Zaire
President: Mobutu Sese Seko (1965)
Prime Minister: Joseph Nsigna (1981)
Area: 905,365 sq mi. (2,344,885 sq km)
Population (est. 1983): 31,250,000 (average annual growth rate: 29%)
Density per square mile: 31.1
Capital: Kinshasa
Largest cities (est. 1982): Kinshasa, 3,000,000; Kananga, 800,000; Lubumbashi, 525,000; Mbuji-Maji, 425,000
Monetary unit: Zaire
Languages: French; Bantu dialects, mainly Swahili, Lingala, Ishiluba, and Kikongo
Religions: Animist, 50%; Roman Catholic, Protestant, Islam
Ethnic groups: Bantu, Sudanese, Nilotics, Pygmies, Hamites
National name: République du Zaïre
Literacy rate (1981): 40%
Economic summary: Gross national product (1980): $6.0 billion. Average annual growth rate (1970–79): —2.6%. Per capita income (1980): $158. Land used for

agriculture: 2%; labor force: 70–80%; principal products: coffee, palm oil, rubber, tea, cotton, cocoa, manioc, bananas, plantains, vegetables, fruits. Major industrial products: processed and unprocessed minerals. Natural resources: copper, cobalt, zinc, industrial diamonds, manganese, tin, gold, rare metals, bauxite, iron, coal, 13% of world hydroelectric potential. Exports: copper, cobalt, diamonds, petroleum, coffee. Imports: consumer goods, foodstuffs, mining and other machinery, transport equipment. Major trading partners: Belgium, West Germany, U.S.

Geography. Zaire is situated in west central Africa and is bordered by the Congo, the Central African Empire, the Sudan, Uganda, Rwanda, Burundi, Tanzania, Zambia, Angola, and the Atlantic Ocean. It is one quarter the size of the U.S.

The principal rivers are the Ubangi and Bomu in the north and the Zaire (Congo) in the west, which flows into the Atlantic. The entire length of Lake Tanganyika lies along the eastern border with Tanzania and Burundi.

Government. Under the Constitution approved by referendum in 1967 and amended in 1974, the third Constitution since 1960, the president and a unicameral Legislature are elected by universal suffrage for five-year terms.

In 1971, the government proclaimed that the Democratic Republic of the Congo would be known as the Republic of Zaire, since the Congo River's name had been changed to the Zaire. In addition, President Joseph D. Mobutu took the name Mobutu Sese Seko and Katanga Province became Shaba.

There is only one political party: the Popular Movement of the Revolution, led by President Mobutu.

History. Formerly the Belgian Congo, this territory was inhabited by ancient Negrito peoples (Pygmies), who were pushed into the mountains by Bantu and Nilotic invaders. The American correspondent Henry M. Stanley navigated the Congo River in 1877 and opened the interior to exploration. Commissioned by King Leopold II of the Belgians, Stanley made treaties with native chiefs that enabled the King to obtain personal title to the territory at the Berlin Conference of 1885.

Criticism of forced labor under royal exploitation prompted Belgium to take over administration of the Congo, which remained a colony until agitation for independence forced Brussels to grant freedom on June 30, 1960. Moise Tshombe, Premier of the then Katanga Province seceded from the new republic on July 11, and another mining province, South Kasai, followed. Belgium sent paratroopers to quell the civil war, and with President Joseph Kasavubu and Premier Patrice Lumumba of the national government in conflict, the United Nations flew in a peacekeeping force.

Kasavubu staged an army coup in 1960 and handed Lumumba over to the Katangan forces. A U.N. investigating commission found that Lumumba had been killed by a Belgian mercenary in the presence of Tshombe. Dag Hammarskjold, U.N. Secretary-General, died in a plane crash en route to a peace conference with Tshombe on Sept. 17, 1961.

U.N. Secretary-General U Thant submitted a national reconciliation plan in 1962 that Tshombe rejected. Tshombe's troops fired on the U.N. force in December, and in the ensuing conflict Tshombe capitulated on Jan. 14, 1963. The peacekeeping force withdrew, and, in a complete about-face, Kasavubu named Tshombe Premier to fight a spreading rebellion. Tshombe used foreign mercenaries and, with the help of Belgian paratroops airlifted by U.S. planes, defeated the most serious opposition, a Communist-backed regime in the northeast.

Kasavubu abruptly dismissed Tshombe in 1965 and was himself ousted by Gen. Joseph-Desiré Mobutu, Army Chief of Staff. The new President nationalized the Union Minière, the Belgian copper mining enterprise that had been a dominant force in the Congo since colonial days. The plane carrying the exiled Tshombe was hijacked in 1967 and he was held prisoner in Algeria until his death from a heart attack was announced June 29, 1969.

Mobutu eliminated opposition to win election in 1970 to a term of seven years, which was renewed in a 1977 election. He invited U.S., South African, and Japanese investment to replace Belgian interests. In 1975, he nationalized much of the economy, barred religious instruction in schools, and decreed the adoption of African names.

In the Angolan civil war of 1975–76, Mobutu backed the National Front for the Liberation of Angola, whose leader, Holden Roberto, is related to him by marriage. The Zairean government opposed the recognition of the Soviet-backed Popular Movement for the Liberation of Angola and reluctantly accepted its victory.

On March 8, 1977, invaders from Angola calling themselves the Congolese National Liberation Front pushed into Shaba and threatened the important mining center of Kolwezi. France and Belgium responded to Mobutu's pleas for help with weapons, but the U.S. gave only nonmilitary supplies.

In April, France flew 1,500 Moroccan troops to Shaba to defeat the invaders, who were, Mobutu charged, Soviet-inspired, and Cuban-led. U.S. intelligence sources, however, confirmed Soviet and Cuban denials of any participation and identified the rebels as former Katanga gendarmes who had fled to Angola after their 1963 defeat.

On May 15, 1978, a new assault from Angola resulted in the capture of Kolwezi and the death of 100 whites and 300 blacks. In this second invasion, France and Belgium intervened directly as 1,000 Foreign Legion paratroopers repelled the Katangese and 1,750 Belgian soldiers helped evacuate 2,000 Europeans. The U.S. supplied 18 air transports for both the troop movement and the evacuation. This time President Carter himself backed Mobutu's renewed assertions of Soviet-Cuban participation.

France led in organizing Western aid for the restoration of the shattered mining operations at Kolwezi, an important part of the Shaba industry that is the mainstay of Zaire's economy.

ZAMBIA

Republic of Zambia
President: Kenneth D. Kaunda (1964)
Prime Minister: Nalumino Mundia (1981)
Area: 290,586 sq mi. (752,618 sq km)
Population (est. 1983): 6,346,000 (average annual growth rate: 3.2%)
Density per square mile: 21.0
Capital: Lusaka

Largest cities (est. 1982): Lusaka, 650,000; Kitwe, 345,000; Ndola, 325,000; Chingola, 195,000
Monetary unit: Kwacha
Languages: English and local dialects
Religions: Animist, Roman Catholic, Protestant, Hindu, Islam
Member of Commonwealth of Nations
Literacy rate (1981): 28%
Economic summary: Gross national product (1981): $3.4 billion. Average annual growth rate (1981): −1.85%. Per capita income (1981): $575. Land used for agriculture: 5%; labor force: 9%; principal products: corn, tobacco, cotton, sugar cane. Labor force in industry: 15%; major products: copper, cobalt, chemicals, textiles, fertilizers. Natural resources: copper, zinc, lead, cobalt, coal. Exports: copper, zinc, lead, cobalt, tobacco. Imports: manufactured goods, machinery and transport equipment, foodstuffs. Major trading partners: Western European countries, Japan, China, South Africa.

Geography. Zambia, a landlocked country in south central Africa, is about one tenth larger than Texas. It is surrounded by Angola, Zaire, Tanzania, Malawi, Mozambique, Zimbabwe, Botswana, and SouthWest Africa (Namibia). The country is mostly a plateau that rises to 8,000 feet (2,434 m) in the east.

Government. Zambia (formerly Northern Rhodesia) is governed by a president, elected by universal suffrage, and a Legislative Assembly, consisting of 105 members elected by universal suffrage and up to 10 additional members nominated by the president.

In 1972, the Assembly passed a law making the ruling United National Independence Party, led by President Kenneth D. Kaunda, the only legal political party.

History. Empire builder Cecil Rhodes obtained mining concessions in 1889 from King Lewanika of the Barotse and sent settlers to the area soon thereafter. It was ruled by the British South Africa Company, which he established, until 1924, when the British government took over the administration.

From 1953 to 1964, Northern Rhodesia was federated with Southern Rhodesia and Nyasaland in the Federation of Rhodesia and Nyasaland. On Oct. 24, 1964, Northern Rhodesia became the independent nation of Zambia.

Kenneth Kaunda, the first president, kept Zambia within the Commonwealth of Nations. The country's economy, dependent on copper exports, was threatened when Rhodesia declared its independence from British rule in 1965 and defied U.N. sanctions, which Zambia supported, an action that deprived Zambia of its trade route through Rhodesia. The U.S., Britain, and Canada organized an airlift in 1966 to ship gasoline into Zambia. In 1967, Britain agreed to finance new trade routes for Zambia.

Kaunda visited China in 1967, and China later agreed to finance a 1,000-mile railroad from the copper fields to Dar es Salaam in Tanzania. A pipeline was opened in 1968 from Ndola in Zambia's copper belt to the Indian Ocean at Dar es Salaam, ending the three-year oil drought.

In 1969, Kaunda announced the nationalization of the foreign copper-mining industry, with Zambia to take 51% (over $1 billion, estimated), and an agreement was reached with the companies on payment. He then announced a similar takeover of foreign oil producers.

Zambia suffered heavy damage from bombing raids by the former Rhodesian air force on Zimbabwean guerrilla bases and on its transportation links. These actions, combined with falling prices for copper and cobalt, forced Kaunda to declare a state of economic austerity in January 1981.

A strike by copper-belt workers, directed partly against cuts in consumer subsidies and partly at UNIP, the regime's single party, brought a quick victory for the workers after they shut down production. In February, Kaunda installed a new Prime Minister and a new party chief, both more acceptable to the powerful copper-belt unions, and in April, UNIP readmitted union leaders who had been expelled at the time of the strike.

ZIMBABWE

President: Rev. Canaan Banana (1980)
Prime Minister: Robert Mugabe (1980)
Area: 150,699 sq mi. (390,308 sq km)
Population (est. 1983): 8,376,000 (average annual growth rate: 3.5%) (black, 96%; white, 4%)
Density per square mile: 52.2
Capital: Harare (Salisbury)
Largest cities (est. 1982 for metropolitan area): Harare, 675,000; Bulawayo, 400,000
Monetary unit: Zimbabwean dollar
Languages: English (official), Sindebele, Shona
Religions: Christian, 20%; Animist
Literacy rate (1981): 30% (blacks), 99% (whites)
Economic summary: Gross national product (1981): $6.0 billion. Average annual growth rate (1980–81): 12%. Per capita income (1981): $780. Land used for agriculture: 6%; labor force: 35%; principal agricultural products: tobacco, corn, sugar, cotton, livestock. Labor force in industry: 25%; major products: steel, textiles, chemicals, vehicles, gold, copper. Natural resources: gold, copper, cobalt, nickel, tin, asbestos. Exports: gold, tobacco, asbestos, copper, meat, chrome, nickel, clothing, sugar. Imports: machinery, petroleum products, wheat, transport equipment. Major trading partner: South Africa.

Geography. Zimbabwe, a landlocked country in south central Africa, is slightly smaller than California. It is bordered by Botswana on the west, Zambia on the north, Mozambique on the east, and South Africa on the south.

A high veld up to 6,000 feet (1,829 m) crosses the country from northeast to southwest. This is flanked by a somewhat lower veld that contains ranching country. Tropical forests that yield hardwoods lie in the southeast.

In the north, on the border with Zambia, is the 175-mile-long (128-m) Kariba Lake, formed by the Kariba Dam across the Zambezi River. It is the site of one of the world's largest hydroelectric projects.

Government. Executive power rests with the 26-member Cabinet, headed by the Prime Minister. The President, elected by a majority of the House of Assembly, exercises formal executive powers. The legislature is composed of a 100-member

House of Assembly, 80 of whom are elected by black voters and 20 by whites, and a 40-member Senate. Black House members elect 14 Senators and whites elect 10. Ten tribal chiefs—five from Mashonaland and five from Matabeleland—are elected by their peers and six appointed by the President complete the Senate membership.

Major political parties are the Zimbabwe African National Union (57 seats in the House of Assembly), led by Prime Minister Robert Mugabe; Zimbabwe African People's Union (20 seats), led by Joshua Nkomo; and the United African National Council (3 seats), led by former Prime Minister Abel Muzorewa. The Republican Front, led by former Prime Minister Ian Smith, holds 17 of the 20 seats reserved for whites.

History. Zimbabwe, formerly called Rhodesia, was colonized by Cecil Rhodes's British South Africa Company at the end of the 19th century. In 1923, European settlers voted in a referendum to become the self-governing British colony of Southern Rhodesia rather than merge with what was then the Union of South Africa. After a brief federation with Northern Rhodesia and Nyasaland in the post-World War II period, Southern Rhodesia chose to remain a colony when its two partners voted for independence in 1963.

On Nov. 11, 1965, the white-minority government of Rhodesia unilaterally declared its independence from Britain.

In 1967, Rhodesia became the first country against which the United Nations ever imposed mandatory sanctions. The U.S. stopped virtually all trade with Rhodesia. The country refused to cave in, but began a slow movement toward meeting the demands of the black Africans. The white-minority regime of Prime Minister Ian Smith withstood British pressure, economic sanctions, guerrilla attacks, and a right-wing assault.

On March 1, 1970, Rhodesia formally proclaimed itself a republic, and within the month nine nations, including the U.S., closed their consulates there.

Heightened guerrilla war and a withdrawal of South African military aid—particularly helicopters—marked the beginning of the collapse of Smith's 11 years of resistance in the spring of 1976. Under pressure from South Africa's Prime Minister, Johannes Vorster, Smith agreed with U.S. Secretary of State Henry A. Kissinger that majority rule should come within two years.

In the fall, Smith met with black nationalist leaders in Geneva. The meeting broke up six weeks later when the Rhodesian Premier insisted that whites must retain control of the police and armed forces during the transition to majority rule. A British proposal called for Britons to take over these powers.

Divisions between Rhodesian blacks—Bishop Abel Muzorewa of the African National Congress and Ndabaningi Sithole as moderates versus Robert Mugabe and Joshua Nkomo of the Patriotic Front as advocates of guerrilla force—sharpened in 1977 and no agreement was reached. In July, with white residents leaving in increasing numbers and the economy showing the strain of war, Smith rejected outside mediation and called for general elections in order to work out an "internal solution" of the transfer of power.

On March 3, 1978, Smith, Muzorewa, Sithole, and Chief Jeremiah Chirau signed an agreement to transfer power to the black majority by Dec. 31, 1978. They constituted themselves an Executive Council, with chairmanship rotating but Smith retaining the title of Prime Minister. Blacks were named to each cabinet ministry, serving as co-ministers with the whites already holding these posts. African nations and the Patriotic Front leaders immediately denounced the action, but Western governments were more reserved, although none granted recognition to the new regime.

Despite continuing fighting, white voters ratified a new constitution on Jan. 30, 1979, enfranchising all blacks, establishing a black majority Senate and Assembly, and changing the country's name to Zimbabwe Rhodesia. A general election on April 24 gave Muzorewa's party 67.3% of the vote, and although the Patriotic Front urged a boycott, more than 60% of the eligible blacks went to the polls.

As black African states refused recognition and the United Nations sanctions remained in force, Muzorewa agreed to negotiate with Mugabe and Nkomo in British-sponsored talks beginning Sept. 9. By December, all parties accepted a new draft constitution, a cease-fire, and a period of British administration pending a general election. Lord Christopher Soames arrived on Dec. 12 to head the government, followed by British and Commonwealth troops who served as peace-keeping forces as Patriotic Front guerrillas were grouped at 40 assembly points throughout the country.

In voting completed on Feb. 29, 1980, Mugabe's ZANU-Patriotic Front party won 57 of the 80 Assembly seats reserved for blacks. Nkomo's ZAPU-Patriotic Front party won 20 seats and Muzorewa's United African National Council only three. In an earlier vote on Feb. 14, the Rhodesian Front won all 20 seats reserved for whites in the Assembly.

At a ceremony on April 18, Prince Charles of Britain handed to President-elect Rev. Canaan Banana the symbols of independence. Mugabe, a Marxist, had already pledged his support for continuation of the existing free-market economy.

In January 1981, Mugabe dismissed Nkomo as Home Minister and his onetime rival left the government in protest. At the same time, the Prime Minister discharged Edgar Z. Tekere, Manpower and Planning Minister, who had been tried and acquitted of the murder of a white farmer.

Mugabe survived both tests and scored an unprecedented triumph when, in response to his appeal for economic aid, Western nations pledged $1.8 billion for the next three years. The United States promised to give $225 million in grants in addition to $50 million in low-interest loans to replace war-damaged housing. Despite the successes of the new government, whites continued to leave the country, threatening Zimbabwe's farm and industrial production.

During 1984 there were several reports of fighting between Mugabe's ruling Zimbabwe African National Union and Nkomo's rival Zimbabwe African People's Union in Matabeleland and Midlands provinces in southern Zimbabwe. A human rights group, the Roman Catholic Justice and Peace Commission, compiled accounts of reported murders, torture, rape and other attrocities by government troops against civilians in Matabeleland, Nkomo's stronghold.

(For late reports, see Current Events of 1983–84)

UNITED NATIONS

The 159 Members of the United Nations

Country	Joined U.N.[1]
Afghanistan	1946
Albania	1955
Algeria	1962
Angola	1976
Antigua and Barbuda	1981
Argentina	1945
Australia	1945
Austria	1955
Bahamas	1973
Bahrain	1971
Bangladesh	1974
Barbados	1966
Belgium	1945
Belize	1981
Benin	1960
Bhutan	1971
Bolivia	1945
Botswana	1966
Brazil	1945
Brunei	1984
Bulgaria	1955
Burma	1948
Burundi	1962
Byelorussian S.S.R.	1945
Cambodia	1955
Cameroon	1960
Canada	1945
Cape Verde	1975
Central African Republic	1960
Chad	1960
Chile	1945
China[2]	1945
Colombia	1945
Comoros	1975
Congo	1960
Costa Rica	1945
Cuba	1945
Cyprus	1960
Czechoslovakia	1945
Denmark	1945
Djibouti	1977
Dominica	1978
Dominican Republic	1945
Ecuador	1945
Egypt	1945
El Salvador	1945
Equatorial Guinea	1968
Ethiopia	1945
Fiji	1970
Finland	1955
France	1945
Gabon	1960
Gambia	1965
Germany, East	1973
Germany, West	1973
Ghana	1957
Greece	1945
Grenada	1974
Guatemala	1945
Guinea	1958
Guinea-Bissau	1974
Guyana	1966
Haiti	1945
Honduras	1945
Hungary	1955
Iceland	1946
India	1945
Indonesia	1950
Iran	1945
Iraq	1945
Ireland	1955
Israel	1949
Italy	1955
Ivory Coast	1960
Jamaica	1962
Japan	1956
Jordan	1955
Kenya	1963
Kuwait	1963
Laos	1955
Lebanon	1945
Lesotho	1966
Liberia	1945
Libya	1955
Luxembourg	1945
Madagascar	1960
Malawi	1964
Malaysia	1957
Maldives	1965
Mali	1960
Malta	1964
Mauritania	1961
Mauritius	1968
Mexico	1945
Mongolia	1961
Morocco	1956
Mozambique	1975
Nepal	1955
Netherlands	1945
New Zealand	1945
Nicaragua	1945
Niger	1960
Nigeria	1960
Norway	1945
Oman	1971
Pakistan	1947
Panama	1945
Papua New Guinea	1975
Paraguay	1945
Peru	1945
Philippines	1945
Poland	1945
Portugal	1955
Qatar	1971
Romania	1955
Rwanda	1962
St. Christopher and Nevis	1983
St. Lucia	1979
St. Vincent and the Grenadines	1980
São Tomé and Príncipe	1975
Saudi Arabia	1945
Senegal	1960
Seychelles	1976
Sierra Leone	1961
Singapore	1965
Solomon Islands	1978
Somalia	1960
South Africa	1945
Spain	1955
Sri Lanka	1955
Sudan	1956
Suriname	1975
Swaziland	1968
Sweden	1946
Syria	1945
Tanzania	1961
Thailand	1946
Togo	1960
Trinidad and Tobago	1962
Tunisia	1956
Turkey	1945
Uganda	1962
Ukrainian S.S.R.	1945
U.S.S.R.	1945
United Arab Emirates	1971
United Kingdom	1945
United States	1945
Upper Volta	1960
Uruguay	1945
Vanuatu	1981
Venezuela	1945
Vietnam	1977
Western Samoa	1976
Yemen Arab Republic	1947
Yemen, People's Dem. Republic of	1967
Yugoslavia	1945
Zaire	1960
Zambia	1964
Zimbabwe	1980

1. The U.N. officially came into existence on Oct. 24, 1945. 2. On Oct. 25, 1971, the U.N. voted membership to the People's Republic of China, which replaced the Republic of China (Taiwan) in the world body.

Six Official Languages Used by U.N.

There are six official working languages recognized by the United Nations. They are Chinese, English, French, Russian, and Spanish, which have been in use since the world body was organized, and Arabic, which was added by the General Assembly in 1973 and by the Security Council in 1982.

Member Countries' Assessments to U.N. Budget, 1984

Country	Total	Country	Total	Country	Total
Afghanistan	$ 64,969	Germany, West	$55,483,141	Papua New Guinea	$ 64,969
Albania	64,969	Ghana	129,937	Paraguay	64,969
Algeria	844,591	Greece	2,598,741	Peru	454,780
Angola	64,969	Grenada	64,969	Philippines	584,717
Antigua and Barbuda	64,969	Guatemala	129,937	Poland	4,677,735
Argentina	4,612,766	Guinea	64,969	Portugal	1,169,434
Australia	10,200,062	Guinea-Bissau	64,969	Qatar	194,905
Austria	4,872,640	Guyana	64,969	Romania	1,234,402
Bahamas	64,969	Haiti	64,969	Rwanda	64,969
Bahrain	64,969	Honduras	64,969	St. Lucia	64,969
Bangladesh	194,905	Hungary	1,494,276	St. Vincent and the Grenadines	64,969
Barbados	64,969	Iceland	194,905	São Tomé and Príncipe	64,969
Belgium	8,315,974	India	2,338,867	Saudi Arabia	5,587,294
Belize	64,969	Indonesia	844,591	Senegal	64,969
Benin	64,969	Iran	3,768,175	Seychelles	64,969
Bhutan	64,969	Iraq	779,623	Sierra Leone	64,969
Bolivia	64,969	Ireland	1,169,434	Singapore	584,717
Botswana	64,969	Israel	1,494,276	Solomon Islands	64,969
Brazil	9,030,627	Italy	24,298,237	Somalia	64,969
Bulgaria	1,169,434	Ivory Coast	194,905	South Africa	2,663,710
Burma	64,969	Jamaica	129,937	Spain	12,538,929
Burundi	64,969	Japan	67,047,543	Sri Lanka	64,969
Byelorussian SSR	2,338,867	Jordan	64,969	Sudan	64,969
Cambodia	64,969	Kenya	64,969	Suriname	64,969
Cameroon	64,969	Kuwait	1,624,214	Swaziland	64,969
Canada	20,010,313	Laos	64,969	Sweden	8,575,848
Cape Verde	64,969	Lebanon	129,937	Syria	194,905
Central African Republic	64,969	Lesotho	64,969	Tanzania	70,094
Chad	64,969	Liberia	64,969	Thailand	519,749
Chile	454,780	Libya	1,689,182	Togo	64,969
China	5,717,232	Luxembourg	389,811	Trinidad and Tobago	194,905
Colombia	714,654	Madagascar	64,969	Tunisia	194,905
Comoros	64,969	Malawi	64,969	Turkey	2,084,594
Congo	64,969	Malaysia	584,717	Uganda	64,969
Costa Rica	129,937	Maldives	64,969	Ukrainian SSR	8,575,848
Cuba	584,717	Mali	64,969	U.S.S.R.	68,476,851
Cyprus	64,969	Malta	64,969	United Arab Emirates	1,039,497
Czechoslovakia	4,937,609	Mauritania	64,969	United Kingdom	30,340,312
Denmark	4,872,640	Mauritius	64,969	United States	190,520,626
Djibouti	64,969	Mexico	5,717,232	Upper Volta	64,969
Dominica	64,969	Mongolia	64,969	Uruguay	259,875
Dominican Republic	194,905	Morocco	324,843	Vanuatu	64,969
Ecuador	129,937	Mozambique	64,969	Venezuela	3,573,269
Egypt	454,780	Nepal	64,969	Vietnam	129,937
El Salvador	64,969	Netherlands	11,571,822	Western Samoa	64,969
Equatorial Guinea	64,969	New Zealand	1,689,182	Yemen Arab Republic	64,969
Ethiopia	64,969	Nicaragua	64,969	Yemen, People's Dem. Republic of	
Fiji	64,969	Niger	64,969		64,969
Finland	3,118,490	Nigeria	1,234,402	Yugoslavia	2,988,552
France	42,294,525	Norway	3,313,395	Zaire	64,969
Gabon	129,937	Oman	64,969	Zambia	64,969
Gambia	64,969	Pakistan	389,811	Zimbabwe	129,937
Germany, East	9,030,627	Panama	129,937		

United Nations Headquarters

The first regular session of the General Assembly held at Central Hall, Westminster, London, voted that interim headquarters of the Organization should be located in New York. From London the U.N. moved to Hunter College in the Bronx. In August 1946, an interim headquarters was set up at Lake Success on Long Island. The New York City building at Flushing Meadows, site of the 1939 World's Fair, was converted for the use of the General Assembly. The search for a permanent home ended in December 1946, when the General Assembly accepted an offer from John D. Rockefeller, Jr., of $8,500,000[1] for the purchase of the present Headquarters site—an 18-acre tract in Manhattan, alongside the East River. The U.S. Government lent the U.N. $65,000,000 interest free, which is being repaid in annual installments.

Architectural plans drawn up by an international Board of Design were approved by the Assembly, and construction began in September 1948. By mid-1950, the 39-story Secretariat Building was ready for occupancy, and in the spring of 1951 "United Nations, New York" became the Organization's permanent address.

1. This amount paid for two-thirds of the land; New York City gave one-third.

Preamble of the United Nations Charter

The Charter of the United Nations was adopted at the San Francisco Conference of 1945. The complete text may be obtained by writing to the United Nations Sales Section, United Nations, New York, N.Y. 10017, and enclosing $1.

We the peoples of the United Nations determined to save succeeding generations from the scourge of war, which twice in our lifetime has brought untold sorrow to mankind, and

To reaffirm faith in fundamental human rights, in the dignity and worth of the human person, in the equal rights of men and women and of nations large and small, and

To establish conditions under which justice and respect for the obligations arising from treaties and other sources of international law can be maintained, and

To promote social progress and better standards of life in larger freedom, and for these ends

To practice tolerance and live together in peace with one another as good neighbors, and

To unite our strength to maintain international peace and security, and

To insure, by the acceptance of principles and the institution of methods, that armed force shall not be used, save in the common interest, and

To employ international machinery for the promotion of the economic and social advancement of all peoples, have resolved to combine our efforts to accomplish these aims.

Accordingly, our respective Governments, through representatives assembled in the city of San Francisco, who have exhibited their full powers found to be in good and due form, have agreed to the present Charter of the United Nations and do hereby establish an international organization to be known as the United Nations.

Principal Organs of the United Nations

Secretariat

This is the directorate on U.N. operations, apart from political decisions. All members contribute to its upkeep. Its staff of over 6,000 specialists is recruited from member nations on the basis of as wide a geographical distribution as possible. The staff works under the Secretary-General, whom it assists and advises.

Secretaries-General

Javier Pérez de Cuéllar, Peru, Jan. 1, 1982.
Kurt Waldheim, Austria, Jan. 1, 1972, to Dec. 31, 1981.
U Thant, Burma, Nov. 3, 1961, to Dec. 31, 1971.
Dag Hammarskjöld, Sweden, April 11, 1953, to Sept. 17, 1961.
Trygve Lie, Norway, Feb. 1, 1946, to April 10, 1953.

General Assembly

The General Assembly is the world's forum for discussing matters affecting world peace and security, and for making recommendations concerning them. It has no power of its own to enforce decisions.

The Assembly is composed of the 51 original member nations and those admitted since, a total of 158. Each nation has one vote. On major questions involving international peace and security, a two-thirds majority of those present and voting is required. Decisions on other questions are made by a simple majority.

The Assembly's agenda can be as broad as the Charter. It can make recommendations to member nations, the Security Council, or both. Emphasis is given questions relating to international peace and security brought before it by any member, the Security Council, or nonmembers.

The Assembly also maintains a broad program of international cooperation in economic, social, cultural, educational, and health fields, and for assisting in human rights and freedoms.

Among other duties, the Assembly has functions relating to the trusteeship system, and considers and approves the U.N. Budget. Every member contributes to operating expenses according to its means.

Security Council

The Security Council is the primary instrument for establishing and maintaining international peace. Its main purpose is to prevent war by settling disputes between nations.

Under the Charter, the Council is permitted to dispatch a U.N. force to stop aggression. All member nations undertake to make available armed forces, assistance, and facilities to maintain international peace and security.

Any member may bring a dispute before the Security Council or the General Assembly. Any nonmember may do so if it accepts the charter obligations of pacific settlement.

The Security Council has 15 members. There are five permanent members: the United States, the Soviet Union, Britain, France, and China, and 10 temporary members elected by the General Assembly for two-year terms, with different regions of the world rotating.

Voting on procedural matters requires a nine-vote majority to carry. However, on questions of substance, the vote of each of the five permanent members is required.

Current temporary members are (term expires Dec. 31, 1984): Malta, Netherlands, Nicaragua, Pakistan, Zimbabwe; (term expires Dec. 31, 1985): Egypt, India, Peru, Ukraine, Upper Volta.

Economic and Social Council

This council is composed of 54 members elected by the General Assembly to 3-year terms. It works closely with the General Assembly as a link with groups formed within the U.N. to help peoples in such fields as education, health, and human rights. It insures that there is no overlapping and sets up commissions to deal with economic conditions and collect facts and figures on conditions over the world. It issues studies and reports and may make recommendations to the Assembly and specialized agencies.

Functional Commissions

Statistical Commission; Population Commission; Commission for Social Development; Commission on Human Rights; Commission on the Status of Women; Commission on Narcotic Drugs.

Regional Commissions

Economic Commission for Europe; Economic and Social Commission for Asia and the Pacific; Economic Commission for Latin America; Economic Commission for Africa; Economic Commission for Western Asia.

Trusteeship Council

This council supervises territories administered by various nations and placed under an international trusteeship system by the United Nations. Each nation is charged with developing the self-government of the territory and preserving and advancing the cultural, political, economic, and other forms of welfare of the people.

The Trusteeship Council is currently composed of 5 members: 1 member—the United States—that administers a trust territory, and 4 members—China, France, the Soviet Union, and the United Kingdom—that are permanent members of the Security Council but do not administer trust territories.

The following countries ceased to be administering members because of the independence of territories they had administered: Italy and France in 1960, Belgium in 1962, New Zealand and the United Kingdom in 1968 and Australia in 1975. France and the U.K. became nonadministering members.

As of December 1980, there was only one trust territory: the Trust Territory of the Pacific Islands (administered by the United States).

International Court of Justice

The International Court of Justice sits at The Hague, the Netherlands. Its 15-judge bench was established to hear disputes among states, which must agree to accept its verdicts. Its judges, charged with administering justice under international law, deal with cases ranging from disputes over territory to those concerning rights of passage.

Following are the members of the Court and the years in which their terms expire:

President: Taslim Olawale Elias, Nigeria (1985)
Vice President: Jose Sette Camara, Brazil (1988)
Manfred Lachs, Poland (1985)
Hermann Mosler, West Germany (1985)
Shigeru Oda, Japan (1985)
Abdallah Fikri El-Khani, Syria (1985)
Platon Dmitrievich Morozov, U.S.S.R. (1988)
Roberto Ago, Italy (1988)
Stephen Schwebel, U.S. (1988)
Mohammed Bedjaoui, Algeria (1988)
Nagendra Singh, India (1991)
Jose Maria Ruda, Argentina (1991)
Robert Y. Jennings, United Kingdom (1991)
Guy Ladreit de Lacharriere, France (1991)
Keba Mbaye, Senegal (1991)

Agencies of the United Nations

INTL. ATOMIC ENERGY AGENCY (IAEA)

Established: Statute for IAEA, approved on Oct. 26, 1956, at a conference held at U.N. Headquarters, New York, came into force on July 29, 1957. The Agency is under the aegis of the U.N., but unlike the following, it is not a specialized agency.

Purpose: To promote the peaceful uses of atomic energy; to ensure that assistance provided by it or at its request or under its supervision or control is not used in such a way as to further any military purpose.

Headquarters: Kaerntnerring, Vienna, 1, Austria.

FOOD AND AGRICULTURE ORGANIZATION OF THE UNITED NATIONS (FAO)

Established: October 16, 1945, when constitution became effective.

Purpose: To raise nutrition levels and living standards; to secure improvements in production and distribution of food and agricultural products.

Headquarters: Via delle Terme di Caracalla, 00100, Rome, Italy.

GENERAL AGREEMENT ON TARIFFS AND TRADE (GATT)

Established: Jan. 1, 1948.

Purpose: An International Trade Organization (ITO) was originally planned. Although this agency has not materialized, some of its objectives have been embodied in an international commercial treaty, the General Agreement on Tariffs and Trade. Its purpose is to sponsor trade negotiations.

Headquarters: Villa le Bocage, Palais des Nations, Geneva 21, Switzerland.

INTERNATIONAL BANK FOR RECONSTRUCTION AND DEVELOPMENT (IBRD) (WORLD BANK)

Established: December 27, 1945, when Articles of Agreement drawn up at Bretton Woods Conference in July 1944 came into force. Began operations on June 25, 1946.

Purpose: To assist in reconstruction and development of economies of members by facilitating capital investment and by making loans to governments and furnishing technical advice.

Headquarters: 1818 H St., N.W., Washington, D.C. 20433.

INTL. CIVIL AVIATION ORGANIZATION (ICAO)

Established: April 4, 1947, after working as a provisional organization since June 1945.

Purpose: To study problems of international civil aviation; to establish international standards and regulations; to promote safety measures, uniform regulations for operation, simpler procedures at international borders, and the use of new technical methods and equipment. It has evolved standards for meteorological services, traffic control, communications, radio beacons and ranges, search and rescue organization, and other facilities. It has brought about much simplification of customs, immigration, and public health regulations as they apply to international air transport. It drafts international air law conventions, and is concerned with economic aspects of air travel.

Headquarters: International Aviation Square, 1000 Sherbrooke St. West, Montreal, Quebec, H3A 2R2, Canada.

INTL. DEVELOPMENT ASSOCIATION (IDA)

Established: Sept. 24, 1960. An affiliate of the World Bank, IDA has the same officers and staff as the Bank.

Purpose: To further economic development of its members by providing finance on terms which bear less heavily on balance of payments of members than those of conventional loans.

Headquarters: 1818 H St., N.W., Washington, D.C. 20433.

INTERNATIONAL FINANCE CORPORATION (IFC)

Established: Charter of IFC came into force on July 20, 1956. Although IFC is affiliated with the World Bank, it is a separate legal entity, and its funds are entirely separate from those of the Bank. However, membership in the Corporation is open only to Bank members.

Purpose: To further economic development by encouraging the growth of productive private enterprise in its member countries, particularly in the less developed areas; to invest in productive private enterprises in association with private investors, without government guarantee of repayment where sufficient private capital is not available on reasonable terms; to serve as a clearing house to bring together investment opportunities, private capital (both foreign and domestic), and experienced management.

Headquarters: 1818 H St., N.W., Washington, D.C. 20433.

INTERNATIONAL FUND FOR AGRICULTURAL DEVELOPMENT (IFAD)

Established: June 18, 1976. Began operations in December 1977.

Purpose: To mobilize additional funds for agricultural and rural development in developing countries through projects and programs directly benefiting the poorest rural populations.

Headquarters: 107 Via del Serafico, 00142, Rome, Italy.

INTERNATIONAL LABOR ORGANIZATION (ILO)

Established: April 11, 1919, when constitution was adopted as Part XIII of Treaty of Versailles. Became specialized agency of U.N. in 1946.

Purpose: To contribute to establishment of lasting peace by promoting social justice; to improve labor conditions and living standards through international action; to promote economic and social stability. The U.S. withdrew from the ILO in 1977 and resumed membership in 1980.

Headquarters: 154 Rue de Lausanne, Geneva, Switzerland.

INTERNATIONAL MARITIME ORGANIZATION (IMO)

Established: March 17, 1958.

Purpose: To give advisory and consultative help to promote international cooperation in maritime navigation and to encourage the highest standards of safety and navigation. Its aim is to bring about a uniform system of measuring ship tonnage; systems now vary widely in different parts of the world. Other activities include cooperation with other U.N. agencies on matters affecting the maritime field.

Headquarters: 101–104 Piccadilly, London, W1V OAE, England.

INTERNATIONAL MONETARY FUND (IMF)

Established: Dec. 27, 1945, when Articles of Agreement drawn up at Bretton Woods Conference in July 1944 came into force. Fund began operations on March 1, 1947.

Purpose: To promote international monetary cooperation and expansion of international trade; to promote exchange stability; to assist in establishment of multilateral system of payments in respect of currency transactions between members.

Headquarters: 700 19th St., N.W., Washington, D.C. 20431.

INTERNATIONAL TELECOMMUNICATION UNION (ITU)

Established: 1865. Became specialized agency of U.N. in 1947.

Purpose: To extend technical assistance to help members keep up with present day telecommunication needs; to standardize communications equipment and procedures; to lower costs. It also works for orderly sharing of radio frequencies and makes studies and recommendations to benefit its members.

Headquarters: Palais des Nations, 1211 Geneva 20, Switzerland.

UNITED NATIONS EDUCATIONAL, SCIENTIFIC, AND CULTURAL ORGANIZATION (UNESCO)

Established: Nov. 4, 1946, when twentieth signatory to constitution deposited instrument of acceptance with government of U.K.

Purpose: To promote collaboration among nations through education, science, and culture in order to further justice, rule of law, and human rights and freedoms without distinction of race, sex, language, or religion.

Headquarters: UNESCO House. Place de Fontenoy, 7e, Paris, France.

UNIVERSAL POSTAL UNION (UPU)

Established: Oct. 9, 1874. Became specialized agency of U.N. in 1947.

Purpose: To facilitate reciprocal exchange of correspondence by uniform procedures by all UPU members; to help governments modernize and speed up mailing procedures.

Headquarters: Case Postale 3000 Berne 15, Switzerland.

WORLD HEALTH ORGANIZATION (WHO)

Established: April 7, 1948, when 26 members of the U.N. had accepted its constitution, adopted July 22, 1946, by the International Health Conference in New York City.

Purpose: To aid attainment by all people of highest possible level of health.

Headquarters: Palais des Nations, 1211 Geneva, Switzerland.

WORLD INTELLECTUAL PROPERTY ORGANIZATION (WIPO)

Established: April 26, 1970, when its Convention came into force. Originated as International Bureau of Paris Union (1883) and Berne Union (1886), later succeeded by United International Bureau for the Protection of Intellectual Property (BIRPI). Became a specialized agency of the U.N. in December 1974.

Purpose: To promote legal protection of intellectual property, including artistic and scientific works, artistic performances, sound recordings, broadcasts, inventions, trademarks, industrial designs, and commercial names.

Headquarters: 32 Chemin des Colombettes, 1211 Geneva 20, Switzerland.

WORLD METEOROLOGICAL ORGANIZATION (WMO)

Established: March 23, 1950, succeeding the International Meteorological Organization, a nongovernmental organization founded in 1878.

Purpose: To promote international exchange of weather reports and maximum standardization of observations; to help developing countries establish weather services for their own economic needs; to fill gaps in observation stations; to promote meterological investigations affecting jet aircraft, satellites, energy resources, etc.

Headquarters: 41 Avenue Giuseppe Motta, Geneva, Switzerland.

CANADA

Sovereign: Queen Elizabeth II
Governor General: Jeanne Sauvé (1984)
Prime Minister: Brian Mulroney (1984)
Area: 3,851,809 sq mi. (9,976,186 sq km)
Population (est. 1983): 24,900,000 (British, 44.6%; French, 28.7%; other European, 23%) (growth rate, 1979–80, 0.9%)
Density per square mile: 6.5
Capital: Ottawa, Ont.
Largest cities (1981 census; metropolitan areas): Toronto, 2,998,947; Montreal, 2,828,349; Vancouver, 1,268,183; Ottawa, 717,978; Edmonton, 657,057; Calgary, 592,743; Winnipeg, 584,842; Quebec, 576,075; Hamilton, 542,095; St. Catherines-Niagara, 304,353; Kitchener, 287,801; London, 283,668; Halifax, 277,727
Monetary Unit: Canadian dollar
Languages: English, French
Religions: Roman Catholic, 47.3%; Protestant, 41.2%; no religion, 7.4%; Eastern Orthodox, 1.5%; Jewish, 1.2%; other, 1.3%
Gross national product (1981): $331.3 billion
Average annual growth rate (1979–82): 0.4%
Literacy rate: 98%

Geography. Covering most of the northern part of the North American continent and with an area larger than that of the United States, Canada has an extremely varied topography. The northeastern region, including most of Quebec, northern Ontario and Manitoba, and the Northwest Territories, with Hudson Bay in the center, is an important source of minerals, wood pulp, and water power. In the east the mountainous maritime provinces have an irregular coast line on the Gulf of St. Lawrence and the Atlantic. The St. Lawrence plain, covering most of southern Quebec and Ontario, and the interior continental plain, covering southern Manitoba and Saskatchewan and most of Alberta, are the principal cultivable areas. They are separated by a forested plateau rising from lakes Superior and Huron.

Westward toward the Pacific, most of British Columbia, Yukon, and part of western Alberta are covered by parallel mountain ranges including the Rockies. The Pacific border of the coast range is ragged with fiords and channels. The highest point in Canada is Mount Logan (19,850 ft; 6,050 m), which is in the Yukon.

Canada has an abundance of large and small lakes. In addition to the Great Lakes on the U.S. border, there are 9 others that are more than 100 miles long (161 km) and 35 that are more than 50 miles long (80 km).

The two principal river systems are the Mackenzie and the St. Lawrence. The St. Lawrence, with its tributaries, is navigable for over 1,900 miles (3,058 km).

Government. Canada, a self-governing member of the Commonwealth of Nations, is a federation of 10 provinces and two territories whose powers were spelled out in the British North America Act of 1867. With the passing of the Constitution Act of 1981, the act and the Constitutional amending power were transferred from the British government to Canada so that the Canadian Constitution is now entirely in the hands of the Canadians.

Actually the Governor General acts only with the advice of the Canadian Prime Minister and the Cabinet, who also sit in the federal Parliament. The Parliament has two houses: a Senate of 104 members appointed for life, and a House of Commons of 282 members apportioned according to provincial population. Elections are held at least every five years or whenever the party in power is voted down in the House of Commons or considers it expedient to appeal to the people. The Prime Minister is the leader of the majority party in the House of Commons—or, if no single party holds a majority, the leader of the party able to command the support of a majority of members of the House. Laws must be passed by both houses of Parliament and signed by the Governor General in the Queen's name.

The 10 provincial governments are nominally headed by Lieutenant Governors appointed by the federal government, but the executive power in each actually is vested in a Cabinet headed by a Premier, who is leader of the majority party. The provincial legislatures are composed of one-house assemblies whose members are elected for four-year terms. They are known as Legislative Assemblies, except in Newfoundland, where it is the House of Assembly, and in Quebec, where it is the National Assembly.

The judicial system consists of a Supreme Court in Ottawa (established in 1875), with appellate jurisdiction, and a Supreme Court in each province, as well as county courts with limited jurisdiction in most of the provinces. The Governor General in Council appoints these judges.

The major political parties are the Progressive Conservative Party (211 of 282 seats in House of Commons), led by Prime Minister Brian Mulroney; Liberal Party (40 seats), led by John T. Turner; and New Democratic Party (30 seats), led by John Edward Broadbent. One Independent holds a seat.

History. The Norse explorer Leif Ericson probably reached the shores of Canada (Labrador or Nova Scotia) in A.D. 1000, but the history of the white man in the country actually began in 1497, when John Cabot, an Italian in the service of Henry VII of England, reached Newfoundland or Nova Scotia. Canada was taken for France in 1534 by Jacques Cartier. The actual settlement of New France, as it was then called, began in 1604 at Port Royal in what is now Nova Scotia; in 1608, Quebec was founded. France's colonization efforts were not very successful, but French explorers by the end of the 17th century had penetrated beyond the Great Lakes to the western prairies and south along the Mississippi to the Gulf of Mexico. Meanwhile, the English Hudson's Bay Company had been established in 1670. Because of the valuable fisheries and fur trade, a conflict developed between the French and English; in 1713, Newfoundland, Hudson Bay, and Nova Scotia (Acadia) were lost to England.

During the Seven Years' War (1756–63), England extended its conquest, and the British Maj. Gen. James Wolfe won his famous victory over Gen. Louis Montcalm outside Quebec on Sept. 13, 1759. The Treaty of Paris in 1763 gave England control.

At that time the population of Canada was almost entirely French, but in the next few decades, thousands of British colonists emigrated to Canada from the British Isles and from the American colo-

Canadian Governors General and Prime Ministers Since 1867

Term of office	Governor General	Term	Prime Minister	Party
1867-1868	Viscount Monck[1]	1867-1873	Sir John A. MacDonald	Conservative
1869-1872	Baron Lisgar	1873-1878	Alexander Mackenzie	Liberal
1872-1878	Earl of Dufferin	1878-1891	Sir John A. MacDonald	Conservative
1878-1883	Marquess of Lorne	1891-1892	Sir John J. C. Abbott	Conservative
1883-1888	Marquess of Lansdowne	1892-1894	Sir John S. D. Thompson	Conservative
1888-1893	Baron Stanley of Preston	1894-1896	Sir Mackenzie Bowell	Conservative
1893-1898	Earl of Aberdeen	1896	Sir Charles Tupper	Conservative
1898-1904	Earl of Minto	1896-1911	Sir Wilfrid Laurier	Liberal
1904-1911	Earl Grey	1911-1917	Sir Robert L. Borden	Conservative
1911-1916	Duke of Connaught	1917-1920	Sir Robert L. Borden	Unionist
1916-1921	Duke of Devonshire	1920-1921	Arthur Meighen	Unionist
1921-1926	Baron Byng of Vinny	1921-1926	W. L. Mackenzie King	Liberal
1926-1931	Viscount Willingdon	1926	Arthur Meighen	Conservative
1931-1935	Earl of Bessborough	1926-1930	W. L. Mackenzie King	Liberal
1935-1940	Baron Tweedsmuir	1930-1935	Richard B. Bennett	Conservative
1940-1946	Earl of Athlone	1935-1948	W. L. Mackenzie King	Liberal
1946-1952	Viscount Alexander	1948-1957	Louis S. St. Laurent	Liberal
1952-1959	Vincent Massey	1957-1963	John G. Diefenbaker	Conservative
1959-1967	George P. Vanier	1963-1968	Lester B. Pearson	Liberal
1967-1973	Roland Michener	1968-1979	Pierre Elliott Trudeau	Liberal
1974-1979	Jules Léger	1979-1980	Charles Joseph Clark	Conservative
1979-1984	Edward R. Schreyer	1980-1984	Pierre Elliott Trudeau	Liberal
1984-	Jeanne Sauvé	1984-1984	John Turner	Liberal
		1984-	Brian Mulroney	Conservative

1. Became Governor General of British North America in 1861. 2. Pending Sept. 4, 1984 election.

nies. In 1849, the right of Canada to self-government was recognized. By the British North America Act of 1867, the Dominion of Canada was created through the confederation of Upper and Lower Canada, Nova Scotia, and New Brunswick. Prince Edward Island joined the Dominion in 1873.

In 1869 Canada purchased from the Hudson's Bay Company the vast middle west (Rupert's Land) from which the provinces of Manitoba (1870), Alberta, and Saskatchewan (1905) were later formed. In 1871, British Columbia joined the Dominion. The country was linked from coast to coast in 1885 by the Canadian Pacific Railway.

During the formative years between 1866 and 1896, the Conservative Party, led by Sir John A. MacDonald, governed the country, except during the years 1873–78. In 1896, the Liberal Party took over and, under Sir Wilfrid Laurier, an eminent French Canadian, ruled until 1911.

In World War I, more than 500,000 Canadian soldiers fought for the Allied cause. After the Treaty of Versailles, Canada, a full-fledged nation, was admitted to the League of Nations and appointed its own representatives in foreign countries. By the Statute of Westminster in 1931 the British Dominions, including Canada, were formally declared to be partner nations with Britain, "equal in status, in no way subordinate to each other," and bound together only by allegiance to a common Crown.

Newfoundland became Canada's 10th province on March 31, 1949, following a plebiscite. Besides the provinces, Canada includes two territories—the Yukon Territory, the area north of British Columbia and east of Alaska, and the Northwest Territories, including all of Canada north of 60° north latitude except Yukon and the northernmost sections of Quebec and Newfoundland. This area includes all of the Arctic north of the mainland, Norway having recognized Canadian sovereignty over the Svendrup Islands in the Arctic in 1931.

The Liberal Party, led by William Lyon Mackenzie King, dominated Canadian politics from 1921 until 1957, when it was succeeded by the Progressive Conservatives. The Liberals, under the leadership of Lester B. Pearson, returned to power in 1963. Pearson remained Prime Minister until 1968, when he retired and was replaced by a former law professor, Pierre Elliott Trudeau. Trudeau maintained Canada's defensive alliance with the United States, but began moving toward a more independent policy in world affairs.

Trudeau set about creating what he termed a "just society," stressing domestic reforms. His election was considered in part a response to the most serious problem confronting the country, the division between French- and English-speaking Canadians, which had led to a separatist movement in the predominantly French province of Quebec. Trudeau, himself a French Canadian, supported programs for bilingualism and an increased measure of provincial autonomy, although he would not tolerate the idea of separatism. In 1974, the provincial government voted to make French the official language of Quebec.

Capturing the Quebec provincial government from the long-entrenched local Liberal Party, René Lévesque and his separatist Parti Québécois pledged that they would seek independence for the province. He shocked English-speaking Canadians with a New York speech two months after his election in which he said the question was not when but *how* Quebec would attain independence.

Conflicts over the law establishing French as the dominant language in Quebec, particularly in schooling, kept separatism as a national issue, but by-elections in 1977 produced easy victories for Trudeau's ruling Liberals in four Quebec seats in the national legislature, and polls showed a decline in separatist support both in the province and elsewhere in Canada. Early in 1978, Trudeau declared that he would use force to prevent any illegal declaration of independence by Lévesque.

Economic problems appeared to take precedence over politics in 1978, as the Sun Life Assurance Company of Canada, the nation's largest insurance firm, announced that it would move its headquarters from Montreal to Toronto. Many businesses had left the province earlier, but Sun Life was the first to cite the language law as the reason for its departure.

Despite Trudeau's removal of price and wage controls in 1978, continuing inflation and a high rate of unemployment caused him to delay elections until May 22, 1979, the first time since 1935 that a Canadian government had retained office for the allowable five-year term. The delay gave Trudeau no advantage—the Progressive Conservatives under Charles Joseph Clark defeated the Liberals everywhere except in Quebec, New Brunswick, and Newfoundland. The Liberals actually won the larger share of the popular vote with 40%, but because their strength was concentrated in Quebec they won only 114 seats to the Conservatives' 136 and 36% of the popular vote.

Clark took office as the head of Canada's fifth minority government in the last 20 years, needing the support of 26 New Democratic Party members and six Social Credit members to obtain an absolute majority in the 282-seat House.

Trudeau's defeat after 11 years in power was attributed to 9.8% inflation, to western opposition to his energy policies, and, in the opinion of some, public distaste over a sensational autobiography written by the Prime Minister's estranged wife. Trudeau's proposed changes in the Canadian constitution aroused the opposition of provincial premiers.

Clark's government collapsed after only six months when a motion to defeat the Tory budget carried by 139-133 on Dec. 13, 1979. On the same day, the Quebec law making French the exclusive official language of the province—an issue which had been expected to provide Clark's first major internal test—was voided by the Canadian Supreme Court.

In national elections Feb. 18, 1980, the resurgent Liberals under Trudeau scored an unexpectedly big victory, winning 146 seats (147 when a vacancy was filled a month later), while the Conservatives fell from 136 to 103 and the New Democrats won 32 seats.

Resolving a dispute that had occupied Trudeau since the beginning of his tenure, Queen Elizabeth II, in Ottawa on April 17, 1982, signed the Constitution Act, cutting the last legal tie between Canada and Britain. Since 1867, the British North America Act required British Parliament approval for any Canadian constitutional change.

The new charter was approved by the federal House of Commons, 246–24, on Dec. 2, 1981, and by a 59–23 vote of the Senate six days later. The Constitution retains Queen Elizabeth as Queen of Canada and keeps Canada's membership in the Commonwealth. A Bill of Rights, subject to overriding provincial legislation, was criticized as deficient in protecting the rights of women and Canada's native peoples, although equality before the law is guaranteed "without discrimination based on race, national or ethnic origin, color, religion, sex, age or mental or physical disability."

Despite assurance of French-language schooling and federal services to French-speaking Canadians anywhere in the nation, Quebec's Premier Lévesque boycotted the signing ceremony and told a crowd of protesters in Montreal, "We are no longer Canadians."

As a concession to Western provinces, the charter granted exclusive jurisdiction over natural resources to provincial governments but forbade the fixing of different prices for energy consumed within a province and energy exported to other provinces.

Ending an era, Trudeau retired on June 30, 1984, after 16 years as prime minister, except for the nine-month interruption in 1979–80.

His successor as Liberal Party leader and Prime Minister, John N. Turner, called an early election for a new Parliament after polls showed the Liberals had made a big comeback from the last months of Trudeau's term, despite Canada's continuing recession and 11.2% unemployment, the highest in 40 years.

Canada's oil and gas industry was hard hit in 1982 by the aftereffects of the 1980 National Energy Program, designed to increase home ownership in a predominately foreign-controlled business, which had slowed investment for new production. Additional blows were the withdrawal of Shell Explorer, Inc., from the multi-billion-dollar Alsands project to extract oil from Alberta tar sands, crippling the project, and the decision by the U.S.-owned Northwest Energy Corporation to delay for two years the building of a gas pipeline from Canada's Prudhoe Bay to the United States.

Population of Canada by Provinces and Territories

Province	1981 (Census)	1983 (June Estimate)	1982 (June Estimate)	1971 (Census)	1961 (Census)
Alberta	2,237,724	2,352,300	2,318,500	1,627,874	1,331,944
British Columbia	2,744,467	2,825,000	2,791,100	2,184,621	1,629,082
Manitoba	1,026,241	1,046,300	1,034,500	988,247	921,686
New Brunswick	696,403	706,600	698,900	634,557	597,936
Newfoundland	567,681	576,200	568,500	522,104	457,853
Nova Scotia	847,442	859,300	851,700	788,960	737,007
Ontario	8,625,107	8,816,000	8,716,100	7,703,106	6,236,092
Prince Edward Island	122,506	123,900	122,700	111,641	104,629
Quebec	6,438,403	6,514,900	6,479,800	6,027,764	5,259,211
Saskatchewan	968,313	992,000	979,100	926,242	925,181
Northwest Territories	45,741	48,600	47,200	34,807	22,998
Yukon Territory	23,153	22,200	23,700	18,388	14,628
Total	**24,343,181**	**24,883,400**	**24,631,800**	**21,568,311**	**18,238,247**
Rural	5,907,254	—	—	5,157,525	5,537,857
Urban	18,435,927	—	—	16,410,785	12,700,390

Source: Statistics Canada.

Partly as a consequence of this, the Liberals' national popularity rating fell to 31% in 1982, the lowest since 1976. Six months before Trudeau's retirement, almost every poll showed the opposition Progressive Conservatives still leading the Liberals by more than 20 percentage points, but by the time Turner took over they showed the Liberals catching up or running slightly ahead.

In the national election on Sept. 4, 1984, the Progressive Conservative Party scored an overwhelming victory, fundamentally changing the country's political landscape. The Conservatives, led by Brian Mulroney, a 45-year-old corporate lawyer, won 211 of the 282 seats in the House of Commons, the highest political majority in Canadian history, Turner's Liberals won only 40 seats while the socialist New Democratic party won 30. An independent, who was expected to join the Conservatives, also was elected. Mulroney was sworn in as Canada's 18th Prime Minister on Sept. 17.

Economy. Agriculture, including horticulture, fruit growing, and the raising of stock and poultry, is the largest single industry. Canada is one of the world's greatest wheat-exporting countries; production is concentrated in Manitoba, Saskatchewan, and Alberta.

Stock raising and dairy farming have grown greatly since 1920. Ontario and Quebec are the most important dairying provinces.

Canadian manufactures rely mainly on domestic raw materials; growing industries that depend largely on material imported in a raw or semifinished state include the manufacture of automobiles, sugar, and rubber goods, as well as the iron and steel industry in Nova Scotia, Quebec, and Ontario. The latter two provinces account for more than 80% of all manufactures. The abundance of cheap water power is one of the chief factors in the growth of Canadian industry.

The most important industries in terms of output are pulp and paper, nonferrous-metals smelting and refining, petroleum products, meatpacking, motor vehicles, and sawmill products.

Canada's mineral resources are both rich and varied. Metals come mainly from two widely separated regions, the mountain ranges of the Pacific coast and the province of Ontario. Copper ore also exists in Quebec, Manitoba, and Newfoundland. Production of petroleum centers in Alberta. There are deposits of uranium in the Northwest Territories.

The total area of land covered by forests is estimated at 1,300,000 square miles (3,367,000 sq km), of which only 435,000 square miles (1,126,650 sq km) are commercially productive and accessible. The manufacture of pulp and paper is one of the leading industries.

Fishing, Canada's oldest industry, is carried on along the Atlantic and Pacific coasts and on the inland lakes.

Chief exports are motor vehicles, machinery, timber, metal ores, crude oil and products, natural gas, chemicals, newsprint, wood pulp, nonferrous metals, cereals. In 1982, exports totaled $84.4 billion, imports $67.6 billion. Leading customers were U.S. (70%), Japan (5.5%). Leading suppliers were U.S. (70%), Japan (9.5%).

In 1982, Canada's inflation rate was 10.8% and unemployment 11%, where it remained through most of 1983 and 1984.

Government of Canada

Governor General: Her Excellency The Governor General Jeanne Sauvé

GOVERNOR GENERAL'S HOUSEHOLD

Secretary to the Governor General and Secretary General of the Order of Canada, and Secretary General of the Order of Military Merit: Esmond U. Butler, Esq., C.V.D.

Comptroller of the Household: D.C. McKinnon, C.V.O.

Director of Honors: Roger de C. C. Nantel, Esq., C.D.

Administrative Secretary: Esmond A.C. Joly de Lotbiniere

Cultural Attaché: Rebecca Sisler

Press Secretary: Vic Wilczur

THE CANADIAN MINISTRY[1]

Prime Minister: John Turner

Deputy Prime Minister and Minister of External Affairs: Jean Chrétien

Government Leader in the Senate: Allan MacEachen

President of the Treasury Board: Herbert Gray

President of the Privy Council, Postmaster General, Minister of State for Regional Economic Development, and Minister of Labor: André Ouellet

Minister of Finance: Marc Lalonde

Minister of Employment and Immigration: John Roberts

Minister of National Health and Welfare: Monique Bégin

Minister of National Defense: Jean-Jacques Blais

Minister of International Trade: Francis Fox

Minister of Energy, Mines and Resources: Gerald Regan

Solicitor-General: Robert Kaplan

Minister of State for Transport: William Rompkey

Minister of Public Works and Minister of Supply and Services: Charles Lapointe

Minister of Regional Industrial Expansion, Minister of State for Science and Technology, and Minister of Communications: Edward Lumley

Minister of Justice: Donald Johnston

Minister of Transport and Minister of State for the Wheat Board: Lloyd Axworthy

Minister of State for Social Development and Minister of State for the Status of Women: Judy Erola

Minister of Environment: Charles Caccia

Secretary of State: Serge Joyal

Minister of Veterans Affairs: Bennett Campbell

Minister of State for Multiculturalism: David Collenette

Minister of State for Small Business and Tourism: David Smith

Minister of National Revenue: Roy MacLaren

Minister of Fisheries and Oceans: Herbert Breau

Minister of State for Regional Development: Rémi Bujold

Minister of State for Youth, Fitness, and Amateur Sport: Jean Lapierre

Minister of Agriculture: Ralph Ferguson

Minister of Indian Affairs and Northern Development: Douglas Frith

1. Prior to Sept. 4, 1984 election of Brian Mulroney as Prime Minister.

Provinces and Territories

ALBERTA

Capital: Edmonton
Lieut. Governor: The Hon. Frank Lynch-Staunton
Premier: The Hon. Peter Lougheed
Provincial Treasurer: Hon. Louis D. Hyndman
Atty. General: Hon. Neil Crawford
Entered Confederation: September 1, 1905
Provincial flower: Wild rose (1930)
Population (est. 1984): 2,361,000
Area: 255,285 sq mi. (661,188 sq km)
Largest cities (est. 1983): Edmonton (metro 682,000); Calgary (metro 620,692); Lethbridge (58,086); Red Deer (50,257); Medicine Hat (41,493)
Provincial parks: 62 (438.03 sq mi.)
Province revenue (Fiscal 1984–85 est.) $9.386 billion[1]
Province expenditure (Fiscal 1984–85 est.) $9.644 billion

1. Excludes funds allocated to Alberta Heritage Trust Fund and Natural Gas Rebates Fund.

Alberta was inhabited by various Indian groups for at least 10,000 years. European explorers first appeared in the 1750s to extend the fur trade. By the last quarter of the 18th century the Hudson's Bay Company and the North West Company had established trading posts. From 1821, when the companies merged, until 1870 the Hudson's Bay Company governed the area. In 1870 it was transferred to the Dominion of Canada, and officially became a province in 1905.

Alberta today has become the most dynamic and fastest growing of Canada's ten provinces. Economic progress, spurred on in recent years by developments in the energy resources sector is rapidly transforming the province into a leading North American economic region. Out of a Gross Domestic Product of $45.9 billion in 1982; the net value of production of commodity producing industries was $18.2 billion. The relative shares of this production were: mining (particularly oil and natural gas) 45.5%; construction, 20.1%; manufacturing, 17.2%; agriculture (including fishing and trapping) 9.5%; utilities 7.3%; forestry, 0.4%.

Among Alberta's attractions are Elk Island National Park, Banff and Jasper National Parks in the Rocky Mountains, Wood Buffalo National Park which straddles the Alberta-Northwest Territories border, Dinosaur Provincial Park, fur trading post of Rocky Mountain House, Provincial Museum and Archives of Alberta in Edmonton, and Heritage Park in Calgary.

BRITISH COLUMBIA

Capital: Victoria
Lieut. Governor: The Hon. Robert Rogers
Premier: The Hon. William R. Bennett
Minister of Finance: The Hon. Hugh A. Curtis
Atty. General: The Hon. Brian Smith
Entered Confederation: July 20, 1871
Provincial flower: Dogwood (1956)
Population (1981 census): 2,744,467
Area: 366,255 sq mi. (948,601 sq km)
Largest cities (1981 census): Vancouver (metro 1,268,-183); Victoria (metro 233,481); **(Oct. 1981 est.):** Burnaby (149,610); Surrey (132,945); Richmond (119,600)
Provincial parks: 356 (19,630 sq mi.)
Province revenue (1982–83): $6.5 billion
Province expenditure (1982–83): $7.5 billion

British Columbia was one of the last regions of the North American continent to be explored and settled, with the impetus coming from the fur trade and the gold that lay in its mountains. Spanish ships visited the coast in 1774, followed by Capt. James Cook, whose account of the fur wealth led to the influx of fur traders. The first trading post was established in 1805 at McLeod Lake. The gold strike of 1858 made Fort Victoria into a city, opened up the mainland to settlement, and resulted in its proclamation as the Colony of British Columbia in 1858. With the arrival of the Canadian Pacific Railway at Port Moody in 1885, a new era opened with permanent railroad and lumbering settlements established along the route.

The chief elements of the province's economy are: forest industries, mining, tourism, shipping, and agriculture, with forest industries the leader. The mining sector is also a large contributor to the economy with copper, crude oil, molybdenum, zinc lead, and natural gas the most valuable products.

Among British Columbia's attractions are the recreated gold rush town of Barkerville, Pacific Rim National Park, the fur trading post of Fort St. James, and Fort Langley where the province's salmon export industry began.

MANITOBA

Capital: Winnipeg
Lieut. Governor: Hon. Pearl McGonigal
Premier: Hon. Howard Pawley
Minister of Finance: Hon. Vic Schroeder
Atty. General: Hon. Roland Penner
Entered Confederation: July 15, 1870
Provincial flower: Prairie crocus (1906)
Population (1984 est.): 1,051,500
Area: 250,946 sq mi. (649,947 sq km)
Largest cities (1981 census): Winnipeg (metro 584,842); Brandon (35,894); Thompson (14,102); Portage la Prairie (12,959); Selkirk (9,949)
Provincial parks: 56 (3,960 sq mi.)
Province revenue (1984–85): $2,969,000,000
Province expenditure (1984–85): $3,457,600,000

Sir Thomas Button, an English explorer, came through Hudson Bay in 1612. After its foundation in 1670, the Hudson's Bay Company began to build forts in the area. Britain's claim to the Hudson Bay region was recognized by the Treaty of Utrecht in 1713, but meanwhile the French entered Manitoba from the east. La Verendrye explored and built several forts in Manitoba between 1733 and 1738. Later, British and French traders from Montreal reopened trade routes in southern and central Manitoba. In 1783, the North West Company based in Montreal began to compete for furs with the Hudson's Bay Company. A fur war ensued which ended in 1821 when the companies merged. The first European settlement of Manitoba came in 1812 when Thomas Douglas, 5th earl of Selkirk, received a grant of land on the Red River from the Hudson's Bay Company. The Dominion of Canada acquired all of the Hudson's Bay Company territory in 1869–70 and part of it became the province of Manitoba under the Manitoba Act of 1870.

Its southern farmlands are the backbone of the province's economy. Wheat is the main crop. Mineral production and forest products are other leading contributors to the economy. The major minerals are nickel, copper, oil, cement, zinc, and sand/gravel. Pulpwood for paper manufacture accounts for 60% of the timber cut. Manufacturing accounts for more than one third of the value of goods and services produced in the province every year.

Among Manitoba's attractions are Lower Fort Garry near Selkirk, restored to recreate a 19th century Hudson's Bay Company post, and Riding Mountain National Park.

NEW BRUNSWICK

Capital: Fredericton
Lieut. Governor: The Hon. Dr. George F.G. Stanley
Premier: The Hon. Richard B. Hatfield
Minister of Finance: The Hon. John B.M. Baxter, Q.C.
Minister of Justice: The Hon. Fernand Dubé, Q.C.
Entered Confederation: July 1, 1867
Provincial flower: Purple violet (1936)
Coat of Arms: Assigned by Queen Victoria in 1868
Motto: Spem Reduxit (Hope Restored)
Provincial flag: Adopted 1965
Provincial tartan: Adopted 1959
Geographic center: Boiestown
Number of counties: 15
Language: French is the first language of 34% of the population. New Brunswick is the only officially bilingual province in Canada.
Population (1984): 710,500
Area: 28,354 sq mi. (73,437 sq km)
Largest cities (1981): St. John (metro 120,900); Moncton (83,900); Fredericton (47,800); Bathurst (15,700); Edmundston (11,800); Campbellton (8,200)
Provincial parks: 57
Province revenue (1982–83): $1,945.2 million
Province expenditure (1982–83): $2,148.0 million

New Brunswick is one of the four original provinces making up the national Confederation in 1867. It was first known to Europeans as a portion of a region called Acadia, settled by the French. By the mid-18th century, British expansion on the neighboring Nova Scotian peninsula led to confrontation with the French. The Acadians were expelled after the British victory of 1755. A British proclamation of 1763 incorporated the area into Nova Scotia but in 1784 it was separated from it and was established as the province of New Brunswick. The first English settlement was established at Maugerville in 1792. During the American Revolution, 14,000 Loyalists settled on the banks of the St. John and St. Croix rivers. Responsible home government was granted by Britain in 1848 and New Brunswick entered the Confederation in 1867.

Since approximately 85% of the province is forested, it is no surprise that New Brunswick's major industries are forest-related, including the manufacture of pulp and paper. Fishing is another economic mainstay on the Bay of Fundy and northeast coasts with herring, lobster, crabs, and cod the top catches. New Brunswick is also an important mining center, ranking first in the nation in the production of bismuth, with zinc antimony, peat and lead following second, silver third, lead fourth, and copper fifth. New Brunswick agriculture and potatoes are synonymous. The dairy industry ranks first, followed by the potato industry. Food processing is a major employer. Tourism is a growing sector.

Among the province's attractions are King's Landing, a recreated Loyalist village where approximately 70 buildings and a costumed staff portray the 1780–1890 era; Village Historique Acadien which depicts the Acadian way of life between 1780–1880; Fundy and Kouchibouguac National Parks; F.D. Roosevelt's summer home on Campobello Island; the N.B. Museum, one of the oldest in the country; more than 90 covered bridges; beaches; golf courses; numerous crafts festivals.

NEWFOUNDLAND

Capital: St. John's
Lieut. Governor: Hon. W. A. Paddon
Premier: The Hon. A. Brian Peckford
Minister of Finance: The Hon. Dr. John Collins
Minister of Justice: The Hon. G. Ottenheimer
Entered Confederation: March 31, 1949
Provincial flower: Pitcher plant (1954)
Population (1981 census): 567,681
Area: 156,185 sq mi. (404,520 sq km)
Largest cities: St. John's (86,576); Corner Brook (35,198); Stephenville (10,284); Mount Pearl (10,193); Conception Bay South (9,743)
Provincial parks: 72 (3,099.0 sq mi.)
Province revenue (1984–85 est.) $2,009,243,000
Province expenditure (1984–85 est.) $2,215,511,000

John Cabot, sailing under the English flag, reached the island of Newfoundland in 1497 and is its official discoverer. His enthusiastic reports led to international rivalries over the region, with English, French, Basque, and Portuguese fishermen contesting for catches. By 1600 England and France were the chief rivals. Attempts at colonization during the 17th century were met with hostility by the English fishermen and after 1634 by the English crown. In 1699 Parliament prohibited settlement except for maintaining fisheries. French-English rivalries were settled by treaties in 1713 and 1783 recognizing British sovereignty. The island's population increased despite repressive legislation, and in 1729 Britain appointed a naval governor and in 1792 established a judicial system. With the appointment of a resident governor and council in 1824, it was acknowledged as a settled colony. A popularly elected assembly was established in 1832 and in 1855 the island was granted full responsible government. Between 1864 and 1869 and again in 1895, the subject of Newfoundland joining the Canadian Confederation was broached but was rejected at the polls. Not until 1948, in the second of two referenda, was there a clear majority for confederation. The administration of Labrador remained unsettled until 1927 when it was awarded to Newfoundland.

Newfoundland's economy is dependent upon mineral production, pulp and paper products, and fish products. Oil has been discovered at the Hybernia Well, some 200 miles offshore from St. John's on Eastern Grand Banks.

Among Newfoundland's attractions are an ancient Indian burial ground at Port aux Choix and a Norse settlement at L'Anse aux Meadows.

NORTHWEST TERRITORIES

Capital: Yellowknife
Commissioner: John H. Parker
Deputy Commissioner: Agnes Semmler
Created: July 15, 1870
Reconstituted: Sept. 1, 1905
Flower: Mountain avens (1959)
Population: 49,431
Area: 1,304,903 sq mi. (3,379,698 sq km)
Largest cities: Yellowknife (10,620); Inuvik (3,599); Hay River (3,121); Frobisher Bay (2,596); Fort Smith (2,347)
Territories revenue (Fiscal 1982–83): $462,114,000
Territories expenditure (Fiscal 1982–83): $475,996,000

The Athabascan Indian people have lived in the forested and barrenland regions of what is now the Northwest Territories during the last 2,500 years. The Inuit (Eskimo) have lived in the Arctic regions for about 1,000 years.

Many believe the first Europeans to visit the Northwest Territories were the Norse. According to their history, they sailed by an icy and mountainous land they called Helluland, which was probably what we now call Baffin Island.

In the late 16th century, British trading companies began searching for a shorter more secure shipping route to the Pacific Ocean and the Orient, and Arctic exploration began. In 1576 Martin Frobisher took possession of Baffin Island. In 1668 the ship *Nonsuch* entered Hudson Bay to establish a trade in furs. This led to the establishment of the Hudson's Bay Company in 1670, a company which continues to this day.

In 1818 the British Admiralty began a serious effort to find the Northwest Passage. Ten expeditions were mounted over the next 30 years. But it wasn't until 1903, when *The Gjoa,* commanded by Norwegian Roald Amundsen, sailed from Europe, that the Passage was finally navigated, after three winters in the Arctic.

Meanwhile land expeditions by Sir John Franklin, Thomas Simpson, and others had resulted in exploration and mapping of the Mackenzie District and northern coastline during the 1820s and 1830s.

Commercial ventures followed in the footsteps of the explorers. Many fur trading posts were established in the Mackenzie Valley. Whaling fleets began in Baffin Bay, Hudson Bay and later the western Arctic.

Not far behind were the missionaries, followed by the Royal Canadian Mounted Police, who were made responsible for maintaining law and order.

In 1920 oil was struck north of Fort Norman. There was a dramatic increase in traffic on the Mackenzie River. The introduction of the airplane increased the demand for fuel and the refinery expanded at Norman Wells in 1939.

The first gold brick was poured in 1938 at Yellowknife and two gold mines are still producing. Mining became the principal industry. Today lead and zinc are the main products. They are mined in Pine Point. Exploration for oil and gas is proceeding at a high pitch with good potential for the future.

There has been an evolution toward more responsible government in the Northwest Territories. In 1967 Yellowknife was named capital of the N.W.T. and the Territorial Government was located there. By 1970 most provincial-type responsibilities had been transferred from the federal government to the Territorial Government. The exception was and still is nonrenewable resources which remain with the federal administration. The Territorial Council has developed from a combination of elected representatives and federal appointees to a fully elected legislative assembly with up to eight of its members responsible for government departments and forming an Executive Council or cabinet along with the Commissioner who is a public servant.

Among the Northwest Territories' attractions are Wood Buffalo National Park, which straddles the Alberta-Northwest Territories border, home of the largest herd of bison on the continent; Nahanni National Park with its spectacular Virginia Falls; and Auyuittuq, on Baffin Island, Canada's first national park above the Arctic Circle.

NOVA SCOTIA

Capital: Halifax
Lieut. Governor: The Hon. Alan Rockwell Abraham
Premier: The Hon. John M. Buchanan
Mayor: His Worship Ron Wallace
Minister of Finance: The Hon. J. Gregory Kerr
Atty. General: The Hon. Ronald C. Giffin
Entered Confederation: July 1, 1867
Provincial flower: Trailing Arbutus (1901) "Mayflower"
Population (1981 census): 847,442
Area: Land 20,402 sq mi.; water, 1,023 sq mi. Total: 21,425 sq mi. (55,491 sq km)
Highest Point: 1,747 ft
Origin of Name: Latin for New Scotland. Derived from the Latin charter by which New Scotland was granted to Sir Wm. Alexander (afterwards Earl of Stirling) in 1621
Slogan: Canada's Ocean Playground
Flag: Consists of the ancient Arms granted in 1625 by King Charles I, with the cross of Saint Andrew extended in a rectangle three-quarters as wide as its length. Colors: Red, yellow, royal blue, and white
Tartan: The Nova Scotia tartan was the first provincial tartan in Canada. Originally designed in 1953, the popular tartan was registered in 1956 in Her Majesty's Register Office in Edinburgh, Scotland. Colors: red, gold, blue, white, and green
No. of counties: 18
Largest cities (1981 census): Halifax (metro 277,727); (1980): Dartmouth (65,341); Sydney (30,645); Glace Bay (21,836); Truro (12,840)
Provincial parks: 103 (25.1 sq mi.)
Province revenue: $1,945,465,007. Recoveries: $173,600,095
Province expenditure: $2,387,755,317

Nova Scotia is one of the four British colonies federated into the Dominion of Canada in 1867. It was the site of the first permanent North American settlement north of Florida, established by the French in 1605. The 17th and 18th centuries were characterized by struggles for power between the British and French. In 1713 the French began construction of Louisbourg fortress and Halifax was founded in 1749 as a counterbalance. In 1848 Nova Scotia became the first British colony to have a government responsible to the people through elected representatives. There was economic and political opposition to the proposed confederation with Ontario, Quebec, and New Brunswick, but the union was carried out in 1867.

The chief components of the province's economy are fisheries, agriculture (livestock, poultry, dairying), the pulp industry, and mining (coal and industrial minerals).

Among Nova Scotia's attractions are Fort Ann, the first national historic park; the restored fortress of Louisbourg; Champlain's habitation at Port Royal; the Halifax Citadel; Alexander Graham Bell National Historic Park; and Cape Breton Highlands National Park.

ONTARIO

Capital: Toronto
Lieut. Governor: The Hon. John Black Aird
Premier: The Hon. William G. Davis
Provincial Treasurer: The Hon. Larry Grossman
Atty. General: The Hon. Roy McMurtry
Entered Confederation: July 1, 1867
Provincial flower: White trillium (1937)
Population (1983): 8,800,000
Area: 413,000 sq mi. (1,070,000 sq km)
Largest cities (1983 census): Toronto (metro 3,067,100); Ottawa (metro 737,600); Hamilton (metro 548,100); **(1981):** North York (559,521); Scarborough (443,353)
Provincial parks: 138 (21,145.8 sq mi.)
Province revenue (1983–84 interim): $22.6 billion
Province expenditure (1983–84 interim): $24.9 billion

The first known white man in the province was the French explorer Étienne Brûlé on an expedition to the Ottawa River in 1610–11. He was followed by Samuel de Champlain, other French explorers, fur traders, and missionaries. France established Fort Frontenac (present-day Kingston) in 1673 to provide military protection to its fur empire. However, no French colonization had taken place, except for a small farming settlement near Detroit, by the time Canada was ceded to Great Britain in 1763. The Quebec Act of 1774 established Ontario as part of an extended colony ruled from Quebec. The Constitution Act of 1791 divided Quebec colony into Lower Canada (French-Quebec) and Upper Canada (Loyalist-Ontario). John Graves Simcoe, the first lieutenant governor of Upper Canada fixed the capital at York (now Toronto). In 1841 the provinces were united. Responsible cabinet government was achieved in 1848. Canadian federation—in 1867—was brought about in large part by John A. MacDonald and George Brown, Ontario politicians.

Leading elements of the province's economy are agriculture, mining (the province mines 51% of the world's nickel), forest products, and manufacturing (steel, automobiles, industrial machinery).

Among Ontario's attractions are Upper Canada Village near Morrisburg, a recreation of a 19th century Ontario community; Fort Henry at Kingston, and Fort George at Niagara Falls; and "Canada's Wonderland," the nation's first theme park located in Maple.

PRINCE EDWARD ISLAND

Capital: Charlottetown
Lieut. Governor: The Hon. J.A. Doiron
Premier: The Hon. James M. Lee
Minister of Finance: The Hon. Lloyd G. MacPhail
Atty. General: The Hon. George R. McMahon
Entered Confederation: July 1, 1873
Provincial flower: Lady's slipper (1947)
Population (1981 census): 122,506
Area: 2,184 sq mi. (5,657 sq km)
Largest cities: Charlottetown (15,282); Summerside (7,828); Sherwood (5,782); St. Eleanors (2,716); Parkdale (2,018)
Provincial parks: 35 (6 sq mi.)
Province revenue (1984–85): $432,222,600
Province expenditure (1984–85): $440,300,700

John Cabot may have seen the island in 1497 but Jacques Cartier, the French navigator, is credited with its discovery in June 1534. Samuel de Champlain claimed it for France in 1603 but it was not colonized until 1720. The British occupied the Island in 1758 and it was formally ceded to Great Britain in 1763. Representative government reached the island in 1851. A conference in 1864 to discuss the possible union of the three Maritime Provinces was the forerunner of the Quebec Conference of 1864 which resulted in the founding of the Dominion of Canada. Thus Prince Edward Island has been known as the "Cradle of Confederation" although it did not join the union until 1873.

Agriculture is the basic element in the Island's economy, followed by the tourist industry and fisheries. Manufacturing and processing are becoming more important, especially electronic equipment and frozen french fries.

Among the province's attractions are Province House in Charlottetown, which is a national historic site; 1,100 miles of pink, sandy beaches; and Fort Amherst-Port LaJoie National Historic Park, with a full-sized reproduction of a Micmac Indian village nearby.

QUEBEC

Capital: Quebec City
Lieut. Governor: The Hon. Gilles Lamontagne
Premier: Rene Levesque
Deputy Prime Minister: Camille Laurin
Minister of Finance: The Hon. Jacques Parizeau
Minister of Justice: The Hon. Pierre-Marc Johnson
Entered Confederation: July 1, 1867
Provincial flower: White garden (Madonna) lily (1963)
Population (1981 census): 6,438,403
Area: 594,860 sq mi. (1,540,687 sq km)
Largest cities (1981 census): Montreal (metro 2,802,-547); Laval (246,243); Quebec (metro 542,158) **(1980):** Longueuil (122,429); St. Léonard (78,452)
Provincial parks, reserves & camping areas: 112
Province revenue (1983): $21,350,000
Province expenditure (1983): $24,630,000

Jacques Cartier landed at present-day Gaspé in 1534 and took possession of the land in the name of the King of France. New France began with the founding of Quebec City by Samuel de Champlain in 1608, Trois-Rivière in 1616, and Montreal in 1642. Following capitulation of the French army to the British in 1760, the land was ceded to Britain in 1763. The Quebec Act of 1774 created what is now Quebec and tried to fuse British and French institutions in the new political entity. In 1791 Canada was divided into Lower Canada (French) and Upper Canada (English). An attempt to unite them in 1822 failed but in 1841 an Act of Union joined the provinces and in 1867 the British North American Act created the Confederation of Canada.

The economy of the province breaks down as follows: 61% service industries, 30% manufacturing-processing industries, 8% agricultural-extractive. Iron ore, electric power, and forest products (pulp and paper plants) are the chief resources.

Among the province's attractions are Montreal,

the second largest French-speaking city in the world; Quebec City, the seat of Parliament, the Plains of Abraham, the restoration of Place Royale (30 buildings of the 18th Century); the Laurentian Mountains with their skiing facilities; and scenic drives along the King's Highway, Beaupré coast, and Gaspé Peninsula.

SASKATCHEWAN

Capital: Regina
Lieut. Governor: The Hon. F. W. Johnson
Premier: The Hon. Grant Devine
Minister of Finance: The Hon. Robert Andrew
Justice Minister: The Hon. Gary Lane
Entered Confederation: September 1, 1905
Provincial flower: Western red lily (1941)
Provincial bird emblem: Prairie sharp-tailed grouse
Population (1983): 990,700
Area: 251,700 sq mi. (651,903 sq km)
Largest cities (1983 estimate): Regina (metro 167,900); Saskatoon (metro 159,000); Moose Jaw (33,357); Prince Albert (30,906); Yorkton (15,158)
Provincial and Regional parks: 116 (2,191 sq mi.)
National Park: 1 (1,500 sq mi.)
Province revenue (1983-84 est.) $2,733,530,000
Province expenditure (1983-84 est.): $3,125,205,940

The first white man known to see the Saskatchewan River was Henry Kelsey in 1691. The area which became the Province of Saskatchewan was first granted to the Hudson's Bay Company. In 1868 it was surrendered back to the British crown by the Rupert's Land Act to be turned over to the newly formed Dominion of Canada, which was done in 1870. In 1873 Canada created the North West Mounted Police to maintain law and order. The territories were granted an executive council in 1875 and by 1897 had won responsible parliamentary government. Saskatchewan entered the Confederation in 1905 under the Saskatchewan Act.

The chief elements of the province's economy are agriculture, oil, gas, potash, coal and uranium.

Among its attractions are Prince Albert National Park, Cypress Hills, Provincial Park, and Fort Walsh, the first headquarters of the North West Mounted police, R.C.M.P. Training Depot, Provincial and Western Development Museums.

YUKON TERRITORY

Capital: Whitehorse
Commissioner: Douglas Bell
Created a separate territory: June 1898
Flower: Fireweed (1957)
Population (1981 census): 23,153
Area: 207,076 sq mi. (536,327 sq km)
Largest cities (1981 census): Whitehorse (14,814); Faro (1,652); Watson Lake (748)
Operating & Maintenance Budget
Government revenue[1] (1983-84): $146,538,000
Government expenditures[1] (1983-84): $143,142,000
Capital Budget
Government revenue (1983-84): $27,136,000
Government expenditures (1983-84): $24,412,000

1. Includes Crown corporations.

The Yukon was among the last areas of the North American continent to be explored by white men. Two explorers for the Hudson's Bay Company, John Bell and Robert Campbell, first entered the region around 1840. Fort Yukon was established in 1847 on the Yukon River in what was Russian territory. It was relocated in 1867 after the United States purchased Alaska from Russia, and it was relocated again in 1890. It was a center for a small fur trade. Gold discoveries in the 1870s brought some prospectors into the area, but it was the discovery of rich deposits in Bonanza Creek in 1896 that led to the gold rush of 1898. In the same year the Canadian Parliament separated the rapidly growing area from the Northwest Territories and gave it separate territorial status.

The territory's economy is dependent upon mining, with tourism, a rapidly expanding industry, second. Logging is carried out in some southern areas.

Among the Yukon's attractions are Klune National Park, (a World Heritage Site) which contains Canada's highest peak, Mount Logan; Dawson City, the old gold rush boom town, which has been restored; and the Dempster Highway, the only publicly accessible land link to the Arctic Ocean.

Party Standings—House of Commons

Thirty-second Parliament—Speaker, Lloyd Francis, The Clerk of the House of Commons, C.B. Koester

Province	Lib.[1]	P.C.[2]	N.D.P.[3]	S.Cr.[4]	Ind.	Vacancies	Seats by provinces
Alberta	0	20	—	—	1	—	21
British Columbia	—	17	11	—	—	—	28
Manitoba	2	5	7	—	—	—	14
New Brunswick	7	3	—	—	—	—	10
Newfoundland	5	2	—	—	—	—	7
Nova Scotia	5	6	—	—	—	—	11
Ontario	51[1]	38	6	—	—	3	95
Prince Edward Island	2	2	—	—	—	—	4
Quebec	74	1	—	—	—	—	75
Saskatchewan	—	7	7	—	—	—	14
Yukon/NWT	1	2	—	—	—	—	3
National totals	**147[5]**	**103**	**31**	—	**1**	**0**	**282**

1. Liberal Party—Leader, John Turner. 2. Progressive Conservative Party—Leader, Brian Mulroney 3. New Democratic Party—Leader, John Edward Broadbent. 4. Social Credit Party—Leader, Fabien Roy. 5. Includes 1 Liberal-Labor member. NOTE: Last three General Elections were held on May 22, 1979, Feb. 18, 1980, and Sept. 4, 1984. The legal duration is five years. Party standings will change with the Thirty-third Parliament as a result of the election.

Principal Trading Partners in 1983

(in millions of Canadian dollars)

Selected countries	Imports	Exports
Algeria	$150.1	$449.3
Australia	357.5	468.7
Belgium/Luxembourg	296.0	714.3
Brazil	500.0	625.3
Denmark	136.9	68.5
France	841.0	654.1
Hong Kong	820.3	229.3
Ireland	107.3	99.1
Italy	798.4	569.3
Japan	4,409.4	4,761.8
Mexico	1,079.2	382.4
Netherlands	349.4	975.7
People's Republic of China	245.8	1,609.0
Saudi Arabia	0.1	369.4
South Korea	791.4	564.1
Taiwan	925.5	345.9
United Kingdom	1,809.8	2,508.8
United States	54,103.3	66,332.5
U.S.S.R.	33.3	1,764.6
Venezuela	1,004.5	309.6
West Germany	1,576.6	1,181.7
Total selected countries	**70,335.8**	**90,113.4**
Total all countries	**75,586.6**	**90,963.9**

National Holidays

	1984	1985	1986
New Year's Day	Jan. 1	Jan. 1	Jan. 1
Good Friday	April 20	April 5	March 28
Easter Monday	April 23	April 8	March 31
Victoria Day	May 21	May 20	May 19
Dominion Day	July 2	July 1	July 1
Labor Day	Sept. 3	Sept. 2	Sept. 1
Thanksgiving	Oct. 8	Oct. 14	Oct. 13
Remembrance Day	Nov. 11	Nov. 11	Nov. 11
Christmas Day	Dec. 25	Dec. 25	Dec. 25
Boxing Day	Dec. 26	Dec. 26	Dec. 26

National Flag and Motto

The National Flag of Canada, otherwise known as the Canadian Flag, was approved by Parliament and proclaimed by Her Majesty the Queen on February 15, 1965, and is described as a red flag of the proportions two by length and one by width, containing in its center a white square the width of the flag, bearing a single red maple leaf.

The Flag is flown on land daily from sunrise to sunset at all federal government buildings, airports, and military bases and establishments within and outside Canada, and may appropriately be flown or displayed by individuals and organizations.

The Canada Shipping Act provides that the National Flag is the proper national colors for all Canadian ships and boats; and it is the flag flown on Canadian Naval vessels.

The motto—*A mari usque ad mare* ("From sea to sea")—is from the Latin version of Psalm LXXII: 8: "He shall have dominion also from sea to sea, and from the river unto the ends of the earth."

Canadian Museums and Related Institutions

Region	Art galleries	History museums	Restorations	Science and technology museums	Living science museums	General museums	Community museums	Archives	Other institutions[1]	Total
Atlantic	10	9	65	8	2	3	44	14	5	160
Quebec	11	19	16	4	11	1	27	11	6	106
Ontario	35	22	73	14	12	3	106	19	9	293
Central	19	39	45	10	8	7	113	12	8	261
British Columbia	11	12	14	9	8	2	49	7	6	118
Yukon and Northwest Territories	—	—	2	—	—	1	3	1	—	7
Total	**86**	**101**	**215**	**45**	**41**	**17**	**342**	**64**	**34**	**945**

1. Aquaria, zoos, botanical gardens, aboretums, and conservatories. 2. Including nature park museums or nature centers. *Source:* Statistics Canada, July 1979, based on a 1976 survey. NOTE: Data are latest available.

Percentage Distribution of Canadian Population by Provinces and Territories

Province or territory	1982 (est.)	1981	1971	1961	1951	1941	1931
Alberta	9.40	9.19	7.55	7.30	6.71	6.92	7.05
British Columbia	11.32	11.29	10.13	8.93	8.32	7.11	6.69
Manitoba	4.20	4.21	4.58	5.05	5.54	6.34	6.75
New Brunswick	2.83	2.86	2.94	3.28	3.68	3.97	3.94
Newfoundland	2.31	2.33	2.42	2.51	2.58	—	—
Nova Scotia	3.45	3.48	3.66	4.04	4.59	5.02	4.94
Ontario	35.38	35.43	35.71	34.19	32.82	32.92	33.07
Prince Edward Island	0.49	0.50	0.52	0.58	0.70	0.83	0.85
Quebec	26.31	26.44	27.95	28.84	28.95	28.96	27.70
Saskatchewan	3.97	3.97	4.29	5.07	5.94	7.79	8.88
Northwest Territories	0.19	0.18	0.16	0.13	0.11	0.10	0.09
Yukon Territory	0.09	0.09	0.09	0.08	0.06	0.04	0.04
Totals	**100.00**	**100.00**	**100.00**	**100.00**	**100.00**	**100.00**	**100.00**

Canadian Motor Vehicle Registrations, 1982

Province or territory	Passenger cars[1]	Motor trucks	Motor buses	Motor cycles	Other motor vehicles[2]	Total motor vehicles
Alberta	1,259,791	460,217	7,845	59,898	(3)	1,787,751
British Columbia	1,406,370	591,925[4]	(5)	74,938[6]	(3)	2,074,530
Manitoba	464,916	187,083	137[7]	17,461[6]	732[8]	670,329
New Brunswick	249,819	99,523	696	12,255[6]	10,503	372,796
Newfoundland	129,387	56,440	n.a.	4,687[6]	n.a.	190,514
Nova Scotia	363,883	147,691	1,529	21,524[6]	745	535,372
Ontario	3,842,743	1,067,535	23,827	126,090[6]	n.a.	5,060,195
Prince Edward Island	48,177	17,397	418	2,104[6]	124	68,220
Quebec	2,376,745	294,706	14,869	138,825[6]	1,005	2,826,150
Saskatchewan	375,165	294,904	4,485	12,269	651	687,474
Northwest Territory	6,480	10,562	93	1,082[6]	57	18,274
Yukon Territory	6,879	11,358	166	709[6]	(3)	19,112
Total	**10,530,355**	**3,239,341**	**54,065**	**473,139**[6]	**13,817**	**14,310,717**

1. Includes taxis and for hire cars. 2. Ambulances, fire trucks, etc. 3. Included with passenger cars or trucks. 4. Includes taxicabs. 5. Included in trucks. 6. Includes mopeds. 7. Excludes school buses which are licensed as passenger cars. 8. Includes only antique vehicles and vehicles for road testing. NOTE: n.a. = not available. *Source:* Statistics Canada.

Canadian Consumer Price Index

(1981 = 100)

Year	Food	Housing	Clothing	Transportation	Health and personal care	Recreation, reading and education	Tobacco and alcohol	All-item index
1965	83.4	77.3	83.8	80.7	79.4	77.9	81.7	80.5
1966	88.7	79.5	87.0	82.6	81.8	80.1	83.7	83.5
1967	89.9	82.9	91.4	86.1	86.0	84.1	85.8	86.5
1968	92.8	86.7	94.1	88.3	89.5	88.3	93.6	90.0
1969	96.7	91.2	96.7	92.4	93.8	93.5	97.2	94.1
1970	98.9	95.7	98.5	96.1	98.0	96.8	98.4	97.2
1971	100.0	100.0	100.0	100.0	100.0	100.0	100.0	100.0
1972	107.6	104.7	102.6	102.6	104.8	102.8	102.7	104.8
1973	123.3	111.4	107.7	105.3	109.8	107.1	106.0	112.7
1974	143.4	121.1	118.0	115.8	119.4	116.4	111.8	125.0
1975	161.9	133.2	125.1	129.4	133.0	128.5	125.3	138.5
1976	166.2	145.7	132.0	143.3	144.3	136.2	134.3	148.9
1977	180.1	161.9	141.0	153.3	155.1	142.7	143.8	160.8
1978	208.0	170.8	146.4	162.2	166.2	148.2	155.5	175.2
1979	235.4	186.2	159.9	178.0	181.2	158.4	166.7	191.2
1980	260.6	201.4	178.7	200.7	199.3	173.5	185.3	210.6
1981	290.4	226.4	191.4	237.6	221.0	191.0	209.2	236.9
1982	107.2	112.5	105.6	114.1	110.6	108.7	115.5	110.8
1983	111.2	120.2	109.8	119.8	118.2	115.8	130.0	117.2

Source: Statistics Canada.

Growth Statistics
(in Canadian dollars)

Year	Exports (including re-exports) (millions of dollars)	Imports (millions of dollars)	Industry selling price indexes for manufacturing (1971 = 100)	Railway gross revenues[1] (millions of dollars)	Railway operating expenses[1] (millions of dollars)	Tons of revenue freight carried one mile[1] (millions)	Freight carried on Welland Canal (thousands of tons)	Vessels other than coastal entered & cleared (thousands of reg net tons)
1921	$ 814	$ 799	n.a.	458	423	26,622	2,792	54,649
1941	1,640	1,449	n.a.	538	404	49,982	12,002	64,766
1951	3,963	4,085	n.a.	1,089	978	64,300	14,696	100,259
1961	5,896	5,771	82.4	1,156	1,053	65,828	28,489	156,987
1965	8,767	8,633	n.a.	1,369	1,288	87,052	53,437	199,454
1966	10,326	9,866	n.a.	1,476	1,367	94,944	59,137	202,170
1967	11,411	11,075	n.a.	1,514	1,438	92,239	52,850	197,422
1968	13,624	12,358	92.3	1,528	1,433	93,147	58,105	204,777
1969	14,890	14,130	95.8	1,579	1,496	94,688	53,532	197,391
1970	16,819	13,952	98.1	1,672	1,570	108,210	57,035	217,621
1971	17,820	15,618	100.0	1,797	1,693	119,412	57,206	228,561
1972	20,140	18,669	104.4	1,843	1,750	119,135	58,236	243,376
1973	25,301	23,303	116.1	2,029	1,935	125,471	60,959	244,466
1974	32,441	31,692	138.1	2,476	2,394	133,554	47,501	227,175
1975	33,245	34,691	153.7	2,619	2,669	131,048	54,295	231,354
1976	38,397	37,444	161.6	3,058	2,927	132,599	58,369	248,502
1977	44,554	42,156	174.3	3,388	3,186	137,745	65,079	264,425
1978	53,183	30,102	190.4	3,723	3,526	141,737	65,671	277,433
1979	65,514	62,724	217.9	4,601	4,259	152,085	66,165	301,562
1980	76,159	69,274	247.2	5,174	4,729	156,248	n.a.	n.a.
1981	83,812	79,482	272.4	5,997	5,468	154,567	n.a.	n.a.
1982	84,535	67,927	288.8	n.a.	n.a.	n.a.	n.a.	n.a.

1. Seven major railways, representing about 95% of the industry in terms of operating revenues and other performance indicators. NOTE: n.a. = not available. *Source:* Statistics Canada.

Growth Statistics
(in Canadian dollars)

Year	Motor vehicle registrations (thousands)	Telephones in use (thousands)	Post office and money order revenue (thousands)	Index numbers of weekly earnings[1] 1961=100	Strikes and lockouts: Employees affected (thousands)	Strikes and lockouts: Time lost working days (thousands)	Federal finance: Total revenue (millions of dollars)	Federal finance: Total expenditure (millions of dollars)	Federal finance: Net debt (millions of dollars)
1921	465	902	26,331	n.a.	28	1,049	436	528	2,341
1931	1,201	1,364	30,416	n.a.	11	204	356	442	2,262
1941	1,573	1,562	40,383	34.1	87	434	872	1,250	3,649
1951	2,872	3,114	90,455	64.0	103	902	3,113	2,901	11,645
1961	5,517	6,014	202,004	100.0	98	1,335	5,618	5,958	12,437
1965	6,669	7,445	263,704	116.2	172	2,350	7,180	7,218	15,504
1966	7,035	7,883	275,994	127.8	411	5,178	7,696	7,735	15,543
1967	7,482	8,358	295,529	130.6	252	3,975	8,358	8,780	15,965
1968	7,877	8,818	337,023	140.3	224	5,083	9,029	9,824	16,760
1969	8,254	9,296	374,902	150.8	307	7,752	10,163	11,938	17,336
1970	8,497	9,750	444,069	162.8	262	6,540	12,321	11,928	16,943
1971	9,022	10,269	432,911	176.7	240	2,867	12,803	13,182	17,322
1972	9,481	10,987	504,211	191.4	706	7,754	14,227	14,841	17,937
1973	10,158	11,677	563,159	205.4	348	5,776	16,602	16,121	17,456
1974	11,002	12,454	591,133	227.6	581	9,255	19,383	20,056	18,128
1975	11,443	13,165	617,743	261.7	506	11,480	24,909	26,055	19,275
1976	11,786	13,885	568,190	295.8	1,571[2]	11,685	29,956	33,978	23,296
1977	12,547	14,488	774,860	326.2	218	3,742	32,721	39,011	29,586
1978	12,975	15,172	945,763	350.3	402	7,393	32,866	42,902	39,622
1979	13,338	15,839	1,108,543	381.6	463	7,834	35,216	46,923	55,807
1980	13,717	16,531	1,483,211	419.6	441	8,975	49,703	57,177	68,595
1981	13,851	16,944	1,529,839	470.6	339	8,878	58,361	67,800	83,491
1982	n.a.	n.a.	1,696,310	520.3	445	5,796	72,532	78,776	94,869

1. In manufacturing. 2. This figure includes 830,000 affected by "day of protest." NOTE: n.a. = not available. *Source:* Statistics Canada.

Estimates of the Civilian Labor Force and Its Main Components, Annual Averages

(in thousands)

Year	Civilian population[1]	Civilian labor force[1]: Employed	Unemployed	Total labor force	Persons not in the labor force[1]	Unemployment rate percent	Participation rate percent
1969	14,638	7,780	382	8,162	6,475	4.7	55.8
1970	15,016	7,879	495	8,374	6,642	5.9	55.8
1971	15,388	8,079	552	8,631	6,757	6.4	56.1
1972	15,747	8,329	562	8,891	6,856	6.3	56.5
1973	16,125	8,759	520	9,279	6,846	5.6	57.5
1974	16,562	9,137	525	9,662	6,900	5.4	58.3
1975	16,470	9,363	697	10,060	6,410	6.9	61.1
1976	16,873	9,572	736	10,308	6,565	7.1	61.1
1977	17,250	9,754	862	10,616	6,634	8.1	61.5
1978[2]	17,381	9,972	911	10,882	6,499	8.4	62.6
1979[2]	17,691	10,369	838	11,207	6,484	7.5	63.3
1980[2]	18,004	10,655	867	11,522	6,483	7.5	64.0
1981[2]	18,295	10,933	898	11,830	6,464	7.6	64.7
1982[2]	18,664	10,644	1,314	11,958	6,706	11.0	64.1
1983[2]	18,917	10,734	1,448	12,183	6,735	11.9	64.4

1. 14 years of age, or over. 2. 15 years of age, or over. *Source:* Statistics Canada.

Highest Elevations

Province or territory	Height in feet	Height in meters
Alberta—Mount Columbia	12,294	3,747
British Columbia—Mt. Fairweather	15,300	4,663
Manitoba—Baldy Mountain	2,729	832
New Brunswick—Mount Carleton	2,690	820
Newfoundland—Cirque Mt., Labrador Penin.	5,160	1,573
Nova Scotia—North Barren Mt., Cape Breton Island	1,747	532
Ontario—Ogidaki Mt.	2,183	665
Prince Edward Island—highest point Queens County	465	142
Quebec—Mt. Jacques Cartier, Gaspé Penin.	4,160	1,268
Saskatchewan—Cypress Hills	4,546	1,386
Northwest Territories—Mt. Sir James MacBrien	9,062	2,762
Yukon Territory—Mount Logan	19,850	6,050

Air Distances Between Cities

(via Air Canada)

From	To	Miles[1]
Gander	Montreal	1,109
Gander	Toronto	1,494
Halifax	Moncton	120
Halifax	Montreal	571
Halifax	North Bay	1,034
Halifax	Ottawa	665
Halifax	Toronto	897
Halifax	Vancouver	3,015
Halifax	Winnipeg	1,893
Lethbridge	Calgary	124
Lethbridge	Edmonton	301
Montreal	Boston	778
Montreal	Edmonton	2,019
Montreal	Goose Bay	824
Montreal	Moncton	451
Montreal	New York	350
Montreal	Ottawa	94
Montreal	Toronto	326
Montreal	Vancouver	2,444
Montreal	Windsor	521
Ottawa	Winnipeg	1,174
St. John's, Nfld.	Montreal	1,147
Sydney	Halifax	200
Toronto	Chicago	435
Toronto	Cleveland	195
Toronto	Edmonton	1,693
Toronto	New York	375
Toronto	Tampa	1,119
Toronto	Vancouver	2,118
Toronto	Winnipeg	942
Vancouver	Victoria	47
Winnipeg	Calgary	750
Winnipeg	Edmonton	753

1. Statute miles. *Source:* Air Canada.

Mileage Between Principal Points in Canada

(via rail or water)

Approximate distances by rail or water	Nfld. St. John's	N.S. Halifax	P.E.I. Charlottetown	N.B. Saint John	N.B. Fredericton	Que. Quebec	Que. Montreal	Ont. Ottawa	Ont. Toronto	Ont. Thunder Bay	Man. Winnipeg	Sask. Regina	Sask. Saskatoon	Alta. Calgary	Alta. Edmonton	B.C. Vancouver	B.C. Victoria	B.C. Pr. Rupert
St. John's	0	930	1,041	1,081	1,094	1,466	1,563	1,675	1,897	2,521	2,797	3,153	3,268	3,531	3,646	4,262	4,362	4,543
Halifax	930	0	239	279	292	664	761	873	1,095	1,719	1,995	2,351	2,466	2,729	2,844	3,460	3,560	3,741
Charlottetown	1,041	239	0	215	230	600	684	795	1,018	1,653	1,950	2,305	2,421	2,772	2,751	3,413	3,498	3,707
Saint John	1,081	279	215	0	67	425	482	594	816	1,470	1,894	2,250	2,374	2,726	2,699	3,368	3,324	3,655
Fredericton	1,094	292	230	67	0	403	454	565	788	1,423	1,753	2,108	2,224	2,575	2,554	3,216	3,301	3,510
Quebec City	1,466	664	600	425	403	0	164	276	498	1,152	1,521	1,877	1,992	2,353	2,323	2,995	2,898	3,279
Montreal	1,563	761	684	482	454	164	0	112	334	988	1,357	1,713	1,828	2,244	2,151	2,886	2,900	3,115
Ottawa	1,675	873	795	594	565	276	112	0	247	887	1,301	1,658	1,772	2,133	2,098	2,775	2,789	3,054
Toronto	1,897	1,095	1,018	816	788	498	334	247	0	809	1,233	1,590	1,704	2,065	2,030	2,707	2,755	2,986
Thunder Bay	2,521	1,719	1,653	1,470	1,423	1,152	988	877	809	0	424	781	895	1,256	1,221	1,898	1,967	2,177
Winnipeg	2,797	1,995	1,950	1,894	1,753	1,521	1,357	1,301	1,233	424	0	356	471	832	797	1,474	1,548	1,753
Regina	3,153	2,351	2,305	2,250	2,108	1,877	1,713	1,658	1,590	781	356	0	161	476	487	1,118	1,193	1,443
Saskatoon	3,268	2,466	2,421	2,374	2,224	1,992	1,828	1,772	1,704	895	471	161	0	399	326	1,097	1,131	1,282
Calgary	3,531	2,729	2,772	2,726	2,575	2,353	2,244	2,133	2,065	1,256	832	476	399	0	195	642	727	1,151
Edmonton	3,646	2,844	2,751	2,699	2,554	2,323	2,151	2,098	2,030	1,221	797	487	326	195	0	771	846	956
Vancouver	4,262	3,460	3,413	3,368	3,216	2,995	2,886	2,775	2,707	1,898	1,474	1,118	1,097	642	771	0	85	546
Victoria	4,362	3,560	3,498	3,324	3,301	2,898	2,900	2,789	2,755	1,967	1,548	1,193	1,131	727	846	85	0	631
Prince Rupert	4,543	3,741	3,707	3,655	3,510	3,279	3,115	3,054	2,986	2,177	1,753	1,443	1,282	1,151	956	546	641	0

Land and Fresh Water Areas of Canada

Province, territory, or district	Land		Fresh water		Total		Percent of total area
	Sq miles	Sq km	Sq miles	Sq km	Sq miles	Sq km	
Alberta	248,800	644,392	6,485	16,976	255,285	661,188	6.6
British Columbia	359,279	930,533	6,976	18,068	366,255	948,601	9.5
Manitoba	211,775	548,497	39,225	101,593	251,000	650,090	6.5
New Brunswick	27,835	72,093	519	1,344	28,354	73,437	0.7
Newfoundland	143,045	370,487	413,140	34,033	156,185	404,520	4.1
Nova Scotia	20,402	52,841	1,023	2,650	21,425	55,491	0.6
Ontario	344,092	891,198	68,490	177,389	412,582	1,068,587	10.7
Prince Edward Island	2,184	5,657	—	—	2,184	5,657	0.1
Quebec	523,860	1,356,797	71,000	183,890	594,860	1,540,687	15.4
Saskatchewan	220,182	570,271	31,518	81,632	251,700	651,903	6.5
Northwest Territories	1,253,438	3,246,404	51,465	133,294	1,304,903	3,379,698	33.9
Franklin	541,753	1,403,140	7,500	19,425	549,253	1,422,565	14.3
Keewatin	218,460	565,811	9,700	25,123	228,160	590,134	5.9
Mackenzie	493,225	1,277,453	34,265	88,746	527,490	1,366,199	13.7
Yukon Territory	205,346	531,846	1,730	4,481	207,076	536,327	5.4
Totals	**3,560,238**	**9,221,017**	**291,571**	**755,169**	**3,851,809**	**9,976,186**	**100.0**

Canada's 20 Tallest Buildings

City	Building	Stories	Height ft	Height m
Toronto	CN Tower	—	1,821	555
Toronto	First Bank Tower	72	952	290
Toronto	Commerce Court West	57	784	239
Toronto	Toronto-Dominion Tower	56	758	231
Calgary	Calgary Tower	—	626	191
Montreal	Place Victoria	47	624	190
Montreal	Place Ville Marie	42	616	188
Montreal	Canadian Imperial Bank of Commerce	43	604	184
Toronto	Royal Trust Tower	46	600	183
Toronto	Royal Bank Plaza—South Tower	41	589	180
Vancouver	Harbour Center (incl. 100-ft pylon)	32	581	177
Toronto	Manulife Centre	53	545	166
Calgary	Scotia Centre	38	504	154
Calgary	Bank of Montreal	45	500	152
Calgary	Nova Building	37	500	152
Montreal	Le Complexe Desjardins La Tour du Sud	40	498	152
Toronto	Two Bloor West	34	486	148
Toronto	Commerce Court North	34	476	145
Toronto	Simpson Tower	33	473	144
Toronto	Sun Life Centre	35	470	143

Average Temperature and Precipitation Data

Station	Temperature° C Mean Jan.	Mean July	Extreme Max.	Extreme Min.	Average frost date Last in spring	First in fall	Average total annual precip. (mm)	Aver. ann. snow-fall (cm)
St. John's A, Nfld.	−3.8	15.3	30.6	−23.3	June 3	Oct. 12	1511.5	363.7
Charlottetown A, P.E.I.	−6.7	18.4	34.4	−27.8	May 17	Oct. 15	1127.8	305.1
Halifax, N.S.	−3.2	18.3	34.4	−25.0	May 1	Nov. 1	1318.8	210.8
Sydney A, N.S.	−4.4	17.9	35.0	−25.6	May 23	Oct. 16	1340.9	288.0
Yarmouth A, N.S.	−2.7	16.4	30.0	−21.0	May 2	Oct. 24	1283.2	204.5
Chatham A, N.B.	−9.3	19.2	37.8	−35.0	May 22	Sept. 21	1051.2	309.4
Moncton A, N.B.	−7.9	18.6	37.2	−32.2	May 23	Sept. 23	1099.3	313.7
Saint John A, N.B.	−7.1	17.1	34.4	−36.7	May 18	Oct. 2	1400.3	204.7
Fort Chimo A, Que.	−23.4	11.4	32.2	−46.7	June 27	Aug. 30	483.8	236.7
Montreal McGill, Que.	−8.9	21.6	36.1	−33.9	April 22	Oct. 23	999.0	243.1
Quebec A, Que.	−11.6	19.2	35.6	−36.1	May 18	Sept. 28	1088.6	326.6
Schefferville (Knob Lake) A, Que.	−22.7	12.6	31.7	−50.6	June 18	Aug. 31	722.5	335.5
Sherbrooke, Que.	−9.6	20.1	36.7	−41.1	May 12	Sept. 27	972.6	244.6
London A, Ont.	−6.0	20.5	36.7	−31.7	May 9	Oct. 6	924.5	201.2
Ottawa A, Ont.	−10.9	20.7	37.8	−36.1	May 11	Oct. 1	850.9	215.6
Thunder Bay A, Ont.	−14.8	17.5	37.2	−41.1	May 31	Sept. 10	738.5	222.0
Toronto, Ont.	−4.4	21.8	40.6	−32.8	April 20	Oct. 30	789.9	141.0
Churchill A., Man.	−27.6	12.0	33.9	−45.0	June 22	Sept. 12	396.6	183.9
The Pas A, Man.	−22.4	17.9	36.7	−49.4	May 28	Sept. 20	449.7	157.2
Winnipeg A, Man.	−18.3	19.7	40.6	−45.0	May 25	Sept. 21	535.2	131.3
Regina A, Sask.	−17.3	18.9	43.3	−50.0	May 27	Sept. 12	397.9	114.8
Saskatoon A, Sask.	−18.7	18.8	40.0	−47.8	May 27	Sept. 15	352.6	112.5
Beaverlodge CDA, Alta.	−14.9	15.6	36.7	−47.8	May 22	Sept. 7	454.7	183.6
Calgary A, Alta.	−10.9	16.5	36.1	−45.0	May 28	Sept. 12	437.1	153.9
Edmonton Ind. A, Alta.	−14.7	17.5	34.4	−48.3	May 14	Sept. 19	446.5	132.1
Kamloops A, B.C.	−6.0	20.9	40.6	−37.2	May 5	Sept. 28	260.6	77.0
Prince George A, B.C.	−11.8	14.9	34.4	−50.0	June 10	Aug. 28	620.7	233.4
Prince Rupert, B.C.	1.8	13.6	32.2	−21.1	April 19	Nov. 5	2414.5	113.0
Vancouver A, B.C.	2.4	17.4	33.3	−17.8	March 31	Oct. 30	1068.1	52.3
Dawson, Y.T.	−28.6	15.5	35.0	−58.3	May 26	Aug. 27	325.5	136.4
Whitehorse A, Y.T.	−18.9	14.1	34.4	−52.2	June 5	Sept. 1	260.3	127.8
Coppermine, N.W.T.	−29.4	9.3	32.2	−50.0	June 27	Aug. 21	216.3	101.9
Fort Simpson A, N.W.T.	−27.6	16.1	35.0	−53.3	May 31	Aug. 29	343.2	137.9
Frobisher Bay A, N.W.T.	−26.2	7.9	24.4	−45.6	June 30	Aug. 29	415.2	246.9
Resolute A, N.W.T.	−32.6	4.3	18.3	−52.2	July 10	July 20	136.4	78.7

A = Airport, Ind. A = Industrial Airport, CDA = Canada Department of Agriculture. *Source: Canada Year Book 1980–81,* Statistics Canada.

Canadian Church Membership

Religious group	Churches	Members	Clergy
Protestant and others[1]	17,744	4,696,182	18,498
Roman Catholics	5,787	10,425,087	12,626
Jewish congregations	112	305,000	n.a.
Eastern churches[2]	118	457,494	75
Polish National Catholic, Armenian churches	20	31,000	17
Buddhist	15	2,543	10
Total	**23,920**	**15,917,306**	**31,324**

1. Includes such groups as Latter-Day Saints and Jehovah's Witnesses. 2. Includes Coptic church. NOTE: n.a. = not available. *Source: Yearbook of American and Canadian Churches, 1984.*

Major Canadian Awards, 1983

Governor General's Literary Awards

Fiction: English: Leon Rooke, *Shakespeare's Dog;* French: Suzanne Jacob, *Laura Laur*
Poetry: English: David Donnell, *Settlements;* French: Suzanne Paradis, *Un Gout de Sel*
Drama: English: Anne Chislett, *Quiet in the Land;* French: René Gingras, *Syncope*
Nonfiction: English: Jeffery Williams, *Byng of Vimy;* French: Maurice Cusson, *Le Controle Social du Crime*

Juno Award Winners[1]

Female Vocalist: Carole Pope
Male Vocalist: Bryan Adams
Group: Loverboy
Country Female Vocalist: Anne Murray
Country Male Vocalist: Eddie Eastman
Country Group: The Good Brothers
Best New Female Vocalist: Lydia Taylor
Best New Male Vocalist: Kim Mitchell
Best New Group: Payola
Instrumental Artist: Liona Boyd
Composer: Bob Rock and Paul Hyie for *Eyes of a Stranger*
Best Jazz Recording: Fraser MacPherson and Oliver Gannon for *I Didn't Know About You*
Best Classical Recording: Glenn Gould, *Bach's Goldberg Variations*

1. For 1982. Beginning in 1984 the award is being presented in December instead of in the spring; therefore, there is no 1983 list of winners available at press time.

Actra Awards

Best Performance by an Actor in a Leading Role on Television: Kenneth Welsh, *Empire, Inc.*
Best Performance by an Actress in a Leading Role in Television: Linda Griffiths, *Empire, Inc.*
Best Performance by an Actor on Radio: Sean Mulcahy, *The Panther and the Jaguar*
Best Performance by an Actress on Radio: Patricia Phillips, *The Diviners*
Best Acting in a Supporting Role on Television: Gabriel Arcand, *Empire, Inc.*
Best Performance in a Continuing Role on Television: Wendy Crewson, *Home Fires*
Best Variety Performance—Television: Richard McMillan, *The Mikado*
Best Variety Performance—Radio: Dinah Christie and Tom Kneebone, *The Entertainers*
Gordon Sinclair Award for Broadcast Journalism (Radio): Elizabeth Gray, *As It Happens*
Foster Hewitt Award for Sportscasting (Radio): Don Cherry and George Young (tie)
Best Host/Interviewer—Television: Barry Callaghan, *Enterprise*
Best Host/Interviewer—Radio: Vicki Gabereau, *Variety Tonight*
Best Writer—Television Drama: Douglas Bowie, *Empire, Inc.*
Best Writer—Radio Drama: Len Peterson, *Erniste Galois*
Best Writer—Television Documentary: Robert Collison, *Prisoners of Debt: Inside a Global Banking Crisis*
Best Writer—Radio Documentary: Jay Ingram, Anita Gordon, and Penny Park, *The World After Nuclear War*
Best Writer—Television Variety: Dick Blasucci, John Candy, Bob Dolman, Joe Flaherty, Paul Flaherty, Eugene Levy, Andrea Martin, John McAndrew, Martin Short, Michael Short, Doug Steckler, and Mary Charlotte Wilcox, *SCTV*
Best Writer—Radio Variety: Roger Abbott, David Broadfoot, Don Fergusin, Gord Holtam, John Morgan, and Rick Olsen, *Air Farce*
Best Children's Television Program: *In the Fall,* Stan Thomas, producer
Best Television Program of the Year: *The Undaunted,* Tom Cahill, producer
Best Radio Program of the Year: *The Panther and the Jaguar,* Fred Diehl, producer
John Drainie Award for Lifetime Achievement in Broadcasting: Robert Christie

The Royal Bank Award

In 1967, as a Canadian centennial project, the Royal Bank of Canada established the Royal Bank Award to honor "a Canadian citizen or person domiciled in Canada whose outstanding achievement is of such importance that it is contributing to human welfare and the common good." The award consists of a gold medal and a cash grant of $100,000.

1967 Dr. Wilder Penfield, neurosurgeon
1968 Dr. C. J. Mackenzie, engineer
1969 His Eminence Paul-Emile Cardinal Léger
1970 Morley Callaghan, novelist
1971 Arthur Erickson, architect
1972 Dr. Gustave Gingras, rehabilitation expert
1973 Dr. J. A. Corry, educationalist
1974 Jean Gascon, actor/director
1975 Dr. R. Keith Downey and Dr. Baldur R. Stefansson, agricultural scientists
1976 Mary Pack, organizer of the Canadian Arthritis and Rheumantism Society
1977 Dr. W. A. Paddon and Dr. Gordon W. Thomas, frontier medical pioneers
1978 Dr. H. Northrop Frye, literary scholar
1979 Dr. Lotta Hitschmanova, founder and executive director, Unitarian Service Committee of Canada
1980 Dr. Jacques Genest, founder and director, Clinical Research Institute of Montreal
1981 Harry E. Foster, founder and president, Canadian Special Olympics Inc.
1982 Rt. Rev. Georges-Henri Levesque, o.p., social scientist
1983 Dr. Henry J. Barnett, brain specialist, and Dr. Charles Drake, brain surgeon
1984 Hugh MacLennam, author

Federal Courts

Federal courts in Canada include the Supreme Court of Canada, the Federal Court of Canada, and various specialized tribunals such as the Tax Review Board, the Court Martial Appeal Court, and the Immigration Appeal Board. These courts and tribunals are created by Parliament.

Aging Children, Elderly Parents—And the Challenges of Growing Old Together

Barry Robinson

American Association of Retired Persons

After suffering a mild heart attack, a 76-year-old man was rushed to a nearby hospital where doctors observed that he also appeared to be somewhat disoriented. He became rational again, however, as soon as his heart function was stabilized. Still, he kept insisting that his "mommy" would soon come and drive him home—an insistence which left his physicians a bit concerned about his over-all mental state.

Once his physical condition had improved to the point where he could be discharged, the doctors decided that he should be kept in the hospital a while longer for psychological observation. A few days later, the medical staff was more than slightly surprised—and undoubtedly a bit relieved—when the man's 95-year-old mother drove to the hospital from a town a hundred miles away, fully prepared to drive her son home.

Don't laugh too hard—it could happen to you!

Sooner or later, depending upon your age now, you could find that you have become either the parent or child in this little anecdote. The most rapid population growth is taking place at present among people over 75 because relatively fewer people than ever before in that age group are dying.

In 1971, the Census Bureau was estimating that, in the year 2000, there would be 28.8 million persons over age 65. By 1975, that estimate had been revised upward to 30.6, and then adjusted upward once more in 1984 to 34.9 million.

Of particular significance is the fact that more than half of these additional older Americans will be at least 80 years old. Where there are now some 5.7 million people who are 80 or older, by the turn of the century there will be nearly ten million—and probably more if the present trend continues as expected.

Thus, there are going to be more and more 76-year-old men and women with 95-year-old mothers and/or fathers, and not all of them are going to be as healthy and self-reliant as the mother in our little story. Hence the inescapable question of who is going to be responsible for their care.

"Can we," asks industrial gerontologist Harold L. Sheppard, "really expect an increasing proportion of Americans in their early 60s to take care of their elderly relatives, especially if they themselves are retired? They might have more time to provide such care, but what about the expenses involved—particularly in relation to retirement income?"

And what happens when the younger, "responsible" relatives are in their 60s, or in their 70s or even 80s?

Then, too, as a result of the lowered birthrates which prevailed through much of the 20th Century, warns demographer Jacob S. Siegel, "elderly persons in the future will have fewer brothers and sisters and fewer children than in the past to provide needed or desirable economic or psychological support."

As a result, we may soon be seeing a redefining of relationships between generations of middle-aged and older adults. According to a new life cycle grid promulgated a few years ago in an effort to relate changing social roles to the increasingly prevalent longer human lifespan, middle age now encompasses the years between 35 and 55. People between the ages of 55 and 75 are now the young-old, and those over 75 are the old-old—and it is the old-old whose population is expanding so rapidly.

Large numbers of people are now living long enough to be able to watch their children growing old along with them. It is no longer unusual, in fact, for people to reach at least the beginnings of old age while one or both of their parents are still alive. While this can be—and often is—a joyful and rewarding experience, it is often accompanied by the distressing intimations of one's own mortality that stem from seeing a parent grown suddenly old.

For anyone unprepared to deal with this new situation, few experiences can be more disconcerting than having to deal with a family crisis involving one's elderly parents who have now grown dependent on an adult child to resolve their problems in the same way the child once depended on them. Unfortunately, some disturbing manifestations of what can happen when this changing relationship doesn't work are becoming visible.

One end result of this process is a syndrome called "battered parents," which usually involves old people who move in with, are perhaps overly dependent on, and are physically abused by their adult children. Little is known about the exact dimensions of this emerging problem. We don't know, for instance, whether the battering of elderly parents is a temporary social quirk typical of

---

Barry Robinson is communication counsel for AARP which, with nearly 17 million members, is the world's largest organization of middle-aged and older individuals. He is the author of *Options for Older Americans, On The Beat: Policemen at Work,* and *The Vision of Aging: Sight and Insight* in *Visual Acuity and Aging.* Founded in 1958, AARP is nonprofit and nonpartisan, providing older Americans with a wide range of membership programs and services, including legislative representation at both federal and state levels.

the troubled times in which we live or a long-term trend with profoundly frightening implications for the future. We also don't know much about the socio-cultural and economic backgrounds of the battered parents, or even how many elderly parents are abused each year. All we know for sure, at this point, is that it happens.

"The battered elderly often refuse to report the abuse for fear of retaliation, lack of alternative shelter, or fear of the unknown," explains Suzanne K. Steinmetz, the University of Delaware professor who first called a Congressional committee's attention to this ugly phenomenon several years ago.

"Besides," comments Eloise Rathbone-McCuan of the University of Vermont, "think of the stigma. What parents would want other people to know that their children beat them?"

What emerges from the case studies cited by Drs. Steinmetz and Rathbone-McCuan is a series of tragic situations in which both parent and child are victims—frequently of circumstances with which neither can cope. For the most part, battered parents tend to be those who are no longer capable of fending for themselves. Unable to function on their own, they are essentially forced to move in with one of their children, an arrangement which neither they nor their children really want, and which results in more stress than either can handle.

"Each family," observes Steinmetz, "has only *x* amount of resources of capacities to deal with stress. The bottom line is that, if you increase the stress on family members without adding supports to help them cope with it, you increase the likelihood of violence because a person and a family can handle only so much."

At this point, it should be noted that this happens only when the relationships between elderly parents and their aging adult children don't work, and that for every relationship that fails, there are literally hundreds—maybe even thousands or tens of thousands—that do indeed work. There are, after all, millions of middle-aged and older people whose lives flow like an unrippled stream until the end.

Nonetheless, old age will probably always be a time of continual loss. The longer one survives, the more one loses in terms of friends, spouses, siblings, pets, social standing, familiar surroundings, etc. Perhaps the most tragic of these losses is the loss of an adult child.

After people reach a certain age, their anticipation of bereavement is usually associated with the probable loss of their spouses or siblings. Thus, the blow is even more crushing when the natural order is reversed and an adult son or daughter dies unexpectedly.

Around the country, there are many self-help and mutual support programs for widowed persons of all ages and for parents whose children die during childhood or adolescence. However, there are few, if any, programs to help older parents who have the tragic misfortune to outlive one or all of their adult children. Because this is a social and psychological phenomenon about which comparatively little research has been done, there is no substantial body of accumulated knowledge to which one can refer when trying to help bereaved parents cope with their distress.

You have probably noticed that throughout this article there have been frequent references to what is not known. The constantly changing relationship between aging adult children and their elderly parents is a relatively new phenomenon about which there are not yet—and may never be—any hard and fast rules. What there are, however, are observations and lessons learned from first-hand experience which those of us who have dealt—or are dealing—with these situations can share with each other.

Know What You're Getting Into. Taking an ailing elderly parent into your home is an immense undertaking and a full-time job—usually for the wife whose career frequently becomes the first casualty. If you need a second salary to keep your household running smoothly, this could represent a serious financial hardship which, if possible, should be considered in advance.

Caring for a parent in your home for more than a brief period is becoming the economic equivalent of putting someone through college and not only are there no scholarships available for those embarking on this mission of mercy, but you don't even receive a diploma of accomplishment. Then, too, you may be part of the "sandwich generation" whose members are literally surrounded by obligations—for the nurturing of their children on one side, the care of their elderly parents on the other, and their own preparations for their later years—and thus have to balance carefully their responsibilities lest none of them be met. If you are not an only child, there may be sibling rivalries over who cares—or escapes from the chores of caring—for the parent-in-need.

Realize now that your lifestyle may be in for some very drastic changes as you attempt to accommodate your parent's needs or desires. Your work habits and schedule may be disrupted, your personal productivity may decline as you begin spending time (which you might otherwise devote to work brought home from the office) on resolving his or her problems. There are thus emotional costs which you should expect and be prepared to bear.

Know Why You're Doing What You're Doing. In *The Best Friend You'll Ever Have*, a tragi-comic memoir of his family's experiences during the final months of his mother's life, Bernard Sloan confesses that, although he and his mother had not had a good relationship for years, he brought her into his home because "we were positive she would relinquish her prejudices in exchange for love and care." If you're thinking about striking such an unspoken bargain (he never bothered to discuss this with his mother), forget it! Sloan's mother didn't change under the circumstances, and it's doubtful if any parent would. Unresolved differences don't usually lend themselves to being resolved in the crucible of family crisis; if such differences are to be breached, they should have been breached long ago instead of being held hostage to a parent's health and well-being.

Don't Be Afraid To Ask for Help. Like most professionals in the field of aging, I have a conceptual understanding of our nation's aging services network, but when it came to seeking assistance in dealing with my late father's problems, my wife and I did what any member of the public should do—we asked his doctor for help and advice. The doctor put us in touch with the local Visiting Nurses Association, which provided still more information. The most important word on the subject of seeking assistance is ask—and keep asking until you get the answers or the help you need. This can often include psychological counseling for you and/or your family since you are undergoing something of an emotional trauma; such counseling may be one of the best ways to prevent parents and their children from becoming battered by life-crushing circumstances.

Read and Heed. A great source of help is the printed word to be found in a steadily growing selection of books about aging child/elderly parent relationships. My personal favorites are *You and Your Aging Parent* by Barbara Silverstone and Helen Kandel Hyman, *When Your Parents Grow Old* by Jane Otten and Florence D. Shelley, and *Aging Parents* by Pauline K. Ragan. Also worth perusing are *Understanding Aging Parents* by Andrew D. and Judith L. Lester, *Your Aging Parents: When and How to Help* by Margaret J. Anderson, and *Caring for Your Aged Parents* by Earl A. and Sharon Hya Grollman.

Don't Expect Miracles. If you do, you and your parent are going to be terribly disappointed. To a great extent, you're going to be fighting a holding action against further deterioration, and trying to make your parent as happy and comfortable as he or she can be under the circumstances. Each case is different so your goal should be established in consultation with a physician (hopefully one with a background in geriatric medicine) and related professionals. If you even get near your goal, you'll be doing well.

Know When To Bail Out. There comes a point when your parent's physical and/or psychological condition may be such that the situation has become potentially damaging for both you and your parent and presumably anyone else who is involved intimately. If you continue, you'll probably end up sacrificing yourself, but without saving your parent. People may tell you you're a saint for what you're doing, but remember that sainthood is usually preceded by martyrdom. It may sound callous, but you have to be realistic at some point, or all of you will go under. Once your parent is out of your home—and, to some extent, off your hands—you may experience some form of decompression, a sort of post partum depression or after-the-battle fatigue. Such reactions are normal, but if they linger too long or interfere with your functioning in any way, don't hesitate to seek professional help.

Anticipation Adds Alternatives. One way of avoiding—or at least alleviating—crisis situations, such as those involving elderly parents, is to find out in advance what they would prefer to have you do if and when they should become incapable of deciding for themselves. For that matter, this is probably a good time for you to begin thinking about your own alternatives should such a situation befall you in the near or distant future.

Perhaps the best key to planning for one's later life is to ignore wholeheartedly the old line about "crossing that bridge when you come to it." Consider the possibility that the bridge may no longer be there upon your arrival, and that you could be stranded on the wrong side of the river unless alternatives are available, having been considered in advance.

Anticipate and plan, but be flexible in expectations. Try to avoid locking yourself into a single lifespan which illness or external events can cancel. If enough options aren't kept open at any age, people may eventually end up on that apocryphal park bench, posturing for the pigeons after the parade has passed.

Characteristics of Persons 65 Years Old and Over

(in percentages)

	1982		1981		1975		1970	
Characteristic	**Male**	**Female**	**Male**	**Female**	**Male**	**Female**	**Male**	**Female**
Marital status:[1]								
Single	4.4	5.6	4.5	5.7	4.7	5.8	7.5	7.7
Married	80.0	40.2	79.3	39.4	79.3	39.1	73.1	35.6
Spouse present	77.6	38.5	77.0	37.8	77.3	37.6	69.9	33.9
Spouse absent	2.4	1.7	2.3	1.6	2.0	1.5	3.2	1.7
Widowed	12.4	50.4	12.8	51.3	13.6	52.5	17.1	54.4
Divorced	3.2	3.8	3.4	3.6	2.5	2.6	2.3	2.3
Family status:[1]								
In families	83.6	56.7	83.4	56.6	83.3	59.3	79.2	58.5
Primary individuals	15.4	42.4	15.2	42.4	15.4	39.4	14.9	35.2
Secondary individuals	1.0	.8	1.3	.9	1.2	1.3	2.4	1.9
Residents of institutions[1]	n.a.	n.a.	n.a.	n.a.	n.a.	n.a.	3.6	4.4
Labor force participation:								
Employed	17.1	7.6	17.8	7.7	21.1	7.8	26.2	10.0
Unemployed	.7	.3	.5	.3	1.2	.4	1.0	.3
Not in labor force	82.2	92.1	81.6	92.0	77.7	91.8	72.8	89.7
Living arrangements:[1]								
Living in household	99.9	99.9	100.0	99.9	99.8	99.8	95.5	95.0
Living alone	14.5	41.4	14.3	41.4	14.8	38.0	14.1	33.8
Spouse present	77.6	38.5	77.0	37.8	77.3	37.6	69.9	33.9
Living with someone else	7.7	19.9	8.7	20.7	7.7	24.2	11.5	27.4
Not in household[2]	.1	.1	—	.1	.2	.2	4.5	5.0

1. Resident population as of March of year indicated. Beginning 1975, excludes institutional population. 2. In institutions and other group quarters. NOTE: n.a. = not available. *Source:* Department of Commerce, Bureau of the Census.

The Facts of Later Life

Income

Most economists estimate that for retirees to maintain their pre-retirement lifestyle within reasonable limits, they need a retirement income equal to 60–70% of their earnings immediately preceding retirement, plus regular adjustments for rising living costs. This is a goal generally beyond the reach of most older Americans who, on average, have half the income of their younger counterparts.

Even with annual Social Security increments, which are supposed to offset inflation, retirees continue to fall farther and farther behind. This is due primarily to the increments coming at least a year after the fact of actual increases in the cost of living, and thus never compensating fully for inflation's inroads.

One seventh of the over-65 population now lives below the poverty level—an improvement over 1970 when a full quarter of all older Americans did, but a disturbing increase over the one-seventh level maintained until 1980. Recent studies by economist Thomas C. Borzilleri indicate that this deterioration can be expected to continue if cash and in-kind (food stamps, Medicaid, etc.) benefits are reduced further.

Actually, points out Dr. Borzilleri, millions of older Americans may be considerably worse off than statistics indicate since they are not quite poor enough to fit below the official poverty line, but are, for all practical purposes, nonetheless impoverished. At the same time, there are, of course, many well-off older persons, but most tend to fall financially somewhere between poverty and affluence, and are haunted by fear of the former in their future.

Most of the aged poor did not become so until they retired, and their incomes dropped by 25–50%. These are essentially middle-class working people, and it is probably harder for them to cope with their newfound poverty than it is for people who have been poor all their lives.

Complicating the financial situations of almost all older Americans is a combination of years of continuously escalating inflation, which has steadily sapped the purchasing power of people living on relatively fixed incomes, and other economic fluctuations which have eroded their traditional income support sources. Although a growing number of retirees are now continuing to work in one way or another, the elderly do not generally possess the ability to increase their income as much as they need to. Thus, they are perenially attempting to cut back and catch up with little hope of ever breaking even again.

Health

Although generally healthier than previous generations of elders, today's older people are still more subject to chronic illness and disability than younger persons. On average, they visit physicians nearly 50% more often, and have health care and medication costs more than double those of younger individuals.

Comprising only 11.6% of the nation's population, older people account for 29% of total personal health care expenditures ($49.4 billion out of $167.9 billion). Yet, most older Americans regard themselves as being comparatively healthy and capable of caring for themselves well enough to continue living independently.

In a 1975 survey, 69% of the older persons questioned described their health as good or excellent in comparison with others of their own age, and 22% said their health was fair. A 1980 study, however came up with these responses: 21% excellent, 39% good, 29% fair, and 12% poor.

Those describing their health as being chronically poor reported suffering from arthritis (38%), hearing loss (29%), and vision impairment, hypertension, and heart disease (20% each). Many suffered from several of these conditions simultaneously.

A 1979 study found that 82% of the older persons polled had not been hospitalized during the previous year. And most persons entering nursing homes returned later to their own residences.

Employment

In 1900, 67% of men and 8% of women over 65 were actively working. By 1981 only 18.2% of older men remained employed, while the percentage of women in the workforce had slipped back to eight after rising to ten in 1974. In general, they are working today at part-time jobs, agricultural labor, or self-employment. There are also indications that, partially in response to economic pressures, a growing number of "retired" workers continue to work after formal retirement, but do not declare themselves officially employed.

Once unemployed, however, older workers usually experience greater difficulty finding new jobs and have longer average periods of unemployment than younger workers. This tendency begins in the mid-to-late 40s and increases with the worker's age.

Some employers have recently begun to recognize the value of older workers already in their employ, and are making efforts to encourage them to remain on the job. This is expected to increase dramatically around the coming turn of the century when fewer young adults will be entering the work force as the result of the sharp birthrate decline which followed the baby boom.

Marital Status

In 1982, 15% of all older men and 40% of all older women were married. Among older women, 54% were widows, a figure which rises to 70% after age 75. It is almost predictable: If the husband is five years younger than his wife, the chances of widowhood are 50%; if the husband and wife are the same age, the chances are two out of three; if the husband is five years older than his wife, the chances are three out of four.

Widows outnumber widowers by 5.3 to 1. Men, however, experience greater difficulty adjusting to the loss of a mate—most likely because they don't expect their wives to die before they do.

In 1977, there were 16,760 brides and 30,721 grooms over 65. For approximately 904 of these older brides and 1,438 older grooms, it was a first marriage. For the rest, remarriage came mostly after widowhood rather than divorce. Interestingly, the actual number of marriages involving people over 65 has decreased in the last few years.

Marriage rates for older men in 1977 were seven times those for older women. The number of older men entering into first marriages was 2.5 times that of older women, while the number of older men remarrying was 8.6 times greater than that of older women.

Living Arrangements

While most older persons live in a family setting—with a husband, wife or other relatives—this frequently decreases with advancing age.

In 1982, more than a third of older Americans—40% of all older women, but only 14% of all older men—live alone or with non-relatives. One reason for this disparity is that women live longer than men, and thus eventually outnumber them in later life.

The majority of older women are widows or divorcees (or, in some cases, both) without adequate means of support and little, if any, preparation for living alone—a circumstance which may in time give rise to new forms of communal living.

Pensions

The newer the retiree, the greater the chances of participation in a company or union pension—and the greater the likelihood of collecting on that pension, thanks to the Employee Retirement Income Security Act (ERISA) of 1974 which regulates pension plans and insures the worker's stake in them.

Prior to that, many workers participated in plans but were unable to collect pensions upon retirement. Thus, most older retirees do not receive private pension payments, but live instead solely on Social Security and whatever savings they have managed to accumulate; some must also depend upon Supplemental Security Income (SSI) payments to assist them in making ends meet.

Of today's active workers, however, it is estimated that nearly half are covered by pension plans, but their future security may be endangered by recession-induced business failures and by efforts to amend ERISA which could result in its providing less protection for individual workers.

Transportation

Most public transportation systems are designed primarily to satisfy the needs of the commuting worker. Older people (whose needs are usually quite different) are thus forced either to rely upon automobiles—which are becoming increasingly expensive to own and maintain—or to surrender their mobility and settle for whatever is within walking distance, no matter how inferior it may be.

Some communities have attempted to provide special transportation services at reduced rates for their older residents, but many of these subsidized systems have fallen victim to their own success. The more they are utilized, the more they cost to operate, and the growing cost often exceeds a community's ability to sustain them. In this age of energy scarcity, this looms large as a major problem.

Crime

While violent crimes against the elderly have been increasing lately and have thus received the most news coverage, they are not nearly as prevalent as "bunco" offenses, in which the victim is defrauded of whatever savings he or she may have managed to accumulate over the course of a lifetime.

Older victims tend to suffer more intensely. A younger victim can recoup a monetary loss by accumulating future earnings, but older victims no longer have that opportunity. Similarly, older victims wounded in crimes of violence require longer to heal, leading to prolonged loss of mobility and the increased possibility of medical complications.

Coping

When You Need Help or Information

Whether your concern is for your own later years or for someone you know with problems, the basic approaches to seeking help or information are essentially the same. In general, your primary sources of information are your local telephone directory and your community's public library.

A good way to begin is to take stock of your resources relating to the problem. This doesn't necessarily mean financial resources, although they can be undeniably important. There are, however, other resources which you may have built up over a lifetime of activity without really being aware of them.

Did you, for instance, serve in the nation's military services? If so, check with the Veterans Administration (listed in the phone book under "U.S. Government") to see if it can help.

Are you a union member? Then, contact your nearest local and find out if the union has any programs to help retirees with your particular problem. This also applies to any civic or fraternal organizations to which you may belong.

Don't forget the many local and national organizations for older people; being a member of one or more of them can prove helpful. These are the major national ones:

AARP (American Association of Retired Persons), 1909 K Street, N.W., Washington, D.C. 20049

National Council of Senior Citizens (NCSC), 925 15th Street, N.W., Washington, D.C. 20005

National Association of Retired Federal Employees (NARFE), 1533 New Hampshire Avenue, N.W., Washington, D.C. 20036

Gray Panthers, 3635 Chestnut Street, Philadelphia, PA 19104

Older Women's League, 1325 G Street, N.W., Lower Level B, Washington, D.C. 20005

There are also organizations of professionals who work with and on behalf of the elderly: National Council on the Aging (NCOA), 600 Maryland Avenue, S.W., Washington, D.C. 20024; Gerontological Society of America, 1411 K Street, N.W., Washington, D.C. 20005; American Geriatric Society, 10 Columbus Circle, New York, N.Y. 10019.

When You Have a Problem . . .

For just about every problem today, there is a private public service organization or government program trying to solve it. The trick is for you to get in touch with the right one.

In this *Almanac* (*see* p. 542), there is a listing of U.S. Societies and Associations in which you might find the name of an organization dealing with your particular problem. Look in your telephone directory to see if there is a branch office in your area; if not, contact the organization's national headquarters at the address given.

To find government agencies that might be able to help, start with your local government (city, town, or village) and move on to county, state, and federal levels only as necessary. Often, the agency nearest home will be the most help. Again, your telephone directory can be your best source of information; if you can't find exactly what you're looking for there, try phoning the municipal or county clerk's office for more specific guidance.

Keys to Finding Help

A few of the sources of assistance or information to which you might turn when dealing with a specific problem are given below. (Unless an address is given, look in your phonebook for the key-word indicated.)

Aging. Administration on Aging, U.S. Department of Health and Human Services, Washington, D.C. 20201. Locally, try state **Offices, Commissions, Departments,** or **Bureaus on Aging** or **Senior Citizens Affairs;** look for county or municipal agencies with similar titles, and for regional **Area Agencies on Aging.**

Career Considerations. If you're unhappy in your present work situation, and are trying to decide whether to stick with it until you can retire gracefully or to attempt to start anew in middle age, these books might provide some helpful insights. *What Color is Your Parachute?* and *The Three Boxes of Life and How to Get Out of Them* by Richard N. Bolles; *The Women's Guide to Re-Entry Employment* by Mary Zimmeth; *What To Do With the Rest of Your Life* by the Catalyst Staff.

Continuing Care. What used to be called "Life care" or "lifetime care" is back in a new, better-planned format. Detailed information about 270 of these retirement facilities offering prepaid medical plans in 37 states can be found in the *National Continuing Care Directory,* edited by Ann Trueblood Raper for the American Association of Homes for the Aging, and published by AARP Books. An introductory pamphlet on *Continuing Care* is available for $2 directly from AAHA, 1050 17th Street, N.W., #770, Washington, D.C. 20036.

Federal Government. Your tie-line and guide to the federal bureaucracy is the **Federal Information Center,** listed in the phonebook under "U.S. Government." If nothing else works, try phoning your Congressional representative's local office; his or her staff can sometimes cut through a lot of red tape.

Food. The key words here are **Food Stamps, Meals on Wheels, National Nutrition Program for the Elderly.** If none of these is listed in your phonebook, check with the agencies listed under Aging.

Funerals. Helpful information and advice about this difficult and potentially expensive purchase may be found in *It's Your Choice: The Practical Guide to Planning a Funeral* by Thomas C. Nelson, Senior Coordinator of AARP's consumer affairs programs.

Health Care. Don't overlook your local health department. If your problem involves a hospital, there is probably a staff social worker to whom you can turn. Also, try local medical and dental societies and schools—the latter frequently provide quality care at relatively low cost. For information about health care at home, contact the National Homecaring Council, 235 Park Ave. South, New York, N.Y. 10003.

Housing. The key agency here is the U.S. Department of Housing and Urban Development; check your phone book for a local office, or write to HUD, Washington, D.C. 20410. If you live in a rural area, contact your agricultural extension agent or write directly to Farmers Home Administration, U.S. Department of Agriculture, 14th Street and Independence Avenue, S.W., Washington, D.C. 20250. Your local **housing authority** can also prove helpful. A good overview can be found in *Planning Your Retirement Housing* by Michael and Marika Sumichrast and Ronald Shafer.

Insurance. Guidance and insight are offered by consumer attorney Nancy C. Chasen in *Policy Wise: The Practical Guide to Insurance Decisions for Older Consumers.*

Legal Problems. Many communities have special legal counseling programs for older residents. Try your local Aging agency, or write to National Senior Citizens Law Center, 1302 18th Street, N.W., #701, Washington, D.C. 20036. Information is also available from the National Resource Center for Consumers of Legal Services, 3254 Jones Court, N.W., Washington, D.C. 20007. Also worth consulting is the *Essential Guide to Wills, Estates, Trusts and Death Taxes* by lawyer-professor Alex J. Soled.

Money. Information about **Social Security** and **Supplemental Security Income** may be found in this *Almanac* or from the **Social Security Administration** office nearest you. Also helpful in special circumstances are the U.S. Office of Personnel Management, Compensation Group, Bureau of Retirement, 1900 E Street, N.W., Washington, D.C. 20415; and the U.S. Railroad Retirement Board, Headquarters office, 844 Rush Street, Chicago, Ill. 60611. For the person who is already retired or on the verge, there is finally a volume just for him or her—*What To Do With What You've Got: The Practical Guide to Money Management in Retirement* by Peter Weaver and Annette Buchanan.

Nursing Homes. Check with your local **health department,** hospital social worker, or the nearest branches of the American Nursing Home Association and the American Association of Homes for the Aging. Some state **Aging** agencies have a **Nursing Home Ombudsman.** Write for the free pamphlet *Thinking About a Nursing Home* to the American Health Care Association, 1200 15th Street, N.W., Washington, D.C. 20005.

Research. If you want to read more about growing older, look in your local library catalog under aging, gerontology, geriatrics, retirement, or write to AARP Books, 1909 K Street, N.W., Washington, D.C., for information about its new books on subjects of special interest and concern to middle-aged and older readers.

Volunteering. If you're interested in working as a volunteer, check with your local **hospitals, non-profit nursing homes, social service agencies,** and **civic organizations.** Or write to: National Center for Citizen Involvement, 1111 North 19th Street, #500, Arlington, VA 22209; ACTION, Older Americans Volunteer Programs, 806 Connecticut Ave., N.W., Washington, D.C. 20525; Service Corps of Retired Executives (SCORE), Small Business Administration, 1129 20th Street, N.W., #410, Washington, D.C. 20416.

Widowhood. For help in coping with the loss of a spouse or long-time companion, write to Widowed Persons Service, 1909 K Street, Washington, D.C. 20049, for the location of the WPS group nearest you or ask your clergyperson or any of the local agencies listed under **Aging.** Considerable comfort and sound advice can be found in Ruth J. Loewinsohn's *Survival Handbook for Widows,* a 1977 classic now being reissued in paperback. No matter what circumstances have left you single, you might be interested in *Alone—Not Lonely: Independent Living for Women over Fifty* by Jane Seskin.

Social Security

The original Social Security Act was passed in 1935 and amended in 1939, 1946, 1950, 1952, 1954, 1956, 1958, 1960, 1961, 1965, 1967, 1969, 1972, 1974, 1977, and 1980-1983.

The act is administered by the Social Security Administration and the Health Care Financing Administration, and other agencies within the Department of Health and Human Services.

For purposes of clarity, the explanations given below will describe the provisions of the act as amended.

Old Age, Disability, and Survivors Insurance

Practically everyone who works fairly regularly is covered by social security. Many state and local government employees are covered under voluntary agreements between states and the Secretary of Health and Human Services. Workers not covered include most federal civilian employees hired prior to January 1984, career railroad workers, and a few other exceptions.

Cash tips count for social security if they amount to $20 or more in a month from employment with a single employer.

To qualify for benefits or make payments possible for your survivors, you must be in work covered by the law for a certain number of "quarters of coverage." Before 1978, a quarter of coverage was earned if a worker was paid $50 or more wages in a 3-month calendar quarter. A self-employed person got 4 "quarters of coverage" for a year in which his net earnings were $400 or more.

In 1978, a worker, whether employed or self-employed, received one quarter of coverage for each $250 of covered annual earnings up to a maximum of four for a year. The quarter of coverage measure was increased to $260 in 1979 and $290 in 1980, $310 in 1981, $340 in 1982, $370 in 1983, $390 in 1984, and will increase automatically in future years to keep pace with increases in average wages. The number of quarters needed differs for different persons and depends on the date of your birth; in general, it is related to the number of years after 1950, or after the year you reach 21, if later, and up to the year you reach 62, become disabled, or die. One "quarter of coverage" is required for each such year in order for you or your family to get benefits. No one will need more than 40 quarters. Your local social security office can tell you how long you need to work.

Who Pays for the Insurance?

Both workers and their employers pay for the workers' insurance. Self-employed persons pay their own social security contributions annually along with their income tax. The rates include the cost of Medicare hospital insurance. The contribution and benefit base is $37,800 for 1984, and will increase automatically in future years as earnings levels rise. The contribution rate schedules under present law are shown in a table in this section.

The separate payroll contribution to finance hospital insurance is placed in a separate trust fund in the U.S. Treasury. In addition, the medical insurance premiums, currently $14.60 for 1984 a month, and the government's shares go into another separate trust fund.

How to Apply for Benefits

You apply for benefits by filing a claim either in

U.S. Population by Age

(in millions)

Age		2000[1]	Percent	1980	Percent	1900	Percent
Under 19		100.9	35	70.5	32	33.7	44
20-34		55.6	19	57.1	26	19.4	26
35-44	Middle age	41.3	14	25.7	11	9.2	12
45-54	Middle age	35.8	12	22.6	10	6.4	8
55-64	Young-old	22.9	8	21.1	10	4.0	5
65-74	Young-old	17.1	6	15.4	7	2.2	3
75 & over	Old-old	13.5	5	9.4	4	.9[2]	1

1. Projected. 2. 899,000. NOTE: Percentages are approximate and because of rounding may not add to 100%.

Social Security Contribution and Rate Schedule

(percent of covered earnings)

Year	Retirement, survivors, and disability insurance	Hospital insurance	Total
EMPLOYERS AND EMPLOYEES			
1978	4.95 %	1.10 %	6.05 %
1979–80	5.08	1.05	6.13
1981	5.35	1.30	6.65
1982–83	5.40	1.30	6.70
1984	5.70	1.30	7.00
1985	5.70	1.35	7.05
1986–87	5.70	1.45	7.15
1988–89	6.06	1.45	7.51
1990 & later	6.20	1.45	7.65
SELF-EMPLOYED			
1978	7.00 %	1.10 %	8.10 %
1979–80	7.05	1.05	8.10
1981	8.00	1.30	9.30
1982	8.05	1.30	9.35
1983	8.05	1.30	9.35
1984	11.40	2.60	14.00
1985	11.40	2.70	14.10
1986–87	11.40	2.90	14.30
1988–89	12.12	2.90	15.02
1990 & later	12.40	2.90	15.30

person, by mail, or by telephone at any social security office. You can get the address either from the post office or from the phone book under the listing, United States Government—Department of Health and Human Services—Social Security Administration. You will need certain kinds of proof, depending upon the type of benefit you are claiming. If it is a retirement benefit, you should provide a birth or baptismal certificate. If you are unable to get these documents, other old documents showing your age or date of birth—such as census records, school records, early naturalization certificate, etc.—may be acceptable. A widow, or widower, 60 or older who is claiming widow's benefits based on his or her spouse's earnings should have both proof of age and a copy of the marriage certificate. If formal proof is not available, the social security office will tell you what kinds of information will be acceptable.

What Does Social Security Offer?

The social security contribution you pay gives you four different kinds of protection: (1) retirement benefits, (2) survivors' benefits, (3) disability benefits, and (4) Medicare hospital insurance benefits.

Retirement benefits A worker becomes eligible for the full amount of his retirement benefits at age 65, if he has retired under the definition in the law. A worker may retire at 62 and get 80% of his full benefit. The closer he is to age 65 when he starts collecting his benefit, the larger is the fraction of his full benefit that he will get.

The amount of the retirement benefit you are entitled to at 65 is the key to all other benefits under the program. The retirement benefit is based on covered earnings, generally those after 1950. Your covered earnings will be updated (indexed) to the second year before you reach age 62, become disabled, or die, and will reflect the increases in average wages that have occurred since the earnings were paid.

A worker who delays his retirement past age 65, or who does not receive a benefit for some months after age 65 because of high earnings will get a special credit that can mean a larger benefit. The credit adds to a worker's benefits 1% (3% for workers age 62 after 1978) for each year (1/12 of 1% for each month) from age 65 to age 70 for which he did not get benefits.

The law provides a special minimum benefit at retirement for people who worked under social security for many years. The provision will help people who had low incomes, but above a specific level, in their working years. The amount of the special minimum depends on the number of years of coverage. For a worker retiring at 65 in Jan. 1984 with 30 or more years of coverage, the special minimum benefit would be $357 (effective December 1983). These benefits are reduced if a worker is under 65 and are increased automatically for increases in the cost of living.

If you retired at age 65 in Jan. 1984 with average earnings, you would get a benefit of $542.

If your spouse is also 65, then he or she will get a spouse's benefit that is equal to half your benefit. So if your benefit is $542.00, your spouse gets $271.00.

If your spouse is between ages 62 and 65, he or she can draw a reduced benefit; the amount depends on the number of months before 65 that he or she starts getting checks. If he or she draws his or her benefit when he or she is 62, he or she will get about 3/8 of your basic benefit, or $203.00. (He or she will get this amount for the rest of his or her life, unless you should die first; then he or she can start getting widow's, or widower's, benefits, described below.)

If the spouse is entitled to a worker's retirement benefit on his or her own earnings, he or she can draw whichever amount is larger. If the spouse is entitled to a retirement benefit which is less than the spouse's benefit, he or she will receive his or her own retirement benefit plus the difference between the retirement benefit and the spouse's benefit.

If you have children under 18 or a child under age 19 attending elementary or secondary school or a son or daughter who became totally disabled prior to reaching age 22, when you retire they will get a benefit equal to half your full retirement benefits (subject to maximum payments that can be made to a family). If your spouse is caring for a child who is under 16 or who became disabled before 22 (and getting benefits too), he or she is eligible for benefits, even if he or she is under 62.

In general, the highest retirement check that can be paid to a worker who retired at 65 in Jan. 1984 is about $703 a month. Maximum payment to the family of this retired worker is about $1,232 in Jan. 1984. When your children reach age 18, their benefits will stop except for children under age 19 attending an elementary or secondary school and except for a benefit that is going to a son or daughter who became totally disabled before attaining age 22. Such a person can continue to get his benefits as long as his disability meets the definition in the law.

If you are divorced, you can get social security benefits (the same as a spouse or widow, or widower), based on your ex-spouse's earnings record if you were married at least 10 years and if your ex-spouse has retired, become disabled, or died.

Survivor benefits. This feature of the social security program gives your family valuable life insurance protection—in some cases benefits to a family could amount to $100,000 or more over a period of years. The amount of protection is again geared to what the worker would be entitled to if he had been age 65 when he died. Your survivors could get:

1. A cash payment to help cover your burial expenses. This "lump-sum death payment" is $255.

2. A benefit for each child until he reaches 18, or 19 if the child is attending elementary or secondary school or at any age if disabled before 22. Each eligible child receives 75% of the basic benefit (subject to reduction for the family maximum). (A disabled child can continue to collect benefits after age 22.) If certain conditions are met, dependent grandchildren of insured workers can receive survivor or dependent benefits.

3. A benefit for your widow, or widower, if she has children under 16 or disabled in her care. Her benefit is also 75% of the basic benefit. She can collect this as long as she has a child under 16 or disabled in her care. Payments stop then (they will start again upon application when she is 60 at a slightly lower amount).

Total family survivor benefits are estimated to be as high as $1,553 a month if the worker dies in 1984.

4. If there are no children either under 16 or disabled, your spouse can get a widow's, or widower's benefit starting at age 60. This would come to 71 1/2% of the basic amount at age 60. A widow, or widower, who first becomes entitled at 65 or later may get 100% of his or her deceased spouse's basic amount (provided neither he nor she ever drew reduced benefits).

5. Dependent parents can sometimes collect survivors' benefits. They are usually eligible if: (a) they were getting at least half their support from the deceased worker at (1) the time of the worker's death if the worker did not qualify for disability benefits before death, or (2) if the worker had been entitled to disability benefits which had not been terminated before death either at the beginning of the period of disability or at the time of death; (b) they have reached 62; and (c) they are not eligible for a greater retirement benefit based on their own earnings. A single surviving parent can then get 82 1/2% of the basic benefit. If two parents are eligible, each would get 75%.

Here is an example of survivors' benefits in one family situation: John Jones died at age 29 in June 1982 leaving a wife and two children aged one and three. He had average covered earnings under social security. Family survivors' benefits would include: (1) a cash lump-sum death payment of $255, and (2) a total monthly benefit of $923 for the family. When the children reach 18, their benefits stop unless they are attending an elementary or secondary school full time, in which case payments continue up to age 19. When the older child no longer collects benefits, the widow and younger child continue to get benefits until that child is 16. If he continues in school, he will still get a benefit, but Mrs. Jones' checks will stop. When Mrs. Jones becomes 60 (assuming she has not remarried), she will be able to get a reduced widow's benefit if she so chooses, or she can wait until age 65 to get a full benefit.

If in addition to your social security benefit as a wife, husband, widow, or widower you receive a pension based on your work in public employment not covered by social security, your benefit as a dependent or survivor will be reduced by the amount of that pension. Under an exception in the law, your government pension will not affect your dependent's or survivor's benefit if you became eligible for that pension before December 1982 and if, at the time you apply or become entitled to your social security benefit as a dependent or survivor, you could have qualified for that benefit if the law in effect in January 1977 had remained in effect. (At that time, men had to prove they were dependent upon their wives for support to be eligible for benefits as a dependent or survivor.) Your government pension, however, currently will not affect any social security benefit based on your own work covered by social security.

Work Credit for Disability Benefits

Born after 1929, become disabled at age	Born before 1930, become disabled before 62 in	Years of work credit you need
42 or younger	1971	5
44	1973	5 1/2
46	1975	6
48	1977	6 1/2
50	1979	7
51	1980	7 1/4
52	1981	7 1/2
54	1983	8
56	1985	8 1/2
58	1987	9
60	1989	9 1/2
62 or older	1991 or later	10

NOTE: Five years of this credit must have been earned in the 10 years ending when you became disabled; years need not be continuous or in units of full years.

Disability Benefits. Disability benefits can be paid to several groups of people:

Disabled workers under 65 and their families.

Persons disabled before 22 who continue to be disabled. These benefits are payable as early as 18 when a parent (or grandparent under certain circumstances) receives social security retirement or disability benefits or when an insured parent dies.

Disabled widows and widowers and (under certain conditions) disabled surviving divorced spouses of workers who were insured at death. These benefits are payable as early as 50.

A disabled person is eligible for Medicare after being entitled to disability payments for 24 months.

If you are a worker and become severely disabled, you will be eligible for monthly benefits if you have worked under social security long enough and recently enough. The amount of work you will need depends on your age when you become disabled:

Before 24: You need credit for 1 1/2 years of work in the 3-year period ending when your disability begins.

24 through 30: You need credit for having worked half the time between 21 and the time you become disabled.

31 or older: All workers disabled at 31 or older—except the blind—need the amount of credit shown in the chart.

To be considered disabled under the social security law you must have a physical or mental condition which: (1) prevents you from doing any substantial gainful work; and (2) is expected to last (or has lasted) for at least 12 months, or is expected to result in death.

If you meet these conditions, you may be able to get payments even if your recovery from the disability is expected.

The medical evidence from your physician or other sources will show the severity of your condition and the extent to which it prevents you from doing substantial gainful work. Your age, education, training, and work experience also may be considered in deciding whether you are able to work.

If you can't do your regular work but can do other substantial gainful work, you will not be considered disabled. A person whose vision is no better than 20/200 even with glasses, or who has a limited visual field of 20 degrees or less, is considered "blind" under the social security law.

While you are receiving benefits as a disabled worker, payments can also be made to certain members of your family. These family members include:

Your unmarried children under 18.

Your children under 19 if they are unmarried and attending an elementary or secondary school full time.

Your unmarried children 18 or older who were disabled before reaching 22 and continue to be disabled.

Your wife at any age if she has in her care a child who is under 16 or disabled and who is getting benefits based on your social security record.

Your wife 62 or older even if there are no children entitled to benefits.

Your husband 62 or older.

A child may be eligible on a grandparent's social security record only if the child's parents are disabled or deceased and the child was living with and dependent upon the grandparent at the time the grandparent qualified for benefits.

Benefits begin after a waiting period of 5 full calendar months. No benefits can be paid for these first 5 months of disability; therefore, the first payment is for the 6th full month. If you are disabled more than 6 full months before you apply, back benefits may be payable, but not before the 6th full month of disability. It is important to apply soon after the disability starts because back payments are limited to the 12 months preceding the month you apply.

Certain disabled people under 65 are eligible for Medicare. They include disabled workers at any age, persons who became disabled before age 22, and disabled widows and widowers age 50 or over who have been entitled to disability checks for 2 years or more.

Medicare protection generally ends when monthly disability benefits end, and can continue an additional 3 years after benefits stop because an individual returns to gainful work.

If a person becomes entitled to disability benefits again, Medicare coverage starts at the same time if a worker becomes disabled again within 5 years after benefits end (or within 7 years for a disabled widow, widower, or person disabled before age 22).

Benefits to workers disabled after 1978 and their dependents are based, in part, on earnings that have been adjusted to take account of increases in average wages since they were earned. The adjusted earnings are averaged together and a formula is applied to the adjusted average to figure the benefit rate.

Monthly benefits in Jan. 1984 or later can be as high as $854 for a worker and as high as $1,281 for a worker with a family. Once a person starts receiving benefits, the amount will increase automatically in future years to keep pace with the rising cost of living.

If you receive benefits as a disabled worker, an adult disabled since childhood, or a disabled widow or widower, you are not subject to the general rule under which some benefits are withheld if you have substantial earnings. There are special rules, which include medical considerations, for determining how any work you do might affect your disability payments.

If one of your dependents who is under 65 and who is not disabled works and earns more than $5,160 in 1984, some of the dependent's benefits may be withheld. In general, $1 in benefits is withheld for each $2 over $5,160. Different rules apply to your dependents who are 65 or over. A person 65 or over can earn $6,960 in 1984 without having benefits withheld.

The amount a person can earn without having any benefits withheld will increase in future years as the level of average wages rises.

If you are receiving disability benefits, you are required by law to let the Social Security Administration know if your condition improves or if you return to work no matter how little you earn.

If at any time medical evidence shows that you no longer meet the requirements for entitlement to disability benefits, you will still receive benefits for a 3-month period of adjustment. Benefits will then be stopped.

Whether or not you report a return to work or that your condition has improved, social security will review your claim periodically to see if you continue to meet the requirements for benefits.

If you are a disabled worker or a person disabled in childhood and you return to work in spite of a severe condition, your benefits may continue to be paid during a trial work period of up to 9 months—not necessarily consecutive months. This will give you a chance to test your ability to work. If after 9 months it is decided that you are able to do substantial gainful work, your benefits will be paid for an adjustment period of 3 additional months.

Thus, if you go to work in spite of your disability, you may continue to receive disability benefits for up to 12 months, even though the work is substantial gainful work. If it is decided that the work you are able to do is not substantial and gainful, you may continue to receive benefits. Of course, should you no longer meet the requirements for entitlement your benefits would be stopped after a 3-month adjustment period even though your trial work period might not be over.

Disabled widows and widowers also can have a trial work period. If your benefits are stopped because you return to work and you become unable to continue working within the next 12 months, your benefits can be restarted automatically. You do not have to file a new disability application.

You Can Earn Income Without Losing Benefits

If you are 72 or over, (70 or over) you can earn any amount and still get all your benefits. If you are under 70, you can receive all benefits if your earnings do not exceed the annual exempt amount. The annual amount for 1984 is $6,960 for people 65 or over and $5,160 for people under 65.

If your earnings go over the annual amount, $1 in benefits is withheld for each $2 of earnings above the limit.

The monthly measure used for 1977 and earlier years to determine whether benefits could be paid for any month during which they earned 1/12 or less of the annual exempt amount and did no substantial work in their business has been eliminated. A person can now use the monthly test only in the first year that he or she has a month in which earnings do not exceed 1/12 of the annual exempt amount or does not perform substantial services in self-employment. If such a month occurs in 1984, a benefit can be paid for any month in which you earn $580 or less (if 65 or older) or $430 (if under 65) and don't perform substantial services in self-employment even though your total yearly earnings exceed the annual amount.

The annual exempt amount will increase automatically as the level of average wages rises.

If a worker's earnings exceed the exempt amount, social security benefits to his dependents may be reduced. However, a dependent's benefits will not be reduced if another dependent has excess earnings.

Anyone earning over the annual exempt amount a year while receiving benefits (and under age 70) must report these earnings to the Social Security Administration. If you continue to work after you have applied for social security, your additional earnings may increase the amount of your monthly payment. This will be done automatically by the Social Security Administration. You need not ask for it.

Medicare

The Medicare program is administered by the Health Care Financing Administration.

Most people 65 and over and many under 65 who have been entitled to disability checks for at least 2 years have Medicare protection. So do insured people and their dependents who need a kidney transplant or dialysis treatment because of permanent kidney failure.

The hospital insurance part of Medicare helps pay the cost of inpatient hospital care and certain kinds of follow-up care. The medical insurance part helps pay for the cost of doctors' services, outpatient hospital services, and for certain other medical items and services.

A person who is eligible for monthly benefits at 65 gets hospital insurance automatically and does not have to pay a premium. He does pay a monthly premium for medical insurance.

Supplemental Security Income

The supplemental security income program started January 1974. These federal payments assure a minimum level of income for aged, blind, and disabled people who have limited income and resources.

This program is administered by the Social Security Administration, but it is financed from general revenues, not from social security contributions. Before 1974, payments to these people were made by state and local public assistance agencies.

Payments of up to $314.00 a month for an individual and up to $472.00 for a couple can be made and States may supplement the federal payments. Further information is available from any social security office.

How to Protect Your Social Security Record

Always show your social security card when you start a new job. In that way you will be sure that your earnings will be credited to *your* social security record and not someone else's. If you lose your social security card, apply for a new one at any social security office. When a woman marries, she should apply for a new card showing her married name (and the same number).

Public Assistance

The Federal government makes grants to the states to help them provide financial assistance, medical care, and social services to certain persons in need, including children dependent because of the death, absence from home, incapacity, or (in some states) unemployment of a parent. In addition, some help is provided from only state and/or local funds to some other needy persons.

Federal sharing in state cash assistance expenditures made in accordance with the Social Security Act is based on formulas which are set forth in the Act. The Social Security Act gives the states the option of using one of two formulas, whichever is to its benefit. One formula limits the amount of assistance payment in which there is federal sharing. The other formula permits federal sharing without a limit on the amount of assistance payment. Administrative costs in all the programs are shared equally by the federal and state governments.

Within these and other general patterns set by the requirements of the Social Security Act and their administrative interpretations, each state initiates and administers its own public assistance programs, including the determination of who is eligible to receive assistance, and how much can be granted and under what conditions. Assistance is in the form of cash payments made to recipients, except that direct payments are used for medical care, and restricted payments may be used in cases of mismanagement. Other social services are provided, in some instances, to help assistance recipients increase their capacity for self-care and self-support or to strengthen family life.

In the medical assistance Medicaid program, federal funds pay 50% to 83% of the costs for medical care. If it is to a state's benefit, it may use the Medicaid formula for federal sharing for its money payment programs, ignoring the maximum on dollar amounts per recipient.

Railroad Workers

These are covered by the federal Railroad Retirement Act which provides retirement and survivor annuities and lump-sum death benefits for aged or disabled employees and their families. Railroad workers are also covered by the Railroad Unemployment Insurance Act, which provides unemployment and sickness benefits as well as a placement service. Both acts are administered by the U.S. Railroad Retirement Board. Those covered by the railroad retirement system also participate in the health insurance program (Medicare) provided by the Social Security Act.

Unemployment Insurance

Unemployment insurance is managed jointly by the states and the federal government. Most states began paying benefits in 1938 and 1939.

Under What Conditions Can the Worker Collect?

The laws vary from state to state. In general, a waiting period of one week is required after a claim is filed before collecting unemployment insurance; the worker must be able to work, must not have quit without good cause or have been discharged for misconduct; he must not be involved in a labor dispute; above all, he must be ready and willing to work. He may be disqualified if he refuses, without good cause, to accept a job which is suitable for him in terms of his qualifications and experience, unless the wages, hours and working conditions offered are substantially less favorable than those prevailing for similar jobs in the community.

The unemployed worker must go to the local state employment security office and register for work. If that office has a suitable opening available, he must accept it or lose his unemployment payments, unless he has good cause for the refusal. If a worker moves out of his own state, he can still collect at his new residence; the state in which he is now located will act as agent for the other state, which will pay his benefits.

Benefits are paid only to unemployed workers who have had at least a certain amount of recent past employment or earnings in a job covered by the state law. The amount of employment or earnings, and the period used to measure them, vary from state to state, but the intent of the various laws is to limit benefits to workers whose recent records indicate that they are members of the labor force. The amount of benefits an unemployed worker may receive for any week is also determined by application to his past wages of a formula specified in the law. The general objective is to provide a weekly benefit which is about half the worker's customary weekly wages, up to a maximum set by the law (see table). In a majority of states, the total benefits a worker may receive in a 12-month period is limited to a fraction of his total wages in a prior 12-month period, as well as to a stated number of weeks. Thus, not all workers in a state are entitled to benefits for the number of weeks shown in the table.

Who Pays for the Insurance?

The total cost is borne by the employer in all but three states. Each state has a sliding scale of rates. The standard rate is set at 2.7% of taxable payroll in most states. But employers with records of less unemployment (that is, with fewer unemployment benefits paid to their former workers) are rewarded with rates lower than the standard 2.7%. The estimated average rate for employers in 1984 was 3.2% of taxable wages or 1.3% of total wages.

State Unemployment Compensation Maximums, 1984

State	Weekly benefit[1]	Maximum duration, weeks
Alabama	120	26
Alaska	156–228	26
Arizona	115	26
Arkansas	136	26
California	166	26
Colorado	202	26
Connecticut	168–252	26
Delaware	165	26
D. C.	206	34
Florida	150	26
Georgia	125	26
Hawaii	188	26
Idaho	159	26
Illinois	161–209	26
Indiana	84–141	26
Iowa	143–176	26
Kansas	175	26
Kentucky	140	26
Louisiana	205	26
Maine	139–203	26
Maryland	165	26
Massachusetts	185–278	30
Michigan	197	26
Minnesota	191	26
Mississippi	115	26
Missouri	105	26
Montana	166	26
Nebraska	120	26
Nevada	158	26
New Hampshire	141	26
New Jersey	170	26
New Mexico	145	26
New York	180	26
North Carolina	166	26
North Dakota	172	26
Ohio	147–233	26
Oklahoma	185	26
Oregon	197	26
Pennsylvania	214–222	26
Puerto Rico	84	20
Rhode Island	174–194	26
South Carolina	118	26
South Dakota	129	26
Tennessee	115	26
Texas	182	26
Utah	166	26
Vermont	146	26
Virgin Islands	130	26
Virginia	150	26
Washington	185	30
West Virginia	223	28
Wisconsin	196	26
Wyoming	157	26

1. Maximum amounts. When two amounts are shown, higher includes dependents' allowances. *Source:* Department of Labor, Employment and Training Administration.

Contributions for 1984 are required on wages up to $7,000 in all States except Conn., $7,100; Ark., $7,500; Ala., Colo., Del., D.C., Ill., Kans., Ky., Ohio, Pa., Vt., V.I., W.Va., $8,000; N.C., $8,200; Mont., $8,400; Mich., $8,500; Wis., $9,500; Wyo., $9,525; N.J., $9,600; Minn., N.Mex., $9,800; R.I., $10,000; Iowa, N.D., $10,400; Nev., $10,700; Wash., $12,000; Oreg., $13,000; Utah, $13,300; Idaho, $14,400; Hawaii, $14,600; Alaska, $21,400; P.R., all wages. Employees as well as employers pay a tax in Alaska ranging from 0.5% to 1.0% in accordance with their employer's tax; in N.J., employees pay 0.5% for unemployment insurance. In Ala., employees pay contributions of 1.0% only when the fund is below a specified amount. In Pa., employees pay contributions of 0.1% of all wages paid for employment.

Employers pay an additional unemployment tax to the federal government—0.7% of the first $7,000 paid to each employee. This money is used for the federal and state costs of administering the employment security program, including both unemployment insurance and the employment service. Any amount over these costs, up to the greater of $550 million or 0.125% of total wages subject to contributions under the state unemployment compensation laws for the calendar year, is put in a special fund on which the states draw when the benefit payment funds are low. Any remaining excess is distributed to the states in proportion to their taxable payrolls. These excess funds may be used for benefit payments, or may be used for administrative expenses if so appropriated by the state legislature.

Requirements vary from state to state, but all states cover firms having at least one employee for 20 weeks or a quarterly payroll of $1,500 in the current or preceding calendar year. In some states, firms with one employee at any time are covered. Certain classes of workers are specifically excluded under some or all state laws—members of the employer's family, insurance agents on commission, student nurses, internes, casual labor, and the self-employed.

During periods of high unemployment on either a state or national level, federal-state extended benefits are available to workers who have exhausted their regular benefits. An unemployed worker may receive benefits equal to the weekly benefit he received under the state program for one half the weeks of his basic entitlement to benefits up to a maximum (including regular benefits) of 39 weeks.

Federal Unemployment Insurance Programs

Amendments to the Social Security Act provided unemployment insurance for Federal civilian employees (1954) and for ex-servicemen (1958). Benefits under these programs are paid by state employment security agencies as agents of the federal government under agreements with the Secretary of Labor. Eligibility for benefits and the amount of benefits paid are determined according to the terms and conditions of the applicable state unemployment insurance law. Thus, federal civilian employees and ex-servicemen are subject to the same eligibility, disqualification, and benefit payment provisions as are claimants for benefits under the state unemployment insurance system.

Medicare Program

The Medicare program is a federal health-insurance program for persons 65 and over, disabled people under 65 who have been entitled to social security disability benefits at least 24 months, and insured workers and their dependents who need dialysis treatment or a kidney transplant because of permanent kidney failure.

Enacted under the Social Security Amendments of 1965, Medicare's official name is Title XVIII of the Social Security Act. These amendments also carried Title XIX, providing federal assistance to state medical-aid programs, which has come to be known as Medicaid.

Medicare

It will be helpful to your understanding of the Medicare program if you keep the following points in mind:

- The federal health-insurance program does not of itself offer medical services. It helps pay hospital, doctor, and other medical bills. You choose your own doctor, who prescribes your treatment and place of treatment. But, you should always make sure that health care facilities or persons who provide you with treatment or services are participating in Medicare. Usually, Medicare cannot pay for care from non-participating health care organizations.
- There are two parts of the program:
  (1) The hospital insurance part for the payment of most of the cost of covered care provided by participating hospitals, skilled nursing facilities, and home health agencies.
  (2) The medical insurance part which helps pay doctors' bills and certain other expenses.
- Another important point to remember: While Medicare pays the major share of the costs of many illnesses requiring hospitalization, it does not offer adequate protection for long-term illness or mental illness.
- Therefore, it may be advisable not to cancel any private health insurance, you now carry. You may wish to cancel a policy whose benefits are duplicated by the federal program, and consider a new policy that will provide for the payment of costs not covered by the federal program. Private insurance companies offer policies supplementing the protection offered by the federal program.

If you want help in deciding whether to buy private supplemental insurance, ask at any social security office for the pamphlet, *Guide to health insurance for people with Medicare.* This free pamphlet describes the various types of supplemental insurance available.

Do You Qualify for Hospital Insurance?

If you're entitled to monthly social security or railroad retirement checks (as a worker, dependent, or survivor), you have hospital insurance protection automatically when you're 65. Disabled people will have hospital insurance automatically after they have been entitled to social security disability benefits for 24 months. (Disabled people who get railroad annuities must meet special requirements.) People 65 or older who are not entitled to monthly benefits need credit for some work under social security to get hospital insurance without paying a monthly premium. If they do not have enough work, they can buy hospital insurance. The premium is $155 a month for the 12-month period starting January 1, 1984.

To be sure your protection will start the month you reach 65, apply for Medicare insurance 3 months before reaching 65, even if you don't plan to retire.

Do You Qualify for Voluntary Medical Insurance?

The voluntary medical insurance plan is a vital supplement to the hospital plan. It helps pay for doctors' and other medical services. Many people have not been able to obtain such insurance from private companies because they could not afford it or because of their medical histories.

One difference between the hospital insurance plan and the medical insurance plan is that you do not have to be under the social security or railroad retirement systems to enroll in the medical plan. Anyone who is 65 or older or who is eligible for hospital insurance can enroll in medical insurance.

People who get social security benefits or retirement benefits under the railroad retirement system will be enrolled automatically for medical insurance—unless they say they don't want it—when they become entitled to hospital insurance. Automatic enrollment does not apply to people who plan to continue working past 65, who are disabled widows or widowers between 50 and 65 who aren't getting disability checks, who are 65 but have not worked long enough to be eligible for hospital insurance, who have permanent kidney failure, or who live in Puerto Rico or foreign countries. These people have to apply for medical insurance if they want it. People who have medical insurance pay a monthly premium covering part of the cost of this protection. The other part is paid from general federal revenues. The basic premium for enrollees is $14.60 a month for the 12-month period starting January 1, 1984.

Is Other Insurance Necessary?

As already indicated, Medicare provides only partial reimbursement. Therefore, you should know how much medical cost you can bear and perhaps arrange for other insurance.

In 1984, for the first 60 days of inpatient hospital care in each benefit period, hospital insurance pays for all covered services except for the first $356. For the 61st through 90th day of a covered inpatient hospital stay, hospital insurance pays for all covered services except for $87 a day. People who need to be in a hospital for more than 90 days in a benefit period can use their 60 inpatient hospital reserve days. Hospital insurance pays for all covered services except for $178 a day for each reserve day used. Hospital insurance also does not pay the full cost of an inpatient stay in a skilled nursing facility.

Under medical insurance, the patient must meet an annual deductible of $75. After the patient has $75 in approved amounts for covered services each year, medical insurance generally pays 80% of the approved amounts for any additional covered services the patient receives during the rest of the year.

How You Obtain Coverage

If you are receiving social security or railroad retirement monthly benefits, you will receive from the government information concerning Medicare about 3 months before you become entitled to hospital insurance.

If you are not receiving benefits or are not covered under social security, contact any social security office to find out how you can get Medicare. People who have permanent kidney failure also should contact a social security office to apply for Medicare.

Aging: Myths and Truths

Myth: You can't teach an old dog new tricks.

Truth: A smart dog can learn new tricks at any age, and so can most people. Research has shown that older people do not necessarily lose their ability to learn, but sometimes learn differently than when younger. Their speed of comprehension, for instance, may decrease somewhat, but their retention and interpretation of new information may improve. Contrary to common belief, senility is not a state of mind that invariably accompanies old age. Rather, it is a serious and complex illness which, in many cases, can be alleviated through proper medical diagnosis and treatment.

Myth: Sex doesn't exist after age 60, and anyone who thinks it does is a "dirty old man" (or woman).

Truth: Normal sexual activity continues well into later life—sometimes even into the 90s—although frequency may decrease somewhat over the years.

Myth: When you grow old, you end up in a nursing home or some other institution.

Truth: Less than 5% of people 65 and over are institutionalized; the rest maintain their independence in a variety of residential situations. The majority of people who enter nursing homes usually do so following a period of hospitalization and eventually return to their homes.

Myth: Like birds in winter, people head south as soon as they retire.

Truth: While some do move south, most don't. Approximately 82.7% of the 65-plus population still live in the same house in which they lived before retiring. Of those who have moved, most moved a relatively short distance—frequently to a smaller residence more suited to their needs—while only 3.6% moved to different states, such as Florida, Arizona, and Nevada.

States With the Largest Population 65 and Over: 1960—1983

(numbers in thousands)

State	1983[1]	1980[2]	1970[2]	1960[2]	% increase, 1960–83
California	2,615	2,414	1,792	1,376	190.0
New York	2,223	2,161	1,951	1,688	31.7
Florida	1,867	1,688	985	553	337.6
Pennsylvania	1,639	1,531	1,267	1,129	45.2
Texas	1,470	1,371	988	745	197.3
Illinois	1,331	1,262	1,089	975	36.5
Ohio	1,250	1,169	993	897	39.4
Michigan	983	912	749	638	54.0
New Jersey	922	860	694	560	64.6
Total U.S.	**27,384**	**25,549**	**19,972**	**16,560**	**65.4**

1. Estimate, July 1, 1983. 2. April 1 census. *Source:* Bureau of the Census, *Current Population Reports,* May 1984.

Medicare—Enrollment and Payments, 1970–1981

Type of insurance	Unit	1981	1980	1979	1978	1977	1975	1970
HOSPITAL INSURANCE								
Enrollment, total	1,000	28,590	28,067	27,459	26,777	26,094	24,640	20,361
Persons aged 65 and over	1,000	25,591	25,104	24,548	23,984	23,475	22,472	20,361
Male	1,000	10,340	10,156	9,945	9,728	9,537	9,168	8,507
Female	1,000	15,250	14,948	14,604	14,256	13,937	13,304	11,855
Disabled persons	1,000	2,999	2,963	2,911	2,793	2,619	2,166	(x)
Male	1,000	1,896	1,871	1,837	1,763	1,654	1,381	(x)
Female	1,000	1,103	1,093	1,073	1,030	965	788	(x)
Benefit payments	Mil. dol.	30,342	25,064	20,623	17,682	15,737	11,315	5,124
MEDICAL INSURANCE								
Enrollment, total	1,000	27,941	27,400	26,757	26,074	25,364	23,904	19,584
Persons aged 65 and over	1,000	25,182	24,680	24,098	23,531	22,991	21,945	19,584
Male	1,000	10,055	9,868	9,645	9,436	9,240	8,873	8,132
Female	1,000	15,127	14,813	14,454	14,094	13,751	13,073	11,452
Disabled persons	1,000	2,759	2,719	2,659	2,543	2,373	1,959	(x)
Male	1,000	1,724	1,695	1,655	1,582	1,475	1,231	(x)
Female	1,000	1,036	1,025	1,004	961	897	729	(x)
Benefit payments	Mil. dol.	13,113	10,635	8,706	7,252	6,038	4,273	1,975

Enrollment as of July 1; payments for calendar year. Benefit payments represent trust fund outlays. Includes Puerto Rico, outlying areas, and enrollees in foreign countries. X = not applicable. *Source:* U.S. Health Care Financing Administration. Published in U.S. Social Security Administration, *Annual Statistical Supplement* to the *Social Security Bulletin.*

Employee-Employer Payroll Tax Rates for Social Security Programs by Selected Countries, 1981

Country	All social security programs			Old-age, disability and survivors insurance		
	Total	Employer	Employee	Total	Employer	Employee
United States	17.60	10.95	6.65	10.70	5.35	5.35
Canada	9.52	5.12[2]	4.40	3.60	1.80	1.80
France	48.55	37.41	11.14	13.00[3]	8.20[3]	4.80[3]
Germany, Fed. Rep.	34.75	18.13	16.63	18.50	9.25	9.25
Italy	55.02	47.57	7.45	24.46	17.31	7.15
Japan	22.85	12.80	10.05	10.60	5.30[4]	5.30[4]
Netherlands	54.86	29.23	25.63	32.45[5]	12.90[5]	19.55[5]
Sweden	32.76	32.65	.11	21.15	21.15	—
Switzerland	17.60	8.45	9.15	9.40	4.70	4.70
United Kingdom	21.45	13.70	7.75	n.a.	n.a.	n.a.

1. In percent. 2. Excludes work-injury compensation program. 3. Disability and survivors benefits financed through sickness insurance. 4. Rate for men in non-contracted-out plan. 5. Disability insurance includes work-injury compensation. n.a. = not available.—Represents zero. *Source:* U.S. Social Security Administration, Office of International Policy.

Manned Space Flight Projects

Mercury. *Project Mercury,* America's first manned space program, was designed to further knowledge about man's capabilities in space. *Mercury 9,* with astronaut Gordon L. Cooper, was the longest flight. It proved conclusively that man can live and work in space for at least 34 hours, despite the high-gravity forces of launch and re-entry, and weightlessness.

Gemini. *Gemini* was an extension of *Project Mercury,* to determine the effects of prolonged space flight on man—two weeks or longer. "Walks in space" provided invaluable information for astronauts' later walks on the Moon. The *Gemini* spacecraft, twice as large as the *Mercury* capsule, accommodated two astronauts.

Apollo. *Apollo* was the designation for the United States' effort to land a man on the Moon and return him safely to Earth. The goal was successfully accomplished with *Apollo 11* on July 20, 1969, culminating eight years of rehearsal and centuries of dreaming. Astronauts Neil A. Armstrong and Col. Edwin E. Aldrin, Jr., scooped up and brought back the first lunar rocks ever seen on Earth—about 47 pounds. Six *Apollo* flights followed, ending with *Apollo 17* in December, 1972. The last three *Apollos* carried mechanized vehicles called lunar rovers for wide-ranging surface exploration of the Moon by astronauts. The rendezvous and docking of an *Apollo* spacecraft with a Russian *Soyuz* craft in Earth orbit on July 18, 1975, closed out the *Apollo* program.

Skylab. America's first Earth-orbiting space station. *Project Skylab* was designed to demonstrate that men can work and live in space for prolonged periods without ill effects. Originally the spent third stage of a Saturn 5 moon rocket, *Skylab* measured 118 feet from stem to stern, and carried the most varied assortment of experimental equipment ever assembled in a single spacecraft. Three three-man crews visited the space stations, spending more than 740 hours observing the Sun and bringing home more than 175,000 solar pictures. These were the first recordings of solar activity above Earth's obscuring atmosphere. *Skylab* also evaluated systems designed to gather information on Earth's resources and environmental conditions. *Skylab* biomedical findings indicated that man adapts well to space for at least a period of three months, provided he has a proper diet and adequately programmed exercise, sleep, work, and recreation periods. *Skylab* orbited Earth at a distance of about 300 miles. Five years after the last *Skylab* mission, the 77-ton space station's orbit began to deteriorate faster than expected, owing to unexpectedly high sunspot activity. On July 11, 1979, the parts of *Skylab* that did not burn up in the atmosphere came crashing down on parts of Australia and the Indian Ocean. No one was hurt.

Space Shuttle. The *Space Shuttle* is America's newest manned space transportation system developed by NASA to reduce the cost of using space for commercial, scientific, and defense needs. The *Shuttle* is a manned rocket which, after depositing its payload in space, can be flown back to Earth like a conventional airplane and be available for re-use. Although most of its cargoes will be unmanned, the *Shuttle* can serve as an inhabited Earth-orbiting laboratory for up to 30 days. The *Space Shuttle Columbia* was successfully launched on April 12, 1981. It made five flights (the first four were test runs), the last completed on November 16, 1982. The second shuttle, *Challenger,* made its maiden flight on April 4, 1983. In April 1984, crew members of the *Challenger* captured, repaired, and returned the Solar Max satellite to orbit, making it the first time a disabled satellite had been repaired in space.

Unmanned Planetary and Lunar Programs

Lunar Orbiter. Series of spacecraft designed to orbit the Moon, taking pictures and obtaining data in support of the subsequent manned Apollo landings. The U.S. launched five *Lunar Orbiters* between Aug. 10, 1966 and Aug. 2, 1967.

Mariner. Designation for a series of spacecraft designed to fly past or orbit the planets, particularly Mercury, Venus, and Mars. *Mariners* provided the early information on Venus and Mars. *Mariner 9,* orbiting Mars in 1971, returned the most startling photographs of that planet to date, and helped pave the way for a *Viking* landing in 1976. *Mariner 10* explored Venus and Mercury in 1973 and was the first probe to use a planet's gravity to whip it toward another.

Pioneer. Designation for the United States' first series of sophisticated interplanetary spacecraft. *Pioneers 10* and *11* reached Jupiter in 1973 and 1974 and continued on to explore Saturn and the other outer planets. *Pioneer 11,* renamed *Pioneer Saturn,* examined the Saturn system in September 1979. Significant discoveries were the finding of a small new moon and a narrow new ring. In 1986, *Pioneer 10* will be the first man-made object to escape the solar system. *Pioneer Venus 1* and *2* reached Venus in 1978 and provided detailed information about that planet's surface and atmosphere.

Ranger. NASA's earliest moon exploration program. Spacecraft were designed for a crash landing on the Moon, taking pictures and returning scientific data up to the moment of impact. Provided the first closeup views of the lunar surface. The *Rangers* provided more than 17,000 closeup pictures, giving us more information about the Moon in a few years than in all the time that had gone before.

Surveyor. Series of unmanned spacecraft designed to land gently on the Moon and provide information on the surface in preparation for the manned lunar landings. Their legs were instrumented to return data on the surface hardness of the Moon. *Surveyor* dispelled the fear that Apollo spacecraft might sink several feet or more into the lunar dust.

Viking. Designation for two spacecraft designed to conduct detailed scientific examination of the planet Mars, including a search for life. *Viking 1* landed on July 20, 1976; *Viking 2,* Sept. 3, 1976. More was learned about the Red Planet in a few short months than in all the time that had gone before. But the question of life on Mars remains unresolved.

Voyager. Designation for two spacecraft designed to explore Jupiter and the other outer planets. *Voyager 1* and *Voyager 2* passed Jupiter in 1979 and sent back startling color TV images of that planet and its moons. They took a total of about 33,000 pictures. *Voyager 2* will continue on a trajectory that will take it to Uranus in 1986. *Voyager 1* passed Saturn November 1980 and *Voyager 2* passed Saturn August 1981.

Notable Unmanned Lunar and Interplanetary Probes

Spacecraft	Launch date	Destination	Remarks
Pioneer 1 (U.S.)	Oct. 11, 1958	Moon	Max. alt.: 71,300 mi. Flight duration: 43 h 17.5 min
Pioneer 3 (U.S.)	Dec. 6, 1958	Moon	Max. alt.: 66,654 mi. Discovered outer Van Allen layer.
Lunik 1 (U.S.S.R.)	Sept. 12, 1959	Moon	Landed in area of Mare Serenitatis.
Pioneer 5 (U.S.)	March 11, 1960	Inter-planetary	Orbited sun between Earth & Venus. Radio transmission over record distance of 20 million miles.
Mariner 2 (U.S.)	Aug. 27, 1962	Venus	Venus probe. Successful mid-course correction. Passed 21,648 mi. from Venus Dec. 14, 1962. Reported 800° F. surface temp. Contact lost Jan. 3, 1963 at 54 million mi.
Ranger 7 (U.S.)	July 28, 1964	Moon	Impacted near Crater Guericke 68.5 h after launch. Sent 4,316 pictures during last 15 min of flight as close as 1,000 ft above lunar surface.
Mariner 4 (U.S.)	Nov. 28, 1964	Mars	After mid-course correction, passed behind Mars July 14, 1965, taking 22 pictures from about 6,000 mi.
Ranger 8 (U.S.)	Feb. 17, 1965	Moon	809 lb. After 64.9 h, crashed into Mare Tranquilitatis, 2.59° N of lunar equator. Sent 7,137 pictures.
Ranger 9 (U.S.)	March 21, 1965	Moon	After 64.5 h, hit Crater Alphonsus. Sent 5,814 pictures.
Zond 3 (U.S.S.R.)	July 18, 1965	Moon	Sent close-ups of 3 million sq mi. of Moon. Now in solar orbit.
Venera 3 (U.S.S.R.)	Nov. 16, 1965	Venus	2,112 lb. Entered Venus atmosphere (March 1, 1966). No data sent.
Pioneer 6 (U.S.)	Dec. 16, 1965	Inter-planetary	Successfully orbiting Sun (every 311 days) to check space conditions between Earth & Venus. Perihelion: 75.6 million mi. Aphelion: 90.7 million mi.
Luna 9 (U.S.S.R.)	Jan. 31, 1966	Moon	3,428 lb. Instrument capsule of 220 lb soft-landed Feb. 3, 1966. Sent back about 30 pictures.
Luna 10 (U.S.S.R.)	March 31, 1966	Moon	540 lb. Orbit achieved April 2, 1966.
Surveyor 1 (U.S.)	May 30, 1966	Moon	Landed June 2, 1966. Sent almost 10,400 pictures, a number after surviving the 14-day lunar night.
Lunar Orbiter 1 (U.S.)	Aug. 10, 1966	Moon	Orbited Moon Aug. 14. 21 pictures sent.
Pioneer 7 (U.S.)	Aug. 17, 1966	Sun Orbit	Orbiting sun (400 days). Perihelion: 92 million mi. Aphelion: 102 million mi.
Luna 11 (U.S.S.R.)	Aug. 24, 1966	Moon	Moon orbit achieved Aug. 27.
Luna 12 (U.S.S.R.)	Oct. 22, 1966	Moon	Moon orbit achieved Oct. 25 for 3.5 h. Transmission
Lunar Orbiter 2 (U.S.)	Nov. 7, 1966	Moon	Orbit achieved Nov. 10. Sent hundreds of excellent pictures.
Luna 13 (U.S.S.R.)	Dec. 21, 1966	Moon	Soft-landed 80 h after launch. Good pictures. Drove spike into Moon's surface.
Lunar Orbiter 3 (U.S.)	Feb. 4, 1967	Moon	Orbited Moon Feb. 8. Terminated Oct. 9, 1967. Excellent pictures.
Surveyor 3 (U.S.)	April 17, 1967	Moon	Soft-landed 65 h after launch on Oceanus Procellarum. Scooped and tested lunar soil.
Lunar Orbiter 4 (U.S.)	May 4, 1967	Moon	Achieved orbit May 7. Changed orbit on command.
Venera 4 (U.S.S.R.)	June 12, 1967	Venus	Arrived Oct. 17. Instrument capsule sent temperature and chemical data.
Mariner 5 (U.S.)	June 14, 1967	Venus	Fly-by Oct. 19, confirming Mariner 2 and Venera 4 findings
Surveyor 4 (U.S.)	July 14, 1967	Moon	Contact lost 2.5 min before landing
Explorer 35 (U.S.)	July 19, 1967	Moon	Orbit July 22. Perilune: 500 mi.; apolune: 4000 mi.
Lunar Orbiter 5 (U.S.)	Aug. 2, 1967	Moon	Orbited Aug. 5, Perilune: 125 mi.; apolune: 3,760 mi. Time 3 h 50 min. After filming, was crashed on Moon.
Surveyor 5 (U.S.)	Sept. 8, 1967	Moon	Landed near lunar equator Sept. 10. Radiological analysis of lunar soil. Mechanical claw for digging soil.
Surveyor 6 (U.S.)	Nov. 7, 1967	Moon	Landed in Sinus Medii Nov. 10. Jumped 8 ft to photograph original position. Sent back 11,524 pictures.
Pioneer 8 (U.S.)	Dec. 12, 1967	Sun Orbit	Achieved Solar orbit. Stopped functioning April 28, 1968.
Pioneer 8 (U.S.)	Dec. 12, 1967	Sun Orbit	Achieved Solar orbit. Stopped functioning April 28, 1968.
Surveyor 7 (U.S.)	Jan. 6, 1968	Moon	Landed near Crater Tycho Jan. 10. Soil analysis. Sent 3,343 pictures.
Zond 4 (U.S.S.R.)	March 2, 1968	Unknown	Achieved parking orbit but was unable to leave. Re-entered March 3.
Zond 5 (U.S.S.R.)	Sept. 14, 1968	Moon	Circumlunar flight
Pioneer 9 (U.S.)	Nov. 8, 1968	Sun Orbit	Achieved orbit. Six experiments returned solar radiation data.
Zond 6 (U.S.S.R.)	Nov. 10, 1968	Moon	Circumlunar flight

Spacecraft	Launch date	Destination	Remarks
Venera 5 (U.S.S.R.)	Jan. 5, 1969	Venus	Landed May 16, 1969. Returned atmospheric data.
Venera 6 (U.S.S.R.)	Jan. 10, 1969	Venus	Landed May 17, 1969. Sent data as Venera 5.
Mariner 6 (U.S.)	Feb. 24, 1969	Mars	Came within 2000 mi. of Mars July 31, 1969. Sent back data & TV pictures.
Mariner 7 (U.S.)	March 27, 1969	Mars	Came within 2000 mi. of Mars Aug. 5, 1969. Sent back data & TV pictures.
Luna 15 (U.S.S.R.)	July 13, 1969	Moon	Lunar orbiter landed on Moon July 21, 1969 after completing varying orbits.
Zond 7 (U.S.S.R.)	Aug. 8, 1969	Moon	Circumlunar. Recovered Aug. 14, 1969.
Pioneer E (U.S.)	Aug. 27, 1969	Inter-planetary	To obtain data on particles and magnetic fields, but failed to achieve orbit.
Venera 7 (U.S.S.R.)	Aug. 17, 1970	Venus	Reached Venus Dec. 15, 1970. Sent data, apparently from surface, for 58 min.
Luna 16 (U.S.S.R.)	Sept. 12, 1970	Moon	Soft-landed Sept. 20, scooped up rock, returned to Earth Sept. 24.
Luna 17 (U.S.S.R.)	Nov. 10, 1970	Moon	Soft-landed on Sea of Rains Nov. 17. Lunokhod 1, self-propelled vehicle, used for first time. Sent TV photos, made soil analysis, etc.
Mars 2 (U.S.S.R.)	May 19, 1971	Mars	Reached Mars Nov. 27. Dropped landing capsule on surface.
Mars 3 (U.S.S.R.)	May 28, 1971	Mars	Like Mars 2. Capsule landed Dec. 2. TV transmission cut short.
Mariner 9 (U.S.)	May 30, 1971	Mars	First craft to orbit Mars, Nov. 13. 7,300 pictures, 1st closeups of Mars' moon. Transmission ended Oct. 27, 1972.
Luna 19 (U.S.S.R.)	Sept. 28, 1971	Moon	Orbited Moon, making measurements & taking photos. Soft-landed Feb. 21 in Sea of Fertility. Returned Feb. 25 with rock samples.
Pioneer 10 (U.S.)	March 3, 1972	Jupiter	620-million-mile flight path through asteroid belt passed Jupiter Dec. 3, 1973, to give man first closeup of planet. In 1986, will become first man-made object to escape solar system.
Venera 8 (U.S.S.R.)	March 27, 1972	Venus	Landed July 22. Sent signals for 50 min. Capsule burned or crushed because of surface heat and pressure. Sent data on atmosphere and surface.
Luna 21 (U.S.S.R.)	Jan. 8, 1973	Moon	Soft-landed Jan. 16. Lunokhod 2 (moon-car) scooped up soil samples, returned them to Earth Jan. 27.
Pioneer 11 (U.S.)	April 6, 1973	Jupiter	Flew by 25,000 mi. from Jupiter Dec. 3, 1974—3 times closer than Pioneer 10.
Mars 4 (U.S.S.R.)	July 21, 1973	Mars	Arrived Feb. 1974, briefly sending back photos
Mars 5 (U.S.S.R.)	July 25, 1973	Mars	Sister craft of Mars 4
Mariner 10 (U.S.)	Nov. 3, 1973	Venus, Mercury	Passed Venus Feb. 5, 1974. Arrived Mercury March 29, 1974, for man's first closeup look at planet. First time gravity of one planet (Venus) used to whip spacecraft toward another (Mercury).
Luna 22 (U.S.S.R.)	May 29, 1974	Moon	Orbited Moon June 2, 1974
Venera 9 (U.S.S.R.)	June 8, 1975	Venus	Soft-landed Oct. 25, 1976. Photographed surface of planet.
Venera 10 (U.S.S.R.)	June 14, 1975	Venus	(See Venera 9)
Viking 1 (U.S.)	Aug. 20, 1975	Mars	Carrying life-detection labs. Landed July 20, 1976, for detailed scientific research, including pictures. Designed to work for only 90 days, it operated for almost 6 1/2 years before it went silent in November 1982.
Viking 2 (U.S.)	Sept. 9, 1975	Mars	Like Viking 1. Landed Sept. 3, 1976. Functioned 3 1/2 years.
Luna 24 (U.S.S.R.)	Aug. 9, 1976	Moon	Soft-landed Aug. 18, 1976. Returned soil samples Aug. 22, 1976.
Voyager 1 (U.S.)	Sept. 5, 1977	Jupiter, Saturn, Uranus	Fly-by mission. Reached Jupiter in March 1979; passed Saturn Nov. 1980; to reach Uranus 1986.
Voyager 2 (U.S.)	Sept. 20, 1977	Jupiter, Saturn, Uranus	Like Voyager 1. Encountered Jupiter in July 1979; flew by Saturn Aug. 1981; to pass Uranus 1986; then perhaps Neptune.
Pioneer Venus 1 (U.S.)	May 20, 1978	Venus	Arrived Dec. 4 and orbited Venus, photographing surface and atmosphere.
Pioneer Venus 2 (U.S.)	Aug. 8, 1978	Venus	Four-part multi-probe, landed Dec. 9.
Venera 11 (U.S.S.R.)	Sept. 9, 1978	Venus	Soft-landed Dec. 25, 1978. Transmitted data for 95 minutes.
Venera 12 (U.S.S.R.)	Sept. 14, 1978	Venus	Like Venera 11. Landed Dec. 21 and transmitted data for 1 hour 50 minutes.
Venera 13 (U.S.S.R.)	Oct. 30, 1981	Venus	Landed March 1, 1982. Took first X-ray fluorescence analysis of the planet's surface. Transmitted data 2 hours 7 minutes.
Venera 14 (U.S.S.R.)	Nov. 4, 1981	Venus	Landed March 5, 1982. Like Venera 13, took X-ray fluorescence analysis of Venusian soil.

Notable Manned Space Flights

Designation and country	Date	Astronauts	Orbit: perigee/apogee (km)	Orbital period (min)	Number of orbits	Flight time (h/min)	Remarks
Vostok 1(U.S.S.R.)	April 12, 1961	Yuri A. Gagarin	181/327	89.1	1	1/48	First manned orbital flight
MR III (U.S.)	May 5, 1961	Alan B. Shepard, Jr.	—	—	([1])	0/15	Range 486 km (302 mi.), peak 187 km (116.5 mi.); capsule recovered
MR IV (U.S.)	July 21, 1961	Virgil I. Grissom	—	—	([1])	0/16	Range 487 km, peak 190 km; capsule lost
Vostok 2 (U.S.S.R.)	Aug. 6–7, 1961	Gherman S. Titov	178/257	88.6	17.5	25/18	First long-duration flight
MA VI (U.S.)	Feb. 20, 1962	John H. Glenn, Jr.	161/261	88.5	3	4/55	First American in orbit
MA VII (U.S.)	May 24, 1962	M. Scott Carpenter	161/268	88.3	3	4/56	Overshot landing area; otherwise fine
MA VIII (U.S.)	Oct. 3, 1962	Walter M. Schirra, Jr.	161/283	88.5	6	9/13	First splashdown close to aiming point
MA IX (U.S.)	May 15–16, 1963	L. Gordon Cooper, Jr.	161/267	88.4	22	34/20	Longest Mercury flight
Vostok 5 (U.S.S.R.)	June 14–19, 1963	Valery F. Bykovsky	180/235	88.4	81	119/6	Longest Russian orbital flight to date
Vostok 6 (U.S.S.R.)	June 16–19, 1963	Valentina V. Tereshkova	183/233	88.3	48	70/50	First orbital flight by female cosmonaut
Voskhod 1 (U.S.S.R.)	Oct. 12, 1964	Vladimir M. Komarov; Konstantin P. Feoktistov; Boris G. Yegorov	177/409	90.1	16	24/17	First 3-man orbital flight; also first flight without space suits
Voskhod 2 (U.S.S.R.)	March 18, 1965	Alexei A. Leonov; Pavel I. Belyayev	174/495	90.9	17	26/2	First "space walk" (by Leonov), 10 min
GT III (U.S.)	March 23, 1965	Virgil I. Grissom; John W. Young	161/224	88.3	3	4/53	First manned test of Gemini spacecraft
GT IV (U.S.)	June 3–7, 1965	James A. McDivitt; Edward H. White, 2d	161/282	89.0	62	97/48	First American "space walk" (by White), lasting slightly over 20 min
GT VI (U.S.)	Dec. 15–16, 1965	Walter M. Schirra, Jr.; Thomas P. Stafford	151/258	88.7	16	25/52	Orbit was extended to 298 km to make rendezvous with orbiting GT VII
GT VIII (U.S.)	March 16–17, 1966	Neil A. Armstrong; David R. Scott	160/270	88.8	6.5	10/42	Only Gemini flight cut short by malfunction; one thruster kept firing after rendezvous and docking with an orbiting Agena rocket had been accomplished
GT XI (U.S.)	Sept. 12–15, 1966	Charles Conrad, Jr.; Richard F. Gordon, Jr.	161/281	89.0	44	71/17	Docking with orbiting Agena on first orbit; apogee of orbit then extended to 1,368 km (850 mi.)
GT XII (U.S.)	Nov. 11–15, 1966	James A. Lovell, Jr.; Edwin E. Aldrin, Jr.	161/282	89.0	59	94/33	Docking with Agena visually, without computer; co-pilot outside spacecraft for total of 5 1/2 hours
Apollo 7 (U.S.)	Oct. 11–22, 1968	Walter M. Schirra, Jr.; Donn F. Eisele; R. Walter Cunningham	233/285	89.9	163	260/9	First manned test of Apollo command module; first live TV transmissions from orbit
Soyuz 3 (U.S.S.R.)	Oct. 26-30, 1968	Georgi T. Bergeovoi	204/224	88.6	64	94/51	First manned rendezvous and possible docking by Soviet cosmonaut
Apollo 8 (U.S.)	Dec. 21-27, 1968	Frank Borman; James A. Lovell, Jr.; William A. Anders	—	—	10[3]	147/00	First spacecraft in circumlunar orbit; TV transmissions from this orbit
Apollo 9 (U.S.)	Mar. 3-13, 1969	James A. McDivitt; David R. Scott; Russell L. Schweikart	197/508	91.5	151	241/1	First manned flight of Lunar Module

Apollo 11 (U.S.)	July 16–24, 1969	Neil A. Armstrong; Edwin E. Aldrin, Jr.; Michael Collins	—	—	—	195/18	First manned landing and EVA on Moon; soil and rock samples collected; experiments left on lunar surface
Soyuz 6 (U.S.S.R.)	Oct. 11–16, 1969	Gorgiy Shonin; Valriy Kabasov	186/221	88.4	80	118/42	Three spacecraft and seven men put into earth orbit simultaneously for first time
Apollo 12 (U.S.)	Nov. 14–24, 1969	Charles Conrad, Jr.; Richard F. Gordon, Jr.; Alan Bean	—	—	—	244/36	Manned lunar landing mission; investigated Surveyor 3 spacecraft; collected lunar samples. EVA time: 15 h 30 min
Soyuz 9 (U.S.S.R.)	June 1–17, 1970	Andreiyan Nikolayez; Vitaly Sevastianov	236/249	89.3	287	424/59	Mission to test man's ability to withstand long periods of weightlessness
Apollo 14 (U.S.)	Jan. 31–Feb. 9, 1971	Alan B. Shepard; Stuart A. Roosa; Edgar D. Mitchell	—	—	—	216/42	Third manned lunar landing: returned largest amount of lunar material
Soyuz 10 (U.S.S.R.)	April 22–24, 1971	Vladimir A. Shatalov; Alexei S. Yeliseyev; Nikolai Rukavishnikov	208/246	88.9	—	47/46	Linked up for 5 1/2 hours with orbiting space station, Salyut 1
Soyuz 11 (U.S.S.R.)	June 6–30, 1971	Georgiy Tomofeyevich Dobrovolskiy; Vladislav Nikolayevich Volkov; Viktor Ivanovich Patsyev	185/217	88.3	—	569/40	Linked up with first space station, Salyut 1. Astronauts died just before re-entry due to loss of pressurization in spacecraft
Apollo 15 (U.S.)	July 26–Aug. 7, 1971	David R. Scott; James B. Irwin; Alfred M. Worden	—	—	—	295/12	Fourth manned lunar landing; first use of Lunar Rover propelled by Scott and Irwin; first live pictures of LM lift-off from Moon; exploration time: 18 hours
Apollo 16 (U.S.)	April 16–27, 1972	John W. Young; Thomas K. Mattingly; Charles M. Duke, Jr.	—	—	—	265/51	Fifth manned lunar landing; second use of Lunar Rover Vehicle, propelled by Young and Duke. Total exploration time on the Moon was 20 h 14 min, setting new record. Mattingly's in-flight "walk in space" was 1 h 23 min. Approximately 213 lb of lunar rock returned
Apollo 17 (U.S.)	Dec. 7-19, 1972	Eugene A. Cernan; Ronald E. Evans; Harrison H. Schmitt	—	—	—	301/51	Sixth and last manned lunar landing; third to carry lunar rover. Cernan and Schmitt, during three EVA's, completed total of 22 h 05 min 3 sec. USS Ticonderoga recovered crew and about 250 lbs of lunar samples.
Skylab SL-2 (U.S.)	May 25-June 22, 1973	Charles Conrad, Jr.; Josep P. Kerwin; Paul J. Weitz	401/424	93.2	—	672/50	First manned Skylab launch. Established Skylab Orbital Assembly and conducted scientific and medical experiments
Skylab SL-3 (U.S.)	July 28-Sept. 25, 1973	Alan L. Bean, Jr.; Jack R. Lousma; Owen K. Garriott	401/424	93.2	—	1427/9	Second manned Skylab launch. New crew remained in space for 59 days, continuing scientific and medical experiments and earth observations from orbit.
Skylab SL-4 (U.S.)	Nov. 16, 1973-Feb. 8, 1974	Gerald Carr; Edward Gibson; William Pogue	401/424	93.2	—	2017/16	Third manned Skylab launch; obtained medical data on crew for use in extending the duration of manned space flight; crews "walked in space" 4 times,

Designation and country	Date	Astronauts	Orbit: perigee/apogee (km)	Orbital period (min)	Number of orbits	Flight time (h/min)	Remarks
							totaling 44 h 40 min. Longest space mission yet—84 d 1 h 16 min. Splashdown in Pacific, Feb. 9, 1974.
Soyuz 13 (U.S.S.R.)	Dec. 18–26, 1973	Pyotr Klimuk; Valentin Lebadev	188/246	88.9	—	188/55	Modified spacecraft to be used for rendezvous with U.S. spacemen in 1975
Soyuz 14 (U.S.S.R.)	July 3–19, 1974	Pavel Popovich; Yuri Artyukhin	201/338	89.9	—	377/29	Crewmen spent two weeks on board Soviet space station Salyut 3
Soyuz 17 (U.S.S.R.)	Jan. 11–Feb. 9, 1975	Col. Aleksey Gubarev; Georgi Grechko				709/20	Crew spent 30 days in Salyut 4 space station, which was launched Dec. 26, 1974 and placed in Earth orbit
Apollo/Soyuz Test Project (U.S. and U.S.S.R.)	July 15–24, 1975 (U.S.)	U.S.: Brig. Gen. Thomas P. Stafford, Vance D. Brand, Donald K. Slayton	152/166	87.7 89.0 (docked)	138 (docked)	216/05	World's first international manned rendezvous and docking in space; aimed at developing a space rescue capability.
	July 15–21, 1975 (U.S.S.R)	U.S.S.R.: Col. A. A. Leonov, V. N. Kubasov	191/218	91.0 89.0 (docked)	138 (docked)	223/35	Apollo and Soyuz docked and crewmen exchanged visits on July 17, 1975. Mission duration for Soyuz: 142 h 31 min. For Apollo: 217 h, 28 min.
Soyuz 21 (U.S.S.R.)	July 6–Aug. 24, 1976	Col. Boris Volynov; Lt. Col. Vitali Zholobov	114/409	89.7	—	1218/24	Crew spent 50 days aboard Salyut 5 space station, which was launched June 22
Soyuz 24 (U.S.S.R.)	Feb. 7–25, 1977	Col. V. Gorbatko; Lt. Col. Yuri Glaszkov	173/323	89.5	—	425/23	Docked and transferred to Salyut 5 on Feb. 8. Returned Feb. 25
Soyuz 31 (U.S.S.R.)	Aug. 26–Nov. 2, 1978	Valery Bykovsky; Sigmund Jaehn	337/353	91.4	—	1632/0[2]	Docked with Salyut 6 and Soyuz 29; crew returned in Soyuz 29 on Sept. 3, 1978
Soyuz 33 (U.S.S.R.)	April 11–12, 1979	N. Rukavishnikov; G. Ivanov	—	—	—	—	Commander veteran of Soyuz 16
Soyuz 35 (U.S.S.R.)	April 9–Oct. 11, 1981	Valery Ryumin; Leonid Popov	—	—	—	—	Docked with Salyut 6; crew set record of 185 days duration in space.
Soyuz T2 (U.S.S.R.)	June 5–9, 1980	Lt. Col. Yuri V. Mayyshev; Vladimir V. Aksenov	—	—	—	—	Docked with Salyut 6; tested new model spacecraft, T2
Columbia (U.S.)	April 12–14, 1981	Capt. Robert L. Crippen; John W. Young	—	—	—	54/20	Maiden voyage of *Space Shuttle*, the first spacecraft designed specifically for re-use up to 100 times.

1. Suborbital flight. 2. Approximate time. 3. Number of orbits around moon. NOTE: The letters MR stand for Mercury (capsule) and Redstone (rocket); MA, for Mercury and Atlas (rocket); GT, for Gemini (capsule) and Titan-II (rocket). The first astronaut listed in the Gemini and Apollo flights is the command pilot. The Mercury capsules had names: MR-III was *Freedom 7*, MR-IV was *Liberty Bell 7*, MA-VI was *Friendship 7*, MA-VII was *Aurora 7*, MA-VIII was *Sigma 7*, and MA-IX was *Faith 7*. The figure 7 referred to the fact that the first group of U.S. astronauts numbered seven men. Only one Gemini capsule had a name: GT-III was called *Molly Brown* (after the Broadway musical *The Unsinkable Molly Brown*); thereafter the practice of naming the capsules was discontinued.

Atomic Energy

Just as the Space Age is said to have started with the orbiting of Sputnik I, the Atomic Age is said to have started with the explosion of a test bomb on July 16, 1945, near Alamogordo, N.M., at 5:30 A.M. local time. The bomb was placed on top of a steel tower, and observers were stationed in bunkers 10,000 yards away. The explosion vaporized the steel tower, produced a mushroom cloud rising to 40,000 feet, and melted the desert sand into glass for distances up to 800 yards from the tower.

The first operational use of an atom bomb took place only three weeks later, when a uranium bomb was exploded over Hiroshima, Japan, on Aug. 6, 1945. The bomb, cylindrical in shape, 10 feet long with a diameter of 2 feet 4 inches, weighed about 9,000 pounds. Its explosive force was equal to 20,000 tons of TNT, hence the term "20-kiloton bomb." Three days later another atomic bomb, this time of plutonium, was exploded over Nagasaki.

Of course, the Atomic Age did not begin with the explosion of the test bomb at Alamogordo, just as the Space Age did not begin with the orbiting of the first artificial satellite. In both cases these visible feats were just experiments that proved the theory that had been built up patiently over decades.

At the turn of the century, scientists began to wonder whether the atoms of the chemical elements might not be composed of smaller particles. This was actually a contradiction in terms, because the Greek word *atomos*, from which the word *atom* was derived, meant "indivisible." But there were some indications of particles smaller than an atom—the electrons. In 1907,* Albert Einstein suggested that matter might just be "condensed energy" and gave the conversion formula $E = mc^2$, in which E represents the energy, m the mass, and c the velocity of light. If this formula was correct, a small piece of matter should represent enormous amounts of energy.

*Einstein's famous formula was first published on May 14, 1907. His special theory of relativity was published in 1905.

Fission and Fusion

Atomic energy can be released in two ways. One is the *fission* of elements with very heavy atoms, such as uranium and plutonium, which will split when struck by a neutron, a sub-atomic particle. The splitting of the heavy atom releases more neutrons, which are then available to split other atoms—the so-called chain reaction. The other way of obtaining atomic energy is *fusion;* four light atoms (hydrogen) are fused together into the next heavier element (helium). The fusion reaction requires enormous heat and very high pressures. These pressures, coupled with very high temperatures, can most easily be produced by exploding a fission bomb.

From about 1910 to 1930, most physicists believed that the release of atomic energy, if it could be done, would be of no practical value. They asserted that causing the release would require more energy than could be obtained. Most astronomers, on the other hand, were convinced that atomic energy was released in the sun and the other stars, because there was no other way to account for the energy the stars radiated into space. Trying to account for the energy radiated by the stars led to theoretical papers predicting what we now call the fusion reaction. At the time (1930), atomic fission was still unknown; it was discovered first by Enrico Fermi in 1934. But nobody yet knew that the sudden bursts of energy observed in the experiments were due to the fission of the uranium-235 atom. This was established (by way of calculation) by Dr. Lise Meitner. Once it was known what happened, the way to a premeditated release of atomic energy was clear.

But nobody could be quite certain whether the release would take the form of an explosion or whether it would be slow enough to be used to generate power. American scientists proceeded under the assumption that the release would be sudden and violent (and the Alamogordo test proved them right), while Professor Heisenberg in Germany thought the slow release to be more likely, which is the reason why the Germans did not start a large-scale atomic energy project.

Atoms for Peace

The *peaceful* Atomic Age can be said to have been born in 1954, when the original U.S. Atomic Energy Act was amended to release many so-called "secrets" of nuclear energy so that nuclear power plants could be built and radioactive isotopes be used in medicine. The next year, the first International Conference on the Peaceful Uses of the Atom was convened at Geneva, bringing together scientists from all over the world to discuss what hitherto had been considered to be secret.

Actually there was little that was really secret about nuclear energy. When the results of the 1938 experiments were brought to the United States, scientists from different parts of the world openly stated that the possibility of atomic bombs was inherent in the scientific findings.

Once the veil of "secrecy" had been dispelled by revision of the Atomic Energy Act and the Geneva meeting, construction of plants to produce electricity by controlled fission of uranium atoms got under way in the United States and several other industrialized nations. Electric power was first produced as a result of nuclear fission in December 1951 at the National Reactor Testing Station in Idaho. When a reactor was connected to a generator, the nuclear power plant produced enough electricity for about 50 homes.

Table of Geological Periods

It is now generally assumed that planets are formed by the accretion of gas and dust in a cosmic cloud, but there is no way of estimating the length of this process. Our earth acquired its present size, more or less, between 4,000 and 5,000 million years ago. Life on earth originated about 2,000 million years ago, but there are no good fossil remains from periods earlier than the Cambrian, which began about 550 million years ago. The largely unknown past before the Cambrian Period is referred to as the Pre-Cambrian and is subdivided into the Lower (or older) and Upper (or younger) Pre-Cambrian—also called the Archaeozoic and Proterozoic Eras.

The known geological history of the earth since the beginning of the Cambrian Period is subdivided into three "eras," each of which comprises a number of "periods." They, in turn, are subdivided into "subperiods." In a subperiod, a certain section may be especially well known because of rich fossil finds. Such a section is called a "formation," and it is usually identified by a place name.

Paleozoic Era

This era began 550 million years ago and lasted for 355 million years. The name was compounded from Greek *palaios* (old) and *zoön* (animal).

Period	Duration[1]	Subperiods	Events
Cambrian (from *Cambria*, Latin name for Wales)	70	Lower Cambrian Middle Cambrian Upper Cambrian	Invertebrate sea life of many types, proliferating during this and the following period
Ordovician (from Latin *Ordovices*, people of early Britain)	85	Lower Ordovician Upper Odovician	
Silurian (from Latin *Silures*, people of early Wales)	40	Lower Silurian Upper Silurian	First known fishes; gigantic sea scorpions
Devonian (from Devonshire in England)	50	Lower Devonian Upper Devonian	Proliferation of fishes and other forms of sea life, land still largely lifeless
Carboniferous (from Latin *carbo* = coal + *fero* = to bear)	85	Lower or Mississippian Upper of Pennsylvanian	Period of maximum coal formation in swampy forests; early insects and first known amphibians
Permian (from district of Perm in Russia)	25	Lower Permian Upper Permian	Early reptiles and mammals; earliest form of turtles

Mesozoic Era

This era began 195 million years ago and lasted for 135 million years. The name was compounded from Greek *mesos* (middle) and *zoön* (animal). Popular name: Age of Reptiles.

Period	Duration[1]	Subperiods	Events
Triassic (from *trias* = triad)	35	Lower or Buntsandstein (from German *bunt* = colorful + *Sandstein* = sandstone) Middle or Muschelkalk (from German *Muschel* = clam + *Kalk* = limestone) Upper or Keuper (old miners' term)	Early saurians
Jurassic (from Jura Mountains)	35	Lower or Black Jurassic, or Lias (from French *liais* = hard stone) Middle or Brown Jurassic, or Dogger (old provincial English for ironstone) Upper or White Jurassic, or Malm (Middle English for sand)	Many sea-going reptiles; early large dinosaurs; somewhat later, flying reptiles (pterosaurs), earliest known birds
Cretaceous (from Latin *creta* = chalk)	65	Lower Cretaceous Upper Cretaceous	Maximum development of dinosaurs; birds proliferating; oppossum-like mammals

Cenozoic Era

This era began 60 million years ago and includes the geological present. The name was compounded from Greek *kainos* (new) and *zoön* (animal). Popular name: Age of Mammals.

Period	Duration[1]	Subperiods	Events
Tertiary (originally thought to be the third of only three periods)	c. 60	Paleocene (from Greek *palaios* = old + *kainos* = new)	First mammals other than marsupials
		Eocene (from Greek *eos* = dawn + *kainos* = new)	Formation of amber; rich insect fauna; early bats
		Oligocene (from Greek *oligos* = few + *kainos* = new)	Steady increase of large mammals
		Miocene (from Greek *meios* = less + *kainos* = new)	
		Pliocene (from Greek *pleios* = more + *kainos* = new)	Mammals closely resembling present types; protohumans
Pleistocene (from Greek *pleistos* = most + *kainos* = new) (popular name: Ice Age)	1	Four major glaciations, named Günz, Mindel, Riss, and Würm, originally the names of rivers. Last glaciation ended 10,000 to 15,000 years ago	Various forms of early man
Holocene (from Greek *holos* = entire + *kainos* = new)		The present	The last 3,000 years are called "history"

1. In millions of years.

Chemical Elements

Element	Symbol	Atomic no.	Atomic weight	Specific gravity	Melting point °C	Boiling point °C	Number of isotopes[1]	Discoverer	Year
Actinium	Ac	89	227[2]	10.07[2]	1050	3200 ±300	11	Debierne	1899
Aluminum	Al	13	26.9815	2.6989	660.37	2467	8	Wöhler	1827
Americium	Am	95	243[6]	13.67	994 ±4	2607	13[3]	Seaborg et al.	1944
Antimony	Sb	51	121.75	6.691	630.74	1750	29	Early historic times	—
Argon	Ar	18	39.948	1.7837[4]	−189.2	−185.7	8	Rayleigh and Ramsay	1894
Arsenic (gray)	As	33	74.9216	5.73	817 (28 atm.)	613[5]	14	Albertus Magnus	1250?
Astatine	At	85	~210	—	302	337	21	Corson et al.	1940
Barium	Ba	56	137.34	3.5	725	1640	25	Davy	1808
Berkelium	Bk	97	247[6]	14.00[7]	—	—	8[3]	Seaborg et al.	1949
Beryllium	Be	4	9.01218	1.848	1278 ±5	2970 (5 mm.)	6	Vauquelin	1798
Bismuth	Bi	83	208.9806	9.747	271.3	1560 ±5	19	Geoffroy	1753
Boron	B	5	10.81	2.37[8]	2300	2550[5]	6	Gay-Lussac and Thénard; Davy	1808
Bromine	Br	35	79.904	3.12[4]	−7.2	58.78	19	Balard	1826
Cadmium	Cd	48	112.40	8.65	320.9	765	22	Stromeyer	1817
Calcium	Ca	20	40.08	1.55	839 ±2	1484	14	Davy	1808
Californium	Cf	98	251[6]	—	—	—	12[3]	Seaborg et al.	1950
Carbon	C	6	12.011	1.8–3.5[9]	~3550	4827	7	Prehistoric	—
Cerium	Ce	58	140.12	6.771	798 ±3	3257	19	Berzelius and Hisinger; Klaproth	1803
Cesium	Cs	55	132.9055	1.873	28.40	678.4	22	Bunsen and Kirchhoff	1860
Chlorine	Cl	17	35.453	1.56[4]	−100.98	−34.6	11	Scheele	1774
Chromium	Cr	24	51.996	7.18–7.20	1857 ±20	2672	9	Vauquelin	1797
Cobalt	Co	27	58.9332	8.9	1495	2870	14	Brandt	c.1735
Copper	Cu	29	63.546	8.96	1083.4±0.2	2567	11	Prehistoric	—
Curium	Cm	96	247[6]	13.51[2]	1340 ±40	—	13[3]	Seaborg et al.	1944
Dysprosium	Dy	66	162.50	8.540	1409	2335	21	Boisbaudran	1886
Einsteinium	Es	99	254[6]	—	—	—	12[3]	Ghiorso et al	1952
Erbium	Er	68	167.26	9.045	1522	2510	16	Mosander	1843
Europium	Eu	63	151.96	5.283	822 ±5	1597	21	Demarcay	1896
Fermium	Fm	100	257[6]	—	—	—	10[3]	Ghiorso et al	1953
Fluorine	F	9	18.9984	1.108[4]	−219.62	−188.14	6	Moissan	1886
Francium	Fr	87	223[6]	—	27[2]	677[2]	21	Perey	1939
Gadolinium	Gd	64	157.25	7.898	1311 ±1	3233	17	Marignac	1880
Gallium	Ga	31	69.72	5.904	29.78	2403	14	Boisbaudran	1875
Germanium	Ge	32	72.59	5.323	937.4	2830	17	Winkler	1886
Gold	Au	79	196.9665	19.32	1064.43	2807	21	Prehistoric	—
Hafnium	Hf	72	178.49	13.31	2227 ±20	4602	17	Coster and von Hevesy	1923
Helium	He	2	4.00260	0.1785[4]	−272.2 (26 atm.)	−268.934	5	Janssen	1868
Holmium	Ho	67	164.9303	8.781	1470	2720	29	Delafontaine and Soret	1878
Hydrogen	H	1	1.0080	0.070[4]	−259.14	−252.87	3	Cavendish	1766

Element	Symbol	Atomic no.	Atomic weight	Specific gravity	Melting point °C	Boiling point °C	Number of isotopes[1]	Discoverer	Year
Indium	In	49	114.82	7.31	156.61	2080	34	Reich and Richter	1863
Iodine	I	53	126.9045	4.93	113.5	184.35	24	Courtois	1811
Iridium	Ir	77	192.22	22.42	2410	4130	25	Tennant	1803
Iron	Fe	26	55.847	7.894	1535	2750	10	Prehistoric	—
Krypton	Kr	36	83.80	3.733[4]	−156.6	−152.30±0.10	23	Ramsay and Travers	1898
Lanthanum	La	57	138.9055	6.166	920±5	3454	19	Mosander	1839
Lawrencium	Lr	103	257[6]	—	—	—	20[3]	Ghiorso et al.	1961
Lead	Pb	82	207.2	11.35	327.502	1740	29	Prehistoric	—
Lithium	Li	3	6.941	0.534	180.54	1347	5	Arfvedson	1817
Lutetium	Lu	71	174.97	9.835	1656±5	3315	22	Urbain	1907
Magnesium	Mg	12	24.305	1.738	648.8±0.5	1090	8	Black	1755
Manganese	Mn	25	54.9380	7.21-7.44[10]	1244±3	1962	11	Gahn, Scheele, and Bergman	1774
Mendelevium	Md	101	256[6]	—	—	—	3[3]	Ghiorso et al.	1955
Mercury	Hg	80	200.59	13.546	−38.87	356.58	26	Prehistoric	—
Molybdenum	Mo	42	95.94	10.22	2617	4612	20	Scheele	1778
Neodymium	Nd	60	144.24	6.80 & 7.004[10]	1010	3127	16	von Welsbach	1885
Neon	Ne	10	20.179	0.89990 (g/1 0°C/1 atm)	−248.67	−246.048	8	Ramsay and Travers	1898
Neptunium	Np	93	237.0482	20.25	640±1	3902	15[3]	McMillan and Abelson	1940
Nickel	Ni	28	58.71	8.902	1453	2732	11	Cronstedt	1751
Niobium (Columbium)	Nb	41	92.9064	8.57	2468±10	4742	24	Hatchett	1801
Nitrogen	N	7	14.0067	0.808[4]	−209.86	−195.8	8	Rutherford	1772
Nobelium	No	102	254[6]	—	—	—	7[3]	Ghiorso et al.	1957
Osmium	Os	76	190.2	22.57	3045±30	5027±100	19	Tennant	1803
Oxygen	O	8	15.9994	1.14[4]	−218.4	−182.962	8	Priestley	1774
Palladium	Pd	46	106.4	12.02	1552	3140	21	Wollaston	1803
Phosphorus	P	15	30.9738	1.82 (white)	44.1	280	7	Brand	1669
Platinum	Pt	78	195.09	21.45	1772	3827±100	32	Ulloa	1735
Plutonium	Pu	94	244[6]	19.84	641	3232	16[3]	Seaborg et al.	1940
Poionium	Po	84	210[6]	9.32	254	962	34	Curie	1898
Potassium	K	19	39.102	0.862	63.65	774	10	Davy	1807
Praseodymium	Pr	59	140.9077	6.772	931±4	3212	15	von Weisbach	1885
Promethium	Pm	61	145[6]	—	≈1080	2460?	14	Marinsky et al.	1945
Protactinium	Pa	91	231.0359	15.37[2]	<1600	—	14	Hahn and Meitner	1917
Radium	Ra	88	226.0254	5.0?	700	1140	15	P. and M. Curie	1898
Radon	Rn	86	222[6]	4.4[4]	−71	−61.8	20	Dorn	1900
Rhenium	Re	75	186.2	21.02	3180	5627[7]	21	Noddack, Berg, and Tacke	1925
Rhodium	Rh	45	102.9055	12.41	1966±3	3727±100	20	Wollaston	1803
Rubidium	Rb	37	85.4678	1.532	38.89	688	20	Bunsen and Kirchoff	1861
Ruthenium	Ru	44	101.07	12.44	2310	3900	16	Klaus	1844
Samarium	Sm	62	150.4	7.536	1072±5	1778	17	Boisbaudran	1879
Scandium	Sc	21	44.9559	2.989	1539	2832	15	Nilson	1879
Selenium	Se	34	78.96	4.79 (gray)	217	684.9±1	20	Berzelius	1817
Silicon	Si	14	28.086	2.33	1410	2355	8	Berzelius	1824
Silver	Ag	47	107.868	10.50	961.93	2212	27	Prehistoric	—
Sodium	Na	11	22.9898	0.971	97.81±0.03	882.9	7	Davy	1807
Strontium	Sr	38	87.62	2.54	769	1384	18	Davy	1808
Sulfur	S	18	32.06	2.07[11]	112.8	444.674	10	Prehistoric	—
Tantalum	Ta	73	180.9479	16.654	2996	5425±100	19	Ekeberg	1801
Technetium	Tc	43	98.9062	11.50[2]	2172	4877	23	Perrier and Segrè	1937
Tellurium	Te	52	127.60	6.24	449.5±0.3	989.8±3.8	29	von Reichenstein	1782
Terbium	Tb	65	158.9254	8.234	1360±4	3041	24	Mosander	1843
Thallium	Tl	81	204.37	11.85	303.5	1457±10	28	Crookes	1861
Thorium	Th	90	232.0381	11.72	1750	4790	12	Berzelius	1828
Thulium	Tm	69	168.9342	9.314	1545±15	1727	18	Cleve	1879
Tin	Sn	50	118.69	7.31 (white)	231.9681	2270	28	Prehistoric	—
Titanium	Ti	22	47.90	4.55	1660±10	3287	9	Gregor	1791
Tungsten (Wolfram)	W	74	183.85	19.3	3410±20	5660	22	J. and F. d'Elhuyar	1783
Uranium	U	92	238.029	–18.95	1132.3±0.8	3818	15	Peligot	1841
Vanadium	V	23	50.9414	6.11	1890±10	3380	9	del Rio	1801
Xenon	Xe	54	131.30	3.52[4]	−111.9	−107.1±3	31	Ramsay and Travers	1898
Ytterbium	Yb	70	173.04	6.972	824±5	1193	16	Marignac	1878
Yttrium	Y	39	88.9059	4.457	1523±8	3337	21	Gadolin	1794
Zinc	Zn	30	65.38	7.133	419.58	907	15	Prehistoric	—
Zirconium	Zr	40	91.22	6.506[2]	1852±2	4377	20	Klaproth	1789

1. Isotopes are different forms of the same element having the same atomic number but different atomic weights. 2. Calculated figure. 3. Artificially produced. 4. Liquid. 5. Sublimation point. 6. Mass number of the isotope of longest known life. 7. Estimated. 8. Amorphous. 9. Depending on whether amorphous, graphite or diamond. 10. Depending on allotropic form. 11. Rhombic. – Is approximately. < Is less than. NOTE: There is a dispute between groups at the Lawrence Berkeley Laboratory of the University of California and at the Dubna Laboratory in the Soviet Union concerning the discovery of elements 104, 105, and 106. The Lawrence Berkeley Laboratory claims that 104 and 105 were discovered in 1969 and 1970, respectively, by Ghiorso et al. and has suggested the names Rutherfordium and Hahnium. The U.S. laboratory claims also that Ghiorso et al. discovered element 106 in 1974. No name has yet been suggested for this element. Names will not be official until the controversy is resolved and they have been approved by the International Union for Pure and Applied Chemistry.

Scientific Inventions, Discoveries, and Theories

Most inventions are the results of the discoveries, theories, experiments, and improvements of many people. This list tries to suggest the development of certain particularly important ideas. In some instances, it tries to connect the fundamental theory with the ultimate practical invention.

Abacus: *See* Calculating machine
Adding machine: *See* Calculating machine; Computer
Adrenaline: (isolation of) Jokichi Takamine, U.S., 1901
Air brake: George Westinghouse, U.S., 1868
Air conditioning: Willis Carrier, U.S., 1911
Airplane: (first powered, sustained, controlled flight) Orville and Wilbur Wright, U.S., 1903. *See also* Jet propulsion, aircraft
Airship: (non-rigid) Henri Giffard, France, 1852; (rigid) Ferdinand von Zeppelin, Germany, 1900
Aluminum manufacture: (by electrolytic action) Charles M. Hall, U.S., 1866
Anesthetic: (first use of anesthetic—ether—on man) Crawford W. Long, U.S., 1842
Antibiotics: (first demonstration of antibiotic effect) Louis Pasteur, Jules-François Joubert, France, 1887; (penicillin, first modern antibiotic) Alexander Fleming, England, 1928
Antiseptic: (surgery) Joseph Lister, England, 1867
Antitoxin, diphtheria: Emil von Behring, Germany, 1890
Atomic theory: (ancient) Leucippus, Democritus, Greece, c.500 B.C.; Lucretius, Rome, c.100 B.C.; (modern) John Dalton, England, 1808
Automobile: (first with internal combustion engine, 250 rpm) Karl Benz, Germany, 1885; (first with practical high-speed internal combustion engine, 900 rpm) Gottlieb Daimler, Germany, 1885; (first true automobile, not carriage with motor) René Panhard, Emile Lavassor, France, 1891; (carburetor, spray) Charles E. Duryea, U.S., 1892
Bacteria: Anton van Leeuwenhoek, The Netherlands, 1683
Bakelite: *See* Plastics
Balloon, hot-air: Joseph and Jacques Montgolfier, France, 1783
Ball-point pen: *See* Pen
Barometer: Evangelista Torricelli, Italy, 1643
Bicycle: Karl D. von Sauerbronn, Germany, 1816; (first modern model) James Starley, England, 1884
Bifocal lens: *See* Lens, bifocal
Blood, circulation of: William Harvey, England, 1628
Braille: Louis Braille, France, 1829
Bullet: (conical) Claude Minié, France, 1849
Calculating machine: (Abacus) China, c.190; (logarithms: made multiplying easier and thus calculators practical) John Napier, Scotland, 1614; (slide rule) William Oughtred, England, 1632; (digital calculator) Blaise Pascal, 1642; (multiplication machine) Gottfried Leibnitz, Germany, 1671; (important 19th-century contributors to modern machine) Frank S. Baldwin, Jay R. Monroe, Dorr E. Felt, W. T. Ohdner, William Burroughs, all U.S.; ("analytical engine" design, included concepts of programming, taping) Charles Babbage, England, 1835. *See also* Computer
Camera: (hand-held) George Eastman, U.S., 1888; (Polaroid Land) Edwin Land, U.S., 1948. *See also* Photography
Carburetor: *See* Automobile
Celanese: *See* Fibers, man-made
Celluloid: *See* Plastics
Classification of plants and animals: (by genera and species) Carolus Linnaeus, Sweden, 1737–53
Clock, pendulum: Christian Huygens, The Netherlands, 1656
Combustion: (nature of) Antoine Lavoisier, France, 1777
Computer: (differential analyzer, mechanically operated) Vannevar Bush, U.S., 1928; (Mark I, first information-processing digital computer) Howard Aiken, U.S., 1944; (ENIAC, Electronic Numerical Integrator and Calculator, first all-electronic) J. Presper Eckert, John W. Mauchly, U.S., 1946; (stored-program concept) John von Neumann, U.S., 1947
Conditioned reflex: Ivan Pavlov, Russia, c.1910
Converter, Bessemer: William Kelly, U.S., 1851
Cosmetics: Egypt, c.4000 B.C.
Cotton gin: Eli Whitney, U.S., 1793
Crossbow: China, c.300 B.C.
Cyclotron: Ernest O. Lawrence, U.S., 1931
Deuterium: (heavy hydrogen) Harold Urey, U.S., 1931
DNA: (deoxyribonucleic acid) Friedrich Meischer, Germany, 1869; (determination of double-helical structure) F. H. Crick, England, James D. Watson, U.S., 1953
Dynamite: Alfred Nobel, Sweden, 1867
Electric generator (dynamo): (laboratory model) Michael Faraday, England, 1832; Joseph Henry, U.S., c.1832; (hand-driven model) Hippolyte Pixii, France, 1833; (alternating-current generator) Nikola Tesla, U.S., 1892
Electric lamp: (arc lamp) Sir Humphrey Davy, England, 1801; (fluorescent lamp) A. E. Becquerel, France, 1867; (incandescent lamp) Sir Joseph Swann, England, Thomas A. Edison, U.S., contemporaneously, 1870s; (carbon arc street lamp) Charles F. Brush, U.S., 1879; (first widely marketed incandescent lamp) Thomas A. Edison, U.S., 1879; (mercury vapor lamp) Peter Cooper Hewitt, U.S., 1903; (neon lamp) Georges Claude, France, 1911; (tungsten filament) Irving Langmuir, U.S., 1915
Electric motor: *See* Motor
Electromagnet: William Sturgeon, England, 1823
Electron: Sir Joseph J. Thompson, England, 1897
Elevator, passenger: (safety device permitting use by passengers) Elisha G. Otis, U.S., 1852; (elevator utilizing safety device) 1857
$E = mc^2$: (equivalence of mass and energy) Albert Einstein, Switzerland, 1905
Engine, internal combustion: No single inventor. Fundamental theory established by Sadi Carnot, France, 1824; (two-stroke) Étienne Lenoir, France, 1860; (ideal operating cycle for four-stroke) Alphonse Beau de Rochet, France, 1862; (operating four-stroke) Nikolaus Otto, Germany, 1876; (diesel) Rudolf Diesel, Germany, 1892; (rotary) Felix Wankel, Germany, 1956. *See also* Automobile
Engine, steam: *See* Steam engine
Evolution: (by natural selection) Charles Darwin, England, 1859
Falling bodies, law of: Galileo Galilei, Italy, 1590
Fermentation: (micro-organisms as cause of) Louis Pasteur, France, c.1860
Fibers, man-made: (nitrocellulose fibers treated to change flammable nitrocellulose to harmless cel-

lulose, precursor of rayon) Sir Joseph Swann, England, 1883; (rayon) Count Hilaire de Chardonnet, France, 1889; (Celanese) Henry and Camille Dreyfuss, U.S., England, 1921; (research on polyesters and polyamides, basis for modern man-made fibers) U.S., England, Germany, 1930s; (nylon) Wallace H. Carothers, U.S., 1935

Fountain pen: *See* Pen

Geometry, elements of: Euclid, Alexandria, Egypt, c.300 B.C.

Gravitation, law of: Sir Isaac Newton, England, c. 1665 (published 1687)

Gunpowder: China, c.700

Gyrocompass: Elmer A. Sperry, U.S., 1905

Gyroscope: Léon Foucault, France, 1852

Helicopter: Igor Sikorsky, U.S., 1939

Helium first observed on sun: Sir Joseph Lockyer, England, 1868

Heredity, laws of: Gregor Mendel, Austria, 1865

Induction, electric: Joseph Henry, U.S., 1828

Insulin: Sir Frederick G. Banting, J. J. R. MacLeod, Canada, 1922

Intelligence testing: Alfred Binet, Theodore Simon, France, 1905

Isotopes: (concept of) Frederick Soddy, England, 1912; (stable isotopes) J. J. Thompson, England, 1913; (existence demonstrated by mass spectrography) Francis W. Ashton, 1919

Jet propulsion, aircraft: Sir Frank Whittle, England, 1930

Laser: (theoretical work on) Charles H. Townes, Arthur L. Schawlow, U.S., N. Basov, A. Prokhorov, U.S.S.R., 1958; (first working model) T. H. Maiman, U.S., 1960

Lens, bifocal: Benjamin Franklin, U.S., c.1760

Light, nature of: (wave theory) Christian Huygens, Denmark, 1678; (electromagnetic theory) James Clerk Maxwell, England, 1873

Light, speed of: (theory that light has finite velocity) Olaus Roemer, Denmark, 1675

Lightning rod: Benjamin Franklin, U.S., 1752

Linotype: *See* Printing

Lithography: *See* Printing

Locomotive: (steam-powered) Richard Trevithick, England, 1804; (first practical, due to multiple-fire-tube boiler) George Stephenson, England, 1829; (largest steam-powered) Union Pacific's "Big Boy," U.S., 1941

Logarithms: *See* Calculating machine

Loom: (horizontal, two-beamed) Egypt, c.4400 B.C.; (Jacquard drawloom, pattern controlled by punch cards) Jacques de Vaucanson, France, 1745, Joseph-Marie Jacquard, 1801; (flying shuttle) John Kay, England, 1733; (power-driven loom) Edmund Cartwright, England, 1785

Machine gun: James Puckle, England, 1718; Richard J. Gatling, U.S., 1861

Match: (phosphorus) François Derosne, France, 1816; (friction) Charles Sauria, France, 1831; (safety) J. E. Lundstrom, Sweden, 1855

Mendelian law: *See* Heredity

Microscope: (compound) Zacharias Janssen, The Netherlands, 1590; (electron) Vladimir Zworykin et al., U.S., Canada, Germany, 1932–1939

Motion pictures: Thomas A. Edison, U.S., 1893

Motion pictures, sound: Product of various inventions. First picture with synchronized musical score: *Don Juan,* 1926; with spoken dialogue: *The Jazz Singer,* 1927; both Warner Bros.

Motor, electric: Michael Faraday, England, 1822; (alternating-current) Nikola Tesla, U.S., 1892

Motor, gasoline: *See* Engine, internal combustion

Motorcycle: (motor tricycle) Edward Butler, England, 1884; (gasoline-engine motorcycle) Gottieb Daimier, Germany, 1885

Neptunium: (first transuranic element, synthesis of) Edward M. McMillan, Philip H. Abelson, U.S., 1940

Neutron: James Chadwick, England, 1932

Neutron-induced radiation: Enrico Fermi et al., Italy, 1934

Nitroglycerin: Ascanio Sobrero, Italy, 1846

Nuclear fission: Otto Hahn, Fritz Strassmann, Germany, 1938

Nuclear reactor: Enrico Fermi et al., U.S., 1942

Nylon: *See* Fibers, man-made

Ohm's law: (relationship between strength of electric current, electromotive force, and circuit resistance) Georg S. Ohm, Germany, 1827

Ozone: Christian Schönbein, Germany, 1839

Paper: China, c.100 B.C.

Parachute: Louis S. Lenormand, France, 1783

Pen: (fountain) Lewis E. Waterman, U.S., 1884; (ball-point, for marking on rough surfaces) John H. Loud, U.S., 1888; (ball-point, for handwriting) Lazlo Biro, Argentina, 1944

Penicillin: *See* Antibiotics

Periodic law: (that properties of elements are functions of their atomic weights) Dmitri Mendeleev, Russia, 1869

Periodic table: (arrangement of chemical elements based on periodic law) Dmitri Mendeleev, Russia, 1869

Phonograph: Thomas A. Edison, U.S., 1877

Photography: (first paper negative, first photograph, on metal) Joseph Nicéphore Niepce, France, 1816–1827; (discovery of fixative powers of hyposulfite of soda) Sir John Herschel, England, 1819; (first direct positive image on silver plate, the daguerreotype) Louis Daguerre, based on work with Niepce, France, 1839; (first paper negative from which a number of positive prints could be made) William Talbot, England, 1841. Work of these four men, taken together, forms basis for all modern photography. (First color images) Alexandre Becquerel, Claude Niepce de Saint-Victor, France, 1848–60; (commercial color film with three emulsion layers, Kodachrome) U.S., 1935. *See also* Camera

Plastics: (first material, nitrocellulose softened by vegetable oil, camphor, precursor to Celluloid) Alexander Parkes, England, 1855; (Celluloid, involving recognition of vital effect of camphor) John W. Hyatt, U.S., 1869; (Bakelite, first completely synthetic plastic) Leo H. Baekeland, U.S., 1910; (theoretical background of macromolecules and process of polymerization on which modern plastics industry rests) Hermann Staudinger, Germany, 1922. *See also* Fibers, man-made

Plow, forked: Mesopotamia, before 3000 B.C.

Plutonium, synthesis of: Glenn T. Seaborg, Edwin M. McMillan, Arthur C. Wahl, Joseph W. Kennedy, U.S., 1941

Polaroid Land camera: *See* Camera

Polio, vaccine against: (vaccine made from dead virus strains) Jonas E. Salk, U.S., 1954; (vaccine made from live virus strains) Albert Sabin, U.S., 1960

Positron: Carl D. Anderson, U.S., 1932

Pressure cooker: (early version) Denis Papin, France, 1679

Printing: (block) Japan, c.700; (movable type) Korea, c.1400; Johann Gutenberg, Germany, c. 1450 (lithography, offset) Aloys Senefelder, Germany, 1796; (rotary press) Richard Hoe, U.S., 1844; (linotype) Ottman Mergenthaler, U.S. 1884

Programming, information: *See* Calculating machine

Propeller, screw: Sir Francis P. Smith, England, 1836; John Ericsson, England, worked independently of and simultaneously with Smith, 1837

Proton: Ernest Rutherford, England, 1919

Psychoanalysis: Sigmund Freud, Austria, c.1904

Quantum theory: Max Planck, Germany, 1901

Rabies immunization: Louis Pasteur, France, 1885

Radar: (limited to one-mile range) Christian Hulsmeyer, Germany, 1904; (pulse modulation, used for measuring height of ionosphere) Gregory Breit, Merle Tuve, U.S., 1925; (first practical radar—radio detection and ranging) Sir Robert Watson-Watt, England, 1934–35

Radio: (electromagnetism, theory of) James Clerk Maxwell, England, 1873; (spark coil, generator of electromagnetic waves) Heinrich Hertz, Germany, 1886; (first practical system of wireless telegraphy) Guglielmo Marconi, Italy, 1895; (vacuum electron tube, basis for radio telephony) Sir John Fleming, England, 1904; (triode amplifying tube) Lee de Forest, U.S., 1906; (regenerative circuit, allowing long-distance sound reception) Edwin H. Armstrong, U.S., 1912; (frequency modulation—FM) Edwin H. Armstrong, U.S., 1933

Radioactivity: (X-rays) Wilhelm K. Roentgen, Germany, 1895; (radioactivity of uranium) Henri Becquerel, France, 1896; (radioactive elements, radium and polonium in uranium ore) Marie Sklodowska-Curie, Pierre Curie, France, 1898; (classification of alpha and beta particle radiation) Pierre Curie, France, 1900; (gamma radiation) Paul-Ulrich Villard, France, 1900; (carbon dating) Willard F. Libby et al., U.S., 1955

Rayon: *See* Fibers, man-made

Reaper: Cyrus McCormick, U.S., 1834

Relativity: (special and general theories of) Albert Einstein, Switzerland, Germany, U.S., 1905–53

Revolver: Samuel Colt, U.S., 1835

Rifle: (muzzle-loaded) Italy, Germany, c.1475; (breech-loaded) England, France, Germany, U.S., c.1866; (bolt-action) Paul von Mauser, Germany, 1889; (automatic) John Browning, U.S., 1918

Roller bearing: (wooden for cartwheel) Germany or France, c.100 B.C.

Rubber: (vulcanization process) Charles Goodyear, U.S., 1839

Safety match: *See* Match

Solar system, universe: (sun-centered universe) Nicolaus Copernicus, Warsaw, 1543; (establishment of planetary orbits as elliptical) Johannes Kepler, Germany, 1609; (infinity of universe) Giordano Bruno, Italian monk, 1584

Spectrum: (heterogeneity of light) Sir Isaac Newton, England, 1665–66

Spermatozoa: Anton van Leeuwenhoek, The Netherlands, 1683

Spinning: (spinning wheel) India, introduced to Europe in Middle Ages; (Saxony wheel, continuous spinning of wool or cotton yarn) England, c.1500–1600; (spinning jenny) James Hargreaves, England, 1764; (spinning frame) Sir Richard Arkwright, England, 1769; (spinning mule, completed mechanization of spinning, permitting production of yarn to keep up with demands of modern looms) Samuel Crompton, England, 1779

Steam engine: (first commercial version based on principles of French physicist Denis Papin) Thomas Savery, England, 1639; (atmospheric steam engine) Thomas Newcomen, England, 1705; (steam engine for pumping water from collieries) Savery, Newcomen, 1725; (modern condensing, doubleacting) James Watt, England, 1782

Steam engine, railroad: *See* Locomotive

Steamship: Claude de Jouffroy d'Abbans, France, 1783; James Rumsey, U.S., 1787; John Fitch, U.S., 1790. All preceded Robert Fulton, U.S., 1807, credited with launching first commercially successful steamship

Sulfa drugs: (parent compound, para-aminobenzenesulfanomide) Paul Gelmo, Austria, 1908; (antibacterial activity) Gerhard Domagk, Germany, 1935

Syphilis, test for: *See* Wassermann test

Tank, military: Sir Ernest Swinton, England, 1914

Telegraph: Samuel F. B. Morse, U.S., 1837

Telephone: Alexander Graham Bell, U.S., 1876

Telescope: Hans Lippershey, The Netherlands, 1608

Television: (mechanical disk-scanning method) successfully demonstrated by J. L. Baird, England, C. F. Jenkins, U.S., 1926; (electronic scanning method) Vladimir K. Zworykin, U.S., 1928; (color, all-electronic) Zworykin, 1925; (color, mechanical disk) Baird, 1928; (color, compatible with black and white) George Valensi, France, 1938; (color, sequential rotating filter) Peter Goldmark, U.S., first introduced, 1951; (color, compatible with black and white) commercially introduced in U.S., National Television Systems Committee, 1953

Thermometer: (open-column) Galileo Galilei, c. 1593; (clinical) Santorio Santorio, Padua, c. 1615; (mercury, also Fahrenheit scale) Gabriel D. Fahrenheit, Germany, 1714; (centigrade scale) Anders Celsius, Sweden, 1742; (absolute-temperature, or Kelvin, scale) William Thompson, Lord Kelvin, England, 1848

Tire, pneumatic: Robert W. Thompson, England, 1845; (bicycle tire) John B. Dunlop, Northern Ireland, 1888

Toilet, flush: Product of Minoan civilization, Crete, c.2000 B.C. Alleged invention by "Thomas Crapper" is untrue.

Tractor: Benjamin Holt, U.S., 1900

Transformer, electric: William Stanley, U.S., 1885

Transistor: John Bardeen, William Shockley, Walter Brattain, U.S., 1948

Uncertainty principle: (that position and velocity of an object cannot both be measured exactly, at the same time) Werner Heisenberg, Germany, 1927

Vaccination: Edward Jenner, England, 1796

Vacuum tube: *See* Radio

Van Allen (radiation) Belt: (around the earth) James Van Allen, U.S., 1958

Vitamins: (hypothesis of disease deficiency) Sir F. G. Hopkins, Casimir Funk, England, 1912; (vitamin A) Elmer V. McCollum, M. Davis, U.S., 1912–14; (vitamin B) Elmer V. McCollum, U.S., 1915–16; (thiamin, B_1) Casimir Funk, England, 1912; (riboflavin, B_2) D. T. Smith, E. G. Hendrick, U.S., 1926; (niacin) Conrad Elvehjem, U.S., 1937; (B_6) Paul Gyorgy, U.S., 1934; (vitamin C) C. A. Hoist, T. Froelich, Norway, 1912; (vitamin D) Elmer V. McCollum, U.S., 1922; (folic acid) Lucy Wills, England, 1933

Wassermann test: (for syphilis) August von Wassermann, Germany, 1906

Weaving, cloth: *See* Loom

Wheel: (cart, solid wood) Mesopotamia, c.3800–3600 B.C.

Windmill: Persia, c.600

X-ray: *See* Radioactivity

Xerography: Chester Carlson, U.S., 1938

Zero: India, c.600; (absolute zero, cessation of all molecular energy) William Thompson, Lord Kelvin, England, 1848

ASTRONOMY

Astronomical Terms

Planet is the term used for a body in orbit around the Sun. Its origin is Greek; even in antiquity it was known that a number of "stars" did not stay in the same relative positions to the others. There were five such restless "stars" known—Mercury, Venus, Mars, Jupiter, and Saturn—and the Greeks referred to them as *planetes*, a word which means "wanderers." That the earth is one of the planets was realized later. The additional planets were discovered after the invention of the telescope.

Satellite (or *moon*) is the term for a body in orbit around a planet. As long as our own Moon was the only moon known, there was no need for a general term for the moons of planets. But when Galileo Galilei discovered the four main moons of the planet Jupiter, Johannes Kepler (in a letter to Galileo) suggested "satellite" (from the Latin *satelles*, which means attendant) as a general term for such bodies. The word is used interchangeably with "moons": astronomers speak and write about the moons of Neptune, Saturn, etc. A satellite may be any size.

Orbit is the term for the path traveled by a body in space. It comes from the Latin *orbis*, which means circle, circuit, etc., and *orbita*, which means a rut or a wheel track. Theoretically, four mathematical figures are possible orbits: two are open (hyperbola and parabola) and two are closed (ellipse and circle), but in reality all closed orbits are ellipses. These ellipses can be nearly circular, as are the orbits of most planets, or very elongated, as are the orbits of most comets. In these orbits, the Sun is in one focal point of the ellipse, and the other focal point is empty. In the orbits of satellites, the planet stands in one focal point of the orbit. The *primary* of an orbit is the body in the focal point. For planets, the point of the orbit closest to the Sun is the *perihelion*, and the point farthest from the Sun is the *aphelion*. For orbits around the Earth, the corresponding terms are *perigee* and *apogee;* for orbits around other planets, corresponding terms are coined when necessary.

Two heavenly bodies are in *inferior* or *superior conjunction* when they have the same Right Ascension, or are in the same meridian; that is, when one is due north or south of the other. If the bodies appear near each other as seen from the Earth, they will rise and set at the same time. They are in *opposition* when they are opposite each other in the heavens: when one rises as the other is setting. *Greatest elongation* is the greatest apparent angular distance from the Sun, when a planet is most favorably suited for observation. Mercury can be seen with the naked eye only at about this time. An *occultation* of a planet or star is an eclipse of it by some other body, usually the Moon.

Stars are the basic units of population in the universe. Our Sun is the nearest star. Stars are very large (our Sun has a diameter of 865,400 miles—a comparatively small star). Stars are composed of intensely hot gasses, deriving their energy from nuclear reactions going on in their interiors.

Galaxies are immense systems containing billions of stars. All that you can see in the sky (with a very few exceptions) belongs to our galaxy—a system of roughly 100 billion stars. The few exceptions are other galaxies. Our own galaxy, the rim of which we see as the "Milky Way," is about 100, 000 light-years in diameter and about 10,000 light-years in thickness. Its shape is roughly that of a thick lens; more precisely it is a "spiral nebula," a term first used for other galaxies when they were discovered and before it was realized that these were separate and distant galaxies. The spiral galaxy nearest to ours is in the constellation An-

Astronomical Constants

Light-year (distance traveled by light in one year)	5,880,000,000,000 mi.
Parsec (parallax of one second, for stellar distances)	3.259 light-yrs.
Velocity of light	186,281.7 mi./sec.
Astronomical unit (A.U.), or mean distance earth-to-sun	ca. 93,000,000 mi.[1]
Mean distance, earth to moon	238,860 mi.
General precession	50".26
Obliquity of the ecliptic	23° 27'8".26–0".4684(t–1900)[2]
Equatorial radius of the earth	3963.34 statute mi.
Polar radius of the earth	3949.99 statute mi.
Earth's mean radius	3958.89 statute mi.
Oblateness of the earth	1/297
Equatorial horizontal parallax of the moon	57' 2".70
Earth's mean velocity in orbit	18.5 mi./sec.
Sidereal year	365d.2564
Tropical year	365d.2422
Sidereal month	27d.3217
Synodic month	29d.5306
Mean sidereal day	23h56m4s.091 of mean solar time
Mean solar day	24h3m56s.555 of sidereal time

1. Actual mean distance derived from radar bounces: 92,935,700 mi. The value of 92,897,400 mi. (based on parallax of 8".80) is used in calculations. 2. *t* refers to the year in question, for example, 1985.

dromeda. It is somewhat larger than our own galaxy and is visible to the naked eye.

Recent developments in radio astronomy have revealed additional celestial objects that are still incompletely understood.

Quasars ("quasi-stellar" objects), originally thought to be peculiar stars in our own galaxy, are now believed to be the most remote objects in the Universe. Spectral studies of quasars indicate that some are 9 billion light years away and moving away from us at the incredible rate of 150,000 miles per second. Quasars emit tremendous amounts of light and microwave radiation. Although they appear to be far smaller than ordinary galaxies, some quasars emit as much as 100 times more energy. Some astronomers believe that quasars are the cores of violently exploding galaxies.

Pulsars are believed to be rapidly spinning neutron stars, so crushed by their own gravity that a million tons of their matter would hardly fill a thimble. Pulsars are so named because they emit bursts of radio energy at regular intervals. Some have pulse rates as rapid as 10 per second.

A *black hole* is the theoretical end-product of the total gravitational collapse of a massive star or group of stars. Crushed even smaller than an incredibly dense neutron star, such a body may become so dense that not even light can escape its gravitational field. It has been suggested that black holes may be detectable in proximity to normal stars when they draw matter away from their visible neighbors. Strong sources of X-rays in our galaxy and beyond may also indicate the presence of black holes. One possible black hole now being studied is the invisible companion to a supergiant star in the constellation Cygnus.

Origin of the Universe

Evidence uncovered in recent years tends to confirm that the universe began its existence about 15 billion years ago as a dense, hot globule of gas expanding rapidly outward. At that time, the universe contained nothing but hydrogen and a small amount of helium. There were no stars and no planets. The first stars probably began to condense out of the primordial hydrogen when the universe was about 100 million years old and continued to form as the universe aged. The Sun arose in this way 4.6 billion years ago. Many stars came into being before the Sun was formed; many others formed after the Sun appeared. This process continues, and through telescopes we can now see stars forming out of compressed pockets of hydrogen in outer space.

Birth and Death of a Star

When a star begins to form as a dense cloud of gas, the individual hydrogen atoms fall toward the center of the cloud under the force of the star's gravity. As they fall, they pick up speed, and their

The Brightest Stars

Star	Constellation	Mag.	Dist. (l.-y.)	Star	Constellation	Mag.	Dist. (l.-y.)
Sirius	Canis Major	−1.6	8	Antares	Scorpius	1.2	170
Canopus	Carina	−0.9	650	Fomalhaut	Piscis Austrinus	1.3	27
Alpha Centauri	Centaurus	+0.1	4	Deneb	Cygnus	1.3	465
Vega	Lyra	0.1	23	Regulus	Leo	1.3	70
Capella	Auriga	0.2	42	Beta Crucis	Crux	1.5	465
Arcturus	Boötes	0.2	32	Eta Carinae	Carina	1–7	—
Rigel	Orion	0.3	545	Alpha-one Crucis	Crux	1.6	150
Procyon	Canis Minor	0.5	10	Castor	Gemini	1.6	44
Achernar	Eridanus	0.6	70	Gamma Crucis	Crux	1.6	—
Beta Centari	Centaurus	0.9	130	Epsilon Canis Majoris	Canis Major	1.6	325
Altair	Aquila	0.9	18	Epsilon Ursae Majoris	Ursa Major	1.7	50
Betelgeuse	Orion	0.9	600	Bellatrix	Orion	1.7	215
Aldebaran	Taurus	1.1	54	Lambda Scorpii	Scorpius	1.7	205
Spica	Virgo	1.2	190	Epsilon Carinae	Carina	1.7	325
Pollux	Gemini	1.2	31	Mira	Cetus	2–10	250

Conversion of Universal Time (U. T.) to Civil Time

U.T.	E.D.T.[1]	E.S.T.[2]	C.S.T.[3]	M.S.T.[4]	P.S.T.[5]	U.T.	E.D.T.[1]	E.S.T.[2]	C.S.T.[3]	M.S.T.[4]	P.S.T.[5]
00	*8P	*7P	*6P	*5P	*4P	**12**	8A	7A	6A	5A	4A
01	*9P	*8P	*7P	*6P	*5P	**13**	9A	8A	7A	6A	5A
02	*10P	*9P	*8P	*7P	*6P	**14**	10A	9A	8A	7A	6A
03	*11P	*10P	*9P	*8P	*7P	**15**	11A	10A	9A	8A	7A
04	M	*11P	*10P	*9P	*8P	**16**	N	11A	10A	9A	8A
05	1A	M	*11P	*10P	*9P	**17**	1P	N	11A	10A	9A
06	2A	1A	M	*11P	*10P	**18**	2P	1P	N	11A	10A
07	3A	2A	1A	M	*11P	**19**	3P	2P	1P	N	11A
08	4A	3A	2A	1A	M	**20**	4P	3P	2P	1P	N
09	5A	4A	3A	2A	1A	**21**	5P	4P	3P	2P	1P
10	6A	5A	4A	3A	2A	**22**	6P	5P	4P	3P	2P
11	7A	6A	5A	4A	3A	**23**	7P	6P	5P	4P	3P

1. Eastern Daylight Time. 2. Eastern Standard Time, same as Central Daylight Time. 3. Central Standard Time, same as Mountain Daylight Time. 4. Mountain Standard Time, same as Pacific Daylight Time. 5. Pacific Standard Time. NOTES: *denotes previous day. N = noon. M = midnight.

Data for Sun, Moon, and Planets

	Mean distance from Sun in millions of miles	Period of revolution around the Sun	Eccentricity of orbit	Inclination to ecliptic ° ′	Diameter (miles)	Period of rotation on axis	Inclination of equator to orbit plane °	Surface gravity (earth = 1)	Density H_2O = 1	Number of satellites	Mean velocity in orbit (mi./sec.)	Max. stellar mag.
Sun	—	—	—	—	865,400	24d.64[2]	7.2	28	1.4	0	—	−26.7
Moon	—	(27d.322)[1]	0.05	5 8	2,160	27d.322	6.7	0.16	3.3	0	0.63	−12.6
Mercury	36.00	87d.969	0.21	7 0	3,100	58.66d	7	0.28	3.8	0	30	−1.2
Venus	67.27	224d.701	0.01	3 24	7,700	243.2d	—	0.85	5.1	0	22	−4.4
Earth	93.00	365d.256	0.02	0 0	7,927[3]	23h 56m	23.4	1.00	5.5	1	18.5	—
Mars	141.71	1y.881	0.09	1 51	4,200	24h 37m	25.2	0.38	4.0	2	15	−2.8
Jupiter	483.88	11y.862	0.05	1 18	88,700[3]	9h 50m[2]	3.1	2.6	1.3	16	8	−2.5
Saturn	887.14	29y.458	0.06	2 29	75,100[3]	16h 39m[2]	26.8	1.2	0.7	21+	6	−0.4
Uranus	1783.98	84y.013	0.05	0 46	32,000	12.8h	98	1.1	1.3	5	4	+5.7
Neptune	2795.46	164y.794	0.01	1 46	27,700	18h.2	29	1.4	2.2	2	3	+7.8
Pluto	3675.27	248y.430	0.25	17 9	1,500(?)	6d 8h(?)	—	—	>1.0	1	<3	+14

1. Period of revolution around the earth. 2. Voyager 1 and 2 data. 3. The equatorial diameters of the earth, Jupiter, and Saturn are given; polar diameters are: earth 7,900.0 mi., Jupiter 82,789 mi., Saturn 67,170 mi. OTHER DATA ON THE EARTH: Equatorial circumference, 24,902.4 mi.; total area, 196,949,970 sq. mi.; mass, 6.6 sextillion tons; mean diameter, 7,917.8 mi.

energy increases. The increase in energy heats the gas. When this process has continued for some millions of years, the temperature reaches about 20 million degrees Fahrenheit. At this temperature, the hydrogen within the star ignites and burns in a continuing series of nuclear reactions in which all the elements in the universe are manufactured from hydrogen and helium. The onset of these reactions marks the birth of a star. When a star begins to exhaust its hydrogen supply, its life nears an end. The first sign of old age is a swelling and reddening of its outer regions. Such an aging, swollen star is called a red giant. The Sun, a middle-aged star, will probably swell to a red giant in 5 billion years, vaporizing the earth and any creatures that may be left on its surface. When all its fuel has been exhausted, a star cannot generate sufficient pressure at its center to balance the crushing force of gravity. The star collapses under the force of its own weight; if it is a small star, it collapses gently and remains collapsed. Such a collapsed star, at its life's end, is called a white dwarf. The Sun will probably end its life in this way. A different fate awaits a large star. Its final collapse generates a violent explosion, blowing the innards of the star out into space. There, the materials of the exploded star mix with the primeval hydrogen of the universe. Later in the history of the galaxy, other stars are formed out of this mixture. The Sun is one of these stars. It contains the debris of countless other stars that exploded before the Sun was born.

Formation of the Solar System

The Sun, like other stars, seems to have been formed 4.6 billion years ago from a cloud of hydrogen mixed with small amounts of other substances that had been manufactured in the bodies of other stars before the Sun was born. This was the parent cloud of the solar system. The dense hot gas at the center of the cloud gave rise to the Sun; the outer regions of the cloud—cooler and less dense—gave birth to the planets.

Our solar system consists of one star (the Sun), nine planets and all their moons, several thousand minor planets called asteroids or planetoids, and an equally large number of comets.

The Sun

All the stars, including our Sun, are gigantic balls of superheated gas, kept hot by atomic reactions in their centers. In our Sun, this atomic reaction is hydrogen fusion: four hydrogen atoms are combined to form one helium atom. The temperature at the core of our Sun must be 20 million degrees centigrade, the surface temperature is around 6,000 degrees centigrade, or about 11,000 degrees Fahrenheit. The diameter of the sun is 865,400 miles, and its surface area is approximately 12,000 times that of the Earth. Compared with other stars, our Sun is just a bit below average in size and temperature. Its fuel supply (hydrogen) is estimated to last for another 5 billion years.

Our Sun is not motionless in space; in fact it has two proper motions. One is a seemingly straight-line motion in the direction of the constellation Hercules at the rate of about 12 miles per second. But since the Sun is a part of the Milky Way system and since the whole system rotates slowly around its own center, the Sun also moves at the rate of 175 miles per second as part of the rotating Milky Way system.

In addition to this motion, the Sun rotates on its axis. Observing the motion of sun spots (darkish areas which look like enormous whirling storms) and solar flares, which are usually associated with sun spots, has shown that the rotational period of our Sun is just short of 25 days. But this figure is valid for the Sun's equator only; the sections near the Sun's poles seem to have a rotational period of 34 days. Naturally, since the Sun generates its own heat and light, there is no temperature difference between poles and equator.

What we call the Sun's "surface" is technically known as the photosphere. Since the whole Sun is a ball of very hot gas, there is really no such thing as a surface; it is a question of visual impression. The next layer outside the photosphere is known as the chromosphere, which extends several thousand miles beyond the photosphere. It is in steady motion, and often enormous prominences can be seen to burst from it, extending as much as 100,000 miles into space. Outside the chromosphere is the corona. The corona consists of very tenuous gases (essentially hydrogen) and makes a magnificent sight when the Sun is eclipsed.

The Moon

Mercury and Venus do not have any moons. Therefore, the Earth is the planet nearest the Sun to be orbited by a moon.

The next planet farther out, Mars, has two very small moons. Jupiter has four major moons and twelve minor ones. Saturn, the ringed planet, has fifteen known moons, of which one (Titan) is larger than the planet Mercury. Uranus has five known moons (four of them large) as well as rings, while Neptune has one large and one small moon. Pluto has one moon, discovered in 1978. Some astronomers still consider Pluto to be a "runaway moon" of Neptune.

Our own Moon, with a diameter of 2,160 miles, is one of the larger moons in our solar system and is especially large when compared with the planet that it orbits. In fact, the common center of gravity of the Earth-Moon system is only about 1,000 miles below the Earth's surface. The closest our Moon can come to us (its perigee) is 221,463 miles; the farthest it can go away (its apogee) is 252,710 miles. The period of rotation of our Moon is equal to its period of revolution around the Earth. Hence from Earth we can see only one hemisphere of the Moon. Both periods are 27 days, 7 hours, 43 minutes and 11.47 seconds. But while the rotation of the Moon is constant, its velocity in its orbit is not, since it moves more slowly in apogee than in perigee. Consequently, some portions near the rim which are not normally visible will appear briefly. This phenomenon is called "libration," and by taking advantage of the librations, astronomers have succeeded in mapping approximately 59% of the lunar surface. The other 41% can never be seen from the earth but has been mapped by American and Russian Moon-orbiting spacecraft.

Though the Moon goes around the Earth in the time mentioned, the interval from new Moon to new Moon is 29 days, 12 hours, 44 minutes and 2.78 seconds. This delay of nearly two days is due to the fact that the Earth is moving around the Sun, so that the Moon needs two extra days to reach a spot in its orbit where no part is illuminated by the Sun, as seen from Earth.

If the plane of the Earth's orbit around the Sun (the ecliptic) and the plane of the Moon's orbit around the Earth were the same, the Moon would be eclipsed by the Earth every time it is full, and the Sun would be eclipsed by the Moon every time the Moon is "new" (it would be better to call it the "black Moon" when it is in this position). But because the two orbits do not coincide, the Moon's shadow normally misses the Earth and the Earth's shadow misses the Moon. The inclination of the two orbital planes to each other is 5 degrees. The tides are, of course, caused by the Moon with the help of the Sun, but in the open ocean they are surprisingly low, amounting to about one yard. The very high tides which can be observed near the shore in some places are due to funnelling effects of the shorelines. At new Moon and at full Moon the tides raised by the Moon are reinforced by the Sun; these are the "spring tides." If the Sun's tidal power acts at right angles to that of the Moon (quarter moons) we get the low "neap tides."

Our Planet Earth

The Earth, circling the Sun at an average distance of 93 million miles, is the fifth largest planet and the third from the Sun. It orbits the Sun at a speed of 67,000 miles per hour, making one revolution in 365 days, 5 hours, 48 minutes, and 45.51 seconds. The Earth completes one rotation on its axis every 23 hours, 56 minutes, and 4.09 seconds. Actually a bit pear-shaped rather than a true sphere, the Earth has a diameter of 7,927 miles at the Equator and a few miles less at the poles. It has an estimated mass of about 6.6 sextillion tons, with an average density of 5.52 grams per cubic centimeter. The Earth's surface area encompasses 196,949, 970 square miles of which about three-fourths is water.

Origin of the Earth. The Earth, along with the other planets, is believed to have been born 4.5 billion years ago as a solidified cloud of dust and gases left over from the creation of the Sun. For perhaps 500 million years, the interior of the Earth stayed solid and relatively cool, perhaps 2000° F. The main ingredients, according to the best available evidence, were iron and silicates, with small amounts of other elements, some of them radioactive. As millions of years passed, energy released by radioactive decay—mostly of uranium, thorium, and potassium—gradually heated the Earth, melting some of its consituents. The iron melted before the silicates, and, being heavier, sank toward the center. This forced upward the silicates that it found there. After many years, the iron reached the center, almost 4,000 miles deep, and began to accumulate. No eyes were around at that time to view the turmoil which must have taken place on the face of the Earth—gigantic heaves and bubbling of the surface, exploding volcanoes, and flowing lava covering everything in sight. Finally, the iron in the center accumulated as the core. Around it, a thin but fairly stable crust of solid rock formed as the Earth cooled. Depressions in the crust were natural basins in which water, rising from the interior of the planet through volcanoes and fissures, collected to form the oceans. Slowly the Earth acquired its present appearance.

The Earth Today. As a result of radioactive heating over millions of years, the Earth's molten *core* is probably fairly hot today, around 11,000° F. By comparison, lead melts at around 800° F. Most of the Earth's 2,100-mile-thick core is liquid, but there is evidence that the center of the core is solid. The liquid outer portion, about 95% of the core, is constantly in motion, causing the Earth to have a magnetic field that makes compass needles point north and south. The details are not known, but the latest evidence suggests that planets which have a magnetic field probably have a solid core or a partially liquid one.

Outside the core is the Earth's *mantle*, 1,800 miles thick, and extending nearly to the surface. The mantle is composed of heavy silicate rock, similar to that brought up by volcanic eruptions. It is somewhere between liquid and solid, slightly yielding, and therefore contributing to an active, moving Earth. Most of the Earth's radioactive material is in the thin *crust* which covers the mantle, but some is in the mantle and continues to give off heat. The crust's thickness ranges from 5 to 25 miles.

Continental Drift. A great deal of recent evidence confirms the long-disputed theory that the continents of the Earth, made mostly of relatively light granite, float in the slightly yielding mantle, like logs in a pond. For many years it had been noticed that if North and South America could be pushed toward western and southern Europe and western Africa, they would fit like pieces in a jigsaw puzzle. Today, there is little question—the continents have drifted widely and continue to do so.

In 10 million years, the world as we know it may be unrecognizable, with California drifting out to sea, Florida joining South America, and Africa moving farther away from Europe and Asia.

The Earth's Atmosphere. The thin blanket of atmosphere that envelops the Earth extends several hundred miles into space. From sea level—the very bottom of the ocean of air—to a height of about 60 miles, the air in the atmosphere is made up of the same gases in the same ratio: about 78% nitrogen, 21% oxygen, and the remaining 1% being a mixture of argon, carbon dioxide, and tiny amounts of neon, helium, krypton, xenon, and other gases. The atmosphere becomes less dense with increasing altitude: more than three-fourths of the Earth's huge envelope is concentrated in the first 5 to 10 miles above the surface. At sea level, a cubic foot of the atmosphere weighs about an ounce and a quarter. The entire atmosphere weighs 5,700,000,000,000,000 tons, and the force with which gravity holds it in place causes it to exert a pressure of nearly 15 pounds per square inch. Going out from the Earth's surface, the atmosphere is divided into five regions. The regions, and the heights to which they extend, are: *Troposphere,* 0 to 7 miles (at middle latitudes); *stratosphere,* 7 to 30 miles; *mesosphere,* 30 to 50 miles; *thermosphere,* 50 to 400 miles; and *exosphere,* above 400 miles. The boundaries between each of the regions are known respectively as the *tropopause, stratopause, mesopause,* and *thermopause.* Alternate terms often used for the layers above the troposhere are *ozonosphere* (for stratosphere) and *ionosphere* for the remaining upper layers.

The Seasons. Seasons are caused by the 23.4 degree tilt of the Earth's axis, which alternately turns the North and South Poles toward the Sun. Times when the Sun's apparent path crosses the Equator are known as *equinoxes.* Times when the Sun's apparent path is at the greatest distance from the Equator are known as *solstices.* The lengths of the days are most extreme at each solstice. If the Earth's axis were perpendicular to the plane of the Earth's orbit around the Sun, there would be no seasons, and the days always would be equal in length. Since the Earth's axis is at an angle, the Sun strikes the Earth directly at the Equator only twice a year: in March (vernal equinox) and September (autumnal equinox). In the Northern Hemisphere, spring begins at the vernal equinox, summer at the summer solstice, fall at the autumnal equinox, and winter at the winter solstice. The situation is reversed in the Southern Hemisphere.

Mercury

Mercury is the planet nearest the Sun. Appropriately named for the wing-footed Roman messenger of the gods, Mercury whizzes around the Sun at a speed of 30 miles per second, completeing one circuit in 88 days. The planet rotates on its axis over a period of nearly 59 days. Daytime on cratered Mercury is hot, about 800 degrees F., although at night the temperature may fall to room temperature. Mercury has no moons, but it does have a trace of atmosphere and a weak magnetic field, according to findings of Mariner 10. Until this spacecraft flew by Mercury in 1974 and 1975, very little was known about the planet, primarily because of its short angular distance from the Sun as seen from Earth, which puts it too close to the Sun to be easily observed.

• Mercury is a naked eye object at morning or evening twilight when it is at greatest elongation.

Venus

Although Venus is Earth's nearest neighbor, little is known about this planet because it is permanently covered by thick clouds. In 1962, Soviet and American space probes, coupled with Earth-based radar and infrared spectroscopy, began slowly unraveling some of the mystery surrounding Venus. According to the latest results, Venus' atmosphere is about 96% carbon dioxide, exerting a pressure at the surface 90.5 times greater than Earth's. Walking on Venus would be as difficult as walking a half-mile beneath the ocean. Because of the thick blanket of carbon dioxide, a "greenhouse effect" exists on Venus: Venus intercepts twice as much of the Sun's light as does the Earth. The light enters freely through carbon dioxide gas and is changed to heat radiation in molecular collisions. But carbon dioxide prevents the heat from escaping. Consequently, the temperature of the surface of Venus is over 800 degrees F., hot enough to melt lead. The atmosphere appears to have five distinct layers and to flash almost continuously with lightning. Radar bounced off the planet recently revealed what appear to be large craters and an immense, 900-mile-long canyon. Venus rotates in retrograde motion for a reason not yet known.

In March 1982, the Soviet *Venera 13* and *14* landing craft made the first actual test samples of the Venusian surface by x-ray fluorescence spectroscopy which gave an element-by-element analysis. The terrestrial samples revealed a terrain of basaltic uplands and lowlands.

The Soviets have announced plans to place two more Venera landers on Venus in 1986.

• Venus is the brightest of all the planets and is often visible in the morning or evening, when it is frequently referred to as the Morning Star or Evening Star. At its brightest, it can sometimes be seen with the naked eye in full daylight, if one knows where to look.

Mars

Mars, on the other side of the Earth from Venus, is Venus' direct opposite in terms of physical properties. Its atmosphere is cold, thin, and transparent, and readily permits observation of the planet's features. We know more about Mars than any other planet except Earth. Mars is a forbidding, rugged planet with huge volcanoes and deep chasms. The largest volcano, Olympus Mons rises 78,000 feet above the surface, higher than Mount Everest. The plains of Mars are pockmarked by the hits of thousands of meteors over the years. Most of our information about Mars comes from the Mariner 9 spacecraft, which orbited the planet in 1971. Mariner 9, photographing 100% of the planet, uncovered spectacular geological formations, including a Martian Grand Canyon that dwarfs the one on Earth. The spacecraft's cameras also recorded what appeared to be dried riverbeds, suggesting the onetime presence of water on the planet. The latter idea gives encouragement to scientists looking for life on Mars, for where there is water, there may be life. However, by 1979, no evidence of life has been found. Temperatures near the equator range from −17 degrees F. in the daytime to −130 degrees F. at night. Mars rotates upon its axis in nearly the same period as Earth—24 hours, 37 minutes—so that a Mars day is almost identical to an Earth day. Mars takes 687 days to make one trip around the Sun. Because of its eccentric orbit Mars' distance from the Sun can vary by about 36 million miles. Its distance from Earth can vary by as much as 200 million miles. The atmosphere of Mars is much thinner than Earth's; atmospheric pressure is about 1% that of our planet. Its gravity is one-third of Earth's. Major constituents are carbon dioxide and nitrogen. Water vapor and oxygen are minor constituents. Mars' polar caps, composed mostly of carbon dioxide, recede and advance according to the Martian seasons. Mars was named for the Roman god of war, because when seen from Earth its distinct red color reminded the ancient people of blood. We know now that the reddish hue reflects the oxidized (rusted) iron in the surface material. The landing of two robot Viking spacecraft on the surface of Mars in 1976 provided more information about Mars in a few months than in all the time that has gone before.

Jupiter

Jupiter, with an equatorial diameter of 88,000 miles, is the largest of a group of planets which differ markedly from the terrestrial planets. The others in the group are Saturn, Uranus, and Neptune. All are large, with very dense atmospheres, and indeed may be giant balls of gas without any perceptible surfaces. They all whirl rapidly around their axes, but more slowly around the Sun, resulting in short days and long years. They have many moons. Majestic Jupiter, named for the king of the Roman gods, rotates so fast that it is greatly flattened at the poles. According to Pioneers 10 and 11, which flew past Jupiter in 1974 and 1975, this planet is a whirling ball of liquid hydrogen with perhaps an Earth-sized iron core. Other atmospheric constituents are helium, methane, and ammonia. Its clouds are probably ammonia ice crystals, becoming ammonia droplets deeper towards the "surface." Temperatures range from perhaps minus 300 degrees F. at the tops of the cloud decks to 100,000 degrees F. or more deep down at the center. The pressure at the center of the planet is estimated to be a crushing 10 million pounds per square inch. The Great Red Spot, a 13,000-mile-wide storm that may have been raging for thousands of years, was found by Voyagers 1 and 2 in 1979 to be cooler at the top than the surrounding clouds, indicating that the Red Spot may tower high above them. Jupiter has 16 satellites. The four largest moons, called Galilean moons, are Europa, Ganymede, Io, and Callisto. *Voyagers 1 and 2* found them to be very different from each other in terms of surface relief, volcanic activity, and other characteristics.

• Even when nearest the Earth, Jupiter is still almost 400 million miles away. But because of its size, it may rival Venus in brilliance when near. Jupiter's four large moons may be seen through field glasses, moving rapidly around Jupiter and changing their position from night to night.

Saturn

Saturn, the second largest planet in the solar system, is the least dense. It would float in an ocean if there were one big enough to hold it. Aside from its rings, Saturn is very similar to Jupiter except that it is probably colder, being twice as far from the Sun. Recent radar observations of Saturn's rings indicate that they are no more than 10 miles thick, and probably composed of chunks of rock and ice averaging a meter in size. Saturn's ring system begins about 7000 miles from the planet's disk, and extends out to about 35,000 miles. Recent observations have shown Saturn to have between 21 and 23 moons, more than any other planet. The two *Voyager* probes that examined Jupiter in 1979 flew by Saturn in 1980 and 1981. *Voyager 2* will encounter Uranus in 1986.

• Saturn is the last of the planets visible to the naked eye. Saturn is never an object of overwhelming brilliance, but it looks like a bright star. The rings can be seen with a small telescope.

Uranus and Neptune

Little is known about the distant giant planets Uranus and Neptune, but they are believed to be similar to Saturn and Jupiter. Being twice as far from the Sun as Saturn, Uranus must be a grim frozen world, and Neptune, 11 A.U. beyond Uranus, must be even colder and darker. The axis of Uranus is tilted at 98 degrees, so it goes around the Sun nearly lying on its side. In 1977, American astronomers made the startling discovery that Uranus has rings, like Saturn. The first Voyager to Uranus may take pictures of the rings in 1986. Uranus has five known moons; Neptune, two. Neptune's Triton, Jupiter's Ganymede and Callisto, and Saturn's Titan are the four largest moons in the solar system.

• Uranus and Neptune can—on rare occasion—become bright enough to be seen with the naked eye, if one knows exactly where to look; normally, they are objects for good field glasses or small portable telescopes.

Pluto

Pluto, the outermost and smallest planet in the solar system, looks more like a terrestrial planet than a gaseous planet. But so little is known about it, that it is difficult to classify. Appropriately named for the Roman god of the underworld, it must be frozen, dark, and dead.

In 1978, light curve studies gave evidence of a moon revolving around Pluto with the same period as Pluto's rotation. Therefore, it stays over the same point on Pluto's surface. In addition, it keeps the same face toward the planet. The discovery of this moon of 500–600 miles in diameter reduces the previously estimated diameter of Pluto to little more than 1,500 miles, making the pair more like a double planet than any other in the solar system. Previously, the Earth-Moon system held this distinction. The density of Pluto is slightly greater than that of water.

Pluto was predicted by calculation when Percival Lowell noticed irregularities in the orbits of Uranus and Neptune. Clyde Tombaugh discovered the planet in 1930, precisely where Lowell predicted it would be. The name Pluto was chosen because the first two letters represent the initials of Percival Lowell.

• Pluto has the most eccentric orbit in the solar system, bringing it at times closer to the Sun

The First Ten Minor Planets (Asteroids)

Name	Year of discovery	Mean distance from sun (millions of miles)	Orbital period (years)	Diameter (miles)	Magnitude
1. Ceres	1801	257.0	4.60	485	7.4
2. Pallas	1802	257.4	4.61	304	8.0
3. Juno	1804	247.8	4.36	118	8.7
4. Vesta	1807	219.3	3.63	243	6.5
5. Astraea	1845	239.3	4.14	50	9.9
6. Hebe	1847	225.2	3.78	121	8.5
7. Iris	1847	221.4	3.68	121	8.4
8. Flora	1847	204.4	3.27	56	8.9
9. Metis	1848	221.7	3.69	78	8.9
10. Hygeia	1849	292.6	5.59	40 (?)	9.5

than Neptune. Pluto is now approaching the perihelion of its orbit, and for the rest of this century will be closer to the Sun than Neptune. Even then, it can be seen only with a large telescope.

The Asteroids

Between the orbits of Mars and Jupiter are an estimated 30,000 pieces of rocky debris, known collectively as the asteroids, or planetoids. The first and, incidentally, the largest was discovered during the New Year's night of 1801 by the Italian astronomer Father Piazzi, and its orbit was calculated by the German mathematician Karl Friedrich Gauss. (Gauss invented a new method of calculating orbits on that occasion.) A German amateur astronomer, the physician Olbers, discovered the second asteroid. The number now known, catalogued, and named is around 1,600; the estimated total is about 20 times that figure. A few asteroids do not move in orbits beyond the orbit of Mars, but in orbits which cross the orbit of Mars. The first of them was named Eros because of this peculiar orbit. It had become the rule to bestow female names on the asteroids, but when it was found that Eros crossed the orbit of a major planet, it received a male name. Since then around two dozen orbit-crossers have been discovered, and they are often referred to as the "male asteroids." A few of them—Albert, Adonis, Apollo, Amor, and Icarus—cross the orbit of the Earth, and two of them may come closer than our Moon; but the crossing is like a bridge crossing a highway, not like two highways intersecting. Hence there is very little danger of collision from these bodies. They are all small, three to five miles in diameter, and therefore very difficult objects to identify, even when quite close. Some scientists believe the asteroids represent the remains of an exploded planet.

Comets

Comets, according to the noted astronomer, Fred L. Whipple, are enormous "snowballs" of frozen gases (mostly carbon dioxide, methane, and water vapor) and contain very little solid material. The whole behavior of comets can then be explained as the behavior of frozen gas being heated by the Sun. When the comet Kohoutek made its first appearance to man in 1973, its behavior seemed to confirm this Whipple theory of the make-up of comets.

Kohoutek will probably not appear in view for another 75,000 years. The next comet large and brilliant enough to be very easily seen is predicted for 1986, when Halley's comet will approach perihelion (the point of its orbit closest to the Sun) again.

Since comets appear in the sky without any warning, people in classical times and especially during the Middle Ages believed that they had a special meaning, which, of course, was bad. Since a natural catastrophe of some sort of a military conflict occurs every year, it was quite simple to blame the comet that happened to be visible. But even in the past, there were some people who used logical reasoning. When, in Roman times, a comet was blamed for the loss of a battle and hence was called a "bad omen," a Roman writer observed that the victors in the battle probably did not think so.

Up until the middle of the sixteenth century, comets were believed to be phenomena of the upper atmosphere; they were usually "explained" as "burning vapors" which had risen from "distant swamps." That nobody had ever actually seen burning vapors rise from a swamp did not matter.

But a large comet which appeared in 1577 was carefully observed by Tycho Brahe, a Danish astronomer who is often, and with the best of reasons, called "eccentric" but who insisted on precise measurements for everything. It was Tycho Brahe's accumulation of literally thousands of precise measurements which later enable his younger collaborator, Johannes Kepler, to discover the laws

21 Famous Comets

Year and no.		Name of comet	Period (years)
1744		De Chéseaux's Comet	—
1806		Biela's Comet	6.7
1811	I	Great Comet of 1811	3000
1812		Di Vico's Comet	70.7
1815		Olbers' Comet	74.0
1819	I	Encke's Comet	3.3
1819		Pons-Winnecke Comet	6.0
1835	III	Halley's Comet	76.3
1843	I	Great Comet of 1843	512.4
1844	II	Great Comet of 1844	102,050
1858	VI	Donati's Comet	2,040(?)
1864	II	Great Comet of 1864	2,800,000
1871	III	Tuttle's Comet	13.8
1874	III	Coggia's Comet	6,000(?)
1879		Brorsen's Comet	5.6
1881	II	Tebbutt's Comet	—
1889	VI	Swift's 2nd Comet	7.0
1892	III	Holmes' Comet	6.9
1923		d'Arrest's Comet	6.6
1925	II	Comet Schwassmann-Wachmann	16.2
1973	I	Comet Kohoutek	75,000(?)

of planetary motion. Measuring the motion of the comet of 1577, Tycho Brahe could show that it had been far beyond the atmosphere, even though he could not give figures for the distance. Tycho Brahe's work proved that comets were astronomical and not meteorological phenomena.

In 1682, the second Astronomer Royal of Great Britain, Dr. Edmond Halley, checked the orbit of a bright comet that was in the sky then and compared it with earlier comet orbits which were known in part. Halley found that the comet of 1682 was the third to move through what appeared to be the same orbit. And the three appearances were roughly 76 years apart. Halley concluded that this was the same comet, moving around the Sun in a closed orbit, like the planets. He predicted that it would reappear in 1758 or 1759. Halley himself died in 1742, but a large comet appeared sixteen years after his death as predicted and was immediately referred to as "Halley's comet."

In the Spring of 1973, the discovery of comet Kohoutek, apparently headed for a close-Christmastime rendezvous with the Sun, created worldwide excitement. The comet was a visual disappointment, but turned out to be a treasure trove of information on these little-understood celestial objects. Given an unprecedented advance notice of nine months on the advent of the fiery object, scientists were able to study the comet in visible, ultraviolet and infrared light; with optical telescopes, radio telescopes, and radar. They observed it from the ground, from high-flying aircraft, with instruments aboard unmanned satellites, with sounding rockets, and telescopes and cameras on the Earth-orbiting Skylab space station.

Astronomers refer to comets as "periodic" or as "non-periodic" comets, but the latter term does not mean that these comets have no period; it merely means that their period is not known. The actual periods of comets run from 3.3 years (the shortest known) to many thousands of years. Their orbits are elliptical, like those of the planets, but they are very eccentric, long and narrow ellipses. Only comet Schwassmann-Wachmann has an orbit which has such a low eccentricity (for a cometary orbit) that it could be the orbit of a minor planet.

When a comet, coming from deep space, approaches the Sun, it is at first indistinguishable from a minor planet. Somewhere between the orbits of Mars and Jupiter its outline becomes fuzzy; it is said to develop a "coma" (the word used here is the Latin word *coma*, which means "hair," not the phonetically identical Greek word which means "deep sleep"). Then, near the orbit of Mars, the comet develops its tail, which at first trails behind. This grows steadily as the comet comes closer and closer to the Sun. As it rounds the Sun (as first noticed by Girolamo Fracastoro) the tail always points away from the Sun so that the comet, when moving away from the Sun, points its tail ahead like the landing lights of an airplane.

The reason for this behavior is that the tail is pushed in these directions by the radiation pressure of the Sun. It sometimes happens that a comet loses its tail at perihelion; it then grows another one. Although the tail is clearly visible against the black of the sky, it is very tenuous. It has been said that if the tail of Halley's comet could be compressed to the density of iron, it would fit into a small suitcase.

Although very low in mass, comets are among the largest members of the solar system. The nucleus of a comet may be up to 10,000 miles in diameter; its coma between 10,000 and 50,000 miles in diameter; and its tail as long as 28 million miles.

Important Meteor Showers

Approx. date	Name of meteor stream	Radiant in constellation
Jan. 1–4	Quadrantids	Boötes
Feb. 5–10	Alpha Aurigids	Auriga
March 10–12	Zeta Boötids	Boötes
April 19–23	Lyrids	Hercules
May 1–6	May Aquarids	Aquarius
May 30	Eta Pegasids	Pegasus
June 27–30	Pons-Winnecke meteors	Draco
July 14	Alpha Cygnids	Cygnus
July 26–31	Delta Aquarids	Aquarius
Aug. 10–14	Perseids	Cassiopeia
Aug. 10–20	Kappa Cygnids	Cygnus
Aug. 21–31	Zeta Draconids	Draco
Sept. 22	Alpha Aurigids	Auriga
Oct. 2	Quadrantids	Boötes
Oct. 9	Giacobinids	Draco
Oct. 18–23	Orionids	Orion
Nov. 14–18	Leonids	Leo
Dec. 10–13	Geminids	Gemini

Meteors and Meteorites

The term "meteor" for what is usually called a "shooting star" bears an unfortunate resemblance to the term "meteorology," the science of weather and weather forecasting. This resemblance is due to an ancient misunderstanding which wrongly considered meteors an atmospheric phenomenon. Actually, the streak of light in the sky that scientists call a meteor is essentially an astronomical phenomenon: the entry of a small piece of cosmic matter into our atmosphere.

The distinction between "meteors" and "fireballs" (formerly also called "bolides") is merely one of convenience; a fireball is an unusually bright meteor. Incidentally, it also means that a fireball is larger than a faint meteor.

Bodies which enter our atmosphere become visible when they are about 60 miles above the ground. The fact that they grow hot enough to emit light is not due to the "friction" of the atmosphere, as one can often read. The phenomenon responsible for the heating is one of compression. Unconfined air cannot move faster than the speed of sound. Since the entering meteorite moves with 30 to 60 times the speed of sound, the air simply cannot get out of the way. Therefore, it is compressed like the air in the cylinder of a Diesel engine and is heated by compression. This heat—or part of it—is transferred to the moving body. The details of this process are now fairly well understood as a result of re-entry tests with ballistic-missile nose cones.

The average weight of a body producing a faint "shooting star" is only a small fraction of an ounce. Even a bright fireball may not weigh more than 2 or 3 pounds. Naturally, the smaller bodies are worn to dust by the passage through the atmosphere; only rather large ones reach the ground. Those that are found are called meteorites. (The "meteor," to repeat, is the term for the light streak in the sky.)

The largest meteorite known is still imbedded in the ground near Grootfontein in SW Africa and is estimated to weight 70 tons. The second largest known is the 34-ton Anighito (on exhibit in the Hayden Planetarium, New York), which was found by Admiral Peary at Cape York in Greenland. The

The 88 Recognized Constellations

In astronomical works, the Latin names of the constellations are used. The letter N or S following the Latin name indicates whether the constellation is located to the north or south of the Zodiac. The letter Z indicates that the constellation is within the Zodiac.

Latin name	Letter	English version
Andromeda	N	Andromeda
Antlia	S	Airpump
Apus	S	Bird of Paradise
Aquarius	Z	Water Bearer
Aquila	N	Eagle
Ara	S	Altar
Aries	Z	Ram
Auriga	N	Charioteer
Boötes	N	Herdsmen
Caelum	S	Sculptor's Tool
Camelopardalis	N	Giraffe
Cancer	Z	Crab
Canes Venatici	N	Hunting Dogs
Canis Major	S	Great Dog
Canis Minor	S	Little Dog
Capricornus	Z	Goat (or Sea-Goat)
Carina	S	Keel (of Argo)[1]
Cassiopeia	N	Cassiopeia
Centaurus	S	Centaur
Cepheus	N	Cepheus
Cetus	S	Whale
Chameleon	S	Chameleon
Circinus	S	Compasses
Columba	S	Dove
Coma Berenices	N	Berenice's Hair
Corona Australis	S	Southern Crown
Corona Borealis	N	Northern Crown
Corvus	S	Crow (Raven)
Crater	S	Cup
Crux	S	Southern Cross
Cygnus	N	Swan

Latin name	Letter	English version
Delphinus	N	Dolphin
Dorado	S	Swordfish (Goldfish)
Draco	N	Dragon
Equuleus	N	Filly
Eridanus	S	Eridanus (river)
Fornax	S	Furnace
Gemini	Z	Twins
Grus	S	Crane
Hercules	N	Hercules
Horologium	S	Clock
Hydra	N	Sea Serpent
Hydrus	S	Water Snake
Indus	S	Indian
Lacerta	N	Lizard
Leo	Z	Lion
Leo Minor	N	Little Lion
Lepus	S	Hare
Libra	Z	Scales
Lupus	S	Wolf
Lynx	N	Lynx
Lyra	N	Lyre (Harp)
Mensa	S	Table (mountain)
Microscopium	S	Microscope
Monoceros	S	Unicorn
Musca	S	Southern Fly
Norma	S	Rule (straightedge)
Octans	S	Octant
Ophiuchus	N	Serpent-Bearer
Orion	S	Orion

Latin name	Letter	English version
Pavo	S	Peacock
Pegasus	N	Pegasus
Perseus	N	Perseus
Phoenix	S	Phoenix
Pictor	S	Painter (or his Easel)
Pisces	Z	Fishes
Piscis Austrinus	S	Southern Fish
Puppis	S	Poop (of Argo)[1]
Pyxis	S	Mariner's Compass
Reticulum	S	Net
Sagitta	N	Arrow
Sagittarius	Z	Archer
Scorpius	Z	Scorpion
Sculptor	S	Sculptor
Scutum	N	Shield
Serpens	N	Serpent
Sextans	S	Sextant
Taurus	Z	Bull
Telescopium	S	Telescope
Triangulum	N	Triangle
Triangulum Australe	S	Southern Triangle
Tucana	S	Toucan
Ursa Major	N	Big Dipper
Ursa Minor	N	Little Dipper
Vela	S	Sail (of Argo)[1]
Virgo	Z	Virgin
Volans	S	Flying Fish
Vulpecula	N	Fox

1. The original constellation Argo Navis (the Ship Argo) has been divided into Carina, Puppis, and Vela. Normally the brightest star in each constellation is designated by alpha, the first letter of the Greek alphabet, the second brightest by beta, the second letter of the Greek alphabet, and so forth. But the Greek letters run through Carina, Puppis, and Vela as if it were still one constellation.

largest meteorite found in the United States is the Willamette meteorite (found in Oregon, weight ca. 15 tons), but large portions of this meteorite weathered away before it was found. Its weight as it struck the ground may have been 20 tons.

All these are iron meteorites (an iron meteorite normally contains about 7% nickel), which form one class of meteorites. The other class consists of the stony meteorites, and between them there are the so-called "stony irons." The so-called "tektites" consist of glass similar to our volcanic glass obsidian, and because of the similarity, there is doubt in a number of cases whether the glass is of terrestrial or of extra-terrestrial origin.

Though no meteorite larger than the Grootfontein is actually known, we do know that the Earth has, on occasion, been struck by much larger bodies. Evidence for such hits are the meteorite craters, of which an especially good example is located near the Cañon Diablo in Arizona. Another meteor crater in the United States is a rather old crater near Odessa, Texas. A large number of others are known, especially in eastern Canada; and for many "probables," meteoric origin has now been proved.

The meteor showers are caused by multitudes of very small bodies travelling in swarms. The Earth travels in its orbit through these swarms like a car driving through falling snow. The point from which the meteors seem to emanate is called the *radiant* and is named for the constellation in that area. The Perseid meteor shower in August is the most spectacular of the year, boasting at peak roughly 60 meteors per hour under good atmospheric conditions. The presence of a bright moon diminishes the number of visible meteors.

The Constellations

Constellations are groupings of stars which form patterns that can be easily recognized and remembered, for example, Orion and the Big Dipper. Actually, the stars of the majority of all constellations do not "belong together." Usually they are at greatly varying distances from the Earth and just happen to lie more or less in the same line of sight as seen from our solar system. But in a few cases the stars of a constellation are actually associated; most of the bright stars of the Big Dipper travel together and form what astronomers call an open cluster.

If you observe a planet, say Mars, for one complete revolution, you will see that it passes successively through twelve constellations. All planets (except Pluto at certain times) can be observed only in these twelve constellations, which form the so-called Zodiac, and the Sun also moves through the Zodiacal signs, though the Sun's apparent

Symbols

☉ the sun	♀ Venus	♃ Jupiter	♆ Neptune	occultation	☽ first quarter
☾ the moon	⊕ the earth	♄ Saturn	♇ Pluto	☍ opposition	○ full moon
☿ Mercury	♂ Mars	♅ Uranus	☌ conjunction	● new moon	☾ last quarter

movement is actually caused by the movement of the Earth.

Although the constellations are due mainly to the optical accident of line of sight and have no real significance, astronomers have retained them as reference areas. It is much easier to speak of a star in Orion than to give its geometrical position in the sky. During the Astronomical Congress of 1928, it was decided to recognize 88 constellations. A description of their agreed-upon boundaries was published at Cambridge, England, in 1930, under the title *Atlas Céleste.*

The Auroras

The "northern lights" *(Aurora borealis)* as well as the "southern lights" *(Aurora australis)* are upper-atmosphere phenomena of astronomical origin. The auroras center around the magnetic (not the geographical) poles of the Earth, which explains why, in the Western Hemisphere, they have been seen as far to the south as New Orleans and Florida while the equivalent latitude in the Eastern Hemisphere never sees an aurora. The northern magnetic pole happens to be in the Western Hemisphere.

The lower limit of an aurora is at about 50 miles. Upper limits have been estimated to be as high as 400 miles. Since about 1880, a connection between the auroras on Earth and the sun spots has been suspected and has gradually come to be accepted. It was said that the sun spots probably eject "particles" (later the word *electrons* was substituted) which on striking the Earth's atmosphere, cause the auroras. But this explanation suffered from certain difficulties. Sometimes a very large sun spot group on the Sun, with individual spots bigger than the Earth itself, would not cause an aurora. Moreover, even if a sun spot caused an aurora, the time that passed between the appearance of the one and the occurrence of the other was highly unpredictable.

This problem of the time lag is, in all probability, solved by the discovery of the Van Allen layer by artificial satellite *Explorer I.* The Van Allen layer is a double layer of charged sub-atomic particles around the Earth. The inner layer, with its center some 1,500 miles from the ground, reaches from about 40° N. to about 40° S. and does not touch the atmosphere. The outer layer, much larger and with its center several thousand miles from the ground, does touch the atmosphere in the vicinity of the magnetic poles.

It seems probable that the "leakage" of electrons from the outer Van Allen layer causes the auroras. A new burst of electrons from the Sun seems to be caught in the outer layer first. Under the assumption that all electrons are first caught in the outer layer, the time lag can be understood. There has to be an "overflow" from the outer layer to produce an aurora.

The Atmosphere

Astronomically speaking, the presence of our atmosphere is deplorable. Though reasonably transparent to visible light, the atmosphere may absorb as much as 60% of the visible and near-visible light. It is opaque to most other wave-lengths, except certain fairly short radio waves. In addition to absorbing much light, our atmosphere bends light rays entering at a slant (for a given observer) so that the true position of a star close to the horizon is not what it seems to be. One effect is that we see the Sun above the horizon before it actually is. And the unsteady movement of the atmosphere causes the "twinkling" of the stars, which may be romantic but is a nuisance when it comes to observing.

The composition of our atmosphere near the ground is 78% nitrogen and 21% oxygen, the remaining 1% consisting of other gases, most of it argon. The composition stays the same to an altitude of at least 70 miles (except that higher up two impurities, carbon dioxide and water vapor, are missing), but the pressure drops very fast. At 18, 000 feet, half of the total mass of the atmosphere is below, and at 100,000 feet, 99% of the mass of the atmosphere is below. The upper limit of the atmosphere is usually given as 120 miles; no definitive figure is possible, since there is no boundary line between the incredibly attenuated gases 120 miles up and space.

Astronomical Telescopes

Optical telescopes used in astronomy are of two basic kinds: refracting and reflecting. In the *refractor telescope,* a lens is used to collect light from a distant object and bring it to a focus. A second lens, the eyepiece, then magnifies the image which may be examined visually or photographed directly. The *reflector telescope* uses a concave mirror instead of a lens, which reflects the light rays back toward the upper end of the telescope where they are magnified and observed or photographed. Most large optical telescopes now being built are reflectors.

Radio telescopes are used to study radio waves coming from outside the Earth's atmosphere. The waves are gathered by an antenna or "dish," which is a parabolic reflecting surface made of metal or finely meshed wire. Radio signals have been received from the Sun, Moon, and planets, and from the center of our galaxy and other galaxies. Radio signals are the means by which the distant and mysterious quasars and pulsars were recently discovered.

Meteorites from Mars? The Moon?

A meteorite recovered from Antarctica in 1975 has been tested and found to bear traces of rare-gas isotopes in ratios similar to those measured by the *Viking* spacecraft on Mars. One question that needs to be resolved is what kind of impact would have caused a chunk of matter from Mars to break free from the planet's gravity?

In another finding, a small piece of rock also found in Antarctica in 1982 may have a lunar origin. The over-all composition of the meteorite is a braccia, made of anorthosite, a type of rock found only on the moon but not in meteorites.

Chinese Calendar

The Chinese lunar year is divided into 12 months of 29 or 30 days. The calendar is adjusted to the length of the solar year by the addition of extra months at regular intervals.

The years are arranged in major cycles of 60 years. Each successive year is named after one of 12 animals. These 12-year cycles are continuously repeated. The Chinese New Year is celebrated at the first new moon after the sun enters Aquarius—sometime between Jan. 21 and Feb. 19.

Rat	Ox	Tiger	Cat (Rabbit)	Dragon	Snake	Horse	Sheep (Goat)	Monkey	Rooster	Dog	Pig
1864	1865	1866	1867	1868	1869	1870	1871	1872	1873	1874	1875
1876	1877	1878	1879	1880	1881	1882	1883	1884	1885	1886	1887
1888	1889	1890	1891	1892	1893	1894	1895	1896	1897	1898	1899
1900	1901	1902	1903	1904	1905	1906	1907	1908	1909	1910	1911
1912	1913	1914	1915	1916	1917	1918	1919	1920	1921	1922	1923
1924	1925	1926	1927	1928	1929	1930	1931	1932	1933	1934	1935
1936	1937	1938	1939	1940	1941	1942	1943	1944	1945	1946	1947
1948	1949	1950	1951	1952	1953	1954	1955	1956	1957	1958	1959
1960	1961	1962	1963	1964	1965	1966	1967	1968	1969	1970	1971
1972	1973	1974	1975	1976	1977	1978	1979	1980	1981	1982	1983
1984	1985	1986	1987	1988	1989	1990	1991	1992	1993	1994	1995

Eclipses of the Sun and the Moon, 1985

May 4: Total eclipse of the Moon. Beginning of umbral phase visible in Antarctica, eastern Europe, Africa except the western part, Asia, the U.S.S.R. except the extreme northeastern part, Australia, New Zealand, and the Indian Ocean; the end visible in eastern South America, Europe, Africa, Asia except the eastern part, western Australia, Antarctica, the South Atlantic Ocean, the Indian Ocean, and western U.S.S.R.

May 19: Partial eclipse of the Sun. Visible in northeastern Asia, Japan, northern part of North America, Arctic regions, Greenland, Iceland, extreme northern part of Scandinavia.

October 28: Total eclipse of the Moon. Beginning of the umbral phase visible in eastern Europe, Asia, U.S.S.R., Alaska, the Arctic regions, Arctic Ocean, eastern Africa, Australia, New Zealand, Indian Ocean, the North Pacific Ocean, northern Greenland, and Wilkes Land part of Antarctica; the end visible in Greenland, Iceland, Europe, Africa, Asia, the U.S.S.R. Australia, the Arctic regions, the Indian Ocean, and Antarctica between Queen Maud Land and Wilkes Land.

November 12: Total eclipse of the Sun. Visible in southern part of South American, and Antarctica.

Phenomena, 1985

Configurations of Sun, Moon, and Planets

NOTE: The hour listings are in Universal Time. For conversion to United States time zones, see conversion table in this section.

JANUARY

d	h	
2	09	Ceres stationary
3	15	Mercury greatest elong. W (23°)
3	20	Earth at perihelion
7	02	FULL MOON
12	03	Moon at perigee
13	05	Mercury 0° 7S of Neptune
13	23	LAST QUARTER
14	22	Jupiter in conjunction with Sun
16	08	Saturn 2° N of Moon
17	19	Uranus 1° 8 N of Moon
18	22	Neptune 4° N of Moon
19	13	Mercury 3° N of Moon
21	02	NEW MOON
22	02	Venus greatest elong. E (47°)
25	00	Venus 5° N of Moon
25	04	Mars 4° N of Moon
27	10	Moon at apogee
29	03	FIRST QUARTER
31	05	Mercury 1° 3 S of Jupiter

FEBRUARY

4	13	Juno stationary
5	15	FULL MOON
8	02	Venus 3° N of Mars
8	04	Moon at perigee
9	11	Juno 1° 3S of Moon
11	10	Pluto stationary
12	08	LAST QUARTER
12	16	Saturn 3° N of Moon
14	02	Uranus 2° N of Moon
15	06	Neptune 4° N of Moon
15	19	Venus 4° N of Mars
17	10	Jupiter 4° N of Moon
19	08	Mercury in superior conjunction
19	19	NEW MOON
23	06	Venus 8° N of Moon
23	08	Mars 3° N of Moon
24	04	Moon at apogee
26	18	Venus greatest brilliancy
28	00	FIRST QUARTER

MARCH

7	02	FULL MOON
7	23	Saturn stationary
8	08	Moon at perigee
8	15	Juno 0° 7N of Moon
10	15	Vesta stationary
11	23	Saturn 3° N of Moon
10	15	Vesta stationary
11	23	Saturn 3° N of Moon
12	08	Venus stationary
13	09	Uranus 2° N of Moon
13	18	LAST QUARTER
14	12	Neptune 5° N of Moon
17	02	Jupiter 5° N of Moon
17	07	Mercury greatest elong. E.(18°)
20	16	Equinox
21	12	NEW MOON
22	18	Mercury 6° N of Moon
22	19	Venus 12° N of Moon
22	22	Uranus stationary
23	02	Mercury 5° S of Venus
23	15	Moon at apogee
24	12	Mars 1° 4N of Moon
24	13	Mercury stationary
25	19	Juno at opposition
29	16	FIRST QUARTER

APRIL

3	14	Mercury in inferior conjunction
3	22	Venus in inferior conjunction
5	01	Neptune stationary

5 03 Pallas in conjunction with Sun
5 12 FULL MOON
5 18 Moon at perigee
8 07 Saturn 3° N of Moon
9 16 Uranus 3° N of Moon
10 19 Neptune 5° N of Moon
12 05 LAST QUARTER
13 17 Jupiter 5° N of Moon
16 00 Mercury stationary
17 23 Venus 10° N of Moon
18 04 Mercury 3° N of Moon
18 21 Vesta at opposition
19 17 Moon at apogee
20 05 NEW MOON
22 11 Venus stationary
22 13 Mars 0° 4S of Moon
23 14 Pluto at opposition
28 04 FIRST QUARTER

MAY

1 15 Mercury greatest elong. W (27°)
4 05 Moon at perigee
4 20 FULL MOON (Eclipse)
5 15 Saturn 3° N of Moon
7 01 Uranus 3° N of Moon
8 04 Neptune 5° N of Moon
9 13 Venus greatest brilliancy
11 05 Jupiter 5° N of Moon
11 13 Mars 6° N of Aldebaran
11 18 LAST QUARTER
15 18 Saturn at opposition
15 23 Venus 3° N of Moon
17 00 Moon at apogee
17 07 Juno stationary
18 01 Mercury 1° 5S of Moon
19 22 NEW MOON
21 10 Mars 1° 9S of Moon
27 13 FIRST QUARTER

JUNE

1 13 Moon at perigee
1 22 Saturn 3° N of Moon
3 04 FULL MOON
3 10 Uranus 2° N of Moon
4 13 Neptune 5° N of Moon
5 08 Jupiter stationary
6 08 Vesta stationary
6 19 Uranus at opposition
7 14 Mercury in superior conjunction
7 16 Jupiter 5° N of Moon
10 08 LAST QUARTER
12 22 Venus greatest elong. W (46°)
13 14 Moon at apogee
14 11 Venus 1° 9S of Moon
18 12 NEW MOON
21 11 Solstice
23 19 Neptune at opposition
25 19 FIRST QUARTER
26 02 Mercury 5° S of Pollux
29 05 Saturn 3° N of Moon
29 09 Moon at perigee
30 18 Uranus 2° N of Moon
30 23 Ceres in conjunction with Sun

JULY

1 22 Neptune 5° N of Moon
2 12 FULL MOON
4 23 Jupiter 5° N of Moon
5 10 Earth at aphelion
10 01 LAST QUARTER
11 08 Moon at apogee
14 01 Mercury greatest elong. E (27°)
14 09 Venus 5° S of Moon
15 13 Venus 3° N of Aldebaran
18 00 NEW MOON
18 03 Mars in conjunction with Sun
18 18 Pluto stationary
19 21 Mercury 7° S of Moon
25 00 FIRST QUARTER
25 18 Moon at perigee
26 10 Saturn 3° N of Moon
26 12 Saturn stationary
27 03 Mercury stationary
28 00 Uranus 2° N of Moon
29 05 Neptune 5° N of Moon
31 22 FULL MOON

AUGUST

1 02 Jupiter 4° N of Moon
4 12 Jupiter at opposition
8 02 Moon at apogee
8 18 LAST QUARTER
10 22 Mercury in inferior conjunction
13 08 Venus 5° S of Moon
14 14 Ceres 1° 0S of Moon
16 10 NEW MOON
20 04 Moon at perigee
20 06 Mercury stationary
22 16 Saturn 3° N of Moon
23 01 Uranus stationary
23 05 FIRST QUARTER
23 08 Venus 7° S of Pollux
24 05 Uranus 3° N of Moon
25 10 Neptune 5° N of Moon
28 04 Jupiter 4° N of Moon
28 12 Mercury greatest elong. W (18°)
30 09 FULL MOON

SEPTEMBER

4 21 Mercury 0° 01S of Mars
4 21 Moon at apogee
6 10 Mercury 1° 0N of Regulus
7 12 LAST QUARTER
9 01 Mars 0° 8N of Regulus
11 21 Ceres 0° 2S of Moon
12 08 Venus 5° S of Moon
12 09 Neptune stationary
13 08 Mars 4° S of Moon
14 19 NEW MOON
16 19 Moon at perigee
19 02 Saturn 3° N of Moon
20 11 Uranus 3° N of Moon
21 11 FIRST QUARTER
21 15 Neptune 5° N of Moon
21 17 Venus 0° 4N of Regulus
22 20 Mercury in superior conjunction
23 02 Equinox
24 06 Jupiter 4° N of Moon
29 00 FULL MOON

OCTOBER

2 13 Moon at apogee
3 10 Jupiter stationary
4 23 Venus 0° 1N. of Mars
7 05 LAST QUARTER
10 04 Ceres 1° 1N. of Moon
12 01 Mars 3° S of Moon
12 09 Venus 3° S of Moon
14 05 NEW MOON
15 01 Moon at perigee
15 05 Mercury 1° 3S of Moon
16 15 Saturn 4° N of Moon
17 21 Uranus 3° N of Moon
18 23 Neptune 5° N of Moon
20 20 FIRST QUARTER
21 13 Jupiter 5° N of Moon
28 04 Pluto in conjunction with Sun
28 18 FULL MOON (Eclipse)
29 22 Moon at apogee
30 21 Mercury 4° S of Saturn

NOVEMBER

1 18 Juno in conjunction with Sun
3 10 Venus 4° N of Spica
5 20 LAST QUARTER
8 09 Mercury greatest elong. E (23°)
8 19 Mercury 1° 8 N. of Antares
9 18 Mars 1° 7 S. of Moon
11 11 Venus 0° 8 N of Moon
11 22 Pallas stationary
12 13 Moon at perigee
12 14 NEW MOON (Eclipse)
14 04 Mercury 0° 5 N of Moon
14 09 Uranus 3° N of Moon
15 09 Neptune 5° N of Moon
18 01 Jupiter 5° N of Moon
18 19 Mercury stationary
19 09 FIRST QUARTER
23 02 Saturn in conjunction with Sun
25 22 Moon at apogee
27 13 FULL MOON

DECEMBER

28 22 Mercury in inferior conjunction
2 11 Mars 3° N. of Spica
4 04 Mercury 1° 6 N of Venus
5 09 LAST QUARTER
5 11 Venus 1° 1 S of Saturn
8 10 Mars 0° 01 S of Moon
8 11 Mercury stationary
10 08 Uranus in conjunction with Sun
10 18 Mercury 5° N of Moon
10 23 Saturn 4° N of Moon
11 01 Moon at perigee
12 01 NEW MOON
15 18 Jupiter 5° N of Moon
16 17 Mercury 0° 5 N of Saturn
17 05 Mercury greatest elong. W (21°)
19 02 FIRST QUARTER
21 10 Mercury 6° N of Antares
21 22 Solstice
22 15 Pallas at opposition
23 07 Moon at apogee
25 05 Neptune in conjunction with Sun
27 08 FULL MOON
29 12 Mercury 0° 7 N of Uranus

WEIGHTS & MEASURES

Measures and Weights

Source: Department of Commerce, National Bureau of Standards.

The International System (Metric)

The International System of Units is a modernized version of the metric system, established by international agreement, i.e. provides a logical and interconnected framework for all measurements in science, industry, and commerce. The system is built on a foundation of seven basic units, and all other units are derived from them. (Use of metric weights and measures was legalized in the United States in 1866, and our customary units of weights and measures are defined in terms of the meter and kilogram.)

Length. Meter. The meter is defined as 1,650,-763.73 wavelengths in vacuum of the orange-red line of the spectrum of krypton-86.

Time. Second. The second is defined as the duration of 9,192,631,770 cycles of the radiation associated with a specified transition of the cesium 133 atom.

Mass. Kilogram. The standard for the kilogram is a cylinder of platinum-iridium alloy kept by the International Bureau of Weights and Measures at Paris. A duplicate at the National Bureau of Standards serves as the mass standard for the United States. The kilogram is the only base unit still defined by a physical object.

Temperature. Kelvin. The kelvin is defined as the fraction 1/273.16 of the thermodynamic temperature of the triple point of water; that is, the point at which water forms an interface of solid, liquid and vapor. This is defined as 0.01° C on the Centigrade or Celsius scale and 32.02° F on the Fahrenheit scale. The temperature 0° K is called "absolute zero."

Electric Current. Ampere. The ampere is defined as that current that, if maintained in each of two long parallel wires separated by one meter in free space, would produce a force between the two wires (due to their magnetic fields) of 2×10^{-7} newton for each meter of length. (A newton is the unit of force which when applied to one kilogram mass would experience an acceleration of one meter per second per second.)

Luminous Intensity. Candela. The candela is defined as the luminous intensity of 1/600,000 of a square meter of a cavity at the temperature of freezing platinum (2,042K).

Amount of Substance. Mole. The mole is the amount of substance of a system that contains as many elementary entities as there are atoms in 0.012 kilograms of carbon-12.

Tables of Metric Weights and Measures

LINEAR MEASURE

10 millimeters (mm) =	1 centimeter (cm)
10 centimeters =	1 decimeter (dm) = 100 millimeters
10 decimeters =	1 meter (m) = 1,000 millimeters
10 meters =	1 dekameter (dam)
10 dekameters =	1 hectometer (hm) = 100 meters
10 hectometers =	1 kilometer (km) = 1,000 meters

AREA MEASURE

100 square millimeters (mm^2) =	1 sq centimeter (cm^2)
10,000 square centimeters =	1 sq meter (m^2) = 1,000,000 sq millimeters
100 square meters =	1 are (a)
100 ares =	1 hectare (ha) = 10,000 sq meters
100 hectares =	1 sq kilometer (km^2) = 1,000,000 sq meters

VOLUME MEASURE

10 milliliters (ml) =	1 centiliter (cl)
10 centiliters =	1 deciliter (dl) = 100 milliliters
10 deciliters =	1 liter (1) = 1,000 milliliters
10 liters =	1 dekaliter (dal)
10 dekaliters =	1 hectoliter (hl) = 100 liters
10 hectoliters =	1 kiloliter (kl) = 1,000 liters

CUBIC MEASURE

1,000 cubic millimeters (mm^3) =	1 cu centimeter (cm^3)
1,000 cubic centimeters =	1 cu decimeter (dm^3) = 1,000,000 cu millimeters
1,000 cubic decimeters =	1 cu meter (m^3) = 1 stere = 1,000,000 cu centimeters = 1,000,000,000 cu millimeters

WEIGHT

10 milligrams (mg) =	1 centigram (cg)
10 centigrams =	1 decigram (dg) = 100 milligrams
10 decigrams =	1 gram (g) = 1,000 milligrams
10 grams =	1 dekagram (dag)
10 dekagrams =	1 hectogram (hg) = 100 grams
10 hectograms =	1 kilogram (kg) = 1,000 grams
1,000 kilograms =	1 metric ton (t)

Tables of Customary U.S. Weights and Measures

LINEAR MEASURE

12 inches (in.) = 1 foot (ft)
3 feet = 1 yard (yd)
5 1/2 yards = 1 rod (rd), pole, or perch (16 1/2 ft)
40 rods = 1 furlong (fur) = 220 yds = 660 ft
8 furlongs = 1 statute mile (mi.) = 1,760 yds = 5,280 ft
3 land miles = 1 league
5,280 feet = 1 statute or land mile
6,076.11549 feet = 1 international nautical mile

AREA MEASURE

144 square inches = 1 sq ft
9 square feet = 1 sq yd = 1,296 sq in.
30 1/4 square yards = 1 sq rd = 272 1/4 sq ft
160 square rods = 1 acre = 4,840 sq yds = 43,560 sq ft
640 acres = 1 sq mi.
1 mile square = 1 section (of land)
6 miles square = 1 township = 36 sections = 36 sq mi.

CUBIC MEASURE

1,728 cubic inches = 1 cu ft
27 cubic feet = 1 cu yd

LIQUID MEASURE

When necessary to distinguish the liquid pint or quart from the dry pint or quart, the word "liquid" or the abbreviation "liq" should be used in combination with the name or abbreviation of the liquid unit.

4 gills (gi) = 1 pint (pt) (= 28.875 cu in.)
2 pints = 1 quart (qt) (= 57.75 cu in.)
4 quarts = 1 gallon (gal) (= 231 cu in.) = 8 pts = 32 gills

APOTHECARIES FLUID MEASURE

60 minims (min.) = 1 fluid dram (fl dr) (= 0.2256 cu in.)
8 fluid drams = 1 fluid ounce (fl oz) (= 1.8047 cu in.)
16 fluid ounces = 1 pt (= 28.875 cu in.) = 128 fl drs
2 pints = 1 qt (= 57.75 cu in.) = 32 fl oz = 256 fl drs
4 quarts = 1 gal (= 231 cu in.) = 128 fl oz = 1,024 fl drs

DRY MEASURE

When necessary to distinguish the dry pint or quart from the liquid pint or quart; the word "dry" should be used in combination with the name or abbreviation of the dry unit.

2 pints = 1 qt (=67.2006 cu in.)
8 quarts = 1 peck (pk) (=537.605 cu in.) = 16 pts
4 pecks = 1 bushel (bu) (= 2,150.42 cu in.) = 32 qts

AVOIRDUPOIS WEIGHT

When necessary to distinguish the avoirdupois dram from the apothecaries dram, or to distinguish the avoirdupois dram or ounce from the fluid dram or ounce, or to distinguish the avoirdupois ounce or pound from the troy or apothecaries ounce or pound, the word "avoirdupois" or the abbreviation "avdp" should be used in combination with the name or abbreviation of the avoirdupois unit.
(The "grain" is the same in avoirdupois, troy, and apothecaries weights.)

27 11/32 grains = 1 dram (dr)
16 drams = 1 oz = 437 1/2 grains
16 ounces = 1 lb = 256 drams = 7,000 grains
100 pounds = 1 hundredweight (cwt)[1]
20 hundredweights = 1 ton (tn) = 2,000 lbs[1]

In "gross" or "long" measure, the following values are recognized:

112 pounds = 1 gross or long cwt[1]
20 gross or long hundredweights = 1 gross or long ton = 2,240 lbs[1]

1. When the terms "hundredweight" and "ton" are used unmodified, they are commonly understood to mean the 100-pound hundredweight and the 2,000-pound ton, respectively; these units may be designated "net" or "short" when necessary to distinguish them from the corresponding units in gross or long measure.

UNITS OF CIRCULAR MEASURE

Second (″) = —
Minute (′) = 60 seconds
Degree (°) = 60 minutes
Right angle = 90 degrees
Straight angle = 180 degrees
Circle = 360 degrees

TROY WEIGHT

24 grains = 1 pennyweight (dwt)
20 pennyweights = 1 ounce troy (oz t) = 480 grains
12 ounces troy = 1 pound troy (lb t) = 240 pennyweights = 5,760 grains

APOTHECARIES WEIGHT

20 grains = 1 scruple (s ap)
3 scruples = 1 dram apothecaries (dr ap) = 60 grains
8 drams apothecaries = 1 ounce apothecaries (oz ap) = 24 scruples = 480 grains
12 ounces apothecaries = 1 pound apothecaries (lb ap) = 96 drams apothecaries = 288 scruples = 5,760 grains

GUNTER'S OR SURVEYOR'S CHAIN MEASURE

7.92 inches = 1 link (li)
100 links = 1 chain (ch) = 4 rods = 66 ft
80 chains = 1 statute mile = 320 rods = 5,280 ft

Metric and U.S. Equivalents

1 angstrom[1] (light wave measurement)	0.1 millimicron 0.000 1 micron 0.000 000 1 millimeter 0.000 000 004 inch
1 cable's length	120 fathoms 720 feet 219.456 meters
1 centimeter	0.3937 inch
1 chain (Gunter's or surveyor's)	66 feet 20.1168 meters
1 decimeter	3.937 inches
1 dekameter	32.808 feet
1 fathom	8 feet 1.8288 meters
1 foot	0.3048 meter
1 furlong	10 chains (surveyor's) 660 feet 220 yards 1/8 statute mile 201.168 meters

1 inch	2.54 centimeters
1 kilometer	0.621 mile
1 league (land)	3 statute miles 4.828 kilometers
1 link (Gunter's or surveyor's)	7.92 inches 0.201 168 meter
1 meter	39.37 inches 1.094 yards
1 micron	0.001 millimeter 0.000 039 37 inch
1 mil	0.001 inch 0.025 4 millimeter
1 mile (statute or land)	5,280 feet 1.609 kilometers
1 mile (nautical international)	1.852 kilometers 1.151 statute miles 0.999 U.S. nautical miles
1 millimeter	0.03937 inch
1 millimicron (mμ)	0.001 micron 0.000 000 039 37 inch
1 nanometer	0.001 micrometer or 0.000 000 039 37 inch
1 point (typography)	0.013 837 inch 1/72 inch (approximately) 0.351 millimeter
1 rod, pole, or perch	16 1/2 feet 5.0292 meters
1 yard	0.9144 meter

AREAS OR SURFACES

1 acre	43,560 square feet 4,840 square yards 0.405 hectare
1 are	119.599 square yards 0.025 acre
1 hectare	2.471 acres
1 square centimeter	0.155 square inch
1 square decimeter	15.5 square inches
1 square foot	929.030 square centimeters
1 square inch	6.4516 square centimeters
1 square kilometer	0.386 square mile 247.105 acres
1 square meter	1.196 square yards 10.764 square feet
1 square mile	258.999 hectares
1 square millimeter	0.002 square inch
1 square rod, square pole or square perch	25.293 square meters
1 square yard	0.836 square meters

CAPACITIES OR VOLUMES

1 barrel, liquid	31 to 42 gallons[2]
1 barrel, standard for fruits, vegetables, and other dry commodities except cranberries	7,056 cubic inches 105 dry quarts 3.281 bushels, struck measure
1 barrel, standard, cranberry	5.286 cubic inches 86 45/64 dry quarts 2.709 bushels, struck measure
1 bushel (U.S.) struck measure	2,150.42 cubic inches 35.238 liters
1 bushel, heaped (U.S.)	2,747.715 cubic inches 1.278 bushels, struck measure[3]
1 cord (firewood)	128 cubic feet
1 cubic centimeter	0.061 cubic inches
1 cubic decimeter	61.024 cubic inches
1 cubic foot	7.481 gallons 28.316 cubic decimeters
1 cubic inch	0.554 fluid ounce 4.433 fluid drams 16.387 cubic centimeters
1 cubic meter	1.308 cubic yards
1 cubic yard	0.765 cubic meter
1 cup, measuring	8 fluid ounces 1/2 liquid pint
1 dram, fluid or liquid (U.S.)	1/8 fluid ounces 0.226 cubic inch 3.697 milliliters 1.041 British fluid drachms
1 dekaliter	2.642 gallons 1.135 pecks
1 gallon (U.S.)	231 cubic inches 3.785 liters 0.833 British gallon 128 U.S. fluid ounces
1 gallon (British Imperial)	277.42 cubic inches 1.201 U.S. gallons 4.546 liters 160 British fluid ounces
1 gill	7.219 cubic inches 4 fluid ounces 0.118 liter
1 hectoliter	26.418 gallons 2.838 bushels
1 liter	1.057 liquid quarts 0.908 dry quart 61.024 cubic inches
1 milliliter	0.271 fluid drams 16.231 minims 0.061 cubic inch
1 ounce, fluid or liquid (U.S.)	1.805 cubic inch 29.574 milliliters 1.041 British fluid ounces

1 peck	8.810 liters
1 pint, dry	33.600 cubic inches 0.551 liter
1 pint, liquid	28.875 cubic inches 0.473 liter
1 quart, dry (U.S.)	67.201 cubic inches 1.101 liters 0.969 British quart
1 quart, liquid (U.S.)	57.75 cubic inches 0.946 liter 0.833 British quart
1 quart (British)	69.354 cubic inches 1.032 U.S. dry quarts 1.201 U.S. liquid quarts
1 tablespoon, measuring	3 teaspoons 4 fluid drams 1/2 fluid ounce
1 teaspoon, measuring	1/3 tablespoon 1 1/3 fluid drams
1 assay ton[4]	29.167 grams
1 carat	200 milligrams 3.086 grains
1 dram, apothecaries	60 grains 3.888 grams
1 dram, avoirdupois	27 11/32 (=27.344) grains 1.772 grams
1 grain	64.798 91 milligrams
1 gram	15.432 grains 0.035 ounce, avoirdupois
1 hundredweight, gross or long[5]	112 pounds 50.802 kilograms
1 hundredweight, net or short	100 pounds 45.359 kilograms
1 kilogram	2.205 pounds
1 microgram [μg (the Greek letter mu in combination with the letter g)]	0.000 001 gram
1 milligram	0.015 grain
1 ounce, avoirdupois	437.5 grains 0.911 troy or apothecaries ounce 28.350 grams
1 ounce, troy or apothecaries	480 grains 1.097 avoirdupois ounces 31.103 grams
1 pennyweight	1.555 grams
1 point	0.01 carat 2 milligrams
1 pound, avoirdupois	7,000 grains 1.215 troy or apothecaries pounds 453.592 37 grams
1 pound, troy or apothecaries	5,760 grains 0.823 avoirdupois pound 373.242 grams
1 ton, gross or long[5]	2,240 pounds 1.12 net tons 1.016 metric tons
1 ton, metric	2,204.623 pounds 0.984 gross ton 1.102 net tons
1 ton, net or short	2,000 pounds 0.893 gross ton 0.907 metric ton

1. The angstrom is basically defined as 10^{-10} meter. 2. There is a variety of "barrels" established by law or usage. For example, federal taxes on fermented liquors are based on a barrel of 31 gallons; many state laws fix the "barrel for liquids" at 31 1/2 gallons; one state fixes a 36-gallon barrel for cistern measurement; federal law recognizes a 40-gallon barrel for "proof spirits"; by custom, 42 gallons comprise a barrel of crude oil or petroleum products for statistical purposes, and this equivalent is recognized "for liquids" by four states. 3. Frequently recognized as 1 1/4 bushels, struck measure. 4. Used in assaying. The assay ton bears the same relation to the milligram that a ton of 2,000 pounds avoirdupois bears to the ounce troy; hence the weight in milligrams of precious metal obtained from one assay ton of ore gives directly the number of troy ounces to the net ton. 5. The gross or long ton and hundredweight are used commercially in the United States to only a limited extent, usually in restricted industrial fields. These units are the same as the British "ton" and "hundredweight."

Miscellaneous Units of Measure

Acre: An area of 43,560 square feet. Originally, the area a yoke of oxen could plow in one day.

Agate: Originally a measurement of type size (5 1/2 points). Now equal to 1/14 inch. Used in printing for measuring column length.

Ampere: Unit of electric current. A potential difference of one volt across a resistance of one ohm produces a current of one ampere.

Astronomical Unit (A.U.): 93,000,000 miles, the average distance of the earth from the sun. Used in astronomy.

Bale: A large bundle of goods. In the U.S., the approximate weight of a bale of cotton is 500 pounds. The weight varies in other countries.

Board Foot (fbm): 144 cubic inches (12 in. × 12 in. × 1 in.). Used for lumber.

Bolt: 40 yards. Used for measuring cloth.

Btu: British thermal unit. Amount of heat needed to increase the temperature of one pound of water by one degree Fahrenheit (252 calories).

Carat (c): 200 milligrams or 3.086 grains troy.

Originally the weight of a seed of the carob tree in the Mediterranean region. Used for weighing precious stones. *See also* Karat.

Chain (ch): a chain 66 feet or one-tenth of a furlong in length, divided into 100 parts called links. One mile is equal to 80 chains. Used in surveying and sometimes called Gunter's or surveyor's chain.

Cubit: 18 inches or 45.72 cm. Derived from distance between elbow and tip of middle finger.

Decibel: Unit of relative loudness. One decibel is the smallest amount of change detectable by the human ear.

Ell, English: 1 1/4 yards or 1/32 bolt. Used for measuring cloth.

Freight Ton (also called Measurement Ton): 40 cubic feet of merchandise. Used for cargo freight.

Great Gross: 12 gross or 1728.

Gross: 12 dozen or 144.

Hand: 4 inches or 10.16 cm. Derived from the width of the hand. Used for measuring the height of horses at withers.

Hertz: Modern unit for measurement of electromagnetic wave frequencies (equivalent to "cycles per second").

Hogshead (hhd): 2 liquid barrels or 14,653 cubic inches.

Horsepower: The power needed to lift 33,000 pounds a distance of one foot in one minute (about 1 1/2 times the power an average horse can exert). Used for measuring power of steam engines, etc.

Karat (kt): A measure of the purity of gold, indicating how many parts out of 24 are pure. For example, 18 karat gold is 3/4 pure. Sometimes spelled *carat.*

Knot: Not a distance, but the rate of speed of one nautical mile per hour. Used for measuring speed of ships.

League: Rather indefinite and varying measure, but usually estimated at 3 miles in English-speaking countries.

Light-Year: 5,880,000,000,000 miles, the distance light travels in a year at the rate of 186,281.7 miles per second. (If an astronomical unit were represented by one inch, a light-year would be represented by about one mile.) Used for measurements in interstellar space.

Magnum: Two-quart bottle. Used for measuring wine, etc.

Ohm: Unit of electrical resistance. A circuit in which a potential difference of one volt produces a current of one ampere has a resistance of one ohm.

Parsec: Approximately 3.26 light-years of 19.2 trillion miles. Term is combination of first syllables of *par*allax and *sec*ond, and distance is that of imaginary star when lines drawn from it to both earth and sun form a maximum angle or parallax of one second (1/3600 degree). Used for measuring interstellar distances.

Pi (π): 3.14159265+. The ratio of the circumference of a circle to its diameter. For practical purposes, the value is used to four decimal places: 3.1416.

Pica: 1/6 inch or 12 points. Used in printing for measuring column width, etc.

Pipe: 2 hogsheads. Used for measuring wine and other liquids.

Point: .013837 (approximately 1/72) inch or 1/12 pica. Used in printing for measuring type size.

Quintal: 100,000 grams or 220.46 pounds avoirdupois.

Quire: Used for measuring paper. Sometimes 24 sheets but more often 25. There are 20 quires in a ream.

Ream: Used for measuring paper. Sometimes 480 sheets, but more often 500 sheets.

Roentgen: Dosage unit of radiation exposure produced by X-rays.

Score: 20 units.

Sound, Speed of: Usually placed at 1,088 ft per second at 32° F at sea level. It varies at other temperatures and in different media.

Span: 9 inches or 22.86 cm. Derived from the distance between the end of the thumb and the end of the little finger when both are outstretched.

Square: 100 square feet. Used in building.

Stone: Legally 14 pounds avoirdupois in Great Britain.

Therm: 100,000 BTU's.

Township: U. S. land measurement of almost 36 square miles. The south border is 6 miles long. The east and west borders, also 6 miles long, follow the meridians, making the north border slightly less than 6 miles long. Used in surveying.

Tun: 252 gallons, but often larger. Used for measuring wine and other liquids.

Watt: Unit of power. The power used by a current of one ampere across a potential difference of one volt equals one watt.

Kelvin Scale

Absolute zero, −273.16° on the Celsius (Centigrade) scale, is 0° Kelvin. Thus, degrees Kelvin are equivalent to degrees Celsius plus 273.16. The freezing point of water, 0° C. and 32° F., is 273.16° K. The conversion formula is K° = C° + 273.16.

Conversion of Miles to Kilometers and Kilometers to Miles

Miles	Kilometers	Miles	Kilometers	Miles	Kilometers	Kilometers	Miles	Kilometers	Miles	Kilometers	Miles
1	1.6	8	12.8	60	96.5	1	0.6	8	4.9	60	37.2
2	3.2	9	14.4	70	112.6	2	1.2	9	5.5	70	43.4
3	4.8	10	16.0	80	128.7	3	1.8	10	6.2	80	49.7
4	6.4	20	32.1	90	144.8	4	2.4	20	12.4	90	55.9
5	8.0	30	48.2	100	160.9	5	3.1	30	18.6	100	62.1
6	9.6	40	64.3	1,000	1609	6	3.7	40	24.8	1,000	621
7	11.2	50	80.4			7	4.3	50	31.0		

Bolts and Screws: Conversion from Fractions of an Inch to Millimeters

Inch	mm	Inch	mm	Inch	mm	Inch	mm
1/64	0.40	17/64	6.75	33/64	13.10	49/64	19.45
1/32	0/79	9/32	7.14	17/32	13.50	25/32	19.84
3/64	1.19	19/64	7.54	35/64	13.90	51/64	20.24
1/16	1.59	5/16	7.94	9/16	14.29	13/16	20.64
5/64	1.98	21/64	8.33	37/64	14.69	53/64	21.03
3/32	2.38	11/32	8.73	19/32	15.08	27/32	21.43
7/64	2.78	23/64	9.13	39/64	15.48	55/64	21.83
1/8	3.18	3/8	9.53	5/8	15.88	7/8	22.23
9/64	3.57	25/64	9.92	41/64	16.27	57/64	22.62
5/32	3.97	13/32	10.32	21/32	16.67	29/32	23.02
11/64	4.37	27/64	10.72	43/64	17.06	59/64	23.42
3/16	4.76	7/16	11.11	11/64	17.46	15/16	23.81
13/64	5.16	29/64	11.51	45/64	17.86	61/64	24.21
7/32	5.56	15/32	11.91	23/32	18.26	31/32	24.61
15/64	5.95	31/64	12.30	47/64	18.65	63/64	25.00
1/4	6.35	1/2	12.70	3/4	19.05	1	25.40

U.S.—Metric Cooking Conversions

U.S. customary system				Metric			
Capacity		Weight		Capacity		Weight	
1/5 teaspoon	1 milliliter	1 fluid oz	30 milliliters	1 milliliter	1/5 teaspoon	1 gram	.035 ounce
1 teaspoon	5 ml		28 grams	5 ml	1 teaspoon	100 grams	3.5 ounces
1 tablespoon	15 ml	1 pound	454 grams	15 ml	1 tablespoon	500 grams	1.10 pounds
1/5 cup	50 ml			34 ml	1 fluid oz	1 kilogram	2.205 pounds
1 cup	240 ml						
2 cups (1 pint)	470 ml			100 ml	3.4 fluid oz		35 oz
4 cups (1 quart)	.95 liter			240 ml	1 cup		
4 quarts (1 gal.)	3.8 liters			1 liter	34 fluid oz 4.2 cups 2.1 pints 1.06 quarts 0.26 gallon		

Cooking Measurement Equivalents

16 tablespoons = 1 cup
12 tablespoons = 3/4 cup
10 tablespoons + 2 teaspoons = 2/3 cup
8 tablespoons = 1/2 cup
6 tablespoons = 3/8 cup
5 tablespoons + 1 teaspoon = 1/3 cup
4 tablespoons = 1/4 cup

2 tablespoons = 1/8 cup
2 tablespoons + 2 teaspoons = 1/6 cup
1 tablespoon = 1/16 cup
2 cups = 1 pint
2 pints = 1 quart
3 teaspoons = 1 tablespoon
48 teaspoons = 1 cup

Prefixes and Multiples

Prefix	Symbol	Equivalent	Multiple/ submultiple	Prefix	Symbol	Equivalent	Multiple/ submultiple
atto	a	quintillionth part	10^{-18}	deci	d	tenth part	10^{-1}
femto	f	quadrillionth part	10^{-15}	deka	da	tenfold	10
pico	p	trillionth part	10^{-12}	hecto	h	hundredfold	10^{2}
nano	n	billionth part	10^{-9}	kilo	k	thousandfold	10^{3}
micro	μ	millionth part	10^{-6}	mega	M	millionfold	10^{6}
milli	m	thousandth part	10^{-3}	giga	G	billionfold	10^{9}
centi	c	hundredth part	10^{-2}	tera	T	trillionfold	10^{12}

Common Formulas

Circumference

Circle: $C=\pi d$, in which π is 3.1416 and d the diameter.

Area

Triangle: $A=\frac{ab}{2}$, in which a is the base and b the height.

Square: $A=a^1$, in which a is one of the sides.

Rectangle: $A=ab$, in which a is the base and b the height.

Trapezoid: $A=\frac{h(a+b)}{2}$, in which h is the height, a the longer parallel side, and b the shorter.

Regular pentagon: $A=1.720a^2$, in which a is one of the sides.

Regular hexagon: $A=2.598a^2$, in which a is one of the sides.

Regular octagon: $A=4.828a^2$, in which a is one of the sides.

Circle: $A=\pi r^2$, in which π is 3.1416 and r the radius.

Volume

Cube: $V=a^3$, in which a is one of the edges.

Rectangular prism: $V=abc$, in which a is the length, b the width, and c the depth.

Pyramid: $V=\frac{Ah}{3}$, in which A is the area of the base and h the height.

Cylinder: $V=\pi r^2h$, in which π is 3.1416, r the radius of the base, and h the height.

Cone: $V=\frac{\pi r^2h}{3}$, in which π is 3.1416, r the radius of the base, and h the height.

Sphere: $V=\frac{4\pi r^3}{3}$, in which π is 3.1416 and r the radius.

Miscellaneous

Speed per second acquired by falling body: $v=32t$, in which t is the time in seconds.

Distance in feet traveled by falling body: $d=16t^2$, in which t is the time in seconds.

Speed of sound in feet per second through any given temperature of air: $V=\frac{1087\sqrt{273+t}}{16.52}$, in which t is the temperature Centigrade.

Cost in cents of operation of electrical device: $C=\frac{Wtc}{1000}$, in which W is the number of watts, t the time in hours, and c the cost in cents per kilowatt-hour.

Conversion of matter into energy (Einstein's Theorem): $E=mc^2$, in which E is the energy in ergs, m the mass of the matter in grams, and c the speed of light in centimeters per second. ($c^2=9.10^{20}$).

Decimal Equivalents of Common Fractions

1/2	.5000	1/10	.1000	2/7	.2857	3/11	.2727	5/9	.5556	7/11	.6364
1/3	.3333	1/11	.0909	2/9	.2222	4/5	.8000	5/11	.4545	7/12	.5833
1/4	.2500	1/12	.0833	2/11	.1818	4/7	.5714	5/12	.4167	8/9	.8889
1/5	.2000	1/16	.0625	3/4	.7500	4/9	.4444	6/7	.8571	8/11	.7273
1/6	.1667	1/32	.0313	3/5	.6000	4/11	.3636	6/11	.5455	9/10	.9000
1/7	.1429	1/64	.0156	3/7	.4286	5/6	.8333	7/8	.8750	9/11	.8182
1/8	.1250	2/3	.6667	3/8	.3750	5/7	.7143	7/9	.7778	10/11	.9091
1/9	.1111	2/5	.4000	3/10	.3000	5/8	.6250	7/10	.7000	11/12	.9167

Conversion Factors

To change	To	Multiply by	To change	To	Multiply by
acres	hectares	.4047	liters	pints (dry)	1.8162
acres	square feet	43,560	liters	pints (liquid)	2.1134
acres	square miles	.001562	liters	quarts (dry)	.9081
atmospheres	cms. of mercury	76	liters	quarts (liquid)	1.0567
BTU	horsepower-hour	.0003931	meters	feet	3.2808
BTU	kilowatt-hour	.0002928	meters	miles	.0006214
BTU/hour	watts	.2931	meters	yards	1.0936
bushels	cubic inches	2150.4	metric tons	tons (long)	.9842
bushels (U.S.)	hectoliters	.3524	metric tons	tons (short)	1.1023
centimeters	inches	.3937	miles	kilometers	1.6093
centimeters	feet	.03281	miles	feet	5280
circumference	radians	6.283	miles (nautical)	miles (statute)	1.1516
cubic feet	cubic meters	.0283	miles (statute)	miles (nautical)	.8684
cubic meters	cubic feet	35.3145	miles/hour	feet/minute	88
cubic meters	cubic yards	1.3079	millimeters	inches	.0394
cubic yards	cubic meters	.7646	ounces avdp.	grams	28.3495
degrees	radians	.01745	ounces	pounds	.0625
dynes	grams	.00102	ounces (troy)	ounces (avdp)	1.09714
fathoms	feet	6.0	pecks	liters	8.8096
feet	meters	.3048	pints (dry)	liters	.5506
feet	miles (nautical)	.0001645	pints (liquid)	liters	.4732
feet	miles (statute)	.0001894	pounds ap or t	kilograms	.3782
feet/second	miles/hour	.6818	pounds avdp	kilograms	.4536
furlongs	feet	660.0	pounds	ounces	16
furlongs	miles	.125	quarts (dry)	liters	1.1012
gallons (U.S.)	liters	3.7853	quarts (liquid)	liters	.9463
grains	grams	.0648	radians	degrees	57.30
grams	grains	15.4324	rods	meters	5.029
grams	ounces avdp	.0353	rods	feet	16.5
grams	pounds	.002205	square feet	square meters	.0929
hectares	acres	2.4710	square kilometers	square miles	.3861
hectoliters	bushels (U.S.)	2.8378	square meters	square feet	10.7639
horsepower	watts	745.7	square meters	square yards	1.1960
hours	days	.04167	square miles	square kilometers	2.5900
inches	millimeters	25.4000	square yards	square meters	.8361
inches	centimeters	2.5400	tons (long)	metric tons	1.016
kilograms	pounds avdp or t	2.2046	tons (short)	metric tons	.9072
kilometers	miles	.6214	tons (long)	pounds	2240
kilowatts	horsepower	1.341	tons (short)	pounds	2000
knots	nautical miles/hour	1.0	watts	BTU/hour	3.4129
knots	statute miles/hour	1.151	watts	horsepower	.001341
liters	gallons (U.S.)	.2642	yards	meters	.9144
liters	pecks	.1135	yards	miles	.0005682

Fahrenheit and Celsius (Centigrade) Scales

Zero on the Fahrenheit scale represents the temperature produced by the mixing of equal weights of snow and common salt.

	F	C
Boiling point of water	212°	100°
Freezing point of water	32°	0°
Absolute zero	−459.6°	−273.1°

Absolute zero is theoretically the lowest possible temperature, the point at which all molecular motion would cease.

To convert Fahrenheit to Celsius (Centigrade), subtract 32 and multiply by 5/9.

To convert Celsius (Centigrade) to Fahrenheit, multiply by 9/5 and add 32.

° Centigrade	° Fahrenheit	° Centigrade	° Fahrenheit
−273.1	−459.6	30	86
−250	−418	35	95
−200	−328	40	104
−150	−238	45	113
−100	−148	50	122
−50	−58	55	131
−40	−40	60	140
−30	−22	65	149
−20	−4	70	158
−10	14	75	167
0	32	80	176
5	41	85	185
10	50	90	194
15	59	95	203
20	68	**100**	**212**
25	77		

Roman Numerals

Roman numerals are expressed by letters of the alphabet and are rarely used today except for formality or variety.

There are three basic principles for reading Roman numerals:

1. A letter repeated once or twice repeats its value that many times. (XXX=30, CC=200, etc.).

2. One or more letters placed after another letter of greater value increases the greater value by the amount of the smaller. (VI=6, LXX=70, MCC=1200, etc.).

3. A letter placed before another letter of greater value decreases the greater value by the amount of the smaller. (IV=4, XC=90, CM=900, etc.).

Letter	Value	Letter	Value	Letter	Value	Letter	Value	Letter	Value
I	1	VII	7	XXX	30	LXXX	80	$\overline{V}$	5,000
II	2	VIII	8	XL	40	XC	90	$\overline{X}$	10,000
III	3	IX	9	L	50	C	100	$\overline{L}$	50,000
IV	4	X	10	LX	60	D	500	$\overline{C}$	100,000
V	5	XX	20	LXX	70	M	1,000	$\overline{D}$	500,000
VI	6							$\overline{M}$	1,000,000

Mean and Median

The mean, also called the average, of a series of quantities is obtained by finding the sum of the quantities and dividing it by the number of quantities. In the series 1,3,5,18,19,20,25, the mean or average is 13—i.e., 91 divided by 7.

The median of a series is that point which so divides it that half the quantities are on one side, half on the other. In the above series, the median is 18.

The median often better expresses the common-run, since it is not, as is the mean, affected by an excessively high or low figure. In the series 1,3,4,7, 55, the median of 4 is a truer expression of the common-run than is the mean of 14.

Prime Numbers Between 1 and 1,000

1	2	3	5	7	11	13	17	19	23
29	31	37	41	43	47	53	59	61	67
71	73	79	83	89	97	101	103	107	109
113	127	131	137	139	149	151	157	163	167
173	179	181	191	193	197	199	211	223	227
229	233	239	241	251	257	263	269	271	277
281	283	293	307	311	313	317	331	337	347
349	353	359	367	373	379	383	389	397	401
409	419	421	431	433	439	443	449	457	461
463	467	479	487	491	499	503	509	521	523
541	547	557	563	569	571	577	587	593	599
601	607	613	617	619	631	641	643	647	653
659	661	673	677	683	691	701	709	719	727
733	739	743	751	757	761	769	773	787	797
809	811	821	823	827	829	839	853	857	859
863	877	881	883	887	907	911	919	929	937
941	947	953	967	971	977	983	991	997	(1009)

Definitions of Gold Terminology

The term "fineness" defines a gold content in parts per thousand. For example, a gold nugget containing 885 parts of pure gold, 100 parts of silver, and 15 parts of copper would be considered 885-fine.

The word "karat" indicates the proportion of solid gold in an alloy based on a total of 24 parts. Thus, 14-karat (14K) gold indicates a composition of 14 parts of gold and 10 parts of other metals.

The term "gold-filled" is used to describe articles of jewelry made of base metal which are covered on one or more surfaces with a layer of gold alloy. No article having a gold alloy portion of less than one twentieth by weight may be marked "gold-filled." Articles may be marked "rolled gold plate" provided the proportional fraction and fineness designations are also shown.

Electroplated jewelry items carrying at least 7 millionths of an inch of gold on significant surfaces may be labeled "electroplate." Plate thicknesses less than this may be marked "gold flashed" or "gold washed."

Portraits and Designs of U.S. Paper Currency[1]

Currency	Portrait	Design on back
$1	Washington	ONE between observe and reverse of Great Seal of U.S.
$2[2]	Jefferson	Monticello
$2[3]	Jefferson	"The Signing of the Declaration of Independence"
$5	Lincoln	Lincoln Memorial
$10	Hamilton	U.S. Treasury Building
$20	Jackson	White House
$50	Grant	U.S. Capitol
$100	Franklin	Independence Hall
$500	McKinley	Ornate FIVE HUNDRED
$1,000	Cleveland	Ornate ONE THOUSAND
$5,000	Madison	Ornate FIVE THOUSAND
$10,000	Chase	Ornate TEN THOUSAND
$100,000[4]	Wilson	Ornate ONE HUNDRED THOUSAND

1. Denominations of $500 and higher were discontinued in 1969. 2. Discontinued in 1966. 3. New issue, April 13, 1976. 4. For use only in transactions between Federal Reserve System and Treasury Department.

CALENDAR & HOLIDAYS

1985

JANUARY

S	M	T	W	T	F	S
—	—	1	2	3	4	5
6	7	8	9	10	11	12
13	14	15	16	17	18	19
20	21	22	23	24	25	26
27	28	29	30	31		

FEBRUARY

S	M	T	W	T	F	S
—	—	—	—	—	1	2
3	4	5	6	7	8	9
10	11	12	13	14	15	16
17	18	19	20	21	22	23
24	25	26	27	28		

MARCH

S	M	T	W	T	F	S
—	—	—	—	—	1	2
3	4	5	6	7	8	9
10	11	12	13	14	15	16
17	18	19	20	21	22	23
24	25	26	27	28	29	30
31						

APRIL

S	M	T	W	T	F	S
—	1	2	3	4	5	6
7	8	9	10	11	12	13
14	15	16	17	18	19	20
21	22	23	24	25	26	27
28	29	30				

1—New Year's Day
6—Epiphany
15—Martin Luther King's Birthday

2—Groundhog Day
12—Lincoln's Birthday
14—St. Valentine's Day
20—Ash Wednesday
22—Washington's Birthday

7—Purim
17—St. Patrick's Day
31—Palm Sunday

5—Good Friday
6—1st Day of Passover
7—Easter
28—Daylight Savings Time begins

MAY

S	M	T	W	T	F	S
—	—	—	1	2	3	4
5	6	7	8	9	10	11
12	13	14	15	16	17	18
19	20	21	22	23	24	25
26	27	28	29	30	31	

JUNE

S	M	T	W	T	F	S
—	—	—	—	—	—	1
2	3	4	5	6	7	8
9	10	11	12	13	14	15
16	17	18	19	20	21	22
23	24	25	26	27	28	29
30						

JULY

S	M	T	W	T	F	S
—	1	2	3	4	5	6
7	8	9	10	11	12	13
14	15	16	17	18	19	20
21	22	23	24	25	26	27
28	29	30	31			

AUGUST

S	M	T	W	T	F	S
—	—	—	—	1	2	3
4	5	6	7	8	9	10
11	12	13	14	15	16	17
18	19	20	21	22	23	24
25	26	27	28	29	30	31

12—Mother's Day
16—Acension Day
21—1st Day of Ramadan
26—Pentecost
26—1st Day of Shabouth
30—Memorial Day

14—Flag Day
16—Father's Day

1—Dominion Day (Canada)
4—Independence Day

SEPTEMBER

S	M	T	W	T	F	S
1	2	3	4	5	6	7
8	9	10	11	12	13	14
15	16	17	18	19	20	21
22	23	24	25	26	27	28
29	30					

OCTOBER

S	M	T	W	T	F	S
—	—	1	2	3	4	5
6	7	8	9	10	11	12
13	14	15	16	17	18	19
20	21	22	23	24	25	26
27	28	29	30	31		

NOVEMBER

S	M	T	W	T	F	S
—	—	—	—	—	1	2
3	4	5	6	7	8	9
10	11	12	13	14	15	16
17	18	19	20	21	22	23
24	25	26	27	28	29	30

DECEMBER

S	M	T	W	T	F	S
1	2	3	4	5	6	7
8	9	10	11	12	13	14
15	16	17	18	19	20	21
22	23	24	25	26	27	28
29	30	31				

2—Labor Day
16—1st Day of Rosh Hashana
25—Yom Kippur
30—1st Day of Sukkoth

12—Columbus Day
14—Thanksgiving Day (Canada)
27—Daylight Savings Time ends
31—Halloween

1—All Saint's Day
5—Election Day
11—Veteran's Day
28—Thanksgiving Day

1—1st Sunday of Advent
8—1st Day of Hanukkah
25—Christmas

Seasons for the Northern Hemisphere, 1985

Eastern Standard Time

March 20, 11:14 a.m., sun enter sign of Aries; spring begins

June 21, 5:44 a.m., sun enters sign of Cancer, summer begins

Sept. 22, 9:07 p.m., sun enters sign of Libra; fall begins

Dec. 21, 5:08 p.m., sun enters sign of Capricorn; winter begins

1984

JANUARY

S	M	T	W	T	F	S
1	2	3	4	5	6	7
8	9	10	11	12	13	14
15	16	17	18	19	20	21
22	23	24	25	26	27	28
29	30	31				

FEBRUARY

S	M	T	W	T	F	S
—	—	—	1	2	3	4
5	6	7	8	9	10	11
12	13	14	15	16	17	18
19	20	21	22	23	24	25
26	27	28	29			

MARCH

S	M	T	W	T	F	S
—	—	—	—	1	2	3
4	5	6	7	8	9	10
11	12	13	14	15	16	17
18	19	20	21	22	23	24
25	26	27	28	29	30	31

APRIL

S	M	T	W	T	F	S
1	2	3	4	5	6	7
8	9	10	11	12	13	14
15	16	17	18	19	20	21
22	23	24	25	26	27	28
29	30					

MAY

S	M	T	W	T	F	S
—	—	1	2	3	4	5
6	7	8	9	10	11	12
13	14	15	16	17	18	19
20	21	22	23	24	25	26
27	28	29	30	31		

JUNE

S	M	T	W	T	F	S
—	—	—	—	—	1	2
3	4	5	6	7	8	9
10	11	12	13	14	15	16
17	18	19	20	21	22	23
24	25	26	27	28	29	30

JULY

S	M	T	W	T	F	S
1	2	3	4	5	6	7
8	9	10	11	12	13	14
15	16	17	18	19	20	21
22	23	24	25	26	27	28
29	30	31				

AUGUST

S	M	T	W	T	F	S
—	—	—	1	2	3	4
5	6	7	8	9	10	11
12	13	14	15	16	17	18
19	20	21	22	23	24	25
26	27	28	29	30	31	

SEPTEMBER

S	M	T	W	T	F	S
—	—	—	—	—	—	1
2	3	4	5	6	7	8
9	10	11	12	13	14	15
16	17	18	19	20	21	22
23	24	25	26	27	28	29
30						

OCTOBER

S	M	T	W	T	F	S
—	1	2	3	4	5	6
7	8	9	10	11	12	13
14	15	16	17	18	19	20
21	22	23	24	25	26	27
28	29	30	31			

NOVEMBER

S	M	T	W	T	F	S
—	—	—	—	1	2	3
4	5	6	7	8	9	10
11	12	13	14	15	16	17
18	19	20	21	22	23	24
25	26	27	28	29	30	

DECEMBER

S	M	T	W	T	F	S
—	—	—	—	—	—	1
2	3	4	5	6	7	8
9	10	11	12	13	14	15
16	17	18	19	20	21	22
23	24	25	26	27	28	29
30	31					

1986

JANUARY

S	M	T	W	T	F	S
			1	2	3	4
5	6	7	8	9	10	11
12	13	14	15	16	17	18
19	20	21	22	23	24	25
26	27	28	29	30	31	

FEBRUARY

S	M	T	W	T	F	S
—	—	—	—	—	—	1
2	3	4	5	6	7	8
9	10	11	12	13	14	15
16	17	18	19	20	21	22
23	24	25	26	27	28	

MARCH

S	M	T	W	T	F	S
—	—	—	—	—	—	1
2	3	4	5	6	7	8
9	10	11	12	13	14	15
16	17	18	19	20	21	22
23	24	25	26	27	28	29
30	31					

APRIL

S	M	T	W	T	F	S
—	—	1	2	3	4	5
6	7	8	9	10	11	12
13	14	15	16	17	18	19
20	21	22	23	24	25	26
27	28	29	30			

MAY

S	M	T	W	T	F	S
—	—	—	—	1	2	3
4	5	6	7	8	9	10
11	12	13	14	15	16	17
18	19	20	21	22	23	24
25	26	27	28	29	30	31

JUNE

S	M	T	W	T	F	S
1	2	3	4	5	6	7
8	9	10	11	12	13	14
15	16	17	18	19	20	21
22	23	24	25	26	27	28
29	30					

JULY

S	M	T	W	T	F	S
—	—	1	2	3	4	5
6	7	8	9	10	11	12
13	14	15	16	17	18	19
20	21	22	23	24	25	26
27	28	29	30	31		

AUGUST

S	M	T	W	T	F	S
—	—	—	—	—	1	2
3	4	5	6	7	8	9
10	11	12	13	14	15	16
17	18	19	20	21	22	23
24	25	26	27	28	29	30
31						

SEPTEMBER

S	M	T	W	T	F	S
—	1	2	3	4	5	6
7	8	9	10	11	12	13
14	15	16	17	18	19	20
21	22	23	24	25	26	27
28	29	30				

OCTOBER

S	M	T	W	T	F	S
—	—	—	1	2	3	4
5	6	7	8	9	10	11
12	13	14	15	16	17	18
19	20	21	22	23	24	25
26	27	28	29	30	31	

NOVEMBER

S	M	T	W	T	F	S
—	—	—	—	—	—	1
2	3	4	5	6	7	8
9	10	11	12	13	14	15
16	17	18	19	20	21	22
23	24	25	26	27	28	29
30						

DECEMBER

S	M	T	W	T	F	S
—	1	2	3	4	5	6
7	8	9	10	11	12	13
14	15	16	17	18	19	20
21	22	23	24	25	26	27
28	29	30	31			

PERPETUAL CALENDAR

1800 ..4	1844 ..9	1888 ..8	1932 .13	1976 .12	2020 .11
1801 ..5	1845 ..4	1889 ..3	1933 ..1	1977 ..7	2021 ..6
1802 ..6	1846 ..5	1890 ..4	1934 ..2	1978 ..1	2022 ..7
1803 ..7	1847 ..6	1891 ..5	1935 ..3	1979 ..2	2023 ..1
1804 ..8	1848 .14	1892 .13	1936 .11	1980 .10	2024 ..9
1805 ..3	1849 ..2	1893 ..1	1937 ..6	1981 ..5	2025 ..4
1806 ..4	1850 ..3	1894 ..2	1938 ..7	1982 ..6	2026 ..5
1807 ..5	1851 ..4	1895 ..3	1939 ..1	1983 ..7	2027 ..6
1808 .13	1852 .12	1896 .11	1940 ..9	1984 ..8	2028 .14
1809 ..1	1853 ..7	1897 ..6	1941 ..4	1985 ..3	2029 ..2
1810 ..2	1854 ..1	1898 ..7	1942 ..5	1986 ..4	2030 ..3
1811 ..3	1855 ..2	1899 ..1	1943 ..6	1987 ..5	2031 ..4
1812 .11	1856 .10	1900 ..2	1944 .14	1988 .13	2032 .12
1813 ..6	1857 ..5	1901 ..3	1945 ..2	1989 ..1	2033 ..7
1814 ..7	1858 ..6	1902 ..4	1946 ..3	1990 ..2	2034 ..1
1815 ..1	1859 ..7	1903 ..5	1947 ..4	1991 ..3	2035 ..2
1816 ..9	1860 ..8	1904 .13	1948 .12	1992 .11	2036 .10
1817 ..4	1861 ..3	1905 ..1	1949 ..7	1993 ..6	2037 ..5
1818 ..5	1862 ..4	1906 ..2	1950 ..1	1994 ..7	2038 ..6
1819 ..6	1863 ..5	1907 ..3	1951 ..2	1995 ..1	2039 ..7
1820 .14	1864 .13	1908 .11	1952 .10	1996 ..9	2040 ..8
1821 ..2	1865 ..1	1909 ..6	1953 ..5	1997 ..4	2041 ..3
1822 ..3	1866 ..2	1910 ..7	1954 ..6	1998 ..5	2042 ..4
1823 ..4	1867 ..3	1911 ..1	1955 ..7	1999 ..6	2043 ..5
1824 .12	1868 .11	1912 ..9	1956 ..8	2000 .14	2044 .13
1825 ..7	1869 ..6	1913 ..4	1957 ..3	2001 ..2	2045 ..1
1826 ..1	1870 ..7	1914 ..5	1958 ..4	2002 ..3	2046 ..2
1827 ..2	1871 ..1	1915 ..6	1959 ..5	2003 ..4	2047 ..3
1828 .10	1872 ..9	1916 .14	1960 .13	2004 .12	2048 .11
1829 ..5	1873 ..4	1917 ..2	1961 ..1	2005 ..7	2049 ..6
1830 ..6	1874 ..5	1918 ..3	1962 ..2	2006 ..1	2050 ..7
1831 ..7	1875 ..6	1919 ..4	1963 ..3	2007 ..2	2051 ..1
1832 ..8	1876 .14	1920 .12	1964 .11	2008 .10	2052 ..9
1833 ..3	1877 ..2	1921 ..7	1965 ..6	2009 ..5	2053 ..4
1834 ..4	1878 ..3	1922 ..1	1966 ..7	2010 ..6	2054 ..5
1835 ..5	1879 ..4	1923 ..2	1967 ..1	2011 ..7	2055 ..6
1836 .13	1880 .12	1924 .10	1968 ..9	2012 ..8	2056 .14
1837 ..1	1881 ..7	1925 ..5	1969 ..4	2013 ..3	2057 ..2
1838 ..2	1882 ..1	1926 ..6	1970 ..5	2014 ..4	2058 ..3
1839 ..3	1883 ..2	1927 ..7	1971 ..6	2015 ..5	2059 ..4
1840 .11	1884 .10	1928 ..8	1972 .14	2016 .13	2060 .12
1841 ..6	1885 ..5	1929 ..3	1973 ..2	2017 ..1	2061 ..7
1842 ..7	1886 ..6	1930 ..4	1974 ..3	2018 ..2	2062 ..1
1843 ..1	1887 ..7	1931 ..5	1975 ..4	2019 ..3	2063 ..2

DIRECTIONS: The number given with each year in the key above is number of calendar to use for that year

1

JANUARY

S	M	T	W	T	F	S
1	2	3	4	5	6	7
8	9	10	11	12	13	14
15	16	17	18	19	20	21
22	23	24	25	26	27	28
29	30	31				

FEBRUARY

S	M	T	W	T	F	S
			1	2	3	4
5	6	7	8	9	10	11
12	13	14	15	16	17	18
19	20	21	22	23	24	25
26	27	28				

MARCH

S	M	T	W	T	F	S
			1	2	3	4
5	6	7	8	9	10	11
12	13	14	15	16	17	18
19	20	21	22	23	24	25
26	27	28	29	30	31	

APRIL

S	M	T	W	T	F	S
						1
2	3	4	5	6	7	8
9	10	11	12	13	14	15
16	17	18	19	20	21	22
23	24	25	26	27	28	29
30						

MAY

S	M	T	W	T	F	S
	1	2	3	4	5	6
7	8	9	10	11	12	13
14	15	16	17	18	19	20
21	22	23	24	25	26	27
28	29	30	31			

JUNE

S	M	T	W	T	F	S
				1	2	3
4	5	6	7	8	9	10
11	12	13	14	15	16	17
18	19	20	21	22	23	24
25	26	27	28	29	30	

JULY

S	M	T	W	T	F	S
						1
2	3	4	5	6	7	8
9	10	11	12	13	14	15
16	17	18	19	20	21	22
23	24	25	26	27	28	29
30	31					

AUGUST

S	M	T	W	T	F	S
		1	2	3	4	5
6	7	8	9	10	11	12
13	14	15	16	17	18	19
20	21	22	23	24	25	26
27	28	29	30	31		

SEPTEMBER

S	M	T	W	T	F	S
					1	2
3	4	5	6	7	8	9
10	11	12	13	14	15	16
17	18	19	20	21	22	23
24	25	26	27	28	29	30

OCTOBER

S	M	T	W	T	F	S
1	2	3	4	5	6	7
8	9	10	11	12	13	14
15	16	17	18	19	20	21
22	23	24	25	26	27	28
29	30	31				

NOVEMBER

S	M	T	W	T	F	S
			1	2	3	4
5	6	7	8	9	10	11
12	13	14	15	16	17	18
19	20	21	22	23	24	25
26	27	28	29	30		

DECEMBER

S	M	T	W	T	F	S
					1	2
3	4	5	6	7	8	9
10	11	12	13	14	15	16
17	18	19	20	21	22	23
24	25	26	27	28	29	30
31						

2

JANUARY

S	M	T	W	T	F	S
	1	2	3	4	5	6
7	8	9	10	11	12	13
14	15	16	17	18	19	20
21	22	23	24	25	26	27
28	29	30	31			

FEBRUARY

S	M	T	W	T	F	S
				1	2	3
4	5	6	7	8	9	10
11	12	13	14	15	16	17
18	19	20	21	22	23	24
25	26	27	28			

MARCH

S	M	T	W	T	F	S
				1	2	3
4	5	6	7	8	9	10
11	12	13	14	15	16	17
18	19	20	21	22	23	24
25	26	27	28	29	30	31

APRIL

S	M	T	W	T	F	S
1	2	3	4	5	6	7
8	9	10	11	12	13	14
15	16	17	18	19	20	21
22	23	24	25	26	27	28
29	30					

MAY

S	M	T	W	T	F	S
		1	2	3	4	5
6	7	8	9	10	11	12
13	14	15	16	17	18	19
20	21	22	23	24	25	26
27	28	29	30	31		

JUNE

S	M	T	W	T	F	S
					1	2
3	4	5	6	7	8	9
10	11	12	13	14	15	16
17	18	19	20	21	22	23
24	25	26	27	28	29	30

JULY

S	M	T	W	T	F	S
1	2	3	4	5	6	7
8	9	10	11	12	13	14
15	16	17	18	19	20	21
22	23	24	25	26	27	28
29	30	31				

AUGUST

S	M	T	W	T	F	S
			1	2	3	4
5	6	7	8	9	10	11
12	13	14	15	16	17	18
19	20	21	22	23	24	25
26	27	28	29	30	31	

SEPTEMBER

S	M	T	W	T	F	S
						1
2	3	4	5	6	7	8
9	10	11	12	13	14	15
16	17	18	19	20	21	22
23	24	25	26	27	28	29
30						

OCTOBER

S	M	T	W	T	F	S
	1	2	3	4	5	6
7	8	9	10	11	12	13
14	15	16	17	18	19	20
21	22	23	24	25	26	27
28	29	30	31			

NOVEMBER

S	M	T	W	T	F	S
				1	2	3
4	5	6	7	8	9	10
11	12	13	14	15	16	17
18	19	20	21	22	23	24
25	26	27	28	29	30	

DECEMBER

S	M	T	W	T	F	S
						1
2	3	4	5	6	7	8
9	10	11	12	13	14	15
16	17	18	19	20	21	22
23	24	25	26	27	28	29
30	31					

3

JANUARY

S	M	T	W	T	F	S
		1	2	3	4	5
6	7	8	9	10	11	12
13	14	15	16	17	18	19
20	21	22	23	24	25	26
27	28	29	30	31		

FEBRUARY

S	M	T	W	T	F	S
					1	2
3	4	5	6	7	8	9
10	11	12	13	14	15	16
17	18	19	20	21	22	23
24	25	26	27	28		

MARCH

S	M	T	W	T	F	S
					1	2
3	4	5	6	7	8	9
10	11	12	13	14	15	16
17	18	19	20	21	22	23
24	25	26	27	28	29	30
31						

APRIL

S	M	T	W	T	F	S
	1	2	3	4	5	6
7	8	9	10	11	12	13
14	15	16	17	18	19	20
21	22	23	24	25	26	27
28	29	30				

MAY

S	M	T	W	T	F	S
			1	2	3	4
5	6	7	8	9	10	11
12	13	14	15	16	17	18
19	20	21	22	23	24	25
26	27	28	29	30	31	

JUNE

S	M	T	W	T	F	S
						1
2	3	4	5	6	7	8
9	10	11	12	13	14	15
16	17	18	19	20	21	22
23	24	25	26	27	28	29
30						

JULY

S	M	T	W	T	F	S
	1	2	3	4	5	6
7	8	9	10	11	12	13
14	15	16	17	18	19	20
21	22	23	24	25	26	27
28	29	30	31			

AUGUST

S	M	T	W	T	F	S
				1	2	3
4	5	6	7	8	9	10
11	12	13	14	15	16	17
18	19	20	21	22	23	24
25	26	27	28	29	30	31

SEPTEMBER

S	M	T	W	T	F	S
1	2	3	4	5	6	7
8	9	10	11	12	13	14
15	16	17	18	19	20	21
22	23	24	25	26	27	28
29	30					

OCTOBER

S	M	T	W	T	F	S
		1	2	3	4	5
6	7	8	9	10	11	12
13	14	15	16	17	18	19
20	21	22	23	24	25	26
27	28	29	30	31		

NOVEMBER

S	M	T	W	T	F	S
					1	2
3	4	5	6	7	8	9
10	11	12	13	14	15	16
17	18	19	20	21	22	23
24	25	26	27	28	29	30

DECEMBER

S	M	T	W	T	F	S
1	2	3	4	5	6	7
8	9	10	11	12	13	14
15	16	17	18	19	20	21
22	23	24	25	26	27	28
29	30	31				

4

JANUARY

S	M	T	W	T	F	S
			1	2	3	4
5	6	7	8	9	10	11
12	13	14	15	16	17	18
19	20	21	22	23	24	25
26	27	28	29	30	31	

FEBRUARY

S	M	T	W	T	F	S
						1
2	3	4	5	6	7	8
9	10	11	12	13	14	15
16	17	18	19	20	21	22
23	24	25	26	27	28	

MARCH

S	M	T	W	T	F	S
						1
2	3	4	5	6	7	8
9	10	11	12	13	14	15
16	17	18	19	20	21	22
23	24	25	26	27	28	29
30	31					

APRIL

S	M	T	W	T	F	S
		1	2	3	4	5
6	7	8	9	10	11	12
13	14	15	16	17	18	19
20	21	22	23	24	25	26
27	28	29	30			

MAY

S	M	T	W	T	F	S
				1	2	3
4	5	6	7	8	9	10
11	12	13	14	15	16	17
18	19	20	21	22	23	24
25	26	27	28	29	30	31

JUNE

S	M	T	W	T	F	S
1	2	3	4	5	6	7
8	9	10	11	12	13	14
15	16	17	18	19	20	21
22	23	24	25	26	27	28
29	30					

JULY

S	M	T	W	T	F	S
		1	2	3	4	5
6	7	8	9	10	11	12
13	14	15	16	17	18	19
20	21	22	23	24	25	26
27	28	29	30	31		

AUGUST

S	M	T	W	T	F	S
					1	2
3	4	5	6	7	8	9
10	11	12	13	14	15	16
17	18	19	20	21	22	23
24	25	26	27	28	29	30
31						

SEPTEMBER

S	M	T	W	T	F	S
	1	2	3	4	5	6
7	8	9	10	11	12	13
14	15	16	17	18	19	20
21	22	23	24	25	26	27
28	29	30				

OCTOBER

S	M	T	W	T	F	S
			1	2	3	4
5	6	7	8	9	10	11
12	13	14	15	16	17	18
19	20	21	22	23	24	25
26	27	28	29	30	31	

NOVEMBER

S	M	T	W	T	F	S
						1
2	3	4	5	6	7	8
9	10	11	12	13	14	15
16	17	18	19	20	21	22
23	24	25	26	27	28	29
30						

DECEMBER

S	M	T	W	T	F	S
	1	2	3	4	5	6
7	8	9	10	11	12	13
14	15	16	17	18	19	20
21	22	23	24	25	26	27
28	29	30	31			

5

JANUARY

S	M	T	W	T	F	S
				1	2	3
4	5	6	7	8	9	10
11	12	13	14	15	16	17
18	19	20	21	22	23	24
25	26	27	28	29	30	31

FEBRUARY

S	M	T	W	T	F	S
1	2	3	4	5	6	7
8	9	10	11	12	13	14
15	16	17	18	19	20	21
22	23	24	25	26	27	28

MARCH

S	M	T	W	T	F	S
1	2	3	4	5	6	7
8	9	10	11	12	13	14
15	16	17	18	19	20	21
22	23	24	25	26	27	28
29	30	31				

APRIL

S	M	T	W	T	F	S
			1	2	3	4
5	6	7	8	9	10	11
12	13	14	15	16	17	18
19	20	21	22	23	24	25
26	27	28	29	30		

MAY

S	M	T	W	T	F	S
					1	2
3	4	5	6	7	8	9
10	11	12	13	14	15	16
17	18	19	20	21	22	23
24	25	26	27	28	29	30
31						

JUNE

S	M	T	W	T	F	S
	1	2	3	4	5	6
7	8	9	10	11	12	13
14	15	16	17	18	19	20
21	22	23	24	25	26	27
28	29	30				

JULY

S	M	T	W	T	F	S
			1	2	3	4
5	6	7	8	9	10	11
12	13	14	15	16	17	18
19	20	21	22	23	24	25
26	27	28	29	30	31	

AUGUST

S	M	T	W	T	F	S
						1
2	3	4	5	6	7	8
9	10	11	12	13	14	15
16	17	18	19	20	21	22
23	24	25	26	27	28	29
30	31					

SEPTEMBER

S	M	T	W	T	F	S
		1	2	3	4	5
6	7	8	9	10	11	12
13	14	15	16	17	18	19
20	21	22	23	24	25	26
27	28	29	30			

OCTOBER

S	M	T	W	T	F	S
				1	2	3
4	5	6	7	8	9	10
11	12	13	14	15	16	17
18	19	20	21	22	23	24
25	26	27	28	29	30	31

NOVEMBER

S	M	T	W	T	F	S
1	2	3	4	5	6	7
8	9	10	11	12	13	14
15	16	17	18	19	20	21
22	23	24	25	26	27	28
29	30					

DECEMBER

S	M	T	W	T	F	S
		1	2	3	4	5
6	7	8	9	10	11	12
13	14	15	16	17	18	19
20	21	22	23	24	25	26
27	28	29	30	31		

6

JANUARY

S	M	T	W	T	F	S
					1	2
3	4	5	6	7	8	9
10	11	12	13	14	15	16
17	18	19	20	21	22	23
24	25	26	27	28	29	30
31						

FEBRUARY

S	M	T	W	T	F	S
	1	2	3	4	5	6
7	8	9	10	11	12	13
14	15	16	17	18	19	20
21	22	23	24	25	26	27
28						

MARCH

S	M	T	W	T	F	S
	1	2	3	4	5	6
7	8	9	10	11	12	13
14	15	16	17	18	19	20
21	22	23	24	25	26	27
28	29	30	31			

APRIL

S	M	T	W	T	F	S
				1	2	3
4	5	6	7	8	9	10
11	12	13	14	15	16	17
18	19	20	21	22	23	24
25	26	27	28	29	30	

MAY

S	M	T	W	T	F	S
						1
2	3	4	5	6	7	8
9	10	11	12	13	14	15
16	17	18	19	20	21	22
23	24	25	26	27	28	29
30	31					

JUNE

S	M	T	W	T	F	S
		1	2	3	4	5
6	7	8	9	10	11	12
13	14	15	16	17	18	19
20	21	22	23	24	25	26
27	28	29	30			

JULY

S	M	T	W	T	F	S
				1	2	3
4	5	6	7	8	9	10
11	12	13	14	15	16	17
18	19	20	21	22	23	24
25	26	27	28	29	30	31

AUGUST

S	M	T	W	T	F	S
1	2	3	4	5	6	7
8	9	10	11	12	13	14
15	16	17	18	19	20	21
22	23	24	25	26	27	28
29	30	31				

SEPTEMBER

S	M	T	W	T	F	S
			1	2	3	4
5	6	7	8	9	10	11
12	13	14	15	16	17	18
19	20	21	22	23	24	25
26	27	28	29	30		

OCTOBER

S	M	T	W	T	F	S
					1	2
3	4	5	6	7	8	9
10	11	12	13	14	15	16
17	18	19	20	21	22	23
24	25	26	27	28	29	30
31						

NOVEMBER

S	M	T	W	T	F	S
	1	2	3	4	5	6
7	8	9	10	11	12	13
14	15	16	17	18	19	20
21	22	23	24	25	26	27
28	29	30				

DECEMBER

S	M	T	W	T	F	S
			1	2	3	4
5	6	7	8	9	10	11
12	13	14	15	16	17	18
19	20	21	22	23	24	25
26	27	28	29	30	31	

7

JANUARY

S	M	T	W	T	F	S
						1
2	3	4	5	6	7	8
9	10	11	12	13	14	15
16	17	18	19	20	21	22
23	24	25	26	27	28	29
30	31					

FEBRUARY

S	M	T	W	T	F	S
		1	2	3	4	5
6	7	8	9	10	11	12
13	14	15	16	17	18	19
20	21	22	23	24	25	26
27	28					

MARCH

S	M	T	W	T	F	S
		1	2	3	4	5
6	7	8	9	10	11	12
13	14	15	16	17	18	19
20	21	22	23	24	25	26
27	28	29	30	31		

APRIL

S	M	T	W	T	F	S
					1	2
3	4	5	6	7	8	9
10	11	12	13	14	15	16
17	18	19	20	21	22	23
24	25	26	27	28	29	30

MAY

S	M	T	W	T	F	S
1	2	3	4	5	6	7
8	9	10	11	12	13	14
15	16	17	18	19	20	21
22	23	24	25	26	27	28
29	30	31				

JUNE

S	M	T	W	T	F	S
			1	2	3	4
5	6	7	8	9	10	11
12	13	14	15	16	17	18
19	20	21	22	23	24	25
26	27	28	29	30		

JULY

S	M	T	W	T	F	S
					1	2
3	4	5	6	7	8	9
10	11	12	13	14	15	16
17	18	19	20	21	22	23
24	25	26	27	28	29	30
31						

AUGUST

S	M	T	W	T	F	S
	1	2	3	4	5	6
7	8	9	10	11	12	13
14	15	16	17	18	19	20
21	22	23	24	25	26	27
28	29	30	31			

SEPTEMBER

S	M	T	W	T	F	S
				1	2	3
4	5	6	7	8	9	10
11	12	13	14	15	16	17
18	19	20	21	22	23	24
25	26	27	28	29	30	

OCTOBER

S	M	T	W	T	F	S
						1
2	3	4	5	6	7	8
9	10	11	12	13	14	15
16	17	18	19	20	21	22
23	24	25	26	27	28	29
30	31					

NOVEMBER

S	M	T	W	T	F	S
		1	2	3	4	5
6	7	8	9	10	11	12
13	14	15	16	17	18	19
20	21	22	23	24	25	26
27	28	29	30			

DECEMBER

S	M	T	W	T	F	S
				1	2	3
4	5	6	7	8	9	10
11	12	13	14	15	16	17
18	19	20	21	22	23	24
25	26	27	28	29	30	31

8

JANUARY

S	M	T	W	T	F	S
1	2	3	4	5	6	7
8	9	10	11	12	13	14
15	16	17	18	19	20	21
22	23	24	25	26	27	28
29	30	31				

FEBRUARY

S	M	T	W	T	F	S
			1	2	3	4
5	6	7	8	9	10	11
12	13	14	15	16	17	18
19	20	21	22	23	24	25
26	27	28	29			

MARCH

S	M	T	W	T	F	S
				1	2	3
4	5	6	7	8	9	10
11	12	13	14	15	16	17
18	19	20	21	22	23	24
25	26	27	28	29	30	31

APRIL

S	M	T	W	T	F	S
1	2	3	4	5	6	7
8	9	10	11	12	13	14
15	16	17	18	19	20	21
22	23	24	25	26	27	28
29	30					

MAY

S	M	T	W	T	F	S
		1	2	3	4	5
6	7	8	9	10	11	12
13	14	15	16	17	18	19
20	21	22	23	24	25	26
27	28	29	30	31		

JUNE

S	M	T	W	T	F	S
					1	2
3	4	5	6	7	8	9
10	11	12	13	14	15	16
17	18	19	20	21	22	23
24	25	26	27	28	29	30

JULY

S	M	T	W	T	F	S
1	2	3	4	5	6	7
8	9	10	11	12	13	14
15	16	17	18	19	20	21
22	23	24	25	26	27	28
29	30	31				

AUGUST

S	M	T	W	T	F	S
			1	2	3	4
5	6	7	8	9	10	11
12	13	14	15	16	17	18
19	20	21	22	23	24	25
26	27	28	29	30	31	

SEPTEMBER

S	M	T	W	T	F	S
						1
2	3	4	5	6	7	8
9	10	11	12	13	14	15
16	17	18	19	20	21	22
23	24	25	26	27	28	29
30						

OCTOBER

S	M	T	W	T	F	S
	1	2	3	4	5	6
7	8	9	10	11	12	13
14	15	16	17	18	19	20
21	22	23	24	25	26	27
28	29	30	31			

NOVEMBER

S	M	T	W	T	F	S
				1	2	3
4	5	6	7	8	9	10
11	12	13	14	15	16	17
18	19	20	21	22	23	24
25	26	27	28	29	30	

DECEMBER

S	M	T	W	T	F	S
						1
2	3	4	5	6	7	8
9	10	11	12	13	14	15
16	17	18	19	20	21	22
23	24	25	26	27	28	29
30	31					

9

JANUARY

S	M	T	W	T	F	S
	1	2	3	4	5	6
7	8	9	10	11	12	13
14	15	16	17	18	19	20
21	22	23	24	25	26	27
28	29	30	31			

FEBRUARY

S	M	T	W	T	F	S
				1	2	3
4	5	6	7	8	9	10
11	12	13	14	15	16	17
18	19	20	21	22	23	24
25	26	27	28	29		

MARCH

S	M	T	W	T	F	S
					1	2
3	4	5	6	7	8	9
10	11	12	13	14	15	16
17	18	19	20	21	22	23
24	25	26	27	28	29	30
31						

APRIL

S	M	T	W	T	F	S
	1	2	3	4	5	6
7	8	9	10	11	12	13
14	15	16	17	18	19	20
21	22	23	24	25	26	27
28	29	30				

MAY

S	M	T	W	T	F	S
			1	2	3	4
5	6	7	8	9	10	11
12	13	14	15	16	17	18
19	20	21	22	23	24	25
26	27	28	29	30	31	

JUNE

S	M	T	W	T	F	S
						1
2	3	4	5	6	7	8
9	10	11	12	13	14	15
16	17	18	19	20	21	22
23	24	25	26	27	28	29
30						

JULY

S	M	T	W	T	F	S
	1	2	3	4	5	6
7	8	9	10	11	12	13
14	15	16	17	18	19	20
21	22	23	24	25	26	27
28	29	30	31			

AUGUST

S	M	T	W	T	F	S
				1	2	3
4	5	6	7	8	9	10
11	12	13	14	15	16	17
18	19	20	21	22	23	24
25	26	27	28	29	30	31

SEPTEMBER

S	M	T	W	T	F	S
1	2	3	4	5	6	7
8	9	10	11	12	13	14
15	16	17	18	19	20	21
22	23	24	25	26	27	28
29	30					

OCTOBER

S	M	T	W	T	F	S
		1	2	3	4	5
6	7	8	9	10	11	12
13	14	15	16	17	18	19
20	21	22	23	24	25	26
27	28	29	30	31		

NOVEMBER

S	M	T	W	T	F	S
					1	2
3	4	5	6	7	8	9
10	11	12	13	14	15	16
17	18	19	20	21	22	23
24	25	26	27	28	29	30

DECEMBER

S	M	T	W	T	F	S
1	2	3	4	5	6	7
8	9	10	11	12	13	14
15	16	17	18	19	20	21
22	23	24	25	26	27	28
29	30	31				

10

JANUARY

S	M	T	W	T	F	S
		1	2	3	4	5
6	7	8	9	10	11	12
13	14	15	16	17	18	19
20	21	22	23	24	25	26
27	28	29	30	31		

FEBRUARY

S	M	T	W	T	F	S
					1	2
3	4	5	6	7	8	9
10	11	12	13	14	15	16
17	18	19	20	21	22	23
24	25	26	27	28	29	

MARCH

S	M	T	W	T	F	S
						1
2	3	4	5	6	7	8
9	10	11	12	13	14	15
16	17	18	19	20	21	22
23	24	25	26	27	28	29
30	31					

APRIL

S	M	T	W	T	F	S
		1	2	3	4	5
6	7	8	9	10	11	12
13	14	15	16	17	18	19
20	21	22	23	24	25	26
27	28	29	30			

MAY

S	M	T	W	T	F	S
				1	2	3
4	5	6	7	8	9	10
11	12	13	14	15	16	17
18	19	20	21	22	23	24
25	26	27	28	29	30	31

JUNE

S	M	T	W	T	F	S
1	2	3	4	5	6	7
8	9	10	11	12	13	14
15	16	17	18	19	20	21
22	23	24	25	26	27	28
29	30					

JULY

S	M	T	W	T	F	S
		1	2	3	4	5
6	7	8	9	10	11	12
13	14	15	16	17	18	19
20	21	22	23	24	25	26
27	28	29	30	31		

AUGUST

S	M	T	W	T	F	S
					1	2
3	4	5	6	7	8	9
10	11	12	13	14	15	16
17	18	19	20	21	22	23
24	25	26	27	28	29	30
31						

SEPTEMBER

S	M	T	W	T	F	S
	1	2	3	4	5	6
7	8	9	10	11	12	13
14	15	16	17	18	19	20
21	22	23	24	25	26	27
28	29	30				

OCTOBER

S	M	T	W	T	F	S
			1	2	3	4
5	6	7	8	9	10	11
12	13	14	15	16	17	18
19	20	21	22	23	24	25
26	27	28	29	30	31	

NOVEMBER

S	M	T	W	T	F	S
						1
2	3	4	5	6	7	8
9	10	11	12	13	14	15
16	17	18	19	20	21	22
23	24	25	26	27	28	29
30						

DECEMBER

S	M	T	W	T	F	S
	1	2	3	4	5	6
7	8	9	10	11	12	13
14	15	16	17	18	19	20
21	22	23	24	25	26	27
28	29	30	31			

11

JANUARY

S	M	T	W	T	F	S
			1	2	3	4
5	6	7	8	9	10	11
12	13	14	15	16	17	18
19	20	21	22	23	24	25
26	27	28	29	30	31	

FEBRUARY

S	M	T	W	T	F	S
						1
2	3	4	5	6	7	8
9	10	11	12	13	14	15
16	17	18	19	20	21	22
23	24	25	26	27	28	29

MARCH

S	M	T	W	T	F	S
1	2	3	4	5	6	7
8	9	10	11	12	13	14
15	16	17	18	19	20	21
22	23	24	25	26	27	28
29	30	31				

APRIL

S	M	T	W	T	F	S
			1	2	3	4
5	6	7	8	9	10	11
12	13	14	15	16	17	18
19	20	21	22	23	24	25
26	27	28	29	30		

MAY

S	M	T	W	T	F	S
					1	2
3	4	5	6	7	8	9
10	11	12	13	14	15	16
17	18	19	20	21	22	23
24	25	26	27	28	29	30
31						

JUNE

S	M	T	W	T	F	S
	1	2	3	4	5	6
7	8	9	10	11	12	13
14	15	16	17	18	19	20
21	22	23	24	25	26	27
28	29	30				

JULY

S	M	T	W	T	F	S
			1	2	3	4
5	6	7	8	9	10	11
12	13	14	15	16	17	18
19	20	21	22	23	24	25
26	27	28	29	30	31	

AUGUST

S	M	T	W	T	F	S
						1
2	3	4	5	6	7	8
9	10	11	12	13	14	15
16	17	18	19	20	21	22
23	24	25	26	27	28	29
30	31					

SEPTEMBER

S	M	T	W	T	F	S
		1	2	3	4	5
6	7	8	9	10	11	12
13	14	15	16	17	18	19
20	21	22	23	24	25	26
27	28	29	30			

OCTOBER

S	M	T	W	T	F	S
				1	2	3
4	5	6	7	8	9	10
11	12	13	14	15	16	17
18	19	20	21	22	23	24
25	26	27	28	29	30	31

NOVEMBER

S	M	T	W	T	F	S
1	2	3	4	5	6	7
8	9	10	11	12	13	14
15	16	17	18	19	20	21
22	23	24	25	26	27	28
29	30					

DECEMBER

S	M	T	W	T	F	S
		1	2	3	4	5
6	7	8	9	10	11	12
13	14	15	16	17	18	19
20	21	22	23	24	25	26
27	28	29	30	31		

12

JANUARY

S	M	T	W	T	F	S
				1	2	3
4	5	6	7	8	9	10
11	12	13	14	15	16	17
18	19	20	21	22	23	24
25	26	27	28	29	30	31

FEBRUARY

S	M	T	W	T	F	S
1	2	3	4	5	6	7
8	9	10	11	12	13	14
15	16	17	18	19	20	21
22	23	24	25	26	27	28
29						

MARCH

S	M	T	W	T	F	S
	1	2	3	4	5	6
7	8	9	10	11	12	13
14	15	16	17	18	19	20
21	22	23	24	25	26	27
28	29	30	31			

APRIL

S	M	T	W	T	F	S
				1	2	3
4	5	6	7	8	9	10
11	12	13	14	15	16	17
18	19	20	21	22	23	24
25	26	27	28	29	30	

MAY

S	M	T	W	T	F	S
						1
2	3	4	5	6	7	8
9	10	11	12	13	14	15
16	17	18	19	20	21	22
23	24	25	26	27	28	29
30	31					

JUNE

S	M	T	W	T	F	S
		1	2	3	4	5
6	7	8	9	10	11	12
13	14	15	16	17	18	19
20	21	22	23	24	25	26
27	28	29	30			

JULY

S	M	T	W	T	F	S
				1	2	3
4	5	6	7	8	9	10
11	12	13	14	15	16	17
18	19	20	21	22	23	24
25	26	27	28	29	30	31

AUGUST

S	M	T	W	T	F	S
1	2	3	4	5	6	7
8	9	10	11	12	13	14
15	16	17	18	19	20	21
22	23	24	25	26	27	28
29	30	31				

SEPTEMBER

S	M	T	W	T	F	S
			1	2	3	4
5	6	7	8	9	10	11
12	13	14	15	16	17	18
19	20	21	22	23	24	25
26	27	28	29	30		

OCTOBER

S	M	T	W	T	F	S
					1	2
3	4	5	6	7	8	9
10	11	12	13	14	15	16
17	18	19	20	21	22	23
24	25	26	27	28	29	30
31						

NOVEMBER

S	M	T	W	T	F	S
	1	2	3	4	5	6
7	8	9	10	11	12	13
14	15	16	17	18	19	20
21	22	23	24	25	26	27
28	29	30				

DECEMBER

S	M	T	W	T	F	S
			1	2	3	4
5	6	7	8	9	10	11
12	13	14	15	16	17	18
19	20	21	22	23	24	25
26	27	28	29	30	31	

13

JANUARY

S	M	T	W	T	F	S
					1	2
3	4	5	6	7	8	9
10	11	12	13	14	15	16
17	18	19	20	21	22	23
24	25	26	27	28	29	30
31						

FEBRUARY

S	M	T	W	T	F	S
	1	2	3	4	5	6
7	8	9	10	11	12	13
14	15	16	17	18	19	20
21	22	23	24	25	26	27
28	29					

MARCH

S	M	T	W	T	F	S
		1	2	3	4	5
6	7	8	9	10	11	12
13	14	15	16	17	18	19
20	21	22	23	24	25	26
27	28	29	30	31		

APRIL

S	M	T	W	T	F	S
					1	2
3	4	5	6	7	8	9
10	11	12	13	14	15	16
17	18	19	20	21	22	23
24	25	26	27	28	29	30

MAY

S	M	T	W	T	F	S
1	2	3	4	5	6	7
8	9	10	11	12	13	14
15	16	17	18	19	20	21
22	23	24	25	26	27	28
29	30	31				

JUNE

S	M	T	W	T	F	S
			1	2	3	4
5	6	7	8	9	10	11
12	13	14	15	16	17	18
19	20	21	22	23	24	25
26	27	28	29	30		

JULY

S	M	T	W	T	F	S
					1	2
3	4	5	6	7	8	9
10	11	12	13	14	15	16
17	18	19	20	21	22	23
24	25	26	27	28	29	30
31						

AUGUST

S	M	T	W	T	F	S
	1	2	3	4	5	6
7	8	9	10	11	12	13
14	15	16	17	18	19	20
21	22	23	24	25	26	27
28	29	30	31			

SEPTEMBER

S	M	T	W	T	F	S
				1	2	3
4	5	6	7	8	9	10
11	12	13	14	15	16	17
18	19	20	21	22	23	24
25	26	27	28	29	30	

OCTOBER

S	M	T	W	T	F	S
						1
2	3	4	5	6	7	8
9	10	11	12	13	14	15
16	17	18	19	20	21	22
23	24	25	26	27	28	29
30	31					

NOVEMBER

S	M	T	W	T	F	S
		1	2	3	4	5
6	7	8	9	10	11	12
13	14	15	16	17	18	19
20	21	22	23	24	25	26
27	28	29	30			

DECEMBER

S	M	T	W	T	F	S
				1	2	3
4	5	6	7	8	9	10
11	12	13	14	15	16	17
18	19	20	21	22	23	24
25	26	27	28	29	30	31

14

JANUARY

S	M	T	W	T	F	S
						1
2	3	4	5	6	7	8
9	10	11	12	13	14	15
16	17	18	19	20	21	22
23	24	25	26	27	28	29
30	31					

FEBRUARY

S	M	T	W	T	F	S
		1	2	3	4	5
6	7	8	9	10	11	12
13	14	15	16	17	18	19
20	21	22	23	24	25	26
27	28	29				

MARCH

S	M	T	W	T	F	S
			1	2	3	4
5	6	7	8	9	10	11
12	13	14	15	16	17	18
19	20	21	22	23	24	25
26	27	28	29	30	31	

APRIL

S	M	T	W	T	F	S
						1
2	3	4	5	6	7	8
9	10	11	12	13	14	15
16	17	18	19	20	21	22
23	24	25	26	27	28	29
30						

MAY

S	M	T	W	T	F	S
	1	2	3	4	5	6
7	8	9	10	11	12	13
14	15	16	17	18	19	20
21	22	23	24	25	26	27
28	29	30	31			

JUNE

S	M	T	W	T	F	S
				1	2	3
4	5	6	7	8	9	10
11	12	13	14	15	16	17
18	19	20	21	22	23	24
25	26	27	28	29	30	

JULY

S	M	T	W	T	F	S
						1
2	3	4	5	6	7	8
9	10	11	12	13	14	15
16	17	18	19	20	21	22
23	24	25	26	27	28	29
30	31					

AUGUST

S	M	T	W	T	F	S
		1	2	3	4	5
6	7	8	9	10	11	12
13	14	15	16	17	18	19
20	21	22	23	24	25	26
27	28	29	30	31		

SEPTEMBER

S	M	T	W	T	F	S
					1	2
3	4	5	6	7	8	9
10	11	12	13	14	15	16
17	18	19	20	21	22	23
24	25	26	27	28	29	30

OCTOBER

S	M	T	W	T	F	S
1	2	3	4	5	6	7
8	9	10	11	12	13	14
15	16	17	18	19	20	21
22	23	24	25	26	27	28
29	30	31				

NOVEMBER

S	M	T	W	T	F	S
			1	2	3	4
5	6	7	8	9	10	11
12	13	14	15	16	17	18
19	20	21	22	23	24	25
26	27	28	29	30		

DECEMBER

S	M	T	W	T	F	S
					1	2
3	4	5	6	7	8	9
10	11	12	13	14	15	16
17	18	19	20	21	22	23
24	25	26	27	28	29	30
31						

The Calendar

History of the Calendar

The purpose of a calendar is to reckon time in advance, to show how many days have to elapse until a certain event takes place—the harvest, a religious festival, or whatever. The earliest calendars, naturally, were crude, and they must have been strongly influenced by the geographical location of the people who made them. In the Scandinavian countries, for example, where the seasons are pronounced, the concept of the year was determined by the seasons, specifically by the end of winter. The Norsemen, before becoming Christians, are said to have had a calendar consisting of ten months of 30 days each.

But in warmer countries, where the seasons are less pronounced, the Moon became the basic unit for time reckoning; an old Jewish book actually makes the statement that "the Moon was created for the counting of the days." All the oldest calendars of which we have reliable information were lunar calendars, based on the time interval from one new moon to the next—a so-called "lunation." But even in a warm climate there are annual events that pay no attention to the phases of the Moon. In some areas it was a rainy season; in Egypt it was the annual flooding of the Nile. It was, therefore, necessary to regulate daily life and religious festivals by lunations, but to take care of the annual event in some other manner.

The calendar of the Assyrians was based on the phases of the Moon. The month began with the first appearance of the lunar crescent, and since this can best be observed in the evening, the day began with sunset. They knew that a lunation was 29 1/2 days long, so their lunar year had a duration of 354 days, falling eleven days short of the solar year.[1] After three years such a lunar calendar would be off by 33 days, or more than one lunation. We know that the Assyrians added an extra month from time to time, but we do not know whether they had developed a special rule for doing so or whether the priests proclaimed the necessity for an extra month from observation. If they made every third year a year of 13 lunations, their three-year period would cover 1,091 1/2 days (using their value of 29 1/2 days for one lunation), or just about four days too short. In one century this mistake would add up to 133 days by their reckoning (in reality closer to 134 days), requiring four extra lunations per century.

We now know that an eight-year period, consisting of five years with 12 months and three years with 13 months would lead to a difference of only 20 days per century, but we do not know whether such a calendar was actually used.

The best approximation that was possible in antiquity was a 19-year period, with seven of these 19 years having 13 months. This means that the period contained 235 months. This, still using the old value for a lunation, made a total of 6,932 1/2 days, while 19 solar years added up to 6,939.7 days, a difference of just one week per period and about five weeks per century. Even the 19-year period required constant adjustment, but it was the period that became the basis of the religious calendar of the Jews. The Arabs used the same calendar at first, but Mohammed forbade shifting from 12 months to 13 months, so that the Islamic religious calendar, even today, has a lunar year of 354 days. As a result the Islamic religious festivals run through all the seasons of the year three times per century.

The Egyptians had a traditional calendar with 12 months of 30 days each. At one time they added five extra days at the end of every year. These turned into a five-day festival because it was thought to be unlucky to work during that time.

When Rome emerged as a world power, the difficulties of making a calendar were well known, but the Romans complicated their lives because of their superstition that even numbers were unlucky. Hence their months were 29 or 31 days long, with the exception of February, which had 28 days. However, four months of 31 days, seven months of 29 days, and one month of 28 days added up to only 355 days. Therefore, the Romans invented an extra month called Mercedonius of 22 or 23 days. It was added every second year.

Even with Mercedonius, the Roman calendar was so far off that Caesar, advised by the astronomer Sosigenes, ordered a sweeping reform in 45 B.C. One year, made 445 days long by imperial decree, brought the calendar back in step with the seasons. Then the solar year (with the value of 365 days and 6 hours) was made the basis of the calendar. The months were 30 or 31 days in length, and to take care of the six hours, every fourth year was made a 366-day year. Moreover, Caesar decreed, the year began with the first of January, not with the vernal equinox in late March.

This was the Julian calendar, named after Julius Caesar. It is still the calendar of the Eastern Orthodox churches.

However, the year is 11 1/2 minutes shorter than the figure written into Caesar's calendar by Sosigenes, and after a number of centuries, even 11 1/2 minutes add up. *See* table.

While Caesar could decree that the vernal equinox should not be used as the first day of the new year, the vernal equinox is still a fact of Nature that could not be disregarded. One of the first (as far as we know) to become alarmed about this was Roger Bacon. He sent a memorandum to Pope Clement IV, who apparently was not impressed. But Pope Sixtus IV (reigned 1471 to 1484) decided that another reform was needed and called the German astronomer Regiomontanus to Rome to advise him. Regiomontanus arrived in 1475, but one year later he died in an epidemic, one of the recurrent outbreaks of the plague. The Pope himself survived, but his reform plans died with Regiomontanus.

Less than a hundred years later, in 1545, the Council of Trent authorized the then Pope, Gregory XIII, to reform the calendar once more. Most of the mathematical and astronomical work was done by Father Christopher Clavius, S.J. The immediate correction, advised by Father Clavius and ordered by Pope Gregory XIII, was that Thursday, Oct. 4, 1582, was to be the last day of the Julian calendar. The next day was Friday, with the date of October 15. For long-range accuracy, a formula suggested by the Vatican librarian Aloysius Giglio (latinized into Lilius) was adopted: every fourth year is a leap year *unless* it is a century year like 1700 or 1800. Century years can be leap years *only* when they are divisible by 400 (e.g., 1600).

1. The correct figures are: lunation: 29 d, 12 h, 44 min, 2.8 sec (29.530585 d); solar year: 365 d, 5 h, 48 min, 46 sec (365.242216 d); 12 lunations: 354 d, 8 h, 48 min, 34 sec (354.3671 d).

Drift of the Vernal Equinox in the Julian Calendar

Date	Julian year	Date	Julian year	Date	Julian year
March 21	325 A.D.	March 17	837 A.D.	March 13	1349 A.D.
March 20	453 A.D.	March 16	965 A.D.	March 12	1477 A.D.
March 19	581 A.D.	March 15	1093 A.D.	March 11	1605 A.D.
March 18	709 A.D.	March 14	1221 A.D.		

This rule eliminates three leap years in four centuries, making the calendar sufficiently correct for all ordinary purposes.

Unfortunately, all the Protestant princes in 1582 chose to ignore the papal bull; they continued with the Julian calendar. It was not until 1698 that the German professor Erhard Weigel persuaded the Protestant rulers of Germany and of the Netherlands to change to the new calendar. In England the shift took place in 1752, and in Russia it needed the revolution to introduce the Gregorian calendar in 1918.

The average year of the Gregorian calendar, in spite of the leap year rule, is about 26 seconds longer than the earth's orbital period. But this discrepancy will need 3,323 years to build up to a single day.

Modern proposals for calendar reform do not aim at a "better" calendar, but at one that is more convenient to use, especially for commercial purposes. A 365-day year cannot be divided into equal halves or quarters; the number of days per month is haphazard; the months begin or end in the middle of a week; a holiday fixed by date (e.g., the Fourth of July) will wander through a week; a holiday fixed in another manner (e.g., Easter) can fall on thirty-five possible dates. The Gregorian calendar, admittedly, keeps the calendar dates in reasonable unison with astronomical events, but it still is full of minor annoyances. Moreover, you need a calendar every year to look up dates; an ideal calendar should be one that you can memorize for one year and that is valid for all other years, too.

In 1834 an Italian priest, Marco Mastrofini, suggested taking one day out of every year. It would be made a holiday and *not* be given the name of a weekday. That would make every year begin with January 1 as a Sunday. The leap-year day would be treated the same way, so that in leap years there would be two unnamed holidays at the end of the year.

About a decade later the philosopher Auguste Comte also suggested a 364-day calendar with an extra day, which he called Year Day.

Since then there have been other unsuccessful attempts at calendar reform.

Time and Calendar

The two natural cycles on which time measurements are based are the year and the day. The year is defined as the time required for the Earth to complete one revolution around the Sun, while the day is the time required for the Earth to complete one turn upon its axis. Unfortunately the Earth needs 365 days plus about six hours to go around the Sun once, so that the year does not consist of so and so many days; the fractional day has to be taken care of by an extra day every fourth year.

But because the Earth, while turning upon its axis, also moves around the Sun there are two kinds of days. A day may be defined as the interval between the highest point of the Sun in the sky on two successive days. This, averaged out over the year, produces the customary 24-hour day. But one might also define a day as the time interval between the moments when a certain point in the sky, say a conveniently located star, is directly overhead. This is called:

Sidereal time. Astronomers use a point which they call the "vernal equinox" for the actual determination. Such a sidereal day is somewhat shorter than the "solar day," namely by about 3 minutes and 56 seconds of so-called "mean solar time."

Apparent solar time is the time based directly on the Sun's position in the sky. In ordinary life the day runs from midnight to midnight. It begins when the Sun is invisible by being 12 hours from its zenith. Astronomers use the so-called "Julian Day," which runs from noon to noon; the concept was invented by the astronomer Joseph Scaliger, who named it after his father Julius. To avoid the problems caused by leap-year days and so forth, Scaliger picked a conveniently remote date in the past and suggested just counting days without regard to weeks, months, and years. The Julian Day 2,440,225.5 is Jan. 1, 1969. The reason for having the Julian Day run from noon to noon is the practical one that astronomical observations usually extend across the midnight hour, which would require a change in date (or in the Julian Day number) if the astronomical day, like the civil day, ran from midnight to midnight.

Mean solar time, rather than apparent solar time, is what is actually used most of the time. The mean solar time is based on the position of a fictitious "mean sun." The reason why this fictitious sun has to be introduced is the following: the Earth turns on its axis regularly; it needs the same number of seconds regardless of the season. But the movement of the Earth around the Sun is not regular because the Earth's orbit is an ellipse. This has the result (as explained in the section The Seasons) that the Earth moves faster in January and slower in July. Though it is the Earth that changes velocity, it looks to us as if the Sun did. In January, when the Earth moves faster, the *apparent* movement of the Sun looks faster. The "mean sun" of time measurements, then, is a sun that moves regularly all year round; the real Sun will be either ahead of or behind the "mean sun." The difference between the real Sun and the fictitious mean sun is called the *equation of time.*

When the real Sun is west of the mean sun we have the "sun fast" condition, with the real Sun crossing the meridian ahead of the mean sun. The opposite is the "sun slow" situation when the real Sun crosses the meridian after the mean sun. Of course, what is observed is the real Sun. The equation of time is needed to establish mean solar time, kept by the reference clocks.

But if all clocks were actually set by mean solar time we would be plagued by a welter of time differences that would be "correct" but a major nuisance. A clock on Long Island, correctly showing mean solar time for its location (this would be *local*

The Names of the Days

Latin	Saxon	English	French	Italian	Spanish	German
Dies Solis	Sun's Day	Sunday	Dimanche	domenica	domingo	Sonntag
Dies Lunae	Moon's Day	Monday	Lundi	lunedi	lunes	Montag
Dies Martis	Tiw's Day	Tuesday	Mardi	martedi	martes	Dienstag
Dies Mercurii	Woden's Day	Wednesday	Mercredi	mercoledi	miércoles	Mittwoch
Dies Jovis	Thor's Day	Thursday	Jeudi	giovedi	jueves	Donnerstag
Dies Veneris	Frigg's Day	Friday	Vendredi	venedri	viernes	Freitag
Dies Saturni	Seterne's Day	Saturday	Samedi	sabato	sábado	Sonnabend

NOTE: The Romans gave one day of the week to each planet known, the Sun and Moon being considered planets in this connection. The Saxon names are a kind of translation of the Roman names: Tiw was substituted for Mars, Woden (Wotan) for Mercury, Thor for Jupiter (Jove), Frigg for Venus, and Seterne for Saturn. The English names are adapted Saxon. The Spanish and Italian names, which are normally not capitalized, and the French are derived from the Latin. The German names follow the Saxon pattern with two exceptions: Wednesday is Mittwoch (Middle of the Week), and Saturday is Sonnabend (Sunday's Eve).

civil time), would be slightly ahead of a clock in Newark, N.J. The Newark clock would be slightly ahead of a clock in Trenton, N.J., which, in turn, would be ahead of a clock in Philadelphia. This condition actually prevailed in the past until 1883, when *standard time* was introduced. Standard time is the correct mean solar time for a designated meridian, and this time is used for a certain area to the east and west of this meridian. In the U.S. four meridians have been designated to supply standard times; they are 75°, 90°, 105°, and 120° west of Greenwich. The 75° meridian determines Eastern Standard Time. It happens to run through Camden, N.J., where standard time, therefore, is also mean solar time and local civil time. The 90° meridian (which happens to pass through the western part of Memphis, Tenn.) determines Central Standard Time, the 105° meridian (passing through Denver) determines Mountain Standard Time, and the 120° meridian (which runs through Lake Tahoe) determines Pacific Standard Time.

Canada, extending over more territory from west to east, adds one time zone on either side: Atlantic Standard Time (based on 60° west of Greenwich) for New Brunswick, Nova Scotia, and Quebec, and Yukon Standard Time (determined by the 135° meridian) for its extreme West. Alaska, extending still farther to the west, adds two more time zones, Alaska Standard Time (determined by the 150° meridian that passes through Anchorage) and Nome Standard Time, based on the 165° meridian just east of Nome.

In general the Earth is divided into 24 such time zones, which run one hour apart. For practical purposes the time zones sometimes show indentations, and there are a few "subzones" that differ from the neighboring zone by only half an hour, e.g., Newfoundland.

The date line. While the time zones are based on the natural event of the Sun crossing the meridian, the date must be an arbitrary decision. The meridians are traditionally counted from the meridian of the observatory of Greenwich in England, which is called the zero meridian. The logical place for changing the date is 12 hours, or 180° from Greenwich. Fortunately, the 180th meridian runs mostly through the open Pacific. The date line makes a zigzag in the north to incorporate the eastern tip of Siberia into the Siberian time system and then another one to incorporate a number of islands into the Alaska time system. In the south there is a similar zigzag for the purpose of tying a number of British-owned islands to the New Zealand time system. Otherwise the date line is the same as 180° from Greenwich. At points to the east of the date line the calendar is one day earlier than at points to the west of it. A traveller going eastward across the date line from one island to another would not have to re-set his watch because he would stay inside the time zone (provided he does so where the date line does *not* coincide with the 180° meridian), but it would be the same time of the previous day.

The Seasons

The seasons are caused by the tilt of the Earth's axis (23.4°) and not by the fact that the Earth's orbit around the Sun is an ellipse. The average distance of the Earth from the Sun is 93 million miles; the difference between aphelion (farthest away) and perihelion (closest to the Sun) is 3 million miles, so that perihelion is about 91.4 million miles from the Sun. The Earth goes through the perihelion point a few days after New Year, just when the northern hemisphere has winter. Aphelion is passed during the first days in July. This by itself shows that the

The Names of the Months

January: named after Janus, protector of the gateway to heaven
February: named after Februalia, a time period when sacrifices were made to atone for sins
March: named after Mars, the god of war, presumably signifying that the campaigns interrupted by the winter could be resumed
April: from *aperire,* Latin for "to open" (buds)
May: named after Maia, the goddess of growth of plants
June: from *juvenis,* Latin for "youth"
July: named after Julius Caesar
August: named after Augustus, the first Roman Emperor
September: from *septem,* Latin for "seven"
October: from *octo,* Latin for "eight"
November: from *novem,* Latin for "nine"
December: from *decem,* Latin for "ten"

NOTE: The earliest Latin calendar was a 10-month one; thus September was the seventh month, October, the eighth, etc. July was originally called Quintilis, as the fifth month; August was originally called Sextilis, as the sixth month.

distance from the Sun is not important within these limits. What is important is that when the Earth passes through perihelion, the northern end of the Earth's axis happens to tilt away from the Sun, so that the areas beyond the Tropic of Cancer receive only slanting rays from a Sun low in the sky.

The tilt of the Earth's axis is responsible for four lines you find on every globe. When, say, the North Pole is tilted away from the Sun as much as possible, the farthest points in the North which can still be reached by the Sun's rays are 23 1/2° from the pole. This is the Arctic Circle. The Antarctic Circle is the corresponding limit 23.4° from the South Pole; the Sun's rays cannot reach beyond this point when we have mid-summer in the North.

When the Sun is vertically above the equator, the day is of equal length all over the Earth. This happens twice a year, and these are the "equinoxes" in March and in September. After having been over the equator in March, the Sun will seem to move northward. The northernmost point where the Sun can be straight overhead is 23.4° north of the equator. This is the Tropic of Cancer; the Sun can never be vertically overhead to the north of this line. Similarly the Sun cannot be vertically overhead to the south of a line 23.4° south of the equator—the Tropic of Capricorn.

This explains the climatic zones. In the belt (the Greek word *zone* means "belt") between the Tropic of Cancer and the Tropic of Capricorn, the Sun can be straight overhead; this is the tropical zone. The two zones where the Sun cannot be overhead but will be above the horizon every day of the year are the two temperate zones; the two areas where the Sun will not rise at all for varying lengths of time are the two polar areas, Arctic and Antarctic.

Holidays

Religious and Secular, 1985

Since 1971, by federal law, Washington's Birthday, Memorial Day, Columbus Day, and Veterans' Day have been celebrated on Mondays to create three-day weekends for federal employees. Many states now observe these holidays on the same Mondays. (*See* page 379). The dates given for the holidays listed below are the traditional ones.

New Year's Day, Tuesday, Jan. 1. A legal holiday in all states and the District of Columbia, New Year's Day has its origin in Roman Times, when sacrifices were offered to Janus, the two-faced Roman deity who looked back on the past and forward to the future.

Epiphany, Sunday, Jan. 6. Falls the twelfth day after Christmas and commemorates the manifestation of Jesus as the Son of God, as represented by the adoration of the Magi, the baptism of Jesus, and the miracle of the wine at the marriage feast at Cana. Epiphany originally marked the beginning of the carnival season preceding Lent, and the evening (sometimes the eve) is known as Twelfth Night.

Martin Luther King, Jr.'s Birthday, Tuesday, Jan. 15. Will become a legal public holiday in 1986 honoring the late civil rights leader.

Lincoln's Birthday, Tuesday, Feb. 12. A legal holiday in many states, this day was first formally observed in Washington, D.C., in 1866, when both houses of Congress gathered for a memorial address in tribute to the assassinated President.

St. Valentine's Day, Thursday, Feb. 14. This day is the festival of two third-century martyrs, both named St. Valentine. It is not known why this day is associated with lovers. It may derive from an old pagan festival about this time of year, or it may have been inspired by the belief that birds mate on this day.

Shrove Tuesday, February 19. Falls the day before Ash Wednesday and marks the end of the carnival season, which once began on Epiphany but is now usually celebrated the last three days before Lent. In France, the day is known as Mardi Gras (Fat Tuesday), and Mardi Gras celebrations are also held in several American cities, particularly in New Orleans. The day is sometimes called Pancake Tuesday by the English because fats, which were prohibited during Lent, had to be used up.

Ash Wednesday, February 20, The first day of the Lenten season, which lasts 40 days. Having its origin sometime before A.D. 1000, it is a day of public penance and is marked in the Roman Catholic Church by the burning of the palms blessed on the previous year's Palm Sunday. With his thumb, the priest then marks a cross upon the forehead of each worshipper. The Anglican Church and a few Protestant groups in the United States also observe the day, but generally without the use of ashes.

Washington's Birthday, Friday, Feb. 22. The birthday of George Washington is celebrated as a legal holiday in every state of the Union, the District of Columbia, and all territories. The observance began in 1796.

Purim (Feast of Lots), Thursday, March 7. A day of joy and feasting celebrating deliverance of the Jews from a massacre planned by the Persian Minister Haman. The Jewish Queen Esther interceded with her husband, King Ahasuerus, to spare the life of her uncle, Mordecai, and Haman was hanged on the same gallows he had built for Mordecai. The holiday is marked by the reading of the Book of Esther (megillah), and by the exchange of gifts, donations to the poor, and the presentation of Purim plays.

St. Patrick's Day, Sunday, March 17. St. Patrick, patron saint of Ireland, has been honored in America since the first days of the nation. There are many dinners and meetings but perhaps the most notable part of the observance is the annual St. Patrick's Day parade on Fifth Avenue in New York City.

Palm Sunday, March 31. Is observed the Sunday before Easter to commemorate the entry of Jesus into Jerusalem. The procession and the ceremonies introducing the benediction of palms probably had their origin in Jerusalem.

First Day of Passover (Pesach), Saturday, April 6.

The Feast of the Passover, also called the Feast of Unleavened Bread, commemorates the escape of the Jews from Egypt. As the Jews fled they ate unleavened bread, and from that time the Jews have allowed no leavening in the houses during Passover, bread being replaced by matzoth.

Good Friday, April 5. This day commemorates the Crucifixion, which is retold during services from the Gospel according to St. John. A feature in Roman Catholic churches is the Liturgy of the Passion; there is no Consecration, the Host having been consecrated the previous day. The eating of hot cross buns on this day is said to have started in England.

Easter Sunday, April 7. Observed in all Christian churches, Easter commemorates the Resurrection of Jesus. It is celebrated on the first Sunday after the full moon which occurs on or next after March 21 and is therefore celebrated between March 22 and April 25 inclusive. This date was fixed by the Council of Nicaea in A.D. 325. The Orthodox Church celebrates Easter on April 14, 1985.

Ascension Day, Thursday, May 16. Took place in the presence of His apostles 40 days after the Resurrection of Jesus. It is traditionally held to have occurred on Mount Olivet in Bethany.

First Day of Shavuot (Hebrew Pentecost), Sunday, May 26. This festival, sometimes called the Feast of Weeks, or of Harvest, or of the First Fruits, falls 50 days after Passover and originally celebrated the end of the seven-week grain harvesting season. In later tradition, it also celebrated the giving of the Law to Moses on Mount Sinai.

Pentecost (Whitsunday), May 26. This day commemorates the descent of the Holy Ghost upon the apostles 50 days after the Resurrection. The sermon by the Apostle Peter, which led to the baptism of 3,000 who professed belief, originated the ceremonies that have since been followed. "Whitsunday" is believed to have come from "white Sunday" when, among the English, white robes were worn by those baptized on the day.

Memorial Day, Thursday, May 30. Also known as Decoration Day, Memorial Day is a legal holiday in most of the states and in the territories, and is also observed by the armed forces. In 1868, Gen. John A. Logan, Commander in Chief of the Grand Army of the Republic, issued an order designating the day as one in which the graves of soldiers would be decorated. The holiday was originally devoted to honoring the memory of those who fell in the Civil War, but is now also dedicated to the memory of all war dead.

Flag Day, Friday, June 14. This day commemorates the adoption by the Continental Congress on June 14, 1777, of the Stars and Stripes as the U.S. flag. Although it is a legal holiday only in Pennsylvania, President Truman, on Aug. 3, 1949, signed a bill requesting the President to call for its observance each year by proclamation.

Independence Day, Thursday, July 4. The day of the adoption of the Declaration of Independence in 1776, celebrated in all states and territories. The observance began the next year in Philadelphia.

Labor Day, Monday, Sept. 2. Observed the first Monday in September in all states and territories, Labor Day was first celebrated in New York in 1882 under the sponsorship of the Central Labor Union, following the suggestion of Peter J. McGuire, of the Knights of Labor, that the day be set aside in honor of labor.

First Day of Rosh Hashana (Jewish New Year), Monday, Sept. 16. This day marks the beginning of the Jewish year 5746 and opens the Ten Days of Penitence closing with Yom Kippur.

Yom Kippur (Day of Atonement), Wednesday, Sept. 25. This day marks the end of the Ten Days of Penitence that began with Rosh Hashana. It is described in *Leviticus* as a "Sabbath of rest," and synagogue services begin the preceding sundown, resume the following morning, and continue to sundown.

First Day of Sukkot (Feast of Tabernacles) Monday, Sept. 30. This festival, also known as the Feast of the Ingathering, originally celebrated the fruit harvest, and the name comes from the booths or tabernacles in which the Jews lived during the harvest, although one tradition traces it to the shelters used by the Jews in their wandering through the wilderness. During the festival many Jews build small huts in their back yards or on the roofs of their houses.

Simhat Torah (Rejoicing of the Law), Tuesday, Oct. 8. This joyous holiday falls on the eighth day of Sukkot. It marks the end of the year's reading of the Torah (Five Books of Moses) in the synagogue every Saturday and the beginning of the new cycle of reading.

Columbus Day, Saturday, Oct. 12. A legal holiday in many states, commemorating the discovery of America by Columbus in 1492. Quite likely the first celebration of Columbus Day was that organized in 1792 by the Society of St. Tammany, or Columbian Order, more widely known as Tammany Hall.

Halloween, Thursday, Oct. 31. Eve of All Saints' Day, formerly called All Hallows and Hallowmass. Halloween is traditionally associated in some countries with old customs such as bonfires, masquerading, and the telling of ghost stories. These are old Celtic practices that marked the beginning of winter.

All Saints' Day, Friday, Nov. 1. A Roman Catholic and Anglican holiday celebrating all saints, known and unknown.

Election Day, (legal holiday in certain states), Tuesday, Nov. 5. Since 1845, by Act of Congress, the first Tuesday after the first Monday in November is the date for choosing Presidential electors. State elections are also generally held on this day.

Veterans Day, Monday, Nov. 11. Armistice Day was established in 1926 to commemorate the signing in 1918 of the Armistice ending World War I. On June 1, 1954, the name was changed to Veterans Day to honor all men and women who have served America in its armed forces.

Thanksgiving, Thursday, Nov. 28. Observed nationally on the fourth Thursday in November by Act of Congress (1941), the first such national proclamation having been issued by President Lincoln in 1863, on the urging of Mrs. Sarah J. Hale, editor of *Godey's Lady's Book.* Most Americans believe that the holiday dates back to the day of thanks ordered by Governor Bradford of Plymouth Colony in New England in 1621, but scholars point out that days of thanks stem from ancient times.

First Sunday of Advent, Dec. 1. Advent is the season in which the faithful must prepare themselves for the advent of the Saviour on Christmas. The four Sundays before Christmas are marked by special church services.

First Day of Hanukkah (Festival of Lights), Saturday, Dec. 8. This festival was instituted by Judas Maccabaeus in 165 B.C. to celebrate the purification of the Temple of Jerusalem, which had been desecrated three years earlier by Antiochus Epiphanes, who set up a pagan altar and offered sacrifices to Zeus Olympius. In Jewish homes, a light is lighted on each night of the eight-day festival.

Christmas (Feast of the Nativity), Wednesday, Dec. 25. The most widely celebrated holiday of the Christian year, Christmas is observed as the anniversary of the birth of Jesus. Christmas customs are centuries old. The mistletoe, for example, comes from the Druids, who, in hanging the mistletoe, hoped for peace and good fortune. Use of such plants as holly comes from the ancient belief that such plants blossomed at Christmas. Comparatively recent is the Christmas tree, first set up in

National Holidays Around the World, 1985

Country	Date	Country	Date	Country	Date
Afghanistan	Aug. 19	Greece	March 25	Papua New Guinea	Sept. 16
Albania	Nov. 29	Grenada	Feb. 7	Paraguay	May 14
Algeria	Nov. 1	Guatemala	Sept. 15	Peru	July 28
Angola	Nov. 11	Guinea	Oct. 2	Philippines	June 12
Antigua and Barbuda	Nov. 1	Guinea-Bissau	Sept. 12	Poland	July 22
Argentina	May 25	Guyana	Feb. 23	Portugal	June 10
Australia	Jan. 26	Haiti	Jan. 1	Qatar	Sept. 3
Austria	Oct. 26	Honduras	Sept. 15	Romania	Aug. 23
Bahamas	July 10	Hungary	April 4	Rwanda	July 1
Bahrain	Dec. 16	Iceland	June 17	St. Lucia	Dec. 13
Bangladesh	March 26	India	Jan. 26	St. Vincent and	
Barbados	Nov. 30	Indonesia	Aug. 17	the Grenadines	Oct. 27
Belgium	July 21	Iran	April 1	Sao Tomé and Príncipe	July 12
Belize	Sept. 20	Iraq	July 14	Saudi Arabia	Sept. 23
Benin	Nov. 30	Ireland	March 17	Senegal	April 4
Bhutan	Dec. 17	Israel	April 25[1]	Seychelles	June 5
Bolivia	Aug. 6	Italy	June 2	Sierra Leone	April 19
Botswana	Sept. 30	Ivory Coast	Dec. 7	Singapore	Aug. 9
Brazil	Sept. 7	Jamaica	Aug. 5[2]	Somalia	Oct. 21
Bulgaria	Sept. 9	Japan	April 29	South Africa	May 31
Burma	Jan. 4	Jordan	May 25	Spain	Oct. 12
Burundi	July 1	Kenya	Dec. 12	Sri Lanka	Feb. 4
Cambodia	April 17	Kuwait	Feb. 25	Sudan	Jan. 1
Cameroon	May 20	Laos	Dec. 2	Suriname	Nov. 25
Canada	July 1	Lebanon	Nov. 22	Swaziland	Sept. 6
Cape Verde	Sept. 12	Lesotho	Oct. 4	Sweden	April 30
Central African Republic	Dec. 1	Liberia	July 26	Syria	April 17
Chad	April 13	Libya	Sept. 1	Tanzania	April 26
Chile	Sept. 18	Luxembourg	June 23	Thailand	Dec. 5
China	Oct. 1	Madagascar	June 26	Togo	April 27
Colombia	July 20	Malawi	July 6	Trinidad and Tobago	Aug. 31
Congo	Aug. 15	Malaysia	Aug. 31	Tunisia	June 1
Costa Rica	Sept. 15	Maldives	July 26	Turkey	Oct. 29
Cuba	Jan. 1	Mali	Sept. 22	Uganda	Oct. 9
Cyprus	Oct. 1	Malta	March 31	U.S.S.R.	Nov. 7
Czechoslovakia	May 9	Mauritania	Nov. 28	United Arab Emirates	Dec. 2
Denmark	April 16	Mauritius	March 12	United States	July 4
Djibouti	June 27	Mexico	Sept. 16	Upper Volta	Dec. 11
Dominican Republic	Feb. 27	Mongolia	July 11	Uruguay	Aug. 25
Ecuador	Aug. 10	Morocco	March 3	Venezuela	July 5
Egypt	July 23	Mozambique	June 25	Vietnam	Sept. 2
El Salvador	Sept. 15	Nepal	Dec. 28	Western Samoa	June 1
Equatorial Guinea	March 5	Netherlands	April 30	Yemen, People's Dem.	
Ethiopia	Sept. 12	New Zealand	Feb. 6	Republic of	Oct. 14
Fiji	Oct. 10	Nicaragua	Sept. 15	Yemen Arab Republic	Sept. 26
Finland	Dec. 6	Niger	Dec. 18	Yugoslavia	Nov. 29
France	July 14	Nigeria	Oct. 1	Zaire	June 30
Gabon	Aug. 17	Norway	May 17	Zambia	Oct. 24
Gambia	Feb. 18	Oman	Nov. 18	Zimbabwe	April 18
Germany, East	Oct. 7	Pakistan	March 23		
Ghana	March 6	Panama	Nov. 3		

1. Changes yearly according to Hebrew calendar. 2. Celebrated on first Monday in August. *Source:* United Nations.

Germany in the 17th century, and the use of candles on trees developed from the belief that candles appeared by miracle on the trees at Christmas. Colonial Manhattan Islanders introduced the name Santa Claus, a corruption of the Dutch name for the 4th-century Asia Minor St. Nicholas.

Legal Holidays in the 50 States, D.C., and Puerto Rico

HOLIDAYS WIDELY OBSERVED

January 1, New Year's Day: All states, D.C., Puerto Rico.

February 12, Lincoln's Birthday: Alaska, California, Connecticut, Florida, Illinois, Indiana, Iowa, Kansas, Kentucky, Maryland, Michigan, Missouri, Montana, New Jersey, New Mexico, New York, Utah, Vermont, Washington, West Virginia.

February (first Monday), Lincoln's Birthday: Delaware, Oregon.

February (second Monday), Lincoln Day: Arizona.

February (third Monday), Washington's Birthday: All states,[3] D.C., Puerto Rico. Called **Washington Day** in Arizona. Called **Presidents' Day** in Hawaii, Nebraska, Pennsylvania, Colorado. Called **Washington-Lincoln Day** in Minnesota, Ohio, South Dakota, Wisconsin, Wyoming.

May 25, Memorial Day: New Mexico.

May 28, Memorial Day: Puerto Rico.

May 30, Memorial Day: Delaware,[2] Illinois, Maryland, New Hampshire, South Dakota, Vermont.

May (last Monday), Memorial Day: All states,[3] D.C., except those listed above, and Alabama, Mississippi, South Carolina.

July 4, Independence Day: All states, D.C., Puerto Rico.

September (1st Monday), Labor Day: All states, D.C., Puerto Rico.

October 12, Columbus Day: Maryland, Puerto Rico.

October (2nd Monday), Columbus Day: All states,[2] D.C., except Alaska, Iowa, Maryland, Mississippi, Nevada, N.J., North Carolina, North Dakota, Oregon, South Carolina, Washington, Puerto Rico. Also called **Fraternal Day** in Alabama. Called **Discoverers' Day** in Hawaii, **Farmers' Day** in Florida, **Pioneers' Day** in South Dakota.

November (4th Thursday), Thanksgiving Day: All states, D.C., Puerto Rico.

November, Day after Thanksgiving: Alabama,[3] Illinois, Nebraska, New Hampshire, Oklahoma, Washington.

November (first Tuesday after the first Monday), Election Day: Arkansas, California, D.C., Delaware, Florida, Hawaii, Idaho, Illinois, Indiana, Kentucky,[5] Louisiana, Maryland, Missouri, Montana, New Hampshire, New Jersey, New York, Oklahoma, Pennsylvania, Rhode Island, South Carolina, Tennessee, Texas, Vermont[6], Virginia, West Virginia, Wisconsin, Wyoming, Puerto Rico.

November 11, Veterans' Day: All states, D.C., Puerto Rico. Called **Armistice Day** and **Veterans' Day** in New Mexico.

December 25, Christmas: All states, D.C., Puerto Rico.

OTHER HOLIDAYS

January 6, Three Kings' Day: Puerto Rico,[3]

January 8, Battle of New Orleans Day: Louisiana.

January 11, De Hostos' Birthday: Puerto Rico.

January 15, Martin Luther King Day: Arkansas,[4] California, Colorado,[7] Connecticut, D.C., Florida, Illinois, Kentucky, Louisiana,[3] Maryland, Massachusetts, New Jersey, Minnesota, Oklahoma, Pennsylvania, South Carolina,[1], Michigan,[2] West Virginia, Wisconsin.

January 19, Robert E. Lee's Birthday: Arkansas[4] Florida, Georgia, Kentucky, Louisiana,[3] South Carolina.[1] Called **Confederate Heroes Day** in Texas.

January (third Sunday), Martin Luther King Day: New York.

January (third Monday), Martin Luther King Day: Kansas, Ohio.

January (third Monday), Robert E. Lee's Birthday: Alabama, Mississippi. **Lee-Jackson Day** in Virginia.

January 30, F. D. Roosevelt's Birthday: Kentucky.

February or March (1 day before Ash Wednesday), Mardi Gras (Shrove Tuesday): Alabama, Louisiana (in some parishes).

February 15, Susan B. Anthony's Birthday: Florida, Minnesota.

February 19, Robert E. Lee Day: Kentucky.

March (first Tuesday), Town Meeting Day: Vermont.

March 2, Texas Independence Day: Texas.

March 17, Evacuation Day: Massachusetts (in Suffolk Co. only).

March or April (2 days before Easter), Good Friday: Connecticut, Delaware, Florida, Hawaii, Indiana, Louisiana, Maryland, New Jersey, North Dakota, Pennsylvania, Tennessee, Wisc. (11 a.m.-3 p.m.).

March or April (1 day after Easter), Easter Monday: North Carolina.

March 20, (First Day of Spring), Youth Day: Oklahoma.

March 22, Abolition Day: Puerto Rico.

March 25, Maryland Day: Maryland.

March 26, Prince Jonah Kuhio Kalanianaole Day: Hawaii.

March (last Monday), Seward's Day: Alaska.

April 2, Pascua Florida Day: Florida.

April 5, Good Friday: Puerto Rico

April 13, Thomas Jefferson's Birthday: Alabama, Oklahoma.

April 16, De Diego's Birthday: Puerto Rico.

April (third Monday), Patriots' Day: Maine, Mass.

April 21, San Jacinto Day: Texas.

April 22, Arbor Day: Nebraska, Delaware.

April 22, Oklahoma Day: Oklahoma.

April 26, Confederate Memorial Day: Florida, Georgia.

April (4th Monday), Fast Day: New Hampshire.

April (last Monday), Confederate Memorial Day: Alabama, Mississippi.

April (last Friday), Arbor Day: Utah.

May (1st Tuesday after the first Monday), Primary Election Day: Indiana.

May (2nd Sunday), Mother's Day: Arizona, Okla.

May 1, Bird Day: Oklahoma.

May 8, Truman Day: Missouri.

May 10, Confederate Memorial Day: South Carolina.[1]

May 11, Minnesota Day: Minnesota.

May 20, Mecklenburg Independence Day: North Carolina.

June (first Monday), Jefferson Davis's Birthday: Alabama, Mississippi.

June (second Sunday), Flag Day: New York.

June (third Sunday), Father's Day: Arizona.

June 3, Jefferson Davis's Birthday: Florida, Georgia, South Carolina, also called **Confederate Memorial Day** in Kentucky and Louisiana.[3]

June 9, Senior Citizens Day: Oklahoma.

June 11, King Kamehameha I Day: Hawaii.
June 14, Flag Day: Pennsylvania.
June 15, Separation Day: Delaware.
June 17, Bunker Hill Day: Massachusetts (in Suffolk Co. only).
June 19, Emancipation Day: Texas.
June 20, West Virginia Day: West Virginia.
July 17, Muñoz Rivera's Birthday: Puerto Rico.
July 24, Pioneer Day: Utah.
July 25, Constitution Day: Puerto Rico.
July 27, Barbosa's Birthday: Puerto Rico.
August (first Sunday), American Family Day: Arizona, Minnesota.
August (first Monday), Colorado Day: Colo.
August (second Monday), Victory Day: Rhode Is.
August 16, Bennington Battle Day: Vermont.
August (third Friday), Admission Day: Hawaii.
August 27, Lyndon B. Johnson's Birthday: Texas.
August 30, Huey P. Long Day: Louisiana.[3]
September (first Tuesday), Primary Election Day: Wisconsin.
September, (second Tuesday), Primary Election Day: Wyoming.
September 9, Admission Day: California.
September 12, Defenders' Day: Maryland.
September 16, Cherokee Strip Day: Oklahoma.
September (1st Saturday after full moon), Indian Day: Oklahoma.
October 10, Oklahoma Historical Day: Oklahoma.
October 18, Alaska Day: Alaska.
October 31, Nevada Day: Nevada.
November 1, All Saints' Day: Louisiana.[3]
November (first Tuesday), Election Day: Montana.
November 4, Will Rogers Day: Oklahoma.
November 8, Return Day: Delaware.
November (week of the 16th), Oklahoma Heritage Week: Oklahoma.
November 19, Discovery Day: Puerto Rico.
November 29, Nellie Tayloe Ross's Birthday: Wyoming.
December 7, Delaware Day: Delaware.
December 10, Wyoming Day: Wyoming.

1. Optional, two of three allowed. 2. Third Monday in Michigan. 3. Observed only if proclaimed by governor. 4. Employee has choice of observing King's or Lee's Birthday. 5. Presidential election only. 6. All even years. 7. Third Monday.

Movable Holidays, 1985–1992

CHRISTIAN AND SECULAR

Year	Ash Wednesday	Easter	Pentecost	Labor Day	Election Day	Thanksgiving	1st Sun. Advent
1985	Feb. 20	April 7	May 26	Sept. 2	Nov. 5	Nov. 28	Dec. 1
1986	Feb. 12	March 30	May 18	Sept. 1	Nov. 4	Nov. 27	Nov. 30
1987	March 4	April 19	June 7	Sept. 7	Nov. 3	Nov. 26	Nov. 29
1988	Feb. 17	April 3	May 22	Sept. 5	Nov. 8	Nov. 24	Nov. 27
1989	Feb. 8	March 26	May 14	Sept. 4	Nov. 7	Nov. 23	Dec. 3
1990	Feb. 28	April 15	June 3	Sept. 3	Nov. 6	Nov. 22	Dec. 2
1991	Feb. 13	March 31	May 19	Sept. 2	Nov. 5	Nov. 28	Dec. 1
1992	March 4	April 19	June 7	Sept. 7	Nov. 3	Nov. 26	Nov. 29

Shrove Tuesday: 1 day before Ash Wednesday
Palm Sunday: 7 days before Easter
Maundy Thursday: 3 days before Easter
Good Friday: 2 days before Easter
Holy Saturday: 1 day before Easter
Ascension Day: 10 days before Pentecost
Trinity Sunday: 7 days after Pentecost
Corpus Christi: 11 days after Pentecost

NOTE: Easter is celebrated on April 14, 1985, by the Orthodox Church.

JEWISH

Year	Purim[1]	1st day Passover[2]	1st day Shavuot[3]	1st day Rosh Hashana[4]	Yom Kippur[5]	1st day Sukkot[6]	Simhat Torah[7]	1st day Hanukkah[8]
1985	March 7	April 6	May 26	Sept. 16	Sept. 25	Sept. 30	Oct. 8	Dec. 8
1986	March 25	April 24	June 13	Oct. 4	Oct. 13	Oct. 18	Oct. 26	Dec. 27
1987	March 15	April 14	June 3	Sept. 24	Oct. 3	Oct. 8	Oct. 16	Dec. 16
1988	March 3	April 2	May 22	Sept. 12	Sept. 21	Sept. 26	Oct. 4	Dec. 4
1989	March 21	April 20	June 9	Sept. 30	Oct. 9	Oct. 14	Oct. 22	Dec. 23
1990	March 11	April 10	May 30	Sept. 20	Sept. 29	Oct. 4	Oct. 12	Dec. 12
1991	Feb. 28	March 30	May 19	Sept. 9	Sept. 18	Sept. 23	Oct. 1	Dec. 2
1992	March 14	April 18	June 7	Sept. 28	Oct. 7	Oct. 12	Oct. 20	Dec. 20

1. Feast of Lots. 2. Feast of Unleavened Bread. 3. Hebrew Pentecost; or Feast of Weeks, or of Harvest, or of First Fruits. 4. Jewish New Year. 5. Day of Atonement. 6. Feast of Tabernacles, or of the Ingathering. 7. Rejoicing of the Law. 8. Festival of Lights.

Length of Jewish holidays (O=Orthodox, C=Conservative, R=Reform):

Passover: O & C, 8 days (holy days: first 2 and last 2); R, 7 days (holy days: first and last)
Shavuot: O & C, 2 days; R, 1 day
Rosh Hashana: O & C, 2 days; R, 1 day.
Yom Kippur: All groups, 1 day
Sukkot: All groups, 7 days (holy days: O & C, first 2; R, first only) O & C observe two additional days: Shemini Atseret (Eighth Day of the Feast) and Simhat Torah R observes Shemini Atseret but not Simhat Torah
Hanukkah: All groups, 8 days

NOTE: All holidays begin at sundown on the evening before the date given.

Major Religions of the World

Judaism

The determining factors of Judaism are: descendance from Israel, the *Torah,* and Tradition.

The name Israel (Jacob, a patriarch) also signifies his descendants as a people. During the 15th–13th centuries B.C., Israelite tribes, coming from South and East, gradually settled in Palestine, then inhabited by Canaanites. They were held together by Moses, who gave them religious unity in the worship of *Jahweh,* the God who had chosen Israel to be his people.

Under Judges, the 12 tribes at first formed an amphictyonic covenant. Saul established kingship (circa 1050 B.C.), and under David, his successor (1000–960 B.C.), the State of Israel comprised all of Palestine with Jerusalem as religio-political center. A golden era followed under Solomon (965–926 B.C.), who built *Jahweh* a temple.

After Solomon's death, the kingdom separated into Israel in the North and Judah in the South. A period of conflicts ensued, which ended with the conquest of Israel by Assyria in 722 B.C. The Babylonians defeated Judah in 586 B.C., destroying Jerusalem and its temple, and deporting many to Babylon.

The era of the kings is significant also in that the great prophets worked in that time, emphasizing faith in *Jahweh* as both God of Israel and God of the universe, and stressing social justice.

When the Persians permitted the Jews to return from exile (539 B.C.), temple and cult were restored in Jerusalem. The Persian rulers were succeeded by the Seleucides. The Maccabaean revolt against these Hellenistic kings gave independence to the Jews in 128 B.C., which lasted till the Romans occupied the country.

Important groups that exerted influence during these times were the Sadducees, priests in the temple in Jerusalem; the Pharisees, teachers of the Law in the synagogues; Essenes, a religious order (from whom Dead Sea Scrolls, discovered in 1947, came); Apocalyptists, who were expecting the heavenly Messiah; and Zealots, who were prepared to fight for national independence.

When the latter turned against Rome in A.D. 66, Roman armies under Titus suppressed the revolt, destroying Jerusalem and its temple in A.D. 70. The Jews were scattered in the *diaspora* (Dispersion), subject to oppressions until the Age of the Enlightenment (18th century) brought their emancipation, although persecutions did not end entirely.

The fall of the Jerusalem temple was an important event in the religious life of the Jews, which now developed around *Torah* (Law) and synagogue. Around A.D. 100 the Sacred Scriptures were codified. Synagogue worship became central, with readings from *Torah* and prophets. Most important prayers are the *Shema* (Hear) and the Prayer of the 18 Benedictions.

Religious life is guided by the commandments contained in the *Torah:* circumcision and *Sabbath,* as well as other ethical and ceremonial commandments.

The *Talmud,* based on the *Mishnah* and its interpretations, took shape over many centuries in the Babylonian and Palestinian Schools. It was a strong binding force of Judaism in the Dispersion.

Estimated Membership of the Principal Religions of the World

Statistics of the world's religions are only very rough approximations. Aside from Christianity, few religions, if any, attempt to keep statistical records; and even Protestants and Catholics employ different methods of counting members. All persons of whatever age who have received baptism in the Catholic Church are counted as members, while in most Protestant Churches only those who "join" the church are numbered. The compiling of statistics is further complicated by the fact that in China one may be at the same time a Confucian, a Taoist, and a Buddhist. In Japan, one may be both a Buddhist and a Shintoist.

Religion	North America[1]	South America	Europe	Asia	Africa	Oceania[2]	World
Total Christian	252,458,670	196,599,780	337,678,150	104,098,695	147,076,000	18,781,550	1,056,692,845
Roman Catholic	138,875,530	185,251,200	178,032,590	57,265,290	56,999,270	5,215,440	621,639,320
Eastern Orthodox	5,648,620	355,250	47,069,040	2,762,810	9,401,840	407,650	65,645,210
Protestant	107,934,520	10,993,330	112,576,520	44,070,595	80,674,890	13,158,460	369,408,315
Jewish[3]	7,611,940	749,580	4,643,810	4,008,850	231,980	73,980	17,320,140
Muslim	1,580,980	406,190	20,190,500	380,068,940	152,943,570	87,000	555,277,180
Zoroastrian	2,750	2,600	14,000	224,370	900	1,000	245,620
Shinto	50,000	—	—	33,000,000	—	—	33,050,000
Taoist	33,250	12,975	13,500	20,500,000	850	2,900	20,563,475
Confucian	99,750	58,925	450,500	162,500,000	2,550	18,390	163,130,115
Buddhist	336,290	241,090	238,300	250,097,200	15,000	23,700	250,951,580
Hindu	309,100	637,400	442,890	459,708,450	1,165,600	326,470	462,589,910
Totals	**262,482,730**	**198,708,540**	**363,671,650**	**1,414,206,505**	**301,436,450**	**19,314,990**	**2,559,820,865**

1. Includes Central America and West Indies. 2. Includes Australia and New Zealand, as well as islands of the South Pacific. 3. Includes total Jewish population, whether or not related to the synagogue. *Source: Britannica Book of the Year, 1984.*

In the 12th century, Maimonides formulated his "13 Articles of Faith," which carried great authority. Fundamental in this creed are: belief in God and his oneness *(Sherma)*, belief in the changeless *Torah*, in the words of Moses and the prophets, belief in reward and punishment, the coming of the Messiah, and the resurrection of the dead.

Judaism is divided into theological schools, the main divisions of which are Orthodox, Conservative, and Reform.

Christianity

Christianity is founded upon Jesus Christ, to whose life the New Testament writings testify. Jesus, a Jew, was born in about 7 B.C. and assumed his public life, after his 30th year, in Galilee. The Gospels tell of many extraordinary deeds that accompanied his ministry. He proclaimed the Kingdom of God, a future reality that is at the same time already present. Nationalistic-Jewish expectations of the Messiah he rejected. Rather, he referred to himself as the "Son of Man," the Christ, who has power to forgive sins now and who shall also come as Judge at the end of time. Jesus set forth the religio-ethical demands for participation in the Kingdom of God as change of heart and love of God and neighbor.

At the Last Supper he signified his death as a sacrifice, which would inaugurate the New Covenant, by which many would be saved. Circa A.D. 30 he died on a cross in Jerusalem. The early Church carried on Jesus' proclamation, the apostle Paul emphasizing his death and resurrection.

The person of Jesus is fundamental to the Christian faith since it is believed that in his life, death, and resurrection, God's revelation became historically tangible. He is seen as the turning point in history, and man's relationship to God as determined by his attitude to Jesus.

Historically Christianity thus arose out of Judaism, claiming fulfillment of the promises of the Old Testament in Jesus. The early Church designated itself as "the true Israel," which expected the speedy return of Jesus. The mother church was at Jerusalem, but churches were soon founded in many other places. The apostle Paul was instrumental in founding and extending a Gentile Christianity that was free from Jewish legalism.

The new religion spread rapidly throughout the eastern and western parts of the Roman Empire. In coming to terms with other religious movements within the Empire, Christianity began to take definite shape as an organization in its doctrine, liturgy, and ministry circa A.D. 200. In the 4th century the Catholic Church had taken root in countries stretching from Spain in the West to Persia and India in the East. Christians had been repeatedly subject to persecution by the Roman state, but finally gained tolerance under Constantine the Great (A.D. 313). Since that time, the Church became favored under his successors and in 380 the Emperor Theodosius proclaimed Christianity the State religion. Paganism was suppressed and public life was gradually molded in accordance with Christian ethical demands.

It was in these years also that the Church was able to achieve a certain unity of doctrine. Due to differences of interpretation of basic doctrines concerning Christ, which threatened to divide the Catholic Church, a standard Christian Creed was formulated by bishops at successive Ecumenical Councils, the first of which was held in A.D. 325 (Nicaea). The chief doctrines formulated concerned the doctrine of the Trinity, i.e., that there is one God in three persons: Father, Son, and Holy Spirit (Constantinople, A.D. 381); and the nature of Christ as both divine and human (Chalcedon, A.D. 541).

Through differences and rivalry between East and West the unity of the Church was broken by schism in 1054. In 1517 a separation occurred in the Western Church with the Reformation. From the major Protestant denominations [Lutheran, Presbyterian, Anglican (Episcopalian)], many Free Churches separated themselves in an age of individualism.

In the 20th century, however, the direction is toward unity. The Ecumenical Movement led to the formation of the World Council of Churches in 1948 (Amsterdam), which has since been joined by many Protestant and Orthodox Churches.

Through its missionary activity Christianity has spread to most parts of the globe.

Eastern Orthodoxy

Eastern Orthodoxy comprises the faith and practice of Churches stemming from ancient Churches in the Eastern part of the Roman Empire. The term covers Orthodox Churches in communion with the See of Constantinople, Uniate Churches in communion with Rome, and Nestorian and Monophysite Churches.

The Orthodox, Catholic, Apostolic Church is the direct descendant of the Byzantine State Church and consists of a series of independent national churches that are united by Doctrine, Liturgy, and Hierarchical organization (deacons and priests, who may either be married or be monks before ordination, and bishops, who must be celibates). The heads of these Churches are patriarchs or metropolitans; the Patriarch of Constantinople is only "first among equals." Rivalry between the Pope of Rome and the Patriarch of Constantinople, aided by differences and misunderstandings that existed for centuries between the Eastern and Western parts of the Empire, led to a schism in 1054. Repeated attempts at reunion have failed in past centuries. The mutual excommunication pronounced in that year was lifted in 1965, however, and because of greater interaction in theology between Orthodox Churches and those in the West, a climate of better understanding has been created in the 20th century. First contacts were with Anglicans and Old Catholics. Orthodox Churches belong to the World Council of Churches.

The Eastern Orthodox Churches recognize only the canons of the seven Ecumenical Councils (325–787) as binding for faith and they reject doctrines that have been added in the West.

The central worship service is called the Liturgy, which is understood as representation of God's acts of salvation. Its center is the celebration of the Eucharist, or Lord's Supper.

In their worship *icons* (sacred pictures) are used that have a sacramental meaning as representation. The Mother of Christ, angels, and saints are highly venerated.

The number of sacraments in the Orthodox Church is the same as in the Western Catholic Church.

Orthodox Churches are found in the Balkans and the Soviet Union also, since the 20th century, in Western Europe and other parts of the world, particularly in America.

Eastern Orthodoxy also includes the Uniate Churches that recognize the authority of the Pope but keep their own traditional liturgies and those Churches dating back to the 5th century that emanicipated themselves from the Byzantine State Church: the Nestorian Church in the Near East and India with approximately half a million members and the Monophysite Churches with some 17 million members (Coptic, Ethiopian, Syrian, Armenian, and the Mar Thoma Church in India).

Roman Catholicism

Roman Catholicism comprises the belief and practice of the Roman Catholic Church. The Church stands under the authority of the Bishop of Rome, the Pope, and is ruled by him and bishops who are held to be, through ordination, successors of Peter and the Apostles, respectively. Fundamental to the structure of the Church is the juridical aspect: doctrine and sacraments are bound to the power of jurisdiction and consecration of the hierarchy. The Pope, as the head of the hierarchy of archbishops, bishops, priests, and deacons, has full ecclesiastical power, granted him by Christ, through Peter. As successor to Peter, he is the Vicar of Christ. The powers that others in the hierarchy possess are delegated.

Roman Catholics believe their Church to be the one, holy, catholic, and apostolic Church, possessing all the properties of the one, true Church of Christ.

The faith of the Church is understood to be identical with that taught by Christ and his Apostles and contained in Bible and Tradition, i.e. the original deposit of faith, to which nothing new may be added. New definitions of doctrines, such as the Immaculate Conception of Mary (1854) and the bodily Assumption of Mary (1950), have been declared by Popes, however, in accordance with the principle of development (implicit-explicit doctrine).

At Vatican Council I (1870) the Pope was proclaimed "endowed with infallibility, *ex cathedra*, i.e., when exercising the office of Pastor and Teacher of all Christians."

The center of Roman Catholic worship is the celebration of the Mass, the Eucharist, which is the commemoration of Christ's sacrificial death and of his resurrection. Other sacraments are Baptism, Confirmation, Confession, Matrimony, Ordination, and Extreme Unction, seven in all. The Virgin Mary and saints, and their relics, are highly venerated and prayers are made to them to intercede with God, in whose presence they are believed to dwell.

The Roman Catholic Church is the largest Christian organization in the world, found in most countries. Some 8 million belong to the Uniate rites, the vast majority to the Latin rite.

Since Vatican Council II (1962–65), and the effort to "update" the Church, many interesting changes and developments have been taking place.

Protestantism

Protestantism comprises the Christian churches that separated from Rome during the Reformation in the 16th century, initiated by an Augustinian monk, Martin Luther. "Protestant" was originally applied to followers of Luther, who protested at the Diet of Spires (1529) against the decree which prohibited all further ecclesiastical reforms. Subsequently, Protestantism came to mean rejection of attempts to tie God's revelation to earthly institutions, and a return to the Gospel and the Word of God as sole authority in matters of faith and practice. Central in the biblical message is the justification of the sinner by faith alone. The Church is understood as a fellowship and the priesthood of all believers stressed.

The Augsburg Confession (1530) was the principal statement of Lutheran faith and practice. It became a model for other Confessions of Faith, which in their turn had decisive influence on Church polity. Major Protestant denominations are the Lutheran, Reformed (Calvinist), Presbyterian, and Anglican (Episcopal). Smaller ones are the Mennonite, Schwenkfeldians, and Unitarians. In Great Britain and America there are the Congregationalists, Baptists, Quakers, Methodists, and other free church types of communities. (In regarding themselves as being faithful to original biblical Christianity, these Churches differ from such religious bodies as Unitarians, Mormons, Jehovah's Witnesses, and Christian Scientists, who either teach new doctrines or reject old ones.)

Since the latter part of the 19th century, national councils of churches have been established in many countries, e.g. the Federal Council of Churches of Christ in America in 1908. Denominations across countries joined in federations and world alliances, beginning with the Anglican Lambeth Conference in 1867.

Protestant missionary activity, particularly strong in the last century, resulted in the founding of many younger churches in Asia and Africa. The Ecumenical Movement, which originated with Protestant missions, aims at unity among Christians and churches.

Islam

Islam is the religion founded in Arabia by Mohammed between 610 and 632. Its more than 600 million adherents are found in countries stretching from Morocco in the West to Indonesia in the East.

Mohammed was born in A.D. 570 at Mecca and belonged to the Quraysh tribe, which was active in caravan trade. At the age of 25 he joined the caravan trade from Mecca to Syria in the employment of a rich widow, Khadiji, whom he married. Critical of the idolatry of the inhabitants of Mecca, he began to lead a contemplative life in the deserts. There he received a series of revelations. Encouraged by Khadiji, he gradually became convinced that he was given a God-appointed task to devote himself to the reform of religion and society. Idolatry was to be abandoned.

The *Hegira (Hijra)* (migration) of Mohammed from Mecca, where he was not honored, to Medina, where he was well received, occurred in 622 and marks the beginning of the Muslim era. In 630 he marched on Mecca and conquered it. He died at Medina in 632. His grave there has since been a place of pilgrimage.

Mohammed's followers, called Moslems, revered him as the prophet of *Allah* (God), beside whom there is no other God. Although he had no close knowledge of Judaism and Christianity, he considered himself succeeding and completing them as the seal of the Prophets. Sources of the Islamic faith are the *Qur'an*, regarded as the uncreated, eternal Word of God, and Tradition *(hadith)* regarding sayings and deeds of the prophet.

Islam means surrender to the will of *Allah*. He is the all-powerful, whose will is supreme and determines man's fate. Good deeds will be rewarded at the Last Judgment in paradise and evil deeds will be punished in hell.

The Five Pillars, primary duties, of Islam are: witness; confessing the oneness of God and of Mohammed, his prophet; prayer, to be performed five times a day; almsgiving to the poor and the mosque (house of worship); fasting during daylight hours in the month of Ramadan; and pilgrimage to Mecca at least once in the Moslem's lifetime.

The practice of Holy War *(jihad),* at first responsible for the rapid growth of the new religion, could not be maintained. Mohammed curtailed the practice of polygamy by limiting it to four wives. In modern times the position of women has improved, due to Western influence. The eating of pork and drinking of intoxicants is forbidden.

Islam, upholding the law of brotherhood, succeeded in uniting an Arab world that had disintegrated into tribes and castes. Disagreements concerning the succession of the prophet caused a great division in Islam between *Sunnis* and *Shias.* Among these, other sects arose *(Wahhabi).* Doctrinal issues also led to the rise of different schools of thought in theology. Nevertheless, since Arab armies turned against Syria and Palestine in 635, Islam has expanded successfully under Mohammed's successors. Its rapid conquests in Asia and Africa are unsurpassed in history. Turning against Europe, Moslems conquered Spain in 713. In 1453 Constantinople fell into their hands and in 1529 Moslem armies besieged Vienna. Since then, Islam has lost its foothold in Europe.

In modern times it has made great gains in Africa.

Hinduism

In India alone there are more than 300 million adherents of Hinduism. In contrast to other religions, it has no founder. Considered the oldest religion in the world, it dates back, perhaps, to prehistoric times.

Hinduism is hard to define, there being no common creed, no one doctrine to bind Hindus together. Intellectually there is complete freedom of belief, and one can be monotheist, polytheist, or atheist. What matters is the social system: a Hindu is one born into a caste.

As a religion, Hinduism is founded on the sacred scriptures, written in Sanskrit and called the *Vedas* (*Yeda*-knowledge). There are four Vedic books, among which the *Rig Veda* is the most important. It speaks of many gods and also deals with questions concerning the universe and creation. The dates of these works are unknown (1000 B.C.?).

The *Upanishads* (dated 1000–300 B.C.), commentaries on the Vedic texts, have philosophical speculations on the origin of the universe, the nature of deity, of *atman* (the human soul), and its relationship to *Brahman* (the universal soul).

Brahman is the principle and source of the universe who can be indicated only by negatives. As the divine intelligence, he is the ground of the visible world, a presence that pervades all beings. Thus the many Hindu deities came to be understood as manifestations of the one *Brahman* from whom everything proceeds and to whom everything ultimately returns. The religio-social system of Hinduism is based on the concept of reincarnation and transmigration in which all living beings, from plants below to gods above, are caught in a cosmic system that is an everlasting cycle of becoming and perishing.

Life is determined by the law of *karma,* according to which rebirth is dependent on moral behavior in a previous phase of existence. The doctrine of transmigration thus provides a rationale for the caste system. In this view, life on earth is regarded as transient *(maya)* and a burden. The goal of existence is liberation from the cycle of rebirth and redeath and entrance into the indescribable state of what in Buddhism is called *nirvana* (extinction of passion).

Further important sacred writings are the Epics *(puranas),* which contain legendary stories about gods and men. They are the *Mahabharata* (composed between 200 B.C. and A.D. 200) and the *Ramayana.* The former includes the *Bhagavad-Gita* (Song of the Lord), its most famous part, that tells of devotion to *Krishna* (Lord), who appears as an *avatar* (incarnation) of the god *Vishnu,* and of the duty of obeying caste rules. The work begins with a praise of the *yoga* (discipline) system.

The practice of Hinduism consists of rites and ceremonies, performed within the framework of the caste system and centering on the main socio-religious occasions of birth, marriage, and death. There are many Hindu temples, which are dwelling places of the deities and to which people bring offerings. There are also places of pilgrimages, the chief one being Benares on the Ganges, most sacred among the rivers in India.

In modern times work has been done to reform and revive Hinduism. One of the outstanding reformers was Ramakrishna (1836–86), who inspired many followers, one of whom founded the Ramakrishna mission, which seeks to convert others to its religion. The mission is active both in India and in other countries.

Buddhism

Founded in the 6th century B.C. in northern India by Gautama Buddha, who was born in southern Nepal as son to a king. His birth is surrounded by many legends, but Western scholars agree that he lived from 563 to 483 B.C. Warned by a sage that his son would become an ascetic or a universal monarch, the king confined him to his home. He was able to escape and began the life of a homeless wanderer in search of peace, passing through many disappointments until he finally came to the Tree of Enlightenment, under which he lived in meditation till enlightenment came to him and he became a Buddha (enlightened one).

Now he understood the origin of suffering, summarized in the *Four Noble Truths,* which constitutes the foundation of Buddhism. The Four are the truth of suffering, which all living beings must endure; of the origin of suffering, which is craving and which leads to rebirth; that it can be destroyed; and of the way that leads to cessation of pain, i.e., the *Noble Eightfold Way,* which is the rule of practical Buddhism: right views, right intention, right speech, right action, right livelihood, right effort, right concentration, and right ecstasy.

Nirvana is the goal of all existence, the state of complete redemption, into which the redeemed enters. Buddha's insight can free every man from the law of reincarnation through complete emptying of the self.

The nucleus of Buddha's church or association was originally formed by monks and lay-brothers, whose houses gradually became monasteries used as places for religious instruction. The worship service consisted of a sermon, expounding of Scripture, meditation, and confession. At a later stage pilgrimages to the holy places associated with the Buddha came into being, as well as veneration of relics.

In the 3rd century B.C., King Ashoka made Buddhism the State religion of India but, as centuries passed, it gradually fell into decay through splits, persecutions, and the hostile Brahmans. Buddhism spread to countries outside India, however.

At the beginning of the Christian era, there occurred a split that gave rise to two main types: *Hinayana* (Little Vehicle), or southern Buddhism, and *Mahayana* (Great Vehicle), or northern Buddhism. The former type, more individualistic, survived in Ceylon and southern Asia. *Hinayana* retained more closely the original teachings of the Buddha, which did not know of a personal god or soul. *Mahayana,* more social, polytheistic, and developing a pluralistic pompous cult, was strong in the Himalayas, Tibet, Mongolia, China, Korea, and Japan.

In the present century, Buddhism has found believers also in the West and Buddhist associations have been established in Europe and the U.S.

Confucianism

Confucius (K'ung Fu-tzu), born in the state of Lu (northern China), lived from 551 to 479 B.C. Tradition, exaggerating the importance of Confucius in life, has depicted him as a great statesman but, in fact, he seems to have been a private teacher. Anthologies of ancient Chinese classics, along with his own Analects *(Lun Yu),* became the basis of Confucianism. These Analects were transmitted as a collection of his sayings as recorded by his students, with whom he discussed ethical and social problems. They developed into men of high moral standing, who served the State as administrators.

In his teachings, Confucius emphasized the importance of an old Chinese concept *(li),* which has the connotation of proper conduct. There is some disagreement as to the religious ideas of Confucius, but he held high the concepts handed down from centuries before him. Thus he believed in Heaven *(T'ien)* and sacrificed to his ancestors. Ancestor worship he indeed encouraged as an expression of filial piety, which he considered the loftiest of virtues.

Piety to Confucius was the foundation of the family as well as the State. The family is the nucleus of the State, and the "five relations," between king and subject, father and son, man and wife, older and younger brother, and friend and friend, are determined by the virtues of love of fellow men, righteousness, and respect.

An extension of ancestor worship may be seen in the worship of Confucius, which became official in the 2nd century B.C. when the emperor, in recognition of Confucius' teachings as supporting the imperial rule, offered sacrifices at his tomb.

Mencius (Meng Tse), who lived around 400 B.C., did much to propagate and elaborate Confucianism in its concern with ordering society. Thus, for two millennia, Confucius' doctrine of State, with its emphasis on ethics and social morality, rooted in ancient Chinese tradition and developed and continued by his disciples, has been standard in China and the Far East.

With the revolution of 1911 in China, however, students, burning Confucius in effigy, called for the removal of "the old curiosity shop."

Shintoism

Shinto, the Chinese term for the Japanese *Kami no Michi,* i.e., the Way of the Gods, comprises the religious ideas and cult indigenous to Japan. *Kami,* or gods, considered divine forces of nature that are worshipped, may reside in rivers, trees, rocks, mountains, certain animals, or, particularly, in the sun and moon. The worship of ancestors, heroes, and deceased emperors was incorporated later.

After Buddhism had come from Korea, Japan's native religion at first resisted it. Then there followed a period of compromise and amalgamation with Buddhist beliefs and ceremonies, resulting, since the 9th century A.D., in a syncretistic religion, a Twofold Shinto. Buddhist deities came to be regarded as manifestations of Japanese deities and Buddhist priests took over most of the Shinto shrines.

In modern times Shinto regained independence from Buddhism. Under the reign of the Emperor Meiji (1868–1912) it became the official State religion, in which loyalty to the emperor was emphasized. The line of succession of emperors is traced back to the first Emperor Jimmu (660 B.C.) and beyond him to the Sun-goddess *Amaterasuomikami.*

The centers of worship are the shrines and temples in which the deities are believed to dwell and believers approach them through *torii* (gateways). Most important among the shrines is the imperial shrine of the Sun-goddess at Ise, where state ceremonies were once held in June and December. The *Yasukuni* shrine of the war dead in Tokyo is also well known.

Acts of worship consist of prayers, clapping of hands, acts of purification, and offerings. On feast days processions and performances of music and dancing take place and priests read prayers before the gods in the shrines, asking for good harvest, the well-being of people and emperor, etc. In Japanese homes there is a god-shelf, a small wooden shrine that contains the tablets bearing the names of ancestors. Offerings are made and candles lit before it.

After World War II the Allied Command ordered the disestablishment of State Shinto. To be distinguished from State Shinto is Sect Shinto, consisting of 13 recognized sects. These have arisen in modern times, gaining large followings. Most important among them is *Tenrikyo* in Tenri City (Nara), in which healing by faith plays a central role.

Taoism

Taoism, a religion of China, was, according to tradition, founded by Lao Tse, a Chinese philosopher, long considered one of the prominent religious leaders from the 6th century B.C.

Data about him are for the most part legendary, however, and the *Tao Te Ching* (the classic of the Way and of its Power), traditionally ascribed to him, is now believed by many scholars to have originated in the 3rd century B.C. The book is composed in short chapters, written in aphoristic rhymes. Central are the word *Tao,* which means way or path and, in a deeper sense, signifies the principle that underlies the reality of this world and manifests itself in nature and in the lives of men, and the word *Te* (power).

The virtuous man draws power from being absorbed in *Tao,* the ultimate reality within an ever-changing world. By non-action and keeping away from human striving it is possible for man to live in harmony with the principles that underlie and govern the universe. *Tao* cannot be comprehended by reason and knowledge, but only by inward quiet.

Besides the *Tao Te Ching,* dating from approximately the same period, there are two Taoist works, written by Chuang Tse and Lieh Tse.

Theoretical Taoism of this classical philosophical movement of the 4th and 3rd centuries B.C. in China differed from popular Taoism, into which it gradually degenerated. The standard of theoretical Taoism was maintained in the classics, of course, and among the upper classes it continued to be alive until modern times.

Religious Taoism is a form of religion dealing with deities and spirits, magic and soothsaying. In the 2nd century A.D. it was organized with temples, cult, priests, and monasteries and was able to hold its own in the competition with Buddhism that came up at the same time.

After the 7th century A.D., however, Taoist religion further declined. Split into numerous sects, which often operate like secret societies, it has become a syncretistic folk religion in which some of the old deities and saints live on.

History of Leading Religious Groups in the United States

(50,000 members or over)

Source: Yearbook of American and Canadian Churches, 1984.

BAPTIST

American Baptist Association: A group of independent Missionary Baptist Churches, mainly in the South, Southeast, and Southwest, organized in 1905. Members (1982): 225,000. Headquarters: 4605 N. State Line Ave., Texarkana, Tex. 75501.

American Baptist Churches in the U.S.A.: Formerly known as the Northern Baptist Convention and the American Baptist Convention, this body changed its name in 1973. Although national missionary organizational developments began in 1814 with the establishment of the American Baptist Foreign Mission Society, the Convention was not formed until 1907. Members (1981): 1,621,795. Headquarters: Valley Forge, Pa. 19481.

Baptist General Conference: Formerly known as the Swedish Baptist General Conference of America. It has operated as a general conference since 1879. Members (1982): 129,928. Headquarters: 2002 S. Arlington Heights Rd., Arlington Heights, Ill. 60005.

Baptist Missionary Association of America: Formerly called the North American Baptist Association. It was organized in 1950 in Little Rock, Ark. Members (1982): 226,953. Office of president: 3674-E McCain Park Dr., Little Rock, Ark. 72216.

Conservative Baptist Association of America: Organized in 1947. Adherents regard the Bible as infallible. Local churches are independent, autonomous, and free from ecclesiastical or political authority. Members (1982): 225,000. Headquarters: 25 W. 560 Geneva Rd., Box 66, Wheaton, Ill. 60187.

Free Will Baptists: A body of evangelical Baptists, organized in 1727 in the South and 1780 in the North. Members (1982): 243,658. Headquarters: 1134 Murfreesboro Rd., Nashville, Tenn. 37217.

General Association of Regular Baptist Churches: Founded in 1932 in Chicago by a group of churches which had withdrawn from the Northern Baptist Convention (now the American Baptist Convention) because of doctrinal differences. Members (1981): 300,839. Headquarters: 1300 N. Meacham Rd., Schaumburg, Ill. 60195.

General Baptists (General Association of): An Arminian group of Baptists, organized in England in 1607 and transplanted to the colonies in 1714. It died out along the Seaboard, but revived in the Midwest in 1823. Members (1981): 75,028. Headquarters: 100 Stinson Dr., Poplar Bluff, Mo. 63901.

National Baptist Convention, U.S.A.: The older and parent convention of Black Baptists. This body is to be distinguished from the National Baptist Convention of America, usually referred to as the "unincorporated" body. Members (1958): 5,500,000. Office of president: 915 Spain St., Baton Rouge, La. 70802.

National Baptist Convention of America: This is a body usually referred to as the "unincorporated" convention, not to be confused with the "incorporated" National Baptist Convention, U.S.A., Inc., from which this body withdrew. Organized in 1880. Members (1956): 2,668,799. Office of president: 954 Kings Rd., Jacksonville, Fla. 32204.

National Primitive Baptist Convention: A group of Baptists having local associations and a National Convention. Organized in 1907. Members (1975): 250,000. Headquarters: Box 2355, Tallahassee, Fla.

North American Baptist Association: *See* Baptist Missionary Association of America.

Primitive Baptists: A large group of Baptists, largely through the South, who are opposed to all centralization and to modern missionary societies. Members (1960): 72,000. Headquarters: Cayce Publishing Co., S. Second St., Thornton, Ariz., 71766.

Progressive National Baptist Convention: A body that held its organizational meeting in Cincinnati in 1961 and its first annual session in Philadelphia in 1962. Members (1967): 521,692. Office of president: New Calvary Baptist Church, 3975 Concord St., Detroit, Mich. 47207.

U. S. Church Membership

Religious group	Members
Protestant bodies and others	76,754,009
Roman Catholics	52,088,774
Jewish congregations[1]	5,725,000
Eastern churches	3,859,668
Old Catholic, Polish National Catholic, Armenian churches	924,861
Buddhist Churches of America	100,000
Miscellaneous	150,747
Total[2]	**139,603,059**

1. Includes Orthodox, Conservative, and Reform. 2. As reported in the *1984 Yearbook* from statistics furnished by 219 religious bodies in the United States.

Southern Baptist Convention: In 1845, Southern Baptists withdrew from the General Missionary Convention over the question of slavery and other matters and formed the Southern Baptist Convention. Members (1982): 13,991,709. Office of recording secretary: 127 9th Ave., N., Nashville, Tenn. 37234.

United Free Will Baptist Church: A body which set up its organization in 1870. Members (1952): 100,000. Headquarters: Kinston College, 1000 University St., Kinston, N.C. 28501.

CATHOLIC AND ORTHODOX

American Carpatho-Russian Orthodox Greek Catholic Church: This church is a self-governing diocese in communion with the Ecumenical Patriarchate of Constantinople. On Sept. 19, 1938, the late Patriarch Benjamin I canonized the diocese in the name of the Orthodox Church of Christ. Members (1976): 100,000. Headquarters: Johnstown, Pa. 15906.

Antiochian Orthodox Christian Archdiocese of North America: Formed in 1975 by merger of the Antiochian Orthodox Christian Archdiocese of New York and All North America (formerly the Syrian Antiochian Orthodox Archdiocese of New York and North America) and the Antiochian Orthodox Archdiocese of Toledo, Ohio, and Dependencies in North America. The new Archdiocese is under the jurisdiction of the Patriarch of Antioch. Members (1977): 152,000. Headquarters: 358 Mountain Rd., Englewood, N.J. 07631.

Armenian Apostolic Church of America: The Armenian Church divided into two separate dioceses in 1933 because of a dispute regarding the political activities of the prelate at that time, and because of the status of the church in Soviet Armenia. Since 1956, this diocese has been under the jurisdiction of the Holy See of Cilicia, Beirut, Lebanon. Members (1972): 125,000. Headquarters: 138 E. 39th St., New York, N.Y. 10016.

Armenian Church of America, Diocese of the (including Diocese of California): The American branch of the Ancient Church of Armenia. Established in the U. S. in 1889. Diocesan organization is under the jurisdiction of the Holy See of Etchmiadzin, Armenia, U.S.S.R. Members (1979): 450,000. Headquarters: St. Vartan Cathedral, 630 Second Ave., New York, N.Y. 10016.

Bulgarian Eastern Orthodox Church (Diocese of North and South America and Australia): A Synod of the Bulgarian Eastern Orthodox Church, established as the Bulgarian Orthodox Mission in 1909. Became a canonical metropolitan archdiocese in 1947. Members (1971): 86,000. Headquarters: 550A W. 50th St., New York, N.Y. 10019; 1953 Stockbridge Rd., Akron, Ohio, 44313.

Coptic Orthodox Church: Part of the ancient Coptic Orthodox Church of Egypt. Egyptian immigrants have formed many parishes in the United States. Members (1980): 100,000. Office of correspondent: 427 West Side Ave., Jersey City, N.J. 07304.

Greek Orthodox Archdiocese of North and South America: Greek-speaking Orthodox Christians have parishes in the U. S., Canada, and South America. These are under the Ecumenical Patriarchate of Constantinople. Members (1977): 1,950,000. Headquarters: 8–10 E. 79th St., New York, N.Y. 10021.

North American Old Roman Catholic Church: A body with the doctrine of the Old Catholics; identical with the Roman Catholic Church in most worship and discipline. It is not under Papal jurisdiction. Members (1982): 62,383. Office of presiding archbishop: 4200 N. Kedvale Áve., Chicago, Ill. 60641.

Orthodox Church in America (The Russian Orthodox Greek Catholic Church of America): This body entered Alaska in 1792. In 1872, its headquarters were moved from Sitka to San Francisco and, in 1905, to New York. Members (1978): 1,000,000. Office of primate: Box 675, Syosset, N.Y. 11791.

Polish National Catholic Church of America: After long dissatisfaction with Roman Catholic administration and ideology, this group was organized in 1897. Members (1960): 282,411. Headquarters: 529 E. Locust St., Scranton, Pa. 18505.

Roman Catholic Church: The largest single group of Christians in the U.S., the Roman Catholic Church is under the spiritual leadership of the Pope. This group dates back to the priests who accompanied Columbus on his second voyage to the New World. A settlement, later discontinued, was made at St. Augustine, Fla. The continuous history of this Church in the colonies began at St. Mary's in 1634, in Maryland. Members (1982): 52,088,774. National Conference of Catholic Bishops, 1312 Massachusetts Ave., N.W., Washington, D.C. 20005.

Russian Orthodox Church in the U.S.A., Patriarchial Parishes of the: This autonomous body is the direct canonical successor of the Orthodox Catholic mission established in Alaska by the Russian Orthodox Church in 1793. It is under the spiritual jurisdiction of the Patriarch of Moscow and all Russia, His Holiness Pimen. In 1962 an administration was established for the Orthodox Mission in Puerto Rico and the Spanish-speaking people in the United States. Members (1975): 51,500. Headquarters: St. Nicholas Patriarchal Cathedral, 15 E. 97th St., New York, N.Y. 10029.

Russian Orthodox Church Outside Russia: The governing body was set up in Constantinople. In 1950, it came to the U.S. Members (1955): 55,000. Headquarters: 75 E. 93rd St., New York, N.Y. 10028.

Serbian Eastern Orthodox Church for the U.S.A. and Canada: This body of the Eastern Orthodox Church is autonomous. Members (1982): 97,123. Chancery: St. Sava Monastery, Box 519, Libertyville, Ill. 60048.

Syrian Antiochian Orthodox Archdiocese of New York and North America: *See* Antiochian Orthodox Christian Archdiocese of New York and All North America.

Ukrainian Orthodox Church in the U.S.A.: This church was organized in the U.S. in 1919. Members (1966): 87,745. Headquarters: South Bound Brook, P.O. Box 495, N.J. 08880.

JEWISH

Jews arrived in the colonies before 1650. The first congregation is recorded in 1654, in New York

City, the Shearith Israel (Remnant of Israel). Members (1982): 5,725,000.

Following are the major Jewish organizations:

Central Conference of American Rabbis (Reform): 21 E. 40th St., New York, N.Y. 10016

Rabbinical Alliance of America (Orthodox): 156 Fifth Ave., New York, N.Y. 10010

Rabbinical Assembly (Conservative): 3080 Broadway, New York, N.Y. 10027

Rabbinical Council of America (Orthodox): 1250 Broadway, New York, N.Y. 10001

Synagogue Council of America: 327 Lexington Ave., New York, N.Y. 10016

Union of American Hebrew Congregations (Reform): 838 Fifth Ave., New York, N.Y. 10021

Union of Orthodox Jewish Congregations of America: 45 W. 36th St., New York, N.Y. 10018

Union of Orthodox Rabbis of the United States and Canada: 235 E. Broadway, New York, N.Y. 10002

United Synagogue of America (Conservative): 155 Fifth Ave., New York, N.Y. 10010

LUTHERAN

American Lutheran Church: This church is the result of the merger in 1960 of the American Lutheran Church, the Evangelical Lutheran Church, and the United Evangelical Lutheran Church. In 1963, the Lutheran Free Church merged with The American Lutheran Church. Members (1982): 2,346,710. Headquarters: 422 S. Fifth St., Minneapolis, Minn. 55415.

Evangelical Lutheran Churches, Association of: Formed in 1976, this group is made up mainly of former affiliates of the Lutheran Church-Missouri Synod, plus some new and some formerly independent congregations. Its members have joined together to be in mission and ministry. Members (1982): 110,934. Headquarters: 12015 Manchester Rd., St. Louis, Mo. 63131.

Lutheran Church—Missouri Synod: This body, the largest constituent part of the Evangelical Lutheran Synodical Conference of North America, was organized in 1847. It is the leader in the conservative group among the Lutherans. Members (1982): 2,630,823. Headquarters: International Center, 1333 S. Kirkwood Rd., St. Louis, Mo. 63102.

Lutheran Church in America: This body was organized in 1962 by the consolidation of the American Evangelical Lutheran Church (1874), the Augustana Evangelical Lutheran Church (1860), the Finnish Evangelical Lutheran Church (1890), and the United Lutheran Church in America (1918). Members (1982): 2,925,655. Headquarters: 231 Madison Ave., New York, N.Y. 10016.

Wisconsin Evangelical Lutheran Synod: This body was organized in Wisconsin in 1850. Members (1982): 412,529. Headquarters: 2929 N. Mayfair Rd., Wauwatosa, Wis. 53222.

METHODIST

African Methodist Episcopal Church: This church began in 1787 in Philadelphia when persons in a Methodist Episcopal Church withdrew. In 1816, the denomination was started. Members (1980): 2,050,000. Office of senior bishop: 1002 Kirkwood Ave., Nashville, Tenn. 37203.

African Methodist Episcopal Zion Church: This group was organized in 1796, having withdrawn from the John Street Methodist Church, New York. Members (1982): 1,134,179. Office of senior bishop: 3752 Springhill Ave., Mobile, Ala. 36608.

Christian Methodist Episcopal Church: In 1870, the General Conference of the M.E. Church, South, approved the request of its black membership for the formation of their conferences into a separate body. Members (1981): 786,707. Office of secretary: Box 3403, Memphis, Tenn. 38103.

Free Methodist Church of North America: This body, organized in 1860, grew out of a movement in the Genesee Conference of the Methodist Episcopal Church about 1850 towards a more original Methodism. Members (1982): 70,657. Headquarters: 901 College Ave., Winona Lake, Ind. 46590.

United Methodist Church: The United Methodist Church was formed in April, 1968, by the union of the Methodist Church and the Evangelical United Brethren Church. The two churches shared a common historical and spiritual heritage. The Methodist Church resulted in 1939 from the unification of three branches of Methodism—the Methodist Episcopal Church; the Methodist Episcopal Church South; and the Methodist Protestant Church. The Methodist movement began in 18th-century England under the preaching of John Wesley, but the so-called Christmas Conference of 1784 in Baltimore is regarded as the date on which the organized Methodist Church was founded as an ecclesiastical organization. The Evangelical United Brethren Church was formed in 1946 with the merger of the Evangelical Church and the Church of the United Brethren in Christ, both of which had their beginnings in Pennsylvania in the evangelistic movement of the 18th and early 19th centuries. Members (1981): 9,457,012. Office of Secretary of General Conference, Perkins School of Theology, Southern Methodist University, Dallas, Tex. 75222.

PRESBYTERIAN

Cumberland Presbyterian Church: An outgrowth of the Great Revival of 1800, the Cumberland Presbytery was organized in 1810 in Tennessee. A union with the Presbyterian Church, U.S.A., in 1906, was only partially successful, and the Cumberland Presbyterian Church continued as a separate denomination. Members (1982): 97,813. Office of moderator: 3331 Preston Hwy., Louisville, Ky. 40213.

Presbyterian Church in America: Formed in Birmingham, Ala., in 1973 after separating from the Presbyterian Church in the United States, this body believes the Bible is the only infallible rule of faith and practice. It is committed to the Reformed Faith as set forth in the Westminster Confession and Catechisms. Members (1982): 149,548. Office of stated clerk: P.O. Box 1428, Decatur, Ga. 30031.

Presbyterian Church in the United States: This body is a branch of the Presbyterian Church established in separate existence in 1861. Members (1982): 814,931. Headquarters: 341 Ponce de Leon Ave., NE, Atlanta, Ga. 30365.

United Presbyterian Church in the United States of America: This group was formed in 1958 by a merger of the Presbyterian Church in the U.S.A. (dating from 1706) and the United Presbyterian Church of North America (established in 1858).

Members (1982): 2,342,441. Headquarters: 475 Riverside Dr., New York, N.Y. 10115.

OTHER RELIGIOUS BODIES

Apostolic Overcoming Holy Church of God: A black body incorporated in Alabama in 1919. It is evangelistic in purpose and emphasizes sanctification, holiness, and divine healing. Members (1956): 75, 000. Office of secretary, 1120 N. 24th St., W., Birmingham, Ala. 35234.

Assemblies of God: A pentecostal, evangelical, missionary denomination which grew out of the spiritual revivals of the early 1900's. The organization is composed of self-governing churches. Founded in Arkansas in 1914. Members (1982): 1,879,182. Headquarters: 1445 Boonville Ave., Springfield, Mo. 65802.

Bahá'í Faith: Baháís are followers of Bahá'u'lláh (1817–1892), whose religion upholds the basic principle of progressive revelation, religious unity and a new world order. There is a spiritual and administrative world center in Haifa, Israel. Headquarters, 536 Sheridan Rd., Wilmette, Ill. 60091.

Buddhist Churches of America: Organized in 1914 as the Buddhist Mission of North America, this body was incorporated in 1942 under the present name and represents the Jodo Shinshu Sect of Buddhism in this country. Members (1983): 100,000. Headquarters: 1710 Octavia St., San Francisco, Calif. 94109.

Christian and Missionary Alliance: An evangelical evangelistic, and missionary movement organized in 1887. It stresses "the deeper Christian life and consecration to the Lord's service." Members (1982): 204,713. Headquarters: 350 N. Highland Ave., Nyack, N.Y. 10960.

Christian Church (Disciples of Christ): In the revival period of the early nineteenth century, a movement resulted in the establishment of a fellowship called "Christians" or "Disciples." This movement calls for the reunion of the church on the basis of a return to New Testament faith and order. It is congregational in government. Members (1982): 1,156,458. Headquarters: 222 S. Downey Ave., Box 1986, Indianapolis, Ind. 46206.

Christian Churches and Churches of Christ: This fellowship, congregational in polity, has its origin in the movement to "restore the New Testament church in doctrine, ordinances and life." Members (1981): 1,063,254. North American Christian Convention, Box 39456, Cincinnati, Ohio 45239.

Christian Congregation: Incorporated in 1887, denomination provides ministerial affiliation for independent clergymen. Members (1982): 100,694. Office of general superintendent: 804 W. Hemlock St., LaFollette, Tenn. 37766.

Christian Reformed Church in North America: A group of Dutch Calvinists which dissented from the Reformed Church in America in 1857 and which was strengthened by later accessions from the same source and by immigration. Members (1982): 223,976. Office of stated clerk: William P. Brink, 2850 Kalamazoo Ave., S.E., Grand Rapids, Mich. 49560.

Church of Christ, Scientist: Founded by Mary Baker Eddy in 1879 to reinstate the healing power of original Christianity. As defined by Mrs. Eddy, her religion is the scientific system of divine healing.[1] Headquarters: Christian Science Church Center, Boston, Mass. 02115.

Church of God: Inaugurated by Bishop A. J. Tomlinson, who served as General Overseer 1903–43. Episcopal in administration. Members (1978): 75,890. Headquarters: 2504 Arrow Wood Dr., S.E., Huntsville, Ala. 35803.

Church of God (Anderson, Ind.): This group is one of the largest of the groups which have taken the name "Church of God." It originated about 1880 and emphasizes Christian unity. Members (1982): 184,685. Headquarters: Box 2420, Anderson, Ind. 46018.

Church of God (Cleveland, Tenn.): This church is one of the large groups which use the name "Church of God." Organized in 1886 in Tennessee as the Christian Union, it was reorganized in 1902 as the Holiness Church, and in 1907 under its present name. Members (1982): 463,992. Headquarters: Keith St. at 25th., N.W., Cleveland, Tenn. 37311.

Church of God in Christ: Organized in Arkansas in 1895, by C. P. Jones and C. H. Mason, who believed there was no salvation without holiness; incorporated 1897. Members (1982): 3,709,661. Headquarters: 939 Mason St., Memphis, Tenn. 38126.

Church of God in Christ, International: Organized in 1969 in Kansas City, Mo., by 14 bishops of the Church of God in Christ of Memphis, Tenn., after disagreement over polity and governmental authority. Church is Wesleyan in theology. Members (1982): 200,000. Headquarters: 170 Adelphi St., Brooklyn, N.Y. 11025.

Church of God of Prophecy: Organized in 1903 at Murphy, N. C. Doctrine stresses justification by faith and the second coming of Christ. Members (1982): 74,084. Headquarters: Bible Place, Cleveland, Tenn. 37311.

Church of the Brethren: German pietists from Krefeld, Germany, under the leadership of Peter Becker, entered the colonies in 1719, and settled at Germantown, Philadelphia, Pa. They hold to the principles of nonviolence, temperance, and the expression of religion through the good life. Members (1982): 168,844. Headquarters: 1451 Dundee Ave., Elgin, Ill. 60120.

Church of the Nazarene: One of the larger holiness bodies, organized in Pilot Point, Tex., in 1908. It is in general accord with the early doctrines of Methodism and emphasizes entire sanctification. Members (1982): 498,491. Headquarters: 6401 The Paseo, Kansas City, Mo. 64131.

Churches of Christ: This body is made up of a large group of churches, formerly reported with the Disciples of Christ but, since the religious census of 1906, reported separately. They are strictly congregational and have no organization larger than the local congregation. Members (1982): 1,605,000.

1. Membership figure not available. The manual of the church forbids "the numbering of people and the reporting of such statistics for publication."

Community Churches, National Council of: This body was formed in 1946 by the merger of the Biennial Council of Community Churches, a black group, with white churches which had the name of the present Council. Its members are ecumenically minded, congregationally governed, noncreedal Protestant churches. Members (1979): 190, 000. Headquarters: 900 Ridge Rd., LL1, Homewood, Ill. 60430.

Congregational Christian Churches: *See* United Church of Christ.

Congregational Christian Churches, National Association of: Organized in Detroit, Mich., in 1955 to continue the Congregational way of faith and order in church life. It has no doctrinal requirements, and participation by member churches is voluntary. Members (1983): 106,460. Headquarters: Box 1620, Oak Creek, Wis. 53154.

Disciples of Christ: *See* Christian Church.

Episcopal Church, The: This group entered the colonies with the earliest settlers as the Church of England. It became autonomous as the Protestant Episcopal Church in the U.S.A. and adopted that name in 1789. It is an integral part of the Anglican Communion. In 1967, the General Convention adopted "The Episocal Church" as an alternate name. Members (1982): 2,794,139. Headquarters: 815 Second Ave., New York, N.Y. 10017.

Evangelical and Reformed Church: *See* United Church of Christ.

Evangelical Covenant Church of America: This church has its roots in historical Christianity as it emerged in the Protestant Reformation in the biblical instruction of the Lutheran State Church of Sweden. Organized in 1885 in Chicago. Prior to 1957, it was known as the Evangelical Mission Covenant Church of America. Members (1982): 81,324. Headquarters: 5101 N. Francisco Ave., Chicago, Ill. 60625.

Evangelical Free Church of America: Organized in the 1880's in Boone, Iowa, as the Swedish Evangelical Free Mission. Later the name was changed to the Evangelical Free Church of America. In 1950, the Evangelical Free Church Association merged with this group. Members (1983): 110,555. Headquarters: 1515 E. 66th St., Minneapolis, Minn. 55423.

Evangelical United Brethren Church: *See* United Methodist Church under Methodist Churches.

Friends United Meeting: The Five Years Meeting of Friends was formed in 1902 by 11 Yearly Meetings entering into a loose confederation. Since then, two of the original Yearly Meetings have withdrawn (Kansas and Oregon) and two American and three Yearly Meetings outside the U. S. have joined. In 1965, the name was changed to Friends United Meeting. Members (1982): 59,338. Office of presiding clerk: 101 Quaker Hill Dr., Richmond, Ind. 47374.

Independent Fundamental Churches of America: Organized in 1930 by representatives of various independent churches. Members (1980): 120,446. Headquarters: 1860 Mannheim Rd., Westchester, Ill. 60153.

International Church of the Foursquare Gospel: An evangelistic missionary body organized by Aimee Semple McPherson in 1927. The parent church is Angelus Temple, 1100 Glendale Blvd., Los Angeles, Calif. 90026. Members (1963): 89,215.

Jehovah's Witnesses: A group calling themselves primitive Christians. They believe that the Kingdom under Christ will replace all earthly governments. Members (1982): 619,188. Headquarters: 25 Columbia Heights, Brooklyn, N.Y. 11201.

Latter-day Saints, Church of Jesus Christ of: Organized in 1830. A group in which the Bible, the Book of Mormon, the Doctrine and Covenants, and the Pearl of Great Price are regarded as the word of God. Their belief is summed up in 13 Articles of Faith written by Joseph Smith. Members (1982): 3,521,000. Headquarters: 50 E. North Temple St., Salt Lake City, Utah 84150.

Latter-day Saints, Reorganized Church of Jesus Christ of: A division among the Latter-day Saints (non-Mormon) occurred on the death of Joseph Smith in 1844. His son, Joseph Smith, became presiding officer of this group, which has headquarters at Independence, Mo. Members (1982): 201,460. Headquarters: the Auditorium, Box 1059, Auditorium, Independence, Mo. 64051.

Mennonite Church: The largest group of the Mennonites who began arriving in the U. S. in 1683, settling in Germantown, Pa. They derive their name from Menno Simons, born 1496. Members (1982): 101,501. Headquarters: 528 E. Madison St., Lombard, Ill. 60148.

Moravian Church in America (Unitas Fratrum): In 1735, Moravian missionaries of the pre-Reformation faith of John Hus came to Georgia, in 1740 to Pennsylvania, and in 1753 to North Carolina. Members: Northern Province (1982): 33,092. Headquarters: 69 W. Church St., P.O. Box 1245, Bethlehem, Pa. 18018; Southern Province (1982): 21,618. Headquarters: 459 S. Church St., Winston-Salem, N.C. 27108.

Old Order Amish Church: Members of this group worship in private homes and adhere to the older forms of worship and attire. Members (1981): 82, 460.

Pentecostal Church of God: Organized in 1919 at Chicago, Ill. The first convention was held in October, 1933. Members (1982): 91,008. Headquarters: Messenger Plaza, 211 Main St., Joplin, Mo. 64801.

Pentecostal Holiness Church: This body grew out of the holiness movement in the South and Middle West from 1895 to 1900. Members (1977): 86,103. Headquarters: Box 12609, Oklahoma City, Okla. 73157.

Plymouth Brethren (also known as Christian Brethren): This orthodox and evangelical movement began in Britain in the 1820s and has since become worldwide. It is made of up two groups—the smaller "exclusive" branch, which stresses the interdependency of congregations, and the "open" branch, in which each assembly is guided by local elders. Members (1983): 98,000.

Reformed Church in America: This group was established by the earliest Dutch settlers of New

York as the Reformed Protestant Dutch Church in 1628. Members (1980): 345,532. Headquarters: 475 Riverside Dr., New York, N.Y. 10115.

Salvation Army: An evangelistic organization, with a military government, first set up by General William Booth in England in 1865 and introduced into the U.S. in 1880. Members (1982): 419,475. Headquarters: 799 Bloomfield Ave., Verona, N.J. 07044.

Seventh-day Adventists: This body developed out of an interdenominational movement in the early decades of the 19th century, but was not formally organized until 1863. Their two cardinal points of faith are belief in the personal, imminent, premillennial return of Christ and observance of the seventh day as the Sabbath. Members (1982): 606,310. Headquarters: 6840 Eastern Ave., N.W., Washington, D.C. 20012.

Triumph the Church and Kingdom of God in Christ (International): Organized by Elder E. D. Smith in Georgia in 1902. This group emphasizes the sanctification and the Second Coming of Christ. Members (1972): 54,307. Headquarters: P.O. Box 77056, Birmingham, Ala. 35228.

Unitarian Universalist Association: This association is the result of a merger in 1961 of the American Unitarian Association, formed in 1825, and the Universalist Church in America, organized in the 1770's. Members (1982): 131,844. Headquarters: 25 Beacon St., Boston, Mass. 02108.

United Church of Christ: A merger in 1961 of the Evangelical and Reformed Church and the Congregational Christian Churches. Members (1982): 1,716,723. Headquarters: 105 Madison Ave., New York, N.Y. 10016.

United Pentecostal Church, International: Pentecostal Church, Inc., and Pentecostal Assemblies of Jesus Christ merged in 1945 at St. Louis. Members (1982): 465,000. Headquarters: 8855 Dunn Rd., Hazelwood, Mo. 63042.

Wesleyan Church: Originated through the uniting of the Pilgrim Holiness Church (1897) and the Wesleyan Methodist Church of America (1843) in 1968. Members (1982): 105,221. Headquarters: Box 2000, Marion, Ind. 46953.

Other Religious Groups

(1,000–50,000 members)

Advent Christian Church (1980: 29,838)
Albanian Orthodox Archdiocese in America (1978: 40,000)
Albanian Orthodox Diocese of America (1982: 5,250)
American Rescue Workers (1978: 2,140)
Anglican Orthodox Church (1972: 2,630)
Apostolic Christian Church (Nazarean) (1981: 2,684)
Apostolic Christian Churches of America (1983: 21,173)
Apostolic Faith (1982: 4,100)
Apostolic Lutheran Church of America (1982: 6,500)
Associate Reformed Presbyterian Church (General Synod) (1980: 31,518)
Beachy Amish Mennonite Church (1981: 5,460)
Berean Fundamental Church (1981: 3,350)
Bethel Ministerial Association (1982: 1,500)
Bible Church of Christ (1983: 4,350)
Bible Protestant Church (1978: 2,077)
Bible Way Church of Our Lord Jesus Christ World Wide (1970: 30,000)
Brethren Church (Ashland, Ohio) (1982: 14,857)
Brethren in Christ Church (1981: 16,201)
Christ Catholic Church (1982: 1,354)
Christadelphians (1964: 15,800)
Christian Catholic Church (Evangelical-Protestant) (1983: 2,500)
Christian Church of North America, General Council (1982: 12,500)
Christian Union (1979: 5,463)
Church of Christ (1972: 2,400)
Church of God General Conference (Oregon, Ill.) (1983: 5,781)
Church of God (7th Day) (1960: 2,000)
Church of God (Seventh Day), Denver (1982: 4,875)
Church of God by Faith (1973: 4,500)
Church of God in Christ (Mennonite) (1981: 10,826)
Church of God of the Mountain Assembly (1977: 3,125)
Church of Illumination (1963: 9,000)
Church of Jesus Christ (Bickertonites) (1981: 2,654)
Church of Our Lord Jesus Christ of the Apostolic Faith (1954: 45,000)
Church of the Lutheran Brethren of America (1982: 10,580)
Church of the Lutheran Confession (1982: 8,986)
Churches of Christ in Christian Union (1980: 11,943)
Churches of God, General Conference (1982: 34,241)
Congregational Holiness Church (1981: 8,347)
Conservative Congregational Christian Conference (1982: 26,008)
Duck River (and Kindred) Association of Baptists (1975: 8,632)
Estonian Evangelical Lutheran Church (1982: 7,995)
Ethical Culture Movement (1982: 4,000)
Evangelical Church of North America (1980: 13,088)
Evangelical Congregational Church (1983: 39,710)
Evangelical Friends Alliance (1982: 24,095)
Evangelical Lutheran Synod (1982: 20,025)
Evangelical Mennonite Brethren Conference (1982: 2,047)
Evangelical Mennonite Church (1982: 3,832)
Evangelical Methodist Church (1974: 10,502)
Free Christian Zion Church of Christ (1956: 22,260)
Free Lutheran Congregations, Association of (1983: 16,759)
Friends General Conference (1974: 26,184)
Full Gospel Assemblies, International (1983: 3,800)
General Church of the New Jerusalem (1971: 2,143)
General Conference of Mennonite Brethren Churches (1981: 17,065)
General Convention, The Swedenborgian Church (1981: 1,820)
General Conference of the Evangelical Baptist Church (1952: 2,200)
Grace Brethren Churches, Fellowship of (1981: 42,023)
Grace Gospel Fellowship (1983: 4,250)
Holy Ukrainian Autocephalic Orthodox Church in Exile (1965: 4,800)
House of God, Which Is the Church of the Living God, the Pillar and Ground of the Truth (1956: 2,350)
Hungarian Reformed Church in America (1982: 11,000)
Hutterian Brethren (1980: 3,684)
International Pentecostal Church of Christ (1983: 2,685)
Latvian Evangelical Lutheran Church in America (1982: 13,526)
Liberal Catholic Church—Province of the United States of America (1973: 2,963)
Mennonite Church, The General Conference (1981: 36,644)
Metropolitan Community Churches, Universal Fellowship of (1983: 32,000)
Missionary Church, The (1982: 25,371)
National Spiritualist Association of Churches (1976: 5,168)
Netherlands Reformed Congregations (1982: 8,760)

New Apostolic Church of North America (1982: 29,638)
North American Baptist Conference (1982: 42,735)
Old German Baptist Brethren (1982: 5,254)
Old Order (Wisler) Mennonite (1980: 9,731)
Open Bible Standard Churches (1983: 46,651)
(Original) Church of God, The (1971: 20,000)
Orthodox Presbyterian Church, The (1981: 17,108)
Pentecostal Assemblies of the World (1960: 4,500)
Pentecostal Free-Will Baptist Church, The (1983: 9,280)
Pillar of Fire (1949: 5,100)
Primitive Methodist Church, U.S.A. (1981: 9,978)
Protestant Conference (Lutheran), The (1982: 1,605)
Protestant Reformed Churches in America (1980: 4,544)
Reformed Church in the United States (1982: 3,710)
Reformed Episcopal Church (1980: 6,200)
Reformed Methodist Union Episcopal Church (1976: 3,800)
Reformed Presbyterian Church of North America (1981: 4,836)
Reformed Zion Union Apostolic Church (1965: 16,000)
Religious Society of Friends (Conservative) (1979: 1,832)
Religious Society of Friends (Unaffiliated Meetings) (1980: 6,386)
Romanian Orthodox Episcopate of America, The (1982: 40,000)
Schwenkfelder Church, The (1982: 2,700)
Second Cumberland Presbyterian Church in U.S. (1959: 30,000)
Separate Baptists in Christ (1982: 8,800)
Seventh-Day Baptist General Conference (1980: 5,008)
Social Brethren (1975: 1,784)
Southern Methodist Church (1977: 11,000)
Syrian Orthodox Church of Antioch (Archdiocese of the U.S.A. and Canada) (1982: 30,000)
Ukrainian Orthodox Church in America (Ecumenical Patriarchate) (1977: 25,000)
United Brethren in Christ (1982: 26,869)
United Holy Church of America (1960: 28,980)
Unity of the Brethren (1964: 6,142)
Vedanta Society of New York (1983: 1,000)
Volunteers of America (1978: 36,634)

Roman Catholic Pontiffs

St. Peter, of Bethsaida in Galilee, Prince of the Apostles, was the first Pope. He lived first in Antioch and then in Rome for 25 years. In AD 64 or 67, he was martyred. St. Linus became the second Pope.

Name	Birthplace	Reigned From	Reigned To
St. Linus	Tuscia	67	76
St. Anacletus (Cletus)	Rome	76	88
St. Clement	Rome	88	97
St. Evaristus	Greece	97	105
St. Alexander I	Rome	105	115
St. Sixtus I	Rome	115	125
St. Telesphorus	Greece	125	136
St. Hyginus	Greece	136	140
St. Pius I	Aquileia	140	155
St. Anicetus	Syria	155	166
St. Soter	Campania	166	175
St. Eleutherius	Epirus	175	189
St. Victor I	Africa	189	199
St. Zephyrinus	Rome	199	217
St. Callistus I	Rome	217	222
St. Urban I	Rome	222	230
St. Pontian	Rome	230	235
St. Anterus	Greece	235	236
St. Fabian	Rome	236	250
St. Cornelius	Rome	251	253
St. Lucius I	Rome	253	254
St. Stephen I	Rome	254	257
St. Sixtus II	Greece	257	258
St. Dionysius	Unknown	259	268
St. Felix I	Rome	269	274
St. Eutychian	Luni	275	283
St. Caius	Dalmatia	283	296
St. Marcellinus	Rome	296	304
St. Marcellus I	Rome	308	309
St. Eusebius	Greece	309[1]	309[1]
St. Meltiades	Africa	311	314
St. Sylvester I	Rome	314	335
St. Marcus	Rome	336	336
St. Julius I	Rome	337	352
Liberius	Rome	352	366
St. Damasus I	Spain	366	384
St. Siricius	Rome	384	399
St. Anastasius I	Rome	399	401
St. Innocent I	Albano	401	417
St. Zozimus	Greece	417	418
St. Boniface I	Rome	418	422
St. Celestine I	Campania	422	432
St. Sixtus III	Rome	432	440
St. Leo I (the Great)	Tuscany	440	461
St. Hilary	Sardinia	461	468
St. Simplicius	Tivoli	468	483
St. Felix III (II)[2]	Rome	483	492
St. Gelasius I	Africa	492	496
Anastasius II	Rome	496	498
St. Symmachus	Sardinia	498	514
St. Hormisdas	Frosinone	514	523
St. John I	Tuscany	523	526
St. Felix IV (III)	Samnium	526	530
Boniface II	Rome	530	532
John II	Rome	533	535
St. Agapitus I	Rome	535	536
St. Silverius	Campania	536	537
Vigilius	Rome	537	555
Pelagius I	Rome	556	561
John III	Rome	561	574
Benedict I	Rome	575	579
Pelagius II	Rome	579	590
St. Gregory I (the Great)	Rome	590	604
Sabinianus	Tuscany	604	606
Boniface III	Rome	607	607
St. Boniface IV	Marsi	608	615
St. Deusdedit (Adeodatus I)	Rome	615	618
Boniface V	Naples	619	625
Honorius I	Campania	625	638
Severinus	Rome	640	640
John IV	Dalmatia	640	642
Theodore I	Greece	642	649
St. Martin I	Todi	649	655
St. Eugene I[3]	Rome	654	657
St. Vitalian	Segni	657	672
Adeodatus II	Rome	672	676
Donus	Rome	676	678
St. Agatho	Sicily	678	681
St. Leo II	Sicily	682	683
St. Benedict II	Rome	684	685

Name	Birthplace	Reigned From	To	Name	Birthplace	Reigned From	To
John V	Syria	685	686	Benedict IX (3rd time)	—	1047	1048
Conon	Unknown	686	687	Damasus II	Bavaria	1048	1048
St. Sergius I	Syria	687	701	St. Leo IX	Alsace	1049	1054
John VI	Greece	701	705	Victor II	Germany	1055	1057
John VII	Greece	705	707	Stephen IX (X)	Lorraine	1057	1058
Sisinnius	Syria	708	708	Nicholas II	Burgundy	1059	1061
Constantine	Syria	708	715	Alexander II	Milan	1061	1073
St. Gregory II	Rome	715	731	St. Gregory VII	Tuscany	1073	1085
St. Gregory III	Syria	731	741	Bl. Victor III	Benevento	1086	1087
St. Zachary	Greece	741	752	Bl. Urban II	France	1088	1099
Stephen II (III)[4]	Rome	752	757	Paschal II	Ravenna	1099	1118
St. Paul I	Rome	757	767	Gelasius II	Gaeta	1118	1119
Stephen III (IV)	Sicily	768	772	Callistus II	Burgundy	1119	1124
Adrian I	Rome	772	795	Honorius II	Flagnano	1124	1130
St. Leo III	Rome	795	816	Innocent II	Rome	1130	1143
Stephen IV (V)	Rome	816	817	Celestine II	Città di Castello	1143	1144
St. Paschal I	Rome	817	824	Lucius II	Bologna	1144	1145
Eugene II	Rome	824	827	Bl. Eugene III	Pisa	1145	1153
Valentine	Rome	827	827	Anastasius IV	Rome	1153	1154
Gregory IV	Rome	827	844	Adrian IV	England	1154	1159
Sergius II	Rome	844	847	Alexander III	Siena	1159	1181
St. Leo IV	Rome	847	855	Lucius III	Lucca	1181	1185
Benedict III	Rome	855	858	Urban III	Milan	1185	1187
St. Nicholas I (the Great)	Rome	858	867	Gregory VIII	Benevento	1187	1187
Adrian II	Rome	867	872	Clement III	Rome	1187	1191
John VIII	Rome	872	882	Celestine III	Rome	1191	1198
Marinus I	Gallese	882	884	Innocent III	Anagni	1198	1216
St. Adrian III	Rome	884	885	Honorius III	Rome	1216	1227
Stephen V (VI)	Rome	885	891	Gregory IX	Anagni	1227	1241
Formosus	Portus	891	896	Celestine IV	Milan	1241	1241
Boniface VI	Rome	896	896	Innocent IV	Genoa	1243	1254
Stephen VI (VII)	Rome	896	897	Alexander IV	Anagni	1254	1261
Romanus	Gallese	897	897	Urban IV	Troyes	1261	1264
Theodore II	Rome	897	897	Clement IV	France	1265	1268
John IX	Tivoli	898	900	Bl. Gregory X	Piacenza	1271	1276
Benedict IV	Rome	900	903	Bl. Innocent V	Savoy	1276	1276
Leo V	Ardea	903	903	Adrian V	Genoa	1276	1276
Sergius III	Rome	904	911	John XXI[7]	Portugal	1276	1277
Anastasius III	Rome	911	913	Nicholas III	Rome	1277	1280
Landus	Sabina	913	914	Martin IV[3]	France	1281	1285
John X	Tossignano	914	928	Honorius IV	Rome	1285	1287
Leo VI	Rome	928	928	Nicholas IV	Ascoli	1288	1292
Stephen VII (VIII)	Rome	928	931	St. Celestine V	Isernia	1294	1294
John XI	Rome	931	935	Boniface VIII	Anagni	1294	1303
Leo VII	Rome	936	939	Bl. Benedict XI	Treviso	1303	1304
Stephen VIII (IX)	Rome	939	942	Clement V	France	1305	1314
Marinus II	Rome	942	946	John XXII	Cahors	1316	1334
Agapitus II	Rome	946	955	Benedict XII	France	1334	1342
John XII	Tusculum	955	964	Clement VI	France	1342	1352
Leo VIII[5]	Rome	963	965	Innocent VI	France	1352	1362
Benedict V[5]	Rome	964	966	Bl. Urban V	France	1362	1370
John XIII	Rome	965	972	Gregory XI	France	1370	1378
Benedict VI	Rome	973	974	Urban VI	Naples	1378	1389
Benedict VII	Rome	974	983	Boniface IX	Naples	1389	1404
John XIV	Pavia	983	984	Innocent VII	Sulmona	1404	1406
John XV	Rome	985	996	Gregory XII	Venice	1406	1415
Gregory V	Saxony	996	999	Martin V	Rome	1417	1431
Sylvester II	Auvergne	999	1003	Eugene IV	Venice	1431	1447
John XVII	Rome	1003	1003	Nicholas V	Sarzana	1447	1455
John XVIII	Rome	1004	1009	Callistus III	Jativa	1455	1458
Sergius IV	Rome	1009	1012	Pius II	Siena	1458	1464
Benedict VIII	Tusculum	1012	1024	Paul II	Venice	1464	1471
John XIX	Tusculum	1024	1032	Sixtus IV	Savona	1471	1484
Benedict IX[6]	Tusculum	1032	1044	Innocent VIII	Genoa	1484	1492
Sylvester III	Rome	1045	1045	Alexander VI	Jativa	1492	1503
Benedict IX (2nd time)	—	1045	1045	Pius III	Siena	1503	1503
Gregory VI	Rome	1045	1046	Julius II	Savona	1503	1513
Clement II	Saxony	1046	1047	Leo X	Florence	1513	1521

Name	Birthplace	Reigned From	To	Name	Birthplace	Reigned From	To
Adrian VI	Utrecht	1522	1523	Innocent XII	Spinazzola	1691	1700
Clement VII	Florence	1523	1534	Clement XI	Urbino	1700	1721
Paul III	Rome	1534	1549	Innocent XIII	Rome	1721	1724
Julius III	Rome	1550	1555	Benedict XIII	Gravina	1724	1730
Marcellus II	Montepulciano	1555	1555	Clement XII	Florence	1730	1740
Paul IV	Naples	1555	1559	Benedict XIV	Bologna	1740	1758
Pius IV	Milan	1559	1565	Clement XIII	Venice	1758	1769
St. Pius V	Bosco	1566	1572	Clement XIV	Rimini	1769	1774
Gregory XIII	Bologna	1572	1585	Pius VI	Cesena	1775	1799
Sixtus V	Grottammare	1585	1590	Pius VII	Cesena	1800	1823
Urban VII	Rome	1590	1590	Leo XII	Genga	1823	1829
Gregory XIV	Cremona	1590	1591	Pius VIII	Cingoli	1829	1830
Innocent IX	Bologna	1591	1591	Gregory XVI	Belluno	1831	1846
Clement VIII	Florence	1592	1605	Pius IX	Senegallia	1846	1878
Leo XI	Florence	1605	1605	Leo XIII	Carpineto	1878	1903
Paul V	Rome	1605	1621	St. Pius X	Riese	1903	1914
Gregory XV	Bologna	1621	1623	Benedict XV	Genoa	1914	1922
Urban VIII	Florence	1623	1644	Pius XI	Desio	1922	1939
Innocent X	Rome	1644	1655	Pius XII	Rome	1939	1958
Alexander VII	Siena	1655	1667	John XXIII	Sotto il Monte	1958	1963
Clement IX	Pistoia	1667	1669	Paul VI	Concesio	1963	1978
Clement X	Rome	1670	1676	John Paul I	Forno di Canale	1978	1978
Bl. Innocent XI	Como	1676	1689	John Paul II	Wadowice, Poland	1978	
Alexander VIII	Venice	1689	1691				

1. Or 310. 2. He should be called Felix II, and his successors of the same name should be numbered accordingly. The discrepancy was caused by the erroneous insertion in some lists of the name of St. Felix of Rome, Martyr. 3. He was elected during the exile of St. Martin I, who endorsed him as Pope. 4. After St. Zachary died, a Roman priest named Stephen was elected but died before his consecration as Bishop of Rome. His name is not included in all lists for this reason. In view of this historical confusion, the *National Catholic Almanac* lists the true Stephen II as Stephen II (III), the true Stephen III as Stephen III (IV), etc. 5. Confusion exists concerning the legitimacy of claims. If the deposition of John was invalid, Leo was an antipope until after the end of Benedict's reign. If the deposition of John was valid, Leo was the legitimate Pope and Benedict an antipope. 6. If the triple removal of Benedict IX was not valid, Sylvester III, Gregory VI, and Clement II were antipopes. 7. Elimination was made of the name of John XX in an effort to rectify the numerical designation of Popes named John. The error dates back to the time of John XV. 8. The names of Marinus I and Marinus II were construed as Martin. In view of these two pontificates and the earlier reign of St. Martin I, this pontiff was called Martin IV. *Source: National Catholic Almanac,* from *Annuarto Pontificio.*

Books of the Bible

OLD TESTAMENT—STANDARD VERSIONS

Genesis
Exodus
Leviticus
Numbers
Deuteronomy
Joshua
Judges
Ruth
I Samuel
II Samuel
I Kings
II Kings
I Chronicles
II Chronicles
Ezra
Nehemiah
Esther
Job
Psalms
Proverbs
Ecclesiastes
Song of Solomon
Isaiah
Jeremiah
Lamentations
Ezekiel
Daniel
Hosea
Joel
Amos
Obadiah
Jonah
Micah
Nahum
Habakkuk
Zephaniah
Haggai
Zechariah
Malachi

NEW TESTAMENT—STANDARD VERSIONS

Matthew
Mark
Luke
John
Acts
Romans
Corinthians
Galatians
Ephesians
Philippians
Colossians
Thessalonians
Timothy
Titus
Philemon
Hebrews
James
Peter
John
Jude
Revelation

OLD TESTAMENT—DOUAY VERSION[1]

Genesis
Exodus
Leviticus
Numbers
Deuteronomy
Josue
Judges
Ruth
I Kings
II Kings
III Kings
IV Kings
I Paralipomenon
II Paralipomenon
I Esdras
II Esdras
Tobias
Judith
Esther
Job
Psalms
Proverbs
Ecclesiastes
Canticle of Canticles
Wisdom
Ecclesiasticus
Isaias
Jeremias
Lamentations
Baruch
Ezechiel
Daniel
Osee
Joel
Amos
Abdias
Jonas
Micheas
Nahum
Habacuc
Sophonias
Aggeus
Zacharias
Malachias
I Machabees
II Machabees

1. In the Douay Version of the Bible, the books of the New Testament are the same as those of the Authorized (King James) Version, except that the Revelation of St. John is called the Apocalypse of St. John in the Douay Version.

U.S. Passport and Customs Information

Source: Department of State, Passport Services and Department of the Treasury, Customs Service.

Passports

With a few exceptions, a passport is required for all United States citizens to depart from and enter the United States and to enter most foreign countries. A United States citizen is not required by United States laws or regulations to have a valid passport for travel to or in North, South, or Central America, except Cuba. It is, however, recommended that a passport be obtained for travel to Central and South America since many of the countries require that United States citizens be in possession of a valid passport. United States travelers should carry documentary evidence of their United States citizenship and identity to facilitate re-entry into the United States. Travelers should check passport and visa requirements with consular officials of the countries to be visited well in advance of their departure date.

Applications for passport may be made to any Passport Agent; to a clerk of any Federal court or State court of record, or a judge or clerk or any probate court, accepting applications; or at a Post Office selected to accept passport applications. Passport agencies are located in Boston; Chicago; Honolulu; Houston; Los Angeles; Miami; New Orleans; New York; Philadelphia; San Francisco; Seattle; Stamford, Conn.; and Washington, D.C.

All persons are required to obtain individual passports in their own names. Neither spouses nor children may be included in each others' passports. Any applicant who is 13 years of age or older must appear in person before the clerk or agent executing the application. For children under the age of 13, a parent or guardian may execute an application for them.

A first passport must be applied for in person. Applicants must present evidence of citizenship (e.g., a birth certificate), personal identification (e. g., driver's license), two identical photographs taken within six months (2 × 2 inches, with the image size measured from the bottom of the chin to the top of the head [including hair] not less than 1 inch nor more than 1 3/8 inches, signed in the center on the reverse; vending machine photographs not acceptable), plus the application. A fee of $35 plus a $7 execution fee is charged for adults 18 years and older. The fee for children under 18 years of age is $20 for a passport and $7 for the execution of the application. No execution fee is payable when using DSP-82, "Application for Passport by Mail."

You may apply by mail if you have been the bearer of a passport issued within eight years prior to the date of a new application; are able to submit your most recent United States passport with your new application; your previous passport was not issued before your 18th birthday. If you are eligible to apply by mail, include your previous passport, completed and signed Application for Passport by Mail, new signed photographs, and the correct passport fee of either $35 or $20 as explained

Expenditures of Visitors in U.S.

(in millions of dollars)

Country or region of permanent residence	1983	1982	1981	1980	1979
Transportation—U.S. Flag Carriers	$2,524	$2,692	$2,575	$2,062	$1,677
Expenditures in U.S.	11,408	12,393	12,913	10,588	8,441
Canada	3,168	2,624	2,672	2,501	2,092
Mexico	1,951	3,098	3,775	2,522	1,975
U.S. border area	1,457	2,308	2,547	1,614	1,266
Overseas Visitors	6,289	6,671	6,466	5,565	4,374
Western Europe	2,157	2,476	2,549	2,192	1,667
United Kingdom	466	547	634	530	375
Germany	542	637	659	564	440
France	254	287	279	244	180
Italy	111	113	114	108	84
Netherlands	133	137	139	122	97
Belgium	n.a.	n.a.	n.a.	n.a.	48
Sweden	n.a.	n.a.	n.a.	n.a.	n.a.
Switzerland	n.a.	n.a.	n.a.	n.a.	n.a.
Other	n.a.	n.a.	n.a.	n.a.	n.a.
Caribbean and Central America	684	525	469	423	375
South America	1,091	1,269	1,273	1,063	793
Other Areas	2,357	2,401	2,175	1,887	1,539
Japan	1,128	1,084	949	824	699
Total expenditures	**13,932**	**15,085**	**15,488**	**12,650**	**10,118**

NOTE: n.a. = not available. *Source:* Department of Commerce, Bureau of Economic Activities.

above. The $7 execution fee is not required when applying by mail.

If you claim citizenship by naturalization, a Certificate of Naturalization is required.

Passports may be amended to show a married name or legal change of name, to correct descriptive data, or to exclude a person previously included.

Any alterations by the bearer other than change of address and notification data appearing in the passport are forbidden.

A passport is valid for ten years from the date of issue for adults over 18 years old and is valid for five years for children under 18 years of age, unless specifically limited by the Secretary of State to a shorter period of validity.

Loss, theft or destruction of passport should be reported immediately to local police authorities and to Passport Services, Washington, D.C., 20520, or, if overseas, to the nearest American embassy or consulate. Your passport is a valuable citizenship and identity document. It should be carefully safeguarded. Its loss could cause you unnecessary travel complications as well as significant expense.

NOTE: This passport information could be subject to change and should be checked with your nearest Passport official.

Customs

United States residents must declare all articles acquired abroad and in their possession at the time of their return. In addition, articles acquired in the U.S. Virgin Islands, American Samoa, or Guam and not accompanying you must be declared at the time of your return. The wearing or use of an article acquired abroad does *not* exempt it from duty. Customs declaration forms are distributed on vessels and planes, and should be prepared in advance of arrival for presentation to the customs inspectors.

If you have not exceeded the duty-free exemption allowed, you may make an oral declaration to the customs inspector. A written declaration is necessary when (1) total fair retail value of articles exceeds $400 (keep your sales slips); (2) over 1 liter of liquor, 200 cigarettes, or 100 cigars are included; (3) items are not intended for your personal or household use, or articles brought home for another person; and (4) when a customs duty or internal revenue tax is collectible on any article in your possession.

An exception to the above are regulations applicable to articles purchased in the U.S. Virgin Islands, American Samoa, or Guam where you may receive a customs exemption of $800. Not more than $400 of this exemption may be applied to merchandise obtained elsewhere than in these islands. Four liters of alcoholic beverages and 1000 cigarettes may be included provided not more than one liter and 200 cigarettes were acquired elsewhere than in these islands. Articles acquired in and sent from these islands to the United States may be claimed under your duty-free personal exemption if properly declared at the time of your return.

Articles accompanying you, in excess of your personal exemption, up to $1000 will be assessed at a flat rate of duty of 10% based on fair retail value in country of acquisition. (If articles were acquired in the insular possessions, the flat rate of duty is 5% and these goods may accompany you or be shipped home.) These articles must be for your personal use or for use as gifts and not for sale. This provision may be used every 30 days, excluding the day of your last arrival. Any items which have a "free" duty rate will be excluded before duty is calculated.

Other exemptions include in part: automobiles, boats, planes, or other vehicles taken abroad for noncommercial use. Foreign-made personal articles (e.g., watches, cameras, etc.) taken abroad should be registered with Customs before departure. Gifts of not more than $50 can be shipped back to the United States tax and duty free ($100 if mailed from the Virgin Islands, American Samoa, or Guam). Household effects and tools of trade which you take out of the United States are duty free at time of return.

Prohibited and restricted articles include in part: absinthe, narcotics and dangerous drugs, obscene articles and publications, seditious and treasonable materials, hazardous articles (e.g., fireworks, dangerous toys, toxic and poisonous substances, and switchblade knives), biological materials of public health or veterinary importance, fruit, vegetables and plants, meats, poultry and products thereof, birds, monkeys, and turtles.

If you understate the value of an article you declare, or if you otherwise misrepresent an article in your declaration, you may have to pay a penalty in addition to payment of duty. Under certain circumstances, the article could be seized and forfeited if the penalty is not paid.

If you fail to declare an article acquired abroad, not only is the article subject to seizure and forfeiture, but you will be liable for a personal penalty in an amount equal to the value of the article in the United States. In addition, you may also be liable to criminal prosecution.

If you carry more than $5,000 into or out of the United States in currency (either United States or foreign money), negotiable instruments in bearer form, or travelers checks, a report must be filed with United States Customs at the time you arrive or depart with such amounts.

As U.S. restrictions on travel to Cuba, North Korea, Vietnam, and Cambodia have been eased, the Office of Foreign Assets Control (FAC) issued a general license, effective March 21, 1977, which allows visitors to those countries to purchase a maximum of $100 worth of goods. This amount is based on retail value in the country where acquired. These articles must be for personal use—not for resale—and must accompany the traveler on his entry into the U.S. This allowance may be used only once every 6 months.

Foreign Currency Exchange

Visitors can usually change their U.S. dollars into the appropriate foreign currency at their point of departure. Most airports have currency exchange facilities, generally open 9:00 A.M. to 10:00 P.M.

The Deak-Perera Group, the largest private organization specializing in foreign money exchange, has offices in some airports. It is generally advisable for an American traveling to a foreign destination to have a small amount of the foreign currency on hand on arrival. Currency can usually be exchanged at foreign entry points.

Price Index Figures for Domestic Travel and Selected Components, 1977–1982

(1967 = 100)

	1982	1981	1980	1979	1978	1977
Travel price index	337.2	319.7	283.2	234.3	203.3	187.8
Gasoline	389.3	410.9	369.1	265.6	196.3	188.2
Common carrier transportation fares						
Taxicab	298.6	283.1	259.5	221.7	203.5	189.9
Intercity train	334.0	297.9	250.1	212.4	194.6	180.6
Air	395.0	358.4	284.8	205.8	190.6	182.0
Bus	368.8	339.8	297.1	260.0	240.2	223.5
Lodging	349.0	312.8	280.7	245.8	212.7	187.0
Food service	306.5	291.0	267.0	242.9	218.4	200.3
Entertainment services	231.8	216.3	201.0	187.6	175.4	166.2
Incidentals	215.4	206.1	193.3	178.0	168.7	161.5

Source: U.S. Travel Data Center.

Expenditures of U.S. Travelers to Foreign Countries

(in millions of dollars)

Type of expense	1983	1982	1981	1980	1975
Transportation fare payments	n.a.	n.a.	n.a.	$6,111	$3,726
Foreign flag carriers	$5,532	$4,772	$4,487	3,607	2,263
U.S. flag carriers	n.a.	n.a.	n.a.	2,504	1,463
Travel payments in foreign countries	13,977	12,374	11,479	10,397	6,417
Canada	2,160	1,936	2,070	1,817	1,306
Mexico	3,576	3,324	2,862	2,564	1,637
Mexican border zone	1,996	2,089	1,648	1,416	1,047
Total overseas areas	8,241	7,134	6,547	6,016	3,474
Europe and Mediterranean[1]	4,412	3,787	3,587	3,412	1,918
Western Europe	3,991	3,413	3,123	3,021	1,709
United Kingdom	1,061	895	952	903	404
France	596	464	375	383	226
Italy	485	490	301	360	194
Switzerland	294	206	127	150	121
West Germany	416	411	361	322	174
Austria	150	145	74	104	65
Denmark	73	48	65	49	43
Sweden	71	45	65	42	29
Norway	60	55	89	51	44
Netherlands	128	97	75	95	60
Belgium and Luxembourg	65	57	45	44	39
Spain	208	153	208	173	135
Portugal	27	45	41	69	19
Ireland	84	104	84	103	55
Greece	225	145	171	139	73
Other Western Europe	48	53	90	34	28
Other Europe and Mediterranean	421	374	464	391	209
Israel	168	166	192	179	57
Other[2]	253	208	272	212	152
Caribbean Area and Central America	1,519	1,349	1,277	1,134	787
Bermuda	220	230	192	191	118
Bahama	402	340	243	262	161
Jamaica	183	153	127	118	118
Other British West Indies	225	188	252	189	103
Netherlands West Indies	200	155	249	157	97
Other West Indies and Central America	289	283	214	217	190
South America	422	380	383	392	242
Other overseas areas	1,888	1,618	1,300	1,078	527
Japan	302	272	214	185	131
Hong Kong	212	197	151	145	75
Australia and New Zealand	492	367	343	234	54
Other	882	782	592	514	267
Total expenses[3]	**n.a.**	**n.a.**	**n.a.**	**16,508**	**10,143**

1. Includes Algeria, Cyprus, Egypt, Israel, Lebanon, Libya, Malta, Morocco, Syria, Tunisia, and Turkey. 2. Includes U.S.S.R. 3. Cruise passenger fare payments included in transportation payments (predominantly foreign flag carriers). Shore expenditures included in regional and country totals. NOTE: n.a. = not available. *Source:* Department of Commerce, Bureau of Economic Analysis.

Average Daily Temperatures (°F) in Tourist Cities

Location	January High	January Low	April High	April Low	July High	July Low	October High	October Low
U.S. CITIES								
(See Weather and Climate Section)								
CANADA								
(See Canadian Section)								
MEXICO								
Acapulco	85	70	87	71	89	75	88	74
Mexico City	66	42	78	52	74	54	70	50
OVERSEAS								
Australia (Sydney)	78	65	71	58	60	46	71	56
Austria (Vienna)	34	26	57	41	75	59	55	44
Bahamas (Nassau)	77	65	81	69	88	75	85	73
Bermuda (Hamilton)	68	58	71	59	85	73	79	69
Brazil (Rio de Janeiro)	84	73	80	69	75	63	77	66
Denmark (Copenhagen)	36	29	50	37	72	55	53	42
Egypt (Cairo)	65	47	83	57	96	70	86	65
France (Paris)	42	32	60	41	76	55	59	44
Germany (Berlin)	35	26	55	38	74	55	55	41
Greece (Athens)	54	42	67	52	90	72	74	60
Hong Kong	64	56	75	67	87	78	81	73
India (Calcutta)	80	55	97	76	90	79	89	74
Italy (Rome)	54	39	68	46	88	64	73	53
Israel (Jerusalem)	55	41	73	50	87	63	81	59
Japan (Tokyo)	47	29	63	46	83	70	69	55
Nigeria (Lagos)	88	74	89	77	83	74	85	74
Netherlands (Amsterdam)	40	34	52	43	69	59	56	48
Puerto Rico (San Juan)	81	67	84	69	87	74	87	73
South Africa (Cape Town)	78	60	72	53	63	45	70	52
Spain (Madrid)	47	33	64	44	87	62	66	48
United Kingdom (London)	44	35	56	40	73	55	58	44
United Kingdom (Edinburgh)	43	35	50	39	65	52	53	44
U.S.S.R. (Moscow)	21	9	47	31	76	55	46	34
Venezuela (Caracas)	75	56	81	60	78	61	79	61
Yugoslavia (Belgrade)	37	27	64	45	84	61	65	47

State and City Tourism Offices

The following is a selected list of state, tourism offices. Where a toll-free 800 number is available, it is given. However, the numbers are subject to change.

ALABAMA
Bureau of Publicity and Information
532 S. Perry St.
Montgomery, AL 36130-2051
205-261-4169 or
1-800-ALABAMA

ALASKA
Alaska Division of Tourism
Pouch E
Juneau, AK 99811
907-465-2010

ARIZONA
Arizona Office of Tourism
Suite 506
3507 N. Central Ave.
Phoenix, AZ 85012
602-255-3618

ARKANSAS
Arkansas Department of Parks and Tourism
1 Capitol Mall
Little Rock, AR 72201
501-371-7777 or
1-800-643-8383

CALIFORNIA
California Office of Tourism
Department of Economic and Business Development
1121 L Street
Suite 103
Sacramento, CA 95814
916-332-1396

COLORADO
Office of Tourism
Colorado Tourism Board
5500 S. Syracuse #267
Englewood, CO 80111

CONNECTICUT
Tourism Promotion Service
Connecticut Department of Economic Development
210 Washington St.
Hartford, CT 06106
203-566-3385 or
1-800-243-1685

DELAWARE
Delaware State Travel Service
Delaware Development Office
99 Kings Highway
P.O. Box 1401
Dover, DE 19901
302-736-4271 or
1-800-441-8846

DISTRICT OF COLUMBIA
Washington Convention and Visitors Association
Suite 250

1575 Eye Street, NW
Washington, D.C. 20005
202-789-7000

FLORIDA
Department of Commerce Visitors Inquiry
126 Van Buren St.
Tallahassee, FL 32301
904-487-1462

GEORGIA
Tourist Division
P.O. Box 1776
Atlanta, GA 30301
404-656-3590

HAWAII
Hawaii Visitors Bureau
2270 Kalakana Ave., Suite 801
Honolulu, HI 96815
808-923-1811

IDAHO
Economic and Community Affairs
State Capitol Bldg., Rm. 108
Boise, ID 83720
208-334-2470 or
1-800-635-7820

ILLINOIS
Office of Tourism
620 East Adams Street
Springfield, IL 62701
217-782-7139

INDIANA
Indiana Dept. of Commerce
Tourism Division
1 North Capitol, Suite 700
Indianapolis, IN 46204-2243
317-232-8860

IOWA
Iowa Development Commission
Visitors and Tourism
600 East Court Ave., Suite A
Des Moines, IA 50309
515-281-3100

KANSAS
Travel & Tourism Division
Department of Economic Development
503 Kansas Ave., 6th Floor
Topeka, KS 66603
913-296-2009

KENTUCKY
Department of Travel Development
Cabinet Tourism
22nd Floor, Capital Plaza Tower
Frankfort, KY 40601
502-564-4930

LOUISIANA
Office of Tourism
P.O. Box 44291, Capitol Station
Baton Route, LA 70804
504-925-3860 or
1-800-231-4730

MAINE
Maine Publicity Bureau
97 Winthrop St.
Hallowell, ME 04347
207-289-2423

MARYLAND
Office of Tourist Development
1748 Forest Dr.
Annapolis, MD 21401
301-269-3517

MASSACHUSETTS
Division of Marketing
100 Cambridge St.
Boston, MA 02202
617-727-3018

MICHIGAN
Travel Bureau
Department of Commerce
P.O. Box 30226
Lansing, MI 48909
517-373-1195 or 1-800-292-2520 (in-state) or 1-800-248-5700
or for latest recorded information on special seasonal activities, 1-800-292-5404 (in-state) or 1-800-248-5708

MINNESOTA
Minnesota Office of Tourism
240 Bremer Bldg., 419 N. Robert St.
St. Paul, MN 55101
612-296-5029 or
1-800-328-1461

MISSISSIPPI
Division of Tourism
Department of Economic Development
P.O. Box 849
Jackson, MS 39205
601-359-3414 or
1-800-647-2290

MISSOURI
Missouri Division of Tourism
301 W. High St.
P.O. Box 1055
Jefferson City, MO 65102
314-751-4133

MONTANA
Travel Promotion
Department of Commerce
1424 9th Ave.
Helena, MT 59620
406-444-2654 or
1-800-548-3390

NEBRASKA
Division of Tourism
Department of Economic Development
P.O. Box 94666, State Office Bldg.
Lincoln, NE 68509
402-471-3111 or
1-800-228-4307

NEVADA
Commission on Tourism
Capitol Complex
Carson City, NV 89710
702-885-4322

NEW HAMPSHIRE
Office of Vacation Travel
P.O. Box 856
Concord, NH 03301
603-271-2666
or for recorded weekly events, ski conditions, foliage reports
1-800-258-3608

NEW JERSEY
Division of Travel and Tourism
CN 384
Trenton, NJ 08625
609-292-2470

NEW MEXICO
Economic Development and Tourism Department
Tourism and Travel Division
Bataan Memorial Bldg.
Santa Fe, NM 87503
505-827-6230 or
1-800-545-2040

NEW YORK
Division of Tourism
1 Commerce Plaza
Albany, NY 12245
Toll free from NYS
1-800-225-5697 or
518-474-4116

NORTH CAROLINA
Travel and Tourism Division
Department of Commerce
430 North Salisbury St.
Raleigh, NC 27611
919-733-4171

NORTH DAKOTA
North Dakota Tourism Promotion
Liberty Memorial Building
Capital Grounds
Bismarck, ND 58505
701-224-2525 or
1-800-437-2077 (out of state)

OHIO
Ohio Office of Travel and Tourism
P.O. Box 1001
Columbus, OH 43216
614-466-8844 or
1-800-Buckeye

OKLAHOMA
Oklahoma Tourism and Recreation Dept.
Literature Distribution Center
215 NE 28th Street
Oklahoma City, OK 73105
405-521-2409

OREGON
Tourism Division
Oregon Economic Development
595 Cottage St., NE
Salem, OR 97310
503-378-6309 or
1-800-547-7842

PENNSYLVANIA
Bureau of Travel Development
416 Forum Building
Harrisburg, PA 17120
717-787-5453

RHODE ISLAND
Department of Economic Development
Tourist Division
7 Jackson Walkway
Providence, RI 02903
401-277-2601 or
1-800-556-2484

SOUTH CAROLINA
South Carolina Division of Tourism
Box 71
Columbia, SC 29202
803-758-8735

SOUTH DAKOTA
South Dakota Division of Tourism
Box 1000
Pierre, SD 57501
605-773-3301 or
1-800-843-1930

TENNESSEE
Department of Tourist Development
P.O. Box 23170
Nashville, TN 37203
615-741-2158

TEXAS
Travel Information Services
State Highway Department
P.O. Box 5064
Austin, TX 78763
512-465-7401

UTAH
Utah Travel Council
Council Hall, Capitol Hill
Salt Lake City, UT 84114
801-533-5681

VERMONT
Agency of Development and Community Affairs
Travel Division
134 State St.
Montpelier, VT 05602
802-828-3236

VIRGINIA
Virginia Division of Tourism
202 North Ninth Street
Suite 500
Richmond, VA 23219
804-786-4484

WASHINGTON
Washington State Dept. of Commerce and Economic Development
General Administration Bldg. G-3
Olympia, WA 98504
206-753-5630 or
1-800-541-9274

WASHINGTON, D.C.
See District of Columbia

WEST VIRGINIA
Travel Development—GOECD
1900 Washington St., East
Charleston, WV 25305
304-348-2286 or
1-800-624-9110

WISCONSIN
Department of Development
Division of Tourism
Box 7606
Madison, WI 53707
Toll free in WI 1-800-escapes
others: 608-266-2161

WYOMING
Wyoming Travel Commission
I-25 at College Drive
Cheyenne, WY 82002-0660
307-777-7777 or
1-800-443-2784

Homes of the Presidents and Presidential Libraries-Museums

Source: American Automobile Association *Tour Books and Information Please* questionnaires. NOTE: Admission fees and visiting hours are subject to change.

GEORGE WASHINGTON

George Washington Birthplace National Monument: RR #1, Box 717, Washington's Birthplace, Va. 22575. Open: daily 9-5 (closed Jan. 1, Dec. 25). Free.

Mount Vernon: on George Washington Memorial Parkway, Mount Vernon, Va. 22121 (16 mi. south of Washington, D.C.). Open: March 1-Oct. 31 daily 9-5; Nov. 1-Feb. 28-daily 9-4. Adm.: $4; 6-11s, $2; senior citizens, $3.
Washington's home.

JOHN ADAMS and JOHN QUINCY ADAMS

John Adams and John Quincy Adams Birthplaces: 133 and 141 Franklin St., Quincy, Mass. 02169. Open: April 19-Oct. 15, daily 9-5. Free. Tour of grounds while houses undergo restoration.
Family home of the Adamses.

Adams National Historic Site: 135 Adams St., Quincy, Mass. 02169. Open: April 19-Nov. 10-daily 9-5. Adm.: 50¢; under 16s, free.
Home of Adams family from 1788 to 1927; built in 1731. Contains furnishings used by four Adams generations.

THOMAS JEFFERSON

Monticello: on Route 53, 3 mi. southeast of Charlottesville, Va. 22902. Open: March 1-Oct. 31-daily 8-5; Nov. 1-Feb. 28-daily. 9-4:30 (closed Dec. 25). Adm.: $4; 6-11s, $1.
Home of Jefferson; begun in 1769; finished in 1809. National shrine contains Jefferson mementos.

JAMES MADISON

Montpelier: Montpelier Station, Va. 22957; on Route 20, 5 mi. west of Orange, Va. Estate not open to public, but graveyard may be visited.
Madison's home.

JAMES MONROE

Ash Lawn: off Route 53, 2 1/2 mi. beyond Monticello, near Charlottesville, Va. 22901. Open: daily, March-Oct. 9-6, Nov.-Feb. 10-5. (closed Jan. 1, Thanksgiving, Dec. 25). Adm.: $3; 6–11s, $1.
Monroe's home from 1799 to 1823; planned by Jefferson; working farm with crafts demonstrations; Summer Music Festival July 4 to mid-August; owned by College of William and Mary.

ANDREW JACKSON

The Hermitage: off I-40 east on U.S. 70N, 12 mi. east of Nashville, 4580 Rachel's Lane, Tenn. 37076. Open: daily 9-5 (closed Dec. 25). Adm.: $3; 6–13s, $1; under 6 years free.
Jackson's home.

MARTIN VAN BUREN

Martin Van Buren National Historic Site (Linden-

wald): on Route 9H, 2 mi. south of Kinderhook, N.Y. 12106. Open: Wed.–Sun., June–Sept.

Van Buren's home from 1839 to 1862. Designated a National Historic Site in 1974, the house is now undergoing restoration by the National Park Service.

WILLIAM HENRY HARRISON

Berkeley Plantation (Harrison's Landing): halfway between Richmond and Williamsburg, Va., on Virginia Route 5. Open daily 8–5 (closed Dec. 25). Adm.: $5; 6–12s, $1.75.

Birthplace of William Henry Harrison and ancestral home of Benjamin Harrison. Site of first official Thanksgiving in America, in 1619.

JOHN TYLER

Sherwood Forest: on Virginia Route 5, 20 mi. west of Colonial Williamsburg, Charles City, Va. 23030. Open: daily 9–5. Adm.: grounds and 5 dependencies, $2; house (by appointment only), $6.75.

Tyler's home; built circa 1730, it is the longest frame residence in America—300 feet in length. Original furnishings. Still occupied by Tyler family. Also owned by President William H. Harrison.

FRANKLIN PIERCE

Franklin Pierce Homestead: near junction of Routes 9 and 31, northwest of Hillsboro, N.H. 03244. Open: Memorial Day–Labor Day, wkds. and hldys., 10–5. Adm.: 50¢; under 18s, free.

Pierce's boyhood home.

JAMES BUCHANAN FOUNDATION

Wheatland: 1120 Marietta Ave., Route 23, Lancaster, Pa. 17603. Open: April 1-Nov. 30, daily, 10–4:15 (closed Thanksgiving). Adm.: $3; under 12s, 75¢; students $1.75; group rate, $1.75.

Restored 1828 mansion of nation's only bachelor President. Contains much of his furniture, china, and silver; also, American Empire and Victorian decorative-arts collections.

ABRAHAM LINCOLN

Lincoln Home National Historic Site: 8th & Jackson Sts., Springfield, Ill. 62703. Open: daily, 8–5 (closed Jan. 1, Dec. 25). Free.

House is only home owned by Lincoln.

ANDREW JOHNSON

Andrew Johnson National Historic Site: College and Depot Sts., Greeneville, Tenn. 37743. Open: daily 9–5 (closed Dec. 25). Adm. to Homestead 50¢; under 16s and senior citizens, free.

Contains two houses where Johnson lived, tailor shop where he worked, and Andrew Johnson National Cemetery.

ULYSSES S. GRANT

U. S. Grant Home State Historic Site: 510 Bouthillier, Galena, Ill. 61036. Open: daily 9–5 (closed Jan. 1, Thanksgiving, Dec. 25). Free.

RUTHERFORD B. HAYES PRESIDENTIAL CENTER

Gilded Age Research Library and Museum; Hayes Residence: Spiegel Grove, 1337 Hayes Ave., Fremont, Ohio 43420. Museum and home open: Sun., Mon., and hldys., 1:30–5; Tues.-Sat. 9–5. Adm. to each: $1.50; 7–12s, 75¢. Library open: Mon.-Sat. 9–5 (closed Sun. and legal hldys.); free. All three sites closed Jan. 1, Thanksgiving, and Dec. 25.

Estate contains Hayes' home, his tomb, and White House gates.

JAMES A. GARFIELD

Lawnfield: 8095 Mentor Ave., Mentor, Ohio 44060. Open: May 1-Oct. 31, Tues.-Sat. 9–5, Sun. and hldys. 1–5. Adm.: $2; 12–17s and senior citizens, $1.

Garfield's home; contains many of his belongings, 1880 campaign office, and replica of his birthplace.

BENJAMIN HARRISON

Benjamin Harrison Memorial Home: 1230 North Delaware St., Indianapolis, Ind. 46202. Open: Mon.-Sat. 10–4, Sun. 12:30–4 (closed month of Jan., Easter, Thanksgiving, Dec. 25). Adm.: $1.50; students, 75¢.

Harrison's home; completed in 1875.

THEODORE ROOSEVELT

Theodore Roosevelt Birthplace National Historic Site: 28 E. 20th St., New York, N.Y. 10003. Open: Wed.-Sun. 9–5 (closed Jan. 1, Thanksgiving, Dec. 25). Adm.: 50¢; under 16s and senior citizens, free.

Sagamore Hill National Historic Site: 3 mi. east of Oyster Bay, L.I., N.Y. 11771, via E. Main St. Home open Tues.-Sun., 9:30–4:30; Mon. **only by appointment** Oct. thru May. The Old Orchard Museum open Mon.-Fri., 9:30–5, 7 days May thru mid-Dec. (closed Jan. 1, Thanksgiving, Dec. 25). Adm.: 50¢; under 16s and senior citizens, free.

Roosevelt's home and rural estate.

WOODROW WILSON

Birthplace of Woodrow Wilson: Coalter and Frederick Sts., Staunton, Va. 24401. Open: daily 9–5 (closed winter Sun., Jan. 1, Thanksgiving, Dec. 25). Adm.: $2.50; 6–16s and students, $1; senior citizens, $2.

Woodrow Wilson House: 2340 S St. N.W., Washington, D.C. 20008. Open: Tues.-Fri. 10–2; Sat., Sun., hldys. 12–4 (closed Jan. 1–March 1, Thanksgiving, Dec. 25). Adm.: $2; students and senior citizens, $1.

Wilson retired to this house after his second term and died here three years later in 1924.

WARREN G. HARDING

Warren G. Harding Home and Museum: 380 Mt. Vernon Ave., Marion, Ohio 43302. Open: Memorial Day to Labor Day, Wed.-Sat. 9:30–5; Sun. 12–5 (closed Mon., Tues.) Sept.-Oct. open Sat. and Sun. only. Adm.: $1.50; 6–12s, $1.

CALVIN COOLIDGE

Calvin Coolidge Birthplace and Historic Plymouth Village: Route 100A, Plymouth, Vt. 05056. Open: mid-May to mid-Oct.—daily 9:30–5:30. Adm.: $1; under 15s, free.

HERBERT HOOVER

Herbert Hoover National Historic Site: 1/2 mi. north of I-80, exit 254, West Branch, Iowa 52358. Grounds open daily 8–5. (closed Jan. 1, Thanksgiving, Dec. 25). Free.

Restored two-room cottage where Hoover was born; replica of his father's blacksmith shop, school, Quaker Meetinghouse, and graves of President and Mrs. Hoover.

Herbert Hoover Presidential Library-Museum: Interstate 80, West Branch, Iowa 52358. Open: Sept.–May, daily 9–5; Memorial Day–Labor Day 8–5, daily except Sun. 9–5. (closed Jan. 1, Thanksgiving, Dec. 25). Adm.: $1; under 16s, free.

Exhibits portray Hoover as mining engineer, public servant, and humanitarian.

International Tourist Arrivals and Receipts, 1982-1983

Area	Arrivals (millions)		Receipts (billions)	
	1982[2]	1983[2]	1982[2]	1983[2]
Africa	6.7	6.7	2.0	2.0
Americas	51.1	50.9	23.5	23.4
East Asia and the Pacific	23.0	23.2	8.9	9.3
Europe	195.0	196.1	55.4	57.0
Middle East	7.0	7.0	3.3	3.3
South Asia	2.4	2.4	1.2	1.2
TOTAL	**285.1**	**286.5**	**94.2**	**96.2**

1. Revised estimates. 2. Preliminary estimates. *Source:* World Tourist Organization.

Volume of Domestic Travel by U.S. Residents

(in millions of person-trips)

Domestic Travel	1983
Mode of Transportation:	
Auto, truck, recreational vehicle	839.8
Airplane	174.2
Bus	26.2
Train	8.6
Other	9.0
Purpose of trip:	
Visiting friends and relatives	384.6
Other pleasures	401.4
Business and convention	146.4
Other	125.4
Type of trip:	
Vacation	642.3
Weekend	485.0
Total person-trips	**1,057.8**

Source: U.S. Travel Data Center, Washington, D.C.

FRANKLIN D. ROOSEVELT

Home of Franklin D. Roosevelt National Historic Site: on U.S. 9, south end of Hyde Park, N.Y. 12538. Open: daily 9–5 (closed Jan. 1, Thanksgiving, Dec. 25). Adm.: $1.50; under 16s and senior citizens, free. Fee includes admission to Vanderbilt Mansion and the Library-Museum. NOTE: As a result of a fire in January 1982, home may not be fully furnished.

Franklin D. Roosevelt Library and Museum: 259 Albany Post Road, Hyde Park, N.Y. 12538. Open: daily 9–5 (closed Jan. 1, Thanksgiving, Dec. 25). Adm.: $2, includes admission to Roosevelt Home and Vanderbilt Mansion; under 16s and senior citizens, free. Archives open Mon.–Fri. 9–5 (closed natl. hldys).

Exhibits feature lives and special interests of Franklin D. and Eleanor Roosevelt. Archives contain historic papers of President and Mrs. Roosevelt and of prominent figures in his Administration. Near the Library are Roosevelt family home, which is open to public, and graves of President and Mrs. Roosevelt.

HARRY S. TRUMAN

Harry S. Truman Birthplace State Historic Site: Truman Ave. & 11th St., Lamar, Mo. 64759. Open: Mon.–Sat. 10–4; Sun. 12–4 (closed Jan. 1, Easter, Thanksgiving, Dec. 25). Free.

Harry S. Truman Library and Museum: U.S. Highway 24 and Delaware St., Independence, Mo. 64050. Open: daily, 9–5 (closed Jan. 1, Thanksgiving, Dec. 25). Adm.: $1; under 15s, free.

Copy of Truman's White House office, United Nations Charter Table, and state gifts. Film programs. Mural by Thomas Hart Benton decorates entrance hall. Truman's gravesite is in the courtyard.

DWIGHT D. EISENHOWER

Eisenhower Birthplace State Historical Site: 208 E. Day St., Denison, Tex. 75020. Open: June 1–Aug. 31, daily, 8–5; Sept. 1–May 31, daily, 10–12, 1–5 (closed Jan. 1, Dec. 25). Adm.: $1; 6–12s, 25¢.

Dwight D. Eisenhower Center: Kansas Highway 15, Abilene, Kan. 67410. Open: daily 9–4:45 (closed Jan. 1, Thanksgiving, Dec. 25). Adm.: Library, free; museum, 75¢.

Exhibits of paintings and memorabilia relating to Eisenhower administration are on display in Library and Museum. Place of Meditation, where Eisenhower is buried, and his boyhood home are nearby and are open to visitors.

JOHN F. KENNEDY

John F. Kennedy National Historic Site: 83 Beals St., Brookline, Mass. 02146. Open: daily 10–4:30 (closed Jan. 1, Thanksgiving, Dec. 25). Adm.: 50¢ under 16s and senior citizens, free.

Kennedy's birthplace.

John Fitzgerald Kennedy Library: Columbia Point on Dorchester Bay, Boston, Mass. 02125. Open: Daily, 9–5 (closed Jan. 1, Thanksgiving, Dec. 25). Adm.: $1.50; under 16s, free.

Exhibits and resources relating to Kennedy's life, his times and administration; research rooms.

LYNDON B. JOHNSON

Lyndon B. Johnson National Historical Park: P.O. Box 329, Johnson City, Tex. 78636. Open: daily 9–5 (closed Jan. 1, Dec. 25); LBJ Ranch, 10–4 (closed Dec. 25). Free.

Site includes LBJ Ranch, birthplace and family cemetery at Stonewall (15 miles west of Johnson City) and his boyhood home and grandfather's ranch headquarters in Johnson City.

Lyndon Baines Johnson Library and Museum: University of Texas campus, Austin, Tex. 78705. Open daily 9–5 (closed Dec. 25). Free.

Documents, photographs, art objects, audio tapes, films, and memorabilia concerning the presidency and four decades of U.S. history. Archives house 31 million documents. Replica of Oval Office during Johnson's presidency is on view.

GERALD R. FORD

Gerald R. Ford Library: 1000 Beal Ave., Ann Arbor, Mich. 48109. Open: Mon.–Fri., 8:45–4:45 (closed Jan. 1, Washington's Birthday, Memorial Day, July 4, Labor Day, Columbus Day, Veterans Day, Thanksgiving, and Dec. 25). Free.

Documents and changing exhibits on Ford's life.

Gerald R. Ford Museum: 303 Pearl St., N.W., Grand Rapids, Mich. 49504. Open: Mon.–Sat. 9–4:45, Sun. 12–4:45 (closed Jan. 1, Thanksgiving, and Dec. 25) Adm.: $1.50; under 16s and school groups, free.

Exhibits relating to Ford's career, the Presidency and American politics.

Road Mileages Between U.S. Cities[1]

Cities	Birming-ham	Boston	Buffalo	Chicago	Cleveland	Dallas	Denver
Birmingham, Ala.	—	1,194	947	657	734	653	1,318
Boston, Mass.	1,194	—	457	983	639	1,815	1,991
Buffalo, N.Y.	947	457	—	536	192	1,387	1,561
Chicago, Ill.	657	983	536	—	344	931	1,050
Cleveland, Ohio	734	639	192	344	—	1,205	1,369
Dallas, Tex.	653	1,815	1,387	931	1,205	—	801
Denver, Colo	1,318	1,991	1,561	1,050	1,369	801	—
Detroit, Mich.	754	702	252	279	175	1,167	1,301
El Paso, Tex.	1,278	2,358	1,928	1,439	1,746	625	652
Houston, Tex.	692	1,886	1,532	1,092	1,358	242	1,032
Indianapolis, Ind.	492	940	510	189	318	877	1,051
Kansas City, Mo.	703	1,427	997	503	815	508	616
Los Angeles, Calif.	2,078	3,036	2,606	2,112	2,424	1,425	1,174
Louisville, Ky.	378	996	571	305	379	865	1,135
Memphis, Tenn.	249	1,345	965	546	773	470	1,069
Miami, Fla.	777	1,539	1,445	1,390	1,325	1,332	2,094
Minneapolis, Minn.	1,067	1,402	955	411	763	969	867
New Orleans, La.	347	1,541	1,294	947	1,102	504	1,305
New York, N.Y.	983	213	436	840	514	1,604	1,780
Omaha, Neb.	907	1,458	1,011	493	819	661	559
Philadelphia, Pa.	894	304	383	758	432	1,515	1,698
Phoenix, Ariz.	1,680	2,664	2,234	1,729	2,052	1,027	836
Pittsburgh, Pa.	792	597	219	457	131	1,237	1,411
St. Louis, Mo.	508	1,179	749	293	567	638	871
Salt Lake City, Utah	1,805	2,425	1,978	1,458	1,786	1,239	512
San Francisco, Calif.	2,385	3,179	2,732	2,212	2,540	1,765	1,266
Seattle, Wash.	2,612	3,043	2,596	2,052	2,404	2,122	1,373
Washington, D.C.	751	440	386	695	369	1,372	1,635

Cities	Detroit	El Paso	Houston	Indian-apolis	Kansas City	Los Angeles	Louisville
Birmingham, Ala.	754	1,278	692	492	703	2,078	378
Boston, Mass.	702	2,358	1,886	940	1,427	3,036	996
Buffalo, N.Y.	252	1,928	1,532	510	997	2,606	571
Chicago, Ill.	279	1,439	1,092	189	503	2,112	305
Cleveland, Ohio	175	1,746	1,358	318	815	2,424	379
Dallas, Tex.	1,167	625	242	877	508	1,425	865
Denver, Colo.	1,310	652	1,032	1,051	616	1,174	1,135
Detroit, Mich.	—	1,696	1,312	290	760	2,369	378
El Paso, Tex.	1,696	—	756	1,418	936	800	1,443
Houston, Tex.	1,312	756	—	1,022	750	1,556	981
Indianapolis, Ind.	290	1,418	1,022	—	487	2,096	114
Kansas City, Mo.	760	936	750	487	—	1,609	519
Los Angeles, Calif.	2,369	800	1,556	2,096	1,609	—	2,128
Louisville, Ky.	378	1,443	981	114	519	2,128	—
Memphis, Tenn.	756	1,095	586	466	454	1,847	396
Miami, Fla.	1,409	1,957	1,237	1,225	1,479	2,757	1,111
Minneapolis, Minn.	698	1,353	1,211	600	466	2,041	716
New Orleans, La.	1,101	1,121	365	839	839	1,921	725
New York, N.Y.	671	2,147	1,675	729	1,216	2,825	785
Omaha, Neb.	754	1,015	903	590	204	1,733	704
Philadelphia, Pa.	589	2,065	1,586	647	1,134	2,743	703
Phoenix, Ariz.	1,986	402	1,158	1,713	1,226	398	1,749
Pittsburgh, Pa.	288	1,778	1,395	360	847	2,456	416
St. Louis, Mo.	529	1,179	799	239	255	1,864	264
Salt Lake City, Utah	1,721	877	1,465	1,545	1,128	728	1,647
San Francisco, Calif.	2,475	1,202	1,958	2,299	1,882	403	2,401
Seattle, Wash.	2,339	1,760	2,348	2,241	1,909	1,150	2,355
Washington, D.C.	526	1,997	1,443	565	1,071	2,680	601

1. These figures represent estimates and are subject to change.

Road Mileages Between U.S. Cities

Cities	Memphis	Miami	Minne-apolis	New Orleans	New York	Omaha	Phila-delphia
Birmingham, Ala.	249	777	1,067	347	983	907	894
Boston, Mass.	1,345	1,539	1,402	1,541	213	1,458	304
Buffalo, N.Y.	965	1,445	955	1,294	436	1,011	383
Chicago, Ill.	546	1,390	411	947	840	493	758
Cleveland, Ohio	773	1,325	763	1,102	514	819	432
Dallas, Tex.	470	1,332	969	504	1,604	661	1,515
Denver, Colo.	1,069	2,094	867	1,305	1,780	559	1,698
Detroit, Mich.	756	1,409	698	1,101	671	754	589
El Paso, Tex.	1,095	1,957	1,353	1,121	2,147	1,015	2,065
Houston, Tex.	586	1,237	1,211	365	1,675	903	1,586
Indianapolis, Ind.	466	1,225	600	839	729	590	647
Kansas City, Mo.	454	1,479	466	839	1,216	204	1,134
Los Angeles, Calif.	1,847	2,757	2,041	1,921	2,825	1,733	2,743
Louisville, Ky.	396	1,111	716	725	785	704	703
Memphis, Tenn.	—	1,025	854	401	1,134	658	1,045
Miami, Fla.	1,025	—	1,801	892	1,328	1,683	1,239
Minneapolis, Minn.	854	1,801	—	1,255	1,259	373	1,177
New Orleans, La.	401	892	1,255	—	1,330	1,043	1,241
New York, N.Y.	1,134	1,328	1,259	1,330	—	1,315	93
Omaha, Neb.	658	1,683	373	1,043	1,315	—	1,233
Philadelphia, Pa.	1,045	1,239	1,177	1,241	93	1,233	—
Phoenix, Ariz.	1,464	2,359	1,644	1,523	2,442	1,305	2,360
Pittsburgh, Pa.	810	1,250	876	1,118	386	932	304
St. Louis, Mo.	295	1,241	559	696	968	459	886
Salt Lake City, Utah	1,556	2,571	1,243	1,743	2,282	967	2,200
San Francisco, Calif.	2,151	3,097	1,997	2,269	3,036	1,721	2,954
Seattle, Wash.	2,363	3,389	1,641	2,606	2,900	1,705	2,818
Washington, D.C.	902	1,101	1,114	1,098	229	1,170	140

Cities	Phoenix	Pitts-burgh	St. Louis	Salt Lake City	San Francisco	Seattle	Wash-ington
Birmingham, Ala.	1,680	792	508	1,805	2,385	2,612	751
Boston, Mass.	2,664	597	1,179	2,425	3,179	3,043	440
Buffalo, N.Y.	2,234	219	749	1,978	2,732	2,596	386
Chicago, Ill.	1,729	457	293	1,458	2,212	2,052	695
Cleveland, Ohio	2,052	131	567	1,786	2,540	2,404	369
Dallas, Tex.	1,027	1,237	638	1,239	1,765	2,122	1,372
Denver, Colo.	836	1,411	871	512	1,266	1,373	1,635
Detroit, Mich.	1,986	288	529	1,721	2,475	2,339	526
El Paso, Tex.	402	1,778	1,179	877	1,202	1,760	1,997
Houston, Tex.	1,158	1,395	799	1,465	1,958	2,348	1,443
Indianapolis, Ind.	1,713	360	239	1,545	2,299	2,241	565
Kansas City, Mo.	1,226	847	255	1,128	1,882	1,909	1,071
Los Angeles, Calif.	398	2,456	1,864	728	403	1,150	2,680
Louisville, Ky.	1,749	416	264	1,647	2,401	2,355	601
Memphis, Tenn.	1,464	810	295	1,556	2,151	2,363	902
Miami, Fla.	2,359	1,250	1,241	2,571	3,097	3,389	1,101
Minneapolis, Minn.	1,644	876	559	1,243	1,997	1,641	1,114
New Orleans, La.	1,523	1,118	696	1,743	2,269	2,626	1,098
New York, N.Y.	2,442	386	968	2,282	3,036	2,900	229
Omaha, Neb.	1,305	932	459	967	1,721	1,705	1,178
Philadelphia, Pa.	2,360	304	886	2,200	2,954	2,818	140
Phoenix, Ariz.	—	2,073	1,485	651	800	1,482	2,278
Pittsburgh, Pa.	2,073	—	599	1,899	2,653	2,517	241
St. Louis, Mo.	1,485	599	—	1,383	2,137	2,164	836
Salt Lake City, Utah	651	1,899	1,383	—	754	883	2,110
San Francisco, Calif.	800	2,653	2,137	754	—	817	2,864
Seattle, Wash.	1,482	2,517	2,164	883	817	—	2,755
Washington, D.C.	2,278	241	836	2,110	2,864	2,755	—

Air Distances Between U.S. Cities in Statute Miles

Cities	Birmingham	Boston	Buffalo	Chicago	Cleveland	Dallas	Denver
Birmingham, Ala.	—	1,052	776	578	618	581	1,095
Boston, Mass.	1,052	—	400	851	551	1,551	1,769
Buffalo, N. Y.	776	400	—	454	173	1,198	1,370
Chicago, Ill.	578	851	454	—	308	803	920
Cleveland, Ohio	618	551	173	308	—	1,025	1,227
Dallas, Tex.	581	1,551	1,198	803	1,025	—	663
Denver, Colo.	1,095	1,769	1,370	920	1,227	663	—
Detroit, Mich.	641	613	216	238	90	999	1,156
El Paso, Tex.	1,152	2,072	1,692	1,252	1,525	572	557
Houston, Tex.	567	1,605	1,286	940	1,114	225	879
Indianapolis, Ind.	433	807	435	165	263	763	1,000
Kansas City, Mo.	579	1,251	861	414	700	451	558
Los Angeles, Calif.	1,802	2,596	2,198	1,745	2,049	1,240	831
Louisville, Ky.	331	826	483	269	311	726	1,038
Memphis, Tenn.	217	1,137	803	482	630	420	879
Miami, Fla.	665	1,255	1,181	1,188	1,087	1,111	1,726
Minneapolis, Minn.	862	1,123	731	355	630	862	700
New Orleans, La.	312	1,359	1,086	833	924	443	1,082
New York, N. Y.	864	188	292	713	405	1,374	1,631
Omaha, Neb.	732	1,282	883	432	739	586	488
Philadelphia, Pa.	783	271	279	666	360	1,299	1,579
Phoenix, Ariz.	1,456	2,300	1,906	1,453	1,749	887	586
Pittsburgh, Pa.	608	483	178	410	115	1,070	1,320
St. Louis, Mo.	400	1,038	662	262	492	547	796
Salt Lake City, Utah	1,466	2,099	1,699	1,260	1,568	999	371
San Francisco, Calif.	2,013	2,699	2,300	1,858	2,166	1,483	949
Seattle, Wash.	2,082	2,493	2,117	1,737	2,026	1,681	1,021
Washington, D.C.	661	393	292	597	306	1,185	1,494

Cities	Detroit	El Paso	Houston	Indianapolis	Kansas City	Los Angeles	Louisville
Birmingham, Ala.	641	1,152	567	433	579	1,802	331
Boston, Mass.	613	2,072	1,605	807	1,251	2,596	826
Buffalo, N. Y.	216	1,692	1,286	435	861	2,198	483
Chicago, Ill.	238	1,252	940	165	414	1,745	269
Cleveland, Ohio	90	1,525	1,114	263	700	2,049	311
Dallas, Tex.	999	572	225	763	451	1,240	726
Denver, Colo.	1,156	557	879	1,000	558	831	1,038
Detroit, Mich.	—	1,479	1,105	240	645	1,983	316
El Paso, Tex.	1,479	—	676	1,264	839	701	1,254
Houston, Tex.	1,105	676	—	865	644	1,374	803
Indianapolis, Ind.	240	1,264	865	—	453	1,809	107
Kansas City, Mo.	645	839	644	453	—	1,356	480
Los Angeles, Calif.	1,983	701	1,374	1,809	1,356	—	1,829
Louisville, Ky.	316	1,254	803	107	480	1,829	—
Memphis, Tenn.	623	976	484	384	369	1,603	320
Miami, Fla.	1,152	1,643	968	1,024	1,241	2,339	919
Minneapolis, Minn.	543	1,157	1,056	511	413	1,524	605
New Orleans, La.	939	983	318	712	680	1,673	623
New York, N. Y.	482	1,905	1,420	646	1,097	2,451	652
Omaha, Neb.	669	878	794	525	166	1,315	580
Philadelphia, Pa.	443	1,836	1,341	585	1,038	2,394	582
Phoenix, Ariz.	1,690	346	1,017	1,499	1,049	357	1,508
Pittsburgh, Pa.	205	1,590	1,137	330	781	2,136	344
St. Louis, Mo.	455	1,034	679	231	238	1,589	242
Salt Lake City, Utah	1,492	689	1,200	1,356	925	579	1,402
San Francisco, Calif.	2,091	995	1,645	1,949	1,506	347	1,986
Seattle, Wash.	1,938	1,376	1,891	1,872	1,506	959	1,943
Washington, D.C.	396	1,728	1,220	494	945	2,300	476

Source: National Geodetic Survey.

Air Distances Between U.S. Cities in Statute Miles

Cities	Memphis	Miami	Minneapolis	New Orleans	New York	Omaha	Philadelphia
Birmingham, Ala.	217	665	862	312	864	732	783
Boston, Mass.	1,137	1,255	1,123	1,359	188	1,282	271
Buffalo, N. Y.	803	1,181	731	1,086	292	883	279
Chicago, Ill.	482	1,188	355	833	713	432	666
Cleveland, Ohio	630	1,087	630	924	405	739	360
Dallas, Tex.	420	1,111	862	443	1,374	586	1,299
Denver, Colo.	879	1,726	700	1,082	1,631	488	1,579
Detroit, Mich.	623	1,152	543	939	482	669	443
El Paso, Tex.	976	1,643	1,157	983	1,905	878	1,836
Houston, Tex.	484	968	1,056	318	1,420	794	1,341
Indianapolis, Ind.	384	1,024	511	712	646	525	585
Kansas City, Mo.	369	1,241	413	680	1,097	166	1,038
Los Angeles, Calif.	1,603	2,339	1,524	1,673	2,451	1,315	2,394
Louisville, Ky.	320	919	605	623	652	580	582
Memphis, Tenn.	—	872	699	358	957	529	881
Miami, Fla.	872	—	1,511	669	1,092	1,397	1,019
Minneapolis, Minn.	699	1,511	—	1,051	1,018	290	985
New Orleans, La.	358	669	1,051	—	1,171	847	1,089
New York, N. Y.	957	1,092	1,018	1,171	—	1,144	83
Omaha, Neb.	529	1,397	290	847	1,144	—	1,094
Philadelphia, Pa.	881	1,019	985	1,089	83	1,094	—
Phoenix, Ariz.	1,263	1,982	1,280	1,316	2,145	1,036	2,083
Pittsburgh, Pa.	660	1,010	743	919	317	836	259
St. Louis, Mo.	240	1,061	466	598	875	354	811
Salt Lake City, Utah	1,250	2,089	987	1,434	1,972	833	1,925
San Francisco, Calif.	1,802	2,594	1,584	1,926	2,571	1,429	2,523
Seattle, Wash.	1,867	2,734	1,395	2,101	2,408	1,369	2,380
Washington, D.C.	765	923	934	966	205	1,014	123

Cities	Phoenix	Pittsburgh	St. Louis	Salt Lake City	San Francisco	Seattle	Washington
Birmingham, Ala.	1,456	608	400	1,466	2,013	2,082	661
Boston, Mass.	2,300	483	1,038	2,099	2,699	2,493	393
Buffalo, N. Y.	1,906	178	662	1,699	2,300	2,117	292
Chicago, Ill.	1,453	410	262	1,260	1,858	1,737	597
Cleveland, Ohio	1,749	115	492	1,568	2,166	2,026	306
Dallas, Tex.	887	1,070	547	999	1,483	1,681	1,185
Denver, Colo.	586	1,320	796	371	949	1,021	1,494
Detroit, Mich.	1,690	205	455	1,492	2,091	1,938	396
El Paso, Tex.	346	1,590	1,034	689	995	1,376	1,728
Houston, Tex.	1,017	1,137	679	1,200	1,645	1,891	1,220
Indianapolis, Ind.	1,499	330	231	1,356	1,949	1,872	494
Kansas City, Mo.	1,049	781	238	925	1,506	1,506	945
Los Angeles, Calif.	357	2,136	1,589	579	347	959	2,300
Louisville, Ky.	1,508	344	242	1,402	1,986	1,943	476
Memphis, Tenn.	1,263	660	240	1,250	1,802	1,867	765
Miami, Fla.	1,982	1,010	1,061	2,089	2,594	2,734	923
Minneapolis, Minn.	1,280	743	466	987	1,584	1,395	934
New Orleans, La.	1,316	919	598	1,434	1,926	2,101	966
New York, N. Y.	2,145	317	875	1,972	2,571	2,408	205
Omaha, Neb.	1,036	836	354	833	1,429	1,369	1,014
Philadelphia, Pa.	2,083	259	811	1,925	2,523	2,380	123
Phoenix, Ariz.	—	1,828	1,272	504	653	1,114	1,983
Pittsburgh, Pa.	1,828	—	559	1,668	2,264	2,138	192
St. Louis, Mo.	1,272	559	—	1,162	1,744	1,724	712
Salt Lake City, Utah	504	1,668	1,162	—	600	701	1,848
San Francisco, Calif.	653	2,264	1,744	600	—	678	2,442
Seattle, Wash.	1,114	2,138	1,724	701	678	—	2,329
Washington, D.C.	1,983	192	712	1,848	2,442	2,329	—

Source: National Geodetic Survey.

Air Distances Between World Cities in Statute Miles

Cities	Berlin	Buenos Aires	Cairo	Calcutta	Cape Town	Caracas	Chicago
Berlin	—	7,402	1,795	4,368	5,981	5,247	4,405
Buenos Aires	7,402	—	7,345	10,265	4,269	3,168	5,598
Cairo	1,795	7,345	—	3,539	4,500	6,338	6,129
Calcutta	4,368	10,265	3,539	—	6,024	9,605	7,980
Cape Town, South Africa	5,981	4,269	4,500	6,024	—	6,365	8,494
Caracas, Venezuela	5,247	3,168	6,338	9,605	6,365	—	2,501
Chicago	4,405	5,598	6,129	7,980	8,494	2,501	—
Hong Kong	5,440	11,472	5,061	1,648	7,375	10,167	7,793
Honolulu, Hawaii	7,309	7,561	8,838	7,047	11,534	6,013	4,250
Istanbul	1,078	7,611	768	3,638	5,154	6,048	5,477
Lisbon	1,436	5,956	2,363	5,638	5,325	4,041	3,990
London	579	6,916	2,181	4,947	6,012	4,660	3,950
Los Angeles	5,724	6,170	7,520	8,090	9,992	3,632	1,745
Manila	6,132	11,051	5,704	2,203	7,486	10,620	8,143
Mexico City	6,047	4,592	7,688	9,492	8,517	2,232	1,691
Montreal	3,729	5,615	5,414	7,607	7,931	2,449	744
Moscow	1,004	8,376	1,803	3,321	6,300	6,173	4,974
New York	3,965	5,297	5,602	7,918	7,764	2,132	713
Paris	545	6,870	1,995	4,883	5,807	4,736	4,134
Rio de Janeiro	6,220	1,200	6,146	9,377	3,773	2,810	5,296
Rome	734	6,929	1,320	4,482	5,249	5,196	4,808
San Francisco	5,661	6,467	7,364	7,814	10,247	3,904	1,858
Shanghai, China	5,218	12,201	5,183	2,117	8,061	9,501	7,061
Stockholm	504	7,808	2,111	4,195	6,444	5,420	4,278
Sydney, Australia	10,006	7,330	8,952	5,685	6,843	9,513	9,272
Tokyo	5,540	11,408	5,935	3,194	9,156	8,799	6,299
Warsaw	320	7,662	1,630	4,048	5,958	5,517	4,667
Washington, D.C.	4,169	5,218	5,800	8,084	7,901	2,059	597

Cities	Hong Kong	Honolulu	Istanbul	Lisbon	London	Los Angeles	Manila
Berlin	5,440	7,309	1,078	1,436	579	5,724	6,132
Buenos Aires	11,472	7,561	7,611	5,956	6,916	6,170	11,051
Cairo	5,061	8,838	768	2,363	2,181	7,520	5,704
Calcutta	1,648	7,047	3,638	5,638	4,947	8,090	2,203
Cape Town, South Africa	7,375	11,534	5,154	5,325	6,012	9,992	7,486
Caracas, Venezuela	10,167	6,013	6,048	4,041	4,660	3,632	10,620
Chicago	7,793	4,250	5,477	3,990	3,950	1,745	8,143
Hong Kong	—	5,549	4,984	6,853	5,982	7,195	693
Honolulu, Hawaii	5,549	—	8,109	7,820	7,228	2,574	5,299
Istanbul	4,984	8,109	—	2,012	1,552	6,783	5,664
Lisbon	6,853	7,820	2,012	—	985	5,621	7,546
London	5,982	7,228	1,552	985	—	5,382	6,672
Los Angeles, Calif.	7,195	2,574	6,783	5,621	5,382	—	7,261
Manila	693	5,299	5,664	7,546	6,672	7,261	—
Mexico City	8,782	3,779	7,110	5,390	5,550	1,589	8,835
Montreal	7,729	4,910	4,789	3,246	3,282	2,427	8,186
Moscow	4,439	7,037	1,091	2,427	1,555	6,003	5,131
New York	8,054	4,964	4,975	3,364	3,458	2,451	8,498
Paris	5,985	7,438	1,400	904	213	5,588	6,677
Rio de Janeiro	11,021	8,285	6,389	4,796	5,766	6,331	11,259
Rome	5,768	8,022	843	1,161	887	6,732	6,457
San Francisco	6,897	2,393	6,703	5,666	5,357	347	6,967
Shanghai, China	764	4,941	4,962	6,654	5,715	6,438	1,150
Stockholm	5,113	6,862	1,348	1,856	890	5,454	5,797
Sydney, Australia	4,584	4,943	9,294	11,302	10,564	7,530	3,944
Tokyo	1,794	3,853	5,560	6,915	5,940	5,433	1,866
Warsaw	5,144	7,355	863	1,715	899	5,922	5,837
Washington, D.C.	8,147	4,519	5,215	3,562	3,663	2,300	8,562

Source: Encyclopaedia Britannica.

Air Distances Between World Cities in Statute Miles

Cities	Mexico City	Montreal	Moscow	New York	Paris	Rio de Janeiro	Rome
Berlin	6,047	3,729	1,004	3,965	545	6,220	734
Buenos Aires	4,592	5,615	8,376	5,297	6,870	1,200	6,929
Cairo	7,688	5,414	1,803	5,602	1,995	6,146	1,320
Calcutta	9,492	7,607	3,321	7,918	4,883	9,377	4,482
Cape Town, South Africa	8,517	7,931	6,300	7,764	5,807	3,773	5,249
Caracas, Venezuela	2,232	2,449	6,173	2,132	4,736	2,810	5,196
Chicago	1,691	744	4,974	713	4,134	5,296	4,808
Hong Kong	8,782	7,729	4,439	8,054	5,985	11,021	5,768
Honolulu	3,779	4,910	7,037	4,964	7,438	8,285	8,022
Istanbul	7,110	4,789	1,091	4,975	1,400	6,389	843
Lisbon	5,390	3,246	2,427	3,364	904	4,796	1,161
London	5,550	3,282	1,555	3,458	213	5,766	887
Los Angeles	1,589	2,427	6,003	2,451	5,588	6,331	6,732
Manila	8,835	8,186	5,131	8,498	6,677	11,259	6,457
Mexico City	—	2,318	6,663	2,094	5,716	4,771	6,366
Montreal	2,318	—	4,386	320	3,422	5,097	4,080
Moscow	6,663	4,386	—	4,665	1,544	7,175	1,474
New York	2,094	320	4,665	—	3,624	4,817	4,281
Paris	5,716	3,422	1,544	3,624	—	5,699	697
Rio de Janeiro	4,771	5,097	7,175	4,817	5,699	—	5,684
Rome	6,366	4,080	1,474	4,281	697	5,684	—
San Francisco	1,887	2,539	5,871	2,571	5,558	6,621	6,240
Shanghai, China	8,022	7,053	4,235	7,371	5,754	11,336	5,677
Stockholm	5,959	3,667	762	3,924	958	6,651	1,234
Sydney, Australia	8,052	9,954	9,012	9,933	10,544	8,306	10,136
Tokyo	7,021	6,383	4,647	6,740	6,034	11,533	6,135
Warsaw	6,365	4,009	715	4,344	849	6,467	817
Washington, D.C.	1,887	488	4,858	205	3,829	4,796	4,434

Cities	San Francisco	Shanghai	Stockholm	Sydney	Tokyo	Warsaw	Washington
Berlin	5,661	5,218	504	10,006	5,540	320	4,169
Buenos Aires	6,467	12,201	7,808	7,330	11,408	7,662	5,218
Cairo	7,364	5,183	2,111	8,952	5,935	1,630	5,800
Calcutta	7,814	2,117	4,195	5,685	3,194	4,048	8,084
Cape Town, South Africa	10,247	8,061	6,444	6,843	9,156	5,958	7,901
Caracas, Venezuela	3,904	9,501	5,420	9,513	8,799	5,517	2,059
Chicago	1,858	7,061	4,278	9,272	6,299	4,667	597
Hong Kong	6,897	764	5,113	4,584	1,794	5,144	8,147
Honolulu	2,393	4,941	6,862	4,943	3,853	7,355	4,519
Istanbul	6,703	4,962	1,348	9,294	5,560	863	5,215
Lisbon	5,666	6,654	1,856	11,302	6,915	1,715	3,562
London	5,357	5,715	890	10,564	5,940	899	3,663
Los Angeles	347	6,438	5,454	7,530	5,433	5,922	2,300
Manila	6,967	1,150	5,797	3,944	1,866	5,837	8,562
Mexico City	1,887	8,022	5,959	8,052	7,021	6,365	1,887
Montreal	2,539	7,053	3,667	9,954	6,383	4,009	488
Moscow	5,871	4,235	762	9,012	4,647	715	4,858
New York	2,571	7,371	3,924	9,933	6,740	4,344	205
Paris	5,558	5,754	958	10,544	6,034	849	3,829
Rio de Janeiro	6,621	11,336	6,651	8,306	11,533	6,467	4,796
Rome	6,240	5,677	1,234	10,136	6,135	817	4,434
San Francisco	—	6,140	5,361	7,416	5,135	5,841	2,442
Shanghai, China	6,140	—	4,825	4,899	1,097	4,951	7,448
Stockholm	5,361	4,825	—	9,696	5,051	501	4,123
Sydney, Australia	7,416	4,899	9,696	—	4,866	9,696	9,758
Tokyo	5,135	1,097	5,051	4,866	—	5,249	6,772
Warsaw	5,841	4,951	501	9,696	5,249	—	4,457
Washington, D.C.	2,442	7,448	4,123	9,758	6,772	4,457	—

Source: Encyclopaedia Britannica.

Average Military Strength—Man Years[1]

(in thousands)

Year	Army	Air Force	Navy	Marine Corps	Total
1941	755	[2]	218	44	1,017
1942	1,992	[2]	416	89	2,498
1943	5,224	[2]	1,206	232	6,662
1944	7,507	[2]	2,386	398	10,290
1945	8,131	[2]	3,205	473	11,809
1950	632	415	412	80	1,539
1951	1,090	584	566	153	2,394
1952	1,597	899	789	219	3,504
1953	1,536	971	809	237	3,554
1954	1,477	939	767	242	3,425
1955	1,311	958	692	217	3,178
1960	871	828	617	173	2,489
1965	966	844	669	190	2,668
1970	1,432	834	732	295	3,293
1971	1,238	763	656	234	2,891
1972	955	749	604	202	2,510
1973	839	706	580	198	2,323
1975	779	628	545	193	2,145
1977	779	577	527	190	2,073
1978	777	570	530	191	2,068
1979	765	565	527	188	2,045
1980	762	561	525	185	2,033
1981	769	561	531	186	2,050
1982	777	570	540	189	2,077
1983[3]	782	592	555	199	2,127
1984[3]	786	597	562	195	2,140

1. Data from 1941 to 1982 represent averages of month-end strengths including both current and preceding fiscal years' figures, each weighted one half. 2. Air Force data prior to June 30, 1948 included with Army data. 3. Data represent actual figures as of March 31 for given year. NOTE: Detail may not add to totals due to rounding. *Source:* Department of Defense.

History of the Armed Services

Source: Department of Defense.

U.S. Army

On June 14, 1775, the Continental Congress "adopted" the New England Army—a mixed force of militia and volunteers besieging the British in Boston—by appointing a committee to draft "Rules and regulations for the government of the Army" and voting to raise 10 rifle companies as a reinforcement. The next day, it appointed Washington commander-in-chief of the "Continental forces to be raised for the defense of liberty," and he took command at Boston on July 3, 1775. The Continental Army that fought the Revolution was our first national military organization, and hence the Army is the senior service. After the war, the Continental Army was radically reduced but enough survived to form a small Regular Army of about 700 men under the Constitution in 1789, a nucleus for expansion in the 1790s to successfully meet threats from the Indians and from France. From these humble beginnings, the U.S. Army has developed, normally expanding rapidly by absorbing citizen soldiers in wartime and contracting just as rapidly after each war.

U.S. Navy

The antecedents of the U.S. Navy go back to September 1775, when Gen. Washington commissioned 7 schooners and brigantines to prey on British supply vessels bound for the Colonies or Canada. On Oct. 13, 1775, a resolve of the Continental Congress called for the purchase of 2 vessels for the purpose of intercepting enemy transports. With its passage a Naval Committee of 7 men was formed, and they rapidly obtained passage of legislation calling for procurement of additional vessels. The Continental Navy was supplemented by privateers and ships operated as state navies, but soon after the British surrender it was disestablished.

In 1794, because of dissatisfaction with the payment of tribute to the Barbary pirates, Congress authorized construction of 6 frigates. The first,

United States, was launched May 10, 1797, but the Navy still remained under the control of the Secretary of War until April 1798, when the Navy Department was created under the Secretary of the Navy with Cabinet rank.

U.S. Air Force

Until creation of the National Military Establishment in September 1947, which united the services under one department, military aviation was a part of the U.S. Army. In the Army, aeronautical operations came under the Signal Corps from 1907 to 1918, when the Army Air Service was established. In 1926, the Army Air Corps came into being and remained until 1941, when the Army Air Forces succeeded it as the Army's air arm. On Sept. 18, 1947, the U.S. Air Force was established as an independent military service under the National Military Establishment. At that time, the name "Army Air Forces" was abolished.

U.S. Coast Guard

Our country's oldest continuous seagoing service, the U.S. Coast Guard, traces its history back to 1790, when the first Congress authorized the construction of ten vessels for the collection of revenue. Known first as the Revenue Marine, and later as the Revenue Cutter Service, the Coast Guard received its present name in 1915 under an act of Congress combining the Revenue Cutter Service with the Life-Saving Service. In 1939, the Lighthouse Service was also consolidated with this unit. The Bureau of Marine Inspection and Navigation was transferred temporarily to the Coast Guard in 1942, permanently in 1946. Through its antecedents, the Coast Guard is one of the oldest organizations under the federal government and, until the Navy Department was established in 1798, served as the only U.S. armed force afloat. In times of peace, it operates under the Department of Transportation, serving as the nation's primary agency for promoting marine safety and enforcing federal maritime laws. In times of war, or on direction of the President, it is attached to the Navy Department.

U.S. Marine Corps

Founded in 1775 and observing its official birthday on Nov. 10, the U.S. Marine Corps was developed to serve on land, on sea, and in the air.

Marines have fought in every U.S. war. From an initial two battalions in the Revolution, the Corps reached a peak strength of six divisions and five aircraft wings in World War II. Its present strength is three active divisions and aircraft wings and a Reserve division/aircraft wing team. In 1947, the National Security Act set Marine Corps strength at not less than three divisions and three aircraft wings.

Service Academies

U.S. Military Academy

Source: U.S. Military Academy.

Established in 1802 by an act of Congress, the U.S. Military Academy is located on the west bank of the Hudson River some 50 miles north of New York City. To gain admission a candidate must first secure a nomination from an authorized source. These sources, and the number of cadetships allocated to each, are:

Congressional

Representatives	5 each
Senators	5 each
Other: Vice Presidential	5
District of Columbia	5
Puerto Rico	6
Am. Samoa, Guam, Virgin Is.	1 each

Military-Service-Connected Nominations (Each Class)

Presidential	100
Enlisted members of Army	85
Enlisted members of Army Reserve/ National Guard	85
Sons and daughters of deceased and disabled veterans (approximately)	10
Honor military, naval schools and ROTC	20
Sons and daughters of persons awarded the Medal of Honor	(unlimited)

Any number of applicants can meet the requirements for a *nomination* in these categories. *Appointments* (offers of admission), however, can only be made to the number of applicants shown above.

Candidates may be nominated for vacancies during the year preceding the day of admission, which occurs in early July. The best time to apply is during the junior year in high school.

Candidates must be citizens of the U.S., be unmarried, be at least 17 but not yet 22 years old on July 1 of the year admitted, have a secondary-school education or its equivalent, and be able to meet the academic, medical, and physical aptitude requirements. Academic qualification is determined by an analysis of entire scholastic record, and performance on either the American College Testing (ACT) Assessment Program Test or the College Entrance Examination Board Scholastic Aptitude Test (SAT). Entrance requirements and procedures for appointment are described in the Admissions Bulletin, available without charge from Admissions, U.S. Military Academy, West Point, N.Y. 10996.

Cadets are members of the Regular Army. As such they receive full scholarships and annual salaries from which they pay for their uniforms, textbooks, and incidental expenses. Upon successful completion of the four-year course, the graduate receives the degree of Bachelor of Science and is commissioned a second lieutenant in the Regular Army with a requirement to serve as an officer for a minimum of five years.

U.S. Naval Academy

Source: U.S. Naval Academy.

The Naval School, established in 1845 at Fort Severn, Annapolis, Md., was renamed the U.S. Naval Academy in 1850. A four-year course was adopted a year later.

The Superintendent is a rear admiral. A civilian academic dean heads the academic program. A captain heads the 4,500-man Brigade of Midshipmen and military, professional, and physical training. The faculty is half military and half civilian.

Graduates are awarded the Bachelor of Science or Bachelor of Science in Engineering and are commissioned as officers in the U.S. Navy or Marine Corps.

Applicants *must* obtain a nomination from an official source in order to be considered by the Naval Academy for an appointment. The principle sources are: U.S. Senators, Representatives, the Vice President, the Mayor of Washington, D. C., and the Resident Commissioner of Puerto Rico may each have 5 midshipmen at the Academy at any one time. Ten candidates may be nominated for each vacancy. Well over half of the more than 1,300 appointments as midshipmen made annually originate from these sources.

The President appoints the 65 best-qualified sons and daughters of deceased or disabled veterans, or sons and daughters of prisoners of war or servicemen missing in action, and the 100 best-qualified sons and daughters of officers and enlisted men in the regular Armed Services. He also appoints sons and daughters of Medal of Honor holders.

The Secretary of the Navy awards 170 (85 + 85) appointments to regular and reserve personnel of the Navy or Marine Corps; 150 to congressional alternate nominees, all on a competitive, best-qualified basis; and 20 outstanding graduates of NROTC or Honor Naval and Military Schools. He may also make additional appointments each year, to bring the Brigade up to authorized strength, from among qualified congressional and competitive nominees, again on a best-qualified basis. Three fourths of these additional appointments must, by law, be congressional nominees.

There are also limited numbers of appointments available from the Philippines, Canal Zone, Virgin Islands, Guam, American Samoa, and the American republics.

To have basic eligibility for admission, candidates must be citizens of the U.S., of good moral character, at least 17 and not more than 22 years of age on July 1 of their entering year, in the top 40% of their high school class, and unmarried.

In order to be considered for admission, a candidate must obtain a nomination from one of the sources of appointments listed above. The Admissions Board at the Naval Academy examines the candidate's school record, College Board or ACT scores, recommendations from school officials, extracurricular activities, and evidence from other sources concerning his or her character, leadership potential, academic preparation, and physical fitness. Qualification for admission is based on all of the above factors.

Tuition, board, lodging, and medical and dental care are provided. Midshipmen receive over $460 a month for books, uniforms, and personal needs.

For a catalogue or answers to specific questions, write: Superintendent, U.S. Naval Academy, (Attention: Candidate Guidance), Annapolis, Md. 21402.

U.S. Air Force Academy

Source: U.S. Air Force Academy

The bill establishing the Air Force Academy was signed by President Eisenhower on April 1, 1954. The first class of 306 cadets was sworn in on July 11, 1955, at Lowry Air Force Base, Denver, the Academy's temporary location. The Cadet Wing moved into the Academy's permanent home north of Colorado Springs in 1958.

Cadets receive four years of academic, military, and physical education to prepare them for leadership as officers in the Air Force. The Academy is authorized a total of 4,417 cadets. Each new class averages 1,500. This includes approximately 1,325 men and 175 women. The candidates for the Academy must be at least 17 but less than 22 on July 1 of the year for which they seek admission, must be a United States citizen, be single, and be able to meet the mental and physical requirements. A candidate is required to take the following examinations and tests: (1) the Service Academies' Qualifying Medical Examination; (2) either the American College Testing (ACT) Assessment Program test or the College Entrance Examination Board Scholastic Aptitude Test (SAT), and (3) a Physical Aptitude Examination.

Cadets receive their entire education at government expense and, in addition, are paid $480 per month base pay. From this sum, they pay for their uniforms, textbooks, tailoring, laundry, entertainment tickets, etc. Upon completion of the four-year course, leading to a Bachelor of Science degree, a cadet who meets the qualifications is commissioned a second lieutenant in the regular U.S. Air Force. Many go on to pilot or navigator training. For details on admissions, write: Director of Cadet Admissions, USAF Academy, Colo. 80840.

U.S. Coast Guard Academy

Source: U.S. Coast Guard Academy.

The U.S. Coast Guard Academy, New London, Conn., was founded on July 31, 1876, to serve as the "School of Instruction" for the Revenue Cutter Service, predecessor to the Coast Guard.

The J.C. Dobbin, a converted schooner, housed the first Coast Guard Academy, and was succeeded in 1878 by the barque Chase, a ship built for cadet training. First winter quarters were in a sail loft at New Bedford, Mass. The school was moved in 1900 to Curtis Bay, Md., to provide a more technical education, and in 1910 was moved back to New England to Fort Trumbull, New London, Conn. In 1932 the Academy moved to its present location in New London.

The Academy today offers a four-year curriculum for the professional and academic training of cadets, which leads to a Bachelor of Science degree and a commission as ensign in the Coast Guard.

Cadets receive appointment through nationwide competition, which includes either the December administration of the College Entrance Examination Board tests, or the American College Testing (ACT) Program tests. Applications must be submitted to the Coast Guard not later than December 15 and to the College Entrance Examination Board, 30 days prior to the tests.

Women were admitted to the Coast Guard Academy for the first time during 1976 as members of the Class of 1980. Candidates must be between 17 and 22 years of age, physically sound, and unmarried. They must agree to remain unmarried until graduation and to serve at least five years on active duty. Cadets receive $5,760 per year to cover their uniform and incidental expenses and are furnished their rations and quarters. Applications may be made to Director of Admissions, U.S. Coast Guard Academy, New London, Conn. 06320.

U.S. Merchant Marine Academy

Source: U.S. Merchant Marine Academy.

The U.S. Merchant Marine Academy, situated at Kings Point, N.Y., on the north shore of Long Island, was dedicated Sept. 30, 1943. It is maintained by the Department of Transportation under direction of the Maritime Administration.

The Academy has a complement of approximately 1,000 men and women representing every state, D.C., the Canal Zone, Puerto Rico, Guam, American Samoa, and the Virgin Islands. It is also authorized to admit up to 12 candidates from the Western Hemisphere and 30 other foreign students at any one time.

Candidates are nominated by Senators and members of the House of Representatives. Nominations to the Academy are governed by a state and territory quota system based on population and the results of the College Entrance Examination Board tests.

A candidate must be a citizen not less than 17 and not yet 22 years of age by July 1 of the year in which admission is sought. Fifteen high school credits, including 3 units in mathematics (from algebra, geometry and/or trigonometry), 1 unit in science (physics or chemistry) and 3 in English are required.

The course is four years and includes one year of practical training aboard a merchant ship. Study includes marine engineering, navigation, satellite navigation and communications, electricity, ship construction, naval science and tactics, economics, business, languages, history, etc.

Upon completion of the course of study, a graduate receives a Bachelor of Science degree, a license as a merchant marine deck or engineering officer, and a commission as an ensign in the Naval Reserve.

The National Guard

Source: Departments of the Army and the Air Force, National Guard Bureau.

The National Guard of the U.S. originated in 1636 with the Old North and East Regiments of the Colonial Militia in Massachusetts. It is the oldest military force in the country. Guardmembers have served this country at home and overseas in every major conflict in which the U.S. has participated.

As of October 1, 1984, the Army and Air National Guard totaled about 535,000 men and women serving in 3,682 Army and Air Guard units in all 50 states, Puerto Rico, Guam, the Virgin Islands, and the District of Columbia. ANG units 332 (current as of June 15, 1984), ARNG units, 3,350.

In peacetime, the National Guard is commanded by the governors of the respective states/territories and may be called to state active duty by the governor to assist in state emergencies, disasters, and civil disturbances. During a war or national emergency, the National Guard may be called to active duty by the President or Congress. The National Guard serves as the primary source of augmentation for the Army and the Air Force.

Budget requests for fiscal 1985 are $4.6 billion for the Army National Guard and $2.8 billion for the Air National Guard. Additional money is appropriated directly for the National Guard by the states. Substantial support is also provided by state, country, and municipal governments in land, police and fire protection, maintenance of roads, and the provision of direct county and municipal fiscal support to local units.

The Army National Guard provides 42% of the Army's divisional combat units. That support consists of 10 combat divisions, 22 separate combat brigades, 4 armored cavalry units, 2 special forces groups, one infantry scout group (arctic recon), 16 major command headquarters, and 1,195 other separate battalions, companies, headquarters, and detachments.

Army National Guard forces are vital to the nation's first-line defenses. For example, the 29th Infantry Brigade in the Hawaii National Guard is a round-out brigade for the active Army's 25th Infantry Division. Under the round-out concept, Army Guard units work and train with the active Army combat divisions of which they would become part upon mobilization. Integral to the total force policy, programs for increasing readiness are continually being improved.

National Guard units also participate in rotational training at the Army's National Training Center, Fort Irwin, Calif. This training with the active forces further develops the readiness of both units and individuals.

Additionally, Army and Air National Guard units participate annually in Joint Chiefs of Staff, active Army and Air Force, and major unified and specified command readiness exercises and deployments held worldwide with other active and reserve counterparts.

A program implemented in the National Guard provides opportunities for military personnel to seek full-time active duty careers in various duty positions with the Guard. The Active Guard/Reserve (AGR) program offers both officer and enlisted (male and female) personnel tours of full-time military duty in an AGR status which could eventually lead to a 20-year active duty retirement identical to that authorized active Army or Air Force personnel. Positions are located in all states at both state and local unit level. Duties encompass the areas of training, supply, administration, and maintenance. Applicants must be members of the Army or Air National Guard to be considered for AGR positions, and generally qualified to perform the duties required of the position for which they apply.

The Air National Guard has 91 flying units and 241 mission support units which, upon mobilization, would be gained by one of six major commands of the USAF. The gaining major commands are Tactical Air Command (TAC), Strategic Air Command (SAC), Military Airlift Command (MAC), Air Force Communications Command (AFCC), Pacific Air Forces (PACAF), and Alaskan Air Command (AAC).

Air National Guard flying units support four mission areas: strategic offense, with aerial refuelers supporting tactical fighter, bomber, and airlift aircraft; strategic defense, with fighter interceptors fulfilling a daily alert mission; general purpose forces equipped with tactical fighters for air to ground and air to air missions, tactical reconnaissance for battlefield assessment, electronic warfare and close air support; mobility with tactical airlift; and defense wide with rescue and recovery.

The National Guard is administered by the National Guard Bureau, a joint Army and Air Force office in the Pentagon. Chief of the Bureau is Lt. Gen. Emmett H. Walker, Jr., of Mississippi.

The Army National Guard offers its young men and women a broad spectrum of educational opportunities. These not only include skill training associated with their military assignment, but in many instances embrace civilian occupations as well. The list of skills is not limited to those that are equipment oriented but includes management, medical, and other career fields. Some of these educational opportunities may even be pursued in civilian institutions, specifically that of the Clinical Specialist, which is compatible with a Licensed Practical Nurse or Licensed Vocational Nurse.

Participation in the military education system by Army National Guard personnel is not limited to initial entry-skill-level training. There are opportunities available to become a qualified aviator, improve managerial and leadership abilities through attending courses designed for middle managers, and, finally, there are the courses offered at the prestigious Senior Service Colleges that address the needs of personnel at the executive level and positions of greater responsibilities.

If openings exist, young men and women between the ages of 17 and 35 may enlist for a period of six years. In certain circumstances the period of active participation may be less than six years. Upon enlistment, they serve a minimum of 12 weeks on active duty, training with the U.S. Army or the U.S. Air Force, depending upon which branch of the National Guard they choose. The remainder of their term of enlistment is spent in part-time training with their Guard unit.

A woman between the ages of 17 and 35 who has no previous military experience may also enlist in the National Guard for a period of six years. Women in the Army National Guard will receive basic training at either Fort McClellan, Ala., Fort Dix, N.J., or Fort Jackson, S.C.; women in the Air National Guard train at Lackland Air Force Base, Tex. Advanced training takes place at appropriate training centers.

Guard members receive a full day's pay of their military rank for each unit training assembly attended. Additionally, they receive a day's pay of their military rank for each day of their 15 days of annual training, plus any other days on active duty for training at military schools or special assignments. All such training counts toward retirement eligibility at age 60 with 20 or more years of qualifying service.

Pay Grades of Enlisted Personnel

Army ranks[1]	Air Force ranks	Marine ranks	Navy and Coast Guard ranks	Pay grades
Command Sergeant Major and Staff Sergeant Major	Chief Master Sergeant	Sergeant Major and Master Gunnery Sergeant	Master Chief Petty Officer	E-9
1st Sergeant and Master Sergeant	Senior Master Sergeant	1st Sergeant and Master Sergeant	Senior Chief Petty Officer	E-8
Sergeant 1st Class	Master Sergeant	Gunnery Sergeant	Chief Petty Officer	E-7
Staff Sergeant	Technical Sergeant	Staff Sergeant	Petty Officer 1st Class	E-6
Sergeant	Staff Sergeant	Sergeant	Petty Officer 2nd Class	E-5
Corporal and Specialist 4th Class	Sergeant and Senior Airman	Corporal	Petty Officer 3rd Class	E-4
Private 1st Class	Airman 1st Class	Lance Corporal	Seaman	E-3
Private	Airman	Private 1st Class	Seaman Apprentice	E-2
Private	Airman/Basic	Private	Seaman Recruit	E-1

1. Army specialist pay grades correspond to numbers: Specialist 4 (E-4), etc. *Source:* Department of Defense

NATO and Warsaw Pact Military Balance, 1983–1984

Category	NATO	(of which) U.S.	Warsaw Pact	(of which) U.S.S.R.
Total manpower in uniform (in thousands)	4,991	2,136	6,068	5,050
Ground forces available in peacetime (division equivalents)	90	5	85	43
Main battle tanks available in peacetime	20,722	5,000	25,490	13,000
Tactical aircraft in operational service:				
Fighter/ground attack	2,186	498	1,685	1,100
Interceptors	647	0	4,382	2,880
Reconnaisance	354	66	564	400
Fighters	368	222	700	700
Bombers	34	0	455	455

Missile strength (all theaters)	Intercontinental ballistic missiles	Submarine launched ballistic missiles	Long-range bombers
United States[1]	1,045	568	272
Soviet Union[1]	1,398	980	143

1. 1983. *Source:* International Institute for Strategic Studies, London.

Extra Pay for Service During Hostilities

Act of March 3, 1847, during the Mexican War, provided for $2 a month extra pay for "distinguished service." This continued beyond the war and applied in the Civil War.

In the Spanish-American War, there was a 20% increase in enlisted men's pay for war service.

In World War I, additional incentive pay was offered for all types of services. Among these items was pay for certificate of merit of $2 a month. By the law passed in 1920, the reasons for additional pay had expanded. Recipients of the Medal of Honor, Distinguished Service Cross, and Distinguished Service Medal received $2 a month extra, while each bar in lieu of these medals also added another $2 a month. Added to this was a foreign service bonus of 20%.

Act of June 30, 1944, authorized $5 a month to enlisted men qualified as expert infantrymen and $10 to those qualified as combat infantrymen. Amounts were payable for the duration of war and 6 months thereafter.

By the Act of July 6, 1945, for the duration of war and for 6 months thereafter, enlisted men entitled to wear Medical Badges received additional pay of $10 a month.

Act of July 10, 1952, authorized $45 a month for each month beginning after May 31, 1950, for which the member was entitled to receive basic pay and during which he was a member of a combat unit in Korea.

The Combat Duty Pay Act of 1952 was repealed by the Uniformed Services Pay Act of 1963, which authorized special pay for duty subject to hostile fire under certain conditions at the rate of $55 (now $65) a month.

Family Separation Allowance

Military members with dependents in grades E-4 (over 4 years of service) and above are entitled to an allowance of $30 a month in addition to allowances or per diem when on a permanent change of station, with movement of dependents not authorized and dependents not residing near his station; or be on board ship or temporary duty for more than 30 days, with dependents not residing near the temporary duty station.

A second type of family separation allowance at the rate equal to the quarters allowance for a member in the same grade without dependents is payable to a member with dependents when assigned to permanent duty outside the United States or in Alaska when government quarters, or quarters under the jurisdiction of a uniformed service, are not available to the member. Further, the member's dependents must not be residing at or near his permanent duty station and are not authorized to movement to or near the permanent duty station at Government expense.

Allowances for Subsistence

Officers receive $102.10 per month. Enlisted personnel receive allowances for subsistence under the following provisions: (1) when rations in kind are not available, $5.50 per day; (2) when on leave or authorized to mess separately, $4.87 per day; (3) when assigned to duty under emergency conditions where no messing facilities of the U.S. are available, $7.28 per day.

Veterans' Benefits

Although benefits of various kinds date back to Colonial days, veterans of World War I were the first to receive disability compensation, allotments for dependents, life insurance, medical care, and vocational rehabilitation. In 1940, these benefits were slowly broadened.

The following benefits available to veterans require certain minimum periods of active duty during qualifying periods of service and, except for service personnel, are applicable only to those whose discharges are not dishonorable.

Unemployment allowances. Every effort is being made to secure employment for Vietnam veterans. Unemployment benefits are administered by the U.S. Department of Labor.

Loans. GI loans are made for a variety of purposes, such as: to buy or build a home; to purchase a mobile home with or without a lot; and to refinance a home presently owned and occupied by the veteran. The VA will guarantee the lender against loss up to 60% of a home loan with a maximum of $27, 500. On mobile home loans, the amount of the guaranty is 50% of the loan with a maximum of $20,000. The interest rate may not exceed the maximum rate set by the VA and in effect when the loan is made.

Compensation and rehabilitation benefits. These are available to those having some service-connected illness or disability.

Disability compensation. The VA pays from $58 to $1,130 per month, and for specific conditions up to $3,223 per month, plus allowances for dependents, where the disability is rated 30% or more.

Vocational rehabilitation. Necessary training expenses, special equipment, etc., toward a definite job objective are paid for, plus a monthly allowance of up to $282, with increased amounts for dependents, in addition to compensation.—

Medical and dental care. This includes care in VA and, in certain instances, in non-VA, or other federal hospitals. It also covers outpatient treatment at a VA field facility or, in some cases, by an approved private physician or dentist. Full domiciliary care is also provided where necessary. Nursing home care may be provided at certain VA medical facilities or in approved community nursing homes. Hospital and other medical care may also be provided for the spouse and child dependents of a veteran who is permanently and totally disabled due to a service-connected disability; or for survivors of a veteran who dies from a service-connected disability; or for survivors of a veteran who at the time of death had a total disability, permanent in nature, resulting from a service-connected disability. These latter benefits are usually provided in nonfederal facilities. Eligibility criteria for these benefits vary, and veterans and/or their dependents or survivors should always apply in advance. Contact the nearest VA medical facility.

Dependents' educational assistance. The VA pays $342 a month for up to 45 months of schooling to sons and daughters of veterans who died of service-connected causes or who were permanently and totally disabled from service-connected causes or died while permanently and totally disabled or who are missing in action, captured in the line of duty, or forcibly detained or interned in line of duty by a foreign power for more than 90 days. Students must usually be between 18 and 26.

Spouses of veterans whose deaths are adjudged to be service-connected, and spouses of veterans who are permanently and totally disabled due to service-connected causes or who are prisoners of war or are missing in action are also eligible for this educational benefit.

Veterans readjustment education. Veterans who served on active duty for at least 181 days after Jan. 31, 1955, but before Jan. 1, 1977, may receive monthly educational assistance under the new GI Bill for post-Korean conflict veterans, varying from $342 for single full-time students to $462 for veterans with two dependents, plus $29 for each additional dependent. Veterans and servicepersons who initially entered the military on or after Jan. 1, 1977, may receive educational assistance under a contributory plan. Individuals contribute $25 to $100 from military pay, up to a maximum of $2, 700. This amount is matched by the Federal Government on a 2 for 1 basis. Participants, while on active duty, may make a lump sum contribution. Participants receive monthly payments for the number of months they contributed, or for 36 months, whichever is less.

Pensions. Pension benefits are payable for wartime veterans totally disabled from non-service-connected causes. These benefits are based on need. Surviving spouses and orphans of wartime veterans have the same eligibility status.

Insurance. The VA life insurance programs have approximately 7.5 million policyholders with total coverage of about $156 billion. Detailed information on NSLI (National Service Life Insurance), USGLI (United States Government Life Insurance), and VMLI (Veterans Mortgage Life Insurance) may be obtained at any VA Office. Information regarding SGLI (Servicemen's Group Life Insurance) and VGLI (Veterans Group Life Insurance) may be obtained from the Office of Servicemen's Group Life Insurance, 213 Washington St., Newark, N.J. 07102

Burial benefits. Burial is provided in any VA national cemetery with available grave space to any deceased veteran of wartime or peacetime service, other than for training, who was discharged under conditions other than dishonorable. Laws of the Congress extended eligibility for burial in a national cemetery to the veteran's spouse, widow, widower, minor children, and under certain conditions, unmarried adult children.

Headstone or marker. A government headstone or marker is furnished for any deceased veteran of wartime or peacetime service, other than for training, who was discharged under conditions other than dishonorable and is interred in a national, state veterans', or private cemetery. VA also will furnish markers to veterans' eligible dependents interred in a national or state veterans' cemetery.

Highest Ranking Officers in the Armed Forces

ARMY[1]

Generals: John W. Vessey, Jr., Chairman of the Joint Chiefs of Staff; John A. Wickham, Jr., Chief of Staff; Bernard W. Rogers, Supreme Allied Commander, Europe; Glenn K. Otis, Donald R. Keith, Richard E. Cavazos, Paul F. Gorman, Maxwell R. Thurman, Robert W. Sennewald.

AIR FORCE

Generals: Wilber L. Creech, James E. Dalton, Bennie L. Davis, Charles A. Gabriel, James V. Hartinger, Andrew P. Iosue, Richard L. Lawson, Robert T. Marsh, Billy M. Minter, James P. Mullins, Jerome F. O'Malley, Thomas M. Ryan, Jr., Lawrence A. Skantze.

NAVY

Admirals: James D. Watkins, Chief of Naval Operations; William J. Crowe, Jr.; William N. Small; Kinnaird R. McKee; Sylvester R. Foley, Jr.; Wesley L. McDonald; Ronald J. Hays; Steven A. White.

MARINE CORPS

Generals: Paul X. Kelley, Commandant of the Marine Corps; John K. Davis, Assistant Commandant of the Marine Corps.

Lieutenant Generals: John H. Miller, Harold A. Hatch, William R. Maloney, William H. Fitch, Charles G. Cooper, D'Wayne Gray, Bernard E. Trainor.

COAST GUARD

Admiral: James S. Gracey, Commandant.

Vice Admirals: Benedict L. Stabile, Vice Commandant; Wayne E. Caldwell, Commander, Atlantic Area; Charles E. Larkin, Commander, Pacific Area.

1. On March 15, 1978, George Washington, the commander of the Continental Army in the American Revolution and our first President, was promoted to the newly-created rank of General of the Armies of the United States. Congress authorized this title to make it clear that Washington is the Army's senior general. *Source:* Department of Defense.

Nuclear Weapons Yield

The most widely used standard for measuring the power of nuclear weapons is "yield," expressed as the quantity of TNT that would produce the same energy release. The first atomic bomb exploded at Hiroshima had a yield of 13 kilotons, or the explosive power of 13,000 tons of TNT.

The largest nuclear detonation was set off by the Soviet Union in 1962 and had a yield of 58 megatons—equivalent to 58 million tons of TNT.

According to the Department of Defense, the United States has withdrawn many large, high-yield weapons since 1960. As a result, the total megatonnage of U.S. nuclear weapons has been reduced by 75% since that time.

Insignia and Ranks of the Armed Forces

Army, Air Force, and Marines		Navy and Coast Guard		
Insignia	**Rank**	**Insignia**	**Rank**	**Stripes[1]**
Five silver stars	General of the Army, AF	Five silver stars	Fleet Admiral	1—4—0
Four silver stars	General	Four silver stars	Admiral	1—3—0
Three silver stars	Lieutenant General	Three silver stars	Vice Admiral	1—2—0
Two silver stars	Major General	Two silver stars	Rear Admiral	1—1—0
One silver star	Brigadier General	One silver star	Commodore[2]	1—0—0
Silver eagle	Colonel	Silver eagle	Captain	0—4—0
Silver oak leaf	Lieutenant Colonel	Silver oak leaf	Commander	0—3—0
Gold oak leaf	Major	Gold oak leaf	Lt. Commander	0—2—1
Two silver bars	Captain	Two silver bars	Lieutenant	0—2—0
One silver bar	First Lieutenant	One silver bar	Lieutenant (jg)	0—1—1
One gold bar	Second Lieutenant	One gold bar	Ensign	0—1—0
Silver bar with 4 enamel bands[3]	Chief Warrant Officer (W-4)	Silver bar with 3 enamel bands[3]	Chief Warrant Officer (W-4)	0—1—0[4]
Silver bar with 3 enamel bands[3]	Chief Warrant Officer (W-3)	Silver bar with 2 enamel bands[3]	Chief Warrant Officer (W-3)	0—1—0[5]
Silver bar with 2 enamel bands[3]	Chief Warrant Officer (W-2)	Gold bar with 3 enamel bands[3]	Chief Warrant Officer (W-2)	0—1—0[6]
Silver bar with 1 enamel band[3]	Warrant Officer (W-1)	Gold bar with 2 enamel bands[3]		

1. Of gold embroidery; first figure is number of 2-in. stripes, second is number of 1/2-inch strips, third is number of 1/4-in. stripes. 2. The Navy rank of Commodore became effective Sept. 15, 1981, however until Fiscal Year 1983, the Navy retained its system of upper-half (0–8) and lower-half (0–7) Rear Admirals. The Coast Guard will continue to have Rear Admirals at both 0–7 and 0–8 grades. 3. Navy and Marine Corps use same size insignia as Army when worn on shoulder straps, but miniature size on shirt collars. Enamel bands are black for Army, scarlet for Marines, medium blue for Air Force, and blue for Navy and Coast Guard. 4. One break. 5. Two breaks. 6. Three breaks.

Pay Grades of Commissioned Officers and Warrant Officers

Rank			
Army, Air Force, and Marine Corps	**Navy, Coast Guard, and National Oceanic and Atmospheric Adm. (NOAA)**	**Public Health Service**	**Pay grade**
General	Admiral[3]	—	0-10
Lieutenant General	Vice Admiral	Surgeon General	0-9
Major General	Rear Admiral (Navy) and Rear Admiral (upper half) (Coast Guard and National Oceanic and Atmospheric Administration	Deputy Surgeon General, Assistant Surgeon General having rank of Major General	0-8
Brigadier General	Commodore (NOAA)[2] (Navy) and Rear Admiral (lower half) (Coast Guard)	Assistant Surgeon General having rank of Brigadier General	0-7
Colonel	Captain	Director Grade	0-6
Lieutenant Colonel	Commander	Senior Grade	0-5
Major	Lieutenant Commander	Full Grade	0-4
Captain	Lieutenant	Senior Assistant Grade	0-3
First Lieutenant	Lieutenant (Junior Grade)	Assistant Grade	0-2
Second Lieutenant	Ensign	Junior Assistant Grade	0-1
Chief Warrant Officer	Chief Warrant Officer[1]	—	W-4
Chief Warrant Officer	Chief Warrant Officer[1]	—	W-3
Chief Warrant Officer	Chief Warrant Officer[1]	—	W-2
Warrant Officer	Warrant Officer[1]	—	W-1

1. Not applicable to the Navy and National Oceanic and Atmospheric Administration (NOAA). 2. The Defense Officer Personnel Management Act (Public Law 96-513;94 Stat. 2835) effective Sept. 15, 1981, established a new officer grade of Commodore in the Navy and assigns officers in that grade to pay grade 0–7. Following a period of transition, attainment of the grade of Rear Admiral will be by selection from officers in the grade of Commodore and officers so selected will be assigned to pay grade 0–8. 3. Not applicable to the National Oceanic and Atmospheric Administration (NOAA). *Source:* Department of Defense.

Navy Proposes Land Burial for Nuclear Subs

The U.S. Navy has decided to bury the defueled nuclear engine compartments of retired nuclear submarines on government-owned land because of strong opposition to ocean-scuttling the vessels by concerned groups who fear contamination of the ocean environment.

The proposed sites for burial are Hanford, Wash., or near Aiken, S.C. There are about 100 nuclear submarines that will be retired in the next 20 to 30 years.

Monthly Basic Pay and Allowance for Quarters Rates by Pay Grades, Effective Jan. 1984

Pay Grade	Pay rates													
	Years of service													
	Under 2	2	3	4	6	8	10	12	14	16	18	20	22	26
COMMISSIONED OFFICERS														
0–10	4874.40	5046.00	5046.00	5046.00	5046.00	5239.50	5239.50	5640.60	5640.60	6044.10	6044.10	6448.50	6448.50	6850.80
0–9	4320.30	4433.40	4527.60	4527.60	4527.60	4642.80	4642.80	4836.00	4836.00	5239.50	5239.50	5640.60	5640.60	6044.10
0–8	3912.90	4030.20	4125.90	4125.90	4125.90	4433.40	4433.40	4642.80	4642.80	4836.00	5046.00	5239.50	5449.50	5449.50
0–7	3251.40	3472.50	3472.50	3472.50	3627.90	3627.90	3838.50	3838.50	4030.20	4433.40	4737.90	4737.90	4737.90	4737.90
0–6	2409.90	2647.80	2821.20	2821.20	2821.20	2821.20	2821.20	2821.20	2916.90	3378.30	3551.10	3627.00	3838.50	4163.10
0–5	1927.50	2263.50	2419.50	2419.50	2419.50	2419.50	2493.30	2627.10	2802.90	3012.60	3185.70	3282.00	3396.60	3396.60
0–4	1624.50	1978.20	2110.50	2110.50	2149.20	2244.60	2397.30	2532.30	2647.80	2763.90	2840.40	2840.40	2840.40	2840.40
0–3	1509.90	1687.80	1804.20	1996.50	2091.90	2167.50	2284.20	2397.30	2456.40	2456.40	2456.40	2456.40	2456.40	2456.40
0–2	1316.40	1437.60	1727.10	1785.30	1822.80	1822.80	1822.80	1822.80	1822.80	1822.80	1822.80	1822.80	1822.80	1822.80
0–1	1143.00	1189.80	1437.60	1437.60	1437.60	1437.60	1437.60	1437.60	1437.60	1437.60	1437.60	1437.60	1437.60	1437.60
COMMISSIONED OFFICERS WITH OVER 4 YEARS ACTIVE DUTY AS AN ENLISTED MEMBER OR WARRANT OFFICER														
0–3E	0.00	0.00	0.00	1996.50	2091.90	2167.50	2284.20	2397.30	2493.30	2493.30	2493.30	2493.30	2493.30	2493.30
0–2E	0.00	0.00	0.00	1785.30	1822.80	1880.40	1978.20	2053.80	2110.50	2110.50	2110.50	2110.50	2110.50	2110.50
0–1E	0.00	0.00	0.00	1437.60	1535.70	1592.40	1650.00	1707.30	1785.30	1785.30	1785.30	1785.30	1785.30	1785.30
WARRANT OFFICERS														
W-4	1538.10	1650.00	1650.00	1687.80	1764.60	1842.30	1919.70	2053.80	2149.20	2224.80	2284.20	2358.30	2437.20	2627.10
W-3	1398.00	1516.50	1516.50	1535.70	1554.00	1667.70	1764.60	1822.80	1880.40	1936.80	1996.50	2073.90	2149.20	2224.80
W-2	1224.60	1324.50	1324.50	1363.20	1437.60	1516.50	1573.80	1631.40	1687.80	1746.90	1804.20	1861.50	1936.80	1936.80
W-1	1020.30	1169.70	1169.70	1267.20	1324.50	1381.50	1437.60	1497.50	1554.00	1611.30	1667.70	1727.10	1727.10	1727.10
ENLISTED MEMBERS														
E-9	0.00	0.00	0.00	0.00	0.00	0.00	1788.90	1829.70	1871.10	1914.00	1956.60	1994.70	2099.70	2303.70
E-8	0.00	0.00	0.00	0.00	0.00	1500.60	1543.20	1583.70	1625.10	1668.00	1708.40	1748.40	1851.00	2057.70
E-7	1047.60	1130.70	1173.00	1213.80	1255.50	1295.10	1336.80	1378.20	1440.60	1481.40	1523.10	1542.90	1646.40	1851.00
E-6	901.20	982.50	1023.60	1067.10	1106.40	1146.90	1188.90	1250.10	1289.40	1331.10	1351.20	1351.20	1351.20	1351.20
E-5	791.10	861.00	902.70	942.00	1003.80	1044.60	1086.30	1126.20	1146.90	1146.90	1146.90	1146.90	1146.90	1146.90
E-4	738.00	779.10	824.70	888.90	924.00	924.00	924.00	924.00	924.00	924.00	924.00	924.00	924.00	924.00
E-3	695.10	732.90	762.60	792.90	792.90	792.90	792.90	792.90	792.90	792.90	792.90	792.90	792.90	792.90
E-2	668.70	668.70	668.70	668.70	668.70	668.70	668.70	668.70	668.70	668.70	668.70	668.70	668.70	668.70
E-1 > 4	596.40	596.40	596.40	596.40	598.40	596.40	596.40	596.40	596.40	596.40	596.40	596.40	596.40	596.40
E-1 < 4	573.60	573.60	573.60	573.60	573.60	573.60	573.60	573.60	573.60	573.60	573.60	573.60	573.60	573.60

The Chairman of the Joint Chiefs and the military heads of each service receive $5,499.90 a month. The senior enlisted persons of the Air Force, Army, Coast Guard, Marine Corps and Navy each get $2,800.20 regardless of length of service. Note: Basic pay is limited to $5,499.90 by Level V of the executive schedule. *Source:* Department of Defense.

Defense Budget by Major Categories

(Current billions of dollars)

Major Missions and Programs	1983 actual	1984 estimate	1985 estimate	1986 estimate	1987 estimate
Strategic forces[1]	19.7	26.3	31.6	33.9	32.7
General purpose forces	98.8	99.7	128.2	151.0	168.7
Intelligence and communications	17.3	20.1	25.8	28.7	30.9
Airlift and sealift	4.3	5.6	7.5	9.6	9.6
Guard and reserve	12.1	12.9	16.5	19.0	21.8
Research and development[2]	18.7	21.4	27.0	30.5	32.0
Central supply and maintenance	21.6	22.5	26.5	29.3	32.1
Training, medical, other general personnel activities[3]	42.2	44.2	35.6	40.1	43.4
Administration and associated activities	4.1	4.8	5.6	6.6	7.1
Support of other nations	.7	.7	.7	.9	.9
Total	**239.5**	**258.2**	**305.0**	**349.6**	**379.2**

1. Excludes strategic systems development included in the research and development category. 2. Excludes research and development in other program areas on systems approved for production. 3. Military retired pay is included in training, medical and other general personal activities through 1984. In 1985 and later years, military retired pay is funded on an accrual basis with costs distributed to all mission categories.

Budget Outlays for National Defense Functions

(in billions of dollars, except as indicated)

Item	1982	1981	1980	1979	1978	1977	1976	1975	1970
Defense Dept., military	182.9	158.6	132.8	115.0	103.0	95.7	88.0	85.0	77.2
Military personnel	42.3	37.0	30.8	28.4	27.1	25.7	25.1	25.0	23.0
Percent of military	23.1	23.3	23.2	24.7	26.3	26.9	28.5	29.4	29.9
Active forces	38.4	33.8	28.5	26.3	25.1	23.9	23.3	23.2	22.0
Reserve forces	3.9	3.2	2.3	2.1	2.0	1.9	1.8	1.7	1.1
Military retirees	14.9	13.8	11.9	10.3	9.2	8.2	7.3	6.2	2.8
Operation, maintenance	59.7	53.8	44.8	36.4	33.6	30.6	27.9	26.3	21.6
Procurement[1]	43.3	34.1	29.0	25.4	20.0	18.2	16.0	16.0	21.6
Army	8.7	6.8	5.4	4.5	3.2	2.6	1.4	2.5	5.2
Navy[2]	16.7	14.3	12.4	11.8	9.2	8.5	8.0	8.1	7.9
Air Force	16.0	12.7	10.9	8.9	7.3	6.9	6.5	5.3	8.4
Research and develop	17.7	15.2	13.1	11.2	10.5	9.8	8.9	8.9	7.2
Military construction	2.9	2.5	2.5	2.1	1.9	1.9	2.0	1.5	1.2
Family housing	2.0	1.9	1.7	1.5	1.4	1.4	1.2	1.1	.6
Civil defense	.1	(7)	(7)	(7)	(7)	.1	.1	.1	.1
Other[3]	4.3	.3	−1.0	−.2	−.8	−.2	−.4	−.1	−1.0
Atomic energy activities[4]	.3	3.6	2.9	2.5	2.1	1.9	1.6	1.5	1.4
Defense-related activities[5]	—	—	.1	.1	.2	−.1	−.1	−.9	—
Total	**187.4**	**162.1**	**135.9**	**117.7**	**105.2**	**97.5**	**89.4**	**85.5**	**78.6**

1. Includes other defense agencies not shown separately. 2. Includes Marine Corps. 3. Revolving and management funds, trust funds, special foreign currency program, allowances, and offsetting receipts. 4. Defense activities only. 5. Includes civil defense activities. *Source:* Office of Management and Budget.

Defense-Related Industries—Selected Shipments

(In millions of dollars)

Military Equipment	1982	1981	1980	1979	1978
Aircraft	7,670	6,393	5,892	4,430	3,719
Aircraft engines	1,668	1,555	1,473	1,113	816
Missile & space vehicle engines and parts	2,360	1,992	1,739	1,294	1,128
Guided missiles and space vehicles	12,181	9,854	8,236	7,507	6,407
Missile systems, excluding propulsion	9,014	7,095	5,754	5,638	4,519
Space vehicle systems, complete	3,167	2,759	2,482	1,869	1,888
Ships, new self-propelled	3,444	3,318	2,903	2,512	2,282
Ship repair	1,321	1,296	1,134	969	912

Source: U.S. Bureau of Industrial Economics, *1982 U.S. Industrial Outlook.*

U.S. Military Actions Other Than Declared Wars

Hawaii (1893): U.S. Marines, ordered to land by U.S. Minister John L. Stevens, aided the revolutionary Committee of Safety in overthrowing the native government. Stevens then proclaimed Hawaii a U.S. protectorate. Annexation, resisted by the Democratic administration in Washington, was not formally accomplished until 1898.

China (1900): Boxers (a group of Chinese revolutionists) occupied Peking and laid siege to foreign legations. U.S. troops joined an international expedition which relieved the city.

Panama (1903): After Colombia had rejected a proposed agreement for relinquishing sovereignty over the Panama Canal Zone, revolution broke out, aided by promoters of the Panama Canal Co. Two U.S. warships were standing by to protect American privileges. The U.S. recognized the Republic of Panama on November 6.

Dominican Republic (1904): When the Dominican Republic failed to meet debts owed to the U.S. and foreign creditors, President Theodore Roosevelt declared the U.S. intention of exercising "international police power" in the Western Hemisphere whenever necessary. The U.S. accordingly administered customs and managed debt payments of the Dominican Republic from 1905 to 1907.

Nicaragua (1911): The possibility of foreign control over Nicaragua's canal route led to U.S. intervention and agreement. The U.S. landed Marines in Nicaragua (Aug. 14, 1912) to protect American interests there. A small detachment remained until 1933.

Mexico (1914): Mexican dictator Victoriano Huerta, opposed by President Woodrow Wilson, had the support of European governments. An incident involving unarmed U.S. sailors in Tampico led to the landing of U.S. forces on Mexican soil. Veracruz was bombarded by the Navy to prevent the landing of munitions from a German vessel. At the point of war, both powers agreed to mediation by Argentina, Brazil, and Chile. Huerta abdicated, and Venustiano Carranza succeeded to the presidency.

Haiti (1915): U.S. Marines imposed a military occupation. Haiti signed a treaty making it a virtual protectorate of the U.S. until troops were withdrawn in 1934.

Mexico (1916): Raids by Pancho Villa cost American lives on both sides of the border. President Carranza consented to a punitive expedition led by Gen. John J. Pershing, but antagonism grew in Mexico. Wilson withdrew the U.S. force when war with Germany became imminent.

Dominican Republic (1916): Renewed intervention in the Dominican Republic with internal administration by U.S. naval officers lasted until 1924.

Korea (1950): In this undeclared war, which terminated with the July 27, 1953, truce at Panmunjom and the establishment of a neutral nations' supervisory commission, the U.S. and 15 member-nations of the U.N. came to the aid of the Republic of South Korea, whose 38th-parallel border was crossed by the invading Russian Communist-controlled North Koreans, who were later joined by the Chinese Communists.

Lebanon (1958): Fearful of the newly formed U.A.R. abetting the rebels of his politically and economically torn country, President Camille Chamoun appealed to the U.S. for military assistance. U.S. troops landed in Beirut in mid-July and left before the end of the year, after internal and external quiet were restored.

Dominican Republic (1965): On April 28, when a political coup-turned-civil war endangered the lives of American nationals, President Lyndon B. Johnson rushed 400 marines into Santo Domingo, the beginning of an eventual U.S. peak-commitment of 30,000 troops, constituting the preponderant military strength of the OAS-created Inter-American Peace Force, and 6,500 troops, including 5,000 Americans, remained until after the peaceful inauguration of President Joaquín Balaguer on July 1, 1966, and the entire force left the country on September 20.

Vietnam: This longest war in U.S. history began with economic and technical assistance after 1954 Geneva accords ending the Indochinese War. By 1964 it had escalated into a major conflict.

This involvement spanning the administrations of five Presidents led to domestic discontent in the late 1960s. By April 1969, U.S. troop strength reached a peak of 543,400. Peace negotiations began in Paris in 1968 but proved fruitless. Finally, on Jan. 27, 1973, a peace accord was signed in Paris by the U.S., North and South Vietnam, and the Vietcong. Within 60 days, U.S. POWs were returned, and the U.S. withdrew all military forces from South Vietnam.

U.S. Casualties in Major Wars

War	Branch of service	Numbers engaged	Battle deaths	Other deaths	Total deaths	Wounds not mortal	Total casualties[1]
Revolutionary War	Army	n.a.	4,044	n.a.	n.a.	6,004	n.a.
1775 to 1783	Navy	n.a.	342	n.a.	n.a.	114	n.a.
	Marines	n.a.	49	n.a.	n.a.	70	n.a.
	Total	**n.a.**	**4,435**	**n.a.**	**n.a.**	**6,188**	**n.a.**
War of 1812	Army	n.a.	1,950	n.a.	n.a.	4,000	n.a.
1812 to 1815	Navy	n.a.	265	n.a.	n.a.	439	n.a.
	Marines	n.a.	45	n.a.	n.a.	66	n.a.
	Total	**286,730**	**2,260**	**n.a.**	**n.a.**	**4,505**	**n.a.**

War	Branch of service	Numbers engaged	Battle deaths	Other deaths	Total deaths	Wounds not mortal	Total casualties
Mexican War 1846 to 1848	Army	n.a.	1,721	11,550	13,271	4,102	17,373
	Navy	n.a.	1	n.a.	n.a.	3	n.a.
	Marines	n.a.	11	n.a.	n.a.	47	n.a.
	Total	**78,718**	**1,733**	**n.a.**	**n.a.**	**4,152**	**n.a.**
Civil War[2] 1861 to 1865	Army	2,128,948	138,154	221,374	359,528	280,040	639,568
	Navy	84,415	2,112	2,411	4,523	1,710	6,233
	Marines		148	312	460	131	591
	Total	**2,213,363**	**140,414**	**224,097**	**364,511**	**281,881**	**646,392**
Spanish-American War 1898	Army	280,564	369	2,061	2,430	1,594	4,024
	Navy	22,875	10	0	10	47	57
	Marines	3,321	6	0	6	21	27
	Total	**306,760**	**385**	2,061	**2,446**	**1,662**	**4,108**
World War I 1917 to 1918	Army	4,057,101	50,510	55,868	106,378	193,663	300,041
	Navy	599,051	431	6,856	7,287	819	8,106
	Marines	78,839	2,461	390	2,851	9,520	12,371
	Total	**4,734,991**	**53,402**	**63,114**	**116,516**	**204,002**	**320,518**
World War II 1941 to 1946	Army[3]	11,260,000	234,874	83,400	318,274	565,861	884,135
	Navy	4,183,466	36,950	25,664	62,614	37,778	100,392
	Marines	669,100	19,733	4,778	24,511	67,207	91,718
	Total	**16,112,566**	**291,557**	**113,842**	**405,399**	**670,846**	**1,076,245**
Korean War 1950 to 1953	Army	2,834,000	27,704	9,429	37,133	77,596	114,729
	Navy	1,177,000	458	4,043	4,501	1,576	6,077
	Marines	424,000	4,267	1,261	5,528	23,744	29,272
	Air Force	1,285,000	1,200	5,884	7,084	368	7,452
	Total	**5,720,000**	**33,629**	**20,617**	**54,246**	**103,284**	**157,530**
War in Southeast Asia[4]	Army	4,386,000	30,867	7,252	38,119	96,802	134,921
	Navy[5]	1,842,000	1,605	911	2,516	4,178	6,694
	Marines	794,000	13,066	1,685	14,749	51,392	66,141
	Air Force	1,740,000	1,715	603	2,318	931	3,249
	Total	**8,744,000**	**47,253**	**10,449**	**57,702**	**153,303**	**211,005**

1. Excludes captured or interned and missing in action who were subsequently returned to military control. 2. Union forces only. Totals should probably be somewhat larger as data or disposition of prisoners are far from complete. Final Confederate deaths, based on incomplete returns, were 133,821, to which should be added 26,000–31,000 personnel who died in Union prisons. 3. Army data include Air Force. 4. As of Sept. 30, 1977. 5. Includes a small number of Coast Guard. NOTE: All data are subject to revision. For wars before World War I, information represents best data from available records. However, due to incomplete records and possible difference in usage of terminology, reporting systems, etc., figures should be considered estimates. n.a. = not available. *Source:* Department of Defense.

Casualties in World War I

Country	Total mobilized forces	Killed or died[1]	Wounded	Prisoners or missing	Total casualties
Austria-Hungary	7,800,000	1,200,000	3,620,000	2,200,000	7,020,000
Belgium	267,000	13,716	44,686	34,659	93,061
British Empire[2]	8,904,467	908,371	2,090,212	191,652	3,190,235
Bulgaria	1,200,000	87,500	152,390	27,029	266,919
France[2]	8,410,000	1,357,800	4,266,000	537,000	6,160,800
Germany	11,000,000	1,773,700	4,216,058	1,152,800	7,142,558
Greece	230,000	5,000	21,000	1,000	27,000
Italy	5,615,000	650,000	947,000	600,000	2,197,000
Japan	800,000	300	907	3	1,210
Montenegro	50,000	3,000	10,000	7,000	20,000
Portugal	100,000	7,222	13,751	12,318	33,291
Romania	750,000	335,706	120,000	80,000	535,706
Russia	12,000,000	1,700,000	4,950,000	2,500,000	9,150,000
Serbia	707,343	45,000	133,148	152,958	331,106
Turkey	2,850,000	325,000	400,000	250,000	975,000
United States	4,734,991	116,516	204,002	—	320,518

1. Includes deaths from all causes. 2. Official figures. NOTE: For additional U.S. figures, *see* the table on U.S. Casualties in Major Wars in this section.

Casualties in World War II

Country	Men in war	Battle deaths	Wounded
Australia	1,000,000	26,976	180,864
Austria	800,000	280,000	350,117
Belgium	625,000	8,460	55,513[1]
Brazil[2]	40,334	943	4,222
Bulgaria	339,760	6,671	21,878
Canada	1,041,080	32,412	53,145
China[3]	17,250,521	1,324,516	1,762,006
Czechoslovakia	—	6,683[4]	8,017
Denmark	—	4,339	—
Finland	500,000	79,047	50,000
France	—	201,568	400,000
Germany	20,000,000	3,250,000[4]	7,250,000
Greece	—	17,024	47,290
Hungary	—	147,435	89,313
India	2,393,891	32,121	64,354
Italy	3,100,000	149,496[4]	66,716
Japan	9,700,000	1,270,000	140,000
Netherlands	280,000	6,500	2,860
New Zealand	194,000	11,625[4]	17,000
Norway	75,000	2,000	—
Poland	—	664,000	530,000
Romania	650,000[5]	350,000[6]	—
South Africa	410,056	2,473	—
U.S.S.R.	—	6,115,000[4]	14,012,000
United Kingdom	5,896,000	357,116[4]	369,267
United States	16,112,566	291,557	670,846
Yugoslavia	3,741,000	305,000	425,000

1. Civilians only. 2. Army and Navy figures. 3. Figures cover period July 7, 1937–Sept. 2, 1945, and concern only Chinese regular troops. They do not include casualties suffered by guerrillas and local military corps. 4. Deaths from all causes. 5. Against Soviet Russia; 385,847 against Nazi Germany. 6. Against Soviet Russia; 169,822 against Nazi Germany. NOTE: The figures in this table are unofficial estimates obtained from various sources.

U.S. Navy Combatant Vessels, 1985

Type	Number	Type	Number
Carriers	13	Mine warfare	4
Destroyers	68	Patrol combatants	6
Cruisers	30	Amphibious warfare	59
Frigates	99	Auxiliaries and sealift	43
Submarines	100	Total	422

Note: Planned for 1985, exact figures are classified. Source: Department of Navy

Strengths of Military Formations, 1981–1982

Type of unit	U.S.	U.S.S.R.	China	West Germany	India	Egypt	Israel
Division: Armored							
Men	18,300	11,000	9,200	17,000	15,000	11,000	—
Tanks	324	335[1]	270	300	200	300	—
Mechanized							
Men	18,500	14,000	12,700[2]	17,500	17,500	12,000	—
Tanks	216	266[1]	30[2]	250	—	190	—
Airborne							
Men	16,800	7,000	9,000	8,000–9,000	—	—	—
Brigade: Armored							
Men	4,500	1,300[3]	1,200[3]	4,500	6,000	3,500	3,500
Tanks	108	95[3]	90[3]	110	150	96	80–100
Mechanized							
Men	4,800	2,300[3]	2,000	5,000	4,500	3,500	3,500
Tanks	54	40[3]	—	54	—	36	36–40
Squadron:							
Fighter Aircraft	18–24	12–15	9–10	15–21	12–20	10–12	15–20

1. Tank strengths are for Soviet division in Eastern Europe: other divisions have fewer. 2. Infantry division. 3. Strength of a regiment, which is equivalent formation in Soviet and Chinese command structures. Particularly in West European countries, "regiment" often describes a battalion-size unit. It is so used here. NOTE: Data are latest available. *Source:* International Institute for Strategic Studies, London.

Military Spending and Strengths of World Nations

Country	Expenditures, 1982				Manpower, 1983					
	Total (millions)	Per capita	% of govt spending	% of GNP[1]	Total in armed forces	Army	Navy	Air Forces	Estimated reservists[2]	Para-military forces
United States	$259,900	$938	29.2	7.2	2,136,400	780,800	763,600[3]	592,000	955,300	158,300
Canada	5,989	247	9.2	2.0	82,855	13,000[4]	5,500[4]	15,300[4]	21,800	1,300
U.S.S.R.	n.a.	n.a.	n.a.	10–20	3,638,000	1,800,000	460,000	365,000	500,000,000	80,450,000
China	n.a.	n.a.	n.a.	n.a.	4,100,000	3,250,000	360,000	490,000	4,300,000	7,700,000
NATO (not including U.S. and Canada)										
Belgium	2,799	283	8.1	3.3	94,717	69,667	4,550	20,500	178,900	16,200
Britain	24,200	432	11.9	5.1	320,600	159,069	71,727	89,827	280,700	—
Denmark	1,122	219	5.5	2.0	31,200	17,500	5,800	7,400	156,200	—
France[5]	21,969	408	17.5	4.1	492,300	311,200	68,000	100,400	457,000	93,100
Germany, West[6]	28,453	461	27.9	4.3	495,000	335,500	36,400	105,900	750,000	20,000
Greece	2,574	265	23.5	6.7	185,000	142,000	19,500	23,500	404,000	29,000
Italy	8,924	156	5.6	2.6	373,100	258,000	44,500	70,600	794,000	206,000
Luxembourg	41	114	3.2	1.2	720	720	—	—	—	500
Netherlands	4,468	315	7.8	3.3	103,000	67,000	17,350[3]	17,500	176,500	8,700
Norway	1,680	410	6.7	3.0	43,200	24,175	8,850	9,860	248,000	—
Portugal	778	79	10.8	3.3	63,500	41,000	13,000[3]	9,500	90,000	37,000
Spain	4,529	116	12.1	2.6	347,000	260,000	54,000[3]	33,000	1,085,000	105,000
Turkey	2,755	59	21.7	5.2	569,000	470,000	46,000[3]	53,000	836,000	125,000
WARSAW PACT[7] (not including U.S.S.R.)										
Bulgaria	1,287	144	5.7	2.2–2.9	162,300	120,000	8,500	33,800	795,000	172,500
Czechoslovakia	3,774	243	7.7	2.8–5.2	204,500	148,000	—	56,500	230,000	131,000
Germany, East	6.163	368	8.4	3.7–6.5	167,000	116,000	14,000	37,000	385,000	411,500
Hungary	1,318	123	4.0	2.4	105,000	84,000	—	21,000	143,000	75,000
Poland	6,254	173	7.1	n.a.	340,000	230,000	22,000	88,000	500,000	635,000
Romania	1,297	57	4.1	1.6	189,500	150,000	7,500	32,000	565,000	1,590,000
OTHER EUROPEAN COUNTRIES										
Austria	787	105	3.9	1.2	50,000	45,400	—	4,600	1,097,000	—
Ireland	296	86	2.7	1.8	15,200	13,431	963	837	37,400	—
Finland	809	168	5.7	1.7	40,400	34,900	2,500	3,000	700,000	4,100
Sweden	3,042	365	6.9	3.1	68,000	48,500	10,000	9,500	735,000	500,500
Switzerland	2,036	320	21.4	2.1	20,000	580,000	—	45,000	605,000	—
Yugoslavia	2,319	102	n.a.	n.a.	239,700	191,000	12,000[3]	36,700	500,000	3–5m
MIDDLE EAST										
Algeria	848	42	4.6	1.9	140,000	120,000	8,000	12,000	100,000	24,600
Egypt	2,495	56	12.0	7.4	447,000	315,000	20,000	27,000	335,000	139,000
Iran	7–13bn	329	31.8	n.a.	n.a.	150,000	20,000[3]	35,000	400,000	2,505,000

Iraq	7,722	568	n.a.	n.a.	517,300	475,000	4,250	38,000	75,000	154,800
Israel	8,242	2,060	40.7	37.9	172,000	135,000	9,000	28,000	326,000	4,500
Jordan	424	139	21.5	11.3	72,800	65,000	300	7,500	35,000	7,500
Libya	709	218	n.a.	n.a.	73,000	58,000	6,500	8,500	40,000	10,000
Saudi Arabia	27,022	2,780	n.a.	n.a.	51,500	35,000	2,500	14,000	—	43,500
Syria	2,548	286	30.0	n.a.	262,500	170,000	2,500	50,000	102,500	9,800
AFRICA										
Ethiopia	n.a.	n.a.	n.a.	n.a.	250,500	244,500	2,500	3,500	200,000	169,000
Morocco	1,328	63	18.0	n.a.	144,000	125,000	6,000	13,000	—	30,000
Nigeria	n.a.	8–23	11.1	2.8	133,000	120,000	4,000	9,000	—	n.a.
South Africa	2,769	94	18.7	3.9	82,400	67,400	5,000[3]	10,000	157,000	145,500
Sudan	234	12	11.6	n.a.	58,000	53,000	2,000	3,000	—	3,500
Zimbabwe	337	45	10.2	n.a.	41,300	40,000	—	1,300	—	13,000
ASIA-OCEANIA (not including Peoples Republic of China)										
Australia	4,497	299	10.2	3.1	72,400	32,850	17,146	22,477	32,700	—
China (Taiwan)	3,323	183	39.4	n.a.	464,000	310,000	77,000[3]	77,000	2,970,000	25,000
India	5,556	8	17.8	n.a.	1,120,000	960,000	47,000	113,000	200,000	262,000
Indonesia	2,926	19	12.4	n.a.	281,000	210,000	42,000[3]	29,000	n.a.	82,000
Japan	10,361	87	5.5	1.0	241,000	156,000	42,000	43,000	41,000	—
Korea, North	1,916	103	16.2	10.2	784,500	700,000	33,500	51,000	270,000	1,798,000
Korea, South	5,173	132	35.0	7.6	622,000	540,000	49,000[3]	33,000	1,540,000	6,220,000
Malaysia	2,077	151	15.2	8.0	99,700	80,000	8,700	11,000	61,000	459,000
New Zealand	493	156	6.2	n.a.	12,900	5,675	2,843	4,425	10,200	—
Pakistan	1,801	20	n.a.	7.0	478,600	450,000	11,000	17,600	513,000	109,100
Philippines	878	17	12.5	2.2	104,800	60,000	28,000[3]	16,800	118,000	108,500
Singapore	852	355	17.0	5.6	55,500	45,000	4,500	6,000	150,000	37,500
Thailand	1,437	29	21.7	3.9	235,300	160,000	32,200[3]	43,100	500,000	72,000
LATIN AMERICA										
Argentina	10,084[8]	360[8]	64.2[8]	8.1[8]	153,000	100,000	36,000[3]	17,000	250,000	42,000
Brazil	1,838	15	13.3	n.a.	277,100	182,800	49,000[3]	45,300	1,115,000	185,000
Colombia	420	16	8.5	n.a.	70,200	57,000	9,000	4,200	70,000	50,000
Cuba	n.a.	n.a.	n.a.	n.a.	153,000	125,000	12,000	16,000	190,000	718,000
Mexico	—	—	—	—	120,500	94,500	20,000[3]	5,500	—	n.a.
Peru	—	—	—	—	135,500	75,000	20,500[3]	40,000	n.a.	31,500
Venezuela	142	78	n.a.	1.6	40,500	27,500	8,500[3]	4,500	—	20,000

1. Based on local currency, GNP estimated where official figures are unavailable. 2. Reservists with recent training. 3. Includes Marine Corps. 4. Includes 49,000 not identified by service. 5. Withdrew from military organization in 1966 but continues as a member of NATO. 6. Includes aid to West Berlin. 7. This section is not directly comparable to others. Difficulty of calculating suitable exchange rates makes conversion to dollars impractical. 8. 1981 figure. NOTE: n.a. = not available, m = million, b = billion. *Source:* International Institute for Strategic Studies, London.

WEATHER & CLIMATE

World and U.S. Extremes of Climate

Highest recorded temperature

	Place	Date	Degree Fahrenheit	Degree Centigrade
World (Africa)	El Azizia, Libya	Sept. 13, 1922	136	58
North America (U.S.)	Death Valley, Calif.	July 10, 1913	134	57
Asia	Tirat Tsvi, Israel	June 21, 1942	129	54
Australia	Cloncurry, Queensland	Jan. 16, 1889	128	53
Europe	Seville, Spain	Aug. 4, 1881	122	50
South America	Rivadavia, Argentina	Dec. 11, 1905	120	49
Antarctica	Esperanza, Palmer Peninsula	Oct. 20, 1956	58	14

Lowest recorded temperature

	Place	Date	Degree Fahrenheit	Degree Centigrade
World (Antarctica)	Vostok	Aug. 24, 1960	−127	−88
Asia	Verkhoyansk/Oimekon	Feb. 6, 1933	−90	−68
Greenland	Northice	Jan. 9, 1954	−87	−66
North America (excl. Greenland)	Snag, Yukon, Canada	Feb. 3, 1947	−81	−63
Europe	Ust 'Shchugor, U.S.S.R.	n.a.	−67	−55
South America	Sarmiento, Argentina	Jan. 1, 1907	−27	−33
Africa	Ifrane, Morocco	Feb. 11, 1935	−11	−24
Australia	Charlotte Pass, N.S.W.	July 22, 1947	−8	−22
United States	Prospect Creek, Alaska	Jan. 23, 1971	−80	−62

Greatest rainfalls

	Place	Date	Inches	Centimeters
1 minute (U.S.)	Unionville, Md.	—	1.23	3.1
20 minutes (Romania)	Curtea-de-Arges	—	8.1	20.6
42 minutes (U.S.)	Holt, Mo.	—	12	30
12 hours (Indian Ocean)	Belouve, La Réunion	—	53	135
24 hours (Indian Ocean)	Cilaos, La Réunion	—	74	188
5 days (Indian Ocean)	Cilaos, La Réunion	—	152	386
1 month (India)	Cherrapunji	—	366	930
1 month (U.S.)	Kukui, Maui, Hawaii	—	460	1,168
12 months (India)	Cherrapunji	—	1,042	2,647

Greatest snowfalls

	Place	Date	Inches	Centimeters
1 month (U.S.)	Tamarack, Calif.	Jan. 1911	390	991
24 hours (U.S.)	Silver Lake, Colo.	April 14–15, 1921	76	193
19 hours (France)	Bessans	—	68	173
1 storm (U.S.)	Mt. Shasta Ski Bowl, Calif.	—	189	480
1 season (U.S.)	Paradise Ranger Sta., Wash.	—	1,122	2,850

NOTE: n.a. = not available. *Source:* National Oceanic and Atmospheric Administration, Environmental Data Service.

Tropical Storms and Hurricanes, 1886–1983

	Jan.–April	May	June	July	Aug.	Sept.	Oct.	Nov.	Dec.	Total
Number of tropical storms (incl. hurricanes)	3	14	53	61	191	274	175	37	5	815
Number of tropical storms that reached hurricane intensity	1	3	22	32	138	177	86	18	2	479

Climate of Selected U.S. Cities, 1983

(T = trace)

Month	Temperature, °F				Precipitation			Percentage possible sunshine	Percentage relative humidity, afternoon
	Average daily maximun	Average daily minimum	Record high	Record low	Rainfall, inches	Snowfall, inches	Days with precipi-tation		
Bakersfield, California (Kern County Air Terminal): lat. 35° 25′ N, long. 119° 03′ W; elevation: 475 ft									
January	54.2	37.1	67	24	0.53	0.0	6	n.a.	57
April	75.2	53.2	90	40	1.07	0.0	4	n.a.	32
July	100.5	73.7	108	63	0.00	0.0	0	n.a.	19
October	79.7	57.7	92	47	0.71	0.0	3	n.a.	37
Annual	76.8	55.6	108	24	7.79	0.0	49	n.a.	41
Caribou, Maine (Municipal Airport): lat. 46° 52′ N, long. 68° 01′ W; elevation: 624 ft									
January	14.6	−6.7	43	−28	2.46	30.9	22	n.a.	53
April	44.3	25.9	73	5	4.01	36.4	19	n.a.	55
July	78.5	54.2	93	39	4.25	0.0	8	n.a.	48
October	54.4	34.4	66	21	1.61	T	9	n.a.	55
Annual	49.0	29.0	93	−28	37.26	135.7	172	n.a.	58
Charleston, South Carolina (Municipal Airport): lat. 32° 54′ N, long. 80° 02′ W; elevation: 40 ft									
January	56.6	33.5	75	10	2.18	T	7	68	53
April	72.6	50.9	83	32	6.51	0.0	11	73	52
July	88.9	73.4	96	66	5.40	0.0	16	n.a.	64
October	74.2	55.9	83	43	2.42	0.0	6	71	61
Annual	75.1	56.1	96	10	47.02	T	120	n.a.	59
Chicago, Illinois (O'Hare International Airport): lat. 41° 59′ N, long. 87° 54′ W; elevation: 658 ft									
January	21.9	2.4	38	−26	2.90	21.1	25	42	61
April	55.3	33.6	73	7	2.78	10.6	12	58	50
July	84.4	63.7	95	46	8.33	0.0	13	66	58
October	65.1	41.3	87	22	1.88	0.0	9	55	54
Annual	57.7	37.8	95	−26	44.68	53.3	143	52	60
Dallas–Ft. Worth, Texas (Regional Airport): lat. 32° 54′ N, long. 97° 02′ W; elevation: 551 ft									
January	57.4	31.8	79	7	2.33	0.8	5	71	54
April	72.3	52.7	90	37	2.71	0.0	10	69	58
July	94.6	74.5	100	68	2.73	0.0	4	83	52
October	77.6	56.3	94	39	3.36	0.0	7	63	52
Annual	75.6	55.1	103	7	40.75	0.8	90	69	56
Denver, Colorado (Stapleton International Airport): lat. 39° 46′ N, long. 104° 52′ W; elevation: 5,282 ft									
January	43.0	17.5	73	−3	0.32	4.8	9	68	47
April	61.6	33.1	80	20	0.34	2.0	7	73	24
July	86.4	58.9	99	50	0.92	0.0	5	79	29
October	62.9	35.0	80	27	1.51	1.2	9	70	37
Annual	62.4	36.2	99	−15	14.45	40.8	106	70	39
Duluth, Minnesota (International Airport): lat. 46° 50′ N, long. 92° 11′ W; elevation: 1,428 ft									
January	7.5	−13.9	34	−38	2.02	34.2	21	41	63
April	45.5	25.9	75	2	2.06	6.3	11	70	52
July	74.0	55.0	90	41	6.21	0.0	14	51	64
October	51.8	38.3	66	25	5.07	0.8	15	39	67
Annual	45.6	27.7	90	−38	34.23	104.5	171	49	64

	Temperature, °F				Precipitation				
Month	Average daily maximum	Average daily minimum	Record high	Record low	Rainfall, inches	Snowfall, inches	Days with precipi-tation	Percentage possible sunshine	Percentage relative humidity, afternoon
Great Falls, Montana (International Airport): lat. 47° 29′ N, long. 111° 22′ W; elevation: 3,663 ft									
January	17.9	−5.4	44	−32	1.09	19.7	20	32	65
April	48.6	27.1	75	4	1.04	18.5	16	58	40
July	80.7	52.8	94	44	0.66	0.0	6	n.a.	32
October	57.8	35.3	74	22	0.75	1.5	9	50	48
Annual	52.3	29.6	94	−32	17.68	109.5	155	n.a.	49
Kansas City, Missouri (International Airport): lat. 39° 19′ N, long. 94° 43′ W; elevation: 973 ft									
January	27.6	9.6	54	−17	2.66	6.0	9	52	57
April	62.4	39.8	81	20	1.55	1.3	10	53	52
July	88.9	69.8	96	62	2.73	0.0	9	63	59
October	67.2	44.0	87	25	3.04	0.0	4	63	54
Annual	61.9	42.9	101	−19	47.21	25.2	122	52	63
Los Angeles, California (International Airport): lat. 33° 56′ N, long. 118° 24′ W; elevation: 97 ft									
January	62.5	46.6	78	35	2.78	T	9	n.a.	57
April	67.3	53.0	83	43	1.61	0.0	3	n.a.	63
July	75.8	62.8	83	58	0.00	0.0	0	n.a.	66
October	78.9	59.5	91	53	0.18	0.0	2	n.a.	55
Annual	70.3	55.8	92	35	13.68	T	47	n.a.	62
Miami, Florida (International Airport): lat. 25° 49′ N, long. 80° 24′ W; elevation: 7 ft									
January	76.8	58.8	87	33	0.44	0.0	6	91	58
April	84.7	71.0	93	60	9.27	0.0	7	77	59
July	90.9	77.7	95	74	3.84	0.0	19	84	59
October	83.8	71.9	92	59	7.12	0.0	14	68	65
Annual	84.3	70.8	96	33	67.41	0.0	149	74	62
New Orleans, Louisiana (International Airport): lat. 29° 59′ N, long. 90° 15′ W; elevation: 4 ft									
January	65.5	43.5	83	15	2.76	T	8	59	62
April	78.3	61.3	86	44	5.86	0.0	14	53	60
July	90.3	72.5	93	67	13.07	0.0	18	61	70
October	79.3	61.4	89	42	3.84	0.0	8	65	61
Annual	78.7	60.5	96	15	65.62	T	123	57	63
New York, New York (Central Park): lat. 40° 47′ N, long. 73° 58′ W; elevation: 132 ft									
January	32.5	19.6	58	0	6.46	11.8	12	n.a.	52
April	60.4	42.0	82	21	5.67	9.6	9	n.a.	44
July	86.1	69.7	98	60	3.14	0.0	5	n.a.	n.a.
October	65.8	51.2	81	38	2.31	0.0	5	n.a.	n.a.
Annual	62.1	47.6	98	0	41.40	25.5	112	n.a.	n.a.
Phoenix, Arizona (Sky Harbor International Airport): lat. 33° 26′ N, long. 112° 01′ W; elevation: 1,110 ft									
January	64.6	43.2	79	34	0.81	0.0	7	81	36
April	85.4	59.5	97	51	T	0.0	0	90	12
July	105.3	82.0	113	73	0.43	0.0	7	84	19
October	87.7	59.3	96	49	T	0.0	0	88	13
Annual	85.0	61.8	113	34	9.94	0.0	54	84	24
Salt Lake City, Utah (International Airport): 40° 47′ N, long. 111° 57′ W; elevation: 4,221 ft									
January	37.7	21.8	62	1	1.08	15.3	17	39	64
April	58.5	34.5	79	19	1.63	9.5	10	73	35

Month	Temperature, °F: Average daily maximum	Average daily minimum	Record high	Record low	Precipitation: Rainfall, inches	Snowfall, inches	Days with precipitation	Percentage possible sunshine	Percentage relative humidity, afternoon
July	88.4	62.5	100	50	2.57	0.0	8	72	30
October	59.4	38.2	71	28	1.87	0.2	9	52	52
Annual	61.9	40.0	100	0	22.86	60.8	132	62	45
San Francisco, California (International Airport): lat. 37° 37′ N, long. 122° 23′ W; elevation: 8 ft									
January	51.8	38.3	58	34	8.81	T	11	n.a.	64
April	62.4	46.8	78	40	3.25	0.0	9	n.a.	59
July	69.8	53.5	84	51	T	0.0	0	n.a.	57
October	70.1	52.0	83	46	1.95	0.0	6	n.a.	53
Annual	63.6	48.2	93	33	34.81	T	78	n.a.	60
Seattle, Washington (Seattle-Tacoma Airport): lat. 47° 27′ N, long. 122° 18′ W; elevation: 400 ft									
January	43.2	35.4	54	14	5.35	7.0	24	17	75
April	55.9	38.8	77	34	2.07	T	12	50	47
July	71.7	53.8	87	49	0.59	0.0	6	59	53
October	59.6	45.8	69	36	4.07	T	14	50	67
Annual	58.7	43.9	94	14	39.32	9.0	150	55	59
Washington, D.C. (National Airport): lat. 38° 51′ N, long. 77° 02′ W; elevation: 10 ft									
January	36.1	20.1	61	−5	2.27	15.3	14	43	60
April	64.9	43.0	82	24	3.19	T	7	67	42
July	88.5	72.0	97	62	2.98	0.0	9	66	51
October	69.4	50.9	84	36	1.75	0.0	7	58	51
Annual	66.4	48.9	97	−5	35.77	27.4	112	57	53

NOTE: n.a. = not available. *Source:* Department of Commerce, NOAA, Environmental Data Service.

Other Recorded Extremes

Highest average annual temperature (World): Dallol, Ethiopia (1960–66), 94° F (34.4° C). **(U.S.):** Key West, Fla. (30-year normal), 78.2° F (25.7° C).

Lowest average annual temperature (Antarctica): Plateau Station −70° F (−56.7° C). **(U.S.):** Barrow, Alaska (30-year normal), 9.3° F (−12.6° C).

Greatest average yearly rainfall (U.S.): Mt. Waialeale, Kauai, Hawaii (1912–58), 460 in. (1,168 cm). **(India):** Cherrapunji (74-year avg), 450 in. (1,143 cm).

Minimum average yearly rainfall (Chile): Arica (59-year avg), 0.03 in. (0.08 cm) (no rainfall for 14 consecutive years). **(U.S.):** Death Valley, Calif. (49-year avg), 1.63 in. (4.14 cm). (Bagdad, Calif., holds the U.S. record for the longest period with no measurable rain, 767 days, from Oct. 3, 1912 to Nov. 8, 1914).

Hottest summer avg in Western Hemisphere (U.S.): Death Valley, Calif., 98° F (36.7° C).

Longest hot spell (W. Australia): Marble Bar, 100° F (37.8° C) (or above) for 162 consecutive days.

Largest hailstone (U.S.): Potter, Neb., 1 1/2 lb (.68 kg).

Lowest recorded temperature (Antarctica): Vostok Station, −127° F (−52.7° C) August 1960.

Wind Chill Factors

Wind speed (mph)	Thermometer reading (degrees Fahrenheit): 35	30	25	20	15	10	5	0	−5	−10	−15	−20	−25	−30	−35	−40	−45
5	33	27	21	19	12	7	0	−5	−10	−15	−21	−26	−31	−36	−42	−47	−52
10	22	16	10	3	−3	−9	−15	−22	−27	−34	−40	−46	−52	−58	−64	−71	−77
15	16	9	2	−5	−11	−18	−25	−31	−38	−45	−51	−58	−65	−72	−78	−85	−92
20	12	4	−3	−10	−17	−24	−31	−39	−46	−53	−60	−67	−74	−81	−88	−95	−103
25	8	1	−7	−15	−22	−29	−36	−44	−51	−59	−66	−74	−81	−88	−96	−103	−110
30	6	−2	−10	−18	−25	−33	−41	−49	−56	−64	−71	−79	−86	−93	−101	−109	−116
35	4	−4	−12	−20	−27	−35	−43	−52	−58	−67	−74	−82	−89	−97	−105	−113	−120
40	3	−5	−13	−21	−29	−37	−45	−53	−60	−69	−76	−84	−92	−100	−107	−115	−123
45	2	−6	−14	−22	−30	−38	−46	−54	−62	−70	−78	−85	−93	−102	−109	−117	−125

NOTES: This chart gives equivalent temperatures for combinations of wind speed and temperatures. For example, the combination of a temperature of 10° Fahrenheit and a wind blowing at 10 mph has a cooling power equal to −9° F. Wind speeds of higher than 45 mph have little additional cooling effect.

Weather Glossary

blizzard: storm characterized by strong winds, low temperatures, and large amounts of snow.
cyclone: circulation of winds rotating counterclockwise in the northern hemisphere and clockwise in the southern hemisphere. Hurricanes and tornadoes are both examples of cyclones.
flash flood: dangerous rapid rise of water levels in streams, rivers, or over land area.
gale warning: winds in the 33–48 knot (38–55 mph) range forecast.
heavy snow warnings: issued when 4 inches or more of snow are expected to fall in a 12-hour period or when 6 inches or more are anticipated in a 24-hour period.
hurricane: devastating cyclonic storm; winds over 74 mph near storm center; usually tropical in origin; called cyclone in Indian Ocean, typhoon in the Pacific.
hurricane warning: winds in excess of 64 knots (74 mph) in connection with hurricane.
snow flurries: snow falling for a short time at intermittent periods; accumulations are usually small.
snow squall: brief, intense falls of snow, usually accompanied by gusty winds.
storm warnings: winds greater than 48 knots (55 mph) are forecast.
temperature-humidity index (THI): measure of personal discomfort based on the combined effects of temperature and humidity. Most people are uncomfortable when the THI is 75. A THI of 80 produces acute discomfort for almost everyone.
tidal waves: series of ocean waves caused by earthquakes; can reach speeds of 600 mph; they grow in height as they reach shore and can crest as high as 100 feet.
tornado: dangerous whirlwind associated with the cumulonimbus clouds of severe thunderstorms; winds up to 300 mph.
tornado warning: tornado has actually been detected by radar or sighted in designated area.
tornado watch: potential exists in the watch area for storms that could contain tornadoes.
tsunami: *see* tidal waves.
warning: the designated condition is imminent.
wind-chill factor: combined effect of temperature and wind speed as compared to equivalent temperature in calm air.

Tornadoes That Caused Outstanding Damage

Date	Number of tornadoes	Deaths	Property losses	States in which storms occurred
1884, Feb. 19	60	800	(1)	Mississippi, Alabama, North and South Carolina, Tennessee, Kentucky, Indiana
1917, May 26–27	(1)	249	$5,555,000	Illinois, Indiana, Arkansas, Kentucky, Tennessee, Alabama, Mississippi
1920, April 20	6	220	3,525,000	Mississippi, Alabama, Tennessee
1924, April 29–30	22	115	4,372,300	Oklahoma, Arkansas, Alabama, Georgia, Louisiana, North and South Carolina, Virginia
1924, June 28	4	96	13,050,000	Ohio and Pennsylvania
1925, March 18	8	792	17,872,000	Missouri, Illinois, Indiana, Kentucky, Tennessee, Alabama
1927, May 8–9	36	227	7,877,000	Texas, Louisiana, Missouri, Nebraska, Indiana, Michigan
1932, March 21	27	321	5,514,000	Alabama, Mississippi, Georgia, Tennessee
1936, April 5–6	22	498	21,800,000	Arkansas, Alabama, Tennessee, Georgia, South Carolina
1944, June 23	4	153	5,160,000	Pennsylvania, West Virginia, Maryland
1947, April 9–10	8	167	10,030,750	Texas, Oklahoma, Kansas
1952, March 21–22	31	343	15,327,100	Arkansas, Tennessee, Missouri, Mississippi, Alabama, Kentucky
1953, June 7–9	12	234	93,230,840	Michigan, Ohio, and New England states
1953, May 11	1	114	39,500,000	Texas
1955, May 25	13	102	11,747,500	Oklahoma and Kansas
1965, April 11–12	47	257	200,000,000	Iowa, Illinois, Wisconsin, Michigan, Indiana, Ohio
1968, May 15	7	63	65,000,000	Arkansas, Iowa, Illinois
1970, May 11	1	26	135,000,000	Texas
1971, Feb. 21	(1)	117	17,000,000	Louisiana, Mississippi
1973, March 31	2	9	115,000,000	Georgia, South Carolina
1973, May 26–28	96	22	(1)	Hawaii and 18 states in South, Southwest, Midwest, and East
1974, April 3–4	144	307	500,000,000 +	13 states in East, South, and Midwest
1975, May 6	3	3	400,000,000 +	Nebraska
1977, April 4	7	22	15,000,000	Alabama
1978, Dec. 3	13	4	100,000,000 +	Louisiana and Arkansas
1979, April 10	10	54	(1)	Texas and Oklahoma
1979, Oct. 3	1	3	200,000,000	Connecticut
1980, May 13	1	5	40,000,000	Michigan
1980, Aug. 9–11	29	0	50,000,000 +	Texas
1981, April 4	1	3	12,900,000	Wisconsin
1983, July 3	22	0	11,000,000 +	Wisconsin

1. Not definitely known; believed to be large. NOTE: Additional storms may be listed in the *Current Events* section. *Source:* Data for 1884–1953, reprinted from *Tornadoes of the United States*, by S. D. Flora, copyright 1954, by University of Oklahoma Press. Used by permission. Also, Department of Commerce, National Oceanic and Atmospheric Administration.

Devastating North Atlantic Hurricanes of the 20th Century

The following is a selected list of North Atlantic hurricanes based on casualties, damage, and general public interest. Facts about each storm are taken from Weather records, although in some cases only estimates of wind speed are available. Data given in this list pertain only to U.S. land areas except where indicated otherwise.

Date	Areas hardest hit	Land stations with highest wind speed	Deaths (U.S. only)	Est. damage (millions)	Remarks
1900, Aug. 27–Sept. 15	Galveston, Tex.	Galveston, Tex. (120[1] mph)	6,000	$30	Damage due to both winds and storm wave. Galveston Is. inundated.
1909, Sept. 10–21	Louisiana and Mississippi	New Orleans, La. (53 mph)	350	5	Winds 50–75 mi. W of New Orleans, where deaths occurred, were stronger than 68 mph.
1915, Aug. 5–23	East Texas and Louisiana	Galveston, Tex. (120 mph)	275	50	Water 5–6 ft deep in Galveston business district. 90% of homes demolished. Warnings issued well ahead of time.
1915, Sept. 22–Oct. 1	Mid-Gulf Coast	Burrwood, La. (140 mph)	275	13	Many casualties due to persons insisting on staying in low-lying areas despite warnings.
1919, Sept. 2–15	Florida, Louisiana, and Texas	Sand Key, Fla. (84[1] mph)	287	22	488 persons drowned at sea.
1926, Sept. 11–22	Florida and Alabama	Miami, Fla. (138 mph)	243	112	Most deaths were in Miami area. Said to have been one of most destructive storms of century.
1928, Sept. 6–20	Southern Florida	Lake Okeechobee, Fla. (75[1] mph)	1,836	25	1,870 injured. Nearly all deaths were in Lake Okeechobee area. Winds estimated as high as 160 mph caused Lake to overflow into populated areas.
1935, Aug. 29–Sept. 10	Southern Florida	Tampa, Fla. (86 mph)	408	6	Sustained winds over Florida Keys est. 150–200 mph. Remembered as "Labor Day Storm."
1938, Sept. 10–22	Long Island and Southern New England	Blue Hills Obs., Mass. (183 mph)	600	306	Unusually destructive. Storm center moved as fast as 56 mph at times. 1,754 injured.
1944, Sept. 9–16	North Carolina to New England	Cape Henry, Va. (150[1] mph)	46	100	344 deaths at sea. Shipping lanes were crowded with war-time activity.
1944, Oct. 12–23	Florida	Dry Tortugas Is. (120 mph)	18	100	About 300 were killed in Cuba area before storm reached U.S. Evacuation of thousands from threatened areas in Fla. prevented higher toll.
1947, Sept. 4–21	Florida and Mid-Gulf Coast	Hillsboro Light, Fla. (155 mph)	51	110	Wind damage especially heavy along Gulf Coast and Florida east coast.
1954, Aug. 25–31	North Carolina to New England	Block Island, R.I. (135 mph)	60	461	"CAROL"—more damage than any other single storm to this date. Water and high waves flooded low-lying areas; 1,000 injuries in Long Island—New England area.
1954, Sept. 2–14	New Jersey to New England	Block Island, R.I. (87 mph)	21	40	"EDNA"—New England again heavily hit. Gusts of 120 mph at Martha's Vineyard, Mass.
1954, Oct. 5–18	South Carolina to New York	New York, N.Y. (113 mph) (See Remarks)	95	252	"HAZEL"—several N.C. localities had winds of 130–150 mph with unusually heavy wave damage resulting. Est. 400–1,000 casualties in Haiti. In Canada there were 78 deaths, mostly due to flooding.
1955, Aug. 7–21	North Carolina to New England	Wilmington, N.C. (83 mph)	184	832	"DIANE"—worst floods in history in Southern New England. 16 in. of rain in Hartford area.
1957, June 25–28	Texas to Alabama	Sabine/Pass, Tex. (100 mph)	390	150	"AUDREY"—gave an early start to the hurricane season and wiped out Cameron, La. Two

Date	Areas hardest hit	Land stations with highest wind speed	Deaths (U.S. only)	Est. damage (millions)	Remarks
					weeks later "BERTHA" struck same area.
1960, Aug. 29–Sept. 13	Florida to New England	Ft. Myers, Fla. (92 mph) Block Island, R.I. (130 mph) (See Remarks)	50	500	"DONNA"—hurricane winds from a single storm swept the entire Atlantic seaboard from Florida to New England for the first time in a 75-year record. Winds estimated near 140 mph with gusts 175–180 mph on Central Keys and lower southwest Florida coast. 115 deaths in Antilles, most from flash floods in Puerto Rico.
1961, Sept. 3–15	Texas coast	Port Lavaca, Tex. (145 mph)	46	408	"CARLA"—devastated Texas Gulf Coast Cities with 15-foot tides and 15-inch rains. Gusts to 175 mph at Port Lavaca.
1964, Aug. 20–Sept. 5	Southern Florida, Eastern Virginia	Miami, Fla. (110 mph)	3	129	"CLEO"—first hurricane in Miami area since 1950. Killed 214 in Caribbean Islands.
1964, Aug. 28–Sept. 16	Northeastern Florida, Southern Georgia	St. Augustine, Fla. (125 mph)	5	250	"DORA"—first storm of full hurricane force on record to move inland from east over northeastern Florida.
1965, Aug. 27–Sept. 12	Southern Florida and Louisiana	Port Sulphur, La. (136 mph)	75	1,420	"BETSY"—Damage in Louisiana, $1.2 billion. 27,000 homes destroyed, 17,500 injured or ill, 300,000 evacuated. Gusts of 165 mph at Pine Key, Fla.
1967, Sept. 5–22	Southern Texas	Brownsville, Texas (109 mph gust)	15	200	"BEULAH"—main damage was caused by torrential rains.
1969, Aug. 14–22	Mississippi, Louisiana, Alabama, Virginia, W. Virginia	Oil drilling rig east of Boothville, La. (172 mph)	256	1,420	"CAMILLE"—68 additional persons missing. One of most destructive killer storms ever to hit U.S.
1970, July 23–Aug. 5	Texas coast	Corpus Christi, Tex. (130 mph)	11	453.8	"CELIA"—Gusts of 161 mph recorded.
1972, June 14–23	Florida to New York	Key West, Fla. (43 mph)	117	3,097	"AGNES"—Devastating floods with many record-breaking river crests. Pa. hardest hit, with 50 deaths.
1975, Sept. 13–24	Florida and Southern Alabama	Ozark, Ala. (104 mph)	21	490	"ELOISE"—Structures destroyed from Panama City Beach, Fla., to Ft. Walton Beach, Fla. Major flooding from rainfall.
1976, Aug. 6–10	New York, New Jersey, and Southern New England	Bridgeport, Conn. (77 mph gust)	5	100	"BELLE"—Crop damage in the Northeast. Considerable Inland stream and road flooding.
1979, Aug. 25–Sept. 7	Florida to New England	Fort Pierce, Fla. (95 mph gust)	5	320	"DAVID"—1200 deaths in the Dominican Republic. Homes 80 percent destroyed in Dominica.
1979, Aug. 29–Sept. 14	Alabama and Mississippi	Dauphin Island, Alabama (145 mph gust)	5	2300	"FREDERIC"—highest dollar damage ever in the United States.
1980, Aug. 3–10	Caribbean Islands to Texas Gulf Coast	Port Mansfield, Texas (120 mph gust.)	28	300	"ALLEN"—Highest tides in 61 years. Over 200 killed in Caribbean Islands. Extensive crop damage in Caribbean.
1983, Aug. 15–21	Texas Coast	Hobby Airport (94 mph)	21	2000	"ALICIA"—Extensive damage in Galveston/Houston area.

1. Wind-measuring equipment disabled at speed indicated. NOTE: Additional hurricanes may be listed in *Current Events*. *Source:* Department of Commerce, National Oceanic and Atmospheric Administration.

STRUCTURES

The Seven Wonders of the World

(Not all classical writers list the same items as the Seven Wonders, but most of them agree on the following.)

The Pyramids of Egypt. A group of three pyramids, *Khufu, Khafra,* and *Menkaura* at Giza, outside modern Cairo, is often called the first wonder of the world. The largest pyramid, built by Khufu (Cheops), a king of the fourth Dynasty, had an original estimated height of 482 ft (now approximately 450 ft). The base has sides 755 ft long. It contains 2,300,000 blocks; the average weight of each is 2.5 tons. Estimated date of construction is 2800 B.C. Of all the Seven Wonders, the pyramids alone survive.

Hanging Gardens of Babylon. Often listed as the second wonder, these gardens were supposedly built by Nebuchadnezzar about 600 B.C. to please his queen, Amuhia. They are also associated with the mythical Assyrian Queen, Semiramis. Archeologists surmise that the gardens were laid out atop a vaulted building, with provisions for raising water. The terraces were said to rise from 75 to 300 ft.

The Walls of Babylon, also built by Nebuchadnezzar, are sometimes referred to as the second (or the seventh) wonder instead of the Hanging Gardens.

Statue of Zeus (Jupiter) at Olympia. The work of Phidias (5th century B.C.), this colossal figure in gold and ivory was reputedly 40 ft high. All trace of it is lost, except for reproductions on coins.

Temple of Artemis (Diana) at Ephesus. A beautiful structure, begun about 350 B.C. in honor of a non-Hellenic goddess who later became identified with the Greek goddess of the same name. The temple, with Ionic columns 60 ft high, was destroyed by invading Goths in A.D. 262.

Mausoleum at Halicarnassus. This famous monument was erected by Queen Artemisia in memory of her husband, King Mausolus of Caria in Asia Minor, who died in 353 B.C. Some remains of the structure are in the British Museum. This shrine is the source of the modern word "mausoleum."

Colossus at Rhodes. This bronze statue of Helios (Apollo), about 105 ft high, was the work of the sculptor Chares, who reputedly labored for 12 years before completing it in 280 B.C. It was destroyed during an earthquake in 224 B.C.

Pharos of Alexandria. The seventh wonder was the Pharos (lighthouse) of Alexandria, built by Sostratus of Cnidus during the 3rd century B.C. on the island of Pharos off the coast of Egypt. It was destroyed by an earthquake in the 13th century.

Famous Structures

Ancient

The *Great Sphinx of Egypt,* one of the wonders of ancient Egyptian architecture, adjoins the pyramids of Giza and has a length of 240 ft. It was built in the 4th dynasty.

Other Egyptian buildings of note include the *Temples of Karnak* and *Edfu* and the *Tombs at Beni Hassan.*

The *Parthenon of Greece,* built on the Acropolis in Athens, was the chief temple to the goddess Athena. It was believed to have been completed by 438 B.C. The present temple remained intact until the 5th century A.D. Today, though the Parthenon is in ruins, its majestic proportions are still discernible.

Other great structures of ancient Greece were the *Temples at Paestum* (about 540 and 420 B.C.); the *Temple of Poseidon* (about 460 B.C.); the *Temple of Apollo* at Corinth (about 540 B.C.); the *Temple of Apollo* at Bassae (about 450–420 B.C.); the famous *Erechtheum* atop the Acropolis (about 421–405 B.C.); the *Temple of Athena Niké* at Athens (about 426 B.C.); the *Olympieum* at Athens (174 B.C.–A.D. 131); the *Athenian Treasury* at Delphi (about 515 B.C.); the *Propylaea* of the Acropolis at Athens (437–432 B.C.); the *Theater of Dionysus* at Athens (about 350–325 B.C.); the *House of Cleopatra* at Delos (138 B.C.) and the *Theater* at Epidaurus (about 325 B.C.).

The *Colosseum (Flavian Amphitheater) of Rome,* the largest and most famous of the Roman amphitheaters, was opened for use A.D. 80. Elliptical in shape, it consisted of three stories and an upper gallery, rebuilt in stone in its present form in the third century A.D. Its seats rise in tiers, which in turn are buttressed by concrete vaults and stone piers. It could seat between 40,000 and 50,000 spectators. It was principally used for gladiatorial combat.

The *Pantheon* at Rome, begun by Agrippa in 27 B.C. as a temple, was rebuilt in its present circular form by Hadrian (A.D. 110–25). Literally the Pantheon was intended as a temple of "all the gods." It is remarkable for its perfect preservation today, and it has served continuously for 20 centuries as a place of worship.

Famous Roman arches include the *Arch of Constantine* (about A.D. 315) and the *Arch of Titus* (about A.D. 80).

Later European

St. Mark's Cathedral in Venice (1063–67), one of the great examples of Byzantine architecture, was begun in the 9th century. Partly destroyed by fire in 976, it was later rebuilt as a Byzantine edifice.

Other famous Byzantine examples of architecture are *St. Sophia* in Istanbul (A.D. 532–37); *San Vitale* in Ravenna (542); *St. Paul's Outside the Walls,* Rome (5th century); the *Kremlin* baptism and marriage church, Moscow (begun in 1397); and *St. Lorenzo Outside the Walls*, Rome, begun in 588.

The *Cathedral Group* at Pisa (1067–1173), one of the most celebrated groups of structures built in Romanesque-style, consists of the cathedral, the cathedral's baptistery, and the *Leaning Tower*. This trio forms a group by itself in the northwest corner of the city. The cathedral and baptistery are built in varicolored marble. The campanile *(Leaning Tower)* is 179 ft. high and leans more than 16 ft out of the perpendicular. There is little reason to believe that the architects intended to have the tower lean.

Other examples of Romanesque architecture include the *Vézelay Abbey* in France (1130); the *Church of Notre-Dame-du-Port* at Clermont-Ferrand in France (1100); the *Church of San Zeno* (begun in 1138) at Verona, and *Durham Cathedral* in England.

The *Alhambra* (1248–1354), located in Granada, Spain, is universally esteemed as one of the greatest masterpieces of Moslem architecture. Designed as a palace and fortress for the Moorish monarchs of Granada, it is surrounded by a heavily fortified wall more than a mile in perimeter. The location of the Alhambra in the Sierra Nevada provides a magnificent setting for this jewel of Moorish Spain.

The *Tower of London* is a group of buildings and towers covering 13 acres along the north bank of the Thames. The central *White Tower*, begun in 1078 during the reign of William the Conqueror, was originally a fortress and royal residence, but was later used as a prison. The *Bloody Tower* is associated with Anne Boleyn and other notables.

Westminster Abbey, in London, was begun in 1045 and completed in 1065. It was rebuilt and enlarged in 1245–50.

Notre-Dame de Paris (begun in 1163), one of the great examples of Gothic architecture, is a twin-towered church with a steeple over the crossing and immense flying buttresses supporting the masonry at the rear of the church.

Other famous Gothic structures are *Chartres Cathedral* (12th century); *Sainte Chapelle*, Paris (1246–48); *Laon Cathedral*, France (1160–1205); *Reims Cathedral* (about 1210–50; rebuilt after its almost complete destruction in World War I); *Rouen Cathedral* (13th–16th centuries); *Amiens Cathedral* (1218–69); *Beauvais Cathedral* (begun 1247); *Salisbury Cathedral* (1220–60); *York Minster* or the *Cathedral of St. Peter* (begun in the 7th century); *Milan Cathedral* (begun 1386); and *Cologne Cathedral* (13th–19th centuries); badly damaged in World War II.

The Duomo (cathedral) in Florence was founded in 1298, completed by Brunelleschi and consecrated in 1436. The oval-shaped dome dominates the entire structure.

The *Vatican* is a group of buildings in Rome comprising the official residence of the Pope. The *Basilica of St. Peter*, the largest church in the Christian world, was begun in 1450. The *Sistine Chapel*, begun in 1473, is noted for the art masterpieces of Michelangelo, Botticelli, and others. The *Basilica of the Savior* (known as *St. John Lateran*) is the first-ranking Catholic Church in the world, for it is the cathedral of the Pope.

Other examples of Renaissance architecture are the *Palazzo Riccardi*, the *Palazzo Pitti* and the *Palazzo Strozzi* in Florence; the *Farnese Palace* in Rome; *Palazzo Grimani* (completed about 1550) in Venice; the *Escorial* (1563–93) near Madrid; the *Town Hall* of Seville (1527–32); the *Louvre*, Paris; the *Château* at Blois, France; *St. Paul's Cathedral*, London (1675–1710; badly damaged in World War II); the *École Militaire*, Paris (1752); the *Pazzi Chapel*, Florence, designed by Brunelleschi (1429); the Palace of *Fontainebleau* and the *Château de Chambord* in France.

The *Palace of Versailles*, containing the famous Hall of Mirrors, was built during the reign of Louis XIV and served as the royal palace until 1793.

Outstanding European buildings of the 18th and 19th centuries are the *Superga* at Turin, the *Hôtel-Dieu* in Lyons, the *Belvedere Palace* at Vienna, the *Royal Palace* of Stockholm, the *Opera House* of Paris (1863–75); the *Bank of England*, the *British Museum*, the *University of London*, and the *Houses of Parliament*, all in London; the *Panthéon*, the *Church of the Madeleine*, the *Bourse*, and the *Palais de Justice* in Paris.

The *Eiffel Tower*, in Paris, was built for the Exposition of 1889 by Alexandre Eiffel. It is 984 ft high.[1]

1. 1,056 ft, including the television tower.

Asiatic and African

The *Taj Mahal* (1632–50), at Agra, India, built by Shah Jahan as a tomb for his wife, is considered by some as the most perfect example of the Mogul style and by others as the most beautiful building in the world. Four slim white minarets flank the building, which is topped by a white dome; the entire structure is of marble.

Other examples of Indian architecture are the temples at Benares and Tanjore.

Among famed Moslem edifices are the *Dome of the Rock* or *Mosque of Omar*, Jerusalem (A.D. 691); the *Citadel* (1166), and the *Tombs of the Mamelukes* (15th century), in Cairo; the *Tomb of Humayun* in Delhi; the *Blue Mosque* (1468) at Tabriz, and the *Tamerlane Mausoleum* at Samarkand.

Angkor Wat, outside the city of Angkor Thom, Cambodia, is one of the most beautiful examples of Cambodian or Khmer architecture. The sanctuary was built during the 12th century.

Great Wall of China (228 B.C.?), designed specifically as a defense against nomadic tribes, has large watch towers which could be called buildings. It was erected by Emperor Ch'in Shih Huang Ti and is 1,400 miles long. Built mainly of earth and stone, it varies in height between 18 and 30 ft.

Typical of Chinese architecture are the pagodas or temple towers. Among some of the better-known pagodas are the *Great Pagoda of the Wild Geese* at Sian (founded in 652); *Nan t'a* (11th century) at Fang Shan; the *Pagoda of Sung Yueh Ssu* (A.D. 523) at Sung Shan, Honan.

Other well-known Chinese buildings are the *Drum Tower* (1273), the *Three Great Halls* in the Purple Forbidden City (1627), *Buddha's Perfume Tower* (19th century), the *Porcelain Pagoda*, and the *Summer Palace*, all at Peking.

United States

Rockefeller Center, in New York City, extends from 5th Ave. to the Avenue of the Americas between 48th and 52nd Sts. (and halfway to 7th Ave. between 47th and 51st Sts.). It occupies more than 22 acres and has 19 buildings.

The Cathedral of St. John the Divine, at 112th St. and Amsterdam Ave. in New York City, was begun in 1892 and is now in the final stages of completion. When completed, it will be the largest cathedral in the world: 601 ft long, 146 ft wide at the nave, 320 ft wide at the transept. The east end is designed in Romanesque-Byzantine style, and the nave and west end are Gothic.

St. Patrick's Cathedral, at Fifth Ave. and 50th St. in New York City, has a seating capacity of 2,500. The nave was opened in 1877, and the cathedral was dedicated in 1879.

Louisiana Superdome, in New Orleans, is the largest arena in the history of mankind. The main area can accommodate up to 95,000 people. It is the world's largest steel-constructed room. Unobstructed by posts, it covers 13 acres and reaches 27 stories at its peak.

World Trade Center, in New York City, was dedicated in 1973. Its twin towers are 110 stories high (1,350 ft), and the complex contains over 9 million sq ft of office space. A restaurant is on the 107th floor of the North Tower.

World's Highest Dams

Name	River, Country or State	Structural height feet	Structural height meters	Gross reservoir capacity thousands of acre feet	Gross reservoir capacity millions of cubic meters	Year completed
Rogun	Vakhsh, U.S.S.R.	1066	325	9,404	11,600	UC
Nurek	Vakhsh, U.S.S.R.	984	300	8,512	10,500	UC
Grande Dixence	Dixence, Switzerland	935	285	324	400	1962
Inguri	Inguri, U.S.S.R.	892	272	801	1,100	UC
Chicoasén	Grijalva, Mexico	869	265	1,346	1,660	1981
Vaiont	Vaiont, Italy	869	265	137	169	1961
Tehri	Bhagirathi, India	856	261	2,869	3,540	UC
Kinshau	Tons, India	830	253	1,946	2,400	UC
Mica	Columbia, Canada	794	242	20,000	24,670	1972
Sayano-Shushensk	Yenisei, U.S.S.R.	794	242	25,353	31,300	1980
Mihoesti	Aries, Romania	794	242	5	6	1983
Chivor	Batá, Colombia	778	237	661	815	1975
Mauvoisin	Drance de Bagnes, Switzerland	777	237	146	180	1957
Oroville	Feather, California	770	235	3,538	4,299	1968
Chirkey	Sulak, U.S.S.R.	764	233	2,252	2,780	1977
Bhakra	Sutlej, India	741	226	8,002	9,870	1963
El Cajón	Humuya, Honduras	741	226	4,580	5,650	UC
Hoover	Colorado, Arizona-Nevada	726	221	28,537	35,200	1936
Contra	Verzasca, Switzerland	722	220	70	86	1965
Dabaklamm	Dorferbach, Austria	722	220	191	235	UC
Piva (Mratinje)	Piva, Yugoslavia	722	220	713	880	1975
Dworshak	N. Fk. Clearwater, Idaho	717	219	3,453	4,259	1974
Glen Canyon	Colorado, Arizona	710	216	27,000	33,305	1964
Toktogul	Naryn, U.S.S.R.	705	215	15,800	19,500	1978
Daniel Johnson	Manicouagan, Canada	703	214	115,000	141,851	1968
San Rogue	Agno, Philippines	689	210	803	990	UC
Luzzone	Brenno di Luzzone, Switzerland	682	208	71	87	1963
Keban	Firat, Turkey	679	207	25,110	31,000	1974
Dez	Dez, Abi, Iran	666	203	2,707	3,340	1963
Almendra	Tormes, Spain	662	202	2,148	2,649	1970
Kölnbrein	Malta, Austria	656	200	166	205	1977
Kārūn	Karun, Iran	656	200	2,351	2,900	1976
Altinkaya	Kizil Irmak, Turkey	640	195	4,672	5,763	UC
New Bullards Bar	No. Yuba, California	637	194	960	1,184	1968
Lakhwar	Yamuna, India	630	192	470	580	UC
New Melones	Stanislaus, California	625	191	2,400	2,960	1979
Itaipu	Paraná, Brazil/Paraguay	623	190	23,510	29,000	UC
Kurobe 4	Kurobe, Japan	610	186	162	199	1964
Swift	Lewis, Washington	610	186	756	932	1958
Mossyrock	Cowlitz, Washington	607	185	1,300	1,603	1968
Oymopinar	Manavgat, Turkey	607	185	251	310	1983
Atatürk	Firat, Turkey	604	184	38,914	48,000	UC
Shasta	Sacramento, California	602	183	4,552	5,615	1945
Bennett WAC	Peace, Canada	600	183	57,006	70,309	1967
Karakaya	Firat, Turkey	591	180	7,767	9,580	UC
Tignes	Isère, France	591	180	186	230	1952
Amir Kabir (Karad)	Karadj, Iran	591	180	166	205	1962
Tachien	Tachia, Taiwan	591	180	207	255	1974
Dartmouth	Mitta-Mitta, Australia	591	180	3,243	4,000	1978
Özköy	Gediz, Turkey	591	180	762	940	UC
Emosson	Barberine, Switzerland	590	180	184	225	1974
Zillergrūndl	Ziller, Austria	590	180	73	90	UC
Los Leones	Los Leones, Chile	587	179	86	106	UC
New Don Pedro	Tuolumne, California	585	178	2,030	2,504	1971
Alpa-Gera	Cormor, Italy	584	178	53	65	1965

Name	River, country, or state	Structural height feet	meters	Gross reservoir capacity Thousands of acre feet	millions of cubic meters	Year completed
Kopperston Tailings 3	Jones Branch, West Virginia	580	177	—	—	1963
Takase	Takase, Japan	577	176	62	76	1979
Nader Shah	Marun, Iran	574	175	1,313	1,620	1978
Hasan Ugurlu	Yesil Irmak, Turkey	574	175	874	1,078	1980
Mazar	Mazar, Ecuador	574	175	405	500	UC
Hungry Horse	S.Fk., Flathead, Montana	564	172	3,468	4,278	1953
Longyangxia	Huanghe, China	564	172	20,025	24,700	1983
Cabora Bassa	Zambezi, Mozambique	561	171	51,075	63,000	1974
Maqarin	Yarmuk, Jordan	561	171	259	320	UC
Amaluza	Paute, Equador	558	170	81	100	1982
Idikki	Periyar, India	554	169	1,618	1,996	1974
Charvak	Chirchik, U.S.S.R.	552	168	1,620	2,000	1970
Gura Apelor Retezat	Riul Mare, Romania	552	168	182	225	1980
Grand Coulee	Columbia, Washington	550	168	9,386	11,578	1942
Boruca	Terraba, Costa Rica	548	167	12,128	14,960	UC
Vidraru	Arges, Romania	545	166	380	465	1965
Kremasta (King Paul)	Achelöus, Greece	541	165	3,850	4,750	1965

NOTE: UC = under construction. *Source:* Department of the Interior, Bureau of Reclamation.

World's Largest Dams

Dam	Location	Volume (thousands) Cubic meters	Cubic yards	Year completed
New Cornelia Tailings	Arizona	209,500	274,015	1973
Pati (Chapetón)	Argentina	200,000	261,590	UC
Tarbella	Pakistan	121,720	159,203	1976
Fort Peck	Montana	96,049	125,628	1940
Yacyretá-Apipe	Paraguay/Argentina	81,000	105,944	UC
Guri (Raul Leoni)	Venezuela	78,000	102,014	UC
Rogun	U.S.S.R.	75,500	98,750	UC
Atatürk	Turkey	75,000	98,096	UC
Oahe	South Dakota	70,339	92,000	1963
Mangla	Pakistan	65,651	85,872	1967
Gardiner	Canada	65,440	85,592	1968
Afsluitdijk	Netherlands	63,400	82,927	1932
Oroville	California	59,639	78,008	1968
San Luis	California	59,383	77,670	1967
Nurek	U.S.S.R.	58,000	75,861	UC
Garrison	North Dakota	50,843	66,500	1956
Cochiti	New Mexico	47,500	62,128	1975
Tabka (Thawra)	Syria	46,000	60,168	1976
Bennett W.A.C.	Canada	43,733	57,201	1967
Tucuruí	Brazil	43,000	56,242	UC
Boruca	Costa Rica	43,000	56,242	UC
High Aswan (Sadd-el-Aali)	Egypt	43,000	56,242	1970
San Rogue	Philippines	43,000	56,242	UC
Kiev	U.S.S.R.	42,841	56,034	1964
Dantiwada Left Embankment	India	41,040	53,680	1965
Saratov	U.S.S.R.	40,400	52,843	1967
Mission Tailings 2	Arizona	40,088	52,435	1973
Fort Randall	South Dakota	38,380	50,200	1956
Kanev	U.S.S.R.	37,860	49,520	1976
Mosul	Iraq	36,000	47,086	1982
Kakhovka	U.S.S.R.	35,640	46,617	1955
Itumbiara	Brazil	35,600	46,563	1980
Lauwerszee	Netherlands	35,575	46,532	1969
Beas	India	35,418	46,325	1974
Oosterschelde	Netherlands	35,000	45,778	UC

NOTE: UC = under construction. *Source:* Department of the Interior, Bureau of Reclamation.

World's Largest Hydroelectric Plants

Name of dam	Location	Rated capacity (MW)		Year of initial operation
		Present	Ultimate	
Itaipu	Brazil/Paraguay	—	12,600	UC
Grand Coulee	Washington	6,280	10,080	1942
Guri (Raul Leoni)	Venezuela	2,800	10,060	1968
Tucuruí	Brazil	—	6,480	UC
Sayano-Shushensk	U.S.S.R.	—	6,400	1980
Krasnoyarsk	U.S.S.R.	6,096	6,096	1968
Corpus-Christi	Argentina/Paraguay	—	6,000	UC
LaGrande 2	Canada	—	5,328	UC
Churchill Falls	Canada	5,225	5,225	1971
Bratsk	U.S.S.R.	4,100	4,600	1964
Ust'—Ilimsk	U.S.S.R.	3,675	4,500	1974
Cabora Bassa	Mozambique	2,075	4,150	1974
Yacyretá-Apipe	Argentina/Paraguay	—	4,050	UC
Rogun	U.S.S.R.	—	3,600	UC
Paulo Afonso	Brazil	1,524	3,409	1955
Pati (Chapetón)	Argentina	—	3,300	UC
Brumley Gap	Virginia	3,200	3,200	1973
Ilha Solteira	Brazil	3,200	3,200	1973
Inga I	Zaire	360	2,820	1974
Gezhouba	China	—	2,715	UC
John Day	Oregon-Washington	2,160	2,700	1969
Nurek	U.S.S.R.	900	2,700	1976
Revelstoke	Canada	—	2,700	UC
Sáo Simao	Brazil	2,680	2,680	1979
LaGrande 4	Canada	—	2,637	UC
Mica	Canada	1,736	2,610	1976
Volgograd—22nd Congress	U.S.S.R.	2,560	2,560	1958
Itaparica	Brazil	—	2,500	UC
Bennett W.A.C.	Canada	2,116	2,416	1969
Chicoasén	Mexico	—	2,400	1980
Atatürk	Turkey	—	2,400	UC
LaGrande 3	Canada	—	2,304	UC
Volga—V.I. Lenin	U.S.S.R.	2,300	2,300	1955
Iron Gates I	Romania/Yugoslavia	2,300	2,300	1970
Fos do Areia	Brazil	2,250	2,250	1983
Bath County	Virginia	—	2,100	UC
High Aswan (Saad-el-Aali)	Egypt	2,100	2,100	1967
Tarbella	Pakistan	1,400	2,100	1977
Piedra de Aquila	Argentina	—	2,100	UC
Itumbiara	Brazil	2,080	2,080	1982
Chief Joseph	Washington	2,069	2,069	1956
Salto Santiago	Brazil	—	2,031	1980
McNary	Oregon	980	2,030	1954
Green River	North Carolina	—	2,000	1980
Tehri	India	—	2,000	UC
Cornwall	New York	—	2,000	1978
Ludington	Michigan	1,979	1,979	1973
Robert Moses—Niagara	New York	1,950	1,950	1961
Salto Grande	Argentina/Uruguay	—	1,890	1979

Note: MW = Megawatts, UC = under construction. *Source:* Department of the Interior, Bureau of Reclamation.

How Old Is Man?

Paleoanthropologists (anthropologists who specialize in the study of fossil man) disagree on when humans first were differentiated from their pre-human ancestors. Estimates range from 2 to 3.8 million years ago, based on such criteria as brain size, knee joints indicating an ability to walk on two legs, and toolmaking ability.

The oldest footprints of a human-like animal were found by Dr. Mary Leakey in 1979 in the Laetoli area of northern Tanzania, East Africa. The 3.6-million-year age of the footprints was determined by radioactive dating of the rock layer in which they were found.

The old concept of a single line of development from ape to man has been replaced by the generally accepted theory that there were at least three different forms of early man and near man in Africa, where most scientists agree humans first emerged.

United States Tallest Buildings

City	Building	Stories	Height ft	Height m	City	Building	Stories	Height ft	Height m
Chicago	Sears Tower	110	1,454	443	Boston	John Hancock Tower	60	790	241
New York	World Trade Center	110	1,377	419	San Francisco	Bank of America	52	779	237
New York	Empire State	102	1,250	381	Minneapolis	IDS Tower	57	775	236
Chicago	Standard Oil (Indiana)	80	1,136	346	New York	One Liberty Plaza	54	775	236
Chicago	John Hancock Center	100	1,127	343	New York	One Penn Plaza	57	774	236
New York	Chrysler	77	1,046	319	Atlanta	Peachtree Plaza	73	754	230
Houston	Texas	75	1,002	305	New York	Exxon	54	750	229
Houston	Allied Bank	71	985	300	Boston	Prudential Tower	52	750	229
New York	American International	66	952	290	Detroit	Detroit Plaza Hotel	73	747	228
New York	Citicorp Center	59	915	279	Dallas	First International	55	744	227
New York	40 Wall Tower	71	900	274	Los Angeles	Security Pacific Plaza	55	743	226
Chicago	Water Tower Place	74	859	262	New York	One Astor Plaza	54	730	222
Los Angeles	United California Bank	62	858	261	Houston	Gulf Tower	52	725	221
San Francisco	Transamerica Pyramid	61	853	260	New York	Marine Midland	52	724	221
Chicago	First National Bank	60	851	259	Houston	One Shell Plaza	50	714	218
New York	RCA	70	850	259	Dallas	First International	56	710	216
Pittsburgh	U.S. Steel Headquarters	64	841	256	Cleveland	Terminal Tower	52	708	216
New York	Chase Manhattan	60	813	248	New York	Union Carbide	52	707	215
New York	Pan Am	59	808	246	New York	General Motors	50	705	215
New York	Woolworth	55	792	241	New York	Metropolitan Life	50	700	213

NOTE: Does not include buildings under construction and not completed in 1982. Height does not include TV towers and antennas. *Source: Information Please* questionnaires to building managements.

Notable Tunnels

Railroad, excluding subways

Name	Location	Length mi.	Length km	Year completed
Seikan	Tsugara Strait, Japan	33.1	53.3	UC
Simplon (I and II)	Alps, Switzerland-Italy	12.3	19.8	1906 & 1922
Kammon Straits	Honshu to Kyoshu Islands, Japan	11.6	18.7	UC
Apennine	Genoa, Italy	11.5	18.5	1934
St. Gotthard	Swiss Alps	9.3	14.9	1881
Lötschberg	Swiss Alps	9.1	14.6	1911
Nakayama	Komochi Mountain, Japan	8.8	14.2	UC
Mont Cénis	French Alps	8.5[1]	13.7	1871
New Cascade	Cascade Mountains, Washington	7.8	12.6	1929
Vosges	Vosges, France	7.0	11.3	1940
Arlberg	Austrian Alps	6.3	10.1	1884
Moffat	Rocky Mountains, Colorado	6.2	9.9	1928
Shimuzu	Shimuzu, Japan	6.1	9.8	1931
Rimutaka	Wairarapa, New Zealand	5.5	8.9	1955

Vehicular

Name	Location	Length mi.	Length km	Year completed
St. Gotthard	Alps, Switzerland	10.2	16.4	1980
Mt. Blanc	Alps, France-Italy	7.5	12.1	1965
Mt. Ena	Japan Alps, Japan	5.3	8.5	1976[2]
Great St. Bernard	Alps, Switzerland-Italy	3.4	5.5	1964
Mount Royal	Montreal, Canada	3.2	5.1	1918
Lincoln	Hudson River, New York-New Jersey	2.5	4.0	1937
Queensway Road	Mersey River, Liverpool, England	2.2	3.5	1934
Brooklyn-Battery	East River, New York City	2.1	3.4	1950
Holland	Hudson River, New York-New Jersey	1.7	2.7	1927
Hampton Roads	Norfolk, Virginia	1.4	2.3	1957
Queens-Midtown	East River, New York City	1.3	2.1	1940
Liberty Tubes	Pittsburgh, Pennsylvania	1.2	1.9	1923
Baltimore Harbor	Baltimore, Maryland	1.2	1.9	1957
Allegheny Tunnels	Pennsylvania Turnpike	1.2	1.9	1940[3]

1. Lengthened to its present 8.5 miles in 1881. 2. Parallel tunnel begun in 1976. 3. Parallel tunnel built in 1965, twin tunnel in 1966. NOTE: UC = under construction. *Source:* American Society of Civil Engineers and International Bridge, Tunnel & Turnpike Association.

Notable Modern Bridges

Suspension

Name	Location	Length of main span, ft	m	Year completed
Humber	Hull, Britain	4,626	1,410	1981
Verrazano-Narrows	Lower New York Bay	4,260	1,298	1964
Golden Gate	San Francisco Bay	4,200	1,280	1937
Mackinac Straits	Michigan	3,800	1,158	1957
Bosporus	Istanbul	3,524	1,074	1973
George Washington	Hudson River at New York City	3,500	1,067	1931
Ponte 25 dé Abril	Tagus River at Lisbon	3,323	1,013	1966
Forth Road	Queensferry, Scotland	3,300	1,006	1964
Severn	Severn River at Beachley, England	3,240	988	1966
Tacoma Narrows	Puget Sound at Tacoma, Wash.	2,800	853	1950
Kanmon Strait	Kyushu-Honshu, Japan	2,336	712	1973
Angostura	Orinoco River at Ciudad Bolivar, Venezuela	2,336	712	1967
Transbay (twin spans)	San Francisco Bay	2,310	704	1936
Bronx-Whitestone	East River, New York City	2,300	701	1939
Pierre Laporte	St. Lawrence River at Quebec, Canada	2,190	668	1970
Delaware Memorial (twin bridges)	Delaware River near Wilmington, Del.	2,150	655	1951, 1968
Seaway Skyway	St. Lawrence River at Ogdensburg, N.Y.	2,150	655	1960
Gas Pipe Line	Atchafalaya River, Louisiana	2,000	610	1951
Walt Whitman	Delaware River at Philadelphia	2,000	610	1957
Tancarville	Seine River at Tancarville, France	1,995	608	1959
Lillebaelt	Lillebaelt Strait, Denmark	1,969	600	1970
Ambassador International	Detroit River at Detroit	1,850	564	1929
Throgs Neck	East River, New York City	1,800	549	1961
Benjamin Franklin	Delaware River at Philadelphia	1,750	533	1926
Skjomen	Narvik, Norway	1,722	525	1972
Kvalsund	Hammerfest, Norway	1,722	525	1977
Kleve-Emmerich	Rhine River at Emmerich, West Germany	1,640	500	1965
Bear Mountain	Hudson River at Peekskill, N.Y.	1,632	497	1924
Wm. Preston Lane, Jr., Memorial (twin bridges)	Near Annapolis, Md.	1,600	488	1952, 1973
Williamsburg	East River, New York City	1,600	488	1903
Newport	Narragansett Bay at Newport, R.I.	1,600	488	1969
Brooklyn	East River, New York City	1,595	486	1883

Cantilever

Name	Location	Length of main span, ft	m	Year completed
Quebec Railway	St. Lawrence River at Quebec, Canada	1,800	549	1917
Forth Railway (twin spans)	Queensferry, Scotland	1,710	521	1890
Minato Ohashi	Osaka, Japan	1,673	510	1974
Commodore John Barry	Chester, Pa.	1,644	501	1974
Greater New Orleans	Mississippi River, Louisiana	1,576	480	1958
Howrah	Hooghly River at Calcutta	1,500	457	1943
Transbay Bridge	San Francisco Bay	1,400	427	1936
Baton Rouge	Mississippi River, Louisiana	1,235	376	1968
Tappan Zee	Hudson River at Tarrytown, N.Y.	1,212	369	1955
Longview	Columbia River at Longview, Wash.	1,200	366	1930
Patapsco River	Baltimore Outer Harbor Crossing	1,200	366	1976
Queensboro	East River, New York City	1,182	360	1909

Steel Arch

Name	Location	Length of main span, ft	m	Year completed
New River Gorge	Fayetteville, W. Va.	1,700	518	1977
Bayonne	Kill Van Kull at Bayonne, N.J.	1,675	510	1931
Sydney Harbor	Sydney, Australia	1,670	509	1932
Fremont	Portland, Ore.	1,255	383	1973
Zdákov	Vltava River, Czechoslovakia	1,244	380	1967
Port Mann	Fraser River at Vancouver, British Columbia	1,200	366	1964
Thatcher Ferry	Panama Canal, Panama	1,128	344	1962
Laviolette	St. Lawrence River, Trois Rivieres, Quebec	1,100	335	1967
Runcorn-Widnes	Mersey River, England	1,082	330	1961
Birchenough	Sabi River at Fort Victoria, Rhodesia	1,080	329	1935

Name	Location	Length of main span, ft	m	Year completed
Cable-Stayed				
Second Hooghly	Calcutta	1,500	457	UC
St.-Nazaire	Loire River, St.-Nazaire, France	1,325	404	1975
Stretto di Rande	Spain	1,312	400	UC
Luling	Missipi River, Luling, La.	1,235	376	UC
Düsseldorf-Flehe	Rhine River, West Germany	1,205	367	UC
Yamatogawa	Osaka, Japan	1,165	355	UC
Duisburg-Neuenkamp	Duisburg, West Germany	1,148	350	1970
Mesopotamia	Corrientes, Argentina	1,116	340	1972
West Gate	Lower Yarra River at Melbourne, Australia	1,102	336	1970
Zárate	Paraná River, Argentina	1,083	330	1976
Brazo Largo	Paraná River, Argentina	1,083	330	1977
Köhlbrand	Hamburg, West Germany	1,066	325	1974
Kniebrücke	Rhine River at Düsseldorf, West Germany	1,050	320	1969
Brotonne[1]	Seine River, France	1,050	320	1976
Erskine	Clyde River at Glasgow, Scotland	1,000	305	1971
Continuous Truss				
Astoria	Columbia River at Astoria, Oregon	1,232	376	1966
Oshima	Oshima Island, Japan	1,066	325	1976
Croton Reservoir	Croton, N.Y.	1,052	321	1970
Tenmon	Kumamoto, Japan	984	300	1966
Kuronoseto	Nagashima-Kyushu, Japan	984	300	1974
Ravenswood	Ohio River, Ravenswood, W. Va.	902	275	UC
Dubuque	Mississippi River at Dubuque, Iowa	845	258	1943
Braga Memorial	Taunton River at Somerset, Mass.	840	256	1966
Graf Spee	Germany	839	256	1936
Concrete Arch				
Jesse H. Jones Memorial	Houston Ship Channel, Texas	1,500	455	1982
KRK	Zagreb, Yugoslavia	1,280	390	1979
Gladesville	Parramatta River at Sydney, Australia	1,000	305	1964
Amizade	Paraná River at Foz do Iguassu, Brazil	951	290	1964
Arrábida	Porto, Portugal	886	270	1963
Sandö	Angerman River at Kramfors, Sweden	866	264	1943
Shibenik	Krka River, Yugoslavia	808	246	1966
Fiumarella	Catanzaro, Italy	758	231	1961
Zaporozhe	Old Dnepr River, U.S.S.R.	748	228	1952
Novi Sad	Danube River, Yugoslavia	692	211	1961

1. Concrete bridge. NOTE: UC = under construction. *Source: Encyclopaedia Britannica,* American Society of Civil Engineers, and International Bridge, Tunnel & Turnpike Association.

Famous Ship Canals

Name	Location	Length (miles)[1]	Width (feet)	Depth (feet)	Locks	Year opened
Albert	Belgium	80.0	53.0	16.5	6	1939
Amsterdam-Rhine	Netherlands	45.0	164.0	41.0	3	1952
Beaumont-Port Arthur	United States	40.0	200.0	34.0	—	1916
Chesapeake and Delaware	United States	19.0	250.0	27.0	—	1927
Houston	United States	43.0	300.0	34.0	—	1914
Kiel (Nord-Ostsee Kanal)	Germany	61.3	144.0	36.0	4	1895
Panama	Canal Zone	50.7	110.0	41.0	12	1914
St. Lawrence Seaway	U.S. and Canada	2,400.0 [2]	([3])	—	—	1959
Montreal to Prescott	U.S. and Canada	11.5	80.0	30.0	7	1959
Welland	Canada	27.5	80.0	27.0	8	1931
Sault Ste. Marie	Canada	1.2	60.0	16.8	1	1895
Sault Ste. Marie	United States	1.6	80.0	25.0	4	1915
Suez	Egypt	100.6 [4]	197.0	36.0	—	1869

1. Statute miles. 2. From Montreal to Duluth. 3. 442–550 feet; there are 11.5 miles of locks, 80 feet wide and 30 feet deep. 4. From Port Said lighthouse to entrance channel in Suez roads. *Source:* American Society of Civil Engineers.

Rules for Correct Punctuation, Capitalization, Abbreviation

Blanche Ormont

Punctuation

Period (.) Use a period: (1) After a statement or command: *Panama is roughly the size of South Carolina. Go to the head of the line.*

(2) After most abbreviations: C.O.D., Ms., U.S. (In familiar abbreviations, where the letters themselves are usually spoken, the period is often omitted: *CIO, NBC, SPCA.*)

(3) With decimals and in dollars and cents: *.05, 22.5, $12.95.* Do not use a period after *percent,* as in *twenty percent;* if cents is written out or the cents sign is used, as in *27 cents, 27¢;* or after Roman numerals, *XXIII, Act III,* except when numbering or listing.

Question Mark (?) Use the question mark after a direct question: *Do you know why the world's climate is changing?* Do not use the question mark after an indirect question or request: *The teacher asked him if he knew the capital of South Dakota. Will you please return this book as soon as possible.*

Exclamation Point (!) Use an exclamation point after an emphatic statement or after a sentence, phrase, or word expressing strong feeling: *You're absolutely wrong! Ouch! That hurts!*

Comma (,) The comma is the most commonly used (and misused) punctuation mark. It indicates a slight separation between words or groups of words and should serve primarily to make the writer's meaning clear. Too many commas may cause the reader to separate words that should be grouped together, or they may unnecessarily slow the movement of a sentence. Too few commas, or misplaced commas, may seriously distort the writer's meaning. Although one should always use good judgment in deciding when and where to use commas, the following rules are generally applicable. Use a comma:

(1) To separate words, phrases, or clauses (a clause is a group of words that has a subject and a predicate) in a series of three or more items: *Tuition, board, lodging, and medical and dental care are provided.* (Note that the comma before the second *and* has been omitted because *medical and dental care* is considered a single unit. However, in some cases it is necessary to insert the comma before *and* to avoid misreading: *The course includes navigation, electricity, ship construction, marine biology, and engineering.*)

Commas are used between two or more adjectives preceding a noun if each separately could modify the noun and if switching the order of the adjectives does not alter the sense: *It was a cold, bleak, rainy day.* Do not use commas if the first adjective qualifies the entire expression following it: *Their constitution established a strong central government.*

Use a comma after *etc.* (abbreviation of *et cetera*) when it is the last of a series within a sentence: *Books, papers, cartons, etc., lay scattered about the room.*

(2) Between independent clauses (clauses that could stand alone as complete sentences) joined by *and, but, for, or, nor: Pluto has the most eccentric orbit in the solar system, and at times it comes closer to the sun than Neptune. A huge fireball appeared in the sky, but the natives were not afraid.* In a short compound sentence—a sentence made up of two or more independent clauses—the comma is often omitted: *The canoe turned over and everyone fell into the water.*

(3) To set off introductory words, phrases, or clauses: *Outraged, he slammed the door behind him. During the wars that followed the French Revolution, Belgium was occupied and later annexed to France. Because Bolivia has no access to the sea, foreign trade must pass through free ports in Chile and river ports on the Amazon.*

If the introductory phrase or clause is very short, or if it is the subject of the sentence, do not use a comma: *Because of its beaches the state is a popular resort area. To cross the sea in ancient times was an extraordinary feat.*

Such introductory transitional words as *yes, no, still, nevertheless, moreover, however, therefore, besides, furthermore,* and weak exclamations like *well, oh,* and *why* should be followed by a comma: *No, I cannot go with you. Well, that's a long story. Why, how nice!*

(4) To set off nonessential elements—words, phrases, or clauses that are not closely related to the rest of the sentence and could be left out without drastically changing its meaning: *Hinduism dates back, perhaps, to prehistoric times. The emperor, in recognition of Confucius' teachings, offered sacrifices at his tomb. Gold, which was responsible for California's settlement boom, is still found in that state.*

To determine whether a modifying expression is restrictive or nonrestrictive (essential or nonessential), see if it can be omitted without significantly changing the meaning. If it is essential to the meaning of the sentence, commas are not used: *Delhi residents who would not limit their families were denied government assistance.* The clause "who would not limit their families" is clearly restrictive; if it were removed, the sentence would indicate that *all* Delhi residents were denied government assistance.

Use the comma before *for, although, though, as, since,* and *because* when these words introduce nonrestrictive clauses or phrases: *The Age of Enlightenment brought about the Jews' emancipa-*

tion, although persecutions did not end entirely. But: The famous Dutch dikes are requisite to the use of much land because half of the country's area is below sea level. (No comma before *because,* which introduces a restrictive clause.)

Appositives are words or phrases that directly follow a noun or pronoun and identify or explain it. If an appositive is nonrestrictive, it is set off by commas: *The fur-bearing chinchilla, a native of the colder plateau regions, is also raised.* If it is restrictive, no commas are used: *The phrase "hot line" refers to the emergency communications link between Washington and Moscow.*

Contrasting expressions introduced by such words and phrases as *not, but not,* and *though not* are usually nonrestrictive and are therefore set off by commas: *Venus, not Mars, is Earth's nearest neighbor.*

When nonrestrictive words, phrases, or clauses occur within a sentence, they must be set off by *two* commas—one before the expression and one after.

(5) In certain conventional places: (a) To separate items in addresses and dates: *He wrote to his aunt at 94 Birch Road, Omaha, Nebraska, on June 12, 1924* (b) With numbers greater than three figures: *1,422, 12,498,620.* (c) In letters, after salutations (in informal letters) and after the complimentary close: *Dear Aunt Mary, Sincerely yours,.* (d) To set off the name of a person addressed: *John, please close the door. Listen carefully, Sarah, because this is important.* (e) To separate degrees and titles from names: *Margaret Harrison, M.D., Ph.D. Frank Simmons, Treasurer.* (f) To set off direct quotations: *"Happiness," someone said, "is a warm puppy."* With exclamations or very short quotations, no comma is necessary: *"Hi there!" she called. He constantly said "like" and "you know."*

(6) Whenever necessary to avoid misunderstanding: *Several months after, he saw his father.* (Without the comma the sentence changes meaning, turning into the clause *Several months after he saw his father.*)

Semicolon (;) The semicolon is a mark of separation that functions like a weak period or a strong comma. Use a semicolon:

(1) Between two independent clauses which are not joined by a conjunction: *The soil is generally poor; high crop yields are dependent upon large-scale use of fertilizers.*

(2) Between two independent clauses containing one or more commas even if a conjunction is used: *After members of the committee have debated the bill, a vote is taken; and if the vote is favorable, the bill is sent back to the floor of the house.*

(3) Between two main clauses linked by such connecting words as *therefore, however, finally, thus, otherwise, nevertheless,* and by such phrases as *for example, in fact, on the contrary: The first game of lawn tennis in the United States was played in 1874; however, it was not until 1880 that standard measurements for the court were established.*

(4) Between items in a series if one or more are subdivided by commas: *Among the great libraries of the world are the British Museum, with more than 6,000,000 printed volumes; the National Diet Library in Tokyo, containing more than 4,100,000 volumes; and, of course, the United States Library of Congress, whose extensive collections total over 72,466,000 volumes.*

Colon (:) The colon is a mark of anticipation introducing material that follows it. Use a colon:

(1) To introduce a long quotation, explanatory statement, or question: *The Declaration of Independence states: "We hold these truths to be self-evident, that all men are created equal, that they are endowed by their Creator with certain unalienable Rights, that among these are Life, Liberty, and the Pursuit of Happiness." In 1976, the World Health Organization accomplished a major goal: It virtually eliminated one of mankind's most ancient enemies—smallpox. The question we discussed was: What are the real differences between Socialism and Communism?*

(2) To introduce a list of items. The colon here is frequently, though not always, preceded by such phrases as *the following* or *as follows: Among the great Gothic structures of Europe are the following: Chartres Cathedral, Notre Dame de Paris. Milan Cathedral, and Cologne Cathedral.*

(3) In these customary places: (Note preceding use of colon.) After a formal salutation in a letter: *Dear Sir:;* between hours and minutes: *10:15 a.m.;* between volume and page in formal footnotes and bibliography: *The Dictionary of Dates 2:120–142;* between chapter and verse in the Bible: *Genesis 1:10;* between numerical elements in ratios: *4:2;* after the name of a speaker in a play: *Lady Macbeth: Out, damned spot!*

Quotation Marks (" ") Use quotation marks:

(1) To enclose a direct quotation: *"Life," said Julia Ward Howe, who lived to be ninety-one, "is like a cup of tea; the sugar is all at the bottom."*

Quotation marks are always used in *pairs,* before the quoted material and after it. However, if you quote two or more paragraphs, place quotation marks at the beginning of each paragraph and at the end of the entire quotation.

Single marks are used to enclose a quotation within a quotation. *"His constant use of such words as 'cool' and 'far out' has become very tiresome," the teacher remarked.*

(2) To enclose the title of a short literary work—a chapter, article, essay, poem, or short story—and titles of paintings, short musical compositions, and radio and television programs. The titles of longer works should be italicized. (Joyce's collection of short stories *Dubliners* includes the famous story "The Dead.")

(3) To enclose all words or phrases that are borrowed, that the writer does not wish to claim as his own, or that he uses ironically: *The term "the chain of being" was for centuries a descriptive name for the universe. For many of the world's poor, "home" is a tarpaper shack or a large oil pipe.*

(4) To enclose words or phrases which themselves are being discussed: *Many women now prefer the term "feminism" to the earlier phrase "women's lib."*

(5) When quotation marks are used with other punctuation, they appear as follows:

Outside a comma or period. *"I'm tired," she said. "It's been a long day."*

Inside the semicolon or colon: *A foreign phrase commonly misused to describe aristocracy is "hoi polloi"; actually, it means "the common people."*

Outside a question mark or exclamation point if either is part of the quotation—otherwise, inside. *"Get out of here!" she shrieked. Who wrote "The Unfinished Symphony"?*

Apostrophe (') Use an apostrophe:

(1) In contractions to indicate the omission of a letter: *haven't.*

(2) Before an *s* to form the plural of figures and

letters: *Two size 12's. Cross your t's and dot your i's.*

(3) To form possessives: *Mary's house, men's clothing.* If a plural ends in *s*, add only the apostrophe: *girls' sports, hostesses' duties.* If a singular ends in *s*, add the apostrophe and *s*: *James's car.* However, the second *s* may be omitted, especially if the word would become more difficult to pronounce: *Socrates' teachings.* Be sure never to use the apostrophe with the possessive pronouns *his, hers, its, yours, ours, theirs.*

Hyphen (-) Use a hyphen:

(1) To link many compound words—two or more words considered as a single unit: *secretary-treasurer, bull's-eye, heavy-hearted, cease-fire.* Do not use a hyphen if a compound modifier follows the noun: *This scientist is well known.* (But note use of hyphen in *a well-known scientist.*) Do not use a hyphen in a compound modifier that includes an adverb ending in *-ly* even if it precedes the noun: *richly deserved praise.*

(2) With certain prefixes and suffixes: *self-support, ex-wife, anti-American, co-worker, president-elect, husband-to-be.* When the parts have become merged in general use, the hyphen may be unnecessary: *midsummer, prehistoric, nonaligned.* (Since usage here is often inconsistent, it is wise, when in doubt, to consult a dictionary.)

(3) In compound numbers from twenty-one to ninety-nine and in fractions: *twenty-five, one-third.*

(4) To divide a word *between syllables* at the end of a line.

(5) Wherever misreading might occur, as in *a navy-blue uniform,* or if a prefix ends with a vowel and the root word begins with the same vowel: *re-elected, anti-inflationary, semi-independent.*

Dash (—) The dash indicates greater separation than a comma but lesser separation than parentheses. Use the dash:

(1) To indicate a sudden change in thought or sentence structure: *We rescheduled the picnic for the following Sunday—we hoped it would be a nice day—but it rained again.*

(2) To emphasize parenthetic, appositive, or explanatory matter. *Imagine a device that is only a cubic foot in size—the size of a hat box—containing 40,000 electronic parts!*

(3) To set off a parenthetic or appositive expression that is itself broken by commas: *She was beset by fears—of heights, open spaces, animals, traffic, strangers—and, as a result, she never left her home.*

Parentheses (()) Generally speaking, dashes add emphasis to the material they enclose, while parentheses tend to subordinate it. Use parentheses:

(1) To enclose incidental or explanatory material that may be relevant but is not strictly necessary: *The rivers, lakes, and surrounding seas (except the Black Sea) are rich in fish. During the reign of Henry VIII (1509–47), the Church of England asserted its independence from the Roman Catholic Church.*

(2) Around figures or letters to enumerate items in a series: *Three qualities of good writing are (1) clarity, (2) consistency, and (3) coherence.*

Parenthetical statements within a sentence begin with a small letter and have no end punctuation, except a question mark or exclamation point if needed. If a comma, semicolon, or colon are necessary after the parenthetical material within a sentence, they are placed outside the closing curve. A complete parenthetic sentence within a paragraph but not within another sentence has an initial capital and end punctuation placed within the closing curve: *Although Nigeria was the world's sixth largest oil producer (its 1974 oil revenues totaled $8 billion), the country's per capita income was only $120 per year. (Even so, it remained black Africa's wealthiest nation.) This problem contributed to continuing government instability.*

Brackets ([]) Use brackets to enclose parenthetic comments inserted in a quotation by the person using the quotation: *In his Nobel Lecture, Martin Luther King said, "In a dark, confused world [where war, poverty, and racism exist] the kingdom of God may yet reign in the hearts of men."*

Capitalization

The use of capital letters is quite standardized in general English. Avoid unnecessary capitals, and when in doubt consult a dictionary. As a rule, capitalize the following:

(1) The first word of a complete sentence: *The modern museum originated during the Renaissance.*; of a quoted sentence: *Freud said, "What does a woman want?"*; of each line of poetry:

Had we but world enough, and time,
This coyness, lady, were no crime.—Andrew Marvell

(2) Proper names. A proper name is the name of a *particular* person, place, or thing. Capitalize all proper names including adjectives and abbreviations derived from proper names. Among the proper names to be capitalized are the names of specific persons or places: *John F. Kennedy, Vermont, China, Central Park;* organizations, institutions, buildings, and monuments: *the Republican Party, the Bank of America, Harvard University, the Museum of Modern Art, the Lincoln Memorial;* peoples, languages, religions, and political groups: *Africans, Indians, French, Caucasian, Methodist, Communist;* days of the week, months, holidays: *Tuesday, August, New Year's Day, Easter;* historical periods, events, or documents: *the Dark Ages, the Renaissance, the Holocaust, the Civil War, the Magna Carta, the Social Security Act;* geographical names and regions: *Yellowstone National Park, Lake Huron, the South Pole, the Northeast* (when words like *south* and *north* refer to directions rather than regions, they are not capitalized); names of departments of government and of institutions: *Department of Commerce, Police Department, the City Council, the English Department, the Graduate School;* stars, planets, constellations, satellites, except the sun, earth, and moon: *Sirius, Venus, Orion, Viking I, Halley's Comet;* words referring to the Deity, the Bible, and other sacred writings: *Jehovah, the Messiah, the Virgin, Genesis, Lamentations, the Koran.*

(3) Titles preceding proper names and titles of high rank used without the name: *Professor Cohen, Mayor Daley, Sergeant Jones, Aunt Ellen, the Pope, the President, the Secretary of State, the Queen Mother.*

(4) First and last words and all other words, except the articles *a, an, the,* conjunctions, and prepositions in titles of books, plays, poems, articles, movies, etc.: *Wild Animals of the World, Ode to the West Wind, All in the Family, Porgy and Bess.*

(5) The pronoun *I* and the exclamation *O*: *If I forget thee, O Jerusalem, let my right hand forget her cunning.*—Psalms

Abbreviations

Abbreviations are useful and appropriate in notetaking, in reference works, in statistical tables, and in certain other situations where speed and space-saving are important. In general writing, however, abbreviations should be avoided. A few standard abbreviations that are correct in all writing are the following:

(1) Titles and names: *Mr., Messrs., Mrs., Dr., Esq., Sr., Jr., Ph.D., M.D., LL.D.* Do not use a title both before and after a name: *Mr. James T. Smith* or *James T. Smith, Ph.D.*, not *Mr. James T. Smith, Ph.D.*

Do not abbreviate civil, professional (except *Dr.*), military, or political titles, except when the person's first name or initials are used: *Professor Downey* or *Prof. Charles Downey, General Marshall* or *Gen. G. C. Marshall*, never *Prof. Downey* or *Gen. Marshall.*

First names should, as a rule, be spelled out: *William Shakespeare*, not *Wm. Shakespeare.*

(2) Certain units of measurements: *a.m., p.m., A.D., B.C., mph,* when used with figures, as in *50 mph; No.* with numbers expressed in figures, as in *No. 8.* Write out other expressions for time, weight, and size, as in *three ounces, two miles, four hours,* unless such expressions appear in directions, recipes, or technical writing: *1/2 tsp salt, 10 ft 2 in.*

(3) Names of organizations, governmental agencies, scientific words, trade names, and other expressions that are familiar to most people and are frequently referred to by their initials: *YMCA, AFL-CIO, FCC, CIA, FBI, NASA, DDT, DNA, CBS, MGM.* Generally no period is used. (Exceptions: *C.O.D., F.O.B.*) Abbreviations like *Co., Inc., Ltd.,* or *Corp.* are correct when they are part of the company name: *Jones Publishing, Inc.*

(4) Certain literary abbreviations: *i.e.* (that is); *e.g.* (for example); *ibid.* (in the same place); *etc.* (and so forth).

In ordinary usage, write out: names of states, countries, months, days of the week; words like *street, road, square* when they are used as part of a proper name: *Maple Street;* and numbers that can be expressed in not more than one or two words: *twenty books, four hundred miles* (but *$3,560.23, 60,211 miles*).

> These are "general" rules of punctuation, capitalization, and abbreviation designed to make writing as clear and "correct" as possible. There are no absolutes. Many publications have modifications of these basic rules that reflect their own special needs.

Forms of Address[1]

By permission. From Webster's Seventh New Collegiate Dictionary. © 1976 by Merriam-Webster Inc., publishers of the Merriam-Webster ® Dictionaries.

Abbot. *Address:* The Right Reverend _____, O.S.B. (or other initials of the order), Abbot of _____. *Begin:* Right Reverend and Dear Father.

Ambassador (U.S.). *Address:* The Honorable _____ _____, American Ambassador; (to the U.S.): His Excellency _____ _____, Ambassador of _____. *Begin:* Sir; *or* Dear Mr. Ambassador.

Archbishop. *Address:* The Most Reverend Archbishop of _____; *or* The Most Reverend _____ _____, Archbishop of _____. *Begin:* Your Excellency; *or* Dear Archbishop _____.

Archdeacon. *Address:* The Venerable the Archdeacon of _____. *Begin:* Venerable Sir.

Armed Forces (U.S.). See *Military and Naval Officers.*

Assemblyman. *Address:* The Honorable _____ _____, The Assembly, State Capitol. *Begin:* Dear Mr. _____.

Associate Justice (Supreme Court). *Address:* Mr. Justice _____, The Supreme Court of the United States. *Begin:* Dear Mr. Justice.

Attorney. *Address:* Mr. _____ _____, Attorney-at-Law; *or* _____ _____, Esq. *Begin:* Dear Mr. _____.

Bishop (Episcopal). *Address:* The Right Reverend _____ _____, Bishop of _____ *Begin:* Right Reverend Sir; *or* Dear Bishop _____.

Bishop (Roman Catholic). *Address:* The Most Reverend _____ _____, Bishop of _____. *Begin:* Your Excellency; *or* Dear Bishop _____.

Bishop (other denominations). *Address:* The Reverend _____ _____. *Begin:* Reverend Sir; *or* Dear Bishop _____.

Brother (Roman Catholic). *Address:* Brother _____ (first name followed by initials of the order). *Begin:* Dear Brother _____.

Cabinet Officer (U.S.). *Address:* The Honorable _____ _____, Secretary of State (or other department); *or* The Honorable _____ _____, Attorney General of the United States. *Begin:* Dear Sir.

Cardinal. *Address:* His Eminence John Cardinal Smith. *Begin:* Your Eminence; *or* Dear Cardinal _____.

Chargé d'Affaires (U.S.). *Address:* _____ _____, Esq., American Chargé d'Affaires. *Begin:* Dear Sir.

Chief Justice (Supreme Court). *Address:* The Chief Justice of the United States. *Begin:* Dear Mr. Chief Justice.

Clergyman (Protestant). *Address:* The Reverend _____ _____; *or* (if a Doctor of Divinity) The Reverend Dr. _____ _____; *Begin:* Dear Sir; *or* Dear Mr. _____; *or* Dear Dr. _____.

Commissioner (of a Department or Bureau). *Address:* The Honorable _____ _____. *Begin:* Dear Mr. _____.

Consul. *Address:* _____ _____, Esq., American Consul. *Begin:* Dear Sir.

Dean (of a Cathedral). *Address:* The Very Reverend _____ _____; *or* Dean _____ _____ *Begin:*

1. Since the relationship between correspondents affects the form of address used in letters, no rigid guidelines can be set down for all occasions. When two salutations are shown, it is to be understood that the formal styling precedes the informal. In salutations where the addressee is a woman, it is to be understood that in formal address Madam may be substituted for Sir, and in informal address Mrs. or Miss or Ms. may be substituted for Mr. 2. From Webster's Seventh New Collegiate Dictionary. NOTE: Forms of Address for foreign dignitaries may be obtained from their United Nations missions in New York City.

Very Reverend Sir; *or* Dear Dean ______.

Dean (of a College or University). *Address:* Dean ______ ______. *Begin:* Dear Dean ______.

Dentist. *Address:* ______ ______, D.D.S. (office address); *or* Dr. ______ ______ (home address). *Begin:* Dear Dr. ______.

Divorced Woman. *Address:* Ordinarily use *Mrs.* with her maiden name as a prename. Some divorced women prefer to resume the *Miss.*[2]

Doctor of Divinity. See *Clergyman.*

Doctor of Philosophy, Laws, etc. *Address:* ______ ______, Ph.D. (LL.D.) (or other degree). *Begin:* Dear Sir; *or* Dear Dr. ______

Governor. *Address:* The Honorable ______ ______, Governor of ______. *Begin:* Dear Governor ______.

Governor-General of Canada. *Address:* His Excellency The Right Honourable ______ ______ (plus personal rank or title, if any). *Begin:* My Lord; *or* Sir (according to rank).[2]

Governor-General's Wife. *Address:* Her Excellency ______ ______ (plus personal rank or title, if any). *Begin:* Madam.[2]

Judge (Federal). *Address:* The Honorable ______ ______, United States District Judge. *Begin:* Dear Judge ______.

Judge (State or Local). *Address:* The Honorable ______ ______, Judge of the Court of Appeals (or other court). *Begin:* Dear Judge ______.

King. *Address:* The King's Most Excellent Majesty; *or* His Most Gracious Majesty, King ______. *Begin:* Sir; *or* May It Please Your Majesty.[2]

Lieutenant Governor. *Address:* The Honorable ______ ______, Lieutenant Governor of ______. *Begin:* Dear Mr. ______.

Mayor (in Canadian Cities and Towns, and English Boroughs and Cities). *Address:* The Right Worshipful the Mayor of ______ (English cities only); His Worship, The Mayor of ______ (other). *Begin:* Sir.[2]

Mayor (U.S.). *Address:* The Honorable ______ ______, Mayor of ______. *Begin:* Dear Mayor ______.

Member of Parliament (or of a Legislative Council). The ordinary form of address followed by M.P. (or M.L.C.).[2]

Military and Naval Officers (U.S.): *Address:* (full rank) ______ ______, U.S.N. (or U.S.A., U.S.A.F., U.S.M.C., U.S.C.G.). *Begin:* Sir (admirals and generals only); *or* Dear (full rank) ______ (other officers, including admirals and generals); *or* Dear Mr. ______ (lieutenant commander, lieutenant, ensign in Coast Guard or Navy only).

Minister (to U.S.). *Address:* The Honorable ______ ______, Minister of ______. *Begin:* Sir; *or* Dear Mr. Minister.

Minister of Religion. See *Clergyman, Priest, Rabbi.*

Monsignor. *Address:* The Right Reverend Monsignor ______. *Begin:* Dear Monsignor ______.

Mother Superior of a Sisterhood. *Address:* The Reverend Mother Superior, O.S.F. (or other initials of the order); *Begin:* Reverend Mother; or Dear Reverend Mother.

Nun. See *Sister of a Religious Order.*

Papal Nuncio or Internuncio or Apostolic Delegate. *Address:* His Excellency, The Papal Nuncio (*or* Internuncio *or* Apostolic Delegate) to ______. *Begin:* Your Excellency.[2]

Patriarch (Eastern Church). *Address:* His Beatitude the Patriarch of ______. *Begin:* Most Reverend Lord.

Physician. *Address:* ______ ______, M.D. (office address); *or* Dr. ______ ______ (home address). *Begin:* Dear Dr. ______

Pope. *Address:* His Holiness Pope ______; *or* His Holiness the Pope. *Begin:* Your Holiness; *or* Most Holy Father.

President of a College or University. *Address:* President ______ ______ *Begin:* Dear President ______.

President of a State Senate. *Address:* The Honorable ______ ______, President of the Senate of ______ *Begin:* Dear Senator ______[2]

President of the U.S. *Address:* The President. *Begin:* Dear Mr. President.

President of the U.S. (Former). *Address:* The Honorable ______ ______ *Begin:* Dear Mr. ______.

Priest (Roman Catholic). *Address:* The Reverend Father ______; *or* The Reverend ______ ______. *Begin:* Dear Father ______; *or* Dear Father.

Prime Minister of Canada. *Address:* The Right Honourable ______ ______, P.C., Prime Minister of Canada. *Begin:* Sir.[2]

Privy Councillor (of Canada). *Address:* The Honourable ______ ______. *Begin:* Sir.[2]

Professor at a College or University. *Address:* Professor ______ ______. *Begin:* Dear Professor ______.

Queen. *Address:* The Queen's Most Excellent Majesty; *or* Her Gracious Majesty, The Queen. *Begin:* Madam; *or* May It Please Your Majesty.[2]

Rabbi. *Address:* Rabbi ______ ______; *or* Rabbi ______ ______, D.D. (if a Doctor of Divinity). *Begin:* Dear Rabbi ______; *or* Dear Dr. ______.

Representative (State). *Address:* The Honorable ______ ______, House of Representatives, State Capitol. *Begin:* Dear Mr. ______.

Representative (U.S.). *Address:* The Honorable ______ ______, The United States House of Representatives. *Begin:* Dear Mr. ______

Secretary-General of the U.N. *Address:* His Excellency ______ ______, Secretary-General of the United Nations. *Begin:* Excellency; *or* Dear Mr. Secretary-General; *or* Dear Mr. ______.

Senator (State). *Address:* The Honorable ______ ______, The State Senate, State Capitol. *Begin:* Dear Senator ______.

Senator (U.S.). *Address:* The Honorable ______ ______, United States Senate. *Begin:* Dear Senator ______.

Sister of a Religious Order. *Address:* Sister ______ ______, S.C. (or other initials of the order). *Begin:* Dear Sister ______ ______; *or* Dear Sister.

Speaker of the House of Commons (Canada). *Address:* The Honourable ______ ______, The Speaker of the House of Commons. *Begin:* Dear Mr. Speaker.[2]

Speaker of the House of Representatives (U.S.). *Address:* The Honorable ______ ______, Speaker of the House of Representatives. *Begin:* Dear Mr. Speaker.

Superior of a Brotherhood. *Address:* Brother ______ (first name followed by initials of the order), Superior. *Begin:* Dear Brother ______.

United Nations Representative (Foreign). *Address:* His Excellency ______ ______, Representative of ______ to the United Nations. *Begin:* Excellency; *or* Dear Mr. Ambassador.[2]

United Nations Representative (U.S.). *Address:* The Honorable ______ ______, United States

Representative to the United Nations. *Begin:* Sir; *or* Dear Mr. Ambassador.[2]

Veterinarian. *Address:* ______ ______, D.V.M. (office address); or Dr. ______ ______ (home address). *Begin:* Dear Dr. ______.

Vice President of the U.S. *Address:* The Vice President, United States Senate. *Begin:* Dear Mr. Vice President.

Widow. Ordinarily addressed by her former title: as, Mrs. John Doe, not Mrs. Jane Doe, unless the latter form is preferred by the person herself.[2]

Foreign Words and Phrases

(The English meanings given are not necessarily literal translations.)

ab ovo: from the beginning
à bon marché: good bargain; cheap
à deux: for two; between two
a priori: from something previous
à votre santé: to your health
ad infinitum: to infinity; with no end
ad valorem: according to its value
al fresco: outdoors
alma mater: one's college or school
alter ego: other self
amicus curiae: friend of the court
ancien regime: the old order
anno Domini: year of our Lord
ante bellum: before the war
au contraire: on the contrary
au courant: current; up-to-date
auf Wiedersehen: goodbye
bête noire: particular nemesis
bienvenue: welcome
bon mot: a funny or witty saying
bon vivant: a gourmet, an epicure
bona fide: in good faith; genuine; honest
carpe diem: enjoy today; seize the day
carte blanche: unlimited authority
cause célèbre: a cause that generates wide interest
caveat emptor: buy at your own risk; let the buyer beware
circa: about; approximately
chacun à son goût: each to his own taste
combien: how much?
corpus delicti: fundamental fact or facts about the commission of a crime
coup de grâce: finishing blow
cum grano salis: with a grain of salt
d'accord: in accord; agreement
de facto: as a matter of fact; actual
de profundis: out of the depths
Deo gratias: thanks be to God
Deo volente: God willing
dernier cri: the last word
deus ex machina: artificially produced to bring a solution to some extreme difficulty
dramatis personae: characters in a play
ecce homo: this is the man
en masse: all together
en passant: in passing
fait accompli: an accomplished fact
faux pas: a false step; a mistake
flagrante delicto: caught in the act
Gesundheit: good health (God bless you)
habeas corpus: common-law writ to bring a person before a court or judge
hoi polloi: the common people
honi soit qui mal y pense: evil to him who thinks evil of it
hors d'oeuvre: appetizer
idée fixe: fixed idea; obsession
in loco parentis: in place of a parent
ipso facto: by the very fact
je ne sais quoi: I don't know what; an elusive quality
jeunesse dorée: gilded youth
laissez faire: noninterference
l'chaim: to life
maven: an expert; connoisseur
mea culpa: I am to blame
mirabile dictu: wonderful to relate
modus operandi: method of operation; way of working
nom de plume: pen name
non compos mentis: not of sound mind
non sequitur: it does not follow
O tempora! O mores!: What sad times and customs
omnia vincit amor: love conquers all
per annum: by the year
per capita: by the head; individually
per diem: by the day; daily
persona non grata: an unwelcome or unacceptable person
plus ça change, plus c'est le même chose: the more things change, the more they remain the same
post mortem: after death
pro bono publico: for the public good
pro tempore (pro tem): for the time being; temporary
quid pro quo: something done or given in exchange for something else
repondez s'il vous plait: please reply; please answer (abbr. R.S.V.P.)
requiescat in pace: rest in peace
sans souci: without worry or care
savoir faire: know-how; manners for all occasions
semper fidelis: always faithful
shalom: peace
sic transit gloria mundi: so passes the glory of the world
s'il vous plait: if you please; please
sine die: with no day set for the next meeting
sine qua non: indispensable
status (in) quo: state in which anything is
sui generis: in a class by itself
tempus fugit: time flies
tout de suite: immediately
veni, vidi, vici: I came, I saw, I conquered
vis-à-vis: face-to-face

Carbon 14 Dating Technique

The old method for determining the age of a fossil by carbon 14 dating usually required samples so large that the fossil being analyzed was often destroyed. The latest technique developed by the University of Rochester uses a special high-voltage generator to directly measure the carbon 14 remaining in the sample. The advantage of this technique is that it requires only a one-milligram sample for testing.

U.S. Motor Vehicle Fuel Consumption

(1982 estimate)

Type of vehicle	Total travel (million vehicle miles)	Number of registered vehicles	Average miles traveled per vehicle	Fuel consumed (thousand gallons)	Average fuel consumption per vehicle (gallons)	Average miles per gallon
All passenger vehicles	1,155,552	130,000,523	8,889	70,849,870	545	16.31
Total personal passenger vehicles	1,148,883	129,441,326	8,876	69,730,000	539	16.48
Cars	1,133,883	123,697,863	9,167	69,430,000	561	16.33
Motorcycles	15,000	5,743,463	2,612	300,000	52	50.00
All buses	6,639	559,197	11,872	1,119,870	2,003	5.93
Commercial	3,577	113,468	31,524	721,170	6,356	4.96
School and other nonrevenue	3,062	445,729	6,870	398,700	894	7.68
All cargo vehicles	436,959	35,252,765	12,395	42,533,767	1,207	10.27
Single unit trucks	376,649	34,042,865	11,064	31,568,267	927	11.93
Combinations	60,310	1,209,900	49,847	10,965,500	9,063	5.50
All motor vehicles	**1,592,481**	**165,253,288**	**9,637**	**113,383,637**	**686**	**14.05**

Source: Department of Transportation, Federal Highway Administration.

Largest Nuclear Power Plants in the United States

(over a million kilowatts)

Location	Operating utility	Capacity (kilowatts)	Year operative
Cowans Ford Dam, NC (Unit 1)	Duke Power Company	1,180,000	1981
Daisy, Tenn. (Unit 1)	Tennessee Valley Authority	1,148,000	1980
Daisy, Tenn. (Unit 2)	Tennessee Valley Authority	1,148,000	1982
Prescott, Ore. (Unit 1)	Portland General Electric Co.	1,130,000	1976
San Clemente, Calif.	Southern Cal. Edison Co.	1,100,000	1983
Bridgman, Mich. (Unit 2)	Indiana & Michigan Electric Co.	1,100,000	1978
Salem, N.J. (Unit 2)	Public Service Electric & Gas, N.J.	1,100,000	1981
Salem, N.J. (Unit 1)	Public Service Electric & Gas, N.J.	1,090,000	1977
Seneca, Ill. (Unit 1)	Commonwealth Edison Co.	1,078,000	1984
Decatur, Ala. (Unit 1)	Tennessee Valley Authority	1,065,000	1974
Decatur, Ala. (Unit 2)	Tennessee Valley Authority	1,065,000	1975
Decatur, Ala. (Unit 3)	Tennessee Valley Authority	1,065,000	1977
Peach Bottom, Pa. (Unit 2)	Philadelphia Electric Co.	1,065,000	1974
Peach Bottom, Pa. (Unit 3)	Philadelphia Electric Co.	1,065,000	1974
Bridgman, Mich. (Unit 1)	Indiana & Michigan Electric Co.	1,054,000	1975
Berwick, Pa. (Unit 1)	Pennsylvania Power & Light	1,050,000	1983
Zion, Ill. (Unit 1)	Commonwealth Edison Co.	1,040,000	1973
Zion, Ill. (Unit 2)	Commonwealth Edison Co.	1,040,000	1974

Source: Nuclear Regulatory Commission.

Radiation Doses

Radiation doses were originally measured in *roentgens,* (r), a unit of exposure to X-ray or gamma-ray radiation in the air. The roentgen drew its name from Wilhelm Konrad Roentgen (1845–1923), who discovered X-rays in 1895 and who received the first Nobel Prize in physics in 1901.

Today, the *rad* (ra) is the unit commonly used for measuring the amount of radiation to which the whole body, as contrasted with a single organ, is exposed.

The *millirad* is one-thousandth of a rad. Most scientists believe that a dose of a few millirads is safe, but there is significant controversy over the threshold at which a dose becomes hazardous.

The *rem* (for "roentgen equivalent, man") is a measure of ionizing radiation of the type that produces the same damage to human beings as one roentgen of approximately 200 kilowatts of X-radiation.

Millirem is the term used to describe the amount of absorption of radiation by humans. The average American is exposed to 100–200 millirems of radiation per year from man-made and natural sources. A normal chest X-ray exposes one to 20–30 millirems.

Petroleum Imports by Country of Origin, 1975–1983

(thousand barrels per day)

Year	Saudi Arabia	Vene-zuela	Indo-nesia	Algeria	Nigeria	Total OPEC[1]	Canada	Mexico	United Kingdom	Virgin Islands
	Organization of Petroleum Exporting Countries (OPEC)									
1975	715	702	390	282	762	3,601	846	71	14	496
1976	1,230	700	539	432	1,025	5,066	599	87	31	510
1977	1,380	690	541	559	1,143	6,193	517	179	126	571
1978	1,144	645	573	649	919	5,751	467	318	180	522
1979	1,356	690	420	636	1,080	5,637	538	439	202	523
1980	1,261	481	348	488	857	4,300	455	533	176	476
1981	1,129	406	366	311	620	3,323	447	522	375	389
1982	552	412	248	170	514	2,146	482	685	456	366
1983[2]	336	414	335	235	294	1,832	542	822	381	323

1. Excludes petroleum imported into the U.S. indirectly from OPEC countries, primarily from Caribbean and West European refining areas, as petroleum products which were refined from crude oil produced in OPEC countries. 2. Preliminary. NOTE: Includes data for individual countries prior to their entrance into OPEC. Data include imports for Strategic Petroleum Reserve, which began in 1977. Sum of components may not equal total due to independent rounding. *Source:* 1975—U.S. Dept. of the Interior, Bureau of Mines; 1976 through 1983—U.S. Dept. of Energy, Energy Information Administration.

Production of Crude Petroleum by Countries

(in thousands of 42-gallon barrels)

Area and country	Est. 1984[1]	1983	Est. percent change
Western Hemisphere	5,911,175	5,899,130	0.9
Argentina	177,390	176,660	1.2
Bolivia	7,300	8,760	–16.7
Brazil	156,950	113,515	38.3
Canada	500,415	471,580	11.3
Chile	14,600	15,695	–7.0
Colombia	59,860	51,830	16.2
Ecuador	90,885	86,505	5.5
Guatemala	1,825	1,825	—
Mexico	993,165	968,710	3.9
Peru	66,065	60,590	8.4
Trinidad and Tabago	58,400	59,860	–2.4
United States	3,159,075	3,172,215	–0.5
Venezuela	625,245	711,385	–12.0
Western Europe	1,331,885	1,157,415	15.7
Austria	8,760	8,030	13.6
Denmark	11,315	13,140	–16.7
France	12,775	12,775	—
West Germany	29,200	29,565	–1.2
Greece	8,760	8,030	–9.1
Italy	16,425	15,695	4.7
Netherlands	22,265	16,790	30.4
Norway	244,550	210,605	11.6
Spain	22,265	17,520	25.0
Turkey	16,425	17,155	–4.3
United Kingdom	939,145	808,110	18.6
Middle East	4,353,355	3,808,045	11.9
Bahrain	15,330	15,330	—
Iran	820,155	971,995	–13.6
Iraq	384,345	292,000	25.0
Israel	365	365	—
Kuwait	336,165	263,165	38.7
Neutral Zone[2]	171,185	92,345	89.7
Oman	146,000	132,130	11.3
Qatar	143,445	83,585	48.5
Saudi Arabia	1,828,650	1,521,320	15.2
Syria	62,050	61,320	1.2
United Arab Emirates	445,665	374,490	11.1
Asia–Pacific	1,077,115	892,790	22.1
Australia	178,485	140,890	25.6
Brunei	58,400	56,575	3.2
Burma	10,950	10,950	—
India	171,550	146,000	17.5
Indonesia	501,145	385,075	33.6
Japan	2,920	3,285	–11.1
Malaysia	135,050	131,400	2.8
New Zealand	5,475	5,475	—
Pakistan	4,380	4,745	–7.7
Philippines	4,015	5,840	–31.3
Taiwan	1,095	1,095	—
Thailand	3,650	1,460	150.0
Africa	1,707,470	1,273,120	36.0
Algeria	238,345	238,345	—
Angola/Cabinda[3]	74,825	54,750	36.7
Cameroon	45,625	39,785	14.7
Congo	32,850	31,755	3.4
Egypt	264,260	242,725	10.5
Gabon	54,750	54,750	—
Ghana	730	730	—
Ivory Coast	9,855	6,935	42.1
Libya	401,500	274,845	46.1
Morocco	365	365	—
Nigeria	531,805	276,305	106.3
Tunisia	43,800	43,800	—
Zaire	8,760	8,030	13.6
Communist bloc	5,422,075	5,461,495	–0.6
China	802,270	761,025	5.4
Romania	93,075	87,600	6.3
U.S.S.R.	4,440,955	4,529,650	–1.8
Other communist	85,775	83,220	3.1
World total	19,803,075	18,491,995	7.1

1. Based on Jan.–Feb. average. 2. Shared by Kuwait and Saudi Arabia. 3. An enclave in West Africa on Atlantic coast between the Congo and Angola. *Source: Oil & Gas Journal,* May 7, 1984.

U.S. Energy Supply and Disposition

(in quadrillion BtUs)

Activity and fuel	1983[1]	1982	1981	1980	1975	1970	1965	1960
SUPPLY								
Production								
Crude Oil and Lease Condensate	18.32	18.31	18.15	18.25	17.73	20.40	16.52	14.93
Natural Gas Plant Liquids	2.20	2.19	2.31	2.27	2.37	2.51	1.88	1.46
Natural Gas[2]	16.34	18.25	19.70	19.70	19.64	21.67	15.78	12.66
Coal[3]	17.29	18.60	18.33	18.88	15.19	15.05	13.38	11.12
Nuclear Power	3.22	3.11	3.01	2.70	1.90	0.24	0.04	0.01
Hydropower	3.51	3.27	2.76	2.91	3.15	2.63	2.06	1.60
Other[4]	0.14	0.11	0.13	0.11	0.07	0.02	0.01	(Z)
Total Production	**61.02**	**63.85**	**64.38**	**64.82**	**60.06**	**62.51**	**49.67**	**41.78**
Imports								
Crude Oil[5]	7.02	7.42	9.34	11.06	8.72	2.81	2.65	2.20
Refined Petroleum Products[6]	3.48	3.36	3.30	3.38	4.23	4.66	2.75	1.80
Natural Gas	0.96	0.95	0.92	1.03	0.98	0.85	0.47	0.16
Other[7]	0.42	0.38	0.42	0.28	0.19	0.07	0.04	0.07
Total Imports	**11.88**	**12.11**	**13.98**	**15.75**	**14.11**	**8.39**	**5.92**	**4.23**
Adjustments[8]	1.28	−0.51	−0.08	−0.54	−1.08	−1.41	−0.74	−0.44
Total Supply	**74.18**	**75.45**	**78.27**	**80.03**	**73.09**	**69.49**	**54.85**	**45.57**
DISPOSITION								
Consumption								
Refined Petroleum Products[9]	29.98	30.23	31.93	34.25	32.73	29.52	23.25	19.92
Natural Gas[2]	17.43	18.51	19.93	20.44	19.95	21.79	15.77	12.39
Coal[5]	15.85	15.29	15.86	15.67	12.82	12.66	11.89	10.12
Nuclear Power	3.22	3.11	3.01	2.70	1.90	0.24	0.04	0.01
Hydropower[10]	3.86	3.59	3.11	3.13	3.22	2.65	2.06	1.65
Other	0.14	0.11	0.13	0.11	0.07	0.02	0.01	(Z)
Net Imports of Coal Coke	−0.02	−0.02	−0.02	−0.04	0.01	−0.06	−0.02	−0.01
Total Consumption	**70.45**	**70.82**	**73.94**	**76.27**	**70.71**	**66.83**	**52.99**	**44.08**
Exports								
Coal[3]	2.04	2.79	2.94	2.47	1.79	1.94	1.38	1.02
Other[11]	1.68	1.85	1.39	1.29	0.60	0.73	0.48	0.46
Total Exports	**3.72**	**4.63**	**4.33**	**3.76**	**2.39**	**2.66**	**1.86**	**1.48**
Total Disposition	**74.18**	**75.45**	**78.27**	**80.03**	**73.09**	**69.49**	**54.85**	**45.57**

1. Preliminary. 2. Dry natural gas. 3. Bituminous coal, subbituminous coal, lignite, and anthracite. 4. Geothermal, wood, refuse, and other vegetal fuels used for electricity generation at utilities. 5. Includes imports of crude oil for the Strategic Petroleum Reserve. 6. Includes imports of unfinished oils and natural gas plant liquids. 7. Includes bituminous coal, subbituminous coal, lignite, anthracite, coal coke, and hydropower. 8. A balancing item. Includes stock changes, losses, gains, misc. blending components, unaccounted for supply, and anthracite shipped overseas to U.S. Armed Forces. 9. Refined petroleum products supplied includes natural gas plant liquids and crude oil burned as fuel. 10. Includes industrial generation of hydropower and net electricity imports. 11. Includes crude oil, refined petroleum products, natural gas, coal coke, and hydropower. (Z)=Less than 0.005 quadrillion Btu. NOTE: Data do not include the consumption of wood-derived fuel (other than that consumed by the electric utility industry) which amounted to an estimated 2.2. quadrillion Btus in 1981. This table also excludes small quantities of other energy forms for which consistent historical data are not available, such as solar energy obtained by the use of thermal and photovoltaic collectors; wind energy; and geothermal, biomass, and waste energy other than that consumed at electric utilities. NOTE: Sum of components may not equal total due to independent rounding. *Source:* Energy Information Administration, *Annual Energy Review 1983.*

Beware of Underinflated Tires

Surveys show that up to 90% of the tires on the road are underinflated, many to the point of being not only wasteful of gas, but of being dangerous.

Improper air pressure not only cuts into gas mileage by about 5% but it also reduces the life of a tire because of heat build-up caused by too much sidewall flexing.

Some motorists try to guess the tire pressure by looking at the tires. That system won't work with radials, which have a natural appearance of being too low, so the car owner becomes accustomed to that look. But put one tire inflated to 24 pounds next to one with 16 pounds, a difference of one third, and the tires will look virtually the same. Therefore, it is important to check the air pressure with a gauge.

Comparing Energy Sources

(converting sources into Btu equivalents)

One British Thermal Unit (BTU) = the amount of heat needed to increase the temperature of one pound of water by 1° F. (252 calories).

	Btu (in thousands)
Bituminous Coal and Lignite	
Production, average/short ton	23,500.0
Consumption, average/short ton	22,800.0
Electricity generation/short ton	21,630.0
Anthracite, short ton	25,400.0
Crude petroleum, barrel (42 gallons)	5,800.0
Natural gas, dry, cubic foot	1.021
Nuclear power, kilowatt-hour	10.66
Hydropower[1] kilowatt-hour	10.38

1. Calculated from national average heat rates for fossil-fueled steam-electric plants.

Household Appliance Data, November 1982

(million households)

	Census region				Area type		Total	
	Northeast	North Central	South	West	Metropolitan	Non-metropolitan		
Appliance	**No.**	**No.**	**No.**	**No.**	**No.**	**No.**	**No.**	**%**
Electric Appliances								
Television set (color)	15.5	18.3	22.8	14.4	54.3	16.7	71.0	84.8
Television set (B/W)	8.9	10.6	13.7	5.8	29.6	9.3	38.9	46.5
Clothes washer (automatic)	11.9	14.5	20.2	11.4	42.4	15.5	57.9	69.1
Clothes washer (wringer)	0.5	1.0	0.9	0.1	1.5	1.0	2.5	3.0
Range (stove-top or burners)	7.6	11.9	16.5	8.7	31.8	12.9	44.7	53.3
Oven (not microwave)[1]	7.0	10.0	15.0	7.7	28.3	11.4	39.7	47.4
Microwave[1]	0.6	1.6	1.3	1.4	3.7	1.1	4.9	5.8
Clothes dryer	6.9	9.7	14.2	7.2	26.3	11.6	37.9	45.3
Separate freezer	5.0	9.1	12.0	4.9	19.9	11.1	31.0	37.0
Dishwasher	5.8	6.8	10.3	7.3	24.7	5.6	30.3	36.1
Humidifier	2.5	6.3	1.7	0.8	7.8	3.5	11.3	13.5
Dehumidifier	2.4	3.9	1.1	0.1	5.5	2.1	7.5	9.0
Window or ceiling fan	5.0	6.5	10.0	1.9	17.6	5.9	23.5	28.0
Whole house cooling fan	1.3	1.8	2.8	0.6	5.0	1.5	6.5	7.8
Evaporative cooler	—	0.1	0.6	2.8	3.0	0.6	3.6	4.2
Gas appliances								
Range (stove-top or burners)	10.3	9.6	11.4	7.7	31.5	7.6	39.0	46.6
Oven[1]	8.9	8.1	9.7	6.9	27.3	6.3	33.7	40.2
Clothes dryer	2.7	4.3	2.4	2.8	10.6	1.6	12.2	14.6
Outdoor piped gas grill	0.7	0.6	1.3	0.5	2.7	0.4	3.0	3.6
Outdoor LPG gas grill	2.4	1.5	1.8	0.7	4.9	1.5	6.4	7.7
Outdoor gas light	0.1	0.5	0.7	0.1	1.2	0.3	1.4	1.7
Swimming pool heater	—	0.1	—	0.1	0.3	—	0.3	0.4
Refrigerators								
One	15.2	17.6	25.1	14.5	54.6	17.8	72.4	86.4
Two or more	2.7	3.6	2.9	1.9	8.5	2.7	11.1	13.3
None	0.1	0.1	0.1	—	0.1	0.1	0.2	0.3
Air Conditioning (A/C)								
Central	2.1	5.9	11.8	3.5	19.2	4.1	23.3	27.8
Individual room units	7.2	6.4	9.5	2.2	19.3	6.0	25.3	30.2
None	8.6	9.0	6.8	10.7	24.7	10.4	35.1	41.9
Total households	**18.0**	**21.3**	**28.1**	**16.5**	**63.2**	**20.6**	**83.8**	**100.0**

1. Data are for the most used oven. NOTE: A dash represents less than 0.05 million households. NOTE: Sum of components may not equal total due to independent rounding. *Source:* Energy Information Administration, Form EIA-457, "The Residential Energy Consumption Survey."

Annual Cost of Fuel

(Based on driving 10,000 miles per year)

	Price Per Gallon						
MPG	**$1.60**	**$1.70**	**$1.80**	**$1.90**	**$2.00**	**$2.10**	**$2.20**
50	320	340	360	380	400	420	440
45	355	377	400	422	444	466	488
40	400	425	450	475	500	525	550
35	458	486	515	543	572	601	629
30	533	566	599	633	666	699	733
25	640	680	720	760	800	840	880
20	800	850	900	950	1,000	1,050	1,100
15	1,067	1,134	1,201	1,267	1,334	1,401	1,467
10	1,600	1,700	1,800	1,900	2,000	2,100	2,200

GREAT DISASTERS

(For later disasters, see Current Events of 1984)

Earthquakes and Volcanic Eruptions

A.D. 79 Aug. 24, Italy: eruption of Mt. Vesuvius buried cities of Pompeii and Herculaneum, killing thousands.

1556 Jan. 24, Shaanxi (Shensi) Province, China: most deadly earthquake in history; 830,000 killed.

1755 Nov. 1, Portugal: one of the most severe of recorded earthquakes leveled Lisbon and was felt as far away as southern France and North Africa; 10,000–20,000 killed in Lisbon.

1883 Aug. 26–28, Netherlands Indies: eruption of Krakatau; violent explosions destroyed two thirds of island. Sea waves occurred as far away as Cape Horn, and possibly England. Estimated 36,000 dead.

1902 May 8, Martinique, West Indies: Mt. Pelée erupted and wiped out city of St. Pierre; 40,000 dead.

1906 April 18, San Francisco: earthquake accompanied by fire razed more than 4 sq mi.; more than 500 dead or missing; property damage about $250–300 million.

1908 Dec. 28, Messina, Sicily: about 85,000 killed and city totally destroyed.

1915 Jan. 13, Avezzano, Italy: earthquake left 29,980 dead.

1920 Dec. 16, Gansu (Kansu) Province, China: earthquake killed 200,000.

1923 Sept. 1, Japan: earthquake destroyed third of Tokyo and most of Yokohama; more than 140,000 killed.

1933 March 10, Long Beach, Calif.: 117 left dead by earthquake.

1935 May 31, India: earthquake at Quetta killed an estimated 50,000.

1939 Jan. 24, Chile: earthquake razed 50,000 sq mi.; about 30,000 killed.

Dec. 27, Northern Turkey: severe quakes destroyed city of Erzingan; about 100,000 casualties.

1946 April 1, Alaska, Hawaii, West Coast: earthquake and tsunami (tidal wave) left 173 dead in Hawaii.

1950 Aug. 15, India: earthquake affected 30,000 sq mi. in Assam; 20,000–30,000 believed killed.

1963 July 26, Skoplje, Yugoslavia: four fifths of city destroyed; 1,011 dead, 3,350 injured.

1964 March 27, Alaska: strongest earthquake ever to strike North America hit 80 miles east of Anchorage; followed by seismic wave 50 feet high that traveled 8,445 miles at 450 miles per hour; 117 killed and damage in Alaska and West Coast $500–750 million.

1970 May 31, Peru: earthquake left 50,000 dead, 17,000 missing.

1971 Feb. 9, Los Angeles: earthquake rocked San Fernando Valley. Death toll 64; damage $1 billion.

1972 April 10, Iran: 5,000 killed in earthquake 600 miles south of Teheran.

Dec. 22, Managua, Nicaragua: earthquake devastated city, leaving up to 6,000 dead.

1976 Feb. 4, Guatemala: earthquake left over 23,000 dead.

July 28, Tangshan, China: earthquake devastated 20-sq-mi. area of city leaving estimated 242,000 dead.

Aug. 17, Mindanao, Philippines: earthquake and tidal wave left up to 8,000 dead or missing.

1977 March 4, Bucharest: earthquake razed most of downtown Bucharest; 1,541 reported dead, over 11,000 injured.

1978 Sept. 16, Tabas, Iran: earthquake destroyed city in eastern Iran, leaving 25,000 dead.

1980 Nov. 23, Naples, Italy: 2,735 killed when earthquake struck southern Italy.

1982 Dec. 13, Yemen: 2,800 reported dead in earthquake.

Floods, Avalanches, and Tidal Waves

1228 Holland: 100,000 persons reputedly drowned by sea flood in Friesland.

1642 China: rebels destroyed Kaifeng seawall; 300,000 drowned.

1889 May 31, Johnstown, Pa.: more than 2,200 died in flood.

1896 June 15, Sanriku, Japan: earthquake and tidal wave killed 27,000.

1928 March 12, Santa Paula, Calif.: collapse of St. Francis Dam left 450 dead.

1953 Northwest Europe: storm followed by floods devastated North Sea coastal areas. Netherlands was hardest hit with 1,794 dead.

1959 Dec. 2, Frejus, France: flood caused by collapse of Malpasset Dam left 412 dead.

1960 Agadir, Morocco: 10,000–12,000 dead as earthquake set off tidal wave and fire, destroying most of city.

1962 Jan. 10, Peru: avalanche down Huascaran, extinct Andean volcano, killed more than 3,000 persons.

1963 Oct. 9, Italy: landslide into the Vaiont Dam; flood killed about 2,000.

1966 Oct. 21, Aberfan, Wales: avalanche of coal, waste, mud, and rocks killed 144 persons, including 116 children in school.

1969 Jan. 18–26, Southern California: floods and mudslides from heavy rains caused widespread property damage; at least 100 dead. Another downpour (Feb. 23–26) caused further floods and mudslides; at least 18 dead.

1970 Nov. 13, East Pakistan: 200,000 killed by cyclone-driven tidal wave from Bay of Bengal. Over 100,000 missing.

1971 Sept. 29, Orissa State, India: cyclone and tidal wave off Bay of Bengal killed as many as 10,000.

1972 Feb. 26, Man, W. Va.: more than 118 died when slag-pile dam collapsed under pressure of torrential rains and flooded 17-mile valley.

June 9–10, Rapid City, S.D.: flash flood caused 237 deaths and $160 million in damage.

June 20, Eastern Seaboard: tropical storm Agnes, in 10-day rampage, caused widespread flash floods. Death toll was 129, 115,000 were left homeless, and damage estimated at $3.5 billion.

1976 Aug. 1, Loveland, Colo.: Flash flood along Route 34 in Big Thompson Canyon left 139 dead.

1977 **Nov. 6, Toccoa, Ga.:** rupture of Kelly Barnes Dam left 39 dead.
Nov. 19, Andhra Pradesh State, India: cyclone and flood from Bay of Bengal left 7,000–10,000 dead.

Storms and Weather

(For U.S. tornadoes and hurricanes, see Index)

1864 **Oct. 5, India:** most of Calcutta denuded by cyclone; 70,000 killed.
1930 **Sept. 3. Santo Domingo:** hurricane killed about 2,000 and injured 6,000.
1934 **Sept. 21, Japan:** hurricane killed more than 4,000 on Honshu.
1942 **Oct. 16, India:** cyclone devastated Bengal; about 40,000 lives lost.
1963 **May 28–29, East Pakistan:** cyclone killed about 22,000 along coast.
Oct. 2–7, Caribbean: Hurricane Flora killed up to 7,000 in Haiti and Cuba.
1965 **May 11–12 and June 1–2, East Pakistan:** cyclones killed about 47,000.
Dec. 15, Karachi, Pakistan: cyclone killed about 10,000.
1974 **Sept. 20, Honduras:** Hurricane Fifi struck northern section of country, leaving 8,000 dead, 100,000 homeless.
Dec. 25, Darwin, Australia: cyclone destroyed nearly the entire city, causing mass evacuation.
1977 **Nov. 19, India:** cyclone struck state of Andhra Pradesh, killing 10,000.

Fires and Explosions

1666 **Sept. 2, England:** "Great Fire of London" destroyed St. Paul's Church, etc. Damage £10 million.
1835 **Dec. 16, New York City:** 530 buildings destroyed by fire.
1871 **Oct. 8, Chicago:** the "Chicago Fire" burned 17,450 buildings, killed 250 persons; $196 million damage.
Oct. 8, Peshtigo, Wis.: 1,152 lives lost; 2 billion trees burned.
1872 **Nov. 9, Boston:** fire destroyed 800 buildings; $75-million damage.
1876 **Dec. 5, New York City:** fire in Brooklyn Theater killed more than 300.
1881 **Dec. 8, Vienna:** at least 620 died in fire at Ring Theatre.
1894 **Sept. 1, Minnesota:** forest fire over 480-square-mile area destroyed six towns and killed 480 people.
1900 **May 1, Scofield, Utah:** explosion of blasting powder in coal mine killed 200.
June 30, Hoboken, N.J.: piers of North German Lloyd Steamship line burned; 326 dead.
1903 **Dec. 30, Chicago:** Iroquois Theatre fire killed 602.
1904 **Feb. 7, Baltimore:** business section burned; estimated $125-million damage.
1906 **March 10, France:** explosion in coal mine in Courrières killed 1,060.
1907 **Dec. 6, Monongha, W. Va.:** coal mine explosion killed 361.
Dec. 19, Jacobs Creek, Pa.: explosion in coal mine left 239 dead.
1909 **Nov. 13, Cherry, Ill.:** explosion in coal mine killed 259.
1911 **March 25, New York City:** fire in Triangle Shirtwaist Factory fatal to 145.
1913 **Oct. 22, Dawson, N.M.:** coal mine explosion left 263 dead.
1917 **April 10, Eddystone, Pa.:** explosion in munitions plant killed 133.
Dec. 6, Canada: explosion and fire at Halifax when ammunition ship collided with a vessel; 1,500 dead.
1930 **April 21, Columbus, Ohio:** fire in Ohio State Penitentiary killed 320 convicts.
1937 **March 18, New London, Tex.:** explosion destroyed schoolhouse; 294 killed.
1942 **April 26, Manchuria:** explosion in Honkeiko Colliery killed 1,549.
Nov. 28, Boston: Cocoanut Grove nightclub fire killed 491.
1943 **Sept. 7, Houston:** fire in Gulf Hotel left 55 dead.
1944 **July 6, Hartford, Conn.:** fire and ensuing stampede in main tent of Ringling Brothers Circus killed 168, injured 487.
July 17, Port Chicago, Calif.: 322 killed as ammunition ships explode.
Oct. 20, Cleveland: liquid-gas tanks exploded, killing 130.
1946 **June 5, Chicago:** fire in La Salle hotel fatal to 61.
Dec. 7, Atlanta: fire in Winecoff Hotel killed 119.
1947 **April 16–18, Texas City, Tex.:** most of city destroyed, 561 dead following explosion on ship.
1949 **Sept. 2, China:** fire on Chongqing (Chungking) waterfront killed 1,700.
1953 **Oct. 16, Boston:** explosion and fire aboard U.S.S. *Leyte* killed 37.
1954 **May 26, off Quonset Point, R.I.:** explosion and fire aboard aircraft *Bennington* killed 103 crewmen.
1956 **Aug. 7, Colombia:** about 1,100 reported killed when seven army ammunition trucks exploded at Cali.
Aug. 8, Belgium: 262 died in coal mine fire at Marcinelle.
1958 **Dec. 1, Chicago:** fire at Our Lady of the Angeles school killed 95.
1960 **Jan. 21, Coalbrook, South Africa:** coal mine explosion killed 437.
Nov. 13, Syria: 152 children killed in moviehouse fire.
Dec. 19. Brooklyn, N.Y.: blaze on aircraft carrier *Constellation* killed 49 workmen.
1961 **Dec. 17, Niteroi, Brazil:** circus fire fatal to 323.
1962 **Feb. 7, Saarland, West Germany:** coal mine gas explosion killed 298.
1963 **Nov. 9, Japan:** explosion in coal mine at Omuta killed 447.
1965 **May 28, India:** coal mine fire in state of Bihar killed 375.
June 1, near Fukuoka, Japan: coal mine explosion killed 236.
1966 **Oct. 26, off South Vietnam:** fire on U.S. carrier *Oriskany* killed 43.
1967 **May 22, Brussels:** fire in L'Innovation, major department store, left 322 dead.
July 29, off North Vietnam: fire on U.S. carrier *Forrestal* killed 134.
1969 **Jan. 14, Pearl Harbor, Hawaii:** nuclear aircraft carrier *Enterprise* ripped by explosions; 27 dead, 82 injured.
April 6, New Orleans: Taiwanese freighter and string of oil-loaded barges collided in fiery explosion on Mississippi River; 25 dead.
1970 **Nov. 1, Saint-Laurent-du-Pont, France:** fire in dance hall killed 146 young people.
Dec. 30, Wooten, Ky.: coal-dust explosion in coal mine killed 38.
1972 **May 2, Kellogg, Idaho:** fire in Sunshine silver mine

killed 91 miners; two men survived.

May 13, Osaka, Japan: 118 people died in fire in nightclub on top floor of Sennichi department store.

June 6, Wankie, Rhodesia: explosion in coal mine killed 427.

1973 **Nov. 29, Kumamoto, Japan:** fire in Taiyo department store killed 101.

1974 **Feb. 1, Sao Paulo, Brazil:** fire in upper stories of bank building killed 189 persons, many of whom leaped to death.

1975 **Dec. 27, Dhanbad, India:** explosion in coal mine followed by flooding from nearby reservoir left 372 dead.

1977 **Feb. 25, Moscow:** fire in 6,000-bed Hotel Rossiya fatal to at least 45 guests.

May 28, Southgate, Ky.: fire in Beverly Hills Supper Club; 167 dead.

June 26, Columbia, Tenn.: fire believed set by inmate was fatal to 42 prisoners and visitors at Maury County Jail.

Dec. 22, Westwego, La.: explosion destroyed Continental Grain Company plant, killing 36.

1978 **July 11, Tarragona, Spain:** 140 killed at coastal campsite when tank truck carrying liquid gas overturned and exploded.

Aug. 20, Abadan, Iran: nearly 400 killed when arsonists set fire to crowded theater.

1979 **July 12, Saragossa, Spain:** fire in 10-story Hotel Corona de Aragon killed more than 72 guests when a pastry machine exploded.

Dec. 31, Chapais, Quebec, Canada: fire at Opemiska Club fatal to 45 New Year's Eve partygoers.

1980 **Oct. 23, Ortuella, Spain:** explosion leveled elementary school, killing 48, nearly all of them children.

Nov. 21, Las Vegas, Nev.: fire in MGM Grand Hotel left 84 dead.

Dec. 4, Harrison, N.Y.: fire in a Stouffer's Inn conference center fatal to 26, most of them corporation executives.

1982 **Dec. 18–21,** Caracas, Venezuela: power-plant fire leaves 128 dead.

Shipwrecks

1833 **May 11, *Lady of the Lake:*** bound from England to Quebec, struck iceberg; 215 perished.

1853 **Sept. 29 *Annie Jane:*** emigrant vessel off coast of Scotland; 348 died.

1865 **April 27, *Sultana:*** boiler explosion on Mississippi River steamboat near Memphis, 1,547 killed.

1898 **Nov. 26, *City of Portland:*** Loss of 157 off Cape Cod.

1904 **June 15, *General Slocum:*** excursion steamer burned in East River, New York; 1,021 perished.

1912 **March 5, *Principe de Asturias:*** Spanish steamer struck rock off Sebastien Point; 500 drowned.

April 15, *Titanic:* sank after colliding with iceberg; 1,513 died.

1914 **May 29, *Empress of Ireland:*** sank after collision in St. Lawrence River; 1,024 perished.

1915 **July 24, *Eastland:*** Great Lakes excursion steamer overturned in Chicago River; 812 died.

1928 **Nov. 12, *Vestris:*** British steamer sank in gale off Virginia; 110 died.

1931 **June 14:** French excursion steamer overturned in gale off St. Nazaire; approximately 450 died.

1934 **Sept. 8, *Morro Castle:*** 134 killed in fire off Asbury Park, N.J.

1939 **May 23, *Squalus:*** submarine with 59 men sank off Hampton Beach, N.H.; 33 saved.

June 1, Submarine *Thetis:* sank in Liverpool Bay, England; 99 perished.

1942 **Oct. 2, *Queen Mary:*** rammed and sank a British cruiser; 338 aboard the cruiser died.

1945 **April 9:** U.S. ship, loaded with aerial bombs, exploded at Bari, Italy; at least 360 killed.

1948 **Dec. 3, *Kiangya:*** Chinese refugee ship wrecked in explosion; about 1,000 believed dead.

1949 **Sept. 17, *Noronic:*** Canadian Great Lakes cruise ship burned at Toronto dock; about 130 died.

1951 **April 16, *Affray:*** British submarine sank in English Channel; 75 dead.

1952 **April 26, *Hobson:*** minesweeper collided with aircraft carrier *Wasp* and sank during night maneuvers in mid-Atlantic; 176 persons lost.

1953 **Jan. 9, *Chang Tyong-Ho:*** South Korean ferry foundered off Pusan; 249 reported dead.

Jan. 31, *Princess Victoria:* British ferry sank in Irish Sea; 133 lost.

1956 **July 25, *Andrea Doria:*** Italian liner collided with Swedish liner *Stockholm* off Nantucket Island, Mass., sinking next day; 52, mostly passengers on Italian ship, dead or unaccounted for; over 1,600 rescued.

1962 **April 8, *Dara,*** British liner, exploded and sank in Persian Gulf; 236 persons dead. Caused by time bomb.

1963 **April 10, *Thresher:*** atomic-powered submarine sank in North Atlantic; 129 dead.

May 4: U.A.R. ferry capsized and sank in upper Nile; over 200 died.

1965 **Nov. 13, *Yarmouth Castle:*** cruise ship burned and sank 60 miles northeast of Nassau en route from Miami to Bahamas; 90 dead.

1968 **Late May, *Scorpion:*** nuclear submarine sank in Atlantic 400 miles S.W. of Azores; 99 dead. (Located Oct. 31.)

1970 **Dec. 15:** ferry in Korean Strait capsized; 261 lost.

1976 **Oct. 20, Luling, La.: *George Prince,*** Mississippi River ferry, rammed by Norwegian tanker *Frosta;* 77 dead.

1983 **May 25, *10th of Ramadan,*** Nile steamer, caught fire and sank in Lake Nasser, near Aswan, Egypt; 272 dead and 75 missing.

Aircraft Accidents

1921 **Aug. 24, England:** *AR-2* British dirigible, broke in two on trial trip near Hull; 62 died.

1925 **Sept. 3, Caldwell, Ohio:** U.S. dirigible *Shenandoah* broke apart; 14 dead.

1930 **Oct. 5, Beauvais, France:** British dirigible R 101 crashed, killing 47.

1933 **April 4, New Jersey Coast:** U.S. dirigible *Akron* crashed; 73 died.

1937 **May 6, Lakehurst, N.J.:** German zeppelin *Hindenburg* destroyed by fire at tower mooring; 36 killed.

1945 **July 28, New York City:** U.S. Army bomber crashed into Empire State Building; 13 dead.

1946 **May 20, New York City:** U.S. Army plane crashed into Manhattan Company building; five dead.

1949 **Nov. 1, Washington, D.C.:** fighter plane rammed airliner, killing 55.

1951 **Dec. 16, Elizabeth, N.J.:** nonscheduled airliner crash killed 56.

1952 **Jan. 22, Elizabeth, N.J.:** 29 killed, including former Secretary of War Robert P. Patterson, when airliner hit apartments; seven of dead were on ground.

Feb. 11, Elizabeth, N.J.: third major air disaster in Elizabeth within two months fatally injured 33.

1953 **June 18, near Tokyo:** crash of U.S. Air Force "Globemaster" killed 129 servicemen.
1955 **Nov. 1, near Longmont, Colo.:** time bomb hidden in luggage destroyed airliner in flight, killing 44.
1956 **June 30, Grand Canyon, Ariz.:** 128 died in collision of TWA Super Constellation and United Airlines DC-7.
1957 **March 17, near Cebu City, Philippines:** President Ramón Magsaysay and 24 others killed in crash.
1959 **Feb. 3, New York City:** American Airlines Lockheed Electra turboprop plane crashed in East River; 65 dead.
1960 **Feb. 25, Rio de Janeiro:** U.S. Navy plane, flying Navy musicians to perform at dinner given by visiting President Eisenhower, collided with Brazilian airliner, killing 61.
Dec. 16, New York City: United and Trans World planes collided in fog, crashed in two boroughs, killing 134 in air and on ground.
1961 **Feb. 15, near Brussels:** 72 on board and farmer on ground killed in crash of Sabena plane; U.S. figure skating team wiped out.
1962 **March 1, New York City:** American Airlines jetliner crashed into Jamaica Bay, near Idlewild Airport, killing all 95 on board.
June 3, Paris: chartered Air France Boeing Jet 707 crashed at Orly Airport; 130 dead.
1965 **Feb. 8, New York City:** Eastern Airlines DC-7B went down in Atlantic shortly after take-off from Kennedy International Airport; 84 dead.
1966 **March 5, Japan:** British airliner caught fire and crashed into Mt. Fuji; 124 dead.
Dec. 24, Binh Thai, South Vietnam: crash of military-chartered plane into village killed 129.
1967 **April 20, Nicosia, Cyprus:** crash of chartered Swiss Turboprop killed 126.
July 19, near Hendersonville, N.C.: Piedmont Airlines Boeing 727 collided with private plane; 82 dead.
1968 **May 3, near Dawson, Tex.:** Braniff airliner crashed; 85 dead.
1969 **March 16, Maracaibo, Venezuela:** Venezuelan jetliner crashed and exploded; 84 crew members and passengers died and 71 were killed on ground.
Sept. 9, Shelbyville, Ind.: Allegheny Airlines jetliner and single-engine plane flown by student pilot collided in air and crashed; 83 dead.
1970 **Feb. 15, Santo Domingo, Dominican Republic:** Dominican Republic jetliner plunged into Caribbean on takeoff; 102 dead.
July 4, Arbucias, Spain: British Comet crashed into mountains while coming in for landing at Barcelona; 112 dead.
July 5, Toronto: Canadian jetliner crashed on landing approach; 109 dead.
Aug. 9, Cuzco, Peru: Peruvian turboprop, with 51 teen-age U.S. students among passengers, crashed shortly after takeoff; 99 dead.
Nov. 14, Huntington, W. Va.: chartered plane carrying 43 players and coaches of Marshall University football team crashed; 75 dead.
1971 **June 6, near Los Angeles:** Air West DC-9 and Navy F-4 fighter collided over San Gabriel Canyon; 49 killed; one Navy crewman parachuted to safety.
July 30, Morioka, Japan: Japanese Boeing 727 and F-86 figher collided in mid-air; toll was 162.
Sept. 4, near Juneau, Alaska: Alaska Airlines Boeing 727 crashed into Chilkoot Mountains; 111 killed.
1972 **June 18, London:** B.E.A. Trident jetliner plunged into field minutes after take-off from Heathrow Airport; all 118 aboard dead.
Aug. 14, East Berlin, East Germany: Soviet-built East German Ilyushin plane crashed, killing 156.
Dec. 3, Santa Cruz de Tenerife, Canary Islands: Spanish charter jet carrying West German tourists crashed on take-off; all 155 aboard killed.
Dec. 30, Miami, Fla.: Eastern Airlines Lockheed 1011 TriStar Jumbo jet crashed into Everglades; 101 killed, 75 survived.
1973 **Jan. 22, Kano, Nigeria:** 171 Nigerian Moslems returning from Mecca and five crewmen died in crash.
April 10, Hochwald, Switzerland: British airliner carrying tourists to Swiss fair crashed in blizzard; 106 dead.
July 11, Paris: Boeing 707 of Varig Airlines, en route to Rio de Janeiro, crashed near airport, killing 122 of 134 passengers.
July 31, Boston: Delta Airlines jet crashed in heavy fog in landing at Logan International Airport killing 88 of 89 aboard.
1974 **Jan. 31, Pago Pago, Samoa:** Pan American 707 crashed while landing; 97 of 101 persons aboard killed.
March 3, Paris: Turkish DC-10 jumbo jet crashed in forest shortly after take-off; all 346 passengers and crew killed in worst single-plane disaster to date.
Dec. 1, Berryville, Va.: all 92 aboard killed in crash of TWA 727 into wooded area.
Dec. 4, Colombo, Sri Lanka: Dutch DC-8 carrying Moslems to Mecca crashed on landing approach, killing all 191 persons aboard.
1975 **April 4, near Saigon, Vietnam:** Air Force Galaxy C-5A crashed after take-off, killing 172, mostly Vietnamese children.
June 24, New York City: Eastern Airlines Boeing 727, arriving from New Orleans, crashed at Kennedy International Airport, killing 113.
Aug. 3, Agadir, Morocco: Chartered Boeing 707, returning Moroccan workers home after vacation in France, plunged into mountainside; all 188 aboard killed.
Aug. 20, Damascus, Syria: Czech airliner crashed while landing, killing 126 of 128 persons aboard.
1976 **Sept. 10, Zagreb, Yugoslavia:** midair collision between British Airways Trident and Yugoslav charter DC-9 fatal to all 176 persons aboard; worst mid-air collision on record.
1977 **March 27, Santa Cruz de Tenerife, Canary Islands:** Pan American and KLM Boeing 747s collided on runway. All 249 on KLM plane and 333 of 394 aboard Pan Am jet killed. Total of 582 is highest for any type of aviation disaster.
1978 **Jan. 1, Bombay:** Air India 747 with 213 aboard exploded and plunged into sea minutes after takeoff.
Sept. 25, San Diego, Calif.: Pacific Southwest plane collided in midair with Cessna. All 135 on airliner, 2 in Cessna, and 7 on ground killed for total of 144.
Nov. 15, Colombo, Sri Lanka: Chartered Icelandic Airlines DC-8, carrying 249 Moslem pilgrims from Mecca, crashed in thunderstorm during landing approach; 183 killed.
1979 **May 25, Chicago:** American Airlines DC-10 lost left engine upon take-off and crashed seconds later, killing all 272 persons aboard and three on the ground in worst U.S. air disaster.
Aug. 15, Ukraine, U.S.S.R.: Two planes collided in mid-air; 150 killed.

Oct. 15, Mexico City: Western Airlines DC-10 crashed on landing, killing 73.

Nov. 26, Jidda, Saudi Arabia: Pakistan International Airlines 707 carrying pilgrims returning from Mecca crashed on take-off; all 156 aboard killed.

Nov. 28, Mt. Erebus, Antarctica: Air New Zealand DC-10 crashed on sightseeing flight; 257 killed.

1980 Jan. 21, near Laskgarak, Iran: Iran Air Boeing 727 crashed into mountains, killing all 128 aboard.

March 14, Warsaw: LOT Polish Airlines Ilyushin 62 crashed while attempting landing; 22 boxers and officials of a U.S. amateur boxing team killed along with 65 others.

April 25, Santa Cruz de Tenerife, Canary Islands: Chartered Boeing 727 carrying 138 British vacationers and crew of 8 crashed into mountain while approaching for landing; all killed.

Aug. 19, Riyadh, Saudi Arabia: all 301 aboard Saudi Arabian jet killed when burning plane made safe landing but passengers were unable to escape.

1981 Dec. 1, Ajaccio, Corsica: Yugoslav DC-9 Super 80 carrying tourists crashed into mountain on landing approach, killing all 178 aboard.

1982 July 9, Kenner, La.: Pan Am 727 crashed minutes after take-off from New Orleans, killing all 145 on board and 9 on ground.

1983 June 28, near Cuenca, Ecuador, Ecuadorean jetliner crashed in mountains, killing 119.

Aug. 30, near island of Sakhalin off Siberia, South Korean civlian jetliner shot shown by Soviet fighter after it strayed off course into Soviet airspace. All 269 people aboard killed.

Railroad Accidents

1904 Aug. 7, Eden, Colo.: Two-train collision killed 96.

1910 March 1, Wellington, Wash.: two trains swept into canyon by avalanche; 96 dead.

1915 May 22, Gretna, Scotland: two passenger trains and troop train collided; 227 killed.

1917 Dec. 12, Modane, France: nearly 550 killed in derailment of troop train near mouth of Mt. Cenis tunnel.

1918 Nov. 1, New York City: derailment of subway train in Malbone St. tunnel in Brooklyn left 92 dead.

1939 Dec. 22, near Magdeburg, Germany: more than 125 killed in collision; 99 killed in another wreck near Friedrichshafen.

1943 Dec. 16, near Rennert, N.C.: 72 killed in derailment and collision of two Atlantic Coast Line trains.

1944 March 2, near Salerno, Italy: 521 suffocated when Italian train stalled in tunnel.

Dec. 31, near Ogden, Utah: 48 killed in collision of two sections of Southern Pacific's Pacific Limited.

1946 April 25, Naperville, Ill.: at least 47 killed in collision of two trains of Burlington Railroad.

1949 Oct. 22, near Nowy Dwor, Poland: more than 200 reported killed in derailment of Danzig-Warsaw express.

1950 Feb. 17, Rockville Centre, N.Y.: head-on crash of two Long Island Rail Road commuter trains killed 30.

Nov. 22, Richmond Hill, N.Y.: 79 died when one Long Island Rail Road communter train crashed into rear of another.

1951 Feb. 6, Woodbridge, N.J.: 85 died when Pennsylvania Railroad commuter train plunged through temporary overpass.

1952 Oct. 8, Harrow-Wealdstone, England: two express trains crashed into commuter train; 112 dead.

1953 Dec. 24, near Sakvice, Czechoslovakia: two trains crashed; over 100 dead.

1957 Sept. 1, near Kendal, Jamaica: about 175 killed when train plunged into ravine.

Sept. 29, near Montgomery, West Pakistan: express train crashed into standing oil train; nearly 300 killed.

Dec. 4, St. John's, England: 92 killed, 187 injured as one commuter train crashed into another in fog.

1958 Sept. 15, near Bayonne, N.J.: over 40 killed when Central Railroad of New Jersey train went through open drawbridge.

1960 Nov. 14, Pardubice, Czechoslovakia: two trains collided; 110 dead, 106 injured.

1962 May 3, near Tokyo: 163 killed and 400 injured when train crashed into wreckage of collision between inbound freight train and outbound commuter train.

1963 Nov. 9, near Yokohama, Japan: two passenger trains crashed into derailed freight, killing 162.

1964 July 26, Custoias, Portugal: passenger train derailed; 94 dead.

1970 Feb. 4, near Buenos Aires:236 killed when express train crashed into standing commuter train.

1972 July 21, Seville, Spain: head-on crash of two passenger trains killed 76.

Oct. 6, near Saltillo, Mexico: train carrying religious pilgrims derailed and caught fire, killing 204 and injuring over 1,000.

Oct. 30, Chicago: two Illinois Central commuter trains collided during morning rush hour; 45 dead and over 200 injured.

1974 Aug. 30, Zagreb, Yugoslavia: train entering station derailed, killing 153 and injuring over 60.

1977 Feb. 4, Chicago: 11 killed and over 180 injured when elevated train hit rear of another, sending two cars to street.

1982 Jan. 26, Algeria: Derailment on Algeirs—Oran line leaves up to 120 dead.

1982 July 11, Tepic, Mexico: Nogales-Guadalajara train plunges down mountain gorge killing 120.

Miscellaneous

1955 June 11, Le Mans, France: Racing car in Grand Prix hurtled into grandstand, killing 82 spectators.

1978 April 27, St. Mary's, W. Va.: Scaffolding in powerplant cooling tower under construction collapsed; killing 57 workmen.

Aug. 4, Lac d'Argent, Quebec: Bus carrying handicapped theatergoers plunged into lake, killing 40.

1980 Jan. 20, Sincolejo, Colombia: Bleachers at a bullring collapsed, leaving 222 dead.

March 30, Stavanger, Norway: Floating hotel in North Sea collapsed, killing 123 oil workers.

May 9, St. Petersburg, Fla.: *Summit Venture,* 606-foot phosphate carrier, struck Sunshine Skyway Bridge in blinding rain squall; 1,300-foot section of roadway fell into Tampa Bay, taking with it several passenger cars and a Greyhound bus; 35 killed.

1981 July 18, Kansas City, Mo.: suspended walkway in Hyatt Regency Hotel collapses; 113 dead, 186 injured.

1982 Feb. 15, off St. John's, Newfoundland: Ocean Ranger, oil-drilling rig, capsizes and sinks in storm 200 miles at sea; 84 lost.

GEOGRAPHY

World Geography

Explorations and Discoveries

(All years are A.D. unless B.C. is specified.)

Country or place	Event	Explorer or discoverer	Date
AFRICA			
Sierra Leone	Visited	Hanno, Carthaginian seaman	c. 520 B.C.
Congo River	Mouth discovered	Diogo Cão, Portuguese	c. 1484
Cape of Good Hope	Rounded	Bartolomeu Diaz, Portuguese	1488
Gambia River	Explored	Mungo Park, Scottish explorer	1795
Sahara	Crossed	Dixon Denham and Hugh Clapperton, English explorers	1822–23
Zambezi River	Discovered	David Livingstone, Scottish explorer	1851
Sudan	Explored	Heinrich Barth, German explorer	1852–55
Victoria Falls	Discovered	Livingstone	1855
Lake Tanganyika	Discovered	Richard Burton and John Speke, British explorers	1858
Congo River	Traced	Sir Henry M. Stanley, British explorer	1877
ASIA			
Punjab (India)	Visited	Alexander the Great	327 B.C.
China	Visited	Marco Polo, Italian traveler	c. 1272
Tibet	Visited	Odoric of Pordenone, Italian monk	c. 1325
Southern China	Explored	Niccolò dei Conti, Venetian traveler	c. 1440
India	Visited (Cape route)	Vasco da Gama, Portuguese navigator	1498
Japan	Visited	St. Francis Xavier of Spain	1549
Arabia	Explored	Carsten Niebuhr, German explorer	1762
China	Explored	Ferdinand Richthofen, German scientist	1868
Mongolia	Explored	Nikolai M. Przhevalsky, Russian explorer	1870–73
Central Asia	Explored	Sven Hedin, Swedish scientist	1890–1908
EUROPE			
Shetland Islands	Visited	Pytheas of Massilia (Marseille)	c. 325 B.C.
North Cape	Rounded	Ottar, Norwegian explorer	c. 870
Iceland	Colonized	Norwegian noblemen	c. 890–900
NORTH AMERICA			
Greenland	Colonized	Eric the Red, Norwegian	c. 985
Labrador; Nova Scotia (?)	Discovered	Leif Ericson, Norse explorer	1000
West Indies	Discovered	Christopher Columbus, Italian	1492
North America	Coast discovered	Giovanni Caboto (John Cabot), for British	1497
Pacific Ocean	Discovered	Vasco Núñez de Balboa, Spanish explorer	1513
Florida	Explored	Ponce de León, Spanish explorer	1513
Mexico	Conquered	Hernando Cortés, Spanish adventurer	1519–21
St. Lawrence River	Discovered	Jacques Cartier, French navigator	1534
Southwest U. S.	Explored	Francisco Coronado, Spanish explorer	1540–42
Colorado River	Discovered	Hernando de Alarcón, Spanish explorer	1540
Mississippi River	Discovered	Hernando de Soto, Spanish explorer	1541
Frobisher Bay	Discovered	Martin Frobisher, English seaman	1576

Country or place	Event	Explorer or discover	Date
Maine Coast	Explored	Samuel de Champlain, French explorer	1604
Jamestown, Va.	Settled	John Smith, English colonist	1607
Hudson River	Explored	Henry Hudson, English navigator	1609
Hudson Bay (Canada)	Discovered	Henry Hudson	1610
Baffin Bay	Discovered	William Baffin, English navigator	1616
Lake Michigan	Navigated	Jean Nicolet, French explorer	1634
Arkansas River	Discovered	Jacques Marquette and Louis Jolliet, French explorers	1673
Mississippi River	Explored	Sieur de La Salle, French explorer	1682
Bering Strait	Discovered	Vitus Bering, Danish explorer	1728
Alaska	Discovered	Vitus Bering	1741
Mackenzie River (Canada)	Discovered	Sir Alexander Mackenzie, Scottish-Canadian explorer	1789
Northwest U. S.	Explored	Meriwether Lewis and William Clark	1804–06
Northeast Passage (Arctic Ocean)	Navigated	Nils Nordenskjöld, Swedish explorer	1879
Greenland	Explored	Robert Peary, American explorer	1892
Northwest Passage	Navigated	Roald Amundsen, Norwegian explorer	1906
SOUTH AMERICA			
Continent	Visited	Columbus, Italian	1498
Brazil	Discovered	Pedro Alvarez Cabral, Portuguese	1500
Peru	Conquered	Francisco Pizarro, Spanish explorer	1532–33
Amazon River	Explored	Francisco Orellana, Spanish explorer	1541
Cape Horn	Discovered	Willem C. Schouten, Dutch navigator	1615
OCEANIA			
Papua New Guinea	Visited	Jorge de Menezes, Portuguese explorer	1526
Australia	Visited	Abel Janszoon Tasman, Dutch navigator	1642
Tasmania	Discovered		
Australia	Explored	John McDouall Stuart, English explorer	1828
Australia	Explored	Robert Burke and William Wills, Australian explorers	1861
New Zealand	Sighted (and named)	Abel Janszoon Tasman	1642
New Zealand	Visited	James Cook, English navigator	1769
ARCTIC, ANTARCTIC, AND MISCELLANEOUS			
Ocean exploration	Expedition	Magellan's ships circled globe	1519–22
Galápagos Islands	Visited	Diego de Rivadeneira, Spanish captain	1535
Spitsbergen	Visited	Willem Barents, Dutch navigator	1596
Antarctic Circle	Crossed	James Cook, English navigator	1773
Antarctica	Discovered	Nathaniel Palmer, U. S. whaler (archipelago) and Fabian Gottlieb von Bellingshausen, Russian admiral (mainland)	1820–21
Antarctica	Explored	Charles Wilkes, American explorer	1840
North Pole	Reached	Robert E. Peary, American explorer	1909
South Pole	Reached	Roald Amundsen, Norwegian explorer	1911

The Continents

A continent is defined as a large unbroken land mass completely surrounded by water, although in some cases continents are (or were in part) connected by land bridges.

The hypothesis first suggested late in the 19th century was that the continents consist of lighter rocks that rest on heavier crustal material in about the same manner that icebergs float on water. That the rocks forming the continents are lighter than the material below them and under the ocean bottoms is now established. As a consequence of this fact, Alfred Wegener (for the first time in 1912) suggested that the continents are slowly moving, at a rate of about one yard per century, so that their relative positions are not rigidly fixed. Many geologists that were originally skeptical have come to accept this theory of Continental Drift.

When describing a continent, it is important to remember that there is a fundamental difference between a deep ocean, like the Atlantic, and shallow seas, like the Baltic and most of the North Sea, which are merely flooded portions of a continent. Another and entirely different point to remember is that political considerations have often overridden geographical facts when it came to naming continents.

Geographically speaking, Europe, including the British Isles, is a large western peninsula of the continent of Asia; and many geographers, when referring to Europe and Asia, speak of the Eurasian Continent. But traditionally, Europe is counted as a separate continent, with the Ural and the Caucasus mountains forming the line of demarcation between Europe and Asia.

To the south of Europe, Asia has an odd-shaped peninsula jutting westward, which has a large number of political subdivisions. The northern section is taken up by Turkey; to the south of Turkey there are Syria, Iraq, Israel, Jordan, Saudi Arabia, and a number of smaller Arab countries. All this is part of Asia. Traditionally, the island of Cyprus in the Mediterranean is also considered to be part of Asia, while the island of Crete is counted as European.

The large islands of Java, Borneo, and Sumatra and the smaller islands near them are counted as part of "tropical Asia," while New Guinea is counted as related to Australia. In the case of the Americas, the problem arises as to whether they should be considered one or two continents. There are good arguments on both sides, but since there is now a land bridge between North and South America (in the past it was often flooded) and since no part of the sea east of the land bridge is deep ocean, it is more logical to consider the Americas as one continent.

Politically, based mainly on history, the Americas are divided into North America (from the Arctic to the Mexican border), Central America (from Mexico to Panama, with the Caribbean islands), and South America. Greenland is considered a section of North America, while Iceland is traditionally counted as a European island because of its political ties with the Scandinavian countries.

The island groups in the Pacific are often called "Oceania," but this name does *not* imply that scientists consider them the remains of a continent.

Volcanoes of the World

About 500 volcanoes have had recorded eruptions within historical times. Almost two thirds of these are in the Northern Hemisphere. Most volcanoes occur at the boundaries of the earth's crustal plates, such as the famous "Ring of Fire" that surrounds the Pacific Ocean plate. Of the world's active volcanoes, about 60% are along the perimeter of the Pacific, about 17% on mid-oceanic islands, about 14% in an arc along the south of the Indonesian islands, and about 9% in the Mediterranean area, Africa, and Asia Minor. Many of the world's volcanoes are submarine and have unrecorded eruptions.

Pacific "Ring of Fire"

NORTHWEST

Japan: At least 33 active vents.

Aso (5,223 ft; 1,592 m), on Kyushu, has one of the largest craters in the world.

Asama (over 8,300 ft; 2,530 m), on Honshu, is continuously active; violent eruption in 1783.

Azuma (nearly 7,700 ft; 2,347 m), on Honshu, erupted in 1900.

Chokai (7,300 ft; 2,225 m), on Honshu, erupted in 1974 after having been quiescent since 1861.

Fujiyama (Fujisan) (12,385 ft; 3,775 m), on Honshu, southwest of Tokyo. Symmetrical in outline, snow-covered. Regarded as a sacred mountain.

On-take (3,668 ft; 1,118 m), on peninsula of Kyushu. Strong smoke emissions and explosions began November 1973 and continued through 1974.

U.S.S.R.: Kamchatka peninsula, 14–18 active volcanoes. Klyuchevskaya (Kluchev) (15,500 ft; 4,724 m) reported active in 1974.

Kurile Islands: At least 13 active volcanoes and several submarine outbreaks.

SOUTHWEST

New Zealand: Mount Tarawera (3,645 ft; 1,112 m), on North Island, had a severe eruption in 1886 that destroyed the famous Pink and White sinter terraces of Rotomahana, a hot lake.

Ngauruhoe (7,515 ft; 2,291 m), on North Island, emits steam and vapor constantly. Erupted 1974.

Papua New Guinea: Karkar Island (4,920 ft; 1,500 m). Mild eruptions 1974.

Philippine Islands: About 100 eruptive centers; Hibok Hibok, on Camiguin, erupted September 1950 and again in December 1951, when about 750 were reported killed or missing; eruptions continued during 1952–53.

Taal (4,752 ft; 1,448 m), on Luzon. Major eruption in 1965 killed 190; erupted again, 1968.

Volcano Islands: Mount Suribachi (546 ft; 166 m), on Iwo Jima. A sulfurous steaming volcano. Raising of U.S. flag over Mount Suribachi was one of the dramatic episodes of World War II.

NORTHEAST

Alaska: Mount Wrangell (14,163 ft; 4,317 m) and Mount Katmai (about 6,700 ft; 2,042 m). On June 6, 1912, a violent eruption (Nova Rupta) of Mount Katmai occurred, during which the "Valley of Ten Thousand Smokes" was formed.

Aleutian Islands: There are 32 active vents known and numerous inactive cones. Akutan Island (over 4,000 ft; 1,220 m) erupted in 1974, with ash and debris rising over 300 ft.

Great Sitkin (5,741 ft; 1,750 m). Explosive activity February–September 1974, accompanied by earthquake originating at volcano that registered 2.3 on Richter scale.

California, Oregon, Washington: Lassen Peak (10,453 ft; 3,186 m) in California is one of two observed active volcanoes in the U.S. outside Alaska and Hawaii. The last period of activity was 1914–17. Mt. St. Helens (9,677 ft; 2,950 m) in the Cascade Range of southwest Washington became active on March 27, 1980, and erupted on May 18. It last erupted in 1857. Other mountains of volcanic origin include Mount Shasta (California), Mount Hood (Oregon), Mount Mazama (Oregon)—the mountain containing Crater Lake, Mount Rainier (Washington), and Mount Baker (Washington), which has been steaming since October 1975, but gives no sign of an impending eruption.

SOUTHEAST

Chile and Argentina: About 25 active or potentially active.

Colombia: Huila (nearly 18,900 ft; 5,760 m), a vapor-emitting volcano, and Tolima (nearly 18,500 ft; 5,640 m). Eruption of Puracé (15,600 ft; 4,755 m) in 1949 killed 17 people.

Ecuador: Cayambe (nearly 19,000 ft; 5,791 m). Almost on the equator.

Cotopaxi (19,344 ft; 5,896 m). Perhaps highest active volcano in the world. Possesses a beautifully formed cone.

Reventador (11,434 ft; 3,485 m). Observed in active state in late 1973.

El Salvador: Izalco ("beacon of Central America") (7,830 ft; 2,387 m) first appeared in 1770 and is still growing (erupted in 1950, 1956; last erupted in October–November 1966). San Salvador (6,187 ft; 1,886 m) had a violent eruption in 1923. Conchagua (about 4100 ft; 1,250 m) erupted with considerable damage early in 1947.

Guatemala: Santa Maria Quezaltenango (12,361 ft; 3,768 m). Frequent activity between 1902–08 and 1922–28 after centuries of quiescence. Most dangerously active vent of Central America. Other volcanoes include Tajumulco (13,814 ft; 4,211 m) and Atitlán (11,633 ft; 3,546 m).

Mexico: Boquerón ("Big Mouth"), on San Benedicto, about 250 mi. south of Lower California. Newest volcano in Western Hemisphere, discovered September 1952.

Colima (about 14,000 ft; 4,270 m), in group that has had frequent eruptions.

Orizaba (Citlaltépetl) (18,701 ft; 5,700 m).

Parícutin (7,450 ft; 2,270 m). First appeared in February 1943. In less than a week, a cone over 140 ft high developed with a crater one quarter mile in circumference. Cone grew more than 1,500 ft (457 m) in 1943. Erupted 1952.

Popocatépetl (17,887 ft; 5,452 m). Large, deep, bell-shaped crater. Not entirely extinct; steam still escapes.

El Chinchonal (7,300 ft; 1,005.6 m) about 15 miles from Pichucalco. Long inactive, it erupted in March 1982.

Nicaragua: Volcanoes include Telica, Coseguina, and Momotombo. Between Momotombo on the west shore of Lake Managua and Coseguina overlooking the Gulf of Fonseca, there is a string of more than 20 cones, many still active. One of these, Cerro Negro, erupted in July 1947, with considerable damage and loss of life, and again in 1971.

Concepción (5,100 ft; 1,555 m). Ash eruptions 1973–74.

Mid-oceanic Islands

Canary Islands: Pico de Teide (12,192 ft; 3,716 m), on Tenerife.

Cape Verde Islands: Fogo (nearly 9,300 ft; 2,835 m). Severe eruption in 1857; quiescent until 1951.

Caribbean: La Soufrière (4,813 ft; 1,467 m), on Basse-Terre, Guadeloupe. Also called La Grande Soufrière. Violent activity in July–August 1976 caused evacuation of 73,000 people; renewed activity in April 1977 again caused thousands to flee their homes.

La Soufrière (4,048 ft; 1,234 m), on St. Vincent. Major eruption in 1902 killed over 1,000 people. Eruptions over 10-day period in April 1979 caused evacuation of northern two thirds of island.

Comoros: One volcano, Karthala (nearly 8,000 ft; 2,440 m), is visible for over 100 miles. Last erupted in 1904.

Hawaii: Mauna Loa ("Long Mountain") (13,680 ft; 4,170 m), on Hawaii, discharges from its high side vents more lava than any other volcano. Largest volcanic mountain in the world in cubic content. Area of crater is 3.7 sq mi. Violent eruption in June 1950, with lava pouring 25 miles into the ocean. Last major eruption in July 1975.

Mauna Kea (13,796 ft; 4,205 m), on Hawaii. Highest mountain in state.

Kilauea (4,090 ft; 1,247 m) is a vent in the side of Mauna Loa, but its eruptions are apparently independent. One of the most spectacular and active craters. Crater has an area of 4.14 sq mi. Earthquake in July 1975 caused major eruption. Eruptions began in September 1977 and reached a height of 980 ft (300 m). Activity ended Oct. 1. Became active again in March 1983.

Iceland: At least 25 volcanoes active in historical times. Very similar to Hawaiian volcanoes. Askja (over 4,700 ft; 1,433 m) is the largest.

Lesser Antilles (West Indian Islands): Mount Pelée (over 4,500 ft; 1,370 m), northwestern Martinique. Eruption in 1902 destroyed town of St. Pierre and killed approximately 40,000 people.

Réunion Island (east of Madagascar): Piton de la Fournaise (Le Volcan) (8,610 ft; 2,624 m). Large lava flows. Last erupted in 1972.

Samoan archipelago: Savai'i Island had an eruption in 1905 that caused considerable damage. Niuafoo (Tin Can), in the Tonga Islands, has a crater that extends 6,000 feet below and 600 feet above water.

Indonesia

Sumatra: Ninety volcanoes have been discovered; 12 are now active. The most famous, Krakatau, is a small volcanic island in the Sunda Strait. Numerous volcanic discharges occurred in 1883. One extremely violent explosion caused the disappearance of the highest peak and the northern part of the island. Fine dust was carried around the world in the upper atmosphere. Over 36,000 persons lost their lives in resultant tidal waves that were felt as far away as Cape Horn. Active in 1972.

Mediterranean Area

Italy: Mount Etna (10,902 ft; 3,323 m), eastern Sicily. Two new craters formed in eruptions of February–March 1947. Worst eruption in 50 years occurred November 1950–January 1951. Erupted again in 1974, 1975, 1977, 1978, 1979, and 1983.

Stromboli (about 3,000 ft; 914 m), Lipari Islands (north of Sicily). Called "Lighthouse of the Mediterranean." Reported active in 1971.

Mount Vesuvius (4,200 ft; 1,280 m), southeast of Naples. Only active volcano on European mainland. Pompeii buried by an eruption, A.D. 79.

Antarctica

The discovery of two small active volcanoes in 1982 brings to five the total number known on Antarctica. The new ones, 30 miles apart, are on the Weddell Sea side of the Antarctic Peninsula. The largest, Mount Erebus (13,000 ft; 3,962 m), rises from McMurdo Sound. Mount Melbourne (9,000 ft; 2,743 m) is in Victoria Land. The fifth, off the northern tip of the Antartic Peninsula, is a crater known as Deception Island.

World Population, Land Areas, and Elevations

Area	Estimated population, 1982	Approximate Land area sq mi.	Percent of total land area	Population density per sq mi.	Elevation, feet: Highest	Elevation, feet: Lowest	Dimensions, miles: East-West	Dimensions, miles: North-South
WORLD	4,586,000,000	58,433,000	100.0	84.4[1]	Mt. Everest, Asia, 29,028	Dead Sea, Asia, 1,290 below sea level	24,902	24,860
ASIA, incl. Philippines, Indonesia, and European and Asiatic Turkey; excl. Asiatic U.S.S.R.	2,672,000,000	10,644,000	18.2	251.0	Mt. Everest, Tibet-Nepal, 29,028	Dead Sea, Israel-Jordan, 1,290 below sea level	5,400[2]	5,300[2]
AFRICA	499,000,000	11,707,000	20.0	42.6	Mt. Kilimanjaro, Tanzania, 19,340	Lake Assal, Djibouti, 571 below sea level	4,600	5,000
NORTH AMERICA, including Hawaii, Central America, and Caribbean region	383,000,000	9,360,000	16.0	40.9	Mt. McKinley; Alaska, 20,320	Death Valley, Calif., 282 below sea level	3,200[5]	4,000[5]
SOUTH AMERICA	252,000,000	6,883,000	11.8	36.6	Mt. Aconcagua, Arg.-Chile, 23,034	Valdes Peninsula, 131 below sea level	3,200	4,600
ANTARCTICA	—	6,000,000	10.3	—	Vinson Massif, Sentinel Range, 16,863	Sea level	—	—
EUROPE, incl. Iceland; excl. European U.S.S.R. and European Turkey	487,000,000	1,905,000	3.3	255.6	Mont Blanc, France, 15,781	Sea level	3,300[3]	2,400[3]
OCEANIA, incl. Australia, New Zealand, Melanesia, Micronesia, and Polynesia[4]	23,500,000	3,284,000	5.6	7.1	Mauna Kea, Hawaii, 13,796	Lake Eyre, Australia, 38 below sea level	—	—
U.S.S.R., both European and Asiatic	271,000,000	8,647,000	14.8	31.3	Communism Peak, Pamir, 24,547	Caspian Sea, 96 below sea level	5,000	2,500

1. In computing density per square mile, the area of Antarctica is omitted. 2. Including Asiatic U.S.S.R. 3. Including European U.S.S.R. 4. Although Hawaii is geographically part of Oceania, its population is included in the population figure for North America. 5. Excludes Hawaii. *Source:* United Nations *Demographic Yearbook, 1982.*

Some Countries With High Population Densities (per square mile)

Monaco	41,095.9	South Korea	1,050.5	Lebanon	672.5	India	569.2
Singapore	10,504.2	Netherlands	1,027.4	West Germany	641.6	Israel	513.0
Bangladesh	1,710.5	Belgium	837.8	Sri Lanka	602.0	Jamaica	510.1
China, Rep. of (Taiwan)	1,350.1	Japan	825.4	United Kingdom	592.6	Italy	485.8

Longitude and Latitude of Foreign Cities

(and time corresponding to 12:00 noon, eastern standard time)

City	Long. °	Long. ′		Lat. °	Lat. ′		Time
Aberdeen, Scotland	2	9	w	57	9	n	5:00 p.m.
Adelaide, Australia	138	36	e	34	55	s	2:30 a.m.[1]
Algiers	3	0	e	36	50	n	6:00 p.m.
Amsterdam	4	53	e	52	22	n	6:00 p.m.
Ankara, Turkey	32	55	e	39	55	n	7:00 p.m.
Asunción, Paraguay	57	40	w	25	15	s	1:00 p.m.
Athens	23	43	e	37	58	n	7:00 p.m.
Auckland, New Zealand	174	45	e	36	52	s	5:00 a.m.[1]
Bangkok, Thailand	100	30	e	13	45	n	midnight[1]
Barcelona	2	9	e	41	23	n	6:00 p.m.
Belém, Brazil	48	29	w	1	28	s	2:00 p.m.
Belfast, Northern Ireland	5	56	w	54	37	n	5:00 p.m.
Belgrade, Yugoslavia	20	32	e	44	52	n	6:00 p.m.
Berlin	13	25	e	52	30	n	6:00 p.m.
Birmingham, England	1	55	w	52	25	n	5:00 p.m.
Bogotá, Colombia	74	15	w	4	32	n	12:00 noon
Bombay	72	48	e	19	0	n	10:30 p.m.
Bordeaux, France	0	31	w	44	50	n	6:00 p.m.
Bremen, W. Germany	8	49	e	53	5	n	6:00 p.m.
Brisbane, Australia	153	8	e	27	29	s	3:00 a.m.[1]
Bristol, England	2	35	w	51	28	n	5:00 p.m.
Brussels	4	22	e	50	52	n	6:00 p.m.
Bucharest	26	7	e	44	25	n	7:00 p.m.
Budapest	19	5	e	47	30	n	6:00 p.m.
Buenos Aires	58	22	w	34	35	s	2:00 p.m.
Cairo	31	21	e	30	2	n	7:00 p.m.
Calcutta	88	24	e	22	34	n	10:30 p.m.
Canton, China	113	15	e	23	7	n	1:00 a.m.[1]
Cape Town, South Africa	18	22	e	33	55	s	7:00 p.m.
Caracas, Venezuela	67	2	w	10	28	n	1:00 p.m.
Cayenne, French Guiana	52	18	w	4	49	n	1:00 p.m.
Chihuahua, Mexico	106	5	w	28	37	n	11:00 a.m.
Chongqing, China	106	34	e	29	46	n	1:00 a.m.[1]
Copenhagen	12	34	e	55	40	n	6:00 p.m.
Córdoba, Argentina	64	10	w	31	28	s	2:00 p.m.
Dakar, Senegal	17	28	w	14	40	n	5:00 p.m.
Darwin, Australia	130	51	e	12	28	s	2:30 a.m.[1]
Djibouti	43	3	e	11	30	n	8:00 p.m.
Dublin	6	15	w	53	20	n	5:00 p.m.
Durban, South Africa	30	53	e	29	53	s	7:00 p.m.
Edinburgh, Scotland	3	10	w	55	55	n	5:00 p.m.
Frankfurt	8	41	e	50	7	n	6:00 p.m.
Georgetown, Guyana	58	15	w	6	45	n	1:15 p.m.
Glasgow, Scotland	4	15	w	55	50	n	5:00 p.m.
Guatemala City, Guatemala	90	31	w	14	37	n	11:00 a.m.
Guayaquil, Ecuador	79	56	w	2	10	s	12:00 noon
Hamburg	10	2	e	53	33	n	6:00 p.m.
Hammerfest, Norway	23	38	e	70	38	n	6:00 p.m.
Havana	82	23	w	23	8	n	12:00 noon
Helsinki, Finland	25	0	e	60	10	n	7:00 p.m.
Hobart, Tasmania	147	19	e	42	52	s	3:00 a.m.[1]
Iquique, Chile	70	7	w	20	10	s	1:00 p.m.
Irkutsk, U.S.S.R.	104	20	e	52	30	n	1:00 a.m.
Jakarta, Indonesia	106	48	e	6	16	s	0:30 a.m.[1]
Johannesburg, South Africa	28	4	e	26	12	s	7:00 p.m.
Kingston, Jamaica	76	49	w	17	59	n	12:00 noon
Kinshasa, Zaire	15	17	e	4	18	s	6:00 p.m.
La Paz, Bolivia	68	22	w	16	27	s	1:00 p.m.
Leeds, England	1	30	w	53	45	n	5:00 p.m.
Leningrad	30	18	e	59	56	n	8:00 p.m.
Lima, Peru	77	2	w	12	0	s	12:00 noon
Lisbon	9	9	w	38	44	n	5:00 p.m.
Liverpool, England	3	0	w	53	25	n	5:00 p.m.
London	0	5	w	51	32	n	5:00 p.m.
Lyons, France	4	50	e	45	45	n	6:00 p.m.
Madrid	3	42	w	40	26	n	6:00 p.m.
Manchester, England	2	15	w	53	30	n	5:00 p.m.
Manila	120	57	e	14	35	n	1:00 a.m.[1]
Marseilles, France	5	20	e	43	20	n	6:00 p.m.
Mazatlán, Mexico	106	25	w	23	12	n	10:00 a.m.
Mecca, Saudi Arabia	39	45	e	21	29	n	8:00 p.m.
Melbourne	144	58	e	37	47	s	3:00 a.m.[1]
Mexico City	99	7	w	19	26	n	11:00 a.m.
Milan, Italy	9	10	e	45	27	n	6:00 p.m.
Montevideo, Uruguay	56	10	w	34	53	s	2:00 p.m.
Moscow	37	36	e	55	45	n	8:00 p.m.
Munich, Germany	11	35	e	48	8	n	6:00 p.m.
Nagasaki, Japan	129	57	e	32	48	n	2:00 a.m.[1]
Nagoya, Japan	136	56	e	35	7	n	2:00 a.m.[1]
Nairobi, Kenya	36	55	e	1	25	s	8:00 p.m.
Nanjing (Nanking), China	118	53	e	32	3	n	1:00 a.m.[1]
Naples, Italy	14	15	e	40	50	n	6:00 p.m.
Newcastle-on-Tyne, Eng.	1	37	w	54	58	n	5:00 p.m.
Odessa, U.S.S.R.	30	48	e	46	27	n	8:00 p.m.
Osaka, Japan	135	30	e	34	32	n	2:00 a.m.[1]
Oslo	10	42	e	59	57	n	6:00 p.m.
Panama City, Panama	79	32	w	8	58	n	12:00 noon
Paramaribo, Surinam	55	15	w	5	45	n	1:30 p.m.
Paris	2	20	e	48	48	n	6:00 p.m.
Peking	116	25	e	39	55	n	1:00 a.m.[1]
Perth, Australia	115	52	e	31	57	s	1:00 a.m.[1]
Plymouth, England	4	5	w	50	25	n	5:00 p.m.
Port Moresby, Papua New Guinea	147	8	e	9	25	s	3:00 a.m.[1]
Prague	14	26	e	50	5	n	6:00 p.m.
Rangoon, Burma	96	0	e	16	50	n	11:30 p.m.
Reykjavik, Iceland	21	58	w	64	4	n	4:00 p.m.
Rio de Janeiro	43	12	w	22	57	s	2:00 p.m.
Rome	12	27	e	41	54	n	6:00 p.m.
Salvador, Brazil	38	27	w	12	56	s	2:00 p.m.
Santiago, Chile	70	45	w	33	28	s	1:00 p.m.
Sao Paulo, Brazil	46	31	w	23	31	s	2:00 p.m.
Shanghai, China	121	28	e	31	10	n	1:00 a.m.[1]
Singapore	103	55	e	1	14	n	0:30 a.m.[1]
Sofia, Bulgaria	23	20	e	42	40	n	7:00 p.m.
Stockholm	18	3	e	59	17	n	6:00 p.m.
Sydney, Australia	151	0	e	34	0	s	3:00 a.m.[1]
Tananarive, Madagascar	47	33	e	18	50	s	8:00 p.m.
Teheran, Iran	51	45	e	35	45	n	8:30 p.m.
Tokyo	139	45	e	35	40	n	2:00 a.m.[1]
Tripoli, Libya	13	12	e	32	57	n	7:00 p.m.
Venice	12	20	e	45	26	n	6:00 p.m.
Veracruz, Mexico	96	10	w	19	10	n	11:00 a.m.
Vienna	16	20	e	48	14	n	6:00 p.m.
Vladivostok, U.S.S.R.	132	0	e	43	10	n	3:00 a.m.[1]
Warsaw	21	0	e	52	14	n	6:00 p.m.
Wellington, New Zealand	174	47	e	41	17	s	5:00 a.m.[1]
Zürich	8	31	e	47	21	n	6:00 p.m.

1. On the following day.

Highest Mountain Peaks of the World

(For U.S. peaks, see Index)

Mountain peak	Range	Location	Height feet	Height meters
Everest[1]	Himalayas	Nepal-Tibet	29,028	8,848
Godwin Austen (K-2)	Karakoram	India	28,741	8,750
Kanchenjunga	Himalayas	Nepal-Sikkim	28,208	8,598
Lhotse	Himalayas	Nepal-Tibet	27,890	8,501
Makalu	Himalayas	Tibet-Nepal	27,790	8,470
Dhaulagiri I	Himalayas	Nepal	26,810	8,172
Manaslu	Himalayas	Nepal	26,760	8,156
Cho Oyu	Himalayas	Nepal	26,750	8,153
Nanga Parbat	Himalayas	India	26,660	8,126
Annapurna I	Himalayas	Nepal	26,504	8,078
Gasherbrum I	Karakoram	India	26,470	8,068
Broad Peak	Karakoram	India	26,400	8,047
Gasherbrum II	Karakoram	India	26,360	8,033
Gosainthan	Himalayas	Tibet	26,291	8,013
Gasherbrum III	Karakoram	India	26,090	7,952
Annapurna II	Himalayas	Nepal	26,041	7,937
Gasherbrum IV	Karakoram	India	26,000	7,925
Kangbachen	Himalayas	Nepal	25,925	7,902
Gyachung Kang	Himalayas	Nepal	25,910	7,897
Himal Chuli	Himalayas	Nepal	25,895	7,893
Disteghil Sar	Karakoram	India	25,868	7,885
Nuptse	Himalayas	Nepal	25,850	7,829
Kunyang Kish	Karakoram	India	25,760	7,852
Dakum (Peak 29)	Himalayas	Nepal	25,760	7,852
Masherbrum	Karakoram	India	25,660	7,821
Nanda Devi	Himalayas	India	25,645	7,817
Chomolonzo	Himalayas	Nepal-Tibet	25,640	7,815
Rakaposhi	Karakoram	India	25,550	7,788
Batura	Karakoram	India	25,540	7,785
Kanjut Sar	Karakoram	India	25,460	7,760
Kamet	Himalayas	India-Tibet	25,447	7,756
Namche Barwa	Himalayas	Tibet	25,445	7,756
Dhaulagiri II	Himalayas	Nepal	25,427	7,750
Saltoro Kangri	Karakoram	India	25,400	7,742
Gurla Mandhata	Himalayas	Tibet	25,355	7,728
Ulugh Muztagh	Kunlun	Tibet	25,341	7,724
Trivor	Karakoram	India	25,330	7,721
Jannu	Himalayas	Nepal	25,294	7,710
Saser Kangri	Karakoram	India	25,170	7,672
Makalu II	Himalayas	Nepal	25,130	7,660
Chogolisa	Karakoram	India	25,110	7,654
Dhaulagiri IV	Himalayas	Nepal	25,064	7,639
Fang	Himalayas	Nepal	25,013	7,624
Kula Gangri	Himalayas	Tibet	24,783	7,554
Changtse	Himalayas	Tibet	24,780	7,553
Muztagh Ata	Muztagh Ata	China	24,757	7,546
Skyang Kangri	Himalayas	Kashmir	24,750	7,544
Communism Peak	Pamir	U.S.S.R.	24,547	7,482
Victory Peak	Pamir	U.S.S.R.	24,406	7,439
Sia Kangri	Himalayas	Kashmir	24,340	7,419
Chamlang	Himalayas	Nepal	24,012	7,319
Alung Gangri	Himalayas	Tibet	23,999	7,315
Chomo Lhari	Himalayas	Tibet-Bhutan	23,996	7,314
Muztagh (K-5)	Kunlun	China	23,891	7,282
Amne Machin	Kunlun	China	23,490	7,160
Gaurisankar	Himalayas	Népal-Tibet	23,440	7,145
Lenin Peak	Pamir	U.S.S.R.	23,405	7,134
Korzhenevski Peak	Pamir	U.S.S.R.	23,310	7,105
Kangto	Himalayas	Tibet	23,260	7,090
Dunagiri	Himalayas	India	23,184	7,066
Pauhunri	Himalayas	India-Tibet	23,180	7,065
Aconcagua	Andes	Argentina-Chile	23,034	7,021
Revolution Peak	Pamir	U.S.S.R.	22,880	6,974
Kangchenjhan	Himalayas	India	22,700	6,919
Siniolchu	Himalayas	India	22,620	6,895
Ojos des Salado	Andes	Argentina-Chile	22,588	6,885

Mountain peak	Range	Location	Height feet	Height meters
Bonete	Andes	Argentina-Chile	22,546	6,872
Simvuo	Himalayas	India	22,346	6,811
Tup	Andes	Argentina	22,309	6,800
Kungpu	Himalayas	Bhutan	22,300	6,797
Falso-Azufre	Andes	Argentina-Chile	22,277	6,790
Moscow Peak	Pamir	U.S.S.R.	22,260	6,785
Veladero	Andes	Argentina	22,244	6,780
Pissis	Andes	Argentina	22,241	6,779
Mercedario	Andes	Argentina-Chile	22,211	6,770
Huascarán	Andes	Peru	22,198	6,766
Tocorpuri	Andes	Bolivia-Chile	22,162	6,755
Karl Marx Peak	Pamir	U.S.S.R.	22,067	6,726
Llullaillaco	Andes	Argentina-Chile	22,057	6,723
Libertador	Andes	Argentina	22,047	6,720
Kailas	Himalayas	Tibet	22,027	6,714
Lingtren	Himalayas	Nepal-Tibet	21,972	6,697
Incahuasi	Andes	Argentina-Chile	21,719	6,620
Carnicero	Andes	Peru	21,689	6,611
Kurumda	Pamir	U.S.S.R.	21,686	6,610
Garmo Peak	Pamir	U.S.S.R.	21,637	6,595
Sajama	Andes	Bolivia	21,555	6,570
Ancohuma	Andes	Bolivia	21,490	6,550
El Muerto	Andes	Argentina-Chile	21,456	6,540
Nacimiento	Andes	Argentina	21,302	6,493
Illimani	Andes	Bolivia	21,184	6,457
Antofalla	Andes	Argentina-Chile	21,129	6,440
Coropuña	Andes	Peru	21,079	6,425
Cuzco (Ausangate)	Andes	Peru	20,995	6,399
Toro	Andes	Argentina-Chile	20,932	6,380
Parinacota	Andes	Bolivia-Chile	20,768	6,330
Chimboraso	Andes	Ecuador	20,702	6,310
Salcantay	Andes	Peru	20,575	6,271
General Manuel Belgrano	Andes	Argentina	20,505	6,250
Chañi	Andes	Argentina	20,341	6,200
Caca Aca	Andes	Bolivia	20,328	6,196
McKinley	Alaska	Alaska	20,320	6,194
Vudor Peak	Pamir	U.S.S.R.	20,118	6,132
Condoriri	Andes	Bolivia	20,095	6,125
Solimana	Andes	Peru	20,069	6,117
Nevada	Andes	Argentina	20,023	6,103

1. The U. S. Air Force Planning Charts list the height of Mt. Everest as 29,141 ft.

Oceans and Seas

Name	Area sq mi.	Area sq km	Average depth feet	Average depth meters	Greatest known depth feet	Greatest known depth meters	Place greatest known depth
Pacific Ocean	64,000,000	165,760,000	13,215	4,028	35,820	10,918	Mindanao Deep
Atlantic Ocean	31,815,000	82,400,000	12,880	3,926	30,246	9,219	Puerto Rico Trough
Indian Ocean	25,300,000	65,526,700	13,002	3,963	24,460	7,455	Sunda Trench
Arctic Ocean	5,440,200	14,090,000	3,953	1,205	18,456	5,625	77° 45′ N; 175° W
Mediterranean Sea[1]	1,145,100	2,965,800	4,688	1,429	15,197	4,632	Off Cape Matapan, Greece
Caribbean Sea	1,049,500	2,718,200	8,685	2,647	22,788	6,946	Off Cayman Islands
South China Sea	895,400	2,319,000	5,419	1,652	16,456	5,016	West of Luzon
Bering Sea	884,900	2,291,900	5,075	1,547	15,659	4,773	Off Buldir Island
Gulf of Mexico	615,000	1,592,800	4,874	1,486	12,425	3,787	Sigsbee Deep
Okhotsk Sea	613,800	1,589,700	2,749	838	12,001	3,658	146° 10′ E; 46° 50′ N
East China Sea	482,300	1,249,200	617	188	9,126	2,782	25° 16′ N; 125° E
Hudson Bay	475,800	1,232,300	420	128	600	183	Near entrance
Japan Sea	389,100	1,007,800	4,429	1,350	12,276	3,742	Central Basin
Andaman Sea	308,100	797,700	2,854	870	12,392	3,777	Off Car Nicobar Island
North Sea	222,100	575,200	308	94	2,165	660	Skagerrak
Red Sea	169,100	438,000	1,611	491	7,254	2,211	Off Port Sudan
Baltic Sea	163,000	422,200	180	55	1,380	421	Off Gotland

1. Includes Black Sea and Sea of Azov. NOTE: For Caspian Sea, *see* Large Lakes of World elsewhere in this section.

World's Greatest Man-Made Lakes[1]

Name of dam	Location	Millions of cubic meters	Thousands of acre-feet	Year completed
Owen Falls	Uganda	204,800	166,000	1954
Kariba	Zimbabwe	181,592	147,218	1959
Bratsk	U.S.S.R.	169,270	137,220	1964
High Aswan (Sadd-el-Aali)	Egypt	168,000	136,200	1970
Akosombo	Ghana	148,000	120,000	1965
Daniel Johnson	Canada	141,851	115,000	1968
Guri (Raul Leoni)	Venezuela	136,000	110,256	UC
Krasnoyarsk	U.S.S.R.	73,300	59,425	1967
Bennett W.A.C.	Canada	70,309	57,006	1967
Zeya	U.S.S.R.	68,400	55,452	UC
Cabora Bassa	Mozambique	63,000	51,075	1974
LaGrande 2	Canada	61,720	50,037	UC
LaGrande 3	Canada	60,020	48,659	UC
Ust'—Ilimsk	U.S.S.R.	59,300	48,075	1980
Volga—V.I. Lenin	U.S.S.R.	58,000	47,020	1955
Caniapiscau	Canada	53,790	43,608	UC
Pati (Chapetón)	Argentina	53,700	43,535	UC
Upper Wainganga	India	50,700	41,103	UC
Sáo Felix	Brazil	50,600	41,022	UC
Bukhtarma	U.S.S.R.	49,740	40,325	1960
Atatürk (Karababa)	Turkey	48,000	38,914	UC
Cerros Colorados	Argentina	48,000	38,914	1973
Irkutsk	U.S.S.R.	46,000	37,290	1956
Tucuruí	Brazil	36,375	29,489	UC
Vilyuy	U.S.S.R.	35,900	29,104	1967
Sanmenxia	China	35,400	28,700	1960
Hoover	Nevada-Arizona	35,200	28,537	1936
Sobridinho	Brazil	34,200	27,726	1981
Glen Canyon	Arizona	33,305	27,000	1964
Jenpeg	Canada	31,790	25,772	1975

1. Formed by construction of dams. NOTE: UC = under construction, *Source:* Department of the Interior, Bureau of Reclamation.

Large Lakes of the World

Name and location	Area		Length		Maximum depth	
	sq mi.	sq km	mi.	km	feet	meters
Caspian Sea, U.S.S.R.-Iran[1]	152,239	394,299	745	1,199	3,104	946
Superior, U.S.-Canada	31,820	82,414	383	616	1,333	406
Victoria, Tanzania—Uganda	26,828	69,485	200	322	270	82
Aral, U.S.S.R.	25,659	66,457	266	428	223	68
Huron, U.S.-Canada	23,010	59,596	247	397	750	229
Michigan, U.S.	22,400	58,016	321	517	923	281
Tanganyika, Tanzania-Zaire	12,700	32,893	420	676	4,708	1,435
Baikal, U.S.S.R.	12,162	31,500	395	636	5,712	1,741
Great Bear, Canada	12,000	31,080	232	373	270	82
Nyasa, Malawi-Mozambique-Tanzania	11,600	30,044	360	579	2,316	706
Great Slave, Canada	11,170	28,930	298	480	2,015	614
Chad,[2] Chad-Niger-Nigeria	9,946	25,760	—	—	23	7
Erie, U.S.-Canada	9,930	25,719	241	388	210	64
Winnipeg, Canada	9,094	23,553	264	425	204	62
Ontario, U.S.-Canada	7,520	19,477	193	311	778	237
Balkash, U.S.S.R.	7,115	18,428	376	605	87	27
Ladoga, U.S.S.R.	7,000	18,130	124	200	738	225
Onega, U.S.S.R.	3,819	9,891	154	248	361	110
Titicaca, Bolivia-Peru	3,141	8,135	110	177	1,214	370
Nicaragua, Nicaragua	3,089	8,001	110	177	230	70
Athabaska, Canada	3,058	7,920	208	335	407	124
Rudolf, Kenya	2,473	6,405	154	248	—	—
Reindeer, Canada	2,444	6,330	152	245	—	—
Eyre, South Australia	2,400[3]	6,216	130	209	varies	varies
Issyk-Kul, U.S.S.R.	2,394	6,200	113	182	2,297	700
Urmia,[2] Iran	2,317	6,001	81	130	49	15
Torrens, South Australia	2,200	5,698	130	209	—	—
Vänern, Sweden	2,141	5,545	87	140	322	98

Name and location	Area		Length		Maximum depth	
	sq mi.	sq km	mi.	km	feet	meters
Winnipegosis, Canada	2,086	5,403	152	245	59	18
Mobutu Sese Seko, Uganda	2,046	5,299	100	161	180	55
Nettilling, Baffin Island, Canada	1,950	5,051	70	113	—	—
Nipigon, Canada	1,870	4,843	72	116	—	—
Manitoba, Canada	1,817	4,706	140	225	22	7
Great Salt, U.S.	1,800	4,662	75	121	15/25	5/8
Kioga, Uganda	1,700	4,403	50	80	about 30	9
Koko-Nor, China	1,630	4,222	66	106	—	—

1. The Caspian Sea is called "sea" because the Romans, finding it salty, named it *Mare Caspium*. Many geographers, however, consider it a lake because it is land-locked. 2. Figures represent high-water data. 3. Varies with the rainfall of the wet season. It has been reported to dry up almost completely on occasion.

Principal Rivers of the World

(For other U.S. rivers, see Index)

River	Source	Outflow	Approx. length	
			miles	km
Nile	Tributaries of Lake Victoria, Africa	Mediterranean Sea	4,180	6,690
Amazon	Glacier-fed lakes, Peru	Atlantic Ocean	3,912	6,296
Mississippi-Missouri-Red Rock	Source of Red Rock, Montana	Gulf of Mexico	3,741	6,020
Yangtze Kiang	Tibetan plateau, China	China Sea	3,602	5,797
Ob	Altai Mts., U.S.S.R.	Gulf of Ob	3,459	5,567
Yellow (Hwang Ho)	Eastern part of Kunlan Mts., west China	Gulf of Chihli	2,900	4,667
Yenisei	Tannu-Ola Mts., western Tuva, U.S.S.R.	Arctic Ocean	2,800	4,506
Paraná	Confluence of Paranaiba and Grande rivers	Río de la Plata	2,795	4,498
Irtish	Altai Mts., U.S.S.R.	Ob River	2,758	4,438
Congo	Confluence of Lualaba and Luapula rivers, Zaire	Atlantic Ocean	2,716	4,371
Amur	Confluence of Shilka (U.S.S.R.) and Argun (Manchuria) rivers	Tatar Strait	2,704	4,352
Lena	Baikal Mts., U.S.S.R.	Arctic Ocean	2,652	4,268
Mackenzie	Head of Finlay River, British Columbia, Canada	Beaufort Sea (Arctic Ocean)	2,635	4,241
Niger	Guinea	Gulf of Guinea	2,600	4,184
Mekong	Tibetan highlands	South China Sea	2,500	4,023
Mississippi	Lake Itasca, Minnesota	Gulf of Mexico	2,348	3,779
Missouri	Confluence of Jefferson, Gallatin, and Madison rivers, Montana	Mississippi River	2,315	3,726
Volga	Valdai plateau, U.S.S.R.	Caspian Sea	2,291	3,687
Madeira	Confluence of Beni and Maumoré rivers, Bolivia-Brazil boundary	Amazon River	2,012	3,238
Purus	Peruvian Andes	Amazon River	1,993	3,207
São Francisco	Southwest Minas Gerais, Brazil	Atlantic Ocean	1,987	3,198
St. Lawrence	Lake Ontario	Gulf of St. Lawrence	1,900	3,058
Yukon	Junction of Lewes and Pelly rivers, Yukon Territory, Canada	Bering Sea	1,900	3,058
Rio Grande	San Juan Mts., Colorado	Gulf of Mexico	1,885	3,034
Brahmaputra	Himalayas	Ganges River	1,800	2,897
Indus	Himalayas	Arabian Sea	1,800	2,897
Danube	Black Forest, W. Germany	Black Sea	1,766	2,842

River	Source	Outflow	Approx. length miles	Approx. length km
Euphrates	Confluence of Murat Nehri and Kara Su rivers, Turkey	Shatt-al-Arab	1,739	2,799
Darling	Central part of Eastern Highlands, Australia	Murray River	1,702	2,739
Zambezi	11°21′S, 24°22′E, Zambia	Mozambique Channel	1,700	2,736
Tocantins	Goiás, Brazil	Pará River	1,677	2,699
Murray	Australian Alps, New South Wales	Indian Ocean	1,609	2,589
Nelson	Head of Bow River, western Alberta, Canada	Hudson Bay	1,600	2,575
Paraguay	Mato Grosso, Brazil	Paraná River	1,584	2,549
Ural	Southern Ural Mts., U.S.S.R.	Caspian Sea	1,574	2,533
Ganges	Himalayas	Bay of Bengal	1,557	2,506
Amu Darya (Oxus)	Nicholas Range, Pamir Mts., U.S.S.R.	Aral Sea	1,500	2,414
Japurá	Andes, Colombia	Amazon River	1,500	2,414
Salween	Tibet, south of Kunlun Mts.	Gulf of Martaban	1,500	2,414
Arkansas	Central Colorado	Mississippi River	1,450	2,333
Colorado	Grand County, Colorado	Gulf of California	1,450	2,333
Dnieper	Valdai Hills, U.S.S.R.	Black Sea	1,419	2,284
Ohio-Allegheny	Potter County, Pennsylvania	Mississippi River	1,306	2,102
Irrawaddy	Confluence of Nmai and Mali rivers, northeast Burma	Bay of Bengal	1,300	2,092
Orange	Lesotho	Atlantic Ocean	1,300	2,092
Orinoco	Serra Parima Mts., Venezuela	Atlantic Ocean	1,281	2,062
Pilcomayo	Andes Mts., Bolivia	Paraguay River	1,242	1,999
Xi Jiang (Si Kiang)	Eastern Yunnan Province, China	China Sea	1,236	1,989
Columbia	Columbia Lake, British Columbia, Canada	Pacific Ocean	1,232	1,983
Don	Tula, R.S.F.S.R., U.S.S.R.	Sea of Azov	1,223	1,968
Sungari	China-North Korea boundary	Amur River	1,215	1,955
Saskatchewan	Canadian Rocky Mts.	Lake Winnipeg	1,205	1,939
Peace	Stikine Mts., British Columbia, Canada	Great Slave River	1,195	1,923
Tigris	Taurus Mts., Turkey	Shatt-al-Arab	1,180	1,899

Highest Waterfalls of the World

Waterfall	Location	River	Height feet	Height meters
Angel	Venezuela	Tributary of Caroni	3,281	1,000
Tugela	Natal, South Africa	Tugela	3,000	914
Cuquenán	Venezuela	Cuquenán	2,000	610
Sutherland	South Island, N.Z.	Arthur	1,904	580
Takkakaw	British Columbia	Tributary of Yoho	1,650	503
Ribbon (Yosemite)	California	Creek flowing into Yosemite	1,612	491
Upper Yosemite	California	Yosemite Creek, tributary of Merced	1,430	436
Gavarnie	Southwest France	Gave de Pau	1,384	422
Vettisfoss	Norway	Mörkedola	1,200	366
Widows' Tears (Yosemite)	California	Tributary of Merced	1,170	357
Staubbach	Switzerland	Staubbach (Lauterbrunnen Valley)	984	300

Waterfall	Location	River	Height feet	Height meters
Middle Cascade (Yosemite)	California	Yosemite Creek, tributary of Merced	909	277
King Edward VIII	Guyana	Courantyne	850	259
Gersoppa	India	Sharavati	829	253
Kaieteur	Guyana	Potaro	822	251
Skykje	Norway	In Skykjedal (valley of Inner Hardinger Fjord)	820	250
Kalambo	Tanzania-Zambia	—	720	219
Fairy (Mount Rainier Park)	Washington	Stevens Creek	700	213
Trummelbach	Switzerland	Trummelbach (Lauterbrunnen Valley)	700	213
Aniene (Teverone)	Italy	Tiber	680	207
Cascata delle Marmore	Italy	Velino, tributary of Nera	650	198
Maradalsfos	Norway	Stream flowing into Ejkisdalsvand (lake)	643	196
Feather	California	Fall River	640	195
Maletsunyane	Lesotho	Maletsunyane	630	192
Bridalveil (Yosemite)	California	Yosemite Creek	620	189
Multnomah	Oregon	Multnomah Creek, tributary of Columbia	620	189
Vøringsfos	Norway	Bjoreia	597	182
Nevada (Yosemite)	California	Merced	594	181
Skjeggedal	Norway	Tysso	525	160
Marina	Guyana	Tributary of Kuribrong, tributary of Potaro	500	152
Tequendama	Colombia	Funza, tributary of Magdalena	425	130
King George's	Cape of Good Hope, South Africa	Orange	400	122
Illilouette (Yosemite)	California	Illilouette Creek, tributary of Merced	370	113
Victoria	Rhodesia-Zambia boundary	Zambezi	355	108
Handöl	Sweden	Handöl Creek	345	105
Lower Yosemite	California	Yosemite	320	98
Comet (Mount Rainier Park)	Washington	Van Trump Creek	320	98
Vernal (Yosemite)	California	Merced	317	97
Virginia	Northwest Territories, Canada	South Nahanni, tributary of Mackenzie	315	96
Lower Yellowstone	Wyoming	Yellowstone	310	94

NOTE: Niagara Falls (New York-Ontario), though of great volume, has parallel drops of only 158 and 167 feet.

Large Islands of the World

Island	Location and status	Area sq mi.	Area sq km
Greenland	North Atlantic (Danish)	839,999	2,175,597
New Guinea	Southwest Pacific (Irian Jaya, Indonesian, west part; Papua New Guinea, east part)	316,615	820,033
Borneo	West mid-Pacific (Indonesian, south part; British protectorate, and Malaysian, north part)	286,914	743,107
Madagascar	Indian Ocean (Malagasy Republic)	226,657	587,042
Baffin	North Atlantic (Canadian)	183,810	476,068
Sumatra	Northeast Indian Ocean (Indonesian)	182,859	473,605
Honshu	Sea of Japan-Pacific (Japanese)	88,925	230,316
Great Britain	Off coast of NW Europe (England, Scotland, and Wales)	88,758	229,883
Ellesmere	Arctic Ocean (Canadian)	82,119	212,688
Victoria	Arctic Ocean (Canadian)	81,930	212,199
Celebes	West mid-Pacific (Indonesian)	72,986	189,034
South Island	South Pacific (New Zealand)	58,093	150,461
Java	Indian Ocean (Indonesian)	48,990	126,884
North Island	South Pacific (New Zealand)	44,281	114,688

Island	Location and status	Area sq mi.	Area sq km
Cuba	Caribbean Sea (republic)	44,218	114,525
Newfoundland	North Atlantic (Canadian)	42,734	110,681
Luzon	West mid-Pacific (Philippines)	40,420	104,688
Iceland	North Atlantic (republic)	39,768	102,999
Mindanao	West mid-Pacific (Philippines)	36,537	94,631
Ireland	West of Great Britain (republic, south part; United Kingdom, north part)	32,597	84,426
Hokkaido	Sea of Japan—Pacific (Japanese)	30,372	78,663
Hispaniola	Caribbean Sea (Dominican Republic, east part; Haiti, west part)	29,355	76,029
Tasmania	South of Australia (Australian)	26,215	67,897
Sri Lanka (Ceylon)	Indian Ocean (republic)	25,332	65,610
Sakhalin (Karafuto)	North of Japan (U.S.S.R.)	24,560	63,610
Banks	Arctic Ocean (Canadian)	23,230	60,166
Devon	Arctic Ocean (Canadian)	20,861	54,030
Tierra del Fuego	Southern tip of South America (Argentinian, east part; Chilean, west part)	18,605	48,187
Kyushu	Sea of Japan—Pacific (Japanese)	16,223	42,018
Melville	Arctic Ocean (Canadian)	16,141	41,805
Axel Heiberg	Arctic Ocean (Canadian)	15,779	40,868
Southampton	Hudson Bay (Canadian)	15,700	40,663

Principal Deserts of the World

Desert	Location	Approximate size	Approx. elevation, ft
Atacama	North Chile	400 mi. long	7,000–13,500
Black Rock	Northwest Nevada	About 1,000 sq mi.	2,000–8,500
Colorado	Southeast California from San Gorgonio Pass to Gulf of California	200 mi. long and a maximum width of 50 mi.	Few feet above to 250 below sea level
Dasht-e-Kavir	Southeast of Caspian Sea, Iran	—	2,000
Dasht-e-Lūt	Northeast of Kerman, Iran	—	1,000
Gobi (Shamo)	Covers most of Mongolia	500,000 sq mi.	3,000–5,000
Great Arabian	Most of Arabia	1,500 mi. long	—
An Nafud (Red Desert)	South of Jauf	400 mi. by avg of 140 mi.	3,000
Dahna	Northeast of Nejd	400 mi. by 30 mi.	—
Rub' al-Khali	South portion of Nejd	Over 200,000 sq. mi.	—
Syrian (Al-Hamad)	North of lat. 30° N	—	1,850
Great Australian	Western portion of Australia	About one half the continent	600–1,000
Great Salt Lake	West of Great Salt Lake to Nevada—Utah boundary	About 110 mi. by 50 mi.	4,500
Kalahari	South Africa—South-West Africa	About 120,000 sq mi.	Over 3,000
Kara Kum (Desert of Kiva)	Southwest Turkmen, U.S.S.R.	115,000 sq mi.	—
Kyzyl Kum	Uzbek and Kazakh, U.S.S.R.	Over 100,000 sq. mi.	160 near Lake Aral to 2,000 in southeast
Libyan	Libya, Egypt, Sudan	Over 500,000 sq mi.	—
Mojave	North of Colorado Desert and south of Death Valley, southeast California	15,000 sq mi.	2,000
Nubian	From Red Sea to great west bend of the Nile, Sudan	—	2,500
Painted Desert	Northeast Arizona	Over 7,000 sq mi.	High plateau, 5,000
Sahara	North Africa to about lat. 15° N and from Red Sea to Atlantic Ocean	3,200 mi. greatest length along lat. 20° N; area over 3,500,000 sq mi.	440 below sea level to 11,000 above; avg elevation, 1,400–1,600
Takla Makan	South central Sinkiang, China	Over 100,000 sq mi.	—
Thar (Indian)	Pakistan-India	Nearly 100,000 sq mi.	Over 1,000

Interesting Caves and Caverns of the World

Aggtelek. In village of same name, northern Hungary. Large stalactitic cavern about 5 miles long.

Altamira Cave. Near Santander, Spain. Contains animal paintings (Old Stone Age art) on roof and walls.

Antiparos. On island of same name in the Grecian Archipelago. Some stalactites are 20 ft long. Brilliant colors and fantastic shapes.

Blue Grotto. On island of Capri, Italy. Cavern hollowed out in limestone by constant wave action. Now half filled with water because of sinking coast. Name derived from unusual blue light permeating the cave. Source of light is a submerged opening, light passing through the water.

Carisbad Caverns. Southeast New Mexico. Largest underground labyrinth yet discovered. Three levels: 754, 900, and 1,320 ft below the surface.

Fingal's Cave. On island of Staffa off coast of western Scotland. Penetrates about 200 ft inland. Contains basaltic columns almost 40 ft high.

Ice Cave. Near Dobsina, Czechoslovakia. Noted for its beautiful crystal effects.

Jenolan Caves. In Blue Mountain plateau, New South Wales, Australia. Beautiful stalactitic formations.

Kent's Cavern. Near Torquay, England. Source of much information on Paleolithic man.

Luray Cavern. Near Luray, Va. Has large stalactitic and stalagmitic columns of many colors.

Mammoth Cave. Limestone cavern in central Kentucky. Cave area is about 10 miles in diameter but has at least 150 miles of irregular subterranean passageways at various levels. Temperature remains fairly constant at 54° F.

Peak Cavern or Devil's Hole. Derbyshire, England. About 2,250 ft into a mountain. Lowest part is about 600 ft below the surface.

Postojna (Postumia) Grotto. Near Postumia in Julian Alps, about 25 miles northeast of Trieste. Stalactitic cavern, largest in Europe. Piuca (Pivka) River flows through part of it. Caves have numerous beautiful stalactites.

Singing Cave. Iceland. A lava cave; name derived from echoes of people singing in it.

Wind Cave. In Black Hills of South Dakota. Limestone caverns with stalactites and stalagmites almost entirely missing. Variety of crystal formations called "boxwork."

Wyandotte Cave. In Crawford County, southern Indiana. A limestone cavern with five levels of passages; one of the largest in North America. "Monumental Mountain," approximately 135 ft high, is believed to be one of the world's largest underground "mountains."

U.S. Geography

Miscellaneous Data for the United States

Source: Department of the Interior, U.S. Geological Survey.

Highest point: Mount McKinley, Alaska	20,320 ft (6,193 m)
Lowest point: Death Valley, Calif.	282 ft (86 m) below sea level
Approximate mean altitude	2,500 ft (762 m)
Points farthest apart (50 states):	
Log Point, Elliot Key, Fla., and Kure Island, Hawaii	5,852 mi. (9,418 km)
Geographic center (50 states):	
In Butte County, S.D. (west of Castle Rock)	44° 58′ N. lat. 103° 46′ W. long.
Geographic center (48 conterminous states):	
In Smith County, Kan. (near Lebanon)	39° 50′ N. lat. 98° 35′ W. long.
Boundaries:	
Between Alaska and Canada	1,538 mi. (2,475 km)
Between the 48 conterminous states and Canada (incl. Great Lakes)	3,987 mi. (6,416 km)
Between the United States and Mexico	1,933 mi. (3,111 km)

Extreme Points of the United States (50 States)

Extreme point	Latitude	Longitude	Distance[1] mi.	Distance[1] km
Northernmost point: Point Barrow, Alaska	71°23′ N	156°29′ W	2,502	4,027
Easternmost point: West Quoddy Head, Me.	44°49′ N	66°57′ W	1,785	2,873
Southernmost point: Ka Lae (South Cape), Hawaii	18°56′ N	155°41′ W	3,456	5,562
Westernmost point: Cape Wrangell, Alaska (Attu Island)	52°55′ N	172°27′ E	3,620	5,826

1. From geographic center of United States (incl. Alaska and Hawaii), west of Castle Rock, S.D., 44°58′ N. lat., 103°46′ W long.

Highest, Lowest, and Mean Altitudes in the United States

State	Altitude, ft[1]	Highest point	Altitude, ft	Lowest point	Altitude, ft
Alabama	500	Cheaha Mountain	2,407	Gulf of Mexico	Sea level
Alaska	1,900	Mount McKinley	20,320	Pacific Ocean	Sea level
Arizona	4,100	Humphreys Peak	12,633	Colorado River	70
Arkansas	650	Magazine Mountain	2,753	Ouachita River	55
California	2,900	Mount Whitney	14,494	Death Valley	282[2]
Colorado	6,800	Mount Elbert	14,433	Arkansas River	3,350
Connecticut	500	Mount Frissell, on south slope	2,380	Long Island Sound	Sea level
Delaware	60	On Ebright Road	442	Atlantic Ocean	Sea level
D.C.	150	Tenleytown, northwest part	410	Potomac River	1
Florida	100	Sec. 30, T6N, R20W[3]	345	Atlantic Ocean	Sea level
Georgia	600	Brasstown Bald	4,784	Atlantic Ocean	Sea level
Hawaii	3,030	Mauna Kea	13,796	Pacific Ocean	Sea level
Idaho	5,000	Borah Peak	12,662	Snake River	710
Illinois	600	Charles Mound	1,235	Mississippi River	279
Indiana	700	Franklin Township, Wayne County	1,257	Ohio River	320
Iowa	1,100	Sec. 29, T100N, R41W[4]	1,670	Mississippi River	480
Kansas	2,000	Mount Sunflower	4,039	Verdigris River	680
Kentucky	750	Black Mountain	4,145	Mississippi River	257
Louisiana	100	Driskill Mountain	535	New Orleans	5[2]
Maine	600	Mount Katahdin	5,268	Atlantic Ocean	Sea level
Maryland	350	Backbone Mountain	3,360	Atlantic Ocean	Sea level
Massachusetts	500	Mount Greylock	3,491	Atlantic Ocean	Sea level
Michigan	900	Mount Arvon	1,979	Lake Erie	572
Minnesota	1,200	Eagle Mountain	2,301	Lake Superior	602
Mississippi	300	Woodall Mountain	806	Gulf of Mexico	Sea level
Missouri	800	Taum Sauk Mountain	1,772	St. Francis River	230
Montana	3,400	Granite Peak	12,799	Kootenai River	1,800
Nebraska	2,600	Johnson Township, Kimball County	5,426	Southeast corner of state	840
Nevada	5,500	Boundary Peak	13,143	Colorado River	470
New Hampshire	1,000	Mount Washington	6,288	Atlantic Ocean	Sea level
New Jersey	250	High Point	1,803	Atlantic Ocean	Sea level
New Mexico	5,700	Wheeler Peak	13,161	Red Bluff Reservoir	2,817
New York	1,000	Mount Marcy	5,344	Atlantic Ocean	Sea level
North Carolina	700	Mount Mitchell	6,684	Atlantic Ocean	Sea level
North Dakota	1,900	White Butte	3,506	Red River	750
Ohio	850	Campbell Hill	1,550	Ohio River	433
Oklahoma	1,300	Black Mesa	4,973	Little River	287
Oregon	3,300	Mount Hood	11,239	Pacific Ocean	Sea level
Pennsylvania	1,100	Mount Davis	3,213	Delaware River	Sea level
Rhode Island	200	Jerimoth Hill	812	Atlantic Ocean	Sea level
South Carolina	350	Sassafras Mountain	3,560	Atlantic Ocean	Sea level
South Dakota	2,200	Harney Peak	7,242	Big Stone Lake	962
Tennessee	900	Clingmans Dome	6,643	Mississippi River	182
Texas	1,700	Guadalupe Peak	8,749	Gulf of Mexico	Sea level
Utah	6,100	Kings Peak	13,528	Beaverdam Creek	2,000
Vermont	1,000	Mount Mansfield	4,393	Lake Champlain	95
Virginia	950	Mount Rogers	5,729	Atlantic Ocean	Sea level
Washington	1,700	Mount Rainier	14,410	Pacific Ocean	Sea level
West Virginia	1,500	Spruce Knob	4,863	Potomac River	240
Wisconsin	1,050	Timms Hill	1,952	Lake Michigan	581
Wyoming	6,700	Gannett Peak	13,804	Belle Fourche River	3,100
United States	2,500	Mount McKinley (Alaska)	20,320	Death Valley (California)	282[2]

1. Approximate mean altitude. 2. Below sea level. 3. Walton County. 4. Osceola County. *Source:* Department of the Interior, U.S. Geological Survey.

Mason and Dixon's Line

Mason and Dixon's Line (often called the Mason-Dixon Line) is the boundary between Pennsylvania and Maryland, running at a north latitude of 39°43′19.11″. The greater part of it was surveyed from 1763–67 by Charles Mason and Jeremiah Dixon, English astronomers who had been appointed to settle a dispute between the colonies. As the line was partly the boundary between the free and the slave states, it has come to signify the division between the North and the South.

Named Summits in the U.S. Over 14,000 Feet Above Sea Level

Name	State	Height	Name	State	Height	Name	State	Height
Mt. McKinley	Alaska	20,320	Mt. Antero	Colo.	14,269	Windom Peak	Colo.	14,087
Mt. St. Elias	Alaska	18,008	Torreys Peak	Colo.	14,267	Mt. Russell	Calif.	14,086
Mt. Foraker	Alaska	17,400	Castle Peak	Colo.	14,265	Mt. Eolus	Colo.	14,084
Mt. Bona	Alaska	16,421	Quandary Peak	Colo.	14,265	Mt. Columbia	Colo.	14,073
Mt. Blackburn	Alaska	16,390	Mt. Evans	Colo.	14,264	Mt. Augusta	Alaska	14,070
Mt. Sanford	Alaska	16,237	Longs Peak	Colo.	14,255	Missouri Mtn.	Colo.	14,067
South Buttress	Alaska	15,885	Mt. Wilson	Colo.	14,246	Humboldt Peak	Colo.	14,064
Mt. Vancouver	Alaska	15,700	White Mtn.	Calif.	14,246	Mt. Bierstadt	Colo.	14,060
Mt. Churchill	Alaska	15,638	North Palisade	Calif.	14,242	Sunlight Peak	Colo.	14,059
Mt. Fairweather	Alaska	15,300	Shavano Peak	Colo.	14,229	Split Mtn.	Calif.	14,058
Mt. Hubbard	Alaska	15,015	Crestone Needle	Colo.	14,197	Handies Peak	Colo.	14,048
Mt. Bear	Alaska	14,831	Mt. Belford	Colo.	14,197	Culebra Peak	Colo.	14,047
East Buttress	Alaska	14,730	Mt. Princeton	Colo.	14,197	Mt. Lindsey	Colo.	14,042
Mt. Hunter	Alaska	14,573	Mt. Yale	Colo.	14,196	Middle Palisade	Calif.	14,040
Mt. Alverstone	Alaska	14,565	Mt. Bross	Colo.	14,172	Little Bear Peak	Colo.	14,037
Browne Tower	Alaska	14,530	Kit Carson Mtn.	Colo.	14,165	Mt. Sherman	Colo.	14,036
Mt. Whitney	Calif.	14,494	Mt. Wrangell	Alaska	14,163	Redcloud Peak	Colo.	14,034
Mt. Elbert	Colo.	14,433	Mt. Shasta	Calif.	14,162	Mt. Langley	Calif.	14,028
Mt. Massive	Colo.	14,421	Mt. Sill	Calif.	14,162	Mt. Tyndall	Calif.	14,018
Mt. Harvard	Colo.	14,420	El Diente Peak	Colo.	14,159	Pyramid Peak	Colo.	14,018
Mt. Rainier	Wash.	14,410	Maroon Peak	Colo.	14,156	Wilson Peak	Colo.	14,017
Mt. Williamson	Calif.	14,375	Tabeguache Mtn.	Colo.	14,155	Mt. Muir	Calif.	14,015
Blanca Peak	Colo.	14,345	Mt. Oxford	Colo.	14,153	Wetterhorn Peak	Colo.	14,015
La Plata Peak	Colo.	14,336	Mt. Sneffels	Colo.	14,150	No. Maroon Pk.	Colo.	14,014
Uncompahgre Pk.	Colo.	14,309	Mt. Democrat	Colo.	14,148	San Luis Peak	Colo.	14,014
Crestone Peak	Colo.	14,294	Capitol Peak	Colo.	14,130	Huron Peak	Colo.	14,005
Mt. Lincoln	Colo.	14,286	Pikes Peak	Colo.	14,110	Mt. of the Holy Cross	Colo.	14,005
Grays Peak	Colo.	14,270	Snowmass Mtn.	Colo.	14,092	Sunshine Peak	Colo.	14,001

Source: Department of the Interior, U.S. Geological Survey.

Post-Eruption Map of Mount St. Helens for Sale

A post-eruption map of Mount St. Helens and vicinity that includes color photographs of the major eruption and aftereffects has been published by the U.S. Geological Survey.

The 30- × 40-inch topographical map shows how the area appears in the wake of the violent eruption of May 18, 1980. Presented at a scale of 1:100, 000 (one inch equals about 1.68 miles), the map denotes land managed by federal and state agencies and includes numerical designations for roads within the Gifford Pinchot National Forest, viewpoints, campgrounds, picnic areas, visitor centers and points of interest.

On the reverse side of the map, the Forest Service has prepared a text and color photographs providing a narrative of recent Mount St. Helens volcanic activities.

The map, "Mount St. Helens and Vicinity, March 1981," may be purchased by mail for $2.10 each, from the Branch of Distribution, U.S. Geological Survey, Box 25286, Federal Center, Denver, Colo. 80225. Map orders *must* specify the correct title given here, and a check or money order made payable to the U.S. Geological Survey must be included with your order.

Rivers of the United States

(350 or more miles long)

Alabama (735 mi.; 1,183 km): From junction of Tallapoosa R. and Coosa R. in Alabama to Mobile R.
Altamaha-Ocmulgee (392 mi.; 631 km): From junction of Yellow R. and South R., Newton Co. in Georgia to Atlantic Ocean.
Apalachicola-Chattahoochee (524 mi.; 843 km): From Towns Co. in Georgia to Gulf of Mexico in Florida.
Arkansas (1,459 mi.; 2,348 km): From Lake Co. in Colorado to Mississippi R. in Arkansas.
Brazos (870 mi.; 1,400 km): From junction of Salt Fork and Double Mountain Fork in Texas to Gulf of Mexico.
Canadian (906 mi.; 1,458 km): From Las Animas Co. in Colorado to Arkansas R. in Oklahoma.
Cimarron (600 mi.; 966 km): From Colfax Co. in New Mexico to Arkansas R. in Oklahoma.
Clark Fork-Pend Oreille (505 mi.; 813 km): From Silver Bow Co. in Montana to Columbia R. in British Columbia.
Colorado (1,450 mi.; 2,333 km): From Rocky Mountain National Park in Colorado to Gulf of California in Mexico.
Colorado (840 mi.; 1,352 km): From Borden Co. in Texas to Matagorda Bay.
Columbia (1,243 mi.; 2,000 km): From Columbia Lake in British Columbia to Pacific Ocean (entering between Oregon and Washington).
Colville (350 mi.; 563 km): From Brooks Range in Alaska to Beaufort Sea.
Connecticut (407 mi.; 655 km): From Third Connecticut Lake in New Hampshire to Long Island Sound in Connecticut.
Cumberland (720 mi.; 1,159 km): From junction of Poor and Clover Forks in Harlan Co. in Kentucky to Ohio R.

Delaware (390 mi.; 628 km): From Schoharie Co. in New York to Liston Point, Delaware Bay.
Gila (630 mi.; 1,014 km): From Catron Co. in New Mexico to Colorado R. in Arizona.
Green (360 mi.; 579 km): From Lincoln Co. in Kentucky to Ohio R. in Kentucky.
Green (730 mi.; 1,175 km): From Sublette Co. in Wyoming to Colorado R. in Utah.
Illinois (420 mi.; 676 km): From St. Joseph Co. in Indiana to Mississippi R. at Grafton in Illinois.
James (sometimes called *Dakota*) (710 mi.; 1,143 km): From Wells Co. in North Dakota to Missouri R. in South Dakota.
Kanawha-New (352 mi.; 566 km): From junction of North and South Forks of New R. in North Carolina, through Virginia and West Virginia (New River becoming Kanawha River), to Ohio River.
Koyukuk (470 mi.; 756 km): From Brooks Range in Alaska to Yukon R.
Kuskokwim (680 mi.; 1,094 km): From Alaska Range in Alaska to Kuskokwim Bay.
Licking (350 mi.; 563 km): From Magoffin Co. in Kentucky to Ohio R. at Cincinnati in Ohio.
Little Missouri (560 mi.; 901 km): From Crook Co. in Wyoming to Missouri R. in North Dakota.
Milk (625 mi.; 1,006 km): From junction of forks in Alberta Province to Missouri R.
Mississippi (2,348 mi.; 3,779 km): From Lake Itasca in Minnesota to mouth of Southwest Pass in La.
Mississippi-Missouri-Red Rock (3,710 mi.; 5,971 km): From source of Red Rock R. in Montana to mouth of Southwest Pass in Louisiana.
Missouri (2,315 mi.; 3,726 km): From junction of Jefferson R., Gallatin R., and Madison R. in Montana to Mississippi R. near St. Louis.
Missouri-Red Rock (2,533 mi.; 4,076 km): From source of Red Rock R. in Montana to Mississippi R. near St. Louis.
Mobile-Alabama-Coosa (780 mi.; 1,255 km): From junction of Etowah R. and Oostanaula R. in Georgia to Mobile Bay.
Neosho (460 mi.; 740 km): From Morris Co. in Kansas to Arkansas R. in Oklahoma.
Niobrara (431 mi.; 694 km): From Niobrara Co. in Wyoming to Missouri R. in Nebraska.
Noatak (350 mi.; 563 km): From Brooks Range in Alaska to Kotzebue Sound.
North Canadian (760 mi.; 1,223 km): From Union Co. in New Mexico to Canadian R. in Oklahoma.
North Platte (618 mi.; 995 km): From Jackson Co. in Colorado to junction with So. Platte R. in Nebraska to form Platte R.
Ohio (981 mi.; 1,579 km): From junction of Allegheny R. and Monongahela R. at Pittsburgh to Mississippi R. between Illinois and Kentucky.
Ohio-Allegheny (1,306 mi.; 2,102 km): From Potter Co. in Pennsylvania to Mississippi R. at Cairo in Illinois.
Osage (500 mi.; 805 km): From east-central Kansas to Missouri R. near Jefferson City in Missouri.
Ouachita (605 mi.; 974 km): From Polk Co. in Arkansas to Red R. in Louisiana.
Pearl (411 mi.; 661 km): From Neshoba County in Mississippi to Gulf of Mexico (Mississippi-Louisiana).
Pecos (735 mi.; 1,183 km): From Mora Co. in New Mexico to Rio Grande in Texas.
Pee Dee-Yadkin (435 mi.; 700 km): From Watauga Co. in North Carolina to Winyah Bay in South Carolina.
Pend Oreille (490 mi.; 789 km): Near Butte in Montana to Columbia R. on Washington-Canada border.
Porcupine (460 mi.; 740 km): From Yukon Territory, Canada, to Yukon R. in Alaska.
Potomac (383 mi.; 616 km): From Garrett Co. in Md. to Chesapeake Bay at Point Lookout in Md.
Powder (375 mi.; 603 km): From junction of forks in Johnson Co. in Wyoming to Yellowstone R. in Montana.
Red (1,270 mi.; 2,044 km): From junction of forks in Harmon Co. in Oklahoma to Mississippi R. in Louisiana.
Red (officially called *Red River of the North*) (545 mi.; 877 km): From junction of Otter Tail R. and Bois de Sioux R. in Minnesota to Lake Winnipeg in Manitoba.
Republican (445 mi.; 716 km): From junction of North Fork and Arikaree R. in Nebraska to junction with Smoky Hill R. in Kansas to form the Kansas R.
Rio Grande (1,885 mi.; 3,034 km): From San Juan Co. in Colorado to Gulf of Mexico.
Roanoke (380 mi.; 612 km): From junction of forks in Montgomery Co. in Virginia to Albemarle Sound in North Carolina.
Sabine (380 mi.; 612 km): From junction of forks in Hunt Co. in Texas to Sabine Lake between Texas and Louisiana.
Sacramento (377 mi.; 607 km): From Siskiyou Co. in California to Suisun Bay.
Saint Francis (425 mi.; 684 km): From Iron Co. in Missouri to Mississippi R. in Arkansas.
Salmon (420 mi.; 676 km): From Custer Co. in Idaho to Snake R.
San Joaquin (350 mi.; 563 km): From junction of forks in Madera Co. in California to Suisun Bay.
San Juan (360 mi.; 579 km): From Archuleta Co. in Colorado to Colorado R. in Utah.
Santee-Wateree-Catawba (538 mi.; 866 km): From McDowell Co. in North Carolina to Atlantic Ocean in South Carolina.
Smoky Hill (540 mi.; 869 km): From Cheyenne Co. in Colorado to junction with Republican R. in Kansas to form Kansas R.
Snake (1,038 mi.; 1,670 km): From Ocean Plateau in Wyoming to Columbia R. in Washington.
South Platte (424 mi.; 682 km): From Park Co. in Colorado to junction with North Platte R. in Nebraska to form Platte R.
Susquehanna (444 mi.; 715 km): From Otsego Lake in New York to Chesapeake Bay in Maryland.
Tanana (620 mi.; 998 km): From Wrangell Mts. in Yukon Territory, Canada, to Yukon R. in Alaska.
Tennessee (652 mi.; 1,049 km): From junction of Holston R. and French Broad R. in Tennessee to Ohio R. in Kentucky.
Tennessee-French Broad (900 mi.; 1,448 km): From Bland Co. in Virginia to Ohio R. at Paducah in Kentucky.
Tombigbee (525 mi.; 845 km): From junction of forks in Itawamba Co. in Mississippi to Mobile R. in Alabama.
Trinity (360 mi.; 579 km): From junction of forks in Dallas Co. in Texas to Galveston Bay.
Wabash (529 mi.; 851 km): From Darke Co. in Ohio to Ohio R. between Illinois and Indiana.
Washita (500 mi.; 805 km): From Hemphill Co. in Texas to Red R. in Oklahoma.
White (720 mi.; 1,159 km): From Madison Co. in Arkansas to Mississippi R.
Wisconsin (430 mi.; 692 km): From Vilas Co. in Wisconsin to Mississippi R.
Yellowstone (671 mi.; 1,080 km): From Park Co. in Wyoming to Missouri R. in North Dakota.
Yukon (1,770 mi.; 2,848 km): From junction of Lewes R. and Pelly R. in Yukon Territory, Canada, to Bering Sea in Alaska.

Longitude and Latitude of U.S. and Canadian Cities

(and time corresponding to 12:00 noon, eastern standard time)

City	Long. w °	Long. w '	Lat. n °	Lat. n '	Time
Albany, N.Y.	73	45	42	40	12:00 noon
Amarillo, Tex.	101	50	35	11	11:00 a.m.
Anchorage, Alaska	149	54	61	13	7:00 a.m.
Atlanta	84	23	33	45	12:00 noon
Atlantic City, N.J.	74	25	39	22	12:00 noon
Austin, Nev.	117	4	39	29	9:00 a.m.
Baker, Ore.	117	50	44	47	9:00 a.m.
Baltimore	76	38	39	18	12:00 noon
Bangor, Me.	68	47	44	48	12:00 noon
Birmingham, Ala.	86	50	33	30	11:00 a.m.
Bismarck, N.D.	100	47	46	48	11:00 a.m.
Boise, Idaho	116	13	43	36	10:00 a.m.
Boston	71	5	42	21	12:00 noon
Buffalo, N.Y.	78	50	42	55	12:00 noon
Calgary, Alberta	114	1	51	1	10:00 a.m.
Carlsbad, N.M.	104	15	32	26	10:00 a.m.
Charleston, S.C.	79	56	32	47	12:00 noon
Charleston, W.Va.	81	38	38	21	12:00 noon
Charlotte, N.C.	80	50	35	14	12:00 noon
Cheyenne, Wyo.	104	52	41	9	10:00 a.m.
Chicago	87	37	41	50	11:00 a.m.
Cincinnati	84	30	39	8	12:00 noon
Cleveland	81	37	41	28	12:00 noon
Columbia, S.C.	81	2	34	0	12:00 noon
Columbus, Ohio	83	1	40	0	12:00 noon
Dallas	96	46	32	46	11:00 a.m.
Denver	105	0	39	45	10:00 a.m.
Des Moines, Iowa	93	37	41	35	11:00 a.m.
Detroit	83	3	42	20	12:00 noon
Dubuque, Iowa	90	40	42	31	11:00 a.m.
Duluth, Minn.	92	5	46	49	11:00 a.m.
Eastport, Me.	67	0	44	54	12:00 noon
El Centro, Calif.	115	33	32	38	9:00 a.m.
El Paso	106	29	31	46	10:00 a.m.
Eugene, Ore.	123	5	44	3	9:00 a.m.
Fargo, N.D.	96	48	46	52	11:00 a.m.
Flagstaff, Ariz.	111	41	35	13	10:00 a.m.
Fresno, Calif.	119	48	36	44	9:00 a.m.
Garden City, Kan.	100	53	37	58	10:00 a.m.
Grand Junction, Colo.	108	33	39	5	10:00 a.m.
Grand Rapids, Mich.	85	40	42	58	12:00 noon
Havre, Mont.	109	43	48	33	10:00 a.m.
Helena, Mont.	112	2	46	35	10:00 a.m.
Honolulu	157	50	21	18	7:00 a.m.
Hoquiam, Wash.	123	54	46	59	9:00 a.m.
Hot Springs, Ark.	93	3	34	31	11:00 a.m.
Idaho Falls, Idaho	112	1	43	30	10:00 a.m.
Indianapolis	86	10	39	46	12:00 noon
Jackson, Miss.	90	12	32	20	11:00 a.m.
Jacksonville, Fla.	81	40	30	22	12:00 noon
Juneau, Alaska	134	24	58	18	9:00 a.m.
Kansas City, Mo.	94	35	39	6	11:00 a.m.
Key West, Fla.	81	48	24	33	12:00 noon
Kingston, Ont.	76	30	44	15	12:00 noon
Klamath Falls, Ore.	121	44	42	10	9:00 a.m.
Knoxville, Tenn.	83	56	35	57	12:00 noon
Lander, Wyo.	108	40	42	50	10:00 a.m.
Las Vegas, Nev.	115	12	36	10	9:00 a.m.
Lewiston, Idaho	117	2	46	24	9:00 a.m.
Lincoln, Neb.	96	40	40	50	11:00 a.m.
London, Ont.	81	34	43	2	12:00 noon
Los Angeles	118	15	34	3	9:00 a.m.
Louisville, Ky.	85	46	38	15	12:00 noon
Manchester, N.H.	71	30	43	0	12:00 noon
Memphis, Tenn	90	3	35	9	11:00 a.m.
Miami, Fla.	80	12	25	46	12:00 noon
Milwaukee	87	55	43	2	11:00 a.m.
Minneapolis	93	14	44	59	11:00 a.m.
Mobile, Ala.	88	3	30	42	11:00 a.m.
Montgomery, Ala.	86	18	32	21	11:00 a.m.
Montpelier, Vt.	72	32	44	15	12:00 noon
Montreal, Que.	73	35	45	30	12:00 noon
Moose Jaw, Sask.	105	31	50	37	10:00 a.m.
Nashville, Tenn.	86	47	36	10	11:00 a.m.
Needles, Calif.	114	36	34	50	9:00 a.m.
Nelson, B.C.	117	17	49	30	9:00 a.m.
New Haven, Conn.	72	55	41	19	12:00 noon
New Orleans	90	4	29	57	11:00 a.m.
New York	73	58	40	47	12:00 noon
Nogales, Ariz.	110	56	31	21	10:00 a.m.
Nome, Alaska	165	30	64	25	6:00 a.m.
North Platte, Neb.	100	46	41	8	11:00 a.m.
Oklahoma City	97	28	35	26	11:00 a.m.
Ottawa, Ont.	75	43	45	24	12:00 noon
Philadelphia	75	10	39	57	12:00 noon
Phoenix, Ariz.	112	4	33	29	10:00 a.m.
Pierre, S.D.	100	21	44	22	11:00 a.m.
Pittsburgh	79	57	40	27	12:00 noon
Port Arthur, Ont.	89	17	48	30	12:00 noon
Portland, Me.	70	15	43	40	12:00 noon
Portland, Ore.	122	41	45	31	9:00 a.m.
Providence, R.I.	71	24	41	50	12:00 noon
Quebec, Que.	71	11	46	49	12:00 noon
Raleigh, N.C.	78	39	35	46	12:00 noon
Reno, Nev.	119	49	39	30	9:00 a.m.
Richfield, Utah	112	5	38	46	10:00 a.m.
Richmond, Va.	77	29	37	33	12:00 noon
Roanoke, Va.	79	57	37	17	12:00 noon
Sacramento, Calif.	121	30	38	35	9:00 a.m.
St. John, N.B.	66	10	45	18	1:00 p.m.
St. Louis	90	12	38	35	11:00 a.m.
Salmon, Idaho	113	54	45	11	10:00 a.m.
Salt Lake City, Utah	111	54	40	46	10:00 a.m.
San Antonio	98	33	29	23	11:00 a.m.
San Diego, Calif.	117	10	32	42	9:00 a.m.
San Francisco	122	26	37	47	9:00 a.m.
San Juan, P.R.	66	10	18	30	1:00 p.m.
Santa Fe, N.M.	105	57	35	41	10:00 a.m.
Sault Ste. Marie, Mich.	84	21	46	30	11:00 a.m.
Savannah, Ga.	81	5	32	5	12:00 noon
Scranton, Pa.	75	39	41	24	12:00 noon
Seattle	122	20	47	37	9:00 a.m.
Shreveport, La.	93	42	32	28	11:00 a.m.
Sioux Falls, S.D.	96	44	43	33	11:00 a.m.
Sitka, Alaska	135	15	57	10	9:00 a.m.
Spokane, Wash.	117	26	47	40	9:00 a.m.
Springfield, Ill.	89	38	39	48	11:00 a.m.
Springfield, Mass.	72	34	42	6	12:00 noon
Springfield, Mo.	93	17	37	13	11:00 a.m.
Syracuse, N.Y.	76	8	43	2	12:00 noon
Tampa, Fla.	82	27	27	57	12:00 noon
Toronto, Ont.	79	24	43	40	12:00 noon
Trinidad, Colo.	104	30	37	10	10:00 a.m.
Victoria, B.C.	123	21	48	25	9:00 a.m.
Watertown, N.Y.	75	55	43	58	12:00 noon
Wichita, Kan.	97	17	37	43	11:00 a.m.
Wilmington, N.C.	77	57	34	14	12:00 noon
Winnipeg, Man.	97	7	49	54	11:00 a.m.

Coastline of the United States

State	Lengths, statute miles General coastline[1]	Tidal shoreline[2]	State	Lengths, statute miles General coastline[1]	Tidal shoreline[2]
Atlantic Coast:			Gulf Coast:		
Maine	228	3,478	Florida (Gulf)	770	5,095
New Hampshire	13	131	Alabama	53	607
Massachusetts	192	1,519	Mississippi	44	359
Rhode Island	40	384	Louisiana	397	7,721
Connecticut	—	618	Texas	367	3,359
New York	127	1,850	Total Gulf coast	1,631	17,141
New Jersey	130	1,792	Pacific Coast:		
Pennsylvania	—	89	California	840	3,427
Delaware	28	381	Oregon	296	1,410
Maryland	31	3,190	Washington	157	3,026
Virginia	112	3,315	Hawaii	750	1,052
North Carolina	301	3,375	Alaska (Pacific)	5,580	31,383
South Carolina	187	2,876	Total Pacific coast	7,623	40,298
Georgia	100	2,344	Arctic Coast:		
Florida (Atlantic)	580	3,331	Alaska (Arctic)	1,060	2,521
Total Atlantic coast	2,069	28,673	Total Arctic coast	1,060	2,521
			States Total	**12,383**	**88,633**

1. Figures are lengths of general outline of seacoast. Measurements made with unit measure of 30 minutes of latitude on charts as near scale of 1:1,200,000 as possible. Coastline of bays and sounds is included to point where they narrow to width of unit measure, and distance across at such point is included. 2. Figures obtained in 1939–40 with recording instrument on largest-scale maps and charts then available. Shoreline of outer coast, offshore islands, sounds, bays, rivers, and creeks is included to head of tidewater, or to point where tidal waters narrow to width of 100 feet. *Source:* Department of Commerce, National Oceanic and Atmospheric Administration, National Ocean Service.

The Continental Divide

The Continental Divide is a ridge of high ground which runs irregularly north and south through the Rocky Mountains and separates eastward-flowing from westward-flowing streams. The waters which flow eastward empty into the Atlantic Ocean, chiefly by way of the Gulf of Mexico; those which flow westward empty into the Pacific.

Mapping Inner Earth

Scientists are now trying to map the structure of the earth's interior by tracking the speeds of earthquake waves. By using the results of data recorded by digital seismometers, a detailed three-dimensional map of the inner geography of the earth is now within the realm of possibility. Present studies are dealing with the earth's mantle and three groups of researchers are involved with the task.

More Serious Earthquakes Reported in 1983

Although the number of "significant" earthquakes increased in 1983 world-wide, there were fewer deaths. A "significant" quake is one that registers 6.5 or more on the Richter scale. There were 70 reported in 1983—14 more than in 1982 and 20 more than in 1981. However, the death toll in 1983 was 2,322, down by 1,016 from the 1982 toll of 3,338 and less than half the number of deaths in 1981.

Emergency Quake Plans for Eastern United States

The strongest earthquakes in the U.S. have occurred in the New Madrid fault system. In 1811 and 1812, three earthquakes took place near New Madrid, Mo., reaching 8.6, 8.4, and 8.7 on the Richter scale. The Mississippi River changed its course in some places and several lakes were created. Property damage was extensive but few lives were lost because of the low population density in the area at that time. The last major quake in that system occurred in 1895.

Scientists believe that another major earthquake in that zone is possible by the end of this century. The Central U.S. Earthquake Consortium received a $300,000 grant from the Federal Emergency Management Agency in April 1984 to use in preparing an emergency response plan in the event a major earthquake occurs in the eastern part of the United States.

The seven states that are most likely to be affected when a major earthquake occurs along the New Madrid fault are: Arkansas, Illinois, Indiana, Kentucky, Missouri, Mississippi, and Tennessee. A successful emergency plan would save lives, minimize transportation and communication problems, and provide medical and social services for the inhabitants of those states.

NORTH AMERICA
LAMBERT AZIMUTHAL EQUAL-AREA PROJECTION
SCALE OF MILES
0 200 400 600 800 1000
SCALE OF KILOMETERS
0 200 400 600 800 1000
Capitals of Countries
International Boundaries
Canals
Copyright by C.S.HAMMOND & Co., N.Y.
North Pole
ARCTIC OCEAN
GREENLAND SEA
Jan Mayen (Nor.)
ASIA
Arctic Circle
Anadyr'
Wrangel I.
BERING SEA
St. Lawrence I.
Bering Str.
BEAUFORT SEA
Pt. Barrow
Axel Heiberg I.
SVERDRUP IS.
Prince Patrick I.
QUEEN ELIZABETH IS.
Melville I.
M'Clure Str.
Banks I.
Parry Channel
Devon I.
Lancaster Sd.
Baffin Bay
Ellesmere I.
PEARY LAND
GREENLAND
(KALAALLIT NUNAAT) (Den.)
KING CHRISTIAN X LAND
KING CHRISTIAN IX LAND
FREDERIK VI COAST
PRUDHOE LAND
Thule Air Base
ICELAND
Reykjavík
Str. of Denmark
Ammassalik
Disko I.
Davis Strait
Nuuk (Godthåb)
Qaqortoq
C. Farewell
Norton Sd.
Seward Pen.
Nome
Yukon
Koyukuk
Kuskokwim
UNITED STATES ALASKA
Fairbanks
Anchorage
Bristol Bay
Alaska Pen.
Kodiak I.
G. of Alaska
Aklavik
Inuvik
Amundsen Gulf
Victoria I.
M'Clintock Chan.
G. of Boothia
Boothia Pen.
Baffin I.
Foxe Basin
Pangnirtung
Cumberland Sd.
Melville Pen.
Norman Wells
Dawson
Mackenzie
Port Radium
Great Bear L.
Wager Bay
Southampton I.
Hudson Str.
C. Chidley
Ft. Simpson
Whitehorse
Yellowknife
Chesterfield Inlet
Coats I.
Mansel I.
Ungava Bay
Labrador
Hamilton Inlet
ALEXANDER ARCH.
Juneau
Liard
Ft. Smith
Great Slave L.
Hudson Bay
Ketchikan
Dixon Entr.
QUEEN CHARLOTTE IS.
Prince Rupert
Peace
Fort McMurray
L. Athabasca
Athabasca
Churchill
Reindeer L.
CANADA
BELCHER IS.
Grande-Rivière de la Baleine
La Grande-Rivière
James Bay
Goose Bay
Battle Harbour
Str. of Belle Isle
Newfoundland
St. John's
C. Race
PACIFIC OCEAN
Fraser
Vancouver I.
Edmonton
Saskatchewan
Prince Albert
Saskatoon
Calgary
Nelson
L. Winnipeg
Albany
Moosonee
Nottaway
G. of St. Lawrence
Sydney
C. Breton I.
Charlottetown
Saint John
Halifax
Str. of Juan de Fuca
Victoria
Vancouver
Lethbridge
Regina
Medicine Hat
L. Manitoba
Winnipeg
Thunder Bay
L. Nipigon
Timmins
Québec
Montréal
Tacoma
Seattle
Spokane
L. Superior
Sault Ste. Marie
Ottawa
Portland
Columbia
Butte
Great Falls
Yellowstone
Fargo
Bismarck
Duluth
St. Paul
L. Huron
Toronto
L. Ontario
Boston
C. Sable
C. Cod
Providence
C. Mendocino
Boise
Snake
Pierre
Minneapolis
L. Michigan
Milwaukee
Detroit
Buffalo
Albany
Pocatello
Missouri
L. Erie
Pittsburgh
New York
Philadelphia
Great Salt Lake
Casper
Sioux City
Chicago
Cleveland
Baltimore
San Francisco
Reno
Sacramento
Oakland
Cheyenne
Salt Lake City
Omaha
Platte
Des Moines
Peoria
Columbus
Indianapolis
Washington
Cincinnati
Louisville
Richmond
Norfolk
Denver
Pueblo
Kansas City
St. Louis
Ohio
Los Angeles
Colorado
UNITED STATES
Wichita
Tulsa
Nashville
Winston-Salem
C. Hatteras
Bermuda (Br.) Hamilton
Chattanooga
Charlotte
Albuquerque
Amarillo
Oklahoma City
Arkansas
Memphis
Atlanta
San Diego
Phoenix
Little Rock
Birmingham
Charleston
Savannah
Mississippi
Tucson
Fort Worth
Dallas
Red
Jackson
Mobile
Jacksonville
El Paso
Brazos
Guadalupe (Mex.)
Lower California
Ciudad Juárez
Hermosillo
Austin
Houston
C. Canaveral
I. Cedros
Gulf of California
Rio Grande
San Antonio
New Orleans
Tampa
BAHAMAS
Yaqui
Chihuahua
Miami
Nassau
Tropic of Cancer
Monterrey
Gulf of Mexico
Strs. of Florida
Torreón
Durango
Windward Pass.
C. San Lucas
Mazatlán
San Luis Potosí
Tampico
Havana
CUBA
DOMINICAN REP.
San Juan
PUERTO RICO (U.S.)
Aguascalientes
Guadalajara
MEXICO
Mérida
Yucatán Chan.
I. de la Juventud
Camagüey
Santiago de Cuba
HAITI
Port-au-Prince
Santo Domingo
Mona Pass.
C. Corrientes
Santiago
Mexico City
Veracruz Llave
Yucatán Pen.
JAMAICA
Kingston
Revillagigedo (Mex.) Is.
Balsas
Villahermosa
Belmopan
BELIZE
Acapulco
Oaxaca
HONDURAS
Tegucigalpa
C. Gracias a Dios
CARIBBEAN SEA
Guatemala
GUATEMALA
San Salvador
EL SALVADOR
Managua
NICARAGUA
Maracaibo
Panama Canal
Clipperton I. (Fr.)
CENTRAL AMERICA
San José
COSTA RICA
Panamá
PANAMA
G. of Panamá
Medellín
Bogotá
Cocos I. (C.R.)
SOUTH AMERICA
Quito
Guayaquil
GALÁPAGOS IS. (Ecuador)
Equator
Longitude 100° West of Greenwich 90°
120°
110°
80°
70°
60°
50°
40°
30°
20°
10°
0°

UNITED STATES
POLYCONIC PROJECTION
SCALE OF MILES
0 50 100 200 300 400
SCALE OF KILOMETERS
0 100 200 300 400
Capitals of Countries
State Capitals
International Boundaries
Railroads
© Copyright HAMMOND INCORPORATED, Maplewood, N. J.
Longitude 95° West of H Greenwich 90°
J 85° K 80° L 75°
95° H 90° J 85° K 80° L 75° M 70° N 65°
45° 40° 35° 30° 25°
2 3 4 5 6
C A N A D A
Lake Superior
Lake Michigan
Lake Huron
Lake Ontario
Lake Erie
James Bay
ATLANTIC OCEAN
GULF OF MEXICO
BAHAMAS
CUBA
Havana
Tropic of Cancer
Straits of Florida
Santarén Channel
Gulf of Maine
MINNESOTA
WISCONSIN
MICHIGAN
IOWA
ILLINOIS
INDIANA
OHIO
PENNSYLVANIA
NEW YORK
NEW JERSEY
MAINE
VT.
N.H.
MASS.
CONN.
RHODE ISLAND
DEL.
MD.
WEST VIRGINIA
VIRGINIA
KENTUCKY
MISSOURI
TENNESSEE
NORTH CAROLINA
SOUTH CAROLINA
GEORGIA
ALABAMA
MISSISSIPPI
ARKANSAS
LOUISIANA
FLORIDA
Montréal
Ottawa
Toronto
Québec
Minneapolis
St. Paul
Duluth
Milwaukee
Madison
Chicago
Detroit
Cleveland
Pittsburgh
Philadelphia
New York
Boston
Albany
Washington
Baltimore
Richmond
Norfolk
Virginia Beach
Raleigh
Charlotte
Columbia
Atlanta
Savannah
Jacksonville
Tallahassee
Orlando
Tampa
Miami
Key West
Montgomery
Birmingham
Jackson
Memphis
Nashville
Knoxville
Louisville
Lexington
Frankfort
Cincinnati
Columbus
Indianapolis
Springfield
St. Louis
Kansas City
Jefferson City
Des Moines
Little Rock
Baton Rouge
New Orleans
Houston
Mobile
Tulsa
Ozark Plat.
Mt. Mitchell 6,684 ft. (2037 m.)
Cape Canaveral
C. Hatteras
C. Lookout
C. Fear
Mississippi Delta

CANADA
CONIC PROJECTION
SCALE OF MILES
0 100 200 300 400 500
SCALE OF KILOMETERS
0 100 200 300 400 500
Capitals of Countries
Provincial & Territorial Capitals
Administrative Centers
© Copyright HAMMOND INCORPORATED, Maplewood, N.J.
GREENLAND
BAFFIN BAY
DAVIS STRAIT
ATLANTIC OCEAN
HUDSON BAY
BEAUFORT SEA
UNITED STATES
ALASKA
YUKON
NORTHWEST TERRITORIES
BRITISH COLUMBIA
ALBERTA
MANITOBA
ONTARIO
QUEBEC
NEWFOUNDLAND
ROCKY MOUNTAINS

MIDDLE AMERICA
BONNE PROJECTION
Copyright by C. S. HAMMOND & Co., N. Y.
SCALE OF MILES
0 200 400 600
KILOMETERS
0 200 400 600
Capitals of Countries
International Boundaries
Canals
Railroads
ATLANTIC OCEAN
Sargasso Sea
Gulf of Mexico
Bay of Campeche
CARIBBEAN SEA
PACIFIC OCEAN
WEST INDIES
GREATER ANTILLES
LESSER ANTILLES
UNITED STATES
MEXICO
CENTRAL AMERICA
CUBA
BAHAMAS
HAITI
DOMINICAN REP.
JAMAICA
PUERTO RICO (U.S.)
GUATEMALA
BELIZE
HONDURAS
EL SALVADOR
NICARAGUA
COSTA RICA
PANAMA
COLOMBIA
VENEZUELA
ECUADOR
BRAZIL
GUYANA
Tropic of Cancer
Equator
Longitude West of Greenwich

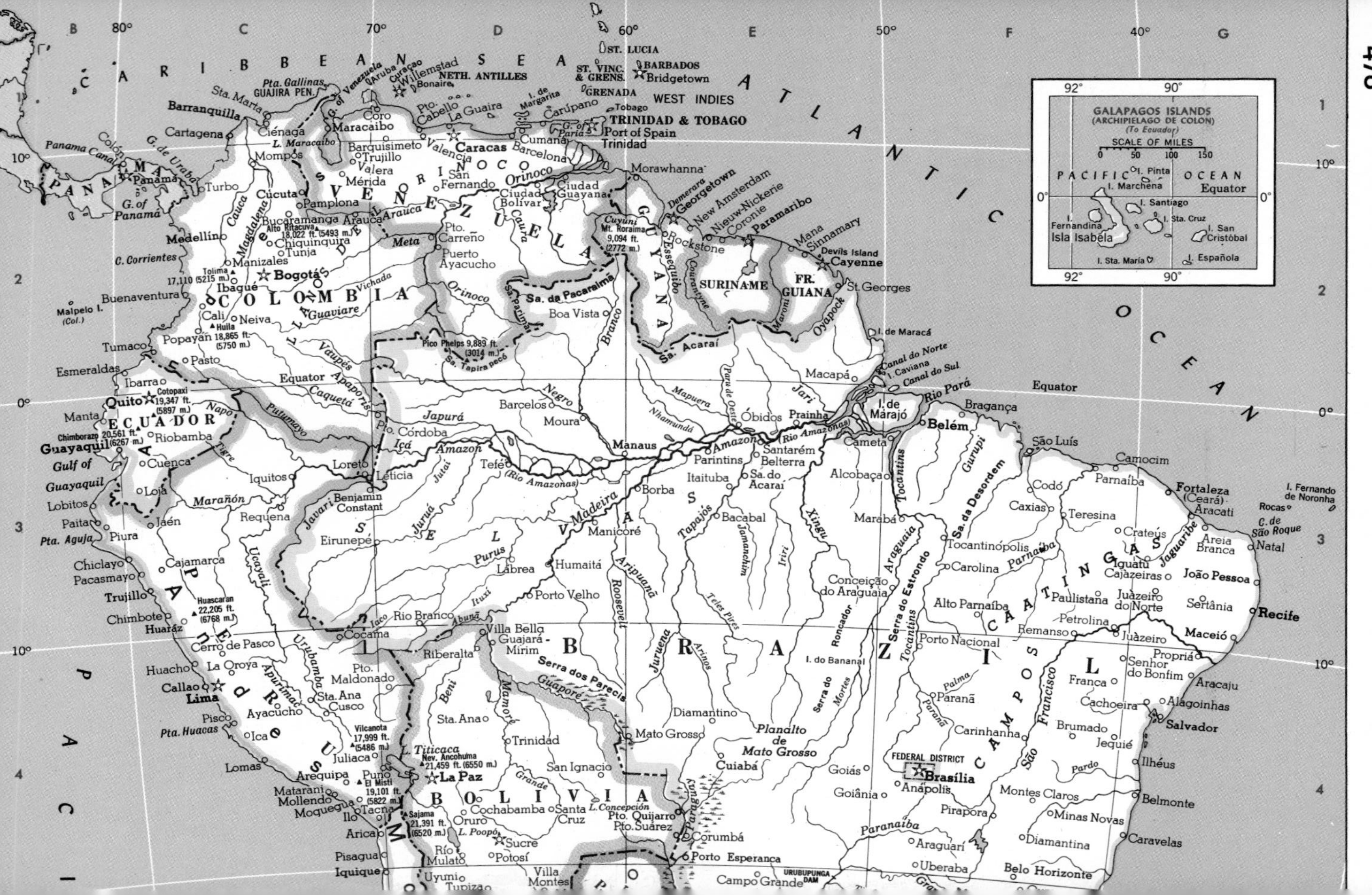

GALAPAGOS ISLANDS
(ARCHIPIELAGO DE COLON)
(To Ecuador)
SCALE OF MILES
PACIFIC OCEAN
Equator
I. Pinta
I. Marchena
I. Santiago
I. Sta. Cruz
I. San Cristóbal
I. Fernandina
Isla Isabela
I. Sta. María
I. Española
CARIBBEAN SEA
ATLANTIC OCEAN
PACIFIC
WEST INDIES
NETH. ANTILLES
TRINIDAD & TOBAGO
BARBADOS
Bridgetown
ST. LUCIA
ST. VINC. & GRENS.
GRENADA
Port of Spain
Trinidad
Tobago
VENEZUELA
Caracas
Maracaibo
L. Maracaibo
Valencia
Barquisimeto
Mérida
Ciudad Bolívar
Ciudad Guayana
Cumaná
Barcelona
Orinoco
Caura
Puerto Ayacucho
LLANOS
GUYANA
Georgetown
New Amsterdam
SURINAME
Paramaribo
FR. GUIANA
Cayenne
Devils Island
St. Georges
Oyapock
Essequibo
Courantyne
Mt. Roraima 9,094 ft. (2772 m.)
Sa. Acaraí
Sa. da Pacaraima
Sa. Parima
Pico Phelps 9,889 ft. (3014 m.)
COLOMBIA
Bogotá
Barranquilla
Cartagena
Sta. Marta
Ciénaga
Cúcuta
Bucaramanga
Medellín
Manizales
Ibagué
Cali
Neiva
Popayán
Pasto
Buenaventura
Tumaco
Magdalena
Cauca
Meta
Guaviare
Vaupés
Caquetá
Putumayo
Apaporis
Huila 18,865 ft. (5750 m.)
Tolima 17,110 (5215 m.)
Pta. Gallinas
GUAJIRA PEN.
PANAMA
Panamá
Colón
Panama Canal
G. of Panamá
G. de Urabá
C. Corrientes
Malpelo I. (Col.)
ECUADOR
Quito
Guayaquil
Gulf of Guayaquil
Cuenca
Riobamba
Esmeraldas
Manta
Ibarra
Loja
Cotopaxi 19,347 ft. (5897 m.)
Chimborazo 20,561 ft. (6267 m.)
Napo
Tigre
PERU
Lima
Callao
Iquitos
Trujillo
Chiclayo
Piura
Paita
Chimbote
Huacho
Pisco
Ica
Arequipa
Cusco
Cerro de Pasco
La Oroya
Cajamarca
Huaráz
Huascarán 22,205 ft. (6768 m.)
Marañón
Ucayali
Urubamba
Apurímac
Puno
Juliaca
Mollendo
Moquegua
Tacna
Ilo
Pta. Aguja
Pta. Huacas
BOLIVIA
La Paz
Sucre
Potosí
Oruro
Cochabamba
Santa Cruz
Trinidad
Riberalta
Titicaca
L. Poopó
Beni
Mamoré
Guaporé
Nev. Ancohuma 21,459 ft. (6550 m.)
Sajama 21,391 ft. (6520 m.)
Villa Montes
Arica
Iquique
Pisagua
BRAZIL
SELVAS
CAATINGAS
CAMPOS
Brasília
FEDERAL DISTRICT
Belém
Manaus
São Luís
Fortaleza (Ceará)
Recife
Natal
João Pessoa
Maceió
Salvador
Aracaju
Teresina
Goiânia
Anápolis
Cuiabá
Corumbá
Campo Grande
Belo Horizonte
Santarém
Óbidos
Macapá
Boa Vista
Porto Velho
Humaitá
Manicoré
Tefé
Benjamin Constant
Leticia
Amazon
Rio Amazonas
Negro
Branco
Madeira
Purus
Juruá
Japurá
Tapajós
Xingu
Tocantins
Araguaia
São Francisco
Paraná
Paranaíba
Paraguay
Jari
I. de Marajó
Rio Pará
Canal do Norte
Canal do Sul
I. Caviana
I. de Maracá
Serra do Estrondo
Sa. da Desordem
Serra dos Parecis
Planalto de Mato Grosso
I. do Bananal
Roncador
Aripuanã
Roosevelt
Juruena
Teles Pires
Jamanchim
Iriri
URUBUPUNGA DAM
I. Fernando de Noronha
Rocas
C. de São Roque
Equator

SOUTH AMERICA
LAMBERT AZIMUTHAL EQUAL-AREA PROJECTION
SCALE OF MILES
0 100 200 400 600
SCALE OF KILOMETERS
0 100 200 400 600
Capitals of Countries
International Boundaries
Canals
Copyright by C.S. HAMMOND & CO., N.Y.
A T L A N T I C
O C E A N
P A C I F I C
O C E A N
Tropic of Capricorn
RIO DE JANEIRO
SÃO PAULO
Asunción
URUGUAY
Montevideo
BUENOS AIRES
Santiago
Valparaíso
Córdoba
Rosario
Porto Alegre
Curitiba
Río de la Plata
FALKLAND ISLANDS
(IS. MALVINAS)
(Br.-claimed by Arg.)
Stanley
East Falkland
West Falkland
Tierra del Fuego
Cape Horn
(Cabo de Hornos)
Strait of Magellan
Punta Arenas
JUAN FERNÁNDEZ IS.
(Chile)
I. Robinson Crusoe
I. Alejandro Selkirk
I. San Félix
(Chile)
I. San Ambrosio
(Chile)
Isla de Chiloé
ARCHIPIÉLAGO de los CHONOS
PEN. TAITAO
Golfo San Jorge
Golfo San Matías
Pen. Valdés
Bahía Blanca
Mar del Plata
Mar Chiquita
L. dos Patos
L. Mirim
Cerro Aconcagua 22,831 ft. (6959 m.)
Vol. Llullaillaco 22,057 ft. (6723 m.)
Nev. Ojos del Salado 22,572 ft. (6880 m.)
Maipo 17,464 ft. (4409 m.)
Longitude 60° West of Greenwich
20°
30°
40°
50°
70°
80°
90°
A
B
C
D
E
F
G
H
5
6
7
8

U. S. S. R.
CASPIAN SEA
BLACK SEA
EUROPE
TURKEY
IRAN
IRAQ
SYRIA
LEBANON
ISRAEL
JORDAN
KUWAIT
Persian Gulf
ASIA
SAUDI ARABIA
Tropic of Cancer
RED SEA
YEMEN ARAB REP.
PEOP. DEM. REP. YEMEN
Gulf of Aden
DJIBOUTI
ETHIOPIA
Ogaden
SOMALIA
KENYA
UGANDA
RWANDA
SUDAN
Nubian Desert
EGYPT
Libyan Desert
LIBYA
Fezzan
Kufra Oasis
CHAD
Tibesti
NIGER
Air (Azbine)
NIGERIA
CAMEROON
CENTRAL AFRICAN REPUBLIC
ZAIRE
GABON
CONGO
EQUATORIAL GUINEA
SÃO TOMÉ E PRÍNCIPE
Gulf of Guinea
Equator
BENIN
TOGO
GHANA
BURKINA FASO
IVORY COAST
LIBERIA
SIERRA LEONE
GUINEA
GUINEA-BISSAU
GAMBIA
SENEGAL
MALI
MAURITANIA
SAHARA
WESTERN SAHARA
ALGERIA
Ahaggar
Tassili n'Ajjer
Tanezrouft
Grand Erg Occidental
Grand Erg Oriental
MOROCCO
Atlas Mountains
TUNISIA
MEDITERRANEAN SEA
SPAIN
PORTUGAL
FRANCE
ITALY
YUGOSLAVIA
ALBANIA
GREECE
BULGARIA
ROMANIA
CYPRUS
MALTA
Tehran
Baghdad
Damascus
Beirut
Riyadh
Mecca
Ankara
Istanbul
Athens
Rome
Naples
Madrid
Lisbon
Tunis
Algiers
Rabat
Casablanca
Tripoli
Benghazi
Cairo
Alexandria
Khartoum
Addis Ababa
Djibouti
Mogadishu
Nairobi
Kampala
N'Djamena
Niamey
Bamako
Dakar
Nouakchott
Lagos
Accra
Abidjan
Monrovia
Freetown
Conakry
Yaoundé
Libreville
Bangui

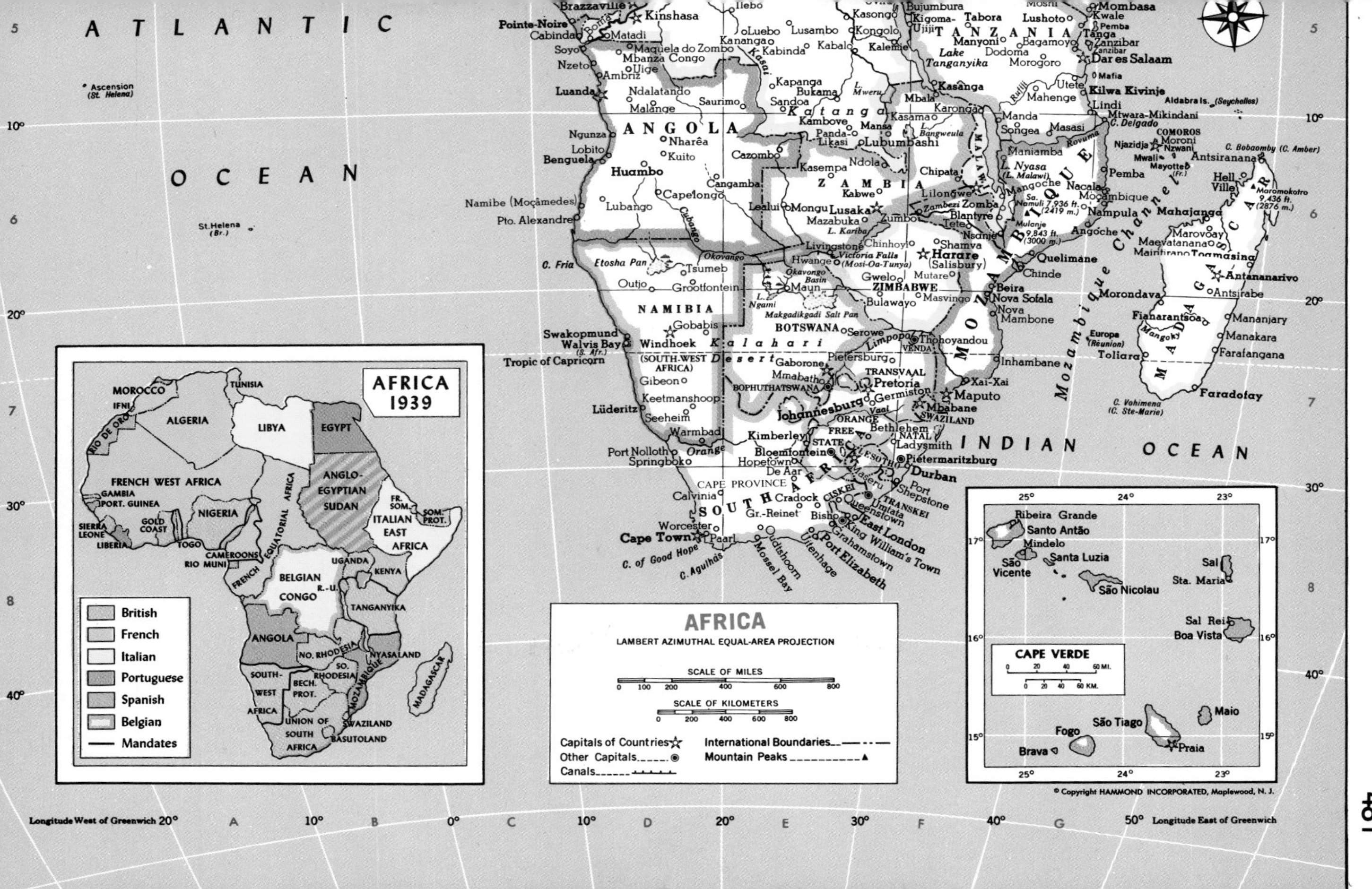
ATLANTIC OCEAN
INDIAN OCEAN
Mozambique Channel
ANGOLA
ZAMBIA
NAMIBIA
BOTSWANA
ZIMBABWE
MOZAMBIQUE
TANZANIA
MADAGASCAR
SOUTH AFRICA
AFRICA 1939
MOROCCO
ALGERIA
LIBYA
EGYPT
ANGLO-EGYPTIAN SUDAN
FRENCH WEST AFRICA
NIGERIA
BELGIAN CONGO
ITALIAN EAST AFRICA
British
French
Italian
Portuguese
Spanish
Belgian
Mandates
AFRICA
LAMBERT AZIMUTHAL EQUAL-AREA PROJECTION
SCALE OF MILES
0 100 200 400 600 800
SCALE OF KILOMETERS
0 200 400 600 800
Capitals of Countries
Other Capitals
Canals
International Boundaries
Mountain Peaks
CAPE VERDE
© Copyright HAMMOND INCORPORATED, Maplewood, N. J.
Longitude West of Greenwich 20°
50° Longitude East of Greenwich

EUROPE
LAMBERT AZIMUTHAL EQUAL AREA PROJECTION
SCALE OF MILES
0 100 200 300 400 500
SCALE OF KILOMETERS
0 100 200 300 400 500
Capitals of Countries
International Boundaries
Canals
Copyright by C. S. HAMMOND & CO., N. Y.
BARENTS SEA
WHITE Sea
BLACK SEA
CASPIAN SEA
Sea of Azov
Sea of Marmara
UNION OF SOVIET SOCIALIST REPUBLICS
RUSSIAN SOVIET FEDERATED SOCIALIST REPUBLIC
UKRAINIAN S.S.R.
WHITE RUSSIAN S.S.R.
ESTONIAN S.S.R.
LATVIAN S.S.R.
LITHUANIAN S.S.R.
MOLDAVIAN S.S.R.
GEORGIAN S.S.R.
ARMENIAN S.S.R.
AZERBAIDZHAN S.S.R.
FINLAND
ROMANIA
BULGARIA
GREECE
TURKEY
SYRIA
IRAN
CYPRUS
CRIMEA
KOLA PEN.
KANIN PEN.
Kolguyev I.
Nordkapp (North Cape)
Bay of Mezen'
Cheshskaya Bay
Gulf of Bothnia
Gulf of Finland
G. of Riga
G. of Kara Bogaz
L. Inari
L. Oulu
L. Onega
L. Ladoga
L. Peipus
L. Il'men
Rybinsk Res.
Gor'kiy Res.
Kama Res.
Votkinsk Res.
Kiev Res.
Kremenchug Res.
Kakhovka Res.
Tsimlyansk Res.
L. Manych-Gudilo
Caucasus
Balkan Mts.
Rhodope
Iron Gate
Ural Mts.
Volga
Ob'
Irtysh
Tobol
Pechora
Usa
Mezen'
Northern Dvina
Onega
Kama
Belaya
Ural
Emba
Oka
Don
Donets
Dnieper
Dniester
Prut
Siret
Danube
Morava
Bug
Wisła
Kizil Irmak
Araks
Torne
Muonio
Tana
Salekhard
Berezovo
Surgut
Khanty-Mansiysk
Tobol'sk
Vorkuta
Naryan Mar
Ust Tsilma
Mezen'
Archangel
Murmansk
Pechenga
Vadsø
Kirovsk
Kandalaksha
Kem'
Onega
Nyandoma
Kotlas
Syktyvkar
Velikiy Ustyug
Petrozavodsk
Sortavala
Joensuu
Kuopio
Vaasa
Oulu
Tornio
Haparanda
Tampere
Turku
Helsinki
Kotka
Vyborg
LENINGRAD
Cherepovets
Vologda
Kirov (Vyatka)
Kotel'nich
Berezniki
Perm'
Izhevsk
Sarapul
Krasnoural'sk
Nizhniy Tagil
Kirovgrad
Sverdlovsk
Tyumen'
Kurgan
Chelyabinsk
Zlatoust
Troitsk
Kustanay
Magnitogorsk
Ufa
Brezhnev
Kuybyshev
Kazan'
Gor'kiy
Dzerzhinsk
Balakhna
Kostroma
Yaroslavl'
Andropov
Ivanovo
Kalinin
MOSCOW (Moskva)
Orekhovo Zuyevo
Serpukhov
Tula
Kaluga
Smolensk
Vitebsk
Velikiye Luki
Pskov
Narva
Kingisepp
Tallinn
Tartu
Pärnu
Hiiumaa
Riga
Cēsis
Jelgava
Rezekne
Daugavpils
Panevežys
Šiauliai
Kaunas
Vilna
Kaliningrad
Minsk
Negoreloye
Grodno
Stolbtsy
Białystok
Pinsk
Brest
Lublin
Gomel'
Bryansk
Orel
Kursk
Michurinsk
Tambov
Penza
Voronezh
Saratov
Engel's
Volgograd (Stalingrad)
Ul'yanovsk
Orenburg
Ural'sk
Aktyubinsk
Temir
Chelkar
Gur'yev
Fort Shevchenko
Astrakhan'
Elista
Millerovo
Voroshilovgrad
Shakhty
Rostov
Taganrog
Zhdanov
Donetsk
Makeyevka
Kramatorsk
Kharkov
Poltava
Kremenchug
Dneprodzerzhinsk
Dnepropetrovsk
Zaporozh'ye
Krivoy Rog
Kirovograd
Kiev
Zhitomir
Rovno
Shepetovka
L'vov
Przemyśl
Ivano-Frankovsk
Vinnitsa
Chernovtsy
Mukachevo
Satu Mare
Debrecen
Oradea
Cluj-Napoca
Roman
Iaşi
Kishinev
Bendery
Tiraspol
Nikolayev
Kherson
Odessa
Belgorod Dnestrovskiy
Galaţi
Brăila
Sulina
Constanţa
Bucharest
Ploieşti
Braşov
Sibiu
Timişoara
Craiova
Ruse
Pleven
Varna
Sliven
Burgas
Sofia
Niš
Plovdiv
Stara Zagora
Edirne
Skopje
Bitola
Kavalla
Thessaloníki
Larisa
Vólos
Trikkala
Lamía
Khalkis
Athens
Piraievs
Pátrai
Corinth
Kalámai
Taínaron
Khania
Iráklion
Crete
Rhodes
Lésvos
Khíos
Sámos
Euboea
Tekirdağ
ISTANBUL
Bosporus
Bursa
Eskişehir
Manisa
İzmir
Afyonkarahisar
Konya
Antalya
Mersin
Tarsus
Adana
Antakya
Aleppo
Latakia
Nicosia
Larnaca
Kayseri
Maraş
Sivas
Ankara
Ereğli
Samsun
Sinop
Trabzon
Erzurum
Kerch
Simferopol'
Sevastopol'
Yalta
Novorossiysk
Krasnodar
Armavir
Tuapse
Sochi
Sukhumi
Maykop
Kislovodsk
Pyatigorsk
Karachayevsk
El'brus 18,510 ft. (5642 m.)
Ordzhonikidze
Groznyy
Makhachkala
Kutaisi
Batumi
Tbilisi
Leninakan
Erivan
Nakhichevan'
Dzhul'fa
Baku
Krasnovodsk

ATLANTIC OCEAN
Greenland
Iceland
Jan Mayen (Nor.)
Faeroe Is. (Den.)
Shetland Is.
Hebrides
Arctic Circle
North Pole
ARCTIC OCEAN
Spitsbergen
Svalbard (Spitsbergen) (Nor.)
Franz Josef Ld.
Severnaya Zemlya
New Siberian Is.
LAPTEV SEA
BARENTS SEA
KARA SEA
Novaya Zemlya
UNITED STATES
ALASKA
Bering Str.
Wrangel I.
Nunivak I.
St. Lawrence I.
BERING SEA
Aleutian Is.
Komandorskiye Is.
PACIFIC OCEAN
SEA OF OKHOTSK
Kamchatka Pen.
Kuril Is.
Sakhalin
Kolyma Range
Sikhote-Alin'
SEA OF JAPAN
JAPAN
TOKYO
Yokohama
Hokkaido
Honshu
Osaka
Kobe
Kyoto
Nagoya
Shikoku
Kyushu
NORTH SEA
BALTIC SEA
G. of Bothnia
WHITE SEA
LONDON
Paris
Brussels
Amsterdam
Hamburg
Copenhagen
Berlin
Stockholm
Oslo
Helsinki
Prague
Vienna
Warsaw
Budapest
Belgrade
Bucharest
Sofia
Rome
Milan
Athens
Istanbul
Ankara
Leningrad
MOSCOW
Kiev
Volgograd (Stalingrad)
UNION OF SOVIET SOCIALIST REPUBLICS
RUSSIAN SOVIET FEDERATED SOCIALIST REPUBLIC
EUROPE
SIBERIA
Ural Mts.
Sverdlovsk
Chelyabinsk
Omsk
Novosibirsk
Krasnoyarsk
Irkutsk
L. Baykal
Yakutsk
Lena
Yenisey
Ob
Irtysh
Amur
BLACK SEA
CASPIAN SEA
Aral Sea
Caucasus
MEDITERRANEAN SEA
ADRIATIC SEA
AEGEAN SEA
RED SEA
TURKEY
SYRIA
IRAQ
IRAN (PERSIA)
SAUDI ARABIA
Tehran
Baghdad
Cairo
Alexandria
AFGHANISTAN
PAKISTAN
KAZAKH S.S.R.
UZBEK S.S.R.
TURKMEN S.S.R.
KIRGIZ S.S.R.
TADZHIK S.S.R.
L. Balkhash
Tashkent
Alma-Ata
MONGOLIA
INNER MONGOLIA
Ulaanbaatar
CHINA
PEKING
SHANGHAI
Tianjin
Shenyang
Harbin
Wuhan
Chongqing
Xi'an
Lanzhou
Seoul
XINJIANG
Tian Shan
Taklimakan Shamo
Kunlun Shan
Altun Shan
TIBET
YELLOW SEA
E. CHINA SEA
Taiwan
Tropic of Cancer

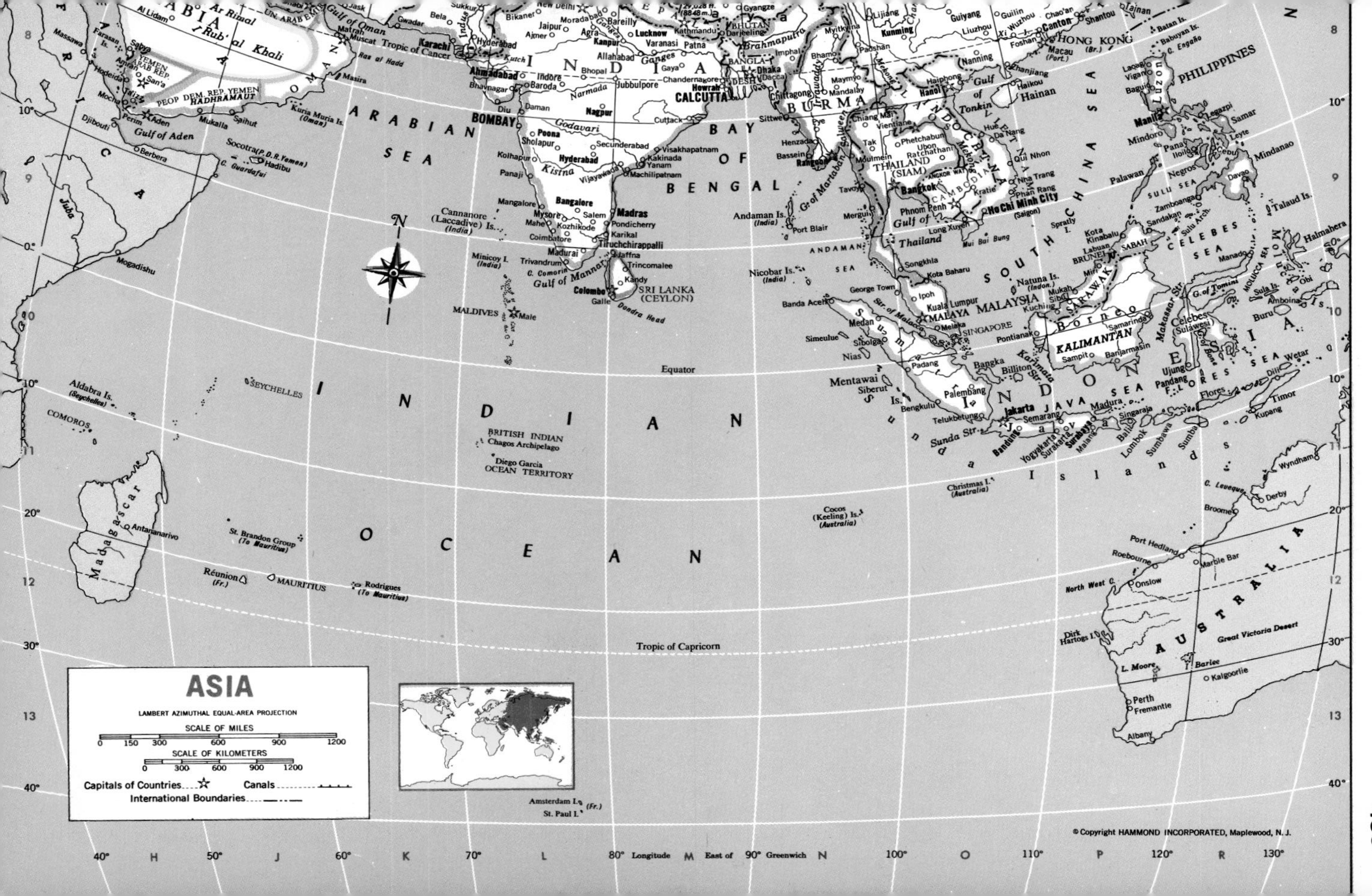
ASIA
LAMBERT AZIMUTHAL EQUAL-AREA PROJECTION
SCALE OF MILES
0 150 300 600 900 1200
SCALE OF KILOMETERS
0 300 600 900 1200
Capitals of Countries
Canals
International Boundaries
INDIAN OCEAN
ARABIAN SEA
BAY OF BENGAL
SOUTH CHINA SEA
JAVA SEA
CELEBES SEA
SULU SEA
ANDAMAN SEA
INDIA
BURMA
THAILAND (SIAM)
CAMBODIA
MALAYSIA
INDONESIA
PHILIPPINES
AUSTRALIA
SRI LANKA (CEYLON)
MALDIVES
BRITISH INDIAN OCEAN TERRITORY
Madagascar
Equator
Tropic of Cancer
Tropic of Capricorn
BOMBAY
CALCUTTA
Madras
Colombo
Jakarta
Manila
Amsterdam I. St. Paul I. (Fr.)
80° Longitude East of 90° Greenwich
© Copyright HAMMOND INCORPORATED, Maplewood, N. J.

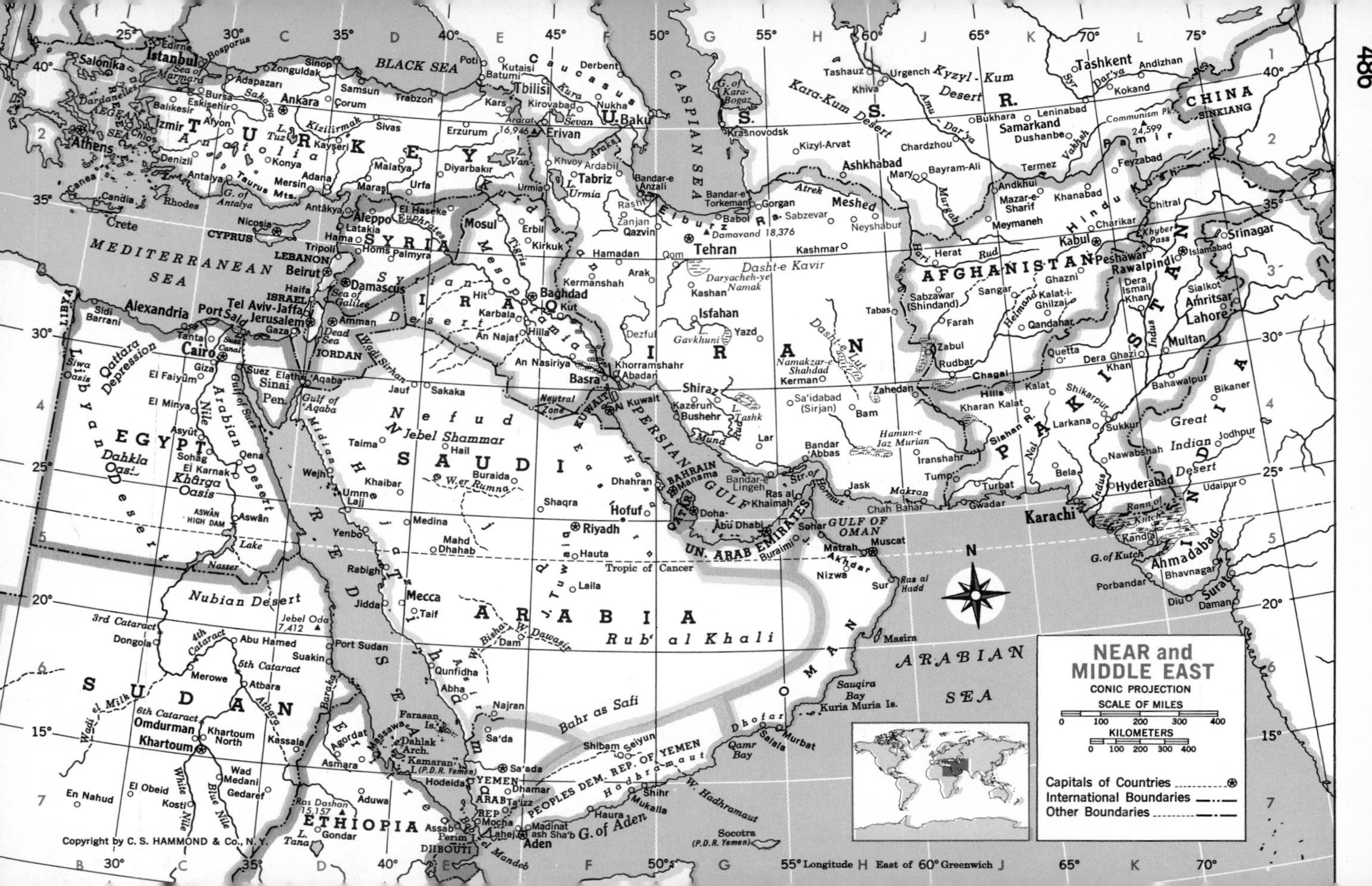
NEAR and MIDDLE EAST
CONIC PROJECTION
SCALE OF MILES
0 100 200 300 400
KILOMETERS
0 100 200 300 400
Capitals of Countries
International Boundaries
Other Boundaries
CASPIAN SEA
BLACK SEA
MEDITERRANEAN SEA
ARABIAN SEA
PERSIAN GULF
GULF OF OMAN
AFGHANISTAN
IRAN
IRAQ
SAUDI ARABIA
SYRIA
TURKEY
EGYPT
SUDAN
ETHIOPIA
JORDAN
LEBANON
ISRAEL
CYPRUS
KUWAIT
BAHRAIN
QATAR
UN. ARAB EMIRATES
OMAN
YEMEN
PEOPLES DEM. REP. OF YEMEN
DJIBOUTI
CHINA
U.S.S.R.
PAKISTAN
INDIA
Tropic of Cancer
55° Longitude East of 60° Greenwich
Copyright by C. S. HAMMOND & Co., N.Y.

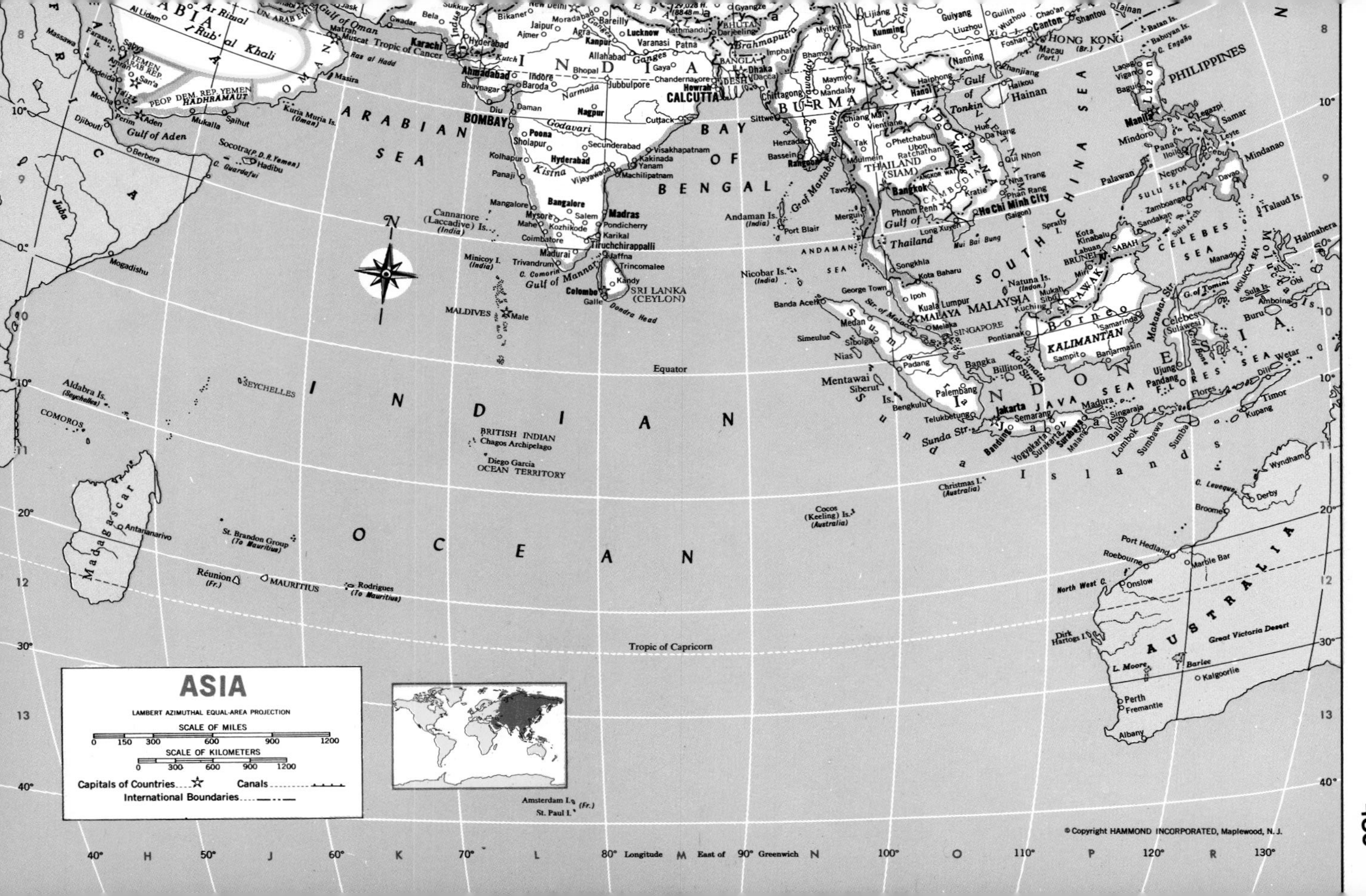
ASIA
LAMBERT AZIMUTHAL EQUAL-AREA PROJECTION
SCALE OF MILES
0 150 300 600 900 1200
SCALE OF KILOMETERS
0 300 600 900 1200
Capitals of Countries
Canals
International Boundaries
© Copyright HAMMOND INCORPORATED, Maplewood, N.J.
80° Longitude East of 90° Greenwich
INDIAN OCEAN
ARABIAN SEA
BAY OF BENGAL
SOUTH CHINA SEA
ANDAMAN SEA
SULU SEA
CELEBES SEA
MOLUCCA SEA
JAVA SEA
FLORES SEA
Equator
Tropic of Capricorn
Tropic of Cancer
INDIA
BURMA
THAILAND (SIAM)
INDOCHINA
CAMBODIA
MALAYSIA
SINGAPORE
INDONESIA
PHILIPPINES
SRI LANKA (CEYLON)
MALDIVES
BRITISH INDIAN OCEAN TERRITORY
Chagos Archipelago
Diego Garcia
SEYCHELLES
MAURITIUS
Réunion (Fr.)
Rodrigues (To Mauritius)
St. Brandon Group (To Mauritius)
Madagascar
Antananarivo
COMOROS
Aldabra Is. (Seychelles)
Amsterdam I. (Fr.)
St. Paul I.
Cocos (Keeling) Is. (Australia)
Christmas I. (Australia)
Andaman Is. (India)
Nicobar Is. (India)
Cannanore (Laccadive) Is. (India)
Minicoy I. (India)
AUSTRALIA
Great Victoria Desert
KALIMANTAN
SARAWAK
SABAH
BRUNEI
HONG KONG (Br.)
Macau (Port.)
Hainan
Luzon
Mindanao
Palawan
Borneo
Celebes (Sulawesi)
Sumatra
Java
Timor
Sunda Islands
BOMBAY
CALCUTTA
Madras
Karachi
Colombo
Bangkok
Rangoon
Jakarta
Manila
Ho Chi Minh City (Saigon)
Hanoi
Kuala Lumpur
Perth
Gulf of Aden
Gulf of Oman
Gulf of Mannar
Gulf of Thailand
Gulf of Tonkin
Str. of Malacca
Sunda Str.
Makassar Str.
G. of Martaban
YEMEN ARAB REP.
PEOP. DEM. REP. YEMEN
HADHRAMAUT
Rub' al Khali
OMAN
Socotra (P.D.R. Yemen)
Kuria Muria Is. (Oman)
Irrawaddy
Ganges
Brahmaputra
Indus
Mekong
Salween
Godavari
Kistna
Narmada
Juba

NEAR and MIDDLE EAST
CONIC PROJECTION
SCALE OF MILES
0 100 200 300 400
KILOMETERS
0 100 200 300 400
Capitals of Countries
International Boundaries
Other Boundaries
Copyright by C. S. HAMMOND & Co., N.Y.
55° Longitude East of 60° Greenwich
TURKEY
SYRIA
LEBANON
ISRAEL
JORDAN
IRAQ
IRAN
AFGHANISTAN
PAKISTAN
INDIA
U.S.S.R.
CHINA
SINKIANG
SAUDI ARABIA
KUWAIT
BAHRAIN
QATAR
UN. ARAB EMIRATES
OMAN
YEMEN ARAB REP.
PEOPLES DEM. REP. OF YEMEN
EGYPT
SUDAN
ETHIOPIA
DJIBOUTI
LIBYA
CYPRUS
BLACK SEA
CASPIAN SEA
MEDITERRANEAN SEA
AEGEAN SEA
RED SEA
PERSIAN GULF
GULF OF OMAN
ARABIAN SEA
G. of Aden
Rub' al Khali
Nefud
Arabian Desert
Nubian Desert
Libyan Desert
Kara-Kum Desert
Kyzyl-Kum Desert
Great Indian Desert
Dasht-e Kavir
Dasht-e Lut
Istanbul
Ankara
Athens
Beirut
Damascus
Amman
Jerusalem
Tel Aviv-Jaffa
Cairo
Alexandria
Baghdad
Tehran
Kabul
Riyadh
Mecca
Medina
Aden
Muscat
Karachi
Khartoum
Omdurman
Baku
Tbilisi
Erivan
Tashkent
Samarkand
Srinagar
Lahore
Islamabad
Rawalpindi

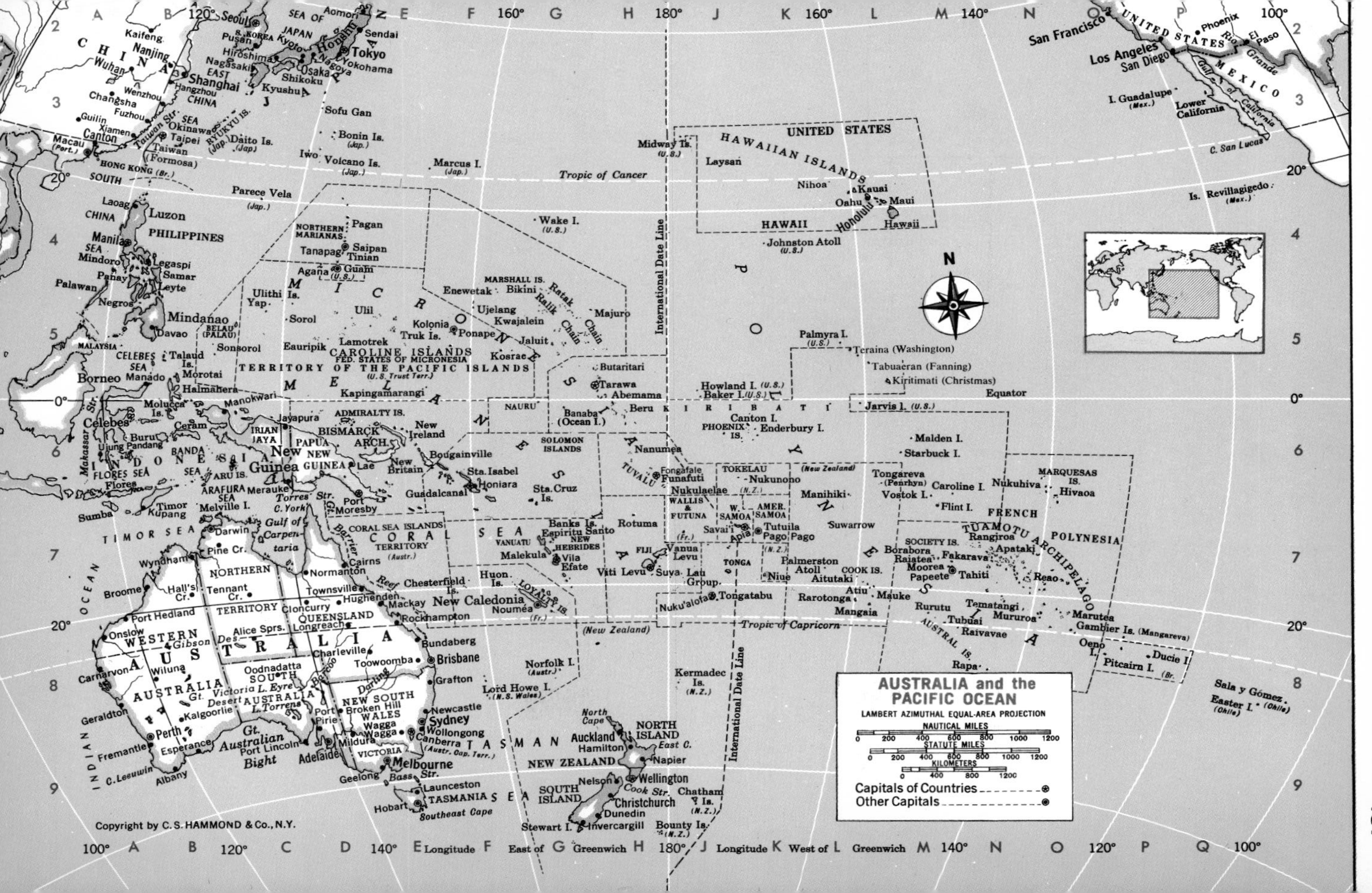
AUSTRALIA and the PACIFIC OCEAN
LAMBERT AZIMUTHAL EQUAL-AREA PROJECTION
NAUTICAL MILES
STATUTE MILES
KILOMETERS
Capitals of Countries
Other Capitals
Copyright by C. S. HAMMOND & Co., N.Y.
UNITED STATES
MEXICO
San Francisco
Los Angeles
San Diego
Phoenix
El Paso
Rio Grande
Gulf of California
Lower California
I. Guadalupe (Mex.)
C. San Lucas
Is. Revillagigedo (Mex.)
HAWAIIAN ISLANDS
HAWAII
Honolulu
Oahu
Kauai
Maui
Hawaii
Nihoa
Laysan
Midway Is. (U.S.)
Johnston Atoll (U.S.)
Tropic of Cancer
International Date Line
Equator
Tropic of Capricorn
Palmyra I. (U.S.)
Teraina (Washington)
Tabuaeran (Fanning)
Kiritimati (Christmas)
Jarvis I. (U.S.)
Malden I.
Starbuck I.
Howland I. (U.S.)
Baker I. (U.S.)
Canton I.
Enderbury I.
PHOENIX IS.
KIRIBATI
POLYNESIA
MICRONESIA
MELANESIA
MARQUESAS IS.
Nukuhiva
Hivaoa
FRENCH POLYNESIA
TUAMOTU ARCHIPELAGO
Rangiroa
Apataki
Fakarava
Reao
Tematangi
Mururoa
Marutea
Gambier Is. (Mangareva)
Pitcairn I. (Br.)
Oeno I.
Ducie I.
Easter I. (Chile)
Sala y Gomez (Chile)
SOCIETY IS.
Borabora
Raiatea
Moorea
Papeete
Tahiti
Flint I.
Caroline I.
Vostok I.
Tongareva (Penrhyn)
Manihiki
Suwarrow
(New Zealand)
COOK IS.
Aitutaki
Palmerston Atoll
Rarotonga
Mangaia
Mauke
Atiu
AUSTRAL IS.
Rurutu
Tubuai
Raivavae
Rapa
Niue
TOKELAU
Nukunono
(N.Z.)
W. SAMOA
AMER. SAMOA
Apia
Pago Pago
Tutuila
Savai'i
TONGA
Nuku'alofa
Tongatabu
WALLIS & FUTUNA
(Fr.)
TUVALU
Funafuti
Fongafale
Nukulaelae
Nanumea
FIJI
Vanua Levu
Viti Levu
Suva
Lau Group
Rotuma
Kermadec Is. (N.Z.)
Chatham Is. (N.Z.)
Bounty Is. (N.Z.)
NEW ZEALAND
NORTH ISLAND
SOUTH ISLAND
Auckland
Hamilton
Napier
Wellington
Cook Str.
Nelson
Christchurch
Dunedin
Invercargill
Stewart I.
North Cape
East C.
TASMAN SEA
Norfolk I. (Austr.)
Lord Howe I. (N.S. Wales)
New Caledonia
Nouméa
LOYALTY IS.
Huon Is.
VANUATU
NEW HEBRIDES
Espiritu Santo
Malekula
Efate
Vila
Banks Is.
Sta. Cruz Is.
SOLOMON ISLANDS
Guadalcanal
Honiara
Sta. Isabel
Bougainville
NAURU
Banaba (Ocean I.)
Tarawa
Abemama
Butaritari
Beru
MARSHALL IS.
Majuro
Jaluit
Kwajalein
Bikini
Enewetak
Ujelang
Ratak Chain
Ralik Chain
Wake I. (U.S.)
Marcus I. (Jap.)
CAROLINE ISLANDS
FED. STATES OF MICRONESIA
TERRITORY OF THE PACIFIC ISLANDS (U.S. Trust Terr.)
Kosrae
Ponape
Kolonia
Truk Is.
Kapingamarangi
Lamotrek
Eauripik
Sorol
Ulithi Is.
Yap
Ulul
NORTHERN MARIANAS
Pagan
Saipan
Tinian
Tanapag
Guam (U.S.)
Agana
Volcano Is. (Jap.)
Iwo
Bonin Is. (Jap.)
Sofu Gan
Parece Vela (Jap.)
BELAU (PALAU)
Sonsorol
ADMIRALTY IS.
BISMARCK ARCH.
New Ireland
New Britain
PAPUA NEW GUINEA
Lae
Port Moresby
IRIAN JAYA
Jayapura
New Guinea
Torres Str.
C. York
Gulf of Carpentaria
ARAFURA SEA
ARU IS.
Merauke
CORAL SEA
CORAL SEA ISLANDS TERRITORY (Austr.)
Chesterfield Is.
Great Barrier Reef
AUSTRALIA
NORTHERN TERRITORY
Darwin
Pine Cr.
Tennant Cr.
Alice Sprs.
QUEENSLAND
Normanton
Cairns
Townsville
Mackay
Rockhampton
Bundaberg
Brisbane
Hughenden
Cloncurry
Longreach
Charleville
Toowoomba
NEW SOUTH WALES
Grafton
Newcastle
Sydney
Wollongong
Canberra (Austr. Cap. Terr.)
Broken Hill
Wagga Wagga
Darling
VICTORIA
Melbourne
Geelong
Mildura
Bass Str.
TASMANIA
Launceston
Hobart
Southeast Cape
SOUTH AUSTRALIA
Adelaide
Port Pirie
Port Lincoln
Oodnadatta
L. Eyre
L. Torrens
Gt. Victoria Desert
Gt. Australian Bight
WESTERN AUSTRALIA
Gibson Des.
Kalgoorlie
Perth
Fremantle
Esperance
Albany
Geraldton
Carnarvon
Onslow
Port Hedland
Broome
Wyndham
Hall's Cr.
Wiluna
C. Leeuwin
INDIAN OCEAN
TIMOR SEA
Timor
Kupang
Melville I.
INDONESIA
BANDA SEA
Ceram
Moluccas
Halmahera
Manokwari
Celebes
Ujung Pandang
Buru
FLORES SEA
Flores
Sumba
Makassar Str.
Borneo
Manado
CELEBES SEA
Talaud Is.
Morotai
MALAYSIA
PHILIPPINES
Mindanao
Davao
Luzon
Manila
Laoag
Legaspi
Samar
Leyte
Panay
Negros
Mindoro
Palawan
SOUTH CHINA SEA
HONG KONG (Br.)
Macau (Port.)
Canton
Taiwan (Formosa)
Taipei
Taiwan Str.
Okinawa
RYUKYU IS. (Jap.)
Daito Is. (Jap.)
CHINA
Shanghai
Hangzhou
Wenzhou
Fuzhou
Xiamen
Guilin
Changsha
Wuhan
Nanjing
Kaifeng
EAST CHINA SEA
S. KOREA
Seoul
Pusan
JAPAN
SEA OF JAPAN
Tokyo
Yokohama
Sendai
Aomori
Honshu
Kyoto
Osaka
Nagoya
Hiroshima
Nagasaki
Kyushu
Shikoku
Longitude East of Greenwich
Longitude West of Greenwich

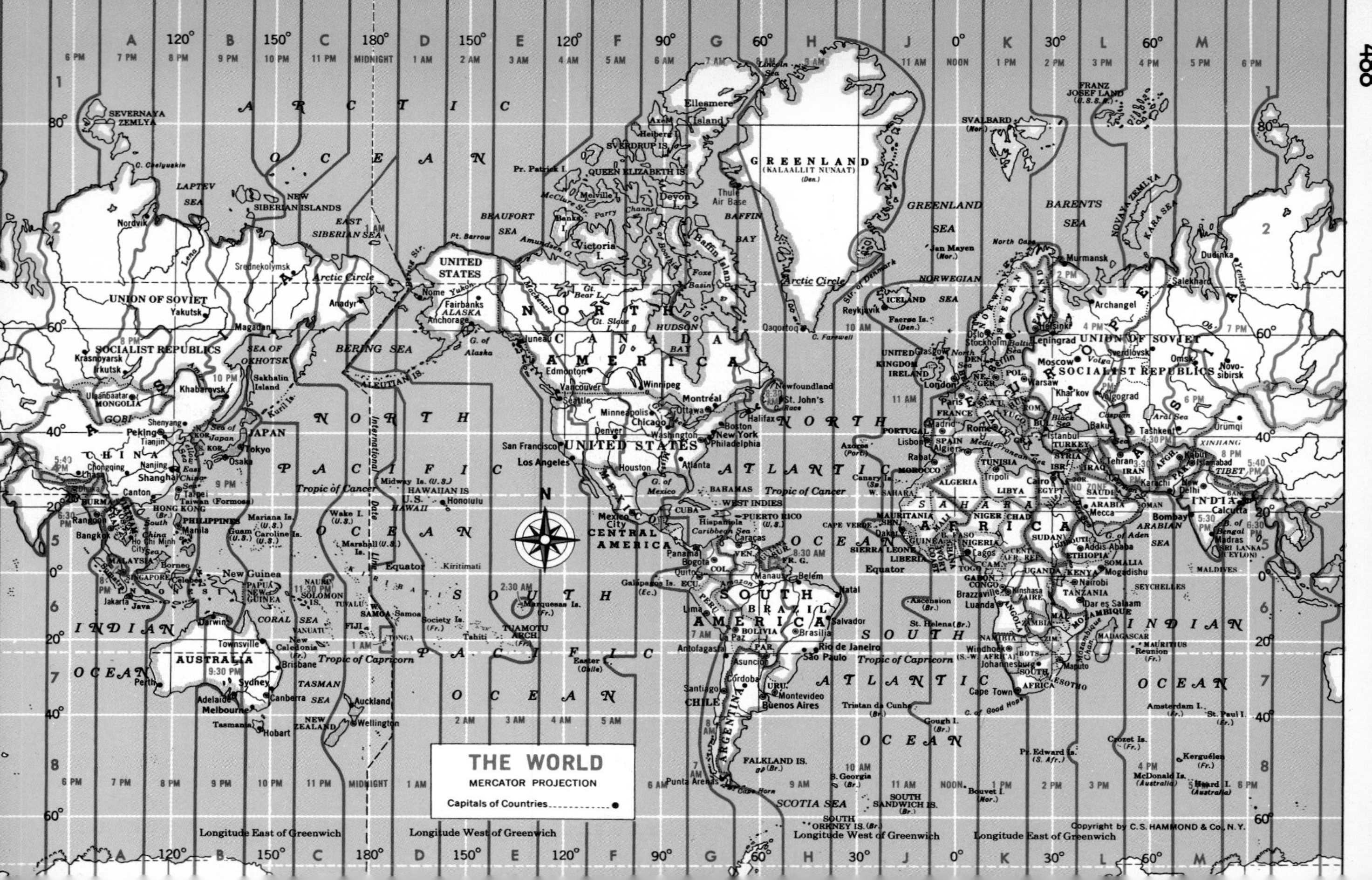
THE WORLD
MERCATOR PROJECTION
Capitals of Countries
Copyright by C.S. HAMMOND & Co., N.Y.
Longitude East of Greenwich
Longitude West of Greenwich
International Date Line
Equator
Tropic of Cancer
Tropic of Capricorn
Arctic Circle
ARCTIC OCEAN
NORTH ATLANTIC
SOUTH ATLANTIC OCEAN
NORTH PACIFIC OCEAN
SOUTH PACIFIC OCEAN
INDIAN OCEAN
NORTH AMERICA
SOUTH AMERICA
AFRICA
AUSTRALIA
UNION OF SOVIET SOCIALIST REPUBLICS
UNITED STATES
CANADA
GREENLAND (KALAALLIT NUNAAT) (Den.)
MIDNIGHT
NOON

1984 Environmental Quality Index

(15 years later)

Source: Copyright 1984 by the National Wildlife Federation.
Reprinted from the February–March issue of *National Wildlife* Magazine.

National Wildlife's annual Environmental Quality Index is a subjective analysis of the state of the nation's natural resources. The information included in each section is based on personal interviews, news reports, and the most current scientific studies. The judgments on resource trends represent the collective thinking of the editors and the National Wildlife Federation staff, based on consultation with government experts, private specialists, and academic researchers.

Wildlife: Same. Because of a proliferation of refuges and a steady infusion of money into many state management programs, dozens of native game animals have enjoyed a population explosion. Federal efforts have helped a number of endangered species to make a comeback including wild turkeys, Atlantic salmon, the ruffed grouse, and the bald eagle. Unfortunately, for lesser-known or non-game animals the story is grimmer. The blue pike, which once flourished in parts of the Great Lakes, was declared officially extinct in 1983—a victim of overfishing and pollution. However, 28 states have adopted tax checkoff programs since 1977 to help fund non-game wildlife programs. On the federal level, many programs suffered in 1983 from lack of funds. In the face of increased human population and administration efforts to open up public lands to development, wildlife habitat continues to shrink nationwide.

Air: Same. Air quality is improving, thanks largely to a cleaner fleet of U.S. automobiles. Today's vehicles emit 90% less carbon monoxide than their 1970 counterparts, meeting for the first time the pollution standards set by the amendments to the Clean Air Act 13 years ago. Unfortunately, ozone, a pervasive pollutant created by a combination of industrial and automobile emissions that is a principal component of urban smog, is proving less tractable. Meanwhile, recent research has discovered new dangers—sulfates, minute particles produced when sulfur dioxide emissions from industries and power plants react in the air. Because they are so easily inhaled, such fine particles are proving far more hazardous to human health than other pollutants. The same sulfates are coming down in the form of acid rain, damaging aquatic life and buildings and threatening forests and crops throughout much of the country.

Minerals: Same. As energy prices skyrocketed over the last 15 years, Americans made major strides in reducing their consumption of electric power and gasoline. Nevertheless, the dream of achieving energy "independence" remains elusive. With the economy picking up, there are signs that the country may be returning to its wasteful ways. In 1983, for the first time in several years, the gasoline efficiency of new U.S. automobiles sold declined. In less than a decade U.S. homeowners cut energy use by 11 percent. Utilities have promoted such savings by offering rebates to consumers who use high efficiency appliances and increase insulation. Yet in 1983, despite legal mandates, the U.S. Department of Energy continued to avoid setting minimum efficiency standards for all common household appliances. The administration continued to press for nuclear power, increasing the budget for nuclear research while cutting it for energy conservation. Congress had to step in to keep programs for renewable energy resources, such as solar energy, from disappearing altogether. The administration also pressed to open public lands to exploration for strategic minerals such as cobalt and chromium, but many experts argued that national stockpiles, not domestic mines, were the appropriate response.

Water: Same. America has made substantial progress in improving the quality of its rivers, streams, and lakes in the past 15 years. Though toxic waste contamination and nonpoint pollution are still severe problems, federal officials report that a majority of U.S. surface waters met the Clean Water Act's 1983 goal of "fishable and swimmable." However, the nation has not begun to resolve one of its most pressing clean-water issues, nonpoint pollution, created by runoff from farming, city streets, and construction sites. Conservationists are also concerned about the depletion and contamination of precious subsurface waters. Americans are tapping underground water supplies much faster than nature can replenish them. In addition, the detritus of modern civilization is seeping downward at an alarming rate, poisoning drinking water supplies for millions of Americans.

Forests: Same. Although forests still cover a third of the nation's land, and Americans continue to grow more wood than they cut, the amount of U.S. forestland is decreasing slightly. What's more, some potentially ominous trends are developing. Among them: Along the Pacific Coast, harvesting of lumber quality "saw timber" has exceeded the annual growth rate for 30 years. Because the large, commercially owned tracts have been heavily harvested in many areas, publicly owned forests have become increasingly under pressure. Every year thousands of forest acres—most privately owned—are being converted to croplands, or developed for housing and recreation. In the Northeast, there is increasing concern about the potential damage to forests from acid rain. In the face of accelerated harvests, reforestation activities have fallen behind. More than a million acres of National Forests need replanting. State and private woodlands may be in worse shape.

Soil: Worse. In 15 years, despite a dramatic increase in the use of conservation tillage practices, the steady loss of topsoil from America's farmlands persists. Even though the U.S. government has spent $20 billion in recent years in an effort to reverse the trend, the erosion continues. The amount of land in cultivation has remained relatively stable, but as more desirable farmland is used for shopping centers, highway construction, and other developments, more and more fragile hillsides and highly erodible prairies are being brought under the plow. What can be done to control erosion? Money has not solved the problem. Now, some experts argue, mandatory controls are necessary.

Living Space: Worse. Recently, a trend almost as old as the nation itself has been reversed: Americans are now increasingly moving from cities to rural areas across the country. As a result the problems of the cities—pollution, development, heavy traffic—have moved with the people. The greatest population growth is expected to occur in the arid Southwest—a trend that will undoubtedly put more pressure on already limited water supplies. The trend to the country will also increase competition between people and wildlife for the limited natural resources of the land. Elsewhere, Americans are continuing to place added strains on the nation's parklands. As a result, Congress allocated more than $114 million in 1983 for new federal parkland acquisitions. By the end of the fiscal year, the Interior Department had spent less than 70% of the funds Congress had earlier committed for new parklands.

Some Endangered Species of the World[1]

Common name	Scientific name	Range
MAMMALS		
Anteater, scaly	*Manis temmincki*	Africa
Bear, brown	*Ursus arctos pruinosus*	China (Tibet)
Bear, brown or grizzly[2]	*Ursus arctos horribilis*	Canada, Western U.S.
Cat, leopard	*Felis bengalensis bengalensis*	Eastern Asia
Cat, tiger	*Felis tigrina*	Costa Rica to northern South America
Cheetah	*Acinonyx jubatus*	Africa to India
Chimpanzee[2]	*Pan troglodytes*	Western and Central Africa
Chinchilla	*Chinchilla brevicaudata boliviana*	Bolivia
Deer, Columbian white-tailed	*Odocoileus virginianus leucurus*	U.S. (Ore., Wash.)
Deer, marsh	*Blastocerus dichotomus*	Argentina, Uruguay, Paraguay, Brazil
Deer, musk	*Moschus moschiferus moschiferus*	Southcentral Asia
Elephant, Asian	*Elephas maximus*	Southcentral and Southeast Asia
Gazelle, Clark's (Dibatag)	*Ammodorcas clarkei*	Somalia, Ethiopia
Gazelle, slender-horned (Rhim)	*Gazella leptoceros*	Sudan, Algeria, Egypt, Libya
Gorilla	*Gorilla gorilla*	Central and western Africa
Ibex, Walia	*Capra walie*	Ethiopia
Jaguar	*Panthera onca*	Central and South America, and U.S. (Texas, N.M., Ariz.)
Kangaroo, red[2]	*Macropus (=Megaleia) rufus*	Australia
Leopard	*Panthera pardus*	Africa, Southern and Eastern Asia
Leopard, snow	*Panthera uncia*	Central Asia
Lion, Asiatic	*Panthera leo persica*	Turkey to India
Mandrill	*Papio sphinx*	Equatorial West Africa
Monkey, black howler[2]	*Alouatta pigra*	Mexico, Guatemala, Belize
Ocelot	*Felis pardalis*	Central and South America, Southwestern U.S.
Orangutan	*Pongo pygmaeus*	Borneo, Sumatra
Otter, southern sea[2]	*Enhydra lutris nereis*	West coast U.S. (Wash.), south to Mexico (Baja Calif.)
Panther, Florida	*Felis concolor coryi*	U.S. (La. and Ark., east to S.C. and Fla.)
Prairie dog, Utah	*Cynomys parvidens*	U.S. (Utah)
Pronghorn, Sonoran	*Antilocapra americana sonoriensis*	U.S. (Ariz.), Mexico
Rat, Morro Bay kangaroo	*Dipodomys heermanni morroensis*	U.S. (Calif.)
Rhinoceros, great Indian	*Rhinoceros unicornis*	India, Nepal
Sloth, Brazilian three-toed	*Bradypus torquatus*	Brazil
Tiger	*Panthera tigris*	Temperate and tropical Asia
Whale, humpback	*Megaptera novaeangliae*	Oceanic
Wolf, gray	*Canis lupus*	U.S. (48 counterminious other than Minn.[2]), Mexico
Zebra, mountain	*Equus zebra zebra*	Southern Africa
BIRDS		
Albatross, short-tailed	*Diomedea albatrus*	North Pacific Ocean: Japan, U.S.S.R., U.S. (Alas., Calif., Hawaii, Ore., Wash.)

Common name	Scientific name	Range
Condor, Andean	*Vultur gryphus*	Colombia to Chile and Argentina
Eagle, bald	*Haliaeetus leucocephalus*	U.S. (except Wash., Ore., Minn., Wis., Mich.[2])
Falcon, Eurasian peregrine	*Falco peregrinus peregrinus*	Europe, Eurasia south to Africa and Mideast
Parakeet, paradise (=beautiful)	*Psephotus pulcherrimus*	Australia
Pelican, brown	*Pelecanus occidentalis*	U.S. (Carolinas to Texas, Calif.), West Indies, Central and South America, coastal
Penguin, Galápagos	*Spheniscus mendiculus*	Ecuador (Galápagos Islands)
Stork, oriental white	*Ciconia ciconia boyciana*	China, Japan, Korea, U.S.S.R.
REPTILES		
Alligator, American	*Alligator mississippiensis*	Southeastern U.S. (except Fla.[2] La., certain areas of Ga., S.C., Texas[2])
Crocodile, American	*Crocodylus acutus*	U.S. (Fla.), Mexico, South America, Central America, Caribbean
Iguana, Anegada ground	*Cyclura pinguis*	West Indies, British Virgin Is. (Anegada Is.)
Python, Indian	*Python molurus molurus*	Sri Lanka, India
Snake, Atlantic salt marsh[2]	*Nerodia fasciata taeniata*	U.S. (Fla.)
Tortoise, Indian flap-shell	*Lissemys punctata punctata*	India, Pakistan, Bangladesh
AMPHIBIANS		
Frog, Israel painted	*Discoglossus nigriventer*	Israel
Toad, African viviparous	*Nectophrynoides* spp.	Tanzania, Guinea
Treefrog, pine barrens	*Hyla andersonii*	U.S. (Fla., Ala., N.C., S.C., N.J.)
FISH		
Catfish, giant	*Pangasianodon gigas*	Thailand
Pike, blue[3]	*Stizostedion vitreum glaucum*	U.S. and Canada (Lakes Erie and Ontario)
Trout, greenback cutthroat[2]	*Salmo clarki stomias*	U.S. (Colo.)

1. Due to space limitations, does not include all mammals, birds, reptiles, amphibians, and fish or any clams, crustaceans, snails, insects, and plants. 2. Threatened. 3. Proposed as extinct, but not yet final. *Source:* Department of the Interior, Fish and Wildlife Service.

Sources of Information

Source: Brooklyn Botanic Garden, *Handbook on The Environment and The Home Gardener.*

Advice on various aspects of conservation programs and problems is available from national, state, and local organizations. Dr. Richard H. Pough, President of the Natural Area Council, has compiled a list of membership organizations that are happy to help smaller groups get started on worthwhile projects in conservation.

America the Beautiful Fund, Inc., 219 Shoreham Building, Washington, D.C. 20005
American Forestry Association, 1319 18th St., N.W., Washington, D.C. 20036
Defenders of Wildlife, 1244 19th St., N.W., Washington, D.C. 20036
Environmental Defense Fund, Inc., 444 Park Ave. South, New York, N.Y. 10016
Friends of the Earth, 208 W. 13th St., New York, N.Y. 10011
Izaak Walton League of America, 1701 North Fort Myer Dr., Arlington, VA. 22209
National Audubon Society, 950 Third Ave., New York, N.Y. 10022
National Park and Conservation Association, 1701 18th St., N.W., Washington, D.C. 20009
National Trust for Historic Preservation, 1785 Massachusetts Ave., N.W., Washington, D.C. 20036
National Wildlife Federation, 1412 16th St., N.W., Washington, D.C. 20036
Natural Science for Youth Foundation, 763 Silvermine Rd., New Canaan, Conn. 06840
The Nature Conservancy, 1800 N. Kent St., Suite 800, Arlington, Va. 22209
Open Space Institute, Inc., Room 4500, 122 East 42nd St., New York, N.Y. 10168
Sierra Club, 530 Bush St., San Francisco, Calif. 94108
The Wilderness Society, 1901 Pennsylvania Ave., N.W., Washington, D.C. 20006
World Wildlife Fund, 1601 Connecticut Ave., N.W., Washington, D.C. 20009

Don't Eat the Flowers

There are more than 700 species of plants that grow in the United States that have been identified as dangerous if eaten. Among them are some that are commonly favored by gardeners—buttercups, daffodils, lily of the valley, sweet peas, oleander, azalea, bleeding heart, delphinium, and rhododendron. According to a survey of the nation's poison control centers, next to medicines, plants are the leading cause of poisoning in children under five years of age. A threefold increase in plant poisoning, from 1971 levels, is attributed to the house plant explosion and back-to-nature dining.

Pollutant Standard Index (PSI) in Standard Metropolitan Statistical Cities—1980–1981

Metropolitan Area	1981 0–99	1981 100–199	1981 200–300	1981 More than 300	1980 0–99	1980 100–199	1980 200–300	1980 More than 300
Buffalo, N.Y.	358	6	—	1	348	12	6	—
Chicago, Ill.	347	18	—	—	318	45	3	—
Denver, Colo.	286	56	22	1	277	62	23	4
Houston, Texas	298	47	20	—	265	80	21	—
Kansas City, Mo.–Kan.	361	4	—	—	329	36	1	—
Los Angeles, Calif.	117	137	111	—	145	109	110	2
Louisville, Ky.–Ind.	345	19	1	—	307	56	3	—
Milwaukee, Wis.	354	10	1	—	350	14	2	—
New York, N.Y.–N.J.	259	102	4	—	235	129	2	—
Philadelphia, Pa.–N.J.	333	31	1	—	303	59	4	—
Portland, Oreg.–Wash.	335	26	4	—	311	42	10	4
Riverside, San Bernardino–Ontario, Calif.	181	92	92	—	195	78	92	1
St. Louis, Mo.–Ill.	339	23	2	1	311	49	6	—
Salt Lake City, Utah	335	29	1	—	312	36	18	—
San Diego, Calif.	296	67	2	—	n.a.	n.a.	n.a.	n.a.
Seattle–Everett, Wash.	330	34	1	—	333	33	—	—
Washington, D.C.–Md.–Va.	344	21	—	—	297	67	2	—

Source: U.S. Council on Environmental Quality, 1980 and unpublished data. PSI is a highly summarized health-related index based on the following criteria pollutants: Carbon monoxide, sulfur dioxide, total suspended particulates, photochemical oxidants or ozone, and nitrogen dioxide. The PSI for one day will rise above 100 when any one of the 5 criteria pollutants (at only one station in an SMSA) reaches a level judged to have adverse short-term effects on human health. Depending on the pollutant, the time to exceed the standard varies from 1 to 24 hours. The health effect labels for PSI intervals are good or moderate for 0–99; unhealthy for 100–199; very unhealthful for 200–300; and hazardous for more than 300.

Federal Outlays for the Environment by Activity, 1978–1982

(In millions of dollars, except percent, for years ending Sept. 30)

Activity	1982[1]	1981	1980	1979	1978
Pollution abatement and control	$6,954	$7,220	$7,632	$6,945	$5,934
Percent Environmental Protection Agency	68.6	72.8	73.4	69.1	68.6
Aid to State and local governments	4,500	4,671	5,177	4,769	3,972
Research and development	800	810	782	795	836
Standard setting and enforcement	750	776	791	537	524
Reduction of pollution from Federal facilities	506	488	471	550	431
Other	398	474	411	294	171
Protection and enhancement	2,266	2,583	2,749	2,614	2,688
Aid to State and local governments[3]	851	1,063	891	856	847
City recreation	196	209	335	338	425
Noncity general recreation	232	253	128	196	158
Historic preservation and rehabilitation	75	106	84	45	39
Direct Federal activities[3]	1,415	1,520	1,858	1,758	1,841
Noncity general recreation	310	319	468	449	372
Preservation and protection[4]	347	382	434	387	647
City recreation	213	206	212	196	132
Historic preservation and rehabilitation	101	100	112	133	63
Understanding, describing, and predicting[3]	2,603	2,698	2,376	2,423	2,155
Observation and prediction[5]	929	902	854	757	744
Locate and describe natural resources	739	902	650	861	688
Research on environmental impact on people	428	398	337	303	266
Ecological and other basic environmental research	181	178	228	266	242
Physical environmental surveys	302	292	281	214	197
Total	**11,823**	**12,501**	**12,757**	**11,982**	**10,777**

1. Estimated. Based on January budget estimates. 2. Includes funds for planning, monitoring and surveillance, and technical assistance. 3. Includes activities not shown separately. 4. Unique natural areas and endangered species. 5. Includes weather, ocean, and earthquakes and other disturbances. *Source: Statistical Abstract of the United States.* 1984.

Water Supply of the World[1]

The Antarctic Icecap is the largest supply of fresh water, nearly 2 percent of the world's total of fresh and salt water. As can be seen from the table below, the amount of water in our atmosphere is over ten times as large as the water in all the rivers taken together. The fresh water actually available for human use in lakes and rivers and the accessible ground water amounts to only about one third of one percent of the world's total water supply.

	Surface area (square miles)	Volume (cubic miles)	Percentage of total
Salt Water			
The oceans	139,500,000	317,000,000	97.2
Inland seas and saline lakes	270,000	25,000	0.008
Fresh Water			
Freshwater lakes	330,000	30,000	0.009
All rivers (average level)	—	300	0.0001
Antarctic Icecap	6,000,000	6,300,000	1.9
Arctic Icecap and glaciers	900,000	680,000	0.21
Water in the atmosphere	197,000,000	3,100	0.001
Ground water within half a mile from surface	—	1,000,000	0.31
Deep-lying ground water	—	1,000,000	0.31
Total (rounded)	—	**326,000,000**	**100.00**

1. All figures are estimated. *Source:* Department of the Interior, Geological Survey.

Speed of Animals

Most of the following measurements are for maximum speeds over approximate quarter-mile distances. Exceptions—which are included to give a wide range of animals—are the lion and elephant, whose speeds were clocked in the act of charging; the whippet, which was timed over a 200-yard course; the cheetah over a 100-yard distance; man for a 15-yard segment of a 100-yard run; and the black mamba, six-lined race runner, spider, giant tortoise, three-toed sloth, and garden snail, which were measured over various small distances.

Animal	Speed mph	Animal	Speed mph	Animal	Speed mph
Cheetah	70	Mongolian wild ass	40	Man	27.89
Pronghorn antelope	61	Greyhound	39.35	Elephant	25
Wildebeest	50	Whippet	35.5	Black mamba snake	20
Lion	50	Rabbit (domestic)	35	Six-line race runner	18
Thomson's gazelle	50	Mule deer	35	Squirrel	12
Quarter horse	47.5	Jackal	35	Pig (domestic)	11
Elk	45	Reindeer	32	Chicken	9
Cape hunting dog	45	Giraffe	32	Spider (Tegenearia atrica)	1.17
Coyote	43	White-tailed deer	30	Giant Tortoise	0.17
Gray fox	42	Wart hog	30	Three-toed sloth	0.15
Hyena	40	Grizzly bear	30	Garden snail	0.03
Zebra	40	Cat (domestic)	30		

Source: Natural History Magazine, March 1974, copyright 1974. The American Museum of Natural History; and James Doherty, Curator of Mammals, N.Y. Zoological Society.

Animal Names: Male, Female, and Young

Animal	Male	Female	Young	Animal	Male	Female	Young	Animal	Male	Female	Young
Ass	Jack	Jenny	Foal	Duck	Drake	Duck	Duckling	Sheep	Ram	Ewe	Lamb
Bear	Boar	Sow	Cub	Elephant	Bull	Cow	Calf	Swan	Cob	Pen	Cygnet
Cat	Tom	Queen	Kitten	Fox	Dog	Vixen	Cub	Swine	Boar	Sow	Piglet
Cattle	Bull	Cow	Calf	Goose	Gander	Goose	Gosling	Tiger	Tiger	Tigress	Cub
Chicken	Rooster	Hen	Chick	Horse	Stallion	Mare	Foal	Whale	Bull	Cow	Calf
Deer	Buck	Doe	Fawn	Lion	Lion	Lioness	Cub	Wolf	Dog	Bitch	Pup
Dog	Dog	Bitch	Pup	Rabbit	Buck	Doe	Bunny				

Source: James Doherty, Curator of Mammals, N.Y. Zoological Society.

Heat Wave in August 1983 Breaks the Record

According to the National Climate Analysis Center, the August 1983 heat wave was the hottest month on record for the United States and also one of the driest.

The unbroken heat wave lasted almost nine weeks, claiming at least 220 lives and destroying $10 billion in crops. The summer of 1983 was only the 17th hottest overall.

Animal Group Terminology

Source: James Doherty, Curator of Mammals, N.Y. Zoological Society, and *Information Please* data.

ants: colony
bears: sleuth, sloth
bees: grist, hive, swarm
birds: flight, volery
cattle: drove
cats: clutter, clowder
chicks: brood, clutch
clams: bed
cranes: sedge, seige
crows: murder
doves: dule
ducks: brace, team
elephants: herd
elks: gang
finches: charm
fish: school, shoal, draught
foxes: leash, skulk
geese: flock, gaggle, skein
gnats: cloud, horde
goats: trip
gorillas: band
hares: down, husk
hawks: cast
hens: brood
hogs: drift
horses: pair, team
hounds: cry, mute, pack
kangaroos: troop
kittens: kindle, litter
larks: exaltation
lions: pride
locusts: plague
magpies: tidings
mules: span
nightingales: watch
oxen: yoke
oysters: bed
parrots: company
partridges: covey
peacocks: muster, ostentation
pheasants: nest, bouquet
pigs: litter
ponies: string
quail: bevy, covey
rabbits: nest
seals: pod
sheep: drove, flock
sparrows: host
storks: mustering
swans: bevy, wedge
swine: sounder
toads: knot
turkeys: rafter
turtles: bale
vipers: nest
whales: gam, pod
wolves: pack, route
woodcocks: fall

Gestation, Incubation, and Longevity of Certain Animals

Animal	Gestation or incubation, in days & (average)	Longevity, in years & (record exceptions)
Ass	365	18–20 (63)
Bear	180–240 [1]	15–30 (47)
Cat	52–69 (63)	10–12 (26+)
Chicken	22	7–8 (14)
Cow	c. 280	9–12 (39)
Deer	197–300 [1]	10–15 (26)
Dog	53–71 (63)	10–12 (24)
Duck	21–35[1](28)	10 (15)
Elephant	510–730 (624) [1]	30–40 (71)
Fox	51–63 [1]	8–10 (14)
Goat	136–160 (151)	12 (17)
Groundhog	31–32	4–9
Guinea pig	58–75 (68)	3 (6)
Hamster, golden	15–17	2 (8)
Hippopotamus	220–255 (240)	30 (49+)
Horse	329–345 (336)	20–25 (50+)
Kangaroo	32–39 [1]	4–6 (23)
Lion	105–113 (108)	10 (29)
Man	253–303	([2])
Monkey	139–270 [1]	12–15[1](29)
Mouse	19–31 [1]	1–3 (4)
Parakeet (Budgerigar)	17–20 (18)	8 (12+)
Pig	101–130 (115)	10 (22)
Pigeon	11–19	10–12 (39)
Rabbit	30–35 (31)	6–8 (15)
Rat	21	3 (5)
Sheep	144–152 (151) [1]	12 (16)
Squirrel	44	8–9 (15)
Whale	365–547 [1]	—
Wolf	60–63	10–12 (16)

1. Depending on kind. 2. For life expectancy charts, *see* Index. *Source:* James Doherty, Curator of Mammals, N.Y. Zoological Society.

Zoological Gardens

North America has more than 30 major zoos, in the United States, Canada, and Mexico. The *Quebec Zoological Society*'s collection is made up of Canadian species; Toronto has many exotic species.

The first zoological garden in the United States was established in Philadelphia in 1874. Since that time nearly every large city in the country has acquired a zoo. Among the largest are San Diego's on the West Coast; Chicago's Brookfield Zoo and those of St. Louis and Kansas City in the Middle West; and, in the East, the New York Zoological Society's park in the Bronx. The *National Zoological Park* in Washington, D.C., in a beautiful setting of hills, woods, and streams, was established in 1890 by an act of Congress. The major U.S. zoos now have created large natural-habitat areas for their collections.

In Europe, zoological gardens have long been popular public institutions. The *Jardin d'Acclimation,* in the Bois de Boulogne, Paris, is the oldest and largest. Others are located at Clères, Ermenonville, Lyons, Marseilles, Maubeuge, Mulhouse, and Nancy.

Germany had about 20 zoological gardens, many of which were developed in the peacetime years between World Wars I and II. Large zoos were located in Berlin and Frankfurt am Main. In Munich, the animals were grouped according to the continent of their origin. At Stellingen near Hamburg, the *Hagenback Garden* became an outstanding show place and distributing center for animals.

The *Schönbrunn* at Vienna is one of the oldest zoos in Europe. The Budapest zoological gardens house a fine collection of European birds. At Antwerp, the *Royal Zoological Society* founded a large menagerie in 1843. It was seriously damaged by German bombs during World War II.

In the British Isles, a popular zoo is in the garden of the *London Zoological Society* in Regent's Park. Although this zoo received a number of direct bomb hits in 1940–41 and again in 1944, it remained open throughout World War II; visitors during this period numbered 6,500,000. Manchester and Clifton have smaller gardens, and the one at Edinburgh is famous for its collection of penguins. The *Dublin Zoo* is noted for its lions, many of which were born there.

The Amsterdam zoo, with its East Indian collection and its aquarium, and the Rotterdam gardens are the two best known in the Netherlands. Built on a high elevation, the *Skansen Zoo* in Stockholm exhibits north European specimens. The most important gardens in the U.S.S.R. are found in Moscow, where northern as well as exotic species are collected. The zoo at Rome has part of its collection confined in barless pits. At Lisbon there is a small zoological garden, and in Madrid a part of the original royal menagerie.

Zoos, Aquariums, and Botanical Gardens

NOTE: The facilities listed are members of, and accredited by, the American Association of Zoological Parks and Aquariums to ensure that they are maintaining professional standards. *Source:* American Association of Zoological Parks and Aquariums.

Arizona-Sonora Desert Museum, Tucson
Audubon Park and Zoological Garden, New Orleans
Baltimore Zoo
Binder Park Zoo, Battle Creek, Mich.
Birmingham (Ala.) Zoo
Brookgreen Gardens, Murrells Inlet, S.C.
Buffalo (N.Y.) Zoological Gardens
Calgary (Alberta, Canada) Zoo
Cheyenne Mountain Zoological Park, Colorado Springs
Cincinnati Zoo
Cleveland Metroparks Zoo
Columbus (Ohio) Zoological Gardens
Denver Zoological Gardens
Discovery Island, Buena Vista, Fla.
Henry Doorly Zoo, Omaha, Neb.
El Paso Zoological Park
Ellen Trout Zoo, Lufkin, Texas
Fort Wayne (Ind.) Children's Zoo
Fort Worth Zoological Park
Glen Oak Zoo, Peoria, Ill.
Greater Baton Rouge (La.) Zoo
Hogle Zoological Garden, Salt Lake City, Utah
Indianapolis Zoo
John Ball Zoological Gardens, Grand Rapids, Mich.
Kings Island (Ohio) Wild Animal Safari
Knoxville (Tenn.) Zoological Park
Lincoln Park Zoological Gardens, Chicago
Living Desert Reserve, Palm Desert, Calif.
Los Angeles Zoo
Louisville (Ky.) Zoological Garden
Marine World Africa USA, Redwood City, Calif.
Memphis (Tenn.) Zoological Gardens and Aquarium
Metropolitan Toronto Zoo
Miller Park Zoo, Bloomington, Ill.
Milwaukee County Zoological Gardens
Minnesota Zoological Garden, Apple Valley, Minn.
National Zoological Park, Washington, D.C.
New England Aquarium, Boston
New York Zoological Park, the Bronx, N.Y.
Oklahoma City Zoo
Philadelphia Zoological Garden
Phoenix (Ariz.) Zoo
Point Defiance Zoo & Aquarium, Tacoma, Wash.
Gladys Porter Zoo, Brownsville, Tex.
Gene Reid Zoological Park, Tucson, Ariz.
Rio Grande Zoological Park, Albuquerque, N.M.
Riverbanks Zoological Park, Columbia, S.C.
Roeding Park Zoo, Fresno, Calif.
Sacramento (Calif.) Zoo
St. Louis Zoological Park
Salisbury (Md.) Zoological Park
San Antonio Zoological Gardens and Aquarium
San Diego Wild Animal Park, Escondido, Calif.
San Diego (Calif.) Zoo
San Francisco Zoological Gardens
Santa Barbara (Calif.) Zoological Gardens
Sea World of Florida, Orlando, Fla.
Sea World of Ohio, Aurora
Sea World of San Diego, Calif.
Seattle Aquarium
Sedgwick County Zoo, Wichita, Kan.
Seneca Park Zoo, Rochester, N.Y.
John G. Shedd Aquarium, Chicago
Toledo (Ohio) Zoological Gardens
Topeka (Kan.) Zoological Park
Tulsa (Okla.) Zoological Park
Vancouver (British Columbia) Public Aquarium
Henry Vilas Park Zoo, Madison, Wis.
Waikiki (Hawaii) Aquarium
Washington Park Zoo, Portland, Ore.
Woodland Park Zoological Gardens, Seattle
Zoo-America at Hershey Park, Hershey, Pa.

The National Park System

Source: Department of the Interior, National Park Service.

The National Park System of the United States is administered by the National Park Service, a bureau of the Department of the Interior. Started with the establishment of Yellowstone National Park in 1872, the system includes not only the most extraordinary and spectacular scenic exhibits in the United States but also a large number of sites distinguished either for their historic or prehistoric importance or scientific interest, or for their superior recreational assets. The number and extent of the various types of areas that make up the system follow.

Type of area	Number	Total acreage[1]	Type of area	Number	Total acreage[1]
National Parks	48	47,946,299.23	National Battlefield Site	1	1.00
National Monuments	78	4,717,372.78	National Historical Parks	26	150,944.35
National Preserves	12	21,106,339.23	National Recreation Areas	17	3,686,982.83
National Lakeshores	4	224,525.55	National Parkways	4	163,225.55
National Rivers[4]	11	553,948.93	National Scenic Trail[5]	1	126,964.09
National Seashores	10	597,023.36	Other Parks[2]	10	32,041.39
National Historic Sites	63	17,792.54	National Capital Parks[3]	1	6,466.88
National Memorials	23	8,227.61	White House	1	18.07
National Military Parks	10	34,668.82	National Mall	1	146.35
National Battlefield Parks	3	8,169.08	Affiliated Areas*	30	45,815.68
National Battlefields	10	11,049.29	**Total**	**335**	**79,392,206.93**

1. Acreage as of Dec. 31, 1983. Ten national cemeteries administered by the National Park Service are administered in conjunction with associated historical units and are not listed separately. 2. Parks without national designation. 3. Comprises 346 units within the District of Columbia, Maryland, and Virginia. 4. Includes Wild and Scenic Rivers and Riverways. 5. Includes Scenic and Historic Trails. *Not included in totals.

National Parks

Name, location, and year authorized	Acreage	Outstanding characteristics
Acadia (Maine), 1919	39,624.76	Rugged seashore on Mt. Desert Island and adjacent mainland
Arches (Utah), 1971	73,378.98	Unusual stone arches, windows, pedestals caused by erosion
Badlands (S.D.), 1978	243,302.33	Arid land of fossils, prairie, bison, deer, bighorn, antelope
Big Bend (Tex.), 1935	741,118.40	Mountains and desert bordering the Rio Grande
Biscayne (Fla.), 1980	172,845.17	Aquatic, coral reef park south of Miami was a national monument, 1968–80
Bryce Canyon (Utah), 1924	35,835.08	Area of grotesque eroded rocks brilliantly colored
Canyonlands (Utah), 1964	337,570.43	Colorful wilderness with impressive red-rock canyons, spires, arches
Capitol Reef (Utah), 1971	241,904.26	Highly colored sedimentary rock formations in high, narrow gorges
Carlsbad Caverns (N.M.), 1930	46,755.33	The world's largest known caves
Channel Islands (Calif.) 1980	249,353.77	Area is rich in marine mammals, sea birds, endangered species and archeology
Crater Lake (Ore.), 1902	160,290.33	Deep blue lake in heart of inactive volcano
Denali (Alaska), 1917	4,700,000.00	Mt. McKinley National Park was renamed and enlarged by Act of Dec. 2, 1980. Contains Mt. McKinley, N. America's highest mountain (20,320 ft)
Everglades (Fla.), 1934	1,398,939.19	Subtropical area with abundant bird and animal life
Gates of the Arctic (Alaska), 1980	7,500,000.00	Diverse north central wilderness contains part of Brooks Range
Glacier (Mont.), 1910	1,013,594.67	Rocky Mountain scenery with many glaciers and lakes
Glacier Bay (Alaska), 1980	3,020,396.00	Park was a national monument (1925–1980) popular for wildlife, whale-watching, glacier-calving, and scenery
Grand Canyon (Ariz.), 1919	1,218,375.24	Mile-deep gorge, 4 to 18 miles wide, 217 miles long
Grand Teton (Wyo.), 1929	310,517.00	Picturesque range of high mountain peaks
Great Smoky Mts. (N.C.-Tenn), 1926	520,269.44	Highest mountain range east of Black Hills; luxuriant plant life
Guadalupe Mountains (Tex.), 1966	76,293.06	Contains highest point in Texas: Guadalupe Peak (8,751 ft)
Haleakala (Hawaii), 1960	28,655.25	World-famous 10,023-ft. Haleakala volcano (dormant)
Hawaii Volcanoes (Hawaii), 1916	229,177.03	Spectacular volcanic area; luxuriant vegetation at lower levels
Hot Springs (Ark.), 1921	5,823.54	47 mineral hot springs said to have therapeutic value
Isle Royale (Mich.), 1931	571.790.11	Largest wilderness island in Lake Superior; moose, wolves, lakes
Katmai (Alaska), 1980	3,716,000.00	Expansion may assure brown bear's preservation. Park was national monument 1918–80; is known for fishing, 1912 eruption, bears
Kenai Fjords (Alaska), 1980	670,000.00	Mountain goats, marine mammals, birdlife are features at this seacoast park near Seward
Kings Canyon (Calif.), 1940	460,136.20	Huge canyons; high mountains; giant sequoias
Kobuk Valley (Alaska), 1980	1,749,037.00	Native culture and anthropology center around the broad Kobuk River in northwest Alaska
Lake Clark (Alaska), 1980	2,874,000.00	Park provides scenic and wilderness recreation across Cook Inlet from Anchorage
Lassen Volcanic (Calif.), 1916	106,372.36	Exhibits of impressive volcanic phenomena
Mammoth Cave (Ky.), 1926	52,369.60	Vast limestone labyrinth with underground river
Mesa Verde (Colo.), 1906	52,085.14	Best-preserved prehistoric cliff dwellings in United States

Name, location, and year authorized	Acreage	Outstanding characteristics
Mount Rainier (Wash.), 1899	235,404.00	Single-peak glacial system; dense forests, flowered meadows
North Cascades (Wash.), 1968	504,780.94	Roadless Alpine landscape; jagged peaks; mountain lakes; glaciers
Olympic (Wash.), 1938	915,425.86	Finest Pacific Northwest rain forest; scenic mountain park
Petrified Forest (Ariz.), 1962	93,492.57	Extensive natural exhibit of petrified wood
Redwood (Calif.), 1968	110,130.63	Coastal redwood forests; contains world's tallest known tree (369.2 ft)
Rocky Mountain (Colo.), 1915	265,192.86	Section of the Rocky Mountains; 107 named peaks over 10,000 ft
Sequoia (Calif.), 1890	402,487.83	Giant sequoias; magnificent High Sierra scenery, including Mt. Whitney
Shenandoah (Va.), 1926	195,072.00	Tree-covered mountains; scenic Skyline Drive
Theodore Roosevelt (N.D.), 1978	70,416.39	Scenic valley of Little Missouri River; T.R. Ranch; Wildlife
Virgin Islands (U.S. V.I.), 1956	14,695.85	Beaches; lush hills; prehistoric Carib Indian relics
Voyageurs (Minn.), 1971	217,892.01	Wildlife, canoeing, fishing, and hiking
Wind Cave (S.D.), 1903	28,292.08	Limestone caverns in Black Hills; buffalo herd
Wrangell-St. Elias (Alaska), 1980	8,945,000.00	Largest Park System area has abundant wildlife, second highest peak in U.S. (Mt. St. Elias); adjoins Canadian park
Yellowstone (Wyo.-Mont.-Idaho), 1872	2,219,822.70	World's greatest geyser area; abundant falls, wildlife, and canyons
Yosemite (Calif.), 1890	760,917.18	Mountains; inspiring gorges and waterfalls; giant sequoias
Zion (Utah), 1919	146,551.10	Multicolored gorge in heart of southern Utah desert

NATIONAL HISTORICAL PARKS

Name and location	*Total acreage*
Appomattox Court House (Va.)	1,325.08
Boston (Mass.)	41.03
Chaco Culture (N.M.)	33,977.82
Chesapeake and Ohio Canal (Md.-W.Va.-D.C.).	20,781.00
Colonial (Va.)	9,315.39
Cumberland Gap (Ky.-Tenn.-Va.)	20,350.90
George Rogers Clark (Ind.)	24.30
Harpers Ferry (W.Va.-Md.)	2,238.37
Independence (Pa.)	44.85
Jean Lafitte (La.)	20,000
Kalaupapa (Hawaii)	10,902.10
Klondike Goldrush (Alaska)	13,272.38
Kaioko-Honokohau (Hawaii)	1,160.91
Lowell (Mass.)	137.08
Lyndon B. Johnson (Tex.)	1,477.78
Minute Man (Mass.)	752.46
Morristown (N.J.)	1,677.65
Nez Perce (Idaho)	2,108.89
Puuhonua o Honaunau (Hawaii)	181,80
San Antonio Missions (Tex.)	477.41
San Juan Island (Wash.)	1,751.99
Saratoga (N.Y.)	3,046.02
Sitka (Alaska)	106.83
Valley Forge (Pa.)	3,464.70
War in the Pacific (Guam)	1,962.25
Women's Rights (N.Y.)	2.45

NATIONAL MONUMENTS

Name and location	*Total acreage*
Agate Fossil Beds (Neb.)	3,055.22
Alibates Flint Quarries (Tex.)	1,370.97
Aniakchak (Alaska)	134,500.00
Aztec Ruins (N.M.)	27.14
Bandelier (N.M.)	36,916.89
Black Canyon (Colo.)	13,672.13
Booker T. Washington (Va.)	223.92
Buck Island Reef (U.S. V.I.)	880.00
Cabrillo (Calif.)	143.94
Canyon de Chelly (Ariz.)	83,840.00
Cape Krusenstern (Alaska)	660,000.00
Capulin Mountain (N.M.)	775.38
Casa Grande (Ariz.)	472.50
Castillo de San Marcos (Fla.)	20.48
Castle Clinton (N.Y.)	1.00
Cedar Breaks (Utah)	6,154.60
Chiricahua (Ariz.)	11,134.80
Colorado (Colo.)	20,453.95
Congaree Swamp (S.C.)	15,138.25
Craters of the Moon (Idaho)	53,545.05
Custer Battlefield (Mont.)	765.34
Death Valley (Calif.-Nev.)	2,067,627.68
Devils Postpile (Calif.)	798.46
Devils Tower (Wyo.)	1,346.91
Dinosaur (Utah-Colo.)	211,141.69
Effigy Mounds (Iowa)	1,474.63
El Morro (N.M.)	1,278.72
Florissant Fossil Beds (Colo.)	5,998.09
Fort Frederica (Ga.)	213.72
Fort Jefferson (Fla.)	64,700.00
Fort Matanzas (Fla.)	298.51
Fort McHenry (Md.)	43.26
Fort Pulaski (Ga.)	5,623.10
Fort Stanwix (N.Y.)	15.52
Fort Sumter (S.C.)	66.77
Fort Union (N.M.)	720.60
Fossil Butte (Wyo.)	8,198.00
George Washington Birthplace (Va.)	538.23
George Washington Carver (Mo.)	210.00
Gila Cliff Dwellings (N.M.)	533.13
Grand Portage (Minn.)	709.97
Great Sand Dunes (Colo.)	38,662.18
Hohokam Pima (Ariz.)	1,690.00
Homestead (Neb.)	194.57
Hovenweep (Utah-Colo.)	785.43
Jewel Cave (S.D.)	1,273.51
John Day Fossil Beds (Ore.)	14,011.90
Joshua Tree (Calif.)	559,959.50
Lava Beds (Calif.)	46,559.87
Lehman Caves (Nev.)	640.00
Montezuma Castle (Ariz.)	857.69
Mound City Group (Ohio)	217.50
Muir Woods (Calif.)	553.55
Natural Bridges (Utah)	7,791.00
Navajo (Ariz.)	360.00
Ocmulgee (Ga.)	683.48
Oregon Caves (Ore.)	487.98
Organ Pipe Cactus (Ariz.)	330,688.86
Pecos (N.M.)	364.80
Pinnacles (Calif.)	16,221.77
Pipe Spring (Ariz.)	40.00
Pipestone (Minn.)	281.78
Rainbow Bridge (Utah)	160.00
Russell Cave (Ala.)	310.45

Name and location	Total acreage
Saguaro (Ariz.)	83,573.88
St. Croix Island (Me.)	35.39
Salinas (N.M.)	1,076.94
Scotts Bluff (Neb.)	2,997.08
Statue of Liberty (N.Y.-N.J.)	58.38
Sunset Crater (Ariz.)	3,040.00
Timpanogos Cave (Utah)	250.00
Tonto (Ariz.)	1,120.00
Tumacacori (Ariz.)	16.52
Tuzigoot (Ariz.)	809.30
Walnut Canyon (Ariz.)	2,249.46
White Sands (N.M.)	144,458.24
Wupatki (Ariz.)	35,253.24
Yucca House (Colo.)	10.00

NATIONAL PRESERVES

Aniakchak (Alaska)	475,500.00
Bering Land Bridge (Alaska)	2,770,000.00
Big Cypress (Fla.)	570,000.00
Big Thicket (Tex.)	35,839.23
Denali (Alaska)	1,330,000.00
Gates of the Arctic (Alaska)	940,000.00
Glacier Bay (Alaska)	55,000.00
Katmai (Alaska)	374,000.00
Lake Clark (Alaska)	1,171,000.00
Noatak (Alaska)	6,560,000.00
Wrangell-St. Elias (Alaska)	4,255,000.00
Yukon-Charley (Alaska)	2,520,000.00

NATIONAL MILITARY PARKS

Chickamauga and Chattanooga (Ga.-Tenn.)	8,102.54
Fort Donelson (Tenn.)	536.66
Fredericksburg and Spotsylvania (Va.)	5,908.64
Gettysburg (Pa.)	3,862.06
Guilford Courthouse (N.C.)	220.25
Horseshoe Bend (Ala.)	2,040.00
Kings Mountain (S.C.)	3,945.29
Pea Ridge (Ark.)	4,300.35
Shiloh (Tenn.)	3,837.50
Vicksburg (Miss.)	1,740.78

NATIONAL BATTLEFIELDS

Antietam (Md.)	3,246.44
Big Hole (Mont.)	655.61
Cowpens (S.C.)	841.56
Fort Necessity (Pa.)	902.80
Monocacy (Md.)	1,659.04
Moores Creek (N.C.)	86.52
Petersburg (Va.)	1,535.38
Stones River (Tenn.)	330.86
Tupelo (Miss.)	1.00
Wilson's Creek (Mo.)	1,749.91

NATIONAL BATTLEFIELD PARKS

Kennesaw Mountain (Ga.)	2,884.38
Manassas (Va.)	4,513.29
Richmond (Va.)	771.41

NATIONAL BATTLEFIELD SITE

Brices Crossroads (Miss.)	1.00

NATIONAL HISTORIC SITES

Abraham Lincoln Birthplace (Ky.)	116.50
Adams (Mass.)	12.17
Allegheny Portage Railroad (Pa.)	1,134.91
Andersonville (Ga.)	475.72
Andrew Johnson (Tenn.)	16.68
Bent's Old Fort (Colo.)	800.00
Carl Sandburg Home (N.C.)	263.52
Christiansted (V.I.)	27.15
Clara Barton (Md.)	8.59
Edgar Allan Poe (Pa.)	0.52
Edison (N.J.)	21.25

Name and location	Total acreage
Eisenhower (Pa.)	690.46
Eleanor Roosevelt (N.Y.)	180.50
Eugene O'Neill (Calif.)	14.00
Ford's Theatre (Lincoln Museum) (D.C.)	0.29
Fort Bowie (Ariz.)	1,000.00
Fort Davis (Tex.)	460.00
Fort Laramie (Wyo.)	832.45
Fort Larned (Kan.)	718.39
Fort Point (Calif.)	29.00
Fort Raleigh (N.C.)	157.27
Fort Scott (Kan.)	16.69
Fort Smith (Ark.-Okla.)	78.36
Fort Union Trading Post (N.D.-Mont.)	436.45
Fort Vancouver (Wash.)	208.89
Frederick Law Olmsted (Mass.)	1.75
Friendship Hill (Pa.)	674.56
Georgia O'Keeffe (N.M.)	4.00
Golden Spike (Utah)	2,735.28
Grant-Kohrs Ranch (Mont.)	1,498.82
Hampton (Md.)	59.44
Harry S. Truman (Mo.)	0.78
Herbert Hoover (Iowa)	186.80
Home of F. D. Roosevelt (N.Y.)	264.01
Hopewell Village (Pa.)	848.06
Hubbell Trading Post (Ariz.)	160.09
James A. Garfield (Ohio)	7.82
Jefferson National Expansion Memorial (Mo.)	90.96
John F. Kennedy (Mass.)	0.09
John Muir (Calif.)	8.90
Knife River Indian Villages (N.D.)	1,293.35
Lincoln Home (Ill.)	12.28
Longfellow (Mass.)	1.98
Maggie L. Walker (Va.)	1.29
Martin Luther King, Jr. (Ga.)	23.16
Martin Van Buren (N.Y.)	39.58
Ninety Six (S.C.)	989.14
Palo Alto Battlefield (Tex.)	50.00
Puukohola Heiau (Hawaii)	76.57
Sagamore Hill (N.Y.)	78.00
Saint-Gaudens (N.H.)	148.33
Salem Maritime (Mass.)	9.10
San Juan (P.R.)	53.20
Saugus Iron Works (Mass.)	8.51
Sewall-Belmont House (D.C.)	0.35
Springfield Armory (Mass.)	54.93
Theodore Roosevelt Birthplace (N.Y.)	0.11
Theodore Roosevelt Inaugural (N.Y.)	1.03
Thomas Stone (Md.)	328.25
Tuskegee Institute (Ala.)	74.39
Vanderbilt Mansion (N.Y.)	211.65
Whitman Mission (Wash.)	98.15
William Howard Taft (Ohio)	3.07

NATIONAL MEMORIALS

Arkansas Post (Ark.)	389.18
Arlington House, the Robert E. Lee Memorial (Va.)	27.91
Chamizal (Tex.)	54.90
Coronado (Ariz.)	4,976.77
Desoto (Fla.)	26.84
Federal Hall (N.Y.)	0.45
Fort Caroline (Fla.)	138.39
Fort Clatsop (Ore.)	125.20
General Grant (N.Y.)	0.76
Hamilton Grange (N.Y.)	0.71
John F. Kennedy Center for Performing Arts (D.C.)	17.50
Johnstown Flood (Pa.)	163.47
Lincoln Boyhood (Ind.)	197.60
Lincoln Memorial (D.C.)	163.63
Lyndon Baines Johnson Memorial Grove on the Potomac (D.C.)	17.00

Name and location	Total acreage
Mount Rushmore (S.D.)	1,278.45
Roger Williams (R.I.)	4.56
Thaddeus Kosciuszko (Pa.)	0.02
Theodore Roosevelt Island (D.C.)	88.50
Thomas Jefferson Memorial (D.C.)	18.36
USS Arizona Memorial (Hawaii)	0.00
Vietnam Veterans, D.C.	2.00
Washington Monument (D.C.)	106.01
Wright Brothers (N.C.)	431.40

NATIONAL CEMETERIES[1]

Name and location	Total acreage
Antietam (Md.)	11.36
Battleground (D.C.)	1.03
Fort Donelson (Tenn.)	15.34
Fredericksburg (Va.)	12.00
Gettysburg (Pa.)	20.58
Poplar Grove (Va.)	8.72
Shiloh (Tenn.)	10.05
Stones River (Tenn.)	20.09
Vicksburg (Miss.)	116.28
Yorktown (Va.)	2.91

NATIONAL SEASHORES

Name and location	Total acreage
Assateague Island (Md.-Va.)	39,630.93
Canaveral (Fla.)	57,627.07
Cape Cod (Mass.)	43,524.00
Cape Hatteras (N.C.)	30,319.43
Cape Lookout (N.C.)	28,414.74
Cumberland Island (Ga.)	36,410.28
Fire Island (N.Y.)	19,578.55
Gulf Islands (Fla.-Miss.)	139,775.46
Padre Island (Tex.)	130,696.83
Point Reyes (Calif.)	71,046.07

NATIONAL PARKWAYS

Name and location	Total acreage
Blue Ridge (Va.-N.C.)	82,117.37
George Washington Memorial (Va.-Md.)	7,141.63
John D. Rockefeller, Jr., Memorial (Wyo.)	23,777.22
Natchez Trace (Miss.-Tenn.-Ala.)	50,189.33

NATIONAL LAKESHORES

Name and location	Total acreage
Apostle Islands (Wis.)	67,884.84
Indiana Dunes (Ind.)	12,721.79
Pictured Rocks (Mich)	72,898.86
Sleeping Bear Dunes (Mich.)	71,020.06

NATIONAL SCENIC RIVERS AND RIVERWAYS

Name and location	Total acreage
Alagnak Wild River (Alaska)	24,038.00
Big South Fork National River & Recreation Area (Ky.-Tenn.)	122,960.00
Buffalo (Ark.)	94,221.08
Delaware (N.Y.-N.J.-Pa.)	1,973.33
Lower St. Croix (Minn.-Wis.)	9,465.14
New River Gorge (W. Va.)	62,024.00
Obed Wild & Scenic River (Tenn.)	5,085.83
Ozark (Mo.)	80,788.34
Rio Grande Wild & Scenic (Tex.)	9,600.00
St. Croix (Minn.-Wis.)	68,793.28
Upper Delaware (N.Y., N.J.-Pa.)	75,000.00

NATIONAL CAPITAL PARKS

Name and location	Total acreage
National Capital Parks (D.C.-Va.-Md.)	6,465.85

WHITE HOUSE

Name and location	Total acreage
White House (D.C.)	18.07

OTHER PARKS

Name and location	Total acreage
Catoctin Mountain (Md.)	5,770.22
Fort Benton (Mont.)	0.0
Fort Washington Park (Md.)	341.00
Frederick Douglass Home (D.C.)	8.08
Greenbelt Park (Md.)	1,175.99
Perry's Victory and International Peace Memorial (Ohio)	25.38
Piscataway (Md.)	4,262.52
Prince William Forest (Va.)	18,571.55
Rock Creek Park (D.C.)	1,754.37
Wolf Trap Farm Park for the Performing Arts (Va.)	130.28

1. The National Cemeteries are not independent areas of the National Park System; each is part of a military park, battlefield, etc., except Battleground. Their acreage is kept separately. Arlington National Cemetery is under the Department of the Army. *See* Index.

NATIONAL RECREATION AREAS

Name and location	Total acreage
Amistad (Tex.)	57,292.44
Bighorn Canyon (Wyo.-Mont.)	120,277.86
Chattahoochee River (Ga.)	8,699.00
Chickasaw (Okla.)	9,500.06
Coulee Dam (Wash.)	100,390.31
Curecanti (Colo.)	42,114.47
Cuyahoga Valley (Ohio)	32,460.19
Delaware Water Gap (Pa.-N.J.)	66,696.79
Gateway (N.Y.-N.J.)	26,310.93
Glen Canyon (Ariz.-Utah)	1,236,880.00
Golden Gate (Calif.)	72,815.04
Lake Chelan (Wash.)	61,890.07
Lake Mead (Ariz.-Nev.)	1,496,600.52
Lake Meredith (Tex.)	44,977.63
Ross Lake (Wash.)	117,574.09
Santa Monica Mountains (Calif.)	150,000.00
Whiskeytown-Shasta-Trinity (Calif.)	42,503.43

NATIONAL SCENIC TRAIL

Name and location	Total acreage
Appalachian (Maine, N.H., Vt., Mass., Conn., N.Y., N.J., Pa., Md., W.Va., Va., N.C., Tenn., Ga.)	115,969.09

NATIONAL MALL

Name and location	Total acreage
National Mall (D.C.)	146.35

AFFILIATED AREAS

(National Historic Sites unless otherwise noted.)

Name and location	Total acreage
Afro-American History and Culture (Ohio)	0.00
American Memorial Park (N. Mariana Is.)	0.00
Benjamin Franklin (Pa.)[1]	0.00
Boston African American (Mass.)	0.00
Cherokee Strip Living Museum (Kan.)	6.00
Chicago Portage (Ill.)	91.20
Chimney Rock (Neb.)	83.36
David Berger (Ohio)[1]	0.00
Ebey's Landing (Wash.)	8,000.00
Father Marquette (Mich.)	52.00
Green Springs Historic District (Va.)	0.00
Gloria Dei Church (Pa.)	3.71
Historic Camden (S.C.)	0.00
Ice Age Scenic Trail (Wisc.)	0.00
Ice Age (Wis.)[2]	32,500.00
Iditarod National Historic Trail (Alaska)	0.00
International Peace Garden (N.D.)	2,330.30
Jamestown (Va.)	20.63
Lewis & Clark Natl. Historic Trail (Ill., Mo., Kan., Neb., Iowa, Idaho, S.D., N.D., Mont., Ore., Wash.)	0.00
M. McLeod Bethune Council House (D.C.)	0.00
McLoughlin House (Ore.)	0.63
Mormon Pioneer Natl. Historic Trail (Ill., Iowa, Neb., Wyo., Utah)	0.00
North Country Nat'l Scenic Trail (N.Y., Pa., Ohio, Mich., Wis., Minn., N.D.)	0.00
Oregon Natl. Historic Trail (Mo., Kan., Neb., Wyo., Idaho, Ore., Wash.)	0.00
Overmountain Victory Trail (Mo. to Ore.)	0.00
Pennsylvania Avenue (D.C.)	0.00
Pinelands Natl. Reserve (N.J.)	[illegible].00
Roosevelt-Campobello International Park (Canada)	[illegible]0
St. Paul's Church (N.Y.)	[illegible]2
Touro Synagogue (R.I.)	[illegible]

1. National Memorial. 2. National Scientific Reser[illegible]

Environmental Glossary

Source: Environmental Protection Agency

abatement: the reduction in degree or intensity of pollution.
acclimation: the physiological and behavioral adjustments of an organism to changes in the environment.
adaptation: a change in structure or habit of an organism that produces better adjustment to its surroundings.
adulterants: chemical impurities or substances that by law do not belong in a food, plant, animal, or pesticide formulation.
aeration: to circulate oxygen through a substance, as in waste water treatment where it aids in purification.
agricultural pollution: the liquid and solid wastes from farming, including: runoff from pesticides, fertilizers, and feedlots; erosion and dust from plowing; animal manure and carcasses, crop residues, and debris.
air pollution: the presence of contaminant substances in the air that do not disperse properly and interfere with human health.
air quality standards: the level of pollutants prescribed by law that cannot be exceeded during a specified time in a defined area.
ambient air: any unconfined portion of the atmosphere; open air.
asbestos: a mineral fiber that can pollute air or water and cause cancer if inhaled or ingested.
A-scale sound level: a measurement of sound approximating the sensitivity of the human ear, used to note the intensity or annoyance of sounds.
attractant: a chemical or agent that lures insects or other pests by stimulating their sense of smell.
biodegradable: any substance that decomposes quickly through the action of microorganisms.
breeder: a nuclear reactor that produces more fuel than it consumes.
carcinogenic: cancer-producing.
catalytic converter: an air pollution abatement device that removes organic contaminants by oxidizing them into carbon dioxide and water.
chilling effect: the lowering of the earth's temperature because of increased particles in the air blocking the sun's rays.
chlorination: the application of chlorine to drinking water, sewage, or industrial waste to disinfect or oxidize undesirable compounds.
combined sewers: a system that carries both sewage and storm water runoff. In dry weather all flow goes to the waste treatment plant. During a storm, only part of the flow is intercepted due to overloading. The remaining mixture of sewage and storm water overflows untreated into the receiving stream.
desalinization: removing salt from ocean or brackish water.
ecological impact: the total effect of an environmental change, natural or man-made, on the community of living things.
ecology: the relationships of living things to one another and to their environment, or the study of such relationships.
effluent: treated or untreated waste material discharged into the environment. Generally refers to water pollution.
emission standard: the maximum amount of discharge legally allowed from a single source, mobile or stationary.
environment: the sum of all external conditions affecting the life, development, and survival of an organism.
fluorocarbons: a gas used as a propellant in aerosols, thought to be modifying the ozone layer in the stratosphere, thereby allowing more harmful solar radiation to reach the earth's surface.
fossil fuels: combustibles—like coal, oil, and natural gas—derived from the remains of ancient plants and animals.
greenhouse effect: the warming of our atmosphere caused by build-up of carbon dioxide, which allows light from the sun's rays to heat the earth, but prevents loss of the heat.
groundwater: the supply of fresh water under the earth's surface that forms a natural reservoir.
habitat: the sum of environmental conditions in a specific place that is occupied by an organism, population, or community.
herbicide: a chemical that controls or destroys undesirable plants.
inversion: an atmospheric condition caused by a layer of warm air preventing the rise of cool air trapped beneath it. This holds down pollutants that might otherwise be dispersed, and can cause an air pollution episode.
nuclear power plant: a device that converts atomic energy into usable power; heat produced by a reactor makes steam to drive electricity-generating turbines.
oil spill: accidental discharge into bodies of water, can be controlled by chemical dispersion, combustion, mechanical containment, and absorption.
organic: referring to or derived from living organisms. In chemistry, any compound containing carbon.
pesticide: any substance used to control pests ranging from rats, weeds, and insects to algae and fungi. Pesticides can accumulate in the food chain and can contaminate the environment if misused.
pollutant: any introduced substance that adversely affects the usefulness of a resource.
pollution: the presence of matter or energy whose nature, location, or quantity produces undesired environmental effects.
radiation: the emission of particles or rays by the nucleus of an atom.
radiation standards: regulations that govern exposure to permissible concentrations of and transportation of radioactive materials.
radioactive: substances that emit rays either naturally or as a result of scientific manipulation.
recycling: converting solid waste into new products by using the resources contained in discarded materials.
refuge, wildlife: an area designated for the protection of wild animals, within which hunting and fishing are either prohibited or strictly controlled.
runoff: water from rain, snow melt, or irrigation that flows over the ground surface and returns to streams. It can collect pollutants from air or land and carry them to the receiving waters.
sanitary landfill, landfilling: protecting the environment when disposing of solid waste. Waste is spread in thin layers, compacted by heavy machinery, and covered with soil daily.
thermal pollution: discharge of heated water from industrial processes that can affect the life processes of aquatic plants and animals.
water pollution: the addition of enough harmful or objectionable material to damage water quality.

POSTAL REGULATIONS

Domestic Mail Service

First Class

First-class consists of letters and written and sealed matter. The rate is 20¢ for the first oz; 17¢ for each additional oz, or fraction of an oz, up to 12 oz. Pieces over 12 oz are subject to priority-mail (heavy pieces) rates. Single postcards, 13¢; double postcards, 26¢ (13¢ for each half). The post office sells prestamped single and double postal cards. Consult your postmaster for information on business-reply mail and presort rates.

The weight limit for first-class mail is 70 lb, and the maximum size is 100 in. in combined length and girth.

Weight	Rates
First oz	$ .20
Over 1 oz, but not over 2	.37
Over 2 oz, but not over 3	.54
Over 3 oz, but not over 4	.71
Over 4 oz, but not over 5	.88
Over 5 oz, but not over 6	1.05
Over 6 oz, but not over 7	1.22
Over 7 oz, but not over 8	1.39
Over 8 oz, but not over 9	1.56
Over 9 oz, but not over 10	1.76
Over 10 oz, but not over 11	1.90
Over 11 oz, but not over 12	2.07
Over 12 oz, *see* Priority Mail	

Priority Mail (over 12 oz to 70 lb)

The zone rate applies to mailable matter over 12 oz of any class carried by air. Such matter shall not exceed 100 in. in length and girth combined. Your local post office will supply free official zone tables appropriate to your location.

Airmail

First-class and priority mail receive airmail service.

Express Mail

Express Mail Service is available for any mailable article up to 70 lb, and guarantees next day delivery between major U.S. cities or your money back.

Articles received by 5 p.m. at a postal facility offering Express Mail Service will be delivered by 3 p.m. the next day or, if you prefer, your shipment can be picked up as early as 10 a.m. the next business day. Rates include Insurance, Shipment Receipt, and Record of Delivery at the destination post office.

Consult Postmaster for other Express Mail Services and rates.

The Postal Service will refund, upon application to originating office, the postage for any Express Mail shipments not meeting the service standard except for those delayed by strike or work stoppage.

Second Class

Second-class mail is used primarily by newspapers, magazines, and other periodicals with second-class mailing privileges. For copies mailed by the public, the rate is:

Weight	Rates	Weight	Rates
0 to 1 oz	$ .19	Over 4 to 5 oz	$ .65
Over 1 to 2 oz	.35	Over 5 to 6 oz	.75
Over 2 to 3 oz	.45	Over 6 to 7 oz	.85
Over 3 to 4 oz	.55	Over 7 to 8 oz	.95
Each additional two ounces over 8 oz, add $ .10			

Third Class (under 16 oz)

Third-class mail is used for circulars, books, printed matter, merchandise, seeds, cuttings, bulbs, roots, scions, and plants, and all other mailable matter not in first or second class. There are two rate structures for this class, a single-piece and a bulk rate.

Many community organizations, as well as businesses, find it economical to use this service. Because of the number of categories of third-class mail, you should consult your postmaster for the one best suited to your needs.

Third-Class, Single-Piece Rates

Weight	Rates	Weight	Rates
0 to 1 oz	$ .20	Over 8 to 10 oz	$ 1.05
Over 1 to 2 oz	.37	Over 10 to 12 oz	1.15
Over 2 to 3 oz	.54	Over 12 to 14 oz	1.25
Over 3 to 4 oz	.71	Over 14 but less than 16 oz	1.35
Over 4 to 6 oz	.85		
Over 6 to 8 oz	.95		

Fourth Class (Parcel Post—16 oz and over)

Fourth-class mail is used for merchandise, books, printed matter, and all other mailable matter not in first, second, or third class. Special fourth-class rates apply to books, library books, publications or records for the blind, and certain controlled-circulation publications.

Packages should be taken to your local post office, where the postage will be determined according to the weight of the package and the distance it is being sent. Information on weight and size limits for fourth-class mail may be obtained there.

Special Fourth-Class Rate

The special fourth-class rate is restricted specifically to books; 16-mm or narrower width films and catalogs of such films (which must be positive prints); printed music, printed objective-test materials, sound recordings, and playscripts and manuscripts for books, periodicals, and music; printed educational reference charts, looseleaf pages, and binders therefor, consisting of medical information for distribution to doctors, hospitals, medical schools, and medical students. The rate is 63¢ for the first lb or fraction, plus 23¢ for each additional lb or fraction through 7 lb, 14¢ for each additional lb or fraction over 7 lb.

Special Services

Registered Mail. When you use registered mail service, you are buying security—the safest way to send valuables. The full value of your mailing must be declared when mailed. You receive a receipt and the movement of your mail is controlled throughout the postal system. For an additional fee, a return receipt showing to whom, when, and where delivered may be obtained.

Fees for articles (in addition to postage)

Value			with Insurance	without Insurance
0.00	to	$ 100	$3.30	$3.25
100.01	to	500	3.60	3.55
500.01	to	1,000	3.90	3.85

For higher values, consult your postmaster.

Certified Mail. Certified mail service provides for a receipt to the sender and a record of delivery at the post office of address. No record is kept at the post office where mailed. It is handled in the ordinary mails and no insurance coverage is provided.

Fee in addition to postage, 75¢.

Return Receipts. Requested at time of mailing:

Showing to whom and date delivered	$ .60
Showing to whom, date, and address where delivered	.70
Requested after mailing:	
Showing to whom and date delivered	3.75

C.O.D. Mail. Consult your postmaster for fees and conditions of mailing.

Insured Mail. Fees, in addition to postage, for coverage against loss or damage:

Liability	Fees
$ .01 to $20	$ .45
$ 20.01 to $50	.85
$ 50.01 to $100	1.25
$ 100.01 to $150	1.70
$ 150.01 to $200	2.05
$ 200.01 to $300	3.45
$ 300.01 to $400[1]	4.70

1. Liability for insured mail is limited to $400.

Special Delivery. The payment of the special-delivery fee entitles mail to the most expeditious transportation and delivery. The fee is in addition to the regular postage.

Class of mail	Weight/Fees: Not more than 2 lb	More than 2 lb but not more than 10 lb	More than 10 lb
First-class	$2.10	$2.35	$3.00
All other classes	2.35	3.00	3.40

Special Handling. Payment of the special-handling fee entitles third- and fourth-class matter to the most expeditious handling and transportation, but not special delivery. The fee is in addition to the regular postage.

Weight	Fees
Not more than 10 lb	$ .75
More than 10 lb	1.30

Money Orders. Money orders are used for the safe transmission of money.

Amount of money order	Fees
$ .01 to $25	$ .75
$ 25.01 to $50	1.10
$ 50.01 to $500	1.55

Minimum Mail Sizes

All mail must be at least 0.007 in. thick and mail that is 1/4 in. or less in thickness must be at least 3 1/2 in. in height, at least 5 in. long, and rectangular in shape.

Adhesive Stamps Available

Purpose	Form	Denomination and prices
Ordinary postage	Single or sheet	1, 2, 3, 4, 5, 6, 10, 11, 12, 13, 14, 15, 16, 17, 18, 20, 25, 28, 30, 35, 37, 40, and 50¢, $1, 2, and $5.
	Book	6 at 20=$1.20 20 at 20=$4.00
	Coil of 100[1]	20¢
	Coil of 500	1, 2, 3, 5, 6, 10, 12, 13, 15, 16, 17, 18, 20, and $1.00.
	Coil of 3,000	1, 2, 3, 5, 6, 9, 10, 15, 16, and 25¢
International airmail postage	Single or sheet	28, 35, and 40¢

1. Dispenser to hold coil of 100 stamps may be purchased for 10¢

"Junk" Mail

The Direct Mail Marketing Association Inc. offers a free service allowing consumers to have their names added or deleted from national advertising lists. Copies of a booklet, "How Did They Get My Name?" which explains consumer mailing lists, are available without charge from DMMA, Dept. M, 6 E. 43rd St., New York, N.Y. 10017.

Non-Standard Mail

All first-class mail weighing one ounce or less and all single-piece rate third-class mail weighing one ounce or less is nonstandard (and subject to a 9¢ surcharge in addition to the applicable postage and fees) if any of the following dimensions are exceeded: length—11 1/2 inches; height—6 1/8 inches; thickness—1/4 inch, or the piece has a height to length (aspect) ratio which does not fall between 1 to 1.3 and 1 to 2.5 inclusive. (The aspect ratio is found by dividing the length by the height. If the answer is between 1.3 and 2.5 inclusive, the piece has a standard aspect ratio).

International Mail Service

Canada and Mexico—Surface Rates

Weight	Letter mail	Printed matter and small packets
1 oz	$ .20	$ .20
2 oz	.37	.37
3 oz	.54	.54
4 oz	.71	.71
6 oz	1.05	.85
8 oz	1.39	.95
10 oz	1.73	1.14
12 oz	2.07	1.36
14 oz	—	1.58
16 oz	2.58	1.81
Postcards	.13	—

Consult your postmaster for rates for heavier items.

International Airmail

Destination	Letters and letter packages[1]	Post-cards	Aero-gramme[2]
Central America Colombia, Venezuela, Caribbean Islands, Bahamas, Bermuda, St. Pierre and Miquelon	35¢ per half oz through 2 oz; 30¢ each additional half oz or fraction	28¢	30¢
All other countries	40¢ per half oz through 2 oz; 35¢ each additional half oz or fraction	28¢	30¢

1. Weight limit, 4 lb. 2. No enclosures permitted.

For Canada and Mexico, *see* Surface Rates.

International Money Order Fees

This service available only to certain countries. Consult post office.

Countries Other Than Canada and Mexico—Surface Rates

Ounces	Letter mail	Printed matter	Small packets
1	$ .30	$ .23	$ .23
2	.47	.37	.37
4	.81	.71	.71
8	1.49	.95	.95
16	2.76	1.81	1.81
32	4.80	2.76	2.76
64	7.80	3.86	—
Each additional 32 oz	—	.96	—

International Surface Parcel Post

Weight through lb	Canada, Mexico, Central America, Caribbean Islands, Bahamas, Bermuda, St. Pierre and Miquelon	All other countries
2	$ 3.10	$ 3.25
3	4.10	4.30
	$1.00 each additional lb or fraction	$1.05 each additional lb or fraction

Consult your postmaster for weight/size limits.

For other international services and rates consult your local postmaster.

United Nations Stamps

United Nations stamps are issued in three different currencies, namely, U.S. dollars, Swiss francs, and Austrian schillings. Stamps in all three currencies are available at face value at each of the U.N. Postal Administration offices in New York, Geneva, and Vienna. They may be purchased over the counter, by mail, or by opening a Customer Deposit Account.

Mail orders for mint (unused) stamps and postal stationery may be sent to the U.N. Postal Administration in New York, Geneva, and Vienna. A special order form, listing all available mint issues, is available on request. Write to: United Nations Postal Administration, P.O. Box 5900, Grand Central Station, New York, N.Y. 10017. All mint stamps and postal stationery are sold by the U.N. Postal Administration at face value.

Authorized 2-Letter State Abbreviations

When the Post Office instituted the ZIP Code for mail in 1963, it also drew up a list of two-letter abbreviations for the states which would gradually replace the traditional ones in use. Following is the official list, including the District of Columbia, Guam, Puerto Rico, and the Virgin Islands (note that only capital letters are used):

Alabama	AL	Kentucky	KY	Ohio	OH
Alaska	AK	Louisiana	LA	Oklahoma	OK
Arizona	AZ	Maine	ME	Oregon	OR
Arkansas	AR	Maryland	MD	Pennsylvania	PA
California	CA	Massachusetts	MA	Puerto Rico	PR
Colorado	CO	Michigan	MI	Rhode Island	RI
Connecticut	CT	Minnesota	MN	South Carolina	SC
Delaware	DE	Mississippi	MS	South Dakota	SD
Dist. of Columbia	DC	Missouri	MO	Tennessee	TN
Florida	FL	Montana	MT	Texas	TX
Georgia	GA	Nebraska	NE	Utah	UT
Guam	GU	Nevada	NV	Vermont	VT
Hawaii	HI	New Hampshire	NH	Virginia	VA
Idaho	ID	New Jersey	NJ	Virgin Islands	VI
Illinois	IL	New Mexico	NM	Washington	WA
Indiana	IN	New York	NY	West Virginia	WV
Iowa	IA	North Carolina	NC	Wisconsin	WI
Kansas	KS	North Dakota	ND	Wyoming	WY

The Mail Order Merchandise Rule

The mail order rule adopted by the Federal Trade Commission in October 1975 provides that when you order by mail:

You must receive the merchandise when the seller says you will.

If you are not promised delivery within a certain time period, the seller must ship the merchandise to you no later than 30 days after your order comes in.

If you don't receive it shortly after that 30-day period, you can cancel your order and get your money back.

How the Rule Works

The seller must notify you if the promised delivery date (or the 30-day limit) cannot be met. The seller must also tell you what the new shipping date will be and give you the option to cancel the order and receive a full refund or agree to the new shipping date. The seller must also give you a free way to send back your answer, such as a stamped envelope or a postage-paid postcard. *If you don't answer, it means that you agree to the shipping delay.*

The seller must tell you if the shipping delay is going to be more than 30 days. You then can agree to the delay or, if you do not agree, the seller must return your money by the end of the first 30 days of the delay.

If you cancel a prepaid order, the seller must mail you the refund within seven business days. Where there is a credit sale, the seller must adjust your account within one billing cycle.

It would be impossible, however, for one rule to apply uniformly to such a varied field as mail order merchandising. For example, the rule does not apply to mail order photo finishing, magazine subscriptions, and other serial deliveries (except for the initial shipment); to mail order seeds and growing plants; to COD orders; or to credit orders where the buyer's account is not charged prior to shipment of the merchandise.

How to Complain About a Postal Problem

When you have a problem with your mail service, complete a Consumer Service Card which is available from letter carriers and at post offices. This will help your postmaster respond to your problem. If you wish to telephone a complaint, a postal employee will fill out the card for you.

The Consumer Advocate represents consumers at the top management level in the Postal Service. If your postal problems cannot be solved by your local post office, then write to the Consumer Advocate. His staff stands ready to serve you. Write to: The Consumer Advocate, U.S. Postal Service, Washington, D.C. 20260-6320. Or phone: 1-202-245-4514.

Pornography

You can stop the mailing of unsolicited sexually oriented advertisements to you by filling out a Form 2201, *Application for Listing Pursuant to 39 USC 3010,* at your local post office. Thirty days after your name has been added to the Postal Service reference listing, any mailer who sends you sexually oriented advertisements is subject to legal action by the United States Government.

You may also stop the mailing of any further advertisements to you which you consider "erotically arousing or sexually provocative." Fill out Form 2150, *Notice for Prohibitory Order Against Sender of Pandering Advertisement in the Mail,* at your post office for this purpose.

MEDIA

Major U.S. Daily Newspapers[1]

City and newspaper	Net paid circulation: Morning[2]	All-Day[2]	Evening[2]	Sunday
Akron, Ohio: *Beacon Journal*	—		167,310	233,230
Albany, N.Y.: *Times-Union* (M & S); *Knickerbocker News* (E)	85,475		37,118[3]	164,744
Albuquerque, N.M.: *Journal* (M & S); *Tribune* (E)	94,420[4]		46,103[4]	133,566[4]
Allentown, Pa.: *Morning Call; Call-Chronicle* (S)	128,756[3]		—	166,476
Amarillo, Tex.: *News* (M); *Globe-Times* (E); *News-Globe* (S)	46,280		29,440[3]	77,850
Asbury Park, N.J.: *Press*	—		120,396	177,950
Atlanta: *Constitution* (M); *Journal* (E); *Journal and Constitution* (S)	226,232[3]		185,278[3]	567,993
Atlantic City, N.J.: *Press*	76,176		—	82,385
Augusta, Ga.: *Chronicle* (M); *Herald* (E); *Chronicle—Herald* (S)	60,677[3]		18,365[3]	83,431
Austin, Tex.: *American-Statesman*	—	154,039[3]	—	182,960
Bakersfield, Calif.: *Californian*	77,585[4]		—	84,553[4]
Baltimore: *Sun*	185,510[3]		163,672[3]	407,436
News American	—		124,354[3]	161,244
Bangor, Me.: *News*	76,522[3]		—	88,417[5]
Baton Rouge, La.: *Advocate* (M & S); *State-Times* (E)	82,071		37,922	132,428
Bergen County (Hackensack), N.J.: *Record* (E); *Sunday Record*	—		153,480[3 4]	223,782[4]
Beaumont, Tex.: *Enterprise*	73,492		—	80,913
Binghamton, N.Y.: *Sun-Bulletin* (M); *Press* (E & S)	30,300[3]		60,821[3]	84,794
Birmingham, Ala.: *Post-Herald* (M); *News* (E & S)	62,807[3]		167,136[3]	211,543
Boston: *Globe*	—	510,261[3]	—	793,151
Herald	325,086[3]		—	276,265
Christian Science Monitor	148,683[3]		—	—
Bridgeport, Conn: *Telegram* (M); *Post* (E); *Sunday Post*	17,539[3 4]		68,694[3 4]	92,110[4]
Buffalo, N.Y.: *News*	—	320,028[3]	—	375,276
Camden, N.J.: *Courier-Post*	—		114,146[3 4]	99,980[4]
Canton, Ohio: *Repository*	—		61,751[4]	78,654[4]
Cedar Rapids, Iowa: *Gazette*	70,639		—	80,332
Charleston, S.C.: *News & Courier* (M); *Evening Post; News & Courier Post* (S)	69,670[3]		38,202[3]	110,819
Charleston, W. Va.: *Gazette* (M); *Daily Mail* (E); *Gazette-Mail* (S)	55,160		53,817	109,327
Charlotte, N.C.: *Observer* (M & S); *News* (E)	184,586		41,904[3]	255,459
Chattanooga, Tenn.: *Times* (M); *News-Free Press* (E & S)	44,950[3]		56,520[3]	104,912
Chicago: *Tribune*	—	762,882[3]	—	1,145,387
Sun-Times	628,285[3]		—	687,386
Daily Herald (M); *Sunday Herald*	61,426		—	60,017
Cincinnati: *Enquirer* (M & S); *Post* (E)	192,106		134,098	300,162
Cleveland: *Plain Dealer*	492,002[3]		—	502,573
Cocoa, Fla.: *Today*	74,284		—	90,014
Colorado Springs, Colo.: *Gazette Telegraph*	52,448[3]		39,848[3]	98,324
Sun	40,595[3]		—	43,465
Columbia, S.C.: *State* (M & S); *Record* (E)	107,968		31,689	139,432
Columbus, Ohio: *Citizen-Journal* (M); *Dispatch* (E & S)	121,232		206,548	358,289
Corpus Christi, Tex.: *Caller* (M); *Times* (E); *Caller-Times* (S)	60,668[3 4]		23,239[3 4]	89,008
Dallas: *News*	340,502		—	437,067
Times Herald	—	282,933	—	381,318
Wall Street Journal (Southwest edition)	241,261[3]		—	—
Davenport, Iowa: *Quad City Times*	—	65,014	—	85,992
Dayton, Ohio: *Journal Herald* (M); *News* (E & S)	101,840		117,286	229,643
Daytona Beach, Fla.: *Journal* (M); *News* (E); *News-Journal* (S)	68,303		31,829	90,052
Denver: *Post*	244,953		—	356,968
News	319,177		—	368,590
Des Moines, Iowa: *Register*	238,609		—	382,745
Detroit: *News*	—	657,015[3]	—	861,004
Free Press	631,087[3]		—	787,300
Duluth, Minn.: *News-Tribune* & *Herald*	62,694		—	82,288
Erie, Pa.: *News* (M); *Times* (E); *Times-News* (S)	25,395[3]		44,026[3]	98,691
El Paso, Tex.: *Times* (M & S); *Herald-Post* (E)	57,062[4]		32,471[4]	88,865[4]
Evansville, Ind.: *Courier* (M); *Press* (E); *Courier & Press* (S)	63,334		41,413	116,979
Flint, Mich.: *Journal*	—		109,438[3]	117,245
Fort Lauderdale, Fla.: *Sun-Sentinel* (M); *News* (E); *News & Sun—Sentinel* (S)	114,868[3]		88,602[3]	259,937

City and newspaper	Net paid circulation			
	Morning[2]	All-Day[2]	Evening[2]	Sunday
Fort Myers, Fla.: *News-Press*	80,943		—	93,705
Fort Wayne, Ind.: *Journal-Gazette* (M & S); *News-Sentinel* (E)	60,219[4]		62,971[4]	123,575[4]
Fort Worth: *Star-Telegram*	117,999[3]		130,948[3]	280,751
Fresno, Calif.: *Bee*	139,958[4]		—	161,197[4]
Gary, Ind.: *Post-Tribune*	—		82,100	94,822
Grand Rapids, Mich.: *Press*	—		132,831	167,636
Greensboro, N.C.: *News* (M & S); *Record* (E)	87,699[3]		23,178	119,744
Greensburg, Pa.: *Tribune-Review*	51,837		—	84,209
Greenville, S.C.: *News* (M): *Piedmont* (E); *News & Piedmont* (S)	86,011[3]		24,122[3]	119,635
Hammond-East Chicago, Ind.: *Times*	—		69,158[3]	76,851
Harrisburg, Pa.: *Patriot* (M); *Evening News; Sunday Patriot News*	47,981[3]		58,235[3]	164,150
Hartford, Conn.: *Courant*	218,830		—	300,767
Honolulu: *Advertiser* (M); *Star-Bulletin* (E); *Star-Bulletin & Advertiser* (S)	87,799		113,608	200,462
Houston: *Chronicle*	—	n.a.	—	n.a.
Post	n.a.		—	n.a.
Indianapolis: *Star* (M & S); *News* (E)	228,319[4]		133,044[4]	388,123
Jackson, Miss.: *Clarion-Ledger* (M); *Daily News* (E); *Clarion Ledger-Daily News* (S)	69,377[3]		37,231[3]	114,450
Jacksonville, Fla.: *Florida Times-Union* (M & S); *Journal* (E)	162,831[3]		42,876[3]	216,373
Kansas City, Mo.: *Times* (M); *Star* (E & S)	288,635		240,142[3]	402,206
Knoxville, Tenn.: *Journal* (M); *News-Sentinel* (E & S)	61,738		98,020	160,994
Lakeland, Fla.: *Ledger*	68,256[4]		—	81,524[4]
Lancaster, Pa.: *Intelligencer-Journal* (M); *New Era* (E); *News* (S)	41,928[4]		57,769[4]	140,647[4]
Lansing, Mich.: *State-Journal*	—		67,458	77,706
Las Vegas, Nev.: *Review-Journal*		101,965[3]	—	114,302
Sun	56,106		—	60,264
Lexington, Ky.: *Herald-Leader*	109,114		—	132,912
Lincoln, Neb.: *Star* (M); *Journal* (E); *Journal & Star* (S)	36,417		45,496	77,863
Little Rock, Ark.: *Arkansas Gazette*	129,040		—	158,056
Arkansas Democrat	78,817		—	144,115
Long Beach, Calif.: *Press-Telegram*	92,769[3]		39,543[3]	141,742
Long Island (Melville), N.Y.: *Newsday*	—		533,384[3]	608,640
Los Angeles: *Times*	1,057,536[3]		—	1,321,244
Herald-Examiner	236,660[3]		—	219,900
Daily News	141,690[3]		—	162,906
Louisville, Ky.: *Courier-Journal* (M & S); *Times* (E)	177,289		135,869	329,998
Lubbock, Tex.: *Avalanche-Journal* (M & S); Journal (E)	59,958[3]		15,141[3]	81,448
Macon, Ga.: *Telegraph and News* (M & S)	68,719		—	89,850
Madison, Wis.: *State Journal* (M & S); *Capital Times* (E)	76,527		30,400	134,740
Memphis, Tenn.: *Commercial Appeal* (M & S); *Press Scimitar* (E)	240,519[6]		66,375	294,175
Miami, Fla.: *Herald* (M & S); *News* (E)	451,206		63,496	545,356
Middletown, N.Y.: *Times-Herald Record* (M); *Sunday Record*	72,132[4]		—	82,582[4]
Milwaukee: *Sentinel* (M); *Journal* (E & S)	180,371		306,055	527,085
Minneapolis: *Star & Tribune* (M); *Tribune* (S)	372,179		—	586,876
Mobile, Ala.: *Register* (M); *Press* (E); *Press-Register* (S)	50,249[3][4]		48,822[3][4]	100,396[4]
Modesto, Calif.: *Bee*	72,400[4]		—	77,133[4]
Naperville, Ill.: *Wall Street Journal* (Midwest edition)	595,381[3]		—	—
Nashville, Tenn.: *Tennessean* (M & S); *Banner* (E)	124,966		72,366	241,717
New Haven, Conn.: *Journal-Courier* (M); *Register* (E & S)	39,189[3]		92,284	142,242
New Orleans: *Times-Picayune/States-Item*	—	279,302[3][4]	—	339,506[4]
New York: *News*	1,374,858[3]		—	1,813,671
Times	970,051[3]		—	1,593,107
Post	—	963,069[3]	—	639,477
Wall Street Journal (Eastern edition)	806,632[3]		—	—
National edition	2,081,995[3]		—	—
Staten Island Advance	—		72,626[3]	82,139
Women's Wear Daily	63,782[3]		—	—
Newark, N.J.: *Star-Ledger*	432,328[3][4]		—	654,446[4]
Newport News—Hampton, Va.: *Daily Press* (M & S); *Times Herald* (E)	62,033[4]		38,932[4]	106,544[4]
Norfolk–Portsmouth–Virginia Beach–Chesapeake, Va.: *Virginian–Pilot* (M); *Ledger–Star* (E); *Virginian–Pilot/Ledger-Star* (S)	139,627[4]		87,099[4]	216,422[4]
Oakland, Calif.: *Tribune* (M & S)	148,033[3]		—	156,185
Oklahoma City: *Oklahoman* (M); *Times* (E); *Sunday Oklahoman*	193,340[3][6]		70,686[3][6]	308,651

City and newspaper	Net paid circulation			
	Morning[2]	All-Day[2]	Evening[2]	Sunday
Omaha, Neb.: *World Herald*	121,967[3]		103,738[3]	284,980
Orange County (Santa Ana), Calif,: *Register*	—	279,452[3]	—	311,062
Orlando, Fla.: *Sentinel Star*	—	233,124[3]	—	287,137
Palo Alto, Calif.: *Wall Street Journal* (Western edition)	438,721[3]		—	—
Times Tribune	—		59,006	59,660
Peoria, Ill.: *Journal Star*	—	100,271	—	120,475
Philadelphia: *Inquirer* (M & S); Daily News (E)	536,065[3]		293,031[3]	1,008,225
Phoenix, Ariz.: *Republic* (M & S); *Gazette* (E)	314,460[4]		121,058[4]	469,179[4]
Pittsburgh: *Post-Gazette* (M); *Press* (E & S)	178,284[3]		255,445[3]	613,795
Pontiac, Mich.: *Press* (E)	—		72,515[3]	81,110
Portland, Me.: *Press-Herald* (M); *Express* (E); *Maine Sunday Telegram*	59,014		28,722	127,826
Portland, Ore.: *Oregonian*	—	288,724[3]	—	410,519
Providence, R.I.: *Journal* (M & S); *Bulletin* (E)	84,336[3]		129,698[3]	252,225
Quincy, Mass.: *Patriot-Ledger*	—		89,111[3,4]	90,216[4,7]
Raleigh, N.C.: *News & Observer* (M & S); *Times* (E)	132,086[4]		34,807[4]	172,426
Reading, Pa.: *Times* (M); *Eagle* (E & S)	45,045		38,205	109,373
Richmond, Va.: *Times-Dispatch* (M & S); *News-Leader* (E)	138,297		113,369	230,545
Riverside, Calif.: *Press-Enterprise* (M & S)	116,198		—	121,942
Roanoke, Va.: *Times & World-News*	75,608[3]		47,736[3]	124,512
Rochester, N.Y.: *Democrat & Chronicle* (M & S); *Times-Union* (E)	132,440[3]		108,474	246,976
Rockford, Ill.: *Register Star*	72,834		—	86,246
Sacramento, Calif.: *Bee*	224,589		—	259,069
Union	99,366		—	98,418
St. Louis: *Post-Dispatch*	—		238,803[3,6]	474,662[6]
Globe-Democrat	251,250[3,6]		—	235,491[5,6]
St. Paul: *Pioneer Press* (M & S); *Dispatch* (E)	105,802[3]		99,729[3]	247,196
St. Petersburg, Fla.: *Times* (M & S); *Independent* (E)	282,653		37,660	357,089
Salt Lake City, Utah: *Tribune* (M & S); *Deseret News* (E & S)	109,157		71,058	202,721[8]
San Antonio: *Express* (M); *News* (E); *Express News* (S)	95,244[3]		79,314[3]	206,817
Light	—		140,374[3]	205,152
San Bernardino, Calif.: *Sun*	77,382		—	81,690
San Diego, Calif.: *Union* (M & S); *Tribune* (E)	220,301[4]		121,670[4]	349,961[4]
San Francisco: *Chronicle* (M); *Examiner* (E); *Examiner & Chronicle* (S)	539,450[3]		152,321[3]	706,150[3]
San Jose, Calif.: *Mercury-News*	—	245,868[3]	—	298,797
Santa Rosa, Calif.: *Press Democrat*	—		71,264[3]	79,736
Sarasota, Fla.: *Herald-Tribune* (M & S); *Journal* (E)	113,332[4]		—	130,087[4]
Seattle: *Post-Intelligencer;* Times	192,494[3]		226,038[3]	473,155
Shreveport, La.: *Times* (M & S); *Journal* (E)	79,462[4]		25,936[4]	110,079[4]
South Bend-Mishawake, Ind.: *Tribune*	—		102,277	123,631
Spokane, Wash.: *Spokesman-Review* (M & S); *Daily Chronicle* (E)	80,275		50,155	138,857
Springfield, Mass.: *Union* (M); *News* (E); *Republican* (S)	71,789		71,847	151,962
Springfield, Mo.: *News* (M); *Leader & Press* (E); *News & Leader* (S)	34,252[3,4]		30,141[3,4]	85,064[4]
Syracuse, N.Y.: *Post-Standard* (M); *Herald-Journal* (E); *Herald-American* (S)	80,376		103,899	234,180
Tacoma, Wash.: *News-Tribune* (E); *News-Tribune & Ledger* (S)	—		106,375	115,925
Tampa, Fla.: *Tribune*	—	216,864	—	282,331
Toledo, Ohio: *Blade*	—		162,780	215,654
Topeka, Kan.: *Capital-Journal*	67,595		—	76,419
Torrance-Redondo Beach-Hermosa Beach Manhattan Beach, Calif.: *Daily Breeze*			88,022	122,898
Tucson, Ariz.: *Daily Star* (M & S); *Citizen* (E)	81,082[4]		65,301[4]	150,743[4]
Tulsa, Okla: *World* (M & S); *Tribune* (E)	136,949[4]		78,003[4]	227,325[4]
Walnut Creek, Calif.: *Contra Costa Times*	80,550		—	82,295
Washington, D.C.: *Post*	768,288[3]		—	1,042,821
West Covina, Calif.; *San Gabriel Valley Tribune*	61,547		—	81,172
West Palm Beach, Fla.: *Post* (M); *Times* (E); *Post-Times* (S)	108,922[3]		27,665[3]	174,760
Wichita, Kan.: *Eagle-Beacon*	123,777		—	188,028
Wilmington, Del.: *News* (M); *Journal* (E); *Sunday News Journal*	64,373[3,4]		60,489[3,4]	123,820[4]
Winston-Salem, N.C.: *Journal* (M & S); *Sentinel* (E)	74,323[3]		32,566[3]	97,613
Worcester, Mass.: *Telegram* (M & S); *Gazette* (E)	55,615[4]		84,796[4]	122,631[4]
Youngstown, Ohio: *Vindicator*	—		99,830[4]	152,081[4]

1. Listing is of cities in which any one edition of a newspaper exceeds an average net paid circulation of 75,000; newspapers of smaller circulation in those cities are also included. 2. Unless otherwise indicated, figures are average Monday-through-Saturday circulation for six month period ending March 31, 1984. 3. Average Monday-through-Friday circulation. 4. Three-month average for period ending March 31, 1984. 5. Weekend edition. 6. Five-month average. 7. Saturday edition. 8. Combined morning and evening edition. NOTE: n.a.—not available. *Source:* Audit Bureau of Circulations.

Leading Magazines: United States and Canada

Magazine	Circulation[1]	Magazine	Circulation[1]
American Hunter, The	1,294,642	Newsweek	3,038,832
Better Homes and Gardens	8,041,951	New Woman	1,055,589
Bon Appetit	1,300,103	Omni	802,528
Boys' Life	1,452,201	1,001 Home Ideas	1,419,953
Business Week	770,414	Organic Gardening	1,399,223
Changing Times, The Kiplinger Magazine	1,375,732	Outdoor Life	1,530,118
Chatelaine	1,108,692	Parents	1,692,553
Consumers Digest	903,034	Penthouse	3,500,275
Cosmopolitan	3,038,400	People Weekly	2,781,542
Country Living	1,033,601	Playboy	4,209,324
Cuisine	766,286	Popular Mechanics	1,624,827
Discover	904,647	Popular Science	1,838,906
Discovery	1,173,305	Prevention	2,769,560
Ebony	1,659,243	Psychology Today	862,015
Family Circle	7,193,079	Reader's Digest	17,937,045
Family Handyman, The	1,250,175	Reader's Digest (Canadian English Edition)	1,327,108
Field and Stream	2,021,360	Redbook Magazine	4,019,611
Glamour	2,275,743	Road & Track	752,780
Globe	1,908,676	Rolling Stone	777,152
Golf Digest	1,183,493	Self	1,091,112
Good Housekeeping	5,393,087	Seventeen	1,688,954
Health	870,123	Smithsonian	1,954,273
Hot Rod	811,610	Southern Living	2,213,878
House Beautiful	864,459	Sport	932,089
Hustler	1,083,744	Sports Illustrated	2,448,486
Jet	871,595	Star, The	3,689,337
Junior Scholastic	827,373	Sunset, The Magazine of Western Living	1,411,609
Ladies' Home Journal	5,252,444	Teen	1,022,552
Life	1,506,953	Time, The Weekly Newsmagazine	4,615,594
Mademoiselle	1,265,081	Travel & Leisure	925,926
McCall's	6,358,293	True Story	1,582,649
Mechanix Illustrated	1,622,821	TV Guide (U.S.)	17,066,126
Michigan Living	805,362	TV Guide (Canada)	804,199
Modern Maturity	9,296,187	U.S. News & World Report	2,122,619
Money	1,374,101	Us	1,083,320
Mother Earth News, The	911,996	Vogue	1,142,542
Motorland	1,426,979	Weekly World News	836,641
Motor Trend	776,239	Weight Watchers Magazine	779,137
National Enquirer	4,706,165	Woman's Day	7,025,290
National Examiner	912,462	Workbasket, The	1,856,805
National Geographic Magazine, The	10,626,224	Workbench	853,071
National News	767,776	Yankee	935,271
Nation's Business	871,201	Young Miss	788,694

1. Average total paid circulation for the six-month period ending December 31, 1983. The table lists magazines of over 750,000 circulation. *Source:* Audit Bureau of Circulations. Publishers' Statements for six-month period ending December 31, 1983.

English Language Daily and Sunday U.S. Newspapers

(number of newspapers as of Feb. 1, 1984; circulation as reported for Sept. 30, 1983)

State	Morning papers and circulation		Evening papers and circulation		Total M and E and circulation		Sunday papers and circulation	
Alabama	12	229,031	15	505,269	27	734,300	19	698,214
Alaska	2	51,842	6	86,649	8	138,473	2	104,120
Arizona	5	387,097	14	277,060	19	664,157	10	638,048
Arkansas[1]	7	280,413	26	208,674	32	489,087	17	501,816
California[1]	39	3,883,090	84	2,110,889	120	5,993,979	59	5,817,519
Colorado	8	723,236	21	230,904	29	954,140	10	1,009,635
Connecticut	6	381,213	18	527,882	24	909,095	10	773,061
Delaware	2	87,808	1	62,074	3	149,882	2	154,661
District of Columbia	3	1,519,937	0	0	3	1,519,937	1	996,621
Florida[1]	24	1,992,910	29	765,446	51	2,758,356	34	3,000,234
Georgia	10	478,831	26	551,465	36	1,030,296	15	1,075,640
Hawaii	2	89,766	5	163,522	7	253,288	2	216,450
Idaho	5	114,084	9	102,784	14	216,868	7	193,183
Illinois[1]	14	1,445,858	63	1,278,109	74	2,723,967	24	2,735,095

State	Morning papers and circulation		Evening papers and circulation		Total M and E and circulation		Sunday papers and circulation	
Indiana	9	465,263	66	1,135,985	75	1,601,248	18	1,218,956
Iowa[1]	8	433,602	31	373,433	38	807,035	9	736,326
Kansas[1]	7	263,735	40	296,862	46	560,597	18	493,488
Kentucky	5	336,769	20	403,044	25	739,813	12	645,491
Louisiana[1]	7	427,416	19	370,795	25	798,211	16	845,127
Maine	5	218,921	4	70,783	9	289,704	3	270,120
Maryland	8	344,756	8	419,640	16	764,396	5	662,929
Massachusetts[1]	6	874,542	40	1,215,911	45	2,090,453	10	1,621,737
Michigan[1]	10	1,000,734	43	1,506,333	52	2,507,067	15	2,498,177
Minnesota	10	605,932	16	316,051	26	921,983	11	997,555
Mississippi	5	137,801	19	277,547	24	415,348	12	336,565
Missouri	9	681,185	39	788,012	48	1,469,197	18	1,162,414
Montana	5	152,205	6	49,326	11	201,531	9	206,282
Nebraska	4	189,403	15	291,034	19	480,437	7	431,032
Nevada[1]	4	159,270	5	79,718	8	238,988	5	249,591
New Hampshire	1	68,295	8	137,994	9	206,289	3	103,120
New Jersey	9	820,917	17	889,881	26	1,710,798	17	1,775,347
New Mexico	2	94,037	18	193,387	20	287,424	13	260,793
New York[1]	24	5,876,147	54	2,262,606	76	8,138,753	33	5,833,268
North Carolina	10	632,143	45	761,135	55	1,393,278	25	1,190,310
North Dakota[1]	3	72,498	8	121,091	10	193,589	5	146,968
Ohio[1]	10	1,013,433	83	2,018,858	92	3,032,291	30	2,675,960
Oklahoma	7	407,359	46	458,130	53	865,489	44	888,399
Oregon[1]	5	287,361	16	340,142	20	627,503	9	646,123
Pennsylvania[1]	33	1,652,919	66	1,817,657	96	3,470,576	21	2,906,296
Rhode Island	1	86,633	6	277,034	7	310,667	2	258,921
South Carolina	8	421,121	9	180,371	17	601,492	8	526,462
South Dakota	2	46,384	10	121,396	12	167,780	4	124,543
Tennessee[1]	10	537,368	21	484,416	39	1,021,784	16	1,027,928
Texas[1]	32	2,113,798	86	1,601,717	114	3,715,425	96	4,276,859
Utah	1	107,183	5	181,019	6	288,202	6	308,633
Vermont	4	89,411	4	30,653	8	120,094	3	79,971
Virginia	14	605,987	24	572,773	38	1,178,760	15	890,573
Washington[1]	8	352,177	21	774,091	28	1,126,268	17	1,090,768
West Virginia	10	243,165	15	224,465	25	467,630	25	406,027
Wisconsin	5	286,624	30	905,700	35	1,192,324	11	965,379
Wyoming	6	70,610	4	32,744	10	103,354	4	74,691
Total	**446**	**33,842,142**	**1,284**	**28,802,461**	**1,701**	**62,644,603**	**772**	**56,747,436**
Total U.S., Sept. 30, 1982	434	33,174,087	1,310	29,313,090	1,711	62,487,177	768	56,260,764
Total U.S., Sept. 30, 1981	408	30,552,316	1,352	30,878,429	1,730	61,430,745	755	55,180,004
Total U.S., Sept. 30, 1980	387	29,414,036	1,388	32,787,804	1,745	62,201,840	736	54,676,173
Total U.S., Sept. 30, 1979	382	28,574,879	1,405	33,648,161	1,763	62,223,040	720	54,379,923
Total U.S., Sept. 30, 1978	355	27,656,739	1,419	34,333,258	1,756	61,989,997	696	53,990,033
Total U.S., Sept. 30, 1977	352	26,742,318	1,435	34,752,822	1,753	61,495,140	668	52,429,234
Total U.S., Sept. 30, 1976	346	25,858,386	1,435	35,118,625	1,762	60,977,011	650	51,565,334
Total U.S., Sept. 30, 1975	339	25,490,186	1,436	35,165,245	1,756	60,655,431	639	51,096,323
Total U.S., Sept. 30, 1974	340	26,144,966	1,449	35,732,231	1,768	61,877,197	641	51,678,726
Total U.S., Sept. 30, 1973	343	26,524,140	1,451	36,623,140	1,774	63,147,280	634	51,717,465

1. "All-day" newspapers are listed in morning and evening columns but only once in the total, and their circulations are divided between morning and evening figures. Adjustments have been made in state and U.S. total figures. *Source: Editor and Publisher Yearbook, 1984.*

See **the Entertainment and Culture section for additional Media information.**

The Pony Express

Established in April 1860, the Pony Express provided fast mail service between St. Joseph, Mo., the westernmost extent of the U.S. telegraph line, and Sacramento, Calif. The freighting and stagecoach firm of Russell, Majors & Waddell hired expert riders to ride fleet horses in relays over the 1,838-mile distance. Along the route, there were 157 stations, spaced about 12 miles apart, at which the riders changed horses. Each man changed horses about six times before being replaced by another. The route, which was covered in about ten days, passed through hostile Indian territory, and, during the Paiute War in the summer of 1860, Indians burned a number of stations and killed the occupants. October 24, 1861, the day the first telegram to San Francisco was transmitted, marked the downfall of the Pony Express. No longer the crucial link to the West, the Pony Express was discontinued. Though a financial failure, it remains one of the most colorful episodes of American history.

Copyrights

Source: Library of Congress, Copyright Office.

The copyright law (Title 17 of the United States Code) was amended by the enactment of a statute for its general revision, Public Law 94-553 (90 Stat. 2541), which was signed by the President on October 19, 1976. The new law superseded the copyright act of 1909, as amended, which remained effective until the new enactment took effect on January 1, 1978.

Under the new law, all copyrightable works, whether published or unpublished, are subject to a single system of statutory protection which gives a copyright owner the exclusive right to reproduce the copyrighted work in copies or phonorecords and distribute them to the public by sale, rental, lease, or lending. Among the other rights given to the owner of a copyright are the exclusive rights to prepare derivative works based upon the copyrighted work, to perform the work publicly if it be literary, musical, dramatic, choreographic, a pantomime, motion picture, or other audiovisual work, and in the case of literary, musical, dramatic, and choreographic works, pantomimes, and pictorial, graphic, or sculptural works, including the individual images of a motion picture or other audiovisual work, to display the copyrighted work publicly. All of these rights are subject to certain exceptions, including the principle of "fair use" which the new statute specifically recognizes.

Special provisions are included which permit compulsory licensing for the recording of musical compositions, noncommercial transmissions by public broadcasters of published musical and graphic works, performances of copyrighted music by jukeboxes, and the secondary transmission of copyrighted works on cable television systems.

Copyright protection under the new law extends to original works of authorship fixed in any tangible medium of expression, now known or later developed, from which they can be perceived, reproduced, or otherwise communicated, either directly or with the aid of a machine or device. Works of authorship include books, periodicals and other literary works, musical compositions with accompanying lyrics, dramas and dramatico-musical compositions, pantomimes and choreographic works, motion pictures and other audiovisual works, and sound recordings.

As a mandatory condition of copyright protection under the law in effect before 1978, all published copies of a work were required to bear a copyright notice. The 1976 Act provides for a notice on published copies, but omission or errors will not immediately result in forfeiture of the copyright, and can be corrected within certain time limits. Innocent infringers misled by the omission or error will be shielded from liability.

Registration in the Copyright Office is not a condition of copyright protection but will be a prerequisite to bringing an action in a court of law for infringement. With certain exceptions, the remedies of statutory damages and attorney's fees will not be available for infringements occurring before registration. Copies or phonorecords published in the United States with notice of copyright are required to be deposited for the collections of the Library of Congress, not as a condition of copyright protection, but under provisions of the law subjecting the copyright owner to certain penalties for failure to deposit after a demand by the Register of Copyrights. Registration is permissive, but may be made either at the time the depository requirements are satisfied or at any other time during the subsistence of the copyright.

For works already under statutory protection, the new law retains the present term of copyright of 28 years from first publication (or from registration in some cases), renewable by certain persons for a second period of protection, but it increases the length of the second period to 47 years. Copyrights in their first term on January 1, 1978, must still be renewed during the last (28th) year of the original copyright term to receive the maximum statutory term of 75 years (a first term of 28 years plus a renewal term of 47 years).

Copyrights in their second term on January 1, 1978, are automatically extended up to a maximum of 75 years, without the need for further renewal. Unpublished works that are already in existence on January 1, 1978, but are not protected by statutory copyright and have not yet gone into the public domain, will generally obtain automatic Federal copyright protection for the author's life, plus an additional 50 years after the author's death, but in any event, for a minimal term of 25 years (that is, until December 31, 2002), and if the work is published before that date, then for an additional term of 25 years, through the end of 2027.

For works created on or after January 1, 1978, the new law provides a term lasting for the author's life, plus an additional 50 years after the author's death. For works made for hire, and for anonymous and pseudonymous works (unless the author's identity is revealed in Copyright Office records), the new term will be 75 years from publication or 100 years from creation, whichever is shorter. The new law provides that all terms of copyright will run through the end of the calendar year in which they would otherwise expire. This will not only affect the duration of copyrights, but also the time-limits for renewal registrations.

Works already in the public domain cannot be protected under the new law. The 1976 Act provides no procedure for restoring protection to works in which copyright has been lost for any reason. In general, works published before January 1, 1910, are not under copyright protection in the United States, at least insofar as any version published before that date is concerned.

The new law requires that all visually perceptible copies published in the United States or elsewhere bear a notice of copyright affixed in such manner and location as to give reasonable notice of the claim of copyright. The notice consists of the symbol © (the letter C in a circle), the word "Copyright," or the abbreviation "Copr.," and the year of first publication of the work, and the name of the owner of copyright in the work. EXAMPLE: © *1985 John Doe.*

The notice of copyright prescribed for sound recordings consists of the symbol ℗ (the letter P in a circle), the year of first publication of the sound recording, and the name of the owner of copyright in the sound recording, placed on the surface of the phonorecord, or on the phonorecord label or container, in such manner and location as to give reasonable notice of the claim of copyright, EXAMPLE: ℗ *1985 Doe Records, Inc.*

A work by a U.S. citizen may obtain copyright protection in all countries that are members of the Universal Copyright Convention (UCC), provided the copyright notice appearing on all copies from the date of first publication includes the symbol ©, together with the name of the copyright owner and the year date of publication. EXAMPLE: © *John Doe 1985.*

Further information and application forms may be obtained free of charge upon request from the Copyright Office, Library of Congress, Washington, D.C. 20559.

Patents

Source: Department of Commerce, Patent and Trademark Office.

A patent, in the most general sense, is a document issued by a government, conferring some special right or privilege. The term is now restricted mainly to patents for inventions; occasionally, land patents.

The grant of a patent for an invention gives the inventor the privilege, for a limited period of time, of excluding others from making, using, or selling a certain article. However, it does not give him the right to make, use, or sell his own invention if it is an improvement on some unexpired patent whose claims are infringed thereby.

In the U.S., the law provides that a patent may be granted, for a term of 17 years, to any person who has invented or discovered any new and useful art, machine, manufacture, or composition of matter, as well as any new and useful improvements thereof. A patent may also be granted to a person who has invented or discovered and asexually reproduced a new and distinct variety of plant (other than a tuber-propagated one) or has invented a new, original and ornamental design for an article of manufacture.

A patent is granted only upon a regularly filed application, complete in all respects; upon payment of the fees; and upon determination that the disclosure is complete and that the invention is new, useful, and, in view of the prior art, unobvious to one skilled in the art. The disclosure must be of such nature as to enable others to reproduce the invention.

A complete application, which must be addressed to the Commissioner of Patents and Trademarks, Washington, D.C. 20231, consists of a specification with one or more claims; oath or declaration; drawing (whenever the nature of the case admits of it); and a basic filing fee of $150.[1] The filing fee is not returned to the applicant if the patent is refused. If the patent is allowed, another fee of $250[1] is required before the patent is issued. The fee for design patent application is $62.50[1]; the issue fee is $87.50[1]. Maintenance fees are required on utility patents at stipulated intervals.

Applications are ordinarily considered in the order in which they are received. Patents are not granted for printed matter, for methods of doing business, or for devices for which claims contrary to natural laws are made. Applications for a perpetual-motion machine have been made from time to time, but until a working model is presented that actually fulfills the claim, no patent will be issued.

1. Fees quoted are for small entities. Fees are double for corporations.

Trademarks

Source: Department of Commerce, Patent and Trademark Office.

A trademark may be defined as a word, letter, device, or symbol, as well as some combination of these, which is used in connection with merchandise and which points distinctly to the origin of the goods.

Certificates of registration of trademarks are issued under the seal of the Patent and Trademark Office and may be registered by the owner if he is engaged in interstate or foreign commerce, since any Federal jurisdiction over trademarks arises under the commerce clause of the Constitution. Trademarks may be registered by foreign owners who comply with our law, as well as by citizens of foreign countries with which the U.S. has treaties relating to trademarks. American citizens may register trademarks in foreign countries by complying with the laws of those countries. The right to registration and protection of trademarks in many foreign countries is guaranteed by treaties.

General jurisdiction in trademark cases involving Federal Registrations is given to Federal courts. Adverse decisions of examiners on applications for registration are appealable to the Trademark Trial and Appeal Board, whose affirmances, and decisions in *inter partes* proceedings, are subject to court review. Before adopting a trademark, a person should make a search of prior marks to avoid infringing unwittingly upon them.

The duration of a trademark registration is 20 years, but it may be renewed indefinitely for 20-year periods, provided the trademark is still in use at the time of expiration.

Birthstones

Month	Stone	Month	Stone
January	Garnet	July	Ruby or Star Ruby
February	Amethyst	August	Peridot or Sardonyx
March	Aquamarine or Bloodstone	September	Sapphire or Star Sapphire
April	Diamond	October	Opal or Tourmaline
May	Emerald	November	Topaz
June	Pearl, Alexandrite, or Moonstone	December	Turquoise or Zircon

Source: Jewelry Industry Council.

CROSSWORD PUZZLE GUIDE

First Aid to Crossword Puzzlers

We cannot begin to list all the odd words you will meet with in your daily and Sunday crossword puzzles, for such words run into many thousands. But we have tried to include those that turn up most frequently, as well as many others that should be of help to you when you are unable to go any further.

Also, we do not guarantee that the definitions in your puzzle will be exactly the same as ours, although we have checked every word with a standard dictionary and have followed its definition.

In nearly every case, we have used as the key word the principal noun of the definition, rather than any adjective, adjective phrase, or noun used as an adjective. And, to simplify your searching, we have grouped the words according to the number of spaces you have to fill.

For a list of Foreign Phrases, *see* Index. For Rulers of England and Great Britain, France, Germany and Prussia, and Russia, *see* Countries of the World.

Words of Two Letters

Ambary, DA
And (French, Latin), ET
Article (Arabic), AL
  (French), LA, LE, UN
  (Spanish), EL, LA, UN
At the (French), AU
  (Spanish), AL
Behold, LO
Bird: Hawaiian, OO
Birthplace: Abraham's, UR
Bone, OS
Buddha, FO
Butterfly: Peacock, IO
Champagne, AY
Chaos, NU
Chief: Burmese, BO
Coin: Roman, AS
  Siamese, AT
Concerning, RE
Dialect: Chinese, WU
Double (Egy. relig.), KA
Drama: Japanese, NO
Egg (comb. form), OO
Esker, OS
Eye (Scotch), EE
Factor: Amplification, MU
Fifty (Greek), NU
Fish: Carplike, ID
Force, OD
Forty (Greek), MU
From (French, Latin, Spanish), DE
  (Latin prefix), AB
From the (French), DU
God: Babylonian, EA, ZU
  Egyptian sun, RA
  Hindu unknown, KA
  Semitic, EL
Goddess: Babylonian, AI
  Greek earth, GE
Gold (heraldry), OR
Gulf: Arctic, OB
Heart (Egy. relig.), AB
Indian: South American, GE
King: Of Bashan, OG
Language: Artificial, RO
  Assamese, AO
Lava: Hawaiian, AA
Letter: Greek, MU, NU, PI, XI
  Hebrew, HE, PE
Lily: Palm, TI
Measure: Annamese, LY
  Chinese, HO, HU, KO, LI, MU, PU,
    TO, TU
  Japanese, GO, JO, MO, RI, SE, TO
  Metric land, AR
  Netherlands, EL
  Portuguese, PE
  Siamese, WA
  Swedish, AM
  Type, EM, EN
Monk: Buddhist, BO
Month: Jewish, AB
Mouth, OS
Mulberry: Indian, AL
Native: Burmese, WA
Note: Of Scale, DO, FA, MI, LA, RE, TI
Of (French, Latin, Spanish), DE
Of the (French), DU
One (Scotch), AE
Pagoda: Chinese, TA
Plant: East Indian fiber, DA
Ridge: Sandy, AS, OS
River: Russian, OB
Sloth: Three-toed, AI
Soul (Egy. relig.), BA
Sound: Hindu mystic, OM
Suffix: Comparative, ER
The. *See* Article
To the: French, AU
  Spanish, AL
Tree: Buddhist sacred, BO
Tribe: Assamese, AO
Type: Jumbled, PI
Weight: Annamese, TA
  Chinese, LI
  Danish, ES
  Japanese, MO
  Roman, AS
Whirlwind: Faeroe Is., OE
Yes (German), JA
  (Italian, Spanish), SI
  (Russian), DA

Words of Three Letters

Adherent: IST
Again, BIS
Age, ERA
Antelope: African, GNU, KOB
Apricot: Japanese, UME
Article (German), DAS, DEM, DEN,
  DER, DES, DIE, EIN
  (French), LES, UNE
  (Spanish), LAS, LOS, UNA
Banana: Polynesian, FEI
Barge, HOY
Bass: African, IYO
Beak, NEB, NIB
Beard: Grain, AWN
Beetle: June, DOR
Being, ENS
Berry: Hawthorn, HAW
Beverage: Hawaiian, AVA
Bird: Australian, EMU
  Crowlike, JAY
  Extinct, MOA
  Fabulous, ROC
  Frigate, IWA
  Parson, POE, TUE, TUI
  Sea, AUK
Blackbird, ANI, ANO
Born, NEE
Bronze: Roman, AES
Bugle: Yellow, IVA
By way of, VIA
Canton: Swiss, URI
Cap: Turkish, FEZ
Catnip, NEP
Character: In "Faerie Queene," UNA
Coin: Afghan, PUL
  Albanian, LEK
  British Guiana, BIT
  Bulgarian, LEV, LEW
  French, ECU, SOU
  Indian, PIE
  Japanese, SEN, YEN
  Korean, WON
  Lithuanian, LIT
  Macao, Timor, AVO
  Palestinian, MIL
  Persian, PUL
  Peruvian, SOL
  Rumanian, BAN, LEU, LEY
  Scandinavian, ORE
  Siamese, ATT
  See also Money of account
Collection: Facts, ANA
Commune: Belgian, ANS, ATH
  Netherlands, EDE, EPE
Community: Russian, MIR
Constellation: Southern, ARA
Contraction: Poetic, EEN, EER, OER
Covering: Apex of roof, EPI
Crab: Fiddler, UCA
Crag: Rocky, TOR
Cry: Crow, rook, raven, CAW
Cup: Wine, AMA
Cymbal, Oriental, TAL, ZEL

Disease: Silkworm, UJI
Division: Danish territorial, AMT
  Geologic, EON
Doctrine, ISM
Dowry, DOT
Dry (French), SEC
Dynasty: Chinese, CHI, HAN, SUI, WEI, YIN
Eagle: Sea, ERN
Earth (comb. form), GEO
Egg: Louse, NIT
Eggs: Fish, ROE
Emmet, ANT
Enzyme, ASE
Equal (comb. form), ISO
Extension: building, ELL
Far (comb. form), TEL
Farewell, AVE
Fiber: Palm, TAL
Finial, EPI
Fish: Carplike, IDE
  Pikelike, GAR
Flatfish, DAB
Fleur-de-lis, LIS, LYS
Food: Hawaiian, POI
Formerly, NEE
Friend (French), AMI
Game: Card, LOO
Garment: Camel-hair, ABA
Gateway, DAR
Gazelle: Tibetan, GOA
Genus: Ducks, AIX
  Grasses, POA
  Grasses (maize), ZEA
  Herbs or shrubs, IVA
  Lizards, UTA
  Rodents (incl. house mice), MUS
  Ruminants (incl. cattle), BOS
  Swine, SUS
Gibbon: Malay, LAR
God: Assyrian, SIN
  Babylonian, ABU, ANU, BEL, HEA, SIN, UTU
  Irish sea, LER
  Phrygian, MEN
  Polynesian, ORO
Goddess: Babylonian, AYA
  Etruscan, UNI
  Hindu, SRI, UMA, VAC
  Teutonic, RAN
Governor: Algerian, DEY
  Turkish, BEY
Grampus, ORC
Grape, UVA
Grass: Meadow, POA
Gypsy, ROM
Hail, AVE
Hare: Female, DOE
Hawthorn, HAW
Hay: Spread for drying, TED
Herb: Japanese, UDO
  Perennial, PIA
  Used for blue dye, WAD
Herd: Whales, GAM, POD
Hero: Spanish, CID
High (music), ALT
Honey (pharm.), MEL
Humorist: American, ADE
I (Latin), EGO
I love (Latin), AMO
Indian: Algonquian, FOX, SAC, WEA
  Chimakuan, HOH
  Keresan, SIA
  Mayan, MAM
  Shoshonean, UTE
  Siouan, KAW, OTO
  South American, ITE, ONA, URO, URU, YAO
  Tierra del Fuego, ONA
  Wakashan, AHT
Ingot, PIG
Inlet: Narrow, RIA
Island: Cyclades, IOS
  Dodecanese, COS, KOS
  (French), ILE
  River, AIT

Jackdaw, DAW
John (Gaelic), IAN
Keelbill, ANI, ANO
Kiln, OST
King: British legendary LUD
Kobold, NIS
Lace: To make, TAT
Lamprey, EEL
Language: Artificial, IDO
  Bantu, ILA
  Siamese, LAO, TAI
Leaf: Palm, OLA, OLE
Leaving, ORT
Left: Cause to turn, HAW
Letter: Greek, CHI, ETA, PHI, PSI, RHO, TAU
  Hebrew, MEM, NUN, SIN, TAV, VAU
Lettuce, COS
Life (comb. form), BIO
Lily: Palm, TOI
Lizard, EFT
Louse: Young, NIT
Love (Anglo-Irish), GRA
Lute: Oriental, TAR
Macaw: Bralizian, ARA
Marble, TAW
Match: Shooting (French), TIR
Meadow, LEA
Measure: Abyssinian, TAT
  Algerian, PIK
  Annamese, GON, MAU, NGU, VUO, SAO, TAO, TAT
  Arabian, DEN, SAA
  Belgian, VAT
  Bulgarian, OKA, OKE
  Chinese, FEN, TOU, YIN
  Cloth, ELL
  Cyprus, OKA, OKE, PIK
  Czech, LAN, SAH
  Danish, FOD, MIL, POT
  Dominican Republic, ONA
  Dutch, old, AAM
  East Indian, KIT
  Egyptian, APT, HEN, PIK, ROB
  Electric, MHO, OHM
  Energy, ERG
  English, PIN
  Estonian, TUN
  French, POT
  German, AAM
  Greek, PIK
  Hebrew, CAB, HIN, KOR, LOG
  Hungarian, AKO
  Icelandic, FET
  Indian, GAZ, GUZ, JOW, KOS
  Japanese, BOO, CHO, KEN, RIN, SHO, SUN, TAN
  Malabar, ADY
  Metric land, ARE
  Netherlands, KAN, KOP, MUD, VAT, ZAK
  Norwegian, FOT, POT
  Persian, GAZ, GUZ, MOU, ZAR, ZER
  Polish, CAL
  Rangoon, DHA, LAN
  Roman, PES, URN
  Russian, FUT, LOF
  Scotch, COP
  Siamese, KEN, NIU, RAI, SAT, SEN, SOK, WAH, YOT
  Somaliland, TOP
  Spanish, PIE
  Straits Settlements, PAU, TUN
  Swedish, ALN, FOT, MIL, REF, TUM
  Swiss, POT
  Tunisian, SAA
  Turkish, OKA, OKE, PIK
  Wire, MIL
  Württemberg, IMI
  Yarn, LEA
  Yugoslavian, OKA, RIF
Milk, LAC
Milkfish, AWA
Moccasin, PAC
Money: Yap stone, FEI
Money of Account: Anglo-Saxon, ORA, ORE
  French, SOU
  Indian, LAC
  Japanese, RIN
  Oman, GAJ
  Virgin Islands, BIT
  See also Coin
Monkey: Capuchin, SAI
Morsel, ORT
Mother: Peer Gynt's, ASE
Mountain: Asia Minor, IDA
Mulberry: Indian, AAL, ACH, AWL
Muttonbird: New Zealand, OII
Nahoor, SNA
Native: Mindanao, ATA
Neckpiece, BOA
Newt, EFT
No (Scotch), NAE
Note: Guido's highest, ELA
  Of scale, SOL
Nursemaid: Oriental, AMA, IYA
Ocher: Yellow, SIL
One (Scotch), YIN
Ornament: Pagoda, TEE
Oven: Polynesian, UMU
Ox: Tibetan, YAK
Pagoda: Chinese, TAA
Parrot: Hawk, HIA
  New Zealand, KEA
Part: Footlike, PES
Particle: Electrified, ION
Pasha, DEY
Pass: Mountain, COL
Paste: Rice, AME
Pea: Indian split, DAL
Peasant: Philippine, TAO
Penpoint, NEB, NIB
Piece out, EKE
Pigeon, NUN
Pine: Textile screw, ARA
Pistol (slang), GAT
Pit: Baking, IMU
Plant: Pepper, AVA
Play: By Capek, RUR
Poem: Old French, DIT
Porgy: Japanese, TAI
Priest: Biblical high, ELI
Prince Ethiopian, RAS
Pseudonym: Dickens', BOZ
Queen: Fairy, MAB
Quince: Bengal, BEL
Record: Ship's, LOG
Refuse: Flax (Scotch), PAB, POB
Resin, LAC
Resort, SPA
Revolver (slang), GAT
Right: Cause to turn, GEE
River: Scotch or English, DEE
  (Spanish), RIO
  Swiss, AAR
Room: Harem, ODA
Rootstock: Fern, ROI
Rose (Persian), GUL
Ruff: Female, REE
Rule: Indian, RAJ
Sailor, GOB, TAR
Saint: Female (abbr.), STE
  Mohammedan, PIR
Salt, SAL
Sash: Japanese, OBI
Scrap, ORT
Seed: Poppy, MAW
  Small, PIP
Self, EGO
Serpent: Vedic sky, AHI
Sesame, TIL
Sheep: Female, EWE
  Indian, SHA
  Male, RAM
Sheepfold (Scotch), REE
Shelter, LEE
Shield, ECU
Shooting match (French), TIR
Shrew: European, ERD
Shrub: Evergreen, YEW
Silkworm, ERI

Snake, ASP, BOA
Soak, RET
Son-in-law: Mohammed's, ALI
Sorrel: Wood, OCA
Spade: Long, narrow, LOY
Spirit: Malignant, KER
Spot: Playing-card, PIP
Spread for drying, TED
Spring: Mineral, SPA
Sprite: Water, NIX
Statesman: Japanese, ITO
Stern: Toward, AFT
Stomach: Bird's, MAW
Street (French), RUE
Summer (French), ETE
Sun, SOL
Swamp, BOG, FEN
Swan: Male, COB
Tea: Chinese, CHA
Temple: Shinto, SHA
The. *See* Article
Thing (law), RES
Title: Etruscan, LAR
  Monk's, FRA
  Portuguese, DOM
  Spanish, DON
  Turkish, AGA, BEY
Tool: Cutting, ADZ, AXE
  Mining, GAD
  Piercing, AWL
Tree: Candlenut, AMA
  Central American, EBO
  East Indian, SAJ, SAL
  Evergreen, YEW
  Hawaiian, KOA, KOU
  Indian, BEL, DAR
  Linden, LIN
  New Zealand, AKE
  Philippine, DAO, TUA, TUI
  Rubber, ULE
  South American, APA
Tribe: New Zealand, ATI
Turmeric, REA
Twice, BIS
Twin: Siamese, ENG
Uncle (dialect), EAM, EME
Veil: Chalice, AER, AIR
Vessel: Wine, AMA
Vestment: Ecclesiastical, ALB
Vetch: Bitter, ERS
Victorfish, AKU
Vine: New Zealand, AKA
  Philippine, IYO
Wallaba, APA
Wapiti, ELK
Water (French), EAU
Waterfall, LIN
Watering place: Prussian, EMS
Weave: Designating plain, UNI
Weight: Annamese, CAN
  Bulgarian, OKA, OKE
  Burmese, MOO, VIS
  Chinese, FEN, HAO, KIN, SSU, TAN, YIN
  Cyprus, OKA, OKE
  Danish, LOD, ORT, VOG
  East Indian, TJI
  Egyptian, KAT, OKA, OKE
  English, for wool, TOD
  German, LOT
  Greek, MNA, OKA, OKE
  Indian, SER
  Japanese, FUN, KIN, RIN, SHI
  Korean, KON
  Malacca, KIP
  Mongolian, LAN
  Netherlands, ONS
  Norwegian, LOD
  Polish, LUT
  Rangoon, PAI
  Roman, BES
  Russian, LOT
  Siamese, BAT, HAP, PAI
  Swedish, ASS, ORT
  Turkish, OKA, OKE
  Yugoslavian, OKA, OKE
Whales: Herd, GAM, POD
Wildebeest, GNU
Wing, ALA
Witticism, MOT
Wolframite, CAL
Worm: African, LOA
Wreath: Hawaiian, LEI
Yale, ELI
Yam: Hawaiian, HOI
Yes (French), OUI
Young: Bring forth, EAN
Z (letter), ZED

Words of Four Letters

Aborigine: Borneo, DYAK
Agave, ALOE
Animal: Footless, APOD
Ant: White, ANAI, ANAY
Antelope: African, ASSE, BISA, GUIB, KOBA, KUDU, ORYX, POKU, PUKU, TOPI, TORA
Apoplexy: Plant, ESCA
Apple, POME
Apricot, ANSU
Ardor, ELAN
Armadillo, APAR, PEBA, PEVA, TATU
Ascetic: Mohammedan, SUFI
Association: Chinese, TONG
Astronomer: Persian, OMAR
Avatar: Of Vishnu, RAMA
Axillary, ALAR
Band: Horizontal (heraldry), FESS
Barracuda, SPET
Bark: Mulberry, TAPA
Base: Column, DADO
Bearing (heraldry), ORLE
Beer: Russian, KVAS
Beige, ECRU
Being, ESSE
Beverage: Japanese rice, SAKE
Bird: Asian, MINA, MYNA
  Egyptian sacred, IBIS
  Extinct, DODO, MAMO
  Flightless, KIWI
  Gull-like, TERN
  Hawaiian, IIWI, MAMO
  Parson, KOKO
  Unfledged, EYAS
Birds: As class, AVES
Black, EBON
  (French), NOIR
Blackbird: European, MERL
Boat: Flat-bottomed, DORY
Bone: Forearm, ULNA
Bones, OSSA
Box, Japanese, INRO
Bravo (rare), EUGE
Buffalo: Indian wild, ARNA
Bull (Spanish), TORO
Burden, ONUS
Cabbage: Sliced, SLAW
Caliph: Mohammedan, OMAR
Canoe: Malay, PRAU, PROA
Cap: Military, KEPI
Cape, NESS
Capital: Ancient Irish, TARA
Case: Article, ETUI
Cat: Wild, BALU, EYRA
Chalcedony, SARD
Chamber: Indian ceremonial, KIVA
Channel: Brain, ITER
Cheese: Dutch, EDAM
Chest: Sepulchral stone, CIST
Chieftain: Arab, EMIR
Church: Part of, APSE, NAVE
  (Scotch), KIRK
Claim (law), LIEN
Cluster: Flower, CYME
Coin: Chinese, TAEL, YUAN
  German, MARK
  Indian, ANNA
  Iranian, RIAL
  Italian, LIRA
  Moroccan, OKIA
  Siamese, BAHT
  South American, PESO
  Spanish, DURO, PESO
  Turkish, PARA
Commune: Belgian, AATH
Composition: Musical, OPUS
Compound: Chemical, DIOL
Constellation: Southern, PAVO
Council: Russian, DUMA
Counsel, REDE
Covering: Seed, ARIL
Cross: Egyptian, ANKH
Cry: Bacchanalian, EVOE
Cup (Scotch), TASS
Cupbearer, SAKI
Dagger, DIRK
  Malay, KRIS
Dam: River, WEIR
Dash, ELAN
Date: Roman, IDES
Dawn: Pertaining to, EOAN
Dean: English, INGE
Decay: In fruit, BLET
Deer: Sambar, MAHA
Disease: Skin, ACNE
Disk: Solar, ATEN
Dog: Hunting, ALAN
Drink: Hindu intoxicating, SOMA
Duck, SMEE, SMEW, TEAL
Dynasty: Chinese, CHEN, CHIN, CHOU, CHOW, HSIA, MING, SUNG, TANG, TSIN
  Mongol, YUAN
Eagle: Biblical, GIER
  Sea, ERNE
Egyptian: Christian, COPT
Ear: Pertaining to, OTIC
Entrance: Mine, ADIT
Esau, EDOM
Escutcheon: Voided, ORLE
Eskers, OSAR
Evergreen: New Zealand, TAWA
Fairy: Persian, PERI
Family: Italian, ESTE
Far (comb. form), TELE
Farewell, VALE
Father (French), PERE
Fennel: Philippine, ANIS
Fever: Malarial, AGUE
Fiber: East Indian, JUTE
Firn, NEVE
Fish: Carplike, DACE
  Hawaiian, ULUA
  Herringlike, SHAD
  Mackerellike, CERO
  Marine, HAKE
  Sea, LING, MERO, OPAH
  Spiny-finned, GOBY
Food: Tropical, TARO
Foot: Metric, IAMB
Formerly, ERST
Founder: Of Carthage, DIDO
France: Southern, MIDI
Furze, ULEX
Gaelic, ERSE
Gaiter, SPAT
Game: Card, FARO, SKAT
Garlic: European wild, MOLY
Garment: Hindu, SARI
  Roman, TOGA
Gazelle, CORA

Gem, JADE, ONYX, OPAL, RUBY
Genus: Amphibians (incl. frogs), RANA
Amphibians (incl. tree toads), HYLA
Antelopes, ORYX
Auks, ALCA, URIA
Bees, APIS
Birds (American ostriches), RHEA
Birds (cranes), CRUS
Birds (magpies), PICA
Birds (peacocks), PAVO
Cetaceans, INIA
Ducks (incl. mallards), ANAS
Fishes (burbots), LOTA
Fishes (incl. bowfins), AMIA
Geese (snow geese), CHEN
Gulls, XEMA
Herbs, ARUM, GEUM
Insects (water scorpions), NEPA
Lilies, ALOE
Mammals (mankind), HOMO
Orchids, DISA
Owls, ASIO, BUBO, OTUS
Palms, NIPA
Sea birds, SULA
Sheep, OVIS
Shrubs, Eurasian, ULEX
Shrubs (hollies), ILEX
Shrubs (incl. Virginia Willow), ITEA
Shrubs, tropical, EVEA
Snakes (sand snakes), ERYX
Swans, OLOR
Trees, chocolate, COLA
Trees (ebony family), MABA
Trees (incl. maples), ACER
Trees (olives), OLEA
Trees, tropical, EVEA
Turtles, EMYS
Goat: Wild, IBEX, KRAS, TAHR, TAIR, THAR
God: Assyrian, ASUR
Babylonian, ADAD, ADDU, ENKI, ENZU, IRRA, NABU, NEBO, UTUG
Celtic, LLEU, LLEW
Hindu, AGNI, CIVA, DEVA, DEWA, KAMA, RAMA, SIVA, VAYU
Phrygian, ATYS
Semitic, BAAL
Teutonic, HLER
Goddess: Babylonian, ERUA, GULA
Hawaiian, PELE
Hindu, DEVI, KALI, SHRI, VACH
Gooseberry: Hawaiian, POHA
Gourd, PEPO
Grafted (heraldry), ENTE
Grandfather (obsolete), AIEL
Grandparents: Pertaining to, AVAL
Grass: Hawaiian, HILO
Gray (French), GRIS
Green (heraldry), VERT
Groom: Indian, SYCE
Half (prefix), DEMI, HEMI, SEMI
Hamlet, DORP
Hammer-head: Part of, PEEN
Handle, ANSA
Harp: Japanese, KOTO
Hartebeest, ASSE, TORA
Hautboy, OBOE
Hawk: Taken from nest (falconry), EYAS
Hearing (law), OYER
Heater: For liquids, ETNA
Herb: Aromatic, ANET, DILL
Fabulous, MOLY
Perennial, GEUM, SEGO
Pot, WORT
Used for blue dye, WADE, WOAD
Hill: Flat-topped, MESA
Sand, DENE, DUNE
Hoarfrost, RIME
Hog: Immature female, GILT
Holly, ILEX
House: Cow, BYRE
(Spanish), CASA
Ice: Floating, FLOE
Image, ICON, IKON
Incarnation: Of Vishnu, RAMA
Indian: Algonquian, CREE, SAUK
Central American, MAYA
Iroquoian, ERIE
Mexican, CORA
Peruvian, CANA, INCA, MORO
Shoshonean, HOPI
Siouan, OTOE
Southwestern, HOPI, PIMA, YUMA, ZUNI
Insect: Immature, PUPA
Instrument: Stringed, LUTE, LYRE
Ireland, EIRE, ERIN
Jacket: English, ETON
Jail (British), GAOL
Jar, OLLA
Judge: Mohammedan, CADI
Juniper: European, CADE
Kiln, OAST, OVEN
King: British legendary, LUDD, NUDD
Kiss, BUSS
Knife: Philippine, BOLO
Koran: Section of, SURA
Laborer: Spanish American, PEON
Lake: Mountain, TARN
(Scotch), LOCH
Lamp: Miner's, DAVY
Landing place: Indian, GHAT
Language: Buddhist, PALI
Japanese, AINU
Latvian, LETT
Layer: Of iris, UVEA
Leaf: Palm, OLAY, OLLA
Legislature: Ukrainian, RADA
Lemur, LORI
Leopard, PARD
Let it stand, STET
Letter: Greek, BETA, IOTA, ZETA
Hebrew, AYIN, BETH, CAPH, KOPH, RESH, SHIN, TETH, YODH
Papal, BULL
Lily, ALOE
Literature: Hindu sacred, VEDA
Lizard, GILA
Monitor, URAN
Loquat, BIWA
Magistrate: Genoese or Venetian, DOGE
Man (Latin), HOMO
Mark: Omission, DELE
armoset: South American, MICO
Meadow: Fertile, VEGA
Measure: Electric, VOLT, WATT
Force, DYNE
Hebrew, OMER
Printing, PICA
Spanish or Portuguese, VARA
Swiss land, IMMI
Medley, OLIO
Merganser, SMEW
Milk (French), LAIT
Molding, GULA
Curved, OGEE
Mongoose: Crab-eating, URVA
Monk: Tibetan, LAMA
Monkey: African, MONA, WAAG
Ceylonese, MAHA
Cochin-China, DOUC
South American, SAKI, TITI
Monkshood, ATIS
Month: Jewish, ADAR, ELUL, IYAR
Mother (French), MERE
Mountain: Thessaly, OSSA
Mouse: Meadow, VOLE
Mythology: Norse, EDDA
Nail (French), CLOU
Native: Philippine, MORO
Nest: Of pheasants, NIDE
Network, RETE
No (German), NEIN
Noble: Mohammedan, AMIR
Notice: Death, OBIT
Novel: By Zola, NANA
Nursemaid: Oriental AMAH, AYAH, EYAH
Nut: Philippine, PILI
Oak: Holm, ILEX
Oil (comb. form), OLEO
Ostrich: American, RHEA
Oven, KILN, OAST
Owl: Barn, LULU
Ox: Celebes wild, ANOE
Extinct wild, URUS
Palm, ATAP, NIPA, SAGO
Parliament, DIET
Parrot: New Zealand, KAKA
Pass: Indian mountain, GHAT
Passage: Closing (music), CODA
Peach: Clingstone, PAVY
Peasant: Indian, RYOT
Old English, CARL
Pepper: Australasian, KAVA
Perfume, ATAR
Persia, IRAN
Person: Extraordinary, ONER
Pickerel or pike, ESOX
Pitcher, EWER
Plant: Aromatic, NARD
Century, ALOE
Indigo, ANIL
Pepper, KAVA
Platform: Raised, DAIS
Plum: Wild, SLOE
Pods: Vegetable, OKRA, OKRO
Poem: Epic, EPOS
Poet: Persian, OMAR
Roman, OVID
Poison, BANE
Arrow, INEE
Porkfish, SISI
Portico: Greek, STOA
Premium, AGIO
Priest: Mohammedan, IMAM
Prima donna, DIVA
Prong: Fork, TINE
Pseudonym: Lamb's, ELIA
Queen: Carthaginian, DIDO
Hindu, RANI
Rabbit, CONY
Race: Of Japan, AINU
Rail: Ducklike, COOT
North American, SORA
Redshank, CLEE
Refuse: After pressing, MARC
Regiment: Turkish, ALAI
Reliquary, ARCA
Resort: Italian, LIDO
Ridges: Sandy, ASAR, OSAR
River: German, ELBE, ODER
Italian, ADDA
Siberian, LENA
Road: Roman, ITER
Rockfish: California, RENA
Rodent: Mouselike, VOLE
South American, PACA
Rootstock, TARO
Salamander, NEWT
Salmon: Silver, COHO
Young, PARR
Same (Greek), HOMO
(Latin), IDEM
Sauce: Fish, ALEC
School: English, ETON
Seaweed, AGAR, ALGA, KELP
Secular, LAIC
Sediment, SILT
Seed: Dill, ANET
Of vetch, TARE
Serf, ILOT
Sesame, TEEL
Settlement: Eskimo, ETAH
Shark: Atlantic, GATA
European, TOPE
Sheep: Wild, UDAD
Sheltered, ALEE
Shield, EGIS
Ship: Jason's, ARGO
Left side of, PORT
Two-masted, BRIG
Shrine: Buddhist, TOPE
Shrub: New Zealand, TUTU
Sign: Magic, RUNE
Silkworm, ERIA
Skin: Beaver, PLEW

Skink: Egyptian, ADDA
Slave, ESNE
Sloth: Two-toed, UNAU
Smooth, LENE
Snow: Glacial, NEVE
Soapstone, TALC
Society: African secret, EGBO, PORO
Son: Of Seth, ENOS
Song (German), LIED
 Unaccompanied, GLEE
Sound: Lung, RALE
Sour, ACID
Sow: Young, GILT
Spike: Brad-shaped, BROB
Spirit: Buddhist evil, MARA
Stake: Poker, ANTE
Star: Temporary, NOVA
Starch: East Indian, SAGO
Stone: Precious, OPAL
Strap: Bridle, REIN
Strewn (heraldry), SEME
Sweetsop, ATES, ATTA
Sword: Fencing, EPEE, FOIL
Tambourine: African, TAAR
Tapir: Brazilian, ANTA
Tax, CESS
Tea: South American, MATE
Therefore (Latin), ERGO
Thing: Extraordinary, ONER
Three (dice, cards, etc.), TREY
Thrush: Hawaiian, OMAO
Tide, NEAP
Tipster: Racing, TOUT
Tissue, TELA
Title: Etruscan, LARS
 Hindu, BABU
 Indian, RAJA
 Mohammedan, EMIR, IMAM
 Persian, BABA
 Spanish, DONA
 Turkish, AGHA, BABA
Toad: Largest-known, AGUA
 Tree, HYLA
Tool: Cutting, ADZE
Track: Deer, SLOT
Tract: Sandy, DENE
Tree: Apple, SORB
 Central American, EBOE
 East Indian, TEAK
 Eucalyptus, YATE
 Guiana and Trinidad, MORA
 Javanese, UPAS
 Linden, LIME, LINN, TEIL, TILL
 Sandarac, ARAR
 Sassafras, AGUE
 Tamarisk salt, ATLE
Tribe: Moro, SULU
Trout, CHAR
Urchin: Street, ARAB
Vessel: Arab, DHOW
Vestment: Ecclesiastical, COPE
Vetch, TARE
Vine: East Indian, SOMA
Violinist: Famous, AUER
Vortex, EDDY
Wampum, PEAG
Wapiti, STAG
Waste: Allowance for, TRET
Watchman: Indian, MINA
Water (Spanish), AGUA
Waterfall, LINN
Wavy (heraldry), ONDE, UNDE
Wax, CERE
 Chinese, PELA
Weed: Biblical, TARE
Weight: Ancient, MINA
 Danish (pl.), ESER
 East Asian, TAEL
 Greek, MINA
 Siamese, BAHT
Well done (rare), EUGE
Whale, CETE
 Killer, ORCA
 White, HUSE, HUSO
Whirlpool, EDDY
Wife: Of Geraint, ENID
Willow: Virginia, ITEA
Wine, PORT
Winged, ALAR
 (Heraldry), AILE
Wings, ALAE
Withered, SERE
Without (French), SANS
Wool: To comb, CARD
Work, OPUS
Wrong: Civil, TORT
Young: Bring forth, YEAN

Words of Five Letters

Abode of dead: Babylonian, ARALU
Aborigine: Borneo DAYAK
Aftersong, EPODE
Aloe, AGAVE
Animal: Footless, APODE
Ant, EMMET
Antelope: African, ADDAX, BEISA, CAAMA, ELAND, GUIBA, ORIBI, TIANG
 Goat, GORAL, SEROW
 Indian, SASIN
 Siberian, SAIGA
Arch: Pointed, OGIVE
Armadillo, APARA, POYOU, TATOU
Arrowroot, ARARU
Artery: Trunk, AORTA
Association: Russian, ARTEL
 Secret, CABAL
Author: English, READE
Automaton, GOLEM, ROBOT
Award: Motion-picture, OSCAR
Basket: Fishing, CREEL
Beer: Russian, KVASS
Bible: Mohammedan, KORAN
Bird: Asian, MINAH, MYNAH
 Indian, SHAMA
 Larklike, PIPIT
 Loonlike, GREBE
 Oscine, VIREO
 South American, AGAMI
 Swimming, GREBE
Black: (French), NOIRE
 (Heraldry), SABLE
Blackbird: European, MERLE, OUSEL, OUZEL
Block: Glacial, SERAC
Blue (heraldry), AZURE
Boat: Eskimo, BIDAR, UMIAK
Bobwhite, COLIN, QUAIL
Bone (comb. form), OSTEO
 Leg, TIBIA
 Thigh, FEMUR
Broom: Twig, BESOM
Brother (French), FRERE
 Moses, AARON
Canoe: Eskimo, BIDAR, KAYAK
Cape: Papal, FANON, ORALE
Caravansary, SERAI
Card: Old playing, TAROT
Caterpillar: New Zealand, AWETO
Catkin, AMENT
Cavity: Stone, GEODE
Cephalopod, SQUID
Cetacean, WHALE
Chariot, ESSED
Cheek: Pertaining to, MALAR
Chieftain: Arab, EMEER
Child (Scotch), BAIRN
Cigar, CLARO
Coating: Seed, TESTA
Cockatoo: Palm, ARARA
Coin: Costa Rican, COLON
 Danish, KRONE
 Ecuadorian, SUCRE
 English, GROAT, PENCE
 French, FRANC
 German, KRONE, TALER
 Hungarian, PENGO
 Icelandic, KRONA
 Indian, RUPEE
 Iraqi, DINAR
 Norwegian, KRONE
 Polish, ZLOTY
 Russian, COPEC, KOPEK, RUBLE
 Swedish, KRONA
 Turkish, ASPER
 Yugoslav, DINAR
Collar: Papal, FANON, ORALE
 Roman, RABAT
Commune: Italian, TREIA
Composition: Choral, MOTET
Compound: Chemical, ESTER
Conceal (law), ELOIN
Council: Ecclesiastical, SYNOD
Court: Anglo-Saxon, GEMOT
 Inner, PATIO
Crest: Mountain, ARETE
Crown: Papal, TIARA
Cuttlefish, SEPIA
Date: Roman, NONES
Decree: Mohammedan, IRADE
 Russian, UKASE
Deposit: Loam, LOESS
Desert: Gobi, SHAMO

Devilfish, MANTA
Disease: Cereals, ERGOT
Disk, PATEN
Dog: Wild, DHOLE, DINGO
Dormouse, LEROT
Drum, TABOR
Duck: Sea, EIDER
Dynasty: Chinese, CHING, LIANG, SHANG
Earthquake, SEISM
Eel, ELVER, MORAY
Ermine: European, STOAT
Ether: Crystalline, APIOL
Fabric: Velvetlike, PANNE
Fabulist, AESOP
Family: Italian, CENCI
Fiber: West Indian, SISAL
Fig: Smyrna, ELEME, ELEMI
Figure: Of speech, TROPE
Finch: European, SERIN
Fish: American small, KILLY
Flower: Garden, ASTER
Friend (Spanish), AMIGO
Fruit: Tropical, MANGO
Fungus: Rye, ERGOT
Furze, GORSE
Gateway, TORAN, TORII
Gem, AGATE, BERYL, PEARL, TOPAZ
Genus: Barnacles, LEPAS
  Bears, URSUS
  Birds (loons), GAVIA
  Birds (nuthatches), SITTA
  Cats, FELIS
  Dogs, CANIS
  Fishes (chiros), ELOPS
  Fishes (perch), PERCA
  Geese, ANSER
  Grasses, STIPA
  Grasses (incl. oats), AVENA
  Gulls, LARUS
  Hares, rabbits, LEPUS
  Hawks, BUTEO
  Herbs, old world, INULA
  Herbs, trailing or climbing, APIOS
  Herbs, tropical, TACCA, URENA
  Horses, EQUUS
  Insects (olive flies), DACUS
  Lice, plant, APHIS
  Lichens, USNEA
  Lizards, AGAMA
  Moles, TALPA
  Mollusks, OLIVA
  Monkeys, CEBUS
  Palms, ARECA
  Pigeons, GOURA
  Plants (amaryllis family), AGAVE
  Ruminants (goats), CAPRA
  Shrubs, Asiatic, SABIA
  Shrubs (heath), ERICA
  Shrubs (incl. raspberry), RUBUS
  Shrubs, tropical, IXORA, TREMA, URENA
  Ticks, ARGAS
  Trees (of elm family), TREMA, ULMUS
  Trees, tropical, IXORA, TREMA
Goat: Bezoar, PASAN
God: Assyrian, ASHIR, ASHUR, ASSUR
  Babylonian, DAGAN, SIRIS
  Gaelic, DAGDA
  Hindu, BHAGA, INDRA, SHIVA
  Japanese, EBISU
  Philistine, DAGON
  Phrygian, ATTIS
  Teutonic, AEGIR, GYMIR
  Welsh, DYLAN
Goddess: Babylonian, ISTAR, NANAI
  Hindu, DURGA, GAURI, SHREE
Group: Of six, HEXAD
Grove: Sacred to Diana, NEMUS
Growing out, ENATE
Guitar: Hindu, SITAR
Gull: PEWEE, PEWIT
Hartebeest, CAAMA
Headdress: Jewish or Persian, TIARA
  Liturgical, MITER, MITRE
Heath, ERICA
Herb: Grasslike marsh, SEDGE
Heron, EGRET
Hog: Young, SHOAT, SHOTE
Image, EIKON
Indian: Cariban, ARARA
  Iroquoian, HURON
  Mexican, AZTEC, OPATA, OTOMI
  Muskhogean, CREEK
  Siouan, OSAGE, TETON
  Spanish American, ARARA, CARIB
Inflorescence: Racemose, AMENT
Insect: Immature, LARVA
Intrigue, CABAL
Iris: Yellow, SEDGE
Juniper, GORSE, RETEM
Kidneys: Pertaining to, RENAL
King: British legendary, LLUDD
Kite: European, GLEDE
Kobold, NISSE
Land: Cultivated, ARADA, ARADO
Landholder (Scotch), LAIRD, THANE
Language: Dravidian, TAMIL
Lariat, LASSO, REATA
Laughing, RIANT
Lawgiver: Athenian, DRACO, SOLON
Leaf: Calyx, SEPAL
  Fern, FROND
Lemur, LORIS
Letter: English, AITCH
  Greek, ALPHA, DELTA, GAMMA, KAPPA, OMEGA, SIGMA, THETA
  Hebrew, ALEPH, CHETH, GIMEL, SADHE, ZAYIN
Lichen, USNEA
Lighthouse, PHARE
Lizard: Old World, AGAMA
Loincloth, DHOTI
Louse: Plant, APHID
Macaw: Brazilian, ARARA
Mahogany: Philippine, ALMON
Mammal: Badgerlike, RATEL
  Civetlike, GENET
  Giraffelike, OKAPI
  Raccoonlike, COATI
Man (French), HOMME
Marble, AGATE
Mark: Insertion, CARET
Market place: Greek, AGORA
Marsupial: Australian, KOALA
Measure: Electric, FARAD, HENRY
  Energy, JOULE
  Metric, LITER, STERE
  Printing, AGATE
  Russian, VERST
Mixture: Smelting, MATTE
Mohicans: Last of, UNCAS
Molding: Convex, OVOLO, TORUS
Mole, TALPA
Monkey: African, PATAS
  Capuchin, SAJOU
  Howling, ARABA
Monkshood, ATEES
Month: Jewish, NISAN, SIVAN, TEBET
Museum (French), MUSEE
Musketeer, ATHOS
Native: Aleutian, ALEUT
  New Zealand, MAORI
Neckpiece: Ecclesiastical, AMICE
Nerve (comb. form), NEURO
Nest: Eagle's or hawk's, AERIE
  Insect's, NIDUS
Net: Fishing, SEINE
Newsstand, KIOSK
Nitrogen, AZOTE
Noble: Mohammedan, AMEER
Nodule: Stone, GEODE
Nostrils, NARES
Notched irregularly, EROSE
Nymph: Mohammedan, HOURI
Official: Roman, EDILE
Oleoresin, ELEMI
Opening: Mouthlike, STOMA
Oration: Funeral, ELOGE
Ostiole, STOMA
Page: Left-hand, VERSO
  Right-hand, RECTO
Palm, ARECA, BETEL
Park: Colorado, ESTES
Perfume, ATTAR

Philosopher: Greek, PLATO
Pillar: Stone, STELA, STELE
Pinnacle: Glacial, SERAC
Plain, LLANO
Plant: Century, AGAVE
Climbing, LIANA
Dwarf, CUMIN
East Asian perennial, RAMIE
Medicinal, SENNA
Mustard family, CRESS
Plate: Communion, PATEN
Poem: Lyric, EPODE
Point: Lowest, NADIR
Poplar, ABELE, ALAMO, ASPEN
Porridge: Spanish American, ATOLE
Post: Stair, NEWEL
Priest: Mohammedan, IMAUM
Protozoan, AMEBA
Queen: (French), REINE
Hindu, RANEE
Rabbit, CONEY
Rail, CRAKE
Red (heraldry), GULES
Religion: Moslem, ISLAM
Resin, ELEMI
Revoke (law), ADEEM
Rich man, MIDAS, NABOB
Ridge: Sandy, ESKAR, ESKER
River: French, LOIRE, SEINE
Rockfish: California, REINA
Rootstock: Fragrant, ORRIS
Ruff: Female, REEVE
Sack: Pack, KYACK
Salt: Ethereal, ESTER
Saltpeter, NITER, NITRE
Salutation: Eastern, SALAM
Sandpiper: Old World, TEREK
Scented, OLENT
School: Fish, SHOAL
French public, LYCEE
Scriptures: Mohammedan, KORAN
Seaweeds, ALGAE
Seed: Aromatic, ANISE
Seraglio, HAREM, SERAI
Serf, HELOT
Sheep: Wild, AUDAD
Sheeplike, OVINE
Shield, AEGIS
Shoe: Wooden, SABOT
Shoots: Pickled bamboo, ACHAR
Shot: Billiard, CAROM, MASSE
Shrine: Buddhist, STUPA
Shrub: Burning bush, WAHOO
Ornamental evergreen, TOYON
Used in tanning, SUMAC
Silk: Watered, MOIRE
Sister (French), SOEUR
(Latin), SOROR
Six: Group of, HEXAD
Skeleton: Marine, CORAL
Slave, HELOT
Snake, ABOMA, ADDER, COBRA, RACER
Soldier: French, POILU
Indian, SEPOY
Sour, ACERB
Spirit: Air, ARIEL
Staff: Shepherd's, CROOK
Starwort, ASTER
Steel (German), STAHL
Stockade: Russian, ETAPE
Stop (nautical), AVAST
Storehouse, ETAPE
Subway: Parisian, METRO
Tapestry, ARRAS
Tea: Paraguayan, YERBA
Temple: Hawaiian, HEIAU
Terminal: Positive, ANODE
Theater: Greek, ODEON, ODEUM
Then (French), ALORS
Thread: Surgical, SETON
Thrush: Wilson's, VEERY
Title: Hindu, BABOO
Indian, RAJAH, SAHEB, SAHIB
Mohammedan, EMEER, IMAUM
Tree: Buddhist sacred, PIPAL
East Indian cotton, SIMAL
Hickory, PECAN
Light-wooded, BALSA
Malayan, TERAP
Mediterranean, CAROB
Mexican, ABETO
Mexican pine, OCOTE
New Zealand, MAIRE
Philippine, ALMON
Rain, SAMAN
South American, UMBRA
Tamarack, LARCH
Tamarisk salt, ATLEE
West Indian, ACANA
Trout, CHARR
Troy, ILION, ILIUM
Twin: Siamese, CHANG
Vestment: Ecclesiastical, STOLE
Violin: Famous, AMATI, STRAD
Volcano: Mud, SALSE
Wampum, PEAGE
War cry: Greek, ALALA
Wavy (heraldry), UNDEE
Weight: Jewish, GERAH
Wen, TALPA
Wheat, SPELT
Wheel: Persian water, NORIA
Whitefish, CISCO
Willow, OSIER
Window: Bay, ORIEL
Wine, MEDOC, RHINE, TINTA, TOKAY
Winged, ALATE
Woman (French), FEMME
Year: Excess of solar over lunar, EPACT
Zoroastrian, PARSI

Words of Six or More Letters

Agave, MAGUEY
Alkaloid: Crystalline, ESERIN, ESERINE
Alligator, CAYMAN
Amphibole, EDENITE, URALITE
Ant: White, TERMITE
Antelope: African, DIKDIK, DUIKER, GEMSBOK, IMPALA, KOODOO
European, CHAMOIS
Indian, NILGAI, NILGAU, NILGHAI, NILGHAU
Ape: Asian or East Indian, GIBBON
Appendage: Leaf, STIPEL, STIPULE
Armadillo, PELUDO, TATOUAY
Arrowroot, ARARAO
Ascetic: Jewish, ESSENE
Ass: Asian wild, ONAGER
Avatar: Of Vishnu, KRISHNA
Babylonian, ELAMITE
Badge: Shoulder, EPAULET
Baldness, ALOPECIA
Barracuda, SENNET
Bark: Aromatic, SINTOC
Bearlike, URSINE
Beetle, ELATER
Bible: Zoroastrian, AVESTA
Bird: Sea, PETREL
South American, SERIEMA
Wading, AVOCET, AVOSET
Bone: Leg, FIBULA
Branched, RAMATE
Brother (Latin), FRATER
Bunting: European, ORTOLAN
Call: Trumpet, SENNET
Canoe: Eskimo, BAIDAR, OOMIAK
Caravansary, IMARET
Cat: Asian or African, CHEETAH
Leopardlike, OCELOT
Cenobite: Jewish, ESSENE
Centerpiece: Table, EPERGNE

Cetacean, DOLPHIN, PORPOISE
Chariot, ESSEDA, ESSEDE
Chief: Seminole, OSCEOLA
Claim: Release as (law), REMISE
Clock: Water, CLEPSYDRA
Cloud, CUMULUS, NIMBUS
Coach: French hackney, FIACRE
Coin: Czech, KORUNA
  Ethiopian, TALARI
  Finnish, MARKKA
  German, THALER
  Greek, DRACHMA
  Haitian, GOURDE
  Honduran, LEMPIRA
  Hungarian, FORINT
  Indo-Chinese, PIASTER
  Netherlands, GUILDER
  Panamanian, BALBOA
  Paraguayan, GUARANI
  Portuguese, ESCUDO
  Russian, COPECK, KOPECK, ROUBLE
  Spanish, PESETA
  Venezuelan, BOLIVAR
Communion: Last holy, VIATICUM
Conceal (law), ELOIGN
Confection, PRALINE
Construction: Sentence, SYNTAX
Convexity: Shaft of column, ENTASIS
Court: Anglo-Saxon, GEMOTE
Cow: Sea, DUGONG, MANATEE
Cylindrical, TERETE
Dagger, STILETTO
  Malay, CREESE, KREESE
Date: Roman, CALENDS, KALENDS
Deer, CARIBOU, WAPITI
Disease: Plant, ERINOSE
Doorkeeper, OSTIARY
Dragonflies: Order of, ODANATA
Drink: Of gods, NECTAR
Drum: TABOUR
  Moorish, ATABAL, ATTABAL
Duck: Fish-eating, MERGANSER
  Sea, SCOTER
Dynasty: Chinese, MANCHU
Eel, CONGER
Edit, REDACT
Envelope: Flower, PERIANTH
Eskimo, AMERIND
Ether: Crystalline, APIOLE
Excuse (law), ESSOIN
Eyespots, OCELLI
Fabric, ESTAMENE, ESTAMIN, ETAMINE
Falcon: European, KESTREL
Figure: Used as column, CARYATID, TELAMON
Fine: For punishment, AMERCE
Fish: Asian fresh-water, GOURAMI
  Pikelike, BARRACUDA
Five: Group of, PENTAD
Fly: African, TSETSE
Foot: Metric, ANAPEST, IAMBUS
Foxlike, VULPINE
Frying pan, SPIDER
Fur, KARAKUL
Galley: Greek or Roman, BIREME, TRIREME
Game: Card, ECARTE
Garment: Greek, CHLAMYS
Gateway, GOPURA, TORANA
Genus: Birds (ravens, crows), CORVUS
  Eels, CONGER
  Fishes, ANABAS
  Foxes, VULPES
  Herbs, ANEMONE
  Insects, CICADA
  Lemurs, GALAGO
  Mints (incl. catnip), NEPETA
  Mollusks, ANOMIA, ASTARTE, TEREDO
  Mollusks (incl. oysters), OSTREA
  Monkeys (spider monkeys), ATELES
  Thrushes (incl. robins), TURDUS
  Trees (of elm family), CELTIS
  Trees (inc. dogwood), CORNUS
  Trees, tropical American, SAPOTA
  Wrens, NANNUS
Gibbon, SIAMANG, WOUWOU
Gland: Salivary, RACEMOSE
Goat: Bezoar, PASANG
Goatlike, CAPRINE
God: Assyrian, ASHSHUR, ASSHUR
  Babylonian, BABBAR, MARDUK, MERODACH, NANNAR, NERGAL, SHAMASH
  Hindu, BRAHMA, KRISHNA, VISHNU
  Tahitian, TAAROA
Goddess: Babylonian, ISHTAR
  Hindu, CHANDI, HAIMAVATI, LAKSHMI, PARVATI, SARASVATI, SARASWATI
Government, POLITY
Governor: Persian, SATRAP
Grandson (Scotch), NEPOTE
Group: Of five, PENTAD
  Of nine, ENNEAD
  Of seven, HEPTAD
Hare: in first year, LEVERET
Harpsichord, SPINET
Herb: Alpine, EDELWEISS
  Chinese, GINSENG
  South African, FREESIA
Hermit, EREMITE
Hero: Legendary, PALADIN
Heron, BITTERN
Horselike, EQUINE
Hound: Short-legged, BEAGLE
House (French), MAISON
Idiot, CRETIN
Implement: Stone, NEOLITH
Incarnation: Hindu, AVATAR
Indian, APACHE, COMANCHE, PAIUTE, SENECA
Inn: Turkish, IMARET
Insects: Order of, DIPTERA
Instrument: Japanese banjolike, SAMISEN
  Musical, CLAVIER, SPINET
Interstice, AREOLA
Ironwood, COLIMA
Juniper: Old Testament, RAETAM
Kettledrum, ATABAL
King: Fairy, OBERON
Kneecap, PATELLA
Knife, MACHETE
Langur: Sumatran, SIMPAI
Legislature: Spanish, CORTES
Lemur: African, GALAGO
  Madagascar, AYEAYE
Letter: Greek, EPSILON, LAMBDA, OMICRON, UPSILON
  Hebrew, DALETH, LAMEDH, SAMEKH
Lighthouse, PHAROS
Lizard, IGUANA
Llama, ALPACA
Lockjaw, TETANUS
Locust, CICADA, CICALA
Macaw: Brazilian, MARACAN
Maid: Of Astolat, ELAINE
Mammal: Madagascar, TENDRAC, TENREC
Man (Spanish), HOMBRE
Marmoset: South American, TAMARIN
Marsupial, BANDICOOT, WOMBAT
Massacre, POGROM
Mayor: Spanish, ALCALDE
Measure: Electric, AMPERE, COULOMB, KILOWATT
Medicine: Quack, NOSTRUM
Member: Religious order, CENOBITE
Molasses, TREACLE
Monkey: African, GRIVET, NISNAS
  Asian, LANGUR
  Philippine, MACHIN
  South American, PINCHE, SAIMIRI, SAMIRI, SAPAJOU
Monster, CHIMERA, GORGON
  (Comb. form), TERATO
  Cretan, MINOTAUR
Month: Jewish, HESHVAN, KISLEV, SHEBAT, TAMMUZ, TISHRI, VEADAR
Mountain: Asia Minor, ARARAT
Mulct, AMERCE
Musketeer, ARAMIS, PORTHOS
Nearsighted, MYOPIC
Net, TRAMMEL
New York City, GOTHAM
Nine: Group of, ENNEAD
Nobleman: Spanish, GRANDEE
Official: Roman, AEDILE
Onyx: Mexican, TECALI
Order: Dragonflies, ODANATA
  Insects, DIPTERA
Organ: Plant, PISTIL

Ornament: Shoulder, EPAULET
Overcoat: Military, CAPOTE
Ox: Wild, BANTENG
Oxidation: Bronze or copper, PATINA
Paralysis: Incomplete, PARESIS
Pear: Alligator, AVOCADO
Persimmon: Mexican, CHAPOTE
Pipe: Peace, CALUMET
Plaid (Scotch), TARTAN
Plain, PAMPAS, STEPPE, TUNDRA
Plant: Buttercup family, ANEMONE
  Century, MAGUEY
  On rocks, LICHEN
Plowing: Fit for, ARABLE
Poem: Heroic, EPOPEE
  Six-lined, SESTET
Point: Highest, ZENITH
Potion: Love, PHILTER, PHILTRE
Protozoan, AMOEBA
Punish, AMERCE
Purple (heraldry), PURPURE
Queen: Fairy, TITANIA
Race: Skiing, SLALOM
Rat, BANDICOOT, LEMMING
Retort, RIPOST, RIPOSTE
Ring: Harness, TERRET
  Little, ANNULET
Rodent: Jumping, JERBOA
  Spanish American, AGOUTI, AGOUTY
Sailor: East Indian, LASCAR
Salmon: Young, GRILSE
Salutation: Eastern, SALAAM
Sandpiper, PLOVER
Sandy, ARENOSE
Sapodilla, SAPOTA, SAPOTE
Saw: Surgical, TREPAN
Seven: Group of, HEPTAD
Sexes: Common to both, EPICENE
Shawl: Mexican, SERAPE
Sheathing: Flower, SPATHE
Sheep: Wild, AOUDAD, ARGALI
Shipworm, TEREDO
Shoes: Mercury's winged, TALARIA
Shortening: Syllable, SYSTOLE
Shrub, SPIRAEA
Sickle-shaped, FALCATE
Silver (heraldry), ARGENT
Snake, ANACONDA
Speech: Loss of, APHASIA
Spiral, HELICAL
Staff: Bishop's, CROSIER, CROZIER
Stalk: Plant, PETIOLE
State: Swiss, CANTON
Studio, ATELIER
Swan: Young, CYGNET
Swimming, NATANT
Sword-shaped, ENSATE
Terminal: Negative, CATHODE
Third (music), TIERCE
Thrust: Fencing, RIPOST, RIPOSTE
Tile: Pertaining to, TEGULAR
Tomb: Empty, CENOTAPH
Tooth (comb. form), ODONTO
Tower: Mohammedan, MINARET
Tree: African timber, BAOBAB
  Black gum, TUPELO
  East Indian, MARGOSA
  Locust, ACACIA
  Malayan, SINTOC
  Marmalade, SAPOTE
Urn: Tea, SAMOVAR
Vehicle, LANDAU, TROIKA
Verbose, PROLIX
Viceroy: Egyptian, KHEDIVE
Vulture: American, CONDOR
Warehouse (French), ENTREPOT
Whale: White, BELUGA
Whirlpool, VORTEX
Will: Addition to, CODICIL
  Having left, TESTATE
Wind, CHINOOK, MONSOON, SIMOOM, SIMOON, SIROCCO
Window: In roof, DORMER
Wine, BARBERA, BURGUNDY, CABERNET, CHABLIS, CHIANTI, CLARET, MUSCATEL, RIESLING, SAUTERNE, SHERRY, ZINFANDEL
Wolfish, LUPINE
Woman: Boisterous, TERMAGANT
Woolly, LANATE
Workshop, ATELIER
Zoroastrian, PARSEE

Old-Testament Names

(We do not pretend that this list is all-inclusive. We include only those names which in our opinion one meets most often in crossword puzzles.)

Aaron: First high priest of Jews; son of Amram; brother of Miriam and Moses; father of Abihu, Eleazer, Ithamar, and Nadab.

Abel: Son of Adam; slain by Cain.

Abigail: Wife of Nabal; later, wife of David.

Abihu: Son of Aaron.

Abimelech: King of Gerar.

Abner: Commander of army of Saul and Ishbosheth; slain by Joab.

Abraham (or Abram): Patriarch; forefather of the Jews; son of Terah; husband of Sarah; father of Isaac and Ishmael.

Absalom: Son of David and Maacah; revolted against David; slain by Joab.

Achish: King of Gath; gave refuge to David.

Achsa (or Achsah): Daughter of Caleb; wife of Othniel.

Adah: Wife of Lamech.

Adam: First man; husband of Eve; father of Cain, Abel, and Seth.

Adonijah: Son of David and Haggith.

Agag: King of Amalek; spared by Saul; slain by Samuel.

Ahasuerus: King of Persia; husband of Vashti and, later, Esther; sometimes identified with Xerxes the Great.

Ahijah: Prophet; foretold accession of Jeroboam.

Ahinoam: Wife of David.

Amasa: Commander of army of David; slain by Joab.

Amnon: Son of David and Ahinoam; ravished Tamar; slain by Absalom.

Amram: Husband of Jochebed; father of Aaron, Miriam and Moses.

Asenath: Wife of Joseph.

Asher: Son of Jacob and Zilpah.

Balaam: Prophet; rebuked by his donkey for cursing God.

Barak: Jewish captain; associated with Deborah.

Baruch: Secretary to Jeremiah.

Bathsheba: Wife of Uriah; later, wife of David.

Belshazzar: Crown prince of Babylon.

Benaiah: Warrior of David; proclaimed Solomon King.

Ben-Hadad: Name of several kings of Damascus.

Benjamin: Son of Jacob and Rachel.

Bezaleel: Chief architect of tabernacle.

Bilbah: Servant of Rachel; mistress of Jacob.

Bildad: Comforter of Job.

Boaz: Husband of Ruth; father of Obed.

Cain: Son of Adam and Eve; slayer of Abel; father of Enoch.

Cainan: Son of Enos.

Caleb: Spy sent out by Moses to visit Canaan; father of Achsa.

Canaan: Son of Ham.

Chilion: Son of Elimelech; husband of Orpah.

Cush: Son of Ham; father of Nimrod.

Dan: Son of Jacob and Bilhah.

Daniel: Prophet; saved from lions by God.

Deborah: Hebrew prophetess; helped Israelites conquer Canaanites.

Delilah: Mistress and betrayer of Samson.

Elam: Son of Shem.

Eleazar: Son of Aaron; succeeded him as high priest.

Eli: High priest and judge; teacher of Samuel; father of Hophni and Phinehas.

Eliakim: Chief minister of Hezekiah.

Eliezer: Servant of Abraham.

Elihu: Comforter of Job.

Elijah (or Elias): Prophet; went to heaven in chariot of fire.

Elimelech: Husband of Naomi; father of Chilion and Mahlon.

Eliphaz: Comforter of Job.

Elisha (or Eliseus): Prophet; successor of Elijah.

Elkanah: Husband of Hannah; father of Samuel.

Enoch: Son of Cain.

Enoch: Father of Methuselah.

Enos: Son of Seth; father of Cainan.

Ephraim: Son of Joseph.

Esau: Son of Isaac and Rebecca; sold his birthright to his brother Jacob.

Esther: Jewish wife of Ahasuerus; saved Jews from Haman's plotting.

Eve: First woman; created from rib of Adam.

Ezra (or Esdras): Hebrew scribe and priest.

Gad: Son of Jacob and Zilpah.

Gehazi: Servant of Elisha.

Gideon: Israelite hero; defeated Midianites.

Goliath: Philistine giant; slain by David.

Hagar: Handmaid of Sarah; concubine of Abraham; mother of Ishmael.

Haggith: Mother of Adonijah.

Ham: Son of Noah; father of Cush, Mizraim, Phut, and Canaan.

Haman: Chief minister of Ahasuerus; hanged on gallows prepared for Mordecai.

Hannah: Wife of Elkanah; mother of Samuel.

Hanun: King of Ammonites.

Haran: Brother of Abraham; father of Lot.

Hazael: King of Damascus.

Hephzi-Bah: Wife of Hezekiah; mother of Mannaseh.

Hiram: King of Tyre.

Holofernes: General of Nebuchadnezzar; slain by Judith.

Hophni: Son of Eli.

Isaac: Hebrew patriarch; son of Abraham and Sarah; half brother of Ishmael; husband of Rebecca; father of Esau and Jacob.

Ishmael: Son of Abraham and Hagar; half brother of Isaac.

Issachar: Son of Jacob and Leah.

Ithamar: Son of Aaron.

Jabal: Son of Lamech and Adah.

Jabin: King of Hazor.

Jacob: Hebrew patriarch, founder of Israel; son of Isaac and Rebecca; husband of Leah and Rachel; father of Asher, Benjamin, Dan, Gad, Issachar, Joseph, Judah, Levi, Naphtali, Reuben, Simeon, and Zebulun.

Jael: Slayer of Sisera.

Japheth: Son of Noah.

Jehoiada: High priest; husband of Jehoshabeath; revolted against Athaliah and made Joash King of Judah.

Jehoshabeath (or Jehosheba): Daughter of Jehoram of Judah; wife of Jehoiada.

Jephthah: Judge in Israel; sacrificed his only daughter because of vow.

Jesse: Son of Obed; father of David.

Jethro: Midianite priest; father of Zipporah.

Jezebel: Phoenician princess; wife of Ahab; mother of Ahaziah, Athaliah, and Jehoram.

Joab: Commander in chief under David; slayer of Abner, Absalom, and Amasa.

Job: Patriarch; underwent many afflictions; comforted by Bildad, Elihu, Eliphaz and Zophar.

Jochebed: Wife of Amram.

Jonah: Prophet; cast into sea and swallowed by great fish.

Jonathan: Son of Saul; friend of David.

Joseph: Son of Jacob and Rachel; sold into slavery by his brothers; husband of Asenath; father of Ephraim and Manassah.

Joshua: Successor of Moses; son of Nun.

Jubal: Son of Lamech and Adah.

Judah: Son of Jacob and Leah.

Judith: Slayer of Holofernes.

Kish: Father of Saul.

Laban: Father of Leah and Rachel.

Lamech: Son of Methuselah; father of Noah.

Lamech: Husband of Adah and Zillah; father of Jabal, Jubal, and Tubal-Cain.

Leah: Daughter of Laban; wife of Jacob.

Levi: Son of Jacob and Leah.

Lot: Son of Haran; escaped destruction of Sodom.

Maacah: Mother of Absalom and Tamar.

Mahlon: Son of Elimelech; first husband of Ruth.

Manasseh: Son of Joseph.

Melchizedek: King of Salem.

Methuselah: Patriarch; son of Enoch; father of Lamech.

Michal: Daughter of Saul; wife of David.

Miriam: Prophetess; daughter of Amram; sister of Aaron and Moses.

Mizraim: Son of Ham.

Mordecai: Uncle of Esther; with her aid, saved Jews from Haman's plotting.

Moses: Prophet and lawgiver; son of Amram; brother of Aaron and Miriam; husband of Zipporah.

Naaman: Syrian captain; cured of leprosy by Elisha.

Nabal: Husband of Abigail.

Naboth: Owner of vineyard; stoned to death because he would not sell it to Ahab.

Nadab: Son of Aaron.

Nahor: Father of Terah.

Naomi: Wife of Elimelech; mother-in-law of Ruth.

Naphtali: Son of Jacob and Bilhah.

Nathan: Prophet; reproved David for causing Uriah's death.

Nebuchadnezzar (or Nebuchadrezzar): King of Babylon; destroyer of Jerusalem.

Nehemiah: Jewish leader; empowered by Artaxerxes to rebuild Jerusalem.

Nimrod: Mighty hunter; son of Cush.

Noah: Patriarch; Son of Lamech; escaped Deluge by building Ark; father of Ham, Japheth and Shem.

Nun (or Non): Father of Joshua.

Obed: Son of Boaz; father of Jesse.

Og: King of Bashan.

Orpah: Wife of Chilion.

Othniel: Kenezite; judge of Israel; husband of Achsa.

Phinehas: Son of Eleazer.

Phinehas: Son of Eli.

Phut (or Put): Son of Ham.

Potiphar: Egyptian official; bought Joseph.

Rachel: Wife of Jacob.

Rebecca (or Rebekah): Wife of Isaac.

Reuben: Son of Jacob and Leah.

Ruth: Wife of Mahlon, later of Boaz; daughter-in-law of Naomi.

Samson: Judge of Israel; famed for strength; betrayed by Delilah.

Samuel: Hebrew judge and prophet; son of Elkanah.

Sarah (or Sara, Sarai): Wife of Abraham.

Sennacherib: King of Assyria.

Seth: Son of Adam; father of Enos.

Shem: Son of Noah; father of Elam.

Simeon: Son of Jacob and Leah.

Sisera: Canaanite captain; slain by Jael.

Tamar: Daughter of David and Maachah; ravished by Amnon.

Terah: Son of Nahor; father of Abraham.

Tubal-Cain: Son of Lamech and Zillah.

Uriah: Husband of Bathsheba; sent to death in battle by David.

Vashti: Wife of Ahasuerus; set aside by him.

Zadok: High priest during David's reign.

Zebulun (or Zabulon): Son of Jacob and Leah.

Zillah: Wife of Lamech.

Zilpah: Servant of Leah; mistress of Jacob.

Zipporah: Daughter of Jethro; wife of Moses.

Zophar: Comforter of Job.

Kings of Judah and Israel

Kings Before Division of Kingdom

Saul: First King of Israel; son of Kish; father of Ish-Bosheth, Jonathan and Michal.

Ish-Bosheth (or Eshbaal): King of Israel; son of Saul.

David: King of Judah; later of Israel; son of Jesse; husband of Abigail, Ahinoam, Bathsheba, Michal, etc.; father of Absalom, Adonijah, Amnon, Solomon, Tamar, etc.

Solomon: King of Israel and Judah; son of David; father of Rehoboam.

Rehoboam: Son of Solomon; during his reign the kingdom was divided into Judah and Israel.

Kings of Judah (Southern Kingdom)

Rehoboam: First King.

Abijah (or Abijam or Abia): Son of Rehoboam.

Asa: Probably son of Abijah.

Jehoshaphat: Son of Asa.

Jehoram (or Joram): Son of Jehoshaphat; husband of Athaliah.

Ahaziah: Son of Jehoram and Athaliah.

Athaliah: Daughter of King Ahab of Israel and Jezebel; wife of Jehoram.

Joash (or Jehoash): Son of Ahaziah.

Amaziah: Son of Joash.

Uzziah (or Azariah): Son of Amaziah.

Jotham: Regent, later King; son of Uzziah.

Ahaz: Son of Jotham.

Hezekiah: Son of Ahaz; husband of Hephzi-Bah.

Manasseh: Son of Hezekiah and Hephzi-Bah.

Amon: Son of Manasseh.

Josiah (or Josias): Son of Amon.

Jehoahaz (or Joahaz): Son of Josiah.

Jehoiachin: Son of Jehoiakim.

Jehoiakim: Son of Josiah.

Zedekiah: Son of Josiah; kingdom overthrown by Babylonians under Nebuchadnezzar.

Kings of Israel (Northern Kingdom)

Jeroboam I: Led secession of Israel.

Nadab: Son of Jeroboam I.

Baasha: Overthrew Nadab.

Elah: Son of Baasha.

Zimri: Overthrew Elah.

Omri: Overthrew Zimri.

Ahab: Son of Omri; husband of Jezebel.

Ahaziah: Son of Ahab.

Jehoram (or Joram): Son of Ahab.

Jehu: Overthrew Jehoram.

Jehoahaz (or Joahaz): Son of Jehu.

Jehoash (or Joash): Son of Jehoahaz.

Jeroboam II: Son of Jehoash.

Zechariah: Son of Jeroboam II.

Shallum: Overthrew Zechariah.

Menahem: Overthrew Shallum.

Pekahiah: Son of Menahem.

Pekah: Overthrew Pekahiah.

Hoshea: Overthrew Pekah; kingdom overthrown by Assyrians under Sargon II.

Prophets

Major.—Isaiah, Jeremiah, Ezekiel, Daniel.

Minor.—Hosea, Obadiah, Nahum, Haggai, Joel, Jonah, Habakkuk, Zechariah, Amos, Micah, Zephaniah, Malachi.

Greek and Roman Mythology

(Most of the Greek deities were adopted by the Romans, although in many cases there was a change of name. In the list below, information is given under the Greek name; the name in parentheses is the Latin equivalent. However, all Latin names are listed with cross references to the Greek ones. In addition, there are several deities which were exclusively Roman.)

Acheron: *See* Rivers.

Achilles: Greek warrior; slew Hector at Troy; slain by Paris, who wounded him in his vulnerable heel.

Actaeon: Hunter; surprised Artemis bathing; changed by her to stag and killed by his dogs.

Admetus: King of Thessaly; his wife, Alcestis, offered to die in his place.

Adonis: Beautiful youth loved by Aphrodite.

Aeacus: One of three judges of dead in Hades; son of Zeus.

Aeëtes: King of Colchis; father of Medea; keeper of Golden Fleece.

Aegeus: Father of Theseus; believing Theseus killed in Crete, he drowned himself, Aegean Sea named for him.

Aegisthus: Son of Thyestes; slew Atreus; with Clytemnestra, his paramour, slew Agamemnon; slain by Orestes.

Aegyptus: Brother of Danaus; his sons, except Lynceus, slain by Danaides.

Aeneas: Trojan; son of Anchises and Aphrodite; after fall of Troy, led his followers eventually to Italy; loved and deserted Dido.

Aeolus: *See* Winds.

Aesculapius: *See* Asclepius.

Aeson: King of Iolcus; father of Jason; overthrown by his brother Pelias; restored to youth by Medea.

Aether: Personification of sky.

Aethra: Mother of Theseus.

Agamemnon: King of Mycenae; son of Atreus; brother of Menelaus; leader of Greeks against Troy; slain on his return home by Clytemnestra and Aegisthus.

Agiaia: *See* Graces.

Ajax: Greek warrior; killed himself at Troy because Achilles' armor was awarded to Odysseus.

Alcestis: Wife of Admetus; offered to die in his place but saved from death by Hercules.

Alcmene: Wife of Amphitryon; mother by Zeus of Hercules.

Alcyone: *See* Pleiades.

Alecto: *See* Furies.

Alectryon: Youth changed by Ares into cock.

Althaea: Wife of Oeneus; mother of Meleager.

Amazons: Female warriors in Asia Minor; supported Troy against Greeks.

Amor: *See* Eros.

Amphion: Musician; husband of Niobe; charmed stones to build fortifications for Thebes.

Amphitrite: Sea goddess; wife of Poseidon.

Amphitryon: Husband of Alcmene.

Anchises: Father of Aeneas.

Ancile: Sacred shield that fell from heavens; palladium of Rome.

Andraemon: Husband of Dryope.

Andromache: Wife of Hector.

Andromeda: Daughter of Cepheus; chained to cliff for monster to devour; rescued by Perseus.

Anteia: Wife of Proetus; tried to induce Bellerophon to elope with her.

Anteros: God who avenged unrequited love.

Antigone: Daughter of Oedipus; accompanied him to Colonus; performed burial rite for Polynices and hanged herself.

Antinoüs: Leader of suitors of Penelope; slain by Odysseus.

Aphrodite (Venus): Goddess of love and beauty; daughter

of Zeus; mother of Eros.

Apollo: God of beauty, poetry, music; later identified with Helios as Phoebus Apollo; son of Zeus and Leto.

Aquilo: *See* Winds.

Arachne: Maiden who challenged Athena to weaving contest; changed to spider.

Ares (Mars): God of war; son of Zeus and Hera.

Argo: Ship in which Jason and followers sailed to Colchis for Golden Fleece.

Argus: Monster with hundred eyes; slain by Hermes; his eyes placed by Hera into peacock's tail.

Ariadne: Daughter of Minos; aided Theseus in slaying Minotaur; deserted by him on island of Naxos and married to Dionysus.

Arion: Musician; thrown overboard by pirates but saved by dolphin.

Artemis (Diana): Goddess of moon; huntress; twin sister of Apollo.

Asclepius (Aesculapius): Mortal son of Apollo; slain by Zeus for raising dead; later deified as god of medicine. Also known as Asklepios.

Astarte: Phoenician goddess of love; variously identified with Aphrodite, Selene, and Artemis.

Astraea: Goddess of Justice; daughter of Zeus and Themis.

Atalanta: Princess who challenged her suitors to a foot race; Hippomenes won race and married her.

Athena (Minerva): Goddess of wisdom; known poetically as Pallas Athene; sprang fully armed from head of Zeus.

Atlas: Titan; held world on his shoulders as punishment for warring against Zeus; son of Iapetus.

Atreus: King of Mycenae; father of Menelaus and Agamemnon; brother of Thyestes, three of whose sons he slew and served to him at banquet; slain by Aegisthus.

Atropos: *See* Fates.

Aurora: *See* Eos.

Auster: *See* Winds.

Avernus: Infernal regions; name derived from small vaporous lake near Vesuvius which was fabled to kill birds and vegetation.

Bacchus: *See* Dionysus.

Bellerophon: Corinthian hero; killed Chimera with aid of Pegasus; tried to reach Olympus on Pegasus and was thrown to his death.

Bellona: Roman goddess of war.

Boreas: *See* Winds.

Briareus: Monster of hundred hands; son of Uranus and Gaea.

Briseis: Captive maiden given to Achilles; taken by Agamemnon in exchange for loss of Chryseis, which caused Achilles to cease fighting, until death of Patroclus.

Cadmus: Brother of Europa; planter of dragon seeds from which first Thebans sprang.

Calliope: *See* Muses.

Calypso: Sea nymph; kept Odysseus on her island Ogygia for seven years.

Cassandra: Daughter of Priam; prophetess who was never believed; slain with Agamemnon.

Castor: *See* Dioscuri.

Celaeno: *See* Pleiades.

Centaurs: Beings half man and half horse; lived in mountains of Thessaly.

Cephalus: Hunter; accidentally killed his wife Procris with his spear.

Cepheus: King of Ethiopia; father of Andromeda.

Cerberus: Three-headed dog guarding entrance to Hades.

Ceres: *See* Demeter.

Chaos: Formless void; personified as first of gods.

Charon: Boatman on Styx who carried souls of dead to Hades; son of Erebus.

Charybdis: Female monster; personification of whirlpool.

Chimera: Female monster with head of lion, body of goat, tail of serpent; killed by Bellerophon.

Chiron: Most famous of centaurs.

Chronos: Personification of time.

Chryseis: Captive maiden given to Agamemnon; his refusal to accept ransom from her father Chryses caused Apollo to send plague on Greeks besieging Troy.

Circe: Sorceress; daughter of Helios; changed Odysseus' men into swine.

Clio: *See* Muses.

Clotho: *See* Fates.

Clytemnestra: Wife of Agamemnon, whom she slew with aid of her paramour, Aegisthus; slain by her son Orestes.

Cocytus: *See* Rivers.

Creon: Father of Jocasta; forbade burial of Polynices; ordered burial alive of Antigone.

Creüsa: Princess of Corinth, for whom Jason deserted Medea; slain by Medea, who sent her poisoned robe; also known as Glaüke.

Creusa: Wife of Aeneas; died fleeing Troy.

Cronus (Saturn): Titan; god of harvests; son of Uranus and Gaea; dethroned by his son Zeus.

Cupid: *See* Eros.

Cybele: Anatolian nature goddess; adopted by Greeks and identified with Rhea.

Cyclopes: Race of one-eyed giants (singular: Cyclops).

Daedalus: Athenian artificer; father of Icarus; builder of Labyrinth in Crete; devised wings attached with wax for him and Icarus to escape Crete.

Danae: Princess of Argos; mother of Perseus by Zeus, who appeared to her in form of golden shower.

Danaïdes: Daughters of Danaüs; at his command, all except Hypermnestra slew their husbands, the sons of Aegyptus.

Danaüs: Brother of Aegyptus; father of Danaïdes; slain by Lynceus.

Daphne: Nymph; pursued by Apollo; changed to laurel tree.

Decuma: *See* Fates.

Deino: *See* Graeae.

Demeter (Ceres): Goddess of agriculture; mother of Persephone.

Diana: *See* Artemis.

Dido: Founder and queen of Carthage; stabbed herself when deserted by Aeneas.

Diomedes: Greek hero; with Odysseus, entered Troy and carried off Palladium, sacred statue of Athena.

Diomedes: Owner of man-eating horses, which Hercules, as ninth labor, carried off.

Dione: Titan goddess; mother by Zeus of Aphrodite.

Dionysus (Bacchus): God of wine; son of Zeus and Semele.

Dioscuri: Twins Castor and Pollux; sons of Leda by Zeus.

Dis: *See* Hades.

Dryads: Wood nymphs.

Dryope: Maiden changed to Hamadryad.

Echo: Nymph who fell hopelessly in love with Narcissus; faded away except for her voice.

Electra: Daughter of Agamemnon and Clytemnestra; sister of Orestes; urged Orestes to slay Clytemnestra and Aegisthus.

Electra: *See* Pleiades.

Elysium: Abode of blessed dead.

Endymion: Mortal loved by Selene.

Enyo: *See* Graeae.

Eos (Aurora): Goddess of dawn.

Epimetheus: Brother of Prometheus; husband of Pandora.

Erato: *See* Muses.

Erebus: Spirit of darkness; son of Chaos.

Erinyes: *See* Furies.

Eris: Goddess of discord.

Eros (Amor or Cupid): God of love; son of Aphrodite.

Eteocles: Son of Oedipus, whom he succeeded to rule alternately with Polynices; refused to give up throne at end of year; he and Polynices slew each other.

Eumenides: *See* Furies.

Euphrosyne: *See* Graces.

Europa: Mortal loved by Zeus, who, in form of white bull, carried her off to Crete.

Eurus: *See* Winds.

Euryale: *See* Gorgons.

Eurydice: Nymph; wife of Orpheus.

Eurystheus: King of Argos; imposed twelve labors on Hercules.

Euterpe: *See* Muses.

Fates: Goddesses of destiny; Clotho (Spinner of thread of life), Lachesis (Determiner of length), and Atropos (Cutter of thread); also called Moirae. Identified by Romans with their goddesses of fate; Nona, Decuma, and Morta; called Parcae.

Fauns: Roman deities of woods and groves.

Faunus: *See* Pan.

Favonius: *See* Winds.

Flora: Roman goddess of flowers.

Fortuna: Roman goddess of fortune.

Furies: Avenging spirits; Alecto, Megaera, and Tisiphone; known also as Erinyes or Eumenides.

Gaea: Goddess of earth; daughter of Chaos; mother of Titans; known also as Ge, Gea, Gaia, etc.

Galatea: Statue of maiden carved from ivory by Pygmalion; given life by Aphrodite.

Galatea: Sea nymph; loved by Polyphemus.

Ganymede: Beautiful boy; successor to Hebe as cupbearer of gods.

Glaucus: Mortal who became sea divinity by eating magic grass.

Glauke: *See* Creüsa.

Golden Fleece: Fleece from ram that flew Phrixos to Colchis; Aeëtes placed it under guard of dragon; carried off by Jason.

Gorgons: Female monsters; Euryale, Medusa, and Stheno; had snakes for hair; their glances turned mortals to stone. *See* Medusa.

Graces: Beautiful goddesses: Aglaia (Brilliance), Euphrosyne (Joy), and Thalia (Bloom); daughters of Zeus.

Graeae: Sentinels for Gorgons; Deino, Enyo, and Pephredo; had one eye among them, which passed from one to another.

Hades (Dis): Name sometimes given Pluto; also, abode of dead, ruled by Pluto.

Haemon: Son of Creon; promised husband of Antigone; killed himself in her tomb.

Hamadryads: Tree nymphs.

Harpies: Monsters with heads of women and bodies of birds.

Hebe (Juventas): Goddess of youth; cupbearer of gods before Ganymede; daughter of Zeus and Hera.

Hecate: Goddess of sorcery and witchcraft.

Hector: Son of Priam; slayer of Patroclus; slain by Achilles.

Hecuba: Wife of Priam.

Helen: Fairest woman in world; daughter of Zeus and Leda; wife of Menelaus; carried to Troy by Paris, causing Trojan War.

Heliades: Daughters of Helios; mourned for Phaëthon and were changed to poplar trees.

Helios (Sol): God of sun; later identified with Apollo.

Helle: Sister of Phrixos; fell from ram of Golden Fleece; water where she fell named Hellespont.

Hephaestus (Vulcan): God of fire; celestial blacksmith; son of Zeus and Hera; husband of Aphrodite.

Hera (Juno): Queen of heaven; wife of Zeus.

Hercules: Hero and strong man; son of Zeus and Alcmene; performed twelve labors or deeds to be free from bondage under Eurystheus; after death, his mortal share was destroyed, and he became immortal. Also known as Herakles or Heracles. Labors: (1) killing Nemean lion; (2) killing Lernaean Hydra; (3) capturing Erymanthian boar; (4) capturing Cerynean hind; (5) killing man-eating Stymphalian birds; (6) procuring girdle of Hippolyte; (7) cleaning Augean stables; (8) capturing Cretan bull; (9) capturing man-eating horses of Diomedes; (10) capturing cattle of Geryon; (11) procuring golden apples of Hesperides; (12) bringing Cerberus up from Hades.

Hermes (Mercury): God of physicians and thieves; messenger of gods; son of Zeus and Maia.

Hero: Priestess of Aphrodite; Leander swam Hellespont nightly to see her; drowned herself at his death.

Hesperus: Evening star.

Hestia (Vesta): Goddess of hearth; sister of Zeus.

Hippolyte: Queen of Amazons; wife of Theseus.

Hippolytus: Son of Theseus and Hippolyte; falsely accused by Phaedra of trying to kidnap her; slain by Poseidon at request of Theseus.

Hippomenes: Husband of Atalanta, whom he beat in race by dropping golden apples, which she stopped to pick up.

Hyacinthus: Beautiful youth accidentally killed by Apollo, who caused flower to spring up from his blood.

Hydra: Nine-headed monster in marsh of Lerna; slain by Hercules.

Hygeia: Personification of health.

Hyman: God of marriage.

Hyperion: Titan; early sun god; father of Helios.

Hypermnestra: Daughter of Danaüs; refused to kill her husband Lynceus.

Hypnos (Somnus): God of sleep.

Iapetus: Titan; father of Atlas, Epimetheus, and Prometheus.

Icarus: Son of Daedalus; flew too near sun with wax-attached wings and fell into sea and was drowned.

Iô: Mortal maiden loved by Zeus; changed by Hera into heifer.

Iobates: King of Lycia; sent Bellerophon to slay Chimera.

Iphigenia: Daughter of Agamemnon; offered as sacrifice to Artemis at Aulis; carried by Artemis to Tauris where she became priestess; escaped from there with Orestes.

Iris: Goddess of rainbow; messenger of Zeus and Hera.

Ismene: Daughter of Oedipus; sister of Antigone.

Iulus: Son of Aeneas.

Ixion: King of Lapithae; for making love to Hera he was bound to endlessly revolving wheel in Tartarus.

Janus: Roman god of gates and doors; represented with two opposite faces.

Jason: Son of Aeson; to gain throne of Ioclus from Pelias, went to Colchis and brought back Golden Fleece; married Medea; deserted her for Creüsa.

Jocasta: Wife of Laius; mother of Oedipus; unwittingly became wife of Oedipus; hanged herself when relationship was discovered.

Juno: *See* Hera.

Jupiter: *See* Zeus.

Juventas: *See* Hebe.

Lachesis: *See* Fates.

Laius: Father of Oedipus, by whom he was slain.

Laocoön: Priest of Apollo at Troy; warned against bringing wooden horse into Troy; destroyed with his two sons by serpents sent by Athena.

Lares: Roman ancestral spirits protecting descendants and homes.

Lavinia: Wife of Aeneas after defeat of Turnus.

Leander: Swam Hellespont nightly to see Hero; drowned in storm.

Leda: Mortal loved by Zeus in form of Swan; mother of Helen, Clytemnestra, Dioscuri.

Lethe: *See* Rivers.

Leto (Latona): Mother by Zeus of Artemis and Apollo.

Lucina: Roman goddess of childbirth; identified with Juno.

Lynceus: Son of Aegyptus; husband of Hypermnestra; slew Danaüs.

Maia: Daughter of Atlas; mother of Hermes.

Maia: *See* Pleiades.

Manes: Souls of dead Romans, particularly of ancestors.

Mars: *See* Ares.

Marsyas: Shepherd; challenged Apollo to music contest and lost; flayed alive by Apollo.

Medea: Sorceress; daughter of Aeëtes; helped Jason obtain Golden Fleece; when deserted by him for Creüsa, killed her children and Creüsa.

Medusa: Gorgon; slain by Perseus, who cut off her head.

Megaera: *See* Furies.

Meleager: Son of Althaea; his life would last as long as brand burning at his birth; Althaea quenched and saved it but destroyed it when Meleager slew his uncles.

Melpomene: *See* Muses.

Memnon: Ethiopian king; made immortal by Zeus; son of Tithonus and Eos.

Menelaus: King of Sparta; son of Atreus; brother of Agamemnon; husband of Helen.

Mercury: *See* Hermes.

Merope: *See* Pleiades.

Mezentius: Cruel Etruscan king; ally of Turnus against Aeneas; slain by Aeneas.

Midas: King of Phrygia; given gift of turning to gold all he touched.

Minerva: *See* Athena.

Minos: King of Crete; after death, one of three judges of dead in Hades; son of Zeus and Europa.

Minotaur: Monster, half man and half beast, kept in Labyrinth in Crete; slain by Theseus.

Mnemosyne: Goddess of memory; mother by Zeus of Muses.

Moirae: *See* Fates.

Momus: God of ridicule.

Morpheus: God of dreams.

Mors: *See* Thanatos.

Morta: *See* Fates.

Muses: Goddesses presiding over arts and sciences: Calliope (epic poetry), Clio (history), Erato (lyric and love poetry), Euterpe (music), Melpomene (tragedy), Polymnia or Polyhymnia (sacred poetry), Terpsichore (choral dance and song), Thalia (comedy and bucolic poetry), Urania (astronomy); daughters of Zeus and Mnemosyne.

Naiads: Nymphs of waters, streams, and fountains.

Napaeae: Wood nymphs.

Narcissus: Beautiful youth loved by Echo; in punishment for not returning her love, he was made to fall in love with his image reflected in pool; pined away and became flower.

Nemesis: Goddess of retribution.

Neoptolemus: Son of Achilles; slew Priam; also known as Pyrrhus.

Neptune: *See* Poseidon.

Nereids: Sea nymphs; attendants on Poseidon.

Nestor: King of Pylos; noted for wise counsel in expedition against Troy.

Nike: Goddess of victory.

Niobe: Daughter of Tantalus; wife of Amphion; her children slain by Apollo and Artemis; changed to stone but continued to weep her loss.

Nona: *See* Fates.

Notus: *See* Winds.

Nox: *See* Nyx.

Nymphs: Beautiful maidens; inferior deities of nature.

Nyx (Nox): Goddess of night.

Oceanids: Ocean nymphs; daughters of Oceanus.

Oceanus: Eldest of Titans; god of waters.

Odysseus (Ulysses): King of Ithaca; husband of Penelope; wandered ten years after fall of Troy before arriving home.

Oedipus: King of Thebes; son of Laius and Jocasta; unwittingly murdered Laius and married Jocasta; tore his eyes out when relationship was discovered.

Oenone: Nymph of Mount Ida; wife of Paris, who abandoned her; refused to cure him when he was poisoned by arrow of Philoctetes at Troy.

Ops: *See* Rhea.

Oreads: Mountain nymphs.

Orestes: Son of Agamemnon and Clytemnestra; brother of Electra; slew Clytemnestra and Aegisthus; pursued by Furies until his purification by Apollo.

Orion: Hunter; slain by Artemis and made heavenly constellation.

Orpheus: Famed musician; son of Apollo and Muse Calliope; husband of Eurydice.

Pales: Roman goddess of shepherds and herdsmen.

Palinurus: Aeneas' pilot; fell overboard in his sleep and was drowned.

Pan (Faunus): God of woods and fields; part goat; son of Hermes.

Pandora: Opener of box containing human ills; mortal wife of Epimetheus.

Parcae: *See* Fates.

Paris: Son of Priam; gave apple of discord to Aphrodite, for which she enabled him to carry off Helen; slew Achilles at Troy; slain by Philoctetes.

Patroclus: Great friend of Achilles; wore Achilles' armor and was slain by Hector.

Pegasus: Winged horse that sprang from Medusa's body at her death; ridden by Bellerophon when he slew Chimera.

Pelias: King of Ioclus; seized throne from his brother Aeson; sent Jason for Golden Fleece; slain unwittingly by his daughters at instigation of Medea.

Pelops: Son of Tantalus; his father cooked and served him to gods; restored to life; Peloponnesus named for him.

Penates: Roman household gods.

Penelope: Wife of Odysseus; waited faithfully for him for ten years while putting off numerous suitors.

Pephredo: *See* Graeae.

Periphetes: Giant; son of Hephaestus; slain by Theseus.

Persephone (Proserpine): Queen of infernal regions; daughter of Zeus and Demeter; wife of Pluto.

Perseus: Son of Zeus and Danaë; slew Medusa; rescued Andromeda from monster and married her.

Phaedra: Daughter of Minos; wife of Theseus; caused the death of her stepson, Hippolytus.

Phaethon: Son of Helios; drove his father's sun chariot and was struck down by Zeus before he set world on fire.

Philoctetes: Greek warrior who possessed Hercules' bow and arrows; slew Paris at Troy with poisoned arrow.

Phineus: Betrothed of Andromeda; tried to slay Perseus but turned to stone by Medusa's head.

Phlegethon: *See* Rivers.

Phosphor: Morning star.

Phrixos: Brother of Helle; carried by ram of Golden Fleece to Colchis.

Pirithous: Son of Ixion; friend of Theseus; tried to carry off Persephone from Hades; bound to enchanted rock by Pluto.

Pleiades: Alcyone, Celaeno, Electra, Maia, Merope, Sterope or Asterope, Taygeta; seven daughters of Atlas; transformed into heavenly constellation, of which six stars are visible (Merope is said to have hidden in shame for loving a mortal).

Pluto (Dis): God of Hades; brother of Zeus.

Plutus: God of wealth.

Pollux: *See* Dioscuri.

Polymnia: *See* Muses.

Polynices: Son of Oedipus; he and his brother Eteocles killed each other; burial rite, forbidden by Creon, performed by his sister Antigone.

Polyphemus: Cyclops; devoured six of Odysseus' men; blinded by Odysseus.

Polyxena: Daughter of Priam; betrothed to Achilles, whom Paris slew at their betrothal; sacrificed to shade of Achilles.

Pomona: Roman goddess of fruits.

Pontus: Sea god; son of Gaea.

Poseidon (Neptune): God of sea; brother of Zeus.

Priam: King of Troy; husband of Hecuba; ransomed Hector's body from Achilles; slain by Neoptolemus.

Priapus: God of regeneration.

Procris: Wife of Cephalus, who accidentally slew her.

Procrustes: Giant; stretched or cut off legs of victims to make them fit iron bed; slain by Theseus.

Proetus: Husband of Anteia; sent Bellerophon to Iobates to be put to death.

Prometheus: Titan; stole fire from heaven for man. Zeus punished him by chaining him to rock in Caucasus where vultures devoured his liver daily.

Proteus: Sea god; assumed various shapes when called on to prophesy.

Psyche: Beloved of Eros; punished by jealous Aphrodite; made immortal and united with Eros.

Pygmalion: King of Cyprus; carved ivory statue of maiden which Aphrodite gave life as Galatea.

Pyramus: Babylonian youth; made love to Thisbe through hole in wall; thinking Thisbe slain by lion, killed himself.

Pyrrhus: *See* Neoptolemus.

Python: Serpent born from slime left by Deluge; slain by Apollo.

Quirinus: Roman war god.

Remus: Brother of Romulus; slain by him.

Rhadamanthus: One of three judges of dead in Hades; son of Zeus and Europa.

Rhea (Ops): Daughter of Uranus and Gaea; wife of Cronus; mother of Zeus; identified with Cybele.

Rivers of Underworld: Acheron (woe), Cocytus (wailing), Lethe (forgetfulness), Phlegethon (fire), Styx (across which souls of dead were ferried by Charon).

Romulus: Founder of Rome; he and Remus suckled in infancy by she-wolf; slew Remus; deified by Romans.

Sarpedon: King of Lycia; son of Zeus and Europa; slain by Patroclus at Troy.

Saturn: *See* Cronus.

Satyrs: Hoofed demigods of woods and fields; companions of Dionysus.

Sciron: Robber; forced strangers to wash his feet, then hurled them into sea where tortoise devoured them; slain by Theseus.

Scylla: Female monster inhabiting rock opposite Charybdis; menaced passing sailors.

Selene: Goddess of moon.

Semele: Daughter of Cadmus; mother by Zeus of Dionysus; demanded Zeus appear before her in all his splendor and was destroyed by his lightnings.

Sibyis: Various prophetesses; most famous, Cumaean sibyl, accompanied Aeneas into Hades.

Sileni: Minor woodland deities similar to satyrs (singular: silenus). Sometimes Silenus refers to eldest of satyrs, son of Hermes or of Pan.

Silvanus: Roman god of woods and fields.

Sinis: Giant; bent pines, by which he hurled victims against side of mountain; slain by Theseus.

Sirens: Minor deities who lured sailors to destruction with their singing.

Sisyphus: King of Corinth; condemned in Tartarus to roll huge stone to top of hill; it always rolled back down again.

Sol: *See* Helios.

Somnus: *See* Hypnos.

Sphinx: Monster of Thebes; killed those who could not answer her riddle; slain by Oedipus. Name also refers to other monsters having body of lion, wings, and head and bust of woman.

Sterope: *See* Pleiades.

Stheno: *See* Gorgons.

Styx: *See* Rivers.

Symplegades: Clashing rocks at entrance to Black Sea; Argo passed through, causing them to become forever fixed.

Syrinx: Nymph pursued by Pan; changed to reeds, from which he made his pipes.

Tantalus: Cruel king; father of Pelops and Niobe; condemned in Tartarus to stand chin-deep in lake surrounded by fruit branches; as he tried to eat or drink, water or fruit always receded.

Tartarus: Underworld below Hades; often refers to Hades.

Taygeta: *See* Pleiades.

Telemachus: Son of Odysseus; made unsuccessful journey to find his father.

Tellus: Roman goddess of earth.

Terminus: Roman god of boundaries and landmarks.

Terpsichore: *See* Muses.

Terra: Roman earth goddess.

Thalia: *See* Graces; Muses.

Thanatos (Mors): God of death.

Themis: Titan goddess of laws of physical phenomena; daughter of Uranus; mother of Prometheus.

Theseus: Son of Aegeus; slew Minotaur; married and deserted Ariadne; later married Phaedra.

Thisbe: Beloved of Pyramus; killed herself at his death.

Thyestes: Brother of Atreus; Atreus killed three of his sons and served them to him at banquet.

Tiresias: Blind soothsayer of Thebes.

Tisiphone: *See* Furies.

Titans: Early gods from which Olympian gods were derived; children of Uranus and Gaea.

Tithonus: Mortal loved by Eos; changed into grasshopper.

Triton: Demigod of sea; son of Poseidon.

Turnus: King of Rutuli in Italy; betrothed to Lavinia; slain by Aeneas.

Ulysses: *See* Odysseus.

Urania: *See* Muses.

Uranus: Personification of Heaven; husband of Gaea; father of Titans; dethroned by his son Cronus.

Venus: *See* Aphrodite.

Vertumnus: Roman god of fruits and vegetables; husband of Pomona.

Vesta: *See* Hestia.

Vulcan: *See* Hephaestus.

Winds: Aeolus (keeper of winds), Boreas (Aquilo) (north wind), Eurus (east wind), Notus (Auster) (south wind), Zephyrus (Favonius) (west wind).

Zephyrus: *See* Winds.

Zeus (Jupiter): Chief of Olympian gods; son of Cronus and Rhea; husband of Hera.

Norse Mythology

Aesir: Chief gods of Asgard.

Andvari: Dwarf; robbed of gold and magic ring by Loki.

Angerbotha (Angrbotha): Giantess; mother by Loki of Fenrir, Hel, and Midgard serpent.

Asgard (Asgarth): Abode of gods.

Ask (Aske, Askr): First man; created by Odin, Hoenir, and Lothur.

Asynjur: Goddesses of Asgard.

Atli: Second husband of Gudrun; invited Gunnar and Hogni to his court, where they were slain; slain by Gudrun.

Audhumia (Audhumbla): Cow that nourished Ymir, created Buri by licking ice cliff.

Balder (Baldr, Baldur): God of light, spring, peace, joy; son of Odin; slain by Hoth at instigation of Loki.

Bifrost: Rainbow bridge connecting Midgard and Asgard.

Bragi (Brage): God of poetry; husband of Ithunn.

Branstock: Great oak in hall of Volsungs; into it, Odin thrust Gram, which only Sigmund could draw forth.

Brynhild: Valkyrie; wakened from magic sleep by Sigurd; married Gunnar; instigated death of Sigurd; killed herself and was burned on pyre beside Sigurd.

Bur (Bor): Son of Buri; father of Odin, Hoenir, and Lothur.

Buri (Bori): Progenitor of gods; father of Bur; created by Audhumla.

Embla: First woman; created by Odin, Hoenir, and Lothur.

Fafnir: Son of Rodmar, whom he slew for gold in Otter's skin; in form of dragon, guarded gold; slain by Sigurd.

Fenrir: Wolf; offspring of Loki; swallows Odin at Ragnarok and is slain by Vitharr.

Forseti: Son of Balder.

Frey (Freyr): God of fertility and crops; son of Njorth; originally one of Vanir.

Freya (Freyja): Goddess of love and beauty; sister of Frey; originally one of Vanir.

Frigg (Frigga): Goddess of sky; wife of Odin.

Garm: Watchdog of Hel; slays, and is slain by, Tyr at Ragnarok.

Gimle: Home of blessed after Ragnarok.

Giuki: King of Nibelungs; father of Gunnar, Hogni, Guttorm, and Gudrun.

Glathsehim (Gladsheim): Hall of gods in Asgard.

Gram (meaning "Angry"): Sigmund's sword; rewelded by Regin; used by Sigurd to slay Fafnir.

Greyfell: Sigmund's horse; descended from Sleipnir.

Grimhild: Mother of Gudrun; administered magic potion to Sigurd which made him forget Brynhild.

Gudrun: Daughter of Giuki; wife of Sigurd; later wife of Atli and Jonakr.

Gunnar: Son of Giuki; in his semblance Sigurd won Brynhild for him; slain at hall of Atli.

Guttorm: Son of Giuki; slew Sigurd at Brynhild's request.

Heimdall (Heimdallr): Guardian of Asgard.

Hel: Goddess of dead and queen of underworld; daughter of Loki.

Hiordis: Wife of Sigmund; mother of Sigurd.

Hoenir: One of creators of Ask and Embla; son of Bur.

Hogni: Son of Giuki; slain at hall of Atli.

Hoth (Hoder, Hodur): Blind god of night and darkness; slayer of Balder at instigation of Loki.

Ithunn (Ithun, Iduna): Keeper of golden apples of youth; wife of Bragi.

Jonakr: Third husband of Gudrun.

Jormunrek: Slayer of Swanhild; slain by sons of Gudrun.

Jotunnheim (Jotunheim): Abode of giants.

Lif and Lifthrasir: First man and woman after Ragnarok.

Loki: God of evil and mischief; instigator of Balder's death.

Lothur (Lodur): One of creators of Ask and Embla.

Midgard (Midgarth): Abode of mankind; the earth.

Midgard Serpent: Sea monster; offspring of Loki; slays, and is slain by, Thor at Ragnarok.

Mimir: Giant; guardian of well in Jotunnheim at root of Yggdrasill; knower of past and future.

Mjollnir: Magic hammer of Thor.

Nagifar: Ship to be used by giants in attacking Asgard at

Ragnarok; built from nails of dead men.

Nanna: Wife of Balder.

Nibelungs: Dwellers in northern kingdom ruled by Giuki.

Niflheim (Nifelheim): Outer region of cold and darkness; abode of Hel.

Njorth: Father of Frey and Freya; originally one of Vanir.

Norns: Demigoddesses of fate: Urth (Urdur) (Past), Verthandi (Verdandi) (Present), Skuld (Future).

Odin (Othin): Head of Aesir; creator of world with Vili and Ve; equivalent to Woden (Wodan, Wotan) in Teutonic mythology.

Otter: Son of Rodmar; slain by Loki; his skin filled with gold hoard of Andvari to appease Rodmar.

Ragnarok: Final destruction of present world in battle between gods and giants; some minor gods will survive, and Lif and Lifthrasir will repeople world.

Regin: Blacksmith; son of Rodmar; foster-father of Sigurd.

Rerir: King of Huns; son of Sigi.

Rodmar: Father of Regin, Otter, and Fafnir; demanded Otter's skin be filled with gold; slain by Fafnir, who stole gold.

Sif: Wife of Thor.

Siggeir: King of Goths; husband of Signy; he and his sons slew Volsung and his sons, except Sigmund; slain by Sigmund and Sinflotli.

Sigi: King of Huns; son of Odin.

Sigmund: Son of Volsung; brother of Signy, who bore him Sinflotli; husband of Hiordis, who bore him Sigurd.

Signy: Daughter of Volsung; sister of Sigmund; wife of Siggeir; mother by Sigmund of Sinflotli.

Sigurd: Son of Sigmund and Hiordis; wakened Brynhild from magic sleep; married Gudrun; slain by Guttorm at instigation of Brynhild.

Sigyn: Wife of Loki.

Sinflotli: Son of Sigmund and Signy.

Skuld: *See* Norns.

Sleipnir (Sleipner): Eight-legged horse of Odin.

Surt (Surtr): Fire demon; slays Frey at Ragnarok.

Svartalfaheim: Abode of dwarfs.

Swanhild: Daughter of Sigurd and Gudrun; slain by Jormunrek.

Thor: God of thunder; oldest son of Odin; equivalent to Germanic deity Donar.

Tyr: God of war; son of Odin; equivalent to Tiu in Teutonic mythology.

Ull (Ullr): Son of Sif; stepson of Thor.

Urth: *See* Norns.

Valhalla (Valhall): Great hall in Asgard where Odin received souls of heroes killed in battle.

Vali: Odin's son: Ragnarok survivor.

Valkyries: Virgins, messengers of Odin, who selected heroes to die in battle and took them to Valhalla; generally considered as nine in number.

Vanir: Early race of gods; three survivors, Njorth, Frey, and Freya, are associated with Aesir.

Ve: Brother of Odin; one of creators of world.

Verthandi: *See* Norns.

Vili: Brother of Odin; one of creators of world.

Vingolf: Abode of goddesses in Asgard.

Vitharr (Vithar): Son of Odin; survivor of Ragnarok.

Volsung: Descendant of Odin, and father of Signy, Sigmund; his descendants were called Volsungs.

Yggdrasill: Giant ash tree springing from body of Ymir and supporting universe; its roots extended to Asgard, Jotunnheim, and Niffheim.

Ymir (Ymer): Primeval frost giant killed by Odin, Vili, and Ve; world created from his body; also, from his body sprang Yggdrasill.

Egyptian Mythology

Aaru: Abode of the blessed dead.

Amen (Amon, Ammdn): One of chief Theban deities; united with sun god under form of Amen-Ra.

Amenti: Region of dead where souls were judged by Osiris.

Anubis: Guide of souls to Amenti; son of Osiris; jackal-headed.

Apis: Sacred bull, an embodiment of Ptah; identified with Osiris as Osiris-Apis or Serapis.

Geb (Keb, Seb): Earth god; father of Osiris; represented with goose on head.

Hathor (Athor): Goddess of love and mirth; cow-headed.

Horus: God of day; son of Osiris and Isis; hawk-headed.

Isis: Goddess of motherhood and fertility; sister and wife of Osiris.

Khepera: God of morning sun.

Khnemu (Khnum, Chnuphis, Chnemu, Chnum): Ram-headed god.

Khonsu (Khensu, Khuns): Son of Amen and Mut.

Mentu (Ment): Solar deity, sometimes considered god of war; falcon-headed.

Min (Khem, Chem): Principle of physical life.

Mut (Maut): Wife of Amen.

Nephthys: Goddess of the dead; sister and wife of Set.

Nu: Chaos from which world was created, personified as a god.

Nut: Goddess of heavens; consort of Geb.

Osiris: God of underworld and judge of dead; son of Geb and Nut.

Ptah (Phtha): Chief deity of Memphis.

Ra: God of the Sun, the supreme god; son of Nut; Pharaohs claimed descent from him; represented as lion, cat, or falcon.

Serapis: God uniting attributes of Osiris and Apis.

Set (Seth): God of darkness or evil; brother and enemy of Osiris.

Shu: Solar deity; son of Ra and Hathor.

Tem (Atmu, Atum, Tum): Solar deity.

Thoth (Dhouti): God of wisdom and magic; scribe of gods; ibis-headed.

Modern Wedding Anniversary Gift List

Anniversary	Gift	Anniversary	Gift	Anniversary	Gift
1st	Clock	10th	Diamond jewelry	19th	Bronze
2nd	China	11th	Fashion jewelry and accessories	20th	Platinum
3rd	Crystal, glass			25th	Sterling Silver Jubilee
4th	Electrical Appliances	12th	Pearls or colored gems	30th	Diamond
5th	Silverware	13th	Textiles, furs	35th	Jade
6th	Wood	14th	Gold jewelry	40th	Ruby
7th	Desk sets, pen and pencil sets	15th	Watches	45th	Sapphire
		16th	Silver hollow ware	50th	Golden Jubilee
8th	Linens, laces	17th	Furniture	55th	Emerald
9th	Leather	18th	Porcelain	60th	Diamond Jubilee

Source: Jewelry Industry Council.

AVIATION

Famous Firsts in Aviation

1782 First balloon flight. Jacques and Joseph Montgolfier of Annonay, France, sent up a small smoke-filled balloon about mid-November.

1783 First hydrogen-filled balloon flight. Jacques A. C. Charles, Paris physicist, supervised construction by A. J. and M. N. Robert of a 13-ft diameter balloon that was filled with hydrogen. It got up to about 3,000 ft and traveled about 16 mi. in a 45-min flight (Aug. 27).

First human balloon flights. A Frenchman, Jean Pilâtre de Rozier made the first captive-balloon ascension (Oct. 15). With the Marquis d'Arlandes, Pilâtre de Rozier made the first free flight, reaching a peak altitude of about 500 ft, and traveling about 5 1/2 mi. in 20 min (Nov. 21).

1784 First powered balloon. Gen. Jean Baptiste Marie Meusnier developed the first propeller-driven and elliptically-shaped balloon—the crew cranking three propellers on a common shaft to give the craft a speed of about 3 mph.

First woman to fly. Mme. Thible, a French opera singer (June 4).

1793 First balloon flight in America. Jean Pierre Blanchard, a French pilot, made it from Philadelphia to near Woodbury, Gloucester County, N.J., in a little over 45 min (Jan. 9).

1794 First military use of the balloon. Jean Marie Coutelle, using a balloon built for the French Army, made two 4-hr observation ascents. The military purpose of the ascents seems to have been to damage the enemy's morale.

1797 First parachute jump. André-Jacques Garnerin dropped from about 6,500 ft over Monceau Park in Paris in a 23-ft diameter parachute made of white canvas with a basket attached (Oct. 22).

1843 First air transport company. In London, William S. Henson and John Stringfellow filed articles of incorporation for the Aerial Transit Company (March 24). It failed.

1852 First dirigible. Henri Giffard, a French engineer, flew in a controllable (more or less) steam-engine powered balloon, 144 ft long and 39 ft in diameter, inflated with 88,000 cu ft of coal gas. It reached 6.7 mph on a flight from Paris to Trappe (Sept. 24).

1860 First aerial photographers. Samuel Archer King and William Black made two photos of Boston, still in existence.

1872 First gas-engine powered dirigible. Paul Haenlein, a German engineer, flew in a semi-rigid-frame dirigible, powered by a 4-cylinder internal-combustion engine running on coal gas drawn from the supporting bag.

1873 First transatlantic attempt. *The New York Daily Graphic* sponsored the attempt with a 400, 000 cu ft balloon carrying a lifeboat. A rip in the bag during inflation brought collapse of the balloon and the project.

1897 First successful metal dirigible. An all-metal dirigible, designed by David Schwarz, a Hungarian, took off from Berlin's Tempelhof Field and, powered by a 16-hp Daimler engine, got several miles before leaking gas caused it to crash (Nov. 13).

1900 First Zeppelin flight. Germany's Count Ferdinand von Zeppelin flew the first of his long series of rigid-frame airships. It attained a speed of 18 mi. per h and got 3 1/2 mi. before its steering gear failed (July 2).

1903 First successful heavier-than-air machine flight. Aviation was really born on the sand dunes at Kitty Hawk, N.C., when Orville Wright crawled to his prone position between the wings of the biplane he and his brother Wilbur had built, opened the throttle of their homemade 12-hp engine and took to the air. He covered 120 ft in 12 sec. Later that day, in one of four flights, Wilbur stayed up 59 sec and covered 852 ft (Dec. 17).

1904 First airplane maneuvers. Orville Wright made the first turn with an airplane (Sept. 15); 5 days later his brother Wilbur made the first complete circle.

1905 First airplane flight over half an hour. Orville Wright kept his craft up 33 min 17 sec (Oct. 4).

1906 First European airplane flight. Alberto Santos-Dumont, a Brazilian, flew a heavier-than-air machine at Bagatelle Field, Paris (Sept. 13).

1908 First airplane fatality. Lt. Thomas E. Selfridge, U.S. Army Signal Corps, was in a group of officers evaluating the Wright plane at Fort Myer, Va. He was up about 75 ft with Orville Wright when the propeller hit a bracing wire and was broken, throwing the plane out of control, killing Selfridge and seriously injuring Wright (Sept. 17).

1910 First licensed woman pilot. Baroness Raymonde de la Roche of France, who learned to fly in 1909, received ticket No. 36 on March 8.

First flight from shipboard. Lt. Eugene Ely, USN, took a Curtiss plane off from the deck of cruiser *Birmingham* at Hampton Roads, Va., and flew to Norfolk (Nov. 14). The following January, he reversed the process, flying from Camp Selfridge to the deck of the armored cruiser *Pennsylvania* in San Francisco Bay (Jan. 18).

1911 First U.S. woman pilot. Harriet Quimby, a magazine writer, who got ticket No. 37.

1913 First multi-engined aircraft. Built and flown by Igor Ivan Sikorsky while still in his native Russia.

1914 First aerial combat. In August, Allied and German pilots and observers started shooting at each other with pistols and rifles—with negligible results.

1915 First air raids on England. German Zeppelins started dropping bombs on four English communities (Jan. 19).

1918 **First U.S. air squadron.** The U.S. Army Air Corps made its first independent raids over enemy lines, in DH-4 planes (British-designed) powered with 400-hp American-designed Liberty engines (April 8).

First regular airmail service. Operated for the Post Office Department by the Army, the first regular service was inaugurated with one round trip a day (except Sunday) between Washington, D.C., and New York City (May 15).

1919 **First transatlantic flight.** The NC-4, one of four Curtiss flying boats commanded by Lt. Comdr. Albert C. Read, reached Lisbon, Portugal, (May 27) after hops from Trepassy Bay, Newfoundland, to Horta, Azores (May 16–17), to Ponta Delgada (May 20). The Liberty-powered craft was piloted by Walter Hinton.

First nonstop transatlantic flight. Capt. John Alcock and Lt. Arthur Whitten Brown, British World War I flyers, made the 1,900 mi. from St. John's, Newfoundland, to Clifden, Ireland, in 16 h 12 min in a Vickers-Vimy bomber with two 350-hp Rolls-Royce engines (June 15–16).

First lighter-than-air transatlantic flight. The British dirigible R-34, commanded by Maj. George H. Scott, left Firth of Forth, Scotland, (July 2) and touched down at Mineola, L.I., 108 h later. The eastbound trip was made in 75 h (completed July 13).

First scheduled passenger service (using airplanes). Aircraft Travel and Transport inaugurated London-Paris service (Aug. 25). Later the company started the first trans-channel mail service on the same route (Nov. 10).

1921 **First naval vessel sunk by aircraft.** Two battleships being scrapped by treaty were sunk by bombs dropped from Army planes in demonstration put on by Brig. Gen. William S. Mitchell (July 21).

First helium balloon. The C-7, non-rigid Navy dirigible was first to use non-inflammable helium as lifting gas, making a flight from Hampton Roads, Va., to Washington, D.C. (Dec. 1).

1922 **First member of Caterpillar Club.** Lt. (later Maj. Gen.) Harold Harris bailed out of a crippled plane he was testing at McCook Field, Dayton, Ohio (Oct. 20), and became the first man to join the Caterpillar Club—those whose lives have been saved by parachute.

1923 **First nonstop transcontinental flight.** Lts. John A. Macready and Oakley Kelly flew a single-engine Fokker T-2 nonstop from New York to San Diego, a distance of just over 2,500 mi. in 26 h 50 min (May 2–3).

First autogyro flight. Juan de la Cierva, a brilliant Spanish mathematician, made the first successful flight in a rotary wing aircraft in Madrid (June 9).

1924 **First round-the-world flight.** Four Douglas Cruiser biplanes of the U.S. Army Air Corps took off from Seattle under command of Maj. Frederick Martin (April 6). 175 days later, two of the planes (Lt. Lowell Smith's and Lt. Erik Nelson's) landed in Seattle after a circuitous route—one source saying 26,345 mi., another saying 27,553 mi.

1926 **First polar flight.** Then-Lt. Cmdr. Richard E. Byrd, acting as navigator, and Floyd Bennett as pilot, flew a trimotor Fokker from Kings Bay, Spitsbergen, over the North Pole and back in 15 1/2 h (May 8–9).

1927 **First solo transatlantic flight.** Charles Augustus Lindbergh lifted his Wright-powered Ryan monoplane, *Spirit of St. Louis,* from Roosevelt Field, L.I., to stay aloft 33 h 39 min and travel 3,600 mi. to Le Bourget Field outside Paris (May 20–21).

First transatlantic passenger. Charles A. Levine was piloted by Clarence D. Chamberlin from Roosevelt Field, L.I., to Eisleben, Germany, in a Wright-powered Bellanca (June 4–5).

1928 **First east-west transatlantic crossing.** Baron Guenther von Huenefeld, piloted by German Capt. Hermann Koehl and Irish Capt. James Fitzmaurice, left Dublin for New York City (April 12) in a single-engine all-metal Junkers monoplane. Some 37 h later, they crashed on Greely Island, Labrador. Rescued.

First U.S.-Australia flight. Sir Charles Kingsford-Smith and Capt. Charles T. P. Ulm, Australians, and two American navigators, Harry W. Lyon and James Warner, crossed the Pacific from Oakland to Brisbane. They went via Hawaii and the Fiji Islands in a trimotor Fokker (May 31–June 8).

First transarctic flight. Sir Hubert Wilkins, an Australian explorer and Carl Ben Eielson, who served as pilot, flew from Point Barrow, Alaska, to Spitsbergen (mid-April).

1929 **First of the endurance records.** With Air Corps Maj. Carl Spaatz in command and Capt. Ira Eaker as chief pilot, an Army Fokker, aided by refueling in the air, remained aloft 150 h 40 min at Los Angeles (Jan. 1–7).

First blind flight. James H. Doolittle proved the feasibility of instrument-guided flying when he took off and landed entirely on instruments (Sept. 24).

First rocket-engine flight. Fritz von Opel, a German auto maker, stayed aloft in his small rocket-powered craft for 75 sec, covering nearly 2 mi. (Sept. 30).

First South Pole flight. Comdr. Richard E. Byrd, with Bernt Balchen as pilot, Harold I. June, radio operator, and Capt. A. C. McKinley, photographer, flew a trimotor Fokker from the Bay of Whales, Little America, over the South Pole and back (Nov. 28–29).

1930 **First Paris–New York nonstop flight.** Dieudonné Coste and Maurice Bellonte, French pilots, flew a Hispano-powered Breguet biplane from Le Bourget Field to Valley Stream, L.I., in 37 h 18 min. (Sept. 2–3).

1931 **First flight into the stratosphere.** Auguste Piccard, a Swiss physicist, and Charles Knipfer ascended in a balloon from Augsburg, Germany, and reached a height of 51,793 ft in a 17-h flight that terminated on a glacier near Innsbruck, Austria (May 27).

First nonstop transpacific flight. Hugh Herndon and Clyde Pangborn took off from Sabishiro Beach, Japan, dropped their landing gear, and flew 4,860 mi. to near Wenatchee, Wash., in 41 h 13 min. (Oct. 4–5).

1932 **First woman's transatlantic solo.** Amelia Earhart, flying a Pratt & Whitney Wasp-powered Lockheed Vega, flew alone from Harbor Grace, Newfoundland, to Ireland in approximately 15 h (May 20–21).

First westbound transatlantic solo. James A. Mollison, a British pilot, took a de Havilland Puss Moth from Portmarnock, Ireland, to Pennfield, N.B. (Aug. 18).

First woman airline pilot. Ruth Rowland Nichols, first woman to hold three international records at the same time—speed, distance, altitude—was employed by N.Y.-New England Airways.

1933 **First round-the-world solo.** Wiley Post took a Lockheed Vega, *Winnie Mae,* 15,596 mi. around the world in 7 d 18 h 49 1/2 min (July 15–22).

1937 **First successful helicopter.** Hanna Reitsch, a German pilot, flew Dr. Heinrich Focke's FW-61 in free, fully controlled flight at Bremen (July 4).

1939 **First turbojet flight.** Just before their invasion of Poland, the Germans flew a Heinkel He-178 plane powered by a Heinkel S3B turbojet (Aug. 27).

1942 **First American jet plane flight.** Robert Stanley, chief pilot for Bell Aircraft Corp., flew the Bell XP-59 *Airacomet* at Muroc Army Base, Calif. (Oct. 1).

1947 **First piloted supersonic flight in an airplane.** Capt. Charles E. Yeager, U.S. Air Force, flew the X-1 rocket-powered research plane built by Bell Aircraft Corp., faster than the speed of sound at Muroc Air Force Base, California (Oct. 14).

1949 **First round-the-world nonstop flight.** Capt. James Gallagher and USAF crew of 13 flew a Boeing B-50A Superfortress around the world nonstop from Ft. Worth, returning to same point: 23,452 mi. in 94 h 1 min, with 4 aerial refuelings enroute (Feb. 27–March 2).

1950 **First nonstop transatlantic jet flight.** Col. David C. Schilling (USAF) flew 3,300 mi. from England to Limestone, Maine, in 10 h 1 min (Sept. 22).

1951 **First solo across North Pole.** Charles F. Blair, Jr., flew a converted P-51 (May 29).

1952 **First jetliner service.** De Havilland Comet flight inaugurated by BOAC between London and Johannesburg, South Africa (May 2). Flight, including stops, took 23 h 38 min.

First transatlantic helicopter flight. Capt. Vincent H. McGovern and 1st Lt. Harold W. Moore piloted 2 Sikorsky H-19s from Westover, Mass., to Prestwick, Scotland (3,410 mi.). Trip was made in 5 steps, with flying time of 42 h 25 min (July 15–31).

First transatlantic round trip in same day. British Canberra twin-jet bomber flew from Aldergrove, Northern Ireland, to Gander, Newfoundland, and back in 7 h 59 min flying time (Aug. 26).

1955 **First transcontinental round trip in same day.** Lt. John M. Conroy piloted F-86 Sabrejet across U.S. (Los Angeles–New York) and back—5,085 mi.—in 11 h 33 min 27 sec (May 21).

1957 **First round-the-world, nonstop jet plane flight.** Maj. Gen. Archie J. Old, Jr., USAF, led a flight of 3 Boeing B-52 bombers, powered with 8 10, 000-lb. thrust Pratt & Whitney Aircraft J57 engines around the world in 45 h 19 min; distance 24,325 mi.; average speed 525 mph. (Completed Jan. 18.)

1958 **First transatlantic jet passenger service.** BOAC, New York to London (Oct. 4). Pan American started daily service, N.Y. to Paris (Oct. 26).

First domestic jet passenger service. National Airlines inaugurated service between New York and Miami (Dec. 10).

1976 **First regularly-scheduled commercial supersonic transport (SST) flights begin.** Air France and British Airways inaugurate service (January 21). Air France flies the Paris-Rio de Janeiro route; B.A., the London-Bahrain. Both airlines begin SST service to Washington, D.C. (May 24).

1977 **First successful man-powered aircraft.** Paul MacCready, an aeronautical engineer from Pasadena, Calif., was awarded the Kremer Prize for creating the world's first successful man-powered aircraft. The *Gossamer Condor* was flown by Bryan Allen over the required 3-mile course on Aug. 23.

1978 **First successful transatlantic balloon flight.** Three Albuquerque, N.M., men, Ben Abruzzo, Larry Newman, and Maxie Anderson, completed the crossing (Aug. 16. Landed, Aug. 17) in their hot air balloon, *Double Eagle II.*

1979 **First man-powered aircraft to fly across the English Channel.** The Kremer Prize for the Channel crossing was won by Bryan Allen who flew the *Gossamer Albatross* from Folkestone, England to Cap Gris-Nez, France, in 2 h 55 min (June 12).

1980 **First successful balloon flight over the North Pole.** Sidney Conn and his wife Eleanor, in hot-air balloon *Joy of Sound* (April 11).

First nonstop transcontinental balloon flight, and also record for longest overland voyage in a balloon. Maxie Anderson and his son, Kris, completed four-day flight from Fort Baker, Calif., to successful landing outside Matane, Quebec, on May 12 in their helium-filled balloon, *Kitty Hawk.*

First long-distance solar-powered flight. Janice Brown, 98-lb former teacher, flew tiny experimental solar-powered aircraft, *Solar Challenger* six miles in 22-min near Marana, Ariz. (Dec. 3). The craft was powered by a 2.75-hp engine.

First solar-powered aircraft to fly across the English Channel. Stephen R. Ptacek flew the 210-lb *Solar Challenger* at the average speed of 30 mph from Cormeilles-en-Vexin near Paris to the Royal Manston Air Force Base on England's southeastern coast in 5 h 30 min (July 7).

Official World Airplane Records

Source: National Aeronatic Association.

Speed Over Measured Straightaway Course

Speed (mph)	Date	Type plane	Pilot	Place
314.32	Dec. 25, 1934	Caudron	Raymond Delmotte (France)	Istres, France
352.39	Sept. 13, 1935	Hughes Special	Howard Hughes (U.S.)	Santa Ana, Calif.
379.63	Nov. 11, 1937	BF-113R	Herman Wurster (Germany)	Augsburg, Germany
469.22	April 26, 1939	ME-109R	Fritz Wendel (Germany)	Augsburg, Germany
606.25	Nov. 7, 1945	Gloster Meteor IV	Group Capt. H. Wilson (U.K.)	Herne Bay, England
615.78	Sept. 7, 1946	Gloster Meteor	Group Capt. E. M. Donalson (U.K.)	Littlehampton, England
650.80	Aug. 25, 1947	Douglas D-558	Maj. Marion Carl, (USMC)	Muroc AFB, Calif.
670.98	Sept. 15, 1948	North American F-86A	Maj. R. L. Johnson (USAF)	Muroc AFB, Calif.
698.51	Nov. 19, 1952	North American F-86D	Capt. James S. Nash (USAF)	Salton Sea, Calif.
755.14	Oct. 29, 1953	North American YF	Lt. Col. F. K. Everest, Jr. (USAF)	Salton Sea, Calif.
822.27	Aug. 20, 1955	North American F-100C	Col. Horace A. Hanes (U.S.)	Palmdale, Calif.
1,132.14	March 10, 1956	Fairey Delta 2	L. Peter Twiss, D.S.C. (U.K.)	Ford-Chichester, England
1,207.60	Dec. 12, 1957	McDonnell F-101A	Maj. Adrian E. Drew (USAF)	Edwards AFB, Calif.
1,404.09	May 16, 1958	Lockheed F104	Capt. Walter W. Irwin (USAF)	Edwards AFB, Calif.
1,483.85	Oct. 31, 1959	Sukhoi S-66	G. Mossolov (U.S.S.R.)	U.S.S.R.
1,525.96	Dec. 15, 1959	F-106A Delta Wing Monoplane	Maj. Joseph W. Rogers (USAF)	Edwards AFB, Calif.
1,606.32	Nov. 22, 1961	McDonnell F4H	Lt. Col. R. B. Robinson (USMC)	Edwards AFB, Calif.
1,665.89	July 7, 1962	E-166 Jet	G. Mossolov (U.S.S.R.)	U.S.S.R.
2,070.101	May 1, 1965	Lockheed YF-12A Jet	Col. R. L. Stephens (USAF)	Edwards AFB, Calif.
2,196.17	July 28, 1976	Lockheed SR-71	Capt. Eldon W. Joersz (USAF)	Beale AFB, Calif.

Fastest U.S. continental: Capt. Robert G. Sowers (USAF)—Convair B-58 "Hustler"—from Long Beach, Calif., to Kennedy International Airport, N.Y.—2,458.58 statute miles—2 h 0 min 58.71 sec—average speed, 1,214.65 mph—March 5, 1962.

Distance, Straight Line

Distance (mi.)	Date	Crew	From	To
4,911.93	Sept. 27–29, 1929	Costes & Bellonte (France)	Le Bourget, France	Manchuria
5,011.35	July 28–30, 1931	Russel N. Boardman, John Polando (U.S.)	New York	Istanbul
5,656.93	Aug. 5–7, 1933	Maurice Rossi, Paul Codos (France)	New York	Ryack, Syria
6,305.66	July 12–14, 1937	Gromov, Youmachev, Daniline (U.S.S.R.)	Moscow	San Jacinto, Calif.
7,158.44	Nov. 5–7, 1938	Sqd. Ldr. R. Kellett (U.K.)	Ismailia, Egypt	Darwin, Australia
7,916.00	Nov. 19–20, 1945	Col. C. S. Irvine & Lt. Col. G. R. Stanley (U.S.)	Guam	Washington, D.C.
11,235.60	Sept. 29–Oct. 1, 1946	Comdr. Thomas D. Davies, Comdrs. Eugene P. Rankin, Walter S. Reid, Lt. Comdr. Ray A. Tabeling (USN)	Perth, Australia	Columbus, Ohio
12,532.28	Jan. 10–11, 1962	Maj. Clyde P. Evely (USAF)	Kadena, Okinawa	Madrid

Longest light airplane (3,858–6,614 lb) distance: Maximillian A. Conrad—U.S. Piper Comanche 250, Lycoming 0-540-AIAS (250 hp), from Casablanca, Morocco, to Los Angeles, 7,668.48 mi.—June 2–4, 1959.

Distance, Closed Circuit

Distance (mi.)	Date	Crew	Place
6,587.441	March 23–26, 1932	Bossoutrot & Rossi (France)	Oran
7,239.588	May 13–15, 1938	Comdr. Fujita & Sgt. Maj. Takahashi (Japan)	Kisarasu, Japan
8,037.899	July 30–Aug. 1, 1939	Angelo Tondi, Roberto Dagasso, Ferrucio Vignoli (Italy)	Rome
8,854.308	Aug. 1–2, 1947	Lt. Col. O. F. Lassiter (U.S.) Capt. W. J. Valentine (U.S.)	Tampa, Fla.
10,078.84	Dec. 13–14, 1960	Lt. Col. J. R. Grissom (USAF)	Edwards AFB, Calif.
11,336.92	June 6–7, 1962	Capt. William Stevenson (USAF)	Seymour-Johnson, N.C.

Altitude

Height (ft)	Date	Crew	Place
44,819	Sept. 28, 1933	G. Lemoine (France)	Villacoublay, France
47,352	April 11, 1934	Comdr. Renato Donati (Italy)	Rome
49,944	Sept. 28, 1936	Sqd. Ldr. F. R. D. Swain (U.K.)	South Farnborough, England
53,937	June 30, 1937	Fl. Lt. M. J. Adam (U.K.)	Farnborough, England
56,046	Oct. 22, 1938	Col. Mario Pezzi (Italy)	Montecelio

Altitude

Height (ft)	Date	Crew	Place
59,445[1]	March 23, 1948	John Cunningham (U.K.)	Hatfield, England
63,668[1]	May 4, 1953	Walter F. Gibb (U.K.)	Bristol, England
65,889[1]	Aug. 29, 1955	Walter F. Gibb (U.K.)	Bristol, England
70,308[1]	Aug. 28, 1957	Michael Randrup (U.K.)	Luton, England
91,243[1]	May 7, 1958	Maj. H. C. Johnson (USAF)	Palmdale, Calif.
103,389[1]	Nov. 14, 1959	Capt. Joe B. Jordan (USAF)	Edwards AFB, Calif.
314,750[2]	July 17, 1962	Maj. Robert M. White (USAF)	Edwards AFB, Calif.
118,898	July 25, 1973	Alexander Fedotov (U.S.S.R.)	U.S.S.R.
123,524	Aug. 31, 1977	Alexander Fedotov (U.S.S.R.)	U.S.S.R.

1. Jet-propelled aircraft. 2. X-15-1-rocket plane.

World's 50 Busiest Airports in 1983

Airport	Passengers[1]
1 O'Hare International: Chicago	42,873,953
2 Hartsfield Atlanta International: Atlanta	37,919,802
3 International: Los Angeles	33,426,731
4 Kennedy International: New York	27,904,474
5 Dallas/Ft. Worth Airport	26,785,852
6 Heathrow Airport: London	26,749,200
7 Stapleton International: Denver	25,247,105
8 International: San Francisco	23,166,500
9 International: Miami	19,321,718
10 La Guardia: New York	18,813,397
11 Boston-Logan International	17,848,797
12 International: Newark	17,411,253
13 Frankfurt/Main: West Germany	17,030,197
14 International: Osaka	16,363,168
15 Orly Airport: Paris	16,258,117
16 Lambert-St. Louis International	16,241,311
17 International: Honolulu	15,261,993
18 National Airport: Washington, D.C.	14,166,345
19 International: Toronto	13,662,828
20 Charles de Gaulle: Paris	13,410,935
21 Intercontinental: Houston	12,984,616
22 Fiumicino Airport: Rome	12,494,694
23 Gatwick Airport: London	12,476,800
24 International: Pittsburgh	11,832,371
25 International: Mexico City	11,699,350
26 Madrid-Barajas Airport	10,157,784
27 Sea-Tac International: Seattle	10,141,737
28 McCarran International: Las Vegas	10,057,479
29 Schiphol Airport: Amsterdam	9,679,792
30 Metropolitan: Detroit	9,606,053
31 International: Philadelphia	9,498,104
32 International: Minneapolis-St. Paul	9,075,531
33 International: Hong Kong	8,850,308
34 Palma Airport: Spain	8,735,716
35 Sky Harbor International: Phoenix	8,605,408
36 Copenhagen Airport Kastrup	8,285,211
37 Zurich Airport	8,255,591
38 International: Tampa	8,228,049
39 King Abdulaziz International: Saudi Arabia	8,101,600
40 International: Orlando	7,990,542
41 Charlotte/Douglas International	7,756,166
42 Changi Airport: Rep. of Singapore	7,635,553
43 Duesseldorf Airport	7,136,112
44 International: Salt Lake City	7,059,964
45 International: San Diego	6,547,439
46 Bombay Airport: India	6,351,567
47 Munich-Riem Airport	6,073,229
48 Linate International: Milan	5,978,559
49 International: New Orleans	5,896,694
50 Ft. Lauderdale-Hollywood International	5,700,618

1. Enplaned, deplaned, and transfer, in millions. *Source:* Airport Operators Council International.

U.S. Airlines Transport Planes, 1984

Manufacturer	Type/Series	Number of passengers	Cruise speed	Range	Wingspan, ft	Length, ft
4-ENGINE JET						
Boeing	707-120B	100–181	615	6,325	142.4	145.1
Boeing	707-320B	145	615	5,750	145.8	152.9
Boeing	747-SP	331	564	6,730	195.7	184.8
Boeing	747 PAX	452	557	6,500	195.7	231.9
Boeing	747 PAX/FRT	238	600	5,500	195.7	231.9
British Aerospace	146-100	88	460	1,450	86.4	85.9
British Aerospace	146-200	100	460	1,450	86.4	93.8
McDonnell Douglas	DC8-30,-40,-50	116/176	544	7,010	142.2	150.3
McDonnell Douglas	DC8-60,-70	259	580	7,150	142.2	187.4
McDonnell Douglas	DC8 PAX/FRT	180/259	600	3,700	142.2	187.4
4-ENGINE TURBOPROP						
DeHavilland	DHC7	50	275	850	93.0	80.0
Lockheed	L188	66/104	405	2,750	99.0	104.5
Lockheed	L382	Cargo	380	2,750	99.0	104.5
4-ENGINE PISTON						
DeHavilland	Heron	14/17	195	750	71.5	46.5
McDonnell Douglas	DC6	90/100	300	3,070	117.5	101.5

Manufacturer	Type/Series	Number of passengers	Cruise speed	Range	Wingspan, ft	Length, ft
3-ENGINE JET						
Boeing	727 All Series	70/131	622	3,000	108.0	133.1
Boeing	727 PAX/FRT	96	600	3,000	108.0	133.1
Boeing	727-200	145	622	2,400	108.0	153.1
Boeing	727F	Cargo	620	1,400	108.0	153.1
Lockheed	L1011	250/400	615	3,450	155.2	177.5
Lockheed	L1011	266/330	580	5,998	155.2	164.2
McDonnell Douglas	DC10-10	250/380	608	6,350	155.2	182.2
McDonnell Douglas	DC10-30	250/380	615	6,350	165.3	181.6
McDonnell Douglas	DC10-40	250/350	615	6,350	165.3	182.3
2-ENGINE JET						
Boeing	737-100	105	577	1,300	93.0	94.0
Boeing	737-200	115/130	573	1,800	92.0	100.1
Boeing	737-200	115/130	577	2,300	93.0	100.1
Boeing	757	178/224	494	2,440	124.5	155.2
Boeing	767	211/290	550	3,200	156.1	159.1
Fokker	F28	85	523	1,055	82.2	96.2
British Aerospace	BAC111	74/79	550	1,430	88.5	93.5
McDonnell Douglas	DC9-10,-20	90	593	2,200	93.2	104.4
McDonnell Douglas	DC9-30,-40	125	593	2,700	93.2	125.5
McDonnell Douglas	DC9-30/40	139	593	2,550	93.2	133.2
McDonnell Douglas	DC9-80	137/172	576	3,060	107.9	147.9
Marcel Dassault	Falcon-10	4–7	600	2,000	42.9	45.5
Marcel Dassault	Falcon-20	12–14	600	3,300	53.5	56.3
2-ENGINE TURBOPROP						
Beechcraft	B-99	15	280	1,150	45.8	44.5
British Aerospace	Jetstream	14/18	250	1,440	52.0	47.0
British Aerospace	748	48	244	2,760	98.5	67.0
CASA	C-212	22/28	230	1,400	62.5	45.9
Convair	CV-580	50	350	1,100	105.2	79.1
DeHavilland	DHC-6	20	209	745	65.0	51.8
Embraer	EMB110	19	212	900	50.1	49.1
Fairchild	F-27	40/56	265	1,450	95.1	82.1
Fairchild Hiller	FH-227	44/52	294	1,520	95.1	83.1
Fokker	FK F27	40/56	265	1,450	95.1	82.1
Fairchild Swrngn	SA226	19	294	2,139	46.2	59.2
Fairchild Swrngn	SA227	21	302	2,139	46.2	59.2
Gulfstream Aerospace	GAG159	18/37	345	2,300	78.3	75.3
Nihon	YS-11	60	292	1,980	105.0	86.2
Nord	ND262	27	240	500	71.9	63.2
Nord	ND STC 262	25	240	500	74.1	63.2
Short Bro-Harland	SH SD3	30	218	1,137	94.7	58.0
2-ENGINE PISTON						
Beechcraft	BE18	7–9	236	1,515	49.7	35.2
Britten-Norman	BN2	10	180	425	49.0	35.7
Britten-Norman	BN 3MK3	18	180	530	53.0	43.7
Cessna	310	4–6	210	600	32.0	37.0
Cessna	402	6–10	239	550	36.0	40.0
Cessna	404	6–11	200	1,500	40.0	46.3
Convair	440	50	270	1,100	105.3	79.1
Curtis Wright	CW46					
Douglas	DC3	21	207	1,330	95.0	64.5
Douglas	DC4	44/60	230	2,750	117.6	94.0
Douglas	DC6	52/80	309	3,070	117.6	106.5
DeHavilland	DH114	20	207	750	65.0	51.8
Grumman	G21	10	160	825	49.0	38.2
Grumman	G73	10	180	1,245	66.6	48.2
Piper	PA23	6	206	1,519	37.2	31.1
Piper	PA31	6	210	925	40.8	34.5
Piper	PA34	6	220	1,036	39.0	28.5
Piper	PA44	4	190	1,000	38.5	27.5

NOTE: Aircraft performance statistics represented here are to be considered only as "typical" of an aircraft type. Due to the various series (models) of individual aircraft types and the engine options available, it is not feasible to show all the various combinations of performance statistics. Data show the most used manufacturers type and model aircraft used by air carriers and commercial operators as of April 1984. *Source:* Federal Aviation Administration.

Important American Aircraft Types (U.S. Air Force)

Abbreviations: GA—Garrett AiResearch; All—Detroit Diesel Allison Div. of General Motors; Con—Continental; GD—General Dynamics; GE—General Electric; Lyc—Lycoming; RI—Rockwell International; P&W—Pratt & Whitney; PWC—Pratt & Whitney Aircraft of Canada, Ltd; Wr—Curtiss Wright; kt—knots.

Type	Manufacturer	Popular name	Power plant	Crew	Wing-span, ft/in.	Length, ft/in.	Height, ft/in.	Gross weight, lb	Speed, mph
ATTACK									
A-70	LTV Aerospace	Corsair II	1 All TF41-A-1	1	38/9	46/1	16/0	42,000	698
A-10A	Fairchild Hiller	Thunderbolt II	2 GE TF34-GE-100	1	57/5	53/3	14/6	46,038	449
A-37B	Cessna	Dragonfly	2 GE J85-GE-17A	1	35/8	29/3	8/9	14,000	507
BOMBERS									
B-52D	Boeing	Stratofortress	8 P&W J57-P-29W	6	185/0	156/6	48/4	450,000	650
B-52G	Boeing	Stratofortress	8 P&W J57-P-43W	6	185/0	161/11	40/8	488,000	650
B-52H	Boeing	Stratofortress	8 P&W TF33-P-3	6	185/0	159/3	40/8	488,000	650
FB-111A	GD/Ft. Worth	—	2 P&W TF30-P-7	2	70/0[3]	73/6	17/0	114,000	Mach 2+
FIGHTERS									
F-4D/E	McDonnell Douglas	Phantom II	2 GEJ79-GE-17	2	38/7	63/0	16/5	61,975	Mach 2.2
F-15A/B/C/D	McDonnell Douglas	Eagle	2 P&W F100-PW-100	1/2	42/8	63/8	18/6	56,000	Mach 2.5
F-5E/F	Northrop	Tiger II	2 J85-GE-21A	1/2	25/3	47/2	13/2	24,676	Mach 1.6
F-16A	GD/Ft. Worth	—	1 P&W F100-PW-200	1	32.10	47/6	16/4	22,000	Mach 2
F-106A	GD/Convair	Delta Dart	1 P&W J75-P-17	1/2	38/3	70/8	20/3	36,000	Mach 2.3
F-111	GD/Ft. Worth	—	2 P&W TF30-P-3/100(F)	2	63/0[4]	73/6	17/0	100,000	Mach 2.5
F-101B	McDonnell Douglas	Voodoo	2 P&W J57-P-55	2	39/8	67/4	18/0	46,500	Mach 1.85
RECONNAISSANCE									
RF-4C	McDonnell Douglas	Phantom II	2 GE J79-GE-17	2	38/7	63/0	16/5	61,795	Mach 2.2
SR-71	Lockheed/Calif.	—	2 P&W J58	2	55/6	107/4	18/5	170,000	Mach 3
U/WU-2	Lockheed/Calif.	—	1 P &W J75	1	80/0	49/6	13/0	19,850	400 kt
OBSERVATION									
0-2A	Cessna		2 Con 10-360-D	2	38/0	29/2	9/5	5,400	199
OV-10A[1]	RI/Columbus	Bronco	2 T76-G-416/417	2	40/0	39/7	15/1	14,466	281
EARLY WARNING COMMAND, CONTROL AND COMMUNICATIONS									
E-3A	Boeing		4 P&W TF33-P-100/A	17	145/9	152/1	42/0	325,000	530
E-4A/B	Boeing	—	4 GE CF6-50E	5	195/7	231/3	63/5	803,000	—
CARGO/TRANSPORT									
C-5A	Lockhead/Georgia	Galaxy	4 GE TF39-GE-1C	7	222/8	245/9	65/1	764,500	550
C-9A	McDonnell Douglas	Nightingale	2 P&W JT8D-9	2-7	93/3	119/3	27/5	108,000	570
C-12A[2]	Beech		2 PWC PT6A-38	2	54/5	43/6	14/6	12,500	260 kt
C-130E/H	Lockheed/Georgia	Hercules	4 All T56-A-7/-15(H)	5	132/6	99/5	38/4	155,000	360
C-140A	Lockheed/Georgia	Jetstar	4 P&W J60-P-5	5	54/4	60/4	20/4	40,921	525
C-141A	Lockheed/Georgia	Starlifter	4 P&W TF33-P-7	4-9	160/7	145/0	39/3	325,000	505
KC-10A	McDonnel Douglas	Extender	3 GE CF6-50C2	5	165.4	182.3	58.1	590,000	528
KC-135A	Boeing	Stratotanker	4 P&W J57-P-59W	4	130/9	136/3	38/4	297,000	530
C-137C	Boeing	Stratoliner	4 P&W JT3D-3B	4	145/9	152/9	42/5	328,000	627
TRAINERS									
CT-39	RI/General Aviation	Sabreliner	2 P&W J60-P-3	2	44/5	43/8	15/9	18,650	595
T-33A	Lockheed/Calif.	Shooting Star	1 All J33-A-35	2	38/9	37/7	11/7	15,100	505
T-37B	Cessna	Tweet	2 CAE J69-T-25	2	33/8	29/3	9/2	6,575	425
T-38A	Northrop	Talon	2 GE J85-5	2	25/3	46/4	12/1	12,500	Mach 1.2
T-41C	Cessna	Mescalero	1 CON 10-360-D	2	36/2	26/5	8/9	2,550	142
T-43A	Boeing	—	2 P&W JT8D-9	2	93/0	100/0	37/0	115,500	Mach .7

1. Air Force/Marines. 2. Air Force/Army. 3. Wing extended; 34 ft fully swept. 4. Wing extended; 31.11 ft fully swept. *Source:* Department of the Air Force.

Lower Ozone Levels for Air Passengers

Ozone in airplanes has been linked with respiratory and skin problems. Air passengers usually encounter high ozone levels in aircraft cabins during transoceanic or high-altitude flights. According to new regulations, the ozone levels within an airplane cannot exceed 0.3 parts per million.

Ozone is a gaseous allotrope of oxygen and is a powerful bleaching, poisonous, oxidizing agent with a pungent, irritating odor. It is used commercially to purify and deodorize air, to sterilize water, and as a bleach.

Helicopter Records

Source: National Aeronautic Association.

Distance in Straight Line
International: 2,213.04 mi.; 3,561.55 km.
Robert G. Ferry (U.S.) in Hughes YOH-6A helicopter powered by Allison T-63-A-5 engine; from Culver City, Calif., to Daytona Beach, Fla., April 6–7, 1966.

Distance, Closed Circuit
International: 1,739.96 mi.; 2,800.20 km.
Jack Schweibold (U.S.) in Hughes YOH-6A helicopter powered by Allison T-62-A-5 engine; Edwards Air Force Base, Calif., March 26, 1966.

Altitude
International: 40,820 ft; 12,442 m.
Jean Boulet (France) in Alouette SA 315-001 "Lama" powered by Artouste IIIB 735 KW engine; Istres, France, June 21, 1972.

Speed Over a 15/25-Km Course
International: 228.91 mph; 368.4 kph.
Gourguen Karapetyan (U.S.S.R.) in A-10 helicopter powered by 2 TB-3-117 engines; Podmoskovnoye, U.S.S.R., Sept. 21, 1978.

Altitude in Horizontal Flight
International: 36,122 ft; 11,010 m.
CWO James K. Church, (U.S.) in Sikorsky CH-54B helicopter powered by 2 P&W JFTD-12 engines; Stratford, CT., Nov. 4, 1971.

Speed Over a 3-Km Course
216,839 mph; 348.971 kph.
Byron Graham (U.S.) at Windsor Locks, CT, Dec. 14, 1970 in Sikorsky S-67 Helicopter powered by 2 GE T-58 turbine engines.

Speed Around the World
35.34 mph; 56.88 kph.
H. Ross Perot, Jr., pilot; J.W. Coburn, co-pilot (U.S.) in Bell 206 L-II Long Ranger, powered by one Allison 250-C28B of 435 hp. Elapsed time: 29 days 3 h 8 min 13 sec, Sept. 1–30, 1982.

Speed for 100 Km (Closed Circuit)
International: 211.35 mph; 340.15 kph.
Boris Galitsky (U.S.S.R.) in MI-6 helicopter powered by 2 TB-2BM turbine engines; Podmoskovnoye, U.S.S.R., Aug. 26, 1964.

Speed for 500 Km (Closed Circuit)
International: 214.84 mph; 345.74 kph.
Thomas Doyle (U.S.) in Sikorsky S-76 helicopter powered by 2 Allison 250-C-30 engines; West Palm Beach, Fla., Feb. 8, 1982.

Speed for 500 Km (Closed Circuit)
International: 205.688 mph; 331.023 kph.
Galina Rastorgoueva (U.S.S.R.) in A-10 helicopter powered by 2 TV2 117A engines; Ramenskoye, U.S.S.R., Aug. 1, 1975.

Speed for 1,000 Km (Closed Circuit)
International: 200.48 mph; 322.646 kph.
Galina Rastorgoueva (U.S.S.R.) in A-10 helicopter powered by 2 TV2 117A engines; Aug. 13, 1975.

Speed for 2,000 Km (Closed Circuit)
International: 146.09 mph; 235.119 kph.
Inna Kopets (U.S.S.R.) in MI-8 helicopter; Sept. 14, 1967.

Active Pilot Certificates Held

(as of January 1)

Year	Total	Airline transport	Commercial	Private
1970	720,028	31,442	176,585	299,491
1975	733,728	41,002	192,425	305,848
1980	814,667	63,652	182,097	343,276
1981	827,071	69,569	183,442	357,479
1982	764,182	70,311	168,580	328,562
1983	733,255	73,471	165,093	322,094
1984	718,004	75,938	159,495	318,643

1. Includes other pilot categories—helicopter, glider and lighter-than-air: and students. *Source:* Department of Transportation, Federal Aviation Administration.

Average Hours and Earnings in Aircraft Industries

Hours and earnings	1983	1982	1981	1980	1975	1970	1965	1960
Average weekly hours								
Aircraft industries	40.8[1]	40.9	41.3	41.8	41.2	40.6	41.7	40.6
Engines and parts industries	41.0	40.7	40.5	41.8	40.9	n.a.	n.a.	n.a.
Average weekly earnings								
Aircraft industries	$513.67[1]	$484.67	$443.56	$403.79	$255.85	$169.30	$131.36	$110.03
Engines and parts industries	$476.01	$454.21	$421.61	$393.76	$247.04	n.a.	n.a.	n.a.
Average hourly earnings								
Aircraft industries	$12.54[1]	$11.85	$10.74	$9.66	$6.21	$4.17	$3.15	$2.71
Engines and parts industries	$11.61	$11.16	$10.41	$9.42	$6.09	n.a.	n.a.	n.a.

1. Ten-month average. NOTE: n.a. = not available. *Source:* U.S. Department of Labor, Bureau of Labor Statistics, July 1984.

WHERE TO FIND OUT MORE

Reference Books And Other Sources

This cannot be a record of all the thousands of available sources of information. Nevertheless, these selected references will enable the reader to locate additional facts about many subjects covered in the *Information Please Almanac.* The editors have chosen sources that they believe will be helpful to the general reader.

General References

Encyclopedias are a unique category, since they attempt to cover most subjects quite thoroughly. The most valuable multivolume encyclopedias are the **Encyclopaedia Britannica** and the **Encyclopedia Americana.** Useful one-volume encyclopedias are the **New Columbia Encyclopedia** and the **Random House Encyclopedia.**

Dictionaries and similar "word books" are also unique: **The American Heritage Dictionary, Second College Edition,** containing 200,000 definitions and specialized usage guidance; **Webster's II New Riverside University Dictionary,** containing 200,000 definitions plus hundreds of word history paragraphs; and the multivolume **Oxford English Dictionary,** providing definitions in historical order. **Roget's II The New Thesaurus,** containing thousands of synonyms grouped according to meaning, assists writers in choosing just the right word. The quick reference set—**The World Book II** (over 40,000 words spelled and divided), **The Right Word II** (a concise thesaurus), and **The Written Word II** (a concise guide to writing, style, and usage)—are based on **The American Heritage Dictionary** and are intended for the busy reader needing information fast. Two excellent books of quotations are **Bartlett's Familiar Quotations** and **The Oxford Dictionary of Quotations.**

There are a number of useful atlases: the **New York Times Atlas of the World,** a number of historical atlases (Penguin Books), **Oxford Economic Atlas of the World, Rand McNally Cosmopolitan World Atlas: New Census Edition,** and **Atlas of the Historical Geography of the United States** (Greenwood). Many contemporary road atlases of the United States and foreign countries are also available.

A source of information on virtually all subjects is the United States Government Printing Office (GPO). For information, write: Superintendent of Documents, Washington, D.C. 20402.

For help on any subject, consult: **Subject Guide to Books in Print, The New York Times Index,** and the **Reader's Guide to Periodical Literature** in your library.

Specific References

America Votes (Congressional Quarterly, Inc.)
American Indian, Reference Encyclopedia of the (B. Klein Publications)
Antiques, Collector's Complete Dictionary of American (Doubleday)
Architecture, Encyclopedia of World (VanNostrand Reinhold)
Art, History of (Prentice-Hall)
Art, Oxford Companion to (Oxford University Press)
Art, Who's Who in American (R.R. Bowker)
Art Directory, American (R.R. Bowker)
Asian-Americans, Who's Who Among (Beacon Presse IA)
Associations, Encyclopedia of (Gale Research Co.)
Auctions and Flea Markets, U.S., Collector's Guide to (Penguin Books)
Authors, 1000–1900, European (H.W. Wilson)
Authors, 1600–1900, American (H.W. Wilson)
Authors, Twentieth Century (H.W. Wilson)
Automobile Facts and Figures (Kallman)
Automobile Year Book of Models (Norton)
Automobile Year Book of Sports Car Racing (Norton)
Banking and Finance, Encyclopedia of (Bankers Publishing Co.)
Baseball Encyclopedia (Macmillan)
(Baseball) **World Series Record Book** (Sporting News)
Basketball, Encyclopedia of (Prentice-Hall)
Biographical Dictionary, Chambers (Littlefield)
Biography Yearbook, Current (H.W. Wilson)
Birds, Field Guide to, Peterson Field Guide Series (Houghton Mifflin)
Black Americans, Who's Who Among (Who's Who Among Black Americans, Inc.)
Book Review Digest, 1905– (H.W. Wilson)
Business and Investment Almanac, Dow Jones-Irwin (Dow Jones-Irwin)
Catholic Encyclopedia, New (Publishers Guild)
Chemistry, Encyclopedia of (VanNostrand Reinehold)
Chemistry and Physics, Handbook of (Chemical Rubber Co. Press)
Christian Church, Oxford Dictionary of the (Oxford University Press)
Churches, Yearbook of American and Canadian (Abingdon Press)
Citizens Band: Radio Service Rules and Regulations (Federal Communications Commission, Government Printing Office)
Communist Affairs, Yearbook on International (Hoover Institution Press)
Composers, Great 1300–1900 (H.W. Wilson)
Composers Since 1900 (H.W. Wilson)
Computer Science and Technology, Encyclopedia of (Dekker)
Computer Terms, Encyclopedia of (Barron)
Condo and Co-op Information Book, Complete (Houghton Mifflin)
Congressional Quarterly Almanac (Congressional Quarterly, Inc.)
(Consumer) **HELP: The Indispensable Almanac of Consumer Information, 1981** (Everest House)
Consumer Reports (Consumers Union)
Drama, Crowell's Handbook of Classical (T.Y. Crowell)
Drama, Crowell's Handbook of Contemporary (T.Y. Crowell)
Ecology Information and Organizations, Guide to (H.W. Wilson)
Energy Factbook (McGraw-Hill)
Environment, Living With Our (U.S. Department of the Interior, Government Printing Office)

Environmental Science (Holt, Rinehart & Winston)
Europa Year Book (Gale Research Co.)
Fact Books, The Rand McNally (Rand)
Facts, Famous First (H.W. Wilson)
Facts on File (Facts on File, Inc.)
Film, Oxford Companion to (Oxford University Press)
Filmgoer's Companion (Avon)
Fishing: An Encyclopedia Guide to Tackle and Tactics for Fresh and Salt Water (Dutton)
Food and Drink, Dictionary of American (Ticknor & Fields)
Football, Encyclopedia of (A.S. Barnes & Co.)
Game, Rules of the (Bantam Books)
Gardening, Encyclopedia of (Houghton Mifflin)
Gardening for Food and Fun (U.S. Department of Agriculture, Government Printing Office)
Geography, Dictionary of (Penguin Books)
Government Manual, U.S. (U.S. Office of the Federal Register, Government Printing Office)
Handicapped Americans, Who's Who Among (Beacon Presse IA)
Hispanic or Spanish-surnamed Americans, Who's Who Among (Beacon Presse IA)
History, Album of American (Scribner's)
History, Dictionary of American (Rowman)
History, Documents of American (Prentice-Hall)
History, Encyclopedia of Latin-American (Greenwood)
History, Encyclopedia of World (Houghton Mifflin)
Ice Hockey A-Z (Lothrop)
Islam, Dictionary of (Orient Book Distributors)
Jazz in the Seventies, Encyclopedia of (Horizon)
Jewish Concepts, Encyclopedia of (Hebrew Publishers)
Job Outlook in Brief, The (U.S. Bureau of Labor Statistics, Government Printing Office)
Legal Word Book, The (Houghton Mifflin)
Libraries, World Guide to (Gale Research Co.)
Library Directory, American (R.R. Bowker)
Literary History of the United States (Macmillan)
Literature, Oxford Companion to American (Oxford University Press)
Literature, Oxford Companion to Classical (Oxford University Press)
Literature, Oxford Companion to English (Oxford University Press)
(Literature) **Reader's Adviser: A Layman's Guide to Literature** (R.R. Bowker)
Literature, Reader's Encyclopedia of American (T.Y. Crowell)
Medical Adviser, Modern Home (Doubleday)
Medical & Health Sciences Word Book, The (Houghton Mifflin)
Museums, Directory of World (Columbia University Press)
Music and Musicians, Handbook of American (Da Capo)
Music, Concise Oxford Dictionary of (Oxford University Press)
Music, Harvard Dictionary of (Harvard University Press)
Musical Terms, Dictionary of (Gordon Press)
Mythology: An Illustrated Encyclopedia (Rizzoli International)
Nations, Handbook of New (T.Y. Crowell)
Nations, Wordmark Encyclopedia of the (Wiley-Interscience)
Native Americans, Who's Who Among (Beacon Presse IA)
Pain, Coping With Chronic (Sister Kenney Institute)
Pocket Data Book, U.S.A. (U.S. Department of Commerce, Bureau of the Census, Government Printing Office)
Poetry, Granger's Index to (Columbia University Press)
Politics, Almanac of American (Gambit, Inc.)
Politics, Who's Who in American (R.R. Bowker)
Private Schools, Handbook of (Porter Sargent)
Publications, Ayer Directory of (IMS Press)
Recreational Vehicle Handbook, The Rand McNally (Rand)
Robert's Rules of Order Revised (Morrow & Co.)
Science, American Men and Women of (R.R. Bowker)
Science and Technology, Asimov's Biographical Encyclopedia of (Doubleday)
Scientific Encyclopedia, VanNostrand's (VanNostrand Reinhold)
Secretary's Handbook, The Professional (Houghton Mifflin)
Sports Talk, Encyclopedia of (Corwin)
Stars and Planets, Field Guide to the (Houghton Mifflin)
States, Book of (Council of State Governments)
Statesman's Year-Book (St. Martin's)
Theater, Oxford Companion to the (Oxford University Press)
Theater, Who's Who in the (Gale Research Co.)
(Travel) **The Birnbaum Guides** (Houghton Mifflin)
United Nations, Demographic Yearbook (U.N. Publishing Service)
United Nations, Statistical Yearbook of the (U.N. Publishing Service)
United States, Historical Statistics of the (U.S. Department of Commerce, Bureau of the Census, Government Printing Office)
United States, Statistical Abstract of the (U.S. Department of Commerce, Bureau of the Census, Government Printing Office)
Washington Information Directory (Congressional Quarterly, Inc.)
Weather Book, The American (Houghton Mifflin)
Who's Who in America (Marquis)
Who's Who in Canada (International Publications Service)
Women, Notable American (Harvard University Press)
Zip Code and Post Office Directory, National (U.S. Postal Service, Government Printing Office)

See the full range of publications of Dun & Bradstreet and Standard & Poor's for corporate financial and stockholder information.

For detailed information on American colleges and universities, see the many publications of the **American Council on Education.**

Also see many other specialized **Who's Who** volumes not listed here for biographies of famous people in many fields.

Working Mothers Are on the Rise

According to the U.S. Department of Labor, about six out of 10 mothers with preschool or school-age children were in the labor force in March 1984. In 1970, only four of 10 mothers were working. Mothers of children under three account for much of the increase.

TOLL-FREE NUMBERS

A Directory of Useful Toll-Free Numbers

The following selection of useful "800" numbers has been compiled to give consumers a valuable source of free information at the federal and private levels. Please note that the numbers and services listed are subject to change.

Should you desire to find out if there are "800" numbers for airlines, hotels, motels, car rentals, and businesses in your area, dial locally 1+800 555-1212 and ask the operator.

AIDS
AIDS Hotline
U.S. Public Health Service
1 800 342-AIDS
1 202 245-6867 (Alaska and Hawaii residents may call collect)
Hours: 8:30–5:30, Mon.–Fri.

A recording provides the latest information to the public about Acquired Immune Deficiency Syndrome (AIDS).

AUTOMOBILE
Auto Safety Hotline
National Highway Traffic Safety Administration
202 426-0123 (Washington, D.C.)
1 800 424-9393 (Elsewhere)
Hours: 8:00–4:00 Mon.–Fri.
Answering service after hours.

Handles complaints on safety-related defects, and receives reports of vehicle safety problems. Provides information and in some cases literature on:

- motor vehicle safety recalls
- car seats
- automobile equipment
- tires
- motor homes
- drunk driving
- gas mileage

BANKING
Federal Deposit Insurance Corporation
202 389-4353 (Washington, D.C.)
1 800 424-5488 (Elsewhere)
Hours: 9:00–5:00, Mon.–Fri.

Receives complaints and provides information on the consumer banking laws.

Federal Home Loan Bank Board
202 377-6988 (Washington, D.C.)
1 800 424-5405 (Elsewhere)
Hours: 24-hour recording

Provides information on federal adjustable mortgage rates.

BLIND
National Federation of the Blind
1 800 638-7518

Provides job information. Concerned about the rights of the blind.

CHILD ABUSE
Parents Anonymous
1 800 352-0386 (California)
1 800 462-6406 (New York)
1 800 421-0353 (Elsewhere)
Hours: 9:00–5:00 Mon.–Fri. however, there is a 24-hour hotline.

Self-help group for parents with abuse problems.

COCAINE ABUSE
1 800 COCAINE
Hours: 24 hours—7days

Provides information on Cocaine and help for Cocaine abusers and drug-related problems.

CONGRESSIONAL LEGISLATION
Toll-Free Number for checking status of bills submitted to Congress.
1 800 342-9860

COOPERATIVE EXTENSION SERVICE
The Cooperative Extension Service is a three-way partnership involving the U.S. Department of Agriculture, the state land-grant universities, and county governments. The Extension staff provides information and education programs for children and adults on food, nutrition, gardening, money management, and a variety of other subjects. To find your toll-free local listing, consult the telephone directory under your state's land-grant university or your county government.

DEPARTMENT OF DEFENSE
1 800 424-9098 (Washington, D.C.)
223-5080 (Autovon Line)
693-5080 (FTS)
Hours: 8:00–5:30

Operated for citizens to report suspected cases of fraud and waste involving the Department of Defense. The anonymity of callers will be respected.

ENERGY
Conservation and Renewable Energy Inquiry and Referral Service
1 800 462-4983 (Pennsylvania)
1 800 233-3071 (Alaska and Hawaii)
1 800 523-2929 (Elsewhere)
Hours: 9:00–5:00 Mon.–Fri.

Provides non-technical information on solar, wind, and other energy heating and cooling technologies, energy conservation, and alcohol fuels.

ENVIRONMENT

Hazardous Waste

Environmental Protection Agency
202 382-3000 (Washington, D.C.)
1 800 424-9346 (Elsewhere)
Hours: 8:30–4:30 Mon.–Fri.

Provides information and interpretation of federal hazardous waste regulations. Will provide referrals regarding other hazardous waste matters.

Pesticide Hotline

National Pesticide Information Clearinghouse
1 800 858-7378
Hours: 24 hours—7 days

Provides information on pesticides.

HANDICAPPED

Library of Congress

202 287-5100 (Washington, D.C.)
1 800 424-8567 (Elsewhere)
Hours: 8:00–4:30, Mon.–Fri.
Answering service after hours.

Provides information on programs and books for the blind and physically handicapped.

HEALTH CARE

Cancer Information Service

National Cancer Institute
National Institutes of Health
Department of Health & Human Services
202 636-5700 (Washington, D.C., and suburbs in Maryland and Virginia)
808 524-1234 (Hawaii) (neighboring islands call collect)
1 800 638-6070 (Alaska)
1 800 422-6237 (National Cancer Institute)
1 800 4-Cancer (Elsewhere)
Hours: 9:00–5:00, Mon.–Fri.

Provides information on cancer treatment and ongoing research; fills requests for pamphlets and other literature on cancer.

National Health Information Clearinghouse

Department of Health & Human Services
703 522-2590 (Washington, D.C., Virginia, Alaska, and Hawaii)
1 800 336-4797 (Elsewhere)
Hours: 8:30–5:00 Mon.–Fri.

Provides referrals to sources of information on health-related issues.

HOUSING

Housing Discrimination Hotline

Fair Housing and Equal Opportunity
Department of Housing & Urban Development
202 426-3500 (Washington, D.C.)
1 800 424-8590 (Elsewhere)
Hours: 8:00–4:30 Mon.–Fri.
Answering service after hours.

Receives housing discrimination complaints due to race, color, religion, sex or national origin.

INSURANCE

Federal Crime Insurance

Federal Emergency Management Administration
202 652-2637 (Washington, D.C. and Maryland—will accept collect calls from MD)
1 800 638-8780 (Elsewhere)
Hours: 9:00–5:00 Mon.–Fri.
Answering service after hours.

Provides information on federal crime insurance for both homes and businesses.

Federal Flood Insurance

Federal Emergency Management Admin.
202 897-5900 (Washington, D.C.)
1 800 492-6605 (Maryland)
1 800 638-6831 (Alaska, Hawaii, Puerto Rico, Virgin Islands, Guam)
1 800 638-6620 (Elsewhere)
Hours: 8:00–5:00 Mon.–Fri.

Provides information on community participation in the flood program (emergency or regular). If the community does not have a program, it is not eligible for government-subsidized insurance relief. Complaints are referred to the proper office within the agency.

PARENTS WITHOUT PARTNERS, INC.

1 800 638-8078
Hours: 8:30-5:00, Mon.-Fri.

Nonprofit organization for all single parents in U.S. and Canada with over 1,000 chapters nationwide. Helps single parents with raising children, has social and educational programs, and sponsors family activities.

PRODUCT SAFETY

Consumer Product Safety Commission

202 492-6800 (Washington, D.C.)
1 800 638-2772 (Elsewhere)
Hours: 8:30–5:00 Mon.–Fri.

Provides information on the safety of consumer products. Receives reports of product-related deaths, illnesses, and injuries. Products are not rated or recommended.

RUNAWAYS

National Runaway Hotline

1 800 231-6946 (U.S.A. except Texas)
1 800 392-3352 (Texas)
Hours: 24 hours—7 days

Helps runaways by referring them to shelters, clinics, local hotlines. Will relay messages from parents to the runaway.

VIETNAM VETERANS

Vietnam Veterans of America

1 800 424-4275
Hours: 24 hours, 7 days

Answering machine takes messages for information and help. Provides information on Agent Orange.

Understanding Computerspeak From A to Z

A Guide to Computer Terminology

Source: Information Please Almanac and Electronic Industries Association

While computers may not yet be for everyone, we are all aware of their rapidly increasing use in business and industry. In addition, more and more families are buying personal home computers, children are being taught to use them in school, and, recently, several institutions of higher learning have required their students to use personal computers for classroom work.

If you are unfamiliar with personal computer terminology and would like to gain some familiarity with it, the following glossary has been prepared by *Information Please Almanac* to help you attain some "computer literacy."

An excellent source of free information is the 50-page booklet published by the Electronic Industries Association, entitled "How To Buy A Home Computer." It covers all the basics about personal computers that you should know in easy-to-understand language. In order to obtain an individual copy, send your request with a self-addressed, stamped (54¢) 6 × 9-in. envelope or larger, to the Electronic Industries Association, Consumer Electronics Group, 2001 "Eye" Street, N.W., Washington, D.C. 20006.

Acoustic Coupler: A portable device for connecting two compatible computers together via the telephone lines using an ordinary telephone. An acoustic coupler is a modem that avoids the need for making a direct connection to the telephone line. (*See* Modem.)
Address: A binary-coded instruction that identifies where a specific unit of information is stored in the computer's memory. Without the address, it would be nearly impossible to find anything that you have stored.
Alphanumeric: Letters and numbers.
ASCII: American Standard Code for Information Interchange, an encoding system for converting keyboard characters and instructions into the binary number code that the computer understands. (*See* Machine Language.)
Assembler: A computer program language that translates assembly language instructions into machine language (the language of 0's and 1's).
BASIC: Beginner's All-Purpose Symbolic Code. This is the most widely used simple and direct language for beginners to use on their home computers. It can inform you when you have made a mistake. BASIC has a broad range of applications and can accept both mathematical formulas and the strings of characters used for word processing. There are many versions of BASIC.
Baud Rate: The speed of data transmission measured in bits per second. Home computers usually have baud rates between 300 and 1500 bits per section.
Binary: A numbering system that uses only two digits, 0 and 1. While computers are marvelous machines and operate at lightning-fast speeds, they are also "stupid" and can *only* add. And they can only add in 0's and 1's.
Bit: (Stands for binary digit). It is the smallest piece of computer information and is either the number 0 or 1. All information is given to the computer in the binary number system. With proper coding, the computer can "understand" any number, letter, punctuation mark, or symbol through an appropriate combination of the numbers 0 and 1.
Boot: To start up a program.
Bug: A malfunction due to an error in the program or a defect in the equipment.
Byte: Most computers use combinations of eight bits to represent one character of data. These eight-bit combinations are called bytes. Bytes can represent data or instructions. For example, the word "cat" has three characters, and it would be represented by three bytes. (NOTE: There are also 16-bit systems.)
Cassette: The least expensive home computer storage device is an ordinary special high quality cassette tape and standard audio cassette recorder. While cassette recorders are convenient, they are also slow. If the information that you want is at the end of the tape, you will have to search at "fast forward" or "reverse" speed before you come to the point you want.
Chip: A tiny wafer of silicon containing miniature electric circuits which can store over eight million bits of information.
COBOL: Common Ordinary Business-Oriented Language. A programming language for large business computers that is intended for record-keeping functions. COBOL programs for home computers are rare.
CP/M[R]: Control Program for Microcomputers. A popular operating system.
CPU: Central Processing Unit. The "brains" or part of a computer where all the incoming information is controlled and executed by its electronic circuitry.
CRT: Cathode Ray Tube. A visual device similar to your television screen that lets the computer operator see what he is doing. Many personal computers are sold without a CRT and allow you to use your home television screen as a CRT.
Cursor: A moving position-indicator displayed on the video screen (CRT) that shows the computer operator where he is working.
Database: A program that enables you to create and update files of information in a well-organized manner.
Debug: Computer slang for finding and correcting in a computer program or equipment malfunction. (*See* Bug).
Disk: A faster, but considerably more expensive mass storage device than the cassette. On large computers, disks are hard and are about the same size as a phonograph record. Home computers use smaller disks, 8 or 5 1/4 inches in diameter. Because they are made from a flexible mylar plastic, they are sometimes called *floppy disks*, or *diskettes.* Floppies can hold between 50K and 1.2 million bytes, but their main advantage is speed. Any information stored on a disk can be located in a fraction of a second with a disk drive.
Disk Drive: The machine that a disk is inserted into so that information may be stored or retrieved from the disk.
Documentation: The instruction manual for a piece of hardware or software.
DOS: Disk Operating System. A program for controlling the storage of information on a disk.

Glitch: The cause of an unexpected malfunction.
Graphics: Pictorial matter such as charts, graphs, and diagrams that can be programmed into a computer's video display.
Graphics Terminal: A specially designed CRT that can display intricate, detailed drawings and diagrams in black and white and in color. (*See* Light Pen.)
Hard Copy: A permanent record of what you have done on the computer in the form of a paper printout.
Hardware: The physical and mechanical components of a computer system. They include electronic circuitry, chips, screens, disk drives, keyboards, and printers.
Hexidecimal: A machine language written in a 16-base number system. In "Hex," the digits are 0 through 9, plus A, B, C, D, E, and F.
I/O: Input/output. Information into or out of a computer.
Input: Data that goes into a computer device.
Interface: A device that connects a computer with a peripheral so that they can communicate with each other.
K: An abbreviation for kilobyte (1024 bytes). Computer memories are measured in terms of the number of bytes they can store. Therefore, a 64K memory means that the computer can handle 64 × 1024 or 65,536 bytes.
Language: A special set of symbols, characters, and numbers that you use to communicate with the computer.
Light Pen: A special pencil-size writing instrument that can be attached to the computer terminal by a cable that allows you to draw on the screen (CRT) with it. You can even erase part of your drawing or text with it and you can enter this information into the computer.
Machine Language: The CPU or "brains" of the computer can only understand instructions written in binary form (bits of 0's and 1's). The commands the operator gives the computer are translated into data by the computer using the two-digit binary number system.
Memory: A computer device or series of devices that store information.
Microcomputer: A small personal computer containing a central processing unit (CPU) and one or more memory circuits. Some personal computers contain a complete microprocessor and memory on a single silicon chip.
Microprocessor: A complete central processing unit (CPU) contained on a single silicon chip.
Modem (modulator-demodulator): A device that will connect two compatible computers together by a direct connection to the telephone line. Modems accomplish this by converting the computer's data into an audio signal.
Mouse: A small hand-held device for controlling the cursor movement on the screen (CRT) by moving the "mouse" back and forth on a desk.
Octal: A machine language that is written in an eight-base number system, 0 through 7.
Output: Data that comes out of a computer device.
Peripherals: Extra equipment for the computer that will extend its usefulness and capability. Most peripherals either increase the computer's storage capacity or permit it to communicate with outside devices.
Printer: A mechanical device for making a permanent printed record of your computer's output on paper.
Program: A precise series of instructions written in a computer language that tells the computer what to do and how to do it. Programs are also called "software."
RAM: Random Access Memory. One of two basic types of memory. RAM is a memory that you can add to, retrieve from, or alter at will. RAM is also called Read/Write Memory. (*See* ROM.)
ROM: Read-Only Memory. One of the two basic types of memory. As its name implies, information in it cannot be altered by the computer operator. It can be transferred out, but not transferred in. ROM contains only permanent information put there by the manufacturer. (*See* RAM.)
Software: The various computer programs. These include the many computer games and business, personal, financial, and educational programs that are available for home computers.
User: The person who is using the computer.
User Friendly: It means that the system and the instructions for it are supposed to be written in simple language and be easy to operate for people with a nontechnical background.

Will Compact Discs Replace LP's?

A revolutionary new technology for recording and playback systems has been developed jointly by Sony Corp. and Philips N.V. that may eventually replace the conventional stereo record and audio turntable. Called the compact disc (CD) player, it utilizes a tiny laser beam in place of the traditional stylus to read recorded audio information from a reflective 4 3/4-inch disc. In addition to the small diameter, the compact disc carries more music than a 12-inch LP and yields up to one whole hour of playing time on only one side.

In some respects the CD player unit operates like a turntable and, in others, it works like a tape deck. In some models, you front load the digital encoded disc into a drawer like a cassette tape. You press a start button and the disc is loaded and cued automatically. There is no stylus to fuss with. A laser beam reads a series of microscopic pits encoded within the disc surface and translates it back into sound. The disc rotates from 200 to 500 rpm's depending on what section of the disc is being played. Some player models have special features such as a search capability. At the touch of a button, an automatic sensor will allow you to leap from song to song, forward or backward. You can even fast forward or reverse while listening to the program. You can repeat the track being played, the entire disc, or only repeat any material between two points that you select.

The discs are made of coated aluminum and have a protective plastic coating that prevents fingerprints or scratches from affecting the quality of sound.

In making the digital recordings, sound is converted into binary bits (yes or no or, in this case, pits or not pits) of information similar to that used in computers. This information is stored in microscopic pits within the disc's surface. There are about 15 million pits in a one-hour recording. A laser beam measuring 1.7 microns (a micron is one millionth of a meter) in diameter aimed at the disc is sensitive enough to discern each tiny pit with unerring accuracy. The resulting sound is free from distortion, hiss, wow, and flutter.

U.S. SOCIETIES & ASSOCIATIONS

Source: Information Please questionnaires to organizations. Names are listed alphabetically according to key word in title; figure in parentheses is year of founding; other figure is membership.

Abortion Federation, National (1976): 900 Pennsylvania Ave. S.E., Washington, D.C., 20003. 285; Barbara Radford, Executive Director.

Abortion Rights Action League, National (1969): 1424 K St., N.W., Washington, D.C. 20005. 145, 000; Nanette Falkenberg, Executive Director.

Accountants, American Institute of Certified Public (1887): 1211 Avenue of the Americas, New York, N.Y. 10036. 207,000; Philip B. Chenok, President.

Accountants, National Association of (1919): 10 Paragon Dr., Montvale, N.J., 07645. 96,000; Robert L. Shultis, Executive Director.

Actors' Equity Association (1913): 165 W. 46th St., New York, N.Y. 10036. 35,000; Alan Eisenberg, Executive Secretary.

Actuaries, Society of (1949): 500 Park Blvd., Itasca, Ill. 60143. 9,300; John E. O'Connor, Jr., Executive Director.

Aeronautic Association, National (1905): 821 15th St., N.W., Washington, D.C. 20005. 200, 000; Ev Langworthy, Executive Director.

Aeronautics and Astronautics, American Institute of (1932): 1633 Broadway, New York, N.Y. 10019. 31,000; James J. Harford, Executive Director.

African-American Institute, The (1953): 833 United Nations Plaza, New York, N.Y. 10017. Donald B. Easum, President.

AFS International/Intercultural Programs (1947): 313 E. 43rd St., New York, N.Y. 10017. 100, 000; William M. Dyal, Jr., President.

Air Force Association (1946): 1501 Lee Highway, Arlington, Va., 22209. 200,000; Russell E. Dougherty, Executive Director.

Air Line Pilots Association (1931): 1625 Massachusetts Ave., N.W., Washington, D.C. 20036. 33, 000; Henry A. Duffy, President.

Air Pollution Control Association (1907): P.O. Box 2861, Pittsburgh, Pa. 15230. 8,000; G. Steve Hart, Executive Vice President.

Alcohol Problems, American Council on (1900): 2908 Patricia Dr., Des Moines, Iowa 50322. 3,500. William N. Plymat, Executive Director.

Alcoholics Anonymous (1935): P.O. Box 459, Grand Central Station, New York, N.Y. 10163. 1,000,000. Address communications to General Service Office.

America-Mideast Educational and Training Services (AMIDEAST) (1951): 1717 Massachusetts Ave., N.W., Washington, D.C. 20036. 350; Orin D. Parker, President.

American Federation of Labor and Congress of Industrial Organizations (AFL-CIO) (1955): 815 16th St., N.W., Washington, D.C. 20006. 14,000, 000; Murray Seeger, Director of Information.

American Friends Service Committee (1917): 1501 Cherry St., Philadelphia, Pa. 19102. Paul E. Brink, Director of Information.

American Indian Affairs, Association on (1923): 432 Park Ave. S., New York, N.Y. 10016. 50, 000; Steven Unger, Executive Director.

American Legion, The (1919): P.O. Box 1055, Indianapolis, Ind. 46206. 2,650,000; Robert W. Spanogle, National Adjutant.

American Legion Auxiliary (1919): 777 N. Meridian St., Indianapolis, Ind. 46204. 950,000; Miriam Junge, National Secretary.

Americans for Democratic Action (1947): 1411 K St., N.W., Washington, D.C. 20005. 75,000; Leon Shull, National Director.

Amnesty International/USA (1966): 304 W. 58th St., New York, N.Y. 10019. 13,000; John G. Healey, Executive Director.

AMVETS (American Veterans of World War II, Korea, and Vietnam) (1944): 4647 Forbes Blvd., Lanham, Md. 20706. 200,000; Morgan S. Ruph, National Executive Director.

AMVETS National Auxiliary (1946): Saco Rd., Old Orchard Beach, Me. 04064. 60,000. Rita J. Potvin, Executive Secretary.

Animal Protection Institute of America (1968): 5894 S. Land Park Dr., P.O. Box 22505, Sacramento, Calif. 95822. Belton P. Mouras, President.

Animals, The American Society for the Prevention of Cruelty to (1866): 441 E. 92nd St., New York, N.Y. 10028. 70,000; John F. Kullberg, President.

Animals, Fund For (1967): 200 W. 57th St., New York, N.Y. 10019. 175,000; Cleveland Amory, President.

Anti-Defamation League of B'nai B'rith (1913): 823 United Nations Plaza, New York, N.Y. 10017. Nathan Perlmutter, National Director, Kenneth Bialkin, Chairman.

Anti-Vivisection Society, The American (1883): Suite 204, Noble Plaza, 801 Old York Rd., Jenkintown, Pa. 19046. 15,000; William A. Cave, President.

Arbitration Association, American (1926): 140 W. 51st St., New York, N.Y. 10020. 4,502; E. W. Dippold, Corporate Secretary.

Architects, American Institute of (1857): 1735 New York Ave., N.W., Washington, D.C. 20006. 38,000; Louis L. Marines, Executive Vice President.

Army, Association of the United States (1950): 2425 Wilson Blvd., Arlington, Va. 22201. 150, 000; Robert F. Cocklin, Executive Vice President.

Arthritis Foundation (1948): 1314 Spring St., N.W., N.E., Atlanta, Ga. 30309. 71 local chapters; Clifford M. Clarke, CAE, President.

Arts and Letters, American Academy and Institute of (1898): 633 W. 155th St., New York, N.Y. 10032. 250; Margaret M. Mills, Executive Director.

Astronomical Society, American (1899): Louisiana State University, Box BK, LSU Observatory, Baton Rouge, La. 70803. 4,000; Arlo U. Landolt, Secretary.

Audubon Society, National (1905): 950 Third Ave., New York, N.Y. 10022. 510,000; Michael Mezo, Information Services.

Authors League of America (1912): 234 W. 44th St., New York, N.Y. 10036. 12,000; Helen A. Stephenson, Administrator.

Automobile Association, American (1902): 8111 Gatehouse Rd., Falls Church, Va. 22047. 24,800, 000; J. B. Creal, President.

Automobile Club, National (1924): One Market Plaza, San Francisco, Calif. 94105. 427,780; Gene Halliburton, President and Chief Executive Officer.

Bar Association, American (1898): 750 N. Lake Shore Dr., Chicago, Ill. 60637. 300,000; Thomas H. Gonser, Executive Director and Chief Operating Officer.

Barber Shop Quartet Singing in America, Society for the Preservation and Encouragement of (1938): 6315 Third Ave., Kenosha, Wis., 53140. 38,000; Hugh Ingraham CAE, Executive Director.

Bible Society, American (1816): 1865 Broadway, New York, N.Y. 10023. 600,000; Charles W. Baas, Alice E. Ball, John D. Erickson, General Officers.

Big Brothers/Big Sisters of America (1977): 117 S. 17th St., Suite 1200, Philadelphia, Pa. 19103. Betty Larkin, Director of Communications.

Blind, National Federation of the (1940): 1800 Johnson St., Baltimore, Md. 21230. 50,000; Kenneth Jernigan, President.

Blindness, National Society to Prevent (1908): 79 Madison Ave., New York, N.Y. 10016. 26 affiliates; Lisa Semple, Executive Director.

Blue Cross and Blue Shield Association (1946 and 1948): 676 St. Clair, Chicago, Ill. 60611. 100 affiliates. Duane R. Carlson, Vice President, Communications.

B'nai B'rith International (1843): 1640 Rhode Island Ave., N.W., Washington, D.C. 20036. 500, 000; Hank Siegel, Press Officer.

Boy Scouts of America (1910): 1325 Walnut Hill Lane, Irving, Tex. 75038. 4,668,953.

Boys Clubs of America (1906): 771 First Ave., New York, N.Y. 10017. 1,200,000.

Broadcasters, National Association of (1922): 1771 N St., N.W., Washington, D.C. 20036. 5,000; Edward Fritts, President.

Brookings Institution, The (1927): 1775 Massachusetts Ave., N.W., Washington, D.C. 20036. Margaret M. Rhoades, Public Affairs Director.

Campers & Hikers Association, National (1949): 7172 Transit Rd., Buffalo, N.Y. 14221. 30,000 families. Fran Opela, National Office Manager.

Camp Fire, Inc. (1910): 4601 Madison Ave., Kansas City, Mo. 64112. 500,000; Arnold E. Sherman, National Executive Director.

Camping Association, The American (1910): Bradford Woods, Martinsville, Ind. 46151. 6,000; Armand Ball, Executive Vice President.

Cancer Society, American (1913): 777 Third Ave., New York, N.Y. 10017. 2,300,000 volunteers; Lane W. Adams, Executive Vice President.

CARE (Cooperative for American Relief Everywhere) (1945): 660 First Ave., New York, N.Y. 10016. 23 agencies plus 14 public members; Philip Johnston, Executive Director.

Catholic Bishops, National Conference of (1966): 1312 Massachusetts Ave., N.W., Washington, D.C. 20005. 340; Most Rev. John R. Roach, President.

Catholic Charities, National Conference of (1910): 1346 Connecticut Ave., N.W., Washington, D.C. 20036. 2,750 individuals, 850 agencies and institutions; Fr. Thomas J. Harvey, Executive Director.

Catholic Conference, United States (1966): 1312 Massachusetts Ave., N.W., Washington, D.C. 20005. Rev. Daniel F. Hoye, General Secretary.

Catholic Daughters of the Americas (1903): 10 W. 71st St., New York, N.Y. 10023. 165,000; Lorraine McMahon, Executive Secretary.

Catholic War Veterans of the U.S.A. (1935): 2 Massachusetts Ave., N.W., Washington, D.C. 20001. 50,000; Edward R. Ross, National Commander.

Cerebral Palsy Associations, United (1949): 66 E. 34th St., New York, N.Y. 10016. 250 affiliates; James E. Introne, Executive Director.

Chamber of Commerce of the U.S. (1912): 1615 H St., N.W., Washington, D.C. 20062. 220,486; Richard L. Lesher, President.

Chartered Life Underwriters, American Society of (1929): 270 Bryn Mawr Ave., Bryn Mawr, Pa. 19010. 30,000; John R. Driskill, Executive Vice President.

Chemical Engineers, American Institute of (1908): 345 E. 47th St., New York, N.Y. 10017. 60,000; J. Charles Forman, Executive Director and Secretary.

Chemical Society, American (1876): 1155 16th St., N.W., Washington, D.C. 20036. 120,000; John K. Crum, Executive Director.

Chess Federation, United States (1939): 186 Rt. 9W, New Windsor, N.Y. 12550. 54,000; Gerard J. Dullea, Executive Director.

Child Welfare League of America (1920): 67 Irving Pl., New York, N.Y. 10003. Zelma J. Felten, Acting Executive Director.

Chiropractic Association, American (1963): 1916 Wilson Blvd., Arlington, Va. 22201. 18,880; G.M. Brassard, Executive Vice President.

Christians and Jews, National Conference of (1928): 71 Fifth Ave., New York, N.Y. 10003. 200,000; Jacqueline G. Wexler, President.

Churches, National Council of (1950): 475 Riverside Drive, New York, N.Y. 10115. 31 Protestant and Orthodox communions; Claire Randall, General Secretary.

Civil Engineers, American Society of (1852): 345 E. 47th St., New York, N.Y. 10017. 95,000; Edward O. Pfrang, Executive Director.

Civil Liberties Union, American (1920): 132 W. 43rd St., New York, N.Y. 10036. 250,000; Alan Reitman, Associate Director.

Colleges, Association of American (1915): 1818 R St., N.W., Washington, D.C. 20009. 600 institutions; Mark H. Curtis, President.

Colored Women's Clubs, National Association of (1896): 5808 16th St., N.W., Washington, D.C. 20011. 40,000; Mrs. Otelia E. Champion, National President.

Common Cause (1970): 2030 M St., N.W., Washington, D.C. 20036. 250,000; Archibald Cox, Chairman.

Composers, Authors, and Publishers, American Society of (ASCAP) (1914): One Lincoln Plaza, New York, N.Y. 10023. 30,000; Hal David, President.

Congress of Racial Equality (CORE) (1942): 1916–38 Park Ave., New York, N.Y. 10037. Nationwide network of chapters; Roy Innis, National Chairman.

Conscientious Objectors, Central Committee for (1948): 2208 South St., Philadelphia, Pa. 19146.

Consumer Federation of America (1968): 1314 14th St., N.W., Washington, D.C. 20005. 220 member organizations; Stephen Brobeck, Executive Director.

Consumers Union (1936): 256 Washington St., Mt. Vernon, N.Y. 10553. 2,800,000 subscribers to *Consumer Reports;* Rhoda H. Karpatkin, Executive Director.

Contract Bridge League, American (1927): P.O. Box 161192, Memphis, Tenn. 38186. 200,000; Ralph Cohen, Executive-Director.

Cooperative League of the U.S.A. (1916): 1828 L St., N.W., Suite 1100, Washington, D.C. 20036.

35,000,000 families; E. Morgan Williams, President.

Country Music Association (1958): Box 22299, Nashville, Tenn. 37202. 7,500; Jo Walker-Meador, Executive Director.

Crime and Delinquency, National Council on (1907): 760 Market St.; Suite 433, San Francisco, Calif. 94102. Nationwide membership; Barry Krisberg, President.

Daughters of the American Revolution, National Society (1890): 1776 D St., N.W., Washington, D.C. 20006. 212,000; Mrs. Walter Hughey King, President General.

Daughters of the Confederacy, United (1894): 328 N. Boulevard, Richmond, Va. 23220. 27,000.

Deaf, National Association of the (1880): 814 Thayer Ave., Silver Spring, Md. 20910. Albert T. Pimentel, Executive Director.

Defenders of Wildlife (1925): 1244 19th St. N.W., Washington, D.C. 20036. 65,000; Daniel C. Smith, Director of Public Information.

Defense Preparedness Association, American (1919): 1700 N. Moore St., Arlington, Va. 22209. 40,000; H.A. Miley, Jr., President.

Democratic Club, National (1834): Chemists Club, 52 E. 41st St., New York, N.Y. 10017. 500; John G. Treacy, Secretary.

Dental Association, American (1859): 211 E. Chicago Ave., Chicago, Ill. 60611. 140,000; John M. Coady, Executive Director.

Diabetes Association, American (1940): 2 Park Ave., New York, N.Y. 10016. Robert S. Bolan, Executive Vice President.

Dignity (1969): 1500 Massachusetts Ave., N.W., Suite 11, Washington, D.C. 20005. 5,000; John Hager, President.

Disabled American Veterans (1922): P.O. Box 14301, Cincinnati, Ohio 45214. 861,000; Richard M. Wilson, Assistant National Adjutant for Public Relations.

Ducks Unlimited (1937): One Waterfowl Way, Long Grove, Ill. 60047. 550,000; Dale E. Whitesell, Executive Vice President.

Eagles, Fraternal Order of (1898): 2401 W. Wisconsin Ave., Milwaukee, Wis. 53233. 795,000; Robert W. Hansen, Publications Editor.

Easter Seal Society, The National (1921): 2023 W. Ogden Ave., Chicago, Ill. 60612. 49 affiliated state societies; John R. Garrison, Executive Director.

Eastern Star, Order of, (1876): 1618 New Hampshire Ave., N.W., Washington, D.C. 20009. 3,000,000; Carol C. Strizek, Most Worthy Grand Matron.

Education Association, National (1857): 1201 16th St., N.W., Washington, D.C. 20036. 1,600,000; Don Cameron, Executive Director.

Electrochemical Society, The (1902): 10 S. Main St., Pennington, N.J. 08534. 5,320; Roque J. Calvo, Assistant Executive Secretary.

Elks of the U.S.A., Benevolent and Protective Order of the (1868): 2750 Lake View Ave., Chicago, Ill. 60614. 1,650,000; Stanley F. Kocur, Grand Secretary.

English-Speaking Union of the United States (1920): 16 E. 69th St., New York, N.Y. 10021. 32,000; John D. Walker, Executive Director.

Exploration Geophysicists, Society of (1930): P.O. Box 3098, Tulsa, Okla. 74101. 19,000; John Hyden, Executive Director.

Family Physicians, American Academy of (1947): 1740 W. 92nd St., Kansas City, Mo. 64114. 56,500; Roger Tusken, Executive Vice President.

Family Service America (1911): 44 E. 23rd St., New York, N.Y. 10010. 268 member agencies; Geneva B. Johnson, President and Chief Executive Officer.

Farm Bureau Federation, American (1919): 225 Touhy Ave., Park Ridge, Ill. 60068. 3.3 million member families; J. Patrick Batts, Director of Information.

Fellowship of Reconciliation (1915): Box 271, Nyack, N.Y. 10960. 33,000; Richard Baggett Deats, Executive Secretary.

Fleet Reserve Association (1924): 1303 New Hampshire Ave., N.W., Washington, D.C. 20036. 163,000; Robert W. Nolan, National Executive Secretary.

Foreign Policy Association (1918): 205 Lexington Ave., New York, N.Y. 10016. Thetis Reavis, Vice President for Public Affairs.

Foreign Relations, Council on (1921): 58 E. 68th St., New York, N.Y. 10021. 2,213; Winston Lord, President.

Foreign Study, American Institute for (1965): 102 Greenwich Ave., Greenwich, Conn. 06830. 250,000; Henry C. Kahn, President.

Foreign Trade Council, Inc., National (1914): 10 Rockefeller Plaza, New York, N.Y. 10020. Over 650 companies; Richard W. Roberts, President.

Foster Parents Plan International (1937). Box 804, East Greenwich, R.I. 02818. George W. Ross, International Executive Director.

4-H Program (early 1900s): Room 5035S, U.S. Department of Agriculture, Washington, D.C. 20250. 5,200,000; Eugene Williams, Deputy Administrator.

Friends of the Earth (1969): 1045 Sansome St., San Francisco, Calif. 94111. 30,000; Rafe Pomerance, President.

Future Farmers of America (1928): 5632 Mt. Vernon Hgwy, Alexandria, Va. 22309. 468,953; Larry D. Case, National Advisor.

Future Homemakers of America (1945): 1910 Association Dr., Reston, Va. 22091. 400,000; Mildred Reel, Executive Director.

Gamblers Anonymous Fellowship: Box 17173, Los Angeles, Calif. 90017. 7,000; Jim Z., National Executive Secretary.

Geographic Society, National (1888): 17th and M Sts., N.W., Washington, D.C. 20036. 10,600,000; Gilbert M. Grosvenor, President.

Gideons International, The (1889): 2900 Lebanon Rd., Nashville, Tenn. 37214. 80,000; M.A. Henderson, Executive Director.

Girls Clubs of America (1945): 205 Lexington Ave., New York, N.Y. 10016. 220,000; Margaret Gates, National Executive Director.

Girl Scouts of the U.S.A. (1912): 830 Third Ave., New York, N.Y. 10022. 2,829,000; Rhoda Pauley, Communications Services.

Hadassah, The Women's Zionist Organization of America (1912): 50 W. 58th St., New York, N.Y. 10019. 370,000; Judith Manelis, Executive Director.

Health, Physical Education, Recreation, and Dance, American Alliance for (1885): 1900 Association Dr., Reston, Va. 22091. 50,000; Dr. Jack E. Razor, Executive Vice President.

Hearing and Speech Action, National Association for (1910): 10801 Rockville Pike, Rockville, Md. 20852. 1500.

Heart Association, American (1924): 7320 Greenville Ave., Dallas, Tex. 75231. 115,000; Dudley Hafner, Executive Vice President.

Hemispheric Affairs, Council on (1975): 1900 L St., N.W., Washington, D.C. 20036. Laurence R. Birns, Director.

Historical Association, American (1884): 400 A St., S.E., Washington, D.C. 20003. 15,000; Samuel R. Gammon, Executive Director.

Home Economics Association, American (1909): 2010 Massachusetts Ave., N.W., Washington, D.C. 20036. 32,000.

Horticultural Society, American (1922): Box 0105, Mt. Vernon, Va. 22121. 45,000; Charles A. Huckins, Executive Director.

Hospital Association, American (1898): 840 N. Lake Shore Dr., Chicago, Ill. 60611, 6271 institutions; J. Alexander McMahon, President.

Humane Association, American (1877): 9725 E. Hampden, Denver, Colo. 80231.

Humane Society of the United States (1954): 2100 L St., N.W., Washington, D.C. 20037. 225, 000; Patrick B. Parkes, Vice President for Field Services.

Indian Rights Association (1882): 1505 Race St., Philadelphia, Pa. 19102. 1,400; Sandra L. Cadwalader, Executive Director.

Interfraternity Conference, National (1909): 3901 W. 86th St., Indianapolis, Ind. 46268. 57; Jonathan J. Brant, Executive Director.

Jaycees, The United States (1920): P.O. Box 7, Tulsa, Okla. 74121. 272,000; Sam Willits, Executive Vice President.

Jewish Appeal, United (1939): 1290 Avenue of the Americas, New York, N.Y. 10104. Stanley B. Horowitz, President.

Jewish Committee, American (1906): 165 E. 56th St., New York, N.Y. 10022. 40,000; Morton Yarmon, Director of Public Relations.

Jewish Community Centers, World Confederation of (1946): 15 E. 26th St., New York, N.Y. 10010. Haim Zipori, Executive Director.

Jewish War Veterans of the U.S.A. (1896): 1811 R Street, N.W., Washington, D.C. 20009.

Jewish Women, National Council of (1893): 15 E. 26th St., New York, N.Y. 10010. Dadie Perlov, Executive Director.

John Birch Society (1958): 395 Concord Ave., Belmont, Mass. 02178. Under 100,000; Charles J. Humphries, Clerk of Corporation.

Journalists, Society of Professional, Sigma Delta Chi (1909): 840 N. Lake Shore Dr., Chicago, Ill. 60611. 30,000; Russell C. Tornabene, Executive Officer.

Judaism, American Council for (1943): 298 Fifth Ave., New York, N.Y. 10001. 10,000; Clarence L. Coleman, Jr., President.

Junior Achievement (1919): 550 Summer St., Stamford, Conn. 06901. 6,750,000; Glenn V. Gardinier, National Public Relations Director.

Junior Leagues, Association of (1921): 825 Third Ave., New York, N.Y. 10022. 160,000.

JWB (1917): 15 E. 26th St., New York, N.Y. 10010. 275 affiliated community centers, YM-YWHAs, and camps; Arthur Rotman, Executive Vice President.

Kennel Club, American (1884): 51 Madison Ave., New York, N.Y. 10010. 438 member clubs; Mark T. Mooty, Secretary.

Kiwanis International (1915): 3636 Woodview Terrace, Indianapolis, Ind. 46286. 300,000; J. William Kleindorfer, International Secretary.

Knights of Columbus (1882): One Columbus Plaza, New Haven, Conn. 06507. 1,395,106; Virgil C. Dechant, Supreme Knight.

Knights of Pythias, Supreme Lodge (1864): 47 N. Grant St., Stockton, Calif. 95202. 104,736; Jule O. Pritchard, Supreme Secretary.

Knights Templar, Grand Encampment of (1816): 14 E. Jackson Blvd., Suite 1700, Chicago, Ill. 60604. 340,000; Paul C. Rodenhauser, Grand Recorder.

La Leche League International (1956): 9616 Minneapolis Ave., Franklin Park, Ill. 60131. 53,543; Betty Wagner, Executive Director.

League of Women Voters of the U.S. (1920): 1730 M St., N.W., Washington, D.C. 20036. 114,000; Carol C. Parr, Executive Director.

Leukemia Society of America (1949): 733 Third Ave., New York, N.Y. 10017. Wallace Dunlap, President.

Library Association, American (1876): 50 E. Huron St., Chicago, Ill. 60611. 38,000; Robert Wedgeworth, Executive Director.

Life Underwriters, National Association of (1890): 1922 F St., N.W., Washington, D.C. 20006. Jack E. Bobo, Executive Vice President.

Lions Clubs International (1917): 300 22nd St., Oak Brook, Ill. 60570. 1,348,142. Roy Schaetzel, Executive Administrator.

Lupus Foundation of America (1976): 11921 A Olive Blvd., St. Louis, Mo. 63141. 201 chapters and groups; Virginia J. Masters, Executive Secretary, 4434 Covington Hwy, Decatur, Ga., 30035.

Management Associations, American (1923): 135 W. 50th St., New York, N.Y. 10020. 80,000; Patricia Conway, Corporate Secretary.

Manufacturers, National Association of (1895): 1776 F St., N.W., Washington, D.C. 20006. 13, 500; Joni C. Hodgson, Secretary.

March of Dimes Birth Defects Foundation (1938): 1275 Mamaroneck Ave., White Plains, N.Y. 10605. 600 chapters; Charles L. Massey, President.

Marine Corps League (1923): 933 N. Kenmore St., Arlington, Va. 22201. 26,000; Raymond B. Butts, Executive Director.

Masons, Ancient and Accepted Scottish Rite, Northern Masonic Jurisdiction, Supreme Council 33 (1867): 33 Marrett Rd., Lexington, Mass. 02173. 490,425; Lynn J. Sanderson, Grand Secretary General.

Masons, Ancient and Accepted Scottish Rite, Southern Jurisdiction, Supreme Council (1801): 1733 16th St., N.W., Washington, D.C. 20009. 654,515; C. Fred Kleinknecht, Grand Secretary General.

Masons, Royal Arch, International General Grand Chapter (1797): Box 55270, Lexington, Ky. 40555. 375,000; Charles K.A. McGaughey, General Grand Secretary.

Mathematical Society, American (1888): P.O. Box 6248, Providence, R.I. 02940. 20,231; William J. LeVeque, Executive Director.

Mayflower Descendants, General Society of (1897): 4 Winslow St., P.O. Box 3297, Plymouth, Mass. 02361. 21,000; Mrs. Clayton M. Merrick Jr., Historian General.

Mechanical Engineers, American Society of (1880): 345 E. 47th St., New York, N.Y. 10017. 110,000; Paul F. Allmendinger, Executive Director.

Medical Association, American (1847): 535 N. Dearborn St., Chicago, Ill. 60610.

Mental Health Association, National (1909): 1021 Prince St., Alexandria, Va., 22314. 1,000,000.

Mining, Metallurgical and Petroleum Engineers, American Institute of (1871): 345 E. 47th St., New York, N.Y. 10017. 98,445; Robert H. Marcrum, Executive Director.

Model Aeronautics, Academy of (1936): 1810 Samuel Morse Dr., Reston Va. 22090. 85,000; John Worth, Executive Director.

Modern Language Association of America (1883):

62 Fifth Avenue., New York, N.Y. 10011. 30,000.

Modern Woodmen of America (1883): Mississippi River at 17th St., Rock Island, Ill. 61201. 550,000; W.B. Foster, President.

Moose, Loyal Order of (1888): Mooseheart, Ill. 60539. 1,747,172; Donald H. Ross, Supreme Secretary.

Motion Picture Arts & Sciences, Academy of (1927): 8949 Wilshire Blvd., Beverly Hills, Calif. 90211. James M. Roberts, Executive Director.

Multiple Sclerosis Society, National (1946): 205 E. 42nd St., New York, N.Y. 10017. Thor Hanson, President.

Muscular Dystrophy Association (1950): 810 Seventh Ave., New York, N.Y. 10019. 1,945,800 volunteers, Jerry Lewis, National Chairman.

Museums, American Association of (1906): 1055 Thomas Jefferson St., N.W., Washington, D.C. 20007. 8,000; Lawrence Reger, Director.

Musicians, American Federation of (1896): 1500 Broadway, New York, N.Y. 10036. 250,000; Victor W. Fuentealba, President.

National Association for the Advancement of Colored People (1909): 186 Remsen St., Brooklyn, N.Y. 11201. 50,000; Benjamin L. Hooks, Executive Director.

National Grange, The (1867): 1616 H St., N.W., Washington, D.C. 20006. 425,000; Edward Andersen, Master.

National PTA (National Congress of Parents and Teachers) (1897): 700 N. Rush St., Chicago, Ill. 60611. 5,413,162; Robert N. Woerner. Executive Administrator.

Newspaper Publishers Association, American (1887): The Newspaper Center, P.O. Box 17407, Dulles International Airport, Washington, D.C. 20041. 1,395; Jerry W. Friedheim, Executive Vice President and General Manager.

Nurses' Association, American (1896): 1101 14th St., N.W. Washington, D.C. 20005. 185,000.

Odd Fellows, Sovereign Grand Lodge, Independent Order of (1819): 422 Trade St., Winston-Salem, N.C. 27101. 1,200,000; Robert W. Wepking, Sovereign Grand Secretary.

Olympic Committee, United States (1921): 1750 Boulder St., Colorado Springs, Colo. 80909. R. Michael Moran, Director of Communications.

Organization of American States, General Secretariat (1890): 1889 F St., N.W., Washington, D.C. 20006. 32 member nations.

ORT Federation, American (1922): 817 Broadway, New York, N.Y. 10003. 160,000; Donald H. Klein, Executive Vice President.

Overeaters Anonymous (1960): 2190 190th St., Torrance, Calif. 90504. 100,000.

Parents Without Partners (1957): 7910 Woodmont Ave., Bethesda, Md. 20814. 209,729; Louise Spaulding, Interim Office Supervisor.

Parks, & Conservation Association, National (1919): 1701 18th St., N.W., Washington, D.C. 20009. 38,000; Paul C. Pritchard, President.

Philatelic Society, American (1886): P.O. Box 8000, State College, Pa. 16803. 53,000; Keith A. Wagner, Executive Director.

Philosophical Society, American (1743): 104 S. 5th St., Philadelphia, Pa. 19106. 600; Herman H. Goldstine, Executive Officer.

Photographic Society of America (1933): 2005 Walnut St., Philadelphia, Pa. 19103. 15,500.

Physical Society, American (1899): 335 E. 45th St., New York, N.Y. 10017. 33,000; W. W. Havens, Jr., Executive Secretary.

Physics, American Institute of (1931): 335 E. 45th St., New York, N.Y. 10017. 58,300; H. William Koch, Director.

Planned Parenthood Federation of America (1916): 810 Seventh Ave., New York, N.Y. 10019. 190 affiliates.

Political Science, Academy of (1880): 2852 Broadway, New York, N.Y. 10025. 11,000; C. Lowell Harriss, Executive Director.

Professional Engineers, National Society of (1934): 2029 K St., N.W., Washington, D.C. 20006. 80,000; Donald G. Weinert, Executive Director.

Psychiatric Association, American (1844): 1400 K St., N.W., Washington, D.C. 20005. 29,513; John Talbott, M.D., President.

Psychological Association, American (1892): 1200 17th St., N.W., Washington, D.C. 20036. 56,000; Michael S. Pallak, Executive Officer.

Public Health Association, American (1872): 1015 15th St., N.W., Washington, D.C. 20005. 30,201; William H. McBeath, M.D., Executive Director.

Puppeteers of America (1937): 5 Cricklewood Path, Pasadena, Calif. 91107. Gayle Schluter, Membership Chairman.

Recording Arts and Sciences, National Academy of (1958): 4444 Riverside Dr., Burbank, Calif. 91505. 6,000; Michael Melvoin, National President.

Red Cross, American (1881): 17th and D Sts., N.W., Washington, D.C. 20006. Over 3,000 chapters; Richard F. Schubert, President.

Rehabilitation Association, National (1925): 633 S. Washington St., Alexandria, Va. 22314. 20,000; David L. Mills, Executive Director.

Reserve Officers Association of the United States (1922): 1 Constitution Ave., N.E., Washington, D.C. 20002. 125,000; Robert H. Spiro, Jr., Executive Director.

Retarded Citizens, Association for (1950): 2501 Avenue J, Arlington, Tex. 76011. 1,600 units; Alan Abeson, National Executive Director.

Retired Federal Employees, National Association of (1921): 1533 New Hampshire Ave., N.W., Washington, D.C. 20036. 495,000; L. J. Andolsek, President.

Retired Persons, American Association of (1958): 1909 K St., N.W., Washington, D.C. 20049. 16,400,000; Cyril F. Brickfield, Executive Director.

RID-USA (Remove Intoxicated Drivers) (1978): Box 520, Schenectady, N.Y. 12301. Over 150 chapters; Doris Aiken, President.

Rifle Association of America, National (1871): 1600 Rhode Island Ave., N.W., Washington, D.C. 20036. 2,900,000; Harlon B. Carter, Executive Vice President.

Right to Life, National Committee (1973): 419 7th St., N.W., Washington, D.C. 20004. Warren Sweeney, Executive Director.

Rotary International (1905): 1600 Ridge Ave., Evanston, Ill. 60201. 915,500; Herbert A. Pigman, General Secretary.

Safety Council, National (1913): 444 N. Michigan Ave., Chicago, Ill. 60611. Charles C. Vance, Director of Public Relations.

Salvation Army, The (1865): 799 Bloomfield Ave., Verona, N.J. 07044. 419,475; Col. James Osborne, National Chief Secretary.

SANE, Committee for a SANE Nuclear Policy (1957): 711 G St., S.E., Washington, D.C. 20003. 80,000; David Cortright, Executive Director.

Save-the-Redwoods League (1918): 114 Sansome St., San Francisco, Calif. 94104. 40,000; John B. Dewitt, Executive Director.

Science, American Association for the Advance-

ment of (1848): 1515 Massachusetts Ave., N.W., Washington, D.C. 20005. 136,000; Carol L. Rogers, Communications.

Screen Actors Guild (1933): 7750 Sunset Blvd., Hollywood, Calif. 90046. 55,000; Kim Fellner, Information Director.

Seeing Eye (1929): Morristown, N.J. 07960. Stuart Grout, Executive Vice President.

Shrine of North America (Shriners Hospitals) (1872): Box 25356, Tampa, Fla. 33622. 900,000; Charles G. Cumpstone, Jr., Executive Secretary.

Sierra Club (1892): 530 Bush St., San Francisco, Calif. 94108. 351,853; Michael McCloskey, Executive Director.

Small Business Association, National (1937): 1604 K St., N.W., Washington, D.C. 20006. 50,000; Herbert Liebenson, President.

Social Welfare, National Conference on (1873): 1730 M St., N.W., Washington, D.C. 20036. 4,000; Benjamin O. Hendrick, Acting Executive Director.

Social Workers, National Association of (1955): 7981 Eastern Ave., Silver Spring, MD 20910. Mark G. Battle, Executive Director.

Sons of Italy in America, Order (1905): 219 E St., N.E., Washington, D.C. 20002. 90,000; Salvatore M. Ambrosino, National Director.

Sons of the American Revolution, National Society of the (1889): 1000 S. 4th St., Louisville, Ky. 40203. 22,000; John C. Davis, Executive Secretary.

Soroptimist International of the Americas (1921): 1616 Walnut St., Philadelphia, Pa. 19103. 40,000; Mary Helen Madden, Executive Director.

Southern Christian Leadership Conference (1957): 334 Auburn Ave., N.E., Atlanta, Ga. 30303. 1,000,000; 350 chapters, 260 affiliated organizations; Dr. Joseph E. Lowery, President.

Speech-Language-Hearing Association, American (1925): 10801 Rockville Pike, Rockville, Md. 20852. 40,000; Frederick T. Spahr, Executive Director.

Sports Car Club of America (1944): 6750 S. Emporia, Englewood, Colo. 80112. 23,000; Mac DeMere, News Department Manager.

Surgeons, American College of (1913): 55 E. Erie, St., Chicago, Ill. 60611. 46,500; C. Rollins Hanlon, Director.

Teachers, American Federation of (1916): 555 New Jersey Ave, N.W., Washington, D.C., 20001. 580,000; Albert Shanker, President.

Television Arts and Sciences, National Academy of: (1948) 110 W. 57th St., New York, N.Y., 10019. 12,000; John Cannon, President.

Travel Agents, American Society of (ASTA) (1931): 4400 MacArthur Blvd., N.W., Washington, D.C. 20007. 20,000; Joseph H. Hallissey, Chairman.

Travelers Aid Services (1905/1982); 2 Lafayette St., New York, N.Y. 10007. Lucy N. Friedman, Executive Director. (Result of merger of Travelers Aid Society of New York and Victim Services Agency in 1982).

United Negro College Fund Inc. (1944): 500 E. 62nd St., New York, N.Y. 10021. Christopher F. Edley, President.

University Women, American Association of (1881): 2401 Virginia Ave., N.W., Washington, D.C. 20037. 190,000; Quincalee Brown, Executive Director.

Urban League, National (1910): 500 E. 62nd St., New York, N.Y. 10021. 116; James D. Williams, Director of Communications.

Veterans Committee, American (AVC) (1944): 1346 Connecticut Ave., N.W., Suite 930, Washington, D.C. 20036. 25,000; June A. Willenz, Executive Director.

Veterans of Foreign Wars of the U.S. (1899): V.F.W. Bldg., 34th and Broadway, Kansas City, Mo. 64111. V.F.W. and Auxiliary, 2,685,000; Howard E. Vander Clute, Jr., Adjutant General.

Veterinary Medical Association, American (1863): 930 N. Meacham Rd., Schaumburg, Ill. 60196. 36,600; Dr. D. A. Price, Executive Vice President.

War Resisters League (1923): 339 Lafayette St., New York, N.Y. 10012. 15,000; Linnea Capps, Chairwoman.

Wildlife Federation, National (1936): 1412 16th St., N.W., Washington, D.C. 20036. 4,600,000; Jay D. Hair, Executive Vice President.

Woman's Christian Temperance Union, National (1874): 1730 Chicago Ave., Evanston, Ill. 60201. 250,000; Martha G. Edgar, President.

Women's American ORT (1927): 315 Park Ave. South, New York, N.Y. 10010. 145,000; Nathan Gould, National Executive Director.

Women's Clubs, General Federation of (1890): 1734 N St., N.W., Washington, D.C. 20036. 500,000; Mildred Baptista, Executive Secretary.

Women's International League for Peace and Freedom (1915): 1213 Race St., Philadelphia, Pa. 19107. 13,000; Libby Frank, Executive Director.

Women's Strike for Peace (1961): 145 S. 13th St., Philadelphia, Pa. 19107. 25,000; Ethel Taylor, National Coordinator.

YMCA of the USA (1844): 101 N. Wacker Dr., Chicago, Ill. 60606. 11,000,000; Solon B. Cousins, Executive Director.

Young Women's Christian Association of the U.S.A. (1858 in U.S.A., 1855 in England): 135 W. 50th St., New York, N.Y. 10020. 2,471,000; Jane Pinkerton, Director of Communications.

Youth Hostels, American (1934): 1332 I St., N.W., Washington, D.C. 20005. 100,000.

Zionist Organization of America (1897): ZOA House, 4 E. 34th St., New York, N.Y. 10016. 135,000; Paul I. Flacks, Executive Vice President and National Secretary.

Continental Drift

A NASA report of a five-year study of land mass movement supports the Continental Drift theory and indicates that the continents are continuing to shift. Their measurements show that the Atlantic Ocean is widening by six-tenths of an inch a year. Hawaii and the Americas are moving apart by two inches a year, while Australia and North America are coming closer together at an annual rate of four-tenths of an inch.

Within the United States, Northern and Southern California are being compressed by 2.6 inches a year. Based on these findings and indications from the past, NASA predicts that all of California west of the San Andreas Fault will become an island in the Pacific in about 20 million years.

PEOPLE

Many public figures not listed here may be found elsewhere in the *Information Please Almanac.*

A name in parentheses is the original name or form of name. Localities are places of birth. Dates of birth appear as month/day/year. **Boldface** years in parentheses are dates of **(birth-death).**
Information has been gathered from many sources, including the individuals themselves. However, the *Information Please Almanac* cannot guarantee the accuracy of every individual item.

A

Aalto, Alvar (architect); Kuortane, Finland **(1898-1976)**
Abbott, Bud (William) (comedian); Asbury Park, N.J. **(1898-1974)**
Abbott, George (stage producer); Forestville, N.Y., 6/25/1887
Abel, Walter (actor); St. Paul, 6/6/1898
Abernathy, Ralph (civil rights leader); Linden, Ala., 3/11/1926
Acheson, Dean (statesman); Middletown, Conn. **(1893-1971)**
Acuff, Roy Claxton (musician); nr. Maynardsville, Tenn. 9/15/1903
Adams, Charles Francis (diplomat); Boston **(1807-1886)**
Adams, Don (actor); New York City, 4/19/1927
Adams, Edie (Edie Enke) (actress); Kingston, Pa., 4/16/1929
Adams, Franklin Pierce (columnist and author); Chicago **(1881-1960)**
Adams, Henry Brooks (historian); Boston **(1838-1918)**
Adams, Joey (comedian); New York City, 1/6/1911
Adams, Maude (Maude Kiskadden) (actress); Salt Lake City, **(1872-1953)**
Adams, Samuel (American Revolutionary patriot); Boston **(1722-1803)**
Adamson, Joy (naturalist); Troppau, Silesia **(1910-1980)**
Addams, Charles (cartoonist); Westfield, N.J., 1/7/1912
Addams, Jane (social worker); Cedarville, Ill. **(1860-1935)**
Adderley, Julian "Cannonball" (jazz saxophonist); Tampa, Fla. **(1928-1975)**
Ade, George (humorist); Kentland, Ind. **(1866-1944)**
Adenauer, Konrad (statesman); Cologne, Germany **(1876-1967)**
Adler, Alfred (psychoanalyst); Vienna **(1870-1937)**
Adler, Larry (musician); Baltimore, 2/10/1914
Adler, Richard (songwriter); New York City, 8/3/1921
Aeschylus (dramatist); Eleusis (Greece) **(525-456 B.C.)**
Aesop (fabulist); birthplace unknown **(lived c. 600 B.C.)**
Aherne, Brian (actor); King's Norton, England, 5/2/1902
Aiken, Conrad (poet); Savannah, Ga. **(1889-1973)**
Ailey, Alvin (choreographer); Rogers, Tex., 1/5/1931
Albanese, Licia (operatic soprano); Bari, Italy, 7/22/1913
Albee, Edward (playwright); Washington, D.C., 3/12/1928
Albers, Josef (painter); Bottrop, Germany **(1888-1976)**
Albert, Eddie (Edward Albert Heimberger) (actor); Rock Island, Ill., 4/22/1908
Albertson, Jack (actor); Malden, Mass. **(1910?-1981)**
Alcott, Louisa May (novelist); Germantown, Pa. **(1832-1888)**
Alda, Alan (actor); New York City, 1/28/1936
Alda, Robert (Alphonso d'Abruzzo) (actor); New York City, 2/26/1914
Alden, John (American Pilgrim); England **(1599?-1687)**
Alexander the Great (monarch and conqueror); Pella, Macedonia (now Greece) **(356-323 B.C.)**
Alger, Horatio (author); Revere, Mass. **(1834-1899)**
Algren, Nelson (novelist); Detroit **(1909-1981)**
Allen, Ethan (American Revolutionary soldier); Litchfield, Conn. **(1738-1789)**
Allen, Fred (John Florence Sullivan) (comedian); Cambridge, Mass. **(1894-1956)**
Allen, Gracie (Grace Ethel Cecile Rosalie Allen) (comedienne); San Francisco **(1906-1964)**
Allen, Mel (Melvin Israel) (sportscaster); Birmingham, Ala., 2/14/1913
Allen, Steve (TV entertainer); New York City, 12/26/1921
Allen, Woody (Allen Stewart Konigsberg) (actor, writer, and director); Brooklyn, N.Y., 12/1/1935
Allison, Fran (actress); LaPorte City, Iowa, 1924(?)
Allman, Gregg (singer); Nashville, Tenn., 12/8/1947
Allyson, June (Jan Allyson) (actress); New York City, 10/7/1923
Alonso, Alicia (ballerina); Havana, 12/21/1921(?)
Alsop, Joseph W., Jr. (journalist); Avon, Conn., 10/11/1910
Alsop, Stewart (journalist); Avon, Conn. **(1914-1974)**
Altman, Robert (film director); Kansas City, Mo., 2/20/1925
Ambler, Eric (suspense writer); London, 6/28/1909
Ameche, Don (Dominic Amici) (actor); Kenosha, Wis., 5/31/1908
Amis, Kingsley (novelist); London, 4/16/1922
Amory, Cleveland (writer and conservationist); Nahant, Mass., 9/2/1917
Amos (Freeman F. Gosden) (radio comedian); Richmond, Va., **(1899-1982)**
Amsterdam, Morey (actor); Chicago, 12/14/1914
Andersen, Hans Christian (author of fairy-tales); Odense, Denmark **(1805-1875)**
Anderson, Eddie. *See* Rochester
Anderson, Jack (journalist); Long Beach, Calif., 10/19/1922
Anderson, Dame Judith (actress); Adelaide, Australia, 2/10/1898
Anderson, Lindsay (Gordon) (director); Bangalore, India, 4/17/1923
Anderson, Lynn (singer); Grand Forks, N.D., 9/26/1947
Anderson, Marian (contralto); Philadelphia, 2/17/1902
Anderson, Maxwell (dramatist); Atlantic, Pa. **(1888-1959)**
Anderson, Robert (playwright); New York City, 4/28/1917
Anderson, Bibi (actress); Stockholm, 11/11/1935
Andress, Ursula (actress); Switzerland, 3/19/1938
Andrews, Dana (actor); Collins, Miss., 1/1/1909
Andrews, Julie (Julia Wells) (actress and singer); Walton-on-Thames, England, 10/1/1935
Andrews, La Verne (singer); Minneapolis **(1916-1967)**
Andrews, Maxene (singer); Minneapolis, 1/3/1918
Andrews, Patti (singer); Minneapolis, 2/16/1920
Andy (Charles J. Correll) (radio comedian); Peoria, Ill. **(1890-1972)**
Angeles, Victoria de los (Victoria Gamez Cima) (operatic soprano); Barcelona, 11/1/1924
Anka, Paul (singer and composer); Ottawa, 7/30/1941
Ann-Margret (Ann-Margret Olsson) (actress); Valsjobyn, Sweden, 4/28/1941
Annabella (actress); Paris, 1912
Anoullh, Jean (playwright); Bordeaux, France, 6/23/1910
Anthony, Susan Brownell (woman suffragist); Adams, Mass. **(1820-1906)**
Antonloni, Michelangelo (director); Ferrara, Italy, 9/29/1912
Antony, Mark (Marcus Antonius) (statesman); Rome **(83?-30 B.C.)**
Anuszkiewicz, Richard (painter); Erie, Pa., 5/23/1930
Aquinas, St. Thomas (philosopher); nr. Aquino (Italy) **(1225?-1274)**
Arbuckle, Roscoe "Fatty" (actor and director); San Jose, Calif. **(1837-1933)**
Archimedes (physicist and mathematician); Syracuse, Sicily **(287?-212 B.C.)**
Archipenko, Alexandre (sculptor); Kiev, Russia **(1887-1964)**
Arden, Elizabeth (Florence Nightingale Graham) (cosmetics executive); Woodbridge, Canada **(1891-1966)**
Arden, Eve (Eunice Quedens) (actress); Mill Valley, Calif., 4/30/1912
Arendt, Hannah (historian); Hannover, Germany **(1906-1975)**
Aristophanes (dramatist); Athens **448?-380 B.C.)**
Aristotle (philosopher); Stagirus, Macedonia **(384-322 B.C.)**
Arkin, Alan (actor and director); New York City, 3/26/1934
Arledge, Roone (TV executive); Forest Hills, N.Y., 7/8/1931
Arlen, Harold (Hyman Arluck) (composer); Buffalo, N.Y., 2/15/1905
Arlen, Richard (actor); Charlottesville, Va. **(1900-1976)**
Arliss, George (actor); London **(1868-1946)**
Armstrong, Louis ("Satchmo") (musician); New Orleans **(1900-1971)**
Armstrong-Jones, Anthony. *See* Snowdon, Earl of
Arnaz, Desi (Desiderio) (actor and producer); Santiago, Cuba, 3/2/1917
Arness, James (James Aurness) (TV actor); Minneapolis, 5/26/1923
Arno, Peter (cartoonist); New York City **(1904-1968)**
Arnold, Benedict (American Revolutionary War General, convicted of treason); Norwich, Conn. **(1741-1801)**
Arnold, Eddy (singer); Henderson, Tenn., 5/15/1918
Arnold, Edward (actor); New York City **(1890-1956)**
Arnold, Matthew (poet and critic); Laleham, England **(1822-1888)**
Arp, Jean (sculptor and painter); Strasbourg (France) **(1887-1966)**

Arquette, Cliff ("Charley Weaver") (actor); Toledo, Ohio (1905-1974)
Arrau, Claudio (pianist); Chillán, Chile, 2/6/1903
Arthur, Bea (Bernice Frankel) (actress); New York City, 5/13/1926(?)
Arthur, Jean (Gladys Greene) (actress); New York City, 10/17/1905
Asch, Sholem (novelist); Kutno, Poland (1880-1957)
Ashkenazy, Vladimir (concert pianist); Gorki, U.S.S.R., 7/6/1937
Ashley, Elizabeth (actress); Ocala, Fla., 8/30/1939
Ashton, Sir Frederick William Mallandaine (choreographer); Guayaquil, Ecuador, 9/17/1904
Asimov, Isaac (author); Petrovichi, Russia, 1/2/1920
Asner, Edward (actor); Kansas City, Mo., 11/15/1929
Astaire, Fred (Frederick Austerlitz) (dancer and actor); Omaha, Neb., 5/10/1899
Astor, John Jacob (financier); Waldorf (Germany) (1763-1848)
Astor, Mary (Lucile Langhanke) (actress); Quincy, Ill., 5/3/1906
Atkins, Chet (guitarist); nr. Luttrell, Tenn., 6/20/1924
Atkinson, Brooks (drama critic); Melrose, Mass. (1894-1984)
Attenborough, Richard (actor-director) Cambridge, England, 8/29/1923
Attila (King of Huns, called "Scourge of God") (406?-453)
Attlee, Clement Richard (statesman); London (1883-1967)
Auchincloss, Louis (author); Lawrence, N.Y., 9/27/1917
Auden, W(ystan) H(ugh) (poet); York, England (1907-1973)
Audubon, John James (naturalist and painter); Haiti (1785-1851)
Auer, Leopold (violinist and teacher); Veszprém, Hungary (1845-1930)
Auer, Mischa (actor); St. Petersburg, Russia (1905-1967)
Augustine, Saint (Aurelius Augustinus) (philosopher); Numidia (Algeria) (354-430)
Augustus (Gaius Octavius) (Roman emperor); Rome (63 B.C.-A.D. 14)
Aumont, Jean-Pierre (actor); Paris, 1/5/1913
Austen, Jane (novelist); Steventon, England (1775-1817)
Autry, Gene (singer and actor); Tioga, Tex., 9/29/1907
Avalon, Frankie (singer); Philadelphia, 9/18/1940
Avedon, Richard (photographer); New York City, 5/15/1923
Avery, Milton (painter); Altmar, N.Y. (1893-1965)
Axelrod, George (playwright); New York City, 6/9/1922
Ayckbourn Alan (playwright); London, 4/12/1939
Ayres, Lew (actor); Minneapolis, 12/28/1908

B

Bacall, Lauren (Betty Joan Perske) (actress); New York City, 9/16/1924
Bach, Johann Sebastian (composer); Eisenach (Germany) (1685-1750)
Bacharach, Burt (songwriter); Kansas City, Mo., 5/12/1929
Backus, Jim (actor); Cleveland, 2/25/1913
Bacon, Francis (painter); Dublin, 1910
Bacon, Francis (philosopher and essayist); London (1561-1626)
Bacon, Roger (philosopher and scientist); Ilchester, England (1214?-1294)
Baedeker, Karl (travel-guidebook publisher); Essen (Germany) (1801-1859)
Baez, Joan (folk singer); Staten Island, N.Y., 1/9/1941
Bagnold, Enid (novelist); Rochester, England (1889-1981)
Bailey, F. Lee (lawyer); Waltham, Mass., 6/10/1933
Bailey, Pearl (singer); Newport News, Va., 3/29/1918
Bainter, Fay (actress); Los Angeles (1891-1968)
Baird, Bill (William B.) (puppeteer); Grand Island, Neb., 8/15/1904
Baker, Josephine (singer and dancer); St. Louis (1906-1975)
Baker, Kenny (singer and actor); Monrovia, Calif., 9/30/1912
Baker, Russell (columnist); Loudoun County, Va., 8/14/1925
Balanchine, George (choreographer); St. Petersburg, Russia (1904-1983)
Balboa, Vasco Nuñez de (explorer); Jerez de los Caballeros (Spain) (1475-1517)
Baldwin, Faith (novelist); New Rochelle, N.Y. (1893-1978)
Baldwin, James (novelist); New York City, 8/2/1924
Balenciaga, Cristóbal (fashion designer); Guetaria, Spain (1895-1972)
Ball, Lucille (Dianne Belmont) (actress and producer); Celoron (nr. Jamestown), N.Y., 8/6/1911
Ballard, Kaye (Catherine Gloria Balotta) (actress); Cleveland, 11/20/1926
Balmain, Pierre (fashion designer); St.-Jean-de-Maurienne, France (1914-1982)
Balsam, Martin (actor); New York City, 11/4/1919
Balzac, Honoré de (novelist); Tours, France (1799-1850)
Bancroft, Anne (Annemarie Italiano) (actress); New York City, 9/17/1931
Bancroft, George (actor); Philadelphia (1882-1956)
Bankhead, Tallulah (actress); Huntsville, Ala. (1903-1963)
Banneker, Benjamin (almanacker and mathematician-astronomer on District of Columbia site survey); Ellicott, Md. (1731-1806)
Bara, Theda (Theodosia Goodman) (actress); Cincinnati (1890-1955)
Barber, Red (Walter Lanier) (sportscaster); Columbus, Miss., 2/17/1908
Barber, Samuel (composer); West Chester, Pa. (1910-1981)
Bardot, Brigitte (actress); Paris, 1935
Barenboim, Daniel (concert pianist and conductor); Buenos Aires, 11/15/1942
Barnard, Christiaan N. (heart surgeon); Beauford West, South Africa, 1923
Barnum, Phineas Taylor (showman); Bethel, Conn. (1810-1891)
Barrie, Sir James Matthew (author); Kirriemuir, Scotland (1860-1937)
Barrie, Wendy (actress); Hong Kong (1913-1978)
Barry, Gene (Eugene Klass) (actor); New York City, 6/4/1922
Barry, John (naval officer); County Wexford, Ireland (1745-1803)
Barrymore, Diana (actress); New York City (1921-1960)
Barrymore, Ethel (Ethel Blythe) (actress); Philadelphia (1879-1959)
Barrymore, Georgiana Drew (actress); Philadelphia (1856-1893)
Barrymore, John (John Blythe) (actor); Philadelphia (1882-1942)
Barrymore, Lionel (Lionel Blythe) (actor); Philadelphia (1878-1954)
Barrymore, Maurice (Herbert Blythe) (actor and playwright); Agra, India (1847-1905)
Bartheime, Donald (novelist); Philadelphia, 4/7/1931
Barthelmess, Richard (actor); New York City (1897-1963)
Bartholomew, Freddie (actor); London, 3/28/1924
Bartók, Béla (composer); Nagyszentmiklos (Romania) (1881-1945)
Barton, Clara (founder of American Red Cross); Oxford, Mass. (1821-1912)
Baruch, Bernard Mannes (statesman), Camden, S.C. (1870-1965)
Baryshnikov, Mikhail Nikolayevich (ballet dancer and artistic director); Riga, Latvia, 1/27/1948
Basehart, Richard (actor); Zanesville, Ohio (1914-1984)
Basie, Count (William) (band leader); Red Bank, N.J. (1904-1984)
Bassey, Shirley (singer); Cardiff, Wales, 1/8/1937
Batchelor, Clarence Daniel (political cartoonist); Osage City, Kan. (1888-1977)
Bates, Alan (actor); Allestree, England, 2/17/1934
Baudelaire, Charles Pierre (poet); Paris (1821-1867)
Baudouin (King); Palace of Laeken, Belgium, 9/7/1930
Baxter, Anne (actress); Michigan City, Ind., 5/7/1923
Baxter, Warner (actor); Columbus, Ohio (1891-1951)
Bean, Orson (Dallas Frederick Burrows) (actor); Burlington, Vt., 7/22/1928
Beardsley, Aubrey Vincent (illustrator); Brighton, England (1872-1898)
Beaton, Cecil (photographer and designer); London (1904-1980)
Beatty, Warren (actor and producer); Richmond, Va., 3/30/1937
Becket, Thomas à (Archbishop of Canterbury); London (1118?-1170)
Beckett, Samuel (playwright); Dublin, 4/13/1906
Beckmann, Max (painter); Leipzig, Germany (1884-1950)
Bede, Saint ("The Venerable Bede") (scholar); Monkwearmouth, England (673-735)
Beecham, Sir Thomas (conductor); St. Helens, England (1879-1961)
Beecher, Henry Ward (clergyman); Litchfield, Conn. (1813-1887)
Beerbohm, Sir Max (author); London (1872-1956)
Beery, Noah, Jr. (actor); New York City, 8/10/1916
Beery, Wallace (actor); Kansas City, Mo. (1886-1949)
Beethoven, Ludwig van (composer); Bonn (Germany) (1770-1827)
Belafonte, Harry (singer and actor); New York City, 3/1/1927
Belasco, David (dramatist and producer); San Francisco (1854-1931)
Bell, Alexander Graham (inventor); Edinburgh, Scotland (1847-1922)
Bellamy, Edward (author); Chicopee Falls, Mass. (1850-1898)
Bellamy, Ralph (actor); Chicago, 6/17/1904
Bellini, Giovanni (painter); Venice (c.1430-1516)
Bellow, Saul (novelist); Lachine, Quebec, Canada, 7/10/1915
Bellows, George Wesley (painter and lithographer); Columbus, Ohio (1882-1925)
Belmonde, Jean-Paul (actor); Neuilly-sur-Seine, France, 4/9/1933
Belushi, John (comedian, actor); Chicago (1949-1982)
Benchley, Peter Bradford (novelist); New York City, 5/8/1940
Benchley, Robert Charles (humorist); Worcester, Mass. (1889-1945)
Bendix, William (actor); New York City (1906-1964)
Benes, Eduard (statesman); Kozlany (Czechoslovakia) (1884-1948)
Benét, Stephen Vincent (poet and story writer); Bethlehem, Pa. (1898-1943)
Benét, William Rose (poet and novelist); Ft. Hamilton, Brooklyn, N.Y. (1886-1950)
Ben-Gurion, David (David Green) (statesman); Plónsk (Poland) (1886-1973)
Benjamin, Richard (actor); New York City, 5/22/1938
Bennett, Constance (actress); New York City (1905-1965)
Bennett, Enoch Arnold (novelist and dramatist); Hanley, England (1867-1931)
Bennett, James Gordon (editor); Keith, Scotland (1795-1872)

Bennett, Joan (actress); Palisades, N.J., 2/27/1910
Bennett, Robert Russell (composer); Kansas City, Mo., **(1894-1981)**
Bennett, Tony (Anthony Benedetto) (singer); Astoria, Queens, N.Y., 8/3/1926
Benny, Jack (Benjamin Kubelsky) (comedian); Chicago **(1894-1974)**
Benton, Thomas Hart (painter); Neosho, Mo. **(1889-1975)**
Berg, Gertrude (writer and actress); New York City **(1899-1966)**
Bergen, Candice (actress); Beverly Hills, Calif., 5/9/1946
Bergen, Edgar (ventriloquist); Chicago, **(1903-1978)**
Bergen, Polly (actress and singer); Knoxville, Tenn., 7/14/1930
Bergman, Ingmar (film director); Uppsala, Sweden, 7/14/1918
Bergman, Ingrid (actress); Stockholm **(1918-1982)**
Berle, Milton (Milton Berlinger) (comedian); New York City, 7/12/1908
Berlin, Irving (Israel Baline) (songwriter); Temum, Russia, 5/11/1888
Berlioz, Louis Hector (composer); La Côte-Saint-André, France **(1803-1869)**
Berman, Lazar (concert pianist); Leningrad, 1930.
Berman, Shelley (Sheldon) (comedian); Chicago, 2/3/1926
Bernhardt, Sarah (Rosine Bernard) (actress); Paris **(1844-1923)**
Bernini, Gian Lorenzo (sculptor and painter); Naples (Italy) **(1598-1680)**
Bernstein, Leonard (conductor); Lawrence, Mass., 8/25/1918
Berry, Chuck (Charles Edward Berry) (singer); San Jose, Calif., 1/15/1926
Betjeman, Sir John (Poet Laureate); London **(1906-1984)**
Bickford, Charles (actor); Cambridge, Mass. **(1889-1967)**
Bierce, Ambrose Gwinnett (journalist); Meigs County, Ohio **(1842-1914?)**
Bikel, Theodore (actor and folk singer); Vienna, 5/2/1924
Bing, Sir Rudolf (opera manager); Vienna, 1/9/1902
Bingham, George Caleb (painter); Augusta Co., Va. **(1811-1879)**
Bishop, Joey (Joseph Gottlieb) (comedian); New York City, 2/3/1919
Bismarck-Schönhausen, Prince Otto Eduard Leopold von (statesman); Schönhausen (Germany) **(1815-1898)**
Bisset, Jacqueline (actress); Weybridge, England, 9/13/1944
Bixby, Bill (actor); San Francisco, 1/22/1934
Bizet, Georges (Alexandre César Léopold Bizet) (composer); Paris **(1838-1875)**
Black, Cilla (singer and actress); Liverpool, England, 5/27/1943
Black, Karen (actress); Park Ridge, Ill., 7/1/1942
Black, Shirley Temple (former actress); Santa Monica, Calif., 4/23/1928
Blackmer, Sidney (actor); Salisbury, N.C. **(1898-1973)**
Blackstone, Sir William (jurist); London **(1723-1780)**
Blaine, Vivian (actress and singer); Newark, N.J., 11/21/1924
Blair, Janet (actress); Altoona, Pa., 4/23/1921
Blake, Amanda (Beverly Louise Neill) (actress); Buffalo, N.Y., 1931
Blake, Eubie (James Hubert) (pianist); Baltimore, **(1883-1983)**
Blake, Robert (Michael Gubitosi) (actor); Nutley, N.J., 9/18/1933
Blake, William (poet and artist); London **(1757-1827)**
Blanc, Mel(vin Jerome) (actor and voice specialist); San Francisco, 5/30/1908
Blass, Bill (fashion designer); Fort Wayne, Ind., 6/22/1922
Bloch, Ernest (composer); Geneva **(1880-1959)**
Blondell, Joan (actress); New York City **(1909-1979)**
Bloom, Claire (actress); London, 2/15/1931
Bloomgarden, Kermit (producer); Brooklyn, N.Y. **(1904-1976)**
Blue, Monte (actor); Indianapolis **(1890-1963)**
Blyth, Ann (actress); New York City, 8/16/1928
Boccaccio, Giovanni (author); Paris **(1313-1375)**
Boccioni, Umberto (painter and sculptor); Reggio di Calabria, Italy **(1882-1916)**
Bock, Jerry (composer); New Haven, Conn., 11/23/1928
Bogarde, Dirk (Derek Van den Bogaerde) (film actor and director); London, 3/28/1921
Bogart, Humphrey DeForest (actor); New York City **(1899-1957)**
Bogdanovich, Peter (producer and director); Kingston, N.Y., 7/30/1939
Bohlen, Charles E. (diplomat); Clayton, N.Y. **(1904-1974)**
Bohr, Niels (atomic physicist); Copenhagen **(1885-1962)**
Bolger, Ray (dancer and actor); Dorchester, Mass., 1/10/1904
Bolivar, Simón (South American liberator); Caracas, Venezuela **(1783-1830)**
Bologna, Giovanni da (sculptor); Douai (France) **(1529-1608)**
Bombeck, Erma (author, columnist); Dayton, Ohio 2/21/1927
Bonaparte, Napoleon (Emperor of the French); Ajaccio, Corsica (France) **(1769-1821)**
Bond, Julian (Georgia legislator); Nashville, Tenn., 1/14/1940
Bondi, Beulah (actress); Chicago **(1883-1981)**
Bonnard, Pierre (painter); Fontenayaux-Roses, France **(1867-1947)**
Bono, Sonny (Salvatore) (singer); Detroit, 2/16/1935
Boone, Daniel (frontiersman); nr. Reading, Pa. **(1734-1820)**
Boone, Pat (Charles) (singer); Jacksonville, Fla., 6/1/1934
Boone, Richard (actor); Los Angeles **(1917-1981)**
Booth, Edwin Thomas (actor); Bel Air, Md. **(1833-1893)**
Booth, Evangeline Cory (religious leader); London **(1865-1950)**
Booth, John Wilkes (actor; assassin of Lincoln); Harford County, Md. **(1838-1865)**
Booth, Shirley (Thelma Booth Ford) (actress); New York City, 8/30/1907
Bordoni, Irene (actress); Ajaccio (France) **(1895-1953)**
Borge, Victor (pianist and comedian); Copenhagen, 1/3/1909
Borgia, Cesare (nobleman and soldier); Rome **(1475?-1507)**
Borgia, Lucrezia (Duchess of Ferrara); Rome **(1480-1519)**
Borgnine, Ernest (actor); Hamden, Conn., 1/24/1917
Borromini, Francesco (architect); Bissone (Italy) **(1599-1667)**
Bosch, Hieronymus (Hieronymus van Aeken) (painter); Hertogenbosch (Netherlands) **(c.1450-1516)**
Bosley, Tom (actor); Chicago, 10/1/1927
Boswell, Connee (singer); New Orleans **(1907-1976)**
Boswell, James (diarist and biographer); Edinburgh, Scotland **(1740-1795)**
Botticelli, Sandro (Alessandro di Mariano dei Filipepi) (painter); Florence (Italy) **(1444?-1510)**
Boulez, Pierre (conductor); Montbrison, France, 3/26/1925
Bow, Clara (actress); Brooklyn, N.Y. **(1905-1965)**
Bowen, Catherine Drinker (biographer); Haverford, Pa. **(1897-1973)**
Bowie, David (David Robert Jones) (actor and musician); London, 1/8/1947(?)
Bowie, James (soldier); Burke County, Ga. **(1799-1836)**
Bowles, Chester (diplomat); Springfield, Mass., 4/5/1901
Boyd, Bill (William) ("Hopalong Cassidy") (actor); Cambridge, Ohio **(1898-1972)**
Boyd, Stephen (Stephen Millar) (actor); Belfast, Northern Ireland **(1928-1977)**
Boyer, Charles (actor); Figeac, France **(1899-1978)**
Bracken, Eddie (actor); Astoria, Queens, N.Y., 2/7/1920
Bradbury, Ray Douglas (science-fiction writer); Waukegan, Ill., 8/22/1920
Bradlee, Benjamin C. (editor); Boston, 8/26/1921
Bradley, Omar N. (5-star general); Clark, Mo. **(1893-1981)**
Bradley, Thomas (Mayor of Los Angeles); Calvert, Tex., 12/29/1917
Brady, Scott (actor); Brooklyn, N.Y., 9/13/1924
Brahms, Johannes (composer); Hamburg **(1833-1897)**
Braille, Louis (teacher of blind); Coupvray, France **(1809-1862)**
Brailowsky, Alexander (pianist); Kiev, Russia **(1896-1976)**
Bramante, Donato D'Agnolo (architect); Monte Asdrualdo (now Fermignano, Italy) **(1444-1514)**
Brancusi, Constantin (sculptor); Pestisansi, Romania **(1876-1957)**
Brando, Marlon (actor); Omaha, Neb., 4/3/1924
Brandt, Willy (Herbert Frahm) (ex-Chancellor); Lübeck, Germany, 12/18/1913
Braque, Georges (painter); Argenteuil, France **(1882-1963)**
Brazzi, Rossano (actor); Bologna, Italy, 9/18/1916
Brecht, Bertolt (dramatist and poet); Augsburg, Bavaria **(1898-1956)**
Brel, Jacques (singer and composer); Brussels, **(1929-1978)**
Brennan, Walter (actor); Lynn, Mass. **(1894-1974)**
Brent, George (actor); Dublin **(1904-1979)**
Breslin, Jimmy (journalist); Jamaica, Queens, N.Y., 10/17/1930
Breuer, Marcel (architect and designer); Pécs, Hungary **(1902-1981)**
Brewer, Teresa (singer); Toledo, Ohio, 5/7/1931
Brewster, Kingman, Jr. (ex-president of Yale); Longmeadow, Mass., 6/17/1919
Brezhnev, Leonid I. (Communist Party Secretary); Dneprodzerzhinsk, Ukraine **(1906-1982)**
Brice, Fanny (Fannie Borach) (comedienne); New York City **(1892-1951)**
Bridges, Beau (actor); Los Angeles, 12/9/1941
Bridges, Lloyd (actor); San Leandro, Calif. 1/15/1913
Brinkley, David (TV newscaster); Wilmington, N.C., 7/10/1920
Britt, May (Maybritt Wilkins) (actress); Sweden, 3/22/1936
Britten, Benjamin (composer); Lowestoft, England **(1913-1976)**
Britton, Barbara (actress); Long Beach, Calif. **(1920-1980)**
Bromfield, Louis (novelist); Mansfield, Ohio **(1896-1956)**
Bronson, Charles (Charles Buchinsky) (actor); Ehrenfield, Pa., 11/3/1922(?)
Brontë, Charlotte (novelist); Thornton, England **(1816-1855)**
Brontë, Emily Jane (novelist); Thornton, England **(1818-1848)**
Bronzino, Agnolo (painter); Monticelli (Italy) **(1503-1572)**
Brook, Peter (director); London, 3/21/1925
Brooke, Rupert (poet); Rugby, England **(1887-1915)**
Brooks, Geraldine (Geraldine Stroock) (actress); New York City **(1925-1977)**
Brooks, Gwendolyn (poet); Topeka, Kan., 6/7/1917
Brooks, Mel (Melvin Kaminsky) (writer and film director); Brooklyn, N.Y., 1926(?)
Broun, Matthew Heywood Campbell (journalist); Brooklyn, N.Y. **(1888-1939)**
Brown, Helen Gurley (author); Green Forest, Ark., 2/18/1922
Brown, James (singer); Augusta, Ga., 5/3/1934
Brown, Joe E. (comedian); Holgate, Ohio **(1892-1973)**
Brown, John (abolitionist); Torrington, Conn. **(1800-1859)**
Brown, John Mason (critic); Louisville, Ky. **(1900-1969)**

Brown, Les (band leader); Reinerton, Pa., 1912
Brown, Pamela (actress); London **(1918-1975)**
Brown, Vanessa (Smylla Brind) (actress); Vienna, 3/24/1928
Browne, Jackson (singer and guitarist); Heidelberg, Germany, 10/9/late 1940s
Browning, Elizabeth Barrett (poet); Durham, England **(1806-1861)**
Browning, Robert (poet); London **(1812-1889)**
Brubeck, Dave (musician); Concord, Calif., 12/6/1920
Bruce, Lenny (comedian); Long Island, N.Y. **(1926-1966)**
Brueghel, Pieter (painter); nr. Breda, Flanders (Netherlands) **(1520?-1569)**
Bruhn, Erik (Belton Evers) (ballet dancer); Copenhagen, 10/3/1928
Brunelleschi, Filippo (architect); Florence (Italy) **(1377-1446)**
Brutus, Marcus Junius (Roman politician); **(85?-42 B.C.)**
Bryan, William Jennings (orator and politician); Salem, Ill. **(1860-1925)**
Bryant, Anita (singer); Barnsdall, Okla., 3/25/1940
Bryant, William Cullen (poet and editor); Cummington, Mass. **(1794-1878)**
Brynner, Yul (Taidje Khan) (actor); Sakhalin Island, Russia, 7/11/1920
Brzezinski, Zbigniew (ex-presidential adviser); Warsaw, 3/28/1928
Buber, Martin (philosopher and theologian); Vienna **(1878-1965)**
Buchanan, Edgar (actor); Humansville, Mo., **(1903-1979)**
Buchholz, Horst (actor); Berlin, 12/4/1933
Buchwald, Art (Arthur) (columnist); Mount Vernon, N.Y., 10/20/1925
Buck, Pearl S(ydenstricker) (author); Hillsboro, W. Va. **(1892-1973)**
Buckley, William F., Jr. (journalist); New York City, 11/24/1925
Buddha. *See* Gautama Buddha
Buffalo Bill (William Frederick Cody) (scout); Scott County, Iowa **(1846-1917)**
Bujold, Genevieve (actress); Montreal, 7/1/1942
Bujones, Fernando (ballet dancer); Miami, Fla., 3/9/1955
Bullins, Ed (playwright); Philadelphia, 7/2/1935
Bumbry, Grace (mezzo-soprano); St. Louis, 1/4/1937
Bunche, Ralph J. (statesman); Detroit **(1904-1971)**
Bundy, McGeorge (educator); Boston, 3/30/1919
Bundy, William Putnam (editor); Washington, D.C., 9/24/1917
Buñuel, Luis (film director); Calanda, Spain, **(1900-1983)**
Bunyan, John (preacher and author); Elstow, England **(1628-1688)**
Burbank, Luther (horticulturist); Lancaster, Mass. **(1849-1926)**
Burke, Adm. Arleigh A. (ex-Chief of Naval Operations); Boulder, Colo., 10/19/1901
Burke, Billie (comedienne); Washington, D.C. **(1885-1970)**
Burke, Edmund (statesman); Dublin **(1729-1797)**
Burne-Jones, Edward Coley (painter); Birmingham, England **(1833-1898)**
Burnett, Carol (comedienne); San Antonio, 4/26/1936
Burns, George (Nathan Birnbaum) (comedian); New York City, 1/20/1896
Burns, Robert (poet); Alloway, Scotland **(1759-1796)**
Burr, Aaron (political leader); Newark, N.J. **(1756-1836)**
Burr, Raymond (William Stacey Burr) (actor); New Westminster, British Columbia, Canada, 5/21/1917
Burroughs, Edgar Rice (novelist); Chicago **(1875-1950)**
Burrows, Abe (playwright and director); New York City, 12/18/1910
Burstyn, Ellen (Edna Rae Gillooly) (actress); Detroit, 12/7/1932
Burton, Richard (Richard Jenkins) (actor); Pontrhydfen, Wales **(1925-1984)**
Bush, Vannevar (scientist); Everett, Mass. **(1890-1974)**
Bushman, Francis X. (actor); Baltimore **(1883-1966)**
Butler, Samuel (author); Langar, England **(1835-1902)**
Buttons, Red (Aaron Chwatt) (actor); New York City, 2/5/1919
Buzzi, Ruth (comedienne); Wequetequock, Conn., 7/24/1936
Byrd, Richard Evelyn (polar explorer); Winchester, Va. **(1888-1957)**
Byrne, Jane (Mayor of Chicago); Chicago, 5/24/1934
Byron, George Gordon (6th Baron Byron) (poet); London **(1788-1824)**

C

Caan, James (actor); The Bronx, N.Y., 3/26/1939
Cabot, John (Giovanni Caboto) (navigator); Genoa (?) **(1450-1498)**
Cabot, Sebastian (navigator); Venice **(1476?-1557)**
Cadmus, Paul (painter and etcher); New York City, 12/17/1904
Caesar, Gaius Julius (statesman); Rome (100?-44 B.C.)
Caesar, Sid (comedian); Yonkers, N.Y., 9/8/1922
Cagney, James (actor); New York City, 7/17/1899
Cahn, Sammy (songwriter); New York City, 6/18/1913
Caine, Michael (Maurice J. Micklewhite) (actor); London, 3/14/1933
Calder, Alexander (sculptor); Lawnton, Pa. **(1898-1976)**
Caldwell, Erskine (novelist); White Oak, Ga., 12/17/1903
Caldwell, Sarah (opera director and conductor); Maryville, Mo., 1928
Caldwell, Taylor (novelist); Manchester, England, 9/7/1900
Caldwell, Zoe (actress); Hawthorn, Australia, 9/14/1933
Calhern, Louis (Carl Henry Vogt) (actor); Brooklyn, N.Y. **(1895-1956)**
Calhoun, John Caldwell (statesman); nr. Calhoun Mills, S.C. **(1782-1850)**
Calisher, Hortense (novelist); New York City, 12/20/1911
Callas, Maria (Maria Calogeropoulos) (dramatic soprano); New York City **(1923-1977)**
Calloway, Cab (Cabell) (band leader); Rochester, N.Y., 12/25/1907
Calvet, Corinne (actress); Paris, 4/30/1926
Calvin, John (Jean Chauvin) (religious reformer); Noyon, Picardy **(1509-1564)**
Cambridge, Godfrey (comedian); New York City **(1933-1976)**
Cameron, Rod (Rod Cox) (actor); Calgary, Alberta, Canada, 12/7/1912
Campbell, Glen (singer); nr. Delight, Ark., 4/22/1938
Camus, Albert (author); Mondovi, Algeria **(1913-1960)**
Caniff, Milton (cartoonist); Hillsboro, Ohio, 2/28/1907
Cannon, Dyan (actress); Tacoma, Wash., 1/4/1937
Canova, Judy (comedienne); Jacksonville, Fla., **(1916-1983)**
Cantinflas (Mario Moreno) (comedian); Mexico City, 8/12/1911
Cantor, Eddie (Edward Iskowitz) (actor); New York City **(1892-1964)**
Cantrell, Lana (singer); Sydney, Australia, 1944
Capote, Truman (novelist); New Orleans **(1924-1984)**
Capp, Al (Alfred Gerald Caplin) (cartoonist); New Haven, Conn. **(1909-1979)**
Capra, Frank (film producer, director); Palermo, Italy, 5/18/1897
Caravaggio, Michelangelo Merisi da (painter); Caravaggio (Italy) **(1573-1610)**
Cardin, Pierre (fashion designer); nr. Venice, 7/7/1922
Cardinale, Claudia (actress); Tunis, Tunisia, 1939
Carey, Harry (actor); New York City **(1878-1947)**
Carey, Macdonald (actor); Sioux City, Iowa, 3/15/1913
Carlisle, Kitty (singer and actress); New Orleans, 9/3/1915
Carlson, Richard (actor); Albert Lea, Minn., **(1912-1977)**
Carlyle, Thomas (essayist and historian); Ecclefechan, Scotland **(1795-1881)**
Carmichael, Hoagy (Hoagland Howard) (songwriter); Bloomington, Ind. **(1899-1981)**
Carne, Judy (Joyce Botterill) (singer); Northampton, England, 1939
Carnegie, Andrew (industrialist); Dunfermline, Scotland **(1835-1919)**
Carney, Art (actor); Mt. Vernon, N.Y., 11/4/1918
Caron, Leslie (actress); Paris, 7/1/1931
Carr, Vikki (singer); El Paso, 7/19/1942
Carracci, Annibale (painter); Bologna (Italy) **(1560-1609)**
Carracci, Lodovico (painter); Bologna (Italy) **(1555-1619)**
Carradine, David (actor); Hollywood, Calif., 12/8/1936
Carradine, John (actor); New York City, 2/5/1906
Carrillo, Leo (actor); Los Angeles **(1881-1961)**
Carroll, Diahann (Carol Diahann Johnson) (singer and actress); Bronx, N.Y., 7/17/1935
Carroll, Leo G. (actor); Weedon, England **(1892-1972)**
Carroll, Lewis (Charles Lutwidge Dodgson) (author and mathematician); Daresbury, England **(1832-1898)**
Carroll, Madeleine (actress); West Bromwich, England, 2/26/1909
Carroll, Pat (comedienne); Shreveport, La., 5/5/1927
Carson, Johnny (TV entertainer); Corning, Iowa, 10/23/1925
Carson, Kit (Christopher) (scout); Madison County, Ky. **(1809-1868)**
Carson, Rachel (biologist and author); Springdale, Pa. **(1907-1964)**
Carter, (Bessie) Lillian (President's mother); Richland, Ga., 8/15/1898
Carter, Jack (comedian); New York City, 1923
Cartier-Brisson, Henri (photographer); Chanteloup, France, 8/22/1908
Cartland, Barbara (author); England, 7/9/1901
Caruso, Enrico (Errico) (tenor); Naples, Italy **(1873-1921)**
Carver, George Washington (botanist); Missouri **(1864-1943)**
Cary, Arthur Joyce Lunel (novelist); Londonderry, Ireland **(1888-1957)**
Casals, Pablo (cellist); Vendrell, Spain **(1876-1973)**
Casanova de Seingalt, Giovanni Jacopo (adventurer); Venice **(1725-1798)**
Cash, Johnny (singer); nr. Kingsland, Ark., 2/26/1932
Cass, Peggy (comedienne); Boston, 5/21/1924
Cassatt, Mary (painter); Allegheny, Pa. **(1844-1926)**
Cassavetes, John (actor and director); New York City, 12/9/1929
Cassidy, David (singer); New York City, 4/12/1950
Cassidy, Jack (actor); Richmond Hill, Queens, N.Y. **(1927-1976)**
Cassini, Oleg (Oleg Lolewski-Cassini) (fashion designer); Paris, 4/11/1913
Castagno, Andrea del (painter); San Martino a Corella (Italy) **(c.1421-1457)**
Castle, Irene (Irene Foote) (actress and dancer); New Rochelle, N.Y. **(1893-1969)**
Castle, Vernon Blythe (dancer and aviator); Norwich, England **(1887-1918)**
Castro Ruz, Fidel (Premier); Mayari, Oriente, Cuba, 8/13/1926
Cather, Willa Sibert (novelist); Winchester, Va. **(1876-1947)**

Cato, Marcus Porcius (called Cato the Elder) (statesman); Tusculum (Italy) (234-149 B.C.)
Catt, Carrie Chapman Lane (woman suffragist); Ripon, Wis. **(1859-1947)**
Catton, Bruce (historian); Petoskey, Mich. **(1899-1978)**
Cavaliaro, Carmen (band leader); New York City, 1913
Cavett, Dick (Richard) (TV entertainer); Gibbon, Neb., 11/19/1936
Cellini, Benvenuto (goldsmith and sculptor); Florence (Italy) **(1500-1571)**
Cervantes Saavedra, Miguel de (novelist); Alcalá de Henares, Spain **(1547-1616)**
Cézanne, Paul (painter); Aix-en-Provence, France **(1839-1906)**
Chagall, Marc (painter); Vitebsk, Russia, 7/7/1887
Chaliapin, Feodor Ivanovitch (operatic basso); Kazan, Russia **(1873-1938)**
Chamberlain, Arthur Neville (statesman); Edgbaston, England **(1869-1940)**
Chamberlain, Richard (actor); Los Angeles, 3/31/1935(?)
Champion, Gower (choreographer); Geneva, Ill. **(1921-1980)**
Champion, Marge (actress and dancer); Los Angeles, 9/2/1923
Champlain, Samuel de (explorer); nr. Rochefort, France **(1567?-1635)**
Chancellor, John (TV commentator); Chicago, 7/14/1927
Chandler, Raymond (writer); Chicago **(1883-1959)**
Chanel, "Coco" (Gabriel Bonheur) (fashion designer); Issoire, France **(1883-1971)**
Chaney, Lon (actor); Colorado Springs, Colo. **(1883-1930)**
Channing, Carol (actress); Seattle, 1/31/1923
Chaplin, Geraldine (actress); Santa Monica, Calif., 7/31/1944
Chaplin, Sir Charles (actor); London **(1889-1977)**
Charisse, Cyd (Tula Finklea) (dancer and actress); Amarillo, Tex., 3/8/1923
Charlemagne (Holy Roman Emperor); birthplace unknown **(742-814)**
Charles, Ray (Ray Charles Robinson) (pianist, singer, and songwriter); Albany Ga., 9/23/1930
Chase, Chevy (Cornelius Crane Chase) (comedian); New York City, 10/8/1943
Chase, Ilka (author and actress); New York City **(1905-1978)**
Chase, Lucia (founder Ballet Theatre [now American Ballet Theatre]); Waterbury, Conn., 3/24/1907
Chatterton, Ruth (actress); New York City **(1893-1961)**
Chaucer, Geoffrey (poet); London **(1340?-1400)**
Chávez, Carlos (composer); nr. Mexico City **(1899-1978)**
Chavez, Cesar (labor leader); nr. Yuma, Ariz., 3/31/1927
Chayefsky, Paddy (Sidney) (playwright); New York City, **(1923-1981)**
Checker, Chubby (Ernest Evans) (performer); Philadelphia, 10/3/1941
Cheever, John (novelist); Quincy, Mass. **(1912-1982)**
Chekhov, Anton Pavlovich (dramatist and short-story writer); Taganrog, Russia **(1860-1904)**
Cher (Cherilyn LaPiere) (singer); El Centro, Calif., 5/20/1946
Chesterton, Gilbert Keith (author); Kensington, England **(1874-1936)**
Chevalier, Maurice (entertainer); Paris **(1888-1972)**
Chiang Kai-shek (Chief of State); Feng-hwa, China **(1887-1975)**
Child, Julia (food expert); Pasadena, Calif., 8/15/1912
Chippendale, Thomas (cabinet-maker); Otley, England **(1718?-1779)**
Chirico, Giorgio de (painter); Vólos, Greece, **(1888-1978)**
Chisholm, Shirley (ex-Representative); Brooklyn, N.Y., 11/30/1924
Chopin, Frédéric François (composer); nr. Warsaw **(1810-1849)**
Chou En-lai. *See* Zhou Enlai
Christian, Linda (Blanca Rosa Welter) (actress); Tampico, Mexico, 11/13/1924
Christie, Agatha (mystery writer); Torquay, England, **(1890-1976)**
Christie, Julie (actress); Chukua, India, 4/14/1941
Christopher, Jordon (actor and musician); Youngstown, Ohio, 1941
Christy, June (singer); Springfield, Ill., 1925
Churchill, Sir Winston Leonard Spencer (statesman); Blenheim Palace, Oxfordshire, England **(1874-1965)**
Cicero, Marcus Tullius (orator and statesman); Arpinum (Italy) **(106-43 B.C.)**
Cilento, Diane (actress); Queensland, Australia, 10/5/1933
Cimabue, Giovanni (painter); Florence (Italy) **(c.1240-c.1302)**
Cimino, Michael (film director); New York City, 1943(?)
Clair, René (René Chomette) (film director); Paris **(1898-1981)**
Claire, Ina (Ina Fagan) (actress); Washington, D.C., 10/15/1895
Clapton, Eric (singer and guitarist); Ripley, England, 3/30/1945
Clark, Dane (Barney Zanville) (actor); New York City, 2/18/1915
Clark, Dick (TV personality); Mt. Vernon, N.Y., 11/30/1929
Clark, Mark W. (general); Madison Barracks, N.Y. **(1896-1984)**
Clark, Petula (singer); Epsom, England, 11/15/1934
Clark, Roy (country music artist); Meherrin, Va., 4/15/1933
Clark, William (explorer); Caroline County, Va. **(1770-1838)**
Claude Lorrain (Claude Gellée) (painter); Champagne, France **(1600-1682)**
Clay, Henry (statesman); Hanover County, Va. **(1777-1852)**
Clay, Lucius D. (banker, ex-general); Marietta, Ga. **(1897-1978)**
Clayburgh, Jill (actress); New York City, 4/30/1944
Clemenceau, Georges (statesman); Mouilleron-en-Pareds, Vondée, France **(1841-1929)**
Clemens, Samuel L. *See* Mark Twain
Cleopatra (Queen of Egypt); Alexandria, Egypt **(69-30 B.C.)**
Cliburn, Van (Harvey Lavan Cliburn, Jr.) (concert pianist); Shreveport, La., 7/12/1934
Clifford, Clark M. (ex-Secretary of Defense); Ft. Scott, Kan., 12/25/1906
Clift, Montgomery (actor); Omaha, Neb. **(1920-1966)**
Clooney, Rosemary (singer); Maysville, Ky., 5/23/1928
Clurman, Harold (stage producer); New York City **(1901-1980)**
Cobb, Irvin Shrewsbury (humorist); Paducah, Ky. **(1876-1944)**
Cobb, Lee J. (Leo Jacob) (actor); New York City **(1911-1976)**
Coburn, Charles Douville (actor); Savannah, Ga. **(1877-1961)**
Coburn, James (actor); Laurel, Neb., 8/31/1928
Coca, Imogene (comedienne); Philadelphia, 11/18/1908
Cocker, Joe (John Robert Cocker) (singer); Sheffield, England, 5/20/1944
Coco, James (actor); New York City, 3/21/1929
Cocteau, Jean (author); Maison-Lafitte, France **(1891-1963)**
Cody, W. F. *See* Buffalo Bill
Cohan, George Michael (actor and dramatist); Providence, R.I. **(1878-1942)**
Cohen, Leonard (singer and songwriter); Montreal, 1935
Colbert, Claudette (Lily Chauchoin) (actress); Paris, 9/13/1903
Colby, William E. (ex-Director of CIA); St. Paul, 1/4/1920
Cole, Nat "King" (singer); Montgomery, Ala. **(1919-1965)**
Cole, Natalie (singer); Los Angeles, 2/6/1950
Cole, Thomas (painter); Lancashire, England **(1801-1848)**
Coleridge, Samuel Taylor (poet); Ottery St. Mary, England **(1772-1834)**
Colette (Sidonie-Gabrielle Colette) (novelist); St.-Sauveur, France **(c. 1873-1954)**
Collingwood, Charles (TV commentator); Three Rivers, Mich., 6/4/1917
Collins, Dorothy (Marjorie Chandler) (singer); Windsor, Ontario, Canada, 11/18/1926
Collins, Joan (actress); London 5/23/1933
Collins, Judy (singer); Seattle, 5/1/1939
Colman, Ronald (actor); Richmond, England **(1891-1958)**
Colonna, Jerry (comedian); Boston, 1905
Columbus, Christopher (Cristoforo Colombo) (discoverer of America); Genoa (Italy) **(1451-1506)**
Comden, Betty (writer); New York City, 5/3/1919
Commager, Henry Steele (historian); Pittsburgh, 10/25/1902
Como, Perry (Pierino) (singer); Canonsburg, Pa., 5/18/1913
Compton, Karl Taylor (physicist); Wooster, Ohio **(1887-1954)**
Conant, James B. (educator and statesman); Dorchester, Mass. **(1893-1978)**
Condon, Eddie (jazz musician); Goodland, Ind. **(1905-1973)**
Confucius (K'ung Fu-tzu) (philosopher); Shantung province, China **(c. 551-479 B.C.)**
Congreve, William (dramatist); nr. Leeds, England **(1670-1729)**
Connelly, Marc (playwright); McKeesport, Pa. **(1890-1980)**
Connery, Sean (actor); Edinburgh, Scotland, 8/25/1930
Conniff, Ray (band leader); Attleboro, Mass., 11/6/1916
Connors, Mike (Krekor Ohanian) (actor); Fresno, Calif., 8/15/1925
Conrad, Joseph (Teodor Jozef Konrad Korzeniowski) (novelist); Berdichev, Ukraine **(1857-1924)**
Conrad, Robert (Conrad Robert Falk) (actor); Chicago, 3/1/1935
Conrad, William (actor); Louisville, Ky., 9/27/1920
Conried, Hans (Frank Foster) (actor); Baltimore **(1915-1982)**
Constable, John (painter); East Bergholt, Suffolk, England **(1776-1837)**
Constantine II (ex-king); Athens, 6/2/1940
Conte, Richard (actor); New York City **(1916-1975)**
Converse, Frank (actor); St. Louis, 1938
Conway, Tim (comedian); Chagrin Falls, Ohio, 12/15/1933
Coogan, Jackie (actor); Los Angeles **(1914-1984)**
Cooke, Alistair (Alfred Alistair); (TV narrator and journalist); Manchester, England, 11/20/1908
Cooley, Denton A(rthur) (heart surgeon); Houston, Tex., 8/22/1920
Coolidge, Rita (singer); Nashville, Tenn., 1944
Cooper, Alice (Vincent Furnier) (rock musician); Detroit, 2/4/1948
Cooper, Gary (Frank James Cooper) (actor); Helena, Mont. **(1901-1961)**
Cooper, Jackie (actor and director); Los Angeles, 9/15/1922
Cooper, James Fenimore (novelist); Burlington, N.J. **(1789-1851)**
Cooper, Peter (industrialist and philanthropist); New York City **(1791-1883)**
Copernicus, Nicolaus (Mikolaj Kopernik) (astronomer); Thorn, Poland **(1473-1543)**
Copland, Aaron (composer); Brooklyn, N.Y., 11/14/1900
Copley, John Singleton (painter); Boston, Mass. **(1738-1815)**
Coppolla, Francis Ford (film director); Detroit, 4/7/1939

Corelli, Franco (operatic tenor); Ancona, Italy, 4/8/1923
Corneille, Pierre (dramatist); Rouen, France **(1606-1684)**
Cornell, Katharine (actress); Berlin **(1893-1974)**
Coret, Jean Baptiste Camille (painter); Paris **(1796-1875)**
Correggio, Antonio Allegri da (painter); Correggio (Italy) **(1494-1534)**
Corsaro, Frank (opera director); New York harbor, 12/22/1924
Cortés (or Cortez), Hernando (explorer); Medellin, Spain **(1485-1547)**
Cosby, Bill (actor); Philadelphia, 7/12/1937
Cosell, Howard (Howard Cohen) (sportscaster); Winston-Salem, N.C., 3/25/1920
Costa-Gavras, Henri (Kostantinos Gavras) (film director); Athens, 1933
Costello, Lou (comedian); Paterson, N.J. **(1908-1959)**
Cotten, Joseph (actor); Petersburg, Va., 5/15/1905
Courbet, Gustave (painter); Ornans, France **(1819-1877)**
Courrèges, André (fashion designer); Pau, France, 3/9/1923
Courtenay, Tom (actor); Hull, England, 2/25/1937
Cousins, Norman (publisher); Union Hill, N.J., 6/24/1915
Cousteau, Jacques-Yves (marine explorer); St. André-de-Cubzac, France, 6/11/1910
Coward, Sir Noel (playwright and actor); Teddington, England **(1899-1973)**
Cowles, Gardner (newspaper publisher); Algona, Iowa, 1/31/1903
Cowper, William (poet); Great Berkhamstead, England **(1731-1800)**
Cozzens, James Gould (novelist); Chicago **(1903-1978)**
Crabbe, Buster (Clarence) (actor); Oakland, Calif. **(1908-1983)**
Crain, Jeanne (actress); Barstow, Calif., 5/25/1925
Cranach, Lucas, the elder (painter); Kronach (Germany) **(1472-1553)**
Crane, Hart (poet); Garrettsville, Ohio **(1899-1932)**
Crane, Stephen (novelist and poet); Newark, N.J. **(1871-1900)**
Crawford, Broderick (actor); Philadelphia, 12/9/1911
Crawford, Cheryl (stage producer); Akron, Ohio, 9/24/1902
Crawford, Joan (Lucille LeSueur) (actress and business executive); San Antonio **(1908-1977)**
Crenna, Richard (actor); Los Angeles, 11/30/1927
Crespin, Régine (operatic soprano); Marseilles, France, 2/23/1929
Crichton, (John) Michael (novelist); Chicago, 10/23/1942
Crisp, Donald (actor); London **(1880-1974)**
Croce, Benedetto (philosopher); Peseasseroli, Aquila, Italy **(1866-1952)**
Croce, Jim (singer); Philadelphia **(1942-1973)**
Crockett, Davy (David) (frontiersman); Greene County, Tenn. **(1786-1836)**
Cromwell, Oliver (statesman); Huntingdon, England **(1599-1658)**
Cronin, A. J. (Archibald J. Cronin) (novelist); Cardross, Scotland **(1896-1981)**
Cronkite, Walter (TV newscaster); St. Joseph, Mo., 11/4/1916
Cronyn, Hume (actor); London, Ontario, Canada, 7/18/1911
Crosby, Bing (Harry Lillis) (singer, actor); Tacoma, Wash. **(1904-1977)**
Crosby, Bob (musician); Spokane, Wash., 8/23/1913
Cross, Milton (opera commentator); New York City **(1897-1975)**
Crouse, Russel (playwright); Findlay, Ohio **(1893-1966)**
Cugat, Xavier (band leader); Barcelona, Spain, 1/1/1900
Cukor, George (film director); New York City **(1899-1983)**
Cullen, Bill (William Lawrence Cullen) (radio and TV entertainer); Pittsburgh, 2/18/1920
Culp, Robert (actor); Berkeley, Calif., 8/16/1930
Cummings, E. E. (Edward Estlin Cummings) (poet); Cambridge, Mass. **(1894-1962)**
Cummings, Robert (actor); Joplin, Mo., 6/9/1910
Curie, Marie (Marja Sklodowska) (physical chemist); Warsaw **(1867-1934)**
Curtin, Phyllis (soprano); Clarksburg, W.Va., 12/3/1927
Curtis, Tony (Bernard Schwartz) (actor); Bronx, N.Y., 6/3/1925
Curzon, Clifford (concert pianist); London **(1907-1982)**
Custer, George Armstrong (army officer); New Rumley, Ohio **(1839-1876)**

D

Dahl, Arlene (actress); Minneapolis, 8/11/1928
Dailey, Dan (actor and dancer); New York City, **(1917-1978)**
Daley, Richard J. (Mayor of Chicago); Chicago **(1902-1976)**
Dali, Salvador (painter); Figueras, Spain, 5/11/1904
Daly, James (actor); Wisconsin Rapids, Wis. **(1918-1978)**
Daly, John (radio and TV news analyst); Johannesburg, South Africa, 2/20/1914
d'Amboise, Jacques (ballet dancer); Dedham, Mass., 7/28/1934
Damone, Vic (Vito Farinola) (singer); Brooklyn, N.Y., 6/12/1928
Damrosch, Walter Johannes (orchestra conductor); Breslau (Poland) **(1862-1950)**
Dana, Charles Anderson (editor); Hinsdale, N.H. **(1819-1897)**
Dandridge, Dorothy (actress); Cleveland **(1923-1965)**
Dangerfield, Rodney (comedian); Babylon, L.I., N.Y., 1921
Daniels, Bebe (Virginia Daniels) (actress); Dallas **(1901-1971)**
Danilova, Alexandra (ballerina); Peterhof, Russia, 1/20/1904
Dannay, Frederic (novelist, pseudonym Ellery Queen); Brooklyn, N.Y. **(1905-1982)**
Danner, Blythe (actress); Philadelphia, 1944(?)
D'Annunzio, Gabriele (soldier and author); Francaville at Mare, Pescara, Italy **(1863-1938)**
Dante (or Durante) Alighieri (poet); Florence (Italy) **(1265-1321)**
Danton, Georges Jacques (French Revolutionary leader); Arcis-sur-Aube, France **(1759-1794)**
Darnell, Linda (actress); Dallas **(1921-1965)**
Darren, James (actor); Philadelphia, 6/8/1936
Darrieux, Danielle (actress); Bordeaux, France, 5/1/1917
Darrow, Clarence Seward (lawyer); Kinsman, Ohio **(1857-1938)**
Darwin, Charles Robert (naturalist); Shrewsbury, England **(1809-1882)**
daSilva, Howard (actor); Cleveland, 5/4/1909
Dassin, Jules (film director); Middletown, Conn., 12/18/1911
Daumier, Honoré (caricaturist); Marseilles, France **(1808-1879)**
Dauphin, Claude (actor); Corbeil, France **(1903-1978)**
David, Jacques-Louis (painter); Paris **(1748-1825)**
David (King of Israel and Judah) **(died c. 973 B.C.)**
Davies, Marion (Marion Douras) (actress); New York City **(1898?-1961)**
da Vinci, Leonardo (painter and scientist); Vinci, Tuscany (Italy) **(1452-1519)**
Davis, Bette (actress); Lowell, Mass., 4/5/1908
Davis, Elmer Holmes (radio commentator); Aurora, Ind. **(1890-1958)**
Davis, Jefferson (President of the Confederacy); Christian (now Todd) County, Ky. **(1808-1889)**
Davis, Mac (singer); Lubbock, Tex., 1/21/1942
Davis, Miles (jazz trumpeter); Alton, Ill., 5/25/1926
Davis, Ossie (actor and writer); Cogdell, Ga., 12/18/1917
Davis, Sammy, Jr. (actor and singer); New York City, 12/8/1925
Davis, Skeeter (Mary Francis Penick) (singer); Dry Ridge, Ky., 12/30/1931
Davis, Stuart (painter); Philadelphia **(1894-1964)**
Day, Dennis (singer); New York City, 5/21/1917
Day, Doris (Doris von Kappelhoff) (singer and actress); Cincinnati, 4/3/1924
Day, Laraine (La Raine Johnson) (actress); Roosevelt, Utah, 10/13/1920
Dayan, Moshe (ex-Defense Minister of Israel); Dagania, Palestine (Jordan) **(1915-1981)**
Dean, James (actor); Marion, Ind. **(1931-1955)**
Dean, Jimmy (singer); Seth Ward, nr. Plainview, Tex., 8/10/1928
De Bakey, Michael E. (heart surgeon); Lake Charles, La., 9/7/1908
de Beauvoir, Simone (novelist and philosopher); Paris, 1/9/1908
Debs, Eugene Victor (Socialist leader); Terre Haute, Ind. **(1855-1926)**
Debussy, Claude Achille (composer); St. Germain-en-Laye, France **(1862-1918)**
De Carlo, Yvonne (Peggy Yvonne Middleton) (actress); Vancouver, B.C., Canada, 9/1/1924
de Chirico, Giorgio (painter); Volos, Greece, **(1888-1978)**
Dee, Ruby (Ruby Ann Wallace) (actress); Cleveland, 10/27/1924(?)
Dee, Sandra (Alexandra Zuck) (actress); Bayonne, N.J., 4/23/1942
Defoe, Daniel (novelist); London **(1659?-1731)**
Degas, Hilaire Germain Edgar (painter); Paris **(1834-1917)**
de Gaulle, Charles André Joseph Marie (soldier and statesman); Lille, France **(1890-1970)**
DeHaven, Gloria (actress); Los Angeles, 7/23/1925
de Havilland, Olivia (actress); Tokyo, 7/1/1916
Dekker, Albert (actor); Brooklyn, N.Y. **(1904-1968)**
de Kooning, Willem (painter); Rotterdam, 4/24/1904
Delacroix, Eugène (painter); Charenton-St. Maurice, France **(1798-1863)**
de la Renta, Oscar (fashion designer); Santo Domingo, Dominican Republic, 7/22/1932
Delaunay, Robert (painter); Paris **(1885-1941)**
De Laurentiis, Dino (film producer); Torre Annunziata, Bay of Naples, Italy, 8/8/1919
Delon, Alain (actor); Sceaux, France, 11/8/1935
Del Rio, Dolores (Dolores Ansunsolo) (actress); Durango, Mexico **(1905-1983)**
DeLuise, Dom (comedian); Brooklyn, N.Y., 8/1/1933
Demarest, William (actor); St. Paul, 2/27/1892
de Mille, Agnes (choreographer); New York City
De Mille, Cecil Blount (film director); Ashfield, Mass. **(1881-1959)**
Demosthenes (orator); Athens **(385?-322 B.C.)**
Deneuve, Catherine (actress); Paris, 10/22/1943
De Niro, Robert (actor); New York City, 8/17/1943
Dennis, Sandy (actress); Hastings, Neb., 4/27/1937
Denver, John (Henry John Deutschendorf, Jr.) (singer); Roswell, N.M., 12/31/1943

Derain, André (painter); Chatou, Seine-et-Oise, France **(1880-1954)**
Descartes, René (philosopher and mathematician); La Haye, France **(1596-1650)**
De Seversky, Alexander P. (aviator); Tiflis, Russia **(1894-1974)**
De Sica, Vittorio (film director); Sora, Italy **(1901-1974)**
Desmond, Johnny (composer); Detroit, 11/14/1921
Desmond, William (actor); Dublin **(1878-1949)**
De Soto, Hernando (explorer); Barcarrota, Spain **(1500?-1542)**
De Valera, Eàmon (ex-President of Ireland); New York City **(1882-1975)**
Devine, Andy (actor); Flagstaff, Ariz. **(1905-1977)**
De Vries, Peter (novelist); Chicago, 2/27/1910
Dewey, George (admiral); Montpelier, Vt. **(1837-1917)**
Dewey, John (philosopher and educator); Burlington, Vt. **(1859-1952)**
Dewey, Thomas E. (politician); Owosso, Mich. **(1902-1971)**
Dewhurst, Colleen (actress); Montreal, 1926(?)
Diamond, Neil (singer); Brooklyn, N.Y., 1/24/1941
Dickens, Charles John Huffam (novelist); Portsea, England **(1812-1870)**
Dickey, James (poet); Atlanta, 2/2/1923
Dickinson, Angie (Angeline Brown) (actress); Kulm, N.D., 9/30/1932
Dickinson, Emily Elizabeth (poet); Amherst, Mass. **(1830-1886)**
Diddley, Bo (Elias McDaniel) (guitarist); McComb, Miss., 12/30/1928
Diefenbaker, John G. (ex-Prime Minister); Grey County, Ontario, Canada **(1895-1979)**
Dietrich, Marlene (Maria Magdalena von Losch) (actress); Berlin, 12/27/1901
Diller, Phyllis (Phyllis Driver) (comedienne); Lima, Ohio, 7/17/1917
Dillinger, John (American bank robber); prob. Indianapolis **(1902-1934)**
Dillman, Bradford (actor); San Francisco, 4/14/1930
Dine, Jim (painter); Cincinnati, 6/16/1935
Diogenes (philosopher); Sinope (Turkey) **(412?-323 B.C.)**
Dion (Dion DiMucci) (singer); Bronx, N.Y., 7/18/1939
Dior, Christian (fashion designer); Granville, France **(1905-1957)**
Disney, Walt(er) Elias (film animator and producer); Chicago **(1901-1966)**
Disraeli, Benjamin (Earl of Beaconsfield) (statesman); London **(1804-1881)**
Dix, Dorothea (civil rights reformer); Hampden, Me. **(1802-1887)**
Dix, Richard (Ernest Carlton Brimmer) (actor); St. Paul **(1894-1949)**
Doctorow, E(dgar) L(aurence) (novelist); New York City, 1/6/1931
Dodgson, C. L. *See* Carroll, Lewis.
Dolin, Anton (dancer); Slinfold, England **(1904-1983)**
Domingo, Placido (tenor); Madrid, 1/21/1941
Domino, Fats (Antoine) (musician); New Orleans, 2/26/1928
Donahue, Phil (television personality); Cleveland, 12/21/1935
Donahue, Troy (Merle Johnson) (actor); New York City, 1/27/1938
Donat, Robert (actor); Withington, England **(1905-1958)**
Donatello (Donato Niccolò di Betto Bardi) (sculptor); Florence (Italy) **(c.1386-1466)**
Donne, John (poet); London **(1573-1631)**
Donovan (Donovan Leitch) (singer and songwriter); Glasgow, Scotland, 2/10/1946
Doolittle, James H. (ex-Air Force general); Alameda, Calif., 12/14/1896
Dorati, Antal (orchestra conductor); Budapest, 4/9/1906
Dorsey, Jimmy (band leader); Shenandoah, Pa. **(1904-1957)**
Dorsey, Tommy (band leader); Mahonoy Plains, Pa. **(1905-1956)**
Dos Passos, John (author); Chicago **(1896-1970)**
Dostoevski, Fyodor Mikhailovich (novelist); Moscow **(1821-1881)**
Douglas, Helen Gahagan (ex-Representative); Boonton, N.J. **(1900-1980)**
Douglas, Kirk (Issur Danielovitch) (actor); Amsterdam, N.Y., 12/9/1916
Douglas, Melvyn (Melvyn Hesselberg) (actor); Macon, Ga., **(1901-1981)**
Douglas, Mike (Michael D. Dowd, Jr.) (TV personality); Chicago, 8/11/1925
Douglas, Paul (actor); Philadelphia **(1907-1959)**
Douglas, Stephen Arnold (politician); Brandon, Vt. **(1813-1861)**
Dowling, Eddie (Edward Goucher) (actor and stage producer); Woonsocket, R.I., **(1894-1976)**
Downs, Hugh (TV entertainer); Akron, Ohio, 2/14/1921
Doyle, Sir Arthur Conan (novelist and spiritualist); Edinburgh, Scotland **(1859-1930)**
Drake, Alfred (singer and actor); New York City, 10/7/1914
Drake, Sir Francis (navigator); Tavistock, England **(1545-1596)**
Dreiser, Theodore (writer); Terre Haute, Ind. **(1871-1945)**
Dressler, Marie (Leila Koeber) (actress); Cobourg, Ontario, Canada **(1869-1934)**
Dreyfus, Alfred (French army officer); Mulhouse (France) **(1859-1935)**
Dreyfuss, Richard (actor); Brooklyn, N.Y., 10/29/1947
Drury, Allen (novelist); Houston, 9/2/1918
Dryden, John (poet); Northamptonshire, England **(1631-1700)**
Dubček, Alexander (ex-President of Czechoslovakia); Uhrovec (Czechoslovakia), 11/27/1921
Dubinsky, David (David Dobnievski) (labor leader); Brest-Litovsk (U.S.S.R.) **(1892-1982)**
Duchamp, Marcel (painter); Blainville, France **(1887-1968)**
Duchin, Peter (pianist and band leader); New York City, 7/28/1937
Duff, Howard (actor); Bremerton, Wash., 11/24/1917
Dufy, Raoul (painter); Le Havre, France **(1877-1953)**
Duke, James B. (industrialist); nr. Durham, N.C. **(1856-1925)**
Duke, Patty (Anna Marie Duke) (actress); New York City, 12/14/1946
Dullea, Keir (actor); Cleveland, 5/30/1936(?)
Dulles, Allen Welsh (ex-Director of CIA); Watertown, N.Y. **(1893-1969)**
Dulles, John Foster (statesman); Washington, D.C. **(1888-1959)**
Dumas, Alexandre (called Dumas fils) (novelist); Paris **(1824-1895)**
Dumas, Alexandre (called Dumas père) (novelist); Villers-Cotterets, France **(1802-1870)**
Du Maurier, Daphine (novelist); London, 5/13/1907
Du Maurier, George Louis Palmella Busson (novelist); Paris **(1834-1896)**
Dumont, Margaret (actress); **(1889-1965)**
Dunaway, Faye (actress); Bascom, Fla., 1/14/1941
Duncan, Isadora (dancer); San Francisco **(1878-1927)**
Duncan, Sandy (actress); Henderson, Tex., 2/20/1946
Dunn, James (actor); Santa Monica, Calif. **(1905-1967)**
Dunne, Irene (actress); Louisville, Ky., 12/20/1904
Dunnock, Mildred (actress); Baltimore, 1/25/1906
Du Pont, Pierre S. (economist); Paris **(1739-1817)**
Durante, Jimmy (comedian); New York City **(1893-1980)**
Durbin, Deanna (Edna Mae) (actress); Winnipeg, Canada, 12/4/1922
Dürer, Albrecht (painter and engraver); Nürnberg (Germany) **(1471-1528)**
Durrell, Lawrence George (novelist); Julundur, India, 2/27/1912
Duse, Eleonora (actress); Chioggia, Italy **(1859-1924)**
Duvalier, Jean-Claude (President; son of "Papa Doc"); Port-au-Prince, Haiti, 7/3/1951
Duvall, Robert (actor); San Diego, Calif., 1931
Dvořák, Antonin (composer); Nelahozeves (Czechoslovakia) **(1841-1904)**
Dylan, Bob (Robert Zimmerman) (folk singer and composer); Duluth, Minn., 5/24/1941

E

Eagels, Joanne (actress); Kansas City, Mo. **(1894-1929)**
Eakins, Thomas (painter and sculptor); Philadelphia, **(1844-1916)**
Earhart, Amelia (aviator); Atchison, Kan. **(1898-1937)**
Eastman, George (inventor); Waterville, N.Y. **(1854-1932)**
Eastwood, Clint (actor); San Francisco, 5/31/1931(?)
Ebsen, Buddy (Christian Ebsen, Jr.) (actor); Belleville, Ill., 4/2/1908
Eckstine, Billy (singer); Pittsburgh, 7/8/1914
Eddy, Mary Baker (founder of Christian Science Church); Bow, N.H. **(1821-1910)**
Eddy, Nelson (baritone and actor); Providence, R.I. **(1901-1967)**
Eden, Sir Anthony (Earl of Avon) (ex-Prime Minister); Durham, England **(1897-1977)**
Eden, Barbara (Barbara Huffman) (actress); Tucson, Ariz., 1934
Edison, Thomas Alva (inventor); Milan, Ohio **(1847-1931)**
Edwards, Ralph (TV and radio producer); Merino, Colo., 1913
Edwards, Vincent (actor); Brooklyn, N.Y., 7/7/1928
Egan, Richard (actor); San Francisco, 7/29/1923
Eglevsky, André (ballet dancer); Moscow **(1917-1977)**
Ehrlich, Paul (bacteriologist); Strzelin (Poland) **(1854-1915)**
Einstein, Albert (physicist); Ulm, Germany **(1879-1955)**
Eisenhower, Milton S. (educator); Abilene, Kan., 9/15/1899
Eisenstaedt, Alfred (photographer and photojournalist); Dirschau (Poland), 12/6/1898
Ekberg, Anita (actress); Malmö, Sweden, 9/29/1931
Eldridge, Florence (Florence McKechnie) (actress); Brooklyn, N.Y., 9/5/1901
Elgar, Sir Edward (composer); Worcester, England **(1857-1934)**
Elgart, Larry (band leader); New London, Conn., 3/20/1922
El Greco (Domenicos Theotocopoulos) (painter); Candia, Crete (Greece) **(c.1541-1614)**
Eliot, George (Mary Ann Evans) (novelist); Chilvers Coton, England **(1819-1880)**
Eliot, Thomas Stearns (poet); St. Louis **(1888-1965)**
Ellington, Duke (Edward Kennedy) (jazz musician); Washington, D.C. **(1899-1974)**
Elliot, "Mama" Cass (Ellen Naomi Cohen) (singer); Baltimore **(1941-1974)**
Elman, Mischa (violinist); Stalnoye, Ukraine **(1891-1967)**
Emerson, Ralph Waldo (philosopher and poet); Boston **(1803-1882)**
Enesco, Georges (composer); Dorohoi, Romania **(1881-1955)**

Engels, Friedrich (Socialist writer); Barmen (Germany) **(1820-1895)**
Entremont, Philippe (concert pianist); Rheims, France, 6/7/1934
Epicurus (philosopher); Samos (Greece) **(341-270 B.C.)**
Epstein, Sir Jacob (sculptor); New York City **(1880-1959)**
Erasmus, Desiderius (Gerhard Gerhards) (scholar); Rotterdam **(1466?-1536)**
Erhard, Ludwig (ex-Chancellor); Furth, Germany **(1897-1977)**
Erickson, Leif (actor); Alameda, Calif., 10/27/1911
Ericson, Leif (navigator); **(c. 10th century A.D.)**
Erikson, Erik H. (psychoanalyst); Frankfurt, Germany, 6/15/1902
Ernst, Max (painter); Bruhl, Germany **(1891-1976)**
Euclid (mathematician); Megara (Greece) **(c. 300 B.C.)**
Euripides (dramatist); Salamis (Greece) **(c.484-407 B.C.)**
Evans, Dale (Frances Butts) (actress and singer); Uvalde, Tex., 10/31/1912
Evans, Dame Edith (actress); London **(1888-1976)**
Evans, Maurice (actor); Dorchester, England, 6/3/1901
Everett, Chad (actor); (Raymon Lee Cramton) South Bend, Ind., 6/11/1936
Evers, Charles (civil rights leader); Decatur, Miss., 9/14/1923(?)
Evers, Medgar (civil rights leader); Decatur, Miss. **(1925-1963)**
Ewell, Tom (Yewell Tompkins) (actor); Owensboro, Ky., 4/29/1909

F

Fabian (Fabian Anthony Forte) (singer); Philadelphia, 2/6/1943
Fabray, Nanette (Nanette Fabarés) (actress); San Diego, Calif., 10/27/1922
Fadiman, Clifton (literary critic); Brooklyn, N.Y., 5/15/1904
Fairbanks, Douglas (Douglas Ulman) (actor); Denver **(1883-1939)**
Fairbanks, Douglas, Jr. (actor); New York City, 12/9/1909
Faith, Percy (conductor); Toronto **(1908-1976)**
Falk, Peter (actor); New York City, 9/16/1927
Falla, Manuel de (composer); Cadiz, Spain **(1876-1946)**
Faraday, Michael (physicist); Newington, England **(1791-1867)**
Farber, Barry (radio-TV broadcaster); Baltimore, Md., 1930
Farmer, James (civil rights leader); Marshall, Tex., 1/12/1920
Farnum, William (actor); Boston **(1876-1953)**
Farrell, Charles (actor); Onset Bay, Mass., 1901
Farrell, Eileen (operatic soprano); Willimantic, Conn., 2/13/1920
Farrell, Glenda (actress); Enid, Okla. **(1904-1971)**
Farrell, James T. (novelist); Chicago **(1904-1979)**
Farrell, Suzanne (Roberta Sue Ficker) (ballerina); Cincinnati, 8/16/1945
Farrow, Mia (actress); Los Angeles, 2/9/1946
Fasanella, Ralph (painter); New York City, 9/2/1914
Fassbinder, Rainer Werner (film and stage director); Bad Worishofen, West Germany **(1946-1982)**
Fast, Howard (novelist); New York City, 11/11/1914
Faulkner, William (novelist); New Albany, Miss. **(1897-1962)**
Fawcett, Farrah (actress); Corpus Christi, Tex., 2/2/1947(?)
Faye, Alice (Ann Leppert) (actress); New York City, 5/5/1915
Feiffer, Jules (cartoonist); New York City, 1/26/1929
Feininger, Lyonel (painter); New York City **(1871-1956)**
Feldon, Barbara (actress); Pittsburgh, 3/12/1941
Feliciano, José (singer); Larez, Puerto Rico, 9/10/1945
Felker, Clay S. (editor and publisher); St. Louis, 10/2/1925(?)
Fellini, Federico (film director); Rimini, Italy, 1/20/1920
Fender, Freddie (Baldemar Huerta) (singer); San Benito, Tex., 1937
Ferber, Edna (novelist); Kalamazoo, Mich. **(1885-1968)**
Ferguson, Maynard (jazz trumpeter); Verdun, Quebec, Canada, 5/4/1928
Fermi, Enrico (atomic physicist); Rome **(1901-1954)**
Fernandel (Fernand Joseph Desire Contandin) (actor); Marseilles, France **(1903-1971)**
Ferrer, José (actor and director); Santurce, Puerto Rico, 1/8/1912
Ferrer, Mel (actor); Eiberon, N.J., 8/25/1917
Fetchit, Stepin (comedian); Key West, Fla., 1902
Fiedler, Arthur (conductor); Boston **(1894-1979)**
Field, Eugene (poet); St. Louis **(1850-1895)**
Field, Marshall (merchant); nr. Conway, Mass. **(1834-1906)**
Field, Sally (actress); Pasadena, Calif., 11/6/1946
Fielding, Henry (novelist); nr. Glastonbury, England **(1707-1754)**
Fields, Gracie (comedienne); Rochdale, England **(1898-1979)**
Fields, Totie (comedienne); Hartford, Conn. **(1931-1978)**
Fields, W. C. (William Claude Dukenfield) (comedian); Philadelphia **(1880-1946)**
Filene, Edward A. (merchant); **(1860-1937)**
Finch, Peter (actor); Kensington, England **(1916-1977)**
Finney, Albert (actor); Salford, England, 5/9/1936
Firkusny, Rudolf (pianist); Napajedia (Czechoslovakia), 2/11/1912
Fischer-Dieskau, Dietrich (baritone); Berlin, 5/28/1925
Fisher, Eddie (Edwin) (singer); Philadelphia, 8/10/1928
Fitzgerald, Barry (William Joseph Shields) (actor); Dublin **(1888-1961)**
Fitzgerald, Edward (radio broadcaster); Troy, N.Y. **(1898(?)-1982)**
Fitzgerald, Ella (singer); Newport News, Va., 4/25/1918
Fitzgerald, F. Scott (Francis Scott Key) (novelist); St. Paul, Minn. **(1896-1940)**
Fitzgerald, Geraldine (actress); Dublin, 11/24/1914
Fitzgerald, Pegeen (radio broadcaster); Norcatur, Kan., 1910
Flack, Roberta (singer); Black Mountain, N.C., 2/10/1940
Flagstad, Kirsten (Wagnerian soprano); Hamar, Norway **(1895-1962)**
Flatt, Lester Raymond (bluegrass musician); Overton County, Tenn. **(1914-1979)**
Flaubert, Gustave (novelist); Rouen, France **(1821-1880)**
Fleming, Sir Alexander (bacteriologist); Lochfield, Scotland **(1881-1955)**
Fleming, Rhonda (Marilyn Louis) (actress); Los Angeles, 8/10/1923
Flynn, Errol (actor); Hobart, Tasmania **(1909-1959)**
Foch, Nina (actress); Leyden, Netherlands, 4/20/1924
Fodor, Eugene (violinist); Turkey Creek, Colo., 3/5/1950
Fonda, Henry (actor); Grand Island, Neb. **(1905-1982)**
Fonda, Jane (actress); New York City, 12/21/1937
Fonda, Peter (actor); New York City, 2/23/1939
Fontaine, Frank (singer and comedian); Cambridge, Mass. **(1920-1979)**
Fontaine, Joan (Joan de Havilland) (actress); Tokyo, 10/22/1917
Fontanne, Lynn (actress); London, **(1887-1983)**
Fonteyn, Dame Margot (Margaret Hookham) (ballerina); Reigate, England, 5/18/1919
Forbes, Malcolm S(tevenson) (publisher and sportsman); Brooklyn, N.Y., 8/19/1919
Ford, Glenn (Gwyllyn Ford) (actor); Quebec, 5/1/1916
Ford, Henry (industrialist); Greenfield, Mich. **(1863-1947)**
Ford, Henry, II (auto maker); Detroit, 9/4/1917
Ford, John (film director); Cape Elizabeth, Me. **(1895-1973)**
Ford, Paul (actor); Baltimore **(1901-1976)**
Ford, Tennessee Ernie (Ernie Jennings Ford) (singer); Bristol, Tenn., 2/13/1919
Forrester, Maureen (contralto); Montreal, 7/25/1930
Forsythe, John (actor); Carney's Point, N.J., 1/29/1918
Fosdick, Harry Emerson (clergyman); Buffalo, N.Y. **(1878-1968)**
Fosse, Bob (Robert Louis) (choreographer and director); Chicago, 6/23/1927
Foster, Jodie (Alicia Christian Foster) (actress); Los Angeles, 11/?/1962
Foster, Stephen Collins (composer); nr. Pittsburgh **(1826-1864)**
Foxx, Redd (John Elroy Sanford) (actor and comedian); St. Louis, 12/9/1922
Foy, Eddie, Jr. (dancer and actor); New Rochelle, N.Y. **(1905-1983)**
Fra Angelico (Giovanni da Fiesole) (painter); Vicchio in the Mugello, Tuscany (Italy) **(c.1387-1455)**
Fracci, Carla (ballerina); Milan, Italy, 8/20/1936
Fragonard, Jean Honoré (painter); Grasse, France **(1732-1806)**
Frampton, Peter (rock musician); Beckenham, England, 4/20/1950
France, Anatole (Jacques Anatole François Thibault) (author); Paris **(1844-1924)**
Francescatti, Zino (violinist); Marseilles, France, 8/9/1905
Franciosa, Anthony (Anthony Papaleo) (actor); New York City, 10/25/1928
Francis, Arlene (Arlene Francis Kazanjian) (actress); Boston, 10/20/1908
Francis, Connie (Concetta Franconero) (singer); Newark, N.J., 12/12/1938
Francis, Kay (Katherine Edwina Gibbs) (actress); Oklahoma City **(1903-1968)**
Franciscus, James (actor); Clayton, Mo., 1/31/1934
Franck, César Auguste (composer); Liège (Belgium) **(1822-1890)**
Franco Bahamonde, Francisco (Chief of State); El Ferrol, Spain **(1892-1975)**
Franklin, Aretha (singer); Memphis, Tenn., 3/25/1942
Franklin, Benjamin (statesman and scientist); Boston **(1706-1790)**
Frazer, Sir James George (anthropologist); Glasgow, Scotland **(1854-1941)**
Freud, Sigmund (psychoanalyst); Moravia (Czechoslovakia) **(1856-1939)**
Friedan, Betty (Betty Noami Goldstein) (feminist); Peoria, Ill., 2/4/1921
Fromm, Erich (psychoanalyst); Frankfurt-am-Main, Germany **(1900-1980)**
Frost, David (TV entertainer); Tenterden, England, 4/7/1939
Frost, Robert Lee (poet); San Francisco **(1874-1963)**
Fry, Christopher (playwright); Bristol, England, 12/18/1907
Frye, David (impressionist); Brooklyn, N.Y., 1934
Fuller, R(ichard) Buckminster (Jr.) (architect and educator); Milton, Mass. **(1895-1983)**
Fulton, Robert (inventor); Lancaster County, Pa. **(1765-1815)**
Furness, Betty (Elizabeth) (ex-actress and consumer advocate); New York City, 1/3/1916

G

Gabel, Martin (actor and producer); Philadelphia, 1912
Gabin, Jean (actor); Paris **(1904-1976)**
Gable, (William) Clark (actor); Cadiz, Ohio **(1901-1960)**
Gabo, Naum (sculptor); Briansk, Russia **(1890-1977)**
Gabor, Eva (actress); Budapest, 2/11/1926(?)
Gabor, Zsa Zsa (Sari) (actress); Budapest, 2/6/1923
Gainsborough, Thomas (painter); Sudbury, Suffolk, England **(1727-1788)**
Galbraith, John Kenneth (economist); Iona Station, Ontario, Canada, 10/15/1908
Galilei, Galileo (astronomer and physicist); Pisa (Italy) **(1564-1642)**
Gallico, Paul (novelist); New York City **(1897-1976)**
Gallup, George H. (poll taker); Jefferson, Iowa **(1901-1984)**
Galsworthy, John (novelist and dramatist); Coombe, England **(1867-1933)**
Galway, James (flutist); Belfast, Northern Ireland, 12/8/1939
Gambling, John A. (radio broadcaster); New York City, 1930
Gandhi, Indira (Indira Nehru) (Prime Minister); Allahabad, India, 11/19/1917
Gandhi, Mohandas Karamchand (called Mahatma Gandhi) (Hindu leader); Porbandar, India **(1869-1948)**
Gannett, Frank E. (editor and publisher); **(1876-1957)**
Garagiola, Joe (Joseph Henry) (sportscaster); St. Louis, 2/12/1926
Garbo, Greta (Greta Gustafsson) (actress); Stockholm, 9/18/1905
Gardner, Ava (Lucy Johnson) (actress); Smithfield, N.C., 12/24/1922
Gardner, Eric Stanley (novelist); Malden, Mass. **(1889-1970)**
Garfield, John (Jules Garfinkle) (actor); New York City **(1913-1952)**
Garfunkel, Art (Arthur) (singer); Newark, N.J., 11/5/1941
Gargan, William (actor); Brooklyn, N.Y., **(1905-1979)**
Garibaldi, Giuseppe (Italian nationalist leader); Nice, France **(1807-1882)**
Garland, Judy (Frances Gumm) (actress and singer); Grand Rapids, Minn. **(1922-1969)**
Garner, Erroll (jazz pianist); Pittsburgh **(1921-1977)**
Garner, James (James Bumgarner) (actor); Norman, Okla., 4/7/1928
Garner, Peggy Ann (actress); Canton, Ohio, 2/3/1932
Garrett, Betty (actress); St. Joseph, Mo., 5/23/1919
Garrick, David (actor); Hereford, England **(1717-1779)**
Garrison, William Lloyd (abolitionist); Newburyport, Mass. **(1805-1879)**
Garroway, Dave (TV host); Schenectady, N.Y. **(1913-1982)**
Garson, Greer (actress); County Down, Northern Ireland, 9/29/1912(?)
Gary, John (singer); Watertown, N.Y., 11/29/1932
Gassman, Vittorio (film actor and director); Genoa, Italy, 9/1/1922
Gaudí, Antonio (architect); Reus, Spain **(1852-1926)**
Gauguin, Eugène Henri Paul (painter); Paris **(1848-1903)**
Gautama Buddha (Prince Siddhartha) (philosopher); Kapilavastu (India) **(563?-?483** B.C.**)**
Gavin, John (actor, diplomat); Los Angeles, 4/8/1935
Gayle, Crystal (Brenda Gayle Webb) (singer); Paintsville, Ky., 1951
Gaynor, Janet (actress); Philadelphia **(1906-1984)**
Gaynor, Mitzi (Francesca Mitzi Marlene de Czanyi von Gerber) (actress); Chicago, 9/4/1931
Gazzara, Ben (Biago Anthony Gazzara) (actor); New York City, 8/28/1930
Gebel-Williams, Gunther (animal trainer); Schweidnitz (Poland), 1934
Geddes, Barbara Bel (actress); New York City, 10/31/1922
Genet, Jean (playwright); Paris, 12/19/1910
Genghis Khan (Temujin) (conqueror); nr. Lake Baikal, Russia **(1162-1227)**
Genn, Leo (actor); London **(1905-1978)**
Gentry, Bobbie (Roberta Streeter) (singer); Chickasaw Co., Miss., 7/27/1944
Gericault, Jean Louis (painter); Rouen, France **(1791-1824)**
Geronimo (Goyathlay) (Apache chieftain); Arizona **(1829-1909)**
Gershwin, George (composer); Brooklyn, N.Y. **(1898-1937)**
Gershwin, Ira (lyricist); New York City, **(1896-1983)**
Getty, J. Paul (oil executive); Minneapolis **(1892-1976)**
Getz, Stan (saxophonist); Philadelphia, 2/2/1927
Ghiberti, Lorenzo (goldsmith and sculptor); Florence **(1378-1455)**
Giacometti, Alberto (sculptor); Switzerland **(1901-1966)**
Giannini, Giancarlo (actor); La Spezia, Italy, 8/1/1942
Gibbon, Edward (historian); Putney, England **(1737-1794)**
Gibson, Charles Dana (illustrator); Roxbury, Mass. **(1867-1944)**
Gibson, Hoot (Edward) (actor); Tememah, Neb. **(1892-1962)**
Gide, André (author); Paris **(1869-1951)**
Gielgud, Sir John (actor); London, 4/14/1904
Gilbert, John (movie actor); Logan, Utah **(1897-1936)**
Gilbert, Sir William Schwenck (librettist); London **(1836-1911)**
Gilels, Emil (concert pianist); Odessa, Ukraine, 1916
Gillespie, Dizzy (John Birks Gillespie) (jazz trumpeter); Cheraw, S.C., 10/21/1917
Gimbel, Bernard F. (merchant); Vincennes, Ind. **(1885-1966)**
Gingold, Hermione (actress and comedienne); London, 12/9/1897
Ginsberg, Allen (poet); Newark, N.J., 6/3/1926
Giorgione (painter); Castelfranco, (Italy) **(c.1477-1510)**
Giotto di Bondone (painter); Vespignamo (Italy) **(c.1266-1337)**
Giovanni, Nikki (poet); Knoxville, Tenn., 6/7/1943
Giroud, Françoise (French government official); Geneva, 9/21/1916
Gish, Dorothy (actress); Massillon, Ohio **(1898-1968)**
Gish, Lillian (Lillian de Guiche) (actress); Springfield, Ohio, 10/14/1896(?)
Givenchy, Hubert (fashion designer); Beauvais, France, 2/21/1927
Gladstone, William Ewart (statesman); Liverpool, England **(1809-1898)**
Gleason, Jackie (comedian); Brooklyn, N.Y., 2/26/1916
Gleason, James (actor); New York City **(1886-1959)**
Gluck, Christoph Willibald (composer); Erasbach (Germany) **(1714-1787)**
Gobel, George (comedian); Chicago, 5/20/1920
Godard, Jean Luc (film director); Paris, 12/3/1930
Goddard, Paulette (Marion Levy) (actress); Great Neck, N.Y., 6/3/1911
Godfrey, Arthur (entertainer); New York City **(1903-1983)**
Goebbels, Joseph Paul (Nazi leader); Rheydt, Germany **(1897-1945)**
Goering, Hermann (Nazi leader); Rosenheim, Germany **(1893-1946)**
Goethals, George Washington (engineer); Brooklyn, N.Y. **(1858-1928)**
Goethe, Johann Wolfgang von (poet); Frankfurt-am-Main, Germany **(1749-1832)**
Gogol, Nikolai Vasilievich (novelist); nr. Mirgorod, Ukraine **(1809-1852)**
Goldberg, Rube (cartoonist); San Francisco **(1883-1970)**
Golden, Harry (Harry Goldhurst) (author); New York City **(1902-1981)**
Goldsmith, Oliver (dramatist and poet); County Longford, Ireland **(1728-1774)**
Goldwyn, Samuel (Samuel Goldfish) (film producer); Warsaw **(1882-1974)**
Golenpaul, Dan (creator of Information Please radio show and editor of almanac of same name); New York City **(1900-1974)**
Gompers, Samuel (labor leader); London **(1850-1924)**
Goodall, Jane (Baroness van Lawick-Goodall) (ethologist); London, 4/3/1934
Goodman, Benny (clarinetist); Chicago, 5/30/1909
Goodyear, Charles (inventor); New Haven, Conn. **(1800-1860)**
Gordimer, Nadine (novelist and short-story writer); Springs, South Africa, 12/20/1923
Gordon, Max (stage producer); New York City; **(1892-1978)**
Gordon, Ruth (actress); Wollaston, Mass., 10/30/1896
Gore, Lesley (singer); Tenafly, N.J., 1946
Goren, Charles H. (bridge expert); Philadelphia, 3/4/1901
Gorki, Maxim (Alexei Maximovich Peshkov) (author); Nizhni Novgorod, Russia **(1868-1936)**
Gorky, Arshile (painter); Armenia **(1904-1948)**
Gormé, Eydie (singer); Bronx, N.Y., 8/16/1932
Gorshin, Frank (actor); Pittsburgh, 4/5/1934
Gosden, Freeman F. *See* Amos
Gould, Chester (cartoonist); Pawnee, Okla., 11/20/1900
Gould, Elliott (Elliott Goldstein) (actor); Brooklyn, N.Y., 8/29/1938
Gould, Glenn (concert pianist); Toronto, **(1932-1982)**
Gould, Morton (composer); Richmond Hill, Queens, N.Y., 12/10/1913
Goulet, Robert (singer); Lawrence, Mass., 11/26/1933
Gounod, Charles François (composer); Paris **(1818-1893)**
Goya y Lucientes, Francisco José de (painter); Fuendetodos, Spain **(1746-1828)**
Grable, Betty (actress); St. Louis **(1916-1973)**
Grace, Princess of Monaco (Grace Kelly) (ex-actress); Philadelphia **(1929-1982)**
Graham, Bill (Wolfgang Grajonca) (rock impresario); Berlin, 1931
Graham, Billy (William F.) (evangelist); Charlotte, N.C., 11/7/1918
Graham, Katharine Meyer (newspaper publisher); New York City, 6/16/1917
Graham, Martha (choreographer); Pittsburgh, 5/11/1894(?)
Grahame, Gloria (Gloria Hallwood) (actress); Los Angeles **(1929-1981)**
Gramm, Donald (Grambach) (bass-baritone); Milwaukee **(1927-1983)**
Granger, Farley (actor); San Jose, Calif., 7/1/1925
Granger, Stewart (James Stewart) (actor); London, 5/6/1913
Grant, Cary (Alexander Archibald Leach) (actor); Bristol, England, 1/18/1904
Grant, Kathryn (actress); Houston, Tex., 1933
Grant, Lee (Lyova Haskell Rosenthal) (actress); New York City, 10/31/1930
Granville, Bonita (actress and producer); New York City, 1923
Grass, Günter (novelist); Danzig (Poland), 10/16/1927
Grauer, Ben (radio and TV announcer); New York City **(1908-1977)**
Graves, Peter (Peter Arness) (actor); Minneapolis, 3/18/1926

Graves, Robert (writer); London, 7/24/1895
Gray, Barry (Bernard Yaroslaw) (radio interviewer); Atlantic City, N.J., 7/2/1916
Gray, Dolores (singer and actress); Chicago, 6/7/1930
Gray, Thomas (poet); London **(1716-1771)**
Grayson, Kathryn (Zelma Hednick) (singer and actress); Winston-Salem, N.C., 2/9/1923
Greco, Buddy (singer); Philadelphia, 8/14/1926
Greco, José (dancer); Montorio nei Frentani, Itály, 12/23/1918
Greeley, Horace (journalist and politician); Amherst, N.H. **(1811-1872)**
Green, Adolph (actor and lyricist); New York City, 12/2/1915
Green, Al (singer); Forrest City, Ark., 4/13/1946
Greene, Graham (novelist); Berkhamsted, England, 10/2/1904
Greene, Lorne (actor); Ottawa, 2/12/1915
Greene, Martyn (actor); London **(1899-1975)**
Greenstreet, Sydney (actor); Sandwich, England **(1879-1954)**
Greenwood, Joan (actress and director); London, 3/4/1921
Greer, Germaine (feminist); Melbourne, 1/29/1939
Gregory, Cynthia (ballerina); Los Angeles, 7/8/1946
Gregory, Dick (comedian); St. Louis, 1932
Greuze, Jean-Baptiste (painter); Tournus, France **(1725-1805)**
Grey, Joel (Joel Katz) (actor); Cleveland, 4/11/1932
Grey, Zane (author); Zanesville, Ohio **(1875-1939)**
Grieg, Edvard Hagerup (composer); Bergen, Norway **(1843-1907)**
Grier, Roosevelt (entertainer and former athlete); Cuthbert, Ga., 7/14/1932
Griffin, Merv (TV entertainer); San Mateo, Calif., 7/6/1925
Griffith, Andy (actor); Mount Airy, N.C., 6/1/1926
Griffith, David Lewelyn Wark (film producer); La Grange, Ky. **(1875-1948)**
Grigorovich, Yuri (choreographer); Leningrad, 1/1/1927
Grimes, Tammy (actress); Lynn, Mass., 1/30/1934
Grimm, Jacob (author of fairy tales); Hanau (Germany) **(1785-1863)**
Grimm, Wilhelm (author of fairy tales); Hanau (Germany) **(1786-1859)**
Gris, Juan (José Victoriano González) (painter); Madrid **(1887-1927)**
Grizzard, George (actor); Roanoke Rapids, N.C., 4/1/1928
Gromyko, Andrei A. (diplomat); Starye Gromyki, Russia, 7/5/1909
Gropius, Walter (architect); Berlin **(1883-1969)**
Gropper, William (painter, illustrator); New York City **(1897-1977)**
Grosz, George (painter); Germany **(1893-1959)**
Guardino, Harry (actor); New York City, 12/23/1925
Guggenheim, Meyer (capitalist); Langnau, Switzerland **(1828-1905)**
Guinness, Sir Alec (actor); London, 4/2/1914
Guitry, Sacha (Alexandre) (actor and film director); St. Petersburg, Russia **(1885-1957)**
Gunther, John (author); Chicago **(1901-1970)**
Gutenberg, Johann (printer); Mainz (Germany) **(1400?-?1468)**
Guthrie, Arlo (singer); New York City, 7/10/1947
Guthrie, Woody (folk singer and composer); Okemah, Okla. **(1912-1967)**
Gwenn, Edmund (actor); London **(1875-1959)**

H

Hackett, Bobby (trumpeter); Providence, R.I. **(1915-1976)**
Hackett, Buddy (Leonard Hacker) (comedian and actor); Brooklyn, N.Y., 8/31/1924
Hackman, Gene (actor); San Bernardino, Calif., 1/30/1931
Hagen, Uta (actress); Göttingen, Germany, 6/12/1919
Haggard, Merle (songwriter); Bakersfield, Calif., 4/6/1937
Hagman, Larry (actor); Weatherford, Tex., 1931
Haig, Alexander Meigs, Jr. (ex-Secretary of State and ex-general); Bala-Cynwyd, Pa., 12/2/1924
Haile Selassie (Ras Tafari Makonnen) (ex-Emperor); Ethiopia **(1892-1975)**
Hailey, Arthur (novelist); Luton, England, 4/5/1920
Halberstam, David (journalist); New York City, 4/10/1934
Hale, Edward Everett (clergyman and author); Boston **(1822-1909)**
Hale, Nathan (American Revolutionary officer); Coventry, Conn. **(1755-1776)**
Haley, Alex (writer); Ithaca, N.Y., 8/11/1921
Hall, Monty (TV personality); Winnipeg, Canada, 1923
Hals, Frans (painter); Antwerp (Netherlands) **(1580?-1666)**
Halsey, William Frederick, Jr. (naval officer); Elizabeth, N.J. **(1882-1959)**
Hamill, Pete (journalist); Brooklyn, N.Y., 6/24/1935
Hamilton, Alexander (statesman); Nevis, British West Indies **(1757?-1804)**
Hamilton, George (actor); Memphis, Tenn., 8/12/1939
Hamilton, Margaret (actress); Cleveland, 9/12/1902
Hamlisch, Marvin (composer and pianist); New York City, 6/2/1944
Hammarskjöld, Dag (U.N. Secretary-General); Jönköping, Sweden **(1905-1961)**
Hammerstein, Oscar, II (librettist and stage producer); New York City **(1895-1960)**
Hampden, Walter (Walter Hampden Dougherty) (actor); Brooklyn, N.Y. **(1879-1955)**
Hampton, Lionel (vibraharpist and band leader); Birmingham, Ala., 4/20/1914
Hancock, John (statesman); Braintree, Mass. **(1737-1793)**
Hand, Learned (jurist); Albany, N.Y. **(1872-1961)**
Handel, George Frederick (Georg Friedrich Händel) (composer); Haile (Germany) **(1685-1759)**
Handy, William Christopher (blues composer); Florence, Ala. **(1873-1958)**
Hannibal (Carthaginian general); North Africa **(247-182 B.C.)**
Hanson, Howard (conductor); Wahoo, Neb., **(1896-1981)**
Harburg, E. Y. "Yip" (songwriter); New York City, 4/8/1896
Harding, Ann (actress); San Antonio, Tex. **(1902-1981)**
Hardwicke, Sir Cedric (actor); Stourbridge, England **(1893-1964)**
Hardy, Oliver (comedian); Atlanta **(1892-1957)**
Hardy, Thomas (novelist); Dorsetshire, England **(1840-1928)**
Harkness, Edward S. (capitalist); Cleveland **(1874-1940)**
Harlow, Jean (Harlean Carpentier) (actress); Kansas City, Mo. **(1911-1937)**
Harnick, Sheldon (lyricist); Chicago, 4/30/1924
Harper, Valerie (actress); Suffern, N.Y., 8/22/1940(?)
Harriman, W. (William) Averell (ex-Governor of New York); New York City, 11/15/1891
Harris, Barbara (actress); Evanston, Ill., 1935
Harris, Emmylou (singer); Birmingham, Ala., 1949
Harris, Julie (actress); Grosse Pointe Park, Mich., 12/2/1925
Harris, Phil (actor and band leader); Linton, Ind., 6/24/1906
Harris, Richard (actor); Limerick, Ireland, 10/1/1933
Harris, Rosemary (actress); Ashby, England, 9/19/1930
Harris, Roy (composer); Lincoln County, Olka. **(1898-1979)**
Harrison, George (singer and songwriter); Liverpool, England, 2/25/1943
Harrison, Rex (Reginald Carey) (actor); Huyton, England, 3/5/1908
Hart, Lorenz (lyricist); New York **(1895-1943)**
Hart, Moss (playwright); New York City **(1904-1961)**
Hart, William S. (actor); Newburgh, N.Y. **(1862-1946)**
Harte, Bret (Francis Brett Harte) (author); Albany, N.Y. **(1836-1902)**
Hartford, Huntington (George Huntington Hartford II) (A.&P. heir); New York City, 4/18/1911
Hartford, John (singer and banjoist); New York City, 12/30/1937
Hartman, Elizabeth (actress); Youngstown, Ohio, 12/23/1941
Harvey, Laurence (Larushka Skikne) (actor); Joniskis, Lithuania **(1928-1973)**
Harvey, William (physician); Folkestone, England **(1578-1657)**
Hasso, Signe (actress); Stockholm, 8/15/1915
Havoc, June (June Hovick) (actress); Seattle, 1916
Hawkins, Jack (actor); London **(1910-1973)**
Hawn, Goldie (actress); Washington, D.C., 11/21/1945
Haworth, Jill (actress); Sussex, England, 1945
Hawthorne, Nathaniel (novelist); Salem, Mass. **(1804-1864)**
Hay, John Milton (statesman); Salem, Ind. **(1838-1905)**
Hayakawa, Sessue (actor); Honshu, Japan **(1890-1973)**
Hayden, Melissa (ballerina); Toronto, 4/25/1923
Hayden, Sterling (Sterling Relyea Walter) (actor and writer); Montclair, N.J., 3/26/1916
Haydn, Franz Joseph (composer); Rohrau (Austria) **(1732-1809)**
Hayes, Helen (Helen Hayes Brown) (actress); Washington, D.C., 10/10/1900
Hayes, Isaac (composer); Covington, Tenn., 8/20/1942
Hayward, Louis (actor); Johannesburg, South Africa, 1909
Hayward, Susan (Edythe Marrener) (actress); Brooklyn, N.Y. **(1919?-1975)**
Hayworth, Rita (Margarita Cansino) (actress); New York City, 10/17/1918
Head, Edith (costume designer); Los Angeles **(1907-1981)**
Hearst, William Randolph (publisher); San Francisco **(1863-1951)**
Hearst, William Randolph, Jr. (publisher); New York City, 1/27/1908
Heath, Edward (ex-Prime Minister); Broadstairs, England, 7/9/1916
Heatherton, Joey (actress); Rockville Centre, N.Y., 9/14/1944
Hecht, Ben (author); New York City **(1894-1964)**
Heckart, Eileen (actress); Columbus, Ohio, 3/29/1919
Heflin, Van (Emmet Evan Heflin) (actor); Walters, Okla. **(1910-1971)**
Hefner, Hugh (publisher); Chicago, 4/9/1926
Hegel, Georg Wilhelm Friedrich (philosopher); Stuttgart (Germany) **(1770-1831)**
Heifetz, Jascha (concert violinist); Vilna, Russia, 2/2/1901
Heine, Heinrich (Harry) (poet); Düsseldorf (Germany) **(1797-1856)**
Heinemann, Gustav (ex-President of Germany); Schweim, Germany **(1899-1976)**
Heller, Joseph (novelist); Brooklyn, N.Y., 5/1/1923
Hellman, Lillian (playwright); New Orleans **(1905-1984)**
Hemingway, Ernest Miller (novelist); Oak Park, Ill. **(1899-1961)**
Hemmings, David (actor); Guilford, England, 11/2/1941

Henderson, Florence (actress); Dale, Ind., 2/14/1934
Henderson, Skitch (Lyle Russell Cedric) (conductor and pianist); Birmingham, England(?), 1/27/1918
Hendrix, Jimi (James Marshall Hendrix) (guitarist); Seattle **(1942-1970)**
Henning, Doug (magician and actor); Winnipeg, Canada, 1947(?)
Henreid, Paul (actor); Trieste, 1/10/1908
Henri, Robert (painter); Cincinnati **(1865-1926)**
Henry, O. (William Sydney Porter) (story writer); Greensboro, N.C. **(1862-1910)**
Henry, Patrick (statesman); Hanover County, Va. **(1736-1799)**
Henson, Jim (puppeteer); Greenville, Miss., 9/24/1936
Hepburn, Audrey (actress); Brussels, Belgium, 5/4/1929
Hepburn, Katharine (actress); Hartford, Conn., 11/8/1909
Hepplewhite, George (furniture designer); England **(?-1786)**
Hepworth, Barbara (sculptor); Wakefield, England **(1903-1975)**
Herbert, Victor (composer); Dublin **(1859-1924)**
Herblock (Herbert L. Block) (political cartoonist); Chicago, 10/13/1909
Herman, Woody (Woodrow Charles) (band leader); Milwaukee, 5/16/1913
Herod (Herodes) (called Herod the Great) (King of Judea) **(73?-4 B.C.)**
Herodotus (historian); Halicarnassus (Turkey) **(c. 484-425 B.C.)**
Hershfield, Harry (humorist and raconteur); Cedar Rapids, Iowa **(1885-1974)**
Hersholt, Jean (actor); Copenhagen **(1886-1956)**
Heston, Charlton (actor); Evanston, Ill., 10/4/1924
Heyerdahl, Thor (ethnologist and explorer); Larvik, Norway, 10/6/1914
Hildegarde (Hildegarde Loretta Sell) (singer); Adell, Wis., 2/1/1906
Hillary, Sir Edmund (mountain climber); New Zealand, 7/20/1919
Hiller, Wendy (actress); Bramhall, England, 8/15/1912
Hilliard, Harriet. *See* Nelson, Harriet
Hindemith, Paul (composer); Hanau, Germany **(1895-1963)**
Hines, Earl "Fatha" (jazz pianist); Duquesne, Pa. **(1905-1983)**
Hines, Jerome (Jerome Heinz) (basso); Los Angeles, 11/8/1921
Hingle, Pat (actor); Denver, 7/19/1924
Hippocrates (physician); Cos, Greece **(c. 460-c. 377 B.C.)**
Hirohito (Emperor); Tokyo, 4/29/1901
Hirschfeld, Al (Albert) (cartoonist); St. Louis, 6/21/1903
Hirschhorn, Joseph Herman (financier, speculator, and art collector); Mitau, Latvia **(1899-1981)**
Hirt, Al (trumpeter); New Orleans, 11/7/1922
Hitchcock, Alfred J. (film director); London **(1899-1980)**
Hitler, Adolf (Adolf Schicklgruber) (German dictator); Braunau, Austria **(1889-1945)**
Hitzig, William Maxwell (physician); Austria, 12/15/1904
Hobson, Laura Z. (Laura K. Zametkin) (novelist); New York City, 1900(?)
Hodges, Eddie (actor); Hattiesburg, Miss., 3/5/1947
Hoffa James R(iddle) (labor leader); Brazil, Ind., 2/14/1913 (presumed dead, 1977)
Hoffman, Dustin (film actor and director); Los Angeles, 8/8/1937
Hofmann, Hans (painter); Germany **(1880-1966)**
Hogarth, William (painter and engraver); London **(1697-1764)**
Holbein, Hans (the Elder) (painter); Augsburg (Germany) **(1465?-1524)**
Holbein, Hans (the Younger) (painter); Augsburg (Germany) **(1497?-1543)**
Holbrook, Hal (actor); Cleveland, 2/17/1925
Holden, William (William Franklin Beedle, Jr.) (actor); O'Fallon, Ill. **(1918-1981)**
Holder, Geoffrey (dancer); Port-of-Spain, Trinidad, 8/1/1930
Holiday, Billie (Eleanora Fagan) (jazz-blues singer); Baltimore **(1915-1959)**
Holiiday, Judy (Judith Tuvim) (comedienne); New York City **(1922-1965)**
Holloway, Stanley (actor); London **(1890-1982)**
Holloway, Sterling (actor); Cedartown, Ga., 1905
Holm, Celeste (actress); New York City, 4/29/1919
Holmes, Oliver Wendell (jurist); Boston **(1841-1935)**
Holt, Jack (actor); Winchester, Va. **(1888-1951)**
Holtz, Lou (comedian); San Francisco **(1898-1980)**
Home, Lord (Alexander Frederick Douglas-Home) (diplomat); London, 7/2/1903
Homeier, Skip (George Vincent Homeier) (actor); Chicago, 10/5/1930
Homer, Winslow (painter); Boston, Mass. **(1836-1910)**
Homer (Greek poet) **(c.850 B.C.?)**
Homolka, Oscar (actor); Vienna **(1898-1978)**
Honegger, Arthur (composer); Le Havre, France **(1892-1955)**
Hook, Sidney (philosopher); New York City, 12/20/1902
Hoover, J. Edgar (FBI director); Washington, D.C. **(1895-1972)**
Hope, Bob (Leslie Townes Hope) (comedian); London, 5/29/1903
Hopkins, Anthony (actor); Port Talbot, Wales, 12/31/1937
Hopkins, Johns (financier); Anne Arundel County, Md. **(1795-1873)**
Hopkins, Miriam (actress); Bainbridge, Ga. **(1902-1972)**
Hopper, Dennis (actor); Dodge City, Kan., 5/17/1936
Hopper, Edward (painter); Nyack, N.Y. **(1882-1967)**
Horace (Quintus Horatius Flaccus) (poet); Venosa (Italy) **(65-8 B.C.)**
Horne, Lena (singer); Brooklyn, N.Y., 6/30/1917
Horne, Marilyn (mezzo-soprano); Bradford, Pa., 1/16/1934
Horowitz, Vladimir (pianist); Kiev, Russia, 10/1/1904
Horton, Edward Everett (comedian); Brooklyn, N.Y. **(1887-1970)**
Houdini, Harry (Ehrich Weiss) (magician); Appleton, Wis. **(1874-1926)**
Houseman, John (Jacques Haussmann) (producer, director, and actor); Bucharest; 9/22/1902
Housman, A(lfred) E(dward) (poet); Fockburg, England **(1859-1936)**
Houston, Samuel (political leader); Rockbridge County, Va. **(1793-1863)**
Howard, Leslie (Leslie Stainer) (actor); London **(1893-1943)**
Howard, Trevor (actor); Kent, England, 9/29/1916
Howe, Elias (inventor); Spencer, Mass. **(1819-1867)**
Howe, Irving (literary critic); New York City, 6/11/1920
Howe, Julia Ward (poet and reformer); New York City **(1819-1910)**
Hudson, Henry (English navigator) **(?-1611)**
Hudson, Rock (born Roy Scherer, Jr.; took Roy Fitzgerald as legal name) (actor); Winnetka, Ill., 11/17/1925
Hughes, Charles Evans (jurist); Glens Falls, N.Y. **(1862-1948)**
Hughes, Howard (industrialist and film producer); Houston **(1905-1976)**
Hughes, Langston (poet); Joplin, Mo. **(1902-1967)**
Hugo, Victor Marie (author); Besançon, France **(1802-1885)**
Hume, David (philosopher); Edinburgh, Scotland **(1711-1776)**
Humperdinck, Engelbert (Arnold Dorsey) (singer); Madras, India, 5/2/1936
Humperdinck, Engelbert (composer); Siegburg (Germany) **(1854-1921)**
Hunt, H. L. (industrialist); nr. Vandalia, Ill. **(1889-1974)**
Hunt, Marsha (actress); Chicago, 10/17/1917
Hunter, Kim (Janet Cole) (actress); Detroit, 11/12/1922
Hunter, Tab (Arthur Andrew Gelien) (actor); New York City, 7/11/1931
Huntley, Chet (TV newscaster); Cardwell, Mont. **(1911-1974)**
Hurok, Sol (Solomon) (impresario); Pogar, Russia **(1884-1974)**
Hurst, Fannie (novelist); Hamilton, Ohio **(1889-1968)**
Hussein I (King); Jordan, 11/14/1935
Huston, John (film director and writer); Nevada, Mo., 8/5/1906
Huston, Walter (Walter Houghston) (actor); Toronto **(1884-1950)**
Hutchins, Robert M. (educator); Brooklyn, N.Y. **(1899-1977)**
Hutton, Barbara (Woolworth heiress); New York City **(1912-1979)**
Hutton, Betty (Betty Thornburg) (actress); Battle Creek, Mich., 2/26/1921
Hutton, Lauren (model and actress); Charleston, S.C., 1944
Huxley, Aldous (author); Godalming, England **(1894-1963)**
Huxley, Sir Julian S. (biologist and author); London **(1887-1975)**
Huxley, Thomas Henry (biologist); Ealing, England **(1825-1895)**

I

Ian, Janis (singer); New York City, 5/7/1951
Ibsen, Henrik (dramatist); Skien, Norway **(1828-1906)**
Inge, William (playwright); Independence, Kan. **(1913-1973)**
Ingres, Jean Auguste Dominique (painter); Montauban, France **(1780-1867)**
Inness, George (painter); nr. Newburgh, N.Y. **(1825-1894)**
Ionesco, Eugene (playwright); Slatina, Romania, 11/26/1912
Ireland, John (actor); Vancouver, B.C., Canada, 1/30/1915
Irving, Washington (author); New York City **(1783-1859)**
Isherwood, Christopher (novelist and playwright); nr. Dilsey and High Lane, England, 8/26/1904
Iturbi, José (concert pianist); Valencia, Spain **(1895-1980)**
Ives, Burl (Icle Ivanhoe) (singer); Hunt, Ill., 6/14/1909
Ives, Charles E(dward) (composer); Danbury, Conn. **(1874-1954)**

J

Jackson, Anne (actress); Millvale, Pa., 9/3/1926
Jackson, Glenda (actress); Hoylake, England, 1937(?)
Jackson, Rev. Jesse (civil rights leader); Greenville, S.C., 10/8/1941
Jackson, Kate (actress); Birmingham, Ala., 10/29/1949
Jackson, Mahalia (gospel singer); New Orleans **(1912-1972)**
Jackson, Michael (singer); Gary, Ind., 8/19/1958
Jackson, Thomas Jonathan ("Stonewall") (general); Clarksburg, Va. (now W. Va.) **(1824-1863)**
Jacobs, Jane (urbanologist); Scranton, Pa., 5/1/1916
Jaffe, Sam (actor); New York City **(1891-1984)**

Jagger, Dean (actor); Lima, Ohio, 11/7/1903
Jagger, Mick (Michael Phillip) (singer); Dartford, England, 7/26/1944
James, Harry (trumpeter); Albany, Ga. **(1916-1983)**
James, Henry (novelist); New York City **(1843-1916)**
James, Jesse Woodson (outlaw); Clay County, Mo. **(1847-1882)**
James, William (psychologist); New York City **(1842-1910)**
Jameson, (Margaret) Storm (novelist); Whitby, England, 1897
Janis, Byron (pianist); McKeesport, Pa., 3/24/1928
Jannings, Emil (actor); Brooklyn, N.Y. **(1886-1950)**
Janssen, David (David Meyer) (actor); Naponee, Neb. **(1930-1980)**
Jay, John (statesman and jurist); New York City **(1745-1829)**
Jeanmaire, Renée (dancer); Paris, 4/29/1924
Jenner, Edward (physician); Berkeley, England **(1749-1823)**
Jennings, Waylon (singer); Littlefield, Tex., 1937
Jessel, George (entertainer); New York City **(1898-1981)**
Jessup, Philip C. (diplomat); New York City, 1/5/1897
Joan of Arc (Jeanne d'Arc) (saint and patriot); Domremy-la-Pucelle, France **(1412-1431)**
Joffrey, Robert (Abdullah Jaffa Bey Khan) (choreographer); Seattle, 12/24/1930
John, Elton (Reginald Kenneth Dwight) (singer and pianist); Pinner, England, 3/25/1947
Johns, Glynis (actress); Pretoria, South Africa, 10/5/1923
Johns, Jasper (painter and sculptor); Augusta, Ga., 5/15/1930
Johnson, James Weldon (author and educator); Jacksonville, Fla. **(1871-1938)**
Johnson, Philip Cortalyou (architect); Cleveland, Ohio, 7/8/1906
Johnson, Samuel (lexicographer and author); Lichfield, England **(1709-1784)**
Johnson, Van (actor); Newport, R.I., 8/20/1916
Joliot-Curie, Frédéric (physicist); Paris **(1900-1958)**
Joliot-Curie, Irène (Irène Curie) (physicist); France **(1897-1956)**
Jolliet (or Joliet), Louis (explorer); Beaupré, Canada **(1645-1700)**
Jolson, Al (Asa Yoelson) (actor and singer); St. Petersburg, Russia **(1886-1950)**
Jones, Carolyn (singer and actress); Amarillo, Tex., **(1933-1983)**
Jones, Dean (actor); Morgan County, Ala., 1/25/1935
Jones, George (singer); Saratoga, Tex., 9/12/1931
Jones, Inigo (architect); London **(1573-1652)**
Jones, James (novelist); Robinson, Ill. **(1921-1977)**
Jones, James Earl (actor); Arkabutla, Miss., 1/17/1931
Jones, Jennifer (Phyllis Isley) (actress); Tulsa, Okla., 3/2/1919
Jones, John Paul (John Paul) (naval officer); Scotland **(1747-1792)**
Jones, Quincy (composer); Chicago, 3/14/1933
Jones, Shirley (singer and actress); Smithtown, Pa., 3/31/1934
Jones, Tom (Thomas Jones Woodward) (singer); Pontypridd, Wales, 6/7/1940
Jong, Erica (writer); New York City, 3/26/1942
Jonson, Ben (Benjamin) (poet and dramatist); Westminster, England **(1572-1637)**
Joplin, Janis (singer); Port Arthur, Tex. **(1943-1970)**
Jory, Victor (actor); Dawson City, Yukon, Canada **(1902-1982)**
Jourdan, Louis (Louis Gendre) (actor); Marseilles, France, 6/19/1920
Joyce, James (novelist); Dublin **(1882-1941)**
Juárez, Benito Pablo (statesman); Guelatao, Mexico **(1806-1872)**
Juliana (Queen); The Hague, Netherlands, 4/30/1909
Jung, Carl Gustav (psychoanalyst); Basel, Switzerland **(1875-1961)**
Jurado, Katy (actress); Guadalajara, Mexico, 1927

K

Kabalevsky, Dmitri (composer); St. Petersburg, Russia, 12/30/1904
Kádár, János (Communist Party leader); Hungary, 1912
Kahn, Gus (songwriter); Coblenz, Germany **(1886-1941)**
Kahn, Louis I. (architect); Oesel Island, Estonia **(1901-1974)**
Kahn, Madeline (actress); Boston, 9/29/1942
Kaminska, Ida (actress); Odessa, Russia **(1899-1980)**
Kandinsky, Wassily (painter); Moscow **(1866-1944)**
Kanin, Garson (playwright); Rochester, N.Y., 11/24/1912
Kant, Immanuel (philosopher); Königsberg (Germany) **(1724-1804)**
Kantor, MacKinlay (novelist); Webster City, Iowa **(1904-1977)**
Kaplan, Gabe (Gabriel) (actor); Brooklyn, N.Y., 3/31/1945
Karloff, Boris (William Henry Pratt) (actor); London **(1887-1969)**
Kaufman, George S. (playwright); Pittsburgh **(1889-1961)**
Kaye, Danny (David Daniel Kominski) (comedian); Brooklyn, N.Y., 1/18/1913
Kaye, Sammy (band leader); Cleveland, 3/13/1910
Kazan, Elia (director); Constantinople, Turkey, 9/7/1909
Kazan, Lainie (Levine) (singer); New York City, 5/15/1940
Keach, Stacy (actor); Savannah, Ga., 6/2/1941
Keaton, Buster (Joseph Frank Keaton) (comedian); Piqua, Kan. **(1896-1966)**
Keaton, Diane (actress); Los Angeles, 1/5/1946
Keats, John (poet); London **(1795-1821)**
Keel, Howard (singer and actor); Gillespie, Ill., 4/13/1919
Keeler, Ruby (Lehy Keeler) (actress and dancer); Halifax, Nova Scotia, Canada, 8/25/1910
Kefauver, Estes (legislator); Madisonville, Tenn. **(1903-1963)**
Keith, Brian (actor); Bayonne, N.J., 11/14/1921
Keller, Helen Adams (author and educator); Tuscumbia, Ala. **(1880-1968)**
Kellerman, Sally (actress); Long Beach, Calif., 6/2/1938
Kelly, Emmett (clown); Sedan, Kan., **(1898-1979)**
Kelly, Gene (dancer and actor); Pittsburgh, 8/23/1912
Kelly, Patsy (actress and comedienne); Brooklyn, N.Y. **(1910-1981)**
Kelly, Walt (cartoonist); Philadelphia **(1913-1973)**
Kemal Ataturk (Mustafa Kemal) (Turkish soldier and statesman); Salonika (Greece) **(1881-1938)**
Kennan, George F. (diplomat); Milwaukee, 2/16/1904
Kennedy, Arthur (actor); Worcester, Mass., 2/17/1914
Kennedy, George (actor); New York City, 2/18/1925
Kennedy, Jacqueline. *See* Onassis, Jacqueline
Kennedy, Joseph P. (financier); Boston **(1888-1969)**
Kennedy, Robert Francis (legislator); Brookline, Mass. **(1925-1968)**
Kennedy, Rose Fitzgerald (President's mother); Boston, 7/22/1890
Kent, Rockwell (painter); Tarrytown Heights, N.Y. **(1882-1971)**
Kenton, Stan (Stanley Newcomb) (jazz musician); Wichita, Kan. **(1912-1979)**
Kepler, Johannes (astronomer); Weil (Germany) **(1571-1630)**
Kerensky, Alexander Fedorovich (statesman); Simbirks, Russia **(1881-1970)**
Kern, Jerome David (composer); New York City **(1885-1945)**
Kerr, Deborah (actress); Helensburgh, Scotland, 9/30/1921
Kesey, Ken (novelist); La Junta, Colo., 9/17/1935
Kettering, Charles F. (engineer and inventor); nr. Loudonville, Ohio **(1876-1958)**
Key, Francis Scott (lawyer and author of national anthem); Frederick (now Carroll) County, Md. **(1779-1843)**
Keyes, Frances Parkinson (novelist); Charlottesville, Va. **(1885-1970)**
Keynes (1st Baron of Tilton) (John Maynard Keynes) (economist); Cambridge, England **(1883-1946)**
Khachaturian, Aram (composer); Tiflis, Russia **(1903-1978)**
Khrushchev, Nikita S. (Soviet leader); Kalinovka, nr. Kursk, Ukraine **(1894-1971)**
Kibbee, Guy (actor); El Paso **(1886-1956)**
Kidd, Michael (choreographer); Brooklyn, N.Y., 1917
Kidd, William (called Captain Kidd) (pirate); Greenock, Scotland **(1645?-1701)**
Kieran, John (writer); New York City **(1892-1981)**
Kiesinger, Kurt Georg (diplomat); Ebingen, Germany, 4/6/1904
Kiley, Richard (actor and singer); Chicago, 3/31/1922
Kilmer, Alfred Joyce (poet); New Brunswick, N.J. **(1886-1918)**
King, Alan (Irwin Alan Kniberg) (entertainer); Brooklyn, N.Y., 12/26/1927
King, B.B. (Riley King) (guitarist); Itta Bena, Miss., 9/16/1925
King, Carole (singer and songwriter); Brooklyn, N.Y., 2/9/1941
King, Coretta Scott (civil rights leader); Marion, Ala., 4/27/1927
King, Martin Luther, Jr. (civil rights leader); Atlanta **(1929-1968)**
King, Pee Wee (Frank) (singer); Abrams, Wis., 2/18/1914
Kingsley, Sidney (Sidney Kirschner) (playwright); New York City, 10/18/1906
Kipling, Rudyard (author); Bombay **(1865-1936)**
Kipnis, Alexander (basso); Ukraine, **(1891-1978)**
Kirby, George (comedian); Chicago, **1923(?)**
Kirk, Grayson (educator); Jeffersonville, Ohio, 10/12/1903
Kirk, Lisa (actress and singer); Charleroi, Pa., 1925
Kirk, Phyllis (actress); Plainfield, N.J., 9/18/1930
Kirkland, Gelsey (ballerina); Bethlehem, Pa., 12/29/1952
Kirkpatrick, Ralph (harpsichordist); Leominster, Mass., 6/10/1911
Kirkwood, James (actor); Grand Rapids, Mich. **(1883-1963)**
Kirsten, Dorothy (soprano); Montclair, N.J., 7/6/1919
Kissinger, Henry (Heinz Alfred Kissinger) (ex-Secretary of State); Furth, Germany, 5/27/1923
Kitt, Eartha (singer); North, S.C., 1/26/1928
Klee, Paul (painter); Münchenbuchsee, nr. Bern, Switzerland **(1879-1940)**
Klein, Calvin (fashion designer); Bronx, N.Y., 11/19/1942
Klemperer, Otto (conductor); Breslau (Poland) **(1885-1973)**
Klemperer, Werner (actor); Cologne, Germany, 3/22/1920
Klugman, Jack (actor); Philadelphia, 4/27/1922
Knievel, Evel (Robert Craig) (daredevil motorcyclist); Butte, Mont., 10/17/1938
Knight, Gladys (singer); Atlanta, 5/28/1944
Knight, Ted (Tadeus Wladyslaw Konopka) (actor); Terryville, Conn., 12/7/1923
Knight, John S. (publisher); Bluefield, W. Va. **(1894-1981)**
Knopf, Alfred A. (publisher); New York City, **(1892-1984)**
Knotts, Don (actor); Morgantown, W.Va., 7/21/1924
Knox, John (religious reformer); Haddington, East Lothian, Scotland **(1505-1572)**
Koch, Robert (physician); Klausthal (Germany) **(1843-1910)**
Koestler, Arthur (novelist); Budapest **(1905-1983)**
Kokoschka, Oskar (painter); Póchlarn Austria **(1886-1980)**

Kooper, Al (singer and pianist); Brooklyn, N.Y., 2/5/1944
Korman, Harvey (actor); Chicago, 2/15/1927
Kosciusko, Thaddeus (Tadeusz Andrzej Bonawentura Kosciuszko) (military officer); Grand Duchy of Lithuania **(1746-1817)**
Kostelanetz, André (orchestra conductor); St. Petersburg, Russia **(1901-1980)**
Kosygin, Aleksei N. (Premier); St. Petersburg, Russia **(1904-1980)**
Koussevitzky, Serge (Sergei) Alexandrovitch (orchestra conductor); Vishni Volochek, Tver, Russia **(1874-1951)**
Kovacs, Ernie (comedian); Trenton, N.J. **(1919-1962)**
Kramer, Stanley E. (film producer and director); New York City, 9/29/1913
Kràus, Lili (pianist); Budapest, 3/4/1905(?)
Kreisler, Fritz (violinist and composer); Vienna **(1875-1962)**
Kresge, S. S. (merchant); Bald Mount, Pa. **(1867-1966)**
Krips, Josef (orchestra conductor); Vienna **(1902-1974)**
Kristofferson, Kris (singer); Brownsville, Tex., 6/22/1936
Kruger, Otto (actor); Toledo, Ohio **(1885-1974)**
Krupa, Gene (drummer); Chicago **(1909-1973)**
Kubelik, Rafael (conductor); Bychory (Czechoslovakia), 6/29/1914
Kublai Khan (Mongol conqueror) **(1216-1294)**
Kubrick, Stanley (producer and director); New York City, 7/26/1928
Kuralt, Charles (TV journalist); Wilmington, N.C., 9/10/1934
Kurosawa, Akira (film director); Tokyo, 3/23/1910
Kurtz, Efrem (conductor); St. Petersburg, Russia, 11/7/1900
Ky, Nguyen Cao (ex-Vice President of South Vietnam); Son Tay (Vietnam), 9/8/1930

L

Ladd, Alan (actor); Hot Springs, Ark. **(1913-1964)**
Ladd, Cheryl (Cheryl Stoppelmoor) (actress); Huron, S.D., 7/12/1951
Lafayette, Marquis de (Marie Joseph Paul Yves Roch Gilbert du Motier) (military officer); Auvergne, France **(1757-1834)**
La Follette, Robert Marin (politician); Primrose, Wis. **(1855-1925)**
La Guardia, Fiorello Henry (Mayor of New York); New York City **(1882-1947)**
Lahr, Bert (Irving Lahrheim) (comedian); New York City **(1895-1967)**
Laine, Frankie (Frank Paul LoVecchio) (singer); Chicago, 3/30/1913
Laird, Melvin (ex-Secretary of Defense); Omaha, Neb., 9/1/1922
Lamarck, Chevalier de (Jean Baptiste Pierre Antoine de Monet) (naturalist); Bazantin, France **(1744-1829)**
Lamarr, Hedy (Hedwig Kiesler) (actress); Vienna, 1915
Lamas, Fernando (actor); Buenos Aires, **(1915-1982)**
Lamb, Charles (Elia) (essayist); London **(1775-1834)**
Lamour, Dorothy (Dorothy Kaumeyer) (actress); New Orleans, 10/10/1914
Lancaster, Burt (actor); New York City, 11/2/1913
Lanchester, Elsa (Elsa Sullivan) (actress); London, 10/28/1902
Landers, Ann (columnist); Sioux City, Iowa, 7/4/1918
Landon, Michael (Eugene Maurice Orowitz) (actor); Forest Hills, Queens, N.Y., 10/31/1936(?)
Lane, Abbe (singer); New York City, 1933
Lang, Fritz (film director); Vienna **(1890-1976)**
Lang, Paul Henry (music critic); Budapest, 8/28/1901
Lange, Hope (actress); Redding Ridge, Conn., 11/28/1933
Langella, Frank (actor); Bayonne, N.J., 1/1/1940
Langford, Frances (singer); Lakeland, Fla., 4/4/1913
Langmuir, Irving (chemist); Brooklyn, N.Y. **(1881-1957)**
Langtry, Lillie (Emily Le Breton) (actress); Island of Jersey **(1852-1929)**
Lansbury, Angela (actress); London, 10/16/1925
Lansing, Robert (Robert Howell Brown) (actor); San Diego, Calif., 6/5/1928
Lanza, Mario (Alfred Arnold Cocozza) (singer and actor); Philadelphia **(1925-1959)**
Lao-Tzu (or Lao-Tse) (Li Erh) (philosopher); Honan Province, China (c. 604-531 B.C.)
Lardner, Ring (Ringgold Wilmar Lardner) (story writer); Niles, Mich. **(1885-1933)**
La Salle, Sieur de (Robert Cavelier) (explorer); Rouen, France **(1643-1687)**
Lasser, Louise (actress); New York City, 1940(?)
Lauder, Sir Harry (Harry MacLennan) (singer); Portobello, Scotland **(1870-1950)**
Laughton, Charles (actor); Scarborough, England **(1899-1962)**
Laurel, Stan (Arthur Jefferson) (comedian); Ulverston, England **(1890-1965)**
Laurents, Arthur (playwright); New York City, 7/14/1918
Laurie, Piper (Rosetta Jacobs) (actress); Detroit, 1/22/1932
Lavoisier, Antoine-Laurent (chemist); Paris **(1743-1794)**
Lawford, Peter (actor); London, 9/7/1923
Lawrence, Carol (Carol Maria Laraia) (dancer and actress); Melrose Park, Ill., 9/5/1932
Lawrence, David Herbert (novelist); Nottingham, England **(1885-1930)**
Lawrence, Gertrude (Gertrud Klasen) (actress); London **(1900-1952)**
Lawrence, Marjorie (singer); Deans Marsh, Australia **(1908-1979)**
Lawrence, Steve (Sidney Leibowitz) (singer); Brooklyn, N.Y., 7/8/1935
Lawrence of Arabia (Thomas Edward Lawrence, later changed to Shaw) (author and soldier); Tremadoc, Wales **(1888-1935)**
Leachman, Cloris (actress); Des Moines, Iowa, 4/30/1926(?)
Lean, David (film director); Croydon, England, 3/25/1908
Lear, Edward (nonsense poet); London **(1812-1888)**
le Carré, John (David John Moore Cornwell) (novelist); Poole, England, 10/19/1931
Le Corbusier (Charles Edouard Jeanneret) (architect); La Chaux-de-Fonds, Switzerland **(1887-1965)**
Lee, Christopher (actor); London, 5/27/1922
Lee, Gypsy Rose (Rose Louise Hovick) (entertainer); Seattle **(1919-1970)**
Lee, Manfred B. (novelist, pseudonym Ellery Queen); Brooklyn, N.Y. **(1905-1971)**
Lee, Peggy (Norma Engstrom) (singer); Jamestown, N.D., 5/26/1920
Lee, Robert Edward (Confederate general); Stratford Estate, Va. **(1807-1870)**
Le Gallienne, Eva (actress); London, 1/11/1899
Lehár, Franz (composer); Komárom (Czechoslovakia) **(1870-1948)**
Lehmah, Herbert H. (Governor and Senator); New York City **(1878-1963)**
Lehmann, Lotte (soprano); Perleberg (Germany) **(1888-1976)**
Leigh, Janet (Jeanetta Morrison) (actress); Merced, Calif., 7/6/1927
Leigh, Vivien (Vivien Mary Hartley) (actress); Darjeeling, India **(1913-1967)**
Leighton, Margaret (actress); nr. Birmingham, England **(1922-1976)**
Leinsdorf, Erich (conductor); Vienna, 2/4/1912
Lemmon, Jack (actor); Boston, 2/8/1925
Lenin, N. (Vladimir Ilich Ulyanov) (Soviet leader); Simbirsk, Russia **(1870-1924)**
Lennon, John (singer and songwriter); Liverpool, England **(1940-1980)**
Lenya, Lotte (Karoline Blamauer) (singer and actress); Vienna, Austria **(1898-1981)**
Leonard, Sheldon (actor and director); New York City, 2/22/1907
Lerner, Alan Jay (lyricist); New York City, 8/31/1918
Lerner, Max (columnist); Minsk, Russia, 12/20/1902
Le Roy, Mervyn (film producer); San Francisco, 10/15/1900
Lessing, Doris (novelist); Kermanshah, Iran, 10/22/1919
Letterman, David (TV personality); Indianapolis, 1944
Levant, Oscar (pianist); Pittsburgh **(1906-1972)**
Levene, Sam (actor); New York City **(1905-1980)**
Levenson, Sam (humorist); New York City **(1911-1980)**
Levi, Carlo (novelist); Turin, Italy **(1902-1975)**
Levine, James (music director, Metropolitan Opera); Cincinnati, 6/23/1943
Levine, Joseph E. (film producer); Boston, 9/9/1905
Lewis, Jerry (Joseph Levitch) (comedian and film director); Newark, N.J., 3/16/1926
Lewis, Jerry Lee (singer); Ferriday, La., 9/29/1935
Lewis, John Llewellyn (labor leader); Lucas, Iowa **(1880-1969)**
Lewis, Meriwether (explorer); Albemarle Co., Va. **(1774-1809)**
Lewis, Shari (Shari Hurwitz) (puppeteer); New York City, 1/17/1934
Lewis, Sinclair (novelist); Sauk Centre, Minn. **(1885-1951)**
Lewis, Ted (entertainer); Circleville, Ohio **(1891-1971)**
Ley, Willy (science writer); Berlin **(1906-1969)**
Liberace (Wladziu Liberace) (pianist); West Allis, Wis., 5/16/1919
Lichtenstein, Roy (painter); New York City, 10/27/1923
Lie, Trygve Halvdan (first U.N. Secretary-General); Oslo **(1896-1968)**
Lightfoot, Gordon (singer and songwriter); Orillia, Ontario, Canada, 11/17/1938
Lillie, Beatrice (Lady Peel) (actress and comedienne); Toronto, 5/29/1898
Lin Yutang (author); Changchow, China **(1895-1976)**
Lind, Jenny (Johanna Maria Lind) (soprano); Stockholm **(1820-1887)**
Lindbergh, Anne Morrow (author); Englewood, N.J., 6/22/1906
Lindbergh, Charles A. (aviator); Detroit **(1902-1974)**
Linden, Hal (Harold Lipshitz) (actor); New York City, 3/20/1931
Lindfors, Viveca (actress); Uppsala, Sweden, 12/29/1920
Lindsay, Howard (playwright); Waterford, N.Y. **(1889-1968)**
Lindsay, John Vliet (ex-Mayor of New York City); New York City, 11/24/1921
Lindstrom, Pia (TV newscaster); Stockholm, 11/?/1938
Linkletter, Art (radio-TV personality); Moose Jaw, Saskatchewan, Canada, 7/17/1912
Lipchitz, Jacques (sculptor); Druskieniki, Latvia **(1891-1973)**
Lippmann, Walter (columnist, author, and political analyst); New York City **(1889-1974)**
Lister, (1st Baron of Lyme Regis) (Joseph Lister) (surgeon); Upton, England **(1827-1912)**

Liszt, Franz (composer and pianist); Raiding (Hungary) **(1811-1886)**
Little, Cleavon (actor and comedian); Chickasha, Okla., 6/1/1939
Little, Rich (impressionist); Ottawa, 11/26/1938
Livesey, Roger (actor); Barry, Wales **(1906-1976)**
Livingstone, David (missionary and explorer); Lanarkshire, Scotland **(1813-1873)**
Livingstone, Mary (Sadye Marks) (comedienne); Seattle **(1909-1983)**
Llewellyn, Richard (novelist); St. David's, Wales
Lloyd, Harold (comedian); Burchard, Neb. **(1894-1971)**
Lloyd George, David (Earl of Dwyfor) (statesman); Manchester, England **(1863-1945)**
Locke, John (philosopher); Somersetshire, England **(1632-1704)**
Lockhart, Gene (actor); London, Ontario, Canada **(1891-1957)**
Lockhart, June (actress); New York City, 6/25/1925
Lockwood, Margaret (actress); Karachi (Pakistan), 9/15/1916
Lodge, Henry Cabot (legislator); Boston **(1850-1924)**
Lodge, Henry Cabot, Jr. (diplomat); Nahant, Mass., 7/5/1902
Loesser, Frank (composer); New York City **(1910-1969)**
Loewe, Frederick (composer); Vienna, 6/10/1904
Logan, Joshua (director and producer); Texarkana, Tex., 10/5/1908
Lollobrigida, Gina (actress); Subiaco, Italy, 1928
Lombard, Carole (Carol Jane Peters) (actress); Ft. Wayne, Ind. **(1908-1942)**
Lombardo, Guy (band leader); London, Ontario, Canada **(1902-1977)**
London, George (baritone); Montreal, 5/30/1920
London, Jack (John Griffith London) (novelist); San Francisco **(1876-1916)**
London, Julie (Julie Peck) (singer and actress); Santa Rosa, Calif., 9/26/1926
Long, Huey Pierce (politician); Winnfield, La. **(1893-1935)**
Longfellow, Henry Wadsworth (poet); Portland, Me. **(1807-1882)**
Longworth, Alice Roosevelt (social figure); New York City **(1884-1980)**
Loos, Anita (novelist); Sissons, Calif., **(1888-1981)**
Lopez, Vincent (band leader); Brooklyn, N.Y. **(1895-1975)**
Lord, Jack (John Joseph Ryan) (actor); New York City, 12/30/1930
Loren, Sophia (Sofia Scicolone) (actress); Rome, 9/20/1934
Lorre, Peter (Laszlo Löewenstein) (actor); Rosenberg (Czechoslovakia) **(1904-1964)**
Louise, Tina (actress); New York City, 2/11/1937
Lowell, Amy (poet); Brookline, Mass. **(1874-1925)**
Lowell, James Russell (poet); Cambridge, Mass. **(1819-1891)**
Lowell, Robert (poet); Boston **(1917-1977)**
Loy, Myrna (Myrna Williams) (actress); nr. Helena, Mont., 8/2/1905
Loyola, St. Ignatius of (Iñigo de Oñez y Loyola) (founder of Jesuits); Gúipuzcoa Province, Spain **(1491-1556)**
Lubitsch, Ernst (film director); Berlin **(1892-1947)**
Luce, Clare Boothe (playwright and former Ambassador); New York City, 4/10/1903
Luce, Henry Robinson (editor and publisher); Tengchow, China **(1898-1967)**
Ludlum, Robert (author); New York City, 5/25/1927
Lugosi, Bela (Bela Lugosi Blasko) (actor); Logos, Hungary **(1888-1956)**
Lukas, Paul (actor); Budapest **(1895-1971)**
Lumet, Sidney (film and TV director); Philadelphia, 6/25/1924
Lunt, Alfred (actor); Milwaukee **(1892-1977)**
Lupino, Ida (actress and director); London, 2/4/1918
Luther, Martin (religious reformer); Eisleben (Germany) **(1483-1546)**
Lynde, Paul (comedian); Mt. Vernon, Ohio **(1926-1982)**
Lynley, Carol (actress); New York City, 2/13/1942
Lynn, Jeffrey (actor); Auburn, Mass., 1909
Lynn, Loretta (singer); Butcher's Hollow, Ky., 4/14/1935

M

Ma, Yo-Yo (cellist); Paris, 10/7/1955
Maazel, Lorin (conductor); Neuilly, France, 3/5/1930
MacArthur, Charles (playwright); Scranton, Pa. **(1895-1956)**
MacArthur, Douglas (five-star general); Little Rock Barracks, Ark. **(1880-1964)**
Macaulay, Thomas Babington (author); Rothley Temple, England **(1800-1859)**
MacDermot, Galt (composer); Montreal, 12/19/1928
MacDonald, James Ramsay (statesman); Lossiemouth, Scotland **(1866-1937)**
MacDonald, Jeanette (actress and soprano); Philadelphia **(1907-1965)**
Macdonald, Ross (Kenneth Millar) (mystery writer); Los Gatos, Calif. **(1915-1983)**
MacDowell, Edward Alexander (composer); New York City **(1861-1908)**
Macfadden, Bernarr (physical culturist); nr. Mill Spring, Mo. **(1868-1955)**
MacGraw, Ali (actress); New York City, 4/1/1939
Machiavelli, Niccolò (political philosopher); Florence (Italy) **(1469-1527)**
Mack, Ted (TV personality); Greeley, Colo. **(1904-1976)**
MacKenzie, Gisele (Marie Marguerite Louise Gisele LaFleche) (singer and actress); Winnipeg, Manitoba, Canada, 1/10/1927
MacLaine, Shirley (Shirley MacLean Beaty) (actress); Richmond, Va., 4/24/1934
MacLeish, Archibald (poet); Glencoe, Ill. **(1892-1982)**
Macmillan, Harold (ex-Prime Minister); London, 2/10/1894
MacMurray, Fred (actor); Kankakee, Ill., 8/30/1908
MacNeil, Cornell (baritone); Minneapolis, 1925
MacRae, Gordon (singer); East Orange, N.J., 3/12/1921
Madison, Guy (Robert Moseley) (actor); Bakersfield, Calif., 1/19/1922
Maeterlinck, Count Maurice (author); Ghent, Belgium **(1862-1949)**
Magellan, Ferdinand (Fernando de Magalhaes) (navigator); Sabrosa, Portugal **(1480?-1521)**
Magnani, Anna (actress); Rome **(1908-1973)**
Magritte, René (painter); Belgium **(1898-1967)**
Magsaysay, Ramón (statesman); Iba, Luzon, Philippines **(1907-1957)**
Mahan, Alfred Thayer (naval historian); West Point, N.Y. **(1840-1914)**
Mahler, Gustav (composer and conductor); Kalischt (Czechoslovakia) **(1860-1911)**
Mailer, Norman (novelist); Long Branch, N.J., 1/31/1923
Mailloi, Aristide (sculptor); Banyuls-sur-Mer, Rousillion, France **(1861-1944)**
Main, Marjorie (Mary Tomlinson Krebs) (actress); Acton, Ind. **(1890-1975)**
Mainbocher (Main Rousseau Bocher) (fashion designer); Chicago **(1891-1976)**
Majors, Lee (actor); Wyandotte, Mich., 4/23/1940
Makarova, Natalia (ballerina); Leningrad, 11/21/1940
Makeba, Miriam (singer); Johannesburg, South Africa, 3/4/1932
Maiamud, Bernard (novelist); Brooklyn, N.Y., 4/26/1914
Maiden, Karl (Miaden Sekulovich) (actor); Chicago, 3/22/1913
Malone, Dorothy (actress); Chicago, 1/30/1925
Malraux, André (author); Paris **(1901-1976)**
Manchester, Melissa (singer); Bronx, N.Y., 2/15/1951
Manchester, William (writer); Attleboro, Mass., 4/1/1922
Mancini, Henry (composer and conductor); Cleveland, 4/16/1924
Manet, Edouard (painter); Paris **(1832-1883)**
Mangano, Silvana (actress); Rome, 4/21/1930
Mangione, Chuck (hornist, pianist, and composer); Rochester, N.Y., 11/29/1940
Manilow, Barry (singer); Brooklyn, N.Y., 6/17/1946
Mankiewicz, Frank F. (columnist); New York City, 5/16/1924
Mankiewicz, Joseph L. (film writer and director); Wilkes-Barre, Pa., 2/11/1909
Mann, Horace (educator); Franklin, Mass. **(1796-1859)**
Mann, Thomas (novelist); Lübeck, Germany **(1875-1955)**
Mannes, Marya (writer); New York City, 11/14/1904
Mansfield, Jayne (Jayne Palmer) (actress); Bryn Mawr, Pa. **(1932-1967)**
Mansfield, Katherine (story writer); Wellington, New Zealand **(1888-1923)**
Mantovani, Annunzio (conductor); Venice **(1905-1980)**
Mao Zedong (Tse-tung) (Chinese leader); Shao Shan, China **(1893-1976)**
Marat, Jean Paul (French revolutionist); Boudry, Neuchâtei, Switzerland **(1743-1793)**
Marceau, Marcel (mime); Strasbourg, France, 3/22/1923
March, Fredric (Frederick Bickel) (actor); Racine, Wis. **(1897-1975)**
Marconi, Guglielmo (inventor); Bologna, Italy **(1874-1937)**
Marcus Aurelius (Marcus Annius Verus) (Roman emperor); Rome **(121-180)**
Marcuse, Herbert (philosopher); Berlin, **(1898-1979)**
Margaret Rose (Princess); Glamis Castle, Angus, Scotland, 8/21/1930
Margrethe II (Queen); Copenhagen, 4/16/1940
Marie Antoinette (Josephe Jeanne Marie Antoinette) (Queen of France); Vienna **(1755-1793)**
Marisol (sculptor); Venezuela, 1930
Markham, Edwin (poet); Oregon City, Ore. **(1852-1940)**
Markova, Dame Alicia (Lilian Alice Marks) (ballerina); London, 12/1/1910
Marley, Bob (reggae singer and songwriter); Kingston, Jamaica **(1945-1981)**
Marlowe, Christopher (dramatist); Canterbury, England **(1564-1593)**
Marlowe, Julia (Sarah Frances Frost) (actress); Cumberlandshire, England **(1866-1950)**
Marquand, J(ohn) P(hillips) (novelist); Wilmington, Del. **(1893-1960)**
Marquette, Jacques (missionary and explorer); Laon, France **(1637-1675)**
Marriner, Neville (conductor); Lincoln, England, 4/15/1924
Marsh, Jean (actress); Stoke Newington, England, 7/1/1934
Marshall, E.G. (actor); Owatonna, Minn., 6/18/1910
Marshall, George Catlett (general); Uniontown, Pa. **(1830-1959)**
Marshall, Herbert (actor); London **(1890-1968)**

Marshall, John (jurist); nr. Germantown, Va. **(1755-1835)**
Marshall, Penny (actress); New York City, 10/15/1942
Martin, Dean (Dino Crocetti) (singer and actor); Steubenville, Ohio, 6/17/1917
Martin, Dick (actor and comedian); Battle Creek, Mich., 1/30/1922
Martin, Mary (singer and actress); Weatherford, Tex., 12/1/1913
Martin, Steve (comedian); Waco, Tex., 1945(?)
Martin, Tony (Alvin Morris) (singer); San Francisco, 12/25/1913
Martinelli, Giovanni (tenor); Montagnana, Italy **(1885-1969)**
Marvin, Lee (actor); New York City, 2/19/1924
Marx, Chico (Leonard) (comedian); New York City **(1891-1961)**
Marx, Groucho (Julius) (comedian); New York City **(1890-1977)**
Marx, Harpo (Arthur) (comedian); New York City **(1893-1964)**
Marx, Karl (Socialist writer); Treves (Germany) **(1818-1883)**
Marx, Zeppo (Herbert) (comedian); New York City **(1901-1979)**
Mary Stuart (Queen of Scotland); Linlithgow, Scotland **(1542-1587)**
Masaryk, Jan Garrigue (statesman); Prague (Czechoslovakia) **(1886-1948)**
Masaryk, Thomas Garrigue (statesman); Hodonin (Czechoslovakia) **(1850-1937)**
Masefield, John (poet); Ledbury, England **(1878-1967)**
Masekela, Hugh (trumpeter); Wilbank, South Africa, 4/4/1939
Mason, James (actor); Huddersfield, England **(1909-1984)**
Massenet, Jules Emile Frédéric (composer); Montaud, France **(1842-1912)**
Massey, Raymond (actor); Toronto, **(1896-1983)**
Massine, Léonide (choreographer); Moscow, **(1895-1979)**
Masters, Edgar Lee (poet); Garnett, Kan. **(1869-1950)**
Mastroianni, Marcello (actor); Fontana Liri, Italy, 9/28/1924
Mathis, Johnny (singer); San Francisco, 9/30/1935
Matisse, Henri (painter); Le Cateau, France **(1869-1954)**
Matthau, Walter (Walter Matuschanskayasky) (actor); New York City, 10/1/1920
Mature, Victor (actor); Louisville, Ky., 1/19/1916
Maugham, W(illiam) Somerset (author); Paris **(1874-1965)**
Mauldin, Bill (political cartoonist); Mountain Park, N.M., 10/29/1921
Maupassant, Henri René Albert Guy de (story writer); Normandy, France **(1850-1893)**
Maurois, André (Emile Herzog) (author); Elbauf, France **(1885-1967)**
Maximilian (Ferdinand Maximilian Joseph) (Emperor of Mexico); Vienna **(1832-1867)**
Maxwell, James Clerk (physicist); Edinburgh, Scotland **(1831-1879)**
May, Elaine (Elaine Berlin) (entertainer-writer); Philadelphia, 4/21/1932
May, Rolio (psychologist); Ada, Ohio, 4/21/1909
Mayall, John (singer and songwriter); Manchester, England, 11/29/1933
Mayo, Charles H. (surgeon); Rochester, Minn. **(1865-1939)**
Mayo, Charles W. (surgeon); Rochester, Minn. **(1898-1968)**
Mayo, William J. (surgeon); Le Sueur, Minn. **(1861-1939)**
McBride, Mary Margaret (radio personality); Paris, Mo. **(1899-1976)**
McBride, Patricia (ballerina); Teaneck, N.J., 8/23/1942
McCallum, David (actor); Glasgow, Scotland, 9/19/1933
McCambridge, Mercedes (actress); Joliet, Ill., 3/17/1918
McCarthy, Eugene J. (ex-Senator); Watkins, Minn., 3/29/1916
McCarthy, Joseph Raymond (Senator); Grand Chute, Wis. **(1908-1957)**
McCarthy, Kevin (actor); Seattle, 2/15/1914
McCarthy, Mary (novelist); Seattle, 6/21/1912
McCartney, Paul (singer and songwriter); Liverpool, England, 6/18/1942
McClellan, George Brinton (general); Philadelphia **(1826-1885)**
McCloy, John J. (lawyer and banker); Philadelphia, 3/31/1895
McCormack, John (tenor); Athione, Ireland **(1884-1945)**
McCormack, John W. (ex-Speaker of House); Boston **(1891-1980)**
McCormack, Patty (actress); New York City, 8/21/1945
McCormick, Cyrus Hall (inventor); Rockbridge County, Va. **(1809-1884)**
McCoy, Col. Tim (actor); Saginaw, Mich. **(1891-1978)**
McCracken, James (dramatic tenor); Gary, Ind., 12/16/1926
McCrea, Joel (actor); Los Angeles, 11/5/1905
McCullers, Carson (novelist); Columbus, Ga. **(1917-1967)**
McDowall, Roddy (actor); London, 9/17/1928
McDowell, Malcolm (actor); Leeds, England, 6/19/1943
McGavin, Darren (actor); San Joaquin, Calif., 5/7/1922
McGinley, Phyllis (poet and writer); Ontario, Ore. **(1905-1978)**
McGoohan, Patrick (actor); Astoria, Queens, N.Y., 1928
McGuire, Dorothy (actress); Omaha, Neb. 6/14/1919
McKenna, Siobhan (actress); Belfast, Northern Ireland, 5/24/1923
McKuen, Rod (singer and composer); Oakland, Calif., 4/29/1933
McLaglen, Victor (actor); Tunbridge Wells, Kent, England **(1886-1959)**
McLaughlin, John (guitarist); Yorkshire, England, 1942
McLean, Don (singer and songwriter); New Rochelle, N.Y., 10/2/1945
McLuhan, Marshall (Herbert Marshall) (communications writer); Edmonton, Canada **(1911-1980)**
McMahon, Ed (TV personality); Detroit, 3/6/1923
McNamara, Robert S. (former president of World Bank); San Francisco, 6/9/1916
McQueen, Steve (Terence Stephen McQueen) (actor); Indianapolis **(1930-1980)**
Mead, Margaret (anthropologist); Philadelphia, **(1901-1978)**
Meadows, Audrey (actress); Wu Chang, China, 1922(?)
Meadows, Jayne (actress); Wu Chang, China 9/27/1926
Meany, George (labor leader); New York City **(1894-1980)**
Medici, Lorenzo de' (called Lorenzo the Magnificent) (Florentine ruler); Florence (Italy) **(1449-1492)**
Meeker, Ralph (Ralph Rathgeber) (actor); Minneapolis, 11/21/1920
Mehta, Zubin (conductor); Bombay, 4/29/1936
Meir, Golda (Golda Myerson, nee Mabovitz) (ex-Premier of Israel); Kiev, Russia **(1898-1978)**
Melanie (Melanie Safka) (singer and songwriter); New York City, 2/3/1947
Melba, Dame Nellie (Helen Porter Mitchell) (soprano); nr. Melbourne **(1861-1931)**
Melchior, Lauritz (Lebrecht Hommel) (heroic tenor); Copenhagen **(1890-1973)**
Mellon, Andrew William (financier); Pittsburgh **(1855-1937)**
Melville, Herman (novelist); New York City **(1819-1891)**
Mencken, Henry Louis (writer); Baltimore **(1880-1956)**
Mendel, Gregor Johann (geneticist); Heinzendorf, Austrian Silesia **(1822-1884)**
Mendeleyev, Dmitri Ivanovich (chemist); Tobolsk, Russia **(1834-1907)**
Mendelssohn-Bartholdy, Jakob Ludwig Felix (composer); Hamburg **(1809-1847)**
Mendès-France, Pierre (ex-Premier); Paris **(1905-1982)**
Menjou, Adolphe (actor); Pittsburgh **(1890-1963)**
Mennin, Peter (Peter Mennini) (composer); Erie, Pa. **(1923-1983)**
Menninger, William C. (psychiatrist); Topeka, Kan. **(1899-1966)**
Menotti, Gian Carlo (composer); Cadegliano, Italy, 7/7/1911
Menuhin, Yehudi (violinist and conductor); New York City, 4/22/1916
Menzies, Robert Gordon (ex-Prime Minister); Jeparit, Australia **(1894-1978)**
Mercer, Johnny (songwriter); Savannah, Ga. **(1909-1976)**
Mercer, Mabel (singer); Burton-on-Trent, England **(1900-1984)**
Mercouri, Melina (actress); Athens, 10/18/1925
Meredith, Burgess (actor); Cleveland, 11/16/1908
Merman, Ethel (Ethel Zimmerman) (singer and actress); Astoria, Queens, N.Y. **(1909-1984)**
Merrick, David (David Margulois) (stage producer); St. Louis, 11/27/1912
Merrill, Dina (actress); New York City, 12/9/1925
Merrill, Gary (actor); Hartford, Conn., 8/2/1914
Merrill, Robert (baritone); Brooklyn, N.Y., 6/4/1919
Merton, Thomas (clergyman and writer); France **(1915-1968)**
Mesmer, Franz Anton (physician); Itzmang, nr. Constance (Germany) **(1733-1815)**
Metternich, Prince Klemens Wenzel Nepomuk Lothar von (statesman); Coblenz (Germany) **(1773-1859)**
Michelangelo Buonarreti (painter, sculptor, and architect); Caprese (Italy) **(1475-1564)**
Michener, James A. (novelist); New York City, 2/3/1907
Midler, Bette (singer); Honolulu, 1945
Mielziner, Jo (stage designer); Paris **(1901-1976)**
Mies van der Rohe, Ludwig (architect and designer); Aachen, Germany **(1886-1969)**
Mikoyan, Anastas I. (diplomat); Sanain, Armenia, **(1895-1978)**
Miles, Sarah (actress); Essex, England, 12/31/1943
Miles, Sylvia (actress); New York City, 9/9/1932
Miles, Vera (Vera Ralston) (actress); nr. Boise City, Okla., 8/23/1930
Milhaud, Darius (composer); Aix-en-Provence, France **(1892-1974)**
Mill, John Stuart (philosopher); London, **(1806-1873)**
Milland, Ray (Reginald Truscott-Jones) (actor); Neath, Wales, 1/3/1907
Millay, Edna St. Vincent (poet); Rockland, Me. **(1892-1950)**
Miller, Ann (Lucille Ann Collier) (dancer and actress); Cherino, Tex., 4/12/1923
Miller, Arthur (playwright); New York City, 10/17/1915
Miller, Glenn (band leader); Clarinda, Iowa **(1909?-1944)**
Miller, Henry (novelist); New York City **(1891-1980)**
Miller, Jason (John Miller) (playwright); New York City, 1939(?)
Miller, Mitch (Mitchell) (musician); Rochester, N.Y., 7/4/1911
Miller, Roger (singer); Fort Worth, 1/2/1936
Millet, Jean François (painter); Gruchy, France **(1814-1875)**
Millett, Kate (feminist); St. Paul, 9/14/1934
Mills, Hayley (actress); London, 4/18/1946
Mills, John (actor); Felixstowe, England, 2/22/1908
Milne, A(lan) A(lexander) (author); London **(1882-1956)**
Milstein, Nathan (concert violinist); Odessa, Russia, 12/31/1904
Milton, John (poet); London **(1608-1674)**
Mimieux, Yvette (actress); Hollywood, Calif., 1/8/1941

Mineo, Sal (actor); New York City **(1939-1976)**
Minnelli, Liza (singer and actress); Hollywood, Calif., 3/12/1946
Minnelli, Vincente (film director); Chicago, 2/28/1913
Minuit, Peter (Governor of New Amsterdam); Wesel (Germany) **(1580-1638)**
Miranda, Carmen (Maria do Carmo da Cunha) (singer and dancer); Lisbon **(1913-1955)**
Miró, Joan (painter); Barcelona **(1893-1983)**
Mitchell, Cameron (actor); Dallastown, Pa., 4/11/1918
Mitchell, Guy (actor); Detroit, 2/27/1927
Mitchell, John N. (former Attorney General); Detroit, 9/15/1913
Mitchell, Joni (Roberta Joan Anderson) (singer and songwriter); Ft. Macleod, Canada, 11/7/1943
Mitchell, Margaret (novelist); Atlanta **(1900-1949)**
Mitchum, Robert (actor); Bridgeport, Conn., 8/6/1917
Mitropoulos, Dimitri (orchestra conductor); Athens **(1896-1960)**
Mix, Tom (actor); Mix Run, Pa. **(1880-1940)**
Modigliani, Amedeo (painter); Leghorn, Italy **(1884-1920)**
Moffo, Anna (soprano); Wayne, Pa., 6/27/1934
Mohammed (prophet); Mecca (Saudi Arabia) **(570-632)**
Molière (Jean Baptiste Poquelin) (dramatist); Paris **(1622-1673)**
Molnar, Ferenc (dramatist); Budapest **(1878-1952)**
Molotov, Vyacheslav M. (V. M. Skryabin) (diplomat); Kukarka, Russia, 3/9/1890
Mondrian, Piet (painter); Amersfoort, Netherlands **(1872-1944)**
Monet, Claude (painter); Paris **(1840-1926)**
Monk, Thelonious (pianist); Rocky Mount, N.C. **(1918-1982)**
Monroe, Marilyn (Norma Jean Mortenson or Baker) (actress); Los Angeles **(1926-1962)**
Monroe, Vaughn (Wilton) (band leader); Akron, Ohio **(1912-1973)**
Monsarrat, Nicholas (novelist); Liverpool, England, **(1910-1979)**
Montaigne, Michel Eyquem de (essayist); nr. Bordeaux, France **(1533-1592)**
Montalban, Ricardo (actor); Mexico City, 11/25/1920
Montand, Yves (Yvo Montand Livi) (actor and singer); Monsummano, Italy, 10/13/1921
Montezuma II (Aztec emperor); Mexico **(1480?-1520)**
Montgomery, Elizabeth (actress); Hollywood, Calif., 4/15/1933
Montgomery, George (George Montgomery Letz) (actor); Brady, Mont., 8/29/1916
Montgomery, Robert (Henry, Jr.) (actor); Beacon, N.Y. **(1904-1981)**
Montgomery of Alamein, 1st Viscount of Hindhead (Sir Bernard Law Montgomery) (military leader); London **(1887-1976)**
Montoya, Carlos (guitarist); Madrid, 12/13/1903
Moore, Clement Clarke (author); New York City **(1779-1863)**
Moore, Garry (Thomas Garrison Morfit) (TV personality); Baltimore, 1/31/1915
Moore, Grace (soprano); Jellico, Tenn. **(1901-1947)**
Moore, Henry (sculptor); Castleford, England, 7/30/1898
Moore, Marianne (poet); Kirkwood, Mo. **(1887-1972)**
Moore, Mary Tyler (actress); Brooklyn, N.Y., 12/29/1937
Moore, Melba (Beatrice) (singer and actress); New York City, 10/27/1945
Moore, Roger (actor); London, 10/14/1927(?)
Moore, Thomas (poet); Dublin **(1779-1852)**
Moore, Victor (actor); Hammonton, N.J. **(1876-1962)**
Moorehead, Agnes (actress); Clinton, Mass. **(1906-1974)**
More, Sir Thomas (statesman and author); London **(1478-1535)**
Moreau, Jeanne (actress); Paris, 1/23/1928
Moreno, Rita (Rosita Dolores Alverio) (actress); Humacao, Puerto Rico, 12/11/1931
Morgan, Dennis (actor); Prentice, Wis., 12/10/1920
Morgan, Helen (singer); Danville, Ohio **(1900?-1941)**
Morgan, Henry (comedian); New York City, 3/31/1915
Morgan, Jane (Florence Currier) (singer); Boston, 1920
Morgan, John Pierpont (financier); Hartford, Conn. **(1837-1913)**
Moriarty, Michael (actor); Detroit, 4/5/1941
Morini, Erica (concert violinist); Vienna, 1/5/1910
Morison, Samuel Eliot (historian); Boston **(1887-1976)**
Morley, Christopher Darlington (novelist); Haverford, Pa. **(1890-1957)**
Morley, Robert (actor); Semley, England, 5/26/1908
Morrison, Jim (James Douglas Morrison) (singer and songwriter); Melbourne, Fla. **(1943-1971)**
Morse, Marston (mathematician); Waterville, Me. **(1892-1977)**
Morse, Robert (actor); Newton, Mass., 5/18/1931
Morse, Samuel Finley Breese (painter and inventor); Charlestown, Mass. **(1791-1872)**
Moses, Grandma (Mrs. Anna Mary Robertson Moses) (painter); Greenwich, N.Y. **(1860-1961)**
Moses, Robert (urban planner); New Haven, Conn., **(1888-1981)**
Mostel, Zero (Samuel Joel Mostel) (actor); Brooklyn, N.Y. **(1915-1977)**
Moussorgsky, Modest Petrovich (composer); Karev, Russia **(1839-1881)**
Moyers, Bill D. (Billy Don) (journalist); Hugo, Okla., 6/5/1934
Moynihan, Daniel Patrick (New York Senator); Tulsa, Okla., 3/16/1927
Mozart, Wolfgang Amadeus (Johannes Chrysostomus Wolfgangus Theophilus Mozart) (composer); Salzburg (Austria) **(1756-1791)**
Mudd, Roger (TV newscaster); Washington, D.C., 2/9/1928
Muggeridge, Malcolm (Thomas) (writer); Croydon, England, 3/24/1903
Muhammad, Elijah (Elijah Poole) (religious leader); Sandersville, Ga. **(1897-1975)**
Mulhare, Edward (actor); Ireland, 1923
Mumford, Lewis (cultural historian and city planner); Flushing, Queens, N.Y., 10/19/1895
Munch, Edvard (painter); Löten, Norway **(1863-1944)**
Muni, Paul (Muni Weisenfreund) (actor); Lemburg (Ukraine) **(1895-1967)**
Munsel, Patrice (soprano); Spokane, Wash., 5/14/1925
Murdoch, Iris (novelist); Dublin, 7/15/1919
Murdoch, Rupert (publisher); Melbourne, 3/11/1931
Murillo, Bartolomé Esteban (painter); Seville, Spain **(1617-1682)**
Murphy, Audie (actor and war hero); Kingston, Tex. **(1924-1971)**
Murphy, George (actor, dancer, and ex-Senator); New Haven, Conn., 7/4/1902
Murray, Arthur (dance teacher); New York City, 4/4/1895
Murray, Ken (Don Court) (producer); New York City, 7/14/1903
Murray, Mae (Marie Adrienne Koenig) (actress); Portsmouth, Va. **(1890-1965)**
Murrow, Edward R. (commentator and government official); Greensboro, N.C. **(1908-1965)**
Mussolini, Benito (Italian dictator); Dovia, Forli, Italy **(1883-1945)**
Myerson, Bess (consumer advocate); Bronx, N.Y., 1924
Myrdal, Gunnar (sociologist and economist); Gustaf Parish, Sweden, 12/6/1898

N

Nabokov, Vladimir (novelist); St. Petersburg, Russia **(1899-1977)**
Nabors, Jim (actor and singer); Sylacauga, Ala., 6/12/1932
Nader, Ralph (consumer advocate); Winsted, Conn., 2/27/1934
Nagel, Conrad (actor); Keokuk, Iowa **(1897-1970)**
Naish, J. Carrol (actor); New York City **(1900-1973)**
Naldi, Nita (Anita Donna Dooley) (actress); New York City **(1899-1961)**
Napoleon Bonaparte. *See* Bonaparte, Napoleon
Nash, Graham (singer); Blackpool, England, 1942
Nash, Ogden (poet); Rye, N.Y. **(1902-1971)**
Nasser, Gamal Abdel (statesman); Beni Mor, Egypt **(1918-1970)**
Nast, Thomas (cartoonist); Landau (Germany) **(1840-1902)**
Nation, Carry Amelia (temperance leader); Garrard County, Ky. **(1846-1911)**
Natwick, Mildred (actress); Baltimore, 6/19/1908
Nazimova, Alla (actress); Yalta, Crimea, Russia **(1879-1945)**
Neagle, Anna (Marjorie Robertson) (actress); London, 10/20/1908
Neal, Patricia (actress); Packard, Ky., 1/20/1926
Neff, Hildegarde (actress); Ulm, Germany, 12/28/1925
Negri, Pola (Appolina Chapulez) (actress); Bromberg (Poland), c. 1897
Nehru, Jawaharlal (first Prime Minister of India); Allahabad, India **(1889-1964)**
Nelson, Barry (Neilsen) (actor); San Francisco, 1920
Nelson, David (actor); New York City, 10/24/1936
Nelson, Harriet Hilliard (Peggy Lou Snyder) (actress); Des Moines, Iowa, 1914
Nelson, Ozzie (Oswald) (actor); Jersey City, N.J. **(1907-1975)**
Nelson, Ricky (Eric) (singer and actor); Teaneck, N.J., 5/8/1940
Nelson, Viscount Horatio (naval officer); Burnham Thorpe, England **(1758-1805)**
Nenni, Pietro (Socialist leader); Faenza, Italy **(1891-1980)**
Nero (Nero Claudius Caesar Drusus Germanicus) (Roman emperor); Antium (Italy) **(37-68)**
Nero, Peter (pianist); New York City, 5/22/1934
Nesbitt, Cathleen (actress); Cheshire, England **(1889-1982)**
Nevelson, Louise (sculptor); Kiev, Russia, 9/23/1900
Newhart, Bob (entertainer); Chicago, 9/5/1929
Newhouse, Samuel I. (publisher); New York City **(1895-1979)**
Newley, Anthony (actor and song writer); London, 9/24/1931
Newman, Edwin (news commentator); New York City, 1/25/1919
Newman, Paul (actor and director); Cleveland, 1/26/1925
Newman, Randy (singer); Los Angeles, 11/28/1943
Newton, Huey (black activist); New Orleans, 2/17/1942
Newton, Sir Isaac (mathematician and scientist); nr. Grantham, England **(1642-1727)**
Newton, Wayne (singer); Norfolk, Va., 4/3/1942
Newton-John, Olivia (singer); Cambridge, England, 9/26/1948
Nichols, Mike (Michael Peschkowsky) (stage and film director); Berlin, 11/6/1931

Nicholson, Jack (actor); Neptune, N.J., 4/22/1937
Nietzsche, Friedrich Wilhelm (philosopher); nr. Lützen (Germany) **(1844-1900)**
Nightingale, Florence (nurse); Florence (Italy) **(1820-1910)**
Nijinsky, Waslaw (ballet dancer); Warsaw **(1890-1950)**
Nilsson, Birgit (soprano); West Karup, Sweden, 5/17/1923
Nilsson, Harry (singer and songwriter); Brooklyn, N.Y., 6/15/1941
Nimitz, Chester W. (naval officer); Fredericksburg, Tex. **(1885-1966)**
Nimoy, Leonard (actor); Boston, 3/26/1931
Nin, Anais (author and diarist); Neuilly, France **(1903-1977)**
Niven, David (actor); Kirriemuir, Scotland, **(1910-1983)**
Nizer, Louis (lawyer and author); London, 2/6/1902
Nobel, Alfred Bernhard (industrialist); Stockholm **(1833-1896)**
Noguchi, Isamu (sculptor); Los Angeles, 11/7/1904
Nolan, Lloyd (actor); San Francisco, 8/11/1902
Nolte, Nick (actor); Omaha, Neb., 1942
Norell, Norman (Norman Levinson) (fashion designer); Noblesville, Ind. **(1900-1972)**
Norstad, Gen. Lauris (ex-commander of NATO forces); Minneapolis, 3/24/1907
North, John Ringling (circus director); Baraboo, Wis., 8/14/1903
Nostradamus (Michel de Notredame) (astrologer); St. Rémy, France **(1503-1566)**
Novaes, Guiomar (pianist); São João de Boa Vista, Brazil **(1895-1979)**
Novak, Kim (Marilyn Novak) (actress); Chicago, 2/13/1933
Novarro, Ramon (Ramon Samaniegoes) (actor); Durango, Mexico **(1899-1968)**
Nugent, Elliott (actor and director); Dover, Ohio, **(1899-1980)**
Nureyev, Rudolf (ballet dancer); U.S.S.R., 3/17/1938
Nuyen, France (actress); Marseilles, France, 7/31/1939
Nyro, Laura (singer and songwriter); Bronx, N.Y., 1947

O

Oakie, Jack (actor); Sedalia, Mo. **(1903-1978)**
Oates, Joyce Carol (novelist); Lockport, N.Y., 6/16/1938
Oberon, Merle (Estelle Merle O'Brien Thompson) (actress); Tasmania **(1911-1979)**
O'Brian, Hugh (Hugh J. Krampe) (actor); Rochester, N.Y., 4/19/1930
O'Brien, Edmond (actor); New York City, 9/10/1915
O'Brien, Margaret (Angela Maxine O'Brien) (actress); San Diego, Calif., 1/15/1937
O'Brien, Pat (William Joseph O'Brien, Jr.) (actor); Milwaukee, **(1899-1983)**
O'Casey, Sean (playwright); Dublin **(1881-1964)**
Ochs, Adolph Simon (publisher); Cincinnati **(1858-1935)**
O'Connor, Carroll (actor); New York City, 8/2/1924
O'Connor, Donald (actor); Chicago, 8/28/1925
Odets, Clifford (playwright); Philadelphia **(1906-1963)**
Odetta (Odetta Holmes) (folk singer and actress); Brimingham, Ala., 12/31/1930
Offenbach, Jacques (composer); Cologne, Germany **(1819-1880)**
O'Hara, John (novelist); Pottsville, Pa. **(1905-1970)**
O'Hara, Maureen (Maureen FitzSimons) (actress); Dublin, 8/17/1921
Oistrakh, David (concert violinist); Odessa, Russia **(1908-1974)**
O'Keeffe, Georgia (painter); Sun Prairie, Wis., 11/15/1887
Oland, Warner (actor); Umea, Sweden **(1880-1938)**
Olav V (King of Norway); Sandringham, England, 7/2/1903
Oldenburg, Claes (painter); Stockholm, Sweden, 1/28/1929
Olivier, Lord (Laurence) (actor); Dorking, England, 5/22/1907
Olmsted, Frederick Law (landscape architect); Hartford, Conn. **(1822-1903)**
Olsen, Ole (John Sigvard Olsen) (comedian); Peru, Ind. **(1892-1963)**
Omar Khayyam (poet and astronomer); Nishapur (Iran) **(died c. 1123)**
Onassis, Aristotle (shipping executive); Smyrna, Turkey **(1906-1975)**
Onassis, Christina (shipping executive); New York City, 12/11/1950
Onassis, Jacqueline Kennedy (Jacqueline Bouvier) (President's widow); Southampton, N.Y., 7/28/1929
O'Neal, Ryan (Patrick) (actor); Los Angeles, 4/20/1941
O'Neal, Tatum (actress); Los Angeles, Calif., 11/5/1963
O'Neill, Eugene Gladstone (playwright); New York City **(1888-1953)**
O'Neill, Jennifer (actress); Rio de Janeiro, 2/20/1949
Oppenheimer, J. Robert (nuclear physicist); New York City **(1904-1967)**
Orff, Carl (composer); Munich, Germany **(1895-1982)**
Orlando, Tony (Michael Anthony Orlando Cassavitis) (singer); New York City, 4/3/1944
Ormandy, Eugene (conductor); Budapest, 11/18/1899
Orozco, José Clemente (painter); Zapotlán, Jalisco, Mexico **(1883-1949)**
Orwell, George (Eric Arthur Blair) (British author); Motihari, India **(1903-1950)**
Osborn, Paul (playwright); Evansville, Ind., 9/4/1901
Osborne, John (playwright); London, 12/12/1929
Osler, Sir William (physician); Bondhead, Ontario, Canada **(1849-1919)**
Osmond, Donny (singer); Ogden, Utah, 12/9/1957
Osmond, Marie (singer); Ogden, Utah, 1959
O'Sullivan, Maureen (actress); County Roscommon, Ireland, 5/17/1911
Otis, Elisha (inventor); Halifax, Vt. **(1811-1861)**
O'Toole, Peter (actor); Connemara, Ireland, 8/2/1933
Ovid (Publius Ovidius Naso) (poet); Sulmona (Italy) **(43 B.C.-?A.D. 17)**
Owens, Buck (Alvis Edgar Owens) (singer); Sherman, Tex., 8/12/1929

P

Paar, Jack (TV personality); Canton, Ohio, 5/1/1918
Pacino, Al (Alfred) (actor); New York City, 4/25/1940
Packard, Vance (author); Granville Summit, Pa., 5/22/1914
Paderewski, Ignace Jan (pianist and statesman); Kurylowka, Russian Podolia **(1860-1941)**
Paganini, Nicolò (violinist); Genoa (Italy) **(1782-1840)**
Page, Geraldine (actress); Kirksville, Mo., 11/22/1924
Page, Patti (Clara Ann Fowler) (singer and entertainer); Claremore, Okla., 11/8/1927
Paige, Janis (actress); Tacoma, Wash., 9/16/1922
Paine, Thomas (political philosopher); Thetford, England **(1737-1809)**
Palance, Jack (Walter Palanuik) (actor); Lattimer, Pa., 2/18/1920
Paley, William S. (broadcasting executive); Chicago, 9/28/1901
Palladio, Andrea (architect); Padua or Vicenza (Italy) **(1508-1580)**
Palmer, Betsy (actress); East Chicago, Ind., 1929
Palmer, Lilli (Lilli Peiser) (actress); Posen (Germany), 5/24/1914
Palmerston, Henry John Templeton (3rd Viscount) (statesman); Broadlands, England **(1784-1865)**
Papanicolaou, George N. (physician); Coumi, Greece **(1883-1962)**
Papas, Irene (actress); Chiliomodion, Greece, 1929
Papp, Joseph (Joseph Papirofsky) (stage producer and director); Brooklyn, N.Y., 6/22/1921
Park, Chung Hee (President of South Korea); Sangmo-ri, Korea **(1917-1979)**
Parker, Dorothy (Dorothy Rothschild) (author); West End, N.J. **(1893-1967)**
Parker, Eleanor (actress); Cedarville, Ohio, 6/26/1922
Parker, Fess (actor); Fort Worth, Tex., 1925
Parker, Suzy (model and actress); San Antonio, 10/28/1933
Parkinson, C(yril) Northcote (historian); Durham, England, 7/30/1909
Parks, Bert (Bert Jacobson) (entertainer); Atlanta, 12/30/1914
Parks, Gordon (film director); Ft. Scott, Kan., 11/30/1912
Parnell, Charles Stewart (statesman); Avondale, Ireland **(1846-1891)**
Parnis, Mollie (Mollie Parnis Livingston) (fashion designer); New York City, 3/18/1905
Parsons, Estelle (actress); Marblehead, Mass., 11/20/1927
Parton, Dolly (singer); Locust Ridge, Tenn. 1/19/1946
Pascal, Blaise (philosopher); Clermont, France **(1623-1662)**
Pasternak, Boris Leonidovich (author); Moscow **(1890-1960)**
Pasternak, Joseph (film producer); Silagy-Somlyo, Romania, 9/19/1901
Pasteur, Louis (chemist); Dôle, France **(1822-1895)**
Patton, George Smith, Jr. (general); San Gabriel, Calif., **(1885-1945)**
Paul, Les (Lester William Polfus) (guitarist); Waukesha, Wis., 6/9/1915
Paul VI (Giovanni Battista Montini) (Pope); Concesio, nr. Brescia, Italy **(1897-1978)**
Pauling, Linus Carl (chemist); Portland, Ore., 2/28/1901
Pavarotti, Luciano (tenor); Modena, Italy, 10/12/1935
Pavlov, Ivan Petrovich (physiologist); Ryazan district, Russia **(1849-1936)**
Pavlova, Anna (ballerina); St. Petersburg, Russia **(1885-1931)**
Payne, John (actor); Roanoke, Va., 1912
Peale, Norman Vincent (clergyman); Bowersville, Ohio, 5/31/1898
Pearl, Minnie (Sarah Ophelia Colley Cannon) (comedienne and singer); Centerville, Tenn., 10/25/1912
Pears, Peter (tenor); Farnham, England, 6/22/1910
Pearson, Drew (Andrew Russel Pearson) (columnist); Evanston, Ill. **(1897-1969)**
Pearson, Lester B. (statesman); Toronto **(1897-1972)**
Peary, Robert Edwin (explorer); Cresson, Pa. **(1856-1920)**
Peck, Gregory (actor); La Jolla, Calif., 4/5/1916
Peckinpah, Sam (film director); Fresno, Calif., 2/21/1925
Peerce, Jan (tenor); New York City, 6/30/1904
Pegler, (James) Westbrook (columnist); Minneapolis, **(1894-1969)**
Pei, I(eoh) M(ing) (architect); Canton, China, 4/26/1917
Penn, Arthur (stage and film director); Philadelphia, 9/27/1922
Penn, William (American colonist); London **(1644-1718)**
Penney, James C. (merchant); Hamilton, Mo. **(1875-1971)**

Peppard, George (actor); Detroit, 10/1/1928
Pepys, Samuel (diarist); Bampton, England **(1633-1703)**
Perelman, S(idney) J(oseph) (writer); Brooklyn, N.Y. **(1904-1979)**
Pericles (statesman); Athens **(died 429 B.C.)**
Perkins, Osgood (actor); West Newton, Mass. **(1892-1937)**
Perkins, Tony (Anthony) (actor); New York City, 4/14/1932
Perlman, Itzhak (violinist); Tel Aviv, Israel, 8/31/1945
Perón, Isabel (María Estela Martínez Cartas) (former chief of state); La Rioja, Argentina, 2/4/1931
Perón, Juan D. (statesman); nr. Lobos, Argentina **(1895-1974)**
Perón, Maria Eva Duarte de (political leader); Los Toldos, Argentina **(1919-1952)**
Perrine, Valerie (actress and dancer); Galveston, Tex., 9/3/1943
Pershing, John Joseph (general); Linn County, Mo. **(1860-1948)**
Peters, Bernadette (Bernadette Lazzara) (actress); New York City, 2/28/1944
Peters, Brock (actor-singer); New York City, 7/2/1927
Peters, Jean (actress); Canton, Ohio, 10/15/1926
Peters, Roberta (Roberta Peterman) (soprano); New York City, 5/4/1930
Petrarch (Francesco Petrarca) (poet); Arezzo (Italy) **(1304-1374)**
Philip (Philip Mountbatten) (Duke of Edinburgh); Corfu, Greece, 6/10/1921
Piaf, Edith (Edith Gassion) (chanteuse); Paris **(1916-1963)**
Piatigorsky, Gregor (cellist); Ekaterinoslav, Russia **(1903-1976)**
Piazza, Ben (actor); Little Rock, Ark., 7/30/1934
Piazza, Marguerite (soprano); New Orleans, 5/6/1926
Picasso, Pablo (painter and sculptor); Málaga, Spain **(1881-1973)**
Pickford, Jack (Jack Smith) (actor); Toronto **(1896-1933)**
Pickford, Mary (Gladys Mary Smith) (actress); Toronto **(1893-1979)**
Picon, Molly (actress); New York City, 6/1/1898
Pidgeon, Walter (actor); East St. John, New Brunswick, Canada, 9/23/1898
Pinter, Harold (playwright); London, 10/10/1930
Pinza, Ezio (basso); Rome **(1892-1957)**
Pirandello, Luigi (dramatist and novelist); nr. Girgenti, Italy **(1867-1936)**
Pissaro, Camille Jacob (painter); St. Thomas (U.S. Virgin Islands) **(1830-1903)**
Piston, Walter (composer); Rockland, Me. **(1894-1976)**
Pitman, Sir (Isaac) James (educator and publisher); Bath, England, 8/14/1901
Pitt, William ("Younger Pitt") (statesman); nr. Bromley, England **(1759-1806)**
Pitts, ZaSu (actress); Parsons, Kan. **(1898-1963)**
Pius XII (Eugenio Pacelli) (Pope); Rome **(1876-1958)**
Pizarro, Francisco (explorer); Trujillo, Spain **(1470?-1541)**
Plato (Aristocles) (philosopher); Athens (?) **(427?-347 B.C.)**
Pleasence, Donald (actor); Worksop, England, 10/5/1919
Pleshette, Suzanne (actress); New York City, 1/31/1937
Plimpton, George (author); New York City, 3/18/1927
Plisetskaya, Maya (ballerina); Moscow, 11/20/1925
Plowright, Joan (actress); Brigg, England, 10/28/1929
Plummer, Christopher (actor); Toronto, 12/13/1929
Plutarch (biographer); Chaeronea (Greece) **(46?-?120)**
Pocahontas (Matoaka) (American Indian princess); Virginia (?) **(1595?-1617)**
Podhoretz, Norman (author); Brooklyn, N.Y., 1/16/1930
Poe, Edgar Allan (poet and story writer); Boston, Mass. **(1809-1849)**
Poitier, Sidney (film actor and director); Miami, Fla., 2/20/1927
Polanski, Roman (film director); Paris, 8/18/1933
Pollard, Michael J. (actor); Passaic, N.J., 5/30/1939
Pollock, Jackson (painter); Cody, Wyo. **(1912-1956)**
Polo, Marco (traveler); Venice **(1254?-?1324)**
Pompey (Gnaeus Pompeius Magnus) (general); Rome (?) **(106-48 B.C.)**
Ponce de León, Juan (explorer); Servas, Spain **(1460?-1521)**
Pons, Lily (coloratura soprano); Cannes, France **(1904-1976)**
Ponti, Carlo (director); Milan, Italy, 12/11/1913
Pope, Alexander (poet); London **(1688-1744)**
Porter, Cole (songwriter); Peru, Ind. **(1891-1964)**
Porter, Katherine Anne (novelist); Indian Creek, Tex. **(1891-1980)**
Post, Wiley (aviator); Grand Plain, Tex. **(1900-1935)**
Potok, Chaim (author); New York City, 2/17/1929
Pound, Ezra (poet); Hailey, Idaho **(1885-1972)**
Powell, Adam Clayton, Jr. (Congressman); New Haven, Conn. **(1908-1972)**
Powell, Dick (actor); Mt. View, Ark. **(1904-1963)**
Powell, Eleanor (actress and tap dancer); Springfield, Mass. **(1912-1982)**
Powell, Jane (Suzanne Burce) (actress and singer); Portland, Ore., 4/1/1929
Powell, William (actor); Pittsburgh, **(1892-1984)**
Power, Tyrone (actor); Cincinnati, Ohio **(1914-1958)**
Powers, Stephanie (Taffy Paul) (actress); Hollywood, Calif., 11/12/1942
Praxiteles (sculptor); Athens **(c.370-c.330 B.C.)**
Preminger, Otto (film director and producer); Vienna, 12/5/1906
Prentiss, Paula (Paula Ragusa) (actress); San Antonio, 1939
Presley, Elvis (singer and actor); Tupelo, Miss. **(1935-1977)**
Preston, Robert (Robert Preston Meservey) (actor); Newton Highlands, Mass., 6/8/1918
Previn, André (conductor); Berlin, 4/6/1929
Previn, Dory (singer); Rahway, N.J., 10/22/1929(?)
Price, Leontyne (Mary) (soprano); Laurel, Miss., 2/10/1927
Price, Ray (country music artist); Perryville, Tex., 1/12/1926
Price, Vincent (actor); St. Louis, 5/27/1911
Pride, Charley (singer); Sledge, Miss., 3/18/1938(?)
Priestley, J. B. (John B.) (author); Bradford, England **(1894-1984)**
Priestley, Joseph (chemist); nr. Leeds, England **(1733-1804)**
Primrose, William (violist); Glasgow, Scotland **(1904-1982)**
Prince, Harold (stage producer); New York City, 1/30/1928
Prinze, Freddie (actor); New York City **(1954-1977)**
Pritchett, V(ictor) S(awdon) (literary critic); Ipswich, England, 12/16/1900
Procter, William (scientist); Cincinnati **(1872-1951)**
Prokofieff, Sergei Sergeevich (composer); St. Petersburg, Russia **(1891-1953)**
Proust, Marcel (novelist); Paris **(1871-1922)**
Prowse, Juliet (actress); Bombay, 9/25/1936
Pryor, Richard (comedian); Peoria, Ill., 12/1/1940
Ptolemy (Claudius Ptolemaeus) (astronomer and geographer); Ptolemais Hermii (Egypt) **(2nd century A.D.)**
Pucci, Emilio (Marchese di Barsento) (fashion designer); Naples, Italy, 11/20/1914
Puccini, Giacomo (composer); Lucca, Italy **(1858-1924)**
Puente, Tito (band leader); New York City, 4/20/1923
Pulaski, Casimir (military officer); Podolia, Poland **(1748-1779)**
Pulitzer, Joseph (publisher); Makó (Hungary) **(1847-1911)**
Pullman, George (inventor); Brockton, N.Y. **(1831-1897)**
Pusey, Nathan M. (educator); Council Bluffs, Iowa, 4/4/1907
Pushkin, Alexander Sergeevich (poet and dramatist); Moscow **(1799-1837)**
Puzo, Mario (novelist); New York City, 10/15/1921
Pyle, Ernest Taylor (journalist); Dana, Ind. **(1900-1945)**
Pythagoras (mathematician and philosopher); Samos (Greece) **(6th century B.C.)**

Q

Quayle, Anthony (actor); Ainsdale, England, 9/7/1913
Queen, Ellery: pen name of the late Frederic Dannay and the late Manfred B. Lee
Quinn, Anthony (actor); Chihuahua, Mexico, 4/21/1916

R

Rabe, David (playwright); Dubuque, Iowa, 3/10/1940
Rabelais, François (satirist); nr. Chinon, France **(1494?-1553)**
Rabi, I(sidor) I(saac) (physicist); Rymanow (Poland), 7/29/1898
Rachmaninoff, Sergei Wassilievitch (pianist and composer); Oneg Estate, Novgorod, Russia **(1873-1943)**
Racine, Jean Baptiste (dramatist); La Ferté-Milon, France **(1639-1699)**
Radner, Gilda (comedienne); Detroit, 6/28/1946
Raft, George (actor); New York City **(1895-1980)**
Rainer, Luise (actress); Vienna, 1912
Rainier III (Prince); Monaco, 5/31/1923
Rains, Claude (actor); London **(1889-1967)**
Raitt, Bonnie (singer); Burbank, Calif., 11/8/1949
Raleigh, Sir Walter (courtier and navigator); London **(1552?-1618)**
Randall, Tony (Leonard Rosenberg) (actor); Tulsa, Okla., 2/26/1920
Randolph, A(sa) Philip (labor leader); Crescent City, Fla. **(1889-1979)**
Raphael (Raffaello Santi) (painter and architect); Urbino (Italy) **(1483-1520)**
Rasputin, Grigori Efimovich (monk); Tobolsk Province, Russia **(1871?-1916)**
Rathbone, Basil (actor); Johannesburg, South Africa **(1892-1967)**
Rather, Dan (TV newscaster); Wharton, Tex., 10/31/1931
Ratoff, Gregory (film director); St. Petersburg, Russia **(1897-1960)**
Rattigan, Terence (playwright); London **(1911-1977)**
Rauschenberg, Robert (painter); Port Arthur, Tex., 10/22/1925
Ravel, Maurice Joseph (composer); Ciboure, France **(1875-1937)**
Rawls, Lou (singer); Chicago, 12/1/1935
Ray, Man (painter); Philadelphia **(1890-1976)**
Ray, Satyajat (film director); Calcutta, 5/2/1922
Rayburn, Gene (TV personality); Christopher, Ill., 12/22/1917
Raye, Martha (Margie Yvonne Reed) (comedienne and actress); Butte, Mont., 8/27/1916

Raymond, Gene (actor); New York City, 8/13/1908
Reasoner, Harry (TV commentator); Dakota City, Iowa, 4/17/1923
Redding, Otis (singer); Dawson, Ga. **(1941-1967)**
Reddy, Helen (singer); Melbourne, 10/25/1941
Redford, Robert (Charles Robert Redford, Jr.) (actor); Santa Monica, Calif., 8/18/1937
Redgrave, Lynn (actress); London, 3/8/1943
Redgrave, Sir Michael (actor); Bristol, England, 3/20/1908
Redgrave, Vanessa (actress); London, 1/30/1937
Reed, Donna (actress); Denison, Iowa, 1/27/1921
Reed, Rex (critic); Ft. Worth, 10/2/1940
Reed, Walter (army surgeon); Belroi, Va. **(1851-1902)**
Reese, Della (Deloreese Patricia Early) (singer); Detroit, 7/6/1932
Reeves, Jim (singer); Panola County, Tex. **(1923-1964)**
Reid, Wallace (actor); St. Louis **(1891-1923)**
Reiner, Carl (actor); New York City, 3/20/1922
Reiner, Fritz (conductor); Budapest **(1888-1963)**
Reiner, Robert (actor); Bronx, N.Y., 1945
Reinhardt, Max (Max Goldmann) (theater producer); nr. Vienna **(1873-1943)**
Remarque, Erich Maria (novelist); Osnabruk, Germany **(1898-1970)**
Rembrandt (Rembrandt Harmensz van Rijn) (painter); Leyden (Netherlands) **(1605-1669)**
Remick, Lee (Ann) (actress); Boston, 12/14/1935
Rennert, Günther (opera director and producer); Essen, Germany, 4/1/1911
Rennie, Michael (actor); Bradford, England **(1909-1971)**
Renoir, Jean (film director and writer); Paris, **(1894-1979)**
Renoir, Pierre Auguste (painter); Limoges, France **(1841-1919)**
Resnais, Alain (film director); Vannes, France, 6/3/1922
Resnik, Regina (mezzo-soprano); New York City, 8/30/1922
Respighi, Ottorino (composer); Bologna, Italy **(1879-1936)**
Reston, James (journalist); Clydebank, Scotland, 11/3/1909
Reuther, Walter (labor leader); Wheeling, W. Va. **(1907-1970)**
Revere, Paul (silversmith and hero of famous ride); Boston **(1735-1818)**
Revson, Charles (business executive); Boston **(1906-1975)**
Reynolds, Burt (actor); Waycross, Ga., 2/11/1936
Renolds, Debbie (Marie Frances Reynolds) (actress); El Paso, 4/1/1932
Reynolds, Sir Joshua (painter); nr. Plymouth, England **(1723-1792)**
Rhodes, Cecil John (South African statesman); Bishop Stortford, England **(1853-1902)**
Rice, Elmer (playwright); New York City **(1892-1967)**
Rice, Grantland (sports writer); Murfreesboro, Tenn. **(1880-1954)**
Rich, Buddy (Bernard) (drummer); Brooklyn, N.Y., 6/30/1917
Rich, Charlie (singer); Colt, Ark., 12/14/1932
Richardson, Elliot L. (ex-Cabinet member); Boston, 7/20/1920
Richardson, Sir Ralph (actor); Cheltenham, England **(1902-1983)**
Richardson, Tony (director); Shipley, England, 6/5/1928
Richelieu, Duc de (Armand Jean du Plessis) (cardinal); Paris **(1585-1642)**
Richter, Charles Francis (seismologist); Hamilton, Canada, 4/26/1900
Richter, Sviatosiav (pianist); Zhitomir, Ukraine, 3/20/1914
Rickenbacker, Edward V. (aviator); Columbus, Ohio **(1890-1973)**
Rickles, Don (comedian); New York City, 5/8/1926
Rickover, Vice Admiral Hyman G. (atomic energy expert); Russia, 1/27/1900
Riddle, Nelson (composer); Hackensack, N.J., 6/1/1921
Ridgway, General Matthew B. (ex-Army Chief of Staff); Ft. Monroe, Va., 3/3/1895
Rigg, Diana (actress); Doncaster, England, 7/20/1938
Riley, James Whitcomb (poet); Greenfield, Ind. **(1849-1916)**
Rimsky-Korsakov, Nikolai Andreevich (composer); Tikhvin, Russia **(1844-1908)**
Rinehart, Mary (née Roberts) (novelist); Pittsburgh **(1876-1958)**
Ritchard, Cyril (actor and director); Sydney, Australia **(1898-1977)**
Ritter, John (Jonathan) (actor); Burbank, Calif., 9/17/1948
Ritter, Tex (Woodward Maurice Ritter) (singer); Panola County, Tex., **(1905-1973)**
Ritz, Al (Al Joachim) (comedian); Newark, N.J. **(1901-1965)**
Rivera, Diego (painter); Guanajuato, Mexico **(1886-1957)**
Rivera, Geraldo (Miguel) (TV newscaster); New York City, 7/3/1943
Rivers, Joan (comedienne); Brooklyn, N.Y., 1935(?)
Rivers, Larry (Yitzroch Loiza Grossberg) (painter); New York City, 8/17/1923
Robards, Jason, Jr. (actor); Chicago, 7/26/1922
Robards, Jason, Sr. (actor); Hillsdale, Mich. **(1892-1963)**
Robbins, Harold (Harold Rubin) (novelist); New York City, 5/21/1916
Robbins, Jerome (Jerome Rabinowitz) (choreographer); New York City, 10/11/1918
Robbins, Marty (singer); Glendale, Ariz., **(1925-1982)**
Roberts, (Granville) Oral (evangelist and publisher); nr. Ada, Okla., 1/24/1918
Robertson, Cliff (actor); La Jolla, Calif., 9/9/1925
Robertson, Dale (Dayle) (actor); Oklahoma City, 7/14/1923
Robeson, Paul (singer and actor); Princeton, N.J., **(1898-1976)**
Robespierre, Maximilien François Marie Isidore de (French Revolutionist); Arras, France **(1758-1794)**
Robinson, Bill "Bojangles" (Luther) (dancer); Richmond, Va. **(1878-1949)**
Robinson, Edward G. (Emanuel Goldenberg) (actor); Bucharest **(1893-1973)**
Robinson, Edwin Arlington (poet); Head Tide, Me. **(1869-1935)**
Robson, Dame Flora (actress); South Shields, England **(1902-1984)**
Rochester (Eddie Anderson) (actor); Oakland, Calif. **(1905-1977)**
Rockefeller, David (banker); New York City, 6/12/1915
Rockefeller, John Davison (capitalist); Richford, N.Y. **(1839-1937)**
Rockefeller, John Davison, Jr. (industrialist); Cleveland **(1874-1960)**
Rockefeller, John D., 3rd (philanthropist); New York City **(1906-1978)**
Rockefeller, Laurance S. (conservationist); New York City, 5/26/1910
Rockwell, Norman (painter and illustrator); New York City, **(1894-1978)**
Rodgers, Jimmie (singer); Meridian, Miss. **(1897-1933)**
Rodgers, Richard (composer); New York City **(1902-1979)**
Rodin, François Auguste René (sculptor); Paris **(1840-1917)**
Roentgen, Wilhelm Konrad (physicist); Lennep, Prussia **(1845-1923)**
Rogers, Buddy (Charles) (actor); Olathe, Kan., 8/13/1904
Rogers, Ginger (Virginia McMath) (dancer and actress); Independence, Mo., 7/16/1911
Rogers, Kenny (singer); Houston, 1939(?)
Rogers, Roy (Leonard Slye) (actor); Cincinnati, 11/5/1912
Rogers, Will (William Penn Adair Rogers) (humorist); Oologah, Okla. **(1879-1935)**
Rogers, Will, Jr. (actor); New York City, 10/20/1911
Rogers, William P. (ex-Secretary of State); Norfolk, N.Y., 6/23/1913
Roland, Gilbert (actor); Juarez, Mexico, 12/11/1905
Rolland, Romain (author); Clamecy, France **(1866-1944)**
Rollins, Sonny (saxophonist); New York City, 9/7/1930
Romberg, Sigmund (composer); Szeged (Hungary) **(1887-1951)**
Rome, Harold (composer); Hartford, Conn., 5/27/1908
Romero, Cesar (actor); New York City, 2/15/1907
Romney, George W. (ex-Secretary of HUD); Chihuahua, Mexico, 7/8/1907
Romulo, Carlos P. (diplomat and educator); Manila, 1/14/1899
Ronstadt, Linda (singer); Tucson, Ariz., 7/30/1946
Rooney, Mickey (Joe Yule, Jr.) (actor); Brooklyn, N.Y., 9/23/1920
Roosevelt, Anna Eleanor (reformer and humanitarian); New York City **(1884-1962)**
Rose, Billy (showman); New York City **(1899-1966)**
Rose, Leonard (concert cellist); Washington, D.C., 7/27/1918
Ross, Diana (singer); Detroit, 3/26/1944
Ross, Katharine (actress); Hollywood, Calif., 1/29/1943
Rossellini, Roberto (film director); Rome **(1906-1977)**
Rossetti, Dante Gabriel (painter and poet); London **(1828-1882)**
Rossini, Gioacchino Antonio (composer); Pesaro (Italy) **(1792-1868)**
Rostand, Edmond (dramatist); Marseilles, France **(1868-1918)**
Rostow, Walt Whitman (economist); New York City, 10/7/1916
Rostropovich, Mstislav (cellist and conductor); Baku, U.S.S.R., 3/12/1927
Roth, Lillian (singer); Boston **(1910-1980)**
Roth, Philip (novelist); Newark, N.J., 3/19/1933
Rothko, Mark (Marcus Rothkovich) (painter); Russia **(1903-1970)**
Rouault, Georges (painter); Paris **(1871-1958)**
Roundtree, Richard (actor); New Rochelle, N.Y., 9/7/1942
Rousseau, Henri (painter); Laval, France **(1844-1910)**
Rousseau, Jean Jacques (philosopher); Geneva **(1712-1778)**
Rovere, Richard H. (journalist); Jersey City, N.J., 5/5/1915
Rowan, Dan (comedian); Beggs, Okla., 7/2/1922
Rowlands, Gena (actress); Cambria, Wis., 6/19/1936(?)
Rubens, Sir Peter Paul (painter); Siegen (Germany) **(1577-1640)**
Rubinstein, Arthur (concert pianist); Lódz (Poland) **(1887-1982)**
Rubinstein, Helena (cosmetics executive); Krakow (Poland) **(1882?-1965)**
Rudel, Julius (conductor); Vienna, 3/6/1921
Ruggles, Charles (actor); Los Angeles **(1892-1970)**
Rule, Janice (actress); Norwood, Ohio, 8/15/1931
Runcie, Robert (Alexander Kennedy) (Archbishop of Canterbury); Liverpool, England, 10/2/1921
Runyon, (Alfred) Damon (journalist); Manhattan, Kan. **(1884-1945)**
Rusk, Dean (ex-Sec. of State); Cherokee County, Ga., 2/9/1909
Ruskin, John (art critic); London **(1819-1900)**
Russell, Lord Bertrand (Arthur William) (mathematician and philosopher); Trelleck, Wales **(1872-1970)**
Russell, Jane (actress); Bemidji, Minn., 6/21/1921
Russell, Leon (pianist and singer); Lawton, Okla., 4/2/1941
Russell, Lillian (Helen Louise Leonard) (soprano); Clinton, Iowa **(1861-1922)**
Russell, Nipsy (comedian); Atlanta, 1924(?)

Russell, Rosalind (actress); Waterbury, Conn. **(1912-1976)**
Rustin, Bayard (civil rights leader); West Chester, Pa., 1910
Rutherford, Dame Margaret (actress); London **(1892-1972)**
Ryan, Robert (actor); Chicago **(1909-1973)**
Rydell, Bobby (singer); Philadelphia, 1942
Rysanek, Leonie (dramatic soprano); Vienna, 11/14/1928

S

Saarinen, Eero (architect); Finland **(1910-1961)**
Sabin, Albert B. (polio researcher); Bialystok (Poland), 8/26/1906
Sadat, Anwar el- (President); Egypt **(1918-1981)**
Sagan, Françoise (novelist); Cajarc, France, 6/21/1935
Sahl, Mort (Morton Lyon Sahl) (comedian); Montreal, 5/11/1927
Saint, Eva Marie (actress); Newark, N.J., 7/4/1924
Saint-Gaudens, Augustus (sculptor); Dublin **(1848-1907)**
St. James, Susan (Susan Miller) (actress); Los Angeles, 8/14/1946
St. John, Jill (actress); Los Angeles, 8/19/1940
St. Johns, Adela Rogers (journalist and author); Los Angeles, 5/20/1894
Saint-Laurent, Yves (Henri Donat Mathieu) (fashion designer); Oran, Algeria, 8/1/1936
Saint-Saens, Charles Camille (composer); Paris **(1835-1921)**
Sainte-Marie, Buffy (Beverly) (folk singer); Craven, Saskatchewan, Canada, 2/20/1942(?)
Salinger, J(erome) D(avid) (novelist); New York City, 1/1/1919
Salisbury, Harrison E. (journalist); Minneapolis, 11/14/1908
Salk, Jonas (polio researcher); New York City, 10/28/1914
Salk, Leo (psychologist); New York City, 1926
Salomon, Haym (American Revolution financier); Leszno, Poland **(1740-1785)**
Sand, George (Amandine Lucille Aurore Dudevant, née Dupin) (novelist); Paris **(1804-1876)**
Sandburg, Carl (poet and biographer); Galesburg, Ill. **(1878-1967)**
Sanders, George (actor); St. Petersburg, Russia **(1906-1972)**
Sands, Tommy (singer); Chicago, 8/27/1937
Sanger, Margaret (birth control leader); Corning, N.Y. **(1883-1966)**
Santayana, George (philosopher); Madrid **(1863-1952)**
Sappo (poet); Lesbos (Greece) (lived c. 600 B.C.)
Sargent, John Singer (painter); Florence, Italy **(1856-1925)**
Sarnoff, David (radio executive); Minsk, Russia **(1891-1971)**
Saroyan, William (novelist); Fresno, Calif. **(1908-1981)**
Sarrazin, Michael (actor); Quebec, 5/22/1940
Sarto, Andrea del (Andrea Domenico d'Agnolo di Francesco) (painter); Florence (Italy) **(1486-1531)**
Sartre, Jean-Paul (existentialist writer); Paris **(1905-1980)**
Sassoon, Vidal (hair stylist); London, 1/(?)/1928
Saul (King of Israel) **(11th century B.C.)**
Savalas, Telly (Aristoteles) (actor); Garden City, N.Y., 1/21/1924(?)
Sayão, Bidú (soprano); Rio de Janeiro, 5/11/1902
Scaasi, Arnold (Arnold Isaacs) (fashion designer); Montreal
Schary, Dore (producer and writer); Newark, N.J. **(1905-1980)**
Schell, Maria (actress); Vienna, 1/15/1926
Schell, Maximilian (actor); Vienna, 12/8/1930
Schiaparelli, Elsa (fashion designer); Rome **(1890?-1973)**
Schiff, Dorothy (newspaper publisher); New York City, 3/11/1903
Schildkraut, Joseph (actor); Vienna **(1896-1964)**
Schiller, Johann Christoph Friedrich von (dramatist and poet); Marbach (Germany) **(1759-1805)**
Schippers, Thomas (conductor); Kalamazoo, Mich. **(1930-1977)**
Schlesinger, Arthur M., Jr. (historian); Columbus, Ohio, 10/15/1917
Schneider, Romy (Rose-Marie Albach) (actress); Vienna **(1938-1982)**
Schoenberg, Arnold (composer); Vienna **(1874-1951)**
Schopenhauer, Arthur (philosopher); Danzig (Poland) **(1788-1860)**
Schubert, Franz Peter (composer); Vienna **(1797-1828)**
Schulberg, Budd (novelist); New York City, 3/27/1914
Schulz, Charles M. (cartoonist); Minneapolis, 11/26/1922
Schuman, Robert (statesman); Luxembourg **(1886-1963)**
Schuman, William (composer); New York City, 8/4/1910
Schumann, Robert Alexander (composer); Zwickau (Germany) **(1810-1856)**
Schwartz, Arthur (song writer); Brooklyn, N.Y. **(1900-1984)**
Schwartz, Maurice (actor); Russia **(1891-1960)**
Schwarzkopf, Elisabeth (soprano); Jarotschin, Poznán (Poland), 12/9/1915
Schweitzer, Albert (humanitarian); Kaysersburg, Upper Alsace **(1875-1965)**
Scofield, Paul (actor); Hurstpierpoint, England, 1/21/1922
Scorsese, Martin (film director); Flushing, N.Y., 11/17/1942
Scott, George C. (actor); Wise, Va., 10/18/1927
Scott, Lizabeth (Emma Matso) (actress); Scranton, Pa., 1923
Scott, Martha (actress); Jamesport, Mo., 9/22/1914
Scott, Randolph (Randolph Crane) (actor); Orange County, Va., 1/23/1903
Scott, Robert Falcon (explorer); Devonport, England **(1868-1912)**
Scott, Sir Walter (novelist); Edinburgh, Scotland **(1771-1832)**
Scott, Zachary (actor); Austin, Tex. **(1914-1965)**
Scotto, Renata (operatic soprano); Savona, Italy, 2/?/1936?
Scruggs, Earl Eugene (bluegrass musician); Cleveland County, N.C., 1/6/1924
Sebastian, John (composer); New York City, 3/17/1944
Seberg, Jean (actress); Marshalltown, Iowa **(1938-1979)**
Sedaka, Neil (singer); Brooklyn, N.Y., 3/13/1939
Seeger, Pete (folk singer); New York City, 5/3/1919
Segal, Erich (novelist); Brooklyn, N.Y., 6/16/1937
Segal, George (actor); New York City, 2/13/1936
Segovia, Andrés (guitarist); Linares, Spain, 2/21/1893
Sellers, Peter (actor); Southsea, England **(1925-1980)**
Selznick, David O. (film producer); Pittsburgh **(1902-1965)**
Sendak, Maurice (Bernard) (children's book author and illustrator); Brooklyn, N.Y., 6/10/1928
Sennett, Mack (Michael Sinnott) (film producer); Richmond, Quebec, Canada **(1880-1960)**
Serkin, Rudolf (pianist); Eger (Hungary), 3/28/1903
Serling, Rod (story writer); Syracuse, N.Y. **(1924-1975)**
Sessions, Roger (composer); Brooklyn, N.Y., 12/28/1896
Seurat, Georges (painter); Paris **(1859-1891)**
Seuss, Dr. (Theodor Seuss Geisel) (author and illustrator); Springfield, Mass., 3/2/1904
Sevareid, Eric (TV commentator); Velva, N.D., 11/26/1912
Severinsen, Doc (Carl) (band leader); Arlington, Ore., 7/7/1927
Sexton, Anne (poet); Newton, Mass. **(1928-1974)**
Shahn, Ben(jamin) (painter); Kaunas, Lithuania **(1898-1969)**
Shakespeare, William (dramatist); Stratford on Avon, England **(1564-1616)**
Shankar, Ravi (sitar player); Benares, India, 4/7/1920
Shanker, Albert (labor leader); New York City, 9/14/1928
Sharif, Omar (Michael Shalhoub) (actor); Alexandria, Egypt, 4/10/1932
Shatner, William (actor); Montreal, 3/22/1931
Shaw, Artie (Arthur Arshawsky) (band leader); New York City, 5/23/1910
Shaw, George Bernard (dramatist); Dublin, **(1856-1950)**
Shaw, Irwin (novelist); Brooklyn, N.Y., **(1913-1984)**
Shaw, Robert (actor); Lancashire, England **(1927-1978)**
Shaw, Robert (chorale conductor); Red Bluff, Calif., 4/30/1916
Shearer, Moira (ballerina); Dunfermline, Scotland, 1/17/1926
Shearer, Norma (actress); Montreal, **(1902?-1983)**
Shearing, George (pianist); London, 8/13/1920
Sheen, Fulton J. (Peter Sheen) (Roman Catholic bishop); El Paso, Ill. **(1895-1979)**
Sheen, Martin (Ramon Estevez) (actor); Dayton, Ohio, 8/3/1940
Shelley, Percy Bysshe (poet); nr. Horsham, England **(1792-1822)**
Shepard, Sam (playwright); Ft. Sheridan, Ill. 11/5/1943
Sheraton, Thomas (furniture designer); Stockton-on-Tees, England **(1751-1806)**
Sheridan, Ann (actress); Denton, Tex. **(1915-1967)**
Sheridan, Philip (army officer); Albany, N.Y. **(1831-1888)**
Sheridan, Richard Brinsley (dramatist); Dublin, **(1751-1816)**
Sherman, William Tecumseh (army officer); Lancaster, Ohio **(1820-1891)**
Sherwood, Robert Emmet (playwright); New Rochelle, N.Y. **(1896-1955)**
Shiref, William L. (journalist and historian); Chicago, 2/23/1904
Sholokhov, Mikhait (novelist); Veshenskaya, Russia **(1905-1984)**
Shore, Dinah (Frances Rose Shore) (singer); Winchester, Tenn., 3/1/1917(?)
Short, Bobby (Robert Waltrip Short) (singer and pianist); Danville, Ill., 9/15/1924
Shostakovich, Dmitri (composer); St. Petersburg, Russia **(1906-1975)**
Shriver, Sargent (Robert Sargent Shriver, Jr.) (business executive); Westminster, Md., 11/9/1915
Shulman, Max (novelist); St. Paul, 3/14/1919
Sibelius, Jean (Johann Julius Christian Sibelius) (composer); Tavastehus (Finland) **(1865-1957)**
Sidney, Sylvia (actress); New York City, 8/8/1910
Siepi, Cesare (basso); Milan, Italy, 2/10/1923
Signoret, Simone (Simone Kaminker) (actress); Wiesbaden, Germany, 3/25/1921
Sikorsky, Igor I. (inventor); Kiev, Russia **(1889-1972)**
Sills, Beverly (Belle Silverman) (soprano, opera director); Brooklyn, N.Y., 5/25/1929
Silone, Ignazio (Secondo Tranquilli) (novelist); Pescina del Marsi, Italy **(1900-1978)**
Silverman, Fred (broadcasting executive); New York City, 9/13/1937
Silvers, Phil (Philip Silversmith) (comedian); Brooklyn, N.Y., 5/11/1912
Sim, Alastair (actor); Edinburgh, Scotland **(1900-1976)**

Simenon, Georges (Georges Sim) (mystery writer); Liège, Belgium, 2/13/1903
Simmons, Jean (actress); Crouch Hill, London, 1/31/1929
Simon, Carly (singer and songwriter); New York City, 6/25/1945
Simon, Neil (playwright); Bronx, N.Y., 7/4/1927
Simon, Norton (business executive); Portland, Ore., 2/5/1907
Simon, Paul (singer and songwriter); Newark, N.J., 11/5/1942
Simon, Simone (actress); Marseilles, France, 4/23/1914
Simone, Nina (Eunice Kathleen Waymoa) (singer and pianist); Tryon, N.C., 2/21/1933
Simpson, Adele (Adele Smithline) (fashion designer); New York City, 12/8/1903
Sinatra, Frank (Francis Albert) (singer and actor); Hoboken, N.J., 12/12/1915
Sinclair, Upton Beall (novelist); Baltimore **(1878-1968)**
Singer, Isaac Bashevis (novelist); Radzymin (Poland), 7/14/1904
Siqueiros, David (painter); Chihuahua, Mexico **(1896-1974)**
Sisley, Alfred (painter); Paris **(1839-1899)**
Sitting Bull (Prairie Sioux Indian Chief); on Grand River, S.D. **(c. 1835-1890)**
Skelton, Red (Richard) (comedian); Vincennes, Ind., 7/18/1913
Skinner, B(urrhus) F(rederic) (psychologist); Susquehanna, Pa., 3/20/1904
Skinner, Cornelia Otis (writer and actress); Chicago, **(1901-1979)**
Skinner, Otis (actor); Cambridge, Mass. **(1858-1942)**
Slezak, Walter (actor); Vienna **(1902-1983)**
Sloan, Alfred P., Jr. (industrialist); New Haven, Conn. **(1875-1965)**
Sloan, John (painter); Lock Haven, Pa. **(1871-1951)**
Smetana, Bedrich (composer); Litomysl (Czechoslovakia) **(1824-1884)**
Smith, Adam (economist); Kirkaldy, Scotland **(1723-1790)**
Smith, Alexis (actress); Penticon, Canada, 6/8/1921
Smith, Alfred Emanuel (politician); New York City **(1873-1944)**
Smith, David (sculptor); Decatur, Ind. **(1906-1965)**
Smith, H. Allen (humorist); McLeansboro, Ill. **(1907-1976)**
Smith, Howard K. (TV commentator); Ferriday, La., 5/12/1914
Smith, Jaclyn (actress); Houston, 10/26/(?)
Smith, John (American colonist); Willoughby, Lincolnshire, England **(1580-1631)**
Smith, Joseph (religious leader); Sharon, Vt. **(1805-1844)**
Smith, Kate (Kathryn) (singer); Greenville, Va., 5/1/1909
Smith, Maggie (actress); Ilford, England, 12/28/1934
Smith, Red (Walter) (sports columnist); Green Bay, Wis. **(1905-1982)**
Smothers, Dick (Richard) (comedian); Governors Island, New York City, 11/20/1939
Smothers, Tom (Thomas) (comedian); Governors Island, New York City, 2/2/1937
Snow, Lord (Charles Percy) (author); Leicester, England **(1905-1980)**
Snowdon, Earl of (Anthony Armstrong-Jones) (photographer); London, 3/7/1930
Snyder, Tom (TV personality); Milwaukee, 5/12/1936
Socrates (philosopher); Athens **(469-399 B.C.)**
Solomon (King of Israel); Jerusalem (?) **(died c. 933 B.C.)**
Solon (lawgiver); Salamis (Greece) **(638?-559 B.C.)**
Solti, Sir Georg (conductor); Budapest, 10/21/1912
Solzhenitsyn, Aleksandr (novelist); Kislovodsk, Russia, 12/11/1918
Sommer, Elke (Elke Schletz) (actress); Berlin, 11/5/1942
Sondheim, Stephen (composer); New York City, 3/22/1930
Sontag, Susan (author and film director); New York City, 1/28/1933
Sophocles (dramatist); nr. Athens **(496?-406 B.C.)**
Sothern, Ann (Harriette Lake) (actress); Valley City, N.D., 1/22/1912
Soul, David (David Solberg) (actor); Chicago, 8/28/(?)
Sousa, John Philip (composer); Washington, D.C. **(1854-1932)**
Soyer, Raphael (painter); Borisoglebsk, Russia, 12/25/1899
Spaak, Paul-Henri (statesman); Brussels **(1899-1972)**
Spacek, Sissy (Mary Elizabeth) (actress); Quitman, Tex., 12/25/1949
Spark, Muriel (novelist); Edinburgh, Scotland, 2/1/1918
Spector, Phil (rock producer); Bronx, N.Y., 12/25/1940
Spencer, Herbert (philosopher); Derby, England **(1820-1903)**
Spender, Stephen (poet); nr. London, 2/28/1909
Spengler, Oswald (philosopher); Blankenburg, Germany **(1880-1936)**
Spenser, Edmund (poet); London **(1552?-1599)**
Spewack, Bella (playwright); Hungary, 3/25/1899
Spiegel, Sam (producer); Jaroslaw (Poland), 11/11/1901
Spielberg, Steven (film director); Cincinnati, 12/18/1947
Spillane, Mickey (Frank Spillane) (mystery writer); Brooklyn, N.Y., 3/9/1918
Spinoza, Baruch (philosopher); Amsterdam (Netherlands) **(1632-1677)**
Spivak, Lawrence (TV producer); Brooklyn, N.Y., 1900
Spock, Benjamin (pediatrician); New Haven, Conn., 5/2/1903
Springsteen, Bruce (singer and songwriter); Freehold, N.J., 9/23/1949
Sproul, Robert G. (educator); San Francisco **(1891-1975)**
Stack, Robert (actor); Los Angeles, 1/13/1919
Stafford, Jo (singer); Coalinga, Calif., 1918
Stalin, Joseph Vissarionovich (Iosif V. Dzhugashvili) (Soviet leader); nr. Tiflis, Russia **(1879-1953)**
Stalina, Svetlana Alliluyeva (Stalin's daughter); Moscow, 2/28/1926
Stallone, Sylvester (actor and writer); New York City, 7/6/1946
Stamp, Terrence (actor); London, 1938
Stang, Arnold (comedian); Chelsea, Mass., 1925
Stanislavski (Konstantin Sergeevich Alekseev) (stage producer); Moscow **(1863-1938)**
Stanley, Sir Henry Morton (John Rowlands) (explorer); Denbigh, Wales **(1841-1904)**
Stanley, Kim (Patricia Reid) (actress); Tularosa, N.M., 2/11/1925
Stans, Maurice H. (ex-Secretary of Commerce); Shakope, Minn., 3/22/1908
Stanton, Frank (broadcasting executive); Muskegon, Mich., 3/20/1908
Stanwyck, Barbara (Ruby Stevens) (actress); Brooklyn, N.Y., 7/16/1907
Stapleton, Jean (Jeanne Murray) (actress); New York City, 1/19/1923
Stapleton, Maureen (actress); Troy, N.Y., 6/21/1925
Starker, Janós (cellist); Budapest 7/5/1926
Starr, Kay (Starks) (singer); Dougherty, Okla., 7/21/1922
Starr, Ringo (Richard Starkey) (singer and songwriter); Liverpool, England, 7/7/1940
Stassen, Harold E. (ex-government official); West St. Paul, Minn., 4/13/1907
Steegmuller, Francis (biographer); New Haven, Conn., 7/3/1906
Steele, Tommy (singer); London, 12/17/1936
Stegner, Wallace (Earle) (novelist and critic); Lake Mills, Iowa, 2/18/1909
Steiger, Rod (Rodney) (actor); Westhampton, N.Y., 4/14/1925
Stein, Gertrude (author); Allegheny, Pa. **(1874-1946)**
Steinbeck, John Ernst (novelist); Salinas, Calif. **(1902-1968)**
Steinberg, David (comedian); Winnipeg, Manitoba, Canada, 8/19/1942
Steinberg, William (conductor); Cologne, Germany **(1899-1978)**
Steinem, Gloria (feminist); Toledo, Ohio, 3/25/1935(?)
Steinmetz, Charles (electrical engineer); Breslau (Poland) **(1865-1923)**
Stendhal (Marie Henri Beyle) (novelist); Grenoble, France **(1783-1842)**
Sterling, Jan (actress); New York City, 4/3/1923
Stern, Isaac (concert violinist); Kreminlecz, Russia, 7/21/1920
Sterne, Laurence (novelist); Clonmel, Ireland **(1713-1768)**
Stevens, Cat (Steven Georgiou) (singer and songwriter); London, 7/?/1947
Stevens, Connie (Concetta Ingolia) (singer); Brooklyn, N.Y., 8/8/1938
Stevens, George (film director); Oakland, Calif. **(1905-1975)**
Stevens, Risë (mezzo-soprano); New York City, 6/11/1913
Stevens, Stella (actress); Yazoo City, Miss., 10/1/1936
Stevenson, Adlai Ewing (statesman); Los Angeles **(1900-1965)**
Stevenson, McLean (actor); Bloomington, Ind., 11/14/1929(?)
Stevenson, Robert Louis Balfour (novelist and poet); Edinburgh, Scotland **(1850-1894)**
Stewart, James (actor); Indiana, Pa., 5/20/1908
Stewart, Rod (Roderick David) (singer); London, 1/10/1945
Stickney, Dorothy (actress); Dickinson, N.D. 6/21/1903
Stills, Stephen (singer and songwriter); Dallas, 1/3/1945
Stokes, Carl (TV newscaster); Cleveland, 6/21/1927
Stokowski, Leopold (conductor); London **(1882-1977)**
Stone, Edward Durell (architect); Fayetteville, Ark. **(1902-1978)**
Stone, Ezra (actor and producer); New Bedford, Mass., 12/2/1917
Stone, I(sidor) F(einstein) (journalist); Philadelphia, 12/24/1907
Stone, Irving (Irving Tennenbaum) (novelist); San Francisco, 7/14/1903
Stone, Lewis (actor); Worcester, Mass. **(1879-1953)**
Stone, Lucy (woman suffragist); nr. West Brookfield, Mass. **(1818-1893)**
Stone, Sly (Sylvester) (rock musician); 1944
Storm, Gale (actress); Bloomington, Tex., 1922
Stout, Rex (mystery writer); Noblesville, Ind. **(1886-1975)**
Stowe, Harriet Elizabeth Beecher (novelist); Litchfield, Conn. **(1811-1896)**
Stradivari, Antonio (violinmaker); Cremona (Italy) **(1644-1737)**
Strasberg, Lee (stage director); Budanov, Austria **(1901-1982)**
Strasberg, Susan (actress); New York City, 5/22/1938
Straus, Oskar (composer); Vienna **(1870-1954)**
Strauss, Johann (composer); Vienna **(1825-1899)**
Strauss, Lewis L. (naval officer and scientist); Charleston, W. Va. **(1896-1974)**
Strauss, Richard (composer); Munich, Germany **(1864-1949)**
Stravinsky, Igor (composer); Orlenbaum, Russia **(1882-1971)**
Streep, Meryl (Mary Louise) (actress); Summit, N.J., 6/22/1949
Streisand, Barbra (singer and actress); Brooklyn, N.Y., 4/24/1942
Stritch, Elaine (actress); Detroit, 2/2/1928
Struthers, Sally Ann (actress); Portland, Ore., 7/28/1948

Stuart, Gilbert Charles (painter); Rhode Island **(1755-1828)**
Stuart, James Ewell Brown (known as Jeb) (Confederate army officer); Patrick County, Va. **(1833-1864)**
Stuyvesant, Peter (Governor of New Amsterdam); West Friesland (Netherlands) **(1592-1672)**
Styne, Jule (Julius Kerwin Stein) (songwriter); London, 12/31/1905
Styron, William (William Clark Styron, Jr.) (novelist); Newport News, Va., 6/11/1925
Sullavan, Margaret Brooke (actress); Norfolk, Va. **(1911-1960)**
Sullivan, Sir Arthur Seymour (composer); London **(1842-1900)**
Sullivan, Barry (Patrick Barry) (actor); New York City, 8/29/1912
Sullivan, Ed (columnist and TV personality); New York City **(1901-1974)**
Sullivan, Francis Loftus (actor); London **(1903-1956)**
Sullivan, Frank (Francis John) (humorist); Saratoga Springs, N.Y. **(1892-1976)**
Sullivan, Louis Henry (architect); Boston, Mass. **(1856-1924)**
Sutzberger, Arthur Ochs (newspaper publisher); New York City, 2/5/1926
Sumac, Yma (singer); Ichocan, Peru, 9/10/1927
Summer, Donna (La Donna Andrea Gaines) (singer); Boston, 12/31/1948
Sun Yat-sen (statesman); nr. Macao **(1866-1925)**
Susann, Jacqueline (novelist); Philadelphia **(1926?-1974)**
Susskind, David (TV producer); New York City, 12/19/1920
Sutherland, Joan (soprano); Sydney, Australia, 11/7/1926
Suzuki, Pat (actress); Cressey, Calif., 1931
Swados, Elizabeth (composer, playwright); Buffalo, N.Y., 2/5/1951
Swanson, Gloria (Gloria May Josephine Svensson) (actress); Chicago, **(1899-1983)**
Swarthout, Gladys (soprano); Deepwater, Mo. **(1904-1969)**
Swayze, John Cameron (news commentator); Wichita, Kan., 4/4/1906
Swift, Jonathan (satirist); Dublin **(1667-1745)**
Swinburne, Algernon Charles (poet); London **(1837-1909)**
Swope, Herbert Bayard (journalist); St. Louis **(1882-1958)**
Sydow, von, Max (Carl Adolf von Sydow) (actor); Lund, Sweden, 4/10/1929
Synge, John Millington (dramatist); nr. Dublin **(1871-1909)**
Szilard, Leo (physicist); Budapest **(1898-1964)**

T

Taft, Robert Alphonso (legislator); Cincinnati **(1889-1953)**
Tagore, Sir Rabindranath (poet); Calcutta **(1861-1941)**
Tallchief, Maria (ballerina); Fairfax, Okla., 1/24/1925
Talleyrand-Périgord, Charles Maurice de (statesman); Paris **(1754-1838)**
Talmadge, Norma (actress); Niagara Falls, N.Y. **(1897-1957)**
Talvela, Martti (basso); Hiitola, Finalnd, 2/4/1935
Tamerlane (Timur) (Mongol conqueror); nr. Samarkand (U.S.S.R.) **(1336?-1405)**
Tandy, Jessica (actress); London, 6/7/1909
Tarkington, (Newton) Booth (novelist); Indianapolis **(1869-1946)**
Tate, Allen (John Orley) (poet and critic); Winchester, Ky., **(1899-1979)**
Tate, Sharon (actress); Dallas **(1943-1969)**
Tati, Jacques (Jacques Tatischeff) (actor); Pecq, France **(1908-1982)**
Taylor, Elizabeth (actress); London, 2/27/1932
Taylor, Estelle (actress); Wilmington, Del. **(1899-1958)**
Taylor, Harold (educator); Toronto, 9/28/1914
Taylor, James (singer and songwriter); Boston, 3/12/1948
Taylor, (Joseph) Deems (composer); New York City **(1885-1966)**
Taylor, Laurette (Laurette Cooney) (actress); New York City **(1884-1946)**
Taylor, Gen. Maxwell D. (former Army Chief of Staff); Keytesville, Mo., 8/26/1901
Taylor, Robert (Spangler Arlington Brugh) (actor); Filley, Neb. **(1911-1969)**
Taylor, Rod (actor); Sydney, Australia, 1/11/1930
Tchaikovsky, Peter (Pëtr) Ilich (composer); Votkinsk, Russia **(1840-1893)**
Teasdale, Sara (poet); St. Louis **(1884-1933)**
Tebaldi, Renata (lyric soprano); Pesaro, Italy, 1/2/1922
Tecumseh (Shawnee Indian chief); nr. Springfield, Ohio **(1768?-1813)**
Teller, Edward (atomic physicist); Budapest, 1/15/1908
Temple, Shirely. *See* Black, Shirley Temple
Tennyson, Alfred (1st Baron Tennyson) (poet); Somersby, England **(1809-1892)**
Terhune, Albert Payson (novelist and journalist); Newark, N.J. **(1872-1942)**
Terry, Ellen Alicia (actress); Coventry, England **(1848-1928)**
Terry-Thomas (Thomas Terry Hoar Stevens) (actor); London, 7/14/1911
Tesia, Nikola (electrician and inventor); Smiljan (Yugoslavia) **(1856-1943)**
Thackeray, William Makepeace (novelist); Calcutta **(1811-1863)**
Thant, U (U.N. statesman); Pantanaw (Burma) **(1909-1974)**
Tharp, Twyla (dancer and choreographer); Portland, Ind., 7/1/1941(?)
Thatcher, Margaret (Prime Minister); Grantham, England, 10/13/1925
Thaxter, Phyllis (actress); Portland, Me., 1921
Thebom, Blanche (mezzo-soprano); Monessen, Pa., 9/19/1919
Theodorakis, Mikis (composer); Chios, Greece, 7/29/1925
Thieu, Nguyen Van (ex-President of South Vietnam); Trithuy (Vietnam) 4/5/1923
Thomas, Danny (Amos Jacobs) (entertainer and TV producer); Deerfield, Mich., 1/6/1914
Thomas, Dylan Marials (poet); Carmarthenshire, Wales **(1914-1953)**
Thomas, Lowell (explorer, commentator); Woodington, Ohio **(1892-1981)**
Thomas, Marlo (actress); Detroit, 11/21/1943
Thomas, Michael Tilson (conductor); Hollywood, Calif., 12/21/1944
Thomas, Norman Mattoon (Socialist leader): Marion, Ohio **(1884-1968)**
Thomas, Richard (actor); New York City, 6/13/1951
Thompson, Dorothy (writer); Lancaster, N.Y. **(1894-1961)**
Thompson, Sada (actress); Des Moines, Iowa, 9/27/1929
Thoreau, Henry David (naturalist and author); Concord, Mass. **(1817-1862)**
Thorndike, Dame Sybil (actress); Gainsborough, England **(1882-1976)**
Thurber, James Grover (author and cartoonist); Columbus, Ohio **(1894-1961)**
Tibbett, Lawrence (baritone); Bakersfield, Calif. **(1896-1960)**
Tierney, Gene (actress); Brooklyn, N.Y., 11/20/1920
Tiffin, Pamela (actress); Oklahoma City, 10/13/1942
Tillstrom, Burr (puppeteer); Chicago, 10/13/1917
Tintoretto, Il (Jacopo Robusti) (painter); Venice **(1518-1594)**
Tiny Tim (Herbert Khaury) (entertainer); New York City, 1923(?)
Tiomkin, Dmitri (composer); St. Petersburg, Russia **(1894-1979)**
Titian (Tiziano Vecelli) (painter); Pieve di Cadore (Italy) **(1477-1576)**
Tito (Josip Broz or Brozovich) (President of Yugoslavia); Croatia (Yugoslavia) **(1892-1980)**
Tocqueville, Alexis de (writer); Verneuil, France **(1805-1859)**
Todd, Thelma (actress); Lawrence, Mass. **(1905-1935)**
Tolstel, Count Leo (Lev) Nikolaevich (novelist); Tula Province, Russia **(1828-1910)**
Tomlin, Lily (comedienne); Detroit, 1939(?)
Tone, Franchot (actor); Niagara Falls, N.Y. **(1905-1968)**
Tormé, Mel (Melvin) (singer); Chicago, 9/13/1925
Torn, Rip (Elmore Torn, Jr.) (actor and director); Temple, Tex., 2/6/1931
Toscanini, Arturo (orchestra conductor); Parma, Italy **(1867-1957)**
Toulouse-Lautrec (Henri Marie Raymond de Toulouse-Lautrec Monfa) (painter); Albi, France **(1864-1901)**
Toynbee, Arnold J. (historian); London **(1889-1975)**
Tracy, Spencer (actor); Milwaukee **(1900-1967)**
Traubei, Helen (Wagnerian soprano); St. Louis **(1903-1972)**
Travolta, John (actor); Englewood, N.J., 2/18/1954
Treacher, Arthur (actor); Brighton, England **(1894-1975)**
Trevor, Claire (actress); New York City, 1911
Trigère, (Pauline (fashion designer); Paris, 11/4/1912
Trilling, Lionel (author and educator); New York City **(1905-1975)**
Trotsky, Leon (Lev Davidovich Bronstein) (statesman); Elisavetgrad, Russia **(1879-1940)**
Trudeau, Pierre Elliott (Prime Minister); Montreal, 10/18/1919
Truffaut, François (film director); Paris, 2/6/1932
Trujillo y Molina, Rafael Leonidas (Dominican Republic dictator); San Cristóbal, Dominican Republic **(1891-1961)**
Truman, Margaret (author); Independence, Mo., 2/17/1924
Tryon, Thomas (actor and novelist); Hartford, Conn., 1/14/1926
Tucker, Forrest (actor); Plainfield, Ind., 2/12/1919
Tucker, Richard (tenor); New York City **(1914-1975)**
Tucker, Sophie (Sophie Abuza) (singer); Europe **(1884?-1966)**
Tudor, Antony (choreographer); London, 4/4/1909
Tune, Tommy (dancer-choreographer); Wichita Falls, Tex., 2/28/1939
Turgenev, Ivan Sergeevich (novelist); Orel, Russia **(1818-1883)**
Turner, Ike (singer); Clarksdale, Miss., 11/?/1931
Turner, Joseph M.W. (painter); London **(1775-1851)**
Turner, Lana (Julia Jean Mildred Frances Turner) (actress); Wallace, Idaho, 2/8/1920
Turner, Nat (civil rights leader); Southampton County, Va. **(1800-1831)**
Turner, Tina (Annie Mae Bullock) (singer); Brownsville, Tex., 1939
Turpin, Ben (comedian); New Orleans **(1874-1940)**
Tushingham, Rita (actress); Liverpool, England, 3/14/1942

Twain, Mark (Samuel Langhorne Clemens) (author); Florida, Mo. **(1835-1910)**
Tweed, William Marcy (politician); New York City **(1823-1878)**
Twiggy (Leslie Hornby) (model); London, 9/19/1949
Twining, Gen. Nathan F. (former Air Force Chief of Staff); Monroe, Wis. **(1897-1982)**
Twitty, Conway (Harold Lloyd Jenkins) (singer and guitarist); Friars Point, Miss., 9/1/1933
Tyson, Cicely (actress); New York City, 12/19/1939(?)

U

Udall, Stewart L. (ex-Secretary of the Interior); St. Johns, Ariz., 1/31/1920
Uggams, Leslie (singer and actress); New York City, 5/25/1943
Ulanova, Galina (ballerina); St. Petersburg, Russia, 1/10/1910
Ullmann, Liv (actress); Tokyo, 12/16/1939
Ulric, Lenore (actress); New Ulm, Minn. **(1894-1970)**
Untermeyer, Louis (anthologist and poet); New York City **(1885-1977)**
Updike, John (novelist); Shillington, Pa., 3/18/1932
Urey, Harold C. (physicist); Walkerton, Ind. **(1893-1981)**
Uris, Leon (novelist); Baltimore, 8/3/1924
Ustinov, Peter (actor and producer); London, 4/16/1921
Utrillo, Maurice (painter); Paris **(1883-1955)**

V

Vaccaro, Brenda (actress); Brooklyn, N.Y., 11/18/1939
Vadim, Roger (Roger Vadim Plemiannikov) (film director); Paris, 1/26/1928
Valentine, Karen (actress); Santa Rosa, Calif., 1947
Valentino, Rudolph (Rodolpho d'Antonguolla) (actor); Castellaneta, Italy **(1895-1926)**
Valentino (Valentino Garavani) (fashion designer); nr. Milan, Italy, 5/11/1932
Vallee, Rudy (Hubert Prior Rudy Vallée) (band leader and singer); Island Pond, Vt., 7/28/1901
Valli, Frankie (Frank Castellaccio) (singer); Newark, N.J., 5/3/1937
Van Allen, James Alfred (space physicist); Mt. Pleasant, Iowa, 9/7/1914
Van Buren, Abigail (Mrs. Morton Phillips) (columnist); Sioux City, Iowa, 7/4/1918
Vance, Vivian (actress); Cherryvale, Kan. **(1912-1979)**
Vanderbilt, Alfred G. (sportsman); London, 9/22/1912
Vanderbilt, Cornelius (financier); Port Richmond, N.Y. **(1794-1877)**
Vanderbilt, Gloria (fashion designer) New York City, 2/20/1924
Van Doren, Carl (writer and educator); Hope, Ill. **(1885-1950)**
Van Doren, Mamie (actress); Rowena, S.D., 2/6/1933
Van Dyke, Dick (actor); West Plains, Mo., 12/13/1925
Vandyke (or Van Dyck), Sir Anthony (painter); Antwerp (Belgium) **(1599-1641)**
Van Eyck, Jan (painter); Maeseyck (Belgium) **(c.1390-1441)**
van Gogh, Vincent (painter); Groot Zundert, Brabant **(1853-1890)**
van Hamel, Martine (ballerina); Brussels, 11/16/1945
Van Heusen, Jimmy (Edward Chester Babcock) (songwriter); Syracuse, N.Y., 1/26/1913
Van Peebles, Melvin (playwright); Chicago, 9/21/1932
Vaughan, Sarah (singer); Newark, N.J., 3/27/1924
Vaughan Williams, Ralph (composer); Down Ampney, England **(1872-1958)**
Vaughn, Robert (actor); New York City, 11/22/1932
Velázquez, Diego Rodriguez de Silva y (painter); Seville, Spain **(1599-1660)**
Velez, Lupe (Guadelupe Velez de Villalobos) (actress); San Luis Potosi, Mexico **(1908-1944)**
Venturi, Robert (Charles) (architect); Philadelphia, 6/25/1925
Verdi, Giuseppe (composer); Roncole (Italy) **(1813-1901)**
Verdon, Gwen (actress); Culver City, Calif., 1/13/1925
Vereen, Ben (actor and singer); Miami, Fla., 10/10/1946
Vermeer, Jan (or Jan van der Meer van Delft) (painter); Delft (Netherlands) **(1632-1675)**
Verne, Jules (author); Nantes, France **(1828-1905)**
Verrazano, Giovanni da (navigator); Florence (Italy) **(1485?-1528)**
Verrett, Shirley (mezzo-soprano); New Orleans, 5/31/1933
Vespucci, Amerigo (navigator); Florence (Italy) **(1454-1512)**
Vickers, Jon (tenor); Prince Albert, Sask, Canada, 10/29/1926
Vidal, Gore (novelist); West Point, N.Y., 10/3/1925
Vidor, King (film director and producer); Galveston, Tex. **(1895-1982)**
Villa, Pancho (Doroteo Arango) (bandit); Rio Grande, Mexico **(1877-1923)**
Villella, Edward (ballet dancer); Bayside, Queens, N.Y., 10/1/1936
Villon, François (François de Montcorbier) (poet); Paris **(1431-1463)**
Vinton, Bobby (singer); Canonsburg, Pa., 4/16/1935(?)
Virgil (or Vergil) (Publius Vergilius Maro) (poet); nr. Mantua (Italy) **(70-19 B.C.)**
Vishnevskaya, Galina (soprano); Leningrad, 10/25/1926
Vlaminck, Maurice de (painter); Paris **(1876-1958)**
Voight, Jon (actor); Yonkers, N.Y., 12/29/1938
Voltaire (François Marie Arouet) (author); Paris **(1694-1778)**
von Braun, Wernher (rocket scientist); Wirsitz, Germany **(1912-1977)**
von Aroldingen, Karin (Karin Awny Hannelore Reinbold von Aroedingen and Eltzinger) (ballet dancer); Greiz, Germany, 7/9/1941
von Furstenberg, Betsy (Elizabeth Caroline Maria Agatha Felicitas Therese von Furstenberg-Hedringen) (actress); Nelheim-Heusen, Germany, 8/16/1935
von Fürstenberg, Diane (Diane Simone Michelle Halfin) (fashion designer); Brussels, 12/31/1946
von Hindenburg, Paul (statesman): Posen (Poland) **(1847-1934)**
von Karajan, Herbert (conductor); Salzburg (Austria), 4/5/1908
Vonnegut, Kurt, Jr. (novelist); Indianapolis, 11/11/1922
Von Stroheim, Erich Oswald Hans Carl Maria von Nordenwall (film actor and director); Vienna **(1885-1957)**
Vreeland, Diana (Diana Dalziel) (fashion journalist and museum consultant); Paris, 1903(?)

W

Wagner, Lindsay (actress); Los Angeles, 6/22/1949
Wagner, Robert (actor); Detroit, 2/10/1930
Wagner, Robert F. (ex-Mayor of New York City); New York City, 4/20/1910
Wagner, Wilhelm Richard (composer); Leipzig (Germany) **(1813-1883)**
Waldheim, Kurt (U.N. Secretary-General); St. Andrae-Wörden, Austria, 12/21/1918
Walker, Clint (actor); Hartford, Ill., 5/30/1927
Walker, Nancy (Ann Myrtle Swoyer); (actress and comedienne); Philadelphia, 5/10/1922
Wallace, DeWitt (publisher); St. Paul **(1889-1981)**
Wallace, Irving (novelist); Chicago, 3/19/1916
Wallace, Mike (Myron Wallace) (TV interviewer and commentator); Brookline, Mass., 5/9/1918
Wallach, Eli (actor); Brooklyn, N.Y., 12/7/1915
Waller, Thomas "Fats" (pianist); New York City **(1904-1943)**
Wallis, Hal (film producer); Chicago, 9/14/1899
Waltari, Mika (novelist); Helsinki, Finland, **(1903-1979)**
Walter, Bruno (Bruno Walter Schlesinger) (orchestra conductor); Berlin **(1876-1962)**
Walters, Barbara (TV commentator); Boston, 9/25/1931
Walton, Izaak (author); Stafford, England **(1593-1683)**
Wambaugh, Joseph (author and screenwriter); East Pittsburgh, Pa., 1/22/1937
Wanamaker, John (merchant); Philadelphia **(1838-1922)**
Ward, Barbara (economist); York, England **(1914-1981)**
Warhol, Andy (artist and producer); Cleveland, 8/8/1930(?)
Waring, Fred (band leader); Tyrone, Pa., **(1900-1984)**
Warner, H. B. (Henry Bryan Warner Lickford) (actor); London **(1876-1958)**
Warren, Robert Penn (novelist); Guthrie, Ky., 4/24/1905
Warwick, Dionne (singer); East Orange, N.J., 1941
Washington, Booker Taliaferro (educator); Franklin County, Va. **(1856-1915)**
Waters, Ethel (actress and singer); Chester, Pa. **(1896-1977)**
Waters, Muddy (McKinley Morganfield) (singer and guitarist); Rolling Fork, Miss. **(1915-1983)**
Watson, Thomas John (industrialist); Campbell, N.Y. **(1874-1956)**
Watt, James (inventor); Greenock, Scotland **(1736-1819)**
Watteau, Jean-Antoine (painter); Valanciennes, France **(1684-1721)**
Watts, André (concert pianist); Nuremberg, Germany, 6/20/1946
Waugh, Alec (Alexander Raban Waugh) (novelist); London **(1898-1981)**
Waugh, Evelyn (satirist); London **(1903-1966)**
Wayne, Anthony (military officer); Waynesboro (family farm), nr. Paoli, Pa. **(1745-1796)**
Wayne, David (David McMeekan); (actor); Traverse City, Mich., 1/30/1914
Wayne, John (Marion Michael Morrison) (actor); Winterset, Iowa, **(1907-1979)**
Weaver, Dennis (actor); Joplin, Mo., 6/4/1925
Weaver, Fritz (actor); Pittsburgh, 1/19/1926
Webb, Clifton (Webb Parmelee Hollenbeck) (actor); Indianapolis **(1893-1966)**
Webb, Jack (film actor and producer); Santa Monica, Calif. **(1920-1982)**

Weber, Karl Maria Friedrich Ernst von (composer); nr. Lübeck (Germany) **(1786-1826)**
Webster, Daniel (statesman); Salisbury, N.H. **(1782-1852)**
Webster, Noah (lexicographer); West Hartford, Conn. **(1758-1843)**
Weill, Kurt (composer); Dessau, Germany **(1900-1950)**
Weizmann, Chaim (statesman); Grodno Province, Russia **(1874-1952)**
Welch, Raquel (Raquel Tejada) (actress); Chicago, 9/5/1942
Weld, Tuesday (Susan) (actress); New York City, 8/27/1943
Welk, Lawrence (band leader); Strasburg, N.D., 3/11/1903
Welles, Orson (actor and producer); Kenosha, Wis., 5/6/1915
Wellington, Duke of (Arthur Wellesley) (statesman); Ireland **(1769-1852)**
Wells, H(erbert) G(eorge) (author); Bromley, England **(1866-1946)**
Welty, Eudora (novelist); Jackson, Miss., 4/13/1909
Werfel, Franz (novelist); Prague **(1890-1945)**
Werner, Oskar (Josef Schliessmayer) (film actor and director); Vienna, 11/13/1922
Wertmuller, Lina (film director); Rome, 1926(?)
Wesley, John (religious leader); Epworth Rectory, Lincolnshire, England **(1703-1791)**
West, Dame Rebecca (Cicily Fairfield); (novelist); County Kerry, Ireland **(1892-1983)**
West, Jessamyn (novelist); nr. North Vernon, Ind. **(1902-1984)**
West, Mae (actress); Brooklyn, N.Y. **(1893-1980)**
West, Nathanael (Nathan Weinstein) (novelist); New York City **(1902-1940)**
Westinghouse, George (inventor); Central Bridge, N.Y. **(1846-1914)**
Westmoreland, William Childs (ex-Army Chief of Staff); Saxon, S.C., 3/26/1914
Wharton, Edith Newbold (née Jones) (novelist); New York City **(1862-1937)**
Wheeler, Bert (Albert Jerome Wheeler) (comedian); Paterson, N.J. **(1895-1968)**
Whistler, James Abbott McNeill (painter and etcher); Lowell, Mass. **(1834-1903)**
White, E(lwyn) B(rooks) (author); Mt. Vernon, N.Y., 7/11/1899
White, Stanford (architect); New York City **(1853-1906)**
White, Theodore H. (historian); Boston, 5/6/1915
White, William Allen (journalist); Emporia, Kan. **(1868-1944)**
Whitehead, Alfred North (mathematician and philosopher); Isle of Thanet, England **(1861-1947)**
Whiteman, Paul (band leader); Denver **(1891-1967)**
Whitman, Walt (Walter) (poet); West Hills, N.Y. **(1819-1892)**
Whitmore, James (actor); White Plains, N.Y., 10/1/1921
Whitney, Cornelius Vanderbilt (sportsman); New York City, 2/20/1899
Whitney, Eli (inventor); Westboro, Mass. **(1765-1825)**
Whitney, John Hay (publisher); Ellsworth, Me. **(1904-1982)**
Whittier, John Greenleaf (poet); Haverhill, Mass. **(1807-1892)**
Widmark, Richard (actor); Sunrise, Minn., 12/26/1914
Wiesel, Elie (Eliezer) (author); Signet, Romania, 9/30/1928
Wilbur, Richard (poet); New York City, 3/1/1921
Wilde, Cornel (film actor and producer); New York City, 10/13/1918
Wilde, Oscar Fingal O'Flahertie Wills (author); Dublin **(1854-1900)**
Wilder, Billy (film producer and director); Vienna, 6/22/1906
Wilder, Gene (Jerome Silberman) (actor); Milwaukee, 6/11/1935(?)
Wilder, Thornton (author); Madison, Wis. **(1897-1975)**
Wilding, Michael (actor); Westcliff, England **(1912-1979)**
Wilkins, Roy (civil rights leader); St. Louis **(1901-1981)**
Williams, Andy (singer); Wall Lake, Iowa, 12/3/1930
Williams, Cindy (actress); Van Nuys, Calif., 8/22/(?)
Williams, Edward Bennett (lawyer); Hartford, Conn., 5/31/1920
Williams, Emlyn (actor and playwright); Mostyn, Wales, 11/26/1905
Williams, Esther (actress); Los Angeles, 8/8/1923
Williams, Gluyas (cartoonist); San Francisco **(1888-1982)**
Williams, Hank, Sr. (Hiram King Williams) (singer); Georgiana, Ala. **(1923-1953)**
Williams, Paul (singer, composer, actor); Omaha, Neb., 9/19/1940
Williams, Robin (comedian); Chicago, 7/?/1952
Williams, Roger (clergyman); London **(1603?-1683)**
Williams, Tennessee (Thomas L. Williams) (playwright); Columbus, Miss. **(1911-1983)**
Wilkie, Wendell Lewis (lawyer); Elwood, Ind. **(1892-1944)**
Wilson, Meredith (composer); Mason City, Iowa **(1902-1984)**
Wilson, Don (radio and TV announcer); Lincoln, Neb. **(1900-1982)**
Wilson, Flip (Clerow) (comedian); Jersey City, N.J., 12/8/1933
Wilson, Harold (ex-Prime Minister); Huddersfield, England, 3/11/1916
Wilson, Nancy (singer); Chillicothe, Ohio, 2/20/1937
Wilson, Sloan (novelist); Norwalk, Conn., 5/8/1920
Winchell, Walter (columnist); New York City **(1897-1972)**
Windsor, Duchess of (Bessie Wallis Warfield); Blue Ridge Summit, Pa., 6/19/1896
Windsor, Duke of (formerly King Edward VIII of England); Richmond Park, England **(1894-1972)**
Winkler, Henry (actor); New York City, 10/30/1945
Winter, Johnny (guitarist); Leland, Miss., 2/23/1944
Winters, Jonathan (comedian); Dayton, Ohio, 11/11/1925
Winters, Shelley (Shirley Schrift) (actress); East St. Louis, Ill., 8/18/1922
Winthrop, John (first Governor, Massachusetts Bay Colony); Suffolk, England **(1588-1649)**
Wise, Stephen Samuel (rabbi); Budapest **(1874-1949)**
Withers, Jane (actress); Atlanta, 1927
Wittgenstein, Ludwig (Josef Johann) (philosopher); Vienna **(1889-1951)**
Wodehouse, P(elham) G(renville) (novelist); Guildford, England **(1881-1975)**
Wolfe, Thomas Clayton (novelist); Asheville, N.C. **(1900-1938)**
Wolfe, Tom (journalist); Richmond, Va., 3/2/1931
Wolsey, Thomas (prelate and statesman); Ipswich, England **(1475?-1530)**
Wonder, Stevie (Steveland Judkins, later Steveland Morris) (singer and songwriter); Saginaw, Mich., 5/13/1950
Wong, Anna May (Lu Tsong Wong) (actress); Los Angeles **(1907-1961)**
Wood, Grant (painter); Anamosa, Iowa **(1892-1942)**
Wood, Natalie (Natasha Gurdin) (film actress); San Francisco **(1938-1981)**
Woodward, Joanne (film actress); Thomasville, Ga., 2/27/1930
Woolf, Adeline Virginia (née Stephens) (novelist); London **(1882-1941)**
Woollcott, Alexander (author-critic); Phalanx, N.J. **(1887-1943)**
Woolley, Monty (Edgar Montillion Woolley) (actor); New York City **(1888-1963)**
Woolworth, Frank (merchant); Rodman, N.Y. **(1852-1919)**
Wordsworth, William (poet); Cockermouth, England **(1770-1850)**
Worley, Jo Anne (actress and singer); Lowell, Ind., 9/6/1937
Wouk, Herman (novelist); New York City, 5/27/1915
Wray, Fay (actress); Alberta, Canada, 1907
Wren, Sir Christopher (architect); East Knoyle, England **(1632-1723)**
Wright, Frank Lloyd (architect); Richland Center, Wis. **(1869-1959)**
Wright, Orville (inventor); Dayton, Ohio **(1871-1948)**
Wright, Richard (novelist); nr. Natchez, Miss. **(1908-1960)**
Wright, Teresa (actress); New York City, 10/27/1918
Wright, Wilbur (inventor); Millville, Ind. **(1867-1912)**
Wyatt, Jane (film actress); Campgaw, N.J., 8/12/1912
Wyeth, Andrew (painter); Chadds Ford, Pa., 7/12/1917
Wyler, William (film director); Mulhouse (France), **(1902-1981)**
Wyman, Jane (Sarah Jane Fulks) (actress); St. Joseph, Mo., 1/4/1914
Wynette, Tammy (Wynette Pugh) (singer); Tupelo, Miss. 5/5/1942
Wynn, Ed (Isaiah Edwin Leopold) (comedian); Philadelphia **(1886-1966)**
Wynn, Keenan (actor); New York City, 7/27/1916
Wynter, Dana (actress); London, 6/8/1930

Y

Yeats, William Butler (poet); nr. Dublin **(1865-1939)**
Yevtushenko, Yevgeny (poet); Zima, U.S.S.R., 7/18/1933
York, Michael (actor); Fulmer, England, 3/27/1942
York, Susannah (Fletcher) (actress); London, 1/9/1942
Yorty, Samuel W. (ex-Mayor of Los Angeles); Lincoln, Neb., 10/1/1909
Young, Alan (actor); North Shield, England, 11/19/1919
Young, Brigham (religious leader); Whitingham, Vt. **(1801-1877)**
Young, Gig (Byron Barr) (actor); St. Cloud, Minn. **(1917-1978)**
Young, Loretta (Gretchen Young) (actress); Salt Lake City, Utah, 1/6/1913
Young, Neil (singer and songwriter); Toronto, 11/12/1945
Young, Robert (actor); Chicago, 2/22/1907
Youngman, Henny (comedian); England, 1906

Z

Zanuck, Darryl F. (film producer); Wahoo, Neb. **(1902-1979)**
Zappa, Frank (Francis Vincent Zappa, Jr.) (singer and songwriter); Baltimore, 12/21/1940
Zeffirelli, Franco (director); Florence, Italy, 2/12/1923
Zhou Enlai (Premier); Hualyin, China **(1898-1976)**
Ziegfeld, Florenz (theatrical producer); Chicago **(1869-1932)**
Zimbalist, Efrem (concert violinist); Rostov-on-Don, Russia, 4/9/1889
Zimbalist, Efrem, Jr. (actor); New York City, 11/30/1923
Zola, Emile (novelist); Paris **(1840-1902)**
Zoroaster (religious leader); Persian Empire **(c. 6th century B.C.)**
Zukerman, Pinchas (violinist); Tel Aviv, Israel 7/16/1948
Zweig, Stefan (author); Vienna **(1881-1942)**

U.S. HISTORY & GOVERNMENT

THE DECLARATION OF INDEPENDENCE

In Congress, July 4, 1776

The unanimous Declaration of the thirteen united States of America.

When in the Course of human events it becomes necessary for one people to dissolve the political bands which have connected them with another, and to assume among the powers of the earth, the separate and equal station to which the Laws of Nature and of Nature's God entitle them, a decent respect to the opinions of mankind requires that they should declare the causes which impel them to the separation.

We hold these truths to be self-evident, that all men are created equal, that they are endowed by their Creator with certain unalienable Rights, that among these are Life, Liberty and the pursuit of Happiness.—That to secure these rights, Governments are instituted among Men, deriving their just powers from the consent of the governed,—That whenever any Form of Government becomes destructive of these ends, it is the Right of the People to alter or to abolish it, and to institute new Government, laying its foundation on such principles and organizing its powers in such form, as to them shall seem most likely to effect their Safety and Happiness. Prudence, indeed, will dictate that Governments long established should not be changed for light and transient causes; and accordingly all experience hath shewn that mankind are more disposed to suffer, while evils are sufferable, than to right themselves by abolishing the forms to which they are accustomed. But when a long train of abuses and usurpations, pursuing invariably the same Object evinces a design to reduce them under absolute Despotism, it is their right, it is their duty, to throw off such Government, and to provide new Guards for their future security.—Such has been the patient sufferance of these Colonies; and such is now the necessity which constrains them to alter their former Systems of Government. The history of the present King of Great Britain is a history of repeated injuries and usurpations, all having in direct object the establishment of an absolute Tyranny over these States. To prove this, let Facts be submitted to a candid world.

He has refused his Assent to Laws, the most wholesome and necessary for the public good.

He has forbidden his Governors to pass Laws of immediate and pressing importance, unless suspended in their operation till his Assent should be obtained; and when so suspended, he has utterly neglected to attend to them.

He has refused to pass other Laws for the accommodation of large districts of people, unless those people would relinquish the right of Representation in the Legislature, a right inestimable to them and formidable to tyrants only.

He has called together legislative bodies at places unusual, uncomfortable, and distant from the depository of their Public Records, for the sole purpose of fatiguing them into compliance with his measures.

He has dissolved Representative Houses repeatedly, for opposing with manly firmness his invasions on the rights of the people.

He has refused for a long time, after such dissolutions, to cause others to be elected; whereby the Legislative Powers, incapable of Annihilation, have returned to the People at large for their exercise; the State remaining in the mean time exposed to all the dangers of invasion from without, and convulsions within.

He has endeavoured to prevent the population of these States; for that purpose obstructing the Laws for Naturalization of Foreigners; refusing to pass others to encourage their migrations hither, and raising the conditions of new Appropriations of Lands.

He has obstructed the Administration of Justice, by refusing his Assent to Laws for establishing Judiciary Powers.

He has made Judges dependent on his Will alone, for the tenure of their offices, and the amount and payment of their salaries.

He has erected a multitude of New Offices, and sent hither swarms of Officers to harass our people, and eat out their substance.

He has kept among us, in times of peace, Standing Armies without the Consent of our legislatures.

He has affected to render the Military independent of and superior to the Civil Power.

He has combined with others to subject us to a jurisdiction foreign to our constitution, and unacknowledged by our laws; giving his Assent to their Acts of pretended Legislation:

For quartering large bodies of armed troops among us:

For protecting them, by a mock Trial, from punishment for any Murders which they should commit on the Inhabitants of these States:

For cutting off our Trade with all parts of the

NOTE: On April 12, 1776, the legislature of North Carolina authorized its delegates to the Continental Congress to join with others in a declaration of separation from Great Britain; the first colony to instruct its delegates to take the actual initiative was Virginia on May 15. On June 7, 1776, Richard Henry Lee of Virginia offered a resolution to the Congress to the effect "that these United Colonies are, and of right ought to be, free and independent States. . . ." A committee, consisting of Thomas Jefferson, John Adams, Benjamin Franklin, Robert R. Livingston, and Roger Sherman was organized to "prepare a declaration to the effect of the said first resolution." The Declaration of Independence was adopted on July 4, 1776.

Most delegates signed the Declaration August 2, but George Wythe (Va.) signed August 27; Richard Henry Lee (Va.), Elbridge Gerry (Mass.), and Oliver Wolcott (Conn.) in September; Matthew Thornton (N.H.), not a delegate until September, in November; and Thomas McKean (Del.), although present on July 4, not until 1781 by special permission, having served in the army in the interim.

world:

For imposing Taxes on us without our Consent:

For depriving us in many cases, of the benefits of Trial by Jury:

For transporting us beyond Seas to be tried for pretended offences:

For abolishing the free System of English Laws in a neighbouring Province, establishing therein an Arbitrary government, and enlarging its Boundaries so as to render it at once an example and fit instrument for introducing the same absolute rule into these Colonies:

For taking away our Charters, abolishing our most valuable Laws and altering fundamentally the Forms of our Governments:

For suspending our own Legislatures, and declaring themselves invested with power to legislate for us in all cases whatsoever.

He has abdicated Government here, by declaring us out of his Protection and waging War against us.

He has plundered our seas, ravaged our Coasts, burnt our towns, and destroyed the lives of our people.

He is at this time transporting large Armies of foreign Mercenaries to compleat the works of death, desolation, and tyranny, already begun with circumstances of Cruelty & Perfidy scarcely paralleled in the most barbarous ages, and totally unworthy the Head of a civilized nation.

He has constrained our fellow Citizens taken Captive on the high Seas to bear Arms against their Country, to become the executioners of their friends and Brethren, or to fall themselves by their Hands.

He has excited domestic insurrections amongst us, and has endeavoured to bring on the inhabitants of our frontiers, the merciless Indian Savages, whose known rule of warfare, is an undistinguished destruction of all ages, sexes and conditions.

In every stage of these Oppressions We have Petitioned for Redress in the most humble terms: Our repeated Petitions have been answered only by repeated injury. A Prince, whose character is thus marked by every act which may define a Tyrant, is unfit to be the ruler of a free people.

Nor have We been wanting in attentions to our Brittish brethren. We have warned them from time to time of attempts by their legislature to extend an unwarrantable jurisdiction over us. We have reminded them of the circumstances of our emigration and settlement here. We have appealed to their native justice and magnanimity, and we have conjured them by the ties of our common kindred to disavow these usurpations, which would inevitably interrupt our connections and correspondence. They too have been deaf to the voice of justice and of consanguinity. We must, therefore, acquiesce in the necessity, which denounces our Separation, and hold them, as we hold the rest of mankind, Enemies in War, in Peace Friends.

We, therefore, the Representatives of the United States of America, in General Congress, Assembled, appealing to the Supreme Judge of the world for the rectitude of our intentions, do, in the Name, and by Authority of the good People of these Colonies, solemnly publish and declare, That these United Colonies are, and of Right ought to be Free and Independent States; that they are Absolved from all Allegiance to the British Crown, and that all political connection between them and the State of Great Britain, is and ought to be totally dissolved; and that as Free and Independent States, they have full Power to levy War, conclude Peace, contract Alliances, establish Commerce, and to do all other Acts and Things which Independent States may of right do.—And for the support of this Declaration, with a firm reliance on the protection of Divine Providence, we mutually pledge to each other our Lives, our Fortunes and our sacred Honor.

—John Hancock

New Hampshire
Josiah Bartlett
Wm. Whipple
Matthew Thornton

Rhode Island
Step. Hopkins
William Ellery

Connecticut
Roger Sherman
Sam'el Huntington
Wm. Williams
Oliver Wolcott

New York
Wm. Floyd
Phil. Livingston
Frans. Lewis
Lewis Morris

New Jersey
Richd. Stockton
Jno. Witherspoon
Fras. Hopkinson
John Hart
Abra. Clark

Pennsylvania
Robt. Morris
Benjamin Rush
Benj. Franklin
John Morton
Geo. Clymer
Jas. Smith
Geo. Taylor
James Wilson
Geo. Ross

Massachusetts-Bay
Saml. Adams
John Adams
Robt. Treat Paine
Elbridge Gerry

Delaware
Caesar Rodney
Geo. Read
Tho. M'Kean

Maryland
Samuel Chase
Wm. Paca
Thos. Stone
Charles Carroll of Carrollton

Virginia
George Wythe
Richard Henry Lee
Th. Jefferson
Benj. Harrison
Ths. Nelson, Jr.
Francis Lightfoot Lee
Carter Braxton

North Carolina
Wm. Hooper
Joseph Hewes
John Penn

South Carolina
Edward Rutledge
Thos. Heyward, Junr.
Thomas Lynch, Junr.
Arthur Middleton

Georgia
Button Gwinnett
Lyman Hall
Geo. Walton

Constitution of the United States of America

(Historical text has been edited to conform to contemporary American usage. The bracketed words are designations for your convenience; they are not part of the Constitution.)

The oldest federal constitution in existence was framed by a convention of delegates from twelve of the thirteen original states in Philadelphia in May, 1787, Rhode Island failing to send a delegate. George Washington presided over the session, which lasted until September 17, 1787. The draft (originally a preamble and seven Articles) was submitted to all thirteen states and was to become effective when ratified by nine states. It went into effect on the first Wednesday in March, 1789, having been ratified by New Hampshire, the ninth state to approve, on June 21, 1788. The states ratified the Constitution in the following order:

Delaware	December 7, 1787	South Carolina	May 23, 1788
Pennsylvania	December 12, 1787	New Hampshire	June 21, 1788
New Jersey	December 18, 1787	Virginia	June 25, 1788
Georgia	January 2, 1788	New York	July 26, 1788
Connecticut	January 9, 1788	North Carolina	November 21, 1789
Massachusetts	February 6, 1788	Rhode Island	May 29, 1790
Maryland	April 28, 1788		

[Preamble]

We the people of the United States, in order to form a more perfect Union, establish justice, insure domestic tranquility, provide for the common defence, promote the general welfare, and secure the blessings of liberty to ourselves and our posterity, do ordain and establish this Constitution for the United States of America.

Article I

Section 1

[Legislative powers vested in Congress.] All legislative powers herein granted shall be vested in a Congress of the United States, which shall consist of a Senate and House of Representatives.

Section 2

[Composition of the House of Representatives.—1.] The House of Representatives shall be composed of members chosen every second year by the people of the several States, and the electors in each State shall have the qualifications requisite for electors of the most numerous branch of the State Legislature.

[Qualifications of Representatives.—2.] No Person shall be a Representative who shall not have attained to the age of twenty-five years, and been seven years a citizen of the United States, and who shall not, when elected, be an inhabitant of that State in which he shall be chosen.

[Apportionment of Representatives and direct taxes—census.[1]—3.] (Representatives and direct taxes shall be apportioned among the several States which may be included within this Union, according to their respective numbers, which shall be determined by adding to the whole number of free persons, including those bound to service for a term of years, and excluding Indians not taxed, three fifths of all other persons.) The actual enumeration shall be made within three years after the first meeting of the Congress of the United States, and within every subsequent term of ten years, in such manner as they shall by law direct. The number of Representatives shall not exceed one for every thirty thousand, but each State shall have at least one Representative; and until such enumeration shall be made, the State of New Hampshire shall be entitled to choose three, Massachusetts eight, Rhode-Island and Providence Plantations one, Connecticut five, New York six, New Jersey four, Pennsylvania eight, Delaware one, Maryland six, Virginia ten, North Carolina five, South Carolina five, and Georgia three.

[Filling of vacancies in representation.—4.] When vacancies happen in the representation from any State, the Executive Authority thereof shall issue writs of election to fill such vacancies.

[Selection of officers; power of impeachment.—5.] The House of Representatives shall choose their Speaker and other officers; and shall have the sole power of impeachment.

Section 3[2]

[The Senate.—1.] The Senate of the United States shall be composed of two Senators from each State, chosen by the Legislature thereof, for six years; and each Senator shall have one vote.

[Classification of Senators; filling of vacancies.—2.] Immediately after they shall be assembled in consequence of the first election, they shall be divided as equally as may be into three classes. The seats of the Senators of the first class shall be vacated at the expiration of the second year, of the second class at the expiration of the fourth year, and of the third class at the expiration of the sixth year, so that one-third may be chosen every second year; and if vacancies happen by resignation, or otherwise, during the recess of the Legislature of any State, the Executive thereof may make temporary appointments (until the next meeting of the Legislature, which shall then fill such vacancies).

[Qualification of Senators.—3.] No person shall be a Senator who shall not have attained to the age of thirty years, and been nine years a citizen of the United States, and who shall not, when elected, be an inhabitant of that State for which he shall be chosen.

[Vice President to be President of Senate.—4.] The Vice President of the United States shall be President of the Senate, but shall have no vote, unless they be equally divided.

[Selection of Senate officers; President pro tempore.—5.] The Senate shall choose their other officers, and also a President pro tempore, in the absence of the Vice President, or when he shall exercise the office of President of the United States.

[Senate to try impeachments.—6.] The Senate

shall have the sole power to try all impeachments. When sitting for that purpose, they shall be on oath or affirmation. When the President of the United States is tried, the Chief Justice shall preside: and no person shall be convicted without the concurrence of two thirds of the members present.

[Judgment in cases of Impeachment.—7.] Judgment in cases of impeachment shall not extend further than to removal from office, and disqualification to hold and enjoy any office of honor, trust, or profit under the United States: but the party convicted shall nevertheless be liable and subject to indictment, trial, judgment and punishment, according to Law.

Section 4

[Control of congressional elections.—1.] The times, places, and manner of holding elections for Senators and Representatives, shall be prescribed in each State by the Legislature thereof; but the Congress may at any time by law make or alter such regulations, except as to the places of choosing Senators.

[Time for assembling of Congress.[3]—2.] The Congress shall assemble at least once in every year, and such meeting shall be on the first Monday in December, unless they shall by law appoint a different day.

Section 5

[Each house to be the judge of the election and qualifications of its members; regulations as to quorum.—1.] Each House shall be the judge of the elections, returns, and qualifications of its own members, and a majority of each shall constitute a quorum to do business; but a smaller number may adjourn from day to day, and may be authorized to compel the attendance of absent members, in such manner, and under such penalties as each House may provide.

[Each house to determine its own rules.—2.] Each House may determine the rules of its proceedings, punish its members for disorderly behavior, and, with the concurrence of two thirds, expel a member.

[Journals and yeas and nays.—3.] Each House shall keep a journal of its proceedings, and from time to time publish the same, excepting such parts as may in their judgment require secrecy; and the yeas and nays of the members of either House on any question shall, at the desire of one fifth of those present, be entered on the journal.

[Adjournment.—4.] Neither House, during the session of Congress, shall, without the consent of the other, adjourn for more than three days, nor to any other place than that in which the two Houses shall be sitting.

Section 6

[Compensation and privileges of members of Congress.—1.] The Senators and Representatives shall receive a compensation for their services, to be ascertained by law, and paid out of the Treasury of the United States. They shall in all cases, except treason, felony, and breach of the peace, be privileged from arrest during their attendance at the session of their respective Houses, and in going to and returning from the same; and for any speech or debate in either House, they shall not be questioned in any other place.

[Incompatible offices; exclusions.—2.] No Senator or Representative shall, during the time for which he was elected, be appointed to any civil office under the authority of the United States, which shall have been created, or the emoluments whereof shall have been increased during such time; and no person holding any office under the United States shall be a member of either House during his continuance in office.

Section 7

[Revenue bills to originate in House.—1.] All bills for raising revenue shall originate in the House of Representatives; but the Senate may propose or concur with amendments as on other bills.

[Manner of passing bills; veto power of President.—2.] Every bill which shall have passed the House of Representatives and the Senate, shall, before it becomes a law, be presented to the President of the United States; if he approve he shall sign it, but if not he shall return it, with his objections to that House in which it shall have originated, who shall enter the objections at large on their journal, and proceed to reconsider it. If after such reconsideration two thirds of that House shall agree to pass the bill, it shall be sent, together with the objections, to the other House, by which it shall likewise be reconsidered, and if approved by two thirds of that House, it shall become a law. But in all such cases the votes of both Houses shall be determined by yeas and nays, and the names of the persons voting for and against the bill shall be entered on the journal of each house, respectively. If any bill shall not be returned by the President within ten days (Sundays excepted) after it shall have been presented to him, the same shall be a law, in like manner as if he had signed it, unless the Congress by their adjournment prevent its return, in which case it shall not be a law.

[Concurrent orders or resolutions, to be passed by President.—3.] Every order, resolution, or vote to which the concurrence of the Senate and House of Representatives may be necessary (except on a question of adjournment) shall be presented to the President of the United States; and before the same shall take effect, shall be approved by him, or being disapproved by him, shall be repassed by two thirds of the Senate and House of Representatives, according to the rules and limitations prescribed in the case of a bill.

Section 8

[General powers of Congress.[4]]

[Taxes, duties, imposts, and excises.—1.] The Congress shall have power to lay and collect taxes, duties, imposts and excises, to pay the debts and provide for the common defense and general welfare of the United States; but all duties, imposts and excises shall be uniform throughout the United States;

[Borrowing of money.—2.] To borrow money on the credit of the United States;

[Regulation of commerce.—3.] To regulate commerce with foreign nations, and among the several States, and with the Indian tribes;

[Naturalization and bankruptcy.—4.] To establish a uniform rule of naturalization, and uniform laws on the subject of bankruptcies throughout the United States;

[Money, weights and measures.—5.] To coin money, regulate the value thereof, and of foreign coin, and fix the standard of weights and measures;

[Counterfeiting.—6.] To provide for the punishment of counterfeiting the securities and current coin of the United States;

[Post offices.—7.] To establish post offices and post roads;

[Patents and copyrights.—8.] To promote the

progress of science and useful arts, by securing for limited times to authors and inventors the exclusive right to their respective writings and discoveries;

[**Inferior courts.—9.**] To constitute tribunals inferior to the Supreme Court;

[**Piracies and felonies.—10.**] To define and punish piracies and felonies committed on the high seas, and offences against the law of nations;

[**War; marque and reprisal.—11.**] To declare war, grant letters of marque and reprisal, and make rules concerning captures on land and water;

[**Armies.—12.**] To raise and support armies, but no appropriation of money to that use shall be for a longer term than two years;

[**Navy.—13.**] To provide and maintain a navy;

[**Land and naval forces.—14.**] To make rules for the government and regulation of the land and naval forces;

[**Calling out militia.—15.**] To provide for calling forth the militia to execute the laws of the Union, suppress insurrections, and repel invasions.

[**Organizing, arming, and disciplining militia.—16.**] To provide for organizing, arming, and disciplining, the militia, and for governing such part of them as may be employed in the service of the United States, reserving to the States, respectively, the appointment of the officers, and the authority of training the militia according to the discipline prescribed by Congress;

[**Exclusive legislation over District of Columbia.—17.**] To exercise exclusive legislation in all cases whatsoever, over such district (not exceeding ten miles square) as may, by cession of particular States, and the acceptance of Congress, become the seat of the Government of the United States, and to exercise like authority over all places purchased by the consent of the Legislature of the State in which the same shall be, for the erection of forts, magazines, arsenals, dock-yards, and other needful buildings;—And

[**To enact laws necessary to enforce Constitution.—18.**] To make all laws which shall be necessary and proper for carrying into execution the foregoing powers, and all other powers vested by this Constitution in the Government of the United States, or in any department or officer thereof.

Section 9

[**Migration or importation of certain persons not to be prohibited before 1808.—1.**] The migration or importation of such persons as any of the States now existing shall think proper to admit, shall not be prohibited by the Congress prior to the year one thousand eight hundred and eight, but a tax or duty may be imposed on such importation, not exceeding ten dollars for each person.

[**Writ of habeas corpus not to be suspended; exception.—2.**] The privilege of the writ of habeas corpus shall not be suspended, unless when in cases of rebellion or invasion the public safety may require it.

[**Bills of attainder and ex post facto laws prohibited.—3.**] No bill of attainder or ex post facto law shall be passed.

[**Capitation and other direct taxes.—4.**] No capitation, or other direct, tax shall be laid, unless in proportion to the census or enumeration herein before directed to be taken.[5]

[**Exports not to be taxed.—5.**] No tax or duty shall be laid on articles exported from any State.

[**No preference to be given to ports of any States; interstate shipping.—6.**] No preference shall be given by any regulation of commerce or revenue to the ports of one State over those of another: nor shall vessels bound to, or from, one State, be obliged to enter, clear, or pay duties in another.

[**Money, how drawn from treasury; financial statements to be published.—7.**] No money shall be drawn from the Treasury, but in consequence of appropriations made by law; and a regular statement and account of the receipts and expenditures of all public money shall be published from time to time.

[**Titles of nobility not to be granted; acceptance by government officers of favors from foreign powers.—8.**] No title of nobility shall be granted by the United States: and no person holding any office of profit or trust under them, shall, without the consent of the Congress, accept of any present, emolument, office, or title, of any kind whatever, from any king, prince, or foreign state.

Section 10

[**Limitations of the powers of the several States.—1.**] No State shall enter into any treaty, alliance, or confederation; grant letters of marque and reprisal; coin money; emit bills of credit; make any thing but gold and silver coin a tender in payment of debts; pass any bill of attainder, ex post facto law, or law impairing the obligation of contracts, or grant any title of nobility.

[**State imposts and duties.—2.**] No State shall, without the consent of the Congress, lay any imposts or duties on imports or exports, except what may be absolutely necessary for executing its inspection laws; and the net produce of all duties and imposts, laid by any State on imports or exports, shall be for the use of the Treasury of the United States; and all such laws shall be subject to the revision and control of the Congress.

[**Further restrictions on powers of States.—3.**] No State shall, without the consent of Congress, lay any duty of tonnage, keep troops, or ships of war in time of peace, enter into any agreement or compact with another state, or with a foreign power, or engage in war, unless actually invaded, or in such imminent danger as will not admit of delay.

Article II

Section 1

[**The President; the executive power.—1.**] The executive power shall be vested in a President of the United States of America. He shall hold his office during the term of four years, and, together with the Vice President, chosen for the same term, be elected, as follows

[**Appointment and qualifications of presidential electors.—2.**] Each State shall appoint, in such manner as the Legislature thereof may direct, a number of electors, equal to the whole number of Senators and Representatives to which the State may be entitled in the Congress: but no Senator or Representative, or person holding an office of trust or profit under the United States, shall be appointed an elector.

[**Original method of electing the President and Vice President.**[6]] (The electors shall meet in their respective States, and vote by ballot for two persons, of whom one at least shall not be an inhabitant of the same State with themselves. And they shall make a list of all the persons voted for, and of the number of votes for each; which list they shall sign and certify, and transmit sealed to the seat of the Government of the United States, directed to the

President of the Senate. The President of the Senate shall, in the presence of the Senate and House of Representatives, open all the certificates, and the votes shall then be counted. The person having the greatest number of votes shall be the President, if such number be a majority of the whole number of electors appointed; and if there be more than one who have such majority, and have an equal number of votes, then the House of Representatives shall immediately choose by ballot one of them for President; and if no person have a majority, then from the five highest on the list the said House shall in like manner choose the President. But in choosing the President, the votes shall be taken by States, the representation from each State having one vote; A quorum for this purpose shall consist of a member or members from two thirds of the States, and a majority of all the states shall be necessary to a choice. In every case, after the choice of the President, the person having the greatest number of votes of the electors shall be the Vice President. But if there should remain two or more who have equal votes, the Senate should choose from them by ballot the Vice President.)

[Congress may determine time of choosing electors and day for casting their votes.—3.] The Congress may determine the time of choosing the electors, and the day on which they shall give their votes; which day shall be the same throughout the United States.

[Qualifications for the office of President.[7]—4.] No person except a natural born citizen, or a citizen of the United States, at the time of the adoption of this Constitution, shall be eligible to the office of President; neither shall any person be eligible to that office who shall not have attained to the age of thirty-five years, and been fourteen years a resident within the United States.

[Filling vacancy in the office of President.[8]—5.] In case of the removal of the President from office, or of his death, resignation, or inability to discharge the powers and duties of the said office, the same shall devolve on the Vice President, and the Congress may by law provide for the case of removal, death, resignation or inability, both of the President and Vice President, declaring what officer shall then act as President, and such officer shall act accordingly, until the disability be removed, or a President shall be elected.

[Compensation of the President.—6.] The President shall, at stated times, receive for his services, a compensation, which shall neither be increased nor diminished during the period for which he shall have been elected, and he shall not receive within that period any other emolument from the United States, or any of them.

[Oath to be taken by the President.—7.] Before he enter on the execution of his office, he shall take the following oath or affirmation:—"I do solemnly swear (or affirm) that I will faithfully execute the office of President of the United States, and will to the best of my ability, preserve, protect, and defend the Constitution of the United States."

Section 2

[The President to be commander in chief of army and navy and head of executive departments; may grant reprieves and pardons.—1.] The President shall be Commander in Chief of the Army and Navy of the United States, and of the militia of the several States, when called into the actual service of the United States; he may require the opinion, in writing, of the principal officer in each of the executive departments, upon any subject relating to the duties of their respective offices, and he shall have power to grant reprieves and pardons for offences against the United States, except in cases of impeachment.

[President may, with concurrence of Senate, make treaties, appoint ambassadors, etc.; appointment of inferior officers, authority of Congress over.—2.] He shall have power, by and with the advice and consent of the Senate, to make treaties, provided two thirds of the Senators present concur; and he shall nominate, and by and with the advice and consent of the Senate, shall appoint ambassadors, other public ministers and consuls, judges of the Supreme Court, and all other officers of the United States, whose appointments are not herein otherwise provided for, and which shall be established by law: but the Congress may by law vest the appointment of such inferior officers, as they think proper, in the President alone, in the courts of law, or in the heads of departments.

[President may fill vacancies in office during recess of Senate.—3.] The President shall have power to fill up all vacancies that may happen during the recess of the Senate, by granting commissions which shall expire at the end of their session.

Section 3

[President to give advice to Congress; may convene or adjourn it on certain occasions; to receive ambassadors, etc.; have laws executed and commission all officers.] He shall from time to time give to the Congress information of the state of the Union, and recommend to their consideration such measures as he shall judge necessary and expedient; he may, on extraordinary occasions, convene both Houses, or either of them, and in case of disagreement between them, with respect to the time of adjournment, he may adjourn them to such time as he shall think proper; he shall receive ambassadors and other public ministers: he shall take care that the laws be faithfully executed, and shall commission all the officers of the United States.

Section 4

[All civil officers removable by impeachment.] The President, Vice President, and all civil officers of the United States shall be removed from office on impeachment for, and conviction of, treason, bribery, or other high crimes and misdemeanors.

Article III

Section 1

[Judicial powers; how vested; term of office and compensation of judges.] The judicial Power of the United States, shall be vested in one Supreme Court, and in such inferior courts as the Congress may from time to time ordain and establish. The judges, both of the supreme and inferior courts, shall hold their offices during good behavior, and shall, at stated times, receive for their services, a compensation, which shall not be diminished during their continuance in office.

Section 2

[Jurisdiction of Federal courts.[9]—1.] The judicial power shall extend to all cases, in law and equity, arising under this Constitution, the laws of the United States, and treaties made, or which shall be made, under their authority; to all cases affecting ambassadors, other public ministers and consuls; to all cases of admiralty and maritime jurisdiction; to controversies to which the United States, shall be a party; to controversies between two or more States; between a State and citizens of another State; between citizens of different States; between citizens of the same State claiming lands under grants of different states, and between a State, or the citizens thereof, and foreign states, citizens, or subjects.

[Original and appellate jurisdiction of Supreme Court.—2.] In all cases affecting ambassadors, other public ministers and consuls, and those in which a State shall be party, the Supreme Court shall have original jurisdiction. In all the other cases before mentioned, the Supreme Court shall have appellate jurisdiction, both as to law and fact, with such exceptions, and under such regulations, as the Congress shall make.

[Trial of all crimes, except impeachment, to be by jury.—3.] The trial of all crimes, except in cases of impeachment, shall be by jury; and such trial shall be held in the State where the said crimes shall have been committed; but when not committed within any State, the trial shall be at such place or places as the Congress may by law have directed.

Section 3

[Treason defined; conviction of.—1.] Treason against the United States, shall consist only in levying war against them, or, in adhering to their enemies, giving them aid and comfort. No person shall be convicted of treason unless on the testimony of two witnesses to the same overt act, or on confession in open court.

[Congress to declare punishment for treason; proviso.—2.] The Congress shall have power to declare the punishment of treason, but no attainder of treason shall work corruption of blood, or forfeiture except during the life of the person attained.

Article IV

Section 1

[Each State to give full faith and credit to the public acts and records of other States.] Full faith and credit shall be given in each State to the public acts, records, and judicial proceedings of every other State. And the Congress may by general laws prescribe the manner in which such acts, records, and proceedings shall be proved, and the effect thereof.

Section 2

[Privileges of citizens.—1.] The citizens of each State shall be entitled to all privileges and immunities of citizens in the several States.

[Extradition between the several States.—2.] A person charged in any State with treason, felony, or other crime, who shall flee from justice, and be found in another State, shall on demand of the Executive authority of the State from which he fled, be delivered up, to be removed to the State having jurisdiction of the crime.

[Persons held to labor or service in one State, fleeing to another, to be returned.—3.] No person held to service or labor in one State, under the laws thereof, escaping into another, shall, in consequence of any law or regulation therein, be discharged from such service or labor, but shall be delivered up on claim of the party to whom such service or labor may be due.

Section 3

[New States.—1.] New States may be admitted by the Congress into this Union; but no new State shall be formed or erected within the jurisdiction of any other State; nor any State be formed by the junction of two or more States, or parts of States, without the consent of the Legislatures of the States concerned as well as of the Congress.

[Regulations concerning territory.—2.] The Congress shall have power to dispose of and make all needful rules and regulations respecting the territory or other property belonging to the United States; and nothing in this Constitution shall be so construed as to prejudice any claims of the United States, or of any particular State.

Section 4

[Republican form of government and protection guaranteed the several States.] The United States shall guarantee to every State in this Union a Republican form of government, and shall protect each of them against invasion; and on application of the Legislature, or of the Executive (when the Legislature cannot be convened) against domestic violence.

Article V

[Ways in which the Constitution can be amended.] The Congress, whenever two thirds of both Houses shall deem it necessary, shall propose amendments to this Constitution, or, on the application of the Legislatures of two thirds of the several States shall call a convention for proposing amendments, which, in either case, shall be valid to all intents and purposes, as part of this Constitution, when ratified by the Legislatures of three fourths of the several States, or by conventions in three fourths thereof, as the one or the other mode of ratification may be proposed by the Congress; provided that no amendment which may be made prior to the year one thousand eight hundred and eight shall in any manner affect the first and fourth clauses in the ninth Section of the first Article; and that no State, without its consent, shall be deprived of its equal suffrage in the Senate.

Article VI

[Debts contracted under the confederation secured.—1.] All debts contracted and engagements entered into, before the adoption of this Constitution, shall be as valid against the United States under this Constitution, as under the Confederation.

[Constitution, laws, and treaties of the United States to be supreme.—2.] This Constitution, and the laws of the United States which shall be made in pursuance thereof; and all treaties made, or which shall be made, under the authority of the United States, shall be the supreme law of the land; and the judges in every State shall be bound thereby, any thing in the Constitution or laws of any

1. The clause included in parentheses is amended by the 14th Amendment, Section 2. 2. The first paragraph of this section and the part of the second paragraph included in parentheses are amended by the 17th Amendment. 3. Amended by the 20th Amendment, Section 2. 4. By the 16th Amendment, Congress is given the power to lay and collect taxes on income. 5. See the 16th Amendment. 6. This clause has been superseded by the 12th Amendment. 7. For qualifications of the Vice President, see 12th Amendment. 8. Amended by the 20th Amendment, Sections 3 and 4. 9. This section is abridged by the 11th Amendment. 10. See the 13th Amendment.

State to the contrary notwithstanding.

[Who shall take constitutional oath; no religious test as to official qualification.—3.] The Senators and Representatives before mentioned, and the members of the several State Legislatures, and all executive and judicial officers, both of the United States and of the several States, shall be bound by oath or affirmation, to support this Constitution; but no religious test shall ever be required as a qualification to any office or public trust under the United States.

Article VII

[Constitution to be considered adopted when ratified by nine States.] The ratification of the conventions of nine States shall be sufficient for the establishment of this Constitution between the States so ratifying the same.

Done in convention by the unanimous consent of the States present the seventeenth day of September in the year of our Lord one thousand seven hundred and eighty-seven and of the independence of the United States of America the Twelfth. In witness whereof we have hereunto subscribed our names.

GEORGE WASHINGTON
President and Deputy from Virginia

NEW HAMPSHIRE
John Langdon — Nicholas Gilman

MASSACHUSETTS
Nathaniel Gorham — Rufus King

CONNECTICUT
Wm. Saml. Johnson — Roger Sherman

NEW YORK
Alexander Hamilton

NEW JERSEY
Wil. Livingston — Wm. Paterson
David Brearley — Jona. Dayton

PENNSYLVANIA
B. Franklin — Thomas Mifflin
Robt. Morris — Geo. Clymer
Thos. FitzSimons — Jared Ingersoll
James Wilson — Gouv. Morris

DELAWARE
Geo. Read — Gunning Bedford Jun.
John Dickinson — Richard Bassett
Jaco. Broom

MARYLAND
James McHenry — Dan. of St. Thos. Jenifer
Danl. Carroll

VIRGINIA
John Blair — James Madison, Jr.

NORTH CAROLINA
Wm. Blount — Richd Dobbs Spaight
Hu. Williamson

SOUTH CAROLINA
J. Rutledge — Charles Cotesworth Pinckney
Charles Pinckney — Pierce Butler

GEORGIA
William Few — Abr. Baldwin

Attest: William Jackson, Secretary

Amendments to the Constitution of the United States

(Amendments I to X inclusive, popularly known as the Bill of Rights, were proposed and sent to the states by the first session of the First Congress. They were ratified Dec. 15, 1791.)

Article I

[Freedom of religion, speech, of the press, and right of petition.] Congress shall make no law respecting an establishment of religion, or prohibiting the free exercise thereof; or abridging the freedom of speech, or of the press; or the right of the people peaceably to assemble, and to petition the Government for a redress of grievances.

Article II

[Right of people to bear arms not to be infringed.] A well regulated militia, being necessary to the security of a free State, the right of the people to keep and bear arms, shall not be infringed.

Article III

[Quartering of troops.] No soldier shall, in time of peace be quartered in any house, without the consent of the owner, nor in time of war, but in a manner to be prescribed by law.

Article IV

[Persons and houses to be secure from unreasonable searches and seizures.] The right of the people to be secure in their persons, houses, papers, and effects, against unreasonable searches and seizures, shall not be violated, and no warrants shall issue, but upon probable cause, supported by oath or affirmation, and particularly describing the place to be searched, and the persons or things to be seized.

Article V

[Trials for crimes; just compensation for private property taken for public use.] No person shall be held to answer for a capital, or otherwise infamous crime, unless on a presentment or indictment of a Grand Jury, except in cases arising in the land or naval forces, or in the militia, when in actual service in time of war or public danger; nor shall any person be subject for the same offence to be twice put in jeopardy of life or limb; nor shall be compelled in any criminal case to be a witness, against himself, nor be deprived of life, liberty, or property, without due process of law; nor shall private property be taken for public use, without just compensation.

Article VI

[Civil rights in trials for crimes enumerated.] In all criminal prosecutions, the accused shall enjoy the right to a speedy and public trial, by an impartial jury of the State and district wherein the crime shall have been committed, which district shall have been previously ascertained by law, and to be informed of the nature and cause of the accusation; to be confronted with the witnesses against him; to have compulsory process for obtaining witnesses in his favor, and to have the assistance of counsel for his defense.

Article VII

[Civil rights in civil suits.] In suits at common law, where the value in controversy shall exceed twenty dollars, the right of trial by jury shall be preserved, and no fact tried by a jury, shall be otherwise re-examined in any court of the United States, than according to the rules of the common law.

Article VIII

[Excessive bail, fines, and punishments prohibited.] Excessive bail shall not be required, nor excessive fines imposed, nor cruel and unusual punishments inflicted.

Article IX

[Reserved rights of people.] The enumeration in the Constitution, of certain rights, shall not be construed to deny or disparage others retained by the people.

Article X

[Powers not delegated, reserved to states and people respectively.] The powers not delegated to the United States by the Constitution, nor prohibited by it to the States, are reserved to the States, respectively, or to the people.

Article XI

(The proposed amendment was sent to the states Mar. 5, 1794, by the Third Congress. It was ratified Feb. 7, 1795.)

[Judicial power of United States not to extend to suits against a State.] The judicial power of the United States shall not be construed to extend to any suit in law or equity, commenced or prosecuted against one of the United States by citizens of another State, or by citizens or subjects of any foreign state.

Article XII

(The proposed amendment was sent to the states Dec. 12, 1803, by the Eighth Congress. It was ratified July 27, 1804.)

[President mode of electing President and Vice-President by electors.[1]] The electors shall meet in their respective states, and vote by ballot for President and Vice President, one of whom, at least, shall not be an inhabitant of the same state with themselves; they shall name in their ballots the person voted for as President, and in distinct ballots the person voted for as Vice President, and they shall make distinct lists of all persons voted for as President, and of all persons voted for as Vice President, and of the number of votes for each, which lists they shall sign and certify, and transmit sealed to the seat of the government of the United States, directed to the President of the Senate; the President of the Senate shall, in the presence of the Senate and House of Representatives, open all the certificates and the votes shall then be counted; the person having the greatest number of votes for President, shall be the President, if such number be a majority of the whole number of electors appointed; and if no person have such majority, then from the persons having the highest numbers not exceeding three on the list of those voted for as President, the House of Representatives shall choose immediately, by ballot, the President. But in choosing the President, the votes shall be taken by states, the representation from each State having one vote; a quorum for this purpose shall consist of a member or members from two thirds of the states, and a majority of all the states shall be necessary to a choice. And if the House of Representatives shall not choose a President whenever the right of choice shall devolve upon them, before the fourth day of March next following, then the Vice President shall act as President, as in the case of the death or other constitutional disability of the President. The person having the greatest number of votes as Vice President, shall be the Vice President, if such number be a majority of the whole number of electors appointed, and if no person have a majority, then from the two highest numbers on the list, the Senate shall choose the Vice President; a quorum for the purpose shall consist of two thirds of the whole number of Senators, and a majority of the whole number shall be necessary to a choice. But no person constitutionally ineligible to the office of President shall be eligible to that of Vice President of the United States.

Article XIII

(The proposed amendment was sent to the states Feb. 1, 1865, by the Thirty-eighth Congress. It was ratified Dec. 6, 1865.)

Section 1

[Slavery prohibited.] Neither slavery nor involuntary servitude, except as a punishment for crime whereof the party shall have been duly convicted, shall exist within the United States, or any place subject to their jurisdiction.

Section 2

[Congress given power to enforce this article.] Congress shall have power to enforce this article by appropriate legislation.

Article XIV

(The proposed amendment was sent to the states June 16, 1866, by the Thirty-ninth Congress. It was ratified July 9, 1868.)

Section 1

[Citizenship defined; privileges of citizens.] All persons born or naturalized in the United States, and subject to the jurisdiction thereof, are citizens of the United States and of the State wherein they reside. No State shall make or enforce any law which shall abridge the privileges or immunities of citizens of the United States; nor shall any State deprive any person of life, liberty, or property, without due process of law; nor deny to any person within its jurisdiction the equal protection of the laws.

Section 2

[Apportionment of Representatives.] Representatives shall be apportioned among the several States according to their respective numbers, counting the whole number of persons in each State, excluding Indians not taxed. But when the right to vote at any election for the choice of electors for President and Vice President of the United States, Representatives in Congress, the executive and judicial officers of a State, or the members of the Legislature thereof, is denied to any of the male inhabitants of such State, being twenty-one years of age, and citizens of the United States, or in any way abridged, except for participation in rebellion, or other crime, the basis of representation therein shall be reduced in the proportion which the number of such male citizens shall bear to the whole number of male citizens twenty-one years of age in such State.

Section 3

[Disqualification for office; removal of disability.] No person shall be a Senator or Representative in Congress, or elector of President and Vice President, or hold any office, civil or military, under the United States, or under any State, who, having previously taken an oath, as a member of Congress, or as an officer of the United States, or as a member of any State Legislature, or as an executive or judicial officer of any State, to support the Constitution of the United States, shall have engaged in insurrection or rebellion against the same, or given aid or comfort to the enemies thereof. But Congress may be a vote of two thirds of each House, remove such disability.

Section 4

[Public debt not to be questioned; payment of debts and claims incurred in aid of rebellion forbidden.] The validity of the public debt of the United States, authorized by law, including debts incurred for payment of pensions and bounties for services in suppressing insurrection or rebellion, shall not be questioned. But neither the United States nor any State shall assume or pay any debt or obligation incurred in aid of insurrection or rebellion against the United States, or any claim for the loss or emancipation of any slave; but all such debts, obligations, and claims shall be held illegal and void.

Section 5

[Congress given power to enforce this article.] The Congress shall have power to enforce, by appropriate legislation, the provisions of this article.

Article XV

(The proposed amendment was sent to the states Feb. 27, 1869, by the Fortieth Congress. It was ratified Feb. 3, 1870.)

Section 1

[Right of certain citizens to vote established.] The right of citizens of the United States to vote shall not be denied or abridged by the United States or by any State on account of race, color, or previous condition of servitude.

Section 2

[Congress given power to enforce this article.] The Congress shall have power to enforce this article by appropriate legislation.

Article XVI

(The proposed amendment was sent to the states July 12, 1909, by the Sixty-first Congress. It was ratified Feb. 3, 1913.)

[Taxes on income; Congress given power to lay and collect.] The Congress shall have power to lay and collect taxes on incomes, from whatever source derived, without apportionment among the several States, and without regard to any census or enumeration.

Article XVII

(The proposed amendment was sent to the states May 16, 1912, by the Sixty-second Congress. It was ratified April 8, 1913.)

[Election of United States Senators; filling of vacancies; qualifications of electors.]

The Senate of the United States shall be composed of two Senators from each State, elected by the people thereof, for six years; and each Senator shall have one vote. The electors in each State shall have the qualifications requisite for electors of the most numerous branch of the State Legislatures.

When vacancies happen in the representation of any State in the Senate, the executive authority of such State shall issue writs of election to fill such vacancies: Provided, that the legislature of any State may empower the executive thereof to make temporary appointment until the people fill the vacancies by election as the legislature may direct.

This amendment shall not be so construed as to affect the election or term of any Senator chosen before it becomes valid as part of the Constitution.

Article XVIII[2]

(The proposed amendment was sent to the states Dec. 18, 1917, by the Sixty-fifth Congress. It was ratified by three quarters of the states by Jan. 16, 1919, and became effective Jan. 16, 1920.)

Section 1

[Manufacture, sale, or transportation of intoxicating liquors, for beverage purposes, prohibited.] After one year from the ratification of this article the manufacture, sale, or transportation of intoxicating liquors within, the importation thereof into, or the exportation thereof from the United States and all territory subject to the jurisdiction thereof for beverage purposes is hereby prohibited.

Section 2

[Congress and the several States given concurrent power to pass appropriate legislation to enforce this article.] The Congress and the several States shall have concurrent power to enforce this article by appropriate legislation.

Section 3

[Provisions of article to become operative, when adopted by three fourths of the States.] This article shall be inoperative unless it shall have been ratified as an amendment to the Constitution by the legislatures of the several States, as provided in the Constitution, within seven years from the date of the submission hereof to the States by Congress.

Article XIX

(The proposed amendment was sent to the states June 4, 1919, by the Sixty-sixth Congress. It was ratified Aug. 18, 1920.)

[The right of citizens to vote shall not be denied because of sex.] The right of citizens of the United States to vote shall not be denied or abridged by the United States or by any State on account of sex.

[Congress given power to enforce this article.] Congress shall have power to enforce this article by appropriate legislation.

Article XX

(The proposed amendment, sometimes called the "Lame Duck Amendment," was sent to the states Mar. 3, 1932, by the Seventy-second Congress. It was ratified Jan. 23, 1933; but, in accordance with Section 5, Sections 1 and 2 did not go into effect until Oct. 15, 1933.)

Section 1

[Terms of President, Vice President, Senators, and Representatives.] The terms of the President and Vice President shall end at noon on the twentieth day of January, and the terms of Senators and Representatives at noon on the third day of January, of the years in which such terms would have ended if this article had not been ratified; and the terms of their successors shall then begin.

Section 2

[Time of assembling Congress.] The Congress shall assemble at least once in every year, and such meeting shall begin at noon on the third day of January, unless they shall by law appoint a different day.

Section 3

[Filling vacancy in office of President.] If, at the time fixed for the beginning of the term of the President, the President-elect shall have died, the Vice President-elect shall become President. If a President shall not have been chosen before the time fixed for the beginning of his term, or if the President-elect shall have failed to qualify, then the Vice President shall have qualified; and the Congress may by law provide for the case wherein neither a President-elect nor a Vice President-elect shall have qualified, declaring who shall then act as President, or the manner in which one who is to act shall be selected, and such person shall act accordingly until a President or Vice President shall have qualified.

Section 4

[Power of Congress in Presidential succession.] The Congress may by law provide for the case of the death of any of the persons from whom the House of Representatives may choose a President whenever the right of choice shall have devolved upon them, and for the case of the death of any of the persons from whom the Senate may choose a Vice President whenever the right of choice shall have devolved upon them.

Section 5

[Time of taking effect.] Sections 1 and 2 shall take effect on the 15th day of October following the ratification of this article.

Section 6

[Ratification.] This article shall be inoperative unless it shall have been ratified as an amendment to the Constitution by the legislatures of three fourths of the several States within seven years from the date of its submission.

Article XXI

(The proposed amendment was sent to the states Feb. 20, 1933, by the Seventy-second Congress. It was ratified Dec. 5, 1933.)

Section 1

[Repeal of Prohibition Amendment.] The eighteenth article of amendment to the Constitution of the United States is hereby repealed.

Section 2

[Transportation of intoxicating liquors.] The transportation or importation into any State, territory, or possession of the United States for delivery or use therein of intoxicating liquors, in violation of the laws thereof, is hereby prohibited.

Section 3

[Ratification.] This article shall be inoperative unless it shall have been ratified as an amendment to the Constitution by convention in the several States, as provided in the Constitution, within seven years from the date of the submission thereof to the States by the Congress.

Article XXII

(The proposed amendment was sent to the states Mar. 21, 1947, by the Eightieth Congress. It was ratified Feb. 27, 1951.)

Section 1

[Limit to number of terms a President may serve.] No person shall be elected to the office of the President more than twice, and no person who has held the office of President, or acted as President, for more than two years of a term to which some other person was elected President shall be elected to the office of the President more than once. But this article shall not apply to any person holding the office of President when this article was proposed by the Congress, and shall not prevent any person who may be holding the office of President, or acting as President, during the term within which this article becomes operative from holding the office of President or acting as President during the remainder of such term.

Section 2

[Ratification.] This article shall be inoperative unless it shall have been ratified as an amendment to the Constitution by the legislatures of three fourths of the several States within seven years from the date of its submission to the States by the Congress.

Article XXIII

(The proposed amendment was sent to the states June 16, 1960, by the Eighty-sixth Congress. It was ratified March 29, 1961.)

Section 1

[Electors for the District of Columbia.] The District constituting the seat of Government of the United States shall appoint in such manner as the Congress may direct:

A number of electors of President and Vice President equal to the whole number of Senators and Representatives in Congress to which the District would be entitled if it were a State, but in no event more than the least populous State; they shall be in addition to those appointed by the States, but they shall be considered, for the purposes of the election of President and Vice President, to be electors appointed by a State; and they shall meet in the District and perform such duties as provided by the twelfth article of amendment.

Section 2

[Congress given power to enforce this article.] The Congress shall have the power to enforce this article by appropriate legislation.

Article XXIV

(The proposed amendment was sent to the states Aug. 27, 1962, by the Eighty-seventh Congress. It was ratified Jan. 23, 1964.)

Section 1

[Payment of poll tax or other taxes not to be prerequisite for voting in federal elections.] The right of citizens of the United States to vote in any primary or other election for President or Vice President, for electors for President or Vice President, or for Senator or Representative in Congress, shall not be denied or abridged by the United States or any State by reasons of failure to pay any poll tax or other tax.

Section 2

[Congress given power to enforce this article.] The Congress shall have the power to enforce this article by appropriate legislation.

Article XXV

(The proposed amendment was sent to the states July 6, 1965, by the Eighty-ninth Congress. It was ratified Feb. 10, 1967.)

Section 1

[Succession of Vice President to Presidency.] In case of the removal of the President from office or of his death or resignation, the Vice President shall become President.

Section 2

[Vacancy in office of Vice President.] Whenever there is a vacancy in the office of the Vice President, the President shall nominate a Vice President who shall take office upon confirmation by a majority vote of both Houses of Congress.

Section 3

[Vice President as Acting President.] Whenever the President transmits to the President pro tempore of the Senate and the Speaker of the House of Representatives his written declaration that he is unable to discharge the powers and duties of his office, and until he transmits to them a written declaration to the contrary, such powers and duties shall be discharged by the Vice President as Acting President.

Section 4

[Vice President as Acting President.] Whenever the Vice President and a majority of either the principal officers of the executive departments or of such other body as Congress may by law provide, transmit to the President pro tempore of the Senate and the Speaker of the House of Representatives their written declaration that the President is unable to discharge the powers and duties of his office, the Vice President shall immediately assume the powers and duties of the office as Acting President.

Thereafter, when the President transmits to the President pro tempore of the Senate and the Speaker of the House of Representatives his written declaration that no inability exists, he shall resume the powers and duties of his office unless the Vice President and a majority of either the principal officers of the executive department or of such other body as Congress may by law provide, transmit within four days to the President pro tempore of the Senate and the Speaker of the House of Representatives their written declaration that the President is unable to discharge the powers and duties of his office. Thereupon Congress shall decide the issue, assembling within forty-eight hours for that purpose if not in session. If the Congress, within twenty-one days after receipt of the latter written declaration, or, if Congress is not in session, within twenty-one days after Congress is required to assemble, determines by two thirds vote of both Houses that the President is unable to discharge the powers and duties of his office, the Vice President shall continue to discharge the same as Acting President; otherwise, the President shall resume the powers and duties of his office.

Article XXVI

(The proposed amendment was sent to the states Mar. 23, 1971, by the Ninety-second Congress. It was ratified July 1, 1971.)

Section 1

[Voting for 18-year-olds.] The right of citizens of the United States, who are 18 years of age or older, to vote shall not be denied or abridged by the United States or by any state on account of age.

Section 2

[Congress given power to enforce this article.] The Congress shall have power to enforce this article by appropriate legislation.

1. Amended by the 20th Amendment, Sections 3 and 4. 2. Repealed by the 21st Amendment.

The White House

Source: Department of the Interior, U.S. National Park Service.

The White House, the official residence of the President, is at 1600 Pennsylvania Avenue in Washington, D.C. The site, covering about 18 acres, was selected by President Washington and Pierre Charles L'Enfant, and the architect was James Hoban. The design of the residence is said to have been suggested by the Duke of Leinster's house in Ireland. The cornerstone was laid Oct. 13, 1792, and the first residents were President and Mrs. John Adams in November 1800. The building was fired by the British in 1814.

From December 1948 to March 1952, the interior of the White House was rebuilt, and the outer walls were strengthened.

The rooms for public functions are on the first floor; on the second and third are the President's apartments. The most celebrated public room is the East Room, where formal receptions take place. Other public rooms are the Red Room, the Green Room, and the Blue Room. The State Dining Room is used for formal dinners. There are 132 rooms.

The Mayflower Compact

On Sept. 6, 1620, the *Mayflower,* a sailing vessel of about 180 tons, started her memorable voyage from Plymouth, England, with about 100[1] pilgrims aboard, bound for Virginia to establish a private permanent colony in North America. Arriving at what is now Provincetown, Mass., on Nov. 11 (Nov. 21, new style calendar), 41 of the passengers signed the famous "Mayflower Compact" as the boat lay at anchor in that Cape Cod harbor. A small detail of the pilgrims, led by William Bradford, assigned to select a place for permanent settlement landed at what is now Plymouth, Mass., on Dec. 21 (n.s.).

The text of the compact follows:

> In the name of God, Amen. We, whose names are underwritten, the Loyal Subjects of our dread Sovereign Lord, King *James,* by the Grace of God, of *Great Britain, France and Ireland,* King, *Defender of the Faith, &*
>
> Having undertaken for the Glory of God, and Advancement of the Christian Faith, and the Honour of our King and Country, a voyage to plant the first colony in the northern Parts of Virginia; do by these Presents, solemnly and mutually in the Presence of God and one of another, covenant and combine ourselves together into a civil Body Politick, for our better Ordering and Preservation, and Furtherance of the Ends aforesaid; And by Virtue hereof to enact, constitute, and frame, such just and equal Laws, Ordinances, Acts, Constitutions and Offices, from time to time, as shall be thought most meet and convenient for the General good of the Colony; unto which we promise all due Submission and Obedience.
>
> In Witness whereof we have hereunto subscribed our names at *Cape Cod* the eleventh of *November,* in the Reign of our Sovereign Lord, King *James* of *England, France* and *Ireland,* the eighteenth, and of *Scotland* the fifty-fourth. *Anno Domini,* 1620

John Carver
Digery Priest
William Brewster
Edmund Margesson
John Alden
George Soule
James Chilton
Francis Cooke
Moses Fletcher
John Ridgate
Christopher Martin
William Mullins
Thomas English
John Howland
Stephen Hopkins
Edward Winslow
Gilbert Winslow
Miles Standish
Richard Bitteridge
Francis Eaton
John Tilly
John Billington
Thomas Tinker
Samuel Fuller
Richard Clark
John Allerton
Richard Warren
Edward Liester
William Bradford
Thomas Williams
Isaac Allerton
Peter Brown
John Turner
Edward Tilly
John Craxton
Thomas Rogers
John Goodman
Edward Fuller
Richard Gardiner
William White
Edward Doten

1. Historians differ as to whether 100, 101, or 102 passengers were aboard.

The Monroe Doctrine

The Monroe Doctrine was announced in President James Monroe's message to Congress, during his second term on Dec. 2, 1823, in part as follows:

"In the discussions to which this interest has given rise, and in the arrangements by which they may terminate, the occasion has been deemed proper for asserting as a principle in which rights and interests of the United States are involved, that the American continents, by the free and independent condition which they have assumed and maintain, are henceforth not to be considered as subjects for future colonization by any European power. . . . We owe it, therefore, to candor and to the amicable relations existing between the United States and those powers to declare that we should consider any attempt on their part to extend their system to any portion of this hemisphere as dangerous to our peace and safety. With the existing colonies or dependencies of any European power we have not interfered and shall not interfere. But with the governments who have declared their independence and maintain it, and whose independence we have, on great consideration and on just principles, acknowledged, we could not view any interposition for the purpose of oppressing them or controlling in any other manner their destiny by any European power in any other light than as the manifestation of an unfriendly disposition toward the United States."

Order of Presidential Succession

1. The Vice President
2. Speaker of the House
3. President pro tempore of the Senate
4. Secretary of State
5. Secretary of the Treasury
6. Secretary of Defense
7. Attorney General
8. Secretary of the Interior
9. Secretary of Agriculture
10. Secretary of Commerce
11. Secretary of Labor
12. Secretary of Health and Human Services
13. Secretary of Housing and Urban Development
14. Secretary of Transportation
15. Secretary of Energy
16. Secretary of Education

NOTE: An official cannot succeed to the Presidency unless that person meets the Constitutional requirements.

The Star-Spangled Banner

Francis Scott Key, 1814

O say, can you see, by the dawn's early light,
What so proudly we hail'd at the twilight's last gleaming?
Whose broad stripes and bright stars, thro' the perilous fight,
O'er the ramparts we watch'd, were so gallantly streaming?
And the rockets' red glare, the bombs bursting in air,
Gave proof thro' the night that our flag was still there.
O say, does that star-spangled banner yet wave
O'er the land of the free and the home of the brave?

On the shore dimly seen thro' the mists of the deep,
Where the foe's haughty host in dread silence reposes,
What is that which the breeze, o'er the towering steep,
As it fitfully blows, half conceals, half discloses?
Now it catches the gleam of the morning's first beam,
In full glory reflected, now shines on the stream:
'T is the star-spangled banner: O, long may it wave
O'er the land of the free and the home of the brave!

And where is that band who so vauntingly swore
That the havoc of war and the battle's confusion,
A home and a country should leave us no more?
Their blood has wash'd out their foul footsteps' pollution.
No refuge could save the hireling and slave
From the terror of flight or the gloom of the grave:
And the star-spangled banner in triumph doth wave
O'er the land of the free and the home of the brave.

O thus be it ever when free-men shall stand
Between their lov'd home and the war's desolation;
Blest with vict'ry and peace, may the heav'n-rescued land
Praise the Pow'r that hath made and preserv'd us a nation!
Then conquer we must, when our cause it is just,
And this be our motto: "In God is our trust!"
And the star-spangled banner in triumph shall wave
O'er the land of the free and the home of the brave!

On Sept. 13, 1814, Francis Scott Key visited the British fleet in Chesapeake Bay to secure the release of Dr. William Beanes, who had been captured after the burning of Washington, D.C. The release was secured, but Key was detained on ship overnight during the shelling of Fort McHenry, one of the forts defending Baltimore. In the morning, he was so delighted to see the American flag still flying over the fort that he began a poem to commemorate the occasion. First published under the title "Defense of Fort M'Henry," and later as "The Star-Spangled Banner," the poem soon attained wide popularity as sung to the tune "To Anacreon in Heaven." The origin of this tune is obscure, but it may have been written by John Stafford Smith, a British composer born in 1750. "The Star-Spangled Banner" was officially made the National Anthem by Congress in 1931, although it had been already adopted as such by the Army and the Navy.

The Emancipation Proclamation

January 1, 1863

By the President of the United States of America:

A Proclamation.

Whereas on the 22d day of September, A.D. 1862, a proclamation was issued by the President of the United States, containing, among other things, the following, to wit:

"That on the 1st day of January, A.D. 1863, all persons held as slaves within any State or designated part of a State the people whereof shall then be in rebellion against the United States shall be then, thenceforward, and forever free; and the executive government of the United States, including the military and naval authority thereof, will recognize and maintain the freedom of such persons and will do not act or acts to repress such persons, or any of them, in any efforts they may make for their actual freedom.

"That the executive will on the 1st day of January aforesaid, by proclamation, designate the States and parts of States, if any, in which the people thereof, respectively, shall then be in rebellion against the United States; and the fact that any State or the people thereof shall on that day be in good faith represented in the Congress of the United States by members chosen thereto at elections wherein a majority of the qualified voters of such States shall have participated shall, in the absence of strong countervailing testimony, be deemed conclusive evidence that such State and the people thereof are not then in rebellion against the United States."

Now, therefore, I, Abraham Lincoln, President

of the United States, by virtue of the power in me vested as Commander-in-Chief of the Army and Navy of the United States in time of actual armed rebellion against the authority and government of the United States, and as a fit and necessary war measure for suppressing said rebellion, do, on this 1st day of January, A.D. 1863, and in accordance with my purpose so to do, publicly proclaimed for the full period of one hundred days from the first day above mentioned, order and designate as the States and parts of States wherein the people thereof, respectively, are this day in rebellion against the United States the following, to wit:

Arkansas, Texas, Louisiana (except the parishes of St. Bernard, Plaquemines, Jefferson, St. John, St. Charles, St. James, Ascension, Assumption, Terrebonne, Lafourche, St. Mary, St. Martin, and Orleans, including the city of New Orleans), Mississippi, Alabama, Florida, Georgia, South Carolina, North Carolina, and Virginia (except the forty-eight counties designated as West Virginia, and also the counties of Berkeley, Accomac, Northhampton, Elizabeth City, York, Princess Anne, and Norfolk, including the cities of Norfolk and Portsmouth), and which excepted parts are for the present left precisely as if this proclamation were not issued.

And by virtue of the power and for the purpose aforesaid, I do order and declare that all persons held as slaves within said designated States and parts of States are, and henceforward shall be, free; and that the Executive Government of the United States, including the military and naval authorities thereof, will recognize and maintain the freedom of said persons.

And I hereby enjoin upon the people so declared to be free to abstain from all violence, unless in necessary self-defense; and I recommend to them that, in all cases when allowed, they labor faithfully for reasonable wages.

And I further declare and make known that such persons of suitable condition will be received into the armed service of the United States to garrison forts, positions, stations, and other places, and to man vessels of all sorts in said service.

And upon this act, sincerely believed to be an act of justice, warranted by the Constitution upon military necessity, I invoke the considerate judgment of mankind and the gracious favor of Almighty God.

The Confederate States of America

State	Seceded from Union	Readmitted to Union[1]	State	Seceded from Union	Readmitted to Union[1]
1. South Carolina	Dec. 20, 1860	July 9, 1868	7. Texas	March 2, 1861	March 30, 1870
2. Mississippi	Jan. 9, 1861	Feb. 23, 1870	8. Virginia	April 17, 1861	Jan. 26, 1870
3. Florida	Jan. 10, 1861	June 25, 1868	9. Arkansas	May 6, 1861	June 22, 1868
4. Alabama	Jan. 11, 1861	July 13, 1868	10. North Carolina	May 20, 1861	July 4, 1868
5. Georgia	Jan. 19, 1861	July 15, 1870[2]	11. Tennessee	June 8, 1861	July 24, 1866
6. Louisiana	Jan. 26, 1861	July 9, 1868			

1. Date of readmission to representation in U.S. House of Representatives. 2. Second readmission date. First date was July 21, 1868, but the representatives were unseated March 5, 1869. NOTE: Four other slave states—Delaware, Kentucky, Maryland, and Missouri—remained in the Union.

Lincoln's Gettysburg Address

The Battle of Gettysburg, one of the most noted battles of the Civil War, was fought on July 1, 2, and 3, 1863. On Nov. 19, 1863, the field was dedicated as a national cemetery by President Lincoln in a two-minute speech that was to become immortal. At the time of its delivery the speech was relegated to the inside pages of the papers, while a two-hour address by Edward Everett, the leading orator of the time, caught the headlines.

The following is the text of the address revised by President Lincoln from his own notes:

Fourscore and seven years ago our fathers brought forth on this continent a new nation conceived in liberty and dedicated to the proposition that all men are created equal. Now we are engaged in a great civil war testing whether that nation, or any nation so conceived and so dedicated, can long endure. We are met on a great battlefield of that war. We have come to dedicate a portion of that field as a final resting-place for those who here gave their lives that that nation might live. It is altogether fitting and proper that we should do this. But, in a larger sense, we cannot dedicate, we cannot consecrate, we cannot hallow this ground. The brave men, living and dead, who struggled here have consecrated it far above our poor power to add or detract. The world will little note nor long remember what we say here, but it can never forget what they did here. It is for us the living rather to be dedicated here to the unfinished work which they who fought here have thus far so nobly advanced. It is rather for us to be here dedicated to the great task remaining before us—that from these honored dead we take increased devotion to that cause for which they gave the last full measure of devotion—that we here highly resolve that these dead shall not have died in vain, that this nation under God shall have a new birth of freedom, and that government of the people, by the people, for the people shall not perish from the earth.

The Early Congresses

At the urging of Massachusetts and Virginia, the First Continental Congress met in Philadelphia on Sept. 5, 1774, and was attended by representatives of all the colonies except Georgia. Patrick Henry of Virginia declared: "The distinctions between Pennsylvanians, New Yorkers and New Englanders are no more. I am not a Virginian but an American." This Congress, which adjourned Oct. 26, 1774, passed intercolonial resolutions calling for extensive boycott by the colonies against British trade.

The following year, most of the delegates from the colonies were chosen by popular election to attend the Second Continental Congress, which assembled in Philadelphia on May 10. As war had already begun between the colonies and England, the chief problems before the Congress were the procuring of military supplies, the establishment of an army and proper defenses, the issuing of continental bills of credit, etc. On June 15, 1775, George Washington was elected to command the Continental army. Congress adjourned Dec. 12, 1776.

Other Continental Congresses were held in Baltimore (1776–77), Philadelphia (1777), Lancaster, Pa. (1777), York, Pa. (1777–78), and Philadelphia (1778–81).

In 1781, the Articles of Confederation, although establishing a league of the thirteen states rather than a strong central government, provided for the continuance of Congress. Known thereafter as the Congress of the Confederation, it held sessions in Philadelphia (1781–83), Princeton, N.J. (1783), Annapolis, Md. (1783–84), and Trenton, N.J. (1784). Five sessions were held in New York City between the years 1785 and 1789.

The Congress of the United States, established by the ratification of the Constitution, held its first meeting on March 4, 1789, in New York City. Several sessions of Congress were held in Philadelphia, and the first meeting in Washington, D.C., was on Nov. 17, 1800.

Presidents of the Continental Congresses

Name	Elected	Born	Died
Peyton Randolph, Va.	Sept. 5, 1774	c.1721	1775
Henry Middleton, S.C.	Oct. 22, 1774	1717	1784
Peyton Randolph, Va.	May 10, 1775	c.1721	1775
John Hancock, Mass.	May 24, 1775	1737	1793
Henry Laurens, S.C.	Nov. 1, 1777	1724	1792
John Jay, N.Y.	Dec. 10, 1778	1745	1829
Samuel Huntington, Conn.	Sept. 28, 1779	1731	1796
Thomas McKean, Del.	July 10, 1781	1734	1817
John Hanson, Md.	Nov. 5, 1781	1715	1783
Elias Boudinot, N.J.	Nov. 4, 1782	1740	1821
Thomas Mifflin, Pa.	Nov. 3, 1783	1744	1800
Richard Henry Lee, Va.	Nov. 30, 1784	1732	1794
John Hancock, Mass.[1]	Nov. 23, 1785	1737	1793
Nathaniel Gorham, Mass.	June 6, 1786	1738	1796
Arthur St. Clair, Pa.	Feb. 2, 1787	1734	1818
Cyrus Griffin, Va.	Jan. 22, 1788	1748	1810

1. Resigned May 29, 1786, never having served, because of continued illness.

The Great Seal of the U.S.

On July 4, 1776, the Continental Congress appointed a committee consisting of Benjamin Franklin, John Adams, and Thomas Jefferson "to bring in a device for a seal of the United States of America." After many delays, a verbal description of a design by William Barton was finally approved by Congress on June 20, 1782. The seal shows an American bald eagle with a ribbon in its mouth bearing the device *E pluribus unum* (One out of many). In its talons are the arrows of war and an olive branch of peace. On the reverse side it shows an unfinished pyramid with an eye (the eye of Providence) above it.

The American's Creed

William Tyler Page

"I believe in the United States of America as a government of the people, by the people, for the people; whose just powers are derived from the consent of the governed; a democracy in a republic; a sovereign Nation of many sovereign States; a perfect union, one and inseparable; established upon those principles of freedom, equality, justice, and humanity for which American patriots sacrificed their lives and fortunes.

"I therefore believe it is my duty to my country to love it, to support its Constitution, to obey its laws, to respect its flag, and to defend it against all enemies."

NOTE: William Tyler Page, Clerk of the U.S. House of Representatives, wrote "The American's Creed" in 1917. It was accepted by the House on behalf of the American people on April 3, 1918.

U.S. Capitol

When the French architect and engineer Maj. Pierre L'Enfant first began to lay out the plans for a new Federal city (now Washington, D.C.), he noted that Jenkins' Hill, overlooking the area, seemed to be "a pedestal waiting for a monument." It was here that the U.S. Capitol would be built. The basic structure as we know it today evolved over a period of more than 150 years. In 1792 a competition was held for the design of a capitol building. Dr. William Thornton, a physician and amateur architect, submitted the winning plan, a simple, low-lying structure of classical proportions with a shallow dome. Later, internal modifications were made by Benjamin Henry Latrobe. After the building was burned by the British in 1814, Latrobe and architect Charles Bulfinch were responsible for its reconstruction. Finally, under Thomas Walter, who was Architect of the Capitol from 1851 to 1865, the House and Senate wings and the imposing cast iron dome topped with the Statue of Freedom were added, and the Capitol assumed the form we see today. It was in the old Senate chamber that Daniel Webster cried out, "Liberty and Union, now and forever, one and inseparable!" In Statuary Hall, which used to be the old House chamber, a small disk on the floor marks the spot where John Quincy Adams was fatally stricken after more than 50 years of service to his country. A whisper from one side of this room can be heard across the vast space of the hall. Visitors can see the original Supreme Court chamber a floor below the Rotunda.

In addition to its historical association, the Capitol Building is also a vast artistic treasure house. The works of such famous artists as Gilbert Stuart, Rembrandt Peale, and John Trumbull are displayed on the walls. The Great Rotunda, with its 180-foot- (54.9-m-) high dome, is decorated with a massive fresco by Constantino Brumidi, which extends some 300 feet (90 m) in circumference. Throughout the building are many paintings of events in U.S. history and sculptures of outstanding Americans. The Capitol itself is situated on a 68-acre (27.5-ha) park designed by the 19th-century landscape architect Frederick Law Olmsted. There are free guided tours of the Capitol, which include admission to the House and Senate galleries. Those who wish to visit the visitors' gallery in either wing without taking the tour may obtain passes from their Senators or Congressmen. Visitors may ride on the monorail subway that joins the House and Senate wings of the Capitol with the Congressional office buildings.

Washington Monument

Construction of this magnificent Washington, D.C., monument, which draws some two million visitors a year, took nearly a century of planning, building, and controversy. Provision for a large equestrian statue of George Washington was made in the original city plan, but the project was soon dropped. After Washington's death it was taken up again, and a number of false starts and changes of design were made. Finally, in 1848, work was begun on the monument that stands today. The design, by architect Robert Mills, then featured an ornate base. In 1854, however, political squabbling and a lack of money brought construction to a halt. Work was resumed in 1880, and the monument was completed in 1884 and opened to the public in 1888. The tapered shaft, faced with white marble and rising from walls 15 feet thick (4.6 m) at the base was modeled after the obelisks of ancient Egypt. The monument, one of the tallest masonry constructions in the world, stands just over 555 feet (169 m). Memorial stones from the 50 States, foreign countries, and organizations line the interior walls. The top, reached only by elevator, commands a panoramic view of the city.

The Liberty Bell

The Liberty Bell was cast in England in 1752 for the Pennsylvania Statehouse (now named Independence Hall) in Philadelphia. It was recast in Philadelphia in 1753. It is inscribed with the words, "Proclaim liberty throughout all the land unto all the inhabitants thereof" (Lev. 25:10). The bell was rung on July 8, 1776, for the first public reading of the Declaration of Independence. Hidden in Allentown during the British occupation of Philadelphia, it was replaced in Independence Hall in 1778. The bell cracked on July 8, 1835, while tolling the death of Chief Justice John Marshall. In 1976 the Liberty Bell was moved to a special exhibition building near Independence Hall.

Arlington National Cemetery

Arlington National Cemetery occupies 617 acres in Virginia on the Potomac River, directly opposite Washington. This land was part of the estate of John Parke Custis, Martha Washington's son. His son, George Washington Parke Custis built the mansion which later became the home of Robert E. Lee. In 1864, Arlington became a military cemetery. Over 189,000 persons, including many thousands of soldiers as well as hundreds of distinguished Americans, are buried there. Expansion of the cemetery began in 1966, using a 180-acre tract of land directly east of the present site.

In 1921, an Unknown American Soldier of World War I was buried in the cemetery; the monument at the Tomb was opened to the public without ceremony in 1932. Two additional Unknowns, one from World War II and one from the Korean War, were buried May 30, 1958. The Unknown Serviceman of Vietnam was buried on May 28, 1984. The inscription carved on the Tomb of the Unknowns reads:

HERE RESTS IN
HONORED GLORY
AN AMERICAN
SOLDIER
KNOWN BUT TO GOD

History of the Flag

Source: Encyclopaedia Britannica.

The first official American flag, the Continental or Grand Union flag, was displayed on Prospect Hill, Jan. 1, 1776, in the American lines besieging Boston. It had 13 alternate red and white stripes, with the British Union Jack in the upper left corner.

On June 14, 1777, the Continental Congress adopted the design for a new flag, which actually was the Continental flag with the red cross of St. George and the white cross of St. Andrew replaced on the blue field by 13 stars, one for each state. No rule was made as to the arrangement of the stars, and while they were usually shown in a circle, there were various other designs. It is uncertain when the new flag was first flown, but its first official announcement is believed to have been on Sept. 3, 1977.

The first public assertion that Betsy Ross made the first Stars and Stripes appeared in a paper read before the Historical Society of Pennsylvania on March 14, 1870, by William J. Canby, a grandson. However, Mr. Canby on later investigation found no official documents of any action by Congress on the flag before June 14, 1777. Betsy Ross's own story, according to her daughter, was that Washington, Robert Morris, and George Ross, as representatives of Congress, visited her in Philadelphia in June 1776, showing her a rough draft of the flag and asking her if she could make one. However, the only actual record of the manufacture of flags by Betsy Ross is a voucher in Harrisburg, Pa., for 14 pounds and some shillings for flags for the Pennsylvania navy.

On Jan. 13, 1794, Congress voted to add two stars and two stripes to the flag in recognition of the admission of Vermont and Kentucky to the Union. By 1818, there were 20 states in the Union, and as it was obvious that the flag would soon become unwieldly, Congress voted April 18 to return to the original 13 stripes and to indicate the admission of a new state simply by the addition of a star the following July 4. The 49th star, for Alaska, was added July 4, 1959; and the 50th star, for Hawaii, was added July 4, 1960.

The first Confederate flag, adopted in 1861 by the Confederate convention in Montgomery, Ala., was called the Stars and Bars; but because of its similarity in colors to the American flag, there was much confusion in the Battle of Bull Run. To remedy this situation, Gen. G. T. Beauregard suggested a battle flag, which was used by the Southern armies throughout the war. The flag consisted of a red field on which was placed a blue cross of St. Andrew separated from the field by a white fillet and adorned with 13[1] white stars for the Confederate states. In May 1863, at Richmond, an official flag was adopted by the Confederate Congress. This flag was white and twice as long as wide; the union, two-thirds the width of the flag, contained the battle flag designed for Gen. Beauregard. A broad transverse stripe of red was added Feb. 4, 1865, so that the flag might not be mistaken for a signal of truce.

1. 11 states formally seceded, and unofficial groups in Kentucky and Missouri adopted ordinances of secession. On this basis, these two states were admitted to the Confederacy, although the official state governments remained in the Union.

The Pledge of Allegiance[1] to the Flag

"I pledge allegiance to the Flag of the United States of America, and to the Republic for which it stands, one Nation under God,[2] indivisible, with liberty and justice for all."

1. The original pledge was published in the Sept. 8, 1892, issue of *The Youth's Companion* in Boston. For years, the authorship was in dispute between James B. Upham and Francis Bellamy of the magazine's staff. In 1939, after a study of the controversy, the United States Flag Association decided that authorship be credited to Bellamy. 2. The phrase "under God" was added to the pledge on June 14, 1954.

The Statue of Liberty

The Statue of Liberty ("Liberty Enlightening the World") is a 225-ton, steel-reinforced copper female figure, 152 ft in height, facing the ocean from Liberty[1] Island in New York Harbor. The right hand holds aloft a torch, and the left hand carries a tablet upon which is inscribed: "July IV MDCCLXXVI."

The statue was designed by Frederic Auguste Bartholdi of Alsace as a gift to the United States from the people of France to memorialize the alliance of the two countries in the American Revolution and their abiding friendship. The French people contributed the $250,000 cost.

The 150-foot pedestal was designed by Richard M. Hunt and built by Gen. Charles P. Stone, both Americans. It contains steel underpinnings designed by Alexander Eiffel of France to support the statue. The $270,000 cost was borne by popular subscription in this country. President Grover Cleveland accepted the statue for the United States on Oct. 28, 1886.

On Sept. 26, 1972, President Richard M. Nixon dedicated the American Museum of Immigration, housed in structural additions to the base of the statue. Some 200 exhibits memorialize the flow of immigrants into the United States, including as many as 5,000 a day on nearby Ellis Island.

On a tablet inside the pedestal is engraved the following sonnet, written by Emma Lazarus (1849–1887):

The New Colossus

Not like the brazen giant of Greek fame.
With conquering limbs astride from land to land;
Here at our sea-washed, sunset gates shall stand
A mighty woman with a torch, whose flame
Is the imprisoned lightning, and her name
Mother of Exiles. From her beacon-hand
Glows world-wide welcome; her mild eyes command
The air-bridged harbor that twin cities frame.
"Keep, ancient lands, your storied pomp!" cries she
With silent lips. "Give me your tired, your poor,
Your huddled masses yearning to breathe free,
The wretched refuse of your teeming shore.
Send these, the homeless, tempest-tost to me,
I lift my lamp beside the golden door!"

1. Called Bedloe's Island prior to 1956.

Item	Unit	1980	1975	1970	1960[2]	1950
1. Population estimates[1]	thousands	226,505	213,540	204,879	180,671	151,684
2. Population abroad		995,546	—	1,737,836	1,374,421	481,545 [17]
3. Population per sq mile		64.0	60.2	57.5	50.6	50.7
4. Median age of population	years	30.0	28.8	28.1	29.5	30.2
5. Number of households	thousands	79,108	71,120	63,401	52,799	43,554
6. Average household size		2.75	2.94	3.14	3.33	3.37
7. Homicides		23,044	21,310	16,848	8,464	7,942
8. Rate per 100,000 population		10.2	10.0	8.3	4.7	5.3
9. Suicides		28,290	27,063	23,480	19,041	17,145
10. Rate per 100,000 population		12.2	12.7	11.6	10.6	11.4
11. Number of immigrants		460,300 [15]	386,200	373,326	265,398	249,187
Immigrants by selected						
12. Professional[4]		39,500 [15]	38,500	46,151	21,940	20,502
13. Farmers[4 5]		800 [15]	900	3,839	3,050	17,642
14. Skilled[4 6]		39,500 [15]	38,500	46,622	34,135	41,450
15. Laborers[4 7]		13,800 [15]	13,000	14,148	12,838	5,693
16. Total Gross National Product—Current prices	billion dollars	2,226.1	1,516.3	977.1	503.7	284.8
17. Per capita Gross National Product—Current prices	dollars	11,536	7,016	4,808	2,788	1,877
Retail prices of selected foods in U.S. cities						
18. Flour—5 lb	¢/unit shown	105	99.5	58.9	55.4	49.1
19. Bread—1 lb	¢/unit shown	50.9	36.0	24.3	20.3	14.3
20. Beef, choice—1 lb	¢/unit shown	237.6	188.5	130.2	105.5	93.6
21. Butter—1 lb	¢/unit shown	187.8	102.5	86.6	74.9	72.9
22. Potatoes—10 lb	¢/unit shown	197.5	134.0	89.7	71.8	46.1
23. Sugar—5 lb	¢/unit shown	213.5	186.0	64.8	58.2	48.7
24. Total labor force[10]	thousands 16 years and over	106,800	94,793	82,049	69,877 [11]	59,643 [11]
25. Percent of population		64.3	61.8	59.0	56.1 [11]	54.1 [11]
26. Percent of civilian labor force unemployed[13]	10 years and over	7.1	8.5	4.9	5.5	5.3
Physical output of selected manufactured commodities						
27. Bitominous coal	mil. short tons	776 [15]	648	603	416	516
28. Beer	thou. bbl.	192,000	158,000	134,654	94,548	88,807
29. Cigarettes	millions	702,000	627,000	562,154	506,127	391,956
30. Total raw steel	thou. short tons	111,800	116,642	131,514	99,282	96,836
31. Total value of new construction put in place	mil. dollars	230,781	132,043	94,855	54,738	33,575
32. Total concerns in business	thousands	2,781	2,679	2,442	2,708	2,687
33. Business failure rate	per 10,000 listed enterprises	42	43	44	57	34
34. Average annual earnings of employees	dollars	14,376 [15]	10,836	7,564	4,743	2,992
Average annual earnings per full time employee in selected industries[23]						
35. Services[19]	current $	12,178 [15]	9,066	5,946	3,513	2,183
36. Agriculture, Forestry, and Fisheries	current $	9,332 [15]	6,232	3,063	1,658	1,282
37. Manufacturing	current $	16,259 [15]	11,903	8,150	5,352	3,302
38. Mining[21]	current $	21,077 [15]	14,765	9,262	5,676	3,460
39. Construction	current $	16,755 [15]	13,448	9,293	5,443	3,333
40. Transportation	current $	22,522 [15]	16,060	9,928	6,185	3,714
41. Communications and public utilities	current $	19,785 [15]	14,020	8,897	5,681	3,346
42. Wholesale and retail trade	current $	13,601 [15]	10,425	7,554	4,597	3,045
43. Finance, insurance, and real estate	current $	14,365 [15]	10,618	8,026	5,030	3,223
44. Government	current $	14,607 [15]	11,451	7,965	4,676	3,014
45. Total farm population	thousands	7,241	8,864	9,712	15,635	23,048
46. Number of farms	thousands	2,428	2,808	2,954	3,962	5,388
47. Total land in farms	mil. acres	1,042	1,086.0	1,102.8	1,176.9	1,161.4
48. Total value of all farm property	mil. dollars	753,608	358,640	215,042	167,564	101,117 [22]
49. Average value per farm of land and buildings	dollars	311,000	142,500	70,485	32,854	14,005
50. Farm wages, per day, with room and board	dollars	20.99 [15]	14.80	9.30	6.50	4.45

1940	1930	1920	1910	1900
132,122	123,188	106,461	92,407	76,094
118,933	2,977,128	2,969,451	2,969,565	2,969,834
44.2	41.2	35.6	31.0	25.6
29.0	26.5	25.3	24.1	22.9
34,949	29,905	24,352	20,256	15,964
3.67	4.11	4.34	4.54	4.76
8,329	10,331	5,815	2,161	230
6.3	8.8	6.8	4.6	1.2
18,907	18,323	8,790	7,283	2,036
14.4	15.6	10.2	15.3	10.2
70,756	241,700	430,001	1,041,570	448,572
6,802	8,585	10,540	9,689	2,392
847	8,375	12,192	11,793	5,433
5,710	32,474	55,991	121,847	54,793
2,120	18,080	83,496	216,909	164,261
99.7	90.4	91.5	35.3	18.7
754	734	860	382	246
21.5	23.0	40.5	18.0	12.5
8.0	8.6	11.5	—	—
36.4	42.6	39.5	17.4	13.2
36.0	46.4	70.1	35.9	26.1
23.9	36.0	63.0	17.0	14.0
26.0	30.5	97.0	30.0	30.5
53,011[11]	48,830[12]	41,614[12]	38,167[12]	29,073[12]
52.9[11]	49.5[12]	50.3[12]	53.3[12]	50.2[12]
14.6	8.7	5.2	5.9	5.0
461	468	569	417	212
54,892	3,681	9,200	59,500	39,500
189,373	124,193	48,091	9,782	3,870
66,983	44,591	46,183	28,330	11,227
8,682	8,741	6,749	3,262	—
2,156	2,183	1,821	1,515	1,174
63	122[16]	48	84	92
1,299	1,368	1,236[18]	517[18]	375[18]
953	1,066	912	447	340
407	388	528	223	178
1,432	1,488	1,532	651	487
1,388	1,424	1,684	668	479
1,330	1,526	1,710	804	593
1,756	1,610	1,645	607	505
1,717	1,499	1,238	516	470
1,382	1,569	1,270	630	508
1,725	1,973	1,758	1,301	1,040
1,344	1,553	1,245	725	584
30,547	30,529	31,974	32,077	29,875
6,102	6,295	6,454	6,366	5,740
1,065.1	990.1	958.7	881.4	841.2
41,829	57,689	78,386	40,959	20,365
5,532	7,624	10,295	5,480	2,895
1.30	1.80	2.80	1.05	.75[23]

Statistical Profile of The United States

1900–1980

There are many ways of looking at American history—at the growth of the United States, its people, and its economy. One of the most interesting is to examine certain aspects of American life "by the numbers." This "Statistical Profile" makes such an examination possible. The data at left and following—stripped of the men and women, events, and technological changes that have shaped American society—reveal much that is often hidden in the complex folds of the fabric of history.

Statistical Profile Table—Footnotes

1. Total, including Armed Forces overseas, as of July 1. 2. Beginning with 1960, figures include Alaska and Hawaii. 3. Based on resident population figures, excluding Armed Forces overseas. 4. Like occupations have been grouped as closely as possible to allow for changing definitions over the years. For example, figures for Professional and Skilled workers are combined for 1975 and following. See sources for definitions and further explanation. 5. Includes "Farmers and Farm Managers." 6. Includes craftsmen, foremen, operatives, and kindred workers. 7. Excludes farm and mine laborers. 8. Earnings are calculated for all types of jobs performed in these industries. 9. Because the Air Deregulation Act of 1978 lifted some restrictions on entering new markets, domestic and international operators are no longer considered separately after 1975. Cargo included. 10. 1940–75, includes Armed Forces. 11. Data for persons 14 years old and over. 12. Data for persons 10 years old and over reporting a gainful occupation. 13. Prior to 1950, figures are for persons 14 years old and over. Annual averages. Unemployment percentages for the Depression years are as follows: 1931, 15.9%; 1932, 23.6%; 1933, 24.9%; 1934, 21.7%; 1935, 20.1%; 1936, 16.9%; 1937, 14.3%; 1938, 19.0%; 1939, 17.2%. 14. In 1918, 2,897,167 people were on active military duty. 15. Figure is for 1979. 16. In 1932, the rate reached a high of 154. 17. Estimate. 18. After deduction for unemployment. 19. Includes workers in personal, medical, and other health services, domestic, nonprofit, educational service industries. 20. Figure is for 1974. 21. Includes workers in anthracite coal, bituminous coal, and metal mining. 22. Figure is for 1949. 23. Figure is for 1899. 24. Liveweight production. 25. Figures are annual averages for 1960–64. 26. Figures are annual averages for 1950–54. 27. Figures are annual averages for 1940–44. 28. Figures are annual averages for 1930–34. 29. Figures are annual averages for 1920–24. 30. Figures are annual averages for 1910–14. 31. Figure is for 1907. 32. Figure is for 1902. 33. Figure is for 1921. 34. Duplication has been eliminated where the same passengers were carried on more than one route of an air carrier, but still exists where the same passengers were carried by more than one air carrier. 35. Includes nonrevenue passengers. 36. Figure is for 1957, the first year for large-scale generation of electricity by nuclear power. 37. Figure is for 1922. 38. Preliminary figures. 39. Figure is for 1913. 40. Includes hospital care, professional services, drugs and sundries, eyeglasses and appliances, nursing home care, expenses for prepayment and administration, government public health activities, other health services, and research and medical facilities construction. 41. Figure is for 1969. 42. Figure is for 1959. 43. Figure is for 1978. 44. Figure is for 1901. 45. Figures for 1970 and following are for both color and monochrome sets. 46. Figures are annual averages for 1975–79. 47. Figures are annual averages for 1970–74. 48. Figures are annual averages for 1965–69. 49. Figures are annual averages for 1955–59. 50. Figures are annual averages for 1945–49. 51. Figures are annual averages for 1935–39. 52. Figures are annual averages for 1925–29. 53. Figures are annual averages for 1915–19. 54. Figures are annual averages for 1910–14. 55. In 1945, 12,123,455 people were on active military duty. *Sources: Historical Statistics of the U.S.* and *Statistical Abstract of the United States,* Department of Commerce, Bureau of the Census; *Crime in the United States,* Department of Justice, Federal Bureau of Investigation; Edison Electric Institute; Bureau of Labor Statistics.

Item	Unit	1980	1975	1970	1960[2]	1950
Farm Productivity						
51. Wheat—yield per acre	bushels	33.4	31.0	31.0	25.2[25]	17.3[26]
52. Wheat—man-hours	100 bushels	9	9	9	12[25]	27[26]
53. Cotton—yield per acre	pounds	404	473	438	475[25]	296[26]
54. Cotton—man-hours	bale	8	23	26	47[25]	107[26]
55. Potatoes—yield per acre	cwt	261	239.0	229.0	194.9[25]	151.2[26]
56. Potatoes—man-hours	ton	—	4	4	5[25]	8[26]
57. Cattle—value	head	502	159	179	137	124
58. Cattle—man-hours	cwt	1.3[46]	1.7[47]	2.1[48]	3.2[49]	4.0[50]
59. Milk cows—milk per cow	pounds	11,000	10,200.0	9,385.0	7,507.0[25]	5,440.0[26]
60. Milk cows—man-hours	cwt of milk	0.4	0.6	0.7	1.2[25]	2.2[26]
61. Total use of electrical energy	mil. kwh	2,286,000	1,918,000	1,641,731	848,723	396,346
62. Residential	mil. kwh	721,000	—	453,015	196,296	72,200
63. Commercial	mil. kwh	510,000	—	295,057	121,437	52,091
64. Industrial	mil. kwh	791,000	—	685,693	415,699	194,835
65. Value of exports	mil. dollars	220,705	107,591	43,265	20,603	10,816
66. Value of imports	mil. dollars	239,944	96,940	40,189	15,046	9,125
67. Passenger car factory sales	thousands	6,400.0	6,713.0	6,546.8	6,674.7	6,665.8
68. Total motor vehicle registrations	millions	159.1	133.7	108.4	73.9	49.2
69. Miles of travel by motor vehicles	mil. miles	1,529,000[15]	1,300,100	1,120,705	718,845	458,246
70. Number of operating railroads		63[15]	341[20]	351	407	471
71. Railroad passengers	thousands	274,200[15]	270,000	289,469	327,172	488,019
Air transportation						
72. Number of operators		63[9]	30	33	42	52
73. Aircraft in service		2,505	2,267	2,437	1,594	960
74. Revenue passengers carried[34]	thousands	273,000	189,000	153,408	56,352	17,345
75. Total school enrollments—elementary and secondary	thousands	48,000[17]	64,872	51,319	41,762	28,492
76. High school graduates	thousands	3,127	3,133	2,906	1,864	1,200
77. Illiteracy[11]	percent	.5[15]	—	1.0[41]	2.2[42]	3.2
78. Total institutions of higher education		2,871[43]	2,747	2,525	1,959	1,863
79. Bachelor's or first professional degrees conferred		1,010,000	988,000	827,234	389,183	432,058
Radio and television						
80. Nuclear plants		75[38]	51	13	4	—
81. Electricity generated by nuclear power	mil. kwh	—	265,200	181,800	21,808	519
82. Television sets produced	thousands	17,508	10,637	9,483[45]	5,708	7,464
83. Households with television sets	thousands	80,000	72,600	63,200	45,750	3,875
84. Books published		42,377	39,372	36,071	15,012	11,022
85. Daily newspapers—number		1,745	1,756	1,748	1,763	1,772
86. Daily newspapers—circulation	thousands	62,202	60,655	62,108	58,882	53,829
87. Telephones per 1,000 population		791.0	695.0	583.4	407.8	280.9
88. Average number of daily telephone conversations	thousands	787,000	633,000	485,200	285,386	170,623
89. Patents issued for inventions		61,800	71,994	64,427	47,170	43,040
90. Currency in circulation	mil. dollars	137,244	92,095.0	54,351.0	32,064.6	27,156.3
91. Total social welfare expenditures under public programs	mil. dollars	428,400[15 38]	290,000	145,893	52,293	23,508
92. Percent of GNP	percent	18.5[15 38]	20	15.3	10.6	8.9
93. Percent of all government expenditures	percent	56.8[15 38]	57.4	47.8	38.0	37.6
94. Per capita (actual prices)	dollars	1,912[15 38]	1336	701	286	153
95. Per capita health expenditure	dollars	1,017	565.00	343.44	146.30	81.86
96. Number of physicians		473,000	409,000	348,328	274,833	191,947
97. Rate per 100,000 population		210	186	166	148	149
Summary of federal government finances						
98. Receipts	mil. dollars	520,100.0	281,000.0	193,700.0	92,500.0	40,900.0
99. Outlays	mil. dollars	579,600.0	324,600.0	196,600.0	92,200.0	43,100.0
100. Total public debt	mil. dollars	907,000.0	533,200.0	370,918.7	286,300.8	257,357.4
101. Per capita public debt	dollars	4,063	2,496	1,811	1,585	1,697
102. Paid civilian employees of the federal government		2,875,866	2,896,944	2,981,574	2,398,704	1,960,708
103. Military personnel on active duty[54]		2,050,000	2,127,000	3,066,294	2,476,435	1,460,261

Item	Unit	1940	1930	1920	1910	1900
Farm Productivity						
51. Wheat—yield per acre	bushels	17.1 [27]	13.5 [28]	13.8 [29]	14.4 [30]	13.9
52. Wheat—man-hours	100 bushels	44 [27]	70 [28]	90 [29]	106 [30]	108
53. Cotton—yield per acre	pounds	260 [27]	184 [28]	155 [29]	201 [30]	189
54. Cotton—man-hours	bale	182 [27]	252 [28]	296 [29]	276 [30]	284
55. Potatoes—yield per acre	cwt	82.1 [27]	64.6 [28]	64.6 [29]	59.8 [30]	—
56. Potatoes—man-hours	ton	17 [27]	21 [28]	23 [29]	25 [30]	—
57. Cattle—value	head	41	56.36	52.64	24.54	26.50
58. Cattle—man-hours	cwt	3.4 [51]	3.3 [52]	3.7 [53]	3.8 [58]	—
59. Milk cows—milk per cow	pounds	4,653.0 [27]	4,289.0 [28]	4,000.0 [29]	3,842.0 [30]	—
60. Milk cows—man-hours	cwt of milk	3.1 [27]	3.4 [28]	3.6 [29]	3.8 [30]	—
61. Total use of electrical energy	mil. kwh	181,706	115,783	57,125	14,262 [31]	6,029 [32]
62. Residential	mil. kwh	24,068	11,018	3,190	—	—
63. Commercial	mil. kwh	22,373	13,944	6,150	—	—
64. Industrial	mil. kwh	92,390	61,023	31,500	—	—
65. Value of exports	mil. dollars	4,030	4,013	8,664	1,919	1,499
66. Value of imports	mil. dollars	7,433	3,500	5,784	1,646	930
67. Passenger car factory sales	thousands	3,717.3	2,787.4	1,905.5	181.0	4.1
68. Total motor vehicle registrations	millions	32.4	26.7	9.2	.5	.008
69. Miles of travel by motor vehicles	mil. miles	302,188	206,320	55,027 [33]	—	—
70. Number of operating railroads		574	775	1,085	1,306	1,224
71. Railroad passengers	thousands	456,088	707,987	1,269,913	971,683	576,831
Air transportation						
72. Number of operators		19	43	—	—	—
73. Aircraft in service		369	497	—	—	—
74. Revenue passengers carried[34]	thousands	2,523	385 [35]	—	—	—
75. Total school enrollments—elementary and secondary	thousands	28,045	28,329	23,278	19,372	16,885
76. High school graduates	thousands	1,221	667	311	156	95
77. Illiteracy[11]	percent	2.9	4.3	6.0	7.7	10.7
78. Total institutions of higher education		1,708	1,409	1,041	951	977
79. Bachelor's or first professional degrees conferred		186,500	122,484	48,622	37,199	27,410
Radio and television						
80. Nuclear plants		—	—	—	—	—
81. Electricity generated by nuclear power	mil. kwh	10 [36]	—	—	—	—
82. Television sets produced	thousands	—	—	—	—	—
83. Households with television sets	thousands	—	—	—	—	—
84. Books published		11,328	10,027	8,422	13,470	6,356
85. Daily newspapers—number		1,878	1,942	2,042	—	—
86. Daily newspapers—circulation	thousands	41,132	39,589	27,791	—	—
87. Telephones per 1,000 population		165.1	162.6	123.4	82.0	17.6
88. Average number of daily telephone conversations	thousands	98,783	83,520	51,814	36,161	7,882
89. Patents issued for inventions		42,238	45,226	37,060	35,141	24,644
90. Currency in circulation	mil. dollars	7,847.5	4,521.0	5,467.6	3,148.7	2,081.2
91. Total social welfare expenditures under public programs	mil. dollars	8,795	4,085	—	1,000 [39]	—
92. Percent of GNP	percent	9.2	4.2	—	2.5 [39]	—
93. Percent of all government expenditures	percent	49.0	—	—	34.0 [39]	—
94. Per capita (actual prices)	dollars	66	33	—	—	—
95. Per capita health expenditure	dollars	29.62	29.49 [14]	—	—	—
96. Number of physicians		165,989	153,803	144,977	151,132	132,002
97. Rate per 100,000 population		126	125	137	164	173
Summary of federal government finances						
98. Receipts	mil. dollars	6,900.0	4,057.9	6,648.9	675.5	567.2
99. Outlays	mil. dollars	9,600.0	3,320.2	6,357.7	693.6	520.9
100. Total public debt	mil. dollars	42,967.5	16,185.3	24,299.3	1,146.9	1,263.4
101. Per capita public debt	dollars	325	132	228	12	17
102. Paid civilian employees of the federal government		1,042,420	601,319	655,265	388,708	239,476 [44]
103. Military personnel on active duty[54]		458,365 [14]	255,648	343,302	139,344 [57]	125,923

Presidents

Name and (party)[1]	Term	State of birth	Born	Died	Religion	Age at inaug.	Age at death
1. Washington (F)[2]	1789–1797	Va.	2/22/1732	12/14/1799	Episcopalian	57	67
2. J. Adams (F)	1797–1801	Mass.	10/30/1735	7/4/1826	Unitarian	61	90
3. Jefferson (DR)	1801–1809	Va.	4/13/1743	7/4/1826	Deist	57	83
4. Madison (DR)	1809–1817	Va.	3/16/1751	6/28/1836	Episcopalian	57	85
5. Monroe (DR)	1817–1825	Va.	4/28/1758	7/4/1831	Episcopalian	58	73
6. J. Q. Adams (DR)	1825–1829	Mass.	7/11/1767	2/23/1848	Unitarian	57	80
7. Jackson (D)	1829–1837	S.C.	3/15/1767	6/8/1845	Presbyterian	61	78
8. Van Buren (D)	1837–1841	N.Y.	12/5/1782	7/24/1862	Reformed Dutch	54	79
9. W. H. Harrison (W)[3]	1841	Va.	2/9/1773	4/4/1841	Episcopalian	68	68
10. Tyler (W)	1841–1845	Va.	3/29/1790	1/18/1862	Episcopalian	51	71
11. Polk (D)	1845–1849	N.C.	11/2/1795	6/15/1849	Methodist	49	53
12. Taylor (W)[3]	1849–1850	Va.	11/24/1784	7/9/1850	Episcopalian	64	65
13. Fillmore (W)	1850–1853	N.Y.	1/7/1800	3/8/1874	Unitarian	50	74
14. Pierce (D)	1853–1857	N.H.	11/23/1804	10/8/1869	Episcopalian	48	64
15. Buchanan (D)	1857–1861	Pa.	4/23/1791	6/1/1868	Presbyterian	65	77
16. Lincoln (R)[4]	1861–1865	Ky.	2/12/1809	4/15/1865	Liberal	52	56
17. A. Johnson (U)[5]	1865–1869	N.C.	12/29/1808	7/31/1875	([6])	56	66
18. Grant (R)	1869–1877	Ohio	4/27/1822	7/23/1885	Methodist	46	63
19. Hayes (R)	1877–1881	Ohio	10/4/1822	1/17/1893	Methodist	54	70
20. Garfield (R)[4]	1881	Ohio	11/19/1831	9/19/1881	Disciples of Christ	49	49
21. Arthur (R)	1881–1885	Vt.	10/5/1830	11/18/1886	Episcopalian	50	56
22. Cleveland (D)	1885–1889	N.J.	3/18/1837	6/24/1908	Presbyterian	47	71
23. B. Harrison (R)	1889–1893	Ohio	8/20/1833	3/13/1901	Presbyterian	55	67
24. Cleveland (D)[7]	1893–1897	—	—	—	—	55	—
25. McKinley (R)[4]	1897–1901	Ohio	1/29/1843	9/14/1901	Methodist	54	58
26. T. Roosevelt (R)	1901–1909	N.Y.	10/27/1858	1/6/1919	Reformed Dutch	42	60
27. Taft (R)	1909–1913	Ohio	9/15/1857	3/8/1930	Unitarian	51	72
28. Wilson (D)	1913–1921	Va.	12/28/1856	2/3/1924	Presbyterian	56	67
29. Harding (R)[3]	1921–1923	Ohio	11/2/1865	8/2/1923	Baptist	55	57
30. Coolidge (R)	1923–1929	Vt.	7/4/1872	1/5/1933	Congregationalist	51	60
31. Hoover (R)	1929–1933	Iowa	8/10/1874	10/20/1964	Quaker	54	90
32. F. D. Roosevelt (D)[3]	1933–1945	N.Y.	1/30/1882	4/12/1945	Episcopalian	51	63
33. Truman (D)	1945–1953	Mo.	5/8/1884	12/26/1972	Baptist	60	88
34. Eisenhower (R)	1953–1961	Tex.	10/14/1890	3/28/1969	Presbyterian	62	78
35. Kennedy (D)[4]	1961–1963	Mass.	5/29/1917	11/22/1963	Roman Catholic	43	46
36. L. B. Johnson (D)	1963–1969	Tex.	8/27/1908	1/22/1973	Disciples of Christ	55	64
37. Nixon (R)[8]	1969–1974	Calif.	1/9/1913	—	Quaker	56	—
38. Ford (R)	1974–1977	Neb.	7/14/1913	—	Episcopalian	61	—
39. Carter (D)	1977–1981	Ga.	10/1/1924	—	Southern Baptist	52	—
40. Reagan (R)	1981–	Ill.	2/6/1911	—	Disciples of Christ	69	—

1. F—Federalist; DR—Democratic-Republican; D—Democratic; W—Whig; R—Republican; U—Union. 2. No party for first election. The party system in the U.S. made its appearance during Washington's first term. 3. Died in office. 4. Assassinated in office. 5. The Republican National Convention of 1864 adopted the name Union Party. It renominated Lincoln for President; for Vice President it nominated Johnson, a War Democrat. Although frequently listed as a Republican Vice President and President, Johnson undoubtedly considered himself strictly a member of the Union Party. When that party broke apart after 1868, he returned to the Democratic Party. 6. Johnson was not a professed church member; however, he admired the Baptist principles of church government. 7. Second nonconsecutive term. 8. Resigned Aug. 9, 1974.

Vice Presidents

Name and (party)[1]	Term	State of birth	Birth and death dates	President served under
1. John Adams (F)[2]	1789–1797	Massachusetts	1735–1826	Washington
2. Thomas Jefferson (DR)	1797–1801	Virginia	1743–1826	J. Adams
3. Aaron Burr (DR)	1801–1805	New Jersey	1756–1836	Jefferson
4. George Clinton (DR)[3]	1805–1812	New York	1739–1812	Jefferson and Madison
5. Elbridge Gerry (DR)[3]	1813–1814	Massachusetts	1744–1814	Madison
6. Daniel D. Tompkins (DR)	1817–1825	New York	1774–1825	Monroe
7. John C. Calhoun[4]	1825–1832	South Carolina	1782–1850	J. Q. Adams and Jackson
8. Martin Van Buren (D)	1833–1837	New York	1782–1862	Jackson
9. Richard M. Johnson (D)	1837–1841	Kentucky	1780–1850	Van Buren
10. John Tyler (W)[5]	1841	Virginia	1790–1862	W. H. Harrison
11. George M. Dallas (D)	1845–1849	Pennsylvania	1792–1864	Polk
12. Millard Fillmore (W)[5]	1849–1850	New York	1800–1874	Taylor
13. William R. King (D)[3]	1853	North Carolina	1786–1853	Pierce
14. John C. Breckinridge (D)	1857–1861	Kentucky	1821–1875	Buchanan

Name and (party)[1]	Term	State of birth	Birth and death dates	President served under
15. Hannibal Hamlin (R)	1861–1865	Maine	1809–1891	Lincoln
16. Andrew Johnson (U)[5]	1865	North Carolina	1808–1875	Lincoln
17. Schuyler Colfax (R)	1869–1873	New York	1823–1885	Grant
18. Henry Wilson (R)[3]	1873–1875	New Hampshire	1812–1875	Grant
19. William A. Wheeler (R)	1877–1881	New York	1819–1887	Hayes
20. Chester A. Arthur (R)[5]	1881	Vermont	1830–1886	Garfield
21. Thomas A. Hendricks (D)[3]	1885	Ohio	1819–1885	Cleveland
22. Levi P. Morton (R)	1889–1893	Vermont	1824–1920	B. Harrison
23. Adlai E. Stevenson (D)	1893–1897	Kentucky	1835–1914	Cleveland
24. Garrett A. Hobart (R)[3]	1897–1899	New Jersey	1844–1899	McKinley
25. Theodore Roosevelt (R)[5]	1901	New York	1858–1919	McKinley
26. Charles W. Fairbanks (R)	1905–1909	Ohio	1852–1918	T. Roosevelt
27. James S. Sherman (R)[3]	1909–1912	New York	1855–1912	Taft
28. Thomas R. Marshall (D)	1913–1921	Indiana	1854–1925	Wilson
29. Calvin Coolidge (R)[5]	1921–1923	Vermont	1872–1933	Harding
30. Charles G. Dawes (R)	1925–1929	Ohio	1865–1951	Coolidge
31. Charles Curtis (R)	1929–1933	Kansas	1860–1936	Hoover
32. John N. Garner (D)	1933–1941	Texas	1868–1967	F. D. Roosevelt
33. Henry A. Wallace (D)	1941–1945	Iowa	1888–1965	F. D. Roosevelt
34. Harry S. Truman (D)[5]	1945	Missouri	1884–1972	F. D. Roosevelt
35. Alben W. Barkley (D)	1949–1953	Kentucky	1877–1956	Truman
36. Richard M. Nixon (R)	1953–1961	California	1913–	Eisenhower
37. Lyndon B. Johnson (D)[5]	1961–1963	Texas	1908–1973	Kennedy
38. Hubert H. Humphrey (D)	1965–1969	South Dakota	1911–1978	Johnson
39. Spiro T. Agnew (R)[6]	1969–1973	Maryland	1918–	Nixon
40. Gerald R. Ford (R)[7]	1973–1974	Nebraska	1913–	Nixon
41. Nelson A. Rockefeller (R)[8]	1974–1977	Maine	1908–1979	Ford
42. Walter F. Mondale (D)	1977–1981	Minnesota	1928–	Carter
43. George Bush (R)	1981–	Massachusetts	1924–	Reagan

1. F—Federalist; DR—Democratic-Republican; D—Democratic; W—Whig; R—Republican; U—Union. 2. No party for first election. The party system in the U.S. made its appearance during Washington's first term as President. 3. Died in office. 4. Democratic-Republican with J. Q. Adams; Democratic with Jackson. Calhoun resigned in 1832 to become a U.S. Senator. 5. Succeeded to presidency on death of President. 6. Resigned Oct. 10, 1973, after pleading no contest to Federal income tax evasion charges. 7. Nominated by Nixon on Oct. 12, 1973, under provisions of 25th Amendment. Confirmed by Congress on Dec. 6, 1973, and was sworn in same day. He became President Aug. 9, 1974, upon Nixon's resignation. 8. Nominated by Ford Aug. 20, 1974; confirmed by Congress on Dec. 19, 1974, and was sworn in same day.

Burial Places of the Presidents

President	Burial place
Washington	Mt. Vernon, Va.
J. Adams	Quincy, Mass.
Jefferson	Charlottesville, Va.
Madison	Montpelier Station, Va.
Monroe	Richmond, Va.
J. Q. Adams	Quincy, Mass.
Jackson	The Hermitage, nr. Nashville, Tenn.
Van Buren	Kinderhook, N.Y.
W. H. Harrison	North Bend, Ohio
Tyler	Richmond, Va.
Polk	Nashville, Tenn.
Taylor	Louisville, Ky.
Fillmore	Buffalo, N.Y.
Pierce	Concord, N.H.
Buchanan	Lancaster, Pa.
Lincoln	Springfield, Ill.
A. Johnson	Greeneville, Tenn.

President	Burial place
Grant	New York City
Hayes	Fremont, Ohio
Garfield	Cleveland, Ohio
Arthur	Albany, N.Y.
Cleveland	Princeton, N.J.
B. Harrison	Indianapolis
McKinley	Canton, Ohio
T. Roosevelt	Oyster Bay, N.Y.
Taft	Arlington National Cemetery
Wilson	Washington National Cathedral
Harding	Marion, Ohio
Coolidge	Plymouth, Vt.
Hoover	West Branch, Iowa
F. D. Roosevelt	Hyde Park, N.Y.
Truman	Independence, Mo.
Eisenhower	Abilene, Kan.
Kennedy	Arlington National Cemetery
L. B. Johnson	Stonewall, Tex.

"In God We Trust"

"In God We Trust" first appeared on U.S. coins after April 22, 1864, when Congress passed an act authorizing the coinage of a 2-cent piece bearing this motto. Thereafter, Congress extended its use to other coins. On July 30, 1956, it became the national motto.

Wives and Children of the Presidents

President	Wife's name	Year and place of wife's birth	Married	Wife died	Children of President[1] Sons	Daughters
Washington	Mrs. Martha Dandridge Custis	1732, Va.	1759	1802	—	—
John Adams	Abigail Smith	1744, Mass.	1764	1818	3	2
Jefferson	Mrs. Martha Wayles Skelton	1748, Va.	1772	1782	1	5
Madison	Mrs. Dorothy "Dolley" Payne Todd	1768, N.C.	1794	1849	—	—
Monroe	Elizabeth "Eliza" Kortright	1768, N.Y.	1786	1830	—	2
J. Q. Adams	Louisa Catherine Johnson	1775, England	1797	1852	3	1
Jackson	Mrs. Rachel Donelson Robards	1767, Va.	1791	1828	—	—
Van Buren	Hannah Hoes	1788, N.Y.	1807	1819	4	—
W. H. Harrison	Anna Symmes	1775, N.J.	1795	1864	6	4
Tyler	Letitia Christian	1790, Va.	1813	1842	3	4
	Julia Gardiner	1820, N.Y.	1844	1889	5	2
Polk	Sarah Childress	1803, Tenn.	1824	1891	—	—
Taylor	Margaret Smith	1788, Md.	1810	1852	1	5
Filmore	Abigail Powers	1798, N.Y.	1826	1853	1	1
	Mrs. Caroline Carmichael McIntosh	1813, N.J.	1858	1881	—	—
Pierce	Jane Means Appleton	1806, N.H.	1834	1863	3	—
Buchanan	(Unmarried)	—	—	—	—	—
Lincoln	Mary Todd	1818, Ky.	1842	1882	4	—
A. Johnson	Eliza McCardle	1810, Tenn.	1827	1876	3	2
Grant	Julia Dent	1826, Mo.	1848	1902	3	1
Hayes	Lucy Ware Webb	1831, Ohio	1852	1889	7	1
Garfield	Lucretia Rudolph	1832, Ohio	1858	1918	5	2
Arthur	Ellen Lewis Herndon	1837, Va.	1859	1880	2	1
Cleveland	Frances Folsom	1864, N.Y.	1886	1947	2	3
B. Harrison	Caroline Lavinia Scott	1832, Ohio	1853	1892	1	1
	Mrs. Mary Scott Lord Dimmick	1858, Pa.	1896	1948	—	1
McKinley	Ida Saxton	1847, Ohio	1871	1907	—	2
T. Roosevelt	Alice Hathaway Lee	1861, Mass.	1880	1884	—	1
	Edith Kermit Carow	1861, Conn.	1886	1948	4	1
Taft	Helen Herron	1861, Ohio	1886	1943	2	1
Wilson	Ellen Louise Axson	1860, Ga.	1885	1914	—	3
	Mrs. Edith Bolling Galt	1872, Va.	1915	1961	—	—
Harding	Mrs. Florence Kling DeWolfe	1860, Ohio	1891	1924	—	—
Coolidge	Grace Anna Goodhue	1879, Vt.	1905	1957	2	—
Hoover	Lou Henry	1875, Iowa	1899	1944	2	—
F. D. Roosevelt	Anna Eleanor Roosevelt	1884, N.Y.	1905	1962	5	1
Truman	Bess Wallace	1885, Mo.	1919	1982	—	1
Eisenhower	Mamie Geneva Doud	1896, Iowa	1916	1979	2	—
Kennedy	Jacqueline Lee Bouvier	1929, N.Y.	1953	—	2	1
L. B. Johnson	Claudia Alta "Lady Bird" Taylor	1912, Tex.	1934	—	—	2
Nixon	Thelma Catherine "Pat" Ryan	1912, Nev.	1940	—	—	2
Ford	Mrs. Elizabeth "Betty" Bloomer Warren	1918, Ill.	1948	—	3	1
Carter	Rosalynn Smith	1928, Ga.	1946	—	3	1
Reagan	Jane Wyman	1914, Mo.	1940[2]	—	1[3]	1
	Nancy Davis	1923, N.Y.	1952	—	1	1

1. Includes children who died in infancy. 2. Divorced in 1948. 3. Adopted.

Elections

How a President is Nominated and Elected

The National Conventions of both major parties are held during the summer of a presidential-election year. Earlier, each party selects delegates by primaries, conventions, committees, etc.

For their 1984 National Convention, the Republicans allowed each state a base of 6 delegates at large; the District of Columbia, 14; Puerto Rico, 14; Guam and the Virgin Islands, 4 each. In addition, each state received 3 district delegates for each of its Representatives in the House. This did not apply to the District of Columbia, Puerto Rico, Guam and the Virgin Islands.

Each state was awarded additional delegates at large on the basis of having supported the Republican candidate for President in 1980 and electing Republican candidates for Senator, Governor, and U.S. Representative in the 1980 and 1982 elections.

The number of delegates at the 1984 convention, held in Dallas starting August 20, was 2,234.

Following was the apportionment of delegates:

Alabama	38	Florida	82	Kentucky	37	Montana	20	Ohio	89	Texas	109
Alaska	18	Georgia	37	Louisiana	41	Nebraska	24	Oklahoma	35	Utah	26
Arizona	32	Guam	4	Maine	20	Nevada	22	Oregon	32	Vermont	19
Arkansas	29	Hawaii	14	Maryland	31	N.H.	22	Pa.	98	V.I.	4
California	176	Idaho	21	Mass.	52	N. Jersey	64	P.R.	14	Virginia	50
Colorado	35	Illinois	93	Michigan	77	New Mexico	24	R.I.	14	Washington	43
Connecticut	35	Indiana	52	Minnesota	32	New York	136	S.C.	35	W. Va.	19
Delaware	19	Iowa	37	Mississippi	30	N.C.	53	S.D.	19	Wisconsin	46
D.C.	14	Kansas	32	Missouri	47	N.D.	18	Tennessee	46	Wyoming	18

The Democrats also based the number of delegates on a state's showing in the 1980 and 1982 elections. At the 1984 convention, held in San Francisco starting July 16, there were 3,923[1] delegates casting votes. Following is the apportionment by states:

Alabama	62	Florida	143	Kentucky	63	Montana	25	Ohio	175	Texas	200
Alaska	14	Georgia	82	Louisiana	68	Nebraska	30	Oklahoma	53	Utah	27
Arizona	39	Guam	7	Maine	27	Nevada	20	Oregon	50	Vermont	17
Arkansas	42	Hawaii	27	Maryland	74	N. H.	22	Pa.	195	V.I.	6
California	345	Idaho	22	Mass.	116	New Jersey	122	P.R.	53	Virginia	78
Colorado	51	Illinois	194	Michigan	155	New Mexico	28	R.I.	27	Washington	70
Connecticut	60	Indiana	88	Minnesota	86	New York	285	S.C.	48	W. Va.	44
Delaware	18	Iowa	58	Mississippi	43	N.C.	88	S.D.	19	Wisconsin	89
D. C.	19	Kansas	44	Missouri	86	N.D.	18	Tennessee	76	Wyoming	15

1. Includes five votes for Democrats abroad and five for the Latin America Regional Democratic Party.

The Conventions

At each convention, a temporary chairman is chosen. After a credentials committee seats the delegates, a permanent chairman is elected. The convention then votes on a platform, drawn up by the platform committee.

By the third or fourth day, presidential nominations begin. The chairman calls the roll of states alphabetically. A state may place a candidate in nomination or yield to another state.

Voting, again alphabetically by roll call of states, begins after all nominations have been made and seconded. A simple majority is required in each party, although this may require many ballots.

Finally, the vice-presidential candidate is selected. Although there is no law saying that the candidates *must* come from different states, it is, practically, necessary for this to be the case. Otherwise, according to the Constitution (*see* Amendment XII), electors from that state could vote for only one of the candidates and would have to cast their other vote for some person of another state. This could result in a presidential candidate's receiving a majority electoral vote and his running mate's failing to.

The Electoral College

The next step in the process is the nomination of electors in each state, according to its laws. These electors must not be Federal office holders. In the November election, the voters cast their votes for electors, not for President. In some states, the ballots include only the names of the presidential and vice-presidential candidates; in others, they include only names of the electors. Nowadays, it is rare for electors to be split between parties. The last such occurrence was in North Carolina in 1968[1]; the last before that, in Tennessee in 1948. On three occasions (1824, 1876, and 1888), the presidential candidate with the largest popular vote failed to obtain an electoral-vote majority.

Each state has as many electors as it has Senators and Representatives. For the 1976 election, the total electors were 538, based on 100 Senators, 435 Representatives, plus 3 electoral votes from the District of Columbia as a result of the 23rd Amendment to the Constitution.

On the first Monday after the second Wednesday in December, the electors cast their votes in their respective state capitols. Constitutionally they may vote for someone other than the party candidate but usually they do not since they are pledged to one party and its candidate on the ballot. Should the presidential or vice-presidential candidate die between the November election and the December meetings, the electors pledged to vote for him could vote for whomever they pleased. However, it seems certain that the national committee would attempt to get an agreement among the state party leaders for a replacement candidate.

The votes of the electors, certified by the states, are sent to Congress, where the president of the Senate opens the certificates and has them counted in the presence of both Houses on January 6. The new President is inaugurated at noon on January 20.

Should no candidate receive a majority of the electoral vote for President, the House of Representatives chooses a President from among the three highest candidates, voting, not as individuals, but as states, with a majority (now 26) needed to elect. Should no vice-presidential candidate obtain the majority, the Senate, voting as individuals, chooses from the highest two.

1. In 1956, 1 of Alabama's 11 electoral votes was cast for Walter B. Jones. In 1960, 6 of Alabama's 11 electoral votes and 1 of Oklahoma's 8 electoral votes were cast for Harry Flood Byrd. (Byrd also received all 8 of Mississippi's electoral votes.)

National Political Conventions Since 1856

Opening date	Party	Where held	Opening date	Party	Where held
June 17, 1856	Republican	Philadelphia	June 10, 1924	Republican	Cleveland
June 2, 1856	Democratic	Cincinnati	June 24, 1924[2]	Democratic	New York City
May 16, 1860	Republican	Chicago	June 12, 1928	Republican	Kansas City
April 23, 1860	Democratic	Charleston and Baltimore	June 26, 1928	Democratic	Houston
			June 14, 1932	Republican	Chicago
June 7, 1864	Republican[1]	Baltimore	June 27, 1932	Democratic	Chicago
Aug. 29, 1864	Democratic	Chicago	June 9, 1936	Republican	Cleveland
May 20, 1868	Republican	Chicago	June 23, 1936	Democratic	Philadelphia
July 4, 1868	Democratic	New York City	June 24, 1940	Republican	Philadelphia
June 5, 1872	Republican	Philadelphia	July 15, 1940	Democratic	Chicago
June 9, 1872	Democratic	Baltimore	June 26, 1944	Republican	Chicago
June 14, 1876	Republican	Cincinnati	July 19, 1944	Democratic	Chicago
June 28, 1876	Democratic	St. Louis	June 21, 1948	Republican	Philadelphia
June 2, 1880	Republican	Chicago	July 12, 1948	Democratic	Philadelphia
June 23, 1880	Democratic	Cincinnati	July 17, 1948	([3])	Birmingham
June 3, 1884	Republican	Chicago	July 22, 1948	Progressive	Philadelphia
July 11, 1884	Democratic	Chicago	July 7, 1952	Republican	Chicago
June 19, 1888	Republican	Chicago	July 21, 1952	Democratic	Chicago
June 6, 1888	Democratic	St. Louis	Aug. 20, 1956	Republican	San Francisco
June 7, 1892	Republican	Minneapolis	Aug. 13, 1956	Democratic	Chicago
June 21, 1892	Democratic	Chicago	July 25, 1960	Republican	Chicago
June 16, 1896	Republican	St. Louis	July 11, 1960	Democratic	Los Angeles
July 7, 1896	Democratic	Chicago	July 13, 1964	Republican	San Francisco
June 19, 1900	Republican	Philadelphia	Aug. 24, 1964	Democratic	Atlantic City
July 4, 1900	Democratic	Kansas City	Aug. 5, 1968	Republican	Miami Beach
June 21, 1904	Republican	Chicago	Aug. 26, 1968	Democratic	Chicago
July 6, 1904	Democratic	St. Louis	July 10, 1972	Democratic	Miami Beach
June 16, 1908	Republican	Chicago	Aug. 21, 1972	Republican	Miami Beach
July 7, 1908	Democratic	Denver	July 12, 1976	Democratic	New York City
June 18, 1912	Republican	Chicago	Aug. 16, 1976	Republican	Kansas City, Mo.
June 25, 1912	Democratic	Baltimore	Aug. 11, 1980	Democratic	New York City
June 7, 1916	Republican	Chicago	July 14, 1980	Republican	Detroit
June 14, 1916	Democratic	St. Louis	Aug. 20, 1984	Republican	Dallas
June 8, 1920	Republican	Chicago	July 16, 1984	Democratic	San Francisco
June 28, 1920	Democratic	San Francisco			

1. The Convention adopted name Union party to attract War Democrats and others favoring prosecution of war. 2. In session until July 10, 1924. 3. States' Rights delegates from 13 Southern states.

National Committee Chairmen Since 1944

Chairman and (state)	Term	Chairman and (state)	Term
REPUBLICAN		**DEMOCRATIC**	
Herbert Brownell, Jr. (N.Y.)	1944–46	Robert E. Hannegan (Mo.)	1944–47
Carroll Reece (Tenn.)	1946–48	J. Howard McGrath (R.I.)	1947–49
Hugh D. Scott, Jr. (Pa.)	1948–49	William M. Boyle, Jr. (Mo.)	1949–51
Guy G. Gabrielson (N.J.)	1949–52	Frank E. McKinney (Ind.)	1951–52
Arthur E. Summerfield (Mich.)	1952–53	Stephen A. Mitchell (Ill.)	1952–54
Wesley Roberts (Kan.)	1953–	Paul M. Butler (Ind.)	1955–60
Leonard W. Hall (N.Y.)	1953–57	Henry M. Jackson (Wash.)	1960–61
Meade Alcorn (Conn.)	1957–59	John M. Bailey (Conn.)	1961–68
Thruston B. Morton (Ky.)	1959–61	Lawrence F. O'Brien (Mass.)	1968–69
William E. Miller (N.Y.)	1961–64	Fred R. Harris (Okla.)	1969–70
Dean Burch (Ariz.)	1964–65	Lawrence F. O'Brien (Mass.)	1970–72
Ray C. Bliss (Ohio)	1965–69	Jean Westwood (Utah)	1972–
Rogers C. B. Morton (Md.)	1969–71	Robert S. Strauss (Tex.)	1972–77
Robert Dole (Kan.)	1971–73	Kenneth M. Curtis (Me.)	1977–
George H. Bush (Tex.)	1973–74	John C. White (Tex.)	1977–81
Mary Louise Smith (Iowa)	1974–77	Charles T. Manatt (Calif.)	1981–
William E. Brock III (Tenn.)	1977–81		
Richard Richards (Utah)	1981–83		
Frank J. Fahrenkopf, Jr. (Nevada)	1983–		

Republican National Committee: 310 First St., S.E., Washington, D. C. 20003.
Democratic National Committee: 1625 Massachusetts Ave., N.W., Washington, D.C. 20036.

Presidential Elections, 1789 to 1980

For the original method of electing the President and the Vice President (elections of 1789, 1792, 1796, and 1800), see Article II, Section 1, of the Constitution. The election of 1804 was the first one in which the electors voted for President and Vice President on separate ballots. (See Amendment XII to the Constitution.)

Year	Presidential candidates	Party	Electoral vote
1789[1]	George Washington	(no party)	69
	John Adams	(no party)	34
	Scattering	(no party)	35
	Votes not cast		8
1792	George Washington	Federalist	132
	John Adams	Federalist	77
	George Clinton	Anti-Federalist	50
	Thomas Jefferson	Anti-Federalist	4
	Aaron Burr	Anti-Federalist	1
	Votes not cast		6
1796	John Adams	Federalist	71
	Thomas Jefferson	Dem.-Rep.	68
	Thomas Pinckney	Federalist	59
	Aaron Burr	Dem.-Rep.	30
	Scattering		48
1800[2]	Thomas Jefferson	Dem.-Rep.	73
	Aaron Burr	Dem.-Rep.	73
	John Adams	Federalist	65
	Charles C. Pinckney	Federalist	64
	John Jay	Federalist	1

Year	Presidential candidates	Party	Electoral vote	Vice-presidential candidates	Party	Electoral vote
1804	Thomas Jefferson	Dem.-Rep.	162	George Clinton	Dem.-Rep.	162
	Charles C. Pinckney	Federalist	14	Rufus King	Federalist	14
1808	James Madison	Dem.-Rep.	122	George Clinton	Dem.-Rep.	113
	Charles C. Pinckney	Federalist	47	Rufus King	Federalist	47
	George Clinton	Dem.-Rep.	6	John Langdon	Ind. (no party)	9
	Votes not cast		1	James Madison	Dem.-Rep.	3
				James Monroe	Dem.-Rep.	3
				Votes not cast		1
1812	James Madison	Dem.-Rep.	128	Elbridge Gerry	Dem.-Rep.	131
	De Witt Clinton	Federalist	89	Jared Ingersoll	Federalist	86
	Votes not cast		1	Votes not cast		1
1816	James Monroe	Dem.-Rep.	183	Daniel D. Tompkins	Dem.-Rep.	183
	Rufus King	Federalist	34	John E. Howard	Federalist	22
	Votes not cast		4	James Ross	Ind. (no party)	5
				John Marshall	Federalist	4
				Robert G. Harper	Ind. (no party)	3
				Votes not cast		4
1820	James Monroe	Dem-Rep	231	Daniel D. Tompkins	Dem.-Rep.	218
	John Quincy Adams	Ind. (no party)	1	Richard Stockton	Ind. (no party)	8
	Votes not cast		3	Daniel Rodney	Ind. (no party)	4
				Richard Rush	Ind. (no party)	1
				Robert G. Harper	Ind. (no party)	1
				Votes not cast		3
1824[3]	John Quincy Adams	(no party)	84	John C. Calhoun	(no party)	182
	Andrew Jackson	(no party)	99	Nathan Sanford	(no party)	30
	William H. Crawford	(no party)	41	Nathaniel Macon	(no party)	24
	Henry Clay	(no party)	37	Andrew Jackson	(no party)	13
				Martin Van Buren	(no party)	9
				Henry Clay	(no party)	2
				Votes not cast		1
1828	Andrew Jackson	Democratic	178	John C. Calhoun	Democratic	171
	John Quincy Adams	Natl. Rep.	83	Richard Rush	Natl. Rep.	83
				William Smith	Democratic	7
1832	Andrew Jackson	Democratic	219	Martin Van Buren	Democratic	189
	Henry Clay	Natl. Rep.	49	John Sergeant	Natl. Rep.	49
	John Floyd	Ind. (no party)	11	Henry Lee	Ind. (no party)	11
	William Wirt	Antimasonic[4]	7	Amos Ellmaker	Antimasonic	7
	Votes not cast		2	William Wilkins	Ind. (no party)	30
				Votes not cast		2

Year	Presidential candidates	Party	Electoral vote	Vice-presidential candidates	Party	Electoral vote
1836	Martin Van Buren	Democratic	170	Richard M. Johnson[5]	Democratic	147
	William H. Harrison	Whig	73	Francis Granger	Whig	77
	Hugh L. White	Whig	26	John Tyler	Whig	47
	Daniel Webster	Whig	14	William Smith	Ind. (no party)	23
	W. P. Mangum	Ind. (no party)	11			
1840	William H. Harrison[6]	Whig	234	John Tyler	Whig	234
	Martin Van Buren	Democratic	60	Richard M. Johnson	Democratic	48
				L. W. Tazewell	Ind. (no party)	11
				James K. Polk	Democratic	1
1844	James K. Polk	Democratic	170	George M. Dallas	Democratic	170
	Henry Clay	Whig	105	Theo. Frelinghuysen	Whig	105
1848	Zachary Taylor[7]	Whig	163	Millard Fillmore	Whig	163
	Lewis Cass	Democratic	127	William O. Butler	Democratic	127
1852	Franklin Pierce	Democratic	254	William R. King	Democratic	254
	Winfield Scott	Whig	42	William A. Graham	Whig	42
1856	James Buchanan	Democratic	174	John C. Breckinridge	Democratic	174
	John C. Fremont	Republican	114	William L. Dayton	Republican	114
	Millard Fillmore	American[8]	8	A. J. Donelson	American[8]	8
1860	Abraham Lincoln	Republican	180	Hannibal Hamlin	Republican	180
	John C. Breckinridge	Democratic	72	Joseph Lane	Democratic	72
	John Bell	Const. Union	39	Edward Everett	Const. Union	39
	Stephen A. Douglas	Democratic	12	H. V. Johnson	Democratic	12
1864	Abraham Lincoln[9]	Union[10]	212	Andrew Johnson	Union[15]	212
	George B. McClellan	Democratic	21	G. H. Pendleton	Democratic	21
1868	Ulysses S. Grant	Republican	214	Schuyler Colfax	Republican	214
	Horatio Seymour	Democratic	80	Francis P. Blair, Jr.	Democratic	80
	Votes not counted[11]		23	Votes not counted[11]		23

Year	Presidential candidates	Party	Electoral vote	Popular vote	Vice-presidential candidates and party
1872	Ulysses S. Grant	Republican	286	3,597,132	Henry Wilson—R
	Horace Greeley	Dem., Liberal Rep.	([12])	2,834,125	B. Gratz Brown—D, LR—(47)
	Thomas A. Hendricks	Democratic	42		Scattering—(19)
	B. Gratz Brown	Dem., Liberal Rep.	18		Votes not counted—(14)
	Charles J. Jenkins	Democratic	2		
	David Davis	Democratic	1		
	Votes not counted		17		
1876[13]	Rutherford B. Hayes	Republican	185	4,033,768	William A. Wheeler—R
	Samuel J. Tilden	Democratic	184	4,285,992	Thomas A. Hendricks—D
	Peter Cooper	Greenback	0	81,737	Samuel F. Cary—G
1880	James A. Garfield[14]	Republican	214	4,449,053	Chester A. Arthur—R
	Winfield S. Hancock	Democratic	155	4,442,035	William H. English—D
	James B. Weaver	Greenback	0	308,578	B. J. Chambers—G
1884	Grover Cleveland	Democratic	219	4,911,017	Thomas A. Hendricks—D
	James G. Blaine	Republican	182	4,848,334	John A. Logan—R
	Benjamin F. Butler	Greenback	0	175,370	A. M. West—G
	John P. St. John	Prohibition	0	150,369	William Daniel—P
1888	Benjamin Harrison	Republican	233	5,440,216	Levi P. Morton—R
	Grover Cleveland	Democratic	168	5,538,233	A. G. Thurman—D
	Clinton B. Fisk	Prohibition	0	249,506	John A. Brooks—P
	Alson J. Streeter	Union Labor	0	146,935	Charles E. Cunningham—UL
1892	Grover Cleveland	Democratic	277	5,556,918	Adlai E. Stevenson—D
	Benjamin Harrison	Republican	145	5,176,108	Whitelaw Reid—R
	James B. Weaver	People's[15]	22	1,041,028	James G. Field—Peo
	John Bidwell	Prohibition	0	264,133	James B. Cranfill—P

	Presidential candidates	Party	Electoral vote	Popular vote	Vice-presidential candidates and party
	Lyndon B. Johnson	Democratic	486	43,129,484	Hubert H. Humphrey—D
	Barry M. Goldwater	Republican	52	27,178,188	William E. Miller—R
	Richard M. Nixon	Republican	301	31,785,480	Spiro T. Agnew—R
	Hubert H. Humphrey	Democratic	191	31,275,166	Edmund S. Muskie—D
	George C. Wallace	American Independent	46	9,906,473	Curtis F. LeMay—AI
	Richard M. Nixon[23]	Republican	520[24]	47,169,911	Spiro T. Agnew—R
	George McGovern	Democratic	17	29,170,383	Sargent Shriver—D
	John G. Schmitz	American	0	1,099,482	Thomas J. Anderson—A
5	Jimmy Carter	Democratic	297	40,830,763	Walter F. Mondale—D
	Gerald R. Ford	Republican	240[25]	39,147,973	Robert J. Dole—R
	Eugene J. McCarthy	Independent	0	756,631	None
0	Ronald Reagan	Republican	489	43,899,248	George Bush—R
	Jimmy Carter	Democratic	49	36,481,435	Walter F. Mondale—D
	John B. Anderson	Independent	0	5,719,437	Patrick J. Lucey—I

nly 10 states participated in the election. The New York legislature chose no electors, and North Carolina and Rhode Island not yet ratified the Constitution. 2. As Jefferson and Burr were tied, the House of Representatives chose the President. vote by states, 10 votes were cast for Jefferson, 4 for Burr; 2 votes were not cast. 3. As no candidate had an electoral-vote ority, the House of Representatives chose the President from the first three. In a vote by states, 13 votes were cast for ams, 7 for Jackson, and 4 for Crawford. 4. The Antimasonic Party on Sept. 26, 1831, was the first party to hold a nominating vention to choose candidates for President and Vice-President. 5. As Johnson did not have an electoral-vote majority, the ate chose him 33–14 over Granger, the others being legally out of the race. 6. Harrison died April 4, 1841, and Tyler ceeded him April 6. 7. Taylor died July 9, 1850, and Fillmore succeeded him July 10. 8. Also known as the Know-Nothing ty. 9. Lincoln died April 15, 1865, and Johnson succeeded him the same day. 10. Name adopted by the Republican National nvention of 1864. Johnson was a War Democrat. 11. 23 Southern electoral votes were excluded. 12. See Election of 1872 *Unusual Voting Results* under Elections, Presidential, in Index. 13. See Election of 1876 in *Unusual Voting Results* under ctions, Presidential, in Index. 14. Garfield died Sept. 19, 1881, and Arthur succeeded him Sept. 20. 15. Members of Peo-'s Party were called Populists. 16. McKinley died Sept. 14, 1901, and Roosevelt succeeded him the same day. 17. James Sherman, Republican candidate for Vice President, died Oct. 30, 1912, and the Republican electoral votes were cast for tler. 18. Harding died Aug. 2, 1923, and Coolidge succeeded him Aug. 3. 19. Roosevelt died April 12, 1945, and Truman cceeded him the same day. 20. One electoral vote from Alabama was cast for Walter B. Jones. 21. Sen. Harry F. Byrd received electoral votes. 22. Kennedy died Nov. 22, 1963, and Johnson succeeded him the same day. 23. Nixon resigned Aug. 1974, and Gerald R. Ford succeeded him the same day. 24. One electoral vote from Virginia was cast for John Hospers, ertarian Party. 25. One electoral vote from Washington was cast for Ronald Reagan.

Characteristics of Voters in 1980 Presidential Election

(in millions)

haracteristic	Persons of voting age	Persons reporting they voted: Total	Persons reporting they voted: Percent	Persons reporting they did not vote
ale	74,082	43,753	59.1	30,329
emale	83,003	49,312	59.4	33,691
Vhite	137,676	83,855	60.9	53,821
lack	16,423	8,287	50.5	8,136
panish origin[1]	8,210	2,453	29.9	5,757
ge: 18–20	12,274	4,387	35.7	7,887
21–24	15,864	6,838	43.1	9,026
25–34	35,733	19,498	54.6	16,235
35–44	25,552	16,460	64.4	9,092
45–54	22,495	15,174	67.5	7,321
55–64	21,074	15,031	71.3	6,043
65–74	15,324	10,622	69.3	4,702
75 and over	8,770	5,055	57.6	3,715

Characteristic	Persons of voting age	Persons reporting they voted: Total	Persons reporting they voted: Percent	Persons reporting they did not vote
Residence:				
Metropolitan	106,627	62,703	58.8	43,924
Nonmetropolitan	50,459	30,363	60.2	20,096
North and West	106,525	64,963	61.0	41,560
South	50,561	28,103	55.6	22,458
Education:				
8 years or less	22,656	9,643	42.6	13,012
9–11 years	22,477	10,246	45.6	12,232
12 years	61,165	35,998	58.9	25,167
More than 12	50,787	37,179	73.2	13,608
Employed	95,041	58,778	61.8	36,262
Unemployed	6,893	2,838	41.2	4,055
Not in labor force	55,151	31,449	57.0	23,702
Total	**157,085**	**93,066**	**59.2**	**64,020**

ersons of Spanish origin may be of any race. *Source:* Department of Commerce, Bureau of the Census.

Facts About Elections

ndidate with highest popular vote: Nixon (1972), 47,169,911.

ndidate with highest electoral vote: F. D. Roosevelt (1936), 523.

ndidate carrying most states: Nixon (1972), 49.

Candidate running most times: Norman Thomas, 6 (1928, 1932, 1936, 1940, 1944, 1948).

Candidate elected, defeated, then reelected: Cleveland (1884, 1888, 1892).

Year	Presidential candidates	Party	Electoral vote	Popular vote	Vice-presidential candidates
1896	William McKinley	Republican	271	7,035,638	Garret A. Hoba
	William J. Bryan	Dem., People's[15]	176	6,467,946	Arthur Sewall—
					Thomas E. Wat
	John M. Palmer	Natl. Dem.	0	133,148	Simon B. Buckn
	Joshua Levering	Prohibition	0	132,007	Hale Johnson—
1900	William McKinley[16]	Republican	292	7,219,530	Theodore Roose
	William J. Bryan	Dem., People's[15]	155	6,358,071	Adlai E. Stevens
	Eugene V. Debs	Social Democratic	0	94,768	Job Harriman—S
1904	Theodore Roosevelt	Republican	336	7,628,834	Charles W. Fairba
	Alton B. Parker	Democratic	140	5,084,491	Henry G. Davis—
	Eugene V. Debs	Socialist	0	402,400	Benjamin Hanford
1908	William H. Taft	Republican	321	7,679,006	James S. Sherman
	William J. Bryan	Democratic	162	6,409,106	John W. Kern—D
	Eugene V. Debs	Socialist	0	402,820	Benjamin Hanford-
1912	Woodrow Wilson	Democratic	435	6,286,214	Thomas R. Marshal
	Theodore Roosevelt	Progressive	88	4,126,020	Hiram Johnson—Pr
	William H. Taft	Republican	8	3,483,922	Nicholas M. Butler-
	Eugene V. Debs	Socialist	0	897,011	Emil Seidel—S
1916	Woodrow Wilson	Democratic	277	9,129,606	Thomas R. Marshall-
	Charles E. Hughes	Republican	254	8,538,221	Charles W. Fairbanks
	A. L. Benson	Socialist	0	585,113	G. R. Kirkpatrick—S
1920	Warren G. Harding[18]	Republican	404	16,152,200	Calvin Coolidge—R
	James M. Cox	Democratic	127	9,147,353	Franklin D. Roosevelt—D
	Eugene V. Debs	Socialist	0	917,799	Seymour Stedman—S
1924	Calvin Coolidge	Republican	382	15,725,016	Charles G. Dawes—R
	John W. Davis	Democratic	136	8,385,586	Charles W. Bryan—D
	Robert M. LaFollette	Progressive, Socialist	13	4,822,856	Burton K. Wheeler—Prog S
1928	Herbert Hoover	Republican	444	21,392,190	Charles Curtis—R
	Alfred E. Smith	Democratic	87	15,016,443	Joseph T. Robinson—D
	Norman Thomas	Socialist	0	267,420	James H. Maurer—S
1932	Franklin D. Roosevelt	Democratic	472	22,821,857	John N. Garner—D
	Herbert Hoover	Republican	59	15,761,841	Charles Curtis—R
	Norman Thomas	Socialist	0	884,781	James H. Maurer—S
1936	Franklin D. Roosevelt	Democratic	523	27,751,597	John N. Garner—D
	Alfred M. Landon	Republican	8	16,679,583	Frank Knox—R
	Norman Thomas	Socialist	0	187,720	George Nelson—S
1940	Franklin D. Roosevelt	Democratic	449	27,244,160	Henry A. Wallace—D
	Wendell L. Willkie	Republican	82	22,305,198	Charles L. McNary—R
	Norman Thomas	Socialist	0	99,557	Maynard C. Krueger—S
1944	Franklin D. Roosevelt[19]	Democratic	432	25,602,504	Harry S. Truman—D
	Thomas E. Dewey	Republican	99	22,006,285	John W. Bricker—R
	Norman Thomas	Socialist	0	80,518	Darlington Hoopes—S
1948	Harry S. Truman	Democratic	303	24,179,345	Alben W. Barkley—D
	Thomas E. Dewey	Republican	189	21,991,291	Earl Warren—R
	J. Strom Thurmond	States' Rights Dem.	39	1,176,125	Fielding L. Wright—SR
	Henry A. Wallace	Progressive	0	1,157,326	Glen Taylor—Prog
	Norman Thomas	Socialist	0	139,572	Tucker P. Smith—S
1952	Dwight D. Eisenhower	Republican	442	33,936,234	Richard M. Nixon—R
	Adlai E. Stevenson	Democratic	89	27,314,992	John J. Sparkman—D
1956	Dwight D. Eisenhower	Republican	457	35,590,472	Richard M. Nixon—R
	Adlai E. Stevenson	Democratic	73[20]	26,022,752	Estes Kefauver—D
1960	John F. Kennedy[22]	Democratic	303	34,226,731	Lyndon B. Johnson—D
	Richard M. Nixon	Republican	219[21]	34,108,157	Henry Cabot Lodge—

Presidential Election of 1968

Principal Candidates for President and Vice President
Republican: Richard M. Nixon; Spiro T. Agnew
Democratic: Hubert H. Humphrey; Edmund S. Muskie
American Independent Party: George C. Wallace; Curtis E. LeMay

		Nixon	Humphrey	Wallace		Electoral Vote			Votes at Natl. Convs.	
State	**Total**	**Rep.**	**Dem.**	**Am. Ind.**	**Plurality**	**R**	**D**	**A**	**Dem.**	**Rep.**
Alabama	1,049,922	146,923	196,579 [1]	691,425 [2]	494,846 A	—	—	10	32	26
Alaska	83,035	37,600	35,411	10,024	2,189 R	3	—	—	22	12
Arizona	486,936	266,721	170,514	46,573	96,207 R	5	—	—	19	16
Arkansas	619,969	190,759	188,228	240,982	50,223 A	—	—	6	33	18
California	7,251,587	3,467,664	3,244,318	487,270	223,346 R	40	—	—	174	86
Colorado	811,199	409,345	335,174	60,813	74,171 R	6	—	—	35	18
Connecticut	1,256,232	556,721	621,561	76,650	64,840 D	—	8	—	44	16
Delaware	214,367	96,714	89,194	28,459	7,520 R	3	—	—	22	12
D.C.	170,578	31,012	139,566	—	108,554 D	—	3	—	23	9
Florida	2,187,805	886,804	676,794	624,207	210,010 R	14	—	—	63	34
Georgia	1,250,266	380,111	334,440	535,550	155,439 A	—	—	12	43	30
Hawaii	236,218	91,425	141,324	3,469	49,899 D	—	4	—	26	14
Idaho	291,183	165,369	89,273	36,541	76,096 R	4	—	—	25	14
Illinois	4,619,749	2,174,774	2,039,814	390,958	134,960 R	26	—	—	118	58
Indiana	2,123,597	1,067,885	806,659	243,108	261,226 R	13	—	—	63	26
Iowa	1,167,931	619,106	476,699	66,422	142,407 R	9	—	—	46	24
Kansas	872,783	478,674	302,996	88,921	175,678 R	7	—	—	38	20
Kentucky	1,055,893	462,411	397,541	193,098	64,870 R	9	—	—	46	24
Louisiana	1,097,450	257,535	309,615	530,300	220,685 A	—	—	10	36	26
Maine	392,936	169,254	217,312	6,370	48,058 D	—	4	—	27	14
Maryland	1,235,039	517,995	538,310	178,734	20,315 D	—	10	—	49	26
Massachusetts	2,331,752	766,844	1,469,218	87,088	702,374 D	—	14	—	72	34
Michigan	3,306,250	1,370,665	1,593,082	331,968	222,417 D	—	21	—	96	48
Minnesota	1,588,506	658,643	857,738	68,931	199,095 D	—	10	—	52	26
Mississippi	654,509	88,516	150,644	415,349	264,705 A	—	—	7	24	20
Missouri	1,809,502	811,932	791,444	206,126	20,488 R	12	—	—	60	24
Montana	274,404	138,835	114,117	20,015	24,718 R	4	—	—	26	14
Nebraska	536,851	321,163	170,784	44,904	150,379 R	5	—	—	30	16
Nevada	154,218	73,188	60,598	20,432	12,590 R	3	—	—	22	12
New Hampshire	297,298	154,903	130,589	11,173	24,314 R	4	—	—	26	8
New Jersey	2,875,395	1,325,467	1,264,206	262,187	61,261 R	17	—	—	82	40
New Mexico	327,350	169,692	130,081	25,737	39,611 R	4	—	—	26	14
New York	6,791,688	3,007,932	3,378,470 [3]	358,864	370,538 D	—	43	—	190	92
North Carolina	1,587,493	627,192	464,113	496,188	131,004 R	12	—	1	59	26
North Dakota	247,882	138,669	94,769	14,244	43,900 R	4	—	—	25	8
Ohio	3,959,698	1,791,014	1,700,586	467,495	90,428 R	26	—	—	115	58
Oklahoma	943,086	449,697	301,658	191,731	148,039 R	8	—	—	41	22
Oregon	819,622	408,433	358,866	49,683	49,567 R	6	—	—	35	18
Pennsylvania	4,747,928	2,090,017	2,259,405	378,582	169,388 D	—	29	—	130	64
Rhode Island	385,000	122,359	246,518	15,678	124,159 D	—	4	—	27	14
South Carolina	666,978	254,062	197,486	215,430	38,632 R	8	—	—	28	22
South Dakota	281,264	149,841	118,023	13,400	31,818 R	4	—	—	26	14
Tennessee	1,248,617	472,592	351,233	424,792	47,800 R	11	—	—	51	28
Texas	3,079,406	1,227,844	1,266,804	584,269	38,960 D	—	25	—	104	56
Utah	422,568	238,728	156,665	26,906	82,063 R	4	—	—	26	8
Vermont	161,404	85,142	70,255	5,104	14,887 R	3	—	—	22	12
Virginia	1,361,491	590,319	442,387	321,833	147,932 R	12	—	—	54	24
Washington	1,304,281	588,510	616,037	96,990	27,527 D	—	9	—	47	24
West Virginia	754,206	307,555	374,091	72,560	66,536 D	—	7	—	38	14
Wisconsin	1,691,538	809,997	748,804	127,835	61,193 R	12	—	—	59	30
Wyoming	127,205	70,927	45,173	11,105	25,754 R	3	—	—	22	12
Total	**73,212,065**	**31,785,480**	**31,275,166**	**9,906,473**	**510,314 R**	**301**	**191**	**46**	**2,622** [4]	**1,333** [5]

1. This vote, cast for Humphrey, is a combination of National Democratic (54,144) and Independent Democratic (142,435).
2. This vote for Wallace was cast as Democratic in Alabama. 3. Contains 3,066,848 Democratic and 311,622 Liberal votes.
4. Includes 23 votes allocated to U.S. territories. 5. Includes 8 votes allocated to U.S. territories.

OTHER CANDIDATES FOR PRESIDENT: New Party, Dick Gregory; Peace and Freedom Party, Eldridge Cleaver, Prohibition Party, E. Harold Munn; Socialist Labor Party, Hennings Blomen; Socialist Workers Party, Fred Halstead.

NATIONAL TOTAL OF OTHER VOTES: 244,946, from 30 states.

Source: America Votes, compiled and edited by Richard M. Scammon.

Presidential Election of 1972

Principal Candidates for President and Vice President
Republican: Richard M. Nixon; Spiro T. Agnew
Democratic: George McGovern; Sargent Shriver
American Party[1]: John G. Schmitz; Thomas J. Anderson

		Nixon	McGovern	Schmitz		Electoral vote			Votes at Natl. Convs.	
State	Total	Republican	Democratic	American	Plurality	R	D	A	Dem.	Rep.
Alabama	1,006,111	728,701	256,923	11,928	471,778 R	9	—	—	37	17
Alaska	95,219	55,349	32,967	6,903	22,382 R	3	—	—	10	12
Arizona	622,926	402,812	198,540	21,208	204,272 R	6	—	—	25	18
Arkansas	651,320	448,541	199,892	2,887	248,649 R	6	—	—	27	18
California	8,367,862	4,602,096	3,475,847	232,554	1,126,249 R	45	—	—	271	96
Colorado	953,884	597,189	329,980	17,269	267,209 R	7	—	—	36	20
Connecticut	1,384,277	810,763	555,498	17,239	255,265 R	8	—	—	51	22
Delaware	235,516	140,357	92,283	2,638	48,074 R	3	—	—	13	12
D.C.	163,421	35,226	127,627	—	92,401 D	—	3	—	15	9
Florida	2,583,283	1,857,759	718,117	—	1,139,642 R	17	—	—	81	40
Georgia	1,174,772	881,496	289,529	812	591,967 R	12	—	—	53	24
Hawaii	270,274	168,865	101,409	—	67,456 R	4	—	—	17	14
Idaho	310,379	199,384	80,826	28,869	118,558 R	4	—	—	17	14
Illinois	4,723,236	2,788,179	1,913,472	2,471	874,707 R	26	—	—	170	58
Indiana	2,125,529	1,405,154	708,568	—	696,586 R	13	—	—	76	32
Iowa	1,225,944	706,207	496,206	22,056	210,001 R	8	—	—	46	20
Kansas	916,095	619,812	270,287	21,808	349,525 R	7	—	—	35	24
Kentucky	1,067,499	676,446	371,159	17,627	305,287 R	9	—	—	47	20
Louisiana	1,051,491	686,852	298,142	52,099	388,710 R	10	—	—	44	8
Maine	417,042	256,458	160,584	—	95,874 R	4	—	—	20	26
Maryland	1,353,812	829,305	505,781	18,726	323,524 R	10	—	—	53	34
Massachusetts	2,458,756	1,112,078	1,332,540	2,877	220,462 D	—	14	—	102	48
Michigan	3,489,727	1,961,721	1,459,435	63,321	502,286 R	21	—	—	132	26
Minnesota	1,741,652	898,269	802,346	31,407	95,923 R	10	—	—	64	26
Mississippi	645,963	505,125	126,782	11,598	378,343 R	7	—	—	25	13
Missouri	1,855,803	1,153,852	697,147	—	456,705 R	12	—	—	73	30
Montana	317,603	183,976	120,197	13,430	63,779 R	4	—	—	17	14
Nebraska	576,289	406,298	169,991	—	236,307 R	5	—	—	24	16
Nevada	181,766	115,750	66,016	—	49,734 R	3	—	—	11	12
New Hampshire	334,055	213,724	116,435	3,386	97,289 R	4	—	—	18	14
New Jersey	2,997,229	1,845,502	1,102,211	34,378	743,291 R	17	—	—	109	40
New Mexico	386,241	235,606	141,084	8,767	94,522 R	4	—	—	18	14
New York	7,165,919	4,192,778	2,951,084	—	1,241,694 R	41	—	—	278	88
North Carolina	1,518,612	1,054,889	438,705	25,018	616,184 R	13	—	—	64	32
North Dakota	280,514	174,109	100,384	5,646	73,725 R	3	—	—	14	12
Ohio	4,094,787	2,441,827	1,558,889	80,067	882,938 R	25	—	—	153	56
Oklahoma	1,029,900	759,025	247,147	23,728	511,878 R	8	—	—	39	22
Oregon	927,946	486,686	392,760	46,211	93,926 R	6	—	—	34	18
Pennsylvania	4,592,106	2,714,521	1,796,951	70,593	917,570 R	27	—	—	182	60
Rhode Island	415,808	220,383	194,645	25	25,738 R	4	—	—	22	8
South Carolina	673,960	477,044	186,824	10,075	290,220 R	8	—	—	32	22
South Dakota	307,415	166,476	139,945	—	26,531 R	4	—	—	17	14
Tennessee	1,201,182	813,147	357,293	30,373	455,854 R	10	—	—	49	26
Texas	3,471,281	2,298,896	1,154,289	6,039	1,144,607 R	26	—	—	130	52
Utah	478,476	323,643	126,284	28,549	197,359 R	4	—	—	19	14
Vermont	186,947	117,149	68,174	—	48,975 R	3	—	—	12	12
Virginia	1,457,019	988,493	438,887	19,721	549,606 R	11[2]	—	—	53	30
Washington	1,470,847	837,135	568,334	58,906	268,801 R	9	—	—	52	24
West Virginia	762,399	484,964	277,435	—	207,529 R	6	—	—	35	18
Wisconsin	1,852,890	989,430	810,174	47,525	179,256 R	11	—	—	67	18
Wyoming	145,570	100,464	44,358	748	56,106 R	3	—	—	11	12
Total	**77,718,554**	**47,169,911**	**29,170,383**	**1,099,482**	**17,999,528 R**	**520**	**17**	**0**	**3,016[3]**	**1,346[4]**

1. Known as American Independent Party and by other names in some states. 2. One Virginia elector cast vote for Libertarian Party. 3. Includes 16 votes allocated to U.S. territories. 4. Includes 11 votes allocated to U.S. territories.
OTHER CANDIDATES FOR PRESIDENT: Communist, Gus Hall, Libertarian Party, John Hospers; People's Party, Benjamin Spock; Prohibition Party, Earle H. Munn; Socialist Labor Party, Louis Fisher; Socialist Workers Party, Linda Jenness.
NATIONAL TOTALS OF OTHER VOTES: People's, 78,756; Social Workers, 66,677; Socialist Labor, 53,814; Communist, 25, 595; Prohibition, 13,505; others and scattered, 40,431.
Source: America Votes 10, compiled and edited by Richard M. Scammon.

Presidential Election of 1976

Principal Candidates for President and Vice President
Democratic: Jimmy Carter; Walter F. Mondale
Republican: Gerald R. Ford; Robert J. Dole
Independent: Eugene J. McCarthy

		Carter	Ford	McCarthy		Electoral Vote		Votes at Natl. Convs.	
State	Total	Demo.	Rep.	Ind.	Plurality	D	R	Dem.	Rep.
Alabama	1,182,850	659,170	504,070	99	155,100 D	9	—	35	37
Alaska	123,574	44,058	71,555	—	27,497 R	—	3	10	19
Arizona	742,719	295,602	418,642	19,229	123,040 R	—	6	25	29
Arkansas	767,535	498,604	267,903	639	230,701 D	6	—	26	27
California	7,867,117	3,742,284	3,882,244	58,412	139,960 R	—	45	280	167
Colorado	1,081,554	460,801	584,278	26,047	123,477 R	—	7	35	31
Connecticut	1,381,526	647,895	719,261	3,759	71,366 R	—	8	51	35
Delaware	235,834	122,596	109,831	2,437	12,765 D	3	—	12	17
D.C.	168,830	137,818	27,873	—	109,945 D	3	—	17	14
Florida	3,150,631	1,636,000	1,469,531	23,643	166,469 D	17	—	81	66
Georgia	1,467,458	979,409	483,743	991	495,666 D	12	—	50	48
Hawaii	291,301	147,375	140,003	—	7,372 D	4	—	17	19
Idaho	344,071	126,549	204,151	1,194	77,602 R	—	4	16	21
Illinois	4,718,914	2,271,295	2,364,269	55,939	92,974 R	—	26	169	101
Indiana	2,220,362	1,014,714	1,183,958	—	169,244 R	—	13	75	54
Iowa	1,279,306	619,931	632,863	20,051	12,932 R	—	8	47	36
Kansas	957,845	430,421	502,752	13,185	72,331 R	—	7	34	34
Kentucky	1,167,142	615,717	531,852	6,837	83,865 D	9	—	46	37
Louisiana	1,278,439	661,365	587,446	6,588	73,919 D	10	—	41	41
Maine	483,216	232,279	236,320	10,874	4,041 R	—	4	20	20
Maryland	1,439,897	759,612	672,661	4,541	86,951 D	10	—	53	43
Massachusetts	2,547,558	1,429,475	1,030,276	65,637	399,199 D	14	—	104	43
Michigan	3,653,749	1,696,714	1,893,742	47,905	197,028 R	—	21	133	84
Minnesota	1,949,931	1,070,440	819,395	35,490	251,045 D	10	—	65	42
Mississippi	769,361	381,309	366,846	4,074	14,463 D	7	—	24	30
Missouri	1,953,600	998,387	927,443	24,029	70,944 D	12	—	71	49
Montana	328,734	149,259	173,703	—	24,444 R	—	4	17	20
Nebraska	607,668	233,293	359,219	9,409	125,926 R	—	5	23	25
Nevada	201,876	92,479	101,273	—	8,794 R	—	3	11	18
New Hampshire	339,618	147,645	185,935	4,095	38,290 R	—	4	17	21
New Jersey	3,014,472	1,444,653	1,509,688	32,717	65,035 R	—	17	108	67
New Mexico	418,409	201,148	211,419	1,161	10,271 R	—	4	18	21
New York	6,534,170	3,389,558	3,100,791	4,303	288,767 D	41	—	274	154
North Carolina	1,678,914	927,365	741,960	780	185,405 D	13	—	61	54
North Dakota	297,188	136,078	153,470	2,952	17,392 R	—	3	13	18
Ohio	4,111,873	2,011,621	2,000,505	58,258	11,116 D	25	—	152	97
Oklahoma	1,092,251	532,442	545,708	14,101	13,266 R	—	8	37	36
Oregon	1,029,876	490,407	492,120	40,207	1,713 R	—	6	34	30
Pennsylvania	4,620,787	2,328,677	2,205,604	50,584	123,073 D	27	—	178	103
Rhode Island	411,170	227,636	181,249	479	46,387 D	4	—	22	19
South Carolina	802,583	450,807	346,149	289	104,658 D	8	—	31	36
South Dakota	300,678	147,068	151,505	—	4,437 R	—	4	17	20
Tennessee	1,476,345	825,879	633,969	5,004	191,910 D	10	—	46	43
Texas	4,071,884	2,082,319	1,953,300	20,118	129,019 D	26	—	130	100
Utah	541,198	182,110	337,908	3,907	155,798 R	—	4	18	20
Vermont	187,765	78,789	100,387	4,001	21,598 R	—	3	12	18
Virginia	1,697,094	813,896	836,554	—	22,658 R	—	12	54	51
Washington	1,555,534	717,323	777,732	36,986	60,409 R	—	8[1]	53	38
West Virginia	750,964	435,914	314,760	113	121,154 D	6	—	33	28
Wisconsin	2,104,175	1,040,232	1,004,987	34,943	35,245 D	11	—	68	45
Wyoming	156,343	62,239	92,717	624	30,478 R	—	3	10	17
Total	**81,555,889**	**40,830,763**	**39,147,793**	**756,631**	**1,682,970 D**	**297**	**240**	**3,008**[2]	**2,259**[3]

1. Ninth Washington elector cast vote for Ronald Reagan. 2. Includes 34 votes allocated to U.S. territories and Democrats abroad. 3. Includes 16 votes allocated to U.S. territories.

OTHER CANDIDATES FOR PRESIDENT: Roger L. MacBride, Libertarian; Lester G. Maddox, American Independent; Thomas J. Anderson, American; Peter Camejo, Socialist Workers; Gus Hall, Communist; Margaret Wright, People's; Lyndon LaRouche, United States Labor; Benjamin C. Bubar, Prohibition; Julius Levin, Socialist Labor; Frank P. Zeidler, Socialist.

NATIONAL TOTALS OF OTHER VOTES: Libertarian, 173,011; American Independent, 170,531; American, 160,773; Socialist Workers, 91,314; Communist, 58,992; People's, 49,024; United States Labor, 40,043; Prohibition, 15,934; Socialist Labor, 9,616; Socialist, 6,038; others and scattered, 45,366.

Source: America Votes 12, compiled and edited by Richard M. Scammon and Alice V. McGillivray.

Presidential Election of 1980

Principal Candidates for President and Vice President
Democratic: Jimmy Carter; Walter F. Mondale
Republican: Ronald Reagan; George Bush
Independent: John B. Anderson; Patrick J. Lucey

		Carter		Reagan		Anderson			Electoral vote		
State	Total	Dem.	Percent	Rep.	Percent	Independent	Percent	Plurality	D	R	I
Alabama	1,341,929	636,730	47	654,192	49	16,481	1	17,462 R	—	9	—
Alaska	157,589	41,842	27	86,112	55	11,156	7	44,270 R	—	3	—
Arizona	873,945	246,843	28	529,688	61	76,952	9	282,845 R	—	6	—
Arkansas	837,582	398,041	48	403,164	48	22,468	3	5,123 R	—	6	—
California	8,585,789	3,083,652	36	4,524,835	53	739,832	9	1,441,183 R	—	45	—
Colorado	1,184,450	368,009	31	652,264	55	130,633	11	284,255 R	—	7	—
Connecticut	1,406,285	541,732	39	677,210	48	171,807	12	135,478 R	—	8	—
Delaware	235,723	105,754	45	111,252	47	16,288	7	5,498 R	—	3	—
D.C.	173,889	130,231	75	23,313	13	16,131	9	106,918 D	3	—	—
Florida	3,686,926	1,419,475	39	2,046,951	56	189,692	5	734,394 R	—	17	—
Georgia	1,596,582	890,733	56	654,168	41	36,055	2	236,565 D	12	—	—
Hawaii	303,287	135,879	45	130,112	43	32,021	11	5,767 D	4	—	—
Idaho	437,431	110,192	25	290,699	67	27,058	6	180,507 R	—	4	—
Illinois	4,749,766	1,981,413	42	2,358,094	50	346,754	7	376,681 —	—	26	—
Indiana	2,242,033	844,197	38	1,255,656	56	111,639	5	411,459 R	—	13	—
Iowa	1,317,661	508,672	39	676,026	51	115,633	9	167,354 R	—	8	—
Kansas	979,786	326,150	33	566,812	58	68,231	7	240,662 R	—	7	—
Kentucky	1,295,627	617,417	48	635,274	49	31,127	2	17,857 R	—	9	—
Louisiana	1,548,591	708,453	46	792,853	51	26,345	2	84,400 R	—	10	—
Maine	523,134	220,974	42	238,522	46	53,450	10	17,548 R	—	4	—
Maryland	1,540,496	726,161	47	680,606	44	119,537	8	45,555 R	10	—	—
Massachusetts	2,524,630	1,053,802	42	1,056,233	42	382,539	15	2,421 R	—	14	—
Michigan	3,909,725	1,661,532	43	1,915,225	49	275,223	7	253,393 R	—	21	—
Minnesota	2,045,780	954,173	47	873,268	43	174,997	9	80,905 D	10	—	—
Mississippi	892,620	429,281	48	441,089	49	12,036	1	11,808 R	—	7	—
Missouri	2,099,824	931,182	44	1,074,181	51	77,920	4	142,999 R	—	12	—
Montana	363,952	118,032	32	206,814	57	29,281	8	88,782 R	—	4	—
Nebraska	639,533	166,424	26	419,214	66	44,854	7	252,790 R	—	5	—
Nevada	243,692	66,666	27	155,017	64	17,651	7	177,026 R	—	3	—
New Hampshire	383,999	108,864	28	221,705	58	49,693	13	112,841 R	—	4	—
New Jersey	2,975,684	1,147,364	39	1,546,557	52	234,632	8	399,193 R	—	17	—
New Mexico	456,237	167,832	37	250,770	55	29,459	6	82,938 R	—	4	—
New York	6,201,959	2,728,372	44	2,893,831	47	467,801	8	165,459 R	—	41	—
North Carolina	1,855,833	875,635	47	915,018	49	52,800	3	39,383 R	—	13	—
North Dakota	301,545	79,189	26	193,695	64	23,640	8	114,506 R	—	3	—
Ohio	4,283,603	1,752,414	41	2,206,545	52	254,472	6	454,131 R	—	25	—
Oklahoma	1,149,708	402,026	35	695,570	60	38,284	3	293,544 R	—	8	—
Oregon	1,181,516	456,890	39	571,044	48	112,389	10	114,154 R	—	6	—
Pennsylvania	4,561,501	1,937,540	42	2,261,872	50	292,921	6	324,332 R	—	27	—
Rhode Island	415,967	198,342	48	154,793	37	59,819	14	43,549 D	4	—	—
South Carolina	893,190	28,220	48	39,277	49	13,868	2	11,456 R	—	8	—
South Dakota	327,703	103,855	32	198,343	61	21,431	7	94,488 R	—	4	—
Tennessee	1,617,616	783,051	48	787,761	49	35,991	2	4,710 R	—	10	—
Texas	4,541,636	1,881,147	41	2,510,705	55	111,613	2	629,558 R	—	26	—
Utah	604,152	124,266	21	439,687	73	30,284	5	315,421 R	—	4	—
Vermont	213,299	81,952	38	94,628	44	31,761	15	12,676 R	—	3	—
Virginia	1,866,032	752,174	40	989,609	53	95,418	5	237,435 R	—	12	—
Washington	1,742,394	650,193	37	865,244	50	185,073	11	215,051 R	—	9	—
West Virginia	737,715	367,462	50	334,206	45	31,691	4	33,256 D	6	—	—
Wisconsin	2,273,221	981,584	43	1,088,845	48	160,657	7	107,261 R	—	11	—
Wyoming	176,713	49,427	28	110,700	63	12,072	7	61,273 R	—	8	—
Total	**86,495,678**	**35,481,435**	**41**	**43,899,248**	**51**	**5,719,437**	**6**	**8,417,813 R**	**49**	**489**	**—**

NATIONAL TOTALS OF OTHER CANDIDATES FOR PRESIDENT: Ed Clark, Libertarian, 920,859; Barry Commoner, Citizens, 230,377; Gus Hall, Communist, 43,871; John Rarick, American Independent, 41,172; Clifton DeBerry, Socialist Workers, 40,105; Ellen McCormack, Respect for Life, 32,319; Margaret Smith, Peace and Freedom, 18,117; Deirdre Griswold, Workers' World, 13,211; others and write-ins, 55,527. *Source:* Federal Election Commission.

1980 Election Had Lowest Voter Turnout in 32 Years

According to the Federal Election Commission, only 53.95% of the eligible voters in the country cast their ballots in the 1980 presidential election. This was the lowest since the Truman-Dewey election of 1948 when only 51.1% of the voters went to the polls.

The highest voter turnout in the last 50 years was in the Kennedy-Nixon contest of 1960 with 62.8% of the electorate participating.

Qualifications for Voting

The Supreme Court decision of March 21, 1972, declared lengthy requirements for voting in state and local elections unconstitutional and suggested that 30 days was an ample period. Most of the states have changed or eliminated their durational residency requirements to comply with the ruling, as shown.

NO DURATIONAL RESIDENCY REQUIREMENT

Alabama, Arkakansas, Connecticut,[14] Delaware,[13] District of Columbia,[17] Florida,[5] Georgia,[2] Hawaii,[2] Idaho, Iowa,[6] Louisiana,[2] Maine, Maryland, Massachusetts,[3] Missouri,[4] Nebraska,[9] New Hampshire,[18] New Mexico,[7] North Carolina, Oklahoma, South Carolina,[2] South Dakota,[10] Tennessee,[12] Texas; Virginia, West Virginia,[2] Wyoming[2]

30-DAY RESIDENCY REQUIREMENT

Alaska,[19] Arizona,[11] Illinois, Indiana, Kentucky,[2] Michigan, Mississippi, Montana, Nevada, New Jersey, New York, North Dakota,[3] Ohio, Pennsylvania, Rhode Island, Utah, Washington

OTHER

California,[20] Colorado,[1] Kansas, Minnesota[16] and Oregon,[16], 20 days; Vermont, 17 days;[15] Wisconsin, 10 days

1. 29-day for Presidential elections, 32 for all other. 2. 30-day registration requirement. 3. 10-day for Presidential elections. 4. Must be registered 28 days prior to vote. 5. 30-day registration requirement for national elections; 45-day for state elections. 6. 10-day registration requirement. 7. 42-day registration requirement. 8. Registration deadline 28 days prior to primary or state elections. 9. Registration requirement, 2nd Friday prior to elections. 10. 15-day registration requirement. 11. 50-day for state. 12. 20-day registration requirement. 13. Must reside in Delaware and register by the last day that the books are open for registration. 14. 21-day registration requirement for elections; 14-day for primaries. 15. Administrative cut-off date for processing applications. 16. Permits registration and voting on election day with approved ID. 17. Must declare residency and D.C. must process within 15 days. Registration stops 30 days before any election and until 15 days after. 18. Registration requirement, 2nd Saturday prior to elections. *Source: Information Please* questionnaires to the states. 19. If otherwise qualified but has not been a resident of the election district for at least 30 days preceding the date of a presidential election, is entitled to register and vote for presidential and vice presidential candidates. 20. Twenty-nine days before an election.

Unusual Voting Results

Election of 1872

The presidential and vice-presidential candidates of the Liberal Republicans and the northern Democrats in 1872 were Horace Greeley and B. Gratz Brown. Greeley died Nov. 29, 1872, before his 66 electors voted. In the electoral balloting for President, 63 of Greeley's votes were scattered among four other men, including Brown.

Election of 1876

In the election of 1876 Samuel J. Tilden, the Democratic candidate, received a popular majority but lacked one undisputed electoral vote to carry a clear majority of the electoral college. The crux of the problem was in the 22 electoral votes which were in dispute because Florida, Louisiana, South Carolina, and Oregon each sent in two sets of election returns. In the three southern states, Republican election boards threw out enough Democratic votes to certify the Republican candidate, Hayes. In Oregon, the Democratic governor disqualified a Republican elector, replacing him with a Democrat. Since the Senate was Republican and the House of Representatives Democratic, it seemed useless to refer the disputed returns to the two houses for solution. Instead Congress appointed an Electoral Commission with five representatives each from the Senate, the House, and the Supreme Court. All but one Justice was named, giving the Commission seven Republican and seven Democratic members. The naming of the fifth Justice was left to the other four. He was a Republican who first favored Tilden but, under pressure from his party, switched to Hayes, ensuring his election by the Commission voting 8 to 7 on party lines.

Minority Presidents

Fifteen candidates have become President of the United States with a popular vote less than 50% of the total cast. It should be noted, however, that in elections before 1872, presidential electors were not chosen by popular vote in all states. Adams' election in 1824 was by the House of Representatives, which chose him over Jackson, who had a plurality of both electoral and popular votes, but not a majority in the electoral college.

Besides Jackson in 1824, only two other candidates receiving the largest popular vote have failed to gain a majority in the electoral college—Samuel J. Tilden (D) in 1876 and Grover Cleveland (D) in 1888.

The "minority" Presidents follow:

Vote Received by Minority Presidents

Year	President	Electoral Percent	Popular vote Percent
1824	John Q. Adams	31.8	29.8
1844	James K. Polk (D)	61.8	49.3
1848	Zachary Taylor (W)	56.2	47.3
1856	James Buchanan (D)	58.7	45.3
1860	Abraham Lincoln (R)	59.4	39.9
1876	Rutherford B. Hayes (R)	50.1	47.9
1880	James A. Garfield (R)	57.9	48.3
1884	Grover Cleveland (D)	54.6	48.8
1888	Benjamin Harrison (R)	58.1	47.8
1892	Grover Cleveland (D)	62.4	46.0
1912	Woodrow Wilson (D)	81.9	41.8
1916	Woodrow Wilson (D)	52.1	49.3
1948	Harry S. Truman (D)	57.1	49.5
1960	John F. Kennedy (D)	56.4	49.7
1968	Richard M. Nixon (R)	56.1	43.4

Government Officials

Cabinet Members With Dates of Appointment

Although the Constitution made no provision for a President's advisory group, the heads of the three executive departments (State, Treasury, and War) and the Attorney General were organized by Washington into such a group; and by about 1793, the name "Cabinet" was applied to it. With the exception of the Attorney General up to 1870 and the Postmaster General from 1829 to 1872, Cabinet members have been heads of executive departments.

A Cabinet member is appointed by the President, subject to the conformation of the Senate; and as his term is not fixed, he may be replaced at any time by the President. At a change in Administration, it is customary for him to tender his resignation, but he remains in office until a successor is appointed.

The table of Cabinet members lists only those members who actually served after being duly commissioned.

The dates shown are those of appointment. "Cont." indicates that the term continued from the previous Administration for a substantial amount of time.

With the creation of the Department of Transportation in 1966, the Cabinet consisted of 12 members. This figure was reduced to 11 when the Post Office Department became an independent agency in 1970 but, with the establishment in 1977 of a Department of Energy, became 12 again. Creation of the Department of Education in 1980 raised the number to 13.

WASHINGTON

Secretary of State	Thomas Jefferson 1789
	Edmund Randolph 1794
	Timothy Pickering 1795
Secretary of the Treasury	Alexander Hamilton 1789
	Oliver Wolcott, Jr. 1795
Secretary of War	Henry Knox 1789
	Timothy Pickering 1795
	James McHenry 1796
Attorney General	Edmund Randolph 1789
	William Bradford 1794
	Charles Lee 1795

J. ADAMS

Secretary of State	Timothy Pickering (Cont.)
	John Marshall 1800
Secretary of the Treasury	Oliver Wolcott, Jr. (Cont.)
	Samuel Dexter 1801
Secretary of War	James McHenry (Cont.)
	Samuel Dexter 1800
Attorney General	Charles Lee (Cont.)
Secretary of the Navy	Benjamin Stoddert 1798

JEFFERSON

Secretary of State	James Madison 1801
Secretary of the Treasury	Samuel Dexter (Cont.)
	Albert Gailatin 1801
Secretary of War	Henry Dearborn 1801
Attorney General	Levi Lincoln 1801
	Robert Smith 1805
	John Breckinridge 1805
	Caesar A. Rodney 1807
Secretary of the Navy	Benjamin Stoddert (Cont.)
	Robert Smith 1801

MADISON

Secretary of State	Robert Smith 1809
	James Monroe 1811
Secretary of the Treasury	Albert Gallatin (Cont.)
	George W. Campbell 1814
	Alexander J. Dallas 1814
	William H. Crawford 1816
Secretary of War	William Eustis 1809
	John Armstrong 1813
	James Monroe 1814
	William H. Crawford 1815
Attorney General	Caesar A. Rodney (Cont.)
	William Pinckney 1811
	Richard Rush 1814
Secretary of the Navy	Paul Hamilton 1809
	William Jones 1813
	B. W. Crowninshield 1814

MONROE

Secretary of State	John Quincy Adams 1817
Secretary of the Treasury	William H. Crawford (Cont.)
Secretary of War	John C. Calhoun 1817
Attorney General	Richard Rush (Cont.)
	William Wirt 1817
Secretary of the Navy	B. W. Crowninshield (Cont.)
	Smith Thompson 1818
	Samuel L. Southard 1823

J. Q. ADAMS

Secretary of State	Henry Clay 1825
Secretary of the Treasury	Richard Rush 1825
Secretary of War	James Barbour 1825
	Peter B. Porter 1828
Attorney General	William Wirt (Cont.)
Secretary of the Navy	Samuel L. Southard (Cont.)

JACKSON

Secretary of State	Martin Van Buren 1829
	Edward Livingston 1831
	Louis McLane 1833
	John Forsyth 1834
Secretary of the Treasury	Samuel D. Ingham 1829
	Louis McLane 1831
	William J. Duane 1833
	Roger B. Taney[3] 1833
	Levi Woodbury 1834
Secretary of War	John H. Eaton 1829
	Lewis Cass 1831
Attorney General	John M. Berrien 1829
	Roger B. Taney 1831
	Benjamin F. Butler 1833
Postmaster General[1]	William T. Barry 1829
	Amos Kendall 1835
Secretary of the Navy	John Branch 1829
	Levi Woodbury 1831
	Mahlon Dickerson 1834

VAN BUREN

Secretary of State	John Forsyth (Cont.)
Secretary of the Treasury	Levi Woodbury (Cont.)
Secretary of War	Joel R. Poinsett 1837
Attorney General	Benjamin F. Butler (Cont.)
	Felix Grundy 1838
	Henry D. Gilpin 1840
Postmaster General	Amos Kendall (Cont.)
	John M. Niles 1840
Secretary of the Navy	Mahlon Dickerson (Cont.)
	James K. Paulding 1838

W. H. HARRISON

Secretary of State	Daniel Webster 1841
Secretary of the Treasury	Thomas Ewing 1841
Secretary of War	John Bell 1841
Attorney General	John J. Crittenden 1841
Postmaster General	Francis Granger 1841
Secretary of the Navy	George E. Badger 1841

TYLER

Secretary of State	Daniel Webster (Cont.)
	Abel P. Upshur 1843
	John C. Calhoun 1844
Secretary of the Treasury	Thomas Ewing (Cont.)

	Walter Forward 1841
	John C. Spencer[3] 1843
	George M. Bibb 1844
Secretary of War	John Bell (Cont.)
	John C. Spencer 1841
	James M. Porter[3] 1843
	William Wilkins 1844
Attorney General	John J. Crittenden (Cont.)
	Hugh S. Legaré 1841
	John Nelson 1843
Postmaster General	Francis Granger (Cont.)
	Charles A. Wickliffe 1841
Secretary of the Navy	George E. Badger (Cont.)
	Abel P. Upshur 1841
	David Henshaw[3] 1843
	Thomas W. Gilmer 1844
	John Y. Mason 1844

POLK

Secretary of State	James Buchanan 1845
Secretary of the Treasury	Robert J. Walker 1845
Secretary of War	William L. Marcy 1845
Attorney General	John Y. Mason 1845
	Nathan Clifford 1846
	Isaac Toucey 1848
Postmaster General	Cave Johnson 1845
Secretary of the Navy	George Bancroft 1845
	John Y. Mason 1846

TAYLOR

Secretary of State	John M. Clayton 1849
Secretary of the Treasury	William M. Meredith 1849
Secretary of War	George W. Crawford 1849
Attorney General	Reverdy Johnson 1849
Postmaster General	Jacob Collamer 1849
Secretary of the Navy	William B. Preston 1849
Secretary of the Interior	Thomas Ewing 1849

FILLMORE

Secretary of State	Daniel Webster 1850
	Edward Everett 1852
Secretary of the Treasury	Thomas Corwin 1850
Secretary of War	Charles M. Conrad 1850
Attorney General	John J. Crittenden 1850
Postmaster General	Nathan K. Hall 1850
	Samuel D. Hubbard 1852
Secretary of the Navy	William A. Graham 1850
	John P. Kennedy 1852
Secretary of the Interior	Thos. M. T. McKennan 1850
	Alex. H. H. Stuart 1850

PIERCE

Secretary of State	William L. Marcy 1853
Secretary of the Treasury	James Guthrie 1853
Secretary of War	Jefferson Davis 1853
Attorney General	Caleb Cushing 1853
Postmaster General	James Campbell 1853
Secretary of the Navy	James C. Dobbin 1853
Secretary of the Interior	Robert McClelland 1853

BUCHANAN

Secretary of State	Lewis Cass 1857
	Jeremiah S. Black 1860
Secretary of the Treasury	Howell Cobb 1857
	Philip F. Thomas 1860
	John A. Dix 1861
Secretary of War	John B. Floyd 1857
	Joseph Holt 1861
Attorney General	Jeremiah S. Black 1857
	Edwin M. Stanton 1860
Postmaster General	Aaron V. Brown 1857
	Joseph Holt 1859
	Horatio King 1861
Secretary of the Navy	Isaac Toucey 1857
Secretary of the Interior	Jacob Thompson 1857

LINCOLN

Secretary of State	William H. Seward 1861
Secretary of the Treasury	Salmon P. Chase 1861
	William P. Fessenden 1864
	Hugh McCulloch 1865
Secretary of War	Simon Cameron 1861
	Edwin M. Stanton 1862
Attorney General	Edward Bates 1861
	James Speed 1864
Postmaster General	Montgomery Blair 1861
	William Dennison 1864
Secretary of the Navy	Gideon Welles 1861
Secretary of the Interior	Caleb B. Smith 1861
	John P. Usher 1863

A. JOHNSON

Secretary of State	William H. Seward (Cont.)
Secretary of the Treasury	Hugh McCulloch (Cont.)
Secretary of War	Edwin M. Stanton (Cont.)
	John M. Schofield 1868
Attorney General	James Speed (Cont.)
	Henry Stanbery 1866
	William M. Evarts 1868
Postmaster General	William Dennison (Cont.)
	Alexander W. Randall 1866
Secretary of the Navy	Gideon Welles (Cont.)
Secretary of the Interior	John P. Usher (Cont.)
	James Harlan 1865
	Orville H. Browning 1866

GRANT

Secretary of State	Elihu B. Washburne 1869
	Hamilton Fish 1869
Secretary of the Treasury	George S. Boutwell 1869
	William A. Richardson 1873
	Benjamin H. Bristow 1874
	Lot M. Morrill 1876
Secretary of War	John A. Rawlins 1869
	William W. Belknap 1869
	Alphonso Taft 1876
	James D. Cameron 1876
Attorney General	Ebenezer R. Hoar 1869
	Amos T. Akerman 1870
	George H. Williams 1871
	Edwards Pierrepont 1875
	Alphonso Taft 1876
Postmaster General	John A. J. Creswell 1869
	Marshall Jewell 1874
	James N. Tyner 1876
Secretary of the Navy	Adolph E. Borie 1869
	George M. Robeson 1869
Secretary of the Interior	Jacob D. Cox 1869
	Columbus Delano 1870
	Zachariah Chandler 1875

HAYES

Secretary of State	William M. Evarts 1877
Secretary of the Treasury	John Sherman 1877
Secretary of War	George W. McCrary 1877
	Alexander Ramsey 1879
Attorney General	Charles Devens 1877
Postmaster General	David M. Key 1877
	Horace Maynard 1880
Secretary of the Navy	Richard W. Thompson 1877
	Nathan Goff, Jr. 1881
Secretary of the Interior	Carl Schurz 1877

GARFIELD

Secretary of State	James G. Blaine 1881
Secretary of the Treasury	William Windom 1881
Secretary of War	Robert T. Lincoln 1881
Attorney General	Wayne MacVeagh 1881
Postmaster General	Thomas L. James 1881
Secretary of the Navy	William H. Hunt 1881
Secretary of the Interior	Samuel J. Kirkwood 1881

ARTHUR

Secretary of State	James G. Blaine (Cont.)
	F. T. Frelinghuysen 1881
Secretary of the Treasury	William Windom (Cont.)
	Charles J. Folger 1881
	Walter Q. Gresham 1884
	Hugh McCulloch 1884
Secretary of War	Robert T. Lincoln (Cont.)
Attorney General	Wayne MacVeagh (Cont.)
	Benjamin H. Brewster 1881
Postmaster General	Thomas L. James (Cont.)
	Timothy O. Howe 1881
	Walter Q. Gresham 1883
	Frank Hatton 1884
Secretary of the Navy	William H. Hunt (Cont.)

	William E. Chandler 1882
Secretary of the Interior	Samuel J. Kirkwood (Cont.)
	Henry M. Teller 1882

CLEVELAND

Secretary of State	Thomas F. Bayard 1885
Secretary of the Treasury	Daniel Manning 1885
	Charles S. Fairchild 1887
Secretary of War	William C. Endicott 1885
Attorney General	Augustus H. Garland 1885
Postmaster General	William F. Vilas 1885
	Don M. Dickinson 1888
Secretary of the Navy	William C. Whitney 1885
Secretary of the Interior	Lucius Q. C. Lamar 1885
	William F. Vilas 1888
Secretary of Agriculture	Norman J. Colman 1889

B. HARRISON

Secretary of State	James G. Blaine 1889
	John W. Foster 1892
Secretary of the Treasury	William Windom 1889
	Charles Foster 1891
Secretary of War	Redfield Proctor 1889
	Stephen B. Elkins 1891
Attorney General	William H. H. Miller 1889
Postmaster General	John Wanamaker 1889
Secretary of the Navy	Benjamin F. Tracy 1889
Secretary of the Interior	John W. Noble 1889
Secretary of Agriculture	Jeremiah M. Rusk 1889

CLEVELAND

Secretary of State	Walter Q. Gresham 1893
	Richard Olney 1895
Secretary of the Treasury	John G. Carlisle 1893
Secretary of War	Daniel S. Lamont 1893
Attorney General	Richard Olney 1893
	Judson Harmon 1895
Postmaster General	Wilson S. Bissell 1893
	William L. Wilson 1895
Secretary of the Navy	Hilary A. Herbert 1893
Secretary of the Interior	Hoke Smith 1893
	David R. Francis 1896
Secretary of Agriculture	Julius Sterling Morton 1893

McKINLEY

Secretary of State	John Sherman 1897
	William R. Day 1898
	John Hay 1898
Secretary of the Treasury	Lyman J. Gage 1897
Secretary of War	Russell A. Alger 1897
	Elihu Root 1899
Attorney General	Joseph McKenna 1897
	John W. Griggs 1898
	Philander C. Knox 1901
Postmaster General	James A. Gary 1897
	Charles E. Smith 1898
Secretary of the Navy	John D. Long 1897
Secretary of the Interior	Cornelius N. Bliss 1897
	Ethan A. Hitchcock 1898
Secretary of Agriculture	James Wilson 1897

T. ROOSEVELT

Secretary of State	John Hay (Cont.)
	Elihu Root 1905
	Robert Bacon 1909
Secretary of the Treasury	Lyman J. Gage (Cont.)
	Leslie M. Shaw 1902
	George B. Cortelyou 1907
Secretary of War	Elihu Root (Cont.)
	William H. Taft 1904
	Luke E. Wright 1908
Attorney General	Philander C. Knox (Cont.)
	William H. Moody 1904
	Charles J. Bonaparte 1906
Postmaster General	Charles E. Smith (Cont.)
	Henry C. Payne 1902
	Robert J. Wynne 1904
	George B. Cortelyou 1905
	George von L. Meyer 1907
Secretary of the Navy	John D. Long (Cont.)
	William H. Moody 1902
	Paul Morton 1904
	Charles J. Bonaparte 1905
	Victor H. Metcalf 1906
	Truman H. Newberry 1908
Secretary of the Interior	Ethan A. Hitchcock (Cont.)
	James R. Garfield 1907
Secretary of Agriculture	James Wilson (Cont.)
Secretary of Commerce and Labor	George B. Cortelyou 1903
	Victor H. Metcalf 1904
	Oscar S. Straus 1906

TAFT

Secretary of State	Philander C. Knox 1909
Secretary of the Treasury	Franklin MacVeagh 1909
Secretary of War	Jacob M. Dickinson 1909
	Henry L. Stimson 1911
Attorney General	George W. Wickersham 1909
Postmaster General	Frank H. Hitchcock 1909
Secretary of the Navy	George von L. Meyer 1909
Secretary of the Interior	Richard A. Ballinger 1909
	Walter L. Fisher 1911
Secretary of Agriculture	James Wilson (Cont.)
Secretary of Commerce and Labor	Charles Nagel 1909

WILSON

Secretary of State	William J. Bryan 1913
	Robert Lansing 1915
	Bainbridge Colby 1920
Secretary of the Treasury	William G. McAdoo 1913
	Carter Glass 1918
	Carter Glass 1918
	David F. Houston 1920
Secretary of War	Lindley M. Garrison 1913
	Newton D. Baker 1916
Attorney General	James C. McReynolds 1913
	Thomas W. Gregory 1914
	A. Mitchell Palmer 1919
Postmaster General	Albert S. Burleson 1913
Secretary of the Navy	Josephus Daniels 1913
Secretary of the Interior	Franklin K. Lane 1913
	John B. Payne 1920
Secretary of Agriculture	David F. Houston 1913
	Edwin T. Meredith 1920
Secretary of Commerce	William C. Redfield 1913
	Joshua W. Alexander 1919
Secretary of Labor	William B. Wilson 1913

HARDING

Secretary of State	Charles E. Hughes 1921
Secretary of the Treasury	Andrew W. Mellon 1921
Secretary of War	John W. Weeks 1921
Attorney General	Harry M. Daugherty 1921
Postmaster General	Will H. Hays 1921
	Hubert Work 1922
	Harry S. New 1923
Secretary of the Navy	Edwin Denby 1921
Secretary of the Interior	Albert B. Fall 1921
	Hubert Work 1923
Secretary of Agriculture	Henry C. Wallace 1921
Secretary of Commerce	Herbert Hoover 1921
Secretary of Labor	James J. Davis 1921

COOLIDGE

Secretary of State	Charles E. Hughes (Cont.)
	Frank B. Kellogg 1925
Secretary of the Treasury	Andrew W. Mellon (Cont.)
Secretary of War	John W. Weeks (Cont.)
	Dwight F. Davis 1925
Attorney General	Harry M. Daughtery (Cont.)
	Harlan F. Stone 1924
	John G. Sargent 1925
Postmaster General	Harry S. New (Cont.)
Secretary of the Navy	Edwin Denby (Cont.)
	Curtis D. Wilbur 1924
Secretary of the Interior	Hubert Work (Cont.)
	Roy O. West 1928
Secretary of Agriculture	Henry C. Wallace (Cont.)
	Howard M. Gore 1924
	William M. Jardine 1925
Secretary of Commerce	Herbert Hoover (Cont.)
	William F. Whiting 1928
Secretary of Labor	James J. Davis (Cont.)

HOOVER

Secretary of State	Frank B. Kellogg (Cont.)

	Henry L. Stimson 1929
Secretary of the Treasury	Andrew W. Mellon (Cont.)
	Ogden L. Mills 1932
Secretary of War	James W. Good 1929
	Patrick J. Hurley 1929
Attorney General	William D. Mitchell 1929
Postmaster General	Walter F. Brown 1929
Secretary of the Navy	Charles F. Adams 1929
Secretary of the Interior	Ray Lyman Wilbur 1929
Secretary of Agriculture	Arthur M. Hyde 1929
Secretary of Commerce	Robert P. Lamont 1929
	Roy D. Chapin 1932
Secretary of Labor	James J. Davis (Cont.)
	William N. Doak 1930

F. D. ROOSEVELT

Secretary of State	Cordell Hull 1933
	E. R. Stettinius, Jr. 1944
Secretary of the Treasury	William H. Woodin 1933
	Henry Morgenthau, Jr. 1934
Secretary of War	George H. Dern 1933
	Harry H. Woodring 1936
	Henry L. Stimson 1940
Attorney General	Homer S. Cummings 1933
	Frank Murphy 1939
	Robert H. Jackson 1940
	Francis Biddle 1941
Postmaster General	James A. Farley 1933
	Frank C. Walker 1940
Secretary of the Navy	Claude A. Swanson 1933
	Charles Edison 1940
	Frank Knox 1940
	James Forrestal 1944
Secretary of the Interior	Harold L. Ickes 1933
Secretary of Agriculture	Henry A. Wallace 1933
	Claude R. Wickard 1940
Secretary of Commerce	Daniel C. Roper 1933
	Harry L. Hopkins 1938
	Jesse H. Jones 1940
	Henry A. Wallace 1945
Secretary of Labor	Frances Perkins 1933

TRUMAN

Secretary of State	E. R. Stettinius, Jr. (Cont.)
	James F. Byrnes 1945
	George C. Marshall 1947
	Dean Acheson 1949
Secretary of the Treasury	Henry Morgenthau, Jr. (Cont.)
	Frederick M. Vinson 1945
	John W. Snyder 1946
Secretary of Defense	James Forrestal 1947
	Louis A. Johnson 1949
	George C. Marshall 1950
	Robert A. Lovett 1951
Attorney General	Francis Biddle (Cont.)
	Tom C. Clark 1945
	J. Howard McGrath 1949
	James P. McGranery 1952
Postmaster General	Frank C. Walker (Cont.)
	Robert E. Hannegan 1945
	Jesse M. Donaldson 1947
Secretary of the Interior	Harold L. Ickes (Cont.)
	Julius A. Krug 1946
	Oscar L. Chapman 1949
Secretary of Agriculture	Claude R. Wickard (Cont.)
	Clinton P. Anderson 1945
	Charles F. Brannan 1948
Secretary of Commerce	Henry A. Wallace (Cont.)
	W. Averell Harriman 1946
	Charles Sawyer 1948
Secretary of Labor	Frances Perkins (Cont.)
	Lewis B. Schwellenbach 1945
	Maurice J. Tobin 1948
Secretary of War[2]	Henry L. Stimson (Cont.)
	Robert P. Patterson 1945
	Kenneth C. Royall 1947
Secretary of the Navy[2]	James Forrestal (Cont.)

EISENHOWER

Secretary of State	John Foster Dulles 1953
	Christian A. Herter 1959
Secretary of the Treasury	George M. Humphrey 1953
	Robert B. Anderson 1957
Secretary of Defense	Charles E. Wilson 1953
	Neil H. McElroy 1957
	Thomas S. Gates, Jr. 1959
Attorney General	Herbert Brownell, Jr. 1953
	William P. Rogers 1958
Postmaster General	Arthur E. Summerfield 1953
Secretary of the Interior	Douglas McKay 1953
	Frederick A. Seaton 1956
Secretary of Agriculture	Ezra Taft Benson 1953
Secretary of Commerce	Sinclair Weeks 1953
	Lewis L. Strauss[3] 1958
	Frederick H. Mueller 1959
Secretary of Labor	Martin P. Durkin 1953
	James P. Mitchell 1953
Secretary of Health, Education, and Welfare	Oveta Culp Hobby 1953
	Marion B. Folsom 1955
	Arthur S. Flemming 1958

KENNEDY

Secretary of State	Dean Rusk 1961
Secretary of the Treasury	C. Douglas Dillon 1961
Secretary of Defense	Robert S. McNamara 1961
Attorney General	Robert F. Kennedy 1961
Postmaster General	J. Edward Day 1961
	John A. Gronouski 1963
Secretary of the Interior	Stewart L. Udall 1961
Secretary of Agriculture	Orville L. Freeman 1961
Secretary of Commerce	Luther H. Hodges 1961
Secretary of Labor	Arthur J. Goldberg 1961
	W. Willard Wirtz 1962
Secretary of Health, Education, and Welfare	Abraham A. Ribicoff 1961
	Anthony J. Celebrezze 1962

L. B. JOHNSON

Secretary of State	Dean Rusk (Cont.)
Secretary of the Treasury	C. Douglas Dillon (Cont.)
	Henry H. Fowler 1965
	Joseph W. Barr[4] 1968
Secretary of Defense	Robert S. McNamara (Cont.)
	Clark M. Clifford 1968
Attorney General	Robert F. Kennedy (Cont.)
	N. de B. Katzenbach 1965
	Ramsey Clark 1967
Postmaster General	John A. Gronouski (Cont.)
	Lawrence F. O'Brien 1965
	W. Marvin Watson 1968
Secretary of the Interior	Stewart L. Udall (Cont.)
Secretary of Agriculture	Orville L. Freeman (Cont.)
Secretary of Commerce	Luther H. Hodges (Cont.)
	John T. Connor 1964
	A. B. Trowbridge 1967
	C. R. Smith 1968
Secretary of Labor	W. Willard Wirtz (Cont.)
Secretary of Health, Education, and Welfare	Anthony J. Celebrezze (Cont.)
	John W. Gardner 1965
	Wilbur J. Cohen 1968
Secretary of Housing and Urban Development	Robert C. Weaver 1966
	Robert C. Wood[4] 1969
Secretary of Transportation	Alan S. Boyd 1966

NIXON

Secretary of State	William P. Rogers 1969
	Henry A. Kissinger 1973
Secretary of the Treasury	David M. Kennedy 1969
	John B. Connally 1971
	George P. Shultz 1972
	William E. Simon 1974
Secretary of Defense	Melvin R. Laird 1969
	Elliot L. Richardson 1973
	James R. Schlesinger 1973
Attorney General	John N. Mitchell 1969
	Richard G. Kleindienst 1972
	Elliot L. Richardson 1973
	William B. Saxbe 1974
Postmaster General[5]	William M. Blount 1969
Secretary of the Interior	Walter J. Hickel 1969
	Rogers C. B. Morton 1971
Secretary of Agriculture	Clifford M. Hardin 1969
	Earl L. Butz 1971
Secretary of Commerce	Maurice H. Stans 1969
	Peter G. Peterson 1972

	Frederick B. Dent 1973
Secretary of Labor	George P. Shultz 1969
	James D. Hodgson 1970
	Peter J. Brennan 1973
Secretary of Health, Education, and Welfare	Robert H. Finch 1969
	Elliot L. Richardson 1970
	Caspar W. Weinberger 1973
Secretary of Housing and Urban Development	George Romney 1969
	James T. Lynn 1973
Secretary of Transportation	John A. Volpe 1969
	Claude S. Brinegar 1973

FORD

Secretary of State	Henry A. Kissinger (Cont.)
Secretary of the Treasury	William E. Simon (Cont.)
Secretary of Defense	James R. Schlesinger (Cont.)
	Donald H. Rumsfeld 1975
Attorney General	William B. Saxbe (Cont.)
	Edward H. Levi 1975
Secretary of the Interior	Rogers C. B. Morton (Cont.)
	Stanley K. Hathaway 1975
	Thomas S. Kleppe 1975
Secretary of Agriculture	Earl L. Butz (Cont.)
	John Knebel 1976
Secretary of Commerce	Frederick B. Dent (Cont.)
	Rogers C. B. Morton 1975
	Elliot L. Richardson 1976
Secretary of Labor	Peter J. Brennan (Cont.)
	John T. Dunlop 1975
	William J. Usery, Jr. 1976
Secretary of Health, Education, and Welfare	Caspar W. Weinberger (Cont.)
	F. David Mathews 1975
Secretary of Housing and Urban Development	James T. Lynn (Cont.)
	Carla A. Hills 1975
Secretary of Transportation	Claude S. Brinegar (Cont.)
	William T. Coleman, Jr. 1975

CARTER

Secretary of State	Cyrus R. Vance 1977
	Edmund S. Muskie 1980
Secretary of the Treasury	W. Michael Blumenthal 1977
	G. William Miller 1979
Secretary of Defense	Harold Brown 1977
Attorney General	Griffin B. Bell 1977
	Benjamin R. Civiletti 1979
Secretary of the Interior	Cecil D. Andrus 1977
Secretary of Agriculture	Bob S. Bergland 1977
Secretary of Commerce	Juanita M. Kreps 1977
	Philip M. Klutznick 1979
Secretary of Labor	F. Ray Marshall 1977
Secretary of Health and Human Services[6]	Joseph A. Califano, Jr. 1977
	Patricia Roberts Harris 1979
Secretary of Housing and Urban Development	Patricia Roberts Harris 1977
	Moon Landrieu 1979
Secretary of Transportation	Brock Adams 1977
	Neil E. Goldschmidt 1979
Secretary of Energy	James R. Schlesinger 1977
	Charles W. Duncan, Jr. 1979
Secretary of Education	Shirley Mount Hufstedler 1979

REAGAN

Secretary of State	Alexander M. Haig, Jr. 1981
	George P. Shultz 1982
Secretary of the Treasury	Donald T. Regan 1981
Secretary of Defense	Caspar W. Weinberger 1981
Attorney General	William French Smith 1981
Secretary of the Interior	James G. Watt 1981
	William P. Clark 1983
Secretary of Agriculture	John R. Block 1981
Secretary of Commerce	Malcolm Baldrige 1981
Secretary of Labor	Raymond J. Donovan 1981
Secretary of Health and Human Services	Richard S. Schweiker 1981
	Margaret M. Heckler 1983
Secretary of Housing and Urban Development	Samuel R. Pierce, Jr. 1981
Secretary of Transportation	Andrew L. Lewis, Jr. 1981
	Elizabeth H. Dole 1983
Secretary of Energy	James B. Edwards 1981
	Donald P. Hodel 1983
Secretary of Education	T. H. Bell 1981

1. The Postmaster General did not become a Cabinet member until 1829. Earlier Postmasters General were: Samuel Osgood (1789), Timothy Pickering (1791), Joseph Habersham (1795), Gideon Granger (1801), Return J. Meigs, Jr. (1814), and John McLean (1823). 2. On July 26, 1947, the Departments of War and of the Navy were incorporated into the Department of Defense. 3. Not confirmed by the Senate. 4. Recess appointment. 5. The Postmaster General is no longer a Cabinet member. 6. Known as Department of Health, Education, and Welfare until May 1980.

How a Bill Becomes a Law

When a Senator or a Representative introduces a bill, he sends it to the clerk of his house, who gives it a number and title. This is the *first reading,* and the bill is referred to the proper committee.

The committee may decide the bill is unwise or unnecessary and *table* it, thus killing it at once. Or it may decide the bill is worthwhile and hold hearings to listen to facts and opinions presented by experts and other interested persons. After members of the committee have debated the bill and perhaps offered amendments, a vote is taken; and if the vote is favorable, the bill is sent back to the floor of the house.

The clerk reads the bill sentence by sentence to the house, and this is known as the *second reading.* Members may then debate the bill and offer amendments. In the House of Representatives, the time for debate is limited by a *cloture rule,* but there is no such restriction in the Senate for cloture, where 60 votes are required. This makes possible a *filibuster,* in which one or more opponents hold the floor to defeat the bill.

The *third reading* is by title only, and the bill is put to a vote, which may be by voice or roll call, depending on the circumstances and parliamentary rules. Members who must be absent at the time but who wish to record their vote may be paired if each negative vote has a balancing affirmative one.

The bill then goes to the other house of Congress, where it may be defeated, or passed with or without amendments. If the bill is defeated, it dies. If it is passed with amendments, a joint Congressional committee must be appointed by both houses to iron out the differences.

After its final passage by both houses, the bill is sent to the President. If he approves, he signs it, and the bill becomes a law. However, if he disapproves, he *vetoes* the bill by refusing to sign it and sending it back to the house of origin with his reasons for the veto. The objections are read and debated, and a roll-call vote is taken. If the bill receives less than a two-thirds vote, it is defeated and goes no farther. But if it receives a two-thirds vote or greater, it is sent to the other house for a vote. If that house also passes it by a two-thirds vote, the President's veto is *overridden,* and the bill becomes a law.

Should the President desire neither to sign nor to veto the bill, he may retain it for ten days, Sundays excepted, after which time it automatically becomes a law without signature. However, if Congress has adjourned within those ten days, the bill is automatically killed, that process of indirect rejection being known as a *pocket veto.*

Figures and Legends in American Folklore

Appleseed, Johnny (John Chapman, 1774–1847): Massachusetts-born nurseryman; reputed to have spread seeds and seedlings from which rose orchards of the Midwest.

Billy the Kid (William H. Bonney, 1859–1881): New York-born desperado; killed his first man before he reached his teens; after short life of crime in Wild West, was gunned down by Sheriff Pat Garrett; symbol of lawless West.

Boone, Daniel (1734–1820): Frontiersman and Indian fighter, about whom legends of early America have been built; figured in Byron's *Don Juan.*

Brodie, Steve (1863–1901): Reputed to have dived off Brooklyn Bridge on July 23, 1886. (Whether he actually did so has never been proved.)

Buffalo Bill (William F. Cody, 1846–1917): Buffalo hunter and Indian scout; much of legend about him and Wild West stems from his own Wild West show, which he operated in late 19th century.

Bunyan, Paul: Mythical lumberjack; subject of tall tales throughout timber country (that he dug Grand Canyon, for example).

Crockett, David (1786–1836): Frontiersman and member of U.S. Congress, about whom legends have been built of heroic feats; died in defense of Alamo.

Fritchie (or Frietchie), Barbara: Symbol of patriotism; in ballad by John Greenleaf Whittier, 90-year-old Barbara Fritchie defiantly waves Stars and Stripes as "Stonewall" Jackson's Confederate troops march through Frederick, Md.

James, Jesse (1847–1882): Bank and train robber; folklore has given him quality of American Robin Hood.

Jones, Casey (John Luther Jones, 1863–1900): Example of heroic locomotive engineer given to feats of prowess; died in wreck with his hand on brake lever when his Illinois Central "Cannonball" express hit freight train at Vaughan, Miss.

Ross, Betsy (1752–1836): Member of Philadelphia flag-making family; reported to have designed and sewn first American flag. (Report is without confirmation.)

Uncle Sam: Personification of United States and its people; origin uncertain; may be based on inspector of government supplies in Revolutionary War and War of 1812.

Assassinations and Attempts in U. S. Since 1865

Cermak, Anton J. (Mayor of Chicago): Shot Feb. 15, 1933, in Miami by Giuseppe Zangara, who attempted to assassinate Franklin D. Roosevelt; Cermak died March 6.

Ford, Gerald R. (President of U.S.): Escaped assassination attempt Sept. 5, 1975, in Sacramento, Calif., by Lynette Alice (Squeaky) Fromm, who pointed but did not fire .45-caliber pistol. Escaped assassination attempt in San Francisco, Calif., Sept. 22, 1975, by Sara Jane Moore, who fired one shot from a .38-caliber pistol that was deflected.

Garfield, James A. (President of U.S.): Shot July 2, 1881, in Washington, D.C., by Charles J. Guiteau; died Sept. 19.

Jordan, Vernon E., Jr. (civil rights leader): Shot and critically wounded in assassination attempt May 29, 1980, in Fort Wayne, Ind.

Kennedy, John F. (President of U.S.): Shot Nov. 22, 1963, in Dallas, Tex., allegedly by Lee Harvey Oswald; died same day. Injured was Gov. John B. Connally of Texas. Oswald was shot and killed two days later by Jack Ruby.

Kennedy, Robert F. (U.S. Senator from New York): Shot June 5, 1968, in Los Angeles by Sirhan Bishara Sirhan; died June 6.

King, Martin Luther, Jr. (civil rights leader): Shot April 4, 1968, in Memphis by James Earl Ray; died same day.

Lincoln, Abraham (President of U.S.): Shot April 14, 1865, in Washington, D.C., by John Wilkes Booth; died April 15.

Long, Huey P. (U.S. Senator from Louisiana): Shot Sept. 8, 1935, in Baton Rouge by Dr. Carl A. Weiss; died Sept. 10.

McKinley, William (President of U.S.): Shot Sept. 6, 1901, in Buffalo by Leon Czolgosz; died Sept. 14.

Reagan, Ronald (President of U.S.): Shot in left lung in Washington by John W. Hinckley, Jr., on March 30, 1981; three others also wounded.

Roosevelt, Franklin D. (President-elect of U.S.): Escaped assassination unhurt Feb. 15, 1933, in Miami. *See* Cermak.

Roosevelt, Theodore (ex-President of U.S.): Escaped assassination (though shot) Oct. 14, 1912, in Milwaukee while campaigning for President.

Seward, William H. (Secretary of State): Escaped assassination (though injured) April 14, 1865, in Washington, D.C., by Lewis Powell (or Paine), accomplice of John Wilkes Booth.

Truman, Harry S. (President of U.S.): Escaped assassination unhurt Nov. 1, 1950, in Washington, D.C., as 2 Puerto Rican nationalists attempted to shoot their way into Blair House.

Wallace, George C. (Governor of Alabama): Shot and critically wounded in assassination attempt May 15, 1972, at Laurel, Md., by Arthur Herman Bremer. Wallace paralyzed from waist down.

Members of the Supreme Court of the United States

Name	Birth		Religious affiliation (*Source:* Library of Congress)	Appointment		Oath taken		Service terminated				Death	
	Place	Date		From	President	Date	Age	Date	Cause	Years served	Age	Date	Age
CHIEF JUSTICES													
John Jay	N.Y.	1745	Episcopal	N.Y.	Washington	1789	44	1795	resigned	5	49	1829	83
John Rutledge	S.C.	1739	Church of England	S.C.	Washington	1795	55	1795	rejected	0	56	1800	60
Oliver Ellsworth	Conn.	1745	Congregational	Conn.	Washington	1796	50	1800	resigned	4	55	1807	62
John Marshall	Va.	1755	Episcopal	Va.	J. Adams	1801	45	1835	death	34	79	1835	79
Roger B. Taney	Md.	1777	Roman Catholic	Md.	Jackson	1836	59	1864	death	28	87	1864	87
Salmon P. Chase	N.H.	1808	Episcopal	Ohio	Lincoln	1864	56	1873	death	8	65	1873	65
Morrison R. Waite	Conn	1816	Episcopal	Ohio	Grant	1874	57	1888	death	14	71	1888	71
Melville W. Fuller	Me.	1833	Episcopal	Ill.	Cleveland	1888	55	1910	death	21	77	1910	77
Edward D. White	La.	1845	Roman Catholic	La.	Taft	1910	65	1921	death	10	75	1921	75
William H. Taft	Ohio	1857	Unitarian	Conn.	Harding	1921	63	1930	retired	8	72	1930	72
Charles E. Hughes	N.Y.	1862	Baptist	N.Y.	Hoover	1930	67	1941	retired	11	79	1948	86
Harlan F. Stone	N.H.	1872	Episcopal	N.Y.	F. Roosevelt	1941	68	1946	death	4	73	1946	73
Frederick M. Vinson	Ky.	1890	Methodist	Ky.	Truman	1946	56	1953	death	7	63	1953	63
Earl Warren	Calif.	1891	Protestant	Calif.	Eisenhower	1953	62	1969	retired	15	78	1974	83
Warren E. Burger	Minn.	1907	Presbyterian	Va.	Nixon	1969	61	—	—	—	—	—	—
ASSOCIATE JUSTICES													
James Wilson	Scotland	1742	Episcopal	Pa.	Washington	1789	47	1798	death	8	55	1798	55
John Rutledge	S.C.	1739	Church of England	S.C.	Washington	1790	50	1791	resigned	1	51	1800	60
William Cushing	Mass.	1732	Unitarian	Mass.	Washington	1790	57	1810	death	20	78	1810	78
John Blair	Va.	1732	Presbyterian	Va.	Washington	1790	58	1796	resigned	5	64	1800	68
James Iredell	England	1751	Episcopal	N.C.	Washington	1790	38	1799	death	9	48	1799	48
Thomas Johnson	Md.	1732	Episcopal	Md.	Washington	1792	59	1793	resigned	0	60	1819	86
William Paterson	Ireland	1745	Protestant	N.J.	Washington	1793	47	1806	death	13	60	1806	60
Samuel Chase	Md.	1741	Episcopal	Md.	Washington	1796	54	1811	death	15	70	1811	70
Bushrod Washington	Va.	1762	Episcopal	Va.	J. Adams	1799	36	1829	death	30	67	1829	67
Alfred Moore	N.C.	1755	Episcopal	N.C.	J. Adams	1800	45	1804	resigned	3	48	1810	55
William Johnson	S.C.	1771	Presbyterian	S.C.	Jefferson	1804	32	1834	death	30	62	1834	62
Brockholst Livingston	N.Y.	1757	Presbyterian	N.Y.	Jefferson	1807	49	1823	death	16	65	1823	65
Thomas Todd	Va.	1765	Presbyterian	Ky.	Jefferson	1807	42	1826	death	18	61	1826	61
Gabriel Duval	Md.	1752	French Protestant	Md.	Madison	1811	58	1835	resigned	23	82	1844	91
Joseph Story	Mass.	1779	Unitarian	Mass.	Madison	1812	32	1845	death	33	65	1845	65
Smith Thompson	N.Y.	1768	Presbyterian	N.Y.	Monroe	1823	55	1843	death	20	75	1843	75
Robert Trimble	Va.	1777	Protestant	Ky.	J. Q. Adams	1826	49	1828	death	2	51	1828	51
John McLean	N.J.	1785	Methodist-Epis.	Ohio	Jackson	1830	44	1861	death	31	76	1861	76
Henry Baldwin	Conn.	1780	Trinity Church	Pa.	Jackson	1830	50	1844	death	14	64	1844	64
James M. Wayne	Ga.	1790	Protestant	Ga.	Jackson	1835	45	1867	death	32	77	1867	77
Philip P. Barbour	Va.	1783	Episcopal	Va.	Jackson	1836	52	1841	death	4	57	1841	57
John Catron	Pa.	1786	Presbyterian	Tenn.	Jackson	1837	51	1865	death	28	79	1865	79

Name	Birth		Religious affiliation (*Source:* Library of Congress)	Appointment		Oath taken		Service terminated				Death	
	Place	Date		From	President	Date	Age	Date	Cause	Years served	Age	Date	Age
John McKinley	Va	1780	Protestant	Ala.	Van Buren	1837	57	1852	death	14	72	1852	72
Peter V. Daniel	Va.	1784	Episcopal	Va.	Van Buren	1841	57	1860	death	18	76	1860	76
Samuel Nelson	N.Y.	1792	Protestant	N.Y.	Tyler	1845	52	1872	retired	27	80	1873	81
Levi Woodbury	N.H.	1789	Protestant	N.H.	Polk	1845	55	1851	death	5	61	1851	61
Robert C. Grier	Pa.	1794	Presbyterian	Pa.	Polk	1846	52	1870	retired	23	75	1870	76
Benjamin R. Curtis	Mass.	1809	(2)	Mass.	Fillmore	1851	41	1857	resigned	5	47	1874	64
John A. Campbell	Ga.	1811	Episcopal	Ala.	Pierce	1853	41	1861	resigned	8	49	1889	77
Nathan Clifford	N.H.	1803	(1)	Maine	Buchanan	1858	54	1881	death	23	77	1881	77
Noah H. Swayne	Va.	1804	Quaker	Ohio	Lincoln	1862	57	1881	retired	18	76	1884	79
Samuel F. Miller	Ky.	1816	Unitarian	Iowa	Lincoln	1862	46	1890	death	28	74	1890	74
David Davis	Md.	1815	(4)	Ill.	Lincoln	1862	47	1877	resigned	14	61	1886	71
Stephen J. Field	Conn.	1816	Episcopal	Calif.	Lincoln	1863	46	1897	retired	34	81	1899	82
William Strong	Conn.	1808	Presbyterian	Pa.	Grant	1870	61	1880	retired	10	72	1895	87
Joseph P. Bradley	N.Y.	1813	Presbyterian	N.J.	Grant	1870	57	1892	death	21	78	1892	78
Ward Hunt	N.Y.	1810	Episcopal	N.Y.	Grant	1872	62	1882	disabled	9	71	1886	75
John M. Harlan	Ky.	1833	Presbyterian	Ky.	Hayes	1877	44	1911	death	33	78	1911	78
William B. Woods	Ohio	1824	Protestant	Ga.	Hayes	1880	56	1887	death	6	62	1887	62
Stanley Matthews	Ohio	1824	Presbyterian	Ohio	Garfield	1881	56	1889	death	7	64	1889	64
Horace Gray	Mass.	1828	(3)	Mass.	Arthur	1882	53	1902	death	20	74	1902	74
Samuel Blatchford	N.Y.	1820	Presbyterian	N.Y.	Arthur	1882	62	1893	death	11	73	1893	73
Lucius Q. C. Lamar	Ga.	1825	Methodist	Miss.	Cleveland	1888	62	1893	death	5	67	1893	67
David J. Brewer	Asia Minor	1837	Protestant	Kan.	Harrison	1889	52	1910	death	20	72	1910	72
Henry B. Brown	Mass.	1836	Protestant	Mich.	Harrison	1890	54	1906	retired	15	70	1913	77
George Shiras, Jr.	Pa.	1832	Presbyterian	Pa.	Harrison	1892	60	1903	retired	10	71	1924	92
Howell E. Jackson	Tenn.	1832	Baptist	Tenn.	Harrison	1893	60	1895	death	2	63	1895	63
Edward D. White	La.	1845	Roman Catholic	La.	Cleveland	1894	48	1910	promoted	16	65	1921	75
Rufus W. Peckham	N.Y.	1838	Episcopal	N.Y.	Cleveland	1895	57	1909	death	13	70	1909	70
Joseph McKenna	Pa.	1843	Roman Catholic	Calif.	McKinley	1898	54	1925	retired	26	81	1926	83
Oliver W. Holmes	Mass.	1841	Unitarian	Mass.	T. Roosevelt	1902	61	1932	retired	29	90	1935	93
William R. Day	Ohio	1849	Protestant	Ohio	T. Roosevelt	1903	53	1922	retired	19	73	1923	74
William H. Moody	Mass.	1853	Episcopal	Mass.	T. Roosevelt	1906	52	1910	disabled	3	56	1917	63
Horace H. Lurton	Ky.	1844	Episcopal	Tenn.	Taft	1909	65	1914	death	4	70	1914	70
Charles E. Hughes	N.Y.	1862	Baptist	N.Y.	Taft	1910	48	1916	resigned	5	54	1948	86
Willis Van Devanter	Ind.	1859	Episcopal	Wyo.	Taft	1910	51	1937	retired	26	78	1941	81
Joseph R. Lamar	Ga.	1857	Ch. of Disciples	Ga.	Taft	1910	53	1916	death	4	58	1916	58
Mahlon Pitney	N.J.	1858	Presbyterian	N.J.	Taft	1912	54	1922	disabled	10	64	1924	66
James C. McReynolds	Ky.	1862	Disciples of Christ	Tenn.	Wilson	1914	52	1941	retired	26	78	1946	84
Louis D. Brandeis	Ky.	1856	Jewish	Mass.	Wilson	1916	59	1939	retired	22	82	1941	84
John H. Clarke	Ohio	1857	Protestant	Ohio	Wilson	1916	59	1922	resigned	5	65	1945	87
George Sutherland	England	1862	Episcopal	Utah	Harding	1922	60	1938	retired	15	75	1942	80
Pierce Butler	Minn.	1866	Roman Catholic	Minn.	Harding	1923	56	1939	death	16	73	1939	73
Edward T. Sanford	Tenn.	1865	Episcopal	Tenn.	Harding	1923	57	1930	death	7	64	1930	64

Harlan F. Stone	N.H.	1872	Episcopal	N.Y.	Coolidge	1925	52	1941	promoted	16	68	1946	73
Owen J. Roberts	Pa.	1875	Episcopal	Pa.	Hoover	1930	55	1945	resigned	15	70	1955	80
Benjamin N. Cardozo	N.Y.	1870	Jewish	N.Y.	Hoover	1932	61	1938	death	6	68	1938	68
Hugo L. Black	Ala.	1886	Baptist	Ala.	F. Roosevelt	1937	51	1971	retired	34	85	1971	85
Stanley F. Reed	Ky.	1884	Protestant	Ky.	F. Roosevelt	1938	53	1957	retired	19	72	1980	95
Felix Frankfurter	Austria	1882	Jewish	Mass.	F. Roosevelt	1939	56	1962	retired	23	79	1965	82
William O. Douglas	Minn.	1898	Presbyterian	Conn.	F. Roosevelt	1939	40	1975	retired	36	77	1980	81
Frank Murphy	Mich.	1890	Roman Catholic	Mich.	F. Roosevelt	1940	49	1949	death	9	59	1949	59
James F. Byrnes	S.C.	1879	Episcopal	S.C.	F. Roosevelt	1941	62	1942	resigned	1	63	1972	92
Robert H. Jackson	N.Y.	1892	Episcopal	Pa.	F. Roosevelt	1941	49	1954	death	13	62	1954	62
Wiley B. Rutledge	Ky.	1894	Unitarian	Iowa	F. Roosevelt	1943	48	1949	death	6	55	1949	55
Harold H. Burton	Mass.	1888	Unitarian	Ohio	Truman	1945	57	1958	retired	13	70	1964	76
Tom C. Clark	Tex.	1899	Presbyterian	Tex.	Truman	1949	49	1967	retired	17	67	1977	78
Sherman Minton	Ind.	1890	Roman Catholic	Ind.	Truman	1949	58	1956	retired	7	65	1965	74
John M. Harlan	Ill.	1899	Presbyterian	N.Y.	Eisenhower	1955	55	1971	retired	16	72	1971	72
William J. Brennan, Jr.	N.J.	1906	Roman Catholic	N.J.	Eisenhower	1956	50	—	—	—	—	—	—
Charles E. Whittaker	Kan.	1901	Methodist	Mo.	Eisenhower	1957	56	1962	disabled	5	61	1973	73
Potter Stewart	Mich.	1915	Episcopal	Ohio	Eisenhower	1958	43	1981	resigned	23	66	—	—
Byron R. White	Colo.	1917	Episcopal	Colo.	Kennedy	1962	44	—	—	—	—	—	—
Arthur J. Goldberg	Ill.	1908	Jewish	Ill.	Kennedy	1962	54	1965	resigned	2	56	—	—
Abe Fortas	Tenn.	1910	Jewish	Tenn.	Johnson	1965	55	1969	resigned	3	58	1982	71
Thurgood Marshall	Md.	1908	Episcopalian	N.Y.	Johnson	1967	59	—	—	—	—	—	—
Harry A. Blackmun	Ill.	1908	Methodist	Minn.	Nixon	1970	61	—	—	—	—	—	—
Lewis F. Powell, Jr.	Va.	1907	Presbyterian	Va.	Nixon	1972	64	—	—	—	—	—	—
William H. Rehnquist	Wis.	1924	Lutheran	Ariz.	Nixon	1972	47	—	—	—	—	—	—
John Paul Stevens	Ill.	1920	Protestant	Ill.	Ford	1975	55	—	—	—	—	—	—
Sandra Day O'Connor	Tex.	1930	Episcopal	Ariz.	Reagan	1981	51	—	—	—	—	—	—

1. Congregationalist; later Unitarian. 2. Unitarian; then Episcopal. 3. Unitarian or Congregational. 4. Not a member of any church.

Impeachments of Federal Officials

Source: Congressional Directory

The procedure for the impeachment of Federal officials is detailed in Article I, Section 3, of the Constitution. See Index.

The Senate has sat as a court of impeachment in the following cases:

William Blount, Senator from Tennessee; charges dismissed for want of jurisdiction, January 14, 1799.

John Pickering, Judge of the U.S. District Court for New Hampshire; removed from office March 12, 1804.

Samuel Chase, Associate Justice of the Supreme Court; acquitted March 1, 1805.

James H. Peck, Judge of the U.S. District Court for Missouri; acquitted Jan. 31, 1831.

West H. Humphreys, Judge of the U.S. District Court for the middle, eastern, and western districts of Tennessee; removed from office June 26, 1862.

Andrew Johnson, President of the United States; acquitted May 26, 1868.

William W. Belknap, Secretary of War; acquitted Aug. 1, 1876.

Charles Swayne, Judge of the U.S. District Court for the northern district of Florida; acquitted Feb. 27, 1905.

Robert W. Archbald, Associate Judge, U.S. Commerce Court; removed Jan. 13, 1913.

George W. English, Judge of the U.S. District Court for eastern district of Illinois; resigned Nov. 4, 1926; proceedings dismissed.

Harold Louderback, Judge of the U.S. District Court for the northern district of California; acquitted May 24, 1933.

Halsted L. Ritter, Judge of the U.S. District Court for the southern district of Florida; removed from office April 17, 1936.

Executive Departments and Agencies

Source: U.S. Government Manual, 1983—1984

Unless otherwise indicated, addresses shown are in Washington, D.C.

CENTRAL INTELLIGENCE AGENCY (CIA)
Washington, D.C. (20505).

Established: 1947.

Director: William J. Casey.

Activities: Coordinates intelligence activities of certain government departments and agencies by making recommendations to the National Security Council; correlates and evaluates intelligence and disseminates the results; performs certain additional services for existing intelligence agencies when the National Security Council determines that these can be more efficiently accomplished centrally.

COUNCIL OF ECONOMIC ADVISERS (CEA)
Executive Office Bldg. (20500).

Members: 3.

Established: Feb. 20, 1946.

Chairman: Martin S. Feldstein.

Activities: Assists President in preparation of economic reports to Congress; studies economic trends; appraises government activities on nation's economy; recommends economic policies.

COUNCIL ON ENVIRONMENTAL QUALITY
722 Jackson Pl., N.W. (20006).

Members: 3.

Established: 1969.

Chairman: A. Alan Hill.

Activities: Develops and recommends to President national policies that promote environmental quality.

NATIONAL SECURITY COUNCIL (NSC)
Old Executive Office Bldg. (20506).

Members: 4.

Established: July 26, 1947.

Chairman: The President.

Other members: Vice President; Secretary of State; Secretary of Defense.

Activities: Assesses and appraises objectives, commitments and risks of United States in relation to our actual and potential military power.

OFFICE OF ADMINISTRATION
Old Executive Office Bldg. (20500).

Established: Dec. 12, 1977.

Director: John F. W. Rogers.

Activities: Provides the common services for the Executive Office of the President such as mail, payroll, dataprocessing and messengers.

OFFICE OF MANAGEMENT AND BUDGET
Executive Office Bldg. (20503).

Established: July 1, 1970.

Director: David A. Stockman.

Activities: Assists President in preparing budget and formulating fiscal program; supervises administration of budget; coordinates advice on proposed legislation; plans improvements in statistical services; keeps President informed of progress of activities by government agencies so that Congressional appropriations are spent most economically.

OFFICE OF SCIENCE AND TECHNOLOGY POLICY
Old Executive Office Building (20506).

Established: May 11, 1976

Director: George A. Keyworth, Jr.

Activities: Advises the President on scientific, engineering and technological aspects of issues requiring his attention.

OFFICE OF THE UNITED STATES TRADE REPRESENTATIVE
600 17th St., N.W. (20506).

Established: Jan. 15, 1963.

Trade Representative: William E. Brock.

Activities: Advises the President on the administration and carrying out of the trade agreements program and on non-tariff barriers to international trade and international commodity agreements; chairs the Trade Expansion Act Advisory Committee.

OFFICE OF POLICY DEVELOPMENT
1600 Pennsylvania Ave., N.W. (20500).

Established: Jan. 21, 1981.

Director: Roger B. Porter.

Activities: Formulates and coordinates domestic policy recommendations for the President.

Executive Departments

DEPARTMENT OF STATE
2201 C St., N.W. (20520).

Established: 1781 as Department of Foreign Affairs; reconstituted, 1789, following adoption of Constitution; name changed to Department of State Sept. 15, 1789.

Secretary: George P. Shultz.

Deputy Secretary: Kenneth W. Dam.

Chief Delegate to U.N.: Jeane J. Kirkpatrick.

Activities: Determines government policy in relation to international problems; formulates measures for promoting friendship with other countries; develops policies and programs for U.S. participation in U.N. and other international organizations; conducts correspondence with our representatives abroad and accredited foreign representatives here; administers Foreign Service.

DEPARTMENT OF THE TREASURY
15th St. & Pennsylvania Ave., N.W. (20220).

Established: Sept. 2, 1789.

Secretary: Donald T. Regan.

Deputy Secretary: Richard McNamar.

Treasurer of the U.S.: Angela M. Buchanan.

Comptroller of the Currency: C. T. Conover.

Activities: Manages national finances; grants warrants for money drawn from Treasury pursuant to legal appropriations; handles collection of revenue; keeps and renders public accounts; prepares plans for improvement of revenue and for support of public credit; controls coinage and printing of money; administers Secret Service, Customs Service, Internal Revenue Service, Bureau of Engraving and Printing, Bureau of the Mint, Federal Law Enforcement Training Center, Bureau of the Public Debt, Bureau of Alcohol, Tobacco, and Firearms, Bureau of Government Financial Operations.

DEPARTMENT OF DEFENSE

The Pentagon (20301).

Established: July 26, 1947, as National Department Establishment; name changed to Department of Defense on Aug. 10, 1949. Subordinate to Secretary of Defense are Secretaries of Army, Navy, Air Force.

Secretary: Caspar W. Weinberger.

Deputy Secretary: Paul Thayer.

Secretary of Army: John O. Marsh, Jr.

Secretary of Navy: John F. Lehman, Jr.

Secretary of Air Force: Verne Orr.

Commandant of Marine Corps: Gen. P. X. Kelly.

Joint Chiefs of Staff:[1] Gen. John W. Vessey, Jr., Chairman; Adm. James D. Watkins, Navy; Gen. Charles A. Gabriel, Air Force: Gen. John A. Wickham, Jr., Army; Gen. P. X. Kelly, Marine Corps.

Activities: Provides for security of U.S. by establishing integrated policies and procedures; coordinates and directs the activities of three separately administered military departments (Army, Navy, and Air Force).

1. Consisting of chairman and chiefs of each service.

DEPARTMENT OF JUSTICE

Constitution Ave. between 9th & 10th Sts., N.W. (20530).

Established: Office of Attorney General was created Sept. 24, 1789. Although he was one of original Cabinet members, he was not executive department head until June 22, 1870, when Department of Justice was established.

Attorney General: William French Smith.

Deputy Attorney General: Edward C. Schmults.

Solicitor General: Rex E. Lee.

Director of FBI: William H. Webster.

Activities: Provides means for enforcing federal laws; investigates and detects violations; represents U.S. in legal matters generally and gives advice and opinions when requested by President or heads of executive departments; directs FBI, Bureau of Prisons, Immigration and Naturalization Service, Drug Enforcement Administration, Marshals Service, Justice System Improvement Act Agencies.

DEPARTMENT OF THE INTERIOR

C St. between 18th & 19th Sts., N.W. (20240).

Established: March 3, 1849.

Secretary: William P. Clark

Under Secretary: Joseph J. Simmons, 3rd.

Activities: Develops and conserves natural resources of U.S. and territories; supervises public business relating to such offices as Bureau of Land Management, Geological Survey, Bureau of Indian Affairs, National Park Service, Bureau of Mines, Fish and Wildlife Service, Bureau of Land Management, Heritage Conservation and Recreation Service, Water and Power Resources Service.

DEPARTMENT OF AGRICULTURE

Independence Ave. between 12th & 14th Sts., S.W. (20250).

Established: May 15, 1862. Administered by Commissioner of Agriculture until 1889, when it was made executive department.

Secretary: John R. Block.

Deputy Secretary: Richard E. Lying.

Activities: Conducts comprehensive research and educational program relating to agriculture; provides crop reports, commodity standards, meat inspection and other marketing services; administers national forests; aids in flood control; administers price-support and production-adjustment programs; makes loans to farmers; supervises Farmers Home Administration, Agricultural Marketing Service, Rural Electrification Administration, Federal Grain Inspection Service, Animal and Plant Health Inspection Service, Food and Nutrition Service; Food Safety and Inspection Service, Commodity Credit Corporation, Federal Crop Insurance Corporation, Science and Education Administration, Soil Conservation Service, Office of Environmental Quality, Forest Service, Foreign Agricultural Service, Agricultural Stabilization and Conservation Service, Office of International Cooperation and Development, Agricultural Research Service, Agricultural Marketing Service.

DEPARTMENT OF COMMERCE

14th St. between Constitution Ave. & E St., N.W. (20230).

Established: Department of Commerce and Labor was created Feb. 14, 1903. On March 4, 1913, all labor activities were transferred out of Department of Commerce and Labor and it was renamed Department of Commerce.

Secretary: Malcolm Baldrige.

Deputy Secretary: Guy W. Fiske.

Activities: Fosters and develops foreign and domestic commerce of U.S.; maintains Bureau of the Census, Economic Development Administration, Bureau of Economic Analysis, Patent and Trademark Office, National Oceanic and Atmospheric Administration (including National Weather Service), National Technical Information Service, National Telecommunications and Information Service, Travel and Tourism Administration, National Bureau of Standards, Minority Business Development Agency, Office of Industrial Economics.

DEPARTMENT OF LABOR

200 Constitution Ave., N.W. (20210).

Established: Bureau of Labor was created in 1884 under Department of the Interior; later became independent department without executive rank. Returned to bureau status in Department of Commerce and Labor, but on March 4, 1913, became independent executive department under its present name.

Secretary: Raymond J. Donovan.

Under Secretary: Ford B. Ford.

Activities: Promotes welfare of wage earners of U.S., improving working conditions and advancing opportunities for profitable employment; directs collection and collation of statistics concerning labor conditions; promulgates and enforces certain maximum-hour, minimum-wage, child-labor, safety and health standards. Maintains Employment and Training Administration, Labor-Management Services Administration, Employment Standards Administration, Occupational Safety and Health Administration, Bureau of Labor Statistics, Women's Bureau, Mine Safety and Health Administration.

DEPARTMENT OF HEALTH AND HUMAN SERVICES[1]

200 Independence Ave., S.W. (20201).

Established: April 11, 1953, replacing Federal Security Agency created in 1939.[1]

Secretary: Margaret M. Heckler.

Under Secretary: John A. Svahn.

Surgeon General: Dr. C. Everett Koop.

Activities: Supervises and coordinates various organizations within the department. Organizations are: Food and Drug Administration, Office of Human Development Services, Public Health Service, Social Security Administration, Alcohol, Drug Abuse and Mental Health Administration, National Institutes of Health, Center for Disease Control, Health Care Financing Administration, Office of Child Support Enforcement, Health Resources Administration, Office of Community Services.

1. Originally Department of Health, Education and Welfare. Name changed in May 1980 when Department of Education was activated.

DEPARTMENT OF HOUSING AND URBAN DEVELOPMENT

451 7th St., S.W. (20410).

Established: 1965, replacing Housing and Home Finance Agency created in 1947.

Secretary: Samuel R. Pierce, Jr.

Under Secretary: Vacant.

Activities: Supervises and coordinates New Community Development Corporation, Government National Mortgage Association.

DEPARTMENT OF TRANSPORTATION

400 7th St., S.W. (20590).

Established: Oct. 15, 1966, as result of Department of Transportation Act, which became effective April 1, 1967.

Secretary: Elizabeth Hanford Dole.

Deputy Secretary: Vacant.

Activities: Supervises and coordinates activities of Coast Guard, Federal Aviation Administration, Federal Highway Administration, Federal Railroad Administration, St. Lawrence Seaway Development Corporation, National Highway Traffic Safety Administration, Urban Mass Transportation Administration, Maritime Administration.

DEPARTMENT OF ENERGY

1000 Independence Ave., S.W. (20585).

Established: Aug. 1977.

Secretary: Donald Paul Hodel.

Deputy Secretary: Vacant.

Activities: Takes over the Federal Energy Administration, the Federal Power Commission, the Energy Research and Development Administration, and functions of other government agencies concerned with energy. Has management responsibility for such projects as Bonneville Dam, the Energy Information Administration, the Energy Regulatory Commission, Economic Regulatory Administration.

DEPARTMENT OF EDUCATION

400 Maryland Avenue, S.W. (20202).

Established: Oct. 17, 1979.

Secretary: Terrel H. Bell.

Under Secretary: Gary L. Jones.

Activities: Administers federally mandated education programs that pertain to elementary and secondary education, post-secondary, vocational and adult education, and special education and rehabilitative services.

Major Independent Agencies

ACTION

806 Connecticut Ave., N.W. (20525).

Established: July 1, 1971.

Director: Thomas Weir Pauken.

Activities: Coordinates a system of volunteer services to people in need at home and abroad; administers Peace Corps and VISTA (Volunteers in Service to America).

CIVIL AERONAUTICS BOARD (CAB)

1825 Connecticut Ave., N.W. (20428).

Members: 4.

Established: June 30, 1940.

Chairman: Dan McKinnon.

Activities: Regulates economic aspects of U.S. air carrier operation; assists in development of international air transportation; promotes safety in civil aviation.

CONSUMER PRODUCT SAFETY COMMISSION

1111 18th St., N.W. (20207).

Members: 5.

Established: Oct. 27, 1972.

Chairman: Nancy Harvey Steorts.

Activities: Protects the public against unreasonable risks of injury associated with consumer products; assists consumers to evaluate the comparative safety of products; develops uniform safety standards for products; promotes research into causes and prevention of product-related deaths, illnesses, and injuries.

ENVIRONMENTAL PROTECTION AGENCY (EPA)

401 M St., S.W. (20460).

Established: Dec. 2, 1970.

Administrator: William D. Ruckelshaus.

Activities: Coordinates governmental action to assure protection of the environment by abating and controlling pollution.

EQUAL EMPLOYMENT OPPORTUNITY COMMISSION (EEOC)

2401 E St., N.W. (20506).

Members: 5.

Established: July 2, 1965.

Chairman: Clarence Thomas.

Activities: Prohibits employment discrimination based on race, color, religion, sex, or national origin.

FARM CREDIT ADMINISTRATION (FCA)

490 L'Enfant Plaza East, S.W. (20578).

Members: 13.

Established: July 17, 1916.

Chairman of Federal Farm Credit Board: John D. Naill.

Activities: Supervises and coordinates cooperative credit system for agriculture; provides long- and short-term credit to farmers and their cooperative marketing, purchasing, and business service organizations.

FEDERAL COMMUNICATIONS COMMISSION (FCC)
1919 M St., N.W. (20554).
Members: 7.
Established: 1934.
Chairman: Mark S. Fowler.
Activities: Regulates interstate and foreign communications by wire and radio, including amateur radio and TV; regulates operator's licenses; classifies radio stations and prescribes their services.

FEDERAL DEPOSIT INSURANCE CORPORATION (FDIC)
550 17th St., N.W. (20429).
Members: 3.
Established: June 16, 1933.
Chairman: William M. Isaac.
Activities: Insures (up to $100,000) deposits in national banks, state banks that are members of the Federal Reserve System, and other state banks that qualify for Federal Deposit Insurance.

FEDERAL ELECTION COMMISSION (FEC)
1325 K St., N.W. (20463).
Members: 6.
Established: 1974.
Chairman: Danny L. McDonald.
Activities: Certifies distribution of public funding of federal elections; regulates compliance with Federal Election Campaign Act; makes available to the public copies of reports filed with the commission.

FEDERAL MARITIME COMMISSION
1100 L St., N.W. (20573).
Members: 4.
Established: Aug. 12, 1961.
Chairman: Alan Green, Jr.
Activities: Regulates waterborne shipping in foreign and domestic offshore commerce of U.S.

FEDERAL MEDIATION AND CONCILIATION SERVICE (FMCS)
2100 K St., N.W. (20427).
Established: 1947.
Director: Kay McMurray.
Activities: Assists in labor-management disputes in industries affecting interstate commerce to reach settlements by mediation or conciliation.

FEDERAL RESERVE SYSTEM (FRS), BOARD OF GOVERNORS OF
20th St. & Constitution Ave., N.W. (20551).
Members: 7.
Established: Dec. 23, 1913.
Chairman: Paul A. Volcker.
Activities: Supervises the 12 Federal Reserve banks, 24 branches and member commercial banks; determines country's monetary policy, including setting maximum interest paid by member banks, amount of credit extended for purchase of securities and discount rates charged by members; handles Government deposits and debt issue; regulates open-market operations; issues Federal Reserve notes.

FEDERAL TRADE COMMISSION (FTC)
Pennsylvania Ave. at 6th St., N.W. (20580).
Members: 5.
Established: Sept. 26, 1914.
Chairman: James C. Miller, 3rd.
Activities: Prevents unfair competition, deceptive practices, false advertising, price discrimination, monopolies.

GENERAL SERVICES ADMINISTRATION (GSA)
18th and F Sts., N.W. (20405).
Established: July 1, 1949.
Administrator: Gerald P. Carmen.
Activities: Establishes policy and provides efficient system for management of the government's property and records, including construction and operation of buildings, procurement and distribution of supplies, stockpiling of strategic materials and utilization and disposal of property. Directs National Archives and Records Service, Federal Supply Service, Public Buildings Service, Federal Preparedness Agency, Automated Data and Telecommunications Service.

INTERSTATE COMMERCE COMMISSION (ICC)
12th St. & Constitution Ave., N.W. (20423).
Members: 11.
Established: Feb. 4, 1887.
Chairman: Reese H. Taylor, Jr.
Activities: Regulates railroads, motor carriers, water carriers, and freight forwarders as to rates, through-routes, services, and bills of lading; authorizes mergers or consolidations; authorizes issue of securities by carriers.

NATIONAL AERONAUTICS AND SPACE ADMINISTRATION (NASA)
400 Maryland Ave., S.W. (20546).
Established: 1958.
Administrator: James M. Beggs.
Activities: Conducts research into problems of flight within and outside earth's atmosphere.

NATIONAL FOUNDATION ON THE ARTS AND THE HUMANITIES
1100 Pennsylvania Ave., N.W., (20506).
Established: 1965.
Chairmen: National Endowment for the Arts, Frank Hodsoll; National Endowment for the Humanities, William J. Bennett.
Activities: Encourages and supports national progress in the humanities and the arts. Also includes National Councils on the Arts and the Humanities, which coordinates activities of the two endowments and related programs of other agencies.

NATIONAL LABOR RELATIONS BOARD (NLRB)
1717 Pennsylvania Ave., N.W. (20570).
Members: 5.
Established: July 5, 1935.
Chairman: Donald L. Dotson.
Activities: Prevents unfair labor practices by employers or labor organizations; conducts secret ballots among employees to determine bargaining representatives.

NATIONAL MEDIATION BOARD
1425 K St., N.W. (20572).
Members: 2
Established: June 21, 1934.
Chairman: Robert O. Harris.
Activities: Mediates railroad and aviation disputes over wages, hours, and working conditions; investigates certification of employee organizations.

NATIONAL SCIENCE FOUNDATION (NSF)
1800 G St., N.W. (20550).
Established: 1950.
Director: Lewis N. Branscomb.
Activities: Awards grants and contracts to sup-

port research in the sciences. Encourages research in areas that can lead to improvements in economic growth, productivity, and environmental quality. Administered by 24-member National Science Board.

NATIONAL TRANSPORTATION SAFETY BOARD
800 Independence Ave., S.W. (20594).
Members: 5
Established: April 1, 1975.
Chairman: James E. Burnett.
Activities: Conducts investigations into accidents, assesses techniques of accident investigation and recommends safety-improvement measures.

NUCLEAR REGULATORY COMMISSION (NRC)
1717 H St., N.W. (20555).
Members: 5.
Established: Jan. 19, 1975.
Chairman: Nunzio J. Pallidino.
Activities: Regulates civilian nuclear facilities to assure protection of public health and safety and the environment, and safeguarding of nuclear materials and facilities.

OFFICE OF PERSONNEL MANAGEMENT (OPM)
1900 E St., N.W. (20415).
Members: 3
Established: Jan. 1, 1979.
Director: Donald J. Devine.
Activities: Provides examinations to test fitness of applicants for positions in competitive service; provides personnel in response to requests from appointing officers; investigates applicants for national security purposes; classifies positions; provides leadership to Federal agencies in personnel matters.

SECURITIES AND EXCHANGE COMMISSION (SEC)
450 5th St., N.W. (20549).
Members: 5.
Established: July 2, 1934
Chairman: John S. R. Shad.
Activities: Registers and issues regulations for securities and exchanges; registers securities offered for public sale; penalizes violators of regulations subject to appeal to U.S. Court of Appeals.

SELECTIVE SERVICE SYSTEM (SSS)
National Headquarters (20435).
Established: Sept. 16, 1940.
Director: Thomas K. Turnage.
Activities: Authorizes registration of male citizens and all other male persons, except aliens in certain categories, for military service. (Authority to induct registrants expired July 1, 1973.)

SMALL BUSINESS ADMINISTRATION (SBA)
1441 L St., N.W. (20416).
Established: July 30, 1953.
Administrator: James C. Sanders.
Activities: Aids and assists the interests of small business firms to insure a fair share of total government contracts; makes loans to small firms and victims of flood and disaster.

TENNESSEE VALLEY AUTHORITY (TVA)
400 West Summit Hill Drive, Knoxville, Tenn. (37902).
Washington office: Capitol Hill Office Bldg., 412 First St., S.E. (20444).
Members of Board of Directors: 3.
Established: May 18, 1933.
Chairman: Charles H. Dean, Jr.
Activities: Provides navigable channel and flood control of Tennessee River and some of its larger tributaries; disposes of surplus electric power, improves, increases, and cheapens fertilizer production.

U.S. ARMS CONTROL AND DISARMAMENT AGENCY
320 21st St., N.W., (20451).
Established: Sept. 26, 1961.
Director: Kenneth L. Adelman.
Special Representative for Negotiations: Edward L. Rowny.
Activities: Conducts studies and provides advice relating to arms control and disarmament policy formulation; prepares for and manages U.S. participation in international negotiations in arms control and disarmament; prepares for, operates, or as needed, directs U.S. participation in international control systems.

U.S. COMMISSION ON CIVIL RIGHTS
1121 Vermont Avenue, N.W. (20425).
Members: 6.
Established: 1957.
Chairman: Clarence M. Pendleton, Jr.
Activities: Collects and studies information concerning discrimination or denial of equal protection of the nation's laws because of race, color, religion, sex, age, handicap, or national origin. Complaints about denials of rights are usually referred to the appropriate Federal agencies for action.

U.S. INFORMATION AGENCY
400 C St., S.W. (20547).
Established: April 1, 1978.
Director: Charles Z. Wick.
Activities: Conducts international communication, educational, cultural, and exchange programs with other peoples of the world.

U.S. INTERNATIONAL DEVELOPMENT COOPERATION AGENCY
320 21st St., N.W. (20523).
Established: Oct. 1, 1979.
Director: M. Peter McPherson.
Activities: Plans and coordinates policy for economic matters affecting relations with developing countries. Administers Agency for International Development, and Overseas Private Investment Corporation.

U.S. INTERNATIONAL TRADE COMMISSION
701 E St., N.W. (20436).
Members: 6.
Established: Sept. 8, 1916.
Chairman: Alfred Eckes.
Activities: Investigates customs laws, unfair competition, and foreign and domestic manufacturing costs; advises the President on duty rates.

U.S. POSTAL SERVICE
475 L'Enfant Plaza West, S.W. (20260).
Postmaster General: William F. Bolger.
Deputy Postmaster General: C. Neil Benson.
Activities: Maintains postal system of U.S.

Established: Office of Postmaster General and temporary post office system created in 1789. Act of Feb. 20, 1792, made detailed provisions for Post Office Department. Postmaster General became Cabinet member in 1829, and Department received executive status in 1872. In 1970 became independent agency headed by 11-member board of governors. Postmaster General, no longer Cabinet member, is chosen by nine governors, who, with Postmaster General, choose Deputy Postmaster General.

VETERANS ADMINISTRATION (VA)
810 Vermont Ave., N.W. (20420).
Established: July 21, 1930.
Administrator: Harry N. Walters.
Activities: Administers laws authorizing benefits for veterans and dependents or beneficiaries. Included are hospitals, pensions, insurance, loans, education, etc.

Other Independent Agencies

Administrative Conference of the United States—2120 L St., N.W. (20037).
American Battle Monuments Commission—5127 Pulaski Bldg. (20314).
Appalachian Regional Commission—1666 Connecticut Ave., N.W. (20235).
Board for International Broadcasting—Suite 1100, 1201 Connecticut Ave., N.W. (20036).
Commission of Fine Arts—708 Jackson Place, N.W. (20006).
Commodity Futures Trading Commission—2033 K St., N.W. (20581).
Export-Import Bank of the United States—811 Vermont Ave., N.W. (20571).
Federal Emergency Management Agency—500 C St., S.W. (20472).
Federal Home Loan Bank Board—1700 G St., N.W. (20552).
Federal Labor Relations Authority—500 C St., S.W. (20472).
Inter-American Foundation—1515 Wilson Blvd., Rosslyn, Va. (22209).
Merit Systems Protection Board—1120 Vermont Ave., N.W. (20419).
National Commission on Libraries and Information Science—7th & D Sts., S.W. (20024).
National Credit Union Administration—1776 G St., N.W. (20456).
Occupational Safety and Health Review Commission—1825 K St., N.W. (20006).
Panama Canal Commission—425 13th St., N.W. (20004).
Peace Corps—806 Connecticut Ave., N.W. (20526).
Pension Benefit Guaranty Corporation—2020 K St., N.W. (20006).
Postal Rate Commission—2000 L St., N.W. (20268).
President's Committee on Employment of the Handicapped—1111 20th St., N.W. (20036).
President's Council on Physical Fitness and Sports—450 5th St., S.W. (20001).
Railroad Retirement Board (RRB)—844 Rush St., Chicago, Ill. (60611); Washington Liaison Office: Room 630, 425 13th St., N.W. (20004).
U.S. Parole Commission—5550 Friendship Blvd., Chevy Chase, Md. (20815).

Legislative Department

ARCHITECT OF THE CAPITOL
U.S. Capitol Building (20515).
Established: First Architect of the Capitol was appointed in 1793; office has been continuous since 1851.
Architect of Capitol: George M. White.
Activities: Architect of the Capitol has charge of structural and mechanical care of Capitol Building and various other government buildings in Washington.

GENERAL ACCOUNTING OFFICE (GAO)
441 G St., N.W. (20548).
Established: 1921.
Comptroller General: Charles A. Bowsher.
Deputy Comptroller General: Vacant.
Activities: Assists Congress in providing legislative control over receipt, disbursement, and application of public funds.

GOVERNMENT PRINTING OFFICE (GPO)
North Capitol & H Sts., N.W. (20401).
Established: June 23, 1860.
Public Printer: Danford L. Sawyer, Jr.
Superintendent of Documents: Michael F. DiMario.
Activities: Executes printing and binding orders for Congress and federal agencies; distributes government publications.

LIBRARY OF CONGRESS
10 First St., S.E. (20540).
Established: April 24, 1800.
Librarian of Congress: Daniel J. Boorstin.
Activities: Extends services to members of government and offers facilities for persons engaged in scholarly research.

OFFICE OF TECHNOLOGY ASSESSMENT
600 Pennsylvania Ave., S.E. (20510).
Established: 1972.
Director: John H. Gibbons.
Activities: Helps Congress anticipate and plan for the consequences of the uses of technology.

UNITED STATES BOTANIC GARDEN
Office of Director, 245 First St., S.W. (20024).
Established: 1820.
Director: George M. White (acting).
Activities: Collects, cultivates, and grows various vegetable products for exhibition and study.

Quasi-Official Agencies

American National Red Cross—17th & D Sts., N.W. (20006).
Legal Services Corporation—733 15th St., N.W. (20005).
National Academy of Sciences, National Academy of Engineering, National Research Council, Institute of Medicine—2101 Constitution Ave., N.W. (20418).
National Railroad Passenger Corporation (Amtrak)—400 N. Capitol St., N.W. (20001).
Smithsonian Institution—1000 Jefferson Dr., S.W. (20560).
U.S. Railway Association—955 L'Enfant Plaza North, S.W. (20595).
U.S. Synthetic Fuels Corporation—2121 K St., N.W. (20586).

Biographies of the Presidents

GEORGE WASHINGTON was born on Feb. 22, 1732 (Feb. 11, 1731/2, old style) in Westmoreland County, Va. While in his teens, he trained as a surveyor, and at the age of 20 he was appointed adjutant in the Virginia militia. For the next three years, he fought in the wars against the French and Indians, serving as Gen. Edward Braddock's aide in the disastrous campaign against Fort Duquesne. In 1759, he resigned from the militia, married Martha Dandridge Custis, a widow, and settled down as a gentleman farmer at Mount Vernon, Va.

As a militiaman, Washington had been exposed to the arrogance of the British officers, and his experience as a planter with British commercial restrictions increased his anti-British sentiment. He opposed the Stamp Act of 1765 and after 1770 became increasingly prominent in organizing resistance. A delegate to the Continental Congress, Washington was selected as commander in chief of the Continental Army and took command at Cambridge, Mass., on July 3, 1775.

Inadequately supported and sometimes covertly sabotaged by the Congress, in charge of troops who were inexperienced, badly equipped, and impatient of discipline, Washington conducted the war on the policy of avoiding major engagements with the British and wearing them down by harrassing tactics. His able generalship, along with the French alliance and the growing weariness within Britain, brought the war to a conclusion with the surrender of Cornwallis at Yorktown, Va., on Oct. 19, 1781.

The chaotic years under the Articles of Confederation led Washington to return to public life in the hope of promoting the formation of a strong central government. He presided over the Constitutional Convention and yielded to the universal demand that he serve as first President. He was inaugurated on April 30, 1789, in New York, the first national capital. In office, he sought to unite the nation and establish the authority of the new government at home and abroad. Greatly distressed by the emergence of the Hamilton-Jefferson rivalry, Washington worked to maintain neutrality but actually sympathized more with Hamilton. Following his unanimous re-election in 1792, his second term was dominated by the Federalists. His Farewell Address on Sept. 17, 1796 (published but never delivered) rebuked party spirit and warned against "permanent alliances" with foreign powers.

He died at Mount Vernon on Dec. 14, 1799.

JOHN ADAMS was born on Oct. 30 (Oct. 19, old style), 1735, at Braintree (now Quincy), Mass. A Harvard graduate, he considered teaching and the ministry but finally turned to law and was admitted to the bar in 1758. Six years later, he married Abigail Smith. He opposed the Stamp Act, served as lawyer for patriots indicted by the British, and be the time of the Continental Congresses, was in the vanguard of the movement for independence. In 1778, he went to France as commissioner. Subsequently he helped negotiate the peace treaty with Britain, and in 1785 became envoy to London. Resigning in 1788, he was elected Vice President under Washington and was re-elected in 1792.

Though a Federalist, Adams did not get along with Hamilton, who sought to prevent his election to the presidency in 1796 and thereafter intrigued against his administration. In 1798, Adam's independent policy averted a war with France but completed the break with Hamilton and the right-wing Federalists; at the same time, the enactment of the Alien and Sedition Acts, directed against foreigners and against critics of the government, exasperated the Jeffersonian opposition. The split between Adams and Hamilton resulted in Jefferson's becoming the next President. Adams retired to his home in Quincy. He and Jefferson died on the same day, July 4, 1826, the 50th anniversary of the signing of the Declaration of Independence.

His *Defence of the Constitutions of Government of the United States* (1787) contains original and striking, if conservative, political ideas.

THOMAS JEFFERSON was born on April 13 (April 2, old style), 1743, at Shadwell in Goochland (now Albemarle) County, Va. A William and Mary graduate, he studied law, but from the start showed an interest in science and philosophy. His literary skill and political clarity brought him to the forefront of the revolutionary movement in Virginia. As delegate to the Continental Congress, he drafted the Declaration of Independence. In 1776, he entered the Virginia House of Delegates and initiated a comprehensive reform program for the abolition of feudal survivals in land tenure and the separation of church and state.

In 1779, he became governor, but constitutional limitations on his power, combined with his own lack of executive energy, caused an unsatisfactory administration, culminating in Jefferson's virtual abdication when the British invaded Virginia in 1781. He retired to his beautiful home at Monticello, Va., to his family. His wife, Martha Wayles Skelton, whom he married in 1772, died in 1782.

Jefferson's *Notes on Virginia* (1784–85) illustrate his many-faceted interests, his limitless intellectual curiosity, his deep faith in agrarian democracy. Sent to Congress in 1783, he helped lay down the decimal system and drafted basic reports on the organization of the western lands. In 1785 he was appointed minister to France, where the Anglo-Saxon liberalism he had drawn from John Locke, the British philosopher, was stimulated by contact with the thought that would soon ferment in the French Revolution. In 1789, Washington appointed him Secretary of State. While favoring the Constitution and a strengthened central government, Jefferson came to believe that Hamilton contemplated the establishment of a monarchy. Growing differences resulted in Jefferson's resignation on Dec. 31, 1793.

Elected vice president in 1796, Jefferson continued to serve as spiritual leader of the opposition to Federalism, particularly to the repressive Alien and Sedition Acts. He was elected President in 1801 by the House of Representatives as a result of Hamilton's decision to throw the Federalist votes to him rather than to Aaron Burr, who had tied him in electoral votes. He was the first President to be inaugurated in Washington, which he had helped to design.

The purchase of Louisiana from France in 1803, though in violation of Jefferson's earlier constitutional scruples, was the most notable act of his administration. Re-elected in 1804, with the Federalist Charles C. Pinckney opposing him, Jefferson tried desperately to keep the United States out of the Napoleonic Wars in Europe, employing to this end the unpopular embargo policy.

After his retirement to Monticello in 1809, he developed his interest in education, founding the University of Virginia and watching its development with never-flagging interest. He died at Monticello on July 4, 1826. Jefferson had an enormous variety of interests and skills, ranging from education and science to architecture and music.

JAMES MADISON was born in Port Conway, Va., on March 16, 1751 (March 5, 1750/1, old style). A Princeton graduate, he joined the struggle for independence on his return to Virginia in 1771. In the 1770s and 1780s he was active in state politics, where he championed the Jefferson reform program, and in the Continental Congress. Madison was influential in the Constitutional Convention as leader of the group favoring a strong central government and as recorder of the debates; and he subsequently wrote, in collaboration with Alexander Hamilton and John Jay, the *Federalist* papers to aid the campaign for the adoption of the Constitution.

Serving in the new Congress, Madison soon emerged as the leader in the House of the men who opposed Hamilton's financial program and his pro-British leanings in foreign policy. Retiring from Congress in 1797, he continued to be active in Virginia and drafted the Virginia Resolution protesting the Alien and Sedition Acts. His intimacy with Jefferson made him the natural choice for Secretary of State in 1801.

In 1809, Madison succeeded Jefferson as President, defeating Charles C. Pinckney. His attractive wife, Dolley Payne Todd, whom he married in 1794, brought a new social sparkle to the executive mansion. In the meantime, increasing tension with Britain culminated in the War of 1812—a war for which the United States was unprepared and for which Madison lacked the executive talent to clear out incompetence and mobilize the nation's energies. Madison was re-elected in 1812, running against the Federalist De Witt Clinton. In 1814, the British actually captured Washington and forced Madison to flee to Virginia.

Madison's domestic program capitulated to the Hamiltonian policies that he had resisted 20 years before and he now signed bills to establish a United States Bank and a higher tariff.

After his presidency, he remained in retirement in Virginia until his death on June 28, 1836.

JAMES MONROE was born on April 28, 1758, in Westmoreland County, Va. A William and Mary graduate, he served in the army during the first years of the Revolution and was wounded at Trenton. He then entered Virginia politics and later national politics under the sponsorship of Jefferson. In 1786, he married Elizabeth (Eliza) Kortright.

Fearing centralization, Monroe opposed the adoption of the Constitution and, as senator from Virginia, was highly critical of the Hamiltonian program. In 1794, he was appointed minister to France, where his ardent sympathies with the Revolution exceeded the wishes of the State Department. His troubled diplomatic career ended with his recall in 1796. From 1799 to 1802, he was governor of Virginia. In 1803, Jefferson sent him to France to help negotiate the Louisiana Purchase and for the next few years he was active in various negotiations on the Continent.

In 1808, Monroe flirted with the radical wing of the Republican Party, which opposed Madison's candidacy; but the presidential boom came to naught and, after a brief term as governor of Virginia in 1811, Monroe accepted Madison's offer to become Secretary of State. During the War of 1812, he vainly sought a field command and instead served as Secretary of War from September 1814 to March 1815.

Elected President in 1816 over the Federalist Rufus King, and re-elected without opposition in 1820, Monroe, the last of the Virginia dynasty, pursued the course of systematic tranquilization that won for his administrations the name "the era of good feeling." He continued Madison's surrender to the Hamiltonian domestic program, signed the Missouri Compromise, acquired Florida, and with the able assistance of his Secretary of State, John Quincy Adams, promulgated the Monroe Doctrine in 1823, declaring against foreign colonization or intervention in the Americas. He died in New York City on July 4, 1831, the third president to die on the anniversary of Independence.

JOHN QUINCY ADAMS was born on July 11, 1767, at Braintree (now Quincy), Mass., the son of John Adams, the second President. He spent his early years in Europe with his father, graduated from Harvard, and entered law practice. His anti-Jeffersonian newspaper articles won him political attention. In 1794, he became minister to the Netherlands, the first of several diplomatic posts that occupied him until his return to Boston in 1801. In 1797, he married Louisa Catherine Johnson.

In 1803, Adams was elected to the Senate, nominally as a Federalist, but his repeated displays of independence on such issues as the Louisiana Purchase and the embargo caused his party to demand his resignation and ostracize him socially. In 1809, Madison rewarded him for his support of Jefferson by appointing him minister to St. Petersburg. He helped negotiate the Treaty of Ghent in 1814, and in 1815 became minister to London. In 1817 Monroe appointed him Secretary of State where he served with great distinction, gaining Florida from Spain without hostilities and playing an equal part with Monroe in formulating the Monroe Doctrine.

When no presidential candidate received a majority of electoral votes in 1824, Adams, with the support of Henry Clay, was elected by the House in 1825 over Andrew Jackson, who had the original plurality. Adams had ambitious plans of government activity to foster internal improvements and promote the arts and sciences, but congressional obstructionism, combined with his own unwillingness or inability to play the role of a politician, resulted in little being accomplished. After being defeated for re-elected by Jackson in 1828, he successfully ran for the House of Representatives in 1830. There though nominally a Whig, he pursued as ever an independent course. He led the fight to force Congress to receive antislavery petitions and fathered the Smithsonian Institution.

Stricken on the floor of the House, he died on Feb. 23, 1848. His long and detailed *Diary* gives a unique picture of the personalities and politics of the times.

ANDREW JACKSON was born on March 15, 1767, in what is now generally agreed to be Waxhaw, S.C. After a turbulent boyhood as an orphan and a British prisoner, he moved west to Tennessee, where he soon qualified for law practice but found time for such frontier pleasures as horse racing, cockfighting, and dueling. His marriage to Rachel Donelson Robards in 1791 was complicated by subsequent legal uncertainties about the status of her divorce. During the 1790s, Jackson served in the Tennessee Constitutional Convention, the United States House of Representatives and Senate, and on the Tennessee Supreme Court.

After some years as a country gentleman, living at the Hermitage near Nashville, Jackson in 1812 was given command of Tennessee troops sent against the Creeks. He defeated the Indians at Horseshoe Bend in 1814; subsequently he became a major general and won the Battle of New Orleans over veteran British troops, though after the treaty of peace had been signed at Ghent. In 1818, Jackson invaded Florida, captured Pensacola, and hanged two Englishmen named Arbuthnot and Ambrister, creating an international incident. A presidential boom began for him in 1821, and to foster it, he returned to the Senate (1823–25). Though he won a plurality of electoral votes in 1824, he lost in the House when Clay threw his strength to Adams. Four years later, he easily defeated Adams.

As President, Jackson greatly expanded the power and prestige of the presidential office and carried through an unprecedented program of domestic reform, vetoing the bill to extend the United States Bank, moving toward a hard-money currency policy, and checking the program of federal internal improvements. He also vindicated federal authority against South Carolina with its doctrine of nullification and against France on the question of debts. The support given his policies by the workingmen of the East as well as by the farmers of the East, West, and South resulted in his triumphant re-election in 1832 over Clay.

After watching the inauguration of his handpicked successor, Martin Van Buren, Jackson retired to the Hermitage, where he maintained a lively interest in national affairs until his death on June 8, 1845.

MARTIN VAN BUREN was born on Dec. 5, 1782, at Kinderhook, N.Y. After graduating from the village school, he became a law clerk, entered practice in 1803, and soon became active in state politics as state senator and attorney general. In 1820, he was elected to the United States Senate. He threw the support of his efficient political organization, known as the Albany Regency, to William H. Crawford in 1824 and to Jackson in 1828. After leading the opposition to Adams's administration in the Senate, he served briefly as governor of New York (1828–29) and resigned to become Jackson's Secretary of State. He was soon on close personal terms with Jackson and played an important part in the Jacksonian program.

In 1832, Van Buren became vice president; in 1836, President. The Panic of 1837 overshadowed his term. He attributed it to the overexpansion of the credit and favored the establishment of an independent treasury as repository for the federal funds. In 1840, he established a 10-hour day on public works. Defeated by Harrison in 1840, he was the leading contender for the Democratic nomination in 1844 until he publicly opposed immediate annexation of Texas, and was subsequently beaten by the Southern delegations at the Baltimore convention. This incident increased his growing misgivings about the slave power.

After working behind the scenes among the antislavery Democrats, Van Buren joined in the movement that led to the Free-Soil Party and became its candidate for President in 1848. He subsequently returned to the Democratic Party while continuing to object to its pro-Southern policy. He died in Kinderhook on July 24, 1862. His *Autobiography* throws valuable sidelights on the political history of the times.

His wife, Hannah Hoes, whom he married in 1807, died in 1819.

WILLIAM HENRY HARRISON was born in Charles City County, Va., on Feb. 9, 1773. Joining the army in 1791, he was active in Indian fighting in the Northwest, became secretary of the Northwest Territory in 1798 and governor of Indiana in 1800. He married Anna Symmes in 1795. Growing discontent over white encroachments on Indian lands led to the formation of an Indian alliance under Tecumseh to resist further aggressions. In 1811, Harrison won a nominal victory over the Indians at Tippecanoe and in 1813 a more decisive one at the Battle of the Thames, where Tecumseh was killed.

After resigning from the army in 1814, Harrison had an obscure career in politics and diplomacy, ending up 20 years later as a county recorder in Ohio. Nominated for President in 1835 as a military hero whom the conservative politicians hoped to be able to control, he ran surprisingly well against Van Buren in 1836. Four years later, he defeated Van Buren but caught penumonia and died in Washington on April 4, 1841, a month after his inauguration. Harrison was the first president to die in office.

JOHN TYLER was born in Charles City County, Va., on March 29, 1790. A William and Mary graduate, he entered law practice and politics, serving in the House of Representatives (1817–21), as governor of Virginia (1825–27), and as senator (1827–36). A strict constructionist, he supported Crawford in 1824 and Jackson in 1828, but broke with Jackson over his United States Bank policy and became a member of the Southern state-rights group that cooperated with the Whigs. In 1836, he resigned from the Senate rather than follow instructions from the Virginia legislature to vote for a resolution expunging censure of Jackson from the Senate record.

Elected vice president on the Whig ticket in 1840, Tyler succeeded to the presidency on Harrison's death. His strict-constructionist views soon caused a split with the Henry Clay wing of the Whig party and a stalemate on domestic questions. Tyler's more considerable achievements were his support of the Webster-Ashburton Treaty with Britain and his success in bringing about the annexation of Texas.

After his presidency he lived in retirement in Virginia until the outbreak of the Civil War, when he emerged briefly as chairman of a peace convention and then as delegate to the provisional Congress of the Confederacy. He died on Jan. 18, 1862. He married Letitia Christian in 1813 and, two years after her death in 1842, Julia Gardiner.

JAMES KNOX POLK was born in Mecklenburg County, N.C., on Nov. 2, 1795. A graduate of the University of North Carolina, he moved west to Tennessee, was admitted to the bar, and soon became prominent in state politics. In 1825, he was elected to the House of Representatives, where he opposed Adams and, after 1829, became Jackson's floor leader in the fight against the Bank. In 1835, he became Speaker of the House. Four years later, he was elected governor of Tennessee, but was beaten in tries for re-election in 1841 and 1843.

The supporters of Van Buren for the Democratic

nomination in 1844 counted on Polk as his running mate; but, when Van Buren's stand on Texas alienated Southern support, the convention swung to Polk on the ninth ballot. He was elected over Henry Clay, the Whig candidate. Rapidly disillusioning those who thought that he would not run his own administration, Polk proceeded steadily and precisely to achieve four major objectives—the acquisition of California, the settlement of the Oregon question, the reduction of the tariff, and the establishment of the independent treasury. He also enlarged the Monroe Doctrine to exclude all non-American intervention in American affairs, whether forcible or not, and he forced Mexico into a war that he waged to a successful conclusion.

His wife, Sarah Childress, whom he married in 1824, was a woman of charm and ability. Polk died in Nashville, Tenn., on June 15, 1849.

ZACHARY TAYLOR was born at Montebello, Orange County, Va., on Nov. 24, 1784. Embarking on a military career in 1808, Taylor fought in the War of 1812, the Black Hawk War, and the Seminole War, meanwhile holding garrison jobs on the frontier or desk jobs in Washington. A brigadier general as a result of his victory over the Seminoles at Lake Okeechobee (1837), Taylor held a succession of Southwestern commands and in 1846 established a base on the Rio Grande, where his forces engaged in hostilities that precipitated the war with Mexico. He captured Monterrey in September 1846 and, disregarding Polk's orders to stay on the defensive, defeated Santa Anna at Buena Vista in February 1847, ending the war in the northern provinces.

Though Taylor had never cast a vote for president, his party affiliations were Whiggish and his availability was increased by his difficulties with Polk. He was elected president over the Democrat Lewis Cass. During the revival of the slavery controversy, which was to result in the Compromise of 1850, Taylor began to take an increasingly firm stand against appeasing the South; but he died in Washington on July 9, 1850, during the fight over the Compromise. He married Margaret Mackall Smith in 1810. His bluff and simple soldierly qualities won him the name Old Rough and Ready.

MILLARD FILLMORE was born at Locke, Cayuga County, N.Y., on Jan. 7, 1800. A lawyer, he entered politics with the Anti-Masonic Party under the sponsorship of Thurlow Weed, editor and party boss, and subsequently followed Weed into the Whig Party. He served in the House of Representatives (1833–35 and 1837–43) and played a leading role in writing the tariff of 1842. Defeated for governor of New York in 1844, he became State comptroller in 1848, was put on the Whig ticket with Taylor as a concession to the Clay wing of the party, and became president upon Taylor's death in 1850.

As president, Fillmore broke with Weed and William H. Seward and associated himself with the pro-Southern Whigs, supporting the Compromise of 1850. Defeated for the Whig nomination in 1852, he ran for president in 1856 as candidate of the American, or Know-Nothing Party, which sought to unite the country against foreigners in the alleged hope of diverting it from the explosive slavery issue. Fillmore opposed Lincoln during the Civil War. He died in Buffalo on March 8, 1874.

He was married in 1826 to Abigail Powers, who died in 1853, and in 1858 to Caroline Carmichael McIntosh.

FRANKLIN PIERCE was born at Hillsboro, N.H., on Nov. 23, 1804. A Bowdoin graduate, lawyer, and Jacksonian Democrate, he won rapid political advancement in the party, in part because of the prestige of his father, Gov. Benjamin Pierce. By 1831 he was Speaker of the New Hampshire House of Representatives; from 1833 to 1837, he served in the federal House and from 1837 to 1842 in the Senate. His wife, Jane Means Appleton, whom he married in 1834, disliked Washington and the somewhat dissipated life led by Pierce; in 1842 Pierce resigned from the Senate and began a successful law practice in Concord, N.H. During the Mexican War, he was a brigadier general.

Thereafter Pierce continued to oppose antislavery tendencies within the Democratic Party. As a result, he was the Southern choice to break the deadlock at the Democratic convention of 1852 and was nominated on the 49th ballot. In the election, Pierce overwhelmed Gen. Winfield Scott, the Whig candidate.

As president, Pierce followed a course of appeasing the South at home and of playing with schemes of territorial expansion abroad. The failure of his foreign and domestic policies prevented his renomination; and he died in Concord on Oct. 8, 1869, in relative obscurity.

JAMES BUCHANAN was born near Mercersburg, Pa., on April 23, 1791. A Dickinson graduate and a lawyer, he entered Pennsylvania politics as a Federalist. With the disappearance of the Federalist Party, he became a Jacksonian Democrat. He served with ability in the House (1821–31), as minister to St. Petersburg (1832–33), and in the Senate (1834–45), and in 1845 became Polk's Secretary of State. In 1853, Pierce appointed Buchanan minister to Britain, where he participated with other American diplomats in Europe in drafting the expansionist Ostend Manifesto.

He was elected president in 1856, defeating John C. Frémont, the Republican candidate, and former President Millard Fillmore of the American Party. The growing crisis over slavery presented Buchanan with problems he lacked the will to tackle. His appeasement of the South alienated the Stephen Douglas wing of the Democratic Party without reducing Southern militancy on slavery issues. While denying the right of secession, Buchanan also denied that the federal government could do anything about it. He supported the administration during the Civil War and died in Lancaster, Pa., on June 1, 1868.

The only president to remain a bachelor throughout his term, Buchanan used his charming niece, Harriet Lane, as White House hostess.

ABRAHAM LINCOLN was born in Hardin (now Larue) County, Ky., on Feb. 12, 1809. His family moved to Indiana and then to Illinois, and Lincoln gained what education he could along the way. While reading law, he worked in a store, managed a mill, surveyed, and split rails. In 1834, he went to the Illinois legislature as a Whig and became the party's floor leader. For the next 20 years he practiced law in Springfield, except for a single term (1847–49) in Congress, where he denounced the Mexican War. In 1855, he was a candidate for senator annd the next year he joined the new Republican Party.

A leading but unsuccessful candidate for the vice-presidential nomination with Frémont, Lincoln gained national attention in 1858 when, as

Republican candidate for senator from Illinois, he engaged in a series of debates with Stephen A. Douglas, the Democratic candidate. He lost the election, but continued to prepare the way for the 1860 Republican convention and was rewarded with the presidential nomination on the third ballot. He won the election over three opponents.

From the start, Lincoln made clear that, unlike Buchanan, he believed the national government had the power to crush the rebellion. Not an abolitionist, he held the slavery issue subordinate to that of preserving the Union, but soon perceived that the war could not be brought to a successful conclusion without freeing the slaves. His administration was hampered by the incompetence of many Union generals, the inexperience of the troops, and the harassing political tactics both of the Republican Radicals, who favored a hard policy toward the South, and the Democratic Copperheads, who desired a negotiated peace. The Gettysburg Address of Nov. 19, 1863, marks the high point in the record of American eloquence. Lincoln's long search for a winning combination finally brought Generals Ulysses S. Grant and William T. Sherman on the top; and their series of victories in 1864 dispelled the mutterings from both Radicals and Peace Democrats that at one time seemed to threaten Lincoln's re-election. He was re-elected in 1864, defeating Gen. George B. McClellan, the Democratic candidate. His inaugural address urged leniency toward the South: "With malice toward none, with charity for all . . . let us strive on to finish the work we are in; to bind up the nation's wounds . . ." This policy aroused growing opposition on the part of the Republican Radicals, but before the matter could be put to the test, Lincoln was shot by the actor John Wilkes Booth at Ford's Theater, Washington, on April 14, 1865. He died the next morning.

Lincoln's marriage to Mary Todd in 1842 was often unhappy and turbulent, in part because of his wife's pronounced instability.

ANDREW JOHNSON was born at Raleigh, N.C., on Dec. 29, 1808. Self-educated, he became a tailor in Greeneville, Tenn., but soon went into politics, where he rose steadily. He served in the House of Representatives (1843–54), as governor of Tennessee (1853–57), and as a senator (1857–62). Politically he was a Jacksonian Democrat and his specialty was the fight for a more equitable land policy. Alone among the Southern Senators, he stood by the Union during the Civil War. In 1862, he became war governor of Tennessee and carried out a thankless and difficult job with great courage. Johnson became Lincoln's running mate in 1864 as a result of an attempt to give the ticket a nonpartisan and nonsectional character. Succeeding to the presidency on Lincoln's death, Johnson sought to carry out Lincoln's policy, but without his political skill. The result was a hopeless conflict with the Radical Republicans who dominated Congress, passed measures over Johnson's vetoes, and attempted to limit the power of the executive concerning appointments and removals. The conflict culminated with Johnson's impeachment for attempting to remove his disloyal Secretary of War in defiance of the Tenure of Office Act which required senatorial concurrence for such dismissals. The opposition failed by one vote to get the two thirds necessary for conviction.

After his presidency, Johnson maintained an interest in politics and in 1875 was again elected to the Senate. He died near Carter Station, Tenn., on July 31, 1875. He married Eliza McCardle in 1827.

ULYSSES SIMPSON GRANT was born (as Hiram Ulysses Grant) at Point Pleasant, Ohio, on April 27, 1822. He graduated from West Point in 1843 and served without particular distinction in the Mexican War. In 1848 he married Julia Dent. He resigned from the army in 1854, after warnings from his commanding officer about his drinking habits, and for the next six years held a wide variety of jobs in the Middle West. With the outbreak of the Civil War, he sought a command and soon, to his surprise, was made a brigadier general. His continuing successes in the western theaters, culminating in the capture of Vicksburg, Miss., in 1863, brought him national fame and soon the command of all the Union armies. Grant's dogged, implacable policy of concentrating on dividing and destroying the Confederate armies brought the war to an end in 1865. The next year, he was made full general.

In 1868, as Republican candidate for president, Grant was elected over the Democrat, Horatio Seymour. From the start, Grant showed his unfitness for the office. His Cabinet was weak, his domestic policy was confused, many of his intimate associates were corrupt. The notable achievement in foreign affairs was the settlement of controversies with Great Britain in the Treaty of London (1871), negotiated by his able Secretary of State, Hamilton Fish.

Running for re-election in 1872, he defeated Horace Greeley, the Democratic and Liberal Republican candidate. The Panic of 1873 graft scandals close to the presidency created difficulties for his second term.

After retiring from office, Grant toured Europe for two years and returned in time to accede to a third-term boom, but was beaten in the convention of 1880. Illness and bad business judgment darkened his last years, but he worked steadily at the *Personal Memoirs*, which were to be so successful when published after his death at Mount McGregor, near Saratoga, N.Y., on July 23, 1885.

RUTHERFORD BIRCHARD HAYES was born in Delaware, Ohio, on Oct. 4, 1822. A graduate of Kenyon College and the Harvard Law School, he practiced law in Lower Sandusky (now Fremont) and then in Cincinnati. In 1852 he married Lucy Webb. A Whig, he joined the Republican party in 1855. During the Civil War he rose to major general. He served in the House of Representatives from 1865 to 1867 and then confirmed a reputation for honesty and efficiency in two terms as Governor of Ohio (1868–72). His election to a third term in 1875 made him the logical candidate for those Republicans who wished to stop James G. Blaine in 1876, and he was nominated.

The result of the election was in doubt for some time and hinged upon disputed returns from South Carolina, Louisiana, Florida, and Oregon. Samuel J. Tilden, the Democrat, had the larger popular vote but was adjudged by the strictly partisan decisions of the Electoral Commission to have one fewer electoral vote, 185 to 184. The national acceptance of this result was due in part to the general understanding that Hayes would pursue a conciliatory policy toward the South. He withdrew the troops from the South, took a conservative position on financial and labor issues, and urged civil service reform.

Hayes served only one term by his own wish and

spent the rest of his life in various humanitarian endeavors. He died in Fremont on Jan. 17, 1893.

JAMES ABRAM GARFIELD, the last president to be born in a log cabin, was born in Cuyahoga County, Ohio, on Nov. 19, 1831. A Williams graduate, he taught school for a time and entered Republican politics in Ohio. In 1858, he married Lucretia Rudolph. During the Civil War, he had a promising career, rising to major general of volunteers; but he resigned in 1863, having been elected to the House of Representatives, where he served until 1880. His oratorical and parliamentary abilities soon made him the leading Republican in the House, though his record was marred by his unorthodox acceptance of a fee in the DeGolyer paving contract case and by suspicions of his complicity in the Crédit Mobilier scandal.

In 1880, Garfield was elected to the Senate, but instead became the presidential candidate on the 36th ballot as a result of a deadlock in the Republican convention. In the election, he defeated Gen. Winfield Scott Hancock, the Democratic candidate. Garfield's administration was barely under way when he was shot by Charles J. Guiteau, a disappointed office seeker, in Washington on July 2, 1881. He died in Elberton, N.J., on Sept. 19.

CHESTER ALAN ARTHUR was born at Fairfield, Vt., on Oct. 5, 1830. A graduate of Union College, he became a successful New York lawyer. In 1859, he married Ellen Herndon. During the Civil War, he held administrative jobs in the Republican state administration and in 1871 was appointed collector of the Port of New York by Grant. This post gave him control over considerable patronage. Though not personally corrupt, Arthur managed his power in the interests of the New York machine so openly that President Hayes in 1877 called for an investigation and the next year Arthur was suspended.

In 1880 Arthur was nominated for vice president in the hope of conciliating the followers of Grant and the powerful New York machine. As president upon Garfield's death, Arthur, stepping out of his familiar role as spoilsman, backed civil service reform, reorganized the Cabinet, and prosecuted political associates accused of post office graft. Losing machine support and failing to gain the reformers, he was not nominated for a full term in 1884. He died in New York City on Nov. 18, 1886.

STEPHEN GROVER CLEVELAND was born at Caldwell, N.J., on March 18, 1837. He was admitted to the bar in Buffalo, N.Y., in 1859 and lived there as a lawyer, with occasional incursions into Democratic politics, for more than 20 years. He did not participate in the Civil War. As mayor of Buffalo in 1881, he carried through a reform program so ably that the Democrats ran him successfully for governor in 1882. In 1884 he won the Democratic nomination for President. The campaign contrasted Cleveland's spotless public career with the uncertain record of James G. Blaine, the Republican candidate, and Cleveland received enough Mugwump (independent Republican) support to win.

As president, Cleveland pushed civil service reform, opposed the pension grab and attacked the high tariff rates. While in the White House, he married Frances Folsom in 1886. Renominated in 1888, Cleveland was defeated by Benjamin Harrison, polling more popular but fewer electoral votes. In 1892, he was elected over Harrison. When the Panic of 1893 burst upon the country, Cleveland's attempts to solve it by sound-money measures alienated the free-silver wing of the party, while his tariff policy alienated the protectionists. In 1894, he sent troops to break the Pullman strike. In foreign affairs, his firmness caused Great Britain to back down in the Venezuela border dispute.

In his last years Cleveland was an active and much-respected public figure. He died in Princeton, N.J., on June 24, 1908.

BENJAMIN HARRISON was born in North Bend, Ohio, on Aug. 20, 1833, the grandson of William Henry Harrison, the ninth president. A graduate of Miami University in Ohio, he took up the law in Indiana and became active in Republican politics. In 1853, he married Caroline Lavinia Scott. During the Civil War, he rose to brigadier general. A sound-money Republican, he was elected senator from Indiana in 1880. In 1888, he received the Republican nomination for President on the eighth ballot. Though behind on the popular vote, he won over Grover Cleveland in the electoral college by 233 to 168.

As President, Harrison failed to please either the bosses or the reform element in the party. In foreign affairs he backed Secretary of State Blaine, whose policy foreshadowed later American imperialism. Harrison was renominated in 1892 but lost to Cleveland. His wife died in the White House in 1892 and Harrison married her niece, Mary Scott (Lord) Dimmick, in 1896. After his presidency, he resumed law practice. He died in Indianapolis on March 13, 1901.

WILLIAM McKINLEY was born in Niles, Ohio, on Jan. 29, 1843. He taught school, then served in the Civil War, rising from the ranks to become a major. Subsequently he opened a law office in Canton, Ohio, and in 1871 married Ida Saxton. Elected to Congress in 1876, he served there until 1891, except for 1883–85. His faithful advocacy of business interests culminated in the passage of the highly protective McKinley Tariff of 1890. With the support of Mark Hanna, a shrewd Cleveland businessman interested in safeguarding tariff protection, McKinley became governor of Ohio in 1892 and Republican presidential candidate in 1896. The business community, alarmed by the progressivism of William Jennings Bryan, the Democratic candidate, spent considerable money to assure McKinley's victory.

The chief event of McKinley's administration was the war with Spain, which resulted in our acquisition of the Philippines and other islands. With imperialism an issue, McKinley defeated Bryan again in 1900. On Sept. 6, 1901, he was shot at Buffalo, N.Y., by Leon F. Czolgosz, an anarchist, and he died there eight days later.

THEODORE ROOSEVELT was born in New York City on Oct. 27, 1858. A Harvard graduate, he was early interested in ranching, in politics, and in writing picturesque historical narratives. He was a Republican member of the New York Assembly in 1882–84, an unsuccessful candidate for mayor of New York in 1886, a U.S. Civil Service Commissioner under Benjamin Harrison, Police Commissioner of New York City in 1895, and Assistant Secretary of the Navy under McKinley in 1897. He resigned in 1898 to help organize a volunteer regiment, the Rough Riders, and take a more direct part in the war with Spain. He was elected governor of New York in 1898 and vice president in 1900, in spite of lack of enthusiasm on the part of the bosses.

Assuming the presidency of the assassinated McKinely in 1901, Roosevelt embarked on a wide-ranging program of government reform and conservation of natural resources. He ordered anti-trust suits against several large corporations, threatened to intervene in the anthracite coal strike of 1902, which prompted the operators to accept arbitration, and, in general, championed the rights of the "little man" and fought the "malefactors of great wealth." He was also responsible for such progressive legislation as the Elkins Act of 1901, which outlawed freight rebates by railroads; the bill establishing the Department of Commerce and Labor; the Hepburn Act, which gave the I.C.C. greater control over the railroads; the Meat Inspection Act; and the Pure Food and Drug Act.

In foreign affairs, Roosevelt pursued a strong policy, permitting the instigation of a revolt in Panama to dispose of Colombian objections to the Panama Canal and helping to maintain the balance of power in the East by bringing the Russo-Japanese War to an end, for which he won the Nobel Peace Prize, the first American to achieve a Nobel prize in any category. In 1904, he decisively defeated Alton B. Parker, his conservative Democratic opponent.

Roosevelt's increasing coldness toward his successor, William Howard Taft, led him to overlook his earlier disclaimer of third-term ambitions and to re-enter politics. Defeated by the machine in the Republican convention of 1912, he organized the Progressive Party (Bull Moose) and polled more votes than Taft, though the split brought about the election of Woodrow Wilson. From 1915 on, Roosevelt strongly favored intervention in the European war. He became deeply embittered at Wilson's refusal to allow him to raise a volunteer division. He died in Oyster Bay, N.Y., on Jan. 6, 1919. He was married twice: in 1880 to Alice Hathaway Lee, who died in 1884, and in 1886 to Edith Kermit Carow.

WILLIAM HOWARD TAFT was born in Cincinnati on Sept. 15, 1857. A Yale graduate, he entered Ohio Republican politics in the 1880s. In 1886 he married Helen Herron. From 1887 to 1890, he served on the Ohio Superior Court; 1890–92, as solicitor general of the United States; 1892–1900, on the federal circuit court. In 1900 McKinley appointed him president of the Phhilippine Commission and in 1901 governor general. Taft had great success in pacifying the Filipinos, solving the problem of the church lands, improving economic conditions, and establishing limited self-government. His period as Secretary of War (1904–08) further demonstrated his capacity as administrator and conciliator, and he was Roosevelt's hand-picked successor in 1908. In the election, he polled 321 electoral votes to 162 for William Jennings Bryan, who was running for the presidency for the third time.

Though he carried on many of Roosevelt's policies, Taft got into increasing trouble with the progressive wing of the party and displayed mounting irritability and indecision. After his defeat in 1912, he became professor of constitutional law at Yale. In 1921 he was appointed Chief Justice of the United States. He died in Washington on March 8, 1930.

THOMAS WOODROW WILSON was born in Staunton, Va., on Dec. 28, 1856. A Princeton graduate, he turned from law practice to post-graduate work in political science at Johns Hopkins University, receiving his Ph.D. in 1886. He taught at Bryan Mawr, Wesleyan, and Princeton, and in 1902 was made president of Princeton. After an unsuccessful attempt to democratize the social life of the university, he welcomed an invitation in 1910 to be the Democratic gubernatorial candidate in New Jersey, and was elected. His success in fighting the machine and putting through a reform program attracted national attention.

In 1912, at the Democratic convention in Baltimore, Wilson won the nomination on the 46th ballot and went on to defeat Roosevelt and Taft in the election. Wilson proceeded under the standard of the New Freedom to enact a program of domestic reform, including the Federal Reserve Act, the Clayton Antitrust Act, the establishment of the Federal Trade Commission, and other measures designed to restore competition in the face of the great monopolies. In foreign affairs, while privately sympathetic with the Allies, he strove to maintain neutrality in the European war and warned both sides against encroachments on American interests.

Re-elected in 1916 as a peace candidate, he tried to mediate between the warring nations; but when the Germans resumed unrestricted submarine warfare in 1917, Wilson brought the United States into what he now believed was a war to make the world safe for democracy. He supplied the classic formulations of Allied war aims and the armistice of Nov. 11, 1918 was negotiated on the basis of Wilson's Fourteen Points. In 1919 he strove at Versailles to lay the foundations for enduring peace. He accepted the imperfections of the Versailles Treaty in the expectation that they could be remedied by action within the League of Nations. He probably could have secured ratification of the treaty by the Senate if he had adopted a more conciliatory attitude toward the mild reservationists; but his insistence on all or nothing eventually caused the diehard isolationists and diehard Wilsonites to unite in rejecting a compromise.

In September 1919 Wilson suffered a paralytic stroke that limited his activity. After leaving the presidency he lived on in retirement in Washington, dying on Feb. 3, 1924. He was married twice—in 1885 to Ellen Louise Axson, who died in 1914, and in 1915 to Edith Bolling Galt.

WARREN GAMALIEL HARDING was born in Morrow County, Ohio, on Nov. 2, 1865. After attending Ohio Central College, Harding became interested in journalism and in 1884 bought the *Marion* (Ohio) *Star*. In 1891 he married a wealthy widow, Florence Kling De Wolfe. As his paper prospered, he entered Republican politics, serving as state senator (1899–1903) and as lieutenant governor (1904–06). In 1910, he was defeated for governor, but in 1914 was elected to the Senate. His reputation as an orator made him the keynoter at the 1916 Republican convention.

When the 1920 convention was deadlocked between Leonard Wood and Frank O. Lowden, Harding became the dark-horse nominee on his solemn affirmation that there was no reason in his past that he should not be. Straddling the League question, Harding was easily elected over James M. Cox, his Democratic opponent. His Cabinet contained some able men, but also some manifestly unfit for public office. Harding's own intimates were mediocre when they were not corrupt. The impending disclosure of the Teapot Dome scandal in the Interior Department and illegal practices in the Justice Department and Veterans' Bureau, as well as political setbacks, profoundly worried him. On his return from Alaska in 1923, he died unexpectedly in San Francisco on Aug. 2.

JOHN CALVIN COOLIDGE was born in Plymouth, Vt., on July 4, 1872. An Amherst graduate, he went into law practice at Northampton, Mass., in 1897. He married Grace Anna Goodhue in 1905. He entered Republican state politics, becoming successively mayor of Northampton, state senator, lieutenant governor and, in 1919, governor. His use of the state militia to end the Boston police strike in 1919 won him a somewhat undeserved reputation for decisive action and brought him the Republican vice-presidential nomination in 1920. After Harding's death Coolidge handled the Washington scandals with care and finally managed to save the Republican Party from public blame for the widespread corruption.

In 1924, Coolidge was elected without difficulty, defeating the Democrat, John W. Davis, and Robert M. La Follette running on the Progressive ticket. His second term, like his first, was characterized by a general satisfaction with the existing economic order. He stated that he did not choose to run in 1928.

After his presidency, Coolidge lived quietly in Northampton, writing an unilluminating *Autobiography* and conducting a syndicated column. He died there on Jan. 5, 1933.

HERBERT CLARK HOOVER was born at West Branch, Iowa, on Aug. 10, 1874, the first president to be born west of the Mississippi. A Stanford graduate, he worked from 1895 to 1913 as a mining engineer and consultant throughout the world. In 1899, he married Lou Henry. During World War I, he served with distinction as chairman of the American Relief Committee in London, as chairman of the Commission for Relief in Belgium, and as U.S. Food Administrator. His political affiliations were still too indeterminate for him to be mentioned as a possibility for either the Republican or Democratic nomination in 1920, but after the election he served Harding and Coolidge as Secretary of Commerce.

In the election of 1928, Hoover overwhelmed Gov. Alfred E. Smith of New York, the Democratic candidate and the first Roman Catholic to run for the presidency. He soon faced the worst depression in the nation's history, but his attacks upon it were hampered by his devotion to the theory that the forces that brought the crisis would soon bring the revival and then by his belief that there were too many areas in which the federal government had no power to act. In a succession of vetoes, he struck down measures proposing a national employment system or national relief, he reduced income tax rates, and only at the end of his term did he yield to popular pressure and set up agencies such as the Reconstruction Finance Corporation to make emergency loans to assist business.

After his 1932 defeat, Hoover returned to private business. In 1946, President Truman charged him with various world food missions; and from 1947 to 1949 and 1953 to 1955, he was head of the Commission on Organization of the Executive Branch of the Government. He died in New York City on Oct. 20, 1964.

FRANKLIN DELANO ROOSEVELT was born in Hyde Park, N.Y., on Jan. 30, 1882. A Harvard graduate, he attended Columbia Law School and was admitted to the New York bar. In 1910, he was elected to the New York State Senate as a Democrat. Reelected in 1912, he was appointed Assistant Secretary of the Navy by Woodrow Wilson the next year. In 1920, his radiant personality and his war service resulted in his nomination for vice president as James M. Cox's running mate. After his defeat, he returned to law practice in New York. In August 1921, Roosevelt was stricken with infantile paralysis while on vacation at Campobello, New Brunswick. After a long and gallant fight, he recovered partial use of his legs. In 1924 and 1928, he led the fight at the Democratic national conventions for the nomination of Gov. Alfred E. Smith of New York, and in 1928 Roosevelt was himself induced to run for governor of New York. He was elected, and was re-elected in 1930.

In 1932, Roosevelt received the Democratic nomination for president and immediately launched a campaign that brought new spirit to a weary and discouraged nation. He defeated Hoover by a wide margin. His first term was characterized by an unfolding of the New Deal program, with greater benefits for labor, the farmers, and the unemployed, and the progressive estrangement of most of the business community.

At an early stage, Roosevelt became aware of the menace to world peace posed by totalitarian fascism, and from 1937 on he tried to focus public attention on the trend of events in Europe and Asia. As a result, he was widely denounced as a warmonger. He was re-elected in 1936 over Gov. Alfred M. Landon of Kansas by the overwhelming electoral margin of 523 to 8, and the gathering international crisis prompted him to run for an unprecedented third term in 1940. He defeated Wendell L. Willkie.

Roosevelt's program to bring maximum aid to Britain and, after June 1941, to Russia was opposed, until the Japanese attack on Pearl Harbor restored national unity. During the war, Roosevelt shelved the New Deal in the interests of conciliating the business community, both in order to get full production during the war and to prepare the way for a united acceptance of the peace settlements after the war. A series of conferences with Winston Churchill and Joseph Stalin laid down the bases for the postwar world. In 1944 he was elected to a fourth term, running against Gov. Thomas E. Dewey of New York.

On April 12, 1945, Roosevelt died of a cerebral hemorrhage at Warm Springs, Ga., shortly after his return from the Yalta Conference. His wife, Anna Eleanor Roosevelt, whom he married in 1905, was a woman of great ability who made significant contributions to her husband's policies.

HARRY S. TRUMAN was born on a farm near Lamar, Mo., on May 8, 1884. During World War I, he served in France as a captain with the 129th Field Artillery. He married Bess Wallace in 1919. After engaging briefly and unsuccessfully in the haberdashery business in Kansas City, Mo., Truman entered local politics. Under the sponsorship of Thomas Pendergast, Democratic boss of Missouri, he held a number of local offices, preserving his personal honesty in the midst of a notoriously corrupt political machine. In 1934, he was elected to the Senate and was re-elected in 1940. During his first term he was a loyal but quiet supporter of the New Deal, but in his second term, an appointment as head of a Senate committee to investigate war production brought out his special qualities of honesty, common sense, and hard work, and he won widespread respect.

Elected vice president in 1944, Truman became president upon Roosevelt's sudden death in April 1945 and was immediately faced with the problems of winding down the war against the Axis and preparing the nation for postwar adjustment.

The years 1947–48 were distinguished by civil-rights proposals, the Truman Doctrine to contain the spread of Communism, and the Marshall Plan to aid in the economic reconstruction of war-ravaged nations. Truman's general record, highlighted by a vigorous Fair Deal campaign, brought about his unexpected election in 1948 over the heavily favored Thomas E. Dewey.

Truman's second term was primarily concerned with the Cold War with the Soviet Union, the implementing of the North Atlantic Pact, the United Nations police action in Korea, and the vast rearmament program with its accompanying problems of economic stabilization.

On March 29, 1952, Truman announced that he would not run again for the presidency. After leaving the White House, he returned to his home in Independence, Mo., to write his memoirs. He further busied himself with the Harry S. Truman Library there. He died in Kansas City, Mo., on Dec. 26, 1972.

DWIGHT DAVID EISENHOWER was born in Denison, Tex., on Oct. 14, 1890. His ancestors lived in Germany and emigrated to America, settling in Pennsylvania, early in the 18th century. His father, David, had a general store in Hope, Kan., which failed. After a brief time in Texas, the family moved to Abilene, Kan.

After graduating from Abilene High School in 1909, Eisenhower did odd jobs for almost two years. He won an appointment to the Naval Academy at Annapolis, but was too old for admittance. Then he received an appointment in 1910 to West Point, from which he graduated as a second lieutenant in 1915.

He did not see service in World War I, having been stationed at Fort Sam Houston, Tex. There he met Mamie Geneva Doud, whom he married in Denver on July 1, 1916, and by whom he had two sons: Doud Dwight (died in infancy) and John Sheldon Doud.

Eisenhower served in the Philippines from 1935 to 1939 with Gen. Douglas MacArthur. Afterward, Gen. George C. Marshall, the Army Chief of Staff, brought him into the War Department's General Staff and in 1942 placed him in command of the invasion of North Africa. In 1944, he was made Supreme Allied Commander for the invasion of Europe.

After the war, Eisenhower served as Army Chief of Staff from November 1945 until February 1948, when he was appointed president of Columbia University.

In December 1950, President Truman recalled Eisenhower to active duty to command the North Atlantic Treaty Organization forces in Europe. He held his post until the end of May 1952.

At the Republican convention of 1952 in Chicago, Eisenhower won the presidential nomination on the first ballot in a close race with Senator Robert A. Taft of Ohio. In the election, he defeated Gov. Adlai E. Stevenson of Illinois.

Through two terms, Eisenhower hewed to moderate domestic policies. He sought peace through Free World strength in an era of new nationalisms, nuclear missiles, and space exploration. He fostered alliances pledging the United States to resist Red aggression in Europe, Asia, and Latin America. The Eisenhower Doctrine of 1957 extended commitments to the Middle East.

At home, the popular president lacked Republican Congressional majorities after 1954, but he was re-elected in 1956 by 457 electoral votes to 73 for Stevenson.

While retaining most Fair Deal programs, he stressed "fiscal responsibility" in domestic affairs. A moderate in civil rights, he sent troops to Little Rock, Ark., to enforce court-ordered school integration.

With his wartime rank restored by Congress, Eisenhower returned to private life and the role of elder statesman, with his vigor hardly impaired by a heart attack, an ileitis operation, and a mild stroke suffered while in office. He died in Washington on March 28, 1969.

JOHN FITZGERALD KENNEDY was born in Brookline, Mass., on May 29, 1917. His father, Joseph P. Kennedy, was Ambassador to Great Britain from 1937 to 1940.

Kennedy was graduated from Harvard University in 1940 and joined the Navy the next year. He became skipper of a PT boat that was sunk in the Pacific by a Japanese destroyer. Although given up for lost, he swam to a safe island, towing an injured enlisted man.

After recovering from a war-aggravated spinal injury, Kennedy entered politics in 1946 and was elected to Congress. In 1952, he ran against Senator Henry Cabot Lodge, Jr., of Massachusetts, and won.

Kennedy was married on Sept. 12, 1953, to Jacqueline Lee Bouvier, by whom he had three children: Caroline, John Fitzgerald, Jr., and Patrick Bouvier (died in infancy).

In 1957 Kennedy won the Pulitzer Prize for a book he had written earlier, *Profiles in Courage.*

After strenuous primary battles, Kennedy won the Democratic presidential nomination on the first ballot at the 1960 Los Angeles convention. With a plurality of only 118,574 votes, he carried the election over Vice President Richard M. Nixon and became the first Roman Catholic president.

Kennedy brought to the White House the dynamic idea of a "New Frontier" approach in dealing with problems at home, abroad, and in the dimensions of space. Out of his leadership in his first few months in office came the 10-year Alliance for Progress to aid Latin America, the Peace Corps, and accelerated programs that brought the first Americans into orbit in the race in space.

Failure of the U.S.-supported Cuban invasion in April 1961 led to the entrenchment of the Communist-backed Castro regime, only 90 miles from United States soil. When it became known that Soviet offensive missiles were being installed in Cuba in 1962, Kennedy ordered a naval "quarantine" of the island and moved troops into position to eliminate this threat to U.S. security. The world seemed on the brink of a nuclear war until Soviet Premier Khrushchev ordered the removal of the missiles.

A sudden "thaw," or the appearance of one, in the cold war came with the agreement with the Soviet Union on a limited test-ban treaty signed in Moscow on Aug. 6, 1963.

In his domestic policies, Kennedy's proposals for medical care for the aged, expanded area redevelopment, and aid to education were defeated, but on minimum wage, trade legislation, and other measures he won important victories.

Widespread racial disorders and demonstrations led to Kennedy's proposing sweeping civil rights legislation. As his third year in office drew to a close, he also recommended an $11-billion tax cut to bolster the economy. Both measures were pending in Congress when Kennedy, looking forward to a second term, journeyed to Texas for a series of speeches.

While riding in a procession in Dallas on Nov. 22, 1963, he was shot to death by an assassin firing from an upper floor of a building. The alleged assassin, Lee Harvey Oswald, was killed two days later in the Dallas city jail by Jack Ruby, owner of a striptease place.

At 46 years of age, Kennedy became the fourth president to be assassinated and the eighth to die in office.

LYNDON BAINES JOHNSON was born in Stonewall, Tex., on Aug. 27, 1908. On both sides of his family he had a political heritage mingled with a Baptist background of preachers and teachers. Both his father and his paternal grandfather served in the Texas House of Representatives.

After his graduation from Southwest Texas State Teachers College, Johnson taught school for two years. He went to Washington in 1932 as secretary to Rep. Richard M. Kleberg. During this time, he married Claudia Alta Taylor, known as "Lady Bird." They had two children: Lynda Bird (Robb) and Luci Baines (Nugent).

In 1935, Johnson became Texas administrator for the National Youth Administration. Two years later, he was elected to Congress as an all-out supporter of Franklin D. Roosevelt, and served until 1949. He was the first member of Congress to enlist in the armed forces after the attack on Pearl Harbor. He served in the Navy in the Pacific and won a Silver Star.

Johnson was elected to the Senate in 1948 after he had captured the Democratic nomination by only 87 votes. He was 40 years old. He became the Senate Democratic leader in 1953. A heart attack in 1955 threatened to end his political career, but he recovered fully and resumed his duties.

At the height of his power as Senate leader, Johnson sought the Democratic nomination for president in 1960. When he lost to John F. Kennedy, he surprised even some of his closest associates by accepting second place on the ticket.

Johnson was riding in another car in the motorcade when Kennedy was assassinated in Dallas on Nov. 22, 1963. He took the oath of office in the presidential jet on the Dallas airfield.

With Johnson's insistent backing, Congress finally adopted a far-reaching civil-rights bill, a voting-rights bill, a Medicare program for the aged, and measures to improve education and conservation. Congress also began what Johnson described as "an all-out war" on poverty.

Amassing a record-breaking majority of nearly 16 million votes, Johnson was elected president in his own right in 1964, defeating Senator Barry Goldwater of Arizona.

The double tragedy of a war in Southeast Asia and urban riots at home marked Johnson's last two years in office. Faced with disunity in the nation and challenges within his own party, Johnson surprised the country on March 31, 1968, with the announcement that he would not be a candidate for re-election. He died of a heart attack suffered at his LBJ Ranch on Jan. 22, 1973.

RICHARD MILHOUS NIXON was born in Yorba Linda, Calif., on Jan. 9, 1913, to Midwestern-bred parents, Francis A. and Hannah Milhous Nixon, who raised their five sons as Quakers.

Nixon was a high school debater and was undergraduate president at Whittier College in California, where he was graduated in 1934. As a scholarship student at Duke University Law School in North Carolina, he graduated third in his class in 1937.

After five years as a lawyer, Nixon joined the Navy in August 1942. He was an air transport officer in the South Pacific and a legal officer stateside before his discharge in 1946 as a lieutenant commander.

Running for Congress in California as a Republican in 1946, Nixon defeated Rep. Jerry Voorhis. As a member of the House Un-American Activities Committee, he made a name as an investigator of Alger Hiss, a former high State Department official, who was later jailed for perjury. In 1950, Nixon defeated Rep. Helen Gahagan Douglas, a Democrat, for the Senate. He was criticized for portraying her as a Communist dupe.

Nixon's anti-Communism, his Western base, and his youth figured in his selection in 1952 to run for vice president on the ticket headed by Dwight D. Eisenhower. Demands for Nixon's withdrawal followed disclosure that California businessmen had paid some of his Senate office expenses. He televised rebuttal, known as "the Checkers speech" (named for a cocker spaniel given to the Nixons), brought him support from the public and from Eisenhower. The ticket won easily in 1952 and again in 1956.

Eisenhower gave Nixon substantive assignments, including missions to 56 countries. In Moscow in 1959, Nixon won acclaim for his defense of U.S. interests in an impromptu "kitchen debate" with Soviet Premier Nikita S. Khrushchev.

Nixon lost the 1960 race for the presidency to John F. Kennedy.

In 1962, Nixon failed in a bid for California's governorship and seemed to be finished as a national candidate. He became a Wall Street lawyer, but kept his old party ties and developed new ones through constant travels to speak for Republicans.

Nixon won the 1968 Republican presidential nomination after a shrewd primary campaign, then made Gov. Spiro T. Agnew of Maryland his surprise choice for vice president. In the election, they edged out the Democratic ticket headed by Vice President Hubert H. Humphrey by 510,314 votes out of 73,212,065 cast.

Committed to wind down the U.S. role in the Vietnamese War, Nixon pursued "Vietnamization"—training and equipping South Vietnamese to do their own fighting. American ground combat forces in Vietnam fell steadily from 540,000 when Nixon took office to none in 1973 when the military draft was ended. But there was heavy continuing use of U.S. air power.

Nixon improved relations with Moscow and reopened the long-closed door to mainland China with a good-will trip there in February 1972. In May of that year, he visited Moscow and signed agreements on arms limitation and trade expansion and approved plans for a joint U.S.-Soviet space mission in 1975.

Inflation was a campaign issue for Nixon, but he failed to master it as president. On Aug. 15, 1971, with unemployment edging up, Nixon abruptly announced a new economic policy: a 90-day wage-price freeze, stimulative tax cuts, a temporary 10% tariff, and spending cuts. A second phase, imposing guidelines on wage, price and rent boosts, was announced October 7.

The economy responded in time for the 1972 campaign, in which Nixon played up his foreign-policy achievements. Played down was the burglary on June 17, 1972, of Democratic national headquarters in the Watergate apartment complex in Washington. The Nixon-Agnew re-election campaign cost a record $60 million and swamped the Democratic ticket headed by Senator George McGovern of South Dakota with a plurality of 17,999,528 out of 77,718,554 votes. Only Massachusetts, with 14 electoral votes, and the District of Columbia, with 3, went for McGovern.

In January 1973, hints of a cover-up emerged at the trial of six men found guilty of the Wtergate burglary. With a Senate investigation under way, Nixon announced on April 30 the resignations of his top aides, H. R. Haldeman and John D. Ehrlichman, and the dismissal of White House counsel John Dean III. Dean was the star witness at televised Senate hearings that exposed both a White House cover-up of Watergate and massive illegalities in Republican fund-raising in 1972.

The hearings also disclosed that Nixon had routinely tape-recorded his office meetings and telephone conversations.

On Oct. 10, 1973, Agnew resigned as vice president, then pleaded no-contest to a negotiated federal charge of evading income taxes on alleged bribes. Two days later, Nixon nominated the House minority leader, Rep. Gerald R. Ford of Michigan, as the new vice president. Congress confirmed Ford on Dec. 6, 1973.

In June 1974, Nixon visited Israel and four Arab nations. Then he met in Moscow with Soviet leader Leonid I. Brezhnev and reached preliminary nuclear arms limitation agreements.

But, in the month after his return, Watergate ended the Nixon regime. On July 24 the Supreme Court ordered Nixon to surrender subpoenaed tapes. On July 30, the Judiciary Committee referred three impeachment articles to the full membership. On August 5, Nixon bowed to the Supreme Court and released tapes showing he halted an FBI probe of the Watergate burglary six days after it occurred. It was in effect an admission of obstruction of justice, and impeachment appeared inevitable.

Nixon resigned on Aug. 9, 1974, the first president ever to do so. A month later, President Ford issued an unconditional pardon for any offenses Nixon might have committed as president, thus forestalling possible prosecution.

In 1940, Nixon married Thelma Catherine (Pat) Ryan. They had two daughters, Patricia (Tricia) Cox and Julie, who married Dwight David Eisenhower II, grandson of the former president.

GERALD RUDOLPH FORD was born in Omaha, Neb., on July 14, 1913, the only child of Leslie and Dorothy Gardner King. His parents were divorced in 1915. His mother moved to Grand Rapids, Mich., and married Gerald R. Ford. The boy was renamed for his stepfather.

Ford captained his high school football team in Grand Rapids, and a football scholarship took him to the University of Michigan, where he starred as varsity center before his graduation in 1935. A job as assistant football coach at Yale gave him an opportunity to attend Yale Law School, from which he graduated in the top third of his class in 1941.

He returned to Grand Rapids to practice law, but entered the Navy in April 1942. He saw wartime service in the Pacific on the light aircraft carrier *Monterey* and was a lieutenant commander when he returned to Grand Rapids early in 1946 to resume law practice and dabble in politics.

Ford was elected to Congress in 1948 for the first of his 13 terms in the House. He was soon assigned to the influential Appropriations Committee and rose to become the ranking Republican on the subcommittee on Defense Department appropriations and an expert in the field.

As a legislator, Ford described himself as "a moderate on domestic issues, a conservative in fiscal affairs, and a dyed-in-the-wool internationalist." He carried the ball for Pentagon appropriations, was a hawk on the war in Vietnam, and kept a low profile on civil-rights issues.

He was also dependable and hard-working and popular with his colleagues. In 1963, he was elected chairman of the House Republican Conference. He served in 1963–64 as a member of the Warren Commission that investigated the assassination of John F. Kennedy. A revolt by dissatisfied younger Republicans in 1965 made him minority leader.

Ford shelved his hopes for the Speakership on Oct. 12, 1973, when Nixon nominated him to fill the vice presidency left vacant by Agnew's resignation under fire. It was the first use of the procedures for filling vacancies in the vice presidency laid down in the 25th Amendment to the Constitution, which Ford had helped enact.

Congress confirmed Ford as vice president on Dec. 6, 1973. Once in office, he said he did not believe Nixon had been involved in the Watergate scandals, but criticized his stubborn court battle against releasing tape recordings of Watergate-related conversations for use as evidence.

The scandals led to Nixon's unprecedented resignation on Aug. 9, 1974, and Ford was sworn in immediately as the 38th president, the first to enter the White House without winning a national election.

Ford assured the nation when he took office that "our long national nightmare is over" and pledged "openness and candor" in all his actions. He won a warm response from the Democratic 93rd Congress when he said he wanted "a good marriage" rather than a honeymoon with his former colleagues. In December 1974 Congressional majorities backed his choice of former New York Gov. Nelson A. Rockefeller as his successor in the again-vacant vice presidency.

The cordiality was chilled by Ford's announcement on Sept. 8, 1974, that he had granted an unconditional pardon to Nixon for any crimes he might have committed as president. Although no formal charges were pending, Ford said he feared "ugly passions" would be aroused if Nixon were brought to trial. The pardon was widely criticized.

To fight inflation, the new president first proposed fiscal restraints and spending curbs and a 5% tax surcharge that got nowhere in the Senate and House. Congress again rebuffed Ford in the spring of 1975 when he appealed for emergency military aid to help the governments of South Vietnam and Cambodia resist massive Communist offensives.

In November 1974, Ford visited Japan, South Korea, and the Soviet Union, where he and Soviet leader Leonid I. Brezhnev conferred in Vladivostok and reached a tentative agreement to limit the number of strategic offensive nuclear weapons. It was Ford's first meeting as president with Brezhnev, who planned a return visit to Washington in the fall of 1975.

Politically, Ford's fortunes improved steadily in the first half of 1975. Badly divided Democrats in Congress were unable to muster votes to override his vetoes of spending bills that exceeded his budget. He faced some right-wing opposition in his own party, but moved to pre-empt it with an early announcement—on July 8, 1975—of his intention to be a candidate in 1976.

Early state primaries in 1976 suggested an easy victory for Ford despite Ronald Reagan's bitter attacks on administration foreign policy and defense programs. But later Reagan primary successes threatened the President's lead. At the Kansas City convention, Ford was nominated by the narrow margin of 1,187 to 1,070. But Reagan had moved the party to the right, and Ford himself was regarded as a caretaker president lacking in strength and vision. He was defeated in November by Jimmy Carter.

In 1948, Ford married Elizabeth Anne (Betty) Bloomer. They had four children, Michael Gerald, John Gardner, Steven Meigs, and Susan Elizabeth.

JAMES EARL CARTER, JR., was born in the tiny village of Plains, Ga., Oct. 1, 1924, and grew up on the family farm at nearby Archery. Both parents were fifth-generation Georgians. His father, James Earl Carter, was known as a segregationist, but treated his black and white workers equally. Carter's mother, Lillian Gordy, was a matriarchal presence in home and community and opposed the then-prevailing code of racial inequality. The future President was baptized in 1935 in the conservative Southern Baptist Church and spoke often of being a "born again" Christian, although committed to the separation of church and state.

Carter married Rosalynn Smith, a neighbor, in 1946. Their first child, John William, was born a year later in Portsmouth, Va. Their other children are James Earl III, born in Honolulu in 1950; Donnel Jeffrey, born in New London, Conn., in 1952, and Amy Lynn, born in Plains in 1967.

In 1946 Carter was graduated from the U.S. Naval Academy at Annapolis and served in the nuclear-submarine program under Adm. Hyman G. Rickover. In 1954, after his father's death, he resigned from the Navy to take over the family's flourishing warehouse and cotton gin, with several thousand acres for growing seed peanuts.

Carter was elected to the Georgia Senate in 1962. In 1966 he lost the race for Governor, but was elected in 1970. His term brought a state government reorganization, sharply reduced agencies, increased economy and efficiency, and new social programs, all with no general tax increase. In 1972 the peanut farmer-politician set his sights on the Presidency and in 1974 built a base for himself as he criss-crossed the country as chairman of the Democratic Campaign Committee, appealing for revival and reform. In 1975 his image as a typical Southern white was erased when he won support of most of the old Southern civil-rights coalition after endorsement by Rep. Andrew Young, black Democrat from Atlanta, who had been the closest aide to the Rev. Martin Luther King, Jr. At Carter's 1971 inauguration as Governor he had called for an end to all forms of racial discrimination.

In the 1976 spring primaries, he won 19 out of 31 with a broad appeal to conservatives and liberals, black and white, poor and well-to-do. Throughout his campaigning Carter set forth his policies in his soft Southern voice, and with his electric-blue stare faced down skeptics who joked about "Jimmy Who?" His toothy smile became his trademark. He was nominated on the first roll-call vote of the 1976 Bicentennial Democratic National Convention in New York, and defeated Gerald R. Ford in November. Likewise, in 1980 he was renominated on the first ballot after vanquishing Senator Edward M. Kennedy of Massachusetts in the primaries. At the convention he defeated the Kennedy forces in their attempt to block a party rule that bound a large majority of pledged delegates to vote for Carter. In the election campaign, Carter attacked his rivals, Ronald Reagan and John B. Anderson, independent, with the warning that a Reagan Republican victory would heighten the risk of war and impede civil rights and economic opportunity. In November Carter lost to Reagan, who won 489 Electoral College votes and 51% of the popular tally, to 49 electoral votes and 41% for Carter.

In his one term, Carter fought hard for his programs against resistance from an independent-minded Democratic Congress that frustrated many pet projects although it overrode only two vetoes. Many of his difficulties were traced to his aides' brusqueness in dealing with Capitol Hill and insensitivity to Congressional feelings and tradition. Observers generally viewed public dissatisfaction with the "stagflation" economy as a principal factor in his defeat. Others included his jittery performance in the debate Oct. 28 with Reagan and the final uncertainties in the negotiations for freeing the Iranians' hostages, along with earlier staff problems, friction with Congress, long gasoline lines, and the months-long Iranian crisis, including the abortive sally in April 1980 to free the hostages. The President, however, did deflect criticism resulting from the activities of his brother, Billy. Yet, assessments of his record noted many positive elements. There was, for one thing, peace throughout his term, with no American combat deaths and with a brake on the advocates of force. Regarded as perhaps his greatest personal achievements were the Camp David accords between Israel and Egypt and the resulting treaty—the first between Israel and an Arab neighbor. The treaty with China and the Panama Canal treaties were also major achievements. Carter worked for nuclear-arms control. His concern for international human rights was credited with saving lives and reducing torture, and he supported the British policy that ended internecine warfare in Rhodesia, now Zimbabwe. Domestically, his environmental record was a major accomplishment. His judicial appointments won acclaim; the Southerner who had forsworn racism made 265 choices for the Federal bench that included minority members and women. On energy, he ended by price decontrols the practice of holding U.S. petroleum prices far below world levels.

RONALD REAGAN, actor turned politician, New Dealer turned conservative, came to the films and politics from a thoroughly middle-American background—middle class, Middle West, and small town. He was born in Tampico, Ill., Feb. 6, 1911, the second son of John Edward Reagan and Nelle Wilson Reagan, and the family later moved to Dixon, Ill. The father, of Irish descent, was a shop clerk and merchant with Democratic sympathies. It was an impoverished family; Ronald sold homemade popcorn at highschool games and worked as a lifeguard to earn money for his college tuition. When the father got a New Deal WPA job, the future President became an ardent Roosevelt Democrat.

Reagan won his B.A. degree in 1932 from Eureka (Ill.) College, where a photographic memory aided in his studies and in debating and college theatricals. In a Depression year, he was making $100 a week as a sports announcer for radio station WHO in Des Moines, Iowa, from 1932 to 1937. His career as a film and TV actor stretched from 1937 to 1966, and his salary climbed to $3,500 a week. As a World War II captain in an Army film studio, Reagan recoiled from what he saw as the laziness of Civil Service workers and soon moved to the Right. As president of the Screen Actors Guild, he resisted what he considered a Communist plot to subvert the film industry. With advancing age, Reagan was eased out of leading-man roles and became a television spokesman for the General Electric Company at $150,000.

With oratorical skill his trademark, Reagan became an active Republican, and in 1964 made a dramatic speech supporting Senator Barry Goldwater, who became the party's Presidential nominee. At the behest of a small group of conservative Southern California businessmen, he ran for Governor with a pledge to cut spending, and was elected by almost a million votes over the political veteran, Democratic Gov. Edmund G. Brown, father of the later Governor. But, bowing to the reality of a depleted state treasury, Reagan sponsored a billion-dollar tax increase, then the largest state tax rise in U.S. history. He later rebated $6 billion in property taxes, although there was a net increase of $15 billion in additional taxes from individuals and businesses in his eight years in office. At the end of his second term in 1974, the state budget had grown by $6 billion.

In 1968 Reagan was nosed out by Richard M. Nixon for the G.O.P. presidential nomination and in 1976 by Gerald Ford. In 1980 Reagan won the nomination after a more aggressively conservative campaign.

In the election battle against Jimmy Carter, Reagan rode a tide of resurgent right-wing sentiment among an electorate battered by the winds of unwanted change, longing for a distant, simpler era. Broadening his appeal by espousing moderate policies, Reagan gained much of his success from crossover votes from disaffected Democrats and blue-collar workers. This was reflected by his winning of Hispanic and blue-collar votes in the California campaigns. In a conciliatory convention speech, he expressed a concern for the poor and urged an end to discrimination against women. His selection of George Bush for Vice President and his overtures to Gerald Ford were viewed as tokens of his outreach to a wider audience, as was his campaign appeal to blacks. In general, the Reagan camp made Carter's record the issue.

The incoming Administration immediately set out to "turn the Government around" with a new economic program. In a few months that program had become reality. Despite strenuous opposition in Congress, Reagan triumphed on the major elements of his "supply side" theory to stimulate production and control inflation through tax cuts and sharp reductions in Government spending. Through adroit and daring maneuvering and the exercise of personal charm in television appeals to the public and direct contacts with Congressmen, he won over the converts needed for massive victories. Thus, he achieved the largest budget and tax cuts in recent United States history; many compared the "Reagan revolution" to the early New Deal of Franklin D. Roosevelt.

The President won high acclaim for his nomination of Sandra Day O'Connor of the Arizona Court of Appeals to be the first woman on the Supreme Court. But the choice encountered some opposition from extreme conservatives over her reported stands on abortion and the equal rights amendment. Critics on the Left questioned her judicial fitness.

Barely three months in office, Reagan was the target of an assassin's bullet. On Monday, March 30, he was shot in the chest by a gunman as he walked to his limousine after addressing a meeting at the Washington Hilton Hotel. James S. Brady, the White House press secretary, and two law officers were also wounded. The President made a good recovery, and by April he was meeting key aides and working on a limited schedule.

The President's courageous comeback won public admiration. In 1982, however, his popularity fell as the country became mired in the worst recession in 40 years, with persistent high unemployment and interest rates. The initial support for his "supply side" economics began to fade despite ebbing inflation. Nevertheless, the President won crucial battles in Congress.

After Republican setbacks in the 1982 midterm elections, the economy turned around, and by 1984 the nation was prospering, with inflation remaining under control.

In foreign policy, the 73-year-old Reagan moderated his attitude toward the Soviet Union by 1984 and tensions seemed to have eased despite running polemics with the Russians over arms control negotiations. The intervention in Lebanon and the withdrawal of the Marines after a disastrous terrorist attack were regarded as a military failure. The invasion of Grenada was a success; Central American affairs were stalemated. Diplomatically and politically, Reagan accomplished much on trips to Asia and Europe.

Earlier in his term, Reagan had faced problems over Israel's invasion of Lebanon; the Argentine invasion of the Falklands, and the precipitate resignation of Alexander M. Haig, Jr., as Secretary of State.

The President and Vice President Bush were renominated by acclamation in August 1984 at a riotously enthusiastic Republican convention at Dallas, Texas.

Reagan is devoted to his wife, Nancy, whom he married after his divorce from the screen actress Jane Wyman. The Reagans spend much time together at the White House and Camp David and at their California home and ranch when Presidential duties permit. Reagan enjoys horseback riding and is a connoisseur of fine wines. The children of the first marriage are Maureen, his daughter by Miss Wyman, and Michael, an adopted son. In the present marriage, the children are Patricia and Ronald. *—A.P.R.*

George Bush

Vice President

Vice President George Bush became Ronald Reagan's running mate for the second time in 1984, in his fifth, second successful, bid for the Vice-Presidential nomination. In the campaign, the 60-year-old Bush faced a new challenge from a younger woman opponent, Geraldine A. Ferraro.

Despite his reputation as a relative liberal, a member of the Northeastern Republican establishment, he earned a reputation for loyalty and devotion to Reagan's conservative policies and for zeal in performance of duty. And by the 1984 Republican convention in Dallas, he had won the acceptance of G.O.P. right-wingers who had jibbed at his earlier membership on the hated "élitist" Trilateral Commission (an international body devoted to discussion of foreign policy and economic issues), support of the proposed equal rights amendment, and opposition to a constitutional ban on abortion. He had, however, won favorable ratings from the conservative Americans for Constitutional Action for his record as a two-term Texas Congressman. Also, he is a former Director of Central Intelligence and in World War II, Bush won the Distinguished Flying Cross as a Navy pilot.

George Bush was born June 12, 1924, in Milton, Mass., to Prescott and Dorothy Bush. The family later moved to Connecticut. Bush attended Phillips Academy at Andover, Mass., and served in the Navy from 1942 to 1945. After the war he earned an economics degree and Phi Beta Kappa key at Yale in 2 1/2 years.

In 1945 he married Barbara Pierce of Rye, N.Y., daughter of a magazine publisher, and in 1948 they left Connecticut for a Texas business career. Bush was cofounder of the Zapata Off-Shore Company, a pioneer in offshore drilling equipment. In 1980 he reported an estimated wealth of some $1.4 million.

After Bush's second unsuccessful Senate race, President Nixon appointed him U.S. delegate to the United Nations with the rank of ambassador, and later he became Republican National Chairman. He served as head of the U.S. liaison office in Peking before becoming Director of Central Intelligence.

His hopes for the Presidential nomination were dashed early in the 1980 campaign. Hard-shell conservatives accepted him as second-place nominee as a pragmatic necessity. It is doubtful, however, that the dominant right-wing leadership would accept him as a G.O.P. Presidential candidate in 1988.

In a subdued way, Bush has been influential in White House decisions, particularly on foreign affairs. He had a key role in the decision to withdraw American forces from Lebanon after that government collapsed early in 1984. In his routine duties as Vice President, Bush has logged more than 566, 000 miles in 59 countries and 48 of the 50 states, speaking at nearly 300 Republican affairs.

The Bushes have lived in 17 cities and 28 homes and have traveled in 26 countries. In her husband's frequent absences, Mrs. Bush has been the "matriarch" of a family of four boys and a girl.

Despite Republican emphasis on Bush's Texas connection, he sold his Houston home several years ago and now lives at the Vice President's quarters in Washington and the family estate at Kennebunkport, Me. *—A.P.R.*

Glossary of Political Terms

Balanced Ticket—A party ticket listing candidates chosen to win support from regional, ethnic, minority, and other elements of the population.

Beauty Contest—The preferential primary in which voters indicate their preference for a candidate in a nonbinding ballot.

Bloc—Group of legislators, usually of both major parties, who vote together for some particular interest.

Brokered Convention—Decisions on candidates and major issues made by party leaders rather than by rank-and-file delegates.

Bullet Vote—Balloting in which the electorate concentrates on single candidates or issues to the neglect of the rest of the slate.

Confirmation—Senate action to validate an appointment, treaty, or other action by the President.

Dark Horse—An entrant into a political contest not previously mentioned. A person unexpectedly nominated, especially at a party convention.

Direct Primary—A party primary in which its members nominate the candidates by direct vote. Also used to choose convention delegates and party leaders. Primaries can be open to members of all parties, making a "crossover" vote possible, or restricted to members of the one party.

Equal Time—The legal right to equivalent time on radio or television to reply to charges in a political campaign made on the same medium.

Favorite Son—A state political leader to whom the party organization pledges its Presidential nominating delegates to avoid early pressure from declared candidates and to increase the state's delegation's bargaining power at the nominating convention.

Gerrymander—The division of a state, county, or other political unit into election districts so as to give one political party a majority in many districts and to concentrate the other party's voting strength into as few districts as possible. In brief, boundary manipulation for political advantage.

Machine Politics—The control of party decisions by the organized group of persons who conduct or direct the activities of a political party or similar organization.

Protest Vote—A vote expressing broad disapproval of an official or party policy, stressing negative reaction.

Slush Fund—A Congressman's office account—contributions are unlimited—the money is used to help run his office, mailings, etc.

Stalking Horse—A candidate used to conceal the candidacy of a more important candidate or to draw votes from a rival.

AWARDS

Nobel Prizes

The Nobel prizes are awarded under the will of Alfred Bernhard Nobel, Swedish chemist and engineer, who died in 1896. The interest of the fund is divided annually among the persons who have made the most outstanding contributions in the fields of physics, chemistry, and physiology or medicine, who have produced the most distinguished literary work of an idealist tendency, and who have contributed most toward world peace.

In 1968, a Nobel Prize of economic sciences was established by Riksbank, the Swedish bank, in celebration of its 300th anniversary. The prize was awarded for the first time in 1969.

The prizes for physics and chemistry are awarded by the Swedish Academy of Science in Stockholm, the one for physiology or medicine by the Caroline Medical Institute in Stockholm, that for literature by the academy in Stockholm, and that for peace by a committee of five elected by the Norwegian Storting. The distribution of prizes was begun on December 10, 1901, the anniversary of Nobel's death. The amount of each prize varies with the income from the fund and currently is about $190,000. No Nobel prizes were awarded for 1940, 1941, and 1942; prizes for Literature were not awarded for 1914, 1918, and 1943.

PEACE

1901 Henri Dunant (Switzerland); Frederick Passy (France)
1902 Elie Ducommun and Albert Gobat (Switzerland)
1903 Sir William R. Cremer (England)
1904 Institut de Droit International (Belgium)
1905 Bertha von Suttner (Austria)
1906 Theodore Roosevelt (U.S.)
1907 Ernesto T. Moneta (Italy) and Louis Renault (France)
1908 Klas P. Arnoldson (Sweden) and Frederik Bajer (Denmark)
1909 Auguste M. F. Beernaert (Belgium) and Baron Paul H. B. B. d'Estournelles de Constant de Rebecque (France)
1910 Bureau International Permanent de la Paix (Switzerland)
1911 Tobias M. C. Asser (Holland) and Alfred H. Fried (Austria)
1912 Elihu Root (U.S.)
1913 Henri La Fontaine (Belgium)
1915 No award
1916 No award
1917 International Red Cross
1919 Woodrow Wilson (U.S.)
1920 Léon Bourgeois (France)
1921 Karl H. Branting (Sweden) and Christian L. Lange (Norway)
1922 Fridtjof Nansen (Norway)
1923 No award
1924 No award
1925 Sir Austen Chamberlain (England) and Charles G. Dawes (U.S.)
1926 Aristide Briand (France) and Gustav Stresemann (Germany)
1927 Ferdinand Buisson (France) and Ludwig Quidde (Germany)
1928 No award
1929 Frank B. Kellogg (U.S.)
1930 Lars O. J. Söderblom (Sweden)
1931 Jane Addams and Nicholas M. Butler (U.S.)
1932 No award
1933 Sir Norman Angell (England)
1934 Arthur Henderson (England)
1935 Karl von Ossietzky (Germany)
1936 Carlos de S. Lamas (Argentina)
1937 Lord Cecil of Chelwood (England)
1938 Office International Nansen pour les Réfugiés (Switzerland)
1939 No award
1944 International Red Cross
1945 Cordell Hull (U.S.)
1946 Emily G. Balch and John R. Mott (U.S.)
1947 American Friends Service Committee (U.S.) and British Society of Friends' Service Council (England)
1948 No award
1949 Lord John Boyd Orr (Scotland)
1950 Ralph J. Bunche (U.S.)
1951 Léon Jouhaux (France)
1952 Albert Schweitzer (French Equatorial Africa)
1953 George C. Marshall (U.S.)
1954 Office of U.N. High Commissioner for Refugees
1955 No award
1956 No award
1957 Lester B. Pearson (Canada)
1958 Rev. Dominique Georges Henri Pire (Belgium)
1959 Philip John Noel-Baker (England)
1960 Albert John Luthuli (South Africa)
1961 Dag Hammarskjöld (Sweden)
1962 Linus Pauling (U.S.)
1963 Intl. Comm. of Red Cross; League of Red Cross Societies (both Geneva)
1964 Rev. Dr. Martin Luther King, Jr. (U.S.)
1965 UNICEF (United Nations Children's Fund)
1966 No award
1967 No award
1968 René Cassin (France)
1969 International Labour Organization
1970 Norman E. Borlaug (U.S.)
1971 Willy Brandt (West Germany)
1972 No award
1973 Henry A. Kissinger (U.S.); Le Duc Tho (North Vietnam)[1]
1974 Eisaku Sato (Japan); Sean MacBride (Ireland)
1975 Andrei D. Sakharov (U.S.S.R.)
1976 Mairead Corrigan and Betty Williams (both Northern Ireland)
1977 Amnesty International
1978 Menachem Begin (Israel) and Anwar el-Sadat (Egypt)
1979 Mother Teresa of Calcutta (India)
1980 Adolfo Pérez Esquivei (Argentina)
1981 Office of the United Nations High Commissioner for Refugees
1982 Alva Myrdal (Sweden)
1983 Lech Walesa (Poland)

1. Le Duc Tho refused prize, charging that peace had not yet been really established in South Vietnam.

LITERATURE

1901 René F. A. Sully Prudhomme (France)
1902 Theodor Mommsen (Germany)

1903 Björnstjerne Björnson (Norway)
1904 Frédéric Mistral (France) and José Echegaray (Spain)
1905 Henryk Sienkiewicz (Poland)
1906 Giosuè Carducci (Italy)
1907 Rudyard Kipling (England)
1908 Rudolf Eucken (Germany)
1909 Selma Lagerlöf (Sweden)
1910 Paul von Heyse (Germany)
1911 Maurice Maeterlinck (Belgium)
1912 Gerhart Hauptmann (Germany)
1913 Rabindranath Tagore (India)
1915 Romain Rolland (France)
1916 Verner von Heidenstam (Sweden)
1917 Karl Gjellerup (Denmark) and Henrik Pontoppidan (Denmark)
1919 Carl Spitteler (Switzerland)
1920 Knut Hamsun (Norway)
1921 Anatole France (France)
1922 Jacinto Benavente (Spain)
1923 William B. Yeats (Ireland)
1924 Wladyslaw Reymont (Poland)
1925 George Bernard Shaw (England)
1926 Grazia Deledda (Italy)
1927 Henri Bergson (France)
1928 Sigrid Undset (Norway)
1929 Thomas Mann (Germany)
1930 Sinclair Lewis (U.S.)
1931 Erik A. Karlfeldt (Sweden)
1932 John Galsworthy (England)
1933 Ivan G. Bunin (Russia)
1934 Luigi Pirandello (Italy)
1935 No award
1936 Eugene O'Neill (U.S.)
1937 Roger Martin du Gard (France)
1938 Pearl S. Buck (U.S.)
1939 Frans Eemil Sillanpää (Finland)
1944 Johannes V. Jensen (Denmark)
1945 Gabriela Mistral (Chile)
1946 Hermann Hesse (Switzerland)
1947 André Gide (France)
1948 Thomas Stearns Eliot (England)
1949 William Faulkner (U.S.)
1950 Bertrand Russell (England)
1951 Pär Lagerkvist (Sweden)
1952 François Mauriac (France)
1953 Sir Winston Churchill (England)
1954 Ernest Hemingway (U.S.)
1955 Halldór Kiljan Laxness (Iceland)
1956 Juan Ramón Jiménez (Spain)
1957 Albert Camus (France)
1958 Boris Pasternak (U.S.S.R.) (declined)
1959 Salvatore Quasimodo (Italy)
1960 St-John Perse (Alexis St.-Léger Léger) (France)
1961 Ivo Andric (Yugoslavia)
1962 John Steinbeck (U.S.)
1963 Giorgios Seferis (Seferiades) (Greece)
1964 Jean-Paul Sartre (France) (declined)
1965 Mikhail Sholokhov (U.S.S.R.)
1966 Shmuel Yosef Agnon (Israel) and Nelly Sachs (Sweden)
1967 Miguel Angel Asturias (Guatemala)
1968 Yasunari Kawabata (Japan)
1969 Samuel Beckett (France)
1970 Aleksandr Solzhenitsyn (U.S.S.R.)
1971 Pablo Neruda (Chile)
1972 Heinrich Böll (Germany)
1973 Patrick White (Australia)
1974 Eyvind Johnson and Harry Martinson (both Sweden)
1975 Eugenio Montale (Italy)
1976 Saul Bellow (U.S.)
1977 Vicente Aleixandre (Spain)
1978 Isaac Bashevis Singer (U.S.)
1979 Odysseus Elytis (Greece)
1980 Czeslaw Milosz (U.S.)
1981 Elias Canetti (Bulgaria)
1982 Gabriel García Márquez (Colombia)
1983 William Golding (England)

PHYSICS

1901 Wilhelm K. Roentgen (Germany), for discovery of Roentgen rays
1902 Hendrik A. Lorentz and Pieter Zeeman (Netherlands), for work on influence of magnetism upon radiation
1903 A. Henri Becquerel (France), for work on spontaneous radioactivity; and Pierre and Marie Curie (France), for study of radiation
1904 John Strutt (Lord Rayleigh) (England), for discovery of argon in investigating gas density
1905 Philipp Lenard (Germany), for work with cathode rays
1906 Sir Joseph Thomson (England), for investigations on passage of electricity through gases
1907 Albert A. Michelson (U.S.), for spectroscopic and metrologic investigations
1908 Gabriel Lippmann (France), for method of reproducing colors by photography
1909 Guglielmo Marconi (Italy) and Ferdinand Braun (Germany), for development of wireless
1910 Johannes D. van der Waals (Netherlands), for work with the equation of state for gases and liquids
1911 Wilhelm Wien (Germany), for his laws governing the radiation of heat
1912 Gustaf Dalén (Sweden), for discovery of automatic regulators used in lighting lighthouses and light-buoys
1913 Heike Kamerlingh-Onnes (Netherlands), for work leading to production of liquid helium
1914 Max von Laue (Germany), for discovery of diffraction of Roentgen rays passing through crystals
1915 Sir William Bragg and William L. Bragg (England), for analysis of crystal structure by X rays
1916 No award
1917 Charles G. Barkla (England), for discovery of Roentgen radiation of the elements
1918 Max Planck (Germany), discoveries in connection with quantum theory
1919 Johannes Stark (Germany), discovery of Doppler effect in Canal rays and decomposition of spectrum lines by electric fields
1920 Charles E. Guillaume (Switzerland), for discoveries of anomalies in nickel steel alloys
1921 Albert Einstein (Germany), for discovery of the law of the photoelectric effect
1922 Niels Bohr (Denmark), for investigation of structure of atoms and radiations emanating from them
1923 Robert A. Millikan (U.S.), for work on elementary charge of electricity and photoelectric phenomena
1924 Karl M. G. Siegbahn (Sweden), for investigations in X-ray spectroscopy
1925 James Franck and Gustav Hertz (Germany), for discovery of laws governing impact of electrons upon atoms
1926 Jean B. Perrin (France), for work on discontinuous structure of matter and discovery of the equilibrium of sedimentation
1927 Arthur H. Compton (U.S.), for discovery of Compton phenomenon; and Charles T. R.

Wilson (England), for method of perceiving paths taken by electrically charged particles

1928 In 1929, the 1928 prize was awarded to Sir Owen Richardson (England), for work on the phenomenon of thermionics and discovery of the Richardson Law

1929 Prince Louis Victor de Broglie (France), for discovery of the wave character of electrons

1930 Sir Chandrasekhara Raman (India), for work on diffusion of light and discovery of the Raman effect

1931 No award

1932 In 1933, the prize for 1932 was awarded to Werner Heisenberg (Germany), for creation of the quantum mechanics

1933 Erwin Schrödinger (Austria) and Paul A. M. Dirac (England), for discovery of new fertile forms of the atomic theory

1934 No award

1935 James Chadwick (England), for discovery of the neutron

1936 Victor F. Hess (Austria), for discovery of cosmic radiation; and Carl D. Anderson (U.S.), for discovery of the positron

1937 Clinton J. Davisson (U.S.) and George P. Thomson (England), for discovery of diffraction of electrons by crystals

1938 Enrico Fermi (Italy), for identification of new radioactivity elements and discovery of nuclear reactions effected by slow neutrons

1939 Ernest Orlando Lawrence (U.S.), for development of the cyclotron

1943 Otto Stern (U.S.), for detection of magnetic momentum of protons

1944 Isidor Isaac Rabi (U.S.), for work on magnetic movements of atomic particles

1945 Wolfgang Pauli (Austria), for work on atomic fissions

1946 Percy Williams Bridgman (U.S.), for studies and inventions in high-pressure physics

1947 Sir Edward Appleton (England), for discovery of layer which reflects radio short waves in the ionosphere

1948 Patrick M. S. Blackett (England), for improvement on Wilson chamber and discoveries in cosmic radiation

1949 Hideki Yukawa (Japan), for mathematical prediction, in 1935, of the meson

1950 Cecil Frank Powell (England), for method of photographic study of atom nucleus, and for discoveries about mesons

1951 Sir John Douglas Cockcroft (England) and Ernest T. S. Walton (Ireland), for work in 1932 on transmutation of atomic nuclei

1952 Edward Mills Purcell and Felix Bloch (U.S.), for work in measurement of magnetic fields in atomic nuclei

1953 Fritz Zernike (Netherlands), for development of "phase contrast" microscope

1954 Max Born (England), for work in quantum mechanics; and Walther Bothe (Germany), for work in cosmic radiation

1955 Polykarp Kusch and Willis E. Lamb, Jr. (U.S.), for atomic measurements

1956 William Shockley, Walter H. Brattain, and John Bardeen (U.S.), for developing electronic transistor

1957 Tsung Dao Lee and Chen Ning Yang (China), for disproving principle of conservation of parity

1958 Pavel A. Cherenkov, Ilya M. Frank, and Igor E. Tamm (U.S.S.R.), for work resulting in development of cosmic-ray counter

1959 Emilio Segre and Owen Chamberlain (U.S.), for demonstrating the existence of the anti-proton

1960 Donald A. Glaser (U.S.), for invention of "bubble chamber" to study subatomic particles

1961 Robert Hofstadter (U.S.), for determination of shape and size of atomic nucleus; Rudolf Mössbauer (Germany), for method of producing and measuring recoil-free gamma rays

1962 Lev D. Landau (U.S.S.R.), for his theories about condensed matter

1963 Eugene Paul Wigner, Maria Goeppert Mayer (both U.S.), and J. Hans D. Jensen (Germany), for research on structure of atom and its nucleus

1964 Charles Hard Townes (U.S.), Nikolai G. Basov, and Aleksandr M. Prochorov (both U.S.S.R.), for developing maser and laser principle of producing high-intensity radiation

1965 Richard P. Feynman, Julian S. Schwinger (both U.S.), and Shinichero Tomonaga (Japan), for research in quantum electrodynamics

1966 Alfred Kastler (France), for work on energy levels inside atom

1967 Hans A. Bethe (U.S.), for work on energy production of stars

1968 Luis Walter Alvarez (U.S.), for study of subatomic particles

1969 Murray Gell-Mann (U.S.), for study of subatomic particles

1970 Hannes Alfvén (Sweden), for theories in plasma physics; and Louis Néel (France), for discoveries in antiferromagnetism and ferrimagnetism

1971 Dennis Gabor (England), for invention of holographic method of three-dimensional imagery

1972 John Bardeen, Leon N. Cooper, and John Robert Schrieffer (all U.S.), for theory of superconductivity, where electrical resistance in certain metals vanishes above absolute zero temperature

1973 Ivar Giaever (U.S.), Leo Esaki (Japan), and Brian D. Josephson (U.K.), for theories that have advanced and expanded the field of miniature electronics

1974 Antony Hewish (England), for discovery of pulsars; Martin Ryle (England), for using radiotelescopes to probe outer space with high degree of precision

1975 James Rainwater (U.S.) and Ben Mottelson and Aage N. Bohr (both Denmark), for showing that the atomic nucleus is asymmetrical

1976 Burton Richter and Samuel C. C. Ting (both U. S.), for discovery of subatomic particles known as J and psi

1977 Philip W. Anderson and John H. Van Vleck (both U.S.), and Nevill F. Mott (U.K.), for work underlying computer memories and electronic devices

1978 Arno A. Penzias and Robert W. Wilson (both U. S.), for work in cosmic microwave radiation; Piotr L. Kapitsa (U.S.S.R.), for basic inventions and discoveries in low-temperature physics

1979 Steven Weinberg and Sheldon L. Glashow (both U.S.) and Abdus Salam (Pakistan), for developing theory that electromagnetism and the "weak" force, which causes radioactive decay in some atomic nuclei, are facets of the same phenomenon

1980 James W. Cronin and Val L. Fitch (both U.S.), for work concerning the assymetry of subatomic particles

1981 Nicolaas Bloembergen and Arthur L. Schawlow (both U.S.) and Kai M. Siegbahn (Sweden), for developing technologies with lasers and other devices to probe the secrets of complex forms of matter

1982 Kenneth G. Wilson (U.S.), for analysis of changes in matter under pressure and temperature

1983 Subrahmanyam Chandrasekhar and William A. Fowler (both U.S.) for complementary research on processes involved in the evolution of stars

CHEMISTRY

1901 Jacobus H. van't Hoff (Netherlands), for laws of chemical dynamics and osmotic pressure in solutions

1902 Emil Fischer (Germany), for experiments in sugar and purin groups of substances

1903 Svante A. Arrhenius (Sweden), for his electrolytic theory of dissociation

1904 Sir William Ramsay (England), for discovery and determination of place of inert gaseous elements in air

1905 Adolf von Baeyer (Germany), for work on organic dyes and hydroaromatic combinations

1906 Henri Moissan (France), for isolation of fluorine, and introduction of electric furnace

1907 Eduard Buchner (Germany), discovery of cellless fermentation and investigations in biological chemistry

1908 Sir Ernest Rutherford (England), for investigations into disintegration of elements

1909 Wilhelm Ostwald (Germany), for work on catalysis and investigations into chemical equilibrium and reaction rates

1910 Otto Wallach (Germany), for work in the field of alicyclic compounds

1911 Marie Curie (France), for discovery of elements radium and polonium

1912 Victor Grignard (France), for reagent discovered by him; and Paul Sabatier (France), for methods of hydrogenating organic compounds

1913 Alfred Werner (Switzerland), for linking up atoms within the molecule

1914 Theodore W. Richards (U.S.), for determining atomic weight of many chemical elements

1915 Richard Willstätter (Germany), for research into coloring matter of plants, especially chlorophyll

1916 No award

1917 No award

1918 Fritz Haber (Germany), for synthetic production of ammonia

1919 No award

1920 Walther Nernst (Germany), for work in thermochemistry

1921 Frederick Soddy (England), for investigations into origin and nature of isotopes

1922 Francis W. Aston (England), for discovery of isotopes in nonradioactive elements and for discovery of the whole number rule

1923 Fritz Pregl (Austria), for method of microanalysis of organic substances discovered by him

1924 No award

1925 In 1926, the 1925 prize was awarded to Richard Zsigmondy (Germany), for work on the heterogeneous nature of colloid solutions

1926 Theodor Svedberg (Sweden), for work on disperse systems

1927 In 1928, the 1927 prize was awarded to Heinrich Wieland (Germany), for investigations of bile acids and kindred substances

1928 Adolf Windaus (Germany), for investigations on constitution of the sterols and their connection with vitamins

1929 Sir Arthur Harden (England) and Hans K. A. S. von Euler-Chelpin (Sweden), for research of fermentation of sugars

1930 Hans Fischer (Germany), for work on coloring matter of blood and leaves and for his synthesis of hemin

1931 Karl Bosch and Friedrich Bergius (Germany), for invention and development of chemical high-pressure methods

1932 Irving Langmuir (U.S.), for work in realm of surface chemistry

1933 No award

1934 Harold C. Urey (U.S.), for discovery of heavy hydrogen

1935 Frédéric and Irène Joliot-Curie (France), for synthesis of new radioactive elements

1936 Peter J. W. Debye (Netherlands), for investigations on dipole moments and diffraction of X rays and electrons in gases

1937 Walter N. Haworth (England), for research on carbohydrates and Vitamin C; and Paul Karrer (Switzerland), for work on carotenoids, flavins, and Vitamins A and B

1938 Richard Kuhn (Germany), for carotinoid study and vitamin research (declined)

1939 Adolf Butenandt (Germany), for work on sexual hormones (declined the prize); and Leopold Ruzicka (Switzerland), for work with polymethylenes

1943 Georg Hevesy De Heves (Hungary), for work on use of isotopes as indicators

1944 Otto Hahn (Germany), for work on atomic fission

1945 Artturi Illmari Virtanen (Finland), for research in the field of conservation of fodder

1946 James B. Sumner (U.S.), for crystallizing enzymes; John H. Northrop and Wendell M. Stanley (U.S.), for preparing enzymes and virus proteins in pure form

1947 Sir Robert Robinson (England), for research in plant substances

1948 Arne Tiselius (Sweden), for biochemical discoveries and isolation of mouse paralysis virus

1949 William Francis Giauque (U.S.), for research in thermodynamics, especially effects of low temperature

1950 Otto Diels and Kurt Alder (Germany), for discovery of diene synthesis enabling scientists to study structure of organic matter

1951 Glenn T. Seaborg and Edwin H. McMillan (U.S.), for discovery of plutonium

1952 Archer John Porter Martin and Richard Laurence Millington Synge (England), for development of partition chromatography

1953 Hermann Staudinger (Germany), for research in giant molecules

1954 Linus C. Pauling (U.S.), for study of forces holding together protein and other molecules

1955 Vincent du Vigneaud (U.S.), for work on pituitary hormones

1956 Sir Cyril Hinshelwood (England) and Nikolai N. Semenov (U.S.S.R.), for parallel research on chemical reaction kinetics

1957 Sir Alexander Todd (England), for research with chemical compounds that are factors in heredity

1958 Frederick Sanger (England), for determining molecular structure of insulin

1959 Jaroslav Heyrovsky (Czechoslovakia), for development of polarography, an electrochemical method of analysis

1960 Willard F. Libby (U.S.), for "atomic time clock" to measure age of objects by measuring their radioactivity

1961 Melvin Calvin (U.S.), for establishing chemical steps during photosynthesis

1962 Max F. Perutz and John C. Kendrew (England), for mapping protein molecules with X-rays

1963 Carl Ziegler (Germany) and Giulio Natta (Italy), for work in uniting simple hydrocarbons into large molecule substances

1964 Dorothy Mary Crowfoot Hodgkin (England), for determining structure of compounds needed in combating pernicious anemia

1965 Robert B. Woodward (U.S.), for work in synthesizing complicated organic compounds

1966 Robert Sanderson Mulliken (U.S.), for research on bond holding atoms together in molecule

1967 Manfred Eigen (Germany), Ronald G. W. Norrish, and George Porter (both England), for work in high-speed chemical reactions

1968 Lars Onsager (U.S.), for development of system of equations in thermodynamics

1969 Derek H. R. Barton (England) and Odd Hassel (Norway), for study of organic molecules

1970 Luis F. Leloir (Argentina), for discovery of sugar nucleotides and their role in biosynthesis of carbohydrates

1971 Gerhard Herzberg (Canada), for contributions to knowledge of electronic structure and geometry of molecules, particularly free radicals

1972 Christian Boehmer Anfinsen, Stanford Moore, and William Howard Stein (all U.S.), for pioneering studies in enzymes

1973 Ernst Otto Fischer (W. Germany) and Geoffrey Wilkinson (U.K.), for work that could solve problem of automobile exhaust pollution

1974 Paul J. Flory (U.S.), for developing analytic methods to study properties and molecular structure of long-chain molecules

1975 John W. Cornforth (Australia) and Vladimir Prelog (Switzerland), for research on structure of biological molecules such as antibiotics and cholesterol

1976 William N. Lipscomb, Jr. (U.S.), for work on the structure and bonding mechanisms of boranes

1977 Ilya Prigogine (Belgium), for contributions to nonequilibrium thermodynamics, particularly the theory of dissipative structures

1978 Peter Mitchell (U.K.), for contributions to the understanding of biological energy transfer

1979 Herbert C. Brown (U.S.) and Georg Wittig (West Germany), for developing a group of substances that facilitate very difficult chemical reactions

1980 Paul Berg and Walter Gilbert (both U.S.) and Frederick Sanger (England), for developing methods to map the structure and function of DNA, the substance that controls the activity of the cell

1981 Roald Hoffmann (U.S.) and Kenichi Fukui (Japan), for applying quantum-mechanics theories to predict the course of chemical reactions

1982 Aaron Klug (U.K.), for research in the detailed structures of viruses and components of life

1983 Henry Taube (U.S.), for research on how electrons transfer between molecules in chemical reactions.

PHYSIOLOGY OR MEDICINE

1901 Emil A. von Behring (Germany), for work on serum therapy against diptheria

1902 Sir Ronald Ross (England), for work on malaria

1903 Niels R. Finsen (Denmark), for his treatment of lupus vulgaris with concentrated light rays

1904 Ivan P. Pavlov (U.S.S.R.), for work on the physiology of digestion

1905 Robert Koch (Germany), for work on tuberculosis

1906 Camillo Golgi (Italy) and Santiago Ramón y Cajal (Spain), for work on structure of the nervous system

1907 Charles L. A. Laveran (France), for work with protozoa in the generation of disease

1908 Paul Ehrlich (Germany), and Elie Metchnikoff (U.S.S.R.), for work on immunity

1909 Theodor Kocher (Switzerland), for work on the thyroid gland

1910 Albrecht Kossel (Germany), for achievements in the chemistry of the cell

1911 Allvar Gullstrand (Sweden), for work on the dioptrics of the eye

1912 Alexis Carrel (France), for work on vascular ligature and grafting of blood vessels and organs

1913 Charles Richet (France), for work on anaphylaxy

1914 Robert Bárány (Austria), for work on physiology and pathology of the vestibular system

1915-1918 No award

1919 Jules Bordet (Belgium), for discoveries in connection with immunity

1920 August Krogh (Denmark), for discovery of regulation of capillaries' motor mechanism

1921 No award

1922 In 1923, the 1922 prize was shared by Archibald V. Hill (England), for discovery relating to heat-production in muscles; and Otto Meyerhof (Germany), for correlation between consumption of oxygen and production of lactic acid in muscles

1923 Sir Frederick Banting (Canada) and John J. R. Macleod (Scotland), for discovery of insulin

1924 Willem Einthoven (Netherlands), for discovery of the mechanism of the electrocardiogram

1925 No award

1926 Johannes Fibiger (Denmark), for discovery of the Spiroptera carcinoma

1927 Julius Wagner-Jauregg (Austria), for use of malaria inoculation in treatment of dementia paralytica

1928 Charles Nicolle (France), for work on typhus exanthematicus

1929 Christiaan Eijkman (Netherlands), for discovery of the antineuritic vitamins; and Sir Frederick Hopkins (England), for discovery of growth-promoting vitamins

1930 Karl Landsteiner (U.S.), for discovery of human blood groups

1931 Otto H. Warburg (Germany), for discovery of the character and mode of action of the respiratory ferment

1932 Sir Charles Sherrington (England) and Edgar D. Adrian (U.S.), for discoveries of the function of the neuron

1933 Thomas H. Morgan (U.S.), for discoveries on hereditary function of the chromosomes

1934 George H. Whipple, George R. Minot, and William P. Murphy (U.S.), for discovery of liver therapy against anemias
1935 Hans Spemann (Germany), for discovery of the organizer-effect in embryonic development
1936 Sir Henry Dale (England) and Otto Loewi (Germany), for discoveries on chemical transmission of nerve impulses
1937 Albert Szent-Györgyi von Nagyrapolt (Hungary), for discoveries on biological combustion
1938 Corneille Heymans (Belgium), for determining importance of sinus and aorta mechanisms in the regulation of respiration
1939 Gerhard Domagk (Germany), for antibacterial effect of prontocilate
1943 Henrik Dam (Denmark) and Edward A. Doisy (U.S.), for analysis of Vitamin K
1944 Joseph Erlanger and Herbert Spencer Gasser (U.S.), for work on functions of the nerve threads
1945 Sir Alexander Fleming, Ernst Boris Chain, and Sir Howard Florey (England), for discovery of penicillin
1946 Herman J. Muller (U.S.), for hereditary effects of X rays on genes
1947 Carl F. and Gerty T. Cori (U.S.), for work on animal starch metabolism; Bernardo A. Houssay (Argentina), for study of pituitary
1948 Paul Mueller (Switzerland), for discovery of insect-killing properties of DDT
1949 Walter Rudolf Hess (Switzerland), for research on brain control of body; and Antonio Caetano de Abreu Freire Egas Moniz (Portugal), for development of brain operation
1950 Philip S. Hench, Edward C. Kendall (both U.S.), and Tadeus Reichstein (Switzerland), for discoveries about hormones of adrenal cortex
1951 Max Theiler (South Africa), for development of anti-yellow-fever vaccine
1952 Selman A. Waksman (U.S.), for co-discovery of streptomycin
1953 Fritz A. Lipmann (Germany-U.S.) and Hans Adolph Krebs (Germany-England), for studies of living cells
1954 John F. Enders, Thomas H. Weller, and Frederick C. Robbins (U.S.), for work with cultivation of polio virus
1955 Hugo Theorell (Sweden), for work on oxidation enzymes
1956 Dickinson W. Richards, Jr., André F. Cournand (both U.S.), and Werner Forssmann (Germany), for new techniques in treating heart disease
1957 Daniel Bovet (Italy), for development of drugs to relieve allergies and relax muscles during surgery
1958 Joshua Lederberg (U.S.), for work with genetic mechanisms; George W. Beadie and Edward L. Tatum (U.S.), for discovering how genes transmit hereditary characteristics
1959 Severo Ochoa and Arthur Kornberg (U.S.), for discoveries related to compounds within chromosomes, which play a vital role in heredity
1960 Sir Macfarlane Burnet (Australia) and Peter Brian Medawar (England), for discovery of acquired immunological tolerance
1961 Georg von Bekesy (U.S.), for discoveries about physical mechanisms of stimulation within cochlea
1962 James D. Watson (U.S.), Maurice H. F. Wilkins, and Francis H. C. Crick (England), for determining structure of deoxyribonucleic acid (DNA)
1963 Alan Lloyd Hodgkin, Andrew Fielding Huxley (both England), and Sir John Carew Eccles (Australia), for research on nerve cells
1964 Konrad E. Bloch (U.S.) and Feodor Lynen (Germany), for research on mechanism and regulation of cholesterol and fatty acid metabolism
1965 François Jacob, André Lwolff, and Jacques Monod (France), for study of regulatory activities in body cells
1966 Charles Brenton Huggins (U.S.), for studies in hormone treatment of cancer of prostate; Francis Peyton Rous (U.S.), for discovery of tumor-producing viruses
1967 Haldan K. Hartline, George Wald, and Ragnar Granit (U.S.), for work on human eye
1968 Robert W. Holley, Har Gobind Khorana, and Marshall W. Nirenberg (U.S.), for studies of genetic code
1969 Max Delbruck, Alfred D. Hershey, and Salvador E. Luria (U.S.), for study of mechanism of virus infection in living cells
1970 Julius Axelrod (U.S.), Ulf S. von Euler (Sweden), and Sir Bernard Katz (England), for studies of how nerve impulses are transmitted within the body
1971 Earl W. Sutherland, Jr. (U.S.), for research on how hormones work
1972 Gerald M. Edelman (U.S.), and Rodney R. Porter (U.K.), for research on the chemical structure and nature of antibodies
1973 Karl von Frisch and Konrad Lorenz (Austria), and Nikolaas Tinbergen (Netherlands), for their studies of individual and social behavior patterns
1974 George E. Palade and Christian de Duve (both U.S.) and Albert Claude (Belgium), for contributions to understanding inner workings of living cells
1975 David Baltimore, Howard M. Temin, and Renato Dulbecco (all U.S.), for work in interaction between tumor viruses and genetic material of the cell
1976 Baruch S. Blumberg and D. Carleton Gajdusek (U.S.), for discoveries concerning new mechanisms for the origin and dissemination of infectious diseases
1977 Rosalyn S. Yalow, Roger C. L. Guillemin, and Andrew V. Schally (all U.S.), for research in role of hormones in chemistry of the body
1978 Daniel Nathans and Hamilton Smith (both U.S.) and Werner Arber (Switzerland), for discovery of restriction enzymes and their application to problems of molecular genetics
1979 Allan McLeod Cormack (U.S.) and Godfrey Newbold Hounsfield (England), for developing computed axial tomography (CAT scan) X-ray technique
1980 Baruj Benacerraf and George D. Snell (both U.S.) and Jean Dausset (France), for discoveries that explain how the structure of cells relates to organ transplants and diseases
1981 Roger W. Sperry and David H. Hubel (both U.S.) and Torsten N. Wiesel (Sweden), for studies vital to understanding the organization and functioning of the brain
1982 Sune Bergstrom and Bengt Samuelsson (Sweden) and John R. Vane (U.K.), for research in prostaglandins, a hormonelike substance involved in a wide range of illnesses

1983 Barbara McClintock (U.S.), for her discovery of mobile genes in the chromosones of a plant that change the future generations of plants they produce

ECONOMIC SCIENCE

1969 Ragnar Frisch (Norway) and Jan Tinbergen (Netherlands), for work in econometrics (application of mathematics and statistical methods to economic theories and problems)
1970 Paul A. Samuelson (U.S.), for efforts to raise the level of scientific analysis in economic theory
1971 Simon Kuznets (U.S.), for developing concept of using a country's gross national product to determine its economic growth
1972 Kenneth J. Arrow (U.S.) and Sir John R. Hicks (U.K.), for theories that help to assess business risk and government economic and welfare policies
1973 Wassily Leontief (U.S.), for devising the input-output technique to determine how different sectors of an economy interact
1974 Gunnar Myrdal (Sweden) and Friedrich A. von Hayek (U.K.), for pioneering analysis of the interdependence of economic, social and institutional phenomena
1975 Leonid V. Kantorovich (U.S.S.R.) and Tjalling C. Koopmans (U.S.), for work on the theory of optimum allocation of resources
1976 Milton Friedman (U.S.), for work in consumption analysis and monetary history and theory, and for demonstration of complexity of stabilization policy
1977 Bertil Ohlin (Sweden) and James E. Meade (U. K.), for contributions to theory of international trade and international capital movements
1978 Herbert A. Simon (U.S.), for research into the decision-making process within economic organizations
1979 Sir Arthur Lewis (England) and Theodore Schultz (U.S.), for work on economic problems of developing nations
1980 Lawrence R. Klein (U.S.), for developing models for forecasting economic trends and shaping policies to deal with them
1981 James Tobin (U.S.), for analyses of financial markets and their influence on spending and saving by families and businesses
1982 George J. Stigler (U.S.), for work on government regulation in the economy and the functioning of industry
1983 Gerard Debreu (U.S.), in recognition of his work on the basic economic problem of how prices operate to balance what producers supply with what buyers want.

Antoinette Perry (Tony) Awards, 1984

Dramatic play: *The Real Thing,* Tom Stoppard
Musical: *La Cage aux Folles*
Actor (play): Jeremy Irons, *The Real Thing*
Actress (play): Glenn Close, *The Real Thing*
Actor (musical): George Hearn, *La Cage aux Folles*
Actress (musical): Chita Rivera, *The Rink*
Actor, featured (play): Joe Mantegna, *Glengarry Glen Ross*
Actress, featured (play): Christine Baranski, *The Real Thing*
Actor, featured (musical): Hinton Battle, *The Tap Dance Kid*
Actress, featured (musical): Lila Kedrova, *Zorba*
Director (play): Mike Nichols, *The Real Thing*
Director (musical): Arthur Laurents, *La Cage aux Folles*
Score: Jerry Herman, *La Cage aux Folles*
Musical book: Harvey Fierstein, *La Cage aux Folles*
Choreography: Danny Daniels, *The Tap Dance Kid*
Scenic design: Tony Straiges, *Sunday in the Park With George*
Costumes: Theoni V. Aldredge, *La Cage aux Folles*
Lighting: Richard Nelson, *Sunday in the Park With George*
Reproduction of a play or musical: Death of a Salesman

Awards of the Society of Professional Journalists, 1983

(Sigma Delta Chi)

General reporting: David Ashenfelter and John Castine, *Detroit Free Press*
Editorial writing: Louis J. Salome, Betsey Willeford, and Ellis Berger, *The Miami News*
Washington correspondence: Michael J. Himowitz, *Baltimore Evening Sun*
Foreign correspondence: William Branigin, *The Washington Post*
News photography: Rich Lipski, United Press International
Editorial cartoon: Rob Lawler, *Philadelphia Daily News*
Public service in newspaper journalism: *The Philadelphia Inquirer*
Magazine reporting: Mike Mallowe, *Philadelphia Magazine*
Public service in magazine journalism: *Memphis Magazine*
Radio reporting: Howard Berkes, National Public Radio
Public service in radio reporting: WMAQ News, Chicago
Editorializing on radio: Gene Slaymaker, WTLC, Indianapolis
Television reporting: Peter Arnett, Cable News Network
Public service in television reporting: WSMV, Nashville, Tenn.
Editorializing on television: KYW, Philadelphia
Research about journalism: Sig Mickelson, for *America's Other Voice,* a definitive book on Radio Free Europe and Radio Liberty

Motion Picture Academy Awards (Oscars)

	Picture	Director	Actress
1928	*Wings,* Paramount	Frank Borzage, *Seventh Heaven;* Lewis Milestone, *Two Arabian Nights*	Janet Gaynor, *Seventh Heaven, Street Angel, Sunrise*
1929	*The Broadway Melody,* M-G-M	Frank Lloyd, *The Divine Lady*	Mary Pickford, *Coquette*
1930	*All Quiet on the Western Front,* Universal	Lewis Milestone, *All Quiet on the Western Front*	Norma Shearer, *The Divorcee*
1931	*Cimarron,* RKO Radio	Norman Taurog, *Skippy*	Marie Dressler, *Min and Bill*
1932	*Grand Hotel,* M-G-M	Frank Borzage, *Bad Girl*	Helen Hayes, *The Sin of Madelon Claudet*
1933	*Cavalcade,* Fox	Frank Lloyd, *Cavalcade*	Katharine Hepburn, *Morning Glory*
1934	*It Happened One Night,* Columbia	Frank Capra, *It Happened One Night*	Claudette Colbert *It Happened One Night*
1935	*Mutiny on the Bounty,* M-G-M	John Ford, *The Informer*	Bette Davis, *Dangerous*
1936	*The Great Ziegfeld,* M-G-M	Frank Capra, *Mr. Deeds Goes to Town*	Luise Rainer, *The Great Ziegfeld*
1937	*The Life of Emile Zola,* Warner Bros.	Leo McCarey, *The Awful Truth*	Luise Rainer, *The Good Earth*
1938	*You Can't Take It with You,* Columbia	Frank Capra, *You Can't Take It with You*	Bette Davis, *Jezebel*
1939	*Gone with the Wind,* Selznick-M-G-M	Victor Fleming, *Gone with the Wind*	Vivien Leigh, *Gone with the Wind*
1940	*Rebecca,* Selznick-UA	John Ford, *The Grapes of Wrath*	Ginger Rogers, *Kitty Foyle*
1941	*How Green Was My Valley,* 20th Century-Fox	John Ford, *How Green Was My Valley*	Joan Fontaine, *Suspicion*
1942	*Mrs. Miniver,* M-G-M	William Wyler, *Mrs. Miniver*	Greer Garson, *Mrs. Miniver*
1943	*Casablanca,* Warner Bros.	Michael Curtiz, *Casablanca*	Jennifer Jones, *The Song of Bernadette*
1944	*Going My Way,* Paramount	Leo McCarey, *Going My Way*	Ingrid Bergman, *Gaslight*
1945	*The Lost Weekend,* Paramount	Billy Wilder, *The Lost Weekend*	Joan Crawford, *Mildred Pierce*
1946	*The Best Years of Our Lives,* Goldwyn-RKO Radio	William Wyler, *The Best Years of Our Lives*	Olivia de Havilland, *To Each His Own*
1947	*Gentleman's Agreement,* 20th Century-Fox	Elia Kazan, *Gentleman's Agreement*	Loretta Young, *The Farmer's Daughter*
1948	*Hamlet,* Rank-Two Cities-U-I	John Huston, *Treasure of Sierra Madre*	Jane Wyman, *Johnny Belinda*
1949	*All the King's Men,* Rossen-Columbia	Joseph L. Mankiewicz, *A Letter to Three Wives*	Olivia de Havilland, *The Heiress*
1950	*All About Eve,* 20th Century-Fox	Joseph L. Mankiewicz, *All About Eve*	Judy Holliday, *Born Yesterday*
1951	*An American in Paris,* M-G-M	George Stevens, *A Place in the Sun*	Vivien Leigh, *A Streetcar Named Desire*
1952	*The Greatest Show on Earth,* DeMille-Paramount	John Ford, *The Quiet Man*	Shirley Booth, *Come Back, Little Sheba*
1953	*From Here to Eternity,* Columbia	Fred Zinnemann, *From Here to Eternity*	Audrey Hepburn, *Roman Holiday*
1954	*On the Waterfront,* Horizon-American Corp., Columbia	Elia Kazan, *On the Waterfront*	Grace Kelly, *The Country Girl*
1955	*Marty,* Hecht and Lancaster, United Artists	Delbert Mann, *Marty*	Anna Magnani, *The Rose Tattoo*
1956	*Around the World in 80 Days,* Michael Todd Co., Inc.-UA	George Stevens, *Giant*	Ingrid Bergman, *Anastasia*
1957	*The Bridge on the River Kwai,* Horizon Picture, Columbia	David Lean, *The Bridge on the River Kwai*	Joanne Woodward, *The Three Faces of Eve*
1958	*Gigi,* Arthur Freed Productions, Inc., M-G-M	Vincente Minnelli, *Gigi*	Susan Hayward, *I Want to Live!*
1959	*Ben-Hur,* M-G-M	William Wyler, *Ben-Hur*	Simone Signoret, *Room at the Top*
1960	*The Apartment,* Mirisch Co., Inc., United Artists	Billy Wilder, *The Apartment*	Elizabeth Taylor, *Butterfield 8*
1961	*West Side Story,* Mirisch Pictures, Inc., and B and P Enterprises, Inc., United Artists	Robert Wise and Jerome Robbins, *West Side Story*	Sophia Loren, *Two Women*

Actor	Supporting Actress	Supporting Actor	
Emil Jannings, *The Way of All Flesh, The Last Command*	—	—	1928
Warner Baxter, *In Old Arizona*	—	—	1929
George Arliss, *Disraeli*	—	—	1930
Lionel Barrymore, *A Free Soul*	—	—	1931
Fredric March, *Dr. Jekyll and Mr. Hyde,* and Wallace Beery, *The Champ*	—	—	1932
Charles Laughton, *The Private Life of Henry VIII*	—	—	1933
Clark Gable, *It Happened One Night*	—	—	1934
Victor McLaglen, *The Informer*	—	—	1935
Paul Muni, *The Story of Louis Pasteur*	Gale Sondergaard, *Anthony Adverse*	Walter Brennan, *Come and Get It*	1936
Spencer Tracy, *Captains Courageous*	Alice Brady, *In Old Chicago*	Joseph Schildkraut, *The Life of Emile Zola*	1937
Spencer Tracy, *Boys Town*	Fay Bainter, *Jezebel*	Walter Brennan, *Kentucky*	1938
Robert Donat, *Goodbye, Mr. Chips*	Hattie McDaniel, *Gone with the Wind*	Thomas Mitchell, *Stagecoach*	1939
James Stewart, *The Philadelphia Story*	Jane Darwell, *The Grapes of Wrath*	Walter Brennan, *The Westerner*	1940
Gary Cooper, *Sergeant York*	Mary Astor, *The Great Lie*	Donald Crisp, *How Green Was My Valley*	1941
James Cagney, *Yankee Doodle Dandy*	Teresa Wright, *Mrs. Miniver*	Van Heflin, *Johnny Eager*	1942
Paul Lukas, *Watch on the Rhine*	Katina Paxinou, *For Whom the Bell Tolls*	Charles Coburn, *The More the Merrier*	1943
Bing Crosby, *Going My Way*	Ethel Barrymore, *None But the Lonely Heart*	Barry Fitzgerald, *Going My Way*	1944
Ray Milland, *The Lost Weekend*	Anne Revere, *National Velvet*	James Dunn, *A Tree Grows in Brooklyn*	1945
Fredric March, *The Best Years of Our Lives*	Anne Baxter, *The Razor's Edge*	Harold Russell, *The Best Years of Our Lives*	1946
Ronald Colman, *A Double Life*	Celeste Holm, *Gentleman's Agreement*	Edmund Gwenn, *Miracle on 34th Street*	1947
Laurence Olivier, *Hamlet*	Claire Trevor, *Key Largo*	Walter Huston, *Treasure of Sierra Madre*	1948
Broderick Crawford, *All the King's Men*	Mercedes McCambridge, *All the King's Men*	Dean Jagger, *Twelve O'Clock High*	1949
José Ferrer, *Cyrano de Bergerac*	Josephine Hull, *Harvey*	George Sanders, *All About Eve*	1950
Humphrey Bogart, *The African Queen*	Kim Hunter, *A Streetcar Named Desire*	Karl Malden, *A Streetcar Named Desire*	1951
Gary Cooper, *High Noon*	Gloria Grahame, *The Bad and the Beautiful*	Anthony Quinn, *Viva Zapata!*	1952
William Holden, *Stalag 17*	Donna Reed, *From Here to Eternity*	Frank Sinatra, *From Here to Eternity*	1953
Marlon Brando, *On the Waterfront*	Eva Marie Saint, *On the Waterfront*	Edmond O'Brien, *The Barefoot Contessa*	1954
Ernest Borgnine, *Marty*	Jo Van Fleet, *East of Eden*	Jack Lemmon, *Mister Roberts*	1955
Yul Brynner, *The King and I*	Dorothy Malone, *Written on the Wind*	Anthony Quinn, *Lust for Life*	1956
Alec Guinness, *The Bridge on the River Kwai*	Miyoshi Umeki, *Sayonara*	Red Buttons, *Sayonara*	1957
David Niven, *Separate Tables*	Wendy Hiller, *Separate Tables*	Burl Ives, *The Big Country*	1958
Charlton Heston, *Ben-Hur*	Shelley Winters, *The Diary of Anne Frank*	Hugh Griffith, *Ben-Hur*	1959
Burt Lancaster, *Elmer Gantry*	Shirley Jones, *Elmer Gantry*	Peter Ustinov, *Spartacus*	1960
Maximilian Schell, *Judgment at Nuremberg*	Rita Moreno, *West Side Story*	George Chakiris, *West Side Story*	1961

	Picture	Director	Actress
1962	*Lawrence of Arabia,* Horizon Pictures, Ltd.-Columbia	David Lean, *Lawrence of Arabia*	Anne Bancroft, *The Miracle Worker*
1963	*Tom Jones,* A Woodfall Production, UA-Lopert Pictures	Tony Richardson, *Tom Jones*	Patricia Neal, *Hud*
1964	*My Fair Lady,* Warner Bros.	George Cukor, *My Fair Lady*	Julie Andrews, *Mary Poppins*
1965	*The Sound of Music,* Argyle Enterprises Production, 20th Century-Fox	Robert Wise, *The Sound of Music*	Julie Christie, *Darling*
1966	*A Man for All Seasons,* Highland Films, Ltd., Production, Columbia	Fred Zinnemann, *A Man for All Seasons*	Elizabeth Taylor, *Who's Afraid of Virginia Woolf?*
1967	*In the Heat of the Night,* Mirisch Corp. Production, United Artists	Mike Nichols, *The Graduate*	Katharine Hepburn, *Guess Who's Coming to Dinner*
1968	*Oliver!,* Columbia Pictures	Sir Carol Reed, *Oliver!*	Katharine Hepburn, *The Lion in Winter, and Barbara Streisand, Funny Girl*
1969	*Midnight Cowboy,* Jerome Hellman-John Schlesinger Production, United Artists	John Schlesinger, *Midnight Cowboy*	Maggie Smith, *The Prime of Miss Jean Brodie*
1970	*Patton,* Frank McCarthy-Franklin J. Schaffner Production, 20th Century-Fox	Franklin J. Schaffner, *Patton*	Glenda Jackson, *Women in Love*
1971	*The French Connection,* D'Antoni Productions, 20th Century-Fox	William Friedkin, *The French Connection*	Jane Fonda, *Klute*
1972	*The Godfather,* Albert S. Ruddy Production, Paramount	Bob Fosse, *Cabaret*	Liza Minnelli, *Cabaret*
1973	*The Sting,* Universal-Bill-Phillips-George Roy Hill Production, Universal	George Roy Hill, *The Sting*	Glenda Jackson, *A Touch of Class*
1974	*The Godfather, Part II,* Coppola Co. Production, Paramount	Francis Ford Coppola, *The Godfather, Part II*	Ellen Burstyn, *Alice Doesn't Live Here Anymore*
1975	*One Flew Over the Cuckoo's Nest,* Fantasy Films Production, United Artists	Milos Forman, *One Flew Over the Cuckoo's Nest*	Louise Fletcher, *One Flew Over the Cuckoo's Nest*
1976	*Rocky,* Robert Chartoff-Irwin Winkler Production, United Artists	John G. Avildsen, *Rocky*	Faye Dunaway *Network*
1977	*Annie Hall,* Jack Rollins-Charles H. Joffe Production, United Artists	Woody Allen, *Annie Hall*	Diane Keaton, *Annie Hall*
1978	*The Deer Hunter,* Michael Cimino Film Production, Universal	Michael Cimino, *The Deer Hunter*	Jane Fonda, *Coming Home*
1979	*Kramer vs. Kramer,* Stanley Jaffe Production, Columbia Pictures	Robert Benton, *Kramer vs. Kramer*	Sally Field, *Norma Rae*
1980	*Ordinary People,* Wildwood Enterprises Production, Paramount	Robert Redford, *Ordinary People*	Sissy Spacek, *Coal Miner's Daughter*
1981	*Chariots of Fire,* Enigma Productions, Ladd Company/Warner Bros.	Warren Beatty, *Reds*	Katharine Hepburn, *On Golden Pond*
1982	*Gandhi,* Indo-British Films Production/Columbia	Richard Attenborough, *Gandhi*	Meryl Streep, *Sophie's Choice*
1983	*Terms of Endearment,* Paramount	James L. Brooks, *Terms of Endearment*	Shirley MacLaine, *Terms of Endearment*

"Oscar"

In 1928, the year-old Academy of Motion Picture Arts and Sciences began the presentation of annual awards for film excellence. Cedric Gibbons, art director of M-G-M, sketched the statue and George Stanley, a sculptor, executed the figure. Unchanged in more than half a century, the statue on its pedestal stands 13 1/2 inches tall and weighs 8 1/2 pounds. Formerly of gold-plated bronze, it is now made of gold-plated britannium, an alloy.

For four years the award endured a nameless existence. In 1931, when Margaret Herrick, the academy's new librarian and later its executive director, first saw the statue, she remarked whimsically that it looked like her Uncle Oscar. A newspaper columnist overheard her, and the next day "Oscar" made its debut in print. Another legend, according to an academy historian, has it that the actress Bette Davis said the statue looked like her first husband, Oscar Nelson. A third yarn credits the late Hollywood columnist Sidney Skolsky with having dubbed the knight Oscar.

Actor	Supporting Actress	Supporting Actor	
Gregory Peck, *To Kill a Mockingbird*	Patty Duke, *The Miracle Worker*	Ed Begley, *Sweet Bird of Youth*	**1962**
Sidney Poitier, *Lilies of the Field*	Margaret Rutherford, *The V.I.P.s*	Melvyn Douglas, *Hud*	**1963**
Rex Harrison, *My Fair Lady*	Lila Kedrova, *Zorba the Greek*	Peter Ustinov, *Topkapi*	**1964**
Lee Marvin, *Cat Ballou*	Shelley Winters, *A Patch of Blue*	Martin Balsam, *A Thousand Clowns*	**1965**
Paul Scofield, *A Man for All Seasons*	Sandy Dennis, *Who's Afraid of Virginia Woolf?*	Walter Matthau, *The Fortune Cookie*	**1966**
Rod Steiger, *In the Heat of the Night*	Estelle Parsons, *Bonnie and Clyde*	George Kennedy, *Cool Hand Luke*	**1967**
Cliff Robertson, *Charly*	Ruth Gordon, *Rosemary's Baby*	Jack Albertson, *The Subject Was Roses*	**1968**
John Wayne, *True Grit*	Goldie Hawn, *Cactus Flower*	Gig Young, *They Shoot Horses, Don't They?*	**1969**
George C. Scott, *Patton*	Helen Hayes, *Airport*	John Mills, *Ryan's Daughter*	**1970**
Gene Hackman, *The French Connection*	Cloris Leachman, *The Last Picture Show*	Ben Johnson, *The Last Picture Show*	**1971**
Marlon Brando, *The Godfather*	Eileen Heckart, *Butterflies Are Free*	Joel Grey, *Cabaret*	**1972**
Jack Lemmon, *Save the Tiger*	Tatum O'Neal, *Paper Moon*	John Houseman, *The Paper Chase*	**1973**
Art Carney, *Harry and Tonto*	Ingrid Bergman, *Murder on the Orient Express*	Robert De Niro, *The Godfather, Part II*	**1974**
Jack Nicholson, *One Flew Over the Cuckoo's Nest*	Lee Grant, *Shampoo*	George Burns, *The Sunshine Boys*	**1975**
Peter Finch, *Network*	Beatrice Straight, *Network*	Jason Robards, *All the President's Men*	**1976**
Richard Dreyfuss, *The Goodbye Girl*	Vanessa Redgrave, *Julia*	Jason Robards, *Julia*	**1977**
Jon Voight, *Coming Home*	Maggie Smith, *California Suite*	Christopher Walken, *The Deer Hunter*	**1978**
Dustin Hoffman, *Kramer vs. Kramer*	Meryl Streep, *Kramer vs. Kramer*	Melvyn Douglas, *Being There*	**1979**
Robert De Niro, *Raging Bull*	Mary Steenburgen, *Melvin and Howard*	Timothy Hutton, *Ordinary People*	**1980**
Henry Fonda, *On Golden Pond*	Maureen Stapleton, *Reds*	John Gielgud, *Arthur*	**1981**
Ben Kingsley, *Gandhi*	Jessica Lange, *Tootsie*	Louis Gossett, Jr., *An Officer and a Gentleman*	**1982**
Robert Duvall, *Tender Mercies*	Linda Hunt, *The Year of Living Dangerously*	Jack Nicholson, *Terms of Endearment*	**1983**

Other Academy Awards for 1983

Art direction: *Fanny and Alexander,* Anna Asp, art direction; Susanne Lingheim, set decoration

Cinematography: Sven Nykvist, *Fanny and Alexander*

Costume design: Marik Vos, *Fanny and Alexander*

Documentary (feature): *He Makes Me Feel Like Dancin';* **short subject:** *Flamenco at 5:15*

Editing (film): Glenn Farr, Lisa Fruchtman, Stephen A. Rotter, Douglas Stewart, and Tom Rolf, *The Right Stuff;* **sound:** Jay Boekelheide, *The Right Stuff*

Foreign-language film: *Fanny and Alexander,* Sweden

Music (original score): Bill Conti, *The Right Stuff;* **adaptation:** Michel Legrand and Alan and Marilyn Bergman, *Yentl*

Screenplay (original): Horton Foote, *Tender Mercies;* **adapted:** James L. Brooks, *Terms of Endearment*

Short subject (live-action): *Boys and Girls;* **animated:** *Sundae in New York*

Song: "Flashdance . . . What a Feeling," Giorgio Moroder, Keith Forsey and Irene Cara, from *Flashdance*

Sound: Mark Berger, Tom Scott, Randy Thom, and David MacMillan, *The Right Stuff*

Visual effects: Richard Edlund, Dennis Muren, Ken Ralston and Phil Tippet, *Return of the Jedi*

Honorary Award: Hal Roach

Jean Hersholt Humanitarian Award: M.J. Frankovich

Gordon E. Sawyer Award: Dr. John G. Frayne

Scientific-Technical Achievement: Dr. Kurt Larché

Major Grammy Awards for Recording in 1983

Source: National Academy of Recording Arts and Sciences.

Record: "Beat It," Michael Jackson (Epic)
Album: "Thriller," Michael Jackson (Epic)
Song: "Every Breath You Take," Sting (Magnetic Publishers/BMI)
New Artist: Culture Club (Epic)
Pop Vocalists: Irene Cara, "Flashdance . . . What a Feeling" (Casablanca); Michael Jackson, "Thriller" (Epic)
Pop Group: The Police, "Every Breath You Take" (A&M)
Pop Instrumentalists: George Benson, "Being With You" (Warner Bros.)
Rock Vocalists: Pat Benatar, "Love Is a Battlefield" (Chrysalis); Michael Jackson, "Beat It" (Epic)
Rock Group: The Police, "Synchronicity" (A&M)
Rock Instrumentalists: Sting, "Brimstone and Treacle" (A&M)
Rhythm and Blues Vocalists: Chaka Khan, "Chaka Khan" (Warner Bros.); Michael Jackson, "Thriller" (Epic)
Rhythm and Blues Group: Rufus and Chaka Khan, "Ain't Nobody" (Warner Bros.)
Rhythm and Blues Instrumentalists: Herbie Hancock, "Rockit" (Columbia)
Rhythm and Blues Song: Michael Jackson, "Billie Jean" (Mijac Music/BMI)
Traditional Blues: B.B. King, "Blues'N'Jazz" (MCA)
Country Vocalists: Anne Murray, "A Little Good News" (Capitol); Lee Greenwood, "I.O.U." (MCA)
Country Group: Alabama, "The Closer You Get . . ." (RCA)
Country Instrumentalist: The New South, "Fireball" (Sugar Hill)
Country Song: Mike Reid, "Stranger in My House" (Lodge Hall Music/ASCAP)
Jazz Vocalists: Ella Fitzgerald, "The Best Is Yet to Come" (Pablo Today); Mel Torme, "Top Drawer" (Concord Jazz)
Jazz Group: Manhattan Transfer, "Why Not!" (Atlantic)
Jazz Instrumentalists: Soloist, Wynton Marsalis, "Think of One" (Columbia); group, Phil Woods Quartet, "At the Vanguard" (Antilles/Island)
Jazz, Big Band: Rob McConnell & the Boss Brass, "All in Good Time" (Dark Orchid)
Jazz Fusion: Pat Metheny Group, "Travels" (ECM/Warner Bros.)
Gospel Vocalists: Amy Grant, "Ageless Medley" (Myrrh/Word); Russ Taff, "Walls of Glass" (Myrrh/Word)
Gospel Group: Sandi Patti and Larnelle Harris, "More Than Wonderful" (Impact/Benson)
Soul Gospel Vocalists: Sandra Crouch, "We Sing Praises" (Light/Lexicon); Al Green, "I'll Rise Again" (Myrrh/Word)
Soul Gospel Group: Bobby Jones & New Life With Barbara Mandrell, "I'm So Glad I'm Standing Here Today" (Myrrh/Word)
Inspirational: Donna Summer, "He's a Rebel" (Mercury)
Ethnic or Traditional: Clifton Chenier & His Red Hot Louisiana Band, "I'm Here" (Alligator)
Latin Pop: José Feliciano, "Me Enamore" (Profono/TPL)
Tropical Latin: Tito Puente & His Latin Ensemble, "On Broadway" (Concord Picante)
Mexican/American: Los Lobos, "Anselma" (Slash/Warner Bros.)
For Children: "E.T. The Extra-Terrestrial," Michael Jackson (MCA)
Comedy: Eddie Murphy, "Comedian" (Columbia)
Spoken Word: William Warfield, "Copland: Lincoln Portrait" (Mercury)
Instrumental Composition: Giorgio Moroder, "Love Theme From 'Flashdance' " (ASCAP)
Instrumental Arrangement: Dave Grusin & the N.Y./L.A. Dream Band, "Summer Sketches '82" (GRP)
Motion Picture Score: "Flashdance," Giorgio Moroder (Casablanca)
Cast Show Album: "Cats" (Geffen/Warner Bros.)
Historical Album: "The Greatest Recordings of Arturo Toscanini Symphonies Vol. 1" (Franklin Mint)
Classical Album: "Mahler: Symphony No. 9 in D Major," Sir Georg Solti (London)
Classical Orchestral Recording: "Mahler: Symphony No. 9 in D Major," Sir Georg Solti (London)
Classical, Soloist Without Orchestra: Glenn Gould, "Beethoven: Sonata for Piano No. 12 in A-Flat Major, Op. 26 & No. 13 in E-Flat Major, Op. 27, No. 1" (CBS)
Classical, Soloist With Orchestra: Wynton Marsalis, "Haydn: Concerto for Trumpet & Orchestra in E-Flat Major/L. Mozart: Concerto for Trumpet & Orchestra in D Major/Hummel: Concerto for Trumpet & Orchestra in E-Flat Major" (CBS)
Chamber Music: Mstislav Rostropovich and Rudolf Serkin, "Brahms: Sonata for Cello & Piano in E Minor, Op. 38 and Sonata in F Major, Op. 99" (DG)
Classical Vocal Soloists: "Leontyne Price and Marilyn Horne In Concert at the Met" (RCA)
Classical, Choral: "Haydn: The Creation," choral director: Margaret Hillis; conductor: Sir Georg Solti (London)
Opera: (a tie) "Mozart: Le Nozzi Di Figaro," Sir Georg Solti, conductor (London); "Verdi: La Traviata," original soundtrack; James Levine, conductor (Elektra)
Producers: Non-classical, Quincy Jones and Michael Jackson; classical, Marc J. Aubort and Joanna Nickrenz

National Book Critics Circle Awards, 1984

(Judged by 200 critics and book-review editors)

Fiction: *Ironweed,* by William Kennedy (Viking Press)
General nonfiction: *The Price of Power: Kissinger in the Nixon White House,* by Seymour Hersh (Summit Books)
Poetry: *The Changing Light at Sandover,* by James Merrill (Atheneum)
Criticism: *Hugging the Shore: Essays in Criticism,* by John Updike (Alfred A. Knopf)
Biography/autobiography: *Minor Characters,* by Joyce Johnson (Houghton Mifflin)

Pulitzer Prize Awards

(For years not listed, no award was made.)

Source: Columbia University.

Pulitzer Prizes in Journalism

MERITORIOUS PUBLIC SERVICE

1918 *New York Times;* also special award to Minna Lewinson and Henry Beetle Hough
1919 *Milwaukee Journal*
1921 *Boston Post*
1922 *New York World*
1923 *Memphis Commercial Appeal*
1924 *New York World*
1926 *Columbus* (Ga.) *Enquirer Sun*
1927 *Canton* (Ohio) *Daily News*
1928 *Indianapolis Times*
1929 *New York Evening World*
1931 *Atlanta Constitution*
1932 *Indianapolis News*
1933 *New York World-Telegram*
1934 *Medford* (Ore.) *Mail Tribune*
1935 *Sacramento Bee*
1936 *Cedar Rapids* (Iowa) *Gazette*
1937 *St. Louis Post-Dispatch*
1938 *Bismarck* (N.D.) *Tribune*
1939 *Miami Daily News*
1940 *Waterbury* (Conn.) *Republican* and *American*
1941 *St. Louis Post-Dispatch*
1942 *Los Angeles Times*
1943 *Omaha World-Herald*
1944 *New York Times*
1945 *Detroit Free Press*
1946 *Scranton* (Pa.) *Times*
1947 *Baltimore Sun*
1948 *St. Louis Post-Dispatch*
1949 (Lincoln) *Nebraska State Journal*
1950 *Chicago Daily News;* and *St. Louis Post-Dispatch*
1951 *Miami Herald;* and *Brooklyn Eagle*
1952 *St. Louis Post-Dispatch*
1953 *Whiteville* (N.C.) *News Reporter;* and *Tabor City* (N.C.) *Tribune*
1954 *Newsday* (Garden City, L.I.)
1955 *Columbus* (Ga.) *Ledger* and *Sunday Ledger-Enquirer*
1956 *Watsonville* (Calif.) *Register-Pajaronian*
1957 *Chicago Daily News*
1958 (Little Rock) *Arkansas Gazette*
1959 *Utica* (N.Y.) *Observer Dispatch* and *Utica Daily Press*
1960 *Los Angeles Times*
1961 *Amarillo* (Tex.) *Globe-Times*
1962 *Panama City* (Fla.) *News-Herald*
1963 *Chicago Daily News*
1964 *St. Petersburg* (Fla.) *Times*
1965 *Hutchinson* (Kan.) *News*
1966 *Boston Globe*
1967 *Louisville Courier-Journal* and *Milwaukee Journal*
1968 *Riverside* (Calif.) *Press-Enterprise*
1969 *Los Angeles Times*
1970 *Newsday* (Garden City, L.I.)
1971 *Winston-Salem* (N.C.) *Journal and Sentinel*
1972 *New York Times*
1973 *Washington Post*
1974 *Newsday* (Garden City, L.I.)
1975 *Boston Globe*
1976 *Anchorage* (Alaska) *Daily News*
1977 *Lufkin* (Tex.) *News*
1978 *Philadelphia Inquirer*
1979 *Point Reyes* (Calif.) *Light*
1980 *Gannett News Service*
1981 *Charlotte* (N.C.) *Observer*
1982 *Detroit News*
1983 *Jackson* (Miss.) *Clarion-Ledger*
1984 *Los Angeles Times*

EDITORIAL

1917 *New York Tribune*
1918 *Louisville Courier-Journal*
1920 Harvey E. Newbranch *(Omaha Evening World-Herald)*
1922 Frank M. O'Brien *(New York Herald)*
1923 William Allen White *(Emporia* [Kan.] *Gazette)*
1924 *Boston Herald* (Frank Buxton); special prize: Frank I. Cobb *(New York World)*
1925 *Charleston* (S.C.) *News and Courier*
1926 *New York Times* (Edward M. Kingsbury)
1927 *Boston Herald* (F. Lauriston Bullard)
1928 Grover Cleveland Hall *(Montgomery* [Ala.] *Advertiser)*
1929 Louis Isaac Jaffe *(Norfolk Virginian-Pilot)*
1931 Charles S. Ryckman *(Fremont* [Neb.] *Tribune)*
1933 *Kansas City* (Mo.) *Star*
1934 E. P. Chase *(Atlantic* [Iowa] *News Telegraph)*
1936 Felix Morley *(Washington Post);* George B. Parker (Scripps-Howard Newspapers)
1937 John W. Owens *(Baltimore Sun)*
1938 W. W. Waymack *(Des Moines Register and Tribune)*
1939 Ronald G. Callvert *(Portland Oregonian)*
1940 Bart Howard *(St. Louis Post-Dispatch)*
1941 Reuben Maury *(New York Daily News)*
1942 Geoffrey Parsons *(New York Herald Tribune)*
1943 Forrest W. Seymour *(Des Moines Register and Tribune)*
1944 *Kansas City* (Mo.) *Star* (Henry J. Haskell)
1945 George W. Potter *(Providence* [R.I.] *Journal-Bulletin)*
1946 Hodding Carter ([Greenville, Miss.] *Delta Democrat-Times*)
1947 William H. Grimes *(Wall Street Journal)*
1948 Virginius Dabney *(Richmond Times-Dispatch)*
1949 John H. Crider *(Boston Herald);* Herbert Elliston *(Washington Post)*
1950 Carl M. Saunders *(Jackson* [Mich.] *Citizen Patriot)*
1951 William H. Fitzpatrick *(New Orleans States)*
1952 Louis LaCoss *(St. Louis Globe-Democrat)*
1953 Vermont C. Royster *(Wall Street Journal)*
1954 *Boston Herald* (Don Murray)
1955 *Detroit Free Press* (Royce Howes)
1956 Lauren K. Soth *(Des Moines Register and Tribune)*
1957 Buford Boone *(Tuscaloosa* [Ala.] *News)*
1958 Harry S. Ashmore *(Arkansas Gazette)*
1959 Ralph McGill *(Atlanta Constitution)*
1960 Lenoir Chambers *(Virginian-Pilot)*
1961 William J. Dorvillier *(San Juan* [P.R.] *Star)*
1962 Thomas M. Storke *(Santa Barbara* [Calif.] *News-Press)*

1963 Ira B. Harkey, Jr. (*Pascagoula* [Miss.] *Chronicle*)
1964 Hazel Brannon Smith (*Lexington* [Miss.] *Advertiser*)
1965 John R. Harrison (*Gainesville* [Fla.] *Daily Sun*)
1966 Robert Lasch (*St. Louis Post-Dispatch*)
1967 Eugene Patterson (*Atlanta Constitution*)
1968 John S. Knight (Knight Newspapers)
1969 Paul Greenberg (*Pine Bluff* [Ark.] *Commercial*)
1970 Phillip L. Geyelin (*Washington Post*)
1971 Horance G. Davis, Jr. (*Gainesville* [Fla.] *Sun*)
1972 John Strohmeyer (*Bethlehem* [Pa.] *Globe Times*)
1973 Roger Bourne Linscott (*Berkshire Eagle* [Pittsfield, Mass.])
1974 F. Gilman Spencer (*Trenton* [N.J.] *Trentonian*)
1975 John Daniell Maurice (*Charleston* [W. Va.] *Daily Mail*)
1976 Philip P. Kerby (*Los Angeles Times*)
1977 Warren L. Lerude, Foster Church and Norman F. Cardoza (*Reno* [Nev.] *Gazette* and *Nevada State Journal*)
1978 Meg Greenfield (*Washington Post*)
1979 Edwin M. Yoder, Jr. (*Washington Star*)
1980 Robert L. Bartley (*Wall Street Journal*)
1981 Not awarded
1982 Jack Rosenthal (*New York Times*)
1983 *Miami Herald*
1984 Albert Scardino (*Georgia Gazette*)

CORRESPONDENCE

1929 Paul Scott Mowrer (*Chicago Daily News*)
1930 Leland Stowe (*New York Hearld Tribune*)
1931 H. R. Knickerbocker (*Philadelphia Public Ledger* and *New York Evening Post*)
1932 Walter Duranty (*New York Times*); Charles G. Ross (*St. Louis Post-Dispatch*)
1933 Edgar Ansel Mowrer (*Chicago Daily News*)
1934 Frederick T. Birchall (*New York Times*)
1935 Arthur Krock (*New York Times*)
1936 Wilfred C. Barber (*Chicago Tribune*)
1937 Anne O'Hare McCormick (*New York Times*)
1938 Arthur Krock (*New York Times*)
1939 Louis P. Lochner (Associated Press)
1940 Otto D. Tolischus (*New York Times*)
1941 Group award[1]
1942 Carlos P. Rornulo (*Philippines Herald*)
1943 Hanson W. Baldwin (*New York Times*)
1944 Ernie Pyle (Scripps-Howard Newspaper Alliance)
1945 Harold V. (Hal) Boyle (Associated Press)
1946 Arnaldo Cortesi (*New York Times*)
1947 Brooks Atkinson (*New York Times*)
1948 Discontinued

EDITORIAL CARTOONING

1922 Rollin Kirby (*New York World*)
1924 Jay Norwood Darling (*New York Tribune*)
1925 Rollin Kirby (*New York World*)
1926 D. R. Fitzpatrick (*St. Louis Post-Dispatch*)
1927 Nelson Harding (*Brooklyn Eagle*)
1928 Nelson Harding (*Brooklyn Eagle*)
1929 Rollin Kirby (*New York World*)
1930 Charles R. Macauley (*Brooklyn Eagle*)
1931 Edmund Duffy (*Baltimore Sun*)
1932 John T. McCutcheon (*Chicago Tribune*)
1933 H. M. Talburt (*Washington Daily News*)
1934 Edmund Duffy (*Baltimore Sun*)
1935 Ross A. Lewis (*Milwaukee Journal*)
1937 C. D. Batchelor (*New York Daily News*)

1. For the public services and the individual achievements of American news reporters in the war zones.

1938 Vaughn Shoemaker (*Chicago Daily News*)
1939 Charles G. Werner (*Daily Oklahoman* [Oklahoma City])
1940 Edmund Duffy (*Baltimore Sun*)
1941 Jacob Burck (*Chicago Times*)
1942 Herbert L. Block (NEA Service)
1943 Jay Norwood Darling (*New York Herald Tribune*)
1944 Clifford K. Berryman (*Washington Evening Star*)
1945 Bill Mauldin (United Features Syndicate)
1946 Bruce Alexander Russell (*Los Angeles Times*)
1947 Vaughn Shoemaker (*Chicago Daily News*)
1948 Reuben L. Goldberg (*New York Sun*)
1949 Lute Pease (*Newark Evening News*)
1950 James T. Berryman (*Washington Evening Star*)
1951 Reg (Reginald W.) Manning (*Arizona Republic* [Phoenix])
1952 Fred L. Packer (*New York Mirror*)
1953 Edward D. Kuekes (*Cleveland Plain Dealer*)
1954 Herbert L. Block (*Washington Post* and *Times-Herald*)
1955 Daniel R. Fitzpatrick (*St. Louis Post-Dispatch*)
1956 Robert York (*Louisville Times*)
1957 Tom Little (*Nashville Tennessean*)
1958 Bruce M. Shanks (*Buffalo Evening News*)
1959 Bill Mauldin (*St. Louis Post-Dispatch*)
1961 Carey Orr (*Chicago Tribune*)
1962 Edmund S. Valtman (*Hartford Times*)
1963 Frank Miller (*Des Moines Register*)
1964 Paul Conrad (formerly of *Denver Post*, later on *Los Angeles Times*)
1966 Don Wright (*Miami News*)
1967 Patrick B. Oliphant (*Denver Post*)
1968 Eugene Gray Payne (*Charlotte* [N.C.] *Observer*)
1969 John Fischetti (*Chicago Daily News*)
1970 Thomas F. Darcy (*Newsday* [Garden City, L.I.])
1971 Paul Conrad (*Los Angeles Times*)
1972 Jeffrey K. MacNelly (*Richmond* [Va.] *News Leader*)
1974 Paul Szep (*Boston Globe*)
1975 Garry Trudeau (Universal Press Syndicate)
1976 Tony Auth (*Philadelphia Inquirer*)
1977 Paul Szep (*Boston Globe*)
1978 Jeffrey K. MacNelly (*Richmond* [Va.] *News Leader*)
1979 Herbert L. Block (*Washington Post*)
1980 Don Wright (*Miami News*)
1981 Mike Peters (*Dayton* [Ohio] *Daily News*)
1982 Ben Sargent (*Austin* [Tex.] *American-Statesman*)
1983 Richard Locher (*Chicago Tribune*)
1984 Paul Conrad (*Los Angeles Times*)

NEWS PHOTOGRAPHY

1942 Milton Brooks (*Detroit News*)
1943 Frank Noel (Associated Press)
1944 Frank Filan (Associated Press); Earle L. Bunker (*Omaha World-Herald*)
1945 Joe Rosenthal (Associated Press)
1947 Arnold Hardy
1948 Frank Cushing (*Boston Traveler*)
1949 Nat Fein (*New York Herald Tribune*)
1950 Bill Crouch (*Oakland Tribune*)
1951 Max Desfor (Associated Press)
1952 John Robinson and Don Ultang (*Des Moines Register & Tribune*)
1953 William M. Gallagher (*Flint* [Mich.] *Journal*)
1954 Mrs. Walter M. Schau

1955 John L. Gaunt, Jr. *(Los Angeles Times)*
1956 *New York Daily News*
1957 Harry A. Trask *(Boston Traveler)*
1958 William C. Beall *(Washington Daily News)*
1959 William Seaman *(Minneapolis Star)*
1960 Andrew Lopez (United Press International)
1961 Yasushi Nagao (Mainichi Newspapers, Tokyo)
1962 Paul Vathis (Harrisburg [Pa.] bureau of Associated Press)
1963 Hector Rondon (*La Republica,* Caracas, Venezuela)
1964 Robert H. Jackson *(Dallas Times Herald)*
1965 Horst Faas (Associated Press)
1966 Kyoichi Sawada (United Press International)
1967 Jack R. Thornell (Associated Press)
1968 News: Rocco Morabito *(Jacksonville* [Fla.] *Journal);* features: Toshio Sakai (United Press International)
1969 Spot news: Edward T. Adams (Associated Press); features: Moneta Sleet, Jr.
1970 Spot news: Steve Starr (Associated Press); features: Dallas Kinney *(Palm Beach Post)*
1971 Spot news: John Paul Filo (*Valley Daily News and Daily Dispatch* [Tarentum and New Kensington, Pa.]); features: Jack Dykinga *(Chicago Sun-Times)*
1972 Spot news: Horst Faas and Michel Laurent (Associated Press); features: Dave Kennerly (United Press International)
1973 Spot News: Huynh Cong Ut *(Associated Press);* features: Brian Lanker *(Topeka Capital-Journal)*
1974 Spot news: Anthony K. Roberts (Associated Press); features: Slava Veder (Associated Press)
1975 Spot news: Gerald H. Gay *(Seattle Times);* features: Matthew Lewis *(Washington Post)*
1976 Spot news: Stanley J. Forman *(Boston Herald-American);* features: photographic staff of *Louisville Courier-Journal* and *Times*
1977 Spot news: Neal Ulevich (Associated Press) and Stanley J. Forman *(Boston Herald-American);* features: Robin Hood *(Chattanooga News-Free Press)*
1978 Spot news: John Blair, freelance, Evansville, Ind.; features: J. Ross Baughman (Associated Press)
1979 Spot news: Thomas J. Kelly, 3rd *(Pottstown* [Pa.] *Mercury);* features: photographic staff of *Boston Herald American*
1980 Features: Erwin H. Hagler *(Dallas Times Herald)*
1981 Spot news: Larry C. Price *(Fort Worth Star-Telegram);* features: Taro M. Yamasaki *(Detroit Free Press)*
1982 Spot news: Ron Edmonds (Associated Press); features: John H. White *(Chicago Sun-Times)*
1983 Spot news: Bill Foley (Associated Press); features: James B. Dickman *(Dallas Times Herald)*
1984 Spot news: Stan Grossfeld *(Boston Globe);* features: Anthony Suau *(Denver Post)*

NATIONAL TELEGRAPHIC REPORTING

1942 Louis Stark *(New York Times)*
1944 Dewey L. Fleming *(Baltimore Sun)*
1945 James Reston *(New York Times)*
1946 Edward A. Harris *(St. Louis Post-Dispatch)*
1947 Edward T. Folliard *(Washington Post)*

NATIONAL REPORTING

1948 Bert Andrews *(New York Herald Tribune);* Nat S. Finney *(Minneapolis Tribune)*
1949 C. P. Trussel *(New York Times)*
1950 Edwin O. Guthman *(Seattle Times)*
1952 Anthony Leviero *(New York Times)*
1953 Don Whitehead (Associated Press)
1954 Richard Wilson (Cowles Newspapers)
1955 Anthony Lewis *(Washington Daily News)*
1956 Charles L. Bartlett *(Chattanooga Times)*
1957 James Reston *(New York Times)*
1958 Relman Morin (Associated Press) and Clark Mollenhoff *(Des Moines Register & Tribune)*
1959 Howard Van Smith *(Miami News)*
1960 Vance Trimble (Scripps-Howard Newspaper Alliance)
1961 Edward R. Cony *(Wall Street Journal)*
1962 Nathan G. Caldwell and Gene S. Graham *(Nashville Tennessean)*
1963 Anthony Lewis *(New York Times)*
1964 Merriman Smith (United Press International)
1965 Louis M. Kohlmeier *(Wall Street Journal)*
1966 Haynes Johnson *(Washington Evening Star)*
1967 Stanley Penn and Monroe Karmin *(Wall Street Journal)*
1968 Howard James *(Christian Science Monitor);* Nathan K. (Nick) Kotz *(Des Moines Register* and *Minneapolis Tribune)*
1969 Robert Cahn *(Christian Science Monitor)*
1970 William J. Eaton *(Chicago Daily News)*
1971 Lucinda Franks and Thomas Powers (United Press International)
1972 Jack Anderson *(United Feature Syndicate)*
1973 Robert Boyd and Clark Hoyt *(Knight Newspapers)*
1974 Jack White *(Providence* [R.I.] *Journal-Bulletin);* and James R. Polk *(Washington Star-News)*
1975 Donald L. Barlett and James B. Steele *(Philadelphia Inquirer)*
1976 James Risser *(Des Moines Register)*
1977 Walter Mears (Associated Press)
1978 Gaylord D. Shaw *(Los Angeles Times)*
1979 James Risser *(Des Moines Register)*
1980 Bette Swenson Orsini and Charles Stafford *(St. Petersburg Times)*
1981 John M. Crewdson *(New York Times)*
1982 Rick Atkinson *(Kansas City* [Mo.] *Times)*
1983 *Boston Globe*
1984 John N. Wilford *(New York Times)*

INTERNATIONAL TELEGRAPHIC REPORTING

1942 Laurence Edmund Allen (Associated Press)
1943 Ira Wolfert (North American Newspaper Alliance, Inc.)
1944 Daniel De Luce (Associated Press)
1945 Mark S. Watson *(Baltimore Sun)*
1946 Homer W. Bigart *(New York Herald Tribune)*
1947 Eddy Gilmore (Associated Press)

INTERNATIONAL REPORTING

1948 Paul W. Ward *(Baltimore Sun)*
1949 Price Day *(Baltimore Sun)*
1950 Edmund Stevens *(Christian Science Monitor)*
1951 Keyes Beech and Fred Sparks *(Chicago Daily News);* Homer Bigart and Marguerite Higgins *(New York Herald Tribune);* Relman Morin and Don Whitehead (Associated Press)
1952 John M. Hightower (Associated Press)
1953 Austin C. Wehrwein *(Milwaukee Journal)*
1954 Jim G. Lucas (Scripps-Howard Newspapers)
1955 Harrison E. Salisbury *(New York Times)*
1956 William Randolph Hearst, Jr. and Frank Conniff (Hearst Newspapers) and Kingsbury Smith (INS)
1957 Russell Jones (United Press)

1958 *New York Times*
1959 Joseph Martin and Philip Santora *(New York Daily News)*
1960 A. M. Rosenthal *(New York Times)*
1961 Lynn Heinzerling (Associated Press)
1962 Walter Lippmann (New York Herald Tribune Syndicate)
1963 Hal Hendrix *(Miami News)*
1964 Malcolm W. Browne (Associated Press) and David Halberstam *(New York Times)*
1965 J. A. Livingston *(Philadelphia Bulletin)*
1966 Peter Arnett (Associated Press)
1967 R. John Hughes *(Christian Science Monitor)*
1968 Alfred Friendly *(Washington Post)*
1969 William Tuohy *(Los Angeles Times)*
1970 Seymour M. Hersh (Dispatch News Service)
1971 Jimmie Lee Hoagland *(Washington Post)*
1972 Peter R. Kann *(Wall Street Journal)*
1973 Max Frankel *(New York Times)*
1974 Hedrick Smith *(New York Times)*
1975 William Mullen and Ovie Carter *(Chicago Tribune)*
1976 Sydney H. Schanberg *(New York Times)*
1978 Henry Kamm *(New York Times)*
1979 Richard Ben Cramer *(Philadelphia Inquirer)*
1980 Joel Brinkley and Jay Mather *(Louisville Courier-Journal)*
1981 Shirley Christian *(Miami Herald)*
1982 John Darnton *(New York Times)*
1983 Thomas L. Friedman *(New York Times)*
1984 Karen E. House *(Wall Street Journal)*

REPORTING

1917 Herbert B. Swope *(New York World)*
1918 Harold A. Littledale *(New York Evening Post)*
1920 John J. Leary, Jr. *(New York World)*
1921 Louis Seibold *(New York World)*
1922 Kirke L. Simpson (Associated Press)
1923 Alva Johnston *(New York Times)*
1924 Magner White *(San Diego Sun)*
1925 James W. Mulroy and Alvin H. Goldstein *(Chicago Daily News)*
1926 William Burke Miller *(Louisville Courier-Journal)*
1927 John T. Rogers *(St. Louis Post-Dispatch)*
1929 Paul Y. Anderson *(St. Louis Post-Dispatch)*
1930 Russell D. Owen *(New York Times);* special award: W. O. Dapping *(Auburn* [N.Y.] *Citizen)*
1931 A. B. MacDonald *(Kansas City* [Mo.] *Star)*
1932 W. C. Richards, D. D. Martin, J. S. Pooler, F. D. Webb, J. N. W. Sloan (all of *Detroit Free Press*
1933 Francis A. Jamieson (Associated Press)
1934 Royce Brier *(San Francisco Chronicle)*
1935 William H. Taylor *(New York Herald Tribune)*
1936 Lauren D. Lyman *(New York Times)*
1937 John J. O'Neill *(New York Herald Tribune);* William Leonard Laurence *(New York Times);* Howard W. Blakeslee (Associated Press); Gobind Behari Lal (Universal Service); David Dietz (Scripps-Howard Newspapers)
1938 Raymond Sprigle *(Pittsburg Post-Gazette)*
1939 Thomas L. Stokes *(New York World-Telegram)*
1940 S. Burton Heath *(New York World-Telegram)*
1941 Westbrook Pegler *(New York World-Telegram)*
1942 Stanton Delaplane *(San Francisco Chronicle)*
1943 George Weller *(Chicago Daily News)*
1944 Paul Schoenstein and associates *(New York Journal-American)*
1945 Jack S. McDowell *(San Francisco Call-Bulletin)*
1946 William Leonard Laurence *(New York Times)*
1947 Frederick Woltman *(New York World-Telegram)*
1948 George E. Goodwin *(Atlanta Journal)*
1949 Malcolm Johnson *(New York Sun)*
1950 Meyer Berger *(New York Times)*
1951 Edward S. Montgomery *(San Francisco Examiner)*
1952 George de Carvalho *(San Francisco Chronicle)*
1953 Editorial staff *(Providence Journal and Evening Bulletin);*[1] Edward J. Mowery *(New York World-Telegram and Sun)*[2]
1954 *Vicksburg* (Miss.) *Sunday Post-Herald;*[1] Alvin Scott McCoy *(Kansas City* [Mo.] *Star)*[2]
1955 Mrs. Caro Brown *(Alice* [Tex.] *Daily Echo);*[1] Roland Kenneth Towery *(Cuero* [Tex.] *Record)*[2]
1956 Lee Hills *(Detroit Free Press);*[1] Arthur Daley *(New York Times)*[2]
1957 *Salt Lake Tribune;*[1] Wallace Turner and William Lambert *(Portland Oregonian)*[2]
1958 *Fargo* [N.D.] *Forum;*[1] George Beveridge *(Washington* [D.C.] *Evening Star)*[2]
1959 Mary Lou Werner *(Washington* [D.C.] *Evening Star);*[1] John Harold Brislin *(Scranton* [Pa.] *Tribune & Scrantonian)*[2]
1960 Jack Nelson *(Atlanta Constitution);*[1] Miriam Ottenberg *(Washington Evening Star)*[2]
1961 Sanche de Gramont *(New York Herald Tribune);*[1] Edgar May *(Buffalo Evening News)*[2]
1962 Robert D. Mullins (*Deseret News,* Salt Lake City);[1] George Bliss *(Chicago Tribune)*[2]
1963 Sylvan Fox, Anthony Shannon, and William Longgood *(New York World-Telegram and Sun);*[1] Oscar Griffin, Jr. (former editor of *Pecos* [Tex.] *Independent and Enterprise,* now on staff of *Houston Chronicle*)[2]

GENERAL LOCAL REPORTING

1964 Norman C. Miller *(Wall Street Journal)*
1965 Melvin H. Ruder (*Hungry Horse News,* Columbia Falls, Mont.)
1966 Staff of *Los Angeles Times*
1967 Robert V. Cox *(Chambersburg* [Pa.] *Public Opinion)*
1968 Staff of *Detroit Free Press*
1969 John Fetterman *(Louisville Times* and *Courier-Journal)*
1970 Thomas Fitzpatrick *(Chicago Sun-Times)*
1971 Staff of *Akron* (Ohio) *Beacon*
1972 Richard Cooper and John Machacek *(Rochester* [N.Y.] *Times-Union)*
1973 *Chicago Tribune*
1974 Arthur M. Petacque and Hugh F. Hough *(Chicago Sun-Times)*
1975 *Xenia* (Ohio) *Daily Gazette*
1976 Gene Miller *(Miami Herald)*
1977 Margo Huston *(Milwaukee Journal)*
1978 Richard Whitt *(Louisville Courier-Journal)*
1979 Staff of *San Diego* (Calif.) *Evening Tribune*
1980 Staff of *Philadelphia Inquirer*
1981 *Longview* (Wash.) *Daily News*
1982 *Kansas City* (Mo.) *Star* and *Kansas City* (Mo.) *Times*
1983 *Fort Wayne* (Ind.) *News-Sentinel*
1984 *Newsday*

SPECIAL LOCAL REPORTING

1964 James V. Magee, Albert V. Gaudiosi, and Frederick A. Meyer *(Philadelphia Bulletin)*
1965 Gene Goltz *(Houston Post)*

1. Reporting under pressure of edition deadlines. 2. Reporting not under pressure of edition deadlines.

1966 John A. Frasca *(Tampa Tribune)*
1967 Gene Miller *(Miami Herald)*
1968 J. Anthony Lukas *(New York Times)*
1969 Albert L. Delugach and Denny Walsh *(St. Louis Globe-Democrat)*
1970 Harold Eugene Martin *(Montgomery Advertiser)*
1971 William Hugh Jones *(Chicago Tribune)*
1972 Timothy Leland, Gerard N. O'Neill, Stephen A. Kurkjian, and Ann DeSantis *(Boston Globe)*
1973 Sun Newspapers of Omaha, Neb.
1974 William Sherman *(New York Daily News)*
1975 *Indianapolis Star*
1976 *Chicago Tribune*
1977 Acel Moore and Wendell Rawls, Jr. *(Philadelphia Inquirer)*
1978 Anthony R. Dolan *(Stamford* [Conn.] *Advocate)*
1979 Gilbert M. Gaul and Elliot G. Jaspin *(Pottsville* [Pa.] *Republican)*
1980 Nils J. Bruzelius, Alexander B. Hawes, Jr., Stephen A. Kurkjian, and Joan Vennochi *(Boston Globe)*
1981 Clark Hallas and Robert B. Lowe (*Arizona Daily Star,* Tucson)
1982 Paul Henderson *(Seattle Times)*
1983 Loretta Tofani *(Washington Post)*
1984 *Boston Globe*

FEATURE WRITING

1979 Jon D. Franklin *(Baltimore Evening Sun)*
1980 Madeleine Blais *(Miami Herald)*
1981 Teresa Carpenter (*Village Voice,* New York)
1982 Saul Pett (Associated Press)
1983 Nan Robertson *(New York Times)*
1984 Peter M. Rinearson *(Seattle Times)*

COMMENTARY

1970 Marquis W. Childs *(St. Louis Post-Dispatch)*
1971 William A. Caldwell (*Record* [Hackensack, N.J.])
1972 Mike Royko *(Chicago Daily News)*
1973 David S. Broder *(Washington Post)*
1974 Edwin A. Roberts, Jr. *(National Observer)*
1975 Mary McGrory *(Washington Star)*
1976 Walter W. (Red) Smith *(New York Times)*
1977 George F. Will (*Washington Post* Writers Group)
1978 William Safire *(New York Times)*
1979 Russell Baker *(New York Times)*
1980 Ellen H. Goodman *(Boston Globe)*
1981 Dave Anderson *(New York Times)*
1982 Art Buchwald (*Los Angeles Times* Syndicate)
1983 Claude Sitton *(Raleigh* [N.C.] *News & Observer)*
1984 Vermont Royster *(Wall Street Journal)*

CRITICISM

1970 Ada Louise Huxtable *(New York Times)*
1971 Harold C. Schonberg *(New York Times)*
1972 Frank Peters, Jr. *(St. Louis Post-Dispatch)*
1973 Ronald Powers *(Chicago Sun-Times)*
1974 Emily Genauer (Newsday Syndicate)
1975 Roger Ebert *(Chicago Sun-Times)*
1976 Alan M. Kriegsman *(Washington Post)*
1977 William McPherson *(Washington Post)*
1978 Walter Kerr *(New York Times)*
1979 Paul Gapp *(Chicago Tribune)*
1980 William A. Henry, 3rd *(Boston Globe)*
1981 Jonathan Yardley *(Washington Star)*
1982 Martin Bernheimer *(Los Angeles Times)*
1983 Manuela Hoelterhoff *(Wall Street Journal)*
1984 Paul Goldberger *(New York Times)*

SPECIAL CITATIONS

1938 *Edmonton* (Alberta) *Journal,* special bronze plaque for editorial leadership in defense of freedom of press in Province of Alberta.
1941 *New York Times* for the public educational value of its foreign news report.
1944 Byron Price, Director of the Office of Censorship, for the creation and administration of the newspaper and radio codes. Mrs. William Allen White, for her husband's interest and services during the past seven years as a member of the Advisory Board of the Graduate School of Journalism, Columbia University. Richard Rodgers and Oscar Hammerstein II for their musical *Oklahoma!*
1945 The cartographers of the American press for their war maps.
1947 (Pulitzer centennial year.) Columbia University and the Graduate School of Journalism for their efforts to maintain and advance the high standards governing the Pulitzer Prize awards. The *St. Louis Post-Dispatch* for its unswerving adherence to the public and professional ideals of its founder and its leadership in American journalism.
1948 Dr. Frank D. Fackenthal for his interest and service.
1951 Cyrus L. Sulzberger *(New York Times)* for his exclusive interview with Archbishop Stepinac in a Yugoslav prison.
1952 *Kansas City Star* for coverage of 1951 floods; Max Kase *(New York Journal-American)* for exposures of bribery in college basketball.
1953 *New York Times* for its 17-year publication of "News of the Week in Review"; and Lester Markel, its founder.
1957 Kenneth Roberts for his historical novels.
1958 Walter Lippmann *(New York Herald Tribune)* for his "wisdom, perception and high sense of responsibility" in his commentary on national and international affairs.
1960 Garrett Mattingly, for *The Armada.*
1961 *American Heritage Picture History of the Civil War,* as distinguished example of American book publishing.
1964 Gannett Newspapers, Rochester, N.Y.
1973 James Thomas Flexner for his biography *George Washington.*
1974 Roger Sessions for his "life's work in music."
1976 John Hohenberg for "services for 22 years as administrator of the Pulitzer Prizes"; Scott Joplin for his contributions to American music.
1977 Alex Haley for his novel, *Roots*
1978 E.B. White of *New Yorker* magazine and Richard L. Strout of *Christian Science Monitor*
1982 Milton Babbitt, "for his life's work as a distinguished and seminal American composer."
1984 Theodor Seuss Geisel (Dr. Seuss) for "books full of playful rhymes, nonsense words and strange illustrations."

Pulitzer Prizes in Letters

FICTION[1]

1918 *His Family.* Ernest Poole
1919 *The Magnificent Ambersons.* Booth Tarkington
1921 *The Age of Innocence.* Edith Wharton
1922 *Alice Adams.* Booth Tarkington
1923 *One of Ours.* Willa Cather
1924 *The Able McLaughlins.* Margaret Wilson
1925 *So Big.* Edna Ferber
1926 *Arrowsmith.* Sinclair Lewis
1927 *Early Autumn.* Louis Bromfield
1928 *The Bridge of San Luis Rey.* Thornton Wilder
1929 *Scarlet Sister Mary.* Julia Peterkin
1930 *Laughing Boy.* Oliver La Farge
1931 *Years of Grace.* Margaret Ayer Barnes
1932 *The Good Earth.* Pearl S. Buck
1933 *The Store.* T. S. Stribling
1934 *Lamb in His Bosom.* Caroline Miller
1935 *Now in November.* Josephine Winslow Johnson
1936 *Honey in the Horn.* Harold L. Davis
1937 *Gone With the Wind.* Margaret Mitchell
1938 *The Late George Apley.* John Phillips Marquand
1939 *The Yearling.* Marjorie Kinnan Rawlings
1940 *The Grapes of Wrath.* John Steinbeck
1942 *In This Our Life.* Ellen Glasgow
1943 *Dragon's Teeth.* Upton Sinclair
1944 *Journey in the Dark.* Martin Flavin
1945 *A Bell for Adano.* John Hersey
1947 *All the King's Men.* Robert Penn Warren
1948 *Tales of the South Pacific.* James A. Michener
1949 *Guard of Honor.* James Gould Cozzens
1950 *The Way West.* A. B. Guthrie, Jr.
1951 *The Town.* Conrad Richter
1952 *The Caine Mutiny.* Herman Wouk
1953 *The Old Man and the Sea.* Ernest Hemingway
1955 *A Fable.* William Faulkner
1956 *Andersonville.* MacKinlay Kantor
1958 *A Death in the Family.* James Agee
1959 *The Travels of Jaimie McPheeters.* Robert Lewis Taylor
1960 *Advise and Consent.* Allen Drury
1961 *To Kill a Mockingbird.* Harper Lee
1962 *The Edge of Sadness.* Edwin O'Connor
1963 *The Reivers.* William Faulkner
1965 *The Keepers of the House.* Shirley Ann Grau
1966 *Collected Stories of Katherine Anne Porter.* Katherine Anne Porter
1967 *The Fixer.* Bernard Malamud
1968 *The Confessions of Nat Turner.* William Styron
1969 *House Made of Dawn.* N. Scott Momaday
1970 *Collected Stories.* Jean Stafford
1972 *Angle of Repose.* Wallace Stegner
1973 *The Optimist's Daughter.* Eudora Welty
1975 *The Killer Angels.* Michael Shaara
1976 *Humboldt's Gift.* Saul Bellow
1978 *Elbow Room.* James Alan McPherson
1979 *The Stories of John Cheever.* John Cheever
1980 *The Executioner's Song.* Norman Mailer
1981 *A Confederacy of Dunces.* John Kennedy Toole
1982 *Rabbit Is Rich.* John Updike
1983 *The Color Purple.* Alice Walker
1984 *Ironweed.* William Kennedy

DRAMA

1918 *Why Marry?* Jesse Lynch Williams
1920 *Beyond the Horizon.* Eugene O'Neill
1921 *Miss Lulu Bett.* Zona Gale
1922 *Anna Christie.* Eugene O'Neill
1923 *Icebound.* Owen Davis
1924 *Hell-Bent Fer Heaven.* Hatcher Hughes
1925 *They Knew What They Wanted.* Sidney Howard
1926 *Craig's Wife.* George Kelly
1927 *In Abraham's Bosom.* Paul Green
1928 *Strange Interlude.* Eugene O'Neill
1929 *Street Scene.* Elmer L. Rice
1930 *The Green Pastures.* Marc Connelly
1931 *Alison's House.* Susan Glaspell
1932 *Of Thee I Sing.* George S. Kaufman, Morrie Ryskind, and Ira Gershwin
1933 *Both Your Houses.* Maxwell Anderson
1934 *Men in White.* Sidney Kingsley
1935 *The Old Maid.* Zöe Akins
1936 *Idiot's Delight.* Robert E. Sherwood
1937 *You Can't Take It With You.* Moss Hart and George S. Kaufman
1938 *Our Town.* Thornton Wilder
1939 *Abe Lincoln in Illinois.* Robert E. Sherwood
1940 *The Time of Your Life.* William Saroyan
1941 *There Shall Be No Night.* Robert E. Sherwood
1943 *The Skin of Our Teeth.* Thornton Wilder
1945 *Harvey.* Mary Chase
1946 *State of the Union.* Russel Crouse and Howard Lindsay
1948 *A Streetcar Named Desire.* Tennessee Williams
1949 *Death of a Salesman.* Arthur Miller
1950 *South Pacific.* Richard Rodgers, Oscar Hammerstein II, and Joshua Logan
1952 *The Shrike.* Joseph Kramm
1953 *Picnic.* William Inge
1954 *The Teahouse of the August Moon.* John Patrick
1955 *Cat on a Hot Tin Roof.* Tennessee Williams
1956 *The Diary of Anne Frank.* Frances Goodrich and Albert Hackett
1957 *Long Day's Journey Into Night.* Eugene O'Neill
1958 *Look Homeward, Angel.* Ketti Frings
1959 *J.B.* Archibald MacLeish
1960 *Fiorello!* George Abbott, Jerome Weidman, Jerry Bock, and Sheldon Harnick
1961 *All the Way Home.* Tad Mosel
1962 *How to Succeed in Business Without Really Trying.* Frank Loesser and Abe Burrows
1965 *The Subject Was Roses.* Frank D. Gilroy
1967 *A Delicate Balance.* Edward Albee
1969 *The Great White Hope.* Howard Sackler
1970 *No Place to Be Somebody.* Charles Gordone
1971 *The Effect of Gamma Rays on Man-in-the-Moon Marigolds.* Paul Zindel
1973 *That Championship Season.* Jason Miller
1975 *Seascape.* Edward Albee
1976 *A Chorus Line.* Conceived by Michael Bennett
1977 *The Shadow Box.* Michael Cristofer
1978 *The Gin Game.* Donald L. Coburn
1979 *Buried Child.* Sam Shepard
1980 *Talley's Folly.* Lanford Wilson
1981 *Crimes of the Heart.* Beth Henley
1982 *A Soldier's Play.* Charles Fuller
1983 *'Night, Mother.* Marsha Norman
1984 *Glengarry Glen Ross.* David Mamet

HISTORY OF UNITED STATES

1917 *With Americans of Past and Present Days.* J. J. Jusserand, Ambassador of France to United States

1. Before 1948, award was for novels only.

1918 *A History of the Civil War, 1861–1865.* James Ford Rhodes
1920 *The War With Mexico.* Justin H. Smith
1921 *The Victory at Sea.* William Sowden Sims in collaboration with Burton J. Hendrick
1922 *The Founding of New England.* James Truslow Adams
1923 *The Supreme Court in United States History.* Charles Warren
1924 *The American Revolution—A Constitutional Interpretation.* Charles Howard Mcilwain
1925 *A History of the American Frontier.* Frederic L. Paxson
1926 *The History of the United States.* Edward Channing
1927 *Pinckney's Treaty.* Samuel Flagg Bemis
1928 *Main Currents in American Thought.* Vernon Louis Parrington
1929 *The Organization and Administration of the Union Army, 1861–1865.* Fred Albert Shannon
1930 *The War of Independence.* Claude H. Van Tyne
1931 *The Coming of the War: 1914.* Bernadotte E. Schmitt
1932 *My Experiences in the World War.* John J. Pershing
1933 *The Significance of Sections in American History.* Frederick J. Turner
1934 *The People's Choice.* Herbert Agar
1935 *The Colonial Period of American History.* Charles McLean Andrews
1936 *The Constitutional History of the United States.* Andrew C. McLaughlin
1937 *The Flowering of New England.* Van Wyck Brooks
1938 *The Road to Reunion, 1865–1900.* Paul Herman Buck
1939 *A History of American Magazines.* Frank Luther Mott
1940 *Abraham Lincoln: The War Years.* Carl Sandburg
1941 *The Atlantic Migration, 1607–1860.* Marcus Lee Hansen
1942 *Reveille in Washington.* Margaret Leech
1943 *Paul Revere and the World He Lived In.* Esther Forbes
1944 *The Growth of American Thought.* Merle Curti
1945 *Unfinished Business.* Stephen Bonsal
1946 *The Age of Jackson.* Arthur M. Schlesinger, Jr.
1947 *Scientists Against Time.* James Phinney Baxter, 3rd
1948 *Across the Wide Missouri.* Bernard DeVoto
1949 *The Disruption of American Democracy.* Roy Franklin Nichols
1950 *Art and Life in America.* Oliver W. Larkin
1951 *The Old Northwest, Pioneer Period 1815–1840.* R. Carlyle Buley
1952 *The Uprooted.* Oscar Handlin
1953 *The Era of Good Feelings.* George Dangerfield
1954 *A Stillness at Appomattox.* Bruce Catton
1955 *Great River: The Rio Grande in North American History.* Paul Horgan
1956 *The Age of Reform.* Richard Hofstadter
1957 *Russia Leaves the War: Soviet-American Relations, 1917–1920.* George F. Kennan
1958 *Banks and Politics in America: From the Revolution to the Civil War.* Bray Hammond
1959 *The Republican Era: 1869–1901.* Leonard D. White, assisted by Jean Schneider
1960 *In the Days of McKinley.* Margaret Leech
1961 *Between War and Peace: The Potsdam Conference.* Herbert Feis
1962 *The Triumphant Empire, Thunder-Clouds Gather in the West.* Lawrence H. Gipson
1963 *Washington, Village and Capital, 1800–1878.* Constance McLaughlin Green
1964 *Puritan Village: The Formation of a New England Town.* Sumner Chilton Powell
1965 *The Greenback Era.* Irwin Unger
1966 *Life of the Mind in America.* Perry Miller
1967 *Exploration and Empire: The Explorer and Scientist in the Winning of the American West.* William H. Goetzmann
1968 *The Ideological Origins of the American Revolution.* Bernard Bailyn
1969 *Origins of the Fifth Amendment.* Leonard W. Levy
1970 *Present at the Creation: My Years in the State Department.* Dean Acheson
1971 *Roosevelt: The Soldier of Freedom.* James McGregor Burns
1972 *Neither Black Nor White. Slavery and Race Relations in Brazil and the United States.* Carl N. Degler
1973 *People of Paradox: An Inquiry Concerning the Origin of American Civilization.* Michael Kammen
1974 *The Americans: The Democratic Experience, Vol. 3.* Daniel J. Boorstin
1975 *Jefferson and His Time.* Dumas Malone
1976 *Lamy of Santa Fe.* Paul Horgan
1977 *The Impending Crisis: 1841–1861.* David M. Potter (posth)
1978 *The Invisible Hand: The Managerial Revolution in American Business.* Alfred D. Chandler, Jr.
1979 *The Dred Scott Case: Its Significance in Law and Politics.* Don E. Fehrenbacher
1980 *Been in the Storm So Long.* Leon F. Litwack
1981 *American Education: The National Experience; 1783–1876.* Lawrence A. Cremin
1982 *Mary Chestnut's Civil War.* C. Vann Woodward, editor
1983 *The Transformation of Virginia, 1740–1790.* Rhys L. Isaac

BIOGRAPHY OR AUTOBIOGRAPHY

1917 *Julia Ward Howe.* Laura E. Richards and Maude Howe Elliott, assisted by Florence Howe Hall
1918 *Benjamin Franklin, Self-Revealed.* William Cabell Bruce
1919 *The Education of Henry Adams.* Henry Adams
1920 *The Life of John Marshall.* Albert J. Beveridge
1921 *The Americanization of Edward Bok.* Edward Bok
1922 *A Daughter of the Middle Border.* Hamlin Garland
1923 *The Life and Letters of Walter H. Page,* Burton J. Hendrick
1924 *From Immigrant to Inventor.* Michael Idvorsky Pupin
1925 *Barrett Wendell and His Letters.* M. A. DeWolfe Howe
1926 *The Life of Sir William Osler.* Harvey Cushing
1927 *Whitman.* Emory Holloway
1928 *The American Orchestra and Theodore Thomas. Charles Edward Russell*
1929 *The Training of an American. The Earlier Life and Letters of Walter H. Page.* Burton J. Hendrick

1930 *The Raven.* Marquis James
1931 *Charles W. Eliot.* Henry James
1932 *Theodore Roosevelt.* Henry F. Pringle
1933 *Grover Cleveland.* Allan Nevins
1934 *John Hay.* Tyler Dennett
1935 *R. E. Lee.* Douglas S. Freeman
1936 *The Thought and Character of William James.* Ralph Barton Perry
1937 *Hamilton Fish.* Allan Nevins
1938 *Pedlar's Progress.* Odell Shepard; *Andrew Jackson.* Marquis James
1939 *Benjamin Franklin.* Carl Van Doren
1940 *Woodrow Wilson. Life and Letters,* Vols. VII and VIII. Ray Stannard Baker
1941 *Jonathan Edwards.* Ola E. Winslow
1942 *Crusader in Crinoline.* Forrest Wilson
1943 *Admiral of the Ocean Sea.* Samuel Eliot Morison
1944 *The American Leonardo: The Life of Samuel F. B. Morse.* Carleton Mabee
1945 *George Bancroft: Brahmin Rebel.* Russel Blaine Nye
1946 *Son of the Wilderness.* Linnie Marsh Wolfe
1947 *The Autobiography of William Allen White*
1948 *Forgotten First Citizen: John Bigelow.* Margaret Clapp
1949 *Roosevelt and Hopkins.* Robert E. Sherwood
1950 *John Quincy Adams and the Foundations of American Foreign Policy.* Samuel Flagg Bemis
1951 *John C. Calhoun: American Portrait.* Margaret Louise Coit
1952 *Charles Evans Hughes.* Merlo J. Pusey
1953 *Edmund Pendleton, 1721–1803.* David J. Mays
1954 *The Spirit of St. Louis.* Charles A. Lindbergh
1955 *The Taft Story.* William S. White
1956 *Benjamin Henry Latrobe.* Talbot F. Hamlin
1957 *Profiles in Courage.* John F. Kennedy
1958 *George Washington.* Douglas Southall Freeman (Vols. 1–6) and John Alexander Carroll and Mary Wells Ashworth (Vol. 7)
1959 *Woodrow Wilson, American Prophet.* Arthur Walworth
1960 *John Paul Jones.* Samuel Eliot Morison
1961 *Charles Sumner and the Coming of the Civil War.* David Donald
1963 *Henry James: Vol. II, The Conquest of London, 1870–1881; Vol. III, The Middle Years, 1881–1895.* Leon Edel
1964 *John Keats.* Walter Jackson Bate
1965 *Henry Adams* (3 Vols.). Ernest Samuels
1966 *A Thousand Days.* Arthur M. Schlesinger, Jr.
1967 *Mr. Clemens and Mark Twain.* Justin Kaplan
1968 *Memoirs, 1925–1950.* George F. Kennan
1969 *The Man From New York.* B. L. Reid
1970 *Huey Long.* T. Harry Williams
1971 *Robert Frost: The Years of Triumph, 1915–1938.* Lawrence Thompson
1972 *Eleanor and Franklin: The Story of Their Relationship Based on Eleanor Roosevelt's Private Papers.* Joseph P. Lash
1973 *Luce and His Empire.* W. A. Swanberg
1974 *O'Neill, Son and Artist.* Louis Sheaffer
1975 *The Power Broker: Robert Moses and the Fall of New York.* Robert A. Caro
1976 *Edith Wharton: A Biography.* Richard W. B. Lewis
1977 *A Prince of Our Disorder.* John E. Mack
1978 *Samuel Johnson.* Walter Jackson Bate
1979 *Days of Sorrow and Pain: Leo Baeck and the Berlin Jews.* Leonard Baker
1980 *The Rise of Theodore Roosevelt.* Edmund Morris
1981 *Peter the Great.* Robert K. Massie
1982 *Grant: A Biography.* William S. McFeely
1983 *Growing Up.* Russell Baker
1984 *Booker T. Washington.* Louis R. Harlan

POETRY[1]

1918 *Love Songs.* Sara Teasdale
1919 *Old Road to Paradise.* Margaret Widdemer; *Corn Huskers.* Carl Sandburg
1922 *Collected Poems.* Edwin Arlington Robinson
1923 *The Ballad of the Harp-Weaver; A Few Figs from Thistles;* eight sonnets in *American Poetry, 1922, A Miscellany.* Edna St. Vincent Millay
1924 *New Hampshire: A Poem With Notes and Grace Notes.* Robert Frost
1925 *The Man Who Died Twice.* Edwin Arlington Robinson
1926 *What's O'Clock.* Amy Lowell
1927 *Fiddler's Farewell.* Leonora Speyer
1928 *Tristram.* Edwin Arlington Robinson
1929 *John Brown's Body.* Stephen Vincent Benét
1930 *Selected Poems.* Conrad Aiken
1931 *Collected Poems.* Robert Frost
1932 *The Flowering Stone.* George Dillon
1933 *Conquistador.* Archibald MacLeish
1934 *Collected Verse.* Robert Hillyer
1935 *Bright Ambush.* Audrey Wurdemann
1936 *Strange Holiness.* Robert P. T. Coffin
1937 *A Further Range.* Robert Frost
1938 *Cold Morning Sky.* Marya Zaturenska
1939 *Selected Poems.* John Gould Fletcher
1940 *Collected Poems.* Mark Van Doren
1941 *Sunderland Capture.* Leonard Bacon
1942 *The Dust Which Is God.* William Rose Benét
1943 *A Witness Tree.* Robert Frost
1944 *Western Star.* Stephen Vincent Benét
1945 *V-Letter and Other Poems.* Karl Shapiro
1947 *Lord Weary's Castle.* Robert Lowell
1948 *The Age of Anxiety.* W. H. Auden
1949 *Terror and Decorum.* Peter Viereck
1950 *Annie Allen.* Gwendolyn Brooks
1951 *Complete Poems.* Carl Sandburg
1952 *Collected Poems.* Marianne Moore
1953 *Collected Poems, 1917–1952.* Archibald MacLeish
1954 *The Waking.* Theodore Roethke
1955 *Collected Poems.* Wallace Stevens
1956 *Poems—North & South.* Elizabeth Bishop
1957 *Things of This World.* Richard Wilbur
1958 *Promises: Poems, 1954–1956.* Robert Penn Warren
1959 *Selected Poems, 1928–1958.* Stanley Kunitz
1960 *Heart's Needle.* William Snodgrass
1961 *Times Three: Selected Verse From Three Decades.* Phyllis McGinley
1962 *Poems.* Alan Dugan
1963 *Pictures From Breughel.* William Carlos Williams
1964 *At the End of the Open Road.* Louis Simpson
1965 *77 Dream Songs.* John Berryman
1966 *Selected Poems.* Richard Eberhart
1967 *Live or Die.* Anne Sexton
1968 *The Hard Hours.* Anthony Hecht
1969 *Of Being Numerous.* George Oppen
1970 *Untitled Subjects.* Richard Howard
1971 *The Carrier of Ladders.* William S. Merwin
1972 *Collected Poems.* James Wright
1973 *Up Country.* Maxine Winokur Kumin

1. This prize was established in 1922. The 1918 and 1919 awards were made from gifts provided by the Poetry Society.

1974 *The Dolphin.* Robert Lowell
1975 *Turtle Island.* Gary Snyder
1976 *Self-Portrait in a Convex Mirror.* John Ashbery
1977 *Divine Comedies.* James Merrill
1978 *Collected Poems.* Howard Nemerov: *Poems, 1976–1978.*
1979 *Now and Then.* Robert Penn Warren.
1980 *Selected Poems.* Donald Rodney Justice
1981 *The Morning of the Poem.* James Schuyler
1982 *The Collected Poems.* Sylvia Plath
1983 *Selected Poems.* Galway Kinnell
1984 *American Primitive.* Mary Oliver

GENERAL NONFICTION

1962 *The Making of the President, 1960.* Theodore H. White
1963 *The Guns of August.* Barbara W. Tuchman
1964 *Anti-intellectualism in American Life.* Richard Hofstadter
1965 *O Strange New World.* Howard Mumford Jones
1966 *Wandering Through Winter.* Edwin Way Teale
1967 *The Problem of Slavery in Western Culture.* David Brion Davis
1968 *Rousseau and Revolution.* Will and Ariel Durant
1969 *So Human an Animal.* Rene Jules Dubos; *The Armies of the Night.* Norman Mailer
1970 *Gandhi's Truth.* Erik H. Erikson
1971 *The Rising Sun.* John Toland
1972 *Stilwell and the American Experience in China, 1911–1945.* Barbara W. Tuchman
1973 *Fire in the Lake: The Vietnamese and the Americans in Vietnam.* Frances FitzGerald; and *Children of Crisis* (Vols. 1 and 2). Robert M. Coles
1974 *The Denial of Death.* Ernest Becker
1975 *Pilgrim at Tinker Creek.* Annie Dillard
1976 *Why Survive? Being Old in America.* Robert N. Butler
1977 *Beautiful Swimmers: Watermen, Crabs and the Chesapeake Bay.* William W. Warner
1978 *The Dragons of Eden.* Carl Sagan
1979 *On Human Nature.* Edward O. Wilson
1980 *Gödel, Escher, Bach: An Eternal Golden Braid.* Douglas R. Hofstadter
1981 *Fin-de-Siecle Vienna: Politics and Culture.* Carl E. Schorske
1982 *The Soul of a New Machine.* Tracy Kidder
1983 *Is There No Place on Earth for Me?* Susan Sheehan
1984 *Social Transformation of American Medicine.* Paul Starr

PULITZER PRIZES IN MUSIC

1943 *Secular Cantata No. 2, A Free Song.* William Schuman
1944 *Symphony No. 4* (Op. 34). Howard Hanson
1945 *Appalachian Spring.* Aaron Copland
1946 *The Canticle of the Sun.* Leo Sowerby
1947 *Symphony No. 3.* Charles Ives
1948 *Symphony No. 3.* Walter Piston
1949 *Louisiana Story* music. Virgil Thomson
1950 *The Consul.* Gian Carlo Menotti
1951 Music for opera *Giants in the Earth.* Douglas Stuart Moore
1952 *Symphony Concertante.* Gail Kubik
1954 *Concerto for Two Pianos and Orchestra.* Quincy Porter
1955 *The Saint of Bleecker Street.* Gian Carlo Menotti
1956 *Symphony No. 3.* Ernst Toch
1957 *Meditations on Ecclesiastes.* Norman Dello Joio
1958 *Vanessa.* Samuel Barber
1959 *Concerto for Piano and Orchestra.* John La Montaine
1960 *Second String Quartet.* Elliott Carter
1961 *Symphony No. 7.* Walter Piston
1962 *The Crucible.* Robert Ward
1963 *Piano Concerto No. 1.* Samuel Barber
1966 *Variations for Orchestra.* Leslie Bassett
1967 *Quartet No. 3.* Leon Kirchner
1968 *Echoes of Time and the River.* George Crumb
1969 *String Quartet No. 3.* Karel Husa
1970 *Time's Encomium.* Charles Wuorinen
1971 *Synchronisms No. 6 for Piano and Electronic Sound.* Mario Davidowsky
1972 *Windows.* Jacob Druckman
1973 *String Quartet No. 3.* Elliott Carter
1974 *Notturno.* Donald Martino
1975 *From the Diary of Virginia Woolf.* Dominick Argento
1976 *Air Music.* Ned Rorem
1977 *Visions of Terror and Wonder.* Richard Wernick
1978 *Déjà Vu for Percussion Quartet and Orchestra.* Michael Colgrass
1979 *Aftertones of Infinity.* Joseph Schwantner
1980 *In Memory of a Summer Day.* David Del Tredici
1981 Not awarded
1982 *Concerto for Orchestra.* Roger Sessions
1983 *Three Movements for Orchestra.* Ellen T. Zwilich
1984 *Canti del Sole.* Bernard Rands

Enrico Fermi Award

Named in honor of Enrico Fermi, the atomic pioneer, the $25,000 award is given in recognition of "exceptional and altogether outstanding" scientific and technical achievement in atomic energy.

1954 Enrico Fermi
1956 John von Neumann
1957 Ernest O. Lawrence
1958 Eugene P. Wigner
1959 Glenn T. Seaborg
1961 Hans A. Bethe
1962 Edward Teller
1963 J. Robert Oppenheimer
1964 Hyman G. Rickover
1966 Otto Hahn, Lise Meitner, and Fritz Strassman
1968 John A. Wheeler
1969 Walter H. Zinn
1970 Norris E. Bradbury
1971 Shields Warren and Stafford L. Warren
1972 Manson Benedict
1976 William L. Russell
1978 Harold M. Agnew and Wolfgang K.H. Panofsky
1980 Alvin M. Weinberg and Rudolf E. Peirls
1982 W. Bennett Lewis

New York Drama Critics' Circle Awards

1935–36
Winterset, Maxwell Anderson
1936–37
High Tor, Maxwell Anderson
1937–38
Of Mice and Men, John Steinbeck
Shadow and Substance, Paul Vincent Carroll[1]
1938–39
(No award) *The White Steed,* Paul Vincent Carroll[1]
1939–40
The Time of Your Life, William Saroyan
1940–41
Watch on the Rhine, Lillian Hellman
The Corn Is Green, Emlyn Williams[1]
1941–42
(No award) *Blithe Spirit,* Noel Coward[1]
1942–43
The Patriots, Sidney Kingsley
1943–44
(No award) *Jacobowsky and the Colonel.* Franz Werfel and S. N. Behrman[1]
1944–45
The Glass Menagerie, Tennessee Williams
1945–46
(No award) *Carousel,* Richard Rodgers and Oscar Hammerstein II[2]
1946–47
All My Sons, Arthur Miller
No Exit, Jean-Paul Sartre[1]
Brigadoon, Alan Jay Lerner and Frederick Loewe[2]
1947–48
A Streetcar Named Desire, Tennessee Williams
The Winslow Boy, Terence Rattigan[1]
1948–49
Death of a Salesman, Arthur Miller
The Madwoman of Chaillot, Jean Giraudoux and Maurice Valency[1]
South Pacific, Richard Rodgers, Oscar Hammerstein II, and Joshua Logan[2]
1949–50
The Member of the Wedding, Carson McCullers
The Cocktail Party, T. S. Eliot[1]
The Consul, Gian Carlo Menotti[2]
1950–51
Darkness at Noon, Sidney Kingsley[3]
The Lady's Not for Burning, Christopher Fry[1]
Guys and Dolls, Abe Burrows, Jo Swerling, and Frank Loesser[2]
1951–52
I Am a Camera, John Van Druten[4]
Venus Observed, Christopher Fry[1]
Pal Joey, Richard Rodgers, Lorenz Hart, and John O'Hara[2]
Don Juan in Hell, George B. Shaw[5]
1952–53
Picnic, William Inge
The Love of Four Colonels, by Peter Ustinov[1]
Wonderful Town, Joseph Fields, Jerome Chodorov, Betty Comden, Adolph Green, and Leonard Bernstein[2]
1953–54
The Teahouse of the August Moon, John Patrick
Ondine, Jean Giraudoux[1]
The Golden Apple, John Latouche and Jerome Moross[2]
1954–55
Cat on a Hot Tin Roof, Tennessee Williams
Witness for the Prosecution, Agatha Christie[1]
The Saint of Bleecker Street, Gian Carlo Menotti[2]
1955–56
The Diary of Anne Frank, Frances Goodrich and Albert Hackett
Tiger at the Gates, Jean Giraudoux and Christopher Fry[1]
My Fair Lady, Frederick Loewe and Alan Jay Lerner[2]
1956–57
Long Day's Journey Into Night, Eugene O'Neill
Waltz of the Toreadors, Jean Anouilh[1]
The Most Happy Fella, Frank Loesser[2] [6]
1957–58
Look Homeward, Angel, Ketti Frings[7]
Look Back in Anger, John Osborne[1]
The Music Man, Meredith Willson[2]
1958–59
A Raisin in the Sun, Lorraine Hansberry
The Visit, Friedrich Duerrenmatt-Maurice Valency[1]
La Plume de ma Tante, Robert Dhery and Gerard Calvi[2]
1959–60
Toys in the Attic, Lillian Hellman
Five Finger Exercise, Peter Shaffer[1]
Fiorello!, Jerome Weidman, George Abbott, Jerry Bock, and Sheldon Harnick[2]
1960–61
All the Way Home, Tad Mosel[3]
A Taste of Honey, Shelagh Delaney[1]
Carnival, Michael Stewart[2]
1961–62
The Night of the Iguana, Tennessee Williams
A Man for All Seasons, Robert Bolt[1]
How to Succeed in Business Without Really Trying, Abe Burrows, Jack Weinstock, Willie Gilbert, and Frank Loesser[2] [9]
1962–63
Who's Afraid of Virginia Woolf?, Edward Albee
Beyond the Fringe, Alan Bennett, Peter Cook, Jonathan Miller, and Dudley Moore[10]
1963–64
Luther, John Osborne
Hello, Dolly!, Michael Stewart and Jerry Herman[2] [11]
The Trojan Women, Euripides[10] [12]
1964–65
The Subject Was Roses, Frank D. Gilroy
Fiddler on the Roof, Joseph Stein, Jerry Bock, and Sheldon Harnick[2] [13]
1965–66
The Persecution and Assassination of Marat as Performed by the Inmates of the Asylum of Charenton Under the Direction of the Marquis de Sade, Peter Weiss
The Man of La Mancha, Dale Wasserman, Mitch Leigh, and Joe Darion
1966–67
The Homecoming, Harold Pinter
Cabaret, Joe Masteroff, John Kander, and Fred Ebb[2] [14]
1967–68
Rosencrantz and Guilderstern Are Dead, Tom Stoppard
Your Own Thing, Donald Driver, Hal Hester, and Danny Apolinar[2]
1968–69
The Great White Hope, Howard Sackler
1776, Sherman Edwards and Peter Stone[2]
1969–70
Borstal Boy, Frank McMahon[15]
The Effect of Gamma Rays on Man-in-the-Moon Marigolds, Paul Zindel[16]
Company, George Furth and Stephen Sondheim[2]
1970–71
Home, David Storey
The House of Blue Leaves, John Guare[16]

Follies, James Goldman and Stephen Sondheim[2]
1971–72
That Championship Season, Jason Miller
Two Gentlemen of Verona, adapted by John Guare and Mel Shapiro[2]
The Screens, Jean Genet[1]
1972–73
The Changing Room, David Storey
The Hot l Baltimore, by Lanford Wilson[16]
A Little Night Music, Hugh Wheeler and Stephen Sondheim[2]
1973–74
The Contractors, David Storey
Short Eyes, Miguel Piñero[16]
Candide, Leonard Bernstein, Hugh Wheeler, and Richard Wilbur[2]
1974–75
Equus, Peter Shaffer
The Taking of Miss Janie, Ed Bullins[16]
A Chorus Line, James Kirkwood and Nicholas Dante[2]
1975–76
Travesties, Tom Stoppard
Streamers, David Rabe[16]
Pacific Overtures, Stephen Sondheim, John Weidman, and Hugh Wheeler[2]
1976–77
Otherwise Engaged, Simon Gray
American Buffalo, David Marmet[16]
Annie, Thomas Meehan, Charles Strouse, and Martin Charnin[2]
1977–78
Da, Hugh Leonard
Ain't Misbehavin', conceived by Richard Maltby, Jr.[2]
1978–79
The Elephant Man, Bernard Pomerance
Sweeney Todd, Hugh Wheeler and Stephen Sondheim[2]
1979–80
Talley's Folly, Lanford Wilson
Evita,[2] Andrew Lloyd Webber and Tim Rice
Betrayal, Harold Pinter[1]
1980–81
A Lesson From Aloes, Athol Fugard
Crimes of the Heart, Beth Henley[16]
1981–82
The Life and Adventures of Nicholas Nickleby, adapted by David Edgar
A Soldier's Play, Charles Fuller[16]
1982–83
Brighton Beach Memoirs, Neil Simon
Plenty, David Hare[1]
Little Shop of Horrors, Alan Menken and Howard Ashman[2] [17]
1983–84
The Real Thing, Tom Stoppard
Glengarry Glen Ross, David Mamet[16]
Sunday in the Park with George, Stephen W Sondheim and James Lapine[2]

1. Citation for best foreign play. 2. Citation for best musical. 3. Based on a novel by Arthur Koestler. 4. Based on Christopher Isherwood's *Berlin Stories.* 5. For "distinguished and original contribution to the theater." 6. Based on Sidney Howard's *They Knew What They Wanted.* 7. Based on a novel by Thomas Wolfe. 8. Based on James Agee's *A Death in the Family.* 9. Based on a book by Shepherd Mead. 10. Special citation. 11. Based on Thornton Wilder's *The Matchmaker.* 12. Translated by Edith Hamilton. 13. Based on Sholem Aleichem's Tevye stories, translated by Arnold Perl. 14. Based on John Van Druten's *I Am a Camera,* which won the award for the best play in 1951–52. 15. Based on Brendan Behan's autobiography. 16. Citation for best American play. 17. Based on a story by Roger Corman.

Major American Book Awards, 1983[1]

Established by Association of American Publishers

Fiction: *The Color Purple,* by Alice Walker (Harcourt Brace Jovanovich)
First novel: *The Women of Brewster Place,* by Gloria Naylor (Viking Press)
General nonfiction: *China: Alive in the Bitter Sea,* by Fox Butterfield (Times Books)
Biography/Autobiography: *Isak Dinesen: The Life of a Storyteller,* by Judith Thurman (St. Martin's Press)
History: *Voices of Protest: Huey Long, Father Coughlin and the Great Depression,* by Alan Brinkley (Alfred A. Knopf)
Science: *'Subtle Is the Lord . . .': The Science and the Life of Albert Einstein,* by Abraham Pais (Oxford University Press)
Poetry: *Selected Poems,* by Galway Kinnell (Houghton Mifflin) and *Country Music,* by Charles Wright (Wesleyan University Press)
Translation: Richard Howarde for Baudelaire's *Les Fleurs du Mal* (David R. Godine)
Children's fiction: *Homesick: My Own Story,* by Jean Fritz (G. B. Putnam's)
Children's nonfiction: *Chimney Sweeps,* by James Cross Giblin (Thomas Y. Crowell)
Children's picture book: *Miss Rumphius,* by Barbara Cooney (Viking Press) and *Doctor De Soto,* by William Steig (Farrar, Straus & Giroux)
Original paperback: *The Red Magician,* by Lisa Goldstein (Timescape/Pocket Books)
Book design (pictorial): Barry Moser and Steve Renick for *Alice's Adventures in Wonderland,* by Lewis Carroll (University of California Press)
Book design (typographical): David Lance Goines and William F. Luckey for *A Constructed Roman Alphabet* (David R. Godine)
Book illustration (original art): Beverly Major, Erick Ingraham, and Cynthia Basil for *Porcupine Stew* (William Morrow Junior Books)
Book illustration (collected art): Howard Morris, Nancy Grubb, and Dana Cole for *John Singer Sargent,* by Carter Ratcliff (Abbeville Press)
Book illustration (photographs): Sarah Greenough, Juan Hamilton, and Eleanor Morris Caponigro for *Alfred Stieglitz: Photographs and Writings* (National Gallery of Art/Callaway Editions)
Cover design: Doris Ettlinger and Neil Stuart for *Bogmail,* by Patrick McGinley (Penguin Books)
Jacket design: Fred Marcellino and Frank Metz for *Souls on Fire,* by Elie Wiesel (Summit Books/Simon & Schuster)

1. Most recent award. Because of a policy change the 1984 award will not be given until November 1984.

Presidential Medal of Freedom

The nation's highest civilian award, the Presidential Medal of Freedom, was established in 1963 by President John F. Kennedy to continue and expand Presidential recognition of meritorious service which, since 1945, had been granted as the Medal of Freedom. Kennedy selected the first recipients, but was assassinated before he could make the presentations. They were made by President Johnson. NOTE: An asterisk following a year denotes a posthumous award.

SELECTED BY PRESIDENT KENNEDY

Marian Anderson (contralto)	1963
Ralph J. Bunche (statesman)	1963
Ellsworth Bunker (diplomat)	1963
Pablo Casals (cellist)	1963
Genevieve Caulfield (educator)	1963
James B. Conant (educator)	1963
John F. Enders (bacteriologist)	1963
Felix Frankfurter (jurist)	1963
Karl Horton (youth authority)	1963
Robert J. Kiphuth (athletic director)	1963
Edwin H. Land (inventor)	1963
Herbert H. Lehman (statesman)	1963*
Robert A. Lovett (statesman)	1963
J. Clifford MacDonald (educator)	1963*
John J. McCloy (banker and statesman)	1963
George Meany (labor leader)	1963
Alexander Meiklejohn (philosopher)	1963
Ludwig Mies van der Rohe (architect)	1963
Jean Monnet (European statesman)	1963
Luis Muñoz-Marin (Governor of Puerto Rico)	1963
Clarence B. Randall (industrialist)	1963
Rudolf Serkin (pianist)	1963
Edward Steichen (photographer)	1963
George W. Taylor (educator)	1963
Alan T. Waterman (scientist)	1963
Mark S. Watson (journalist)	1963
Annie D. Wauneka (public health worker)	1963
E. B. White (author)	1963
Thornton N. Wilder (author)	1963
Edmund Wilson (author and critic)	1963
Andrew Wyeth (artist)	1963

AWARDED BY PRESIDENT JOHNSON

Dean G. Acheson (statesman)	1964
Eugene R. Black (banker)	1969
Detlev W. Bronk (neurophysiologist)	1964
McGeorge Bundy (government service)	1969
Elisworth Bunker (diplomat)	1968
Clark Clifford (statesman)	1969
Aaron Copland (composer)	1964
Michael E. DeBakey (surgeon)	1969
Willem de Kooning (artist)	1964
Walt Disney (cartoon film producer)	1964
J. Frank Dobie (author)	1964
David Dubinsky (labor leader)	1969
Lena F. Edwards (physician and humanitarian)	1964
Thomas Stearns Eliot (poet)	1964
Ralph Ellison (author)	1969
Lynn Fontanne (actress)	1964
Henry Ford II (industrialist)	1969
John W. Gardner (educator)	1964
W. Averell Harriman (statesman)	1969
Rev. Theodore M. Hesburgh (educator)	1964
Bob Hope (comedian)	1969
John XXIII (Pope)	1963*
Clarence L. Johnson (aircraft engineer)	1964
Edgar F. Kaiser (industrialist)	1969
Frederick R. Kappel (telecommunications executive)	1964
Helen A. Keller (educator)	1964
John Fitzgerald Kennedy (U.S. President)	1963*
Robert W. Komer (government service)	1968
Mary Lasker (philanthropist)	1969
John L. Lewis (labor leader)	1964
Walter Lippmann (journalist)	1964
Eugene M. Locke (diplomat)	1968
Alfred Lunt (actor)	1964
John W. Macy, Jr. (government service)	1969
Ralph McGill (journalist)	1964
Robert S. McNamara (government service)	1968
Samuel Eliot Morison (historian)	1964
Lewis Mumford (urban planner and critic)	1964
Edward R. Murrow (radio-TV commentator)	1964
Reinhold Niebuhr (theologian)	1964
Gregory Peck (actor)	1969
Leontyne Price (soprano)	1964
A. Philip Randolph (labor leader)	1964
Laurance S. Rockefeller (conservationist)	1969
Walt Whitman Rostow (government service)	1969
Deak Rusk (statesman)	1969
Carl Sandburg (poet and biographer)	1964
Merriman Smith (journalist)	1969
John Steinbeck (author)	1964
Helen B. Taussig (pediatrician)	1964
Cyrus R. Vance (government service)	1969
Carl Vinson (legislator)	1964
Thomas J. Watson, Jr. (industrialist)	1964
James E. Webb (NASA administrator)	1968
Paul Dudley White (physician)	1964
William S. White (journalist)	1969
Roy Wilkins (social welfare executive)	1969
Whitney M. Young, Jr. (social welfare executive)	1969

AWARDED BY PRESIDENT NIXON

Edwin E. Aldrin (astronaut)	1969
Apollo 13 Mission Operations Team	1970
Neil A. Armstrong (astronaut)	1969
Earl Charles Behrens (journalist)	1970
Manlio Brosio (NATO secretary general)	1971
Michael Collins (astronaut)	1969
Edward K. "Duke" Ellington (musician)	1969
Edward T. Folliard (journalist)	1970
John Ford (film director)	1973
Samuel Goldwyn (film producer)	1971
Fred Wallace Haise, Jr. (astronaut)	1970
William M. Henry (journalist)	1970*
Paul G. Hoffman (statesman)	1974
William J. Hopkins (White House service)	1971
Arthur Krock (journalist)	1970
Melvin R. Laird (government service)	1974
David Lawrence (journalist)	1970
George Gould Lincoln (journalist)	1970
James A. Lovell, Jr. (astronaut)	1970
Dr. Charles L. Lowman (orthopedist)	1974
Raymond Moley (journalist)	1970
Eugene Ormandy (conductor)	1970
William P. Rogers (diplomat)	1973
Adela Rogers St. Johns (journalist)	1970
John Leonard Swigert, Jr. (astronaut)	1970
John Paul Vann (adviser, Vietnam war)	1972*
DeWitt and Lila Wallace (founders, *Reader's Digest*)	1972

AWARDED BY PRESIDENT FORD

I. W. Abel (labor leader)	1977
John Bardeen (physicist)	1977
Irving Berlin (composer)	1977
Norman Borlaug (agricultural scientist)	1977
Omar N. Bradley (national security)	1977
David K. E. Bruce (diplomat)	1976
Arleigh Burke (national security)	1977
Alexander Calder (sculptor)	1977
Bruce Catton (historian)	1977
Joseph P. DiMaggio (baseball star)	1977
Ariel Durant (author)	1977

Will Durant (author)	1977
Arthur Fiedler (conductor)	1977
Henry J. Friendly (jurist)	1977
Martha Graham (dancer-choreographer)	1976
Claudia "Lady Bird" Johnson (service to U.S. scenic beauty)	1977
Henry A. Kissinger (statesman)	1977
Archibald MacLeish (poet)	1977
James A. Michener (author)	1977
Georgia O'Keeffe (artist)	1977
Jesse Owens (track champion)	1976
Nelson A. Rockefeller (government service)	1977
Norman Rockwell (illustrator)	1977
Arthur Rubinstein (pianist)	1976
Donald H. Rumsfeld (government service)	1977
Katherine Filene Shouse (service to the performing arts)	1977
Lowell Thomas (radio-TV commentator)	1977
James D. Watson (biochemist)	1977

AWARDED BY PRESIDENT CARTER

Ansel Adams (photographer)	1980
Horace M. Albright (government service)	1980
Roger Baldwin (civil libertarian)	1981
Harold Brown (government service)	1981
Zbigniew Brzezinski (government service)	1981
Rachel Carson (author)	1980*
Lucia Chase (ballet director)	1980
Warren M. Christopher (government service)	1981
Walter Cronkite (TV newscaster)	1981
Kirk Douglas (actor)	1981
Arthur J. Goldberg (government service)	1978
Hubert H. Humphrey (government service)	1980*
Archbishop Iakovos (churchman)	1980
Lyndon B. Johnson (U.S. President)	1980*
Rev. Dr. Martin Luther King, Jr. (civil rights leader)	1977*
Margaret Craig McNamara (educator)	1981
Margaret Mead (anthropologist)	1979*
Karl Menninger (psychiatrist)	1981
Clarence Mitchell, Jr. (civil rights leader)	1980
Edmund S. Muskie (government service)	1981
Esther Peterson (government service)	1981
Roger Tory Peterson (ornithologist)	1980
Adm. Hyman Rickover (national security)	1980
Jonas Salk (medical research)	1977
Beverly Sills (opera singer)	1980
Gerard C. Smith (government service)	1981
Robert S. Strauss (government service)	1981
Elbert Parr Tuttle (government service)	1981
Earl Warren (government service)	1981*
Robert Penn Warren (author and poet)	1980
John Wayne (actor)	1980*
Eudora Welty (author)	1980
Tennessee Williams (playwright)	1980
Andrew M. Young (government service)	1981

AWARDED BY PRESIDENT REAGAN

Howard H. Baker, Jr. (government service)	1984
George Balanchine (choreographer)	1983
James H. (Eubie) Blake (composer-pianist)	1981
Paul W. (Bear) Bryant (football coach)	1983*
James Burnham (editor-historian)	1983
James Francis Cagney (actor)	1984
Whittaker Chambers (public servant)	1984*
James Cheek (educator)	1983
Leo Cherne (economist-humanitarian)	1984
Terence Cardinal Cooke, His Eminence (theologian)	1984*
Denton Arthur Cooley, M.D. (heart surgeon)	1984
Tennessee Ernie Ford (singer)	1984
R. Buckminster Fuller (architect-geometrician)	1983
Hector P. Garcia, M.D. (humanitarian)	1984
Gen. Andrew J. Goodpaster (soldier-diplomat)	1984
Rev. Billy Graham (evangelist)	1983
Ella T. Grasso (Connecticut governor)	1981*
Philip C. Habib (diplomat)	1982
Bryce N. Harlow (government service)	1981
Eric Hoffer (philosopher-longshoreman)	1983
Jacob K. Javits (government service)	1983
Walter H. Judd (government service)	1981
Lincoln Kirstein (ballet director)	1984
Louis L'Amour (author)	1984
Morris I. Leibman (lawyer)	1981
Clare Booth Luce (author-diplomat)	1983
Dumas Malone (historian)	1983
Mabel Mercer (jazz singer)	1983
Norman Vincent Peale (theologian)	1984
Simon Ramo (industrialist)	1983
Gen. Carlos P. Romulo (Philippino statesman)	1984
Jack Roosevelt Robinson (baseball player)	1984*
Mohamed Anwar el-Sadat (statesman)	1984*
Eunice Kennedy Shriver (humanitarian)	1984
Kate Smith (singer)	1982
Charles B. Thornton (industrialist)	1981

Recipients of Kennedy Center Honors

The Kennedy Center for the Performing Arts in Washington, D.C., created its Honors awards in 1978 to recognize the achievements of five distinguished contributors to the performing arts. Following are the recipients:

1978: Marian Anderson (contralto), Fred Astaire (dancer-actor), Richard Rodgers (Broadway composer), Arthur Rubinstein (pianist), George Balanchine (choreographer).

1979: Ella Fitzgerald (jazz singer), Henry Fonda (actor), Martha Graham (dancer-choreographer), Tennessee Williams (playwright), Aaron Copland (composer).

1980: James Cagney (actor), Leonard Bernstein (composer-conductor), Agnes de Mille (choreographer), Lynn Fontanne (actress), Leontyne Price (soprano).

1981: Count Basie (jazz composer-pianist), Cary Grant (actor), Helen Hayes (actress), Jerome Robbins (choreographer), Rudolf Serkin (pianist).

1982: George Abbott (Broadway producer), Lillian Gish (actress), Benny Goodman (jazz clarinetist), Gene Kelly (dancer-actor), Eugene Ormandy (conductor).

1983: Katherine Dunham (dancer-choreographer), Elia Kazan (director-author), James Stewart (actor), Virgil Thomson (music critic-composer), Frank Sinatra (singer).

Labors of Hercules

Hercules, was the son of Zeus and Alcmene. He performed twelve labors to be free from bondage under Eurystheus. After his death, he became immortal. His labors were: (1) killing the Nemean Lion; (2) killing the Lernaean Hydra; (3) capturing the Cerynean Stag; (4) capturing the Erymanthian Boar; (5) cleaning the Augean Stables; (6) killing the Stymphalian Birds; (7) capturing the Cretan Bull; (8) capturing the Mares of Diomedes; (9) procuring the Girdle of Hippolyta; (10) capturing the Cattle of Geryon; (11) procuring the golden Apples of Hesperides; (12) bringing Cerberus up from Hades.

American Library Association Awards for Children's Books, 1984

John Newbery Medal for best book: *Dear Mr. Henshaw,* Beverly Cleary (Morrow)

Newbery Honor Books: *Sign of the Beaver,* by Elizabeth George Speare (Houghton Mifflin); *Solitary Blue,* by Cynthia Voigt (Atheneum); *Sugaring Time,* by Kathryn Lasky (MacMillian); *Wish Giver,* by Bill Brittain (Harper)

Randolph Caldecott Medal for best picture book: *The Glorious Flight; Across the Channel With Louis Bleriot,* written and illustrated by Alice and Martin Provensen (Viking)

Caldecott Honor Books: *Little Red Riding Hood,* retold and illustrated by Trina Schart Hyman (Holiday House); *Ten, Nine and Eight,* written and illustrated by Molly Bang (Greenwillow Books)

George Foster Peabody Awards for Broadcasting, 1983

Radio

WCCO, Minneapolis: *Debbie Pielow: Waiting for a Heart That Never Came*
South Carolina Educational Radio Network: *Piano Jazz*
WMAL, Washington, D.C. *The Jeffersonian World of Dumas Malone*
Don McGannon, Westinghouse Broadcasting Corporation
KMOX, St. Louis: *Times Beach: Born 1925, Died 1983*
Thomas Looker, Montague Center, Mass.: *New England Almanac: Portraits in Sound of New England Life and Landscape*
WRAL, Raleigh, N.C.: *Victims*
WSM, Nashville: *The Grand Ole Opry*

Television

CBS News, New York: *The Plane That Fell from the Sky* and *60 Minutes: Lenell Geter's in Jail*
Cable News Network, Atlanta: *Significant News and Information Programming*
WNBC, New York: *Asylum in the Streets*
WCCO, Minneapolis: *I-Team: Ambulances*
NBC and Motown Productions: *Motown 25: Yesterday, Today, Forever*
WTTW, Chicago: *The Merry Widow*
Chrysalis-Yellen Productions and NBC: *Prisoner Without a Name, Cell Without a Number*
WTTW, Chicago and the British Broadcasting Corporation: *The Making of a Continent*
WTBS, Atlanta, *Portrait of America*
WGBH, Central Independent Television, London, and Antenne-2, Paris: *Vietnam: A Television History*
Sunbow Productions, New York: *The Great Space Coaster*
CBS Entertainment and Smith-Hemion Productions: *Romeo and Juliet on Ice*
ABC and Dick Clark Productions: *The Woman Who Willed a Miracle*
CBS Entertainment and Mendelson-Melendez Productions: *What Have We Learned, Charlie Brown?*
WBBM, Chicago, *Studebaker: Less Than They Promised*
WBRZ, Baton Rouge, La.: *Give Me That Bigtime Religion*
KRON, San Francisco: *Climate of Death*
WGBH, Boston: *Nova: The Miracle of Life*
NBC and Edgar J. Scherick Associates: *He Makes Me Feel Like Dancin'*
KCTS, Seattle: *Diagnosis: Aids*

Poets Laureate of England

Edmund Spenser	1591–1599	Nicholas Rowe	1715–1718	William Wordsworth	1843–1850
Samuel Daniel	1599–1619	Laurence Eusden	1718–1730	Alfred Lord Tennyson	1850–1892
Ben Jonson	1619–1637	Colley Cibber	1730–1757	Alfred Austin	1896–1913
William Davenant	1638–1668	William Whitehead	1757–1785	Robert Bridges	1913–1930
John Dryden[1]	1670–1689	Thomas Warton	1785–1790	John Masefield	1930–1967
Thomas Shadwell	1689–1692	Henry James Pye	1790–1813	C. Day Lewis	1967–1972
Nahum Tate	1692–1715	Robert Southey	1813–1843	Sir John Betjeman	1972–1984

1. First to bear the title officially. *Source: Encyclopedia Britannica.*

Winners of Bollingen Prize in Poetry

($5,000 award is given biennially. It is administered by Yale University and the Bollingen Foundation.)

Year	Winner
1949	Ezra Pound
1950	Wallace Stevens
1951	John Crowe Ransom
1952	Marianne Moore
1953	Archibald MacLeish and William Carlos Williams
1954	W. H. Auden
1955	Léonie Adams and Louise Bogan
1956	Conrad Aiken
1957	Allen Tate
1958	E.E. Cummings
1959	Theodore Roethke
1960	Delmore Schwartz
1961	Yvor Winters
1962	John Hall Wheelock and Richard Eberhart
1963	Robert Frost
1965	Horace Gregory
1967	Robert Penn Warren
1969	John Berryman and Karl Shapiro
1971	Richard Wilbur and Mona Van Duyn
1973	James Merrill
1975	Archie Randolph Ammons
1977	David Ignatow
1979	W. S. Merwin
1981	Howard Nemerov and May Swenson
1983	Anthony Hecht and John Hollander

A List of Books Some People Consider Dangerous

Source: Selected from a list compiled by the staff of the American Booksellers Association.

Before the birth of Christ, even before the time of Homer (approximately 850 B.C.), writers and their writings were questioned. Although objections vary, foremost grounds have usually been religious, political or obscene, or pornographic. Penalties have ranged from censure and removal of books, to fines and/or imprisonment for writers, booksellers, and publishers, to the burning of books and even a few authors.

Where possible, the following list is coded (*see* legend) to indicate the reason(s) that have been given to seek the banning of each title. In the case of juvenile titles, many were questioned as to suitability at particular grade levels. With regard to obscenity, that category includes some titles thought to be objectionable if not actually obscene. Uncoded titles came from several sources and the reasons were not specified. In each instance the number(s) immediately follows the title. Books are listed by title, code, author, and publisher(s).

Legend: 1. Ethnic; 2. Inappropriate for young readers; including improper grade level; 3. Objectionable language; 4. Obscene; 5. Political; 6. Pornographic; 7. Religious; 8. Special interest groups; 9. Cultural; 10. Ethical; 11. Literary standards.

American Heritage Dictionary (2,3,4) Dell, Houghton Mifflin

The Gospel (7) Arbor House, Baker Books

The Koran (7) Penguin, Tahrike Tarsile Quran

The Talmud (5) Soncino Press

Lysistrata (4) *Aristophanes,* New American Library, Penguin, University Press of Virginia

The Wizard of Oz (2,11) *Frank L. Baum,* Grosset & Dunlap

The Living Bible (7) *William C. Bower,* Arno

The Good Earth (2) *Pearl S. Buck,* Crowell, Harper & Row, Pocket Books

Alice's Adventures in Wonderland (9,10,11) *Lewis Carroll,* Ace, Bantam, Crown, Delacorte, Dover, New American Library, Norton, Penguin, Random House, St. Martin's

Don Quixote (7,10) *Miguel de Saavedra Cervantes,* Methuen, New American Library, Norton, Random House

On The Origin of Species (2,7) *Charles B. Darwin,* Harvard University Press, Littlefield, Macmillan, New American Library, Norton, Rowman

Adventures of Robinson Crusoe (1) *Daniel Defoe,* Bantam, Grosset & Dunlap, New American Library, Norton

The Adventures of Sherlock Holmes (7) *Sir Arthur Conan Doyle,* Avon, Berkley, Harper & Row

Silas Marner (2) *George Eliot,* Bantam, New American Library, Zodiac Press

The Great Gatsby (3,4) *F. Scott Fitzgerald,* Scribner

Madame Bovary (4,9,10) *Gustave Flaubert,* Bantam, Houghton Mifflin, Modern Library, New American Library, Norton, Penguin

Anne Frank: The Diary of a Young Girl (2,4) *Anne Frank,* Doubleday, Pocket Books, Random House

The Art of Loving (2) *Erich Fromm,* Harper & Row

History of The Decline and Fall of the Roman Empire (5,7) *Edward Gibbon,* Modern Library

Faust (5,7) *Johann Wolfgang von Goethe,* Doubleday, Macmillan, Norton, Oxford University Press, Penguin

I Claudius (4) *Robert Graves,* Random House

Across the River and Into the Trees (4), **A Farewell to Arms** (2), **For Whom the Bell Tolls** (4), **The Old Man and the Sea** (2), **The Sun Also Rises** (2, 4), **To Have and Have Not** (4) *Ernest Hemingway,* Scribner

Mein Kampf (5) *Adolf Hitler,* Houghton Mifflin

The Odyssey (2,5) *Homer,* Airmont, Doubleday, Harper & Row, Macmillan, New American Library, Oxford University Press, Penguin

Les Miserables (7) *Victor Hugo,* Dodd Mead, Fawcett, Penguin

Brave New World (2,5,6,7) *Aldous Huxley,* Harper & Row

The Voyages of Dr. Dolittle, *Hugh Lofting,* Lippincott/Harper & Row

The Call of The Wild (5) *Jack London,* Ace, Bantam, Grosset & Dunlap, Macmillan, New American Library, Penguin, Pocket Books, Raintree, Tempo

The Prince (5) *Niccolo Machiavelli,* Bantam, New American Library, Penguin

Das Kapital (5) *Karl Marx,* Imported Publishers, Random House, Regnery-Gateway

Paradise Lost (2,7) *John Milton,* Airmont, Holt Rinehart & Winston, Modern Library/Random House, New American Library, Norton

Gone With the Wind (2) *Margaret Mitchell,* Avon, Macmillan

The Naked Ape (7,10,11) *Desmond Morris,* Dell, McGraw-Hill

Animal Farm (2) *George Orwell,* Harcourt, Brace Jovanovich, New American Library

All Quiet On the Western Front (4,5) *Erich Maria Remarque,* Fawcett, Little

The Merchant of Venice (1,2,7) *William Shakespeare,* Airmont, Cambridge University Press, Methuen, New American Library, Penguin, Pocket Books, Washington Square Press, Wiley

Man and Superman (4) *George Bernard Shaw,* Airmont, Penguin

Prometheus Unbound (5,7,10) *Percy Bysshe Shelley*

Mrs. Warren's Profession (4) *George Bernard Shaw,* Garland

Grapes of Wrath (2,3,4,5,7) *John Steinbeck,* Penguin, Viking

Gulliver's Travels (4,5) *Jonathan Swift,* Airmont, Bantam, Bobbs Merrill, Dell, Grosset & Dunlap, Houghton Mifflin, New American Library, Norton, Oxford University Press, Pocket Books

Mary Poppins (2) *P.L. Travers,* Harcourt Brace Jovanovich

Leaves of Grass (3) *Walt Whitman,* Adler, Doubleday, Holt Rinehart & Winston, Norton, Penguin

J' Accuse (5) *Emile Zola,* French & European

NOTE: The opinions about the books stated here are not those of the Publisher or editorial staff of *Information Please Almanac.*

Should you desire to have a complete copy of the latest annotated "List of Books Some People Consider Dangerous," write to: American Booksellers Association, 122 East 42nd. Street, New York, N.Y. 10168.

U.S. STATES & CITIES

States and Territories

State flower, bird, etc., are official unless otherwise indicated; dates in parentheses are those of adoption. Largest cities include incorporated places only. For secession and readmission dates of the former Confederate states, *see* Index. For lists of Governors, Senators, and Representatives, *see* Index. For additional state information, *see* the sections on "Business and the Economy," "Taxes," and "U.S. Statistics."

ALABAMA

Capital: Montgomery
Governor: George Corley Wallace, D (to Jan. 1987)
Lieut. Governor: William J. Baxley, D (to Jan. 1987)
Secy. of State: Don Seigleman, D (to Jan. 1987)
Comptroller: Tom Brassell
Atty. General: Charles A. Graddick, D (to Jan. 1987)
Organized as territory: March 3, 1817
Entered Union & (rank): Dec. 14, 1819 (22)
Present constitution adopted: 1901
Motto: *Audemus jura nostra defendere* (We dare defend our rights)
State flower: Camellia (1959)
State bird: Yellowhammer (1927)
State song: "Alabama" (1931)
State tree: Southern pine (longleaf) (1949)
Nickname: Yellowhammer State
Origin of name: May come from Choctaw meaning "thicket-clearers" or "vegetation-gatherers"
1980 population (1980 census) & (rank): 3,893,888 (22)
1983 est. population (July) & (rank): 3,959,000 (22)
1984 land area & (rank): 50,767 sq mi. (131,487 sq km) (28)
Geographic center: In Chilton Co., 12 mi. SW of Clanton
Number of counties: 67
Largest cities (1980 census): Birmingham, 284,413; Mobile, 200,452; Montgomery, 178,157; Huntsville, 142,513; Tuscaloosa, 75,143; Gadsden, 47,565
State forests: 8 (14,248.58 ac.)
State parks: 22 (45,614 ac.)
Gross receipts (1982–83): $11,666,316,492
Net receipts (1982–83): $9,512,274,579
Net disbursements (1982–83): $9,745,469,063

Spanish explorers are believed to have arrived at Mobile Bay in 1519, and the territory was visited in 1540 by the explorer Hernando de Soto. The first permanent European settlement in Alabama was founded by the French at Fort Louis in 1702. The British gained control of the area in 1763 by the Treaty of Paris, but had to cede almost all the Alabama region to the U.S. after the American Revolution. The Confederacy was founded at Montgomery in February 1861 and, for a time, the city was the Confederate capital.

During the last part of the 19th century, the economy of the state slowly improved. At Tuskegee Institute, founded in 1881 by Booker T. Washington, Dr. George Washington Carver carried out his famous agricultural research.

In the 1950s and '60s, Alabama was the site of such landmark civil-rights actions as the bus boycott in Montgomery (1955–56) and the "Freedom March" from Selma to Birmingham (1965).

Today, Alabama is the leading heavy-industry state in the South. Textiles, iron, and steel lead its manufacturing, which centers around Birmingham, the "Pittsburgh of the South." Industry is growing rapidly in other areas, including the Tennessee River Valley, with its great Muscle Shoals power plant. Manufacturing also includes cement, feed, fertilizer, chemical, rubber, and aluminum products. The state ranks high in the output of poultry, cotton, cattle, hogs, corn, potatoes, peanuts, and fruit.

Points of interest include the George C. Marshall Space Flight Center at Huntsville, Russell Cave National Monument near Bridgeport, and the White House of the Confederacy in Montgomery.

ALASKA

Capital: Juneau
Governor: Bill Sheffield, D (to Dec. 1986)
Lieut. Governor: Stephen McAlpine, D (to Dec. 1986)
Commissioner of Administration: Lisa Rudd, D (to Dec. 1986)
Atty. General: Norman C. Gorsuch, D (to Dec. 1986)
Organized as territory: 1912
Entered Union & (rank): Jan. 3, 1959 (49)
Constitution ratified: April 24, 1956
Motto: North to the Future
State flower: Forget-me-not
State tree: Sitka spruce
State bird: Willow ptarmigan
State fish: King salmon
State song: "Alaska's Flag"
Nickname: The state is commonly called "The Last Frontier" or "Land of the Midnight Sun"
Origin of name: Corruption of Aleut word meaning "great land" or "that which the sea breaks against"
1980 population (1980 census) & (rank): 401,851 (50)
1983 est. population (July) & (rank): 479,000 (50)
1984 land area & (rank): 570,833 sq mi. (1,478,458 sq km) (1)
Geographic center: 60 mi. NW of Mt. McKinley
Number of boroughs: 10
Largest cities (1980 census): Anchorage, 174,431; Fairbanks, 22,645; Juneau, 19,528; Sitka, 7,803; Ketchikan, 7,198; Kodiak, 4,756; Bethel, 3,576
State forests: None
State parks: 5; 59 waysides and areas (3.3 million ac.)
General revenue (1982–83): $4,024,700,000
General expenditures (1982–83): $4,295,636,000

Vitus Bering, a Dane working for the Russians, and Alexei Chirikov discovered the Alaskan mainland and the Aleutian Islands in 1741. The tremendous land mass of Alaska—equal to one fifth of the continental U.S.—was unexplored in 1867 when Secretary of State William Seward arranged for its purchase from the Russians for $7,200,000. The transfer of the territory took place on Oct. 18, 1867. Despite a price of about two cents an acre, the purchase was widely ridiculed as "Seward's Folly." The first official census (1880) reported a total of 33,426 Alaskans, all but 430 being of aboriginal stock. The Gold Rush of 1898 resulted in a mass influx of more than 30,000 people. Since then, Alaska has returned billions of dollars' worth of products to the U.S.

In 1968, a large oil and gas reservoir near Prudhoe Bay on the Arctic Coast was found. The Prudhoe Bay reservoir, with an estimated recoverable 10 billion barrels of oil and 27 trillion cubic feet of gas, is twice as large as any other oil field in North America. The Trans-Alaska pipeline was completed in 1977 at a cost of $7.7 billion. On June 20, oil started flowing through the 800-mile-long pipeline from Prudhoe Bay to the port of Valdez.

Other industries important to Alaska's economy are fisheries, wood and wood products, and furs.

Denali National Park and Mendenhall Glacier in North Tongass National Forest are of interest, as is the large totem pole collection at Sitka National Historical Park. The Katmai National Park includes the "Valley of Ten Thousand Smokes," an area of active volcanoes.

ARIZONA

Capital: Phoenix
Governor: Bruce Babbitt, D (to Jan. 1987)
Secy. of State: Rose Mofford, D (to Jan. 1987)
Atty. General: Bob Corbin, R (to Jan. 1987)
State Treasurer: Ray Rottas, R (to Jan. 1987)
Organized as territory: Feb. 24, 1863
Entered Union & (rank): Feb. 14, 1912 (48)
Present constitution adopted: 1911
Motto: *Ditat Deus* (God enriches)
State flower: Flower of saguaro cactus (1931)
State bird: Cactus wren (1931)
State colors: Blue and old gold (1915)
State song: "Arizona," a march song (1919)
State tree: Paloverde (1957)
Nickname: Grand Canyon State
Origin of name: From the Indian "Arizonac," meaning "little spring"
1980 population (1980 census) & (rank): 2,718,425 (29)
1983 est. population (July) & (rank): 2,963,000 (28)
1984 land area & (rank): 113,508 sq mi. (293,986 sq km) (6)
Geographic center: In Yavapai Co., 55 mi. ESE of Prescott
Number of counties: 15
Largest cities (1980 census): Phoenix, 789,704; Tucson, 330,537; Mesa, 152,453; Tempe, 106,743; Glendale, 97,172; Scottsdale, 86,622; Yuma, 42,481
State forests: None
State parks: 16
State revenue (1983): $2,621,508,141
State expenditure (1983): $2,526,546,677

Marcos de Niza, a Spanish Franciscan friar, was the first European to explore Arizona. He entered the area in 1539 in search of the mythical Seven Cities of Gold. Although he was followed a year later by another gold seeker, Francisco Vásquez de Coronado, most of the early settlement was for missionary purposes. In 1776 the Spanish established Fort Tucson. In 1848, after the Mexican War, most of the Arizona territory became part of the U.S., and the southern portion of the territory was added by the Gadsden Purchase in 1853.

In 1973 the world's biggest dam, the New Cornelia Tailings, was completed near Ajo.

Arizona history is rich in legends of America's Old West. It was here that the great Indian chiefs Geronimo and Cochise led their people against the frontiersmen. Tombstone, Ariz., was the site of the West's most famous shoot-out—the gunfight at the O.K. Corral. Today, Arizona has the largest U.S. Indian population; more than 14 tribes are represented on 19 reservations.

Manufacturing has become Arizona's most important industry. Principal products include electrical, communications, and aeronautical items. The state produces over half the country's copper. Agriculture is also important to the state's economy.

State attractions include such famous scenery as the Grand Canyon, the Petrified Forest, and the Painted Desert. Hoover Dam, Lake Mead, Fort Apache, and the reconstructed London Bridge at Lake Havasu City are of particular interest.

ARKANSAS

Capital: Little Rock
Governor: Bill Clinton, D (to Jan. 1985)
Lieut. Governor: Winston Bryant, D (to Jan. 1985)
Secy. of State: Paul Reviere, D (to Jan. 1985)
Atty. General: Steve Clark (to Jan. 1985)
Auditor of State: Julia Highes Jones, D (to Jan. 1985)
Treasurer of State: Jimmie Lou Fisher, D (to Jan. 1985)
Land Commissioner: Bill McCuen, D (to Jan. 1985)
Organized as territory: March 2, 1819
Entered Union & (rank): June 15, 1836 (25)
Present constitution adopted: 1874
Motto: *Regnat populus* (The people rule)
State flower: Apple Blossom (1901)
State tree: Pine (1939)
State bird: Mockingbird (1929)
State insect: Honeybee
State song: "Arkansas" (1963)
Nickname: Land of Opportunity
Origin of name: From the Quapaw Indians
1980 population (1980 census) & (rank): 2,286,435 (33)
1983 est. population (July) & (rank): 2,328,000 (33)
1984 land area & (rank): 52,078 sq mi. (134,883 sq km) (27)
Geographic center: In Pulaski Co., 12 mi. NW of Little Rock
Number of counties: 75
Largest cities (1980 census): Little Rock, 158,461; Fort Smith, 71,626; North Little Rock, 64,288; Pine Bluff, 56,636; Fayetteville, 36,608; Hot Springs, 35,781
State forests: None
State parks: 44
State tax receipts (1982): $1,092,094,538
Taxes from all sources (1982): $2,202,889,587
State general expenditure (1982): $2,198,286,251

Hernando de Soto, in 1541, was among the early European explorers to visit the territory. It was a Frenchman, Henri de Tonty, who in 1686 founded the first permanent white settlement—the Arkansas Post. In 1803 the area was acquired by the U.S. as part of the Louisiana Purchase.

Food products are the state's largest employing sector, with lumber and wood products a close second. Arkansas is also a leader in the production of cotton, rice, and soybeans. The state produces 97% of the nation's high-grade domestic bauxite ore—the source of aluminum. It also has the country's only active diamond mine; located near Murfreesboro, it is operated as a tourist attraction.

Hot Springs National Park is a major state attraction. Its 47 curative springs flow at an average temperature of 147° F year round. Blanchard Springs Caverns, the Arkansas Territorial Capitol Restoration at Little Rock, and Dogpatch U.S.A. near Harrison are of interest. There are two large national forests in Arkansas—the Ouachita and the Ozark—and one of the nation's smallest—the St. Francis.

CALIFORNIA

Capital: Sacramento
Governor: George Deukmejian, R (to Jan. 1987)
Lieut. Governor: Leo McCarthy, D (to Jan. 1987)
Secy. of State: March Fong Eu, D (to Jan. 1987)
Controller: Ken Cory, D (to Jan. 1987)
Atty. General: John Van de Kamp, D (to Jan. 1987)
Treasurer: Jesse M. Unruh, D (to Jan. 1987)
Entered Union & (rank): Sept. 9, 1850 (31)
Present constitution adopted: 1879
Motto: *Eureka* (I have found it)
State flower: Golden poppy (1903)
State tree: California redwoods *(Sequoia sempervirens & Sequoia gigantea)* (1937 & 1953)
State bird: California valley quail (1931)
State animal: California grizzly bear (1953)
State fish: California golden trout (1947)
State insect: California dog-face butterfly (1972)
State colors: Blue and gold (1951)
State song: "I Love You, California" (1951)
Nickname: Golden State
Origin of name: From a book, *Las Sergas de Esplandián,* by Garcia Ordóñez de Montalvo, c. 1500
1980 population (1980 census) & (rank): 23,667,565 (1)
1983 est. population (July) & (rank): 25,174,000 (1)
1984 land area & (rank): 156,299 sq mi. (404,815 sq km) (3)
Geographic center: In Madera Co., 35 mi. NE of Madera
Number of counties: 58
Largest cities (1980 census): Los Angeles, 2,966,850; San Diego, 875,538; San Francisco, 678,974; San Jose, 629,442; Long Beach, 361,334; Oakland, 339,337
State forests: 8 (70,283 ac.)
State parks and beaches: 180 (723,000 ac.)
State general revenue (1981–82): $26,026,000,000
State general expenditure (1981–82): $25,758,105,000

Although California was sighted by Spanish navigator Juan Rodríguez Cabrillo in 1542, its first Spanish mission (at San Diego) was not established until 1769. California became a U.S. Territory in 1847 when Mexico surrendered it to John C. Frémont. On Jan. 24, 1848, James W. Marshall discovered gold at Sutter's Mill, starting the California Gold Rush and bringing settlers to the state in large numbers.

In 1964, the U.S. Census Bureau estimated that California had become the most populous state, surpassing New York. California also leads the country in personal income and consumer expenditures.

Leading industries include manufacturing (transportation equipment, machinery, and electronic equipment), agriculture, and tourism. Principal natural resources include petroleum, cement, and natural gas.

The Bank of America National Trust and Savings Association, founded by the Giannini family, ranks first or second in the world.

Death Valley, in the southeast, is 282 feet below sea level, the lowest point in the nation; and Mt. Whitney (14,495 ft) is the highest point in the contiguous 48 states. Lassen Peak is one of two active U.S. volcanos outside of Alaska and Hawaii; its last eruptions were recorded in 1917. The General Sherman Tree in Sequoia National Park is estimated to be about 3,500 years old and a stand of bristlecone pine trees in the White Mountains may be over 4,000 years old.

Other points of interest include Yosemite National Park, Disneyland, Hollywood, the Golden Gate Bridge, San Simeon State Park, and Point Reyes National Seashore.

COLORADO

Capital: Denver
Governor: Richard D. Lamm, D (to Jan. 1987)
Lieut. Governor: Nancy E. Dick, D (to Jan. 1987)
Secy. of State: Natalie Meyer, R (to Jan 1987)
Treasurer: Roy Romer, D (to Jan. 1987)
Controller: James A. Stroup
Atty. General: Duane Woodard, R (to Jan. 1987)
Organized as territory: Feb. 28, 1861
Entered Union & (rank): Aug. 1, 1876 (38)
Present constitution adopted: 1876
Motto: *Nil sine Numine* (Nothing without Providence)
State flower: Rocky Mountain columbine (1899)
State tree: Colorado blue spruce (1939)
State bird: Lark bunting (1931)
State animal: Rocky Mountain bighorn sheep
State colors: Blue and white (1911)
State gemstone: Aquamarine (1971)
State song: "Where the Columbines Grow" (1915)
Nickname: Centennial State
Origin of name: From the Spanish, "ruddy" or "red"
1980 population (1980 census) & (rank): 2,889,735 (28)
1983 est. population (July) & rank: 3,139,000 (26)
1984 land area & (rank): 103,595 sq mi. (268,311 sq km) (8)
Geographic center: In Park Co., 30 mi. NW of Pikes Peak
Number of counties: 63
Largest cities (1980 census): Denver, 492,365; Colorado Springs, 214,821; Aurora, 158,588; Lakewood, 113,808; Pueblo, 101,686; Arvada, 84,576; Boulder, 76,685
State forests: 1 (71,000 ac.)
Total state revenue (1981–82): $2,304,308,443
Total state expenditure (1981–82): $2,358,266,761

First visited by Spanish explorers in the 1500s, the territory was claimed for Spain by Juan de Ulibarri in 1706. The U.S. obtained eastern Colorado as part of the Louisiana Purchase in 1803, the central portion in 1845 with the admission of Texas as a state, and the western part in 1848 as a result of the Mexican War.

Colorado has the highest mean elevation of any state, with more than 1,000 Rocky Mountain peaks over 10,000 feet high and 54 towering above 14, 000 feet. Pikes Peak, the most famous of these mountains, was discovered by U.S. Army Lieut. Zebulon M. Pike in 1806.

Gold was first discovered near present-day Denver in 1858 and at Cripple Creek in 1891. Rich silver deposits were also found in 1875.

Once primarily a mining and agricultural state, today Colorado draws the largest segment of its income from manufacturing. Denver is a leader in electronics and space-age industry. Pueblo, the "Pittsburgh of the West," makes iron, steel, brick, tile, and foundry products.

Rich in natural resources, Colorado now produces most of the world's molybdenum. Uranium, vanadium, gold, silver, lead, tin, zinc, and other minerals are also mined. Colorado's highly developed irrigation system promotes farming of wheat, hay, beans, sugar beets, corn, potatoes, barley, and truck vegetables. Cattle and sheep raising is also important.

Tourism has developed into a major industry largely because of Colorado's magnificent scenery. Among the major attractions are Rocky Mountain National Park, Garden of the Gods, Great Sand Dunes and Dinosaur National Monuments, Pikes Peak and Mt. Evans Highways, and Mesa Verde National Park (prehistoric cliff dwellings).

Colorado Springs, with the nearby U.S. Air Force Academy, is probably the most popular tourist center in the Rocky Mountains, while Aspen and Vail have become leading ski resorts.

CONNECTICUT

Capital: Hartford
Governor: William A. O'Neill, D (to Jan. 1987)
Lieut. Governor: Joseph J. Fauliso, D (to Jan. 1987)
Secy. of State: Julia H. Tashjian, D (to Jan. 1987)
Comptroller: J. Edward Caldwell, D (to Jan. 1987)
Treasurer: Henry E. Parker, D (to Jan. 1987)
Atty. General: Joseph I. Lieberman, D (to Jan. 1987)
Entered Union & (rank): Jan. 9, 1788 (5)
Present constitution adopted: Dec. 30, 1965
Motto: *Qui transtulit sustinet* (He who transplanted still sustains)
State flower: Mountain laurel (1907)
State tree: White Oak (1947)
State animal: Sperm whale (1975)
State bird: American robin (1943)
State insect: Praying mantis (1977)
State mineral: Garnet (1977)
State song: "Yankee Doodle" (1978)
State ship: USS Nautilus (SSN571) (1983)
Official designation: *Constitution State* (1959)
Nickname: Nutmeg State
Origin of name: From an Indian word (Quinnehtukqut) meaning "beside the long tidal river"
1980 population (1980 census) & (rank): 3,107,576 (25)
1983 est. population (July) & (rank): 3,138,000 (27)
1984 land area & (rank): 4,872 sq mi. (12,618 km) (48)
Geographic center: In Hartford Co., at East Berlin
Number of counties: 8
Largest cities (1980 census): Bridgeport, 142,546; Hartford, 136,392; New Haven, 126,109; Waterbury, 103,266; Stamford, 102,453; Norwalk, 77,767
State forests: 30 (138,029 ac.)
State parks: 87 (29,214 ac.)
State general revenue (1982–83): $7,210,000,000
State general expenditure (1982–83): $7,134,000,000

The Dutch navigator, Adriaen Block, was the first European of record to explore the area, sailing up the Connecticut River in 1614. In 1633, Dutch colonists built a fort and trading post near present-day Hartford, but soon lost control to English Puritans migrating south from the Massachusetts Bay Colony.

English settlements, established in the 1630s at Windsor, Wethersfield, and Hartford, united in 1639 to form the Connecticut Colony and adopted the *Fundamental Orders,* considered the world's first written constitution.

The colony's royal charter of 1662 was exceptionally liberal. When Gov. Edmund Andros tried to seize it in 1687, it was hidden in the Hartford Oak, commemorated in Charter Oak Place.

Connecticut played a prominent role in the Revolutionary War, serving as the Continental Army's major supplier. Sometimes called the "Arsenal of the Nation," the state became one of the most industrialized in the nation. Its early business and industrial pioneers included Eli Whitney, Samuel Colt, and Charles Goodyear.

Today, Connecticut factories produce weapons, sewing machines, jet engines, helicopters, motors, hardware and tools, cutlery, clocks, locks, ball bearings, silverware, and submarines. Hartford, which has the oldest U.S. newspaper still being published—the *Courant,* established 1764—is the insurance capital of the nation.

Poultry, fruit, and dairy products account for the largest portion of farm income, and Connecticut shade-grown tobacco is acknowledged to be the nation's most valuable crop, per acre.

Connecticut is a popular resort area with its 250-mile Long Island Sound shoreline and many inland lakes. Among the major points of interest are the American Shakespeare Theatre in Stratford, Yale University's Gallery of Fine Arts and Peabody Museum. Other famous museums include the P.T. Barnum, Winchester Gun, and American Clock and Watch. The town of Mystic features a recreated 19th-century New England seaport and the Mystic Marinelife Aquarium.

DELAWARE

Capital: Dover
Governor: Pierre S. du Pont IV, R (to Jan. 1985)
Lieut. Governor: Michael N. Castle (to Jan. 1985)
Secy. of State: Glenn C. Kenton, R (Pleasure of Governor)
State Treasurer: Janet C. Rzewnicki, R (to Jan. 1986)
Atty. General: Charles M. Oberly III, D (to Jan. 1986)
Entered Union & (rank): Dec. 7, 1787 (1)
Present constitution adopted: 1897
Motto: Liberty and independence
State colors: Colonial blue and buff
State flower: Peach blossom
State tree: American holly
State bird: Blue Hen chicken
State insect: Ladybug
State song: "Our Delaware"
Nicknames: Diamond State; First State
Origin of name: From Delaware River and Bay; named in turn for Sir Thomas West, Lord De La Warr
1980 population (1980 census) & (rank): 594,317 (47)
1983 est. population (July) & (rank): 606,000 (47)
1984 land area & (rank): 1,932 sq mi. (5,005 sq km) (49)
Geographic center: In Kent Co., 11 mi. S of Dover
Number of counties: 3
Largest cities (1980 census): Wilmington, 70,195; Newark, 25,247; Dover, 23,512; Elsmere, 6,493; Milford, 5,356; Seaford, 5,256; New Castle, 4,709; Lewes, 2,197
State forests: 3 (6,149 ac.)
State parks: 10
State receipts (1983): $686,649,000[1]
State disbursements (1983): $688,548,600[1]

1. General Funds, do not include Federal funds.

Henry Hudson, sailing under the Dutch flag, is credited with Delaware's discovery in 1609. The following year, Capt. Samuel Argall of Virginia named Delaware for his colony's governor, Thomas West, Baron De La Warr. An attempted Dutch settlement failed in 1631. Swedish colonization began at Fort Christina (now Wilmington) in 1638, but New Sweden fell to Dutch forces led by New Netherlands' Gov. Peter Stuyvesant in 1655.

England took over the area in 1664 and it was transferred to William Penn as the southern Three Counties in 1682. Semiautonomous after 1704, Delaware fought as a separate state in the American Revolution and became the first state to ratify the constitution in 1787.

During the Civil War, although a slave state, Delaware did not secede from the Union.

In 1802, Éleuthère Irénée du Pont established a gunpowder mill near Wilmington that laid the foundation for Delaware's huge chemical industry. Delaware's manufactured products now also include vulcanized fiber, glazed kid and morocco leathers, textiles, paper, dental supplies, metal products, machinery, machine tools, and automobiles.

Delaware also grows a great variety of fruits and vegetables and is a U.S. pioneer in the food-canning industry. Corn, soybeans, potatoes, and hay are important crops. Delaware's broiler chicken farms supply the big Eastern markets, and fishing is another major industry.

Points of interest include the Fort Christina Monument, Hagley Museum, Holy Trinity Church (erected in 1698, the oldest Protestant church in the United States still in use), and Winterthur Museum, in and near Wilmington; central New Castle, an almost unchanged late 18th-century capital; and the Delaware Museum of Natural History.

Popular recreation areas include Cape Henlopen, Delaware Seashore, Trapp Pond State Park, and Rehoboth Beach.

DISTRICT OF COLUMBIA

See listing at end of *50 Largest Cities of the United States.*

FLORIDA

Capital: Tallahassee
Governor: Bob Graham, D (to Jan. 1987)
Lieut. Governor: Wayne Mixson, D (to Jan. 1987)
Secy. of State: George Firestone, D (to Jan. 1987)
Comptroller: Gerald Lewis, D (to Jan. 1987)
Commissioner of Agriculture: Doyle Connor, D (to Jan. 1987)
Atty. General: Jim Smith, D (to Jan. 1987)
Organized as territory: March 30, 1822
Entered Union & (rank): March 3, 1845 (27)
Present constitution adopted: 1969
Motto: In God we trust (1868)
State flower: Orange blossom (1909)
State bird: Mockingbird (1927)
State song: "Suwannee River" (1935)
Nickname: Sunshine State (1970)
Origin of name: From the Spanish, meaning "feast of flowers" (Easter)
1980 population (1980 census) & (rank): 9,746,342 (7)
1983 est. population (July) & (rank): 10,680,000 (7)
1984 land area & (rank): 54,153 sq mi. (140,256 sq km) (26)
Geographic center: In Hernando Co., 12 mi. NNW of Brooksville
Number of counties: 67
Largest cities (1980 census): Jacksonville, 540,920; Miami, 346,865; Tampa, 271,523; St. Petersburg, 238,647; Fort Lauderdale, 153,279; Hialeah, 159,887
State forests: 4 (306,881 ac.)
State parks: 88 (215,820 ac.)
State tax receipts (1982–83): $6,339,483,236
Other state revenue (1982–83): $14,519,005,260
State expenditures (1982–83): $20,681,611,074

In 1513, Ponce de Leon, seeking the mythical "Fountain of Youth," named Florida and claimed it for Spain. Later, Florida would be held at different times by Spain, France, and England until Spain finally sold it to the United States in 1819.

Florida's early 19th-century history as a U.S. territory was scarred by savage wars with the Seminole Indians that did not end until 1842.

One of the nation's fastest-growing states, Florida's population has gone from 2.8 million in 1950 to more than 10.6 million today.

Florida's economy rests on a solid base of tourism, manufacturing, and agriculture. The state entertained more than 35.9 million visitors, who spent about $16.5 billion, in 1979.

Oranges and grapefruit lead Florida's crop list, followed by sugar cane, tomatoes, beans, celery, potatoes, field corn, honey, watermelons, limes, and mangoes. Forestry, truck gardening, commercial fishing, and cattle raising are leading industries. Deep-sea fishing for sport is a leading tourist industry.

Florida is expanding in all industrial areas with the greatest development taking place in the research-oriented Space Age manufacturing. The state produces 80% of the nation's phosphate.

Major tourist attractions are Miami Beach, Palm Beach, St. Augustine (founded in 1565 and the oldest, permanent city in the U.S.), Daytona Beach, and Fort Lauderdale, on the East Coast. West Coast resorts include Sarasota, Tampa, Key West, and St. Petersburg. Disney World, located on a 27, 000-acre site near Orlando, is a popular attraction.

The John F. Kennedy Space Center at Cape Canaveral, and Everglades National Park, a 5,000-square-mile preserve, also draw many visitors.

GEORGIA

Capital: Atlanta
Governor: Joe Frank Harris, D (to Jan. 1987)
Lieut. Governor: Zell Miller, D (to Jan. 1987)
Secy. of State: Max Cleland, D (to Jan. 1987)
Comptroller General: Johnnie Caldwell, D (to Jan. 1987)
Atty. General: Michael J. Bowers, D (to Jan. 1987)
Entered Union & (rank): Jan. 2, 1788 (4)
Present constitution adopted: 1977
Motto: Wisdom, justice, and moderation
State flower: Cherokee rose (1916)
State tree: Live oak (1937)
State bird: Brown thrasher (1935)
State song: "Georgia on my Mind" (1922)
Nicknames: Peach State, Empire State of the South
Origin of name: In honor of George II of England
1980 population (1980 census) & (rank): 5,463,105 (13)
1983 est. population (July) & (rank): 5,732,000 (12)
1984 land area & (rank): 58,056 sq mi. (150,365 sq km) (21)
Geographic center: In Twiggs Co., 18 mi. SE of Macon
Number of counties: 159
Largest cities (1980 census): Atlanta, 425,022; Columbus, 169,441; Savannah, 141,634; Macon, 116,860; Albany, 74,550; Augusta, 47,532; Athens, 42,549; Warner Robins, 39,893
State forests: 25,258,000 ac. (67% of total state area)
State parks: 53 (42,600 ac.)
State revenue receipts (1983): $3,593,462,746
State revenue distribution (1983): $3,674,432,157

Hernando de Soto, the Spanish explorer, first traveled parts of Georgia in 1540. British claims later conflicted with those of Spain. After obtaining a royal charter, Gen. James Oglethorpe established the first permanent settlement in Georgia in 1733 as a refuge for English debtors. In 1742, Oglethorpe defeated Spanish invaders in the Battle of Bloody Marsh.

A Confederate stronghold, Georgia was the scene of extensive military action during the Civil War. Union General William T. Sherman burned Atlanta and destroyed a 60-mile wide path to the coast where he captured Savannah in 1864.

The largest state east of the Mississippi, Georgia is typical of the changing South with an ever-increasing industrial development. Atlanta, largest city in the state, is the communications and transportation center for the Southeast and the area's chief distributor of goods.

Georgia leads the nation in the production of paper and board, tufted textile products, and processed chicken. Other major manufactured products are transportation equipment, food products, apparel, and chemicals.

Important agricultural products are corn, cotton, tobacco, soybeans, eggs, and peaches. Georgia produces twice as many peanuts as the next leading state. From its vast stands of pine come more than half the world's resins and turpentine and 74.4% of the U.S. supply. Georgia is also a leader in the production of marble, kaolin, barite, and bauxite.

Principal tourist attractions in Georgia include the Okefenokee National Wildlife Refuge, Andersonville Prison Park and National Cemetery, Chickamauga and Chattanooga National Military Park, the Little White House at Warm Springs where Pres. Franklin D. Roosevelt died in 1945, Sea Island, the enormous Confederate Memorial at Stone Mountain, Kennesaw Mountain National Battlefield Park, and Cumberland Island National Seashore.

HAWAII

Capital: Honolulu (on Oahu)
Governor: George R. Ariyoshi, D (to Dec. 1986)
Lieut. Governor: John Waihee, D (to Dec. 1986)
Comptroller: Hideo Murakami, (to Dec. 1986)
Atty. General: Tany S. Hong, (to Dec. 1986)
Organized as territory: 1900
Entered Union & (rank): Aug. 21, 1959 (50)
Motto: *Ua Mau Ke Ea O Ka Aina I Ka Pono* (The life of the land is perpetuated in righteousness)
State flower: Hibiscus
State song: "Hawaii Ponoi"
State bird: Nene (Hawaiian goose)
Nickname: Aloha State
Origin of name: Uncertain. The islands may have been named by Hawaii Loa, their traditional discoverer. Or they may have been named after Hawaii or Hawaiki, the traditional home of the Polynesians.
1980 population (1980 census) & (rank): 964,691 (39)
1983 est. population (July) & (rank): 1,023,000 (39)
1984 land area & (rank): 6,425 sq mi. (16,641 sq km) (47)
Geographic center: In Hawaii Co., off Maui Island
Number of counties: 4
Largest cities (1980 census): Honolulu, 365,048; Hilo, 37,017[1]
State parks and historic sites: 72
Total state government revenues (1981–82): $1,989,461,000
Total state government expenditures (1981–82): $1,958,473,000

1. There are no political boundaries to Honolulu or any other place, but statistical boundaries are assigned under state law.

First settled by Polynesians sailing from other Pacific islands in the 6th century, Hawaii was visited in 1778 by British Captain James Cook who called the group the Sandwich Islands.

Hawaii was a native kingdom throughout most of the 19th century when the expansion of the vital sugar industry (pineapple came after 1898) meant increasing U.S. business and political involvement. In 1893, Queen Liliuokalani was deposed and a year later the Republic of Hawaii was established with Sanford B. Dole as president. Then, following its annexation in 1898, Hawaii became a U.S. Territory in 1900.

The Japanese attack on the naval base at Pearl Harbor on Dec. 7, 1941, was directly responsible for U.S. entry into World War II.

Hawaii, 2,100 miles west-southwest of San Francisco, is a 1,600-mile chain of islets and eight main islands—Hawaii, Kahoolawe, Maui, Lanai, Molokai, Oahu, Kauai, and Niihau. Kure Atoll, an islet in the Northwestern Hawaiian Islands, is administratively part of Hawaii.

The temperature is mild and Hawaii's soil is fertile for tropical fruits and vegetables. Cane sugar and pineapple are the chief products. Hawaii also grows coffee, bananas and nuts. The tourist business is Hawaii's largest source of outside income.

Hawaii's highest peak is Mauna Kea (13,796 ft.). Mauna Loa (13,677 ft.) is the largest volcanic mountain in the world in cubic content.

Among the major points of interest are Hawaii Volcanoes National Park (Hawaii), Haleakala National Park (Maui), Puuhonua o Honaunau National Historical Park (Hawaii), Polynesian Cultural Center (Oahu), the U.S.S. *Arizona* Memorial at Pearl Harbor, and Iolani Palace (the only royal palace in the U.S.), Bishop Museum, and Waikiki Beach (all in Honolulu).

IDAHO

Capital: Boise
Governor: John V. Evans, D (to Jan. 1986)
Lieut. Governor: David Leroy, R (to Jan. 1986)
Secy. of State: Pete T. Cenarrusa, R (to Jan. 1986)
State Auditor: Joe R. Williams, D (to Jan. 1986)
Atty. General: James Jones, R (to Jan. 1986)
Organized as territory: March 3, 1863
Entered Union & (rank): July 3, 1890 (43)
Present constitution adopted: 1890
Motto: *Esto perpetua* (May you last forever)
State flower: Syringa (1931)
State tree: White pine (1935)
State bird: Mountain bluebird (1931)
State horse: Appaloosa (1975)
State gem: Star garnet (1967)
State song: "Here We Have Idaho"
Nicknames: Gem State; Spud State; Panhandle State
Origin of name: Means "Gem of the Mountains"
1980 population (1980 census) & (rank): 944,038 (41)
1983 est. population (July) & (rank): 989,000 (40)
1984 land area & (rank): 82,413 sq mi. (213,449 sq km) (11)
Geographic center: In Custer Co., at Custer, SW of Challis
Number of counties: 44, plus small part of Yellowstone National Park
Largest cities (1980 census): Boise, 102,160; Pocatello, 46,340; Idaho Falls, 39,590; Lewiston, 27,986; Twin Falls, 26,209; Nampa, 25,112; Coeur d'Alene, 20,054
State forests: 881,000 ac.
State parks: 21 (38,487 ac.)
State revenue (Fiscal 1983): $4,218,000,000
State expenditure (Fiscal 1983): $4,236,000,000

After its acquisition by the U.S. as part of the Louisiana Purchase in 1803, the region was explored by Meriwether Lewis and William Clark in 1805–06. Northwest boundary disputes with Great Britain were settled by the Oregon Treaty in 1846 and the first permanent U.S. settlement in Idaho was established by the Mormons at Franklin in 1860.

After gold was discovered on Orofino Creek in 1860, prospectors swarmed into the territory, but left little more than a number of ghost towns.

In the 1870s, growing white occupation of Indian lands led to a series of battles between U.S. forces and the Nez Percé, Bannock, and Sheepeater tribes.

Mining, lumbering, and irrigation farming have been important for years. Idaho produces more than one third of all the silver mined in the U.S. It also ranks high among the states in antimony, lead, cobalt, garnet, phosphate rock, vanadium, zinc, and mercury.

Idaho's most impressive growth began when World War II military needs made processing agricultural products a big industry, particularly the dehydrating and freezing of potatoes. The state produces about one fourth of the nation's potato crop, as well as wheat, apples, corn, barley, sugar beets, and hops. More money is made from livestock in the state than from all agricultural products.

With the growth of winter sports, tourism now outranks mining in dollar revenue. Idaho's many streams and lakes provide fishing, camping, and boating sites. The nation's largest elk herds draw hunters from all over the world and the famed Sun Valley resort attracts thousands of visitors to its swimming and skiing facilities.

Other points of interest are the Craters of the Moon National Monument; Nez Percé National Historic Park, which includes many sites visited by Lewis and Clark; and the State Historical Museum in Boise.

ILLINOIS

Capital: Springfield
Governor: James R. Thompson, R (to Jan. 1987)
Lieut. Governor: George H. Ryan, R (to Jan. 1987)
Secy. of State: Jim Edgar, R (to Jan. 1987)
Comptroller: Roland J. Burris, D (to Jan. 1987)
Atty. General: Neil F. Hartigan, D (to Jan. 1987)
Treasurer: James H. Donnewald, D (to Jan. 1987)
Organized as territory: Feb. 3, 1809
Entered Union & (rank): Dec. 3, 1818 (21)
Present constitution adopted: 1970
Motto: State sovereignty, national union
State flower: Violet (1908)
State tree: White oak (1973)
State bird: Cardinal (1929)
State insect: Monarch butterfly
State song: "Illinois" (1925)
State slogan: Land of Lincoln
State mineral: Fluorite (1965)
Nickname: Prairie State
Origin of name: From an Indian word and French suffix meaning "tribe of superior men"
1980 population (1980 census) & (rank): 11,426,518 (5)
1983 est. population (July) & (rank): 11,486,000 (5)
1984 land area & (rank): 55,645 sq mi. (144,120 sq km) (24)
Geographic center: In Logan Co., 28 mi. NE of Springfield
Number of counties: 102
Largest cities (1980 census): Chicago, 3,005,072; Rockford, 139,712; Peoria, 124,160; Springfield, 100,054; Decatur, 94,081; Aurora, 81,293; Joliet, 77, 956
Public use areas: 187 (275,000 ac.), incl. state parks, memorials, forests and conservation areas
Total state revenue, all funds, all sources (Fiscal 1983): $14,575,000,000
Total state expenditures, all funds (Fiscal 1983): $14,671,000,000

French explorers Marquette and Joliet, in 1673, were the first Europeans of record to visit the region. In 1699 French settlers established the first permanent settlement at Cahokia, near present-day East St. Louis.

Great Britain obtained the region at the end of the French and Indian War in 1763. The area figured prominently in frontier struggles during the Revolutionary War and in Indian wars during the early 19th century.

Significant episodes in the state's early history include the growing migration of Eastern settlers following the opening of the Erie Canal in 1825; the Black Hawk War, which virtually ended the Indian troubles in the area; and the rise of Abraham Lincoln from farm laborer to President-elect.

Today, Illinois stands high in manufacturing, coal mining, agriculture, and oil production. The sprawling Chicago district (including a slice of Indiana) is a great iron and steel producer, meat packer, grain exchange, and railroad center. Chicago is also famous as a busy long-flight airport city and Great Lakes port.

Illinois ranks first in the nation in export of agricultural products and second in hog production. An important dairying state, Illinois is also a leader in corn, oats, wheat, barley, rye, truck vegetables, and the nursery products.

The state manufactures a great variety of industrial and consumer products: railroad cars, clothing, furniture, tractors, liquor, watches, and farm implements are just some of the items made in its factories and plants.

Central Illinois is noted for shrines and memorials associated with the life of Abraham Lincoln. In Springfield are the Lincoln Home, the Lincoln Tomb, and the restored Old State Capitol. Other points of interest are the home of Mormon leader Joseph Smith in Nauvoo and, in Chicago: the Art Institute, Field Museum, Museum of Science and Industry, Shedd Aquarium, Adler Planetarium, Merchandise Mart, and Chicago Portage National Historic Site.

INDIANA

Capital: Indianapolis
Governor: Robert D. Orr, R (to Jan. 1985)
Lieut. Governor: John M. Muntz, R (to Jan. 1985)
Secy. of State: Edwin J. Simcox, R (to Dec. 1986)
Treasurer: Julian L. Ridlen, R (to Feb. 1987)
Atty. General: Linley E. Pearson, R (to Jan. 1985)
Auditor: Otis E. Cox, D (to Dec. 1986)
Organized as territory: May 7, 1800
Entered Union & (rank): Dec. 11, 1816 (19)
Present constitution adopted: 1851
Motto: The Crossroads of America
State flower: Peony (1957)
State tree: Tulip tree (1931)
State bird: Cardinal (1933)
State song: "On the Banks of the Wabash, Far Away" (1913)
Nickname: Hoosier State
Origin of name: Meaning "land of Indians"

1980 population (1980 census) & (rank): 5,490,260 (12)
1983 est. population (July) & (rank): 5,479,000 (14)
1984 land area & (rank): 35,932 sq mi. (93,064 sq km) (38)
Geographic center: In Boone Co., 14 mi. NNW of Indianapolis
Number of Counties: 92
Largest cities (1980 census): Indianapolis, 700,807; Fort Wayne, 172,028; Gary, 151,953; Evansville, 130,496; South Bend, 109,727; Hammond, 93,714; Muncie, 77,216
State parks: 19 (54,126 ac.)
State memorials: 16 (941.977 ac.)
State general revenue (1982–83): $2,463,000,000
State general expenditure (1982–83): $1,178,000,000

First explored for France by La Salle in 1679–80, the region figured importantly in the Franco-British struggle for North America that culminated with British victory in 1763.

George Rogers Clark led American forces against the British in the area during the Revolutionary War and, prior to becoming a state, Indiana was the scene of frequent Indian uprisings until the victory of Gen. William Henry Harrison at Tippecanoe in 1811.

Indiana's 41-mile Lake Michigan waterfront—one of the world's great industrial centers—turns out iron, steel, and oil products. Products include automobile parts and accessories, mobile homes and recreational vehicles, truck and bus bodies, aircraft engines, farm machinery, and fabricated structural steel. Phonograph records, wood office furniture, and pharmaceuticals are also manufactured.

The state is a leader in agriculture with corn the principal crop. Hogs, soybeans, wheat, oats, rye, tomatoes, onions, and poultry also contribute heavily to Indiana's agricultural output. Much of the building limestone used in the U.S. is quarried in Indiana which is also a large producer of coal.

Wyandotte Cave, one of the largest in the U.S., is located in Crawford County in southern Indiana and West Baden and French Lick are well known for their mineral springs. Other attractions include Indiana Dunes National Lakeshore, Indianapolis Motor Speedway, Lincoln Boyhood National Memorial, and the George Rogers Clark National Historical Park.

IOWA

Capital: Des Moines
Governor: Terry E. Branstad, R (to Jan. 1987)
Lieut. Governor: Robert T. Anderson, D (to Jan. 1987)
Secy. of State: Mary Jane Odell, R (to Jan. 1987)
Treasurer: Michael L. Fitzgerald, D (to Jan. 1987)
Atty. General: Tom Miller, D (to Jan. 1987)
Organized as territory: June 12, 1838
Entered Union & (rank): Dec. 28, 1846 (29)
Present constitution adopted: 1857
Motto: Our liberties we prize and our rights we will maintain
State flower: Wild rose (1897)
State bird: Eastern goldfinch (1933)
State colors: Red, white, and blue (in state flag)
State song: "Song of Iowa"
Nickname: Hawkeye State
Origin of name: Probably from an Indian word meaning "I-o-w-a, this is the place," or "The Beautiful Land"
1980 population (1980 census) & (rank): 2,913,808 (27)
1983 est. population (July) & (rank): 2,905,000 (29)
1984 land area & (rank): 55,965 sq mi. (144,950 sq km) (23)
Geographic center: In Story Co., 5 mi. NE of Ames
Number of counties: 99
Largest cities (1980 census): Des Moines, 191,003; Cedar Rapids, 110,243; Davenport, 103,264; Sioux City, 82,003; Waterloo, 75,985; Dubuque, 62,321; Council Bluffs, 56,449; Iowa City, 50,508; Ames, 45,775
State forests: 5 (28,000 ac.)
State parks: 95 (49,237)
Total revenue (1983): $4,961,100,000[1]
Total expenditures (1983): $4,817,300,000[1]

1. From all sources including state university tuition fees.

The first Europeans to visit the area were the French explorers, Father Jacques Marquette and Louis Joliet in 1673. The U.S. obtained control of the area in 1803 as part of the Louisiana Purchase.

During the first half of the 19th century, there was heavy fighting between white settlers and Indians. Lands were taken from the Indians after the Black Hawk War in 1832 and again in 1836 and 1837.

When Iowa became a state in 1846, its capital was Iowa City; the more centrally located Des Moines became the new capital in 1857. At that time, the state's present boundaries were also drawn.

Although Iowa produces a tenth of the nation's food supply, the value of Iowa's manufactured products is three times that of its agriculture. Major industries are food and associated products, non-electrical machinery, electrical equipment, printing and publishing, and fabricated products.

Iowa stands in a class by itself as an agricultural state. Its farms sell over $10 billion worth of crops and livestock annually. Iowa leads the nation in all livestock and hog marketings, with about 26% of the pork supply and 11% of the grain-fed cattle. Iowa's forests produce hardwood lumber, particularly walnut, and its mineral products include cement, limestone, sand, gravel, gypsum, and coal.

Tourist attractions include the Herbert Hoover birthplace and library near West Branch; the Amana Colonies; Fort Dodge Historical Museum, Fort, and Stockade; the Iowa State Fair at Des Moines in August; and the Effigy Mounds National Monument at Marquette, a prehistoric Indian burial site.

KANSAS

Capital: Topeka
Governor: John W. Carlin, D (to Jan. 1987)
Lieut. Governor: Tom Docking, D (to Jan. 1987)
Secy. of State: Jack H. Brier, R (to Jan. 1987)
Treasurer: Joan Finney, D (to Jan. 1987)
Atty. General: Robert T. Stephan, R (to Jan. 1987)
Organized as territory: May 30, 1854
Entered Union & (rank): Jan. 29, 1861 (34)
Present constitution adopted: 1859
Motto: *Ad astra per aspera* (To the stars through difficulties)
State flower: Sunflower (1903)
State tree: Cottonwood (1937)
State bird: Western meadow lark (1937)
State animal: Buffalo (1955)
State song: "Home on the Range" (1947)
State march: "The Kansas March" (1935)
Nicknames: Sunflower State; Jayhawk State
Origin of name: From a Siouan word meaning "people of the south wind"
1980 population (1980 census) & (rank): 2,364,236 (32)
1983 est. population (July) & (rank): 2,425,000 (32)

1984 land area & (rank): 81,781 sq mi. (211,814 sq km) (13)
Geographic center: In Barton Co., 15 mi. NE of Great Bend
Number of counties: 105
Largest cities (1980 census): Wichita, 279,835; Kansas City, 161,148; Topeka, 115,266; Overland Park, 81,784; Lawrence, 52,738; Salina, 41,843; Hutchinson, 40,284
State parks: 22 (14,394 ac.)
State operating revenue (1982-83): $3,045,456,000
State operating expenditure (1982-83): $2,921,865,000

Spanish explorer Francisco de Coronado, in 1541, is considered the first European to have traveled this region. La Salle's extensive land claims for France (1682) included present-day Kansas. Ceded to Spain by France in 1763, the territory reverted back to France in 1800 and was sold to the U.S. as part of the Louisiana Purchase in 1803.

Lewis and Clark, Zebulon Pike, and Stephen H. Long explored the region between 1803 and 1819. The first permanent settlements in Kansas were outposts—Fort Leavenworth (1827), Fort Scott (1842), and Fort Riley (1853)—established to protect travelers along the Santa Fe and Oregon Trails.

Just before the Civil War, the conflict between the pro- and anti-slavery forces earned the region the grim title "Bleeding Kansas."

Today, wheat fields, oil well derricks, herds of cattle, and grain storage elevators are chief features of the Kansas landscape. A leading wheat-growing state, Kansas also raises corn, sorghums, oats, barley, soybeans, and potatoes. Kansas stands high in petroleum production and mines zinc, coal, salt, and lead. It is also the nation's leading producer of helium.

Wichita is one of the nation's leading aircraft manufacturing centers, ranking first in production of private aircraft. Kansas City is an important transportation, milling, and meat-packing center.

Points of interest include the Kansas State Historical Society Museum at Topeka, the Eisenhower boyhood home and the new Eisenhower Memorial Museum and Presidential Library at Abilene, John Brown's cabin at Osawatomie, recreated Front Street in Dodge City, Fort Larned (once the most important military post on the Santa Fe Trail), and Fort Leavenworth and Fort Riley.

KENTUCKY

Capital: Frankfort
Governor: Martha Layne Collins, D (to Dec. 1987)
Lieut. Governor: Steven L. Beshear, D (to Dec. 1987)
Secy. of State: Drexell R. Davis, D (to Jan. 1988)
State Treasurer: Frances Jones Mills, D (to Jan. 1988)
State Auditor: Mary Ann Tobin, D (to Jan. 1988)
Atty. General: David Armstrong, D (to Jan. 1988)
Entered Union & (rank): June 1, 1792 (15)
Present constitution adopted: 1891
Motto: United we stand, divided we fall
State tree: Coffeetree
State flower: Goldenrod
State bird: Kentucky cardinal
State song: "My Old Kentucky Home"
Nickname: Bluegrass State
Origin of name: From an Iroquoian word "Ken-tah-ten" meaning "land of tomorrow"
1980 population (1980 census) & (rank): 3,660,257 (23)
1983 est. population (July) & (rank): 3,714,000 (23)
1984 land area & (rank): 39,669 sq mi. (102,743 sq km) (37)
Geographic center: In Marion Co., 3 mi. NNW of Lebanon
Number of counties: 120
Largest cities (1980 census): Louisville, 298,840; Lexington, 204,165; Owensboro, 54,450; Covington, 49,563; Bowling Green, 40,450; Paducah, 29,315; Hopkinsville, 27,318
State forests: 9 (44,173 ac.)
State parks: 43 (40,574 ac.)
Total state revenue (1982-83): $4,217,427,440[1]
Total state expenditure (1982-83): $4,408,696,698

1. Operating funds only.

Kentucky was the first region west of the Allegheny Mountains settled by American pioneers. James Harrod established the first permanent settlement at Harrodsburg in 1774; the following year Daniel Boone, who had explored the area in 1767, blazed the Wilderness Trail and founded Boonesboro.

Politically, the Kentucky region was originally part of Virginia, but early statehood was gained in 1792.

During the Civil War, as a slaveholding state with a considerable abolitionist population, Kentucky was caught in the middle of the conflict, supplying both Union and Confederate forces with thousands of troops.

In recent years, manufacturing has shown important gains, but agriculture and mining are still vital to Kentucky's economy. Kentucky prides itself on producing some of the nation's best tobacco, horses, and whiskey. Corn, soybeans, wheat, fruit, hogs, cattle, and dairy farming are also important.

Among the manufactured items produced in the state are furniture, aluminum ware, brooms, shoes, lumber products, machinery, textiles, and iron and steel products. Kentucky also produces significant amounts of petroleum, natural gas, fluorspar, clay, and stone. However, coal accounts for 90% of the total mineral income.

Louisville, the largest city, famed for the Kentucky Derby at Churchill Downs, is also the location of a large state university, whiskey distilleries, and cigarette factories. The Bluegrass country around Lexington is the home of some of the world's finest race horses. Other attractions are Mammoth Cave, the George S. Patton, Jr., Military Museum at Ft. Knox, and Old Ft. Harrod State Park.

LOUISIANA

Capital: Baton Rouge
Governor: Edwin W. Edwards, R (to March 1986)
Lieut. Governor: Robert L. Freeman, D (to March 1986)
Secy. of State: James H. Brown, Jr., D (to March 1986)
Treasurer: Mary Evelyn Parker, D (to March 1986)
Atty. General: William J. Guste, Jr., D (to March 1986)
Organized as territory: March 26, 1804
Entered Union & (rank): April 30, 1812 (18)
Present constitution adopted: 1974
Motto: Union, justice, and confidence
State flower: Magnolia (1900)
State tree: Bald cypress
State bird: Pelican
State song: "Give Me Louisiana," and "You Are My Sunshine"
Nicknames: Pelican State; Sportsman's Paradise; Creole State; Sugar State
Origin of name: In honor of Louis XIV of France
1980 population (1980 census) & (rank): 4,206,312 (19)
1983 est. population (July) & (rank): 4,438,000 (18)
1984 land area & (rank): 44,521 sq mi. (115,310 sq km) (33)

Geographic center: In Avoyelles Parish, 3 mi. SE of Marksville
Number of parishes (counties): 64
Largest cities (1980 census): New Orleans, 557,927; Baton Rouge, 219,419; Shreveport, 205,820; Lafayette, 81,961; Lake Charles, 75,226; Monroe, 57,597; Alexandria, 51,565
State forests: 1 (8,000 ac.)
State parks: 30 (13,932 ac.)
State general revenue (1983–84 est.): $5,872,515,000
Capital outlay: (1983–84 est): $1,423,859,000
State general expenditure (1983–84 est): $6,096,944,000

Louisiana has a rich, colorful historical background. Early Spanish explorers were Piñeda, 1519; Cabeza de Vaca, 1528; and de Soto in 1541. La Salle reached the mouth of the Mississippi and claimed all the land drained by it and its tributaries for Louis XIV of France in 1682.

Louisiana became a French crown colony in 1731, was ceded to Spain in 1763, returned to France in 1800, and sold by Napoleon to the U.S. as part of the Louisiana Purchase (with large territories to the north and northwest) in 1803.

In 1815, Gen. Andrew Jackson's troops defeated a larger British army in the Battle of New Orleans, neither side aware that the treaty ending the War of 1812 had been signed.

As to total value of its mineral output, Louisiana is a leader in natural gas, salt, petroleum, and sulfur production. Much of the oil and sulfur comes from offshore deposits. The state also produces large crops of sweet potatoes, rice, sugarcane, pecans, soybeans, corn, and cotton.

Leading manufactures include chemicals, processed food, petroleum and coal products, paper, lumber and wood products, transportation equipment, and apparel.

Louisiana marshes supply most of the nation's muskrat fur as well as that of opossum, raccoon, mink, and otter, and large numbers of game birds.

Major points of interest include New Orleans with its French Quarter and Superdome, plantation homes near Natchitoches and New Iberia, Cajun country in the Mississippi delta region, Chalmette National Historical Park, and the state capital at Baton Rouge.

MAINE

Capital: Augusta
Governor: Joseph E. Brennan, D (to Jan. 1987)
Secy. of State: Rodney F. Quinn, D (to Jan. 1987)
Controller: Donald A. Brown (term indefinite)
Atty. General: James Tierney, D (to Jan. 1987)
Entered Union & (rank): March 15, 1820 (23)
Present constitution adopted: 1820
Motto: *Dirigo* (I direct)
State flower: White pine cone and tassel (1895)
State tree: White pine tree (1945)
State bird: Chickadee (1927)
State fish: Landlocked salmon (1969)
State mineral: Tourmaline (1971)
State song: "State of Maine Song" (1937)
Nickname: Pine Tree State
Origin of name: First used to distinguish the mainland from the offshore islands. It has been considered a compliment to Henrietta Maria, Queen of Charles I of England. She was said to have owned the province of Mayne in France.
1980 population (1980 census) & (rank): 1,125,027 (38)
1983 est. population (July) & (rank): 1,146,000 (38)
1984 land area & (rank): 30,995 sq mi. (80,277 sq km) (39)
Geographic center: In Piscataquis Co., 18 mi. N of Dover-Foxcroft
Number of counties: 16
Largest cities (1980 census): Portland, 61,572; Lewiston, 40,481; Bangor, 31,643; Auburn, 23,128; South Portland, 22,712; Augusta, 21,819; Biddeford, 19,638
State forests: 1 (21,000 ac.)
State parks: 26 (247,627 ac.)
State historic sites: 18 (403 ac.)
State total revenue (1982): $1,305,870,287
State total expenditure (1982): $1,314,622,632

John Cabot and his son, Sebastian, are believed to have visited the Maine coast in 1498. However, the first permanent English settlements were not established until more than a century later, in 1623.

The first naval action of the Revolutionary War occurred in 1775 when colonials captured the British sloop *Margaretta* off Machias on the Maine coast. In that same year, the British burned Falmouth (now Portland).

Long governed by Massachusetts, Maine became the 23rd state as part of the Missouri Compromise in 1820.

Maine produced 26.5 million hundred weight of potatoes or 9.4% of the national production in 1981 and 95% of the nation's low-bush blueberries. Farm income is also derived from apples, sweet corn, peas, and beans, with poultry and eggs the largest items.

The state is one of the world's largest pulp-paper producers. It ranks fifth in boot-and-shoe manufacturing. With more than 90% of its area forested, Maine turns out wood products from boats to toothpicks.

Maine leads the world in the production of the familiar flat tins of sardines, producing more than 100 million of them annually. Lobstermen normally catch 80–90% of the nation's true total of lobsters.

A scenic seacoast, beaches, lakes, mountains, and resorts make Maine a popular vacationland. There are more than 2,500 lakes and 5,000 streams, plus 26 state parks, to attract hunters, fishermen, skiers, and campers.

Major points of interest are: Bar Harbor, Allagash National Wilderness Waterway, the Wadsworth-Longfellow House in Portland, Roosevelt Campobello International Park, and the St. Croix Island National Monument.

MARYLAND

Capital: Annapolis
Governor: Harry Hughes, D (to Jan. 1987)
Lieut. Governor: J. Joseph Curran, D (to Jan. 1987)
Secy. of State: Lorraine M. Sheehan, D (appointed by governor)
Comptroller of the Treasury: Louis L. Goldstein, D (to Jan. 1987)
Treasurer: William S. James, D (to Jan. 1987)
Atty. General: Stephen H. Sachs, D (to Jan. 1987)
Entered Union & (rank): April 28, 1788 (7)
Present constitution adopted: 1867
Motto: *Fatti maschii, parole femine* (Manly deeds, womanly words)
State flower: Black-eyed susan (1918)
State tree: White oak (1941)
State bird: Baltimore oriole (1947)
State dog: Chesapeake Bay retriever (1964)

State fish: Rockfish (1965)
State insect: Baltimore checkerspot butterfly (1973)
State sport: Jousting (1962)
State song: "Maryland! My Maryland!" (1939)
Nicknames: Free State; Old Line State
Origin of name: In honor of Henrietta Maria (Queen of Charles I of England)
1980 population (1980 census) & (rank): 4,216,975 (18)
1983 est. population (July) & (rank): 4,304,000 (19)
1984 land area & (rank): 9,837 sq mi. (25,477 sq km) (42)
Geographic center: In Prince Georges Co., 4 1/2 mi. NW of Davidsonville
Number of counties: 23, and 1 independent city
Largest cities (1980 census): Baltimore, 786,775; Rockville, 43,811; Hagerstown, 34,132; Bowie, 33,695; Annapolis, 31,740; Frederick, 28,086; Gaithersburg, 26,424
State forests: 10 (120,921 ac.)
State parks: 42 (70,302 ac.)
State general revenue (1984 est.): $3,397,779,000
State general expenditure (1984 est.): $3,449,526,363

In 1608, Chesapeake Bay was explored by Capt. John Smith. Charles I granted a royal charter to Cecil Calvert, Lord Baltimore, in 1632 and English Roman Catholics landed on St. Clement's (now Blakistone Island) in 1634. Religious freedom, granted all Christians in the Toleration act passed by the Maryland assembly in 1649, was ended by a Puritan revolt, 1654–58.

In 1814, when the British unsuccessfully tried to capture Baltimore, the bombardment of Fort McHenry inspired Francis Scott Key to write *The Star Spangled Banner.*

Maryland is almost cut in two by the Chesapeake Bay, and the many estuaries and rivers create one of the longest waterfronts of any state. The Bay produces more seafood—oysters, crabs, clams, fin fish—than any comparable body of water. Important agricultural products, in order of cash value, are chickens, dairy products, corn, cattle, tobacco, and vegetables. Maryland is a leader in vegetable canning. Sand, gravel, lime and cement, stone, coal, and clay are the chief mineral products.

Manufacturing industries produce missiles, airplanes, steel, clothing, and chemicals. Baltimore, home of The Johns Hopkins University and Hospital, ranks as the nation's second port in foreign tonnage. Annapolis, site of the U.S. Naval Academy, has one of the earliest state houses (1772–79) still in regular use by a State government.

Among the popular attractions in Maryland are the Fort McHenry National Monument, Harpers Ferry and Chesapeake and Ohio Canal National Historical Parks, St. Marys City restoration near Leonardtown, USS *Constellation* at Baltimore, U.S. Naval Academy in Annapolis, Assateague Island National Seashore, and Catoctin Mountain and Piscataway parks.

MASSACHUSETTS

Capital: Boston
Governor: Michael S. Dukakis, D (to Jan. 1987)
Lieut. Governor: John F. Kerry, D (to Jan. 1987)
Secy. of the Commonwealth: Michael Joseph Connolly, D (to Jan. 1987)
Treasurer & Receiver-General: Robert Q. Crane, D (to Jan. 1987)
Auditor of the Commonwealth: John J. Finnegan, D (to Jan. 1987)
Atty. General: Francis X. Bellotti (to Jan. 1987)
Entered Union & (rank): Feb. 6, 1788 (6)
Motto: *Ense petit placidam sub libertate quietem* (By the sword we seek peace, but peace only under liberty)
State flower: Mayflower (1918)
State tree: American elm (1941)
State bird: Chickadee (1941)
State colors: Blue and gold
State song: "All Hail to Massachusetts" (1966)
State beverage: Cranberry juice (1970)
State horse: Morgan horse (1970)
State insect: Ladybug (1974)
Nicknames: Bay State; Old Colony State
Origin of name: From two Indian words meaning "Great mountain place"
1983 est. population (July) & (rank): 5,767,000 (11)
1984 land area & (rank): 7,824 sq mi. (20,265 sq km) (45)
Geographic center: In Worcester Co., in S part of city of Worcester
Number of counties: 14
Largest cities (1980 census): Boston, 562,994; Worcester, 161,799; Springfield, 152,319; New Bedford, 98,478; Cambridge, 95,322; Brockton, 95,172; Fall River, 94,574
State forests and parks: 129 (242,000 ac.)[1]
State general revenue (1981–82): $7,207,000,000
State general expenditure (1981–82): $7,640,000,000

1. The Metropolitan District Commission, an agency of the Commonwealth serving municipalities in the Boston area, has about 14,000 acres of parkways and reservations under its jurisdiction.

Massachusetts has played a significant role in American history since the Pilgrims, seeking religious freedom, founded Plymouth Colony in 1620.

As one of the most important of the 13 colonies, Massachusetts became a leader in resisting British oppression. In 1773, the Boston Tea Party protested unjust taxation. The Minutemen started the American Revolution by battling British troops at Lexington and Concord on April 19, 1775.

During the 19th century, Massachusetts was famous for the vigorous intellectual activity of famous writers and educators and for its expanding commercial fishing, shipping, and manufacturing interests.

Massachusetts pioneered in the manufacture of textiles and shoes. Today, these industries have been replaced in importance by activity in the electronics and communications equipment fields.

The state's cranberry crop is the nation's largest. Also important are dairy and poultry products, nursery and greenhouse produce, vegetables, and fruit.

Tourism has become an important factor in the economy of the state because of its numerous recreational areas and historical landmarks.

Cape Cod has summer theaters, water sports, and an artists' colony at Provincetown. Tanglewood, in the Berkshires, features the summer concerts of the Boston Symphony.

Among the many other points of interest are Old Sturbridge Village, Minute Man National Historical Park between Lexington and Concord, and, in Boston: Old North Church, Old State House, Faneuil Hall, the USS *Constitution* and the John F. Kennedy Library.

MICHIGAN

Capital: Lansing
Governor: James J. Blanchard, D (to Jan. 1986)
Lieut. Governor: Martha W. Griffiths, D (to Jan. 1986)

Secy. of State: Richard H. Austin, D (to Jan. 1986)
Atty. General: Frank J. Kelley, D (to Jan. 1986)
Organized as territory: Jan. 11, 1805
Entered Union & (rank): Jan. 26, 1837 (26)
Present constitution adopted: April 1, 1963, (effective Jan. 1, 1964)
Motto: *Si quaeris peninsulam amoenam circumspice* (If you seek a pleasant peninsula, look around you)
State flower: Apple blossom (1897)
State bird: Robin
State fish: Brook trout (1965)
State gem: Isle Royal Greenstone (Chlorastrolite) (1972)
State stone: Petoskey stone (1965)
Nickname: Wolverine State
Origin of name: From two Indian words meaning "great lake"
1980 population (1980 census) & (rank): 9,262,078 (8)
1983 est. population (July) & (rank): 9,069,000 (8)
1984 land area & (rank): 56,954 sq mi. (147,511 sq km) (22)
Geographic center: In Wexford Co., 5 mi. NNW of Cadillac
Number of counties: 83
Largest cities (1980 census): Detroit, 1,203,339; Grand Rapids, 181,843; Warren, 161,134; Flint, 159,611; Lansing, 130,414; Sterling Heights, 108,999; Ann Arbor, 107,966
State forests: 33 (3,762,184 ac.)
State parks and recreation areas: 92 (216,857 ac.)
State general revenue (1982): $10,253,753,000
State general expenditure (1982): $10,577,291,000

Indian tribes were living in the Michigan region when the first European, Étienne Brulé of France, arrived in 1618. Other French explorers, including Marquette, Joliet, and La Salle, followed, and the first permanent settlement was established in 1668 at Sault Ste. Marie. France was ousted from the territory by Great Britain in 1763, following the French and Indian War.

After the Revolutionary War, the U.S. acquired most of the region, which remained the scene of constant conflict between the British and U.S. forces and their respective Indian allies through the War of 1812.

Bordering on four of the five Great Lakes, Michigan is divided into Upper and Lower Peninsulas by the Straits of Mackinac, which link Lakes Michigan and Huron. The two parts of the state are connected by the Mackinac Bridge, one of the world's longest suspension bridges. To the north, connecting Lakes Superior and Huron are the busy Sault Ste. Marie Canals.

While Michigan ranks first among the states in production of motor vehicles and parts, it is also a leader in many other manufacturing and processing lines including prepared cereals, machine tools, airplane parts, refrigerators, hardware, steel springs, and furniture.

The state produces important amounts of iron, copper, iodine, gypsum, bromine, salt, lime, gravel, and cement. Michigan's farms grow apples, cherries, pears, grapes, potatoes, and sugar beets and the annual value of its forest products is estimated at $2 billion. With over 36,000 miles of streams, some 11,000 lakes, and a 2,000 mile shoreline, Michigan is a prime area for both commercial and sport fishing.

Points of interest are the automobile plants in Dearborn, Detroit, Flint, Lansing, and Pontiac; Mackinac Island; Pictured Rocks and Sleeping Bear Dunes National Lakeshores, Greenfield Village near Dearborn; and the many summer resorts along both the inland and Great Lakes.

MINNESOTA

Capital: St. Paul
Governor: Rudy Perpich, D (to Jan. 1987)
Lieut. Governor: Marlene Johnson, D (to Jan. 1987)
Secy. of State: Joan Growe (to Jan. 1987)
State Auditor: Arne Carlson, R (to Jan. 1987)
Atty. General: Hubert H. Humphrey III, D (to Jan. 1987)
State Treasurer: Robert Mattson, D (to Jan. 1987)
Organized as territory: March 3, 1849
Entered Union & (rank): May 11, 1858 (32)
Present constitution adopted: 1858
Motto: L'Etoile du Nord (The North Star)
State flower: Showy lady slipper (1902)
State tree: Red (or Norway) pine
State bird: Common loon (also called Great Northern Diver)
State song: "Hail Minnesota"
Nicknames: North Star State; Gopher State; Land of 10,000 Lakes
Origin of name: From a Dakota Indian word meaning "sky-tinted water"
1980 population (1980 census) & (rank): 4,075,970 (21)
1983 est. population (July) & (rank): 4,144,000 (21)
1984 land area & (rank): 79,548 sq mi. (206,030 sq km) (14)
Geographic center: In Crow Wing Co., 10 mi. SW of Brainerd
Number of counties: 87
Largest cities (1980 census): Minneapolis, 370,951; St. Paul, 270,230; Duluth, 92,811; Bloomington, 81,831; Rochester, 57,890; Edina, 46,073
State forests: 55 (2,984,000 ac.)
State parks: 92 (202,205 ac.)
Total revenue (Fiscal 1982): $5,593,186,000
Total expenditures (Fiscal 1982): $6,169,926,000

Following the visits of several French explorers, fur traders, and missionaries, including Marquette and Joliet and La Salle, the region was claimed for Louis XIV by Daniel Greysolon, Sieur Duluth, in 1679.

The U.S. acquired eastern Minnesota from Great Britain after the Revolutionary War and 20 years later bought the western part from France in the Louisiana Purchase of 1803. Much of the region was explored by U.S. Army Lt. Zebulon M. Pike before cession of the northern strip of Minnesota bordering Canada by Britain in 1818.

The state is rich in natural resources. A few square miles of land in the north in the Mesabi, Cuyuna, and Vermillion ranges, produce more than 60% of the nation's iron ore. The state's farms rank high in yields of corn, wheat, rye, alfalfa, and sugar beets. Other leading farm products include butter, eggs, milk, potatoes, green peas, barley, and livestock.

Minnesota's factory production includes non-electrical machinery, fabricated metals, flour-mill products, plastics, electronic computers, scientific instruments, and processed foods.

Minneapolis is the trade center of the Northwest; St. Paul is the nation's biggest publisher of calendars and law books. These "twin cities" are the nation's third largest trucking center. Duluth has the nation's largest inland harbor and now handles a significant amount of foreign trade. Rochester is the home of the Mayo Clinic, an internationally famous medical center.

Today, tourism is a major revenue producer in Minnesota, with fishing, hunting, water sports, and winter sports bringing in millions of visitors each year.

Among the most popular attractions are the St.

Paul Winter Carnival; the Tyrone Guthrie Theatre, the Institute of Arts, Walker Art Center, and Minnehaha Park, in Minneapolis; Voyageurs National Park; North Shore Drive; and the Minnesota Zoological Gardens.

MISSISSIPPI

Capital: Jackson
Governor: William A. Allain, D (to Jan. 1988)
Lieut. Governor: Brad Dye, D (to Jan. 1988)
Secy. of State: Dick Molpus, D (to Jan. 1988)
Treasurer: Bill Cole, D (to Jan. 1988)
Atty. General: Edwin Lloyd Pittman, D (to Jan. 1988)
Organized as territory: April 7, 1798
Entered Union & (rank): Dec. 10, 1817 (20)
Present constitution adopted: 1890
Motto: *Virtute et armis* (By valor and arms)
State flower: Flower or bloom of the magnolia or evergreen magnolia (1952)
State tree: Magnolia (1938)
State bird: Mockingbird (1944)
State song: "Go, Mississippi" (1962)
Nickname: Magnolia State
Origin of name: From an Indian word meaning "Father of Waters"
1980 population (1980 census) & (rank): 2,520,638 (31)
1983 est. population (July) & (rank): 2,587,000 (31)
1984 land area & (rank): 47,233 sq mi. (122,333 sq km) (31)
Geographic center: In Leake Co., 9 mi. WNW of Carthage
Number of counties: 82
Largest cities (1980 census): Jackson, 202,895; Biloxi, 49,311; Hattiesburg, 40,829; Greenville, 40,613; Gulfport, 39,676; Pascagoula, 29,318
State forest: 1 (1,760 ac.)
State parks: 27 (16,763 ac.)
State general revenue (Fiscal 1983): $2,590,264,359[1]
State general expenditure (Fiscal 1983): $2,679,986,700[1]

1. Ending June 30, 1983.

First explored for Spain by Hernando de Soto who discovered the Mississippi River in 1540, the region was later claimed by France. In 1699, a French group under Sieur d'Iberville established the first permanent settlement near present-day Biloxi.

Great Britain took over the area in 1763 after the French and Indian War, ceding it to the U.S. in 1783 after the Revolution. Spain did not relinquish its claims until 1798, and in 1810 the U.S. annexed West Florida from Spain, including what is now southern Mississippi.

Mississippi, the stronghold of the Old South, has until the past decade been one of the least industrialized states, with more than half its population making a living from the soil. However, a recent industrialization program has attracted manufacturing industries such as lumber, furniture, paper, food processing, apparel, chemicals, transportation equipment, and machinery.

Cotton, nevertheless, is still king with the state ranking second to Texas in cotton production, though soybeans have become Mississippi's largest crop. Other important farm products are corn, peanuts, pecans, rice, sugarcane, sweet potatoes, and hay. Poultry and eggs are also important.

The state abounds in historical landmarks and is the home of the Vicksburg National Military Park where visitors may see the remains of forts, trenches, and other military relics used in the 1863 Union-army siege of the city. Other National Park Service areas are Brices Cross Roads National Battlefield Site, Tupelo National Battlefield, and part of Natchez Trace National Parkway. Pre-Civil War mansions are the special pride of Natchez, Oxford, Hattiesburg, and Jackson.

MISSOURI

Capital: Jefferson City
Governor: Christopher S. Bond, R (to Jan. 1985)
Lieut. Governor: Kenneth J. Rothman, D (to Jan. 1985)
Secy. of State: James C. Kirkpatrick, D (to Jan. 1985)
Auditor: James F. Antonio, R (to Jan. 1987)
Treasurer: Mel Carnahan, D (to Jan. 1985)
Atty. General: John D. Ashcroft, R (to Jan. 1985)
Organized as territory: June 4, 1812
Entered Union & (rank): Aug. 10, 1821 (24)
Present constitution adopted: 1945
Motto: *Salus populi suprema lex esto* (The welfare of the people shall be the supreme law)
State flower: Hawthorn (1923)
State bird: Bluebird (1927)
State colors: Red, white, and blue (1913)
State song: "Missouri Waltz" (1949)
State rock: Mozarkite (1967)
State mineral: Galena (1967)
Nickname: Show-me State
Origin of name: Named after a tribe called Missouri Indians. "Missouri" means "town of the large canoes."
1980 population (1980 census) & (rank): 4,916,759 (15)
1983 est. population (July) & (rank): 4,970,000 (15)
1984 land area & (rank): 68,945 sq mi. (178,568 sq km) (18)
Geographic center: In Miller Co., 20 mi. SW of Jefferson City
Number of counties: 114, plus 1 independent city
Largest cities (1980 census): St. Louis, 453,085; Kansas City, 448,159; Springfield, 133,116; Independence, 111,806; Columbia, 62,061; Florissant, 55,372
State forests and Tower sites: 93 (265,000 ac.)
State parks: 71 (97,314 ac.)[1]
State cash receipts (1983): $4,116,081,622
State general expenditure (1983): $3,976,559,739

1. Includes 24 historic sites and 1 archaeological site.

De Soto visited the Missouri area in 1541. France's claim to the entire region was based on La Salle's travels in 1682. French fur traders established Ste. Genevieve in 1735 and St. Louis was first settled in 1764.

The U.S. gained Missouri from France as part of the Louisiana Purchase in 1803, and the territory was admitted as a state following the Missouri Compromise of 1820. Throughout the pre-Civil War period and during the war, Missourians were sharply divided in their opinions about slavery and in their allegiances, supplying both Union and Confederate forces with troops. However, the state itself remained in the Union.

Historically, Missouri played a leading role as a gateway to the West, St. Joseph being the eastern starting point of the Pony Express, while the much-traveled Santa Fe and Oregon Trails began in Independence. Now a popular vacationland, Missouri has 11 major lakes and numerous fishing streams, springs, and caves. Bagnell Dam, across the Osage River in the Ozarks, completed in 1931, created one of the largest man-made lakes in the world, covering 65,000 acres of surface area.

Manufacturing, paced by the aerospace industry, provides more income and jobs than any other segment of the economy. Missouri is also a leading producer of transportation equipment, shoes, lead, and beer. Among the major crops are corn, soybeans, wheat, oats, barley, potatoes, tobacco, and cotton.

Points of interest include Mark Twain's boyhood home and Mark Twain Cave (Hannibal), the Harry S. Truman Library and Museum (Independence), the house where Jesse James was killed in St. Joseph, Jefferson National Expansion Memorial (St. Louis), and the Ozark National Scenic Riverway.

MONTANA

Capital: Helena
Governor: Ted Schwinden, D (to Jan. 1985)
Lieut. Governor: George Turman, D (to Jan. 1985)
Secy. of State: Jim Waltermire, R (to Jan. 1985)
Auditor: E. V. "Sonny" Omholt, R (to Jan. 1985)
Atty. General: Michael Greely, D (to Jan. 1985)
Organized as territory: May 26, 1864
Entered Union & (rank): Nov. 8, 1889 (41)
Present constitution adopted: 1972
Motto: *Oro y plata* (Gold and silver)
State flower: Bitterroot (1895)
State tree: Ponderosa pine (1949)
State stones: Sapphire and agate (1969)
State bird: Western meadow lark (1931)
State song: "Montana" (1945)
Nickname: Treasure State
Origin of name: Chosen from Latin dictionary by J. M. Ashley. It is a Latinized Spanish word.
1983 est. population (July) & (rank): 817,000 (44)
1984 land area & (rank): 145,392 sq mi. (376,564 sq km) (4)
Geographic center: In Fergus Co., 12 mi. W of Lewistown
Number of counties: 56, plus small part of Yellowstone National Park
Largest cities (1980 census): Billings, 66,824; Great Falls, 56,725; Butte-Silver Bow, 37,205; Missoula, 33,388; Helena, 23,938; Bozeman, 21,645; Havre, 10,891
State forests: 7 (214,000 ac.)
State parks and recreation areas: 77 (18,273 ac.)
State general revenue (1982–83): $321,944,764
State general expenditure (1982–83): $302,043,072

First explored for France by Frânçois and Louis-Joseph Verendrye in the early 1740s, much of the region was acquired by the U.S. from France as part of the Louisiana Purchase in 1803. Before western Montana was obtained from Great Britain in the Oregon Treaty of 1846, American trading posts and forts had been established in the territory.

The major Indian wars (1867–1877) included the famous 1876 Battle of the Little Big Horn, better known as "Custer's Last Stand," in which Cheyennes and Sioux killed George A. Custer and more than 200 of his men in southeastern Montana.

Much of Montana's early history was concerned with mining with copper, lead, zinc, silver, coal, and oil as principal products.

Butte, sitting on the "richest hill in the world," is the center of the area that once supplied half of the U.S. copper.

Fields of grain cover much of Montana's plains; it ranks high among the states in wheat and barley, with rye, oats, flaxseed, sugar beets, and potatoes other important crops. Sheep and cattle raising make significant contributions to the state's economy.

Tourist attractions include hunting, fishing, skiing, and dude ranching. Glacier National Park, on the Continental Divide, is a scenic and vacation wonderland with 60 glaciers, 200 lakes, and many streams with good trout fishing.

Other major points of interest include the Custer Battlefield National Monument, Virginia City, Yellowstone National Park, Museum of the Plains Indians at Browning, and the Fort Union Trading Post and Grant-Kohr's Ranch National Historic Sites.

NEBRASKA

Capital: Lincoln
Governor: Bob Kerrey, D (to Jan. 1987)
Lieut. Governor: Donald L. McGinley, D (to Jan. 1987)
Secy. of State: Allen J. Beerman, R (to Jan. 1987)
Atty. General: Paul L. Douglas, R (to Jan. 1987)
Auditor: Ray A. C. Johnson, R (to Jan. 1987)
Treasurer: Kay A. Orr, R (to Jan. 1987)
Organized as territory: May 30, 1854
Entered Union & (rank): March 1, 1867 (37)
Present constitution adopted: Nov. 1, 1875 (extensively amended 1919–20)
Motto: Equality before the law
State flower: Goldenrod (1895)
State tree: Cottonwood (1972)
State bird: Western meadow lark (1929)
State insect: Honey Bee (1975)
State gemstone: Blue agate (1967)
State rock: Prairie agate (1967)
State fossil: Mammoth (1967)
State song: "Beautiful Nebraska" (1967)
Nicknames: Cornhusker State; Beef State; Tree Planters State
Origin of name: From an Oto Indian word meaning "flat water"
1980 population (1980 census) & (rank): 1,570,006 (35)
1983 est. population (July) & (rank): 1,597,000 (36)
1984 land area & (rank): 76,644 sq mi. (198,508 sq km) (15)
Geographic center: In Custer Co., 10 mi. NW of Broken Bow
Number of counties: 93
Largest cities (1980 census): Omaha, 313,911; Lincoln, 171,932; Grand Island, 33,180; North Platte, 24,479; Fremont, 23,979; Hastings, 23,045; Bellevue, 21,813
State forests: None
State parks: 93 areas, 4 categories, 5 major areas
State general revenue (1982–83): $1,544,109,227
State general expenditure (1982–83): $1,614,519,359

French fur traders first visited Nebraska in the early 1700s. Part of the Louisiana Purchase in 1803, Nebraska was explored by Lewis and Clark in 1804–06.

Robert Stuart pioneered the Oregon Trail across Nebraska in 1812–13 and the first permanent settlement was established at Bellevue in 1823. Western Nebraska was acquired by treaty following the Mexican War in 1848. The Union Pacific began its transcontinental railroad at Omaha in 1865. In 1937, Nebraska became the only state in the Union to have a unicameral (one-house) legislature. Members are elected to it without party designation.

Nebraska is a leading grain-producer with bumper crops of rye, corn, and wheat. More varieties of grass, valuable for forage, grow in this state than in any other in the nation.

The state's sizable cattle and hog industries make

Omaha with its surrounding area the nation's largest meat-packing center and the second-largest cattle market in the world.

Manufacturing has become diversified in Nebraska, strengthening the state's economic base. Firms making electronic components, auto accessories, pharmaceuticals, and mobile homes have joined such older industries as clothing, farm machinery, chemicals, and transportation equipment. Oil was discovered in 1939 and natural gas in 1949.

Among the principal attractions are Agate Fossil Beds, Homestead, and Scotts Bluff National Monuments; Chimney Rock National Historic Site; a recreated pioneer village at Minden; the Union stockyards in Omaha; the Stuhr Museum of the Prairie Pioneer with 57 original 19th-century buildings near Grand Island; and the Sheldon Memorial Art Gallery at the University of Nebraska in Lincoln.

NEVADA

Capital: Carson City
Governor: Richard H. Bryan, D (to Jan. 1987)
Lieut. Governor: Robert A. Cashell, R (to Jan. 1987)
Secy. of State: Wm. D. Swackhamer, D (to Jan. 1987)
State Treasurer: Patty D. Cafferata, R (to Jan. 1987)
Controller: Darrel R. Daines, R (to Jan. 1987)
Atty. General: Brian McKay, R (to Jan. 1987)
Organized as territory: March 2, 1861
Entered Union & (rank): Oct. 31, 1864 (36)
Present constitution adopted: 1864
Motto: All for Our Country
State flower: Sagebrush (1967)
State tree: Single-leaf pinon (1953)
State bird: Mountain bluebird (1967)
State animal: Desert bighorn sheep (1973)
State colors: Silver and blue (unofficial)
State song: "Home Means Nevada" (1933)
Nicknames: Sagebrush State; Silver State; Battle-born State
Origin of name: Spanish: "snowcapped"
1980 population (1980 census) & (rank): 800,493 (43)
1983 est. population (July) & (rank): 891,000 (43)
1984 land area & (rank): 109,893 sq mi. (284,624 sq km) (7)
Geographic center: In Lander Co., 26 mi. SE of Austin
Number of counties: 16, plus 1 independent city
Largest cities (1980 census): Las Vegas, 164,674; Reno, 100,756; North Las Vegas, 42,739; Sparks, 40,780; Carson City, 32,022; Henderson, 24,363; Boulder City, 9,590
State forests: None
State parks: 20 (150,000 ac., including leased lands)
General fund revenue (1983–84): $404,970,729
General fund expenditure (1981–82): $381,792,794

Trappers and traders, including Jedediah Smith, and Peter Skene Ogden, entered the Nevada area in the 1820s. In 1843–45, John C. Fremont and Kit Carson explored the Great Basin and Sierra Nevada.

In 1848 following the Mexican War, the U.S. obtained the region and the first permanent settlement was a Mormon trading post near present-day Genoa.

The driest state in the nation with an average annual rainfall of only 3.73 inches, much of Nevada is uninhabited, sagebrush-covered desert.

Nevada was made famous by the discovery of the fabulous Comstock Lode in 1859 and its mines have produced large quantities of gold, silver, copper, lead, zinc, mercury, barite, and tungsten. Oil was discovered in 1954. Copper now far exceeds all other minerals in value of production.

In 1931, the state created two industries, divorce and gambling. For many years, Reno and Las Vegas were the "divorce capitals of the nation." More liberal divorce laws in many states have ended this distinction, but Nevada is the gambling and entertainment capital of the U.S. State gambling taxes account for 45% of tax revenues. Although Nevada leads the nation in per capita gambling revenue, it ranks only fourth in total gambling revenue.

Near Las Vegas, on the Colorado River, stands Hoover Dam, which impounds the waters of Lake Mead, one of the world's largest artificial lakes.

The state's agricultural crop consists mainly of hay, alfalfa seed, barley, and wheat.

Nevada manufactures gaming devices, chemicals, forest products, suntan lotion, and stone-clay-glass products.

Major resort areas flourish in Lake Tahoe, Reno, and Las Vegas. Recreation areas include those at Pyramid Lake, Lake Tahoe, and Lake Mead and Lake Mohave, both in Lake Mead National Recreation Area. Among the other attractions are Hoover Dam, Virginia City, and Lehman Caves National Monument.

NEW HAMPSHIRE

Capital: Concord
Governor: John H. Sununu, R (to Jan. 1985)
Secy. of State: William M. Gardner, D (to Dec. 1984)
Commissioner: Thomas Roy, Jr.
Atty. General: Gregory Smith
Entered Union & (rank): June 21, 1788 (9)
Present constitution adopted: 1784
Motto: Live free or die
State flower: Purple lilac (1919)
State tree: White birch (1947)
State bird: Purple finch (1957)
State songs: "Old New Hampshire" (1949) and "New Hampshire, My New Hampshire" (1963)
Nickname: Granite State
Origin of name: From the English county of Hampshire
1980 population (1980 census) & (rank): 920,610 (42)
1983 est. population (July) & (rank): 959,000 (41)
1984 land area & (rank): 8,993 sq mi. (23,292 sq km) (44)
Geographic center: In Belknap Co., 3 mi. E of Ashland
Number of counties: 10
Largest cities (1980 census): Manchester, 90,936; Nashua, 67,865; Concord, 30,400; Portsmouth, 26,254; Dover, 22,377; Rochester, 21,560; Keene, 21,449
State forests & parks: 175 (96,975 ac.)
State revenue (1983): $767,510,175
State expenditure (1983): $814,814,048

Under an English land grant, Capt. John Smith sent settlers to establish a fishing colony at the mouth of the Piscataqua River, near present-day Rye and Dover, in 1623. Capt. John Mason, who participated in the founding of Portsmouth in 1630, gave New Hampshire its name.

After a 38-year period of union with Massachusetts, New Hampshire was made a separate royal colony in 1679. As leaders in the revolutionary cause, New Hampshire delegates received the honor of being the first to vote for the Declaration of Independence on July 4, 1776. New Hampshire is the only state that ever played host at the formal conclusion of a foreign war when, in 1905,

Portsmouth was the scene of the treaty ending the Russo-Japanese War.

Abundant water power early turned New Hampshire into an industrial state and manufacturing is the principal source of income in the state. The most important industrial products are leather goods, electrical and other machinery, textiles, and pulp and paper products.

Dairy and poultry farming and growing fruit, truck vegetables, corn, potatoes, and hay are the major agricultural pursuits.

Tourism, because of New Hampshire's scenic and recreational resources, now brings over $400 million into the state annually.

Vacation attractions include Lake Winnipesaukee, largest of 1,300 lakes and ponds; the 724,000-acre White Mountain National Forest; Daniel Webster's birthplace near Franklin; Strawberry Banke, restored building of the original settlement at Portsmouth; and the famous "Old Man of the Mountain" granite head profile, the state's official emblem, at Franconia.

NEW JERSEY

Capital: Trenton
Governor: Thomas H. Kean, R (to Jan. 1986)
Secy. of State: Jane Burgio, R (to Jan. 1986)
Treasurer: Kenneth Biederman, R (to Jan. 1986)
Atty. General: Irwin I. Kimmelman, R (to Jan. 1986)
Entered Union & (rank): Dec. 18, 1787 (3)
Present constitution adopted: 1947
Motto: Liberty and prosperity
State flower: Purple violet (1913)
State bird: Eastern goldfinch (1935)
State insect: Honeybee
State tree: Red oak (1950)
State animal: Horse (1977)
State colors: Buff and blue (1965)
Nickname: Garden State
Origin of name: From the Channel Isle of Jersey
1980 population (1980 census) & (rank): 7,364,823 (9)
1983 est. population (July) & (rank): 7,468,000 (9)
1984 land area & (rank): 7,468 sq mi. (19,342 sq km) (46)
Geographic center: In Mercer Co., 5 mi. SE of Trenton
Number of counties: 21
Largest cities (1980 census): Newark, 329,248; Jersey City, 223,532; Paterson, 137,970; Elizabeth, 106,201; Trenton, 92,124; Camden, 84,910; Clifton, 77,690
State forests: 11
State parks: 40 (73,483 ac.)
State general revenue (Fiscal est. 1985): $7,437,200,000
State appropriations (Fiscal est. 1985): $7,574,630,000

New Jersey's early colonial history was involved with that of New York (New Netherlands), of which it was a part. One year after the Dutch surrender to England in 1664, New Jersey was organized as an English colony under Gov. Philip Carteret.

In the late 1600s the colony was divided between Carteret and William Penn; later it would be administered by the royal governor of New York. Finally, in 1738, New Jersey was separated from New York under its own royal governor, Lewis Morris.

Because of its key location between New York City and Philadelphia, New Jersey saw much fighting during the American Revolution.

Today, New Jersey, an area of wide industrial diversification, is known as the Crossroads of the East. Products from over 15,000 factories can be delivered overnight to almost 60 million people, representing 12 states and the District of Columbia. The greatest single industry is chemicals and New Jersey is one of the foremost research centers in the world. Many large oil refineries are located in northern New Jersey and other important manufactures are pharmaceuticals, instruments, machinery, electrical goods, and apparel.

Of the total land area, 43% is forested and about 24% is devoted to agriculture. The state ranks high in production of almost all garden vegetables. Tomatoes, asparagus, corn, and blueberries are important crops, and poultry farming and dairying make significant contributions to the state's economy.

Tourism is the second largest industry in New Jersey. The state has numerous resort areas on 127 miles of Atlantic coastline. In 1977, New Jersey voters approved legislation allowing legalized casino gambling in Atlantic City. Points of interest include the Walt Whitman House in Camden, the Delaware Water Gap, the Edison National Historic Site in West Orange, and Princeton University.

NEW MEXICO

Capital: Santa Fe
Governor: Toney Anaya, D (to Jan. 1987)
Lieut. Governor: Mike Runnels, D (to Jan. 1987)
Secy. of State: Clara Jones, D (to Jan. 1987)
Atty. General: Paul Bardacke, D (to Jan. 1987)
State Auditor: Albert Romero, D (to Jan. 1987)
State Treasurer: Earl Hartley, D (to Jan. 1987)
Commissioner of Public Lands: Jim Baco, D (to Jan. 1987)
Organized as territory: Sept. 9, 1850
Entered Union & (rank): Jan. 6, 1912 (47)
Present constitution adopted: 1911
Motto: *Crescit eundo* (It grows as it goes)
State flower: Yucca (1927)
State tree: Pinon (1949)
State animal: Black bear (1963)
State bird: Roadrunner (1949)
State fish: Cutthroat trout (1955)
State vegetables: Chile and frijol (1965)
State gem: Turquoise (1967)
State colors: Red and yellow of old Spain (1925)
State song: "O Fair New Mexico" (1917)
Spanish language state song: "Asi Es Nuevo Mejico" (1971)
Nicknames: Land of Enchantment; Sunshine State
Origin of name: From the country of Mexico
1980 population (1980 census) & (rank): 1,302,981 (37)
1983 est. population (July) & (rank): 1,399,000 (37)
1984 land area & (rank): 121,335 sq mi. (314,258 sq km) (5)
Geographic center: In Torrance Co., 12 mi. SSW of Willard
Number of counties: 33
Largest cities (1980 census): Alburquerque, 331,767; Santa Fe, 48,953; Las Cruces, 45,086; Roswell, 39,676; Farmington, 31,222; Clovis, 31,194; Hobbs, 29,153
State-owned forested land: 933,000 ac.
State parks: 29 (105,012 ac.)
State general revenue (1983): $1,342,600,000
State general expenditure (1983): $1,385,400,000

Francisco Vásquez de Coronado, Spanish explorer searching for gold, traveled the region that became New Mexico in 1540–42. In 1598 the first Spanish settlement was established on the Rio

Grande River by Juan de Onate and in 1610 Santa Fe was founded and made the capital of New Mexico.

The U.S. acquired most of New Mexico in 1848, as a result of the Mexican War, and the remainder in the 1853 Gadsden Purchase. Union troops captured the territory from the Confederates during the Civil War. With the surrender of Geronimo in 1886, the Apache Wars and most of the Indian troubles in the area were ended.

Since 1945, New Mexico has been a leader in energy research and development with extensive experiments conducted at Los Alamos Scientific Laboratory and Sandia Laboratories in the nuclear, solar, and geothermal areas.

Minerals are the state's richest natural resource and New Mexico leads the U.S. in output of uranium and potassium salts. Petroleum, natural gas, copper, gold, silver, zinc, lead, and molybdenum also contribute heavily to the state's income.

The principal manufacturing industries include food products, chemicals, transportation equipment, lumber, electrical machinery, and stone-clay-glass products. More than two thirds of New Mexico's farm income comes from livestock products, especially sheep. Cotton, pecans, and sorghum are the most important field crops. Corn, peanuts, beans, onions, and lettuce are also grown.

Tourist attractions in New Mexico include the Carlsbad Caverns National Park, Inscription Rock at El Morro National Monument, the ruins at Fort Union, Billy the Kid mementos at Lincoln, and the White Sands and Gila Cliff Dwellings National Monuments.

NEW YORK

Capital: Albany
Governor: Mario M. Cuomo, D (to Jan. 1987)
Lieut. Governor: Alfred B. Del Bello, D (to Jan. 1987)
Secy. of State: Gail S. Shaffer, D (to Jan. 1987)
Comptroller: Edward V. Regan, R (to Jan. 1987)
Atty. General: Robert Abrams, D (to Jan. 1987)
Entered Union & (rank): July 26, 1788 (11)
Present constitution adopted: 1777 (last revised 1938)
Motto: *Excelsior* (Ever upward)
State animal: Beaver (1975)
State fish: Brook trout (1975)
State gem: Garnet (1969)
State flower: Rose (1955)
State tree: Sugar maple (1956)
State bird: Bluebird
State song: "I Love New York" (1980)
Nickname: Empire State
Origin of name: In honor of the English Duke of York
1980 population (1980 census) & (rank): 17,558,072 (2)
1983 est. population (July) & (rank): 17,667,000 (2)
1984 land area & (rank): 47,377 sq mi. (122,707 sq km) (30)
Geographic center: In Madison Co., 12 mi. S of Oneida and 26 mi. SW of Utica
Number of counties: 62
Largest cities (1980 census): New York, 7,071,639; Buffalo, 357,870; Rochester, 241,741; Yonkers, 195,351; Syracuse, 170,105; Albany, 101,727; Utica, 75,632
State forest preserves: Adirondacks, 2,500,000 ac., Catskills, 250,000 ac.
State parks: 150 (250,000 ac.)
State general fund income (1984–85): $20,668,000,000
State general fund outgo (1984–85): $20,617,000,000

Giovanni da Verrazano, Italian-born navigator sailing for France, discovered New York Bay in 1524. Henry Hudson, an Englishman employed by the Dutch, reached the bay and sailed up the river now bearing his name in 1609, the same year that northern New York was explored and claimed for France by Samuel de Champlain.

In 1624 the first permanent Dutch settlement was established at Fort Orange (now Albany); one year later Peter Minuit is said to have purchased Manhattan Island from the Indians for trinkets worth about $24 and founded the Dutch colony of New Amsterdam (now New York City), which was surrendered to the English in 1664.

For a short time, New York City was the U.S. capital and George Washington was inaugurated there as first President on April 30, 1789.

New York's extremely rapid commercial growth may be partly attributed to Governor De Witt Clinton, who pushed through the construction of the Erie Canal (Buffalo to Albany), which was opened in 1825. Today, the 559-mile Governor Thomas E. Dewey Thruway connects New York City with Buffalo and with Connecticut, Massachusetts, and Pennsylvania express highways. Two toll-free superhighways, the Adirondack Northway (linking Albany with the Canadian border) and the North-South-Expressway (crossing central New York from the Pennsylvania border to the Thousand Isalnds) have been opened.

New York, with the great metropolis of New York City, is the spectacular nerve center of the nation. It is a leader in manufacturing, foreign trade, commercial and financial transactions, book and magazine publishing, and theatrical production.

New York City is not only a national but an international leader. A leading seaport, its John F. Kennedy International Airport is one of the busiest airports in the world. The largest manufacturing center in the country, in 1978 its manufacturing establishments employed almost 610,000 persons and reported $15.2 billion of value added by manufacture. The apparel industry is the city's largest manufacturing employer, with printing and publishing second.

Nearly all the rest of the state's manufacturing is done on Long Island, along the Hudson River north to Albany and through the Mohawk Valley, Central New York, and Southern Tier regions to Buffalo. The St. Lawrence seaway and power projects have opened the North Country to industrial expansion and have given the state a second seacoast. In 1962, the Niagara power development was completed, giving the state the largest hydroelectric installation in the free world.

The state ranks second in the nation in manufacturing with 1,537,500 employees and $48.3 billion in value added by manufacture in 1978. The principal industries are machinery, printing and publishing, instruments, apparel, and chemicals.

The convention and tourist business is one of the state's most important sources of income.

New York farms are famous for dairying, truck gardening, and the raising of potatoes, onions, cabbage, fruits, and poultry. The state is a leading wine producer.

Among the major points of interest are Castle Clinton, Fort Stanwix, and Statue of Liberty National Monuments; Niagara Falls; U.S. Military Academy at West Point; National Historic Sites that include homes of Franklin D. Roosevelt at Hyde Park and Theodore Roosevelt in Oyster Bay and New York City; National Memorials, including Grant's Tomb and Federal Hall in New York City;

Fort Ticonderoga; the Baseball Hall of Fame in Cooperstown; and the United Nations, skyscrapers, museums, theaters, and parks in New York City.

NORTH CAROLINA

Capital: Raleigh
Governor: James B. Hunt, Jr., D (to Jan. 1985)
Lieut. Governor: James C. Greene (to Jan. 1985).
Secy. of State: Thad Eure, D (to Jan. 1985)
Treasurer: Harlan E. Boyles (to Jan. 1985)
Auditor: Edward Renfrow, D (to Jan. 1985)
Atty. General: Rufus Edmisten, D (to Jan. 1985)
Entered Union & (rank): Nov. 21, 1789 (12)
Present constitution adopted: 1971
Motto: *Esse quam videri* (To be rather than to seem)
State flower: Dogwood (1941)
State tree: Pine (1963)
State bird: Cardinal (1943)
State mammal: Gray Squirrel (1969)
State insect: Honeybee (1973)
State Reptile: Turtle (1979)
State gemstone: Emerald (1973)
State shell: Scotch bonnet (1965)
State song: "The Old North State" (1927)
State colors: Red and blue (1945)
Nickname: Tar Heel State
Origin of name: In honor of Charles I of England
1980 population (1980 census) & (rank): 5,881,813 (10)
1983 est. population (July) & (rank): 6,082,000 (10)
1984 land area & (rank): 48,843 sq mi. (126,504 sq km) (29)
Geographic center: In Chatham Co., 10 mi. NW of Sanford
Number of counties: 100
Largest cities (1980 census): Charlotte, 314,447; Greensboro, 155,642; Raleigh, 150,255; Winston-Salem, 131,885; Durham, 100,538; High Point, 63,808
State forests: 1
State parks: 26 (115,051 ac.)
State revenues (1982–83): $3,982,000,000[1]
State expenditure (1982–83): $4,010,000,000[2]

1. Excludes all Federal revenues and expenditures. 2. All expenditures: operating and capital improvements.

English colonists, sent by Sir Walter Raleigh, unsuccessfully attempted to settle Roanoke Island in 1585 and 1587. Virginia Dare, born there in 1587, was the first child of English parentage born in America.

In 1653 the first permanent settlements were established by English colonists from Virginia near the Roanoke and Chowan Rivers.

The region was established as an English proprietary colony in 1663–65 and its early history was the scene of Culpepper's Rebellion (1677), the Quaker-led Cary Rebellion of 1708, the Tuscarora Indian War in 1711–13, and many pirate raids.

During the American Revolution, there was relatively little fighting within the state, but many North Carolinians saw action elsewhere. Despite considerable pro-Union, anti-slavery sentiment, North Carolina joined the Confederacy.

North Carolina is the nation's largest furniture, tobacco, brick, and textile producer. It holds second place in the Southeast in population and first place in the value of its industrial and agricultural production. This production is highly diversified, with metalworking, chemicals, and paper constituting enormous industries. Tobacco, corn, cotton, hay, peanuts, and truck and vegetable crops are of major importance. It is the country's leading producer of mica and lithium.

Tourism is also important, with travelers and vacationers spending more than $1 billion annually in North Carolina. Sports include year-round golfing, skiing at mountain resorts, both fresh and salt water fishing, and hunting.

Among the major attractions are the Great Smoky Mountains, the Blue Ridge National Parkway, the Cape Hatteras and Cape Lookout National Seashores, the Wright Brothers National Memorial at Kitty Hawk, Guilford Courthouse and Moores Creek National Military Parks, Carl Sandburg's home near Hendersonville, and the Old Salem Restoration in Winston-Salem.

NORTH DAKOTA

Capital: Bismarck
Governor: Allen I. Olson, R (to Jan. 1985)
Lieut. Governor: Ernest M. Sands, R (to Jan. 1985)
Secy. of State: Ben Meier, R (to Jan. 1985)
Auditor: Robert W. Peterson, R (to Jan. 1985)
State Treasurer: John Lesmeister, R (to Jan. 1985)
Atty. General: Bob Wefald, R (to Jan. 1985)
Organized as territory: March 2, 1861
Entered Union & (rank): Nov. 2, 1889 (39)
Present constitution adopted: 1889
Motto: Liberty and union, now and forever: one and inseparable
State tree: American Elm (1947)
State bird: Western meadow lark (1947)
State song: "North Dakota Hymn" (1947)
Nicknames: Sioux State; Flickertail State
Origin of name: From the Dakotah tribe, meaning "allies"
1980 population (1980 census) & (rank): 652,717 (46)
1983 est. population (July) & (rank): 680,000 (46)
1984 land area & (rank): 70,665 sq mi (183,113 sq km) (17)
Geographic center: In Sheridan Co., 5 mi. SW of McClusky
Number of counties: 53
Largest cities (1980 census): Fargo, 61,383; Bismarck, 44,485; Grand Forks, 43,765; Minot, 32,843; Jamestown, 16,280; Dickinson, 15,924; Mandan, 15,513
State forests: None
State parks: 14 (14,922.6 ac.)
Total state collections (Fiscal 1983): $732,349,302
Total state disbursements (Fiscal 1983): $865,862,752

North Dakota was explored in 1738–40 by French Canadians led by Vérendrye. In 1803, the U.S. acquired most of North Dakota from France in the Louisiana Purchase. Lewis and Clark explored the region in 1804–06 and the first settlements were made at Pembina in 1812 by Scottish and Irish families while this area was still in dispute between the U.S. and Great Britain.

In 1818, the U.S. obtained the northeastern part of North Dakota by treaty with Great Britain and took possession of Pembina in 1823.

North Dakota is the most rural of all the states, with farms covering more than 90% of the land. Only Kansas produces more wheat, and the state's coal and oil reserves are plentiful.

Other agricultural products include barley, rye, oats, and flaxseed, sugar beets, and hay; beef cattle, sheep, and hogs are also important to the state's economy.

Recently, manufacturing industries have grown, especially food processing and farm equipment. The state also produces natural gas, lignite, salt, clay, sand, and gravel.

The Garrison Dam on the Missouri River provides extensive irrigation and produces 400,000 kilowatts of electricity for the Missouri Basin areas.

Known for its waterfowl, grouse, and deer hunting and bass, trout, and northern pike fishing, North Dakota has 20 state parks and recreation areas. Points of interest include the International Peace Garden near Dunseith, Fort Union Trading Post National Historic Site, the State Capitol at Bismarck, the Badlands, and Fort Lincoln, now a state park, from which Gen. George Custer set out on his last campaign in 1876.

OHIO

Capital: Columbus
Governor: Richard F. Celeste, D (to Jan. 1987)
Lieut. Governor: Myrl H. Shoemaker, D (to Jan. 1987)
Secy. of State: Sherrod Brown, D (to Jan. 1987)
Auditor: Thomas E. Ferguson (to Jan. 1987)
Treasurer: Mary Ellen Withrow, D (to Jan. 1987)
Atty. General: Anthony J. Celebrezze, Jr., D (to Jan. 1987)
Entered Union & (rank): March 1, 1803 (17)
Present constitution adopted: 1851
Motto: With God, all things are possible
State flower: Scarlet carnation (1904)
State tree: Buckeye (1953)
State bird: Cardinal (1933)
State insect: Ladybug (1975)
State gemstone: Flint (1965)
State song: "Beautiful Ohio"
State drink: Tomato juice (1965)
Nickname: Buckeye State
Origin of name: From an Iroquoian word meaning "great river"
1980 population (1980 census) & (rank): 10,797,624 (6)
1983 est. population (July) & (rank): 10,746,000 (6)
1984 land area & (rank): 41,004 sq mi. (106,201 sq km) (35)
Geographic center: In Delaware Co., 25 mi. NNE of Columbus
Number of counties: 88
Largest cities (1980 census): Cleveland, 573,822; Columbus, 565,032; Cincinnati, 385,457; Toledo, 354,635; Akron, 237,177; Dayton, 203,371; Youngstown, 115,436
State forests: 19 (172,744 ac.)
State parks: 71 (198,027 ac.)
State actual revenue (1982–83): $11,562,171,075
State actual expenditure (1982–83): $11,599,117,511

First explored for France by La Salle in 1669, the Ohio region became British property after the French and Indian War. Ohio was acquired by the U.S. after the Revolutionary War in 1783 and, in 1788, the first permanent settlement was established at Marietta, capital of the Northwest Territory.

The 1790s saw severe fighting with the Indians in Ohio; a major battle was won by Maj. Gen. Anthony Wayne at Fallen Timbers in 1794. In the War of 1812, Commodore Oliver H. Perry defeated the British in the Battle of Lake Erie on Sept. 10, 1813.

Ohio is one of the nation's industrial leaders, ranking third in the value of manufactured products. Important manufacturing centers are located in or near Ohio's major cities. Akron is known for rubber; Canton for roller bearings; Cincinnati for jet engines and machine tools; Cleveland for auto assembly and parts, refining, and steel; Dayton for office machines, refrigeration, and heating and auto equipment; Youngstown and Steubenville for steel; and Toledo for glass and auto parts.

The state's thousands of factories almost overshadow its importance in agriculture and mining. Its fertile soil produces soybeans, corn, oats, grapes, and clover. More than half of Ohio's farm receipts come from dairying and sheep and hog raising. Ohio is the top state in lime production and among the leaders in coal, clay, salt, sand, and gravel. Petroleum, gypsum, cement, and natural gas are also important.

Tourism is a valuable revenue producer, bringing in over $3 billion annually. Attractions include the Indian burial grounds at Mound City Group National Monument, Perry's Victory International Peace Memorial, the Pro Football Hall of Fame at Canton, and the homes of Presidents Grant, Taft, Hayes, Harding, and Garfield.

OKLAHOMA

Capital: Oklahoma City
Governor: George P. Nigh, D (to Jan. 1987)
Lieut. Governor: Spencer Bernard, D (to Jan. 1987)
Secy. of State: Jeannette Edmondson, D (to Jan. 1987)
Treasurer: Leo Winters, D (to Jan. 1987)
Atty. General: Michael C. Turpen, D (to Jan. 1987)
Organized as territory: May 2, 1890
Entered Union & (rank): Nov. 16, 1907 (46)
Present constitution adopted: 1907
Motto: *Labor omnia vincit* (Labor conquers all things)
State flower: Mistletoe (1893)
State tree: Redbud (1937)
State bird: Scissor-tailed flycatcher (1951)
State animal: Bison (1972)
State reptile: Mountain boomer lizard (1969)
State stone: Rose Rock (barite rose) (1968)
State colors: Green and white (1915)
State song: "Oklahoma" (1953)
Nickname: Sooner State
Origin of name: From two Choctaw Indian words meaning "red people"
1980 population (1980 census) & (rank): 3,025,290 (26)
1983 est. population (July) & (rank): 3,298,000 (24)
1984 land area & (rank): 68,655 sq mi. (177,817 sq km) (19)
Geographic center: In Oklahoma Co., 8 mi. N of Oklahoma City
Number of counties: 77
Largest cities (1980 census): Oklahoma City, 403,213; Tulsa, 360,919; Lawton, 80,054; Norman, 68,020; Enid, 50,363; Midwest City, 49,559; Muskogee, 40,011
State forests: None
State parks: 36 (57,487 ac.)
Total state revenue (1983): $4,839,433,462
Total state expenditure (1983): $4,790,504,400

Francisco Vásquez de Coronado first explored the region for Spain in 1541. The U.S. acquired most of Oklahoma in 1803 in the Louisiana Purchase from France; the Western Panhandle region became U.S. territory with the annexation of Texas in 1845.

In 1834, Oklahoma was set aside as Indian Territory. It remained so until April 22, 1889, when it was opened to homestead settlement. On that one day 50,000 people swarmed in and the term "Sooners" was applied to those who tried to beat the noon starting gun. Other Oklahoma "Land Rushes" took place through 1901.

Oil has made Oklahoma a rich state and Tulsa one of the world's wealthiest cities per capita. Oil refining, meat packing, food processing, and machinery manufacturing (especially construction and oil equipment) are important industries.

Other minerals produced in Oklahoma include natural gas, helium, gypsum, zinc, cement, coal, copper, and silver.

Oklahoma's rich plains produce bumper yields of wheat, as well as large crops of sorghum, corn, cotton, and peanuts. Its beef cattle herd is among the largest in the nation; more than half of Oklahoma's annual farm receipts are contributed by livestock products.

Tourist attractions include the National Cowboy Hall of Fame in Oklahoma City, the Will Rogers Memorial in Claremore, the Cherokee Cultural Center with a restored Cherokee village, the restored Fort Gibson Stockade near Muskogee, and the Lake Texoma recreation area.

OREGON

Capital: Salem
Governor: Victor G. Atiyeh, R (to Jan. 1987)
Secy. of State: Norma Paulus, R (to Jan. 1985)
Treasurer: Bill Rutherford, R (to Jan. 1985)
Atty. General: David B. Frohnmayer, R (to Jan. 1985)
Organized as territory: Aug. 14, 1848
Entered Union & (rank): Feb. 14, 1859 (33)
Present constitution adopted: 1859
Motto: The Union (1957)
State flower: Oregon grape (1899)
State tree: Douglas fir (1939)
State animal: Beaver (1969)
State bird: Western meadow lark (1927)
State fish: Chinook salmon (1961)
State rock: Thunderegg (1965)
State colors: Navy blue and gold (1959)
State song: "Oregon, My Oregon" (1927)
Nickname: Beaver State
Origin of name: Unknown. However, it is generally accepted that the name, first used by Jonathan Carver in 1778, was taken from the writings of Maj. Robert Rogers, an English army officer.
1980 population (1980 census) & (rank): 2,633,105 (30)
1983 est. population (July) & (rank): 2,662,000 (30)
1984 land area & (rank): 96,184 sq mi. (249,117 sq km) (10)
Geographic center: In Crook Co., 25 mi. SSE of Prineville
Number of counties: 36
Largest cities (1980 census): Portland, 366,383; Eugene, 105,624; Salem, 89,233; Springfield, 41,621; Corvallis, 40,960; Medford, 39,603; Gresham, 33,005
State forests: 820,000 ac.
State parks: 240 (93,330 ac.)
State general revenue (1983–85 est.): $3,184,077,600
State general expenditure (1983–85 est.): $3,139,102,829

Spanish and English sailors are believed to have sighted the Oregon coast in the 1500s and 1600s. Capt. James Cook, seeking the Northwest Passage, charted some of the coastline in 1778. In 1792, Capt. Robert Gray, in the *Columbia,* discovered the river named after his ship and claimed the area for the U.S.

In 1805 the Lewis and Clark expedition explored the area and John Jacob Astor's fur depot, Astoria, was founded in 1811. Disputes for control of Oregon between American settlers and the Hudson Bay Company were finally resolved in the 1846 Oregon Treaty in which Great Britain gave up claims to the region.

Oregon, with the greatest U.S. reserve of standing timber, has a five-billion-dollar wood processing industry. Its salmon-fishing industry, centered at Astoria at the mouth of the Columbia, is one of the world's largest.

In agriculture, the state leads in growing peppermint, winter pears, fresh plums, prunes, blackberries, boysenberries, filberts, Blue Lake beans, and cover seed crops, and also raises strawberries, hops, wheat and other grains, sugar beets, potatoes, green peas, fiber flax, dairy products, livestock and poultry, apples, pears, and cherries. Oregon is the source of all the nickel produced in the U.S.

With the low-cost electric power provided by Bonneville Dam, McNary Dam, and other dams in the Pacific Northwest, Oregon has developed steadily as a manufacturing state. Leading manufactures are lumber and plywood, metalwork, machinery, aluminum, chemicals, paper, food packing, and electronic equipment.

Crater Lake National Park, Mount Hood, and Bonneville Dam on the Columbia are major tourist attractions. Oregon Dunes National Recreation Area has been established near Florence. Other points of interest include the Oregon Caves National Monument, Cape Perpetua in Siuslaw National Forest, Columbia River Gorge between The Dalles and Troutdale, and Hells Canyon.

PENNSYLVANIA

Capital: Harrisburg
Governor: Richard L. Thornburgh, R (to Jan. 1987)
Lieut. Governor: William W. Scranton III, R (to Jan. 1987)
Secy. of the Commonwealth: William R. Davis (apptd. by the Governor)
Auditor General: Al Benedict, D (to Jan. 1985)
Atty. General: Leroy S. Zimmerman, R (to Jan. 1985)
Entered Union & (rank): Dec. 12, 1787 (2)
Present constitution adopted: 1968
Motto: Virtue, liberty, and independence
State flower: Mountain laurel (1933)
State tree: Hemlock (1931)
State bird: Ruffed grouse (1931)
State insect: Firefly (1974)
State dog: Great Dane (1965)
State colors: Blue and gold
State song: None
Nickname: Keystone State
Origin of name: In honor of Adm. Sir. William Penn, father of William Penn. It means "Penn's Woodland."
1980 population (1980 census) & (rank): 11,866,728 (4)
1983 est. population (July) & (rank): 11,895,000 (4)
1984 land area & (rank): 44,888 sq mi. (116,260 sq km) (32)
Geographic center: In Centre Co., 2 1/2 mi. SW of Bellefonte
Number of counties: 67
Largest cities (1980 census): Philadelphia, 1,688,210; Pittsburgh, 423,938; Erie, 119,123; Scranton, 88,117; Reading, 78,686; Bethlehem, 70,419
State forests: 1,945,503 ac.
State parks: 112 (278,909 ac.)
Total estimated revenue subject to general appropriations (1984–85): $8,503,889,000
Total est. appropriations (1984–85): $8,500,456,000

Rich in historic lore, Pennsylvania territory was disputed in the early 1600s among the Dutch, the Swedes, and the English. England acquired the region in 1664 with the capture of New York and in 1681 Pennsylvania was granted to William Penn, a Quaker, by King Charles II.

Philadelphia was the seat of the federal government almost continuously from 1776 to 1800; there the Declaration of Independence was signed in 1776 and the U.S. Constitution drawn up in 1787. Valley Forge, of Revolutionary War fame, and Gettysburg, the turning-point of the Civil War, are both in Pennsylvania. The Liberty Bell is located in Independence Hall in Philadelphia.

Approximately 23% of all American pig iron steel is made in Pennsylvania, which ranks first among the states in steel wire and structural metal production. Other manufactures include machinery, chemicals, storage batteries, motor vehicles and trailers, computers, textiles and apparel, shoes, plastics, and explosives. Pennsylvania produces almost all the nation's anthracite coal. Also important are bituminous coal, cement, stone, petroleum, natural gas, lime, clays, zinc, and iron.

Prosperous farms brought in total receipts of more than $1.3 billion in 1973. The state ranked high in milk cows, chickens, and turkeys. Agricultural products include apples, peaches, potatoes, corn, wheat, barley, buckwheat, and mushrooms.

Tourists now spend approximately $6 billion in Pennsylvania annually. Among the chief attractions: the Gettysburg National Military Park, Valley Forge National Historical Park, Independence National Historical Park in Philadelphia, the Pennsylvania Dutch region, the Eisenhower farm near Gettysburg, and the Delaware Water Gap National Recreation Area.

RHODE ISLAND

Capital: Providence
Governor: J. Joseph Garrahy, D (to Jan. 1985)
Lieut. Governor: Thomas R. Di Luglio, D (to Jan. 1985)
Secy. of State: Susan Farmer, R (to Jan. 1985)
Controller: James A. Carter (civil service)
Atty. General: Dennis J. Roberts II, D (to Jan. 1985)
Entered Union & (rank): May 29, 1790 (13)
Present constitution adopted: 1843
Motto: Hope
State flower: Violet (unofficial)
State tree: Red maple (official)
State bird: Rhode Island Red (official)
State colors: Blue, white, and gold (in state flag)
State song: "Rhode Island" (1946)
Nickname: The Ocean State
Origin of name: From the Greek Island of Rhodes
1980 population (1980 census) & (rank): 947,154 (40)
1983 est. population (July) & (rank): 955,000 (42)
1984 land area & (rank): 1,055 sq mi. (2,732 sq km) (50)
Geographic center: In Kent Co., 1 mi. SSW of Crompton
Number of counties: 5
Largest cities (1980 census): Providence, 156,804; Warwick, 87,123; Cranston, 71,992; Pawtucket, 71,204; East Providence, 50,980; Woonsocket, 45,914
State forests: 11 (20,900 ac.)
State parks: 17 (8,200 ac.)
State general revenue (1982–83): $1,160,806,905
State general expenditure (1982–83): $1,170,913,932

From its beginnings, Rhode Island has been distinguished by its support for freedom of conscience and action, started by Roger Williams, who was exiled by the Massachusetts Bay Colony Puritans in 1636, and was the founder of the present state capital, Providence. Williams was followed by other religious exiles who founded Pocasset, now Portsmouth, in 1638 and Newport in 1639.

The first Baptist church in the U.S. was established in Providence in 1638 and Rhode Island provided a haven for Quakers in 1657 and for Jews from Holland in 1659.

Rhode Island's rebellious, authority-defying nature was further demonstrated by the burnings of the British revenue cutters *Liberty* and *Gaspee* prior to the Revolution, by its early declaration of independence from Great Britain in May 1776, its refusal to participate actively in the War of 1812, and by Dorr's Rebellion of 1842, which protested property requirements for voting.

Rhode Island, smallest of the 50 states, is densely populated and highly industrialized. The state pioneered in the manufacture of jewelry and silverware and still retains first place in the U.S. Other leading industries are primary metal processing, metal products, machinery, rubber and plastics, food processing, chemicals, transportation equipment and electronic equipment.

With more than eight tenths of the population living in urban areas, adjacent areas of the state are involved in dairying and poultry and truck farming. Nursery and greenhouse products, potatoes, corn, apples, oats, and hay lead the crop list.

Newport became famous as the summer capital of society in the mid-19th century. Touro Synagogue (1763) is the oldest in the U.S. Other points of interest include the Roger Williams National Memorial in Providence, Samuel Slater's Mill in Pawtucket, the General Nathaniel Greene Homestead in Coventry, Block Island, and Narragansett Pier.

SOUTH CAROLINA

Capital: Columbia
Governor: Richard W. Riley, D (to Jan. 1987)
Lieut. Governor: Mike Daniel, D (to Jan. 1987)
Secy. of State: John T. Campbell, D (to Jan. 1987)
Comptroller General: Earl E. Morris, Jr. (to Jan. 1987)
Atty. General: T. Travis Medlock, D (to Jan. 1987)
Entered Union & (rank): May 23, 1788 (8).
Present constitution adopted: 1895
Mottoes: *Animis opibusque parati* (Prepared in mind and resources) and *Dum spiro spero* (While I breathe, I hope)
State flower: Carolina yellow jessamine (1924)
State tree: Palmetto tree (1939)
State bird: Carolina wren (1948)
State song: "Carolina" (1911)
Nickname: Palmetto State
Origin of name: In honor of Charles I of England
1980 population (1980 census) & (rank): 3,121,833 (24)
1983 est. population (July) & (rank): 3,264,000 (25)
1984 land area & (rank): 30,203 sq mi. (78,227 sq km) (40)
Geographic center: In Richland Co., 13 mi. SE of Columbia
Number of counties: 46
Largest cities (1980 census): Columbia, 100,385; Charleston, 69,510; North Charleston, 62,534; Greenville, 58,242; Spartanburg, 43,826; Rock Hill, 35,344
State forests: 4 (124,052 ac.)
State parks: 50 (61,726 ac.)
State general fund revenue (1983–84 est.): $2,143,710,610[1]
State general expenditures (1983–84 est.): $2,121,900,556[1]

1. Highway Department has separate funding and expenditures.

Following exploration of the coast in 1521 by De Gordillo, the Spanish tried unsuccessfully to establish a colony near present-day Georgetown in 1526 and the French also failed to colonize Parris Island near Fort Royal in 1562.

The first English settlement was made in 1670 at Albemarle Point on the Ashley River, but poor conditions drove the settlers to the site of Charleston (originally called Charles Town). South Carolina, officially separated from North Carolina in 1729, was the scene of extensive military action during the Revolution and again during the Civil War. The Civil War began in 1861 as South Carolina troops fired on federal Fort Sumter in Charleston Harbor and the state was the first to secede from the Union.

Once primarily agricultural, South Carolina has built so many large textile and other mills that today its factories produce eight times the output of its farms in cash value. Charleston makes asbestos, wood, pulp, and steel products; chemicals, machinery, and apparel are also important.

Farms have become fewer but larger in recent years. South Carolina grows more peaches than any other state except California; it ranks fourth in tobacco. Other farm products include cotton, peanuts, sweet potatoes, soybeans, corn, and oats. Poultry and dairy products are also important revenue producers.

Points of interest include Fort Sumter National Monument, Fort Moultrie, Fort Johnson, and aircraft carrier USS *Yorktown* in Charleston Harbor; the Middleton, Magnolia, and Cypress Gardens in Charleston; Cowpens National Battlefield; and the Hilton Head resorts.

SOUTH DAKOTA

Capital: Pierre
Governor: William J. Janklow, R (to Jan. 1987)
Lieut. Governor: Lowell C. Hansen II, R (to Jan. 1987)
Atty. General: Mark Meierhenry, R (to Jan. 1987)
Secy. of State: Alice Kundert, R (to Jan. 1987)
State Auditor: Vern Larson, R (to Jan. 1987)
State Treasurer: David L. Volk, R (to Jan. 1987)
Organized as territory: March 2, 1861
Entered Union & (rank): Nov. 2, 1889 (40)
Present constitution adopted: 1889
Motto: Under God the people rule
State flower: American pasqueflower (1903)
State grass: Western wheat grass (1970)
State tree: Black Hills spruce (1947)
State bird: Ring-necked pheasant (1943)
State insect: Honeybee (1978)
State animal: Coyote (1949)
State mineral stone: Rose quartz (1966)
State gemstone: Fairburn agate (1966)
State colors: Blue and gold (in state flag)
State song: "Hail! South Dakota" (1943)
State fish: Walleye (1982)
Nicknames: Sunshine State; Coyote State
Origin of name: Same as for North Dakota
1980 population (1980 census) & (rank): 690,768 (45)
1983 est. population (July) & (rank): 700,000 (45)
1984 land area & (rank): 75,952 sq mi. (196,715 sq km) (16)
Geographic center: In Hughes Co., 8 mi. NE of Pierre
Number of counties: 67 (64 county governments)
Largest cities (1980 census): Sioux Falls, 81,343; Rapid City, 46,492; Aberdeen, 25,851; Watertown, 15,649; Brookings, 14,951; Mitchell, 13,916; Huron, 13,000
State forests: None[1]
State parks: 13 plus 39 recreational areas (87,269 ac.)[2]
State general revenue (1983): $273,721,454
State general expenditure (1983): $276,364,217

1. No designated state forests; about 13,000 ac. of state land is forestland. 2. Acreage includes 39 recreation areas and 80 roadside parks, in addition to 12 state parks.

Exploration of this area began in 1743 when Louis-Joseph and François Verendrye came from France in search of a route to the Pacific.

The U.S. acquired the region as part of the Louisiana Purchase in 1803 and it was explored by Lewis and Clark in 1804–06. Fort Pierre, the first permanent settlement, was established in 1817 and, in 1831, the first Missouri River steamboat reached the fort.

Settlement of South Dakota did not begin in earnest until the arrival of the railroad in 1873 and the discovery of gold in the Black Hills the following year.

Agriculture is South Dakota's basic industry today. It normally ranks first in the U.S. in the size of its rye crop and high in spring wheat, flaxseed, oats, and barley. In 1983 South Dakota had 4,220, 000 cattle, 730,000 sheep, and 1,650,000 hogs.

South Dakota is the nation's second leading producer of gold (Nevada ranks first) and the Homestake Mine is the richest in the U.S. Other minerals produced include berylium, bentonite, granite, silver, petroleum, and uranium.

Processing of foods produced by farms and ranches is the largest South Dakota manufacturing industry, followed by lumber, wood products, and machinery, including farm equipment.

The Black Hills are the highest mountains east of the Rockies. Mt. Rushmore, in this group, is famous for the likenesses of Washington, Jefferson, Lincoln, and Theodore Roosevelt, which were carved in granite by Gutzon Borglum. The Badlands offer scenic masses of bare rock and clay unrelieved by any vegetation. Other points of interest are Deadwood, where Wild Bill Hickok was killed in 1876; the Crazy Horse Memorial near Custer; and the Corn Palace in Mitchell.

TENNESSEE

Capital: Nashville
Governor: Lamar Alexander, R (to Jan. 1987)
Lieut. Governor: John S. Wilder, D (to Jan. 1985)
Secy. of State: Gentry Crowell, D (to Jan. 1985)
Atty. General: William M. Leech, Jr., D (to Sept. 1986)
State Treasurer: Harlan Mathews, D (to Jan. 1985)
Entered Union & (rank): June 1, 1796 (16)
Present constitution adopted: 1870; amended 1953, 1960, 1965, and 1973
Motto: "Tennessee—America at its best!" (1965)
State flower: Iris (1933)
State tree: Tulip poplar (1947)
State bird: Mockingbird (1933)
State horse: Tennessee walking horse
State animal: Raccoon
State wild flower: Passion flower
State song: "Tennessee Waltz" (1965)
Nickname: Volunteer State
Origin of name: Of Cherokee origin; the exact meaning is unknown
1980 population (1980 census) & (rank): 4,591,120 (17)
1983 est. population (July) & (rank): 4,685,000 (17)
1984 land area & (rank): 41,155 sq mi. (106,591 sq km) (34)
Geographic center: In Rutherford Co., 5 mi. NE of Murfreesboro
Number of counties: 95
Largest cities (1980 census): Memphis, 646,174; Nashville, 455,651; Knoxville, 175,045; Chattanooga, 169,558; Clarksville, 54,777; Jackson, 49,131
State forests: 14 (155,752 ac.)
State parks: 21 (130,000 ac.)
State general revenue (1982): $4,521,000,000
State general expenditure (1982): $4,298,000,000

First visited by the Spanish explorer de Soto in 1541, the Tennessee area would later be claimed by both France and England as a result of the 1670s and 1680s explorations of Marquette and Jolliet, La Salle, and the Englishmen James Needham and Gabriel Arthur.

Great Britain obtained the region following the French and Indian War in 1763 and it was rapidly occupied by settlers moving in from Virginia and the Carolinas.

During 1784–87, the settlers formed the "state" of Franklin, which was disbanded when the region was allowed to send representatives to the North Carolina legislature. In 1790 Congress organized the territory south of the Ohio River and Tennessee joined the Union in 1796.

Although Tennessee joined the Confederacy during the Civil War, there was much pro-Union sentiment in the state, which was the scene of extensive military action.

The state is now predominantly industrial; in 1970, 58.8% of its population lived in urban areas. Among the most important products are chemicals, textiles, apparel, electrical machinery, furniture, and leather goods. Other lines include food processing, lumber, primary metals, and metal products. The state is known as the U.S. hardwood-flooring center and ranks first in the production of marble, zinc, pyrite, and ball clay.

Tennessee is one of the leading tobacco-producing states in the nation and its farming income is also derived from livestock and dairy products as well as corn, cotton, and soybeans.

With six other states, Tennessee shares the extensive federal reservoir developments on the Tennessee and Cumberland River systems. The Tennessee Valley Authority operates a number of dams and reservoirs in the state.

Among the major points of interest: the Andrew Johnson National Historic Site at Greenville, American Museum of Atomic Energy at Oak Ridge, Great Smoky Mountains National Park, The Hermitage (home of Andrew Jackson near Nashville), Rock City Gardens near Chattanooga, and three National Military Parks.

TEXAS

Capital: Austin
Governor: Mark White, D (to Jan. 1987)
Lieut. Governor: William P. Hobby, D (to Jan. 1986)
Secy. of State: John Fainter, D (to Jan. 1987)
Comptroller: Bob Bullock (to Jan. 1987)
Atty. General: Jim Mattox, D (to Jan. 1987)
Entered Union & (rank): Dec. 29, 1845 (28)
Present constitution adopted: 1876
Motto: Friendship
State flower: Bluebonnet (1901)
State tree: Pecan (1919)
State bird: Mockingbird (1927)
State song: "Texas, Our Texas" (1930)
Nickname: Lone Star State
Origin of name: From an Indian word meaning "friends"
1980 population (1980 census) & (rank): 14,229,288 (3)
1983 est. population (July) & (rank): 15,724,000 (3)
1984 land area & (rank): 262,017 sq mi. (678,623 sq km) (2)
Geographic center: In McCulloch Co., 15 mi. NE of Brady
Number of counties: 254
Largest cities (1980 census): Houston, 1,595,138; Dallas, 904,078; San Antonio, 785,023; El Paso, 425,259; Fort Worth, 385,164; Austin, 345,496
State forests: 4 (6,306 ac.)
State parks: 83 (64 developed)
State revenue receipts (1981–82): $27,549,944,302
State government cost (1981–82): $26,949,609,825
Total net revenue: (1982–83): $14,619,602,768
Total net expenditures (1982–83): $13,642,028,058

Spanish explorers, including Cabeza de Vaca and Coronado, were the first to visit the region in the 16th and 17th centuries, settling at Ysleta near present-day El Paso in 1682. In 1685, La Salle established a short-lived French colony at Matagorda Bay.

Americans, led by Stephen F. Austin, began to settle along the Brazos River in 1821 when Texas was controlled by Mexico, recently independent from Spain. In 1836, following a brief war between the American settlers in Texas and the Mexican government, and famous for the battles of the Alamo and San Jacinto, the Independent Republic of Texas was proclaimed with Sam Houston as president.

After Texas became the 28th U.S. state in 1845, border disputes led to the Mexican War of 1846–48.

Today, Texas, second only to Alaska in land area, leads all other states in such categories as oil, cattle, sheep, and cotton. Possessing enormous natural resources, Texas is a major agricultural state and an industrial giant.

Sulfur, salt, helium, asphalt, graphite, bromine, natural gas, cement, and clays give Texas first place in mineral production—nearly $8 billion in 1973. Chemicals, oil refining, food processing, machinery, and transportation equipment are among the major Texas manufacturing industries.

Texas ranches and farms produce beef cattle, poultry, rice, pecans, peanuts, sorghum, and an extensive variety of fruits and vegetables.

Millions of tourists spend well over $2 billion annually visiting more than 70 state parks, recreations areas, and points of interest such as the Gulf Coast resort area, the Lyndon B. Johnson Space Center in Houston, the Alamo in San Antonio, the state capital in Austin, and the Big Bend and Guadalupe Mountains National Parks.

UTAH

Capital: Salt Lake City
Governor: Scott M. Matheson, D (to Jan. 1985)
Lieut. Governor: David S. Monson, R (to Jan. 1985)
Atty. General: David Wilkison, R (to Jan. 1985)
Organized as territory: Sept. 9, 1850
Entered Union & (rank): Jan. 4, 1896 (45)
Present constitution adopted: 1896
Motto: Industry
State flower: Sego lily (1911)
State tree: Blue spruce (1933)
State bird: Seagull (1955)
State emblem: Beehive
State song: "Utah, We Love Thee"
Nickname: Beehive State
Origin of name: From the Ute tribe, meaning "people of the mountains"
1980 population (1980 census) & (rank): 1,461,037 (36)
1983 est. population (July) & (rank): 1,619,000 (35)
1984 land area & (rank): 82,073 sq mi. (212,569 sq km) (12)

Geographic center: In Sanpete Co., 3 mi. N. of Manti
Number of counties: 29
Largest cities (1980 census): Salt Lake City, 163,697; Provo, 52,210; Ogden, 64,407; Orem, 52,399; Sandy City, 52,210; Bountiful, 32,877; West Jordan, 27,192; Logan, 26,844; Murray, 25,750
State forests: None
State parks: 44 (64,097 ac.)
Total state revenues (Fiscal 1983): $1,601,010,000
Total state expenditures (Fiscal 1983): $1,715,606,000
Cash balance—Unappropriated general fund balance (Fiscal 1983): $11,585,000

The region was first explored for Spain by Franciscan friars, Escalante and Dominguez in 1776. In 1824 the famous American frontiersman Jim Bridger discovered the Great Salt Lake.

Fleeing the religious persecution encountered in eastern and middle-western states, the Mormons reached the Great Salt Lakes in 1847 and began to build Salt Lake City. The U.S. acquried te Utah region in the treaty ending the Mexican War in 1848 and the first transcontinental railroad was completed with the driving of a golden spike at Promontory Point in 1869.

Mormon difficulties with the federal government about polygamy did not end until the Mormon Church renounced the practice in 1890, six years before Utah became a state.

In recent years, manufacturing has become Utah's most important industry, ahead of mining, agriculture, and tourism. The state's factories produce transportation equipment, food products, machinery, metal products, and electrical equipment. Utah has also become an important aerospace research and production center and is a leading warehousing and distribution point for much of the western U.S.

Rich in natural resources, Utah has long been a leading producer of copper, gold, silver, lead, zinc, and molybdenum. Oil has also become a major product; with Colorado and Wyoming, Utah shares what have been called the world's richest oil shale deposits.

Ranked eighth among the states in number of sheep in 1973, Utah also produces large crops of apricots and cherries as well as sugar beets, potatoes, onions, alfalfa, winter wheat, and beans. Utah's farmlands and crops require extensive irrigation.

Utah is a great vacationland with 11,000 miles of fishing streams and 147,000 acres of lakes and reservoirs. Among the many tourist attractions are Arches, Bryce Canyon, Canyonlands, Capitol Reef, and Zion National Parks; Dinosaur, Natural Bridges, and Rainbow Bridge National Monuments; the Mormon Tabernacle in Salt Lake City; and Monument Valley.

VERMONT

Capital: Montpelier
Governor: Richard A. Snelling, R (to Jan. 1985)
Lieut. Governor: Peter Smith (to Jan. 1985)
Secy. of State: James H. Douglas (to Jan. 1985)
Treasurer: Emory A. Hebard, R (to Jan. 1985)
Auditor of Accounts: Alexander V. Acebo (to Jan. 1985)
Atty. General: John J. Easton, Jr. (to Jan. 1985)
Entered Union & (rank): March 4, 1791 (14)
Present constitution adopted: 1793
Motto: Vermont, Freedom, and Unity
State flower: Red clover (1894)
State tree: Sugar maple (1949)
State bird: Hermit thrush (1941)
State animal: Morgan horse (1961)
State insect: Honeybee (1978)
State song: "Hail, Vermont!" (1938)
Nickname: Green Mountain State
Origin of name: From the French "vert mont," meaning "green mountain"
1980 population (1980 census) & (rank): 511,456 (48)
1983 est. population (July) & (rank): 525,000 (48)
1984 land area & (rank): 9,273 sq mi. (24,017 sq km) (43)
Geographic center: In Washington Co., 3 mi. E of Roxbury
Number of counties: 14
Largest cities (1980 census): Burlington, 37,712; Rutland, 18,436; South Burlington, 10,679; Barre, 9,824; Montpelier, 8,241; St. Albans, 7,308; Winooski, 6,318
State forests: 34 (113,953 ac.)
State parks: 45 (31,325 ac.)
State receipts (1983): $690,778,567
State disbursements (1983): $745,879,191

The Vermont region was explored and claimed for France by Samuel de Champlain in 1609 and the first French settlement was established at Fort Ste. Anne in 1666. The first English settlers moved into the area in 1724 and built Fort Drummer on the site of present-day Brattleboro. England gained control of the area in 1763 after the French and Indian War.

First organized to drive settlers from New York out of Vermont, the Green Mountain Boys, led by Ethan Allen, won fame by capturing Fort Ticonderoga from the British on May 10, 1775, in the early days of the Revolution.

In 1777 Vermont adopted its first constitution abolishing slavery and providing for universal male suffrage without property qualifications. In 1791 Vermont became the first state after the original 13 to join the Union.

Vermont leads the nation in the production of monument granite, marble, and maple syrup. It is also a leader in the production of asbestos and talc.

In ratio to population, Vermont keeps more dairy cows than any other state. Vermont's soil is devoted to dairying, truck farming, and fruit growing because the rugged, rocky terrain discourages extensive farming.

Principal manufactured goods are machine tools, computer components, stone and clay products, lumber, furniture, and paper.

Tourism is a major industry in Vermont. Vermont's many famous ski areas include Stowe, Killington, Mt. Snow, Bromley, Jay Peak, and Sugarbush. Hunting and fishing also attract many visitors to Vermont each year. Among the many points of interest are the Green Mountain National Forest, Bennington Battle Monument, the Calvin Coolidge Homestead at Plymouth, and the Marble Exhibit in Proctor.

VIRGINIA

Capital: Richmond
Governor: Charles S. Robb, D (to Jan. 1986)
Lieut. Governor: Richard J. Davis, D (to Jan. 1986)
Secy. of the Commonwealth: Frederick T. Gray, D (apptd. by Governor)
Acting Comptroller: Vincent Pross, Jr. (apptd. by Governor)
Atty. General: Gerald L. Baliles, D (to Jan. 1986)

Entered Union & (rank): June 25, 1788 (10)
Present constitution adopted: 1970
Motto: *Sic semper tyrannis* (Thus always to tyrants)
State flower: American dogwood (1918)
State bird: Cardinal (1950)
State dog: American foxhound (1966)
State shell: Oyster shell
State song: "Carry Me Back to Old Virginia" (1940)
Nicknames: The Old Dominion; Mother of Presidents
Origin of name: In honor of Elizabeth "Virgin Queen" of England
1980 population (1980 census) & (rank): 5,346,818 (14)
1983 est. population (July) & (rank): 5,550,000 (13)
1984 land area & (rank): 39,703 sq mi. (102,832 sq km) (36)
Geographic center: In Buckingham Co., 5 mi. SW of Buckingham
Number of counties: 95, plus 41 independent cities
Largest cities (1980 census): Norfolk, 266,979; Virginia Beach, 262,199; Richmond, 219,214; Newport News, 144,903; Hampton, 122,617; Chesapeake, 114,486
State forests: 8 (49,566 ac.)
State parks and recreational parks: 22, plus 3 in process of acquisition and/or development (42,722 ac.)[1]
State revenue (1981–82): $5,919,100,000
State expenditure (1981–82): $6,095,400,000

1. Does not include portion of Breaks Interstate Park (Va.-Ky., 1,200 ac.) which lies in Virginia.

The history of America is closely tied to that of Virginia, particularly in the Colonial period. Jamestown, founded in 1607, was the first permanent English settlement in North America and slavery was introduced there in 1619. The surrenders ending both the American Revolution (Yorktown) and the Civil War (Appomattox) occurred in Virginia. The state is called the "Mother of Presidents" because eight chief executives of the United States were born there.

Today, Virginia has a large number of diversified manufacturing industries including chemicals, textiles, food products, and clothing. Other important lines are lumber, paper, furniture, cigarettes, electrical machinery, transportation equipment, and stone-glass-clay products.

Agriculture remains an important sector in the Virginia economy and the state ranks among the leaders in the U.S. in tobacco, peanuts, apples, and sweet potatoes. Other crops include corn, vegetables, barley, and peaches. Famous for its turkeys and Smithfield hams, Virginia also has a large dairy industry.

Coal mining accounts for roughly 70% of Virginia's mineral output, and lime, zinc, and stone are also mined.

Points of interest include Mt. Vernon and other places associated with George Washington; Monticello, home of Thomas Jefferson; Stratford, home of the Lees; Richmond, capital of the Confederacy and of Virginia; and Williamsburg, the restored Colonial capital.

The Chesapeake Bay Bridge-Tunnel spans the mouth of Chesapeake Bay, connecting Cape Charles with Norfolk. Consisting of a series of low trestles, two bridges and two mile-long tunnels, the complex is 18 miles (29 km) long. It was opened in 1964.

Other attractions are the Shenandoah National Park, Fredericksburg and Spotsylvania National Military Park, the Booker T. Washington birthplace near Roanoke, Arlington House (the Robert E. Lee Memorial), the Skyline Drive, and the Blue Ridge National Parkway.

WASHINGTON

Capital: Olympia
Governor: John Spellman (to Jan. 1985)
Lieut. Governor: John A. Cherberg, (to Jan. 1985)
Secy. of State: Ralph Munro (to Jan. 1985)
State Treasurer: Robert S. O'Brien (to Jan. 1985)
Atty. General: Kenneth O. Eikenberry (to Jan. 1985)
Organized as territory: March 2, 1853
Entered Union & (rank): Nov. 11, 1889 (42)
Present constitution adopted: 1889
Motto: *Al-Ki* (Indian word meaning "by and by")
State flower: Rhododendron (1949)
State tree: Western hemlock (1947)
State bird: Willow goldfinch (1951)
State fish: Steelhead trout (1969)
State gem: Petrified wood (1975)
State colors: Green and gold (1925)
State song: "Washington, My Home" (1959)
State dance: Square dance (1979)
Nicknames: Evergreen State; Chinook State
Origin of name: In honor of George Washington
1980 population (1980 census) & (rank): 4,132,180 (20)
1983 est. population (July) & (rank): 4,300,000 (20)
1984 land area & (rank): 66,511 sq mi (172,264 sq km) (20)
Geographic center: In Chelan Co., 10 mi. WSW of Wenatchee
Number of countries: 39
Largest cities (1980 census): Seattle, 493,846; Spokane, 171,300; Tacoma, 158,501; Bellevue, 73,903; Everett, 54,413; Yakima, 49,826; Bellingham, 45,794
State forest lands: 1,922,880 ac.
State parks: 202 (171,700 ac.)[1]
State revenue (1983–85 projected): $14,361,400,000
State expenditure (1983–85 projected): $14,788,100,000

1. Parks and undeveloped areas administered by Parks and Recreation Dept. Game Dept. administers wildlife and recreation areas totaling 762,895 acres.

As part of the vast Oregon Country, Washington territory was visited by Spanish, American, and British explorers—Bruno Heceta for Spain in 1775, the American Capt. Robert Gray in 1792, and Capt. George Vancouver for Britain in 1792–94. Lewis and Clark explored the Columbia River region and coastal areas for the U.S. in 1805–06.

Rival American and British settlers and conflicting territorial claims threatened war in the early 1840s. However, in 1846 the Oregon Treaty set the boundary at the 49th parallel and war was averted.

Washington is a leading lumber producer. Its rugged surface is rich in stands of Douglas fir, hemlock, ponderosa and white pine, spruce, larch, and cedar. The state holds first place in apples, blueberries, hops, and red raspberries and it ranks high in potatoes, winter wheat, pears, grapes, apricots, and strawberries. Livestock and livestock products make important contributions to total farm revenue and the commercial fishing catch of salmon, halibut, and bottomfish makes a significant contribution to the state's economy.

Manufacturing industries in Washington include aircraft and missiles, shipbuilding and other transportation equipment, lumber, food processing, metals and metal products, chemicals, and machinery.

The Columbia River contains one third of the potential water power in the U.S., harnessed by such dams as the Grand Coulee, one of the greatest power producers in the world. Washington has 90 dams throughout the state built for irrigation, power, flood control, and water storage. Its abundance of electrical power makes Washington the nation's largest producer of refined aluminum.

Among the major points of interest: Mt. Rainier, Olympic, and North Cascades. In 1980, Mount St. Helens, a peak in the Cascade Range in Southwestern Washington erupted on May 18th. Also of interest are National Parks; Whitman Mission and Fort Vancouver National Historic Sites; and the Pacific Science Center and Space Needle in Seattle.

WEST VIRGINIA

Capital: Charleston
Governor: John D. Rockefeller IV, D (to Jan. 1985)
Secy. of State: James A. Manchin, D (to Jan. 1985)
State Auditor: Glen Gainer (to Jan. 1985)
Atty. General: Chauncey H. Browning, Jr., D (to Jan. 1985)
Entered Union & (rank): June 20, 1863 (35)
Present constitution adopted: 1872
Motto: *Montani semper liberi* (Mountaineers are always free)
State flower: Rhododendron (1903)
State tree: Sugar maple (1949)
State bird: Cardinal (1949)
State animal: Black bear
State colors: Blue and gold (unofficial)
State songs: "West Virginia, My Home Sweet Home," "The West Virginia Hills," and "This Is My West Virginia" (adopted by Legislature in 1947, 1961 and 1963 as official state songs)
Nickname: Mountain State
Origin of name: Same as for Virginia
1980 population (1980 census) & (rank): 1,950,279 (34)
1983 est. population (July) & (rank): 1,965,000 (34)
1984 land area & (rank): 24,119 sq mi. (62,468 sq km) (41)
Geographic center: In Braxton Co., 4 mi. E of Sutton
Number of counties: 55
Largest cities (1980 census): Charleston, 63,968; Huntington, 63,684; Wheeling, 43,070; Parkersburg, 39,967; Morgantown, 27,605; Weirton, 25,371
State forests: 9 (77,000 ac.)
State parks: 34 (65,861 ac.)
Total state revenue (1982–83): $4,469,285,023
Total state expenditure (1982–83): $4,537,009,760

West Virginia's early history from 1609 until 1863 is largely shared with Virginia, of which it was a part until Virginia seceded from the Union in 1861. Then the delegates of 40 western counties formed their own government, which was granted statehood in 1863.

First permanent settlement dates from 1731 when Morgan Morgan founded Mill Creek. In 1742 coal was discovered on the Coal River, an event that would be of great significance in determining West Virginia's future.

The state usually ranks first in bituminous coal production with about 20% of the U.S. total. It also is a leader in steel, glass, aluminum, and chemical manufactures; natural gas, oil, quarry products, and hardwood lumber.

Poultry, dairy products, cattle, and sheep account for the major portion of farm receipts. Apples, peaches, wheat, corn, and hay are profitable crops. More than 75% of West Virginia is covered with forests.

Tourism is increasingly popular in mountainous West Virginia and visitors spend over $750 million annually. More than a million acres have been set aside in 34 state parks and recreation areas and in 9 state forests.

Major points of interest include Harpers Ferry and Chesapeake and Ohio Canal National Historical Parks, White Sulphur Springs and Berkeley Springs resorts, the scenic railroad at Cass, and the historic homes at Charles Town.

WISCONSIN

Capital: Madison
Governor: Anthony S. Earl, D (to Jan. 1987)
Lieut. Governor: James T. Flynn, D (to Jan. 1987)
Secy. of State: Douglas J. La Follette, D (to Jan. 1987)
State Treasurer: Charles P. Smith, D (to Jan. 1987)
Atty. General: Bronson C. La Follette, D (to Jan. 1987)
Superintendent of Public Instruction: Herbert J. Grover, Nonpartisan (to July 1985)
Organized as territory: July 4, 1836
Entered Union & (rank): May 29, 1848 (30)
Present constitution adopted: 1848
Motto: Forward
State flower: Wood violet
State tree: Sugar maple
State bird: Robin
State animal: Badger; "wild life" animal: white-tailed deer; "domestic" animal: dairy cow
State insect: Honeybee (1977)
State fish: Musky (Muskellunge)
State song: "On Wisconsin"
State mineral: Galena (1971)
State rock: Red Granite (1971)
Nickname: Badger State
Origin of name: French corruption of an Indian word whose meaning is disputed
1980 population (1980 census) & (rank): 4,705,521 (16)
1983 est. population (July) & (rank): 4,751,000 (16)
1984 land area & (rank): 54,426 sq mi. (140,964 sq km) (25)
Geographic center: In Wood Co., 9 mi. SE of Marshfield
Number of counties: 72
Largest cities (1980 census): Milwaukee, 636,236; Madison, 170,616; Green Bay, 87,899; Racine, 85,725; Kenosha, 77,685; West Allis, 63,982; Appleton, 58,913
State forests: 9 (465,926 ac.)
State parks & scenic trails: 47 parks, 8 trails (61,573 ac.)
State revenue (1982–83): $9,941,960,925
State expenditure (1982–83): $8,591,378,779

The Wisconsin region was first explored for France by Jean Nicolet, who landed at Green Bay in 1634. In 1660 a French trading post and Roman Catholic mission were established near present-day Ashland.

Great Britain obtained the region in settlement of the French and Indian War in 1763; the U.S. acquried it in 1783 after the Revolutionary War. However, Great Britain retained actual control until after the War of 1812. The region was successively governed as part of the territories of Indiana, Illinois, and Michigan between 1800 and 1836, when it became a separate territory.

Wisconsin leads the nation in milk and cheese production. In 1983 the state ranked first in the number of milk cows (1,830,000) and produced 17% of the nation's total output of milk. Other important farm products are peas, beets, corn, potatoes, cabbage, maple sugar, and cranberries.

The chief industrial products of the state are automobiles, machinery, furniture, paper, beer, and processed foods. Wisconsin ranks second among the 47 paper-producing states.

Wisconsin pioneered in social legislation, providing pensions for the blind (1907), aid to dependent children (1913), and old-age assistance (1925). In labor legislation, the state was the first to enact an unemployment compensation law (1932) and the first in which a workman's compensation law actually took effect. Wisconsin had the first state-wide primary-election law and the first successful income-tax law. In April 1984, Wisconsin became the first state to adopt the Uniform Marital Property Act. The act will take effect on January 1, 1986.

The state has over 8,500 lakes, of which Winnebago is the largest. Water sports, ice-boating, and fishing are popular, as are skiing and hunting. Public parks and forests take up one seventh of the land, with 47 state parks, 9 state forests, 8 state trails, and 2 national forests.

Among the many points of interest are the Apostle Islands National Lakeshore; Ice Age National Scientific Reserve; the Circus World Museum at Baraboo; the Wolf, St. Croix, and Lower St. Croix national scenic riverways; and the Wisconsin Dells.

WYOMING

Capital: Cheyenne
Governor: Ed Herschler, D (to Jan. 1987)
Secy. of State: Thyra G. Thomson, R (to Jan. 1987)
Auditor: James B. Griffith, Jr., R (to Jan. 1987)
Treasurer: Stan Smith, R (to Jan. 1987)
Atty. General: A. G. McClintock, D (apptd. by Governor)
Organized as territory: May 19, 1869
Entered Union & (rank): July 10, 1890 (44)
Present constitution adopted: 1890
Motto: Equal rights (1955)
State flower: Indian paintbrush (1917)
State tree: Cottonwood (1947)
State bird: Meadow lark (1927)
State gemstone: Jade (1967)
State insignia: Bucking horse (unofficial)
State song: "Wyoming" (1955)
Nickname: Equality State
Origin of name: From the Delaware Indian word, meaning "mountains and valleys alternating"; the same as the Wyoming Valley in Pennsylvania
1980 population (1980 census) & (rank): 469,557 (49)
1983 est. population (July) & (rank): 514,000 (49)
1984 land area & (rank): 96,989 sq mi. (251,201 sq km) (9)
Geographic center: In Fremont Co., 58 mi. ENE of Lander
Number of counties: 23, plus Yellowstone National Park
Largest cities (1980 census): Casper, 51,016; Cheyenne, 47,283; Laramie, 24,410; Rock Springs, 19,458; Sheridan, 15,146; Green River, 12,807; Gillette, 12,134
State forests: None
State parks: 9 (44,732 ac.)
Estimated income (1985-86): $784,400,000
Estimated expenditure (1985-86): $892,768,288

The U.S. acquired the territory from France as part of the Louisiana Purchase in 1803. John Colter, a fur-trapper, is the first white man known to have entered present Wyoming. In 1807 he explored the Yellowstone area and brought back news of its geysers and hot springs.

Robert Stuart pioneered the Oregon Trail across Wyoming in 1812–13 and, in 1834, Fort Laramie, the first permanent trading post in Wyoming, was built. Western Wyoming was obtained by the U.S. in the 1846 Oregon Treaty with Great Britain and as a result of the treaty ending the Mexican War in 1848.

When the Wyoming Territory was organized in 1869 Wyoming women became the first in the nation to obtain the right to vote. In 1925 Mrs. Nellie Tayloe Ross was elected first woman governor in the United States.

Wyoming's towering mountains and vast plains provide spectacular scenery, grazing lands for sheep and cattle, and rich mineral deposits.

Mining, particularly oil and natural gas, is the most important industry. In January 1981, Wyoming led the nation in sodium carbonate (natrona) and bentonite production, and was second in uranium.

Wyoming ranks second among the states in wool production. In January 1981, its sheep numbered 1,110,000, exceeded only by Texas and California; it also had 1,350,000 cattle. Principal crops include wheat, oats, sugar beets, corn, potatoes, barley, and alfalfa.

Second in mean elevation to Colorado, Wyoming has many attractions for the tourist trade, notably Yellowstone National Park. Cheyenne is famous for its annual "Frontier Days" celebration. Flaming Gorge, the Fort Laramie National Historic Site, and Devils Tower and Fossil Butte National Monuments are other National points of interest.

Self-Governing Areas

PUERTO RICO

Capital: San Juan
Governor: Carlos Romero Barceló, New Progressive Party (to Jan. 1985)
Song: "La Borinqueña"
1970 population: 2,712,033
1980 population: 3,196,520
1980 land area: 3,459 sq mi. (8,958 sq km)
Largest cities (1980 census): San Juan, 424,600; Bayamón, 185,087; Ponce, 161,739; Carolina, 147,835; Caguas, 87,214; Mayagüez, 82,968

Puerto Rico is an island about 100 miles long and 35 miles wide at the northeastern end of the Caribbean Sea. It is a self-governing Commonwealth freely and voluntarily associated with the U.S. Under its Constitution, a Governor and a Legislative Assembly are elected by direct vote for a four-year period. The judiciary is vested in a Supreme Court and lower courts established by law. The people elect a Resident Commissioner to the U.S. House of Representatives, where he has a voice but no vote. The island was formerly an unincorporated territory of the U.S. after being ceded by Spain as a result of the Spanish-American War.

The Commonwealth, established in 1952, has one of the highest standards of living in Latin America. Featuring Puerto Rican economic development is Operation Bootstrap. There are now over 1,600 manufacturing plants which have been created by this program. It has also greatly increased transportation and communications facilities, electric power, housing, and other industries.

The island's chief exports are chemicals, apparel, fish products and electronic products.

Columbus discovered the island on his second voyage to America in 1493.

GUAM

Capital: Agaña
Governor: Ricardo J. Bordallo
1950 population: 59,498
1960 population: 67,044
1970 population: 84,996
1980 population: 105,979
1980 land area: 209 sq mi. (541 sq km)

Guam, the largest of the Mariana Islands, is independent of the trusteeship assigned to the U.S. in 1947. It was acquired by the U.S. from Spain in 1898 (occupied 1899) and was placed under the Navy Department.

In World War II, Guam was seized by the Japanese on Dec. 11, 1941; but on July 21, 1944, it was once more in U.S. hands.

On Aug. 1, 1950, President Truman signed a bill which granted U.S. citizenship to the people of Guam and established self-government. However, the people do not vote in national elections. In 1972 Guam elected its first delegate to the U.S. Congress. The Executive Branch of the Guam government is under the general supervision of the U.S. Secretary of the Interior. In November 1970, Guam elected its first Governor.

Military installations and tourism are important factors in Guam's economy.

Non-Self-Governing Territories

AMERICAN SAMOA

Capital: Fagatogo (on Tutuila Island)
Governor: Peter Tali Coleman
Lieut. Governor: Tufele Liá
1960 population: 20,051
1970 population: 27,159
1980 population: 32,297
1980 land area: 77 sq mi (199 sq km)

American Samoa, a group of five volcanic islands and two coral atolls located some 2,600 miles south of Hawaii in the South Pacific Ocean, is an unincorporated, unorganized territory of the U.S., administered by the Department of the Interior.

By the Treaty of Berlin, signed Dec. 2, 1899, and ratified Feb. 16, 1900, the U.S. was internationally acknowledged to have rights extending over all the islands of the Samoa group east of longitude 171° west of Greenwich. On April 17, 1900, the chiefs of Tutuila and Aunu'u ceded those islands to the U.S. In 1904, the King and chiefs of Manu'a ceded the islands of Ofu, Olosega and Tau (composing the Manu'a group) to the U.S. Swains Island, some 214 miles north of Samoa, was included as part of the territory by Act of Congress March 4, 1925; and on Feb. 20, 1929, Congress formally accepted sovereignty over the entire group and placed the responsibility for administration in the hands of the President. From 1900 to 1951, by Presidential direction, the Department of the Navy governed the territory. On July 1, 1951, administration was transferred to the Department of the Interior. The first Constitution for the territory was signed on April 27, 1960, and became effective on Oct. 17, 1960. It was revised in 1967.

Congress has provided for a non-voting delegate to sit in the House of Representatives in 1981.

The principal products are canned tuna, pet food, fish meal, mats, and handicrafts.

BAKER, HOWLAND, AND JARVIS ISLANDS

These Pacific islands were not to play a role in the extraterritorial plans of the U.S. until May 13, 1936. President F. D. Roosevelt, at that time, placed them under the control and jurisdiction of the Secretary of the Interior for administration purposes.

Baker Island is a saucer-shaped atoll with an area of approximately one square mile. It is about 1,650 miles from Hawaii.

Howland Island, 36 miles to the northeast, is approximately one and a half miles long and half a mile wide.

Jarvis Island is several hundred miles to the east and is approximately two miles long by one and an eighth mile wide.

Baker, Howland, and Jarvis have been uninhabited since 1942. In 1974, these islands became part of the National Wildlife Refuge System, administered by the U.S. Fish & Wildlife Service, Department of the Interior.

CANTON AND ENDERBURY ISLANDS

Canton and Enderbury islands, the largest of the Phoenix group, are jointly administered by the U.S. and Great Britain after an agreement signed April 6, 1939. The status of Canton and Enderbury was the subject of negotiations between the U.S., U.K., and Gilbert Islands Governments in 1979. The negotiations resulted in the signing on September 20, 1979, of a Treaty of Friendship between the U.S. and the Republic of Kiribati, which, once ratified by the U.S. Senate, will formally renounce the U.S. claim to Canton and Enderbury. The Republic of Kiribati declared its independence on July 12, 1979.

Canton is triangular in shape and the largest of the eight islands of this group. It lies about 1,600 miles southwest of Hawaii and was discovered at the turn of the 18th century by U.S. whalers. After World War II it served as an aviation support facility, and later as a missile tracking station. Since 1967, the island has been utilized by the U.S. Air Force Space and Missile Test Center.

Enderbury is rectangular in shape and is 3.5 miles long by 1.5 miles wide. It is unpopulated and lies about 32 miles southeast of Canton.

JOHNSTON ATOLL

Johnston is a coral atoll about 700 miles southwest of Hawaii. It consists of four small islands—Johnston Island, Sand Island, Hikina Island, and Akau Island—which lie on a reef about 9 miles long in a northeast-southwest direction.

The atoll was discovered by Capt. Charles James Johnston of *H.M.S. Cornwallis* in 1807. In 1858 it was claimed by Hawaii, and later became a U.S. possession.

Johnston Atoll is a Naval Defense Sea Area and Airspace Reservation and is closed to the public.

The administration of Johnston Atoll is under the jurisdiction of the Defense Nuclear Agency, Commander, Johnston Atoll (FCDNA), APO San Francisco, CA 96305.

KINGMAN REEF

Kingman Reef, located about 1,000 miles south of Hawaii, was discovered by Capt. E. Fanning in 1798, but named for Capt. W. E. Kingman, who rediscovered it in 1853. The reef, drying only on its northeast, east and southeast edges, is of atoll character. The reef is triangular in shape, with its apex northward; it is about 9.5 miles long, east and west, and 5 miles wide, north and south, within the 100-fathom curve.

A United States possession, Kingman Reef is a Defense Sea Area and Airspace Reservation, and is closed to the public. The Airspace Entry Control has been suspended, but is subject to immediate reinstatement without notice. No vessel or aircraft, except those authorized by the Secretary of the Navy, shall be navigated in or above the area within the 3-mile limit.

MIDWAY ISLANDS

Midway Islands, lying about 1,200 miles west-northwest of Hawaii, were discovered by Captain N. C. Brooks of the Hawaiian bark *Gambia* on July 5, 1859, in the name of the United States. The atoll was formally declared a U.S. possession in 1867, and in 1903 Theodore Roosevelt made it a naval reservation.

Midway Islands consist of a circular atoll, 6 miles in diameter, and enclosing two islands. Eastern Island, on its southeast side, is triangular in shape, and about 1.2 miles long. Sand Island on its south side, is about 2 miles long in a northeast-southwest direction.

The Midway Islands are within a naval defensive sea area. The Navy Department maintains an installation and has jurisdiction over the atoll. Permission to enter the Naval Defense Sea Area must be obtained in advance from the Commanding Officer, Naval Air Facility, Midway Islands, FPO San Francisco, CA 96614.

U.S. VIRGIN ISLANDS

Capital: Charlotte Amalie (on St. Thomas)
Governor: Juan Luis
1970 population: 62,468
1982 population: 99,670 (St. Croix, 51,830; St. Thomas, 45,350; St. John, 2,490)
1980 land area: 132 sq mi (342 sq km): St. Croix, 80 sq mi. (207 sq km), St. Thomas, 32 sq mi. (83 sq km), St. John, 20 sq mi. (52 sq km)

The Virgin Islands, consisting of nine main islands and some 75 islets, were discovered by Columbus in 1493. Since 1666, England has held six of the main islands; the other three (St. Croix, St. Thomas, and St. John), as well as about 50 of the islets, were eventually acquired by Denmark, which named them the Danish West Indies. In 1917, these islands were purchased by the U.S. from Denmark for $25 million.

Congress granted U.S. citizenship to Virgin Islanders in 1927; and, in 1931, administration was transferred from the Navy to the Department of the Interior. Universal suffrage was given in 1936 to all persons who could read and write the English language. The Governor was elected by popular vote for the first time in 1970; previously he had been appointed by the President of the U.S. A unicameral 15-man legislature serves the Virgin Islands, and Congressional legislation gave the islands a non-voting Representative in Congress.

The "Constitution" of the Virgin Islands is the Revised Organic Act, of 1954 in which the U.S. Congress defines the three branches of the territorial government, i.e., the Executive Branch, the Legislative Branch, and the Judicial Branch. Residents of the islands substantially enjoy the same rights as those enjoyed by mainlanders with one important exception: citizens of the U.S. who are residents may not vote in presidential elections.

About 80% of the population is black, and there is limited farming, fishing, and cattle raising. Industrial products include rum, watches, costume jewelry, alumina, pharmaceuticals, and petroleum products. Tourism is the principal industry.

WAKE ISLAND

Wake Island, about halfway between Midway and Guam, is an atoll comprising the three islets of Wilkes, Peale, and Wake. They were discovered by the British in 1796 and annexed by the U.S. in 1899. The entire area comprises 3 square miles and has no native population. In 1938, Pan American Airways established a seaplane base and Wake Island has been used as a commercial base since then. On Dec. 8, 1941, it was attacked by the Japanese, who finally took possession on Dec. 23. It was surrendered by the Japanese on Sept. 4, 1945.

The President, acting pursuant to the Hawaii Omnibus Act, assigned responsibility for Wake to the Secretary of the Interior in 1962. The Department of Transportation exercised civil administration of Wake through an agreement with the Department of the Interior until June 1972.

Trust Territory of the Pacific Islands (Micronesia)

In 1885, Germany assumed a protectorate over the Marshall Islands; and, in 1899, she purchased the Northern Mariana and Caroline Islands from Spain. These islands were occupied by the Japanese in 1914 and were mandated to Japan by the League of Nations in 1919. On April 2, 1947, the U.N. Security Council approved a trusteeship agreement proposed by the U.S. under which the Northern Mariana, Caroline, and Marshall Islands became a Strategic Trust Territory under the administration of the U.S. The measure was approved by the President, with the agreement of Congress, on July 18, 1947. Administration was transferred from the Navy to the Department of the Interior on July 1, 1951. However, during 1953, administration of the islands of the Northern Marianas, except

Rota, was transferred back to the Navy. The Department of the Interior again took over administration of these islands in July, 1962. The 1980 population of the Northern Marianas was 16,780.

In February 1975 a covenant was signed by the U.S. and the Marianas Political Status Commission that would make the 14 islands in the Northern Marianas a commonwealth under American sovereignty. The covenant was overwhelmingly ratified by the people of the islands and was approved by President Ford on March 24, 1976.

On April 9, 1978, in Hilo, Hawaii, the heads of the three Micronesian political status commissions and the U.S. negotiator signed a statement of agreed principles which is intended to form the basis of a free association relationship between the U.S. and Micronesia. Compact of Free Association was signed by the U.S. and the respective Micronesian commissions in 1982. The document now must be approved by the people of the three Micronesian entities, the U.S. Congress, and the United Nations.

The entire group with a 1980 population of 116, 149, comprises more than 2,000 islands, but the total land area is only 533 sq mi. (1,381 sq km), many of the islands being only tiny coral reefs. There are six administrative districts: Kosrae, Marshall Islands, Palau, Ponape, Truk, and Yap.

The Micronesians are the main ethnic group; however, the inhabitants of two outlying islands, Kapingamarangi and Nukuoro, are Polynesian.

MARIANA ISLANDS

The Mariana Islands, east of the Philippines and south of Japan, include the islands of Guam, Rota, Saipan, Tinian, Pagan, Guguan, Agrihan, and Aguijan. Guam, the largest, is independent of the trusteeship, having been acquired by the U.S. from Spain in 1898. (For more information, *see* the entry on Guam in this section.) The remaining islands, referred to as the Northern Mariana Islands, will become a commonwealth of the United States, pursuant to P.L. 94-241, upon termination of the trusteeship agreement.

Chief crops are copra and fresh fruits and vegetables.

CAROLINE ISLANDS

The Caroline Islands, east of the Philippines and south of the Marianas, include the Yap, Truk, and the Palau groups and the islands of Ponape and Kosrae, as well as many coral atolls.

The islands are composed chiefly of volcanic rock, and their peaks rise 2,000 to 3,000 feet above sea level. Chief exports of the islands are copra, fish products, and handicrafts.

MARSHALL ISLANDS

The Marshall Islands, east of the Carolines, are divided into two chains: the western or Ralik group, including the atolls Jaluit, Kwajalein, Wotho, Bikini, and Enewetak; and the eastern or Ratak group, including the atolls Mili, Majuro, Maloelap, Wotje, and Likiep.

The islands are of the coral-reef type and rise only a few feet above sea level. The chief crop is coconuts; exports include copra, tortoise shell, mother-of-pearl, etc.

Bikini and Enewetak were the scene of several atom-bomb tests after World War II: Enewetak was returned to Trust Territory administration in August 1976. In April 1977, some 55 original inhabitants, the forerunner of 450 returnees, were resettled after an absence of 30 years.

1983 Estimated Population of States by Rank

State	Population	Rank	State	Population	Rank
California	25,174,000	1	Colorado	3,139,000	26
New York	17,667,000	2	Connecticut	3,138,000	27
Texas	15,724,000	3	Arizona	2,963,000	28
Pennsylvania	11,895,000	4	Iowa	2,905,000	29
Illinois	11,486,000	5	Oregon	2,662,000	30
Ohio	10,746,000	6	Mississippi	2,587,000	31
Florida	10,680,000	7	Kansas	2,425,000	32
Michigan	9,069,000	8	Arkansas	2,328,000	33
New Jersey	7,468,000	9	West Virginia	1,965,000	34
North Carolina	6,082,000	10	Utah	1,619,000	35
Massachusetts	5,767,000	11	Nebraska	1,597,000	36
Georgia	5,732,000	12	New Mexico	1,399,000	37
Virginia	5,550,000	13	Maine	1,146,000	38
Indiana	5,479,000	14	Hawaii	1,023,000	39
Missouri	4,970,000	15	Idaho	989,000	40
Wisconsin	4,751,000	16	New Hampshire	959,000	41
Tennessee	4,685,000	17	Rhode Island	955,000	42
Louisiana	4,438,000	18	Nevada	891,000	43
Maryland	4,304,000	19	Montana	817,000	44
Washington	4,300,000	20	South Dakota	700,000	45
Minnesota	4,144,000	21	North Dakota	680,000	46
Alabama	3,959,000	22	Delaware	606,000	47
Kentucky	3,714,000	23	Vermont	525,000	48
Oklahoma	3,298,000	24	Wyoming	514,000	49
South Carolina	3,264,000	25	Alaska	479,000	50

As of July 1, 1983. *Source:* Bureau of the Census, Current Population Reports, January 1984.

Tabulated Data on State Governments

	Governor		Legislature[1]						Highest Court[2]		
State	Term, years	Annual salary	Membership U[3]	Membership L[4]	Term, yrs. U[3]	Term, yrs. L[4]	Salaries of members[5]		Members	Term, years	Annual salary[6]
Alabama	4[10]	63,839[16]	35	105	4	4	95	per diem[16 22]	9	6	$58,000
Alaska	4	77,760	20	40	4	2	50,800	per annum	5	([8])	77,760
Arizona	4	56,000	30	60	2	2	15,000	per annum	5	6	57,500
Arkansas	2	35,000	35	100	4	2	7,500	per annum[25]	7	8	46,214
California	4	49,100	40	80	4	2	28,110	per annum	7	12	62,935[25]
Colorado	4	60,000	35	65	4	2	17,500	per annum[26]	7	10	63,000
Connecticut	4	65,000	36	151	2	2	21,000	per biennium	6	8	61,800
Delaware	4[9]	70,000	21	41	4	2	12,720	per annum	5	12	59,000
Florida	4[10]	60,498	40	120	4	2	12,000	per annum	7	6	60,453
Georgia	4[9]	68,571	56	180	2	2	7,200	per annum	7	6	55,462
Hawaii	4	59,400	25	51	4	2	15,600	per session	5	10	56,430
Idaho	4	50,000	35	70	2	2	4,200	per annum	5	6	38,000
Illinois	4	58,000	59	118	4–2	2	28,000	per annum	7	10	75,000
Indiana	4[10]	48,000	50	100	4	2	11,600	per annum	5	([24])	60,000
Iowa	4	64,000	50	100	4	2	14,600	per annum	9	8	60,900
Kansas	4	49,500	40	125	4	2	42	per diem[22]	7	6	59,143
Kentucky	4[7]	60,000	38	100	4	2	100	per diem[22]	7	8	56,664
Louisiana	4	73,400	39	105	4	4	16,800	per annum	7	10	66,566
Maine	4	35,000	33	151	2	2	10,000	per biennium[16]	7	7	44,431
Maryland	4[10]	75,000	47	141	4	4	21,000	per annum	7	10	62,500
Massachusetts	4	75,000	40	160	2	2	30,000	per annum	7	Life	65,000
Michigan	4	76,000	38	110	4	2	33,200	per annum[16]	7	8	74,000
Minnesota	4	72,000	67	134	4	2	18,500	per annum[16]	9	6	56,000
Mississippi	4[7]	63,000	52	122	4	4	8,100	per session[5]	9	8	59,000
Missouri	4[10]	55,000	34	163	4	2	15,000	per annum[5]	7	12	50,000
Montana	4	47,963	50	100	4	2	49.20	per diem[16]	6	8	47,963
Nebraska	4[10]	40,000	49[11]	—	4[11]	—	4,800	per annum	7	6	48,315
Nevada	4	65,000	21	42	4	2	6,240	per biennium	5	6	61,500
New Hampshire	2	59,885	24	([12])	2	2	200	per biennium	5	([13])	57,025
New Jersey	4[10]	85,000	40	80	4[14]	2	25,000	per annum	7	7[15]	78,000
New Mexico	4[7]	50,000	42	70	4	2	40	per diem	5	8	55,000
New York	4	100,000	61	150	2	2	32,960	per annum	7	14	80,892
North Carolina	4[9]	85,000	50	120	2	2	6,936	per annum[16]	7	8	61,128
North Dakota	4	60,862[16]	53	106	4	2	62.5	per diem[16 23]	5	10	53,900
Ohio	4	65,000	33	99	4	2	22,500	per annum	7	6	68,000
Oklahoma	4	70,000	48	101	4	2	20,000[16]	per annum	([19])	6	59,136
Oregon	4[10]	55,423	30	60	4	2	8,400[26]	per annum	7	6	54,637
Pennsylvania	4[10]	85,000	50	203	4	2	35,000	per annum	7	10	76,500
Rhode Island	2	49,500	50	100	2	2	5	per diem[17]	5	([18])	60,594
South Carolina	4[7]	60,000	46	124	4	2	10,000	per annum	5	10	47,000
South Dakota	4[10]	50,975	35	70	2	2	6,000	per biennium	5	3	48,775
Tennessee	4	68,226	33	99	4	2	12,500	per annum	5	8	60,000
Texas	4	90,700	31	150	4	2	7,200	per annum	([20])	6	76,500
Utah	4	52,000	29	75	4	2	25	per diem[16]	5	10	50,000
Vermont	2	60,000	30	150	2	2	80	per week[21]	5	6	41,000
Virginia	4[7]	75,000	40	100	4	2	8,000	per annum	7	12	63,000
Washington	4	63,000	49	98	4	2	12,850	per annum	9	6	51,500
West Virginia	4	72,000	34	100	4	2	5,136	per annum	5	12	55,000
Wisconsin	4	75,337	33	99	4	2	27,202	per annum	7	10	68,000
Wyoming	4	70,000	30	62	4	2	60	per diem[16]	5	8	63,500

1. General Assembly in Ark., Colo., Conn., Del., Ga., Ind., Ky., Md., Mo., N.C., Ohio, Pa., R.I., S.C., Tenn., Vt., Va., Legislative Assembly in N.D., Ore.; General Court in Mass., N.H.; Legislature in other states. Meets biennially in Calif., Ky., Me., Mont., Nev., N.H., N.J., N.C., N.D., Ore., Pa., Texas, Wash. and Wyo.; meets annually in other states. 2. Court of Appeals in Md., N.Y., Supreme Court of Virginia in Va., Supreme Judicial Court in Me., Mass.; Supreme Court in other states. 3. Upper house: Senate in all states. 4. Lower house: Assembly in Calif., Nev., N.Y., Wis.; House of Delegates in Md., Va., W.Va.; General Assembly in N.J.; House of Representatives in other states. 5. Does not include additional payments for expenses, mileage, special sessions, etc., or additional per diem payments beyond salary shown. 6. In some states, Chief Justice receives a higher salary. 7. Cannot succeed himself. 8. Appointed for 3 years; thereafter subject to approval or rejection on a nonpartisan ballot for 10-year term. 9. May serve only 2 terms, consecutive or otherwise. 10. May not serve 3rd consecutive term. 11. Unicameral legislature. 12. Constitutional number: 375–400. 13. Until 70 years old. 14. When term begins in Jan. of 2nd year following U.S. census, term shall be 2 years. 15. 2nd term receive tenure, mandatory retirement at 70. 16. Plus additional expenses. 17. For 60 days only. 18. Term of good behavior. 19. 9 members in Supreme Court, highest in civil cases; 3 in Court of Criminal Appeals. 20. 9 members in Supreme Court, highest in civil cases; 9 in Court of Criminal Appeals. 21. To limit of $9,500 per biennium; $2,000 for special session. 22. When in session. 23. Plus $180 per month. 24. Appointed for 2 years; thereafter elected popularly for 10-year term. 25. To receive cost of living increase not to exceed 10% in the two year period. 26. Plus $300 per month when performing official duties. *Source: Information Please* questionnaires to the states.

50 Largest Cities of the United States

Source of population and land area: Bureau of the Census. Telephones; *source:* American Telephone & Telegraph Co. Other data were supplied by the cities in response to *Information Please* questionnaires.

ALBUQUERQUE, N.M.

Incorporated as city: 1891
Mayor: Harry Kinney (to Dec. 1985)
1970 population & (rank): 244,501 (58)
1980 population (1980 census) & (rank): 331,767 (44)
1982 est. population & (rank): 341,978 (46)
1984 land area: 95.3 sq mi. (247 sq km)
Altitude: 4,958 ft.
Location: Central part of state on Rio Grande River
County: Bernalillo
Churches: 211
City-owned parks: 135
Telephones (Jan. 1, 1982): 323,935
Radio stations: 14
Television stations: 5
Assessed valuation (1983): $1,459,998,479
City tax rate (1983): $21.223 per $1,000
Bonded debt (1983): $110,475,000
Revenue (1983): $121,535,394
Expenditures (1983): $106,681,898
Chamber of Commerce: Albuquerque Chamber of Commerce, 401 2nd St., N.W., Albuquerque, N.M. 87102. Hispanic Chamber of Commerce, 407 Rio Grande Blvd., N.W. Albuquerque, N.M. 87104

ATLANTA, GA.

Incorporated as city: 1847
Mayor: Andrew Young (to Jan. 1986)
1970 population & (rank): 495,039 (27)
1980 population (1980 census) & (rank): 425,022 (29)
1982 est. population & (rank): 428,153 (30)
1984 city land area: 136 sq mi. (339 sq km)
Altitude: Highest, 1,050 ft; lowest, 940
Location: In northwest central part of state, near Chattahoochee River
Counties: Fulton and De Kalb
Churches (15-county area): 1,500+
City-owned parks: 297 (3,178 ac.)
Telephones (Jan. 1, 1982): 959,000
Radio stations (15-county area): AM, 29; FM, 16
Television stations (15-county area): 6 commercial; 2 PBS
Gross assessed valuation (city, 1983): $4,369,276,287
City tax rate (1983): $46.50 per $1,000
Total bonded debt (1983): $166,397,732
Revenue (incl. General Fund, Airport Revenues, Water/Sewer Fund) (1983): $344,166,698
Expenditures (1983): $175,392,725
Chamber of Commerce: Atlanta Chamber of Commerce, 1300 N Omni International, Atlanta, Ga. 30303
Information is gathered on 2 geographic areas:
City of Atlanta, and 18 county SMSA

AUSTIN, TEX.

Incorporated as city: 1839
Mayor: Ron Mullen (to May 1985)
1970 population & (rank): 253,539 (56)
1980 population (1980 census) & (rank): 345,496 (42)
1982 est. population & (rank): 368,135 (39)
1984 land area: 116.0 sq mi. (300 sq km)
Altitude: Highest, 425 ft
Location: In south central part of state, on the Colorado River
County: Seat of Travis Co.
Churches: 353 churches, representing 45 denominations
City-owned parks and playgrounds: 150
Telephones (Jan. 1, 1983): 292,105
Radio stations: AM, 6; FM, 12
Television stations: 3 commercial; 1 PBS
Assessed valuation (1983): $9,863,239,245
Tax rate (1983): $19.60 per $1,000 at 100% assessed valuation
Bonded debt (1982–83): $947,998,663
Revenue (1983–84): $175,687,326
Expenditures (1983–84): $161,354,656
Chamber of Commerce: Austin Chamber of Commerce, 901 W Riverside Dr., Austin, Tex. 78704

BALTIMORE, MD.

Incorporated as city: 1797
Mayor: William D. Schaefer (to Dec. 1987)
1970 population & (rank): 905,787 (7)
1980 population (1980 census) & (rank): 786,775 (10)
1982 est. population & (rank): 774,113 (12)
1984 land area: 80.3 sq mi. (208 sq km)
Altitude: Highest, 490 ft; lowest, sea level
Location: On Patapsco River, about 12 mi. from Chesapeake Bay
County: Independent city
Churches: Roman Catholic, 72; Jewish, 50; Protestant and others, 344
City-owned parks: 347 park areas and tracts (6,314 ac.)
Telephones (Jan. 1, 1982): 1,528,116
Radio stations: AM, 11; FM, 9
Television stations: 5
Assessed valuation (1984): $4,628,207,000
City tax rate (1983): $5.99 per $100.00
Net bonded debt (April 1984): $367,650,000
Revenue (1984): $1,240,119,356
Expenditures (1983): $1,379,539,000
Chamber of Commerce: Greater Baltimore Committee, 2 Hopkins Plaza, Baltimore, Md. 21201

BIRMINGHAM, ALA.

Incorporated as city: 1871
Mayor: Richard Arrington, Jr. (to Nov. 1987)
1970 population & (rank): 300,910 (48)
1980 population (1980 census) & (rank): 284,413 (50)
1982 est. population & (rank): 283,239 (53)
1984 land area: 98.5 sq mi. (255 sq km)
Altitude: Highest, 1,200 ft.; lowest, 583
Location: In north central part of state in Jones Valley.
County: Seat of Jefferson Co.
Churches: 1,100
City-owned parks and playgrounds: 100 (1,684 ac.)
Telephones (Jan. 1, 1982): 496,017
Radio stations: AM, 16; FM, 4
Television stations: 5

Assessed valuation (1983): $933,016,246
City tax rate (1983): $28.50 per $1,000 assessed value
Bonded debt (June 1983): $157,605,000
Revenue (1983): $96,883,327
Expenditures (1983): $93,615,158
Chamber of Commerce: Chamber of Commerce, 1st Ave. and 21st St., Birmingham, Ala.

BOSTON, MASS.

Incorporated as city: 1822
Mayor: Raymond L. Flynn (to Jan. 1988)
1970 population & (rank): 641,071 (16)
1980 population (1980 census) & (rank): 562,994 (20)
1982 est. population & (rank): 560,847 (21)
1985 land area: 47.2 sq mi. (122 sq km)
Altitude: Highest, 330 ft; lowest, sea level
Location: On Massachusetts Bay, at mouths of Charles and Mystic Rivers
County: Seat of Suffolk Co.
Churches: Protestant, 187; Roman Catholic, 73; Jewish, 28; others, 100
City-owned parks, playgrounds, etc.: 2,276.36 ac.
Telephones (Jan. 1, 1984): 614,430
Radio stations: AM, 9; FM, 8
Television stations: 7
Assessed valuation (1984): $13,024,000,000
City tax rate (1984): $17.10 residential, $32.54 commercial, per $1000
Gross direct bonded debt (July 1, 1984): $503,794,000
Revenue (1984): $939,300,000
Expenditures (1984): $939,300,000
Chamber of Commerce: Boston Chamber of Commerce, 125 High St., Boston, Mass. 02110

BUFFALO, N.Y.

Incorporated as city: 1832
Mayor: James Griffin (to Dec. 1985)
1970 population & (rank): 462,768 (28)
1980 population (1980 census) & (rank): 357,870 (39)
1982 est. population & (rank): 348,035 (44)
1984 land area: 41.8 sq mi. (198 sq km)
Altitude: Highest, 698 ft; lowest, 571
Location: At east end of Lake Erie, on Niagara River
County: Seat of Erie Co.
Churches: 60 denominations, with over 1,100 churches
County-owned parks: 9 public parks (3,000 ac.)
Telephones (Jan. 1, 1983): 473,504
Radio stations: AM, 10; FM, 13
Television stations: 5 (plus reception from 4 Canadian stations)
Assessed valuation (1981–82): $1,009,174,754
City tax rate (1981–82): $87.00 per $1,000
Total funded debt (long-term, Oct. 31, 1982): $90,803,448
Revenue (general fund, Fiscal 1982): $219,801,000
Expenditures (Fiscal 1982): $210,646,000
Chamber of Commerce: Buffalo Area Chamber of Commerce, 107 Delaware Ave., Buffalo, N.Y. 14202

CHARLOTTE, N.C.

Incorporated as city: 1768
Mayor: Harvey Gantt (to Nov. 1985)
1970 population & (rank): 241,420 (60)
1980 population (1980 census) & (rank): 314,447 (47)
1982 est. population & (rank): 323,972 (48)
1984 land area: 149 sq mi. (372 sq km)
Altitude: 765 ft
Location: In the southern part of state near the border of South Carolina
County: Seat of Mecklenburg Co.
Churches: Protestant, over 400; Roman Catholic, 8; Jewish, 3; Greek Orthodox, 1
City-owned parks and parkways: 87
Telephones (June 1984): 147,271 (residential)
Radio stations: AM, 8; FM, 4
Television stations: 4 commercial; 2 PBS
Assessed valuation (1984): $12,243,210,400
City tax rate (includes county 1984): $.64 per $100
Bonded debt (June 30, 1984): $217,175,000
Revenue (Fiscal 1985): $236,236,391
Expenditures (Fiscal 1985): $236,236,391
Chamber of Commerce: Greater Charlotte Chamber of Commerce, P.O. Box 32785, Charlotte, N.C., 28232

CHICAGO, ILL.

Incorporated as city: 1837
Mayor: Harold Washington (to April 1987)
1970 population & (rank): 3,369,357 (2)
1980 population (1980 census) & (rank): 3,005,072 (2)
1982 est. population & (rank): 2,997,155 (3)
1984 land area: 228.1 sq mi. (591 sq km)
Altitude: Highest, 672 ft; lowest, 578.5
Location: On lower west shore of Lake Michigan
County: Seat of Cook Co.
Churches: Protestant, 850; Roman Catholic, 263; Jewish, 51
City-owned parks: 578
Telephones (Jan. 1, 1982): 2,757,128
Radio stations: AM, 18, FM, 19
Television stations: 9
Assessed valuation (1981): $13,202,914,826
Total Chicago tax rate (1981): $9.538 per $100
Total gross bonded debt (1981): $346,790,000
Revenue (est. 1984): $1,889,410,525
Expenditures (est. 1984): $1,886,219,324
Chamber of Commerce: Chicago Association of Commerce & Industry, 130 S Michigan Ave., Chicago, Ill. 60603

CINCINNATI, OHIO

Incorporated as city: 1819
Mayor: Arn Bortz (to Dec. 1984)
City Manager: Sylvester Murray
1970 population & (rank): 453,514 (30)
1980 population (1980 census) & (rank): 385,457 (32)
1982 est. population & (rank): 380,118 (35)
1984 land area: 78.1 sq mi. (202 sq km)
Altitude: Highest, 960 ft; lowest, 441
Location: In southwestern corner of state on Ohio River
County: Seat of Hamilton Co.
Churches: 850
City-owned parks: 96 (4,345 ac.)
Telephones (Jan. 1, 1982): 777,300
Radio stations: AM, 9; FM, 15 (Greater Cincinnati)
Television stations: 6
Assessed valuation (1983): $2,745,795,230
City tax rate (1983): $11.12 per $1,000
Bonded debt (1983): $176,210,120
Revenue (general fund, 1983): $142,940,628
Expenditures (general fund, 1983): $145,733,758
Chamber of Commerce: Cincinnati Chamber of Commerce, 120 W Fifth St., Cincinnati, Ohio 45202

CLEVELAND, OHIO

Incorporated as city: 1836
Mayor: George V. Voinovich (to Dec. 1985)
1970 population & (rank): 750,879 (10)

1980 population (1980 census) & (rank): 573,822 (18)
1982 est. population & (rank): 558,869 (22)
1984 land area: 79.0 sq mi. (205 sq km)
Altitude: Highest, 1048 ft.; lowest, 573
Location: On Lake Erie at mouth of Cuyahoga River
County: Seat of Cuyahoga Co.
Churches: [1] Protestant, 980; Roman Catholic, 187; Jewish, 31; Eastern Orthodox, 22
City-owned parks: 41 (1,930 ac.)
Telephones (Jan. 1, 1982): 912,245
Radio stations: AM, 15; FM, 17
Television stations: 7
Assessed valuation (1983): 3,706,234,148
City tax rate (1984): $77.40 per $1,000
Bonded debt (Dec. 31, 1983): $407,320,000[2]
Revenue (est. 1984): $231,184,000
Expenditures (est. 1984): $231,173,000
Chamber of Commerce: Greater Cleveland Growth Association, 690 Union Commerce Building, Cleveland, Ohio 44115

1. 100-mile area. 2. Includes general obligation bonded debt and also mortgage revenue bonded debt.

COLUMBUS, OHIO

Incorporated as city: 1834
Mayor: Dana G. Rinehart (to Jan. 1988)
1970 population & (rank): 540,025 (21)
1980 population (1980 census) & (rank): 565,032 (19)
1982 est. population & (rank): 570,588 (19)
1984 land area: 185.18 sq mi. (469 sq km)
Altitude: Highest, 902 ft; lowest, 702
Location: In central part of state, on Scioto River
County: Seat of Franklin Co.
Churches: Protestant, 412; Roman Catholic, 43; Jewish, 5
City-owned parks: 135 (10,931 ac.)
Telephones (Jan. 1, 1982): 477,599
Radio stations: AM, 8; FM, 6
Television stations: 3 commercial, 2 PBS
Assessed valuation (1983): $4,659,938
City tax rate (1983): $38.62 per $1,000
Bonded debt (May 31, 1984): $680,361
Revenue (1983): $389,031,167
Expenditures (1983): $410,257,967
Chamber of Commerce: Columbus Area Chamber of Commerce, P.O. Box 1527, Columbus, Ohio 43216

DALLAS, TEX.

Incorporated as city: 1856
Mayor: Starke Taylor (to April 1985)
City Manager: Charles Anderson (apptd. Oct. 1981)
1970 population & (rank): 844,401 (8)
1980 population (1980 census) & (rank): 904,078 (7)
1982 est. population & (rank): 943,848 (7)
1984 land area: 333.0 sq mi. (862 sq km)
Altitude: Highest, 750 ft; lowest, 375
Location: In northeastern part of state, on Trinity River
County: Seat of Dallas Co.
Churches: 1,200 (in Dallas Co.)
City-owned parks: 283 (21,012 ac.)
Telephones (Jan. 1, 1982): 1,000,014
Radio stations: AM, 14; FM, 15
Television stations: 7
Assessed valuation (1981–82): $35,911,521,000
City tax rate (1981–82): $.5131 per $100 valuation
Bonded debt (Sept. 30, 1982): $757,076,000
Revenue (1982): 449,111,000
Expenditures (1982): $479,579,000
Chamber of Commerce: Dallas Chamber of Commerce. 1507 Pacific, Dallas, Tex. 75201

DENVER, COLO.

Incorporated as city: 1861
Mayor: Federico Pena (to July 1987)
1970 population & (rank): 514,678 (24)
1980 population (1980 census) & (rank): 492,365 (24)
1982 est. population & (rank): 505,563 (24)
1984 land area: 110.6 sq mi. (287 sq km)
Altitude: Highest, 5,470 ft; lowest, 5,130
Location: In northeast central part of state, on South Platte River
County: Coextensive with Denver Co.
Churches:[1] Protestant, 815; Roman Catholic, 63; Jewish, 13
City-owned parks: 155 (3,600 ac.)
City-owned mountain parks: 40 (13,448 ac.)
Telephones (Jan. 1, 1982): 1,491,069
Radio stations: AM, 18; FM, 13[1]
Television stations: 5
Assessed valuation (1983): $2,698,991,800
City tax rate (1983): $28.11 per $1,000[2]
Bonded debt (1983): $334,622,000[2]
Revenue (1983): $699,483,000[2]
Expenditures (1983): $678,206,000[2]
Chamber of Commerce: Denver Chamber of Commerce, 1301 Welton, Denver, Colo. 80204

1. Metropolitan area. 2. Excluding school district.

DETROIT, MICH.

Incorporated as city: 1815
Mayor: Coleman A. Young (to Jan. 1986)
1970 population & (rank): 1,514,063 (5)
1980 population (1980 census) & (rank): 1,203,339 (6)
1982 est. population & (rank): 1,138,717 (6)
1984 land area: 135.6 sq mi. (351 sq km)
Altitude: Highest, 685 ft; lowest, 574
Location: In southeastern part of state, on Detroit River
County: Seat of Wayne Co.
Churches: [1]Protestant, 2,204; Roman Catholic, 333; Jewish, 40
City-owned parks: 52 parks (3,843 ac.); 350 sites (5,838 ac.)
Telephones (Jan. 1, 1982): 1,484,740
Radio stations: AM, 17; FM, 37 (7-county area)
Television stations: 11 (incl. Windsor, Ontario, Canada)[1]
Assessed valuation (1982): $5,366,753,613
City tax rate (1982–83): $32.68 per $1,000
Net bonded debt (April 1983): General obligations, (net): $396,201,000
Revenue (1983–84): $1,566,788,953[2]
Expenditures (1983–84): $1,566,788,953[2]
Chamber of Commerce: Greater Detroit Chamber of Commerce, 150 Michigan Ave., Detroit, Mich. 48226

1. Six-county metropolitan area. 2. Excludes utilities.

EL PASO, TEX.

Incorporated as city: 1873
Mayor: Jonathan Rogers (to April 1985)
1970 population & (rank): 322,261 (45)
1980 population (1980 census) & (rank): 425,259 (28)
1982 est. population & (rank): 445,071 (28)
1984 land area: 239.2 sq mi. (620 sq km)
Altitude: 4,000 ft
Location: In far western part of state, on Rio Grande
County: Seat of El Paso Co.
Churches: Protestant, 212; Roman Catholic, 36; Jewish, 2; others, 13
City-owned parks: 83 (4,694 ac.)
Telephones (Jan. 1, 1982): 286,324

Radio stations: AM, 9; FM, 5
Television stations: 5
Assessed valuation (1983): $7,397,149,965
City tax rate (1983): $5.31 per $1,000, city; $7.26, El Paso Independent School District; $7.36, Ysleta Independent School District
Bonded debt (1983): $42,440,000
Revenue (1982–83): $101,705,000
Expenditures (1982–83): $101,705,000
Chamber of Commerce: El Paso Chamber of Commerce, 10 Civic Center Plaza, El Paso, Tex. 79944

FORT WORTH, TEX.

Incorporated as city: 1873
Mayor: Bob Bolen (to April 1985)
City Manager: Robert L. Herchert
1970 population & (rank): 393,455 (33)
1980 population (1980 census) & (rank): 385,164 (33)
1982 est. population & (rank): 401,402 (33)
1984 land area: 240.1 sq mi. (622 sq km)
Altitude: Highest, 780 ft; lowest, 520
Location: In north central part of state, on Trinity River
County: Seat of Tarrant Co.
Churches: Protestant, 392; Roman Catholic, 16; Jewish, 2
City-owned parks: 136 (8,189 ac.; 3,500 ac. in Nature Center)
Telephones (Jan. 1, 1982): 368,058
Radio stations: AM, 6; FM, 8
Television stations: 6 (2 local)
Assessed valuation (1983–84): $7,173,140,999
City tax rate (1983–84): $9.25 per $1,000
Bonded debt (1983–84): $185,359,330
Revenue (1983–84): $150,535,087
Expenditures (1983–84): $150,535,087
Chamber of Commerce: Fort Worth Chamber of Commerce, 700 Throckmorton, Fort Worth, Tex. 76102

HONOLULU, HAWAII

Incorporated as city and county: 1907
Mayor: Eileen R. Anderson (to Jan. 1985)
1970 population & (rank): 324,871 (44)
1980 population (1980 census) & (rank): 365,048[1] (36)
1982 est. population & (rank): 781,899[1] (11)
1984 land area: 617 sq. mi (1,600 sq km)[1]
Altitude: Highest, 4,025 ft; lowest, sea level
Location: The city and county government's jurisdiction includes the entire island of Oahu
Churches: Roman Catholic, 33; Buddhist, 32; Jewish, 2; Protestant and others, 328
City-owned parks: 5,279 ac.
Telephones (Jan. 1, 1982): 403,821
Radio stations: AM, 17; FM, 9
Television stations: 6
Assessed valuation (1983): $15,000,000,000) (60% of market value.)
City and county tax rate (1983): $13.44 per $1,000
Bonded debt (June 1983): $181,752,980
Net revenue (1982–83): $344,451,577
Net expenditures (1982–83): $351,080,341
Chamber of Commerce: Chamber of Commerce of Hawaii, 735 Bishop St., Honolulu, Hawaii 96813

1. City and county area.

HOUSTON, TEX.

Incorporated as city: 1837
Mayor: Kathryn J. Whitmire (to Dec. 1985)
1970 population & (rank): 1,233,535 (6)
1980 population (1980 census) & (rank): 1,595,138 (5)
1982 est. population & (rank): 1,725,617 (4)
1984 land area: 556.4 sq mi. (1,441 sq km)
Altitude: Highest, 120 ft; lowest, sea level
Location: In southeastern part of state, near Gulf of Mexico
County: Seat of Harris Co.
Churches: 1,750[2]
City-owned parks: 259 (5,742 ac., not including parkways)
Telephones (Jan. 1, 1982): 1,562,990
Radio stations: AM, 14; FM, 16[1]
Television stations: 6
Assessed valuation (1983): $63,060,561,843
City tax rate (1983): $.495 per $100
Bonded debt (1983): $630,304,000
Revenue (1983): $1,136,790,000
Expenditures (1983): $1,005,597,000
Chamber of Commerce: Houston Chamber of Commerce, 1100 Milam Building, Houston, Tex. 77002

1. Includes annexations since 1970. 2. Metropolitan area (Harris County).

INDIANAPOLIS, IND.

Incorporated as city: 1832 (reincorporated 1838)
Mayor: William H. Hudnut III (to Jan. 1988)
1970 population & (rank): 736,856 (11)
1980 population (1980 census) & (rank): 700,807 (12)
1982 est. population & (rank): 707,655 (13)
1984 land area: 352.0 sq mi. (912 sq km)
Altitude: Highest, 840 ft; lowest, 700
Location: In central part of the state, on West Fork of White River
County: Seat of Marion Co.
Churches: 1,200[1]
City-owned parks: 188 (8,992 ac.)
Telephones (Jan. 1, 1982): 656,300
Radio stations: AM, 9; FM, 13[1]
Television stations: 7[1]
Assessed valuation (1983): (consolidated city), $3,611, 645,940; (Marion County) $3,876,885,192
City tax rate (Center Township, 1983): $114.08 per $1,000
Gross debt (consolidated city, Dec. 31, 1983): $214,-880,000
Revenue (1983): $250,750,936
Expenditures (1983): $247,457,121
Chamber of Commerce: Indianapolis Chamber of Commerce, 320 N Meridian St., Indianapolis, Ind. 46202

1. Marion County.

JACKSONVILLE, FLA.

Incorporated as city: 1822
Mayor: Jake M. Godbold (to July 1, 1987)
1970 population & (rank): 504,265 (26)
1980 population (1980 census) & (rank): 540,920 (22)
1982 est. population & (rank): 556,370 (23)
1984 land area: 759.6 sq mi. (1,967 sq km)
Altitude: Highest, 71 ft; lowest, sea level
Location: On St. Johns River, 20 miles from Atlantic Ocean
County: Duval
Churches: Protestant, 525; Roman Catholic, 20; Jewish, 4; others, 11
City-owned parks and playgrounds: 138 (1,522 ac.)
Telephones (Jan. 1, 1982): 448,835
Radio stations: AM, 15; FM, 10
Television stations: 6 commercial, 1 PBS
Assessed valuation (1982): $7,196,460,820
City tax rate (1982–83): $17.00 per $1,000 (old county area); $17.56 per $1,000 (old city area)
Bonded debt (1982): $54,871,683
Revenue (1982–83): $1,086,987,492

Expenditures (1982–83): $1,086,987,492
Chamber of Commerce: Jacksonville Area Chamber of Commerce, Jacksonville, Fla. 32202

KANSAS CITY, MO.

Incorporated as city: 1850
Mayor: Richard L. Berkley (April 10, 1987)
City Manager: A. J. Wilson, (apptd. Oct. 1983)
1970 population & (rank): 507,330 (25)
1980 population (1980 census) & (rank): 448,159 (27)
1982 est. population & (rank): 445,222 (27)
1984 land area: 316.3 sq mi. (819 sq km)
Altitude: Highest, 1,014 ft; lowest, 722
Location: In western part of state, at juncture of Missouri and Kansas Rivers
County: Located in Jackson, Clay, and Platte Co.
Churches: 1,100 churches of all denominations
City-owned parks and playgrounds: 174 (7,600 ac.)
Telephones (Dec., 1982): 408,857
Radio stations: AM, 14; FM, 13[1]
Television stations: 6[1]
Assessed valuation (1981–82): $1,801,388,903
City tax rate (1981–82): $15.20 per $1,000
Bonded debt (1981–82): $61,040,000
Revenue (1981–82): $286,272,451
Expenditures (1981–82): $285,319,539
Budget (gross total, 1982–83): $359,160,641
Chamber of Commerce: Chamber of Commerce of Greater Kansas City, 920 Main St., Kansas City, Mo. 64105

1. Metropolitan area.

LONG BEACH, CALIF.

Founded: 1881
Mayor: Ernie Kell (to July 1986)
City Manager: John E. Dever (apptd. Jan. 1, 1977)
1970 population & (rank): 358,879 (40)
1980 population (1980 census) & (rank): 361,334 (37)
1982 est. population & (rank): 371,426 (37)
1984 land area: 49.8 sq mi. (129 sq km)
Altitude: Highest, 170 ft; lowest, sea level
Location: On San Pedro Bay, south of Los Angeles
County: In Los Angeles Co.
Churches: 236
City-owned parks: 43 (1,620 ac.)
Telephones: (Jan. 1982): 384,294
Radio stations: AM, 2; FM, 6
Television stations: 1 (cable)
Assessed valuation (1984): $12,452,576,965
City tax rate (1981–82): none; county, $10 per $1,000
Bonded debt (1984): $214,205,000[1]
Revenue (1983–84): $1,050,369,180[2]
Expenditures (1983–84): $1,006,051,272[2]
Chamber of Commerce: Long Beach Chamber of Commerce, 50 Oceangate Plaza, Long Beach, Calif. 90802

1. Includes redevelopment funds. 2. unaudited.

LOS ANGELES, CALIF.

Incorporated as city: 1850
Mayor: Tom Bradley (to June 1985)
1970 population & (rank): 2,811,801 (3)
1980 population (1980 census) & (rank): 2,966,850 (3)
1982 est. population & (rank): 3,022,247 (2)
1984 land area: 464.7 sq mi. (1,204 sq km)
Altitude: Highest, 5,081 ft; lowest, sea level
Location: In southwestern part of state, on Pacific Ocean
County: Seat of Los Angeles Co.
Churches: 1,963 of all denominations
City-owned parks: 296 (14,489 ac.)
Telephones (Jan. 1982): 1,978,561[1]
Radio stations: AM, 32; FM, 40
Television stations: 18
Assessed valuation (1983–84): $86,537,949,814
City tax rate (1981–82): $0.016 per $1,000
Gross debt (June 30, 1983): general obligation bonds, $62,275,000; revenue bonds, $2,359,906,000
Revenue (1982–83): $1,472,315,166
Expenditures (1982–83): $1,444,456,149
Chamber of Commerce: Los Angeles Chamber of Commerce, 404 S Bixel St., Los Angeles, Calif. 90017

1. Does not include Long Beach, Calif.

LOUISVILLE, KY.

Incorporated as city: 1828
Mayor: Harvey I. Sloane (to Dec. 1985)
1970 population & (rank): 361,706 (38)
1980 population (1980 census) & (rank): 298,840 (49)
1982 est. population & (rank): 293,531 (50)
1984 land area: 60.0 sq mi. (155 sq km)
Altitude: Highest, 565 ft; lowest, 477
Location: In north central part of state, on Ohio River
County: Seat of Jefferson Co.
Churches: 678[1]
City-owned parks and playgrounds: 166 (over 7,000 ac.)
Telephones (Jan. 1, 1982): 571,703
Radio stations: 16
Television stations: 5
Assessed valuation (1981): $3,591,678,150
City tax rate (1983): 1.25% occupational; 49.5¢ per $100; 56.6¢ per $100 personal property
Net bonded debt (Jan. 1, 1983): $33,280,000
Revenue (1982–83): $93,200,000
Expenditures (1982–83): $93,172,690
Chamber of Commerce: Louisville Area Chamber of Commerce, 300 W Liberty St., Louisville, Ky. 40202

1. Metropolitan area.

MEMPHIS, TENN.

Incorporated as city: 1826
Mayor: Richard C. Hackett (to Dec. 1987)
1970 population & (rank): 623,988 (17)
1980 population (1980 census) & (rank): 646,174 (14)
1982 est. population & (rank): 645,760 (16)
1984 land area: 264.1 sq mi. (684 sq km)
Altitude: Highest, 331 ft
Location: In southwestern corner of state, on Mississippi River
County: Seat of Shelby Co.
Churches: 1,000
Parks and playgrounds: 169 (5,400 ac.)
Telephones (Jan. 1982): 640,431
Radio stations: AM, 13; FM, 8
Television stations: 5
Assessed valuation (1983): $3,020,397,139
City tax rate (1983): $36.70 per $1,000
Bonded debt (June 30, 1983): $476,065,589
Revenue (1983): $703,108,193[1]
Expenditures (1983): $665,460,134[1]
Chamber of Commerce: Memphis Area Chamber of Commerce, P.O. Box 224, Memphis, Tenn. 38103

1. Includes Board of Education figures.

MIAMI, FLA.

Incorporated as city: 1896
Mayor: Maurice A. Ferre (to Nov. 1985)
City manager: Howard V. Gary (apptd. April 1981)

1970 population & (rank): 334,859 (42)
1980 population (1980 census) & (rank): 346,865 (41)
1982 est. population & (rank): 382,726 (34)
1984 land area: 34.3 sq mi. (89 sq km)
Altitude: Average, 12 ft
Location: In southeastern part of state, on Biscayne Bay
County: Seat of Dade Co.
Churches: Protestant, 592; Roman Catholic, 53; Jewish, 48
City-owned parks: 94
Telephones (Jan. 1, 1982): 1,265,110
Radio stations: AM, 18; FM, 20
Television stations: 5 commercial, 2 PBS
Assessed valuation (1983–84): $8,491,885,880
City tax rate (1983–84): $9.5514 per $1,000
Bonded debt (1983–84): $131,020,000
Revenue (1983–84): $170,552,499
Expenditures (1983–84): $170,552,499
Chamber of Commerce: Greater Miami Chamber of Commerce, 391 N.E. 15th St., Miami, Fla. 33132

MILWAUKEE, WIS.

Incorporated as city: 1846
Mayor: Henry W. Maier (to April 1988)
1970 population & (rank): 717,372 (12)
1980 population (1980 census) & (rank): 636,236 (16)
1982 est. population & (rank): 631,509 (18)
1984 land area: 95.8 sq mi. (248 sq km)
Altitude: 580.60 ft
Location: In southeastern part of state, on Lake Michigan
County: Seat of Milwaukee Co.
Churches: 411
County-owned parks: 14,061 ac.
Telephones (Jan. 1, 1982): 873,718
Radio stations: AM, 9; FM, 14
Television stations: 8
Assessed valuation (1983): $10,542,257,409
City tax rate (1983): $33.47 per $1,000
Gross debt (1983): $242,040,000
Revenue (1983): $529,504,330
Expenditures (1983): $536,738,139
Chamber of Commerce: Metropolitan Milwaukee Association of Commerce, 828 N. Broadway, Milwaukee, Wis. 53202

MINNEAPOLIS, MINN.

Incorporated as city: 1867
Mayor: Donald M. Fraser (to Jan. 1986)
1970 population & (rank): 434,400 (31)
1980 population (1980 census) & (rank): 370,951 (34)
1982 est. population & (rank): 369,161 (38)
1984 land area: 55.1 sq mi. (143 sq km)
Altitude: Highest, 945 ft; lowest, 695
Location: In southeast central part of state, on Mississippi River
County: Seat of Hennepin Co.
Churches: 419
City-owned parks: 153
Telephones (incl. St. Paul, Jan. 1, 1982): 1,697,467
Radio stations: AM, 17; FM, 15 (metro area)
Television stations: 6 (metro area)
Assessed valuation (1983): $2,585,775,870
City tax rate (1983): $34.835 per $1,000
Net debt (Dec. 31, 1983): $62,955,000
Revenue (1983): $329,608,732
Expenditures (1983): $323,037,251
Chamber of Commerce: Greater Minneapolis Chamber of Commerce, 15 S Fifth Street, Minneapolis, Minn. 55402

1. Assessed valuations on majority of properties now range from 16% (homesteads) to 43% (commercial, industrial) of actual market value.

NASHVILLE, TENN.

Incorporated as city: 1806
Mayor: Richard H. Fulton (to Sept. 1987)
1970 population & (rank): 426,029 (32)
1980 population (1980 census) & (rank): 455,651 (25)
1982 est. population & (rank): 455,252 (26)
1984 land area: 479.4 sq mi. (1,242 sq km)
Altitude: Highest, 1,100 ft; lowest, approx. 400 ft
Location: In north central part of state, on Cumberland River
County: Davidson
Churches: Protestant, 739; Roman Catholic, 16; Jewish, 3
City-owned parks: 68 (6,650 ac.)
Telephones (Jan. 1, 1982): 425,903
Radio stations: AM, 11; FM, 8
Television stations: 5
Assessed valuation (1983): $2,060,292,993
City tax rate (1983): $68.30 per $1,000
Bonded debt (June 1983): $225,522,000
Revenue (1983): $367,602,373
Expenditures (1983): $368,881,285
Chamber of Commerce: Nashville Area Chamber of Commerce, 161 Fourth Ave. North, Nashville, Tenn. 37219

NEWARK, N.J.

Incorporated as city: 1836
Mayor: Kenneth A. Gibson (to June 1986)
1970 population & (rank): 381,930 (35)
1980 population (1980 census) & (rank): 329,248 (46)
1982 est. population & (rank): 320,512 (49)
1984 land area: 24.1 sq mi. (62 sq km)
Altitude: Highest, 273.4 ft; lowest, sea level
Location: In northeastern part of state, on Passaic River and Newark Bay
County: Seat of Essex Co.
Churches: Roman Catholic, 32; Jewish, 4; Protestant and others, 250
City-owned parks: 40 (and 20 mini parks); (39.3 ac.)
County-governed parks in city: 7 (743.97 ac.)
Telephones (Jan. 1, 1982): 330,982
Radio stations: AM, 2; FM, 4
Television stations: 2
Assessed valuation (1984): $1,023,476,000
City tax rate (1984): $125.80 per $1,000
Net bonded debt (1984): $44,491,000
Revenue (est. 1984): $306,853,954
Expenditures (est. 1984): $306,853,954
Chamber of Commerce: Greater Newark Chamber of Commerce, 50 Park Place, Newark, N.J. 07102

NEW ORLEANS, LA.

Incorporated as city: 1805
Mayor: Ernest N. Morial (to May 1986)
1970 population & (rank): 593,471 (19)
1980 population (1980 census) & (rank): 557,927 (21)
1982 est. population & (rank): 564,561 (20)
1984 land area: 199.4 sq mi. (516 sq km)
Altitude: Highest, 15 ft; lowest, –4
Location: In southeastern part of state, between Mississippi River and Lake Ponchartrain
Parish: Seat of Orleans Parish
Churches: 644
City-owned parks: 69 (21,000 ac.)
Telephones (Jan. 1, 1982): 801,040
Radio stations: AM, 12; FM, 10
Television stations: 5
Assessed valuation (1983): $1,200,000,000
City tax rate (1984): $102.57 per $10,000
Bonded debt (1983): $237,000,000

Revenue (est. 1984): $362,000,000
Expenditures (est. 1984): $362,000,000
Chamber of Commerce: New Orleans and the River Region Chamber of Commerce, 301 Camp Street, New Orleans, La. 70130

NEW YORK, N.Y.

Chartered as "Greater New York": 1898
Mayor: Edward Koch (to Dec. 31, 1985)
Borough Presidents: Bronx, Stanley Simon; Brooklyn, Howard Golden; Manhattan, Andrew Stein; Queens, Donald R. Manes; Staten Island, Anthony Gaeta
1970 population & (rank): 7,895,563 (1)[1]
1980 population (1980 census) & (rank): 7.071,639 (1)[1]
1982 est. population & (rank): 7,086,096 (1)[1]
1984 land area: 301.5 sq mi. (781 sq km) (Queens, 109; Brooklyn, 72; Staten Island, 55; Bronx, 42.5; Manhattan, 23.0)
Altitude: Highest, 410 ft; lowest, sea level
Location: In south of state, at mouth of Hudson River (also known as the North River as it passes Manhattan)
Counties: Consists of 5 counties: Bronx, Kings (Brooklyn), New York (Manhattan), Queens, Richmond (Staten Island)
Churches: Protestant, 1,766; Jewish, 1,256; Roman Catholic, 437; Orthodox, 66
City-owned parks: 1,588 (37,372 ac.)
Telephones (Jan. 1, 1982): 5,751,006
Radio stations: AM and FM, 7; AM only, 10; FM only, 12
Television stations: 6 commercial
Assessed valuation (1983–84): $45,795,143,358
City tax rate (1984–85): $9.323 commercial, $.0910 residential, per $100
Expenditures (1983–84): $16,834,120,760
Chamber of Commerce: New York Chamber of Commerce and Industry, 65 Liberty St., New York, N.Y. 10005

1. For population of boroughs, *see* Index.

OAKLAND, CALIF.

Incorporated as city: 1854
Mayor: Lionel J. Wilson (to June 30, 1985)
City Manager: Henry L. Gardner (apptd. June 1981)
1970 population & (rank): 361,561 (39)
1980 population (1980 census) & (rank): 339,337 (43)
1982 est. population & (rank): 344,652 (45)
1984 land area: 53.9 sq mi.
Altitude: Highest, 1,700 ft; lowest, sea level
Location: In west central part of state, on east side of San Francisco Bay
County: Seat of Alameda Co.
Churches: 374, representing over 78 denominations in the City; over 500 churches in Alameda County
City-owned parks: 2,196 ac.
Telephones (Jan. 1, 1982): 615,845
Radio stations: AM, 3; FM, 2
Television stations: 9 commercial; 3 PBS
Assessed valuation (1982–83): $8,441,549,990 (25% of appraised value)
City tax rate (1982–83): $1.3288%[2]
Bonded debt (est. June 1983): $1,783,000
Revenue (1982–83 est.): $219,109,000
Expenditures (1982–83): $206,999,000
Chamber of Commerce: Oakland Chamber of Commerce, 1939 Harrison St., Suite 400, Oakland, Calif. 94612

1. In East Bay Exchange, which includes Oakland. 2. Code area 17001.

OKLAHOMA CITY, OKLA.

Incorporated as city: 1890
Mayor: Andy Coars (to April 1987)
City Manager: Scott Johnson
1970 population & (rank): 368,164 (37)
1980 population (1980 census) & (rank): 403,213 (31)
1982 est. population & (rank): 427,714 (31)
1984 land area: 621.5 sq mi. (1,563 sq km)
Altitude: Highest, 1,320 ft; lowest, 1,140
Location: In central part of state, on North Canadian River
County: Seat of Oklahoma Co.
Churches: Roman Catholic, 15; Jewish, 2; Protestant and others, 741
City-owned parks: 138 (3,944 ac.)
Telephones (Jan. 1, 1982): 731,918
Television stations: 8
Radio stations: AM, 10; FM, 14
Assessed valuation (1983–84): $1,305,440,435
City tax rate (1983–84): $16.51 per $1,000
Bonded debt (1983–84): $189,442,670
Revenue (general fund, 1982–83): $113,859,362
Expenditures (general fund, 1982–83): $98,724,280
Chamber of Commerce: Oklahoma City Chamber of Commerce, 1 Santa Fe Plaza, Oklahoma City, Okla. 73102

OMAHA, NEB.

Incorporated as city: 1857
Mayor: Mike Boyle (to June 1985)
1970 population & (rank): 346,929 (41)
1980 population (1980 census) & (rank): 313,911 (48)
1982 est. population & (rank): 328,557 (47)
1984 land area: 90.9 sq mi. (235 sq km)
Altitude: Highest, 1,270 ft
Location: In eastern part of state, on Missouri River
County: Seat of Douglas Co.
Churches: Protestant, 246; Roman Catholic, 44; Jewish, 4
City-owned parks: 99 (3,671.6 ac.)
Telephones (Jan. 1, 1982): 504,975
Radio stations: AM, 7; FM, 6
Television stations: 4
Assessed valuation (1984): $6,124,006,220
City tax rate (1984): $0.7524 per $100
Bonded debt (1983): $93,334,600
Revenue (1983): $135,981,606
Expenditures (1983): $131,309,111
Chamber of Commerce: Omaha Chamber of Commerce, 1620 Dodge St., Omaha, Neb. 68102

PHILADELPHIA, PA.

First charter as city: 1701
Mayor: W. Wilson Goode (to Jan. 1988)
1970 population & (rank): 1,949,996 (4)
1980 population (1980 census) & (rank): 1,688,210 (4)
1982 est. population & (rank): 1,665,382 (5)
1984 land area: 136.0 sq mi. (352 sq km)
Altitude: Highest, 440 ft; lowest, sea level
Location: In southeastern part of state, at junction of Schuylkill and Delaware Rivers
County: Seat of Philadelphia Co. (coterminous)
Churches: Roman Catholic, 139; Jewish, 70; Protestant and others, 830
City-owned parks: 630 (10,252 ac.)
Telephones (Jan. 1, 1982): 1,710,113
Radio stations: AM, 20; FM, 22
Television stations: 8
Assessed valuation (1984): $6,036,000,000
City and school district tax rate (1984): $74.75 per $1,000
Net bonded debt (June 30, 1983): $2,114,000,000 (incl. revenue bonds of $666,700,000 for water and sewer; $355,000,000 for gas works; $67,000,000 for aviation)

Revenue (1983): $1,287,100,000
Expenditures (1983): $1,342,300,000
Chamber of Commerce: Greater Philadelphia Chamber of Commerce, 1617 John F. Kennedy Blvd., Philadelphia, Pa. 19103

PHOENIX, ARIZ.

Incorporated as city: 1881
Mayor: Terry Goddard (to Jan. 1986)
City Manager: Marvin A. Andrews (appt. Oct. 1976)
1970 population & (rank): 584,303 (20)
1980 population (1980 census) & (rank): 789,704 (9)
1982 est. population & (rank): 824,230 (9)
1983 land area: 344.4 sq mi.
Altitude: Highest, 2,740 ft.; lowest, 1,017
Location: In center of state, on Salt River
County: Seat of Maricopa Co.
City-owned parks: 142 (26,647 ac.)
Telephones (Sept. 1983): 1,298,935
Radio stations: AM, 19; FM, 15
Television stations: 8 commercial; 1 PBS
Assessed valuation (1983–84): $3,345,840,212
City tax rate (1983–84): $15.90 per $1,000
Bonded debt (Oct. 1983): $743,625,000
Revenues (est. 1983–84): $586,485,000
Expenditures (est. 1983–84): $559,115,000
Chamber of Commerce: Phoenix Chamber of Commerce, 805 N Second St., Phoenix, Ariz. 85004

PITTSBURGH, PA.

Incorporated as city: 1816
Mayor: Richard S. Caliguiri (to Jan. 1986)
1970 population & (rank): 520,089 (23)
1980 population (1980 census) & (rank): 423,959 (30)
1982 est. population & (rank): 414,936 (32)
1984 land area: 55.4 sq mi. (144 sq km)
Altitude: Highest, 1,240 ft; lowest, 715
Location: In southwestern part of state, at beginning of Ohio River
County: Seat of Allegheny Co.
Churches: Protestant, 348; Roman Catholic, 86; Jewish, 28; Orthodox, 26
City-owned parks and playgrounds: 88 (2,471 ac.)
Telephones (Jan. 1, 1982): 818,641
Radio stations: AM, 18; FM, 9
Television stations: 4
Assessed valuation (1982): land, $343,582,636; buildings, $1,162,089,145
City tax rate (1983): $27 per $1,000 buildings; $155.50 per $1,000 land
Net bonded debt (Dec. 1981): $205,552,314
Revenue (1982): $235,500,000
Expenditures (1982): $219,800,000
Chamber of Commerce: The Chamber of Commerce of Greater Pittsburgh, 411 Seventh Ave., Pittsburgh, Pa. 15222

PORTLAND, ORE.

Incorporated as city: 1851
Mayor: John (Bud) Clark (to Dec. 1988)
1970 population & (rank): 379,967 (36)
1980 population (1980 census) & (rank): 366,383 (35)
1982 est. population & (rank): 367,530 (40)
1984 land area: 103.3 sq mi. (267.5 sq km)
Altitude: Highest, 1,073 ft; lowest, sea level
Location: In northwestern part of state, on Willamette River
County: Seat of Multnomah Co.
Churches: Protestant, 332; Roman Catholic, 27; Jewish, 4; Buddhist, 4; Vedanta Society, 1
City-owned parks: 228 (8,718 ac.)
Telephones (Jan. 1, 1982): 527,974
Radio stations: AM, 12; FM, 12
Television stations: 5
Assessed valuation (1983–84): $11,866,835,000 (at 100% of cash value)
City tax rate (1983–84): $6.58 per $1,000
Bonded debt (July 1, 1984): $300,290,944
Revenue (est. 1984–85): $722,079,084
Expenditures (est. 1984–85): $722,079,084
Chamber of Commerce: Portland Chamber of Commerce, 824 SW Fifth Ave., Portland, Ore. 97204

ST. LOUIS, MO.

Incorporated as city: 1822
Mayor: Vincent Schoemehl, Jr. (to April 1985)
1970 population & (rank): 622,236 (18)
1980 population (1980 census) & (rank): 453,085 (26)
1982 est. population & (rank): 437,354 (29)
1984 land area: 61.4 sq mi. (159 sq km)
Altitude: Highest, 616 ft; lowest, 413
Location: In east central part of state, on Mississippi River
County: Independent city
Churches: 900[1]
City-owned parks: 89 (2,639 ac.)
Telephones (Jan. 1, 1982): 589,056
Radio stations: AM, 18; FM, 20[1]
Television stations: 5 commercial; 1 PBS
Assessed valuation (1983): $1,453,573,097
City tax rate (1983): $61.40 per $1,000
Bonded debt (1983–84): $23,834,545
Revenue (1983–84): $271,807,714
Expenditures (1983–84): $256,959,487
Chamber of Commerce: St. Louis Regional Commerce and Growth Association, 10 Broadway, St. Louis, Mo. 63102

1. Metropolitan area.

SAN ANTONIO, TEX.

Incorporated as city: 1837
Mayor: Henry Cisneros (to May 1985)
City Manager: Louis J. Fox (apptd. Jan. 1982)
1970 population & (rank): 654,153 (15)
1980 population (1980 census) & (rank): 786,023 (11)
1982 est. population & (rank): 819,021 (10)
1984 land area: 262.7 sq mi. (680 sq km)
Altitude: 700 ft
Location: In south central part of state, on San Antonio River
County: Seat of Bexar Co.
City-owned parks: Approximately 5,881 ac.
Telephones (Jan. 1, 1982): 429,350
Radio stations: AM, 13; FM, 12
Television stations: 5
Assessed valuation (1983): $6,738,454,216
City tax rate (1983): $.7575 per $100
Net funded debt (1983): $153,440,651
Revenue (est. 1982–83): $209,338,000[1]
Expenditures (est. 1982–83): $225,240,000[1]
Chamber of Commerce: Greater San Antonio Chamber of Commerce, P.O. Box 1628, 602 E Commerce, San Antonio, Tex. 78296

1. General Fund only.

SAN DIEGO, CALIF.

Incorporated as city: 1850
Mayor: Roger Hedgecock (to Dec. 1984)

City Manager: Ray T. Blair, Jr. (apptd. May 1978)
1970 population & (rank): 697,471 (14)
1980 population (1980 census) & (rank): 875,538 (8)
1982 est. population & (rank): 915,956 (8)
1984 land area: 323.4 sq mi. (837 sq km)
Altitude: Highest, 1,591 ft; lowest, sea level
Location: In southwesternmost part of state, on San Diego Bay
County: Seat of San Diego Co.
Churches: Roman Catholic, 80; Jewish, 8; Protestant 334; Eastern Orthodox, 7; other, 6
City park and recreation facilities: 266 (24,531 ac.)
Telephones (Jan. 1, 1982): 562,021
Radio stations: AM, 13; FM, 20
Television stations: 5
Assessed valuation (1984): $26,787,213,436
City tax rate (1984): $10.16 per $1,000 (includes county and school district)
Bonded debt (1984): $22,765,000
Revenue (est. 1984): $426,102,815
Expenditures (est. 1984): $426,102,815
Chamber of Commerce: San Diego Chamber of Commerce, 110 W. C St., Suite 1600, San Diego, Calif. 92101

SAN FRANCISCO, CALIF.

Incorporated as city: 1850
Mayor: Dianne Feinstein (to Jan. 1988)
1970 population & (rank): 715,674 (13)
1980 population (1980 census) & (rank): 678,974 (13)
1982 est. population & (rank): 691,637 (14)
1984 land area: 46.4 sq mi. (120 sq km)
Altitude: Highest, 925 ft; lowest, sea level
Location: In northern part of state between Pacific Ocean and San Francisco Bay
County: Coextensive with San Francisco Co.
Churches: 540 of all denominations
City-owned parks and squares: 120
Telephones (Jan. 1, 1982): 892,015
Radio stations: 22
Television stations: 7
Assessed valuation (1983–84): $21,748,512,000 (100% of valuation)
City and county tax rate (1983–84): $1.15 per $100
Bonded debt (June 30, 1983): $907,251,000
Revenue (1983–84): $1,358,000,000
Expenditures (1983–84): $1,540,000,000
Chamber of Commerce: Greater San Francisco Chamber of Commerce, 465 California St., San Francisco, Calif. 94104

SAN JOSE, CALIF.

Incorporated as city: 1850
Mayor: Thomas McEnery (to Dec. 31, 1986)
1970 population & (rank): 459,913 (29)
1980 population (1980 census) & (rank): 629,546 (17)
1982 est. population & (rank): 659,181 (15)
1983 land area: 162.75 sq. mi (421 sq km)
Altitude: 100 ft
Location: In northern part of state, on south San Francisco Bay, 50 miles from San Francisco
County: Santa Clara
Churches: Protestant, 195; Roman Catholic, 29; Jewish, 4; others, 24
City-owned parks and playgrounds: 142 (2,939 ac.)
Telephones (Jan. 1, 1982): 707,692
Radio stations: AM, 5; FM, 6
Television stations: 5 commercial; 1 PBS
Assessed valuation (1983–84): $18,709,393,731 (100% of valuation)
City tax rate (1982–83): $1.55 per $1,000
Bonded debt (June 1983): $24,502,000
Revenue (1983–84): $552,260,000
Expenditures (1983–84): $552,260,000
Chamber of Commerce: San Jose Chamber of Commerce, One Paseo de San Antonio, San Jose, Calif. 95113

SEATTLE, WASH.

Incorporated as city: 1869
Mayor: Charles Royer (to Nov. 1985)
1970 population & (rank): 530,831 (22)
1980 population (1980 census) & (rank): 493,846 (23)
1982 est. population & (rank): 490,077 (25)
1984 land area: 144.6 sq mi. (375 sq km)
Altitude: Highest, 540 ft; lowest, sea level
Location: In west central part of state, on Puget Sound
County: Seat of King Co.
Churches: Roman Catholic, 36; Jewish, 13; Protestant and others, 535
City-owned parks, playgrounds, etc.: 278 (4,773.4 ac.)
Telephones (Jan. 1, 1982): 697,116
Radio stations: AM, 22; FM, 26
Television stations: 3 commercial; 1 educational
Assessed valuation (1984): $21,039,060,319
City tax rate (1984): $10.01 per $1,000
Bonded debt (1982): $649,495,000
Revenue (1982): $281,765,060
Expenditures (1982): $268,332,860
Chamber of Commerce: Seattle Chamber of Commerce, 215 Columbia Street, Seattle, Wash. 98104

TOLEDO, OHIO

Incorporated as city: 1837
Mayor: Donna Owens (to Dec. 1985)
City Manager: David Boston (apptd. Sept. 1981)
1970 population & (rank): 383,062 (34)
1980 population (1980 census) & (rank): 354,635 (40)
1982 est. population & (rank): 350,565 (43)
1984 land area: 84.2 sq mi. (218 sq km)
Altitude: 630 ft
Location: In northwestern part of state, on Maumee River at Lake Erie
County: Seat of Lucas Co.
Churches: Protestant, 301; Roman Catholic, 55; Jewish, 4; others, 98
City-owned parks and playgrounds: 134 (2,650.90 ac.)
Telephones (Jan. 1, 1982): 315,378
Radio stations: AM, 8; FM, 8
Television stations: 4
Assessed valuation (1984): $2,661,746,397
City tax rate (1982): $58.80 per $1,000
Bonded debt (1982): $175,728,000
Revenue (est. 1983): $173,303,000
Expenditures (est. 1983): $167,369,000
Chamber of Commerce: Toledo Area Chamber of Commerce, 218 Huron St., Toledo, Ohio 43604

TUCSON, ARIZ.

Incorporated as city: 1877
Mayor: Lewis C. Murphy (to Dec. 1987)
1970 population & (rank): 262,933 (53)
1980 population (1980 census) & (rank): 330,537 (45)
1982 est. population & (rank): 352,455 (42)
1984 land area: 98.8 sq mi. (256 sq km)
Altitude: 2,500 ft
Location: In southeastern part of state, on the Santa Cruz River

County: Seat of Pima Co.
Churches: Protestant, 181; Roman Catholic, 24; other, 136
City-owned parks and parkways: (2,001.75 ac.)
Telephones (Jan. 1, 1982): 423,575
Radio stations: AM, 12; FM, 7
Television stations: 3 commercial; 1 educational; 2 other
Assessed valuation (1983): $1,130,996
City tax rate (1983): $6.60 per $1,000
Net bonded debt (1983): $151,688,538
Revenue (1983): $196,699,626
Expenditures (1983): $196,670,001
Chamber of Commerce: Tucson Chamber of Commerce, P.O. Box 991, Tucson, Ariz. 85702

TULSA, OKLA.

Incorporated as city: 1898
Mayor: Terry Young (to May 1986)
1970 population & (rank): 330,350 (43)
1980 population (1980 census) & (rank): 360,919 (38)
1982 est. population & (rank): 375,300 (36)
1984 land area: 185.6 sq mi. (481 sq km)
Altitude: 674 ft
Location: In northeastern part of state, on Arkansas River
County: Seat of Tulsa Co.
Churches: Protestant, 593; Roman Catholic, 32; Jewish, 2; others, 4
City parks and playgrounds: 113 (5,050 ac.)
Telephones (Jan. 1, 1984): 275,234 access lines
Radio stations: AM, 7; FM, 10
Television stations: 5 commercial; 1 PBS; 1 cable
Assessed valuation (1983–84): $1,277,602,753
City tax rate (1983–84): $74.80 per $1,000
Bonded debt (July 1983): $83,990,000
Revenue (1982–83): $249,413,766
Expenditures (1982–83): $236,671,635
Chamber of Commerce: Metropolitan Tulsa Chamber of Commerce, 616 S Boston, Tulsa, Okla. 74119

WASHINGTON, D.C.

Land ceded to Congress: 1788 by Maryland; 1789 by Virginia (retroceded to Virginia Sept. 7, 1846)
Seat of government transferred to D. C.: Dec. 1, 1800
Created municipal corporation: Feb. 21, 1871
Mayor: Marion Barry, Jr. (to Jan. 1987)
Motto: *Justitia omnibus* (Justice to all)
Flower: American beauty rose
Tree: Scarlet oak
Origin of name: In honor of Columbus
1980 population (1980 census) & (rank): 638,432 (15)
1982 est. population & (rank): 633,425 (17)
1984 land area: 62.7 sq mi. (162 sq km)
Geographic center: Near corner of Fourth and L Sts., NW
Altitude: Highest, 420 ft; lowest, sea level
Location: Between Virginia and Maryland, on Potomac River
Churches: Protestant, 446; Roman Catholic, 23; Jewish, 10; others, 23
City parks: 753 (7,725 ac.)
Telephones (Jan. 1, 1982): 1,091,787
Radio stations: AM, 15; FM, 16
Television stations: 6 (including 2 UHF stations)
Assessed valuation (1984): $20,724,685,004[1]
City tax rate (1983–84): $21.30 per $1,000 (commercial)
Bonded debt: None
Revenue (est. 1985): $2,842,128,000
Expenditures (est. 1985): $2,836,815,000
Chamber of Commerce: D.C. Chamber of Commerce, 1319 F St., NW, Washington, D.C. 20004

1. On taxable property only. More than 50% of all land in District of Columbia is owned by the Federal government and tax-exempt organizations, and therefore is nontaxable.

The District of Columbia—identical with the City of Washington—is the capital of the United States and the first carefully planned capital in the world.

D.C. history began in 1790 when Congress directed selection of a new capital site, 10 miles square, along the Potomac. When the site was determined, it included 30.75 square miles on the Virginia side of the river. In 1846, however, Congress returned that area to Virginia.

The city was planned and partly laid out by Major Pierre Charles L. 'Enfant, a French engineer. This work was perfected and completed by Major Andrew Ellicott. In 1814, during the War of 1812, a British force fired the capital, and it was from the white paint applied to cover fire damage that the President's home was called the White House.

Until Nov. 3, 1967, the District of Columbia was administered by three commissioners appointed by the President. On that day, a government consisting of a mayor-commissioner and a 9-member Council, all appointed by the President with the approval of the Senate, took office. On May 7, 1974, the citizens of the District of Columbia approved the Home Rule Charter, giving them their first form of elected government in over 100 years. The District also has one non-voting member in the House of Representatives.

On Aug. 22, 1978, the Senate passed a proposed constitutional amendment to give Washington, D.C., voting representation in the Congress. The House had approved the legislation in the spring. The amendment must be ratified by at least 28 state legislatures within seven years to become effective. As of 1984, 11 states voted for it.

How the Census Bureau Ranks the 50 Largest Cities

The 1982 population estimates for the fifty largest cities were prepared by the Commerce Department's Census Bureau using procedures that rely on resident births and deaths to measure net natural change; federal tax data to estimate net internal migration; counts of inmates of institutions, college students living in dormitories, and armed forces members living in barracks to measure changes in special populations; and estimates of legal immigration.

The population estimates are used in the federal government's General Revenue Sharing Program and other federal funds distribution programs.

According to the Census Bureau, 176 cities in the United States had populations over 100,000 in 1982. Newcomers to the 1982 list are the cities of Abline, Tex., pop. 104,302; Odessa, Tex., pop. 102,-465; Pomona, Calif., pop. 100,465; and Houma, La., pop. 100,346.

The City of Honolulu, coextensive with Honolulu County, is a federal general revenue sharing area not recognized as a city for census purposes.

Tabulated Data on City Governments

City	Mayor: Term, years	Mayor: Salary[1]	City manager's salary[2]	Council or Commission: Name	Members	Term, years	Salary[3]
Albuquerque, N.M.	4	$47,840	47,840[4]	Council	9	4	$4,600
Atlanta	4	50,000	—	Council	19	4	12,500
Austin, Tex.	2	18,200	89,500	Council	6	2	22,000
Baltimore	4	53,000	—	Council	19	4	23,000
Birmingham, Ala.	4	52,500	—	Council	9	4	6,900
Boston	4	60,000	—	Council	9	2	32,500
Buffalo, N.Y.	4	55,000	—	Council	13	2[5]	25,000
Charlotte, N.C.	2	12,000	75,000	Council	11	2	6,000
Chicago	4	60,000	—	Council	50	4	27,600
Cincinnati	2	29,581	77,220	Council	9	2	26,081
Cleveland	4	57,881	—	Council	21	4	23,958
Columbus, Ohio	4	65,000	—	Council	7	4	10,000
Dallas	2	50[6]	—	Council	11	2	50[6]
Denver	4	59,879	—	Council	13	4	21,890
Detroit	4	75,172	—	Council	9	4	40,771
El Paso	2	25,000	—	Council	7[7]	2	15,000
Fort Worth	2	10[8]	78,784	Council	9	2	10[8]
Honolulu	4	69,792	63,444	Council	9	4	17,500[9]
Houston	2	81,560	—	Council	14	2	21,750
Indianapolis	4	57,270	—	Council	29	4	9,200[10]
Jacksonville, Fla.	4	40,000	—	Council	19	4	10,000
Kansas City, Mo.	4	40,000	94,500	Council	13[7]	4	12,500
Long Beach, Calif.	2	674[12]	—	Council	9[13]	4	674[12]
Los Angeles	4	80,708	—	Council	15	4	43,755
Louisville, Ky.	4	47,310	—	Board of Aldermen	12	2	14,290
Memphis, Tenn.	4	60,000[14]	54,000	Council	13	4	6,000
Miami, Fla.	2	5,000[15]	106,861	Commission	3	4	5,000
Milwaukee	4	68,781	—	Council	16	4	31,391
Minneapolis	4	51,871	62,879	Council	13	2	37,250
Nashville, Tenn.	4	50,000	—	Council	41	4	5,400
Newark, N.J.	4	52,500	50,000[17]	Council	9	4	24,500
New Orleans	4	75,905	67,644	Council	7	4	29,500
New York	4	110,000	76,650[16]	Council	35	4	47,500
Oakland, Calif.	4	15,000	59,500	Council	9[7]	4	([18])
Oklahoma City	4	2,000	75,000	Council	8	4	20[19]
Omaha, Neb.	4	47,280	—	Council	7	4	12,600
Philadelphia	4	70,000	62,500[20]	Council	17	4	40,000
Phoenix, Ariz.	2	37,500	92,404	Council	9	2	18,000
Pittsburgh	4	57,000	—	Council	9	4	([21])
Portland, Ore.	4	55,395	—	Commission	4	4	44,412
St. Louis	4	59,758	—	Board of Aldermen	29	4	12,500
San Antonio	2	3,000[22]	83,655	Council	11[7]	2	20[23]
San Diego, Calif.	4	46,000	83,448	Council	8	4	32,500
San Francisco	4	84,225	83,180	Board of Supervisors	11	4	9,600
San Jose, Calif.	4	31,750	90,251	Council	10	4	24,000
Seattle	4	78,410	—	Council	9	4	52,432
Toledo, Ohio	2	36,900	61,500	Council	9[13]	2	7,800
Tucson, Ariz.	4	25,000	72,000	Council	7	4	12,000
Tulsa, Okla.	2	50,000	—	Commission	4	2	38,500
Washington, D.C.	4	78,630	69,600	Council	13	4	45,655

1. Annual salary unless otherwise indicated. 2. Annual salary. City Manager's term is indefinite and at will of Council. 3. Annual salary unless otherwise indicated. In some cities, President of Council receives a higher salary. 4. City Administrative Officer appointed by Mayor, approved by Council. 5. For 9 District Councilmen; 4 years for 5 Councilmen-at-Large. 6. Per Council meeting; not over $2,600 per year. 7. Including Mayor. 8. Per week and per Council meeting. 9. Managing Director appointed by Mayor; no Council approval required. 10. Plus $40 per meeting for three meetings a month. 11. Chief Administrative Officer appointed by Mayor; not subject to Council confirmation. 12. Per month. 13. Including Mayor and Vice-Mayor. 14. Plus $5,000 expense account. 15. Plus $2,500 expense account. 16. No City Manager; salary is for Deputy Mayor. 17. Business Administrator, appointed by Mayor and confirmed by Council. 18. Flat $500 per month, or $6,000 annually. 19. Per Council meeting; not to exceed 5 meetings a month. 20. Appointed by Mayor, with title of Managing Director. 21. 4 members at $32,500; 5 members at $27,500. 22. Plus Council pay. 23. Per Council meeting; not over $1,040 per year. 24. $10,000 additional for Chairman. 25. City manager replaced by 3 deputy mayors with salaries of $56,301. *Source: Information Please* questionnaires to the cities.

EDUCATION

School Enrollment, October 1983

(in thousands)

Age	White		Black		Spanish origin[1]		All races	
	Enrolled	Percent	Enrolled	Percent	Enrolled	Percent	Enrolled	Percent
3 and 4 years	2,132	37.6	387	36.2	151	23.5	2,624	37.5
5 and 6 years	5,094	95.7	915	94.7	564	95.1	6,214	95.4
7 to 9 years	7,642	98.9	1,405	99.1	880	98.5	9,408	98.9
10 to 13 years	11,292	99.3	2,065	99.7	1,259	99.7	13,870	99.4
14 and 15 years	5,857	98.4	1,035	97.8	591	96.0	7,093	98.3
16 and 17 years	5,492	91.4	1,002	92.6	498	88.6	6,698	91.7
18 and 19 years	3,285	50.9	523	46.1	254	44.3	3,938	50.4
20 and 21 years	2,253	33.4	258	23.4	147	24.0	2,609	32.5
22 to 24 years	1,753	16.4	254	15.6	105	12.5	2,111	16.6
25 to 29 years	1,641	9.4	193	7.8	120	8.2	1,976	9.6
30 to 34 years	981	6.2	164	7.6	49	3.8	1,203	6.4
Total	**47,423**	**47.7**	**8,200**	**50.8**	**4,617**	**49.3**	**57,744**	**48.4**

1. Persons of Spanish origin may be of any race. NOTE: Figures include persons enrolled in nursery school, kindergarten, elementary school, high school, and college. *Source:* Department of Commerce, Bureau of the Census.

Persons Not Enrolled in School, October 1983

(in thousands)

Age	Population	Total not enrolled		High school graduate		Not high school graduate (dropouts)[1]	
		Number	Percent	Number	Percent	Number	Percent
14 and 15 years	7,214	121	1.7	—	—	121	1.7
16 and 17 years	7,304	606	8.3	111	1.5	494	6.8
18 and 19 years	7,819	3,881	49.6	2,748	35.1	1,132	14.5
20 and 21 years	8,039	5,430	67.5	4,143	51.1	1,287	16.0
22 to 24 years	12,722	10,611	83.4	8,620	67.8	1,991	15.7

1. Persons who are not enrolled in school and who are not high school graduates are considered dropouts. *Source:* Department of Commerce, Bureau of the Census.

School Enrollment by Grade, Control, and Race

(in thousands)

Grade level and type of control	White			Black			All races[1]		
	Oct. 1983[3]	Oct. 1980[4]	Oct. 1970	Oct. 1983[3]	Oct. 1980[4]	Oct. 1970	Oct. 1983[3]	Oct. 1980[4]	Oct. 1970
Nursery school: Public	563	432	198	215	180	129	809	633	333
Private	1,369	1,205	695	111	115	49	1,541	1,354	763
Kindergarten: Public	2,181	2,172	2,233	427	440	374	2,706	2,690	2,674
Private	588	423	473	48	50	53	656	486	536
Grades 1–8: Public	19,340	19,743	24,923	3,964	4,058	4,668	24,203	24,398	30,001
Private	2,714	2,768	3,715	189	202	200	2,994	3,051	3,949
Grades 9–12: Public	10,339	12,056[2]	11,599	2,057	2,200[2]	1,794	12,792	14,556[2]	13,545
Private	1,086	—	1,124	86	—	41	1,218	—	1,170
College: Public	6,949	8,875[2]	5,168	858	1,007[2]	422	8,185	10,180[2]	5,699
Private	2,293	—	1,591	245	—	100	2,640	—	1,714
Total: Public	39,372	—	44,121	7,521	—	7,387	48,695	—	52,225
Private	8,050	—	7,598	679	—	443	9,049	—	8,132
Grand Total	**47,422**	**47,673**	**51,719**	**8,200**	**8,251**	**7,830**	**57,744**	**57,348**	**60,357**

1. Includes persons of Spanish origin. 2. Total public and private. Breakdown not available. 3. Estimates controlled to 1980 census base. 4. Estimates controlled to 1970 census base. *Source:* Department of Commerce, Bureau of the Census.

State Compulsory School Attendance Laws

State	Enactment[1]	Age limits	State	Enactment[1]	Age limits
Alabama	1915	7-16	Montana	1883	7-16
Alaska	1929	7-16	Nebraska	1887	7-16
Arizona	1899	8-16	Nevada	1873	7-17
Arkansas	1909	7-15	New Hampshire	1871	6-16
California	1874	6-16	New Jersey	1875	6-16
Colorado	1889	7-16	New Mexico	1891	8-17
Connecticut	1872	7-16	New York	1874	6-16
Delaware	1907	6-16	North Carolina	1907	7-16
D. C.	1864	7-16	North Dakota	1883	7-16
Florida	1915	7-16	Ohio	1877	6-18
Georgia	1916	7-16	Oklahoma	1907	7-16
Hawaii	1896	6-18	Oregon	1889	7-18
Idaho	1887	7-16	Pennsylvania	1895	8-17
Illinois	1883	7-16	Rhode Island	1883	7-16
Indiana	1897	7-16	South Carolina	1915	7-16
Iowa	1902	7-16	South Dakota	1883	7-16
Kansas	1874	7-16	Tennessee	1905	7-16
Kentucky	1896	7-16	Texas	1915[2]	7-17
Louisiana	1910	7-15	Utah	1890	6-18
Maine	1875	7-17	Vermont	1867	7-16
Maryland	1902	6-16	Virginia	1908	6-17
Massachusetts	1852	6-16	Washington	1871	8-18
Michigan	1871	6-16	West Virginia	1897	7-16
Minnesota	1885	7-16	Wisconsin	1879	7-16
Mississippi	1918	6-14	Wyoming	1876	7-16
Missouri	1905	7-16			

1. Date of enactment of first compulsory attendance law. 2. A compulsory school attendance law was contained in a law of 1873 establishing free public schools. However, the provision was omitted in superseding legislation passed in 1876. *Source:* Department of Education, National Center for Educational Statistics.

High School and College Graduates

Year of graduation	High School			College[1]		
	Men	Women	Total	Men	Women	Total
1900	38,075	56,808	94,883	22,173	5,237	27,410
1910	63,676	92,753	156,429	28,762	8,437	37,199
1920	123,684	187,582	311,266	31,980	16,642	48,622
1929-30	300,376	366,528	666,904	73,615	48,869	122,484
1939-40	578,718	642,757	1,221,475	109,546	76,954	186,500
1949-50	570,700	629,000	1,199,700	328,841	103,217	432,058
1959-60	898,000	966,000	1,864,000	254,063	138,377	392,440
1962-63	959,000	991,000	1,950,000	273,169	174,453	447,622
1963-64	1,121,000	1,169,000	2,290,000	296,676	197,477	494,153
1964-65	1,314,000	1,351,000	2,665,000	316,286	213,717	530,003
1965-66	1,308,000	1,324,000	2,632,000	328,853	222,194	551,047
1966-67	1,332,000	1,348,000	2,679,000	353,349	237,198	590,547
1967-68	1,341,000	1,361,000	2,702,000	390,507	276,203	666,710
1968-69	1,402,000	1,427,000	2,829,000	444,380	319,805	764,185
1969-70	1,433,000	1,463,000	2,896,000	484,174	343,060	827,234
1970-71	1,456,000	1,487,000	2,943,000	511,138	366,538	877,676
1971-72	1,490,000	1,518,000	3,008,000	541,313	389,371	930,684
1972-73	1,501,000	1,536,000	3,037,000	564,680	407,700	972,380
1973-74	1,515,000	1,565,000	3,080,000	575,843	423,749	999,592
1974-75	1,541,000	1,599,000	3,140,000	533,797	425,052	978,849
1975-76	1,554,000	1,601,000	3,155,000	557,817	430,578	988,395
1976-77	1,548,000	1,606,000	3,154,000	547,919	435,989	983,908
1977-78	1,535,000	1,599,000	3,134,000	487,000	434,000	921,000
1978-79	1,531,800	1,602,400	3,134,200	529,996	460,242	990,238
1979-80	1,500,000	1,558,000	3,058,000	526,327	473,221	999,548
1980-81	1,485,000[2]	1,541,000[2]	4,214,000[2]	522,675	484,421	1,007,096

1. Includes bachelor's and first-professional degrees. 2. Preliminary data. NOTE: Includes graduates from public and private schools. Beginning in 1959-60, figures include Alaska and Hawaii. Because of rounding, details may not add to totals. Most recent data available. *Source:* Department of Education, National Center for Education Statistics.

Institutions of Higher Education—Faculty and Enrollment Characteristics and Projections to 1988

(in thousands except for institutions)

Item	1988	1985	1980	1978[2]	1977[2]	1976[2]	1975	1974	1973	1972	1971
Institutions	n.a.	n.a.	3,152	2,871	2,826	2,785	2,765	2,747	2,720	2,665	2,606
4-year	n.a.	n.a.	1,957	1,816	1,808	1,783	1,767	1,744	1,717	1,701	1,675
2-year	n.a.	n.a.	1,195	1,055	1,018	1,002	998	1,003	1,003	964	931
Resident instructional staff	n.a.	696	730	809	812	793	670	622	599	590	590
ENROLLMENT											
Degree credit	11,048	11,358	11,611	n.a.	n.a.	n.a.	9,731	9,023	8,518	8,265	8,116
Male	5,631	5,802	5,907	5,641	5,789	5,811	5,321	4,969	4,771	4,701	4,717
Female	5,417	5,556	5,704	5,619	5,497	5,201	4,410	4,055	3,747	3,564	3,399
4-year institutions	6,694	6,968	7,302	7,232	7,243	7,129	7,223	6,825	6,597	6,473	6,391
2-year institutions	4,354	4,390	4,039	4,027	4,043	3,883	2,508	2,198	1,921	1,792	1,725
Full-time	6,185	6,460	6,847	6,668	6,793	6,717	6,147	5,817	5,683	5,647	5,676
Part-time	4,863	4,898	4,764	4,592	4,493	4,295	3,584	3,206	2,835	2,618	2,440
Public	8,754	8,974	9,124	8,786	8,847	8,653	7,426	6,838	6,389	6,159	6,014
Private	2,294	2,384	2,487	2,474	2,439	2,359	2,306	2,185	2,130	2,106	2,102
Graduate	1,358	1,382	1,365	1,081	1,085	1,085	1,263	1,190	1,123	1,066	1,012
Undergraduate[1]	9,417	9,698	9,981	10,179	10,201	9,927	8,468	7,833	7,395	7,199	7,104
Male	4,713	4,870	4,996	5,057	5,193	5,209	4,621	4,306	4,124	4,074	4,102
Female	4,704	4,828	4,985	5,122	5,008	4,719	3,847	3,527	3,271	3,125	3,002
4-year institutions	5,063	5,308	5,672	6,152	6,158	6,045	5,960	5,635	5,474	5,407	5,379
Full-time	3,823	4,048	4,404	4,678	4,703	4,622	4,619	4,429	4,350	4,350	4,358
Part-time	1,240	1,260	1,262	1,474	1,456	1,423	1,341	1,206	1,124	1,057	1,021
2-year institutions	4,354	4,390	4,309	4,028	4,043	3,883	2,508	2,198	1,921	1,792	1,725
Public	7,708	7,910	8,079	8,083	8,128	7,924	6,520	5,986	5,589	5,401	5,302
Private	1,709	1,788	1,902	2,096	2,073	2,003	1,948	1,847	1,806	1,799	1,802
1st time enrolled	n.a.	n.a.	n.a.	2,422	2,432	2,377	1,910	1,854	1,757	1,740	1,766
Nondegree credit	n.a.	n.a.	n.a.	n.a.	n.a.	n.a.	1,453	1,200	1,084	950	833
Total	**11,048**	**11,104**	**11,611**	**11,260**	**11,286**	**11,012**	**11,184**	**10,223**	**9,602**	**9,215**	**8,949**

1. Includes first-professional enrollment. 2. Total enrollment, degree and nondegree credit. NOTE: As of fall. Covers universities, colleges, professional schools, junior and teachers colleges, and normal schools, both publicly and privately controlled, regular session. n.a. = not available. *Source:* Department of Education, National Center for Educational Statistics.

Major U.S. College and University Libraries

(Top 50 based on number of volumes in library)

Institution	Volumes	Microforms[1]
Harvard	10,567,240	3,021,292
Yale	7,880,025	1,716,933
U of Illinois	6,411,948	1,978,872
U of California, Berkeley	6,336,301	2,696,778
U of California, Los Angeles	5,744,144	2,695,219
U of Michigan	5,597,266	2,490,143
Columbia	5,270,432	2,771,509
U of Texas	5,057,649	2,859,799
Stanford	5,040,940	2,606,866
U of Chicago	4,688,361	911,979
Cornell	4,516,717	2,953,693
U of Wisconsin	4,281,749	2,271,769
U of Washington	4,168,079	3,910,104
Indiana	4,105,734	1,267,234
U of Minnesota	4,037,478	1,686,647
Ohio State	3,779,819	2,029,478
Princeton	3,519,262	1,603,912
Duke	3,261,222	1,055,627
U of Pennsylvania	3,120,976	1,522,668
Northwestern	2,973,100	1,278,889
North Carolina	2,952,859	1,845,576
Michigan State	2,898,698	1,871,763
U of Arizona	2,853,707	2,479,283
New York	2,756,470	1,676,461
U of Virginia	2,550,064	2,859,945
U of Iowa	2,494,680	2,074,442
U of Pittsburgh	2,472,489	1,713,068
Pennsylvania State	2,402,938	2,493,017
Johns Hopkins	2,393,572	1,070,066
U of Florida	2,349,473	2,348,774
U of Kansas	2,323,678	1,272,088
U of Southern California	2,247,063	1,480,342
U of Georgia	2,226,090	2,787,338
SUNY, Buffalo	2,181,241	2,550,694
U of Missouri	2,160,287	2,720,052
Rutgers	2,083,310	1,672,761
Syracuse	2,065,873	2,181,160
U of Utah	2,045,797	1,942,337
Louisiana State	2,017,365	1,712,189
U of South Carolina	2,003,347	1,972,448
U of Oklahoma	1,981,440	1,450,350
U of Colorado	1,972,172	2,476,185
Washington U, St. Louis	1,953,047	1,259,184
Wayne State	1,941,348	1,324,228
U of Massachusetts	1,938,833	1,148,684
Rochester	1,925,138	2,064,509
U of Hawaii	1,914,846	1,536,824
MIT	1,906,374	1,279,067
U of Kentucky	1,894,632	2,555,680
Brown	1,847,736	788,595

1. Includes reels of microfilm and number of microcards, microprint sheets, and microfiches. *Source:* Association of Research Libraries.

College and University Endowments, 1982–83

(top 75 in millions of dollars)

Institution	Endowment (market value)	Voluntary support[1]	Expenditures[2]	Institution	Endowment (market value)	Voluntary support[1]	Expenditures[2]
Harvard U	$2,440.9	$126.2	$ n.a.	Vassar	138.8	9.3	25.4
Princeton U	1,281.0	58.2	136.8	Trinity U	137.4	9.5	27.3
Yale U	1,098.0	60.3	325.5	Oberlin C	137.4	6.2	33.0
Stanford U	965.0	91.8	467.1	Amherst C	136.7	8.2	24.8
Columbia U	918.3	62.0	416.8	Berea C	131.7	6.3	11.5
Massachusetts Inst. of Tech.	806.9	60.7	372.2	U of Richmond	130.3	8.7	21.7
U of Rochester	664.6	19.7	177.8	Rensselaer Polytech Inst.	127.0	12.6	82.4
U of California	593.1	135.8	2,296.6	Grinnell C	125.6	4.2	14.2
U of Chicago	540.9	45.6	225.0	U of Pittsburgh	125.2	9.6	274.5
Northwestern U	494.7	39.2	230.1	Wake Forest U	124.8	11.9	92.8
Rice U	490.1	21.3	63.7	Loyola U of New Orleans	124.0	3.4	26.7
Cornell U	486.0	61.5	467.9	Ohio State U	122.3	20.1	441.0
Washington U	470.6	41.7	220.8	Baylor U	121.1	14.7	55.2
Emory U	402.4	15.8	132.0	Tulane U	116.7	25.6	116.4
Dartmouth C	354.6	28.4	102.0	George Washington U	115.4	6.7	140.9
Johns Hopkins U	354.5	41.0	n.a.	Pomona C	113.9	15.5	20.1
New York U	350.3	43.6	374.3	U of Texas–Austin	108.6	32.5	215.5
Rockefeller U	347.4	20.8	56.2	Loyola U of Chicago	107.9	22.2	90.3
U of Notre Dame	279.2	27.0	65.0	Texas Christian U	106.2	10.9	43.5
U of Pennsylvania	256.0	50.9	372.3	Middlebury C	104.5	4.4	33.4
Vanderbilt U	225.0	21.0	127.0	Lehigh U	102.5	14.8	61.4
U of Southern California	217.6	54.4	315.8	U of Wisconsin–Madison	99.2	43.4	445.1
Duke U	216.3	36.0	203.6	Boston U	96.9	21.0	243.4
California Inst. of Tech.	208.3	21.7	90.3	Lafayette C	96.7	7.4	21.3
U of Michigan	200.7	50.5	474.7	Georgetown U	95.3	21.3	128.6
Case Western Reserve U	200.4	28.4	131.3	Brandeis U	94.0	15.9	72.6
Brown U	193.3	25.4	102.0	Baylor C of Medicine	92.9	16.2	139.9
U of Virginia	187.6	28.9	n.a.	Harvard Law School	92.3	5.8	n.a.
Smith C	183.2	16.4	32.4	Syracuse U	87.3	9.2	150.7
U of Kansas	177.7	14.8	121.6	Thomas Jefferson U	86.6	7.4	69.3
Wellesley C	177.4	14.9	33.7	U of Washington	85.3	30.4	375.5
Princeton Theol. Seminary	176.8	5.3	10.5	Carleton C	84.3	6.8	18.5
Carnegie-Mellon U	173.4	13.6	53.0	U of Cincinnati	83.9	17.8	211.2
U of Delaware	162.9	9.0	120.3	Mount Holyoke C	83.7	7.5	23.5
Wesleyan U	162.7	7.4	37.8	Rochester Inst. of Tech.	81.3	7.4	93.7
Williams C	162.6	13.8	26.2	U of Nebraska	79.4	21.0	215.6
Southern Methodist U	150.7	18.6	70.9	U of Illinois	77.2	49.0	616.6
U of Minnesota	143.8	62.6	580.5				

1. Gifts from business, alumni, religious denominations, and others. 2. Figure represents about 80% of typical operating budget. Does not include auxiliary enterprises and capital outlays. NOTE: C = College; U = University; n.a. = not available. *Source:* Council for Financial Aid to Education.

Federal Funds for Some Major Programs for Education, Fiscal Year 1984[1]

Program	Amount in thousands
Elementary–secondary education	$ 4,226,205
Educationally disadvantaged	3,502,054
Special programs and populations	581,100
Bilingual education[2]	143,051
School assistance in federally affected areas	593,621
Higher education	7,889,897
Library programs	880
Strengthening institutions	137,296
Student assistance	
Educational opportunity grants	3,279,830
Work-study and cooperative education	569,400
Direct loans to students	184,260
Guaranteed student loans	3,531,660
Special program for the disadvantaged	168,740
Other	17,831
Higher education facilities	231,022
Vocational education	911,468
Education personnel training	89,090
Grants to institutions and individuals	33,550
Special education	55,540
Education for the handicapped	1,348,127
State grant programs	1,186,276
Early childhood education	54,251
Special centers, projects, and research	93,600
Captioned films and media services	14,000
Adult basic and secondary education	100,000
Indian education	70,718
Total	**15,460,148**

1. Estimated outlay for fiscal year 1984. 2. Includes bilingual vocational education training. *Source: Digest of Education Statistics* 1983–84, National Center for Education Statistics.

Community, Junior, and Technical Colleges

ALABAMA

Publicly controlled

Alabama Aviation and Tech. College	Ozark
Alabama Technical College	East Gadsden
Alexander City State Junior College	Alexander City
Atmore State Technical Institute	Atmore
Bessemer State Technical College	Bessemer
Brewer State Junior College	Fayette
C. A. Fredd State Tech. Coll.	Tuscaloosa
Carver State Technical College	Mobile
Chattahoochee Valley State Comm. Coll.	Phenix City
Chauncey Sparks State Tech. Coll.	Eufaula
Community College of the Air Force	Maxwell AFB
Douglas-MacArthur St. Tech. Coll.	Opp
Enterprise State Junior College	Enterprise
Gadsden State Junior College	East Gadsden
Gadsden State Technical Institute	Gadsden
George C. Wallace State Comm. College	Dothan
George C. Wallace State Comm. College	Hanceville
George Corley Wallace St. Comm. Coll.	Selma
Harry M. Ayers State Tech. College	Anniston
Hobson State Technical College	Thomasville
James H. Faulkner State Junior College	Bay Minette
Jefferson Davis State Junior College	Brewton
Jefferson State Junior College	Birmingham
J. F. Drake State Technical College	Huntsville
J. F. Ingram State Tech. Inst.	Deatsville
John C. Calhoun State Comm. College	Decatur
John M. Patterson State Tech. College	Montgomery
Lawson State Community College	Birmingham
Lurleen B. Wallace State Junior College	Andalusia
Muscle Shoals State Tech. College	Muscle Shoals
N.F. Nunnelley State Tech. College	Childersburg
Northeast Alabama State Junior College	Rainsville
Northwest Alabama State Junior College	Phil Campbell
Northwest Alabama State Tech. College	Hamilton
Opelika State Technical College	Opelika
Patrick Henry State Junior College	Monroeville
Reid State Technical College	Evergreen
S. D. Bishop State Junior College	Mobile
Shelton State Community College	Tuscaloosa
Snead State Junior College	Boaz
Southern Union State Junior College	Wadley
Southwest State Technical College	Mobile
Trenholm State Technical College	Montgomery
Walker State Technical College	Sumiton

Privately controlled

Concordia College	Selma
Marion Military Institute	Marion
Walker College	Jasper

ALASKA

Publicly controlled

Univ. of Alaska Community Colleges	Fairbanks
Anchorage Community College	Anchorage
Islands Community College	Sitka
Kenai Peninsula Community College	Soldotna
Ketchikan Community College	Ketchikan
Kodiak Community College	Kodiak
Kuskokwim Community College	Bethel
Matanuska Susitna Community College	Palmer
Northwest Community College	Nome
Prince William Sound Comm. Coll.	Valdez
Tanana Valley Community College	Fairbanks

Privately controlled

Sheldon Jackson College	Sitka

ARIZONA

Publicly controlled

Arizona Western College	Yuma
Central Arizona College District	Coolidge
Aravaipa Campus	Winkleman
Signal Peak Campus	Coolidge
Cochise College	Douglas
Eastern Arizona College	Thatcher
Maricopa County Comm. Coll. District	Phoenix
Glendale Community College	Glendale
Maricopa Technical Community Coll.	Phoenix
Mesa Community College	Mesa
Phoenix College	Phoenix
Rio Salado Community College	Phoenix
Scottsdale Community College	Scottsdale
South Mountain Comm. College	Phoenix
Mohave Community College	Kingman
Navajo Community College	Tsaile
Northland Pioneer College	Holbrook
Pima Community College	Tucson
Community Campus	Tucson
Downtown Campus	Tucson
East Campus	Tucson
West Campus	Tucson
Yavapai College	Prescott

Privately controlled

Ganado, College of	Ganado

ARKANSAS

Publicly controlled

Arkansas State Univ.—Beebe Branch	Beebe
East Arkansas Community College	Forrest City
Garland County Community College	Hot Springs
Mississippi County Community College	Blytheville
North Arkansas Community College	Harrison
Phillips County Community College	Helena
Rich Mountain Community College	Mena
Southern Arkansas University	Magnolia
El Dorado Branch	El Dorado
Technical Branch	East Camden
Westark Community College	Fort Smith

Privately controlled

Shorter College	North Little Rock
Southern Baptist College	Walnut Ridge

CALIFORNIA

Publicly controlled

Allan Hancock College	Santa Maria
Antelope Valley College	Lancaster
Barstow Community College	Barstow
Butte College	Oroville
Cabrillo College	Aptos
Canyons, College of the	Valencia
Cerritos College	Norwalk
Chabot College	Hayward
Chaffey College	Alta Loma
Citrus College	Azusa
Coast Community College District	Costa Mesa
Coastline Community College	Fountain Valley
Golden West College	Huntington Beach
Orange Coast College	Costa Mesa
Compton Community College	Compton
Contra Costa Community Coll. District	Martinez
Contra Costa College	San Pablo
Diablo Valley College	Pleasant Hill

Los Medanos College	Pittsburg
Cuesta College	San Luis Obispo
Desert, College of the	Palm Desert
El Camino College	Via Torrance
Foothill-Deanza Comm. Coll. District	Los Altos Hills
De Anza College	Cupertino
Foothill College	Los Altos Hills
Gavilan College	Gilroy
Glendale Community College	Glendale
Grossmont Community College District	El Cajon
Cuyamaca College	El Cajon
Grossmont College	El Cajon
Hartnell College	Salinas
Imperial Valley College	Imperial
Kern Community College District	Bakersfield
Bakersfield College	Bakersfield
Cerro Coso Community College	Ridgecrest
Porterville College	Porterville
Lake Tahoe Community College	South Lake Tahoe
Lassen College	Susanville
Long Beach City College	Long Beach
Los Angeles Community College District	Los Angeles
East Los Angeles College	Monterey Park
Los Angeles City College	Los Angeles
Los Angeles Harbor College	Wilmington
Los Angeles Metropolitan College	Los Angeles
Los Angeles Mission College	San Fernando
Los Angeles Pierce College	Woodland Hills
Los Angeles Southwest College	Los Angeles
Los Angeles Trade-Technical College	Los Angeles
Los Angeles Valley College	Van Nuys
West Los Angeles College	Culver City
Los Rios Community College District	Sacramento
American River College	Sacramento
Cosumnes River College	Sacramento
Sacramento City College	Sacramento
Marin Community Colleges, The	Kentfield
Indian Valley Colleges	Novato
Marin, College of	Kentfield
Mendocino College	Ukiah
Merced College	Merced
Mira Costa College	Oceanside
Monterey Peninsula College	Monterey
Mt. San Antonio College	Walnut
Mt. San Jacinto College	San Jacinto
Napa Valley College	Napa
North Orange County Comm. Coll. District	Fullerton
Cypress College	Cypress
Fullerton College	Fullerton
Ohlone College	Fremont
Palo Verde College	Blythe
Palomar College	San Marcos
Pasadena City College	Pasadena
Peralta Community College District	Oakland
Alameda, College of	Alameda
Feather River College	Quincy
Laney College	Oakland
Merritt College	Oakland
Vista College	Berkeley
Redwoods, College of the	Eureka
Rio Hondo College	Whittier
Riverside City College	Riverside
Saddleback Community Coll. District	Mission Viejo
San Bernardino Community Coll. District	San Bernardino
Crafton Hills College	Yucaipa
San Bernardino Valley College	San Bernardino
San Diego Community College District	San Diego
San Diego City College	San Diego
San Diego Mesa College	San Diego
San Diego Miramar College	San Diego
San Francisco Community Coll. District	San Francisco
Community College Centers	San Francisco
San Francisco, City College of	San Francisco
San Joaquin Delta College	Stockton
San Jose Community College District	San Jose
Evergreen Valley College	San Jose
San Jose City College	San Jose
San Mateo County Comm. Coll. District	San Mateo
Canada College	Redwood City
San Mateo, College of	San Mateo
Skyline College	San Bruno
Santa Ana College	Santa Ana
Santa Barbara City College	Santa Barbara
Santa Monica College	Santa Monica
Santa Rosa Junior College	Santa Rosa
Shasta College	Redding
Sequoias, College of the	Visalia
Sierra College	Rocklin
Siskiyous, College of the	Weed
Solano Community College	Suisun City
Southwestern College	Chula Vista
State Center Community College District	Fresno
Fresno City College	Fresno
Kings River Community College	Reedley
Taft College	Taft
Ventura County Community Coll. District	Ventura
Moorpark College	Moorpark
Oxnard College	Oxnard
Ventura College	Ventura
Victor Valley College	Victorville
West Hills Community College	Coalinga
West Valley Joint Comm. Coll. District	Saratoga
Mission College	Santa Clara
West Valley College	Saratoga
Yosemite Community College District	Modesto
Columbia College	Columbia
Modesto Junior College	Modesto
Yuba College	Marysville

Privately controlled

Brooks College	Long Beach
Don Bosco Technical Institute	Rosemead
Fashion Institute of Design/Merch.	Los Angeles
Heald Institute of Technology	Santa Clara
Humphreys College	Stockton
Marymount Palos Verdes College	Rancho Palos Verdes
Queen of the Holy Rosary College	Mission San Jose

COLORADO

Publicly controlled

Aims Community College	Greeley
Arapahoe Community College	Littleton
Colorado Mountain College	Glenwood Springs
Community Education Unit	Glenwood Springs
East Campus	Leadville
West Campus	Glenwood Springs
Colorado Northwestern Comm. College	Rangely
Community College of Aurora	Aurora
Community College of Denver System	Denver
Denver Auraria Community College	Denver
Front Range Community College	Westminster
Red Rocks Community College	Golden
Lamar Community College	Lamar
Morgan Community College	Fort Morgan
Northeastern Junior College	Sterling
Otero Junior College	La Junta
Pikes Peak Community College	Colorado Springs
Pueblo Community College	Pueblo
Trinidad State Junior College	Trinidad

CONNECTICUT

Publicly controlled

Asnuntuck Community College	Enfield
Greater Hartford Community College	Hartford
Greater New Haven State Tech. Coll.	North Haven
Hartford State Technical College	Hartford
Housatonic Community College	Bridgeport
Manchester Community College	Manchester
Mattatuck Community College	Waterbury
Middlesex Community College	Middletown
Mohegan Community College	Norwich
Northwestern Connecticut Comm. College	Winsted
Norwalk Community College	Norwalk
Norwalk State Technical College	Norwalk
Quinebaug Valley Community College	Danielson
South Central Community College	New Haven
Thames Valley State Technical College	Norwich
Tunxis Community College	Farmington
Waterbury State Technical College	Waterbury

Privately controlled

Hartford College for Women	Hartford
Mitchell College	New London

DELAWARE

Publicly controlled

Delaware Technical and Comm. College	Dover
Southern Campus	Georgetown
Stanton/Wilmington Campuses	Wilmington
Terry Campus	Dover

Privately controlled

Brandywine College	Wilmington

FLORIDA

Publicly controlled

Brevard Community College	Cocoa
Broward Community College	Ft. Lauderdale
Central Florida Community College	Ocala
Chipola Junior College	Marianna
Daytona Beach Community College	Daytona Beach
Edison Community College	Ft. Myers
Florida Junior Coll. at Jacksonville	Jacksonville
Downtown Campus	Jacksonville
Fred H. Kent Campus	Jacksonville
North Campus	Jacksonville
South Campus	Jacksonville
Florida Keys Community College	Key West
Gulf Coast Community College	Panama City
Hillsborough Community College	Tampa
Indian River Community College	Ft. Pierce
Lake City Community College	Lake City
Lake-Sumter Community College	Leesburg
Manatee Junior College	Bradenton
Miami-Dade Community College	Miami
Medical Center Campus	Miami
New World Center Campus	Miami
North Campus	Miami
South Campus	Miami
North Florida Junior College	Madison
Okaloosa-Walton Junior College	Niceville
Palm Beach Junior College	Lake Worth
Pasco-Hernando Community College	Dade City
Pensacola Junior College	Pensacola
Polk Community College	Winter Haven
St. Johns River Community College	Palatka
St. Petersburg Junior College	St. Petersburg
Santa Fe Community College	Gainesville
Seminole Community College	Sanford
South Florida Junior College	Avon Park
Tallahassee Community College	Tallahassee
Valencia Community College	Orlando

Privately controlled

Bauder Fashion College	Ft. Lauderdale
Florida College	Temple Terrace
International Fine Arts College	Miami
Webber College	Babson Park

GEORGIA

Publicly controlled

Abraham Baldwin Agricultural College	Tifton
Albany Junior College	Albany
Atlanta Junior College	Atlanta
Bainbridge Junior College	Bainbridge
Brunswick Junior College	Brunswick
Clayton Junior College	Morrow
Dalton Junior College	Dalton
DeKalb Community College	Clarkston
Emanuel County Junior College	Swainsboro
Floyd Junior College	Rome
Gainesville Junior College	Gainesville
Gordon Junior College	Barnesville
Macon Junior College	Macon
Middle Georgia College	Cochran
South Georgia College	Douglas
Waycross Junior College	Waycross

Privately controlled

Andrew College	Cuthbert
Brewton-Parker College	Mt. Vernon
Draughon's Junior College	Savannah
Georgia Military College	Milledgeville
Oxford College of Emory University	Oxford
Reinhardt College	Waleska
Truett-McConnell College	Cleveland
Young Harris College	Young Harris

HAWAII

Publicly controlled

Univ. of Hawaii Community Coll. System	Honolulu
Hawaii Community College	Hilo
Honolulu Community College	Honolulu
Kapiolani Community College	Honolulu
Kauai Community College	Lihue Kauai
Leeward Community College	Pearl City
Maui Community College	Kahului
Windward Community College	Kaneohe

IDAHO

Publicly controlled

North Idaho College	Coeur d'Alene
Southern Idaho, College of	Twin Falls

Privately controlled

Ricks College	Rexburg

ILLINOIS

Publicly controlled

Belleville Area College	Belleville
Black Hawk College	Moline
East Campus	Kewanee
Quad Cities Campus	Moline
Carl Sandburg College	Galesburg
Chicago, City Colleges of	Chicago
Chicago City-Wide College	Chicago
Chicago Urban Skills Institute	Chicago
Kennedy-King College	Chicago
Loop College	Chicago
Malcolm X College	Chicago
Olive Harvey College	Chicago
Richard J. Daley College	Chicago
Truman College	Chicago
Wilbur Wright College	Chicago
Danville Area Community College	Danville
DuPage, College of	Glen Ellyn
Dupage Open College	Glen Ellyn
Main Campus	Glen Ellyn
Elgin Community College	Elgin
Highland Community College	Freeport

Illinois Central College	East Peoria
Illinois Eastern Community College	Olney
Frontier Community College	Fairfield
Lincoln Trail College	Robinson
Olney Central College	Olney
Wabash Valley College	Mt. Carmel
Illinois Valley Community College	Oglesby
John A. Logan College	Carterville
John Wood Community College	Quincy
Joliet Junior College	Joliet
Kankakee Community College	Kankakee
Kaskaskia College	Centralia
Kishwaukee College	Malta
Lake County, College of	Grayslake
Lake Land College	Mattoon
Lewis and Clark Community College	Godfrey
Lincoln Land Community College	Springfield
McHenry County College	Crystal Lake
Moraine Valley Community College	Palos Hills
Morton College	Cicero
Oakton Community College	Des Plaines
Parkland College	Champaign
Prairie State College	Chicago Heights
Rend Lake College	Ina
Richland Community College	Decatur
Rock Valley College	Rockford
Sauk Valley College	Dixon
Shawnee Community College	Ullin
Southeastern Illinois College	Harrisburg
Spoon River College	Canton
State Comm. College of East St. Louis	East St. Louis
Thornton Community College	South Holland
Triton College	River Grove
Waubonsee Community College	Sugar Grove
William Rainey Harper College	Palatine
Privately controlled	
Felician College	Chicago
Lincoln College	Lincoln
MacCormac College	Chicago
St. Augustine College	Chicago
Springfield College in Illinois	Springfield

INDIANA

Publicly controlled	
Indiana Vocational Technical College	Indianapolis
Central Indiana Region	Indianapolis
Columbus Technical Inst.	Columbus
East Central Tech. Inst.	Muncie
Kokomo Technical Inst.	Kokomo
Lafayette Technical Inst.	Lafayette
North Central Tech. Inst.	South Bend
Northeast Technical Inst.	Fort Wayne
Northwest Region	Gary
South Central Tech. Inst.	Sellersburg
Southeast Region	Madison
Southwest Technical Inst.	Evansville
Wabash Valley Region	Terre Haute
Whitewater Technical Inst.	Richmond
Vincennes University	Vincennes
Privately controlled	
Ancilla College	Donaldson

IOWA

Publicly controlled	
Des Moines Area Community College	Ankeny
Ankeny Campus	Ankeny
Boone Campus	Boone
Urban Campus	Des Moines
Eastern Iowa Community Coll. District	Davenport
Clinton Community College	Clinton
Muscatine Community College	Muscatine
Scott Community College	Bettendorf
Hawkeye Institute of Technology	Waterloo
Indian Hills Community College	Ottumwa
Centerville Center	Ottumwa
Ottumwa Airport Center	Ottumwa
Ottumwa Heights Center	Ottumwa
Iowa Central Community College	Fort Dodge
Iowa Lakes Community College	Estherville
Iowa Valley Community Coll. District	Marshalltown
Ellsworth Community College	Iowa Falls
Marshalltown Community College	Marshalltown
Iowa Western Community College	Council Bluffs
Kirkwood Community College	Cedar Rapids
North Iowa Area Community College	Mason City
Northeast Iowa Technical Institute	Calmar
Northwest Iowa Technical College	Sheldon
Southeastern Community College	West Burlington
North Campus	West Burlington
South Campus	Keokuk
Southwestern Community College	Creston
Western Iowa Tech. Community College	Sioux City
Privately controlled	
Sioux Empire College	Hawarden
Waldorf College	Forest City

KANSAS

Publicly controlled	
Allen County Community College	Iola
Barton County Community Junior Coll.	Great Bend
Butler County Community College	El Dorado
Cloud County Community College	Concordia
Coffeyville Community College	Coffeyville
Colby Community Junior College	Colby
Cowley County Community College	Arkansas City
Dodge City Community College	Dodge City
Fort Scott Community College	Fort Scott
Garden City Community College	Garden City
Haskell Indian Junior College	Lawrence
Highland Community College	Highland
Hutchinson Community College	Hutchinson
Independence Community College	Independence
Johnson County Community College	Overland Park
Kansas City, Kan., Community Coll.	Kansas City
Kansas Technical Institute	Salina
Labette Community College	Parsons
Neosho County Community College	Chanute
Pratt Community College	Pratt
Seward County Community Junior Coll.	Liberal
Privately controlled	
Brown Mackie College, The	Salina
Central College	McPherson
Donnelly College	Kansas City
Hesston College	Hesston

KENTUCKY

Publicly controlled	
Eastern Kentucky Univ.—Office of Community College Programs	Richmond
Kentucky, Univ. of, Comm. Coll. System	Lexington
Ashland Community College	Ashland
Elizabethtown Community College	Elizabethtown
Hazard Community College	Hazard
Henderson Community College	Henderson
Hopkinsville Community College	Hopkinsville
Jefferson Community College	Louisville
Lexington Technical Institute	Lexington
Madisonville Community College	Madisonville
Maysville Community College	Maysville
Paducah Community College	Paducah
Prestonsburg Community College	Prestonsburg
Somerset Community College	Somerset
Southeast Community College	Cumberland

Privately controlled

Lees Junior College	Jackson
Lindsey Wilson College	Columbia
Midway College	Midway
St. Catharine College	St. Catharine
Sue Bennett College	London

LOUISIANA

Publicly controlled

Bossier Parish Community College	Bossier City
Delgado Community College	New Orleans
Louisiana State University	Baton Rouge
Alexandria Campus	Alexandria
Eunice Campus	Eunice
Southern University at Shreveport	Shreveport

MAINE

Publicly controlled

Central Maine Vocational Tech. Inst.	Auburn
Eastern Maine Vocational Tech. Inst.	Bangor
Kennebec Valley Vocational Tech. Inst.	Fairfield
Maine, University of	Bangor
Augusta Branch	Augusta
Bangor Community College	Bangor
Northern Maine Vocational Tech. Inst.	Presque Isle
Southern Maine Vocational Tech. Inst.	South Portland
Washington County Voc. Tech. Inst.	Calais

MARYLAND

Publicly controlled

Allegany Community College	Cumberland
Anne Arundel Community College	Arnold
Catonsville Community College	Baltimore
Cecil Community College	North East
Charles County Community College	La Plata
Chesapeake College	Wye Mills
Community College of Baltimore	Baltimore
Dundalk Community College	Dundalk
Essex Community College	Baltimore Co.
Frederick Community College	Frederick
Garrett Community College	McHenry
Hagerstown Junior College	Hagerstown
Harford Community College	Bel Air
Howard Community College	Columbia
Montgomery College	Rockville
Germantown Campus	Germantown
Rockville Campus	Rockville
Takoma Park Campus	Takoma Park
Prince George's Community College	Largo
Wor-Wic Tech. Community College	Salisbury

Privately controlled

Villa Julie College	Stevenson

MASSACHUSETTS

Publicly controlled

Berkshire Community College	Pittsfield
Blue Hills Technical Institute	Canton
Bristol Community College	Fall River
Bunker Hill Community College	Boston
Cape Cod Community College	W. Barnstable
Greenfield Community College	Greenfield
Holyoke Community College	Holyoke
Massachusetts Bay Community College	Wellesley
Massasoit Community College	Brockton
Middlesex Community College	Bedford
Mount Wachusett Community College	Gardner
North Shore Community College	Beverly
Northern Essex Community College	Haverhill
Quincy Junior College	Quincy
Quinsigamond Community College	Worcester
Roxbury Community College	Boston
Springfield Technical Community Coll.	Springfield

Privately controlled

Aquinas Junior College	Milton
Aquinas Junior College	Newton
Bay Path Junior College	Longmeadow
Becker Junior College	Worcester
Leicester Campus	Leicester
Worcester Campus	Worcester
Chamberlayne Junior College	Boston
Dean Junior College	Franklin
Endicott College	Beverly
Fisher Junior College	Boston
Franklin Institute of Boston	Boston
Laboure Junior College	Boston
Lasell Junior College	Newton
Mount Ida Junior College	Newton Centre
Newbury Junior College	Boston
Worcester Junior College	Worcester

MICHIGAN

Publicly controlled

Alpena Community College	Alpena
Bay de Noc Community College	Escanaba
Charles Stewart Mott Community Coll.	Flint
Delta College	University Center
Glen Oaks Community College	Centreville
Gogebic Community College	Ironwood
Grand Rapids Junior College	Grand Rapids
Henry Ford Community College	Dearborn
Highland Park Community College	Highland Park
Jackson Community College	Jackson
Kalamazoo Valley Community College	Kalamazoo
Kellogg Community College	Battle Creek
Kirtland Community College	Roscommon
Lake Michigan College	Benton Harbor
Lansing Community College	Lansing
Macomb Community College	Warren
Mid Michigan Community College	Harrison
Monroe County Community College	Monroe
Montcalm Community College	Sidney
Muskegon Community College	Muskegon
North Central Michigan College	Petoskey
Northwestern Michigan College	Traverse City
Oakland Community College	Bloomfield Hills
Auburn Hills Campus	Auburn Heights
Highland Lakes Campus	Union Lake
Orchard Ridge Campus	Farmington
Southeast Campus	Southfield
St. Clair County Community College	Port Huron
Schoolcraft College	Livonia
Southwestern Michigan College	Dowagiac
Washtenaw Community College	Ann Arbor
Wayne County Community College	Detroit
West Shore Community College	Scottville

Privately controlled

Davenport College of Business	Grand Rapids
Suomi College	Hancock

MINNESOTA

Publicly controlled

Austin Community College	Austin
Brainerd Community College	Brainerd
Clearwater Comm. Coll. Region	Fergus Falls
Fergus Falls Community College	Fergus Falls
Northland Community College	Thief River Falls
Inver Hills Community College	Inver Grove Heights
Lakewood Community College	White Bear Lake
Minneapolis Community College	Minneapolis
Minnesota, Univ. of, Technical Coll.	Minneapolis
Crookston Campus	Crookston

Waseca Campus	Waseca
Minnesota Comm. Coll. System	St. Paul
Alexandria Vocational Tech. Inst.	Alexandria
Anoka-Ramsey Community College	Coon Rapids
Arrowhead Community College	Hibbing
Hibbing Community College	Hibbing
Itasca Community College	Grand Rapids
Mesabi Community College	Virginia
Rainy River Community College	Intl. Falls
Vermilion Community College	Ely
Normandale Community College	Bloomington
North Hennepin Community College	Brooklyn Park
Rochester Community College	Rochester
Willmar Area Technical Institute	Willmar
Willmar Community College	Willmar
Worthington Community College	Worthington
Privately controlled	
Bethany Lutheran College	Mankato
Crosier Seminary Junior College	Onamia
Golden Valley Lutheran College	Minneapolis
St. Mary's Junior College	Minneapolis

MISSISSIPPI

Publicly controlled	
Coahoma Junior College	Clarksdale
Copiah-Lincoln Junior College	Wesson
East Central Junior College	Decatur
East Mississippi Junior College	Scooba
Hinds Junior College District	Raymond
Utica Campus	Utica
Holmes Junior College	Goodman
Itawamba Junior College	Fulton
Jones County Junior College	Ellisville
Meridian Junior College	Meridian
Mississippi Delta Junior College	Moorhead
Mississippi Gulf Coast Junior College	Perkinston
Jackson County Campus	Gautier
Jefferson Davis Campus	Gulfport
Perkinston Campus	Perkinston
Northeast Mississippi Junior College	Booneville
Northwest Mississippi Junior College	Senatobia
Pearl River Junior College	Poplarville
Southwest Mississippi Junior College	Summit
Privately controlled	
Clarke College	Newton
Mary Holmes College	West Point
Wood Junior College	Mathiston

MISSOURI

Publicly controlled	
Crowder College	Neosho
East Central College	Union
Jefferson College	Hillsboro
Metropolitan Community Colleges, The	Kansas City
Longview Community College	Lee's Summit
Maple Woods Community College	Kansas City
Penn Valley Community College	Kansas City
Pioneer Community College	Kansas City
Mineral Area College	Flat River
Moberly Junior College	Moberly
St. Louis Community College	St. Louis
St. Louis C.C.—Florissant Valley	St. Louis
St. Louis C.C. at Forest Park	St. Louis
St. Louis C.C.—Meramec	St. Louis
State Fair Community College	Sedalia
Three Rivers Community College	Poplar Bluff
Trenton Junior College	Trenton
Privately controlled	
Cottey College	Nevada
Kemper Military School and College	Boonville
St. Mary's College of O'Fallon	O'Fallon
St. Paul's College	Concordia
Wentworth Military Academy	Lexington

MONTANA

Publicly controlled	
Blackfeet Community College	Browning
Dawson Community College	Glendive
Flathead Valley Community College	Kalispell
Miles Community College	Miles City
Privately controlled	
Dullknife Memorial Comm. Coll.	Lame Deer
Salish Kootenai Comm. College	Pablo

NEBRASKA

Publicly controlled	
Central Community College	Grand Island
Grand Island Campus	Grand Island
Hastings Campus	Hastings
Platte Campus	Columbus
Metropolitan Technical Community Coll.	Omaha
Mid-Plains Technical Comm. Coll. Area	North Platte
McCook Community College	McCook
Mid-Plains Community College	North Platte
Nebraska, Univ. of, Sch. of Tech. Agri.	Curtis
Northeast Technical Community College	Norfolk
Southeast Community College	Lincoln
Beatrice Campus	Beatrice
Lincoln Campus	Lincoln
Milford Campus	Milford
Western Technical Comm. Coll. Area	Scottsbluff
Nebraska Western College	Scottsbluff
Western Nebraska Technical Coll.	Sidney
Privately controlled	
York College	York

NEVADA

Publicly controlled	
Nevada, Univ. of, Comm. Coll. System	Reno
Clark County Community College	North Las Vegas
Northern Nevada Community College	Elko
Truckee Meadows Community College	Reno
Western Nevada Community College	Carson City

NEW HAMPSHIRE

Publicly controlled	
New Hampshire Technical Institute	Concord
New Hampshire Vocational Technical Coll.	Berlin
Berlin Campus	Berlin
Claremont Campus	Claremont
Laconia Campus	Laconia
Manchester Campus	Manchester
Nashua Campus	Nashua
Stratham Campus	Stratham
Privately controlled	
White Pines College	Chester

NEW JERSEY

Publicly controlled	
Atlantic Community College	Mays Landing
Bergen Community College	Paramus
Brookdale Community College	Lincroft
Burlington County College	Pemberton
Camden County College	Blackwood
County College of Morris	Randolph
Cumberland County College	Vineland
Essex County College	Newark
Gloucester County College	Sewell
Hudson County Community College	Jersey City
Mercer County Community College	Trenton
Middlesex County College	Edison
Ocean County College	Toms River
Passaic County Community College	Paterson
Salem Community College	Carneys Point

Somerset County College	Somerville
Union County College	Cranford
Warren County Community College	Belvidere

NEW MEXICO

Publicly controlled

Albuquerque Tech. Voc. Institute	Albuquerque
Eastern New Mexico University	Portales
Clovis Campus	Clovis
Roswell Campus	Roswell
Inst. of American Indian Arts	Santa Fe
Luna Vocational Technical Institute	Las Vegas
New Mexico, University of	Albuquerque
Gallup Campus	Gallup
Los Alamos	Los Alamos
New Mexico Junior College	Hobbs
New Mexico Military Institute	Roswell
New Mexico State University	Las Cruces
Alamogordo Campus	Alamogordo
Carlsbad Campus	Carlsbad
Dona Ana Branch	Las Cruces
Grants Campus	Grants
Northern New Mexico Community Coll.	El Rito
San Juan College	Farmington
Sante Fe Community College	Santa Fe

NEW YORK

Publicly controlled

Adirondack Community College	Glens Falls
Borough of Manhattan Community Coll.	New York
Bramson ORT Technical Institute	New York
Bronx Community College	Bronx
Broome Community College	Binghamton
Cayuga County Community College	Auburn
Clinton Community College	Plattsburgh
Columbia-Greene Community College	Hudson
Comm. Coll. of the Finger Lakes	Canandaigua
Corning Community College	Corning
Dutchess Community College	Poughkeepsie
Erie Community College	Buffalo
City Campus	Buffalo
North Campus	Williamsville
South Campus	Orchard Park
Fashion Institute of Technology	New York
Fulton-Montgomery Community College	Johnstown
Genesee Community College	Batavia
Herkimer County Community College	Herkimer
Hostos Community College	Bronx
Hudson Valley Community College	Troy
Jamestown Community College	Jamestown
Jefferson Community College	Watertown
Kingsborough Community College	Brooklyn
Laguardia Community College	Long Island City
Mohawk Valley Community College	Utica
Monroe Community College	Rochester
Nassau Community College	Garden City
New York City Technical College	Brooklyn
Niagara County Community College	Sanborn
North Country Community College	Saranac Lake
Onondaga Community College	Syracuse
Orange County Community College	Middletown
Queensborough Community College	Bayside
Rockland Community College	Suffern
Schenectady County Community College	Schenectady
SUNY Agricultural & Technical Colleges	
Alfred Campus	Alfred
Canton Campus	Canton
Cobleskill Campus	Cobleskill
Delhi Campus	Delhi
Farmingdale Campus	Farmingdale
Morrisville Campus	Morrisville
Suffolk County Community College	Selden
Sullivan County Community College	Loch Sheldrake
Tompkins-Cortland Community College	Dryden
Ulster County Community College	Stone Ridge
Westchester Community College	Valhalla

Privately controlled

Aeronautics, Academy of	Flushing
Albany, Junior College of	Albany
Cazenovia College	Cazenovia
Elizabeth Seton College	Yonkers
Hilbert College	Hamburg
Lab Inst. of Merchandising	New York
Maria College	Albany
Maria Regina College	Syracuse
Mater Dei College	Ogdensburg
Paul Smith's Coll. of Arts & Science	Paul Smiths
Trocaire College	Buffalo
Villa Maria College of Buffalo	Buffalo

NORTH CAROLINA

Publicly controlled

Albemarle, College of the	Elizabeth City
Anson Technical College	Ansonville
Asheville-Buncombe Technical College	Asheville
Beaufort County Community College	Washington
Bladen Technical College	Dublin
Blue Ridge Technical College	Flat Rock
Caldwell Comm. Coll. and Tech. Inst.	Hudson
Cape Fear Technical Institute	Wilmington
Carteret Technical College	Morehead City
Catawba Valley Technical College	Hickory
Central Carolina Technical College	Sanford
Central Piedmont Community College	Charlotte
Cleveland Technical College	Shelby
Coastal Carolina Community College	Jacksonville
Craven Community College	New Bern
Davidson County Community College	Lexington
Durham Technical Institute	Durham
Edgecombe Technical College	Tarboro
Fayetteville Technical Institute	Fayetteville
Forsyth Technical Institute	Winston Salem
Gaston College	Dallas
Guilford Technical Institute	Jamestown
Halifax Community College	Weldon
Haywood Technical College	Clyde
Isothermal Community College	Spindale
James Sprunt Technical College	Kenansville
Johnston Technical College	Smithfield
Lenoir Community College	Kinston
Martin Community College	Williamston
Mayland Technical College	Spruce Pine
McDowell Technical College	Marion
Mitchell Community College	Statesville
Montgomery Technical Institute	Troy
Nash Technical Institute	Rocky Mount
Pamlico Technical College	Grantsboro
Piedmont Technical College	Roxboro
Pitt Community College	Greenville
Randolph Technical College	Asheboro
Richmond Technical College	Hamlet
Roanoke-Chowan Technical College	Ahoskie
Robeson Technical College	Lumberton
Rockingham Community College	Wentworth
Rowan Technical College	Salisbury
Sampson Technical College	Clinton
Sandhills Community College	Carthage
Southeastern Community College	Whiteville
Southwestern Technical College	Sylva
Stanly Technical Institute	Albemarle
Surry Community College	Dobson
Technical College of Alamance	Haw River
Tri-County Community College	Murphy
Vance-Granville Community College	Henderson
Wake Technical College	Raleigh

Wayne Community College	Goldsboro
Western Piedmont Community College	Morganton
Wilkes Community College	Wilkesboro
Wilson County Technical Institute	Wilson
Privately controlled	
Brevard College	Brevard
Chowan College	Murfreesboro
Lees-McRae College	Banner Elk
Louisburg College	Louisburg
Montreat-Anderson College	Montreat
Mount Olive College	Mount Olive
Peace College	Raleigh
St. Mary's College	Raleigh

NORTH DAKOTA

Publicly controlled	
Bismarck Junior College	Bismarck
Lake Region Junior College	Devils Lake
North Dakota, Univ. of—Williston	Williston
North Dakota State School of Science	Wahpeton
North Dakota State Univ.—Bottineau	Bottineau
Turtle Mountain Comm. College	Belcourt
Privately controlled	
Standing Rock Comm. College	Fort Yates

OHIO

Publicly controlled	
Akron, Univ. of, Comm. and Tech. Coll.	Akron
Wayne General & Technical Coll.	Orrville
Applied Science & Technology, Coll. of	Youngstown
Belmont Technical College	St. Clairsville
Bowling Green Univ.—Firelands Campus	Huron
Central Ohio Technical College	Newark
Cincinnati, University of	Cincinnati
Clermont General & Technical Coll.	Batavia
Omi-College of Applied Science	Cincinnati
Raymond Walters Gen. & Tech. Coll.	Cincinnati
University College	Cincinnati
Cincinnati Technical College	Cincinnati
Clark Technical College	Springfield
Columbus Technical Institute	Columbus
Cuyahoga Community College District	Cleveland
Eastern Campus	Warrensville Twnsp.
Metropolitan Campus	Cleveland
Western Campus	Parma
Edison State Community College	Piqua
Hocking Technical College	Nelsonville
Jefferson Technical College	Steubenville
Kent State University	Kent
Ashtabula Campus	Ashtabula
East Liverpool Regional Campus	East Liverpool
Geauga Campus	Burton
Salem Campus	Salem
Stark Regional Campus	Canton
Trumbull Campus	Warren
Tuscarawas Campus	New Philadelphia
Lakeland Community College	Mentor
Lima Technical College	Lima
Lorain County Community College	Elyria
Marion Technical College	Marion
Miami University	Oxford
Hamilton Campus	Hamilton
Middletown Campus	Middletown
Muskingum Area Technical College	Zanesville
North Central Technical College	Mansfield
Northwest Technical College	Archbold
Ohio State University	Columbus
Agricultural Technical Institute	Wooster
Lima Campus	Lima
Mansfield Campus	Mansfield
Marion Campus	Marion
Newark Campus	Newark
Ohio University	Athens
Belmont County Campus	St. Clairsville
Chillicothe Campus	Chillicothe
Ironton Campus	Ironton
Lancaster Campus	Lancaster
Zanesville Campus	Zanesville
Owens Technical College	Toledo
Rio Grande Coll. & Comm. Coll.	Rio Grande
Shawnee State Community College	Portsmouth
Sinclair Community College	Dayton
Southern State Community College	Hillsboro
Stark Technical College	Canton
Terra Technical College	Fremont
Toledo, Univ. of, Comm. & Tech. Coll.	Toledo
Washington Technical College	Marietta
Wright State Univ.—Western Branch	Celina
Privately controlled	
Chatfield College	St. Martin
Kettering College of Medical Arts	Kettering

OKLAHOMA

Publicly controlled	
Carl Albert Junior College	Poteau
Connors State College	Warner
Eastern Oklahoma State College	Wilburton
El Reno Junior College	El Reno
Murray State College	Tishomingo
Northeastern Oklahoma A&M College	Miami
Northern Oklahoma College	Tonkawa
Oklahoma City Community College	Oklahoma City
Oklahoma State U. Technical Institute	Oklahoma City
Rogers State College	Claremore
Rose State College	Midwest City
Sayre Junior College	Sayre
Seminole Junior College	Seminole
Tulsa Junior College	Tulsa
Western Oklahoma State College	Altus
Privately controlled	
Bacone College	Muskogee
Hillsdale Free Will Baptist	Moore
St. Gregory's College	Shawnee

OREGON

Publicly controlled	
Blue Mountain Community College	Pendleton
Central Oregon Community College	Bend
Chemeketa Community College	Salem
Clackamas Community College	Oregon City
Clatsop Community College	Astoria
Lane Community College	Eugene
Linn-Benton Community College	Albany
Mt. Hood Community College	Gresham
Portland Community College	Portland
Rogue Community College	Grants Pass
Southwestern Oregon Community Coll.	Coos Bay
Tillamook Bay Comm. Coll. Service Dist.	Bay City
Treasure Valley Community College	Ontario
Umpqua Community College	Roseburg
Privately controlled	
Bassist College	Portland

PENNSYLVANIA

Publicly controlled	
Bucks County Community College	Newtown
Butler County Community College	Butler
Community Coll. of Allegheny County	Pittsburgh
Allegheny Campus	Pittsburgh
Boyce Campus	Monroeville
College Center—North	Pittsburgh
South Campus	West Mifflin
Community College of Beaver County	Monaca

Comm. College of Philadelphia — Philadelphia
Delaware County Community College — Media
Harrisburg Area Community College — Harrisburg
Lehigh County Community College — Schnecksville
Luzerne County Community College — Nanticoke
Montgomery County Community College — Blue Bell
Northhampton County Area Comm. Coll. — Bethlehem
Reading Area Community College — Reading
Westmoreland County Community Coll. — Youngwood
Williamsport Area Community College — Williamsport

Privately controlled

Center for Degree Studies — Scranton
Central Penn. Business School — Summerdale
Harcum Junior College — Bryn Mawr
Keystone Junior College — La Plume
Lackawanna Junior College — Scranton
Manor Junior College — Jenkintown
Mount Aloysius Junior College — Cresson
Northeastern Christian Junior College — Villanova
Peirce Junior College — Philadelphia
Pennsylvania Institute of Technology — Media
Pinebrook Junior College — Coopersburg
Valley Forge Military Junior College — Wayne
Wheeler School — Pittsburgh

PUERTO RICO

Publicly controlled

Puerto Rico, Univ. of, Regional Colleges — Rio Piedras
  Aguadilla Regional College — Ramey
  Arecibo Technical Univ. College — Arecibo
  Bayamon U. Technological Coll. — Bayamon
  Carolina Regional College — Carolina
  La Montana Regional College — Utuado
  Ponce Technical University College — Ponce

Privately controlled

Catholic University of Puerto Rico — Ponce
  Arecibo Regional Campus — Arecibo
  Guayama Center — Guayama
  Mayaguez Center — Mayaguez
  Ponce Center — Ponce
ICPR Junior College — Hato Rey
Interamerican University of Puerto Rico — San Juan
  Aguadilla Regional College — Aguadilla
  Arecibo Regional College — Arecibo
  Barranquitas Regional College — Barranquitas
  Fajardo Regional Campus — Fajardo
  Guayama Regional College — Guayama
  Ponce Regional College — Ponce
Puerto Rico Junior College — Rio Piedras
Ramirez Coll. of Business Tech. — Santurce

RHODE ISLAND

Publicly controlled

Community Coll. of Rhode Island — Warwick
  Knight Campus — Warwick
  Flanagan Campus — Lincoln

SOUTH CAROLINA

Publicly controlled

State System of Technical Colleges: — Columbia
  Aiken Technical College — Aiken
  Beaufort Technical College — Beaufort
  Chesterfield-Marlboro Technical Coll. — Cheraw
  Denmark Technical College — Denmark
  Florence-Darlington Technical Coll. — Florence
  Greenville Technical College — Greenville
  Horry-Georgetown Technical College — Conway
Midlands Technical College — Columbia
Orangeburg-Calhoun Technical College — Orangeburg
Piedmont Technical College — Greenwood
South Carolina, University of — Columbia
  Beaufort Campus — Beaufort
  Lancaster Regional Campus — Lancaster
  Salkehatchie Regional Campus — Allendale
  Sumter Regional Campus — Sumter
  Union Campus — Union
Spartanburg Technical College — Spartanburg
Sumter Area Technical College — Sumter
Tri-County Technical College — Pendleton
Trident Technical College — Charleston
Williamsburg Technical College — Kingstree
York Technical College — Rock Hill

Privately controlled

Anderson College — Anderson
North Greenville College — Tigerville
Spartanburg Methodist College — Spartanburg

SOUTH DAKOTA

Privately controlled

Oglala Sioux Community College — Kyle
Presentation College — Aberdeen
Sinte Gleska College Center — Rosebud

TENNESSEE

Publicly controlled

Chattanooga State Tech. Comm. Coll. — Chattanooga
Cleveland State Community College — Cleveland
Columbia State Community College — Columbia
Dyersburg State Community College — Dyersburg
Jackson State Community College — Jackson
Motlow State Community College — Tullahoma
Nashville State Technical Institute — Nashville
Roane State Community College — Harriman
Shelby State Community College — Memphis
State Technical Inst. at Knoxville — Knoxville
State Technical Inst. at Memphis — Memphis
Tri-Cities State Tech. Inst. — Blountville
Volunteer State Community College — Gallatin
Walters State Community College — Morristown

Privately controlled

Aquinas Junior College — Nashville
Hiwassee College — Madisonville
John A. Gupton College — Nashville
Martin College — Pulaski
Morristown College — Morristown
Tomlinson College — Cleveland

TEXAS

Publicly controlled

Alamo Comm. Coll. District — San Antonio
  St. Philip's College — San Antonio
  San Antonio College — San Antonio
Alvin Community College — Alvin
Amarillo College — Amarillo
Angelina College — Lufkin
Austin Community College — Austin
Bee County College — Beeville
Blinn College — Brenham
Brazosport College — Lake Jackson
Central Texas College — Killeen
Cisco Junior College — Cisco
Clarendon College — Clarendon
Cooke County College — Gainesville
Dallas County Community Coll. District — Dallas
  Brookhaven College — Farmers Branch
  Cedar Valley College — Lancaster
  Eastfield College — Mesquite
  El Centro College — Dallas
  Mountain View College — Dallas
  North Lake College — Irving
  Richland College — Dallas
Del Mar College — Corpus Christi
El Paso County Comm. Coll. District — El Paso
  Rio Grande Campus — El Paso
  Transmountain Campus — El Paso

Valle Verde Campus	El Paso
Frank Phillips College	Borger
Galveston College	Galveston
Grayson County Junior College	Denison
Henderson County Junior College	Athens
Hill Junior College	Hillsboro
Houston Community College System	Houston
Howard County Junior Coll. District	Big Spring
Howard College	Big Spring
SW Collegiate Inst. for the Deaf	Big Spring
Kilgore College	Kilgore
Lamar University	Beaumont
Orange County Center	Orange
Port Arthur Branch	Port Arthur
Laredo Junior College	Laredo
Lee College	Baytown
Mainland, College of the	Texas City
McLennan Community College	Waco
Midland College	Midland
Navarro College	Corsicana
North Harris County College	Houston
Odessa College	Odessa
Panola Junior College	Carthage
Paris Junior College	Paris
Ranger Junior College	Ranger
San Jacinto College District	Pasadena
Central Campus	Pasadena
North Campus	Houston
South Campus	Houston
South Plains College	Levelland
Southwest Texas Junior College	Uvalde
Tarrant County Junior Coll. District	Fort Worth
Northeast Campus	Hurst
Northwest Campus	Fort Worth
South Campus	Fort Worth
Temple Junior College	Temple
Texarkana Community College	Texarkana
Texas Southmost College	Brownsville
Texas State Technical Institute	Waco
Amarillo Campus	Amarillo
Harlingen Campus	Harlingen
Sweetwater Campus	Sweetwater
Waco Campus	Waco
Tyler Junior College	Tyler
Vernon Regional Junior College	Vernon
Victoria College	Victoria
Weatherford College	Weatherford
Western Texas College	Snyder
Wharton County Junior College	Wharton
Privately controlled	
Jacksonville College	Jacksonville
Lon Morris College	Jacksonville
Southwestern Christian College	Terrell
Southwestern Junior College	Waxahachie

UTAH

Publicly controlled	
Dixie College	St. George
Eastern Utah, College of	Price
Snow College	Ephraim
Utah Technical College at Provo	Provo
Utah Technical College at Salt Lake	Salt Lake City

VERMONT

Publicly controlled	
0Community College of Vermont	Waterbury
Vermont Technical College	Randolph Center
Privately controlled	
Champlain College	Burlington
Vermont College of Norwich University	Montpelier

VIRGINIA

Publicly controlled	
Blue Ridge Community College	Weyers Cave
Central Virginia Community College	Lynchburg
Dabney S. Lancaster Community Coll.	Clifton Forge
Danville Community College	Danville
Eastern Shore Community College	Melfa
Germanna Community College	Locust Grove
J. Sargeant Reynolds Community Coll.	Richmond
Downtown Campus	Richmond
Parham Road Campus	Richmond
Western Campus	Richmond
John Tyler Community College	Chester
Lord Fairfax Community College	Middletown
Mountain Empire Community College	Big Stone Gap
New River Community College	Dublin
Northern Virginia Community College	Annandale
Alexandria Campus	Alexandria
Annandale Campus	Annandale
Loudoun Campus	Sterling
Manassas Campus	Manassas
Woodbridge Campus	Woodbridge
Patrick Henry Community College	Martinsville
Paul D. Camp Community College	Franklin
Piedmont Virginia Community College	Charlottesville
Rappahannock Community College	Glenns
North Campus	Warsaw
South Campus	Glenns
Richard Bland College	Petersburg
Southside Virginia Community College	Alberta
Christanna Campus	Alberta
John H. Daniel Campus	Keysville
Southwest Virginia Community College	Richlands
Thomas Nelson Community College	Hampton
Tidewater Community College	Portsmouth
Chesapeake Campus	Chesapeake
Frederick Campus	Portsmouth
Virginia Beach Campus	Virginia Beach
Virginia Highlands Community College	Abingdon
Virginia Western Community College	Roanoke
Wytheville Community College	Wytheville
Privately controlled	
Southern Seminary Junior College	Buena Vista

WASHINGTON

Publicly controlled	
Bellevue Community College	Bellevue
Big Bend Community College	Moses Lake
Clark College	Vancouver
Columbia Basin College	Pasco
Community College District XII	Centralia
Centralia College	Centralia
Olympia Tech. Comm. Coll.	Olympia
Community Colleges of Spokane	Spokane
Spokane Community College	Spokane
Spokane Falls Comm. Coll.	Spokane
Edmonds Community College	Lynnwood
Everett Community College	Everett
Fort Steilacoom Comm. Coll.	Tacoma
Grays Harbor College	Aberdeen
Green River Comm. College	Auburn
Highline Community College	Midway
Lower Columbia College	Longview
Olympic College	Bremerton
Peninsula College	Port Angeles
Seattle Comm. Coll. District VI	Seattle
North Seattle Comm. Coll.	Seattle
Seattle Central Comm. Coll.	Seattle
South Seattle Comm. Coll.	Seattle
Shoreline Community College	Seattle
Skagit Valley College	Mount Vernon
Tacoma Community College	Tacoma
Walla Walla Community College	Walla Walla

Wenatchee Valley College	Wenatchee
Whatcom Community College	Bellingham
Yakima Valley Community College	Yakima

WEST VIRGINIA

Publicly controlled

Fairmont Community College	Fairmont
Marshall Univ.—Community College	Huntington
Parkersburg Community College	Parkersburg
Potomac State College	Keyser
Shepherd College—Community College Component	Shepherdstown
Southern West Virginia Comm. College	Logan
Logan Campus	Logan
Williamson Campus	Williamson
West Virginia Institute of Technology—Community and Technical College	Montgomery
West Virginia Northern Comm. College	Wheeling
West Virginia State Comm. College	Institute

Privately controlled

Beckley College	Beckley
Ohio Valley College	Parkersburg

WISCONSIN

Publicly controlled

University Center System	Madison
Baraboo-Sauk County Campus	Baraboo
Barron County Campus	Rice Lake
Fond du Lac Campus	Fond du Lac
Fox Valley Campus	Menasha
Manitowoc County Campus	Manitowoc
Marathon County Campus	Wausau
Marinette County Campus	Marinette
Marshfield-Wood County Campus	Marshfield
Richland Campus	Richland Center
Rock County Campus	Janesville
Sheboygan Campus	Sheboygan
Washington County Campus	West Bend
Waukesha County Campus	Waukesha
Vocational Tech. & Adult Education Sys.	Madison
Blackhawk Technical Institute	Janesville
District One Technical Institute	Eau Claire
Fox Valley Technical Institute	Appleton
Appleton Campus	Appleton
Oshkosh Campus	Oshkosh
Gateway Technical Institute	Kenosha
Elkhorn Campus	Elkhorn
Kenosha Campus	Kenosha
Racine Campus	Racine
Lakeshore Technical Institute	Cleveland
Madison Area Technical College	Madison
Mid-State Technical Institute	Wisconsin Rapids
Marshfield Campus	Marshfield
Stevens Point Campus	Stevens Point
Wisconsin Rapids Campus	Wisconsin Rapids
Milwaukee Area Technical College	Milwaukee
Central Campus	Milwaukee
North Campus	Mequon
South Campus	Oak Creek
West Campus	West Allis
Moraine Park Technical Institute	Fond du Lac
Beaver Dam Campus	Beaver Dam
Fond du Lac Campus	Fond du Lac
West Bend Campus	West Bend
Nicolet College and Tech. Institute	Rhinelander
North Central Technical Institute*	Wausau
Antigo Campus	Antigo
Wausau Campus	Wausau
Northeast Wisconsin VTAE District	Green Bay
Green Bay Campus	Green Bay
Marinette Campus	Marinette
Sturgeon Bay Campus	Sturgeon Bay
Southwest Wisconsin Voc.—Tech. Inst.	Fennimore
Waukesha County Technical Institute	Pewaukee
Western Wisconsin Technical Institute	La Crosse
Wisconsin Indianhead VTAE District	Shell Lake
Ashland Campus	Ashland
New Richmond Campus	New Richmond
Rice Lake Campus	Rice Lake
Superior Campus	Superior

WYOMING

Publicly controlled

Casper College	Casper
Central Wyoming College	Riverton
Eastern Wyoming College	Torrington
Laramie County Community College	Cheyenne
Northwest Community College	Powell
Sheridan College	Sheridan
Western Wyoming Community College	Rock Springs

AMERICAN SAMOA

Publicly controlled

American Samoa Community College	Pago Pago

CANADA

Publicly controlled

Grande Prairie Regional College	G.P.Alberta
Grant MacEwan Community College	Edmonton, Alberta
Keyano College	Alberta
Medicine Hat College	Medicine Hat, Alberta
Mount Royal College	Calgary, Albta.
Red Deer College	Alberta

GUAM

Publicly controlled

Guam Community College	Guam

MICRONESIA

Publicly controlled

Community Coll. of Micronesia	East Caroline Isl.
Northern Marianas College	Saipan

PANAMA

Privately controlled

Panama Canal College	APO Miami

OTHER COUNTRIES

Privately controlled

American College of Switzerland	Leysin, Switz.
Schiller International-Univ.	Heidelberg, W. Ger.
Shin-Gu Junior Coll.	Korea
St. Johns College	British Honduras

Institutional Accreditation

Accreditation is attained through a process of evaluation and periodic review of total institutions conducted by the commission in accord with policies and procedures approved by the Council on Postsecondary Accreditation.

Accredited U.S. Senior Colleges and Universities, Spring 1984

Source: Information Please questionnaires to Colleges and Universities

Schools listed are those that offer at least a Bachelor's degree, and are fully accredited by one of the institutional and professional accrediting associations recognized by the Council on Post-secondary Accreditation. Also included are accredited colleges outside the U.S. The number of students is for full-time, matriculated, undergraduate and graduate students who are working for a degree. Actual enrollment, including part-time students, may be much higher. Number of faculty also is full-time.

Tuition, room, and board listed are average annual figures (including fees), subject to fluctuation, usually covering two semesters, two out of three trimesters, or three out of four quarters, depending on school calendar.

For further information, write to the Registrar of the school concerned.

NOTE: An asterisk (*) indicates that the college has not supplied up-to-date information. A dash (—) means the information does not apply. n.a. = information not available.

Abbreviations used for controls:

AB	American Baptist
AC	Advent Christian
AG	Assemblies of God
AL	American Lutheran
AME	African Methodist Episcopal
B	Baptist
BC	Brethren in Christ
CB	Church of Brethren
CC	Church of Christ
CE	Christian Evangelical
CG	Church of God
ChC	Christian Church
CMA	Christian & Missionary Alliance
CME	Christian Methodist Episcopal
Cong	Congregational
CP	Cumberland Presbyterian
CR	Christian Reformed
DC	Disciples of Christ
E	Episcopal
EC	Evangelical Covenant
ECh	Evangelical Christian
EFC	Evangelical Free Church
EL	Evangelical Lutheran
F	Friends
Fed	Federal
FG	Foursquare Gospel
FGB	Fellowship of Grace Brethren Churches
FM	Free Methodist
FWB	Free Will Baptist
GGF	Grace Gospel Fellowship
ID	Interdenominational
IND	Independent
J	Jewish
L	Lutheran
LCA	Lutheran Church of America
LDS	Latter Day Saints
M	Methodist
MB	Mennonite Brethren
MC	Missionary Church
Men	Mennonite
Mor	Moravian
Mun	Municipal
Naz	Nazarene
ND	Non-denominational
OBS	Open Bible Standard
P	Private
PH	Pentecostal Holiness
Pres	Presbyterian
Pub	Public
PUS	Presbyterian, U.S.
RC	Roman Catholic
RCA	Reformed Church in America
RP	Reformed Presbyterian
S	State
SB	Southern Baptist
SDA	Seventh Day Adventist
SOF	Society of Friends
Sw	Swedenborgian
UCC	United Church of Christ
UM	United Methodist
UP	United Presbyterian
W	Wesleyan

	Enrollment				Tuition ($)		
Institution and location	**Male**	**Female**	**Faculty**	**Control**	**Res.**	**Nonres.**	**Rm/Bd ($)**
Abilene Christian University; Abilene, Tex. 79699	1,935[1]	1,857[1]	175	P	3,168	3,168	1,900
Adams State College; Alamosa, Colo. 81102	894[1]	1,193[1]	100	S	1,000	3,000	2,500
Adelphi University; Garden City, N.Y. 11530	1,476	3,267	331	P	5,114	5,114	2,704
Adrian College; Adrian, Mich. 49221	580[1]	513[1]	65	P/UM	5,522	5,522	2,022
Agnes Scott College; Decatur, Ga. 30030	—	531	67	P	6,590	6,590	2,700
Akron, The University of; Akron, Ohio 44325	8,103[1]	7,141[1]	745[2]	S	1,344	2,688	2,270
Alabama, The University of*; University, Ala. 35486	8,699	8,220	836	S	994	2,119	1,687
Alabama, The University of, in Birmingham*; Birmingham, Ala. 35294	3,796	4,452	385	S	1,245	2,445	—
Alabama, The University of, in Huntsville*; Huntsville, Ala. 35899	2,829	2,630	222	S	966	1,932	2,240
Alabama A&M University; Normal, Ala. 35762	1,827[1]	1,538[1]	245	S	800	1,532	1,650
Alabama State University*; Montgomery, Ala 36195	1,704	2,330	174	S	660	1,320	1,320
Alaska, University of, Anchorage*; Anchorage, Alaska 99504	1,297	2,287	128	S	681	1,851	—
Alaska, University of, Fairbanks; Fairbanks, Alaska 99701	1,719[1]	1,399[1]	330	S	720	1,920	2,390
Alaska Bible College; Glennallen, Alas. 99588	26	10	8	ND	1,600	1,600	2,850
Alaska Pacific University; Anchorage, Alaska 99508	58	142	21	P/UM	3,360	3,360	3,335
Albany College of Pharmacy; Albany, N.Y. 12208	221	305	30	P	3,700	3,700	2,800
Albany Law School of Union University; Albany, N.Y. 12208	412[3]	284[3]	25	P	6,500	6,500	3,200
Albany Medical College*; Albany, N.Y. 12208	344	172	224	P	14,200	14,200	2,600
Albany State College*; Albany, Ga. 31705	771	1,125	135	S	2,898	4,383	2,160
Albertus Magnus College; New Haven, Conn. 06511	1[1]	313[1]	29	P/RC	3,990	3,990	3,340
Albion College; Albion, Mich. 49224	856	724	118	P/UM	5,436	5,436	2,630

Institution and location	Enrollment		Faculty	Control	Tuition ($)		Rm/Bd ($)
	Male	Female			Res.	Nonres.	
Albright College; Reading, Pa. 19603	617 [1]	796 [1]	92	P/UM	6,720 [3]	6,720 [3]	2,525 [3]
Albuquerque, University of; Albuquerque, N.M. 87140	643	907	78	P/RC	3,900 [3]	3,900 [3]	—
Alcorn State University; Lorman, Miss. 39096	1,071	1,331	157	S	1,200 [4]	1,663 [4]	—
Alderson-Broaddus College; Philippi, W. Va. 26416	297 [1]	481 [1]	65	P/AB	4,916 [3]	4,916 [3]	1,804 [3]
Alfred University[5]; Alfred, N.Y. 14802	1,259	1,189	150	P	7,910	7,910	2,860
Alice Lloyd College; Pippa Passes, Ky. 41844	174	247	22	P	2,390	2,390	1,550
Allegheny College; Meadville, Pa. 16335	984	925	130	P	5,835	5,835	7,986
Allentown College of St. Francis de Sales; Center Valley, Pa. 18034	450	525	53	P/RC	4,370	4,370	2,600
Alliance College; Cambridge Springs, Pa. 16403	174 [1]	96 [1]	16	P	3,000	3,000	2,150
Alma College; Alma, Mich. 48801	473	536	78	P	5,980	5,980	2,516
Alvernia College; Reading, Pa. 19607	136	241	36	P/RC	2,990	2,990	2,540
Alverno College; Milwaukee, Wis. 53215	—	635	65	P	4,362 [3]	4,362 [3]	1,900 [3]
Amber University*; Garland, Tex. 75041	547	462	15	P	2,040	2,040	—
American Baptist College*; Nashville, Tenn. 37207	145	20	5	P/B	1,094	1,094	986
American College, The*; Bryn Mawr, Pa. 19010	14,336	2,370	31	P	220	220	—
American College in Paris, The*; Paris, France 75007	850		23	P	4,800	4,800	—
American College of Puerto Rico*; Bayamón, P.R. 00619	1,516	1,919	n.a.	P	n.a.	n.a.	n.a.
American College of Switzerland, The; Leysin, Switzerland CH-1854	133	130	26	P	11,870 [4]	11,870 [4]	—
American Conservatory of Music; Chicago, Ill. 60603	140	151	291	P	5,000	5,000	4,500 [6]
American Grad. School of Intl. Mgt.; Glendale, Ariz. 85306	655	341	68	P	8,300	8,300	4,000
American International College; Springfield, Mass. 01109	705	543	93	P	4,620	4,620	2,435
American Technological University*; Killeen, Tex. 76540[7]	362	171	12	P	2,376	2,376	2,516
American University, The; Washington, D.C. 20016	2,899 [1]	3,219 [1]	385	P	7,600	7,600	2,220
American University in Cairo, The; Cairo, Egypt	1,042	1,507	184	P	1,205	5,625 [8]	4,950
Americas, University of the*; Puebla, Mexico 72820	1,290	808	76	P	1,377	1,733	n.a.
Amherst College; Amherst, Mass. 01002	885	607	154	P	9,400 [3]	9,400 [3]	3,000
Ana G. Méndez Educational Foundation; Rio Piedras, P.R. 00928:							
Colegio Universitario Metropolitano; San Juan, P.R. 00928	1,636	2,987	102	P	1,500	1,500	n.a.
Turabo University College; Caguas, P.R. 00625	2,554	3,755	90	P	1,500	1,500	2,400
Anderson College*; Anderson, Ind. 46012	752	935	101	P/CG	4,160	4,160	1,660
Andrews University; Berrien Springs, Mich. 49104	1,378 [1]	944 [1]	210	P/SDA	5,625	5,625	2,880
Angelo State University; San Angelo, Tex. 76909	2,302 [3]	2,298 [3]	195	S	420	1,500	2,624
Anna Maria College; Paxton, Mass. 01612	212 [1]	354 [1]	30	P	4,690	4,690	2,860
Antillian College; Mayaguez, P.R. 00709	365	546	50	P/SDA	1,792	1,792	1,440
Antioch University; Yellow Springs, Ohio 45387	1,292 [1]	2,221 [1]	172	P	n.a. [9]	n.a. [9]	n.a.
Appalachian Bible College; Bradley, W. Va. 25818	105	84	13	P/ND	2,300	2,300	2,000
Appalachian State University. *See* North Carolina, University System of							
Aquinas College; Grand Rapids, Mich. 49506	716 [3]	917 [3]	85	P/RC	4,790	4,790	2,308
Arizona, The University of; Tucson, Ariz. 85721	12,386 [1]	10,958 [1]	1,433	S	950	3,700	2,372
Arizona College of the Bible; Phoenix, Ariz. 85021	61	35	9	P/Ind	2,600	2,600	1,150
Arizona State University*; Tempe, Ariz. 85287	20,119	19,200	1,163	S	755	3,420	2,600
Arkansas, Univ. of, at Fayetteville*; Fayetteville, Ark. 72701	7,708	5,139	693	S	660	1,690	1,695
Arkansas, Univ. of, at Little Rock*; Little Rock, Ark. 72204	4,369	5,412	397	S	800	1,940	—
Arkansas, Univ. of, at Monticello; Monticello, Ark. 71655	878 [1]	1,026 [1]	96	S	850	1,850	1,530
Arkansas, Univ. of, at Pine Bluff; Pine Bluff, Ark. 71601	1,024	1,394	151	S	780	2,040	1,640
Arkansas College; Batesville, Ark. 72501	166	252	33	P/PUS	3,950	3,950	1,900
Arkansas State University;' State University, Ark. 72467	2,879	2,878	310	S	790	1,790	1,700
Arkansas Tech. University; Russellville, Ark. 72801	1,580	1,508	150	S	750	1,450	1,600
Arlington Baptist College; Arlington, Tex. 76012	167	118	16	P	1,200	1,200	1,750
Armstrong College*; Berkeley, Calif. 94704[7]	500		30	P	2,178	2,178	—
Armstrong State College; Savannah, Ga. 31419	1,137	1,650	169	S	990	2,700	—
Arnold & Marie Schwartz Coll. of Pharmacy & Health Sciences. *See* Long Island Univ. Center, Brooklyn Center							
Art Academy of Cincinnati; Cincinnati, Ohio 45202	112	113	14	P	3,000	3,000	—
Art Center College of Design; Pasadena, Calif. 91103	690	450	44	P	4,390	4,390	3,100
Arthur D. Little Management Education Institute*; Cambridge, Mass. 02140	51	6	26	P	10,100	10,100	—
Art Institute of Chicago, School of the; Chicago, Ill. 60603	406	541	120	P	6,150	6,150	3,780
Asbury College; Wilmore, Ky. 40390	475	529	81	P/ND	3,459	3,459	2,334
Ashland College*; Ashland, Ohio 44805	650	651	114	P/BC	5,586	5,586	2,394
Assemblies of God Graduate School; Springfield, Mo. 65802	144 [1]	14 [1]	8	P/AG	2,400	2,400	—
Associated Arts, School of the; St. Paul, Minn. 55102	40	41	3 [10]	P	3,150 [3]	3,150 [3]	—
Assumption College; Worcester, Mass. 01609	690	780	87	P/RC	5,230	5,230	2,785
Athens State College; Athens, Ala. 35611	518	589	38	S	1,200	2,400	2,318
Atlanta Christian College; East Point, Ga. 30344	84	61	15	P	1,750	1,750	1,800
Atlanta College of Art; Atlanta, Ga. 30309	125 [1]	113 [1]	20	P	4,650	4,650	1,200
Atlanta University; Atlanta, Ga. 30314	507	588	108	P	3,600	3,600	3,532
Atlantic, College of the; Bar Harbor, Maine 04609	57	57	13	P	6,500 [3]	6,500 [3]	1,500 [11]
Atlantic Christian College; Wilson, N.C. 27893	461 [1]	924 [1]	88	P/DC	3,500	3,500	1,700
Atlantic Union College; South Lancaster, Mass. 01561	210 [1]	343 [1]	54	P/SDA	5,386	5,386	1,200
Auburn University; Auburn University, Ala. 36849	9,419 [1]	6,730 [1]	1,036	S	1,080	2,490	2,300
Auburn University at Montgomery*; Montgomery, Ala. 36193	2,320	2,749	181	S	795	1,830	2,220
Augsburg College*; Minneapolis, Minn. 55454	603	640	90	P/AL	4,820	4,820	2,277
Augusta College*; Augusta, Ga. 30910	1,624	2,386	185	S	741	2,226	—

Institution and location	Enrollment Male	Enrollment Female	Faculty	Control	Tuition ($) Res.	Tuition ($) Nonres.	Rm/Bd ($)
Augustana College; Rock Island, Ill. 61201	960	1,017	117	P/LCA	5,154	5,154	2,337
Augustana College; Sioux Falls, S.D. 57197	586[1]	990[1]	117	P/AL	5,200	5,200	1,795
Aurora College; Aurora, Ill. 60506	349[1]	415[1]	54	P/AC	4,650	4,650	2,625
Austin College*; Sherman, Tex. 75090	655	531	100	P/Pres	4,000	4,000	1,950
Austin Peay State University; Clarksville, Tenn. 37044[12]	1,396[1]	1,774[1]	235	S	810	2,568	1,900
Averett College; Danville, Va. 24541	343	651	53	P/B	3,750	3,750	2,650
Avila College; Kansas City, Mo. 64145	160	534	69[13]	P/RC	4,200	4,200	2,000
Azusa Pacific University; Azusa, Calif. 91702	776[1]	816[1]	86	P/ID	5,170	5,170	2,550
Babson College*; Babson Park, Mass. 02157	1,149	597	95	P	6,364	6,364	2,000
Baker University; Baldwin City, Kan. 66006	368[1]	394[1]	51	P/UM	3,950[3]	3,950[3]	2,200[3]
Baldwin-Wallace College; Berea, Ohio 44017	871[1]	895[1]	135	P/M	5,859	5,859	2,700
Ball State University; Muncie, Ind. 47306	7,461[1]	9,313[1]	830	S	1,562	3,120	1,926
Baltimore, University of; Baltimore, Md. 21201	1,208[1]	936[1]	145	S	1,305	2,505	—
Baltimore Hebrew College*; Baltimore, Md. 21215	62	142	16	P	970	970	—
Bank Street College of Education; New York, N.Y. 10025	14	103	50	P	([14])	([14])	—
Baptist Bible College; Springfield, Mo. 65803	668	499	39	P/B	495	495	985
Baptist Bible Institute; Graceville, Fla. 32440	314[1]	75[1]	17	SB	990	990	800[11]
Baptist College at Charleston*; Charleston, S.C. 29411	728	821	73	SB	3,950	3,950	2,374
Barat College; Lake Forest, Ill. 60045	80	394	32	P	4,995	4,995	2,700
Barber-Scotia College*; Concord, N.C. 28025	142	205	24	Pres	4,302	4,302	1,879
Bard College; Annandale-on-Hudson, N.Y. 12504	300[1]	381[1]	49	P	9,980	9,980	3,260
Barnard College; New York, N.Y. 10027[15]	—	2,209	140	P	8,590[3]	8,590[3]	4,000
Barrington College; Barrington, R.I. 02806	165[1]	208[1]	26	P	5,930	5,930	2,650
Barry University*; Miami Shores, Fla. 33161	318	864	90	P	4,400	4,400	2,900
Bartlesville Wesleyan College; Bartlesville, Okla. 74006	194[1]	192[1]	25	P/W	3,150	3,150	2,150
Bates College; Lewiston, Maine 04240	705[1]	709[1]	119	P	11,500[4]	11,500[4]	—
Bayamón Central University*; Bayamón, P.R. 00619	917	707	35	P/RC	1,915	1,915	—
Baylor College of Dentistry; Dallas, Tex. 75246	440[1]	181[1]	120[16]	P	750	3,600	—
Baylor College of Medicine*; Houston, Tex 77030	635	228	n.a.	P	n.a.	n.a.	n.a.
Baylor University; Waco, Tex. 76798	4,922	5,312	524	P/B	3,210	3,210	2,570
Beacon College*; Washington, D.C. 20009	56	89	n.a.	P	2,400	2,400	—
Beaver College*; Glenside, Pa. 19038	168	555	79	P	5,800	5,800	2,600
Behrend College. *See* Pennsylvania State University							
Belhaven College; Jackson, Miss. 39202	217	259	27	P/Pres	3,400	3,400	1,790
Bellarmine College; Louisville, Ky. 40205	540[1]	650[1]	92	RC	3,600	3,600	2,000
Bellevue College; Bellevue, Neb. 68005	1,200	1,500	30	P	1,440	1,440	—
Belmont Abbey College*; Belmont, N.C. 28012	436	314	40	P/RC	2,000	4,000	2,000
Belmont College; Nashville, Tenn. 37203	954	976	95	P/B	2,900	2,900	2,220
Beloit College; Beloit, Wis. 53511	567[1]	512[1]	n.a.	P	7,300	7,300	2,375
Bemidji State Univ. *See* Minnesota State University System							
Benedict College; Columbia, S.C. 29204	511	904	87	P/B	3,000	3,000	1,700
Benedictine College*; Atchison, Kan. 66002	427	410	68	P/RC	4,000	4,000	2,090
Benjamin Franklin University*; Washington, D.C. 20036	214	194	18	P	2,700	2,700	—
Bennett College; Greensboro, N.C. 27420	—	495	41	P	4,650[4]	4,650[4]	—
Bennington College; Bennington, Vt. 05201	190	372	63	P	11,720	11,720	2,870
Bentley College; Waltham, Mass. 02154	1,811	1,724	189	P	6,100	6,100	3,340
Berea College; Berea, Ky. 40404	688[1]	823[1]	120	P	—	—	1,700
Berklee College of Music; Boston, Mass. 02215	2,361		212	P	3,990	3,990	3,290
Berkshire Christian College; Lenox, Mass. 01240	49	60	8	P/AC	3,700	3,700	2,600
Bernard M. Baruch Coll. *See* New York, City Univ. of							
Berry College; Mount Berry, Ga. 30149	532[1]	760[1]	81	P	3,975	3,975	1,800
Bethany Bible College; Santa Cruz, Calif. 95066	215	196	37	P/AG	3,182	3,182	2,380
Bethany College*; Bethany, W. Va. 26032	394	342	64	P/DC	5,380	5,380	2,155
Bethany College*; Lindsborg, Kan. 67456	417	403	50	P/LCA	2,740	2,740	1,655
Bethany Nazarene College; Bethany, Okla. 73008	495	577	70	P/Naz	2,820	2,820	2,190
Bethel College; McKenzie, Tenn. 38201	167	181	25	P/CP	2,640	2,640	1,770
Bethel College; Mishawaka, Ind. 46545	197	323	25	P/MC	3,968	3,968	2,160
Bethel College; North Newton, Kan. 67117	256	255	40	P/Men	4,098[3]	4,098[3]	2,258[3]
Bethel College; St. Paul, Minn. 55112	710	896	111	P/B	5,395	5,395	2,445
Bethune-Cookman College; Daytona Beach, Fla. 32015	686	944	108	M	3,337	3,337	2,270
Biola University; La Mirada, Calif. 90639	1,211[1]	1,210[1]	151	P/ND	4,894	4,894	2,710
Birmingham-Southern College; Birmingham, Ala. 35254	698[3]	889[3]	93	UM	4,600	4,600	2,100
Biscayne College*; Miami, Fla. 33054	1,763	1,394	104	P/RC	3,400	3,400	2,700
Bishop College*; Dallas, Tex. 75241	654	260	52	P/B	2,400	2,400	1,580
Blackburn College; Carlinville, Ill. 62626	260	285	36	P	3,990	3,990	1,419
Black Hills State College; Spearfish, S.D. 57783	986[1]	1,232[1]	89	S	944	2,000	1,556
Bloomfield College; Bloomfield, N.J. 07003	316[1]	605[1]	54	P	5,040	5,040	2,600
Bloomsburg State College. *See* Bloomsburg University							
Bloomsburg University; Bloomsburg, Pa. 17815	1,902	2,954	381	S	1,614	2,724	1,592
Bluefield College*; Bluefield, Va. 24605	190	164	22	P/B	1,615	1,615	1,515
Bluefield State College; Bluefield, W. Va. 24701	700	800	80	S	800	2,200	—
Blue Mountain College; Blue Mountain, Miss. 38610	52[1]	202[1]	26	P/B	1,980	1,980	1,620

Institution and location	Enrollment		Faculty	Control	Tuition ($)		Rm/Bd ($)
	Male	Female			Res.	Nonres.	
Bluffton College; Bluffton, Ohio 45817	303[1]	307[1]	52	P/Men	4,563	4,563	1,917
Boise State University; Boise, Idaho 83725	5,400	5,564	426	S	1,016	3,236	4,500
Boricua College; New York, N.Y. 10032	458	686	54[17]	P	3,500	3,500	—
Borromeo College of Ohio*; Wickliffe, Ohio 44092	75	—	14	RC	2,375	2,375	1,200
Boston Architectural Center*; Boston, Mass. 02115	562		150	P	1,240	1,240	—
Boston College*; Chestnut Hill, Mass. 02167	3,797	5,080	550	P/RC	6,800	6,800	3,555
Boston Conservatory of Music; Boston, Mass. 02215	121	255	28	P	5,800	5,800	3,300
Boston University*; Boston, Mass. 02215	9,336	10,116	1,454	P	7,175	7,175	3,400
Bowdoin College; Brunswick, Maine 04011	769[1]	591[1]	109	P	8,635	8,635	3,155
Bowie State College*; Bowie, Md. 20715	1,243	1,636	109	S	n.a.	n.a.	n.a.
Bowling Green State University; Bowling Green, Ohio 43403	6,020	7,614	731	S	1,800	1,800	1,888
Bradford College; Bradford, Mass. 01830	162[1]	174[1]	26	P	6,615[3]	6,615[3]	3,560[3]
Bradley University; Peoria, Ill. 61625	2,640[1]	1,855[1]	311	P	5,750[3]	5,750[3]	2,800[3]
Brandeis University; Waltham, Mass. 02254	1,316	1,294	356	P	9,350	9,350	4,041
Brenau College; Gainesville, Ga. 30501	566	1,027	90	P	3,927	3,927	3,123
Brescia College; Owensboro, Ky. 42301	182	254	55	RC	3,090	3,090	1,895
Briar Cliff College; Sioux City, Iowa 51104	368[1]	492[1]	60	P/RC	4,125	4,125	1,899
Bridgeport, The University of; Bridgeport, Conn. 06601	3,400	3,435	450	P	6,760	6,760	3,540
Bridgeport Engineering Institute; Bridgeport, Conn. 06606	820[1]	61[1]	108	P	2,330	2,330	—
Bridgewater College; Bridgewater, Va. 22812	361	400	60	P	3,690	3,690	2,385
Bridgewater State College; Bridgewater, Mass. 02324	2,194[1]	3,029[1]	263	S	850	2,800	2,000
Briercrest Bible College; Caronport, Sask., Canada SOH OSO	374[1]	302[1]	24	P/ID	1,536	1,536	1,770
Brigham Young University; Provo, Utah 84602	16,079	11,632	1,237	P/LDS	1,340[18]	2,010[19]	2,000
Hawaii Campus*; Laie, Hawaii 96762	819	967	86	P/LDS	1,438[18]	2,158[19]	2,450
Bristol College; Bristol, Tenn. 37620	240	380	32	P	2,400	2,400	1,000[11]
Brooklyn Center. *See* Long Island University Center							
Brooklyn College. *See* New York, City University of							
Brooklyn Law School*; Brooklyn, N.Y. 11201	680	517	39	P	5,200	5,200	—
Brooks Institute of Photography; Santa Barbara, Calif. 93108	453	209	30	P	5,250[3]	5,250[3]	—
Brown University; Providence, R.I. 02912	3,642[1]	3,178[1]	450	P	9,940[3]	9,940[3]	3,510[3]
Bryan College; Dayton, Tenn. 37321	213[1]	301[1]	37	P/ID	3,250	3,250	2,450
Bryant College; Smithfield, R.I. 02917	1,757[1]	1,428[1]	102	P	4,525	4,525	3,095
Bryn Mawr College; Bryn Mawr, Pa. 19010	91[1]	1,359[1]	144	P	8,345	8,345	3,655
Bucknell University; Lewisburg, Pa. 17837	1,637	1,502	213	P	9,025[3]	9,025[3]	2,285
Buena Vista College; Storm Lake, Iowa 50588	593	560	65	P	5,885	5,885	2,109
Burlington College; South Burlington, Vt. 05602	51	86	—	P	4,050	4,050	—
Butler University; Indianapolis, Ind. 46208	1,100	900	n.a.	P	5,640	5,640	2,566
Cabrini College; Radnor, Pa. 19087	156	483	36	P/RC	4,200	4,200	2,900
Caldwell College; Caldwell, N.J. 07006	—	323	42	P	4,200	4,200	2,750
California, University of; Berkeley, Calif. 94720:							
UC, Berkeley; Berkeley, Calif. 94720	16,413	12,640	2,205[20]	S	1,346	4,910	3,300
UC, Davis; Davis, Calif. 95616	9,688[1]	9,281[1]	2,000	S	1,350	4,850	2,400
UC, Hastings College of Law*; San Francisco, Calif. 94102	898	572	n.a.	S	n.a.	n.a.	n.a.
UC, Irvine*; Irvine, Calif. 92717	4,942	4,748	377	S	768	2,400	2,434
UC, Los Angeles; Los Angeles, Calif. 90024	17,610[3]	15,872[3]	2,150[20]	S	1,290	4,854	2,540
UC, Riverside; Riverside, Calif. 92521	2,302[1]	2,089[1]	435	S	1,307	4,871	3,000
UC, San Diego; La Jolla, Calif. 92093	7,010	5,309	870	S	1,332	4,896	4,000
UC, San Francisco*; San Francisco, Calif. 94143	1,151	1,257	800	S	1,282	4,425	5,400
UC, Santa Barbara; Santa Barbara, Calif. 93106	8,335	8,416	616[21]	S	1,677	5,037	2,972
UC, Santa Cruz; Santa Cruz, Calif. 95064	3,267	3,222	346	S	1,458	4,818	2,885
California Baptist College; Riverside, Calif. 92504	247	274	39	P/SB	1,505	1,505	1,100
California College of Arts and Crafts; Oakland, Calif. 94618	281	570	75[20]	P	5,690[22]	5,190[23]	1,155[11]
California College of Podiatric Medicine; San Francisco, Calif. 94115	283	76	20	P	9,000	9,000	4,000[6]
California Institute of Integral Studies; San Francisco, Calif. 94110	45	55	19	P	4,500	4,500	—
California Institute of Technology*; Pasadena, Calif. 91125	1,467	221	386	P	6,249	6,249	2,110
California Institute of the Arts*; Valencia, Calif. 91355	397	380	84	P	6,200	6,200	3,500
California Lutheran College*; Thousand Oaks, Calif. 91360	611	675	85	P/AL	4,900	4,900	2,400
California Maritime Academy; Vallejo, Calif. 94590	424	30	50	S	645	2,463	1,053
California Polytechnic State University*; San Luis Obispo, Calif. 93407[24]	9,269	6,594	820	S	n.a.	n.a.	n.a.
California School of Professional Psychology; San Francisco, Calif. 94123:							
Berkeley Campus*; Berkeley, Calif. 94704	99	150	30	P	7,440	7,440	—
Fresno Campus*; Fresno, Calif. 93712	78	46	11	P	7,740	7,740	—
Los Angeles Campus*; Los Angeles, Calif. 90057	97	175	24	P	7,440	7,440	—
San Diego Campus*; San Diego, Calif. 92121	130	123	19	P	7,740	7,740	—
California State Coll. (Pa.). *See* California Univ. of Pennsylvania							
California State College, Bakersfield; Bakersfield, Calif. 93311[24]	1,283	1,928	133	S	648	3,888	2,687
California State College, San Bernardino; San Bernardino, Calif. 92407[24]	1,216[1]	1,630[1]	212	S	727	3,275	2,628
California State Coll., Stanislaus; Turlock, Calif. 95381[24]	1,791	2,296	192	S	718	2,770	2,500
California State Polytechnic University, Pomona; Pomona, Calif. 91768[24]	9,347	6,284	989	S	700	2,600	2,970
California State University, Chico; Chico, Calif. 95929[25]	6,976[1]	7,153[1]	632	S	722	722[26]	2,484
California State University, Consortium of the*; Long Beach, Calif. 90815	2,500		n.a.	S	n.a.	n.a.	—
California St. Univ., Dominguez Hills*; Carson, Calif. 90747[24]	1,999	2,781	280	S	330	3,350	5,600

Institution and location	Enrollment		Faculty	Control	Tuition ($)		Rm/Bd ($)
	Male	Female			Res.	Nonres.	
California State Univ., Fresno; Fresno, Calif. 93740[25]	7,942[1]	8,351[1]	771	S	716	3,956	2,625
California State Univ., Fullerton; Fullerton, Calif. 92634[24]	7,297	8,206	700	S	694	3,286	5,300
California State Univ., Hayward; Hayward, Calif. 94542[24]	4,794	6,155	637	S	668	3,500	—
California State University, Long Beach*; Long Beach, Calif. 90840[24]	7,933	8,904	871	S	297	3,347	2,300
California State University, Los Angeles; Los Angeles, Calif. 90032[24]	5,549	6,969	610	S	690	3,930	—
California State University, Northridge*; Northridge, Calif. 91330[24]	12,177	14,646	1,000	S	450	3,150	7,200
California State University, Sacramento; Sacramento, Calif. 95819[24]	10,064	11,317	900	S	678	2,838	3,500
California Univ. of Pennsylvania; California, Pa. 15419	2,325[1]	2,146[1]	302	S	1,480	2,590	1,800
California Western School of Law; San Diego, Calif. 92101	464	167	25	P	6,900[3]	6,900[3]	—
Calumet College; Whiting, Ind. 46394	196[1]	217[1]	31	P/RC	2,723	2,723	—
Calvary Bible College; Kansas City, Mo. 64147	149	129	21	ND	2,240[3]	2,240[3]	2,160
Calvin College; Grand Rapids, Mich. 49506	1,741[1]	1,837[1]	215	P/CR	3,900	3,900	1,980
Cambridge College/Institute of Open Education; Cambridge, Mass. 02138	139[1]	194[1]	15	P	6,200	6,200	—
Cameron University; Lawton, Okla. 73505	1,430	1,358	235	S	568	1,549	1,700
Campbellsville College; Campbellsville, Ky. 42718	287	369	44	P/SB	3,000	3,000	1,520
Campbell University*; Buie's Creek. N.C. 27506	1,920	1,390	170	P/SB	4,022	4,072	1,585
Canadian Bible College*; Caronport, Sask., Canada S4T OH8	246	186	n.a.	P/CMA	n.a.	n.a.	n.a.
Canisius College*; Buffalo, N.Y. 14208	1,651	1,161	155	P	4,100	4,100	2,300
Capital University; Columbus, Ohio 43209	1,336[1]	1,201[1]	130	P/AL	6,335	6,335	2,620
Capitol Institute of Technology; Laurel, Md. 20708	390	31	26	P	3,507	3,507	—
Cardinal Newman College; Normandy, Mo. 63121	64	44	17	P/RC	4,100	4,100	2,330
Cardinal Stritch College; Milwaukee, Wis. 53217	443[1]	545[1]	50	P/RC	3,900	3,900	2,300
Caribbean Center for Advanced Studies; Santurce, P.R. 00940	50	124	9	P	2,665	2,665	—
Caribbean University College; Bayamón, P.R. 00619	1,006[1]	1,737[1]	33	P	1,425	1,425	—
Carleton College; Northfield, Minn. 55057	913[1]	944[1]	137	P	7,810	7,810	2,339
Carlow College; Pittsburgh, Pa. 15213	18[1]	652[1]	52	P/RC	5,740	5,740	3,145
Carnegie–Mellon University; Pittsburgh, Pa. 19213	3,770[1]	1,621[1]	471	P	8,400	8,400	3,344
Carroll College; Helena, Mont. 59625	447	627	80	P/RC	3,220	3,220	2,164
Carroll College; Waukesha, Wis. 53186	552[1]	608[1]	76	P/PUS	6,160[3]	6,160[3]	2,310
Carson–Newman College; Jefferson City, Tenn. 37760	783[1]	827[1]	94	P/B	3,300	3,400	1,650
Carthage College; Kenosha, Wis. 53140	470	518	75	P/LCA	4,865	4,865	2,130
Case Western Reserve University; Cleveland, Ohio 44106	4,384[1]	2,156[1]	1,800	P	7,650[3]	7,650[3]	3,050[3]
Castleton State College*; Castleton, Vt. 05735	581	724	n.a.	S	1,380	3,360	2,614
Catawba College; Salisbury, N.C. 28144	471	378	70	UCC	3,970	3,970	1,925
Cathedral College of the Immaculate Conception; Douglaston, N.Y. 11362	99[1]	—	17	RC	3,300	3,300	2,000
Catholic University of America, The; Washington, D.C. 20064	2,214[1]	2,059[1]	375	P	6,650[3]	6,650[3]	3,800[3]
Catholic University of Puerto Rico*; Ponce, P.R. 00731	3,048	5,524	n.a.	P/RC	n.a.	n.a.	n.a.
Cayey University College. *See* **Puerto Rico, University of**							
Cedar Crest College; Allentown, Pa. 18104	3	620	62	P	6,600[3]	6,600[3]	2,930[3]
Cedarville College; Cedarville, Ohio 45314	704	840	97	P/B	3,120	3,120	2,190
Centenary College*; Hackettstown, N.J. 07840	—	683	45	P	4,000	4,000	3,250
Centenary College of Louisiana; Shreveport, La. 71134	485	459	64	P/M	3,750	3,750	1,400
Center for Advanced Studies on Puerto Rico and the Caribbean; Old San Juan, P.R. 00904	40	23	2[27]	P	1,500	1,500	1,600
Center for Early Education, College of The*; Los Angeles, Calif. 90048	15	55	20	P	2,400	2,400	—
Central Arkansas, University of*; Conway, Ark. 72032	2,442	3,433	295	S	740	1,480	1,688
Central Baptist College*; Conway, Ark. 72032	100	81	18	P/B	800	800	1,200
Central Bible College; Springfield, Mo. 65803	556	340	33	P/AG	2,330	2,330	2,100
Central Christian College of the Bible; Moberly, Mo. 65270	60[1]	51[1]	7	P/ChC	1,340	1,340	1,600
Central Connecticut State University; New Britain, Conn. 06050	3,726[1]	3,350[1]	396	S	1,124	2,944	2,546
Central Florida, University of; Orlando, Fla. 32816	4,381	4,003	546	S	795[28]	2,355[28]	2,521
Central Methodist College; Fayette, Mo. 65248	296[1]	317[1]	48	P/UM	4,400	4,400	2,150
Central Michigan University; Mt. Pleasant, Mich. 48859	6,446[1]	7,813[1]	670	S	1,507	3,770	2,220
Central Missouri State University; Warrensburg, Mo. 64093	4,352[1]	4,001[1]	426	S	836	1,546	2,070
Central New England College of Technology*; Worcester, Mass. 01610	494	130	18	P	4,000	4,000	—
Central State University*; Edmond, Okla. 73034	5,521	6,788	350	S	500	1,500	1,500
Central State University; Wilberforce, Ohio 45384	1,029	1,123	134	S	1,290	2,301	2,607
Central University of Iowa; Pella, Iowa 50219	649[1]	829[1]	72	P/RCA	5,049	5,049	2,019
Central University of the Caribbean, Cayey School of Medicine*; Cayey, P.R. 00633	228	90	n.a.	P	n.a.	n.a.	n.a.
Central Washington University; Ellensburg, Wash. 98926	3,295	3,333	319	S	1,017	3,510	3,500
Central Wesleyan College; Central, S.C. 29630	160[1]	189[1]	28	P/W	4,120	4,120	2,150
Centre College of Kentucky; Danville, Ky. 40422	416[1]	343[1]	66	P/Pres	6,335	6,335	2,625
Chadron State College; Chadron, Neb. 69337	617	610	86	S	825	1,380	1,300
Chaminade University of Honolulu; Honolulu, Hawaii 96816	1,418	876	60	P/RC	3,600	3,600	5,800
Chapman College*; Orange, Calif. 92666	569	592	95	P	5,570	5,570	2,500
Charleston, The College of; Charleston, S.C. 29424	2,425	2,860	385	Mun/S	1,220	2,020	1,200
Charleston, The University of; Charleston, W. Va. 25304	452[1]	678[1]	58	P	3,498	3,498	2,470
Chatham College; Pittsburgh, Pa. 15102	—	547[1]	45	P	6,390	6,390	3,110
Chestnut Hill College; Philadelphia, Pa. 19118	—	924	45	P RC	3,900	3,900	2,575
Cheyney University of Pennsylvania*; Cheyney, Pa. 19319	1,050	850	175	S	1,450	2,400	1,550
Chicago, The University of; Chicago, Ill. 60637	5,882[1]	3,100[1]	1,055	P	8,824	8,824	6,950

Institution and location	Enrollment Male	Enrollment Female	Faculty	Control	Tuition ($) Res.	Tuition ($) Nonres.	Rm/Bd ($)
Chicago College of Osteopathic Medicine; Chicago, Ill. 60615	210	90	150	P	9,100	12,050	10,000
Chicago State University; Chicago, Ill. 60628	956	1,654	300	S	1,147	3,442	—
Christ College Irvine; Irvine, Calif. 92715	153 [1]	175 [1]	20	P/L	3,360	3,360	1,230
Christian Brothers College; Memphis, Tenn. 38104	751 [1]	514 [1]	71	P/RC	3,890	3,890	2,720
Christopher Newport College*; Newport News, Va. 23606	847	1,084	112	S	1,120	1,453	—
Church College of Hawaii. *See* Brigham Young University—Hawaii Campus							
Cincinnati, University of; Cincinnati, Ohio 45221	10,381	8,485	1,898	S	1,803	4,329	2,817
Cincinnati Bible College; Cincinnati, Ohio 45204	291 [1]	213 [1]	24	P	1,728	1,728	2,200
Circleville Bible College; Circleville, Ohio 43113	128 [1]	97 [1]	16	P/CC	2,550	2,550	1,850
Citadel, The*; Charleston, S.C. 29409	2,568	817	200	S	125	385	1,420
City College (NYC). *See* New York, City University of							
City University*; Bellevue, Wash. 98008	1,509	1,032	220	P	1,800	1,800	—
Claflin College*; Orangeburg, S.C. 29115	108	487	46	P/UM	2,552	2,552	1,665
Claremont Colleges:							
Claremont Graduate School*; Claremont, Calif. 91711	433	186	58	P	4,050	4,050	—
Claremont McKenna College; Claremont, Calif. 91711	559	252	73	P	8,650	8,650	2,300
Claremont Men's College. *See* Claremont McKenna College							
Harvey Mudd College; Claremont, Calif 91711	427	77	57	P	8,500 [3]	8,500 [3]	3,650 [3]
Pitzer College; Claremont, Calif. 91711	330 [1]	352 [1]	50	P	8,600	8,600	3,424
Pomona College*; Claremont, Calif. 91711	650	650	n.a.	P	6,250	6,250	2,650
Scripps College; Claremont, Calif. 91711	—	584	55	P	7,900	7,900	3,560
Clarion State College. *See* Clarion University of Pennsylvania							
Clarion University of Pennsylvania; Clarion, Pa. 16214	2,600	2,900	425	S	1,750	2,500	1,800
Clark College; Atlanta, Ga. 30314	692 [1]	1,244 [1]	128	P	3,350	3,350	1,935
Clarke College; Dubuque, Iowa 52001	249	647	50	P/RC	5,000	5,000	2,050
Clarkson College of Technology. *See* Clarkson University							
Clarkson University; Potsdam, N.Y. 13676	2,953	890	244	P	7,690	7,690	3,400
Clark University; Worcester, Mass. 01610	1,052 [1]	1,202 [1]	154	P	8,400	8,400	2,800
Cleary College; Ypsilanti, Mich. 48197	225 [1]	864 [1]	48	P	2,925	2,925	1,700
Clemson University; Clemson, S.C. 29631	6,356 [1]	4,450 [1]	721	S	1,652	3,580	1,990
Cleveland Chiropractic College; Kansas City, Mo. 64113	311	83	n.a.	P	5,400	5,400	n.a.
Cleveland Institute of Art, The; Cleveland, Ohio 44106	232	249	50	P	4,950	4,950	3,390
Cleveland Institute of Music, The; Cleveland, Ohio 44106	97 [1]	114 [1]	25	P	7,050 [3]	7,050 [3]	3,050
Cleveland State University; Cleveland, Ohio 44115	5,368 [1]	3,856 [1]	522	S	1,635	3,270	2,290
Clinch Valley College. *See* Virginia, University of							
Coe College; Cedar Rapids, Iowa 52402	505 [1]	540 [1]	75	P/Pres	5,810	5,810	2,020
Cogswell College; San Francisco, Calif. 94108	320	49	22	P	3,600	3,600	—
Coker College; Hartsville, S.C. 29550	144	199	45	P	4,600 [3]	4,600 [3]	2,410
Colby College; Waterville, Me. 04901	885 [1]	819 [1]	109	P	8,660 [3]	8,660 [3]	3,320
Colby-Sawyer College; New London, N.H. 03257	—	405	50	P	7,300	7,300	3,130
Colegio Universitario Metropolitano. *See* Ana G. Méndez Educational Foundation							
Coleman College*; La Mesa, Calif. 92041	645	206	n.a.	P	n.a.	n.a.	n.a.
Colgate University; Hamilton, N.Y. 13346	1,423	1,127	169	P	9,075	9,075	3,265
College Misericordia; Dallas, Pa. 18612	150	692	70	P/RC	1,850	1,850	1,125
Colorado, University of; Boulder, Colo. 80302:							
U. of Colorado at Boulder*; Boulder, Colo. 80309	11,934	10,243	939	S	981	4,490	2,062
U. of Colorado at Colorado Springs; Colorado Springs, Colo. 80933	1,402 [1]	1,445 [1]	160	S	950	3,800	—
U. of Colorado Health Sciences Center; Denver, Colo. 80262	507 [1]	922 [1]	1,015	S	6,046	26,337	—
U. of Colorado at Denver; Denver, Colo. 80202	2,674	2,366	367	S	1,017	4,213	—
Colorado College, The*; Colorado Springs, Colo. 80907	983	962	137	P	6,400	6,400	2,100
Colorado School of Mines; Golden, Colo. 80401	2,357 [1]	574 [1]	210	S	2,310	6,318	2,730
Colorado State University; Fort Collins, Colo. 80523	8,363 [1]	7,804 [1]	1,120	S	1,446	4,698	2,793
Colorado Technical College; Colorado Springs, Colo. 80907	353	77	34	P	2,970	2,970	—
Columbia Bible College; Columbia, S.C. 29230	510	265	25	P	3,000	3,000	2,000
Columbia Christian College; Portland, Ore. 97220	112	103	18	P	3,420	3,420	2,175
Columbia College*; Chicago, Ill. 60605	1,369	1,171	39	P	3,000	3,000	—
Columbia College*; Columbia, Mo. 65216	255	307	45	P	4,425	4,425	2,200
Columbia College*; Columbia, S.C. 29203	—	822	66	P/M	3,700	3,700	2,100
Columbia College-Hollywood; Los Angeles, Calif. 90038	243	87	38 [29]	P	3,000	3,000	4,070
Columbia Union College; Takoma Park, Md. 20912	402	513	65	SDA	4,810	4,810	2,350
Columbia University in the City of New York*; New York, N.Y. 10027	11,669	3,020	1,727	P	8,042	8,042	5,800
Columbus College; Columbus, Ga. 31993	978	1,288	202	S	852	2,559	—
Combs College of Music; Bryn Mawr, Pa. 19010	47 [3]	40 [3]	8	P	4,070	4,070	2,550
Concord College; Athens, W. Va. 24712	758 [1]	920 [1]	89	S	800 [3]	2,200 [3]	2,237
Concordia College; Ann Arbor, Mich. 48105	215	255	42	L	3,448	3,448	2,648
Concordia College; Bronxville, N.Y. 10708	200 [1]	212 [1]	35	L	3,690	3,690	2,545
Concordia College; Moorhead, Minn. 56560	1,037 [1]	1,406 [1]	148	P/AL	5,590	5,590	1,910
Concordia College; River Forest, Ill. 60305	356 [1]	704 [1]	88	P/L	3,700	3,700	2,355
Concordia College*; St. Paul, Minn. 55104	321	342	54	P/L	3,855	3,855	1,830
Concordia College-Wisconsin; Mequon, Wis. 53092	261 [1]	346 [1]	30	P/L	3,600	3,600	2,200
Concordia Lutheran College; Austin, Tex. 78705	186	179	n.a.	P/L	2,650	2,650	2,375
Concordia Teachers College; Seward, Neb. 68434	396 [1]	495 [1]	87	P/L	3,744	3,744	2,044

Institution and location	Enrollment		Faculty	Control	Tuition ($)		Rm/Bd ($)
	Male	Female			Res.	Nonres.	
Connecticut, University of; Storrs, Conn. 06268	8,003[1]	8,450[1]	1,208	S	876	3,280	2,174
Connecticut College; New London, Conn. 06320	624	1,026	138	P	9,500	9,500	2,750
Conservatory of Music of Puerto Rico; Hato Rey, P.R. 00918	183[3]	76[3]	22	S	230	230	—
Converse College; Spartanburg, S.C. 29301	—	716[1]	75	P	8,200[4]	8,200[4]	—
Cooper Union, The; New York, N.Y. 10003	700	300	55	P	—	—	—
Coppin State College*; Baltimore, Md. 21216	490	1,198	113	S	1,135	2,175	—
Cornell College; Mt. Vernon, Iowa 52314	516[1]	446[1]	65	P	6,166	6,166	2,446
Cornell University; Ithaca, N.Y. 14853	10,159[1]	7,492[1]	1,534	P	3,740[30]	6,050[30]	3,250
Cornish Institute; Seattle, Wash. 98102	196[1]	341[1]	11	P	4,850	4,850	2,500
Corpus Christi State University. *See* South Texas, University System of							
Covenant College; Lookout Mountain, Tenn./Ga. 37350	232[1]	240[1]	34	P/PUS	4,440[3]	4,440[3]	2,500[3]
Cranbrook Academy of Art; Bloomfield Hills, Mich. 48013	73	70	9	P	5,600	5,600	2,600
Creative Studies, Center for; Detroit, Mich. 48202	307[1]	241[1]	40	P	5,200	5,200	2,206[11]
Creighton University; Omaha, Neb. 68178	3,406[1]	2,895[1]	991	P	4,800	4,800	2,402
Criswell Bible College. *See* Criswell Center for Biblical Studies							
Criswell Center for Biblical Studies; Dallas, Tex. 75201	286	29	16	P/SB	1,150	1,150	—
Culver-Stockton College; Canton, Mo. 63435	316	333	38	P	4,280	4,280	1,840
Cumberland College; Williamsburg, Ky. 40769	855[1]	1,159[1]	92	P/SB	2,528	2,528	1,676
Curry College*; Milton, Mass. 02186	425	365	66	P	6,300	6,300	3,500
Curtis Institute of Music, The; Philadelphia, Pa. 19103	92	75	70	P	—	—	4,500
C. W. Post Center. *See* Long Island Univ. Center							
Daemen College; Amherst, N.Y. 14226	373[1]	821[1]	73	P	4,900	4,900	2,600
Dakota Northwestern Univ.; Minot, N.D. 58701	981[1]	1,510[1]	125	S	891	1,608	1,380
Dakota State College; Madison, S.D. 57042	454[1]	636[1]	59	S	519	2,000	1,560
Dakota Wesleyan University; Mitchell, S.D. 57301	188	305	41	P/M	3,280	3,280	2,625
Dallas, University of*; Irving, Tex. 75061	852	593	94	P/RC	1,815	1,815	1,160
Dallas Baptist College; Dallas, Tex. 75211	397[3]	342[3]	51	P/B	3,150	3,150	2,322
Dallas Bible College; Dallas, Tex. 75228	143	69	10	P	2,560	2,560	1,856
Dallas Christian College; Dallas, Tex. 75234	62[1]	44[1]	11	P/ChC	n.a.	n.a.	n.a.
Dana College; Blair, Neb. 68008	258[1]	237[1]	34	P/AL	4,500[3]	4,500[3]	1,955
Daniel Webster College; Nashua, N.H. 03063	657	443	19	P	5,590	5,590	1,300
Dartmouth College; Hanover, N.H. 03755	2,032	1,501	495	P	9,810[3]	9,810[3]	1,992
David Lipscomb College; Nashville, Tenn. 37203	1,049	1,075	116	P/CC	2,832	2,832	2,085
Davidson College; Davidson, N.C. 28036	830	525	110	P/PUS	9,090[4]	9,090[4]	—
Davis and Elkins College; Elkins, W. Va. 26241	378[1]	460[1]	51	P/Pres	4,828	4,828	2,398
Dayton, University of; Dayton, Ohio 45469	3,942	2,939	375	P/RC	4,500	4,500	2,370
Defiance College, The; Defiance, Ohio 43512	358	329	50	P	4,700	4,700	2,200
Delaware, University of; Newark, Del. 19716	6,155[1]	7,555[1]	793	S[31]	1,590	4,200	2,390
Delaware Law School of Widener University*; Wilmington, Del. 19803	595	218	28	P	4,100	4,100	—
Delaware State College*; Dover, Del. 19901	757	876	141	S	650	1,600	1,850
Delaware Valley College of Science and Agriculture; Doylestown, Pa. 18901	813[1]	378[1]	71	P	4,900	4,900	2,400
DeLourdes College; Des Plaines, Ill. 60016	—	62	n.a.	P/RC	n.a.	n.a.	n.a.
Delta State University*; Cleveland, Miss. 38733	1,011	1,183	157	S	n.a.	n.a.	n.a.
Denison University; Granville, Ohio 43023	1,028	1,020	160	P	7,700[3]	7,700[3]	2,710
Denver, University of; Denver, Colo. 80208	2,784[1]	2,807[1]	439	P	6,984[3]	6,984[3]	3,000[3]
DePaul University; Chicago, Ill. 60604	6,408	6,037	402	P	4,950	4,950	3,452
Goodman School of Drama; Chicago, Ill. 60614	101	105	19	P/RC	5,265	5,265	2,793
De Paul University; Greencastle, Ind. 46135	1,127[1]	1,286[1]	155	P/M	7,100	7,100	2,970
Deree College, The American College of Greece; Aghia Paraskevi, Greece GR-153 10	453	759	47	P	1,240	1,240	534
Detroit, University of; Detroit, Mich. 48221	2,325[1]	1,180[1]	250	P/RC	5,400	5,400	2,300
Detroit Bible College. *See* William Tyndale College							
Detroit College of Law; Detroit, Mich. 48226	265	141	27	P	4,800	4,800	—
DeVry Institute of Technology; Atlanta, Ga. 30341	2,041	463	57	P	3,500	3,500	—
DeVry Institute of Technology; Chicago, Ill. 60618	4,082[1]	759[1]	n.a.	P	3,200	3,200	—
DeVry Institute of Technology; Columbus, Ohio 43209	2,942	444	73	P	1,725	1,725	—
DeVry Institute of Technology; Irving, Tex. 75062	1,753[1]	274[1]	55	P	4,500	4,500	—
DeVry Institute of Technology; Kansas City, Mo. 64131	1,622	224	50	P	3,500	3,500	—
DeVry Institute of Technology; Phoenix, Ariz. 85016	3,699	542	72	P	3,500	3,500	—
Dickinson College*; Carlisle, Pa. 17013	805	940	145	P	5,840	5,840	2,150
Dickinson School of Law; Carlisle, Pa. 17013	311	194	21	P	4,900[3]	4,900[3]	2,600
Dickinson State College*; Dickinson, N.D. 58601	434	549	75	S	735	1,296	1,600
Dillard University*; New Orleans, La. 70122	320	822	99	P	3,000	3,000	2,100
District of Columbia, University of the; Washington, D.C. 20008	5,484	6,904	611	S	364	1,614	—
Divine Word College; Epworth, Iowa 52045	86	—	21	P	3,500	3,500	1,200
Doane College; Crete, Neb. 68333	299	316	43	P	4,175	4,175	1,710
Dr. Martin Luther College; New Ulm, Minn. 56073	173	428	68	P/EL	1,775	1,775	1,550
Dr. William M. Scholl Coll. of Podiatric Medicine; Chicago, Ill. 60610	439	70	154	P	9,500	9,500	—
Dominican College of Blauvelt; Orangeburg, N.Y. 10962	577	1,152	60	P/Ind	3,150	3,150	2,800
Dominican College of San Rafael; San Rafael, Calif. 94901	105[1]	333[1]	62	P/RC	5,200	5,200	3,600
Dordt College*; Sioux Center, Iowa 51250	503	595	68	P/CR	3,400	3,400	1,410
Dowling College; Oakdale, N.Y. 11786	745[1]	728[1]	66	P	4,350	4,350	2,748

Institution and location	Enrollment		Faculty	Control	Tuition ($)		Rm/Bd ($)
	Male	Female			Res.	Nonres.	
Drake University; Des Moines, Iowa 50311	2,826[1]	3,182[1]	300	P	6,200	6,200	2,800
Drew University*; Madison, N.J. 07940	779	853	130	P/UM	4,700	4,700	1,820
Drexel University; Philadelphia, Pa. 19104	5,217	2,299	375	P	5,268[3]	5,268[3]	2,800
Dropsie College, The; Merion, Pa. 19066	45	1	5	P	4,700	4,700	—
Drury College; Springfield, Mo. 65802	359	460	76	P/ChC	4,250	4,250	1,990
Dubuque, Univ. of–Coll. of Liberal Arts; Dubuque, Iowa 52001	415[1]	200[1]	52	P/Pres	4,500	4,500	1,900
Duke University*; Durham, N.C. 27706	5,313	3,737	1,442	P	6,780	6,780	3,441
Duquesne University; Pittsburgh, Pa. 15282	2,269	2,328	295	P/RC	5,430	5,430	2,610
Dyke College; Cleveland, Ohio 44114	288	613	26	P	2,850	2,850	—
D'Youville College; Buffalo, N.Y. 14201	139[1]	831[1]	72	P	4,550	4,550	2,470
Earlham College*; Richmond, Ind. 47374	515	603	76	P/SOF	6,333	6,333	2,180
East Carolina Univ. *See* North Carolina, Univ. System of							
East Central Oklahoma State University; Ada, Okla. 74820	1,469[1]	1,689[1]	183	S	450	1,000	1,800
Eastern College; St. Davids, Pa. 19087	201	326	42	P/AB	5,190	5,190	2,120
Eastern Connecticut State University; Willimantic, Conn. 06226	1,181[1]	1,296[1]	124	S	650	2,120	2,542
Eastern Illinois University; Charleston, Ill. 61920	4,380	5,015	668	S	966	2,898	2,060
Eastern Kentucky University; Richmond, Ky. 40475	4,554[1]	5,494[1]	670	S	900	2,560	2,000
Eastern Mennonite College; Harrisonburg, Va. 22801	300[3]	487[3]	66	P/Men	4,820	4,820	2,176
Eastern Michigan University; Ypsilanti, Mich. 48197	8,480[1]	10,409[1]	620	S	1,098	2,688	2,490
Eastern Montana College; Billings, Mont. 59101	964	1,411	160	S	768	1,956	2,500
Eastern Nazarene College; Quincy, Mass. 02170	318[1]	419[1]	69	P/Naz	3,996[3]	3,996[3]	2,300[3]
Eastern New Mexico University*; Portales, N.M. 88130	1,760	1,815	152	S	714	2,000	1,702
Eastern Oregon State College; La Grande, Ore. 97850	675[1]	675[1]	148	S	1,338	1,338	2,200
Eastern Washington University*; Cheney, Wash. 99004	3,580	3,570	365	S	1,017	4,218	2,208
East Stroudsburg University; East Stroudsburg, Pa. 18301	1,623[1]	1,755[1]	226	S	1,650	2,760	1,734
East Tennessee State University; Johnson City, Tenn. 37614[12]	3,127[1]	3,735[1]	427	S	786	2,544	1,600
East Texas Baptist University; Marshall, Tex. 75670	271	263	49	P/SB	2,400	2,400	2,587
East Texas State University*; Commerce, Tex. 75428	2,368	2,233	325	S	440	1,540	1,940
East Texas State University—Texarkana; Texarkana, Tex. 75505	407	724	30	S	450	1,200	—
Eckerd College; St. Petersburg, Fla. 33733	503[1]	526[1]	74	P/Pres	6,685	6,685	2,700
Edgewood College; Madison, Wis. 53711	64	299	64	P/RC	4,200	4,200	2,220
Edinboro University of Pennsylvania; Edinboro, Pa. 16444	2,258[1]	2,474[1]	339	S	1,480	2,590	1,690
Edward Waters College*; Jacksonville, Fla. 32209	274	593	39	P/AME	2,100	2,100	7,000
Elizabeth City State University. *See* North Carolina, University System of							
Elizabethtown College; Elizabethtown, Pa. 17022	563[1]	907[1]	103	P/CB	5,260	5,260	2,490
Elmhurst College*; Elmhurst, Ill. 60126	1,426	1,973	102	P	4,040	4,040	2,260
Elmira College; Elmira, N.Y. 14901	352[1]	677[1]	70	P	5,990	5,990	2,380
Elon College; Elon College, N.C. 27244	1,513[1]	1,202[1]	92	P/UCC	3,250[3]	3,250[3]	1,275[3]
Embry-Riddle Aeronautical University; Daytona Beach, Fla. 32014	4,304[1]	315[1]	250	P	4,313	4,313	2,711
Prescott Campus; Prescott, Ariz. 86301	704	93	42	P	3,450	3,450	2,000
Emerson College; Boston, Mass. 02116	745[1]	1,028[1]	84	P	6,990	6,990	4,450
Emmanuel Bible College; Kitchener, Ont., Canada N2A 2H2	90	75	8	P/MC	1,500	1,500	1,800
Emmanuel College; Boston, Mass. 02115	5	608	60	P/RC	5,700	5,700	3,100
Emory and Henry College; Emory, Va. 24327	416	308	60	UM	3,936	3,936	2,265
Emory University; Atlanta, Ga. 30322	3,713	3,114	1,172	P	7,550	7,550	3,050
Emporia State University; Emporia, Kan. 66801	1,678[1]	1,963[1]	230	S	940[3]	1,960[3]	1,950
Erskine College; Due West, S.C. 29639	272[1]	260[1]	53	P/RP	4,330	4,330	2,450
Eureka College; Eureka, Ill. 61530	264[1]	234[1]	32	P	3,350	3,350	2,150
Evangel College*; Springfield, Mo. 65802	720	872	76	P/AG	2,600	2,600	2,020
Evansville, University of; Evansville, Ind. 47702	1,304[1]	1,544[1]	197	P/UM	5,478	5,478	2,568
Evergreen State College, The; Olympia, Wash. 98505	2,280[1]		140	S	1,017	3,486	993
Fairfield University; Fairfield, Conn. 06430	1,430[1]	1,457[1]	175	P/RC	6,100	6,100	3,400
Fairleigh Dickinson University*:							
Madison, N.J. 07940; Rutherford, N.J. 07070; Teaneck, N.J. 07666	3,260	2,915	525	P	5,024	5,024	2,925
Fairmont State College; Fairmont, W. Va. 26554	2,229[1]	2,644[1]	171	S	754	2,124	2,152
Faith Baptist Bible College; Ankeny, Iowa 50021	197[1]	210[1]	17	P/B	2,600	2,600	1,980
Fashion Institute of Technology; New York, N.Y. 10001[32]	628	3,116	201	S	1,350[3]	2,700[3]	3,200[3]
Fayetteville State U. *See* North Carolina, U. System of							
Felician College; Lodi, N.J. 07644	—	231	47	P	2,720	2,720	—
Ferris State College; Big Rapids, Mich. 49307	6,409[1]	4,358[1]	480	S	1,671	3,381	2,190
Ferrum College; Ferrum, Va. 24088	813	446	84	P/M	3,350	3,350	1,725
Fielding Institute*; Santa Barbara, Calif. 93101	360		n.a.	P	n.a.	n.a.	n.a.
Findlay College; Findlay, Ohio 45840	420[1]	419[1]	61	P	4,740	4,740	2,181
Fisk University; Nashville, Tenn. 37203	219	430	55	P	6,325	6,535	2,085
Fitchburg State College; Fitchburg, Mass. 01420	1,532[1]	2,255[1]	233	S	936	2,976	2,080
Flagler College*; St. Augustine, Fla. 32084	425	525	38	P	2,830	2,830	1,800
Florida, University of; Gainesville, Fla. 32611	17,190[1]	12,335[1]	3,006	S	850	2,735	2,500
Florida A&M University*; Tallahassee, Fla. 32308	1,912	1,897	372	S	795	2,355	924
Florida Atlantic University; Boca Raton, Fla. 33431	4,560	4,940	415	S	900	2,400	2,450
Florida Institute of Technology; Melbourne, Fla. 32901	2,505	835	221	P	2,460	2,460	2,190
Florida International University; Miami, Fla. 33199	7,125	8,124	463	S	883	2,527	1,954
Florida Memorial College*; Miami, Fla. 33054	419	508	44	P/B	4,060	4,060	1,620
Florida Southern College*; Lakeland, Fla. 33802	847	1,013	102	P/UM	2,430	2,430	1,850

Institution and location	Enrollment		Faculty	Control	Tuition ($)		Rm/Bd ($)
	Male	Female			Res.	Nonres.	
Florida State University; Tallahassee, Fla. 32304	9,848 [1]	11,217 [1]	1,140	S	848	2,408	2,283
Fontbonne College*; St. Louis, Mo. 63105	173	732	62	P	4,100	4,100	2,200
Fordham University; Bronx, N.Y. 10458	3,263 [1]	3,673 [1]	500	P/RC	5,950	5,950	3,200
Fort Hays State University; Hays, Kan. 67601	2,379 [1]	3,097 [1]	283	S	1,020	2,040	1,860
Fort Lauderdale College*; Fort Lauderdale, Fla. 33301	598	493	28	P	1,822	1,822	4,500
Fort Lewis College; Durango, Colo. 81301	2,125 [1]	1,560 [1]	160	S	698	3,012	1,960
Fort Valley State College; Fort Valley, Ga. 31030	713	868	117	S	990	2,466	1,710
Framingham State College*; Framingham, Mass. 01701	1,026	2,045	161	S	845	2,792	1,743
Francis Marion College; Marion, S.C. 29571	1,090 [1]	1,110 [1]	102	S	940 [3]	1,880 [3]	2,300 [3]
Franklin and Marshall College; Lancaster, Pa. 17604	1,000	950	134	P	8,160	8,160	2,890
Franklin College of Indiana; Franklin, Ind. 46131	327 [1]	258 [1]	43	P/AB	5,390	5,390	n.a.
Franklin Pierce College*; Rindge, N.H. 03461	996	838	52	P	5,850	5,850	2,640
Franklin University; Columbus, Ohio 43215	2,354 [1]	2,503 [1]	63	P	2,550	2,550	—
Freed-Hardeman College; Henderson, Tenn. 38340	553	615	83	P/CC	2,830	2,830	2,120
Free Will Baptist Bible College; Nashville, Tenn. 37205	186 [1]	186 [1]	20	P/FWB	1,920	1,920	2,020
Fresno Pacific College*; Fresno, Calif. 93702	357	464	28	P/MB	3,600	3,600	2,085
Friends Bible College; Haviland, Kan. 67059	48	50	10	P/SOF	3,500	3,500	1,550
Friends University; Wichita, Kan. 67213	300	290	44	P/SOF	3,900	3,900	1,790
Frostburg State College; Frostburg, Md. 21532	1,416 [1]	1,390 [1]	184	S	1,030	2,100	2,170
Furman University; Greenville, S.C. 29613	1,100	1,032	158	P/B	4,800	4,800	1,312
Gallaudet College; Washington, D.C. 20002	616 [1]	1,002 [1]	283	P	1,684 [32]	2,526 [33]	2,846
Gannon University; Erie, Pa. 16541	1,500 [1]	1,202 [1]	137	P/RC	4,400	4,400	2,115
Gardner-Webb College; Boiling Springs, N.C. 28017	762 [1]	746 [1]	95	P/SB	3,530	3,530	1,870
General Motors Institute. *See* GMI Engineering and Management Institute							
Geneva College; Beaver Falls, Pa. 15010	658 [1]	412 [1]	52	P/RP	4,470	4,470	2,340
George Fox College; Newberg, Ore. 97132	272 [1]	385 [1]	41	P/SOF	5,380	5,380	2,595
George Mason University; Fairfax, Va. 22030	6,570 [1]	7,975 [1]	460	S	1,512 [3]	2,928 [3]	3,382
Georgetown College; Georgetown, Ky. 40324	467 [1]	446 [1]	67	P/SB	3,582	3,582	2,876
Georgetown University; Washington, D.C. 20057	5,250 [1]	4,141 [1]	1,015	P/RC	8,500 [3]	8,500 [3]	3,340
George Washington University, The*; Washington, D.C. 20052	9,248	7,721	861	P	6,248	6,248	3,690
George Williams College; Downers Grove, Ill. 60515	185	339	55	P	5,382	5,382	2,304
Georgia, University of; Athens, Ga. 30602	10,631 [1]	10,532 [1]	1,802	S	1,407	3,669	2,248
Georgia College*; Milledgeville, Ga. 31061	1,469	1,998	130	S	771	2,061	1,395
Georgia Institute of Technology; Atlanta, Ga. 30332	8,040	2,128	n.a.	S	1,401	4,161	2,850
Georgian Court College; Lakewood, N.J. 08701	10	623	56	P	3,900	3,900	2,450
Georgia Southern College; Statesboro, Ga. 30460	2,782 [1]	3,037 [1]	364	S	852	2,559	1,860
Georgia Southwestern College; Americus, Ga. 31709	839 [3]	1,040 [3]	111	S	1,053	2,760	1,731
Georgia State University; Atlanta, Ga. 30303	9,486 [1]	12,026 [1]	738	S	1,185	3,885	—
Gettysburg College; Gettysburg, Pa. 17325	944	914	132	P/L	7,740	7,740	2,520
Glassboro State College; Glassboro, N.J. 08028	2,342	2,852	374	S	960	1,560	2,450
Glenville State College; Glenville, W. Va. 26351	560	603	73	S	800	2,200	2,264
GMI Engineering & Management Institute; Flint, Mich. 48502	1,752 [1]	741 [1]	145	P	4,400	4,400	2,000
Goddard College; Plainfield, Vt. 05667	126	124	13	P	6,500	6,500	2,400
Golden Gate University; San Francisco, Calif. 94105	912 [1]	642 [1]	71	P	3,000	3,000	—
Goldey Beacom College; Wilmington, Del. 19808	184	542	28	P	3,150 [3]	3,150 [3]	1,950
Gonzaga University; Spokane, Wash. 99258	1,606 [1]	1,206 [1]	151	P	5,800	5,800	2,620
Goodman School of Drama. *See* **DePaul University**							
Gordon College; Wenham, Mass. 01984	438 [3]	597 [3]	52	P	6,015	6,015	2,916
Goshen College*; Goshen, Ind. 46526	428	585	70	P/Men	4,165	4,165	1,925
Goucher College; Towson, Md. 21204	—	902 [1]	90	P	7,700	7,700	3,960
Governors State University; University Park, Ill. 60466	339 [1]	367 [1]	145	S	966	2,898	—
Grace Bible College; Grand Rapids, Mich. 49509	61 [1]	70 [1]	10	P/GGF	1,780	1,780	2,100
Grace College*; Winona Lake, Ind. 46590	327	383	39	P/FGB	3,286	3,286	2,186
Grace College of the Bible; Omaha, Neb. 68108	159	131	21	P/ID	2,640	2,640	1,920
Graceland College; Lamoni, Iowa 50140	415	459	70	P	4,410	4,410	1,935
Graduate School and University Center (NYC). *See* New York, City University of							
Grambling State University; Grambling, La. 71245	3,850		195	S	620	1,300	944
Grand Canyon College; Phoenix, Ariz. 85017	455	507	55	P/SB	2,490	2,490	1,700
Grand Rapids Baptist College; Grand Rapids, Mich. 49505	313 [1]	358 [1]	34	P/B	3,310	3,310	2,466
Grand Valley State College; Allendale, Mich. 49401	2,920 [34]	3,299 [34]	210	S	2,370	3,582	2,630
Grand View College; Des Moines, Iowa 50316	440 [1]	502 [1]	68	P/LCA	3,990 [3]	3,990 [3]	1,850
Grantham College of Engineering*; Los Angeles, Calif. 90034	741	7	n.a.	P	700	700	—
Gratz College; Philadelphia, Pa. 19141	59 [1]	152 [1]	7	P/J	575	575	—
Great Falls, College of; Great Falls, Mont. 59405	576	642	36	P/RC	3,300	3,300	1,800
Great Lakes Bible College; Lansing, Mich. 48901	85	59	11	CC	1,950	1,950	2,213
Green Mountain College; Poultney, Vt. 05764	133 [1]	178 [1]	18	P	5,302	5,302	3,150
Greensboro College; Greensboro, N.C. 27401	189	332	33	P/M	4,130	4,130	2,170
Greenville College; Greenville, Ill. 62246	278 [1]	324 [1]	47	P/FM	4,587	4,587	2,170
Grinnell College; Grinnell, Iowa 50112	576	596	105	P	7,805	7,805	2,345
Grove City College; Grove City, Pa. 16127	1,110 [1]	1,041 [1]	101	P	3,060	3,060	1,800
Guam, University of; Mangilao, Guam 96913	861	943	171	S	684	1,548	2,200

Institution and location	Enrollment Male	Enrollment Female	Faculty	Control	Tuition ($) Res.	Tuition ($) Nonres.	Rm/Bd ($)
Guilford College; Greensboro, N.C. 27410	720[1]	541[1]	83	P/SOF	5,114[3]	5,114[3]	2,474[3]
Gulf Coast Bible College; Houston, Tex. 77270	191	132	20	P/CG	2,700	2,700	1,800
Gustavus Adolphus College; St. Peter, Minn. 56082	912	1,129	181	P/LCA	8,150[4]	8,150[4]	—
Gwynedd Mercy College; Gwynedd Valley, Pa. 19437	257	1,820	110	P/RC	4,100	4,100	2,600
Hahnemann University*; Philadelphia, Pa. 19102	865	1,122	395	P	n.a.	n.a.	—
Hamilton College; Clinton, N.Y. 13323	895	685	135	P	9,300	9,300	3,050
Hamline University; St. Paul, Minn. 55104	893[3]	763[3]	88	P/UM	6,400	6,400	2,550
Hampden-Sydney College; Hampden-Sydney, Va. 23943	787[1]	2[1]	56	P	7,050	7,050	2,310
Hampshire College; Amherst, Mass. 01002	480	495	100	P	10,175	10,175	3,245
Hampton Institute; Hampton, Va. 23668	1,611[1]	2,452[1]	220	P	3,225	3,225	1,620
Hannibal-LaGrange College; Hannibal, Mo. 63401	234[1]	340[1]	31	P/SB	2,780	2,780	1,666
Hanover College; Hanover, Ind. 47243	491[1]	493[1]	70	P/Pres	3,890	3,890	2,025
Harding University; Searcy, Ark. 72143	1,234	1,250	160	P/CC	3,300	3,300	2,100
Hardin-Simmons University; Abilene, Tex. 79698	933[1]	994[1]	95	P	3,140	3,140	2,120
Harris-Stowe State College; St. Louis, Mo. 63103	248	407	28	S	650	1,241	—
Hartford, University of*; West Hartford, Conn. 06117	2,527	2,117	328	P	6,000	6,000	3,610
Hartford Graduate Center, The*; Hartford, Conn. 06120	1,108	264	18	P	n.a.	n.a.	—
Hartwick College; Oneonta, N.Y. 13820	589[1]	770[1]	102	P	7,450[3]	7,450[3]	2,800[3]
Harvard University*; Cambridge, Mass. 02138	10,020	6,007	3,595	P	8,195	8,195	3,905
Radcliffe College*; Cambridge, Mass. 02167	—	2,377	—	P	8,195	8,195	n.a.
Harvey Mudd College. *See* Claremont Colleges							
Hastings College; Hastings, Neb. 68901	360[1]	388[1]	56	P/Pres	4,550	4,550	2,000
Haverford College; Haverford, Pa. 19041	642[1]	398[1]	113	P	8,640	8,640	3,130
Hawaii, University of, at Hilo; Hilo, Hawaii 96720[35]	1,328[1]	1,400[1]	183	S	760	2,870	2,000
Hawaii, University of, at Manoa; Honolulu, Hawaii 96822[35]	7,060[1]	8,083[1]	1,551	S	850	3,060	5,257
Hawaii Loa College; Kaneohe, Hawaii 96744	188	171	25	P	4,400	4,400	3,000
Hawaii Pacific College; Honolulu, Hawaii 96813	1,929[1]	1,105[1]	72	P	3,050	3,050	3,800
Hawthorne College*; Antrim, N.H. 03440[7]	309	61	16	P	4,640	4,640	1,550
Health Sciences, University of/College of Osteopathic Medicine*; Kansas City, Mo. 64124	519	103	50	P	11,000	11,000	—
Health Sciences, Univ. of—The Chicago Medical School, *See* Illinois, Univ. of							
Hebrew College*; Brookline, Mass. 02146	58	87	12	P	810	810	—
Heidelberg College; Tiffin, Ohio 44883	455	333	63	P	6,230	6,230	1,100
Henderson State University; Arkadelphia, Ark. 71923	1,013[1]	1,111[1]	117	S	810	1,620	1,480
Hendrix College; Conway, Ark. 72032	507	483	62	P/M	3,900	3,900	1,785
Herbert H. Lehman College. *See* New York, City University of							
High Point College; High Point, N.C. 27262	643[1]	716[1]	55	P/UM	3,600	3,600	1,790
Hillsdale College; Hillsdale, Mich. 49242	488[1]	497[1]	72	P	5,800	5,800	2,830
Hiram College; Hiram, Ohio 44234	585[1]	647[1]	82	P	6,424	6,424	2,019
Hobart and William Smith Colleges; Geneva, N.Y. 14456	1,072	753	135	P	8,835[3]	8,835[3]	3,303[3]
Hofstra University; Hempstead, N.Y. 11550	5,249	5,180	364	P	5,050	5,050	2,150
Hollins College; Hollins College, Va. 24020	9[1]	856[1]	72	P	7,100	7,100	3,300
Holy Apostles College*. Cromwell, Conn. 06416	113	28	20	P/RC	4,550	4,550	4,550
Holy Cross, College of the; Worcester, Mass. 01610	1,275[1]	1,261[1]	172	P/RC	7,700[3]	7,700[3]	3,300[3]
Holy Family College*; Mission San Jose, Calif. 94538	n.a.	n.a.	n.a.	P/RC	n.a.	n.a.	n.a.
Holy Family College; Philadelphia, Pa. 19114	76	527	49	P	3,600	3,600	—
Holy Names College; Oakland, Calif. 94553	128	216	49	P/RC	5,650	5,650	3,000
Holy Redeemer College; Waterford, Wis. 53185	56	—	21	RC	2,370	2,370	1,935
Hood College*; Frederick, Md. 21701	106	958	85	P	5,510	5,510	2,765
Hope College; Holland, Mich. 49423	1,187[1]	1,332[1]	150	P/RCA	5,756	5,756	2,500
Houghton College; Houghton, N.Y. 14744	453	632	n.a.	P/W	4,170	4,170	2,100
Buffalo Suburban Campus; West Seneca, N.Y. 14224	55	46	22	P/W	3,000	3,000	1,594
Houston, University of, System; Houston, Tex. 77023:							
U. of Houston—Clear Lake; Houston, Tex. 77058	667	1,054	198	S	456	1,316	—
U. of Houston—Downtown*; Houston, Tex. 77002	3,022	2,575	124	S	400	1,260	2,550
U. of Houston—University Park; Houston, Tex. 77004	9,058[1]	6,724[1]	941	S	400	1,300	2,775
U. of Houston—Victoria; Victoria, Tex. 77901	324	587	23	S	316	1,492	—
Houston Baptist University*; Houston, Tex. 77074	1,114	1,463	110	P/SB	3,048	3,048	1,700
Howard Payne University; Brownwood, Tex. 76801	451[1]	454[1]	77	P/SB	2,400	2,400	2,100
Howard University; Washington, D.C. 20059	4,399	5,179	1,200	P	3,045	3,045	2,882
Humboldt State University*; Arcata, Calif. 95521[24]	3,744	3,303	500	S	675	3,000	2,400
Hunter College. *See* New York, City University of							
Huntingdon College; Montgomery, Ala. 36194	248[1]	341[1]	43	P/UM	3,080[3]	3,080[3]	2,470[3]
Huntington College; Huntington, Ind. 46750	195	161	32	P/BC	4,620	4,620	2,120
Huron College*; Huron, S.D. 57350	159	175	22	P/Pres	3,270	3,270	2,128
Husson College*; Bangor, Me. 04401	343	391	34	P	4,200	4,200	2,500
Huston-Tillotson College; Austin, Tex. 78702	354	161	30	P	2,340	2,340	2,340
Idaho, The College of; Caldwell, Idaho 83605	278[1]	239[1]	43	P	5,072	5,072	2,500
Idaho, University of; Moscow, Idaho 83843	5,171[1]	3,249[1]	531	S	970	2,970	2,071
Idaho State University; Pocatello, Idaho 83209	1,912[1]	1,714[1]	305	S	1,010	1,910	3,700
Illinois, Univ. of, at Chicago; Chicago, Ill. 60680	13,685[1]	10,966[1]	1,807	S	1,533	3,741	3,177
Illinois, Univ. of, at Urbana-Champaign; Urbana-Champaign, Ill. 61801	17,950[1]	13,298[1]	2,051	S	1,248	3,744	2,910

Institution and location	Enrollment		Faculty	Control	Tuition ($)		Rm/Bd ($)
	Male	Female			Res.	Nonres.	
Illinois, Univ. of, at Chicago, Health Sciences Center; Chicago, Ill. 60612	2,313 [1]	1,697 [1]	n.a.	S	1,104	3,312	3,650
Illinois Benedictine College; Lisle, Ill. 60532	519	400	71	P/RC	4,500	4,500	1,000
Illinois College; Jacksonville, Ill. 62650	415 [1]	346 [1]	44	P	3,600	3,600	2,160
Illinois College of Optometry; Chicago, Ill. 60616	426	116	35	P	8,100	8,100	1,455 [11]
Illinois Coll. of Podiatric Medicine. *See* Dr. William M. Scholl Coll. of Podiatric Medicine							
Illinois Institute of Technology*; Chicago, Ill. 60616	6,939		275	P	6,390	6,390	3,000
Illinois School of Professional Psychology; Chicago, Ill. 60604	148	150	9	P	6,900	6,900	—
Illinois State University; Normal, Ill. 61761	9,135 [1]	10,682 [1]	846	S	864	2,592	2,088
Illinois Wesleyan University; Bloomington, Ill. 61702	697 [1]	937 [1]	125	P/M	6,140	6,140	2,600
Immaculata College; Immaculata, Pa. 19345	10	569	55	P/RC	3,650	3,650	2,670
Incarnate Word College; San Antonio, Tex. 78209	190	634	70	P/RC	3,872	3,872	2,016
Indiana Central University; Indianapolis, Ind. 46227	422	600	115	P/UM	4,930 [3]	4,930 [3]	2,260
Indiana Institute of Technology*; Fort Wayne, Ind. 46803	430	124	34	P	3,750	3,750	2,200
Indiana State Univ.—Evansville; Evansville, Ind. 47712	1,677 [1]	2,129 [1]	103	S	1,271	3,100	—
Indiana State Univ.—Terre Haute; Terre Haute, Ind. 47809	5,679	5,275	689	S	1,454	1,962	2,006
Indiana University; Bloomington, Ind. 47405:							
Indiana Univ. at Kokomo; Kokomo, Ind. 46902	298 [1]	450 [1]	60	S	1,275	3,127	—
Indiana Univ. at South Bend*; South Bend, Ind. 46615	1,273	1,650	200	S	975	2,280	—
Indiana Univ.-Bloomington; Bloomington, Ind. 47405	16,456 [1]	16,653 [1]	1,355	S	1,304	3,678	2,164
Indiana University Northwest; Gary, Ind. 46408	675	1,069	140	S	1,200	2,920	—
I.U.-Purdue U. at Fort Wayne; Fort Wayne, Ind. 46805	1,976 [1]	1,809 [1]	300	S	1,275	3,165	—
I.U.-Purdue U. at Indianapolis; Indianapolis, Ind. 46202	4,999 [1]	4,973 [1]	1,200	S	697	1,852	1,078 [11]
Indiana University Southeast; New Albany, Ind. 47150	873 [1]	1,096 [1]	103	S	994	1,294	—
Indiana University of Pennsylvania; Indiana, Pa. 15705	4,786 [1]	6,206 [1]	650	S	1,480	2,590	1,868
Instituto Technológico*; Monterrey, Mexico	n.a.	n.a.	n.a.	P	n.a.	n.a.	n.a.
Insurance, The College of; New York, N.Y. 10007	214 [1]	90 [1]	30	P	4,500	4,500	4,180
Inter American University of Puerto Rico*; San Juan, P.R. 00936:	10,014	15,337	588	P	1,395	1,395	—
Arecibo Regional College*; Arecibo, P.R. 00612	1,454	2,049	54	P	n.a.	n.a.	n.a.
Metropolitan Campus*; Hato Rey, P.R. 00919	5,640	8,778	237	P	540	540	—
San Germán Campus; San Germán, P.R. 00753	2,739 [1]	3,648 [1]	161	P	1,650	1,650	1,400
School of Law; Santurce, P.R. 00924	454	297	23	P	3,600	3,600	—
School of Optometry; San Juan, P.R. 00936	n.a.	n.a.	n.a.	P	n.a.	n.a.	n.a.
International College of the Cayman Islands; Newlands, Grand Cayman, B.W.I.	78 [1]	187 [1]	10	P	1,294	1,294	1,838
International Correspondence Institute*; Brussels, Belgium	5,745		—	P	n.a.	n.a.	—
International Institute of the Americas*; Hato Rey, P.R. 00917	n.a.	n.a.	n.a.	P	n.a.	n.a.	n.a.
International Training, The School for; Brattleboro, Vt. 05301	275	381	n.a.	P	5,940	5,940	([36])
Iona College; New Rochelle, N.Y. 10801	2,023 [1]	1,478 [1]	183	P	4,800	4,800	3,150
Iowa, University of; Iowa City, Iowa 52242	13,752 [1]	12,283 [1]	1,600	S	1,242	3,450	2,051
Iowa State University of Science and Technology; Ames, Iowa 50011	16,253 [1]	9,767 [1]	1,919	S	1,242	3,450	1,848
Iowa Wesleyan College; Mount Pleasant, Iowa 52641	209 [1]	282 [1]	41	P/UM	5,300	5,300	2,270
Ithaca College; Ithaca, N.Y. 14850	2,229 [1]	2,819 [1]	318	P	6,026	6,026	2,688
Jackson College for Women. *See* Tufts University							
Jackson State University; Jackson, Miss. 39217	2,337 [1]	2,723 [1]	307	S	972	1,948	1,824
Jacksonville State University; Jacksonville, Ala. 36265	2,263 [1]	2,465 [1]	263	S	800	1,050	1,390
Jacksonville University; Jacksonville, Fla. 32211	1,073 [1]	770 [1]	100	P	4,500	4,500	1,290
James Madison University*; Harrisonburg, Va. 22807	3,657	4,297	443	S	1,660	2,590	2,338
Jamestown College; Jamestown, N.D. 58401	259 [1]	265 [1]	40	P/Pres	5,120	5,120	1,785
Jarvis Christian College*; Hawkins, Tex. 75765	214	217	50	P/DC	2,250	2,250	1,750
Jersey City State College; Jersey City, N.J. 07305	1,654	1,688	250	S	1,180	1,780	1,000
John Brown University; Siloam Springs, Ark. 72761	434 [1]	404 [1]	45	P	2,700	2,700	2,100
John Carroll University; Cleveland, Ohio 44118	1,333 [1]	1,215 [1]	183	P/RC	4,768	4,768	2,750
John F. Kennedy University; Orinda, Calif. 94549	253 [1]	399 [1]	224 [37]	P	2,520	2,520	—
John Jay College of Criminal Justice. *See* New York, City University of							
John Marshall Law School, The; Chicago, Ill. 60604	663 [1]	293 [1]	47	P	5,600	5,600	5,900
Johns Hopkins University, The; Baltimore, Md. 21218	3,447 [1]	2,096 [1]	1,454	P	8,600 [3]	8,600 [3]	3,500
Johnson and Wales College*; Providence, R.I. 02903	2,145	1,755	135	P	4,320	4,320	2,940
Johnson Bible College; Knoxville, Tenn. 37998	198 [1]	141 [1]	15	P/ChC	1,560	1,560	1,940
Johnson C. Smith University; Charlotte, N.C. 28216	576	612	89	P	2,580	2,580	1,640
Johnson State College; Johnson, Vt. 05656	376	329	43	S	1,530	3,560	2,734
Johnston College, Calif. *See* Redlands, University of							
John Wesley College; High Point, N.C. 27260	56	24	5	P/Ind	2,000	2,000	1,500 [11]
Jones College; Jacksonville, Fla. 32211	549	676	20	P	2,314	2,314	—
Jones College Medical Education Center*; Jacksonville, Fla. 32204	15	235	n.a.	P	n.a.	n.a.	n.a.
Judson College; Elgin, Ill. 60120	205 [1]	225 [1]	23	AB	4,980	4,980	2,730
Judson College*; Marion, Ala. 36756	—	565	26	P/B	2,140	2,140	1,460
Juilliard School, The*; New York, N.Y. 10023	670	650	137	P	4,000	4,000	—
Juniata College*; Huntingdon, Pa. 16652	696	573	76	P	5,985	5,985	2,340
Kalamazoo College; Kalamazoo, Mich. 49007	548 [3]	582 [3]	69	P/B	7,275	7,275	2,721
Kansas, University of; Lawrence, Kan. 66045	27,742 [1]	23,938 [1]	1,313	S	1,148	2,828	2,000
Kansas City Art Institute; Kansas City, Mo. 64111	234 [1]	218 [1]	41	P	6,250	6,250	1,355 [11]
Kansas Newman College*; Wichita, Kan. 67213	173	241	40	P/RC	3,450	3,450	1,890
Kansas State University; Manhatten, Kan. 66506	10,219 [1]	7,973 [1]	892	S	1,181	2,861	2,016

Institution and location	Enrollment Male	Enrollment Female	Faculty	Control	Tuition ($) Res.	Tuition ($) Nonres.	Rm/Bd ($)
Kansas Wesleyan University; Salina, Kan. 67401	178[1]	127[1]	32	P/UM	3,977	3,977	2,449
Kean College of New Jersey; Union, N.J. 07083	4,509	6,616	337	S	1,245	1,845	n.a.
Kearney State College; Kearney, Neb. 68849	2,643[1]	3,362[1]	252	S	725[3]	1,380[3]	1,676[3]
Keene State College*; Keene, N.H. 03431	1,151	1,533	160	S	625	1,600	1,751
Keller Graduate School of Management; Chicago, Ill. 60606	1,012	338	5	P	3,712	3,712	n.a.
Kendall College; Evanston, Ill. 60201	114	213	21	P	4,290	4,290	2,500
Kendall School of Design; Grand Rapids, Mich. 49503	277[1]	377[1]	26	P	4,035	4,035	2,966
Kennesaw College; Marietta, Ga. 30161	1,929	2,875	170	S	936	2,643	—
Kent State University; Kent, Ohio 44242	8,836[1]	10,851[1]	754	S	1,890	3,090	2,070
Kentucky, University of; Lexington, Ky. 40506	9,255[1]	7,527[1]	1,524	S	1,124	3,202	2,394
Kentucky Christian College; Grayson, Ky. 41143	341[1]	216[1]	23	P/ChC	1,666	1,666	1,960
Kentucky State University; Frankfort, Ky. 40601	606	552	102	S	388	1,163	885
Kentucky Wesleyan College; Owensboro, Ky. 42301	372[1]	385[1]	53	P/UM	3,930[3]	3,930[3]	2,130[3]
Kenyon College; Gambier, Ohio 43022	733[1]	665[1]	98	P	8,250	8,250	2,717
Keuka College*; Keuka Park, N.Y. 14478	—	482	50	P	5,480	5,480	1,980
King College; Bristol, Tenn. 37620	221[1]	213[1]	30	P/Pres	3,740	3,740	2,640
King's College; Wilkes-Barre, Pa. 18711	894[1]	694[1]	100	RC	4,750	4,750	2,600
King's College, The; Briarcliff Manor, N.Y. 10510	278[1]	453[1]	49	P/ND	5,250	5,250	2,050
Kirksville College of Osteopathic Medicine; Kirksville, Mo. 63501	443	78	82	P	14,000	14,000	4,950
Knox College; Galesburg, Ill. 61401	483[1]	404[1]	85	P	7,338[3]	7,338[3]	2,520[3]
Knoxville College*; Knoxville, Tenn. 37921[7]	260	167	32	UP	2,400	2,400	1,671
Kutztown State College; Kutztown, Pa. 19530	2,053	2,478	282	S	1,250	1,250	1,652
Laboratory Institute of Merchandising; New York, N.Y. 10022	12[1]	209[1]	5	P	4,800[3]	4,800[3]	2,450
Lafayette College; Easton, Pa. 18042	1,159[1]	833[1]	159	P	8,350[3]	8,350[3]	3,025
LaGrange College; LaGrange, Ga. 30240	220	302	52	P/M	2,565	2,565	4,300
Lake Erie College*; Painesville, Ohio 44077	77	381	47	P	5,630	5,630	2,970
Lake Forest College; Lake Forest, Ill. 60045	502[3]	510[3]	85	P	7,580	7,580	2,300
Lake Forest School of Management; Lake Forest, Ill. 60045	321	118	—	P	2,520	2,520	—
Lakeland College; Sheboygan, Wis. 53082	235[1]	176[1]	29	P/UCC	7,460	7,460	2,400
Lake Superior State College; Sault Ste. Marie, Mich. 49783	1,277[1]	986[1]	105	S	1,455	2,760	2,568
Lamar University; Beaumont, Tex. 77710	4,612	4,579	465	S	240	2,016	3,912
Lambuth College; Jackson, Tenn. 38301	226[3]	369[3]	48	P/UM	3,600	3,600	1,900
Lancaster Bible College; Lancaster, Pa. 17601	154[1]	97[1]	18	P	3,800	3,800	2,150
Lander College; Greenwood, S.C. 29646	680[1]	1,085[1]	97	S	1,270	1,870	875
Lane College; Jackson, Tenn. 38301	332	334	40	P/CME	2,200	2,200	1,520
Langston University*; Langston, Okla. 73050	1,177	1,025	59	S	546	1,071	2,257
Laredo State Univ. *See* South Texas, Univ. System of							
La Roche College; Pittsburgh, Pa. 15237	241[1]	472[1]	33	P	3,800	3,800	2,600
La Salle College; Philadelphia, Pa. 19141	1,828	1,365	212	P/RC	4,990	4,990	1,585
La Verne, University of; La Verne, Calif. 91750	2,178	2,171	95	P/CB	5,900[3]	5,900[3]	3,440
Lawrence Institute of Technology; Southfield, Mich. 48075	3,108[1]	680[1]	60	P	2,100	2,100	—
Lawrence University*; Appleton, Wis. 54912	515	517	105	P	7,176	7,176	2,214
Lebanon Valley College; Annville, Pa. 17003	393	407	71	P/UM	5,850	5,850	2,710
Lee College*; Cleveland, Tenn. 37311	534	527	60	P/CG	2,200	2,200	1,600
Lehigh University; Bethlehem, Pa. 18015	3,520[1]	1,470[1]	345	P	8,000	8,000	2,900
Le Moyne College; Syracuse, N.Y. 13214	887	888	113	P	5,140	5,140	2,420
LeMoyne-Owen College*; Memphis, Tenn. 38126	331	642	52	P	3,450	3,450	—
Lenoir-Rhyne College; Hickory, N.C. 28603	465[1]	701[1]	n.a.	P/LCA	4,190[3]	4,190[3]	1,755
Lesley College*; Cambridge, Mass. 02238	253	943	n.a.	P	6,000	6,000	3,745
LeTourneau College; Longview, Tex. 75607	850	120	63	P	4,490	4,490	2,500
Lewis and Clark College; Portland, Ore. 97219	1,291	1,257	135	P	7,800	7,800	2,811
Lewis-Clark State College*; Lewiston, Idaho 83501	884	1,164	87	S	740	2,640	1,920
Lewis University; Romeoville, Ill. 60441	1,479[1]	1,171[1]	90	P/RC	4,896	4,896	2,360
Liberty Baptist College; Lynchburg, Va. 24506	2,231[1]	1,976[1]	182	P	2,500	2,500	2,800
L.I.F.E. Bible College; Los Angeles, Calif. 90026	151	72	23	FG	1,980	1,980	2,225
Lifelong Learning, School for, University System of New Hampshire*; Durham, N.H. 03824	465	564	—	S	n.a.	n.a.	—
Limestone College; Gaffney, S.C. 29340	777[1]	759[1]	n.a.	P	4,960	4,960	2,240
Lincoln Christian College; Lincoln, Ill. 62656	163	127	17	P/ChC	2,700	2,700	1,610
Lincoln Memorial University; Harrogate, Tenn. 37752	487[1]	931[1]	50	P	2,400	2,400	1,800
Lincoln University; Jefferson City, Mo. 65101	731	700	151	S	700	1,400	2,088
Lincoln University*; Lincoln University, Pa. 19352	568	643	n.a.	P	n.a.	n.a.	n.a.
Lindenwood College, The; St. Charles, Mo. 63301	712	1,066	55	P	4,600	4,600	3,000
Linfield College*; McMinnville, Ore. 97128	542	548	80	P	2,205	2,205	1,920
Livingstone College; Salisbury, N.C. 28144	403[1]	377[1]	49	P/AME	2,840	2,840	1,956
Livingston University; Livingston, Ala. 35470	623[1]	894[1]	82	S	810	810	1,563
Lock Haven University of Pennsylvania*; Lock Haven, Pa. 17745	1,117	1,292	169	S	1,480	2,590	1,648
Logan College of Chiropractic; Chesterfield, Mo. 63017	487	138	45	P	5,400	5,400	18,700
Loma Linda University; Loma Linda, Calif. 92350	1,673	1,535	595	P/SDA	1,925	1,925	870
La Sierra Campus; Riverside, Calif. 92515	2,415[1]	2,438[1]	721	SDA	5,775	5,775	2,520
Long Island University Center; Greenvale, N.Y. 11548:							
Arnold and Marie Schwartz College of Pharmacy and Health Services. *See* Brooklyn Center.							

Institution and location	Enrollment		Faculty	Control	Tuition ($)		Rm/Bd ($)
	Male	Female			Res.	Nonres.	
Brooklyn Center*; Brooklyn, N.Y. 11201	1,654	2,090	n.a.	P	4,150	4,150	1,340
C.W. Post Center; Greenvale, N.Y. 11548	2,657 [1]	2,873 [1]	362	P	5,550	5,550	2,938
Southampton College*; Southampton, N.Y. 11968	581	488	69	P	5,240	5,240	2,730
Longwood College; Farmville, Va. 23901	772	1,631	136	S	930	1,680	2,190
Loras College*; Dubuque, Iowa 52001	815	600	125	P	4,300	4,300	1,150
Loretto Heights College; Denver, Colo. 80236	136	523	64	P	5,800	5,800	3,100
Los Angeles Baptist College; Newhall, Calif. 91322	134 [1]	170 [1]	28	P/B	1,800	1,800	1,265
Los Angeles College of Chiropractic*; Glendale, Calif. 91205	501	149	43	P	5,500	5,500	—
Louise Salinger Academy of Fashion*; San Francisco, Calif. 94105	n.a.	n.a.	n.a.	P	5,940	5,940	—
Louisiana College; Pineville, La. 71359	360	486	67	SB	1,416	1,416	700
Louisiana State University and A&M College; Baton Rouge, La. 70803	13,220 [1]	10,866 [1]	1,116	S	971	2,471	1,954
LSU in Shreveport; Shreveport, La. 71115	2,020	2,389	156	S	780	2,010	—
LSU Medical Center at New Orleans; New Orleans, La. 70112	1,208	1,058	825	S	2,200	7,450	2,500 [11]
Louisiana Tech University; Ruston, La. 71270	4,765 [1]	3,238 [1]	430	S	894	1,575	2,961
Louisville, University of; Louisville, Ky. 40292	10,192 [1]	9,558 [1]	989	S	1,135	3,213	2,400
Lowell, University of; Lowell, Mass. 01854	6,241 [1]	3,411 [1]	443	S	1,100	3,600	2,600
Loyola College; Baltimore, Md. 21210	1,403	1,345	164	P/RC	4,950	4,950	3,055
Loyola Marymount University; Los Angeles, Calif. 90045	2,384	2,570	n.a.	P/RC	6,050 [3]	6,050 [3]	2,824
Loyola University, New Orleans; New Orleans, La. 70118	1,571 [1]	1,869 [1]	210	P/RC	4,390 [3]	4,390 [3]	3,116
Loyola University of Chicago; Chicago, Ill. 60011	4,147 [1]	4,393 [1]	776	P	5,090	5,090	2,695
Lubbock Christian College; Lubbock, Tex. 79407	463 [1]	374 [1]	45	P/CC	3,100	3,100	2,000
Lutheran Bible Institute of Seattle; Issaquah, Wash. 98011	102	92	13	P/L	2,379	2,379	2,879
Luther College; Decorah, Iowa 52101	893	1,168	128	P/AL	5,975	5,975	2,025
Lycoming College; Williamsport, Pa. 17701	640 [1]	560 [1]	82	P	6,200 [3]	6,200 [3]	2,550 [3]
Lynchburg College*; Lynchburg, Va. 24501	700	955	122	P/DC	4,900	4,900	2,400
Lyndon State College*; Lyndonville, Vt. 05851	544	427	59	S	1,250	3,050	2,396
Macalester College; St. Paul, Minn. 55105	796	797	125	P	7,520 [3]	7,520 [3]	2,600 [3]
MacMurray College; Jacksonville, Ill. 62650	183 [1]	403 [1]	58	P/UM	5,200	5,200	2,300
Madonna College; Livonia, Mich. 48150	871	2,814	90	P	2,120	2,120	2,260
Maharishi International Univ.; Fairfield, Iowa 52556	558 [1]	251 [1]	90	P	4,368	4,368	1,200
Maine, Univ. of, at Farmington*; Farmington, Me. 04938	406	1,138	85	S	1,170	3,270	2,110
Maine, Univ. of, at Fort Kent; Fort Kent, Me. 04743	275	371	22	S	1,412	3,630	2,600
Maine, Univ. of, at Machias*; Machias, Me. 04654	185	235	40	S	930	2,900	1,950
Maine, Univ. of, at Orono; Orono, Me. 04469	5,279 [1]	4,028 [1]	648	S	1,509	4,560	2,921
Maine, Univ. of, at Presque Isle; Presque Isle, Me. 04769	581 [1]	717 [1]	55	S	1,413	3,630	2,542
Maine Maritime Academy; Castine, Me. 04420	640 [1]	17 [1]	43	S	2,000	3,630	2,955
Malone College; Canton, Ohio 44709	356	454	40	P/F	4,433	4,433	2,250
Manchester College; North Manchester, Ind. 46962	419	487	76	CB	4,860	4,860	2,040
Manhattan Christian College; Manhattan, Kan. 66502	87 [1]	50 [1]	13	P/Ind	1,700	1,700	2,020
Manhattan College; Riverdale, Bronx, N.Y. 10471	2,413	1,087	250	P	4,500	4,500	3,400
Manhattan School of Music*; New York, N.Y. 10027	235	280	n.a.	P	4,000	4,000	—
Manhattanville College; Purchase, N.Y. 10577	270 [1]	666 [1]	78	P	7,700 [3]	7,700 [3]	3,800
Mankato State University. *See* Minnesota State University System							
Mannes College of Music*; New York, N.Y. 10024	101	132	n.a.	P	4,500	4,500	4,000
Mansfield University of Pennsylvania; Mansfield, Pa. 16933	1,187 [1]	1,181 [1]	184	S	1,480	2,590	1,764
Marian College; Indianapolis, Ind. 46222	262 [1]	686 [1]	62	P/RC	3,790	3,790	2,025
Marian College of Fond du Lac; Fond du Lac, Wis. 54935	65 [1]	392 [1]	45	P/RC	3,780	3,780	1,600
Marietta College; Marietta, Ohio 45750	725	407	82	P	6,500	6,500	2,250
Marion College; Marion, Ind. 46953	488 [1]	671 [1]	65	P/W	4,290	4,290	2,150
Marist College; Poughkeepsie, N.Y. 12601	1,488 [1]	1,127 [1]	92	P	5,360	5,360	3,330
Marlboro College; Marlboro, Vt. 05344	90	76	24	P	8,100	8,100	3,110
Marquette University*; Milwaukee, Wis. 53233	n.a.	n.a.	n.a.	P/RC	n.a.	n.a.	n.a.
Marshall University; Huntington, W. Va. 25701	5,310 [1]	6,457 [1]	461	S	846	2,396	2,405
Mars Hill College; Mars Hill, N.C. 28754	655 [1]	826 [1]	84	P/SB	3,635 [3]	3,635 [3]	1,635 [3]
Mary Baldwin College; Staunton, Va. 24401	27 [1]	780 [1]	56	P/PUS	9,750 [3]	9,750 [3]	n.a.
Mary College*; Bismarck, N.D. 58501	255	577	60	P/RC	2,960	2,960	1,607
Marycrest College; Davenport, Iowa 52804	171 [3]	415 [3]	50	P/RC	4,140	4,140	1,990
Marygrove College; Detroit, Mich. 48221	149 [1]	620 [1]	49	P/RC	4,352	4,352	2,230
Mary Hardin-Baylor, University of; Belton, Tex. 76513	289	516	69	SB	2,550	2,550	1,890
Maryland, University of (System); College Park, Md. 20742:							
UM at Baltimore (UMAB)*; Baltimore, Md. 21201	1,752	2,153	746	S	870	2,835	1,409
UM, Baltimore County (UMBC)*; Baltimore, Md. 21228	2,691	2,928	276	S	1,362	3,758	5,600
UM–College Park (UMCP)*; College Park, Md. 20742	19,410	17,636	1,862	S	1,185	3,303	1,294
UM Eastern Shore (UMES); Princess Anne, Md. 21853	554 [1]	669 [1]	79	S	1,252	3,496	2,620
UM University College (UMUC)*; College Park, Md. 20742	383	326	13	S	1,690	1,690	—
Maryland Institute College of Art*; Baltimore, Md. 21217	323	499	43	P	5,300	5,300	—
Marylhurst College for Lifelong Learning; Marylhurst, Ore. 97036	300	600	35	P	1,140	1,140	—
Marymount College*; Tarrytown, N.Y. 10591	42	952	n.a.	P	n.a.	n.a.	n.a.
Marymount College of Kansas; Salina, Kan. 67401	188	432	41	P/RC	3,950	3,950	2,200
Marymount College of Virginia; Arlington, Va. 22207	350	1,350	60	P	4,600	4,600	2,800
Marymount Manhattan College; New York, N.Y. 10021	62 [1]	674 [1]	51	P	4,810	4,810	1,550
Maryville College*; Maryville, Tenn. 37801	278	270	47	P/UP	3,920	3,920	1,995

Institution and location	Enrollment Male	Enrollment Female	Faculty	Control	Tuition ($) Res.	Tuition ($) Nonres.	Rm/Bd ($)
Maryville College; St. Louis, Mo. 63141	318[1]	625[1]	61	P	4,890	4,890	2,510
Mary Washington College; Fredericksburg, Va. 22401	497	1,744	137	S	1,326	2,896	2,636
Marywood College*; Scranton, Pa. 18509	365	1,804	136	P/RC	3,000	3,000	2,100
Massachusetts, Univ. of at Amherst; Amherst, Mass. 01003	11,082	9,770	1,214	S	1,129[1]	3,686[1]	2,480
Massachusetts, Univ. of, at Boston*; Boston, Mass. 02125	2,897	3,131	322	S	1,129	1,434	—
Massachusetts College of Art*; Boston, Mass. 02215	809	1,213	49	S	845	2,792	—
Massachusetts College of Optometry. *See* New England College of Optometry							
Massachusetts College of Pharmacy and Allied Health Sciences*; Boston, Mass. 02115	513	473	70	P	4,410	4,410	3,900
Massachusetts Institute of Technology*; Cambridge, Mass. 02139	7,046	1,853	1,089	P	9,600	9,600	3,880
Massachusetts Maritime Academy; Buzzards Bay, Mass. 02532	748	52	59	S	845	845	2,464
Mayo Medical School*; Rochester, Minn. 55901[38]	120	42	25	P	5,000	5,000	4,500
Mayville State College; Mayville, N.D. 58257	303	329	49	S	858	1,506	1,440
McKendree College*; Lebanon, Ill. 62254	257	206	32	P/M	n.a.	n.a.	1,850
McMurry College; Abilene, Tex. 79697	375	408	67	P/M	3,000	3,000	1,710
McNeese State University; Lake Charles, La. 70609	2,598[1]	2,907[1]	250	S	793	1,473	1,600
McPherson College; McPherson, Kan. 67460	224[3]	194[3]	37	P/CB	3,900	3,900	2,225
Medaille College; Buffalo, N.Y. 14214	249[1]	383[1]	38	P	4,140	4,140	1,250
Medgar Evers College. *See* New York, City College of							
Medical College of Georgia; Augusta, Ga. 30912	848	850	665	S	1,944	5,832	980
Medical College of Ohio; Toledo, Ohio 43699	380	190	237	S	4,950	6,950	—
Medical College of Wisconsin, The; Milwaukee, Wis. 53226	548[1]	261[1]	565	P	7,500[3]	13,000[3]	3,960[3]
Medical University of South Carolina*; Charleston, S.C. 29425	1,311	1,249	700	S	1,000	1,738	2,200
Medicine and Dentistry, University of, of New Jersey*; Newark, N.J. 07103	1,342	754	735	S	5,500	6,875	—
New Jersey Dental School; Newark, N.J. 07103	239	91	72	S	6,825	8,530	—
New Jersey Medical School*; Newark, N.J. 07103	n.a.	n.a.	n.a.	S	n.a.	n.a.	n.a.
New Jersey School of Osteopathic Medicine; Camden, N.J. 08301	147	43	n.a.	S	6,825	8,530	7,000
Rutgers Medical School; Piscataway, N.J. 08854	361	152	251	S	6,825	8,530	—
Meharry Medical College*; Nashville, Tenn. 37208	489	395	246	P	7,500	7,500	5,000
Memphis Academy of Arts, The; Memphis, Tenn. 38118	77	100	16	P	4,100	4,100	1,125
Memphis State University; Memphis, Tenn. 38152[12]	10,450	11,590	700	S	832	2,590	1,000[11]
Menlo College School of Business Administration; Atherton, Calif. 94025	404	187	47	P	7,120[3]	7,120[3]	3,825
Mercer University College of Liberal Arts*; Macon, Ga. 31207	1,100	1,100	120	P/B	3,669	3,669	1,785
Mercer University in Atlanta; Atlanta, Ga. 30341	1,023	848	64	P/SB	3,600	3,600	—
Southern School of Pharmacy; Atlanta, Ga. 30312	188	130	34	P/B	5,298	5,298	—
Mercy College; Dobbs Ferry, N.Y. 10522	2,757[1]	3,231[1]	237	P	3,060	3,060	—
Mercy College of Detroit; Detroit, Mich. 48219	175[1]	1,096[1]	90	P/RC	3,680	3,680	1,540
Mercyhurst College; Erie, Pa. 16546	506[1]	717[1]	74	P/RC	4,950	4,950	2,115
Meredith College*; Raleigh, N.C. 27607	27	1,507	76	P/SB	3,350	3,350	1,450
Merrimack College; North Andover, Mass. 01845	1,091[1]	899[1]	125	P/RC	5,150	5,150	3,150
Mesa College; Grand Junction, Colo. 81501	1,565	1,629	121	S	1,240	3,584	2,070
Messiah College; Grantham, Pa. 17027	581	909	72	P	4,770	4,770	2,400
Methodist College*; Fayetteville, N.C. 28301	371	344	46	P/M	2,500	2,500	1,650
Metropolitan State College; Denver, Colo. 80204	3,574	2,969	354	S	962	3,504	—
Metropolitan State University, Minn. *See* Minnesota State University System							
Miami, University of*; Coral Gables, Fla. 33124	6,716	4,656	n.a.	P	n.a.	n.a.	n.a.
Miami University; Oxford, Ohio 45056	6,460	7,593	787	S	2,385	2,150	2,225
Michigan, The University of; Ann Arbor, Mich. 48109	19,779[1]	11,899[1]	2,763	S	2,474	6,346	2,648
Univ. of Michigan—Dearborn*; Dearborn, Mich. 48128	1,884	1,567	181	S	1,528	4,692	1,392[11]
Univ. of Michigan—Flint; Flint, Mich. 48502	1,254	1,399	144	S	1,472	4,768	—
Michigan Christian College; Rochester, Mich. 48063	153[1]	199[1]	23	P/ND	2,610	2,610	2,110
Michigan State University; East Lansing, Mich. 48824	17,393[1]	16,391[1]	2,426	S	1,884	4,112	2,412
Michigan Technological University; Houghton, Mich. 49931	5,631[1]	1,783[1]	400	S	1,692	3,636	2,336
Mid-America Nazarene College*; Olathe, Kan. 66062	597	621	61	P/Naz	2,394	2,394	1,998
Middlebury College; Middlebury, Vt. 05753	950	950	162	P	12,600[4]	12,600[4]	—
Middle Tennessee State Univ.; Murfreesboro, Tenn. 37132[12]	4,341[1]	4,309[1]	410	S	760	2,518	1,520
Midland Luthern College; Fremont, Neb. 68025	335	492	60	P/L	4,650	4,650	2,645
Mid-South Bible College*; Memphis, Tenn. 38182	90	41	8	P/ND	2,330	2,330	1,900
Midwest Christian College*; Oklahoma City, Okla. 73111	41	27	9	P	1,350	1,350	1,767
Midwest College of Engineering[39]; Lombard, Ill. 60148	41[1]	1[1]	—	P	5,280	5,280	—
Midwestern State University; Wichita Falls, Tex. 76308	1,142	1,234	146	S	435	1,515	1,750
Miles College; Birmingham, Ala. 35208	295	247	39	P/CME	3,000	3,000	1,850
Millersville University of Pennsylvania; Millersville, Pa. 17551	2,309[1]	2,658[1]	304	S	1,480	2,590	1,790
Milligan College; Milligan College, Tenn. 37682	307[1]	387[1]	43	P/ChC	3,998	3,998	2,292
Millikin University; Decatur, Ill. 62522	691[1]	726[1]	101	P	5,000	5,000	2,255
Millsaps College; Jackson, Miss. 39210	537[1]	494[1]	69	P/M	4,980	4,980	2,100
Mills College; Oakland, Calif. 94613	20	779	65	P	7,700	7,700	3,800
Milton S. Hershey Medical Center. *See* Pennsylvania State University							
Milwaukee Institute of Art and Design; Milwaukee, Wis. 53202	129[1]	132[1]	15	P	3,300	3,300	—
Milwaukee School of Engineering; Milwaukee, Wis. 53201	2,425[1]	224[1]	84	P	5,670	5,670	2,505
Minneapolis College of Art and Design*; Minneapolis, Minn. 55404	217	287	44	P	4,070	4,070	1,040
Minnesota, The University of; Minneapolis, Minn. 55455	21,333[1]	16,301[1]	1,690	S	1,795	4,504	2,447

Institution and location	Enrollment		Faculty	Control	Tuition ($)		Rm/Bd ($)
	Male	Female			Res.	Nonres.	
Univ. of Minnesota, Duluth*; Duluth, Minn. 55804	4,029	3,705	434	S	1,290	3,550	2,295
Univ. of Minnesota, Morris; Morris, Minn. 56267	827[1]	776[1]	102	S	1,650	4,560	2,172
Minnesota Bible College; Rochester, Minn. 55902	49	41	9	ChC	2,100	2,100	1,675
Minnesota State University System; St. Paul, Minn. 55101:							
Bemidji State University; Bemidji, Minn. 56601	2,131[1]	1,938[1]	194	S	1,390	2,598	1,510
Mankato State University; Mankato, Minn. 56001	5,181[1]	5,155[1]	483	S	1,485	2,775	1,620
Metropolitan State University[40]; St. Paul, Minn. 55101	190[1]	254[1]	n.a.	S	1,056	2,112	—
Moorhead State University; Moorhead, Minn. 56560	2,431[1]	2,972[1]	280	S	1,280	2,241	1,491
St. Cloud State University; St. Cloud, Minn. 56301	4,946[1]	4,882[1]	478	S	1,288[3]	2,577[3]	1,674[3]
Southwest State University; Marshall, Minn. 56258	870[1]	679[1]	107	S	1,121	2,242	1,656
Winona State University; Winona, Minn. 55987	1,722[1]	2,384[1]	230	S	1,120	1,891	1,707
Minot State Coll. *See* Dakota Northwestern Univ.							
Mississippi, The University of; University, Miss. 38677	4,896[1]	4,340[1]	367	S	1,321	2,297	1,644
Medical Center; Jackson, Miss. 39216	1,005[1]	754[1]	400	S	1,185	2,161	4,800
Mississippi College*; Clinton, Miss. 39058	877	818	127	P/B	2,250	2,250	4,550
Mississippi State University*; Mississippi State, Miss. 39762	6,434	4,100	725	S	1,132	2,058	1,870
Mississippi University for Women; Columbus, Miss. 39701	309[1]	1,969[1]	150	S	825	1,801	1,660
Mississippi Valley State University*; Itta Bena, Miss. 38941	1,002	1,226	145	S	800	926	1,256
Missouri, University of; Columbia, Mo. 65201:							
Univ. of Missouri—Columbia; Columbia, Mo. 65211	12,630[1]	11,429[1]	1,851	S	1,355	3,931	2,004
Univ. of Missouri—Kansas City*; Kansas City, Mo. 64110	2,329	2,129	693	S	1,294	3,646	1,938
Univ. of Missouri—Rolla; Rolla, Mo. 65401	5,005[1]	1,189[1]	349	S	1,550	4,125	2,855
Univ. of Missouri—St. Louis; St. Louis, Mo. 63121	3,021[1]	2,741[1]	446	S	1,288	3,864	—
Missouri Baptist College; St. Louis, Mo. 63141	141	113	24	P/B	2,950	2,950	n.a.
Missouri Institute of Technology*; Kansas City, Mo. 64114	1,656	190	n.a.	P	n.a.	n.a.	n.a.
Missouri Southern State College; Joplin, Mo. 64801	1,824	2,131	152	S	770	1,506	1,550
Missouri Valley College*; Marshall, Mo. 65340	288	192	35	P/Pres	3,400	3,400	1,880
Missouri Western State College; St. Joseph, Mo. 64506	1,844	2,079	149	S	880	1,670	1,670
Mobile College; Mobile, Ala. 36572	214	460	65	P/SB	2,200	2,200	1,860
Molloy College; Rockville Centre, N.Y. 11570	110[1]	1,203[1]	110	P/RC	3,970	3,970	1,100
Monmouth College; West Long Branch, N.J. 07764	866	872	170	P	5,660[41]	5,660[41]	2,867
Monmouth College, The*; Monmouth, Ill. 61462	312	266	49	P/Pres	5,139	5,139	2,160
Montana, University of*; Missoula, Mont. 59812	3,853	3,390	400	S	825	2,265	2,081
Montana College of Mineral Science and Technology; Butte, Mont. 59701	1,184	483	105	S	775	1,467	2,240
Montana State University; Bozeman, Mont. 59717	6,559[1]	4,888[1]	576	S	884	2,576	2,476
Montclair State College*; Upper Montclair, N.J. 07043	5,453	8,883	583	S	432	752	3,000
Monterey Institute of International Studies; Monterey, Calif. 93940	148[1]	239[1]	35	P	5,750	5,750	—
Montevallo, University of*; Montevallo, Ala. 35115	789	1,328	151	S	1,030	1,630	1,804
Montserrat School of Visual Art*; Beverly, Mass. 01915	16	40	7	P	3,200	3,200	—
Moody Bible Institute; Chicago, Ill. 60610	841[1]	524[1]	71	P/ND	—	—	2,790
Moore College of Art; Philadelphia, Pa. 19103	—	438[1]	39	P	6,000	6,000	3,300
Moorhead State University. See Minnesota State University System							
Moravian College; Bethlehem, Pa. 18018	649[1]	550[1]	92	P/Mor	6,275	6,275	2,480
Morehead State University*; Morehead, Ky. 40351	2,236	2,480	283	S	586	1,740	1,080
Morehouse College*; Atlanta, Ga. 30314	1,931	—	98	P	3,100	3,100	2,206
Morehouse School of Medicine; Atlanta, Ga. 30310	46[1]	52[1]	n.a.	P	9,000	9,000	—
Morgan State University; Baltimore, Md. 21239	1,605	1,850	275	S	1,111	2,146	1,215
Morningside College; Sioux City, Iowa 51106	425	494	n.a.	P/M	5,581	5,581	1,950
Morris Brown College*; Atlanta, Ga. 30314	616	769	153	P/AME	2,700	2,700	1,626
Morris College; Sumter, S.C. 29150	223	361	53	P	2,722	2,722	1,784
Mount Holyoke College*; South Hadley, Mass. 01075	—	1,942	171	P	7,750	7,750	2,950
Mount Marty College; Yankton, S.D. 57078	118[1]	303[1]	46	P/RC	3,750	3,750	2,010
Mount Mary College*; Milwaukee, Wis. 53222	—	1,111	69	P/RC	3,900	3,900	2,100
Mount Mercy College*; Cedar Rapids, Iowa 52402	255	668	54	P/RC	3,970	3,970	1,825
Mount Saint Clare College*; Clinton, Iowa 52732	103	174	11	P/RC	2,990	2,990	2,000
Mount St. Joseph, College of; Mount St. Joseph, Ohio 45051	229[1]	1,003[1]	59	P/RC	4,554	4,554	2,634
Mount Saint Mary College; Newburgh, N.Y. 12550	192	803	51	P	3,930	3,930	2,380
Mount Saint Mary's College; Emmitsburg, Md. 21727	917[1]	635[1]	91	P/RC	5,150	5,150	2,550
Mount St. Mary's College; Los Angeles, Calif. 90049	15[1]	931[1]	69	P/RC	5,500	5,500	3,290
Mount Saint Vincent, College of*; Riverdale, N.Y. 10471	50	700	65	P	4,550	4,550	3,000
Mount Senario College*; Ladysmith, Wis. 54848	180	218	29	P	3,520	3,520	1,930
Mount Sinai School of Medicine. *See* New York, City University of							
Mount Union College; Alliance, Ohio 44601	526[1]	398[1]	71	P	7,160	7,160	2,190
Mount Vernon College; Washington, D.C. 20007	—	428	23	P	6,400	6,400	4,100
Mount Vernon Nazarene College*; Mount Vernon, Ohio 43050	505	522	46	P	2,813	2,813	1,777
Muhlenberg College; Allentown, Pa. 18104	764[1]	738[1]	103	P/L	7,025	7,025	2,315
Multnomah School of the Bible; Portland, Ore. 97220	366	237	39	P	3,480	3,480	1,930
Mundelein College; Chicago, Ill. 60660	12	432	70	P	5,040	5,040	2,412
Murray State University; Murray, Ky. 42071	2,909[1]	3,180[1]	348	S	890	2,550	1,690
Museum Art School, Portland. *See* Pacific Northwest College of Art							
Museum of Fine Arts, School of the; Boston, Mass. 02115	176	380	50	P	5,850[3]	5,850[3]	—
Muskingum College; New Concord, Ohio 43762	516[1]	478[1]	65	P/PUS	6,450	6,450	2,420

Institution and location	Enrollment Male	Enrollment Female	Faculty	Control	Tuition ($) Res.	Tuition ($) Nonres.	Rm/Bd ($)
Nathaniel Hawthorne College. *See* Hawthorne College							
National College of Chiropractic; Lombard, Ill. 60148	535	191	66	P	4,530	4,530	—
National College of Education*; Evanston, Ill. 60201	1,004	3,434	79	P	4,620	4,620	2,565
National University*; San Diego, Calif. 92108	3,155	1,527	37	P	4,320	4,320	—
Naval Postgraduate School*; Monterey, Calif. 93940	1,341	102	200	Fed	—	—	—
Nazareth College*; Nazareth, Mich. 49074	67	343	43	P/RC	4,790	4,790	2,370
Nazareth College of Rochester; Rochester, N.Y. 14610	255 [1]	1,031 [1]	104	P	4,925	4,925	2,850
Nebraska, University of–Lincoln; Lincoln, Neb. 68588	11,351 [1]	8,034 [1]	1,064	S	1,211	2,981	1,860
Univ. of Nebraska at Omaha*; Omaha, Neb. 68182	3,979	3,344	470	S	1,050	2,800	—
Univ. of Nebraska Medical Center; Omaha, Neb. 68105	1,049 [1]	941 [1]	593	S	966	2,618	—
Nebraska Wesleyan University; Lincoln, Neb. 68504	490	489	75	P/M	4,590	4,590	2,050
Neumann College*; Aston, Pa. 19014	41	338	39	P/RC	1,487	1,487	—
Nevada, University of, System; Reno, Nev. 89557:							
Univ. of Nevada, Las Vegas; Las Vegas, Nev. 89154	2,989 [1]	2,517 [1]	307	S	1,080	3,280	2,470
Univ. of Nevada—Reno; Reno, Nev. 89557	3,453 [1]	2,889 [1]	350	S	1,152	3,352	2,650
Newberry College; Newberry, S.C. 29108	381 [1]	223 [1]	44	P/LCA	5,000	5,000	2,300
New Church, Academy of the*; Bryn Athyn, Pa. 19009	51	53	28	P/SW	1,500	1,500	1,796
New College of California; San Francisco, Calif. 94110	199 [1]	228 [1]	5	P	3,200	3,200	—
New College of the University of South Florida. *See* South Florida, University of							
Newcomb College. *See* Tulane University							
New England, University of; Biddeford, Me. 04005	398 [1]	450 [1]	43	P	4,950	4,950	2,780
College of Osteopathic Medicine*; Biddeford, Me. 04005	201	60	17	P	11,000	11,000	—
New England College*; Henniker, N.H. 03242	714	561	94	P	5,900	5,900	2,380
New England College of Optometry; Boston, Mass. 02115	240	119	60	P	9,984	9,984	5,733
New England Conservatory of Music*; Boston, Mass. 02115	341	271	55	P	5,500	5,500	3,125
New England School of Law*; Boston, Mass. 02116	703	351	25	P	4,200	4,200	—
New Hampshire, University of; Durham, N.H. 03824	4,282 [1]	5,096 [1]	518	S	1,925	5,250	2,334
New Hampshire College; Manchester, N.H. 03104	2,141 [1]	1,938 [1]	78	P	6,266	6,266	3,456
New Haven, University of*; West Haven, Conn. 06516	1,498	617	143	P	5,040	5,040	2,850
New Jersey Dental School. *See* Medicine and Dentistry, College of, of New Jersey							
New Jersey Institute of Technology; Newark, N.J. 07102	3,247 [1]	547 [1]	284	S	1,596	2,192	1,876 [3]
New Jersey Medical School. *See* Medicine and Dentistry, College of, of New Jersey							
New Jersey School of Osteopathic Medicine. *See* Medicine and Dentistry, College of, of New Jersey							
New Mexico, The University of*; Albuquerque, N.M. 87131	7,327	6,682	1,015	S	768	2,448	1,900
New Mexico Highlands University; Las Vegas, N.M. 87701	758	774	127	S	555	2,110	1,650
New Mexico Institute of Mining and Technology; Socorro, N.M. 87801	855 [1]	285 [1]	85	S	802	2,431	2,330
New Mexico State University; Las Cruces, N.M. 88003	6,552	5,543	589	S	870	2,838	1,986
New Orleans, University of*; New Orleans, La. 70148 [42]	4,236	3,960	597	S	864	2,174	1,428
New Rochelle, College of*; New Rochelle, N.Y. 10801	n.a.	n.a.	n.a.	P	n.a.	n.a.	n.a.
New School for Social Research; New York, N.Y. 10011	349 [1]	345 [1]	70	P	6,250	6,250	3,690
Parsons School of Design; New York, N.Y. 10011	616 [1]	1,234 [1]	21	P	6,800	6,800	3,690
New School of Music, The*; Philadelphia, Pa. 19103	35	34	35	P	3,435	3,435	2,350
New York, City University of; New York, N.Y. 10021:							
Bernard M. Baruch College; New York, N.Y. 10010	3,635 [1]	4,889 [1]	461	S	1,250	2,550	—
Brooklyn College; Brooklyn, N.Y. 11210	4,198 [43]	4,917 [43]	775 [1]	S	1,306 [1]	2,106 [1]	—
City College; New York, N.Y. 10031	5,239 [1]	3,049 [1]	504	S	1,320	2,620	—
College of Staten Island*; Staten Island, N.Y. 10301	5,043	6,079	375	S	1,100	1,600	—
Graduate School and University Center; New York, N.Y. 10036	1,412 [1]	1,291 [1]	n.a.	Mun	1,900	3,200	—
Herbert H. Lehman College; Bronx, N.Y. 10468	1,879	3,396	357	S	1,225	2,025	—
Hunter College; New York, N.Y. 10021	2,469 [1]	6,607 [1]	600	Mun/S	1,875	2,050	1,100
John Jay College of Criminal Justice; New York, N.Y. 10019	1,984 [1]	1,916 [1]	271	Mun/S	1,025	2,025	—
Medgar Evers College; Brooklyn, N.Y. 11225	754	1,860	261	Mun	612	1,012	—
Mount Sinai School of Medicine; New York, N.Y. 10029	298 [1]	169 [1]	1,029	P	13,000	13,000	6,000
New York City Technical Coll.*; Brooklyn, N.Y. 11201	4,033	3,923	n.a.	Mun	n.a.	n.a.	n.a.
Queens College; Flushing, N.Y. 11367	15,434		900	Mun	1,392	2,192	—
York College*; Jamaica, N.Y. 11451	1,237	1,556	188 [20]	Mun	1,075	1,075	—
New York, State University of; Albany, N.Y. 12246:							
SUNY at Albany; Albany, N.Y. 12222	7,536 [1]	8,461 [1]	673	S	1,350	3,200	2,583
SUNY at Binghamton; Binghamton, N.Y. 13901	4,250 [1]	5,227 [1]	482	S	1,350	3,200	2,750
SUNY at Buffalo*; Buffalo, N.Y. 14260	11,705	7,555	1,457	S	1,350	2,650	2,700
SUNY at Stony Brook; Stony Brook, N.Y. 11794	6,890 [1]	6,100 [1]	1,039	S	1,350	2,650	2,500
SUNY College at Brockport; Brockport, N.Y. 14420	5,395 [1]		350	S	1,350	2,650	2,700
SUNY College at Buffalo; Buffalo, N.Y. 14222	4,560	6,840	465	S	1,350	2,650	2,700
SUNY College at Cortland; Cortland, N.Y. 13045	2,529 [1]	3,741 [1]	269	S	1,350	2,625	2,640
SUNY College at Fredonia; Fredonia, N.Y. 14063	2,073 [1]	2,147 [1]	273	S	1,350	2,650	2,800
SUNY College at Geneseo*; Geneseo, N.Y. 14454	1,577	3,193	259	S	1,050	1,750	2,110
SUNY College at New Paltz; New Paltz, N.Y. 12561	2,272 [1]	2,660 [1]	413	S	1,350	2,650	2,670
SUNY College at Old Westbury*; Old Westbury, N.Y. 11568	1,306	1,393	121	S	1,350	2,650	2,400
SUNY College at Oneonta; Oneonta, N.Y. 13820	2,247 [1]	3,198 [1]	581	S	1,350	3,200	2,740
SUNY College at Oswego; Oswego, N.Y. 13126	3,217 [1]	3,314 [1]	345	S	1,050	3,200	2,660
SUNY College at Plattsburgh; Plattsburgh, N.Y. 12901	2,486 [1]	3,431 [1]	278	S	1,350	2,650	2,864
SUNY College at Potsdam; Potsdam, N.Y. 13676	1,874 [1]	2,104 [1]	264	S	1,375	3,225	2,810

Institution and location	Enrollment Male	Enrollment Female	Faculty	Control	Tuition ($) Res.	Tuition ($) Nonres.	Rm/Bd ($)
SUNY College at Purchase; Purchase, N.Y. 10960	1,100 [1]	1,100 [1]	150	S	1,350	2,200	1,500
SUNY College of Environmental Science and Forestry; Syracuse, N.Y. 13210	855	300	105	S	1,350	2,650	3,600
SUNY College of Optometry*; New York, N.Y. 10010	161	98	40	S	4,300	6,300	8,500
SUNY College of Technology; Utica, N.Y. 13502	908	438	86	S	1,350	2,700	2,950
SUNY Downstate Medical Center*; Brooklyn, N.Y. 11203	761	547	441	S	3,100	4,500	2,800
SUNY Empire State College; Saratoga Springs, N.Y. 12866[44]	404 [1]	634 [1]	108	S	1,350	3,200	—
SUNY Maritime College*; Fort Schuyler, Bronx, N.Y. 10465	n.a.	n.a.	n.a.	S	n.a.	n.a.	n.a.
SUNY Upstate Medical Center*; Syracuse, N.Y. 13210	483	370	248	S	1,132	1,832	2,400
New York, University of the State of,							
Regents External Degree Program; Albany, N.Y. 12230	7,813 [1]	6,833 [1]	200	P	375	375	—
New York City Technical Coll. *See* New York, City Univ. of							
New York College of Podiatric Medicine*; New York, N.Y. 10035	407	100	55	P	8,880	8,880	5,000
New York Institute of Technology*; Old Westbury, N.Y. 11568	5,215	1,766	232	P	3,680	3,680	2,690
New York Law School; New York, N.Y. 10013	543	297	51	P	6,300	6,300	—
New York Medical College*; Valhalla, N.Y. 10595	n.a.	n.a.	n.a.	P	n.a.	n.a.	n.a.
New York University; New York, N.Y. 10003	8,937 [1]	9,076 [1]	n.a.	P	7,850 [3]	7,850 [3]	4,138 [3]
Niagara University*; Niagara University, N.Y. 14109	1,620	1,937	159	P/RC	4,590	4,590	2,800
Nicholls State University; Thibodaux, La. 70310	2,615 [1]	2,751 [1]	279	S	787	1,417	1,625
Nichols College; Dudley, Mass. 01570	446 [1]	265 [1]	35	P	4,725	4,725	2,790
Norfolk State University; Norfolk, Va. 23504	2,437 [1]	3,407 [1]	345	S	1,090	1,910	2,190
North Adams State College; North Adams, Mass. 01247	1,038 [1]	1,204 [1]	103	S	845	2,790	2,320
North Alabama, University of; Florence, Ala. 35632	1,826 [1]	2,180 [1]	192	S	940	1,340	1,896
North American Baptist College; Edmonton, Alta., Canada T6J 4T3	109	87	16	P/B	1,440	1,440	2,424
North Carolina, University System of; Chapel Hill, N.C. 27514:							
Appalachian State University*; Boone, N.C. 28608	5,081	5,432	468	S	732	2,532	1,730
East Carolina University; Greenville, N.C. 27834	4,993 [1]	5,971 [1]	846	S	410	2,722	1,894
Elizabeth City State University; Elizabeth City, N.C. 27909	603 [1]	759 [1]	93	S	738	2,772	1,832
Fayetteville State University*; Fayetteville, N.C. 28301	1,081	1,328	143	S	689	2,271	n.a.
North Carolina Agricultural and Technical State University*; Greensboro, N.C. 27411	3,131	2,158	324	S	372	2,160	1,772
North Carolina Central University*; Durham, N.C. 27707	n.a.	n.a.	n.a.	S	n.a.	n.a.	n.a.
North Carolina School of the Arts; Winston-Salem, N.C. 27107	380 [1]	239 [1]	97	S	732	2,752	2,252
N.C. State Univ. at Raleigh; Raleigh, N.C. 27695	14,515 [1]	8,117 [1]	1,272	S	726	3,088	2,250
Pembroke State University; Pembroke, N.C. 28372	850 [1]	984 [1]	118	S	630	2,664	1,430
Univ. of N.C. at Asheville*; Asheville, N.C. 28814	1,228 [1]	1,420 [1]	98	S	704	2,738	1,900
Univ. of N.C. at Chapel Hill; Chapel Hill, N.C. 27514	8,615	10,310	1,917	S	436	2,260	2,300
Univ. of N.C. at Charlotte; Charlotte, N.C. 28223	3,783 [1]	3,274 [1]	469	S	669	2,981	2,252
Univ. of N.C. at Greensboro; Greensboro, N.C. 27412	3,055	6,273	542	S	808	3,170	1,950
Univ. of N.C. at Wilmington; Wilmington, N.C. 28403	2,462 [1]	2,727 [1]	281	S	645	2,227	2,025
Western Carolina University; Cullowhee, N.C. 28723	2,334 [1]	2,164 [1]	310	S	410	2,722	1,690
Winston-Salem State University*; Winston-Salem, N.C. 27110	858	1,308	175	S	754	2,336	1,821
North Carolina Central Univ. *See* North Carolina, Univ. System of							
North Carolina School of the Arts. *See* North Carolina, Univ. System of							
North Carolina State University at Raleigh. *See* North Carolina, Univ. System of							
North Carolina Wesleyan College; Rocky Mount, N.C. 27801	292 [1]	239 [1]	50	P/M	4,000	4,000	1,090
North Central College; Naperville, Ill. 60566	508	440	69	P	5,112	5,112	2,442
North Dakota, University of; Grand Forks, N.D. 58202	4,889 [1]	4,004 [1]	504	S	1,080	1,986	1,738
North Dakota State University; Fargo, N.D. 58105	5,713 [3]	3,764 [3]	450	S	1,008	1,914	1,644
Northeastern Bible College*; Essex Fells, N.J. 07021	193	128	17	P	2,800	2,800	1,900
Northeastern Illinois University; Chicago, Ill. 60625	2,012 [45]	2,390 [45]	370	S	1,014 [3]	3,042 [3]	—
Northeastern Louisiana University*; Monroe, La. 71209	4,833	6,467	367	S	527	1,157	1,544
Northeastern Ohio Universities, College of Medicine; Rootstown, Ohio 44272	249 [1]	130 [1]	38	S	3,750	7,500	—
Northeastern Oklahoma State University; Tahlequah, Okla. 74464	2,935	3,787	220	S	736	2,070	2,036
Northeastern University*; Boston, Mass. 02115	11,548	6,891	830	P	4,725	4,725	3,300
Northeast Louisiana University*; Monroe, La. 71209	3,819	4,275	406	S	660	1,290	2,008
Northeast Missouri State University; Kirksville, Mo. 63501	3,044 [1]	3,946 [1]	350	S	620	1,240	1,400
Northern Arizona University; Flagstaff, Ariz. 86011	6,096 [1]	5,405 [1]	512	S	950	3,200	1,072
Northern Colorado, University of; Greeley, Colo. 80639	3,907 [1]	5,101 [1]	444	S	1,158	4,182	1,308
Northern Illinois University*; DeKalb, Ill. 60115	8,039	9,248	1,100	S	780	2,340	1,045
Northern Iowa, University of; Cedar Falls, Iowa 50614	3,713 [1]	4,339 [1]	578	S	1,184	2,700	1,812
Northern Kentucky University; Highland Heights, Ky. 41076	2,389 [1]	2,375 [1]	279	S	890	2,550	1,240 [11]
Northern Michigan University; Marquette, Mich. 49855	4,216 [3]	4,013 [3]	304	S	1,472	3,392	2,316
Northern Montana College; Havre, Mont. 59501	1,028	714	90	S	651	1,839	2,130
Northern State College; Aberdeen, S.D. 57401	968	1,242	115	S	944	2,000	1,475
North Florida, University of*; Jacksonville, Fla. 32216	2,502	3,009	180	S	840	2,730	—
North Georgia College; Dahlonega, Ga. 30597	781 [1]	910 [1]	110	S	852	2,559	1,575
Northland College; Ashland, Wis. 54806	337 [1]	285 [1]	43	P	4,900	4,900	2,565
North Park College*; Chicago, Ill. 60625	600	600	75	P/EC	4,680	4,680	2,313
Northrop University*; Inglewood, Calif. 90306	1,418	187	90	P	4,725	4,725	3,210
North Texas State University; Denton, Tex. 76203	9,868 [1]	10,366 [1]	890	S	465	1,600	2,578
Northwest Bible College; Minot, N.D. 58701	96	64	6	P/CG	7,650	7,650	1,600
Northwest Christian College; Eugene, Ore. 97401	124 [1]	90 [1]	16	P/ChC	3,690	3,690	2,168
Northwest College of the Assemblies of God*; Kirkland, Wash. 98033	382	259	24	AG	2,670	2,670	1,824

Institution and location	Enrollment		Faculty	Control	Tuition ($)		Rm/Bd ($)
	Male	Female			Res.	Nonres.	
Northwestern College; Orange City, Iowa 51041	420[1]	446[1]	62	P/RCA	4,752	4,752	1,868
Northwestern College; Roseville, Minn. 55113	386	410	34	P/ID	4,260	4,260	1,950
Northwestern College; Watertown, Wis. 53094	248	—	20	P/EL	1,540	1,540	1,550
Northwestern Coll. of Chiropractic; Bloomington, Minn. 55431	209	92	32	P	4,900	4,900	6,000
Northwestern Oklahoma State University*; Alva, Okla. 73717	841	1,017	73	S	590	1,530	1,360
Northwestern State University of Louisiana*; Natchitoches, La. 71497	1,248	1,737	240	S	340	655	795
Northwestern University*; Evanston, Ill. 60201	8,366	7,335	1,300	P	8,085	8,085	1,300
Northwest Missouri State University; Maryville, Mo. 64468	2,074[1]	2,092[1]	245	S	875	1,590	1,770
Northwest Nazarene College*; Nampa Idaho 83651	549	599	76	P/Naz	3,495	3,495	1,965
Northwood Institute; Midland, Mich. 48640	1,100[3]	680[3]	50	P	4,100	4,100	2,400
Norwich University; Northfield, Vt. 05663	1,673[1]	938[1]	180	P	7,750	7,750	2,500
Vermont College of Norwich Univ.*; Montpelier, Vt. 05663	52	366	44	P	8,400[4]	8,400[4]	—
Notre Dame, College of*; Belmont, Calif. 94002	308	505	64	P/RC	4,700	4,700	2,800
Notre Dame, University of*; Notre Dame, Ind. 46556	6,499	2,527	774	P/RC	5,950	5,950	2,200
Notre Dame College; Manchester, N.H. 03104	39	371	37	P/RC	3,870	3,870	2,670
Notre Dame College of Ohio; South Euclid, Ohio 44121	—	405[1]	33	P/RC	3,850[3]	3,850[3]	2,150
Notre Dame of Maryland, College of; Baltimore, Md. 21210	—	535	62	P	5,200	5,200	3,200
Nova University; Ft. Lauderdale, Fla. 33314	2,757[1]	3,402[1]	83	P	4,320	4,320	3,500
Nyack College; Nyack, N.Y. 10960	347	353	51	P/CMA	4,260	4,260	2,440
Oakland City College; Oakland City, Ind. 47660	300[1]	236[1]	35	P/B	3,600	3,600	1,100
Oakland University; Rochester, Mich. 48063	4,511	6,617	360	S	1,545	3,917	2,486
Oakwood College; Huntsville, Ala. 35896	657	664	76	P/SDA	3,966	3,966	2,025
Oberlin College; Oberlin, Ohio 44074	1,255[1]	1,490[1]	240	P	9,175	9,175	3,340
Occidental College; Los Angeles, Calif. 90041	812[1]	793[1]	120	P	7,752	7,752	3,300
Oglethorpe University; Atlanta, Ga. 30319	415[1]	615[1]	40	P	4,940	4,940	2,710
Ohio Dominican College; Columbus, Ohio 43219	297[1]	344[1]	50	P/RC	4,610	4,610	2,650
Ohio Institute of Technology, Columbus. *See* DeVry Institute of Technology, Columbus							
Ohio Northern University; Ada, Ohio 45810	1,509[1]	965[1]	167	P/UM	5,415	5,415	2,280
Ohio State University, The; Columbus, Ohio 43210	22,734	17,539	3,087	S	1,557	3,984	2,625
Columbus Campus*; Columbus, Ohio 43210	24,603	18,548	2,969	S	1,458	3,726	2,514
Lima Campus; Lima, Ohio 45807	291[1]	400[1]	43	S	1,509	3,936	—
Mansfield Campus; Mansfield, Ohio 44906	384	540	37	S	4,554	7,787	2,625
Marion Campus*; Marion, Ohio 43302	213	222	25	S	1,413	3,681	—
Newark Campus*; Newark, Ohio 43055	260	295	29	S	1,413	3,681	—
Ohio University; Athens, Ohio 45701	7,407	5,684	739	S	1,917	3,858	2,595
Ohio Wesleyan University; Delaware, Ohio 43015	801[1]	747[1]	139	P/M	6,785	6,785	2,425
Oklahoma, University of; Norman, Okla. 73019	9,749[1]	6,579[1]	888	S	858	2,484	2,293
Oklahoma Baptist University; Shawnee, Okla. 74801	731	796	102	P/B	2,480	2,480	1,820
Oklahoma Christian College; Oklahoma City, Okla. 73111	615[1]	657[1]	56	P/CC	2,550	2,550	1,900
Oklahoma City Southwestern College. *See* Southwestern College of Christian Ministries							
Oklahoma City University; Oklahoma City, Okla. 73106	843[1]	659[1]	116	P/M	3,240	3,240	2,700
Oklahoma College of Osteopathic Medicine and Surgery*; Tulsa, Okla. 74101	212	38	30	S	2,500	2,500	—
Oklahoma Panhandle State University; Goodwell, Okla. 73939	512	458	54	S	550	981	1,600
Oklahoma State University*; Stillwater, Okla. 74078	n.a.	n.a.	n.a.	S	n.a.	n.a.	n.a.
Old Dominion University; Norfolk, Va. 23508	9,877[1]		717	S	1,504	2,800	3,000
Olivet College; Olivet, Mich. 49021	359[1]	246[1]	36	P/UCC	5,080	5,080	2,350
Olivet Nazarene College; Kankakee, Ill. 60901	690[1]	820[1]	85	P/Naz	3,704	3,704	2,106
Ontario Bible College; Willowdale, Ont., Canada M2M 4B3	166[1]	163[1]	17	ID	1,836	1,836	2,160
Open Bible College; Des Moines, Iowa 50321	40	23	10	P/OBS	2,250	2,250	2,500
Oral Roberts University; Tulsa, Okla. 74171	2,296[1]	2,064[1]	385	P/ID	3,600	3,600	2,400
Oregon, University of; Eugene, Ore. 97403	7,899[1]	7,579[1]	885	S	1,432	4,057	2,250
Oregon College of Education. *See* Western Oregon State College							
Oregon Graduate Center; Beaverton, Ore. 97006	55	11	30	P	6,000	6,000	—
Oregon Health Sciences University*; Portland, Ore. 97201	687	653	n.a.	S	n.a.	n.a.	n.a.
Oregon Institute of Technology*; Klamath Falls, Ore. 97601	1,517	592	186	S	1,370	3,995	2,195
Oregon State University; Corvallis, Ore. 97331	8,860[1]	5,941[1]	837	S	1,410	4,035	2,040
Orlando College*; Orlando, Fla. 32810	413	365	n.a.	P	n.a.	n.a.	n.a.
Osteopathic Medicine, College of, of the Pacific; Pomona, Calif. 91766	249	82	30	P	11,500	11,500	4,270
Otis Art Institute of Parsons School of Design; Los Angeles, Calif. 90057	236[1]	377[1]	15	P	5,870	5,870	1,732
Ottawa University; Ottawa, Kan. 66067	276[3]	168[3]	25	P/AB	3,830	3,830	1,064
Otterbein College; Westerville, Ohio 43081	487[1]	659[1]	100	P/UM	6,309	6,309	2,544
Ouachita Baptist University; Arkadelphia, Ark. 71923	748	756	85	P/B	2,700	2,700	1,700
Our Lady of Angels College. *See* Neumann College							
Our Lady of Holy Cross College; New Orleans, La. 70114	175	478	36	P/RC	3,000	3,000	—
Our Lady of the Elms, College of*; Chicopee, Mass. 01013	—	595	57	P/RC	4,350	4,350	2,480
Our Lady of the Lake University of San Antonio; San Antonio, Tex. 78285	400[1]	610[1]	80	P/RC	3,660	3,660	2,000
Ozarks, The College of the; Clarksville, Ark. 72830	288[3]	318[3]	41	P/Pres	1,425	1,425	1,450
Ozarks, The School of the; Point Lookout, Mo. 65726	533	536	80	P	([46])	([46])	([46])
Pace University; New York, N.Y. 10038	1,290[1]	1,578[1]	175	P	4,800	4,800	3,200
Pace University at White Plains; White Plains, N.Y. 10603	687[1]	1,148[1]	65	P	5,000	5,000	3,050
University College of Pace University*; Pleasantville, N.Y. 10570	1,151	1,324	125	P	3,648	3,648	2,700
Pacific, University of the; Stockton, Calif. 95211	2,662[1]	2,149[1]	367	P	7,780	7,780	3,282

Institution and location	Enrollment Male	Enrollment Female	Faculty	Control	Tuition ($) Res.	Tuition ($) Nonres.	Rm/Bd ($)
Pacific Christian College; Fullerton, Calif. 92631	163	125	15	P/ChC	2,900	2,900	2,500
Pacific Lutheran University; Tacoma, Wash. 98447	1,513 [1]	2,020 [1]	221	P	5,950	5,950	2,815
Pacific Northwest College of Art; Portland, Ore. 97205	68 [1]	126 [1]	16	P	3,550	3,550	—
Pacific Oaks College*; Pasadena, Calif. 91103	21	241	22	P	n.a.	n.a.	—
Pacific Union College; Angwin, Calif. 94508	678 [1]	765 [1]	113	P/SDA	5,775	5,775	2,175
Pacific University; Forest Grove, Ore. 97116	618 [1]	414 [1]	n.a.	P/UCC	5,650	5,650	2,750
Paine College; Augusta, Ga. 30910	231	496	65	P/UM	2,700	2,700	1,650
Palm Beach Atlantic College; West Palm Beach, Fla. 33401	333 [1]	378 [1]	30	P/SB	3,450	3,450	2,150
Pan American University; Edinburg, Tex. 78539	2,421	3,048	375	S	508	2,018	2,880
Paper Chemistry, The Institute of; Appleton, Wis. 54915	73	11	37	P	3,000	3,000	2,220
Park College; Parkville, Mo. 64152	220 [1]	191 [1]	25	P/LDS	4,110	4,110	2,140
Parks College of St. Louis University; Cahokia, Ill. 62206	610	51	50	P/RC	5,565	5,565	3,630
Parsons School of Design. *See* New School for Social Research							
Patten College; Oakland, Calif. 94601	60	90	12	P/CE	2,412	2,412	2,417
Paul Quinn College*; Waco, Tex. 76704	211	209	28	P	1,800	1,800	1,500
Peabody Institute of The Johns Hopkins University, Conservatory of Music; Baltimore, Md. 21202	173 [1]	166 [1]	51	P	7,150	7,150	3,000
Pembroke State University. *See* North Carolina, University System of							
Pennsylvania, University of*; Philadelphia, Pa. 19104	n.a.	n.a.	n.a.	P	n.a.	n.a.	n.a.
Pennsylvania College of Optometry; Philadelphia, Pa. 19141	380	212	n.a.	P	6,500	6,500	4,000
Pennsylvania College of Podiatric Medicine; Philadelphia, Pa. 19107	361	97	33	P	9,500	9,500	4,820
Pennsylvania State University, The; University Park, Pa. 16870	18,740	14,182	1,886	S [47]	2,312	4,644	2,610
Behrend College; Erie, Pa. 16563	1,179	610	100	P	2,312	4,254	2,274
Capitol Campus*; Middletown, Pa. 17057	n.a.	n.a.	n.a.	S	n.a.	n.a.	n.a.
College of Medicine at The Milton S. Hershey Medical Center; Hershey, Pa. 17033	269 [3]	116 [3]	280	S	7,296	11,397	n.a.
King of Prussia Graduate Center*; King of Prussia, Pa. 19406	15	15	n.a.	S	n.a.	n.a.	n.a.
Peppardine University*; Malibu, Calif. 90265	2,472	1,997	180	P/CC	7,520	7,520	3,400
Peru State College; Peru, Neb. 68421	386 [1]	386 [1]	48	S	825	1,380	1,735
Pfeiffer College; Misenheimer, N.C. 28109	352 [1]	300 [1]	52	P/UM	3,465	3,465	1,985
Philadelphia College of Art; Philadelphia, Pa. 19102	397	496	73	P	6,375	6,375	2,000 [11]
Philadelphia College of Bible; Langhorne, Pa. 19047	246 [1]	182 [1]	40	P	3,520	3,520	2,330
Philadelphia College of Osteopathic Medicine; Philadelphia, Pa. 19131	619	214	108	P	10,300	10,600	—
Philadelphia College of Pharmacy and Science; Philadelphia, Pa. 19104	520 [1]	561 [1]	149	P	5,400	5,400	2,640
Philadelphia College of Textiles and Science*; Philadelphia, Pa. 19144	649	920	92	P	4,400	4,400	2,550
Philadelphia College of the Performing Arts; Philadelphia, Pa. 19102	146 [1]	198 [1]	15	P	5,720	5,720	2,000 [11]
Philander Smith College*; Little Rock, Ark. 72202	263	263	30	P/UM	1,300	1,300	2,000
Phillips University; Enid, Okla. 73701	377 [1]	298 [1]	68	P	3,680	3,680	2,330
Phoenix, University of; Phoenix, Ariz. 85004	4,300		n.a.	P	3,600	3,600	—
Piedmont Bible College*; Winston-Salem, N.C. 27101	240	150	20	P/B	2,136	2,136	1,680
Piedmont College, Demorest, Ga. 30535	170 [1]	180 [1]	20	P/Cong	1,200	1,925	2,400
Pikeville College; Pikeville, Ky. 41501	117	247	35	P/Pres	3,300	3,300	2,100
Pine Manor College; Chestnut Hill, Mass. 02167	—	545	28	P	7,200	7,200	4,200
Pittsburgh, University of; Pittsburgh, Pa. 15260	15,620 [1]	13,805 [1]	2,142	P/S	2,650	5,300	2,732
U. of Pittsburgh at Bradford*; Bradford, Pa. 16701	929		n.a.	S	2,210	4,420	2,500
U. of Pittsburgh at Johnstown; Johnstown, Pa. 15904	1,654	1,394	118	P/S	2,420	4,840	2,302
Pittsburgh State University; Pittsburg, Kan. 66762	2,712 [1]	2,559 [1]	229	S	908	1,928	2,124
Pitzer College. *See* Claremont Colleges							
Plymouth State College; Plymouth, N.H. 03264	1,567 [1]	1,341 [1]	142	S	1,450	3,800	2,180
Point Loma Nazarene College; San Diego, Calif. 92106	659	854	80	P/Naz	4,272	4,272	2,260
Point Park College; Pittsburgh, Pa. 15222	615 [1]	469 [1]	78	P	4,762	4,762	3,350
Polytechnic Institute of New York; Brooklyn, N.Y. 11201	4,284	634	235	P	3,550	3,550	1,500
Pomona College. *See* Claremont Colleges							
Ponce School of Medicine; Ponce, P.R. 00732	138	45	41	P	11,000	13,000	6,600
Portland, University of; Portland, Ore. 97232	952 [1]	968 [1]	109	P	4,740	4,740	2,400
Portland School of Art; Portland, Me. 04101	82 [1]	153 [1]	15	P	5,500	5,500	2,900
Portland State University; Portland, Ore. 97068	7,075 [1]	7,422 [1]	671	S	1,404	4,029	2,718
Post College; Waterbury, Conn. 06708	221 [3]	404 [3]	31	P	4,536	4,536	2,835
Potsdam Coll. of Arts & Science. *See* New York, State Univ. of							
Prairie View A&M Univ. *See* Texas A&M Univ. System							
Pratt Institute; Brooklyn, N.Y. 11205	2,245 [1]	1,551 [1]	139	P	6,500	6,500	1,800
Presbyterian College; Clinton, S.C. 29325	520 [1]	375 [1]	56	P	4,580	4,580	2,170
Princeton University; Princeton, N.J. 08544	3,916 [1]	6,305 [1]	617	P	9,450	9,450	3,460
Principia College; Elsah, Ill. 62028	318	431	93	P	6,516	6,516	3,468
Providence College; Providence, R.I. 02918	1,865	1,877	218	P	6,328	6,328	3,550
Puerto Rico, University of; Río Piedras, P.R. 00931:							
Cayey University College*; Cayey, P.R. 00633	1,178	2,141	n.a.	S	n.a.	n.a.	n.a.
Humacao University College*; Humacao, P.R. 00661	913	1,624	n.a.	S	n.a.	n.a.	n.a.
Mayaguez Campus*; Mayaguez, P.R. 00708	n.a.	n.a.	n.a.	S	n.a.	n.a.	n.a.
Medical Sciences Campus*; San Juan, P.R. 00936	1,034	1,985	n.a.	S	700	2,000	—
Río Piedras Campus; Río Piedras, P.R. 00931	4,857	9,403	1,098	S	435	([48])	902
Puget Sound, University of; Tacoma, Wash. 98416	1,289 [1]	1,563 [1]	170	P	6,248 [3]	6,248 [3]	3,000 [3]

Institution and location	Enrollment		Faculty	Control	Tuition ($)		Rm/Bd ($)
	Male	Female			Res.	Nonres.	
Puget Sound College of the Bible; Edmonds, Wash. 98020	60	44	7	P/ChC	2,187	2,187	2,055
Purdue University; West Lafayette, Ind. 47907	15,872	10,376	2,058	S	1,532	4,556	2,362
Calumet Campus; Hammond, Ind. 46323	1,666 [1]	1,599 [1]	305	S	500	1,223	—
Indiana University–Purdue University at Indianapolis. *See* Indiana University							
Queens College*; Charlotte, N.C. 28274	97	650	480	P/Pres	4,200	4,200	2,360
Queens College (NYC). *See* New York, City University of							
Quincy College*; Quincy, Ill. 62301	365	377	73	P/RC	4,200	4,200	2,130
Quinnipiac College; Hamden, Conn. 06518	779 [1]	1,519 [1]	200	P	5,950	5,950	2,800
Radcliffe College. *See* Harvard University							
Radford University; Radford, Va. 24142	2,115	4,170	289	S	1,485	2,235	2,424
Ramapo College of New Jersey; Mahwah, N.J. 07430	2,017	1,938	135	S	969	1,569	2,000 [11]
Rand Graduate Institute; Santa Monica, Calif. 90406	53 [1]	7 [1]	—	P	7,500	7,500	10,000
Randolph–Macon College; Ashland, Va. 23005	504	360	74	P	6,000 [3]	6,000 [3]	2,750 [3]
Randolph–Macon Women's College; Lynchburg, Va. 24503	—	739	64	P/UM	7,000	7,000	3,300
Redlands, University of; Redlands, Calif. 92374	1,124 [1]	1,016 [1]	115	P	7,800	7,800	3,250
Reed College; Portland, Ore. 97202	625 [3]	471 [3]	117	P	8,190	8,190	2,830
Reformed Bible College; Grand Rapids, Mich. 49506	117	74	14	P	3,000	3,000	2,200
Regis College; Denver, Colo. 80221	1,683 [1]	1,330 [1]	75	P/RC	2,915	2,915	1,785
Regis College; Weston, Mass. 02193	—	814 [1]	55	P/RC	5,150	5,150	3,100
Rensselaer Polytechnic Institute; Troy, N.Y. 12181	4,749	1,150	380	P	9,050	9,050	3,378
Rhode Island, University of; Kingston, R.I. 02881	5,378	4,939	730	S	1,386	4,862	3,223
Rhode Island College; Providence, R.I. 02908	1,709 [1]	3,055 [1]	376	S	998	3,330	2,910
Rhode Island School of Design; Providence, R.I. 02903	660	1,054	92	P	8,150	8,150	3,500
Rice University; Houston, Tex. 77251	2,343	1,420	450	P	3,900	3,900	3,250
Richmond, University of; Richmond, Va. 23173	1,619	1,419	200	P/B	6,800	6,800	2,200
Richmond College, The American International College of London; London, England TW10 6JP	320	440	25	P	([49])	([49])	([50])
Rider College*; Lawrenceville, N.J. 08648	1,592	1,698	209	P	4,500	4,500	2,420
Ringling School of Art and Design; Sarasota, Fla. 33580	180 [1]	237 [1]	30	P	3,900	3,900	2,680
Ripon College; Ripon, Wis. 54971	475	355	71	P	6,542	6,542	1,960
Rivier College; Nashua, N.H. 03060	30	515	50	P/RC	4,200	4,200	2,700
Roanoke Bible College; Elizabeth City, N.C. 27909	85 [1]	76 [1]	9	P	1,000	1,000	1,480
Roanoke College; Salem, Va. 24153	537 [1]	625 [1]	72	P/LCA	5,200	5,200	7,450
Robert Morris College; Corapolis, Pa. 15108	1,429	1,595	96	P	2,880 [3]	2,880 [3]	2,000 [3]
Roberts Wesleyan College; Rochester, N.Y. 14624	214	378	47	P/FM	4,878	4,878	2,338
Rochester, The University of; Rochester, N.Y. 14627	4,057 [1]	2,546 [1]	1,189	P	8,240	8,240	3,545
Rochester Institute of Technology; Rochester, N.Y. 14623	4,857	2,470	642	P	6,255	6,255	3,321
Rockford College; Rockford, Ill. 61108	287 [1]	370 [1]	77	P	5,390	5,390	2,500
Rockhurst College; Kansas City, Mo. 64110	654 [1]	694 [1]	86	P/RC	5,000	5,000	2,550
Rockmont College; Denver, Colo. 80226	101	99	16	P/ID	3,734	3,734	1,355
Rocky Mountain College; Billings, Mont. 59102	198	191	40	P[51]	3,690	3,690	2,385
Roger Williams College*; Bristol, R.I. 02809	1,230	739	97	P	4,496	4,496	2,842
Rollins College; Winter Park, Fla. 32789	680	680	130	P	6,586	6,586	3,000
Roosevelt University; Chicago, Ill. 60605	1,028 [1]	990 [1]	180	P	3,432	3,432	3,060
Rosary College; River Forest, Ill. 60305	177 [1]	599 [1]	70	P/RC	5,200	5,200	2,550
Rose–Hulman Institute of Technology; Terre Haute, Ind. 47803	1,261	—	96	P	6,000	6,000	2,670
Rosemont College; Rosemont, Pa. 19010	—	506	36	P/RC	5,210	5,210	3,395
Rush University*; Chicago, Ill. 60612	443	729	636	P	n.a.	n.a.	n.a.
Russell Sage College; Troy, N.Y. 12180	—	1,400	133	P	6,200	6,200	n.a.
Rust College; Holly Springs, Miss. 38635	377	474	33	P	3,900 [4]	3,900 [4]	—
Rutgers, The State University of New Jersey; New Brunswick, N.J. 08903	15,596 [1]	15,693 [1]	2,533	S	1,490	2,980	2,270
Rutgers Medical School. *See* Medicine and Dentistry, College of, of New Jersey							
Sacred Heart, Univ. of the; Santurce, P.R. 00914	3,346	4,827	126	P/RC	1,804	1,804	1,500
Sacred Heart College; Belmont, N.C. 28012	75 [1]	244 [1]	19	P/RC	2,300	2,300	2,080
Sacred Heart University; Bridgeport, Conn. 06606	761 [1]	1,151 [1]	93	P	4,150	4,150	—
Saginaw Valley State College; University Center, Mich. 48710	1,104 [1]	1,150 [1]	123	S	1,627	3,162	2,280
St. Ambrose College; Davenport, Iowa 52803	730 [1]	446 [1]	82	P/RC	4,368	4,368	2,020
St. Andrews Presbyterian College; Laurinburg, N.C. 28352	327 [3]	338 [3]	51	P/Pres	5,350	5,350	2,645
St. Anselm College*; Manchester, N.H. 03102	870	883	130	P/RC	5,200	5,200	2,700
St. Augustine's College; Raleigh, N.C. 27611	659 [3]	937 [3]	67	P/E	1,800	1,800	1,600
St. Benedict, College of; St. Joseph, Minn. 56374	—	1,948 [1]	107	P/RC	4,760	4,760	2,055
St. Bonaventure University St. Bonaventure N.Y. 14778	1,238 [3]	1,111 [3]	163	P	4,990	4,990	2,750
St. Catherine, The College of; St. Paul, Minn. 55105	21 [1]	2,263 [1]	121	P/RC	4,960	4,960	2,360
St. Cloud State University. *See* Minnesota State University System							
St. Edward's University; Austin, Tex. 78704	1,206	1,000	73	P/RC	3,250	3,250	2,480
St. Elizabeth, College of*; Convent Station, N.J. 07961	3	509	50	P/RC	4,500	4,500	2,500
St. Francis, College of; Joliet, Ill. 60435	264	408	40	P/RC	4,148	4,148	2,660
St. Francis College; Brooklyn, N.Y. 11201	777	683	65	P	3,854	3,854	—
St. Francis College; Fort Wayne, Ind. 46808	134 [1]	301 [1]	45	RC	3,300	3,300	2,300
St. Francis College; Loretto, Pa. 15940	502 [1]	512 [1]	61	P/RC	4,576	4,576	2,550
St. John Fisher College; Rochester, N.Y. 14618	838 [1]	715 [1]	100	P	5,325 [3]	5,325 [3]	2,830 [3]

Institution and location	Enrollment Male	Enrollment Female	Faculty	Control	Tuition ($) Res.	Tuition ($) Nonres.	Rm/Bd ($)
St. John's College; Annapolis, Md. 21404	223	173	52	P	8,250	8,250	2,900
St. John's College*; Santa Fe, N.M. 87501	154	126	35	P	7,200	7,200	2,700
Saint John's College*; Camarillo, Calif. 93010	n.a.	n.a.	n.a.	P/RC	n.a.	n.a.	n.a.
Saint John's University; Collegeville, Minn. 56321	1,923 [1]	22 [1]	124	P/RC	4,760	4,760	2,295
St. John's University; Jamaica, N.Y. 11439	7,114 [1]	6,335 [1]	601	P/RC	4,000 [3]	4,000 [3]	—
St. Joseph College*; West Hartford, Conn. 06117	4	575	64	P	4,750	4,750	2,900
St. Joseph in Vermont, College of*; Rutland, Vt. 05701	39	117	10	P/RC	3,990	3,990	2,470
St. Joseph's College; Brooklyn, N.Y. 11205	107 [1]	343 [1]	115	P	3,200	3,200	—
St. Joseph's College; North Windham, Me. 04062	152	322	35	P/RC	3,950	3,950	2,400
St. Joseph's College; Rensselaer, Ind. 47978	608 [1]	370 [1]	51	P/RC	4,990	4,990	2,470
St. Joseph's University; Philadelphia, Pa. 19131	2,016 [1]	1,937 [1]	140	P/RC	5,140	5,140	3,230
St. Joseph the Provider, College of. *See* St. Joseph in Vermont, College of							
St. Lawrence University; Canton, N.Y. 13617	1,144 [1]	1,074 [1]	157	P	7,800	7,800	2,710
St. Leo College*; St. Leo, Fla. 33574	620	538	55	P/RC	3,530	3,530	1,620
St. Louis Christian College*; Florissant, Mo. 63033	68	75	13	P/ChC	1,400	1,400	1,260
St. Louis College of Pharmacy*; St. Louis, Mo. 63110	306	327	31	P	3,730	3,730	2,250
St. Louis Conservatory of Music*; St. Louis, Mo. 63130	n.a.	n.a.	n.a.	P	n.a.	n.a.	n.a.
St. Louis University; St. Louis, Mo. 63103	3,699 [1]	2,629 [1]	900	P	4,990	4,990	2,500
St. Martin's College*; Lacey, Wash. 98503	n.a.	n.a.	n.a.	P/RC	n.a.	n.a.	n.a.
St. Mary, College of; Omaha, Neb. 68124	16	444	42	P/RC	4,290	4,290	2,000
St. Mary College*; Leavenworth, Kan. 66048	—	650	45	P/RC	2,700	2,700	1,900
St. Mary of the Plains College; Dodge City, Kan. 67801	232 [1]	443 [1]	62	P/RC	3,600	3,600	2,200
St. Mary-of-the-Woods College; St. Mary-of-the-Woods, Ind. 47876	—	466 [1]	53	P/RC	4,720	4,720	2,290
St. Mary's College; Notre Dame, Ind. 46566	20 [1]	1,776 [1]	119	P/RC	5,850	5,850	3,038
St. Mary's College*; Orchard Lake, Mich. 48033	72	48	16	P	2,100	2,100	2,580
St. Mary's College*; Winona, Minn. 55987	638	598	72	P/RC	4,700	4,700	2,160
St. Mary's College of California; Moraga, Calif. 94575	823	1,061	124	P/RC	5,896	5,896	3,146
St. Mary's College of Maryland; St. Mary's City, Md. 20686	557	650	71	S	1,220	2,220	2,780
St. Mary's Dominican College*; New Orleans, La. 70118	5	363	30	P/RC	3,690	3,690	2,600
St. Mary's University; San Antonio, Tex. 78284	1,714 [3]	1,518 [3]	179	P/RC	4,384	4,384	2,200
St. Michael's College; Winooski, Vt. 05404	796 [1]	805 [1]	105	P/RC	7,575	7,575	7,575
St. Norbert College; De Pere, Wis. 54115	777 [1]	884 [1]	101	P/RC	5,220	5,220	2,500
St. Olaf College; Northfield, Minn. 55057	1,310 [1]	1,565 [1]	218	P/AL	6,550 [3]	6,550 [3]	2,200
St. Patrick's College, Mountain View, Calif. *See* St. Joseph's College							
St. Paul Bible College; Bible College, Minn. 55375	295 [1]	305 [1]	40	P/CMA	2,970	2,970	2,450
St. Paul's College; Lawrenceville, Va. 23868	341	346	46	P	2,690	2,690	2,250
St. Peter's College; Jersey City, N.J. 07306	1,361	1,191	135	P/RC	2,085	2,085	—
St. Rose, The College of; Albany, N.Y. 12203	246	858	105	P	2,200	2,200	1,200
St. Scholastica, College of; Duluth, Minn. 55811	240	766	75	P/RC	4,545	4,545	2,221
St. Teresa, College of*; Winona, Minn. 55987	10	600	62	P/RC	4,500	4,500	1,800
St. Thomas, College of*; St. Paul, Minn. 55105	3,378	2,252	150	P/RC	4,160	4,160	2,000
St. Thomas, University of; Houston, Tex. 77006	873 [1]	1,195 [1]	109	RC	3,200	3,200	3,000
St. Thomas Aquinas College; Sparkill, N.Y. 10976	557 [1]	600 [1]	100	P	3,600	3,600	1,500
Saint Vincent College; Latrobe, Pa. 15650	703	122	51	P/RC	4,380	4,380	2,200
St. Xavier College; Chicago, Ill. 60655	347 [1]	910 [1]	140	P/RC	4,870	4,870	2,728
Salem College; Salem, W. Va. 26426	362	373	45	P	4,440	4,440	2,460
Salem College; Winston-Salem, N.C. 27108	—	553	55	P	4,600	4,600	3,100
Salem State College; Salem, Mass. 01970	2,234	3,071	279	S	1,045	3,085	1,990
Salisbury State College; Salisbury, Md. 21801	1,378 [1]	1,711 [1]	183	S	1,030	2,140	2,400
Salve Regina—The Newport College*; Newport, R.I. 02840	222	1,054	83	P/RC	4,800	4,800	2,800
Samford University; Birmingham, Ala. 35229	1,890 [1]	2,196 [1]	n.a.	P/B	3,616	3,616	2,198
Sam Houston State University; Huntsville, Tex. 77341	4,914	4,860	390	S	404	1,264	2,378
San Diego, University of; San Diego, Calif. 92110	1,805 [1]	2,219 [1]	250	P/RC	6,250	6,250	2,600
San Diego State University; San Diego, Calif. 92182[24]	9,844	10,273	1,500	S	700	4,210	3,780
San Francisco, University of; San Francisco, Calif. 94117	1,822	1,918	237	P/RC	5,400	5,400	3,500
San Francisco Art Institute; San Francisco, Calif. 94133	283	314	28	P	5,720	5,720	6,000
San Francisco Conservatory of Music, The; San Francisco, Calif. 94122	73 [1]	94 [1]	13	P	5,300	5,300	—
San Francisco State Univ.; San Francisco, Calif. 94132[24]	17,373		1,000	S	345	345 [52]	2,500
Sangamon State University; Springfield, Ill. 62708	549 [1]	450 [1]	175	S	1,136	3,076	1,950
San Jose Bible College; San Jose, Calif. 95108	81	77	7	P/ChC	3,570	3,570	1,950
San Jose State University; San Jose, Calif. 95192[24]	7,460 [1]	7,511 [1]	990	S	612	4,122	2,600
Santa Clara, University of*; Santa Clara, Calif. 95053	2,223	2,055	282	P/RC	5,607	5,607	3,030
Santa Fe, College of; Santa Fe, N.M. 87501	235	322	41	P/RC	2,640	2,640	1,177
Sarah Lawrence College*; Bronxville, N.Y. 10708	162	799	69	P	8,150	8,150	3,600
Savannah State College; Savannah, Ga. 31404	895	1,045	132	S	1,092	2,799	1,770
Science and Arts, University of, of Oklahoma; Chickasha, Okla. 73018	289 [1]	445 [1]	55	S	608	1,696	1,500
Scranton, University of; Scranton, Pa. 18510	3,025	1,421	130	P/RC	4,384	4,384	2,475
Scripps College. *See* **Claremont Colleges**							
Seattle Pacific University; Seattle, Wash. 98119	763	1,088	165	P/FM	5,400	5,400	2,900
Seattle University; Seattle, Wash. 98122	2,217 [1]	2,469 [1]	283	P/RC	5,625	5,625	3,000
Seton Hall University*; South Orange, N.J. 07079	3,615	3,381	n.a.	P/RC	n.a.	n.a.	n.a.

Institution and location	Enrollment		Faculty	Control	Tuition ($)		Rm/Bd ($)
	Male	Female			Res.	Nonres.	
Seton Hall University School of Law; Newark, N.J. 07102	425	313	35	P	6,600	6,600	—
Seton Hill College; Greensburg, Pa. 15601	—	651[1]	51	P	5,250	5,250	2,650
Shaw University*; Raleigh, N.C. 27611	n.a.	n.a.	n.a.	P/B	n.a.	n.a.	n.a.
Sheldon Jackson College; Sitka, Alaska 99835	90[1]	98[1]	26	P	3,246	3,246	3,400
Shenandoah College and Conservatory of Music; Winchester, Va. 22601	317[1]	610[1]	75	P	4,600	4,600	2,500
Shepherd College; Shepherdstown, W. Va. 25443	938[1]	1,143[1]	106	S	800	2,200	2,040
Sherwood Conservatory of Music; Chicago, Ill. 60605	20	20	4[53]	P	2,500	2,500	3,200
Sherwood Music School. *See* Sherwood Conservatory of Music							
Shippensburg University of Pennsylvania; Shippensburg, Pa. 17257	2,269[1]	2,635[1]	275	S/Pub	2,960	5,180	3,420
Shorter College; Rome, Ga. 30161	291[1]	418[1]	49	P	2,525	3,250	2,000
Siena College; Loudonville, N.Y. 12211	1,371	1,234	134	P	4,470	4,470	2,860
Siena Heights College*; Adrian, Mich. 49221	296	355	68	P/RC	3,720	3,720	2,200
Sierra Nevada College; Incline Village, Nev. 89450	69	51	15	P	2,400	2,400	3,700
Silver Lake College; Manitowoc, Wis. 54220	58[1]	162[1]	30	P/RC	4,000[3]	4,000[3]	—
Simmons College*; Boston, Mass. 02115	—	2,000	150	P	7,104	7,104	3,488
Simon's Rock of Bard College; Great Barrington, Mass. 01230	124	170	32	P	8,100	8,100	2,800
Simpson College; Indianola, Iowa 50125	410[1]	353[1]	57	P	5,375	5,375	1,875
Simpson College; San Francisco, Calif. 94134	140[1]	126[1]	28	CMA	3,200	3,200	2,100
Sinte Gleska College*; Rosebud, S.D. 57570	62	105	n.a.	P	n.a.	n.a.	n.a.
Sioux Falls College; Sioux Falls, S.D. 57105	238[1]	327[1]	38	P/B	4,250	4,250	2,095
Skidmore College; Saratoga Springs, N.Y. 12866	743[1]	1,395[1]	184	P	8,050	8,050	3,450
Slippery Rock State College. *See* Slippery Rock University of Pennsylvania							
Slippery Rock University of Pennsylvania; Slippery Rock, Pa. 16057	2,955[1]	3,204[1]	330	S	1,480	2,590	1,754
Smith College; Northampton, Mass. 01063	—	2,486	250	P	9,170	9,170	3,570
Sojourner-Douglass College*; Baltimore, Md. 21205	170		n.a.	P	n.a.	n.a.	n.a.
Sonoma State University; Rohnert Park, Calif. 94928[24]	1,501[1]	1,887[1]	232	S	700	4,210	4,500
South, The University of the; Sewanee, Tenn. 37375	621[1]	435[1]	116	P/E	7,700[3]	7,700[3]	2,060[3]
South Alabama, University of; Mobile, Ala. 36688	3,359[1]	3,320[1]	346	S	1,389	1,989	1,935
Southampton College. *See* Long Island Univ. Center							
South Carolina, University of; Columbia, S.C. 29208	8,336[1]	7,602[1]	956	S	1,440	2,970	2,300
USC at Aiken; Aiken, S.C. 29801	739[1]	1,196[1]	81	S	1,000	2,140	—
USC at Spartanburg*; Spartanburg, S.C. 29303	782	1,826	130	S	850	1,840	—
USC–Coastal Carolina; Conway, S.C. 29526	843[1]	899[1]	115	S	1,000	2,140	2,100[6]
South Carolina State College*; Orangeburg, S.C. 29117	1,536	1,900	224	S	n.a.	n.a.	684
South Dakota, University of; Vermillion, S.D. 57069	2,681[1]	2,484[1]	407	S	976	2,224	936
University of South Dakota at Springfield*; Springfield, S.D. 57062	518	147	60	S	816	1,692	1,414
South Dakota School of Mines and Technology*; Rapid City, S.D. 57701	1,730	490	116	S	920	2,200	1,500
South Dakota State University; Brookings, S.D. 57007	3,479[1]	2,652[1]	370	S	915	2,072	1,540
Southeastern Bible College; Birmingham, Ala. 35256	88	44	17	P/ND	2,720	2,720	2,070
Southeastern College of Osteopathic Medicine*; North Miami Beach, Fla. 33162	n.a.	n.a.	n.a.	P	n.a.	n.a.	n.a.
Southeastern College of the Assemblies of God; Lakeland, Fla. 33801	598[1]	425[1]	31	P/AG	1,800	1,800	1,368
Southeastern Louisiana University*; Hammond, La. 70402	3,838	5,682	286	S	740	1,370	1,410
Southeastern Massachusetts University*; North Dartmouth, Mass. 02747	2,683	2,681	297	S	983	2,989	2,988
Southeastern Oklahoma State Univ.; Durant, Okla. 74701	1,823	1,841	150	S	619	1,702	1,856
Southeastern University*; Washington, D.C. 20024	554	308	3	P	n.a.	n.a.	n.a.
Southeast Missouri State University; Cape Girardeau, Mo. 63701	4,210[3]	4,883[3]	412	S	720	1,400	2,250
Southern Arkansas University; Magnolia, Ark. 71753	981[1]	1,184[1]	116	S	780	1,250	1,530
Southern Bible College*; Houston, Tex. 77213	70	51	n.a.	P/CG	1,560	1,560	1,680
Southern California, Univ. of; Los Angeles, Calif. 90089	18,337[1]	10,655[1]	1,811	P	8,625	8,625	n.a.
Southern California College; Costa Mesa, Calif. 92626	367[1]	304[1]	35	AG	3,800	3,800	1,200
Southern California College of Optometry; Fullerton, Calif. 92631	260	122	35	P	7,500	7,500	—
Southern California Institute of Architecture; Santa Monica, Calif. 90404	274	89	32	P	5,040	5,040	—
Southern College of Optometry; Memphis, Tenn. 38104	397[1]	81[1]	25	P	7,152	11,552	4,296
Southern College of Seventh-Day Adventists; Collegedale, Tenn. 37315	657[1]	968[1]	122	P/SDA	4,840[3]	4,840[3]	2,260
Southern Colorado, University of; Pueblo, Colo. 81001	2,717[1]	2,265[1]	196	S	950	3,744	2,544
Southern Connecticut State University; New Haven, Conn. 06515	2,915[1]	3,927[1]	407	S	1,061	2,881	1,316
Southern Illinois University at Carbondale; Carbondale, Ill. 62901	14,960[1]	8,423[1]	1,770	S	1,430	3,338	2,316
Southern Illinois University at Edwardsville*; Edwardsville, Ill. 62026	5,066	5,192	600	S	1,190	2,650	1,800
Southern Maine, University of; Gorham, Me. 04038	3,376	4,494	n.a.	S	1,623	4,902	2,475
Southern Methodist University; Dallas, Tex. 75275	3,556	3,175	467	P/M	6,100	6,100	3,380
Southern Missionary College. *See* Southern College of Seventh-Day Adventists							
Southern Mississippi, Univ. of*; Hattiesburg, Miss. 39406	5,059	5,733	500	S	1,040	1,966	770
Southern Oregon State College; Ashland, Ore. 97520	1,462	1,498	240	S	1,428	3,672	2,300
Southern School of Pharmacy. *See* Mercer Univ.							
Southern Technical Institute*; Marietta, Ga. 30060	2,758	242	100	S	660	1,710	3,929
Southern University and A&M College System; Baton Rouge, La. 70813:							
Southern University and A&M College*; Baton Rouge, La. 70813	4,407	4,770	570	S	750	1,380	2,160
Southern University in New Orleans*; New Orleans, La. 70126	857	1,843	110	S	618	1,248	—
Southern Utah State College; Cedar City, Utah 84720	1,224[1]	1,319[1]	118	S	285	758	1,800
Southern Vermont College; Bennington, Vt. 05201	114	129	17	P	3,540	3,540	2,620
South Florida, The University of; Tampa, Fla. 33620	12,690[1]	14,611[1]	1,052	S	845	2,405	2,290

Institution and location	Enrollment Male	Enrollment Female	Faculty	Control	Tuition ($) Res.	Tuition ($) Nonres.	Rm/Bd ($)
New College Campus; Sarasota, Fla. 33580	170	160	48	S	1,012	3,280	1,440 [11]
St. Petersburg Campus*; St. Petersburg, Fla. 33701	n.a.	n.a.	n.a.	S	n.a.	n.a.	n.a.
South Texas, University System of:							
Corpus Christi State University; Corpus Christi, Tex. 78412	462	619	109	S	405	1,485	1,800
Laredo State University; Laredo, Tex. 78040	404	498	30	S	120	1,200	—
Texas A&I University; Kingsville, Tex. 78363	2,724	2,578	215	S	636	1,926	2,582
South Texas College of Law*; Houston, Tex. 77002	381	174	27	P	4,300	4,300	6,100 [6]
Southwest, College of this; Hobbs, N.M. 88240	40	72	10	P	1,170	1,170	720 [11]
Southwest Baptist University*; Bolivar, Mo. 65613	643	782	72	P/SB	2,620	2,620	1,260
Southwestern Adventist College*; Keene, Tex. 76059	329	335	50	P/SDA	4,084	4,084	2,074
Southwestern at Memphis; Memphis, Tenn. 38112	493 [1]	492 [1]	95	P	6,330	6,330	2,920
Southwestern Baptist Bible College; Phoenix, Ariz. 85032	59 [1]	44 [1]	8	P/B	2,330	2,330	2,070
Southwestern College; Winfield, Kan. 67156	347	287	45	P/UM	3,400	3,400	2,107
Southwestern College of Christian Ministries; Oklahoma City, Okla. 73008	39	34	3	P/PH	1,950	1,950	1,640
Southwestern Louisiana, University of; Lafayette, La. 70504	8,150 [1]	8,116 [1]	621	S	653	1,280	1,682
Southwestern Oklahoma State University; Weatherford, Okla. 73096	1,899 [1]	1,896 [1]	203	S	604	1,687	1,240
Southwestern University; Georgetown, Tex. 78626	424 [1]	542 [1]	68	P/UM	4,300	4,300	2,675
Southwestern University School of Law*; Los Angeles, Calif. 90005	1,000	555	40	P	n.a.	n.a.	n.a.
Southwest Missouri State Univ.; Springfield, Mo. 65804	5,175 [1]	5,401 [1]	529	S	996 [3]	1,992 [3]	1,590 [3]
Southwest State Univ. *See* Minnesota State Univ. System							
Southwest Texas State Univ.; San Marcos, Tex. 78666	7,054 [1]	7,290 [1]	580 [20]	S	506	1,659	2,023
Spalding University; Louisville, Ky. 40203	49	383	56	P/RC	3,680	3,680	2,360
Spelman College; Atlanta, Ga. 30314	—	1,541	90	P	3,350	3,350	2,730
Spertus College of Judaica; Chicago, Ill. 60605	35	37	8	P	2,640	2,640	—
Spring Arbor College; Spring Arbor, Mich. 49283	572	405	45	P	4,590	4,590	2,008
Springfield College; Springfield, Mass. 01109	970 [1]	1,105 [1]	132	P	4,500	4,500	1,640
Spring Garden College; Philadelphia, Pa. 19118	600	120	60	P	4,700	4,700	3,600
Spring Hill College*; Mobile, Ala. 36608	435	412	55	P/RC	4,750	4,750	2,770
Stanford University; Stanford, Calif. 94305	3,736 [1]	2,818 [1]	1,219	P	9,705 [3]	9,705 [3]	4,146 [3]
Staten Island, College of (NYC). *See* New York, City University of							
Stephen F. Austin State Univ.; Nacogdoches, Tex. 75961	5,835 [1]	6,687 [1]	375	S	120	1,200	2,500
Stephens College; Columbia, Mo. 65215	21 [1]	1,054 [1]	99	P	6,270	6,270	2,830
Sterling College; Sterling, Kan. 67579	143	154	25	P/PUS	3,850	3,850	1,850
Stetson University College of Law; St. Petersburg, Fla. 33707	300	210	23	P	5,580	5,580	3,163
Steubenville, University of; Steubenville, Ohio 43952	261	355	49	P/RC	4,680	4,680	2,700
Stevens Institute of Technology; Hoboken, N.J. 07030	1,881	288	145	P	8,000 [3]	8,000 [3]	3,150 [3]
Stillman College; Tuscaloosa, Ala. 35403	269 [1]	334 [1]	47	P/PUS	2,300	2,300	2,200
Stockton State College*; Pomona, N.J. 08240	2,093	1,690	156	P	1,136	1,776	2,260
Stonehill College; North Easton, Mass. 02357	802 [1]	930 [1]	85	P/RC	5,515	5,515	3,000
Strayer College; Washington, D.C. 20005	576 [1]	1,147 [1]	34	P	2,640	2,640	—
Suffolk University; Boston, Mass. 02108	1,196	1,163	200	P	4,500	4,500	—
Sul Ross State University; Alpine, Tex. 79832	1,001	751	109	S	540	1,692	2,530
Susquehanna University; Selinsgrove, Pa. 17870	741	644	113	P/L	9,990	9,990	2,685
Swain School of Design; New Bedford, Mass. 02740	79	81	11	P	4,700	4,700	2,000 [6]
Swarthmore College*; Swarthmore, Pa. 19081	689	586	135	P	8,430	8,430	3,260
Sweet Briar College; Sweet Briar, Va. 24595	1	705	70	P	7,220 [1]	7,220 [1]	2,430 [1]
Syracuse University; Syracuse, N.Y. 13210	6,326 [1]	5,750 [1]	858	P	7,140	7,140	3,520
Tabor College; Hillsboro, Kan. 67063	211	159	30	MB	3,630	3,630	2,190
Talladega College*; Talladega, Ala. 35160	n.a.	n.a.	n.a.	P	n.a.	n.a.	n.a.
Tampa, The University of*; Tampa, Fla. 33606	771	644	88	P	4,356	4,356	2,000
Tampa College*; Tampa, Fla. 33607	740	900	n.a.	P	1,620	1,620	—
Tarkio College; Tarkio, Mo. 64491	320	207	30	P/UP	4,000	4,000	2,800
Tarleton State University*; Stephenville, Tex. 76402[54]	1,944	1,784	144	S	120	1,200	1,648
Taylor University; Upland, Ind. 46989	685	722	86	P/ID	5,240	5,240	2,224
Teachers College of Columbia University*; New York, N.Y. 10027	520	1,092	147	P	7,040	7,040	7,200
Temple University; Philadelphia, Pa. 19122	9,734 [1]	8,145 [1]	1,140	P/S	2,890	5,074	3,156
Tennessee State University; Nashville, Tenn. 37203[12]	2,099	2,376	441	S	792	2,550	2,016
Tennessee System, University of; Knoxville, Tenn. 37996:							
U. of Tennessee at Chattanooga*; Chattanooga, Tenn. 37402	2,327	2,335	265	S	620	1,840	n.a.
U. of Tennessee at Knoxville; Knoxville, Tenn. 37996	14,399 [1]	12,619 [1]	1,181	S	999	2,973	2,200
U. of Tennessee at Martin; Martin, Tenn. 38238	2,046	1,957	223	S	948	3,159	1,005 [11]
U. of Tennessee Center for the Health Sciences; Memphis, Tenn. 38163	1,137 [1]	777 [1]	523	S	2,300	4,500	1,200 [11]
Tennessee Technological Univ.*; Cookeville, Tenn. 38505[12]	3,920	2,629	351	S	771	2,532	1,620
Tennessee Wesleyan College; Athens, Tenn. 37303	168 [1]	187 [1]	22	P/UM	3,000	3,000	2,415
Texas, University of, System; Austin, Tex. 78701:							
U. of Texas at Arlington; Arlington, Tex. 76019	8,078 [1]	5,741 [1]	610	S	932	3,092	3,200
U. of Texas at Austin; Austin, Tex. 78712	25,960 [1]	21,671 [1]	1,910	S	462	1,542	2,851
U. of Texas at Dallas*; Richardson, Tex. 75080	1,162	1,091	210	S	394	1,254	—
U. of Texas at El Paso*; El Paso, Tex. 79968	4,858	4,342	439	S	400	1,480	2,005
U. of Texas at San Antonio; San Antonio, Tex. 78285	5,724 [1]	6,166 [1]	275	S	450	860	—
U. of Texas at Tyler; Tyler, Tex. 75701	444	675	91	S	420	1,500	—
U. of Texas Health Science Center at Dallas*; Dallas, Tex. 75235	823	461	730	S	120	1,200	—

Institution and location	Enrollment Male	Enrollment Female	Faculty	Control	Tuition ($) Res.	Tuition ($) Nonres.	Rm/Bd ($)
U. of Texas Health Science Center at Houston*; Houston, Tex. 77025	1,255	1,033	700	S	400	1,200	5,000
U. of Texas Health Science Center at San Antonio; San Antonio, Tex. 78284	1,109[1]	877[1]	709	S	400	1,200	—
U. of Texas Medical Branch; Galveston, Tex. 77550	752	891	558	S	4,00	1,200	6,652
U. of Texas of the Permian Basin; Odessa, Tex. 79762	938	1,047	67	S	360	1,440	—
Texas A&I University. *See* South Texas, Univ. System of							
Texas A&M University System; College Station, Tex. 77843:							
Prairie View Agricultural & Mechanical University*; Prairie View, Tex. 77445	2,268	2,227	200	S	471	1,767	2,141
Texas A&M University; College Station, Tex. 77843	19,998[1]	12,250[1]	2,182	S	120	1,200	3,220
Texas A&M Univ. at Galveston; Galveston, Tex. 77553	379	133	47	S	120	1,200	2,952
Texas Chiropractic College; Pasadena, Tex. 77505	361[1]	108[1]	34	P	5,100	5,100	—
Texas Christian University; Fort Worth, Tex. 76129	3,142[1]	3,736[1]	314	P/DC	4,500	4,500	2,000
Texas College; Tyler, Tex. 75702	360	227	37	P/CME	2,100	2,100	1,952
Texas College of Osteopathic Medicine; Fort Worth, Tex. 76107	264	114	139	S	400	900	4,122
Texas Lutheran College; Seguin, Tex. 78155	456[1]	446[1]	n.a.	P	3,225	3,225	2,100
Texas Southern University; Houston, Tex. 77004	4,536	4,296	400	S	550	1,690	2,270
Texas Tech University; Lubbock, Tex. 79409	10,084	7,125	930	S	120	600	2,467
Texas Wesleyan College; Fort Worth, Tex. 76105	628	848	89	P/M	1,825	1,825	1,300
Texas Woman's University; Denton, Tex. 76204	308[1]	3,969[1]	395	S	472	1,624	2,230
Thiel College; Greenville, Pa. 16125	341	391	65	P/LCA	5,620	5,620	2,720
Thomas Aquinas College; Santa Paula, Calif. 93060	60	56	14	P/RC	5,795	5,795	2,935
Thomas College; Waterville, Me. 04901	180[1]	199[1]	20	P	5,350	5,350	3,150
Thomas Jefferson University; Philadelphia, Pa. 19107	1,530		535	P	6,800	6,800	n.a.
Thomas M. Cooley Law School; Lansing, Mich. 48933	806	351	27	P	4,770	4,770	—
Thomas More College*; Crestview Hills, Ky. 41017	430	343	69	RC	4,000	4,000	2,400
Tift College; Forsyth, Ga. 31029	125	540	25	P/B	900	900	830
Toledo, The University of; Toledo, Ohio 43606	8,209[1]	7,888[1]	614	S	1,512	3,429	2,304
Tougaloo College*; Tougaloo, Miss. 39174	245	453	67	P	2,450	2,450	1,320
Touro College*; New York, N.Y. 10001	735	1,111	123	P	3,200	3,200	1,300
Towson State University*; Baltimore, Md. 21204	4,017	5,102	366	S	1,205	2,245	2,324
Transylvania University; Lexington, Ky. 40508	297	332	64	P/DC	5,675	5,675	2,550
Trenton State College; Trenton, N.J. 08625	1,946	3,933	355	S	1,024	1,664	2,725
Trevecca Nazarene College*; Nashville, Tenn. 37203	426	443	50	P/Naz	2,805	2,805	2,025
Tri–College University*; Moorhead, Minn. 26260	220		4	S	n.a.	n.a.	—
Trinity Bible Institute; Ellendale, N.D. 58436	159	153	24	P	1,904	1,904	1,836
Trinity Christian College; Palos Heights, Ill. 60463	177[1]	229[1]	31	P/CR	4,670	4,670	2,200
Trinity College; Burlington, Vt. 05401	12	361	44	P/RC	5,040	5,040	2,851
Trinity College; Deerfield, Ill. 60015	157	196	22	EFC	4,515	4,515	1,350
Trinity College*; Hartford, Conn. 06106	922	865	135	P	7,100	7,100	1,850
Trinity College; Washington, D.C. 20017	—	495[1]	55	P/RC	6,500	6,500	4,000
Trinity University; San Antonio, Tex. 78284	1,280[1]	1,452[1]	225	P	5,490	5,490	2,875
Tri-State University*; Angola, Ind. 46703	761	229	80	P	4,272	4,272	2,100
Troy State University; Troy, Ala. 36082	1,568	2,024	200	S	990	1,485	1,540
Tufts University; Medford, Mass. 02155	3,580[1]	3,313[1]	525	P	8,534	8,534	4,000
Tulane University; New Orleans, La. 70118	4,970	3,109	667	P	8,000	8,000	3,270
Tulsa, The University of; Tulsa, Okla. 74104	2,199[1]	1,748[1]	311	P	3,700	3,700	2,250
Turabo University College. *See* Ana G. Méndez Educational Foundation							
Tusculum College[7]; Greeneville, Tenn. 37743	180[1]	190[1]	30	P/Pres	3,500	3,500	2,390
Tuskegee Institute; Tuskegee Institute, Ala. 36088	1,551	1,560	368	P	3,500	3,500	2,000
Union College*; Barbourville, Ky. 40906	187	236	n.a.	P/UM	n.a.	n.a.	n.a.
Union College; Lincoln, Neb. 68506	424[1]	464[1]	n.a.	P/SDA	5,800	5,800	2,180
Union College; Schenectady, N.Y. 12308	1,398[1]	799[1]	161	P	8,710[3]	8,710[3]	3,070[3]
Union University; Jackson, Tenn. 38305	443[1]	686[1]	71	SB	2,650	2,650	1,450
U.S. Air Force Academy; Colorado Springs, Colo. 80840	3,718	484	573	Fed	—	—	—
U.S. Army Command and General Staff College*; Fort Leavenworth, Kan. 66027	978	11	n.a.	Fed	—	—	—
U.S. Coast Guard Academy; New London, Conn. 06320	671	91	110	Fed	—	—	—
U.S. International University; San Diego, Calif. 92131	1,982	1,293	150	P	7,080	7,080	4,852
U.S. Merchant Marine Academy; Kings Point, N.Y. 11024	953	86	83	Fed	—	—	—
U.S. Military Academy*; West Point, N.Y. 10996	4,013	426	639	Fed	—	—	—
U.S. Naval Academy; Annapolis, Md. 21402	4,103	307	600	Fed	—	—	—
Unity College; Unity, Me. 04988[7]	210	80	23	P	4,620	4,620	2,600
Upper Iowa University; Fayette, Iowa 52142	183	163	28	P	4,600	4,600	2,300
Upsala College*; East Orange, N.J. 07019	673	423	74	P/L	4,212	4,212	2,000
Urbana College; Urbana, Ohio 43078	288	235	29	P	4,500	4,500	2,460
Ursinus College; Collegeville, Pa. 19426	571[1]	491[1]	78	P	5,975[3]	5,975[3]	2,750
Ursuline College; Pepper Pike, Ohio 44124	15	586	46	P/RC	3,920	3,920	2,200
Utah, University of; Salt Lake City, Utah 84112	14,809[1]	10,102[1]	957	S	1,050	2,973	2,682
Utah State University; Logan, Utah 84322	7,026[1]	4,823[1]	508[20]	S	1,002	2,820	2,148
Utica College of Syracuse University; Utica, N.Y. 13502	573	717	105	P	5,975	5,975	2,500

Institution and location	Enrollment Male	Enrollment Female	Faculty	Control	Tuition ($) Res.	Tuition ($) Nonres.	Rm/Bd ($)
Valdosta State College; Valdosta, Ga. 31698	2,546[1]	3,289[1]	250	S	1,092	2,799	1,572
Valley City State College; Valley City, N.D. 58072	419[1]	475[1]	53	S	771	1,488	1,566
Valley Forge Christian College; Phoenixville, Pa. 19460	291	218	16	P/AG	2,208	2,208	2,000
Valparaiso University; Valparaiso, Ind. 46383	1,615	1,778	275	P/L	5,300	5,300	2,290
Vanderbilt University; Nashville, Tenn. 37240	4,751[1]	4,284[1]	1,297	P	7,500	7,500	3,250
VanderCook College of Music*; Chicago, Ill. 60616	65	25	12	P	4,300	4,300	3,000
Vassar College; Poughkeepsie, N.Y. 12601	919[1]	1,325[1]	208	P	8,800	8,800	3,720
Vennard College*; University Park, Iowa 52595	103	98	7	P/ID	1,900	1,900	1,760
Vermont, University of; Burlington, Vt. 05405	3,691[1]	4,577[1]	764	S	2,550[3]	6,760[3]	2,902
Vermont College. *See* **Norwich University**							
Vermont Law School; South Royalton, Vt. 05068	247	140	26	P	6,750	6,750	—
Villa Maria College; Erie, Pa. 16505	10	420	63	P	4,650	4,650	2,600
Villanova University*; Villanova, Pa. 19085	3,487	2,753	477	P/RC	5,040	5,040	1,498
Virginia, University of; Charlottesville, Va. 22903	8,203[1]	7,275[1]	1,447	S	1,826[3]	4,336[3]	2,570
Clinch Valley College; Wise, Va. 24293	370[1]	393[1]	43	S	960	1,608	1,800
Virginia Commonwealth University*; Richmond, Va. 23284	8,423	11,394	1,408	S	920	1,890	2,074
Virginia Intermont College; Bristol, Va. 24201	132[3]	448[3]	44	P/B	3,850	3,850	2,400
Virginia Military Institute; Lexington, Va. 24450	1,309.[1]	—	96	S	1,380[55]	3,700[55]	1,990[55]
Virginia Polytechnic Institute and State University; Blacksburg, Va. 24061	11,969[1]	8,127[1]	1,380	S	1,812	3,642	1,683
Virginia State University; Petersburg, Va. 23803	1,771[1]	2,185[1]	237	S	1,455	2,036	2,200
Virginia Union University; Richmond, Va. 23220	511[1]	656[1]	55	P/B	3,340	3,340	2,310
Virginia Wesleyan College; Norfolk, Va. 23502	345[1]	457[1]	47	P/UM	4,750	4,750	2,700
Virgin Islands, College of the; St. Thomas, V.I. 00802	207	565	81	S	528	1,584	1,183
Visual Arts, School of; New York, N.Y. 10010	1,344[1]	1,163[1]	61[56]	P	5,500	5,500	4,600
Viterbo College; La Crosse, Wis. 54601	129[1]	693[1]	72	P/RC	4,390	4,390	1,950
Voorhees College; Denmark, S.C. 29042	223	345	37	P/E	2,742	2,742	2,142
Wabash College; Crawfordsville, Ind. 47933	774[1]	—	68	P	5,700	5,700	2,500
Wagner College; Staten Island, N.Y. 10301	1,037	1,110	83	P/L	5,560	5,560	3,410
Wake Forest University; Winston-Salem, N.C. 27109	1,887	1,199	641	P/B	5,550	5,550	2,170
Walla Walla College; College Place, Wash. 99324	886[1]	781[1]	134	P/SDA	5,640	5,640	2,295
Walsh College; Canton, Ohio 44720	358[1]	317[1]	64	P/RC	3,650	3,650	1,950
Walsh College of Accountancy and Business Administration; Troy, Mich. 48084	168[1]	189[1]	11	P	2,286	2,286	—
Warner Pacific College; Portland, Ore. 97215	193[1]	157[1]	40	P/CG	4,500	4,500	2,205
Warner Southern College; Lake Wales, Fla. 33853	119[1]	176[1]	16	P/CG	3,650	3,650	1,900
Warren Wilson College*; Swannanoa, N.C. 28778	246	284	50[20]	P/UP	3,950	3,950	1,608
Wartburg College; Waverly, Iowa 50677	508	542	68	P/AL	5,420[3]	5,420[3]	2,110
Washburn University of Topeka; Topeka, Kan. 66621	1,801[1]	1,766[1]	225	Mun	1,643	2,418	2,300
Washington, University of; Seattle, Wash. 98199	12,412	10,576	2,500	S	1,302	3,618	3,303
Washington and Jefferson College*; Washington, Pa. 15301	654	404	85	P	5,900	5,900	2,190
Washington and Lee University; Lexington, Va. 24450	1,600[1]	119[1]	168	P	6,515	6,515	2,850
Washington Bible College; Lanham, Md. 20706	152	87	16	P	2,824	2,824	2,450
Washington College; Chestertown, Md. 21620	336[1]	348[1]	63	P	6,130[3]	6,130[3]	2,720[3]
Washington State University; Pullman, Wash. 99164	9,653[1]	6,750[1]	1,031	S	1,308	3,624	2,300
Washington University in St. Louis; St. Louis, Mo. 63130	5,084[1]	3,378[1]	1,325	P	8,600[3]	8,600[3]	3,594
Wayland Baptist University*; Plainview, Tex. 79072	279	264	49	SB	1,700	1,700	1,730
Waynesburg College; Waynesburg, Pa. 15370	343	278	42	P	4,850	4,850	2,250
Wayne State College; Wayne, Neb. 68787	843[1]	1,016[1]	93	S	1,912	3,002	1,806
Wayne State University; Detroit, Mich. 48202	14,687[1]	14,952[1]	1,300	S	1,720	3,820	n.a.
Webber College; Babson Park, Fla. 33827	120	132	14	P	5,850	5,850	2,320
Webb Institute of Naval Architecture; Glen Cove, N.Y. 11542	70[1]	12[1]	10	P	—	—	2,730
Weber State College; Ogden, Utah 84408	5,689[1]	4,625[1]	387	S	876	2,367	2,589
Webster University*; St. Louis, Mo. 63119	952	682	70	P	3,600	3,600	1,900
Wellesley College; Wellesley, Mass. 02181	2[1]	1,954[1]	245	P	9,260	9,260	3,570
Wells College; Aurora, N.Y. 13026	—	460[1]	55	P	7,970	7,970	2,930
Wentworth Institute of Technology*; Boston, Mass. 02115	2,830	196	164	P	3,990	3,990	3,000
Wesleyan College; Macon, Ga. 31297	8	385	44	P/M	3,000	3,800	2,450
Wesleyan University; Middletown, Conn. 06457	1,511[1]	1,302[1]	262	P	9,250	9,250	1,680
Wesley College; Dover, Del. 19901	193	271	44	P/UM	5,070	5,070	2,620
Wesley College; Florence, Miss. 39073	24	26	8	P/M	1,300	1,300	1,850
Westbrook College; Portland, Me. 04103	63[1]	481[1]	55	P	6,050	6,050	2,915
West Chester University of Pennsylvania; West Chester, Pa. 19380	2,854	3,754	459	P	1,480	2,590	1,888
West Coast Christian College; Fresno, Calif. 93710	167[1]	85[1]	9	P/CG	2,040	2,040	1,888
West Coast University*; Los Angeles, Calif. 90020	776	180	200	P	2,850	2,850	—
Western Baptist College; Salem, Ore. 97301	127	139	20	P/B	3,660	3,660	2,340
Western Bible College; Morrison, Colo. 80465	120[1]	83[1]	11	P	2,848	2,848	2,226
Western Carolina University. *See* North Carolina, University System of							
Western Connecticut State University; Danbury, Conn. 06810	1,323[1]	1,802[1]	183	S	830	2,650	2,448
Western Illinois University; Macomb, Ill. 61455	5,834[1]	5,065[1]	663	S	1,328	3,260	2,070
Western Kentucky University; Bowling Green, Ky. 42101	4,146	4,264	608	S	900	2,560	2,500
Western Maryland College; Westminster, Md. 21157	576[1]	670[1]	82	P	6,175	6,175	2,460
Western Michigan University; Kalamazoo, Mich. 49008	9,656	8,886	842	S	1,600	2,000	2,300

Institution and location	Enrollment Male	Female	Faculty	Control	Tuition ($) Res.	Nonres.	Rm/Bd ($)
Western Montana College; Dillon, Mont. 59725	352	247	33	S	791	2,123	2,300
Western New England College; Springfield, Mass. 01119	1,400	800	110	P	4,650	4,650	3,100
Western New Mexico University*; Silver City, N.M. 88026	710	753	68	S	530	1,816	1,600
Western Oregon State College; Monmouth, Ore. 97361	887	1,242	162	S	1,395	3,642	2,190
Western Pentecostal Bible College; Clayburn, B.C., Canada VOX 1EO	154	90	10	P/AG	1,200	1,200	2,150
Western State College of Colorado; Gunnison, Colo. 81230	1,691 [1]	1,145 [1]	130	S	798	2,394	1,800
Western State University College of Law*; Fullerton, Calif. 92631	265	156	12	P	3,762	3,762	—
Western State University College of Law of San Diego; San Diego, Calif. 92110	158 [1]	53 [1]	11	P	5,550	5,550	—
Western Washington University; Bellingham, Wash. 98225	4,309 [1]	4,376 [1]	428	S	1,017	3,486	2,182
Westfield State College*; Westfield, Mass. 01086	1,129	1,692	165	S	845	2,545	1,700
West Florida, The University of*; Pensacola, Fla. 32504	2,579	2,830	251	S	840	2,730	2,221
West Georgia College*; Carrollton, Ga. 30118	2,372	3,225	242	S	834	2,124	1,865
West Liberty State College; West Liberty, W. Va. 26074	1,027 [1]	1,050 [1]	131	S	754	2,124	2,171
West Los Angeles, Univ. of; Los Angeles, Calif. 90066	615		4	P	2,025	2,025	—
Westmar College; LeMars, Iowa 51031	290	195	43	P/UM	4,526	4,526	2,158
Westminster Choir College; Princeton, N.J. 08540	150 [1]	210 [1]	37	P	5,580	5,580	1,355
Westminster College; Fulton, Mo. 65251	475	135	58	P	4,600	4,600	2,300
Westminster College; New Wilmington, Pa. 16172	613 [1]	684 [1]	102	P/UP	5,500	5,500	2,134
Westminster College of Salt Lake City; Salt Lake City, Utah 84105	247	291	47	P	4,050	4,050	3,200
Westmont College; Santa Barbara, Calif. 93108	450 [1]	542 [1]	62	P	6,494	6,494	3,220
West Oahu College, University of Hawaii; Pearl City, Hawaii 96782[35]	82	77	10	S	630	2,200	—
West Texas State University; Canyon, Tex. 79016	2,881	3,134	224	S	120	1,200	2,100
West Virginia College of Graduate Studies*; Institute, W. Va. 25112	393	657	53	S	450	1,830	—
West Virginia Institute of Technology*; Montgomery, W. Va. 25136	1,734	692	142	S	478	1,498	1,956
West Virginia School of Osteopathic Medicine; Lewisburg, W. Va. 24901	180	53	25	S	1,892	4,512	—
West Virginia State College; Institute, W. Va. 25112	1,252 [1]	1,024 [1]	127	S	800	2,200	2,310
West Virginia University; Morgantown, W. Va. 26506	9,578 [1]	6,957 [1]	1,346	S	1,160 [3]	3,140 [3]	2,802
West Virginia Wesleyan College; Buckhannon, W. Va. 26201	604 [1]	804 [1]	94	P/UM	4,380	4,380	2,620
Wheaton College*; Norton, Mass. 02766	1	1,229	95	P	8,420	8,420	3,325
Wheaton College; Wheaton, Ill. 60187	1,100 [1]	1,193 [1]	150	P	5,916	5,916	2,660
Wheeling College*; Wheeling, W. Va. 26003	492	497	65	P	4,575	4,575	2,575
Wheelock College*; Boston, Mass. 02215	9	598	56	P	4,900	4,900	2,700
White Plains, Coll. of, Pace Univ. *See* Pace Univ.							
Whitman College; Walla Walla, Wash. 99362	617	559	84	P	6,380	6,380	2,710
Whittier College; Whittier, Calif. 90608	486 [1]	468 [1]	90	P	7,300	7,300	2,910
Whitworth College; Spokane, Wash. 99251	580 [1]	636 [1]	67	P/Pres	6,040	6,040	2,469
Wichita State University; Wichita, Kan. 67208	3,745	3,102	585	S	1,156 [3]	2,836 [3]	1,948 [3]
Widener University; Chester, Pa. 19013	1,300	1,100	75	P	6,200	6,200	2,820
Wilberforce University; Wilberforce, Ohio 45384	371 [1]	510 [1]	55	P/AME	5,700	5,700	3,060
Wiley College*; Marshall, Tex. 75670	220	286	36	P/UM	2,100	2,100	1,754
Wilkes College; Wilkes-Barre, Pa. 18766	998 [1]	864 [1]	145	P	2,700 [3]	2,700 [3]	575
Willamette University*; Salem, Ore. 97301	1,030	783	105	P	4,860	4,860	2,150
William and Mary, College of; Williamsburg, Va. 23185	2,833 [1]	2,912 [1]	424	S	888	2,345	1,170
William Carey College; Hattiesburg, Miss. 39401	348 [1]	474 [1]	52	P	2,370	2,370	1,900
William Jewell College; Liberty, Mo. 64068	846 [1]	1,007 [1]	89	B	4,120	4,120	2,020
William Mitchell College of Law; St. Paul, Minn. 55105	671	439	30	P	5,250	5,250	—
William Paterson College of New Jersey; Wayne, N.J. 07470	2,747	3,068	365	S	1,245	1,845	2,400
William Penn College; Oskaloosa, Iowa 52577	299 [1]	149 [1]	30	P/SOF	5,440 [3]	5,440 [3]	1,980 [3]
Williams College; Williamstown, Mass. 01267	1,169 [1]	883 [1]	174	P	9,200 [3]	9,200 [3]	3,254
William Smith College. *See* Hobart and William Smith Colleges							
William Tyndale College*; Farmington Hills, Mich. 48071	93	61	15	P/ID	2,396	2,396	2,200
William Woods College; Fulton, Mo. 65251	—	729 [1]	55	P	5,500	5,500	2,240
Wilmington College; New Castle, Del. 19720	332 [1]	274 [1]	11	P	([57])	([57])	1,200 [11]
Wilmington College of Ohio; Wilmington, Ohio 45177	482 [1]	304 [1]	60	P/SOF	5,115 [3]	5,115 [3]	1,431 [3]
Wilson College; Chambersburg, Pa. 17201	232		33	P/Pres	6,676	6,676	2,674
Wingate College; Wingate, N.C. 28174	713 [1]	854 [1]	68	SB	2,750	2,750	1,920
Winnipeg Bible College; Otterburne, Man., Canada ROA 1GO	141	114	11	P/ND	1,940	1,940	1,700
Winona State Univ. *See* Minnesota State Univ. System							
Winston-Salem State University. *See* North Carolina, University System of							
Winthrop College; Rock Hill, S.C. 29733	1,223 [1]	2,742 [1]	259	S	1,212	2,110	1,556
Wisconsin, University of; Madison, Wis. 53706:							
U. of Wisconsin—Eau Claire; Eau Claire, Wis. 54701	4,307 [1]	5,391 [1]	471	S	1,103	3,500	1,914
U. of Wisconsin—Green Bay; Green Bay, Wis. 54301	2,112 [1]	2,768 [1]	172	S	1,100	3,630	2,200
U. of Wisconsin—La Crosse; La Crosse, Wis. 54601	3,532 [1]	4,237 [1]	550	S	886	3,283	1,656
U. of Wisconsin —Madison; Madison, Wis. 53706	23,459 [1]	19,616 [1]	2,155	S	1,279	4,191	2,510
U. of Wisconsin—Milwaukee; Milwaukee, Wis. 53201	9,028 [1]	9,868 [1]	840	S	1,300	2,000	2,600
U. of Wisconsin—Oshkosh*; Oshkosh, Wis. 54901	4,825	5,375	450	S	950	3,100	1,550
U. of Wisconsin—Parkside; Kenosha, Wis. 53141	1,549	1,269	208	S	1,039	3,436	—
U. of Wisconsin—Platteville; Platteville, Wis. 53818	3,275	1,447	329	S	1,120	3,520	1,730
U. of Wisconsin—River Falls; River Falls, Wis. 54022	2,500 [1]	2,400 [1]	260	S	1,109	3,506	1,974
U. of Wisconsin—Stevens Point; Stevens Point, Wis. 54481	3,820 [1]	3,629 [1]	450	S	1,240	3,720	2,082

Institution and location	Enrollment Male	Enrollment Female	Faculty	Control	Tuition ($) Res.	Tuition ($) Nonres.	Rm/Bd ($)
U. of Wisconsin—Stout; Menomonie, Wis. 54751	3,697[1]	3,168[1]	328	S	1,111	3,508	1,776
U. of Wisconsin—Superior; Superior, Wis. 54880	1,296[3]	1,534[3]	103	S	1,065	3,462	4,275
U. of Wisconsin—Whitewater*; Whitewater, Wis. 53190	4,243	4,024	414	S	1,037	3,368	1,522
Wittenberg University*; Springfield, Ohio 45501	982	1,138	149	P/LCA	6,774	6,774	2,385
Wofford College; Spartanburg, S.C. 29301	740[1]	268[1]	57	P/EM	4,595	4,595	2,455
Woodbury University*; Los Angeles, Calif. 90017	n.a.	n.a.	n.a.	P	n.a.	n.a.	n.a.
Wooster, The College of*; Wooster, Ohio 44691	909	817	140	P	6,030	6,030	1,900
Worcester Polytechnic Institute*; Worcester, Mass. 01609	2,129	425	190	P	5,850	5,850	2,400
Worcester State College; Worcester, Mass. 01602	1,502	1,761	165	S	936	2,976	1,922
World College West; San Rafael, Calif. 94912	24	48	10	P	5,100	5,100	2,700
Wright Institute, The; Berkeley, Calif. 94704[7]	79[1]	116[1]	—	P	6,900	6,900	—
Wright State University; Dayton, Ohio 45435	7,248[1]	7,296[1]	571	S	1,623	3,246	2,184
Wyoming, University of; Laramie, Wyo. 82071	5,791[1]	4,457[1]	822	S	716	2,226	2,470
Xavier University; Cincinnati, Ohio 45207	1,760[1]	2,365[1]	218	P	5,080	5,080	5,430
Xavier University of Louisiana*; New Orleans, La. 70125	741	1,435	123	P	3,400	3,400	2,000
Yale University; New Haven, Conn. 06520	5,914[1]	4,403[1]	1,302	P	9,750	9,750	4,200
Yankton College; Yankton, S.D. 57078	131	99	26	P/UCC	3,840	3,840	2,080
Yeshiva University; New York, N.Y. 10033	2,001[1]	1,736[1]	1,278	P	6,430	6,430	3,320
York College (NYC). *See* New York, City University of							
York College of Pennsylvania; York, Pa. 17405	969[1]	1,437[1]	113	P	2,980	2,980	1,972
Youngstown State Univ.; Youngstown, Ohio 44555	5,735[1]	4,602[1]	434	S	1,335	2,310	2,190

1. Fall 1983. 2. Plus 229 general, non-teaching. 3. Fall 1984. 4. Comprehensive fee covering tuition, room, and board. 5. Includes SUNY College of Ceramics. 6. Off campus. 7. Accreditation on probation. 8. Non-Egyptians. 9. Varies, depending on branch. 10. Plus 24 part-time. 11. Room only. 12. Member State University and Community College System. 13. FTE 133. 14. $200 per credit. 15. Affiliate of Columbia University. 16. Plus 112 part-time. 17. Plus 47 adjunct faculty. 18. LDS members. 19. Non-LDS members. 20. FTE. 21. FTE 717. 22. New students. 23. Continuing students. 24. Member California State University and Colleges. 25. Member California State University System. 26. Plus $117 per unit. 27. Plus 13 part-time. 28. Spring 1983. 29. Part-time. 30. Endowed, $8,900. 31. State assisted. 32. Under SUNY supervision. 32. National residents. 33. International residents. 34. Includes part-time. 35. Member University of Hawaii System. 36. $89 per week. 37. Plus 222 part-time. 38. Affiliated academically with University of Minnesota. 39. Evening school—most students are part-time: FTE male 124, female 8. 40. Total head count 3,529—most students are part-time. 41. Effective June 1984. 42. Part of Louisiana State University System. 43. Fall 1982. 44. Total enrollment 4,902; 79% of students are part-time. 45. Total enrollment 9,626. 46. Tuition, room, and board paid for by work-study program, 960 hours per year. 47. State related. 48. Special rate according to the state. 49. 3,790 pounds Sterling. 50. 1,200 pounds Sterling. 51. UM/UP/UCC. 52. Plus $117 per unit. 53. Plus 30 part-time. 54. Member Texas A&M System. 55. Other required fees, $1,360. 56. Plus 379 part-time. 57. $325 per course.

A Testing Dictionary

In recent years, increasing attention has been paid to *testing*—for admission to schools, for employment, and for increased self-awareness. This listing of established, frequently used achievement, intelligence, and psychological tests from a broad range of test publishers was compiled by the Educational Testing Service. It briefly describes what these tests measure, and how they are used.

Advanced Placement Program. These tests are designed to measure advanced student achievement in a variety of subject areas. They are generally taken by the student in grades 10–12 who is entering college and who wishes to receive credit for college-level work completed during high school. Most colleges in the United States give credit or advanced-placement standing or both for college-level courses taken in the student's own high school.

American College Testing Program (ACT). A series of measures in English, mathematics, social sciences, and natural sciences, which is designed to measure the academic development of the college-bound student who takes these tests in grades 11–13. Scores are reported to the individual student, as well as to the secondary school and designated colleges. Results provide information helpful in formulating educational plans.

Basic Skills Assessment Program. This program for students in grades 8–12 measures student mastery of basic skills in reading, writing, and mathematics. By determining the competency of each student, this program assists the teacher in identifying the need for additional educational assistance.

California Achievement Tests. The tests of this series may be administered by the classroom teacher to measure the achievement growth of pupils at various levels, from kindergarten through high school. The subject areas include: pre-reading, reading, spelling, language, mathematics, and reference skills. Scores indicate both achievement level and mastery of curriculum goals. Score reports are furnished for the individual student and for the teacher as class lists.

California Psychological Inventory. The purpose of this test is to measure specific personality characteristics considered important for social living. Essentially self-administered, the test may be used in schools, colleges, businesses, or counseling agencies. Test results are reported as profiles representing the degree to which individuals exhibit each trait.

CIRCUS. CIRCUS assesses the skills of young children (pre-school to second grade) in language, mathematics, perception, information processing, attitudes and interests, and divergent production. Results aid in determining the child's readiness for academic instruction and in identifying particular needs. Scores are reported to the teacher numerically and in sentence format.

College Board Achievement Tests. A series of achievement tests that measure knowledge in each of fifteen subject areas. They are designed for the college-bound student and are administered in group sessions. The number of tests taken is decided by the student, and scores are reported to designated colleges.

College-Level Examination Program (CLEP). CLEP enables people of all ages to earn college credit by successful achievement on examinations. Two types of tests are offered—General Examinations and Subject Examinations. The General Examinations are based on materials covered in the first two years of college and focus on achievement in five basic areas of the liberal arts: English composition, humanities, mathematics, natural sciences, and social sciences-history. The 47 Subject Examinations measure achievement in specific college courses and are essentially end-of-course tests.

Comprehensive Tests of Basic Skills (CTBS). CTBS measures basic academic skills as well as the ability to apply knowledge to everyday living from kindergarten through high school. The general areas of assessment include reading, language, arithmetic, and study skills. Test results may prove useful to school administrators for educational planning and guidance and for determining minimum competency in necessary life-skills.

Differential Aptitude Tests. The purpose of this test battery is to measure student potential in each of eight areas. Test results may be used as a basis for educational or vocational planning. It is administered in group sessions, and scores, reported separately for each area, yield a profile of relative strengths and weaknesses for each student.

Edwards Personal Preference Schedule. Administered primarily for personal counseling or guidance, this test is used to measure the basic motivations and needs of the individual. The responses may be hand- or machine-scored, and are plotted on an individual profile depicting which of fifteen possible needs are most characteristic of that individual.

Flanagan Aptitude Classification Tests. A series of separate tests for senior high school students and adults that may be used in various combinations to evaluate the potential for success in specific careers. Each test measures a different job-related skill and may be self-scored. Tests are generally administered in the course of vocational counseling or to job applicants.

General Aptitude Test Battery. This battery of tests is available only for use by State Employment Service offices or approved organizations. Each test measures a specific ability associated with a number of occupations. Test scores provide a basis upon which vocational plans may be made.

Graduate Management Admission Test. This test is specifically intended for students who are interested in attending graduate business schools. Verbal, quantitative, and total scores are reported for each student and may be used by the school in screening applicants. Test questions are designed to measure the general abilities associated with success in business and management studies.

Graduate Record Examinations (GRE). The purpose of these tests is to determine the scholastic ability of college seniors who wish to continue their education beyond the college level. The scores are typically used by graduate schools to screen applicants. There is a test of general aptitude, which covers verbal, quantitative, and analytical skills. There are also advanced tests available to measure ability in each of twenty specific subject areas. Some of these tests offer subscores that may be used for guidance and placement by the graduate school.

Henmon-Nelson Tests of Mental Ability. This series is designed for students from kindergarten through high school to provide an evaluation of the abilities considered important for academic success. Appropriate for classroom testing, the scores are reported as group lists. Individual student scores may prove helpful to parents and teachers as indications of future progress.

Kuder Preference Record. To assist high school students and adults in choosing a suitable profession, this test measures the individual's preference for the types of social situations that may influence vocational choice. It is scored by hand, and test results are reported as profiles depicting relative preference for group activities, familiar situations, working with ideas, avoiding conflict, and directing others.

Kuhlmann-Anderson Intelligence Test, Seventh Edition. Designed to measure the mental capacities of the student in grades K–12 as an indication of academic potential. Verbal and quantitative abilities are measured in tests for grade 7 and above. All tests may be administered and scored by the school teacher. Student score-reports depict an intelligence quotient, as well as the student's standing in relation to others of the same age.

Law School Admission Test. This examination is given to college seniors who are considering application to law school. A general measure of the academic skills related to success in the study of law, score reports are made available to the student and to the schools under consideration. They may be used by law schools in the selection and counseling of applicants for admission.

Medical College Admission Test. College seniors wishing to study medicine take this examination to fulfill admissions requirements. Scores are reported to the schools in biology, chemistry, physics, science problems, and skills analysis—reading and quantitative skills.

Metropolitan Achievement Tests. This battery of tests is intended to measure academic achievement from kindergarten through junior high. Areas of assessment include: reading, mathematics, word knowledge, language, spelling, science, and social studies. The test may be administered by the teacher to student groups. Score reports are made to each pupil, and group lists are provided to assist teachers and school administrators.

Minnesota Multiphasic Personality Inventory. This test is designed for ages 16 through adult to evaluate the personality characteristics that affect social and personal adjustment. It may be used, in conjunction with other measures, in personnel selection or in clinical therapy. It is required, however, that the test administrator have training and experience in testing. A tape-recorded version of the test is available for use with semiliterate and disabled persons.

National Teachers Examination. Designed for college students who have completed degree programs in teaching, the tests measure general knowledge within the field of education and readiness for the profession of teaching. Some 26 subject area tests are also available to measure knowledge within specialized fields. Scores are used by school boards in the selection of teaching staff and by states for certification.

Otis-Lennon Mental Ability Tests. A test of general mental ability or scholastic aptitude that may be administered to groups by the classroom teacher. There are various levels appropriate for use from kindergarten through high school. The score for each student is reported within a group list, which indicates an intelligence quotient, as well as the student's relative status by age and grade.

Preliminary Scholastic Aptitude Test (PSAT)/-National Merit Scholarship Qualifying Tests. As an abbreviated version of the *Scholastic Aptitude Test,* this examination is designed to provide sophomores, juniors, or seniors in high school with an indication of their ability to handle college work. Consisting of general verbal and mathematical measures, a third score is also reported that is considered for National Merit Scholarship Programs. Scores are reported to the student, the school principal, and/or the school system.

Rorschach Technique. This well-known test is primarily used in clinical therapy for ages 3-up, and may be interpreted only by an experienced examiner. It is designed to identify aspects of the individual's personality through responses to each of a series of inkblots.

Scholastic Aptitude Test (SAT). Designed to measure scholastic ability, the SAT is generally required for admission to college. As an indication of the student's readiness for college curricula, verbal and mathematical reasoning skills are assessed. Scores are reported to each student and to designated college admissions offices, where they are used for selecting applicants.

Stanford Achievement Tests. This achievement battery is useful for assessing the academic performance of students within the classroom (grades 1–9) or within the entire school system. Skills are measured in the areas of reading comprehension, language, science, social science, and auditory proficiency. The scoring system allows for both individual and group reporting.

Stanford-Binet Intelligence Scale. An individually administered test of intelligence that consists of different performance tasks for ages 2-up. Responses may only be recorded and interpreted by an experienced examiner. The test results are reported as an intelligence quotient, which takes into consideration both the age and the performance of the individual being tested.

STEP III. The Sequential Tests of Educational Progress are achievement tests for grades 3–12 that measure the extent of student learning in reading, mathematics computation and concepts, writing skills, listening, study skills, science, and social studies. The tests are designed for out-of-level testing within a single classroom.

The Strong-Campbell Interest Inventory. A test used to determine the occupational interests of students 16 years and older and adults. Feelings about specific occupations, occupational activities, hobbies, amusements, school subjects, and types of people are analyzed to produce an individual profile. Scores are reported on each os 23 basic Interest Scales, as well as each of 125 Occupational Scales to demonstrate the over-all orientation of the individual.

Tests of General Educational Development (GED). These tests measure the educational competency of adults who have not graduated from high school. They provide a means of demonstrating abilities comparable to those of a high school graduate. Measures of language, usage, mathematics, and reading interpretation are available in English, Spanish, and French.

Wechsler Intelligence Scale for Children. This test measures general intelligence. The subtests focus on performance tasks and verbal responses. Appropriate for both children and adolescents, the test is administered individually by persons with extensive training in psychological measurement. Analysis of responses yields an intelligence quotient for the individual tested.

Wonderlic Personnel Test. In the process of gathering information, a business or industrial personnel office may use this brief test to determine the general mental ability of job applicants. It may be administered either on an individual basis or in groups, and the final score is determined by the number of questions answered correctly. Actual score interpretation is limited to those persons who are experienced in psychological testing procedures.

Selected Degree Abbreviations

Source: This material has been taken from *American Universities and Colleges,* 10th and 11th editions, published by the American Council on Education.

A.B. Bachelor of Arts
Ae.E. Aeronautical Engineer
A.M. Master of Arts
A.M.T. Master of Arts in Teaching

B.A. Bachelor of Arts
B.A.E. Bachelor of Arts in Education, or Bachelor of Art Education, Aeronautical Engineering, Agricultural Engineering, or Architectural Engineering
B.Ag. Bachelor of Agriculture
B.Arch. Bachelor of Architecture
B.B.A. Bachelor of Business Administration
B.C.E. Bachelor of Civil Engineering or Bachelor of Christian Education
B.Ch.E. Bachelor of Chemical Engineering
B.D. Bachelor of Divinity
B.E. Bachelor of Education or Bachelor of Engineering
B.E.E. Bachelor of Electrical Engineering
B.F. Bachelor of Forestry
B.F.A. Bachelor of Fine Arts
B.J. Bachelor of Journalism
B.L.S. Bachelor of Liberal Studies or Bachelor of Library Science
B.Litt. Bachelor of Literature
B.M. Bachelor of Medicine or Bachelor of Music
B.Mus. Bachelor of Music
B.N. Bachelor of Nursing
B.Pharm. Bachelor of Pharmacy
B.R.E. Bachelor of Religious Education
B.S. Bachelor of Science
B.S.Ed. Bachelor of Science in Education
C.E. Civil Engineer
Chem.E. Chemical Engineer
D.B.A. Doctor of Business Administration
D.D. Doctor of Divinity[1]
D.D.S. Doctor of Dental Surgery or Doctor of Dental Science
D.L.S. Doctor of Library Science
D.M.D. Doctor of Dental Medicine
D.O. Doctor of Osteopathy
D.M.S. Doctor of Medical Science
D.P.A. Doctor of Public Administration[2]
D.P.H. Doctor of Public Health
D.R.E. Doctor of Religious Education
D.S.W. Doctor of Social Welfare or Doctor of Social Work
D.Sc. Doctor of Science[3]
D.V.M. Doctor of Veterinary Medicine
Ed.D. Doctor of Education[2]
Ed.S. Education Specialist
E.E. Electrical Engineer
E.M. Engineer of Mines or Mining Engineer
E.Met. Engineer of Metallurgy
I.E. Industrial Engineer
J.D. Doctor of Jurisprudence[2]
J.S.D. Doctor of the Science of Law
L.H.D. Doctor of Humane Letters[3]
Litt.M. Master of Letters[4]
LL.B. Bachelor of Laws
LL.D. Doctor of Laws[3]
LL.M. Master of Laws
M.A. Master of Arts
M.Aero.E. Master of Aeronautical Engineering
M.B.A. Master of Business Administration
M.C.E. Master of Christian Education or Master of Civil Engineering
M.C.S. Master of Commercial Science or Master of Computer Science
M.D. Doctor of Medicine
M.Div. Master of Divinity
M.E. Master of Engineering
M.Ed. Master of Education
M.Eng. Master of Engineering
M.F. Master of Forestry
M.F.A. Master of Fine Arts
M.L.S. Master of Library Science
M.M. Master of Music
M.M.E. Master of Mechanical Engineering or Master of Music Education
M.Mus. Master of Music
M.Nurs. Master of Nursing
M.R.E. Master of Religious Education
M.S. Master of Science
M.S.W. Master of Social Work
M.Th. Master of Theology
Nuc.E. Nuclear Engineer
O.D. Doctor of Optometry
Pharm.D. Doctor of Pharmacy[2]
Ph.B. Bachelor of Philosophy
Ph.D. Doctor of Philosophy
S.B. Bachelor of Science
Sc.D. Doctor of Science[3]
S.J.D. Doctor of Juridical Science or Doctor of the Science of Law
S.Sc.D Doctor of Social Science
S.T.B. Bachelor of Sacred Theology
S.T.D. Doctor of Sacred Theology
S.T.M. Master of Sacred Theology
Th.B. Bachelor of Theology
Th.D. Doctor of Theology
Th.M. Master of Theology

1. Honorary. 2. Earned and honorary. 3. Usually honorary. 4. Sometimes honorary.

Academic Costume: Colors Associated With Fields

Field	Color
Agriculture	Maize
Arts, Letters, Humanities	White
Commerce, Accountancy, Business	Drab
Dentistry	Lilac
Economics	Copper
Education	Light Blue
Engineering	Orange
Fine Arts, Architecture	Brown
Forestry	Russet
Journalism	Crimson
Law	Purple
Library Science	Lemon
Medicine	Green
Music	Pink
Nursing	Apricot
Oratory (Speech)	Silver gray
Pharmacy	Olive green
Philosophy	Dark blue
Physical Education	Sage green
Public Admin. including Foreign Service	Peacock blue
Public Health	Salmon pink
Science	Golden yellow
Social Work	Citron
Theology	Scarlet
Veterinary Science	Gray

Population

Colonial Population Estimates (in round numbers)

Year	Population	Year	Population	Year	Population	Year	Population
1610	350	1660	75,100	1710	331,700	1760	1,593,600
1620	2,300	1670	111,900	1720	466,200	1770	2,148,100
1630	4,600	1680	151,500	1730	629,400	1780	2,780,400
1640	26,600	1690	210,400	1740	905,600		
1650	50,400	1700	250,900	1750	1,170,800		

National Censuses[1]

Year	Resident population[2]	Land area, sq mi.	Pop. per sq mi.	Year	Resident population[2]	Land area, sq mi.	Pop. per sq mi.
1790	3,929,214	864,746	4.5	1890	62,947,714	2,969,640	21.2
1800	5,308,483	864,746	6.1	1900	75,994,575	2,969,834	25.6
1810	7,239,881	1,681,828	4.3	1910	91,972,266	2,969,565	31.0
1820	9,638,453	1,749,462	5.5	1920	105,710,620	2,969,451	35.6
1830	12,866,020	1,749,462	7.4	1930	122,775,046	2,977,128	41.2
1840	17,069,453	1,749,462	9.8	1940	131,669,275	2,977,128	44.2
1850	23,191,876	2,940,042	7.9	1950	150,697,361	2,974,726	50.7
1860	31,443,321	2,969,640	10.6	1960	179,323,175	3,540,911	50.6
1870	39,818,449	2,969,640	13.4	1970	203,302,031	3,540,023	57.4
1880	50,155,783	2,969,640	16.9	1980	226,545,805	3,618,770	62.6

1. Beginning with 1960, figures include Alaska and Hawaii. 2. Excludes armed forces overseas. NOTE: n.a. = not available. *Source:* Department of Commerce, Bureau of the Census.

Population Distribution by Age, Race, Nativity, and Sex

	Age						Race and nativity				
							White[1]				
Year	Total	Under 5	5–19	20–44	45–62	65 and over	Total	Native born	Foreign born	Black	Other races[1]
PERCENT DISTRIBUTION											
1860[2]	100.0	15.4	35.8	35.7	10.4	2.7	85.6	72.6	13.0	14.1	0.3
1870[2]	100.0	14.3	35.4	35.4	11.9	3.0	87.1	72.9	14.2	12.7	0.2
1880[2]	100.0	13.8	34.3	35.9	12.6	3.4	86.5	73.4	13.1	13.1	0.3
1890[3]	100.0	12.2	33.9	36.9	13.1	3.9	87.5	73.0	14.5	11.9	0.3
1900	100.0	12.1	32.3	37.7	13.7	4.1	87.9	74.5	13.4	11.6	0.5
1910	100.0	11.6	30.4	39.0	14.6	4.3	88.9	74.4	14.5	10.7	0.4
1920	100.0	10.9	29.8	38.4	16.1	4.7	89.7	76.7	13.0	9.9	0.4
1930	100.0	9.3	29.5	38.3	17.4	5.4	89.8	78.4	11.4	9.7	0.5
1940	100.0	8.0	26.4	38.9	19.8	6.8	89.8	81.1	8.7	9.8	0.4
1950	100.0	10.7	23.2	37.6	20.3	8.1	89.5	82.8	6.7	10.0	0.5
1960	100.0	11.3	27.1	32.2	20.1	9.2	88.6	83.4	5.2	10.5	0.9
1970[2]	100.0	8.4	29.5	31.7	20.6	9.8	87.6	83.4	4.3	11.1	1.4
1980	100.0	7.2	24.8	37.1	19.6	11.3	83.1	n.a.	n.a.	11.7	5.2
MALES PER 100 FEMALES											
1860[2]	104.7	102.4	101.2	107.9	111.5	98.3	105.3	103.7	115.1	99.6	260.8
1870[2]	102.2	102.9	101.2	99.2	114.5	100.5	102.8	100.6	115.3	96.2	400.7
1880[2]	103.6	103.0	101.3	104.0	110.2	101.4	104.0	102.1	115.9	97.8	362.2
1890[3]	105.0	103.6	101.4	107.3	108.3	104.2	105.4	102.9	118.7	99.5	165.2
1900	104.4	102.1	100.9	105.8	110.7	102.0	104.9	102.8	117.4	98.6	185.2
1910	106.0	102.5	101.3	108.1	114.4	101.1	106.6	102.7	129.2	98.9	185.6
1920	104.0	102.5	100.8	102.8	115.2	101.3	104.4	101.7	121.7	99.2	156.6
1930	102.5	103.0	101.4	100.5	109.1	100.5	102.9	101.1	115.8	97.0	150.6
1940	100.7	103.2	102.0	98.1	105.2	95.5	101.2	100.1	111.1	95.0	140.5

Year	Age						Race and nativity				
							White[1]				
	Total	Under 5	5–19	20–44	45–62	65 and over	Total	Native born	Foreign born	Black	Other races[1]
1950	98.6	103.9	102.5	96.2	100.1	89.6	99.0	98.8	102.0	93.7	129.7
1960	97.1	103.4	102.7	95.6	95.7	82.8	97.4	97.6	94.2	93.3	109.7
1970[2]	94.8	104.0	103.3	95.1	91.6	72.1	95.3	95.9	83.8	90.8	100.2
1980	94.5	104.7	104.0	98.1	90.7	67.6	94.8	n.a.	n.a.	89.6	100.3

1. The 1980 census data for white and other races categories are not directly comparable to those shown for the preceding years because of the changes in the way some persons reported their race, as well as changes in 1980 procedures relating to racial classification. 2. Excludes persons for whom age is not available. 3. Excludes persons enumerated in the Indian Territory and on Indian reservations. NOTES: Data exclude Armed Forces overseas. Beginning in 1960, includes Alaska and Hawaii, n.a. = not available. *Source:* Department of Commerce, Bureau of the Census.

Population and Rank of Large Metropolitan Areas, 1970–1980

(over 150,000)

Standard metropolitan statistical area	1980 Census		1970 Census		Change, 1970–80	
	Number	Rank	Number	Rank	Number	%
Akron, Ohio	660,328	57	679,239	52	−18,911	−2.7
Albany–Schenectady–Troy, N.Y.	795,019	50	777,977	43	17,042	2.2
Albuquerque, N.M.	454,499	86	333,266	102	121,233	36.4
Alexandria, La.	151,985	205	131,749	203	20,236	15.4
Allentown–Bethlehem–Easton, Pa.-N.J.	636,714	62	594,382	60	42,332	7.2
Amarillo, Tex.	173,699	188	144,396	192	29,303	20.3
Anaheim–Santa Ana–Garden Grove, Calif.	1,931,570	18	1,421,233	20	510,337	36.0
Anchorage, Alaska	173,017	191	126,385	211	46,632	36.9
Ann Arbor, Mich.	264,748	145	234,103	141	30,645	13.1
Appleton–Oshkosh, Wis.	291,325	129	276,948	121	14,377	5.2
Asheville, N.C.	177,761	184	161,059	181	16,702	10.4
Atlanta	2,029,618	16	1,595,517	18	434,101	27.3
Atlantic City, N.J.	194,119	171	175,043	168	19,076	10.9
Augusta, Ga.–S.C.	327,372	113	275,787	122	51,585	18.8
Austin, Tex.	536,450	70	360,463	93	175,987	48.9
Bakersfield, Calif.	403,089	97	330,234	104	72,855	22.1
Baltimore	2,174,023	14	2,071,016	13	103,007	5.0
Baton Rouge, La.	493,973	80	375,628	87	118,345	31.6
Battle Creek, Mich.	187,338	177	180,129	164	7,209	4.1
Beaumont–Port Arthur, Tex.	375,497	104	347,568	97	27,929	8.1
Biloxi–Gulfport, Miss.	191,918	174	160,070	183	31,848	19.9
Binghamton, N.Y.-Pa.	301,336	126	302,672	111	−1,336	−0.4
Birmingham, Ala.	847,360	45	767,230	44	80,130	10.5
Boise, Idaho	173,036	190	112,230	232	60,806	54.2
Boston	2,763,357	10	2,899,101	8	−135,744	−4.6
Bridgeport, Conn.	395,455	98	401,752	82	−6,297	−1.5
Brockton, Mass.	169,374	196	150,416	186	18,958	12.7
Brownsville–Harlingen–San Benito, Tex.	209,680	164	140,368	194	69,312	49.4
Buffalo, N.Y.	1,242,573	31	1,349,211	24	−106,638	−7.9
Canton, Ohio	404,421	96	393,789	83	10,632	2.7
Cedar Rapids, Iowa	169,775	194	163,213	179	6,562	4.1
Champaign–Urbana–Rantoul, Ill.	168,392	197	163,281	178	5,111	3.2
Charleston–North Charleston, S.C.	430,301	91	336,036	100	94,265	28.1
Charleston, W. Va.	269,595	142	257,140	133	12,455	4.9
Charlotte–Gastonia, N.C.	637,218	61	557,785	62	79,433	14.3
Chattanooga, Tenn.-Ga.	426,540	92	370,857	90	55,683	15.1
Chicago	7,102,328	3	6,974,755	3	127,573	1.9
Cincinnati, Ohio-Ky.-Ind.	1,401,403	27	1,387,207	22	14,196	1.1
Clarksville–Hopkinsville, Tenn.-Ky.	150,220	209	118,945	220	31,275	26.3
Cleveland	1,898,720	19	2,063,729	14	−165,009	−7.9
Colorado Springs, Colo.	317,458	120	239,288	139	78,170	32.7
Columbia, S.C.	408,176	95	322,880	107	85,296	26.5
Columbus, Ga.-Ala.	239,196	154	238,584	140	612	0.3
Columbus, Ohio	1,093,293	35	1,017,847	33	75,446	7.5
Corpus Christi, Tex.	326,228	114	284,832	118	41,396	14.6

Standard metropolitan statistical area	1980 Census		1970 Census		Change, 1970–80	
	Number	Rank	Number	Rank	Number	%
Dallas-Fort Worth	2,974,878	8	2,377,623	12	597,255	25.2
Davenport-Rock Island-Moline, Iowa-Ill.	383,958	100	362,638	91	21,320	5.9
Dayton, Ohio	830,070	47	852,531	40	−22,461	−2.6
Daytona Beach, Fla.	258,762	148	169,487	174	89,275	52.7
Denver-Boulder, Colo.	1,619,921	22	1,239,545	27	380,376	30.7
Des Moines, Iowa	338,048	111	313,562	109	24,486	7.9
Detroit	4,352,762	5	4,435,051	5	−82,289	−1.8
Duluth-Superior, Minn.-Wis.	266,650	143	265,350	126	1,300	0.5
El Paso	479,899	82	359,291	94	120,608	33.6
Erie, Pa.	279,780	135	263,654	128	16,126	6.2
Eugene-Springfield, Ore.	275,226	138	215,401	151	59,825	27.8
Evansville, Ind.-Ky.	309,408	123	284,959	117	24,449	8.6
Fall River, Mass.-R.I.	176,831	185	169,549	173	7,282	4.3
Fayetteville-Springdale, Ark.	177,850	183	127,846	208	50,004	39.2
Fayetteville, N.C.	247,160	152	212,042	152	35,118	16.6
Flint, Mich.	521,589	77	508,664	69	12,925	2.6
Fort Lauderdale-Hollywood, Fla.	1,014,043	37	620,100	58	393,943	63.6
Fort Myers-Cape Coral, Fla.	205,266	166	105,216	238	100,050	95.1
Fort Smith, Ark.-Okla.	203,269	167	160,421	182	42,848	26.8
Fort Wayne, Ind.	382,961	101	361,984	92	20,977	5.8
Fresno, Calif.	515,013	78	413,329	77	101,684	24.7
Gainesville, Fla.	151,348	208	104,764	239	46,584	44.5
Galveston-Texas City, Tex.	195,940	170	169,812	172	26,128	15.4
Gary-Hammond-East Chicago, Ind.	642,781	58	633,367	54	9,414	1.5
Grand Rapids, Mich.	601,680	64	539,225	67	62,455	11.6
Green Bay, Wis.	175,280	187	158,244	185	17,036	10.8
Greensboro-Winston-Salem-High Point, N.C.	827,385	48	724,129	47	103,256	14.3
Greenville-Spartanburg, S.C.	568,758	68	473,454	71	95,304	20.2
Hamilton-Middletown, Ohio	258,787	147	226,207	145	32,580	14.5
Harrisburg, Pa.	446,072	88	410,505	80	35,567	8.7
Hartford, Conn.	726,114	54	720,581	48	5,533	0.8
Honolulu	762,874	52	630,528	55	132,346	21.0
Houston	2,905,350	9	1,999,316	16	906,034	45.4
Huntington-Ashland, W. Va.-Ky.-Ohio	311,350	122	286,935	116	24,415	8.6
Huntsville, Ala.	308,593	124	282,450	119	26,143	9.3
Indianapolis	1,166,929	34	1,111,352	29	55,577	5.1
Jackson, Mich.	151,495	207	143,274	193	8,221	5.8
Jackson, Miss.	320,425	117	258,906	130	61,519	23.8
Jacksonville, Fla.	737,519	53	621,827	57	115,692	18.7
Jersey City, N.J.	556,972	69	607,839	59	−50,867	−8.3
Johnson City-Kingsport-Bristol, Tenn.-Va.	433,638	90	373,591	88	60,047	16.1
Johnstown, Pa.	264,506	146	262,822	129	1,684	0.7
Kalamazoo-Portage, Mich.	279,192	137	257,723	132	21,469	8.4
Kansas City, Mo.-Kan.	1,327,020	29	1,273,926	25	53,094	4.2
Killeen-Temple, Tex.	214,656	162	159,794	184	54,862	34.4
Knoxville, Tenn.	476,517	83	409,409	81	67,108	16.4
Lafayette, La.	150,017	210	111,643	233	38,374	34.4
Lake Charles, La.	167,048	198	145,415	189	21,633	14.9
Lakeland-Winter Haven, Fla.	321,652	116	228,515	143	93,137	40.8
Lancaster, Pa.	362,346	108	320,079	108	42,267	13.3
Lansing-East Lansing, Mich.	468,482	84	424,271	75	44,211	10.5
Las Vegas, Nev.	461,816	85	273,288	123	188,528	69.0
Lawrence-Haverhill, Mass.-N.H.	281,981	133	258,564	131	23,417	9.1
Lexington-Fayette, Ky.	318,136	119	266,701	125	51,435	19.3
Lima, Ohio	218,244	160	210,074	153	8,170	3.9
Lincoln, Neb.	192,884	173	167,972	176	24,912	14.9
Little Rock-North Little Rock, Ark.	393,494	99	323,296	106	70,198	21.8
Long Branch-Asbury Park, N.J.	503,173	79	461,849	72	41,324	9.0
Longview-Marshall, Tex.	151,752	206	120,770	217	30,982	25.7
Lorain-Elyria, Ohio	274,909	139	256,843	134	18,066	7.1
Los Angeles-Long Beach, Calif.	7,477,657	2	7,041,980	2	435,677	6.2
Louisville, Ky.-Ind.	906,240	43	867,330	39	38,910	4.5
Lowell, Mass.-N.H.	233,410	155	218,268	149	15,142	7.0
Lubbock, Tex.	211,651	163	179,295	165	32,356	18.1
Lynchburg, Va.	153,260	204	134,744	198	18,516	13.8
Macon, Ga.	254,623	149	226,782	144	27,841	12.3
Madison, Wis.	323,545	115	290,272	114	33,273	11.5
Manchester, N.H.	160,767	202	132,512	201	28,255	21.4
McAllen-Pharr-Edinburg, Tex.	283,229	132	181,535	162	101,694	56.1

Standard metropolitan statistical area	1980 Census		1970 Census		Change, 1970–80	
	Number	Rank	Number	Rank	Number	%
Melbourne-Titusville-Cocoa, Fla.	272,959	140	230,006	142	42,953	18.7
Memphis, Tenn.-Ark.-Miss.	912,887	42	834,103	41	78,784	9.5
Miami, Fla.	1,625,979	21	1,267,792	26	358,187	28.3
Milwaukee	1,397,143	28	1,403,884	21	−6,741	−0.4
Minneapolis-St. Paul	2,114,256	15	1,965,391	17	148,865	7.6
Mobile, Ala.	442,819	89	376,690	86	66,129	17.6
Modesto, Calif.	265,902	144	194,506	158	71,396	36.8
Montgomery, Ala.	272,687	141	225,911	146	46,776	20.8
Muskegon-Norton Shores-Muskegon Heights, Mich.	179,591	182	175,410	166	4,181	2.4
Nashville-Davidson, Tenn.	850,505	44	699,271	50	151,234	21.7
Nassau-Suffolk, N.Y.	2,605,813	11	2,555,868	9	49,945	2.0
Newark, N.J.	1,965,304	17	2,057,468	15	−92,164	−4.4
New Bedford, Mass.	169,425	195	161,288	180	8,137	5.1
New Brunswick-Perth Amboy-Sayreville, N.J.	595,893	65	583,813	61	12,080	2.1
New Haven-West Haven, Conn.	417,592	93	411,287	79	6,305	1.6
New London-Norwich, Conn.-R.I.	248,554	151	241,862	138	6,692	2.8
New Orleans	1,186,725	33	1,046,470	32	140,255	13.5
Newport News-Hampton, Va.	364,449	107	333,140	103	31,309	9.4
New York, N.Y.-N.J.	9,119,737	1	9,973,716	1	−853,979	−8.5
Norfolk-Virginia Beach-Portsmouth, Va.-N.C.	806,691	49	732,600	46	74,091	10.2
Northeast Pennsylvania	640,396	60	621,882	56	18,514	3.0
Oklahoma City	834,088	46	699,092	51	134,996	19.4
Omaha, Neb.-Iowa	570,399	67	542,646	65	27,753	5.2
Orlando, Fla.	700,699	55	453,270	74	247,429	54.6
Oxnard-Simi Valley-Ventura, Calif.	529,899	75	378,497	85	151,402	40.1
Parkersburg-Marietta, W. Va.-Ohio	162,836	201	148,132	187	14,704	10.0
Paterson-Clifton-Passaic, N.J.	447,585	87	460,782	73	−13,197	−2.8
Pensacola, Fla.	289,782	131	243,075	137	46,707	19.3
Peoria, Ill.	365,864	106	341,979	98	23,885	7.0
Philadelphia, Pa.-N.J.	4,716,818	4	4,824,110	4	−107,292	−2.2
Phoenix, Ariz.	1,508,030	26	971,228	35	536,802	55.3
Pittsburgh	2,263,894	13	2,401,362	11	−137,468	−5.7
Portland, Me.	183,625	181	170,081	171	13,544	8.0
Portland, Ore.-Wash.	1,242,187	32	1,007,131	34	235,057	23.4
Poughkeepsie, N.Y.	245,055	153	222,295	147	22,760	10.3
Providence-Warwick-Pawtucket, R.I.-Mass.	919,216	41	908,887	37	10,329	1.2
Provo-Orem, Utah	218,106	161	137,776	196	80,330	58.4
Racine, Wis.	173,132	189	170,838	170	2,294	1.4
Raleigh-Durham, N.C.	530,673	73	419,254	76	111,419	26.6
Reading, Pa.	312,509	121	296,382	112	16,127	5.5
Reno, Nev.	193,623	172	121,068	216	72,555	60.0
Richmond, Va.	632,015	63	547,542	64	84,473	15.5
Riverside-San Bernardino-Ontario, Calif.	1,557,080	25	1,139,149	28	417,931	36.7
Roanoke, Va.	224,548	159	203,153	157	21,395	10.6
Rochester, N.Y.	971,879	39	961,516	36	10,363	1.1
Rockford, Ill.	279,514	136	272,063	124	7,451	2.8
Sacramento, Calif.	1,014,002	38	803,793	42	210,209	26.2
Saginaw, Mich.	228,059	158	219,743	148	8,316	3.8
St. Cloud, Minn.	163,256	199	134,585	199	28,671	21.4
St. Louis, Mo.-Ill.	2,355,276	12	2,410,884	10	−55,608	−2.3
Salem, Ore.	249,895	150	186,658	160	63,237	33.9
Salinas-Seaside-Monterey-Calif.	290,444	130	247,450	136	42,994	17.4
Salt Lake City-Ogden, Utah	936,255	40	705,458	49	230,797	32.8
San Antonio	1,071,954	36	888,179	38	183,775	20.7
San Diego, Calif.	1,861,846	20	1,357,854	23	503,992	37.2
San Francisco-Oakland, Calif.	3,252,721	6	3,109,249	6	143,472	4.7
San Jose, Calif.	1,295,071	30	1,065,313	31	229,758	21.6
Santa Barbara-Santa Maria-Lompoc, Calif.	298,660	128	264,324	127	34,336	13.0
Santa Cruz, Calif.	188,141	175	123,790	213	64,351	52.0
Santa Rosa, Calif.	299,827	127	204,885	156	94,942	46.4
Sarasota, Fla.	202,251	168	120,413	218	81,838	68.0
Savannah, Ga.	230,728	156	207,987	154	22,741	11.0
Seattle-Everett, Wash.	1,606,765	23	1,424,605	19	182,160	12.8
Shreveport, La.	376,646	103	336,000	101	40,646	12.1
South Bend, Ind.	280,772	134	279,813	120	959	0.4
Spokane, Wash.	341,835	110	287,487	115	54,348	19.0
Springfield, Ill.	187,789	176	171,020	169	16,769	9.9

Standard metropolitan statistical area	1980 Census		1970 Census		Change, 1970–80	
	Number	Rank	Number	Rank	Number	%
Springfield-Chicopee-Holyoke, Mass.-Conn.	530,668	74	541,752	66	−11,084	−2.0
Springfield, Mo.	207,704	165	168,053	175	39,651	23.6
Springfield, Ohio	183,885	180	187,606	159	−3,721	−1.9
Stamford, Conn.	198,854	169	206,340	155	−7,486	−3.6
Steubenville-Weirton, Ohio-W. Va.	163,099	200	166,385	177	−3,286	−1.9
Stockton, Calif.	347,342	109	291,073	113	56,269	19.4
Syracuse, N.Y.	642,375	59	636,596	53	5,779	1.0
Tacoma, Wash.	485,643	81	412,344	78	73,299	17.8
Tallahassee, Fla.	159,542	203	109,355	235	50,187	45.9
Tampa-St. Petersburg, Fla.	1,569,492	24	1,088,549	30	480,943	44.2
Terre Haute, Ind.	176,583	186	175,143	167	1,440	0.9
Toledo, Ohio-Mich.	791,599	51	762,658	45	28,941	3.8
Topeka, Kan.	185,442	179	180,619	163	4,823	2.7
Trenton, N.J.	307,863	125	304,116	110	3,747	1.3
Tucson, Ariz.	531,263	72	351,667	95	179,596	51.1
Tulsa, Okla.	689,628	56	549,154	63	140,474	25.6
Utica-Rome, N.Y.	320,180	118	340,477	99	−20,297	−5.9
Vallejo-Fairfield-Napa, Calif.	334,402	112	251,129	135	83,273	33.2
Waco, Tex.	170,755	193	147,553	188	23,202	15.8
Washington, D.C.-Md.-Va.	3,060,240	7	2,910,111	7	150,129	5.2
Waterbury, Conn.	228,178	157	216,808	150	11,370	5.3
West Palm Beach-Boca Raton, Fla.	573,125	66	348,993	96	224,132	64.3
Wheeling, W. Va.-Ohio	185,566	178	181,954	161	3,612	2.0
Wichita, Kan.	411,313	94	389,352	84	21,961	5.7
Wilmington, Del.-N.J.-Md.	524,108	76	499,493	70	24,615	5.0
Worcester, Mass.	372,940	105	372,144	89	796	0.3
Yakima, Wash.	172,508	192	145,212	191	27,296	18.8
York, Pa.	381,255	102	329,540	105	51,715	15.7
Youngstown-Warren, Ohio	531,350	71	537,124	68	−5,774	−1.0

NOTE: The general concept of a standard metropolitan statistical area (SMSA) is one of a large population nucleus together with adjacent communities that have a high degree of economic and social integration with that nucleus. *Source:* Department of Commerce, Bureau of the Census.

Population by Age, Sex, Race, and Spanish Origin, 1980

(in thousands)

Age	White		Black		Spanish origin		Other races		All persons	
	Male	Female	Male	Female	Male	Female	Male	Female	Male	Female
Under 5	6,484	6,150	1,228	1,208	848	815	650	627	8,362	7,986
5–9	6,685	6,347	1,255	1,235	783	754	598	578	8,539	8,160
10–14	7,408	7,053	1,344	1,329	747	728	563	544	9,316	8,926
15–19	8,634	8,327	1,489	1,496	827	779	632	588	10,755	10,412
20–24	8,683	8,605	1,300	1,424	819	767	680	625	10,663	10,655
25–29	8,005	7,979	1,084	1,237	697	679	615	599	9,705	9,815
30–34	7,299	7,345	871	1,018	558	570	506	521	8,676	8,884
35–39	5,831	5,930	662	795	416	438	368	378	6,861	7,108
40–44	4,849	4,976	566	684	345	367	292	300	5,708	5,961
45–49	4,638	4,818	515	628	300	321	234	255	5,388	5,701
50–54	4,918	5,239	504	624	270	294	198	226	5,620	6,089
55–59	4,852	5,385	466	570	217	237	163	178	5,481	6,133
60–64	4,173	4,802	385	486	147	174	111	130	4,669	5,418
65–69	3,481	4,331	331	445	116	148	90	104	3,902	4,879
70–74	2,552	3,543	234	329	85	109	67	72	2,853	3,944
75–79	1,650	2,660	153	235	59	77	45	52	1,847	2,946
80–84	923	1,762	75	125	27	39	21	28	1,019	1,915
85 and over	614	1,430	53	106	19	30	14	23	681	1,558
All ages	91,685	96,686	12,519	13,977	7,280	7,329	5,847	5,829	110,052	116,492
15 and over	71,095	77,124	8,689	10,200	4,901	5,030	4,035	4,080	83,819	91,404
20 and over	62,463	68,798	7,345	8,871	4,153	4,302	3,450	3,492	74,504	82,478
65 and over	9,222	13,726	847	1,240	305	404	236	277	10,304	15,245
Median age	30.0	32.5	23.5	26.1	22.6	23.8	24.1	25.7	28.8	31.2

Source: Department of Commerce, Bureau of the Census.

Population by State

State	1980	Percent change, 1970–80	Pop. per sq. mi., 1980	Pop. rank, 1980	1970	1950	1900	1790
Alabama	3,893,888	+13.1	76.7	22	3,444,354	3,061,743	1,828,697	—
Alaska	401,851	+32.8	0.7	50	302,583	128,643	63,592	—
Arizona	2,718,425	+53.1	23.9	29	1,775,399	749,587	122,931	—
Arkansas	2,286,435	+18.9	43.9	33	1,923,322	1,909,511	1,311,564	—
California	23,667,565	+18.5	151.4	1	19,971,069	10,586,223	1,485,053	—
Colorado	2,889,735	+30.8	27.9	28	2,209,596	1,325,089	539,700	—
Connecticut	3,107,576	+ 2.5	637.8	25	3,032,217	2,007,280	908,420	237,946
Delaware	594,317	+ 8.4	307.6	47	548,104	318,085	184,735	59,096
D.C.	638,432	−15.6	—	—	756,668	802,178	278,718	—
Florida	9,746,324	+43.5	180.0	7	6,791,418	2,771,305	528,542	—
Georgia	5,463,105	+19.1	94.1	13	4,587,930	3,444,578	2,216,331	82,548
Hawaii	964,691	+25.3	150.1	39	769,913	499,794	154,001	—
Idaho	944,038	+32.4	11.5	41	713,015	588,637	161,772	—
Illinois	11,426,518	+ 2.8	205.3	5	11,110,285	8,712,176	4,821,550	—
Indiana	5,490,260	+ 5.7	152.8	12	5,195,392	3,934,224	2,516,462	—
Iowa	2,913,808	+ 3.1	52.1	27	2,825,368	2,621,073	2,231,853	—
Kansas	2,364,236	+ 5.1	28.9	32	2,249,071	1,905,299	1,470,495	—
Kentucky	3,660,257	+13.7	92.3	23	3,220,711	2,944,806	2,147,174	73,677
Louisiana	4,206,312	+15.4	94.5	19	3,644,637	2,683,516	1,381,625	—
Maine	1,125,027	+13.2	36.3	38	993,722	913,774	694,466	96,540
Maryland	4,216,975	+ 7.5	428.7	18	3,923,897	2,343,001	1,188,044	319,728
Massachusetts	5,737,037	+ 0.8	733.3	11	5,689,170	4,690,514	2,805,346	378,787
Michigan	9,262,078	+ 4.3	162.6	8	8,881,826	6,371,766	2,420,982	—
Minnesota	4,075,970	+ 7.1	51.2	21	3,806,103	2,982,483	1,751,394	—
Mississippi	2,520,638	+13.7	53.4	31	2,216,994	2,178,914	1,551,270	—
Missouri	4,916,759	+ 5.1	71.3	15	4,677,623	3,954,653	3,106,665	—
Montana	786,690	+13.3	5.4	44	694,409	591,024	243,329	—
Nebraska	1,569,825	+ 5.7	20.5	35	1,485,333	1,325,510	1,066,300	—
Nevada	800,493	+63.8	7.3	43	488,738	160,083	42,335	—
New Hampshire	920,610	+24.8	102.4	42	737,681	533,242	411,588	141,885
New Jersey	7,364,823	+ 2.7	986.2	9	7,171,112	4,835,329	1,883,669	184,139
New Mexico	1,302,981	+28.1	10.7	37	1,017,055	681,187	195,310	—
New York	17,558,072	− 3.7	370.6	2	18,241,391	14,830,192	7,268,894	340,120
North Carolina	5,881,813	+15.7	120.4	10	5,084,411	4,061,929	1,893,810	393,751
North Dakota	652,717	+ 5.7	9.4	46	617,792	619,636	319,146	—
Ohio	10,797,624	+ 1.3	263.3	6	10,657,423	7,946,627	4,157,545	—
Oklahoma	3,025,290	+18.2	44.1	26	2,559,463	2,233,351	790,391[1]	—
Oregon	2,633,149	+25.9	27.4	30	2,091,533	1,521,341	413,536	—
Pennsylvania	11,863,895	+ 0.5	264.3	4	11,800,766	10,498,012	6,302,115	434,373
Rhode Island	947,154	− 0.3	897.8	40	949,723	791,896	428,556	68,825
South Carolina	3,121,833	+20.5	103.4	24	2,590,713	2,117,027	1,340,316	249,073
South Dakota	690,768	+ 3.7	9.1	45	666,257	652,740	401,570	—
Tennessee	4,591,120	+16.9	111.6	17	3,926,018	3,291,718	2,020,616	35,691
Texas	14,229,288	+27.1	54.3	3	11,198,655	7,711,194	3,048,710	—
Utah	1,461,037	+37.9	17.8	36	1,059,273	688,862	276,749	—
Vermont	511,456	+15.0	55.2	48	444,732	377,747	343,641	85,425
Virginia	5,346,818	+14.9	134.7	14	4,651,448	3,318,680	1,854,184	747,610[2]
Washington	4,132,180	+21.1	62.1	20	3,413,244	2,378,963	518,103	—
West Virginia	1,950,279	+11.8	80.8	34	1,744,237	2,005,552	958,800	—
Wisconsin	4,705,521	+ 6.5	86.5	16	4,417,821	3,434,575	2,069,042	—
Wyoming	469,557	+41.3	4.8	49	332,416	290,529	92,531	—
Total U.S.	**226,545,805**	+11.4	**62.6**	—	**203,302,031**	**151,325,798**	**76,212,168**	**3,929,214**

1. Includes population of Indian Territory: 1900, 392,960. 2. Until 1863, Virginia included what is now West Virginia. *Source:* Department of Commerce, Bureau of the Census.

F.B.I. Reports Violent Crime Receding in the U.S.

According to the F.B.I.'s 1982 annual *Uniform Crime Reports,* the number of serious crimes in the United States reported to the police dropped 3% in 1982, and the over-all crime rate declined 4%, the lowest in six years. Murder was down 7%, robbery 6%, and forcible rape dropped 5%. Burglaries decreased 9%, motor vehicle theft 2%, and larceny-theft decreased by 1%.

The F.B.I. reported that the number of serious crimes in 1982 was estimated at 12.9 million as compared with 13.3 million in 1983.

Incorporated Places Over 25,000 Population

Asterisk denotes more than one ZIP code for a city and refers to Postmaster. To find the ZIP code for a particular address, consult the ZIP code directory available in every post office. For latest population figures of many cities, see listing for individual states in the United States section.

City and major ZIP code	1980 census	1970 census
Aberdeen, SD (57401)	25,851	26,476
Abilene, TX (79604*)	98,315	89,653
Addison, IL (60101)	29,759	24,482
Akron, OH (44309*)	237,177	275,425
Alameda, CA (94501)	63,852	70,968
Albany, GA (31706*)	74,550	72,623
Albany, NY (12212*)	101,727	115,781
Albany, OR (97321)	26,678	18,181
Albuquerque, NM (87101*)	331,767	244,501
Alexandria, LA (71301*)	51,565	41,811
Alexandria, VA (22313*)	103,217	110,927
Alhambra, CA (91802*)	64,615	62,125
Allen Park, MI (48101)	34,196	40,747
Allentown, PA (18101*)	103,758	109,871
Alton, IL (62002)	34,171	39,700
Altoona, PA (16603*)	57,078	63,115
Amarillo, TX (79120*)	149,230	127,010
Ames, IA (50010)	45,775	39,505
Anaheim, CA (92803*)	219,311	166,408
Anchorage, AK (99502*)	174,431	48,081
Anderson, IN (46018*)	64,695	70,787
Anderson, SC (29621*)	27,965	27,556
Annapolis, MD (21401*)	31,740	30,095
Ann Arbor, MI (48106*)	107,966	100,035
Anniston, AL (36201*)	29,523	31,533
Antioch, CA (94509)	42,683	28,060
Appleton, WI (54911*)	58,913	56,377
Arcadia, CA (91006)	45,994	45,138
Arlington, TX (76010*)	160,113	90,229
Arlington Heights, IL (60004*)	66,116	65,058
Arvada, CO (80001*)	84,576	49,844
Asheville, NC (28810*)	53,583	57,820
Ashland, KY (41101)	27,064	29,245
Athens, GA (30603*)	42,549	44,342
Atlanta, GA (30304*)	425,022	495,039
Atlantic City, NJ (08401*)	40,199	47,859
Attleboro, MA (02703)	34,196	32,907
Auburn, AL (36830)	28,471	22,767
Auburn, NY (13021)	32,548	34,599
Auburn, WA (98002*)	26,417	21,653
Augusta, GA (30901*)	47,532	59,864
Aurora, CO (80010*)	158,588	74,974
Aurora, IL (60507*)	81,293	74,389
Austin, TX (78710*)	345,496	253,539
Azusa, CA (91702)	29,380	25,217
Bakersfield, CA (93302*)	105,735	69,515
Baldwin Park, CA (91706)	50,554	47,285
Baltimore, MD (21233*)	786,775	905,787
Bangor, ME (04401)	31,643	33,168
Barberton, OH (44203)	29,751	33,052
Bartlesville, OK (74003*)	34,568	29,683
Baton Rouge, LA (70821*)	219,419	165,921
Battle Creek, MI (49016*)	35,724	38,931
Bay City, MI (48706)	41,593	49,449
Bayonne, NJ (07002)	65,047	72,743
Baytown, TX (77520*)	56,923	43,980
Beaumont, TX (77704*)	118,102	117,548
Beavercreek, OH (45401)	31,589	—
Beaverton, OR (97005*)	30,582	18,577
Bell, CA (90201)	25,450	21,836
Belleville, IL (62220*)	41,580	41,223
Belleville, NJ (07109)	35,367	37,629
Bellevue, WA (98009*)	73,903	61,196
Bellflower, CA (90706)	53,441	52,334
Bell Gardens, CA (90201)	34,117	29,308
Bellingham, WA (98225*)	45,794	39,375
Beloit, WI (53511)	35,207	35,729
Bergenfield, NJ (07621)	25,568	29,000
Berkeley, CA (94704*)	103,328	114,091
Berwyn, IL (60402)	46,840	52,502
Bessemer, AL (35020*)	31,729	33,428
Bethel Park, PA (15102)	34,755	34,758
Bethlehem, PA (18016*)	70,419	72,686
Bettendorf, IA (52722)	27,381	22,126
Beverly, MA (01915)	37,655	38,348
Beverly Hills, CA (90213*)	32,367	33,416
Billings, MT (59101*)	66,842	61,581
Biloxi, MS (39530*)	49,311	48,486
Binghamton, NY (13902*)	55,860	64,123
Birmingham, AL (35203*)	284,413	300,910
Bismarck, ND (58501)	44,485	34,703
Blacksburg, VA (24060)	30,638	9,384
Blaine, MN (55433)	28,558	20,573
Bloomfield, NJ (07003)	47,792	52,029
Bloomington, IL (61701)	44,189	39,992
Bloomington, IN (47401)	52,044	43,262
Bloomington, MN (55420*)	81,831	81,970
Blue Springs, MO (64015)	25,927	6,779
Boca Raton, FL (33432*)	49,505	28,506
Boise, ID (83708*)	102,160	74,990
Bolingbrook, IL (60439)	37,261	7,651
Bossier City, LA (71111*)	50,817	43,769
Boston, MA (02205*)	562,994	641,071
Boulder, CO (80302*)	76,685	66,870
Bountiful, UT (84010)	32,877	27,751
Bowie, MD (20715)	33,695	35,028
Bowling Green, KY (42101)	40,450	36,705
Bowling Green, OH (43402)	25,728	14,656
Boynton Beach, FL (33435*)	35,624	18,115
Bradenton, FL (33506*)	30,170	21,040
Brea, CA (92621)	27,913	18,447
Bremerton, WA (98310*)	36,208	35,307
Bridgeport, CT (06602*)	142,546	156,542
Bristol, CT (06010)	57,370	55,487
Brockton, MA (02403*)	95,172	89,040
Broken Arrow, OK (74012)	35,761	11,018
Brookfield, WI (53005)	34,035	31,761
Brooklyn Center, MN (55429*)	31,230	35,173
Brooklyn Park, MN (55007)	43,332	26,230
Brook Park, OH (44142)	26,195	30,774
Brownsville, TX (78520*)	84,997	52,522
Brunswick, OH (44212)	28,104	15,852
Bryan, TX (77801*)	44,337	33,719
Buena Park, CA (90622*)	64,165	63,646
Buffalo, NY (14240*)	357,870	462,768
Burbank, CA (91505*)	84,625	88,871
Burbank, IL (60459)	28,462	—
Burlingame, CA (94010)	26,173	27,320
Burlington, IA (52601)	29,529	32,366
Burlington, NC (27215)	37,266	35,930
Burlington, VT (05401)	37,712	38,633
Burnsville, MN (55337)	35,674	19,940
Burton, MI (48502)	29,976	—
Butte, MT (59701)	37,205	23,368
Calumet City, IL (60409)	39,697	33,107
Camarillo, CA (93010)	37,797	19,219
Cambridge, MA (02140)	95,322	100,361
Camden, NJ (08101*)	84,910	102,551

City and major ZIP code	1980 census	1970 census
Campbell, CA (95008)	27,067	23,797
Canton, OH (44711*)	93,077	110,053
Cape Coral, FL (33910)	32,103	—
Cape Girardeau, MO (63701)	34,361	31,282
Carbondale, IL (62901)	26,414	22,816
Carlsbad, CA (92008)	35,490	14,944
Carlsbad, NM (88220)	25,496	21,297
Carrollton, TX (75006*)	40,595	13,855
Carson, CA (90749)	81,221	71,150
Carson City, NV (89701)	32,022	15,468
Casper, WY (82601*)	51,016	39,361
Cedar Falls, IA (50613)	36,322	29,597
Cedar Rapids, IA (52401*)	110,243	110,642
Cerritos, CA (90701)	53,020	15,856
Champaign, IL (61820*)	58,133	56,837
Chandler, AZ (85224)	29,673	13,763
Chapel Hill, NC (27514)	32,421	26,199
Charleston, SC (29401*)	69,510	66,945
Charleston, WV (25301*)	63,968	71,505
Charlotte, NC (28228*)	314,447	241,420
Charlottesville, VA (22906*)	39,916	38,880
Chattanooga, TN (37401*)	169,558	119,923
Chelsea, MA (02150)	25,431	30,625
Chesapeake, VA (23320*)	114,486	89,580
Chester, PA (19013*)	45,794	56,331
Cheyenne, WY (82001*)	47,283	41,254
Chicago, IL (60607*)	3,005,072	3,369,357
Chicago Heights, IL (60411)	37,026	40,900
Chico, CA (95926)	26,603	19,580
Chicopee, MA (01021*)	55,112	66,676
Chino, CA (91710)	40,165	20,411
Chula Vista, CA (92010*)	83,927	67,901
Cicero, IL (60650)	61,232	67,058
Cincinnati, OH (45234*)	385,457	453,514
Claremont, GA (91711)	30,950	24,776
Clarksville, TN (37040*)	54,777	31,719
Clearwater, FL (33575*)	85,528	52,074
Cleveland, OH (44101*)	573,822	750,879
Cleveland, TN (37311)	26,415	21,446
Cleveland Heights, OH (44118)	56,438	60,767
Clifton, NJ (07015*)	74,388	82,437
Clinton, IA (52732)	32,828	34,719
Clovis, CA (93612)	33,021	13,856
Clovis, NM (88101)	31,194	28,495
College Station, TX (77840)	37,272	17,676
Colorado Springs, CO (80901*)	214,821	135,517
Columbia, MO (65201*)	62,061	58,812
Columbia, SC (29201*)	100,385	113,542
Columbia, TN (38401)	26,571	21,471
Columbus, GA (31908*)	169,441	155,028
Columbus, IN (47201*)	30,614	26,457
Columbus, MS (39701*)	27,383	25,795
Columbus, OH (43216*)	565,032	540,025
Compton, CA (90220*)	81,286	78,547
Concord, CA (94520*)	103,255	85,164
Concord, NH (03301*)	30,400	30,022
Coon Rapids, MN (55433)	35,826	30,505
Coral Gables, FL (33114)	43,241	42,494
Coral Springs, FL (33065)	37,349	1,489
Corona, CA (91720)	37,791	27,519
Corpus Christi, TX (78408*)	231,999	204,525
Corvallis, OR (97333*)	40,960	35,056
Costa Mesa, CA (92626*)	82,562	72,660
Council Bluffs, IA (51501)	56,449	60,348
Covina, CA (91722*)	33,751	30,395
Covington, KY (41011*)	49,563	52,535
Cranston, RI (02910*)	71,992	74,287
Crystal, MN (55428*)	25,543	30,925
Culver City, CA (90230)	38,139	34,451
Cumberland, MD (21502)	25,933	29,724
Cupertino, CA (95014)	34,015	17,895
Cuyahoga Falls, OH (44222*)	43,890	49,815
Cypress, CA (90630)	40,391	31,569
Dallas, TX (75260*)	904,078	844,401
Daly City, CA (94015*)	78,519	66,922
Danbury, CT (06810*)	60,470	50,781
Danville, IL (61832)	38,985	42,570
Danville, VA (24541*)	45,642	46,391
Davenport, IA (52802*)	103,264	98,469
Davis, CA (95616)	36,640	23,488
Dayton, OH (45401*)	193,444	243,023
Daytona Beach, FL (32015*)	54,176	45,327
Dearborn, MI (48120*)	90,660	104,199
Dearborn Heights, MI (48127)	67,706	80,069
Decatur, AL (35602*)	42,002	38,044
Decatur, IL (62521*)	94,081	90,397
Deerfield Beach, FL (33441)	39,193	16,662
De Kalb, IL (60115)	33,099	32,949
Del City, OK (73155*)	28,424	27,133
Delray Beach, FL (33444*)	34,325	19,915
Del Rio, TX (78840)	30,034	21,330
Denton, TX (76201*)	48,063	39,874
Denver, CO (80202*)	492,365	514,678
Des Moines, IA (50318*)	191,003	201,404
Des Plaines, IL (60018*)	53,568	57,239
Detroit, MI (48233*)	1,203,339	1,514,063
Dothan, AL (36303*)	48,750	36,733
Downers Grove, IL (60515*)	42,572	32,544
Downey, CA (90241*)	82,602	88,573
Dubuque, IA (52001)	62,321	62,309
Duluth, MN (55806*)	92,811	100,578
Duncanville, TX (75138*)	27,781	14,105
Dunedin, FL (33528)	30,203	17,639
Durham, NC (27701*)	100,538	95,438
East Chicago, IN (46312)	39,786	49,982
East Cleveland, OH (44112)	36,957	39,660
East Detroit, MI (48021)	38,280	45,920
East Lansing, MI (48823)	51,392	47,540
Easton, PA (18042)	26,027	29,450
East Orange, NJ (07019*)	77,690	75,471
East Point, GA (30364)	37,486	39,315
East Providence, RI (02914)	50,980	48,207
East St. Louis, IL (62201*)	55,200	70,169
Eau Claire, WI (54701*)	51,509	44,619
Edina, MN (55424*)	46,073	44,046
Edmond, OK (73034)	34,637	16,633
Edmonds, WA (98020)	27,679	23,684
El Cajon, CA (92020*)	73,892	52,273
El Dorado, AR (71730)	25,270	25,283
Elgin, IL (60120)	63,798	55,691
Elizabeth, NJ (07207*)	106,201	112,654
Elk Grove, IL (60007)	28,907	20,346
Elkhart, IN (46515*)	41,305	43,152
Elmhurst, IL (60126)	44,276	46,392
Elmira, NY (14901*)	35,327	39,945
El Monte, CA (91734*)	79,494	69,892
El Paso, TX (79910*)	425,259	322,261
Elyria, OH (44035*)	57,538	53,427
Emporia, KS (66801)	25,287	23,327
Englewood, CO (80110*)	30,021	33,695
Enid, OK (73701)	50,363	44,986
Erie, PA (16515*)	119,123	129,265
Escondido, CA (92025*)	64,355	36,792
Euclid, OH (44117)	59,999	71,552
Eugene, OR (97401*)	105,624	79,028
Evanston, IL (60204*)	73,706	80,113
Evansville, IN (47708*)	130,496	138,764
Everett, MA (02149)	37,195	42,485
Everett, WA (98201*)	54,413	53,622
Fairborn, OH (45324)	29,702	32,267
Fairfield, CA (94533)	58,099	44,146
Fairfield, OH (45014)	30,777	14,680

City and major ZIP code	1980 census	1970 census
Fair Lawn, NJ (07410)	32,229	38,040
Fall River, MA (02722*)	92,574	96,898
Fargo, ND (58102*)	61,383	53,365
Farmington, NM (87401)	31,222	21,979
Farmington Hills, MI (48024)	58,056	—
Fayetteville, AR (72701)	36,608	30,729
Fayetteville, NC (28302*)	59,507	53,510
Ferndale, MI (48220)	26,227	30,850
Findlay, OH (45840)	35,594	35,800
Fitchburg, MA (01420)	39,580	43,343
Flagstaff, AZ (86001)	34,743	26,117
Flint, MI (48502*)	159,611	193,317
Florence, AL (35631*)	37,029	34,031
Florence, SC (29501)	29,176	25,997
Florissant, MO (63033*)	55,372	65,908
Fond du Lac, WI (54935)	35,863	35,515
Fontana, CA (92335)	37,107	20,673
Fort Collins, CO (80521*)	65,092	43,337
Fort Dodge, IA (50501)	29,423	31,263
Fort Lauderdale, FL (33310*)	153,279	139,590
Fort Lee, NJ (07024)	32,449	30,631
Fort Myers, FL (33906*)	36,638	27,351
Fort Pierce, FL (33454*)	33,802	29,721
Fort Smith, AR (72901*)	71,626	62,802
Fort Wayne, IN (46802*)	172,028	178,269
Fort Worth, TX (76101*)	385,164	393,455
Fountain Valley, CA (92708)	55,080	31,886
Frankfort, KY (40601)	25,973	21,902
Frederick, MD (21701)	28,086	23,641
Freeport, IL (61032)	26,266	27,736
Freeport, NY (11520)	38,272	40,374
Fremont, CA (94538*)	131,945	100,869
Fresno, CA (93706*)	218,202	165,655
Fridley, MN (55432)	30,228	29,233
Fullerton, CA (92631*)	102,034	85,987
Gadsden, AL (35901*)	47,565	53,928
Gainesville, FL (32602*)	81,371	64,510
Gaithersburg, MD (20877*)	26,424	8,344
Galesburg, IL (61401)	35,305	36,290
Galveston, TX (77553*)	61,902	61,809
Gardena, CA (90247*)	45,165	41,021
Garden City, MI (48135)	35,640	41,864
Garden Grove, CA (92640*)	123,307	121,155
Garfield, NJ (07026)	26,803	30,797
Garfield Heights, OH (44125)	34,938	41,417
Garland, TX (75040*)	138,857	81,437
Gary, IN (46401*)	151,953	175,415
Gastonia, NC (28052)	47,333	47,322
Glendale, AZ (85301*)	97,172	36,228
Glendale, CA (91209*)	139,060	132,664
Glendora, CA (91740)	38,500	32,143
Glenview, IL (60025)	32,060	24,880
Gloucester, MA (01930)	27,768	27,941
Goldsboro, NC (27530)	31,871	26,960
Grand Forks, ND (58201)	43,765	39,008
Grand Island, NE (68801)	33,180	32,358
Grand Junction, CO (81501*)	27,956	20,170
Grand Prairie, TX (75051*)	71,462	50,904
Grand Rapids, MI (49501*)	181,843	197,649
Granite City, IL (62040)	36,815	40,685
Great Falls, MT (59403*)	56,725	60,091
Greeley, CO (80631*)	53,006	38,902
Green Bay, WI (54305*)	87,899	87,809
Greenfield, WI (53220)	31,467	24,424
Greensboro, NC (27420*)	155,642	144,076
Greenville, MS (38701*)	40,613	39,648
Greenville, NC (27834)	35,740	29,063
Greenville, SC (29602*)	58,242	61,436
Gresham, OR (97030)	33,005	10,030
Gulfport, MS (39503*)	39,676	40,791
Hackensack, NJ (07602*)	36,039	36,008
Hagerstown, MD (21740)	34,132	35,862
Hallandale, FL (33009)	36,517	23,849
Haltom City, TX (76117)	29,014	28,127
Hamilton, OH (45012*)	63,189	67,865
Hammond, IN (46320*)	93,714	107,983
Hampton, VA (23670*)	122,617	120,779
Hanover Park, IL (60103)	28,850	11,735
Harlingen, TX (78550*)	43,543	33,503
Harrisburg, PA (17105*)	53,264	68,061
Hartford, CT (06101*)	136,392	158,017
Harvey, IL (60426)	35,810	34,636
Hattiesburg, MS (39401)	40,829	38,277
Haverhill, MA (01830)	46,865	46,120
Hawthorne, CA (90250)	56,447	53,304
Hayward, CA (94544*)	94,342	93,058
Hazleton, PA (18201)	27,318	30,426
Hempstead, NY (11551*)	40,404	39,411
Hendersonville, TN (37075)	26,561	412
Hialeah, FL (33010*)	145,254	102,452
Highland, IN (46322)	25,935	24,947
Highland Park, IL (60035)	30,611	32,263
Highland Park, MI (48203)	27,909	35,444
High Point, NC (27260*)	63,808	63,229
Hillsboro, OR (97123*)	27,664	14,675
Hilo, HI (96720)	35,269	26,353
Hobbs, NM (88240)	29,153	26,025
Hoboken, NJ (07030)	42,460	45,380
Hoffman Estates, IL (60195)	37,272	22,238
Holland, MI (49423)	26,281	26,479
Hollywood, FL (33022*)	121,323	106,873
Holyoke, MA (01040)	44,678	50,112
Honolulu, HI (96820*)	365,048	324,871
Hopkinsville, KY (42240)	27,318	21,395
Hot Springs, AR (71901*)	35,781	35,631
Houma, LA (70360)	32,602	30,922
Houston, TX (77001*)	1,595,138	1,233,535
Huber Heights, OH (45424)	35,480	—
Huntington, WV (25704*)	63,684	74,315
Huntington Beach, CA (92647*)	170,505	115,960
Huntington Park, CA (90255)	46,223	33,744
Huntsville, AL (35804*)	142,513	139,282
Hurst, TX (76053)	31,420	27,215
Hutchinson, KS (67501)	40,284	36,885
Idaho Falls, ID (83401*)	39,590	35,776
Independence, MO (64051*)	111,806	111,630
Indianapolis, IN (46206*)	700,807	736,856
Inglewood, CA (90311*)	94,245	89,985
Inkster, MI (48141)	35,190	38,595
Iowa City, IA (52240*)	50,508	46,850
Irvine, CA (92713)	62,134	—
Irving, TX (75061*)	109,943	97,260
Irvington, NJ (07111)	61,493	59,743
Ithaca, NY (14850)	28,732	26,226
Jackson, MI (49201*)	39,739	45,484
Jackson, MS (39205*)	202,895	153,968
Jackson, TN (38301*)	49,131	39,996
Jacksonville, AR (72076)	27,589	19,832
Jacksonville, FL (32203*)	540,920	504,265
Jamestown, NY (14701)	35,775	39,795
Janesville, WI (53545*)	51,071	46,426
Jefferson City, MO (65101)	33,619	32,407
Jersey City, NJ (07303*)	223,532	260,350
Johnson City, TN (37601)	39,753	33,770
Johnstown, PA (15901*)	35,496	42,476
Joliet, IL (60436*)	77,956	78,827
Jonesboro, AR (72401)	31,530	27,050
Joplin, MO (64801)	39,023	39,256
Kalamazoo, MI (49001*)	79,722	85,555
Kankakee, IL (60901)	30,141	30,944

City and major ZIP code	1980 census	1970 census
Kansas City, KS (66110*)	161,148	168,213
Kansas City, MO (64108*)	448,159	507,330
Kearny, NJ (07032)	35,735	37,585
Kenner, LA (70062*)	66,382	29,858
Kennewick, WA (99336)	34,397	15,212
Kenosha, WI (53141*)	77,685	78,805
Kent, OH (44240)	26,164	28,183
Kentwood, MI (49508)	30,438	20,310
Kettering, OH (45429)	61,186	71,864
Killeen, TX (76541*)	46,296	35,507
Kingsport, TN (37662*)	32,027	31,938
Kingsville, TX (78363)	28,808	28,915
Kinston, NC (28501)	25,234	23,020
Kirkwood, MO (63122)	27,987	31,679
Knoxville, TN (37901*)	175,045	174,587
Kokomo, IN (46902*)	47,808	44,042
La Crosse, WI (54601*)	48,347	50,286
Lafayette, IN (47901*)	43,011	44,955
Lafayette, LA (70501*)	81,961	68,908
La Habra, CA (90631)	45,232	41,350
Lake Charles, LA (70601*)	75,226	77,998
Lakeland, FL (33802*)	47,406	42,803
Lakewood, CA (90714*)	74,654	83,025
Lakewood, CO (80215)	113,808	92,743
Lakewood, OH (44107)	61,963	70,173
Lake Worth, FL (33461*)	27,048	23,714
La Mesa, CA (92041)	50,308	39,178
La Mirada, CA (90638)	40,986	30,808
Lancaster, CA (93534*)	48,027	—
Lancaster, OH (43130)	34,953	32,911
Lancaster, PA (17604*)	54,725	57,690
Lansing, IL (60438)	29,039	25,805
Lansing, MI (48924*)	130,414	131,403
La Puente, CA (91747*)	30,882	31,092
Laredo, TX (78041*)	91,449	69,024
Largo, FL (33540*)	58,977	24,230
Las Cruces, NM (88001*)	45,086	37,857
Las Vegas, NV (89114*)	164,674	125,787
Lauderdale Lakes, FL (33313)	25,426	10,577
Lauderhill, FL (33313)	37,271	8,465
Lawrence, IN (46226)	25,591	16,353
Lawrence, KS (66044)	52,738	45,698
Lawrence, MA (01842*)	63,175	66,915
Lawton, OK (73501*)	80,054	74,470
Leavenworth, KS (66048)	33,656	25,147
Lebanon, PA (17042)	25,711	28,572
Lee's Summit, MO (64063)	28,741	16,230
Leominster, MA (01453)	34,508	32,939
Lewiston, ID (83501)	27,986	26,068
Lewiston, ME (04240)	40,481	41,779
Lexington, KY (40511*)	204,165	108,137
Lima, OH (45802*)	47,381	53,734
Lincoln, NE (68501*)	171,932	149,518
Lincoln Park, MI (48146)	45,105	52,984
Linden, NJ (07036)	37,836	41,409
Lindenhurst, NY (11757)	26,919	28,359
Little Rock, AR (72231*)	158,461	132,483
Littleton, CO (80120*)	28,631	26,466
Livermore, CA (94550)	48,349	37,703
Livonia, MI (48150*)	104,814	110,109
Lodi, CA (95240)	35,221	28,691
Logan, UT (84321)	26,844	22,333
Lombard, IL (60148)	37,295	34,043
Lompoc, CA (93436)	26,267	25,284
Long Beach, CA (90809*)	361,334	358,879
Long Beach, NY (11561)	34,073	33,127
Long Branch, NJ (07740)	29,819	31,774
Longmont, CO (80501)	42,942	23,209
Longview, TX (75602*)	62,762	45,547
Longview, WA (98632)	31,052	28,373
Lorain, OH (44052*)	75,416	78,185
Los Altos, CA (94022)	25,769	25,062
Los Angeles, CA (90052*)	2,966,850	2,811,801
Los Gatos, CA (95030)	26,906	22,613
Louisville, KY (40231*)	298,840	361,706
Loveland, CO (80537)	30,244	16,220
Lowell, MA (01853*)	92,418	94,239
Lubbock, TX (79408*)	173,979	149,101
Lufkin, TX (75901)	28,562	23,049
Lynchburg, VA (24506*)	66,743	54,083
Lynn, MA (01901*)	78,471	90,294
Lynwood, CA (90262)	48,548	43,354
Macon, GA (31213*)	116,896	122,423
Madisón, WI (53707*)	170,616	171,809
Madison Heights, MI (48071)	35,375	38,599
Malden, MA (02148)	53,386	56,127
Manchester, NH (03103*)	90,936	87,754
Manhattan, KS (66502)	32,644	27,575
Manhattan Beach, CA (90266)	31,542	35,352
Manitowoc, WI (54220)	32,547	33,430
Mankato, MN (56001)	28,651	30,895
Mansfield, OH (44901*)	53,927	55,047
Maple Heights, OH (44137)	29,735	34,093
Maplewood, MN (55109)	26,990	25,186
Margate, FL (33063*)	35,900	8,867
Marietta, GA (30060*)	30,829	27,216
Marion, IN (46952*)	35,874	39,607
Marion, OH (43302)	37,040	38,646
Marlborough, MA (01752)	30,617	27,936
Marshalltown, IA (50158)	26,938	26,219
Mason City, IA (50401)	30,144	30,279
Massillon, OH (44646)	30,557	32,539
Maywood, IL (60153)	27,998	29,019
McAllen, TX (78501)	66,281	37,636
McKeesport, PA (15134*)	31,012	37,977
Medford, MA (02155)	58,076	64,397
Medford, OR (97501)	39,603	28,973
Melbourne, FL (32901*)	46,536	40,236
Melrose, MA (02176)	30,055	33,180
Memphis, TN (38101*)	646,174	623,988
Menlo Park, CA (94025)	26,369	26,826
Menomonee Falls, WI (53051)	27,845	31,697
Mentor, OH (44060)	42,065	36,912
Merced, CA (95340)	36,499	22,670
Meriden, CT (06450)	57,118	55,959
Meridian, MS (39301)	46,577	45,083
Merrillville, IN (46410)	27,677	—
Mesa, AZ (85201*)	152,453	63,049
Mesquite, TX (75149*)	67,053	55,131
Miami, FL (33152*)	346,865	334,859
Miami Beach, FL (33139)	96,298	87,072
Michigan City, IN (46360)	36,850	39,369
Middletown, CT (06457)	39,040	36,924
Middletown, OH (45042)	43,719	48,767
Midland, MI (48640)	37,250	35,176
Midland, TX (79702*)	70,525	59,463
Midwest City, OK (73140*)	49,559	48,212
Milford, CT (06460)	49,101	50,858
Milpitas, CA (95035)	37,820	26,561
Milwaukee, WI (53201*)	636,236	717,372
Minneapolis, MN (55401*)	370,951	434,400
Minnetonka, MN (55343)	38,683	35,776
Minot, ND (58701)	32,843	32,290
Miramar, FL (33023)	32,813	23,997
Mishawaka, IN (46544*)	40,201	36,060
Missoula, MT (59806*)	33,388	29,497
Mobile, AL (36601*)	200,452	190,026
Modesto, CA (95350*)	106,602	61,712
Moline, IL (61265)	45,709	46,237
Monroe, LA (71203*)	57,597	56,374
Monroeville, PA (15146)	30,977	29,011
Monrovia, CA (91016)	30,531	30,562

City and major ZIP code	1980 census	1970 census
Montclair, NJ (07042*)	38,321	44,043
Montebello, CA (90640)	52,929	42,807
Monterey, CA (93940)	27,558	26,302
Monterey Park, CA (91754)	54,338	49,166
Montgomery, AL (36119*)	177,857	133,386
Moore, OK (73153*)	35,063	18,761
Moorhead, MN (56560)	29,998	29,687
Morgantown, WV (26505)	27,605	29,431
Mountain View, CA (94042*)	58,655	54,132
Mount Prospect, IL (60056)	52,634	34,995
Mount Vernon, NY (10551*)	66,713	72,778
Muncie, IN (47302*)	77,216	69,082
Murfreesboro, TN (37130)	32,845	26,360
Murray, UT (84107)	25,750	21,206
Muskegon, MI (49440*)	40,823	44,631
Muskogee, OK (74401)	40,011	37,331
Nacogdoches, TX (75961)	27,149	22,544
Nampa, ID (83651)	25,112	20,768
Napa, CA (94558*)	50,879	36,103
Naperville, IL (60566*)	42,330	22,794
Nashua, NH (03061*)	67,865	55,820
Nashville, TN (37202*)	455,651	426,029
National City, CA (92050)	48,772	43,184
Naugatuck, CT (06770)	26,456	23,034
New Albany, IN (47150)	37,103	38,402
Newark, CA (94560)	32,126	27,153
Newark, DE (19711*)	25,247	21,298
Newark, NJ (07102*)	329,248	381,930
Newark, OH (43055)	41,200	41,836
New Bedford, MA (02741*)	98,478	101,777
New Berlin, WI (53151)	30,529	26,910
New Britain, CT (06050*)	73,840	83,441
New Brunswick, NJ (08901*)	41,442	41,885
New Castle, PA (16101*)	33,621	38,559
New Haven, CT (06511*)	126,109	137,707
New Iberia, LA (70560)	32,766	30,147
New London, CT (06320)	28,842	31,630
New Orleans, LA (70113*)	557,927	593,471
Newport, RI (02840)	29,259	34,562
Newport Beach, CA (92660*)	62,556	49,582
Newport News, VA (23607*)	144,903	138,177
New Rochelle, NY (10802*)	70,794	75,385
Newton, MA (02158)	83,622	91,263
New York, NY (10001*)	7,071,639	7,895,563
Bronx borough (10451*)	1,168,972	1,471,701
Brooklyn borough (11201*)	2,230,936	2,602,012
Manhattan borough (10001*)	1,428,285	1,539,233
Queens borough[1]	1,891,325	1,987,174
Staten Island borough (10314*)	352,121	295,443
Niagara Falls, NY (14302*)	71,384	85,615
Niles, IL (60648)	30,363	31,432
Norfolk, VA (23501*)	266,979	307,951
Normal, IL (61761)	35,672	26,396
Norman, OK (73070*)	68,020	52,117
Norristown, PA (19401*)	34,684	38,169
Northampton, MA (01060)	29,286	29,664
Northbrook, IL (60062)	30,778	25,422
North Charleston, SC (29406)	62,534	—
North Chicago, IL (60064)	38,774	47,275
Northglenn, CO (80233)	29,847	27,785
North Las Vegas, NV (89030)	42,739	46,067
North Little Rock, AR (72114*)	64,288	60,040
North Miami, FL (33161)	42,566	34,767
North Miami Beach, FL (33160)	36,553	30,544
North Olmsted, OH (44070)	36,486	34,861
North Richland Hills, TX (76118)	30,592	16,514
North Tonawanda, NY (14120)	35,760	36,012
Norwalk, CA (90650)	85,286	90,164
Norwalk, CT (06856*)	77,767	79,288
Norwich, CT (06360)	38,074	41,739

City and major ZIP code	1980 census	1970 census
Norwood, OH (45212*)	26,342	30,420
Novato, CA (94947)	43,916	31,006
Nutley, NJ (07110)	28,998	31,913
Oak Forest, IL (60452)	26,096	19,271
Oakland, CA (94615*)	339,337	361,561
Oak Lawn, IL (60454*)	60,590	60,305
Oak Park, IL (60301*)	54,887	62,511
Oak Park, MI (48237)	31,537	36,762
Oak Ridge, TN (37830)	27,662	28,319
Ocala, FL (32678*)	37,170	22,583
Oceanside, CA (92054*)	76,698	40,494
Odessa, TX (79760*)	90,027	78,380
Ogden, UT (84401*)	64,407	69,478
Oklahoma City, OK (73125*)	403,136	368,164
Olathe, KS (66061*)	37,258	17,917
Olympia, WA (98501*)	27,447	23,296
Omaha, NE (68108*)	313,911	346,929
Ontario, CA (91761*)	88,820	64,118
Orange, CA (92667*)	91,788	77,365
Orange, NJ (07051*)	31,136	32,566
Orem, UT (84057*)	52,399	25,729
Orlando, FL (32802*)	128,291	99,006
Oshkosh, WI (54901)	49,620	53,082
Ottumwa, IA (52501)	27,381	29,610
Overland Park, KS (66204)	81,784	77,934
Owensboro, KY (43201)	54,450	50,329
Oxnard, CA (93030*)	108,195	71,225
Pacifica, CA (94044)	36,866	36,020
Paducah, KY (42001)	29,315	31,627
Palatine, IL (60067*)	32,166	26,050
Palm Springs, CA (92263*)	32,366	20,936
Palo Alto, CA (94303*)	55,225	56,040
Panama City, FL (32401*)	33,346	32,096
Paramount, CA (90723)	36,407	34,734
Paramus, NJ (07652)	26,474	28,381
Paris, TX (75460)	25,498	23,441
Parkersburg, WV (26101*)	39,967	44,208
Park Forest, IL (60466)	26,222	30,638
Park Ridge, IL (60068)	38,704	42,614
Parma, OH (44129)	92,548	100,216
Pasadena, CA (91109*)	118,550	112,951
Pasadena, TX (77501*)	112,560	89,957
Pascagoula, MS (39567)	29,318	27,264
Passaic, NJ (07055)	52,463	55,124
Paterson, NJ (07510*)	137,970	144,824
Pawtucket, RI (02860*)	71,204	76,984
Peabody, MA (01960)	45,976	48,080
Pembroke Pines, FL (33024)	35,776	15,496
Pensacola, FL (32501*)	57,619	59,507
Peoria, IL (61601*)	124,160	126,963
Perth Amboy, NJ (08861*)	38,951	38,798
Petaluma, CA (94952)	33,834	24,870
Petersburg, VA (23804*)	41,055	36,103
Phenix City, AL (36867)	26,928	25,281
Philadelphia, PA (19104*)	1,688,210	1,949,996
Phoenix, AZ (85026*)	789,704	584,303
Pico Rivera, CA (90660)	53,387	54,170
Pine Bluff, AR (71601*)	56,636	57,389
Pinellas Park, FL (33565)	32,811	22,287
Pittsburg, CA (94565)	33,034	21,423
Pittsburgh, PA (15219*)	423,959	520,089
Pittsfield, MA (01201)	51,974	57,020
Placentia, CA (92670)	35,041	21,948
Plainfield, NJ (07061*)	45,555	46,862
Plano, TX (75074*)	72,331	17,872
Plantation, FL (33318)	48,653	23,523
Pleasant Hill, CA (94523)	25,124	24,610
Pleasanton, CA (94566)	35,160	18,328
Plum, PA (15239)	25,390	21,932

City and major ZIP code	1980 census	1970 census
Plymouth, MN (55447*)	31,615	18,077
Pocatello, ID (83201)	46,340	40,036
Pomona, CA (91766*)	92,742	87,384
Pompano Beach, FL (33060*)	52,618	38,587
Ponca City, OK (74601*)	26,238	25,940
Pontiac, MI (48056*)	76,715	85,279
Portage, IN (46368)	27,409	19,127
Portage, MI (49081)	38,157	33,590
Port Arthur, TX (77640)	61,251	57,371
Port Huron, MI (48060)	33,981	35,794
Portland, ME (04101*)	61,572	65,116
Portland, OR (97208*)	366,383	379,967
Portsmouth, NH (03801)	26,254	25,717
Portsmouth, OH (45662)	25,943	27,633
Portsmouth, VA (23705*)	104,577	110,963
Poughkeepsie, NY (12601*)	29,757	32,029
Prichard, AL (36610*)	39,541	41,578
Providence, RI (02940*)	156,804	179,116
Provo, UT (84603*)	74,108	53,131
Pueblo, CO (81003*)	101,686	97,774
Quincy, IL (62301)	42,554	45,288
Quincy, MA (02269)	84,743	87,966
Racine, WI (53401*)	85,725	95,162
Rahway, NJ (07065*)	26,723	29,114
Raleigh, NC (27611*)	150,255	122,830
Rancho Cucamonga, CA (91730)	55,250	—
Rancho Palos Verdes, CA (90274)	36,577	—
Rapid City, SD (57701)	46,492	43,836
Raytown, MO (64133*)	31,759	33,306
Reading, PA (19603*)	78,686	87,643
Redding, CA (96001*)	41,995	16,659
Redlands, CA (92373)	43,619	36,355
Redondo Beach, CA (90277*)	57,102	57,451
Redwood City, CA (94064*)	54,951	55,686
Reno, NV (89510*)	100,756	72,863
Renton, WA (98057*)	30,612	25,878
Revere, MA (02151)	42,423	43,159
Rialto, CA (92376)	37,474	28,370
Richardson, TX (75080*)	72,496	48,405
Richfield, MN (55423)	37,851	47,231
Richland, WA (99352)	33,578	26,290
Richmond, CA (94802*)	74,676	79,043
Richmond, IN (47374)	41,349	43,999
Richmond, VA (23232*)	219,214	249,332
Ridgewood, NJ (07451*)	25,208	27,547
Riverside, CA (92507*)	170,591	140,089
Riviera Beach, FL (33404)	26,489	21,401
Roanoke, VA (24022*)	100,220	92,115
Rochester, MN (55901*)	57,890	53,766
Rochester, NY (14692*)	241,741	295,011
Rockford, IL (61125*)	139,712	147,370
Rock Hill, SC (29730)	35,344	33,846
Rock Island, IL (61201)	47,036	50,166
Rockville, MD (20850*)	43,811	42,739
Rockville Centre, NY (11570)	25,412	27,444
Rocky Mount, NC (27801)	41,283	34,284
Rome, GA (30161)	29,654	30,759
Rome, NY (13440)	43,826	50,148
Rosemead, CA (91770)	42,604	40,972
Roseville, MI (48066)	54,311	60,529
Roseville, MN (55113*)	35,820	34,438
Roswell, NM (88201)	39,676	33,908
Royal Oak, MI (48068*)	70,893	86,238
Sacramento, CA (95813*)	275,741	257,105
Saginaw, MI (48065*)	77,508	91,849
St. Charles, MO (63301)	36,087	31,834
St. Clair Shores, MI (48080*)	76,210	88,093
St. Cloud, MN (56301)	42,566	39,691
St. Joseph, MO (64501*)	76,691	72,748
St. Louis, MO (63155*)	453,085	622,236
St. Louis Park, MN (55426*)	42,931	48,883

City and major ZIP code	1980 census	1970 census
St. Paul, MN (55101*)	270,230	309,866
St. Petersburg, FL (33730*)	238,647	216,159
Salem, MA (01970)	38,220	40,556
Salem, OR (97301*)	89,233	68,725
Salina, KS (67401)	41,843	37,714
Salinas, CA (93907*)	80,479	58,896
Salt Lake City, UT (84119*)	163,697	175,885
San Angelo, TX (76902*)	73,240	63,884
San Antonio, TX (78284*)	786,023	654,153
San Bernardino, CA (92403*)	118,794	106,869
San Bruno, CA (94066)	35,417	36,254
San Buenaventura (Ventura), CA (93002*)	74,393	57,964
San Clemente, CA (92672)	27,325	17,063
San Diego, CA (92199*)	875,538	697,471
Sandusky, OH (44870)	31,360	32,674
Sandy City, UT (84070*)	52,210	6,438
San Francisco, CA (94188*)	678,974	715,674
San Gabriel, CA (91776*)	30,072	29,336
San Jose, CA (95101*)	629,546	459,913
San Leandro, CA (94577*)	63,952	68,698
San Luis Obispo, CA (93401)	34,252	28,036
San Mateo, CA (94402*)	77,561	78,991
San Rafael, CA (94901*)	44,700	38,977
Santa Ana, CA (92711*)	204,023	155,710
Santa Barbara, CA (93102*)	74,414	70,215
Santa Clara, CA (95050*)	87,746	86,118
Santa Cruz, CA (95060*)	41,483	32,076
Santa Fe, NM (87501*)	48,953	41,167
Santa Maria, CA (93456*)	39,685	32,749
Santa Monica, CA (90406*)	88,314	88,289
Santa Rosa, CA (95402*)	83,320	50,006
Sarasota, FL (33578*)	48,868	40,237
Saratoga, CA (95070)	29,261	26,810
Savannah, GA (31401*)	141,390	118,349
Sayreville, NJ (08872)	29,969	32,508
Schaumburg, IL (60194)	53,305	18,531
Schenectady, NY (12301*)	67,972	77,958
Scottsdale, AZ (85251*)	88,622	67,823
Scranton, PA (18505*)	88,117	102,696
Seal Beach, CA (90740)	25,975	24,441
Seaside, CA (93955)	36,567	36,883
Seattle, WA (98109*)	493,846	530,831
Selma, AL (36701)	26,684	27,379
Shaker Heights, OH (44120)	32,487	36,306
Shawnee, KS (66202*)	29,653	20,946
Shawnee, OK (74801)	26,506	25,075
Sheboygan, WI (53081)	48,085	48,484
Shelton, CT (06484)	31,314	27,165
Sherman, TX (75090)	30,413	29,061
Shreveport, LA (71102*)	205,820	182,064
Simi Valley, CA (93065*)	77,500	59,832
Sioux City, IA (51101*)	82,003	85,925
Sioux Falls, SD (57101*)	81,343	72,488
Skokie, IL (60076*)	60,278	68,322
Slidell, LA (70458)	26,718	16,101
Somerville, MA (02143)	77,372	88,779
Somerville, NJ (08876)	29,969	32,508
South Bend, IN (46624*)	109,727	125,580
South Euclid, OH (44121)	25,713	29,579
Southfield, MI (48037*)	75,568	69,285
South Gate, CA (90280)	66,784	56,909
Southgate, MI (48195)	32,058	33,909
South San Francisco, CA (94080)	49,393	46,646
Sparks, NV (89431)	40,780	24,187
Spartanburg, SC (29301*)	43,826	44,546
Spokane, WA (99210*)	171,300	170,516
Springfield, IL (62703*)	100,054	91,753
Springfield, MA (01101*)	152,319	163,905
Springfield, MO (65801*)	133,116	120,096
Springfield, OH (45501*)	72,563	81,941

City and major ZIP code	1980 census	1970 census
Springfield, OR (97477*)	41,621	26,874
Stamford, CT (06904*)	102,453	108,798
State College, PA (16801*)	36,130	32,833
Sterling Heights, MI (48077)	108,999	61,365
Steubenville, OH (43952)	26,400	30,771
Stillwater, OK (74074*)	38,268	31,126
Stockton, CA (95208*)	149,779	109,963
Stow, OH (44224)	25,303	20,061
Strongsville, OH (44136)	28,577	15,182
Suffolk, VA (23434*)	47,621	9,858
Sunnyvale, CA (94086*)	106,618	95,976
Sunrise, FL (33338)	39,681	7,403
Superior, WI (54880)	29,571	32,237
Syracuse, NY (13220*)	170,105	197,297
Tacoma, WA (98413*)	158,501	154,407
Tallahassee, FL (32301*)	81,548	72,624
Tamarac, FL (33320)	29,376	5,193
Tampa, FL (33630*)	271,523	277,714
Taunton, MA (02780)	45,001	43,756
Taylor, MI (48180)	77,568	70,020
Tempe, AZ (85282*)	106,743	63,550
Temple, TX (76501*)	42,354	33,431
Temple City, CA (91780)	28,972	31,034
Terre Haute, IN (47808*)	61,125	70,335
Texarkana, TX (75501*)	31,271	30,497
Texas City, TX (77590*)	41,403	38,908
Thornton, CO (80229)	40,343	13,326
Thousand Oaks, CA (91360*)	77,072	35,873
Tinley Park, IL (60477)	26,171	12,572
Titusville, FL (32780)	31,910	30,515
Toledo, OH (43601*)	354,635	383,062
Topeka, KS (66603*)	115,266	125,011
Torrance, CA (90510*)	129,881	134,968
Torrington, CT (06790)	30,987	31,952
Trenton, NJ (08650*)	92,124	104,786
Troy, MI (48099*)	67,102	39,419
Troy, NY (12180*)	56,638	62,918
Tucson, AZ (85726*)	330,537	262,933
Tulsa, OK (74101*)	360,919	330,350
Turlock, CA (95380)	26,287	13,992
Tuscaloosa, AL (35403*)	75,211	65,773
Tustin, CA (92680)	32,317	22,313
Twin Falls, ID (83301)	26,209	21,914
Tyler, TX (75712*)	70,508	57,770
Union City, CA (94587)	39,406	14,724
Union City, NJ (07087)	55,593	57,305
University City, MO (63130)	42,738	47,527
Upland, CA (91786)	47,647	32,551
Upper Arlington, OH (43221)	35,648	38,727
Urbana, IL (61801)	35,978	33,976
Utica, NY (13504*)	75,632	91,373
Vacaville, CA (95688)	43,367	21,690
Valdosta, GA (31601)	37,596	32,303
Vallejo, CA (94590*)	80,303	71,710
Valley Stream, NY (11580*)	35,769	40,413
Vancouver, WA (98661*)	42,834	41,859
Vicksburg, MS (39180)	25,434	25,478
Victoria, TX (77901*)	50,695	41,349
Vineland, NJ (08360)	53,753	47,399
Virginia Beach, VA (23450*)	262,199	172,106
Visalia, CA (93277*)	49,729	27,130
Vista, CA (92083)	35,834	24,688
Waco, TX (76701*)	101,261	95,326
Walla Walla, WA (99362)	25,618	23,619
Walnut Creek, CA (94596*)	53,643	39,844
Waltham, MA (02154)	58,200	61,582
Warner Robins, GA (31093)	39,893	33,491
Warren, MI (48089*)	161,134	179,260
Warren, OH (44481*)	56,629	63,494
Warwick, RI (02887*)	87,123	83,694
Washington, DC (20013*)	638,432	756,668
Waterbury, CT (06701*)	103,266	108,033
Waterloo, IA (50701*)	75,985	75,533
Watertown, NY (13601)	27,861	30,787
Waukegan, IL (60085*)	67,653	65,134
Waukesha, WI (53186)	50,365	39,695
Wausau, WI (54401)	32,426	32,806
Wauwatosa, WI (53213)	51,308	58,676
Weirton, WV (26062)	25,371	27,131
West Allis, WI (53213)	63,982	71,649
West Covina, CA (91793*)	80,291	68,034
Westfield, MA (01085)	36,465	31,433
Westfield, NJ (07091*)	30,447	33,720
West Haven, CT (06516)	53,184	52,851
West Jordan, UT (84084)	27,192	4,221
Westland, MI (48185)	84,603	86,749
West Memphis, AR (72301)	28,138	26,070
West Mifflin, PA (15122)	26,279	28,070
Westminster, CA (92683)	71,133	60,076
Westminster, CO (80030*)	50,211	19,512
West New York, NJ (07093)	39,194	40,627
West Orange, NJ (07052)	39,510	43,715
West Palm Beach, FL (33401*)	63,305	57,375
Wheaton, IL (60187)	43,043	31,138
Wheat Ridge, CO (80033)	30,293	29,778
Wheeling, WV (26003)	43,070	48,188
White Plains, NY (10602*)	46,999	50,346
Whittier, CA (90605*)	69,717	72,863
Wichita, KS (67276*)	279,835	276,554
Wichita Falls, TX (76307*)	94,201	96,265
Wilkes-Barre, PA (18701*)	51,551	58,856
Williamsport, PA (17701)	33,401	37,918
Wilmette, IL (60091)	28,229	32,134
Wilmington, DE (19850*)	70,195	80,386
Wilmington, NC (28402*)	44,000	46,169
Wilson, NC (27893)	34,424	29,347
Winona, MN (55987)	25,075	26,438
Winston-Salem, NC (27102*)	131,885	133,683
Woburn, MA (01801)	36,626	37,406
Woodland, CA (95695)	30,235	20,677
Woonsocket, RI (02895)	45,914	46,820
Worcester, MA (01613*)	161,799	176,572
Wyandotte, MI (48192)	34,006	41,061
Wyoming, MI (49509)	59,616	56,560
Yakima, WA (98903*)	49,826	45,588
Yonkers, NY (10701*)	195,351	204,297
Yorba Linda, CA (92686)	28,254	11,856
York, PA (17405*)	44,619	50,335
Youngstown, OH (44501*)	115,436	140,909
Yuma, AZ (85364*)	42,481	29,007
Zanesville, OH (43701)	28,655	33,045

1. Queens has four major ZIP codes: 11690*—Far Rockaway; 11351*—Flushing; 11431*—Jamaica; 11101*—Long Island City. *Sources:* Department of Commerce, Bureau of the Census; *1983 National ZIP Code & Post Office Directory.*

Annual Pay Levels in Metropolitan Areas

According to the U.S. Bureau of Labor Statistics' estimates, out of 315 metropolitan areas in 1983, Anchorage, Alaska, had the highest annual pay level of $27,570, followed by Flint Mich., with $23,271. San Jose, Calif., was third with $22,288. Jacksonville, N.C., had the lowest annual pay level at $11,654.

Territorial Expansion

Accession	Date	Area[1]
United States	—	3,618,770
Territory in 1790	—	891,364
Louisiana Purchase	1803	831,321
Florida	1819	69,866
Texas	1845	384,958
Oregon	1846	283,439
Mexican Cession	1848	530,706
Gadsden Purchase	1853	29,640
Alaska	1867	591,004
Hawaii	1898	6,471
Other territory	—	4,693
Philippines	1898	115,600[2]
Puerto Rico	1899	3,515
Guam	1899	209
American Samoa	1900	77
Canal Zone[4]	1904	553
Corn Islands[3]	1914	4
Virgin Islands of U.S.	1917	133
Trust Territory of Pacific Islands	1947	717[5]
All other	—	42
Total, 1980	—	**3,623,463**

1. Total land and water area in square miles. 2. Became independent in 1946. 3. Leased from Nicaragua for 99 years in 1914, but returned April 25, 1971. 4. Reverted to Panama. 5. Land area only; includes Northern Mariana Islands. *Source:* Department of Commerce, Bureau of the Census.

Total Population

Area	1960	1970	1980
50 states of U.S.	179,323,175	203,302,031	226,545,805
48 coterminous	178,464,236	202,229,535	225,179,263
Alaska	226,167	302,583	401,851
Hawaii	632,772	769,913	964,691
American Samoa	20,051	27,159	32,297
Canal Zone	42,122	44,198	(1)
Canton Island	320	n.a.	—
Corn Islands	1,872	(2)	—
Guam	67,044	84,996	105,979
Johnston Atoll	156	1,007	327
Midway	2,356	2,220	453
Puerto Rico	2,349,544	2,712,033	3,196,520
Swan Islands	28	22	n.a.
Trust Ter. of Pac. Is.	70,724	90,940	132,929[3]
Virgin Is. of U.S.	32,099	62,468	96,569
Wake Island	1,097	1,647	302
Population abroad	1,374,421	1,737,836	995,546
Armed forces	609,720	1,057,776	515,408
Other[4]	n.a.	n.a.	n.a.
Total	**183,285,009**	**208,066,557**	**231,106,727**

1. Granted independence on Oct. 1, 1979. 2. Returned to Nicaragua April 25, 1971. 3. Includes Northern Mariana Islands. 4. Includes Baker Island, Enderbury Island, Howland Island, and Jarvis Island, all uninhabited. NOTE: n.a. = unavailable. *Source:* Department of Commerce, Bureau of the Census.

Population by Race, 1980 Census

State	White	Black	Spanish origin	Other
Ala.	2,869,688	995,623	33,100	24,750
Alaska	308,455	13,619	9,497	78,407
Ariz.	2,240,033	75,034	440,915	402,799
Ark.	1,890,002	373,192	17,873	22,319
Calif.	18,031,689	1,819,282	4,543,770	3,817,591
Colo.	2,570,596	101,702	339,300	216,517
Conn.	2,799,420	217,433	124,499	90,723
Del.	488,543	95,971	9,671	10,711
D.C.	171,796	488,229	17,652	17,626
Fla.	8,178,387	1,342,478	857,898	219,127
Ga.	3,948,007	1,465,457	61,261	50,801
Hawaii	318,608	17,352	71,479	629,040
Idaho	901,641	2,716	36,615	39,578
Ill.	9,225,575	1,675,229	635,525	517,657
Ind.	5,004,567	414,732	87,020	70,880
Iowa	2,838,805	41,700	25,536	32,882
Kan.	2,167,752	126,127	63,333	69,329
Ky.	3,379,648	259,490	27,403	22,295
La.	2,911,243	1,237,263	99,105	55,466
Me.	1,109,850	3,128	5,005	11,682
Md.	3,158,412	958,050	64,740	99,984
Mass.	5,362,836	221,279	141,043	152,922
Mich.	7,868,956	1,198,710	162,388	190,678
Minn.	3,936,948	53,342	32,124	86,858
Miss.	1,615,190	887,206	24,731	18,242
Mo.	4,346,267	514,274	51,667	56,903
Mont.	740,148	1,786	9,974	44,756
Neb.	1,490,569	48,389	28,020	31,048
Nev.	699,377	50,791	53,786	49,016
N.H.	910,099	3,990	5,587	6,521
N.J.	6,127,090	924,786	491,867	312,282
N.M.	976,465	24,042	476,089	299,461
N.Y.	13,961,106	2,401,842	1,659,245	1,194,340
N.C.	4,453,010	1,316,050	56,607	105,369
N.D.	625,536	2,568	3,903	24,591
Ohio	9,597,266	1,076,734	119,880	123,419
Okla.	2,597,783	204,658	57,413	222,825
Ore.	2,490,192	37,059	65,833	105,412
Pa.	10,654,325	1,047,609	154,004	164,794
R.I.	896,692	27,584	19,707	22,878
S.C.	2,145,122	948,146	33,414	25,940
S.D.	638,955	2,144	4,028	49,079
Tenn.	3,835,078	725,949	34,081	29,723
Tex.	11,197,663	1,710,250	2,985,643	1,320,470
Utah	1,382,550	9,225	60,302	69,262
Vt.	506,736	1,135	3,304	3,585
Va.	4,229,734	1,008,311	79,873	108,234
Wash.	3,777,296	105,544	119,986	247,323
W. Va.	1,874,751	65,051	12,707	9,842
Wis.	4,442,598	182,593	62,981	80,144
Wyo.	447,716	3,364	24,499	19,736
Total	**188,340,790**	**26,488,218**	**14,605,883**	**11,675,817**

Source: Department of Commerce, Bureau of the Census.

One-Parent Families Increase

Families headed by one parent have doubled since 1970 according to a Census Bureau report. The number of single-parent families rose from 3.3 million to 6.6 million from 1970 to 1981. Divorce is cited as the primary cause for the increase.

Immigration to U.S. by Country of Origin

(Figures are totals, not annual averages, and were tabulated as follows: 1820–67, alien passengers arrived; 1868–91 and 1895–97, immigrant aliens arrived; 1892–94 and 1898 to present, immigrant aliens admitted. Data before 1906 relate to country whence alien came; since 1906, to country of last permanent residence.) 1981 data based on country of birth.

Countries	1981	1820–1981	1961–70	1951–60	1941–50	1931–40	1971–80	1820–1930
Europe: Albania[1]	11	2,622	98	59	85	2,040	329	—
Austria[2]	367	4,318,845	20,621	67,106	24,860	3,563	9,478	3,658,978
Belgium	467	203,957	9,192	18,575	12,189	4,817	5,329	153,388
Bulgaria[3]	124	68,226	619	104	375	938	1,188	64,918
Czechoslovakia[1]	793	139,367	3,273	918	8,347	14,393	6,023	105,620
Denmark	506	365,548	9,201	10,984	5,393	2,559	4,439	332,466
Estonia[1]	22	1,179	163	185	212	506	91	—
Finland[1]	317	34,398	4,192	4,925	2,503	2,146	2,868	17,447
France	1,745	756,979	45,237	51,121	38,809	12,623	25,069	582,375
Germany[2]	6,552	6,998,056	190,796	477,765	226,578	114,058	74,414	5,907,893
Great Britain: England	14,997	4,978,524	174,452	156,171	112,252	21,756	137,374	2,619,435
Scotland	—	—	29,849	32,854	16,131	6,887	—	726,887
Wales	—	—	2,052	2,589	3,209	735	—	85,659
Not specified[4]	—	—	3,675	3,884	—	—	—	793,741
Greece	4,361	669,888	85,969	47,608	8,973	9,119	92,369	421,489
Hungary[2]	581	—	5,401	36,637	3,469	7,861	6,550	473,373
Ireland	902	4,692,856	37,461	57,332	26,967	13,167	11,490	4,578,941
Italy	4,662	5,310,516	214,111	185,491	57,661	68,028	129,368	4,651,195
Latvia[1]	39	2,661	510	352	361	1,192	207	—
Lithuania[1]	44	3,980	562	242	683	2,201	248	—
Luxembourg[1]	18	2,950	556	684	820	565	307	—
Netherlands	999	362,993	30,606	52,277	14,860	7,150	10,492	246,609
Norway[5]	331	857,646	15,484	22,935	10,100	4,740	3,941	800,115
Poland[6]	5,014	528,098	53,539	9,985	7,571	17,026	37,234	397,729
Portugal	7,049	467,879	76,065	19,588	7,423	3,329	101,710	252,715
Romania[7]	1,974	175,958	2,531	1,039	1,076	3,871	12,393	153,074
Spain	1,711	266,426	44,659	7,894	2,898	3,258	34,141	166,865
Sweden[5]	832	1,274,289	17,116	21,697	10,665	3,960	6,531	1,213,488
Switzerland	601	351,191	18,453	17,675	10,547	5,512	8,235	290,168
U.S.S.R.[8]	9,223	3,394,999	2,336	584	548	1,356	38,961	3,341,991
Yugoslavia[3]	2,048	119,557	20,381	8,225	1,576	5,835	30,540	50,952
Other Europe	405	56,324	4,203	8,155	3,983	2,361	4,049	33,699
Total Europe	66,695	36,405,952	1,123,363	1,325,640	621,124	347,552	800,368	32,121,210
Asia: China[9]	25,803	593,432	34,764	9,657	16,709	4,928	124,326	377,245
India	21,522	226,452	27,189	1,973	1,761	496	164,154	9,377
Japan[10]	3,896	419,055	39,988	46,250	1,555	1,948	49,775	275,643
Turkey	2,766	391,860	10,142	3,519	798	1,065	13,399	360,171
Other Asia	210,356	1,906,371	315,688	88,707	11,537	7,644	1,236,544	35,895
Total Asia[11]	264,343	3,537,170	427,771	150,106	32,360	16,081	1,588,178	1,058,331
America: Canada and Newfoundland[12]	11,191	4,149,838	413,310	377,952	171,718	108,527	169,939	2,897,201
Central America	24,509	376,049	101,330	44,751	21,665	5,861	134,640	43,293
Mexico[13]	101,268	2,334,154	453,937	299,811	60,589	22,319	640,294	755,936
South America	35,913	824,369	257,954	91,628	21,831	7,803	295,741	113,499
West Indies	73,301	1,904,427	470,213	123,091	49,725	15,502	741,126	431,469
Other America[13]	158	109,620	19,630	59,711	29,276	25	789	31
Total America	246,340	9,698,457	1,716,374	996,944	354,804	160,037	1,982,529	4,241,429
Africa	15,029	172,281	28,954	14,092	7,367	1,750	80,779	24,310
Australia and New Zealand	1,947	125,140	19,562	11,506	13,805	2,231	23,788	52,301
Pacific Islands[14]	108	24,963	1,769	4,698	5,437	780	1,806	10,365
Countries not specified[15]	2,138	288,589	3,884	12,493	142	—	15,866	254,066
Total all countries	**596,600**	**50,252,552**	**3,321,677**	**2,515,479**	**1,035,039**	**528,431**	**4,493,314**	**37,762,012**

1. Countries established since beginning of World War I are included with countries to which they belonged. 2. Data for Austria-Hungary not reported until 1861. Austria and Hungary recorded separately after 1905, Austria included with Germany 1938–45. 3. Bulgaria, Serbia, Montenegro first reported in 1899. Bulgaria reported separately since 1920. In 1920, separate enumeration for Kingdom of Serbs, Croats, Slovenes; since 1922, recorded as Yugoslavia. 4. United Kingdom not specified; for 1901–51, included in "Other Europe." 5. Norway included with Sweden 1820–68. 6. Included with Austria-Hungary, Germany, and Russia 1899–1919. 7. No record of immigration until 1880. 8. From 1931–63, the U.S.S.R. was broken down into European U.S.S.R. and Asian U.S.S.R. Since 1964, total U.S.S.R. has been reported in Europe. 9. Beginning in 1957, China includes Taiwan. 10. No record of immigration until 1861. 11. From 1952, Asia included Philippines. From 1934–51, Philippines were included in Pacific Islands; before 1934, recorded in separate tables as insular travel. 12. Includes all British North American possessions, 1820–98. 13. No record of immigration, 1886–93. 14. Included with "Countries not specified" prior to 1925. 15. Includes 32,897 persons returning in 1906 to their homes in U.S. *Source:* Department of Justice, Immigration and Naturalization Service. NOTE: Data are latest available.

Immigrant and Nonimmigrant Aliens Admitted to U.S.

Period[1]	Immigrants	Non-immigrants	Total	Period[1]	Immigrants	Non-immigrants	Total
1901-10	8,795,386	1,007,909	9,803,295	1966-70	1,871,365	16,227,660	18,099,025
1911-20	5,735,811	1,376,271	7,112,082	1971-75	1,936,281	29,545,190	31,481,471
1921-30	4,107,209	1,774,896	5,882,090	1976	398,613	7,654,491	8,053,104
1931-40	528,431	1,574,071	2,102,502	1977[2]	462,315	8,036,916	8,499,231
1941-50	1,035,039	2,461,359	3,496,398	1978	601,442	9,343,710	9,945,152
1951-55	1,087,638	2,654,461	3,742,009	1979[3]	460,348	7,060,082	7,520,430
1956-60	1,427,841	4,458,562	5,886,403	1980	530,639	n.a.	—
1961-65	1,450,312	7,879,564	9,329,876	1981	596,600	n.a.	—

1. Fiscal year ending June 30, except as noted. 2. Starting 1977, for fiscal year ending Sept. 30. 3. Figures for October 1978–June 1979. Nonimmigrant aliens include visitors for business or pleasure, students, foreign government officials, and others temporarily in the U.S. NOTE: n.a. = not available. *Source:* Department of Justice, Immigration and Naturalization Service.

Persons Naturalized Since 1907

Period[1]	Civilian	Military	Total	Period[1]	Civilian	Military	Total
1907-30	2,713,389	300,506	3,013,895	1977[2]	154,568	5,305	159,873
1931-40	1,498,573	19,891	1,518,464	1978	168,409	5,126	173,535
1941-50	1,837,229	149,799	1,987,028	1979	158,276	5,874	164,150
1951-60	1,148,241	41,705	1,189,946	1980	153,343	4,595	157,938
1961-70	1,084,195	36,068	1,120,263	1981	162,227	4,090	166,317
1971-80	1,397,846	66,926	1,464,772	1907-81	9,841,700	618,985	10,460,685

1. Fiscal year ending June 30, except as noted. 2. Fiscal year, Oct. 1976–Sept. 1977. *Source:* Department of Justice, Immigration and Naturalization Service. NOTE: Data are latest available.

Population of Largest Indian Reservations, 1981

Navajo (Ariz., N.M., Utah)	160,722	Shawnee (Okla.)	11,636	Fort Apache (Ariz.)	8,010
Cherokee (Okla.)	42,992	Gila River (Ariz.)	9,592	Standing Rock (N.D., S.D.)	7,958
Creek (Okla.)	37,679	Rosebud (S.D.)	9,484	Northern Pueblos (N.M.)	7,383
Choctaw (Okla.)	19,660	Turtle Mountain (N.D.)	8,656	Pawnee (Okla.)	7,178
Papago (Ariz.)	17,651	Chickasaw (Okla.)	8,507	Zuni (N.M.)	6,999
South Pueblos (N.M.)	15,633	Yakima (Wash.)	8,502	Blackfeet (Mont.)	6,632
Pine Ridge (S.D.)	13,417	Hopi (Ariz.)	8,439	Wind River (Wyo.)	5,705

NOTE: The Bureau of Indian Affairs lists 734,895 Indians residing on or near Federal reservations as of December 1981. The total Indian population of the United States, according to the 1980 census, is 1,418,195. *Source:* Department of the Interior, Bureau of Indian Affairs.

Income of Households by Age of Head, 1982

Age of head	Households (thousands)	Income (per cent) Under $5,000	$5,000 to $7,499	$7,500 to $9,999	$10,000 to $14,999	$15,000 to $24,999	$25,999 and over	Total
15-24 years	5,695	10.5	8.7	9.8	10.1	8.1	3.0	6.8
25-34 years	19,104	17.2	14.9	17.2	23.1	28.5	23.1	22.8
35-44 years	16,020	11.9	10.3	11.1	14.1	18.4	26.1	19.1
45-54 years	12,354	9.9	7.2	9.4	10.1	12.6	21.2	14.7
55-64 years	13,074	14.0	12.6	13.6	15.0	14.8	17.6	15.6
65 years and over	17,671	36.5	46.3	38.9	27.6	17.7	9.0	21.0
Total	**83,918**	**100.0**	**100.0**	**100.0**	**100.0**	**100.0**	**100.0**	**100.0**

Source: Department of Commerce, Bureau of the Census.

Population Projections to 2050[1]

(in millions)

Sex, race, age group	1995	2000	2025	2050
MALE, WHITE	106.3	108.8	117.3	115.1
Up to 19 years	30.3	30.5	28.9	27.7
20 to 39 years	33.3	31.2	30.5	29.3
40 to 59 years	26.4	30.5	29.1	28.9
60 to 79 years	13.7	13.8	24.8	22.2
80 and over	2.5	2.8	4.0	7.0
FEMALE, WHITE	111.3	114.0	123.4	123.0
Up to 19 years	28.8	29.0	27.5	26.3
20 to 39 years	32.4	30.2	29.4	28.3
40 to 59 years	27.1	31.1	29.1	28.7
60 to 79 years	17.4	17.4	28.9	25.4
80 and over	5.5	6.3	8.5	14.3
MALE, BLACK	16.0	17.1	22.0	25.0
Up to 19 years	6.1	6.4	6.9	6.8
20 to 39 years	5.5	5.4	6.5	7.0
40 to 59 years	3.0	3.8	5.2	6.2
60 to 79 years	1.2	1.3	3.1	4.0
80 and over	0.2	0.2	0.4	1.0
FEMALE, BLACK	17.7	18.7	23.9	27.2
Up to 19 years	6.0	6.2	6.7	6.7
20 to 39 years	5.7	5.5	6.5	7.0
40 to 59 years	3.7	4.4	5.5	6.5
60 to 79 years	1.8	2.0	4.2	4.9
80 and over	0.5	0.6	1.0	2.2
TOTALS[2]	259.6	268.0	301.0	308.8
Up to 19 years	73.7	74.9	73.7	72.1
20 to 39 years	79.7	75.2	76.8	76.3
40 to 59 years	62.4	72.4	72.4	74.9
60 to 79 years	35.0	35.4	63.7	59.8
80 and over	8.9	10.1	14.4	15.7
Males	126.3	130.4	146.1	148.8
Females	133.3	137.6	154.9	160.1
White	217.6	222.8	240.7	238.1
Black	33.6	35.7	45.9	52.1
Median age	34.7	36.3	40.0	41.6

1. Based on average of 1.9 lifetime births per woman. 2. Includes all races. NOTE: Zero population growth is expected to be reached by 2050. Details may not add because of rounding. *Source:* Department of Commerce, Bureau of the Census.

Marriage and Divorce

Marriages and Divorces

Year	Marriage Number	Marriage Rate[2]	Divorce[1] Number	Divorce[1] Rate[2]
1900	709,000	9.3	55,751	.7
1905	842,000	10.0	67,976	.8
1910	948,166	10.3	83,045	.9
1915	1,007,595	10.0	104,298	1.0
1920	1,274,476	12.0	170,505	1.6
1925	1,188,334	10.3	175,449	1.5
1930	1,126,856	9.2	195,961	1.6
1935	1,327,000	10.4	218,000	1.7
1940	1,595,879	12.1	264,000	2.0
1944	1,452,394	10.9	400,000	2.9
1945	1,612,992	12.2	485,000	3.5
1946	2,291,045	16.4	610,000	4.3
1947	1,991,878	13.9	483,000	3.4
1948	1,811,155	12.4	408,000	2.8
1949	1,579,798	10.6	397,000	2.7
1950	1,667,231	11.1	385,144	2.6
1951	1,594,694	10.4	381,000	2.5
1952	1,539,318	9.9	392,000	2.5
1953	1,546,000	9.8	390,000	2.5
1954	1,490,000	9.2	379,000	2.4
1955	1,531,000	9.3	377,000	2.3
1956	1,585,000	9.5	382,000	2.3
1957	1,518,000	8.9	381,000	2.2
1958	1,451,000	8.4	368,000	2.1
1959	1,494,000	8.5	395,000	2.2
1960	1,523,000	8.5	393,000	2.2
1961	1,548,000	8.5	414,000	2.3
1962	1,577,000	8.5	413,000	2.2
1963	1,654,000	8.8	428,000	2.3
1964	1,725,000	9.0	450,000	2.4
1965	1,800,000	9.3	479,000	2.5
1966	1,857,000	9.5	499,000	2.5
1967	1,927,000	9.7	523,000	2.6
1968	2,069,258	10.4	584,000	2.9
1969	2,145,438	10.6	639,000	3.2
1970	2,158,802	10.6	708,000	3.5
1971	2,190,481	10.6	773,000	3.7
1972	2,282,154	11.0	845,000	4.1
1973	2,284,108	10.9	915,000	4.4
1974	2,229,667	10.5	977,000	4.6
1975	2,152,662	10.1	1,036,000	4.9
1976	2,154,807	10.0	1,083,000	5.0
1977	2,178,367	10.1	1,091,000	5.0
1978	2,282,272	10.5	1,130,000	5.2
1979	2,341,799	10.6	1,181,000	5.4
1980	2,406,708	10.6	1,182,000	5.2
1981[3]	2,438,000	10.6	1,219,000	5.3
1982[3]	2,495,000	10.8	1,180,000	5.1

1. Includes annulments. 2. Per 1,000 population. Divorce rates for 1941–46 are based on population including armed forces overseas. Marriage rates are based on population excluding armed forces overseas. 3. Provisional. NOTE: Marriage and divorce figures for most years include some estimated data. Alaska is included beginning 1959, Hawaii beginning 1960. *Source:* Department of Health and Human Services, National Center for Health Statistics.

Marriage Information by State

State	Legal minimum marriage age: With parental consent[3] M	With parental consent[3] F	Without parental consent M	Without parental consent F	Blood test required	Waiting period[1] Before license	Waiting period[1] After license	Marriages[2] 1982[4]	Marriages[2] 1981[4]
Alabama	14	14	18	18	yes	none	none	47,431	47,318
Alaska	16	16	18	18	yes	3 d [26]	none	6,436	5,809
Arizona	16	16	18	18	yes	none	none	31,408	31,784
Arkansas	18	16	18	18	no	3 d	none	28,000	26,724
California	18	16	18	18	yes	none	none	230,694	214,708
Colorado	16 [19]	16 [19]	18	18	yes[17]	none	none	35,340	36,461
Connecticut	16	16	18	18	yes	4 d	none	26,867	25,517
Delaware	18 [25]	16 [25]	18	18	no	none	24 h [5]	4,826	4,561
D. C.	16–17 [7]	16–17 [7]	18	18	yes[7]	5 d [6]	none	5,698	5,310
Florida	18	16	18	18	yes	3 d	none	115,414	111,660
Georgia	16 [25]	16 [25]	18	18 [25]	yes[21]	3 d	none	71,704	70,486
Hawaii	16	16	18	18	yes	none	none	13,483	12,309
Idaho	18	16	18	18	yes	3 d [24]	none	13,964	14,372
Illinois	16	16	18	18	yes	none	1 d	106,861	109,449
Indiana	17	17 [20]	18	18	yes	3 d	none	55,924	55,699
Iowa	16	16	18	18	yes	3 d	none	27,187	27,063
Kansas	([23])	([23])	18	18	no	3 d	none	26,660	26,254
Kentucky	([18])	([18])	18	18	no	3 d	none	35,141	35,201
Louisiana	18	16	18	18	no	none	72 h	43,284	44,139
Maine	16	16	18	18	no	5 d	none	12,388	12,552
Maryland	16 [15]	16 [15]	18	18	no	48 h	none	47,467	46,840
Massachusetts	14–17 [12]	12–15 [12]	18	18	yes	3 d	none	50,565	46,274
Michigan	18	16 [8]	18	18	yes	3 d	none	84,045	85,814
Minnesota	16	16	18	18	no	5 d	none	37,409	37,945
Mississippi	17	15	21	21	yes	3 d	none	27,584	27,530
Missouri	15 [12]	15 [12]	18	18	yes	3 d	none	53,836	53,265
Montana	16 [22]	16 [22]	18	18	yes	5 d	3 d	8,185	8,221
Nebraska	17	17	19	19	yes	2 d	none	14,081	14,418
Nevada	16	16	18	18	no	none	none	106,256	n.a.
New Hampshire	14 [12, 15]	13 [12, 15]	18	18	no	3 d	none	12,536	9,916
New Jersey	18	16	18	18	yes	72 h	none	60,228	57,555
New Mexico	16	16	18	18	yes	none	none	17,453	17,130
New York	16	14 [9]	21	18	yes	none	([10])	162,486	150,007
North Carolina	16	16	18	18	yes	none	none	51,058	48,040
North Dakota	16	16	18	18	yes	none	none	6,166	6,182
Ohio	18	16	18	18	yes	5 d	none	102,905	99,617
Oklahoma	16 [11]	16 [19]	18	18	yes	none [14]	none	47,660	48,127
Oregon	17	17	18	18	no	3 d	none	24,186	22,747
Pennsylvania	16	16	18	18	yes	3 d	none	92,622	92,370
Rhode Island	18	16 [9]	18	18	yes	none	none	7,515	7,539
South Carolina	16	14	18	18	no	24 h	none	53,507	55,008
South Dakota	16	16	18	18	yes	none	none	8,343	8,708
Tennessee	16	16	18	18	yes	none [14]	none	58,543	59,865
Texas	16 [13]	16 [13]	18	18	yes	none	none	198,647	192,368
Utah	14	14	16	16	no	none	none	18,702	18,346
Vermont	14 [19]	14 [19]	18	18	yes	none	3 d [16]	5,570	5,207
Virginia	16	16	18	18	yes	none	none	62,099	61,460
Washington	17	17	18	18	no	3 d	none	46,972	48,901
West Virginia	18	16	18	18	yes	3 d	none	16,467	16,734
Wisconsin	16	16	18	18	no	5 d	none	42,146	40,934
Wyoming	18	16 [19]	19	19	yes	none	none	6,685	7,052

1. In some states, waiting period may be waived or reduced by court order. 2. By place of occurrence. 3. In most states, persons younger than the age shown may be married by court permission. 4. Provisional figures; data represent marriages reported, marriage intentions filed, or marriage licenses issued. 5. 96 hours if nonresidents. 6. Day of application and day of pickup are included in 5-day waiting period. 7. No exceptions granted under this age. 8. Consent of one parent or guardian necessary for female only. 9. Females 14 to 16 years old must also have consent of judge of Family Court. 10. Marriage may not be solemnized within 3 days from date on which specimen was taken for serological test, and not until 24 hours after issuance of marriage license. Waiting period may be waived by court order. 11. If under 16, need court order and a doctor's statement relating to pregnancy. 12. Need court order. 13. Parent must appear in person or provide doctor's affidavit of his or her illness. 14. 3 days if either party is under legal age. 15. If pregnant. 16. After date on which marriage application has been filed with town clerk, excluding date of filing. 17. Blood test for rubella and RH type not required of females over 45 years or found by physician to be incapable of bearing children. 18. No age limit. 19. If under 16 need court order. 20. 15 for pregnancy or maternity. 21. Prior to issuance of license, a medical examination for rubella is required. 22. With judicial approval. 23. Under 18 with parental consent only. 24. Only for those under 18. 25. May marry at any age with proof of pregnancy signed by physician or if marrying father of child born out of wedlock. 26. If a three-day waiting period would result in undue hardship or delay in an individual case, the licensing officer may waive the three-day requirement. *Sources:* Legal information, *Information Please* questionnaires to states; marriage statistics, Department of Health and Human Services, National Center for Health Statistics.

Percent of Population Ever Married

Age group, years[1]	1983	1980	1970	1960	1950	1940	1930	1920	1910	1900
Males: 15 to 19	1.9	2.7	2.6	3.3	2.9	1.5	1.5	1.8	1.0	0.9
20 to 24	26.8	31.2	45.3	46.9	41.0	27.8	29.0	29.1	24.7	22.2
25 to 29	61.8	67.0	80.9	79.2	76.2	64.0	63.2	60.5	57.1	54.1
30 to 34	80.4	84.1	90.6	88.1	86.8	79.3	78.8	75.8	73.9	72.3
35 to 44	91.4	92.5	93.3	91.9	90.4	86.0	85.7	83.8	83.3	83.0
45 to 54	94.0	93.9	92.5	92.6	91.5	88.9	88.6	88.0	88.8	89.7
Females: 15 to 19	6.6	8.8	9.7	13.5	14.4	10.0	10.9	10.8	9.8	9.4
20 to 24	44.5	49.8	64.2	71.6	67.7	52.8	53.9	54.4	51.5	48.4
25 to 29	75.2	79.1	89.5	89.5	86.7	77.2	78.3	76.9	75.0	72.4
30 to 34	87.0	90.5	93.8	93.1	90.7	85.3	86.8	85.1	83.8	83.4
35 to 44	93.7	94.5	94.8	93.9	91.7	89.6	90.0	88.6	88.6	88.9
45 to 54	95.5	95.3	95.1	93.0	92.2	91.3	90.9	90.4	91.4	92.2

1. 1980 and 1983: 15 years and over; previous years: 14 and older. *Source:* Department of Commerce, Bureau of the Census.

Persons Living Alone, by Sex and Age

(numbers in thousands)

	1983		1980		1975		1970		1960	
Sex and age[1]	Number	Percent	Number	Percent	Number	Percent	Number	Percent	Number	Percent
BOTH SEXES										
15 to 24 years	1,303	6.8	1,726	9.4	1,111	8.0	556	5.1	234	3.3
25 to 44 years	5,576	29.0	4,729	25.8	2,744	19.7	1,604	14.8	1,212	17.2
45 to 64 years	4,515	23.5	4,514	24.7	4,076	29.2	3,622	33.4	2,720	38.5
65 years and over	7,856	40.8	7,328	40.1	6,008	43.1	5,071	46.7	2,898	41.0
Total, 15 years and over	**19,250**	**100.0**	**18,296**	**100.0**	**13,939**	**100.0**	**10,851**	**100.0**	**7,063**	**100.0**
MALE										
15 to 24 years	672	9.0	947	13.6	610	4.4	274	2.5	124	1.8
25 to 44 years	3,441	46.2	2,920	41.9	1,689	12.1	933	8.6	686	9.7
45 to 64 years	1,714	23.0	1,613	23.2	1,329	9.5	1,152	10.6	965	13.7
65 years and over	1,624	21.8	1,486	21.3	1,290	9.3	1,174	10.8	853	12.1
Total, 15 years and over	**7,451**	**100.0**	**6,966**	**100.0**	**4,918**	**35.3**	**3,532**	**32.5**	**2,628**	**37.2**
FEMALE										
15 to 24 years	631	5.3	779	6.9	501	3.6	282	2.6	110	1.6
25 to 44 years	2,135	18.1	1,809	16.0	1,055	7.6	671	6.2	526	7.4
45 to 64 years	2,801	23.7	2,901	25.6	2,747	19.7	2,470	22.8	1,755	24.8
65 years and over	6,232	52.8	5,842	51.6	4,718	33.8	3,897	35.9	2,045	29.0
Total, 15 years and over	**11,799**	**100.0**	**11,330**	**100.0**	**9,021**	**64.7**	**7,319**	**67.5**	**4,436**	**62.8**

1. Prior to 1980, data are for persons 14 years and older. *Source:* Department of Commerce, Bureau of the Census.

Characteristics of Unmarried-Couple Households: 1983

(number in thousands)

Characteristics	Number	Percent	Characteristics	Number	Percent
Unmarried-couple households	1,891	100.0	Presence of children:		
			No children under 15 years	1,366	72.2
Age of Householders:			Some children under 15 years	325	27.8
Under 25 years	455	24.1			
25–44 years	1,082	57.2	Sex of householders:		
45–64 years	233	12.3	Male	1,151	60.9
65 years and over	121	6.4	Female	740	39.1

Source: U.S. Bureau of the Census.

Divorce Information by State

State	Residence for divorce	Period before parties may remarry: Plaintiff	Defendant	Divorce rate[1] 1982[3]	1981	1980	1979
Alabama	6 mo	60 d	60 d	6.2	6.8	7.1	7.0
Alaska	([24])	none	none	8.3	8.6	8.4	8.6
Arizona	90 d	none	none	7.0	7.4	7.8	8.2
Arkansas	90 d	none	none	6.9	8.0	9.9	9.3[2]
California	6 mo	none	none	5.6	5.6	5.8	6.1
Colorado	90 d[19]	none	none	5.6	6.2	6.4	6.0
Connecticut	1 yr	none	none	3.4	3.8	3.8	4.5
Delaware	6 mo[19]	none[12]	none[12]	5.3	4.9	4.0	5.3
D.C.	6 mo	60 d	60	5.4	5.8	5.5	6.8
Florida	6 mo	none	none	6.9	7.4	7.8	7.9
Georgia	6 mo	none	none	5.7	6.3	6.4	6.5
Hawaii	6 mo	none	none	4.3	4.3	4.7	5.5
Idaho	6 wk	none	none	6.6	7.0	7.3	7.1
Illinois	1 yr	none	none	4.4	4.5	4.5	4.6
Indiana	6 mo[4 6]	none	none	n.a.	n.a.	n.a.	7.7
Iowa	1 yr[11]	none	none	3.7	4.2	4.0	3.9
Kansas	60 d	30 d	30 d	5.3	6.1	5.6	5.4
Kentucky	6 mo[4 22]	none	none	4.6	4.8	4.8	4.5[2]
Louisiana	1 yr	none[8]	none[8]	n.a.	n.a.	n.a.	3.8[2]
Maine	6 mo	none	none	5.1	5.6	5.7	5.6
Maryland	1 yr[23]	none	none	3.5	3.8	3.9	4.1
Massachusetts	1 yr	none	none	3.6	3.3	2.9	3.0
Michigan	1 yr	none	none	4.2	4.7	4.4	4.8
Minnesota	180 d	none	none	3.5	3.9	3.7	3.7[3]
Mississippi	6 mo	([10])	([10])	5.2	5.2	5.5	5.6[3]
Missouri	90 d	none	none	5.3	5.7	5.7	5.7
Montana	1 yr	none	none	5.8	6.3	6.3	6.5
Nebraska	1 yr[5]	none	none	4.1	4.3	4.1	4.0
Nevada	6 wk	none	none	13.1	17.6	18.6	16.8
New Hampshire	1 yr	none	none	5.3	5.5	5.8	5.9
New Jersey	1 yr	none	none	3.9	3.9	3.5	3.2
New Mexico	6 mo[13]	30d	30d	7.0	8.0	8.1	8.0
New York	([14])	none	none	3.6	3.6	3.1	3.7
North Carolina	6 mo	none	none	4.9	5.0	5.0	4.9
North Dakota	1 yr	([9])	([9])	3.3	3.5	3.3	3.2
Ohio	6 mo[6]	none	none	4.9	5.4	5.4	5.5
Oklahoma	6 mo[21]	6 mo[20]	6 mo[20]	7.5	8.1	8.2	7.9
Oregon	6 mo	30 d	30 d	6.3	6.7	7.0	7.0
Pennsylvania	6 mo	none	none	3.2	3.3	3.0	3.4
Rhode Island	2 yr	none	none	3.7	3.7	3.9	3.9
South Carolina	1 yr	none	none	4.3	4.5	4.7	4.7
South Dakota	([7])	none	none	3.7	4.1	4.1	3.9
Tennessee	1 yr	none[15]	none[15]	6.4	6.9	6.8	6.8
Texas	6 mo	30 d[15]	30 d[15]	6.6	6.7	7.1	6.9
Utah	3 mo	3 mo[12]	3 mo[12]	5.4	5.4	5.6	5.6
Vermont	6 mo[18]	none	none	5.1	4.6	5.0	4.6
Virginia	6 mo	none	none	4.8	4.7	4.5	4.5
Washington	none [18]	none	none	6.5	6.9	7.0	6.9
West Virginia	1 yr[16]	([17])	([17])	5.3	5.7	5.3	5.3
Wisconsin	6 mo	6 mo	6 mo	3.7	3.9	3.7	3.6
Wyoming	60 d	none	none	8.1	8.4	8.5	7.8

1. By place of occurrence, including reported annulments. 2. Incomplete. 3. Estimated. 4. Only one party must have resided in the state for 180 days. 5. Decree not final until 6 months after trial and decision. 6. 6-month residence in state; 90-day residence in county. 7. Physical presence plus intent to make state the place of residence. 8. In case of adultery, guilty party cannot marry correspondent. 9. At discretion of court. 10. Until court that grants the divorce is adjourned. 11. No time required if both parties are residents of state and intend to make state their place of residence. 12. 30 days between first and final judgment. 13. Servicemen acquire residence by being continuously stationed at military base in state for 6 months. 14. Action for divorce may be maintained only where (1) parties were married in the state and either has been a resident for one year preceding the action; (2) parties have resided in the state as husband and wife and either has been a resident for one year preceding the action; (3) cause for divorce occurred in the state and either party has been a resident for one year preceding the action; (4) cause for divorce occurred in the state and both parties are residents at time of the action; (5) either party is a resident for at least 2 years preceding the action. 15. Parties may remarry each other at any time. 16. 2 years if residence is acquired after cause of divorce action arose. 17. Court can lengthen waiting period if desired. 18. Court must find resumption of marital relations not reasonably probable. 19. Must be domiciled in state. 20. 30 days from date of judgment of appeal. 21. 5 years if on grounds of insanity and insane spouse is in institution. 22. No decree shall be entered until parties have lived apart for 60 days. 23. When cause for divorce occurred out of state. 24. No residency requirement but action will not be heard by court until 30 days after filing for divorce. NOTE: n.a. = not available. *Sources:* Legal information, *Information Please* questionnaires to states; divorce statistics, Department of Health and Human Services, National Center for Health Statistics.

Grounds for Divorce

State	Adultery	Cruelty	Desertion	Alcoholism	Impotence	Felony conviction	Neglect to provide	Insanity	Pregnancy marriage[1]	Bigamy	Separation	Indignities	Drug addiction	Violence	Fraudulent contract	Others
Alabama	yes	yes	yes[2]	yes	yes	yes[16]	yes[3]	yes[6]	yes[1]	—	yes[3]	—	yes	yes	—	(27 29 34)
Alaska	yes	yes	yes[2]	yes	yes	yes	—	yes[9]	—	—	—	yes	yes	yes	—	—
Arizona	—	—	—	—	—	—	—	—	—	—	—	—	—	—	—	(29)
Arkansas	yes	yes	yes[2]	yes	yes	yes	yes	yes	—	yes	yes[4]	yes	—	yes	yes	(12 31 48)
California	—	—	—	—	—	—	—	—	—	—	—	—	—	—	—	(28)
Colorado	—	—	—	—	—	—	—	—	—	—	—	—	—	—	—	(29 52)
Connecticut	yes	yes	yes[2]	yes	—	yes[20]	—	yes[6]	—	—	—	—	—	—	yes	(13 23 30 42 46)
Delaware	yes	yes	yes[2]	yes[3]	yes[61]	yes	yes	yes[6]	—	yes	yes[9]	—	yes	yes	yes	(27 68)
D.C.	yes	yes[53]	—	—	—	—	—	—	—	—	yes[2]	—	—	—	—	(63)
Florida	—	—	—	—	—	—	—	—	—	—	—	—	—	—	—	(49 52)
Georgia	yes	yes	yes[2]	yes	yes	yes[15]	yes	yes	yes	yes	yes	yes	yes	yes	yes	(27 31 44 49)
Hawaii	—	—	—	—	—	—	—	—	—	—	yes[3]	—	—	—	—	(29)
Idaho	yes	yes	yes	—	—	yes	yes	yes[4]	—	yes	—	—	—	—	—	(26 28 42)
Illinois	yes	yes	yes[2]	yes[3]	yes	yes	—	—	—	yes[51]	—	—	yes[3]	yes	—	(32 37 56)
Indiana	—	—	—	—	yes	—	—	yes[3]	—	—	—	—	—	—	—	(29 33 52)
Iowa	—	—	—	—	—	—	—	—	—	—	—	—	—	—	—	(49)
Kansas	yes	yes	yes[2]	yes	—	yes	yes	yes[6]	—	—	—	—	—	—	yes	(28 31 48 69 70)
Kentucky	—	—	—	—	—	—	—	—	—	—	—	—	—	—	—	(49)
Louisiana	yes	yes	yes	yes	—	yes	yes	—	—	yes	yes[3]	—	yes	yes	—	(37 58)
Maine	yes	yes	yes[4]	yes	yes	yes[20]	yes	yes[36]	yes[61]	yes[61]	—	yes	yes	yes	yes[61]	(28)
Maryland[65]	yes	—	—	—	yes	yes[18]	—	yes[66]	—	—	yes[10]	—	—	—	—	(28 35 67)
Massachusetts	yes	yes	yes[2]	yes	yes	yes[19]	yes	—	—	—	—	—	yes	—	—	(29 49)
Michigan	—	—	—	—	—	—	—	—	—	—	—	—	—	—	—	(29)
Minnesota	—	—	—	—	—	—	—	—	—	—	—	—	—	—	—	(29 49 52)
Mississippi	yes	yes	yes	yes	yes	yes[22]	—	yes[47]	yes	yes	yes[2]	—	yes	yes	—	(10 28 31 49)
Missouri	yes	yes	yes	yes	yes	yes	—	—	yes	yes	—	yes		—	—	(10 30 32 52)
Montana	—	—	—	—	—	—	—	—	—	—	—	—	—	—	—	(29 52)
Nebraska	—	—	—	—	—	—	—	—	—	—	—	—	—	—	—	(49)
Nevada	—	—	—	—	—	—	—	yes[3]	—	—	yes[2]	—	—	—	—	(27)
New Hampshire	yes	yes	yes[3]	yes[3]	yes	yes[14]	yes[3]	—	—	—	—	—	—	yes	—	(25 28 40 57 60)
New Jersey	yes	yes	yes[2]	yes[2]	yes[51]	yes[44]	—	yes[3]	—	yes[51]	yes[9]	—	yes[2]	—	yes[51]	(34 49)
New Mexico	yes	yes	yes	—	—	—	—	—	—	—	—	—	—	—	—	(27)
New York	yes	yes	yes[2]	—	—	yes[17]	—	—	—	—	yes[2]	—	—	—	—	—
North Carolina	yes	—	—	—	yes	—	—	yes[6]	yes	—	yes[2]	—	—	—	—	(34)
North Dakota	yes	yes	yes[2]	yes[2]	—	yes	yes[2]	yes[6]	—	—	—	—	—	—	—	(28)
Ohio	yes	yes	yes	yes[4]	yes	yes	yes	yes[5]	—	yes	yes[2]	—	—	—	yes	(12 24 41 55)
Oklahoma	yes	yes	yes[2]	yes	yes	yes[21]	yes	yes[6]	yes	—	—	—	—	—	yes	(27 41 55)
Oregon	—	—	—	—	—	—	—	—	—	—	—	—	—	—	yes	(49)
Pennsylvania	yes	yes	yes[2]	—	yes[45]	yes[15]	—	yes	—	yes	yes[4]	yes	—	yes	yes	(29 31)
Rhode Island	yes	yes	yes[6]	yes	yes	yes[7]	yes[2]	yes[48]	—	yes	yes[3]	—	yes	yes	yes	(13 38)
South Carolina	yes	yes[39]	yes[2]	yes	—	—	—	—	—	—	yes[2]	—	yes	—	—	(50)
South Dakota	yes	yes	yes[2]	yes[2]	Yes[6]	yes	yes[2]	yes[6]	—	yes[61]	—	—	—	—	yes[61]	—
Tennessee	yes	yes	yes[2]	yes[43]	yes	yes	yes	—	yes	yes	—	yes	—	—	—	(28 32 37 59)
Texas	yes	yes	yes[2]	—	—	yes[54]	—	yes[4]	—	—	yes[4]	yes	—	—	—	(28)
Utah	yes	yes	yes[2]	yes	yes	yes	yes	yes	—	—	yes[4]	—	—	—	—	—
Vermont	yes	yes	yes[7]	—	—	yes[17]	yes	yes[6]	—	—	yes[8]	—	—	—	—	(29)
Virginia	yes	yes	yes[2]	—	yes[51]	yes	—	—	yes[51]	yes[51]	yes[71]	—	—	—	yes[51]	—
Washington	—	—	—	—	—	—	—	—	—	—	—	—	—	—	—	(29)
West Virginia	yes	yes	yes[8]	yes	—	yes	yes	yes	—	—	yes[3]	—	yes	yes	—	(62)
Wisconsin	—	—	—	—	—	—	—	—	—	—	—	—	—	—	—	(29 64)
Wyoming	yes	yes	yes[2]	yes	yes	yes	yes[2]	yes[3]	yes	—	yes[3]	yes	—	—	—	(11 25 28)

1. If unknown to husband. 2. 1 year. 3. 2 years. 4. 3 years. 5. 4 years. 6. 5 years. 7. 7 years. 8. 6 months. 9. 18 months. 10. Absence of 1 year. 11. Absence of 1 year voluntarily, or under legal separation judgment. 12. Absence of 3 years. 13. Absence of one spouse; presumption of death. 14. With imprisonment of 1 year. 15. With imprisonment of 2 years. 16. With imprisonment of 2 years, sentence being for 7 years or more. 17. With imprisonment of 3 years. 18. With imprisonment of three years, or an indeterminate sentence, twelve months of which have been served. 19. With imprisonment of 5 years. 20. With imprisonment for life. 21. Imprisonment of other party in state or federal penal institution under sentence thereto for commission of felony at time the petition is filed. 22. Unless pardoned before beginning sentence. 23. Noncohabitation for 18 months. Grounds for annulment in Maine. 24. Court of Common Pleas may grant a dissolution of marriage—6 months residency required. 25. Noncohabitation for 2 years. 26. Noncohabitation for 5 years. 27. Incompatibility. 28. Irreconcilable differences. 29. Irretrievable breakdown of marriage relationship. 30. Irretrievably broken upon proof, decree of dissolution. 31. Relationship within prohibited degree. 32. Infamous crime. 33. Infamous crime subsequent to marriage. 34. Crime against nature. 35. Excessively vicious conduct; any cause which, by laws of state, renders marriage null and void at its inception. 36. Requiring confinement in mental institution for at least 7 years prior to commencement of action. 37. Attempt by one party on life of other. 38. Any other gross misbehavior or wickedness. 39. Physical cruelty only. 40. Treatment such as to injure health or endanger reason. 41. Gross neglect of duty. 42. Habitual intemperance. 43. Habitual drunkenness contracted

after marriage. 44 With imprisonment of 18 months. 45. If at time of marriage and incurable. 46. Infamous crime involving violation of conjugal duty and punishable by imprisonment of more than 1 year. 47. Incurable, regardless when it occurs. 48. Insanity at time of marriage. 49. No-fault divorce. 50. No-fault divorce after 1 year's separation. 51. Grounds for nullity. 52. The term divorce is no longer used. The term now used is Dissolution of Marriage. 53. Limited divorce; may be enlarged into absolute divorce after separation of 1 year. 54. Suit for divorce cannot be sustained until 12 months after final judgment of conviction. Divorce cannot be obtained if plaintiff's testimony contributed toward conviction. 55. Defendant obtained divorce from plaintiff in any other state or country. 56. Infected other party with communicable venereal disease. 57. Joining a religious cult disbelieving in marriage. 58. Public defamation. 59. Wife's refusal to remove with husband to this state and willfully absenting herself for 2 years. 60. Wife gone to reside outside state and absent 10 years. 61. Annulment. 62. Abuse of a child. 63. Modified "no-fault" law enacted April 6, 1977. 64. Voluntary noncohabitation for 1 year. 65. Maryland grants two types of divorce—vinculo and mensa. The information here applies to vinculo divorce. 66. Only after confined 3 years, plus other requirements. 67. Abandonment after 12 months, or living separately for 3 years. 68. If wife was under 16 or husband was under 18 at time of marriage, unless marriage was confirmed by each after arriving at such age. 69. Failure to perform a marital duty or obligation. 70. Incompatibility by reason of mental illness or mental incapacity of one or both spouses. 71. One year or 6 months if no minor child is involved. *Source: Information Please* questionnaires to the states.

Households, Families, and Married Couples

	Households		Families		Married couples
Date	Number	Average population per household	Number	Average population per family	Number
June 1890	12,690,000	4.93	—	—	—
April 1930	29,905,000	4.11	—	—	25,174,000
April 1940	34,949,000	3.67	32,166,000	3.76	28,517,000
April 1950	43,554,000	3.37	39,303,000	3.54	36,091,000
April 1955	47,874,000	3.33	41,951,000	3.59	37,556,000
March 1960[1]	52,799,000	3.33	45,111,000	3.67	40,200,000
March 1965	57,436,000	3.29	47,956,000	3.70	42,478,000
March 1970	63,401,000	3.14	51,586,000	3.58	45,373,000
March 1975	71,120,000	2.94	55,712,000	3.42	47,547,000
March 1980	80,776,000	2.76	59,550,000	3.29	49,714,000
March 1981	82,368,000	2.73	60,309,000	3.27	49,896,000
March 1982	83,527,000	2.72	61,019,000	3.25	50,294,000
March 1983	83,918,000	2.73	61,393,000	3.26	50,666,000

1. First year in which figures for Alaska and Hawaii are included. *Source:* Department of Commerce, Bureau of the Census.

Families Maintained by Women

(numbers in thousands)

	1983		1980		1975		1970		1960	
	Number	Percent	Number	Percent	Number	Percent	Number	Percent	Number	Percent
Age of women:										
Under 35 years	3,172	33.5	3,015	34.6	2,356	32.5	1,364	24.4	796	17.7
35 to 44 years	2,325	24.6	1,916	22.0	1,510	20.9	1,074	19.2	940	20.9
45 to 64 years	2,639	37.9	2,514	28.9	2,266	31.3	2,021	36.1	1,731	38.5
65 years and over	1,335	14.1	1,260	14.5	1,108	15.3	1,131	20.2	1,027	22.9
Median age	41.2	n.a.	41.7	—	43.4	—	48.5	—	50.1	—
Presence of children:										
No own children under 18 years	3,751	39.6	3,260	37.4	2,838	39.2	2,665	47.7	2,397	53.3
With own children under 18 years	5,718	60.4	5,445	62.6	4,404	60.8	2,926	52.3	2,097	46.7
Total own children under 18 years	10,366	n.a.	10,204	—	9,227	—	6,694	—	4,674	—
Average per family	1.09	n.a.	1.17	—	1.27	—	1.20	—	1.04	—
Average per family with children	1.81	n.a.	1.87	—	2.10	—	2.29	—	2.24	—
Race:										
White	6,507	68.7	6,052	69.5	5,212	72.0	4,165	74.5	3,547	78.9
Black[1]	2,734	28.9	2,495	28.7	1,940	26.8	1,382	24.7	947	21.1
Other	228	2.4	158	1.8	90	1.2	44	0.8	n.a.	n.a.
Marital status:										
Married, husband absent	1,765	18.6	1,769	20.3	1,647	22.7	1,326	23.7	1,099	24.5
Widowed	2,548	26.9	2,570	29.5	2,559	35.3	2,396	42.9	2,325	51.7
Divorced	3,433	36.3	3,008	34.6	2,110	29.1	1,259	22.5	694	15.4
Single	1,724	18.2	1,359	15.6	926	12.8	610	10.9	376	8.4
Total families maintained by women	**9,469**	**100.0**	**8,705**	**100.0**	**7,242**	**100.0**	**5,591**	**100.0**	**4,494**	**100.0**

1. Includes other races in 1960. NOTE: n.a. = not available. *Source:* Department of Commerce, Bureau of the Census.

Selected Family Characteristics

Characteristics	1982 Number (thousands)	1982 Median income
ALL RACES		
All families	61,393	23,433
Type of residence		
Nonfarm	59,777	23,565
Farm	1,617	18,756
Location of residence		
Inside metropolitan areas	41,145	25,423
1,000,000 or more	22,925	26,449
Inside central cities	8,135	20,878
Outside central cities	14,789	29,973
Under 1,000,000	18,271	24,164
Inside central cities	8,082	22,489
Outside central cities	10,139	25,511
Outside metropolitan areas	20,248	20,100
Region		
Northeast	12,975	24,918
North Central	15,721	24,219
South	21,111	21,500
West	11,586	24,624
Type of family		
Married-couple family	49,908	26,019
Wife in paid labor force	25,480	30,342
Wife not in paid labor force	24,428	21,299
Male householder, no wife present	2,016	20,140
Female householder, no husband present	9,469	11,484
Number of earners[2]		
No earners	8,943	9,911
1 earner	18,761	18,913
2 earners	24,776	28,073
3 earners	5,477	35,798
4 earners	2,697	44,409
Size of family		
2 persons	24,392	19,816
3 persons	14,189	24,186
4 persons	13,039	27,619
5 persons	5,970	27,144
6 persons	2,329	27,012
7 persons or more	1,475	23,569
Occupation group of longest job of householder	46,847	26,686
White-collar workers		
Professional, technical, and kindred workers	n.a.	n.a.
Salaried	n.a.	n.a.
Self-employed	n.a.	n.a.
Managers and administrators, except farm	n.a.	n.a.
Salaried	n.a.	n.a.
Self-employed	n.a.	n.a.
Sales workers	4,963	30,192
Clerical and kindred workers	3,984	23,718
Blue-collar workers		
Craft and kindred workers	9,128	26,724
Operatives, incl. transport	n.a.	n.a.
Operatives, except transport	4,150	22,641
Transport equip. oper.	3,077	24,055
Laborers, except farm	1,795	20,131
Service workers		
Private household workers	177	8,205
Service workers, exc. private household	4,057	18,496
Farm workers	2,108	15,508
Tenure status		
Owner occupied	44,475	26,798
Renter occupied	15,929	15,546
Occupier paid no cash rent	990	13,708
Educational attainment of householder		
Elementary	8,883	13,443
High school	28,024	22,069
College	21,050	33,121
1 to 3 years	8,965	27,440
4 years or more	12,085	38,255
4 years	6,393	35,778
5 years or more	5,691	41,587
Total, 25 years and over	57,957	24,185
WHITE		
All families	53,407	24,603
Type of residence		
Nonfarm	51,839	24,799
Farm	1,568	19,042
Location of residence		
Inside metropolitan areas	35,000	26,743
1,000,000 or more	19,013	28,242
Inside central cities	5,516	23,528
Outside central cities	13,496	30,421
Under 1,000,000	15,987	25,237
Inside central cities	6,628	24,179
Outside central cities	9,360	25,941
Outside metropolitan areas	18,407	20,867
Region		
Northeast	11,563	25,815
North Central	14,295	24,903
South	17,426	23,089
West	10,122	25,249
Type of family		
Married-couple families	45,252	26,443
Wife in paid labor force	22,692	30,801
Wife not in paid labor force	22,580	21,849
Male householder, no wife present	1,648	21,416
Female householder, no husband present	6,507	13,496
Number of earners[2]	52,776	24,654
No earners	7,370	11,364
1 earner	16,097	20,244
2 earners	22,016	28,628
3 earners	4,870	36,824
4 earners or more	2,424	45,052
BLACK		
All families	6,530	13,599
Type of residence		
Nonfarm	6,490	13,648
Farm	40	n.a.
Location of residence		
Inside metropolitan areas	4,998	14,580
1,000,000 or more	3,148	15,012
Inside central cities	2,265	13,362
Outside central cities	883	20,063
Under 1,000,000	1,850	13,958
Inside central cities	1,273	12,517
Outside central cities	577	17,292

Characteristics	1982 Number (thousands)	1982 Median income
Outside metropolitan areas	1,531	11,532
Region		
Northeast	1,203	14,735
North Central	1,237	12,374
South	3,443	13,044
West	646	16,508
Type of family		
Married-couple families	3,486	20,586
Wife in paid labor force	2,315	25,359
Wife not in paid labor force	1,372	12,469
Male householder, no wife present	309	14,661
Female householder, no husband present	2,734	7,458
Number of earners[2]	6,460	13,507
No earners	1,409	4,886
1 earner	2,240	11,062
2 earners	2,148	23,249
3 earners	465	26,992
4 earners or more	198	37,463
SPANISH ORIGIN OF HOUSEHOLDER[3]		
All families	3,369	16,228
Type of residence		
Nonfarm	3,345	16,274
Farm	24	(8)
Location of residence		
Inside metropolitan areas	2,901	16,339
1,000,000 or more	1,898	16,119
Inside central cities	1,061	13,733
Outside central cities	837	19,567
Under 1,000,000	1,003	16,699
Inside central cities	668	15,981
Outside central cities	335	17,954
Outside metropolitan areas	468	15,510
Region		
Northeast	655	12,369
North Central	220	20,841
South	1,096	16,087
West	1,397	17,193
Type of family		
Married-couple families	2,448	19,338
Wife in paid labor force	1,123	24,491
Wife not in paid labor force	1,325	15,180
Male householder, no wife present	153	17,263
Female householder, no husband present	767	7,436
Number of earners[2]	3,324	16,254
No earners	493	5,574
1 earner	1,126	12,399
2 earners	1,258	21,449
3 earners	294	26,255
4 earners or more	153	37,118

1. Family data are as of March 1983. 2. Excludes families with members in the Armed Forces. 3. Persons of Spanish origin may be of any race. *Source:* Department of Commerce, Bureau of the Census. NOTE: Data are the latest available.

Births

Live Births and Birth Rates

Year	Births[1]	Rate[2]	Year	Births[1]	Rate[2]	Year	Births[1]	Rate[2]
1910	2,777,000	30.1	1952[3]	3,913,000	25.1	1968	3,501,564	17.5
1915	2,965,000	29.5	1953[3]	3,965,000	25.1	1969	3,600,206	17.8
1920	2,950,000	27.7	1954[3]	4,078,000	25.3	1970	3,731,386	18.4
1925	2,909,000	25.1	1955	4,104,000	25.0	1971	3,555,970	17.2
1930	2,618,000	21.3	1956[3]	4,218,000	25.2	1972	3,258,411	15.6
1935	2,377,000	18.7	1957[3]	4,308,000	25.3	1973	3,136,965	14.9
1940	2,559,000	19.4	1958[3]	4,255,000	24.5	1974	3,159,958	14.9
1943	3,104,000	22.7	1959[3]	4,295,000	24.3	1975	3,144,198	14.8
1944	2,939,000	21.2	1960[3]	4,257,850	23.7	1976	3,167,788	14.8
1945	2,858,000	20.4	1961[3]	4,268,326	23.3	1977	3,326,632	15.4
1946	3,411,000	24.1	1962[3]	4,167,362	22.4	1978	3,333,279	15.3
1947	3,817,000	26.6	1963[3]	4,098,020	21.7	1979	3,494,398	15.9
1948	3,637,000	24.9	1964[3]	4,027,490	21.0	1980	3,612,258	15.9
1949	3,649,000	24.5	1965[3]	3,760,358	19.4	1981	3,629,238	15.8
1950	3,632,000	24.1	1966[3]	3,606,274	18.4	1982[4]	3,704,000	16.0
1951[3]	3,823,000	24.9	1967	3,520,959	17.8	1983[4]	3,614,000	15.5

1. Figures through 1959 include adjustment for underregistration; beginning 1960, figures represent number registered. For comparison, the 1959 registered count was 4,245,000. 2. Rates are per 1,000 population estimated as of July 1 for each year except 1940, 1950, 1960, 1970, and 1980, which are as of April 1, the census date; for 1942–46 based on population including armed forces overseas. 3. Based on 50% sample of births. 4. Provisional. NOTE: Alaska is included beginning 1959; Hawaii beginning 1960. Since 1972, based on 100% of births in selected states and on 50% sample in all other states. *Sources:* Department of Commerce, Bureau of the Census; and Department of Health and Human Services, National Center for Health Statistics.

Median Age at First Marriage

Year	Males	Females	Year	Males	Females	Year	Males	Females	Year	Males	Females
1900	25.9	21.9	1930	24.3	21.3	1960	22.8	20.3	1981	24.8	22.3
1910	25.1	21.6	1940	24.3	21.5	1970	23.2	20.8	1982	25.2	22.5
1920	24.6	21.2	1950	22.8	20.3	1980	24.7	22.0	1983	25.4	22.8

Source: Department of Commerce, Bureau of the Census.

Live Births by Age of Mother

		Age of mother							
Year[1] and race	Total	Under 15 yr	15–19 yr	20–24 yr	25–29 yr	30–34 yr	35–39 yr	40–44 yr	45 yr and over
1940	2,558,647	3,865	332,667	799,537	693,268	431,468	222,015	68,269	7,558
1945	2,858,449	4,028	298,868	832,746	785,299	554,906	296,852	78,853	6,897
1950	3,631,512	5,413	432,911	1,155,167	1,041,360	610,816	302,780	77,743	5,322
1955	4,014,112	6,181	493,770	1,290,939	1,133,155	732,540	352,320	89,777	5,430
1960	4,257,850	6,780	586,966	1,426,912	1,092,816	687,722	359,908	91,564	5,182
1965	3,760,358	7,768	590,894	1,337,350	925,732	529,376	282,908	81,716	4,614
1970	3,731,386	11,752	644,708	1,418,874	994,904	427,806	180,244	49,952	3,146
1975	3,144,198	12,642	582,238	1,093,676	936,786	375,500	115,409	26,319	1,628
1977	3,326,632	11,455	559,154	1,146,491	1,016,231	446,939	120,900	24,117	1,345
1978	3,333,279	10,772	543,407	1,139,524	1,015,183	474,318	126,196	22,627	1,252
1979	3,494,398	10,699	549,472	1,188,663	1,069,246	516,999	135,096	23,018	1,205
1980	3,612,258	10,169	552,161	1,226,200	1,108,291	550,354	140,793	23,090	1,200
1981	3,629,238	9,632	527,392	1,212,000	1,128,188	581,454	146,056	23,326	1,190
White	2,908,669	3,970	370,013	967,770	945,776	484,965	117,496	17,827	852
Black	587,797	5,425	143,278	208,194	139,536	67,310	19,867	3,970	217
Other	132,772	237	14,101	36,036	42,876	29,179	8,693	1,529	121

1. Data for 1940–55 are adjusted for underregistration. Beginning 1960, registered births only are shown. Data for 1960–70 based on a 50% sample of births. Since 1972, based on 100% of births in selected states and on 50% sample in all other states. Beginning 1960, including Alaska and Hawaii. NOTE: Data refer only to births occurring within the U.S. Figures are shown to the last digit as computed for convenience in summation. They are not assumed to be accurate to the last digit. Figures for age of mother not stated are distributed. *Sources:* Department of Commerce, Bureau of the Census; and Department of Health and Human Services, National Center for Health Statistics. NOTE: Data are latest available.

Births to Unmarried Women

(in thousands, except as indicated)

Age and race	1981	1980	1975	1970	1965	1960	1955	1950	1940
By age of mother:									
Under 15 years	8.6	9.0	11.0	9.5	6.1	4.6	3.9	3.2	2.1
15–19 years	259.2	262.8	222.5	190.4	123.1	87.1	68.9	56.0	40.5
20–24 years	246.9	237.3	134.0	126.7	90.7	68.0	55.7	43.1	27.2
25–29 years	109.2	99.6	50.2	40.6	36.8	32.1	28.0	20.9	10.5
30–34 years	45.3	41.0	19.8	19.1	19.6	18.9	16.1	10.8	5.2
35–39 years	14.3	13.2	8.1	9.4	11.4	10.6	8.3	6.0	3.0
40 years and over	3.1	2.9	2.3	3.0	3.7	3.0	2.4	1.7	1.0
By race:									
White	337.1	320.1	186.4	175.1	123.7	82.5	64.2	53.5	40.3
Black and other	349.6	345.7	261.6	223.6	167.5	141.8	119.2	88.1	49.2
Total of above births	**686.7**	**665.8**	**447.9**	**398.7**	**291.2**	**224.3**	**183.4**	**141.6**	**89.5**
Percent of all births[1]	18.9	18.4	14.2	10.7	7.7	5.3	4.5	3.9	3.5
Rate[2]	29.6	29.4	24.8	26.4	23.4	21.8	19.3	14.1	7.1

1. Through 1955, based on data adjusted for underregistration; thereafter, registered births. 2. Rate per 1,000 unmarried (never married, widowed, and divorced) women, 15–44 years old. *Sources:* Department of Commerce, Bureau of the Census; and Department of Health and Human Services, National Center for Health Statistics. NOTE: Data are latest available.

Live Births and Birth Rates

State	1982[1] number	1982[1] rate	1981[1] number	1981[1] rate	State	1982[1] number	1982[1] rate	1981[1] number	1981[1] rate
Alabama	61,040	15.5	61,139	15.6	Montana	14,222	17.8	13,939	17.6
Alaska	11,068	25.3	9,928	24.1	Nebraska	26,849	16.9	27,155	17.2
Arizona	52,565	18.4	51,322	18.4	Nevada	13,023	14.8	14,162	16.8
Arkansas	34,166	14.9	35,386	15.4	New Hampshire	13,849	14.6	13,501	14.4
California	435,019	17.6	422,066	17.4	New Jersey	96,401	13.0	93,529	12.6
Colorado	55,116	18.1	52,654	17.8	New Mexico	23,711	17.4	28,262	21.3
Connecticut	40,125	12.7	37,604	12.0	New York	249,171	14.1	242,873	13.8
Delaware	9,510	15.8	9,372	15.7	North Carolina	86,692	14.4	84,470	14.2
D.C.	18,638	29.5	17,801	28.2	North Dakota	13,608	20.3	13,415	20.4
Florida	144,246	13.8	138,204	13.6	Ohio	163,767	15.2	169,986	15.8
Georgia	91,924	16.3	91,991	6.5	Oklahoma	55,494	17.5	51,252	16.5
Hawaii	18,807	18.9	18,241	18.6	Oregon	42,129	15.9	44,425	16.8
Idaho	19,351	20.1	19,379	20.2	Pennsylvania	162,884	13.7	161,356	13.6
Illinois	180,423	15.8	181,560	15.8	Rhode Island	13,003	13.6	12,849	13.5
Indiana	83,453	15.3	84,634	15.5	South Carolina	49,418	15.4	49,605	15.7
Iowa	45,631	15.7	46,617	16.1	South Dakota	12,665	18.3	12,679	18.5
Kansas	40,244	16.7	40,239	16.9	Tennessee	71,744	15.4	71,696	15.5
Kentucky	57,055	15.6	58,047	15.9	Texas	315,147	20.6	287,272	19.5
Louisiana	85,100	19.5	81,995	19.0	Utah	43,188	27.8	41,973	27.7
Maine	16,425	14.5	16,482	14.5	Vermont	7,772	15.1	7,655	14.8
Maryland	57,063	13.4	54,137	12.7	Virginia	77,783	14.2	76,266	14.0
Massachusetts	75,908	13.1	76,075	13.2	Washington	66,327	15.6	70,274	16.7
Michigan	135,585	14.9	138,988	15.1	West Virginia	28,203	14.5	28,503	14.6
Minnesota	66,645	16.1	66,943	16.4	Wisconsin	76,973	16.2	73,518	15.5
Mississippi	45,597	17.9	45,842	18.1	Wyoming	10,050	20.0	10,162	20.7
Missouri	78,843	15.9	77,883	15.8	**Total**	**3,693,620**	**n.a.**	**3,635,306**	**15.9**

1. Provisional NOTE: Based on 100% of births in selected states and 50% sample in others. Rates are per 1,000 population. *Source:* Department of Health and Human Services, National Center for Health Statistics.

Live Births and Birth Rates by Race

Race	Births 1981[1]	Rates 1981	Rates 1980	Rates 1979	Race	Births 1981[1]	Rates 1981	Rates 1980	Rates 1979
White	2,908,669	14.8	14.9	14.5	Chinese	13,900	n.a.	n.a.	n.a.
Black	587,797	21.6	22.1	22.2	Filipino	15,965	n.a.	n.a.	n.a.
Indian	37,162	n.a.	n.a.	n.a.	Other	56,882	n.a.	n.a.	n.a.
Japanese	8,863	n.a.	n.a.	n.a.	**All races**	**3,629,238**	**15.8**	**15.9**	**15.6**

1. Based on all births in selected states and on a 50% sample of births in all other states. NOTES: Rates per 1,000 population in each specified group. n.a. = not available; Data are latest available. *Source:* Department of Health and Human Services, National Center for Health Statistics.

Live Births by Sex and Sex Ratio[1]

Year	Total[2] Male	Total[2] Female	Total[2] Males per 1,000 females	White Male	White Female	White Males per 1,000 females	Black Male	Black Female	Black Males per 1,000 females
1970[3]	1,915,378	1,816,008	1,055	1,590,140	1,501,124	1,059	290,508	281,854	1,031
1974[4]	1,622,114	1,537,844	1,055	1,325,019	1,250,773	1,059	257,277	249,885	1,030
1975[4]	1,613,135	1,531,063	1,054	1,312,308	1,239,688	1,059	259,610	251,971	1,030
1976[4]	1,624,436	1,543,352	1,053	1,319,717	1,247,897	1,058	260,661	253,818	1,027
1977[4]	1,705,916	1,620,716	1,053	1,383,440	1,307,630	1,058	275,556	268,665	1,026
1978[4]	1,709,394	1,623,885	1,053	1,378,222	1,302,894	1,058	279,598	271,942	1,028
1979[4]	1,791,267	1,703,131	1,052	1,442,981	1,365,439	1,057	293,013	284,842	1,029
1980[4]	1,852,616	1,759,642	1,053	1,490,140	1,408,592	1,058	299,033	290,583	1,029
1981[4]	1,860,272	1,768,966	1,052	1,494,451	1,414,232	1,057	297,864	289,923	1,027

1. Excludes births to nonresidents of U.S. 2. Includes races other than white and black. 3. Based on 50% sample of births. 4. Based on 100% of births for selected states and 50% sample in all others. *Source:* Department of Health and Human Services, National Center for Health Statistics. NOTE: Data are latest available.

Mortality

Death Rates for Selected Causes

Cause of death	Death rates per 100,000							
	1982[1]	1981	1980	1950	1945–49	1940–44	1920–24	1900–04
Typhoid fever	n.a.	0.0	0.0	0.1	0.2	0.6	7.3	26.7
Communicable diseases of childhood	n.a.	0.0	0.0	1.3	2.3	4.6	33.8	65.2
Measles	—	0.0	0.0	0.3	0.6	1.1	7.3	10.0
Scarlet fever	n.a.	0.0	0.0	0.2	0.1	0.4	4.0	11.8
Whooping cough	—	0.0	0.0	0.7	1.0	2.2	8.9	10.7
Diphtheria	n.a.	—	0.0	0.3	0.7	1.0	13.7	32.7
Pneumonia and influenza	21.8	23.4	23.3	31.3	41.3	63.7	140.3	184.3
Influenza	0.3	1.3	1.1	4.4	5.0	13.0	34.8	22.8
Pneumonia	21.5	22.1	22.0	26.9	37.2	50.7	105.5	161.5
Tuberculosis	0.9	0.8	0.8	22.5	33.3	43.4	96.7	184.7
Cancer	188.1	184.0	182.5	139.8	134.0	123.1	86.9	67.7
Diabetes mellitus	14.3	15.1	15.0	16.2	24.1	26.2	17.1	12.2
Major cardiovascular diseases	420.5	424.2	434.5	510.8	493.1	490.4	369.9	359.5
Diseases of the heart	327.8	328.7	335.2	356.8	325.1	303.2	169.8	153.0
Cerebrovascular diseases	68.9	71.3	74.6	104.0	93.8	91.7	93.5	106.3
Nephritis and nephrosis	7.9	7.5	7.6	16.4	48.4	72.1	81.5	84.3
Syphilis	0.0	0.1	0.1	5.0	8.4	12.7	17.6	12.9
Appendicitis	0.2	0.3	0.3	2.0	3.5	7.2	14.0	9.4
Accidents, all forms	41.3	43.9	46.0	60.6	67.6	73.0	70.8	79.2
Motor vehicle accidents	20.1	22.4	23.0	23.1	22.3	22.7	12.9	n.a.
Infant mortality[2]	11.2	11.9	12.5	29.2	33.3	42.4	76.7	n.a.
Neonatal mortality[2]	7.6	8.0	8.4	20.5	22.9	26.2	39.7	n.a.
Fetal mortality[2]	n.a.	9.0	n.a.	22.9	24.3	28.5	39.2[3]	n.a.
Maternal mortality[2]	0.1	0.1	0.1	0.8	1.4	2.8	6.9	n.a.
All causes	**857.6**	**862.4**	**874.2**	**963.8**	**1,003.3**	**1,062.0**	**1,196.6**	**1,621.6**

1. Provisional. Based on a 10% sample of deaths. 2. Rates per 1,000 live births. 3. 1922–24. NOTE: Includes only deaths occurring within the registration areas. Beginning with 1940, area includes the entire United States; beginning with 1960, Alaska and Hawaii are included. Rates per 100,000 population residing in areas, enumerated as of April 1 for 1940 and 1950 and estimated as of July 1 for all other years. Due to changes in statistical methods, death rates are not strictly comparable. n.a. = not available. *Source:* Department of Health and Human Services, National Center for Health Statistics.

Accidental Deaths by Principal Types

Year	Motor vehicle	Falls	Drowning	Fire burns	Ingestion of food or object	Firearms	Poison (solid, liquid)	Poison by gas
1970	54,633	16,926	7,860	6,718	2,753	2,406	3,679	1,620
1975	45,853	14,896	8,000	6,071	3,106	2,380	4,694	1,577
1978	52,411	13,690	7,026	6,163	3,063	1,806	3,035	1,737
1979	53,524	13,216	6,872	5,991	3,243	2,004	3,165	1,472
1980	53,300	12,600	7,100	5,600	2,900	1,800	3,000	1,300
1981	51,500	12,000	6,100	5,100	2,900	1,900	2,800	1,400
1982	46,000	11,600	6,200	5,000	2,900	1,900	3,000	1,400

NOTE: Figures are latest available. *Source:* Department of Health and Human Services, National Center for Health Statistics and National Safety Council.

Accident Rates, 1982

(eleven accidental deaths every hour)

Class of accident		One every	Class of accident		One every
All accidents	Deaths	9 minutes	Workers off-job	Deaths	15 minutes
	Injuries	4 seconds		Injuries	12 seconds
Motor-vehicle	Deaths	11 minutes	Home	Deaths	25 minutes
	Injuries	19 seconds		Injuries	10 seconds
Work	Deaths	47 minutes	Public non-motor-vehicle	Deaths	28 minutes
	Injuries	17 seconds		Injuries	13 seconds

NOTE: Data are latest available. *Source:* National Safety Council.

Motor-Vehicle Deaths by Type of Accident

	Deaths from collisions with—								
Year	Pedes-trians	Other motor vehicles	Railroad trains	Street cars	Pedalcycles	Animal-drawn vehicle or animal	Fixed objects	Deaths from non-collision accidents	Total deaths[1]
1960	7,860	14,800	1,368	5	460	80	1,700	11,900	38,137
1965	8,900	20,800	1,556	5	680	120	2,200	14,900	1,113
1970	9,900	23,200	1,459	3	780	100	3,800	15,400	54,633
1975	8,400	19,550	979	1	1,000	100	3,130	12,700	45,853
1980	9,700	22,000	800	—	1,200	100	4,400	15,100	53,300
1981	9,000	20,700	900	—	1,200	100	3,800	15,100	50,800
1982	8,600	18,900	600	—	1,100	100	3,600	13,100	46,000

NOTE: Figures are latest available. 1. Yearly totals do not quite equal sums of various types because totals for most types are estimated, and these have been made to nearest 10 deaths for some types and to nearest 50 deaths for others. *Source:* National Safety Council.

Improper Driving as Factor in Accidents, 1982

	Fatal accidents			Injury accidents			All accidents[1]		
Kind of improper driving	Total	Urban	Rural	Total	Urban	Rural	Total	Urban	Rural
Improper driving	61.2	62.3	60.6	67.8	70.5	63.6	66.6	67.7	64.5
Speed too fast[2]	30.5	31.5	30.2	24.4	20.7	30.2	21.0	17.6	28.1
Right of way	12.1	17.8	9.6	24.3	30.7	14.3	23.7	27.6	15.7
Drove left of center	11.8	6.0	14.3	4.2	2.4	7.1	3.5	2.1	6.3
Improper overtaking	1.5	1.0	1.6	1.4	1.1	1.9	2.1	1.7	2.7
Made improper turn	0.7	0.8	0.6	2.2	2.5	1.8	3.7	4.2	2.7
Followed too closely	0.5	0.7	0.4	6.2	7.8	3.6	6.5	7.6	4.4
Other improper driving	4.1	4.5	3.9	5.1	5.3	4.7	6.1	6.9	4.6
Total	**100.0%**	**100.0%**	**100.0%**	**100.0%**	**100.0%**	**100.0%**	**100.0%**	**100.0%**	**100.0%**

1. Principally property-damage accidents, but also includes fatal and injury accidents. 2. Includes "speed too fast for conditions." *Source:* Urban and rural reports from ten state traffic authorities to National Safety Council. NOTE: Figures are latest available.

Deaths and Death Rates

	Total deaths[1]		Motor vehicle traffic deaths[2]				Total deaths[1]		Motor vehicle traffic deaths[2]		
State	1982 rate	1981 rate	1982 number	1981 rate	1980 rate	State	1982 rate	1981 rate	1982 number	1981 rate	1980 rate
Alabama	8.9	9.0	845	3.4	3.3	Montana	8.2	8.4	254	4.8	4.9
Alaska	4.0	4.4	107	3.4	3.3	Nebraska	9.3	9.1	261	3.3	3.5
Arizona	7.9	8.0	724	4.9	5.0	Nevada	7.7	7.7	280	4.5	5.7
Arkansas	9.6	9.7	550	3.2	3.6	New Hamshire	7.8	8.1	173	2.3	3.0
California	7.8	7.8	4,609	3.2	3.5	New Jersey	8.9	9.0	1,061	2.3	2.2
Colorado	6.6	6.8	664	3.4	3.2	New Mexico	6.1	6.7	575	4.7	5.4
Connecticut	8.1	8.3	521	2.7	3.0	New York	9.4	9.6	2,147	3.2	3.4
Delaware	8.5	8.6	123	2.5	3.7	North Carolina	8.1	8.4	1,320	3.6	3.7
D.C.	13.4	14.1	36	1.5	1.4	North Dakota	8.5	8.8	148	3.1	2.9
Florida	10.5	10.9	2,711	4.1	3.6	Ohio	8.7	9.1	1,618	2.5	2.8
Georgia	7.9	8.5	1,227	3.2	3.5	Oklahoma	9.0	9.0	1,064	3.6	3.5
Hawaii	5.5	5.4	161	2.6	3.3	Oregon	8.2	8.2	518	3.3	3.4
Idaho	6.9	6.9	255	4.2	4.8	Pennsylvania	10.0	10.1	1,848	2.9	3.0
Illinois	8.5	8.6	1,671	2.8	3.1	Rhode Island	9.5	9.8	109	2.0	2.4
Indiana	8.6	8.8	964	3.0	3.2	South Carolina	7.6	7.8	730	3.7	3.8
Iowa	9.2	9.2	474	3.2	3.3	South Dakota	9.4	9.2	148	2.9	3.7
Kansas	8.8	8.9	498	3.3	3.4	Tennessee	9.3	9.3	1,074	3.2	n.a.
Kentucky	8.9	9.1	836	3.3	3.3	Texas	7.6	7.6	4,271	3.9	4.0
Louisiana	8.3	8.4	1,093	4.9	5.2	Utah	5.8	5.6	296	3.4	3.5
Maine	8.9	9.2	163	2.8	3.5	Vermont	8.7	8.7	106	3.1	3.6
Maryland	7.8	7.9	660	2.8	2.8	Virginia	7.5	7.6	881	2.6	2.7
Massachusetts	9.8	8.6	655	2.1	2.5	Washington	7.9	7.9	757	2.9	3.4
Michigan	8.2	8.2	1,417	2.6	2.9	West Virginia	9.8	10.0	452	4.2	5.0
Minnesota	8.1	7.9	581	2.7	3.0	Wisconsin	8.8	8.4	775	2.8	3.2
Mississippi	9.0	9.1	728	4.4	4.2	Wyoming	6.0	6.0	201	5.1	4.9
Missouri	9.9	10.1	908	3.0	3.5	**Total U.S.**	**n.a.**	**n.a.**	**46,000**	**3.3**	**3.5**

1. Provisional rates per 1,000 population, by place of occurrence. 2. Per 100 million vehicle-miles. *Sources:* Department of Health and Human Services, National Center for Health Statistics; National Safety Council.

Annual Death Rates

Year	Rate	Year	Rate	Year	Deaths	Rate
1900	17.2	1939	10.6	1962	1,756,720	9.5
1905	15.9	1940	10.8	1963	1,813,549	9.6
1910	14.7	1941	10.5	1964	1,798,051	9.4
1915	13.2	1942	10.3	1965	1,828,136	9.4
1918	18.1[1]	1943	10.9	1966	1,863,149	9.5
1920	13.0	1944	10.6	1967	1,851,323	9.4
1923	12.1	1945	10.6	1968	1,930,082	9.7
1924	11.6	1946	10.0	1969	1,921,990	9.5
1925	11.7	1947	10.1	1970[2]	1,921,031	9.5
1926	12.1	1948	9.9	1971	1,927,542	9.3
1927	11.3	1949	9.7	1972	1,963,944	9.4
1928	12.0	1950	9.6	1973	1,973,003	9.3
1929	11.9	1951	9.7	1974	1,934,388	9.1
1930	11.3	1952	9.6	1975	1,892,879	8.8
1931	11.1	1953	9.6	1976	1,909,440	8.8
1932	10.9	1954	9.2	1977	1,899,597	8.6
1933	10.7	1955	9.3	1978	1,927,788	8.7
1934	11.1	1956	9.4	1979	1,913,841	8.5
1935	10.9	1957	9.6	1980	1,989,841	8.7
1936	11.6	1958	9.5	1981	1,977,981	8.7
1937	11.3	1959	9.4	1982[3]	1,986,000	8.6
1938	10.6	1960	9.5	1983[3]	2,010,000	8.6

1. Year of influenza epidemic. 2. First year for which deaths of nonresidents are excluded. 3. Provisional. NOTE: Includes only deaths occurring within the registration area. Beginning with 1933, area includes entire U.S.; with 1959 includes Alaska, and with 1960 includes Hawaii. Excludes fetal deaths. Rates per 1,000 population residing in area, as of April 1 for 1940, 1950, 1960, 1970, and 1980, and estimated as of July 1 for all other years. *Sources:* Department of Commerce, Bureau of the Census; and Department of Health and Human Services, National Center for Health Statistics.

Death Rates by Age, Color, and Sex

Age	1982[1]	1981	1980	1975[2]	1970[2]	1960	1982[1]	1981	1980	1975[2]	1970[2]	1960
	White males						White females					
Under 1 year	11.3	11.8	12.3	15.9	21.1	26.9	9.1	9.4	9.6	12.2	16.1	20.1
1–4	0.6	0.6	0.7	0.7	0.8	1.0	0.4	0.5	0.5	0.6	0.8	0.9
5–14	0.3	0.3	0.4	0.4	0.5	0.5	0.2	0.2	0.2	0.3	0.3	0.3
15–24	1.5	1.5	1.7	1.7	1.7	1.4	0.5	0.5	0.6	0.6	0.6	0.5
25–34	1.6	1.7	1.7	1.7	1.8	1.6	0.6	0.6	0.7	0.7	0.8	0.9
35–44	2.4	2.5	2.6	3.0	3.4	3.3	1.3	1.3	1.4	1.6	1.9	1.9
45–54	6.7	6.9	7.0	7.9	8.8	9.3	3.6	3.7	3.7	4.1	4.6	4.6
55–64	16.5	16.9	17.3	19.5	22.0	22.3	8.6	8.7	8.8	9.4	10.1	10.8
65–74	38.9	39.3	40.4	43.6	48.1	48.5	20.3	20.3	20.7	21.5	24.7	27.8
75–84	85.1	85.7	88.3	96.1	101.0	103.0	50.9	51.8	54.0	60.3	67.0	77.0
85 and over	183.3	184.5	191.0	182.6	185.5	217.5	142.8	144.4	149.8	144.9	159.8	194.8
	All other males						All other females					
Under 1 year	18.2	19.3	23.5	30.0	40.2	51.9	14.4	16.3	19.4	25.2	31.7	40.7
1–4	1.0	1.0	1.0	1.1	1.4	2.1	0.6	0.8	0.8	0.9	1.2	1.7
5–14	0.5	0.4	0.4	0.6	0.6	0.8	0.2	0.3	0.3	0.3	0.4	0.5
15–24	1.9	1.8	2.0	2.4	3.0	2.1	0.6	0.6	0.7	0.9	1.1	1.1
25–34	3.3	3.4	3.6	4.5	5.0	3.9	1.3	1.3	1.4	1.6	2.2	2.6
35–44	5.1	5.7	5.9	7.4	8.7	7.3	2.5	2.7	2.9	3.6	4.9	5.5
45–54	11.8	12.6	13.1	14.2	16.5	15.5	6.3	6.5	6.9	7.8	9.8	11.4
55–64	24.4	25.2	26.1	28.1	30.5	31.5	13.1	13.8	14.2	16.4	18.9	24.1
65–74	47.1	46.3	47.5	49.7	54.7	56.6	26.0	27.2	28.6	31.7	36.8	39.8
75–84	81.1	80.6	86.9	86.0	89.8	86.6	52.6	54.6	58.6	59.8	63.9	67.1
85 and over	155.1	146.9	157.7	116.9	114.1	152.4	112.0	113.7	119.2	91.8	102.9	128.7

1. Provisional. Based on a 10% sample of deaths. 2. Excludes deaths of nonresidents of U.S. 3. Based on enumerated population adjusted for age bias in nonwhite population at ages 55–69 years. NOTE: For 1920, data are from only 10 selected states and the District of Columbia; for 1940, from D.C. and the former 48 states; for 1960, from D.C. and all 50 states. Excludes fetal deaths. Rates are per 1,000 population in each group, enumerated as of April 1 for 1940, 1950, and 1960, and estimated as of July 1 for all other years. NOTE: Data are latest available. *Sources:* Department of Commerce, Bureau of the Census; and Department of Health and Human Services, National Center for Health Statistics.

Expectation of Life

Expectation of Life in the United States

Calendar period	Age 0	10	20	30	40	50	60	70	80
WHITE MALES									
1850[1]	38.3	48.0	40.1	34.0	27.9	21.6	15.6	10.2	5.9
1890[1]	42.50	48.45	40.66	34.05	27.37	20.72	14.73	9.35	5.40
1900–1902[2]	48.23	50.59	42.19	34.88	27.74	20.76	14.35	9.03	5.10
1909–1911[2]	50.23	51.32	42.71	34.87	27.43	20.39	13.98	8.83	5.09
1919–1921[3]	56.34	54.15	45.60	37.65	29.86	22.22	15.25	9.51	5.47
1929–1931	59.12	54.96	46.02	37.54	29.22	21.51	14.72	9.20	5.26
1939–1941	62.81	57.03	47.76	38.80	30.03	21.96	15.05	9.42	5.38
1949–1951	66.31	58.98	49.52	40.29	31.17	22.83	15.76	10.07	5.88
1959–1961	67.55	59.78	50.25	40.98	31.73	23.22	16.01	10.29	5.89
1969–1971	67.94	59.69	50.22	41.07	31.87	23.34	16.07	10.38	6.18
1979	70.8	62.0	52.5	43.3	34.0	25.3	17.6	11.5	6.9
1980	70.7	61.9	52.4	43.2	34.0	25.2	17.5	11.3	6.7
1981[5]	71.0	62.1	52.6	43.4	34.2	25.4	17.7	11.5	6.8
1982[5]	71.4	62.5	53.0	43.7	34.4	25.6	17.8	11.6	6.9
WHITE FEMALES									
1850[1]	40.5	47.2	40.2	35.4	29.8	23.5	17.0	11.3	6.4
1890[1]	44.46	49.62	42.03	35.36	28.76	22.09	15.70	10.15	5.75
1900–1902[2]	51.08	52.15	43.77	36.42	29.17	21.89	15.23	9.59	5.50
1909–1911[2]	53.62	53.57	44.88	36.96	29.26	21.74	14.92	9.38	5.35
1919–1921[3]	58.53	55.17	46.46	38.72	30.94	23.12	15.93	9.94	5.70
1929–1931	62.67	57.65	48.52	39.99	31.52	23.41	16.05	9.98	5.63
1939–1941	67.29	60.85	51.38	42.21	33.25	24.72	17.00	10.50	5.88
1949–1951	72.03	64.26	54.56	45.00	35.64	26.76	18.64	11.68	6.59
1959–1961	74.19	66.05	56.29	46.63	37.13	28.08	19.69	12.38	6.67
1969–1971	75.49	66.97	57.24	47.60	38.12	29.11	20.79	13.37	7.59
1979	78.4	69.4	59.7	50.0	40.4	31.2	22.7	15.2	9.0
1980	78.1	69.1	59.7	49.7	40.1	30.9	22.4	14.8	8.6
1981[5]	78.5	69.4	59.6	49.9	40.3	31.1	22.7	15.2	9.0
1982[5]	78.7	69.6	59.8	50.1	40.5	31.3	22.8	15.2	9.0
ALL OTHER MALES[4]									
1900–1902[2]	32.54	41.90	35.11	29.25	23.12	17.34	12.62	8.33	5.12
1909–1911[2]	34.05	40.65	33.46	27.33	21.57	16.21	11.67	8.00	5.53
1919–1921[3]	47.14	45.99	38.36	32.51	26.53	20.47	14.74	9.58	5.83
1929–1931	47.55	44.27	35.95	29.45	23.36	17.92	13.15	8.78	5.42
1939–1941	52.33	48.54	39.74	32.25	25.23	19.18	14.38	10.06	6.46
1949–1951	58.91	52.96	43.73	35.31	27.29	20.25	14.91	10.74	7.07
1959–1961	61.48	55.19	45.78	37.05	28.72	21.28	15.29	10.81	6.87
1969–1971	60.98	53.67	44.37	36.20	28.29	21.24	15.35	10.68	7.57
1979	65.4	57.3	47.7	39.0	30.6	23.0	16.7	11.6	7.5
1980	65.3	57.1	47.5	38.8	30.3	22.6	16.2	11.1	6.9
1981[5]	66.1	57.7	48.1	39.4	30.9	23.1	16.7	11.5	7.2
1982[5]	66.5	58.1	48.5	39.7	31.1	23.2	16.6	11.4	7.2
ALL OTHER FEMALES[4]									
1900–1902[2]	35.04	43.02	36.89	30.70	24.37	18.67	13.60	9.62	6.48
1909–1911[2]	37.67	42.84	36.14	29.61	23.34	17.65	12.78	9.22	6.05
1919–1921[3]	46.92	44.54	37.15	31.48	25.60	19.76	14.69	10.25	6.58
1929–1931	49.51	45.33	37.22	30.67	24.30	18.60	14.22	10.38	6.90
1939–1941	55.51	50.83	42.14	34.52	27.31	21.04	16.14	11.81	8.00
1949–1951	62.70	56.17	46.77	38.02	29.82	22.67	16.95	12.29	8.15
1959–1961	66.47	59.72	50.07	40.83	32.16	24.31	17.83	12.46	7.66
1969–1971	69.05	61.49	51.85	42.61	33.87	25.97	19.02	13.30	9.01
1979	74.1	65.8	56.1	46.6	37.4	28.9	21.3	14.8	9.8
1980	73.6	65.3	55.5	46.0	36.8	28.3	20.7	14.2	9.0
1981[5]	74.5	65.9	56.1	46.7	37.4	28.9	21.2	14.7	9.3
1982[5]	75.2	66.6	56.8	47.3	38.0	29.3	21.7	15.0	9.6

1. Massachusetts only; white and nonwhite combined, the latter being about 1% of the total. 2. Original Death Registration States. 3. Death Registration States of 1920. 4. Data for periods 1900–1902 to 1929–1931 relate to blacks only. 5. Provisional. *Sources:* Department of Health and Human Services, National Center for Health Statistics; Department of Commerce, Bureau of the Census. NOTE: Data are latest available.

Expectation of Life and Mortality Probabilities, 1980

Age	Expectation of life in years					Mortality probability per 1,000				
	Total persons	White		All other		Total persons	White		All other	
		Male	Female	Male	Female		Male	Female	Male	Female
0	73.7	70.7	78.1	65.3	73.6	12.7	12.3	9.7	20.9	17.6
1	73.7	70.6	77.9	65.7	73.9	.9	1.0	.6	1.3	1.0
2	72.7	69.6	76.9	64.7	73.0	.7	.7	.5	1.1	.8
3	71.8	68.7	76.0	63.8	72.1	.5	.5	.4	.9	.9
4	70.8	67.7	75.0	62.9	71.1	.4	.4	.4	.7	.6
5	69.8	66.8	74.0	61.9	70.2	.4	.4	.3	.6	.5
6	68.9	65.8	73.1	60.9	69.2	.3	.4	.3	.5	.4
7	67.9	64.8	72.1	60.0	68.2	.3	.3	.2	.5	.3
8	66.9	63.8	71.1	59.0	67.2	.3	.3	.2	.4	.3
9	65.9	62.8	70.1	58.0	66.3	.2	.2	.2	.3	.2
10	64.9	61.9	69.1	57.1	65.3	.2	.2	.2	.3	.2
11	64.0	60.9	68.1	56.1	64.3	.2	.2	.2	.3	.3
12	63.0	59.9	67.1	55.1	63.3	.3	.3	.2	.4	.3
13	62.0	58.9	66.2	54.1	62.3	.4	.5	.3	.5	.3
14	61.0	57.9	65.2	53.1	61.3	.5	.7	.3	.7	.3
15	60.0	57.0	64.2	52.2	60.4	.7	1.0	.4	.9	.4
16	59.1	56.0	63.2	51.2	59.4	.9	1.3	.5	1.1	.4
17	58.1	55.1	62.3	50.3	58.4	1.0	1.5	.6	1.3	.5
18	57.2	54.2	61.3	49.3	57.4	1.1	1.7	.6	1.6	.6
19	56.3	53.3	60.3	48.4	56.5	1.2	1.7	.6	1.9	.6
20	55.3	52.4	59.4	47.5	55.5	1.3	1.8	.6	2.3	.7
21	54.4	51.5	58.4	46.6	54.5	1.3	1.9	.6	2.6	.8
22	53.5	50.5	57.4	45.7	53.6	1.4	2.0	.6	2.9	.9
23	52.5	49.6	56.5	44.9	52.6	1.4	2.0	.6	3.0	1.0
24	51.6	48.7	55.5	44.0	51.7	1.4	1.9	.6	3.1	1.0
25	50.7	47.8	54.5	43.1	50.7	1.3	1.8	.6	3.2	1.1
26	49.7	46.9	53.6	42.3	49.8	1.3	1.8	.6	3.2	1.2
27	48.8	46.0	52.6	41.4	48.8	1.3	1.7	.6	3.3	1.2
28	47.9	45.1	51.6	40.5	47.9	1.3	1.7	.6	3.4	1.3
29	46.9	44.2	50.6	39.7	47.0	1.3	1.7	.6	3.5	1.3
30	46.0	43.2	49.7	38.8	46.0	1.3	1.7	.6	3.6	1.4
31	45.1	42.3	48.7	38.0	45.1	1.4	1.6	.7	3.7	1.4
32	44.1	41.4	47.7	37.1	44.2	1.4	1.7	.7	3.9	1.5
33	43.2	40.4	46.8	36.2	43.2	1.4	1.7	.8	4.1	1.6
34	42.2	39.5	45.8	35.4	42.3	1.5	1.8	.8	4.3	1.7
35	41.3	38.6	44.9	34.5	41.4	1.6	1.8	.9	4.5	1.9
36	40.4	37.6	43.9	33.7	40.4	1.7	1.9	1.0	4.7	2.0
37	39.4	36.7	42.9	32.8	39.5	1.8	2.1	1.1	5.0	2.2
38	38.5	35.8	42.0	32.0	38.6	2.0	2.2	1.2	5.3	2.4
39	37.6	34.9	41.0	31.2	37.7	2.1	2.4	1.3	5.6	2.7
40	36.7	34.0	40.1	30.3	36.8	2.3	2.6	1.4	6.0	3.0
41	35.7	33.0	39.1	29.5	35.9	2.5	2.8	1.6	6.4	3.3
42	34.8	32.1	38.2	28.7	35.0	2.8	3.1	1.7	6.9	3.6
43	33.9	31.2	37.3	27.9	34.2	3.0	3.4	1.9	7.5	4.0
44	33.0	30.3	36.3	27.1	33.3	3.4	3.8	2.1	8.1	4.3
45	32.1	29.4	35.4	26.3	32.4	3.7	4.2	2.3	8.8	4.7
46	31.3	28.6	34.5	25.6	31.6	4.0	4.6	2.6	9.6	5.1
47	30.4	27.7	33.6	24.8	30.7	4.4	5.2	2.8	10.4	5.6
48	29.5	26.8	32.7	24.1	29.9	4.9	5.7	3.1	11.4	6.0
49	28.7	26.0	31.8	23.3	29.1	5.4	6.4	3.4	12.4	6.5
50	27.8	25.2	30.9	22.6	28.3	5.9	7.1	3.8	13.4	7.0
51	27.0	24.3	30.0	21.9	27.5	6.5	7.8	4.1	14.5	7.6
52	26.1	23.5	29.1	21.2	26.7	7.1	8.6	4.5	15.7	8.2
53	25.3	22.7	28.2	20.6	25.9	7.7	9.5	4.9	16.8	8.8
54	24.5	21.9	27.4	19.9	25.1	8.4	10.4	5.3	18.0	9.5
55	23.7	21.2	26.5	19.3	24.4	9.1	11.4	5.8	19.2	10.2
56	22.9	20.4	25.7	18.6	23.6	9.9	12.4	6.3	20.5	10.9
57	22.2	19.6	24.8	18.0	22.9	10.7	13.6	6.9	21.9	111.7
58	21.4	18.9	24.0	17.4	22.1	11.7	14.9	7.5	23.4	12.7
59	20.6	18.2	23.2	16.8	21.4	12.7	16.3	8.2	25.1	13.6
60	19.9	17.5	22.4	16.2	20.7	13.8	17.8	9.0	26.8	14.7
61	19.2	16.8	21.6	15.7	20.0	15.0	19.3	9.8	28.6	15.9
62	18.5	16.1	20.8	15.1	19.3	16.3	21.1	10.7	30.5	17.0
63	17.8	15.4	20.0	14.6	18.6	17.7	23.1	11.6	32.3	18.1
64	17.1	14.8	19.2	14.0	18.0	19.2	25.2	12.6	34.2	19.2
65	16.4	14.2	18.5	13.5	17.3	20.8	27.5	13.7	36.2	20.4

Age	Expectation of life in years: Total persons	White: Male	White: Female	All other: Male	All other: Female	Mortality probability per 1,000: Total persons	White: Male	White: Female	All other: Male	All other: Female
66	15.7	13.6	17.1	13.0	16.7	22.4	30.0	14.9	38.3	21.6
67	15.1	13.0	17.0	12.5	16.0	24.3	32.6	16.2	40.6	23.2
68	14.4	12.4	16.2	12.0	15.4	26.3	35.4	17.7	43.1	25.1
69	13.8	11.8	15.5	11.5	14.8	28.5	38.5	19.4	45.8	27.4
70	13.2	11.3	14.8	11.1	14.2	30.9	41.8	21.2	48.7	29.9
71	12.6	10.7	14.1	10.6	13.6	33.5	45.4	23.2	51.7	32.5
72	12.0	10.2	13.5	10.2	13.0	36.3	49.1	25.4	54.9	35.1
73	11.5	9.7	12.8	9.7	12.5	39.2	53.1	27.9	58.1	37.5
74	10.9	9.3	12.2	9.3	12.0	42.3	57.4	30.7	61.5	39.8
75	10.4	8.8	11.5	8.9	11.4	45.7	61.9	33.7	65.0	42.2
76	9.9	8.3	10.9	8.5	10.9	45.5	66.9	37.2	68.8	45.0
77	9.3	7.9	10.3	8.1	10.4	53.6	72.2	41.0	73.1	48.1
78	8.9	7.5	9.1	7.7	9.9	58.2	78.1	45.2	77.9	51.9
79	8.4	7.1	9.2	7.3	9.4	63.3	84.5	50.0	83.3	56.2
80	7.9	6.7	8.6	6.9	9.0	69.0	91.5	55.6	89.4	61.1
81	7.5	6.3	8.1	6.5	8.5	75.5	99.2	61.9	96.2	66.7
82	7.0	6.0	7.6	6.2	8.1	82.9	107.5	69.4	103.9	73.0
83	6.6	5.6	7.1	5.8	7.7	91.4	116.6	78.2	112.6	79.9
84	6.2	5.3	6.7	5.5	7.3	101.3	126.4	88.9	122.4	87.6
85	5.9	5.0	6.3	5.3	7.0	—	—	—	—	—

Source: Department of Health and Human Services, National Center for Health Statistics. NOTE: Data are latest available.

Law Enforcement and Crime

Full-Time Law Enforcement Employees, 1982

City	Officers	Civilians	Total	Percent change 81-82
Atlanta	1,340	283	1,623	−1.4
Baltimore	3,056	525	3,581	−.3
Birmingham, Ala.	659	138	797	−.6
Boston	1,737	392	2,129	+10.0
Buffalo, N.Y.	1,034	112	1,146	−.1
Chicago	12,562	2,463	15,025	+2.4
Cincinnati	991	154	1,145	−2.8
Cleveland	1,947	331	2,278	+4.7
Columbus, Ohio	1,216	337	1,553	+10.5
Dallas	1,996	573	2,569	+7.7
Denver	1,388	303	1,691	+3.0
Detroit	4,092	613	4,705	+1.4
El Paso	651	180	831	+1.9
Fort Worth	719	233	952	+2.8
Honolulu	1,549	346	1,895	+2.3
Houston	3,345	1,074	4,419	+1.3
Indianapolis	937	315	1,252	+.8
Jacksonville, Fla.	903	664	1,567	+1.3
Kansas City, Mo.	1,145	527	1,672	+.2
Long Beach, Calif.	633	305	938	+7.4
Los Angeles	6,861	2,441	9,302	−2.1
Louisville, Ky.	682	188	870	−3.7
Memphis, Tenn.	1,200	298	1,498	−2.3
Miami, Fla.	979	346	1,325	+6.7
Milwaukee	2,087	305	2,392	+3.0
Minneapolis	690	92	782	−3.5
New Orleans	1,355	503	1,858	+3.9
New York	22,855	5,876	28,731	+3.2
Newark, N.J.	1,166	246	1,412	−4.9
Norfolk, Va.	590	73	663	−1.4
Oakland, Calif.	625	278	903	+6.1
Oklahoma City	767	216	983	+5.3
Omaha, Neb.	572	159	731	+5.4
Philadelphia	7,377	904	8,281	−.8
Pheonix, Ariz.	1,621	694	2,315	+1.6
Pittsburgh	1,278	130	1,408	−2.8
Portland, Ore.	699	190	889	+3.2
Rochester, N.Y.	603	127	730	−4.1
St. Louis	1,808	543	2,351	−3.7
St. Paul	482	105	587	−12.1
San Antonio	1,132	258	1,390	+4.3
San Diego, Calif.	1,395	491	1,886	+9.4
San Francisco	1,971	508	2,479	+6.8
San Jose, Calif.	891	206	1,097	+4.6
Seattle	1,007	371	1,378	−.5
Tampa, Fla.	660	194	854	+1.1
Toledo, Ohio	655	40	695	+1.7
Tuscon, Ariz.	557	182	739	−2.4
Tulsa, Okla.	700	172	872	+4.5
Washington, D.C.	3,861	524	4,385	+8.9

NOTE: As of Oct. 31, 1982. *Source:* Department of Justice, Federal Bureau of Investigation, *Uniform Crime Reports for the United States, 1982.*

Estimated Arrests, 1982[1]

Murder and non-negligent manslaughter	18,475	Weapons—carrying, possession, etc.	163,461
Forcible rape	28,179	Prostitution and commercial vice	110,713
Robbery	137,562	Sex offenses, except forcible rape and prostitution	66,083
Aggravated assault	257,607	Drug abuse violations	562,390
Burglary	433,774	Gambling	36,539
Larceny—theft	1,137,329	Offenses against family and children	45,260
Motor vehicle theft	108,279	Driving under the influence	1,379,180
Arson	16,810	Liquor laws	402,690
Total violent crime	441,823	Drunkenness	1,033,385
Total property crime	1,696,192	Disorderly conduct	760,687
Other assaults	448,166	Vagrancy	32,127
Forgery and counterfeiting	79,772	All other offenses, except traffic	1,949,405
Fraud	268,969	Curfew and loitering law violations	78,564
Embezzlement	7,288	Runaways	114,334
Stolen property—buying, receiving, possessing	114,007	**Total**	**10,000,078**
Vandalism	200,208		

1. Arrest totals based on all reporting agencies and estimates for unreported areas. *Source:* Department of Justice, Federal Bureau of Investigation, *Uniform Crime Reports for the United States,* 1982.

Number of Arrests by Sex and Age

	Male				Female			
	Total		Under 18		Total		Under 18	
Offense	1982	1981	1982	1981	1982	1981	1982	1981
Serious crimes	1,372,226	1,377,210	437,761	471,262	349,134	337,474	100,800	105,558
Murder[1]	11,655	12,659	1,006	1,235	1,900	1,882	94	121
Forcible rape	21,445	21,888	3,139	3,127	189	192	46	46
Robbery	88,080	89,942	21,810	23,440	7,290	7,243	1,644	1,913
Aggravated assault	179,702	176,085	22,521	23,702	27,132	25,771	4,345	4,329
Burglary—breaking or entering	332,847	349,198	133,816	149,835	24,794	24,761	9,820	10,624
Larceny—theft	652,742	634,636	224,069	231,997	278,290	267,731	80,763	83,957
Motor vehicle theft	73,429	79,792	26,704	32,095	7,718	8,258	3,462	3,997
Arson	12,326	13,010	4,696	5,831	1,821	1,636	626	571
All other								
Other assaults	302,862	296,386	44,084	44,267	51,876	49,439	12,082	12,134
Forgery and counterfeiting	45,662	43,976	4,598	4,738	22,458	20,886	2,151	2,051
Fraud	122,558	126,622	3,053	3,733	93,724	93,926	1,413	1,572
Embezzlement	4,416	4,596	364	528	1,921	1,881	132	192
Stolen property—buying, receiving, possessing	82,869	84,266	21,852	23,984	11,024	10,410	2,215	2,327
Vandalism	147,633	153,393	66,420	73,825	15,478	15,433	6,075	6,662
Weapons—carrying, possessing, etc.	113,003	112,983	16,462	17,916	9,278	8,923	1,166	1,125
Prostitution and commercialized vice	22,053	19,177	600	641	47,019	46,075	1,408	1,416
Sex offenses, except forcible rape and prostitution	51,402	49,612	8,374	8,284	4,215	4,060	564	600
Drug abuse violations	374,833	373,299	51,099	61,432	62,034	59,359	10,267	12,258
Gambling	18,079	19,807	463	569	2,227	2,071	29	33
Offenses against family and children	34,113	34,576	866	1,246	3,925	4,149	475	899
Driving under the influence	1,118,190	1,043,117	20,228	20,867	135,658	118,588	2,616	2,598
Liquor laws	278,893	268,855	75,934	77,389	51,704	49,246	23,491	23,573
Drunkenness	830,644	845,739	25,041	27,327	76,415	72,868	4,181	4,476
Disorderly conduct	365,095	363,679	54,131	56,865	70,917	71,481	12,331	13,103
Vagrancy	18,106	20,920	2,146	2,636	3,056	4,635	463	501
All other offenses, except traffic	1,067,113	1,006,159	145,185	149,892	209,370	194,689	39,507	39,899
Curfew and loitering law violations	57,158	62,034	57,158	62,034	16,217	16,964	16,217	16,964
Runaways	37,696	39,086	37,696	39,086	51,723	52,996	51,723	52,996
Total	**6,464,604**	**6,345,492**	**1,073,515**	**1,148,521**	**1,289,373**	**1,235,553**	**289,306**	**300,937**

1. Includes non-negligent manslaughter. NOTE: 1982 figures represent arrests reported by 8,443 agencies serving a population of 153,255,000 as estimated by FBI. *Source:* Department of Justice, Federal Bureau of Investigation, *Uniform Crime Reports for the United States, 1982.*

Arrests by Race, 1982

(in thousands)

Offense	White	Black	Other	Total
Serious crimes				
Murder[1]	9.1	9.2	0.2	18.5
Forcible rape	13.7	13.1	0.5	28.2
Robbery	52.5	83.6	2.0	137.6
Aggravated assault	154.0	99.8	3.7	257.6
Burglary	290.7	137.5	6.7	433.8
Larceny—theft	736.0	379.4	21.9	1,137.5
Arson	12.4	4.2	0.2	16.8
All other				
Other assaults	286.5	155.1	6.5	448.2
Forgery and counterfeiting	50.6	28.5	0.7	79.7
Fraud	179.3	87.7	2.0	269.0
Embezzlement	5.4	1.7	0.1	7.3
Stolen property—buying, receiving, possessing	71.3	41.8	0.9	114.0
Vandalism	159.9	37.7	2.6	200.2
Weapons—carrying, possession, etc.	100.8	60.9	1.8	163.5
Prostitution and commercial vice	56.2	53.1	1.4	110.7
Sex offenses, except forcible rape and prostitution	51.3	13.7	1.0	66.1
Drug abuse violation	400.7	156.4	2.2	562.4
Gambling	12.8	22.3	1.4	36.5
Offenses against family and children	28.5	16.3	0.4	45.3
Driving under the influence	1,209.7	148.2	21.2	1,379.2
Liquor laws	356.4	37.4	8.9	402.7
Drunkenness	848.3	162.3	22.7	1,033.4
Disorderly conduct	449.2	303.2	8.3	760.7
Vagrancy	20.7	10.8	0.6	32.1
All other offenses except traffic	1,285.6	636.5	27.3	1,949.4
Suspicion	6.9	1.7	0.3	8.9
Curfew and loitering law violations	53.7	24.0	0.9	78.6
Runaways	95.7	16.4	2.2	114.3
Total	**7,070.4**	**2,777.1**	**152.6**	**10,000.1**

1. Includes non-negligent manslaughter. NOTE: Figures represent arrests reported by 9,789 agencies serving a total 1982 population of 186,480,000 as estimated by FBI. *Source:* Department of Justice, Federal Bureau of Investigation, *Uniform Crime Reports for the United States, 1982.*

Total Arrests, by Age Groups, 1982

Age	Arrests	Age	Arrests	Age	Arrests	Age	Arrests	Age	Arrests
Under 15	550,901	18	557,292	22	487,494	30–34	1,068,314	50–54	242,080
15	318,775	19	559,922	23	442,606	35–39	667,773	55 and over	369,718
16	427,310	20	536,360	24	421,755	40–44	447,450	**Total**	**10,062,343**
17	507,702	21	521,816	25–29	1,623,271	45–49	311,804		

NOTE: Based on reports furnished to the FBI by 9,832 agencies covering a 1982 estimated population of 187,346,000. *Source:* Department of Justice, Federal Bureau of Investigation, *Uniform Crime Reports for the United States, 1982.*

Federal Prisoners Under Sentence, by Offense and Race: 1981

(Represents more than 89 percent of the sentenced Federal prisoner population)

	White		Other races		
Offense	Number	Average sentence (mo.)	Number	Average sentence (mo.)	Total
Drug laws	4,030	75.8	1,357	104.5	5,387
Robbery	2,152	178.3	2,160	178.3	4,312
Larceny/theft	1,345	60.5	881	49.2	2,225
Firearms	603	59.1	201	52.4	804
Immigration	934	15.3	20	15.0	954
Forgery	229	55.1	310	48.8	539
Securities violations[2]	73	79.3	29	71.5	102
Counterfeiting	310	59.5	79	48.0	389
Fraud	597	50.3	142	37.8	739
Kidnaping	276	373.7	140	400.2	416
Juvenile delinquency	4	14.5	5	68.4	9
Burglary	41	94.8	29	112.9	70
Government[3]	592	298.3	1,732	213.4	2,342
Total[1]	**12,758**	**102.4**	**7,600**	**144.2**	**20,358**

1. Includes offenses not shown separately. 2. Transporting false or forged securities. 3. Includes offenses committed on government reservations, the high seas, territories, and the District of Columbia. NOTE: These data pertain only to the Federal offender population housed in Federal institutions during or on the last day of the fiscal year ending Sept. 30. *Source:* U.S. Bureau of Prisons, *Statistical Report,* annual.

Crime Rates for Population Groups and Selected Cities

(offenses known to the police per 100,000 population, as of July 1)

Group and city	Violent crime: Murder	Forcible rape	Robbery	Aggravated assault	Total	Property crime: Burglary—breaking or entering	Larceny—theft	Motor vehicle theft	Total	Total all crimes
Cities over 250,000	9,205	1,354	21.7	69	773	491	7,851	2,426	4,328	1,097
100,000–249,999	8,355	779	11.5	51	321	395	7,576	2,203	4,802	571
50,000–99,999	6,579	561	6.8	37	212	306	6,019	1,712	3,794	513
25,000–49,999	5,984	431	5.7	27	139	260	5,553	1,460	3,699	393
10,000–24,999	4,866	320	4.3	18	80	218	4,546	1,162	3,097	286
Under 10,000	4,498	284	4.1	16	50	214	4,214	1,008	2,986	221
Total, 8,033 cities	**6,899**	**723**	**10.8**	**40**	**335**	**337**	**6,177**	**1,754**	**3,827**	**596**
Suburbs	4,515	351	5.4	24	99	223	4,164	1,207	2,647	311
Rural areas	2,225	184	6.8	15	20	142	2,041	788	1,133	120
Selected cities:										
Dallas	11,937	1,345	31.5	114	587	613	10,592	3,433	6,416	743
Phoenix	9,293	667	11.7	53	295	307	8,626	2,639	5,448	540
Detroit	12,942	2,009	43.4	99	1,357	510	10,933	4,200	4,061	2,672
San Francisco	9,685	1,640	15.7	84	1,010	530	8,045	1,935	5,210	900
New York	9,703	2,028	23.5	50	1,352	603	7,674	2,435	3,726	1,514
Washington, D.C.	10,411	2,123	30.7	67	1,448	578	8,288	2,341	5,299	648
Los Angeles	10,328	1,739	27.4	87	968	657	8,589	2,740	4,273	1,575
Baltimore	9,134	2,090	28.4	69	1,171	822	7,044	2,044	4,442	558
San Diego	7,131	635	7.8	47	342	239	6,496	1,764	3,883	849
Memphis	8,476	1,153	18.5	108	667	359	7,322	2,560	3,984	778
San Antonio	7,814	695	22.4	47	258	367	7,119	2,358	4,127	635
Chicago	6,041	877	22.2	37	542	276	5,164	1,071	3,068	1,025
Philadelphia	5,608	1,038	19.7	50	628	340	4,571	1,370	2,376	824
Indianapolis	7,508	938	14.9	84	431	409	6,570	2,161	3,782	627

1. Agencies also included in other city groups. *Source:* U.S. Federal Bureau of Investigation, *Crime in the United States,* annual.

Percent of Firearms Usage in Selected Crimes, by Region: 1980–1982

Region	Murder[1] 1980	1981	1982	Aggravated assault 1980	1981	1982	Robbery 1980	1981	1982
Northeast	54.2	53.4	52.2	15.5	16.9	14.9	32.6	34.6	33.2
North Central	62.8	62.8	60.6	25.0	22.5	23.1	42.0	38.3	38.9
South	68.4	68.0	65.8	27.6	27.8	26.1	46.7	46.9	47.3
West	57.8	57.6	55.1	24.5	23.3	22.0	43.2	42.0	41.2
U.S. Total	**62.4**	**62.4**	**60.2**	**23.9**	**23.6**	**22.4**	**40.3**	**40.1**	**39.9**

1. Murder includes non-negligent manslaughter. *Source:* U.S. Federal Bureau of Investigation, *Crime in the United States,* annual.

Reported Child Neglect and Abuse Cases: 1979 to 1981

Division	1981 population (1,000)	Total number of reports (1,000): 1981	1980	1979	Reports per 1,000 population: 1981	1980	1979
New England	12,448	39.0	48.3	41.3	3.1	3.9	3.3
Middle Atlantic	36.893	101.9	91.8	85.5	2.8	2.5	2.3
North Central	59,856	196.2	183.0	171.4	7.7	7.0	6.4
South Atlantic	37.695	174.8	154.5	126.2	4.6	4.2	3.5
South Central	39,160	154.5	127.9	112.4	8.1	6.9	6.9
Mountain	11,706	37.3	27.7	38.6	3.2	3.3	2.9
Pacific	32,489	142.5	141.8	111.7	4.4	4.4	4.1
U.S. Total	**229,348**	**846.2**	**785.1**	**707.4**	**3.7**	**3.5**	**3.2**

Source: American Humane Association, *National Analysis of Official Child Neglect and Abuse Reporting,* annual.

Prisoners Under Sentence of Death

Characteristic	1982	1981	1980
White	604	488	427
Black and other	446	350	287
Under 20 years	18	15	11
20–24 years	195	171	173
25–34 years	531	415	334
35–54 years	294	224	186
55 years and over	12	13	10
Schooling completed:			
7 years or less	81	74	68
8 years	105	83	74
9–11 years	318	247	204
12 years	258	199	162
More than 12 years	78	57	43
Unknown	210	178	163

Characteristic	1982	1981	1980
Marital status:			
Never married	413	327	268
Married	317	259	229
Divorced or separated[1]	320	252	217
Time elapsed since sentencing:			
6 months or less } 7–12 months	264	227	185
13–47 months	525	416	389
48–71 months[2]	150	110	102
72 months and over	111	85	38
Legal status at arrest:			
Not under sentence	556	433	384
On parole or probation	182	147	115
In prison or escaped	53	46	45
Unknown	259	212	170
Total	**1,050**	**838**	**714**

1. Includes widows, widowers, and unknown. 2. 4–8 years, more than 8 years prior to 1980. NOTE: As of Dec. 31. Excludes prisoners under sentence of death confined in local correctional systems pending appeal or who had not been committed to prison. *Source:* Department of Justice, Law Enforcement Assistance Administration; after 1978 U.S. Bureau of Justice Statistics, *Capital Punishment,* annual.

Methods of Execution[1]

State	Method
Alabama[2]	Electrocution
Alaska	No death penalty
Arizona[2]	Lethal gas
Arkansas[2]	Electrocution
California*	Lethal gas
Colorado[2]	Lethal gas
Connecticut[2,*]	Electrocution
Delaware	Hanging
D.C.	No death penalty
Florida*	Electrocution
Georgia[2]	Electrocution
Hawaii	No death penalty
Idaho[2]	Lethal injection
Illinois	Electrocution
Indiana[2]	Electrocution
Iowa	No death penalty
Kansas	No death penalty
Kentucky[2]	Electrocution
Louisiana[2,*]	Electrocution
Maine	No death penalty
Maryland[2]	Lethal gas
Massachusetts[6]	No death penalty
Michigan	No death penalty
Minnesota	No death penalty
Mississippi[2]	Lethal injection
Missouri	Lethal gas
Montana[2]	Hanging, or lethal injection[7]
Nebraska[2]	Electrocution
Nevada[2]	Lethal injection
New Hampshire[2]	Hanging
New Jersey	Lethal injection
New Mexico*	Lethal injection
New York	No death penalty
North Carolina[2]	Lethal gas or injection
North Dakota	No death penalty
Ohio[2]	Electrocution
Oklahoma	Lethal injection
Oregon	No death penalty
Pennsylvania[2,*]	Electrocution
Rhode Island	No death penalty([3])
South Carolina[2,*]	Electrocution
South Dakota	Electrocution
Tennessee[2]	Electrocution
Texas[2]	Lethal injection
Utah[2,*]	Firing squad
Vermont	Electrocution
Virginia*	Electrocution
Washington[2,*]	Hanging or lethal injection
West Virginia	No death penalty
Wisconsin	No death penalty
Wyoming	Lethal gas
U.S. (Fed. Govt.)	([4])
American Samoa	([5])
Guam	No death penalty
Puerto Rico	No death penalty
Virgin Islands	No death penalty

1. On July 1, 1976, by a 7-2 decision, the U.S. Supreme Court upheld the death penalty as not being "cruel or unusual." However, in another ruling the same day, the Court, by a 5-4 vote, stated that states may not impose "mandatory" capital punishment on every person convicted of murder. These decisions left uncertain the fate of condemned persons throughout the U.S. On Oct. 4, the Court refused to reconsider its July ruling, which allows some states to proceed with executions of condemned prisoners. The first execution in this country since 1967 was in Utah on Jan. 17, 1977. Gary Mark Gilmore was executed by shooting. 2. Voted to restore death penalty after June 29, 1972, Supreme Court decision ruling capital punishment unconstitutional. 3. Person shall be executed by gas if he commits murder while serving a prison term. 4. Method shall be that used by state in which sentence is imposed. If state does not have death penalty, federal judge shall prescribe method for carrying out sentence. 5. New criminal code re-establishes death penalty but at this time prescribes no method. 6. Death penalty has been passed, but not been used. 7. Defendent may choose between hanging and a lethal injection. *Source: Information Please* questionnaires to the states. NOTE: An asterisk after the name of the state indicates non-reply.

Motor Vehicle Laws, 1984

State	Date new license plates can be used	Age for driver's license[1]			State gasoline tax	Percent state tax[3]	Annual safety inspection required
		Regular	Learner's	Restrictive			
Alabama	On issue	16	16	14[10]	$.11	1 1/2	no[24]
Alaska	On issue	18		14[6]	.08	—	no[24]
Arizona	On issue	18		16[6]	.12	4	no[25]
Arkansas	On issue	18	([5])	14[6]	.095	3	yes
California	On issue	18	15[4,7]	16[4]	.09	6	no[24]
Colorado	On issue	21	15 1/2[5]	16[6]	.12	3	no[26]
Connecticut	On issue	18		16[4]	.16	7 1/2	yes[27,28]
Delaware	On issue	18	16	16[4]	.11	([16])	yes
D. C.	On issue	18	([5])	16[6]	.13	([17])	yes
Florida	On issue	16	([5])	15[6]	.08	5	no
Georgia	Jan. 1	18	15	16[6]	.075	3	no
Hawaii	On issue	18	([5])	15[6]	([13])	([18])	yes[29]
Idaho	On issue	16	([5])	14[4]	.145	4 1/2	no
Illinois	On issue	18	([5])	16[4,6]	.075	4	no[30]
Indiana	On issue	18	16[8]	16 1/2[4,6]	.105[14]	5	no
Iowa	On issue	18	14	16[4]	.13	4	([31])
Kansas	On issue	16	([5])	14	.08	3	([24,31])
Kentucky	On issue	18	([5])	16[6]	.10	5	no
Louisiana	On issue	17		15[11]	.08	3	yes
Maine	On issue	17	([5])	15[4]	.09	5	yes
Maryland	March 1	18	([5])	16[4,6]	.13	5	no[32]
Massachusetts	On issue	18	([5])	16[4,6]	.104	5	6 mos.
Michigan	On issue	18		16[4,6]	.13	4	no[24]
Minnesota	On issue	18	([5])	16[4]	.17	6	no[24]
Mississippi	On issue	15	([5])	16	.09	3	yes
Missouri	On issue	16		15[4]	.07	4	yes
Montana	On issue	18	([5])	15[4,6]	.09	1 1/2[19]	no
Nebraska	On issue	16	15[5]	14	.137	4	no
Nevada	On issue	18	15 1/2[5]	16[6]	.12	2[20]	no
New Hampshire	On issue	18		16[4]	.14	—	6 mos.
New Jersey	On issue	17		16	.08	6	2 yrs.
New Mexico	Dec. 15	16	15	14[12]	.11	2	no
New York	On issue	17[4]		16[6]	.08[15]	4	yes
North Carolina	On issue	18		15[4,6]	.12	2[21]	yes
North Dakota	Feb. 1	16	([5])	14[4,6]	.13	4	no[24]
Ohio	1st day/mo. of exp.	18	16[5,6]	14[3]	.12	5	no[24]
Oklahoma	On issue	16		15 1/2[4]	.0658	2	yes
Oregon	On issue	16	15[5]	14	.09	—	no[24]
Pennsylvania	On issue	17[4]	17[8]	16[6]	.12	6	yes
Rhode Island	On issue	18	([5])	16[4]	.11	6	yes
South Carolina	On issue	16	15[9]	15	.13	4	yes
South Dakota	Jan. 1	16	([5])	14	.13	4[22]	no
Tennessee	On issue	16	([5])	15	.10	4 1/2[23]	no
Texas	On issue	16[4]	15[7]	15[3]	.05	4	yes
Utah	On issue	16[4]	([5])		.11	4	yes
Vermont	On issue	18	15[5]	16[7]	.13	4	yes
Virginia	On issue	18	15 3/4[5,6]	16[4,6]	.11	2	yes
Washington	On issue	18	15[8]	16[4]	.135	5 1/2	no[24]
West Virginia	On issue	18	([5])	16[6]	.105	5	yes
Wisconsin	On issue	18	([5])	16[4]	.15	5	no
Wyoming	Jan. 1	18	15[6,7]	16[6]	.08	3	no

1. Full driving privileges at age given in "Regular" column. A license restricted or qualified in some manner may be obtained at age given in "Restricted" column. 2. Applicable to car sales (local and county sales taxes extra where applicable). 3. Upon proof of hardship. 4. Must have completed approved driver education course. 5. Learner's permit required. 6. Guardian's or parental consent required. 7. Driver with learner's permit must be accompanied by locally licensed operator 18 years or older. 8. Must be enrolled in driver education course. 9. Driver with learner's permit must be accompanied by locally licensed operator 21 years or older. 10. Restricted to mopeds. 11. All persons under 17 are prohibited from operating vehicles between 11 p.m. and 5 a.m. 12. For use while enrolled in driver education course. Must be accompanied by instructor. 13. 8.5–13.5¢ varies by county. 14. 8% of retail price plus 4% sales tax. 15. New York City leaded gasoline tax, 1¢ extra per gallon. 16. Document fee of 2% of cost of car. 17. 4–7% depending on weight of car. 18. 4% on cars purchased out of state only. 19. Periodic reductions for cars purchased later in year. 20. Plus 1 1/2% school support tax and 2 1/4% city and county relief tax in all counties. 21. $120 maximum. 22. Tax on first registration. 23. Some counties have an additional 1 to 2 1/4% county tax. 24. State troopers are authorized to inspect at their discretion. 25. Arizona emission inspection fee $5.26. Annual emissions test in some counties. 27. Used motor vehicles being registered in Connecticut from out-of-state are required to be inspected and approved and Connecticut cars 10 years old and older must be inspected upon being sold or transferred. 28. Annual emissions test. 29. If car is 10 years or older, every 6 months. 30. Trucks and buses only. 31. Prior to first registration and transfers. 32. All used vehicles upon resale or transfer. NOTES: A driver's license is required in every state. The national speed limit is 55 miles per hour. All states have an *implied consent* Chemical Test Law for alcohol. *Source:* American Automobile Association.

Law Enforcement Officers Killed in Line of Duty

(beginning 1973, includes federal officers)

Area	1982	1981	1980	1979	1978	1977	1976	1975	1970	1965	1960
New England	5	5	3	—	3	2	4	4	2	3	3
Middle Atlantic	12	12	20	13	9	12	15	24	29	10	7
East North Central	32	16	8	13	5	10	19	32	38	10	9
West North Central	9	13	7	3	5	14	11	8	6	3	3
South Atlantic	29	35	21	23	15	31	34	31	23	15	13
East South Central	13	21	9	15	13	11	14	18	5	9	2
West South Central	33	24	15	11	19	21	21	22	15	14	6
Mountain	11	8	5	8	5	3	4	14	4	7	0
Pacific	16	19	9	15	15	15	13	22	24	12	5
Puerto Rico and Virgin Islands	4	3	7	3	4	2	4	9	n.a.	n.a.	n.a.
CAUSE											
By felons	92	91	104	106[4]	93	93	111	129[1]	100	53	n.a.
In accidents	72	66	61	59	53	30[3]	29	56	46	30	n.a.
Total	**164**	**157**	**165**[3]	**165**[4]	**146**	**123**[3]	**140**[2]	**185**[1]	**146**	**83**	**48**

1. Includes one officer in Guam. 2. Includes one officer killed in Bogota, Colombia. 3. Includes one officer killed in Virgin Islands. 4. Includes two officers killed on Guam. NOTE: n.a. = not available. *Source:* Department of Justice, Federal Bureau of Investigation, *Law Enforcement Officers Killed and Assaults,* annual.

Minimum Legal Age for Purchase of Liquor, Wine, and Beer

State	Liquor	Wine	Beer
Alabama	19	19	19
Alaska	21	21	21
Arizona	21	21	21
Arkansas	21	21	21
California	21	21	21
Colorado	21	21	21[1]
Connecticut	20	20	20
Delaware	21	21	21
D.C.	21	21[2]	18
Florida	19	19	19
Georgia	19	19	19
Hawaii	18	18	18
Idaho	19	19	19
Illinois	21	21	21
Indiana	21	21	21
Iowa	19	19	19
Kansas	21	21	21[1]
Kentucky	21	21	21
Louisiana	18	18	18
Maine	20	20	20
Maryland	21	21	21
Massachusetts	20	20	20
Michigan	21	21	21
Minnesota	19	19	19
Mississippi	21	21[2]	21[3]
Missouri	21	21	21
Montana	19	19	19
Nebraska	21	21	21
Nevada	21	21	21
New Hampshire	20	20	20
New Jersey	21	21	21
New Mexico	21	21	21
New York	19	19	19
North Carolina	21	21[4]	19
North Dakota	21	21	21
Ohio	21	21	19
Oklahoma	21	21	21
Oregon	21	21	21
Pennsylvania	21	21	21
Rhode Island	21	21	21
South Carolina	21	18	18
South Dakota	21	21	21[5]
Tennessee	21	21	21
Texas	19	19	19
Utah	21	21	21
Vermont	18	18	18
Virginia	21	21	19
Washington	21	21	21
West Virginia[6]	19	19	19
Wisconsin	19	19	19
Wyoming	19	19	19

1. 3.2 beer: 18. 2. Light wine: 18. 3. Up to 4% alcohol by weight: 18. 4. 19 for light wine. 5. 3.2 beer: 19. 6. 19 for all beverages for in-state residents; 21 for out-of-state residents. *Source:* Distilled Spirits Council of the United States.

Guns and Suicide

In the past three decades since 1953, the number of suicides committed with guns has increased at twice the rate of the other two common means of suicide, gas and poison. The study, conducted by Dr. Jeffrey H. Boyd of the National Institute of Mental Health in Rockville, Md., also noted that pistols accounted for 83% of the firearms used in suicide. The study raises the possibility that by restricting the sale of handguns the suicide rate might be reduced.

U.S. District Courts—Criminal Cases Commenced and Defendants Disposed of, by Nature of Offense: 1981 and 1982

[For years ending June 30]

		DISPOSITION OF DEFENDANTS, 1982								1981	
		Not convicted		Convicted			Sentenced				
Nature of offense	1982 cases commenced[1]	Total	Acquitted	Total	Guilty plea	Court or jury	Imprisonment	Probation	Fine and other	Cases commenced[1]	Defendants disposed of
General offenses:											
Homicide	151	42	13	130	79	51	89	14	27	186	168
Robbery	1,427	219	50	1,526	1,195	331	1,431	91	4	1,415	1,514
Assault	579	195	45	411	326	85	271	121	19	559	630
Burglary	143	33	2	141	111	30	100	40	1	125	143
Larceny—theft	2,887	688	97	2,869	2,597	272	1,265	1,434	170	3,030	3,753
Embezzlement and fraud	6,781	1,175	224	6,801	5,922	879	2,700	3,911	190	6,580	7,631
Auto theft	369	90	9	429	362	67	306	120	3	350	543
Forgery, counterfeiting	2,128	371	43	1,909	1,724	185	1,075	825	9	1,810	2,102
Sex offenses	135	36	6	107	71	36	81	19	7	152	156
DAPCA[3]	4,193	1,645	285	6,336	4,798	1,538	4,586	1,617	133	3,697	7,008
Misc. general offenses	8,757	2,596	248	6,591	5,707	884	2,177	1,942	2,472	8,416	8,395
Total[2]	**31,623**	**8,214**	**1,163**	**32,252**	**27,392**	**4,860**	**15,857**	**12,723**	**3,672**	**30,355**	**38,127**

1. Excludes transfers. 2. Includes items not shown separately. 3. All marijuana, narcotics, and controlled substances under the Drug, Abuse, Prevention and Control Act. *Source: Statistical Abstract of the United States,* 1984.

Murder Victims by Weapons Used

		Weapons used or cause of death						
		Guns						
Year	Murder victims, total	Total	Percent	Cutting or stabbing	Blunt object[1]	Strangulation and hands, fists, feet	Drownings, arson, etc.	All other[2]
1965	8,773	5,015	57.2	2,021	505	894	226	112
1968	12,503	8,105	64.8	2,317	713	936	294	138
1969	13,575	8,876	65.4	2,534	613	1,039	322	191
1970	13,649	9,039	66.2	2,424	604	1,031	353	198
1971	16,183	10,712	66.2	3,017	645	1,295	314	200
1972	15,832	10,379	65.6	2,974	672	1,291	331	185
1973	17,123	11,249	65.7	2,985	848	1,445	173[3]	423
1974	18,632	12,474	66.9	3,228	976	1,417	153[3]	384
1975	18,642	12,061	64.7	3,245	1,001	1,646	193[3]	496
1976	16,605	10,592	63.8	2,956	806	1,330	227[3]	694
1977	18,033	11,274	62.5	3,440	849	1,431	252[3]	787
1978	18,714	11,910	63.6	3,526	896	1,422	255[3]	705
1979	20,591	13,040	63.3	3,954	997	1,557	276[3]	767
1980	21,860	13,650	62.0	4,212	1,094	1,666	291[3]	947
1981	20,053	12,523	62.4	3,886	1,038	1,469	258[3]	658
1982	19,485	11,721	60.2	4,065	957	1,657	279[3]	630

1. Refers to club, hammer, etc. 2. Includes poison, explosives, unknown, and not stated; for 1973 to 1976, includes drowning. 3. Arson only. *Source:* Department of Justice, Federal Bureau of Investigation, *Uniform Crime Reports for the United States, 1983.*

1982 Prison Population Hits an All-Time High

The prison population increased by 42,915 in 1982, bringing the total number of inmates to a record high of 412,303. Of these, 29,673 were in federal prisons; the remaining 382,630 were in state prisons. Officials believe that tougher sentencing and more restrictive parole laws accounted for the rise, the largest in absolute numbers since 1925 when the first count was made.

Average Time Served by Prisoners Released from Federal Institutions for First Time: 1965 to 1982[1]

(For years ending June 30; except beginning 1977, years ending September 30)

Year and offense	All first releases[1]			Parole[1]		
		Average time (mo.)			Average time (mo.)	
	Number	Sentence	Served	Number	Sentence	Served
1965, all offenses.	12,100	32.6	19.9	3,394	42.6	18.3
1970, all offenses.	8,487	38.6	19.7	2,754	55.0	20.0
1975, all offenses.	11,313	39.8	18.5	4,367	73.7	27.8
1976, all offenses.	10,463	32.3	15.1	3,114	74.3	26.9
1977, all offenses.	10,953	30.7	15.5	2,688	70.8	26.5
1978, all offenses.	12,132	37.2	18.7	3,318	78.5	30.0
1979, all offenses.	10,925	44.1	21.0	3,766	85.1	32.6
1980, all offenses.	9,069	33.9	15.9	2,440	83.8	31.0
1981, all offenses.	9,884	41.0	17.9	3,495	83.9	30.2
1982, all offenses[2]	**11,348**	**36.6**	**16.3**	**3,554**	**81.7**	**29.1**
Counterfeiting	242	30.9	15.8	99	51.8	18.7
Drug laws	2,496	46.3	20.3	1,114	73.4	26.6
Embezzlement	300	18.1	8.7	79	41.7	15.9
Escape, flight, or harboring a fugitive	104	28.7	16.6	33	49.2	23.8
Firearms	492	29.4	15.8	116	60.5	24.4
Forgery	401	31.0	15.5	167	48.1	19.9
Fraud	748	20.4	10.5	204	43.2	16.8
Immigration	2,625	6.3	4.2	116	33.2	13.5
Income tax	244	12.0	7.0	44	31.5	12.3
Juvenile delinquency	2	44.5	26.5	1	31.0	10.0
Kidnaping	47	217.0	64.7	35	258.1	67.3
Larceny—theft	1,445	31.7	16.2	521	52.1	21.3
Motor vehicle, interstate	252	44.6	23.1	123	57.3	23.9
Liquor laws	7	20.1	11.2	3	38.0	19.3
Robbery	742	138.3	50.3	539	165.1	53.6
Securities, transporting false	46	58.7	29.3	19	99.0	42.4
White slave traffic	20	50.6	26.1	7	74.2	36.0
Military court-martial cases	28	93.8	45.0	12	142.6	59.1
Govt. reservation, high seas, territories, and D.C.	518	55.8	23.0	192	116.8	40.7

1. Excludes prisoners sentenced under Youth Corrections Act. 2. Includes other offenses not shown separately. Excludes 585 releases (escapes, pardons, etc.) other than by parole, expiration of sentence, and mandatory release; also excludes 278 second or subsequent releases. *Source:* U.S. Bureau of Prisons, *Statistical Report,* annual.

Drug Use by Type of Drug and by Age Group: 1982

Type of drug	Percent of youths		Percent of young adults		Percent of adults	
	Ever used	Current user	Ever used	Current user	Ever used	Current user
Marihauna	26.7	11.5	64.1	27.4	23.0	6.6
Inhalants	n.a.	n.a.	n.a.	n.a.	n.a.	n.a.
Hallucinogens	5.2	1.4	21.1	1.7	6.4	1.2
Cocaine	6.5	1.6	28.3	6.8	8.5	n.a.
Heroin	(Z)	(Z)	1.2	(Z)	1.1	0.6

Current users are those who used drugs at least once within month prior to this study. The study is based on national samples of 1,581 youths (12–17 years old), 1,283 young adults (18–25 years old), and 2,760 older adults (26 years old and over). Z = less than 5%. n.a. = not available. *Source:* National Institute of Drug Abuse, *National Survey on Drug Abuse: Main Findings, 1982.*

Marihuana and Alcohol—Percent of Population Who Are Current Users: 1976–1982

Characteristics	Youths			Young adults			Adults		
	1976	1979	1982	1976	1979	1982	1976	1979	1982
MARIHUANA									
Current users, total	12	17	12	25	35	27	4	6	7
Male	14	19	13	31	45	36	6	9	10
Female	11	14	10	19	20	19	2	3	3
ALCOHOL									
Current users, total	32	37	27	69	76	68	56	61	57
Male	36	39	27	79	84	75	63	72	69
Female	29	36	27	58	68	61	49	52	46

Source: U.S. Institute on Drug Abuse, *National Survey on Drug Abuse: Main Findings, 1982.*

Federal Prosecutions of Public Corruption: 1973 to 1982

(Prosecution of persons who have corrupted public office in violation of Federal Criminal Statutes. As of Dec. 31, 1982)

Prosecution status	1982	1981	1980	1979	1978	1977	1976	1975	1974	1973
Total:[1] Indicted	729	878	721	687	557	507	563	255	291	244
Convicted	671	730	552	555	409	440	380	179	217	181
Awaiting trial	186	231	213	187	205	210	199	27	5	18
Federal officials: Indicted	158	198	123	128	133	129	111	53	59	60
Convicted	147	159	131	115	91	94	101	43	51	48
Awaiting trial	38	23	16	21	42	32	1	5	1	2
State officials: Indicted	49	87	72	58	55	50	59	36	36	19
Convicted	43	66	51	32	56	38	35	18	23	17
Awaiting trial	18	36	28	30	20	33	30	5	—	—
Local officials: Indicted	257	244	247	212	171	157	194	139	130	85
Convicted	232	211	168	156	127	164	100	94	87	64
Awaiting trial	58	102	82	67	72	62	98	15	4	2

1. Includes individuals who are neither public officials nor employees, but who were involved with public officials or employees in violating the law, now shown separately. NOTE:—represents zero. *Source:* U.S. Department of Justice, *Federal Prosecutions of Corrupt Public Officials, 1970–1980,* and *Report to Congress on the Activities and Operations of the Public Integrity Section, 1981.*

Legal Abortions—Estimated Number, Rate, and Ratio by Race: 1972 to 1980

Year	White				Black and other			
	Women 15–44 yr[1] old (1,000)	Number of abortions (1,000)	Abortion rate per 1,000 women	Abortion rate per 1,000 live births	Women 15–44 yr[1] old (1,000)	Number of abortions (1,000)	Abortion rate per 1,000 women	Abortion rate per 1,000 live births
1972	38,532	455.3	11.8	175	6,056	131.5	21.7	223
1975	40,857	701.2	17.2	275	6,749	333.0	49.3	562
1976	41,721	784.9	18.8	306	7,000	394.4	56.3	657
1977	42,567	888.8	20.9	330	7,247	427.9	59.0	673
1978	43,427	969.4	22.3	362	7,493	440.2	58.7	675
1979	44,266	1,062.4	24.0	378	7,750	435.3	56.2	635
1980	44,942	1,093.6	24.3	376	8,106	460.3	56.8	642

1. Refers to women 15–44 years old at time of abortion. NOTE: n.a. = not available. *Source:* The Alan Guttmacher Institute, New York, N.Y., unpublished data.

Firsts in America

This selection is based on our editorial judgment. Other sources may list different firsts.

Admiral in U.S. Navy: David Glasgow Farragut, 1866.

Air-mail route, first transcontinental: Between New York City and San Francisco, 1920.

Assembly, representative: House of Burgesses, founded in Virginia, 1619.

Bank established: Bank of North America, Philadelphia, 1781.

Birth in America to English parents: Virginia Dare, born Roanoke Island, N.C., 1587.

Botanic garden: Established by John Bartram in Philadelphia, 1728. (Oldest still existing was established in Cambridge, Mass., in 1807.)

Cartoon, colored: "The Yellow Kid," by Richard Outcault, in *New York World,* 1895.

College: Harvard, founded 1636.

College to confer degrees on women: Oberlin (Ohio) College, 1841.

College to establish coeducation: Oberlin (Ohio) College, 1833.

Electrocution of a criminal: William Kemmler in Auburn Prison, Auburn, N.Y., Aug. 6, 1890.

Five and Ten Cents Store: Founded by Frank Woolworth, Utica, N.Y., 1879 (moved to Lancaster, Pa., same year).

Fraternity: Phi Beta Kappa; founded Dec. 5, 1776, at College of William and Mary.

Law to be declared unconstitutional by U.S. Supreme Court: Judiciary Act of 1789. Case: *Marbury* v. *Madison,* 1803.

Library, circulating: Philadelphia, 1731.

Newspaper, illustrated daily: *New York Daily Graphic,* 1873.

Newspaper published daily: *Pennsylvania Packet and General Advertiser,* Philadelphia, Sept., 1784.

Newspaper published over a continuous period: *The Boston News-Letter,* April, 1704.

Newsreel: Pathé Frères of Paris, in 1910, circulated a weekly issue of their *Pathé Journal.*

Oil well, commercial: Titusville, Pa., 1859.

Panel quiz show on radio: *Information Please,* May 17, 1938.

Postage stamps issued: 1847.

Railroad, transcontinental: Central Pacific and Union Pacific railroads, joined at Promontory, Utah, May 10, 1869.

Savings bank: The Provident Institute for Savings, Boston, 1816.

Science museum: Founded by Charleston (S.C.) Library Society, 1773.

Skyscraper: Home Insurance Co., Chicago, 1885 (10 floors, 2 added later).

Slaves brought into America: At Jamestown, Va., 1619, from a Dutch ship.

Sorority: Kappa Alpha Theta, at De Pauw University, 1870.

State to abolish capital punishment: Michigan, 1847.

State to enter Union after original 13: Vermont, 1791.

Steam-heated building: Eastern Hotel, Boston, 1845.

Steam railroad (carried passengers and freight): Baltimore & Ohio, 1830.

Strike on record by union: Journeymen Printers, New York City, 1776.

Subway: Opened in Boston, 1897.

"Tabloid" picture newspaper: *The Illustrated Daily News* (now *The Daily News*), New York City, 1919.

Vaudeville theater: Gaiety Museum, Boston, 1883.

Woman cabinet member: Frances Perkins, Secretary of Labor, 1933.

Woman candidate for President: Victoria Claflin Woodhull, nominated by National Woman's Suffrage Assn. on ticket of Nation Radical Reformers, 1872.

Woman candidate for Vice-President: Geraldine A. Ferraro, nominated by a major party on ticket of the Democratic Party, 1984.

Woman doctor of medicine: Elizabeth Blackwell; M.D. from Geneva Medical College of Western New York, 1849.

Woman elected governor of a state: Mrs. Nellie Tayloe Ross, Wyoming, 1925.

Woman elected to U.S. Senate: Mrs. Hattie Caraway, Arkansas; elected Nov., 1932.

Woman graduate of law school: Mrs. Ada H. Kepley, Union College of Law, Chicago, 1870.

Woman member of U.S. House of Representatives: Jeannette Rankin; elected Nov., 1916.

Woman member of U.S. Senate: Mrs. Rebecca Latimer Felton of Georgia; appointed Oct. 3, 1922.

Woman member of U.S. Supreme Court: Mrs. Sandra Day O'Connor; appointed July 1981.

Woman suffrage granted: Wyoming Territory, 1869.

Written constitution: *Fundamental Orders of Connecticut,* 1639.

ENTERTAINMENT & CULTURE

Notable Books, 1983

This list has been compiled by the Notable Books Council, Reference and Adult Services, a division of the American Library Association for use by the general reader and by librarians who work with adult readers. The titles were selected for their significant contribution to the expansion of knowledge or for the pleasure they can provide to adult readers. Criteria include wide general appeal and literary merit.

Bradford, Sarah, **Disraeli,** Stein & Day
Bricktop, with James Haskins, **Bricktop,** Atheneum
Carver, Raymond, **Cathedral: Stories,** Knopf
Chase, Joan, **During the Reign of the Queen of Persia: A Novel,** Harper
Chatwin, Bruce, **On the Black Hill,** Viking
Clampitt, Amy, **The Kingfisher: Poems,** Knopf
Didion, Joan, **Salvador,** Simon & Schuster
Down & Out in the Great Depression: Letters from the "Forgotten Man," edited by Robert S. McElvaine, University of North Carolina Press
Drew, Elizabeth, **Politics and Money: The New Road to Corruption,** Macmillan
Dubus, Andre, **The Times Are Never So Bad: A Novella & Eight Short Stories,** Godine
Egerton, John, **Generations: An American Family,** University Press of Kentucky
Fossey, Dian, **Gorillas in the Mist,** Houghton
Gage, Nicholas, **Eleni,** Random
García Márquez, Gabriel, **Chronicle of a Death Foretold,** translated from the Spanish by Gregory Rabassa, Knopf
Heat Moon, William Least, **Blue Highways: A Journey into America,** Atlantic/Little
Helprin, Mark, **Winter's Tale,** Harcourt
Hersh, Seymour M., **The Price of Power: Kissinger in the Nixon White House,** Summit
Hilts, Philip J., **Scientific Temperaments: Three Lives in Contemporary Science,** Simon & Schuster
Isaacs, Arnold R., **Without Honor: Defeat in Vietnam and Cambodia,** Johns Hopkins University Press
Jensen, Robert, and Patricia Conway, **Ornamentalism: The New Decorativeness in Architecture & Design,** Potter
Kennedy, William, **Ironweed: A Novel,** Viking
Lamb, David, **The Africans,** Random
LeVot, André, **F. Scott Fitzgerald: A Biography,** translated from the French by William Byron, Doubleday
Liang Heng and Judith Shapiro, **Son of the Revolution,** Knopf
Loewinsohn, Ron, **Magnetic Field(s): A Novel,** Knopf
MacLaverty, Bernard, **Cal,** Braziller
Malamud, Bernard, **The Stories of Bernard Malamud,** Farrar
Murdoch, Iris, **The Philosopher's Pupil,** Viking
Page, Joseph A., **Peron: A Biography,** Random
Pancake, Breece D'J., **The Stories of Breece D'J Pancake,** Atlantic/Little
Parry, Linda, **William Morris Textiles,** Viking/Studio
Petrosky, Anthony, **Jurgis Petraskas: Poems,** Louisiana State University Press
Porter, Eliot, **All Under Heaven: The Chinese World,** text by Jonathan Porter, Pantheon
Radosh, Ronald, and Joyce Milton, **The Rosenberg File: A Search for the Truth,** Holt
Rockwell, John, **All American Music: Composition in the Twentieth Century,** Knopf
Rushdie, Salman, **Shame,** Knopf
Silverman, Jonathan, **For the World to See: The Life of Margaret Bourke-White,** Viking/Studio
Song, Cathy, **Picture Bride,** Yale University Press
Theroux, Paul, **The London Embassy,** Houghton
Updike, John, **Hugging the Shore: Essays and Criticism,** Knopf
Warner, William W., **Distant Water: The Fate of the North Atlantic Fisherman,** Atlantic/Little
Wideman, John Edgar, **Send for You Yesterday,** Avon
Wilcox, Fred A., **Waiting for an Army to Die: The Tragedy of Agent Orange,** Random
Wright, Stephen, **Meditations in Green,** Scribner

Source: Reprinted by permission of the American Library Association. Issued as a pamphlet by ALA, 50 E. Huron St., Chicago, Ill. 60611, annually in the spring for the preceding year © American Library Association 1984.

Major U.S. Symphony Orchestras and Their Music Directors

Source: American Symphony Orchestra League.

Atlanta Symphony: Robert Shaw
Baltimore Symphony: David Zinman
Boston Symphony: Seiji Ozawa
Buffalo Philharmonic: Julius Rudel
Chicago Symphony: Georg Solti
Cincinnati Symphony: Michael Gielen
Cleveland Orchestra: Christoph von Dohnanyi
Dallas Symphony: Eduardo Mata
Denver Symphony: Gaetano Delogu
Detroit Symphony: Gunther Herbig
Houston Symphony: Sergiu Comissiona[1]
Indianapolis Symphony: John Nelson
Los Angeles Philharmonic: André Previn
Milwaukee Symphony: Lukas Foss
Minnesota Orchestra: Neville Marriner
National Symphony: (Washington, D.C.): Mstislav Rostropovich
New Orleans Philharmonic Symphony Orchestra: Philippe Entremont
New York Philharmonic: Zubin Mehta
Oregon Symphony: James DePreist
Philadelphia Orchestra: Riccardo Muti
Pittsburgh Symphony: André Previn
Rochester Philharmonic: David Zinman
Saint Louis Symphony: Leonard Slatkin
Saint Paul Chamber Orchestra: Pinchas Zukerman
San Antonio Symphony: Lawrence Smith
San Diego Symphony: David Atherton
San Francisco Symphony: Herbert Blamstedt
Seattle Symphony: Gerard Schwarz
Syracuse Symphony: Christopher Keene
Utah Symphony: Joseph Silverstein

1. Artistic Advisor.

Major Public Libraries

City (branches)	Volumes	Circulation	Budget (in millions)
Akron–Summit County, Ohio (18)	994,079	2,063,625	$ 4.8
Albuquerque, N.M. (8)	404,782	1,745,636	3.1
Annapolis, Md. (12)	1,154,763	3,774,619	5.2
Atlanta (26)	1,600,000	4,218,210	8.3
Austin, Tex. (15)	775,850	1,986,909	7.4
Baltimore (33)	1,946,942[1]	2,095,895	10.7
Baton Rouge, La. (9)	466,782	1,514,257	2.4
Birmingham, Ala. (18)	1,100,118	2,000,158	4.3
Boston (24)	4,950,123	1,454,414	11.1
Buffalo–Erie County, N.Y. (60)	3,426,033	6,231,371	13.1
Charleston–Kanawha County, W.Va. (11)	519,736	931,770	2.2
Charlotte, N.C. (15)	762,250	2,118,501	6.0
Chicago (88)	4,302,505	8,309,797	47.9
Cincinnati (40)	3,380,203	6,380,265	15.9
Cleveland (31)	2,420,871	3,938,249	19.0
Columbus–Franklin County, Ohio (21)	1,282,583	4,005,808	10.2
Dallas (18)	1,762,621	3,950,601	12.9
Dayton–Montgomery County Ohio (19)	1,344,584	5,075,320	6.7
Denver (21)	1,875,420	2,623,921	10.2
Des Moines, Iowa (5)	493,724	1,270,312	2.3
Detroit (24)	2,421,578	1,442,435	14.5
D.C. (26)	1,359,788	1,624,225	11.5
El Paso (9)	1,060,000	1,170,000	3.0
Erie, Pa. (6)	420,355	1,409,932	1.8
Evansville–Vanderburgh County Ind. (7)	501,806	1,596,806	2.7
Fort Wayne–Allen County, Ind. (12)	1,634,106	2,126,375	5.4
Fort Worth (8)	798,544	2,920,351	3.7
Grand Rapids, Mich. (5)	617,835	795,280	2.3
Greenville City–County S.C. (10)	525,624	1,155,055	2.6
Honolulu (23)	1,525,727	3,647,015	12.4
Houston (29)	2,802,949	6,331,119	15.3
Independence, Mo. (25)	1,280,631	3,128,600	4.4
Indianapolis–Marion County (23)	1,455,602	3,937,289	11.2
Jackson, Miss. (37)	959,545	1,317,170	2.9
Jacksonville, Fla. (11)	1,370,302	1,945,370	3.9
Kansas City, Mo. (13)	1,320,332	949,972	4.7
Knoxville, Tenn. (19)	622,612	1,765,128	2.9
Lincoln, Neb. (9)	432,325	1,260,977	2.4
Long Beach, Calif. (11)	769,256	2,189,365	7.3
Los Angeles (County) (100)	5,101,872	10,080,479	32.9
Louisville, Ky. (20)	1,128,926	2,897,997	5.4
Madison, Wis. (7)	559,432	1,870,571	4.0
Memphis, Tenn. (22)	2,904,692	2,462,189	6.8
Miami–Dade County, Fla. (20)	1,983,312	3,399,787	18.1
Milwaukee (12)	2,261,904	3,522,534	11.6
Minneapolis (14)	1,654,717	2,569,652	10.8
Nashville–Davidson County, Tenn. (15)	560,451	1,590,012	4.3
Newark, N.J. (11)	1,231,560	1,520,544	5.5
New Orleans (11)	828,364	1,168,051	4.4
New York City (82)	3,448,799	8,887,285	40.8
Research	7,582,385	—	26.9
Brooklyn (60)	4,029,237	7,687,104	25.1
Queens (60)	4,638,201	7,663,376	24.0
Norfolk, Va. (11)	724,840	1,130,202	3.2
Oklahoma City–County (10)	669,360	1,968,562	5.9
Omaha, Neb. (9)	560,931	1,670,513	3.4
Philadelphia (52)	2,992,528	5,045,308	20.9
Phoenix, Ariz. (9)	1,173,000	3,833,320	7.9
Pittsburgh (20)	1,886,245	2,981,773	9.5
Portland–Multnomah County, Ore. (16)	1,170,830	3,228,616	5.4
Providence, R.I. (7)	1,203,028	720,056	3.0
Richmond, Va. (7)	687,558	968,670	2.4
Rochester, N.Y. (10)	1,193,690	1,422,859	6.1
Sacramento, Calif. (26)	1,201,438	3,706,083	7.6
St. Louis (14)	1,468,603	1,205,542	6.2
St. Paul (11)	1,118,108	1,925,582	4.2
St. Petersburg, Fla. (4)	460,647	1,218,450	1.7
Salt Lake City–County, Utah (14)	921,788	3,025,685	6.3
San Antonio (12)	1,352,645	2,331,912	6.7
San Diego, Calif. (30)	1,775,900	4,307,634	8.0
San Francisco (26)	1,850,148	2,613,154	13.2
San Jose, Calif. (16)	1,372,000	2,797,400	7.9
Seattle (22)	1,566,424	4,270,919	12.3
Springfield, Mass. (8)	712,414	950,000	3.1
Tampa, Fla. (14)	2,122,137	2,179,402	6.5
Tucson, Ariz. (15)	760,000	3,700,000	6.4
Tulsa City–County, Okla. (20)	577,406	2,021,350	6.9
Wichita, Kan. (11)	552,981	1,214,696	2.7
Winston-Salem–Forsyth County, N.C. (8)	334,098	1,457,672	2.7
Worcester, Mass. (6)	599,327	782,623	2.4
Youngstown–Mahoning County, Ohio (23)	759,949	1,633,963	3.5

Source: Information Please questionnaires to the libraries. 1. Does not include fiction paperbacks.

Glossary of Art Movements

Abstract Expressionism. American art movement of the 1940s that emphasized form and color within a nonrepresentational framework. Jackson Pollock initiated the revolutionary technique of splattering the paint directly on canvas to achieve the subconscious interpretation of the artist's inner vision of reality.

Art Deco. A 1920s style characterized by setbacks, zigzag forms, and the use of chrome and plastic ornamentation. New York's Chrysler Building is an architectural example of the style.

Art Nouveau. An 1890s style in architecture, graphic arts, and interior decoration characterized by writhing forms, curving lines, and asymmetrical organization. Some critics regard the style as the first stage of modern architecture.

Ashcan School. A group of New York realist artists, formed in 1908, who abandoned decorous subject matter and portrayed the more common as well as the sordid aspects of city life.

Assemblage (Collage). Forms of modern sculpture and painting utilizing readymades, found objects, and pasted fragments to form an abstract composition. Louise Nevelson's boxlike enclosures, each with its own composition of assembled objects, illustrate the style in sculpture. Pablo Picasso developed the technique of cutting and pasting natural or manufactured materials to a painted or unpainted surface.

Barbizon School (Landscape Painting). A group of painters who, around the middle of the 19th century, reacted against classical landscape and advocated a direct study of nature. They were influenced by English and Dutch landscape masters. Theodore Rousseau, one of the principal figures of the group, led the fight for outdoor painting. In this respect, the school was a forerunner of Impressionism.

Baroque. European art and architecture of the 17th and 18th centuries. Giovanni Bernini, a major exponent of the style, believed in the union of the arts of architecture, painting, and sculpture to overwhelm the spectator with ornate and highly dramatized themes. Although the style originated in Rome as the instrument of the Church, it spread throughout Europe in such monumental creations as the Palace of Versailles.

Beaux Arts. Elaborate and formal architectural style characterized by symmetry and an abundance of sculptured ornamentation. New York's old Custom House at Bowling Green is an example of the style.

Black or Afro-American Art. The work of American artists of African descent produced in various styles characterized by a mood of protest and a search for identity and historical roots.

Classicism. A form of art derived from the study of Greek and Roman styles characterized by harmony, balance, and serenity. In contrast, the Romantic Movement gave free rein to the artist's imagination and to the love of the exotic.

Constructivism. A form of sculpture using wood, metal, glass, and modern industrial materials expressing the technological society. The mobiles of Alexander Calder are examples of the movement.

Cubism. Early 20th-century French movement marked by a revolutionary departure from representational art. Pablo Picasso and Georges Bracque penetrated the surface of objects, stressing basic abstract geometric forms that presented the object from many angles simultaneously.

Dada. A product of the turbulent and cynical post-World War I period, this anti-art movement extolled the irrational, the absurd, the nihilistic, and the nonsensical. The reproduction of Mona Lisa adorned with a mustache is a famous example. The movement is regarded as a precursor of Surrealism. Some critics regard HAPPENINGS as a recent development of Dada. This movement incorporates environment and spectators as active and important ingredients in the production of random events.

Expressionism. A 20th-century European art movement that stresses the expression of emotion and the inner vision of the artist rather than the exact representation of nature. Distorted lines and shapes and exaggerated colors are used for emotional impact. Vincent Van Gogh is regarded as the precursor of this movement.

Fauvism. The name "wild beasts" was given to the group of early 20th-century French painters because their work was characterized by distortion and violent colors. Henri Matisse and Georges Roualt were leaders of this group.

Futurism. This early 20th-century movement originating in Italy glorified the machine age and attempted to represent machines and figures in motion. The aesthetics of Futurism affirmed the beauty of technological society.

Genre. This French word meaning "type" now refers to paintings that depict scenes of everyday life without any attempt at idealization. Genre paintings can be found in all ages, but the Dutch productions of peasant and tavern scenes are typical.

Impressionism. Late 19th-century French school dedicated to defining transitory visual impressions painted directly from nature, with light and color of primary importance. If the atmosphere changed, a totally different picture would emerge. It was not the object or event that counted but the visual impression as caught at a certain time of day under a certain light. Claude Monet and Camille Pissarro were leaders of the movement.

Mannerism. A mid-16th century movement, Italian in origin, although El Greco was a major practitioner of the style. The human figure, distorted and elongated, was the most frequent subject.

Neoclassicism. An 18th-century reaction to the excesses of Baroque and Rococo, this European art movement tried to recreate the art of Greece and Rome by imitating the ancient classics both in style and subject matter.

Op Art. The 1960s movement known as Optical Painting is characterized by geometrical forms that create an optical illusion in which the eye is required to blend the colors at a certain distance.

Pop Art. In this return to representational art, the artist returns to the world of tangible objects in a reaction against abstraction. Materials are drawn from the everyday world of popular culture—comic strips, canned goods, and science fiction.

Rococo. A French style of interior decoration developed during the reign of Louis XV consisting mainly of asymmetrical arrangements of curves in paneling, porcelain, and gold and silver objects. The characteristics of ornate curves, prettiness, and gaiety can also be found in the painting and sculpture of the period.

Surrealism. A further development of Collage, Cubism, and Dada, this 20th-century movement stresses the weird, the fantastic, and the dream-world of the subconscious.

Celebration for a Lady

On the evening of November 7, 1983, at the New York State Theater in New York City, a gala gathering of stars was on hand for the Inaugural Event for the Statue of Liberty-Ellis Island Centennial. The event was the first in an undertaking to fund the repair and rehabilitation of the Statue of Liberty in time for her centennial celebration in 1986.

Scaffolding went up in the spring of 1984, and on July 4th the torch was lowered during a ceremony on Ellis Island. A plastic model of the torch was lit, and will burn at the base of the statue until the new one is in place.

Top 10 Classical Albums, 1983

1. **Bach: Goldberg Variations,** Glen Gould (CBS)
2. **Pachelbel: Kanon,** Paillard Chamber Orchestra (RCA Red Seal)
3. **Perhaps Love,** Placido Domingo (CBS)
4. **Vivaldi: The Four Seasons,** (Pinnock) (Deutsche Grammophon)
5. **Pachelbel: Canon,** Academy of Ancient Music (Hogwood) (L'Oiseau Lyre)
6. **In Concert at the Met,** Leontyne Price and Marilyn Horne, (Levine) (RCA)
7. **My Life for a Song,** Placido Domingo (CBS)
8. **Canteloube: Songs of the Auvergne,** Kiri Te Kanawa, English Chamber Orchestra (Tate) (London)
9. **Mozart Arias,** Kiri Te Kanawa (Davis) (Philips)
10. **Gladrags,** Labeque Sisters (Angel)

Source: Billboard. © 1983 by Billboard Publications, Inc., Compiled by the Billboard Research Department and reprinted with permission.

Artists of the Year, 1983

Based on combined singles and albums chart performance—through sales and radio play—during the year.

Single of the Year: Every Breath You Take, The Police
Album of the Year: Thriller, Michael Jackson
Female Artist of the Year: Irene Cara
Male Artist of the Year: Michael Jackson
Group of the Year: Men at Work
New Artist of the Year: Culture Club
Country Artist of the Year: Charley Pride
Disco Artist of the Year: Michael Jackson
Adult Contemporary Artist of the Year: Lionel Richie
Jazz Artist of the Year: Al Jarreau
Classical Artist of the Year: Placido Domingo
Soundtrack of the Year: Flashdance

Source: Billboard. © 1983 by Billboard Publications, Inc. Compiled by the Billboard Research Department and reprinted with permission.

Top 10 Pop Albums, 1983

1. **Thriller,** Michael Jackson (Epic)
2. **Business As Usual,** Men at Work (Columbia)
3. **Synchronicity,** The Police (A&M)
4. **H_2O,** Daryl Hall & John Oates (RCA)
5. **1999,** Prince (Warner Bros.)
6. **Lionel Richie,** Lionel Richie (Motown)
7. **Jane Fonda's Workout Record,** Jane Fonda (Columbia)
8. **Pyromania,** Def Leppard (Mercury)
9. **Kissing to be Clever,** Culture Club (Virgin/Epic)
10. **Olivia's Greatest Hits, Vol. 2,** Olivia Newton-John (MCA)

Source: Billboard. © 1983 by Billboard Publications, Inc. Compiled by the Billboard Research Department and reprinted by permission.

Manufacturers' Dollar Shipments of Phonograph Records

(in millions)

	Singles		Albums[3]	
Year	Units	Dollars[1]	Units	Dollars[1]
1977	190	245	344	2,195
1978	190	260	341	2,473
1979[2]	196	275	318	2,136
1980[2]	164	269	323	2,290
1981[2]	155	256	295	2,342
1982[2]	137	283	244	1,925
1983[2]	125	269	210	1,690

1. List price value. 2. Figures based on new data and methodology developed by NPD Research for RIAA. 3. Includes EPs-extended play. *Source:* Recording Industry Association of America, Inc.

Top 10 Country Single Recordings, 1983

1. **Jose Cuervo,** Shelly West (Warner/Viva)
2. **You're Gonna Ruin My Bad Reputation,** Ronnie McDowell (Epic)
3. **Whatever Happened to Old Fashion Love,** B.J. Thomas (Cleveland Int'l/Epic)
4. **He's a Heartache (Looking for a Place to Happen),** Janie Fricke (Columbia)
5. **A Fire I Can't Put Out,** George Strait (MCA)
6. **Pancho & Lefty,** Willie Nelson & Merle Haggard (Epic)
7. **You're the First Time I've Thought About Leaving,** Reba McEntire (Mercury)
8. **I'm Only in It for the Love,** John Conlee (MCA)
9. **Swingin',** John Anderson (Warner Bros.)
10. **Night Games,** Charley Pride (RCA)

Source: Billboard. © 1983 by Billboard Publications, Inc. Compiled by the Billboard Research Department and reprinted with permission.

Top 10 Pop Single Recordings, 1983

1. **Every Breath You Take,** The Police (A&M)
2. **Billie Jean,** Michael Jackson (Epic)
3. **Flashdance-What a Feeling,** Irene Cara (Casablanca)
4. **Down Under,** Men at Work (Columbia)
5. **Beat It,** Michael Jackson (Epic)
6. **Total Eclipse of the Heart,** Bonnie Tyler (Columbia)
7. **Maneater,** Daryl Hall & John Oates (RCA)
8. **Baby Come to Me,** Patti Austin with James Ingram (Quest)
9. **Maniac,** Michael Sembello (Casablanca)
10. **Sweet Dreams (Are Made of This),** Eurythmics (RCA)

Source: Billboard. © 1983 by Billboard Publications, Inc. Compiled by the Billboard Research Department and reprinted with permission.

Top 10 Black Single Recordings, 1983

1. **Sexual Healing,** Marvin Gaye Columbia
2. **Billie Jean,** Michael Jackson, Epic
3. **Juicy Fruit,** Mtaime, Epic
4. **Cold Blooded,** Rick James, Gordy
5. **Atomic Dog,** George Clinton, Capitol
6. **The Girl Is Mine,** Michael Jackson & Paul McCartney, Epic
7. **She Works Hard for Her Money,** Donna Summer, Mercury
8. **Save the Overtime for Me,** Gladys Knight & The Pips, Columbia
9. **Outstanding,** The Gap Band, Total Experience
10. **I Like It,** DeBarge, Gordy

Source: Billboard. © 1983 by Billboard Publications, Inc. Compiled by the Billboard Research Department and reprinted with permission.

Audience Composition of Selected Prime Time Program Types[1]

	General drama	Suspense and mystery drama	Situation comedy	Adventure	Feature films	All regular network programs 7–11 p.m.
Women (18 and over)	11,830,000	12,710,000	10,760,000	10,790,000	12,510,000	11,210,000
Men (18 and over)	7,070,000	9,890,000	7,080,000	9,260,000	9,540,000	8,560,000
Teens (12–17)	1,430,000	1,810,000	2,380,000	2,910,000	2,230,000	2,010,000
Children (2–11)	1,500,000	1,820,000	3,450,000	4,710,000	1,610,000	2,330,000
Total	**21,830,000**	**26,230,000**	**23,670,000**	**27,670,000**	**25,890,000**	**24,110,000**

1. All figures are estimated for the period November 1983. *Source:* A. C. Nielsen Company, Nielsen Television Index Audience Estimates.

Top 15 Regular Prime Time TV Programs of 1983–84[1]

Rank	Program name (network)	Total percent of TV households
1.	ABC Sunday Night Movie[2]	27.7
2.	Dallas (CBS)	26.3
3.	60 Minutes (CBS)	24.8
4.	A Team (NBC)	24.6
5.	Simon & Simon (CBS)	24.3
6.	Falcon Crest (CBS)	22.9
7.	Magnum, P.I. (CBS)	22.8
8.	Dynasty (ABC)	22.4
9.	Hotel (ABC)	20.8
10.	Aftermash (CBS)	20.7
11.	Knots Landing (CBS)	20.0
12.	Newhart (CBS)	19.6
13.	Fall Guy (ABC)	19.4
14.	Love Boat (ABC)	18.9
15.	CBS NFL Football Game 1	18.9
	Total U.S. TV households	**83,971,800**

1. Oct. 24, 1983, through Nov. 20, 1983. NOTE: Percentages are calculated from average audience viewings, 15 minutes or longer and 2 or more telecasts. 2. Includes "Day After" regular episode of ABC Sunday movie. *Source:* A. C. Nielsen Company, Nielsen Television Index Audience Estimates.

Television Network Addresses

American Broadcasting Companies (ABC)
1330 Avenue of the Americas
New York, N.Y. 10019

Canadian Broadcasting Corporation (CBC)
1500 Bronson Avenue
Ottawa, Ontario, Canada K1G 3J5

Columbia Broadcasting System (CBS)
51 W. 52nd Street
New York, N.Y. 10019

Metromedia, Inc. (WNEW)
655 3rd Avenue
New York, N.Y. 10017

National Broadcasting Company (NBC)
30 Rockefeller Plaza
New York, N.Y. 10020

Public Broadcasting Service (PBS)
475 L'Enfant Plaza West, S.W.
Washington, D.C. 20024

Westinghouse Broadcasting (Group W)
90 Park Avenue
New York, N.Y. 10016

Source of Household Viewing—Prime Time

Pay Cable, Basic Cable, and Non-Cable Households

	Nov. 1983			Nov. 1982			Nov. 1981		
	Pay cable	Basic cable	Non-cable	Pay cable	Basic cable	Non-cable	Pay cable	Basic cable	Non-cable
% TV Usage[1]	71.4	63.7	60.5	67.2	60.9	60.1	70.6	60.5	62.0
Pay Cable	13.6	—	—	12.5	—	—	12.0	—	—
Cable-originated programming	6.7	5.4	—	4.9	3.8	—	3.2	2.6	—
Other-on-air stations	11.5	12.9	10.3	13.4	12.5	10.3	13.3	10.7	9.5
Network affiliated stations	48.1	48.4	53.8	43.5	47.3	52.7	45.8	49.0	53.7
Network share[2]	(67)	(76)	(89)	(65)	(78)	(88)	(65)	(81)	(87)

1. May be less than sum of reception sources because of simultaneous viewing. 2. Percent Network/Sum of Sources. *Source:* A. C. Nielsen Company, Nielsen Television Index Estimates.

Weekly TV Viewing by Age
(in hours and minutes)

	Time per week	
	1983	1982
Women 18–34 years old	30 h 19 min	26 h 56 min
Women 35–54	33 h 23 min	33 h 23 min
Women 55 and over	41 h 13 min	37 h 14 min
Men 18–34	28 h 30 min	24 h 39 min
Men 35–54	27 h 50 min	26 h 56 min
Men 55 and over	35 h 53 min	32 h 59 min
Female Teens	24 h 16 min	21 h 20 min
Male Teens	25 h 17 min	23 h 40 min
Children 6–11	24 h 50 min	24 h 00 min
Children 2–5	27 h 09 min	25 h 29 min
Total Persons	**30 h 47 min**	**28 h 22 min**

NOTE: All figures are estimates based on National Audience Demographics Report, November 1983. *Source:* A. C. Nielsen Company, Nielsen Television Index Audience Estimates.

Persons Viewing Nightly Prime Time TV[1]
(in millions)

	Total persons[2]
Monday	94.4
Tuesday	93.7
Wednesday	93.4
Thursday	96.9
Friday	93.1
Saturday	91.7
Sunday	106.9
Total average	**95.7**

1. Average minute audiences. 2. Based on National Demographics Report (November 1983). NOTE: Prime time is 8–11 p.m. (EST), except 7–11 p.m. Sunday. *Source:* A. C. Nielsen Company, Nielsen Television Index Audience Estimates.

Top 10 Syndicated TV Programs of 1983–84

Rank	Program	Rating (% U.S.)[1]
1.	Family Feud (P.M.)	12.3
2.	Wheel of Fortune	12.1
3.	M*A*S*H	11.2
4.	Three's Company	10.3
5.	PM Magazine	9.8
6.	People's Court	9.1
7.	Hee Haw	9.0
8.	Entertainment Tonight	8.8
9.	Jeffersons	8.3
10.	Solid Gold	7.6

1. During November 1983. Ranked on the basis of average 15-minute audience ratings. *Source:* A.C. Nielsen Company, Nielsen Television Index Audience Estimates.

Average Hours of Household TV Usage
(in hours and minutes per day)

	Yearly average	February	July
1965–66	5 h 30 min	6 h 28 min	4 h 23 min
1970–71	6 h 01 min	6 h 53 min	5 h 08 min
1975–76	6 h 11 min	6 h 49 min	5 h 33 min
1976–77	6 h 13 min	6 h 55 min	5 h 13 min
1977–78	6 h 13 min	7 h 00 min	5 h 32 min
1978–79	6 h 26 min	7 h 11 min	5 h 46 min
1979–80	6 h 35 min	7 h 22 min	5 h 48 min
1980–81	6 h 44 min	7 h 32 min	6 h 08 min
1981–82	6 h 48 min	7 h 22 min	6 h 09 min
1982–83	6 h 55 min	7 h 33 min	6 h 23 min

NOTE: Estimates are based on total U.S. TV households, excluding unusual days. *Source:* A. C. Nielsen Company, Nielsen Television Index Audience Estimates.

Selected Characteristics of Cable T.V.: 1979 to 1981

		Financial Entities		Subscribers		Pay cable	
Year	Communities (number)	Total number	Percent reporting	Number (1,000)	Avg. Rate per month in $	Net income $ millions[1]	revenue $ millions
1979	8,539	2,992	94	15,760	7.37	199	355
1980	8,678	2,868	96	16,913	7.69	168	575
1981	11,944	3,600	88	23,565	7.94	40	1,172

1. Before tax. *Source:* U.S. Federal Communications Commission, *Cable Television Revenues,* annual.

Longest Broadway Runs[1]

1. A Chorus Line (M) (1974–)	3,744
2. Grease (M) (1972–80)	3,388
3. Oh! Calcutta! (M) (1976–) (revival)	3,359
4. Fiddler on the Roof (1964–72)	3,242
5. Life with Father (1939–47)	3,224
6. Tobacco Road (1933–41)	3,182
7. Hello, Dolly! (M) (1964–71)	2,844
8. My Fair Lady (M) (1956–62)	2,717
9. Annie (M) (1977–1983)	2,377
10. Man of La Mancha (M) (1965–71)	2,329
11. Abie's Irish Rose	2,327
12. Oklahoma! (M) (1943–48)	2,212
13. South Pacific (M) (1949–54)	1,925
14. The Magic Show (M) (1974–78)	1,920
15. Pippin (M) (1971–77)	1,908
16. Gemini (1977–81)	1,819
17. Deathtrap (1978–1982)	1,793
18. Harvey (1944–49)	1,775
19. Dancin' (M) (1978–82)	1,774
20. 42nd Street (M) (1980–)	1,752
21. Hair (M) (1968–72)	1,742
22. The Wiz (M) 1975–79)	1,672
23. Born Yesterday (1946–49)	1,642
24. Ain't Misbehavin' (M) (1978–82)	1,604
25. The Best Little Whorehouse in Texas (M) (1978–82)	1,584

1. As of Aug. 5, 1984. M = musical. Years are those of opening and closing.

Major U.S. Fairs and Expositions

1853 Crystal Palace Exposition, New York City: modeled on similar fair held in London.

1876 Centennial Exposition, Philadelphia: celebrating 100th year of independence.

1893 World's Columbian Exposition, Chicago: commemorating 400th anniversary of Columbus' voyage to America.

1894 Midwinter International Exposition, San Francisco: promoting business revival after Depression of 1893.

1898 Trans-Mississippi and International Exposition, Omaha, Neb.: exhibiting products, resources, industries, and civilization of states and territories west of the Mississippi River.

1901 Pan-American Exposition, Buffalo, N.Y.: promoting social and commercial interest of Western Hemisphere nations.

1904 Louisiana Purchase Exposition, St. Louis: marking 100th anniversary of major land acquisition from France and opening up of the West.

1905 Lewis and Clark Centennial Exposition, Portland, Ore.: commemorating 100th anniversary of exploration of a land route to the Pacific.

1907 Jamestown Ter Centennial Exposition, Hampton Roads, Va.: marking 300th anniversary of first permanent English settlement in America.

1909 Alaska-Yukon-Pacific Exposition, Seattle: celebrating growth of the Puget Sound area.

1915–16 Panama-Pacific International Exposition, San Francisco: celebrating opening of the Panama Canal.

1915–16 Panama-California Exposition, San Diego: promoting resources and opportunities for development and commerce of the Western states.

1926 Sesquicentennial Exposition, Philadelphia: marking 150th year of independence.

1933–34 Century of Progress International Exposition, Chicago: celebrating 100th anniversary of incorporation of Chicago as a city.

1935 California Pacific International Exposition, San Diego: marking 400 years of progress since the first Spaniard landed on the West Coast.

1939–40 New York World's Fair, New York City: "The World of Tomorrow," symbolized by Trylon and Perisphere. Officially commemorating 150th anniversary of inauguration of George Washington as President in New York.

1939–40 Golden Gate International Exposition, Treasure Island, San Francisco: celebrating new Golden Gate Bridge and Oakland Bay Bridge.

1962 The Century 21 Exposition, Seattle: "Man in the Space Age," symbolized by 600-foot steel space needle.

1964–65 New York World's Fair, New York City: "Peace Through Understanding."

1974 Expo '74, Spokane: "Tomorrow's Fresh, New Environment."

1982 World's Fair, Knoxville, Tenn.: "Energy Turns the World," symbolized by the bronze-globed Sunsphere.

1984 Louisiana World Exposition, New Orleans: "The World of Rivers."

Motion Picture Revenues

Top Money Makers

1. E.T. The Extra-Terrestrial (Universal, 1982)	$209,567,000
2. Star Wars (20th Century-Fox, 1977)	193,500,000
3. Return of the Jedi (20th Century Fox, 1983)	165,500,000
4. The Empire Strikes Back (20th Century-Fox)	141,600,000
5. Jaws (Universal, 1975)	133,435,000
6. Raiders of the Lost Ark (Paramount)	115,598,000
7. Grease (Paramount, 1978)	96,300,000
8. Tootsie (Columbia, 1982)	94,571,613
9. The Exorcist (Warner Bros., 1973)	89,000,000
10. The Godfather (Paramount, 1972)	86,275,000
11. Close Encounters of the Third Kind (Columbia, 1977/80)	83,452,000
12. Superman (Warner Bros., 1978)	82,800,000
13. The Sound of Music (20th Century-Fox, 1965)	79,748,000
14. The Sting (Universal, 1973)	79,419,900
15. Gone With the Wind (M-G-M/United Artists, 1939)	76,700,000
16. Saturday Night Fever (Paramount, 1977)	74,100,000
17. National Lampoon's Animal House (Universal, 1978)	74,000,000
18. Nine to Five (20th Century-Fox, 1980)	66,200,000
19. Rocky III (M-G-M/United Artists, 1982)	65,763,177
20. Superman II (Warner Bros., 1981)	65,100,000
21. On Golden Pond (Universal/Associated Film Distribution, 1981)	63,000,000
22. Kramer vs. Kramer (Columbia, 1979)	61,734,000
23. Smokey and the Bandit (Universal, 1977)	61,055,000
24. One Flew Over the Cuckoo's Nest (United Artists, 1975)	59,205,793
25. Stir Crazy (Columbia, 1980)	58,408,000

Top Rentals 1983

1. Return of the Jedi (20th Century-Fox)	$165,500,000
2. Tootsie (Columbia)	94,571,613
3. Trading Places (Paramount)	40,600,000
4. WarGames (M-G-M/United Artists)	36,595,975
5. Superman III (Warner Bros.)	36,400,000
6. Flashdance (Paramount)	36,180,000
7. Staying Alive (Paramount)	33,650,000
8. Octopussy (M-G-M/United Artists)	33,203,999
9. Mr. Mom (20th Century-Fox)	31,500,000
10. 48 Hours (Paramount)	30,328,000
11. National Lampoon's Vacation (Warner Bros.)	29,500,000
12. Risky Business (Geffen/Warner Bros.)	28,500,000
13. The Verdict (20th Century-Fox)	26,650,000
14. Jaws 3-D (Universal)	26,439,000
15. Never Say Never Again (Warner Bros.)	25,000,000
16. Terms of Endearment (Paramount)	25,000,000
17. The Toy (Columbia)	24,512,935
18. Gandhi (Columbia)	24,364,472
19. Dark Crystal (Universal)	23,375,000
20. Sudden Impact (Warner Bros.)	23,000,000
21. E.T. The Extra-Terrestrial (reissue)	22,567,000
22. Blue Thunder (Columbia)	21,784,119
23. Best Friends (Warner Bros.)	19,000,000
24. Porky's II: The Next Day (20th Century Fox)	17,500,000
25. The Big Chill (Columbia)	16,814,095

NOTE: United States and Canada only. 1. Figures are total rentals collected by film distributors as of Dec. 31, 1982. 2. Figures are not to be confused with gross box-office receipts from sale of tickets. *Source: Variety.*

Museums of the United States

Source: Information Please questionnaires to museums. NOTE: Admission fees and visiting hours are subject to change.

Washington, D.C.

Anacostia Neighborhood Museum, Smithsonian Institution: 2405 Martin Luther King, Jr., Ave. SE, Washington, D.C. 20020. Open: Mon.-Fri. 10–6, Sat. and Sun. 1–6 (closed Dec. 25). Free.

Exhibits on Afro-American history, art shows, programs for children.

Arts and Industries Building, Smithsonian Institution: 900 Jefferson Dr. SW, Washington, D.C. 20560. Open: daily 10–5:30 (closed Dec. 25). Free.

Constructed to house exhibits from 1876 Centennial Exhibition, building has been restored as nearly as possible to original appearance.

Corcoran Gallery of Art: 17th St. and New York Ave. NW, Washington, D.C. 20006. Open: Tues.-Sun. 10–4:30, until 9 on Thurs. (closed Mon.; also Jan. 1, July 4, Thanksgiving, Dec. 25). Free.

American paintings, sculpture, graphics. European art.

Dumbarton Oaks: 1703 32nd St. NW, Washington, D.C. 20007. Museum open: Tues.-Sun. 2–5 (closed natl. hldys.). Free. Gardens open: daily (except hldys.). Apr.–Oct. 2–6. Adm. $1, children free, senior citizens free Wed.; Sept.–Mar. 2–5 free. Closed during inclement weather.

Byzantine and Pre-Columbian art collections.

Freer Gallery of Art, Smithsonian Institution: Jefferson Dr. at 12th St. SW, Washington, D.C. 20560. Open: daily 10–5:30 (closed Dec. 25). Free.

Oriental paintings, sculpture, bronzes, pottery, and metal work. Early Christian manuscripts. Largest Whistler collection in the U.S.

Hirshhorn Museum and Sculpture Garden, Smithsonian Institution: Eighth St. at Independence Ave. SW, Washington, D.C. 20560. Open: daily, 10–5:30; extended hours in summer announced annually. (closed Dec. 25). Free.

More than 7,000 works tracing development of modern painting and sculpture since 19th century. Rodin, Moore, Picasso, Calder, Miró, Eakins, and Matisse among those represented.

National Air and Space Museum, Smithsonian Institution: Independence Ave. bet. 4th and 7th Sts. SW, Washington, D.C. 20560. Open: daily 10–5:30; extended hours in summer announced annually. (closed Dec. 25). Free.

Exhibits on aviation and space age; Wright Brothers' 1903 Flyer, *Lindbergh's* Spirit of St. Louis.

National Gallery of Art: Constitution Ave. bet. 3rd and 7th Sts. NW, Washington, D.C. 20565. Open: Mon.-Sat. 10–5, Sun. 12–9[1] (closed Jan. 1, Dec. 25). Free.

Paintings, sculpture, drawings, prints, decorative arts Works by Raphael, Jan Van Eyck, Vermeer, Rembrandt, Van Gogh, Renoir, Monet, and Cassatt.

National Museum of African Art, Smithsonian Institution: 318 A St., N.E., Washington, D.C. 20002. Open: Mon.-Fri. 10–5; Sat. and Sun. 12–5 (closed Dec. 25). Free.

Only U.S. museum devoted solely to African art through collection of almost 7,000 objects.

National Museum of American Art, Smithsonian Institution: Eighth and G Sts. NW, Washington, D.C. 20560. Open: daily 10–5:30 (closed Dec. 25). Free.

Paintings, sculptures, and graphics.

National Museum of American History, Smithsonian Institution: 14th St. and Constitution Ave. NW, Washington, D.C. 20560. Open: daily 10–5:30; extended hours in summer announced annually. (closed Dec. 25). Free.

Exhibits showing scientific, technological, and cultural development feature original Star-Spangled Banner, furnishings, gowns of First Ladies, inventions, stamps, coins, musical instruments, ceramics, and crafts.

National Museum of Natural History/National Museum of Man, Smithsonian Institution: 10th St. and Constitution Ave. NW, Washington, D.C. 20560. Open: daily 10–5:30; extended hours in summer announced annually. (closed Dec. 25). Free.

Origin, development, and physical characteristics of man. Dioramas of peoples and animals in natural settings. Land and sea mammals, birds, fish, reptiles, and gems, minerals, meteorites, volcanoes, prehistoric animals, fossils. Hope Diamond. Insect Zoo.

National Portrait Gallery, Smithsonian Institution: Eighth and F Sts. NW, Washington, D.C. 20560. Open: daily 10–5:30 (closed Dec. 25). Free.

Only major museum in hemisphere devoted exclusively to portraiture. Exhibits likenesses in all media of persons who have made significant contributions to U.S. history and culture.

Renwick Gallery, Smithsonian Institution: 17th St. and Pennsylvania Ave. NW, Washington, D.C. 20560. Open: daily 10–5:30 (closed Dec. 25). Free.

American crafts, decorative arts, and design, housed in a mid-19th-century building restored to its original appearance.

Smithsonian Institution Building: 1000 Jefferson Dr. SW, Washington, D.C. 20560. Open: daily 10–5:30; extended hours in summer announced annually. (closed Dec. 25). Free.

Information center and James Smithson's tomb are in original building. Institution maintains the museums and art galleries indicated above; also Cooper-Hewitt Museum in New York City, National Zoological Park in Washington, D.C., and research facilities elsewhere.

New York City

American Academy and Institute of Arts and Letters: Audubon Terrace, west side of Broadway between 155th and 156th Sts., NYC 10032. Open: Tues.-Sun. 1–4 during exhibitions (closed Mon. and natl. hldys.). Free.

Annual exhibitions of work of recipients of awards and honors, and paintings eligible for purchase under Hassam and Speicher Funds. Memorial exhibition of work of deceased members.

American Museum of Natural History: Central Park West at 79th St., NYC 10024. Open: Mon., Tues., Thurs., Sun., 10–5:45; Wed., Fri., Sat., 10–9. Suggested adm.: $3.00; children, $1.50. Fri., Sat. evenings free.

All branches of natural sciences with exhibits including astronomy at American Museum-Hayden Planetarium.

Brooklyn Museum, The: Eastern Pkwy., Brooklyn, N.Y. 11238. Open: Mon., Wed., Fri., 10–5, Sat. 11–6, Sun. 1–6, hldys. 1–6 (closed Jan. 1, Dec. 25). Suggested adm.: $3; students $1; under 12s and senior citizens, free.

Egyptian and classical art, American and European paintings, decorative arts and period rooms, prints, drawings, costumes, and textiles. Arts of Africa, Oceania, Orient, Middle East, Islam, and New World. Two reference libraries.

Cloisters, The: Ft. Tryon Pk., NYC 10040. Open: Tues.-Sun. 9:30–5:15 (closed Mon.). Suggested adm.: $4; students and senior citizens, $2.

Cloisters, chapel, chapter house, apse. The various cloisters are reconstituted from elements of 12–15th-century French cloisters. Apse has been relocated here in its entirety. Frescoes, polychromed statues, stained glass, tapestries, paintings, ivories, precious metalwork. Medieval branch of The Metropolitan Museum of Art.

Cooper-Hewitt Museum, the Smithsonian Institution's National Museum of Design: 2 E. 91st St., NYC 10128. Open: Tues. 10–9, Wed.-Sat. 10–5, Sun. 12–5 (closed Mon.; also Jan. 1, July 4, Thanksgiving, Dec. 25). Adm.: $2 (free on Tues. after 5).

Regularly changing exhibitions devoted to some aspect of design.

Frick Collection: 1 E. 70th St., NYC 10021. Open: Tues.-Sat. 10–6, Sun. and most hldys. 1–6 (closed Mon.; also Jan. 1, Thanksgiving, Dec. 24–25, July 4). Adm.: Tues.-Sat. $1; students and senior citizens, 50¢; Sun. $2. Children under 10 not admitted.

Paintings, prints, drawings of 14th to 19th centuries, Italian Renaissance and French sculpture and furniture. Chinese and French porcelain. Concerts, lectures.

Guggenheim Museum, Solomon R.: 1071 Fifth Ave. at 88th St., NYC 10128. Open: Tues. 11–8; Wed.-Sun. and hlyds. 11–5 (closed Mon., except hldys., and Dec. 25). Adm.: $2.50; under 7s, free; College students with ID's, and senior citizens, $1.50; student groups of more than 10 with a teacher and appointment $1.

Works of leading 20th-century foreign and American painters and sculptors.

Hayden Planetarium. *See* American Museum of Natural History.

Hispanic Society of America, The (Museum and Library): Broadway and W. 155th St., NYC 10032. Museum open: Tues.-Sat. 10–4:30, Sun. 1–4 (closed Mon.; also Jan. 1, Feb. 12, Feb. 22, Good Friday, Easter, May 30, July 4, Thanksgiving, Dec. 25). During Christmas Week, museum is open for three consecutive days from Dec. 26 through Dec. 31. Library open: Tues.-Fri. 1–4:30, Sat. 10:30–4:30 (closed Sun., Mon.; also hldys., Good Friday, month of Aug., and for two weeks beginning Tues. before Christmas Eve). Free.

Paintings, sculpture, decorative arts, manuscripts, and incunabula, representative of Hispanic culture. Works on Hispanic art, history, literature.

Jewish Museum, The: 1109 Fifth Ave. at 92nd St., NYC 10128. Open: Mon., Wed., Thurs., 12–5, Tues., 12–8, (closed Fri. and Sat., major Jewish hldys and certain legal hldys). Adm.: $2.50, 6–16s, students with ID's, senior citizens $1.50. Members, free.

Former Warburg mansion and adjoining Albert A. List building house most extensive collection of Jewish ceremonial objects in Western Hemisphere. Changing exhibitions of sculpture, paintings, photography and architecture illuminate Jewish experience, culture, and tradition.

Metropolitan Museum of Art, The: Fifth Ave. at 82nd St., NYC 10128. Open: Tues. 9:30–8:45, Wed.-Sun. 9:30–5:15 (closed Mon.). Discretionary admission fee.

European and American paintings, drawings, sculpture, decorative arts, prints. Egyptian, Greek, Roman, Islamic, and Near and Far Eastern art. Arts of Africa, Pacific islands and pre-Columbian and native America. Musical instruments, arms and armor. European period rooms. Costumes and textiles. See also *Cloisters.*

Museum of the American Indian, Heye Foundation: Broadway at 155th St., NYC 10032. Open: Tues.-Sat. 10–5; Sun. 1–5 (closed Mon., also Jan. 1, 2; Easter, July 4, Thanksgiving, Dec. 25). Adm.: $2; students and senior citizens, $1. Museum members and American Indians free. Group rates.

Archeology, ethnology, and primitive-to-20th-century arts and artifacts of North, Central, and South America.

Museum of the City of New York: 1220 Fifth Ave. at 103rd St., NYC 10029. Open: Tues.-Sat. 10–4:45, Sun. and hldys. 1–4:45 (closed Mon.; also Jan. 1, Thanksgiving, Dec. 25). Free.

History and life of New York City. Period costumes, furniture, miniature scenes, portraits, paintings, prints, manuscripts, theater and music collection, silver, dolls and doll houses.

Museum of Modern Art, The: 11 W. 53rd St., NYC 10019. Open: Mon., Tues., Fri., Sat. and Sun. 11–6, Thurs. 11–9 (closed Wed.; also Dec. 25). Adm.: $4. 50, students with IDs, $3, children free when accompanied by an adult, senior citizens, $2. Tuesday, pay what you wish.

Founded 1929 to help people enjoy and understand the art of our times. Changing exhibitions of contemporary painting, sculpture, drawings, prints, photography, architecture, industrial and graphic design, films, video.

National Academy of Design: 1083 Fifth Ave. at 89th St., NYC 10128. Open: Tues. 12–8, Wed.-Sun. 12–5.

Exhibitions from permanent collection of American paintings, sculptures and graphics; exhibitions of contemporary art, 19th and 20th century European and American art.

New-York Historical Society: 170 Central Park West at 77th St., NYC 10024. Museum open: Tues.-Fri. 11–5, Sat. 10–5, Sun. 1–5. Library open to adults: Tues.-Sat. 10–5. (Both closed Mon.; also Jan. 1, July 4, Thanksgiving, Dec. 25). Summer hrs. (Memorial Day-Labor Day): Library Mon. Fri. 10–5 (Closed Sat.). Museum, $2; library adm. an additional $1;

New York city and state historical exhibits. Early American paintings and portraits. Tiffany lamps and windows. Audubon watercolors. Gallery of American silver.

Pierpont Morgan Library: 29 E. 36th St. NYC 10016. Open: Tues.-Sat. 10:30–5, Sun. 1–5 (closed Mon.; also legal hldys., Sundays in July, and month of August). Suggested adm.: $2.

Medieval and Renaissance illuminated manuscripts, rare books, music and autograph manuscripts, old master drawings, bindings, early children's books, ancient written records.

Whitney Museum of American Art: 945 Madison Ave. at 75th St., NYC 10021. Open: Wed.-Sat. 11–6, Tues. 11–8 (free 6–8), Sun. and hldys. 12–6 (closed Mon.; also Dec. 25). Adm.: $2.50; senior citizens, $1.25; college students with ID, and under 12s accompanied by an adult, free.

Sculpture, paintings, watercolors, drawings, and prints by 20th-century American artists. Exhibitions of contemporary and historical American art. Daily film and video showings. Downtown Branch at Federal Hall National Memorial, 26 Wall St. (at Broad); Midtown Branch at Philip Morris, 120 Park Ave. (at 42nd St.)

Chicago

Art Institute of Chicago, The: Michigan Ave. at Adams St., Chicago, Ill. 60603. Open: Mon.-Wed. and Fri. 10:30–4:30, Thurs. 10:30–8, Sat. 10–5,

Sun. and hldys. 12–5 (Closed Dec. 25). Voluntary admission fee.

Paintings, sculpture, prints, drawings, textiles, photography. Oriental arts; European, American decorative arts; primitive art, architectural drawings and fragments, Thorne Miniature Rooms. Junior Museum. Goodman Theatre, Art School.

Beverly Art Center: 2153 W. 111th St., Chicago, Ill. 60643. Open: daily 8–6.

Permanent John H. Vanderpoel Collection plus monthly exhibits.

Chicago Academy of Sciences, Museum of Ecology: Lincoln Park—2001 North Clark St., Chicago, Ill. 60614. Open: daily 10–5 (closed Dec. 25). Adm.: $1; 6–17s and senior citizens, 50¢. Free on Monday. Groups with prior reservations free.

Exhibits of ecology of animal and plant life, minerals and fossils of Great Lakes region. Walk-through coal forest, cave, and canyon. Lectures, field trips, movies.

Chicago Historical Society: Clark St. and North Ave., Chicago, Ill. 60614. Open: Mon.-Sat. 9:30–4:30, Sun. 12–5 (closed Jan. 1, Thanksgiving, Dec. 25). Adm.: $1.50; 6–17s, 50¢; senior citizens, 50¢. Free on Monday. Research collection open Tues.-Sat. 9:30–4:30.

Exhibits and collections relating to Chicago and Illinois history, Illinois pioneer crafts, American history, Lincoln.

Field Museum of Natural History: Roosevelt Rd. at Lake Shore Dr., Chicago, Ill. 60605. Open: Daily 9–5. (closed Jan. 1, Thanksgiving, Dec. 25). Adm.: $2; families, $4; 6–17s and students with ID's, $1; senior citizens, 50¢. Free on Thurs.

Dioramas of plants, and animals; displays of fossils, rocks, and gems; anthropology exhibits from Egypt, China, Africa, Oceania, and the Americas. New exhibit "Maritime Peoples of the Arctic and Northwest Coast."

Museum of Science and Industry: 57th St. and Lake Shore Dr., Chicago, Ill. 60637. Open: Memorial Day-Labor Day 9:30–5:30; rest of year, Mon.-Fri. 9:30–4, Sat., Sun. and hldys. 9:30–5:30. Free (small fee to four exhibits).

Operating coal mine, captured German submarine, giant heart, Paul Bunyan house, Colleen Moore's Fairy Castle, The Farm, the Apollo 8 spacecraft, Sears' Cinema Circus, computerized "Food for Life," historic and advanced forms of planes, ships, trains, and cars.

Oriental Institute Museum of the University of Chicago: 1155 E. 58th St., Chicago, Ill. 60637. Open: Tues.-Sat. 10–4, Sun. 12–4 (closed Mon. and hldys.). Free.

Ancient Near Eastern objects, including 40-ton human-headed winged bull from Khorsabad in Assyria, 16-ft. statue of Tutankhamen from Egypt, colossal bull's head from Persepolis; glyptic, bronze, and ivory artifacts.

Philadelphia

Academy of Natural Sciences of Philadelphia: 19th St. and the Ben Franklin Parkway, Philadelphia, Pa. 19103. Natural history museum. Open: Mon.-Fri. 10–4; Sat. and Sun. 10–5 (closed Jan. 1, Thanksgiving, Dec. 25). Adm.: $2.75 (students, senior citizens, military, $2.50; 3–12s, $2.25, under 3 free.

Exhibits on dinosaurs and extinct species; animal, bird, and gem displays. Live animal shows.

Franklin Institute, The: 20th St. and the Ben Franklin Parkway, Philadelphia, Pa. 19103. Open: Mon.-Sat. 10–5, Sun. 12–5 (closed Jan. 1, Memorial Day, July 4, Thanksgiving, Dec. 24–25). Adm.: $3.50; students, $3; 4–11s, $2.50; senior citizens, $2.

Operating science museum, planetarium, library, and research laboratories. "Hands-on" science and technology exhibits.

Pennsylvania Academy of the Fine Arts: Broad and Cherry Sts., Philadelphia, Pa. 19102. Open: Tues.-Sat. 10–4, Sun. 12–4; (closed Jan. 1, July 4, Thanksgiving, Dec. 25). Adm.: $2; students, $1; senior citizens, $1.50. Free on Tues.

Oldest art museum and school in U.S. Collection devoted to American art. Lectures, concerts.

Philadelphia Museum of Art: 26th St. and the Ben Franklin Parkway, Philadelphia, Pa. 19130. Open: Wed. 10–5, partially open Tues., (closed major hldys.). Adm.: $3; students, children 5–18 and senior citizens, $1.50. Reduced charge Tues. Free Sun. 10–1.

Paintings, drawings, prints, from old masters to present. Sculpture, decorative arts, period rooms and armor. Oriental collections. American Wing. Rodin Museum at Parkway and 22nd St. Colonial Houses in Fairmount Park. Samuel S. Fleisher Art Memorial, 715–19 Catharine St.

Museums In Other Cities

Addison Gallery of American Art: Phillips Academy, Andover, Mass. 01810. Open: Tues.-Sat. 10–5, Sun. 2:30–5 (closed Mon.; also natl. hldys. and month of Aug.). Free.

Paintings, sculpture, graphics, photographs of 18th, 19th, and 20th centuries. Changing contemporary exhibitions.

Alabama, Museum of Natural History of: Smith Hall, on campus of U. of Alabama. Tuscaloosa, Ala. 35486. Open: Mon.-Fri. 8–4:45. Free.

All phases of natural history. See also *Mound State Monument Museum.*

Albright-Knox Art Gallery: 1285 Elmwood Ave., Buffalo, N.Y. 14222. Open: Tues.-Sat. 11–5; Sun. 12–5 (closed Mon.; also Jan. 1, Thanksgiving, Dec. 25). Voluntary admission fee.

Comprehensive collection of contemporary paintings; 18th-19th-century English, French, and American paintings. Sculpture since 3000 B.C.

Atomic Energy, American Museum of: *See* Science and Energy, American Museum of.

Baltimore Museum of Art: Art Museum Dr., Baltimore, Md. 21218. Open: Tues.-Fri. 10–4; Thurs. evening 6–10 (except summer); Sat.-Sun. 11–6 (closed Mon.). Adm.: $2; members, under 22s, and Thurs. free.

Paintings, sculpture, graphics, tribal arts, decorative arts, sculpture garden.

Baseball Hall of Fame and Museum, National: Main St., Cooperstown, N.Y. 13326. Open: May-Oct. 9–9, Nov.-Apr. 9–5 (closed Jan. 1, Thanksgiving, Dec. 25). Adm.: $4; 7–15s, $1.50.

Memorabilia, pictures, documents of baseball history. Bronze plaques of game's immortals. Baseball movies shown daily. See also *Hall of Fame in index.*

Berkshire Museum, The: 39 South St., Pittsfield, Mass. 01201. Open: Tues.-Sat. 10–5, Sun. 1–5 (closed Mon.). Open Mon. in July and Aug. Free.

Painting, sculpture, decorative arts—ancient to modern. Loan exhibits. Galleries on biology, birds, man, minerals, and American history. Live animal exhibits. Movies, lectures.

Birmingham Museum of Art: 2000 Eighth Ave. North, Birmingham, Ala. 35203. Open: Tues.-Wed., Fri. and Sat. 10–5, Thurs. 10–9, Sun. 2–6 (closed Mondays; also Jan. 1, Dec. 25). Free.

Kress Collection of Italian art; 17th-century Dutch, Flemish, and English paintings; 19th-century American paintings; Beeson Wedgwood Collection; art of Old West, including Remington bronzes; modern American paintings; silver, porcelain; Oriental art; African art.

(Boston) Museum of Fine Arts: Huntington Ave., Boston, Mass. 02115. Open: (entire museum): Tues. and Thurs.-Sun. 10–5; Wed. 10–10; (West Wing only): Thurs. and Fri. 5–10 (closed Mon.; also Jan. 1, July 4, Labor Day, Thanksgiving, and Dec. 24–25). Adm.: $4 when entire museum is open; $3 when only West Wing is open. Members and children 16 and under free; senior citizens $2.50. Free to all Sat. 10–12.

European and American paintings, sculpture, furniture, interiors, tapestries, textiles, silver, costumes, musical instruments. Prints, drawings, watercolors. Egyptian, Asiatic, contemporary collections.

Buffalo Museum of Science: Humboldt Parkway, Buffalo, N.Y. 14211. Open: Mon.-Thurs. and Sat. 10–5; Fri. 10–10 (Sept. thru May only), Sun. and hldys. 10–5 (Jan. 1 and July 4, 1–5) (closed Dec. 25). Adm.: $1; 3–18s, students, and senior citizens, 50¢.

Exhibits of astronomy, geology, zoology, botany, anthropology. Kellogg Observatory.

California Academy of Sciences: Golden Gate Park, San Francisco, Calif. 94118. Open: daily 10–5. Adm.: $2, 6–11s, 75¢; 12–17s and senior citizens $1. under 6 free. Free adm. first Wed. of month.

North American and African habitat groups. Astronomical exhibits, earthquake experience, minerals, fossils, plants. Steinhart Aquarium, Morrison Planetarium, Wattis Hall of Man.

California Palace of the Legion of Honor: 34th Ave. and Clement St., Lincoln Park, San Francisco, Calif. 94121. Open: Wed.-Sun. 10–5. Adm.: $2; 5–17s and senior citizens, 50¢; under 5, free. Free adm. first Wed. of month.

Devoted to arts of France: paintings, sculpture, and decorative arts; prints and drawings of all periods and nationalities.

Carnegie Institute: 4400 Forbes Ave., Pittsburgh, Pa. 15213. Open: Tues.-Sat. 10–5, Sun. 1–5 (closed Mon. and major hldys.). Suggested contributions: Adults, $2; children and students, $1. Sat. free to students and children.

Museum of Art: European and American paintings, sculpture, and decorative arts. Carnegie Museum of Natural History. Hillman Hall of Minerals and Gems. Home of the Dinosaurs.

Cincinnati Art Museum: Eden Park, Cincinnati, Ohio 45202. Open: wkdys. 10–5, Sun. 1–5 (closed Mon. and major hldys.). Adm.: $2; 12–18s and senior citizens, $1; 3–11, 25¢. Free to everyone on Sat.

European and American painting, prints, photographs, decorative arts, sculpture, costumes. Egyptian, Greco-Roman, Medieval, Near and Far Eastern arts. Ancient musical instruments.

Clark (Sterling and Francine) Art Institute: Williamstown, Mass. 01267. Open: daily except Monday, 10–5 (closed Jan. 1, Thanksgiving, Dec. 25). Free.

Paintings from 14th to 19th centuries, including works by Corot, Renoir, Degas, Toulouse-Lautrec, Homer, sculpture, antique silver, prints and drawings.

Cleveland Museum of Art: 11150 East Boulevard, Cleveland, Ohio 44106. Open: Tues. 10–6, Wed. 10–10, Thurs. and Fri. 10–6, Sat. 9–5, Sun. 1–6 (closed Mon.; also Jan. 1, July 4, Thanksgiving, Dec. 25). Free.

Paintings, sculpture, graphic arts, furniture, silver, gold, arms, armor, textiles, ceramics from all cultures and periods, arranged historically.

Cleveland Museum of Natural History: Wade Oval, University Circle, Cleveland, Ohio 44106. Open: Mon.-Sat. 10–5, Sun. 1–5:30 (closed Jan. 1, Memorial Day, July 4, Labor Day, Thanksgiving, Dec. 24–25). Adm.: $2.50, 6–18s and senior citizens, $1. Free Tues. and Thurs. after 3.

Dinosaurs, area fossils, minerals, birds, mammals, insects, reptiles, plants. American Indian and Eskimo displays. Planetarium, observatory. Hall of Man's Ecology, Hall of Earth Science.

Colonial Williamsburg: Williamsburg, Va. 23187. Open: daily. Adm.: $10 and $15; 6–12s, half price; under 6 free.

Restored 18th-century capital of Colonial Virginia; 173 acres of colonial city with more than 40 exhibition homes, craft shops, and public buildings; 90 acres of gardens; outdoor events; colonial lodging and dining.

Colorado Springs Fine Arts Center: 30 W. Dale St., Colorado Springs, Colo. 80903. Open: Tues.-Sat. 10–5; Sun. 1–5 (closed Mon.; also selected hldys.). Free.

Native American and Hispanic art; 19th- and 20th century American art; touring exhibits.

Columbus Museum of Art: 480 E. Broad St., Columbus, Ohio 43215. Open: Tues.-Fri., and Sun. 11–5; Sat. 10–5 (closed Mon.). Adm.: $2.50; 6–17s, students, and senior citizens, $1: Fri. free.

European paintings from 16th to 20th century; 19th- and 20th-century American and European paintings, sculpture, and works on paper. Chinese and Japanese ceramics. European and American decorative arts. Sculpture Park and Garden.

Corning Glass Center: Dept. IP, Corning, N.Y. 14831. Open daily 9–5 (closed Jan. 1, Thanksgiving, Dec. 24–25). Adm.: $2.50; 6–17s and senior citizens, $2; children with adult, free; family maximum, $6.

Museum of Glass, Hall of Science and Industry, Glass Factory.

Currier Gallery of Art, The: 192 Orange St., Manchester, N.H. 03104. Open: Tues., Wed., Fri., and Sat. 10–4; Sun. 2–5; Thurs. 10–10 (closed Mon. and major hldys.). Free.

European and American paintings and sculpture. 13th-20th century. American decorative arts, 17th-19th century, including furniture, silver, pewter, and early glass.

Delaware Art Museum, The: 2301 Kentmere Pkwy., Wilmington, Del. 19806. Open: Mon.-Sat. 10–5, Sun. 1–5. Free.

Major collection of works by Howard Pyle, founder of Brandywine School; English pre-Raphaelite and 19th- and 20th-century American art. Paintings by Wyeth, Homer, and Hooper. Art reference library.

Denver Art Museum, The: 100 W. 14th Ave. Parkway, Denver, Colo. 80204. Open: Tues.-Sat. 9–5; Sun.-Mon. 12–5; Wed. 9–8.

Art from nearly every culture and period.

Denver Museum of Natural History: City Park, Denver, Colo. 80205. Open: daily 9–5 (closed Dec. 25). Adm.: $3; senior citizens, $1.50; 6–15s, $1; under 6s free.

Seventy life-size ecological habitat dioramas. Animals from four continents, earth-science exhibits, displays of fossil mammals and historic native Americans. Planetarium and IMAX Theater (small charge).

Des Moines Art Center: Greenwood Park, 45th St. and Grand Ave., Des Moines, Iowa 50312. Open:

Tues.-Sat. 11–5, Sun. 12–5. Free.

Permanent collection includes Calder, Rodin, Arp, Bellows, Johns, Hopper, Giacometti, David Smith, Bacon, and Brancusi, among others.

Detroit Historical Museum: 5401 Woodward Ave., Detroit, Mich. 48202. Open: Wed.-Sun. 9:30–5 (closed Mon. Tues. and legal hldys.).

"Streets of Old Detroit" recreates periods of 1840, 1870, and 1905; historic fashions, period rooms, automobile collection. Marine exhibits at Dossin Great Lakes Museum on Belle Isle; military history exhibits at historic Ft. Wayne.

Detroit Institute of Arts, The: 5200 Woodward Ave., Detroit, Mich. 48202. Open: Tues.-Sun. 9:30–5:30 (closed Mon.; also legal hldys.). Free.

Paintings, sculpture, decorative arts from ancient times to modern.

Dickson Mounds Museum: off Route 97-78 near Lewistown, Ill. 61542. Open: Daily 8:30–5 (closed Jan. 1, Easter, Thanksgiving, Dec. 25). Free.

Museum of anthropology with exhibits relating to prehistoric American Indian.

Farmers' Museum: Lake Rd., Route 80, P.O. Box 800, Cooperstown, N.Y. 13326. Open: May 1-Oct. 31, daily. 9–5; restricted schedule for fall and winter. (closed Mon.; also Jan. 1, Thanksgiving, Dec. 25). Adm.: $4[2]; 7–15s, $1.50.

Re-created village crossroads. Early farm and handicraft tools. School house, country store, smithy, print shop, doctor's and lawyer's offices, pharmacy, tavern, church, farm unit. Cardiff Giant. Operated by New York State Historical Association.

Fenimore House: Lake Rd., Route 80 P.O. Box 800, Cooperstown, N.Y. 13326. Open: summer season, daily 9–5; Nov., Dec., and April, Tues.-Sat. 9–5, Sun. 1–5 (closed Mon.; also Jan., Feb., March, Dec. 25). Adm.: $3.50[2]; 7–15s, $1.25.

American folk art, 19th-century fine art portraits, genre landscapes. Browere life masks of Founding Fathers. James Fenimore Cooper memorabilia. Library. Operated by New York State Historical Association.

Florida State Museum, University of Florida: Museum Road, Gainesville, Fla. 32611. Open: Mon.-Fri. 9–5, Sat. 9–5, Sun. 1–5 (closed Dec. 25). Free.

State and University museum with research and exhibition emphasis on natural and anthropological history of Florida, southeastern United States, and Caribbean area.

Fogg Art Museum: Harvard University, 32 Quincy St., Cambridge, Mass. 02138. Open: Mon.-Fri. 9–5, Sat. 10–5, Sun. 1–5 (closed natl. hldys.). Adm.: $2; students and senior citizens, $1; under 18s, free. Free Sat. mornings.

Collections illustrate evolution of Eastern and Western art from ancient to modern times. Chinese sculpture and bronzes; Romanesque sculpture; Italian primitives; French 19th-century paintings; European drawings and prints.

Gardner (Isabella Stewart) Museum: 2 Palace Road, Boston, Mass. 02115. Open: Wed.-Sun. 12–5; Tues. 12–9 (July and Aug. 12–5). (closed Mon., natl. hldys.). Adm.: Suggested contribution, $2.

Paintings, 14th-20th centuries, in building of Venetian palace style. Sculpture, tapestries, furniture. Flowering courtyard. Free tours on Thursday at 2:30 p.m.

Getty (J. Paul) Museum, The: 17985 Pacific Coast Hgwy., Malibu, Calif. 90265. Open: Tues.-Sun. 10–5 (closed all major hldys). Free. Parking reservations are required (213 459-8402).

Re-creation of ancient Roman country house, the Villa dei Papiri, houses Greek and Roman antiquities, Western European paintings, 18th-century European decorative arts, old master drawings, Medieval and Renaissance manuscripts.

Heard Museum: 22 East Monte Vista Rd., Phoenix, Ariz. 85004. Open: Mon.-Sat. 10–4:45, Sun. 1–4:45 (closed hldys.). Adm,: senior citizens, $1.50; children and students, 75¢.

Anthropology and primitive arts, with emphasis on rich heritage of Southwest.

High Museum of Art: 1280 Peachtree St. NE, Atlanta, Ga. 30309. Open: Tues.-Sat. 10–5, Sun. 12–5 (closed Mon.; natl. hldys.). Adm. $2; students and senior citizens $1; under 12s free. Free Thurs. 1–5.

Paintings and sculpture from 14th to 18th century in Samuel H. Kress Collection. 19th and 20th century American paintings, sculpture, and decorative arts. Richman Collection of African Art; 18th-century European porcelains; photography, contemporary art.

(Houston) Museum of Fine Arts, The: 1001 Bissonnet at Main, Houston, Tex. 77005. Open: Tues.-Sat. 10–5, Sun. 1–6 (closed Mon.; also Jan. 1, July 4, Thanksgiving, Dec. 25). Free.

American and European art through 20th century; Southwest American Indian art and artifacts; early American furniture and decorative arts; pre-Columbian and Far Eastern art; native arts from Africa, Australia, South Pacific. Impressionist and post-Impressionist paintings. 20th-century photography.

Huntington Library, Art Collection and Botanical Gardens: 1151 Oxford Rd., San Marino, Calif. 91108. Open: Tues.-Sun. 1–4:30; (reservations required on Sun.) (closed Mon.; Jan. 1, Easter, Memorial Day, July 4, Labor Day, Thanksgiving, Dec. 24–25). Free.

18th-century British and European paintings, including Gainsborough's "Blue Boy" and Lawrence's "Pinkie." American art 1730–1930. Manuscript and rare-book exhibits include Gutenberg Bible, Franklin's Autobiography *in his handwriting. Botanical gardens. Research library.*

Illinois State Museum: Spring and Edwards Sts., Springfield, Ill. 62706. Open: Mon.-Sat. 8:30–5, Sun. 1:30–5 (closed Jan. 1, Easter, Thanksgiving, Dec. 25). Free.

Museum of natural history, anthropology, and art native to Illinois. "Hands-on" room for visitors to examine scientific specimens and artifacts.

Indianapolis Museum of Art: 1200 W. 38th St., Indianapolis, Ind. 46208. Krannert and Clowes Pavilions open: Tues.-Sun. 11–5 (closed Mon.; also Jan. 1, Thanksgiving, Dec. 25). Free. Lilly Pavilion of Decorative Arts open Tues.-Sun. 1–4 (closed Mon. and major hldys.). Free.

Pre-Columbian through contemporary art in all media. British and American paintings of 19th century; J.M.W. Turner collection. Dutch and Flemish paintings of 17th century; textiles, decorative arts of 18th-century Germany, England, France, and Italy. Oriental collection. Clowes Fund Collection of old masters.

Los Angeles County Museum of Art: 5905 Wilshire Blvd., Los Angeles, Calif. 90036. Open: Tues.-Fri. 10–5; Sat.-Sun. 10–6 (closed Mon.; also Jan. 1, Thanksgiving, Dec. 25). Adm.: $1.50; students with ID, senior citizens, and children 5–17, 75¢. Under 5 free. Free second Tues. of month.

Permanent collection in Ahmanson Gallery; special exhibitions in Frances and Armand Hammer Wing.

(Los Angeles County) Natural History Museum: Exposition Park, 900 Exposition Blvd., Los Angeles, Calif. 90007. Open: Tues.-Sun. 10–5 (closed Mon.; also Jan. 1, Thanksgiving, Dec. 25). Adm.: $1.50; 5–17s, 75¢. Free first Tues. of month.

Exhibits in Pre-Columbian archeology, Pacific Islands and African ethnology, Southern California botany, evolution of life, marine biology, insects, mineralogy. Dinosaur and Cenozoic fossil reconstructions. North American and African animal habitat groups. U.S., California, Western, Plains, and West Coast Indian history. Rancho La Brea tar pits, a designated natural history landmark, are at 5801 Wilshire Blvd., Hancock Park, with satellite George C. Page Museum of La Brea. Pleistocene fossil reconstructions. Open: same as parent museum. Free to all second Tues. of month.

Milwaukee Art Museum: War Memorial Center, 750 North Lincoln Memorial Dr., Milwaukee, Wis. 53202. Open: Tues., Wed., Fri., and Sat. 10–5; Thurs. 12–9; Sun. 1–6 (closed Mon.). Adm.: $2; students, senior citizens, $1; under 12s, free.

Paintings, sculpture, graphics, and decorative arts from ancient to modern; Bradley Collection of 19th- and 20th-century American art. The Flagg Tanning Corp. Collection of Haitian Art; the von Schleinitz Collection of 19th-century German paintings, Mettlachsteins and Meissen china.

Milwaukee Public Museum: 800 W. Wells St., Milwaukee, Wis. 53233. Open: daily 9–5 (closed Jan. 1, July 4, Labor Day, Thanksgiving, Dec. 25). Adm.: $2; under 18s, $1; max. family rate, $5.

American Indian and West African art, pre-Columbian collections. Natural history and history displays that include Streets of Old Milwaukee. Urban Habitat, Earth Sciences Hall, and European Village.

Minneapolis Institute of Arts, The: 2400 Third Ave. South, Minneapolis, Minn. 55404. Open: Tues., Wed. Sat. 10–5; Thurs.-Fri. 10–9; Sun. 12–5 (closed Mon.; also Dec. 25). Adm.: $2; 12–18s, $1; senior citizens and children under 12, free.

European and American paintings, sculpture, decorative arts, period rooms, prints and drawings, photography; Oriental, African, Oceanic, ancient and native North and South American arts.

Mint Museum, Art Museum: 501 Hempstead Pl., Charlotte, N.C. 28207. Closed for construction of new wing. Reopening mid-Sept. 1985 with hrs. Tues. -Sat. 10–5; Sun. 2–5 (closed Mon. and hldys.). Free.

Paintings, sculpture, decorative arts, prints (Renaissance-20th century), pre-Columbian Collection, Delhom Gallery and Institute for Study and Research in Ceramics. Coins and artifacts from 19th-century Charlotte branch of U.S. Mint.

Mound State Monument Archaeological Museum: Rte. 69, Moundville, Ala. 35474. Open: daily 9–5 (closed Dec. 25). Adm.: $2 (children $1).

Twenty prehistoric Indian mounds, excavated artifacts, re-created temple and village of Moundville Indians. Trailer and tent campgrounds. Operated by Alabama Museum of Natural History. The University of Alabama.

Mystic Seaport: Mystic, Conn. 06355. Open: daily. May-Oct. 9–5; Nov.-April 9–4 (closed Dec. 25). Adm.: $8.50 (5–15s, $4.25). Two-day tickets and group rates available.

Maritime museum emphasizing Age of Sail. Tall ships, including Charles W. Morgan, 1841 whaling ship. Waterfront village with working craftsmen and demonstrations of maritime skills. Small boat collection and exhibits of figureheads and marine art. Working shipyard; planetarium. Summer steamboat rides at additional charge.

Nelson-Atkins Museum of Art, The: 4525 Oak St., Kansas City, Mo. 64111. Open: Tues.-Sat. 10–5, Sun. 1–5 (closed Mon.; also Jan. 1, Memorial Day, July 4, Thanksgiving, Dec. 25). Adm.: $2; students and under 18s, free. Free on Sun.

Egyptian, Oriental, classic, and European art. American paintings and decorative arts; five Early American rooms. Pre-Columbian and Indian art. Children's Museum, lectures, films, musical programs.

Newark Museum: 49 Washington St., Newark, N.J. 07101. Open: daily 12–5 (closed Jan. 1, July 4, Thanksgiving, Dec. 25). Free.

Collections: American painting, sculpture; Tibetan, Chinese, Japanese arts; decorative arts, ancient glass and ceramics; natural science, ethnology. Planetarium. Ballantine House restoration. Fire Museum. Sculpture garden. Junior Museum. Newark's oldest schoolhouse (1784).

New Mexico, Museum of: Admin. bldg. at 113 Lincoln St., P.O. Box 2087, Santa Fe, N.M. 87503. Museum of Fine Arts, Museum of International Folk Art, Palace of the Governors. Open: daily 9–4:45 (closed Mon. Oct. 15-March 15; also state hldys). Laboratory of Anthropology. Open: Mon.-Fri. 9–4:45 (closed Sat., Sun., and hldys.). Adm. Free; donation requested.

Exhibits of fine arts, folk arts; history of Southwest and of American Indian; archeology; ethnology.

New Orleans Museum of Art: Lelong Ave., City Park, New Orleans, La. 70179. Open: Tues.-Sun. 10–5 (closed Mon.).

Old master paintings from 14th to 19th centuries, including Kress Collection of Italian Art; 20th-century European and American art; African, Oriental and pre-Columbian collections; Latin American Colonial painting and sculpture; prints and photographs, jewels by Fabergé.

New York State Historical Associations: Lake Rd., P.O. Box 800, Rte. 80, Cooperstown, N.Y. 13326.

Administers Farmers' Museum and Fenimore House. See those entries. Also, Cooperstown Graduate Program in history museum studies.

Norton Simon Museum of Art at Pasadena: Colorado Blvd. at Orange Grove, Pasadena, Calif. 91105. Open: Thurs.-Sun. 12–6. Adm.: Thurs.-Sat. $2; students and senior citizens, 75¢; under 12s, free; Sun. $3 for all.

Paintings by old masters and from Italian Renaissance; Dutch 17th-century school; paintings and sculpture by Impressionist and early 20th-century masters; Southeast Asian stone sculptures and bronzes.

Peabody Museum: East India Sq., Salem, Mass. 01970. Open: Mon.-Sat. 10–5, Sun. and hldys., 1–5 (closed Jan. 1, Thanksgiving, Dec. 25). Adm.: $3 students with IDs and senior citizens, $2; 6–16s, $1.50.

Maritime history, ethnology, and natural history. Navigational instruments, Japanese household arts and crafts.

Putnam Museum: 1717 W. 12th St., Davenport, Iowa 52804. Open: Tues.-Sat. 9–5, Sun. 1–5 (closed Mon.; also Jan. 1, Memorial Day, July 4, Labor Day, Thanksgiving, Dec. 25). Adm.: $1.50; 13–18s, and senior citizens, $1. Free Sat. 9–12.

Art, history and natural history; ethnology; archaeology; botany; paleontology; anthropology. Arts of Asia, Africa, Oceania, the American In-

dian and pre-Columbian era.

Ringling Museums: P.O. Box 1838, Sarasota, Fla. 33578. John and Mable Ringling Museum of Art, Asolo Theater, Ringling Residence, Museum of the Circus. Open: Mon.-Fri. 9–7, Sat. 9–5, Sun. 11–6. Adm.: $4.50; 6–12s, $1.75; groups, $4.

Extensive collection of Rubens and Baroque art. Asolo is only 18th-century Italian theater in America. Circus Museum contains gilded wagons and memorabilia.

Rosicrucian Egyptian Museum and Art Gallery: Park and Naglee Aves., San Jose, Calif. 95191. Open: Tues.-Fri. 9–4:40, Sat.-Mon. 12–4:40 (closed Jan. 1, Aug. 2, Thanksgiving, Dec. 25). Guided tours for school groups weekdays. No charge, by appointment.

Egyptian and Oriental antiquities. Mummies, statuary, jewelry, utensils, clothing. Reproduction of Egyptian rock tomb. Babylonian and Assyrian collection. Art gallery.

St. Louis Art Museum, The: Forest Park, St. Louis, Mo. 63110. Open: Tues. 1:30–8:30, Wed.-Sun. 10–5 (closed Mon.; also Jan. 1, Dec. 25). Free.

American, European, African, Oceanic, pre-Columbian, American Indian, and Chinese arts.

San Diego Museum of Art: Balboa Park, San Diego, Calif. 92101. Open: Tues.-Sun. 10–5 (closed Mon.; also Jan. 1, Thanksgiving, Dec. 25). Adm.: $2.50. Free on Tuesday.

European paintings, Renaissance to 20th century; American paintings and decorative arts. Oriental arts, including Indian and Persian miniatures. Contemporary sculpture.

San Diego Museum of Man: 1350 El Prado, Balboa Park, San Diego, Calif. 92101. Open: daily 10–4:30 (closed Jan. 1, Thanksgiving, Dec. 25). Adm.: $2; students, 50¢; 6–16s, 25¢. Free first Tues. of month.

Exhibits on Man of the Western Americas, early man, Indians' life style, and Mayan civilization.

San Diego Society of Natural History—Natural History Museum: Balboa Park, San Diego, Calif. 92112. Open: wkdys. and Sun. 10–4:30 (closed Jan. 1, Thanksgiving, Dec. 25). Adm.: $2.50; 6–17s 50¢; under 6 free.

Mammals, birds, fossils, shells, plants, insects, minerals, marine biology. Emphasis on Southwestern U.S., and Sonora and Baja California.

San Francisco, The Fine Arts Museums of, M.H. de Young Memorial Museum: Kennedy Dr. and Eighth Ave., Golden Gate Park, San Francisco, Calif. 94118.Open: Wed.-Sun. 10–5. Adm.: $2; 6–17s and senior citizens, 50¢. Free first Wed. of month.

Art of Europe, America, Ancient Egypt, Greece, and Rome; traditional arts of Africa, Oceania, and the Americas. See also *California Palace of the Legion of Honor.*

San Francisco Museum of Modern Art: Van Ness at McAllister, San Francisco, Calif. 94102. Open: Tues., Wed., and Fri. 10–6, Thurs. 10–10, Sat. and Sun. 10–5 (closed Mon.; also Jan. 1, Memorial Day, Labor Day, Thanksgiving, Dec. 25). Adm.: $3; under 16s and senior citizens, $1.50. Free Thurs. 6–10.

American and international paintings, sculpture, graphics, photography, and ceramics from entire 20th century.

Science and Energy, American Museum of: 300 South Tulane St., Oak Ridge, Tenn. 37830. Open: Sept-May, Mon.-Sat. 9–5, Sun. 12:30–5; June–Aug., Mon.-Sat. 9–6, Sun. 12:30–6 (closed Jan. 1, Thanksgiving, Dec. 25). Free.

Demonstrations, exhibits, motion pictures, models, etc., relating to all forms of energy.

Seattle Art Museum: Volunteer Park, Seattle, Wash. 98112 and the Pavilion at Seattle Center, Seattle, Wash. 98109. Both open: Tues.-Sat. 10–5 (Thurs. to 9), Sun. 12–5 (closed Mon.; also Jan. 1, Thanksgiving, Dec. 25). Adm.: $2; students and senior citizens, $1; under 6s, free. Free on Thurs.

Asian art and jade; Greek and Roman art; Samuel H. Kress Collection of 14th–18th-century European painting and sculpture. European and American modern art; African art.

Southwest Museum: 234 Museum Dr., Los Angeles, Calif. 90065. Open: Tues.-Sat. 11–5; Sun. 1–5 (closed Mon., major hldys). Adm.: $1.50; students and senior citizens $1; 7–18s 75¢.

American Indian exhibits, ancient and modern. Research library. Casa de Adobe, reproduction of adobe hacienda, at 4605 N. Figueroa St.; 1850s Spanish.

J. B. Speed Art Museum, The: 2035 S. 3rd St., Louisville, Ky. 40208. Open: Tues.-Sat. 10–4; Sun. 2–6 (closed Mon. and hldys.). Contribution $2; students free.

Ancient relics to modern art. Sculpture court.

Toledo Museum of Art, The: Monroe St. at Scottwood Ave., Toledo, Ohio 43697. Open: Tues.-Sat. 9–5, Sun. 1–5 (closed Mon. and legal hldys.). Free.

European and American paintings and decorative arts. Ancient and medieval art; books, prints, graphics. Ancient and American glass.

Virginia Museum of Fine Arts: Boulevard and Grove Ave., Richmond, Va. 23221. Open: Tues.-Sat. 11–5, Sun. 1–5 (closed Mon.; also Jan. 1, July 4, Thanksgiving, Dec. 25). Adm.: Suggested donation of $1.

World art of all periods, Lillian Thomas Pratt Collection of Fabergé objects, South Asian art.

Wadsworth Atheneum: 600 Main St., Hartford, Conn. 06103. Open: Tues.-Sun. 11–5 Tues.-Fri. 5–7 (1st fl. galleries only) (closed Mon.; and most major hldys.) Adm.: $2; 13–18s and senior citizens, $1; under 13s, free. Free on Thurs.

European and American paintings and drawings. Sculpture. Bronzes, silver, porcelain, American period furniture, art library.

Walker Art Center: Vineland Pl., Minneapolis, Minn. 55403. Open: Tues.-Sat. 10–5 (special exhibition galleries, 5–8), Sun. 11–5 (closed Mon.; also major hldys.). Free.

Collection of major 20th-century paintings, sculpture, drawings, and prints. Music, dance, film, theater, and educational programs.

Walters Art Gallery: 600 North Charles St., Baltimore, Md. 21201. Open: Tues.-Sun. 11–5. (closed Mon., Jan. 1, July 4, Thanksgiving, Dec. 24–25). Adm.: $2; students and senior citizens, $1; under 18s, free. Free on Wednesday.

Art from ancient empires through 19th-century Europe.

Wheelwright Museum of the American Indian: 704 Camino Lejo, Santa Fe, N.M. 87502. Open: May-Oct., Mon.-Sat. 10–4:45, Sun. 1–4:45; Nov.-April, same as above except closed Mon. (closed Jan. 1, Easter, Thanksgiving, Dec. 25). Free.

Baskets, textiles, pottery, jewelry. Historic and contemporary Indian art.

Worcester Art Museum: 55 Salisbury St., Worcester, Mass. 01608. Open: Tues.-Sat. 10–5, Sun. 1–5 (closed Mon.; also Jan. 1, July 4, Thanksgiving, Dec. 25). Free.

Second largest museum in New England with art spanning 50 centuries.

1. Summer hours (June 10-Labor Day), Mon.-Sat. 10–9, Sun. 12–9. 2. Combination rates are available for Farmers' Museum, Fenimore House, and National Baseball Hall of Fame.

SPORTS

Sports Personalities

A name in parentheses is the original name or form of name. Localities are places of birth. Dates of birth appear as month/day/year. **Boldface** years in parentheses are dates of **(birth-death).**
Information has been gathered from many sources, including the individuals themselves. However, the *Information Please Almanac* cannot guarantee the accuracy of every individual item.

Aaron, Hank (Henry) (baseball); Mobile, Ala., 2/5/1934
Abdul-Jabbar, Kareem (Lewis Ferdinand Alcindor, Jr.) (basketball); New York City, 4/16/1947
Adderly, Herbert A. (football); Philadelphia, 6/8/1939
Alcindor, Lew. *See* Abdul-Jabbar
Ali, Muhammad (Cassius Clay) (boxing); Louisville, Ky., 1/18/1942
Allen, Dick (Richard Anthony) (baseball); Wampum, Pa., 3/8/1942
Alworth, Lance (football); Houston, 8/3/1940
Anderson, Donny (Gary Donny) (football); Brooklyn, N.Y., 4/3/1949
Anderson, Ken (football); Batavia, Ill., 2/15/1949
Anderson, Sparky (George) (baseball); Bridgewater, S.D., 2/22/1934
Anthony, Earl (bowling); Kent, Wash., 4/27/1938
Appling, Luke (baseball); High Point, N.C., 4/2/1907
Arcaro, Eddie (George Edward) (jockey); Cincinnati, 2/19/1916
Ashe, Arthur (tennis); Richmond, Va., 7/10/1943
Austin, Tracy (tennis); Rolling Hills, Calif., 12/2/1962
Babashoff, Shirley (swimming); Whittier, Calif., 1/31/1957
Baer, Max (boxer); Omaha, Neb. **(1909-1959)**
Bakken, Jim (James Leroy) (football); Madison, Wis., 11/2/1940
Banks, Ernie (baseball); Dallas, 1/31/1931
Bannister, Roger (runner); Harrow, England, 3/24/1929
Barry, Rick (Richard) (basketball); Elizabeth, N.J., 3/28/1944
Bauer, Hank (Henry) (baseball); East St. Louis, Ill., 7/31/1922
Baugh, Sammy (football); Temple, Tex., 3/17/1914
Bayi, Filbert (runner); Karratu, Tanganyika, 6/23/1953
Baylor, Elgin (basketball); Washington, D.C., 9/16/1934
Beamon, Bob (long jumper); New York City, 8/2/1946
Beliveau, Jean (hockey); Three Rivers, Quebec, Canada, 8/31/1931
Beman, Deane (golf); Washington, D.C., 4/22/1938
Bench, Johnny (Johnny Lee) (baseball); Oklahoma City, 12/7/1947
Berg, Patty (Patricia Jane) (golf); Minneapolis, 2/13/1918
Berning, Susie Maxwell (golf); Pasadena, Calif., 7/22/1941
Berra, Yogi (Lawrence) (baseball); St. Louis, 5/12/1925
Biletnikoff, Frederick (football); Erie, Pa., 2/23/1943
Bird, Larry (basketball); French Lick, Ind., 12/7/1956
Blaik, Earl H. (football); Detroit, 2/15/1897
Blanda, George Frederick (football); Youngwood, Pa., 9/17/1927
Blue, Vida (baseball); Mansfield, La., 7/28/1949
Borg, Björn (tennis); Stockholm, 6/6/1956
Boros, Julius (golf); Fairfield, Conn., 3/3/1920
Bossy, Mike (hockey); Montreal, 1/22/1957
Boston, Ralph (long jumper); Laurel, Miss., 5/9/1939
Bradley, Bill (William Warren) (basketball); Crystal City, Mo., 7/28/1943
Bradshaw, Terry (football); Shreveport, La., 9/2/1948
Brett, George (baseball); Glendale, W. Va., 5/15/1953
Brock, Louis Clark (baseball); El Dorado, Ark., 6/18/1939
Brown, Jimmy (football); St. Simon Island, Ga., 2/17/1936
Brown, Larry (football); Clairton, Pa., 9/19/1947
Brumel, Valeri (high jumper); Tolbuzino, Siberia, 4/14/1942
Bryant, Rosalyn Evette (track); Chicago, 1/7/1956
Burton, Michael (swimming); Des Moines, Iowa, 7/3/1947
Butkus, Dick (Richard Marvin) (football); Chicago, 12/9/1942
Campanella, Roy (baseball); Homestead, Pa., 11/19/1921
Campbell, Earl (football); Tyler, Tex., 3/29/1955
Caponi, Donna Maria (golf); Detroit, 1/29/1945
Cappelletti, Gino (football); Keewatin, Minn., 3/26/1934
Carew, Rod (Rodney Cline) (baseball); Gatun, Panama, 10/1/1945
Carlos, John (sprinter); New York City, 6/5/1945
Carlton, Steven Norman (baseball); Miami, Fla., 12/22/1944
Carner, Joanne Gunderson (Mrs. Don) (golf); Kirkland, Wash., 3/4/1939
Casals, Rosemary (tennis); San Francisco, 9/16/1948
Casper, Billy (golf); San Diego, Calif., 6/24/1931
Caulkins, Tracy (swimming); Wimona, Minn., 1/11/63
Cauthen, Steve (jockey); Covington, Ky., 5/1/1960
Chamberlain, Wilt (Wilton) (basketball); Philadelphia, 8/21/1936
Chinaglia, Giorgio (soccer); Carrara, Italy, 1/24/1947
Clarke, Bobby (Robert Earle) (hockey); Flin Flon, Manitoba, Canada, 8/13/1949
Clay, Cassius. *See* Ali, Muhammad
Clemente, Roberto Walker (baseball); Carolina, Puerto Rico **(1934-1972)**
Cobb, Tyrus Raymond (Ty) (baseball); Narrows, Ga. **(1886-1961)**
Cochran, Barbara Ann (skiing); Claremont, N.H., 1/4/1951
Cochran, Marilyn (skiing); Burlington, Vt., 2/7/1950
Cochran, Robert (skiing); Claremont, N.H., 12/11/1951
Coe, Sebastian Newbold (track); London, England, 9/29/1956
Colavito, Rocky (Rocco Domenico) (baseball); New York City, 8/10/1933
Comaneci, Nadia (gymnast); Onesti, Romania, 11/12/1961
Connors, Jimmy (James Scott) (tennis); East St. Louis, Ill., 9/2/1952
Cordero, Angel (jockey); Santurce, Puerto Rico, 5/8/1942
Cournoyer, Yvan Serge (hockey); Drummondville, Quebec, Canada, 11/22/1943
Court, Margaret Smith (tennis); Albury, New South Wales, Australia, 7/16/1942
Cousy, Bob (basketball); New York City, 8/9/1928
Crenshaw, Ben (golf); Austin, Tex., 1/11/1952
Cronin, Joe (baseball executive); San Francisco, 10/12/1906
Cruyff, Johan (soccer); Amsterdam, Netherlands, 4/25/47
Csonka, Larry (Lawrence Richard) (football); Stow, Ohio, 12/25/1946
Dancer, Stanley (harness racing); New Egypt, N.J., 7/25/1927
Dark, Alvin (baseball); Comanche, Okla., 1/7/1922
Davenport, Willie (track); Troy, Ala., 6/6/1943
Dawson, Leonard Ray (football); Alliance, Ohio, 6/20/1935
Dean, Dizzy (Jay Hanna) (baseball); Lucas, Ark. **(1911-1974)**
DeBusschere, Dave (basketball); Detroit, 10/16/1940
Delvecchio, Alex Peter (hockey); Fort William, Ontario, Canada, 12/4/1931
Demaret, Jim (golf); Houston, 5/10/1910
Dempsey, Jack (William H.) (boxing); Manassa, Colo. **(1895-1983)**
DeVicenzo, Roberto (golf); Buenos Aires, 4/14/1923
Dietz, James W. (rowing); New York, N.Y., 1/12/1949
DiMaggio, Joe (baseball); Martinez, Calif., 11/25/1914
Dionne, Marcel (hockey); Drummondville, Quebec, Canada, 8/3/1951
Dominguín, Luis Miguel (matador); Madrid, 12/9/1926
Dorsett, Tony (football); Rochester, Pa., 4/7/1954
Dryden, Kenneth (hockey); Hamilton, Ontario, Canada, 8/4/1947
Drysdale, Don (baseball); Van Nuys, Calif., 7/23/1936
Duran, Roberto (boxing); Panama City, 6/16/1951
Durocher, Leo (baseball); West Springfield, Mass., 7/27/1906
Durr, François (tennis); Algiers, Algeria, 12/25/1942
El Cordobés, (Manuel Benítez Pérez) (matador); Palma del Río, Córdoba, Spain, 5/4/1936(?)
Elder, Lee (golf); Dallas, 7/14/1934
Emerson, Roy (tennis); Kingsway, Australia, 11/3/1936
Ender, Kornelia (swimming); Plauen, East Germany, 10/25/1958
Erving, Julius (Dr. J) (basketball); Roosevelt, N.Y., 2/22/1950
Esposito, Phil (Philip Anthony) (hockey); Sault Ste. Marie, Ontario, Canada, 2/20/1942
Ewbank, Weeb (football); Richmond, Ind., 5/6/1907
Feller, Robert (Bobby) (baseball); Van Meter, Iowa, 11/3/1918
Feuerbach, Allan Dean (track); Preston, Iowa, 1/12/1948
Finley, Charles O. (sportsman); Ensley, Ala., 2/22/1918
Fischer, Bobby (chess); Chicago, 3/9/1943
Fitzsimmons, Bob (Robert Prometheus) (boxer); Cornwall, England **(1862-1917)**
Fleming, Peggy Gale (ice skating); San Jose, Calif., 7/27/1948
Ford, Whitey (Edward) (baseball); New York City, 10/21/1928
Foreman, George (boxing); Marshall, Tex., 1/10/1949
Fosbury, Richard (high jumper); Portland, Ore., 3/6/1947
Fox, Nellie (Jacob Nelson) (baseball); St. Thomas, Pa. **(1927-1975)**
Foxx, James Emory (baseball); Sudlersville, Md., **(1907-1967)**
Foyt, A. J. (auto racing); Houston, 1/16/1935
Francis, Emile (hockey); North Battleford, Sask., 9/13/1926
Fratianne, Linda (figure skating); Los Angeles, 8/2/1960
Frazier, Joe (boxing); Beauford, S.C., 1/17/1944
Frazier, Walt (basketball); Atlanta, 3/29/1945
Frick, Ford C. (baseball); Wawaka, Ind., **(1894-1978)**
Furniss, Bruce (swimming); Fresno, Calif., 5/27/1957

Gabriel, Roman (football); Wilmington, N.C., 8/5/1940
Gallagher, Michael Donald (skiing); Yonkers, N.Y., 10/3/1941
Gehrig, Lou (Henry Louis Gehrig) (baseball); New York City **(1903-1941)**
Geoffrion, Bernie (Boom Boom) (hockey); Montreal, 2/14/1931
Gerulaitis, Vitas (tennis); Brooklyn, N.Y., 7/26/1954
Giacomin, Ed (hockey); Sudbury, Ontario, Canada, 6/6/1939
Gibson, Bob (baseball); Omaha, Neb., 11/9/1935
Gifford, Frank (football); Santa Monica, Calif., 8/16/1930
Gilbert, Rod (Rodrique) (hockey); Montreal, 7/1/1941
Gilmore, Artis (basketball); Chipley, Fla., 9/21/1949
Glance, Harvey (track); Phenix City, Ala., 3/28/1957
Gonzalez, Pancho (tennis); Los Angeles, 5/9/1928
Goodell, Brian Stuart (swimming); Stockton, Calif., 4/2/1959
Goodrich, Gail (basketball); Los Angeles, 4/23/1943
Goolagong Cawley, Evonne (tennis); Griffith, Australia, 7/31/1951
Gottfried, Brian (tennis); Baltimore, Md., 1/27/1952
Graham, David (golf); Windson, Australia, 5/23/1946
Graham, Otto Everett (football); Waukegan, Ill., 12/6/1921
Grange, Red (Harold) (football); Forksville, Pa., 6/13/1904
Green, Hubert (golf); Birmingham, Ala., 12/28/1946
Greene, Charles E. (sprinter); Pine Bluff, Ark., 3/21/1945
Gretzky, Wayne (hockey); Brantford, Ont., 1/26/1961
Griese, Bob (Robert Allen) (football); Evansville, Ind., 2/3/1945
Grove, Lefty (Robert Moses) (baseball); Lonaconing, Md., **(1900-1975)**
Groza, Lou (football); Martins Ferry, Ohio, 1/25/1924
Guidry, Ronald Ames (baseball); Lafayette, La., 8/28/1950
Gunter, Nancy Richey (tennis); San Angelo, Tex., 8/23/1942
Halas, George (football); Chicago **(1895-1983)**
Hall, Gary (swimming); Fayetteville, N.C., 8/7/1951
Hamill, Dorothy (figure skater); Chicago, 1956(?)
Hammond, Kathy (runner); Sacramento, Calif., 11/2/1951
Harris, Franco (football); Ft. Dix, N.J., 3/7/1950
Hartack, William, Jr. (jockey); Colver, Pa., 12/9/1932
Haughton, William (harness racing); Gloversville, N.Y., 11/2/1923
Havlicek, John (basketball); Martins Ferry, Ohio, 4/8/1940
Hayes, Elvin (basketball); Rayville, La., 11/17/1945
Heiden, Eric (speed skating); Madison, Wis., 6/14/1958
Hencken, John (swimming); Culver City, Calif., 5/29/1954
Henderson, Rickey (baseball); Chicago, 12/25/1958
Henie, Sonja (ice skater); Oslo **(1912-1969)**
Hernandez, Keith (baseball); San Francisco, 10/20/1953
Hines, James (sprinter); Dumas, Ark., 9/10/1946
Hodges, Gil (baseball); Princeton, Ind. **(1924-1972)**
Hogan, Ben (golf); Dublin, Tex., 8/13/1912
Holmes, Larry (boxing); Cuthert, Ga., 11/3/1949
Hornsby, Rogers (baseball); Winters, Tex. **(1896-1963)**
Hornung, Paul (football); Louisville, Ky., 12/23/1935
Houk, Ralph (baseball); Lawrence, Kan., 8/9/1919
Howard, Elston (baseball); St. Louis **(1929-1980)**
Howe, Gordon (hockey); Floral, Sask., Canada, 3/31/1928
Howell, Jim Lee (football); Lonoke, Ark., 9/27/1914
Hubbell, Carl (baseball); Carthage, Mo., 6/22/1903
Huff, Sam (Robert Lee) (football); Morgantown, W. Va., 10/4/1934
Hull, Bobby (hockey); Point Anne, Ontario, Canada, 1/3/1939
Hunter, Jim (Catfish) (baseball); Hertford, N.C., 4/8/1946
Huntley, Joni (track); McMinnville, Ore., 8/4/1956
Hutson, Donald (football); Pine Bluff, Ark., 1/31/1913
Insko, Del (harness racing); Amboy, Minn., 7/10/1931
Irwin, Hale (golf); Joplin, Mo., 6/3/1945
Jackson, Reggie (baseball); Wyncote, Pa., 5/18/1946
Jeffries, James J. (boxer); Carroll, Ohio **(1875-1953)**
Jenkins, Ferguson Arthur (baseball); Chatham, Ontario, Canada, 12/13/1943
Jenner, (W.) Bruce (track); Mt. Kisco, N.Y., 10/28/1949
Jezek, Linda (swimming); Palo Alto, Calif., 3/10/1960
Johnson, Earvin (Magic) (basketball); E. Lansing, Mich., 8/14/1959
Johnson, Anthony (rowing); Washington, D.C., 11/16/1940
Johnson, Jack (John Arthur Johnson) (boxer); Galveston, Tex. **(1876-1946)**
Johnson, Rafer (decathlon); Hillsboro, Tex., 8/18/1935
Jones, Deacon (David) (football); Eatonville, Fla., 12/9/1938
Juantoreno, Alberto (track); Santiago, Cuba, 12/3/1951
Jurgensen, Sonny (football); Wilmington, N.C., 8/23/1934
Kaat, Jim (baseball); Zeeland, Mich., 11/7/1938
Kaline, Al (Albert) (baseball); Baltimore, 12/19/1934
Keino, Kipchoge (runner); Kapchemoiymo, Kenya, 1/?/1940
Kelly, Leroy (football); Philadelphia, 5/20/1942
Kelly, Red (Leonard Patrick) (hockey); Simcoe, Ontario, Canada, 7/9/1927
Killebrew, Harmon (baseball); Payette, Idaho, 6/29/1936
Killy, Jean-Claude (skiing); Saint-Cloud, France, 8/30/1943
King, Billie Jean (Billie Jean Moffitt) (tennis); Long Beach, Calif., 11/22/1943
Kinsella, John (swimming); Oak Park, Ill., 8/26/1952
Kodes, Jan (tennis); Prague, 3/1/1946
Kolb, Claudia (swimming); Hayward, Calif., 12/19/1949
Koosman, Jerry Martin (baseball); Appleton, Minn., 12/23/1942
Korbut, Olga (gymnast); Grodno, Byelorussia, U.S.S.R., 5/16/1955
Koufax, Sandy (Sanford) (baseball); Brooklyn, N.Y., 12/30/1935
Kramer, Jack (tennis); Las Vegas, Nev., 8/1/1921
Kramer, Jerry (football); Jordan, Mont., 1/23/1936
Kuhn, Bowie Kent (baseball); Takoma Park, Md., 10/28/1926
Kwalik, Ted (Thaddeus John) (football); McKees Rocks, Pa., 4/15/1947
Lafleur, Guy Damien (hockey); Thurson, Quebec, Canada, 8/20/1951
Laird, Ronald (walker); Louisville, Ky., 5/31/1935
Lamonica, Daryle (football); Fresno, Calif., 7/17/1941
Landis, Kenesaw Mountain (1st baseball commissioner); Millville, Ohio **(1866-1944)**
Landry, Tom (football); Mission, Tex., 9/11/1924
Landy, John (runner); Australia, 4/4/1930
Larrieu, Francie (track); Palo Alto, Calif., 11/28/1952
Lasorda, Tom (baseball); Norristown, Pa., 9/22/1927
Laver, Rod (tennis); Rockhampton, Australia, 8/9/1938
Lendl, Ivan (tennis); Prague, 3/7/1960
Leonard, Benny (Benjamin Leiner) (boxer); New York City **(1896-1947)**
Leonard, Sugar Ray (boxing); Wilmington, N.C., 5/17/1956
Lewis, Carl (track); Willingboro, N.J., 7/1/1961
Linehan, Kim (swimming); Bronxville, N.Y., 12/11/1962
Liquori, Marty (runner); Montclair, N.J., 9/11/1949
Little, Floyd Douglas (football); New Haven, Conn., 7/4/1942
Little, Lou (football); Leominster, Mass., **(1893-1979)**
Littler, Gene (golf); San Diego, Calif., 11/16/1920
Lloyd, Chris Evert (Christine Marie) (tennis); Fort Lauderdale, Fla., 12/21/1954
Lombardi, Vince (football); Brooklyn, N.Y. **(1913-1970)**
Longden, Johnny (horse racing); Wakefield, England, 2/14/1907
Lopez, Al (baseball); Tampa, Fla., 8/20/1908
Lopez, Nancy (golf); Torrance, Calif., 1/6/1957
Louis, Joe (Joe Louis Barrow) (boxing); Lafayette, Ala. **(1914-1981)**
Lynn, Frederic Michael (baseball); Chicago, Ill., 2/3/1952
Mack, Connie (Cornelius Alexander McGillicuddy) (baseball executive); East Brookfield, Mass. **(1862-1956)**
Mackey, John (football); New York City, 9/24/1941
Mahovlich, Frank (Francis William) (hockey); Timmins, Ontario, Canada, 1/10/1938
Mann, Carol (golf); Buffalo, N.Y., 2/3/1941
Manning, Madeline (runner); Cleveland, 1/11/1948
Mantle, Mickey Charles (baseball); Spavinaw, Okla., 10/20/1931
Marciano, Rocky (boxing); Brockton, Mass. **(1923-1969)**
Marichal, Juan (baseball); Laguna Verde, Montecristi, Dominican Republic, 10/20/1937
Maris, Roger (baseball); Hibbing, Minn., 9/10/1934
Martin, Billy (Alfred Manuel) (baseball); Berkeley, Calif., 5/16/1928
Martin, Rick (Richard Lionel) (hockey); Verdun, Quebec, Canada, 7/26/1951
Mathews, Ed (Edwin) (baseball); Texarkana, Tex., 10/13/1931
Matson, Randy (shot putter); Kilgore, Tex., 3/5/1945
Mays, Willie (baseball); Westfield, Ala., 5/6/1931
McAdoo, Bob (basketball); Greensboro, N.C., 9/25/1951
McCarthy, Joe (Joseph Vincent) (baseball); Philadelphia **(1887-1978)**
McCovey, Willie Lee (baseball); Mobile, Ala., 1/10/1938
McEnroe, John Patrick, Jr. (tennis); Wiesbaden, Germany, 2/16/1959
McGraw, John Joseph (baseball); Truxton, N.Y. **(1873-1934)**
McLain, Dennis (baseball); Chicago, 3/24/1944
McMillan, Kathy Laverne (track); Raeford, N.C., 11/7/1957
Merrill, Janice (track); New London, Conn., 6/18/1962
Meyer, Deborah (swimming); Haddonfield, N.J., 8/14/1952
Middlecoff, Cary (golf); Halls, Tenn., 1/6/1921
Mikita, Stan (hockey); Sokolce, Czechoslovakia, 5/20/1940
Milburn, Rodney, Jr. (hurdler); Opelousas, La., 5/18/1950
Miller, Johnny (golf); San Francisco, 4/29/1947
Montgomery, Jim (swimming); Madison, Wis., 1/24/1955
Moore, Archie (boxing); Benoit, Miss., 12/13/1916
Morgan, Joe Leonard (baseball); Bonham, Tex., 9/19/1943
Morrall, Earl (football); Muskegon, Mich., 5/17/1934
Morton, Craig L. (football); Flint, Mich., 2/5/1943
Mosconi, Willie (pocket billiards); Philadelphia, 6/27/1913
Moser, Annemarie. *See* Proell, Annemarie
Moses, Edward Corley (track); Dayton, Ohio, 8/31/1958
Munson, Thurman (baseball); Akron, Ohio, **(1947-1979)**
Murphy, Calvin (basketball), Norwalk, Conn., 5/9/1948
Musial, Stan (baseball); Donora, Pa., 11/21/1920
Naber, John (swimming); Evanston, Ill., 1/20/1956
Namath, Joe (Joseph William) (football); Beaver Falls, Pa., 5/31/1943
Nastase, Ilie (tennis); Bucharest, 7/19/1946

Navratilova, Martina (tennis); Prague, 10/18/1956
Nehemiah, Renaldo (track); Newark, N.J., 3/24/1959
Newcombe, John (tennis); Sydney, Australia, 5/23/1943
Niekro, Phil (baseball); Lansing, Ohio, 4/1/1939
Nicklaus, Jack (golf); Columbus, Ohio, 1/21/1940
North, Lowell (yachting); Springfield, Mo., 12/2/1929
Oerter, Al (discus thrower); New York City, 9/19/1936
Okker, Tom (tennis); Amsterdam, 2/22/1944
Oldfield, Barney (racing driver); Fulton County, Ohio **(1878-1946)**
Oliva, Tony (Pedro) (baseball); Pinar Del Rio, Cuba, 7/20/1940
Olsen, Merlin Jay (football); Logan, Utah, 9/15/1940
Orantes, Manuel (tennis); Granada, Spain, 2/6/1949
Orr, Bobby (hockey); Parry Sound, Ontario, Canada, 3/20/1948
Ovett, Steve (track); Brighton, England, 10/9/1955
Owens, Jesse (track); Decatur, Ala. **(1914-1980)**
Pace, Darrell (archery); Cincinnati, 10/23/1956
Paige, Satchel (Leroy) (baseball); Mobile, Ala., **(1906-1982)**
Palmer, Arnold (golf); Latrobe, Pa., 9/10/1929
Palmer, James Alvin (baseball); New York City, 10/15/1945
Parent, Bernard Marcel (hockey); Montreal, 4/3/1945
Park, Brad (Douglas Bradford) (hockey); Toronto, Ontario, Canada, 7/6/1948
Parseghian, Ara (football); Akron, Ohio, 5/21/1923
Pasarell, Charles (tennis); San Juan, Puerto Rico, 2/12/1944
Patterson, Floyd (boxing); Waco, N.C., 1/4/1935
Peete, Calvin (golf); Detroit, Mich., 7/18/1943
Pelé (Edson Arantes do Nascimento) (soccer); Tres Coracoes, Brazil, 10/23/1940
Perry, Gaylord (baseball); Williamston, N.C., 9/15/1938
Perry, Jim (baseball); Williamston, N.C., 9/15/1938
Pettit, Bob (basketball); Baton Rouge, La., 12/12/1932
Petty, Richard Lee (auto racing); Randleman, N.C., 7/2/1937
Plante, Jacques (hockey); Shawinigan Falls, Quebec, Canada, 1/17/1929
Player, Gary (golf); Johannesburg, South Africa, 11/1/1935
Plunkett, Jim (football); San Jose, Calif., 12/5/1947
Potvin, Denis Charles (hockey); Hull, Quebec, Canada, 10/29/1953
Powell, Boog (John) (baseball); Lakeland, Fla., 8/17/1941
Prefontaine, Steve Roland (runner); Coos Bay, Ore. **(1951-1975)**
Proell, Annemarie Moser (Alpine skier); Kleinarl, Austria, 3/27/1953
Ralston, Dennis (tennis); Bakersfield, Calif., 7/27/1942
Rankin, Judy Torluemke (golf); St. Louis, Mo., 2/18/1945
Ratelle, Jean (Joseph Gilbert Yvon Jean) (hockey); St. Jean, Quebec, Canada, 10/29/1953
Reed, Willis (basketball); Hico, La., 6/25/1942
Reese, Pee Wee (Harold) (baseball); Ekron, Ky., 7/23/1919
Richard, Maurice (hockey); Montreal, 8/14/1924
Riessen, Martin (tennis); Hinsdale, Ill., 12/4/1941
Rigney, William (baseball); Alameda, Calif., 1/29/1918
Rizzuto, Phil (baseball); New York City, 9/25/1918
Roark, Helen Wills Moody (tennis); Centerville, Calif., 10/6/1906
Robertson, Oscar (basketball); Charlotte, Tenn., 11/24/1938
Robinson, Arnie (track); San Diego, Calif., 4/7/1948
Robinson, Brooks (baseball); Little Rock, Ark., 5/18/1937
Robinson, Frank (baseball); Beaumont, Tex., 8/31/1935
Robinson, Jackie (baseball); Cairo, Ga. **(1919-1972)**
Robinson, Larry Clark (hockey); Marvelville, Ontario, Canada, 6/2/1951
Robinson, (Sugar) Ray (boxing); Detroit, 5/3/1920
Rockne, Knute Kenneth (football); Voss, Norway **(1888-1931)**
Rono, Harry (track); Kiptaragon, Kenya, 2/12/1952
Rose, Pete (Peter Edward) (baseball); Cincinnati, 4/14/1942
Rosenbloom, Maxie (boxing); New York City **(1904-1976)**
Rosewall, Ken (tennis); Sydney, Australia, 11/2/1934
Rote, Kyle (football); San Antonio, 10/27/1928
Rozelle, Pete (Alvin Ray) (commissioner of National Football League); South Gate, Calif., 3/1/1926
Rudolph, Wilma Glodean (sprinter); St. Bethlehem, Tenn., 6/23/1940
Russell, Bill (basketball); Monroe, La., 2/12/1934
Ruth, Babe (George Herman Ruth) (baseball); Baltimore **(1895-1948)**
Rutherford, Johnny (auto racing); Fort Worth, 3/12/1938
Ryan, Nolan (Lynn Nolan, Jr.) (baseball); Refugio, Tex., 1/31/1947
Ryun, Jim (runner); Wichita, Kan., 4/29/1947
Salazar, Alberto (track); Havana, 8/7/1958
Santana, Manuel (Manuel Santana Martinez) (tennis); Chamartín, Spain, 5/10/1938
Sayers, Gale (football); Wichita, Kan., 5/30/1943
Schmidt, Mike (baseball); Dayton, Ohio, 9/27/1949
Schoendienst, Al (Albert) (baseball); Germantown, Ill., 2/2/1923
Schollander, Donald (swimming); Charlotte, N.C., 4/30/1946
Seagren, Bob (Robert Lloyd) (pole vaulter); Pomona, Calif., 10/17/1946
Seaver, Tom (baseball); Fresno, Calif., 11/17/1944
Seidler, Maren (track); Brooklyn, N.Y., 6/11/1962
Shoemaker, Willie (jockey); Fabens, Tex., 8/19/1931
Shorter, Frank (runner); Munich, Germany, 10/31/1947
Shula, Don (Donald Francis) (football); Grand River, Ohio, 1/4/1930
Silvester, Jay (discus thrower); Tremonton, Utah, 2/27/1937
Simpson, O. J. (Orenthal James) (football); San Francisco, 7/9/1947
Sims, Billy (football); St. Louis, 9/18/1955
Smith, Bubba (Charles Aaron) (football); Orange, Tex., 2/28/1945
Smith, Ronnie Ray (sprinter); Los Angeles, 3/28/1949
Smith, Stanley Roger (tennis); Pasadena, Calif., 12/14/1946
Smith, Tommie (sprinter); Clarksville, Tex., 6/5/1944
Smoke, Marcia Jones (canoeing); Oklahoma City, 7/18/1941
Snead, Sam (golf); Hot Springs, Va., 5/27/1912
Sneva, Tom (auto racing); Spokane, Wash., 6/1/1948
Snider, Duke (Edwin) (baseball); Los Angeles, 9/19/1926
Solomon, Harold (tennis); Washington, D.C., 9/17/1952
Spahn, Warren (baseball); Buffalo, N.Y., 4/23/1921
Speaker, Tristram (baseball); Hubbard City, Tex. **(1888-1958)**
Spinks, Leon (boxing); St. Louis, 7/11/1953
Spitz, Mark (swimming); Modesto, Calif., 2/10/1950
Stabler, Kenneth (football); Foley, Ala., 12/25/1945
Stagg, Amos Alonzo (football); West Orange, N.J. **(1862-1965)**
Stargell, Willie (Wilver Dornell) (baseball); Earlsboro, Okla., 3/6/1941
Starr, Bart (football); Montgomery, Ala., 1/9/1934
Staubach, Roger (football); Cincinnati, 2/5/1942
Steinkraus, William C. (equestrian); Cleveland, 10/12/1925
Stenerud, Jan (football); Fetsund, Norway, 11/26/1942
Stengel, Casey (Charles Dillon) (baseball); Kansas City, Mo. **(1891-1975)**
Stenmark, Ingemar (Alpine skier); Tarnaby, Sweden, 3/18/1956
Stockton, Richard LaClede (tennis); New York City, 2/18/1951
Stones, Dwight Edwin (track); Los Angeles, 12/6/1953
Sullivan, John Lawrence (boxer); Boston **(1858-1918)**
Sutton, Don (Donald Howard) (baseball); Clio, Ala., 4/2/1945
Swann, Lynn (football); Alcoa, Tenn., 3/7/1952
Tanner, Leonard Roscoe III (tennis); Chattanooga, Tenn., 10/15/1951
Tarkenton, Fran (Francis) (football); Richmond, Va., 2/3/1940
Tebbetts, Birdie (George R.) (baseball); Nashua, N.H., 11/10/1914
Thoeni, Gustavo (Alpine skier); Trafoi, Italy, 2/28/1951
Thompson, David (basketball); Shelby, N.C., 7/13/1954
Thorpe, Jim (James Francis Thorpe) (all-around athlete); nr. Prague, Okla. **(1888-1953)**
Tilden, William Tatem II (tennis); Philadelphia **(1893-1953)**
Tittle, Y. A. (Yelberton Abraham) (football); Marshall, Tex., 10/24/1926
Trevino, Lee (golf); Dallas, 12/1/1939
Tunney, Gene (James J.) (boxing); New York City **(1898-1978)**
Tyus, Wyomia (runner); Griffin, Ga., 8/29/1945
Unitas, John (football); Pittsburgh, 5/7/1933
Unser, Al (auto racing); Albuquerque, N. Mex., 5/29/1939
Unser, Bobby (auto racing); Albuquerque N. Mex., 2/20/1934
Valenzuela, Fernando (baseball); Sonora, Mexico, 11/1/1960
Van Brocklin, Norm (football); Eagle Butte, S. Dak. **(1926-1983)**
Vilas, Guillermo (tennis); Mar del Plata, Argentina, 8/17/1952
Viren, Lasse (track); Myrskyla, Finland, 7/12/1949
Wade, Virginia (tennis); Bournemouth, England, 7/10/1945
Wagner, Honus (John Peter Honus) (baseball); Carnegie, Pa. **(1867-1955)**
Walcott, Jersey Joe (Arnold Cream) (boxing); Merchantville, N.J., 1/31/1914
Walton, Bill (basketball); La Mesa, Calif., 11/5/1952
Watson, Martha Rae (track); Long Beach, Calif., 8/19/1946
Watson, Tom (golf); Kansas City, Mo., 9/4/1949
Weaver, Earl (baseball); St. Louis, 8/14/1930
Webster, Alex (football); Kearny, N.J., 4/19/1931
Weiskopf, Tom (golf); Massillon, Ohio, 11/9/1942
Weiss, George (baseball executive); New Haven, Conn. **(1895-1972)**
Weissmuller, Johnny (swimmer and actor); Windber, Pa. **(1904-1984)**
West, Jerry (basketball); Cheylan, W. Va., 5/28/1938
White, Willye B. (long jumper); Money, Miss., 1/1/1936
Whitworth, Kathy (golf); Monahans, Tex., 9/27/1939
Wilkens, Mac Maurice (track); Eugene, Ore., 11/15/1950
Wilkins, Lennie (basketball); 11/25/1937
Wilkinson, Bud (football); Minneapolis, 4/23/1916
Williams, Dick (baseball); St. Louis, 5/7/1929
Williams, Ted (baseball); San Diego, Calif., 8/30/1918
Wills, Maury (baseball); Washington, D.C., 10/2/1932
Winfield, Dave (baseball); St. Paul, Minn., 10/3/1951
Wohlhuter, Richard C. (runner); Geneva, Ill. 12/23/1945
Woodhead, Cynthia (swimming); Riverside, Calif., 2/7/1964
Wottle, David James (runner); Canton, Ohio, 8/7/1950
Wright, Mickey (Mary Kathryn) (golf); San Diego, Calif., 2/14/1935
Yarborough, Cale (William Caleb) (auto racing); Timmonsville, S.C., 3/27/1939
Yastrzemski, Carl (baseball); Southampton, N.Y., 8/22/1939
Young, Cy (Denton True Young) (baseball); Gilmore, Ohio **(1867-1955)**

THE OLYMPIC GAMES

(W)—Site of Winter Games. (S)—Site of Summer Games

1896	Athens	1936	Garmisch-Partenkirchen (W)	1968	Mexico City (S)
1900	Paris	1936	Berlin (S)	1972	Sapporo, Japan (W)
1904	St. Louis	1948	St. Moritz (W)	1972	Munich (S)
1906	Athens	1948	London (S)	1976	Innsbruck, Austria (W)
1908	London	1952	Oslo (W)	1976	Montreal (S)
1912	Stockholm	1952	Helsinki (S)	1980	Lake Placid (W)
1920	Antwerp	1956	Cortina d'Ampezzo, Italy (W)	1980	Moscow (S)
1924	Chamonix (W)	1956	Melbourne (S)	1984	Sarajevo, Yugoslavia (W)
1924	Paris (S)	1960	Squaw Valley, Calif. (W)	1984	Los Angeles (S)
1928	St. Moritz (W)	1960	Rome (S)	1988	Calgary, Alberta (W)
1928	Amsterdam (S)	1964	Innsbruck, Austria (W)	1988	Seoul, South Korea (S)
1932	Lake Placid (W)	1964	Tokyo (S)		
1932	Los Angeles (S)	1968	Grenoble, France (W)		

The first Olympic Games of which there is record occurred in 776 B.C. and consisted of one event, a great foot race of about 200 yards held on a plain by the River Alpheus (now the Ruphia) just outside the little town of Olympia in Greece. It was from that date that the Greeks began to keep their calendar by "Olympiads," the four-year spans between the celebrations of the famous games.

The modern Olympic Games, which started in Athens in 1896, are the result of the devotion of a French educator, Baron Pierre de Coubertin, to the idea that, since young people and athletics have gone together down the ages, education and athletics might well go hand-in-hand toward a better international understanding.

At the top of the organization responsible for the Olympic movement and the staging of the Games every four years is the International Olympic Committee (IOC). Other important roles are played by National Olympic Committees in each participating country, international sports federations, and the Organizing Committee of the host city.

In 1979, the IOC consisted of 89 members, elected by the IOC itself. Its headquarters are in Lausanne, Switzerland. The president of the IOC is Juan Antonio Samaranch of Spain.

The Olympic motto is "Citius, Altius, Fortius"—"Faster, Higher, Stronger." The Olympic symbol is five interlocking circles colored blue, yellow, black, green, and red, on a white background, representing the five continents. At least one of these colors appears in the national flag of every country.

Summer Games

TRACK AND FIELD—MEN

100-Meter Dash

1896	Thomas Burke, United States	12s
1900	Francis W. Jarvis, United States	10.8s
1904	Archie Hahn, United States	11s
1906	Archie Hahn, United States	11.2s
1908	Reginald Walker, South Africa	10.8s
1912	Ralph Craig, United States	10.8s
1920	Charles Paddock, United States	10.8s
1924	Harold Abrahams, Great Britain	10.6s
1928	Percy Williams, Canada	10.8s
1932	Eddie Tolan, United States	10.3s
1936	Jesse Owens, United States	10.3s[1]
1948	Harrison Dillard, United States	10.3s
1952	Lindy Remigino, United States	10.4s
1956	Bobby Morrow, United States	10.5s
1960	Armin Hary, Germany	10.2s
1964	Robert Hayes, United States	10s
1968	James Hines, United States	9.9s
1972	Valery Borzov, U.S.S.R.	10.14s
1976	Hasely Crawford, Trinidad and Tobago	10.06s
1980	Allan Wells, Britain	10.25s
1984	Carl Lewis, United States	9.99s

1. Wind assisted.

200-Meter Dash

1900	John Tewksbury, United States	22.2s
1904	Archie Hahn, United States	21.6s
1908	Robert Kerr, Canada	22.6s
1912	Ralph Craig, United States	21.7s
1920	Allan Woodring, United States	22s
1924	Jackson Scholz, United States	21.6s
1928	Percy Williams, Canada	21.8s
1932	Eddie Tolan, United States	21.2s
1936	Jesse Owens, United States	20.7s
1948	Melvin E. Patton, United States	21.1s
1952	Andrew Stanfield, United States	20.7s
1956	Bobby Morrow, United States	20.6s
1960	Livio Berruti, Italy	20.5s
1964	Henry Carr, United States	20.3s
1968	Tommie Smith, United States	19.8s
1972	Valery Borzov, U.S.S.R.	20s
1976	Don Quarrie, Jamaica	20.23s
1980	Pietro Mennea, Italy	20.19s
1984	Carl Lewis, United States	19.80s

400-Meter Dash

1896	Thomas Burke, United States	54.2s
1900	Maxwell Long, United States	49.4s
1904	Harry Hillman, United States	49.2s
1906	Paul Pilgrim, United States	53.2s
1908	Wyndham Halswelle, Great Britain (walkover)	50s
1912	Charles Reidpath, United States	48.2s
1920	Bevil Rudd, South Africa	49.6s
1924	Eric Liddell, Great Britain	47.6s
1928	Ray Barbuti, United States	47.8s
1932	William Carr, United States	46.2s
1936	Archie Williams, United States	46.5s
1948	Arthur Wint, Jamaica, B.W.I.	46.2s
1952	George Rhoden, Jamaica, B.W.I.	45.9s
1956	Charles Jenkins, United States	46.7s
1960	Otis Davis, United States	44.9s
1964	Mike Larrabee, United States	45.1s

1968	Lee Evans, United States	43.8s
1972	Vincent Matthews, United States	44.66s
1976	Alberto Juantorena, Cuba	44.26s
1980	Viktor Markin, U.S.S.R.	44.60s
1984	Alonzo Babers, United States	44.27s

800-Meter Run

1896	Edwin Flack, Australia	2m11s
1900	Alfred Tysoe, Great Britain	2m1.4s
1904	James Lightbody, United States	1m56s
1906	Paul Pilgrim, United States	2m1.2s
1908	Mel Sheppard, United States	1m52.8s
1912	Ted Meredith, United States	1m51.9s
1920	Albert Hill, Great Britain	1m53.4s
1924	Douglas Lowe, Great Britain	1m52.4s
1928	Douglas Lowe, Great Britain	1m51.8s
1932	Thomas Hampson, Great Britain	1m49.8s
1936	John Woodruff, United States	1m52.9s
1948	Malvin Whitfield, United States	1m49.2s
1952	Malvin Whitfield, United States	1m49.2s
1956	Tom Courtney, United States	1m47.7s
1960	Peter Snell, New Zealand	1m46.3s
1964	Peter Snell, New Zealand	1m45.1s
1968	Ralph Doubell, Australia	1m44.3s
1972	David Wottle, United States	1m45.9s
1976	Alberto Juantorena, Cuba	1m43.5s
1980	Steve Ovett, Britain	1m45.4s
1984	Joaquin Cruz, Brazil	1m43.0s

1,500-Meter Run

1896	Edwin Flack, Australia	4m33.2s
1900	Charles Bennett, Great Britain	4m6s
1904	James Lightbody, United States	4m5.4s
1906	James Lightbody, United States	4m12s
1908	Mel Sheppard, United States	4m3.4s
1912	Arnold Jackson, Great Britain	3m56.8s
1920	Albert Hill, Great Britain	4m1.8s
1924	Paavo Nurmi, Finland	3m53.6s
1928	Harry Larva, Finland	3m53.2s
1932	Luigi Beccali, Italy	3m51.2s
1936	Jack Lovelock, New Zealand	3m47.8s
1948	Henri Eriksson, Sweden	3m49.8s
1952	Joseph Barthel, Luxembourg	3m45.2s
1956	Ron Delany, Ireland	3m41.2s
1960	Herb Elliott, Australia	3m35.6s
1964	Peter Snell, New Zealand	3m38.1s
1968	Kipchoge Keino, Kenya	3m34.9s
1972	Pekka Vasala, Finland	3m36.3s
1976	John Walker, New Zealand	3m39.17s
1980	Sebastian Coe, Britain	3m38.4s
1984	Sebastian Coe, Britain	3m32.53s

1,500 meter wheelchair

1984	Paul Van Winkel, Belgium	3m58.50s

5,000-Meter Run

1912	Hannes Kolehmainen, Finland	14m36.6s
1920	Joseph Guillemot, France	14m55.6s
1924	Paavo Nurmi, Finland	14m31.2s
1928	Willie Ritola, Finland	14m38s
1932	Lauri Lehtinen, Finland	14m30s
1936	Gunnar Hockert, Finland	14m22.2s
1948	Gaston Reiff, Belgium	14m17.6s
1952	Emil Zatopek, Czechoslovakia	14m6.6s
1956	Vladimir Kuts, U.S.S.R.	13m39.6s
1960	Murray Halberg, New Zealand	13m43.4s
1964	Bob Schul, United States	13m48.8s
1968	Mohamed Gammoudi, Tunisia	14m.05s
1972	Lasse Viren, Finland	13m26.4s
1976	Lasse Viren, Finland	13m24.76s
1980	Miruts Yifter, Ethiopia	13m21s
1984	Savd Advita, Morocco	13m5.59s

5-Mile Run

1906	H. Hawtrey, Great Britain	26m26.2s
1908	Emil Voigt, Great Britain	25m11.2s

10,000-Meter Run

1912	Hannes Kolehmainen, Finland	31m20.8s
1920	Paavo Nurmi, Finland	31m45.8s
1924	Willie Ritola, Finland	30m23.2s
1928	Paavo Nurmi, Finland	30m18.8s
1932	Janusz Kusocinski, Poland	30m11.4s
1936	Ilmari Salminen, Finland	30m15.4s
1948	Emil Zatopek, Czechoslovakia	29m59.6s
1952	Emil Zatopek, Czechoslovakia	29m17s
1956	Vladimir Kuts, U.S.S.R.	28m45.6s
1960	Peter Bolotnikov, U.S.S.R.	28m32.2s
1964	Billy Mills, United States	28m24.4s
1968	Naftali Temu, Kenya	29m27.4s
1972	Lasse Viren, Finland	27m38.4s
1976	Lasse Viren, Finland	27m40.38s
1980	Miruts Yifter, Ethiopia	27m42.7s
1984	Alberto Cova, Italy	27m47.5s

Marathon

1896	Spiridon Loues, Greece	2h58m50s
1900	Michel Teato, France	2h59m45s
1904	Thomas Hicks, United States	3h28m53s
1906	William J. Sherring, Canada	2h51m23.65s
1908	John J. Hayes, United States	2h55m18.4s
1912	Kenneth McArthur, South Africa	2h36m54.8s
1920	Hannes Kolehmainen, Finland	2h32m35.8s
1924	Albin Stenroos, Finland	2h41m22.6s
1928	A. B. El Quafi, France	2h32m57s
1932	Juan Zabala, Argentina	2h31m36s
1936	Kitei Son, Japan	2h29m19.2s
1948	Delfo Cabrera, Argentina	2h34m51.6s
1952	Emil Zatopek, Czechoslovakia	2h23m3.2s
1956	Alain Mimoun, France	2h25m
1960	Abebe Bikila, Ethiopia	2h15m16.2s
1964	Abebe Bikila, Ethiopia	2h12m11.2s
1968	Mamo Wold, Ethiopia	2h20m26.4s
1972	Frank Shorter, United States	2h12m19.8s
1976	Walter Cierpinski, East Germany	2h09m55s
1980	Walter Cierpinski, East Germany	2h11m3s
1984	Carlos Lopes, Portugal	2hr9m.55s

110-Meter Hurdles

1896	Thomas Curtis, United States	17.6s
1900	Alvin Kraenzlein, United States	15.4s
1904	Frederick Schule, United States	16s
1906	R. G. Leavitt, United States	16.2s
1908	Forrest Smithson, United States	15s
1912	Frederick Kelly, United States	15.1s
1920	Earl Thomson, Canada	14.8s
1924	Daniel Kinsey, United States	15s
1928	Sydney Atkinson, South Africa	14.8s
1932	George Saling, United States	14.6s
1936	Forrest Towns, United States	14.2s
1948	William Porter, United States	13.9s
1952	Harrison Dillard, United States	13.7s
1956	Lee Calhoun, United States	13.5s
1960	Lee Calhoun, United States	13.8s
1964	Hayes Jones, United States	13.6s
1968	Willie Davenport, United States	13.3s
1972	Rodney Milburn, United States	13.24s
1976	Guy Drut, France	13.30s
1980	Thomas Munkett, East Germany	13.39s
1984	Roger Kingdom, United States	13.20s

200-Meter Hurdles

1900	Alvin Kraenzlein, United States	25.4s
1904	Harry Hillman, United States	24.6s

400-Meter Hurdles

1900	John Tewksbury, United States	57.6s
1904	Harry Hillman, United States	53s
1908	Charles Bacon, United States	55s
1920	Frank Loomis, United States	54s
1924	F. Morgan Taylor, United States	52.6s
1928	Lord David Burghley, Great Britain	53.4s
1932	Robert Tisdall, Ireland	51.8s[1]
1936	Glenn Hardin, United States	52.4s
1948	Roy Cochran, United States	51.1s
1952	Charles Moore, United States	50.8s
1956	Glenn Davis, United States	50.1s
1960	Glenn Davis, United States	49.3s
1964	Rex Cawley, United States	49.6s
1968	David Hemery, Great Britain	48.1s
1972	John Akii-Bua, Uganda	47.8s
1976	Edwin Moses, United States	47.64s
1980	Volker Beck, East Germany	48.70s
1984	Edwin Moses, United States	47.75s

1. Record not allowed.

2,500-Meter Steeplechase

1900	George Orton, United States	7m34s
1904	James Lightbody, United States	7m39.6s

3,000-Meter Steeplechase

1920	Percy Hodge, Great Britain	10m0.4s
1924	Willie Ritola, Finland	9m33.6s
1928	Toivo Loukola, Finland	9m21.8s
1932	Volmari Iso-Hollo, Finland	10m33.4s[1]
1936	Volmari Iso-Hollo, Finland	9m3.8s
1948	Thure Sjoestrand, Sweden	9m4.6s
1952	Horace Ashenfelter, United States	8m45.4s
1956	Chris Brasher, Great Britain	8m41.2s
1960	Zdzislaw Krzyskowiak, Poland	8m34.2s
1964	Gaston Roelants, Belgium	8m30.8s
1968	Amos Biwott, Kenya	8m51s
1972	Kipchoge Keino, Kenya	8m23.6s
1976	Anders Gardervd, Sweden	8m08.02s
1980	Bronislaw Malinowski, Poland	8m9.7s
1984	Julius Korir, Kenya	8m11.80s

1. About 3,450 meters—extra lap by error.

Cross-Country

1912	Hannes Kolehmainen, Finland (8,000 meters)	45m11.6s
1920	Paavo Nurmi, Finland (10,000 meters)	27m15s
1924	Paavo Nurmi, Finland (10,000 meters)	32m54.8s

Cross-Country Team Races

		Pts
1912	Sweden (8,000 meters)	10
1920	Finland (10,000 meters)	10
1924	Finland (10,000 meters)	11

1,500-Meter Walk

1906	George V. Bonhag, United States	7m12.6s

3,000-Meter Walk

1920	Ugo Frigerio, Italy	13m14.2s

10,000-Meter Walk

1912	George Goulding, Canada	46m28.4s
1920	Ugo Frigerio, Italy	48m6.2s
1924	Ugo Frigerio, Italy	47m49s
1948	John Mikaelsson, Sweden	45m13.2s
1952	John Mikaelsson, Sweden	45m2.8s

20,000-Meter Walk

1956	Leonid Spirin, U.S.S.R.	1h31m27.4s
1960	Vladimir Golubnichy, U.S.S.R.	1h34m7.2s
1964	Ken Mathews, Great Britain	1h29m34s
1968	Vladimir Golubnichy, U.S.S.R.	1h33m58.4s
1972	Peter Frenkel, East Germany	1h26m42.4s
1976	Daniel Bautista, Mexico	1h24m40.6s
1980	Maurizio Damiliano, Italy	1h23m35.5s
1984	Ernesto Conto, Mexico	1m23.13s

50,000-Meter Walk

1932	Thomas W. Green, Great Britain	4h50m10s
1936	Harold Whitlock, Great Britain	4h30m41.1s
1948	John Ljunggren, Sweden	4h41m52s
1952	Giuseppe Dordoni, Italy	4h28m7.8s
1956	Norman Read, New Zealand	4h30m42.8s
1960	Donald Thompson, Great Britain	4h25m30s
1964	Abdon Pamich, Italy	4h11m12.4s
1968	Christoph Hohne, East Germany	4h20m13.6s
1972	Bern Kannernberg, West Germany	3h56m11.6s
1980	Hartwig Gauder, East Germany	3h49m24s
1984	Raul Gonzalez, Mexico	3hr47m26s

400-Meter Relay (4 × 100)

1912	Great Britain	42.4s
1920	United States	42.2s
1924	United States	41s
1928	United States	41s
1932	United States	40s
1936	United States	39.8s
1948	United States	40.6s
1952	United States	40.1s
1956	United States	39.5s
1960	Germany	39.5s
1964	United States	39s
1968	United States	38.2s
1972	United States	38.19s
1976	United States	38.33s
1980	U.S.S.R.	38.26s
1984	United States	37.83s

1,600-Meter Relay (200–200–400–800)

1908	United States	3m29.4s

1,600-Meter Relay (4 × 400)

1912	United States	3m16.6s
1920	Great Britain	3m22.2s
1924	United States	3m16s
1928	United States	3m14.2s
1932	United States	3m8.2s
1936	Great Britain	3m9s
1948	United States	3m10.4s
1952	Jamaica, B.W.I.	3m3.9s
1956	United States	3m4.8s
1960	United States	3m2.2s
1964	United States	3m0.7s
1968	United States	2m56.1s
1972	Kenya	2m59.8s
1976	United States	2m58.65s
1980	U.S.S.R.	3m01.1s
1984	United States	2m57.91s

Team Race

		Pts
1900	Great Britain (5,000 meters)	26
1904	United States (4 miles)	27
1908	Great Britain (3 miles)	6
1912	United States (3,000 meters)	9
1920	United States (3,000 meters)	10
1924	Finland (3,000 meters)	9

Standing High Jump

1900	Ray Ewry, United States	5 ft 5 in.
1904	Ray Ewry, United States	4 ft 11 in.
1906	Ray Ewry, United States	5 ft 1 5/8 in.
1908	Ray Ewry, United States	5 ft 2 in.
1912	Platt Adams, United States	5 ft 4 1/8 in.

Running High Jump

1896	Ellery Clark, United States	5 ft 11 1/4 in.
1900	Irving Baxter, United States	6 ft 2 3/4 in.
1904	Samuel Jones, United States	5 ft 11 in.
1906	Con Leahy, Ireland	5 ft 9 7/8 in.
1908	Harry Porter, United States	6 ft 3 in.
1912	Alma Richards, United States	6 ft 4 in.
1920	Richmond Landon, United States	6 ft 4 1/4 in.
1924	Harold Osborn, United States	6 ft 5 15/16 in.
1928	Robert W. King, United States	6 ft 4 3/8 in.
1932	Duncan McNaughton, Canada	6 ft 5 5/8 in.
1936	Cornelius Johnson, United States	6 ft 7 15/16 in.
1948	John Winter, Australia	6 ft 6 in.
1952	Walter Davis, United States	6 ft 8 5/16 in.
1956	Charles Dumas, United States	6 ft 11 1/4 in.
1960	Robert Shavlakadze, U.S.S.R.	7 ft 1 in.
1964	Valeri Brumel, U.S.S.R.	7 ft 1 3/4 in.
1968	Dick Fosbury, United States	7 ft 4 1/4 in.
1972	Yuri Tarmak, U.S.S.R.	7 ft 3 3/4 in.
1976	Jacek Wszola, Poland	(2.25m) 7 ft 4 1/2 in.
1980	Gerd Wessig, East Germany	7 ft 8 3/4 in.
1984	Dietmar Mogenburg, West Germany	7 ft 8 1/2 in.

Standing Long Jump

1900	Ray Ewry, United States	10 ft 6 2/5 in.
1904	Ray Ewry, United States	11 ft 4 7/8 in.
1906	Ray Ewry, United States	10 ft 10 in.
1908	Ray Ewry, United States	10 ft 11 1/4 in.
1912	Constantin Tsicilitiras, Greece	11 ft 1/4 in.

Long Jump

1896	Ellery Clark, United States	20 ft 9 3/4 in.
1900	Alvin Kraenzlein, United States	23 ft 6 7/8 in.
1904	Myer Prinstein, United States	24 ft 1 in.
1906	Myer Prinstein, United States	23 ft 7 1/2 in.
1908	Frank Irons, United States	24 ft 6 1/2 in.
1912	Albert Gutterson, United States	24 ft 11 1/4 in.
1920	William Petterssen, Sweden	23 ft 5 1/2 in.
1924	DeHart Hubbard, United States	24 ft 5 1/8 in.
1928	Edward B. Hamm, United States	25 ft 4 3/4 in.
1932	Edward Gordon, United States	25 ft 3/4 in.
1936	Jesse Owens, United States	26 ft. 5 5/16 in.
1948	Willie Steele, United States	25 ft 8 in.
1952	Jerome Biffle, United States	24 ft 10 in.
1956	Gregory Bell, United States	25 ft 8 1/4 in.
1960	Ralph Boston, United States	26 ft 7 3/4 in.
1964	Lynn Davies, Great Britain	26 ft 5 3/4 in.
1968	Bob Beamon, United States	29 ft 2 1/2 in.
1972	Randy Williams, United States	27 ft 1/2 in.
1976	Arnie Robinson, United States	(8.35m) 24 ft 7 3/4 in.
1980	Lutz Dombrowski, E. Germany	28 ft 1/4 in.
1984	Carl Lewis, United States	28 ft 1/4 in.

Standing Triple Jump

1900	Ray Ewry, United States	34 ft 8 1/2 in.
1904	Ray Ewry, United States	34 ft 7 1/4 in.

Triple Jump

1896	James B. Connolly, United States	45 ft
1900	Myer Prinstein, United States	47 ft 4 1/4 in.
1904	Myer Prinstein, United States	47 ft
1906	P. G. O'Connor, Ireland	46 ft 2 in.
1908	Timothy Ahearne, Great Britain	48 ft 11 1/4 in.
1912	Gustaf Lindblom, Sweden	48 ft 5 1/8 in.
1920	Vilho Tuulos, Finland	47 ft 6 7/8 in.
1924	Archie Winter, Australia	50 ft 11 1/8 in.
1928	Mikio Oda, Japan	49 ft 10 13/16 in.
1932	Chuhei Nambu, Japan	51 ft 7 in.
1936	Naoto Tajima, Japan	52 ft 5 7/8 in.
1948	Arne Ahman, Sweden	50 ft 6 1/4 in.
1952	Adhemar da Silva, Brazil	53 ft 2 1/2 in.
1956	Adhemar da Silva, Brazil	53 ft 7 1/2 in.
1960	Jozef Schmidt, Poland	55 ft 1 3/4 in.
1964	Jozef Schmidt, Poland	55 ft 3 1/4 in.
1968	Viktor Saneyev, U.S.S.R.	57 ft 3/4 in.
1972	Viktor Saneyev, U.S.S.R.	56 ft 11 in.
1976	Viktor Saneyev, U.S.S.R.	(17.29m) 56 ft 8 3/4 in.
1980	Jaak Uudmae, U.S.S.R.	56 ft 11 1/8 in.
1984	Al Joyner, United States	56 ft 7 1/2 in.

Pole Vault

1896	William Hoyt, United States	10 ft 9 3/4 in.
1900	Irving Baxter, United States	10 ft 9 7/8 in.
1904	Charles Dvorak, United States	11 ft 6 in.
1906	Fernand Gouder, France	11 ft 6 in.
1908	Alfred Gilbert, United States, and Edward Cook, United States (tie)	12 ft 2 in.
1912	Harry Babcock, United States	12 ft 11 1/2 in.
1920	Frank Foss, United States	13 ft 5 9/16 in.
1924	Lee Barnes, United States	12 ft 11 1/2 in.
1928	Sabin W. Carr, United States	13 ft 9 3/8 in.
1932	William Miller, United States	14 ft 1 7/8 in.
1936	Earle Meadows, United States	14 ft 3 1/4 in.
1948	Guinn Smith, United States	14 ft 1 1/4 in.
1952	Robert Richards, United States	14 ft 11 1/8 in.
1956	Robert Richards, United States	14 ft 11 1/2 in.
1960	Don Bragg, United States	15 ft 5 1/8 in.
1964	Fred Hansen, United States	16 ft 8 3/4 in.
1968	Bob Seagren, United States	17 ft 8 1/2 in.
1972	Wolfgang Nordwig, East Germany	18 ft 1/2 in.
1976	Tadeusz Slusarski, Poland	(5.50m) 18 ft 1/2 in.
1980	Wladyslaw Kozakiewicz, Poland	18 ft 11 1/2 in.
1984	Pierre Quinon, France	18 ft 10 1/4 in.

16-lb Shot-Put

1896	Robert Garrett, United States	36 ft 9 3/4 in.
1900	Richard Sheldon, United States	46 ft 3 1/8 in.
1904	Ralph Rose, United States	48 ft 7 in.
1906	Martin Sheridan, United States	40 ft 4 4/5 in.
1908	Ralph Rose, United States	46 ft 7 1/2 in.
1912	Pat McDonald, United States	50 ft 4 in.
1920	Ville Porhola, Finland	48 ft 7 1/8 in.
1924	Clarence Houser, United States	49 ft 2 1/2 in.
1928	John Kuck, United States	52 ft 11 11/16 in.
1932	Leo Sexton, United States	52 ft 6 3/16 in.
1936	Hans Woellke, Germany	53 ft 1 3/4 in.
1948	Wilbur Thompson, United States	56 ft 2 in.
1952	Parry O'Brien, United States	57 ft 1 1/2 in.
1956	Parry O'Brien, United States	60 ft 11 in.
1960	Bill Nieder, United States	64 ft 6 3/4 in.
1964	Dallas Long, United States	66 ft 8 1/4 in.
1968	Randy Matson, United States	67 ft 4 3/4 in.
1972	Wladyslaw Komar, Poland	69 ft 6 in.
1976	Udo Beyer, East Germany	(21.05m) 69 ft 3/4 in.
1980	Vladimir Kiselyov, U.S.S.R.	70 ft 1/2 in.
1984	Alessandro Andrei, Italy	69 ft 9 in.

16-lb Shot-Put (Both Hands)

1912	Ralph Rose, United States	90 ft 5 3/8 in.

Discus Throw

1896	Robert Garrett, United States	95 ft 7 1/2 in.
1900	Rudolf Bauer, Hungary	118 ft 2 7/8 in.
1904	Martin Sheridan, United States	128 ft 10 1/2 in.
1906	Martin Sheridan, United States	136 ft 1/3 in.
1908	Martin Sheridan, United States	134 ft 2 in.
1912	Armas Taipale, Finland	145 ft 9/16 in.
1920	Elmer Niklander, Finland	146 ft 7 in.
1924	Clarence Houser, United States	151 ft 5 1/4 in.
1928	Clarence Houser, United States	155 ft 2 4/5 in.
1932	John Anderson, United States	162 ft 4 7/8 in.
1936	Ken Carpenter, United States	165 ft 7 3/8 in.
1948	Adolfo Consolini, Italy	173 ft 2 in.
1952	Simeon Iness, United States	180 ft 6 1/2 in.

1956	Al Oerter, United States	184 ft 10 1/2 in.
1960	Al Oerter, United States	194 ft 2 in.
1964	Al Oerter, United States	200 ft 1 1/2 in.
1968	Al Oerter, United States	212 ft 6 in.
1972	Ludvik Danek, Czechoslovakia	211 ft 3 in.
1976	Mac Wilkins, United States	(67.5m) 221 ft 5 in.
1980	Viktor Rashchupkin, U.S.S.R.	218 ft 8 in.
1984	Rolf Dannenberg, West Germany	218 ft 6 in.

Discus Throw—Greek Style

1906	Werner Jaervinen, Finland	115 ft 4 in.
1908	Martin Sheridan, United States	124 ft 8 in.

Discus Throw (Both Hands)

1912	Armas Taipale, Finland	271 ft 10 1/8 in.

Javelin Throw

1906	Eric Lemming, Sweden	175 ft 6 in.
1908	Eric Lemming, Sweden	179 ft 10 1/2 in.
1912	Eric Lemming, Sweden	198 ft 11 1/4 in.
1920	Jonni Myyra, Finland	215 ft 9 3/4 in.
1924	Jonni Myyra, Finland	206 ft 6 3/4 in.
1928	Eric Lundquist, Sweden	218 ft 6 1/8 in.
1932	Matti Jarvinen, Finland	238 ft 7 in.
1936	Gerhard Stoeck, Germany	235 ft 8 5/16 in.
1948	Kaj Rautavaara, Finland	228 ft 10 1/2 in.
1952	Cy Young, United States	242 ft 3/4 in.
1956	Egil Danielsen, Norway	281 ft 2 1/4 in.
1960	Viktor Tsibulenko, U.S.S.R.	277 ft 8 3/8 in.
1964	Pauli Nevala, Finland	271 ft 2 1/4 in.
1968	Janis Lusis, U.S.S.R.	295 ft 7 in.
1972	Klaus Wolfermann, West Germany	296 ft 10 in.
1976	Miklos Nemeth, Hungary	(94.58m) 310 ft 4 in.
1980	Dainis Kula, U.S.S.R.	299 ft 2 3/8 in.
1984	Arto Haerkoenen, Finland	284 ft 8 in.

Javelin Throw—Free Style

1908	Eric Lemming, Sweden	178 ft 7 1/2 in.

Javelin Throw (Both Hands)

1912	Julius Saaristo, Finland	358 ft 11 1/2 in.

16-lb Hammer Throw

1900	John Flanagan, United States	167 ft 4 in.
1904	John Flanagan, United States	168 ft 1 in.
1908	John Flanagan, United States	170 ft 4 1/4 in.
1912	Matt McGrath, United States	179 ft 7 1/8 in.
1920	Pat Ryan, United States	173 ft 5 5/8 in.
1924	Fred Tootell, United States	174 ft 10 1/4 in.
1928	Patrick O'Callaghan, Ireland	168 ft 7 1/2 in.
1932	Patrick O'Callaghan, Ireland	176 ft 11 1/8 in.
1936	Karl Hein, Germany	185 ft 4 in.
1948	Imre Nemeth, Hungary	183 ft 11 1/2 in.
1952	Jozsef Csermak, Hungary	197 ft 11 9/16 in.
1956	Harold Connolly, United States	207 ft 2 3/4 in.
1960	Vasily Rudenkov, U.S.S.R.	220 ft 1 5/8 in.
1964	Romuald Klim, U.S.S.R.	228 ft 9 1/2 in.
1968	Gyula Zsivotzky, Hungary	240 ft 8 in.
1972	Anatoly Bondarchuk, U.S.S.R.	247 ft 8 1/2 in.
1976	Yuri Sedykh, U.S.S.R.	(77.52m) 254 ft 4 in.
1980	Yuri Sedykh, U.S.S.R.	(81.80m) 268 ft 4 1/2 in.
1984	Juha Tiainen, Finland	256 ft 2 in.

Throwing the Stone (14 lbs.)

1906	Nicolas Georgantas, Greece	65 ft 4 1/5 in.

56-lb Weight Throw

1904	Etienne Desmarteau, Canada	34 ft 4 in.
1920	Pat McDonald, United States	36 ft 11 5/8 in.

All-Around

1904	Thomas Kiely, Great Britain	6,036 pts.

Pentathlon

1906	H. Mellander, Sweden	24 pts.
1912	Jim Thorpe, United States	
	Ferdinand Bie, Norway	—
1920	Eero Lehtonen, Finland	14 pts.
1924	Eero Lehtonen, Finland	16 pts.

Decathlon

1912	Jim Thorpe, United States	—
	Hugo Wieslander, Sweden	—
1920	Helge Lovland, Norway	6,804.35 pts.
1924	Harold Osborn, United States	7,710.775 pts.
1928	Paavo Yrjola, Finland	8,053.29 pts.
1932	James Bausch, United States	8,462.23 pts.
1936	Glenn Morris, United States	7,900 pts.[1]
1948	Robert B. Mathias, United States	7,139 pts.
1952	Robert B. Mathias, United States	7,887 pts.
1956	Milton Campbell, United States	7,937 pts.
1960	Rafer Johnson, United States	8,392 pts.
1964	Willi Holdorf, Germany	7,887 pts.[1]
1968	Bill Toomey, United States	8,193 pts.
1972	Nikolai Avilov, U.S.S.R.	8,454 pts.
1976	Bruce Jenner, United States	8,618 pts.
1980	Daley Thompson, Britain	8,495 pts.
1984	Daley Thompson, Britain	8,797 pts.

1. Point system revised.

Tug of War

1904	United States	1912	Sweden
1906	Germany	1920	Great Britain
1908	Great Britain		

TRACK AND FIELD—WOMEN

100-Meter Dash

1928	Elizabeth Robinson, United States	12.2s
1932	Stella Walsh, Poland	11.9s
1936	Helen Stephens, United States	11.5s
1948	Fanny Blankers-Koen, Netherlands	11.9s
1952	Marjorie Jackson, Australia	11.5s
1956	Betty Cuthbert, Australia	11.5s
1960	Wilma Rudolph, United States	11s
1964	Wyomia Tyus, United States	11.4s
1968	Wyomia Tyus, United States	11s
1972	Renate Stecher, East Germany	11.07s
1976	Annegret Richter, West Germany	11.08s
1980	Lyudmila Kondratyeva, U.S.S.R.	11.06s

200-Meter Dash

1948	Fanny Blankers-Koen, Netherlands	24.4s
1952	Marjorie Jackson, Australia	23.7s
1956	Betty Cuthbert, Australia	23.4s
1960	Wilma Rudolph, United States	24s
1964	Edith McGuire, United States	23s
1968	Irena Szewinska, Poland	22.5s
1972	Renate Stecher, East Germany	22.4s
1976	Baerbel Eckert, East Germany	22.37s
1980	Barbara Wockel, East Germany	22.03s
1984	Valerie Brisco-Hooks, United States	21.81s

400-Meter Dash

1964	Betty Cuthbert, Australia	52s
1968	Colette Besson, France	52s
1972	Monika Zehrt, East Germany	51.08s
1976	Irena Szewinska, Poland	49.29s
1980	Marita Koch, East Germany	48.88s
1984	Valerie Brisco-Hooks, United States	48.83s

800-Meter Run

1928	Lina Radke, Germany	2m16.8s
1960	Ljudmila Shevcova, U.S.S.R.	2m4.3s
1964	Ann Packer, Great Britain	2m1.1s
1968	Madeline Manning, United States	2m0.9s
1972	Hildegard Falck, West Germany	1m58.6s
1976	Tatiana Kazankina, U.S.S.R.	1m54.94s
1980	Nadezhda Olizarenko, U.S.S.R.	1m53.5s
1984	Doina Melinte, Romania	1m57.60s

1,500-Meter Run

1972	Ludmila Bragina, U.S.S.R.	4m01.4s
1976	Tatiana Kazankina, U.S.S.R.	4m05.48s

80-Meter Hurdles

1932	Mildred Didrikson, United States	11.7s
1936	Trebisonda Valla, Italy	11.7s
1948	Fanny Blankers-Koen, Netherlands	11.2s
1952	Shirley S. de la Hunty, Australia	10.9s
1956	Shirley S. de la Hunty, Australia	10.7s
1960	Irina Press, U.S.S.R.	10.8s
1964	Karin Balzer, Germany	10.5s[1]
1968	Maureen Caird, Australia	10.3s

1. Wind assisted.

100-Meter Hurdles

1972	Annelie Ehrhardt, East Germany	12.59s
1976	Johanna Schaller, East Germany	12.77s
1980	Vera Komisova, U.S.S.R.	12.56s
1984	Benita Fitzgerald-Brown, United States	12.84s

400-Meter Relay

1928	Canada	48.4s
1932	United States	47s
1936	United States	46.9s
1948	Netherlands	47.5s
1952	United States	45.9s
1956	Australia	44.5s
1960	United States	44.5s
1964	Poland	43.6s
1968	United States	42.8s
1972	West Germany	42.81s
1976	East Germany	42.55s
1980	East Germany	41.60s
1984	United States	41.65s

1,600-Meter Relay

1972	East Germany	3m23s
1976	East Germany	3m19.23s
1980	U.S.S.R.	3m20.2s
1984	United States	3m18.29s

Marathon

1984	Joan Benoit, United States	2 hr 24 m 52s

Running High Jump

1928	Ethel Catherwood, Canada	5 ft 3 in.
1932	Jean Shiley, United States	5 ft 5 1/4 in.
1936	Ibolya Csak, Hungary	5 ft 3 in.
1948	Alice Coachman, United States	5 ft 6 1/8 in.
1952	Ester Brand, South Africa	5 ft 5 3/4 in.
1956	Mildred McDaniel, United States	5 ft 9 1/4 in.
1960	Iolanda Balas, Romania	6 ft 3/4 in.
1964	Iolanda Balas, U.S.S.R.	6 ft 2 3/4 in.
1968	Miloslava Rezkova, Czechoslovakia	5 ft 11 3/4 in.
1972	Ulrike Meyfarth, West Germany	6 ft 3 5/8 in.
1976	Rosemarie Ackerman, E. Germany	(1.93m) 6 ft 4 in.
1980	Sara Simeoni, Italy	6 ft 5 1/2 in.
1984	Ulrike Meyfarth, West Germany	6 ft 7 1/2 in.

Long Jump

1948	Olga Gyarmati, Hungary	18 ft 8 1/4 in.
1952	Yvette Williams, New Zealand	20 ft 5 3/4 in.
1956	Elzbieta Krzesinska, Poland	20 ft 9 3/4 in.
1960	Vera Krepkina, U.S.S.R.	20 ft 10 3/4 in.
1964	Mary Rand, Great Britain	22 ft 2 in.
1968	Viorica Ciscopoleanu, Romania	22 ft 4 1/2 in.
1972	Heidemarie Rosendahl, West Germany	22 ft 3 in.
1976	Angela Voigt, East Germany	(6.72m) 22 ft 1/2 in.
1980	Tatiana Kolpakova, U.S.S.R.	23 ft 2 in.
1984	Anisoara Stanciu, Romania	22 ft 10 in.

Shot-Put

1948	Micheline Ostermeyer, France	45 ft 1 1/2 in.
1952	Galina Zybina, U.S.S.R.	50 ft 1 1/2 in.
1956	Tamara Tishkyevich, U.S.S.R.	54 ft 5 in.
1960	Tamara Press, U.S.S.R.	56 ft 9 7/8 in.
1964	Tamara Press, U.S.S.R.	59 ft 6 in.
1968	Margitta Gummel, East Germany	64 ft 4 in.
1972	Nadezhda Chizhova, U.S.S.R.	69 ft
1976	Ivanka Christova, Bulgaria	(21.16m) 69 ft 5 in.
1980	Ilona Sluplanek, East Germany	73 ft 6 in.
1984	Claudia Losch, West Germany	67 ft 2 1/4 in.

Discus Throw

1928	Helena Konopacka, Poland	129 ft 11 7/8 in.
1932	Lillian Copeland, United States	133 ft 2 in.
1936	Gisela Mauermayer, Germany	156 ft 3 3/16 in.
1948	Micheline Ostermeyer, France	137 ft 6 1/2 in.
1952	Nina Romaschkova, U.S.S.R.	168 ft 8 7/16 in.
1956	Olga Fikotova, Czechoslovakia	176 ft 1 1/2 in.
1960	Nina Ponomareva, U.S.S.R.	180 ft 8 1/4 in.
1964	Tamara Press, U.S.S.R.	187 ft 10 3/4 in.
1968	Lia Manoliu, Romania	191 ft 2 1/2 in.
1972	Faina Melnik, U.S.S.R.	218 ft 7 in.
1976	Evelin Schlaak, East Germany	(69.0m) 226 ft 4 in.
1980	Evelin Jahl, East Germany	229 ft 6 1/2 in.
1984	Ria Stalman Netherlands	214 ft 5 in.

Javelin Throw

1932	Mildred Didrikson, United States	143 ft 4 in.
1936	Tilly Fleischer, Germany	148 ft 2 3/4 in.
1948	Herma Bauma, Austria	149 ft 6 in.
1952	Dana Zatopek, Czechoslovakia	165 ft 7 in.
1956	Inessa Janzeme, U.S.S.R.	176 ft 8 in.
1960	Elvira Ozolina, U.S.S.R.	183 ft 8 in.
1964	Mihaela Penes, Romania	198 ft 7 1/2 in.
1968	Angela Nemeth, Hungary	198 ft 0 in.
1972	Ruth Fuchs, East Germany	209 ft 7 in.
1976	Ruth Fuchs, East Germany	(65.94m) 216 ft 4 in.
1980	Maria Colon, Cuba	224 ft 5 in.
1984	Tessa Sanderson, Britain	228 ft 2 in.

Pentathlon

1964	Irina Press, U.S.S.R.	5,246 pts.
1968	Ingrid Becker, West Germany	5,098 pts.
1972	Mary Peters, Britain	4,801 pts.
1976	Siegrun Siegl, East Germany	4,745 pts.
1980	Nadyezhda Tkachenko, U.S.S.R.	5,083 pts.
1984	Daniele Masala, Italy	5,469 pts.

400-Meter Hurdle

1984	Nawai El Moutawakel, Morocco	54.61s

3,000-Meter Run

1984	Maricica Puica, Romania	8m35.96s

SWIMMING—MEN

50-Yard Freestyle

1904	Zoltan de Halmay, Hungary	28s

100 Meters Freestyle

1896	Alfred Hajos, Hungary	1m22.2s
1904	Zoltan de Halmay, Hungary	1m2.8s[1]
1906	Charles Daniels, United States	1m13s
1908	Charles Daniels, United States	1m5.6s
1912	Duke P. Kahanamoku, United States	1m3.4s
1920	Duke P. Kahanamoku, United States	1m1.4s
1924	John Weissmuller, United States	59s
1928	John Weissmuller, United States	58.6s
1932	Yasuji Miyazaki, Japan	58.2s
1936	Ferenc Csik, Hungary	57.6s
1948	Walter Ris, United States	57.3s
1952	Clarke Scholes, United States	57.4s
1956	Jon Henricks, Australia	55.4s
1960	John Devitt, Australia	55.2s
1964	Don Schollander, United States	53.4s
1968	Michael Wenden, Australia	52.2s
1972	Mark Spitz, United States	51.22s
1976	Jim Montgomery, United States	49.99s
1980	Jorg Woithe, East Germany	50.40s
1984	Rowdy Gaines, United States	49.80s

1. 100 yards.

200-Meter Freestyle

1900	Frederick Lane, Australia	2m25.2s
1904	Charles Daniels, United States	2m44.2s[1]
1968	Michael Wenden, Australia	1m55.2s
1972	Mark Spitz, United States	1m52.78s
1976	Bruce Furniss, United States	1m50.29s
1980	Sergei Kopliakov, U.S.S.R.	1m49.81s
1984	Michael Gross, West Germany	1m47.44s

1. 220 yards

400-Meter Freestyle

1896	Paul Neumann, Austria	8m12.6s[1]
1904	Charles Daniels, United States	6m16.2s[2]
1906	Otto Sheff, Austria	6m23.8s
1908	Henry Taylor, Great Britain	5m36.8s
1912	George Hodgson, Canada	5m24.4s
1920	Norman Ross, United States	5m26.8s
1926	Jonn Weissmuller, United States	5m4.2s
1928	Albert Zorilla, Argentina	5m1.6s
1932	Clarence Crabbe, United States	4m48.4s
1936	Jack Medica, United States	4m44.5s
1948	William Smith, United States	4m41s
1952	Jean Boiteux, France	4m30.7s
1956	Murray Rose, Australia	4m27.3s
1960	Murray Rose, Australia	4m18.3s
1964	Don Schollander, United States	4m12.2s
1968	Mike Burton, United States	4m9s
1972	Bradford Cooper, Australia	4m00.27s[3]
1976	Brian Goodell, United States	3m51.93s
1980	Vladimir Salnikov, U.S.S.R.	3m51.31s
1984	George DiCarlo, United States	3m51.23s

1. 500 meters. 2. 440 yards. 3. Rick DeMont, United States, won but was disqualified following day for medical reasons.

1,200-Meter Freestyle

1896	Alfred Hajos, Hungary	18m22.2s

1,500 Meter Freestyle

1904	Emil Rausch, Germany	27m18.2s[1]
1906	Henry Taylor, Great Britain	28m28s[2]
1908	Henry Taylor, Great Britain	22m48.4s
1912	George Hodgson, Canada	22m
1920	Norman Ross, United States	22m23.2s
1924	Andrew Charlton, Australia	20m6.6s
1928	Arne Borg, Sweden	19m51.8s
1932	Kusuo Kitamura, Japan	19m12.4s
1936	Noboru Terada, Japan	19m13.7s
1948	James McLane, United States	19m18.5s
1952	Ford Konno, United States	18m30s
1956	Murray Rose, Australia	17m58.9s
1960	Jon Konrads, Australia	17m19.6s
1964	Robert Windle, Australia	17m1.7s
1968	Michael Burton, United States	16m38.9s
1972	Mike Burton, United States	15m52.58s
1976	Brian Goodell, United States	15m02.4s
1980	Vladimir Salnikov, U.S.S.R.	14m58.27s
1984	Michael O'Brien, United States	15m05.2s

1. One mile. 2. 1,600 meters

4,000-Meter Freestyle

1900	John Jarvis, Great Britain	58m24s

100-Meter Backstroke

1904	Walter Brack, Germany	1m16.8s[1]
1908	Arno Bieberstein, Germany	1m24.6s
1912	Harry Hebner, United States	1m21.2s
1920	Warren Kealoha, United States	1m15.2s
1924	Warren Kealoha, United States	1m13.2s
1928	George Kojac, United States	1m8.2s
1932	Masaji Kiyokawa, Japan	1m8.6s
1936	Adolph Kiefer, United States	1m5.9s
1948	Allen Stack, United States	1m6.4s
1952	Yoshinobu Oyakawa, United States	1m5.4s
1956	David Thiele, Australia	1m2.2s
1960	David Thiele, Australia	1m1.9s
1968	Roland Matthes, East Germany	58.7s
1972	Roland Matthes, East Germany	56.58s
1976	John Naber, United States	55.49s
1980	Bengt Baron, Sweden	56.53s
1984	Rick Carey, United States	55.79s

1. 100 yards

200-Meter Backstroke

1900	Ernst Hoppenberg, Germany	2m47s
1964	Jed Graef, United States	2m10.3s
1968	Roland Matthes, East Germany	2m9.6s
1972	Roland Matthes, East Germany	2m2.82s
1976	John Naber, United States	1m59.19s
1980	Sandor Wladar, Hungary	2:01.93s
1984	Rick Carey, United States	2m00.23s

100-Meter Breaststroke

1968	Donald McKenzie, United States	1m7.7s
1972	Nobutaka Taguchi, Japan	1m4.94s
1976	John Hencken, United States	1m03.11s
1980	Duncan Goodhew, Britain	1m03.34s
1984	Steve Lindquist, United States	1m01.65s

200-Meter Breaststroke

1908	Frederick Holman, Great Britain	3m9.2s
1912	Walter Bathe, Germany	3m1.8s
1920	Haken Malmroth, Sweden	3m4.4s
1924	Robert Skelton, United States	2m56.6s
1928	Yoshiyuki Tsuruta, Japan	2m48.8s
1932	Yoshiyuki Tsuruta, Japan	2m45.4s
1936	Tetsuo Hamuro, Japan	2m41.5s
1948	Joseph Verdeur, United States	2m39.3s
1952	John Davies, Australia	2m34.4s
1956	Masura Furukawa, Japan	2m34.7s
1960	Bill Mulliken, United States	2m37.4s
1964	Ian O'Brien, Australia	2m27.8s
1968	Felipe Munoz, Mexico	2m28.7s

1972	John Hencken, United States	2m21.55s
1976	David Willkie, Britain	2m15.11s
1980	Robertas Zulpa, U.S.S.R.	2m15.85s
1984	Victor Davis, Canada	2m13.34s

400-Meter Breaststroke

1904	Georg Zacharias, Germany	7m23.6s[1]
1912	Walter Bathe, Germany	6m29.6s
1920	Haken Malmroth, Sweden	6m31.8s

1. 440 yards.

100-Meter Butterfly

1968	Douglas Russell, United States	55.9s
1972	Mark Spitz, United States	54.27s
1976	Matt Vogel, United States	54.35s
1980	Par Arvidsson, Sweden	54.92s
1984	Michael Gross, West Germany	53.08s

200-Meter Butterfly

1956	Bill Yorzyk, United States	2m19.3s
1960	Mike Troy, United States	2m12.8s
1964	Kevin Berry, Australia	2m6.6s
1968	Carl Robie, United States	2m8.7s
1972	Mark Spitz, United States	2m00.7s
1976	Mike Bruner, United States	1m59.23s
1980	Sergei Fesenko, U.S.S.R.	1m59.76s
1984	Jon Sieben, Australia	1m57.0s

200-Meter Individual Medley

1968	Charles Hickcox, United States	2m12s
1972	Gunnar Larsson, Sweden	2m7.17s

400-Meter Individual Medley

1964	Dick Roth, United States	4m45.4s
1968	Charles Hickcox, United States	4m48.4s
1972	Gunnar Larsson, Sweden	4m31.98s
1976	Rod Strachan, United States	4m23.68s
1980	Aleksandr Sidorenko, U.S.S.R.	4m22.8s
1984	Alex Baumann, Canada	4m17.41s

60-Meter Underwater

1900	de Vaudeville, France	1m53.4s

200-Meter Obstacle

1900	Frederick Lane, Australia	2m38.4s

Relays

1900	Germany (200 meters, 5 men)	32 pts.
1904	United States (200 yards)	2m4.6s
1906	Hungary (1,000 meters)	16m52.4s

400-Meter Freestyle Relay

1964	United States	3m32.2s
1968	United States	3m31.7s
1972	United States	3m26.42s

800-Meter Freestyle Relay

1908	Great Britain	10m55.6s
1912	Australia	10m11.2s
1920	United States	10m4.4s
1924	United States	9m53.4s
1928	United States	9m36.2s
1932	Japan	8m58.4s
1936	Japan	8m51.5s
1948	United States	8m46s
1952	United States	8m31.1s
1956	Australia	8m23.6s
1960	United States	8m10.2s
1964	United States	7m52.1s
1968	United States	7m52.3s
1972	United States	7m35.78s
1976	United States	7m23.22s
1980	U.S.S.R.	7m23.50s
1984	United States	7m16.59s

400-Meter Medley Relay

1960	United States	4m5.4s
1964	United States	3m58.4s
1968	United States	3m54.9s
1972	United States	3m48.16s
1976	United States	3m42.22s
1980	Australia	3m45.70s
1984	United States	3m39.30s

Springboard Dive

		Points
1908	Albert Zuerner, Germany	85.5
1912	Paul Guenther, Germany	79.23
1920	Louis Kuehn, United States	675
1924	Albert White, United States	696.4
1928	Pete Desjardins, United States	185.04
1932	Michael Galitzen, United States	161.38
1936	Richard Degener, United States	163.57
1948	Bruce Harlan, United States	163.64
1952	David Browning, United States	205.59
1956	Robert Clotworthy, United States	159.56
1960	Gary Tobian, United States	170.00
1964	Ken Sitzberger, United States	159.90
1968	Bernard Wrightson, United States	170.15
1972	Vladimir Vasin, U.S.S.R.	594.09
1976	Phil Boggs, United States	619.05
1980	Alexsandr Portnov, U.S.S.R.	905.02
1984	Greg Louganis, United States	754.41

Platform Dive

		Points
1904	G. E. Sheldon, United States	12.75
1906	Gottlob Walz, Germany	156
1908	Hialmar Johansson, Sweden	83.75
1912	Erik Adlerz, Sweden	73.94
1920	Clarence Pinkston, United States	100.67
1924	Albert White, United States	487.3
1928	Pete Desjardins, United States	98.74
1932	Harold Smith, United States	124.80
1936	Marshall Wayne, United States	113.58
1948	Samuel Lee, United States	130.05
1952	Samuel Lee, United States	156.28
1956	Joaquin Capilla, Mexico	152.44
1960	Bob Webster, United States	165.56
1964	Bob Webster, United States	148.58
1968	Klaus Dibiasi, Italy	164.18
1972	Klaus Dibiasi, Italy	504.12
1976	Klaus Dibiasi, Italy	600.51
1980	Falk Hoffman, E. Germany	835.65
1984	Greg Louganis, United States	710.91

Plain High Dive

		Points
1912	Erik Adlerz, Sweden	40
1920	Arvid Wallman, Sweden	7
1924	Richard Eve, Australia	160

Plunge for Distance

1904	W. E. Dickey, United States	62 ft 6 in.

SWIMMING—WOMEN

100-Meter Freestyle

1912	Fanny Durack, Australia	1m22.2s
1920	Ethelda Bleibtrey, United States	1m13.6s
1924	Ethel Lackie, United States	1m12.4s
1928	Albina Osipowich, United States	1m11s
1932	Helene Madison, United States	1m6.8s

1936	Hendrika Mastenbroek, Netherlands	1m5.9s
1948	Greta Andersen, Denmark	1m6.3s
1952	Katalin Szoke, Hungary	1m6.8s
1956	Dawn Fraser, Australia	1m2s
1960	Dawn Fraser, Australia	1m1.2s
1964	Dawn Fraser, Australia	59.5s
1968	Marge Jan Henne, United States	1m
1972	Sandra Neilson, United States	58.59s
1976	Kornelia Ender, East Germany	55.65s
1980	Barbara Krause, East Germany	54.79s
1984	Carrie Steinseifer, United States	55.92s

200-Meter Freestyle

1968	Debbie Meyer, United States	2m10.5s
1972	Shane Gould, Australia	2m3.56s
1976	Kornelia Ender, East Germany	1m59.26s
1980	Barbara Krause, East Germany	1m58.33s
1984	Mary Wayle, United States	1m59.23s

400-Meter Freestyle

1920	Ethelda Bleibtrey, United States	4m34s[1]
1924	Martha Norelius, United States	6m2.2s
1928	Martha Norelius, United States	5m42.8s
1932	Helene Madison, United States	5m28.5s
1936	Hendrika Mastenbroek, Netherlands	5m26.4s
1948	Ann Curtis, United States	5m17.8s
1952	Valerie Gyenge, Hungary	5m12.1s
1956	Lorraine Crapp, Australia	4m54.6s
1960	Chris von Saltza, United States	4m50.6s
1964	Ginny Duenkel, United States	4m43.3s
1968	Debbie Meyer, United States	4m31.8s
1972	Shane Gould, Australia	4m19.04s
1976	Petra Thumer, East Germany	4m09.89s
1980	Ines Diers, East Germany	4m08.76s
1984	Tiffany Cohen, United States	4m07.10s

1. 300 meters.

800-Meter Freestyle

1968	Debbie Meyer, United States	9m24s
1972	Keena Rothhammer, United States	8m53.68s
1976	Petra Thumer, East Germany	8m37.14s
1980	Michelle Ford, Australia	8m28.90s
1984	Tiffany Cohen, United States	8m24.95s

100-Meter Backstroke

1924	Sybil Bauer, United States	1m23.2s
1928	Marie Braun, Netherlands	1m22s
1932	Eleanor Holm, United States	1m19.4s
1936	Dina Senff, Netherlands	1m18.9s
1948	Karen Harup, Denmark	1m14.4s
1952	Joan Harrison, South Africa	1m14.3s
1956	Judy Grinham, Great Britain	1m12.9s
1960	Lynn Burke, United States	1m9.3s
1964	Cathy Ferguson, United States	1m7.7s
1968	Kaye Hall, United States	1m6.2s
1972	Melissa Belote, United States	1m5.78s
1976	Ulrike Richter, East Germany	1m01.83s
1980	Rica Reinisch, East Germany	1m00.86s
1984	Theresa Andrews, United States	1m02.55s

200-Meter Backstroke

1968	Pokey Watson, United States	2m24.8s
1972	Melissa Belote, United States	2m19.19s
1976	Ulrike Richter, East Germany	2m13.43s
1980	Rica Reinisch, East Germany	2m11.77s
1984	Jolanda DeRover, Netherlands	2m12.38s

100-Meter Breaststroke

1968	Djurdjica Bjedov, Yugoslavia	1m15.8s
1972	Catherine Carr, United States	1m13.58s
1976	Hannelore Anke, East Germany	1m11.16s
1980	Ute Geweniger, East Germany	1m10.22s
1984	Petra Van Staveren, Netherlands	1m09.88s

200-Meter Breaststroke

1924	Lucy Morton, Great Britain	3m33.2s
1928	Hilde Schrader, Germany	3m12.6s
1932	Clare Dennis, Australia	3m6.3s
1936	Hideko Maehata, Japan	3m3.6s
1948	Nel van Vliet, Netherlands	2m57.2s
1952	Eva Szekely, Hungary	2m51.7s
1956	Ursala Happe, Germany	2m53.1s
1960	Anita Lonsbrough, Great Britain	2m49.5s
1964	Galina Prozumenschikova, U.S.S.R.	2m46.4s
1968	Sharon Wichman, United States	2m44.4s
1972	Beverly Whitfield, Australia	2m41.71s
1976	Marina Koshevaia, U.S.S.R.	2m33.35s
1980	Lina Kachushite, U.S.S.R.	2m29.54s
1984	Anne Ottenbrite, Canada	2m30.38s

100-Meter Butterfly

1956	Shelley Mann, United States	1m11s
1960	Carolyn Schuler, United States	1m9.5s
1964	Sharon Stouder, United States	1m4.7s
1968	Lynn McClements, Australia	1m5.5s
1972	Mayumi Aoki, Japan	1m3.34s
1976	Kornelia Ender, East Germany	1m00.13s
1980	Caren Metschuck, East Germany	1m00.42s
1984	Mary Meagher, United States	59.26s

200-Meter Butterfly

1968	Ada Kok, Netherlands	2m24.7s
1972	Karen Moe, United States	2m15.57s
1976	Andrea Pollack, East Germany	2m11.41s
1980	Ines Geissler, East Germany	2m10.44s
1984	Mary Meagher, United States	2m06.90s

200-Meter Individual Medley

1968	Claudia Kolb, United States	2m24.7s
1972	Shane Gould, Australia	2m23.07s
1984	Tracy Caulkins, United States	1m12.64s

400-Meter Individual Medley

1964	Donna de Varona, United States	5m18.7s
1968	Claudia Kolb, United States	5m8.5s
1972	Gail Neall, Australia	5m2.97s
1976	Ulrike Tauber, East Germany	4m42.77s
1980	Petra Schneider, East Germany	4m36.29s
1984	Tracy Caulkins, United States	4m39.21s

400-Meter Freestyle Relay

1912	Great Britain	5m52.8s
1920	United States	5m11.6s
1924	United States	4m58.8s
1928	United States	4m47.6s
1932	United States	4m38s
1936	Netherlands	4m36s
1948	United States	4m29.2s
1952	Hungary	4m24.4s
1956	Australia	4m17.1s
1960	United States	4m8.9s
1964	United States	4m3.8s
1968	United States	4m2.5s
1972	United States	3m55.19s
1976	United States	3m44.82s
1980	East Germany	3m42.71s
1984	United States	3m44.43s

400-Meter Medley Relay

1960	United States	4m41.1s
1964	United States	4m33.9s
1968	United States	4m28.3s
1972	United States	4m20.75s
1976	East Germany	4m07.95s

1980	East Germany	4m06.67s
1984	United States	4m08.34s

Springboard Dive

		Points
1920	Aileen Riggin, United States	539.90
1924	Elizabeth Becker, United States	474.5
1928	Helen Meany, United States	78.62
1932	Georgia Coleman, United States	87.52
1936	Marjorie Gestring, United States	89.27
1948	Victoria M. Draves, United States	108.74
1952	Patricia McCormick, United States	147.30
1956	Patricia McCormick, United States	142.36
1960	Ingrid Kramer, Germany	155.81
1964	Ingrid Kramer Engel, Germany	145.00
1968	Sue Gossick, United States	150.77
1972	Micki King, United States	450.03
1976	Jennifer Chandler, United States	506.19
1980	Irina Kalinina, U.S.S.R.	725.91
1984	Sylvie Bernier, Canada	530.70

Platform Dive

		Points
1912	Greta Johansson, Sweden	39.9
1920	Stefani Fryland, Denmark	34.60
1924	Caroline Smith, United States	166
1928	Elizabeth B. Pinkston, United States	31.60
1932	Dorothy Poynton, United States	40.26
1936	Dorothy Poynton Hill, United States	33.92
1948	Victoria M. Draves, United States	68.87
1952	Patricia McCormick, United States	79.37
1956	Patricia McCormick, United States	84.85
1960	Ingrid Kramer, Germany	91.28
1964	Lesley Bush, United States	99.80
1968	Milena Duchkova, Czechoslovakia	109.59
1972	Ulrika Knape, Sweden	390.00
1976	Elena Vaytsekhovskaia, U.S.S.R.	406.59
1980	Martina Jaschke, East Germany	596.25
1984	Zhou Jihong, China	435.51

BOXING

(U.S. winners only)

(U.S. boycotted Olympics in 1980)

Flyweight—112 pounds (51 kilograms)

1904	George V. Finnegan	1952	Nate Brooks
1920	Frank De Genaro	1976	Leo Randolph
1924	Fidel La Barba	1984	Steve McCrory

Bantamweight—119 (54 kg)

1904 O.L. Kirk

Featherweight—126 pounds (57 kg)

1904	O.L. Kirk	1984	Meldrick Taylor
1924	Jackie Fields		

Lightweight—132 pounds (60 kg)

1904	H.J. Spanger	1976	Howard Davis
1920	Samuel Mosberg	1984	Pernell Whitaker
1968	Ronnie Harris		

Light Welterweight—140 pounds (63.5 kg)

1952	Charles Adkins	1976	Ray Leonard
1972	Ray Seales	1984	Jerry Page

Welterweight—148 pounds (67 kg)

1904	Al Young	1984	Mark Breland
1932	Edward Flynn		

Light Middleweight—157 pounds (71 kg)

1960	Wilbert McClure	1984	Frank Tate

DISTRIBUTION OF MEDALS 1984 SUMMER GAMES

Country	Gold	Silver	Bronze	Total
United States	83	61	30	174
West Germany	17	19	23	59
Rumania	20	16	17	53
Canada	10	18	16	44
Britain	5	10	22	37
China	15	8	9	32
Italy	14	6	12	32
Japan	10	8	14	32
France	5	7	15	27
Australia	4	8	12	24
South Korea	6	6	7	19
Sweden	2	11	6	19
Yugoslavia	7	4	7	18
Netherlands	5	2	6	13
Finland	4	3	6	13
New Zealand	8	1	2	11
Brazil	1	5	2	8
Switzerland	0	4	4	8
Mexico	2	3	1	6
Denmark	0	3	3	6
Spain	1	2	2	5
Belgium	1	1	2	4
Austria	1	1	1	3
Portugal	1	0	2	3
Jamaica	0	1	2	3
Norway	0	1	2	3
Turkey	0	0	3	3
Venezuela	0	0	3	3
Morocco	2	0	0	2
Kenya	1	0	1	2
Greece	0	1	1	2
Nigeria	0	1	1	2
Puerto Rico	0	1	1	2
Algeria	0	0	2	2
Pakistan	1	0	0	1
Colombia	0	1	0	1
Egypt	0	1	0	1
Ireland	0	1	0	1
Ivory Coast	0	1	0	1
Peru	0	1	0	1
Syria	0	1	0	1
Thailand	0	1	0	1
Cameroon	0	0	1	1
Dominican Republic	0	0	1	1
Iceland	0	0	1	1
Taiwan	0	0	1	1
Zambia	0	0	1	1

Middleweight—165 pounds (75 kg)

1904	Charles Mayer	1960	Eddie Cook
1932	Carmen Barth	1976	Michael Spinks
1952	Floyd Patterson		

Light Heavyweight—179 pounds (81 kg)

1920	Edward Eagan	1960	Cassius Clay
1952	Norvel Lee	1976	Leon Spinks
1956	James Boyd		

Heavyweight—201 pounds

1904	Sam Berger	1964	Joe Frazier
1952	Edward Sanders	1968	George Foreman
1956	Pete Rademacher	1984	Henry Tillman

Super Heavyweight (unlimited)

1984 Tyrell Biggs

BASKETBALL—MEN

1904	United States	1964	United States
1936	United States	1968	United States
1948	United States	1972	U.S.S.R.
1952	United States	1976	United States
1956	United States	1980	Yugoslavia
1960	United States	1984	United States

BASKETBALL—WOMEN

1976	U.S.S.R.
1980	U.S.S.R.
1984	United States

Winter Games

FIGURE SKATING—MEN

1908	Ulrich Salchow, Sweden
1920	Gillis Grafstrom, Sweden
1924	Gillis Grafstrom, Sweden
1928	Gillis Grafstrom, Sweden
1932	Karl Schaefer, Austria
1936	Karl Schaefer, Austria
1948	Richard Button, United States
1952	Richard Button, United States
1956	Hayes Alan Jenkins, United States
1960	David Jenkins, United States
1964	Manfred Schnelldorfer, Germany
1968	Wolfgang Schwartz, Austria
1972	Ondrej Nepela, Czechoslovakia
1976	John Curry, Great Britain
1980	Robin Cousins, Great Britain
1984	Scott Hamilton, United States

FIGURE SKATING—WOMEN

1908	Madge Syers, Britain
1920	Magda Julin-Maurey, Sweden
1924	Herma Szabo-Planck, Austria
1928	Sonja Henie, Norway
1932	Sonja Henie, Norway
1936	Sonja Henie, Norway
1948	Barbara Ann Scott, Canada
1952	Jeannette Altwegg, Great Britain
1956	Tenley Albright, United States
1960	Carol Heiss, United States
1964	Sjoukje Dijkstra, Netherlands
1968	Peggy Fleming, United States
1972	Beatrix Schuba, Austria
1976	Dorothy Hamill, United States
1980	Anett Poetzsch, East Germany
1984	Katarina Witt, East Germany

SPEED SKATING—MEN

(U.S. winners only)

500 Meters

1924	Charles Jewtraw	44.0
1932	John A. Shea	43.4
1952	Kenneth Henry	43.2
1964	Terrence McDermott	40.1
1980	Eric Heiden	38.03

1,000 Meters

1976	Peter Mueller	1:19.32
1980	Eric Heiden	1:15.18

1,500 Meters

1932	John A. Shea	2:57.5
1980	Eric Heiden	1:55.44

5,000 Meters

1932	Irving Jaffee	9:40.8
1980	Eric Heiden	7:02.29

10,000 Meters

1932	Irving Jaffee	19:13.6
1980	Eric Heiden	14:28.13

SPEED SKATING—WOMEN

500 Meters

1972	Anne Henning	43.33
1976	Sheila Young	42.76

1,500 Meters

1972	Dianne Holum	2:20.85

SKIING, ALPINE—MEN

Downhill

1948	Henri Oreiller, France	2m55.0s
1952	Zeno Colo, Italy	2m30.8s
1956	Anton Sailer, Austria	2m52.2s
1960	Jean Vuarnet, France	2m06.2s
1964	Egon Zimmermann, Austria	2m18.16s
1968	Jean-Claude Killy, France	1m59.85s
1972	Bernhard Russi, Switzerland	1m51.43s
1976	Franz Klammer, Austria	1m45.72s
1980	Leonhard Stock, Austria	1m45.50s
1984	Bill Johnson, United States	1m45.59s

Slalom

1948	Edi Reinalter, Switzerland	2m10.3s
1952	Othmar Schneider, Austria	2m00.0s
1956	Anton Sailer, Austria	194.7 pts.
1960	Ernst Hinterseer, Austria	2m08.9s
1964	Josef Stiegler, Austria	2m10.13
1968	Jean-Claude Killy, France	1m39.73s
1972	Francisco Fernandez Ochoa, Spain	1m49.27s
1976	Piero Gros, Italy	2m03.29s
1980	Ingemar Stenmark, Sweden	1m44.26s
1984	Phil Mahre, United States	1m39.41s

Giant Slalom

1952	Stein Eriksen, Norway	2m25.0s
1956	Anton Sailer, Austria	3m00.1s
1960	Roger Staub, Switzerland	1m48.3s
1964	François Bonlieu, France	1m46.71s
1968	Jean-Claude Killy, France	3m29.28s
1972	Gustavo Thoeni, Italy	3m09.52s
1976	Heini Hemmi, Switzerland	3m26.97s
1980	Ingemar Stenmark, Sweden	2m40.74s
1984	Max Julen, Switzerland	1m20.54s

DISTRIBUTION OF MEDALS 1984 WINTER GAMES

(Sarajevo, Yugoslavia)

	Gold	Silver	Bronze	Total
Soviet Union	6	10	9	25
East Germany	9	9	6	24
Finland	4	3	6	13
Norway	3	2	4	9
United States	4	4	0	8
Sweden	4	2	2	8
Czechoslovakia	0	2	4	6
Switzerland	2	2	1	5
Canada	2	1	1	4
West Germany	2	1	1	4
France	0	1	2	3
Italy	2	0	0	2
Liechtenstein	0	0	2	2
Britain	1	0	0	1
Yugoslavia	0	1	0	1
Austria	0	0	1	1

SKIING, ALPINE—WOMEN

Downhill

1948 Hedi Schlunegger, Switzerland 2m28.3s
1952 Trude Jochum-Beiser, Austria 1m47.1s
1956 Madeleine Berthod, Switzerland 1m40.1s
1960 Heidi Biebl, Germany 1m37.6s
1964 Christl Haas, Austria 1m55.39s
1968 Olga Pall, Austria 1m40.87s
1972 Marie-Therese Nadig, Switzerland 1m36.68s
1976 Rosi Mittermeier, West Germany 1m46.16s
1980 Annemarie Proell Moser, Austria 1m37.52s
1984 Michela Figini, Switzerland 1m13.36s

Slalom

1948 Gretchen Fraser, United States 1m57.2s
1952 Andrea Mead Lawrence, United States 2m10.6s
1956 Renee Colliard, Switzerland 112.3 pts.
1960 Anne Heggtveigt, Canada 1m49.6s
1964 Christine Goitschel, France 1m29.86s
1968 Marielle Goitschel, France 1m25.86s
1972 Barbara Cochran, United States 1m31.24s
1976 Rosi Mittermeier, West Germany 1m30.54s
1980 Hanni Wenzel, Liechtenstein 1m25.09s
1984 Paoletta Magoni, Italy 1m36.47s

Giant Slalom

1952 Andrea M. Lawrence, United States 2m06.8s
1956 Ossi Reichert, Germany 1m56.5s
1960 Yvonne Ruegg, Switzerland 1m39.9s
1964 Marielle Goitschel, France 1m52.24s
1968 Nancy Greene, Canada 1m51.97s
1972 Marie-Therese Nadig, Switzerland 1m29.90s
1976 Kathy Kreiner, Canada 1m29.13s
1980 Hanni Wenzel, Liechtenstein 2m41.66s
1984 Debbie Armstrong, United States 2m20.98s

ICE HOCKEY

1920 Canada
1924 Canada
1928 Canada
1932 Canada
1936 Great Britain
1948 Canada
1952 Canada
1956 U.S.S.R.
1960 United States
1964 U.S.S.R.
1968 U.S.S.R.
1972 U.S.S.R.
1976 U.S.S.R.
1980 United States
1984 Soviet Union

SKIING, NORDIC, JUMPING

90-Meter Hill

		Points
1924	Jacob T. Thams, Norway	227.5
1928	Alfred Andersen, Norway	230.5
1932	Birger Ruud, Norway	228.0
1936	Birger Ruud, Norway	232.0
1948	Peter Hugsted, Norway	228.1
1952	A. Bergmann, Norway	226.0
1956	Antti Hyvarinen, Finland	227.0
1960	Helmut Recknagel, Germany	227.2
1964	Toralf Engan, Norway	230.7
1968	Vladimir Beloussov, U.S.S.R.	231.3
1972	Wojciech Fortuna, Poland	219.9
1976	Karl Schnabl, Austria	234.8
1980	Jouko Tormanen, Finland	271.0
1984	Matti Nykaenen, Finland	231.2

Small Hill (70 meters)

1964 Veikko Kankkonen, Finland 229.9
1968 Jiri Raska, Czechoslovakia 216.5
1972 Yukio Kasaya, Japan 244.2
1976 Hans-Georg Aschenbach, East Germany 252.0
1980 Anton Innauer, Austria 266.3
1984 Jens Weissflog, East Germany 215.2

FINAL OVER-ALL 1984 OLYMPIC HOCKEY STANDINGS

GROUP A

	W	L	T	Pts	GF	GA
Soviet Union	7	0	0	14	48	5
West Germany	4	1	0	9	34	21
Sweden	4	2	1	9	33	16
Italy	1	4	0	2	15	31
Yugoslavia	1	4	0	2	8	37
Poland	1	5	0	2	20	44

GROUP B

	W	L	T	Pts	GF	GA
Czechoslovakia	6	1	0	12	40	9
Canada	4	3	0	8	24	16
United States	2	2	2	6	23	21
Finland	2	3	1	5	31	26
Austria	1	4	0	2	13	37
Norway	0	4	1	1	15	43

Seventh Place

United States 7, Poland 4

Fifth Place

West Germany 7, Finland 4

Medal Round

Czechoslovakia 2, Sweden 0
Soviet Union 4, Canada 0

Third place

Sweden 2, Canada 0

Championship

Soviet Union 2, Czechoslovakia 0

Other 1984 Olympic Games Champions

SUMMER

Archery
Men—Darrell Pace, United States
Women—Hyang-Soun Seo, South Korea

Boxing
106 lb—Paul Gonzalez, United States
112 lb—Steve McCrory, United States
119 lb—Maurizio Stecca, Italy
126 lb—Meldrick Taylor, United States
132 lb—Pernell Whitaker, United States
139 lb—Jerry Page, United States
148 lb—Mark Breland, United States
157 lb—Frank Tate, United States
165 lb—Joun-Sup Shin, South Korea
179 lb—Anton Josipovic, Yugoslavia
201 lb—Henry Tillman, United States
Over 201—Tyrell Biggs, United States

Canoeing
500 m—Larry Cain, Canada
1,000 m—Ulrich Eiche, West Germany
500-m pairs—Yugoslavia (Matija Ljubekt and Mirko Nisovic)
1,000-m pairs—Romania (Ivan Potzaichin and Toma Simionov)

Kayak—Men
500 m—Ian Ferguson, New Zealand
1,000 m—Alan Thompson, New Zealand
500-m pairs—New Zealand (Ian Ferguson and Paul MacDonald)
1,000-m pairs—Canada (Hugh Fisher and Alwyn Moris)
1,000-m fours—New Zealand (Grant Bramwell, Ian Ferguson, Paul MacDonald, Alan Thompson)

Kayak—Women
500 m—Agneta Andersson, Sweden
500-m pairs—Sweden (Agneta Andersson and Anna Olsson)
500-m fours—Romania (Agafia Constantin, Nastasia Ionescu, Tecia Marinescu, Maria Stefan)

Cycling—Men
4,000-m Individual pursuit—Steve Hegg, United States
Individual road race—Alexi Grewal, United States
1,000-m Time trials—Fredy Schmidtke, West Germany
4,000-m Team pursuit—Australia
Sprint—Mark Gorski, United States
Points race—Roger Ilegems, Belgium
100-km road team trials—Italy

Cycling—Women
Individual road race—Connie Carpenter, United States

Equestrian
Dressage—Dr. Reiner Klimke, West Germany
Dressage team—West Germany
Jumping—Joe Fargia, United States
Jumping, team—United States
Three-day event—Mark Todd, New Zealand
Team three-day event—United States

Fencing
Foil—Mauro Numa, Italy
Team foil—Italy
Epee—Philippe Boisse, France
Team epee—West Germany
Sabre—Jean-Francois Lamour, France
Team sabre—Italy
Women's foil—Luan Jujie, China
Women's team foil—West Germany

Gymnastics—Men
All-around—Koji Gushiken, Japan
Floor exercises—Li Ning, China
Horizontal bar—Shinji Morisue, Japan
Parallel bars—Bart Conner, United States
Pommel horse—Li Ning, China and Peter Vidmar, United States
Rings—Koji Gushiken, Japan and Li Ning, China
Vault—Lou Yun, China
Team—United States

Gymnastics—Women
All-around—Mary Lou Retton, United States
Balance beam—Simona Pauca, Romania, and Ecaterina Szabo, Romania
Floor exercises—Ecaterina Szabo, Romania
Uneven bars—Ma Yanhonjg, China
Vault—Evaterina Szabo, Romania
Team—Romania

Judo
Lightweight—Byeong-Keun Ahn, South Korea
Extra lightweight—Shinji Hosokawa, Japan
Half lightweight—Yoshiyuki Matsuoka, Japan
Half middleweight—Frank Wieneke, West Germany
Middleweight—Peter Seisenbacher, Austria
Half heavyweight—Hyoung-Za Ha, South Korea
Heavyweight—Hitoshi Saito, Japan

Modern Pentathlon
Individual—Daniele Masala, Italy
Team—Italy

Rowing—Men
Singles—Pertti Karppinen, Finland
Doubles—United States (Bradley Lewis and Paul Enquist)
Quadruples—West Germany (Albert Hedderich, Raimond Hormann, Dieter Wiedenmann, Michael Dursch)
Pairs—Romania (Petru Iosub, Valer Toma)
Pairs with coxswain—Italy (Carmine Abbaginale, Giuseppe Abbaginale)
Fours—New Zealand (Leslie O'Connell, Conrad Robertson, Shane O'Brien, Keith Trask)
Fours with coxswain—Britain (Martin Cross, Richard Budgett, Andrew Holmes, Steve Redgrave)
Eights—Canada (Pat Turner, Kevin Neufield, Mark Evans, Grant Main, Paul Steele, Mike Evans, Dean Crawford, Blair Horm, Brian McMahon)

Rowing—Women
Singles—Valeria Racila, Romania
Doubles—Romania
Pairs—Romania
Pairs with coxswain—Romania
Fours with coxswain—Romania
Quadruple sculls—Romania
Eights—United States

Shooting—Men
Free pistol—Xu Haifeng, China
Rapid-fire pistol—Takeo Kamachi, Japan
Small-bore rifle—Ed Etzel, United States
Small-bore rifle, 3 positions—Malcolm Cooper, Britain
Rifle running game target—Li Yuwei, China
Trap—Luciano Giovanetti, Italy
Skeet—Matthew Dryke, Canada
Air rifle—Philippe Heberle, France

Shooting—Women
Air rifle—Pat Spurgin, United States
Small-bore rifle, 3 positions—Wu Xiaoxuan, China
Sport pistol—Linda Thom, Canada

Synchronized Swimming
Solo—Tracie Ruiz, United States
Duet—United States (Candy Costie and Tracie Ruiz)

Weight Lifting
115 lb—Zeng Guoqiang, China
123 lb—Wu Shude, China
132 lb—Chen Weiqang, China
149 lb—Yao Jingyuang, China
165 lb—Karl Heinz Radschinsky, West Germany
182 lb—Petre Becheru, Romania
198 lb—Nicu Vlad, Romania
220 lb—Rolf Miller, West Germany
242 lb—Noberto Oberburger, Italy
Over 242—Dinko Lukim, Australia

Wrestling—Freestyle
106 lb—Bobby Weaver, United States
114.5 lb—Saban Trstena, Yugoslavia
125.5 lb—Hideaki Tomiyama, Japan
136.5 lb—Randy Lewis, United States
149.5 lb—In-Tak You, South Korea
163 lb—David Schultz, United States
181 lb—Mark Schultz, United States
198.5 lb—Ed Banach, United States
220 lb—Lou Banach, United States
Over 220—Bruce Baumgartner, United States

Wrestling—Greco-Roman
106 lb—Vincenzo Maenza, Italy
114.5 lb—Atsuji Miyahara, Japan
125.5 lb—Pasquale Passarelli, West Germany
136.5 lb—Weon Kee Kim, South Korea
150 lb—Viado Lisjak, Yugoslavia
163 lb—Jouko Salomaki, Finland
181 lb—Ion Draica, Romania
198.5 lb—Steven Fraser, United States
220 lb—Vasile Andrei, Romania
Over 220—Jeff Blatnick, United States

Yachting
Windglider—Stephan Van Den Berg, Netherlands
Finn—Russell Coutts, New Zealand

Flying Dutchmen—United States (Jonathan McKee, Bill Buchan)
470 Class—Spain
Soling—United States (Robert Haines Jr., Ed Trevelyan, Rod Davis)
Star—United States (William Buchan, Steve Erickson)
Tornado—New Zealand

Team Champions

Field hockey, men—Pakistan
Field hockey, women—Netherlands
Handball, men—Yugoslavia
Handball, women—Yugoslavia
Soccer—France
Volleyball, men—United States
Volleyball, women—China
Water polo—Yugoslavia

WINTER

Biathlon

Individual—Eirik Kvalfoss, Norway (10 km); P. Angerer, West Germany (20 km)
Relay—Soviet Union (Dmitry Vassiliev, Youry Kachkarov, Algulmantas Shalna, Serguey Bouliguin)

Bobsledding

2-man—East Germany (Wolfgang Hoppe, captain)
4-man—East Germany (Wolfgang Hoppe, Roland Wetzig, Dietmar Schauerhanmer, Andreas Kirchner)

Figure Skating

Men—Scott Hamilton, United States
Women—Katarina Witt, East Germany
Pairs—Elena Valova and Oleg Vasiliev, Soviet Union
Dance—Jayne Torvill and Christopher Dean, Britain

Speed Skating—Men

500 m—Sergei Fokicheu, Soviet Union
1,000 m—Gaetan Boucher, Canada
1,500 m—Gaetan Boucher, Canada
5,000 m—Tomas Gustafson, Sweden
10,000 m—Igor Malkov, Soviet Union

Speed Skating—Women

500 m—Christina Rothernberger, East Germany
1,000 m—Karin Enke, East Germany
1,500 m—Karin Enke, East Germany
3,000 m—Andrea Schoene, East Germany

Hockey

Team—Soviet Union

Luge

Men—Paul Hildgartner, Italy
Doubles—Hans Stangassinger and Franz Wembacher, West Germany
Women—Steffi Martin, East Germany

Skiing, Nordic—Men

Combined—Tom Sandberg, Norway
70-m jump—Jens Weissflog, East Germany
90-m jump—Matti Nykaenen, Finland

Cross-Country Skiing—Men

15 km—Gunde Svan, Sweden
30 km—Nikolai Zimiatov, Soviet Union
50 km—Thomas Wassberg, Sweden
40-km relay—Sweden (Thomas Wassberg, Benny Kohlberg, Jan Ottoson, Gunde Svan)

Cross-Country Skiing—Women

5 km—Marja-Liisa Hamalainen, Finland
10 km—Marja-Liisa Hamalainen, Finland
20 km—Marja-Liisa Hamalainen, Finland
20-km relay—Norway (Inger Helene Nybraaten, Anne Jahra, Brit Petersen, Berit Aunli)

JAMES E. SULLIVAN MEMORIAL AWARD WINNERS

(Amateur Athlete of Year Chosen in Amateur Athletic Union Poll)

1930	Robert Tyre Jones, Jr.	Golf
1931	Bernard E. Berlinger	Track and field
1932	James A. Bausch	Track and field
1933	Glenn Cunningham	Track and field
1934	William R. Bonthron	Track and field
1935	W. Lawson Little, Jr.	Golf
1936	Glenn Morris	Track and field
1937	J. Donald Budge	Tennis
1938	Donald R. Lash	Track and field
1939	Joseph W. Burk	Rowing
1940	J. Gregory Rice	Track and field
1941	Leslie MacMitchell	Track and field
1942	Cornelius Warmerdam	Track and field
1943	Gilbert L. Dodds	Track and field
1944	Ann Curtis	Swimming
1945	Felix (Doc) Blanchard	Football
1946	Y. Arnold Tucker	Football
1947	John B. Kelly, Jr.	Rowing
1948	Robert B. Mathias	Track and field
1949	Richard T. Button	Figure skating
1950	Fred Wilt	Track and field
1951	Robert E. Richards	Track and field
1952	Horace Ashenfelter	Track and field
1953	Major Sammy Lee	Diving
1954	Malvin Whitfield	Track and field
1955	Harrison Dillard	Track and field
1956	Patricia McCormick	Diving
1957	Bobby Jo Morrow	Track and field
1958	Glenn Davis	Track and field
1959	Parry O'Brien	Track and field
1960	Rafer Johnson	Track and field
1961	Wilma Rudolph Ward	Track and field
1962	Jim Beatty	Track and field
1963	John Pennel	Track and field
1964	Don Schollander	Swimming
1965	Bill Bradley	Basketball
1966	Jim Ryun	Track and field
1967	Randy Matson	Track and field
1968	Debbie Meyer	Swimming
1969	Bill Toomey	Decathlon
1970	John Kinsella	Swimming
1971	Mark Spitz	Swimming
1972	Frank Shorter	Marathon
1973	Bill Walton	Basketball
1974	Rick Wohlhuter	Track
1975	Tim Shaw	Swimming
1976	Bruce Jenner	Track and field
1977	John Naber	Swimming
1978	Tracy Caulkins	Swimming
1979	Kurt Thomas	Gymnastics
1980	Eric Heiden	Speed skating
1981	Carl Lewis	Track and field
1982	Mary Decker Tabb	Track and field

FOOTBALL

The pastime of kicking around a ball goes back beyond the limits of recorded history. Ancient savage tribes played football of a primitive kind. There was a ball-kicking game played by Athenians, Spartans, and Corinthians 2500 years ago, which the Greeks called *Episkuros.* The Romans had a somewhat similar game called *Harpastum* and are supposed to have carried the game with them when they invaded the British Isles in the First Century, B.C.

Undoubtedly the game known in the United States as Football traces directly to the English game of Rugby, though the modifications have been many. Informal football was played on college lawns well over a century ago, and an annual Freshman-Sophomore series of "scrimmages" began at Yale in 1840. The first formal intercollegiate football game was the Princeton-Rutgers contest at New Brunswick, N.J., on Nov. 6, 1869, with Rutgers winning by 6 goals to 4.

In those days, games were played with 25, 20, 15, or 11 men on a side. In 1880, there was a convention at which Walter Camp of Yale persuaded the delegates to agree to a rule calling for 11 players on a side. The game grew so rough that it was attacked as brutal, and some colleges abandoned the sport. Conditions were so bad in 1906 that President Theodore Roosevelt called a meeting of Yale, Harvard, and Princeton representatives at the White House in the hope of reforming and improving the game. The outcome was that the game, with the forward pass introduced and some other modifications of the rules inserted, became faster and cleaner.

The first professional game was played in 1895 at Latrobe, Pa. The National Football League was founded in 1921. The All-American Conference went into action in 1946. At the end of the 1949 season the two circuits merged, retaining the name of the older league. In 1960, the American Football League, began operations. In 1970, the leagues merged. The United States Football League played its first season in 1983, from March to July.

College Football

NATIONAL COLLEGE FOOTBALL CHAMPIONS

The "National Collegiate A. A. Football Guide" recognizes as unofficial national champion the team selected each year by press association polls. Where The Associated Press poll (of writers) does not agree with the United Press International poll (of coaches), the guide lists both teams selected.

1937 Pittsburgh
1938 Texas Christian
1939 Texas A & M
1940 Minnesota
1941 Minnesota
1942 Ohio State
1943 Notre Dame
1944 Army
1945 Army
1946 Notre Dame
1947 Notre Dame
1948 Michigan
1949 Notre Dame
1950 Oklahoma
1951 Tennessee
1952 Michigan State
1953 Maryland
1954 Ohio State and U.C.L.A.
1955 Oklahoma
1956 Oklahoma
1957 Auburn and Ohio State
1958 Louisiana State
1959 Syracuse
1960 Minnesota
1961 Alabama
1962 So. California
1963 Texas
1964 Alabama
1965 Alabama and Michigan State
1966 Notre Dame
1967 So. California
1968 Ohio State
1969 Texas
1970 Texas and Nebraska
1971 Nebraska
1972 So. California
1973 Notre Dame
1974 Oklahoma and So. California
1975 Oklahoma
1976 Pittsburgh
1977 Notre Dame
1978 Alabama and So. California
1979 Alabama
1980 Georgia
1981 Clemson
1982 Penn State
1983 Miami

ARMY-NAVY SERIES RECORD SINCE 1962

1962 Navy 34, Army 14
1963 Navy 21, Army 15
1964 Army 11, Navy 8
1965 Army 7, Navy 7
1966 Army 20, Navy 7
1967 Navy 19, Army 14
1968 Army 21, Navy 14
1969 Army 27, Navy 0
1970 Navy 11, Army 7
1971 Army 24, Navy 23
1972 Army 23, Navy 15
1973 Navy 51, Army 0
1974 Navy 19, Army 0
1975 Navy 30, Army 6
1976 Navy 38, Army 10
1977 Army 17, Navy 14
1978 Navy 28, Army 0
1979 Navy 31, Army 7
1980 Navy 33, Army 6
1981 Army 3, Navy 3
1982 Navy 24, Army 7
1983 Navy 42, Army 13

RECORD OF ANNUAL MAJOR BOWL COLLEGE FOOTBALL GAMES

Rose Bowl
(At Pasadena, Calif.)

1902 Michigan 49, Stanford 0
1916 Washington State 14, Brown 0
1917 Oregon 14, Pennsylvania 0
1918 Mare Island Marines 19, Camp Lewis 7
1919 Great Lakes 17, Mare Island Marines 0
1920 Harvard 7, Oregon 6
1921 California 28, Ohio State 0
1922 Washington and Jefferson 0, California 0
1923 So. California 14, Penn State 3
1924 Navy 14, Washington 14
1925 Notre Dame 27, Stanford 10
1926 Alabama 20, Washington 19
1927 Alabama 7, Stanford 7
1928 Stanford 7, Pittsburgh 6
1929 Georgia Tech 8, California 7
1930 So. California 47, Pittsburgh 14
1931 Alabama 24, Washington State 0
1932 So. California 21, Tulane 12
1933 So. California 35, Pittsburgh 0
1934 Columbia 7, Stanford 0
1935 Alabama 29, Stanford 13
1936 Stanford 7, So. Methodist 0
1937 Pittsburgh 21, Washington 0
1938 California 13, Alabama 0
1939 So. California 7, Duke 3
1940 So. California 14, Tennessee 0

1941 Stanford 21, Nebraska 13
1942 Oregon State 20, Duke 16[1]
1943 Georgia 9, U.C.L.A. 0
1944 So. California 29, Washington 0
1945 So. California 25, Tennessee 0
1946 Alabama 34, So. California 14
1947 Illinois 45, U.C.L.A. 14
1948 Michigan 49, So. California 0
1949 Northwestern 20, California 14
1950 Ohio State 17, California 14
1951 Michigan 14, California 6
1952 Illinois 40, Stanford 7
1953 So. California 7, Wisconsin 0
1954 Michigan State 28, U.C.L.A. 20
1955 Ohio State 20, So. California 7
1956 Michigan State 17, U.C.L.A. 14
1957 Iowa 35, Oregon State 19
1958 Ohio State 10, Oregon 7
1959 Iowa 38, California 12
1960 Washington 44, Wisconsin 8
1961 Washington 17, Minnesota 7
1962 Minnesota 21, U.C.L.A. 3
1963 So. California 42, Wisconsin 37
1964 Illinois 17, Washington 7
1965 Michigan 34, Oregon State 7
1966 U.C.L.A. 14, Michigan State 12
1967 Purdue 14, So. California 13
1968 So. California 14, Indiana 3
1969 Ohio State 27, So. California 16
1970 So. California 10, Michigan 3
1971 Stanford 27, Ohio State 17
1972 Stanford 13, Michigan 12
1973 So. California 42, Ohio State 17
1974 Ohio State 42, So. California 21
1975 So. California 18, Ohio State 17
1976 U.C.L.A. 23, Ohio State 10
1977 So. California 14, Michigan 6
1978 Washington 27, Michigan 20
1979 So. California 17, Michigan 10
1980 So. California 17, Ohio State 16
1981 Michigan 23, Washington 6
1982 Washington 28, Iowa 0
1983 U.C.L.A. 24, Michigan 14
1984 U.C.L.A. 45, Illinois 9

1. Played at Durham, N.C.

Orange Bowl

(At Miami)

1933 Miami (Fla.) 7, Manhattan 0
1934 Duquesne 33, Miami (Fla.) 7
1935 Bucknell 26, Miami (Fla.) 0
1936 Catholic 20, Mississippi 19
1937 Duquesne 13, Mississippi State 12
1938 Auburn 6, Michigan State 0
1939 Tennessee 17, Oklahoma 0
1940 Georgia Tech 21, Missouri 7
1941 Mississippi State 14, Georgetown 7
1942 Georgia 40, Texas Christian 26
1943 Alabama 37, Boston College 21
1944 Louisiana State 19, Texas A&M 14
1945 Tulsa 26, Georgia Tech 12
1946 Miami (Fla.) 13, Holy Cross 6
1947 Rice 8, Tennessee 0
1948 Georgia Tech 20, Kansas 14
1949 Texas 41, Georgia 28
1950 Santa Clara 21, Kentucky 13
1951 Clemson 15, Miami (Fla.) 14
1952 Georgia Tech 17, Baylor 14
1953 Alabama 61, Syracuse 6
1954 Oklahoma 7, Maryland 0
1955 Duke 34, Nebraska 7
1956 Oklahoma 20, Maryland 6
1957 Colorado 27, Clemson 21
1958 Oklahoma 48, Duke 21
1959 Oklahoma 21, Syracuse 6
1960 Georgia 14, Missouri 0
1961 Missouri 21, Navy 14
1962 Louisiana State 25, Colorado 7
1963 Alabama 17, Oklahoma 0
1964 Nebraska 13, Auburn 7
1965 Texas 21, Alabama 17
1966 Alabama 39, Nebraska 28
1967 Florida 27, Georgia Tech 12
1968 Oklahoma 26, Tennessee 24
1969 Penn State 15, Kansas 14
1970 Penn State 10, Missouri 3
1971 Nebraska 17, Louisiana State 12
1972 Nebraska 38, Alabama 6
1973 Nebraska 40, Notre Dame 6
1974 Penn State 16, Louisiana State 9
1975 Notre Dame 13, Alabama 11
1976 Oklahoma 14, Michigan 6
1977 Ohio State 27, Colorado 10
1978 Arkansas 31, Oklahoma 6
1979 Oklahoma 31, Nebraska 24
1980 Oklahoma 24, Florida State 7
1981 Oklahoma 18, Florida State 17
1982 Clemson 22, Nebraska 15
1983 Nebraska 21, Louisiana State 20
1984 Miami 31, Nebraska 30

Sugar Bowl

(At New Orleans)

1935 Tulane 20, Temple 14
1936 Texas Christian 3, Louisiana State 2
1937 Santa Clara 21, Louisiana State 14
1938 Santa Clara 6, Louisiana State 0
1939 Texas Christian 15, Carnegie Tech 7
1940 Texas A & M 14, Tulane 13
1941 Boston College 19, Tennessee 13
1942 Fordham 2, Missouri 0
1943 Tennessee 14, Tulsa 7
1944 Georgia Tech 20, Tulsa 18
1945 Duke 29, Alabama 26
1946 Oklahoma A & M 33, St. Mary's (Calif.) 13
1947 Georgia 20, North Carolina 10
1948 Texas 27, Alabama 7
1949 Oklahoma 14, North Carolina 6
1950 Oklahoma 35, Louisiana State 0
1951 Kentucky 13, Oklahoma 7
1952 Maryland 28, Tennessee 13
1953 Georgia Tech 24, Mississippi 7
1954 Georgia Tech 42, West Virginia 19
1955 Navy 21, Mississippi 0
1956 Georgia Tech 7, Pittsburgh 0
1957 Baylor 13, Tennessee 7
1958 Mississippi 39, Texas 7
1959 Louisiana State 7, Clemson 0
1960 Mississippi 21, Louisiana State 0
1961 Mississippi 14, Rice 6
1962 Alabama 10, Arkansas 3
1963 Mississippi 17, Arkansas 13
1964 Alabama 12, Mississippi 7
1965 Louisiana State 13, Syracuse 10
1966 Missouri 20, Florida 18
1967 Alabama 34, Nebraska 7
1968 Louisiana State 20, Wyoming 13
1969 Arkansas 16, Georgia 2
1970 Mississippi 27, Arkansas 22
1971 Tennessee 34, Air Force Academy 13
1972 Oklahoma 40, Auburn 22
1973 Oklahoma 14, Penn State 0
1974 Notre Dame 24, Alabama 23
1975 Nebraska 13, Florida 10
1976 Alabama 13, Penn State 6
1977 Pittsburgh 27, Georgia 3
1978 Alabama 35, Ohio State 6
1979 Alabama 14, Penn State 7
1980 Alabama 24, Arkansas 9
1981 Georgia 17, Notre Dame 10
1982 Pittsburgh 24, Georgia 20
1983 Penn State 27, Georgia 23
1984 Auburn 9, Michigan 7

Cotton Bowl

(At Dallas)

1937 Texas Christian 16, Marquette 6
1938 Rice 28, Colorado 14
1939 St. Mary's (Calif.) 20, Texas Tech. 13
1940 Clemson 6, Boston College 3
1941 Texas A & M 13, Fordham 12
1942 Alabama 29, Texas A & M 21
1943 Texas 14, Georgia Tech 7
1944 Randolph Field 7, Texas 7
1945 Oklahoma A & M 34, Texas Christian 0
1946 Texas 40, Missouri 27
1947 Louisiana State 0, Arkansas 0
1948 So. Methodist 13, Penn State 13
1949 So. Methodist 21, Oregon 13
1950 Rice 27, North Carolina 13
1951 Tennessee 20, Texas 14
1952 Kentucky 20, Texas Christian 7
1953 Texas 16, Tennessee 0
1954 Rice 28, Alabama 6
1955 Georgia Tech 14, Arkansas 6
1956 Mississippi 14, Texas Christian 13
1957 Texas Christian 28, Syracuse 27
1958 Navy 20, Rice 7
1959 Air Force 0, Texas Christian 0
1960 Syracuse 23, Texas 14
1961 Duke 7, Arkansas 6
1962 Texas 12, Mississippi 7
1963 Louisiana State 13, Texas 0
1964 Texas 28, Navy 6
1965 Arkansas 10, Nebraska 7
1966 Louisiana State 14, Arkansas 7
1967 Georgia 24, So. Methodist 9
1968 Texas A & M 20, Alabama 16
1969 Texas 36, Tennessee 13
1970 Texas 21, Notre Dame 17
1971 Notre Dame 24, Texas 11
1972 Penn State 30, Texas 6
1973 Texas 17, Alabama 13
1974 Nebraska 19, Texas 3
1975 Penn State 41, Baylor 20
1976 Arkansas 31, Georgia 10
1977 Houston 30, Maryland 21
1978 Notre Dame 38, Texas 10
1979 Notre Dame 35, Houston 34
1980 Houston 17, Nebraska 14
1981 Alabama 30, Baylor 2
1982 Texas 14, Alabama 12
1983 Southern Methodist 7, Pittsburgh 3
1984 Georgia 10, Texas 9

Gator Bowl

(At Jacksonville, Fla. Played on Saturday nearest New Year's Day of year indicated)

1953 Florida 14, Tulsa 13
1954 Texas Tech 35, Auburn 13
1955 Auburn 33, Baylor 13

1956 Vanderbilt 25, Auburn 13
1957 Georgia Tech 21, Pittsburgh 14
1958 Tennessee 3, Texas A & M 0
1959 Mississippi 7, Florida 3
1960 Arkansas 14, Georgia Tech 7
1961 Florida 13, Baylor 12
1962 Penn State 30, Georgia Tech 15
1963 Florida 17, Penn State 7
1964 No. Carolina 35, Air Force 0
1965 Florida State 36, Oklahoma 19
1966 Georgia Tech 31, Texas Tech 21
1967 Tennessee 18, Syracuse 12
1968 Penn State 17, Florida State 17
1969 Missouri 35, Alabama 10
1970 Florida 14, Tennessee 13
1971 Auburn 35, Mississippi 28
1972 Georgia 7, North Carolina 3
1973 Auburn 24, Colorado 3
1974 Texas Tech 28, Tennessee 19
1975 Auburn 27, Texas 3
1976 Maryland 13, Florida 0
1977 Notre Dame 20, Penn State 9
1978 Pittsburgh 34, Clemson 3
1979 Clemson 17, Ohio State 15
1980 North Carolina 17, Michigan 15
1981 Pittsburgh 37, South Carolina 9
1982 North Carolina 31, Arkansas 27
1983 Florida State 31, West Virginia 12
1984 Florida 14, Iowa 6

RESULTS OF OTHER 1983 SEASON BOWL GAMES

Aloha (Honolulu, Dec. 26)—Penn State 13, Washington 10
Bluebonnet (Houston, Dec. 31)—Oklahoma State 24, Baylor 14
California (Fresno, Dec. 17)—Northern Illinois 20, Fullerton State 13
Fiesta (Tempe, Ariz., Jan. 2)—Ohio State 28, Pittsburgh 23
Florida Citrus (Orlando, Fla., Dec. 17)—Tennessee 30, Maryland 23
Hall of Fame (Birmingham, Ala., Dec. 22)—West Virginia 20, Kentucky 16
Holiday (San Diego, Dec. 23)—Brigham Young 21, Missouri 17
Independence (Shreveport, La., Dec. 10)—Air Force 9, Mississippi 3
Liberty (Memphis, Tenn., Dec. 29)—Notre Dame 19, Boston College 18
Peach (Atlanta, Dec. 30)—Florida State 28, North Carolina 3
Sun (El Paso, Tex., Dec. 24)—Alabama 28, Southern Methodist 7

HEISMAN MEMORIAL TROPHY WINNERS

The Heisman Memorial Trophy is presented annually by the Downtown Athletic Club of New York City to the nation's outstanding college football player, as determined by a poll of sportswriters and sportscasters.

1935 Jay Berwanger, Chicago
1936 Larry Kelley, Yale
1937 Clinton Frank, Yale
1938 Davey O'Brien, Texas Christian
1939 Nile Kinnick, Iowa
1940 Tom Harmon, Michigan
1941 Bruce Smith, Minnesota
1942 Frank Sinkwich, Georgia
1943 Angelo Bertelli, Notre Dame
1944 Leslie Horvath, Ohio State
1945 Felix Blanchard, Army
1946 Glenn Davis, Army
1947 Johnny Lujack, Notre Dame
1948 Doak Walker, So. Methodist
1949 Leon Hart, Notre Dame
1950 Vic Janowicz, Ohio State
1951 Dick Kazmaier, Princeton
1952 Billy Vessels, Oklahoma
1953 Johnny Lattner, Notre Dame
1954 Alan Ameche, Wisconsin
1955 Howard Cassady, Ohio State
1956 Paul Hornung, Notre Dame
1957 John Crow, Texas A & M
1958 Pete Dawkins, Army
1959 Billy Cannon, Louisiana State
1960 Joe Bellino, Navy
1961 Ernie Davis, Syracuse
1962 Terry Baker, Oregon State
1963 Roger Staubach, Navy
1964 John Huarte, Notre Dame
1965 Mike Garrett, Southern California
1966 Steve Spurrier, Florida
1967 Gary Beban, U.C.L.A.
1968 O. J. Simpson, Southern California
1969 Steve Owens, Oklahoma
1970 Jim Plunkett, Stanford
1971 Pat Sullivan, Auburn
1972 Johnny Rodgers, Nebraska
1973 John Cappelletti, Penn State
1974–75 Archie Griffin, Ohio State
1976 Tony Dorsett, Pittsburgh
1977 Earl Campbell, Texas
1978 Billy Sims, Oklahoma
1979 Charles White, Southern California
1980 George Rogers, South Carolina
1981 Marcus Allen, Southern California
1982 Hershel Walker, Georgia
1983 Mike Rozier, Nebraska

COLLEGE FOOTBALL HALL OF FAME

(Kings Island, Interstate 71, Kings Mills, Ohio)

(Date given is player's last year of competition)

Players

Abell, Earl—Colgate, 1915
Agase, Alex—Purdue/Illinois, 1946
Agganis, Harry—Boston Univ., 1952
Albert, Frank—Stanford, 1941
Aldrich, Chas. (Ki)—T.C.U., 1938
Aldrich, Malcolm—Yale, 1921
Alexander, John—Syracuse, 1920
Alworth, Lance—Arkansas, 1961
Ameche, Alan (Horse)—Wisconsin, 1954
Amling, Warren—Ohio State, 1946
Anderson, H. (Hunk)—Notre Dame, 1921
Bacon, C. Everett—Wesleyan, 1912
Bagnell, Francis (Reds)—Penn, 1950
Baker, Hobart (Hobey)—Princeton, 1913
Baker, John—So. Calif., 1931
Baker, Terry—Oregon State, 1962
Ballin, Harold—Princeton, 1914
Banker, Bill—Tulane, 1929
Barnes, Stanley—S. California, 1921
Barrett, Charles—Cornell, 1915
Baston, Bert—Minnesota, 1916
Battles, Cliff—W. Va. Wesleyan, 1931
Baugh, Sammy—Texas Christian U., 1936
Bausch, James—Kansas, 1930
Beckett, John—Oregon, 1913
Bednarik, Chuck—Pennsylvania, 1948
Bellini, Joe—Navy, 1960
Benbrook, A.—Michigan, 1911
Bertelli, A.—Notre Dame, 1943
Berry, Charlie—Lafayette, 1924
Berwanger, John (Jay)—Chicago, 1935
Bettencourt, Larry—St. Mary's, 1927
Blanchard, Felix (Doc)—Army, 1946
Bock, Ed—Iowa State, 1938
Bomar, Lynn—Vanderbilt, 1924
Bomeisler, Doug (Bo)—Yale, 1913
Booth, Albie—Yale, 1931
Borries, Fred—Navy, 1934
Bosely, Bruce—West Virginia, 1955

Bottari, Vic—California, 1939
Boynton, Ben—Williams, 1920
Brewer, Charles—Harvard, 1895
Bright, John—Drake, 1951
Brooke, George—Pennsylvania, 1895
Brown, Gordon—Yale, 1900
Brown, John, Jr.—Navy, 1913
Brown, Johnny Mack—Alabama, 1925
Brown, Raymond (Tay)—So. California, 1932
Bunker, Paul—Army, 1902
Butkus, Dick—Illinois, 1964
Butler, Robert—Wisconsin, 1912
Cafego, George—Tennessee, 1939
Cagle, Chris—SW La./Army, 1929
Cain, John—Alabama, 1932
Cameron, Eddie—Wash. & Lee, 1924
Campbell, David C.—Harvard, 1901
Cannon, Billy—L.S.U., 1959
Cannon, Jack—Notre Dame, 1929
Carideo, Frank—Notre Dame, 1930
Caroline, J.C.—Illinois, 1954
Carney, Charles—Illinois, 1921
Carpenter, Bill—Army, 1959
Carpenter, C. Hunter—VPI, 1905
Carroll, Charles—Washington, 1928
Casey, Edward L.—Harvard, 1919
Cassady, Howard—Ohio State, 1955
Chamberlain, Guy—Nebraska, 1915
Chapman, Sam—Cal.-Berkeley, 1938
Christman, Paul—Missouri, 1940
Clark, Earl (Dutch)—Colo. College, 1929
Clevenger, Zora—Indiana, 1903
Cochran, Gary—Princeton, 1895
Cody, Josh—Vanderbilt, 1920
Coleman, Don—Mich. State, 1951
Conerly, Chuck—Mississippi, 1947
Connor, George—Notre Dame, 1947
Corbin, W.—Yale, 1888
Corbus, William—Stanford, 1933
Cowan, Hector—Princeton, 1889
Coy, Edward H. (Tad)—Yale, 1909
Crawford, Fred—Duke, 1933
Crow, John D.—Texas A&M, 1957
Crowley, James—Notre Dame, 1924
Cutter, Slade—Navy, 1934
Czarobski, Ziggie—Notre Dame, 1947
Dalrymple, Gerald—Tulane, 1931
Daniell, James—Ohio State, 1941
Dawkins, Pete—Army, 1958
Dalton, John—Navy, 1912
Daly, Charles—Harvard/Army, 1902
Daniell, Averell—Pittsburgh, 1936
Davies, Tom—Pittsburgh, 1921
Davis, Ernest—Syracuse, 1961
Davis, Glenn—Army, 1946
Davis, Robert T.—Georgia Tech, 1947
DesJardien, Paul—Chicago, 1914
Devino, Aubrey—Iowa, 1921
DeWitt, John—Princeton, 1903
Dobbs, Glenn—Tulsa, 1942
Dodd, Bobby—Tennessee, 1930
Donan, Holland—Princeton, 1950
Donchess, Joseph—Pittsburgh, 1929
Dougherty, Nathan—Tennessee, 1909
Drahos, Nick—Cornell, 1940
Driscoll, Paddy—Northwestern, 1917
Drury, Morley—So. California, 1927
Dudley, William (Bill)—Virginia, 1941
Eckersall, Walter—Chicago, 1906
Edwards, Turk—Washington State, 1931
Edwards, William—Princeton, 1900
Eichenlaub, R.—Notre Dame, 1913
Evans, Ray—Kansas, 1947
Exendine, Albert—Carlisle, 1908
Falaschi, Nello—Santa Clara, 1937
Fears, Tom—Santa Clara/UCLA, 1947
Feathers, Beattie—Tennessee, 1933
Fenimore, Robert—Oklahoma State, 1947
Fenton, G.E. (Doc)—La. State U., 1910
Ferraro, John—So. California, 1944
Fesler, Wesley—Ohio State, 1930
Fincher, Bill—Georgia Tech, 1920
Fischer, Bill—Notre Dame, 1948
Fish, Hamilton—Harvard, 1909
Fisher, Robert—Harvard, 1911
Flowers, Abe—Georgia Tech, 1920
Fortmann, Daniel—Colgate, 1935
Francis, Sam—Nebraska, 1936
Franco, Edmund (Ed)—Fordham, 1937
Frank, Clint—Yale, 1937
Franz, Rodney—California, 1949
Friedman, Benny—Michigan, 1926
Gain, Bob—Kentucky, 1950
Galiffa, Arnold—Army, 1949
Gallarneau, Hugh—Stanford, 1941
Garbisch, Edgar—Army, 1924
Gelbert, Charles—Pennsylvania, 1896
Geyer, Forest—Oklahoma, 1915
Giel, Paul—Minnesota, 1953
Gifford, Frank—So. California, 1951
Gilbert, Walter—Auburn, 1936
Gipp, George—Notre Dame, 1920
Gladchuk, Chet—Boston College, 1940
Goldberg, Marshall—Pittsburgh, 1938
Goodreault, Gene—Boston College, 1940
Gordon, Walter—California, 1918
Graham, Otto—Northwestern, 1943
Grange, Harold (Red)—Illinois, 1925
Grayson, Robert—Stanford, 1935
Green, Joe—North Texas State, 1968
Griese, Bob—Purdue, 1966
Gulick, Merel—Hobart, 1929
Guyon, Joe—Georgia Tech, 1919
Hale, Edwin—Mississippi Col, 1921
Hamilton, Robert (Bones)—Stanford, 1935
Hamilton, Tom—Navy, 1925
Hanson, Vic—Syracuse, 1926
Hardwick, H. (Tack)—Harvard, 1914
Hare, T. Truxton—Pennsylvania, 1900
Harley, Chick—Ohio State, 1919
Harmon, Tom—Michigan, 1940
Harpster, Howard—Carnegie Tech, 1928
Hart, Edward J.—Princeton, 1911
Hart, Leon—Notre Dame, 1949
Hartman, Bill—Georgia, 1937
Hazel, Homer—Rutgers, 1924
Healey, Ed—Dartmouth, 1916
Heffelfinger, W. (Pudge)—Yale, 1891
Hein, Mel—Washington State, 1930
Henry, Wilber—Wash. & Jefferson, 1919
Herschberger, Clarence—Chicago, 1899
Herwig, Robert—California, 1937
Heston, Willie—Michigan, 1904
Hickman, Herman—Tennessee, 1931
Hickok, William—Yale, 1895
Hill, Dan—Duke, 1938
Hillebrand, A.R. (Doc)—Princeton, 1900
Hinkey, Frank—Yale, 1894
Hinkle, Carl—Vanderbilt, 1937
Hinkle, Clark—Bucknell, 1932
Hirsch, Elroy—Wis./Mich., 1943
Hitchcock, James—Auburn, 1932
Hoffman, Frank—Notre Dame, 1931
Hogan, James J.—Yale, 1904
Holland, Jerome (Brud)—Cornell, 1938
Hollenbeck, William—Penn., 1908
Holovak, Michael—Boston College, 1942
Horrell, Edwin—California, 1924
Horvath, Les—Ohio State, 1944
Howe, Arthur—Yale, 1911
Howell, Millard (Dixie)—Alabama, 1934
Hubbard, Cal—Centenary, 1926
Hubbard, John—Amherst, 1906
Hubert, Allison—Alabama, 1925
Huff, Robert Lee (Sam)—W. Va., 1955
Humble, Weldon G.—Rice, 1946
Hunt, Joel—Texas A&M, 1927
Huntington, Ellery—Colgate, 1914
Hutson, Don—Alabama, 1934
Ingram, James—Navy, 1906
Isbell, Cecil—Purdue, 1937
Jablonsky, Harvey—Wash. U./Army, 1933
Janowicz, Vic—Ohio State, 1951
Jenkins, Darold—Missouri, 1941
Jensen, Jack—Cal-Berkeley, 1948
Joesting, Herbert—Minnesota, 1927
Johnson, James—Carlisle, 1903
Jones, Calvin—Iowa, 1955
Jones, Gomer—Ohio State, 1935
Jordan, Lee Roy—Alabama, 1962
Juhan, Frank—Univ. of South, 1910
Justice, Charlie—North Carolina, 1949
Kaer, Mort—So. California, 1926
Kavanaugh, Kenneth—La. State U., 1939
Kaw, Edgar—Cornell, 1922
Kazmaier, Richard—Princeton, 1951
Keck, James—Princeton, 1921
Kelley, Larry—Yale, 1936
Kelly, William—Montana, 1926
Kenna, Ed—Syracuse, 1966
Kern, George—Boston College, 1941
Ketcham, Henry—Yale, 1913
Killinger, William—Penn State, 1922
Kimbrough, John—Texas A&M, 1940
Kinard, Frank—Mississippi, 1937
King, Phillip—Princeton, 1893
Kinnick, Nile—Iowa, 1939
Kipke, Harry—Michigan, 1923
Kirkpatrick, John Reed—Yale, 1910
Kitzmiller, John—Oregon, 1929
Koch, Barton—Baylor, 1931
Kitner, Malcolm—Texas, 1942
Kramer, Ron—Michigan, 1956
Krueger, Charlie—Texas A&M, 1957
Lach, Steve—Duke, 1941
Lane, Myles—Dartmouth, 1927
Lattner, Joseph J.—Notre Dame, 1953
Lauricella, Hank—Tennessee, 1952
Lautenschlaeger—Tulane, 1925
Layden, Elmer—Notre Dame, 1924
Layne, Bobby—Texas, 1947
Lea, Langdon—Princeton, 1895
LeBaron, Eddie—Univ. of Pacific, 1949
Leech, James—Va. Mil. Inst., 1920
Lilly, Bob—Texas Christian, 1960
Little, Floyd—Syracuse, 1966
Lio, Augie—Georgetown, 1940
Locke, Gordon—Iowa, 1922
Lourie, Don—Princeton, 1921
Luckman, Sid—Columbia, 1938
Lujack, John—Notre Dame, 1947
Lund, J.L. (Pug)—Minnesota, 1934
Macomber, Bart—Illinois, 1915
MacLeod, Robert—Dartmouth, 1938
Maegle, Dick—Rice, 1954
Mahan, Edward W.—Harvard, 1915
Mallory, William—Yale, 1893
Mann, Gerald—So. Methodist, 1927
Markov, Vic—Washington, 1937
Marshall, Robert—Minnesota, 1907
Matson, Ollie—San Fran. U., 1952
Matthews, Ray—Texas Christ. U., 1928
Maulbetsch, John—Michigan, 1914
Mauthe, J.L. (Pete)—Penn State, 1912
Maxwell, Robert—Chi./Swarthmore, 1906
McAfee, George—Duke, 1939
McColl, William F.—Stanford, 1951
McCormick, James B.—Princeton, 1907
McDowall, Jack—No. Car. State, 1927
McElhenny, Hugh—Washington, 1951
McEver, Gene—Tennessee, 1931
McEwan, John—Minn./Army, 1916
McFadden, J.B.—Clemson, 1939
McFadin, Bud—Texas, 1950
McClung, Thomas L.—Yale, 1891
McGinley, Edward—Pennsylvania, 1924
McGovern, J.—Minnesota, 1910
McGraw, Thurman—Colorado State, 1949
McLaren, George—Pittsburgh, 1918
McMillan, Dan—U.S.C./Calif., 1922
McMillin, A.N. (Bo)—Centre, 1921
McWhorter, Robert—Georgia, 1913
Mercer, Leroy—Pennsylvania, 1912
Meredith, Don—Southern Methodist, 1959
Metzger, Bert—Notre Dame, 1930
Mickal, Abe—La. State U., 1935
Miller, Creighton—Notre Dame, 1943
Miller, Don—Notre Dame, 1925
Miller, Edgar (Rip)—Notre Dame, 1924
Miller, Eugene—Penn State, 1913
Milstead, Century—Wabash, Yale, 1923
Minds, John—Pennsylvania, 1897
Moffatt, Alex—Princeton, 1884
Montgomery, Cliff—Columbia, 1933
Moomaw, Donn—U.C.L.A., 1952
Morley, William—Columbia, 1903
Morris, George—Georgia Tech, 1952
Morton, William—Dartmouth, 1931

Muller, Harold (Brick)—Calif., 1922
Nagurski, Bronko—Minnesota, 1929
Nevers, Ernie—Stanford, 1925
Newell, Marshall—Harvard, 1893
Newman, Harry—Michigan, 1932
Nobis, Tommy—Texas, 1965
Nomellini, Leo—Minnesota, 1949
Oberlander, Andrew—Dartmouth, 1925
O'Brien, Davey—Texas Christ. U., 1938
O'Dea, Pat—Wisconsin, 1899
O'Hearn, J.—Cornell, 1915
Oliphant, Elmer—Purdue/Army, 1917
Olsen, Merlin—Utah State, 1961
Oosterbaan, Ben—Michigan, 1927
O'Rourke, Charles—Boston College, 1940
Orsi, John—Colgate, 1931
Osgood, W.D.—Cornell/Penn, 1895
Osmanski, William—Holy Cross, 1938
Owen, George—Harvard, 1922
Owens, Jim—Oklahoma, 1949
Parilli, Vito (Babe)—Kentucky, 1951
Parker, Clarence (Ace)—Duke, 1936
Parker, Jackie—Miss. State, 1953
Parker, James—Ohio State, 1956
Pazzetti, V.J.—Wes./Lehigh, 1912
Peabody, Endicott—Harvard, 1941
Peck, Robert—Pittsburgh, 1916
Pennock, Stanley B.—Harvard, 1914
Pfann, George—Cornell, 1923
Phillips, H.D.—U. of South, 1904
Pingel, John—Michigan State, 1938
Pihos, Pete—Indiana, 1945
Pinckert, Ernie—So. California, 1931
Poe, Arthur—Princeton, 1899
Pollard, Fritz—Brown, 1916
Poole, Barney—Miss./Army, 1947
Pregulman, Merv—Michigan, 1943
Price, Eddie—Tulane, 1949
Pund, Henry—Georgia Tech, 1928
Ramsey, Gerrard—Wm. & Mary, 1942
Reeds, Claude—Oklahoma, 1913
Reid, William—Harvard, 1900
Rentner, Ernest—Northwestern, 1932
Reynolds, Robert—Nebraska, 1952
Reynolds, Robert—Stanford, 1935
Richter, Les—California, 1951
Rinehart, Charles—Lafayette, 1897
Rodgers, Ira—West Virginia, 1919
Rogers, Edward L.—Minnesota, 1903
Romig, Joe—Colorado, 1961
Rosenberg, Aaron—So. California, 1934
Rote, Kyle—So. Methodist, 1950
Routt, Joe—Texas A&M, 1937
Salmon, Louis—Notre Dame, 1904
Sauer, George—Nebraska, 1933
Sayers, Gale—Kansas, 1964
Scarbath, Jack—Maryland, 1952
Scarlett, Hunter—Pennsylvania, 1909
Schoonover, Wear—Arkansas, 1929
Schreiner, Dave—Wisconsin, 1942
Schultz, Adolf (Germany)—Mich., 1908
Schwab, Frank—Lafayette, 1922
Schwartz, Marchmont—Notre Dame, 1931
Schwegler, Paul—Washington, 1931
Scott, Clyde—Arkansas, 1949
Scott, Tom—Virginia, 1953
Seibels, Henry—Sewanee, 1899
Shakespeare, Bill—Notre Dame, 1935
Shelton, Murray—Cornell, 1915
Shevlin, Tom—Yale, 1905
Shively, Bernie—Illinois, 1926
Simons, Claude—Tulane, 1934
Simpson, O.J.—So. Calif., 1968
Sington, Fred—Alabama, 1930
Sinkwich, Frank—Georgia, 1942
Sitko, Emil—Notre Dame, 1949
Skladany, Joe—Pittsburgh, 1933
Slater, F.F. (Duke)—Iowa, 1921
Smith, Bruce—Minnesota, 1941
Smith, Ernie—So. California, 1932
Smith, Harry—So. California, 1939
Smith, John (Clipper)—Notre Dame, 1927
Smith, Vernon—Georgia, 1931
Snow, Neil—Michigan, 1901
Sparlis, Al—U.C.L.A., 1945
Spears, Clarence W.—Dartmouth, 1915
Spears, W.D.—Vanderbilt, 1927
Sprackling, William—Brown, 1911
Sprague, M. (Bud)—Texas/Army, 1928
Stafford, Harrison—Texas, 1932
Stagg, Amos Alonzo—Yale, 1889
Staubach, Roger—Navy, 1963
Steffen, Walter—Chicago, 1908
Stein, Herbert—Pittsburgh, 1921
Steuber, Robert—Missouri, 1943
Stevens, Mal—Yale, 1923
Stinchcomb, Gaylord—Ohio State, 1920
Stevenson, Vincent—Pennsylvania, 1905
Strong, Ken—New York Univ., 1928
Strupper, George—Georgia Tech, 1917
Stuhldreher, Harry—Notre Dame, 1924
Stydahar, Joe—West Virginia, 1935
Suffridge, Robert—Tennessee, 1940
Sundstrom, Frank—Cornell, 1923
Swanson, Clarence—Nebraska, 1921
Swiacki, Bill—Holy Cross/Colombia, 1947
Swink, Jim—Texas Christian, 1956
Taliafarro, George—Indiana, 1948
Taylor, Charles—Stanford, 1942
Thompson, Joe—Pittsburgh, 1907
Thorne, Samuel B.—Yale, 1906
Thorpe, Jim—Carlisle, 1912
Ticknor, Ben—Harvard, 1930
Tigert, John—Vanderbilt, 1904
Tinsley, Gaynell—La. State U., 1936
Tipton, Eric—Duke, 1938
Tonnemaker, Clayton—Minnesota, 1949
Torrey, Robert—Pennsylvania, 1906
Travis, Ed Tarkio—Missouri, 1920
Trippi, Charles—Georgia, 1946
Tryon, J. Edward—Colgate, 1925
Utay, Joe—Texas A&M, 1907
Van Brocklin, Norm—Oregon, 1948
Van Sickel, Dale—Florida, 1929
Van Surdam, Henderson—Wesleyan, 1905
Very, Dexter—Penn State, 1912
Vessels, Billy—Oklahoma, 1931
Vick, Ernie—Michigan, 1921
Wagner, Huber—Pittsburgh, 1913
Walker, Doak—So. Methodist, 1949
Wallace, Bill—Rice, 1935
Walsh, Adam—Notre Dame, 1924
Warburton, I. (Cotton)—So. Calif., 1934
Ward, Robert (Bob)—Maryland, 1951
Warner, William—Cornell, 1903
Washington, Ken—U.C.L.A., 1939
Wedemeyer, Herman J.—St. Mary's, 1947
Weekes, Harold—Columbia, 1902
Weir, Ed—Nebraska, 1925
Welch, Gus—Carlisle, 1914
Weller, John—Princeton, 1935
Wendell, Percy—Harvard, 1913
West, D. Belford—Colgate, 1919
Weyand, Alex—Army, 1915
Wharton, Charles—Pennsylvania, 1896
Wheeler, Arthur—Princeton, 1894
White, Byron (Whizzer)—Colorado, 1937
Whitmire, Don—Alabama/Navy, 1944
Wickhorst, Frank—Navy, 1926
Widseth, Ed—Minnesota, 1936
Wildung, Richard—Minnesota, 1942
Williams, James—Rice, 1949
Willis, William—Ohio State, 1945
Wilson, George—Washington, 1925
Wilson, Harry—Penn State/Army, 1923
Wistert, Albert A.—Michigan, 1942
Wistert, Al—Michigan, 1949
Wistert, Frank (Whitey)—Mich., 1933
Wood, Barry—Harvard, 1931
Wojciechowicz, Alex—Fordham, 1936
Wyant, Andrew—Bucknell/Chicago, 1894
Wyatt, Bowden—Tennessee, 1938
Wyckoff, Clint—Cornell, 1896
Yoder, Lloyd—Carnegie Tech, 1926
Young, Claude (Buddy)—Illinois, 1946
Young, Harry—Wash. & Lee, 1916
Zarnas, Gus—Ohio State, 1937

Coaches

Bill Alexander
Dr. Ed Anderson
Ike Armstrong
Matty Bell
Hugo Bezdek
Dana X. Bible
Bernie Bierman
Earl (Red) Blaik
Frank Broyles
Charles W. Caldwell
Walter Camp
Len Casanova
Frank Cavanaugh
Fritz Crisler
Duffy Daugherty
Bob Devaney
Gil Dobie
Michael Donohue
Gus Dorais
Charles (Rip) Engle
Don Faurot
Jake Gaither
Ernest Godfrey
Jack Harding
Edward K. Hall
Richard Harlow
Jesse Harper
Percy Haughton
Woody Hayes
John W. Heisman
R. A. (Bob) Higgins
Orin E. Hollingberry
William Ingram
Morley Jennings
Howard Jones
L. (Biff) Jones
Thomas (Tad) Jones
Ralph (Shug) Jordan
Andy Kerr
Frank Leahy
George E. Little
Lou Little
El (Slip) Madigan
Herbert McCracken
Daniel McGugin
DeOrmond (Tuss) McLaughry
L. R. (Dutch) Meyer
Bernie Moore
Scrappy Moore
Ray Morrison
George A. Munger
Clarence Munn
Frank Murray
William Murray
Ed (Hooks) Mylin
Earle (Greasy) Neale
Jess Neely
Robert Neyland
Homer Norton
Frank (Buck) O'Neill
Bennie Owen
Ara Parseghian
James Phalea
E. N. Robinson
Knute Rockne
E. L. (Dick) Romney
William W. Roper
Darrell Royal
George F. Sanford
Francis A. Schmidt
Floyd (Ben) Schwartzwalder
Clark Shaughnessy
Buck Shaw
Andrew L. Smith
Carl Snavely
Amos A. Stagg
Jock Sutherland
James Tatum
Frank W. Thomas
John H. Vaught
Wallace Wade
Lynn Waldorf
Glenn (Pop) Warner
E. E. (Tad) Wieman
John W. Wilce
Bud Wilkinson
Henry L. Williams
George W. Woodruff
Fielding H. Yost
Robert Zuppke

MAJOR COLLEGE FOOTBALL RECORDS (1940–1982)

(Opposing teams are listed in parentheses. *Source:* National Collegiate Sports Services)

LONGEST PLAYS

Rushing

	Yards
Kelsey Finch, Tennessee (Florida) 1977	99
Ralph Thompson, W. Tex. State (Wichita State) 1970	99
Max Anderson, Arizona State (Wyoming) 1967	99
Gale Sayers, Kansas (Nebraska) 1963	99
Granville Amos, Virginia M. I. (Wm. & Mary) 1964	98
Jim Thacker, Davidson (George Washington) 1952	98
Bill Powell, California (Oregon State) 1951	98
Al Yannelli, Bucknell (Delaware) 1946	98
Meredith Warner, Iowa State (Iowa Pre-Flight) 1943	98
Stanley Howell, Miss. State (Southern Miss.) 1979	98
Mark Malone, Arizona State (Utah State) 1979	98
Steve Atkins, Maryland (Clemson) 1978	98

Punt Returns

	Yards
Jimmy Campagna, Georgia (Vanderbilt) 1952	100
Hugh McElhenny, Washington (So. Cal.) 1951	100
Frank Brady, Navy (Maryland) 1951	100
Bert Rechichar, Tennessee (Wash. & Lee) 1950	100
Eddie Macon, Pacific (Boston U.) 1950	100
Richie Luzzi, Clemson (Georgia) 1968	100[1]
Don Guest, California (Washington State) 1966	100[1]

1. Return of a field goal attempt.

Passing

	Yards
Chris Collingsworth—Derrick Gaffney, Florida (Rice) 1977	99
Terry Peel—Robert Ford, Houston (San Diego St.) 1972	99
Terry Peel—Robert Ford, Houston (Syracuse) 1970	99
Colin Clapton—Eddie Jenkins, Holy Cross (Boston U.) 1970	99
Bo Burris—Warren McVea, Houston (Wash. St.) 1966	99
Fred Owens—Jack Ford, Portland (St. Mary's) 1947	99
Jeff Martin—Mark Flaker, Drake (N.M. State) 1976	98
Pete Woods—Joe Stewart, Missouri (Nebraska) 1976	98
Dan Hagemann—Jack Steptoe, Utah (New Mexico) 1976	98
Bruce Shaw—Pat Kenny, N.C. State (Penn State) 1972	98
Jerry Rhome—Jeff Jordan, Tulsa (Wichita State) 1963	98
Bob Dean—Norman Dawson, Cornell (Navy) 1947	98

Punts

	Yards
Pat Brady, Nevada-Reno (Loyola, L. A.) 1950	99
George O'Brien, Wisconsin (Iowa) 1952	96
John Hadi, Kansas (Oklahoma) 1959	94
Carl Knox, Texas Christian (Oklahoma State) 1947	94
Preston Johnson, SMU (Pittsburgh) 1940	94

Field Goals

	Yards
Joe Williams, Wichita State (So. Illinois) 1978	67
Steve Little, Arkansas (Texas) 1977	67
Russell Erxleben, Texas (Rice) 1977	67
Tony Franklin, Texas A&M (Baylor) 1976	65
Russell Erxleben, Texas (Oklahoma) 1977	64
Tony Franklin, Texas A&M (Baylor) 1976	64
Morten Andersen, Mich. State (Ohio State) 1981	63
Clark Kemble, Colorado State (Arizona) 1975	63
Dan Christopulos, Wyoming (Colorado State) 1977	62
Iseed Khoury, North Texas State (Richmond) 1977	62
Dave Lawson, Air Force Academy (Iowa State) 1975	62
Ralf Mojsiejenko, Mich. State (Illinois) 1982	61
Steve Little, Arkansas (Tulsa) 1976	61
Wayne Latimer, Virginia Tech (Florida State) 1975	61
Ray Guy, Southern Mississippi (Utah State) 1972	61

CAREER LEADERS

Rushing

	Years	Plays	Yds	Avg
Tony Dorsett, Pittsburgh	1973–76	1,074	6,082[1]	5.66
Charles White, So. Calif.	1976–79	1,023	5,598	5.47
Hershel Walker, Georgia	1980–82	994	5,259	5.29
Archie Griffin, Ohio State	1972–75	845	5,177	6.13
George Rogers, So. Carolina	1977–80	902	4,958	5.50
Mike Rozier, Nebraska	1981–83	668	4,780	7.16
Ed Marinaro, Cornell	1969–71	918	4,715	5.14
Marcus Allen, So. Calif.	1978–81	893	4,682	5.24
Ted Brown, No. Carolina St.	1975–78	860	4,602	5.35
Terry Miller, Oklahoma St.	1974–77	847	4,582	5.24
Eric Dickerson, S.M.U.	1979–82	790	4,450	5.63
Earl Campbell, Texas	1974–77	765	4,443	5.81
Amos Lawrence, No. Carolina	1977–80	881	4,391	4.98
Jon Morris, Syracuse	1978–81	813	4,299	5.29
Jerome Persell, W. Mich.	1976–78	842	4,190	4.98

1. Record.

Passing Yards, Career

	Years	Comp	Yds	Td
Ben Bennett, Duke	1980–83	820[1]	9,614[1]	53
Jim McMahon, Brigham Young	1977–78 1980–81	653	9,536	84[1]
John Elway, Stanford	1979–82	774	9,349	78
Mark Hermann, Purdue	1977–80	717	9,188	62
Joe Adams, Tennessee State	1977–80	604	8,649	81
Dan Marino, Pittsburgh	1979–82	626	7,905	74
John Holman, Nev-Las Vegas	1979–82	593	7,827	51
Jack Thompson, Washington State	1975–78	601	7,818	53
Steve Young, Brigham Young	1981–83	592	7,733	56
Marc Wilson, Brigham Young	1977–79	535	7,637	61
John Reaves, Florida	1969–71	603	7,549	54
Jim Plunkett, Stanford	1968–70	530	7,544	52

1. Record.

Total Offense

	Years	Plays	Yds	Avg
Jim McMahon, Brigham Young	1977–78 1980–81	1,325	9,723[1]	7.34[2]
John Elway, Stanford	1979–82	1,505	9,070	6.03
Ben Bennett, Duke	1980–83	1,582	9,061	5.73
Steve Young, Brigham Young	1981 83	1,177	8,817	7.49
Mark Hermann, Purdue	1977–80	1,354	8,444	6.24
Gene Swick, Toledo	1972–75	1,579[1]	8,074	5.11
Joe Adams, Tennessee State	1977–80	1,256	7,972	6.35
Jim Plunkett, Stanford	1968–70	1,174	7,887	6.72
Art Schlichter, Ohio State	1978–81	1,316	7,869	5.98
John Holman, Northeast Louisiana	1979–82	1,376	7,802	5.67
Jack Thompson, Washington State	1975–78	1,345	7,698	5.72
Dan Marino, Pittsburgh	1979–82	1,185	7,635	6.44
Marc Wilson, Brigham Young	1977–79	1,183	7,602	6.43
John Reaves, Florida	1969–71	1,258	7,283	5.79
Matt Dunigan, Louisiana Tech	1979–82	1,483	7,167	4.83
Steve Brown, Appalachian State	1977–80	1,160	7,129	6.15
Steve Clarkson, San Jose State	1979–82	1,124	6,995	6.22

1. Record. 2. Record for a minimum of 6,500 yards.

Pass Receiving

	Years	Rec	Yds	Td
Howard Twilley, Tulsa	1963–65	261[1]	3,343	32
Darrin Nelson, Stanford	1977–78 1980–81	214	2,368	16
Ron Sellers, Florida State	1966–68	212	3,598[1]	23
Gerald Harp, Western Carolina	1977–80	197	3,305	26
Jeff Champine, Colorado State	1980–83	184	2,811	21
Phil Odle, Brigham Young	1965–67	183	2,548	25
Tim Delaney, San Diego State	1968–70	180	2,535	22

1. Record.

BEST SINGLE-GAME PERFORMANCES

Most yards, rushing—356, Eddie Lee Ivery, Georgia Tech (Air Force) 1978

Most yards, total offense—599, Virgil Carter, Brigham Young (Texas-El Paso) 1966

Most yards, passing—621, Dave Wilson, Illinois (Ohio State) 1980

Most yards, pass receiving—349, Chuck Hughes, Texas-El Paso (North Texas State) 1965

Most points scored—43, Jim Brown, Syracuse (Colgate) 1956

Most passes attempted—71, Sandy Schwab, Northwestern (Michigan) 1982

Most passes completed—45, Sandy Schwab, Northwestern (Michigan) 1982

Most passes caught—22, Jay Miller, Brigham Young (New Mexico) 1973

Scoring

	Years	Td	Pat	Fg	Pts
Tony Dorsett, Pittsburgh	1973–76	59[1]	2	0	356[1]
Glenn Davis, Army	1943–46	59[1]	0	0	354
Art Luppino, Arizona	1953–56	48	49	0	337
Steve Owens, Oklahoma	1967–69	56	0	0	336
Wilford White, Arizona State	1947–50	48	27	4	327
Ed Marinaro, Cornell	1969–71	52	6	0	318
Pete Johnson, Ohio State	1973–76	53	0	0	318
Herschel Walker, Georgia	1980–82	52	2	0	314
Ted Brown, North Carolina State	1975–78	51	6	0	312
Mike Rozier, Nebraska	1981–83	52	0	0	312
Eddie Talboom, Wyoming	1948–50	34	99	0	303

1. Record.

N.C.A.A. DIVISION II AND III FOOTBALL RECORDS (1942–1983)

LONGEST PLAYS

Rushing

	Yards
Don Patria, Rensselaer Polytech (Lowell) 1981	99
Kevin Doherty, Mass. Maritime (New Haven) 1980	99
Fred Deutsch, Springfield (Wagner) 1977	99
Sam Hallston, Albany State, N.Y. (Norwich) 1977	99
Sammy Croom, San Diego (Azusa Pacific) 1972	99
John Stenger, Swarthmore (Widener) 1970	99
Jed Knuttila, Hamline (St. Thomas) 1968	99
Dave Lanoha, Colorado College (Texas Lutheran) 1967	99
Tom Pabst, Cal—Riverside (Cal. Tech) 1965	99
George Phillips, Concord (Davis and Elkins) 1961	99
Gerry White, Connecticut (Rhode Island) 1960	99
Leo Williams, St. Augustine's (Morris) 1960	99
George Phelps, Cornell College (Monmouth) 1959	99
Mark Lydon, Tufts (Bowdoin) 1958	99
David Wells, Tufts (Williams) 1956	99
Jack Moskal, Western Reserve (Case Tech) 1956	99
Lou Mariano, Kent State (Western Reserve) 1954	99
Ron Temple, Chico State (Southern Oregon) 1953	99
Ellis Horton, Eureka, (Rose-Hulman) 1952	99
Pat Abbruzzi, Rhode Island (New Hampshire) 1951	99

Field Goals

Joe Duren, Arkansas State (McNeese State) 1974	63
Dom Antonini, Glassboro State (Salisbury State) 1976	62
Mike Flater, Colorado Mines (Western State) 1973	62
Duane Christian, Cameron (Southwestern Oklahoma) 1976	61
Mike Wood, Southeast Missouri (Lincoln) 1975	61
Bill Shear, Cortland State (Hobart) 1966	61

Passing

	Yards
Nick Pannunzio–Herman Heard, Southern Colorado (Adams State) 1982	99
Tim Ebersole–Ed Noon, Shippensburg (Pa.) State (Indiana, Pa.) 1982	99
John Guercio—Tom Bennett, C.W. Post (Juniata) 1980	99
Mike Moroski—Calvin Ellison, California-Davis (Puget Sound) 1978	99
Rich Boling—Lewis Borsellino, DePauw (Valparaiso) 1976	99
John Wicinski—Donnell Lipford, John Carroll (Allegheny) 1975	99
Jack Berry—Mercer West, Washington and Lee (Hampden-Sydney) 1974	99
Gary Shope—Rick Rudolph, Juniata (Moravian) 1973	99
Gary Dusenberg—Harvey King, North Park (Illinois Wesleyan) 1970	99
Bob Janesko—Frank Stankiewicz, Emporia (Pittsburg State) 1969	99
John Williams—Bill Carter, N.M. Highlands (North Colorado) 1964	99
Carl Meyers—Roger Sayers, Nebraska-Omaha (Drake) 1963	99

Punts

Earl Hurst, Emporia State (Central Missouri) 1964	97
Gary Frens, Hope (Olivet) 1966	96
Jim Jarrett, North Dakota (South Dakota) 1957	96
Elliot Mills, Carleton (Monmouth) 1970	93
Kaspar Fitins, Taylor (Georgetown, Ky.) 1966	93
Leeroy Sweeney, Pomona (Cal-Riverside) 1960	93

CAREER LEADERS

Rushing

	Years	Plays	Yds	Avg
Chris Cobb, Eastern Illinois	1976–79	930	5,042[1]	5.42
Jerry Linton, Panhandle State	1959–62	648	4,839	7.47
John VanWagner, Mich. Tech.	1973–76	958	4,788	5.00
Rich Kowalski, Hobart	1972–75	907	4,631	5.11
Don Aleksiewicz, Hobart	1969–72	819	4,525	5.53
Dale Mills, NE Missouri	1957–60	751	4,502	5.99
Leo Lewis, Lincoln (Mo.)	1951–54	623	4,458	7.16
Bernie Peeters, Luther	1968–71	1,072[1]	4,435	4.14
Larry Schreiber, Tenn. Tech.	1966–69	878	4,421	5.04
Brad Rowland, McMurry	1947–50	683	4,347	6.36
Vincent Allen, Indiana State	1973–77	832	4,335	5.21
Bill Rhodes, Colorado Western	1953–56	506	4,294	8.49[1]
Lem Harkey, Col. of Emporia	1951–54	502	4,232	8.43

1. Record.

Scoring

	Years	Td	Pat	Fg	Pts
Walter Payton, Jackson State	1971–74	66[1]	53	5	464[1]

Dale Mills, NE Missouri	1957–60	64	0	23	407
Garney Henley, Huron	1956–59	63	0	16	394
Leo Lewis, Lincoln (Mo.)	1951–54	64	0	0	384
Billy Johnson, Widener	1971–73	62	0	0	372
Tank Younger, Grambling	1945–48	60	0	9	369

1. Record.

Passing

	Years	Comp	Pct	Yds	Td
Jim Lindsey, Abilene Chr.	1967–70	642[1]	.519	8,521[1]	61
Doug Williams, Grambling	1974–77	484	.480	8,411	93[1]
Steve Wray, Franklin	1978–82	592	.481	8,123	62
Tom Bertoldi, North Mich.	1980–83	524	.531	7,330	45
Craig Solomon, SW Tennessee	1975–78	542	.530	7,314	71
Bob Caress, Bradley	1962–65	610	.528	7,115	64
Kim McQuilken, Lehigh	1971–73	516	.538	6,996	37
Bruce Upstill, Col. of Emporia	1960–63	438	.570	6,935	48
Ken O'Brien, Sacramento	1978				
St.–Calif.–Davis	1980–82	496	.539	6,848	45
Mike Houston, St. Joseph's	1978–81	576	.559	6,815	60
George Bork, N. Illinois	1960–63	577	.640	6,782	60
Dan Miles, So. Oregon	1964–67	577	.662[1]	6,531	52

1. Record.

Pass Receiving

	Years	Rec	Yards	Td
Bill Stromberg, Johns Hopkins	1978–81	258[1]	3,776	39
Chris Myers, Kenyon	1967–70			
Bruce Cerone, Yankton–	1966–67	253	3.897	33
Emporia St.	1968–1969	241[1]	4,354[1]	49[1]
Harold Roberts, Austin Peay	1967–70	232	3,005	31
Jerry Hendren, Idaho	1967–69	230	3,435	27
John Ward, Cornell (Iowa)	1979–82	211	3,085	30
Terry Fredenberg, Wis.-Milwaukee	1965–68	206	2,789	24

Rich Ott, NE Missouri St.	1980–83	202	2,821	16
Rick Fry, Occidental	1974–77	200	3,073	18
Jay True, DePauw	1977–80	195	2,567	12
Bill Wick, Carroll (Wis.)	1966–69	190	2,967	20
Don Hutt, Boise State	1971–73	187	2,716	30

1. Record.

MOST POINTS IN SEASON

	Yards	Tds	PAT	Fg	Pts
Terry Metcalf, Long Beach St.	1971	29[1]	4	0	178
Jim Switzer, Coll. Emporia	1963	28	0	0	168
Carl Herakovich, Rose–Hulman	1958	25	18	0	168
Ted Scown, Sul Ross State	1948	28	0	0	168
Eddie McGovern, Rose–Hulman	1942	23	27	0	165
Leon Burns, Long Beach State	1969	27	2	0	164

1. Record.

Total Offense

	Years	Plays	Yds
Jim Lindsey, Abilene Christian	1967–70	1,510[1]	8,385[1]
Doug Williams, Grambling	1974–77	1,072	8,195
Steve Wray, Franklin	1978–82	1,370	7,606
Tom Nelson, St. Cloud State	1980–83	1,421	7,430
Donald Smith, Langston	1958–61	998	7,376
Bruce Upstill, Coll. Emporia	1960–63	922	7,122
Mike Houston, St. Joseph's (Ind.)	1978–81	1,298	7,104
Craig Solomon, SW Tennessee	1975–78	1,261	7,055
Clay Sampson, Denison	1977–80	1,225	6,920
Kim McQuilken, Lehigh	1971–73	991	6,878
Tom Bertoldi, North Mich.	1980–83	1,147	6,807
Bob Caress, Bradley	1962–65	1,361	6,757

1. Record.

N.C.A.A. 1983 CHAMPIONSHIP PLAYOFFS

DIVISION I-AA

Quarterfinals

Southern Illinois 23, Indiana State 7
Western Carolina 28, Holy Cross 21
Nevada–Reno 20, North Texas State 17 (OT)
Furman 35, Boston University 16

Semifinals

Western Carolina 14, Furman 7
Southern Illinois 23, Nevada-Reno 7

Championship

Southern Illinois 43, Western Carolina 7

DIVISION II

Quarterfinals

Central Ohio 24, Southwest Texas State 16
Calif.-Davis 25, Butler 6
North Alabama 16, Virginia Union 14
North Dakota State 24, Towson State 17

Semifinals

Central Ohio 27, North Alabama 24
North Dakota State 26, Calif.–Davis 17

Championship

North Dakota State 41, Central Ohio 21

DIVISION III

Quarterfinals

Augustana (Ill.) 22, Adrian 21
Wisconsin–LaCrosse 43, Occidental 42
Union (N.Y.) 51, Hofstra 19
Salisbury State 16, Carnegie-Mellon 14

Semifinals

Union 23, Salisbury State 21
Augustana 21, Wisconsin–LaCrosse 15

Championship

Augustana 21, Union 17

NATIONAL ASSOCIATION OF INTERCOLLEGIATE ATHLETICS 1983 CHAMPIONSHIPS

DIVISION I

Semifinals

Carson–Newman 41, Saginaw Valley 7
Mesa 34, Central Arkansas 17

Championship

Carson–Newman 36, Mesa 28

DIVISION II

Semifinals

Northwestern 30, William Jewell 12
Pacific Lutheran 16, Westminster 13

Championship

Northwestern 25, Pacific Lutheran 21

Professional Football

NATIONAL FOOTBALL LEAGUE FINAL STANDING 1983

AMERICAN CONFERENCE

Eastern Division

	W	L	T	Pct	Pts	OP
Miami	12	4	0	.750	389	250
Buffalo	8	8	0	.500	283	351
New England	8	8	0	.500	274	289
New York Jets	7	9	0	.438	313	331
Baltimore	7	9	0	.438	264	354

Central Division

	W	L	T	Pct	Pts	OP
Pittsburgh	10	6	0	.625	355	303
Cleveland	9	7	0	.563	356	342
Cincinnati	7	9	0	.438	346	302
Houston	2	14	0	.125	284	460

Western Division

	W	L	T	Pct	Pts	OP
Los Angeles Raiders	12	4	0	.750	442	338
Denver[1]	9	7	0	.563	302	327
Seattle[1]	9	7	0	.563	403	397
Kansas City	6	10	0	.375	386	367
San Diego	6	10	0	.375	358	462

1. Wild card qualifier for playoffs.

Playoffs: Seattle 31, Denver 7; Seattle 27, Miami 20; Los Angeles Raiders 38, Pittsburgh 10.
Conference championship: Los Angeles Raiders 30, Seattle 14

NATIONAL CONFERENCE

Eastern Division

	W	L	T	Pct	Pts	OP
Washington	14	2	0	.875	541	332
Dallas[1]	12	4	0	.750	479	360
St. Louis	8	7	1	.533	374	428
Philadelphia	5	11	0	.313	233	322
New York Giants	3	12	1	.219	267	347

Central Division

	W	L	T	Pct	Pts	OP
Detroit	9	7	0	.563	346	286
Chicago	8	8	0	.500	311	301
Green Bay	8	8	0	.500	429	439
Minnesota	8	8	0	.500	316	348
Tampa Bay	2	14	0	.125	241	380

Western Division

	W	L	T	Pct	Pts	OP
San Francisco	10	6	0	.625	432	293
Los Angeles Rams[1]	9	7	0	.563	361	344
New Orleans	8	8	0	.500	319	337
Atlanta	7	9	0	.438	370	389

1. Wild card qualifier for playoffs.

Playoffs: Los Angeles 24, Dallas 17; San Francisco 24, Detroit 23; Washington 51, Los Angeles Rams 7.
Conference championship: Washington 24, San Francisco 21.

LEAGUE CHAMPIONSHIP—SUPER BOWL XVIII

(Jan. 22, 1984; at Tampa Stadium, Tampa, Fla.; Attendance 72,920)

Scoring

	1st Q	2nd Q	3rd Q	4th Q	Final
Washington (NFC)	0	3	6	0	9
Los Angeles (AFC)	7	14	14	3	38

Scoring—Los Angeles: Touchdowns: Jensen, recovery of blocked punt in end zone; Branch, 12-yard pass from Plunkett; Squirek, 5-yard return of interception; Allen, 5-yard run; Allen, 74-yard run. Conversions: Bahr, 5 (kicks). Field goal: Bahr, 21 yards. Washington: Touchdown: Riggins, 1-yard run. Conversion: Mosley, 1 (kick). Field goal: Mosley, 24-yards.

Statistics of the Game

	Washington	Los Angeles
First downs	19	18
Yards gained rushing	90	231
Yards gained passing	193	154
Passes completed	16	16
Passes intercepted by	0	2
Punts	8-32	7-43
Fumbles lost	1	2
Yards penalized	62	56

SUPER BOWLS I–XVIII

Game	Date	Winner	Loser	Site	Attendance
XVIII	Jan. 22, 1984	Los Angeles Raiders (AFC) 38	Washington 9	Tampa Stadium, Tampa, Fla	72,920
XVII	Jan. 30, 1983	Washington (NFC) 27	Miami (AFC) 17	Rose Bowl, Pasadena, Calif.	103,667
XVI	Jan. 24, 1982	San Francisco (NFC) 26	Cincinnati (AFC) 21	Silverdome, Pontiac, Mich.	81,270
XV	Jan. 25, 1981	Oakland (AFC) 27	Philadelphia (NFC) 10	Superdome, New Orleans	75,500
XIV	Jan. 20, 1980,	Pittsburgh (AFC) 31	Los Angeles (NFC) 19	Rose Bowl, Pasadena	103,985
XIII	Jan. 21, 1979	Pittsburgh (AFC) 35	Dallas (NFC) 31	Orange Bowl, Miami	79,484
XII	Jan. 15, 1978	Dallas (NFC) 27	Denver (AFC) 10	Superdome, New Orleans	75,583
XI	Jan. 9, 1977	Oakland (AFC) 32	Minnesota (NFC) 14	Rose Bowl, Pasadena	103,424
X	Jan. 18, 1976	Pittsburgh (AFC) 21	Dallas (NFC) 17	Orange Bowl, Miami	80,187
IX	Jan. 12, 1975	Pittsburgh (AFC) 16	Minnesota (NFC) 6	Tulane Stadium, New Orleans	80,997
VIII	Jan. 13, 1974	Miami (AFC) 24	Minnesota (NFC) 7	Rice Stadium, Houston	71,882
VII	Jan. 14, 1973	Miami (AFC) 14	Washington (NFC) 7	Memorial Coliseum, Los Angeles	90,182
VI	Jan. 16, 1972	Dallas (NFC) 24	Miami (AFC) 3	Tulane Stadium, New Orleans	81,591
V	Jan. 17, 1971	Baltimore (AFC) 16	Dallas (NFC) 13	Orange Bowl, Miami	79,204
IV	Jan. 11, 1970	Kansas City (AFL) 23	Minnesota (NFL) 7	Tulane Stadium, New Orleans	80,562
III	Jan. 12, 1969	New York (AFL) 16	Baltimore (NFL) 7	Orange Bowl, Miami	75,389
II	Jan. 14, 1968	Green Bay (NFL) 33	Oakland (AFL) 14	Orange Bowl, Miami	75,546
I	Jan. 15, 1967	Green Bay (NFL) 35	Kansas City (AFL) 10	Memorial Coliseum, Los Angeles	61,946

1. Super Bowls I to IV were played before the American Football League and National Football League merged into the NFL, which was divided into two conferences, the NFC and AFC.

NATIONAL LEAGUE CHAMPIONS

Year	Champion (W-L-T)
1921	Chicago Bears (Staley's) (10–1–1)
1922	Canton Bulldogs (10–0–2)
1923	Canton Bulldogs (11–0–1)
1924	Cleveland Indians (7–1–1)
1925	Chicago Cardinals (11–2–1)
1926	Frankford Yellow Jackets (14–1–1)
1927	New York Giants (11–1–1)
1928	Providence Steamrollers (8–1–2)
1929	Green Bay Packers (12–0–1)
1930	Green Bay Packers (10–3–1)
1931	Green Bay Packers (12–2–0)
1932	Chicago Bears (7–1–6)

Year	Eastern Conference winners (W-L-T)	Western Conference winners (W-L-T)	League champion playoff results
1933	New York Giants (11–3–0)	Chicago Bears (10–2–1)	Chicago Bears 23, New York 21
1934	New York Giants (8–5–0)	Chicago Bears (13–0–0)	New York 30, Chicago Bears 13
1935	New York Giants (9–3–0)	Detroit Lions (7–3–2)	Detroit 26, New York 7
1936	Boston Redskins (7–5–0)	Green Bay Packers (10–1–1)	Green Bay 21, Boston 6
1937	Washington Redskins (8–3–0)	Chicago Bears (9–1–1)	Washington 28, Chicago Bears 21
1938	New York Giants (8–2–1)	Green Bay Packers (8–3–0)	New York 23, Green Bay 17
1939	New York Giants (9–1–1)	Green Bay Packers (9–2–0)	Green Bay 27, New York 0
1940	Washington Redskins (9–2–0)	Chicago Bears (8–3–0)	Chicago Bears 73, Washington 0
1941	New York Giants (8–3–0)	Chicago Bears (10–1–1)[2]	Chicago Bears 37, New York 9
1942	Washington Redskins (10–1–1)	Chicago Bears (11–0–0)	Washington 14, Chicago Bears 6
1943	Washington Redskins (6–3–1)[2]	Chicago Bears (8–1–1)	Chicago Bears 41, Washington 21
1944	New York Giants (8–1–1)	Green Bay Packers (8–2–0)	Green Bay 14, New York 7
1945	Washington Redskins (8–2–0)	Cleveland Rams (9–1–0)	Cleveland 15, Washington 14
1946	New York Giants (7–3–1)	Chicago Bears (8–2–1)	Chicago Bears 24, New York 14
1947	Philadelphia Eagles (8–4–0)[2]	Chicago Cardinals (9–3–0)	Chicago Cardinals 28, Philadelphia 21
1948	Philadelphia Eagles (9–2–1)	Chicago Cardinals (11–1–0)	Philadelphia 7, Chicago Cardinals 0
1949	Philadelphia Eagles (11–1–0)	Los Angeles Rams (8–2–2)	Philadelphia 14, Los Angeles 0
1950[1]	Cleveland Browns (10–2–0)[2]	Los Angeles Rams (9–3–0)[2]	Cleveland 30, Los Angeles 28
1951[1]	Cleveland Browns (11–1–0)	Los Angeles Rams (8–4–0)	Los Angeles 24, Cleveland 17
1952[1]	Cleveland Browns (8–4–0)	Detroit Lions (9–3–0)[2]	Detroit 17, Cleveland 7
1953	Cleveland Browns (11–1–0)	Detroit Lions (10–2–0)	Detroit 17, Cleveland 16
1954	Cleveland Browns (9–3–0)	Detroit Lions (9–2–1)	Cleveland 56, Detroit 10
1955	Cleveland Browns (9–2–1)	Los Angeles Rams (8–3–1)	Cleveland 38, Los Angeles 14
1956	New York Giants (8–3–1)	Chicago Bears (9–2–1)	New York 47, Chicago Bears 7
1957	Cleveland Browns (9–2–1)	Detroit Lions (8–4–0)[3]	Detroit 59, Cleveland 14
1958	New York Giants (9–3–0)[2]	Baltimore Colts (9–3–0)	Baltimore 23, New York 17[3]
1959	New York Giants (10–2–0)	Baltimore Colts (9–3–0)	Baltimore 31, New York 16
1960	Philadelphia Eagles (10–2–0)	Green Bay Packers (8–4–0)	Philadelphia 17, Green Bay 13
1961	New York Giants (10–3–1)	Green Bay Packers (11–3–0)	Green Bay 37, New York 0
1962	New York Giants (12–2–0)	Green Bay Packers (13–1–0)	Green Bay 16, New York 7
1963	New York Giants (11–3–0)	Chicago Bears (11–1–2)	Chicago 14, New York 10
1964	Cleveland Browns (10–3–1)	Baltimore Colts (12–2–0)	Cleveland 27, Baltimore 0
1965	Cleveland Browns (11–3–0)	Green Bay Packers (11–3–1)[2]	Green Bay 23, Cleveland 12
1966	Dallas Cowboys (10–3–1)	Green Bay Packers (12–2–0)	Green Bay 34, Dallas 27
1967	Dallas Cowboys (9–5–0)[2]	Green Bay Packers (9–4–1)[2]	Green Bay 21, Dallas 17
1968	Cleveland Browns (10–4–0)[2]	Baltimore Colts (13–1–0)[2]	Baltimore 34, Cleveland 0
1969	Cleveland Browns (10–3–1)[2]	Minnesota Vikings (12–2–0)[2]	Minnesota 27, Cleveland 7

1. League was divided into American and National Conferences, 1950–52 and again in 1970, when leagues merged. 2. Won divisional playoff. 3. Won at 8:15 of sudden death overtime period.

NATIONAL CONFERENCE CHAMPIONS

Year	Eastern Division	Central Division	Western Division	Champion
1970	Dallas Cowboys (10–4–0)	Minnesota Vikings (12–2–0)	San Francisco 49ers (10–3–1)	Dallas
1971	Dallas Cowboys (11–3–0)	Minnesota Vikings (11–3–0)	San Francisco 49ers (9–5–0)	Dallas
1972	Washington Redskins (11–3–0)	Green Bay Packers (10–4–0)	San Francisco 49ers (8–5–1)	Washington
1973	Dallas Cowboys (10–4–0)	Minnesota Vikings (12–2–0)	Los Angeles Rams (12–2–0)	Minnesota
1974	St. Louis Cardinals (10–4–0)	Minnesota Vikings (10–4–0)	Los Angeles Rams (10–4–0)	Minnesota
1975	St. Louis Cardinals (11–3–0)	Minnesota Vikings (12–2–0)	Los Angeles Rams (10–4–0)	Dallas
1976	Dallas Cowboys (11–3–0)	Minnesota Vikings (11–2–1)	Los Angeles Rams (10–3–1)	Minnesota
1977	Dallas Cowboys (12–2–0)	Minnesota Vikings (9–5–0)	Los Angeles Rams (10–4–0)	Dallas
1978	Dallas Cowboys (12–4–0)	Minnesota Vikings (8–7–1)	Los Angeles Rams (12–4–0)	Dallas
1979	Dallas Cowboys (11–5–0)	Tampa Bay Buccaneers (10–6–0)	Los Angeles Rams (9–7–0)	Los Angeles
1980	Philadelphia Eagles (12–4–0)	Minnesota Vikings (9–7–0)	Atlanta Falcons (12–4–0)	Philadelphia
1981	Dallas Cowboys (12–4–0)	Tampa Bay Buccaneers (9–7–0)	San Francisco 49ers (13–3–0)	San Francisco
1982*	Washington Redskins won conference title and also had best regular-season record (8–1–0)			
1983	Washington Redskins (14–2–0)	Detroit Lions (8–8–0)	San Francisco 49ers (10–6–0)	Washington

*Schedule reduced to 9 games from usual 16, with no standings kept in Eastern, Central, and Western Divisions, because of 57-day player strike.

AMERICAN CONFERENCE CHAMPIONS

Year	Eastern Division	Central Division	Western Division	Champion
1970	Baltimore Colts (11–2–1)	Cincinnati Bengals (8–6–0)	Oakland Raiders (8–4–2)	Baltimore
1971	Miami Dolphins (10–3–1)	Cleveland Browns (9–5–0)	Kansas City Chiefs (10–3–1)	Miami
1972	Miami Dolphins (14–0–0)	Pittsburgh Steelers (11–3–0)	Oakland Raiders (10–3–1)	Miami
1973	Miami Dolphins (12–2–0)	Cincinnati Bengals (10–4–0)	Oakland Raiders (9–4–1)	Miami
1974	Miami Dolphins (11–3–0)	Pittsburgh Steelers (10–3–1)	Oakland Raiders (12–2–0)	Pittsburgh
1975	Baltimore Colts (10–4–0)	Pittsburgh Steelers (12–2–0)	Oakland Raiders (12–2–0)	Pittsburgh
1976	Baltimore Colts (11–3–0)	Pittsburgh Steelers (10–4–0)	Oakland Raiders (13–1–0)	Oakland
1977	Baltimore Colts (10–4–0)	Pittsburgh Steelers (9–5–0)	Denver Broncos (12–2–0)	Denver
1978	New England Patriots (11–5–0)	Pittsburgh Steelers (14–2–0)	Denver Broncos (10–6–0)	Pittsburgh
1979	Miami Dolphins (10–6–0)	Pittsburgh Steelers (12–4–0)	San Diego Chargers (12–4–0)	Pittsburgh
1980	Buffalo Bills (11–5–0)	Cleveland Browns (11–5–0)	San Diego Chargers (11–5–0)	Oakland
1981	Miami Dolphins (11–4–1)	Cincinnati Bengals (12–4–0)	San Diego Chargers (10–6–0)	Cincinnati
1982*	Miami Dolphins won the conference title, but the Los Angeles Raiders had best regular-season record (8–1–0).			
1983	Miami (12–4–0)	Pittsburgh (10–6–0)	Los Angeles Raiders (12–4–0)	Los Angeles Raiders

*Schedule reduced to 9 games from usual 16, with no standings kept in Eastern, Central, and Western Divisions, because of 57-day player strike.

AMERICAN LEAGUE CHAMPIONS

Year	Eastern Division (W-L-T)	Western Division (W-L-T)	League champion, playoffs results
1960	Houston Oilers (10-4-0)	Los Angeles Chargers (10-4-0)	Houston 24, Los Angeles 16
1961	Houston Oilers (10-3-1)	San Diego Chargers (12-2-0)	Houston 10, San Diego 3
1962	Houston Oilers (11-3-0)	Dallas Texans (11-3-0)	Dallas 20, Houston 17[1]
1963	Boston Patriots (8-6-1)[2]	San Diego Chargers (11-3-0)	San Diego 51, Boston 10
1964	Buffalo Bills (12-2-0)	San Diego Chargers (8-5-1)	Buffalo 20, San Diego 7
1965	Buffalo Bills (10-3-1)	San Diego Chargers (9-2-3)	Buffalo 23, San Diego 0
1966	Buffalo Bills (9-4-1)	Kansas City Chiefs (11-2-1)	Kansas City 31, Buffalo 7
1967	Houston Oilers (9-4-1)	Oakland Raiders (13-1-0)	Oakland 40, Houston 7
1968	New York Jets (11-3-0)	Oakland Raiders (12-2-0)[2]	New York 27, Oakland 23
1969	New York Jets (10-4-0)	Oakland Raiders (12-1-1)	Kansas City 17, Oakland 7[3]

1. Won at 2:45 of second sudden death overtime period. 2. Won divisional playoff. 3. Kansas City defeated New York, 13–6, and Oakland defeated Houston, 56–7, in interdivisional playoffs.

NATIONAL FOOTBALL LEAGUE GOVERNMENT

Commissioner's Office: Pete Rozelle, commissioner; Don Weiss, executive director; Bill Ray, treasurer; Jay Moyer, counsel to commissioner; Jan Van Duser, director of operations; Jim Heffernan, director of public relations; Joe Browne, director of information; Warren Welsh, director of security; Charles R. Jackson, assistant director of security; Joel Bussert, director of player personnel; Art McNally, supervisor of officials; Joe Rhein, administrative coordinator; Wayne Rosen, director of personnel; Buddy Young, director of player relations; Jim Steeg, director of special events.

American Conference: Lamar Hunt, president; Al Ward, assistant to the president; Fran Connors, director of information.

National Conference: George Halas, president; Bill Granholm, assistant to the president; Dick Maxwell, director of information.

PRO FOOTBALL HALL OF FAME

(National Football Museum, Canton, Ohio)

Teams named are those with which player is best identified; figures in parentheses indicate number of playing seasons.

Adderley, Herb, defensive back, Packers, Cowboys (12)	1961–72
Alworth, Lance, wide receiver, Chargers, Cowboys (11)	1962–72
Atkins, Doug, defensive end, Browns, Bears, Saints (17)	1953–69
Badgro, Morris, end, N.Y. Yankees, Giants, Bklyn. Dodgers (8)	1927, 1930–36
Battles, Cliff, back, Redskins (6)	1932–37
Baugh, Sammy, quarterback, Redskins (16)	1937–52
Bednarik, Chuck, center-lineback, Eagles (14)	1949–62
Bell, Bert, N.F.L. founder, owner Eagles and Steelers, N.F.L. Commissioner	1946–59
Bell, Bobby, linebacker, Chiefs (12)	1963–74
Berry, Raymond, end, Colts (13)	1955–67
Bidwell, Charles W., owner Chicago Cardinals	1933–47
Blanda, George, quarterback-kicker, Bears, Oilers, Raiders (27)	1949–75
Brown, Jim, fullback, Browns (9)	1957–65
Brown, Paul E., coach, Browns (1946–62), Bengals (1968–75)	1946–75
Brown, Roosevelt, tackle, Giants (13)	1953–65
Brown, Willie, cornerback, Broncos, Raiders (16)	1963–78
Butkus, Dick, linebacker, Bears (19)	1965–73
Canadeo, Tony, back, Packers (11)	1941–52
Carr, Joe, president N.F.L. (18)	1921–39
Chamberlin, Guy, end 4 teams (9)	1919–27
Christiansen, Jack, defensive back, Lions (8)	1951–58
Clark, Earl (Dutch), Qback, Spartans, Lions (7)	1931–38
Connor, George, tackle, linebacker, Bears (8)	1948–55
Conzelman, Jimmy, Qback 5 teams (10), owner	1921–48
Davis, Willie, defensive end, Packers (10)	1960–69
Donovan, Art, defensive tackle, Colts (12)	1950–61
Driscoll, John (Paddy), Qback, Cards, Bears (11)	1919–29
Dudley, Bill, back, Steelers, Lions, Redskins (9)	1942–53
Edwards, Albert Glen (Turk), tackle, Redskins (9)	1932–40
Ewbank, Weeb, coach Colts, Jets (20)	1954–73
Fears, Tom, end, Rams (9); coach, Saints	1948–56

Flaherty, Ray, end, Yankees, Giants (9); coach, Redskins, Yankees (14) 1928–49
Ford, Len, end, def. end, Browns, Packers (11) 1948–58
Fortmann, Daniel J., guard, Bears (8) 1936–43
George, Bill, linebacker, Bears, Rams (15) 1952–66
Gifford, Frank, back, Giants (12) 1952–64
Gillman, Sid, coach, Rams, Chargers, Oilers (18) 1955–70, 73–74
Graham, Otto, quarterback, Browns (10) 1946–55
Grange, Harold (Red), back, Bears, Yankees (9) 1925–34
Gregg, Forrest, tackle, Packers (15) 1956–71
Groza, Lou, place-kicker, tackle, Browns (21) 1946–67
Guyon, Joe, back, 6 teams (8) 1919–27
Halas, George, N.F.L. founder, owner and coach, Staleys and Bears, end (11) 1919–67
Healey, Ed, tackle, Bears (8) 1920–27
Hein, Mel, center, Giants (15) 1931–45
Henry, Wilbur (Pete), tackle, Bulldogs, Giants (8) 1920–28
Herber, Arnie, Qback, Packers, Giants (13) 1930–45
Hewitt, Bill, end, Bears, Eagles (9) 1932–43
Hinkle, Clarke, fullback, Packers (10) 1932–41
Hirsch, Elroy (Crazy Legs), back, end, Rams (12) 1946–57
Hubbard, R. (Cal), tackle, Giants, Packers (9) 1927–36
Huff, Sam, linebacker, Giants, Redskins (13) 1956–67, 1969
Hunt, Lamar, Founder A.F.L., owner Texans, Chiefs 1959–
Hutson, Don, end, Packers (11) 1935–45
Jones, David (Deacon), defensive end, Rams, Chargers, Redskins (14) 1961–74
Jurgensen, Sonny, quarterback, Eagles, Redskins (18) 1957–74
Kiesling, Walt, guard 6 teams (13) 1926–38
Kinard, Frank (Bruiser), tackle, Dodgers (9) 1938–47
Lambeau, Earl (Curly), N.F.L. founder, coach, end, back, Packers (11) 1919–53
Lane, Richard (Night Train), defensive back, Rams, Cardinals, Lions (14) 1952–65
Lary, Yale, defensive back, punter, Lions (11) 1952–64
Laveill, Dante, end, Browns (11) 1946–56
Layne, Bobby, Qback, Bears, Lions, Steelers (15) 1948–62
Leemans, Alphonse (Tuffy), back, Giants (8) 1936–43
Lilly, Bob, defensive tackle, Cowboys (14) 1961–74
Lombardi, Vince, coach, Packers, Redskins (11) 1959–70
Luckman, Sid, quarterback, Bears (12) 1939–50
Lyman, Roy (Link), tackle, Bulldogs, Bears (11) 1922–34
Mara, Tim, N.F.L. founder, owner Giants 1925–59
Marchetti, Gino, defensive end, Colts (14) 1952–66
Marshall, George P., N.F.L. founder, owner Redskins 1932–65
Matson, Ollie, back, Cardinals, Rams, Lions, Eagles (14) 1952–66
McAfee, George, back, Bears (8) 1940–50
McCormack, Mike, tackle, N.Y. Yankees, Cleveland Browns (10) 1951–1962
McElhenny, Hugh, back, 49ers, Vikings, Giants (13) 1952–64
McNally, John (Blood), back, 7 teams (15) 1925–39
Michalske, August, guard, Yankees, Packers (11) 1926–37
Millner, Wayne, end, Redskins (7) 1936–45
Mitchell, Bobby, wide receiver, Browns, Redskins (11) 1958–68
Mix, Ron, tackle, Chargers (11) 1960–71
Moore, Lenny, back, Colts (12) 1956–67
Motley, Marion, fullback, Browns, Steelers (9) 1946–55
Musso, George, guard-tackle, Bears (12) 1933–44
Nagurski, Bronko, fullback, Bears (9) 1930–43
Neale, Earle (Greasy), coach, Eagles 1941–50
Nevers, Ernie, fullback, Chicago Cardinals (5) 1926–31
Nitschke, Ray, linebacker, Packers (15) 1958–72
Nomellini, Leo, defensive tackle, 49ers (14) 1950–63
Olsen, Merlin, defensive tackle, Rams (15) 1962–76
Otto, Jim, center, Raiders (15) 1960–74
Owen, Steve, tackle, Giants (9), coach, Giants (13) 1924–53
Parker, Clarence (Ace), quarterback, Dodgers (7) 1937–46
Parker, Jim, guard, tackle, Colts (11) 1957–67
Perry, Joe, fullback, 49ers, Colts (16) 1948–63
Pihos, Pete, end, Eagles (9) 1947–55
Ray, Hugh, Shorty, N.F.L. advisor 1938–52
Reeves, Dan, owner Rams 1941–71
Ringo, Jim, center, Packers (15) 1963–67
Robustelli, Andy, def. end, Rams, Giants (14) 1951–64
Rooney, Art, N.F.L. founder, owner Steelers 1933–
Sayers, Gale, back, Bears (7) 1965–71
Schmidt, Joe, linebacker, Lions (13) 1953–65
Starr, Bart, quarterback, coach, Packers (16) 1956–71
Stautner, Ernie, defensive tackle, Steelers (14) 1950–63
Strong, Ken, back, Giants, Yankees (14) 1929–47
Stydahar, Joe, tackle, Bears (9); coach, Rams, Cardinals (5) 1936–54
Taylor, Charlie, wide receiver, Redskins (14) 1964–77
Taylor, Jim, fullback, Packers, Saints (10) 1958–67
Thorpe, Jim, back, 7 teams (12) 1915–28
Tittle, Y. A., Qback, Colts, 49ers, Giants (17) 1948–64
Trafton, George, center, Bears (13) 1920–32
Trippi, Charley, back, Chicago Cardinals (9) 1947–55
Tunnell, Emlen, def. back, Giants, Packers (14) 1948–61
Turner, Clyde (Bulldog), center, Bears (13) 1940–52
Unitas, John, quarterback, Colts (18) 1956–73
Van Brocklin, Norm, Qback, Rams, Eagles (12) 1949–60
Van Buren, Steve, back, Eagles (8) 1944–51
Warfield, Paul, wide receiver, Browns, Dolphins (13) 1964–74, 76–77
Waterfield, Bob, quarterback, Rams (8) 1945–52
Weinmeister, Arnie, tackle, N.Y. Yankees, Giants (6) 1948–53
Willis, Bill, Guard, Browns (8) 1946–53
Wilson, Larry, defensive back, Cardinals (13) 1960–72
Wojciechowicz, Alex, center, Lions, Eagles (13) 1938–50

N.F.L. INDIVIDUAL LIFETIME, SEASON, AND GAME RECORDS

(American Football League records were incorporated into N.F.L. records after merger of the leagues)

All-Time Leading Touchdown Scorers

	Yrs	Rush	Pass rec	Returns	TD
Jim Brown	9	106	20	0	126
Lenny Moore	12	63	48	2	113
Don Hutson	11	3	99	3	105
Franco Harris	12	91	9	0	100
Jim Taylor	10	83	10	0	93
Bobby Mitchell	11	18	65	8	91
Leroy Kelly	10	74	13	3	90
Charley Taylor	13	11	79	0	90
Don Maynard	15	0	88	0	88
Lance Alworth	11	2	85	0	87

All-Time Leading Passers

	Comp	Pct comp	Yds	TD	Int	Rating
Joe Montana	1,045	63.5	11,979	78	44	90.0
Danny White	1,029	60.2	13,174	98	79	84.2
Roger Staubach	1,685	57.0	22,700	153	109	83.4
Sonny Jurgensen	2,433	57.1	32,224	255	189	82.6
Len Dawson	2,136	57.1	28,711	239	183	82.6
Ken Anderson	2,452	59.2	30,390	184	146	82.0
Dan Fouts	2,268	58.6	30,114	182	168	80.9
Bart Starr	1,808	57.4	24,718	152	138	80.5
Fran Tarkenton	3,686	57.0	47,003	342	266	80.5
Bert Jones	1,430	56.1	18,190	124	101	78.2
Johnny Unitas	2,830	54.6	40,239	290	253	78.2

The passing ratings are based on performance standards established for completion percentage, interception percentage, touchdown percentage, and average pass gain. Passers are allocated points according to how their marks compare with those standards. This listing is based on 1,500 or more pass attempts.

All-Time Leading Receivers

	Yrs	Pass rec	Yds	Avg
Charley Taylor	13	649	9,110	14.0
Don Maynard	15	633	11,834	18.7

Raymond Berry	13	631	9,275	14.7
Charlie Joiner	15	596	9,981	16.7
Fred Biletnikoff	14	589	8,974	12.7
Harold Carmichael	13	589	8,978	15.2
Harold Jackson	16	579	10,410	17.9
Lionel Taylor	10	567	7,195	12.7
Lance Alworth	11	542	10,266	18.9
Bobby Mitchell	11	521	7,954	15.3

All-Time Leading Rushers

	Yrs	Att	Yds	Avg
Jim Brown	9	2,359	12,312	5.2
Franco Harris	12	2,881	11,950	4.1
Walter Payton	9	2,666	11,625	4.3
O.J. Simpson	11	2,404	11,236	4.7
John Riggins	12	2,413	9,436	3.9
Jim Taylor	10	1,941	8,597	4.4
Joe Perry	14	1,737	8,378	4.8
Tony Dorsett	7	1,834	8,336	4.5
Larry Csonka	11	1,891	8,081	4.3
Leroy Kelly	10	1,727	7,274	4.2

All-Time Leading Scorers

	Yrs	TD	FG	PAT	Pts
George Blanda	26	9	335	943	2,002
Jan Stenerud	17	0	324	509	1,459
Jim Turner	16	1	304	521	1,439
Jim Bakken	17	0	282	534	1,380
Fred Cox	15	0	282	519	1,365
Lou Groza	17	1	234	641	1,349
Gino Cappelletti	11	42	176	350	1,130[1]
Don Cockroft	13	0	216	432	1,080
Garo Yepremian	14	0	210	444	1,074
Bruce Gossett	11	0	219	374	1,031

1. Includes four 2-point conversions.

Scoring

Most points scored, lifetime—2,002, George Blanda, Chicago Bears, 1949–58; Baltimore, 1950; Houston, 1960–66; Oakland, 1967–75 (9tds, 943 pat, 335 fgs).
Most points, season—176, Paul Hornung, Green Bay, 1960 (15 td, 41 pat, 15 fg).
Most points, game—40, Ernie Nevers, Chicago Cardinals, 1929 (6 td, 4 pat).
Most points, per quarter—29, Don Hutson, Green Bay, 1945 (4 td, 5 pat).
Most touchdowns, lifetime—126, Jim Brown, Cleveland, 1957–65.
Most touchdowns, season—23, O.J. Simpson, Buffalo, 1975.
Most touchdowns, game—6, Ernie Nevers, Chicago Cardinals, 1929; William Jones, Cleveland, 1951; Gale Sayers, Chicago Bears, 1965.
Most points after touchdown, lifetime—943, George Blanda, Chicago Bears, 1949–58; Baltimore, 1950; Houston, 1960–66; Oakland, 1967–75.
Most points after touchdown, game—9, Pat Harder, Chicago Cardinals, 1948; Bob Waterfield, Los Angeles, 1950; Charlie Gogolak, Washington, 1966.
Most consecutive points after touchdown—234, Tommy Davis, San Francisco, 1959–65.
Most points after touchdown, no misses, season—56, Danny Villanueva, Dallas, 1966.
Most field goals, lifetime—335, George Blanda, Chicago Bears 1949–58; Baltimore, 1950; Houston, 1960–66; Oakland 1967–75.
Most field goals, season—34, Jim Turner, New York Jets, 1968.
Most field goals, game—7, Jim Bakken, St. Louis, 1967.
Longest field goal—63 yards, Tom Dempsey, New Orleans, 1970.

Rushing

Most yards gained, lifetime—12,312, Jim Brown, Cleveland, 1957–65.
Most yards gained, season—2,003, O. J. Simpson, Buffalo, 1973.
Most yards gained, game—275, Walter Payton, Chicago, 1977.
Most touchdowns, lifetime—106, Jim Brown, Cleveland, 1957–65.
Most touchdowns, season—19, Earl Campbell, Houston, 1979; Jim Taylor, Green Bay, 1962; Chuck Muncie, San Diego, 1981.
Most touchdowns, game—6, Ernie Nevers, Chicago Cardinals, 1929.
Longest run from scrimmage—99 yards, Tony Dorsett, Dallas, 1982 (touchdown).

Passing

Most passes completed, lifetime—3,686, Fran Tarkenton, Minnesota, 1961–66, 72–78; New York Giants, 1967–71.
Most passes completed, season—360, Dan Fouts, San Diego, 1981.
Most passes completed, game—42, Richard Todd, New York Jets, 1980.
Most consecutive passes completed—17, Bert Jones, Baltimore, 1974.
Most yards gained, lifetime—47,003, Fran Tarkenton, Minnesota, 1961–66, 72–78; New York Giants, 1967–71.
Most yards gained, season—4,802, Dan Fouts, San Diego, 1981.
Most yards gained, game—554, Norm Van Brocklin, Los Angeles, 1951.
Most touchdown passes, lifetime—342, Fran Tarkenton, Minnesota, 1961–66, 72–78; New York Giants, 1967–71.
Most touchdown passes, season—36, George Blanda, Houston, 1961; Y. A. Tittle, New York Giants, 1963.
Most touchdown passes, game—7, Sid Luckman, Chicago Bears, 1943; Adrian Burk, Philadelphia, 1954; George Blanda, Houston 1961; Y.A. Tittle, New York Giants, 1963; Joe Kapp, Minnesota, 1969.
Most consecutive games, touchdown passes—47, John Unitas, Baltimore.
Most consecutive passes attempted, none intercepted—294, Bart Starr, Green Bay, 1964–65.
Longest pass completion—99 yards, Frank Filchock (to Andy Farkas), Washington, 1939; George Izo (to Bob Mitchell), Washington, 1963; Karl Sweetan (to Pat Studstill), Detroit, 1966; Sonny Jurgensen (to Gerry Allen), Washington, 1968, (all for touchdowns).
Most pass receptions, lifetime—649, Charley Taylor, Washington, 1964–75, 1977.
Most pass receptions, season—101, Charley Hennigan, Houston, 1964.
Most pass receptions, game—18, Tom Fears, Los Angeles, 1950.
Most consecutive games, pass receptions—127, Harold Carmichael, Philadelphia, 1972–80.
Most yards gained, pass receptions, lifetime—11,834, Don Maynard, New York Giants, 1958; New York Jets, 1960–72; St. Louis, 1973.
Most yards gained receptions, season—1,746, Charley Hennigan, Houston, 1961.
Most yards gained receptions, game—303, Jim Benton, Cleveland Rams, 1945.
Most touchdown pass receptions, lifetime—99, Don Hutson, Green Bay, 1935–45.
Most touchdown pass receptions, season—17, Don Hutson, Green Bay, 1942; Elroy Hirsch, Los Angeles, 1951; Bill Groman, Houston, 1961.

Most touchdown pass receptions, game—5, Bob Shaw, Chicago Cards, 1950.
Most consecutive games, touchdown pass receptions—11, Elroy Hirsch, Los Angeles, 1950–51; Buddy Dial, Pittsburgh, 1959–60.
Most pass interceptions, lifetime—81, Paul Krause, Washington, 1964–67; Minnesota, 1968–79.
Most pass interceptions, season—14, Richard (Night Train) Lane, Los Angeles, 1952.
Most pass interceptions, game—4, by 15 players.
Longest pass interception return—102 yards, Bob Smith, Chicago Bears, 1949; Erich Barnes, New York Giants, 1961; Gary Barbaro, Kansas City, 1977; Louis Breeden, Cincinnati, 1981.

Kicking

Longest punt—98 yards, Steve O'Neal, New York Jets, 1969.
Highest average punting, lifetime—45.10 yards, Sammy Baugh, Washington, 1937–52.
Longest punt return—98 yards, Gil LeFebvre, Cincinnati Reds, 1933; Charlie West, Minnesota, 1968; Dennis Morgan, Dallas, 1974.
Longest kick-off return—106 yards, Roy Green, St. Louis, 1979; Al Carmichael, Green Bay, 1956; Noland Smith, Kansas City, 1967.

UNITED STATES FOOTBALL LEAGUE

The United States Football League played its inaugural season in the spring and summer of 1983. The league originated with the concept of not competing directly with the established National Football League, and scheduled its games between March and July. Television contracts from ABC-TV and ESPN helped finance the league at the start by guaranteeing two years of network coverage and paying the U.S.F.L. $12 million annually. The league, which started with 12 teams, added six more in 1984 and began serious bidding for established N.F.L. players and top college prospects.

UNITED STATES FOOTBALL LEAGUE FINAL STANDINGS 1984

EASTERN CONFERENCE
Atlantic Division

	W	L	T	Pct	Pts	OP
Philadelphia	16	2	0		479	225
New Jersey	14	4	0		430	312
Pittsburgh	3	15	0		259	379
Washington	3	15	0		270	492

Southern Division

	W	L	T	Pct	Pts	OP
Birmingham	14	4	0		557	316
Tampa Bay	14	4	0		498	337
New Orleans	8	10	0		348	395
Memphis	7	11	0		320	455
Jacksonville	6	12	0		327	455

WESTERN CONFERENCE
Central Division

	W	L	T	Pct	Pts	Op
Houston	13	5	0		618	400
Michigan	10	8	0		400	382
San Antonio	7	11	0		309	325
Oklahoma	6	12	0		251	459
Chicago	5	13	0		340	466

Pacific Division

	W	L	T	Pct	Pts	Op
Los Angeles	10	8	0		338	373
Arizona	10	8	0		502	284
Denver	9	9	0		356	413
Oakland	7	11	0		242	348

Playoffs

Quarterfinals

Philadelphia 28, New Jersey 7
Los Angeles 27, Michigan 21 OT
Birmingham 36, Tampa Bay 17
Arizona 17, Houston 16

Semifinals

Arizona 35, Los Angeles 23
Philadelphia 20, Birmingham 10

Championship

Philadelphia 23, Arizona 3

TEAM NICKNAMES AND HOME FIELD CAPACITIES

AMERICAN CONFERENCE
Eastern Division

Buffalo Bills	Rich Stadium (AT)	80,020
Indianapolis Colts[1]	Hoosier Dome (AT)	61,500
Miami Dolphins	Orange Bowl (G)	75,059
New England Patriots	Sullivan Stadium (ST)	61,297
New York Jets[2]	Giants Stadium (AT)	76,891

Central Division

Cincinnati Bengals	Riverfront Stadium (AT)	59,754
Cleveland Browns	Municipal Stadium (G)	80,322
Houston Oilers	Astrodome (AT)	50,496
Pittsburgh Steelers	Three Rivers Stadium (AT)	59,000

Western Division

Denver Broncos	Mile High Stadium (G)	75,103
Kansas City Chiefs	Arrowhead Stadium (TT)	78,067
Los Angeles Raiders[3]	Memorial Coliseum (G)	92,498
San Diego Chargers	Jack Murphy Stadium (G)	53,675
Seattle Seahawks	Kingdome (AT)	64,757

1. Moved franchise from Baltimore prior to 1984 season. 2. Moved to Giants Stadium; East Rutherford, N.J. prior to 1984 season. 3. Moved franchise to Los Angeles for 1982 season. Shift is still being argued in courts, as city of Oakland tries to regain franchise.

NATIONAL CONFERENCE
Eastern Division

Dallas Cowboys	Texas Stadium (TT)	65,101
New York Giants	Giants Stadium (AT)[1]	76,891
Philadelphia Eagles	Veterans Stadium (AT)	72,204
St. Louis Cardinals	Busch Memorial Stadium (AT)	51,392
Washington Redskins	R.F. Kennedy Stadium (G)	55,045

Central Division

Chicago Bears	Soldier Field (AT)	65,793
Detroit Lions	Pontiac Silverdome (AT)	80,638
Green Bay Packers	Lambeau Field (G)	56,189
	Milwaukee Stadium (G)	55,958
Minnesota Vikings	Hubert Humphrey Metrodome (ST)	62,212
Tampa Bay Buccaneers	Tampa Stadium	72,812

Western Division

Atlanta Falcons	Atlanta-Fulton Stadium	60,748
Los Angeles Rams	Anaheim Stadium	69,007
New Orleans Saints	Louisiana Superdome	71,330
San Francisco 49ers	Candlestick Park	61,185

1. At East Rutherford, N.J. NOTE: Stadium playing surfaces in parentheses: (AT) Astro Turf; (G) Grass; (ST) Super Turf; (TT) Tartan Turf.

FISHING

WORLD ALL-TACKLE FISHING RECORDS

Caught With Rod and Reel in Fresh Water

Source: International Game Fish Association

Species	lb-oz	Where caught	Year	Angler
Barramundi	59-12	Point Stuart, Australia	1983	Andrew Davern
Bass, Largemouth	22-4	Montgomery Lake, Ga.	1932	George W. Perry
Bass, Peacock	26-8	Mataveni River, Columbia	1982	Rod Neubert
Bass, Redeye	8-3	Flint River, Ga.	1977	David A. Hubbard
Bass, Rock	3-0	York River, Ontario	1974	Peter Gulgin
Bass, Smallmouth	11-15	Dale Hollow Lake, Ky.	1955	David L. Hayes
Bass, Spotted	8-15	Smith Lake, Ala.	1978	Philip C. Terry, Jr.
Bass, Striped	78-8	Atlantic City, N.J.	1982	Albert McReynolds
Bass, Striped (landlocked)	59-12	Colorado River, Ariz.	1977	Frank W. Smith
Bass, White	5-9	Colorado River, Texas	1977	David S. Cordill
Bass, Whiterock	20-6	Savannah River, Ga.	1978	Danny Wood
Bass, Yellow	2-4	Lake Monroe, Ind.	1977	Donald L. Stalker
Bluegill	4-12	Ketona Lake, Ala.	1950	T.S. Hudson
Bowfin	21-8	Florence, S.C.	1980	Robert L. Harmon
Buffalo, Bigmouth	70-5	Bussey Brake, Bastrop, La.	1980	Delbert Sisk
Buffalo, Smallmouth	51-0	Lawrence, Kan.	1979	Scott Butler
Bullhead, Black	8-0	Lake Waccabuc, N.Y.	1951	Kani Evans
Bullhead, Brown	5-8	Veal Pond, Ga.	1975	Jimmy Andrews
Bullhead, Yellow	3-0	Nelson Lake, Wisc.	1977	Mark Nessman
Burbot	18-4	Pickford, Mich.	1980	Tom Courtemanche
Carp	57-13	Potomac River, Wash., D.C.	1983	David Nikolow
Catfish, Blue	97-0	Missouri River, S.D.	1959	Edward B. Elliott
Catfish, Channel	58-0	Santee–Cooper Res., S.C.	1964	W.B. Whaley
Catfish, Flathead	91-4	Lake Lewisville, Texas	1982	Mike Rogers
Catfish, White	17-7	Success Lake, Tulare, Calif.	1981	Chuck Idell
Char, Arctic	29-11	Arctic River, N.W.T., Canada	1968	Jeanne Branson
Crappie, Black	6-0	Seaplane Canal, Westwego, La.	1969	Lettie Robertson
Crappie, White	5-3	Enid Dam, Mississippi	1957	Fred L. Bright
Dolley Varden	4-0	Togiak National Wildlife Refuge, Alaska	1982	Jonathan Olch
Dorado	48-11	Ita–Ibate, Corrientes, Argentina	1982	Sindo Farina
Drum, Freshwater	54-8	Nickajack Lake, Tenn.	1972	Benny E. Hull
Gar, Alligator	279	Rio Grande River, Tex.	1951	Bill Valverde
Gar, Florida	21-3	Boca Raton, Fla.	1981	Jeff Sabol
Gar, Longnose	50-5	Trinity River, Texas	1954	Townsend Miller
Gar, Shortnose	3-5	Lake Francis Case, S.D.	1977	J. Pawlowski
Grayling, Arctic	5-15	Katseyedie River, N.W.T.	1967	Jeanne P. Branson
Huchen	70-12	Carinthia, Austria	1980	Martin F. Esterl
Inconnu	38-2	Kobuk River, Alaska	1982	Mark L. Feldman
Kokanee	6-9	Priest Lake, Idaho	1975	Jerry Verge
Muskellunge	69-15	St. Lawrence River, N.Y.	1957	Arthur Lawton
Muskellunge, Tiger	51-3	Lac-Vieux-Desert, Wisc.-Mich.	1919	John A. Knobla
Perch, White	4-12	Messalonskee Lake, Maine	1949	Mrs. Earl Small
Perch, Yellow	4-3	Bordentown, N.J.	1865	Dr. C.C. Abbot
Pickerel, Eastern Chain	9-6	Homerville, Ga.	1961	Baxley McQuaig, Jr.
Redhorse, Northern	3-11	Missouri River, S.D.	1977	Phillip Laumeyer
Redhorse, Silver	9-11	Winnipeg River, Canada	1982	John D. Richards
Salmon, Atlantic	79-2	Tana River, Norway	1928	Henrik Henriksen
Salmon, Chinook	93-0	Kelp Bay, Alaska	1977	Howard C. Rider
Salmon, Chum	27-3	Raymond Cove, Alaska	1977	Robert A. Jahnke
Salmon, Coho	31-0	Cowichan Bay, B.C., Canada	1947	Mrs. Lee Hallberg
Salmon, Landlocked	22-8	Sebago Lake, Mich.	1907	Edward Blakely
Salmon, Pink	12-9	Moose & Kenai Rivers, Alaska	1974	Steven Alan Lee
Salmon, Sockeye	12-8	Situk River, Yakutat, Alaska	1983	Mike Boswell
Sauger	8-12	Lake Sakakawea, N.D.	1971	Mike Fischer
Shad, American	9-4	Delaware River, Pa.	1979	J. Edward Whitman
Splake	16-12	Island Lake, Colo.	1973	Del Canty
Sturgeon	468-0	Benicia, Calif.	1983	Joey Pallotta III

Sturgeon, White	380-0	Snake River, Idaho	1973	Del Canty
Sunfish, Green	2-2	Stockton Lake, Missouri	1971	Paul M. Dilley
Sunfish, Redbreast	1-8	Suwannee River, Fla.	1977	Tommy D. Cason, Jr.
Sunfish, Redear	4-8	Chase City, Va.	1970	Maurice E. Ball
Tigerfish	46-4	Lake Tanganika, Zambia	1981	Giorgio Cuturi
Trout, Brook	14-8	Nipigon River, Ontario	1916	Dr. W.J. Cook
Trout, Brown	35-15	Nahuel Huapi, Argentina	1952	Eugenio Cavaglia
Trout, Bull	32-0	Lake Pend Orielle, Idaho	1949	N.L. Higgins
Trout, Cutthroat	41-0	Pyramid Lake, Nev.	1925	John Skimmerhorn
Trout, Golden	11-0	Cook's Lake, Wyoming	1948	Charles S. Reed
Trout, Lake	65-0	Great Bear Lake, N.W.T., Canada	1970	Larry Daunis
Trout, Rainbow	42-2	Bell Island, Alaska	1970	David Robert White
Trout, Tiger	20-13	Lake Michigan, Wisc.	1978	Peter M. Friedland
Walleye	25-0	Old Hickory Lake, Tenn.	1960	Mabry Harper
Warmouth	2-2	Souglas Swamp, S.C.	1973	William Singletary
Whitefish, Lake	13-5	Meaford, Ontario	1981	Wayne Caswell
Whitefish, Mountain	5-0	Athabasca River, Alberta, Canada	1963	Orville Welch
Whitefish, Round	3-4	Leland Harbor, Mich.	1977	Vernon A. Bauer

Caught With Rod and Reel in Salt Water

Source: International Game Fish Association

Species	lb-oz	Where caught	Year	Angler
Albacore	88-2	Canary Islands	1977	Siegfried Dickemann
Amberjack	155-10	Challenger Bank, Bermuda	1981	Joseph Dawson
Barracuda	83	Lagos, Nigeria	1952	K. J. W. Hackett
Bass, Black Sea	8-12	Oregon Inlet, N.C.	1979	Joe W. Mizelle, Sr.
Bass, Giant Sea	563-8	Anacapa Island, Calif.	1968	J. D. McAdam, Jr.
Bass, Striped	78-8	Atlantic City, N.J.	1982	Albert J. McReynolds
Blackfish (Tautog)	21-6	Cape May, N.J.	1954	R. N. Sheafer
Bluefish	31-12	North Carolina	1972	James M. Hussey
Bonefish	19	Zululand, S. Africa	1962	Brian W. Batchelor
Bonito, Atlantic	16-12	Canary Islands	1980	Rolf Fedderies
	16-12	Garajau, Portugal	1982	Winfried Hobelmann
Bonito, Pacific	23-8	Victoria, Mahe	1975	Mrs. Anne Cochain
Cobia	110-5	Mombasa, Kenya	1964	Eric Tinworth
Cod, Atlantic	98-12	Isle of Shoals, N.H.	1969	Alphonse Bielevich
Cod, Pacific	9-8	Adak, Alaska	1983	Gordon L. Votruba
Conger	102-8	Plymouth, Devon, England	1983	Raymond Ewart Street
Dolphin	87	Papagallo Gulf, Costa Rica	1976	Manual Salazar
Drum, Black	113-1	Lewes, Del.	1975	G. M. Townsend
Drum, Red	90	Rodanthe, N.C.	1973	Elvin Hooper
Flounder, Summer	22-7	Montauk, N.Y.	1975	Charles Nappi
Halibut, Atlantic	250	Gloucester, Mass.	1981	Louis P. Sirard
Halibut, California	45	Santa Cruz Island, Calif.	1982	Jack C. Meserve
Hailbut, Pacific	350	Homer, Alaska	1982	Vern S. Foster
Jack, Crevalle	54-7	Port Michel, Gabon	1982	Thomas F. Gibson, Jr.
Jack, Horse-eye	24-8	Miami, Fla.	1982	Tito Schnau
Jack, Pacific Crevalle	16-15	Zihuatanejo, Mexico	1983	H. Clay Johnson
Jewfish	680	Fernandina Beach, Fla.	1961	Lynn Joyner
Kawakawa	26	Merimbula, N.S.W., Australia	1980	Wally Elfring
Lingcod	46-0	Hakai Pass, British Columbia, Canada	1983	Betty I. Moore
Mackerel, King	90	Key West, Florida	1976	Norton I. Thomton
Mackerel, Spanish	10-15	Oak Bluffs, Mass.	1983	Heather J. Wadsworth
Marlin, Atlantic Blue	1282	St. Thomas, Virgin Islands	1977	Larry Martin
Marlin, Black	1560	Cabo Blanco, Peru	1953	A. C. Glassel, Jr.
Marlin, Pacific Blue	1376	Kaaiwi Point, Kona, Hawaii	1982	Jay Wm. deBeaubien
Marlin, Striped	455-4	Mayor Island, New Zealand	1982	Bruce Jenkinson
Marlin, White	181-14	Victoria, Brazil	1979	Evandro Luiz Coser
Permit	51-8	Lake Worth, Fla.	1978	William M. Kenney
Pollack	26	Ile de Ouessant, France	1981	Loik Le Chat
Pollack (virens)	46-7	Brielle, N.J.	1975	John T. Holton
Pompano, African	41-8	Fort Lauderdale, Fla.	1979	Wayne Sommers
Roosterfish	114	La Paz, Mexico	1960	Abe Sackheim
Runner, Rainbow	33-10	Clarion Island, Mexico	1976	R. A. Mikkelsen

Sailfish, Atlantic	128-1	Luanda, Angola, Africa	1974	Harm Steyn
Sailfish, Pacific	221	Santa Cruz Is., Galapagos Is.	1947	C. W. Stewart
Seabass, White	83-12	San Felipe, Mexico	1953	L. C. Baumgardner
Seatrout, Spotted	16	Mason's Beach, Va.	1977	William G. Katko
Shark, Blue	437	Catherine Bay, Australia	1976	Peter Hyde
Shark, Hammerhead	991	Sarasota, Fla.	1982	Allen Ogle
Shark, Mako	1080	Montauk, N.Y.	1979	James L. Melanson
Shark, Porbeagle	465	Padstow, Cornwall, England	1976	Jorge Potier
Shark, Thresher	802	Tutukaka, New Zealand	1981	Dianne North
Shark, Tiger	1780	Cherry Grove, S.C.	1964	Walter Maxwell
Shark, White	2664	South Australia	1959	Alfred Dean
Skipjack, Black	20-2	Clarion Island, Mexico	1982	Whitey Patterson
Snapper, Cubera	121-8	Cameron, La.	1982	Mike Hebert
Snook	53-10	Costa Rica	1978	Gilbert Ponzi
Spearfish	90-13	Madeira Island, Portugal	1980	Joseph Larkin
Swordfish	1182	Iquique, Chile	1953	L. E. Marron
Tanguigue	99	Scottburgh, Natal, South Africa	1982	Michael John Wilkinson
Tarpon	283	Lake Maracalbo, Venezuela	1956	M. Salazar
Tautog (see Blackfish)				
Tope	71-10	Knysna, South Africa	1982	William F. De Wet
Trevally, Bigeye	9-12	Pinas Bay, Panama	1983	Roy K. Gushiken
Trevally, Giant	137-9	McKenzie State Park, Hawaii	1983	Roy K. Gushiken
Tuna, Atlantic Bigeye	375-8	Ocean City, Md.	1977	Cecil Browne
Tuna, Blackfin	42	Bermuda	1978	Alan J. Card
Tuna, Bluefin	1496	Nova Scotia, Canada	1979	Ken Fraser
Tuna, Dog-tooth	194	Kwan-Tall Island, Korea	1980	Kim Chul
Tuna, Longtail	79-2	Montague Island, Australia	1982	Tim Simpson
Tuna, Pacific Big-Eyed	435	Cobo Blanco, Peru	1957	R.V. A. Lee
Tuna, Skipjack	41-12	Black River, Mauritius	1982	Bruno de Ravel
Tuna, Southern Bluefin	348-5	Whakatane, New Zealand	1981	Rex Wood
Tuna, Yellowfin	388-12	Mexico	1977	Curt Wiesenmutter
Tunny, Little	27	Key Largo, Fla.	1976	William E. Allison
Wahoo	149	Cat Cay, Bahamas	1962	John Pirovano
Weakfish	19-0	Chesapeake Bay, Va.	1983	Philip W. Halstead
Yellowtail, California	71-15	Alijos Rocks, Mexico	1979	Michael Carpenter
Yellowtail, Southern	111	Bay of Islands, New Zealand	1961	A. F. Plim

SQUASH RACQUETS

1984 U.S. SQUASH RACQUETS CHAMPIONSHIPS

Men's Events

Singles—Kenton Jernigan, Newport, R.I.
Singles, 35 and over—Scott Ryan, Rosemont, Pa.
Singles, 40 and over—Robert Hetherington, Buffalo, N.Y.
Singles, 45 and over—Gerry Shugar, Toronto
Singles, 50 and over—Les Harding, Seattle, Wash.
Singles, 55 and over—Henri Salauni, Needham, Mass.
Singles, 60 and over—Richard Daly, Mercer Island, Wash.
Singles, 65 and over—Edward Hobler, Wilmette, Ill.
Singles, 70 and over—H. Ashton Crosby, Franconia, N.H.
Class B singles Insilco—Diniar Alikajn, Atlanta, Ga.
Class C singles Insilco—Marwan Mustakin, Denver, Colo.
Class D singles Insilco—Reed Ballon, London, Ontario
Doubles—Rob Hill, Denver, Colo., and Andrea MacDonald, Vancouver, B.C.
Veterans doubles, 40 and over—Andy Pastor, Toronto, and Peter Hall, Toronto
Senior doubles, 50 and over—Don Leggat, Hamilton, and Chuck Wright, Toronto
Masters doubles, 60 and over—Newton B. Mead, Jr., Philadelphia, and Tom Schweizer, Baltimore, Md.
Intercollegiate A singles—Kenton Jernigan, Harvard University
Intercollegiate B singles—Richard Jackson, Harvard University
Intercollegiate C singles—Bill Ullman, Harvard University
Intercollegiate team—Harvard University
United States 5-man team—Mexico
Lapham Cup (singles)—Canada 9, United States 6
Grant Trophy (doubles)—Canada 8, United States 1
North American Open singles—Jahangir Khan, Pakistan

Women's Events

Singles—Alicia McConnell, Brooklyn, N.Y.
Singles, 35 and over—Mariann Greenberg, Mamaroneck, N.Y.
Singles, 35 and over B tournament—Sharon Schwarze, Wayne, Pa.
Singles, 40 and over—Marigold Edwards, Pittsburgh, Pa.
Class B singles—Marjorie Wall, Portland, Ore.
Class C singles—Melinda Kahle, Buffalo, N.Y.
Doubles—Barbara Savage and Heather McKay, Toronto
Senior doubles—Joyce Davenport, King of Prussia, Pa., and Jane Young, Narberth, Pa.
Mixed doubles—Joyce Davenport, King of Prussia, Pa., and Peter Briggs, Greenwich, Conn.
Intercollegiate singles—Alicia McConnell, Brooklyn, N.Y.

BASKETBALL

Basketball may be the one sport whose exact origin is definitely known. In the winter of 1891–92, Dr. James Naismith, an instructor in the Y.M.C.A. Training College (now Springfield College) at Springfield, Mass., deliberately invented the game of basketball in order to provide indoor exercise and competition for the students between the closing of the football season and the opening of the baseball season. He affixed peach baskets overhead on the walls at opposite ends of the gymnasium and organized teams to play his new game in which the purpose was to toss an association (soccer) ball into one basket and prevent the opponents from tossing the ball into the other basket. The game is fundamentally the same today, though there have been improvements in equipment and some changes in rules.

Because Dr. Naismith had eighteen available players when he invented the game, the first rule was; "There shall be nine players on each side." Later the number of players became optional, depending upon the size of the available court, but the five-player standard was adopted when the game spread over the country. United States soldiers brought basketball to Europe in World War I, and it soon became a world-wide sport.

College Basketball

NATIONAL COLLEGIATE A.A. CHAMPIONS

1939	Oregon	1949	Kentucky	1959	California	1975	U.C.L.A.
1940	Indiana	1950	C.C.N.Y.	1960	Ohio State	1976	Indiana
1941	Wisconsin	1951	Kentucky	1961	Cincinnati	1977	Marquette
1942	Stanford	1952	Kansas	1962	Cincinnati	1978	Kentucky
1943	Wyoming	1953	Indiana	1963	Loyola (Chicago)	1979	Michigan State
1944	Utah	1954	La Salle	1964	U.C.L.A.	1980	Louisville
1945	Oklahoma A & M	1955	San Francisco	1965	U.C.L.A.	1981	Indiana
1946	Oklahoma A & M	1956	San Francisco	1966	Texas Western	1982	North Carolina
1947	Holy Cross	1957	North Carolina	1967–73	U.C.L.A.	1983	North Carolina State
1948	Kentucky	1958	Kentucky	1974	No. Carolina State	1984	Georgetown

NATIONAL INVITATION TOURNAMENT (NIT) CHAMPIONS

1939	Long Island U.	1952	La Salle	1964	Bradley	1976	Kentucky
1940	Colorado	1953	Seton Hall	1965	St. John's (N.Y.C.)	1977	St. Bonaventure
1941	Long Island U.	1954	Holy Cross	1966	Brigham Young	1978	Texas
1942	West Virginia	1955	Duquesne	1967	So. Illinois	1979	Indiana
1943–44	St. John's (N.Y.C.)	1956	Louisville	1968	Dayton	1980	Virginia
1945	DePaul	1957	Bradley	1969	Temple	1981	Tulsa
1946	Kentucky	1958	Xavier (Cincinnati)	1970	Marquette	1982	Bradley
1947	Utah	1959	St. John's (N.Y.C.)	1971	North Carolina	1983	Fresno State
1948	St. Louis	1960	Bradley	1972	Maryland	1984	Michig
1949	San Francisco	1961	Providence	1973	Virginia Tech		
1950	C.C.N.Y.	1962	Dayton	1974	Purdue		
1951	Brigham Young	1963	Providence	1975	Princeton		

N.C.A.A. MAJOR COLLEGE INDIVIDUAL SCORING RECORDS

Single Season Averages

Player, Team	Year	G	FG	FT	Pts	Avg
Pete Maravich, Louisiana State	1969–70	31	522 [1]	337	1381 [1]	44.5 [1]
Pete Maravich	1968–69	26	433	282	1148	44.2
Pete Maravich	1967–68	26	432	274	1138	43.8
Frank Selvy, Furman	1953–54	29	427	355 [1]	1209	41.7
Johnny Neumann, Mississippi	1970–71	23	366	191	923	40.1
Freeman Williams, Portland State	1976–77	26	417	176	1010	38.8
Billy McGill, Utah	1961–62	26	394	221	1009	38.8
Calvin Murphy, Niagara	1967–68	24	337	242	916	38.2
Austin Carr, Notre Dame	1969–70	29	444	218	1106	38.1

1. Record.

N.C.A.A. CAREER SCORING TOTALS

Division I

Player, Team	Last year	G	FG	FT	Pts	Avg
Pete Maravich, Louisiana State	1970	83	1387[1]	893[1]	3667[1]	44.2[1]
Austin Carr, Notre Dame	1971	74	1017	526	2560	34.6
Oscar Robertson, Cincinnati	1960	88	1052	869	2973	33.8
Calvin Murphy, Niagara	1970	77	947	654	2548	33.1
Dwight Lamar[2]	1973	57	768	326	1862	32.7
Frank Selvy, Furman	1954	78	922	694	2538	32.5
Rick Mount, Purdue	1970	72	910	503	2323	32.3
Darrel Floyd, Furman	1956	71	868	545	2281	32.1
Nick Werkman, Seton Hall	1964	71	812	649	2273	32.0

1. Record. 2. Also played two seasons in college division.

Division II

Player, Team	Last year	G	FG	FT	Pts	Avg
Travis Grant, Kentucky State	1972	121	1760[1]	525	4045[1]	33.4[1]
John Rinka, Kenyon	1970	99	1261	729	3251	32.8
Florindo Vierira, Quinnipiac	1957	69	761	741	2263	32.8
Willie Shaw, Lane	1964	76	960	459	2379	31.3
Mike Davis, Virginia Union	1969	89	1014	730	2758	31.0
Henry Logan, Western Carolina	1968	107	1263	764	3290	30.7
Willie Scott, Alabama State	1969	103	1277	601	3155	30.6
Gregg Northington, Alabama State	1972	75	894	403	2191	29.2
Bob Hopkins, Grambling	1956	126	1403	953	3759	29.8

1. Record.

TOP SINGLE-GAME SCORING MARKS

Player, Team (Opponent)	Yr	Pts	Player, Team (Opponent)	Yr	Pts
Selvy, Furman (Newberry)	1954	100[1]	Floyd, Furman (Morehead)	1955	67
Williams, Portland State (Rocky Mtn.)	1978	81	Maravich, LSU (Tulane)	1969	66
Mlkvy, Temple (Wilkes)	1951	73	Handlan, W & L (Furman)	1951	66
Williams, Portland State (So. Oregon)	1977	71	Roberts, Oral Roberts (N.C. A&T)	1977	66
Maravich, LSU (Alabama)	1970	69	Williams, Portland State (Geo. Fox Coll.)	1978	66
Murphy, Niagara (Syracuse)	1969	68	Roberts, Oral Roberts (Oregon)	1977	65

1. Record.

MEN'S N.C.A.A. BASKETBALL CHAMPIONSHIPS—1984

DIVISION I

First Round—East

Temple 65, St. John's 63
Richmond 72, Auburn 71
Virginia Commonwealth 70, Northeastern 69
Virginia 58, Iona 57

First Round—Mideast

Brigham Young 84, Alabama-Birmingham 68
Louisville 72, Morehead State 69
West Virginia 64, Oregon State 62
Villanova 84, Marshall 72

First Round—Midwest

Illinois State 49, Alabama 48
Kansas 57, Alcorn State 56
Memphis State 92, Oral Roberts 83
Louisiana Tech 66, Fresno State 56

First Round—West

Southern Methodist 83, Miami (Ohio) 69
Nevada-Las Vegas 68, Princeton 56
Washington 64, Nevada-Reno 54
Dayton 74, Louisiana State 66

Second Round—East

North Carolina 77, Temple 66
Indiana 75, Richmond 67
Syracuse 78, Virginia Commonwealth 63
Virginia 53, Arkansas 51 (overtime)

Second Round—Mideast

Kentucky 93, Brigham Young 68
Louisville 69, Tulsa 67
Maryland 102, West Virginia 77
Illinois 64, Villanova 56

Second Round—Midwest

DePaul 75, Illinois State 61
Wake Forest 69, Kansas 59
Memphis State 66, Purdue 48
Houston 77, Louisiana Tech 69

Second Round—West

Georgetown 37, Southern Methodist 36
Nevada-Las Vegas 73, UTEP 60
Washington 80, Duke 78
Dayton 89, Oklahoma 85

Third Round—East

Indiana 72, North Carolina 68
Virginia 63, Syracuse 55

Third Round—Mideast

Kentucky 72, Louisville 67
Illinois 72, Maryland 70

Third Round—Midwest

Wake Forest 73, DePaul 71 (overtime)
Houston 78, Memphis State 71

Third Round—West

Georgetown 62, Nevada-Las Vegas 48
Dayton 64, Washington 58

Regional Finals

East—Virginia 50, Indiana 48
Mideast—Kentucky 54, Illinois 51
Midwest—Houston 68, Wake Forest 63
West—Georgetown 61, Dayton 49

National Semifinals

(Seattle, March 31, 1984)

Georgetown 53, Kentucky 40
Houston 49, Virginia 47 (overtime)

National Final

(Seattle, April 2, 1984)

Georgetown 84, Houston 75

DIVISION II
Semifinals

Central Missouri State 89, North Alabama 85
St. Augustine's (N.C.) 89, Kentucky Wesleyan 80

Championship

Central Missouri State 81, St. Augustine's 77

DIVISION III
Semifinals

Clark (Mass.) 69, Upsala (N.J.) 68
Wisconsin-Whitewater 85, Depauw 69

Championship

Wisconsin-Whitewater 103, Clark 87

JUNIOR COLLEGES
Men's Championship

San Jacinto (Tex.) 86, Independence (Kan.) 82

Women's Championship

Roane State (Tenn.) 69, Northwest Mississippi 53

WOMEN'S N.C.A.A. BASKETBALL CHAMPIONSHIPS—1984

DIVISION I
First Round—East

Old Dominion 87, Penn State 65
North Carolina 81, St. John's (NY) 79 (overtime)
Cheyney State 92, Maryland 64
North Carolina State 86, Virginia 73

First Round—Mideast

Georgia 112, Louisville 69
Tennessee 70, Middle Tennessee 52
Mississippi 77, Ohio State 55
Alabama 78, Central Michigan 70

First Round—Midwest

Northeast Louisiana 78, Kansas State 73
Texas 96, Drake 60
Louisiana Tech 94, Texas Tech 68
Louisiana State 92, Missouri 82

First Round—West

San Diego State 70, Oregon 63
Southern California 97, Brigham Young 72
Long Beach State 78, Nevada-Las Vegas 58
Montana 56, Oregon State 47

Second Round—East

Cheyney State 73, North Carolina 72
Old Dominion 73, North Carolina State 71 (overtime)

Second Round—Mideast

Tennessee 65, Alabama 58
Georgia 73, Mississippi 63

Second Round—Midwest

Texas 99, Northeast Louisiana 91
Louisiana Tech 92, Louisiana State 67

Second Round—West

Southern California 76, Montana 51
Long Beach State 91, San Diego State 73 (overtime)

Regional Finals

East—Cheyney State 80, Old Dominion 71
Mideast—Tennessee 73, Georgia 61
Midwest—Louisiana Tech 85, Texas 60
West—Southern California 90, Long Beach State 74

NATIONAL SEMIFINALS

(Los Angeles, Calif., March 30, 1984)

Southern California 62, Louisiana Tech 57
Tennessee 82, Cheyney State 73

CHAMPIONSHIP

(Los Angeles, Calif., April 1, 1984)

Southern California 72, Tennessee 61

DIVISION II
Championship

Central Missouri State 80, Virginia Union 73

DIVISION III
Championship

Rust College 51, Elizabethtown 49

LEADING N.C.A.A. SCORERS—1983-1984

Division I

	FG	FT	Pts	Avg
Joe Jakubick, Akron	304	206	814	30.1
Lewis Jackson, Alabama State	305	202	812	29.0
Devin Durrant, Brigham Young	312	242	866	27.9
Alfrederick Hughes, Loyola (Ill.)	326	148	800	27.6
Wayman Tisdale, Oklahoma	369	181	919	27.0
Joe Dumars, McNeese State	275	267	817	26.4
Brett Crawford, U.S. Int'l	257	100	614	24.6
Michael Cage, San Diego State	250	186	686	24.5
Steve Burtt, Iona	309	131	749	24.2
Leon Wood, Cal. State-Fullerton	254	211	719	24.0
Willie Jackson, Centenary	260	143	663	23.7

Butch Graves, Yale	246	117	609	23.4
Napoleon Johnson, Grambling State	255	168	678	23.4
Derrick Gervin, Texas-San Antonio	239	148	626	23.2
Chris Mullin, St John's (N.Y.)	225	169	619	22.9
Tom Sewell, Lamar	287	136	710	22.9
Al McClain, New Hampshire	265	108	638	22.8
Charlie Bradley, South Florida	253	119	625	22.3
Barry Stevens, Iowa State	257	130	644	22.2
Carlos Yates, George Mason	200	174	574	22.1

NATIONAL ASSOCIATION OF INTERCOLLEGIATE ATHLETICS—1984

MEN'S TOURNAMENT

Round of 16

Wisconsin-Stevens Point 51, Arkansas College 46
St. Thomas Aquinas (N.Y.) 74, Central Washington 59
Waynesburg (Pa.) 61, St. Mary's (Tex.) 59
Chicago State 105, Kearney State (Neb.) 104 (2 overtimes)
Westmont (Calif.) 63, Pembroke State (N.C.) 54
Fort Hays State (Kan.) 76, Central Wesleyan (S.C.) 68
West Virginia Wesleyan 86, William Carey (Miss.) 68
Chaminade (Hawaii) 86, Cumberland (Ky.) 77

Quarterfinals

Westmont 78, St. Thomas Aquinas 65
Fort Hays State 87, Waynesburg 55
Wisconsin-Stevens Point 77, West Virginia Wesleyan 50
Chicago State 68, Chaminade 66

Semifinals

Wisconsin-Stevens Point 79, Westmont 53
Fort Hays State 86, Chicago State 84 (overtime)

Third Place

Chicago State 86, Westmont 82 (overtime)

Championship

Fort Hays State 48, Wisconsin-Stevens Point 46 (overtime)

WOMEN'S TOURNAMENT

Semifinals

North Carolina-Asheville 81, Dillard (La.) 64
U. of Portland (Ore.) 72, Berry (Ga.) 58

Third Place

Dillard 70, Berry 58

Championship

North Carolina-Asheville 72, U. of Portland 70 (overtime)

NATIONAL INVITATION TOURNAMENT (N.I.T.)—1984

Semifinals

(March 26, 1984, Madison Square Garden, New York)

Michigan 78, Virginia Tech 75
Notre Dame 65, Southwestern Louisiana 59

Third Place

Virginia Tech 71, Southwestern Louisiana 70

Championship

(March 28, 1984, Madison Square Garden, New York)

Michigan 83, Notre Dame 63

MEN'S A.A.U. CHAMPIONSHIP—1984

(Las Vegas, Nevada, March 29–April 1, 1984)

Championship

Las Vegas Paul-son Dice 100, Houston Flyers 97

Semifinals

Houston Flyers 103, Oklahoma City (Okla.) 101
Las Vegas Paul-son Dice 106, Topeka Hughes (Kan.) 97

Professional Basketball

NATIONAL BASKETBALL ASSOCIATION CHAMPIONS

Source: Matt Winick, Director of Media Information, National Basketball Association.

The National Basketball Association was originally the Basketball Association of America. It took its current name in 1949 when it merged with the National Basketball League.

Season	Eastern Conference (W-L)	Western Conference (W-L)	Playoff Champions[1]
1946–47	Washington Capitols (49–11)	Chicago Stags (39–22)	Philadelphia Warriors
1947–48	Philadelphia Warriors (27–21)	St. Louis Bombers (29–19)	Baltimore Bullets
1948–49	Washington Capitols (38–22)	Rochester Royals (45–15)	Minneapolis Lakers
1949–50	Syracuse Nationals (51–13)	Indianapolis Olympians (39–25)	Minneapolis Lakers
1950–51	Philadelphia Warriors (40–26)	Minneapolis Lakers (44–24)	Rochester Royals
1951–52	Syracuse Nationals (40–26)	Rochester Royals (41–25)	Minneapolis Lakers
1952–53	New York Knickerbockers (47–23)	Minneapolis Lakers (48–22)	Minneapolis Lakers
1953–54	New York Knickerbockers (44–28)	Minneapolis Lakers (46–26)	Minneapolis Lakers
1954–55	Syracuse Nationals (43–29)	Ft. Wayne Pistons (43–29)	Syracuse Nationals
1955–56	Philadelphia Warriors (45–27)	Ft. Wayne Pistons (37–35)	Philadelphia Warriors
1956–57	Boston Celtics (44–28)	St. Louis Hawks (38–34)	Boston Celtics
1957–58	Boston Celtics (48–23)	St. Louis Hawks (41–31)	St. Louis Hawks
1958–59	Boston Celtics (52–20)	St. Louis Hawks (49–23)	Boston Celtics
1959–60	Boston Celtics (59–16)	St. Louis Hawks (46–29)	Boston Celtics
1960–61	Boston Celtics (57–22)	St. Louis Hawks (51–28)	Boston Celtics
1961–62	Boston Celtics (60–20)	Los Angeles Lakers (54–26)	Boston Celtics
1962–63	Boston Celtics (58–22)	Los Angeles Lakers (53–27)	Boston Celtics
1963–64	Boston Celtics (59–21)	San Francisco Warriors (48–32)	Boston Celtics
1964–65	Boston Celtics (62–18)	Los Angeles Lakers (49–31)	Boston Celtics

Season	Eastern Conference (W-L)	Western Conference (W-L)	Playoff Champions[1]
1965–66	Philadelphia 76ers (55–25)	Los Angeles Lakers (45–35)	Boston Celtics
1966–67	Philadelphia 76ers (68–13)	San Francisco Warriors (44–37)	Philadelphia 76ers
1967–68	Philadelphia 76ers (62–20)	St. Louis Hawks (56–26)	Boston Celtics
1968–69	Baltimore Bullets (57–25)	Los Angeles Lakers (55–27)	Boston Celtics
1969–70	New York Knickerbockers (60–22)	Atlanta Hawks (48–34)	New York Knicks
1970–71	Baltimore Bullets (42–40)	Milwaukee Bucks (66–16)	Milwaukee Bucks
1971–72	New York Knickerbockers (48–34)	Los Angeles Lakers (69–13)	Los Angeles Lakers
1972–73	New York Knickerbockers (57–25)	Los Angeles Lakers (69–22)	New York Knicks
1973–74	Boston Celtics (56–26)	Milwaukee Bucks (59–23)	Boston Celtics
1974–75	Washington Bullets (60–22)	Golden State Warriors (48–34)	Golden State Warriors
1975–76	Boston Celtics (54–28)	Phoenix Suns (42–40)	Boston Celtics
1976–77	Philadelphia 76ers (50–32)	Portland Trail Blazers (49–33)	Portland Trail Blazers
1977–78	Washington Bullets (44–38)	Seattle Super Sonics (47–35)	Washington Bullets
1978–79	Washington Bullets (54–28)	Seattle Super Sonics (52–30)	Seattle Super Sonics
1979–80	Philadelphia 76ers (59–23)	Los Angeles Lakers (60–22)	Los Angeles Lakers
1980–81	Boston Celtics (62–20)	Phoenix Suns (57–25)	Boston Celtics
1981–82	Boston Celtics (63–19)	Los Angeles Lakers (57–25)	Los Angeles Lakers
1982–83	Philadelphia 76ers (65–17)	Los Angeles Lakers (58–24)	Philadelphia 76ers
1983–84	Boston Celtics (56–26)	Los Angeles Lakers (58–24)	Boston Celtics

1. Playoffs may involve teams other than conference winners.

INDIVIDUAL N.B.A. SCORING CHAMPIONS

Season	Player, Team	G	FG	FT	Pts	Avg
1953–54	Neil Johnston, Philadelphia Warriors	72	591	577	1759	24.4
1954–55	Neil Johnston, Philadelphia Warriors	72	521	589	1631	22.7
1955–56	Bob Pettit, St. Louis Hawks	72	646	557	1849	25.7
1956–57	Paul Arizin, Philadelphia Warriors	71	613	591	1817	25.6
1957–58	George Yardley, Detroit Pistons	72	673	655	2001	27.8
1958–59	Bob Pettit, St. Louis Hawks	72	719	667	2105	29.2
1959–60	Wilt Chamberlain, Philadelphia Warriors	72	1065	577	2707	37.6
1960–61	Wilt Chamberlain, Philadelphia Warriors	79	1251	531	3033	38.4
1961–62	Wilt Chamberlain, Philadelphia Warriors	80	1597	835	4029	50.4
1962–63	Wilt Chamberlain, San Francisco Warriors	80	1463	660	3586	44.8
1963–64	Wilt Chamberlain, San Francisco Warriors	80	1204	540	2948	36.9
1964–65	Wilt Chamberlain, San Francisco Warriors-Phila. 76ers	73	1063	408	2534	34.7
1965–66	Wilt Chamberlain, Philadelphia 76ers	79	1074	501	2649	33.5
1966–67	Rick Barry, San Francisco Warriors	78	1011	753	2775	35.6
1967–68	Dave Bing, Detroit Pistons	79	835	472	2142	27.1
1968–69	Elvin Hayes, San Diego Rockets	82	930	467	2327	28.4
1969–70	Jerry West, Los Angeles Lakers	74	831	647	2309	31.2
1970–71	Lew Alcindor,[1] Milwaukee Bucks	82	1063	470	2596	31.7
1971–72	Kareem Abdul-Jabbar, Milwaukee Bucks	81	1159	504	2822	34.8
1972–73	Nate Archibald, Kansas City-Omaha Kings	80	1028	663	2719	34.0
1973–74	Bob McAdoo, Buffalo Braves	74	901	459	2261	30.8
1974–75	Bob McAdoo, Buffalo Braves	82	1095	641	2831	34.5
1975–76	Bob McAdoo, Buffalo Braves	78	934	559	2427	31.1
1976–77	Pete Maravich, New Orleans Jazz	73	886	501	2273	31.1
1977–78	George Gervin, San Antonio Spurs	82	864	504	2232	27.2
1978–79	George Gervin, San Antonio	80	947	471	2365	29.6
1979–80	George Gervin, San Antonio	78	1024	505	2585	33.1
1980–81	Adrian Dantley, Utah Jazz	80	909	632	2452	30.7
1981–82	George Gervin, San Antonio	79	993	555	2551	32.3
1982–83	Alex English, Denver Nuggets	82	959	406	2326	28.4
1983–84	Adrian Dantley, Utah Jazz	79	802	813	2418	30.6

1. (Kareem Abdul-Jabbar).

N.B.A. LIFETIME LEADERS

(Through 1983–1984 season)

Scoring

	Yrs	FG	FT	Pts
(a) Kareem Abdul–Jabbar	15	13,006	5,515	31,527
Wilt Chamberlain	14	12,681	6,057	31,419
(a) Elvin Hayes	16	10,976	5,356	27,313
Oscar Robertson	14	9,508	7,694	26,710
(a) Dan Issel*	14	10,058	6,334	26,498
John Havlicek	16	10,513	5,369	26,395
(a) Julius Erving*	13	10,287	5,438	26,120
Rick Barry*	14	9,695	5,713	25,279
Jerry West	14	9,016	7,160	25,192
(a) George Gervin*	12	10,243	5,130	23,746
Elgin Baylor	14	8,693	5,763	23,149

Hal Greer	15	8,504	4,578	21,586
Walt Bellamy	14	7,914	5,113	20,941
Bob Pettit	11	7,349	6,182	20,880

(a) Active player. *Includes statistics compiled in the American Basketball Association.

Scoring Average
(400 games or 10,00 points minimum)

	Games	Pts	Avg
Wilt Chamberlain	1,045	31,419	30.1
Elgin Baylor	846	23,149	27.4
Jerry West	932	25,192	27.0
(a) Kareem Abdul-Jabbar	1,170	31,527	26.9
Bob Pettit	792	20,880	26.4
(a) George Gervin*	906	23,746	26.2
(a) Adrian Dantley	546	14,207	26.0
Oscar Robertson	1,040	26,710	25.7
(a) Julius Erving*	1,031	26,120	25.3
Rick Barry*	1,020	25,279	24.8
Pete Maravich	658	15,948	24.2
(a) Moses Malone	615	14,636	23.8
(a) Bob McAdoo	757	17,803	23.5

(a) Active player. Includes statistics compiled in the American Basketball Association.

Rebounds

Wilt Chamberlain	23,924
Bill Russell	21,620
(a) Elvin Hayes	16,279
(a) Kareem Abdul-Jabbar	15,005
Nate Thurmond	14,464
Walt Bellamy	14,241
Wes Unseld	13,769
Jerry Lucas	12,942
Bob Pettit	12,849
Paul Silas	12,357

(a) Active player.

N.B.A. ALL-DEFENSIVE TEAM—1984

Forwards—Bobby Jones, Philadelphia, Michael Cooper, Los Angeles
Center—Wayne "Tree" Rollins, Atlanta
Guards—Sidney Moncrief, Milwaukee, Maurice Cheeks, Philadelphia

Free-Throw Percentage
(1,200 free throws made minimum)

	FTA	FTM	Pct
Rick Barry	4,243	3,818	.900
Calvin Murphy	3,864	3,445	.892
Bill Sharman	3,557	3,143	.884
Mike Newlin	3,456	3,005	.870
(a) Larry Bird	1,907	1,637	.858
(a) Fred Brown	2,211	1,896	.858
Larry Siegfried	1,945	1,662	.854
James Silas	1,690	1,440	.852
Flynn Robinson	1,881	1,597	.849
(a) Ricky Sobers	2,408	2,030	.843

(a) Active player.

Field-Goal Percentage
(2,000 field goals minimum)

	FGA	FGM	Pct
(a) Artis Gilmore	7,271	4,332	.596
(a) Darryl Dawkins	5,239	2,970	.567
(a) Cedric Maxwell	4,607	2,585	.561
(a) Kareem Abdul-Jabbar	23,207	13,006	.560
(a) Bill Cartwright	4,639	2,582	.557
(a) Bobby Jones	5,476	3,016	.551
(a) Adrian Dantley	9,227	5,074	.550
Wilt Chamberlain	23,497	12,681	.540
(a) Bernard King	8,245	4,448	.539
(a) Swen Nater	4,528	2,432	.537

(a) Active player.

Assists

Oscar Robertson	9,887
Lenny Wilkens	7,211
Bob Cousy	6,955
Guy Rodgers	6,917
(a) Nate Archibald	6,476
Jerry West	6,238
John Havlicek	6,114
Dave Bing	5,397
Kevin Porter	5,314
Norm Van Lier	5,217

(a) Active player.

N.B.A. MOST VALUABLE PLAYERS

1956	Bob Pettit
1957	Bob Cousy
1958	Bill Russell
1959	Bob Pettit
1960	Wilt Chamberlain
1961–63	Bill Russell
1964	Oscar Robertson
1965	Bill Russell
1966–68	Wilt Chamberlain
1969	Wes Unseld
1970	Willis Reed
1971–72	Lew Alcindor (Kareem Abdul-Jabbar)
1973	Dave Cowens
1974	Kareem Abdul-Jabbar, Milwaukee
1975	Bob McAdoo, Buffalo
1976–77	Kareem Abdul-Jabbar, Los Angeles
1978	Bill Walton, Portland
1979	Moses Malone, Houston
1980	Kareem Abdul-Jabbar, Los Angeles
1981	Julius Erving, Philadelphia
1982	Moses Malone, Houston
1983	Moses Malone, Philadelphia
1984	Larry Bird, Boston

N.B.A. TEAM RECORDS

Most points, game—186, Detroit vs. Denver, 3 overtimes, 1983
Most points, quarter—58, Buffalo vs. Boston, 1968
Most points, half—97, Atlanta vs. San Diego, 1970
Most points, overtime period—22, Detroit vs. Cleveland, 1973
Most field goals, game—74, Detroit, 1983
Most field goals, quarter—23, Boston, 1959; Buffalo, 1972
Most field goals, half—40, Boston, 1959; Syracuse, 1963; Atlanta, 1979
Most assists, game—53, Milwaukee, 1978
Most rebounds, game—109, Boston 1960
Most points, both teams, game—370 (Detroit 186, Denver 184) 3 overtimes, Denver, December 13, 1983
Most points, both teams, quarter—96 (Boston 52, Minneapolis 44), 1959; (Detroit 53, Cincinnati 43), 1972
Most points, both teams, half—170 (Philadelphia 90, Cincinnati 80), Philadelphia, 1971
Longest winning streak—33, Los Angeles, 1971–72
Longest losing streak—20, Philadelphia, 1973
Longest winning streak at home—36, Philadelphia, 1966–67
Most games won, season—69, Los Angeles, 1971–72
Most games lost, season—73, Philadelphia, 1972–73
Highest average points per game—126.5, Denver, 1981–82

N.B.A. INDIVIDUAL RECORDS

Most points, game—100, Wilt Chamberlain, Philadelphia vs. New York at Hershey, Pa., 1962
Most points, quarter—33, George Gervin, San Antonio, 1978
Most points, half—59, Wilt Chamberlain, Philadelphia, 1962
Most free throws, game—28, Wilt Chamberlain, Philadelphia, vs. New York at Hershey, Pa. 1962; 28, Adrian Dantley, Utah, vs. Houston, 1984
Most free throws, quarter—14, Rick Barry, San Francisco, 1966
Most free throws, half—19, Oscar Robertson, Cincinnati, 1964
Most field goals, game—36, Wilt Chamberlain, Philadelphia, 1962
Most consecutive field goals, game—18, Wilt Chamberlain, San Francisco, 1963; Wilt Chamberlain, Philadelphia, 1967
Most assists, game—29, Kevin Porter, New Jersey Nets, 1978
Most rebounds, game—55, Wilt Chamberlain, Philadelphia, 1963

NATIONAL BASKETBALL ASSOCIATION FINAL STANDINGS OF THE CLUBS—1983–1984

EASTERN CONFERENCE

Atlantic Division

	W	L	Pct	Scoring Avg For	Scoring Avg Agst
Boston Celtics	62	20	.756	112.1	105.6
Philadelphia 76ers	52	30	.634	107.8	105.6
New York Knicks	47	35	.573	106.9	103.0
New Jersey Nets	45	37	.549	110.0	108.9
Washington Bullets	35	47	.427	102.7	105.6

Central Division

	W	L	Pct	Scoring Avg For	Scoring Avg Agst
Milwaukee Bucks	50	32	.610	105.7	101.5
Detroit Pistons	49	33	.598	117.1	113.5
Atlanta Hawks	40	42	.488	101.5	102.8
Cleveland Cavaliers	28	54	.341	102.3	106.5
Chicago Bulls	27	55	.329	103.7	108.9
Indiana Pacers	26	56	.317	104.5	109.3

WESTERN CONFERENCE

Midwest Division

	W	L	Pct	Scoring Avg For	Scoring Avg Agst
Utah Jazz	45	37	.549	115.0	113.8
Dallas Mavericks	43	39	.524	110.4	110.0
Denver Nuggets	38	44	.463	123.7	124.8
Kansas City Kings	38	44	.463	110.0	111.5
San Antonio Spurs	37	45	.451	120.3	120.5
Houston Rockets	29	53	.354	110.6	113.7

Pacific Division

	W	L	Pct	Scoring Avg For	Scoring Avg Agst
Los Angeles Lakers	54	28	.659	115.6	111.8
Portland Trail Blazers	48	34	.585	113.1	109.6
Seattle Super Sonics	42	40	.512	108.1	108.3
Phoenix Suns	41	41	.500	111.0	110.1
Golden State Warriors	37	45	.451	109.9	113.3
San Diego Clippers	30	52	.366	110.7	114.0

N.B.A. PLAYOFFS—1984

EASTERN CONFERENCE

First Round

Boston defeated Washington, 3 games to 1
New York defeated Detroit, 3 games to 2
Milwaukee defeated Atlanta, 3 games to 2
New Jersey defeated Philadelphia, 3 games to 2

Semifinal Round

Boston defeated New York, 4 games to 3
Milwaukee defeated New Jersey, 4 games to 2

Conference Finals

Boston defeated Milwaukee, 4 games to 1
May 15—Boston 119, Milwaukee 96
May 17—Boston 125, Milwaukee 110
May 19—Boston 109, Milwaukee 100
May 21—Milwaukee 122, Boston 113
May 23—Boston 115, Milwaukee 108

WESTERN CONFERENCE

First Round

Los Angeles defeated Kansas City, 3 games to 0
Dallas defeated Seattle, 3 games to 2
Utah defeated Denver, 3 games to 2
Phoenix defeated Portland, 3 games to 2

Semifinal Round

Los Angeles defeated Dallas, 4 games to 1
Phoenix defeated Utah, 4 games to 2

Conference Finals

Los Angeles defeated Phoenix, 4 games to 2
May 12—Los Angeles 110, Phoenix 94
May 15—Los Angeles 118, Phoenix 102
May 18—Phoenix 135, Los Angeles 127 (overtime)
May 20—Los Angeles 126, Phoenix 115
May 23—Phoenix 126, Los Angeles 121
May 25—Los Angeles 99, Phoenix 97

Championship

Boston defeated Los Angeles, 4 games to 3
May 27—Los Angeles 115, Boston 109
May 31—Boston 124, Los Angeles 121 (overtime)
June 3—Los Angeles 137, Boston 104
June 6—Boston 129, Los Angeles 125 (overtime)
June 8—Boston 121, Los Angeles 103
June 10—Los Angeles 119, Boston 108
June 12—Boston 111, Los Angeles 102

FIELD-GOAL LEADERS—1983–1984

(Minimum 300 FG made)

	FG	Att	Pct
Artis Gilmore, San Antonio	351	556	.631
Jim Donaldson, San Diego	360	604	.596
Mike McGee, Los Angeles	347	584	.594
Darryl Dawkins, New Jersey	507	855	.593
Calvin Natt, Portland	500	857	.583
Jeff Ruland, Washington	599	1,035	.579
Kareem Abdul-Jabbar, Los Angeles	716	1,238	.578
Larry Nance, Phoenix	601	1,044	.576
Bob Lanier, Milwaukee	392	685	.572
Bernard King, New York	795	1,391	.572

FREE-THROW LEADERS—1983–1984

(Minimum 125 FT made)

	FT	Att	Pct
Larry Bird, Boston	374	421	.888
John Long, Detroit	243	275	.884
Bill Laimbeer, Detroit	316	365	.866

Walter Davis, Phoenix	233	270	.863
Ricky Pierce, San Diego	149	173	.861
Adrian Dantley, Utah	813	946	.859
Billy Knight, Kansas City	243	283	.859
Jack Sikma, Seattle	411	480	.856
Kiki Vanderweghe, Denver	494	580	.852
Dennis Johnson, Boston	281	330	.852

LEADING SCORERS—1983–1984

	G	FG	FT	Pts	Avg
Adrian Dantley, Utah	79	802	813	2,418	30.6
Mark Aquirre, Dallas	79	925	465	2,330	29.5
Kiki Vandeweghe, Denver	78	895	494	2,295	29.4
Alex English, Denver	82	907	352	2,167	26.4
Bernard King, New York	77	795	437	2,027	26.3
George Gervin, San Antonio	76	765	427	1,967	25.9
Larry Bird, Boston	79	758	374	1,908	24.2
Mike Mitchell, San Antonio	79	779	275	1,839	23.3
Terry Cummings, San Diego	81	737	380	1,854	22.9
Purvis Short, Golden State	79	714	353	1,803	22.8
Moses Malone, Philadelphia	71	532	545	1,609	22.7
Julius Erving, Philadelphia	77	678	364	1,727	22.4
Rolando Blackman, Dallas	81	721	372	1,815	22.4
World B. Free, Cleveland	75	626	395	1,669	22.3
Jeff Ruland, Washington	75	599	466	1,665	22.2
Eddie Johnson, Kansas City	82	753	268	1,794	21.9
Dominque Wilkins, Atlanta	81	684	382	1,750	21.6
Kareem Abdul-Jabbar, Los Angeles	80	716	285	1,717	21.5
Isiah Thomas, Detroit	82	669	388	1,748	21.3
Kelly Tripucka, Detroit	76	595	426	1,618	21.3

BLOCKED-SHOTS LEADERS—1983–1984

(Minimum 70 games or 100 blocked shots)

	GP	No.	Avg
Mark Eaton, Utah	82	351	4.28
Wayne Rollins, Atlanta	77	277	3.60
Ralph Sampson, Houston	82	197	2.40
Larry Nance, Phoenix	82	173	2.11
Artis Gilmore, San Antonio	64	132	2.06
Roy Hinson, Cleveland	80	145	1.81
LaSalle Thompson, Kansas City	80	145	1.81
Julius Erving, Philadelphia	77	139	1.81
Kareem Abdul-Jabbar, Los Angeles	80	143	1.79
Joe Barry Carroll, Golden State	80	142	1.78

ASSISTS LEADERS—1983–1984

(Minimum 70 games or 400 assists)

	G	No.	Avg
Earvin Johnson, Los Angeles	67	875	13.1
Norm Nixon, San Diego	82	914	11.1
Isiah Thomas, Detroit	82	914	11.1
John Lucas, San Antonio	63	673	10.7
John Moore, San Antonio	59	566	9.6
Rickey Green, Utah	81	748	9.2
Gus Williams, Seattle	80	675	8.4
Ennis Whatley, Chicago	80	662	8.3
Larry Drew, Kansas City	73	558	7.6
Brad Davis, Dallas	81	561	6.9

STEALS LEADERS—1983–1984

(Minimum 70 games or 125 steals)

	GP	No.	Avg
Ricky Green, Utah	81	215	2.65
Isiah Thomas, Detroit	82	204	2.49
Gus Williams, Seattle	80	189	2.36
Maurice Cheeks, Philadelphia	75	171	2.28
Eddie Johnson, Kansas City	67	150	2.24
T.R. Dunn, Denver	80	173	2.16
Ray Williams, New York	76	162	2.13
Darwin Cook, New Jersey	82	164	2.00
Dennis Conner, Golden State	82	162	1.98
Julius Erving, Philadelphia	77	141	1.83

3-POINT FIELD-GOAL LEADERS—1983–1984

(Minimum 25 made)

	FG	Att	Pct
Darrell Griffith, Utah	91	252	.361
Mike Evans, Denver	32	89	.360
Johnny Moore, San Antonio	28	87	.322
Michael Cooper, Los Angeles	38	121	.314
Ray Williams, New York	25	81	.309
Ricky Sobers, Washington	29	111	.261

REBOUND LEADERS—1983–1984

(Minimum 70 games or 800 rebounds)

	G	Off	Def	Total	Avg
Moses Malone, Philadelphia	71	352	598	950	13.4
Buck Williams, New Jersey	81	355	645	1000	12.3
Jeff Ruland, Washington	75	265	657	922	12.3
Bill Laimbeer, Detroit	82	329	674	1003	12.2
Ralph Sampson, Houston	82	293	620	913	11.1
Jack Sikma, Seattle	82	225	686	911	11.1
Robert Parish, Boston	80	243	614	857	10.7
Cliff Robinson, Cleveland	73	156	597	753	10.3
David Greenwood, Chicago	78	214	572	786	10.1
Larry Bird, Boston	79	181	615	796	10.1

N.B.A. ALL-STAR TEAM—1984

First Team	Pos.	Second Team
Larry Bird, Boston	F	Julius Erving, Philadelphia
Bernard King, New York	F	Adrian Dantley, Utah
Kareem Abdul-Jabbar, Los Angeles	C	Moses Malone, Philadelphia
Earvin (Magic) Johnson, Los Angeles	G	Sidney Moncrief, Milwaukee
Isiah Thomas, Detroit	G	Jim Paxson, Portland

VOLLEYBALL

U.S. VOLLEYBALL ASSOCIATION CHAMPIONSHIPS

National Champions

Men—Nautilus Pacifica, Long Beach, Calif.; runnerup: Riunite, Westwood, Calif.

Women—Carlsen Chrysler, Palo Alto, Calif.; runnerup: X-Tecs, San Diego, Calif.

Senior men—Outrigger Canoe Club, Honolulu; runnerup: Chuck's Steak House, Los Angeles.

Golden masters—The Legends, Long Beach, Calif.; runnerup: Kansas City Masters, Kansas City, Mo.

N.C.A.A. CHAMPIONSHIPS

Men

Final—U.C.L.A. defeated Pepperdine.
Third place—George Mason defeated Ball State.

Women

Division I—Hawaii defeated U.C.L.A.
Division II—California State-Northridge defeated Portland State.
Division III—Elmhurst (Ill.) defeated California State-San Diego.

N.A.I.A. CHAMPIONSHIPS

Women

Hawaii Hilo defeated St. Mary's of California.

HOCKEY

Ice hockey, by birth and upbringing a Canadian game, is an offshoot of field hockey. Some historians say that the first ice hockey game was played in Montreal in December 1879 between two teams composed almost exclusively of McGill University students, but others assert that earlier hockey games took place in Kingston, Ontario, or Halifax, Nova Scotia. In the Montreal game of 1879, there were fifteen players on a side, who used an assortment of crude sticks to keep the puck in motion. Early rules allowed nine men on a side, but the number was reduced to seven in 1886 and later to six.

The first governing body of the sport was the Amateur Hockey Association of Canada, organized in 1887. In the winter of 1894–95, a group of college students from the United States visited Canada and saw hockey played. They became enthused over the game and introduced it as a winter sport when they returned home. The first professional league was the International Hockey League, which operated in northern Michigan in 1904–06.

Until 1910, professionals and amateurs were allowed to play together on "mixed teams," but this arrangement ended with the formation of the first "big league," the National Hockey Association, in eastern Canada in 1910. The Pacific Coast League was organized in 1911 for western Canadian hockey. The league included Seattle and later other American cities. The National Hockey League replaced the National Hockey Association in 1917. Boston, in 1924, was the first American city to join that circuit. The league expanded to include western cities in 1967. The Stanley Cup was competed for by "mixed teams" from 1894 to 1910, thereafter by professionals. It was awarded to the winner of the N.H.L. playoffs from 1926–67 and now to the league champion. The World Hockey Association was organized in October 1972 and was dissolved after the 1978–79 season when the N.H.L. absorbed four of the teams.

STANLEY CUP WINNERS

Emblematic of World Professional Championship; N.H.L. Championship after 1967

Year	Winner
1894	Montreal A.A.A.
1895	Montreal Victorias
1896	Winnipeg Victorias
1897–99	Montreal Victorias
1900	Montreal Shamrocks
1901	Winnipeg Victorias
1902	Montreal A.A.A.
1903–05	Ottawa Silver Seven
1906	Montreal Wanderers
1907	Kenora Thistles[1]
1907	Mont. Wanderers[2]
1908	Montreal Wanderers
1909	Ottawa Senators
1910	Montreal Wanderers
1911	Ottawa Senators
1912–13	Quebec Bulldogs
1914	Toronto
1915	Vancouver Millionaires
1916	Montreal Canadiens
1917	Seattle Metropolitans
1918	Toronto Arenas
1919	No champion
1920–21	Ottawa Senators
1922	Toronto St. Patricks
1923	Ottawa Senators
1924	Montreal Canadiens
1925	Victoria Cougars
1926	Montreal Maroons
1927	Ottawa Senators
1928	N.Y. Rangers
1929	Boston Bruins
1930–31	Montreal Canadiens
1932	Toronto Maple Leafs
1933	N.Y. Rangers
1934	Chicago Black Hawks
1935	Montreal Maroons
1936–37	Detroit Red Wings
1938	Chicago Black Hawks
1939	Boston Bruins
1940	N.Y. Rangers
1941	Boston Bruins
1942	Toronto Maple Leafs
1943	Detroit Red Wings
1944	Montreal Canadiens
1945	Toronto Maple Leafs
1946	Montreal Canadiens
1947–49	Toronto Maple Leafs
1950	Detroit Red Wings
1951	Toronto Maple Leafs
1952	Detroit Red Wings
1953	Montreal Canadiens
1954–55	Detroit Red Wings
1956–60	Montreal Canadiens
1961	Chicago Black Hawks
1962–64	Toronto Maple Leafs
1965–66	Montreal Canadiens
1967	Toronto Maple Leafs
1968–69	Montreal Canadiens
1970	Boston Bruins
1971	Montreal Canadiens
1972	Boston Bruins
1973	Montreal Canadiens
1974–75	Philadelphia Flyers
1976–79	Montreal Canadiens
1980–83	New York Islanders
1984	Edmonton Oilers

1. January. 2. March.

NATIONAL HOCKEY LEAGUE YEARLY TROPHY WINNERS

The Hart Trophy—Most Valuable Player

Year	Winner
1924	Frank Nighbor, Ottawa
1925	Billy Burch, Hamilton
1926	Nels Stewart, Montreal Maroons
1927	Herb Gardiner, Montreal Canadiens
1928	Howie Morenz, Montreal Canadiens
1929	Roy Worters, New York Americans
1930	Nels Stewart, Montreal Maroons
1931–32	Howie Morenz, Montreal Canadiens
1933	Eddie Shore, Boston
1934	Aurel Joliat, Montreal Canadiens
1935–36	Eddie Shore, Boston
1937	Babe Siebert, Montreal Canadiens
1938	Eddie Shore, Boston
1939	Toe Blake, Montreal Canadiens
1940	Ebbie Goodfellow, Detroit
1941	Bill Cowley, Boston
1942	Tom Anderson, New York Americans
1943	Bill Cowley, Boston
1944	Babe Pratt, Toronto
1945	Elmer Lach, Montreal Canadiens
1946	Max Bentley, Chicago
1947	Maurice Richard, Montreal Canadiens
1948	Buddy O'Connor, New York Rangers
1949	Sid Abel, Detroit
1950	Chuck Rayner, New York Rangers
1951	Milt Schmidt, Boston
1952–53	Gordon Howe, Detroit
1954	Al Rollins, Chicago
1955	Ted Kennedy, Toronto
1956	Jean Belveau, Montreal Canadiens
1957–58	Gordon Howe, Detroit
1959	Andy Bathgate, New York Rangers
1960	Gordon Howe, Detroit
1961	Bernie Geoffrion, Montreal Canadiens
1962	Jacques Plante, Montreal Canadiens
1963	Gordon Howe, Detroit
1964	Jean Beliveau, Montreal Canadiens
1965–66	Bobby Hull, Chicago

1967–68	Stan Mikita, Chicago
1969	Phil Esposito, Boston
1970–72	Bobby Orr, Boston
1973	Bobby Clarke, Philadelphia
1974	Phil Esposito, Boston
1975–76	Bobby Clarke, Philadelphia
1977–78	Guy Lafleur, Montreal
1979	Bryan Trottier, N.Y. Islanders
1980	Wayne Gretzky, Edmonton
1981	Wayne Gretzky, Edmonton
1982	Wayne Gretzky, Edmonton
1983	Wayne Gretzky, Edmonton
1984	Wayne Gretzky, Edmonton

Vezina Trophy—Leading Goalkeeper

1956–60	Jacques Plante, Montreal
1961	Johnny Bower, Toronto
1962	Jacques Plante, Montreal
1963	Glenn Hall, Chicago
1964	Charlie Hodge, Montreal
1965	Terry Sawchuk—Johnny Bower, Toronto
1966	Lorne Worsley—Charlie Hodge, Montreal
1967	Glenn Hall—Denis DeJordy, Chicago
1968	Lorne Worsley—Rogatien Vachon, Montreal
1969	Glenn Hall—Jacques Plante, St. Louis
1970	Tony Esposito, Chicago
1971	Ed Giacomin—Gilles Villemure, New York
1972	Tony Esposito—Gary Smith, Chicago
1973	Ken Dryden, Montreal
1974	Bernie Parent, Philadelphia, and Tony Esposito, Chicago
1975	Bernie Parent, Philadelphia
1976	Ken Dryden, Montreal
1977–79	Ken Dryden—Michel Larocque, Montreal
1980	Bob Sauve—Don Edwards, Buffalo
1981	Richard Sevigny, Denis Herron and Michel Larocque, Montreal
1982	Billy Smith, New York Islanders
1983	Pete Peeters, Boston
1984	Tom Barrasso, Buffalo

James Norris Trophy—Defenseman

1954	Red Kelly, Detroit
1955–58	Doug Harvey, Montreal
1959	Tom Johnson, Montreal
1960–62	Doug Harvey, Montreal, New York (62)
1963–65	Pierre Pilote, Chicago
1966	Jacques Laperriere, Montreal
1967	Harry Howell, New York
1968–75	Bobby Orr, Boston
1976	Denis Potvin, N.Y. Islanders
1977	Larry Robinson, Montreal
1978	Denis Potvin, N.Y. Islanders
1980	Larry Robinson, Montreal
1981	Randy Carlyle, Pittsburgh
1982	Doug Wilson, Chicago
1983–84	Rod Langway, Washington

Lady Byng Trophy—Sportsmanship

1960	Don McKenney, Boston
1961	Red Kelly, Detroit
1962–63	Dave Keon, Toronto
1964	Ken Wharram, Chicago
1965	Bobby Hull, Chicago
1966	Alex Delvecchio, Detroit
1967–68	Stan Mikita, Chicago
1969	Alex Delvecchio, Detroit
1970	Phil Goyette, St. Louis
1971	John Bucyk, Boston
1972	Jean Ratelle, New York
1973	Gil Perreault, Buffalo
1974	John Buyck, Boston
1975	Marcel Dionne, Detroit
1976	Jean Ratelle, N.Y. Rangers–Boston
1977	Marcel Dionne, Los Angeles
1978	Butch Goring, Los Angeles
1979	Bob MacMillan, Atlanta
1980	Wayne Gretzky, Edmonton
1981	Rick Kehoe, Pittsburgh
1982	Rick Middleton, Boston
1983–84	Mike Bossy, N.Y. Islanders

Calder Trophy—Rookie

1962	Bobby Rousseau, Montreal
1963	Kent Douglas, Toronto
1964	Jacques Laperriere, Montreal
1965	Roger Crozier, Detroit
1966	Brit Selby, Toronto
1967	Bobby Orr, Boston
1968	Derek Sanderson, Boston
1969	Danny Grant, Minnesota
1970	Tony Esposito, Chicago
1971	Gilbert Perreault, Buffalo
1972	Ken Dryden, Montreal
1973	Steve Vickers, New York Rangers
1974	Denis Potvin, N.Y. Islanders
1975	Eric Vail, Atlanta
1976	Bryan Trottier, N.Y. Islanders
1977	Willi Plett, Atlanta
1978	Mike Bossy, N.Y. Islanders
1979	Bobby Smith, Minnesota
1980	Ray Bourque, Boston
1981	Peter Stastny, Quebec
1982	Dale Hawerchuk, Winnipeg
1983	Steve Larmer, Chicago
1984	Tom Barrasso, Buffalo

Art Ross Trophy—Leading scorer

1955	Bernie Geoffrion, Montreal
1956	Jean Beliveau, Montreal
1957	Gordie Howe, Detroit
1958–59	Dickie Moore, Montreal
1960	Bobby Hull, Chicago
1961	Bernie Geoffrion, Montreal
1962	Bobby Hull, Chicago
1963	Gordie Howe, Detroit
1964–65	Stan Mikita, Chicago
1966	Bobby Hull, Chicago
1967–68	Stan Mikita, Chicago
1969	Phil Esposito, Boston
1970	Bobby Orr, Boston
1971–74	Phil Esposito, Boston
1975	Bobby Orr, Boston
1976–78	Guy Lafleur, Montreal
1979	Bryan Trottier, N.Y. Islanders
1980	Marcel Dionne, Los Angeles
1981–84	Wayne Gretzky, Edmonton

N.H.L. CHAMPIONS
Prince of Wales Trophy

1939	Boston
1940	Boston
1941	Boston
1942	New York
1943	Detroit
1944–47	Montreal
1948	Toronto
1948–55	Detroit
1956	Montreal
1957	Detroit
1958–62	Montreal
1963	Toronto
1964	Montreal
1965	Detroit
1966	Montreal
1967	Chicago

Eastern Division

1968–69 Montreal
1970 Chicago
1971 Boston
1972 Boston
1973 Montreal
1974 Boston

Prince of Wales Conference

1975 Buffalo
1976–79 Montreal
1980 Buffalo
1981 Montreal
1982 New York Islanders
1983 New York Islanders
1984 New York Islanders

CAMPBELL BOWL
Western Division

1968 Philadelphia
1969 St. Louis
1970 St. Louis
1971–73 Chicago
1974 Philadelphia

Clarence Campbell Conference

1975 Philadelphia
1976–77 Philadelphia
1978–79 N.Y. Islanders
1980 Philadelphia
1981 New York Islanders
1982 Edmonton
1983 Edmonton
1984 Edmonton

NATIONAL HOCKEY LEAGUE
Final Standing of the Clubs—1983–84

PRINCE OF WALES CONFERENCE
Patrick Division

	W	L	T	GF	GA	Pts
New York Islanders	50	26	4	357	269	104
Washington Capitals	48	27	5	308	226	101
Philadelphia Flyers	44	26	10	350	290	98
New York Rangers	42	29	9	314	304	93
New Jersey Devils	17	56	7	231	350	41
Pittsburgh Penguins	16	58	6	254	390	38

Adams Division

	W	L	T	GF	GA	Pts
Boston Bruins	49	25	6	336	261	104
Buffalo Sabres	48	25	7	315	257	103
Quebec Nordiques	42	28	10	360	278	94
Montreal Canadiens	35	40	5	286	295	75
Hartford Whalers	28	42	10	288	320	66

CLARENCE CAMPBELL CONFERENCE
Norris Division

	W	L	T	GF	GA	Pts
Minnesota North Stars	39	31	10	345	344	88
St. Louis Blues	32	41	7	293	316	71
Detroit Red Wings	31	42	7	298	323	69
Chicago Black Hawks	30	42	8	277	311	68
Toronto Maple Leafs	26	45	9	303	387	61

Smythe Division

	W	L	T	GF	GA	Pts
Edmonton Oilers	57	18	5	446	314	119
Calgary Flames	34	32	14	311	314	82
Vancouver Canucks	32	39	9	306	328	73
Winnipeg Jets	31	38	11	340	374	73
Los Angeles Kings	23	44	13	309	376	59

Stanley Cup Playoffs—1984

Preliminary Round

New York Islanders defeated New York Rangers, 3 games to 2
Washington Capitals defeated Philadelphia Flyers, 3 games to 0
Quebec Nordiques defeated Buffalo Sabres, 3 games to 0
Montreal Canadiens defeated Boston Bruins, 3 games to 0
Minnesota North Stars defeated Chicago Black Hawks, 3 games to 2
St. Louis Blues defeated Detroit Red Wings, 3 games to 1
Edmonton Oilers defeated Winnipeg Jets, 3 games to 0
Calgary Flames defeated Vancouver Canucks, 3 games to 1

Quarterfinal Round

New York Islanders defeated Washington Capitals, 4 games to 1
Montreal Canadiens defeated Quebec Nordiques, 4 games to 2
Minnesota North Stars defeated St. Louis Blues, 4 games to 3
Edmonton Oilers defeated Calgary Flames, 4 games to 3

Semifinal Round

New York Islanders defeated Montreal Canadiens, 4 games to 2
April 24—Montreal 3, New York 0
April 26—Montreal 4, New York 2
April 28—New York 5, Montreal 2[1]
May 1—New York 3, Montreal 1[1]
May 3—New York 3, Montreal 1
May 5—New York 4, Montreal 1[1]
1. At Nassau Coliseum, Uniondale, New York

Edmonton Oilers defeated Minnesota North Stars, 4 games to 0
April 24—Edmonton 7, Minnesota 1[1]
April 26—Edmonton 4, Minnesota 3[1]
April 28—Edmonton 8, Minnesota 5
May 1—Edmonton 3, Minnesota 1
1. At Edmonton.

Championship

Edmonton Oilers defeated New York Islanders, 4 games to 1
May 10—Edmonton 1, New York 0[1]
May 12—New York 6, Edmonton 2[1]
May 15—Edmonton 7, New York 2
May 17—Edmonton 7, New York 2
May 19—Edmonton 5, New York 2
1. At Nassau Coliseum, Uniondale, New York.

N.H.L. LEADING SCORERS—1983–84

	GP	G	A	Pts
Wayne Gretzky, Edmonton	74	87	118	205
Paul Coffey, Edmonton	80	40	86	126
Michel Goulet, Quebec	75	56	65	121
Peter Stastny, Quebec	80	46	73	119
Mike Bossy, New York Islanders	67	51	67	118
Barry Pederson, Boston	80	39	77	116

Jari Kurri, Edmonton	64	52	61	113
Bryan Trottier, New York Islanders	68	40	71	111
Bernie Federko, St. Louis	79	41	66	107
Rick Middleton, Boston	80	47	58	105
Dale Hawerchuk, Winnipeg	80	37	65	102
Mark Messier, Edmonton	73	37	64	101
Glenn Anderson, Edmonton	80	54	45	99
Ray Borque, Boston	78	31	65	96
Bernie Nicholls, Los Angeles	78	41	54	95
Denis Savard, Chicago	75	37	57	94
Tim Kerr, Philadelphia	79	54	39	93
Rick Vaive, Toronto	76	52	41	93
Mike Bullard, Pittsburgh	76	51	41	92
Charlie Simmer, Los Angeles	79	44	48	92
Marcel Dionne, Los Angeles	66	39	53	92
Brian Prepp, Philadelphia	79	39	53	92

OTHER N.H.L. AWARDS—1984

Selke (Best defensive forward)—Doug Jarvis, Washington
Smythe (Most valuable in playoffs)—Mark Messier, Edmonton

N.H.L. LEADING GOALTENDERS—1983-84

(Minimum 1,400 minutes)

	G	Min	GA	Avg
Pat Riggin, Washington	41	2,299	102	2.66
Tom Barrasso, Buffalo	42	2,475	117	2.84
Al Jensen, Washington	43	2,414	117	2.91
Doug Keans, Boston	33	1,779	92	3.10
Bob Froese, Philadelphia	48	2,863	150	3.14
Pete Peeters, Boston	50	2,868	151	3.16
Dan Bouchard, Quebec	57	3,373	180	3.20
Roland Melanson, New York Islanders	37	2,019	110	3.27
Murray Bannerman	56	3,335	188	3.38
Richard Sevigny, Montreal	40	2,203	124	3.38
Billy Smith, New York Islanders	42	2,279	130	3.42
Mike Liut, St. Louis	58	3,425	197	3.45
Bob Suave, Buffalo	40	2,375	138	3.49
Rejean Lemelin, Calgary	51	2,568	150	3.50
Glen Hanlon, New York Rangers	50	2,837	166	3.51

Top Team Averages

Washington (Riggin, Jensen, Mason, Parro)	80	4,834	226	2.81
Buffalo (Barrasso, Suave)	80	4,850	257	3.18

N.H.L. CAREER SCORING LEADERS

(Listed in order of total points scored; figures in parentheses indicate the top 10 in goals scored)

	Yrs	Games	G	A	Pts
Gordie Howe (1)	26	1,767	801	1,049	1,850
Phil Esposito (2)	18	1,282	717	873	1,590
Stan Mikita (6)	22	1,394	541	926	1,467
Marcel Dionne (4)[1]	13	1,003	583	796	1,379
John Bucyk (5)	23	1,540	556	813	1,369
Alex Delvecchio	24	1,549	456	825	1,281
Jean Ratelle (10)	21	1,281	491	776	1,267
Guy Lafleur (8)[1]	13	942	516	725	1,241
Norm Ullman	20	1,410	490	739	1,229
Jean Beliveau (9)	20	1,215	507	712	1,219
Bobby Clarke	15	1,144	358	852	1,210
Bobby Hull (3)	16	1,063	610	560	1,170
Gil Perreault[1]	14	1,021	452	715	1,167
Frank Mahovlich (7)	18	1,181	533	570	1,103
Darryl Sittler[1]	14	1,035	473	621	1,094
Henri Richard	20	1,256	358	688	1,046
Rod Gilbert	18	1,065	406	615	1,021
Dave Keon	18	1,296	396	590	986

1. Still active in N.H.L.

N.H.L. ALL-STAR TEAMS—1984

First Team	Pos.	Second Team
Tom Barrasso, Buffalo	G	Pat Riggin, Washington
Rod Langway, Washington	D	Paul Coffey, Edmonton
Ray Borque, Boston	D	Denis Potvin, New York Islanders
Wayne Gretzky, Edmonton	C	Bryan Trottier, New York Islanders
Michel Goulet, Quebec	LW	Mark Messier, Edmonton
Mike Bossy, New York Islanders	RW	Jari Kurri, Edmonton

AMATEUR LEAGUES—1984

Ontario League—Regular season: Leyden Division: Ottawa; Emms Division: Kitchener. Playoffs: Ottawa defeated Kitchener 8-2 in points (Ottawa won 3 games and 2 were tied in 5-game series).

Quebec Major League—Regular season: Robert LeBel Division: Laval; Frank Dilio Division: Shawinigan. Playoffs: Laval defeated Longueuil 4 games to 2 in 7-game final series

Western League—Regular season: Eastern Division: Regina; Western Division: Kamloops. Playoffs: Kamloops defeated Regina 4 games to 3 in 7-game final series.

International League—Regular season: Toledo. Playoffs: Flint defeated Toledo 4 games to 0 in 7-game series.

Memorial Cup—Ottawa.

MINOR LEAGUE HOCKEY CHAMPIONS
American League—1983-1984

	W	L	T	GF	GA	Pts
Northern Division						
Fredericton Express	45	30	5	340	262	95
Adirondack Red Wings	37	29	14	346	328	88
Maine Mariners	33	36	11	310	312	77
Nova Scotia Voyageurs	32	37	11	277	288	75
Moncton Alpines	32	40	8	251	278	72
Sherbrooke Jets	22	53	5	301	419	49
Southern Division						
Baltimore Skipjacks	46	24	10	384	299	102
Rochester Americans	46	32	2	363	300	94
St. Catherines Saints	43	31	6	364	346	92
Springfield Indians	39	35	6	344	340	84
New Haven Nighthawks	36	40	4	365	371	76
Binghamton Whalers	33	43	4	359	388	70
Hershey Bears	28	42	10	320	383	66

CALDER CUP PLAYOFFS

Quarterfinals

Nova Scotia defeated Fredericton, 4 games to 3
Maine defeated Adirondack, 4 games to 3
Baltimore defeated Springfield, 4 games to 0
Rochester defeated St. Catherines, 4 games to 3

Semifinals

Maine defeated Nova Scotia, 4 games to 1
Rochester defeated Baltimore, 4 games to 2

Final

Maine defeated Rochester, 4 games to 1

Central League—1983-1984

	W	L	T	GF	GA	Pts
Colorado Flames	48	25	3	343	287	99
Tulsa Oilers[2]	36	27	5	252	248	77

Salt Lake City Golden Eagles	35	35	2	334	330	72
Indianapolis Checkers	34	36	2	308	289	70
Montana Magic	20	52	4	276	381	44
United States Olympic Team[1]	6	4	0	48	31	12
Canadian Olympic Team[1]	5	5	0	34	29	10

1. During the 1983–84 season, both the United States and the Canadian Olympic ice hockey teams played 10 games against Central League teams which were counted in the league standings. 2. The Tulsa Oilers left Tulsa midway through the 1983–84 season due to financial problems. The team played the remainder of its schedule on the road and was known simply as "The Oilers." The Central League ceased operation completely following the 1983–84 season.

ADAMS CUP PLAYOFFS

Semifinals

Indianapolis defeated Colorado, 4 games to 2.
The Oilers defeated Salt Lake City, 4 games to 1.

Final

The Oilers defeated Indianapolis, 4 games to 0.

COLLEGE CHAMPIONS—1984

N.C.A.A. Division I—Final: Bowling Green defeated Minnesota-Duluth, 5–4 in 4 overtimes. Third place: North Dakota defeated Michigan State, 6–5. Semifinals: Bowling Green defeated Michigan State, 2–1; Minnesota-Duluth defeated North Dakota, 2–1.

E.C.A.C. Division I—Final: RPI defeated Boston University, 5–2. Third place: Clarkson defeated Boston College, 3–1. Semifinals: Boston University defeated Boston College, 6–4; RPI defeated Clarkson, 5–4.

W.C.H.A.—Final: Minnesota-Duluth defeated North Dakota, 12–6, in 2-game total-goals series. Semifinals: North Dakota defeated Minnesota, 9–7, in 2-game, total-goals series; Minnesota-Duluth defeated Wisconsin, 15–3, in 2-game, total-goals series.

C.C.H.A.—Final: Michigan State defeated Western Michigan, 5–0. Third place: Ohio State defeated Bowling Green, 3–2. Semifinals: Michigan State defeated Ohio State, 8–1; Western Michigan defeated Bowling Green, 5–4.

BOWLING

AMERICAN BOWLING CONGRESS CHAMPIONS

Year	Singles	All-events	Year	Singles	All-events
1959	Ed Lubanski	Ed Lubanski	1973	Ed Thompson	Ron Woolet
1960	Paul Kulbaga	Vince Lucci	1974	Gene Krause	Bob Hart
1961	Lyle Spooner	Luke Karen	1975	Jim Setser	Bobby Meadows
1962	Andy Renaldo	Billy Young	1976	Mike Putzer	Jim Lindquist
1963	Fred Delello	Bus Owalt	1977	Frank Gadaleto	Bud Debenham
1964	Jim Stefanich	Les Zikes, Jr.	1978	Rich Mersek	Chris Cobus
1965	Ken Roeth	Tom Hathaway	1979	Rick Peters	Bob Basacchi
1966	Don Chapman	John Wilcox	1980	Mike Eaton	Steve Fehr
1967	Frank Perry	Gary Lewis	1981	Rob Vital	Rod Toft
1968	Wayne Kowalski	Vince Mazzanti	1982	Bruce Bohm	Rich Wonders
1969	Greg Campbell	Eddie Jackson	1983	Rick Kendrick	Tony Cariello
1970	Jake Yoder	Mike Berlin	1984	Bob Antczak and Neal Young (tie)	Bob Goike
1971	Al Cohn	Al Cohn			
1972	Bill Pointer	Mac Lowry			

PROFESSIONAL BOWLERS ASSOCIATION

National Championship Tournament

1960 Don Carter
1961 Dave Soutar
1962 Carmen Salvino
1963 Billy Hardwick
1964 Bob Strampe
1965 Dave Davis
1966 Wayne Zahn
1967 Dave Davis
1968 Wayne Zahn
1969 Mike McGrath
1970 Mike McGrath
1971 Mike Lemongello
1972 Johnny Guenther
1973 Earl Anthony
1974 Earl Anthony
1975 Earl Anthony
1976 Paul Colwell
1977 Tommy Hudson
1978 Warren Nelson
1979 Mike Aulby
1980 Johnny Petraglia
1981 Earl Anthony
1982 Earl Anthony
1983 Earl Anthony
1984 Bob Chamberlain

BOWLING PROPRIETORS' ASSOCIATION OF AMERICA—MEN

United States Open[1]

1971 Mike Lemongello
1972 Don Johnson
1973 Mike McGrath
1974 Larry Laub
1975 Steve Neff
1976 Paul Moser
1977 Johnny Petraglia
1978 Nelson Burton, Jr.
1979 Joe Berardi
1980 Steve Martin
1981 Marshall Holman
1982 Dave Husted
1983 Gary Dickinson
1984 Mark Roth

1. Replaced All-Star tournament and is rolled as part of B.P.A. tour.

WOMEN'S INTERNATIONAL BOWLING CONGRESS CHAMPIONS

Year	Singles	All-events	Year	Singles	All-events
1959	Mae Bolt	Pat McBride	1972	D. D. Jacobson	Mildred Martorella
1960	Marge McDaniels	Judy Roberts	1973	Bobby Buffaloe	Toni Calvery
1961	Elaine Newton	Evelyn Teal	1974	Shirley Garms	Judy C. Soutar
1962	Martha Hoffman	Flossie Argent	1975	Barbara Leicht	Virginia Norton
1963	Dot Wilkinson	Helen Shablis	1976	Bev Shonk	Betty Morris
1964	Jean Havlish	Jean Havlish	1977	Akiko Yamaga	Akiko Yamaga
1965	Doris Rudell	Donna Zimmerman	1978	Mae Bolt	Annese Kelly
1966	Gloria Bouvia	Kate Helbig	1979	Betty Morris	Betty Morris
1967	Gloria Paeth	Carol Miller	1980	Betty Morris	Cheryl Robinson
1968	Norma Parks	Susie Reichley	1981	Virginia Norton	Virginia Norton
1969	Joan Bender	Helen Duval	1982	Gracie Freeman	Aleta Rzepecki
1970	Dorothy Fothergill	Dorothy Fothergill	1983	Aleta Rzepecki	Virginia Norton
1971	Mary Scruggs	Lorrie Nichols	1984	Freida Gates	Shinobu Saitoh

WIBC QUEENS TOURNAMENT CHAMPIONS

1961	Janet Harman	1967	Mildred Martorella	1973	Dorothy Fothergill	1979	Donna Adamek
1962	Dorothy Wilkinson	1968	Phyllis Massey	1974	Judy Soutar	1980	Donna Adamek
1963	Irene Monterosso	1969	Ann Feigel	1975	Cindy Powell	1981	Katsuko Sugimoto
1964	D.D. Jacobson	1970	Mildred Martorella	1976	Pamela Buckner	1982	Katsuko Sugimoto
1965	Betty Kuczynski	1971	Mildred Martorella	1977	Dana Stewart	1983	Aleta Rzepecki
1966	Judy Lee	1972	Dorothy Fothergill	1978	Loa Boxberger	1984	Kazue Inahashi

BOWLING PROPRIETORS' ASSOCIATION OF AMERICA—WOMEN

United States Open[1]

1971	Paula Carter	1975	Paula Carter	1979	Diana Silva	1983	Dana Miller
1972	Lorrie Nichols	1976	Patty Costello (Pa.)	1980	Pat Costello (Calif.)	1984	Karen Ellingsworth
1973	Mildred Martorella	1977	Betty Morris	1981	Donna Adamek		
1974	Pat Costello (Calif.)	1978	Donna Adamek	1982	Shinobu Saitoh		

AMERICAN BOWLING CONGRESS TOURNAMENT—1984

(Reno, Nev., Feb. 3–May 25, 1984)

Regular Division

Singles—Bob Antczak, Chicago, and Neal Young, Louisville, Ky. (tie)	764
Doubles—Chris Cobus and John Megna, Milwaukee, Wis.	1,383
All events—Bob Goike, Detroit	2,142
Team—Minnesota Loons No. 1, St. Paul, Minn.	3,228
Team all events—Minnesota Loons No. 1, St. Paul, Minn.	9,562
Booster Team—J&D Lawn Service, Lincoln, Neb.	2,820

WIBC QUEENS TOURNAMENT—1984

Winner—Kazue Inahashi, Tokyo, Japan (defeated Aleta Sill, Cocoa Beach, Fla., 248–222, in final)

COLLEGIATE
Association of College Unions-International

Singles—Michelle Elkienbaum, University of Florida	624
Doubles—Jan Schmidt, Indiana State, and Suzette Mitchell, Virginia Tech	1,152
All events—Suzette Mitchell, Virginia Tech	1,680

WOMEN'S INTERNATIONAL BOWLING CONGRESS—1984

(Niagara Falls, N.Y., April 5–June 9, 1984)

Open Division

Singles—Freida Gates, North Syracuse, N.Y.	712
Doubles—Bea Hoffman and Sue Reese, Novato, Calif.	1,292
All events—Shinobu Saitoh, Tokyo, Japan	1,921
Team—All Japan, Tokyo, Japan	3,019

Division I

Singles—Cathy Sartwell, Morgan City, La.	690
Doubles—Diane Wilde and Shirley Heppner, Oskosh, Wis.	1,255
All events—Verona Gloudeman, Kimberly, Wash.	1,749
Team—Dave Diomedi's Lanes, Ann Arbor, Mich.	2,721

Division II

Singles—Lorraine Hands, Lucan, Ontario	635
Doubles—Ursula Schroeder and Janice Daniels, Elizabethtown, Ky.	1,125
All events—Janet Marsteller, Sandy Lake, Pa.	1,711
Team—Spirit of Ely II, Ely, Nev.	2,511

MASTERS TOURNAMENT—1984

(Reno, Nev., May 8–12, 1984)

Singles—Earl Anthony, Dublin, Calif. (defeated Gil Sliker, Washington, N.J., 191–175, in final)
Third place—Rick Minier, Vancouver, Wash.
Fourth place—George Pappas, Charlotte, N.C.
Fifth place—Mark Baker, Garden Grove, Calif.

SKIING

ALPINE WORLD CUP OVERALL WINNERS

Year	Men	Women	Team
1967	Jean-Claude Killy, France	Nancy Greene, Canada	France
1968	Jean-Claude Killy, France	Nancy Greene, Canada	France
1969	Karl Schranz, Austria	Gertrude Gabl, Austria	Austria
1970	Karl Schranz, Austria	Michel Jacot, France	France
1971	Gustavo Thoeni, Italy	Annemarie Proell, Austria	France
1972	Gustavo Thoeni, Italy	Annemarie Proell, Austria	France
1973	Gustavo Thoeni, Italy	Annemarie Proell Moser, Austria	Austria
1974	Piero Gros, Italy	Annemarie Proell Moser, Austria	Austria
1975	Gustavo Thoeni, Italy	Annemarie Proell Moser, Austria	Austria
1976	Ingemar Stenmark, Sweden	Rosi Mittermaier, West Germany	Austria
1977	Ingemar Stenmark, Sweden	Lise-Marie Morerod, Switzerland	Austria
1978	Ingemar Stenmark, Sweden	Hanni Wenzel, Liechtenstein	Austria
1979	Peter Luescher, Switzerland	Annemarie Proell Moser, Austria	Austria
1980	Andreas Wenzel, Liechtenstein	Hanni Wenzel, Liechtenstein	Liechtenstein
1981	Phil Mahre, United States	Marie-Theres Nadig, Switzerland	Switzerland
1982	Phil Mahre, United States	Erika Hess, Switzerland	Austria
1983	Phil Mahre, United States	Tamara McKinney, United States	
1984	Pirman Zurbriggen, Switzerland	Erika Hess, Switzerland	

UNITED STATES CHAMPIONSHIPS—1984

ALPINE

Men's Events

Downhill—Bill Johnson, Van Nuys, Calif. 1:51.64
Slalom—Steve Mahre, Yakima, Wash. 1:29.00
Giant slalom—Steve Mahre, Yakima, Wash. 2:13.52

Women's Events

Downhill—Lisa Wilcox, Ithaca, N.Y. 1:36.27
Slalom—Tamara McKinney, Olympic Valley, Calif. 1:18.72
Giant slalom—Christin Cooper, Sun Valley, Idaho 2:06.75

NORDIC

Men's Cross Country

15 kilometers—Audun Endestad, Alaska 46:20.4
30 kilometers—Jum Galanes, Brattleboro, Vt. 1:19:26.8
50 kilometers—Audun Endestad, Alaska 2:15:59.6
Relay—Alaska "A" (Auden Endestad, David Michael, John Svennson) 1:33:44.2
Veterans 10 km—Dan Simoneau 26:48.2

Women's Cross Country

5 kilometers—Judy Rabinowitz, Fairbanks, Alaska 17:33.5
10 kilometers—Sue Long, Manchester Centre, Vt. 30:07.7
20 kilometers—Sue Long, Manchester Centre, Vt. 1:01:22.1
Relay—Alaska (Alice Tower, Jay Jay Peoti, Sue Strutz) 56:32.6

FREESTYLE

Men's Events

Ballet—Lane Spina
Moguls—Steve Desovitch
Aerials—Tim Hadfield
Combined—Dan Herby

Women's Events

Ballet—Jan Bucher
Moguls—Hillary Engisch
Aerials—Betsy Reid
Combined—Betsy Reid

COLLEGIATE

(Attitash Mountain, New Hampshire, March 7–10, 1984)

Men—N.C.A.A.

Slalom—James Marceau, Colorado
Giant slalom—Andrew Shaw, Vermont
Cross country—John Aalberg, Utah
Cross country relay—Utah
Team—Utah

Women—N.C.A.A.

Slalom—Bente Dahlum, Utah
Giant slalom—Bente Dahlum, Utah
Cross country—Heidi Sorenson, New Mexico
Cross country relay—Vermont
Team—Utah

WORLD CHAMPIONSHIPS—1982

The World Championships of Skiing are held every four years in even numbered, non-Olympic years. The last World Championships were held in Schladming, Austria from Jan. 31 to Feb. 7, 1982. There were no World Championships in 1984 because of the Olympics. The next scheduled World Championships will be held in February 1986.

ALPINE

Men's Events

Downhill—Harti Weirather, Austria 1:55.10
Slalom—Ingemar Stenmark, Sweden 1:48.48
Giant slalom—Steve Mahre, Yakima, Wash. 2:38.80
Combined—Michel Vion, France 12.64 pts

Women's Events

Downhill—Gerry Sorensen, Canada 1:37.47
Slalom—Erika Hess, Switzerland 1:41.60
Giant slalom—Erika Hess 2:37.17
Combined—Erika Hess 8.99 pts

NORDIC

(Oslo, Norway, Feb. 17–27, 1982)

Jumping

70-meter—Armin Kogler, Austria (237 ft 11 in. and 241-2) 249.3 pts
90-meter—Matti Nykanen, Finland (355-9, 336-3) 257.9 pts

Combined

70-meter jump—Hubert Schwartz, West Germany 221.7 pts
15-km cross-country—Tom Sandberg, Norway 40:06
Combined—Tom Sandberg, Norway (13th in jump, 1st in run) 426.600 pts

Men's Cross-Country

15 kilometers—Oddvar Bra, Norway	38:52.5
30 kilometers—Thomas Eriksson, Sweden	1:21:52.3
50 kilometers—Thomas Wassberg, Sweden	2:32:00.9
40-km relay—Norway and Soviet Union (tie)	1:56:27.6

Women's Cross-Country

5 kilometers—Berit Aunli, Norway	14:30.2
10 kilometers—Berit Aunli, Norway	29:25.9
20 kilometers—Raisa Smetanina, Soviet Union	1:06:16.9
20-km relay—Norway	1:02.15.9

ALPINE WORLD CUP—1984

Overall—Men	**Pts**
Pirman Zurbriggen, Switzerland	256
Ingemar Stenmark, Sweden	230
Marc Girardelli, Luxemberg	222
Bill Johnson, United States	87

Overall—Women	**Pts**
Erika Hess, Switzerland	247
Hanni Wenzel, Liechenstein	238
Tamara McKinney, United States	195

Event Leaders—Men	**Pts**
Downhill—Urs Raeber, Switzerland	94
2—Erwin Rasch, Austria	91
3—Bill Johnson, United States	87
Slalom—Marc Girardelli, Luxemburg	125
2—Ingemar Stenmark, Sweden	115
3—Franz Gruber, Austria	82
9—Phil Mahre, United States	44
Giant slalom—Ingemar Stenmark, Sweden	115[1]
2—Pirman Zurbriggen, Switzerland	115
3—Han Enni, Austria	105
19—Phil Mahre, United States	29
Combined—Andreas Wenzel, Liechtenstein	90
2—Pirman Zurbriggen, Switzerland	65
3—Anton Steiner, Austria	54
11—Phil Mahre, United States	5

1. Stenmark declared the winner because of more individual races won.

Event Leaders—Women	**Pts**
Downhill—Maria Walliser, Switzerland	95
2—Irene Epple, West Germany	94
3—Hanni Wenzel, Liechenstein	77
6—Holly Flanders, United States	64
Slalom—Tamara McKinney, United States	110
2—Roswitha Steiner, Austria	100
3—Perrine Pelen, France	96
Giant slalom—Erika Hess, Switzerland	115
2—Christin Cooper, United States	90
3—Tamara McKinney, United States	85
Combined—Erika Hess, Switzerland	79
2—Irene Epple, West Germany	77
3—Olga Charvatova, Czechoslovakia	76
9—Tamara McKinney, United States	31

NORDIC WORLD CUP—1984

Overall—Men	**Pts**
Cross-country	
1—Gunde Svan, Sweden	145
2—Thomas Wassberg, Sweden	96
3—Harri Kirvesniemi, Finland	93
21—Jim Galanes, United States	42
Jumping	
1—Jens Wiesflog, East Germany	230
2—Matti Nykaenen, Finland	217
3—Pavel Ploc, Czechoslovakia	150
4—Jeff Hastings, United States	123
Overall—Women	
1—Marja-Liisa Hamalanen, Finland	134
2—Raisa Smetanina, Soviet Union	114
3—Anne Jahren, Norway	104
31—Sue Long, United States	21
Combined—Men	
1—Tom Sandberg, Norway	103
2—Uwe Dotzauer, East Germany	89
3—Geir Anderson, Norway	82
8—Kerry Lynch, United States	43

ALPINE NATIONS CUP—1984

	Pts
Overall—Switzerland	1,871
Austria	1,677
United States	779
West Germany	603
Italy	501
Liechtenstein	499
France	462
Sweden	435
Canada	408
Yugoslavia	344

LACROSSE

NATIONAL INTERCOLLEGIATE CHAMPIONS

1946	Navy	1958	Army	1972	Virginia
1947–48	Johns Hopkins	1959	Army, Johns Hopkins, Maryland	1973	Maryland
1949	Johns Hopkins, Navy	1960	Navy	1974	Johns Hopkins
1950	Johns Hopkins	1961	Army, Navy	1975	Maryland
1951	Army, Princeton	1962–66	Navy	1976–77	Cornell
1952	Virginia, R.P.I.	1967	Johns Hopkins, Maryland, Navy	1978–80	Johns Hopkins
1953	Princeton	1968	Johns Hopkins	1981	North Carolina
1954	Navy	1969	Army, Johns Hopkins	1982	North Carolina
1955–56	Maryland	1970	Johns Hopkins, Navy, Virginia	1983	Syracuse
1957	Johns Hopkins	1971[1]	Cornell	1984	Johns Hopkins

1. First year of N.C.A.A. Championship Tournaments.

N.C.A.A. CHAMPIONSHIPS—1984

DIVISION I
Final
(University of Delaware, May 26, 1984)

Johns Hopkins 13, Syracuse 10

DIVISION III
Final
(Geneva, N.Y., May 9, 1984)

Hobart 12, Washington College 5

SPEED SKATING

U.S. OUTDOOR CHAMPIONS

Men

1959–60	Ken Bartholomew
1961	Ed Rudolph
1962	Floyd Bedbury
1963	Tom Gray
1964	Neil Blatchford
1965–66	Rich Wurster
1967	Mike Passarella
1968–70	Peter Cefalu
1971	Jack Walters
1972	Barth Levy
1973	Mike Woods
1974	Leigh Barczewski, Mike Passarella
1975	Rich Wurster
1976	John Wurster
1977	Jim Chapin
1978	Bill Heinkel
1979	Erik Henriksen
1980	Greg Oly
1981	Tom Grannes
1982	Greg Oly
1983	Michael Ralston
1984	Michael Ralston

Women

1960	Mary Novak
1961	Jean Ashworth
1962	Jean Omelenchuk
1963	Jean Ashworth
1964	Diane White
1965	Jean Omelenchuk
1966	Diane White
1967	Jean Ashworth
1968	Helen Lutsch
1969	Sally Blatchford
1970–71	Sheila Young
1972	Ruth Moore, Nancy Thorne
1973	Nancy Class
1974	Kris Garbe
1975	Nancy Swider
1976	Connie Carpenter
1977	Liz Crowe
1978	Paula Class, Betsy Davis
1979	Gretchen Byrnes
1980	Shari Miller
1981	Lisa Merrifield
1982	Lisa Merrifield
1983	Janet Hainstock
1984	Janet Hainstock

WORLD SPEED SKATING RECORDS

Men

Distance	Time	Skater	Place	Year
500 m	0:36.57	Pavel Pegov	Medeo, U.S.S.R.	1983
1,000 m	1:12.58	Pavel Pegov	Medeo, U.S.S.R.	1983
1,500 m	1:53.26	Oleg Bojiev	Medeo, U.S.S.R.	1984
3,000 m	4:04.01	Eric Heiden, U.S.A.	Inzell, Austria	1978
5,000 m	6:49.15	Victor Shasherin	Medeo, U.S.S.R.	1984
10,000 m	14:21.51	Igor Malkov, U.S.S.R.	Medeo, U.S.S.R.	1984
All-Around	160.807	Victor Shasherin	Medeo, U.S.S.R.	1984

Women

Distance	Time	Skater	Place	Year
500 m	0:39.69	Christa Rothenburger, E. Germany	Medeo	1983
1,000 m	1:19.31	Natalya Petruseva, U.S.S.R.	Medeo	1983
1,500 m	2:03.34	Andrea Schone, E. Germany	Medeo	1984
3,000 m	4:20.91	Andrea Schone, E. Germany	Medeo	1984
5,000 m	7:34.52	Andrea Schone, E. Germany	Medeo	1984
All-around	171.760	Andrea Schone, E. Germany	Medeo	1984

U.S. OUTDOOR CHAMPIONS

(Milwaukee, Wis., Feb. 4–5, 1984)

Men—Michael Ralston, Streamwood, Ill.
Women—Janet Hainstock, Alpena, Mich.
Intermediate men—Marty Pierce, St. Francis, Wis.
Intermediate women—Anne Hills, St. Paul, Minn.
Junior boys—Frank Filardi, Park Ridge, Ill.
Junior girls—Michelle Kline, Circle Pines, Minn.

U.S. INDOOR CHAMPIONS

(Lake Placid, N.Y., March 10–11, 1984)

Men—David Besteman, Madison, Wis.
Women—Bonnie Blair, Champaign, Ill.
Intermediate men—Eric Flaim, Pembroke, Mass.
Intermediate women—Michelle Fang, Arlington Heights, Ill.
Junior boys—David Cruikshank, Northbrook, Ill.
Junior girls—Maura D'Andrea, Saratoga Springs, N.Y., and Beth Nowell, Winchester, Mass. (tie)

NORTH AMERICAN OUTDOOR CHAMPIONS

(St. Paul, Minn., Feb. 11–12, 1984)

Men—Michael Ralston, Streamwood, Ill.
Women—No competition held, insufficient entrants
Intermediate men—Pat Seltsam, Pembroke, Mass.
Intermediate women—Anne Hills, St. Paul, Minn.
Junior boys—Frank Filardi, Park Ridge, Ill.
Junior girls—Michelle Kline, Circle Pines, Minn.

NORTH AMERICAN INDOOR CHAMPIONS

(St. John, New Brunswick, Canada, March 31–April 1, 1984)

Men—Gordon Goplen, Saskatoon, Canada, and Michael Holmes, St. John, Canada (tie)
Women—Kathy Vogt, Winnipeg, Manitoba, Canada
Intermediate men—Sebastian Rioux, Quebec
Intermediate women—Marge Stapley, Winnipeg
Junior boys—Jean Moein, Quebec
Junior girls—Angel Cutrone, Montreal

WORLD CHAMPIONSHIPS 1984

(Gothenburg, Sweden, Feb. 25 26, 1984)

Men

Overall champion—Oleg Bojiev, Soviet Union	169.663 pts
500 m—Hilbert van der Duim, Holland	0:39.06
1,500 m—Oleg Bojiev, Soviet Union	1:59.62
5,000 m—Geir Karlstad, Norway	7:17.62
10,000 m—Michael Hadgchieff, Austria	15:00.30

Women
(Deventer, Holland, Jan. 28–29, 1984)

Overall champion—Karin Enke, East Germany	175.510 pts
500 m—Karin Enke	0:42.04
1,500 m—Karin Enke	2:05.59
3,000 m—Karin Enke	4:28.20
5,000 m—Andrea Schone, East Germany	7:46.04

SPORTS ORGANIZATIONS AND INFORMATION BUREAUS

(Note: Addresses are subject to change)

Amateur Athletic Union of the U.S. 3400 West 86th St., Indianapolis, Indiana 46862

Amateur Hockey Association of the U.S. 2997 Broadmoor Valley Road, Colorado Springs, Colo. 80906

Amateur Skating Union of the U.S. 1033 Shady Lane, Glen Ellyn, Ill. 60137

Amateur Softball Association. 2801 N.E. 50th St., Oklahoma City, Okla. 73111

Amateur Trapshooting Association of America. Vandalia, Ohio 45377

American Amateur Baseball Congress. 215 East Green, Box 467, Marshall, Mich. 49068

American Association of Professional Baseball Clubs. P.O. Box 382, Wichita, Kan. 67201

American Bowling Congress. 5301 South 76th St., Greendale, Wis. 53129

American Canoe Association. P.O. Box 248, Lorton, Va. 22079

American Hockey League. 31 Elm St., Suite 533, Springfield, Mass. 01103

American Horse Shows Association. 527 Madison Ave., New York, N.Y. 10022

American Kennel Club. 51 Madison Ave., New York, N.Y. 10010

American League (baseball). 280 Park Ave., New York, N.Y. 10017

American Motorcycle Association. 33 Collingwood Rd., Westerville, Ohio, 43081

American Power Boat Association. 17640 East 9-Mile Rd., P.O. Box 377, East Detroit, Mich. 48021

American Water Ski Association. 799 Overlook Drive, P.O. Box 191, Winter Haven, Fla. 33882

Association of Intercollegiate Athletics for Women. 1201 16th St., N.W., Washington, D.C.

Athletics Congress/USA, The. 200 South Capitol Ave., Suite 140, Indianapolis, Ind. 46225

Baseball Commissioner. 350 Park Ave., New York, N.Y. 10022

Baseball Hall of Fame. Cooperstown, N.Y. 13326

Bowling Proprietors' Association of America. P.O. Box 5802, Arlington, Texas 76011

Championship Auto Racing Teams (CART). 2655 Woodward Ave., Suite 275, Bloomfield Hills, Mich. 48013

Eastern College Athletic Conference. P.O. Box 3, Centerville, Mass. 02632

Elias Sports Bureau. 500 Fifth Ave., New York, N.Y. 10036

Fish and Wildlife Service. Department of the Interior, Washington, D.C. 20240

Football Hall of Fame (college). Kings Island, Ohio 45034

Football Hall of Fame (pro). Canton, Ohio 44708

Intercollegiate (Big Ten) Conference (1896). 1111 Plaza Dr., Schaumburg, Ill. 60195

International Game Fish Association. 3000 East Las Olas Blvd., Fort Lauderdale, Fla. 33316

International League (baseball). Box 608, Grove City, Ohio 43123

International Olympic Committee. Chateau de Vidy, Lausanne, Switzerland

International Tennis Hall of Fame. Newport, R.I. 02840

The Jockey Club. 300 Madison Ave., New York, N.Y. 10017

Ladies Professional Golf Association. 1250 Shoreline Drive, Suite 200, Sugar Laud, Texas, 77478

Little League Baseball. Williamsport, Pa. 17701

National Archery Association. 1750 E. Boulder St., Colorado Springs, Colo. 80909

National Association of Intercollegiate Athletics. 1221 Baltimore St., Kansas City, Mo. 64105

National Association of Professional Baseball Leagues (minors). P.O. Box A, St. Petersburg, Fla. 33731

National Association for Stock Car Auto Racing. P.O. Box K, Daytona Beach, Fla. 32015—9947

National Baseball Congress. P.O. Box 1420, Wichita, Kan. 67201

National Basketball Association. Olympic Tower, 645 Fifth Ave., New York, N.Y. 10022

National Collegiate Athletic Association. P.O. Box 1906, Mission, Kan. 66201

National Duck Pin Bowling Congress. Fairview Avenue, Baltimore, Md. 21090

National Field Archery Association. Rt. 2, Box 514, Redlands, Calif. 92373

National Football Foundation. 201 East 42nd St., New York, N.Y. 10017. *See also:* Football Hall of Fame (college)

National Football League. 410 Park Ave., New York, N.Y. 10022

National Hockey League. 1155 Metcalfe St., Suite 960, Montreal, Que., Canada H3B 2W2

National Horseshoe Pitchers Association. Box 810, Circleville, Ohio, 43113

National Hot Rod Association. P.O. Box 150, North Hollywood, Calif. 91603

National Junior College Athletic Association. P.O. Box 1586, Hutchinson, Kan. 67504—1586

National League (baseball). 350 Park Ave., New York, N.Y. 10022

National Rifle Association of America. 1600 Rhode Island Ave., N.W., Washington, D.C. 20036

National Skeet Shooting Association. P.O. Box 28188, San Antonio, Tex. 78228

New York Racing Association. P.O. Box 90, Jamaica, N.Y. 11417

New York State Athletic Commission (boxing and wrestling). 270 Broadway, New York, N.Y. 10007

National Shuffleboard Association. 26 Central Terrace, Cincinnati, Ohio 45215

North American Yacht Racing Union. *See* United States Yacht Racing Union

North American Soccer League. 1133 Avenue of the Americas, New York, N.Y. 10036

Pacific Coast League (baseball). 2101 E. Broadway, Suite 35, Tempe, Ariz., 85282

Professional Bowlers Association. 1720 Merriman Road, Akron, Ohio 44313

Professional Golfers' Association of America. Sawgrass, Ponte Vedra, Fla. 32082

Roller Skating Rink Operators Association. P.O. Box 81846, Lincoln, Neb. 68501
Sports Car Club of America. 6750 S. Emporia St., Englewood, Colo. 80112
Thoroughbred Racing Assn. of N. America. 3000 Marcus Ave., Lake Success, N.Y. 11042
Track and Field Hall of Fame. Charleston, W. Va.
United States Amateur Confederation of Roller Skating. 7700 "A" St., Lincoln, Neb. 68501
United States Auto Club. 4910 West 16th St., Speedway, Ind. 46224
United States Badminton Association. P.O. Box 456, Waterford, Mich. 48095
U.S. Chess Federation. 186 Route 9W, New Windsor, N.Y. 12550
U.S. Cycling Federation. Box 669, Wall Street Station, New York, N.Y. 10005
U.S. Fencing Assn., 1750 E. Boulder St., Colorado Springs, Colo. 80909
U.S. Figure Skating Association. 200 First Street, Colorado Springs, Colo. 80906
U.S. Football League. 52 Vanderbilt Ave., New York, N.Y. 10017
U.S. Golf Association. Far Hills, N.J. 07931
U.S. Handball Association. 930 N. Benton Ave., Tucson, Ariz. 85711
U.S. Men's Curling Association. 12822 Water Street, Duluth, Minn. 55008
U.S. Olympic Committee. 1750 East Boulder Street, Colorado Springs, Colo. 80909
U.S. Olympic Training Center. 1776 E. Boulder St., Colorado Springs, Colo. 80909—5793
U.S. Parachute Association. 806–15th St., N.W., Washington, D.C. 20005
U.S. Polo Association. 1301 W. 22nd St., Oak Brook, Ill. 60521
U.S. Rowing Assn., 4 Boathouse Row, Philadelphia, Pa. 19130
U.S. Ski Association. c/o U.S. Olympic Complex, 1750 E. Boulder St., Colorado Springs, Colo. 80909
U.S. Ski Team. P.O. Box 100, Park City, Utah 84060
U.S. Soccer Federation. 350 Fifth Ave., Suite 4010, New York, N.Y. 10001
U.S. Squash Racquets Association. 211 Ford Road, Bala-Cynwyd, Pa. 19004
U.S. Table Tennis Association. c/o U.S. Olympic Complex, 1750 E. Boulder St., Colorado Springs, Colo. 80909
U.S. Tennis Association. 51 E. 42nd St., New York, N.Y. 10017
U.S. Touch and Flag Football Association. 2705 Normandy Drive, Youngstown, Ohio, 49511
U.S. Trotting Association. 750 Michigan Ave., Columbus, Ohio 43215
U.S. Volleyball Association. 1750 East Boulder St., Colorado Springs, Colo. 80909
U.S. Women's Curling Association. 635 Chatham Road, Glenview, Ill. 60025
U.S. Yacht Racing Union. P.O. Box 209, Goat Island, Newport, R.I. 02840
Women's International Bowling Congress. 5301 S. 76th St., Greendale, Wis. 53129

STANDARD MEASUREMENTS IN SPORTS

BASEBALL

Home plate to pitcher's box: 60 feet 6 inches.
Plate to second base: 127 feet 3 3/8 inches.
Distance from base to base (home plate included): 90 feet.
Size of bases: 15 inches by 15 inches.
Pitcher's plate: 24 inches by 6 inches.
Batter's box: 4 feet by 6 feet.
Home plate: 17 inches by 12 inches by 12 inches, cut to a point at rear.
Home plate to backstop: Not less than 60 feet (recommended).
Weight of ball: Not less than 5 ounces nor more than 5 1/4 ounces.
Circumference of ball: Not less than 9 inches nor more than 9 1/4 inches.
Bat: Must be round, not over 2 3/4 inches in diameter at thickest part, nor more than 42 inches in length, and of solid wood in one piece or laminated wood.

FOOTBALL

(N.C.A.A.)

Length of field: 120 yards. (including 10 yards of end zone at each end).
Width of field: 53 1/3 yards (160 feet).
Height of goal posts: At least 20 feet.
Height of crossbar: 10 feet.
Width of goal posts (above crossbar): 23 feet 4 inches, inside to inside, and not more than 24 feet, outside to outside.
Length of ball: 10 7/8 to 11 7/16 inches (long axis).
Circumference of ball: 20 3/4 to 21 1/4 inches (middle); 27 3/4 to 28 1/2 inches (long axis).

LAWN TENNIS

Size of court: Rectangle 78 feet long and 27 feet wide (singles); 78 feet long and 36 feet wide (doubles).
Height of net: 3 feet in center, gradually rising to reach 3-foot 6-inch posts at a point 3 feet outside each side of court.
Ball: Shall be more than 2 1/2 inches and less than 2 5/8 inches in diameter and weigh more than 2 ounces and less than 2 1/16 ounces.
Service line: 21 feet from net.

HOCKEY

Size of rink: 200 feet long by 85 feet wide surrounded by a wooden wall not less than 40 inches and not more than 48 inches above level of ice.
Size of goal: 6 feet wide by 4 feet in height.
Puck: 1 inch thick and 3 inches in diameter, made of vulcanized rubber; weight 5 1/2 to 6 ounces.
Length of stick: Not more than 58 inches from heel to end of shaft nor 12 1/2 inches from heel to end of blade. Blade should not be more than 3 inches in width but not less than 2 inches, except goal keeper's stick, which shall not exceed 3 1/2 inches in width except at the heel, where it must not exceed 4 1/2 inches.

BOWLING

Lane dimensions: Overall length 62 feet 10 3/16 inches, measuring from foul line to pit (not including tail plank), with 1/2 inch tolerance permitted. Foul line to center of No. 1 pinspot 60 feet, with 1/2 inch tolerance permitted. Lane width, 41 1/2 inches with a tolerance of 1/2 inch permitted. Approach, not less than 15 feet. Gutters, 9 5/16 inches wide with 3/16 plus or 5/16 minus tolerances permitted.
Ball: Circumference, not more than 27 inches. Weight, 16 pounds maximum.

GOLF

The ball, specifications: Broadened to require that the ball be designed to perform as if it were spherically symmetrical. The weight of the ball shall not be greater than 1.620 ounces avoirdupois, and the size shall not be less than 1.680 inches in diameter.

Velocity of ball: Not greater than 250 feet per second when tested on U.S.G.A. apparatus, with 2 percent tolerance.

Hole: 4 1/4 inches in diameter and at least 4 inches deep.

Clubs: 14 is the maximum number permitted.

BASKETBALL

(National Collegiate A.A. Rules)

Playing court: College: 94 feet long by 50 feet wide (ideal dimensions). High School: 84 feet long by 50 feet wide (ideal inside dimensions).

Baskets: Rings 18 inches in inside diameter, with white cord 12-mesh nets, 15 to 18 inches in length. Each ring is made of metal, is not more than 5/8 of an inch in diameter, and is bright orange in color.

Height of basket: 10 feet (upper edge).

Weight of ball: Not less than 20 ounces nor more than 22.

Circumference of ball: No greater than 30 inches and not less than 29 1/2.

Free-throw line: 15 feet from the face of the backboard, 2 inches wide.

BOXING

Ring: Professional matches take place in an area not less than 18 nor more than 24 feet square including apron. It is enclosed by four covered ropes, each not less than one inch in diameter. The floor has a 2-inch padding of Ensolite (or equivalent) underneath ring cover that extends at least 6 inches beyond the roped area in the case of elevated rings. For U.S.A./A.B.F. boxing, not less than 16 nor more than 20 feet square within the ropes. The floor must extend beyond the ring ropes not less than 2 feet. The ring posts shall be connected to the three ring ropes with the extension not shorter than 18 inches and must be properly padded.

Gloves: In professional fights, not less than 8-ounce gloves generally are used. U.S.A./A.B.F., not less than 10 ounces for all divisions; for international competition not less than 8 ounces.

FIGURE SKATING

WORLD CHAMPIONS

Men

1960	Alain Giletti, France
1961	No competition
1962	Donald Jackson, Canada
1963	Don McPherson, Canada
1964	Manfred Schnelldorfer, West Germany
1965	Alain Calmat, France
1966–68	Emmerich Danzer, Austria
1969–70	Tim Wood, United States
1971–73	Ondrej Nepela, Czechoslovakia
1974	Jan Hoffman, East Germany
1975	Sergei Yolkov, U.S.S.R.
1976	John Curry, Britain
1977	Vladimir Kovelov, U.S.S.R.
1978	Charles Tickner, United States
1979	Vladimir Kovalev, U.S.S.R.
1980	Jan Hoffman, East Germany
1981	Scott Hamilton, United States
1982	Scott Hamilton, United States
1983	Scott Hamilton, United States
1984	Scott Hamilton, United States

Women

1956–60	Carol Heiss, United States
1961	No competition
1962–64	Sjoukje Dijkstra, Netherlands
1965	Petra Burka, Canada
1966–68	Peggy Fleming, United States
1969–70	Gabriele Seyfert, East Germany
1971–72	Beatrix Schuba, Austria
1973	Karen Magnusson, Canada
1974	Christine Errath, East Germany
1975	Dianne de Leeuw, Netherlands
1976	Dorothy Hamill, United States
1977	Linda Fratianne, United States
1978	Anett Poetzsch, East Germany
1979	Linda Fratianne, United States
1980	Anett Poetzsch, East Germany
1981	Denise Beillmann, Switzerland
1982	Elaine Zayak, United States
1983	Rosalynn Sumners, United States
1984	Katarina Witt, East Germany

U.S. CHAMPIONS

Men

1946–52	Richard Button
1953–56	Hayes Jenkins
1957–60	David Jenkins
1961	Bradley Lord
1962	Monty Hoyt
1963	Tommy Litz
1964	Scott Allen
1965	Gary Visconti
1966	Scott Allen
1967	Gary Visconti
1968–70	Tim Wood
1971	John M. Petkevich
1972	Ken Shelley
1973–75	Gordon McKellen
1976	Terry Kubicka
1977–80	Charles Tickner
1981	Scott Hamilton
1982	Scott Hamilton
1983	Scott Hamilton
1984	Scott Hamilton

Women

1943–48	Gretchen Merrill
1949–50	Yvonne Sherman
1951	Sonya Klopfer
1952–56	Tenley Albright
1957–60	Carol Heiss
1961	Laurence Owen
1962	Barbara Roles Pursley
1963	Lorraine Hanlon
1964–68	Peggy Fleming
1969–73	Janet Lynn
1974–76	Dorothy Hamill
1977–80	Linda Fratianne
1981	Elaine Zayak
1982	Rosalynn Sumners
1983	Rosalynn Sumners
1984	Rosalynn Sumners

UNITED STATES CHAMPIONS—1984

(Salt Lake City, Utah, Jan. 17–22, 1984)

Men's singles—Scott Hamilton, Denver, Colo.
Women's singles—Rosalynn Sumners, Edmonds, Wash.
Pairs—Peter and Caitlin Carruthers, Wilmington, Del.
Dance—Judy Blumberg, Tarzana, Calif., and Michael Seibert, Washington, Pa.
Junior dance—Christina and Keith Yatsuhashi, Boston, Mass.

WORLD CHAMPIONS—1983

(Helsinki, Finland, March 7–12, 1983)

Men's singles—Scott Hamilton, Denver, Colo.
Women's singles—Katarina Witt, East Germany
Pairs—Barbara Underhill and Paul Martini, Canada
Dance—Jayne Torvill and Christopher Dean, Britain

SWIMMING

WORLD RECORDS—MEN

(Through Sept. 5, 1984)
Approved by the International Swimming Federation (F.I.N.A.)
(F.I.N.A. discontinued acceptance of records in yards in 1968)
Source: United States Swim Team.

Distance	Record	Holder	Country	Year made
Freestyle				
50 Meters	0:22.54	Robin Leamy	United States	1981
100 Meters	0:49.36	Rowdy Gaines	United States	1981
200 Meters	1:47.44	Michael Gross	West Germany	1984
400 Meters	3:48.32	Vladimir Salnikov	U.S.S.R.	1983
800 Meters	7:52.33	Vladimir Salnikov	U.S.S.R.	1983
1,500 Meters	14:54.76	Vladimir Salnikov	U.S.S.R.	1983
Backstroke				
100 Meters	0:55.19	Rick Carey	United States	1983
200 Meters	1:01.65	Sergey Zabolotnov	U.S.S.R.	1984
Breaststroke				
100 Meters	1:01.65	Steve Lundquist	United States	1984
200 Meters	2:13.34	Victor Davis	Canada	1984
Butterfly				
100 Meters	0:53.08	Michael Gross	West Germany	1984
200 Meters	1:57.04	John Sieben	Australia	1984
Individual Medley				
200 Meters	2:01.42	Alex Baumann	Canada	1984
400 Meters	4:17.41	Alex Baumann	Canada	1984
Freestyle Relays				
400 Meters	3:19.03	United States National Team	United States	1984
800 Meters	7:15.69	United States National Team	United States	1984
Medley Relay				
400 Meters	3:39.30	United States National Team	United States	1984

WORLD RECORDS—WOMEN

Distance	Record	Holder	Country	Year made
Freestyle				
50 Meters	0:25.61	Dara Torres	United States	1984
100 Meters	0:54.79	Barbara Krause	East Germany	1980
200 Meters	1:57.75	Kristin Otto	East Germany	1984
400 Meters	4:06.28	Tracy Wickham	Australia	1978
800 Meters	8:24.62	Tracy Wickham	Australia	1978
1,500 Meters	16:04.49	Kim Linehan	United States	1979
Backstroke				
100 Meters	1:00.59	Ina Kleber	East Germany	1984
200 Meters	2:09.91	Cornelia Sirch	East Germany	1982
Breaststroke				
100 Meters	1:08.29	Sylvia Gerasch	East Germany	1984
200 Meters	2:28.36	Lina Kachushite	U.S.S.R.	1979
Butterfly				
100 Meters	0:57.93	Mary T. Meagher	United States	1982
200 Meters	2:05.96	Mary T. Meagher	United States	1982

Individual Medley

200 Meters	2:11.73	Ute Geweniger	East Germany	1981
400 Meters	4:36.10	Petra Schneider	East Germany	1982

Freestyle

400 Meters	3:42.41	East German National Team	East Germany	1984
800 Meters	8:02.27	East German National Team	East Germany	1983

Medley Relay

400 Meters	4:05.79	East German National Team	East Germany	1983

U.S. SHORT-COURSE SWIMMING RECORDS

Source: United States Swim Team.

MEN

Freestyle

50 yards—Robin Leamy, 1981	0:19.36
100 yards—Rowdy Gaines, 1981	0:42.38
100 yards—Rowdy Gaines, 1980	0:43.16
100 yards—Andy Coan, 1979	0:43.25
100 yards—Jonty Skinner, 1978	0:43.29
100 yards—Joe Bottom, 1977	0:43.49
200 yards—Rowdy Gaines, 1981	1:33.80
200 yards—Rowdy Gaines, 1980	1:34.57
200 yards—Andy Coan, 1979	1:35.62
200 yards—Jim Montgomery, 1977	1:35.67
500 yards—George DiCarlo, 1984	4:15.36
500 yards—Brian Goodell, 1978	4:16.40
500 yards—Brian Goodell, 1979	4:16.43
1,000 yards—Jeff Kostoff, 1983	8:48.57
1,000 yards—Jeff Kostoff, 1982	8:49.97
1,650 yards—Jeff Kostoff, 1984	14:38.22
1,650 yards—Brian Goodell, 1979	14:47.27
1,650 yards—Rafael Escalas, 1981	14:53.90
1,650 yards—Brian Goodell, 1979	14:54.13
1,650 yards—Brian Goodell, 1978	14:54.54

Backstroke

100 yards—Rick Carey, 1983	0:48.25
100 yards—Dave Bottom, 1982	0:48.94
200 yards—Rick Carey, 1983	1:44.43
200 yards—Wladar Sandor, 1982	1:45.22

Breaststroke

100 yards—Steve Lundquist, 1983	0:52.48
100 yards—Steve Lundquist, 1980	0:53.59
100 yards—Steve Lundquist, 1979	0:54.08
100 yards—Graham Smith, 1977	0:54.91
100 yards—Scott Spann, 1977	0:55.19
200 yards—Steve Lundquist, 1981	1:55.01
200 yards—Bill Barrett, 1980	1:58.43
200 yards—Steve Lundquist, 1979	1:59.18
200 yards—Graham Smith, 1977	2:00.05
200 yards—Nick Nevid, 1978	2:00.53

Butterfly

100 yards—Pablo Morales, 1984	0:47.02
100 yards—Scott Spann, 1981	0:47.22
100 yards—Par Arvidsson, 1980	0:47.34
100 yards—Par Arvidsson, 1979	0:47.76
100 yards—Joe Bottom, 1977	0:47.77
200 yards—Craig Beardsley, 1982	1:43.81
200 yards—Craig Beardsley, 1982	1:44.10
200 yards—Craig Beardsley, 1981	1:44.15
200 yards—Par Arvidsson, 1980	1:44.43

Individual Medley

200 yards—Bill Barrett, 1982	1:45.00
200 yards—Bill Barrett, 1981	1:45.01
400 yards—Pat Kennedy, 1984	3:47.79
400 yards—Ricardo Prado, 1982	3:47.97

Relays

200-yard freestyle—Mission Viejo, 1981	1:18.55
400-yard freestyle—U.C.L.A., 1982	2:53.15
400-yard freestyle—Mission Viejo, 1981	2:53.86
400-yard freestyle—Tennessee, 1979	2:54.54
400-yard freestyle—Gatorade S.C., 1978	2:55.27
800-yard freestyle—Florida Aquatic Club, 1979	6:25.42
800-yard freestyle—Auburn, 1981	6:26.49
800-yard freestyle—Florida A.C., 1978	6:29.81
400-yard medley—S.M.U., 1983	3:12.63
400-yard medley—Texas, 1981	3:12.93
400-yard medley—California-Berkeley, 1979	3:15.22 [1]
400-yard medley—Indiana, 1977	3:17.14 [1]
400-yard medley—Auburn, 1977	3:17.62

WOMEN

Freestyle

50 yards—Tammy Thomas, 1983	0:22.13
50 yards—Jill Sterkel, 1981	0:22.41
100 yards—Tammy Thomas, 1983	0:48.40
100 yards—Jill Sterkel, 1982	0:48.61
100 yards—Jill Sterkel, 1980	0:48.76
100 yards—Cynthia Woodhead, 1979	0:49.39
100 yards—Jill Sterkel, 1979	0:49.55
100 yards—Tracy Caulkins, 1978	0:49.58
200 yards—Cynthia Woodhead, 1979	1:44.10
200 yards—Marybeth Linzmeier, 1982	1:45.82
500 yards—Tracy Caulkins, 1979	4:36.25
500 yards—Cynthia Woodhead, 1978	4:39.94
1000 yards—Kim Linehan, 1981	9:29.91
1,650 yards—Tiffany Cohen, 1983	15:46.54
1,650 yards—Kim Linehan, 1979	15:49.10

Backstroke

100 yards—Sue Walsh, 1983	0:54.74
100 yards—Sue Walsh, 1982	0:54.81
200 yards—Tracy Caulkins, 1981	1:57.02

Breaststroke

100 yards—Tracy Caulkins, 1981	1:01.13
100 yards—Tracy Caulkins, 1979	1:01.82
100 yards—Tracy Caulkins, 1979	1:02.06
100 yards—Tracy Caulkins, 1978	1:02.20
200 yards—Tracy Caulkins, 1980	2:11.46
200 yards—Tracy Caulkins, 1978	2:14.07

Butterfly

100 yards—Jill Sterkel, 1981	0:52.99
100 yards—Mary T. Meagher, 1980	0:53.18
100 yards—Jill Sterkel, 1979	0:53.76
100 yards—Diane Johannigman, 1978	0:54.11
200 yards—Mary T. Meagher, 1981	1:52.99

Individual Medley

200 yards—Tracy Caulkins, 1984	1:57.06
200 yards—Tracy Caulkins, 1979	1:57.86
200 yards—Tracy Caulkins, 1978	1:59.33
400 yards—Tracy Caulkins, 1981	4:04.63
400 yards—Tracy Caulkins, 1979	4:08.04

Relays

200-yard freestyle—Stanford, 1981	1:31.12
400-yard freestyle—Florida, 1984	3:18.52
400-yard freestyle—Stanford, 1981	3:19.70
400-yard freestyle—Nashville A.C., 1979	3:20.51
400-yard freestyle—Nashville A.C., 1978	3:20.69
800-yard freestyle—Florida, 1984	7:06.98
800-yard freestyle—Mission Viejo S.C., 1979	7:15.14
800-yard freestyle—U.S. Team, 1976	7:15.64
200-yard medley—Florida, 1982	1:42.10
400-yard medley—Florida, 1982	3:40.99

1. Open American record by non-U.S. competitors.

U.S. INDOOR CHAMPIONSHIPS—1984

(Short-Course Championships not held in Olympic Years)
(Indianapolis, Ind., March 27–31, 1984)

Men's Events

50-m freestyle—Robin Leamy, Rancho Palosverde, Calif.	0:22.90
100-m freestyle—Rowdy Gaines, Winter Haven, Fla.	0:50.23
200-m freestyle—Mike Heath, Dallas, Tex.	1:50.18
400-m freestyle—Gary Brinkman, South Africa	3:55.27
800-m freestyle—Jeff Kostoff, Upland, Calif.	8:02.60
1,500-m freestyle—Jeff Kostoff, Upland, Calif.	15:25.25
100-m backstroke—Dave Wilson, Cincinnati, Ohio	0:56.89
200-m backstroke—Jesse Vassallo, Miami, Fla.	2:01.48
100-m breaststroke—John Moffit, Costa Mesa, Calif.	1:03.15
200-m breaststroke—Doug Soltis, Tarpon Springs, Fla.	2:19.84
100-m butterfly—Pablo Morales, Santa Clara, Calif.	0:53.91
200-m butterfly—Craig Beardsley, Harrington Park, N.J.	1:58.77
200-m individual medley—Bill Barrett, Los Angeles, Calif.	2:03.23
400-m individual medley—Matt Rankin, Portland, Ore.	4:24.56
400-m freestyle relay—Florida Aquatic Swim Team	3:22.58
800-m freestyle relay—Florida Aquatic Swim Team	7:26.49
400-m medley relay—Florida Aquatic Swim Team	3:47.40
Team champion: 1. Mission Viejo.	447 pts
2. Florida Aquatic Swim Team.	394 pts
3. Bruin Swim Association.	392 pts

Women's Events

50-m freestyle—Dara Torres, Mission Viejo, Calif.	0:25.88
100-m freestyle—Nancy Hogshead, Jacksonville, Fla.	0:55.99
200-m freestyle—Mary T. Meagher, Louisville, Ky.	2:00.91
400-m freestyle—Tiffany Cohen, Mission Viejo, Calif.	4:08.47
800-m freestyle—Tiffany Cohen, Mission Viejo, Calif.	8:28.39
1,500-m freestyle—Michele Richardson, Miami, Fla.	16:12.57
100-m backstroke—Betsy Mitchell, Marietta, Ohio	1:02.88
200-m backstroke—Amy White, Mission Viejo, Calif.	2:14.91
100-m breaststroke—Jeanne Childs, Denver, Col.	1:10.94
200-m breaststroke—Jeanne Childs, Denver, Col.	2:35.26
100-m butterfly—Mary T. Meagher, Louisville, Ky.	0:59.93
200-m butterfly—Mary T. Meagher, Louisville, Ky.	2:07.87
200-m individual medley—Tracy Caulkins, Nashville, Tenn.	2:15.26
400-m individual medley—Channon Hermstad, Mission Viejo	4:49.03
400-m freestyle relay—Concord-Pleasant Hills	3:47.57
800-m freestyle relay—Mission Viejo	8:11.44
400-m medley relay—Mission Viejo	4:13.50
Team champion: 1. Mission Viejo.	795.5 pts
2. Concord-Pleasant Hills.	259.5 pts
3. Florida Aquatic Swim Team.	232 pts

U.S. LONG-COURSE CHAMPIONSHIPS

(Fort Lauderdale, Fla., Aug. 14–18, 1984)

Men's Events

50-m freestyle—Mark Stockwell, Australia	0:22.83
100-m freestyle—Mark Stockwell, Australia	0:50.38
200-m freestyle—Bruce Hayes, Dallas, Tex.	1:51.39
400-m freestyle—Matt Cetlinski, Lake Worth, Fla.	3:51.43
800-m freestyle—John Mykkanen, Placentia, Calif.	7:58.24[1]
1,500-m freestyle—John Mykkanen, Placentia, Calif.	15:22.10
100-m backstroke—Dan Veatch, Rockville, Md.	0:57.17
200-m backstroke—Dan Veatch, Rockville, Md.	2:03.43
100-m breaststroke—Bob Jackson, Tacoma, Wash.	1:03.46
200-m breaststroke—Brett Beedle, Los Altos, Calif.	2:18.73
100-m butterfly—Duffy Dillon, Fort Lauderdale, Fla.	0:54.81
200-m butterfly—Chris Rives, Houston, Tex.	2:07.05
200-m individual medley—Duffy Dillon, Fort Lauderdale, Fla.	2:04.51
400-m individual medley—Rob Woodhouse, Australia	4:19.97
400-m freestyle relay—Holmes Lumber Gators	3:25.24
800-m freestyle relay—Holmes Lumber Gators	7:26.26
400-m medley relay—Holmes Lumber Gators	3:39.46
Team champion: 1. Holmes Lumber Gators.	454 pts
2. Mission Viejo.	258 pts
3. Cincinnati Pepsi Marlins.	170 pts

Women's Events

50-m freestyle—Jenna Johnson, Lahabre, Calif.	0:26.09
100-m freestyle—Jenna Johnson, Lahabre, Calif.	0:53.36
200-m freestyle—Michelle Pearson, Australia	2:00.65
400-m freestyle—Michele Richardson, Miami, Fla.	4:11.40
800-m freestyle—Tami Bruce, San Diego, Calif.	8:34.77
1,500-m freestyle—Michele Richardson, Miami, Fla.	16.18.80
100-m backstroke—Susan O'Brien, Rockville, Md.	1:03.05
200-m backstroke—Amy White, Mission Viejo	2:14.95
100-m breaststroke—Terri Baxster, Concord, Calif.	1:12.27
200-m breaststroke—Polly Winde, Ellicot City, Md.	2:35.51
100-m butterfly—Jenna Johnson, Lahabre, Calif.	0:59.25
200-m butterfly—Erika Hansen, King of Prussia, Pa.	2:12.08
200-m individual medley—Michelle Pearson, Australia	2:16.07
400-m individual medley—Erika Hansen, King of Prussia, Pa.	4:45.58
400-m freestyle relay—Cincinnati Pepsi Marlins	3:52.11
800-m freestyle relay—Mission Viejo	8:19.58
400-m medley relay—Cincinnati Pepsi Marlins	4:17.17
Team champions: 1. Mission Viejo.	385 pts
2. Cincinnati Pepsi Marlins.	209 pts
3. Holmes Lumber Gators.	74 pts

1. American Record.

U.S. DIVING CHAMPIONSHIPS—1984

INDOOR

(Gainesville, Fla., April 10–14, 1984)

Men's Events	Pts
1-meter—Greg Louganis, Mission Viejo, Calif.	659.16
3-meter—Greg Louganis	643.86

Platform—Bruce Kimball, Ann Arbor, Mich. 622.14
Hight point winner—Bruce Kimball
Team—Mission Viejo

Women's Events

1-meter—Megan Neyer, Mission Viejo, Calif. 459.27
3-meter—Kelly McCormick, Columbus, Ohio 529.50
Platform—Wendy Nyland, Mission Viejo, Calif. 406.62
High point winner—none
Team—Mission Viejo

OUTDOOR
(Santa Clara, Calif., Aug. 21-25, 1984)
Men's Events

1-meter—Greg Louganis, Mission Viejo, Calif. 663.09
3-meter—Greg Louganis 7:07.01
Platform—Greg Louganis[1] 6.83.19
Team—Mission Viejo

1. Louganis set American record with 29 national titles in this event.

Women's Events

1-meter—Wendy Lucero, Denver. Col. 460.53
3-meter—Wendy Williams, Mission Viejo, Calif. 449.61
Platform—Michelle Mitchell, Mission Viejo, Calif. 432.78
Team—Mission Viejo, Calif.

NATIONAL COLLEGIATE ATHLETIC ASSOCIATION

(Cleveland, Ohio, March 22-24, 1984)

Division I

50-yd freestyle—Tom Jager, U.C.L.A.	0:19.55
100-yd freestyle—Tom Jager	0:42.85
200-yd freestyle—Mike Heath, Florida	1:35.21
500-yd freestyle—George DiCarlo, Arizona	4:15.36[1]
1,650-yd freestyle—Jeff Kostoff, Stanford	14:38.22[1]
100-yd backstroke—Rick Carey, Texas	0:48.63
200-yd backstroke—Rick Carey, Texas	1:44.82
100-yd breaststroke—John Moffet, Stanford	0:54.38
200-yd breaststroke—John Moffet	1:57.99
100-yd butterfly—Pablo Morales, Stanford	0:47.02[1]
200-yd butterfly—Pablo Morales	1:44.33
200-yd individual medley—Ricardo Prado, SMU	1:47.95
400-yd individual medley—Ricardo Prado	3:46.86
400-yd freestyle relay—U.C.L.A.	2:54.11
800-yd freestyle relay—Florida	6:21.29[1]
400-yd medley relay—Texas	3:13.35
1-m dive—Matt Scoggins, Texas	528.85 pts
3-m dive—Kent Ferguson, Michigan	560.85 pts
Team—Florida	287 1/2 pts

1. American record.

NATIONAL COLLEGIATE ATHLETIC ASSOCIATION WOMEN'S CHAMPIONSHIPS

(Indianapolis, Ind., March 15-17, 1984)

50-yd freestyle—Krissie Bush, Stanford	0:22.98
100-yd freestyle—Agneta Eriksson, Texas	0:49.63
200-yd freestyle—Marybeth Linzmeter, Stanford	1:45.47
500-yd freestyle—Marybeth Linzmeter	4:38.91
1,650-yd freestyle—Marybeth Linzmeter	16:02.38
100-yd backstroke—Sue Walsh, North Carolina	0:55.32
200-yd backstroke—Sue Walsh	1:59.84
100-yd breaststroke—Tracy Caulkins, Florida	1:01.37
200-yd breaststroke—Susan Rapp, Stanford	2:12.84
100-yd butterfly—Joan Pennington, Texas	0:53.70
200-yd butterfly—Tracy Caulkins, Florida	1:55.55
200-yd individual medley—Tracy Caulkins	1:57.06[1]
400-yd individual medley—Tracy Caulkins	4:08.37
200-yd freestyle relay—Texas	1:31.95
400-yd freestyle relay—Florida	3:18.52[1]
800-yd freestyle relay—Florida	7:06.98[1]
200-yd medley relay—Stanford	1:42.81
400-yd medley relay—Texas	3:41.80
1-m dive—Megan Neyer, Florida	450.40 pts
3-m dive—Megan Neyer	498.05 pts
Team—Texas	392 pts

1. American record.

NATIONAL ASSOCIATION OF INTERCOLLEGIATE ATHLETICS—1984

(Arkadelphia, Ark., March 1-3, 1984)

50-m freestyle—Gerald Kollross, Wisconsin-LaCrosse	0:20.77
100-m freestyle—Gerald Kollross	0:45.70
200-m freestyle—Greg Remmert, Denver	1:41.19
500-m freestyle—Eugene Gyorfi, Simon Fraser	4:31.22
1,650-m freestyle—Eugene Gyorfi	15:52.05
100-m backstroke—Ron Staab, Drury	0:51.50
200-m backstroke—John Sayre, Central Washington	1:52.05
100-m breaststroke—John Sayre	0:57.70
200-m breaststroke—John Bryant, Central Washington	2:07.39
100-m butterfly—Kurt Keuser, Drury	0:50.00
200-m butterfly—Eric Hooyschuur, Hendrix	1:52.18
200-m individual medley—John Sayre	1:52.94
400-m individual medley—Alain Steenbeeke, Denver	4:06.38
400-m freestyle relay—Central Washington	3:04.45
800-m freestyle relay—Simon Fraser	6:53.30
1-m dive—Kip Strate, Drury	450.10 pts
Team—Central Washington	292 pts

PLATFORM TENNIS

UNITED STATES CHAMPIONS—1984

American Platform Tennis Association

Open singles* (New York City, April 7-8, 1984)—Bob Kleinert, New York City, defeated Doug Russell, New York City, 6-4, 6-7, 6-1 in final

Men's doubles (Cleveland, Ohio, March 10-11, 1984)—Bob Kleinert and Doug Russell, New York City, defeated Steve Baird, Harrison, N.Y., and Rich Maier, Nyack, N.Y., 3-6, 5-7, 7-5, 6-3, 6-2 in final

Women's doubles (Cleveland, Ohio, March 10-11, 1984)—Robin Fulton, Norwalk, Conn., and Yvonne Hackenberg, Kalamazoo, Mich., defeated Pat Butterfield, Stamford, Conn., and Diane Tucker, Bedford, N.Y., 6-1, 7-5 in final

Mixed doubles (March 24-25, 1984)—Robin Fulton, Norwalk, Conn., and Tom Smith, Nyack, N.Y., defeated Muffin Slonaker, Summit, N.J., and Bob Kleinert, New York City, 2-6, 6-4, 6-2 in final

*Open is for men and women.

PADDLE TENNIS

Source: Murray Geller, Executive Secretary, U.S. Paddle Tennis Association.

NATIONAL OPEN CHAMPIONSHIPS—1984

(Venice Beach, Calif., May 19-20, 1984)

Men's singles—Mark Rifenbark, Los Angeles
Women's singles—Kathy Paben, Los Angeles

GYMNASTICS

WORLD CHAMPIONSHIPS—1983

(Budapest, Hungary, Oct. 23–30, 1983)

Men's Events

	Pts
All-around—Dimitri Belozerchev, Soviet Union	119.200
Floor exercises—Tong Fei, China	19.9
Pommel horse—Dimitri Belozerchev, Soviet Union	20.0
Still rings—Tie: Dimitri Belozerchev, Soviet Union, Koji Gushiken, Japan	19.925
Parallel bars—Tie: Lou Yun, China, Vladimir Astemov, Soviet Union	19.95
Vault—Artour Akopien, Soviet Union	19.875
Horizontal bars—Dimitri Belozerchev, Soviet Union	19.85
Team—China	591.45

Women's Events

	Pts
All-around—Natalia Iourcherlco, Soviet Union	79.35
Floor exercises—Ecaterina Szebo, Romania	19.975
Balance beam—Olga Mostepanova, Soviet Union	19.775
Uneven parallel bars—Maxi Gnauck, East Germany	19.925
Vault—Boriana Stoyanova, Bulgaria	19.825
Team—Soviet Union	393.45

NATIONAL COLLEGIATE ATHLETIC ASSOCIATION

Men's Division I

(Los Angeles, Calif., April 14, 1984)

	Pts
All-around—Mitch Gaylord, U.C.L.A.	116.95
Floor exercise—Kevin Ekburg, Northern Illinois	9.85
Pommel horse—Tim Daggett, U.C.L.A.	9.9
Still rings—Tim Daggett, U.C.L.A.	9.8
Vault—Chris Riegel, Nebraska	10.0
Horizontal bars—Charles Lakes, Illinois	9.95
Parallel bars—Tim Daggett, U.C.L.A.	9.7
Team—U.C.L.A.	285.05

Women's Division I

(Los Angeles, Calif., April 6, 1984)

	Pts
All around—Megan Marsden, Utah	37.9
Balance beam—Heidi Anderson, Oregon State	9.7
Floor exercise—Maria Anz, Florida	9.7
Vault—Megan Marsden, Utah	9.575
Uneven parallel bars—Jackie Brummer, Arizona St.	9.7
Team—Utah	186.05

UNITED STATES CHAMPIONSHIPS—1984

(Evanston, Ill., May 5–12, 1984)

Men's Events

	Pts
All-around—Mitch Gaylord, Van Nuys, Calif.	117.85
Floor exercise—Peter Vidmar, Los Angeles, Calif.	9.7
Horizontal bars—Peter Vidmar and Tim Daggett, West Springfield, Mass.	9.95
Still rings—Mitch Gaylord	9.9
Pommel horse—Tim Daggett	9.95
Parallel bars—Peter Vidmar and Tim Daggett	9.8
Vault—Chris Riegel, Reading, Pa.	9.7

Women's Events

	Pts
All-around—Mary Lou Retton, Houston, Texas	77.02
Floor exercise—Mary Lou Retton	10.0
Balance beam—Pam Bileck, San Jose, Calif., and Tracy Talavera, Walnut Creek, Calif.	9.8
Vault—Mary Lou Retton	9.85
Uneven parallel bars—Julianne McNamara, San Ramon, Calif.	9.95

WORLD CUP

(Zagneb, Yugoslavia, Oct. 20–24, 1982)

Men's Events

	Pts
All-around—Ning Li, China	59.45
Floor exercise—Ning Li, China	19.80
Horizontal bar—Fei Tong, China	19.90
Still rings—Ning Li, China	19.80
Pommel horse—Ning Li, China	19.85
Parallel bars—Yori Korolev, Soviet Union	19.80
Vault—Ning Li, China	197.20

Women's Events

	Pts
All-around—Tie, Olga Bicherova, Soviet Union, and Natalia Jurchenko, Soviet Union	39.95
Floor exercise—Olga Bicherova, Soviet Union	19.80
Balance beam—Natalia Jurchenko, Soviet Union	19.80
Vault—Stella Zakhavrova, Soviet Union	19.70
Uneven parallel bars—Maxi Gnauck, East Germany	19.85

DUCKPIN BOWLING

NATIONAL CHAMPIONSHIPS—1984

(Baltimore, Md., April 28-May 27, 1984)

National Duckpin Bowling Congress

Men's singles—Frank Frieman, Salisbury, Md.	580
Women's singles—Mary Fran Kinzey, Columbia, Md.	548
Men's doubles—Jim Berube, Rhode Island, and Jeff Farrand, Salisbury, Md	1,054
Women's doubles—Laurie Gardner and Debbie Page, Charlotte Hall, Md.	884
Mixed doubles—Pat Malthan and Butch Banon, Towson, Md.	935
Class A Teams—Jeff Farrand Eastwood Trophies, Salisbury, Md.	2,229
Class B Teams—Bowl America Westwood, Bethesda, Md.	1,912
Class C Teams—Bowl America Westwood, Bethesda, Md.	935

BOXING

Whether it be called pugilism, prize fighting or boxing, there is no tracing "the Sweet Science" to any definite source. Tales of rivals exchanging blows for fun, fame or money go back to earliest recorded history and classical legend. There was a mixture of boxing and wrestling called the "pancratium" in the ancient Olympic Games and in such contests the rivals belabored one another with hands fortified with heavy leather wrappings that were sometimes studded with metal. More than one Olympic competitor lost his life at this brutal exercise.

There was little law or order in pugilism until Jack Broughton, one of the early champions of England, drew up a set of rules for the game in 1743. Broughton, called "the father of English boxing," also is credited with having invented boxing gloves. However, these gloves—or "mufflers" as they were called—were used only in teaching "the manly art of self-defense" or in training bouts. All professional championship fights were contested with "bare knuckles" until 1892, when John L. Sullivan lost the heavyweight championship of the world to James J. Corbett in New Orleans in a bout in which both contestants wore regulation gloves.

The Broughton rules were superseded by the London Prize Ring Rules of 1838. The 8th Marquis of Queensberry, with the help of John G. Chambers, put forward the "Queensberry Rules" in 1866, a code that called for gloved contests. Amateurs took quickly to the Queensberry Rules, the professionals slowly.

HISTORY OF WORLD HEAVYWEIGHT CHAMPIONSHIP FIGHTS

(Bouts in which a new champion was crowned)

Source: Nat Fleischer's Ring *Boxing Encyclopedia and Record Book*, published and copyrighted by The Ring Book Shop, Inc., 120 West 31st St., New York, N.Y. 10001.

Date	Where held	Winner, weight, age	Loser, weight, age	Rounds	Referee
Sept. 7, 1892	New Orleans, La.	James J. Corbett, 178 (26)	John L. Sullivan, 212 (33)	21	Prof. John Duffy
March 17, 1897	Carson City, Nev.	Bob Fitzsimmons, 167 (34)	James J. Corbett, 183 (30)	KO 14	George Siler
June 9, 1899	Coney Island, N.Y.	James J. Jeffries, 206 (24)[1]	Bob Fitzsimmons, 167 (37)	KO 11	George Siler
Feb. 23, 1906	Los Angeles	Tommy Burns, 180 (24)[2]	Marvin Hart, 188 (29)	20	James J. Jeffries
Dec. 26, 1908	Sydney, N.S.W.	Jack Johnson, 196 (30)	Tommy Burns, 176 (27)	KO 14	Hugh McIntosh
April 5, 1915	Havana, Cuba	Jess Willard, 230 (33)	Jack Johnson, 205 1/2 (37)	KO 26	Jack Welch
July 4, 1919	Toledo, Ohio	Jack Dempsey, 187 (24)	Jess Willard, 245 (37)	KO 3	Ollie Pecord
Sept. 23, 1926	Philadelphia	Gene Tunney, 189 (28)[3]	Jack Dempsey, 190 (31)	10	Pop Reilly
June 12, 1930	New York	Max Schmeling, 188 (24)	Jack Sharkey, 197 (27)	WF 4	Jim Crowley
June 21, 1932	Long Island City	Jack Sharkey, 205 (29)	Max Schmeling, 188 (26)	15	Gunboat Smith
June 29, 1933	Long Island City	Primo Carnera, 260 1/2 (26)	Jack Sharkey, 201 (30)	KO 6	Arthur Donovan
June 14, 1934	Long Island City	Max Baer, 209 1/2 (25)	Primo Carnera, 263 1/4 (27)	KO 11	Arthur Donovan
June 13, 1935	Long Island City	Jim Braddock, 193 3/4 (29)	Max Baer, 209 1/2 (26)	15	Jack McAvoy
June 22, 1937	Chicago	Joe Louis, 197 1/4 (23)	Jim Braddock, 197 (31)	KO 8	Tommy Thomas
June 22, 1949	Chicago	Ezzard Charles, 181 3/4 (27)[4]	Joe Walcott, 195 1/2 (35)	15	Davey Miller
Sept. 27, 1950	New York	Ezzard Charles, 184 1/2 (29)[5]	Joe Louis, 218 (36)	15	Mark Conn
July 18, 1951	Pittsburgh	Joe Walcott, 194 (37)	Ezzard Charles, 182 (30)	KO 7	Buck McTiernan
Sept. 23, 1952	Philadelphia	Rocky Marciano, 184 (29)[6]	Joe Walcott, 196 (38)	KO 13	Charley Daggert
Nov. 30, 1956	Chicago	Floyd Patterson, 182 1/4 (21)	Archie Moore, 187 3/4 (42)	KO 5	Frank Sikora
June 26, 1959	New York	Ingemar Johansson, 196 (26)	Floyd Patterson, 182 (24)	KO 3	Ruby Goldstein
June 20, 1960	New York	Floyd Patterson, 190 (25)	Ingemar Johansson, 194 3/4 (27)	KO 5	Arthur Mercante
Sept. 25, 1962	Chicago	Sonny Liston, 214 (28)	Floyd Patterson, 189 (27)	KO 1	Frank Sikora
Feb. 25, 1964	Miami Beach, Fla.	Cassius Clay, 210 (22)[7]	Sonny Liston, 218 (30)	KO 7	Barney Felix
March 4, 1968	New York	Joe Frazier, 204 1/2 (24)[8]	Buster Mathis, 243 1/2 (23)	KO 11	Arthur Mercante
April 27, 1968	Oakland, Calif.	Jimmy Ellis, 197 (28)[9]	Jerry Quarry, 195 (22)	15	Elmer Costa
Feb. 16, 1970	New York	Joe Frazier, 205 (26)[10]	Jimmy Ellis, 201 (29)	KO 5	Tony Perez
Jan. 22, 1973	Kingston, Jamaica	George Foreman, 217 1/2 (24)	Joe Frazier, 214 (29)	KO 2	Arthur Mercante
Oct. 30, 1974	Kinshasa, Zaire	Muhammad Ali, 216 1/2 (32)	George Foreman, 220 (26)	KO 8	Zack Clayton
Feb. 15, 1978	Las Vegas, Nev.	Leon Spinks, 197 (25)	Muhammad Ali, 224 1/2 (36)	15	Howard Buck
June 9, 1978	Las Vegas, Nev.	Larry Holmes, 212 (28)[11]	Ken Norton, 220 (32)	15	Mills Lans
Sept. 15, 1978	New Orleans	Muhammad Ali, 221 (36)[12]	Leon Spinks, 201 (25)	15	Lucien Joubert
Oct. 20, 1979	Pretoria, S. Africa	John Tate, 240 (24)[13]	Gerrie Coetzee, 222 (24)	15	Carlos Berrocal
March 31, 1980	Knoxville, Tenn.	Mike Weaver, 207 1/2 (27)	John Tate, 232 (25)	KO 15	Ernesto Magana Ansorena
Dec. 10, 1982	Las Vegas, Nev.	Michael Dokes, 216 (24)	Mike Weaver, 209 1/2 (30)	KO 1	Joey Curtis
Sept. 23, 1983	Richfield, Ohio	Gerrie Coetzee, 215 (28)	Michael Dokes, 217 (25)	KO 10	Tony Perez
March 9, 1984	Las Vegas, Nev.	Tim Witherspoon, 220 1/2 (26)[14]	Greg Page, 239 1/2 (25)	12	
August 31, 1984	Las Vegas, Nev.	Pinklon Thomas, 216 (26)	Tim Witherspoon, 217 (26)	12	Richard Steele

1. Jeffries retired as champion in March 1905. He named Marvin Hart and Jack Root as leading contenders and agreed to referee their fight in Reno, Nev., on July 3, 1905, with the stipulation that he would term the winner the champion. Hart, 190 (28), knocked out Root, 171 (29), in the 12th round. 2. Burns claimed the title after defeating Hart. 3. Tunney retired as champion after defeating Tom Heeney on July 26, 1928. 4. After Louis announced his retirement as champion on March 1, 1949, Charles won recognition from the National Boxing Association as champion by defeating Walcott. 5. Charles gained undisputed recognition as champion by defeating Louis, who came out of retirement. 6. Retired as champion April 27, 1956. 7. The World Boxing Association later withdrew its recognition of Clay as champion and declared the winner of a bout between

Ernie Terrell and Eddie Machen would gain its version of the title. Terrell, 199 (25), won a 15-round decision from Machen, 192 (32), in Chicago on March 5, 1965. Clay, 212 1/4 (25) and Terrell, 212 1/2 (27) met in Houston on Feb. 6, 1967, Clay winning a 15-round decision. 8. Winner recognized by New York, Massachusetts, Maine, Illinois, Texas and Pennsylvania to fill vacated title when Clay was stripped of championship for failing to accept U. S. Induction. 9. Bout was final of eight-man tournament to fill Clay's place and is recognized by World Boxing Association. 10. Bout settled controversy over title. 11. Holmes won World Boxing Council title after WBC had withdrawn recognition of Spinks, March 18, 1978, and awarded its title to Norton, WBC, said Spinks had reneged on agreement to fight Norton 12. Ali regained World Boxing Association championship. 13. Tate won WBA title after Ali retired and left it vacant. 14. Tim Witherspoon and Greg Page fought for the WBC heavyweight title vacated by Larry Holmes, who could not come to agreement on a deal to fight Page, the No. 1 contender. Holmes declared he would fight under the banner of the International Boxing Federation. Several dates were set and postponed for fights between Holmes and Gerry Coetzee, the WBA champ, the latest being Nov. 16, 1984.

CHAMPIONSHIP BOUTS—1984

(Through Sept. 15, 1984)

Junior Flyweight

(108 pound limit)

Junhkoo Chang of South Korea retained his World Boxing Council championship by stopping Japan's Katsuo Tokashiki in the ninth round of a bout held in Pohang, South Korea.

Francisco Quiroz of the Dominican Republic defended his World Boxing Association title on August 18 in Panama City with a second round knockout of Victor Sierra of Panama.

The World Boxing Council (WBC) refers to this division as Light Flyweight.

Flyweight

(112 pound limit)

Candido Teller registered a third round knockout of Ian Clyde on January 18 to retain his American Boxing Federation title. Teller knocked out Clyde with a hard left with 2:22 remaining in the third round.

Gabriel Bernal defeated Koji Kobayashy with a second round knockout on April 4 to capture the WBC crown. Kobayashi was the defending champion, having knocked out Frank Cedeno in the second round of their fight in January in Tokyo.

Santos Benigno Laciar retained the WBA crown with a 15-round split decision over Juan Herrera in January in Marsala, Italy.

Super Flyweight

(115 pound limit)

Payao Pooltarat of Thailand registered a technical knockout of Gustavo Espadas of Mexico to retain the WBC title on March 28. Jiro Watanabe of Japan is the reigning WBA champion.

Junior Bantamweight

(115 pound limit)

WBA champion Jiro Watanabe defended his title on March 17 with a 15th round knockout of Celso Chavez in Osaka, Japan. On July 28, he captured the undisputed championship when he won a split decision over WBC super flyweight Payao Pooltarat.

Chun Choo Do of South Korea won the International Boxing Federation version of the title on May 26 with a unanimous decision over Felix Marquez

Bantamweight

(118 pound limit)

Jeff Chandler retained his WBA championship on Dec. 17, 1983, with a seventh round knockout of Oscar Muniuz. Chandler opened a cut over Muniuz's left eye in the second round and kept working on it until the fight was called with 23 seconds remaining in the seventh.

The title was not Chandler's for long, however. On April 28, Richie Sandoval won the title from Chandler with a 15th round technical knockout.

Albert Davila's 11th round knockout of Enrique Sanchez in Miami Beach retained for him the WBC title.

Junior Featherweight (Super Bantamweight)

(122 pound limit)

Jaime Garza captured the W.B.C. title on Nov. 17, 1983 with a fifth round knockout of Bteo Perez in Los Angeles.

Loris Stecca won the WBA crown with a 12th round technical knockout of Leo Cruz in Milan, Italy.

Featherweight

(128 pound limit)

Wilfred Gomez won the WBC title on March 31, dethroning defending champion Juan LaPorte in a unanimous decision. Gomez took control of the fight in the sixth round with a series of rights and lefts to the head and body in the 12-round boat in San Juan.

Eusebo Pedroza defended the W.B.A. version of the title with a knockout of Gerald Heges (cq) on June 23. The knockout came with 41 seconds remaining in the 12-round fight.

The title defense was the second for Pedroza in less than a month. On May 27 he defended his title by decisioning Angel Mayor of Venezuela. Pedroza had now defended his title successfully 19 times.

Junior Lightweight

(130 pound limit)

Rocky Lockridge knocked out Roger Mayweather 1:31 into the first round to win the W.B.A. championship. Lockridge hit Mayweather with an overhand right to record the victory in Beaumont, Texas.

Hector Comacho knocked out Royard Solls (cq) in the fifth round on Nov. 18, 1983 to capture the WBC championship.

Lockridge defended his WBA title on June 12, knocking out Tae-Jin Moon of South Korea 31 seconds into the 11th round in Anchorage, Alaska.

Lightweight

(135 pound limit)

Ray "Boom Boom" Mancini retained his title in Reno, Nev., with a knockout of Bobby Chacon 1:17 into the third round of the WBA title bout on Jan. 4. Later in the year, however, Mancini was upset by Livingston Bramble, who recorded a 14th-round technical knockout of Mancini on June 1 in Buffalo, N.Y.

Edwin Rosario of Puerto Rico defended his WBC title with a first-round knockout of Roberto Elizondo on March 17. Elizondo went down just 1:57 into the first round in San Juan.

Rosario defended his title successfully again on June 23, taking a split decision from Howard Davis, Jr. A left hook by Rosario knocked Davis down in the final round with 15 seconds remaining and saved the fight for the defending champ in San Juan.

Harry Arroyo took the International Boxing Federation's title on April 15, knocking out Charlie "Choo Choo" Brown at 2:07 of the 15th and final round. Arroyo defended that title on Sept. 1 with another knockout—this time 41 seconds into the eighth round against

Junior Welterweight (Super Lightweight)

(140 pound limit)

Johnny Bumphus took a 15-round unanimous decision from Lorenzo Garcia in the WBA title bout Jan. 18 in Atlantic City, in a title fight for the crown left vacant by the temporary retirement of Aaron Pryor. On June 1, however, Gene Hatcher took the title away from Bumphus, with a knockout 2:35 into the 11th round in Buffalo.

Pryor, meanwhile, decided to come out of retirement and fight under the banner of the International Boxing Federation, the same group that took in Larry Holmes when he vacated his title as heavyweight champ in December 1983.

Pryor was victorious in his return, taking a 15-round unanimous decision from Nicky Furlano.

Billy Costello won the WBC title, called the super lightweight championship, from Bruce Curry on Jan. 29, when he recorded a 10th-round knockout in a scheduled 12-round bout.

On July 15, Costello retained his title with a 12-round decision over Ronnie Shields in Kingston, N.Y. Costello has a record of 28-0, 17 by knockout.

Welterweight

(147 pound limit)

Milton McCrory retained his WBC title in January with a sixth-round knockout of Milton Guest in Sterling Heights, Mich. On April 15, he defended it again, this time knocking out Gilles Elbilia of France in the sixth round.

Don Curry took a 15-round unanimous decision from Marling Starling to capture the WBA championship in Atlantic City in January. The fight was also recognized by the International Boxing Federation.

Curry defended his title on April 21 when Elio Diaz failed to answer the bell for the eight round of their title fight in Fort Worth, Texas.

Starling could take solace from the fact he won the United States Boxing Association crown on April 17 against Lupe Aquino.

Super Welterweight (Junior Middleweight)

(154 pound limit)

Thomas Hearns retained the WBC championship with a 12-round decision over Luigi Michillo on February 11. The decision was unanimous and gave Hearns a 38–1 career record—the only loss coming to Sugar Ray Leonard in September 1981.

Hearns defended the title on June 15, when he knocked out Roberto Duran 1:07 into the second round. Duran had surrendered the WBA title in order to fight Hearns.

Hearns defended his title a third time in 1984 on Sept. 15, when he registered a third round knockout of Fred Hutchings.

Middleweight

(160 pound limit)

Marvin Hagler retained his undisputed championship, one of the rare divisions recognized by both the WBA and WBC on March 30 in Las Vegas, when he stopped Juan Domingo Roldan 39 seconds into the 10th round. Roldan won the first two rounds, but Hagler came on strong. He has not lost since March 1986, when he was decisioned by Willie Monroe.

Light Heavyweight (Super Middleweight)

(175 pound limit)

Michael Spinks retained his undisputed championship with a unanimous but close decision over Eddie Davis on Feb. 26 in Atlantic City. The fight was extremely close, and Davis complained bitterly that he should have been awarded the decision. Both the WBA and WBC recognized the title.

The International Boxing Federation calls this division the Super Middleweight. Murray Sutherland took a 16-round decision from Ernie Singletag to win the title on March 28.

Junior Heavyweight (Cruiserweight)

(190 pound limit)

Osvaldo Ocasio retained his WBA title with a 15th-round knockout of John Oahiambo in San Juan, Puerto Rico.

The WBC calls this division Cruiserweight. Carlos DeLeon decisioned Anthony Davis in March to retain his title, and then decisioned Bash Ali on June 3 to retain it again.

Heavyweight

(unlimited)

Larry Holmes, the undefeated W.B.C. champion, vacated his title on Dec. 11, 1983, over a dispute with the W.B.C., which wanted him to fight No. 1 contender Greg Page. The money wasn't big enough to suit Holmes, so he surrendered his title, and declared he would fight with the fledgling International Boxing Federation. Several dates were announced in 1984 for fights between Holmes and W.B.A. champion Gerry Coetzee, the latest and still uncertain being Nov. 16.

Neither Holmes nor Coetzee had fought in 1984 up to that time. Holmes' last W.B.C. title defense came on Nov. 25, 1983, when he knocked out Marvis Frazier, son of former heavyweight champion Joe Frazier, in the first round.

On March 9, 1984, Tim Witherspoon won a decision over Greg Page for the vacated W.B.C. championship. The bout went 12 rounds and Witherspoon won a majority decision—two judges voted for the winner, the third had the fight even in Las Vegas.

Witherspoon's grasp on the title was short lived, however. In Las Vegas on Aug. 31, Pinklon Thomas won a 12-round majority decision from Witherspoon to capture the W.B.C. heavyweight crown.

JOE LOUIS' TITLE FIGHTS

Date	Opponent	Result	Round
June 22, 1937[1]	Jim Braddock, Chicago	KO	8
Aug. 30, 1937	Tommy Farr, Yankee Stadium	W	15
Feb. 23, 1938	Nathan Mann, Mad. Sq. Garden	KO	3
April 1, 1938	Harry Thomas, Chicago	KO	5
June 22, 1938[2]	Max Schmeling, Yankee Stadium	KO	1
Jan. 25, 1939	John Henry Lewis, Mad. Sq. Garden	KO	1
April 17, 1939	Jack Roper, Los Angeles	KO	1
June 28, 1939	Tony Galento, Yankee Stadium	KO	4
Sept. 30, 1939	Bob Pastor, Detroit	KO	11
Feb. 9, 1940	Arturo Godoy, Mad. Sq. Garden	W	15
March 29, 1940	Johnny Paycheck, Mad. Sq. Garden	KO	2
June 20, 1940	Arturo Godoy, Yankee Stadium	KO	8
Dec. 16, 1940	Al McCoy, Boston	KO	6
Jan. 31, 1941	Red Burman, Mad. Sq. Garden	KO	5
Feb. 17, 1941	Gus Dorazio, Philadelphia	KO	2
March 21, 1941	Abe Simon, Detroit	KO	13
April 8, 1941	Tony Musto, St. Louis	KO	9
May 23, 1941	Buddy Baer, Washington, D.C.	W disq.	7
June 18, 1941	Billy Conn, Polo Grounds	KO	13
Sept. 29, 1941	Lou Nova, Polo Grounds	KO	6
Jan. 9, 1941	Buddy Baer, Madison Sq. Garden	KO	1
March 27, 1942	Abe Simon, Madison Sq. Garden	KO	6
June 19, 1946	Billy Conn, Yankee Stadium	KO	8
Sept. 8, 1946	Tami Mauriello, Yankee Stadium	KO	1
Dec. 5, 1947	Joe Walcott, Madison Sq. Garden	W	15
June 25, 1948	Joe Walcott, Yankee Stadium	KO	11
Sept. 27, 1950[3]	Ezzard Charles, Yankee Stadium	L	15

1. Won title. 2. Schmeling had stopped Louis in 12th round of non-title fight, June 19, 1936. 3. After announcing retirement as champion on March 1, 1949, Louis returned to boxing and sought to regain title in bout with Charles.

OTHER WORLD BOXING TITLEHOLDERS

(Through Aug. 20, 1984)

Light Heavyweight

Year	Titleholder
1903	Jack Root, George Gardner
1903–05	Bob Fitzsimmons
1905–12	Philadelphia Jack O'Brien[1]
1912–16	Jack Dillon
1916–20	Battling Levinsky
1920–22	Georges Carpentier
1923	Battling Siki
1923–25	Mike McTigue
1925–26	Paul Berlenbach
1926–27	Jack Delaney[2]
1927	Mike McTigue
1927–29	Tommy Loughran
1930	Jimmy Slattery
1930–34	Maxie Rosenbloom
1934–35	Bob Olin
1935–39	John Henry Lewis
1939	Melio Bettina
1939–41	Billy Conn[2]
1941	Anton Christoforidis (NBA)
1941–48	Gus Lesnevich
1948–50	Freddie Mills
1950–52	Joey Maxim
1952–61	Archie Moore[3]
1961–63	Harold Johnson
1963–65	Willie Pastrano
1965–66	José Torres
1966–67	Dick Tiger
1968	Dick Tiger, Bob Foster
1969–70	Bob Foster
1971	Vicente Rondon (WBA), Bob Foster (WBC)
1972–73	Bob Foster (WBA, WBC)
1974	John Conteh (WBA), Bob Foster (WBC)[14]
1975–76	Victor Galindez (WBA), John Conteh (WBC)
1977	Victor Galindez (WBA), John Conteh (WBC)[4], Miguel Cuello (WBC)
1978	Victor Galindez (WBA), Mike Rossman (WBA), Miguel Cuello (WBC), Mate Parlov (WBC), Marvin Johnson (WBC)
1979	Mike Rossman (WBA), Vict Galindez (WBA), Marvin Johnson (WBC), Matthew (Franklin) Saad Muhammad (WBC)
1980	Matthew Saad Muhammad (WBC), Marvin Johnson (WBA), Eddie (Gregory) Mustafa Muhammad (WBA)
1981	Matthew Saad Muhammad (WBC), Eddie Mustafa Muhammad (WBA), Michael Spinks (WBA), Dwight Braxton (WBC)
1982	Dwight Braxton (WBC), Michael Spinks (WBA)
1983	Michael Spinks (undisputed)
1984	Michael Spinks (undisputed)

1. Retired. 2. Abandoned title. 3. NBA withdrew recognition in 1961, New York Commission in 1962; recognized thereafter only by California and Europe. 4. WBC withdrew recognition.

Middleweight

Year	Titleholder
1867–72	Tom Chandler
1872–81	George Rooke
1881–82	Mike Donovan[1]
1884–91	Jack (Nonpareil) Dempsey
1891–97	Bob Fitzsimmons[2]
1908	Stanley Ketchel, Billy Papke
1908–10	Stanley Ketchel[3]
1913	Frank Klaus
1913–14	George Chip
1914–17	Al McCoy
1917–20	Mike O'Dowd
1920–23	Johnny Wilson
1923–26	Harry Greb
1926	Tiger Flowers
1926–31	Mickey Walker[2]
1931–41	Gorilla Jones, Ben Jeby, Marcel Thil, Lou Brouillard, Vince Dundee, Teddy Yarosz, Babe Risko, Freddy Steele, Al Hostak, Solly Kreiger, Fred Apostoli, Ceferino Garcia, Ken Overlin, Billy Soose, Tony Zale[4]
1941–47	Tony Zale
1947–48	Rocky Graziano
1948	Tony Zale
1948–49	Marcel Cerdan
1949–51	Jake LaMotta
1952	Ray Robinson, Randy Turpin
1951–52	Ray Robinson[1]
1953–55	Carl Olson
1955–57	Ray Robinson[5]
1957	Gene Fullmer, Ray Robinson
1957–58	Carmen Basilio
1958–60	Ray Robinson[6]
1960–61	Paul Pender[7]
1959–62	Gene Fullmer (NBA)
1961–62	Terry Downes[1]
1962	Paul Pender[1]
1962–63	Dick Tiger
1963–65	Joey Giardello
1965–66	Dick Tiger
1966	Emile Griffith
1967	Nino Benvenuti, Emile Griffith
1968	Emile Griffith, Nino Benvenuti
1969	Nino Benvenuti
1970	Nino Benvenuti, Carlos Monzon
1971–73	Carlos Monzon
1974–75	Carlos Monzon (WBA), Rodrigo Valdez (WBC)
1976	Carlos Monzon (WBA, WBC), Rodrigo Valdez (WBC)
1977	Carlos Monzon (WBA, WBC)[1], Rodrigo Valdez (WBA, WBC)
1978	Rodrigo Valdez, Hugo Corro
1979	Hugo Corro, Vito Antuofermo
1980	Vito Antuofermo, Alan Minter, Marvin Hagler
1981	Marvin Hagler
1982–84	Marvelous Marvin Hagler (undisputed)

1. Retired. 2. Abandoned title. 3. Died. 4. National Boxing Association and New York Commission disagreed on champions. Those listed were accepted by one or the other until Zale gained world-wide recognition. 5. Ended retirement in 1954. 6. NBA withdrew recognition. 7. Recognized by New York, Massachusetts, and Europe.

Welterweight

Year	Titleholder
1892–94	Mysterious Billy Smith
1894–96	Tommy Ryan
1896	Kid McCoy[2]
1896–1900	Mysterious Billy Smith
1900	Rube Ferns
1900–01	Matty Matthews
1901	Ruby Ferns
1901–04	Joe Walcott
1904	Dixie Kid[2]
1933	Young Corbett 3rd
1933–34	Jimmy McLarnin, Barney Ross
1934–35	Jimmy McLarnin
1935–38	Barney Ross
1938–40	Henry Armstrong
1940–41	Fritzie Zivic
1941–46	Freddie Cochrane
1946	Marty Servo[1]
1946–51	Ray Robinson[2]
1951	Johnny Bratton (NBA)
1951–54	Kid Gavilan
1969	Curtis Cokes, José Napoles
1970	José Napoles, Billy Backus
1971	Billy Backus, José Napoles
1972–74	José Napoles
1975	José Napoles (WBA, WBC)[3], Angel Espada (WBA), John Stracey (WBC)
1976	Angel Espada (WBA), José Cuevas (WBA), John Stracey (WBC), Carlos Palomino (WBC)

1904–06 Joe Walcott
1906–07 Honey Mellody
1907 Mike (Twin) Sullivan[2]
1915–19 Ted Lewis
1919–22 Jack Britton
1922–26 Mickey Walker
1926–27 Pete Latzo
1927–29 Joe Dundee
1929–30 Jackie Fields
1930 Young Jack Thompson
1930–31 Tommy Freeman
1931 Young Jack Thompson
1931–32 Lou Brouillard
1932–33 Jackie Fields
1954–55 Johnny Saxton
1955 Tony DeMarco
1955–56 Carmen Basilio
1956 Johnny Saxton
1956–57 Carmen Basilio[2]
1958 Virgil Akins
1959–60 Don Jordan
1960–61 Benny (Kid) Paret
1961 Emile Griffith
1961–62 Benny (Kid) Paret
1962–63 Emile Griffith, Luis Rodriguez
1963–66 Emile Griffith[2]
1966–69 Curtis Cokes
1977–78 José Cuevas (WBA), Carlos Palomino (WBC)
1979 José Cuevas (WBA), Carlos Palomino (WBC), Wilfredo Benitez (WBC)
1980 Jose Cuevas (WBA), Sugar Ray Leonard (WBC), Roberto Duran (WBC), Thomas Hearns (WBA)
1981 Ray Leonard (WBC), Thomas Hearns (WBA), Ray Leonard (WBC,WBA)
1982 Ray Leonard
1983–84 Donald Curry (WBA)
1983–84 Milton McCrory (WBC)

1. Retired. 2. Abandoned title. 3. WBA withdrew recognition.

Lightweight

1869–99 Kid Lavigne
1899–1902 Frank Erne
1902–08 Joe Gans
1908–10 Battling Nelson
1910–12 Ad Wolgast
1912–14 Willie Ritchie
1914–17 Freddy Welsh
1917–25 Benny Leonard[1]
1925 Jimmy Goodrich
1925–26 Rocky Kansas
1926–30 Sammy Mandell
1930 Al Singer
1930–33 Tony Canzoneri
1933–35 Barney Ross[2]
1935–36 Tony Canzoneri
1936–38 Lou Ambers
1938–39 Henry Armstrong
1939–40 Lou Ambers
1940–41 Lew Jenkins
1941–42 Sammy Angott[1]
1943–47 Beau Jack (N.Y.), Bob Montgomery (N.Y.), Sammy Angott (NBA), Juan Zurita (NBA), Ike Williams (NBA)
1947–51 Ike Williams
1951–52 James Carter
1952 Lauro Salas
1952–54 James Carter
1954 Paddy DeMarco
1954–55 James Carter
1955–56 Wallace Smith
1956–62 Joe Brown
1962–65 Carlos Ortiz
1965 Ismael Laguna
1965–68 Carlos Ortiz
1968 Teo Cruz
1969 Teo Cruz, Mando Ramos
1970 Mando Ramos, Ismael Laguna, Ken Buchanan
1971 Ken Buchanan (WBA), Mando Ramos (WBC), Pedro Carrasco (WBC)
1972 Ken Buchanan (WBA), Roberto Duran (WBA), Pedro Carrasco (WBC), Mando Ramos (WBC), Chango Carmona (WBC), Rodolfo Gonzalez (WBC)
1973 Roberto Duran (WBA), Rodolfo Gonzalez (WBC))
1974 Roberto Duran (WBA), Rodolfo Gonzalez (WBC), Guts Ishimatsu (WBC)
1975 Roberto Duran (WBA), Guts Ishimatsu (WBC)
1976 Roberto Duran (WBA), Guts Ishimatsu (WBC), Esteban De Jesus (WBC)
1977 Roberto Duran (WBA), Esteban De Jesus (WBC)
1978 Roberto Duran (WBA, WBC)
1979 Roberto Duran[2], Jim Watt (WBC), Ernesto Espana (WBA)
1980 Ernesto Espana (WBA), Hilmer Kenty (WBA), Jim Watt (WBC)
1981 Hilmer Kenty (WBA), Sean O'Grady (WBA), James Watt (WBC), Alexis Arguello (WBC), Arturo Frias (WBA)
1982 Arturo Frias (WBA), Ray Mancini (WBA), Alexis Arguello (WBC)
1983 Edwin Rosario (WBC), Ray Mancini (WBA)
1984 Edwin Rosario (WBC), Livingstone Bramble (WBA)

1. Retired. 2. Abandoned title.

Featherweight

1889 Dal Hawkins[1]
1890 Billy Murphy
1892–1900 George Dixon
1900–01 Terry McGovern
1901 Young Corbett[1]
1901–12 Abe Attell
1912–23 Johnny Kilbane
1923 Eugene Criqui
1923–25 Johnny Dundee[1]
1925–27 Louis (Kid) Kaplan[1]
1927–28 Benny Bass
1928 Tony Canzoneri
1928–29 Andre Routis
1929–32 Battling Battalino[1]
1932 Tommy Paul (NBA), Kid Chocolate (N.Y.)
1933–36 Freddie Miller
1936–37 Petey Sarron
1937–38 Henry Armstrong[1]
1938–40 Joey Archibald
1940–41 Harry Jefra, Joey Archibald
1941–42 Chalky Wright
1942–48 Willie Pep
1948–49 Sandy Saddler[2]
1949–50 Willie Pep
1950–57 Sandy Saddler
1957–59 Kid Bassey
1959–63 Davey Moore
1963–64 Sugar Ramos
1964–67 Vicente Saldivar[2]
1968 Howard Winstone, José Legra,[3] Paul Rojas (WBA), Sho Saijo (WBA)
1969 Sho Saijo (WBA), Johnny Famechon[3]
1970 Sho Saijo (WBA), Johnny Famechon,[3] Vicente Salvidar,[3] Kuniaki Shibata[3]
1971 Sho Saijo (WBA), Antonio Gomez (WBA), Kuniaki Shibata (WBC)
1972 Antonio Gomez (WBA), Ernesto Marcel (WBA), Kuniaki Shibata (WBC), Clemente Sanchez (WBC), José Legra (WBC)
1973 Ernesto Marcel (WBA), José Legra (WBC), Eder Jofre (WBC)
1974 Ernesto Marcel (WBA)[2], Ruben Olivares (WBA), Alexis Arguello (WBA), Eder Jofre (WBC), Bobby Chacon (WBC)

Year	Champion
1975	Alexis Arguello (WBA), Bobby Chacon (WBC), Ruben Olivares (WBC), David Kotey (WBC)
1976	Alexis Arguello (WBA),[2] David Kotey (WBC), Danny Lopez (WBC)
1977	Rafael Ortega (WBA), Danny Lopez (WBC)
1978	Rafael Ortega (WBA), Cecilio Lastra (WBA), Eusebio Pedrosa (WBA), Danny Lopez (WBC)
1979	Eusebio Pedrosa (WBA), Danny Lopez (WBC)
1980	Eusebio Pedroza (WBA), Danny Lopez (WBC), Salvador Sanchez (WBC)
1981	Eusebio Pedroza (WBA), Salvador Sanchez (WBC)
1982	Eusebio Pedroza (WBA), Salvador Sanchez (WBC)[4]
1983	Juan Laporte (WBC) Eusebio Pedroza (WBA)
1984	Wilfred Gomez (WBC), Eusebio Pedroza (WBA)

1. Abandoned title. 2. Retired. 3. Recognized in Europe, Mexico, and Orient. 4. Killed in auto accident.

Bantamweight

Year	Champion
1890–92	George Dixon[1]
1894–99	Jimmy Barry[2]
1899–1900	Terry McGovern[1]
1901	Harry Harris[1]
1902–03	Harry Forbes
1903–04	Frankie Neil
1904	Joe Bowker[1]
1905–07	Jimmy Walsh[1]
1910–14	Johnny Coulon
1914–17	Kid Williams
1917–20	Pete Herman
1920	Joe Lynch
1920–21	Joe Lynch, Pete Herman, Johnny Buff
1922	Johnny Buff, Joe Lynch
1923	Joe Lynch
1924	Joe Lynch, Abe Goldstein
1924	Abe Goldstein, Eddie (Cannonball) Martin
1925	Eddie (Cannonball) Martin, Charlie (Phil) Rosenberg[3]
1927–28	Bud Taylor (NBA)[1]
1929–34	Al Brown
1935	Al Brown, Baltazar Sangchili
1936	Baltazar Sangchili, Tony Marino, Sixto Escobar
1937	Sixto Escobar, Harry Jeffra
1938	Harry Jeffra, Sixto Escobar
1939–40	Sixto Escobar[2]
1940–42	Lou Salica
1942–46	Manuel Ortiz
1947	Manuel Ortiz, Harold Dade
1948–50	Manuel Ortiz
1950–52	Vic Toweel
1952–54	Jimmy Carruthers[2]
1954–55	Robert Cohen
1956	Robert Cohen, Mario D'Agata, Raul Macias (NBA)
1957	Mario D'Agata, Alphonse Halimi
1958–59	Alphonse Halimi
1959–60	Jose Becerra[2]
1960–61	Alphonse Halimi[4]
1961–62	Johnny Caldwell[4]
1961–65	Eder Jofre
1965–68	Masahika (Fighting) Harada
1968	Masahika (Fighting) Harada, Lionel Rose
1969	Lionel Rose, Ruben Olivares
1970	Ruben Olivares, Chucho Castillo
1971	Chucho Castillo, Ruben Olivares
1972	Ruben Olivares, Rafael Herrera, Enrique Pinder
1973	Enrique Pinder (WBA), Romeo Anaya (WBA), Arnold Taylor (WBA), Rodolfo Martinez (WBC), Rafael Herrera
1974	Arnold Taylor (WBA), Soo Hwan Hong (WBA), Rafael Herrera (WBC), Rodolfo Martinez (WBC)
1975	Soo Hwan Hong (WBA), Alfonso Zamora (WBA), Rodolfo Martinez (WBC)
1976	Alfonso Zamora (WBA), Rodolfo Martinez (WBC), Carlos Zarate (WBC)
1977	Alfonso Zamora (WBA), Jorge Lujan (WBA), Carlos Zarate (WBC)
1978	Jorge Lujan (WBA), Carlos Zarate (WBC)
1979	Jorge Lujan (WBA), Carlos Zarate (WBC), Lupe Pinto (WBC)
1980	Jorge Lujan (WBA), Lupe Pintor (WBC), Julian Solis (WBA), Jeff Chandler (WBA)
1981	Lupe Pintor (WBC), Jeff Chandler (WBA)
1982	Lupe Pintor (WBC), Jeff Chandler (WBA)
1983	Jeff Chandler (WBA), Albert Dauila (WBC)
1984	Richie Sandqual (WBA), Albert Dauila (WBC)

1. Abandoned title. 2. Retired. 3. Deprived of title for failing to make weight. 4. Recognized in Europe.

Flyweight

Year	Champion
1916–23	Jimmy Wilde
1923–25	Pancho Villa[1]
1925	Frankie Genaro
1925–27	Fidel La Barba[2]
1927–31	Corporal Izzy Schwartz, Frankie Genaro, Emile (Spider) Pladner, Midget Wolgast, Young Perez[3]
1932–35	Jackie Brown
1935–38	Bennie Lynch[4]
1939	Peter Kane[4]
1943–47	Jackie Paterson[1]
1947–50	Rinty Monaghan[2]
1950	Terry Allen
1950–52	Dado Marino
1952–54	Yoshio Shirai
1954–60	Pascual Perez
1960–62	Pone Kingpetch
1962–63	Masahika (Fighting) Harada
1963–64	Hiroyuki Ebihara
1964–65	Pone Kingpetch
1965–66	Salvatore Burrini
1966	Walter McGown, Chartchai Chionoi
1966–68	Charchai Chionoi
1969	Bernabe Villacampa, Efran Torres (WBA)
1970	Bernabe Villacampa, Chartchai Chionoi, Erbito Salavarria, Berkrerk Chartvanchai (WBA), Masao Ohba (WBA)
1971	Masao Ohba (WBA), Erbito Salavarria (WBC)
1972	Masao Ohba (WBA), Erbito Salavarria (WBC), Betulio Gonzalez (WBC), Venice Borkorsor (WBC)
1973	Masao Ohba (WBA), Chartchai Chionoi (WBA), Venice Borkorsor (WBC), Betulio Gonzalez (WBC)
1974	Chartchai Chionoi (WBA), Susumu Hanagata (WBA), Betulio Gonzalez (WBC), Shoji Oguma (WBC)
1975	Susumu Hanagata (WBA), Erbito Salavarria (WBA), Shoji Oguma (WBC), Miguel Canto (WBC)
1976	Erbito Salavarria (WBA), Alfonso Lopez (WBA), Guty Espadas (WBA), Miguel Canto (WBC)
1977	Guty Espadas (WBA), Miguel Canto (WBC)
1978	Guty Espadas (WBA), Betulio Gonzalez (WBA), Miguel Canto (WBC)
1979	Betulio Gonzalez (WBA), Miguel Canto (WBC), Park Chan-Hee (WBC)
1980	Luis Ibarra (WBA), Kim Tae Shik (WBA), Park Chan-Hee (WBC), Shoji Oguma (WBC) Peter
1983	Frank Cedeno (WBC), Santos Lacia (WBA)
1984	Koji Kobayashy (WBC), Gabriel Bernal (WBC), Santos Laciar (WBA)

1. Died. 2. Retired. 3. Claimants to NBA and New York Commission titles. 4. Abandoned title.

FIGHTER OF THE YEAR

Selected by *The Ring* Magazine.

1928	Gene Tunney	1941	Joe Louis	1955	Rocky Marciano	1969	Jose Napoles
1929	Tommy Loughran	1942	Ray Robinson	1956	Floyd Patterson	1970–71	Joe Frazier
1930	Max Schmeling	1943	Fred Apostoli	1957	Carmen Basilio	1972	Carlos Monzon and Muhammad Ali
1931	Tommy Loughran	1944	Beau Jack	1958	Ingemar Johansson		
1932	Jack Sharkey	1945	Willie Pep	1959	Ingemar Johansson	1973	George Foreman
1933	No award	1946	Tony Zale	1960	Floyd Patterson	1974–75	Muhammad Ali
1934	Barney Ross and Tony Canzoneri	1947	Gus Lesnevich	1961	Joe Brown	1976	George Foreman
		1948	Ike Williams	1962	Dick Tiger	1977	Carlos Zarate
1935	Barney Ross	1949	Ezzard Charles	1963	Cassius Clay	1978	Muhammad Ali
1936	Joe Louis	1950	Ezzard Charles	1964	Emile Griffith	1979	Sugar Ray Leonard
1937	Henry Armstrong	1951	Ray Robinson	1965	Dick Tiger	1980	Thomas Hearns
1938	Joe Louis	1952	Rocky Marciano	1966	No award	1981	Sugar Ray Leonard
1939	Joe Louis	1953	Bobo Olson	1967	Joe Frazier	1982	Aaron Pryor
1940	Billy Conn	1954	Rocky Marciano	1968	Nino Benvenuti	1983	Marvin Hagler

MARCIANO WAS UNBEATEN AS A PRO

Rocky Marciano, heavyweight boxing champion of the world and winner of each of his 49 fights as a professional, announced his retirement from the ring on Apr. 27, 1956. He was the only heavyweight champion ever to retire without losing a professional fight.

Marciano won the title on Sept. 23, 1952, in Philadelphia, by knocking out Joe Walcott in the 13th round.

Marciano, born in Brockton, Mass., on Sept. 1, 1924, was killed in a plane crash, Aug. 31, 1969.

These were Marciano's championship fights:

Sept. 23, 1952[1]	Joe Walcott, Philadelphia	KO	13
May 15, 1953	Joe Walcott, Chicago	KO	1
Sept. 24, 1953	Roland LaStarza, Polo Grounds	KO	11
June 17, 1954	Ezzard Charles, Yankee Stad.	W	15
Sept. 17, 1954	Ezzard Charles, Yankee Stad.	KO	8
May 16, 1955	Don Cockell, San Francisco	KO	9
Sept. 21, 1955	Archie Moore, Yankee Stad.	KO	9

1. Won title.

BOXING—AMATEUR

U.S. AMATEUR CHAMPIONSHIPS—1983

(Colorado Springs, Colo., Nov. 7–12, 1983)

106 lb—Paul Gonzalez, Los Angeles, Calif.
112 lb—Steve McCrory, Detroit, Mich.
119 lb—Jesse Benavides, Corpus Christi, Texas
125 lb—Andrew Minsker, Milwaukee, Wisc.
132 lb—Clifford Gray, Boynton Beach, Fla.
139 lb—Zachary Padila, Azosa, Calif.
147 lb—Mark Breland, Brooklyn, N.Y.
156 lb—Frank Tate, Detroit, Mich.
165 lb—Michael Grogan, Atlanta, Ga.
178 lb—Ricky Womack, Detroit, Mich.
201 lb—Henry Milligan Hockessin, Detroit, Mich.
Over 201 lb—Tyrell Biggs, Philadelphia, Pa.

WORLD CHAMPIONSHIPS—1984

(Los Angeles, Calif., April 13, 1984)

106 lb—Rafael Sainz, Cuba
112 lb—Pedro Reyes, Cuba
119 lb—Floyd Favors, United States
125 lb—Adolfo Horta, Cuba
132 lb—Pernell Whitaker, United States
139 lb—Carlos Garcia, Cuba
147 lb—Mark Breland, United States
158 lb—Frank Tate, United States
165 lb—Bernardo Comas, Cuba
178 lb—Ricky Womack, United States
Heavyweight—Willie deWit, Canada
Super heavyweight—Tyrell Biggs, United States

NATIONAL GOLDEN GLOVES

CHAMPIONS—1984

106 lb—Israel Acosta, Milwaukee, Wisc.
112 lb—Les Fabri, California
119 lb—Robert Shannon, Las Vegas, Nev.
125 lb—Victor Levine, Indianapolis, Ind.
132 lb—Marvin Chambers. St. Louis, Mo.
139 lb—Timothy Rabon, Louisiana
147 lb—Mylon Watkins, Las Vegas, Nev.
156 lb—Ronnie Essett, Indianpolis, Ind.
165 lb—Virgil Hill, Minneapolis, Minn.
178 lb—Evander Holyfield, Knoxville, Tenn.
Heavyweight—Michael Tyason, New York, N.Y.
Superheavyweight—Michael Williams, Louisiana

POWERBOAT RACING

AMERICAN POWER BOAT ASSOCIATION

World Championship—1983

(Key West, Fla., Nov. 6–10, 1983)

Open Class I—George Morales, Ft. Lauderdale, Fla., "Mercrusier Special." Average speed: 90.9 mph.

Sports Class II—Henry Ryan, Grosseile, Mich., "Express." Average speed: 86.059 mph.

Modified Class III—Robert Kahrig, New Baltimore, Mich., "Cougar." Average speed: 77.65 mph.

Modified Class IV—Peter Aitkin, South Norwalk, Conn., "Black Duck." Average speed: 74.32 mph.

Class V-B—Franz Kneissl, Newport, R.I., "Newport Is Sports." Average speed: 64.74 mph.

Class V-A—Nicky Cutro, Jr., Lake George, N.Y., "Boardwalk." Average speed: 57.99 mph.

HORSE RACING

Ancient drawings on stone and bone prove that horse racing is at least 3000 years old, but Thoroughbred Racing is a modern development. Practically every thoroughbred in training today traces its registered ancestry back to one or more of three sires that arrived in England about 1728 from the Near East and became known, from the names of their owners, as the Byerly Turk, the Darley Arabian, and the Godolphin Arabian. The Jockey Club (English) was founded at Newmarket in 1750 or 1751 and became the custodian of the Stud Book as well as the court of last resort in deciding turf affairs.

Horse racing took place in this country before the Revolution, but the great lift to the breeding industry came with the importation in 1798, by Col. John Hoomes of Virginia, of Diomed, winner of the Epsom Derby of 1780. Diomed's lineal descendants included such famous stars of the American turf as American Eclipse and Lexington. From 1800 to the time of the Civil War there were race courses and breeding establishments plentifully scattered through Virginia, North Carolina, South Carolina, Tennessee, Kentucky, and Louisiana.

The oldest stake event in North America is the Queen's Plate, a Canadian fixture that was first run in the Province of Quebec in 1836. The oldest stake event in the United States is The Travers, which was first run at Saratoga in 1864. The gambling that goes with horse racing and trickery by jockeys, trainers, owners, and track officials caused attacks on the sport by reformers and a demand among horse racing enthusiasts for an honest and effective control of some kind, but nothing of lasting value to racing came of this until the formation in 1894 of The Jockey Club.

"TRIPLE CROWN" WINNERS IN THE UNITED STATES[1]

(Kentucky Derby, Preakness and Belmont Stakes)

Year	Horse	Owner	Year	Horse	Owner
1919	Sir Barton	J. K. L. Ross	1946	Assault	Robert J. Kleberg
1930	Gallant Fox	William Woodward	1948	Citation	Warren Wright
1935	Omaha	William Woodward	1973	Secretariat	Meadow Stable
1937	War Admiral	Samuel D. Riddle	1977	Seattle Slew	Karen Taylor
1941	Whirlaway	Warren Wright	1978	Affirmed	Louis Wolfson
1943	Count Fleet	Mrs. John Hertz			

1. Statistics relative to thoroughbred racing in this publication are reproduced from the *American Racing Manual*, by special permission of the copyright owners. TRIANGLE PUBLICATIONS, INC. Reproduction prohibited.

KENTUCKY DERBY

Churchill Downs; 3-year-olds; 1 1/4 miles.

Year	Winner	Jockey	Wt.	Win val.	Year	Winner	Jockey	Wt.	Win val.
1875	Aristides	O. Lewis	100	$2,850	1909	Wintergreen	V. Powers	117	$4,850
1876	Vagrant	R. Swim	97	2,950	1910	Donau	F. Herbert	117	4,850
1877	Baden Baden	W. Walker	100	3,300	1911	Meridian	G. Archibald	117	4,850
1878	Day Star	J. Carter	100	4,050	1912	Worth	C. H. Shilling	117	4,850
1879	Lord Murphy	C. Schauer	100	3,550	1913	Donerail	R. Goose	117	5,475
1880	Fonso	G. Lewis	105	3,800	1914	Old Rosebud	J. McCabe	114	9,125
1881	Hindoo	J. McLaughlin	105	4,410	1915	Regret	J. Notler	112	11,450
1882	Apollo	B. Hurd	102	4,560	1916	George Smith	J. Loftus	117	9,750
1883	Leonatus	W. Donohue	105	3,760	1917	Omar Khayyam	C. Borel	117	16,600
1884	Buchanan	I. Murphy	110	3,990	1918	Exterminator	W. Knapp	114	14,700
1885	Joe Cotton	E. Henderson	110	4,630	1919	Sir Barton	J. Loftus	112 1/2	20,825
1886	Ben Ali	P. Duffy	118	4,890	1920	Paul Jones	T. Rice	126	30,375
1887	Montrose	I. Lewis	118	4,200	1921	Behave Yourself	C. Thompson	126	38,450
1888	Macbeth II	G. Covington	115	4,740	1922	Morvich	A. Johnson	126	46,775
1889	Spokane	T. Kiley	118	4,970	1923	Zev	E. Sande	126	53,600
1890	Riley	I. Murphy	118	5,460	1924	Black Gold	J. D. Mooney	126	52,775
1891	Kingman	I. Murphy	122	4,680	1925	Flying Ebony	E. Sande	126	52,950
1892	Azra	A. Clayton	122	4,230	1926	Bubbling Over	A. Johnson	126	50,075
1893	Lookout	E. Kunze	122	4,090	1927	Whiskery	L. McAtee	126	51,000
1894	Chant	F. Goodale	122	4,020	1928	Reigh Count	C. Lang	126	55,375
1895	Halma	J. Perkins	122	2,970	1929	Clyde Van Dusen	L. McAtee	126	53,950
1896	Ben Brush	W. Simms	117	4,850	1930	Gallant Fox	E. Sande	126	50,725
1897	Typhoon H	F. Garner	117	4,850	1931	Twenty Grand	C. Kurtsinger	126	48,725
1898	Plaudit	W. Simms	117	4,850	1932	Burgoo King	E. James	126	52,350
1899	Manuel	F. Taral	117	4,850	1933	Brokers Tip	D. Meade	126	48,925
1900	Lieut. Gibson	J. Boland	117	4,850	1934	Cavalcade	M. Garner	126	28,175
1901	His Eminence	J. Winkfield	117	4,850	1935	Omaha	W. Saunders	126	39,525
1902	Alan-a-Dale	J. Winkfield	117	4,850	1936	Bold Venture	I. Hanford	126	37,725
1903	Judge Himes	H. Booker	117	4,850	1937	War Admiral	C. Kurtsinger	126	52,050
1904	Elwood	F. Prior	117	4,850	1938	Lawrin	E. Arcaro	126	47,050
1905	Agile	J. Martin	122	4,850	1939	Johnstown	J. Stout	126	46,350
1906	Sir Huon	R. Troxler	117	4,850	1940	Gallahadion	C. Bierman	126	60,150
1907	Pink Star	A. Minder	117	4,850	1941	Whirlaway	E. Arcaro	126	61,275
1908	Stone Street	A. Pickens	117	4,850	1942	Shut Out	W. D. Wright	126	64,225

Year	Winner	Jockey	Wt.	Win val.	Year	Winner	Jockey	Wt.	Win val.
1943	Count Fleet	J. Longden	126	$ 60,725	1964	Northern Dancer	W. Hartack	126	114,300
1944	Pensive	C. McCreary	126	64,675	1965	Lucky Debonair	W. Shoemaker	126	112,000
1945	Hoop Jr.	E. Arcaro	126	64,850	1966	Kauai King	D. Brumfield	126	120,500
1946	Assault	W. Mehrtens	126	96,400	1967	Proud Clarion	R. Ussery	126	119,700
1947	Jet Pilot	E. Guerin	126	92,160	1968	Forward Pass[1]	I. Valenzuela	126	122,600
1948	Citation	E. Arcaro	126	83,400	1969	Majestic Prince	W. Hartack	126	113,200
1949	Ponde	S. Brooks	126	91,600	1970	Dust Commander	M. Manganello	126	127,800
1950	Middleground	W. Boland	126	92,650	1971	Canonero II	G. Avila	126	145,500
1951	Count Turf	C. McCreary	126	98,050	1972	Riva Ridge	R. Turcotte	126	140,300
1952	Hill Gail	E. Arcaro	126	96,300	1973	Secretariat	R. Turcotte	126	155,050
1953	Dark Star	H. Moreno	126	90,050	1974	Cannonade	A. Cordero, Jr.	126	274,000
1954	Determine	R. York	126	102,050	1975	Foolish Pleasure	J. Vasquez	126	209,600
1955	Swaps	W. Shoemaker	126	108,400	1976	Bold Forbes	A. Cordero, Jr.	126	165,200
1956	Needles	D. Erb	126	123,450	1977	Seattle Slew	J. Cruguet	126	214,700
1957	Iron Liege	W. Hartack	126	107,950	1978	Affirmed	S. Cauthen	126	186,900
1958	Tim Tam	I. Valenzuela	126	116,400	1979	Spectacular Bid	R. Franklin	126	228,650
1959	Tomy Lee	W. Shoemaker	126	119,650	1980	Genuine Risk	J. Vasquez	126	250,550
1960	Venetian Way	W. Hartack	126	114,850	1981	Pleasant Colony	J. Velasquez	126	317,200
1961	Carry Back	J. Sellers	126	120,500	1982	Gato del Sol	E. Delahoussaye	126	417,600
1962	Decidedly	W. Hartack	126	119,650	1983	Sunny's Halo	E. Delahoussaye	126	426,000
1963	Chateauguay	B. Baeza	126	$108,900	1984	Swale	L. Pincay Jr.	126	537,400

1. Dancer's Image finished first but was disqualified after traces of drug were found in system.

PREAKNESS STAKES

Pimlico; 3-year-olds; 1 3/16 miles; first race 1873.

Year	Winner	Jockey	Wt.	Win Val.	Year	Winner	Jockey	Wt.	Win val.
1919	Sir Barton	J. Loftus	126	$24,500	1957	Bold Ruler	E. Arcaro	126	$65,250
1930	Gallant Fox	E. Sande	126	51,925	1958	Tim Tam	I. Valenzuela	126	97,900
1931	Mate	G. Ellis	126	48,225	1959	Royal Orbit	W. Harmatz	126	136,200
1932	Burgoo King	E. James	126	50,375	1960	Bally Ache	R. Ussery	126	121,000
1933	Head Play	C. Kurtsinger	126	26,850	1961	Carry Back	J. Sellers	126	126,200
1934	High Quest	R. Jones	126	25,175	1962	Greek Money	J. Rotz	126	135,800
1935	Omaha	W. Saunders	126	25,325	1963	Candy Spots	W. Shoemaker	126	127,500
1936	Bold Venture	G. Woolf	126	27,325	1964	Northern Dancer	W. Hartack	126	124,200
1937	War Admiral	C. Kurtsinger	126	45,600	1965	Tom Rolfe	R. Turcotte	126	128,100
1938	Dauber	M. Peters	126	51,875	1966	Kauai King	D. Brumfield	126	129,000
1939	Challedon	G. Seabo	126	53,710	1967	Damascus	W. Shoemaker	126	141,500
1940	Bimelech	F.A. Smith	126	53,230	1968	Forward Pass	I. Valenzuela	126	142,700
1941	Whirlaway	E. Arcaro	126	49,365	1969	Majestic Prince	W. Hartack	126	129,500
1942	Alsab	B. James	126	58,175	1970	Personality	E. Belmonte	126	151,300
1943	Count Fleet	J. Longden	126	43,190	1971	Canonero II	G. Avila	126	137,400
1944	Pensive	C. McCreary	126	60,075	1972	Bee Bee Bee	E. Nelson	126	135,300
1945	Polynesian	W.D. Wright	126	66,170	1973	Secretariat	R. Turcotte	126	129,900
1946	Assault	W. Mehrtens	126	96,620	1974	Little Current	M. Rivera	126	156,000
1947	Faultless	D. Dodson	126	98,005	1975	Master Derby	D. McHargue	126	158,100
1948	Citation	E. Arcaro	126	91,870	1976	Elocutionist	J. Lively	126	129,700
1949	Capot	T. Atkinson	126	79,985	1977	Seattle Slew	J. Cruguet	126	138,600
1950	Hill Prince	E. Arcaro	126	56,115	1978	Affirmed	S. Cauthen	126	136,200
1951	Bold	E. Arcaro	126	83,110	1979	Spectacular Bid	R. Franklin	126	165,300
1952	Blue Man	C. McCreary	126	86,135	1980	Codex	A. Cordero	126	180,600
1953	Native Dancer	E. Guerin	126	65,200	1981	Pleasant Colony	J. Velasquez	126	270,800
1954	Hasty Road	J. Adams	126	91,600	1982	Aloma's Ruler	J. Kaenel	126	209,900
1955	Nashua	E. Arcaro	126	67,550	1983	Deputed Testimony	D. Miller	126	251,200
1956	Fabius	W. Hartack	126	84,250	1984	Gate Dancer	A. Cordero	126	243,600

BELMONT STAKES

Belmont Park; 3-year-olds; 1 1/2 miles.

Run at Jerome Park 1867 to 1890; at Morris Park 1890–94; at Belmont Park 1905–62; at Aqueduct 1963–67. Distance 1 5/8 miles prior to 1874; reduced to 1 1/2 miles, 1874; reduced to 1 1/4 miles, 1890; reduced to 1 1/8 miles, 1893; increased to 1 1/4 miles, 1895; increased to 1 3/8 miles, 1896; reduced to 1 1/4 miles in 1904; increased to 1 1/2 miles, 1926.

Year	Winner	Jockey	Wt.	Win val.	Year	Winner	Jockey	Wt.	Win val.
1919	Sir Barton	J. Loftus	126	$11,950	1940	Bimelech	F.A. Smith	126	$35,030
1930	Gallant Fox	E. Sande	126	66,040	1941	Whirlaway	E. Arcaro	126	39,770
1931	Twenty Grand	C. Kurtsinger	126	58,770	1942	Shut Out	E. Arcaro	126	44,520
1932	Faireno	T. Malley	126	55,120	1943	Count Fleet	J. Longden	126	35,340
1933	Hurryoff	M. Garner	126	49,490	1944	Bounding Home	G.L. Smith	126	55,000
1934	Peace Chance	W.D. Wright	126	43,410	1945	Pavot	E. Arcaro	126	56,675
1935	Omaha	W. Saunders	126	35,480	1946	Assault	W. Mehrtens	126	75,400
1936	Granville	J. Stout	126	29,800	1947	Phalanx	R. Donoso	126	78,900
1937	War Admiral	C. Kurtsinger	126	38,020	1948	Citation	E. Arcaro	126	77,700
1938	Pasteurized	J. Stout	126	34,530	1949	Capot	T. Atkinson	126	60,900
1939	Johnstown	J. Stout	126	37,020	1950	Middleground	W. Boland	126	61,350

Year	Winner	Jockey	Wt.	Win val.	Year	Winner	Jockey	Wt.	Win val.
1951	Counterpoint	D. Gorman	126	$ 82,000	1968	Stage Door Johnny	H. Gustines	126	$117,700
1952	One Count	E. Arcaro	126	82,400	1969	Arts and Letters	B. Baeza	126	104,050
1953	Native Dancer	E. Guerin	126	82,500	1970	High Echelon	J. Rotz	126	115,000
1954	High Gun	E. Guerin	126	89,000	1971	Pass Catcher	R. Blum	126	97,710
1955	Nashua	E. Arcaro	126	83,700	1972	Riva Ridge	R. Turcotte	126	93,540
1956	Needles	D. Erb	126	83,600	1973	Secretariat	R. Turcotte	126	90,120
1957	Gallant Man	W. Shoemaker	126	77,300	1974	Little Current	M. Rivera	126	101,970
1958	Cavan	P. Anderson	126	73,440	1975	Avatar	W. Shoemaker	126	116,160
1959	Sword Dancer	W. Shoemaker	126	93,525	1976	Bold Forbes	A. Cordero, Jr.	126	117,000
1960	Celtic Ash	W. Hartack	126	96,785	1977	Seattle Slew	J. Cruguet	126	109,080
1961	Sherluck	B. Baeza	126	104,900	1978	Affirmed	S. Cauthen	126	110,580
1962	Jaipur	W. Shoemaker	126	109,550	1979	Coastal	R. Hernandez	126	161,400
1963	Chateauguay	B. Baeza	126	101,700	1980	Temperence Hill	E. Maple	126	176,220
1964	Quadrangle	M. Ycaza	126	110,850	1981	Summing	G. Martens	126	170,580
1965	Hail to All	J. Sellers	126	104,150	1982	Conquistador Cielo	L. Pincay, Jr.	126	159,720
1966	Amberoid	W. Boland	126	117,700	1983	Caveat	L. Pincay, Jr.	126	215,100
1967	Damascus	W. Shoemaker	126	104,950	1984	Swale	L. Pincay, Jr.	126	310,020

TRIPLE CROWN RACES—1984

(For 3-year-olds, carrying 126 pounds, jockeys in parentheses)

Kentucky Derby (Churchill Downs, Louisville, Ky., May 5; gross purse $712,400; 1 1/4 miles)—1. Swale (Laffit Pincay, Jr.), owned by Claiborne Farm, Paris, Ky.; mutuel returns: $8.80, 4.80, 3.40. 2. Coax Me Chad (McCauley) $8.00, 4.00. 3. At The Threshold (Maple) $13.80. 4. Gate Dancer (Delhssye). 5. Fall Time (Hawley). 6. Pine Circle (Smith). 7. Fight Over (Vergara). 8. Life's Magic (Brumfield). 9. Silent King (Shoemaker). 10. Reyson's Hope (Gaffglione). 11. So Vague (Cooksey). 12. Biloxi Indian (Patterson). 13. Taylor's Special (S. Maple). 14. Raja's Shark (Wilson). 15. Bedouin (Sibille). 16. Valandingham (Day). 17. Secret Prince (Perret). 18. Bear Hunt (MacBeth). 19. Althea (McCarron). 20. Majestic Shore (Lively). Time: 2:02 2/5. Winner's purse: $537, 400. Margin of victory: 3 1/2 lengths. Attendance: 126,453.

Belmont Stakes (Elmont, N.Y., June 9; gross purse: $516,700; 1 1/2 miles)—1. Swale (Laffit Pincay, Jr.) owned by Claiborne Farm, Paris, Ky.; mutuel returns: $5.00, 4.40, 3.60. 2. Pine Circle (Day) $15.00, 7.00. 3. Morning Bob (Velasquez) $4.00. 4. Play On (Samyn). 5. Coax Me Chad (McCauley). 6. Gate Dancer (Cordero). 7. Silent King (Brumfield). 8. Exattic (Davis). 9. Romantic Tradition (Hernandez). 10. Back Bay Barrister (MacBeth). 11. Minstrel Star (Bailey). Time: 2:27. Winner's purse: $310, 020. Margin of victory: 4 lengths. Attendance: 47,369.

Preakness Stakes (Pimlico, Md., May 19; gross purse: $338,600; 1 3/16 miles)—1. Gate Dancer (Angel Cordero, Jr.), owned by Kenneth Opstein; mutuel returns: $11.60, 5.00, 4.20. 2. Play On (Jean-Luc Samyn) $7.20, 5.00. 3. Fight Over (Vergara) $5.60. 4. Taylor's Special (Shoemaker). 5. Pine Circle (Smith). 6. Wind Flyer (Murphy). 7. Swale (Pincay, Jr.). 8. Raja's Shark (Wilson). 9. Pac Soldier (Byrnes). 10. Hot Sauce (Miller). Time: 1:53.[1] Winner's purse: $243,600. Margin of victory: 1 1/2 lengths. Attendance: 80,566.

1. Track record.

ECLIPSE AWARDS—1983

The Eclipse Awards in thoroughbred racing are given on the basis of voting by three groups: the Daily Racing Form, the National Turf Writers Association, and the racing secretaries at tracks who are members of the Thoroughbred Racing Association.

Horse of the year	All Along
2-year-old colt	Devil's Bag
2-year-old filly	Althea
3-year-old colt	Slew O'Gold
3-year-old filly	Heartlight No. One
Older colt or gelding	Bates Motel
Older filly or mare	Ambassador of Luck
Male turf horse	John Henry
Female turf horse	All Along
Sprinter	Chinook Pass
Steeplechase	Flatteier
Jockey	Angel Cordero
Trainer	Woody Stephens

FENCING

UNITED STATES CHAMPIONS—1984

U.S. Fencing Association

Men's foil—Michael McCahey, New York Fencers Club, New York City
Men's epee—Paul Soter, Halberstadt Fencers Club, San Francisco
Men's sabre—Peter Westbrook, New York Fencers Club, New York City
Women's foil—Vincent Bradford, Pentathlon Center, San Antonio, Tex.
Women's epee—Vincent Bradford, Pentathlon Center, San Antonio, Tex.
Men's foil team—The Fencing Center, San Jose, Calif.
Men's sabre team—New York Fencers Club, New York City
Men's epee team—New York Athletic Club, New York City
Women's foil—New York Fencer's Club, New York City

WORLD CHAMPIONSHIPS—1983[1]

Men's foil—Alexcander Romankov, Soviet Union
Men's epee—Elmar Borrman, West Germany
Men's sabre—Vassil Etropolski, Bulgaria
Women's foil—Donna Vaccaroni, Italy
Men's foil team—West Germany
Men's epee team—France
Men's sabre team—Soviet Union
Women's foil team—Italy

1. World champions not held in 1984, an Olympic year.

WORLD UNIVERSITY GAMES—1983[1]

Men's foil—Mauro Numa, Italy
Men's epee—Stefano Bellone, Italy
Men's sabre—Marco Marin, Italy
Women's foil—Elisabeta Guzganu, Romania
Men's foil team—Italy
Men's epee team—Italy
Men's sabre team—Soviet Union
Women's foil team—China

1. World University Games held every other year. Next games scheduled for Japan in 1985.

TRACK AND FIELD

Running, jumping, hurdling and throwing weights—track and field sports, in other words—are as natural to young people as eating, drinking and breathing. Unorganized competition in this form of sport goes back beyond the Cave Man era. Organized competition begins with the first recorded Olympic Games in Greece, 776 B.C., when Coroebus of Elis won the only event on the program, a race of approximately 200 yards. The Olympic Games, with an ever-widening program of events, continued until "the glory that was Greece" had faded and "the grandeur that was Rome" was tarnished, and finally were abolished by decree of Emperor Theodosius I of Rome in A.D. 394. The Tailteann Games of Ireland are supposed to have antedated the first Olympic Games by some centuries, but we have no records of the specific events and winners thereof.

Professional contests of speed and strength were popular at all times and in many lands, but the widespread competition of amateur athletes in track and field sports is a comparatively modern development. The first organized amateur athletic meet of record was sponsored by the Royal Military Academy at Woolwich, England, in 1849. Oxford and Cambridge track and field rivalry began in 1864, and the English amateur championships were established in 1866. In the United States such organizations as the New York Athletic Club and the Olympic Club of San Francisco conducted track and field meets in the 1870s, and a few colleges joined to sponsor a meet in 1874. The success of the college meet led to the formation of the Intercollegiate Association of Amateur Athletes of America and the holding of an annual set of championship games beginning in 1876. The Amateur Athletic Union, organized in 1888, has been the ruling body in American amateur athletics since that time. In 1980, The Athletics Congress of the U.S.A. took over the governing of track and field from the A.A.U.

WORLD RECORDS—MEN

(Through Sept. 19, 1984)

Recognized by the International Athletic Federation.

The I.A.A.F. decided late in 1976 not to recognize records in yards except for the one-mile run.

The I.A.A.F. also requires automatic timing for all records for races of 400 meters or less.

Event	Record	Holder	Home Country	Where Made	Date
Running					
100 m	0:09.93	Calvin Smith	U.S.	Colorado Springs	July 3, 1983
200 m	0:19.72	Pietro Mennea	Italy	Mexico City	Sept. 17, 1979
400 m	0:43.86	Lee Evans	U.S.	Mexico City	Oct. 18, 1968
800 m	1:41.8	Sebastian Coe	England	Florence, Italy	June 10, 1981
1,000 m	2:12.40	Sebastian Coe	England	Oslo, Norway	July 11, 1981
1,500 m	3:30.77	Steve Ovett	England	Rieti, Italy	Sept. 4, 1983
1 mile	3:47.33	Sebastian Coe	England	Brussels	Aug. 28, 1981
2,000 m	4:51.4	John Walker	New Zealand	Oslo	June 30, 1976
3,000 m	7:32.1	Henry Rono	Kenya	Oslo	June 27, 1978
3,000-m steeplechase	8:05.1	Henry Rono	Kenya	Seattle, Wash.	May 13, 1978
5,000 m	13:00.12	David Moorcroft	England	Oslo	July 7, 1982
10,000 m	27:13.81	Fernando Mamede	Portugal	Stockholm, Swe.	July 2, 1984
25,000 m	1:13:55.8	Toshihiko Seko	Japan	Christchurch, N.Z.	March 22, 1981
30,000 m	1:29:18.8	Toshihiko Seko	Japan	Christchurch, N.Z.	March 22, 1981
20,000 m	57:24.2	Jos Hermans	Netherlands	Papandal, Neth.	May 1, 1976
1 hour	13 mi. 24 yd	Jos Hermans	Netherlands	Papandal, Neth.	May 1, 1976
Walking					
20,000 m	1:18:39.9	Ernesto Canto	Mexico	Fana, Norway	May 5, 1984
2 hours	17 mi. 1,092 yd	Ralph Kowalsky	East Germany	East Berlin	March 28, 1982
30,000 m	2:06.54	Ralph Kowalsky	East Germany	East Berlin	March 28, 1982
50,000 m	3:41:39	Raul Gonzales	Mexico	Bergen, Norway	May 25, 1979
Hurdles					
110 m	0:12.93	Renaldo Nehemiah	U.S.	Zurich, Switzerland	Aug. 19, 1981
400 m	0:47.02	Edwin Moses	U.S.	Koblenz, W. Ger.	Aug. 31, 1983
Relay Races					
400 m (4×100)	0:37.83	Olympic Team	U.S.	Los Angeles, Ca.	Aug. 11, 1984
800 m (4×200)	1:20.26	So. California	U.S.	Tempe, Ariz.	May 27, 1978
		(Joel Andrews, James Sanford, Billy Mullins, Clancy Edwards)			
1,600 m (4×400)	2:56.16	National Team	U.S.	Mexico City	Oct. 20, 1968
		(Vince Matthews, Ron Freeman, Larry James, Lee Evans)			
3,200 m (4×800)	7:03.89	National Team	Britain	London	Aug. 30, 1982
		(Peter Elliot, Garry Cook, Steve Cram, Sebastian Coe)			

Field Events

High jump	7 ft. 10 in.	Zhu Jianhua	China	Eberstadt, W. Ger.	June 10, 1984
Long jump	29 ft 2 1/2 in.	Bob Beamon	U.S.	Mexico City	Oct. 18, 1968
Triple jump	58 ft 8 1/4 in.	Joao Oliveirn	Brazil	Mexico City	Oct. 15, 1975
Pole vault	19 ft 5 3/4 in.	Sergey Bubka	U.S.S.R.	Rome	Aug. 31, 1984
Shot put	72 ft 10 3/4 in.	Udo Beyer	E. Germany	Los Angeles, Cal.	June 25, 1983
Discus throw	235 ft 9 in.	Yuriy Dumchev	U.S.S.R.	Moscow	May 29, 1983
Hammer throw	283 ft 3 in.	Yuriy Syedikh	U.S.S.R.	Cork, Ire.	July 3, 1984
Javelin throw	343 ft 10 in.	Uwe Hohn	E. Germany	Oslo, Norway	July 20, 1984
Decathlon	8,798 pts	Jurgen Hingsen	W. Germany	Mannheim, W. Ger.	June 8–9, 1984

WORLD RECORDS—WOMEN

Event	Record	Holder	Home Country	Where Made	Date
Running					
100 m	0:10.76	Evelyn Ashford	U.S.	Zurich, Switz.	Aug. 22, 1984
200 m	0:21.71	Marita Koch	E. Germany	Karl Marx Stadt	June 10, 1979
400 m	0:47.99	Jarmila Kratochvilova	Czechoslovakia	Helsinki, Fin.	Aug. 10, 1983
800 m	1:53.28	Jarmila Kratochvilova	Czechoslovakia	Munich, W. Ger.	July 26, 1983
1,500 m	3:52.47	Tatyana Kazankina	U.S.S.R.	Zurich, Switz.	Aug. 13, 1980
1 mile	4:17.44	Maricica Puica	Rumania	Rieti, Italy	Sept. 16, 1982
3,000 m	8:22.62	Tatyana Kazankina	U.S.S.R.	Moscow	Aug. 26, 1984
5,000 m	14:58.89	Ingrid Kristiansen	Norway	Oslo, Nor.	June 28, 1984
10,000 m	31:13.78	Olga Bondarenko	U.S.S.R.	Kiev, U.S.S.R.	June 24, 1984
Hurdles					
100 m	0:12.36	Grazyna Rabsztyn	Poland	Warsaw, Pol.	June 13, 1980
400 m	0:53.58	Margarita Ponomaryeva	U.S.S.R.	Kiev, U.S.S.R.	June 22, 1984
Relay Races					
400 m (4×100)	0:41.53	East Germany	E. Germany	Berlin, E. Ger.	July 31, 1983
800 m (4×200)	1:28.15	East Germany	E. Germany	Jena, E. Ger.	Aug. 9, 1980
1,600 m (4×400)	3:15.92	East Germany	E. Germany	Erfurt, E. Ger.	June 3, 1984
3,200 m (4×800)	7:52.3	Soviet Union	U.S.S.R.	Podolsk, U.S.S.R.	Aug. 16, 1976
Field Events					
High jump	6 ft 9 in.	Lyudmila Andonova	Bulgaria	Oslo, Norway	July 20, 1984
Long jump	24 ft 4 1/2 in.	Anisoara (Cusmir) Stanciu	Rumania	Bucharest, Rum.	June 4, 1983
Shot put	73 ft 11 in.	Natalya Lisovskaya	U.S.S.R.	Sochi, U.S.S.R.	May 27, 1984
Discus throw	244 ft 11 in.	Zdena Silhava	Czechoslovakia	Prague, Czech.	Aug. 26, 1984
Javelin throw	245 ft 3 in.	Tiina Lillak	Finland	Tampere, Fin.	June 13, 1983
Heptathlon	6,867 pts	Sabine Paetz	East Germany	Potsdam, E. Ger.	May 5–6, 1984

AMERICAN RECORDS—MEN

Officially approved by The Athletics Congress.

Event	Record	Holder	Where Made	Date
Running				
100 m	0:09.93	Calvin Smith	Colorado Springs, Colo.	July 3, 1983
200 m	0:19.75	Carl Lewis	Indianapolis, Ind.	June 19, 1983
400 m	0:43.86	Lee Evans	Mexico City	Oct. 16, 1968
800 m	1:43.28	Johnny Gray	Cologne, W. Ger.	Aug. 26, 1984
1,000 m	2:13.9	Richard Wohlhuter	Oslo, Norway	July 30, 1974
1,500 m	3:31.96	Steve Scott	Koblenz, W. Ger.	Aug. 26, 1981
1 mile	3:47.69	Steve Scott	Oslo, Norway	July 7, 1982
2,000 m	4:54.71	Steve Scott	Ingelhelm, W. Ger.	Aug. 31, 1982
3,000 m	7:35.84	Doug Padilla	Oslo, Norway	July 9, 1983
5,000 m	13:11.93	Alberto Salazar	Stockholm, Swe.	July 6, 1982
10,000 m	27:25.61	Alberto Salazar	Oslo, Norway	June 28, 1982
20,000 m	58:15.0	Bill Rodgers	Boston, Mass.	Aug. 9, 1977
25,000 m	1:14:11.8	Bill Rodgers	Saratoga, Cal.	Feb. 21, 1979
30,000 m	1:31:49	Bill Rodgers	Saratoga, Cal.	Feb. 21, 1979
1 hour	12 mi., 1351 yds	Bill Rodgers	Boston, Mass.	Aug. 9, 1977
3,000-m steeplechase	8:12.37	Henry Marsh	Berlin, W. Ger.	Aug. 17, 1983

Hurdles

110 m	0:12.93	Renaldo Nehemiah	Zurich, Switz.	Aug. 19, 1981
400 m	0:47.02	Edwin Moses	Koblenz, W. Ger.	Aug. 31, 1983

Relay Races

400 m (4×100)	0:37.83	U.S. Olympic Team	Los Angeles, Cal.	Aug. 11, 1984
800 m (4×200)	1:20.26	Southern California	Tempe, Ariz.	May 27, 1978
1,600 m (4×400)	2:56.16	U.S. Olympic Team	Mexico City	Oct. 20, 1968
3,200 m (4×800)	7:08.96	Arizona State	Tempe, Ariz.	Apr. 7, 1984

Field Events

High jump	7 ft 8 in.	Dwight Stones	Los Angeles, Cal.	June 24, 1984
Long jump	29 ft 2 1/2 in.	Bob Beamon	Mexico City	Oct. 18, 1968
Triple jump	57 ft 7 1/2 in.	Willie Banks	Sacramento, Cal.	June 21, 1981
Pole vault	19 ft 3/4 in.	Mike Tully	Los Angeles, Cal.	June 21, 1984
Shot put	72 ft 9 3/4 in.	Brian Oldfield	San Jose, Cal.	May 26, 1984
Discus throw	237 ft 4 in.	Ben Plucknett	Stockholm, Swe.	July 7, 1981
Javelin throw	327 ft 2 in.	Tom Petranoff	Los Angeles, Cal.	May 15, 1983
Hammer throw	248 ft 0 in.	Bill Green	Los Angeles, Cal.	Aug. 6, 1984
Decathlon	8,617 pts	Bruce Jenner	Montreal, Can.	July 29–30, 1976

AMERICAN RECORDS—WOMEN

Event	Record	Holder	Where Made	Date
Running				
100 m	0:10.76	Evelyn Ashford	Zurich, Switz.	Aug. 22, 1984
200 m	0:21.81	Valerie Brisco-Hooks	Los Angeles, Cal.	Aug. 9, 1984
400 m	0:48.83	Valerie Brisco-Hooks	Los Angeles, Cal.	Aug. 6, 1984
800 m	1:57.61	Mary Decker	Gateshead, Eng.	July 31, 1983
1,500 m	3:57.12	Mary Decker	Stockholm, Swe.	July 26, 1983
1 mile	4:18.08	Mary Decker	Paris, France	July 9, 1982
3,000 m	8:29.71	Mary Decker	Oslo, Norway	July 7, 1982
5,000 m	15:08.26	Mary Decker	Eugene, Ore.	June 5, 1982
10,000 m	31:35.3	Mary Decker	Eugene, Ore.	July 16, 1982
Hurdles				
100 m	12.79	Stephanie Hightower	Karl-Marx-Stadt, E. Ger.	July 10, 1982
400 m	54.93	Judi Brown	Los Angeles, Cal.	June 21, 1984
Relay Races				
400 m (4×100)	0:41.61	U.S. National Team	Colorado Springs, Col.	July 3, 1983
800 m (4×200)	1:32.6	U.S. National Team	Bourges, France	June 24, 1979
1,600 m (4×400)	3:18.29	U.S. Olympic Team	Los Angeles, Cal.	Aug. 11, 1984
Field Events				
High jump	6 ft 7 in.	Louise Ritter	Rome, Italy	Sept. 1, 1983
Long Jump	22 ft 11 3/4 in.	Jodi Anderson	Eugene, Ore.	June 28, 1980
Shot put	62 ft 7 3/4 in.	Maren Seidler	Walnut, Cal.	June 16, 1979
Discus throw	213 ft 11 in.	Leslie Demiz	Tempe, Ariz.	Apr. 7, 1984
Javelin throw	227 ft 5 in.	Kate Schmidt	Furth, W. Ger.	Sept. 10, 1977
Heptathlon	6,520 pts	Jackie Joyner	Los Angeles, Cal.	June 16–17, 1984

HISTORY OF THE RECORD FOR THE MILE RUN

Time	Athlete	Country	Year	Location
4:36.5	Richard Webster	England	1865	England
4:29.0	William Chinnery	England	1868	England
4:28.8	Walter Gibbs	England	1868	England
4:26.0	Walter Slade	England	1874	England
4:24.5	Walter Slade	England	1875	London

4:23.2	Walter George	England	1880	London
4:21.4	Walter George	England	1882	London
4:18.4	Walter George	England	1884	Birmingham, England
4:18.2	Fred Bacon	Scotland	1894	Edinburgh, Scotland
4:17.0	Fred Bacon	Scotland	1895	London
4:15.6	Thomas Conneff	United States	1895	Travers Island, N.Y.
4:15.4	John Paul Jones	United States	1911	Cambridge, Mass.
4:14.4	John Paul Jones	United States	1913	Cambridge, Mass.
4:12.6	Norman Taber	United States	1915	Cambridge, Mass.
4:10.4	Paavo Nurmi	Finland	1923	Stockholm
4:09.2	Jules Ladoumegue	France	1931	Paris
4:07.6	Jack Lovelock	New Zealand	1933	Princeton, N.J.
4:06.8	Glenn Cunningham	United States	1934	Princeton, N.J.
4:06.4	Sydney Wooderson	England	1937	London
4:06.2	Gundar Hägg	Sweden	1942	Göteborg, Sweden
4:06.2	Arne Andersson	Sweden	1942	Stockholm
4:04.6	Gunder Hägg	Sweden	1942	Stockholm
4:02.6	Arne Andersson	Sweden	1943	Göteborg, Sweden
4:01.6	Arne Andersson	Sweden	1944	Malmö, Sweden
4:01.4	Gunder Hägg	Sweden	1945	Malmö, Sweden
3:59.4	Roger Bannister	England	1954	Oxford, England
3:58.0	John Landy	Australia	1954	Turku, Finland
3:57.2	Derek Ibbotson	England	1957	London
3:54.5	Herb Elliott	Australia	1958	Dublin
3:54.4	Peter Snell	New Zealand	1962	Wanganui, N.Z.
3:54.1	Peter Snell	New Zealand	1964	Auckland, N.Z.
3:53.6	Michel Jazy	France	1965	Rennes, France
3:51.3	Jim Ryun	United States	1966	Berkeley, Calif.
3:51.1	Jim Ryun	United States	1967	Bakersfield, Calif.
3:51.0	Filbert Bayi	Tanzania	1975	Kingston, Jamaica
3:49.4	John Walker	New Zealand	1975	Göteborg, Sweden
3:49.0	Sebastian Coe	England	1979	Oslo
3:48.8	Steve Ovett	England	1980	Oslo
3:48.53	Sebastian Coe	England	1981	Zurich, Switzerland
3:48.40	Steve Ovett	England	1981	Koblenz, W. Ger.
3:47.33	Sebastian Coe	England	1981	Brussels

WORLD'S FASTEST INDOOR MILES

Time	Athlete	Country	Date	Location
3:49.78	Eamonn Coghlan	Ireland	Feb. 27, 1983	East Rutherford, N.J.
3:50.6	Eamonn Coghlan	Ireland	Feb. 20, 1981	San Diego
3:51.2	Ray Flynn[1]	Ireland	Feb. 27, 1983	East Rutherford, N.J.
3:51.8	Steve Scott[1]	United States	Feb. 20, 1981	San Diego
3:52.28	Steve Scott[2]	United States	Feb. 27, 1983	East Rutherford, N.J.
3:52.56	Jose Abascal[3]	Spain	Feb. 27, 1983	East Rutherford, N.J.
3:52.6	Eamonn Coghlan	Ireland	Feb. 16, 1979	San Diego
3:52.8	John Walker[2]	New Zealand	Feb. 20, 1981	San Diego
3:52.8	John Walker	New Zealand	Feb. 19, 1982	San Diego
3:52.9	Eamonn Coghlan	Ireland	Feb. 15, 1980	Los Angeles
3:53.0	Steve Scott[1]	United States	Feb. 15, 1980	Los Angeles
3:53.0	Eamonn Coghlan	Ireland	Feb. 6, 1981	New York
3:53.1	Eamonn Coghlan	Ireland	Feb. 18, 1983	San Diego
3:53.6	Ray Flynn[3]	Ireland	Feb. 20, 1981	San Diego
3:53.6	Tom Byers[3]	United States	Feb. 19, 1982	San Diego
3:53.7	Steve Scott	United States	Jan. 30, 1981	Los Angeles
3:53.8	Ray Flynn	Ireland	Feb. 6, 1981	New York
3:54.1	Steve Scott[1]	United States	Feb. 16, 1979	San Diego
3:54.1	Ray Flynn[2]	Ireland	Feb. 19, 1982	San Diego
3:54.3	Eamonn Coghlan[4]	Ireland	Jan. 30, 1981	Los Angeles
3:54.4	Ray Flynn[2]	Ireland	Jan. 30, 1981	Los Angeles
3:54.4	Eamonn Coghlan[1]	Ireland	Jan. 20, 1983	New York
3:54.4	Jay Wards	United States	Feb. 20, 1983	East Rutherford, N.J.
3:54.5	Filbert Bayi[2]	Tanzania	Feb. 15, 1980	Los Angeles
3:54.7	Steve Lacy[2]	United States	Feb. 16, 1979	San Diego
3:54.7	Thomas Wessinghage[2]	West Germany	Feb. 6, 1981	New York

3:54.9	Ray Flynn	Ireland	Feb. 13, 1981	Inglewood, Calif.
3:55.0	Tony Waldrop	United States	Feb. 17, 1979	San Diego
3:55.0	Dick Buerkle	United States	Jan. 13, 1978	College Park, Md.
3:55.0	Eamonn Coghlan	Ireland	Feb. 9, 1979	New York
3:55.0	Steve Scott[3]	United States	Feb. 6, 1981	New York
3:55.0	Steve Scott[3]	United States	Feb. 19, 1982	San Diego
3:55.2	John Walker[1]	New Zealand	Feb. 13, 1981	Inglewood, Calif.
3:55.3	Steve Scott	United States	Feb. 21, 1981	Daly City, Calif.
3:55.37	Steve Scott	United States	Feb. 12, 1982	New York
3:55.4	Niall O'Shaughnessy	Ireland	Jan. 28, 1977	Columbia, Mo.
3:55.41	Tom Byers[1]	United States	Feb. 12, 1982	New York
3:55.5	Filbert Bayi[1]	Tanzania	Feb. 22, 1980	San Diego
3:55.5	Sydney Maree[1]	South Africa	Feb. 21, 1981	Daly City, Calif.
3:55.55	Eamonn Coghlan	Ireland	Jan. 31, 1981	Dallas

1. Finished second. 2. Finished third. 3. Finished fourth. 4. Finished fifth.

WORLD'S FASTEST OUTDOOR MILES

Time	Athlete	Country	Date	Location
3:47.33	Sebastian Coe	England	Aug. 28, 1981	Brussels
3:47.69	Steve Scott	United States	July 7, 1982	Oslo
3:48.40	Steve Ovett	England	Aug. 26, 1981	Koblenz, W. Ger.
3:48.53	Sebastian Coe	England	Aug. 19, 1981	Zurich
3:48.53	Steve Scott	United States	June 26, 1982	Oslo
3:48.8	Steve Ovett	England	July 1, 1980	Oslo
3:48.83	Sydney Maree	United States	Sept. 9, 1981	Rieti, Italy
3:48.85	Sydney Maree[1]	United States	June 26, 1982	Oslo
3:48.95	Sebastian Coe	England	July 17, 1979	Oslo
3:49.08	John Walker[1]	New Zealand	July 7, 1982	Oslo
3:49.25	Steve Ovett	England	July 11, 1981	Oslo
3:49.34	David Moorcroft[2]	England	June 26, 1982	Oslo
3:49.4	John Walker	New Zealand	Aug. 12, 1975	Goteborg, Sweden
3:49.44	Sydney Maree	United States	July 13, 1982	Cork, Eire
3:49.45	Mike Boit[1]	Kenya	Aug. 28, 1981	Brussels
3:49.50	John Walker[3]	New Zealand	June 26, 1982	Oslo
3:49.57	Steve Ovett	England	Aug. 31, 1979	London
3:49.66	Steve Ovett	England	July 14, 1981	Lausanne, Switz.
3:49.67	Jose-Luis Gonzalez[1]	Spain	July 11, 1981	Oslo
3:49.68	Steve Scott[2]	United States	July 11, 1981	Oslo
3:49.72	Steve Scott	United States	Aug. 25, 1982	Koblenz, W. Ger.
3:49.74	Mike Boit[1]	Kenya	Aug. 19, 1981	Zurich
3:49.75	Sydney Maree[1]	United States	Aug. 25, 1982	Koblenz, W. Ger.
3:49.77	Ray Flynn[2]	Eire	July 7, 1982	Oslo
3:49.92	Steve Cram[1]	England	July 13, 1982	Cork, Eire
3:49.93	Sydney Maree	United States	Sept. 16, 1981	Aichach, W. Ger.
3:49.95	Steve Cram[2]	England	Aug. 19, 1981	Zurich
3:50.03	John Walker[2]	New Zealand	July 13, 1982	Cork, Eire
3:50.12	John Walker[3]	New Zealand	Aug. 19, 1981	Zurich
3:50.19	Thomas Wessinghage[2]	West Germany	Aug. 25, 1982	Koblenz, W. Ger.
3:50.23	Steve Ovett[1]	England	Sept. 9, 1981	Rieti, Italy
3:50.26	John Walker[3]	New Zealand	July 11, 1981	Oslo
3:50.34	Todd Harbour[4]	United States	July 11, 1981	Oslo
3:50.38	Steve Cram[5]	England	July 11, 1981	Oslo
3:50.38	Pierre Deleze[3]	Switzerland	Aug. 25, 1982	Koblenz, W. Ger.
3:50.51	Mike Boit[1]	Kenya	Sept. 16, 1981	Aichach, W. Ger.
3:50.54	Ray Flynn[4]	Eire	June 26, 1982	Oslo
3:50.55	Ray Flynn[4]	Eire	Aug. 25, 1982	Koblenz, W. Ger.
3:50.56	Thomas Wessinghage[1]	West Germany	Aug. 31, 1979	London
3:50.58	John Walker	New Zealand	Mar. 19, 1981	Auckland, N.Z.
3:50.65	Graham Williamson[3]	England	July 13, 1982	Cork, Eire
3:50.84	Tom Byers[5]	United States	Aug. 25, 1982	Koblenz, W. Ger.
3:50.87	Jose-Luis Gonzalez[1]	Spain	July 14, 1981	Lausanne, Switz.
3:50.91	Thomas Wessinghage[6]	West Germany	July 11, 1981	Oslo
3:50.95	Thomas Wessinghage[4]	West Germany	Aug. 19, 1981	Zurich
3:51.0	Filbert Bayi	Tanzania	May 17, 1975	Kingston, Jamaica
3:51.1	Jim Ryun	United States	June 23, 1967	Bakersfield, Calif.

1. Finished second. 2. Finished third. 3. Finished fourth. 4. Finished fifth. 5. Finished sixth. 6. Finished seventh. NOTE: Professional marks not included.

HISTORY OF THE POLE VAULT

(Some of early dates are the winning heights of A.A.U. champion for that year, used to show progression from one foot level to the next. Figures from A.A.U. records and *Track & Field News.*)

Bamboo Poles

1877	G. McNichol	9 ft 7 in.
1879	W. J. Van Houten	10 ft 4 3/4 in.
1883	Hugh Baxter	11 ft 0 1/2 in.
1904	Norman Dole	12 ft 1 3/10 in.
1912	Robert Gardner	13 ft 1 in.
1927	Sabin Carr	14 ft 0 in.
1940	Cornelius Warmerdam	15 ft 1 in.
1942	Cornelius Warmerdam	15 ft 7 3/4 in.

Metal Poles

1957	Bob Gutowski	15 ft 8 1/4 in.
1960	Don Bragg	15 ft 9 1/4 in.

Fiberglas Poles

1961	George Davis	15 ft 10 1/4 in.
1962	John Uelses	16 ft 0 3/4 in.
1962	Dave Tork	16 ft 2 in.
1962	Pentti Nikula	16 ft 2 1/2 in.
1963	John Pennel	16 ft 4 in.
1963	Brian Sternberg	16 ft 5 in.
1963	John Pennel	16 ft 6 3/4 in.
1963	Brian Sternberg	16 ft 8 in.
1963	John Pennel	16 ft 10 in.
1963	John Pennel	17 ft 0 3/4 in.
1964	Fred Hansen	17 ft 4 in.
1966	Bob Seagren	17 ft 5 1/2 in.
1966	John Pennel	17 ft 6 1/4 in.
1967	Bob Seagren	17 ft 7 in.
1967	Paul Wilson	17 ft 7 3/4 in.
1968	Bob Seagren	17 ft 9 in.
1969	John Pennel	17 ft 10 1/4 in.
1970	Wolfgang Norwig	17 ft 10 1/2 in.
1970	Chris Papanicolaou	18 ft 0 1/4 in.
1972	Kjell Isaksson	18 ft 1 in.
1972	Kjell Isaksson	18 ft 2 in.
1972	Kjell Isaksson, Bob Seagren	18 ft 4 1/4 in.
1972	Bob Seagren	18 ft 5 3/4 in.
1975	Dave Roberts	18 ft 6 1/2 in.
1976	Earl Bell	18 ft 7 1/4 in.
1976	Dave Roberts	18 ft 8 1/4 in.
1980	Thierry Vigneron	18 ft 10 1/4 in.
1980	Philippe Houvion	18 ft 11 in.
1980	Wladyslaw Kozakiewicz	18 ft 11 1/2 in.
1981	Thierry Vigneron	19 ft 1/4 in.
1981	Vladimir Polyakov	19 ft 3/4 in.
1983	Pierre Quinon	19 ft 1/2 in.
1983	Thierry Vigneron	19 ft 1 1/2 in.
1984	Sergey Bubka	19 ft 1 1/2 in.
1984	Sergey Bubka	19 ft 2 1/4 in.
1984	Sergey Bubka	19 ft 3 1/2 in.
1984	Sergey Bubka	19 ft 4 1/4 in.
1984	Thierry Vigneron	19 ft 4 3/4 in.
1984	Sergey Bubka	19 ft 5 3/4 in.

UNITED STATES MARATHON CHAMPIONS

(26 miles, 385 Yards)

Boston Marathon

1970	Ron Hill, England	2:10:30
1971	Alvaro Meija, Colombia	2:18:45
1972	Olavi Suomalainen, Finland	2:15:39
1973	Jon Anderson, Eugene, Ore.	2:16:03
1974	Neil Cusack, Ireland	2:13:39
1975	William H. Rodgers, Boston	2:09:55
1976	Jack Fultz, Arlington, Va.	2:20:19
1977	Jerome Drayton, Toronto	2:14:46
1978	William H. Rodgers, Melrose, Mass.	2:10:13
1979	William H. Rodgers, Melrose, Mass.	2:09:27
1980	William H. Rodgers, Melrose, Mass.	2:12:11
1981	Toshihiko Seko, Japan	2:09:26
1982	Alberto Salazar, Eugene, Ore.	2:08:51
1983	Greg Meyer, Wellesley, Mass.	2:09:00
1984	Geoff Smith, England	2:10:34

Amateur Athletic Union

1970	Bob Fitts, Wisconsin	2:24:11
1971	Ken Moore, Portland, Ore.	2:16:49
1972	Edmund Norris, Brockton, Mass.	2:24:42.8
1973	Doug Schmenk	2:15:48
1974	Ron Wayne, Eugene, Ore.	2:18:52
1975	Gary Tuttle, Beverly Hills Strider	2:17:27
1976	Gary Tuttle, Los Angeles	2:15:15
1977	Not Held	
1978	Carl Hatfield, West Va. T.C.	2:17.20
1979	Tom Antczak, Rockford, Ill.	2:15.28

The Athletics Congress

1980	Frank Richardson, Ames, Iowa	2:14:04
1981	Not contested	
1982	Joel Menges, Birmingham, Ala.	2:32:29
1983	Pete Pfitzinger, Boston, Mass.	2:14:45
1984	Not contested	

(Replaced by U.S. Olympic Marathon Trials Pete Pfitzinger, West Newton, M 2:11:43).

CROSS COUNTRY RACE CHAMPIONS

The Athletics Congress

(A.A.U. before 1980)

(10,000 Meters)

1971	Frank Shorter, Gainesville, Fla.; Florida T.C.
1972	Frank Shorter, Gainesville, Fla.; Florida T.C.
1973	Frank Shorter, Gainesville, Fla.; Florida T.C.
1974	John Ngeno, Kenya; Colorado T.C.
1975	Greg Fredericks, Philadelphia; Colorado T.C.
1976	Rick Rojas, San Diego; Jamul Toads
1977	Nick Rose, England; Colorado T.C.
1978	Greg Meyer, Boston; Mason Dixon A.C.
1979	Alberto Salazar, Boston; Greater Boston T.C.

1980 Jon Sinclair, Boulder, Colo. Victory A.C.
1981 Adrian Royle, Reno, Nev.; Athletics West
1982 Pat Porter, Eugene, Ore.; Athletics West
1983 Pat Porter, Alamosa, Colo.; Athletics West

N.C.A.A. (University)

(10,000 meters)

1973 Steve Prefontaine, Oregon; Oregon
1974 Nick Rose, Western Kentucky; Oregon
1975 Craig Virgin, Illinois; Texas-El Paso
1976 Henry Rono, Wash. State; Texas-El Paso
1977 Henry Rono, Wash. State; Oregon
1978 Alberto Salazar, Oregon; Texas-El Paso
1979 Henry Rono, Washington State; Texas-El Paso
1980 Suleiman Nyambui, Texas-El Paso, Texas-El Paso
1981 Matthews Motshwarateu, Texas-El Paso; Texas-El Paso
1982 Mark Scrutton, Colorado; Wisconsin
1983 Zackariah Barie, Texas-El Paso; Texas-El Paso

N.C.A.A. (College)

(10,000 meters)

1975 Div. II: Ralph Serna, Calif.-Irvine; Calif.-Irvine
Div. III: Vin Fleming, Lowell; N. Central Illinois
1976 Div. II: Ralph Serna, Calif.-Irvine; Calif.-Irvine
Div. III: Dale Cramer, Carleton; N. Central Illinois
1977 Div. II: Michael Bollman, N.D. State; E. Illinois
Div. III: Dale Kramer, Carleton; Occidental
1978 Div. II: Jim Schankel, Cal Poly, San Luis Opisbo; Cal Poly, San Luis Opisbo
Div. III: Dan Henderson, Wheaton; N. Cent. Illinois
1979 Div. II: Jim Schankel, Cal Poly, San Luis Opisbo
Div. III: Steve Hunt, Boston State; North Central, Ill.
1980 Div. II: Gary Henry, Pembroke State; Humboldt State
Div. III: Jeff Millman, North Central; Carleton
1981 Div. II: Mark Conover, Humboldt State; Millersville State
Div. III: Mark Whalley, Principia; North Central
1982 Div. II: Greg Beardsley, Edinboro State; Eastern Washington
Div. III: Nicolae Manciu, St. Thomas; North Central
1983 Div. II: Brian Ferrari, California of Pennsylvania; California-Poly/Pomoma
Div. III: Tony Bluell, North Central; Brandeis

N.A.I.A.

(5 Miles)

1973 Tony Brien, Marymount; Eastern New Mexico
1974 Mike Boit, Eastern New Mexico; Eastern New Mexico
1975 Mike Boit, Eastern New Mexico; Edinboro State
1976 John Kebiro, Eastern New Mexico; Edinboro State
1977 Garry Henry, Pembroke State; Adams State
1978 Kelly Jensen, So. Oregon; Pembroke State
1979 Sam Montoya, Adams State; Adams State
1980 Pat Porter, Adams State; Adams State
1981 Pat Porter, Adams State; Adams State
1982 Steve Delano, Southwestern Kansas; Simon Fraser, Canada
1983 Steve Delano, Southwestern Kansas; Adams State (Colo.)

WORLD CROSS-COUNTRY CHAMPIONSHIPS—1984

(EAST RUTHERFORD, NEW JERSEY, MARCH 25, 1984)

Men—Carlos Lopes, Portugal	33:25
Women—Maricica Puica, Rumania	15:56
Junior men—Pedro Casacuberta, Spain	21:32
Men's team—Ethiopia	134 pts
Women's team—United States	52 pts
Junior men's team—Ethiopia	21 pts

WORLD AND AMERICAN BEST PERFORMANCES IN INDOOR TRACK

The International Amateur Athletic Union does not recognize indoor records. The following best performances, often called world records, are from lists provided by The Athletics Congress of the United States.

MEN

Running

50 yards—Stanley Floyd, Los Angeles, 1982	0:05.22
60 yards—Carl Lewis, Dallas, 1983	0:06.02
70 yards—Herb McFarland, Louisville, Ky.	0:06.7
100 yards—Don Quarrie, Pocatello, Idaho, 1971	0:09.3
Carl Lawson, Pocatello, Idaho, 1971	0:09.3
Cliff Branch, Pocatello, Idaho, 1972	0:09.3
300 yards—Terron Wright, Bloomington, Ind., 1981	0:29.26
440 yards—Tommie Smith, Louisville, Ky., 1967	0:46.2
Deon Hogan (Am.), Lincoln, Neb., 1981	0:47.20
500 yards—Lee Evans, College Park, Md., 1971	0:54.4
Pro—Larry James, Salt Lake City, Utah, 1973	0:53.9
600 yards—Martin McGrady, New York, 1970	1:07.6
880 yards—Ralph Doubell, Albuquerque N.M., 1969	1:47.9
Mark Belger (Am.), College Park, Md., 1978	1:48.1
Tom Von Ruden (Am.), College Park, Md., 1971	1:48.5
1,000 yards—Don Paige, Inglewood, Calif., 1982	2:04.7
Mile—Eamonn Coghlan, East Rutherford, N.J., 1983	3:49.78
Steve Scott (Am.), San Diego, 1981	3:51.8
2 miles—Emiel Puttemans, Pentin, Belgium, 1976	8:13.2
Doug Padilla (Am.), San Diego, 1983	8:16.5
3 miles—Emiel Puttemans, Pentin, Belgium, 1976	12:54.6
Alberto Salazar (Am.), New York, 1981	12:56.6

Running—Metric Distances

50 meters—Manfred Koket, East Germany, 1971	0:05.4
Bill Gaines (Am.), Highland Park, N.J., 1968	0:05.4
James Sanford (Am.), San Diego, 1981	0:05.61
60 meters—Houston McTear, New York, 1978	0:06.11
70 meters—Helmut Kornig, Germany, 1932	0:07.5
Ira Murchison (Am.), United States	0:07.5
Pro—John Carlos, Pocatello, Idaho, 1974	0:07.3
100 meters—Eugen Ray, East Berlin, 1976	0:10.16
Pro—Warren Edmonson, Pocatello, Idaho, 1973	0:10.2

Walking

1,500 meters—Jim Helring, East Rutherford, N.J., 1982	5:27.1
Mile—Ray Sharp, New York, 1983	5:46.21
3,000 meters—Yevgeny Yavsyukov, Montreal, 1979	11:31.1
Jim Heiring (Am.), Rosemont, Ill., 1983	11:32.15
2 miles—Jim Heiring, New York, 1984	12:11.21
3 miles—Antoll Soloman, Toronto, 1978	19:40.0

Relays

1,600 meters—West Germany, Dortmund, West Germany, 1981	3:34.38
880 yards—Idaho State, Pocatello, Idaho, 1979	1:26.9

800 meters—Italy, Turin, Italy, 1984 1:22.32
Morgan State (Am.), Fairfax, Va., 1984 1:25.92
Mile—Pacific Coast Club, Pocatello, Idaho, 1971 3:09.4
2 miles—Univ. of Chicago, T.C., Louisville, Ky., 1974 7:20.8
4 miles—Villanova, Hanover, N.H., 1976 16:19
Spring medley—Eastern Michigan, Kalamazoo, Mich., 1984 3:18.70
Distance medley—Arkansas, Boston, Mass., 1984 9:35.29

Field Events

High jump—Carlo Thranhardt, Berlin, W. Germany 1984 7 ft 9 1/4 in.
Jeff Woodard (Am.), New York, 1981 7 ft 7 3/4 in.
Long jump—Carl Lewis, NY, NY, 1984 28 ft 10 1/4 in.
Triple jump—Willie Banks, San Diego, 1982 57 ft 1 1/2 in.
Pole vault—Thierry Vigneron, Goteborg, Sweden, 1984 19 ft 2 1/4 in.
35-lb weight throw—Tore Johnsen, Texas-El Paso 70 ft 3 1/4 in.
Pro—Steve Smith, New York, 1975 18 ft 5 in.
Billy Olson (Am.), Inglewood, Calif., 1984 19 ft 1/4 in.
Shotput—George Woods, Inglewood, Calif., 1974 72 ft 2 3/4 in.
Brian Oldfield (pro), El Paso, Tex., 1975 72 ft 6 1/2 in.
35-pound weight throw—Tore Johnsen, Air Force Academy, Colo, 1984 78 ft. 6 1/2 in.
Jud Logan (Am.), Princeton, N.J. 75 ft 3 1/4 in.
Penthathlon—Daley Thompson, Canyon, Tex., 1982 4.314 pts
200 meters—Ralf Lubke, Stuttgart, West Germany, 1984 0:20.57
Mel Lattany (Am.), Stuttgart, W. Germany, 1984 0:20.84
300 meters—Pietro Mennea, Italy, 1978 0:32.83
Elliot Quow (Am.), Boston, 1983 0:33.19
400 meters—Antonio McKay, Gainesville, Florida, 1984 (World and American record) 0:45.79
500 meters—Herman Frazier, Long Beach, Calif., 1979 1:01.2
Pro—Lee Evans, Pocatello, Idaho, 1973 1:02
600 meters—Donato Sabia, Genoa, Italy, 1984 1:15.77
Pro—Lee Evans, Pocatello, Idaho, 1977 1:16.7
800 meters—Sebastian Coe, Cosford, England, 1983 1:44.91
Ted Nelson (Am.), Berlin, 1965 1:47.4
1,000 meters—Sebastian Coe, Oslo, Norway, 1983 2:18.58
Don Paige (Am.), East Rutherford, New Jersey, 1984 2:18.88
Pro—Chris Fisher, Daly City, Calif., 1973 2:19.7
1,500 meters—Eamonn Coghlan, San Diego, 1981 3:35.6
Steve Smith (Am.), San Diego, 1981 3:36.0
2,000 meters—Steve Scott, Louisville, Ky., 1981 4:58.6
3,000 meters—Emiel Puttemans, Berlin, 1973 7:39.2
Doug Padilla, (Am.), San Diego, 1983 7:44.9
5,000 meters—Suleiman Nyambul, New York, 1981 13:20.4
Doug Pedilla (Am.), New York, 1982 13:20.55

Hurdles

50 yards—Renaldo Nehemiah, Toronto, 1982 0:05.92
60 yards—Renaldo Nehemiah, Dallas, 1982 0:06.82
50 meters—Renaldo Nehemiah, Edmonton, 1979 0:06.36
60 meters—Thomas Munkelt, Budapest, 1983 0:07.48
Tonie Campbell (Am.), Cosford, Great Britain, 1984 0:07.58

WOMEN

Running

50 yards—Evelyn Ashford, San Diego, 1983 0:05.74
60 yards—Evelyn Ashford, New York, 1982 0:06.54
100 yards—Marlies Gohr, Senftenberg, East Germany, 1983 0:10.29
Wilma Rudolph (Am.), Tennessee State, 1960 0:10.70
220 yards—Chandra Cheeseborough, New York, 1982 0:23.25
300 yards—Merlene Ottey, Cedar Falls, Neb., 1982 0:32.63
Diane Dixon (Am.), Madison, Wis., 1983 0:33.83
440 yards—Rosalyn Bryant, New York, 1977 0:53.20
Lori McCauley (Am.), Cambridge, Mass., 1983 0:53.29
500 yards—Rosalyn Bryant, San Diego, 1977 1:03.30
Janine MacGregor, Inglewood, Calif., 1982 1:03.30
600 yards—Delisa Walton, Cedar Falls, Neb., 1982 1:17.38
880 yards—Mary Decker, San Diego, 1980 1:59.70
1,000 yards—Mary Decker, Inglewood, Calif., 1978 2:23.80
Mile—Mary Decker Tabb, San Diego, 1982 4:20.5
2 miles—Mary Decker Tabb, Los Angeles, 1983 9:31.7

Running—Metric Distances

50 meters—Jeanette Bolden, Edmonton, Alberta, 1981 0:06.13
60 meters—Marita Koch, Senftenberg, East Germany, 1983 0:07.08
Alice Brown, Tokyo, Japan, 1984 0:07.18
100 meters—Marlies Gohr, East Berlin, 1979 0:11.30
Mamie Rallins (Am.), San Diego, 1975 0:12.40
200 meters—Marita Koch, Budapest, 1983 0:22.39
300 meters—Merlene Ottey, Lincoln, Neb., 1981 0:33.12
Diane Dixon, (Am.), Normal, Ill., 1983 0:37.50
400 meters—Jarmila Kratochvilova, Milan, Italy, 1982 0:49.59
Diane Dixon (Am.), East Rutherford, N.J., 1983 0:53.17
Cathy Rattray, Gainesville, Fla. 1984 1:09.38
Edna Brown (Am.), Hanover, N.H., 1984 1:11.10
600 meters—Anita Weiss, East Berlin, 1980 1:26.20
Chris Muller (Am.), Columbia, Mo., 1980 1:28.80
800 meters—Jarmila Kratochvilova, Jablonec, Czechoslovakia, 1983 1:58.33
Mary Decker (Am.), San Diego, 1980 1:58.90
1,000 meters—Bridgette Kraus, West Germany 1978 2:34.80
Diana Richburg (Am.), New London, Conn., 1983 2:40.1
1,500 meters—Mary Decker, New York, 1980 4:00.80
2,000 meters—Yekaterina Podkopayeva, Moscow, 1983 5:43.30
Francie Larrieu (Am.), Edmonton, Alberta, 1981 5:55.2
3,000 meters—Mary Decker Tabb, Inglewood, Calif., 1982 8:47.3

Hurdles

50 yards—Johanna Klier, Toronto, 1978 0:06.20
Debv LaPlante (Am.), Toronto, 1978 0:06.37
60 yards—Stephanie Hightower, New York, 1983 0:07.36
70 yards—Mamie Rallins, Chicago, 1970 0:08.80
Deby LaPlante, Louisville, Ky., 1976 0:08.80
50 meters—Annelie Ehrhardt, Berlin, 1973 0:06.74
Sofia Bielczyzk, Grenoble, France, 1981 0:06.74
Candy Young (Am.), Rosemont, Ill., 1983 0:06.85
60 meters—Bettine Jahn, Budapest, 1983 0:07.75
Stephanie Hightower (Am.), Louisville, Ky., 1983 0:08.02
100 meters—Annelie Ehrhardt, East Germany, 1976 0:13.12
Patty van Wolvelaere (Am.), New York, 1974 0:13.20

Walking

Mile—Susan Brodock, New York, 1978 7:01.70
1,500 meters—Susan Brodock, Toronto, 1976 6:42.90

Relays

640 yards—Tennessee State, New York, 1981 1:08.99
800 meters—Italy, Turin, Italy, 1984 1:34.05
880 yards—Tennessee State, Louisville, Ky., 1980 1:37.80
880 yard medley relay—Tennessee State, New York, 1981 1:42.17
Mile—Atoms T.C., New York, 1984 3:38.15
1,500 meters—Tennessee, Syracuse, NY, 1984 3:37.04
2 miles—Soviet Union, 1972 8:41.60
3,200 meters—Tennessee, Syracuse, NY, 1984 8:40.17
Distance medley—Virginia, Princeton, N.J., 1982 11:19.39

Field Events

Long jump—Heike Dante, Senftenberg, East Germany, 1984 — 22 ft 11 1/4 in.
Carol Lewis (Am.), Dallas, TX, 1984 — 22 ft 2 1/4 in.
High jump—Tamara Bykova, Budapest, 1983 — 6 ft 8 in.
Shotput—Helena Fibingerova, Czechoslovakia, 1977 — 73 ft 9 3/4 in.
Maren Seidler (Am.), West Germany, 1978 — 61 ft 2 1/4 in.

THE ATHLETICS CONGRESS NATIONAL CHAMPIONSHIPS

INDOOR

(Madison Square Garden, New York, Feb. 24, 1984)

Men's Events

60 yd—Emmit King, New Balance T.C.	0:06.08
600 yd—Mark Rowe, Tiger International	1:09.60
1,000 yd—Don Paige, Athletic Attic	2:08.20
440 yd—Clinton Davis, New Image T.C.	0:48.10[a]
Mile—Steve Scott, SUB-4 TC	4:00.06
3 miles—Doug Padilla, Athletics West,	13:09.01
60-yd hurdles—Greg Foster, World Class Athletic Club	0:06.95
2-mile walk—Jim Heiring, Bud Light Track America	12:11.21[1]
Sprint medley relay—Tiger International (Michael Paul, Bill Collins, Anthony Ketchum, Rudy Levarity)	2:00.25
2-mile relay—Arizona State (Mike Stahr, Eddie Davis, Pete Richardson, Treg Scott)	7:25.44
Mile relay—Tiger International (David Walker, Greg Moore, Michael Paul, Mark Rowe)	3:13.18
High jump—Dennis Lewis, New Balance T.C.	7 ft 7 in.
Pole Vault—Sergey Bubka, Soviet Union,	18 ft 6 in.
Long jump—Carl Lewis, Santa Monica T.C.	27 ft 10 3/4 in.
Triple jump—Ajayi Agbebaku, El Paso T.C.	55 ft 7 in.
Shotput—Augie Wolf (NYAC)	69 ft 3/4 in.
35-lb. weight throw—Jud Logan, Univ. of Chicago T.C.	75 ft. 3 1/4 in.[2]
Team—Bud Light Track America	24 1/2 pts

a. Walter McCoy finished first in 0:48.10 but was disqualified for bumping. 1. World Indoor Record. 2. American Indoor Record.

Women's Events

60 yd—Alice Brown, World Class AC	0:06.62
220 yd—Valerie Brisco-Hooks, World Class AC	0:23.97
440 yd—Diane Dixon, Atoms TC	0:53.82
880 yd—Lyubov Gurina, Soviet Union,	2:05.34
Mile—Brit McRoberts, Canada	4:33.91
2 miles—Cathy Branta, Wisconsin	9:49.39
60-yd hurdles—Stephanie Hightower, Bud Light Track America	0:07.43
Mile walk—Teresa Vaill, Island T.C.	7:12.85
640-yd relay—Tennessee State (Angela Williams, Wanda Fort, Jackie Vanzant, Barbara Frazier)	1:09.87
Sprint medley relay—Tennessee State (Maxine McMillan, Wanda Fort, Barbara Frazier, Angela Williams)	1:44.12
Mile relay—Atoms T.C. (Tonya McIntosh, Edie Brown, Grace Jackson, Diane Dixon)	3:38.15
High jump—Tamara Bykova, Soviet Union	6 ft 6 3/4 in.[1]
Long jump—Carol Lewis, Univ. of Houston	21 ft 8 in.[1]
Shotput—Meg Ritchie, adidas	58 ft 6 3/4 in.
Teams—Atoms Track Club	12 pts

1. Meet record.

THE ATHLETICS CONGRESS NATIONAL CHAMPIONSHIPS—1984

(San Jose, California, June 7–9, 1984)

OUTDOOR

Men's Events

100 m—Sam Graddy, adidas	0:10.28
200 m—Brady Crain, NY Pioneer Club	0:20.09
400 m—Mark Rowe, Tiger International	0:45.34
800 m—James Robinson, Inner City AC	1:47.46
1,500 m—Jim Spivey, Athletics West	3:40.54
3,000-m steeplechase—Henry Marsh, Athletics West	8:26.70
5,000 m—Sydney Maree, Reebok Racing team	13:51.31
10,000 m—Jon Sinclair, Brooks Racing team	28:42.54
110-m hurdles—Tonie Campbell, Stars and Stripes TC	0:13.26
400-m hurdles—David Patrick, adidas	0:49.08
20,000-m walk—Ray Funkhouser, Shore AC	1:31.47.1
High jump—Jimmy Howard, Pacific Coast Club	7 ft 7 1/4 in.
Pole vault—Earl Bell, Pacific Coast Club	19 ft 1/4 in.[1,2]
Long jump—Mike McRae, Bay Area Striders	27 ft 1 3/4 in.
Triple jump—Al Joyner, Bud Light Track America	55 ft 6 1/4 in.
Shotput—Augie Wolf, Bud Light Track America	70 ft 5 3/4 in.
Discus—John Powell, Bud Light Track America	233 ft 9 in.[2]
Hammer throw—Jud Logan, Univ. of Chicago TC	240 ft 6 in.
Javelin—Curt Ransford, Puma Energizer	276 ft 11 in.
Team—Bud Light Track America	83 1/2 pts

1. American record. 2. Meet record.

Women's Events

100 m—Merlene Ottey, unattached	0:11.12
200 m—Merlene Ottey, unattached	0:22.20
400 m—Valerie Brisco-Hooks, Tiger World Class AC	0:49.83[1,2]
800 m—Kim Gallagher, Puma Energizer	1:59.87
1,500 m—Kim Gallagher, Puma Energizer	4:08.08
3,000 m—Jan Merrill, Age Group AA	9:01.31
5,000 m—Katie Ishmael, Wisconsin Univ.	16:07.50
10,000 m—Bonnie Sons, Iowa St.	35:03.36
100-m hurdles—Stephanie Hightower, Bud Light Track America	0:12.99
400-m hurdles—Judi Brown, Nike TC	0:54.99[1,2]
10,000-m walk—Debbie Lawrence, Roos TC	51:00.30
440-yd relay—Hawkeye TC (Vivien, McKenzie, Elaine Jones, Brenda Calhoun, Davera Taylor)	0:45.04
Mile relay—Puma Energizer Red (Sherri Howard, Denean Howard, June Griffith, Robin Campbell)	3:30.83
2-mile relay—Los Angeles Mercurettes (Andrea Ward, Laurel Hacche, Trescia Palmer, Cindy Cumbess)	8:50.15
Sprint medley relay—Atoms TC (Diane Dixon, Helena Nelson, Grace Jackson, Edna Brown)	1:40.69
High jump—Pam Spencer, Puma Energizer	6 ft 4 in.
Long jump—Shonel Ferguson, unattached	22 ft 1/4 in.
Discus—Ria Stalman, Adidas-Holland	221 ft 9 in.[2]
Shot put—Ria Stalman, adidas-Holland	59 ft 1 1/2 in.
Javelin—Karin Smith, Athletics West	198 ft 11 in.

1. American record. 2. meet record.

N.C.A.A. CHAMPIONSHIPS—1984

INDOOR

(Carrier Dome, Syracuse, N.Y., March 9–10, 1984)

Men's Events

55 m—Rod Richardson, Texas A&M	0:06.14
400 m—Antonio McKay, Georgia Tech	0:46.46
500 m—Robin Thomas, Southeast Missouri	1:02.06
800 m—Gareth Brown, Iowa State	1:49.47
1,000 m—William Wuyke, Alabama	2:24.27
1,500 m—Bob Verbeeck, Iowa State	3:52.85
3,000 m—Peter Koech, Washington State	8:04.20
55-m hurdles—Roger Kingdom, Pitt	0:07.08
1,600-m relay—Oklahoma, Aubrey Jones, Fonnie Kemp, Danny Carter, Don Bly	3:08.55
Distance medley relay—Eastern Michigan, Codrington, Frederick, Shamiyeh, Jones	9:40.18
High jump—Nick Saunders, Boston Univ.	7 ft 5 1/4 in.
Pole vault—Joe Dial, Oklahoma St.	18 ft 0 in.
Long jump—Mike Conley, Arkansas	25 ft 8 1/4 in.
Triple jump—Mike Conley, Arkansas	55 ft 7 3/4 in.
Shotput—Michael Carter, Southern Methodist Univ.	66 ft 1 1/2 in.
35-lb weight throw—Tore Johnsen, Univ. Texas-El Paso	72 ft 3 1/2 in.
Team—Arkansas	38 pts

OUTDOOR

(Eugene, Oregon, May 28–June 2, 1984)

Men's Events

100 m—Sam Graddy, Tennessee	0:10.25
200 m—Kirk Baptiste, Houston	0:20.16
400 m—Antonio McKay, Georgia Tech	0:44.83
800 m—Joaquim Cruz, Oregon	1:45.10
1,500 m—Joaquim Cruz, Oregon	3:36.48
3,000-m Steeplechase—Farley Gerber, Weber State	8:19.27
5,000 m—Julius Korir, Washington St.	13:47.77
10,000 m—Ed Eyestone, B.Y.U.	28:05.30
110-m hurdles—Albert Lane, Missouri	0:13.61
400-m hurdles—Danny Harris, Iowa St.	0:48.81 [1]
400-m relay—Georgia (Neal Jessie, Sam Palmer, Stanley Blalock, Lester Benjamin)	0:39.39
1,600-m relay—Oklahoma (Aubrey Jones, Fonnie Kemp, Dannie Carter, Don Bly)	3:03.06 [2]
High jump—Jake Jacoby, Boise State	7 ft 5 1/4 in.
Pole vault—Joe Dial, Oklahoma State	18 ft 2 1/2 in.
Long jump—Mike Conley, Arkansas	27 ft 0 in.
Triple jump—Mike Conley, Arkansas	56 ft 11 1/2 in.
Discus—John Brenner, UCLA	208 ft 2 in.
Shotput—John Brenner, UCLA	71 ft 11 in. [3]
Javelin—Einar Vilhjalmsson, Texas	294 ft 0 in.
Hammer throw—Matt Mileham, Fresno St.	241 ft 11 in.
Decathlon—Rob Muzzio, George Mason	8,227 pts [2,3]
Team—Oregon	113 pts

1. World and American Junior record. 2. Meet record. 3. Collegiate record.

Women's Events

100 m—Randy Givens, Florida St.	0:11.06
200 m—Randy Givens, Florida St.	0:22.87
400 m—Marita Payne, Florida St.	0:51.05
800 m—Joetta Clark, Tennessee	2:02.60
1,500 m—Claudette Groenendaal, Oregon	4:14.31 [1]
3,000 m—Cathy Branta, Wisconsin	8:59.57
5,000 m—Patti Sue Plumer, Stanford	15:39.38
10,000 m—Kathy Hayes, Oregon	32:43.81 [1,2]
100-m hurdles—Kim Turner, El Paso	0:13.02
400-m hurdles—Nawal El Moutawakil, Iowa St.	0:55.84 [1]
400-m relay—Florida St. (Michelle Finn, Marita Payne, Brenda Cliette, Randy Givens)	0:43.72
1,600-m relay—Florida St. (Janet Davis, Brenda Cliette, Randy Givens, Marita Payne)	3:28.93 [1,2]
High jump—Tonya Alston, UCLA	6 ft 1 1/4 in.
Long jump—Gwen Loud, Hawaii	22 ft 5 3/4 in.
Triple jump—Terri Turner, Texas	44 ft 4 1/4 in. [3]
Shotput—Ramona Pagel, San Diego	56 ft 8 in. [1]
Discus—Carol Cady, Stanford	198 ft 5 in.
Javelin—Iris Gronfeldt, Alabama	184 ft 2 in.
Heptathlon—Sheila Tarr, UNLV	5,856 pts
Teams—Florida St.	145 pts.

1. Meet record. 2. College record. 3. World best; new event.

NATIONAL ATHLETICS CONGRESS

Relay Championships

(Piscataway, N.J., July 1, 1984)

400 m—Westchester/Puma and Energizer (Rouse, McKnight, Barnwell, Gabriel)	0:41.6
800 m—Shore AC (Abernathy, Brown, Valmon, Chambliss)	1:26.5
1,600 m—Shore AC (Brown, Jenkins, Chambliss, Valmon)	3:14.1
3,200 m—New York Athletic Club (Speranza, Borgese, Foley, Keyworth)	7:27.8 [1]
Sprint medley—Westchester/Puma and Energizer (Sessoms, McKnight, Rouse, Barr)	3:25.6
6,000 m—Mine Mt.	15:43.6
Distance medley—NYAC (Speranza, Majeski, Keyworth, Foley)	9:49.2
440-m shuttle hurdles—New York Pioneer Club (Jeremiah, Jackson, Allen, Pendergrass)	0:60.0
Team—Westchester/Puma and Energizer	46 pts

1. Meet record.

AMERICAN SWIMMERS RACE AGAINST OLYMPIC CLOCK IN 1980

Forty-eight hours after the 1980 Olympic swimming competition in Moscow ended, United States swimmers, who had boycotted the Games, protesting the Soviet intervention in Afghanistan, took to the water at Irvine, Calif., hoping to shatter records in the United States Championships and Olympic Trials. Organizers erected a huge scoreboard showing the Olympic times in each event so swimmers and spectators could make comparisons as to how the Americans would have fared had they chosen to go to Moscow.

In a sport they usually dominated, the Americans registered three world records, and on a basis of comparative times, showed they would have won six of 11 gold medals in men's events and four of 11 in women's events had they competed in the Olympics. The world records shattered at Irvine were by Craig Beardsley of Gainesville, Fla., in the 200-meter butterfly (1:58.46); Bill Barrett of Alpharetta, Ga., in the 200 individual medley (2:03.24); and Mary T. Meagher, a 15-year-old from Cincinnati, in the 200 butterfly (2:06.37).

TENNIS

Lawn tennis is a comparatively modern modification of the ancient game of court tennis. Major Walter Clopton Wingfield thought that something like court tennis might be played outdoors on lawns, and in December, 1873, at Nantclwyd, Wales, he introduced his new game under the name of *Sphairistike* at a lawn party. The game was a success and spread rapidly, but the name was a total failure and almost immediately disappeared when all the players and spectators began to refer to the new game as "lawn tennis." In the early part of 1874, a young lady named Mary Ewing Outerbridge returned from Bermuda to New York, bringing with her the implements and necessary equipment of the new game, which she had obtained from a British Army supply store in Bermuda. Miss Outerbridge and friends played the first game of lawn tennis in the United States on the grounds of the Staten Island Cricket and Baseball Club in the spring of 1874.

For a few years, the new game went along in haphazard fashion until about 1880, when standard measurements for the court and standard equipment within definite limits became the rule. In 1881, the U.S. Lawn Tennis Association (whose name was changed in 1975 to U.S. Tennis Association) was formed and conducted the first national championship at Newport, R.I. The international matches for the Davis Cup began with a series between the British and United States players on the courts of the Longwood Cricket Club, Chestnut Hill, Mass., in 1900, with the home players winning.

Professional tennis, which got its start in 1926 when the French star Suzanne Lenglen was paid $50,000 for a tour, received full recognition in 1968. Staid old Wimbledon, the London home of what are considered the world championships, let the pros compete. This decision ended a long controversy over open tennis and changed the format of the competition. The United States championships were also opened to the pros and the site of the event, long held at Forest Hills, N.Y., was shifted to the National Tennis Center in Flushing Meadows, N.Y., in 1978. Pro tours for men and women became worldwide in play that continued throughout the year.

DAVIS CUP CHAMPIONSHIPS

No matches in 1901, 1910, 1915–18, and 1940–45.

1900	United States 3, British Isles 0
1902	United States 3, British Isles 2
1903	British Isles 4, United States 1
1904	British Isles 5, Belgium 0
1905	British Isles 5, United States 0
1906	British Isles 5, United States 0
1907	Australasia 3, British Isles 2
1908	Australasia 3, United States 2
1909	Australasia 5, United States 0
1911	Australasia 5, United States 0
1912	British Isles 3, Australasia 2
1913	United States 3, British Isles 2
1914	Australasia 3, United States 2
1919	Australasia 4, British Isles 1
1920	United States 5, Australasia 0
1921	United States 5, Japan 0
1922	United States 4, Australasia 1
1923	United States 4, Australasia 1
1924	United States 5, Australasia 0
1925	United States 5, France 0
1926	United States 4, France 1
1927	France 3, United States 2
1928	France 4, United States 1
1929	France 3, United States 2
1930	France 4, United States 1
1931	France 3, Great Britain 2
1932	France 3, United States 2
1933	Great Britain 3, France 2
1934	Great Britain 4, United States 1
1935	Great Britain 5, United States 0
1936	Great Britain 3, Australia 2
1937	United States 4, Great Britain 1
1938	United States 3, Australia 2
1939	Australia 3, United States 2
1946	United States 5, Australia 0
1947	United States 4, Australia 1
1948	United States 5, Australia 0
1949	United States 4, Australia 1
1950	Australia 4, United States 1
1951	Australia 3, United States 2
1952	Australia 4, United States 1
1953	Australia 3, United States 2
1954	United States 3, Australia 2
1955	Australia 5, United States 0
1956	Australia 5, United States 0
1957	Australia 3, United States 2
1958	United States 3, Australia 2
1959	Australia 3, United States 2
1960	Australia 4, Italy 1
1961	Australia 5, Italy 0
1962	Australia 5, Mexico 0
1963	United States 3, Australia 2
1964	Australia 3, United States 2
1965	Australia 4, Spain 1
1966	Australia 4, India 1
1967	Australia 4, Spain 1
1968	United States 4, Australia 1
1969	United States 5, Romania 0
1970	United States 5, West Germany 0
1971	United States 3, Romania 2
1972	United States 3, Romania 2
1973	Australia 5, United States 0
1974	South Africa (Default by India)
1975	Sweden 3, Czechoslovakia 2
1976	Italy 4, Chile 1
1977	Australia 3, Italy 1
1978	United States 4, Britain 1
1979	United States 5, Italy 0
1980	Czechoslovakia 3, Italy 2
1981	United States 3, Argentina 1
1982	United States 3, France 0
1983	Australia 3, Sweden 2

FEDERATION CUP CHAMPIONSHIPS

World team competition for women conducted by International Lawn Tennis Federation.

1963	United States 2, Australia 1
1964	Australia 2, United States 1
1965	Australia 2, United States 1
1966	United States 3, West Germany 0
1967	United States 2, Britain 0
1968	Australia 3, Netherlands 0
1969	United States 2, Australia 1
1970	Australia 3, West Germany 0
1971	Australia 3, Britain 0
1972	South Africa 2, Britain 1
1973	Australia 3, South Africa 0
1974	Australia 2, United States 1
1975	Czechoslovakia 3, Australia 0
1976	United States 2, Australia 1
1977	United States 2, Australia 1
1978	United States 2, Australia 1
1979	United States 3, Australia 0
1980	United States 3, Australia 0
1981	United States 3, Britain 0
1982	United States 3, West Germany 0
1983	Czechoslovakia 2, West Germany 1
1984	Czechoslovakia 2, Australia 1

U.S. CHAMPIONS

Singles—Men

NATIONAL

Year	Champion
1881–87	Richard D. Sears
1888–89	Henry Slocum, Jr.
1890–92	Oliver S. Campbell
1893–94	Robert D. Wrenn
1895	Fred H. Hovey
1896–97	Robert D. Wrenn
1898–1900	Malcolm Whitman
1901–02	William A. Larned
1903	Hugh L. Doherty
1904	Holcombe Ward
1905	Beals C. Wright
1906	William J. Clothier
1907–11	William A. Larned
1912–13	Maurice McLoughlin[1]
1914	R. N. Williams II
1915	William Johnston
1916	R. N. William II
1917–18	R. Lindley Murray[2]
1919	William Johnston
1920–25	Bill Tilden
1926–27	Jean Rene Lacoste
1928	Henri Cochet
1929	Bill Tilden
1930	John H. Doeg
1931–32	Ellsworth Vines
1933–34	Fred J. Perry
1935	Wilmer L. Allison
1936	Fred J. Perry
1937–38	Don Budge
1939	Robert L. Riggs
1940	Donald McNeill
1941	Robert L. Riggs
1942	Fred Schroeder
1943	Joseph Hunt
1944–45	Frank Parker
1946–47	Jack Kramer
1948–49	Richard Gonzales
1950	Arthur Larsen
1951–52	Frank Sedgman
1953	Tony Trabert
1954	Vic Seixas
1955	Tony Trabert
1956	Ken Rosewall
1957	Mal Anderson
1958	Ashley Cooper
1959–60	Neale Fraser
1961	Roy Emerson
1962	Rod Laver
1963	Rafael Osuna
1964	Roy Emerson
1965	Manuel Santana
1966	Fred Stolle
1967	John Newcombe
1968	Arthur Ashe
1969	Rod Laver

OPEN

Year	Champion
1968	Arthur Ashe
1969	Rod Laver
1970	Ken Rosewall
1971	Stan Smith
1972	Ilie Nastase
1973	John Newcombe
1974	Jimmy Connors
1975	Manuel Orantes
1976	Jimmy Connors
1977	Guillermo Vilas
1978	Jimmy Connors
1979	John McEnroe
1980–81	John McEnroe
1982	Jimmy Connors
1983	Jimmy Connors
1984	John McEnroe

Singles—Women

NATIONAL

Year	Champion
1887	Ellen F. Hansel
1888–89	Bertha Townsend
1890	Ellen C. Roosevelt
1891–92	Mabel E. Cahill
1893	Aline M. Terry
1894	Helen R. Helwig
1895	Juliette P. Atkinson
1896	Elisabeth H. Moore
1897–98	Juliette P. Atkinson
1899	Marion Jones
1900	Myrtle McAteer
1901	Elisabeth H. Moore
1902	Marion Jones
1903	Elisabeth H. Moore
1904	May Sutton
1905	Elisabeth H. Moore
1906	Helen Homans
1907	Evelyn Sears
1908	Maud Bargar-Wallach
1909–11	Hazel V. Hotchkiss
1912–14	Mary K. Browne
1915–18	Molla Bjurstedt
1919	Hazel Hotchkiss Wightman
1920–22	Molla Bjurstedt Mallory
1923–25	Helen N. Wills
1926	Molla B. Mallory
1927–29	Helen N. Wills
1930	Betty Nuthall
1931	Helen Wills Moody
1932–35	Helen Jacobs
1936	Alice Marble
1937	Anita Lizana
1938–40	Alice Marble
1941	Sarah Palfrey Cooke
1942–44	Pauline Betz
1945	Sarah Cooke
1946	Pauline Betz
1947	Louise Brough
1948–50	Margaret Osborne duPont
1951–53	Maureen Connolly
1954–55	Doris Hart
1956	Shirley Fry
1957–58	Althea Gibson
1959	Maria Bueno
1960–61	Darlene Hard
1962	Margaret Smith
1963–64	Maria Bueno
1965	Margaret Smith
1966	Maria Bueno
1967	Billie Jean King
1968–69	Margaret Smith Court[3]

OPEN

Year	Champion
1968	Virginia Wade
1969–70	Margaret Court
1971–72	Billie Jean King
1973	Margaret Court
1974	Billie Jean King
1975–78	Chris Evert
1979	Tracy Austin
1980	Chris Evert Lloyd
1981	Tracy Austin
1982	Chris Evert Lloyd
1983–84	Martina Navratilova

Doubles—Men

NATIONAL

1920	Bill Johnston–C. J. Griffin
1921–22	Bill Tilden–Vincent Richards
1923	Bill Tilden–B. I. C. Norton
1924	H. O. Kinsey—R. G. Kinsey
1925–26	Vincent Richards—R. N. Williams II
1927	Bill Tilden—Frank Hunter
1928	G. M. Lott, Jr.-V. Hennessy
1929–30	G. M. Lott, Jr.-J. H. Doeg
1931	W. L. Allison–John Van Ryn
1932	E. H. Vines, Jr.–Keith Gledh
1933–34	G. M. Lott, Jr.–L. R. Stoefen
1935	W. L. Allison–John Van Ryn
1936	Don Budge—Gene Mako
1937	G. von Cramm–H. Henkel
1938	Don Budge–Gene Mako
1939	A. K. Quist–J. E. Bromwich
1940–41	Jack Kramer–F. R. Schroeder
1942	Gardnar Mulloy–Bill Talbert
1943	Jack Kramer—Frank Parker
1944	Don McNeill—Bob Falkenburg
1945	Gardnar Mulloy–Bill Talbert
1946	Gardnar Mulloy–Bill Talbert
1947	Jack Kramer–Fred Schroeder
1948	Gardnar Mulloy–Bill Talbert
1949	John Bromwich–William Sidwell
1950	John Bromwich–Frank Sedgman
1951	Frank Sedgman–Ken McGregor
1952	Vic Seixas-Mervyn Rose
1953	Mervyn Rose–Rex Hartwig
1954	Vic Seixas–Tony Trabert
1955	Kosei Kamo–Atsushi Miyagi
1956	Lewis Hoad–Ken Rosewall
1957	Ashley Cooper–Neale Fraser
1958	Ham Richardson–Alex Olmedo
1959–60	Neale Fraser–Roy Emerson
1961	Chuck McKinley–Dennis Ralston
1962	Rafael Osuna–Antonio Palafox
1963–64	Chuck McKinley–Dennis Ralston
1965–66	Fred Stolle–Roy Emerson
1967	John Newcombe–Tony Roche
1968	Stan Smith–Bob Lutz[3]
1969	Richard Crealy–Allan Stone[3]

OPEN

1968	Stan Smith–Bob Lutz	1975	Jimmy Connors–Ilie Nastase	1982	Kevin Curren–Steve Denton
1969	Fred Stolle–Ken Rosewall	1976	Marty Riessen–Tom Okker	1983	John McEnroe–Peter Fleming
1970	Nikki Pilic–Fred Barthes	1977	Frew McMillan–Bob Hewitt	1984	John Fitzgerald–Tomas Smid
1971	John Newcombe–Roger Taylor	1978	Bob Lutz–Stan Smith		
1972	Cliff Drysdale–Roger Taylor	1979	John McEnroe–Peter Fleming		
1973	John Newcombe–Owen Davidson	1980	Stan Smith–Bob Lutz		
1974	Bob Lutz–Stan Smith	1981	John McEnroe–Peter Fleming		

1. Challenge round abandoned in 1912. 2. Patriotic Tournament in 1917. 3. With the inaugural of the Open Tournament in 1968, the United States Lawn Tennis Association held a national championship at Longwood, Chestnut Hill, Mass. which barred contract professionals in 1968 and 1969.

Doubles—Women

NATIONAL

1924	G. W. Wightman–Helen Wills
1925	Mary K. Browne–Helen Wills
1926	Elizabeth Ryan–Eleanor Goss
1927	L. A. Godfree–Ermyntrude Harvey
1928	Hazel Hotchkiss Wightman–Helen Wills
1929	Phoebe Watson–L. R. C. Michell
1930	Betty Nuthall–Sarah Palfrey
1931	Betty Nuthall–E. B. Wittingstall
1932	Helen Jacobs–Sarah Palfrey
1933	Betty Nuthall–Freda James
1934	Helen Jacobs–Sarah Palfrey
1935	Helen Jacobs–Sarah Palfrey Fabyan
1936	Marjorie G. Van Ryn–Carolin Babcock
1937–40	Sarah Palfrey Fabyan–Alice Marble
1941	Sarah Palfrey Cooke–Margaret Osborne
1942–47	A. Louise Brough–Margaret Osborne
1948–50	A. Louise Brough–Margaret O. duPont
1951–54	Doris Hart–Shirley Fry
1955–57	A. Louise Brough–Margaret O. duPont
1958–59	Darlene Hard–Jeanne Arth
1960	Darlene Hard–Maria Bueno
1961	Darlene Hard–Lesley Turner
1962	Darlene Hard–Maria Bueno
1963	Margaret Smith–Robyn Ebbern
1964	Karen Hantze Susman–Billie Jean Moffitt
1965	Nancy Richey–Carole Caldwell Graebner
1966	Nancy Richey–Maria Bueno
1967	Billie Jean King–Rosemary Casals
1968	Margaret Court–Maria Bueno[3]
1969	Margaret Court–Virginia Wade[3]

OPEN

1968	Maria Bueno–Margaret Court
1969	Darlene Hard–Francoise Durr
1970	Margaret Court–Judy Dalton
1971	Rosemary Casals–Judy Dalton
1972	Francoise Durr–Betty Stove
1973	Margaret Court–Virginia Wade
1974	Billie Jean King–Rosemary Casals
1975	Margaret Court–Virginia Wade
1976	Linky Boshoff–Ilana Kloss
1977	Martina Navratilova–Betty Stove
1978	Billie Jean King–Martina Navratilova
1979	Betty Stove–Wendy Turnbull
1980	Billie Jean King–Martina Navratilova
1981	Kathy Jordan–Anne Smith
1982	Rosemary Casals–Wendy Turnbull
1983–84	Martina Navratilova–Pam Shriver

1. Challenge round abandoned in 1912. 2. Patriotic Tournament in 1917. 3. With the inaugural of the Open Tournament in 1968, the United States Lawn Tennis Association held a national championship at Longwood, Chestnut Hill, Mass. which barred contract professionals in 1968 and 1969.

U.S. INDOOR CHAMPIONS

Singles—Men

1964	Charles McKinley
1965	Erik Lundquist
1966	Charles Pasarell
1967	Charles Pasarell
1968	Cliff Richey
1969	Stan Smith
1970	Ilie Nastase
1971	Clark Graebner
1972	Stan Smith
1973–75	Jimmy Connors
1976	Ilie Nastase
1977	Bjorn Borg
1978–79	Jimmy Connors
1980	John McEnroe
1981	Gene Mayer
1982	Johan Kriek
1983–84	Jimmy Connors

Singles—Women

1964	Mary Ann Eisel
1965	Nancy Richey
1966	Billie Jean King
1967	Billie Jean King
1968	Billie Jean King
1969	Mary Ann Eisel
1970	Mary Ann Curtis
1971	Billie Jean King
1972	Not held
1973	Evonne Goolagong
1974	Billie Jean King
1975	Martina Navratilova
1976	Virginia Wade
1977	Chris Evert
1978	Chris Evert
1979	Evonne Goolagong
1980	Tracy Austin
1981	Martina Navratilova
1982	Barbara Potter
1983	Kim Shaefer
1984	Martina Navratilova

Doubles—Men

1967	Arthur Ashe–Charles Pasarell
1968	Thomas Koch–Tom Okker
1969	Stan Smith–Bob Lutz
1970	Arthur Ashe–Stan Smith
1971	Manuel Orantes–Juan Gisbert
1972	Manuel Orantes–Andres Gimeno
1973	Juan Gisbert–Jurgen Fassbender
1974	Jimmy Connors–Frew McMillan
1975	Jimmy Connors–Ilie Nastase
1976–77	Sherwood Stewart–Fred McNair
1978	Brian Gottfried–Raul Ramirez
1979	Wojtek Fibak–Tom Okker
1980	John McEnroe–Brian Gottfried
1981	Gene Mayer–Sandy Mayer
1982	Kevin Curren–Steve Denton
1983	Peter McNamara–Paul McNamee
1984	Fritz Bushning–Peter Fleming

Doubles—Women

1967	Carol Aucamp–Mary Ann Eisel
1968	Rosemary Casals–Billie Jean King
1969	Mary Ann Eisel–Valerie Ziegenfuss
1970	Peaches Bartkowicz–Nancy Richey
1971	Billie Jean King–Rosemary Casals
1972	Not held
1973	Olga Morozova–Marina Kroshina
1974	Not held
1975	Billie Jean King—Rosemary Casals
1976	Rosemary Casals–Francoise Durr
1977	Martina Navratilova–Betty Stove
1978	Kerry Reid–Wendy Turnbull
1979	Billie Jean King–Martina Navratilova
1980	Ann Kiyomora–Candy Reynolds
1981	Martina Navratilova–Pam Shriver
1982	Rosemary Casals–Wendy Turnbull
1983	Billie Jean King–Sharon Walsh
1984	Martina Navratilova–Pam Shriver

BRITISH (WIMBLEDON) CHAMPIONS

(Amateur from inception in 1877 through 1967)

Singles—Men

1908–09	Arthur Gore	1930	Bill Tilden	1952	Frank Sedgman	1968–69	Rod Laver
1910–13	A. F. Wilding	1931	S. B. Wood	1953	Vic Siexas	1970–71	John Newcombe
1914	N. E. Brookes	1932	Ellsworth Vines	1954	Jaroslav Drobny	1972	Stan Smith
1919	G. L. Patterson	1933	J. H. Crawford	1955	Tony Trabert	1973	Jan Kodes
1920–21	Bill Tilden	1934–36	Fred Perry	1956–57	Lewis Hoad	1974	Jimmy Connors
1922	G. L. Patterson	1937–38	Don Budge	1958	Ashley Cooper	1975	Arthur Ashe
1923	William Johnston	1939	Robert L. Riggs	1959	Alex Olmedo	1976–80	Bjorn Borg
1924	Jean Borotra	1946	Yvon Petra	1960	Neale Fraser	1981	John McEnroe
1925	Rene Lacoste	1947	Jack Kramer	1961–62	Rod Laver	1982	Jimmy Connors
1926	Jean Borotra	1948	R. Falkenburg	1963	Chuck McKinley	1983–84	John McEnroe
1927	Henri Cochet	1949	Fred Schroeder	1964–65	Roy Emerson		
1928	Rene Lacoste	1950	Budge Patty	1966	Manuel Santana		
1929	Jean Cochet	1951	Richard Savitt	1967	John Newcombe		

Singles—Women

1919–23	Lenglen	1938	Helen Wills Moody	1962	Karen Susman	1976	Chris Evert
1924	Kathleen McKane	1939	Alice Marble	1963	Margaret Smith	1977	Virginia Wade
1925	Lenglen	1946	Pauline M. Betz	1964	Maria Bueno	1978–79	Martina Navratilova
1926	Godfree	1947	Margaret Osborne	1965	Margaret Smith	1980	Evonne Goolagong Cawley
1927–29	Helen Wills	1948–50	A. Louise Brough	1966–67	Billie Jean King	1981	Chris Evert Lloyd
1930	Helen Wills Moody	1951	Doris Hart	1968	Billie Jean King	1982–84	Martina Navratilova
1931	Frl. C. Aussen	1952–54	Maureen Connolly	1969	Ann Jones		
1932–33	Helen Wills Moody	1955	A. Louise Brough	1970	Margaret Court		
1934	D. E. Round	1956	Shirley Fry	1971	Evonne Goolagong		
1935	Helen Wills Moody	1957–58	Althea Gibson	1972–73	Billie Jean King		
1936	Helen Jacobs	1959–60	Maria Bueno	1974	Chris Evert		
1937	D. E. Round	1961	Angela Mortimer	1975	Billie Jean King		

Doubles—Men

1953	K. Rosewall–L. Hoad	1965	John Newcombe–Tony Roche	1979	Peter Fleming–John McEnroe
1954	R. Hartwig–M. Rose	1966	John Newcombe–Ken Fletcher	1980	Peter McNamara–Paul McNamee
1955	R. Hartwig–L. Hoad	1967	Bob Hewitt–Frew McMillan	1981	John McEnroe–Peter Fleming
1956	L. Hoad–K. Rosewall	1968–70	John Newcombe–Tony Roche	1982	Paul McNamee–Peter McNamara
1957	Gardnar Mulloy–Budge Patty	1971	Rod Laver–Roy Emerson	1983–84	John McEnroe–Peter Fleming
1958	Sven Davidson–Ulf Schmidt	1972	Bob Hewitt–Frew McMillan		
1959	Roy Emerson–Neale Fraser	1973	Jimmy Connors–Ilie Nastase		
1960	Dennis Ralston–Rafael Osuna	1974	John Newcombe–Tony Roche		
1961	Roy Emerson–Neale Fraser	1975	Vitas Gerulaitis–Sandy Mayer		
1962	Fred Stolle–Bob Hewitt	1976	Brian Gottfried–Raul Ramirez		
1963	Rafael Osuna–Antonio Palafox	1977	Ross Case–Geoff Masters		
1964	Fred Stolle–Bob Hewitt	1978	Fred McMillan–Bob Hewitt		

Doubles-Women

1956	Althea Gibson–Angela Buxton	1966	Nancy Richey–Maria Bueno	1979	Billie Jean King–Martina Navratilova
1957	Althea Gibson–Darlene Hard	1967–68	Billie Jean King–Rosemary Casals	1980	Kathy Jordan–Anne Smith
1958	Althea Gibson–Maria Bueno	1969	Margaret Court–Judy Tegart	1981	Martina Navratilova–Pam Shriver
1959	Darlene Hard–Jeanne Arth	1970–71	Billie Jean King–Rosemary Casals	1982–84	Pam Shriver–Martina Navratilova
1960	Darlene Hard–Maria Bueno	1972	Billie Jean King–Betty Stove		
1961	Karen Hantze–Billie Jean Moffitt	1973	Billie Jean King–Rosemary Casals		
1962	Karen Hantze Susman–Billie Jean Moffitt	1974	Evonne Goolagong–Peggy Michel		
		1975	Ann Kiyomura–Kazuko Sawamatsu		
1963	Darlene Hard–Maria Bueno	1976	Chris Evert–Martina Navratilova		
1964	Margaret Smith–Les Turnerley	1977	Helen Cawley–JoAnne Russell		
1965	Billie Jean Moffitt–Maria Bueno	1978	Wendy Turnbull–Kerry Reid		

UNITED STATES CHAMPIONSHIPS—1984

Open

(Flushing Meadows, N.Y., Aug. 28–Sept. 9, 1984)

Men's singles—Final: John McEnroe, Douglaston, N.Y., defeated Ivan Lendl, Czechoslovakia, 6–3, 6–4, 6–1. Semifinals: McEnroe defeated Jimmy Connors, Sanibel Island, Fla., 6–4, 4–6, 7–5, 4–6, 6–3; Lendl defeated Pat Cash, Australia, 3–6, 6–3, 6–4, 6–7 (5–7), 7–6 (7–4).

Women's singles—Final: Martina Navratilova, Dallas, Tex., defeated Chris Evert Lloyd, Fort Lauderdale, Fla., 4–6, 6–4, 6–4. Semifinals: Navratilova defeated Wendy Turnbull, Australia, 6–4, 6–1; Evert Lloyd defeated Carling Bassett, Canada, 6–2, 6–2.

Men's doubles—Final: John Fitzgerald, Australia, and Tomas Smid, Czechoslovakia, defeated Stefan Edberg and Anders Jarryd, Sweden, 7–6, 6–3, 6–3.

Women's doubles—Martina Navratilova, Dallas Tex., and Pam Shriver, Baltimore, Md., defeated Anne Hobbs, Britain, and Wendy Turnbull, Australia, 6–2, 6–4.

Mixed doubles—Manuela Maleeva, Bulgaria, and Tom Gullikson, United States, defeated Elizabeth Sayers and John Fiztgerald, Australia, 2–6, 7–5, 6–4.

National Clay Court

(Indianapolis, Aug. 7–13, 1984)

Men's singles final—Andres Gomez, Ecuador, defeated Balazs Taroczy, Hungary, 6–0, 7–6.

Women's singles final—Manuela Maleeva, Bulgaria, defeated Lisa Bonder, Saline, Mich., 6–4, 6–3.

Men's doubles final—Ken Flach, St. Louis, Mo., and Robert Seguso, Sunrise, Fla., defeated Balazs Taroczy, Hungary, and Heinz Gunthardt, Switzerland, 7–6, 6–5, disq.

Women's doubles final—Beverly Mould, South Africa, and Paula Smith, LaJolla, Calif., defeated Elise Burgin, Baltimore, Md., and Jo Anne Russell, Naples, Fla., 6–2, 7–5.

World Championship Tennis

(Forest Hills, N.Y., May 6–13, 1984)

Final—John McEnroe, Douglaston, N.Y., defeated Ivan Lendl, Czechoslovakia, 6–4, 6–2.

U.S. National Indoor

(Memphis, Tenn., Feb. 6–12, 1984)

Singles final—Jimmy Connors, Sanibel Island, Fla., defeated Henri LeConte, Paris, France, 6–3, 4–6, 7–5. Doubles final—Fritz Buehning, Short Hills, N.J., and Peter Fleming, Seabrook Island, S.C., defeated Heinz Gunthardt, Switzerland, and Tomas Smid, Czechoslovakia, 6–3, 6–0.

U.S. Pro Indoor

(Philadelphia, Jan. 23–30, 1984)

Final—John McEnroe, Douglaston, N.Y., defeated Ivan Lendl, Czechoslovakia 6–3, 3–6, 6–3, 7–6. Doubles final—McEnroe and Peter Fleming, Seabrook Island, S.C., defeated Henri LeConte and Yannick Noah, France, 6–2, 6–3.

U.S. Pro

(Brookline, Mass., July 15–23, 1984)

Singles final—Aaron Krickstein, Grosse Pointe, Mich., defeated Jose-Luis Clerc, Argentina, 7–6, 3–6, 6–4. Doubles final—Ken Flach, St. Louis, Mo., and Robert Seguso, Sunrise, Fla., defeated Gary Donnelly and Ernie Fernandez, Puerto Rico, 6–4, 6–4.

OTHER 1984 CHAMPIONS

Wimbledon Open

Men's singles—John McEnroe, New York, defeated Jimmy Connors, Sanibel Harbor, Fla., 6–1, 6–1, 6–2.

Women's singles—Martina Navratilova, Dallas, defeated Chris Evert Lloyd, Ft. Lauderdale, Fla., 7–6 (7–5), 6–2.

Men's Doubles—Peter Fleming and John McEnroe, United States, defeated Pat Cash and Paul McNamee, Australia, 6–2, 5–7, 6–2, 3–6, 6–3

Women's doubles—Pam Shriver and Martina Navratilova, United States, defeated Kathy Jordan and Anne Smith, United States, 6–3, 6–4.

Mixed doubles—John Lloyd, Britain, and Wendy Turnbull, Australia, defeated Steve Denton and Kathy Jordan, United States, 6–3, 6–3.

French Open

Men's singles—Ivan Lendl, Czechoslovakia, defeated John McEnroe, New York, 3–6, 2–6, 6–4, 7–5, 7–5.

Women's singles—Martina Navratilova, Dallas, defeated Chris Evert Lloyd, Ft. Lauderdale, Fla. 6–3, 6–1.

Men's doubles—Yannick Noah and Henri LeConte, France, defeated Pavel Slozil and Tomas Smid, Czechoslovakia, 6–4, 2–6, 3–6, 6–3, 6–2.

Women's doubles—Pam Shriver and Martina Navratilova, United States, defeated Claudia Kohde-Kilsch and Hana Mandilkova, Czechoslovakia, 5–7, 6–3, 6–2.

Mixed doubles—Dick Stockton and Anne Smith, United States, defeated Anne Miller and Laurie Warder, Australia, 6–2, 6–4.

Australian Open

Men's singles—Mats Wilander, Sweden, defeated Ivan Lendl, Czechoslovakia, 6–1, 6–4, 6–4.

Women's singles—Martina Navratilova, Dallas, defeated Kathy Jordan, King of Prussia, Pa., 6–2, 7–6.

Men's doubles—Paul McNamee and Mark Edmundson, Australia, defeated Steve Denton and Sherwood Stewart, United States, 6–3, 7–6.

Women's doubles—Pam Shriver and Martina Navratilova, United States, defeated Wendy Turnbull and Anne Hobbs, 6–4, 6–7, 6–2.

DAVIS CUP RESULTS—1983

Australia 3, Sweden 2 (at Melbourne, Australia)

Singles—Mats Wilander (S) defeated Pat Cash (A), 6–3, 4–6, 9–7, 6–3; John Fitzgerald (A) defeated Joakim (S), 6–4, 6–2, 4–6, 6–4; Pat Cash (A) defeated Joakim Nystrom (S), 6–4, 6–1, 6–1; Mats Wilander (S) defeated John Fitzgerald (A), 6–3, 6–0, 6–1.

Doubles—Paul McNamee and Mark Edmundson (A) defeated Anders Jarryd and Hans Simonsson (S), 6–4, 6–4, 6–2.

MEN'S FINAL TENNIS EARNINGS—1983

Player and Amount: Ivan Lendl, $1,747,128; John McEnroe, 1,-206,844; Mats Wilander, 1,119,650; Guillermo Villas, 677,035; Jimmy Connors, 598,047; Tomas Smid, 457,886; Yannick Noah, 377,394; Jimmy Arias, 340,033; Brian Teacher, 332,948; Kevin Curren, 306,852.

WOMEN'S FINAL TENNIS EARNINGS—1983

Player and Amount: Martina Navratilova, $1,456,030; Chris Evert Lloyd, 430,436; Pam Shriver, 312,216; Andrea Jaeger, 261,954; Kathy Jordan, 211,786; Jo Durie, 211,342; Wendy Turnbull, 206,-391; Andrea Temesvari, 168,301; Sylvia Hanika, 154,950; Hana Mandilkova, 151,762.

ROWING

Rowing goes back so far in history that there is no possibility of tracing it to any particular aboriginal source. The oldest rowing race still on the calendar is the "Doggett's Coat and Badge" contest among professional watermen of the Thames (England) that began in 1715. The first Oxford-Cambridge race was held at Henley in 1829. Competitive rowing in the United States began with matches between boats rowed by professional oarsmen of the New York water front. They were oarsmen who rowed the small boats that plied as ferries from Manhattan Island to Brooklyn and return, or who rowed salesmen down the harbor to meet ships arriving from Europe. Since the first salesman to meet an incoming ship had some advantage over his rivals, there was keen competition in the bidding for fast boats and the best oarsmen. This gave rise to match races.

Amateur boat clubs sprang up in the United States between 1820 and 1830 and seven students of Yale joined together to purchase a four-oared lap-streak gig in 1843. The first Harvard-Yale race was held Aug. 3, 1852, on Lake Winnepesaukee, N.H. The first time an American college crew went abroad was in 1869 when Harvard challenged Oxford and was defeated on the Thames. There were early college rowing races on Lake Quinsigamond, near Worcester, Mass., and on Saratoga Lake, N.Y., but the Intercollegiate Rowing Association in 1895 settled on the Hudson, at Poughkeepsie, as the setting for the annual "Poughkeepsie Regatta." In 1950 the I.R.A. shifted its classic to Marietta, Ohio, and in 1952 it was moved to Syracuse, N.Y. The National Association of Amateur Oarsmen, organized in 1872, has conducted annual championship regattas since that time.

INTERCOLLEGIATE ROWING ASSOCIATION REGATTA

(Varsity Eight-Oared Shells)

Rowed at 4 miles, Poughkeepsie, N.Y., 1895–97, 1899–1916, 1925–32, 1934–41. Rowed at 3 miles, Saratoga, N.Y., 1898; Poughkeepsie, 1921–24, 1947–49; Syracuse, N.Y., 1952–1963, 1965–67. Rowed at 2,000 meters, Syracuse, N.Y., 1964 and from 1968 on. Rowed at 2 miles, Ithaca, N.Y., 1920; Marietta, Ohio, 1950–51. Suspended 1917–19, 1933, 1942–46.

Year	Time	First	Second
1895	21:25	Columbia	Cornell
1896	19:59	Cornell	Harvard
1897	20:47 4/5	Cornell	Columbia
1898	15:51 1/2	Pennsylvania	Cornell
1899	20:04	Pennsylvania	Wisconsin
1900	19:44 3/5	Pennsylvania	Wisconsin
1901	18:53 1/5	Cornell	Columbia
1902	19:03 3/5	Cornell	Wisconsin
1903	18:57	Cornell	Georgetown
1904	20:22 3/5	Syracuse	Cornell
1905	20:29	Cornell	Syracuse
1906	19:36 4/5	Cornell	Pennsylvania
1907	20:02 2/5	Cornell	Columbia
1908	19:24 1/5	Syracuse	Columbia
1909	19:02	Cornell	Columbia
1910	20:42 1/5	Cornell	Pennsylvania
1911	20:10 4/5	Cornell	Columbia
1912	19:31 2/5	Cornell	Wisconsin
1913	19:28 3/5	Syracuse	Cornell
1914	19:37 4/5	Columbia	Pennsylvania
1915	19:36 3/5	Cornell	Stanford
1916	20:15 2/5	Syracuse	Cornell
1920	11:02 3/5	Syracuse	Cornell
1921	14:07	Navy	California
1922	13:33 3/5	Navy	Washington
1923	14:03 1/5	Washington	Navy
1924	15:02	Washington	Wisconsin
1925	19:24 4/5	Navy	Washington
1926	19:28 3/5	Washington	Navy
1927	20:57	Columbia	Washington
1928	18:35 4/5	California	Columbia
1929	22:58	Columbia	Washington
1930	21:42	Cornell	Syracuse
1931	18:54 1/5	Navy	Cornell
1932	19:55	California	Cornell
1934	19:44	California	Washington
1935	18:52	California	Cornell
1936	19:09 3/5	Washington	California
1937	18:33 3/5	Washington	Navy
1938	18:19	Navy	California
1939	18:12 3/5	California	Washington
1940	22:42	Washington	Cornell
1941	18:53 3/10	Washington	California
1947	13:59 1/5	Navy	Cornell
1948	14:06 2/5	Washington	California
1949	14:42 3/5	California	Washington
1950	8:07.5	Washington	California
1951	7:50.5	Wisconsin	Washington
1952	15:08.1	Navy	Princeton
1953	15:29.6	Navy	Cornell
1954	16:04.4	Navy[1]	Cornell
1955	15:49.9	Cornell	Pennsylvania
1956	16:22.4	Cornell	Navy
1957	15:26.6	Cornell	Pennsylvania
1958	17:12.1	Cornell	Navy
1959	18:01.7	Wisconsin	Syracuse
1960	15:57	California	Navy
1961	16:49.2	California	Cornell
1962	17:02.9	Cornell	Washington
1963	17:24	Cornell	Navy
1964	6:31.1	California	Washington
1965	16:51.3	Navy	Cornell
1966	16:03.4	Wisconsin	Navy
1967	16:13.9	Pennsylvania	Wisconsin
1968	6:15.6	Pennsylvania	Washington
1969	6:30.4	Pennsylvania	Dartmouth
1970	6:39.3	Washington	Wisconsin
1971	6:06	Cornell	Washington
1972	6:22.6	Pennsylvania	Brown
1973	6:21	Wisconsin	Brown
1974	6:33	Wisconsin	Mass. Inst. of Technology
1975	6:08.2	Wisconsin	M.I.T.
1976	6:31	California	Princeton
1977	6:32.4	Cornell	Pennsylvania
1978	6:39.5	Syracuse	Brown
1979	6:26.4	Brown	Wisconsin
1980	6:46	Navy	Northeastern
1981	5:57.3	Cornell	Navy
1982	5:57.5	Cornell	Princeton
1983	6:14.4	Brown	Navy
1984	5:54.7	Navy	Pennsylvania

1. Disqualified.

COLLEGIATE—1984

Intercollegiate Rowing Association
(Lake Onondoga, Syracuse, N.Y.)
(All races at 2,000 meters)

Eights—1. Navy 5 minutes 54.7 seconds. 2. Pennsylvania, 5:57.5. 3. California–Berkeley, 6:02.2. 4. Syracuse, 6:02.3. 5. Cornell, 6:03.2. 6. Brown, 6:04.2.

Junior varsity eights—Brown	6:04.5
Freshman eights—Princeton	6:04.8
Pairs without coxswain—Wisconsin	7:32.0
Fours with coxswain—Temple	7:01.3
Fours without coxswain—Princeton	6:44.1
Freshman fours—Navy	7:36.4
Open fours—Mass. Institute of Technology	7:16.6

U.S. MEN'S CHAMPIONSHIPS

U.S. Rowing Association
(Los Gatos, Calif., July 12–15, 1984)

Lightweight 1/4-mile dash—Paul Fuchs, Detroit Rowing Club	1:21.3
Intermediate pair without coxswain—Stanford Rowing Club (Mark Wogulis, Dan Cornew)	7:16.94
Intermediate doubles—Marin Rowing Club (Raoul Wertz, Dan Louis)	7:04.15
Intermediate lightweight doubles—Detroit (Tim O'Hara, Brian Benz)	7:05.34
Intermediate Four with coxswain—Los Gatos Rowing Club (Paul Duryea, Victor Bruni, Walt Edberg, Russ Forbes)	6:58.
Elite lightweight four without coxswain—Mexico (Luis Amexcua, Juan Chavez, Renato Chavez, Alfonso Castro)	6:36.7
Senior pair without coxswain—California R.C. (Craig Amerkhanian, Brian Ettlin)	7:16.06
Elite lightweight single—Detroit, Paul Fuchs	7:49.17
Intermediate lightweight single—Kennebecasis R.C., Brain Flood	8:04.05
Intermediate single—Marin, Dan Louis	7:38.53
Senior Four with coxswain—Dirty Dozen (Tom Drengacz, Steve Rocconi, Kevin Dugan, Dell Turner)	6:56.3
Senior lightweight eight—Lake Washington/-Pacific Lutheran	6:59.97
Elite lightweight quad—Malta/LWRC (Dave Poley, Mike Brown, Bill Kalenius, Tom Pounds)	6:55.2
Intermediate lightweight eight—West Side	6:51.01
Intermediate Eight—Marin "A"	6:23.64
Elite four without coxswain—Australia (Duncan Fisher, Jim Lowe, David Doyle, John Bentley)	6:19.34
Elite single—Burnaby Lake, Patrick Walter	7:06.7
1/2-mile dash—Burnaby Lake, Patrick Walter	1:22.12
Elite lightweight pair without coxswain—LWRC "C" (Chet North, Willie Black)	7:26.5
Senior double—CYC/LBRA (Robert Salonites, Steve Nowinski)	6:51.9
Senior lightweight double—Detroit (Tim O'Hara, Brian Benz)	7:30.5
Elite four with coxswain—Stanford (Mark Wogulis, Dan Cornew, William Fink, Richard Lyon)	7:12.0
Senior lightweight four without coxswain—Marina (Luis Amezcua, Juan Chavez, Alfonso Castro, Renato Chavez)	7:14.4
Senior quad—Espana (David Pastor, Ricardo Gonzalez, Joaquin Gomez, Luis Miguel Garcia)	unavailable
Elite pair without coxswain—Australia (James Stride, Robert Booth)	7:28.0
Elite lightweight four with coxswain—LWRC (Bill Kalenius, James Schacht, Steve Amorosi, Tom Pounds)	7:29.0
Elite double—LBRA (Steve Meckna, Steve Messner)	7:41.5
Senior eight—Dirty dozen	6:57.0
Elite pair with coxswain—Stanford (Mark Wogulis, Dan Cornew)	8:41.2
Senior single—Marin, Dan Louis	8:35.1
Elite lightweight doubles—Detroit (Tim O'Hara, Brian Benz)	7:53.3
Elite lightweight eight—West Side	6:56.5
Elite quadruple sculls—Australia (Paul Reedy, Gary Gullock, Tim McLaren, Tony Lourich)	6:34.4
Senior lightweight single—Kennebecasis, Brian Flood	8:46.0
Elite eight—Australia/Burnaby/Los Gatos	6:14.7
Barnes Point Trophy—Marin	188 pts

U.S. WOMEN'S CHAMPIONSHIPS
(Oak Ridge, Tenn., June 14–17, 1984)

Flyweight four—Westside Boat Club	3:51.7
Junior single—Durham Boat Club	4:20.03
Elite four—Pioneer Valley Rowing Association	3:47.90
Senior double—Vesper "A"	3:54.67
Lightweight pair—Pioneer Valley "B"	4:01.25
Junior quadruple sculls—Durham	3:47.54
Late bloomers four—Minnesota/Minneapolis	4:26.32
Senior eight—Wisconsin	3:23.68
Lightweight single dash—Boston "A", Barbara Trafton	1:32.45
Elite single dash—PGRC, Elizabeth Hud-Broderick	1:30.98
Lightweight straight four—Pioneer Valley	3:31.97
High school four—Durham "A"	3:43.55
Senior pair—Boston "B"	3:53.44
Lightweight double sculls—Boston	3:41.59
Elite quadruple sculls—Vesper	3:32.87
Lightweight eight—PVRA "A"	3:12.49
Elite single—PGRC, Elizabeth Hud-Broderick	4:00.84
Junior doubles—ZLAC/MBRA "A"	4:18.40
Lightweight four with coxswain—Minnesota "B"	3:47.30
Elite pair—Boston	4:02.72
High school eight—Durham	3:28.19
Mixed Masters four with coxswain—SDRC/-Bachelors/Cambridge/MIT	3:56.40
Senior single—Vesper, Anne Keeler	4:11.52
Lightweight single—Boston, Anne Martin	4:09.84
Senior four—Boston	3:56.28
Junior pair—Durham	4:13.75
Elite double—Vesper	3:53.75
Lightweight quad—Boston/Cambridge/PVRA	3:43.77
Elite eight—PVRA	3:26.31
The Best Cup—Pioneer Valley	183.25 pts

WORLD CHAMPIONSHIPS—1983
(Duisbourg, Aug. 27–September 4, 1983)

Men

Fours with coxswain—New Zealand	6:13.89
Double sculls—East Germany	6:20.17
Pairs without coxswain—East Germany	6:35.85
Single sculls—West Germany	6:49.88
Pairs with coxswain—East Germany	6:49.75
Fours without coxswain—Romania	6:14.83
Quadruple sculls—West Germany	5:45.97
Eights—New Zealand	5:34.39

Women

Fours with coxswain—East Germany	3:11.18
Double sculls—East Germany	3:13.44
Four without coxswain—East Germany	3:26.68
Single sculls—East Germany	3:36.51
Quadruple sculls—Soviet Union	3:02.48
Eights—Soviet Union	2:56.22

MOTORCYCLE RACING

WORLD CHAMPION—1984

500 c.c.—Andre Malherbe, Belgium (HONDA)

1983 PAN-AMERICAN GAMES CHAMPIONSHIPS

Archery

Men—Darrell Pace, United States
Women—Ruth Rowe, United States

Boxing

106 lb—Rafael Ramos, Puerto Rico
112 lb—Pedro Reyes, Cuba
119 lb—Manuel Vilchez, Venezuela
126 lb—Adolfo Horta, Cuba
132 lb—Pernell Whitaker, United States
140 lb—Candelario Duvergel, Cuba
148 lb—Louis Howard, United States
157 lb—Orestes Solano, Cuba
165 lb—Bernardo Comas, Cuba
179 lb—Pedro Romero, Cuba
201 lb—Aurello Toyo, Cuba
Over 201 lb—Jorge Gonzalez, Cuba

Cycling

Sprint—Nelson Vails, United States
Pursuit—David Grylls, United States
Team pursuit—United States
Road race—Luis Rosendo, Mexico
Team road race—United States
50,000 meter points race—John Beckman, United States

Equestrian

Dressage—Carole Grant, United States
Dressage team—United States
Jumping—Anne Kursinski, United States
Team jumping—United States

Fencing

Foil—Efigenio Favier, Cuba
Team foil—Cuba
Epee—Agapito Nussa, Cuba
Sabre—Peter Westbrook, United States
Women's foil—Margarita Rodriguez, Cuba
Women's team foil—Cuba

Gymnastics—Men

All-around—Casimiro Suarez, Cuba
Floor exercises—Casimiro Suarez, Cuba
Horizontal bar—Casimiro Suarez, Cuba
Parallel bars—Roberto Richard, Cuba
Pommel horse—Amador Lazaro, Cuba
Rings—Casimiro Suarez, Cuba
Vault—Casimiro Suarez, Cuba
Team—Cuba

Gymnastics—Women

All-around—Orisel Martinez, Cuba
Balance beam—Elsa Chivas, Cuba
Floor exercises—Yumi Mordre, United States
Uneven bars—Lucy Wener, United States
Vault—Orisel Martinez, Cuba
Team all-around—United States

Judo—Men

132 lb—Rafael Rodriguez, Cuba
143 lb—Gerardo Padilla, Mexico
157 lb—Guillermo D'Nelson, Cuba
172 lb—Brett Barron, United States
189 lb—Louis Jani, Canada
209 lb—Isaac Azcuy, Cuba
Over 209—Mark Berger, Canada
Open—Venacio Gomez, Cuba

Judo—Women

106 lb—Darlene Anaya, United States
114 lb—Mary Lewis, United States
123 lb—Annmaria Burns, United States
134 lb—Robin Chapman, United States
145 lb—Christine Penick, United States
158 lb—Allinson Henri, Venezuela
Over 158 lb—Margaret Castro, United States
Open—Heidi Bauersachs, United States

Rowing—Men

Singles—Ricardo Ibarra, Argentina
Doubles—Canada
Pairs—Brazil
Pairs with coxswain—Cuba
Fours—Cuba
Fours without coxswain—Canada
Eights—United States

Rowing—Women

Singles—Chris Ernst, United States
Doubles—United States

Shooting—Men

Free pistol—Eric Buljung, United States
Rapid-fire pistol—Terry Anderson, United States
Air pistol—Carlos Hura, Peru
Rifle, Running Game Target—Helmuth Bellingrode, Columbia
Skeet—Matt Dryke, United States
Trap—Dan Carlisle, United States

Shooting—Women

Air rifle—Pat Spurgin, United States
Free rifle, three position—Wanda Jewell, United States
Air pistol—Cathy Graham, United States

SWIMMING—Men

100-meter freestyle—Rowdy Gaines, United States
200-meter freestyle—Bruce Hayes, United States
400-meter freestyle—Bruce Hayes, United States
1,500-meter freestyle—Jeff Kostkoff, United States
100-meter breaststroke—Steve Lundquist, United States
200-meter breaststroke—Steve Lundquist, United States
100-meter backstroke—Rick Carey, United States
200-meter backstroke—Rick Carey, United States
100-meter butterfly—Matt Gribble, United States
200-meter butterfly—Craig Beardsley, United States
200-meter Individual Medley—Ricardo Prado, Brazil
400-meter freestyle relay—United States
400-meter Individual Medley—Ricardo Prado, Brazil
400-meter medley relay—United States
800-meter freestyle relay—United States

Swimming—Women

100-meter freestyle—Carrie Steinseifer, United States
200-meter freestyle—Sippy Woodhead, United States
400-meter freestyle—Tiffany Cohen, United States
800-meter freestyle—Tiffany Cohen, United States
100-meter breaststroke—Ann Ottenbrite, Canada
200-meter breaststroke—Kathy Bald, Canada
100-meter butterfly—Laurie Lehner, United States
200-meter butterfly—Mary Meagher, United States
200-meter individual medley—Tracy Caulkins, United States
400-meter individual Medley—Tracy Caulkins, United States
400-meter freestyle relay—United States
400-meter medley relay—United States

Weight Lifting

52 kg—Juan Hernandez, Cuba
56 kg—Cristoteles Soler, Cuba
67.5 kg—Julio Loscos, Cuba
75 kg—Julio Echenique, Cuba
90 kg—Ciro Ibanez, Cuba
More than 100 kg—Reinaldo Chavez, Cuba

Wrestling—Freestyle

106 lb—Cristobal Gonzalez, Cuba
115 lb—Ray Takahashi, Canada
126 lb—Barry Davis, United States
137 lb—Randy Lewis, United States
150 lb—Raul Cascaret, Cuba
163 lb—Leroy Kemp, United States
181 lb—Jose Damian, Cuba
198 lb—Roberto Limonta, Cuba
220 lb—Greg Gibson, United States
Unlimited—Candido Meza, Cuba

Wrestling—Greco-Roman

106 lb—Reinaldo Jimenez, Cuba
115 lb—Edmundo Miranda, Cuba
126 lb—Jesus Tejada, Cuba
137 lb—Rene Rodriguez, Cuba
150 lb—Antonio Lopez, Cuba
163 lb—Jeff Stuebing, Canada
181 lb—Orlando Perez, Canada
198 lb—Steve Frazier, United States
220 lb—Rene Vidat, Cuba
Over 220 lb—Candido Meza, Cuba

Yachting

470 Class—Brazil
Snipe—United States
Laser—Brazil
Lightning—Brazil
J-24—United States
Soling—Brazil
Star—United States

Team sports

Baseball—Cuba
Basketball, men—United States
Basketball, women—United States
Field hockey—Canada

1983 PAN-AMERICAN GAMES—DISTRIBUTION OF MEDALS

	Gold	Silver	Bronze	Total[1]
United States	136	92	56	284
Cuba	79	53	43	175
Canada	18	44	47	109
Venezuela	12	26	35	73
Brazil	14	20	22	56
Mexico	7	11	24	42
Argentina	2	11	22	35
Colombia	1	7	13	21
Puerto Rico	2	7	6	15
Dominican Republic	0	5	9	14
Chile	1	3	9	13
Peru	1	1	4	6
Jamaica	0	0	6	6
Uruguay	1	0	2	3
Panama	0	0	3	3
Trinidad	0	1	2	3
Ecuador	1	0	0	1
Bahamas	0	1	0	1
Nicaragua	0	1	0	1
Guatemala	0	0	1	1
Belize	0	0	1	1
Virgin Islands	0	0	1	1

1. Table reflects vacated medals relative to athletes who won medals then were tested positive for the use of banned substances. Medals were vacated, not re-awarded.

Soccer—Uruguay
Softball, men—Canada
Softball, women—United States
Volleyball, men—Brazil
Volleyball, women—Cuba
Water polo—United States

COLLEGE BASEBALL

1984 CHAMPIONS

N.C.A.A. Division I—California State University at Fullerton defeated Texas 3–1 in championship game

NAIA—Lewis & Clark State (Idaho) defeated Azusa Pacific (California), 15–2, in title game

SHUFFLEBOARD

U.S. INTERNATIONAL PRO WORLD CHAMPIONSHIP

(Hollywood, Fla., Feb. 9–11, 1984)

Men—Fred Berger, New York, and Horace Lancellotta, Rhode Island
Women—Eva Jackson, Florida, and Anna Carabetta, Connecticut

CHESS

WORLD CHAMPIONS

1894–1921	Emanuel Lasker, Germany
1921–27	Jose R. Capablanca, Cuba
1927–35	Alexander A. Alekhine, U.S.S.R.
1935–37	Dr. Max Euwe, Netherlands
1937–46	Alexander A. Alekhine, U.S.S.R.[1]
1948–57	Mikhail Botvinnik, U.S.S.R.
1957–58	Vassily Smyslov, U.S.S.R.
1958–60	Mikhail Botvinnik, U.S.S.R.
1960–61	Mikhail Tal, U.S.S.R.
1961–63	Mikhail Botvinnik, U.S.S.R.
1963–68	Tigran Petrosian, U.S.S.R.
1969–71	Boris Spassky, U.S.S.R.
1972–74	Bobby Fischer, Los Angeles
1975	Bobby Fischer[2], Anatoly Karpov, U.S.S.R.
1976–84	Anatoly Karpov, U.S.S.R.[3]

1. Alekhine, a French citizen, died while champion. 2. Relinquished title. 3. In 1978, Karpov defeated Viktor Korchnoi 6 games to 5.

UNITED STATES CHAMPIONS

1909–36	Frank J. Marshall, New York
1936–44	Samuel Reshevsky, New York[1]
1944–46	Arnold S. Denker, New York
1946	Samuel Reshevsky, Boston
1948	Herman Steiner, Los Angeles
1951–52	Larry Evan, New York
1954–57	Arthur Bisguier, New York
1958–61	Bobby Fischer, Brooklyn, N.Y.
1962	Larry Evans, New York
1963–67	Bobby Fischer, New York
1968	Larry Evans, New York
1969–71	Samuel Reshevsky, Spring Valley, N.Y.
1972	Robert Byrne, Ossining, N.Y.
1973	Lubomir Kavelek, Washington; John Grefe, San Francisco
1974–77	Walter Browne, Berkeley, Calif.
1978–79	Lubomir Kavalek, New York
1980	Tie, Walter Browne, Berkeley, Calif. Larry Christiansen, Modesto, Calif. Larry Evans, Reno, Nev.
1981–82[2]	Tie, Walter Browne, Berkeley, Calif. Yasser Seirawan, Seattle, Wash.
1983	Tie, Walter Browne, Berkeley, Calif. Larry Christiansen, Los Angeles, Calif., Roman Dzindzichashvili, Corona, N.Y.
1984	Lev Aiburt, New York City

1. In 1942, Isaac I. Kashdan of New York was co-champion for a while because of a tie with Reshevsky in that year's tournament. Reshevsky won the play-off. 2. Championship not contested in 1982.

HARNESS RACING

Oliver Wendell Holmes, the famous Autocrat of the Breakfast Table, wrote that the running horse was a gambling toy but the trotting horse was useful and, furthermore, "horse-racing is not a republican institution; horse-trotting is." Oliver Wendell Holmes was a born-and-bred New Englander, and New England was the nursery of the harness racing sport in America. Pacers and trotters were matters of local pride and prejudice in Colonial New England, and, shortly after the Revolution, the Messenger and Justin Morgan strains produced many winners in harness racing "matches" along the turnpikes of New York, Connecticut, Rhode Island, Massachusetts, Vermont, and New Hampshire.

There was English thoroughbred blood in Messenger and Justin Morgan, and, many years later, it was blended in Rysdyk's Hambletonian, foaled in 1849. Hambletonian was not particularly fast under harness but his descendants have had almost a monopoly of prizes, titles, and records in the harness racing game. Hambletonian was purchased as a foal with its dam for a total of $124 by William Brysdyk of Goshen, N.Y., and made a modest fortune for the purchaser.

Trotters and pacers often were raced under saddle in the old days, and, in fact, the custom still survives in some places in Europe. Dexter, the great trotter that lowered the mile record from 2:19 3/4 to 2:17 1/4 in 1867, was said to handle just as well under saddle as when pulling a sulky. But as sulkies were lightened in weight and improved in design, trotting under saddle became less common and finally faded out in this country.

WORLD RECORDS

Established in a Race or Against Time at One Mile

Source: Research Specialist, United States Trotting Association

Trotting on Mile Track

	Record	Holder	Driver	Where Made	Year
All Age	1:54*	Arndon	Del Miller	Lexington, Ky.	1982
	1:54 4/5[1]	Lindy's Crown	Howard Beissinger	Du Quoin, Ill.	1980
2-year-old	1:56[1]	TV Yankee	Tom Haughton	Lexington, Ky.	1982
	1:55 4/5*	Fancy Crown	George Sholte	Lexington, Ky.	1983
3-year-old	1:54*	Arndon	Del Miller	Lexington, Ky.	1982
	1:55[1]	Speedy Somolli	Howard Beissinger	Du Quoin, Ill.	1978
	1:55[1]	Florida Pro	George Sholty	Du Quoin, Ill.	1978
	1:55[1]	Jazz Cosmos	Mickey McNichol	Lexington, Ky.	1982
4-year-old	1:54 4/5[1]	Lindy's Crown	Howard Beissinger	Du Quoin, Ill.	1980
	1:54 4/5*	Nevele Pride	Stanely Dancer	Indianapolis	1969

Trotting on Five-Eighths Mile Track

	Record	Holder	Driver	Where Made	Year
All Age	1:57 1/5[1]	Lindy's Crown	Howard Beissinger	Wilmington, Del.	1980
2-year-old	1:58 2/5[1]	Mr. Drew	Jan Nordin	Wilmington, Del.	1982
3-year-old	1:57 2/5[1]	Arndon	Del Miller	Montreal, Quebec	1982
4-year-old	1:57 1/5[1]	Lindy's Crown	Howard Beissinger	Wilmington, Del.	1980

Trotting on Half-Mile Track

	Record	Holder	Driver	Where Made	Year
All Age	1:56 4/5[1]	Nevele Pride	Stanley Dancer	Saratoga Springs, N.Y.	1969
2-year-old	2:00[1]	Incredible Nevele	Glen Garnsey	Delaware, Ohio	1981
3-year-old	1:58[1]	Incredible Nevele	Glen Garnsey	Saratoga Springs, N.Y.	1982
4-year-old	1:56 4/5[1]	Nevele Pride	Stanley Dancer	Saratoga Springs, N.Y.	1969

Pacing on Mile Track

	Record	Holder	Driver	Where Made	Year
All Age	1:51 3/5[1]	Trenton	Tommy Haughton	Springfield, Ill.	1982
	1:49 1/5*	Niatross	Clint Galbraith	Lexington, Ky.	1980
2-year-old	1:53 3/5[1]	Trim The Tree	Dick Macomber	Lexington, Ky.	1982
3-year-old	1:51 3/5[1]	Trenton	Tommy Haughton	Springfield, Ill.	1982
	1:49 1/5*	Niatross	Clint Galbraith	Lexington, Ky.	1980
4-year-old	1:50 4/5*	Fan Hanover	Glen Garnsey	Lexington, Ky.	1982
	1:51 4/5[1]	It's Fritz	Martin Allen	Lexington, Ky.	1983

Pacing on Five-Eighths Mile Track

	Record	Holder	Driver	Where Made	Year
All Age	1:52 1/5[1]	It's Fritz	Martin Allen	Meadow Lands, Pa.	1983
2-year-old	1:56 1/5[1]	French Chef	Stanley Dancer	Columbus, Ky.	1980
3-year-old	1:53 2/5[1]	Storm Damage	Joe O'Brien	Meadow Lands, Pa.	1980
4-year-old	1:52 1/5[1]	It's Fritz	Martin Allen	Meadow Lands, Pa.	1983

Pacing on Half-Mile Track

	Record	Holder	Driver	Where Made	Year
All Age	1:53 3/5[1]	It's Fritz	Martin Allen	Louisville, Ky.	1983
2-year-old	1:56 1/5[1]	Temujin	Clarence Martin	Louisville, Ky.	1981
	1:56 1/5[1]	Signed N. Sealed	Bill O'Donnell	Louisville, Ky.	1983
3-year-old	1:54 3/5[1]	Temujin	Clarence Martin	Delaware, Ohio	1982
4-year-old	1:53 3/5[1]	It's Fritz	Martin Allen	Louisville, Ky.	1983

1. Record set in race. *Record set in time trial.

HARNESS RACING RECORDS FOR THE MILE

Trotters

Time	Trotter, age, driver	Year
2:00	Lou Dillon, 5, Millard Sanders	1903
1:58 1/2	Lou Dillon, 5, Millard Sanders	1903
1:58	Uhlan, 8, Charles Tanner	1912
1:58	Peter Manning, 5, T. W. Murphy	1921
1:57 3/4	Peter Manning, 5, T. W. Murphy	1921
1:57	Peter Manning, 6, T. W. Murphy	1922
1:56 3/4	Peter Manning, 6, T. W. Murphy	1922
1:56 3/4	Greyhound, 5, Sep Palin	1937
1:56	Greyhound, 5, Sep Palin	1937
1:55 1/4	Greyhound, 6, Sep Palin	1938
1:54 4/5	Nevele Pride, 4, Stanley Dancer	1969
1:54 4/5	Lindy's Crown, 4, Howard Beissinger	1980
1:54	Arndon, 3, Del Miller	1982

Pacers

Time	Pacer, age, driver	Year
2:00 1/2	John R. Gentry, 7, W.J. Andrews	1896
1:59 1/4	Star Pointer, 8, D. McClary	1897
1:59	Dan Patch, 7, M. E. McHenry	1903
1:56 1/4	Dan Patch, 7, M. E. McHenry	1903
1:56	Dan Patch, 8, H. C. Hersey	1904
1:55	Billy Direct, 4, Vic Fleming	1938
1:55	Adios Harry, 4, Luther Lyons	1955
1:54 3/5	Adios Butler, 4, Paige West	1960
1:54	Bret Hanover, 4, Frank Ervin	1966
1:53 3/5	Bret Hanover, 4, Frank Ervin	1966
1:52	Steady Star, 4, Joe O'Brien	1971
1:49 1/5	Niatross, 3, Clint Galbraith	1980

HISTORY OF TRADITIONAL HARNESS RACING STAKES

The Hambletonian

Three-year-old trotters. One mile. Guy McKinney won first race at Syracuse in 1926; held at Goshen, N.Y., 1930–1942, 1944–1956; at Yonkers, N.Y., 1943; at Du Quoin, Ill., 1957–1980. In 1981–83 the race was held at the Meadowlands in East Rutherford, N.J.

Year	Winner	Driver	Best time	Total purse
1967	Speedy Streak	Del Cameron	2:00	122,650
1968	Nevele Pride	Stanley Dancer	1:59 2/5	116,190
1969	Lindy's Pride	Howard Beissinger	1:57 3/5	124,910
1970	Timothy T.	John Simpson, Jr.	1:58 2/5[1]	143,630
1971	Speedy Crown	Howard Beissinger	1:57 2/5	129,770
1972	Super Bowl	Stanley Dancer	1:56 2/5	119,090
1973	Flirth	Ralph Baldwin	1:57 1/5	144,710
1974	Christopher T	Billy Haughton	1:58 3/5	160,150
1975	Bonefish	Stanely Dancer	1:59[2]	232,192
1976	Steve Lobell	Billy Haughton	1:56 2/5	263,524
1977	Green Speed	Billy Haughton	1:55 3/5	284,131
1978	Speedy Somolli	Howard Beissinger	1:55[3]	241,280
1979	Legend Hanover	George Sholty	1:56 1/5	300,000
1980	Burgomeister	Billy Haughton	1:56 3/5	293,570
1981	Shiaway St. Pat	Ray Remmen	2:01 1/5[4]	838,000
1982	Speed Bowl	Tommy Haughton	1:56 4/5	875,750
1983	Duenna	Stanley Dancer	1:57 2/5	1,000,000

1. By Formal Notice. 2. By Yankee Bambino. 3. By Speedy Somolli and Florida Pro. 4. By Super Juan.

Little Brown Jug

Three-year-old pacers. One Mile. Raced at Delaware County Fair Grounds, Delaware, Ohio.

Year	Winner	Driver	Best time	Total purse
1967	Best of All	Jim Hackett	1:59[1]	84,778
1968	Rum Customer	Billy Haughton	1:59 3/5	104,226
1969	Laverne Hanover	Billy Haughton	2:00 2/5	109,731
1970	Most Happy Fella	Stanley Dancer	1:57 1/5	100,110
1971	Nansemond	Herve Filion	1:57 2/5	102,994
1972	Strike Out	Keith Waples	1:56 3/5	104,916
1973	Melvin's Woe	Joe O'Brien	1:57 3/5	120,000
1974	Ambro Omaha	Billy Haughton	1:57	132,630
1975	Seatrain	Ben Webster	1:57[2]	147,813
1976	Keystone Ore	Stanley Dancer	1:56 4/5[3]	153,799
1977	Governor Skipper	John Chapman	1:56 1/5	150,000
1978	Happy Escort	William Popfinger	1:55 2/5[4]	186,760
1979	Hot Hitter	Herve Filion	1:55 3/5	226,455
1980	Niatross	Clint Galbraith	1:54 4/5	207,361
1981	Fan Hanover	Glen Garnsey	1:56[5]	243,799
1982	Merger	John Campbell	1:56 3/5	328,900
1983	Ralph Hanover	Ron Waples	1:55 3/5	358,800

1. By Nardin's Byrd. 2. By Armbro Ranger. 3. By Falcon Almahurst. 4. By Falcon Almahurst. 5. By Seahawk Hanover.

HARNESS HORSE OF THE YEAR

Chosen in poll conducted by United States Trotting Association in conjunction with the U.S. Harness Writers Assn.

1959	Bye Bye Byrd, Pacer
1960	Adios Butler, Pacer
1961	Adios Butler, Pacer
1962	Su Mac Lad, Trotter
1963	Speedy Scot, Trotter
1964	Bret Hanover, Pacer
1965	Bret Hanover, Pacer
1966	Bret Hanover, Pacer
1967	Nevele Pride, Trotter
1968	Nevele Pride, Trotter
1969	Nevele Pride, Trotter
1970	Fresh Yankee, Trotter
1971	Albatross, Pacer
1972	Albatross, Pacer
1973	Sir Dalrae, Pacer
1974	Delmonica Hanover, Trotter
1975	Savoir, Trotter
1976	Keystone Ore, Pacer
1977	Green Speed, Trotter
1978	Abercrombie, Pacer
1979	Niatross, Pacer
1980	Niatross, Pacer
1981	Fan Hanover, Pacer
1982	Cam Fella, Pacer
1983	Cam Fella, Pacer

ARCHERY

NATIONAL ARCHERY ASSOCIATION CHAMPIONSHIPS

(Aurora, Ill., July 23–27, 1984)

Men's Division

	Pts
Freestyle—Dennis Barnes, Oklahoma	2,741
Freestyle limited—Charles Langston, Texas	2,632
Barebow—Dennis Cline, Virginia	2,593
Bow hunter—Ben Rogers, California	2,519
Bow hunter freestyle—James Bibee, Tennessee	2,667
Bow hunter freestyle limited—Larry Davis, Kentucky	2,613

Women's Division

Freestyle—Roseann Jackson, Canada	2,686
Freestyle limited—Paulette Podratz, Montana	2,522
Barebow—Gloria Shelly, Connecticut	2,483
Bow hunter—Carolyn Phillips, Oregon	2,296
Bow hunter freestyle—Ruth Price, Alabama	2,502
Bow hunter freestyle limited—Marge Stelck, Montana	2,185

Young Adult Division (15–17 years old)

Male freestyle—Joe Peidle, Ohio	2,668
Female freestyle—Theresa Fazio, Ohio	2,613
Male freestyle limited—Mark DuPont, Louisiana	2,601
Female freestyle limited—Trina Whitefield, Texas	2,155
Male barebow—Tim Kloss, Wisconsin	2,232

Youth Division (12–14 years old)

Male freestyle—Steve Gorby, West Virginia	2,716
Female freestyle—Rebecca Dunn, Virginia	2,296
Male freestyle limited—Chad Hensky, Mississippi	2,502
Female freestyle limited—Michelle Kelly, Michigan	2,185
Male barebow—Donald Blebins, West Virginia	2,272

WRESTLING

U.S.A. NATIONAL CHAMPIONSHIPS—1984

Freestyle

(Stillwater, Okla., March 22–24, 1984)

105.5 lb—Rich Salamone, New York Athletic Club
114.5 lb—Charlie Heard, Sunkist Kids
125.5 lb—Joe Corso, New York Athletic Club
136.5 lb—Rick Dellagatta, New York Athletic Club
149.5 lb—Andre Metzger, unattached, North Carolina
163 lb—Dave Schultz, Sunkist Kids
180.5 lb—Mark Schultz, Sunkist Kids
198 lb—Steve Fraser, Michigan Wrestling Club
220 lb—Harold Smith, Wildcat Wrestling Club
Unlimited—Bruce Baumgartner, New York Athletic Club
Team—Sunkist Kids, 101 pts
Outstanding wrestler—Dave Schultz

Greco-Roman

(Chicago, Ill., May 11–12, 1984)

105.5 lb—T.J. Jones, United States Navy
114.5 lb—Mark Fuller, Little C Wrestling Club
125.5 lb—Frank Samiano, ATWA
136.5 lb—Dan Mello, United States Marines
149.5 lb—Jim Martinez, Minnesota Wrestling Club
163 lb—John Matthews, Michigan Wrestling Club
180.5 lb—Tom Press, Minnesota Wrestling Club
198 lb—Mike Houck, Minnesota Wrestling Club
220 lb—Dennis Koslowski, Minnesota Wrestling Club
Heavyweight—Ron Carlisle and Gary Albright both disqualified in finals. No champion.
Team—ATWA 69, Minnesota Wrestling Club 66, United States Marines 46
Outstanding wrestler—Jim Martinez

WORLD CUP CHAMPIONSHIPS—1984

Freestyle

(Toledo, Ohio, April 1, 1984)

105.5 lb—Bob Weaver, United States
114.5 lb—Joe Gonzales, United States
125.5 lb—Anatoli Belaglazou, Soviet Union
136.5 lb—Steven Sarkisyan, Soviet Union
149.5 lb—Mikhail Kharachura, Soviet Union
163 lb—Vladimir Dzhuton, Soviet Union
180.5 lb—Chris Campbell, United States
198 lb—Sanasar Oganasyan, Soviet Union
220 lb—Magomad Magomadov, Soviet Union
Heavyweight—Bruce Baumgartner, United States
Team—1. Soviet Union; 2. United States; 3. Bulgaria

N.C.A.A. CHAMPIONSHIPS—1984

(East Rutherford, N.J., March 9–11, 1984)

118 lb—Carl DeStefanis, Penn State
126 lb—Kevin Darkus, Iowa State
134 lb—Scott Lynch, Penn State
142 lb—Jesse Reyes, Cal State at Bakersfield
150 lb—Kenny Monday, Oklahoma State
158 lb—Jim Zaleski, Iowa
167 lb—Mike Sheets, Oklahoma State
177 lb—Jim Sherr, Nebraska
198 lb—Bill Scherr, Nebraska
Heavyweight—Tab Thacker, North Carolina State
Team—Iowa 123.75; Oklahoma State 98; Penn State 70.5

GOLF

It may be that golf originated in Holland—historians believe it did—but certainly Scotland fostered the game and is famous for it. In fact, in 1457 the Scottish Parliament, disturbed because football and golf had lured young Scots from the more soldierly exercise of archery, passed an ordinance that "futeball and golf be utterly cryit doun and nocht usit." James I and Charles I of the royal line of Stuarts were golf enthusiasts, whereby the game came to be known as "the royal and ancient game of golf."

The golf balls used in the early games were leather-covered and stuffed with feathers. Clubs of all kinds were fashioned by hand to suit individual players. The great step in spreading the game came with the change from the feather ball to the guttapercha ball about 1850. In 1860, formal competition began with the establishment of an annual tournament for the British Open championship. There are records of "golf clubs" in the United States as far back as colonial days but no proof of actual play before John Reid and some friends laid out six holes on the Reid lawn in Yonkers, N.Y., in 1888 and played there with golf balls and clubs brought over from Scotland by Robert Lockhart. This group then formed the St. Andrews Golf Club of Yonkers, and golf was established in this country.

However, it remained a rather sedate and almost aristocratic pastime until a 20-year-old ex-caddy, Francis Ouimet of Boston, defeated two great British professionals, Harry Vardon and Ted Ray, in the United States Open championship at Brookline, Mass., in 1913. This feat put the game and Francis Ouimet on the front pages of the newspapers and stirred a wave of enthusiasm for the sport. The greatest feat so far in golf history is that of Robert Tyre Jones, Jr., of Atlanta, who won the British Open, the British Amateur, the U.S. Open, and the U.S. Amateur titles in one year, 1930.

THE MASTERS TOURNAMENT WINNERS

Augusta National Golf Club, Augusta, Ga.

Year	Winner	Score	Year	Winner	Score	Year	Winner	Score
1934	Horton Smith	284	1953	Ben Hogan	274	1970	Billy Casper[1]	279
1935	Gene Sarazen[1]	282	1954	Sam Snead[1]	289	1971	Charles Coody	279
1936	Horton Smith	285	1955	Cary Middlecoff	279	1972	Jack Nicklaus	286
1937	Byron Nelson	283	1956	Jack Burke	289	1973	Tommy Aaron	283
1938	Henry Picard	285	1957	Doug Ford	283	1974	Gary Player	278
1939	Ralph Guldahl	279	1958	Arnold Palmer	284	1975	Jack Nicklaus	276
1940	Jimmy Demaret	280	1959	Art Wall, Jr.	284	1976	Ray Floyd	271
1941	Craig Wood	280	1960	Arnold Palmer	282	1977	Tom Watson	276
1942	Byron Nelson[1]	280	1961	Gary Player	280	1978	Gary Player	277
1943–45	No Tournaments		1962	Arnold Palmer[1]	280	1979	Fuzzy Zoeller[1]	280
1946	Herman Keiser	282	1963	Jack Nicklaus	286	1980	Severiano Ballesteros	275
1947	Jimmy Demaret	281	1964	Arnold Palmer	276	1981	Tom Watson	280
1948	Claude Harmon	279	1965	Jack Nicklaus	271	1982	Craig Stadler[1]	284
1949	Sam Snead	282	1966	Jack Nicklaus[1]	288	1983	Severiano Ballesteros	280
1950	Jimmy Demaret	283	1967	Gay Brewer, Jr.	280	1984	Ben Crenshaw	277
1951	Ben Hogan	280	1968	Bob Goalby	277			
1952	Sam Snead	286	1969	George Archer	281			

1. Winner in playoff.

U.S. OPEN CHAMPIONS

Year	Winner	Score	Where played	Year	Winner	Score	Where played
1895	Horace Rawlins	173	Newport	1919	Walter Hagen[2]	301	Brae Burn
1896	James Foulis	152	Shinnecock Hills	1920	Edward Ray	295	Inverness
1897	Joe Lloyd	162	Chicago	1921	Jim Barnes	289	Columbia
1898[3]	Fred Herd	328	Myopia	1922	Gene Sarazen	288	Skokie
1899	Willie Smith	315	Baltimore	1923	R. T. Jones, Jr.[1,2]	296	Inwood
1900	Harry Vardon	313	Chicago	1924	Cyril Walker	297	Oakland Hills
1901	Willie Anderson[1]	331	Myopia	1925	Willie Macfarlane[1]	291	Worcester
1902	Laurie Auchterlonie	307	Garden City	1926	R. T. Jones, Jr.[2]	293	Scioto
1903	Willie Anderson[1]	307	Baltusrol	1927	Tommy Armour[1]	301	Oakmont
1904	Willie Anderson	303	Glen View	1928	Johnny Farrell[1]	294	Olympia Fields
1905	Willie Anderson	314	Myopia	1929	R. T. Jones, Jr.[1,2]	294	Winged Foot
1906	Alex Smith	295	Onwentsia	1930	R. T. Jones, Jr.[2]	287	Interlachen
1907	Alex Ross	302	Philadelphia	1931	Billy Burke[1]	292	Inverness
1908	Fred McLeod[1]	322	Myopia	1932	Gene Sarazen	286	Fresh Meadow
1909	George Sargent	290	Englewood	1933	John Goodman[2]	287	North Shore
1910	Alex Smith[1]	298	Philadelphia	1934	Olin Dutra	293	Merion
1911	John McDermott[1]	307	Chicago	1935	Sam Parks, Jr.	299	Oakmont
1912	John McDermott	294	Buffalo	1936	Tony Manero	282	Baltusrol
1913	Francis Ouimet[1,2]	304	Brookline	1937	Ralph Guldahl	281	Oakland Hills
1914	Walter Hagen	290	Midlothian	1938	Ralph Guldahl	284	Cherry Hills
1915	Jerome D. Travers[2]	297	Baltusrol	1939	Byron Nelson[1]	284	Philadelphia
1916	Charles Evans, Jr.[2]	286	Minikahda	1940	Lawson Little[1]	287	Canterbury
1917–18	No tournaments[4]			1941	Craig Wood	284	Colonial

Year	Winner	Score	Where played	Year	Winner	Score	Where played
1942–45	No tournaments[5]			1965	Gary Player[1]	282	Bellerive
1946	Lloyd Mangrum[1]	284	Canterbury	1966	Bill Casper[1]	278	Olympic
1947	Lew Worsham[1]	282	St. Louis	1967	Jack Nicklaus	275	Baltusrol
1948	Ben Hogan	276	Riviera	1968	Lee Trevino	275	Oak Hill
1949	Cary Middlecoff	286	Medinah	1969	Orville Moody	281	Champions G. C.
1950	Ben Hogan[1]	287	Merion	1970	Tony Jacklin	281	Hazeltine
1951	Ben Hogan	287	Oakland Hills	1971	Lee Trevino[1]	280	Merion
1952	Julius Boros	281	Northwood	1972	Jack Nicklaus	290	Pebble Beach
1953	Ben Hogan	283	Oakmont	1973	Johnny Miller	279	Oakmont
1954	Ed Furgol	284	Baltusrol	1974	Hale Irwin	287	Winged Foot
1955	Jack Fleck[1]	287	Olympic	1975	Lou Graham[1]	287	Medinah
1956	Cary Middlecoff	281	Oak Hill	1976	Jerry Pate	277	Atlanta A.C.
1957	Dick Mayer[1]	298	Inverness	1977	Hubert Green	278	Southern Hills
1958	Tommy Bolt	283	Southern Hills	1978	Andy North	285	Cherry Hills
1959	Bill Casper, Jr.	282	Winged Foot	1979	Hale Irwin	284	Inverness
1960	Arnold Palmer	280	Cherry Hills	1980	Jack Nicklaus	272	Baltusrol
1961	Gene Littler	281	Oakland Hills	1981	David Graham	273	Merion
1962	Jack Nicklaus[1]	283	Oakmont	1982	Tom Watson	282	Pebble Beach
1963	Julius Boros[1]	293	Country Club	1983	Larry Nelson	280	Oakmont
1964	Ken Venturi	278	Congressional	1984	Fuzzy Zoeller[1]	276	Winged Foot

1. Winner in playoff. 2. Amateur. 3. In 1898, competition was extended to 72 holes. 4. In 1917, Jock Hutchison, with a 292, won an Open Patriotic Tournament for the benefit of the American Red Cross at Whitemarsh Valley Country Club. 5. In 1942, Ben Hogan, with a 271 won a Hale American National Open Tournament for the benefit of the Navy Relief Society and USO at Ridgemoor Country Club.

U.S. AMATEUR CHAMPIONS

Year	Winner	Year	Winner	Year	Winner	Year	Winner
1895	Charles B. Macdonald	1921	Jesse P. Guilford	1947	Robert Riegel	1967	Bob Dickson
1896–97	H. J. Whigham	1922	Jess W. Sweetser	1948	Willie Turnesa	1968	Bruce Fleisher
1898	Findlay S. Douglas	1923	Max R. Marston	1949	Charles Coe	1969	Steven Melnyk
1899	H. M. Harriman	1924–25	R. T. Jones, Jr.	1950	Sam Urzetta	1970	Lanny Wadkins
1900–01	Walter J. Travis	1926	George Von Elm	1951	Billy Maxwell	1971	Gary Cowan
1902	Louis N. James	1927–28	R. T. Jones, Jr.	1952	Jack Westland	1972	Vinny Giles 3d
1903	Walter J. Travis	1929	H. R. Johnston	1953	Gene Littler	1973[3]	Craig Stadler
1904–05	H. Chandler Egan	1930	R. T. Jones, Jr.	1954	Arnold Palmer	1974	Jerry Pate
1906	Eben M. Byers	1931	Francis Ouimet	1955–56	Harvie Ward	1975	Fred Ridley
1907–08	Jerome D. Travers	1932	Ross Somerville	1957	Hillman Robbins	1976	Bill Sander
1909	Robert A. Gardner	1933	G. T. Dunlap, Jr.	1958	Charles Coe	1977	John Fought
1910	W. C. Fownes, Jr.	1934–35	Lawson Little	1959	Jack Nicklaus	1978	John Cook
1911	Harold H. Hilton	1936	John W. Fischer	1960	Deane Beman	1979	Mark O'Meara
1912–13	Jerome D. Travers	1937	John Goodman	1961	Jack Nicklaus	1980	Hal Sutton
1914	Francis Ouimet	1938	Willie Turnesa	1962	Labron Harris, Jr.	1981	Nathaniel Crosby
1915	Robert A. Gardner	1939	Marvin H. Ward	1963	Deane Beman	1982	Jay Sigel
1916	Charles Evans, Jr.	1940	R. D. Chapman	1964	Bill Campbell	1983	Jay Sigel
1919	S. D. Herron	1941	Marvin H. Ward	1965[2]	Robert Murphy, Jr.	1984	Scott Verplank
1920	Charles Evans, Jr.	1946	Ted Bishop	1966	Gary Cowan[1]		

1. Winner in playoff. 2. Tourney switched to medal play through 1972. 3. Return to match play.

U.S. P.G.A. CHAMPIONS

Year	Winner	Year	Winner	Year	Winner	Year	Winner
1916	Jim Barnes	1939	Henry Picard	1955	Doug Ford	1970	Dave Stockton
1919	Jim Barnes	1940	Byron Nelson	1956	Jack Burke, Jr.	1971	Jack Nicklaus
1920	Jock Hutchison	1941	Victor Ghezzi	1957	Lionel Hebert	1972	Gary Player
1921	Walter Hagen	1942	Sam Snead	1958[2]	Dow Finsterwald	1973	Jack Nicklaus
1922–23	Gene Sarazen	1944	Bob Hamilton	1959	Bob Rosburg	1974	Lee Trevino
1924–27	Walter Hagen	1945	Byron Nelson	1960	Jay Hebert	1975	Jack Nicklaus
1928–29	Leo Diegel	1946	Ben Hogan	1961	Jerry Barber[1]	1976	Dave Stockton
1930	Tommy Armour	1947	Jim Ferrier	1962	Gary Player	1977	Lanny Wadkins[1]
1931	Tom Creavy	1948	Ben Hogan	1963	Jack Nicklaus	1978	John Mahaffey
1932	Olin Dutra	1949	Sam Snead	1964	Bobby Nichols	1979	David Graham[1]
1933	Gene Sarazen	1950	Chandler Harper	1965	Dave Marr	1980	Jack Nicklaus
1934	Paul Runyan	1951	Sam Snead	1966	Al Geiberger	1981	Larry Nelson
1935	Johnny Revolta	1952	Jim Turnesa	1967	Don January[1]	1982	Ray Floyd
1936–37	Denny Shute	1953	Walter Burkemo	1968	Julius Boros	1983	Hal Sutton
1938	Paul Runyan	1954	Chick Harbert	1969	Ray Floyd	1984	Lee Trevino

1. Winner in playoff. 2. Switched to medal play.

U.S. WOMEN'S AMATEUR CHAMPIONS

Year	Winner	Year	Winner	Year	Winner	Year	Winner
1916	Alexa Stirling	1937	Mrs. J. A. Page, Jr.	1957	JoAnne Gunderson	1972	Mary Ann Budke
1919–20	Alexa Stirling	1938	Patty Berg	1958	Anne Quast	1973	Carol Semple
1921	Marion Hollins	1939–40	Betty Jameson	1959	Barbara McIntire	1974	Cynthia Hill
1922	Glenna Collett	1941	Mrs. Frank Newell	1960	JoAnne Gunderson	1975	Beth Daniel
1923	Edith Cummings	1946	Mildred Zaharias	1961	Anne Quast Decker	1976	Donna Horton
1924	Dorothy Campbell Hurd	1947	Louise Suggs	1962	JoAnne Gunderson	1977	Beth Daniel
		1948	Grace Lenczyk	1963	Anne Quast Welts	1978	Cathy Sherk
1925	Glenna Collett	1949	Mrs. D. G. Porter	1964	Barbara McIntire	1979	Carolyn Hill
1926	Helen Stetson	1950	Beverly Hanson	1965	Jean Ashley	1980	Juli Inkster
1927	Mrs. M. B. Horn	1951	Dorothy Kirby	1966	JoAnne Gunderson	1981	Juli Inkster
1928–30	Glenna Collett	1952	Jacqueline Pung	1967	Lou Dill	1982	Juli Inkster
1931	Helen Hicks	1953	Mary Lena Faulk	1968	JoAnne G. Carner	1983	Joanne Pacillo
1932–34	Virginia Van Wie	1954	Barbara Romack	1969	Catherine LaCoste	1984	Deb Richard
1935	Glenna Collett Vare	1955	Patricia Lesser	1970	Martha Wilkinson		
1936	Pamela Barton	1956	Marlene Stewart	1971	Laura Baugh		

U.S. WOMEN'S OPEN CHAMPIONS

Year	Winner	Score	Year	Winner	Score	Year	Winner	Score
1946	Patty Berg (match play)	—	1959	Mickey Wright	287	1972	Susie Berning	299
1947	Betty Jameson	295	1960	Betsy Rawls	291	1973	Susie Berning	290
1948	Mildred D. Zaharias	300	1961	Mickey Wright	293	1974	Sandra Haynie	295
1949	Louise Suggs	291	1962	Murle Lindstrom	301	1975	Sandra Palmer	295
1950	Mildred D. Zaharias	291	1963	Mary Mills	289	1976	JoAnne Carner	292
1951	Betsy Rawls	293	1964	Mickey Wright[1]	290	1977	Hollis Stacy	292
1952	Louise Suggs	284	1965	Carol Mann	290	1978	Hollis Stacy	289
1953	Betsy Rawls[1]	302	1966	Sandra Spuzich	297	1979	Jerilyn Britz	284
1954	Mildred D. Zaharias	291	1967	Catherine LaCoste	294	1980	Amy Alcott	280
1955	Fay Crocker	299	1968	Susie Berning	289	1981	Pat Bradley	279
1956	Katherine Cornelius[1]	302	1969	Donna Caponi	294	1982	Janet Alex	283
1957	Betsy Rawls	299	1970	Donna Caponi	287	1983	Jan Stephenson	290
1958	Mickey Wright	290	1971	JoAnne Carner	288	1984	Hollis Stacy	290

1. Winner in playoff. 2. Amateur.

BRITISH OPEN CHAMPIONS

(First tournament, held in 1860, was won by Willie Park, Sr.)

Year	Winner	Score	Year	Winner	Score	Year	Winner	Score
1920	George Duncan	303	1946	Sam Snead	290	1966	Jack Nicklaus	282
1921	Jock Hutchison[1]	296	1947	Fred Daly	294	1967	Roberto de Vicenzo	278
1922	Walter Hagen	300	1948	Henry Cotton	283	1968	Gary Player	289
1923	A. G. Havers	295	1949	Bobby Locke[1]	283	1969	Tony Jacklin	280
1924	Walter Hagen	301	1950	Bobby Locke	279	1970	Jack Nicklaus[1]	283
1925	Jim Barnes	300	1951	Max Faulkner	285	1971	Lee Trevino	278
1926	R. T. Jones, Jr.	291	1952	Bobby Locke	287	1972	Lee Trevino	278
1927	R. T. Jones, Jr.	285	1953	Ben Hogan	282	1973	Tom Weiskopf	276
1928	Walter Hagen	292	1954	Peter Thomson	283	1974	Gary Player	282
1929	Walter Hagen	292	1955	Peter Thomson	281	1975	Tom Watson[1]	279
1930	R. T. Jones, Jr.	291	1956	Peter Thomson	286	1976	Johnny Miller	279
1931	Tommy Armour	296	1957	Bobby Locke	279	1977	Tom Watson	268
1932	Gene Sarazen	283	1958	Peter Thomson[1]	278	1978	Jack Nicklaus	281
1933	Denny Shute[1]	292	1959	Gary Player	284	1979	Severiano Ballesteros	283
1934	Henry Cotton	283	1960	Kel Nagle	278	1980	Tom Watson	271
1935	A. Perry	283	1961	Arnold Palmer	284	1981	Bill Rogers	276
1936	A. H. Padgham	287	1962	Arnold Palmer	276	1982	Tom Watson	284
1937	Henry Cotton	290	1963	Bob Charles[1]	277	1983	Tom Watson	275
1938	R. A. Whitcombe	295	1964	Tony Lema	279	1984	Severiano Ballesteros	276
1939	R. Burton	290	1965	Peter Thomson	285			

1. Winner in playoff.

MEN'S U.S. AMATEUR

(Edmond, Okla., Aug. 29–Sept. 2, 1984)

Final (36 holes)—Scott Verplank, Dallas, Tex., defeated Sam Randolph, Santa Barbara, Calif., 4 and 3 in final

Semifinals—Verplank defeated Randy Sonnier, Houston, Tex., 1 up, and Randolph defeated Jerry Haas, Belleville, Ill., 7 and 5

WOMEN'S U.S. AMATEUR

(Broadmoor Golf Club, Seattle, Wash., Aug. 15–18, 1984)

Final (37 holes)—Deb Richard, Manhattan, Kan., defeated Kimberly Williams, Bethesda, Md., 1 up in final

Semifinals—Richard defeated Carol Slane, Auburn, Calif., 4 and 3, and Williams defeated Jody Rosenthal, Adina, Minn., 1 up

MEN'S U.S. OPEN—1984

(Winged Foot Golf Club, Mamaroneck, N.Y., June 14–17, 1984)

Fuzzy Zoeller[1]	71	66	69	70—276	$94,000
Greg Norman	70	68	69	69—276	47,000
Curtis Strange	69	70	74	68—281	36,000
Johnny Miller	74	68	70	70—282	22,335
Jim Thorpe	68	71	70	73—282	22,335
Hale Irwin	68	68	69	79—284	16,238
Peter Jacobsen	72	73	73	67—285	14,237
Mark O'Meara	71	74	71	69—285	14,237
Fred Couples	69	71	74	72—286	12,122
Lee Trevino	71	72	69	74—286	12,122

1. won 18-hole playoff with Greg Norman.

Leaders—18 holes, Hale Irwin, Jim Thorpe, Hubert Green, Mike Donald, 68; 36 holes, Hale Irwin, 136; 54 holes, Hale Irwin, 205.

U.S. WOMEN'S OPEN—1984

(Salem Country Club, Peabody, Mass., July 13–16, 1984)

Hollis Stacy	74	72	75	69—290	$36,000
Rosie Jones	73	71	75	72—291	19,500
Lori Garbacz	74	76	72	70—292	13,008
Amy Alcott	71	74	73	74—292	13,008
Patty Sheehan	73	77	74	70—294	7,389
Penny Pulz	75	69	78	72—294	7,389
Betsy King	74	72	75	73—294	7,389
Avaki Okamoto	72	74	74	75—295	5,511
Donna White	75	71	72	77—295	5,511
Beth Daniel	76	76	73	72—297	4,746
Kathy Whitworth	73	75	76	74—297	4,746

BRITISH OPEN—1984

(St. Andrews, Scotland, July 19–22, 1984)

Severiano Ballesteros	69	68	70	69—276	$71,500
Bernhard Langer	71	68	68	71—278	41,470
Tom Watson	71	68	66	73—278	41,470
Fred Couples	70	69	74	68—281	25,740
Lanny Wadkins	70	69	73	69—281	25,740
Nick Faldo	69	68	76	69—282	21,307
Greg Norman	67	74	74	67—282	21,307
Mark McCumber	74	67	74	70—283	18,590
Hugh Balocchi	72	70	70	72—284	14,643
Ian Baker Finch	68	66	71	79—284	14,643
Graham Marsh	70	74	73	67—284	14,643
Ronan Rafferty	74	72	67	71—284	14,643
Sam Torrance	74	74	66	70—284	14,643

P.G.A CHAMPIONSHIP—1984

(Shoal Creek Golf Club, Birmingham, Ala., Aug. 16–19, 1984)

Lee Trevino	69	68	67	69—273	$125,000
Lanny Wadkins	68	69	68	72—277	62,500
Gary Player	74	63	69	71—277	62,500
Calvin Peete	71	70	69	68—278	35,000
Severiano Ballesteros	70	69	70	70—279	25,000
Gary Hallberg	69	71	68	72—280	17,125
Larry Mize	71	69	67	73—280	17,125
Scott Simpson	69	69	72	70—280	17,125
Hal Sutton	74	73	64	69—280	15,125

L.P.G.A. CHAMPIONSHIP—1984

(Jack Nicklaus Sports Center, Kings Island, Ohio, May 31–June 3, 1984)

Patty Sheehan	71	70	63	68—272	$37,500
Beth Daniel	71	73	70	68—282	19,375
Pat Bradley	71	72	70	69—282	19,375
Patti Rizzo	74	71	68	70—283	13,750
Lisa Young	72	72	71	69—284	11,250
Penny Pulz	72	72	70	72—286	9,375
Juli Inkster	75	71	72	69—287	5,811
Ayako Okamoto	72	71	74	70—287	5,811
Robin Walton	73	69	75	70—287	5,811
Alice Ritzman	73	69	74	71—287	5,811
Betsy King	72	67	76	72—287	5,811

MASTERS TOURNAMENT—1984

(Augusta, Ga., April 12–15, 1984)

Ben Crenshaw	67	72	70	68—277	$108,000
Tom Watson	74	67	69	69—279	64,800
Dave Edwards	71	70	72	67—280	34,800
Gil Morgan	73	71	69	67—280	34,800
Larry Nelson	76	69	66	70—281	24,000
Ronnie Black	71	74	69	68—282	19,425
Tom Kite	70	68	69	75—282	19,425
Mark Lye	69	66	73	74—282	19,425
David Graham	69	70	70	73—282	19,425
Fred Couples	71	73	67	72—283	16,200

FINAL 1983 LEADING L.P.G.A. EARNINGS

Player	Amount	Player	Amount
JoAnne Carner	$291,404	Beth Daniel	$167,403
Patty Sheehan	250,399	Alice Miller	157,321
Pat Bradley	240,207	Amy Alcott	153,721
Jan Stephenson	193,364	Hollis Stacy	149,036
Kathy Whitworth	191,492	Ayako Okamoto	131,214

FINAL 1983 LEADING P.G.A. EARNINGS

Player	Amount	Player	Amount
Hal Sutton	$426,668	Rex Caldwell	$284,434
Fuzzy Zoeller	417,597	Ben Crenshaw	275,474
Lanny Wadkins	319,271	Mark McCumber	268,254
Calvin Peete	313,845	Tom Kite	257,066
Gil Morgan	306,133	Jack Nicklaus	256,158

1984 LEADING P.G.A. EARNINGS

(Through Sept. 9, 1984)

Player	Amount	Player	Amount
Tom Watson	$438,785	Andy Bean	$305,475
Tom Kite	343,744	Bruce Lietzke	302,404
Fred Couples	321,201	Peter Jacobsen	295,025
Mark O'Meara	316,236	Lee Trevino	282,907
Greg Norman	310,230	Gil Morgan	281,948

1984 LEADING L.P.G.A. EARNINGS

(Through Sept. 9, 1984)

Player	Amount	Player	Amount
Patty Sheehan	$247,672	Amy Alcott	$183,738
Betsy King	234,067	Juli Inkster	182,525
Ayako Okamoto	196,359	JoAnne Carner	144,900
Pat Bradley	189,114	Donna White	114,320
Nancy Lopez	183,756	Alice Miller	111,533

OTHER 1984 L.P.G.A. TOUR WINNERS

(Through September 4, 1984)

Mazda Classic—Silvia Bertolaccini (280)	$30,000
Elizabeth Arden Classic—Patty Sheehan (280)	26,250
Sarasota Classic—Alice Miller (280)	26,250
LPGA Invitational—Nancy Lopez (284)	45,000
Samaritan Turqoise Classic—Chris Johnson (276)	22,500
Tucson LPGA Open—Chris Johnson (272)	22,500
Women's Kemper Open—Betsy King (283)	30,000
Dinah Shore Invitational—Juli Inkster (280)	55,000
J&B Scotch Pro-Am—Ayako Okamoto (275)	30,000
S&H Golf Classic—Vicki Fergon (275)	22,500
Freedom Orlando Classic—Betsy King (202)	22,500
Potamkin Cadillac Classic—Sharon Barrett (213)	30,000
United Virginia Bank Classic—Amy Alcott (210)	26,250
Chrysler-Plymouth Classic—Barb Bunkowsky (209)	26,250
Corning Classic—JoAnne Carner (281)	22,500
LPGA Championship—Patty Sheehan (272)	37,500
MacDonald's Kids Classic—Patty Sheehan (281)	52,500
Mayflower Classic—Ayako Okamoto (281)	37,500
Boston Classic—Laurie Rinker (286)	33,750
Lady Keystone Open—Amy Alcott (208)	30,000
Jamie Farr Toledo Classic—Lauri Peterson (278)	26,250
Rochester International—Kathy Whitworth (281)	30,000
Maurier Classic—Juli Inkster (279)	41,250
West Virginia Classic—Alice Miller (209)	22,500
Henredon Classic—Patty Sheehan (277)	27,000
World Championship of Golf—Nancy Lopez (281)	65,000
Mastercard Pro-Am—Sally Quinlan (284)	15,287
Columbia Savings Classic—Betsy King (281)	30,000
Rail Charity Classic—Cindy Hill (207)	26,250

OTHER 1984 PGA TOUR WINNERS

(Through September 4, 1984)

Bob Hope Desert Classic—John Mahaffey (340)	$72,000
Phoenix Open—Tom Purtzer (268)	72,000
San Diego Open—Gary Koch (272)	72,000
Bing Crosby National Pro-Am—Hale Irwin (278)	72,000
Hawaiian Open—Jack Renner (271)	90,000
Los Angeles Open—Dave Edwards (279)	72,000
Honda Classic—Bruce Lietzke (280)	90,000
Doral-Eastern Open—Tom Kite (272)	72,000
Bay Hill Classic—Gary Koch (272)	72,000
USF&G Classic—Bob Eastwood (272)	72,000
Tournament Players Championship—Fred Couples (277)	144,000
Greater Greensboro Open—Andy Bean (280)	72,000
Sea Pines Heritage Classic—Nick Faldo (270)	72,000
Houston Open—Corey Pavin (274)	90,000
MONY Tournament of Champions—Tom Watson (274)	72,000
Byron Nelson Classic—Craig Stadler (276)	90,000
Colonial National Invitational—Peter Jacobsen (270)	90,000
Memorial Tournament—Jack Nicklaus (280)	90,000
Kemper Open—Greg Norman (280)	72,000
Westchester Classic—Scott Simpson (269)	90,000
Atlanta Classic—Tom Kite (269)	72,000
Canadian Open—Greg Norman (278)	72,000
Western Open—Tom Watson (280)	72,000
Anheuser-Busch Classic—Ronnie Black (267)	63,000
Miller High Life Quadcities—Scott Hoch (266)	36,000
Greater Hartford Open—Peter Jacobsen (269)	72,000
Memphis Classic—Bob Eastwood (280)	90,000
Buick Open—Denis Watson (271)	72,000
World Series of Golf—Denis Watson (271)	126,000
B.C. Open—Wayne Levi (275)	54,000

SOCCER

WORLD CUP

1930 Uruguay
1934 Italy
1938 Italy
1942 No competition
1946 No competition
1950 Uruguay
1954 West Germany
1958 Brazil
1962 Brazil
1966 England
1970 Brazil
1974 West Germany
1978 Argentina
1982 Italy

WORLD CUP—1982 SEMIFINALS

(Madrid, Spain, July 8, 1982)

Italy 2, Poland 0
West Germany 5, France 4 (penalty kicks)

FINAL

(Madrid, Spain July 11, 1982)

Italy 3, West Germany 1

THIRD PLACE

(Madrid, Spain, July 10, 1982)

Poland 3, France 2

The following are the results of matches played by the four teams which reached the semifinals:

Italy (Group C)

Italy 0, Poland 0
Italy 1, Peru 1
Italy 1, Cameroon 1
Italy 2, Argentina 1
Italy 3, Brazil 2

Poland (Group A)

Poland 0, Italy 0
Poland 0, Cameroon 0
Poland 5, Peru 1
Poland 3, Belgium 0
Poland 0, Soviet Union 0

West Germany (Group B)

West Germany 1, Algeria 2
West Germany 4, Chile 1
West Germany 1, Austria 0
West Germany 0, England 0
West Germany 2, Spain 1

France (Group D)

France 1, England 3
France 4, Kuwait 1
France 1, Czechoslovakia 1
France 1, Austria 0
France 4, Northern Ireland 1

MAJOR INDOOR SOCCER LEAGUE
FINAL STANDING—1984

EASTERN DIVISION

	W	L	Pct	GB
Baltimore Blast	34	14	.708	—
Pittsburgh Spirit	32	16	.667	2
Cleveland Force	31	17	.646	3
New York Arrows	20	28	.417	14
Memphis	18	30	.375	16
Buffalo Stallions	14	33	.313	19

WESTERN DIVISION

	W	L	Pct	GB
St. Louis Steamers	26	22	.542	—
Wichita Wings	25	23	.521	1
Kansas City Comets	24	24	.500	2
Los Angeles Lazers	24	24	.500	2
Tacoma	22	26	.458	4
Phoenix Inferno	18	30	.375	8

CHAMPIONSHIP PLAYOFFS

Quarterfinal Round

Baltimore defeated New York, 3 games to 1
Cleveland defeated Pittsburgh, 3 games to 1
Wichita defeated Los Angeles, 3 games to 1
St. Louis defeated Kansas City, 3 games to 2

Semifinal Round

Baltimore defeated Cleveland, 3 games to 0
St. Louis defeated Wichita, 3 games to 0

Final

Baltimore defeated St. Louis, 4 games to 1

N.A.S.L. INDOOR SOCCER—1984
FINAL STANDING

	W	L	Pct	GB
San Diego Sockers	21	11	.656	—
Chicago Sting	20	12	.625	1
Cosmos	20	12	.625	1
Golden Bay Earthquakes	19	13	.594	2
Vancouver Whitecaps	12	20	.375	9
Tulsa Roughnecks	11	21	.344	10
Tampa Bay Rowdies	9	23	.281	12

CHAMPIONSHIP PLAYOFFS
Semifinal Round

Cosmos defeated Chicago, 2 games to 1
San Diego defeated Golden Bay, 2 games to 0

Final

San Diego defeated Cosmos, 3 games to 0

LEADING N.A.S.L. SCORERS—1984

	GP	G	A	Pts
Steve Zungul, Golden Bay	24	20	10	50
Franco Segota, Golden Bay	24	18	11	47
Ron Futcher, Tulsa	23	18	8	44
Karl Granitza, Chicago	24	16	12	44
Peter Ward, Vancouver	24	16	10	42
Ade Coker, San Diego	22	16	7	39
David Byrne, Toronto	20	12	13	37
Alan Willey, Minnesota	24	15	4	34
Jean Willrich, San Diego	22	5	20	30
Roberta Bettega, Toronto	23	8	13	29

OUTDOOR SOCCER
NORTH AMERICAN SOCCER LEAGUE—1984
Final Standing—1984

	W	L	GF	GA	BP[1]	Pts
EASTERN DIVISION						
Chicago Sting	13	11	50	49	44	120
Toronto Blizzard	14	10	46	33	35	117
Cosmos	13	10	43	41	39	115
Tampa Bay Rowdies	9	15	43	61	35	87
WESTERN DIVISION						
San Diego Sockers	14	10	51	42	40	118
Vancouver Whitecaps	13	11	51	48	43	117
Minnesota	14	10	40	44	35	115
Tulsa Roughnecks	10	14	42	46	38	98
Golden Bay	8	16	60	62	49	95

1. A bonus point is awarded for each goal scored to a maximum of three a game, excluding overtimes and shootouts; team receives six points for each victory in regulation time or overtime, but only four points for winning a game decided by s shootout.

CHAMPIONSHIP PLAYOFF—1984

Semifinals

Chicago defeated Vancouver, 2 games to 1
Toronto defeated San Diego, 2 games to 0

Championship

Chicago defeated Toronto, 2 games to 0

NORTH AMERICAN SOCCER LEAGUE CHAMPIONS

1968—Atlanta Chiefs
1969—Kansas City Stars
1970—Rochester Lancers
1971—Dallas Tornado
1972—New York Cosmos
1973—Philadelphia Atoms
1974—Los Angeles Aztecs
1975—Tampa Bay Rowdies
1976—Toronto Metro-Croatia
1977—New York Cosmos
1978—New York Cosmos
1979—Vancouver Whitecaps
1980—New York Cosmos
1981—Chicago Sting
1982—New York Cosmos
1983—Tulsa Roughnecks
1984—Chicago Sting

SKEET SHOOTING

UNITED STATES CHAMPIONSHIPS

(San Antonio, Texas, July 23–27, 1984)

	Pts
12 gauge—Wayne Mayes, Cleveland, Tenn.	250
20 gauge—Alan Clark, Carlsbad, Calif.	100
28 gauge—Tal Sprinkles, Manor, Texas	100
410 bore—Dave Starrett, New Boston, Ohio	100
Overall champion—Bob Unkalis, Philadelphia, Pa.	550

YACHTING

AMERICA'S CUP RECORD

First race in 1851 around Isle of Wight, Cowes, England. First defense and all others through 1920 held 30 miles off New York Bay. Races since 1930 held 30 miles off Newport, R.I. Conducted as one race only in 1851 and 1870; best four-of-seven basis, 1871; best two-of-three, 1876–1887; best three-of-five, 1893–1901; best four-of-seven, since 1930. Figures in parentheses indicate number of races won.

Year	Winner and owner	Loser and owner
1851	AMERICA (1), John C. Stevens, U.S.	AURORA, T. Le Marchant, England[1]
1870	MAGIC (1), Franklin Osgood, U.S.	CAMBRIA, James Ashbury, England[2]
1871	COLUMBIA (2), Franklin Osgood, U.S.[3]	LIVONIA (1), James Ashbury, England
	SAPPHO (2), William P. Douglas, U.S.	
1876	MADELEINE (2), John S. Dickerson, U.S.	COUNTESS OF DUFFERIN, Chas. Gifford, Canada
1881	MISCHIEF (2), J. R. Busk, U.S.	ATALANTA, Alexander Cuthbert, Canada
1885	PURITAN (2), J. M. Forbes-Gen. Charles Paine, U.S.	GENESTA, Sir Richard Sutton, England
1886	MAYFLOWER (2), Gen. Charles Paine, U.S.	GALATEA, Lt. William Henn, England
1887	VOLUNTEER (2), Gen. Charles Paine, U.S.	THISTLE, James Bell et al, Scotland
1893	VIGILANT (3), C. Oliver Iselin et al., U.S.	VALKYRIE II, Lord Dunraven, England
1895	DEFENDER (3), C. O. Iselin-W. K. Vanderbilt-E. D. Morgan, U.S.	VALKYRIE III, Lord Dunraven-Lord Lonsdale-Lord Wolverton, England
1899	COLUMBIA (3), J. P. Morgan-C. O. Iselin, U.S.	SHAMROCK I, Sir Thomas Lipton, Ireland
1901	COLUMBIA (3), Edwin D. Morgan, U.S.	SHAMROCK II, Sir Thomas Lipton, Ireland
1903	RELIANCE (3), Cornelius Vanderbilt et al., U.S.	SHAMROCK III, Sir Thomas Lipton, Ireland
1920	RESOLUTE (3), Henry Walters et al., U.S.	SHAMROCK IV (2), Sir Thomas Lipton, Ireland
1930	ENTERPRISE (4), Harold S. Vanderbilt et al., U.S.	SHAMROCK V, Sir Thomas Lipton, Ireland
1934	RAINBOW (4), Harold S. Vanderbilt, U.S.	ENDEAVOUR (2), T. O. M. Sopwith, England
1937	RANGER (4), Harold S. Vanderbilt, U.S.	ENDEAVOUR II, T. O. M. Sopwith, England
1958	COLUMBIA (4), Henry Sears et al., U.S.	SCEPTRE, Hugh Goodson et al., England
1962	WEATHERLY (4), Henry D. Mercer et al., U.S.	GRETEL (1), Sir Frank Packer et al., Australia
1964	CONSTELLATION (4), New York Y.C. Syndicate, U.S.	SOVEREIGN (0), J. Anthony Bowden, England
1967	INTREPID (4), New York Y.C. Syndicate, U.S.	DAME PATTIE (0), Sydney (Aust.) Syndicate
1970	INTREPID (4), New York Y.C. Syndicate, U.S.	GRETEL II (1), Sydney (Aust.) Syndicate
1974	COURAGEOUS (4), New York, N.Y. Syndicate, U.S.	SOUTHERN CROSS (0), Sydney (Aust.) Syndicate
1977	COURAGEOUS (4), New York, N.Y. Syndicate, U.S.	AUSTRALIA (0), Sun City (Aust.) Syndicate
1980	FREEDOM (4), New York, N.Y. Syndicate, U.S.	AUSTRALIA (1), Alan Bond et al, Australia
1983	AUSTRALIA II (4) Alan Bond et al, Australia,	LIBERTY (3) New York, N.Y. Syndicate, U.S.

1. Fourteen British yachts started against America; Aurora finished second. 2. Cambria sailed against 23 U.S. yachts and finished tenth. 3. Columbia was disabled in the third race, after winning the first two; Sappho substituted and won the fourth and fifth.

LONGEST WINNING STREAK IN SPORT'S HISTORY OVER

The victory of Australia II in the 1983 America's Cup race snapped a 132-year continuous victory streak by American 12-meter yachts. The end of U.S. yachting supremacy came on September 26th. in an unprecedented seventh race in the best-of-seven finals.

Australia II was the first challenger to win the 33-1/2-inch silver cup since the schooner America won the inaugral race around England's Isle of Wight in 1851. Australia is planning its first defense of the America Cup trophy most likely in 1987.

CURLING

WORLD CHAMPIONSHIPS—1984

Men (Duluth, Minnesota, April 2-8, 1984)—Norway, Eigil Ramsfjell, skip (defeated Switzerland, 8–5, in final)

Women (Perth, Scotland, March 25–30, 1984)—Canada, Connie Laliberte, skip (defeated Switzerland, 10–0, in final)

UNITED STATES CHAMPIONSHIPS—1984

Men (Hibbing, Minnesota, March 25–30, 1984)—Minnesota, Bruce Roberts, skip (defeated Wisconsin, 13–5, in final)

Women (Wauwautosa, Wisconsin, March 18–23, 1984)—Duluth, Minnesota, Amy Hatten, skip, (won round robin tournament with 5–1 record)

JIM THORPE'S OLYMPIC MEDALS ARE RETURNED

More than 70 years after he won the pentathlon and decathlon at Stockholm, Sweden, Jim Thorpe's Olympic gold medals were returned posthumously to him by the International Olympic Committee. Thorpe, an Oklahoma Sac and Fox Indian, became one of the greatest all-around athletes ever produced in America. He was an all-American football player at the Carlisle Institute, an Indian trade school in Pennsylvania, and starred in baseball and track and field. After winning the medals in the 1912 Olympics, he was forced to give them up when he admitted he had played two seasons for money as a semipro baseball player in 1909 and 1910. Under the rules, he had lost his amateur status by taking money and thus was theoretically ineligible for the Olympics. In October of 1982, after many years of vigorous efforts by his family and other officials in athletics, the I.O.C. reinstated Thorpe in its archives as a co-winner of the two events. At ceremonies in Los Angeles in January 1983, Antonio Samaranch, president of the I.O.C., presented Thorpe's children with gold medals to replace those he had turned back. Thorpe, who later in his career played major-league baseball and pro football, died at the age of 65 in 1953.

AUTO RACING

INDIANAPOLIS 500

Year	Winner	Car	Time	mph	Second place
1911	Ray Harroun	Marmon	6:42:08	74.59	Ralph Mulford
1912	Joe Dawson	National	6:21:06	78.72	Teddy Tetzloff
1913	Jules Goux	Peugeot	6:35:05	75.93	Spencer Wishart
1914	René Thomas	Delage	6:03:45	82.47	Arthur Duray
1915	Ralph DePalma	Mercedes	5:33:55.51	89.84	Dario Resta
1916[1]	Dario Resta	Peugeot	3:34:17	84.00	Wilbur D'Alene
1919	Howard Wilcox	Peugeot	5:40:42.87	88.05	Eddie Hearne
1920	Gaston Chevrolet	Monroe	5:38:32	88.62	René Thomas
1921	Tommy Milton	Frontenac	5:34:44.65	89.62	Roscoe Sarles
1922	Jimmy Murphy	Murphy Special	5:17:30.79	94.48	Harry Hartz
1923	Tommy Milton	H. C. S. Special	5:29.50.17	90.95	Harry Hartz
1924	L. L. Corum–Joe Boyer	Dusenberg Special	5:05:23.51	98.23	Earl Cooper
1925	Peter DePaolo	Dusenberg Special	4:56:39.45	101.13	Dave Lewis
1926[2]	Frank Lockhart	Miller Special	4:10:14.95	95.904	Harry Hartz
1927	George Souders	Dusenberg Special	5:07:33.08	97.54	Earl DeVore
1928	Louis Meyer	Miller Special	5:01:33.75	99.48	Lou Moore
1929	Ray Keech	Simplex Special	5:07:25.42	97.58	Louis Meyer
1930	Billy Arnold	Miller–Hartz Special	4:58:39.72	100.448	Shorty Cantlon
1931	Louis Schneider	Bowes Special	5:10:27.93	96.629	Fred Frame
1932	Fred Frame	Miller–Hartz Special	4:48:03.79	104.144	Howard Wilcox
1933	Louis Meyer	Tydol Special	4:48:00.75	104.162	Wilbur Shaw
1934	Bill Cummings	Boyle Products Special	4:46:05.20	104.863	Mauri Rose
1935	Kelly Petillo	Gilmore Special	4:42:22.71	106.240	Wilbur Shaw
1936	Louis Meyer	Ring Free Special	4:35:03.39	109.069	Ted Horn
1937	Wilbur Shaw	Shaw–Gilmore Special	4:24:07.80	113.580	Ralph Hepburn
1938	Floyd Roberts	Burd Piston Ring Special	4:15:58.40	117.200	Wilbur Shaw
1939	Wilbur Shaw	Boyle Special	4:20:47.39	115.035	Jimmy Snyder
1940	Wilbur Shaw	Boyle Special	4:22:31.17	114.277	Rex Mays
1941	Floyd Davis–Mauri Rose	Noc–Out Hose Clamp Special	4:20:36.24	115.117	Rex Mays
1946	George Robson	Thorne Engineering Special	4:21:26.71	114.820	Jimmy Jackson
1947	Mauri Rose	Blue Crown Special	4:17:52.17	116.338	Bill Holland
1948	Mauri Rose	Blue Crown Special	4:10:23.33	119.814	Bill Holland
1949	Bill Holland	Blue Crown Special	4:07:15.97	121.327	Johnny Parsons
1950[3]	Johnnie Parsons	Wynn's Friction Proof Special	2:46:55.97	124.002	Bill Holland
1951	Lee Wallard	Belanger Special	3:57:38.05	126.244	Mike Nazaruk
1952	Troy Ruttman	Agajanian Special	3:52:41.88	128.922	Jim Rathmann
1953	Bill Vukovich	Fuel Injection Special	3:53:01.69	128.740	Art Cross
1954	Bill Vukovich	Fuel Injection Special	3:49:17.27	130.840	Jim Bryan
1955	Bob Sweikert	John Zink Special	3:53:59.13	128.209	Tony Bettenhausen
1956	Pat Flaherty	John Zink Special	3:53:28.84	128.490	Sam Hanks
1957	Sam Hanks	Belond Exhaust Special	3:41:14.25	135.601	Jim Rathmann
1958	Jimmy Bryan	Belond A–P Special	3:44:13.80	133.791	George Amick
1959	Rodger Ward	Leader Card 500 Roadster	3:40:49.20	135.857	Jim Rathmann
1960	Jim Rathmann	Ken–Paul Special	3:36:11.36	138.767	Rodger Ward
1961	A. J. Foyt	Bowes Special	3:35:37.49	139.130	Eddie Sachs
1962	Rodger Ward	Leader Card Special	3:33:50.33	140.293	Len Sutton
1963	Parnelli Jones	Agajanian Special	3:29:35.40	143.137	Jim Clark
1964	A. J. Foyt	Offenhauser Special	3:23:35.83	147.350	Rodger Ward
1965	Jim Clark	Lotus–Ford	3:19:05.34	150.686	Parnelli Jones
1966	Graham Hill	Lola–Ford	3:27:52.53	144.317	Jim Clark
1967[4]	A. J. Foyt	Coyote–Ford	3:18:24.22	151.207	Al Unser
1968	Bobby Unser	Eagle–Offenhauser	3:16:13.76	152.882	Dan Gurney
1969	Mario Andretti	STP Hawk–Ford	3:11:14.71	156.867	Dan Gurney
1970	Al Unser	P. J. Colt–Ford	3:12:37.04	155.749	Mark Donohue
1971	Al Unser	P. J. Colt–Ford	3:10:11.56	157.735	Peter Revson
1972	Mark Donohue	McLaren–Offenhauser	3:04:05.54	162.962	Al Unser
1973[5]	Gordon Johncock	Eagle–Offenhauser	2:05:26.59	159.036	Bill Vukovich
1974	Johnny Rutherford	McLaren–Offenhauser	3:09:10.06	158.589	Bobby Unser
1975[6]	Bobby Unser	Eagle–Offenhauser	2:54:55.08	149.213	Johnny Rutherford
1976[7]	Johnny Rutherford	McLaren–Offenhauser	1:42:52.48	148.725	A. J. Foyt
1977	A. J. Foyt	Coyote–Foyt	3:05:57.16	161.331	Tom Sneva
1978	Al Unser	Lola–Cosworth	3:05:54.99	161.363	Tom Sneva
1979	Rick Mears	Penske–Cosworth	3:08:27.97	158.899	A. J. Foyt
1980	Johnny Rutherford	Chaparral–Cosworth	3:29:59.56	142.862	Tom Sneva
1981[8]	Bobby Unser	Eagle–Offenhauser	3:35:41.78	139.029	Mario Andretti

1982	Gordon Johncock	Wildcat–Cosworth	3:05:09.14	162.029	Rick Mears
1983	Tom Sneva	March–Cosworth	3:05:03.06	162.117	Al Unser
1984	Rick Mears	March–Cosworth	3:03:21.00	162.962	Roberto Guerrero

1. 300 miles. 2. Race ended at 400 miles because of rain. 3. Race ended at 345 miles because of rain. 4. Race, postponed after 18 laps because of rain on May 30, was finished on May 31. 5. Race postponed May 28 and 29 was cut to 332.5 miles because of rain, May 30. 6. Race ended at 435 miles because of rain. 7. Race ended at 255 miles because of rain. 8. Andretti was awarded the victory the day after the race after Bobby Unser, whose car finished first, was penalized one lap and dropped from first place to second for passing other cars illegally under a yellow caution flag. Unser appealed the decision to the U.S. Auto Club and was upheld. A panel ruled the penalty was too severe and instead fined Unser $40,000, but restored the victory to him.

U.S. AUTO CLUB NATIONAL CHAMPIONS

1910	Ray Harroun	1926	Harry Hartz	1950	Henry Banks	1968	Bobby Unser
1911	Ralph Mulford	1927	Peter DePaolo	1951	Tony Bettenhausen	1969	Mario Andretti
1912	Ralph DePalma	1928–29	Louis Meyer	1952	Chuck Stevenson	1970	Al Unser
1913	Earl Cooper	1930	Billy Arnold	1953	Sam Hanks	1971–72	Joe Leonard
1914	Ralph DePalma	1931	Louis Schneider	1954	Jimmy Bryan	1973	Roger McCluskey
1915	Earl Cooper	1932	Bob Carey	1955	Bob Sweikert	1974	Bobby Unser
1916	Dario Resta	1933	Louis Meyer	1956–57	Jimmy Bryan	1975	A. J. Foyt
1917	Earl Cooper	1934	Bill Cummings	1958	Tony Bettenhausen	1976	Gordon Johncock
1918	Ralph Mulford	1935	Kelly Petillo	1959	Rodger Ward	1977–78	Tom Sneva
1919	Howard Wilcox	1936	Mauri Rose	1960–61	A. J. Foyt	1979	A. J. Foyt
1920	Gaston Chevrolet	1937	Wilbur Shaw	1962	Rodger Ward	1980	Johnny Rutherford
1921	Tommy Milton	1938	Floyd Roberts	1963–64	A. J. Foyt	1981–82	George Snider
1922	James Murphy	1939	Wilbur Shaw	1965–66	Mario Andretti	1983	Tom Sneva
1923	Eddie Hearne	1940–41	Rex Mays	1967	A. J. Foyt	1984	Rick Mears
1924	James Murphy	1946–48	Ted Horn				
1925	Peter DePaolo	1949	Johnnie Parsons				

NATIONAL ASSOCIATION FOR STOCK CAR AUTO RACING (NASCAR) GRAND NATIONAL CHAMPIONS

1949	Red Byron	1956–57	Buck Baker	1966	David Pearson	1976–78	Cale Yarborough
1950	Bill Rexford	1958–59	Lee Petty	1967	Richard Petty	1979	Richard Petty
1951	Herb Thomas	1960	Rex White	1968–69	David Pearson	1980	Dale Earnhardt
1952	Tim Flock	1961	Ned Jarrett	1970	Bobby Isaac	1981	Darrell Waltrip
1953	Herb Thomas	1962–63	Joe Weatherly	1971–72	Richard Petty	1982	Darrell Waltrip
1954	Lee Petty	1964	Richard Petty	1973	Benny Parsons	1983	Bobby Allison
1955	Tim Flock	1965	Ned Jarrett	1974–75	Richard Petty		

WORLD GRAND PRIX DRIVER CHAMPIONS

1950	Giuseppe Farina, Italy, Alfa Romeo	1968	Graham Hill, England, Lotus-Ford
1951	Juan Fangio, Argentina, Alfa Romeo	1969	Jackie Stewart, Scotland, Matra-Ford
1952	Alberto Ascari, Italy, Ferrari	1970	Jochen Rindt, Austria, Lotus-Ford
1953	Alberto Ascari, Italy, Ferrari	1971	Jackie Stewart, Scotland, Tyrrell-Ford
1955	Juan Fangio, Argentina, Maserati, Mercedes-Benz	1972	Emerson Fittipaldi, Brazil, Lotus-Ford
1955	Juan Fangio, Argentina, Mercedes-Benz	1973	Jackie Stewart, Scotland, Tyrrell-Ford
1956	Juan Fangio, Argentina, Lancia-Ferrari	1974	Emerson Fittipaldi, Brazil, McLaren-Ford
1957	Juan Fangio, Argentina, Masserati	1975	Niki Lauda, Austria, Ferrari
1958	Mike Hawthorn, England, Ferrari	1976	James Hunt, Britain, McLaren-Ford
1959	Jack Brabham, Australia, Cooper	1977	Niki Lauda, Austria, Ferrari
1960	Jack Brabham, Australia, Cooper	1978	Mario Andretti, Nazareth, Pa., Lotus
1961	Phil Hill, United States, Ferrari	1979	Jody Scheckter, South Africa
1962	Graham Hill, England, BRM	1980	Alan Jones, Australia
1963	Jim Clark, Scotland, Lotus-Ford	1981	Nelson Piquet, Brazil
1964	John Surtees, England, Ferrari	1982	Kiki Rosberg, Finland
1965	Jim Clark, Scotland, Lotus-Ford	1983	Nelson Piquet, Brazil
1966	Jack Brabham, Australia, Brabham-Repco		
1967	Denis Hulme, New Zealand, Brabham-Repco		

GRAND PRIX RACING EVENTS—1984

(Through Sept. 9, 1984)

Formula One Competition

Brazil (Rio de Janiero, March 25)—Alain Prost, France, driving a McLaren-Porsche turbo; 1 hour 42 minutes 34.49 seconds; 111.5 miles per hour

South Africa (Kyalami, April 7)—Niki Lauda, Austria, McLaren-Porsche turbo; 1:29.23; 128.37 mph

Belgium (Zolder, April 29)—Michale Alboreto, Italy, Ferrari V-6 turbo; 1:36.32; 115.245 mph

Italy (San Marino Grand Prix, Imola, Italy, May 6)—Alain Prost, France, McLaren-Porsche turbo; 1:36.53; 113.09 mph

France (Dijon, May 20)—Niki Lauda, Austria, McLaren-Porsche turbo;

1:31.11;125,535 mph

Monaco (Monte Carlo, June 3)—Alain Prost, France, McLaren-Porsche turbo; 1:01.7;62.62 mph

Canada (Montreal, June 17)—Nelson Piquet, Brazil, Brabham BMW 4-cylinder turbo; 1:46.23; 108.17 mph

Detroit (Detroit, Mich., June 24)—Nelson Piquet, Brabham, BMW 4-cylinder turbo; 1:55.41; 81.679 mph

Dallas (Dallas, Texas, July 8)—Keke Rosberg, Finland, Williams Honda V-6 turbo; 2:01.22; 80.283 mph

Britain (Brands Hatch, July 22)—Niki Lauda, Austria, McLaren-Porsche turbo; 1:29.28; 124.406 mph

West Germany (Hockenheim, Aug. 5)—Alain Prost, France, McLaren-Porsche turbo; 1:24.43; 131.612 mph

Austria (Osterreichring, Aug. 19)—Niki Lauda, Austria, McLaren-Porsche turbo; 1:21.12; 139.0 mph

Holland (Zandboort, Aug. 26)—Alain Prost, France, McLaren-Porsche turbo; 1:37.21; 115.60 mph

U.S. AUTO CLUB

1984 Triple Crown Races

Indianapolis 500 (Indianapolis Motor Speedway, May 30, 1984, 500 miles)—1. Rick Mears, Bakersfield, Calif.; Pennzoil Z-7 March 84 CC; 200 laps; 3:03.21.66; 163.612 mph; first place prize—$434, 061. 2. Roberto Guerrero, Medellin, Colombia; Master Mechanic Tools March 84 CC; 198 laps. 3. Al Unser, Albuquerque, N.M.; Miller High Life March 84 CC; 198 laps. 4. Al Holbert, Warrington, Pa.; CRC Chemicals/Red Roof Inns March 84 CC; 198 laps. 5. Michael Andretti, Nazareth, Pa.; Electrolux/Kraco March 84 CC; 198 laps.

Pocono 500 (Pocono International Raceway, Long Pond, Pa., Aug., 1984, 500 miles)—1. Danny Sullivan, Louisville, Ky.; Domino's Pizza "Hot One" Lola T800 C; 3:38.29.69; 137.308 mph; 200 laps; $72,290. 2. Rick Mears, Bakersfield, Calif.; Penzoil Z-7 March 84CC; 200 laps. 3. Bobby Rahal, Dublin, Ohio; 7-Eleven/Red Roof Inns March 84 CC; 200 laps. 4. Tom Sneva, Paradise Valley, Ariz.; Texaco Star March 84 CC; 200 laps. 5. Danny Ongais, Santa Ana, Calif.; Interscope March 84 CC; 200 laps.

OTHER 1984 CHAMPIONSHIP AUTO RACES

Championship Auto Racing Team (CART) Events

Grand Prix of Long Beach (Long Beach, Calif., April 1, 1984, 187.04 miles)—Mario Andretti, Nazareth, Pa.; Newman/Haas Budweiser Lola T800 C; 2 hours 15 minutes, 23 seconds; 82.898 mph; $78, 524

Dana 150 (Phoenix, Ariz., April 15, 1984, 150 miles)—Tom Sneva, Paradise Valley, Ariz.; Texaco Star March 84 CC; 1:14.39.42; 120. 555 mph; $23,160

Dana/Rex Mays 200 (West Allis, Wis., June 3, 1984, 200 miles)—Tom Sneva, Paradise Valley, Ariz.; Texaco Star March 84 CC; 1:41. 41.128; 118.030 mph; $24,040

Stroh's G.I. Joe's 200 (Portland, Ore., June 17, 1984, 199.16 miles)—Al Unser, Jr., Albuquerque, N.M.; Coors Light Silver Bullet G-March 84C C; 1:53.17.39; 105.484 mph; $50,250

Meadowlands Grand Prix (East Rutherford, N.J., July 1, 1984, 168.2 miles)—Mario Andretti, Nazareth, Pa; Newman Haas Budweiser Lola T800 C; 2:04.59.4; 80.742 mph; $73,121

Cleveland Grand Prix (Cleveland, Ohio, July 8, 1984, 218.24 miles)—Danny Sullivan, Louisville, Ky.; Domino's Pizza "Hot One" Lola T800 C; 1:50.17; 118.734 mph; $38,450

Michigan 500 (Brooklyn, Mich., July 22, 1984, 500 miles)—Mario Andretti, Nazareth, Pa.; Newman Haas Budweiser Lola T800 C; 3:44.45; 133.482 mph; $81,776

Provimi Veal 200 (Elkhart Lake, Wis., Aug. 5, 1984, 200 miles)—Mario Andretti, Nazareth, Pa.; Newman Haas Budweiser Lola T800 C; 1:43.8.4; 116.347 mph; $43,110

Escort Radar Warning 500 (Lexington, Ohio, Sept. 2, 1984, 200 miles)—Mario Andretti, Nazareth, Pa.; Newman Haas Budwesier Lola T800 C; 1:59.50.11; 100.388 mph; $46,970

Molson Indy (St. Pie, Quebec, Sept. 9, 1984, 185.85 miles)—Danny Sullivan, Louisville, Ky.; Domino's Pizza "Hot One" Lola T800 C; 1:39.49.43; 111.707 mph; $55,543

NATIONAL ASSOCIATION FOR STOCK CAR RACING (NASCAR)—1984

(Through Sept. 9, 1984)

Daytona 500 (Daytona Beach, Fla., Feb. 19, 1984, 500 miles)—Cale Yarborough, Sardis, S.C.; Hardee's Chevrolet; 3 hours 18 minutes 41 seconds; average speed 150.994 mph; total purse $1,172, 131; winners purse $160,300

Richmond 400 (Richmond, Va., Feb. 26, 1984) 400 miles—Ricky Rudd, Chesapeake, Va.; Budweiser Chevrolet; 2:09.31; 76.736 mph; $243,256; $31,775

Carolina 500 (Rockingham, N.C., March 4, 1984, 500 miles)—Bobby Allison, Hueytown, Ala.; Miller High Life Buick; 4:03.55; 122.931 mph; $290,191; $33,150

Coca-Cola 500 (Hampton, Ga., March 18, 1984, 500 miles)—Benny Parsons, Ellerbee, N.C.; Copenhagen Chevrolet; 3:26.39; 144.945 mph; $359,315; $51,110

Valleydale 500 (Bristol, Tenn., April 1, 1984, 500 miles)—Darrell Waltrip, Franklin, Tenn.; Budweiser Chevrolet; 2:50.10; 93.967 mph; $219,165; $31,670

Northwestern Bank 400 (North Wilkesboro, N.C., April 8, 1984, 250 miles)—Tim Richmond, Ashland, Ohio; Old Milwaukee Pontiac; 2:33.19; 97.83 mph; $227,290; $24,780

Transouth 500 (Darlington, S.C., April 15, 1984, 500 miles)—Darrell Waltrip, Franklin, Tenn.; Budweiser Chevrolet; 4:18.16; 119.925 mph; $311,865; $39,450

Sovran Bank 500 (Martinsville, Va., April 29, 1984, 262.5 miles)—Geoff Bodine, Chemung, N.Y.; Northwestern Security Chevrolet; 3:35.23; 73.264 mph; $29,880

Winston 500 (Talladega, Ala., May 6, 1984, 500 miles)—Cale Yarborough, Sardis, S.C.; Hardee's Chevrolet; 2:53.27; 172.988 mph; $475,715; $42,300

Coors 420 (Nashville, Tenn., May 12, 1984, 250 miles)—Darrell Waltrip, Franklin, Tenn.; Budweiser Chevrolet; 2:55.15; 85.702 mph; $217,465; $29,300

Budwesier 500 (Dover, Delaware, May 20, 1984, 500 miles)—Richard Petty, Rundleman, N.C.; STP Pontiac; 4:12.42; 118.717 mph; $276,490; $28,105

World 600 (Harrisburg, N.C.; May 27, 1984, 600 miles)—Bobby Allison, Hueytown, Ala.; Miller High Life Buick; 4:38.34; 129,233 mph; $538,965; $88,500

Budweiser 400 (Riverside, Calif., June 3, 1984, 400 kilometers)—Terry Labonte, Corpus Christi, Tex.; Piedmont Airlines Chevrolet; 2:25.7; 102.910 mph; $266,140; $31,955

Van Scoy Diamond Mines 500 (Pocono, Pa., June 10, 1984, 500 miles)—Cale Yarborough; Hardee's Chevrolet; 3:37.08; 138.164 mph; $341,140; $30,850

Miller High Life 400 (Brooklyn, Mich., June 17, 1984, 400 miles)—Bill Elliott, Dawsonville, Ga.; Coors Ford; 2:58.10; 134.705 mph; $373,855; $41,600

Firecracker 400 (Daytona Beach, Fla., July 4, 1984, 400 miles)—Richard Petty, Randleman, N.C.; STP Pontiac; 2:19.59; 171.204 mph; $387,300; $43,755

Pepsi 420 (Nashville, Tenn., July 14, 1984, 250 miles)—Geoff Bodine, Chemung, N.Y.; Northwestern Security Chevrolet; 3:05.38; 80.908 mph; $206,800; $25,800

Like Cola 500 (Long Pond, Pa., July 22, 1984, 500 miles)—Harry Gant, Taylorsville, N.C.; Skoal Bandit Chevrolet; 4:07.21; 121.351 mph; $347,975; $34,605

Talladega 500 (Talladega, Ala., July 29, 1984, 500 miles)—Dale Earnhardt, Kannapolis, N.C.; Wrangler Jeans Chevrolet; 3:12.04; 155.485 mph; $415,725; $47,100

Champion Spark Plug 400 (Brooklyn, Mich., Aug. 12, 1984, 400 miles)—Darrell Waltrip, Franklin, Tenn.; Budweiser Chevrolet; 2:35. 59; 153.863 mph; $351,715; $40,800

Busch 500 (Bristol, Tenn., Aug. 25, 1984, 266.5 miles)—Terry Labonte, Corpus Christi, Tex.; Piedmont Airlines Chevrolet; 3:07. 19; 85.365 mph; $228,800; $28,480

Southern 500 (Darlington, S.C., Sept. 2, 1984, 500 miles)—Harry Gant, Taylorsville, N.C.; Skoal Bandit Chevrolet; 3:54.02; 128,270 mph; $377,510; $46,180

Wrangler Sanforset 400 (Richmond, Va., Sept. 9, 1984, 216.8 miles)—Darrell Waltrip, Franklin, Tenn.; Budweiser, Chevrolet; 2:53.57; 74.780 mph; $244,640; $46,550

FINAL 1983 NASCAR LEADING MONEY WINNERS

Bobby Allison	$828,355
Darrell Waltrip	824,858
Richard Petty	491,022
Bill Elliott	479,960
Neil Bennett	455,662
Dale Earnhardt	446,272
Harry Gant	390,189
Terry Labonte	362,790
Dave Marcis	309,355
Morgan Shepard	270,851

FINAL 1983 WINSTON CUP GRAND NATIONAL POINT LEADERS

Bobby Allison	4,667
Darrell Waltrip	4,620
Bill Elliott	4,279
Richard Petty	4,042
Terry Labonte	4,004
Neil Bennett	3,842
Harry Gant	3,790
Dale Earnhardt	3,732
Ricky Rudd	3,693
Tim Richmond	3,612

BASEBALL—MINOR LEAGUES—1984

CLASS AAA

AMERICAN ASSOCIATION

	W	L	Pct
Indianapolis (Expos)	91	63	.591
Iowa (Cubs)	80	74	.519
Denver (White Sox)	79	75	.513
*Louisville (Cardinals)	78	76	.506
Wichita (Reds)	78	76	.506
Evansville (Tigers)	72	82	.471
Oklahoma City (Rangers)	70	84	.455
Omaha (Royals)	68	86	.442

*Won 4th place playoff with Wichita.

Playoffs

League championship—Louisville defeated Denver, 4 games to 1

INTERNATIONAL LEAGUE

	W	L	Pct
Columbus (Yankees)	82	57	.590
Maine (Indians)	77	59	.566
Toledo (Twins)	74	63	.540
Pawtucket (Red Sox)	75	65	.536
Tidewater (Mets)	71	69	.507
Richmond (Braves)	66	73	.475
Syracuse (Blue Jays)	58	81	.417
Rochester (Orioles)	52	88	.371

Playoffs

Semifinals—Pawtucket defeated Columbus, 3 games to 1. Maine defeated Toledo, 3 games to 0

Final—Pawtucket defeated Maine, 3 games to 2

PACIFIC COAST LEAGUE

Northern Division

First half winner—Edmonton (Angels)
Second half winner—Salt Lake City (Mariners)
Playoff—Edmonton defeated Salt Lake, 3 games to 1

Southern Division

First half winner—Las Vegas (Padres)
Second half winner—Hawaii (Pirates)
Playoff—Hawaii defeated Las Vegas, 3 games to 0
Championship playoff—Edmonton defeated Hawaii, 2 games to 0

CLASS AA

Eastern League—Regular season champion: Albany (A's). Playoffs—Waterbury (Angels) defeated Glens Falls (White Sox), 3 games to 1. Vermont (Reds) defeated Albany (A's) 3 games to 0. Championship—Vermont defeated Waterbury, 3 games to 2.

Southern League—Eastern Division, first half: Greenville (Braves); second half: Charlotte (Orioles) won division playoff with Orlando. Western Division, first half: Knoxville (Blue Jays); second half: Nashville (Yankees) defeated Birmingham (Tigers) in division playoff. Division championships—East: Charlotte defeated Greenville 3 games to 1. West: Knoxville defeated Nashville, 3 games to 1. League championship: Charlotte defeated Knoxville, 3 games to 0.

Texas League—Eastern Division, first half: Jackson (Mets); second half: Jackson (Mets). Western division, first half: Beaumont (Padres); second half: Beaumont (Padres). League championship: Jackson defeated Beaumont, 4 games to 2.

CLASS A

California League—Northern Division, first half: Modesto (A's); second half: Redwood (Angels); playoff: Modesto. Southern Division, first half: Fresno (Giants); second half: Bakersfield (Dodgers); playoff: Bakersfield. League championship: Modesto defeated Bakersfield, 3 games to 1.

Midwest League—Northern Division: Appleton (White Sox); Central Division: Beloit (Brewers); Southern Division: Springfield (Cardinals). Playoffs: Semifinals: Appleton defeated Madison (A's, wild card team) 2 games to 1; Springfield defeated Beloit, 2 games to 0. League championship: Appleton defeated Springfield, 3 games to 2.

Carolina League—Northern Division, first half: Lynchburg (Mets); second half: Lynchburg (Mets). Southern Division, first half: Durham (Braves); second half: Peninsula (Phillies). Playoff: Durham. League championship: Lynchburg defeated Durham, 3 games to 1.

Florida State League—Northern Division, first half: Tampa (Reds); second half: Daytona Beach (Astros); playoff: Tampa. Southern Division, first half: Fort Meyers (Royals); second half: Fort Lauderdale (Yankees); playoff: Fort Lauderdale. League championship: Fort Lauderdale defeated Tampa, 3 games to 2.

South Atlantic League—Northern Division, first half: Greensboro (Yankees); second half: Asheville (Astros); playoff: Ashville. Southern Division, first half: Charlston (Royals); second half: Savannah (Cardinals); playoff: Charleston. League championship: Asheville defeated Charleston, 3 games to 0.

New York-Penn League—Yawkey Division: Little Falls (Mets); Wrigley Division: Newark (Orioles). League championship: Little Falls defeated Newark, 2 games to 1.

Northwest League—Washington Division: Tri Cities (Rangers); Oregon Division: Medford (A's). League championship: Tri Cities defeated Medford, 17-8.

AAA WORLD SERIES

First year of a new round robin between the league champions of the American Association, the International League, and the Pacific Coast League. Each team played the other team twice, the team with the best record was the winner.[1]

	W	L
Tidewater (Mets)	3	1
Portland (Phillies)	2	2
Denver (White Sox)	1	3

Champion—Tidewater
1. World Series not held in 1984.

ROOKIE LEAGUES

Appalachian—Northern Division: Pulaski (Braves); Southern Division: Elizabethtown (Twins). League champion: Elizabethtown defeated Pulaski 7-4 in championship game.

Gulf Coast—Northern Division: Rangers; Southern Division: White Sox. League champion: Rangers defeated White Sox 6-5 in championship game.

Pioneer—Northern Division: Helena (Co-op); Southern Division: Billings (Reds). League championship: Helena defeated Billins, 3 games to 1.

LITTLE LEAGUE WORLD SERIES

1947	Williamsport, Pa.
1948	Lock Haven, Pa.
1949	Hammonton, N.J.
1950	Houston, Tex.
1951	Stamford, Conn.
1952	Norwalk, Conn.
1953	Birmingham, Ala.
1954	Schenectady, N.Y.
1955	Morrisville, Pa.
1956	Roswell, N.M.
1957	Monterrey, Mexico
1958	Monterrey, Mexico
1959	Hamtramck, Mich.
1960	Levittown, Pa.
1961	El Cajon, Calif.
1962	San Jose, Calif.
1963	Granada Hills, Calif.
1964	Staten Island, N.Y.
1965	Windsor Locks, Conn.
1966	Houston, Tex.
1967	West Tokyo, Japan
1968	Wakayama, Japan
1969	Taiwan (Nationalist China)
1970	Wayne, N.J.
1971	Taiwan (National China)
1972	Taiwan (National China)
1973	Taiwan (Nationalist China)
1974	Taiwan (Nationalist China)
1975	Lakewood Township, N.J.
1976	Tokyo, Japan
1977	Tapei, Taiwan
1978–79	Pintung, Taiwan
1980	Hua Lian, Taiwan
1981	Taiwan
1982	Kirkland, Wash.
1983	Marietta, Ga.
1984	South Korea

HANDBALL

U.S.H.A. NATIONAL FOUR-WALL CHAMPIONS

Singles

1960	Jimmy Jacobs
1961	John Sloan
1962–63	Oscar Obert
1964–65	Jimmy Jacobs
1966–67	Paul Haber
1968	Simon (Stuffy) Singer
1969–71	Paul Haber
1972	Fred Lewis
1973	Terry Muck
1974	Fred Lewis
1975	Jay Bilyeu
1976	Vern Roberts, Jr.
1977	Naty Alvarado
1978	Fred Lewis
1979	Naty Alvarado
1980	Naty Alvarado
1981	Fred Lewis
1982	Naty Alvarado
1983	Naty Alvarado
1984	Naty Alvarado

Doubles

1960	Jimmy Jacobs–Dick Weisman
1961	John Sloan–Vic Hershkowitz
1962–63	Jimmy Jacobs–Marty Decatur
1964	John Sloan–Phil Elbert
1965	Jimmy Jacobs–Marty Decatur
1966	Pete Tyson–Bob Lindsay
1967–68	Jimmy Jacobs–Marty Decatur
1969	Lou Kramberg–Lou Russo
1970	Karl and Ruby Obert
1971	Ray Neveau–Simie Fein
1972	Kent Fusselman–Al Drews
1973–74	Ray Neveau–Simie Fein
1975	Marty Decatur–Steve Lott
1976	Gary Rohrer–Dan O'Connor
1977	Skip McDowell–Matt Kelly
1978	Stuffy Singer–Marty Decatur
1979	Stuffy Singer–Marty Decatur
1980	Skip McDowell–Harry Robertson
1981	Tom Kopatich–Jack Roberts
1982	Naty Alvarado–Vern Roberts
1983	Naty Alvarado–Vern Roberts
1984	Naty Alvarado–Vern Roberts

U.S. HANDBALL ASSOCIATION FOUR-WALL CHAMPIONS

(Baltimore, Md., June 16–23, 1984)

Men's open singles—Naty Alvarado, Hesperia, Calif. (defeated John Sabo, Summit, N.J., 21-4, 21-9, in final)

Men's open doubles—Naty Alvarado and Vern Roberts, Tucson, Ariz. (defeated Dennis Haynes, Orange, Calif., and Jaime Paredes, San Diego, 21-14, 21-17, in final)

Women's open singles—Rosemary Bellini, New York (defeated Diane Harmon, Long Beach, Calif., 21-17, 21-12, in final)

Women's open doubles—Allison Roberts, Cincinnati, and Peanut Motal, Houston (defeated Rosemary Bellini and Diane Harmon, 21-14, 21-7, in final)

23 and under singles—Tim Labey, St. Paul, Minn. (defeated Kris Schaumann, Air Force Academy, 21-13, 21-16, in final)

35 and over singles—Fred Bancalari, Pleasanton, Calif. (defeated Jerry Fagundes, San Leandro, Calif., 21-18, 18-21, 11-7, in final)

40 and over singles—Pat Kirby, Tucson, Ariz. (defeated Neal Manning, Tucson, 21-12, 21-13, in final)

40 and over doubles—Stuffy Singer, Los Angeles, and Marty Decatur, Happauge, N.Y. (defeated Pat Kirby and Fred Munsch, Pearl River, N.Y., 9-21, 21-18, 11-5, in final)

50 and over singles—Tom Rohrback, Canoga Park, Calif. (defeated Dick Miller, Orlando, Fla., 21-14, 21-3, in final)

50 and over doubles—Arnie Aguilar and Del Mora, Santa Barbara, Calif. (defeated Tom Schoendorf and Bert Dinan, Milwaukee, Wis., 17-21, 21-3, 11-8, in final)

60 and over super singles—Ray Barrett, Virginia Beach, Va. (defeated John Scopis, Atlanta, 4-21, 21-10, 11-10, in final)

60 and over doubles—Rudy Stadlberger, San Francisco, and Chuck Harris, Independence, Mo. (defeated Julie Rothman and Ed Miskie, New York, 21-16, 21-8, in final)

70 and over diamond doubles—Steve Subak, Minneapolis, Minn., and Chuck Housman, Des Moines, Iowa (defeated Marty Grossman and Dave Okun, New York, 21-14, 21-11, in final)

SOFTBALL

Source: Amateur Softball Association.

AMATEUR CHAMPIONS

1959 Aurora (Ill.) Sealmasters
1960 Clearwater (Fla.) Bombers
1961 Aurora (Ill.) Sealmasters
1962–63 Clearwater (Fla.) Bombers
1964 Burch Gage & Tool, Detroit
1965 Aurora (Ill.) Sealmasters
1966 Clearwater (Fla.) Bombers
1967 Aurora (Ill.) Sealmasters
1968 Clearwater (Fla.) Bombers
1969 Raybestos Cardinals, Stratford, Conn.
1971 Welty Way, Cedar Rapids, Iowa
1972 Raybestos Cardinals, Stratford, Conn.
1973 Clearwater (Fla.) Bombers
1974 Santa Rosa (Calif.)
1975 Rising Sun Hotel, Reading, Pa.
1976 Raybestos Cardinals, Stratford, Conn.
1977 Billard Barbell, Reading, Pa.
1978 Reading, Pa.
1979 Midland, Mich.
1980 Peterbilt Western, Seattle
1981 Archer Daniels Midland, Decatur, Ill.
1982 Peterbilt Western, Seattle
1983 Franklin Cardinals, West Haven, Conn.
1984 California Coors Kings, Merced, Calif.

YOUTH TOURNAMENTS—1984

Boys 18-and-under fast pitch—Rice Lake, Rice Lake, Wis.
Boys 18-and-under slow pitch—Mavericks, Tifton, Ga.
Boys 15-and-under fast pitch—Brennan Insurance, Sioux Falls, S.D.
Boys 15-and-under slow pitch—Little Rascals, Jasper, Ind.
Boys 12-and-under fast pitch—Excutone Bombers, Baton Rouge, La.
Boys 12-and-under slow pitch—Royal Pharmacy, Tifton, Ga.
Girls 18-and-under fast pitch—California Raiders, Santa Monica, Calif.
Girls 18-and-under slow pitch—Florida Sharks, Melbourne, Fla.
Girls 15 and under fast pitch—Inland Cities Panthers, LaPalma, Calif.
Girls 15-and-under slow pitch—Pembroke Pines Cardinals, Pembroke Pines, Fla.
Girls 12-and-under fast pitch—Tri-City Gamblers, Cyprus, Ind.
Girls 12-and-under slow—Pacers, Pembroke Pines, Fla.

WORLD CHAMPIONS—1984

Men's fast pitch—New Zealand
Women's fast pitch—not contested in 1984. Next scheduled tournament, 1986, Auckland, New Zealand. New Zealand reigning champion from 1982.
Men's church slow pitch—Palatka First Baptist Church, Palatka, Fla.
Women's church slow pitch—CME Crushettes, Warner Robbins, Ga.
Women's modified slow pitch—Alibi Inn, Staten Island, N.Y.

AMATEUR SOFTBALL ASSOCIATION CHAMPIONS—1984

Men's major fast pitch—California Coors Kings, Merced, Calif.
Women's major fast pitch—California Diamond Blazers, Los Angeles
Women's Class A fast pitch—Arrow Butane Flames, Las Cruces, N.M.
Men's Class A fast pitch—Hudson Supply, Bakersville, Calif.
Men's major slow pitch—Lilly Air, Chicago, Ill.
Women's major slow pitch—Spooks, Anoka, Minn.
Men's major industrial slow pitch—Sikorsky Aircraft, Stratford, Conn.
Women's industrial slow pitch—Cargill Gold, Mound, Minn.
Men's Class A slow pitch—Bender Plumming, New Haven, Conn.
Women's Class A slow pitch—Mr. A's Express, Sacramento, Calif.
Men's Class A industrial slow pitch—Brown & Williamson, Macon, Ga.
Men's super slow pitch—Howard's Western Steer, Denver, N.C.
Women's modified fast pitch—Alibi Inn, Staten Island, N.Y.

WEIGHTLIFTING

U.S. WEIGHTLIFTING FEDERATION MEN'S NATIONAL CHAMPIONSHIPS

(York, Pa., March 10–11, 1984)

	Snatch	C&J[1]	Total[2]
114 lb—Brian Okada, Wailuku, Hawaii	90[3]	115[3]	205[3]
123 lb—Albert Hood, Los Angeles, Calif.	102.5	130	232.5
132 lb—Phil Sanderson, Billings, Mont.	105	130	235
148 lb—Don Abrahamson	120	155	275
165 lb—Chuck Jambliter, Jamestown, N.Y.	127.5	172.5	300
181 lb—Mark Levell, Chicago, Ill.	130	180	310
198 lb—Kevin Winter, San Jose, Calif.	160	187.5	347.5
220 lb—Ken Clark, Pacifica, Calif.	160	200	360
242 lb—Guy Carlton, Colorado Springs, Col.	160	202.5	362.5
Over 242 lb—Mario Martinez, San Francisco	180	220	400

1. Clean and Jerk. 2. All results in kilograms. 3. American record.

WOMEN'S NATIONAL CHAMPIONSHIPS

(Atlanta, Ga., May 5, 1984)

	Snatch	C&J[1]	Total[2]
97 lb—DeeAnna Hammock, Cumming, Ga.	35.0	50.0	85.0
105.8 lb—Mary Carr, Wichita, Kan.	52.5[3]	65.0	117.5[3]
114.5 lb—Rachel Silverman, San Francisco	57.5	67.5	125.0
123 lb—Colleene Colley, Chamblee, Ga.	65.0	92.5	157.5[3]
132 lb—Jane Camp, College Park, Ga.	62.5	92.5[3]	155.0[3]
148.75 lb—Judy Glenney, Farmington, New Mexico	77.5	90.0	167.5
165.25 lb—Jody Anderson, Geneva, Ill.	70.0[3]	100.0[3]	170.0[3]
181.75 lb—Benita Carswell, Atlanta, Ga.	72.5	87.5	160.0
Over 181.75 lb—Karyn Tarter, New Rochelle, N.Y.	87.5	115.0	202.5[3]

1. Clean and jerk. 2. All results in kilograms. 3. American record.

BASEBALL

The popular tradition that baseball was invented by Abner Doubleday at Cooperstown, N.Y., in 1839 has been enshrined in the Hall of Fame and National Museum of Baseball erected in that town, but research has proved that a game called "Base Ball" was played in this country and England before 1839. The first team baseball as we know it was played at the Elysian Fields, Hoboken, N.J., on June 19, 1846, between the Knickerbockers and the New York Nine. The next fifty years saw a gradual growth of baseball and an improvement of equipment and playing skill.

Historians have it that the first pitcher to throw a curve was William A. (Candy) Cummings in 1867. The Cincinnati Red Stockings were the first all-professional team, and in 1869 they played 64 games without a loss. The standard ball of the same size and weight, still the rule, was adopted in 1872. The first catcher's mask was worn in 1875. The National League was organized in 1876. The first chest protector was worn in 1885. The three-strike rule was put on the books in 1887, and the four-ball ticket to first base was instituted in 1889. The pitching distance was lengthened to 60 feet 6 inches in 1893, and the rules have been modified only slightly since that time.

The American League, under the vigorous leadership of B. B. Johnson, became a major league in 1901. Judge Kenesaw Mountain Landis, by action of the two major leagues, became Commissioner of Baseball in 1921, and upon his death (1944), Albert B. Chandler, former United States Senator from Kentucky, was elected to that office (1945). Chandler failed to obtain a new contract and was succeeded by Ford C. Frick (1951), the National League president. Frick retired after the 1965 season, and William D. Eckert, a retired Air Force lieutenant general, was named to succeed him. Eckert resigned under pressure in December, 1968. Bowie Kuhn, a New York attorney, became interim commissioner for one year in February. His appointment was made permanent with two seven-year contracts until August 1983. In August 1983, Kuhn's contract was not renewed, and a search begun for his successor. Peter Ueberroth was named new Commissioner and took office Oct. 1, 1984.

MAJOR LEAGUE ALL-STAR GAME

Year	Date	Winning league and manager	Runs	Losing league and manager	Runs	Winning pitcher	Losing pitcher	Site	Paid attendance
1933	July 6	A.L. (Mack)	4	N.L. (McGraw)	2	Gomez	Hallahan	Chicago A.L.	47,595
1934	July 10	A.L. (Cronin)	9	N.L. (Terry)	7	Harder	Mungo	New York N.L.	48,363
1935	July 8	A.L. (Cochrane)	4	N.L. (Frisch)	1	Gomez	Walker	Cleveland A.L.	69,831
1936	July 7	N.L. (Grimm)	4	A.L. (McCarthy)	3	J. Dean	Grove	Boston N.L.	25,556
1937	July 7	A.L. (McCarthy)	8	N.L. (Terry)	3	Gomez	J. Dean	Washington A.L.	31,391
1938	July 6	N.L. (Terry)	4	A.L. (McCarthy)	1	Vander Meer	Gomez	Cincinnati N.L.	27,067
1939	July 11	A.L. (McCarthy)	3	N.L. (Hartnett)	1	Bridges	Lee	New York A.L.	62,892
1940	July 9	N.L. (McKechnie)	4	A.L. (Cronin)	0	Derringer	Ruffing	St. Louis N.L.	32,373
1941	July 8	A.L. (Baker)	7	N.L. (McKechnie)	5	E. Smith	Passeau	Detroit A.L.	54,674
1942	July 6	A.L. (McCarthy)	3	N.L. (Durocher)	1	Chandler	Cooper	New York N.L.	34,178
1943	July 13[1]	A.L. (McCarthy)	5	N.L. (Southworth)	3	Leonard	Cooper	Philadelphia A.L.	31,938
1944	July 11[1]	N.L. (Southworth)	7	A.L. (McCarthy)	1	Raffensberger	Hughson	Pittsburgh N.L.	29,589
1946	July 9	A.L. (O'Neill)	12	N.L. (Grimm)	0	Feller	Passeau	Boston A.L.	34,906
1947	July 8	A.L. (Cronin)	2	N.L. (Dyer)	1	Shea	Sain	Chicago N.L.	41,123
1948	July 13	A.L. (Harris)	5	N.L. (Durocher)	2	Raschi	Schmitz	St. Louis A.L.	34,009
1949	July 12	A.L. (Boudreau)	11	N.L. (Southworth)	7	Trucks	Newcombe	Brooklyn N.L.	32,577
1950	July 11	N.L. (Shotton)	4	A.L. (Stengel)	3[3]	Blackwell	Gray	Chicago A.L.	46,127
1951	July 10	N.L. (Sawyer)	8	A.L. (Stengel)	3	Maglie	Lopat	Detroit A.L.	52,075
1952	July 8	N.L. (Durocher)	3	A.L. (Stengel)	2[4]	Rush	Lemon	Philadelphia N.L.	32,785
1953	July 14	N.L. (Dressen)	5	A.L. (Stengel)	1	Spahn	Reynolds	Cincinnati N.L.	30,846
1954	July 13	A.L. (Stengel)	11	N.L. (Alston)	9	Stone	Conley	Cleveland A.L.	68,751
1955	July 12	N.L. (Durocher)	6	A.L. (Lopez)	5[3]	Conley	Sullivan	Milwaukee N.L.	45,643
1956	July 10	N.L. (Alston)	7	A.L. (Stengel)	3	Friend	Pierce	Washington A.L.	28,843
1957	July 9	A.L. (Stengel)	6	N.L. (Alston)	5	Bunning	Simmons	St. Louis N.L.	30,693
1958	July 8	A.L. (Stengel)	4	N.L. (Haney)	3	Wynn	Friend	Baltimore A.L.	48,829
1959[2]	July 7	N.L. (Haney)	5	A.L. (Stengel)	4	Antonelli	Ford	Pittsburgh N.L.	35,277
	Aug. 3	A.L. (Stengel)	5	N.L. (Haney)	3	Walker	Drysdale	Los Angeles N.L.	55,105
1960[2]	July 11	N.L. (Alston)	5	A.L. (Lopez)	3	Friend	Monbouquette	Kansas City A.L.	30,619
	July 13	N.L. (Alston)	6	A.L. (Lopez)	0	Law	Ford	New York A.L.	38,362
1961[2]	July 11	N.L. (Murtaugh)	5	A.L. (Richards)	4[6]	Miller	Wilhelm	San Francisco N.L.	44,115
	July 31	N.L (Murtaugh)	1	A.L. (Richards)	1[7]	—	—	Boston A.L.	31,851
1962[2]	July 10	N.L. (Hutchinson)	3	A.L. (Houk)	1	Marichal	Pascual	Washington A.L.	45,480
	July 30	A.L. (Houk)	9	N.L. (Hutchinson)	4	Herbert	Mahaffey	Chicago N.L.	38,359
1963	July 9	N.L. (Dark)	5	A.L. (Houk)	3	Jackson	Bunning	Cleveland A.L.	44,160
1964	July 7	N.L. (Alston)	7	A.L. (Lopez)	4	Marichal	Radatz	New York N.L.	50,850
1965	July 13	N.L. (March)	6	A.L. (Lopez)	5	Koufax	McDowell	Minnesota A.L.	46,706
1966	July 12	N.L. (Alston)	2	A.L. (Mele)	1[6]	Perry	Rickert	St. Louis N.L.	49,926
1967	July 11	N.L. (Alston)	2	A.L. (Bauer)	1[8]	Drysdale	Hunter	Anaheim A.L.	46,309
1968	July 9	N.L. (Schoendienst)	1	A.L. (Williams)	0	Drysdale	Tiant	Houston N.L.	48,321
1969	July 23	N.L. (Schoendienst)	9	A.L. (M. Smith)	3	Carlton	Stottlemyre	Washington A.L.	45,259
1970	July 14	N.L. (Hodges)	5	A.L. (Weaver)	4	Osteen	Wright	Cincinnati N.L.	51,838
1971	July 13	A.L. (Weaver)	6	N.L. (Anderson)	4	Blue	Ellis	Detroit A.L.	53,559

1972	July 25	N.L. (Murtaugh)	4	A.L. (Weaver)	3[6]	McGraw	McNally	Atlanta N.L.	53,107
1973	July 24[1]	N.L. (Anderson)	7	A.L. (Williams)	1	Wise	Blyleven	Kansas City A.L.	40,849
1974	July 23[1]	N.L. (Berra)	7	A.L. (Williams)	2	Brett	Tiant	Pittsburgh N.L.	50,706
1975	July 15[1]	N.L. (Alston)	6	A.L. (Dark)	3	Matlack	Hunter	Milwaukee A.L.	51,540
1976	July 13	N.L. (Anderson)	7	A.L. (D. Johnson)	1	R. Jones	Fidrych	Philadelphia N.L.	63,974
1977	July 19[1]	N.L. (Anderson)	7	A.L. (Martin)	5	Sutton	Palmer	New York A.L.	56,683
1978	July 11[1]	N.L. (Lasorda)	7	A.L. (Martin)	3	Sutter	Gossage	San Diego N.L.	51,549
1979	July 17[1]	N.L. (Lasorda)	7	A.L. (Lemon)	6	Sutter	Kern	Seattle A.L.	58,905
1980	July 8[1]	N.L. (Tanner)	4	A.L. (Weaver)	2	Reuss	John	Los Angeles N.L.	56,088
1981	Aug. 9[1]	N.L. (Green)	5	A.L. (Frey)	4	Blue	Fingers	Cleveland* A.L.	72,086
1982	July 13[1]	N.L. (Lasorda)	4	A.L. (Martin)	1	Rogers	Eckersley	Montreal N.L.	59,057
1983	July 6[1]	A.L. (Kuenn)	13	N.L. (Herzog)	3	Steib	Soto	Chicago A.L.	43,801
1984	July 11[1]	N.L. (Owens)	3	A.L. (Altobelli)	1	Leg	Steib	San Francisco, N.L.	57,756

1. Night game. 2. Two games. 3. Fourteen innings. 4. Five innings, rain. 5. Twelve innings. 6. Ten innings. 7. Called because of rain after nine innings. 8. Fifteen innings. NOTE: No game in 1945. *Game was originally scheduled for July 14, but was put off because of players' strike.

NATIONAL BASEBALL HALL OF FAME

Cooperstown, N.Y.

Fielders

Member	Active years
Aaron, Henry (Hank)	1954–1976
Anson, Adrian (Cap)	1876–1897
Aparicio, Luis	1956–1973
Appling, Lucius (Luke)	1930–1950
Averill, H. Earl	1929–1941
Baker, J. Frank (Home Run)	1908–1922
Bancroft, David	1915–1930
Banks, Ernest	1953–1971
Beckley, Jacob	1888–1907
Bell, James (Cool Papa)[1]	1920–1947
Berra, Lawrence (Yogi)	1946–1965
Bottomley, James	1922–1937
Boudreau, Louis	1938–1952
Bresnahan, Roger	1897–1915
Brouthers, Dennis	1879–1896
Burkett, Jesse	1890–1905
Campanella, Roy	1948–1957
Carey, Max	1910–1929
Chance, Frank	1898–1914
Charleston, Oscar[1]	1915–1954
Clarke, Fred	1894–1915
Clemente, Roberto	1955–1972
Cobb, Tyrus	1905–1928
Cochrane, Gordon (Mickey)	1925–1937
Collins, Edward	1906–1930
Collins, James	1895–1908
Comiskey, Charles	1882–1894
Combs, Earle	1924–1935
Connor, Roger	1880–1897
Crawford, Samuel	1899–1917
Cronin, Joseph	1926–1945
Cuyler, Hazen (Kiki)	1921–1938
Delahanty, Edward	1888–1903
Dickey, William	1928–1946
Dihigo, Martin[1]	1923–1945
DiMaggio, Joseph	1936–1951

Member	Active years
Duffy, Hugh	1888–1906
Eyers, John	1902–1919
Ewing, William	1880–1897
Flick, Elmer	1898–1910
Foxx, James	1925–1945
Frisch, Frank	1919–1937
Gehrig, H. Louis (Lou)	1923–1939
Gehringer, Charles	1924–1942
Gibson, Josh[1]	1929–1946
Goslin, Leon (Goose)	1921–1938
Greenberg, Henry (Hank)	1933–1947
Hafey, Charles (Chick)	1924–1937
Hamilton, William	1888–1901
Hartnett, Charles (Gabby)	1922–1941
Heilmann, Harry	1914–1932
Herman, William	1931–1947
Hooper, Harry	1909–1925
Hornsby, Rogers	1915–1937
Irvin, Monford (Monte)[1]	1939–1956
Jackson, Travis	1922–1936
Jennings, Hugh	1891–1918
Johnson, William (Judy)[1]	1921–1937
Kaline, Albert W.	1953–1974
Keeler, William (Wee Willie)	1892–1910
Kell, George	1943–1957
Kelley, Joseph	1891–1908
Kelly, George	1915–1932
Kelly, Michael (King)	1878–1893
Killebrew, Harmon	1954–1975
Kiner, Ralph	1946–1955
Klein, Charles H. (Chuck)	1928–1944
Lajoie, Napoleon	1896–1916
Leonard, Walter (Buck)[1]	1933–1955
Lindstrom, Frederick	1924–1936
Lloyd, John Henry[1]	1905–1931
Mantle, Mickey	1951–1968
Manush, Henry (Heinie)	1923–1939

Member	Active years
Maranville, Walter (Rabbit)	1912–1935
Mathews, Edwin	1952–1968
Mays, Willie	1951–1973
McCarthy, Thomas	1884–1896
McGraw, John J.	1891–1906
Medwick, Joseph (Ducky)	1932–1948
Mize, John (The Big Cat)	1936–1953
Musial, Stanley	1941–1963
O'Rourke, James	1876–1894
Ott, Melvin	1926–1947
Reese, Harold (Pee Wee)	1940–1958
Rice, Edgar (Sam)	1915–1934
Robinson, Brooks	1955–1977
Robinson, Frank	1956–1976
Robinson, Jack	1947–1956
Robinson, Wilbert	1886–1902
Roush, Edd	1913–1931
Ruth, George (Babe)	1914–1935
Schalk, Raymond	1912–1929
Sewell, Joseph	1920–1933
Simmons, Al	1924–1944
Sisler, George	1915–1930
Snider, Edwin D. (Duke)	1947–1964
Speaker, Tristram	1907–1928
Terry, William	1923–1936
Thompson, Samuel	1885–1906
Tinker, Joseph	1902–1916
Traynor, Harold (Pie)	1920–1937
Wagner, John (Honus)	1897–1917
Wallace, Roderick (Bobby)	1894–1918
Waner, Lloyd	1927–1945
Waner, Paul	1926–1945
Ward, John (Monte)	1878–1894
Wheat, Zachariah	1909–1927
Williams, Theodore	1939–1960
Wilson, Lewis R. (Hack)	1923–1934
Youngs, Ross (Pep)	1917–1926

Pitchers

Alexander, Grover	1911–1930
Bender, Charles (Chief)	1903–1925

Brown, Mordecai (3-Finger)	1903–1916
Chesbro, John	1899–1909

Clarkson, John	1882–1894
Coveleski, Stanley	1912–1928
Dean, Jerome (Dizzy)	1930–1947

Name	Years
Drysdale, Don	1956–1969
Faber, Urban (Red)	1914–1933
Feller, Robert	1936–1956
Ferrell, Rick	1929–1947
Ford, Edward (Whitey)	1950–1967
Foster, Andrew (Rube)	1897–1926
Galvin, James (Pud)	1876–1892
Gibson, Bob	1959–1975
Gomez, Vernon (Lefty)	1930–1943
Griffith, Clark	1891–1914
Grimes, Burleigh	1916–1934
Grove, Robert (Lefty)	1925–1941
Haines, Jesse	1918–1937
Hoyt, Waite	1918–1938
Hubbell, Carl	1928–1943
Johnson, Walter	1907–1927
Joss, Adrian	1902–1910
Keefe, Timothy	1880–1893
Koufax, Sanford (Sandy)	1955-1966
Lemon, Robert	1946–1958
Lyons, Theodore	1923–1946
Marichal, Juan	1960–1975
Marquard, Richard (Rube)	1908–1924
Mathewson, Christopher	1900–1916
McGinnity, Joseph	1899–1908
Nichols, Charles (Kid)	1890–1906
Paige, Leroy (Satchel)[1]	1926–1965
Pennock, Herbert	1912–1934
Plank, Edward	1901–1917
Radbourn, Charles (Hoss)	1880–1891
Rixey, Eppa	1912–1933
Roberts, Robert (Robin)	1948–1966
Ruffing, Charles (Red)	1924–1947
Rusie, Amos	1889-1901
Spahn, Warren	1942–1965
Vance, Arthur (Dazzy)	1915–1935
Waddell, George	1897–1910
Walsh, Edward	1904–1917
Welch, Michael (Mickey)	1880–1892
Wynn, Early	1939–1963
Young, Denton (Cy)	1890–1911

Officials and Others

Alston, Walter[2]
Barrow, Edward[2, 3]
Bulkeley, Morgan G.[3]
Cartwright, Alexander[3]
Chadwick, Henry[4]
Chandler, A.B.[7]
Conlan, John[3]
Connolly, Thomas[5]
Cummings, William A.[6]
Evans, William G.[5, 3]
Frick, Ford C.[7, 3]
Giles, Warren C.[3]
Gowdy, Curt[9]
Harridge, William[3]
Harris, Stanley R.[8]
Hubbard, R. Calvin[5]
Higgins, Miller J.[2]
Johnson, B. Bancroft[3]
Klem, William[5]
Landis, Kenesaw M.[7]
Lopez, Alfonso R.[8]
Mack, Connie[2, 3]
MacPhail, Leland S.[3]
McCarthy, Joseph V.[2]
McKechnie, William B.[2]
Rickey, W. Branch[2, 3]
Smith, Ken[10]
Spalding, Albert G.[5]
Stengel, Charles D.[8]
Weiss, George M.[3]
Wright, George[6]
Wright, Harry[6, 2]
Yawkey, Thomas[3]

1. Negro league player selected by special committee. 2. Manager. 3. Executive. 4. Writer-statistician. 5. Umpire. 6. Early player. 7. Commissioner. 8. Player-manager. 9. Broadcaster. 10. Sportswriter.

OTHER LIFETIME BATTING, PITCHING, AND BASE-RUNNING RECORDS

(An asterisk indicates active player)

Sources: Baseball Record Book, published and copyrighted by The Sporting News, St. Louis, Mo. 63166; *The Book of Baseball Records,* published and copyrighted by Seymour Siwoff, New York, N.Y. 10036; and *The Complete Handbook of Baseball,* published and copyrighted by New American Library, New York, N.Y. 10019.

Hits (3,000 or more)

Ty Cobb	4,191
Pete Rose*	4,097
Henry Aaron	3,771
Stan Musial	3,630
Tris Speaker	3,515
Honus Wagner	3,430
Carl Yastrzemski	3,419
Eddie Collins	3,311
Willie Mays	3,283
Nap Lajoie	3,251
Paul Waner	3,152
Cap Anson	3,081
Lou Brock	3,023
Al Kaline	3,007
Roberto Clemente	3,000

Earned Run Average[1]

Walter Johnson	2.37
Grover Alexander	2.56
Tom Seaver*	2.73
Whitey Ford	2.74
Jim Palmer*	2.83
Stanley Coveleski	2.88
Juan Marichal	2.89
Wilbur Cooper	2.89
Bob Gibson	2.91
Carl Mays	2.92
Don Drysdale	2.95
Carl Hubbell	2.98
Ron Guidry*	2.99
Gaylord Perry	2.99
Steve Carlton*	3.01
Bert Blyleven*	3.01

1. Through 1983 season.

Runs Scored

Ty Cobb	2,245
Henry Aaron	2,174
Babe Ruth	2,174
Pete Rose*	2,091
Willie Mays	2,062
Stan Musial	1,949
Lou Gehrig	1,888
Tris Speaker	1,881
Mel Ott	1,859
Frank Robinson	1,829
Eddie Collins	1,816
Carl Yastrzemski	1,816
Ted Williams	1,798
Charlie Gehringer	1,774
Jimmie Foxx	1,751
Honus Wagner	1,740
Willie Keeler	1,720
Cap Anson	1,712
Jesse Burkett	1,708
Billy Hamilton	1,690
Mickey Mantle	1,677
John McPhee	1,674
George Van Haltren	1,650

*Active player through 1984

Strikeouts, Pitching

Nolan Ryan*	3,874
Steve Carlton*	3,872
Gaylord Perry	3,534
Walter Johnson	3,508
Tom Seaver*	3,429
Don Sutton*	3,208
Ferguson Jenkins	3,192
Bob Gibson	3,117
Phil Niekro*	3,048
Jim Bunning	2,855
Mickey Lolich	2,832
Cy Young	2,819
Warren Spahn	2,583
Bob Feller	2,581
Tim Keefe	2,538
Christy Mathewson	2,505

Home Runs (350 or More)

Henry Aaron	755
Babe Ruth	714
Willie Mays	660
Frank Robinson	586
Harmon Killebrew	573
Mickey Mantle	536
Jimmie Foxx	534
Ted Williams	521
Willie McCovey	521
Eddie Matthews	512
Ernie Banks	512
Mel Ott	511
Reggie Jackson*	503
Lou Gehrig	493
Stan Musial	475
Willie Stargell	475
Carl Yastrzemski	452
Billy Williams	426
Mike Schmidt*	425
Duke Snider	406
Al Kaline	399
Johnny Bench	389
Frank Howard	382
Orlando Cepeda	379
Norm Cash	377
Dave Kingman	377
Rocky Colavito	374
Gil Hodges	370
Ralph Kiner	369
Tony Perez	369
Joe DiMaggio	361
Lee May	360

Johnny Mize	359
Yogi Berra	358
Dick Allen	351

*Active player through 1984.

Don Sutton*	56
Bob Gibson	56
Steve Carlton*	55
Jim Palmer	53
Gaylord Perry	53
Juan Marichal	52

1. Through 1983 season.

Shutouts[1]

Walter Johnson	110
Grover Alexander	90
Christy Mathewson	83
Cy Young	77
Ed Plank	64
Warren Spahn	63
Ed Walsh	58
James Galvin	57
Tom Seaver*	56

Strikeouts, Batting[1]

Reggie Jackson*	2,106
Willie Stargell	1,912
Bobby Bonds	1,757
Tony Perez*	1,799
Lou Brock	1,730
Mickey Mantle	1,710

Harmon Killebrew	1,699
Dick Allen	1,556
Lee May	1,552
Willie McCovey	1,550
Frank Robinson	1,532
Willie Mays	1,526
Eddie Matthews	1,487
Frank Howard	1,460
Jim Wynn	1,427

1. Through 1983 season.

Bases on Balls[1]

Babe Ruth	2,056
Ted Williams	2,019
Carl Yastrzemski	1,845
Joe Morgan*	1,799
Mickey Mantle	1,734
Mel Ott	1,708
Eddie Yost	1,614
Stan Musial	1,599
Harmon Killebrew	1,559
Lou Gehrig	1,508
Willie Mays	1,464
Jimmie Foxx	1,452
Eddie Mathews	1,444
Frank Robinson	1,420
Henry Aaron	1,402

1. Through 1983 season.

RECORD OF WORLD SERIES GAMES

Source: The Book of Baseball Records, published by Seymour Siwoff, New York City.

Figures in parentheses for winning pitchers (WP) and losing pitchers (LP) indicate the game number in the series.

1903—Boston A.L. 5 (Jimmy Collins); Pittsburgh N.L. 3 (Fred Clarke). WP—Bos.: Dinneen (2, 6, 8), Young (5, 7); Pitts.: Phillippe (1, 3, 4). LP—Bos.: Young (1), Hughes (3), Dinneen (4); Pitts.: Leever (2, 6), Kennedy (5), Phillippe (7, 8).

1904—No series.

1905—New York N.L. 4 (John J. McGraw); Philadelphia A.L. 1 (Connie Mack). WP—N.Y.: Mathewson (1, 3, 5); McGinnity (4); Phila.: Bender (2). LP—N.Y.: McGinnity (2); Phila.: Plank (1, 4), Coakley (3), Bender (5).

1906—Chicago A.L. 4 (Fielder Jones); Chicago N.L. 2 (Frank Chance). WP—Chi.: A.L.: Altrock (1), Walsh (3, 5), White (6); Chi.: N.L.: Reulbach (2), Brown (4). LP—Chi. A.L.: White (2), Altrock. (4); Chi.: N.L.: Brown (1, 6), Pfeister (3, 5).

1907—Chicago N.L. 4 (Frank Chance); Detroit A.L. 0 (Hugh Jennings). First game tied 3–3, 12 innings. WP—Pfeister (2), Reulbach (3), Overall (4), Brown (5). LP—Mullin (2, 5), Siever (3), Donovan (4).

1908—Chicago N.L. 4 (Frank Chance); Detroit A.L. 1 (Hugh Jennings). WP—Chi.: Brown (1, 4), Overall (2, 5); Det.: Mullin (3). LP—Chi.: Pfeister (3); Det.: Summers (1, 4), Donovan (2, 5).

1909—Pittsburgh N.L. 4 (Fred Clarke); Detroit A.L. 3 (Hugh Jennings). WP—Pitts.: Adams (1, 5, 7), Maddox (3); Det.: Donovan (2), Mullin (4, 6). LP—Pitts.: Camnitz (2), Leifield (4), Willis (6); Det.: Mullin (1), Summers (3, 5), Donovan (7).

1910—Philadelphia A.L. 4 (Connie Mack); Chicago N.L. 1 (Frank Chance). WP—Phila.: Bender (1), Coombs (2, 3, 5); Chi.: Brown (4). LP—Phila.: Bender (4); Chi.: Overall (1), Brown (2, 5), McIntyre (3).

1911—Philadelphia A.L. 4 (Connie Mack); New York N.L. 2 (John J. McGraw). WP—Phila.: Plank (2), Coombs (3), Bender (4, 6); N.Y.: Mathewson (1), Crandall (5). LP—Phila.: Bender (1), Plank (5); N.Y.: Marquard (2), Mathewson (3, 4), Ames (6).

1912—Boston A.L. 4 (J. Garland Stahl); New York N.L. 3 (John J. McGraw). Second game tied, 6–6, 11 innings. WP—Bos.: Wood (1, 4, 8), Bedient (5); N.Y.: Marquard (3, 6), Tesreau (7). LP—Bos.: O'Brien (3, 6), Wood (7); N.Y.: Tesreau (1, 4), Mathewson (5, 8).

1913—Philadelphia A.L. 4 (Connie Mack); New York N.L. 1 (John J. McGraw). WP—Phila.: Bender (1, 4), Bush (3), Plank (5); N.Y.: Mathewson (2); LP—Phila.: Plank (2); N.Y.: Marquard (1), Tesreau (3), Demaree (4), Mathewson (5).

1914—Boston N.L. 4 (George Stallings); Philadelphia A.L. 0 (Connie Mack). WP—Rudolph (1, 4), James (2, 3). LP—Bender (1), Plank (2), Bush (3), Shawkey (4).

1915—Boston A.L. 4 (Bill Carrigan); Philadelphia N.L. 1 (Pat Moran). WP—Bos.: Foster (2, 5), Leonard (3), Shore (4); Phila.: Alexander (1). LP—Bos.: Shore (1); Phila.: Mayer (2), Alexander (3), Chalmers (4), Rixey (5).

1916—Boston A.L. 4 (Bill Carrigan); Brooklyn N.L. 1 (Wilbert Robinson). WP—Bos.: Shore (1, 5), Ruth (2), Leonard (4); Bklyn.: Coombs (3). LP—Bos.: Mays (3); Bklyn.: Marquard (1, 4), Smith (2), Pfeffer (5).

1917—Chicago A.L. 4 (Clarence Rowland); New York N.L. 2 (John J. McGraw). WP—Chi.: Cicotte (1), Faber (2, 5, 6); N.Y.: Benton (3), Schupp (4), LP—Chi.: Cicotte (3), Faber (4); N.Y.: Sallee (1, 5), Anderson (2), Benton (6).

1918—Boston A.L. 4 (Ed Barrow); Chicago N.L. 2 (Fred Mitchell). WP—Bos.: Ruth (1, 4), Mays (3, 6); Chi.: Tyler (2), Vaughn (5). LP—Bos.: Bush (2), Jones (5); Chi.: Vaughn (1, 3), Douglas (4), Tyler (6).

1919—Cincinnati N.L. 5 (Pat Moran); Chicago A.L. 3 (William Gleason). WP—Cin.: Ruether (1), Sallee (2), Ring (4), Eller (5, 8); Chi.: Kerr (3, 6), Cicotte (7). LP—Cin.: Fisher (3), Ring (6), Sallee (7); Chi.: Cicotte (1, 4), Williams (2, 5, 8).

1920—Cleveland A.L. 5 (Tris Speaker); Brooklyn N.L. 2 (Wilbert Robinson). WP—Cleve.: Coveleski (1, 4, 7), Bagby (5), Mails (6); Bklyn.: Grimes (2), Smith (3). LP—Cleve.: Bagby (2), Caldwell (3). Bklyn.: Marquard (1), Cadore (4), Grimes (5, 7), Smith (6).

1921—New York N.L. 5 (John J. McGraw); New York A.L. 3 (Miller Huggins). WP—N.Y. N.L.: Barnes (3, 6), Douglas (4, 7), Nehf (8); N.Y. A.L.: Mays (1), Hoyt (2, 5). LP—N.Y. N.L.: Nehf (2, 5), Douglas (1). N.Y. A.L.: Quinn (3), Mays (4, 7), Shawkey (6), Hoyt (8).

1922—New York N.L. 4 (John J. McGraw); New York A.L. 0 (Miller Huggins). Second game tied 3–3, 10 innings. WP—Ryan (1), Scott (3), McQuillan (4), Nehf (5); LP—Bush (1, 5), Hoyt (3), Mays (4).

1923—New York A.L. 4 (Miller Huggins); New York N.L. 2 (John J. McGraw). WP—N.Y. A.L.: Pennock (2, 6), Shawkey (4), Bush (5); N.Y. N.L.: Ryan (1), Nehf (3). LP—N.Y. A.L.: Bush (1), Jones (3); N.Y. N.L.: McQuillan (2), Scott (4), Bentley (5), Nehf (6).

1924—Washington A.L. 4 (Bucky Harris); New York N.L. 3 (John J. McGraw). WP—Wash.: Zachary (2, 6), Mogridge (4), Johnson (7); N.Y.: Nehf (1), McQuillan (3), Bentley (5). LP—Wash.: Johnson (1, 5), Marberry (3); N.Y.: Bentley (2, 7), Barnes (4), Nehf (6).

1925—Pittsburgh N.L. 4 (Bill McKechnie); Washington A.L. 3 (Bucky Harris). WP—Pitts.: Aldridge (2, 5), Kremer (6, 7); Wash.: Johnson (1, 4), Ferguson (3). LP—Pitts.: Meadows (1), Kremer (3), Yde (4); Wash.: Coveleski (2, 5), Ferguson (6), Johnson (7).

1926—St. Louis N.L. 4 (Rogers Hornsby); New York A.L. 3 (Miller Huggins). WP—St. L.: Alexander (2, 6), Haines (3, 7); N.Y.: Pennock (1, 5), Hoyt (4). LP—St. L.: Sherdel (1, 5), Reinhart (4); N.Y.: Shocker (2), Ruether (3), Shawkey (6), Hoyt (7).

1927—New York A.L. 4 (Miller Huggins); Pittsburgh N.L. 0 (Donie Bush). WP—Hoyt (1), Pipgras (2), Pennock (3), Moore (4). LP—Kremer (1), Aldridge (2), Meadows (3), Miljus (4).

1928—New York A.L. 4 (Miller Huggins); St. Louis N.L. 0 (Bill McKechnie). WP—Hoyt (1, 4), Pipgras (2), Zachary (3). LP—Sherdel (1, 4), Alexander (2), Haines (3).

1929—Philadelphia A.L. 4 (Connie Mack); Chicago N.L. 1 (Joe McCarthy). WP—Phila.: Ehmke (1), Earnshaw (2), Rommel (4), Walberg (5); Chi.: Bush (3). LP—Phila.: Earnshaw (3) Chi.: Root (1), Malone (2, 5), Blake (4).

1930—Philadelphia A.L. 4 (Connie Mack); St. Louis N.L. 2 (Gabby Street). WP—Phila.: Grove (1, 5), Earnshaw (2, 6); St. L.: Hallahan (3), Haines (4). LP—Phila.: Walberg (3), Grove (4); St. L.: Grimes (1, 5), Rhem (2), Hallahan (6).

1931—St. Louis N.L. 4 (Gabby Street); Philadelphia A.L. 3 (Connie Mack). WP—St. L.: Hallahan (2, 5), Grimes (3, 7); Phila.: Grove (1, 6), Earnshaw (4). LP—St. L.: Derringer (1, 6), Johnson (4); Phila.: Earnshaw (2, 7), Grove (3), Hoyt (5).

1932—New York A.L. (Joe McCarthy); Chicago N.L. 0 (Charles Grimm). WP—Ruffing (1), Gomez (2), Pipgras (3), Moore (4). LP—Bush (1), Warneke (2), Root (3), May (4).

1933—New York N.L. 4 (Bill Terry); Washington A.L. 1 (Joe Cronin.). WP—N.Y.: Hubbell (1, 4), Schumacher (2), Luque (5); Wash.: Whitehill (3). LP—N.Y.: Fitzsimmons (3); Wash.: Stewart (1), Crowder (2), Weaver (4), Russell (5).

1934—St. Louis N.L. 4 (Frank Frisch); Detroit A.L. 3 (Mickey Cochrane). WP—St. L.: J. Dean (1, 7), P. Dean (3, 6); Det.: Rowe (2), Auker (4), Bridges (5). LP—St. L.: W. Walker (2, 4), J. Dean (5); Det.: Crowder (1), Bridges (3), Rowe (6), Auker (7).

1935—Detroit A.L. 4 (Mickey Cochrane); Chicago N.L. 2 (Charles Grimm). WP—Det.: Bridges (2, 6), Rowe (3), Crowder (4); Chi.: Warneke (1, 5); LP—Det.: Rowe (1, 5), Chi.: Root (2), French (3, 6), Carleton (4).

1936—New York A.L. 4 (Joe McCarthy); New York N.L. 2 (Bill Terry). WP—N.Y. A.L.: Gomez (2, 6), Hadley (3), Pearson (4); N.Y. N.L.: Hubbell (1), Schumacher (5); LP—N.Y. A.L.: Ruffing (1), Malone (5); N.Y. N.L.: Schumacher (2), Fitzsimmons (3, 6), Hubbell (4).

1937—New York A.L. 4 (Joe McCarthy); New York N.L. 1 (Bill Terry). WP—N.Y. A.L.: Gomez (1, 5), Ruffing (2), Pearson (3); N.Y. N.L.: Hubbell (4). LP—N.Y. A.L.: Hadley (4); N.Y. N.L.: Hubbell (1), Melton (2, 5), Schumacher (3).

1938—New York A.L. 4 (Joe McCarthy); Chicago N.L. 0 (Gabby Hartnett). WP—Ruffing (1, 4), Gomez (2), Pearson (3) LP—Lee (1, 4), Dean (2), Bryant (3).

1939—New York A.L. 4 (Joe McCarthy); Cincinnati N.L. 0 (Bill McKechnie). WP—Ruffing (1), Pearson (2), Hadley (3), Murphy (4). LP—Derringer (1), Walters (2, 4), Thompson (3).

1940—Cincinnati N.L. 4 (Bill McKechnie); Detroit A.L. 3 (Del Baker). WP—Cin.: Walters (2, 6), Derringer (4, 7); Det.: Newsom (1, 5), Bridges (3). LP—Cin.: Derringer (1), Turner (3), Thompson (5); Det.: Rowe (2, 6), Trout (4), Newsom (7).

1941—New York A.L. 4 (Joe McCarthy); Brooklyn N.L. 1 (Leo Durocher). WP—N.Y.: Ruffing (1), Russo (3), Murphy (4), Bonham (5); Bklyn: Wyatt (2). LP—N.Y.: Chandler (2); Bklyn: Davis (1), Casey (3, 4), Wyatt (5).

1942—St. Louis N.L. 4 (Billy Southworth); New York A.L. 1 (Joe McCarthy). WP—St. L.: Beazley (2, 5), White (3), Lanier (4); N.Y.: Ruffing (1). LP—St. L.: Cooper (1); N.Y.: Bonham (2), Chandler (3), Donald (4), Ruffing (5).

1943—New York A.L. 4 (Joe McCarthy); St. Louis N.L. 1 (Billy Southworth). WP—N.Y.: Chandler (1, 5), Borowy (3), Russo (4); St. L.: Cooper (2). LP—N.Y.: Bonham (2); St. L.: Lanier (1), Brazle (3), Brecheen (4), Cooper (5).

1944—St. Louis N.L. 4 (Billy Southworth); St. Louis A.L. 2 (Luke Sewell). WP—St. L. N.L.: Donnelly (2), Brecheen (4), Cooper (5), Lanier (6); St. L. A.L.: Galehouse (1), Kramer (3). LP—St. L. N.L.: Cooper (1), Wilks (3); St. L. A.L.: Muncrief (2), Jakucki (4), Galehouse (5), Potter (6).

1945—Detroit A.L. 4 (Steve O'Neill); Chicago N.L. 3 (Charles Grimm). WP—Det.: Trucks (2), Trout (4), Newhouser (5, 7); Chi.: Borowy (1, 6), Passeau (3). LP—Det.: Newhouser (1), Overmire (3), Trout (6); Chi.: Wyse (2), Prim (4), Borowy (5, 7).

1946—St. Louis N.L. 4 (Eddie Dyer); Boston A.L. 3 (Joe Cronin). WP—St. L.: Brecheen (2, 6, 7), Munger (4); Bos.: Johnson (1), Ferriss (3), Dobson (5). LP—St. L.: Pollet (1), Dickson (3), Brazle (5); Bos.: Harris (2, 6), Hughson (4), Klinger (7).

1947—New York A.L. 4 (Bucky Harris); Brooklyn N.L. 3 (Burt Shotton). WP—N.Y.: Shea (1, 5), Reynolds (2), Page (7); Bklyn.: Casey (3, 4), Branca (6). LP—N.Y.: Newsom (3), Bevens (4), Page (6); Bklyn.: Branca (1), Lombardi (2), Barney (5), Gregg (7).

1948—Cleveland A.L. 4 (Lou Boudreau); Boston N.L. 2 (Billy Southworth). WP—Cleve.: Lemon (2, 6), Bearden (3), Gromek (4); Bos.: Sain (1), Spahn (5). LP—Cleve.: Feller (1, 5); Bos.: Spahn (2), Bickford (3), Sain (4), Voiselle (6).

1949—New York A.L. 4 (Casey Stengel); Brooklyn N.L. 1 (Burt Shotton). WP—N.Y.: Reynolds (1), Page (3), Lopat (4), Raschi (5); Bklyn.: Roe (2). LP—N.Y.: Raschi (2); Bklyn.: Newcombe (1, 4), Branca (3), Barney (5).

1950—New York A.L. 4 (Casey Stengel); Philadelphia N.L. 0 (Eddie Sawyer). WP—Raschi (1), Reynolds (2), Ferrick (3), Ford (4). LP—Konstanty (1), Roberts (2), Meyer (3), Miller (4).

1951—New York A.L. 4 (Casey Stengel); New York N.L. 2 (Leo Durocher). WP—N.Y. A.L.: Lopat (2, 5), Reynolds (4), Raschi (6); N.Y. N.L.: Koslo (1), Hearn (3). LP—N.Y. A.L.: Reynolds (1), Raschi (3); N.Y. N.L.: Jansen (2, 5), Maglie (4), Koslo (6).

1952—New York A.L. 4 (Casey Stengel); Brooklyn N.L. 3 (Chuck Dressen). WP—N.Y.: Raschi (2, 6), Reynolds (4, 7); Bklyn.: Black (1), Roe (3), Erskine (5). LP—N.Y.: Reynolds (1), Lopat (3), Sain (5); Bklyn.: Erskine (2), Black (4, 7), Loes (6).

1953—New York A.L. 4 (Casey Stengel); Brooklyn N.L. 2 (Chuck Dressen). WP—N.Y.: Sain (1), Lopat (2), McDonald (5), Reynolds (6); Bklyn.: Erskine (3), Loes (4). LP—N.Y.: Raschi (3), Ford (4); Bklyn.: Labine (1, 6), Roe (2), Podres (5).

1954—New York N.L. 4 (Leo Durocher); Cleveland A.L. 0 (Al Lopez). WP—Grissom (1), Antonelli (2), Gomez (3), Liddie (4). LP—Lemon (1, 4), Wynn (2), Garcia (3).

1955—Brooklyn N.L. 4 (Walter Alston); New York A.L. 3 (Casey Stengel). WP—Bklyn.: Podres (3, 7), Labine (4), Craig (5); N.Y.: Ford (1, 6), Byrne (2). LP—Bklyn.: Newcombe (1), Loes (2), Spooner (6); N.Y.: Turley (3), Larsen (4), Grim (5), Byrne (7).

1956—New York A.L. 4 (Casey Stengel); Brooklyn N.L. 3 (Walter Alston). WP—N.Y.: Ford (3), Sturdivant (4), Larsen (5), Kucks (7); Bklyn.: Maglie (1), Bessent (2), Labine (6). LP—N.Y.: Ford (1), Morgan (2), Turley (6); Bklyn.: Craig (3), Erskine (4), Maglie (5), Newcombe (7).

1957—Milwaukee N.L. 4 (Fred Haney); New York A.L. 3 (Casey Stengel). WP—Mil.: Burdette (2, 5, 7), Spahn (4); N.Y.: Ford (1), Larsen (3), Turley (6). LP—Mil.: Spahn (1), Buhl (3), Johnson (6); N.Y.: Shantz (2), Grim (4), Ford (5), Larsen (7).

1958—New York A.L. 4 (Casey Stengel); Milwaukee N.L. 3 (Fred Haney). WP—N.Y.: Larsen (3), Turley (5, 7), Duren (6); Mil.: Spahn (1, 4), Burdette (2). LP—N.Y.: Duren (1), Turley (2), Ford (4); Mil.: Rush (3), Burdette (5, 7), Spahn (6).

1959—Los Angeles N.L. 4 (Walter Alston); Chicago A.L. 2 (Al Lopez). WP—L.A.: Podres (2), Drysdale (3), Sherry (4, 6); Chi.: Wynn (1), Shaw (5). LP—L.A.: Craig (1), Koufax (5); Chi.: Shaw (2), Donovan (3), Staley (4), Wynn (6).

1960—Pittsburgh N.L. 4 (Danny Murtaugh); New York A.L. 3 (Casey Stengel). WP—Pitts.: Law (1, 4), Haddix (5, 7); N.Y.: Turley (2), Ford (3, 6). LP—Pitts.: Friend (2, 6), Mizell (3); N.Y.: Ditmar (1, 5), Terry (4, 7).

1961—New York A.L. 4 (Ralph Houk); Cincinnati N.L. 1 (Fred Hutchinson). WP—N.Y.: Ford (1, 4), Arroyo (3), Daley (5); Cin.: Jay (2). LP—N.Y.: Terry (2); Cin.: O'Toole (1, 4), Purkey (3), Jay (5).

1962—New York A.L. 4 (Ralph Houk); San Francisco N.L. 3 (Al Dark). WP—N.Y.: Ford (1), Stafford (3), Terry (5, 7); S.F. Sanford (2), Larsen (4), Pierce (6). LP—N.Y.: Terry (2), Coates (4), Ford (6); S.F.: O'Dell (1), Pierce (3), Sanford (5, 7).

1963—Los Angeles N.L. 4 (Walter Alston); New York A.L. 0 (Ralph Houk). WP—Koufax (1, 4), Podres (2), Drysdale (3). LP—Ford (1, 4), Downing (2), Bouton (3).

1964—St. Louis N.L. 4 (Johnny Keane); New York A.L. 3 (Yogi Berra). WP—St. L.: Sadecki (1), Craig (4), Gibson (5, 7); N.Y.: Stottlemyre (2), Bouton (3, 6). LP—St. L.: Gibson (2), Schultz (3), Simmons (6); N.Y.: Ford (1), Downing (4), Mikkelsen (5), Stottlemyre (7).

1965—Los Angeles N.L. 4 (Walter Alston); Minnesota A.L. 3 (Sam Mele). WP—L.A.: Osteen (3), Drysdale (4), Koufax (5, 7); Minn.: Grant (1, 6), Kaat (2). LP—L.A.: Drysdale (1), Koufax (2), Osteen (6); Minn.: Pascual (3), Grant (4), Kaat (5, 7).

1966—Baltimore A.L. 4 (Hank Bauer); Los Angeles N.L. 0 (Walter Alston). WP—Drabowsky (1), Palmer (2), Bunker (3), McNally (4). LP—Drysdale (1, 4), Koufax (2), Osteen (3).

1967—St. Louis N.L. 4 (Red Schoendienst); Boston A.L. 3 (Dick Williams). WP—St. L.: Gibson (1, 4, 7), Briles (3); Bos.: Lonborg (2, 5); Wyatt (6). LP—St. L.: Hughes (2), Carlton (5), Lamabe (6); Bos.: Santiago (1, 4), Bell (3), Lonborg (7).

1968—Detroit A.L. 4 (Mayo Smith); St. Louis N.L. 3 (Red Schoendienst). WP—Det.: Lolich (2, 5, 7), McLain (6); St. L.: Gibson (1, 4), Washburn (3), LP—Det.: McLain (1, 4), Wilson (3); St. L.: Briles (2), Hoerner (5), Washburn (6), Gibson (7).

1969—New York N.L. 4 (Gil Hodges); Baltimore A.L. 1 (Earl Weaver). WP—N.Y.: Koosman (2, 5), Gentry (3), Seaver (4); Balt.: Cuellar (1). LP—N.Y.: Seaver (1); Balt.: McNally (2), Palmer (3), Hall (4), Watt (5).

1970—Baltimore A.L. 4 (Earl Weaver); Cincinnati N.L. 1 (Sparky Anderson) 1. WP—Balt.: Palmer (1), Phoebus (2), McNally (3), Cuellar (5); Cin.: Carroll (4). LP—Cin.: Nolan (1), Wilcox (2), Cloninger (3), Merritt (5); Balt.: Watt (4).

1971—Pittsburgh N.L. 4 (Danny Murtaugh); Baltimore A.L. 3 (Earl Weaver). WP—Pitts.: Blass (3, 7), Kison (4), Briles (5); Balt.: McNally (1, 6), Palmer (2). LP—Pitts.: Ellis (1), R. Johnson (2), Miller (6); Balt.: Cuellar (3, 7), Watt (4) McNally (5).

1972—Oakland A.L. 4 (Dick Williams); Cincinnati N.L. (Sparky Anderson) 3. WP—Oakland: Holtzman (1), Hunter (2, 7), Fingers (4); Cincinnati: Billingham (3), Grimsley (5, 6). LP—Oakland: Odom (3), Fingers (5), Blue (6); Cincinnati: Nolan (1), Grimsley (2), Carroll (4), Borbon (7).

1973—Oakland A.L. 4 (Dick Williams): New York N.L. 3 (Yogi Berra). WP—Oakland: Holtzman (1, 7), Lindblad (3), Hunter (6). New York: McGraw (2), Matlack (4), Koosman (5). LP—Oakland: Fingers (2), Holtzman (4), Blue (5). New York: Matlack (1, 7) Parker (3), Seaver (6).

1974—Oakland A.L. 4 (Al Dark); Los Angeles N.L. 1 (Walter Alston). WP—Oakland: Fingers (1), Hunter (3), Holtzman (4), Odom (5). Los Angeles: Sutton (2). LP—Oakland: Blue (2), Los Angeles: Messersmith (1, 4), Downing (3), Marshall (5).

1975—Cincinnati N.L. 4 (Sparky Anderson); Boston A.L. 3 (Darrell Johnson). WP—Cincinnati: Eastwick (2–3), Gullett (5), Carroll (7); Boston: Tiant (1–4), Wise (6). LP—Cincinnati: Gullett (1), Norman (4), Darcy (6); Boston: Drago (2), Willoughby (3), Cleveland (5), Burton (7).

1976—Cincinnati N.L. 4 (Sparky Anderson); New York A.L. 0 (Billy Martin). WP—Gullett (1), Billingham (2), Zachry (3), Nolan (4). LP—Alexander (1), Hunter (2), Ellis (3), Figueroa (4).

1977—New York A.L. 4 (Billy Martin); Los Angeles N.L. 2 (Tom Lasorda). WP—New York: Lyle (1), Torrez (3, 6), Guidry (4); Los Angeles: Hooton (2), Sutton (5). LP—New York: Hunter (2), Gullett (5); Los Angeles: Rhoden (1), John (3), Rau (4), Hooton (6).

1978—New York A.L. 4 (Bob Lemon), Los Angeles N.L. 2 (Tom Lasorda); WP—New York: Guidry (3), Gossage (4); Beattie (5), Hunter (6); Los Angeles: John (1), Hooton (2). LP—New York: Figuero (1), Hunter (2); Los Angeles: Sutton (3–6), Welch (4), Hooton (5).

1979—Pittsburgh N.L. 4 (Chuck Tanner), Baltimore A.L. 3 (Earl Weaver); WP—Pittsburgh: D. Robinson (2), Blyleven (5), Candelaria (6), Jackson (7); Baltimore: Flanagan (1), McGregor (3), Stoddard (4). LP—Pittsburgh: Kison (1), Candelaria (3), Tekulve (4); Baltimore: Stanhouse (2), Flanagan (5), Palmer (6), McGregor (7).

1980—Philadelphia N.L. 4 (Dallas Green), Kansas City A.L. 2 (Jim Frey); WP—Philadelphia: Walk (1), Carlton (2), McGraw (5), Carlton (6); Kansas City: Quisenberry (3), Leonard (4). LP—Philadelphia: McGraw (3), Christenson (4); Kansas City: Leonard (1), Quisenberry (2), Quisenberry (5), Gale (6).

1981—Los Angeles N.L. 4 (Tom Lasorda), New York A.L. 2 (Bob Lemon); WP—Los Angeles: Valenzuela (3), Howe (4), Reuss (5), Hooton (6); New York: Guidry (1), John (2). LP—Los Angeles: Reuss (1), Hooton (2); New York: Frazier (3), Frazier (4), Guidry (5), Frazier (6).

1982—St. Louis N.L. 4 (Whitey Herzog), Milwaukee A.L. (Harvey Kuenn); WP—St. Louis: Sutter (2), Andujar (3), Stuper (6), Andujar (7). Milwaukee: Caldwell (1), Slaton (4), Caldwell (5). LP—St. Louis: Forsch (1), Bair (4), Forsch (5). Milwaukee: McClure (2), Vuckovich (3), Sutton (6), McClure (7).

1983—Baltimore A.L. 4 (Joe Altobelli), Philadelphia N.L. 1 (Paul Owens); WP—Baltimore: Boddicker (2), Palmer (3), Davis (4), McGregor (5). Philadelphia: Denny (1).

1984—Detroit A.L. 4 (Sparky Anderson), San Diego N.L. 1 (Dick Williams); WP—Det.: Morris (1,4), Wilcox (3), Lopez (5), San Diego: Hawkins (2). LP—Det.: Petry (2), San Diego: Thurmond (1), Lollar (3), Show (4), Hawkins (5).

BASEBALL PLAYERS' STRIKE HALTED 1981 SEASON FOR 7 WEEKS

A seven-week strike by major league players began on June 12 and disrupted the 1981 baseball season, canceled 713 games, caused heavy financial losses in all 26 big-league cities, and created confusion and ill-feelings among fans, players, and officials.

The major issue stemmed from a disagreement between the players and the club owners over compensation for the signing of free agents. The two sides finally worked out an agreement and the strike ended on Aug. 1. A pool arrangement under which teams losing a ranking free agent would receive a professional player as compensation as well as a selection in the amateur free-agent draft was the key to the accord. It also resolved a service credit issue for the players for the time lost during the strike. Service credit is used to determine eligibility for free agency and salary arbitration.

The players were allowed a week to get into condition and the season resumed on Aug. 10. The All-Star Game at Cleveland, postponed from its original date of July 14 because of the strike, was played on Aug. 9. Rescheduling the championship season became a problem. Normally the regular-season winners in the two divisions—Eastern and Western—in the National and American leagues meet in a best-of-five-game playoff series for their respective league pennants.

Because the 162-game regular season was shortened, officials decided to split the season into two halves. The four leaders in the two leagues when the strike began were declared champions of the first half. The four leaders in the second half were also declared champions. Those teams played off in a preliminary, or miniseries, playoff round. The survivors played off for their respective league pennants and the right to move on to the World Series, which started on Oct. 20, much later than usual.

WORLD SERIES CLUB STANDING (THROUGH 1984)

	Series	Won	Lost	Pct.
Oakland (A)	3	3	0	1.000
Pittsburgh (N)	7	5	2	.714
St. Louis (N)	13	9	4	.692
New York (A)	33	22	11	.667
Cleveland (A)	3	2	1	.667
Boston (A)	8	5	3	.625
Philadelphia (A)	8	5	3	.625
Los Angeles (N)	8	4	4	.500
New York (N-Mets)	2	1	1	.500
Milwaukee (N)	2	1	1	.500
Boston (N)	2	1	1	.500
Chicago (A)	4	2	2	.500
Cincinnati (N)	8	4	4	.500
Baltimore (A)	6	3	3	.500
Detroit (A)	9	4	5	.444
New York (N-Giants)	14	5	9	.357
Washington (A)	3	1	2	.333
Philadelphia (N)	4	1	3	.250
Chicago (N)	10	2	8	.200
Brooklyn (N)	9	1	8	.111
St. Louis (A)	1	0	1	.000
San Francisco (N)	1	0	1	.000
Minnesota (A)	1	0	1	.000
Kansas City (A)	1	0	1	.000
Milwaukee (A)	1	0	1	.000
San Diego (N)	1	0	1	.000

Recapitulation

	Won
American League	46
National League	34

SINGLE GAME AND SINGLE SERIES RECORDS

Most hits game—5, Paul Molitor, Milwaukee A.L., first game vs. St. Louis, N.L., 1982.

Most 4-hit games, series—2, Robin Yount, Milwaukee A.L., first and fifth games vs. St. Louis N.L., 1982.

Most hits inning—2, held by many players.

Most hits series—13 (7 games) Bobby Richardson, New York A.L., 1964; Lou Brock, St. Louis N.L., 1968; 12 (6 games) Billy Martin, New York A.L., 1953; 12 (8 games) Buck Herzog, New York N.L., 1912; Joe Jackson, Chicago A.L., 1919; 10 (4 games) Babe Ruth, New York A.L., 1928; 9 (5 games) held by 8 players.

Most home runs, series—5 (6 games) Reggie Jackson, New York A.L., 1977; 4 (7 games) Babe Ruth, New York A.L., 1926; Duke Snider, Brooklyn N.L., 1952, 1955; Hank Bauer, New York A.L., 1958; Gene Tenace, Oakland A.L., 1972; 4 (4 games) Lou Gehrig, New York A.L., 1928; 3 (6 games) Babe Ruth, New York A.L., 1923; Ted Kluszewski, Chicago A.L., 1959; 3 (5 games) Donn Clendenon, New York Mets N.L., 1969.

Most home runs, game—3, Babe Ruth, New York A.L., 1926 and 1928; Reggie Jackson, New York A.L., 1977.

Most strikeouts, series—12 (6 games) Willie Wilson, Kansas City A.L., 1980; 11 (7 games) Ed Mathews, Milwaukee N.L., 1958; Wayne Garrett, New York N.L., 1973: 10 (8 games) George Kelly, New York N.L., 1921; 9 (6 games) Jim Bottomley, St. Louis N.L., 1930; 9 (5 games) Carmelo Martinez, San Diego, N.L., 1984; Duke Snider, Brooklyn N.L., 1949; 7 (4 games) Bob Muesel, New York A.L., 1927.

Most stolen bases, game—3, Honus Wagner, Pittsburgh N.L., 1909; Willie Davis, Los Angeles N.L., 1965; Lou Brock, St. Louis N.L., 1967 and 1968.

Most strikeouts by pitcher, game—17, Bob Gibson, St. Louis N.L. 1968.

Most strikeouts by pitcher in succession—6, Horace Eller, Cincinnati N.L., 1919; Moe Drabowsky, Baltimore A.L., 1966.

Most strikeouts by pitcher, series—35 (7 games) Bob Gibson, St. Louis N.L., 1968; 28 (8 games) Bill Dinneen, Boston A.L., 1903; 23 (4 games) Sandy Koufax, Los Angeles, 1963; 20 (6 games) Chief Bender, Philadelphia A.L., 1911; 18 (5 games) Christy Mathewson, New York N.L., 1905.

Most bases on balls, series—11 (7 games) Babe Ruth, New York A.L., 1926; Gene Tenace, Oakland A.L., 1973; 9 (6 games) Willie Randolph, New York A.L., 1981; 7 (5 games) James Sheckard, Chicago N.L., 1910; Mickey Cochrane, Philadelphia A.L., 1929; Joe Gordon, New York A.L., 1941; 7 (4 games) Hank Thompson, New York N.L., 1954.

Most consecutive scoreless innings one series—27, Christy Mathewson, New York N.L., 1905.

LIFETIME WORLD SERIES RECORDS

Most hits—71, Yogi Berra, New York A.L., 1947, 1949-53, 1955-58, 1960-63.

Most runs—42, Mickey Mantle, New York A.L., 1951-53, 1955-58, 1960-64.

Most runs batted in—40, Mickey Mantle, New York A.L., 1951-53, 1955-58, 1960-64.

Most home runs—18, Mickey Mantle, New York A.L., 1951-53, 1955-58, 1960-64.

Most bases on balls—43, Mickey Mantle, New York A.L., 1951-53, 1955-58, 1960-64.

Most strikeouts—54, Mickey Mantle, New York A.L., 1951-53, 1955-58, 1960-64.

Most stolen bases—14, Eddie Collins, Philadelphia A.L. 1910-11, 13-14; Chicago A.L., 1917, 1919. Lou Brock, St. Louis N.L., 1964, 67-68.

Most victories, pitcher—10, Whitey Ford, New York A.L., 1950, 1953, 1955-58, 1960-64.

Most times member of winning team—10, Yogi Berra, New York A.L., 1947, 1949-53, 1956, 1958, 1961-62.

Most victories, no defeats—6, Vernon Gomez, New York A.L., 1932, 1936(2), 1937(2), 1938.

Most shutouts—4, Christy Mathewson, New York N.L., 1905 (3), 1913.

Most innings pitched—146, Whitey Ford, New York A.L., 1950, 1953, 1955-58, 1960-1964.

Most consecutive scoreless innings—33 2/3, Whitey Ford, New York A.L., 1960 (18), 1961 (14), 1962 (1 2/3).

Most strikeouts by pitcher—94, Whitey Ford, New York A.L., 1950, 1953, 1955-58, 1960-64.

AMERICAN LEAGUE HOME RUN CHAMPIONS

Year	Player, team	No.
1901	Nap Lajoie, Phila.	13
1902	Ralph Seybold, Phila.	16
1903	Buck Freeman, Bost.	13
1904	Harry Davis, Phila.	10
1905	Harry Davis, Phila.	8
1906	Harry Davis, Phila.	12
1907	Harry Davis, Phila.	8
1908	Sam Crawford, Det.	7
1909	Ty Cobb, Det.	9
1910	J. Garland Stahl, Bost.	10
1911	Franklin Baker, Phila.	9
1912	Franklin Baker, Phila.	10
1913	Franklin Baker, Phila.	12
1914	Franklin Baker, Phila., and Sam Crawford, Det.	8
1915	Robert Roth, Chi.-Cleve.	7
1916	Wally Pipp, N.Y.	12
1917	Wally Pipp, N.Y.	9
1918	Babe Ruth, Bost., and Clarence Walker, Phila.	11
1919	Babe Ruth, Bost.	29
1920	Babe Ruth, N.Y.	54
1921	Babe Ruth, N.Y.	59
1922	Ken Williams, St. L.	39
1923	Babe Ruth, N.Y.	41
1924	Babe Ruth, N.Y.	46
1925	Bob Meusel, N.Y.	33
1926	Babe Ruth, N.Y.	47
1927	Babe Ruth, N.Y.	60
1928	Babe Ruth, N.Y.	54
1929	Babe Ruth, N.Y.	46
1930	Babe Ruth, N.Y.	49
1931	Lou Gehrig, N.Y., and Babe Ruth, N.Y.	46
1932	Jimmy Foxx, Phila.	58
1933	Jimmy Foxx, Phila.	48
1934	Lou Gehrig, N.Y.	49
1935	Jimmy Foxx, Phila., and Hank Greenberg, Det.	36
1936	Lou Gehrig, N.Y.	49
1937	Joe DiMaggio, N.Y.	46
1938	Hank Greenberg, Det.	58
1939	Jimmy Foxx, Bost.	35
1940	Hank Greenberg, Det.	41
1941	Ted Williams, Bost.	37
1942	Ted Williams, Bost.	36
1943	Rudy York, Det.	34
1944	Nick Etten, N.Y.	22
1945	Vern Stephens, St. L.	24
1946	Hank Greenberg, Det.	44
1947	Ted Williams, Bost.	32
1948	Joe DiMaggio, N.Y.	39
1949	Ted Williams, Bost.	43
1950	Al Rosen, Cleve.	37
1951	Gus Zernial, Chi.-Phila.	33
1952	Larry Doby, Cleve.	32
1953	Al Rosen, Cleve.	43
1954	Larry Doby, Cleve.	32
1955	Mickey Mantle, N.Y.	37
1956	Mickey Mantle, N.Y.	52
1957	Roy Sievers, Wash.	42
1958	Mickey Mantle, N.Y.	42
1959	Rocky Colavito, Cleve., and Harmon Killebrew, Wash.	42
1960	Mickey Mantle, N.Y.	40
1961	Roger Maris, N.Y.	61
1962	Harmon Killebrew, Minn.	48
1963	Harmon Killebrew, Minn.	45
1964	Harmon Killebrew, Minn.	49
1965	Tony Conigliaro, Bost.	32
1966	Frank Robinson, Balt.	49
1967	Carl Yastrzemski, Bost., and Harmon Killebrew, Minn.	44
1968	Frank Howard, Wash.	44
1969	Harmon Killebrew, Minn.	49
1970	Frank Howard, Wash.	44
1971	Bill Melton, Chicago	33
1972	Dick Allen, Chicago	37
1973	Reggie Jackson, Oak.	32
1974	Dick Allen, Chicago	32
1975	Reggie Jackson, Oak., and George Scott, Mil.	36
1976	Graig Nettles, N.Y.	32
1977	Jim Rice, Boston	39
1978	Jim Rice, Boston	46
1979	Gorman Thomas, Milwaukee	45
1980	Reggie Jackson, N.Y., and Ben Oglivie, Mil.	41
1981*	Tony Armas, Oak., Dwight Evans, Bost., Bobby Grich, Calif., and Eddie Murray, Balt. (tie)	22
1982	Gorman Thomas, Mil., and Reggie Jackson, Calif.	39
1983	Jim Rice, Boston	39
1984	Tony Armas, Boston	43

AMERICAN LEAGUE BATTING CHAMPIONS

Year	Player, team	Avg
1901	Nap Lajoie, Phila.	.422
1902	Ed Delahanty, Wash.	.376
1903	Nap Lajoie, Cleve.	.355
1904	Nap Lajoie, Cleve.	.381
1905	Elmer Flick, Cleve.	.306
1906	George Stone, St. L.	.358
1907	Ty Cobb, Det.	.350
1908	Ty Cobb, Det.	.324
1909	Ty Cobb, Det.	.377
1910	Ty Cobb, Det.	.385
1911	Ty Cobb, Det.	.420
1912	Ty Cobb, Det.	.410
1913	Ty Cobb, Det.	.390
1914	Ty Cobb, Det.	.368
1915	Ty Cobb, Det.	.369
1916	Tris Speaker, Cleve.	.386
1917	Ty Cobb, Det.	.383
1918	Ty Cobb, Det.	.382
1919	Ty Cobb, Det.	.384
1920	George Sisler, St. L.	.407
1921	Harry Heilmann, Det.	.394
1922	George Sisler, St. L.	.420
1923	Harry Heilmann, Det.	.403
1924	Babe Ruth, N.Y.	.378
1925	Harry Heilmann, Det.	.393
1926	Heinie Manush, Det.	.378
1927	Harry Heilmann, Det.	.398
1928	Goose Goslin, Wash.	.379
1929	Lew Fonseca, Cleve.	.369
1930	Al Simmons, Phila.	.381
1931	Al Simmons, Phila.	.390
1932	Dale Alexander, Det.-Bost.	.367
1933	Jimmy Foxx, Phila.	.356
1934	Lou Gehrig, N.Y.	.363
1935	Buddy Myer, Wash.	.349
1936	Luke Appling, Chi.	.388
1937	Charley Gehringer, Det.	.371
1938	Jimmy Foxx, Bost.	.349
1939	Joe DiMaggio, N.Y.	.381
1940	Joe DiMaggio, N.Y.	.352
1941	Ted Williams, Bost.	.406
1942	Ted Williams, Bost.	.356
1943	Luke Appling, Chi.	.328
1944	Lou Boudreau, Cleve.	.327
1945	George Sternweiss, N.Y.	.309
1946	Mickey Vernon, Wash.	.353
1947	Ted Williams, Bost.	.343
1948	Ted Williams, Bost.	.369
1949	George Kell, Det.	.343
1950	Billy Goodman, Bost.	.354
1951	Ferris Fain, Phila.	.344
1952	Ferris Fain, Phila.	.327
1953	Mickey Vernon, Wash.	.337
1954	Bobby Avila, Cleve.	.341
1955	Al Kaline, Det.	.340
1956	Mickey Mantle, N.Y.	.353
1957	Ted Williams, Bost.	.388
1958	Ted Williams, Bost.	.328
1959	Harvey Kuenn, Det.	.353
1960	Pete Runnels, Bost.	.320
1961	Norman Cash, Det.	.361
1962	Pete Runnels, Bost.	.326
1963	Carl Yastrzemski, Bost.	.321
1964	Tony Oliva, Minn.	.323
1965	Tony Oliva, Minn.	.321
1966	Frank Robinson, Balt.	.316
1967	Carl Yastrzemski, Bost.	.326
1968	Carl Yastrzemski, Bost.	.301
1969	Rod Carew, Minn.	.332
1970	Alex Johnson, Calif.	.329
1971	Tony Oliva, Minn.	.337
1972	Rod Carew, Minn.	.318
1973	Rod Carew, Minn.	.350
1974	Rod Carew, Minn.	.364
1975	Rod Carew, Minn.	.359
1976	George Brett, Kansas City	.333
1977	Rod Carew, Minn.	.388
1978	Rod Carew, Minn.	.333
1979	Fred Lynn, Boston	.333
1980	George Brett, Kansas City	.390
1981*	Carney Lansford, Bost.	.336
1982	Willie Wilson, Kansas City	.332
1983	Wade Boggs, Boston	.361
1984	Don Maltingly, New York	.343

*Split season because of player strike.

NATIONAL LEAGUE HOME RUN CHAMPIONS

Year	Player, team	No.	Year	Player, team	No.	Year	Player, team	No.
1876	George Hall, Phila. Athletics	5	1913	Cliff Cravath, Phila.	19	1948	Ralph Kiner, Pitts., and John Mize, N.Y.	40
1877	George Shaffer, Louisville	3	1914	Cliff Cravath, Phila.	19	1949	Ralph Kiner, Pitts.	54
1878	Paul Hines, Providence	4	1915	Cliff Cravath, Phila.	24	1950	Ralph Kiner, Pitts.	47
1879	Charles Jones, Bost.	9	1916	Davis Robertson, N.Y., and Fred Williams, Chi.	12	1951	Ralph Kiner, Pitts.	42
1880	James O'Rourke, Bost., and Harry Stovey, Worcester	6	1917	Davis Robertson, N.Y., and Cliff Cravath, Phila.	12	1952	Ralph Kiner, Pitts., and Hank Sauer, Chi.	37
1881	Dan Brouthers, Buffalo	8	1918	Cliff Cravath, Phila.	8	1953	Ed Mathews, Mil.	47
1882	George Wood, Det.	7	1919	Cliff Cravath, Phila.	12	1954	Ted Kluszewski, Cin.	49
1883	William Ewing, N.Y.	10	1920	Cy Williams, Phila.	15	1955	Willie Mays, N.Y.	51
1884	Ed Williamson, Chi.	27	1921	George Kelly, N.Y.	23	1956	Duke Snider, Bklyn.	43
1885	Abner Dalrymple, Chi.	11	1922	Rogers Hornsby, St. L.	42	1957	Henry Aaron, Mil.	44
1886	Arthur Richardson, Det.	11	1923	Cy Williams, Phila.	41	1958	Ernie Banks, Chi.	47
1887	Roger Conoor, N.Y., and Wm. O'Brien, Wash.	17	1924	Jacques Fournier, Bklyn.	27	1959	Ed Mathews, Mil.	46
1888	Roger Connor, N.Y.	14	1925	Rogers Hornsby, St. L.	39	1960	Ernie Banks, Chi.	41
1889	Sam Thompson, Phila.	20	1926	Hack Wilson, Chi.	21	1961	Orlando Cepeda, San Fran.	46
1890	Tom Burns, Bklyn, and Mike Tiernan, N.Y.	13	1927	Hack Wilson, Chi., and Cy Williams, Phila.	30	1962	Willie Mays, San Fran.	49
1891	Harry Stovey, Bost., and Mike Tiernan, N.Y.	16	1928	Hack Wilson, Chi., and Jim Bottomley, St. L.	31	1963	Henry Aaron, Mil., and Willie McCovey, San Fran.	44
1892	Jim Holliday, Cin.	13	1929	Chuck Klein, Phila.	43	1964	Willie Mays, San Fran.	47
1893	Ed Delahanty, Phila.	19	1930	Hack Wilson, Chi.	56	1965	Willie Mays, San Fran.	52
1894	Hugh Duffy, Bost., and Robert Lowe, Bost.	18	1931	Chuck Klein, Phila.	31	1966	Henry Aaron, Atlanta	44
1895	Bill Joyce, Wash.	17	1932	Chuck Klein, Phila., and Mel Ott, N.Y.	38	1967	Henry Aaron, Atlanta	39
1896	Ed Delhanty, Phila., and Sam Thompson, Phila.	13	1933	Chuck Klein, Phila.	28	1968	Willie McCovey, San Fran.	36
1897	Nap Lajoie, Phila.	10	1934	Mel Ott, N.Y., and Rip Collins, St. L.	35	1969	Willie McCovey, San Fran.	45
1898	James Colins, Bost.	14	1935	Wally Berger, Bost.	34	1970	Johnny Bench, Cin.	45
1899	John Freeman, Wash.	25	1936	Mel Ott, N.Y.	33	1971	Willie Stargell, Pitts.	48
1900	Herman Long, Bost.	12	1937	Mel Ott, N.Y., and Joe Medwick, St. L.	31	1972	Johnny Bench, Cin.	40
1901	Sam Crawford, Con.	16	1938	Mel Ott, N.Y.	36	1973	Willie Stargell, Pitts.	44
1902	Tom Leach, Pitts.	6	1939	John Mize, St. L.	28	1974	Mike Schmidt, Phila.	36
1903	James Sheckard, Bklyn.	9	1940	John Mize, St. L.	43	1975	Mike Schmidt, Phila.	38
1904	Harry Lumley, Bklyn.	9	1941	Dolph Camilli, Bklyn.	34	1976	Mike Schmidt, Phila.	38
1905	Fred Odwell, Cin.	9	1942	Mel Ott, N.Y.	30	1977	George Foster, Cin.	52
1906	Tim Jordan, Bklyn	12	1943	Bill Nicholson, Chi.	29	1978	George Foster, Cin.	40
1907	David Brain, Bost.	10	1944	Bill Nicholson, Chi.	33	1979	Dave Kingman, Chicago	48
1908	Tim Jordan, Bklyn.	12	1945	Tommy Holmes, Bost.	28	1980	Mike Schmidt, Phila.	48
1909	John Murray, N.Y.	7	1946	Ralph Kiner, Pitts.	23	1981*	Mike Schmidt, Phila.	31
1910	Fred Beck, Bost., and Frank Schulte, Chi.	10	1947	Ralph Kiner, Pitts., and John Mize, N.Y.	51	1982	Dave Kingman, N.Y.	37
1911	Frank Schulte, Chi.	21				1983	Mike Schmidt, Phila.	40
1912	Henry Zimmerman, Chi.	14				1984	Mike Schmidt, Phila. and Dale Murphy, Atlanta	36

*Split season because of player strike.

NATIONAL LEAGUE BATTING CHAMPIONS

Year	Player, Team	Avg	Year	Player, Team	Avg	Year	Player, Team	Avg
1876	Roscoe Barnes, Chicago	.404	1894	Hugh Duffy, Boston	.438	1912	Henry Zimmerman, Chicago	.372
1877	Jim White, Boston	.385	1895	Jesse Burkett, Cleveland	.423	1913	Jake Daubert, Brooklyn	.350
1878	Abner Dalrymple, Mil.	.356	1896	Jesse Burkett, Cleveland	.410	1914	Jake Daubert, Brooklyn	.329
1879	Cap Anson, Chicago	.407	1897	Willie Keeler, Baltimore	.432	1915	Larry Doyle, New York	.320
1880	George Gore, Chicago	.365	1898	Willie Keeler, Baltimore	.379	1916	Hal Chase, Cincinnati	.339
1881	Cap Anson, Chicago	.399	1899	Ed Delahanty, Phila.	.408	1917	Edd Roush, Cincinnati	.341
1882	Dan Brouthers, Buffalo	.367	1900	Honus Wagner, Pittsburgh	.381	1918	Jack Wheat, Brooklyn	.335
1883	Dan Brouthers, Buffalo	.371	1901	Jesse Burkett, St. Louis	.382	1919	Edd Roush, Cincinnati	.321
1884	James O'Rourke, Buffalo	.350	1902	Clarence Beaumont, Pitts.	.357	1920	Rogers Hornsby, St. Louis	.370
1885	Roger Connor, N. Y.	.371	1903	Honus Wagner, Pittsburgh	.355	1921	Rogers Hornsby, St. Louis	.397
1886	King Kelly, Chicago	.388	1904	Honus Wagner, Pittsburgh	.349	1922	Rogers Hornsby, St. Louis	.401
1887	Cap Anson, Chicago	.421	1905	Cy Seymour, Cincinnati	.377	1923	Rogers Hornsby, St. Louis	.384
1888	Cap Anson, Chicago	.343	1906	Honus Wagner, Pittsburgh	.339	1924	Rogers Hornsby, St. Louis	.424
1889	Dan Brouthers, Boston	.373	1907	Honus Wagner, Pittsburgh	.350	1925	Rogers Hornsby, St. Louis	.403
1890	John Glasscock, N. Y.	.336	1908	Honus Wagner, Pittsburgh	.354	1926	Gene Hargrave, Cincinnati	.353
1891	William Hamilton, Phila.	.338	1909	Honus Wagner, Pittsburgh	.339	1927	Paul Waner; Pittsburgh	.380
1892	Dan Brouthers, Bklyn., and Clarence Childs, Cleve.	.335	1910	Sherwood Magee, Philadelphia	.331	1928	Rogers Hornsby, Boston	.387
						1929	Lefty O'Doul, Phila.	.398
1893	Hugh Duffy, Boston	.378	1911	Honus Wagner, Pittsburgh	.334	1930	Bill Terry, N.Y.	.401

Year	Player, Team	Avg	Year	Player, Team	Avg	Year	Player, Team	Avg
1931	Chick Hafey, St. Louis	.349	1949	Jackie Robinson, Brooklyn	.342	1967	Roberto Clemente, Pitts.	.357
1932	Lefty O'Doul, Brooklyn	.368	1950	Stan Musial, St. Louis	.346	1968	Pete Rose, Cincinnati	.335
1933	Chuck Klein, Phila.	.368	1951	Stan Musial, St. Louis	.355	1969	Pete Rose, Cincinnati	.348
1934	Paul Waner, Pittsburgh	.362	1952	Stan Musial, St. Louis	.336	1970	Rico Carty, Atlanta	.366
1935	Arky Vaughan, Pittsburgh	.385	1953	Carl Furillo, Brooklyn	.344	1971	Joe Torre, St. Louis	.363
1936	Paul Waner, Pittsburgh	.373	1954	Willie Mays, N. Y.	.345	1972	Billy Williams, Chicago	.333
1937	Joe Medwick, St. Louis	.374	1955	Richie Ashburn, Phila.	.338	1973	Pete Rose, Cincinnati	.338
1938	Ernie Lombardi, Cin.	.342	1956	Henry Aaron, Mil.	.328	1974	Ralph Garr, Atlanta	.353
1939	John Mize, St. Louis	.349	1957	Stan Musial, St. Louis	.351	1975	Bill Madlock, Chicago	.354
1940	Debs Garms, Pittsburgh	.355	1958	Richie Ashburn, Phila.	.350	1976	Bill Madlock, Chicago	.339
1941	Pete Reiser, Brooklyn	.343	1959	Henry Aaron, Mil.	.355	1977	Dave Parker, Pittsburgh	.338
1942	Ernie Lombardi, Boston	.330	1960	Dick Groat, Pittsburgh	.325	1978	Dave Parker, Pittsburgh	.334
1943	Stan Musial, St. Louis	.357	1961	Roberto Clemente, Pitts.	.351	1979	Keith Hernandez, St. Louis	.344
1944	Dixie Walker, Brooklyn	.357	1962	Tommy Davis, L. A.	.346	1980	Bill Buckner, Chicago	.324
1945	Phil Cavarretta, Chicago	.355	1963	Tommy Davis, L. A.	.326	1981*	Bill Madlock, Pittsburgh	.341
1946	Stan Musial, St. Louis	.365	1964	Roberto Clemente, Pitts.	.339	1982	Al Oliver, Montreal	.331
1947	Harry Walker, St. L.-Phila.	.363	1965	Roberto Clemente, Pitts.	.329	1983	Bill Madlock, Pittsburgh	.323
1948	Stan Musial, St. Louis	.376	1966	Matty Alou, Pittsburgh	.342	1984	Tony Gwynn, San Diego	.351

AMERICAN LEAGUE PENNANT WINNERS

Year	Club	Manager	Won	Lost	Pct	Year	Club	Manager	Won	Lost	Pct
1901	Chicago	Clark C. Griffith	83	53	.610	1944	St. Louis	Luke Sewell	89	65	.578
1902	Philadelphia	Connie Mack	83	53	.610	1945[1]	Detroit	Steve O'Neill	88	65	.575
1903[1]	Boston	Jimmy Collins	91	47	.659	1946	Boston	Joseph E. Cronin	104	50	.675
1904[2]	Boston	Jimmy Collins	95	59	.617	1947[1]	New York	Stanley R. Harris	97	57	.630
1905	Philadelphia	Connie Mack	92	56	.622	1948[1]	Cleveland	Lou Boudreau	97	58	.626
1906[1]	Chicago	Fielder A. Jones	93	58	.616	1949[1]	New York	Casey Stengel	97	57	.630
1907	Detroit	Hugh A. Jennings	92	58	.613	1950[1]	New York	Casey Stengel	98	56	.636
1908	Detroit	Hugh A. Jennings	90	63	.588	1951[1]	New York	Casey Stengel	98	56	.636
1909	Detroit	Hugh A. Jennings	98	54	.645	1952[1]	New York	Casey Stengel	95	59	.617
1910[1]	Philadelphia	Connie Mack	102	48	.680	1953[1]	New York	Casey Stengel	99	52	.656
1911[1]	Philadelphia	Connie Mack	101	50	.669	1954	Cleveland	Al Lopez	111	43	.721
1912[1]	Boston	J. Garland Stahl	105	47	.691	1955	New York	Casey Stengel	96	58	.623
1913[1]	Philadelphia	Connie Mack	96	57	.627	1956[1]	New York	Casey Stengel	97	57	.630
1914	Philadelphia	Connie Mack	99	53	.651	1957	New York	Casey Stengel	98	56	.636
1915[1]	Boston	William F. Carrigan	101	50	.669	1958[1]	New York	Casey Stengel	92	62	.597
1916[1]	Boston	William F. Carrigan	91	63	.591	1959	Chicago	Al Lopez	94	60	.610
1917[1]	Chicago	Clarence H. Rowland	100	54	.649	1960	New York	Casey Stengel	97	57	.630
1918[1]	Boston	Ed Barrow	75	51	.595	1961[1]	New York	Ralph Houk	109	53	.673
1919	Chicago	William Gleason	88	52	.629	1962[1]	New York	Ralph Houk	96	66	.593
1920[1]	Cleveland	Tris Speaker	98	56	.636	1963	New York	Ralph Houk	104	57	.646
1921	New York	Miller J. Huggins	98	55	.641	1964	New York	Yogi Berra	99	63	.611
1922	New York	Miller J. Huggins	94	60	.610	1965	Minnesota	Sam Mele	102	60	.630
1923[1]	New York	Miller J. Huggins	98	54	.645	1966[1]	Baltimore	Hank Bauer	97	53	.606
1924[1]	Washington	Stanley R. Harris	92	62	.597	1967	Boston	Dick Williams	92	70	.568
1925	Washington	Stanley R. Harris	96	55	.636	1968[1]	Detroit	Mayo Smith	103	59	.636
1926	New York	Miller J. Huggins	91	63	.591	1969	Baltimore[3]	Earl Weaver	109	53	.673
1927[1]	New York	Miller J. Huggins	110	44	.714	1970[1]	Baltimore[3]	Earl Weaver	108	54	.667
1928[1]	New York	Miller J. Huggins	101	53	.656	1971	Baltimore[4]	Earl Weaver	101	57	.639
1929[1]	Philadelphia	Connie Mack	104	46	.693	1972[1]	Oakland[5]	Dick Williams	93	62	.600
1930[1]	Philadelphia	Connie Mack	102	52	.662	1973[1]	Oakland[6]	Dick Williams	94	68	.580
1931	Philadelphia	Connie Mack	107	45	.704	1974[1]	Oakland[6]	Alvin Dark	90	72	.556
1932[1]	New York	Joseph V. McCarthy	107	47	.695	1975	Boston[4]	Darrell Johnson	95	65	.594
1933	Washington	Joseph E. Cronin	99	53	.651	1976	New York[7]	Billy Martin	97	62	.610
1934	Detroit	Gordon Cochrane	101	53	.656	1977[1]	New York[7]	Billy Martin	100	62	.617
1935[1]	Detroit	Gordon Cochrane	93	58	.616	1978[1]	New York[7]	Billy Martin and Bob Lemon	100	63	.613
1936[1]	New York	Joseph V. McCarthy	102	51	.667						
1937[1]	New York	Joseph V. McCarthy	102	52	.662	1979	Baltimore[8]	Earl Weaver	102	57	.642
1938[1]	New York	Joseph V. McCarthy	99	53	.651	1980	Kansas City[9]	Jim Frey	97	65	.599
1939[1]	New York	Joseph V. McCarthy	106	45	.702	1981	New York[10]	Gene Michael-Bob Lemon	59	48	.551*
1940	Detroit	Delmar D. Baker	90	64	.584						
1941[1]	New York	Joseph V. McCarthy	101	53	.656	1982	Milwaukee[11]	Harvey Kuenn	95	67	.586
1942	New York	Joseph V. McCarthy	103	51	.669	1983	Baltimore[12]	Joe Altobelli	98	64	.605
1943[1]	New York	Joseph V. McCarthy	98	56	.636	1984	Detroit[13]	Sparky Anderson	104	58	.642

*Split season because of player strike. 1. World Series winner. 2. No World Series. 3. Defeated Minnesota, Western Division winner, in playoff. 4. Defeated Oakland, Western Division Leader, in playoff. 5. Defeated Detroit, Eastern Division winner, in playoff. 6. Defeated Baltimore, Eastern Division winner, in playoff. 7. Defeated Kansas City, Western Division winner, in playoff. 8. Defeated California, Western Division winner, in playoff. 9. Defeated New York, Eastern Division winner, in playoff. 10. Defeated Oakland, Western Division winner, in playoff. 11. Defeated California, Western Division winner, in playoff. 12. Defeated Chicago, Western Division winner in playoff. 13. Defeated Kansas City, Western Division winner, in playoff.

NATIONAL LEAGUE PENNANT WINNERS

Year	Club	Manager	Won	Lost	Pct
1876	Chicago	Albert G. Spalding	52	14	.788
1877	Boston	Harry Wright	31	17	.646
1878	Boston	Harry Wright	41	19	.683
1879	Providence	George Wright	55	23	.705
1880	Chicago	Adrian C. Anson	67	17	.798
1881	Chicago	Adrian C. Anson	56	28	.667
1882	Chicago	Adrian C. Anson	55	29	.655
1883	Boston	John F. Morrill	63	35	.643
1884	Providence	Frank C. Bancroft	84	28	.750
1885	Chicago	Adrian C. Anson	87	25	.777
1886	Chicago	Adrian C. Anson	90	34	.726
1887	Detroit	W. H. Watkins	79	45	.637
1888	New York	James J. Mutrie	84	47	.641
1889	New York	James J. Mutrie	83	43	.659
1890	Brooklyn	William H. McGunnigle	86	43	.667
1891	Boston	Frank G. Selee	87	51	.630
1892	Boston	Frank G. Selee	102	48	.680
1893	Boston	Frank G. Selee	86	44	.662
1894	Baltimore	Edward H. Hanlon	89	39	.695
1895	Baltimore	Edward H. Hanlon	87	43	.669
1896	Baltimore	Edward H. Hanlon	90	39	.698
1897	Boston	Frank G. Selee	93	39	.705
1898	Boston	Frank G. Selee	102	47	.685
1899	Brooklyn	Edward H. Hanlon	88	42	.677
1900	Brooklyn	Edward H. Hanlon	82	54	.603
1901	Pittsburgh	Fred C. Clarke	90	49	.647
1902	Pittsburgh	Fred C. Clarke	103	36	.741
1903	Pittsburgh	Fred C. Clarke	91	49	.650
1904	New York[2]	John J. McGraw	106	47	.693
1905	New York[1]	John J. McGraw	105	48	.686
1906	Chicago	Frank L. Chance	116	36	.763
1907	Chicago[1]	Frank L. Chance	107	45	.704
1908	Chicago[1]	Frank L. Chance	99	55	.643
1909	Pittsburgh[1]	Fred C. Clarke	110	42	.724
1910	Chicago	Frank L. Chance	104	50	.675
1911	New York	John J. McGraw	99	54	.647
1912	New York	John J. McGraw	103	48	.682
1913	New York	John J. McGraw	101	51	.664
1914	Boston[1]	George T. Stallings	94	59	.614
1915	Philadelphia	Patrick J. Moran	90	62	.592
1916	Brooklyn	Wilbert Robinson	94	60	.610
1917	New York	John J. McGraw	98	56	.636
1918	Chicago	Fred L. Mitchell	84	45	.651
1919	Cincinnati[1]	Patrick J. Moran	96	44	.686
1920	Brooklyn	Wilbert Robinson	93	61	.604
1921	New York[1]	John J. McGraw	94	59	.614
1922	New York[1]	John J. McGraw	93	61	.604
1923	New York	John J. McGraw	95	58	.621
1924	New York	John J. McGraw	93	60	.608
1925	Pittsburgh[1]	William B. McKechnie	95	58	.621
1926	St. Louis[1]	Rogers Hornsby	89	65	.578
1927	Pittsburgh	Donie Bush	94	60	.610
1928	St. Louis	William B. McKechnie	95	59	.617
1929	Chicago	Joseph V. McCarthy	98	54	.645
1930	St. Louis	Gabby Street	92	62	.597
1931	St. Louis[1]	Gabby Street	101	53	.656
1932	Chicago	Charles J. Grimm	90	64	.584
1933	New York[1]	William H. Terry	91	61	.599
1934	St. Louis[1]	Frank F. Frisch	95	58	.621
1935	Chicago	Charles J. Grimm	100	54	.649
1936	New York	William H. Terry	92	62	.597
1937	New York	William H. Terry	95	57	.625
1938	Chicago	Gabby Hartnett	89	63	.586
1939	Cincinnati	William B. McKechnie	97	57	.630
1940	Cincinnati[1]	William B. McKechnie	100	53	.654
1941	Brooklyn	Leo E. Durocher	100	54	.649
1942	St. Louis[1]	William H. Southworth	106	48	.688
1943	St. Louis	William H. Southworth	105	49	.682
1944	St. Louis[1]	William H. Southworth	105	49	.682
1945	Chicago	Charles J. Grimm	98	56	.636
1946	St. Louis[1]	Edwin H. Dyer	98	58	.628
1947	Brooklyn	Burton E. Shotton	94	60	.610
1948	Boston	William H. Southworth	91	62	.595
1949	Brooklyn	Burton E. Shotton	97	57	.630
1950	Philadelphia	Edwin M. Sawyer	91	63	.591
1951	New York	Leo E. Durocher	98	59	.624
1952	Brooklyn	Charles W. Dressen	96	57	.630
1953	Brooklyn	Charles W. Dressen	105	49	.682
1954	New York[1]	Leo E. Durocher	97	57	.630
1955	Brooklyn[1]	Walter Alston	98	55	.641
1956	Brooklyn	Walter Alston	93	61	.604
1957	Milwaukee[1]	Fred Haney	95	59	.617
1958	Milwaukee	Fred Haney	92	62	.597
1959	Los Angeles[1]	Walter Alston	88	68	.564
1960	Pittsburgh[1]	Danny Murtaugh	95	59	.617
1961	Cincinnati	Fred Hutchinson	93	61	.604
1962	San Francisco	Alvin Dark	103	62	.624
1963	Los Angeles[1]	Walter Alston	99	63	.611
1964	St. Louis[1]	Johnny Keane	93	69	.574
1965	Los Angeles[1]	Walter Alston	97	65	.599
1966	Los Angeles	Walter Alston	95	67	.586
1967	St. Louis[1]	Red Schoendienst	101	60	.627
1968	St. Louis	Red Schoendienst	97	65	.599
1969	New York[1 3]	Gil Hodges	100	62	.617
1970	Cincinnati[4]	Sparky Anderson	102	60	.630
1971	Pittsburgh[1 5]	Danny Murtaugh	97	65	.599
1972	Cincinnati[4]	Sparky Anderson	95	59	.617
1973	New York[6]	Yogi Berra	82	79	.509
1974	Los Angeles[6]	Walter Alston	102	60	.630
1975	Cincinnati[1 4]	Sparky Anderson	108	54	.667
1976	Cincinnati[7 1]	Sparky Anderson	102	60	.630
1977	Los Angeles[7]	Tom Lasorda	98	64	.605
1978	Los Angeles[7]	Tom Lasorda	95	67	.586
1979[1]	Pittsburgh[6]	Chuck Tanner	98	64	.605
1980[1]	Philadelphia[4]	Dallas Green	91	71	.562
1981	Los Angeles[1 9]	Tom Lasorda	63	47	.573*
1982[1]	St. Louis[10]	Whitey Herzog	92	70	.568
1983	Philadelphia[11]	Paul Owens	90	72	.556
1984	San Diego[12]	Dick Williams	92	70	.568

*Split season because of player strike. 1. World Series winner. 2. No World Series. 3. Defeated Atlanta, Western Division winner, in playoff. 4. Defeated Pittsburgh, Eastern Division winner, in playoff. 5. Defeated San Francisco, Western Division winner, in playoff. 6. Defeated Cincinnati, Western Division winner, in playoff. 7. Defeated Philadelphia, Eastern Division winner, in playoff. 8. Defeated Houston, Western Division winner, in playoff. 9. Defeated Montreal, Eastern Division winner, in playoff. 10. Defeated Atlanta, Western Division winner, in playoff. 11. Defeated Los Angeles, Western Division in playoff. 12. Defeated Chicago, Eastern Division champion in playoff.

MOST VALUABLE PLAYERS

(Baseball Writers Association selections)

American League

1931 Lefty Grove, Philadelphia
1932–33 Jimmy Foxx, Philadelphia
1934 Mickey Cochrane, Detroit
1935 Hank Greenberg, Detroit
1936 Lou Gehrig, New York
1937 Charlie Gehringer, Detroit
1938 Jimmy Foxx, Boston
1939 Joe DiMaggio, New York
1940 Hank Greenberg, Detroit
1941 Joe DiMaggio, New York
1942 Joe Gordon, New York
1943 Spurgeon Chandler, New York
1944–45 Hal Newhouser, Detroit
1946 Ted Williams, Boston
1947 Joe DiMaggio, New York
1948 Lou Boudreau, Cleveland
1949 Ted Williams, Boston
1950 Phil Rizzuto, New York
1951 Yogi Berra, New York
1952 Bobby Shantz, Philadelphia
1953 Al Rosen, Cleveland
1954–55 Yogi Berra, New York
1956–57 Mickey Mantle, New York
1958 Jackie Jensen, Boston
1959 Nellie Fox, Chicago
1960–61 Roger Maris, New York
1962 Mickey Mantle, New York
1963 Elston Howard, New York
1964 Brooks Robinson, Baltimore
1965 Zoilo Versalles, Minnesota
1966 Frank Robinson, Baltimore
1967 Carl Yastrzemski, Boston
1968 Dennis McLain, Detroit
1969 Harmon Killebrew, Minnesota
1970 John (Boog) Powell, Baltimore
1971 Vida Blue, Oakland
1972 Dick Allen, Chicago
1973 Reggie Jackson, Oakland
1974 Jeff Burroughs, Texas
1975 Fred Lynn, Boston
1976 Thurman Munson, New York
1977 Rod Carew, Minnesota
1978 Jim Rice, Boston
1979 Don Baylor, California
1980 George Brett, Kansas City
1981 Rollie Fingers, Milwaukee
1982 Robin Yount, Milwaukee
1983 Cal RipKen, Jr., Baltimore

National League

1931 Frank Frisch, St. Louis
1932 Chuck Klein, Philadelphia
1933 Carl Hubbell, New York
1934 Dizzy Dean, St. Louis
1935 Gabby Hartnett, Chicago
1936 Carl Hubbell, New York
1937 Joe Medwick, St. Louis
1938 Ernie Lombardi, Cincinnati
1939 Bucky Walters, Cincinnati
1940 Frank McCormick, Cincinnati
1941 Dolph Camilli, Brooklyn
1942 Mort Cooper, St. Louis
1943 Stan Musial, St. Louis
1944 Marty Marion, St. Louis
1945 Phil Cavarretta, Chicago
1946 Stan Musial, St. Louis
1947 Bob Elliott, Boston
1948 Stan Musial, St. Louis
1949 Jackie Robinson, Brooklyn
1950 Jim Konstanty, Philadelphia
1951 Roy Campanella, Brooklyn
1952 Hank Sauer, Chicago
1953 Roy Campanella, Brooklyn
1954 Willie Mays, New York
1955 Roy Campanella, Brooklyn
1956 Don Newcombe, Brooklyn
1957 Henry Aaron, Milwaukee
1958–59 Ernie Banks, Chicago
1960 Dick Groat, Pittsburgh
1961 Frank Robinson, Cincinnati
1962 Maury Wills, Los Angeles
1963 Sandy Koufax, Los Angeles
1964 Ken Boyer, St. Louis
1965 Willie Mays, San Francisco
1966 Roberto Clemente, Pittsburgh
1967 Orlando Cepeda, St. Louis
1968 Bob Gibson, St. Louis
1969 Willie McCovey, San Francisco
1970 Johnny Bench, Cincinnati
1971 Joe Torre, St. Louis
1972 Johnny Bench, Cincinnati
1973 Pete Rose, Cincinnati
1974 Steve Garvey, Los Angeles
1975–76 Joe Morgan, Cincinnati
1977 George Foster, Cincinnati
1978 Dave Parker, Pittsburgh
1979 Willie Stargell, Pittsburgh
1979 Keith Hernandez, St. Louis
1980 Mike Schmidt, Philadelphia
1981 Mike Schmidt, Philadelphia
1982 Dale Murphy, Atlanta
1983 Dale Murphy, Atlanta

CY YOUNG AWARD

1956 Don Newcombe, Brooklyn N.L.
1957 Warren Spahn, Milwaukee N.L.
1958 Bob Turley, New York A.L.
1959 Early Wynn, Chicago A.L.
1960 Vernon Law, Pittsburgh, N.L.
1961 Whitey Ford, New York A.L.
1962 Don Drysdale, Los Angeles N.L.
1963 Sandy Koufax, Los Angeles N.L.
1964 Dean Chance, Los Angeles A.L.
1965 Sandy Koufax, Los Angeles N.L.
1966 Sandy Koufax, Los Angeles N.L.
1967 Jim Lonborg, Boston A.L.; Mike McCormick, San Francisco N.L.
1968 Dennis, McLain, Detroit A.L.; Bob Gibson, St. Louis N.L.
1969 Mike Cuellar, Baltimore, and Dennis McLain, Detroit, tied in A.L.; Tom Seaver, N.Y. N.L.
1970 Jim Perry, Minnesota A.L; Bob Gibson, St. Louis N.L.
1971 Vida Blue, Oakland A.L.; Ferguson Jenkins, Chicago N.L.
1972 Gaylord Perry, Cleveland A.L.; Steve Carlton, Phila. N.L.
1973 Jim Palmer, Baltimore A.L.; Tom Seaver, New York N.L.
1974 Catfish Hunter, Oakland A.L.; Mike Marshall, Los Angeles N.L.
1975 Jim Palmer, Baltimore A.L.; Tom Seaver, New York N.L.
1976 Jim Palmer, Baltimore A.L.; Randy Jones, San Diego N.L.
1977 Sparky Lyle, N.Y., A.L.; Steve Carlton, Philadelphia N.L.
1978 Ron Guidry, N.Y., A.L.; Gaylord Perry, San Diego N.L.
1979 Mike Flanagan, Baltimore, A.L.; Bruce Sutter, Chicago, N.L.
1980 Steve Stone, Baltimore, A.L.; Steve Carlton, Philadelphia, N.L.
1981 Rollie Fingers, Milwaukee, A.L.; Fernando Valenzuela, Los Angeles, N.L.
1982 Pete Vuckovich, Milwaukee, A.L., Steve Carlton, Philadelphia, N.L.
1983 LaMarr Hoyt, Chicago, A.L.; John Denny, Philadelphia, N.L.

ROOKIE OF THE YEAR

(Baseball Writers Association selections)

American League

1949 Roy Sievers, St. Louis
1950 Walt Dropo, Boston
1951 Gil McDougald, New York
1952 Harry Byrd, Philadelphia
1953 Harvey Kuenn, Detroit
1954 Bob Grim, New York
1955 Herb Score, Cleveland
1956 Luis Aparicio, Chicago
1957 Tony Kubek, New York
1958 Albie Pearson, Washington
1959 Bob Allison, Washington
1960 Ron Hansen, Baltimore
1961 Don Schwall, Boston
1962 Tom Tresh, New York
1963 Gary Peters, Chicago
1964 Tony Oliva, Minnesota
1965 Curt Blefary, Baltimore
1966 Tommy Agee, Chicago
1967 Rod Carew, Minnesota
1968 Stan Bahnsen, New York
1969 Lou Piniella, Kansas City
1970 Thurman Munson, New York
1971 Chris Chambliss, Cleveland

1972 Carlton Fisk, Boston
1973 Alonzo Bumbry, Baltimore
1974 Mike Hargrove, Texas
1975 Fred Lynn, Boston
1976 Mark Fidrych, Detroit
1977 Eddie Murray, Baltimore
1978 Lou Whitaker, Detroit
1979 Alfredo Griffin, Toronto
1979 John Castino, Minnesota
1980 Joe Charboneau, Cleveland
1981 Dave Righetti, New York
1982 Cal Ripken, Jr., Baltimore
1983 Ron Kittle, Chicago

National League

1949 Don Newcombe, Brooklyn
1950 Sam Jethroe, Boston
1951 Willie Mays, New York
1952 Joe Black, Brooklyn
1953 Jim Gilliam, Brooklyn
1954 Wally Moon, St. Louis
1955 Bill Virdon, St. Louis
1956 Frank Robinson, Cincinnati
1957 Jack Sanford, Philadelphia
1958 Orlando Cepeda, San Francisco
1959 Willie McCovey, San Francisco
1960 Frank Howard, Los Angeles
1961 Billy Williams, Chicago
1962 Ken Hubbs, Chicago
1963 Pete Rose, Cincinnati
1964 Richie Allen, Philadelphia
1965 Jim Lefebvre, Los Angeles
1966 Tommy Helms, Cincinnati
1967 Tom Seaver, New York
1968 Johnny Bench, Cincinnati
1969 Ted Sizemore, Los Angeles
1970 Carl Morton, Montreal
1971 Earl Williams, Atlanta
1972 Jon Matlack, New York
1973 Gary Matthews, San Francisco
1974 Bake McBride, St. Louis
1975 John Montefusco, San Francisco
1976 Pat Zachry, Cincinnati
1977 Andre Dawson, Montreal
1978 Bob Horner, Atlanta
1979 Rick Sutcliffe, Los Angeles
1980 Steve Howe, Los Angeles
1981 Fernando Valenzuela, Los Angeles
1982 Steve Sax, Los Angeles
1983 Darryl Strawberry, New York

BASEBALL'S PERFECTLY PITCHED GAMES[1]

(no opposing runner reached base)

John Richmond—Worcester vs. Cleveland (NL) June 12, 1880	1-0
John M. Ward—Providence vs. Buffalo (NL) June 17, 1880	5-0
Cy Young—Boston vs. Philadelphia (AL) May 5, 1904	3-0
Addie Joss—Cleveland vs. Chicago (AL) Oct. 2, 1908	1-0
Ernest Shore[2]—Boston vs. Washington (AL) June 23, 1917	4-0
Charles Robertson—Chicago vs. Detroit (AL) April 30, 1922	2-0
Don Larsen[3]—New York (AL) vs. Brooklyn (NL) Oct. 8, 1956	2-0
Jim Bunning—Philadelphia vs. New York (NL) June 21, 1964	6-0
Sandy Koufax—Los Angeles vs. Chicago (NL) Sept. 9, 1965	1-0
Jim Hunter—Oakland vs. Minnesota (AL) May 8, 1968	4-0
Len Barker—Cleveland vs. Toronto (AL) May 15, 1981	3-0
Mike Witt—California vs. Texas (AL) Sept. 30, 1984	1-0

1. Harvey Haddix, of Pittsburgh, pitched 12 perfect innings against Milwaukee (NL), May 26, 1959 but lost game in 13th on error and hit. 2. Shore, relief pitcher for Babe Ruth who walked first batter before being ejected by umpire, retired 26 batters who faced him and baserunner was out stealing. 3. World Series.

MAJOR LEAGUE LIFETIME RECORDS

Source: The Book of Baseball Records, published and copyrighted by Seymour Siwoff, New York, N.Y. 10036.

Leading Batters, by Average

(Over 2,000 Hits)

	Years	At Bats	Hits	Avg
Ty Cobb	24	11,429	4,191	.367
Rogers Hornsby	23	8,173	2,930	.358
Dan Brouthers	19	6,725	2,349	.349
Ed Delahanty	16	7,493	2,593	.346
Tris Speaker	22	10,196	3,515	.345
Willie Keeler	19	8,564	2,955	.345
Ted Williams	19	7,706	2,654	.345
Billy Hamilton	14	6,262	2,157	.344
Harry Heilmann	17	7,787	2,660	.342
Babe Ruth	22	8,399	2,873	.342
Jesse Burkett	16	8,389	2,872	.342
Bill Terry	14	6,428	2,193	.341
Lou Gehrig	17	8,001	2,721	.340
George Sisler	15	8,267	2,812	.340
Nap Lajoie	21	9,589	3,251	.339
Cap Anson	22	9,084	3,081	.339
Sam Thompson	15	6,004	2,016	.336
Al Simmons	20	8,761	2,927	.334
Eddie Collins	25	9,949	3,311	.333
Paul Waner	20	9,459	3,152	.333
Stan Musial	22	10,972	3,630	.331
Rod Carew*	18	8,872	2,929	.330
Heinie Manush	17	7,653	2,524	.330
Hugh Duffy	17	6,999	2,307	.330
Honus Wagner	21	10,427	3,430	.329
Joe DiMaggio	13	6,821	2,214	.325
Jimmie Foxx	20	8,134	2,646	.325

*Active player.

Leading Pitchers

(Over 250 Victories)

	Years	W	L	Pct
Cy Young	22	511	315	.619
Walter Johnson	21	416	279	.599
Grover Alexander	20	373	208	.642
Christy Mathewson	17	373	188	.665
James Galvin	15	365	309	.542
Warren Spahn	21	363	245	.597
Charles Nichols	15	360	202	.641
Tim Keefe	14	346	225	.606
John Clarkson	12	328	175	.652
Eddie Plank	17	325	190	.631
Mickey Welch	13	316	214	.596
Gaylord Perry*	22	314	265	.542
Steve Carlton*	20	313	207	.602
Hoss Radbourne	11	308	191	.617
Lefty Grove	20	300	141	.680

	Years	W	L	Pct
Early Wynn	23	300	244	.551
Tom Seaver*	18	288	181	.614
Robin Roberts	19	286	245	.539
Phil Niekro*	21	284	238	.544
Ferguson Jenkins	19	284	226	.557
Jim Kaat	25	283	236	.545
Tony Mullane	14	282	221	.561
Don Sutton	19	280	218	.562
Red Ruffing	22	273	225	.548
Burleigh Grimes	19	270	212	.560
Jim Palmer*	18	268	149	.643
Bob Feller	18	266	162	.621
Eppa Rixey	21	266	251	.515
Gus Weyhing	14	265	236	.529
Jim McCormick	10	264	217	.549
Ted Lyons	21	260	230	.531
Red Faber	20	254	212	.545
Carl Hubbell	16	253	154	.622
Bob Gibson	17	251	174	.591

*Active player.

MAJOR LEAGUE ALL-TIME PITCHING RECORDS

Most Games Won—511, Cy Young, Cleveland N.L., 1890–98, St. Louis N.L., 1899–1900, Boston A.L., 1901–08, Cleveland A.L., 1909–11, Boston N.L., 1911.

Most Games Won, Season—60, Hoss Radbourne, Providence N.L., 1884. (Since 1900—41, Jack Chesbro, New York A.L., 1904.)

Most Consecutive Games Won—24, Carl Hubbell, New York N.L., 1936 (16) and 1937 (8).

Most Consecutive Games Won, Season—19, Tim Keefe, New York N.L., 1888; Rube Marquard, New York N.L., 1912.

Most Years Won 20 or More Games—16, Cy Young, Cleveland N.L., 1891–98, St. Louis N.L., 1899–1900, Boston A.L., 1901–04, 1907–08.

Most Shutouts—113, Walter Johnson, Wash. A.L., 1907–27.

Most Shutouts, Season—16, Grover Alexander, Philadelphia N.L., 1916.

Most Consecutive Shutouts—6, Don Drysdale, Los Angeles, N.L., 1968.

Most Consecutive Scoreless Innings—58, Don Drysdale, Los Angeles, N.L., 1968.

Most Strikeouts—3,874, Nolan Ryan, New York N.L., California A.L., Houston N.L., 1968–1984 (Still active)

Most Strikeouts, Season—505, Matthew Kilroy, Baltimore A.A., 1886. (Since 1900—383, Nolan Ryan, California, A.L., 1973.)

Most Strikeouts, Game—21, Tom Cheney, Washington A.L., 1962, 16 innings. Nine innings: 19, Charles McSweeney, Providence N.L., 1884; Hugh Dailey, Chicago U.A., 1884. (Since 1900—19, Steve Carlton, St. Louis N.L. vs. New York, Sept. 15, 1969; Tom Seaver, New York N.L. vs. San Diego, April 22, 1970; Nolan Ryan, California A.L. vs. Boston, Aug. 12, 1974.)

Most Consecutive Strikeouts—10, Tom Seaver, New York N.L. vs. San Diego, April 22, 1970.

Most Games, Season—106, Mike Marshall, Los Angeles, N.L., 1974.

Most Complete Games, Season—74, William White, Cincinnati N.L., 1879. (Since 1900—48, Jack Chesbro, New York A.L., 1904.)

MAJOR LEAGUE INDIVIDUAL ALL-TIME RECORDS

Highest Batting Average—442, James O'Neill, St. Louis, A.A., 1887; .438, Hugh Duffy, Boston, N.L., 1894 (Since 1900—.424, Rogers Hornsby, St. Louis, N.L., 1924; .422, Nap Lajoie, Phil., A.L., 1901)

Most Times at Bat—12,364, Henry Aaron, Milwaukee N.L., 1954–65; Atlanta N.L., 1966–74; Milwaukee A.L., 1975–76.

Most Years Batted .300 or Better—23, Ty Cobb, Detroit A.L., 1906–26, Philadelphia A.L., 1927–28.

Most hits—4,191, Ty Cobb, Detroit A.L., 1905–26, Philadelphia A.L., 1927–28.

Most Hits, Season—257, George Sisler, St. Louis A.L., 1920.

Most Hits, Game (9 innings)—7, Wilbert Robinson, Baltimore N.L., 6 singles, 1 double, 1892. Rennie Stennett, Pittsburgh N.L., 4 singles, 2 doubles, 1 triple, 1975.

Most Hits, Game (extra innings)—9, John Burnett, Cleveland A.L., 18 innings, 7 singles, 2 doubles, 1932.

Most Hits in Succession—12, Mike Higgins, Boston A.L., in four games, 1938; Walt Dropo, Detroit A.L., in three games, 1952.

Most Consecutive Games Batted Safely—56, Joe DiMaggio, New York A.L., 1941.

Most Runs—2,244, Ty Cobb, Detroit A.L., 1905–26, Philadelphia A.L., 1927–28.

Most Runs, Season—196, William Hamilton, Philadelphia N.L., 1894. (Since 1900—177, Babe Ruth, New York A.L., 1921.)

Most Runs, Game—7, Guy Hecker, Louisville A.A., 1886. (Since 1900—6, by Mel Ott, New York N.L., 1934, 1944; Johnny Pesky, Boston A.L., 1946; Frank Torre, Milwaukee N.L., 1957.)

Most Runs Batted in—2,297, Henry Aaron, Milwaukee N.L., 1954–1965; Atlanta N.L., 1966–74; Milwaukee A.L., 1975–76.

Most Runs Batted in, Season—190, Hack Wilson, Chicago N.L., 1930.

Most Runs Batted In, Game—12, Jim Bottomley, St. Louis N.L., 1924.

Most Home Runs—755, Henry Aaron, Milwaukee N.L., 1954–1965; Atlanta N.L., 1966–74; Milwaukee A.L., 1975–76.

Most Home Runs, Season—61, Roger Maris, New York A.L., 1961 (162-game season); 60, Babe Ruth, New York A.L., 1927 (154-game season)

Most Home Runs with Bases Filled—23, Lou Gehrig, New York A.L., 1927–39.

Most 2-Base Hits—793, Tris Speaker, Boston A.L., 1907–15, Cleveland A.L., 1916–26, Washington A.L., 1927, Philadelphia A.L., 1928.

Most 2-Base Hits, Season—67, Earl Webb, Boston A.L., 1931.

Most 2-base Hits, Game—4, by many.

Most 3-Base Hits—312, Sam Crawford, Cincinnati N.L., 1899–1902, Detroit A.L., 1903–17.

Most 3-Base Hits, Season—36, Owen Wilson, Pittsburgh N.L., 1912.

Most 3-Base Hits, Game—4, George Strief, Philadelphia A.A., 1885; William Joyce, New York N.L., 1897. (Since 1900—3, by many.)

Most Games Played—3,298, Henry Aaron, Milwaukee N.L., 1954–1965; Atlanta, N.L., 1966–74; Milwaukee A.L., 1975–76.

Most Consecutive Games Played—2,130, Lou Gehrig, New York A.L., 1925–39.

Most Bases on Balls—2,056, Babe Ruth, Boston A.L., 1914–19; New York A.L., 1920–34, Boston N.L., 1935.

Most Bases on Balls, Season—170, Babe Ruth, New York A.L., 1923.

Most bases on Balls, Game—6, Jimmy Foxx, Boston A.L., 1938.

Most Strikeouts, Season—189, Bobby Bonds, San Francisco N.L., 1970.

Most Strikeouts, Game (9 innings)—5, by many.

Most Strikeouts, Game (extra innings)—6, Carl Weilman, St. Louis A.L., 15 innings, 1913; Don Hoak, Chicago N.L., 17 innings, 1956; Fred Reichardt, California A.L., 17, innings, 1966; Billy Cowan, California A.L., 20, 1971; Cecil Cooper, Boston A.L., 15, 1974.
Most pinch—hits, lifetime—150, Manny Mota, S.F., 1962; Pitt., 1963-68; Montreal, 1969; L.A., 1969-80, N.L.
Most Pinch-hits, season—25, Jose Morales, Montreal N.L., 1976.
Most consecutive pinch-hits—9, Dave Philley, Phil., N.L., 1958 (8), 1959 (1).
Most pinch-hit home runs, lifetime—18, Gerald Lynch, Pitt.-Cin. N.L., 1957-66.
Most pinch-hit home runs, season—6, Johnny Frederick, Brooklyn, N.L., 1932.
Most stolen bases, lifetime (since 1900)—938, Lou Brock, Chicago N.L. 1961-64; St. Louis, N.L. 1964-79.
Most stolen bases, season—156, Harry Stovey, Phil., A.A., 1888. Since 1900: 130, Rickey Henderson, Oak., A.L., 1982; 118, Lou Brock, St. Lou., 1974.
Most stolen bases, game—7, George Gore, Chicago N.L. 1881; William Hamilton, Philadelphia N.L. 1894. (Since 1900—6, Eddie Collins, Philadelphia A.L., 1912.)
Most time stealing home, lifetime—35, Ty Cobb, Detroit-Phil. A.L., 1905-28.

MAJOR LEAGUE ATTENDANCE RECORDS

Single game—78,672, San Francisco at Los Angeles (N.L.), April 18, 1958. (At Memorial Coliseum.)
Doubleheader—84,587, New York at Cleveland (A.L.), Sept. 12, 1954.
Night—78,382, Chicago at Cleveland (A.L.), Aug. 20, 1948.
Season, home—3,608,881, Los Angeles (N.L.), 1982.
Season, road—2,461,240, New York (A.L.), 1980.
Season, league—23,988,661, American League, 1983.
Season, both leagues—45,557,582, 1983.
World Series, single game—92,706, Chicago (A.L.) at Los Angeles (N. L.), Oct. 6, 1959.
World Series, all games (6)—420,784, Chicago (A.L.) and Los Angeles (N.L.), 1959.

MOST HOME RUNS IN ONE SEASON

(45 or More)

HR	Player/Team	Year
61	Roger Maris, New York (AL)	1961
60	Babe Ruth, New York (AL)	1927
59	Babe Ruth, New York (AL)	1921
58	Jimmy Foxx, Philadelphia (AL)	1932
58	Hank Greenberg, Detroit (AL)	1938
56	Hack Wilson, Chicago (NL)	1930
54	Babe Ruth, New York (AL)	1920
54	Babe Ruth, New York (AL)	1928
54	Ralph Kiner, Pittsburgh (NL)	1949
54	Mickey Mantle, New York (AL)	1961
52	Mickey Mantle, New York (AL)	1956
52	Willie Mays, San Francisco (NL)	1965
52	George Foster, Cincinnati (NL)	1977
51	Ralph Kiner, Pittsburgh (NL)	1947
51	John Mize, New York (NL)	1947
51	Willie Mays, New York (NL)	1955
50	Jimmy Foxx, Boston (AL)	1938
49	Babe Ruth, New York (AL)	1930
49	Lou Gehrig, New York (AL)	1934
49	Lou Gehrig, New York (AL)	1936
49	Ted Kluszewski, Cincinnati (NL)	1954
49	Willie Mays, San Francisco (NL)	1962
49	Harmon Killebrew, Minnesota (AL)	1964
49	Frank Robinson, Baltimore (AL)	1966
49	Harmon Killebrew, Minnesota (AL)	1969
48	Jimmy Foxx, Philadelphia (AL)	1933
48	Harmon Killebrew, Minnesota (AL)	1962
48	Willie Stargell, Pittsburgh (NL)	1971
48	Dave Kingman, Chicago (NL)	1979
48	Mike Schmidt, Philadelphia (NL)	1980
47	Babe Ruth, New York (AL)	1926
47	Ralph Kiner, Pittsburgh (NL)	1950
47	Ed Mathews, Milwaukee (NL)	1953
47	Ernie Banks, Chicago (NL)	1958
47	Willie Mays, San Francisco (NL)	1964
47	Henry Aaron, Atlanta (NL)	1971
47	Reggie Jackson, Oakland (AL)	1969
46	Babe Ruth, New York (AL)	1924
46	Babe Ruth, New York, (AL)	1929
46	Babe Ruth, New York (AL)	1931
46	Lou Gehrig, New York (AL)	1931
46	Joe DiMaggio, New York (AL)	1937
46	Ed Mathews, Milwaukee (NL)	1959
46	Orlando Cepeda, San Francisco (NL)	1961
46	Jim Rice, Boston (AL)	1978
45	Harmon Killebrew, Minnesota (AL)	1963
45	Willie McCovey, San Francisco (NL)	1969
45	Johnny Bench, Cincinnati (NL)	1970
45	Gorman Thomas, Milwaukee (AL)	1979
45	Henry Aaron, Milwaukee (NL)	1962

RODEO

PROFESSIONAL RODEO COWBOY ASSOCIATION, ALL AROUND COWBOY

1953	Bill Linderman
1954	Buck Rutherford
1955	Casey Tibbs
1956-59	Jim Shoulders
1960	Harry Tompkins
1961	Benny Reynolds
1962	Tom Nesmith
1963-65	Dean Oliver
1966-70	Larry Mahan
1971-72	Phil Lyne
1973	Larry Mahan
1974	Tom Ferguson
1975	Leo Camarillo and Tom Ferguson
1976-79	Tom Ferguson
1980	Paul Tierney
1981	Jimmie Cooper
1982	Chris Lybbert
1983	Roy Cooper

MAJOR LEAGUE BALL PARK STATISTICS*

lf—Left-field foul line; cf—center field; rf—right-field foul line

Club, nickname, and grounds	Distance, feet			Seating capacity	Record Attendance[4]		
	lf	cf	rf		Day game	Double-header[3]	Night game
American League							
Baltimore Orioles—Memorial Stadium	309	405	309	53,208	51,956	46,796	51,883
Boston Red Sox—Fenway Park	315	390	302	33,465	36,388	41,995	36,228
California Angels—Anaheim Stadium	333	404	333	67,335	62,020	41,723	61,640
Chicago White Sox—Comiskey Park	341	401	341	43,651	54,215	55,555	53,940
Cleveland Indians—Municipal Stadium	320	400	320	74,208	74,420	84,587	78,382
Detroit Tigers—Tiger Stadium	340	440	325	52,687	57,888	58,369	56,586
Kansas City Royals—Royals Stadium	330	410	330	40,635	41,095	40,525	41,860
Milwaukee Brewers—County Stadium	315	402	315	53,192	55,120	54,630	55,716
Minnesota Twins—Hubert H. Humphrey Metrodome	343	408	327	55,122	46,463	43,419	52,299
New York Yankees—Yankee Stadium[1]	312	417	310	57,545	69,755	81,841	74,747
Oakland A's—Oakland Coliseum	330	397	330	50,219	48,758	48,562	49,300
Seattle Mariners—Kingdome	316	410	316	59,438	47,353	25,344	57,762
Texas Rangers—Arlington Stadium	330	400	330	41,284	40,078	42,163	41,097
Toronto Blue Jays—Exhibition Stadium	330	400	330	43,737	44,649	41,308	39,347
National League							
Atlanta Braves—Atlanta Stadium	330	402	330	52,934	51,275	46,489	53,775
Chicago Cubs—Wrigley Field	355	400	353	37,272	46,572	46,965	No lights
Cincinnati Reds—Riverfront Stadium	330	404	330	52,392	53,390	52,147	53,328
Houston Astros—Astrodome	340	406	340	45,000	49,442	45,115	50,908
Los Angeles Dodgers—Dodger Stadium[2]	330	400	330	56,000	78,672	53,856	72,140
Montreal Expos—Olympic Stadium	325	404	325	58,838	57,592	59,282	57,121
New York Mets—Shea Stadium	338	410	338	55,300	56,738	57,175	56,658
Philadelphia Phillies—Veterans Stadium	330	408	330	66,507	63,283	40,720	63,501
Pittsburgh Pirates—Three Rivers Stadium	335	400	335	54,598	51,695	49,341	48,846
St. Louis Cardinals—Busch Memorial Stadium	330	414	330	50,222	50,548	49,743	50,340
San Diego Padres—Jack Murphy Stadium	330	405	330	51,319	36,750	43,473	50,569
San Francisco Giants—Candlestick Park	335	400	335	58,000	56,197	50,924	55,920

*At end of 1982 season. 1. Distance and capacity after rebuilding; attendance records prior to rebuilding. 2. Played also in Los Angeles Coliseum. 3. Two day games. 4. Through 1982 season.

MAJOR LEAGUE FRANCHISE SHIFTS AND ADDITIONS

1953—Boston Braves (N.L.) became Milwaukee Braves. Home attendance, last season in Boston (1952), 281,278; first season in Milwaukee (1953), 1,826,397.

1954—St. Louis Browns (A.L.) became Baltimore Orioles. Home attendance, last season in St. Louis (1953), 297,238; first season in Baltimore (1954), 1,060,910.

1955—Philadelphia Athletics (A.L.) became Kansas City Athletics. Home attendance, last season in Phila. (1954), 627,100; first season in K.C. (1955), 1,393,054.

1958—New York Giants (N.L.) became San Francisco Giants. Home attendance, last season in New York (1957), 653,923; first season in San Francisco (1958), 1,272,625.

1958—Brooklyn Dodgers (N.L.) became Los Angeles Dodgers. Home attendance, last season in Brooklyn (1957), 1,028,258; first season in Los Angeles (1958), 1,845,556.

1961—Washington Senators (A.L.) became Minnesota Twins. Home attendance, last season in Washington (1960), 743,404; first season in Minneapolis-St. Paul (1961), 1,256,722.

1961—Los Angeles Angels (later renamed the California Angels) enfranchised by the American League.

1961—Washington Senators enfranchised by the American League (a new team, replacing the former Washington club, whose franchise was moved to Minneapolis-St. Paul).

1962—Houston Colt .45's (later renamed the Houston Astros) enfranchised by the National League.

1962—New York Mets enfranchised by the National League. Home attendance, first season (1962), 922,530.

1966—Milwaukee Braves (N.L.) became Atlanta Braves. Home attendance, last season in Milwaukee (1965), 555,584; first season in Atlanta (1966), 1,539,801.

1968—Kansas City Athletics (A.L.) became Oakland Athletics.

1969—Two major leagues each added two teams for totals of 12 and split into two divisions. American League additions: Kansas City Royals and Seattle Pilots; National League additions: Montreal Expos and San Diego Padres. The Division leaders met for the league championship and the two league winners met in the World Series.

1970—Seattle franchise was shifted to Milwaukee, with final court approval coming on March 31. Club was renamed Milwaukee Brewers.

1971—Washington franchise-shifted at end of season to Dallas-Fort Worth Texas. Rangers with field at Arlington, Tex.

1977—Seattle and Toronto began play in American League.

MAJOR LEAGUE BASEBALL BREAKS ATTENDANCE RECORD IN 1983

Major league baseball attendance rose to 45,557,582 in 1983, breaking a record set in 1982 when the 26 teams drew 44,584,943 fans to the ball parks. The American League also broke a mark it set in 1982, drawing 23,948,661 in 1983 compared with the previous record of 23,080,440.

MAJOR LEAGUE BASEBALL—1984

AMERICAN LEAGUE
(Final Standing—1984)

EASTERN DIVISION

Team	W	L	Pct	GB
Detroit Tigers	104	58	.642	—
Toronto Blue Jays	89	73	.549	15
New York Yankees	87	75	.537	17
Boston Red Sox	86	76	.531	18
Baltimore Orioles	85	77	.525	19
Cleveland Indians	75	87	.463	29
Milwaukee Brewers	67	94	.416	36 1/2

WESTERN DIVISION

Team	W	L	Pct	GB
Kansas City Royals	84	78	.519	—
California Angels	81	81	.500	3
Minnesota Twins	81	81	.500	3
Oakland Athletics	77	85	.475	7
Chicago White Sox	74	88	.457	10
Seattle Mariners	74	88	.457	10
Texas Rangers	69	92	.429	14 1/2

AMERICAN LEAGUE PLAYOFFS—1984
1st game, Kansas City, Kan., Oct. 2

Detroit	200	110	121	—	8	14	0
Kansas City	000	000	100	—	1	5	1

Morris, Hernandez (8); Black, Huismann (6), Jones (8). Winner: Morris. Loser: Black. Home runs: Detroit: Herndon, Trammell, Parrish. Attendance: 41,973.

2nd game, Kansas City, Kan. Oct. 3

Detroit	201	000	000	02	—	5	8	1
Kansas City	000	100	110	00	—	3	10	3

Petry, Hernandez (8), Lopez (9); Saberhagen, Quisenberry (9). Winner: Lopez. Loser: Quisenberry. Home runs: Detroit: Kirk Gibson. Attendance: 42,019.

3rd game, Detroit, Mich. Oct. 5

Kansas City	000	000	000	—	0	3	3
Detroit	010	000	00X	—	1	3	0

Lebrant; Wilcox, Hernandez (9), Winner Wilcox. Loser: Lebrant. Attendance: 52,168.

NATIONAL LEAGUE
(Final Standing—1984)

EASTERN DIVISION

Team	W	L	Pct	GB
Chicago Cubs	96	65	.596	—
New York Mets	90	72	.556	6 1/2
St. Louis Cardinals	84	78	.519	12 1/2
Philadelphia Phillies	81	81	.500	15 1/2
Montreal Expos	78	83	.484	18
Pittsburgh Pirates	75	87	.463	21 1/2

WESTERN DIVISION

Team	W	L	Pct	GB
San Diego Padres	92	70	.568	—
Atlanta Braves	80	82	.494	12
Houston Astros	80	82	.494	12
Los Angeles Dodgers	79	83	.488	13
Cincinnati Reds	70	92	.432	22
San Francisco Giants	66	96	.407	26

NATIONAL LEAGUE PLAYOFFS—1984
1st game, Chicago, Ill., Oct. 2

San Diego	000	000	000	—	0	6	1
Chicago	203	062	00X	—	13	16	0

Show, Harris (6), Booker (7); Sutcliffe, Brusstar (8). Winner: Sutcliffe. Loser: Harris. Home runs: Chicago: Dernier, Matthews 2, Cey, Sutcliffe. Attendance: 36,282.

2nd game, Chicago, Ill., Oct. 3

San Diego	000	101	000	—	2	5	0
Chicago	102	100	00X	—	4	8	1

Thurmond, Hawkins (4), Dravecky (6), Lefferts (8); Trout, Smith (9). Winner: Trout. Loser: Thurmond. Home runs: none. Attendance: 36, 282

3rd game, San Diego, Calif., Oct. 4

Chicago	010	000	000	—	1	5	0
San Diego	000	034	00X	—	7	11	0

Eckersly, Frazier (6), Stoddard (8); Whitson, Gossage (9). Winner: Whitson. Loser: Eckersly. Homeruns: San Diego: McReynolds S. Attendance: 58,346.

4th game, San Diego, Calif., Oct. 6

Chicago	000	300	020	—	5	8	1
San Diego	002	010	202	—	7	11	0

Sanderson, Brosstar (5), Stoddard (7) Smith (8); Lollar, Hawkins (5), Dravecky (6), Gossage (8) Lefferts (9). Winner: Lefferts. Loser: Smith. Home runs: Chicago: Davis, Durham; San Diego: Garvey. Attendance: 58,354.

5th game, San Diego, Calif. Oct. 7

Chicago	210	000	000	—	3	5	1
San Diego	000	002	40X	—	6	6	0

Sutcliffe, Trout (7), Brusstar (8); Show, Hawkins (2), Dravecky (4), Lefferts (6), Gossage (8). Winner: Lefferts. Loser: Sutcliffe. Home runs: Chicago: Durham, Davis. Attendance: 58,359.

AMERICAN LEAGUE LEADERS—1984

Batting—Don Mattingly, New York	.343
Runs—Darrell Evans, Boston	121
Hits—Don Mattingly, New York	207
Runs batted in—Tony Armas, Boston	123
Triples—Dave Collins, Toronto	15
Doubles—Don Mattingly, New York	44
Home runs—Tony Armas, Boston	43
Stolen bases—Rickey Henderson, Oakland	66
Game winning RBI—Eddie Murray, Baltimore	19

Pitching

Victories—Mike Boddicker, Baltimore	20
Earned run average—Mike Boddicker, Baltimore	2.79
Strikeouts—Mark Langston, Seattle	204
Shutouts—Bob Ojeda, Boston	5
Complete games—Charlie Hough, Texas	17
Saves—Dan Quisenberry, Kansas City	44

NATIONAL LEAGUE LEADERS—1984

Batting—Tony Gwynn, San Diego	.351
Runs—Ryne Sandberg, Chicago	114
Hits—Tony Gwynn	213
Runs batted in—Gary Carter, Montreal	106
Doubles—Tim Raines, Montreal	38
Triples—Juan Samuel, Philadelphia	19
Home runs—Dale Murphy, Atlanta, and Mike Schmidt, Philadelphia	36
Stolen bases—Tim Raines, Montreal	75

Pitching

Victories—Joaquin Andujar, St. Louis	20
Earned run average—Alejandro Pena, Los Angeles	2.48
Strikeouts—Dwight Gooden, New York	276
Shutouts—Joaquin Andujar, St. Louis	4
Complete games—Mario Soto, Cincinnati	12
Saves—Bruce Sutter, St. Louis	45

AMERICAN LEAGUE AVERAGES—1984

Batting—Club

	AB	R	H	HR	RBI	Pct
Boston	5599	801	1579	180	756	.282
New York	5665	758	1559	129	724	.275
Toronto	5657	741	1546	141	693	.273
Detroit	5644	829	1530	187	788	.271
Kansas City	5543	673	1487	117	639	.268
Cleveland	5609	755	1486	123	699	.265
Minnesota	5563	673	1472	113	635	.265
Milwaukee	5474	638	1436	95	595	.262
Texas	5526	646	1438	120	612	.260
Oakland	5417	732	1401	158	689	.259
Seattle	5504	676	1415	127	628	.257
Baltimore	5426	679	1370	160	641	.252
California	5436	689	1353	148	641	.249
Chicago	5486	679	1358	172	640	.248

Batting Leaders
(300 or more at bats)

Player/Team	AB	R	H	HR	RBI	Pct
Mattingly, New York	603	91	207	23	110	.343
Winfield, New York	567	106	193	19	100	.340
Beniquez, California	354	60	119	8	39	.336
Boggs, Boston	625	109	203	6	55	.325
Mulliniks, Toronto	343	41	111	3	42	.324
Bell, Texas	552	88	174	11	83	.315
Trammel, Detroit	555	85	174	14	69	.314
Easler, Boston	601	87	188	27	91	.313
Hrbek, Minnesota	559	80	174	27	107	.311
Collins, Toronto	441	59	136	2	44	.308
Murray, Baltimore	588	97	180	29	110	.306
Baines, Chicago	569	72	173	29	94	.304
Johnson, Toronto	359	51	109	16	61	.304
Ripken, Baltimore	641	103	195	27	86	.304
Vukovich, Cleveland	437	38	133	9	60	.304
Barrett, Boston	475	56	144	3	45	.303
McRae, Kansas	317	30	96	3	42	.303
Hatcher, Minnesota	576	61	174	5	69	.302
Bradley, Seattle	322	49	97	0	24	.301
Wilson, Kansas	541	81	163	2	44	.301
Lansford, Oakland	597	70	179	14	74	.300
Rivers, Texas	313	40	94	4	33	.300
Orta, Kansas	403	50	120	9	50	.298
Yount, Milwaukee	624	105	186	16	80	.298
Puckett, Min.	557	63	165	0	31	.296
Carew, California	329	42	97	3	31	.295
Evans, Boston	630	121	186	32	104	.295

Leading Pitchers
(10 or more decisions)

Player/Team	IP	H	BB	SO	W	L	ERA
Hernandez, Detroit	140	96	36	112	9	3	1.92
Righetti, New York	96	79	37	90	5	6	2.34
Camacho, Cleveland	100	83	37	47	5	9	2.43
Schmidt, Texas	70	69	20	46	6	6	2.56
Howell, New York	104	86	33	109	9	4	2.69
Caudill, Oakland	96	77	31	89	9	7	2.71
Boddicker, Baltimore	261	218	82	128	20	11	2.79
Stieb, Toronto	267	215	88	198	16	8	2.83
Blyleven, Cleveland	245	204	74	169	19	7	2.87
Lopez, Detroit	138	109	52	94	10	1	2.94
Niekro, New York	216	219	76	136	16	8	3.00
Zahn, California	199	200	48	61	13	10	3.12
Black, Kansas	257	226	64	140	17	12	3.12
Davis, Baltimore	225	205	71	105	14	9	3.12
Alexander, Toronto	262	238	59	137	17	6	3.13
Burris, Oakland	212	193	90	93	13	10	3.15
Waddell, Cleveland	97	68	37	59	7	4	3.15
Viola, Min.	258	225	73	149	18	12	3.21
Petry, Detroit	233	231	66	143	18	8	3.24
Tanana, Texas	246	234	81	141	15	15	3.25
Stewart, Baltimore	93	80	47	56	7	4	3.29
Sanchez, California	84	84	33	62	9	7	3.33
Beckwith, Kansas	101	92	26	75	8	4	3.40
Langston, Seattle	225	188	118	204	17	10	3.40
Beattie, Seattle	211	206	75	119	12	16	3.41

NATIONAL LEAGUE AVERAGES—1984

Batting—Club

	AB	R	H	HR	RBI	Pct
Philadelphia	5547	712	1479	145	665	.267
San Francisco	5576	673	1476	112	637	.265
Houston	5511	686	1451	79	634	.263
Chicago	5438	762	1415	136	703	.260
San Diego	5502	686	1425	109	629	.259
New York	5405	649	1391	107	602	.257
Pittsburgh	5503	607	1400	98	576	.254
St. Louis	5433	652	1368	74	610	.252
Montreal	5438	593	1364	96	553	.251
Atlanta	5390	627	1330	110	573	.247
Los Angeles	5399	580	1316	102	531	.244
Cincinnati	5496	627	1338	106	578	.243

Batting Leaders
(300 or more at bats)

Player/Team	AB	R	H	HR	RBI	Pct
Gladden, San Francisco	342	71	120	4	31	.351
Gwynn, South Dakota	606	88	213	5	71	.351
Lacy, Pittsburgh	474	66	152	12	70	.321
C. Davis, San Francisco	499	87	157	21	81	.315
Sandberg, Chicago	636	114	200	19	84	.314
Cruz, Houston	600	96	187	12	95	.312
Ray, Pittsburgh	555	75	173	6	67	.312
Hernandez, New York	550	83	171	15	94	.311
Cabell, Houston	436	52	135	8	44	.310
Raines, Mon.	622	106	192	8	60	.309
Guerrero, Los Angeles	535	85	162	16	72	.303
Leonard, San Francisco	514	76	155	21	86	.302
Oliver, Philadelphia	432	36	130	0	48	.301
Puhl, Houston	449	66	135	9	55	.301
G. Carter, Mon.	596	75	175	27	106	.294
V. Hayes, Philadelphia	561	85	164	16	67	.292
Brenly, San Francisco	506	74	147	20	80	.291
Matthews, Chicago	491	101	143	14	82	.291
McGee, St. Louis	571	82	166	5	50	.291
Mumphrey, Houston	524	65	152	9	83	.290
Murphy, Atlanta	607	94	176	36	100	.290
Washington, Atlanta	415	62	119	17	61	.287
Morrison, Pittsburgh	304	38	87	11	45	.286

Rose, Cincinnati	374	44	107	0	34 .286
T. Pena, Pittsburgh	546	77	156	15	78 .286

Leading Pitchers
(10 or more decisions)

Player/Team	IP	H	BB	SO	W	L	ERA
Sutter, St. Louis	123	108	23	77	5	7	1.54
Dawley, Houston	98	82	35	47	11	4	1.93
Bedrosian, Atlanta	84	65	33	81	9	6	2.37
Andersen, Philadelphia	91	85	26	52	3	7	2.38
Denny, Philadelphia	154	122	29	94	7	7	2.45
A. Pena, Los Angeles	199	186	46	135	12	6	2.48
Scurry, Pittsburgh	46	28	22	48	5	6	2.53
Orosco, New York	87	58	34	85	10	6	2.59
Gooden, New York	218	161	73	276	17	9	2.60
Hershiser, Los Angeles	190	160	50	150	11	8	2.66
Tekulve, Pittsburgh	88	86	33	36	3	9	2.66
Sutcliffe, Chicago	150	123	39	155	16	1	2.69
Schatzeder, Mon.	136	112	36	89	7	7	2.71
Rhoden, Pittsburgh	238	216	62	136	14	9	2.72
Candiria, Pittsburgh	185	179	34	133	12	11	2.72
Power, Cincinnati	109	93	46	81	9	7	2.82
Honeycutt, Los Angeles	184	180	51	75	10	9	2.84
Lea, Mon.	224	198	68	123	15	10	2.89
Reardon, Mon.	87	70	37	77	7	7	2.90
Gossage, South Dakota	102	75	36	84	10	6	2.90
Dravecky, South Dakota	157	125	51	71	9	8	2.93
McWilliams, Pittsburgh	227	226	78	149	12	11	2.93
Thurmond, South Dakota	179	174	55	57	14	8	2.97
D. Robison, Pittsburgh	122	99	49	110	5	6	3.02
Eckersley, Chicago	160	152	36	81	10	8	3.03

WORLD SERIES—1984

Detroit Tigers (AL) defeated San Diego Padres (NL), 4 games to 1

1st Game—San Diego, Oct. 9

DETROIT (A)	AB	R	H	BI	SAN DIEGO (N)	AB	R	H	BI
Whitaker, 2b	4	1	1	0	Wiggins, 2b	4	0	1	0
Trammell, ss	5	0	2	1	Gwynn, rf	2	0	1	0
Gibson, rf	4	0	0	0	Garvey, 1b	4	1	1	0
Parrish, c	3	1	2	0	Nettles, 3b	2	1	2	0
Herndon, lf	3	1	2	2	Salazar, 3b	1	0	0	0
Garbey, dh	4	0	0	0	Kennedy, c	4	0	2	2
Lemon, cf	4	0	1	0	Brown, cf	4	0	0	0
Evans, 1b	3	0	0	0	Martinez, lf	4	0	0	0
Bergman, 1b	0	0	0	0	Templeton, ss	4	0	0	0
Castillo, 3b	2	0	0	0	Bevacqua, dh	3	0	1	0
Grubb, ph	0	0	0	0					
Brookens, 3b	1	0	0	0					
Total	**33**	**3**	**8**	**3**	**Total**	**32**	**2**	**8**	**2**

Detroit	**100 020 000**	**3**
San Diego	**200 000 000**	**2**

Game-winning RBI—Herndon (1). E—Martinez. DP—Detroit 1, San Diego 1. LOB—Detroit 9, San Diego 6. 2B—Whitaker, Kennedy, Parrish, Bevacqua. HR—Herndon (1).SB—Trammell (1), Gwynn (1).

	IP	H	R	ER	BB	SO
Detroit						
Morris W, 1–0	9	8	2	2	3	9
San Diego						
Thurmond L, 0–1	5	7	3	3	3	2
Hawkins	2 2/3	1	0	0	3	0
Dravecky	1 1/3	0	0	0	0	1

Time of game—3:18. Attendance—57,908.

2nd Game—San Diego, Oct. 10

DETROIT (A)	AB	R	H	BI	SAN DIEGO (N)	AB	R	H	BI
Whitaker, 2b	4	1	1	0	Wiggins, 2b	5	1	3	0
Trammell, ss	4	1	2	0	Gwynn, rf	3	0	1	0
Gibson, rf	4	1	2	1	Garvey, 1b	3	0	0	0
Parrish, c	3	0	0	1	Nettles, 3b	1	1	0	1
Evans, 3b	4	0	1	1	Kennedy, c	4	1	1	0
Jones, lf	2	0	0	0	Bevacqua, dh	4	2	3	3
Herndon, lf	2	0	0	0	Martinez, lf	3	0	0	0
Grubb, dh	2	0	1	0	Templeton, ss	4	0	3	0
Kuntz, ph	1	0	0	0	Brown, cf	3	0	0	1
Lemon, cf	3	0	0	0	Salazar, cf	1	0	0	0
Bergman, 1b	2	0	0	0					
Brookens, 3b	1	0	0	0					
Total	**32**	**3**	**7**	**3**	**Total**	**31**	**5**	**11**	**5**

Detroit	**300 000 000—3**
San Diego	**100 130 00x—5**

Game-winning RBI—Bevacqua (1).

E—Trammell, Gibson. DP—Detroit 1, San Diego 1. LOB—Detroit 3, San Diego 8. HR—Bevacqua (1). SB—Gibson (1). S—Garvey. SF—Parrish, Nettles.

	IP	H	R	ER	BB	SO
Detroit						
Petry L, 0–1	4 1/3	8	5	5	3	2
Lopez	2/3	1	0	0	1	0
Scherrer	1 1/3	2	0	0	0	0
Bair	2/3	0	0	0	0	1
Hernandez	1	0	0	0	0	0
San Diego						
Whitson	2/3	5	3	3	0	0
Hawkins W, 1–0	5 1/3	1	0	0	0	3
Lefferts S, 1	3	1	0	0	0	5

Balk—Petry. Time of game—2:44. Attendance—57,908.

3rd game—Detroit, Oct. 12

SAN DIEGO (N)	AB	R	H	BI	DETROIT (A)	AB	R	H	BI
Wiggins, 2b	5	1	2	0	Whitaker, 2b	3	1	0	0
Gwynn, rf	5	1	2	0	Trammell, ss	3	1	2	1
Garvey, 1b	5	0	1	1	Gibson, rf	2	0	0	1
Nettles, 3b	2	0	0	1	Parrish, c	3	0	1	0
Kennedy, c	3	0	0	0	Herndon, lf	4	0	1	1
Bevacqua, dh	4	0	1	0	Garbey, dh	5	0	0	0
Martinez, lf	4	0	1	0	Lemon, cf	5	1	2	0
Templeton, ss	4	0	2	0	Evans, 1b	2	1	0	0
Brown, cf	3	0	0	0	Bergman, 1b	0	0	0	0
Salazar, ph	1	0	1	0	Castillo, 3b	4	1	1	2
Total	**36**	**2**	**10**	**2**	**Total**	**31**	**5**	**7**	**5**

San Diego	**001 000 100—2**
Detroit	**041 000 00x—5**

Game Winning RBI—Castillo (1). LOB—San Diego 10, Detroit 14.2B—Wiggins, Trammell, Garvey. HR—Castillo (1). SB—Gibson (2). SF—Nettles.

	IP	H	R	ER	BB	SO
San Diego						
Lollar L, 0–1	1 2/3	4	4	4	4	0
Booker	1	0	1	1	4	0
Harris	5 1/3	3	0	0	3	5
Detroit						
Wilcox W, 1–0	6	7	1	1	2	4
Scherrer	2/3	2	1	1	0	0
Hernandez S 1	2 1/3	1	0	0	0	0

HBP—Gibson by Harris. Time of game—3:11. Attendance—51, 970.

4th Game—Detroit, Oct. 13

SAN DIEGO (N)	AB	R	H	BI	DETROIT (A)	AB	R	H	BI
Wiggins, 2b	3	0	0	0	Whitaker, 2b	4	2	2	0
Summers, ph	1	0	0	0	Trammell, ss	4	2	3	4
Roenicke, lf	0	0	0	0	Gibson, rf	4	0	1	0
Gwynn, rf	4	0	1	0	Parrish, c	4	0	0	0
Garvey, lb	4	1	0	0	Evans, 3b	2	0	0	0
Nettles, 3b	4	0	0	0	Brookens, 3b	1	0	0	0
Kennedy, c	4	1	1	1	Grubb, dh	1	0	0	0
Bevacqua, dh	3	0	1	0	Garbey, dh	2	0	0	0
Martinez, lf	2	0	0	0	Jones, lf	1	0	0	0
Flannery, 2b	1	0	1	0	Herndon, lf	2	0	1	0
Templeton, ss	3	0	0	0	Lemon, cf	2	0	0	0
Brown, cf	3	0	0	0	Bergman, lb	3	0	0	0
Total	**32**	**2**	**5**	**1**	**Total**	**30**	**4**	**7**	**4**

San Diego 010 000 001—2
Detroit 202 000 00x—4

Game Winning RBI—Trammell (2). E—Wiggins, Gwynn, DP—San Diego 2. LOB—San Diego 3, Detroit 4. 2B—Bevacqua, Whitaker, Garvey. HR—Trammell 2 (2), Kennedy (1). SB—Gibson (3), Lemon (1).

	IP	H	R	ER	BB	SO
San Diego						
Snow L, 0–1	2 2/3	4	4	3	1	2
Dravecky	3 1/3	3	0	0	1	4
Lefferts	1	0	0	0	0	0
Gossage	1	0	0	0	0	0
Detroit						
Morris W, 2–0	9	5	2	2	0	4

Wild pitch—Morris (2). Time of game—2:20. Attendance—52,130.

5th Game—Detroit, Oct. 14

SAN DIEGO (N)	AB	R	H	BI	DETROIT (A)	AB	R	H	BI
Wiggins, 2b	5	0	2	1	Whitaker, 2b	4	1	1	0
Gwynn, rf	5	0	0	0	Trammell, ss	4	1	0	0
Garvey, lb	4	0	1	1	Gibson, rf	4	3	3	5
Nettles, 3b	3	0	1	0	Parrish, c	5	2	2	1
Kennedy, c	4	0	0	0	Herndon, lf	4	0	1	0
Bevacqua, dh	3	2	1	1	Lemon, cf	3	0	2	1
Martinez, lf	4	0	2	0	Garbey, dh	1	0	0	0
Salazar, cf	0	0	0	0	Grubb, ph	0	0	0	0
Templeton, ss	4	1	1	0	Kuntz, ph	0	0	0	1
Brown, cf	2	1	1	1	Johnson, ph	1	0	0	0
Bochy, ph	1	0	1	0	Evans, lb	4	0	0	0
Roenicke, pr	0	0	0	0	Bergman, lb	0	0	0	0
					Castillo, 3b	3	1	2	0
Total	**35**	**4**	**10**	**4**	**Total**	**33**	**8**	**11**	**8**

San Diego 001 200 010—4
Detroit 300 010 13x—8

Game-winning RBI—Kuntz (1).

E—Parrish, Wiggins. DP—San Diego 1. LOB—San Diego 7, Detroit 9. 2B—Templeton. HR—Gibson 2 (2), Parrish (1), Bevacqua (2). SB—Wiggins (1), Parrish (1), Lemon (1). S—Trammell. SF—Brown, Kuntz.

	IP	H	R	ER	BB	SO
San Diego						
Thurmond	1/3	5	3	3	0	0
Hawkins L, 1–1	4	2	1	1	3	1
Lefferts	2	1	0	0	1	2
Gossage	1 2/3	3	4	4	1	2
Detroit						
Petry	3 2/3	6	3	3	2	2
Scherrer	1	1	0	0	0	0
Lopez W, 1–0	2 1/3	0	0	0	0	4
Hernandez S, 2	2	3	1	1	0	0

HBP—by Hawkins (Grubb). Wild pitch (Hawkins). Time of game—2:55. Attendance—51,901.

HOME RUN RECORDS OF HENRY AARON AND BABE RUTH

Henry Aaron broke Babe Ruth's career home run record, April 8, 1974, by hitting the ball over the left-center field fence at Atlanta for his 715th homer. He had tied Ruth's mark, April 4, at Cincinnati. Aaron, of the Atlanta Braves, hit 20 homers during the 1974 season, raising the mark to 733. Playing for Milwaukee, he added 22 in the next two seasons for a 755 total. He made 3,771 hits and scored 2,174 runs.

BABE RUTH'S RECORD

Year	Club	HR
1914	Boston (AL)	0
1915	Boston (AL)	4
1916	Boston (AL)	3
1917	Boston (AL)	2
1918	Boston (AL)	11
1919	Boston (AL)	29
1920	New York (AL)	54
1921	New York (AL)	59
1922	New York (AL)	35
1923	New York (AL)	41
1924	New York (AL)	46
1925	New York (AL)	25
1926	New York (AL)	47
1927	New York (AL)	60
1928	New York (AL)	54
1929	New York (AL)	46
1930	New York (AL)	49
1931	New York (AL)	46
1932	New York (AL)	41
1933	New York (AL)	34
1934	New York (AL)	22
1935	Boston (NL)	6

World Series

Year	Club	HR
1915	Boston (AL)	0
1916	Boston (AL)	0
1918	Boston (AL)	0
1921	New York (AL)	1
1922	New York (AL)	0
1923	New York (AL)	3
1926	New York (AL)	4
1927	New York (AL)	2
1928	New York (AL)	3
1932	New York (AL)	2

Totals

Regular season	714
World Series	15
All-Star	1

(Ruth was a pitcher mainly until 1918, when he also played outfield. That was the first year he appeared at bat over 150 times. He became a regular outfielder in 1919.)

HENRY AARON'S RECORD

Year	Club	HR
1954	Milwaukee (NL)	13
1955	Milwaukee (NL)	27
1956	Milwaukee (NL)	26
1957	Milwaukee (NL)	44
1958	Milwaukee (NL)	30
1959	Milwaukee (NL)	39
1960	Milwaukee (NL)	40
1961	Milwaukee (NL)	34
1962	Milwaukee (NL)	45
1963	Milwaukee (NL)	44
1964	Milwaukee (NL)	24
1965	Milwaukee (NL)	32
1966	Atlanta (NL)	44
1967	Atlanta (NL)	39
1968	Atlanta (NL)	29
1969	Atlanta (NL)	44
1970	Atlanta (NL)	38
1971	Atlanta (NL)	47
1972	Atlanta (NL)	34
1973	Atlanta (NL)	40
1974	Atlanta (NL)	20
1975	Milwaukee (AL)	12
1976	Milwaukee (AL)	10

Totals

Regular Season	755
World Series	2
Playoff Games	3
All-Star Games	2
	762

World's Series Most Valuable Players

1955	Johnny Podres, Brooklyn (NL)
1956	Don Larsen, New York (AL)
1957	Lew Burdette, Milwaukee (NL)
1958	Bob Turley, New York (AL)
1959	Larry Sherry, Los Angeles (NL)
1960	Bobby Richardson, New York (AL)
1961	Whitey Ford, New York (AL)
1962	Ralph Terry, New York (AL)
1963	Sandy Koufax, Los Angeles (NL)
1964	Bob Gibson, St. Louis (NL)
1965	Sandy Koufax, Los Angeles (NL)
1966	Frank Robinson, Baltimore (AL)
1967	Bob Gibson, St. Louis (NL)
1968	Mickey Lolich, Detroit (AL)
1969	Donn Clendenon, New York (NL)
1970	Brooks Robinson, Baltimore (AL)
1971	Roberto Clemente, Pittsburgh (NL)
1972	Gene Tenace, Oakland (AL)
1973	Reggie Jackson, Oakland (AL)
1974	Rollie Fingers, Oakland (AL)
1975	Pete Rose, Cincinnati (NL)
1976	Johnny Bench, Cincinnati (NL)
1977	Reggie Jackson, New York (AL)
1978	Bucky Dent, New York (AL)
1979	Willie Stargell, Pittsburgh (NL)
1980	Mike Schmidt, Philadelphia (NL)
1981	Ron Cey, Pedro Guerrero, Steve Yeager, Los Angeles (NL)
1982	Darrell Porter, St. Louis (NL)
1983	Rick Dempsey, Baltimore (AL)
1984	Alan Trammell, Detroit (AL)

STEVE CARLTON JOINS 300 VICTORY CLUB

Steve Carlton, the 39-year-old left hander for the Philadelphia Phillies, became only the 16th pitcher in baseball history to record 300 victories in 1983. Carlton, who had played in the major leagues for 20 years through 1984 (seven with St. Louis, 13 with the Phillies), won his 300th on Sept. 23 against St. Louis. In 1983 he led the National League in strikeouts for the fifth time, and in 1984 he broke Warren Spahn's record for most seasons with 100 or more strikeouts at 18.

Currently in ongoing battle with Houston Astros pitcher Nolan Ryan for the all-time career strike-out record. He surpassed Walter Johnson's record of 3,508 and ended the 1983 season on top with 3,709.

HENDERSON OF A'S SETS STOLEN-BASES RECORD

Rickey Henderson of the Oakland A's broke the major league record for stolen bases in one season on Aug. 27, 1982, at Milwaukee when he stole his 119th base in the third inning. The previous record of 118 was held by Lou Brock of St. Louis and was set in 1974. Henderson had broken the American League stolen-bases mark in 1980 when he surpassed Ty Cobb's record of 96, set in 1915. Henderson finished the 1980 season with 100 stolen bases. In 1982 he completed the season with 130. The major league record for career stolen bases is held by Brock with 938.

EQUESTRIAN EVENTS—1984

World Cup Jumping (Gothenburg, Sweden)—Mari Deslauriers, Canada, riding Aramis. Runnerup: Norman Dello Jio, United States, riding I Love You

Olympic Games[1]

Team—United States (J. Michael Plumb, Karen Stives, Torrance Fleischmann, Bruce Davidson)
Team jumping—United States (Joe Fargis, Conrad Hamfeld, Leslie Burr, Melanie Smith)
Individual—Mark Todd, New Zealand
Individual dressage—Dr. Reiner Klimke, West Germany

1. World championships not held in 1984 because of Olympics. Next world championship scheduled for 1986.

BILLIARDS—1983

Men's world pocket billiards champion—Steve Mizerak, Fords, N.J.
Women's world pocket billiards champion—Jean Balukas, Brooklyn, N.Y.

RUGBY—1984

Five Nations—Scotland
United States Men's Champions—"The Colonials," Eastern Rugby Union of America
United States Women's Champions—Florida State University Women
United States college—Harvard University
Professional and graduate school—Life Chiropractic College of Georgia
Military—Fort Stewart, Georgia

ROLLER SKATING

NATIONAL CHAMPIONSHIPS

Speed—1984

Senior men—Jeff Foster, Marleton, N.J.
Senior women—Kim Turner, Livonia, Mich.
Senior two-man relay—Chris Snyder, Mike Vouklizas, Irving, Tex.
Senior two-woman relay—Linda Barnhizer, Mary Hemmingson, Des Moine, Iowa
Senior four-man relay—Chuck, Marty, and Steve Laufer, Gary Boldt, Butler, Wis.
Senior four-woman relay—Tracy Conn, Angie Stepro, Angela Durbin, Darlene Kessinger, Louisville, Ky.
Two mixed—Linda Barnhizer, Dante Muse, Des Moine, Iowa
Four mixed—Robin Bradshaw, Kathy Gomez, Chris Snyder, Mike Vouklizas, Irving, Tex.

Artistic—1984

Men's singles—Scott Cohen, Hamilton, N.J.
Women's singles—Tina Kneisley, Maumee, Ohio
Men's figures—Tony St. Jacques, Virginia Beach, Va.
Women's figures—Debbie Erdmann, Austin, Tex.
World class dance—David Golub and Angela Famiano, East Meadow, N.Y.
World class pairs—Ken Benson and Robyn Young, Hurst, Tex.
American dance—Curt Craton and Theresa Tilson, Fountain Valley, Calif.
Free dance—Larry Blackstone and Julie Brantly, Orlando, Fla.

COMPREHENSIVE INDEX

A

B

D

F

H

I

J

K

L

M

O

P

S

T

U

V

X

Y

Z